March 14–18, 2015
Vancouver, BC, Canada

Association for Computing Machinery

Advancing Computing as a Science & Profession

CSCW'15

Proceedings of the 2015 ACM International Conference on Computer Supported Cooperative Work and Social Computing

Sponsored by:

ACM SIGCHI

Supported by:

NSF, Facebook, GRAND, Microsoft Research, Bloomberg, Northwestern University School of Communication, IBM Research, Google and Simon Fraser University

Vol. 2 of 2

Association for Computing Machinery

Advancing Computing as a Science & Profession

The Association for Computing Machinery
2 Penn Plaza, Suite 701
New York, New York 10121-0701

Notice to Past Authors of ACM-Published Articles

ACM intends to create a complete electronic archive of all articles and/or other material previously published by ACM. If you have written a work that has been previously published by ACM in any journal or conference proceedings prior to 1978, or any SIG Newsletter at any time, and you do NOT want this work to appear in the ACM Digital Library, please inform permissions@acm.org, stating the title of the work, the author(s), and where and when published.

ISBN: 978-1-4503-2922-4 (Digital)

ISBN: 978-1-4503-3767-0 (Print)

Additional copies may be ordered prepaid from:

ACM Order Department
PO Box 30777
New York, NY 10087-0777, USA

Phone: 1-800-342-6626 (USA and Canada)
+1-212-626-0500 (Global)
Fax: +1-212-944-1318
E-mail: acmhelp@acm.org
Hours of Operation: 8:30 am – 4:30 pm ET

Printed in the USA

Welcome from the General Chairs

We are excited to welcome the CSCW community to Vancouver, British Columbia, Canada, for the 2015 ACM Conference on Computer Supported Cooperative Work and Social Computing!

CSCW is the premier venue for research on computer-mediated collaboration, social computing, and social media, from the design of technical systems for collaboration to ethnographic studies of systems in the wild. The mission of the conference is to share research that advances the state of human knowledge and improves both the design of systems and the ways they are used. The diversity of work in our conference program reflects the diversity of technology use in people's work, social, and civic lives as well as the geographic and cultural diversity of contributors.

This diversity and quality is reflected in CSCW's submissions, which have once again surpassed prior years. Technical chairs David McDonald and Luigina Ciolfi have continued to refine our revise and resubmit process for papers, with 161 of 575 submissions accepted. In addition, we will feature 11 workshops, 32 posters, 18 demos, and 5 panels.

Our featured speakers also testify to the quality and varied interests of CSCW. Jeff Hancock of Cornell University will open the conference, speaking on "The Facebook Study: A Personal Account of Data Science, Ethics and Change." Our closing plenary will feature Zeynep Tufekci, University of North Carolina, Chapel Hill, speaking on "Algorithms in our Midst: Information, Power and Choice when Software is Everywhere."

We are also honored to welcome Wanda Orlikowski of MIT as the recipient of this year's CSCW Lasting Impact award for her influential 1992 paper, "Learning from Notes: organizational issues in groupware implementation."

This year, CSCW has some unique new features. One of our innovations was the institution of a reviewer mentorship program, organized by Pernille Bjørn, to help increase the number of well-trained reviewers and keep pace with our growth. We are also excited to be co-located with ACM's Learning at Scale (L@S) conference. We invite L@S conference goers to attend our opening keynote on Monday morning and encourage our attendees to attend the L@S closing keynote (Peter Norvig, Director of Research at Google) on Sunday. L@S will take place during our preconference and there will be plenty of opportunities for attendees to mingle during breaks and evening hours.

Every year, putting together CSCW is a massive collaborative effort. We especially thank all the CSCW authors for contributing the intellectual and technical innovation at the core of our excellent program this year. We are grateful to the program committee and reviewers, who worked hard in providing detailed feedback for authors and improving the quality of the program. We thank our entire hard-working conference committee, an amazing group of people who volunteered many hours of their time and every one of whom helped innovate, solve problems, and bring together the scientific content and social experience of CSCW 2015. We also thank Lisa Tolles at Sheridan Communications, Yvonne Lopez at Executive Events, and Ashley Cozzi and Stephanie Sabal from ACM for all of their assistance with arrangements, registration, and publications. Special thanks go out to John and Joanne Lateulere for their invaluable help with conference planning and management. Finally, we thank our sponsors ACM and SIGCHI, as well as our early sponsors Facebook, National Science Foundation, Microsoft Research, GRAND, Bloomberg, IBM Research, Northwestern University, Simon Fraser University and SFU School of Interactive Arts & Technology, and Google for their generosity.

Finally, thank you, conference goers, for your part in making CSCW what it is today. We hope you will enjoy not only the conference, but everything the beautiful city of Vancouver has to offer in spring.

Dan Cosley
CSCW'15 General Chair
Cornell University, USA

Andrea Forte
CSCW'15 General Chair
Drexel University, USA

From the Papers & Notes Co-Chairs

The CSCW community continues to grow. This year we received 575 papers which represents a 13% increase over the total submissions for the prior year. We had submissions from 24 countries covering all continents.

This year was the fourth year of the "Revise and Resubmit" (R&R) process. Over the last four years the CSCW conference community has been conducting the review process in two rounds. In the first round reviewers are encouraged to review papers with an eye to improving the intellectual strength and contributions of the paper, making it clear which changes would be helpful and which are likely required to make the paper acceptable. In the second round, the same reviewers see the same paper and review to understand whether or not the revised paper now meets the standards of the CSCW community as acceptable. This two-round review model, with encouraging and intellectual give-and-take, is designed to improve papers of good quality but in need of work that might otherwise slip just below the bar in the more common one-shot reviewing conferences. As the Papers Co-Chairs we received numerous email commenting on the high quality of the reviewing, even from some authors whose work was not accepted.

Of all the submissions, 262 were offered the opportunity to R&R, representing a little over 45% of the original submissions. A very small number of authors either withdrew their papers or otherwise declined to resubmit their papers. The Program Committee accepted 161 papers for an acceptance rate of 28% of the total.

The R&R process would not have been possible without the work of 96 Program Committee (PC) members, making up the largest ever PC for a CSCW conference (a 50% increase in committee members over 2014). This represents the substantial increase in the number of CSCW researchers actively involved in the intellectual decision making for the community. Our work to expand the PC included reaching out to more junior researchers, industry researchers, as well as our more established colleagues. This year's PC is one of the most diverse to date and is testament to the richness within the CSCW community in terms of countries, institutions and areas of expertise.

We also wish to acknowledge the 720 external reviewers that have generously volunteered their time and expertise to ensure the quality of the CSCW 2015 program.

We hope you enjoy!

Luigina Ciolfi
Sheffield Hallam University

David W. McDonald
University of Washington

Table of Contents

Volunteerism

Teamwork Challenges

Politics and Social Networks

Motivating Peer Production

My Mobile, My Friends

Is There a Doctor in the Room?

Collaborating Around Crisis

Location, Location, Location

Communities for Individual Behavior Change

Wikipedia: Structure & Function

The Powers of Co-location

Collaborative Design Approaches

Collaborating Under Constraints

Civic Participation

Experiencing Social Media

Children and Families

Motivating Crowdwork

There's Just Something About Hands

Games and Virtual Worlds

Motivation and Dynamics of the Open Classroom

Closing Keynote

CSCW 2015 Conference Organization

General Co-Chairs:	Dan Cosley *(Cornell University, USA)* Andrea Forte *(Drexel University, USA)*
Papers Co-Chairs:	Luigina Ciolfi *(Sheffield Hallam University, UK)* David McDonald *(University of Washington, USA)*
Posters Co-Chairs:	Karyn Moffat *(McGill University, Canada)* Aleksandra Sarcevic *(Drexel University, USA)*
Panels Co-Chairs:	Louise Barkhuus *(Stockholm University, Sweden)* Anatoliy Gruzd *(Ryerson University, Canada)*
Workshops Co-Chairs:	Laura Dabbish *(Carnegie Mellon University, USA)* Jenn Thom *(Amazon.com, USA)*
Demos Co-Chairs:	Tomoo Inoue *(University of Tsukuba, Japan)* Tony Tang *(University of Calgary, Canada)*
Publicity Co-Chairs:	Moira Burke *(Facebook, USA)* Elizabeth Gerber *(Northwestern University, USA)* Andrés Monroy-Hernandez *(Microsoft Research & University of Washington, USA)* Dario Taraborelli *(Wikimedia Foundation, USA)*
Doctoral Consortium Co-Chairs:	Carl Gutwin *(University of Saskatchewan, Canada)* Abigail Sellen *(Microsoft Research Cambridge, USA)*
Student Volunteer Co-Chairs:	Erin Brady *(University of Rochester, USA)* Syavash Nobarany *(University of British Columbia, Canada)*
Treasurer:	Jeremy Birnholtz *(Northwestern University, USA)*
Proceedings Co-Chairs:	Jacqueline Pike *(Duquesne University, USA)* Andrea Wiggins *(University of Maryland, USA)*
Local Arrangements & Accessibiity Co-Chairs:	Serena Hillman *(Simon Fraser University, Canada)* Carman Neustaedter *(Simon Fraser University, Canada)*
Sponsorship Co-Chairs:	Sean Goggins *(University of Missouri, USA)* Steven Poltrock *(USA)*
Graphic Design & Webmastering:	Xiaohui Eva Luo *(Georgia Institute of Technology, USA)* Elizabeth Murnane *(Cornell University, USA)*

Best of CSCW Committee:

Loren Terveen *(University of Minnesota, USA)*
Danyel Fisher *(Microsoft Research, USA)*
Myriam Lewkowicz *(Troyes University of Technology, France)*
Jeremy Birnholtz *(Northwestern University, USA)*
Jacki O'Neill *(Microsoft Research India, India)*
Aleksandra Sarcevic *(Drexel University, USA)*
Carla Simone *(University of Milano-Bicocca, Italy)*
Josh Introne *(Michigan State University, USA)*

CSCW Lasting Impact Award Committee:

Jakob Bardram *(IT University of Copenhagen, Denmark)*
Susan Fussell *(Cornell University, USA)*
Elizabeth Churchill *(Google, USA)*
John Tang *(Microsoft Research, USA)*
Luigina Ciolfi *(Sheffield Hallam University, UK)*
David McDonald *(University of Washington, USA)*

CSCW Reviewer Mentors:

Pernille Bjørn, Chair *(IT University of Copenhagen, Denmark)*
Morgan Ames *(University of California, Irvine, USA)*
Tone Bratteteig *(University of Oslo, Norway)*
John M. Carroll *(The Pennsylvania State University, USA)*
Dan Cosley *(Cornell University, USA)*
Giorgio De Michelis *(University of Milan-Bicocca, Italy)*
Paul Dourish *(University of California, Irvine, USA)*
Rosta Farzan *(University of Pittsburgh, USA)*
Fernando Figueira Filho *(Federal University of Rio Grande do Norte, Brazil)*
Joel Fischer *(University of Nottingham, UK)*
Morten Fjeld *(Chalmers University of Technology, Sweden)*
Benjamim Fonseca *(University of Trás-os-Montes e Alto Douro, Portugal)*
Andrea Forte *(Drexel University, USA)*
Wai-Tat Fu *(University of Illinois, Urbana-Champaign, USA)*
Joanne Hinds *(University of Bath, UK)*
Gary Hsieh *(University of Washington, USA)*
Jina Huh *(Michigan State University, USA)*
James Howison *(University of Texas, Austin, USA)*
Adriana Iamnitchi *(University of South Florida, USA)*
Pertti Järvinen *(University of Tampere, Finland)*
Jofish Kaye *(Yahoo!, USA)*
Rajiv Krishnamurthy *(Facebook, USA)*
Wayne Lutters *(University of Maryland, Baltimore County, USA)*
Winter Mason *(Stevens Institute of Technology, USA)*
Victoria Pammer-Schindler *(Graz University of Technology, Austria)*
Dave Randall *(University of Siegen, Germany)*
Lionel P. Robert, Jr. *(University of Michigan, USA)*
Duncan Sanderson *(Téléuniversité Montréal, Canada)*
Sarita Yardi Schoenebeck *(University of Michigan, USA)*
Gunnar Stevens *(University of Siegen, Germany)*

CSCW Reviewer Mentors (continued):

Deborah Tatar *(Virginia Institute of Technology, USA)*
Jamie Teevan *(Microsoft Research, USA)*
Loren Terveen *(University of Minnesota, USA)*

CSCW Reviewer Mentees:

Elena Agapie *(University of Washington, USA)*
Karin Ahlin *(Mid Sweden University, Sweden)*
Syed Ishtiaque Ahmed *(Cornell University, USA)*
Tawfiq Ammari *(University of Michigan, USA)*
Nazanin Andalibi *(Drexel University, USA)*
Milena Araujo *(Federal University of Campina Grande, Brazil)*
Mariam Asad *(Georgia Institute of Technology, USA)*
Amir Azarbakht *(Oregon State University, USA)*
Andrea Barbarin *(University of Michigan, USA)*
Nils Bornoe *(Aalborg University, Denmark)*
Amira Chalbi *(University of Paris-Sud, France)*
Shuo Chang *(University of Minnesota, USA)*
Nan-Chen Chen *(University of Washington, USA)*
Stella Christodoulaki *(University of Paris-Sud, France)*
António Correia *(University of Trás-os-Montes e Alto Douro, Portugal)*
Anahita Davoudi *(University of Central Florida, USA)*
Wenfei Don *(Uppsala University, Sweden)*
Alison E. Doub *(The Pennsylvania State University, USA)*
Toni Ferro *(University of Washington, USA)*
Cédric Foucault *(University of Paris-Sud & ENS Cachan, France)*
Anita Marie Gilbert *(University of California, Irvine, USA)*
Francisco J. Gutierrez *(University of Chile, Chile)*
Oliver Haimson *(University of California, Irvine, USA)*
Susanna Heyman *(KTH Royal Institute of Technology, Sweden)*
Syed Ali Hussain *(Michigan State University, USA)*
Maia Jacobs *(Georgia Institute of Technology, USA)*
Rasmus Eskild Jensen *(IT University of Copenhagen, Denmark)*
Imrul Kayes *(University of South Florida, USA)*
Elizabeth Kaziunas *(University of Michigan, USA)*
Na Li *(The Pennsylvania State University, USA)*
Katherine Lo *(University of California, Irvine, USA)*
Angela Locoro *(University of Milan-Bicocca, Italy)*
Claudia López *(University of Pittsburgh, USA)*
Haley MacLeod *(Indiana University, USA)*
Jamie Mahoney *(University of Lincoln, UK)*
Jennifer Marlow *(Carnegie Mellon University, USA)*
Stina Matthiessen *(IT University of Copenhagen, Denmark)*
Tien T. Nguyen *(University of Minnesota, USA)*
Nigini Abilio Oliveira *(Federal University of Campina Grande, Brazil)*
Pinar Ozturk *(Stevens Institute of Technology, USA)*
Yushan Pan *(University of Oslo, Norway)*
Michelle Purcell *(Drexel University, USA)*

CSCW Reviewer Mentees (continued):

Katherine Ringland *(University of California, Irvine, USA)*
Thijs Roumen *(National University of Singapore, Singapore)*
Saiph Savage *(University of California, Santa Barbara, USA & National Autonomous University of Mexico, Mexico)*
Sophie KyoungHee Son *(Korea Advanced Institute of Science and Technology, South Korea)*
Oliver Stickel *(University of Siegen, Germany)*
Minhyang Suh *(University of Washington, USA)*
Athanasios Taousakos *(University of Paris-Sud, France)*
Jimmy Ti *(Queensland University of Technology, Australia)*
Luis Contreras Toledo *(University of Bristol, UK)*
Emma Tonkin *(University of Bristol, UK)*
Stela Valchovska *(University of Nottingham, UK)*
Hanna Vrzakova *(University of Eastern Finland, Finland)*
Joanne White *(University of Colorado, Boulder, USA)*
Christine Wolf *(University of California, Irvine, USA)*
Pawel Woźniak *(Chalmers University of Technology, USA)*
Yu Wu *(The Pennsylvania State University, USA)*
Sangseok You *(University of Michigan, USA)*
Alyson Young *(University of Maryland, Baltimore County, USA)*
Amy X. Zhang *(Massachusetts Institute of Technology, USA)*
Saijing Zheng *(The Pennsylvania State University, USA)*

CSCW 2015 Program Committee Members

*Committee members whose names appear in **bold** are being recognized by fellow Associate Chairs for one or more excellent reviews*

Joanna Abraham, *University of Illinois,* USA
Judd Antin, *Yahoo! Research,* USA
Daniel Avrahami, *FXPAL,* USA
Louise Barkhuus, *Stockholm University,* Sweden
Jacob Biehl, *FX Palo Alto Laboratory,* USA
Jeffrey Bigham, *Carnegie Mellon University,* USA
Jeremy Birnholtz, *Northwestern University,* USA
Pernille Bjørn, *IT University of Copenhagen,* Denmark
Alexander Boden, *Fraunhofer Institute for Applied Information Technology (FIT)*, Germany
Claus Bossen, *Aarhus University,* Denmark
Nina Boulus, *IT University of Copenhagen,* Denmark
Tone Bratteteig, *University of Oslo,* Norway
Barry Brown, *University of California, San Diego,* USA
Amy Bruckman, *Georgia Institute of Technology,* USA
Moira Burke, *Facebook,* USA
Alan Chamberlain, *The University of Nottingham,* UK
Yunan Chen, *University of California, Irvine,* USA
Coye Cheshire, *University of California, Berkeley,* USA
Lars Rune Christensen, *IT University of Copenhagen,* Denmark
Gregorio Convertino, *Xerox Research Center Europe,* France
Dan Cosley, *Cornell University,* USA
Edward Cutrell, *Microsoft Research India,* India
Antonella De Angeli, *University of Trento,* Italy
Cleidson de Souza, *Universidade Federal do Pará,* Brazil
Xianghua Ding, *Fudan University,* China
Steven Dow, *Carnegie Mellon University,* USA
Arvid Engström, *Mobile Life at Interactive Institute,* Sweden
Ingrid Erickson, *Rutgers University,* USA
Rosta Farzan, *University of Pittsburgh,* USA
Andrew Fiore, *Facebook,* USA
Danyel Fisher, *Microsoft Research,* USA
Morten Fjeld, *Chalmers University of Technology,* Sweden
Benjamim Fonseca, *University of Trás-os-Montes e Alto Douro (UTAD)*, Portugal
Susan Fussell, *Cornell University,* USA
Elizabeth Gerber, *Northwestern University,* USA
Alain GIBOIN, *INRIA,* France
Eric Gilbert, *Georgia Institute of Technology,* USA
Sukeshini Grandhi, *Eastern Connecticut State University,* USA
Antonietta Grasso, *Xerox Research Centre Europe,* France
Carl Gutwin, *University of Saskatchewan,* Canada
Ido Guy, *Yahoo! Labs,* Israel
Aaron Halfaker, *University of Minnesota,* USA
Christine Halverson, *IBM T.J. Watson Research Center,* USA
Mark Handel, *The Boeing Company,* USA
Jina Huh, *Michigan State University,* USA
Claudia-Lavinia Ignat, *INRIA Lorraine,* France
Joshua Introne, *Michigan State University,* USA
Michal Jacovi, *IBM Research Lab in Haifa,* Israel
Brian Keegan, *Northwestern University,* USA
Wendy Kellogg, *IBM T.J. Watson Research Center,* USA
Cliff Lampe, *University of Michigan,* USA
Edith Law, *Harvard University,* USA
Gilly Leshed, *Cornell University,* USA
Myriam Lewkowicz, *UTT,* France
Kurt Luther, *Virginia Tech,* USA
Wayne Lutters, *University of Maryland, Baltimore County,* USA
Gloria Mark, *University of California, Irvine,* USA
Andres Monroy-Hernandez, *Massachusetts Institute of Technology,* USA
Michael Muller, *IBM Research*, USA
Maria Normark, *Södertörn University,* Sweden
Jacki O'Neill, *Microsoft Research India*, India
Volkmar Pipek, *University of Siegen,* Germany
Anne Marie Piper, *Northwestern University,* USA
Erika Poole, *Penn State University,* USA
Michael Prilla, *Institute for Applied Work Science Bochum,* Germany
Emilee Rader, *Michigan State University,* USA
David Randall, *University of Siegen*, Germany
Madhu Reddy, *Pennsylvania State University,* USA
David Redmiles, *University of California, Irvine,* USA
David Ribes, *Georgetown University,* USA
Lionel Robert, *University of Michigan,* USA
Daniela Rosner, *University of Washington,* USA
Aleksandra Sarcevic, *Drexel University,* USA
Steve Sawyer, *Syracuse University,* USA

m.c. schraefel, *University of Southampton*, UK
Bryan Semaan, *Syracuse University,* USA
David A. Shamma, *Yahoo!,* USA
Aaron Shaw, *Northwestern University,* USA
Patrick Shih, *The Pennsylvania State University,* USA
Irina Shklovski, *IT University of Copenhagen,* Denmark
Carla Simone, *DISCO-Universita' di Milano-Bicocca -Italy,* Italy
Gunnar Stevens, *Institute of Information Systems / University of Siegen,* Germany
Norman Su, *Indiana University*, USA
John Tang, *Microsoft Research,* USA
Hilda Tellioglu, *Vienna University of Technology,* Austria
Loren Terveen, *University of Minnesota,* USA
Jennifer Thom, *Amazon,* USA
Zachary Toups, *New Mexico State University,* USA
Sarah Vieweg, *Qatar Computing Research Institute,* Qatar
Jessica Vitak, *University of Maryland,* USA
Hao-Chuan Wang, *National Tsing Hua University,* Taiwan
Yang Wang, *Syracuse University,* USA
Rick Wash, *Michigan State University,* USA
Svetlana Yarosh, *University of Minnesota,* USA
Xiaomu Zhou, *Rutgers University,* USA

CSCW 2015 Paper Reviewers

*Reviewers whose names appear in **bold** are being recognized by the Associate Chairs for one or more excellent reviews*

Margunn Aanestad
Lada Adamic
Phil Adams
Elena Agapie
Karin Ahlin
Syed Ishtiaque Ahmed
June Ahn
Warren Allen
Jens Allwood
Peter Alston
Morgan Ames
Tawfiq Ammari
Nazanin Andalibi
Lars Bo Andersen
Paul André
Craig Anslow
Panayotis Antoniadis
Milena Araujo
Rosa Arriaga
Henrik Artman
Mattias Arvola
Mariam Asad
Marcos Baez
Naveen Bagalkot
Brian Bailey
Saeideh Bakhshi
Eytan Bakshy
Elizabeth Bales
Dawna Ballard
Stinne Ballegaard
Liam Bannon
Andrea Barbarin
Flore Barcellini
Jakob Bardram
Jeffrey Bardzell
Jordan Barlow
Scott Bateman
Eric Baumer
Natalie Bazarova
Roman Bednarik
Andrew Begel
Bo Begole
Marek Bell
Aurélien Bénel
Frank Bentley
Laura Benton
Michael Bernstein
Nadia Bianchi-Berthouze
Matthew Bietz
Dorrit Billman
Igor Bilogrevic
Jan Boehmer
Elizabeth Bonsignore
Silvia Bordin
Alan Borning
Nis Bornoe
Nathan Bos
Guillaume Bouchard
Kristy Boyer
Alessandro Bozzon
Erin Brady
Robin Brewer
Pam Briggs
Christopher Brooks
Jed Brubaker
Elizabeth Buie
Jean-marie Burkhardt
Jenna Burrell
Richard Byrne
Federico Cabitza
Béatrice Cahour
Stefan Carmien
Stefania Castellani
Marcelo Cataldo
Teresa Cerratto Pargman
Meeyoung Cha
Abdelberi Chaabane
Y.-L. Betty Chang
Chen Chen
Francine Chen
Mike Chen
Nan-Chen Chen
Nicholas Chen
Xiang 'Anthony' Chen
Shiwei Cheng
Marshini Chetty
Ed Chi
Parmit Chilana
Eun Kyoung Choe
Ming Ki Chong
Tanzeem Choudhury
Stella Christodoulaki
Hao-Hua Chu
Tyng-Ruey Chuang
Chia-Fang Chung
Giovanni Luca Ciampaglia
Adrian Clear
D Coetzee
Benjamin Collier
Tommaso Colombino
Rob Comber
Bernard Conein
António Correia
Lynne Coventry
Henriette Cramer
Justin Cranshaw
Alma Leora Culen
Aron Culotta
Chandrika Cycil
Mary Czerwinski
Laura Dabbish
Peter Danholt
Sauvik Das
Anahita Davoudi
Munmun De Choudhury
Fiorella De Cindio
Giorgio De Michelis
Laura Devendorf
Nicholas Diakopoulos
Tawanna Dillahunt
Jill Dimond
Yvonne Dittrich
Wenfei Dong
Brian Dorn
Honglu Du
Nicolas Ducheneaut
Paul Dunphy
Serge Egelman
Kate Ehrlich
Michael Ekstrand
Yasmine El-Glaly
Nicole Ellison
Niklas Elmqvist
Jennifer Englert
Sheena Erete

Thomas Erickson
David Evans
Robert Farrell
Toni Ferro
Oliver Ferschke
Bruce Ferwerda
Casey Fiesler
Fernando Figueira Filho
Flavio Figueiredo
Ailbhe Finnerty
Joel Fischer
Colin Fitzpatrick
Heather Ford
Cédric Foucault
Amy Franklin
Guo Freeman
Samantha Fried
Wai-Tat Fu
Ge Gao
Jayden Garner
Daniel Gatica-Perez
R.Stuart Geiger
Bluma Gelley
Darren Gergle
Kathrin Gerling
Marco Gerosa
Werner Geyer
Anita Gilbert
Mareike Glöss
Gerard Goggin
Sean Goggins
Jennifer Golbeck
Richard Gomer
Amy Gonzales
Joseph Gonzales
Elizabeth Goodman
Mary Gray
Rebecca Gray
Anders Green
William Green
Michael Greenberg
Christian Greiffenhagen
Catherine Grevet
Nir Grinberg
Miria Grisot
Erik Grönvall
Kristina Groth
Dan Gruen
Ning Gu
Shion Guha
Julien Guibourdenche
Philip Guo
Francisco Gutierrez
Joshua Hailpern
Oliver Haimson
Julia Haines
Maria Håkansson
Megan Halpern
William Hamilton
Jessica Hammer
Kyungsik (Keith) Han
Jeff Hancock
Mark Hancock
Benjamin Hanrahan
Emily Harburg
Ellie Harmon
Franklin Harper
Richard Harper
Christopher Harris
Drew Harry
Björn Hartmann
Mark Hartswood
Andrea Hartzler
Ari Hautasaari
Gillian Hayes
Brent Hecht
Tomi Heimonen
Libby Hemphill
David Hendry
Thomas Herrmann
Morten Hertzum
Susanna Heyman
Benjamin Mako Hill
Brian Hilligoss
Serena Hillman
Jon Hindmarsh
Chaya Hiruncharoenvate
Christopher Hoadley
Bernie Hogan
Naja Holten Møller
Hwajung Hong
Jason Hong
Lichan Hong
Juan Pablo Hourcade
Aaron Houssian
James Howison
Gary Hsieh
Jochen Huber
David Huffaker
Amanda Hughes
Julie Hui
Jessica Hullman
Syed Hussain
Alice Hutchings
Helge Hüttenrauch
Inseok Hwang
Kori Inkpen
Shamsi Iqbal
Lilly Irani
Petra Isenberg
Corey Jackson
Steven Jackson
Abigail Jacobs
Maia Jacobs
Mattias Jacobsson
Mohammad Hossein Jarrahi
Tom Jenkins
Rasmus Jensen
Haiyan Jia
Lian Jian
Hongxia Jin
Christopher Jones
Jasmine Jones
Fatima Jonsson
Anirudha Joshi
Suhas Govind Joshi
David Joyner
Wendy Ju
Oskar Juhlin
Malte Jung
Yumi Jung
Sasa Junuzovic
Sanjay Kairam
Yoram Kalman
Santosh Kalwar
Noreen Kamal
Bridget Kane
Ruogu Kang
Thomas Kannampallil
Anne Marie Kanstrup
Karrie Karahalios
David Kaufman
Andrea Kavanaugh
Joseph 'Jofish' Kaye
Elizabeth Kaziunas
Lyndon Kennedy
M. Laeeq Khan
Donnie Kim
Jeeeun Kim
Juho Kim
Sung-Hee Kim
Sunyoung Kim
Taemie Kim

David Kirk
Reuben Kirkham
Spyros Kitsiou
Funda Kivran-Swaine
Styliani Kleanthous
Mark Klein
Scott Klemmer
Kristina Knaving
Benjamin Koehne
Joseph Konstan
Matthias Korn
Yubo Kou
Yong Ming Kow
Sven Kratz
Robert Kraut
Pavel Kucherbaev
Katie Kuksenok
Anand Kulkarni
Chinmay Kulkarni
Neha Kumar
Diana Kusunoki
Harris Kyriakou
Jarmo Laaksolahti
Ben Lafreniere
Nicolas LaLone
Shyong Lam
Airi Lampinen
James Landay
Monica Landoni
Walter Lasecki
Thomas LaToza
Yann Laurillau
Christopher Le Dantec
Alex Leavitt
Charlotte Lee
Seungyon Claire Lee
Benedikt Ley
Jia Li
Na Li
Daniel Liebling
Michael Liegl
Christopher Lima
Rhema Linder
Siân Lindley
Conor Linehan
Wang Ling
Jessica Lingel
Lars Lischke
Eden Litt
Leslie Liu
Sophia Liu
Angela Locoro
Thomas Lodato
Claudia López
Zhihan Lu
Thomas Ludwig
Johan Lundin
zhihan lv
Christopher MacLellan
Haley MacLeod
Rachel Magee
Jamie Mahoney
Lena Mamykina
Nicolas Mangano
Jennifer Mankoff
Sampada Marathe
Gabriela Marcu
Drew Margolin
Annette Markham
Jennifer Marlow
David Martin
Paulo Martins
Misa Maruyama
Christopher Mascaro
Jorge Matias
Tara Matthews
Stina Matthiesen
Hanna Maurin
Matthieu Mazzega
Victoria McArthur
Joe McCarthy
David McDonald
Poppy McLeod
Donald McMillan
Richard Medland
Yevgeniy Medynskiy
David Mellis
Maria Menendez
Amanda Menking
Samantha Merritt
Enza Messina
Solomon Messing
Ronald Metoyer
Tommi Mikkonen
David Millen
Andrew Miller
Gregor Miller
Robert Miller
Tanushree Mitra
Manas Mittal
Wendy Moncur
Peter Mooney
Jonathan Morgan
Jonathan Morgan
Meredith Morris
Robert Morris
Dan Morrow
Gabriel Mugar
Claudia Müller
Sean Munson
David Murakami Wood
Elizabeth Murnane
Alison Murphy
Brad Myers
Mor Naaman
Lennart Nacke
Mathieu Nancel
Bonnie Nardi
Carman Neustaedter
Duyen Nguyen
Tien Nguyen
Syavash Nobarany
Sylvie Noël
Oded Nov
Francisco Nunes
Mohammad Obaid
Brendan O'Connor
Erick Oduor
Anne Oeldorf-Hirsch
Alice Oh
Nigini Oliveira
Gary Olson
Judith Olson
Thomas Olsson
Robert On
Babajide Osatuyi
Myle Ott
Pinar Ozturk
Stefano Padilla
Xinru Page
Drew Paine
Chankyung Pak
Joyojeet Pal
Leysia Palen
Yushan Pan
Katherine Panciera
Hugo Paredes
Daniel Pargman
Albert Park
Souneil Park
Kayur Patel
Jessica Pater
Sharoda Paul

Joslenne Pena
Wei Peng
Adam Perer
Simon Perrault
Mark Perry
Tamara Peyton
Antonio Piccinno
Hannah Pileggi
Tamar Pincus
Kathleen Pine
Valerie Polichar
Andreas Poller
Wanda Pratt
Nuno Preguica
Reid Priedhorsky
Jason Procyk
Michelle Purcell
Yin Qu
Alexander Quinn
Irene Rae
David Randall
Matt Ratto
Ilaria Redaelli
Daniel Rees Lewis
Stuart Reeves
Katharina Reinecke
Christian Reuter
Corinne Ribert-Van De Weerdt
Alexander Richter
Scott Robertson
Tom Rodden
John Rooksby
Asta Roseway
Luca Rossi
Chiara Rossitto
Mary Beth Rosson
Thijs Roumen
Mark Rouncefield
Jeffrey Rzeszotarski
Alan Said
Pascal Salembier
Mohamed Sarwat
Saiph Savage
Florian Schaub
Chris Schmandt
Jodi Schneider
Raz Schwartz
Tobias Schwartz
Lauren Scissors
Jeremy Scott
Mark Selby
Shilad Sen
Bernard Senach
Leslie Setlock
Burr Settles
N. Sadat Shami
Nikhil Sharma
Sarika Sharma
Wes Sharrock
Scott Sherwood
Frank Shipman
Liz Sillence
Leif Singer
Petr Slovák
Madeline Smith
Jaime Snyder
Jacob Solomon
Eduardo Solteiro Pires
KyoungHee Son
Vladimir Soroka
Tasos Spiliotopoulos
Emma Spiro
Janaki Srinivasan
Kevin Stanley
Kate Starbird
Luke Stark
Bogdan State
Martin Stein
Stephanie Steinhardt
Igor Steinmacher
Erik Stolterman
Simone Stumpf
Masanori Sugimoto
Minhyang (Mia) Suh
Maoyuan Sun
Alistair Sutcliffe
Anthony Tang
Charlotte Tang
Athanasios Taousakos
Dario Taraborelli
Yla Tausczik
Rannie Teodoro
Elizabeth Thiry
Jakob Tholander
John Thomas
Bart Thomee
Jimmy Ti
Matthieu Tixier
Peter Tolmie
Catalina Toma
Stephanie Tong
Erik Trainer
Stefano Tranquillini
Khai Truong
Hsin-yi Tsai
Jason Tsay
Zeynep Tufekci
Michael Twidale
Heli Väätäjä
Rajan Vaish
Stela Valchovska
Kami Vaniea
Julita Vassileva
Tiffany Veinot
Gina Venolia
Nervo Verdezoto
Guri Verne
Chris Vincent
John Vines
Gianluigi Viscusi
Tatiana Vlahovic
Juergen Vogel
Dirk Vom Lehn
Hana Vrzakova
Ina Wagner
Judy Wajcman
James Wallace
Jillian Wallis
William Yang Wang
Yi-Chia Wang
Yiran Wang
Peter Wardrip
Morten Warncke-Wang
Nic Weber
Carolyn Wei
Nadir Weibel
Joanne White
Kevin White
Andrea Wiggins
Lauren Wilcox
Hiroko Wilensky
Jutta Willamowski
Wesley Willett
Michele Williams
Matt Willis
Max Wilson
Fredrik Winberg
Susan Winter
Pamela Wisniewski
Donghee Yvette Wohn
Christine Wolf
Anita Woll
Paweł Woźniak

Yu Wu
Volker Wulf
Susan Wyche
Lu Xiao
Bin Xu
Naomi Yamashita
Huahai Yang
Jiang Yang
Sarita Yardi Schoenebeck
Ming Yin
Chuang-wen You
Sangseok You
Alyson Young
Lixiu Yu
Chien Wen Yuan
Hideto Yuzawa
Mark Zachry
Gabriela Zago
Amy Zhang
Haoqi Zhang
Dejin Zhao
Saijing Zheng
Haiyi Zhu
Mengxiao Zhu
Ann Zimmerman
John Zimmerman
Philippe Zimmermann
Moustafa Zouinar
Arkaitz Zubiaga
Kathryn Zyskowski
Douglas Zytko

CSCW 2015 Sponsor & Supporters

Sponsor: SIGCHI

Champions: NSF facebook

Benefactors: Graphisme, animation et nouveaux médias grand Graphics, Animation and New Media

Microsoft Research

Bloomberg

Contributors: Northwestern University School of Communication

IBM Research

Friends: Google™

SFU SIMON FRASER UNIVERSITY ENGAGING THE WORLD

Toward Collaborative Ideation at Scale — Leveraging Ideas from Others to Generate More Creative and Diverse Ideas

Pao Siangliulue[1] Kenneth C. Arnold[1] Krzysztof Z. Gajos[1] Steven P. Dow[2]

[1]Harvard School of Engineering and Applied Sciences
Cambridge, MA USA
{paopow, kcarnold, kgajos}@seas.harvard.edu

[2]Carnegie Mellon University
Pittsburgh, PA USA
spdow@cs.cmu.edu

ABSTRACT
A growing number of large collaborative idea generation platforms promise that by generating ideas together, people can create better ideas than any would have alone. But how might these platforms best leverage the number and diversity of contributors to help each contributor generate even better ideas? Prior research suggests that seeing particularly creative or diverse ideas from others can inspire you, but few scalable mechanisms exist to assess diversity. We contribute a new scalable crowd-powered method for evaluating the diversity of sets of ideas. The method relies on similarity comparisons (is idea A more similar to B or C?) generated by non-experts to create an abstract spatial *idea map*. Our validation study reveals that human raters agree with the estimates of dissimilarity derived from our idea map as much or more than they agree with each other. People seeing the diverse sets of examples from our idea map generate more diverse ideas than those seeing randomly selected examples. Our results also corroborate findings from prior research showing that people presented with creative examples generated more creative ideas than those who saw a set of random examples. We see this work as a step toward building more effective online systems for supporting large scale collective ideation.

Author Keywords
Collaborative ideation, inspirational examples, creativity

ACM Classification Keywords
H.5.m. Information Interfaces and Presentation (e.g. HCI): Miscellaneous

INTRODUCTION
The "lone inventor" is a myth: even geniuses benefit from exposure to ideas of others [29]. Seeing ideas different from their own broadens people's perspectives, sheds light on obscure connections, and inspires people to come up with ideas they might not have thought of alone [14, 19, 5]. By generating ideas together, people can produce more diverse ideas than if each person ideated alone, and this diversity can lead to more creative overall solutions [23, 27].

CSCW '15, March 14 - 18 2015, Vancouver, BC, Canada

ACM 978-1-4503-2922-4/15/03...$15.00
http://dx.doi.org/10.1145/2675133.2675239

Various online platforms have emerged as spaces where people can share their ideas and get inspired by other people's ideas. For example, AllOurIdeas.org hosts more than 200,000 ideas addressing 4,500 problems, Quirky.com receives hundreds of new product ideas every day from its 500,000 inventors, and OpenIDEO.com hosts an archive of more than 1,000 ideas to solve 24 pertinent societal problems. Contributors to these platforms can browse other people's ideas in search of inspiration. The mix of perspectives and expertise among the participants allows creative solutions to emerge in a way unimaginable in the lone-innovator or small-group settings.

But the large-scale idea generation paradigm also introduces a new challenge: how to find the most inspiring ideas in a sea of hundreds? Existing approaches are to either help people parametrically browse and search for examples [19, 17] or extract schemas from examples and search for the schema that allows analogical transfer for a new idea [38, 36]. Even with such strategies, the users still have to wade through many examples to either find an inspiring idea or to find the right set of ideas to allow schema induction. Ideators may get overwhelmed by a large number of mundane or redundant ideas before they encounter ideas that genuinely inspire them.

Alternatively, a system can select appropriate sets of inspiring examples for its users. The challenges of algorithmically identifying inspiring ideas from a large pool of ideas are twofold.

Firstly, picking out a set of inspiring ideas calls for finesse. People are easily influenced by ideas they encounter [15, 30, 22, 16]. A set of uninspiring examples may fixate ideators on ordinary or a relatively narrow set of ideas. In contrast, a set of unique examples might prompt people to explore semantically different paths from their original ones, potentially yielding ideas from unexplored parts of the solution space. Our literature review reveals two criteria for an inspiring set of example ideas: creativity of individual examples and diversity of the *set* of examples. Compared to seeing a random selection of examples (as one might see when simply browsing ideas), seeing particularly creative (i.e., novel and valuable) ideation examples has been shown to improve both the creativity and diversity of ideas one generates [22, 26, 20]. Similarly, if the set of examples is diverse (i.e., if the ideas within the set were substantially different from each other), the diversity of generated ideas should also increase [25]. An effective ideation system should be able to assess the creativity of ideas and diversity of sets of ideas to be able to present inspiring ideas to promote creativity.

Secondly, there is a question of scalability. Even a human expert might struggle to find a set of creative and diverse ideas from a large idea archive in a reasonable amount of time. Our approach needs to effectively identify a promising set of inspiration from a pool of thousands of ideas.

Scalable crowd-powered mechanisms for assessing creativity of individual ideas have already been developed [28, 32, 35, 40, 37, 39]. However, automated or crowd-powered methods for assessing semantic diversity of sets of ideas are less well developed. To enable selection of diverse sets, we built on prior work on multidimensional scaling and active similarity learning techniques [31, 34] to develop a technique that "embeds" all ideas in a two-dimensional space, creating an abstract spatial map from as few human queries as possible. As input, our technique takes triplet comparisons ("Is idea A more similar to B or to C?"), which non-experts can provide easily and reliably. The distance between a pair of ideas on the generated map reflects the collective perception of the semantic difference between these ideas. This map allows us to estimate the relative diversity of subsets of ideas: sets where all ideas are close to each other on the map will be perceived as less diverse than sets where ideas are far apart.

We conducted a study to test whether the effects of creativity and diversity of examples on generated ideas still hold when we sampled examples using our scalable mechanisms. We presented ideators with sets of ideation examples that varied in creativity (as measured by a conventional method) and diversity (as measured by our idea map metric). Our results demonstrated that more creative examples led to more creative ideas being generated and that more diverse sets of examples led to more diverse sets of ideas being generated. However, we did not observe any impact of creative examples on the diversity of generated ideas or diversity of examples on the average creativity of generated ideas.

In this work, we made the following contributions:

- We developed and validated a crowd-powered method for automatically constructing an "idea map" that can be used to extract diverse sets of examples at scale.
- We conducted a study demonstrating that participants generated more diverse ideas when seeing diverse sets of examples generated using our idea map approach than when seeing randomly selected examples. The study also corroborated results from prior research by showing that people presented with particularly creative examples generated more creative ideas than those who saw set of random examples.

Together, these results can inform the design of systems to support large-scale collective ideation. Instead of leaving people to explore ideas of others haphazardly, future systems can help contributors to quickly find manageable sets of particularly creative and diverse ideas. Some existing systems already include mechanisms (such as voting mechanism used by OpenIDEO.com) for finding particularly creative ideas. We extend the state of the art by contributing a scalable crowd-powered approach that enables selection of sets of diverse ideas.

PRIOR WORK

How creative and diverse examples affect ideation

Seeing others' ideas can have positive effects on one's own ideation as it can help people come up with ideas that they would not have thought of otherwise. Teams where members can see ideas of others generate more ideas (and sometimes of higher quality) compared to teams where each member generates ideas alone without seeing ideas of others [8, 9, 4]. Exposure to others' ideas also accelerates the generation of ideas across different semantic categories, increasing productivity overall [25].

However, seeing other people's ideas may have unintended side effects. Specifically, people tend to generate ideas that borrow concepts from presented examples [15, 30, 22, 16]. If the examples were mundane or represented only a narrow slice of the solution space, seeing them may actually constrain rather than stimulate idea generation. This phenomenon has been referred to as *design fixation.*

Conversely, presenting people with sets of diverse and creative ideas may stimulate pursuit of new directions of thought. Empirical work suggests that exposing people to novel ideas, as opposed to common ones, can result in more novel ideas [22]. This result might be attributable to the conforming effect: influenced by the novel examples, people incorporate the novel elements into their own ideas. An example with unfamiliar semantic properties prompt people to investigate ideas with those properties. Meanwhile, they might incorporate the ideas of their own with the examples, producing ideas in a new category that has not been explored by prior contributors. Building on this work, we looked into the effects of creativity — which combines novelty and value of ideas — and diversity of examples on idea generation. Our results support this finding: when presented with creative examples, people not only integrate examples into their ideas but also add their own spin to them and innovate in other ways.

The value of exposing people to diverse sets of examples is also supported by cognitive models of creativity. For example, the model known as *search for ideas in associative memory* (SIAM) describes idea generation as a two-stage process: knowledge activation and idea production [25, 24]. Ideas generated by others can act as external stimuli, activating material retrieval from memory for idea production. If the examples are diverse, one will retrieve a diverse set of raw material for idea synthesis and will be more likely to generate a diverse set of ideas. On the flip side, if the stimulus examples are homogenous, the generated ideas are likely to be homogenous, an exploration of semantically similar ideas in depth. Similar to SIAM, the Geneplore model [7] also views examples as an activator of preinventive forms, a raw material for ideas in the exploration phase. If the set of stimulus examples is diverse, the generated ideas are likely to be diverse. This prediction from both models is supported by empirical evidence: people generated more diverse ideas when exposed to ideas from a wide range of semantic categories [25].

Another mechanism at play may be social influence. Results from a study of social influence processes in group brainstorming suggested that people are affected by information about the performance of others [26, 20]. One can infer the overall performance of others from ideas that one sees and try to match with ideas of the same calibre. We expect that exposing people to high quality, creative examples generated by peers will raise their aspirations while showing them less creative examples would likely lower the quality of subsequent ideas.

To summarize, prior research suggests that exposing people to ideas of others may positively impact one's own ideation outcomes especially if 1) each idea is individually of high quality, meaning that it is both novel and appropriate; 2) the *set* of ideas that a person is exposed to covers many semantic categories.

These insights lead us to propose two interventions that a collective ideation system might employ: show examples of particularly good ideas generated by others, and show a diverse sets of examples. In line with prior work, we hypothesize that both of these interventions will increase both the *creativity* and the *diversity* of ideas generated. Our research seeks to integrate appropriate methods for applying these interventions at scale in a way that does not require expert intervention.

Prior work has already produced a number of scalable mechanisms for evaluating the quality of individual ideas. Some of them are already used in existing online idea generation platforms. For example, Quirky.com and OpenIDEO.com have used simple binary voting mechanisms to identify promising ideas. AllOurIdeas.org finds top ideas by deriving ranks of ideas from users' ranking of pairs of ideas [28]. In other works where more refined measures are needed, users rate creativity of ideas on different Likert scales [40, 32]. Xu and Bailey demonstrated a mechanism that helps ensure that voting results from non-experts match those of experts [35].

Scalably assessing the diversity of a set of ideas, however, has not been as well studied. We next dive into prior work on this branch of research.

Prior approaches for assessing diversity

Two approaches to quantifying diversity are common in prior work: labeling items with semantic categories, or evaluating subjective similarity between items independent of semantic categories.

Semantic categories

Manually created semantic categories have been used in prior research in creativity, either as ways to select a diverse set of ideas [25], or as a way to evaluate the diversity of creative artifacts [10, 15].

Efficient crowd-based mechanisms exist to label large collections of items with semantic categories or tags. Some take the approach of generating labels or tags for each individual item [18], while others produce hierarchical taxonomies capturing the semantic structure of the concepts represented in the item set [3, 2, 1]. Differences in contributors' mental models have been a persistent difficulty in semantic categorization even for experts [3]. A complete system for organizing ideas should include elements of both discrete semantic categories and continuous quantitative similarity, but because of difficulties we encountered with categorization approaches in pilot experiments, we chose to focus on continuous similarity in this work. Compared to these methods, our approach offers more fine-grained assessment of similar ideas.

Figure 1. An idea map generated by our system, showing emergent clusters of ideas around different themes and sentiments.

Idea similarity

An alternative approach to quantifying diversity is quantifying how items are *related*, such as evaluating the diversity of creative artifacts by collecting similarity judgements on a numerical scale between pairs of ideas [6]. However this approach requires on the order of the square of the number of ideas, making it less feasible for large idea collections. Moreover, accurate measures require that ratings be calibrated. Alternative approaches, like ours, consider pairwise rankings, which ask evaluators to choose one pair of items over the other and thus do not require calibration.

Machine learning techniques can help scale human judgments by inferring a latent structure for the items, such as clusters [13, 11] or a Euclidean space [31, 34]. Like the semantic categorization approaches, these approaches seek a compact representation of items rather than explicitly encoding all relationships, but the latent structure has no intrinsic semantics. In the next section, we detail how we build our method on top of these non-semantic techniques.

SCALABLE MECHANISM FOR IDENTIFYING DIVERSE SETS OF IDEAS USING AN IDEA MAP

We need a way to construct sets of diverse ideas, and ideally also to systematically compare the relative diversity of pairs of sets. We only consider methods that incorporate human input, because fully automated methods currently tend to capture only superficial similarity [1]. Because we intend to use this measure in systems that support collaborative ideation in large groups, it also must scale to a large pool of ideas. We seek approaches that can be sustained by a large number of small contributions from non-experts. Moreover, it should be robust to between-rater differences in mental models and judgment calibration.

We chose to adapt an existing machine-learning–based method [31] that uses triplet similarity comparisons to place ideas in a two-dimensional map. The map is constructed such that ideas perceived by people to be similar to each other are placed close together, while ideas perceived to be very different are placed far apart. Figure 1 shows an example of such an idea map generated with our system.

To generate an idea map, we first present groups of three ideas to human judges and ask them to pick which of B or C is more similar to A. Compared to similarity rating query (how similar is A to B), this triplet based representation of relative similarity is less cognitively taxing to judges [31]. We use t-Distributed Stochastic Triplet Embedding (t-STE) [34] to find an arrangement of ideas in a two-dimensional space (an "embedding") that is most consistent with the comparisons that people made. To minimize the number of comparisons that we ask people, we use an active learning heuristic [31] that estimates the expected gain in information about the position of an idea when comparing it to a particular pair of other ideas.

Informally, we expect the number of comparisons required to embed n ideas to be between $O(n)$ (scaling with the number of parameters of the model: 2 coordinates per idea) and $O(n \log n)$ (scaling with the number of comparisons required to find the closest existing idea for each new idea). For the most common ideas, even fewer comparisons should be required to determine that it is a common idea and thus unlikely to contribute much to the diversity of a set.

Because our idea maps are constructed such that the distances in the map reflect human perceptions of dissimilarity, we can use the maps to assess the uniqueness of an individual idea or the diversity of a subset of ideas. For example, we might define a unique idea as one that is far from other ideas. We use a simple metric of diversity: the diversity of a set of ideas is the mean distance between all pairs of those ideas.

IDEATION TASK AND SEED IDEAS

We collected an initial set of ideas from pilot studies. We used these ideas to validate our diversity measurement mechanism. We also used a subset of these as ideation examples for other participants in our main experiment.

Ideation Task

The ideation task we chose for this study was to generate birthday messages for a greeting card for Mary, a female firefighter who is about to turn 50. The instruction for the task is included in the appendix. We chose this task because it is short and simple, yet similar to the tasks of real creative professionals. Previous work in brainstorming and creativity has also used similar kinds of simple tasks [12, 33, 30, 22, 21].

Pilot experiments showed that the task was accessible to untrained participants, and that it elicited a wide variety of ideas of varying quality. We encouraged participants to generate lots of ideas within a 4-minute time limit and not to worry about the quality of the ideas. When they finished generating ideas, participants were asked to select a diverse set of up to 5 of their best ideas.

Participants

For our pilot ideation study, we recruited 209 participants from 2 sources: our own social networks (63 participants) and MTurk (146 participants). For all MTurk studies in this paper, we limited recruitment to U.S. residents who had completed at least 1,000 HITs[1] with greater than 95% approval rate. A participant could do the task only once. MTurk participants were paid $1.50 for their participation, while uncompensated participants were given feedback on how the quantity and diversity of the ideas they generated compared to that of other participants.

IDEA MAP ELICITATION AND VALIDATION

We then randomly selected 52 seed ideas from the 932 messages generated in the pilot studies from which to build an idea map.

Collecting Data to Build the Idea Map

We presented three birthday messages to each worker and asked him/her to pick which of the latter two ideas is more similar to/different from the first. We collected 2818 comparisons for 778 different triplets from 145 different people. We asked for multiple comparisons for the same triplets to enable subsequent analysis of inter-rater agreement. Many fewer comparisons would have been needed just to generate the idea map. The generated idea map is illustrated in Figure 1.

We then computed diversity scores for random subsets of the seed ideas. To illustrate, here are examples of idea sets to which our metric assigns *low* diversity scores:

- *"After 50 years your light is still burning strong", "We were worried you wouldn't be home on time, so we set your kitchen on fire.", "How many firefighters does it take to put out fifty candles?"*
- *"Wishing you a happy birthday!", "May the second 50 be as good as the first one!", "Happy Birthday!"*

While these idea sets get high diversity scores:

- *"Your cake is more lit up than a forest fire.", "Happy Birthday, Mary! 50 years is quite an accomplishment.", "Thank you for being there for us. Happy BD"*
- *"Have a fiery birthday bash!", "Time for Mary to start rolling down the hill!", "You have been one of a kind. Happy Birthday!"*

[1]For triplet comparison tasks, only a minimum of 100 approved HITs were required.

Validating the Idea Map

To validate the diversity ratings created by the idea map, we collected similarity ratings [6] for randomly chosen pairs of ideas in the example set. We then evaluated how well the measures of similarity captured in the idea map agreed with the perceptions of similarity provided by human raters.

We recruited 32 MTurk workers to rate similarity of pairs of messages on a scale of 1 (not at all similar) to 7 (very similar). Each rater rated about 30 pairs of messages. Each pair of messages was rated by three raters. We normalized (i.e., converted to z-scores) the ratings within each rater prior to aggregating the results. After excluding 4 workers whose answers to gold standard items indicated that they were not paying close attention to the task, we were left with 791 similarity ratings.

Krippendorff's alpha for the triplet comparison responses used to generate the idea map was 0.623 (nominal data) while the Krippendorff's alpha for the similarity ratings was 0.352 (interval data) indicating that comparison queries are, indeed, easier for participants to reach agreement on than rating queries.

Comparing mean human similarity ratings and our algorithm's diversity measure we found a significant correlation (Spearman correlation, $\rho = -0.5284$, $p < .0001$). Note that our measure captured diversity while the participants were asked to assess similarity, so the negative correlation coefficient is the desirable outcome.

Krippendorff's alpha between mean z-scored similarity ratings (standardized, sign of similarity inverted) and the diversity measure generated by our algorithm was 0.55. This is a high level of agreement considering that human raters agreed with each other only with alpha = 0.35.

MAIN EXPERIMENT

We designed our main experiment to explore the possibility of having a large scale collaborative idea generation system where judiciously chosen ideas from previous contributors are used as ideation examples for newcomers. Namely, we want to look at the effects of creativity and the diversity of ideation examples–algorithmically sampled from a pool of ideas based on intended intervention–on the creativity and diversity of ideas produced by later participants.

Tasks

We used the same ideation task as in the pilot study: generate birthday messages for Mary, a firefighter who is turning 50. With 20% probability, participants were asked to perform exactly the same task as in the pilot study, while the others were presented with an intervention: At the beginning of the ideation task, they were shown a set of 3 example ideas (which remained visible throughout the idea generation phase).

Interventions

We used the same set of 52 ideas generated in the pilot study as possible ideation examples. We varied the individual creativity of the ideation examples as well as the diversity of the sets of examples to investigate how these manipulations impacted individual idea generation.

Two trained coders from our research team independently rated the creativity of each birthday message on the scale from 1 (not creative) to 3 (very creative). We marked as "creative" the eleven messages that received scores of at least 2 from both coders. To illustrate, some of the most creative messages were: *"We were worried you wouldn't be home on time, so we set your kitchen on fire."* and *"How many firefighters does it take to put out a birthday cake?"*, while some of the least creative were: *"Hey Mary, It's Your Birthday, Happy Birthday!"* and *"Love and Happiness to Mary, one of the best!"*

Half of the participants who were presented with ideation examples saw messages sampled only from the pool of 11 creative messages (*Creative examples only* condition), while those in the other group saw ideation examples drawn uniformly from the entire pool of 52 ideas (*All examples* condition).

To investigate the impact of diversity of ideation examples on individual ideation outcomes, we used the diversity metric introduced in the previous section to assess the diversity of each randomly generated set of ideation examples presented in either of the creativity conditions. The mean diversity score in the All examples condition (M=9.85) was higher than in the Creative examples only condition (M=8.71), but the difference was small (Cohen's $d = 0.36$). The variances of diversity scores in the two creativity conditions were similar. There is no statistically significant difference of diversity of examples between the two conditions (t(116)=1.84, n.s.)

Procedure

As in the pilot experiment, each participants had 4 minutes to generate as many messages as they could, and they selected up to 5 as a diverse set of their best ideas.

To measure whether participants paid attention to the given examples (and thus could have been influenced by our manipulation), at the end of the experiment we showed them five ideation examples and asked them to select the ideas they saw during the ideation tasks. Three of the five ideas were the ideas that had been shown at the previous stage while the other two were distractors.

Design And Analysis

For the primary analysis we used a 2×2 full factorial between-subject design with the following factors and levels:

- *Creativity of ideation examples* {All examples, Creative examples only}
- *Diversity of ideation examples* (modeled as a continuous variable).

Our measures were:

- *Creativity of generated ideas* assessed by expert raters.

  Five experts from oDesk rated creativity of generated ideas. All experts were professional writers or editors. Each expert rated at least 300 messages on a scale from

1 (not at all creative) to 7 (very creative). Each message was rated by three experts. Our creativity measure is the average of each expert's normalized rating for each message.

- *Diversity of generated ideas* assessed by MTurk workers.

  We chose to use an established measure of diversity for our outcomes: as in the validation experiment, we used average pairwise similarity [6]. We randomly selected 15 participants from the baseline condition, 30 participants from the All examples conditions and 30 participants from the Creative examples only condition. For this measure, we only included participants who generated more than one idea. We only analyzed messages that participants included in their diverse sets of best messages. For each participant, we asked 3 workers to rate the similarity of each pair of generated ideas. As before, we converted worker ratings into z-scores prior to analysis. We flipped the sign of z-scored similarity ratings to derive diversity scores.

For each measure, we conducted an analysis of covariance including both factors and their interaction.

We also compared our interventions to the baseline condition. For the *Creativity of ideation examples* factor, we conducted an analysis of variance with one factor with three levels: baseline, All examples and Creative examples only. For the *Diversity of ideation examples* factor, we first created two discrete diversity conditions: Low diversity (which included the ideas generated by participants who saw the 25% least diverse sets of ideation examples) and High diversity. We then conducted an analysis of variance with one factor with three levels: baseline, Low diversity and High diversity.

Participants
We recruited 138 participants via MTurk to generate the ideas under the same recruitment limitation as in the pilot experiment.

Three participants did not complete the task and were excluded from further analysis. There were 27 participants in the baseline condition, 49 in the All examples condition and 59 in the Creative only examples condition.

Adjustments of Data
We filtered out participants who did not pay attention to the examples — those who answered correctly fewer than four out of five questions when asked which ideation examples they saw while ideating. After the exclusion, there were 27 participants in the baseline condition, 48 in the All examples condition and 52 in the Creative only examples conditions.

Results
127 participants generated 723 ideas and selected 564 ideas to be their best ideas. We only analyzed the 564 self-selected ideas. For the similarity assessment, 52 workers generated 1,581 ratings.

Creativity of generated ideas
We observed a significant main effect of creativity of ideation examples on the mean creativity of generated ideas, $F(1,96)=6.95, p = 0.0098$. Participants who were presented with Creative only ideation examples produced ideas that received higher mean creativity scores (M=0.21) than participants who were presented with randomly selected ideation examples (M=-0.079). However, the example diversity had no significant effect on the creativity of generated ideas ($F(1,96)=1.13$, n.s.).

In a three-way comparison between the baseline condition and the two creativity conditions (Figure 2a), we observed a significant main effect of condition on creativity of generated ideas ($F(2,124)=3.91$, $p = 0.0227$). Participants who were presented with Creative only ideation examples had higher scores (M=0.21) than people in the baseline condition (M=0.0912), while participants who were presented with random examples had lower scores (M=−0.079) than participants in the baseline condition. A post hoc Tukey HSD test showed that neither of these two pairwise differences was significant, however. The significant difference responsible for the main effect was between the Creative only and All examples conditions.

In a comparison of the baseline condition to participants who saw the High diversity and Low diversity example sets (Figure 2b), participants who saw diverse examples generated ideas with slightly lower creativity scores (M=0.0406) than participants in the baseline condition (M=0.0912) while those who saw least diverse examples had higher creativity scores (M=0.249) than participants in the baseline condition. However, this effect was not significant ($F(2,75) = 0.99$, n.s.).

Diversity of generated ideas
We observed a significant main effect of the example diversity on the mean diversity of generated examples ($F(1,56)=2.26$, $p = 0.028$) with diversity of generated ideas increasing with the increase in the diversity of examples. However, we observed no significant effect of diversity of examples on the creativity of generated ideas ($F(1,56)=3.33$, n.s.)

In a three-way comparison between the baseline condition and the two creativity conditions (Figure 2c), we observe no significant effect of the creativity of examples on the diversity of generated ideas ($F(2,72) = 0.34$, n.s.). The three way comparison including the baseline condition and the participants who saw the High diversity and the Low diversity examples (Figure 2d) also produced no significant effect ($F(2,41) = 1.56$, n.s.)

Additional Analyses
The results so far show that people generate creative ideas when they see creative examples and that they generate a diverse set of ideas when they see a set of diverse examples. But are people genuinely motivated and inspired by the examples (as suggested by [22, 26, 20]), or do they simply produce ideas that closely imitate the examples?

To answer this question, we measured how similar the generated ideas were to provided examples. Specifically, we asked 130 MTurk workers to rate similarity of generated messages to the examples using the same procedure as in the validation experiment. For each generated idea, we found the closest example out of the three examples that the participant saw. High

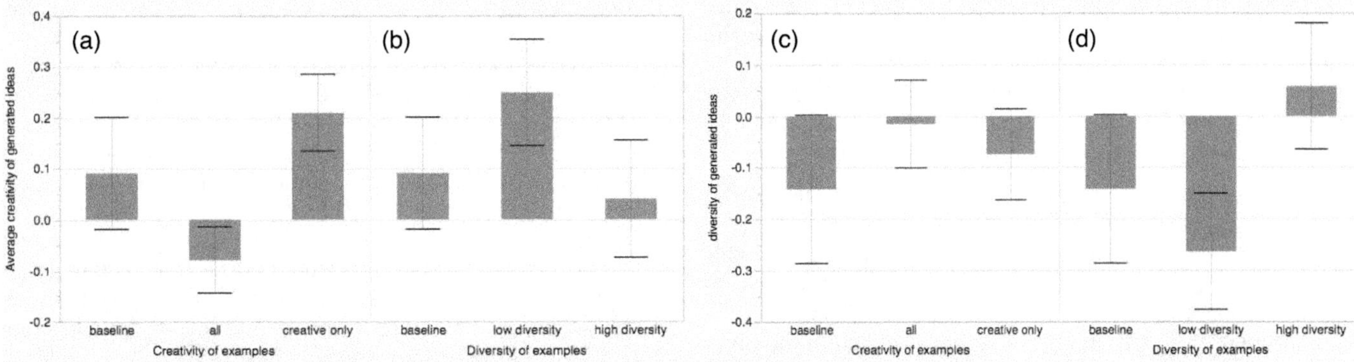

Figure 2. (a) Participants in the Creative Only condition generated more creative ideas than participants in the All condition. (b) There is no difference in average creativity of generated ideas across groups seeing different levels of diversity. (c) There is no difference in the diversity of generated ideas across groups seeing different levels of creativity. (d) Participants who saw examples with high diversity generated more diverse sets of ideas than those who saw examples with low diversity.

similarity to the closest example indicates high degree of fixation. Averaging similarity to the closest example for each of the participant's ideas, we get a measure of how similar the ideas this participant generated were to provided examples.

For the baseline condition (where no examples were given), we measured *self-fixation* [24] instead: that is, we measured how similar each new idea was to the closest of the ideas the participant had already generated. While not directly comparable to the fixation induced by externally-provided examples, this measure provides an informative baseline for evaluating how much external examples influenced each participant's ideas.

Rather than fixating participants, we found that good example sets actually did the opposite. Participants in the 'Creative only' condition generated ideas that were rated less similar to the examples (M=0.43) than the participants in the 'All examples' condition (M=0.65, t(98)=2.49, p=0.0143) (Figure 3a). Likewise, participants in the 'High diversity' condition generated ideas with lower similarity to most similar example (M=0.41) than the participants in the 'Low diversity' condition (M=0.68, t(46)=2.30, p=0.0260) (Figure 3b). In both interventions, the similarity to examples was lower than the self-fixation observed in the baseline condition (M=0.79).

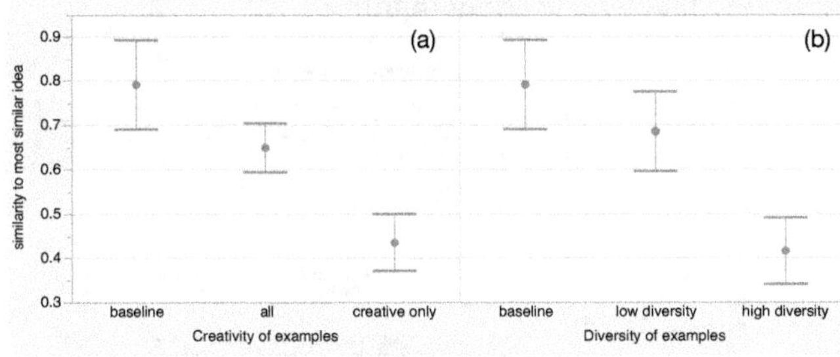

Figure 3. (a) Participants in the Creative only condition were less fixated than those in the baseline and the All examples condition. (b) Participants who saw a set of diverse examples were less fixated those in the baseline condition and those who saw a set of examples with low diversity.

We also manually inspected the ideas generated by 20 participants randomly sampled from all but the baseline condition and we compared the ideas they generated to the examples they were shown. The results suggest that participants often generated ideas seemingly entirely unrelated to the examples or added a new spin on an example (e.g., a participant who saw *"How many firefighters does it take to put out fifty candles?"* generated *"Get ready to call the fire department, we are about to light the 50 candles!!"*). They sometimes tried to combine ideas from more than one examples (e.g., a participant who saw *"We were worried you wouldn't be home on time, so we set your kitchen on fire."* and *"Remember, blow out the candles on your cake, don't use the hydrant!"* generated *"Mary! That's a lot of candles! If the place catches on fire, at least we won't have to call anyone!"*). There were cases of surface feature borrowing (e.g., a participant who saw *"Mary you could rescue me any day!"* generated *"mary you could put out fires for me any day"*), but such cases were rare.

These additional analyses suggest that there is no evidence that presenting participants with examples stifled their creativity. Instead, the results provide additional evidence that presenting people with particularly creative or particularly diverse ideas may help: those participants generated ideas that were more original (i.e., less similar to the examples) than the participants who saw more mundane examples.

DISCUSSION

Our studies demonstrate that we can select sets of diverse examples using a scalable method, and that people presented with the examples so selected generate more diverse ideas than those presented with random examples. Similarly, seeing examples of ideas that others deemed as particularly creative improves the creativity of generated ideas compared to seeing randomly selected examples.

Neither intervention resulted in ideation outcomes that were statistically different from not showing any examples at all, but the trends were illuminating: participants who saw creative ideation examples produced more creative ideas than those who saw no examples at all, but participants who saw randomly selected examples produced the least creative ideas. We observed a similar trend for diversity: participants who saw the 25% most diverse sets of examples produced more diverse ideas than participants in the baseline condition, while participants who saw the 25% least diverse sets of examples produced the least diverse sets of ideas of all participants.

Two possible explanations of the results arise. One explanation is that people get inspired by example ideas and incorporate these examples in their own idea generation. This explanation implies that we can guide how a community explores the space of possible ideas by exposing people to ideas in particular areas of interest. Another explanation involves social influence. People might infer the desirable properties of a set of ideas from the example set that they saw. Here, an example set provides information about the performance of others, encouraging participants to match the properties of their own ideas to example sets [26, 20]. While the two explanations involve very different mechanisms, they both support the value of presenting ideators with sets of creative and diverse examples. In order to understand which is the more likely cause, we need to conduct further investigation. For example, a future study can ask participants about the desirable properties of a set of generated ideas and how they use examples to infer whether they just try to match the properties of an example set or whether they actually incorporate the content of the examples into their own ideation.

Despite contrasting explanations, our results demonstrate the feasibility and value of using scalable crowd-powered mechanisms to improve large-scale online collaborative ideation platforms: instead of leaving contributors to manually browse through hundreds or thousands of previously generated ideas, these systems can help contributors by selecting manageable sets of particularly creative and diverse ideas.

One limitation of our work is that we have only studied the effect of showing people the raw ideas that others generated. Alternative interventions include presenting categories or schemas (as in [37]), or giving specific instructions about what kind of idea to generate.

Another limitation of our work is timing: the best time to present people with inspirational examples might be when they run out of their own ideas, not right at the beginning of the ideation process.

Finally, we suspect that the 4-minute time limit might prevent some participants from putting in enough cognitive effort to process examples deeply enough to benefit from them.

CONCLUSION

One challenge in designing large-scale collaborative online ideation platforms is how to leverage the ideas generated by others to effectively inspire future (or returning) contributors. As prior research suggests and as our results corroborate, showing people random examples of prior ideas has little positive impact on what new ideas people generate. However, prior research suggests that presenting people with sets of particularly creative or particularly diverse ideas is likely to improve the creativity and diversity of generated ideas.

These prior findings were not easy to act on: while there exist scalable crowd-powered methods for identifying the most creative ideas among thousands, the same is not true for finding sets of *diverse* ideas. In this paper, we contribute a scalable method for evaluating *diversity* of sets of examples by using simple similarity comparisons from non-expert contributors (members of the ideation community or an external crowd) to create an *idea map*. An idea map is a two-dimensional embedding of the ideas such that the pairwise distances between ideas on a map correspond to human perception of dissimilarity. Idea maps make it possible to sample sets of ideas of varying levels of diversity by picking ideas that are close to or far from each other.

The results of our study show that this method is indeed effective: participants who saw sets of diverse examples generated using our method produced more diverse ideas than participants who saw randomly selected examples. Our study also corroborates previous findings that showing people examples that others consider particularly creative results in more creative ideas than showing random ideas.

The goal of this work was to inform the design of future systems for supporting collaborative ideation at large scale. Our scalable method for assessing diversity, together with existing creativity metrics [28, 40, 32, 35], can enable creativity support systems to adjust which examples are shown to contributors and thus, as we have shown, modulate the quality and diversity of the ideas that they contribute. These methods, thanks to their lightweight nature, can be either outsourced to external micro-task market or embedded in the ideation workflow where contributors provide information about the example ideas for succeeding ideators.

ACKNOWLEDGMENTS

This work was funded in part by a Sloan Research Fellowship, gifts from Google and Adobe and awards from the National Science Foundation (IIS-1208382 and IIS-1217096). We thank Ofra Amir and Joel Chan for feedback on the manuscript.

APPENDIX

The figure below shows the instructions we used in the ideation task.

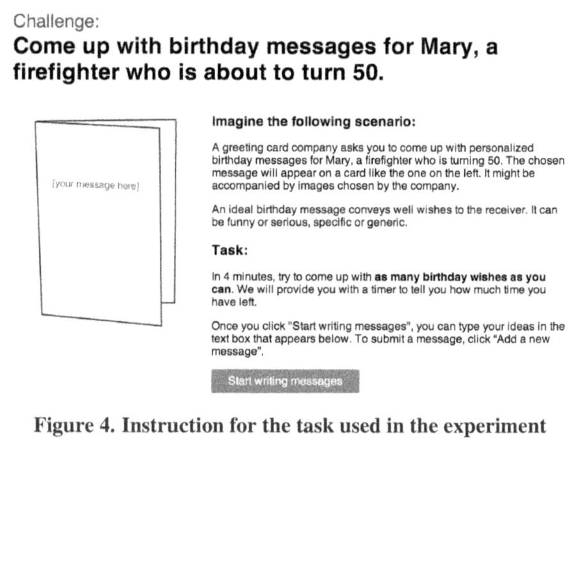

Figure 4. Instruction for the task used in the experiment

REFERENCES

1. André, P., Kittur, A., and Dow, S. P. Crowd synthesis: Extracting categories and clusters from complex data. In *Proceedings of the 17th ACM Conference on Computer Supported Cooperative Work & Social Computing*, CSCW '14, ACM (New York, NY, USA, 2014), 989–998.
2. Chilton, L. B., Kim, J., André, P., Cordeiro, F., Landay, J. A., Weld, D. S., Dow, S. P., Miller, R. C., and Zhang, H. Frenzy: Collaborative data organization for creating conference sessions. In *Proceedings of the 32Nd Annual ACM Conference on Human Factors in Computing Systems*, CHI '14, ACM (New York, NY, USA, 2014), 1255–1264.
3. Chilton, L. B., Little, G., Edge, D., Weld, D. S., and Landay, J. A. Cascade: Crowdsourcing taxonomy creation. In *Proceedings of the 2013 ACM annual conference on Human factors in computing systems*, ACM (2013), 1999–2008.
4. Dennis, A. R., and Valacich, J. S. Computer brainstorms: More heads are better than one. *Journal of Applied Psychology 78*, 4 (1993), 531.
5. Dow, S., Fortuna, J., Schwartz, D., Altringer, B., Schwartz, D., and Klemmer, S. Prototyping dynamics: Sharing multiple designs improves exploration, group rapport, and results. In *Proceedings of the SIGCHI Conference on Human Factors in Computing Systems*, CHI '11, ACM (New York, NY, USA, 2011), 2807–2816.
6. Dow, S., Glassco, A., Kass, J., Schwarz, M., Schwartz, D., and Klemmer, S. Parallel prototyping leads to better design results, more divergence, and increased self-efficacy. *Transactions on Computer-Human Interaction (TOCHI 17*, 4 (2010).
7. Finke, R. A., Ward, T. B., and Smith, S. M. *Creative cognition: Theory, research, and applications*. MIT press Cambridge, MA, 1992.
8. Gallupe, R. B., Bastianutti, L. M., and Cooper, W. H. Unblocking brainstorms. *Journal of Applied Psychology 76*, 1 (1991), 137.
9. Gallupe, R. B., Dennis, A. R., Cooper, W. H., Valacich, J. S., Bastianutti, L. M., and Nunamaker, J. F. Electronic brainstorming and group size. *Academy of Management Journal 35*, 2 (1992), 350–369.
10. Goldenberg, O., Larson, J. R., and Wiley, J. Goal instructions, response format, and idea generation in groups. *Small Group Research 44*, 3 (2013), 227–256.
11. Gomes, R. G., Welinder, P., Krause, A., and Perona, P. Crowdclustering. In *Advances in Neural Information Processing Systems 24*, J. Shawe-Taylor, R. Zemel, P. Bartlett, F. Pereira, and K. Weinberger, Eds. Curran Associates, Inc., 2011, 558–566.
12. Guilford, J. P. The nature of human intelligence.
13. Heikinheimo, H., and Ukkonen, A. The Crowd-Median Algorithm. *First AAAI Conference on Human ...* (2013), 69–77.
14. Herring, S., Chang, C.-C., Krantzler, J., and Bailey, B. Getting inspired!: understanding how and why examples are used in creative design practice. *CHI '09: Proceedings of the 27th international conference on Human factors in computing systems* (2009).
15. Jansson, D. G., and Smith, S. M. Design fixation. *Design Studies 12*, 1 (1991), 3–11.
16. Kohn, N. W., and Smith, S. M. Collaborative fixation: Effects of others' ideas on brainstorming. *Applied Cognitive Psychology 25*, 3 (2011), 359–371.
17. Kumar, R., Satyanarayan, A., Torres, C., Lim, M., Ahmad, S., Klemmer, S. R., and Talton, J. O. Webzeitgeist: design mining the web. In *CHI '13: Proceedings of the SIGCHI Conference on Human Factors in Computing Systems*, ACM Request Permissions (Apr. 2013).
18. Law, E., and Von Ahn, L. Input-agreement: a new mechanism for collecting data using human computation games. In *Proceedings of the SIGCHI Conference on Human Factors in Computing Systems*, ACM (2009), 1197–1206.
19. Lee, B., Srivastava, S., Kumar, R., Brafman, R., and Klemmer, S. R. Designing with interactive example galleries. In *CHI '10: Proceedings of the SIGCHI Conference on Human Factors in Computing Systems*, ACM Request Permissions (Apr. 2010).
20. Leggett Dugosh, K., and Paulus, P. B. Cognitive and social comparison processes in brainstorming. *Journal of Experimental Social Psychology 41*, 3 (May 2005), 313–320.
21. Lewis, S., Dontcheva, M., and Gerber, E. Affective computational priming and creativity. In *Proceedings of the SIGCHI Conference on Human Factors in Computing Systems*, ACM (2011), 735–744.
22. Marsh, R. L., Landau, J. D., and Hicks, J. L. How examples may (and may not) constrain creativity. *Memory & Cognition 24*, 5 (1996), 669–680.
23. Nagasundaram, M., and Dennis, A. R. When a group is not a group the cognitive foundation of group idea generation. *Small Group Research 24*, 4 (1993), 463–489.
24. Nijstad, B. A., and Stroebe, W. How the group affects the mind: A cognitive model of idea generation in groups. *Personality and Social Psychology ...* (2006).
25. Nijstad, B. A., Stroebe, W., and Lodewijkx, H. F. M. Cognitive stimulation and interference in groups: Exposure effects in an idea generation task. *Journal of Experimental Social Psychology 38*, 6 (2002), 535–544.
26. Paulus, P. B., and Dzindolet, M. T. Social influence processes in group brainstorming. *Journal of Personality and Social Psychology 64*, 4 (1993), 575.
27. Paulus, P. B., Kohn, N. W., and Arditti, L. E. Effects of quantity and quality instructions on brainstorming. *The Journal of Creative Behavior 45*, 1 (2011), 38–46.
28. Salganik, M. J., and Levy, K. E. Wiki surveys: Open and quantifiable social data collection. *arXiv preprint arXiv:1202.0500* (2012).
29. Singh, J., and Fleming, L. Lone inventors as sources of breakthroughs: Myth or reality? *Management Science 56*, 1 (2010), 41–56.
30. Smith, S. M., Ward, T. B., and Schumacher, J. S. Constraining effects of examples in a creative generation task. *Memory & Cognition 21*, 6 (1993), 837–845.
31. Tamuz, O., Liu, C., Belongie, S., Shamir, O., and Kalai, A. T. Adaptively Learning the Crowd Kernel. *arXiv.org* (May 2011).
32. Tanaka, Y., Sakamoto, Y., and Kusumi, T. conceptual combination versus critical combination: devising creative solutions using the sequential application of crowds. In *Proceedings of the 33rd Annual Conference of the Cognitive Science Society* (2011).
33. Torrance, E. P. *Torrance tests of creative thinking*. Personnel Press, Incorporated, 1968.
34. van der Maaten, L., and Weinberger, K. Stochastic triplet embedding. *Machine Learning for Signal Processing (MLSP), 2012 IEEE International Workshop on* (2012), 1–6.
35. Xu, A., and Bailey, B. A reference-based scoring model for increasing the findability of promising ideas in innovation pipelines. In *Proceedings of the ACM 2012 conference on Computer Supported Cooperative Work*, ACM (2012), 1183–1186.
36. Yu, L., Kittur, A., and Kraut, R. E. Distributed analogical idea generation: inventing with crowds. In *Proceedings of the 32nd annual ACM conference on Human factors in computing systems*, ACM (2014), 1245–1254.
37. Yu, L., Kittur, A., and Kraut, R. E. Distributed analogical idea generation: Inventing with crowds. In *Proceedings of the SIGCHI Conference on Human Factors in Computing Systems*, CHI '14, ACM (New York, NY, USA, 2014), 1245–1254.
38. Yu, L., Kittur, A., and Kraut, R. E. Searching for analogical ideas with crowds. In *Proceedings of the 32Nd Annual ACM Conference on Human Factors in Computing Systems*, CHI '14, ACM (New York, NY, USA, 2014), 1225–1234.
39. Yu, L., Kittur, A., and Kraut, R. E. Searching for analogical ideas with crowds. In *Proceedings of the 32Nd Annual ACM Conference on Human Factors in Computing Systems*, CHI '14, ACM (New York, NY, USA, 2014), 1225–1234.
40. Yu, L., and Nickerson, J. Cooks or cobblers?: crowd creativity through combination. *CHI '11: Proceedings of the 2011 annual conference on Human factors in computing systems* (2011).

Towards an Appropriable CSCW Tool Ecology: Lessons from the Greatest International Scavenger Hunt the World Has Ever Seen

Joseph A. Gonzales, Casey Fiesler, Amy Bruckman
GVU Center
Georgia Institute of Technology
85 5th St. NW, Atlanta, GA 30332 USA
jgonzales8@gatech.edu, casey.fiesler@gatech.edu, asb@cc.gatech.edu

ABSTRACT

If you could accomplish a complex, collaborative work task with one tool or many tools working together, which would you choose? In this paper, we present a case study of GISHWHES (the "Greatest International Scavenger Hunt the World Has Ever Seen"), an annual event in which teams spend one week completing complex, creative tasks. Building on the literature of IT ecosystems, we show how teams used different collections of tools to meet their communication needs. We interviewed team members, finding that most teams used multiple tools during GISHWHES. By analyzing which tools they chose over others for each function, we gain insight into the strengths and weaknesses of these tools, and the complexity surrounding work processes. In light of this complexity, this research highlights the importance of designing appropriable tools that can work with unanticipated workflows and mesh well with other tools in a communicative ecology.

Author Keywords
Collaboration, GISHWHES, Communicative Ecology, Appropriability, Pipeline, Facebook

ACM Classification Keywords
H.5.3 **[Information Interfaces and Presentation]**: Group and Organization Interfaces --- *collaborative computing; computer-supported cooperative work; theory and models; web-based interaction.*

General Terms
Human Factors, Management, Theory

ACM 978-1-4503-2922-4/15/03…$15.00.
http://dx.doi.org/10.1145/2675133.2675240

INTRODUCTION

As CSCW researchers and designers, we often handcraft tools and applications for specific environments. We meticulously gather requirements and analyze needs. We pour sweat equity into building these systems and then reach out to communities to adopt our software. Then we collect data in hopes of gaining insight into the efficacy of our creations.

In the wild, however, collaborators often use several tools. Lightweight tools like email or spreadsheets might complement special-purpose systems. In this study, we interviewed participants in a massive online scavenger hunt. In a thematic analysis of this data, we focus on how these groups coordinated and collaborated in order to accomplish tasks. All but one of our interview participants reported the use of multiple tools in the course of the scavenger hunt. These included familiar tools such as Facebook, Excel, email, and Google Docs, as well as Pipeline, a tool designed specifically to help teams manage online creative collaborations. We conclude that it is increasingly anachronistic to think of user needs as being supported by a single tool, and that key design challenges lie in understanding the complexity of these communicative ecologies.

This paper offers a detailed account of tool use for a complex, creative-collaboration environment. Additionally, we contribute a rich description of that environment, GISHWES (pronounced "GISH-wehz"[1]), as an intriguing example of Internet-supported, collaborative creativity. Using GISHWHES as an example, we demonstrate how to analyze sources of complexity within CSCW environments based on research from the information technology literature. Finally, we point out appropriation design principles in action, and suggest ways those principles can help improve support for complex collaboration.

---

1 http://whatisgishwhes.wordpress.com/frequently-asked-questions/

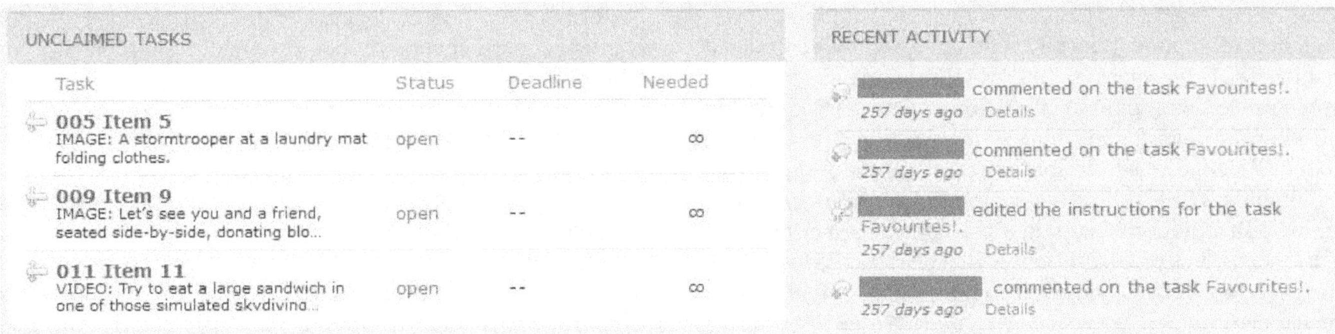

Figure 1. In Pipeline, tasks are tracked on the left, while team member activity is shown on the right.

BACKGROUND

GISHWHES

GISHWHES[2] (or The Greatest Scavenger Hunt the World Has Ever Seen) was created in 2011 by Misha Collins, a popular actor from the television show *Supernatural*. The scavenger hunt functions in part to raise money and awareness for Collins' non-profit organization Random Acts, which is dedicated to spreading "one random act of kindness at a time." Since it began in 2011 there have been three GISHWHES competitions. For this study, we focused on GISHWHES 2013, which included 155 scavenger hunt items (also referred to as *tasks*). Each item is a request for an image or a video with a focus on producing art and/or helping others. For example, item #19 was:

> IMAGE: Attend a ballet class or "spinning" cycling class wearing full scuba gear -flippers, mask, tanks and all. *(70 points)*

While item #21 was:

> VIDEO: Find an example of someone who engages in sustained generosity in your community and then do something nice for them. For example there is an 82-year-old Connecticut barber who always offers free haircuts to the homeless in exchange for hugs. You could find this barber and polish his shoes. Find someone similar in your own community and do something nice for them. In the video, you must describe what the person does for their community, and then show what your kind gesture toward them is. *(32 points)*

GISHWHES draws a global audience of individuals who want to have fun and help others. As explained on its 'What Is? ' page:

> Gishwhes believes that "normalcy" is overrated and that true "living" can be found hidden under the rocks of community artistic creation and in acts of artistic sublime public performances. More importantly, we are all artists and have gifts for society no matter what our capabilities or talents. And most importantly, cheese is not a good sewing material.[3]

GISHWHES is also a highly collaborative activity. Everyone who participates in GISHWHES does so on a team and in 2013 teams consisted of fifteen participants. Participants joined as groups or individuals, and the GISHWHES staff would combine these until each team had fifteen members. Teams had one week to complete as many items as possible. After GISHWHES ended, a panel of judges scored each submitted item for creativity and completeness. The first-place team for 2013 received "a trip to Vancouver, Canada for a chartered seaplane flight to a majestic island with Misha Collins for fish stew, a séance, and a Viking surprise."

At the end of the hunt photo submissions that impressed the judges were published in a coffee table book. While official participation numbers for the 2013 hunt have not been released, the previous year's hunt had 14,580 participants, and at the time of this writing is recognized by the Guinness Book of World Records as the world's largest media scavenger hunt.[4]

Pipeline

We became interested in GISHWHES in 2012 when participants adopted a tool called Pipeline[5] (see Figure 1). Pipeline was created to support collaboration by non-co-located groups in order to study teams of artists who created Flash animations for the website Newgrounds [13]. Pipeline helped meet the needs of Flash animators and was later released as free and open-source software so that it could benefit other communities that relied on creative collaboration.

One of the authors of this study participated in GISHWHES 2012, using Pipeline to coordinate with her team, and word of mouth resulted in four additional teams making at least

[2] http://www.gishwhes.com

[3] http://www.gishwhes.com/g_blog/what-is-gishwhes/

[4] http://www.guinnessworldrecords.com/world-records/1000/largest-media-scavenger-hunt

[5] http://pipeline.cc.gatech.edu

some use of Pipeline. The Flash animators that Pipeline was designed to support typically work in a highly centralized fashion [12]. In contrast, GISHWHES teams are typically decentralized with individuals claiming particular items and working on them largely independently. Since one design goal of Pipeline was to enable a more decentralized process, we thought GISHWHES would provide insight into how online collaboration occurs in other contexts. We therefore did a needs analysis based on 2012 GISHWHES use, with an eye towards a more in depth study of a future GISHWHES.

As part of this needs analysis, we interviewed four of these scavenger hunt participants whose teams used Pipeline. Based on feedback about their use, we added features that we thought would better support their processes. For example, we noticed that some teams would use lightweight chat applications to keep in touch during GISHWHES, so we built in a minimalistic chat room. We also redesigned the way that tasks showed in the dashboard in order to provide clarity on tasks statuses, and we created a utility that would allow us to upload the GISHWHES task list for teams, saving them the trouble of having to create each task manually.

Following our feature additions to Pipeline, we decided to explore these issues further by studying GISHWHES 2013. Interested more broadly in the communicative ecology of each team, we did not limit our analysis to only participants who used Pipeline.

RELATED WORK

Scavenger Hunts

Arguably the most famous CSCW-related scavenger hunt was the 2009 DARPA Network Challenge. During this challenge teams had to locate ten red balloons, which were dispersed around the United States. Teams demonstrated that they could solve "impossible" problems [19] with the use of multiple online tools and strategies. Although financial incentives were used during this scavenger hunt [16], one of the key findings by DARPA was that "altruistic motives" were enough to initiate "successful recruitment and mobilization efforts" [19].

Besides tackling geo-location problems, scavenger hunts have furthered education efforts and provided entertainment. Universities have created initiatives to create interest in CS for K-12 students [24] and to address CS retention in undergraduate students [22]. Other schools like the University of Chicago and MIT have used scavenger hunts[6,7] to build light-hearted and beloved traditions. Computer-supported scavenger hunts are an interesting example of a complex, collaborative task. Hunts are often performed by non-co-located individuals, and typically challenge participants to be resourceful in their use of CSCW tools.

Sources of Ecosystem Complexity

An important feature in computer-supported scavenger hunts is the complexity introduced by multiple tools and collaboration requirements. In a study of complexity in information technology environments, Lentz et al. studied how these environments evolved into complex ecosystems over time [11]. They found that four factors caused complexity in IT ecosystems. These factors inform our analysis of complexity in the GISHWHES environment.

(1) *Poorly interlocked job responsibilities.* Job responsibilities and degree of worker specialization differ within and across organizations, resulting in tool capabilities that rarely map well to actual practices.

(2) *Ad-hoc organizational procedures.* Similar to job responsibilities, processes and organizational structures can develop organically.

(3) *Environment diversity.* IT environments are a mixture of many tools published by different vendors. This introduces a challenge when designing a new tool to join the mix.

(4) *Specialized tool preferences.* Users often have strong preferences for particular types of tools—for example, GUI interfaces versus command-line versions. Two workers with the same responsibilities may accomplish their work in different ways.

Volunteers participating in a scavenger hunt are clearly different from IT workers; however, as we will see, similar issues describe the complexity within GISHWHES teams.

Communicative Ecology

One source of this complexity is that GISHWHES teams typically use many tools in accomplishing tasks. The field of communicative ecology [20] sheds light on how groups of people use multiple tools for their communication needs. Researchers like Turner et al. have used communication ecology to explain how tool use is shaped by other tools used in the workplace [23]. Additionally, Dittrich and Giuffrida have built off of Turner et al.'s work to show that instant messaging applications can act as a glue between communication channels [5], while Johri has shown that blogs and IRC can mostly replace email in a small technology firm [10]. An ecologies approach is not limited to the digital world but can also provide insights into interaction that bridges digital and embodied modes [14].

[6] http://scavhunt.uchicago.edu/index.html

[7] http://www.mit.edu/~puzzle/

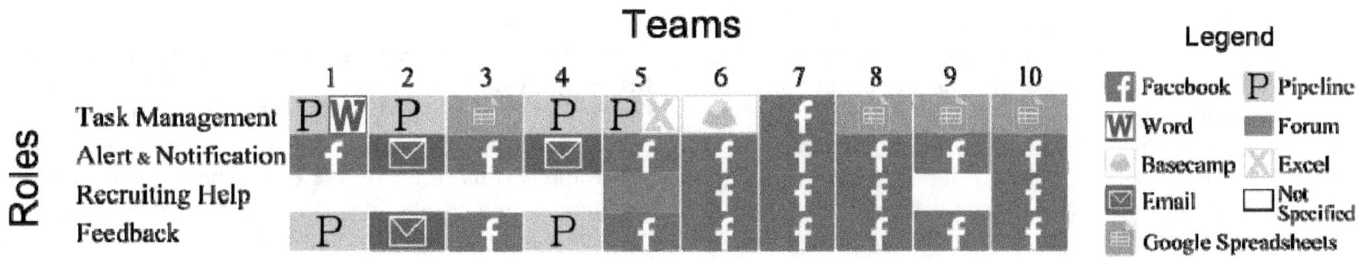

Figure 2. Matrix of tools used during GISHWHES.

While several of the studies above include all communication channels (including face-to-face and telephone use), for this study we focused on the software tools used within each GISHWHES group.

Appropriation

Designing software for complex, creative-collaboration environments is challenging. One promising approach is designing for *appropriation*. Appropriation is the study of how technology is often adapted or repurposed to solve problems it was never intended to address [6,7,21]. Appropriation is important because it acknowledges both the social and technical reasons that people adopt certain technologies [7,15]. There have been a number of studies of appropriation, such as Orlikowski's early work on Lotus Notes [15]. Quinones studied how workers adopted different tools, and observed that an individual taking on the role of a "shepherd" helped support tool adoption [17]. Additionally, Dix presented heuristics for supporting appropriation:

- Allow interpretation: Provide system elements without a fixed meaning.
- Provide visibility: Make how the system works clear to the user, so the user can devise his/her own uses.
- Expose intentions: Make the purpose of the system clear, to make it easier for users to subvert that purpose.
- Support not control: "Provide necessary functions so the user can achieve the task, but not drive the users through the steps."
- Plugability and configuration: Allow parts to be combined in different ways.
- Encourage sharing: Help users to share appropriation success stories.
- Learn from appropriation. [6]

Dix's ideas about appropriation shed light on user behavior we observed in GISHWHES, and also highlight ways we could better support this kind of collaborative practice in the future.

METHODS

For this study, we performed ten semi-structured interviews with fourteen individuals who participated in GISHWHES 2013. These individuals represented ten different teams. Interviews were one-on-one with the exception of one team for which five team members participated in a group interview. Initial interviews were conducted by phone/voice chat, and follow-up questions sent by email. Because GISHWHES is a creative activity and many of our participants view themselves as artists, it would be potentially unethical to deny them credit for this work [3]. Therefore, we used real names instead of pseudonyms if requested by our participants. Pseudonyms are denoted with an asterisk (*). We also analyzed their online activity and artifacts they created, where possible.

We recruited participants from Tumblr and other personal blogs if they showed evidence that they participated in GISHWHES 2013. We also emailed teams with an invitation to be interviewed if they used Pipeline during GISHWHES. Out of the seven teams who used Pipeline to participate in GISHWHES, representatives from four teams agreed to participate in an interview. Interview participants also came from six additional teams that did not use Pipeline, for a total of ten represented teams.

Our participants consisted of thirteen females and one male, between the ages of seventeen and forty-nine. According to our participants, the majority of GISHWHES participants found out about the scavenger hunt through Misha Collins because they or a friend were members of the fandom community for his television show. This gender breakdown is not unusual for these types of communities. Previous work has shown similar fandoms had female membership composition as high as ninety percent [1] , while other work has shown the predominant contribution by women to media fandom [18]. Although the Internet has caused these demographics to become more diverse over time [18], the demographics of our study reflects the target audience of *Supernatural's* parent network [4].

Our semi-structured interviews contained questions regarding the following topics: tasks, team composition, team dynamics, leadership, tool use, team workflows, conflict resolution, and public perceptions. Our goal was to gain a better understanding of how GISHWHES teams interact with tools, workflows, and each other during the competition. After transcribing the interviews, the first part of our analysis was to break up tool use by team. Next, we conducted a thematic analysis [2] to determine the *software roles* that each tool provided for the teams. One researcher performed the coding, which underwent multiple iterations. All of the researchers discussed the codes during the thematic analysis. Although our sample size is small, Guest et al. have shown that saturation can occur with "high-level, overarching themes" in as few as six interviews [9].

RESULTS

The ten teams we studied made use of various combinations of eight different tools (see Figure 2). These included three productivity tools (Microsoft Word, Microsoft Excel, Google Spreadsheets), three communication tools (Facebook, neighborhood online forum, email), and two more comprehensive collaboration tools: Basecamp, which is a web-based project management tool, and Pipeline.

Pipeline was designed specifically to help leaders in online collaborative groups by redistributing some of their responsibilities among the group [13]. Its major functionality is as a task management and feedback system. Every team that used Pipeline for GISHWHES created a new project for their team. The projects were all private, which meant that only invited members would be able to participate in the project. Team members would create *tasks*, which mirrored the GISHWHES item list. Within a task, team members could claim a task, and upload an image or a video as a *contribution.* While they could leave feedback at the contribution level, several teams used the chat room to leave feedback for their team. Statuses such as *open* or *closed* could be specified at the task level. Each project also came with a discussion forum to facilitate communication.

In the overall GISHWHES task completion workflow we observed, first teams must determine which team member will complete a given task. Next, one or more team members must actually perform the task, leading to the generation of either images or video. Task performers may then solicit feedback. In some cases, this step is skipped—particularly towards the end of the GISHWHES window as time runs short. Finally, someone must upload the task to Imgur (for images) or YouTube (for videos), and then officially submit to the GISHWHES webpage.

In analyzing this workflow, we observed four primary software roles:

- Task management
- Alert and notification
- Soliciting help
- Feedback

We will now look at these roles in detail and describe how teams incorporated each.

Task Management

Since teams were managing a list of 155 items, shared by fifteen individuals, every team mentioned a need to keep track of which tasks were claimed by whom and the status of each task (e.g., in progress, submitted, etc.). Interestingly, this software role experienced a shift in tools for some of our teams. Figure 3 illustrates tool use at the beginning of GISHWHES compared to the tools being used by the end of GISHWHES.

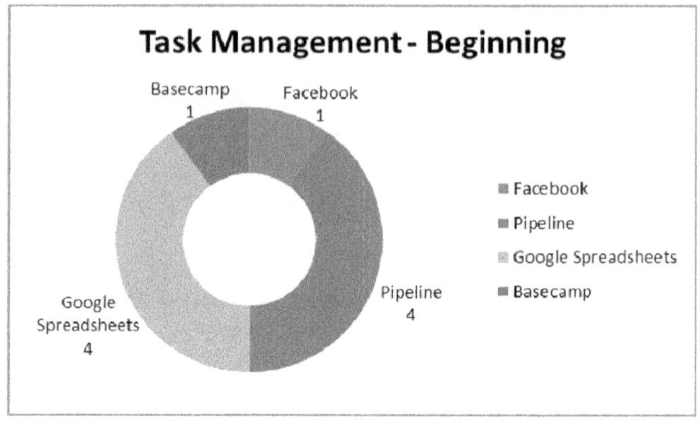

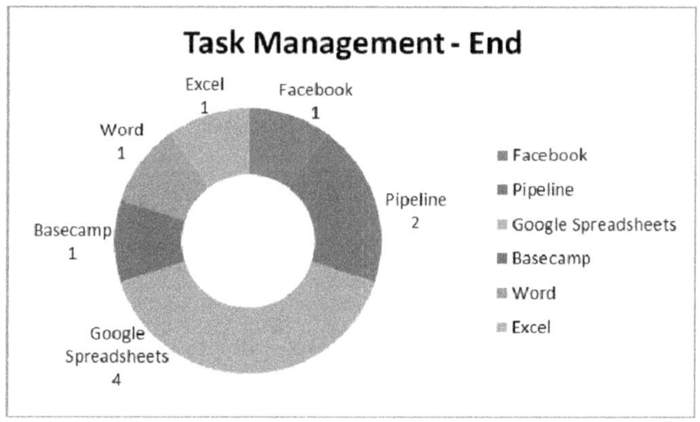

Figure 3. Task Management Tools Throughout GISHWHES.

The teams that we interviewed who used Pipeline to track task management reported a positive experience. For example, when Amy (Team 2) was asked to describe her experience with Pipeline, she responded:

I felt that it was really cool, because otherwise, I don't know how we would have kept track of who was doing what tasks because it was such a long list. This way, it was separated out. So, it told me what I had said I would do and it told me what had already been claimed. So, it was just very easy. ~ Amy (Team 2)

However, even though participants reported a good experience with Pipeline, we noticed that use of the tool broke down over the course of GISHWHES. Team 1, for example, eventually reduced their use of Pipeline because as the deadline for GISHWHES loomed near they shifted focus to submitting images and videos—completely omitting the step where they would request feedback before submitting their tasks:

Pipeline was fantastic. It was nice to see them [pictures] all there and everything. I think towards the end, we were so busy that we stopped using it. We ended up sending them [pictures] directly to Imgur. I'd say like maybe after the last third of the week, those last couple of days, because tasks stopped getting closed on Pipeline. We ended up just skipping straight to where the submission was, because people weren't having the time to go on there and look at photos anymore. ...So, unfortunately, we ran out of time to be reviewing each other, and we just trusted each other's judgment. ...On Facebook we'd say, "I got this item done," and, "I got this item done," and Sarah would be updating every single time on the Word document.* ~ Rae (Team 1)

Team 1 originally used Pipeline for two different software roles (task management and feedback), but because they stopped using Pipeline for one of these roles (feedback), the cost of maintaining use for the one remaining role was too great. Consequently, Team 1 switched to a more lightweight tool (Microsoft Word) to handle task management.

Team 5 also decreased their use of Pipeline during GISHWHES when half of their team experienced issues using Pipeline. Team 5 was composed of two sub-teams—one located in the U.S. and one located in Canada. The Canadian sub-team expressed difficulty with uploading images/videos to Pipeline, as well as with performing workflows like assigning a task. As a result, both sub-teams shared an Excel spreadsheet stored on a Google Drive to handle task management, using color coding to denote sub-teams.

It is worth noting that the Excel spreadsheet assigned each task to one of the sub-teams instead of individuals. This is something that is not currently supported by Pipeline (all tasks must be assigned to an individual). It is also interesting to note that the U.S. sub-team did not completely abandon Pipeline, as they still were using it up until the completion of GISHWHES.

Besides Excel, other teams chose to use spreadsheets for task management. Four teams used Google Spreadsheets, largely because of the ability to co-edit. Similar to Team 5, multiple teams reported using color coding in their spreadsheets:

It [task list] was a document that we could edit. Carol [team leader] was real organized. She had it all color-coded. So, when you chose it, you typed it in red and put your name. Then when you accomplished it, you changed it to green and put the date.* ~ Deborah (Team 10)

Team 9 displayed an amazing amount of effort in constructing a Google spreadsheet for task management:

It took us two months of work into the Google Doc, because we wanted to know how the layout is and how easy it is to read. We also did a test run with a few of our friends here. If they couldn't get it, then we fixed it and, you know, asked their opinions. It was like color coordinated. ... If you wanted to do an item, you would like claim it by putting your name beside it and changing the color of the item on the Google Doc. So, the color code was like red/yellow/green, and they all meant something different. Then you just have your name with it. If more than one person was doing it, there were multiple names. Whoever got it done, we would look at it and we would choose which one was best if there were multiples of one. ~ Team 9

The other project management tool that was used to help teams keep track of assignment and progression was Basecamp. The only team to use Basecamp was Team 6, and they reported a positive experience:

... the Basecamp worked fantastically. I actually found that I did start a Pipeline account before GISHWHES started because I had intended on using it. Then somebody brought up Basecamp and they had used it before. So we wound up using it. ~ Ashley (Team 6)

The interesting difference between Pipeline use and Basecamp use was that the team who used Basecamp only created one account for the entire team, instead of individual accounts for each team member:

We used the same email or password for our YouTube channel, for our Imgur account, and for the Basecamp and anything else just so it was easier for everybody to say, 'Okay. Well, we can log on and have all of the same information.' ~ Ashley (Team 6)

Team 6 was able to use Basecamp effectively as a productivity tool even though they could not rely on automatically tracking each user's unique activity. Sharing login credentials was common for other teams when creating Imgur, YouTube and Google accounts.

Team 7 was the only team that used Facebook to handle task management. They accomplished this by creating a Facebook document on their private group page. The Facebook document was a simple list of every GISHWHES task. Facebook documents do not allow co-editing like Google Spreadsheets; however, this was not a problem because most of the members were in different time zones and were not online at the same time. While Team 7 had a positive experience using Facebook for task management, Team 9 reported trying to use Facebook for task management with suboptimal results. This was due to information that would get "buried" over the duration of GISHWHES. This caused Team 9 to adopt Google Spreadsheets, which offered more functionality and reportedly a better experience.

Alert and Notification

Besides tracking the progress of every task, team members also need a way to communicate status changes with the group. They have to communicate when tasks are claimed, or when a team member will not be able to complete a task that they had previously claimed.

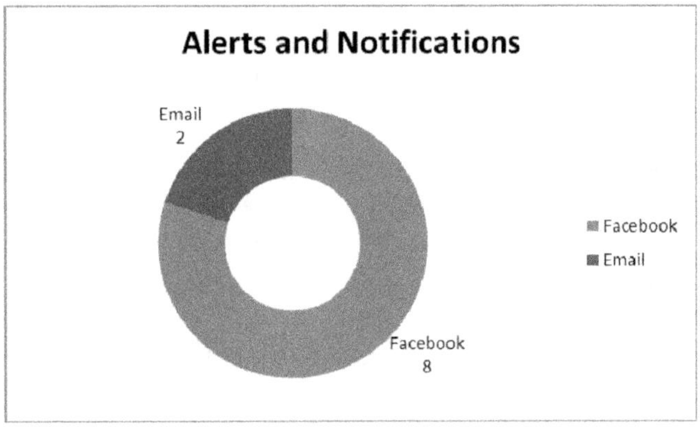

Figure 4. Alert and Notification Tools.

Eight out of ten teams reported using Facebook (see Figure 4) for alerts and notifications, making it the most popular tool for teams to communicate.

We used it [Facebook] to communicate with people because with the time difference, and sometimes people just don't get emails or just don't check their email. I'm pretty diligent about checking all my email, but I don't trust everyone else to be as diligent as I am. But everyone checks their Facebook, especially if you get the little notification saying something's been posted. So, we used that just to keep everyone updated on what we had done and remind people to update the excel spreadsheet as we were going. ~ Sandra* (Team 5)

One factor that may be able to account for Facebook's popularity involves the convenience of receiving Facebook updates on mobile phones:

And with the Facebook page, I have Facebook connected to my phone. So, whenever somebody would post something, it would go off, and I could check it. If it was important, I could get back. If not, whenever I get a chance. ~ Ashley (Team 6)

So, there's a lot of time where someone's sleeping and someone's up. People on my team really like to communicate. There's a lot of communication happening. So, my phone was going off all the time where people were communicating across Facebook. ~ Amy S. (Team 3)

It was mostly through posts, but everybody had Facebook on their phone. We were able to keep in almost instant contact like chat through doing posts, because we were all carrying our phones around and doing Facebook on our phone while we were doing items. ~ Deborah (Team 10)

The remaining two teams who participated in our interviews mentioned using emails for alerts and notifications. Team 2, for example, explained how staying connected through email was helpful for sending updates, as well as receiving feedback:

She [team leader] kind of made sure from the beginning when the team list came out, she was the first person to email everybody. When the list itself actually came up, she was like trying to get everybody to be organized and see who was going to take what task. Let's see. Then like throughout the day, she would just like send out updates of what she was doing, like email us, and show us what she had done, and ask if we liked it. ~ Amy (Team 2)

Soliciting Help

Another key software role is soliciting help. Many of the GISHWHES tasks required access to unusual items or places (for example, item #14 was a photograph of someone dressed as The Flash inside the large hadron collider tunnel), and could not be accomplished without a geographically diverse group. Therefore, participants leveraged their networks of strong and weak ties [8] to provide information, loan items, and solicit participation from others. To support this process, the most popular tool was Facebook, which four teams reported using (see Figure 5). One team mentioned that they created a post on a neighborhood online forum, but did not receive any responses. Five of the teams did not specify the act of recruiting help online, but we do not believe this omission is conclusive that another team member did not solicit help.

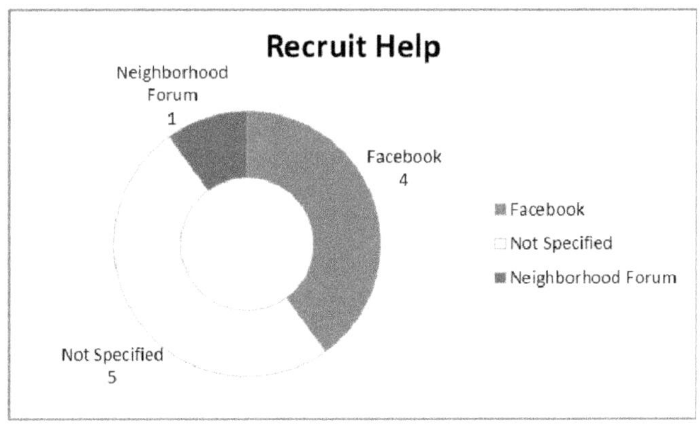

Figure 5. Recruitment Tools.

Soliciting help for a GISHWHES task from your social network can offer the additional benefit of strengthening existing relationships. As an example, item #119 requires access to an old typewriter:

Item #119 - *IMAGE: Type out your team's one-page manifesto on an old, mechanical typewriter. The page must be legible and the bottom of it must be partially fed into the typewriter. (16 POINTS)*

Jenna(Team 7) described how she completed this challenge:

I use Facebook for a lot of stuff. So, one of them was writing your team's manifesto on an old typewriter, a manual typewriter. So, I got on Facebook and just said... Actually, it happened multiple times that I needed something. I'd be like, "Hey, I'm asking for more help with GISHWHES. Who has an old typewriter that you can bring over to my house? I'll make you coffee in payment." ~ Jenna (Team 7)

Figure 6. Submission by Team 7 for Item #119 – Type out your team's one page manifesto on an old, mechanical typewriter. *(16 points)* ©Jenna Boring

After soliciting help on Facebook, it did not take long before one of her friends volunteered to help out:

... first my mother-in-law said she had one. But then she couldn't find it. Then another friend of mine who's pretty hipster (she's into the old stuff and we hadn't seen each other for a long time), she's like, "I'll bring it over if you make lunch and we can hang out for a little. (Laughter)" ~ Jenna (Team 7)

By reconnecting with her friend, she was able to nurture a weak tie [8] that had remained inactive for a while. Other teams also mentioned using Facebook to gather support from both their strong and weak ties:

I would go on Facebook and I'd say, "Okay, everybody. I desperately need a trench coat" or whatever I needed. Then people could... I mean, there were some things that people just didn't have and we weren't able to use. But a lot of things, somebody in my Facebook family and local friends were able to help me find. ~ Deborah (Team 10)

In another example, Ashley (Team 6) recounted how she was able to convince her Facebook connections to follow the account of an imaginary alarm clock that she created on Twitter, for completion of a task:

My favorite thing that we did with social media was we had to do the Twitter alarm clock. So, I was the Twitter alarm clock. So, I went on Facebook and I posted it, because I had warned everybody, like all my friends and family like, "Listen. Things are going to get crazy and I'm going to demand that you do things, and you need to do them." (Laughter) So, I went on Facebook and I was like, "Listen. I need you to go follow me at Misha, the Alarm Clock." They're like, "What?" I was like, "I'm an alarm clock. Just go with it." (Laughter) Like I had teachers from when I was in high school, family, everybody. They went to Twitter and they followed me for all my crazy tweets as an alarm clock just so I could get to my 200 followers that I needed. I wound up with like 400. I still have 415 followers. (Laughter) ~ Ashley (Team 6)

Notice that even though the participant was soliciting participation on Twitter, she used Facebook to recruit those participants.

Besides using Facebook to reach friends and family, some teams also used Facebook to identify completely new social networks to ask for help. Item #5 required teams to take a picture of a member at a Laundromat wearing a *Star Wars* Stormtrooper costume. When Deborah (Team 10) reached out in person to a local game store, they were pointed back to social media instead:

So, I went to our local gamer store. I said, "Hey, any of you guys have a Stormtrooper costume?" I think was actually how I approached it. They were like, "No, but you want to check out..." And they told me the name of the group, which I guess is an international group, or Star Wars costume enthusiasts or whatever. So, I put that on the Facebook group while I was still out and about at stores for a different thing. By the time I got home, someone was like, "Yeah! So, I got in touch with the local group, and they're going to call me back." So, we went on with other things and we were accomplishing other tasks while that one waited on a call back that didn't arrive. ~ Lauren (Team 8)

These are just a couple of the ways in which Facebook was utilized to complete tasks. In the next section we will discuss how Facebook was used as a way for teams to share feedback about GISHWHES submissions.

Feedback

Finally, all teams reported using a process that allowed an individual to receive feedback from the rest of the team before an image or video was submitted. Seven out of the ten teams reported using Facebook in order to give feedback to other members (see Figure 7).

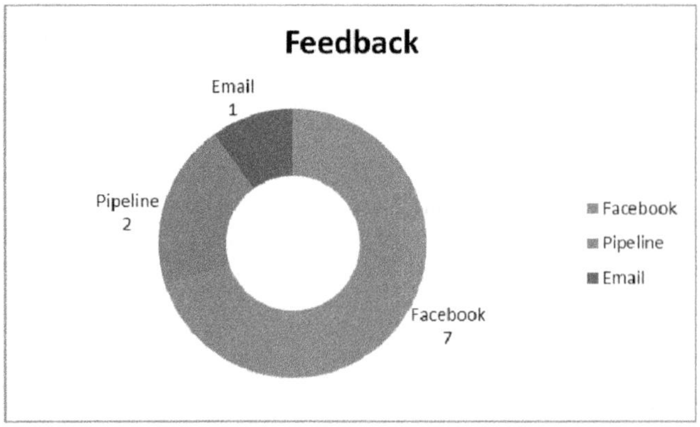

Figure 7. Feedback Tools

Two teams mentioned using Pipeline in order to leave feedback for other team members. However, those who used Pipeline did not always use the features that were specifically designed for giving and receiving feedback. Instead, they repurposed the team chat room for this function:

So, it was really easy for them to leave their feedback in that chat box. ...We rarely ever actually left feedback where it suggests you leave feedback, perhaps like in the actual threads that you can create. We never used those hardly ever. I know that there's a checkbox where you can select that you would like feedback on that photo. I think people would select it, but actual comments were rarely left. It was more of everyone would just leave a chat note on the item they had reviewed. ~ Rae (Team 1)

Team 2 was the only team that reported using email in order to give feedback. In the first version of their feedback workflow, team members who completed a task emailed their team to request that everyone approve their contribution before it was submitted to GISHWHES. This workflow proved inefficient and team members did not know how many approvals to wait for before submitting a task. The team leader of Team 2 quickly adjusted the workflow to allow team members to turn in submissions as soon as they received three approvals from fellow team members. This welcomed change had a positive impact for Team 2.

DISCUSSION

Our interviews revealed how teams used multiple tools to serve different software roles. Looking at the bigger picture, Lentz et al.'s model of complexity can extend our understanding of these particular tool ecosystems. We will use these categories to identify successful examples of appropriation, and to point out where appropriation inspired design could benefit the collaborative process.

Poorly Interlocked Job Responsibilities

Similar to IT environments, participant roles in GISHWHES are ambiguous and dynamic. Some teams had explicit leaders, and others did not. Job responsibilities also differed between teams. For example, some teams required that the person who completed an item perform any necessary modifications and then submit the image to GISHWHES, while other teams had team members who only acquired images/videos with the expectation that other members would handle post-processing and submission. Tool choice was shaped by work patterns, and those patterns differed across teams. Even within a single team, the patterns were not static over the course of the week.

Tools to support this activity need to adapt to this complexity. As a result, a software design process that began with analyzing user roles and developing software to match a given set of roles would be unlikely to function as planned, because actual roles will be different in practice. Instead, it would be preferable to design appropriable software that assumes dynamic roles. In Dix's terms, we need to allow interpretation, and support but not control the process [6].

Ad-Hoc Organizational Procedures

The concept of ad-hoc organizational procedures is relevant to both the policies or procedures mandated by GISHWHES organizers, and those constructed by individual teams. One example of a GISHWHES mandated policy was that participants were not allowed to post any of their items to any "social media platform" (special rules were written for posting videos to YouTube, which was a requirement).[8] Many of our interview participants interpreted the spirit of this law as allowing them to post images to private Facebook groups so that they could collaborate during GISHWHES. However, Team 5 interpreted this rule explicitly and did their best to enforce the rule among their team. In this case, tool choice was shaped by rule interpretation.

An example of a team procedure naturally evolving was the feedback workflow that Team 2 instituted. During GISHWHES they realized that it took too long to wait for every team member's feedback, and instead they set up an approval process that required only three team members to approve. A software solution that tried to codify the idea of "approval" would not be able to adapt to this change in what approval meant. Software that in Dix's terms supports the process without controlling it can allow for this change easily.

Finally, a creative procedure that evolved over time was Team 9's mandate that all submitted photos receive a team watermark, and all videos start with an intro screen displaying their team name. Team 9 created this procedure after realizing that submissions (from a previous GISHWHES) that were distributed via the GISHWHES coffee-table book, or shared online, did not credit the originating teams. As a result, one team member was

[8] http://www.gishwhes.com/g_blog/updates/

responsible for applying these identifying marks before submitting anything to GISHWHES.

In each of these three examples, Dix's principle to support the process but not control it is key. The way the process was implemented changed across teams and for individual teams across time. A software solution that tried to control the process could not meet this challenge.

IT Environment Diversity

We presented an overview of all the tools used to fulfill the software roles in Figure 7. Besides these tools, teams also used Imgur and YouTube for storing images and videos, tools like Photoshop or Kdenlive for editing images and videos, and services like Google Drive and Dropbox for storing team materials. With respect to hardware, cell phones were used by some participants to capture photos or as a way to stay connected with the team while they were away from a computer. Altogether, a communicative ecology of software and hardware was used to help teams navigate GISHWHES. The plugability and configurability of tools used are key features to make them appropriable in this context.

Specialized Tool Preference

We found several examples of specialized tool preference within the GISHWHES teams. Team 4, for example developed a workflow where Jake* would download all of the video files from Pipeline to a Dropbox folder. This was because he would often work in a Windows environment, but when he edited the teams' videos, he liked to use a free and open-source video called Kdenlive, which was only available on Linux.

Another example of tool specialization was the Google spreadsheet Team 9 lovingly referred to as "their baby". This Google spreadsheet took two months to build. It was color coordinated and its purpose was to optimize the "layout" in order to make it "easy to read". Through iterative rounds of testing, they ran friends not associated with GISHWHES through so they could iron out the areas that people found confusing. The amount of effort reportedly put into their task management tool was more than any other team reported. Unsurprisingly, they considered this spreadsheet to be a secret asset, and chose not to share it during the interviews.

The Google Spreadsheet is an excellent example of an appropriable tool. Being highly configurable and open to interpretation, it allowed Team 9 to build a tool that met the level of sophistication they were looking for. Software to support complex collaboration should look into providing tools that (to paraphrase Dix) allow the user to do more for themselves.

Designing for Complexity

A professional IT organization is a different setting from a wacky, volunteer scavenger hunt. This makes it perhaps more striking that we found similar sources of complexity in interacting software platforms and user roles. Lentz et. al. conclude that "Simplistic design approaches centered on point problems or averaged concepts of static user roles are ill suited to tackling these complexity issues. Simplification will require sophisticated design approaches that consider the role of design elements in the larger context of multiple ecosystems of interacting subsystems.[11]" An appropriability perspective takes this further to suggest that rather than trying to understand/model/anticipate features of such a dynamic system, it makes sense to design appropriable solutions that will be used in diverse ways. By embracing an appropriation-inspired approach to software development, we will create more robust solutions for complex, communicative ecologies.

CONCLUSION

Would you be able to dress a rooster in a GISHWHES tank top? What about borrow a nun's habit, and wear it down a water slide? How would you make your country's flag out of food or food packaging (Figure 8)? Could you get your grandfather (or other elderly gentleman) to dress like a teenage girl from Jersey Shore? These were all tasks from the 2013 GISHWHES. How would you accomplish 155 of these tasks in one week? This paper, first, provides a detailed description of GISHWHES and how its participants attempted a complex, creative, time-limited collaborative task.

Figure 8. **Submission by Team 7 for Item # 127. Make your country's flag from food or food packaging.** ***(49 points)*** **©Jenna Boring**

As CSCW designers, we often think in terms of creating a new tool or platform for a task. In our fieldwork on tool use in GISHWHES, we found that a communicative ecologies approach better captured key features of user activity. All teams used multiple tools, and tool choice shifted as the pace of work accelerated over the course of the week.

This phenomenon is not unique to GISHWHES. For example, in ongoing work we are studying tool use in our institution's online degree program. We have observed that faculty supporting online classes are using not one tool but several. Those tools include our institute's official grading software, a vendor's content delivery system, our standard course support software designed for on-campus classes, a third-party site that supports class discussion, and email. The challenge is in making all these tools work together, and planning appropriable new tools as a harmonious part of a dynamic communicative ecology.

In our analysis of GISHWHES, we found four primary software roles: task management, alert and notification, soliciting help, and feedback. We were surprised at the extent to which teams used Facebook. While one might be tempted to view Facebook as a social platform, it has notable affordances for group work. In particular, it offers the ability to reach out to social networks for help, instant notification on mobile platforms, and smooth desktop/mobile integration. Additionally, it proved to be a key advantage that participants all already had Facebook accounts and were familiar with the platform. Team members were often reluctant to try a new tool like Basecamp or Pipeline. However, even the groups most dedicated to Facebook found that information "got buried" in a single-threaded Facebook group, and needed to rely on tools like email and spreadsheets to track complex information.

Moving forward, we must look for opportunities to increase the appropriability of the new technologies we create. Users will invent creative ways to use our tools, and our technology will rarely exist in isolation. While the environments that will arise will be complex, designing for appropriation can provide the flexibility needed for meeting the needs of these communicative ecologies.

ACKNOWLEDGMENTS

We would like to thank the participants in this study along with Jessica Pater, Catherine Grevet, and our anonymous reviewers for their helpful feedback. We would like to thank Kurt Luther who is the creator of Pipeline for his generous support and guidance. This research was made possible by NSF award CreativeIT-0855952.

REFERENCES

1. Bacon-Smith, C. *Enterprising women: Television fandom and the creation of popular myth*. University of Pennsylvania Press, 1992.
2. Braun, V. and Clarke, V. Using thematic analysis in psychology. *Qualitative Research in Psychology 3*, 2 (2006), 77–101.
3. Bruckman, A. Studying the amateur artist : A perspective on disguising data collected in human subjects research on the Internet. *Ethics and Information Technology 4*, 3 (2002), 217–231.
4. Dana, R. It's No Gossip, Ratings Slip Threatens CW Network. *The Wall Street Journal*, 2008, 1. http://online.wsj.com/news/articles/SB121089546043097065.
5. Dittrich, Y. and Giuffrida, R. Exploring the Role of Instant Messaging in a Global Software Development Project. *2011 IEEE Sixth International Conference on Global Software Engineering*, (2011), 103–112.
6. Dix, A. Designing for Appropriation. *Proceedings of the 21st BCS HCI Group Conference*, (2007), 27–30.
7. Dourish, P. The Appropriation of Interactive Technologies : Some Lessons from Placeless Documents. *Computer Supported Cooperative Work (CSCW) 12*, 4 (2003), 465–490.
8. Granovetter, M.S. Granovetter 1973 The Strength of Weak Ties.pdf. *American Journal of Sociology 78*, 6 (1973), 1360–1380.
9. Guest, G., Bunce, A., and Johnson, L. How Many Interviews Are Enough?: An Experiment with Data Saturation and Variability. *Field Methods 18*, 1 (2006), 59–82.
10. Johri, A. Look Ma , No Email ! Blogs and IRC as Primary and Preferred Communication Tools in a Distributed Firm. *Proceedings of the ACM 2011 Conference on Computer Supported Cooperative Work*, (2011), 305–308.
11. Lentz, J.L. and Bleizeffer, T.M. IT Ecosystems : Evolved Complexity and Unintelligent Design. *Symposium on Computer-Human Interaction for Management of Information Technology*, (2007).
12. Luther, K., Caine, K., Ziegler, K., and Bruckman, A. Why it works (when it works): success factors in online creative collaboration. *ACM International Conference on Supporting Group Work*, (2010), 1–10.
13. Luther, K., Fiesler, C., and Bruckman, A. Redistributing leadership in online creative collaboration. *Proceedings of the 2013 conference on Computer supported cooperative work - CSCW '13*, ACM Press (2013), 1007.
14. Memarovic, N., Langheinrich, M., Rubegni, E., David, A., and Elhart, I. Designing "interacting places" for a student community using a communicative ecology approach. *Proceedings of the 11th International Conference on Mobile and Ubiquitous Multimedia - MUM '12*, ACM Press (2012), 43:1–43:10.
15. Orlikowski, W.J. Using Technology and Constituting Structures : A Practice Lens for Studying Technology in Organizations. *Organization Science 11*, 4 (2000), 404–428.
16. Pickard, G., Pan, W., Rahwan, I., et al. Time-critical social mobilization. *Science (New York, N.Y.) 334*, 6055 (2011), 509–12.

17. Quiñones, P. Cultivating Practice & Shepherding Technology Use : Supporting Appropriation Among Unanticipated Users. *Proceedings of the 17th ACM conference on Computer supported cooperative work & social computing*, (2014), 305–318.
18. Reid, R.A. *Women in Science Fiction and Fantasy: Overviews*. ABC-CLIO, 2009.
19. Report, P. *DARPA NETWORK CHALLENGE*. 2010.
20. Slater, D., Tacchi, J., and Lewis, P. *Ethnographic monitoring and evaluation of community multimedia centres: A study of Kothmale community radio internet project, Sri Lanka*. 2002.
21. Stevens, G., Pipek, V., and Wulf, V. Appropriation Infrastructure : Supporting the. In *End-user development*. Springer, 2009, 50–69.
22. Talton, J.O., Peterson, D.L., and Al-muhtadi, J. Scavenger Hunt : Computer Science Retention Through Orientation. *Special Interest Group on Computer Science Education*, (2006), 443–447.
23. Turner, T., Qvarfordt, P., Biehl, J.T., et al. Exploring the Workplace Communication Ecology. *ACM SIGCHI Conference on Human Factors in Computing Systems*, (2010), 841–850.
24. Wahba, S.K., Feaster, Y., Hallstrom, J.O., Computers, K., and Computer, E. A Technology-Assisted Scavenger Hunt for Introducing K-12 Students to Sensor Networks. *Annual Conference on Innovation and Technology in Computer Science Education*, (2011), 73–77.

Digital Entanglements: Craft, Computation and Collaboration in Fine Art Furniture Production

Amy Cheatle
Cornell University
Ithaca, NY
ac2288@cornell.edu

Steven J. Jackson
Information Science, Cornell University
208 Gates Hall, Ithaca, NY 14853
sjj54@cornell.edu

ABSTRACT
This paper joins a growing body of CSCW and HCI work exploring questions of creativity and collaboration at the intersection of digital and material practices of craft. Drawing on studio visits and interviews with fine art furniture maker Wendell Castle and his team, we investigate one studio's experience with integrating digital fabrication tools into their studio practice, and its implications for the collective organization of work and creativity. We explore how the introduction of new computational and industrial machine objects (here, Computer Numerical Controllers) remediates traditional relations of craft and the forms of human-object value, care, and creativity built around them. We also chart new forms of creative practice and material flow that emerge from this encounter, and show how remediations of craft in the Castle studio may pose questions and opportunities for wider CSCW concerns around craft, creativity, and design.

Author Keywords
Craft; fine art; studio; digital fabrication; post-digital; computer-aided design; handwork

ACM Classification Keywords
H.5.m. Information interfaces and presentation

INTRODUCTION
...in the Machine lies the only future of art and craft - as I believe, a glorious future; that the machine is, in fact, the metamorphosis of ancient art and craft; that we are at last face to face with the machine - the modern Sphinx-whose riddle the artist must solve if he would that art live.... Frank Lloyd Wright, 1901

The pace of technological creation and its incorporation into everyday life alters the power, shape, and meaning of human practice. Relationships between people, social and natural environments, work and leisure, and how we conceptualize and interact with the material world are being (re)mixed as a result of this encounter. Artists, as sophisticated makers, are often at the forefront of this process. They act as creative and critical users of tools – both computational and otherwise – whose practice has the potential to reveal new insights and understandings about the world in which we live, while also generating new theoretical frameworks that may apply to other contexts of human-computer interaction [3]. Digital fabrication tools such as 3D scanning and printing and Computer Numerical Controlled (CNC) robotics can expand the practice of artists by enlarging artistic repertoires and opening up design to new physical possibilities. New computational tools may also enter into and remix sites of ideation and imagination themselves, (re)imagining concepts and outcomes and redistributing collaborative practices and relations within complex work environments. These processes may at the same time challenge and restructure relationships and values at the interface of technology, design, and creative production.

ACM 978-1-4503-2922-4/15/03...$15.00.
http://dx.doi.org/10.1145/2675133.2675291

In this paper we explore the studio practice of American fine art furniture maker Wendell Castle, who for more than forty years has kept his studio precariously balanced on the edges of contemporary technological practice and traditional woodworking techniques. Referred to as "post-digital" [28] by contemporary craft scholars, Castle is internationally regarded as both an innovator and master craftsman whose work bridges the fields of industrial design, fine art furniture production, and sculpture. Castle's studio couples highly complex computational tools (including Computer Numerical Controllers) with traditional woodworking practices in innovative, playful and interdisciplinary ways.

From a CSCW perspective, Castle's studio presents an intriguing case study around the adoption of complex computational tools in collaborative and creative work environments. It brings to the fore larger questions and concerns around the nature of creativity and innovation, and what it means to design, create, and make in an increasingly computational world.

The paper that follows analyzes Castle's evolving studio practice in light of theories of craft, creativity, and materiality drawn from CSCW, HCI, and the social sciences. It seeks answers to three basic questions. How has the integration of complex computational design tools and manufacturing robotics maintained or expanded Castle's conceptual and imaginative practices? How have collaborations in the studio been remixed as a result of these new tools (and what does it mean to do craft under such conditions)? And what can this experience teach us about relations of creativity, craft, and collaboration under the shifting conditions of digital production?

BACKGROUND AND LITERATURE REVIEW

The incorporation of mechanical tools meant to replace, augment, or assist human labor and skill have long played a central and contested role in the evolution and meaning of art, craft, and handwork processes. From the English silk weavers of the 1800's who destroyed Jacquard's loom to the birth of artistic genres such as the Arts and Crafts movement, controversies around the use of machines as crafters of artifacts recur throughout history. Englishman William Morris, founder of the Arts and Crafts movement, advocated for a return to the simple beauty of handcrafted, utilitarian objects as a way of staying true to materials and labor. Morris and others of similar mind saw artists transitioning into servants of the machine, and they sought to free both artisan and artifact from the dehumanizing effects of mass-produced, machine made goods [17]. Other artists and craftsmen of the era however welcomed the revolutionary power of the machine as aid and extension to the craft process. In a 1901 speech, architect and designer Frank Lloyd Wright explicitly rejected Morris' concerns, arguing that the machine, once it could be freed from its role as solider of industry, represented the very future of art and craft making. Artists were in the best position to realize this ambition. According to Wright artists, as well as craftspeople, were graced with a type of creativity and openness well suited to *embrace* the machine, not as contested outsider or interlocutor, but as "best friend" and ally to the art making process [26].

The same rough opposition continues to inform values surrounding machines and craft processes today, as new computational tools and infrastructures enter into "traditional" processes of artistic and craft-based production. This question has been taken up by a small but growing body of HCI and CSCW work exploring the dynamics and tensions surrounding the integration of new technological systems and practices into craft and creative design environments. Some of this work has looked towards expanded and "active" concepts of materiality as a mode of analysis for gaining deeper insights into the interplay between objects and humans at the heart of the creative process. The work of Tholander et al [25] for example has sought to reconceptualize materials as agents with unique properties and abilities to constrain or enable design outcomes. Material agency is witnessed and enacted through dialogues that unfold between human and material elements within complex sociomaterial practices. In this way, the agency of materials and objects is seen as *becoming* through human/object negotiation and sociomaterial interaction [25]. In a similar light, Rosner et al [22] find that materials, information, techniques, and human relationships are bound and rebound in a "cross-bred" (or interdisciplinary) network, which blurs and reconciles the ontological "gap" between digital and physical environments. In separate work, Rosner [21] explores the ways in which the active property of materials "unfold through collaborations with people, workspaces, and even each other" – fixing and transforming all parties to the encounter. Jackson and Barbrow [12] find that the introduction of new computational tools into existing partnerships remediates (read: challenges, disrupts, expands, remixes) the complex relationships between human agents, objects, and the wider infrastructures to which they are intimately joined. Dourish and Mazmanian [7] point to similar instances of remediation, arguing that materiality carries both symbolic weight and human value – and that transitions from one material to another can therefore shift experiences of identity at both the individual and community levels.

Recent work has connected these interests in turn to more specific questions of materiality and collaboration in creative work processes. Countering individualistic and human-centered notions of creativity, Jackson and Kang [13] argue instead for an *entangled* notion of creativity and design, built on recognition of how creativity may be embedded, constituted and completed within a world of things. Through such processes, materials (with all their affordances and limitations) and people (with their complex value systems) are intertwined in and through the creative process. It is precisely these forms of entanglement that generate the push and pull that moves creativity forward. Such a view shifts ontological understandings away from those that privilege human actants toward ones that recognize materials as integral to the way we live, act, and create in the world. In sum, "we think and imagine in concert with things, not just through them or about them. Creativity is something we do *in* and *with* the world, not just to it."

These arguments build in turn on a broader body of work around materiality and social life growing in the organizational and social sciences. Orlikowski [18] finds that materiality is integral to organizational life and that developing new ways of dealing with material is critical if one is to understand the multiple, emergent, shifting and interdependent technologies at the heart of contemporary practice. Orlikowski sees humans and technology as bound through acts of 'recursive intertwining' or 'constitutive entanglement' that eschew pre-ordered hierarchies or dualisms. Rather, human actors and technological practices are enmeshed and co-constituted, emerging *together* from entangled networks that are always shifting and co-emerging in time.

Drawing on the design notebooks of painter Paul Klee, social anthropologist Tim Ingold [10, 11] argues that the essence of matter lies in form-taking activity, movements and variations "swept up in the generative currents of the world" [10:95] that collectively constitute time, history, and forward trajectory. In such a world, the role of the artist is not to make (in its ex nihilo sense), but to follow and to bend, to "...join with and follow the forces and flows of material that bring the form of the work into being" [10:97]. In this way, "artists – as also artisans – are itinerant wayfarers... bringing forth their work as they press on with their own lives" [10:97].

As the materials, tools and practices of creative wayfarers move into abstracted spaces, tensions can surface. Matthew Crawford [6: 24] finds that integrating the computer into craft-based workflows may shift making into a type of algorithmic "rule following" that requires a different sort of cognitive disposition than the embodied manipulations of analog tools. For this reason, hybrid practices that intertwine computation and handwork without an embodied, sensual knowledge can be "technologically correct" but otherwise "disastrous", occupying a contested landscape that challenges the aura of rusticity and traditionalism sometimes attached to craft in the modern imagination [23]. However Malcolm McCullough [16] takes another path. He sees computational tools as 'extending' tools that allow forms and ideas to be materialized in new and concrete ways. [16:81]. Richard Sennet [23] seconds this position, tracing craft's theoretical, material, and social development from ancient weavers to Linux programmers, arguing that 'good craft' can be found in any human undertaking – from carpentry to parenting to software engineering – wherever material engagements are deep and commitments to quality for its own sake are high.

Parallels to these lines of HCI and social science work around materiality and craft – and the anxieties and shifting values that digital production may occasion – can be found in recent scholarship in art theory and history. Craft and design historian Ron Labaco, curator at the Museum of Arts and Design in New York, has mapped areas where fine arts and design intersect with digital tools and processes. In a series of upcoming exhibitions (which includes the work of Wendell Castle described further below), he explores the developing genre within digital art practice referred to as the 'post-digital' [9]. Being post-digital (a term that "sucks but is useful" according to art theorist Florian Cramer [5]) differs from the "digital art" that preceded it. The post-digital emerges from a blended digital practice that does *not* pay undue attention (positive or negative) to the technological means by which it was produced. It marks a period in time when our unquenchable fascination with computational systems and gadgets has become historical [1:1]. For artists and theorists such as Mel Axenburg [1] post-digital art is a humanizing one, restoring balance and the possibility of a more constructive and even-handed aesthetic relationship between creative handwork and digital work. In a post-digital studio, technological tools and methods are just one of the toolsets artists use (or might), without any particular fascination or anxiety either way. It is the digital made ordinary, even boring – until enlivened by the flow and possibilities of a vibrant aesthetic process.

The literatures reviewed above raise important questions and possibilities around the shifting relations between craft, computation and collaboration in the fine arts furniture environment (and other spaces of collaborative creative endeavor). Tholander [25], Rosner [21,22], and Jackson and Kang [13] all point to the formative agencies of materials, and how these may be brought out and revealed through human-object interaction and use. Dourish and Mazmanian [7] and Jackson and Barbrow [12] point to the crucial effects of remediation, and the important ways in which tools and material choices may shift human values and practices, including those central to individual and collective experiences of collaboration. Crawford [6] and McCullough [16], like Morris and Frank Lloyd Wright before them, point to the somewhat ambivalent remediations of craft that new digital tools may produce, with contradictory effects on the nature and understanding of craft itself. Orlikowski [18], Ingold [10,11] and post-digital concepts from the arts [1] suggest a more measured and ontologically neutral account of the forces and changes at play here: recognizing the real and formative effects of digital tools and other material changes on collaborative creative process, without overweighting their contributions.

The sections that follow test and develop these claims against the experience of digital tool adoption in the Wendell Castle studio, a fine arts furniture studio in upstate New York, long at the forefront of the American art furniture movement. Drawing on a series of studio visits, observations, and interviews with Castle and his collaborative team conducted during spring and summer of 2014, we follow the processes by which a new computational intermediary – a Computer-Numerical Controller sourced from the U.S. Postal Service and referred to as "the robot" – was integrated into the collaborative work practices and material flows that collectively constitute the processes of imagination and production that define the Castle studio and its unique creative process and vision. Here we seek answers to three basic questions. How has the integration of complex computational tools such as 'the Robot' maintained or expanded Castle's conceptual and imaginative practices? How has collaborative studio work been remixed as a result of this addition? And what lessons might this story bring to the field of CSCW regarding the nature of creativity, craft, and collaboration under the shifting conditions of digital production?

ACCESSING PRACTICE: FINE ART FURNITURE MAKER WENDELL CASTLE

Our case study of the Castle workshop unfolded during studio visits which were designed to facilitate observation, structured and unstructured interviews (about 8 hours of interviews were recorded, transcribed, and analyzed), and the collection of photographic materials illustrating evolving fine art furniture design as well as tools and methods. We interviewed 4 full time studio employees who gave us permission to use their first names. Due to the public nature of Castle's work we did not attempt to anonymize the research – a fact made clear to our informants prior to and during the research process. Our interviews included conversations with Wendell Castle, who's original design concepts the studio collaboratively executes, Marvin, or Marv, Castle's longtime associate who now acts as the studio's manager and computational programmer and technician, Terry, one of two studio carvers/woodworkers, and Bryon, who with his apprentice, finishes each piece by preparing it's final surface.

Figure 1. Original *Long Night* chair by Wendell Castle

We focused our fieldwork on one area of the studio's ongoing practice, progressing towards completion during our visits. Our line of questioning circulated around the studio's first attempt to fulfill Castle's Paris gallery's request for an edition of 8 identical chairs (which were part of a larger order for 25 pieces). The chair to be multiplied, *Long Night* (*see figure 1*) originated with Castle's 2013 "Leap of Faith" series. This is the first instance in the studio's history where an edition of nearly identical wood furniture pieces has been possible to complete. "*There's no way we could have done that before [the robot)*" says Castle. "*We'd never be able to get the chairs to match*". Our research looks back to tell the story of one studio's history with technological integration over five years' time, and shares how they see that integration affecting their creative and collaborative work. Through observation, we witnessed the collaborative mastery of form, process and material flow grow from early concept drawings, evolving into finished work. Key moments from this process are described further below.

Formal Analysis of Castle's Work

Castle, who is considered the founding father of fine art furniture design, crafts large, playful and intriguing sculptures one is meant to interact with as furniture pieces. They are said to invoke grace, beauty, humor and comfort while unifying form and function, aesthetics and utility. "From the mechanic to the organic, his forms often reference natural or biomorphic shapes that almost seem to grow directly from the gallery floor" [27:1]. The work is said to be both "practical and transcendent" [8]. The literature shows that since the early 1960's, Castle's aim as a maker and creative thinker has not been tied to the materiality, expression or beauty of wood. Instead he is motivated by a desire to "...free wood forms from structural convention..." [2:8].

The data we gathered from conversations with the studio craftsmen as well as the literature surrounding Castle's career, reveal him as a fine art furniture maker whose work neutralizes categorical boundaries between fine art, the decorative arts, industrial design, and craft [24]. His latest series of one-off pieces are darker, more dreamlike and mysterious than earlier pieces, and some work, such as his large-scale installation *A New Environment,* from 2013, incorporate private nooks that the viewer can curl up or escape into. This new work stems in part from Castle's playful and conceptual interest in defying gravity. Pieces from *A New Environment* have been finished in an inky dark stain, simultaneously both severe and entrancing. One feels the invitation to run a hand slowly over the piece's organic contours, and because this work is meant for bodies to interact with, one *is* permitted touch, or even to rest, in the seat. Its easy to imagine spending moments sinking into these dark and edgy yet nurturing pieces, losing one's self in their onyx wishing-well depths. Pieces with nest-like seats are comfortable – and comforting. "*They sit okay*", says Castle, "*I think that's important - so we find a way to make them sit pretty well*" [4].

Introduction to Studio Process

"*In some ways,*" Castle says regarding his practice, "*things here are not vastly different from the way they were in the 1960s*" [4]. And, in many ways, Castle's process has remained relatively stable over the decades. Pieces start with a drawing. A form evolves and is sculpted into a small-scale model. Castle commits to the design. Slabs of wood are then cut into cross sections, stacked, clamped, and glued together. The stack is carved with a variety of tools, from chainsaw to grinder, revealing a final form. The surface of the piece is refined and finished and the work is then numbered, signed, and delivered to the collector or gallery.

Yet in 2009, the process that had been relatively stable for nearly 50 years began to evolve as Castle began introducing digital fabrication technologies into the workflow. According to Castle [4], the implementation of these tools created a disruption to the artisanal woodcraft process not seen since the Industrial Revolution. This technological integration was driven by necessity. Says Castle, "*We absolutely needed to work in a different way. We needed to get an accurate model of these cross sections. If we glued up the pieces accurately, it would greatly reduce carving*" [4]. Today, five years after the first integration of digital design tools, the studio's workflow is tight, complex, and technologically innovative. It is a process continuously reflected upon and redesigned by Castle and studio collaborators. "*Wendell is always interested in and encouraging us to tweak the process, or shape the workflow in the name of efficiency or precision,*" says Bryon, who is responsible for finishing the work. He notes that Castle is not as keen to allow others to influence design however: *"He'll listen to ideas regarding concept, but not too warmly"* [14].

Castle juxtaposes his use of digital fabrication tools with artists such as Joris Laarman, whom Castle believes allows technology to drive his design. For Castle, the work is all about form. "*I don't want this to be about how the work is made, or even what it's made of. I'm not even that interested in wood as a material. I want the work to be about form – and if the technology used to make the object is too apparent, the form starts to get lost…I'm very interested in technology but I just want it to help.*"

General Methods and Evolution of Process: 1960-2014

Today's process as reported by Castle, Marv, Terry, and Bryon, and as we witnessed it, generally unfolds as explained below; though there is evidence that the workflow is flexible and varies from piece to piece. Factors such as artist's intent, material constraints, unforeseen limitations, or collaborative suggestions from studio workers all contribute to the modification of the process.

Castle, who draws daily with paper and pencil, conceptualizes form by creating a number of uncomplicated 2D sketches. These sketches are numerous, and can be seen hanging on walls and covering work surfaces throughout the studio. These drawings guide his production of small, but accurately scaled, foam models informing the larger wood piece to come. These hand-sized models are carved from thin planks of urethane foam glued together (a process that mirrors the large-scale wood lamination stage which we discuss further below). The small foam laminates are sent off-site to a woodworker unaffiliated with the Castle workshop who utilizes 3D scanning tools to digitize the model, creating a CAD drawing of the piece. The offsite scanning facility also adds line work to the image, marking the future wood laminate layers. This image is then sent to Marv, who manages the studio's computational practices.

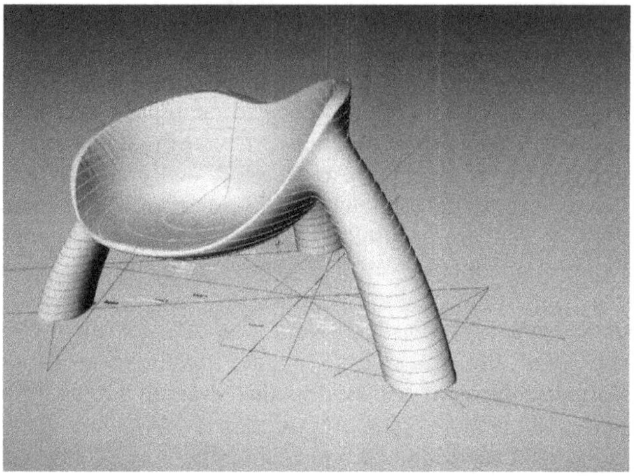

Figure 2. Digital Long Night

We sit with Marv as he reviews the digital file of the chair *(see figure 2)*. He points to the 1 ¼" thick "stacks" or hairlines, shown on the digital image. These cross sections will be individually printed out on paper using the studio's plotter, resulting in large patterns meant to inform both the shape of the wood planks to come, as well as their order within the developing laminate block. The layers that make up the laminate block will be cut from Ash, a hard and scratch-resistant wood. Ash is an appropriate if not extravagant choice for furniture. It is inexpensive, yet often overlooked and, says Castle, "*super common*".

Evolution of Laminates and 3D Scanning: 2009-2014

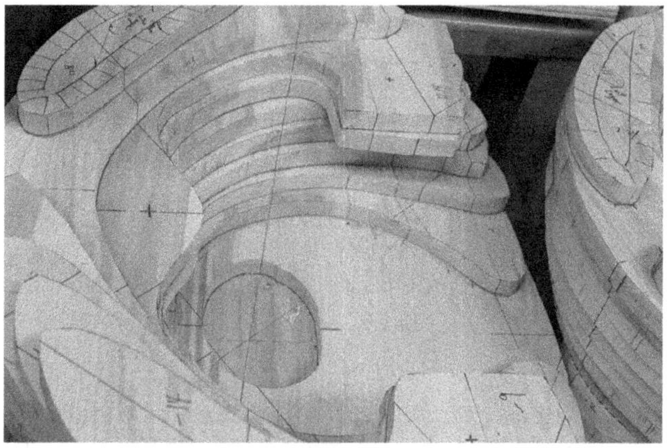

Figure 3. *Long Night* showing laminate layers

Castle references 1960's sculptor Leonard Baskin as the force responsible for introducing him to the stack lamination process. Castle explains, "anybody who ever glued two pieces of wood together, laminated. But what I brought to the table was the idea of large pieces with the cross sections pre-planned, so that you bandsaw out each layer to roughly its right size before you glue it on. That means you can only glue one layer at a time, but then you can see the form developing and you can actually make some small changes. And you can make really big things. You just keep throwing the wood on" *(see figure 3)* [15].

In the days before 3D scanning was the studio norm, sketches of Castle's forms were placed upon an opaque projector and beamed onto the wall. These projections were meant to aid the carver's estimation of stacks. Additional large drawings would also hang for the carver's reference. This process, however innovative in the larger practice of furniture making, was not accurate enough for Castle's needs. Cross sections were informally imagined rather than precisely mapped, and the result was a high potential for error, combined with the probable and costly loss of time and material.

"*What I would do before was just imagine a cross section in a piece, and begin at a point where it was the easiest to imagine, and start there...you can't get terribly complex...it becomes so much work it just gets ridiculous*" says Castle. "*We absolutely needed to get an accurate cross section*".

The 2009 implementation of 3D scanning combined with accurately printed paper patterns "*...improved things*", says Bryon "*...because the large scale mockups...translated Wendell's instructions more clearly. That clear translation allowed him to get much more complex in the design*". In Castle's words, the technology "freed up" the design, while greatly increasing accuracy. Fewer errors were made and less materials, time and energy were lost.

The new digital process came with an unanticipated benefit. Within the digital environment maintained by Marv, Castle is afforded the ability to consider the furniture object in 3D virtual space before large-scale physical shaping begins. He can make slight adjustments (IE raising or lowering a seat while instantly exploring the digital result) by tweaking the files with Marv's help.

Once decided upon, the patterns and laminates are accurately cut, stacked, glued and clamped into place. A chainsaw wielded by carvers Castle, Terry, or Peter becomes the first physical tool used to reveal the final form.

Finding the form – Carver's Technique

A carver's ability to 'find the form' within the rough laminates is a high-level skill often mentioned to us during our interviews. Castle, Marv and Bryon all speak of an innate difference in skill between woodworker and carver. "*Carvers know how to be reductive to reveal the final form, and then know when to stop. They somehow see "it" in their mind*" [4] says Castle. Traditionally trained woodworkers, while familiar with wood's physical opportunities and constraints, may not necessarily 'see' positive and negative space as a sculptor/carver does. They may not have the embodied knowledge needed to understand the delicate boundary between taking away or leaving too much material. While the patterns greatly improve accuracy, the next step of the work demands the skill of a master carver versed in the material properties of wood. (This need for skill, finesse and accuracy has challenged Castle to experiment with non-traditional crafting processes and tools, and as we discuss further below, was a motivation for the implementation of the CNC router).

Finishing the Work

Once the initial carving of the laminate block is completed, it is taken through a series of sanders and grinders that continue to refine and reveal the final form. When this shaping is finished the work is sent to Bryon, who sands or perhaps wire brushes the piece, depending on the predetermined surface. Not including this finishing time, the shaping, carving and refinement of the piece takes the studio 4 or 5 days to complete.

Says Bryon regarding the finish of each piece, "*In our art here at the studio, it's a normal thing to strive for balance. Subtlety is always what we are after. Wendell is really all about the form, the design, not really about the wood. So we don't want to draw too much attention to the wood with the style of finish. But, we still need to leave the evidence of wood. We could make these look like giant plastic works, but we don't*".

Figure 4. *Long Night* finished surface

According to Bryon, the 8 commissioned chairs we followed went through a "*complex and labor intensive finishing process*". Due to the gallery's request for clearly revealed and deep grain patterns (referred to as the "open" finish - a style popular in the European market) each seat required hand finishing with a wire brush meant to reveal the grain while also opening the wood's pores. After wire brushing, Bryon sanded the surface with a number of paper grains. He applied alternating coats of black lacquer and an oil filler capable of reaching deep into the grain. Finally, he applied layers of an abrasive polish in a satin finish, treating the surface until it achieved its dark, deep, and lustrous aura *(see figure 4)*. The process is especially regimented for these pieces, as there can be no deviation among the edition. Once cured, the finished chairs are signed and stamped and then moved into the studio's waiting area until it is time to package and ship.

The tightly knit teamwork responsible for crafting a Castle piece took another technological leap in 2013 with the integration of the CNC machine, as discussed below.

Implementing the Robotic Carving Arm: 2013

"How the technology comes into this is something I'm very interested in…but I don't think of this as a 'crafting' technology. I think the end product is more important, and if any of these things stand out– like the technology – then it's too much. You may not even think we are using any technology, even though we are. It won't be obvious, the work that the Robot does… in the end no one will know that the robot will do anything"[4] – Wendell Castle.

It was a sense of need, play and adventure (as well as a hunch that it might help with some of the work) that led to Castle's purchase of the studio's latest digital fabrication tool, a computer numerical control (CNC) machine. The industrial orange machine, who's name is evolving through use (The Robot/Mr. Chips) was repurposed by the studio from its pick-and-place past in service of the US mail system. The machine was hacked (or released from it's proprietary purposes) by Marv, who transformed it into a 6-axis carving arm. The robot's new mission in pursuit of art is to mill several feet of laminated wood stack quickly and accurately, using the X and Y reference points that Marv identifies and enters into its RAPID code. Marv, who is tasked with the building, programing, care, and execution of the CNC's process, speaks of this new aspect of his work as "*exciting*" while also expressing other initial emotions such as uneasiness or apprehension.

Figure 5. CNC with Long Night

In 2013 Castle hired Marv, his long-time associate who was at the time working with another studio running its 3-axis CNC machine, to come back and devise a system for running a yet to be purchased 6-axis CNC. As a professional woodworker and carver, Marv understands the properties of wood, and as a mechanical engineer he understands the constraints and possibilities of software designed primarily to be used by the aerospace and automobile industries (where most CNC robots are utilized). His intrinsic knowledge of wood and woodcarving gives him an access point into the process. Marv states that he has the ability to "*…tailor the software driving the CNC to fit the shop's specific needs. Differentials such as feed speeds and types of cutters are all issues here.*" [19].

```
MoveL [[-176.961,-171.635,616.684],[0,0,1,0],
MoveL [[-178.541,-168.842,616.788],[0,0,1,0],
MoveL [[-180.554,-165.286,616.674],[0,0,1,0],
MoveL [[-182.567,-161.73,616.386],[0,0,1,0],[
MoveL [[-184.579,-158.174,616.36],[0,0,1,0],[
MoveL [[-186.592,-154.618,616.175],[0,0,1,0],
MoveL [[-188.539,-151.177,616.111],[0,0,1,0],
MoveL [[-190.91,-146.988,615.88],[0,0,1,0],[-
MoveL [[-192.629,-143.95,615.686],[0,0,1,0],[
MoveL [[-194.642,-140.394,615.535],[0,0,1,0],
MoveL [[-196.654,-136.838,615.362],[0,0,1,0],
MoveL [[-198.667,-133.282,615.155],[0,0,1,0],
MoveL [[-200.679,-129.726,614.957],[0,0,1,0],
MoveL [[-202.692,-126.17,614.726],[0,0,1,0],[
```

Figure 6. *Long Night* in RAPID code

It took Marv over a year to assemble all the CNC add-on parts and locate the translation software that redirected the robot into becoming a milling machine. He describes the current CNC workflow: it begins with a CAD (mac) file delivered to him by the outsourced 3D scanning studio. The file must be translated into a set of CAM (Computer Aided Manufacturing) (windows) M and G codes using Rhinocam. These codes are then translated into RAPID code *(see figure 6)*, the proprietary software language used by the *ABB Robotics* CNC machine. In Marv's estimate, the amount of RAPID code needed to drive the movements of the CNC machine (which is fit with routers of varying size depending on the stage of the carving process), is in the realm of hundreds of thousands of lines. These lines of RAPID code are broken into sections, which are lined up to be run at carving time.

Once the RAPID codes are ready, the laminate block must be placed properly in the "blank" space that surrounds the carving reach of the machine. "*We don't start with an industrial material, and we don't start with an industrial form such as a rectangle or a cylinder. The first thing the RAPID program asks you is, 'What is the blank size?' well, if I just glued up a big cube of wood the machine would know where your blank is, just X, and Y and Z…we don't do that. It would take days for it to cut down to that form and waste an awful lot of wood as well…so the difference between a piece that goes to the robot and a piece that goes to a human carver is that the robot doesn't care…it has no thought. It goes through the motions and does what you tell it to do. To work around this I make a judgment call and make the laminate bigger – maybe an inch here, an inch and a half over here, so that I know it will fall within a range where we need it. The other thing I did was place a laser on the robot and have a program written that allows it to trace the grid work lines we put in the 3D drawing. While the program is running it's just tracing those lines. I then pick those lines on the work piece itself and I move the work piece around on the bed until the X and Y lines of the virtual space and the lines of the actual piece match up. Its an act of faith. You hit that go button and you hold your breath and you hope you haven't made a mistake somewhere. I copy and paste the software code and run it again, bringing the carving tool closer and closer to the final form until its maybe 1/32 of an inch away from it... and that is going to give us a surface you can start sanding on.*

The CNC in action is "*mesmerizing*" for both he and Castle to watch. But according to Marv, integrating the machine into the studio practice also came with a sense of hesitation and caution. "*This machine can move 2 meters a second. Safety is a huge issue. When I told my brother, who used to work in the automobile industry about the robot, he had real safety concerns for us*".

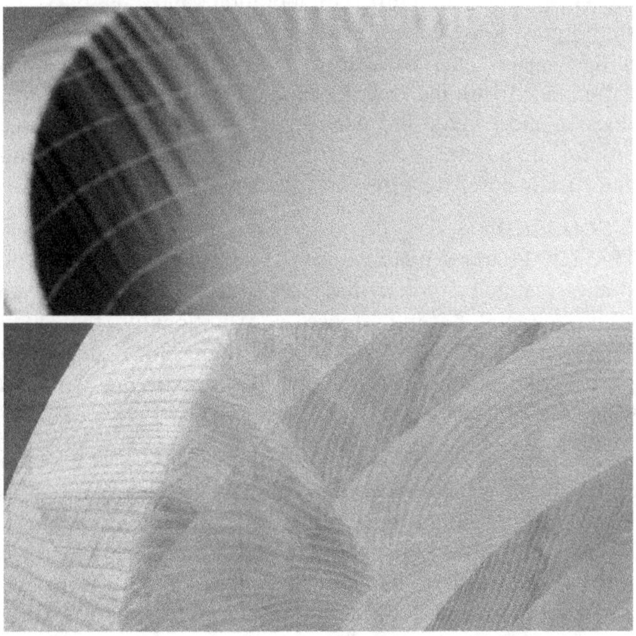

Figure 7. Scanning anomalies replicated in wood

As we completed our initial site visits, the studio had pulled 8 identical chairs off of the machine. Marv was still working with perfecting his process. He shared his current challenge of removing anomalies from the scanning process that were rendered as wavelike artifacts carved into the surface of the wood *(see figure 7)*. Marv points to the virtual image and says, "*See these waves on the surface right here? Well, The Robot carves exactly what you tell it to, and these waves are carved out perfectly.*" Marv attributes the waves to the outdated scanning technology used by the offsite firm, but doesn't want to resolve the issue by changing technicians. "*We have a long relationship with them. They are woodworkers too, so we can speak the same language. They know what I mean when I ask them for something, so because of that we'll work around the anomalies*".

After a year of non-recurring manufacturing on the part of Marv - building, hacking, tweaking, writing code, purchasing random parts on ebay, devising a complete workflow and then finally, running the machine to pull off the chairs, Marv remains mostly unromantic about the machine. *"All the robot is doing is executing functions that could otherwise be performed by hand. But there is a degree of repeatability here, that could never be achieved manually*". It was this degree of repeatability that enabled the studio to produce their first edition of wood furniture pieces.

Robot Reorganizes, and Saves the Studio from (some) Grunt Work

All of the workers we spoke with saw the robot as a machine capable of sharing the carver's workload. In fact it seemed to have taken over some of the more tedious parts of the carving job. Says Castle, "*The robot worked for four hours without a break and never got bored! That really helps our carver out a lot*". Terry, to whom Castle was referring, traditionally spends most of his workday rough carving and then refining the laminate shape. He mirrors Castle's statement. *"The robot helps. When Wendell said he was getting a robot, I expected it to do more complex work. Instead, it does the rough cuts, but very fast. So it saves me a step. It saves me a lot of time actually. It can carve the seat of a chair in a day, and that would have taken me 2 or 3 days. It can do a whole edition at the same time. If I were to do an edition at the same time, that would be boring and, well, I'm not sure I would know the best way to manage that."* [20].

Says Marv, "*It allows us to better use our human labor where most needed. If it were up to Wendell, every piece would be pulled off the carver. But to be cost effective, multiple pieces need to be pulled to make the initial time investment worth it economically. It takes ...a bit... of planning...and it's sometimes a challenge to explain that to the boss.*"

Bryon estimates that the CNC machine has removed 30 percent of the work from Terry's process. This frees him up to work more efficiently on the refinement of the finished pieces, where his skill and expertise as a carver makes him most suited to be placed. "*It removes the grunt work from Terry and speeds up the process, saving probably weeks of work for the entire series by the end*" Says Bryon.

While the machine can mill the laminates in much less time, it can never address the sensitivities of an organic material the way a human carver can. Marv: "*If you see the wood, a good woodworker can tell you what areas of the wood had a knot. The grain will deviate around that knot. A guy who has a tool can say, 'I have a problem here, I can go this way or this way'... but the machine never can. Natural materials will always represent constraints with the CNC, as it was designed for industrial materials - for steel, or plastic.*" Wood must therefore be carefully preselected for the CNC machine. If the CNC were to meet a knot, the laminate could potentially crack or split.

"*At the end of the day, it's the physical properties of the material that drives our process*", says Marv as he describes the way the wood grain of a Castle piece can be read to determine the orientation of the tree's growth within the forest. *I always say, this tree is now dead, but its wood is not - and it's important to know that going into this.*" Bryon understands this in a similar way, "*There's a lot of tension in wood. When you start cutting it up, that tension is released, free to do as it will. And form changes. Things crack, they bend, and warp*" [16].

Bryon reports that his work has not drastically changed since the robot has been implemented as a carver, except that there is now more work to be finished. He isn't quick to attribute this to the robot, finding the increased finishing work more representative to an influx in gallery sales. "*To avoid getting backed up we're training Matt now.*"

The Robot and its Conversation with Castle: Expanding Design Vocabulary

As described below, the robot expands design in three important ways: by extending reach, allowing for more complex joinery, and creating hollows in solid form. Besides sharing the workload of the carvers by assuming the rough, boring, strenuous cuts, the carving arm of the CNC machine can reach underneath, around and within the wood block to shape a sculpture in ways a human arm could not due to the limited reach of arm and chainsaw. This expanded reach frees Castle's design from some of the historical constraints of the material. As Castle explains, the CNC robot has allowed him to remediate or "free up the vocabulary" of his design. Castle plans to combine this extended reach with the robot's ability to hollow laminates to go bigger with the work than ever before.

"*We were never able to do anything as complex as this before. Things can be made so much larger now because we can hollow out the form and we can break it down due to the new cuts and joints we can make...and the idea is to get gigantic. We're making a floor lamp for a Paris exhibition that's 9 feet tall...like a big tree.*"

Additionally, the mechanical arm allows for seamless, previously impossible joinery to be realized. "*No one will ever know how these pieces are attached.*" Says Castle. The improved seam potential allows Castle to conceptualize form in new ways, facilitating his current explorations into crafting sculptural forms that seem to defy gravity.

Despite the opportunities created through Mr. Chip's introduction into the studio, not all of the attention generated has been without caution. While the Paris gallery's request for an edition of *The Long Night* shows its comfort with wood editions of previous one-off collector objects, one unnamed dealer was still deciding how to address the implementation of the robot to the larger craft audience and community of buyers. "*They're not yet completely comfortable discussing the robot,*" says Castle. "*They weren't sure if it should be more secretive than not.*" Castle is quick to assure that the robot could never overstep its bounds and assume too much of the crafting. He says frankly, "*I don't think it can cross over into my space...but besides, I just want it to be a helper. I don't want it to lead me.*"

Five years of technological implementation has shifted the nature and location of collaboration, creativity and craft within the studio. The process, growth trajectory and eventual implications of adopting computational tools and systems are still very much in the process of being worked out, both by the collaborative team in the Castle studio and the wider worlds of art and craft they touch. Under the wrong circumstances, this could challenge and undermine the core values of craft, collaboration, and creativity the studio has long depended on. But where such changes unfold against the backdrop of a tightly knit workplace experienced with the techniques and expressions of balance, finesse, and beauty and where human ties to collaborative process are strongly forged, forms of innovation that extend and sustain core strengths and values may result.

DISCUSSION

Through the implementation of 3D scanning technology, the studio realized improved speed, precision and accuracy within certain crafting processes. Additionally, the studio began interfacing with its designs in digital form, a step that gave Castle another entry point to the evolving work via Marv's 3D software.

In a more powerful way, Mr. Chips can be seen as a collaborator capable of remediating Castle's relationship with creative wood design forms. While extending the reach of a human carver, the robot entered the process in such a way that Castle's pursuit to "free wood from its conventional form" took an evolutionary leap. Form could be conceptualized in a larger, more complex way not possible before the CNC entered the process.

In this way, the role and significance of Mr. Chips within the design and craft process help us expand Jackson and Kang's argument that creativity is emergent and performative, happening in and with the world of things. In the Castle studio, creativity can be found emerging within and through the use of a remediating tool, meeting the artist and his medium and sparking a creative capacity not possible before such computational and robotic intervention. Mr. Chips collaborates with the design work of Castle in a way no other studio member does. And in doing so, it reduces the ontological gap some see between the human/object relationship.

In this light we begin to see Orlikowski's notion of the constitutive entanglement in action. Suddenly, not only are materials understood as performative and unfolding through collaborative actions, they are also understood as entangled within sociomaterial "flows" comprised of all the various entities of the work process - studio members, wood, Mr. Chips, RAPID, collectors of art, glue, 3D scanners, wood clamps, galleries, patterns, etc. Together, these actors create an object through a full orchestra of players uniquely different from any that could otherwise be formed. Though it was not Castle's intent for the tool to '...cross over into [his] space', it has surely met him there and offered a way to collaboratively evolve design together.

The piece-by-piece building, hacking and appropriation of the CNC machine relies on the creative repurposing, and in some way reimagining, of the tool from its expected or proprietary roots. It's working the tool against its grain, exploiting its material form and propensities in ways that can be bent to the intentions of the work. In this way it's not so different than the chainsaw must have looked and felt when it showed up in Castle's practice several decades ago.

Perhaps less romantically, Mr. Chips collaborates with and reorganizes labor within the studio by assuming some of the more specialized and repetitive grunt work, which frees other studio employees to focus on work best suited for crafting capabilities and human skill. Marv, as the studio worker who must deal with the precise work requirements necessary to translate the non-native languages into RAPID code, understands that it is not yet practical for the CNC to work each studio piece. As a result, he must choose projects most suited to the machine. He is cognizant that although the robot can carve quickly and accurately without tiring, amplifying technicalities of repeatability, diligence, precision and efficiency, it cannot respond to the materiality of wood in the same way a human carver can. As a tool built for industrial labor, the CNC is not devised to know the properties of organic crafting material like wood. It does not know how much force it can absorb or which way it will bend under pressure. It cannot analyze growth patterns to read how to approach a cut, nor bring out the Ash grain using a wire brush. It does not "see" form, but precisely executes a set of commands fed to it linearly. In this regard, it is unlikely that the machine will soon replace the handwork of the artisans working within the studio and as we saw, even those pieces tweaked in the computer and roughly-carved by the machine begin and end with the hand.

At the same time, because of the machine's ability to store libraries, The Robot enables the studio to reimagine wood pieces as reproducible parts of a larger edition, where they were once relegated and honored as completely unique pieces. This development affords new market opportunities, as shown by the gallery's request for the *Long Night* series. One of the more interesting contributions of digital fabrication tools may in fact be to provoke new questions around authenticity and authorship that challenge the very assumptions behind such terms. Now that new forms of technology make editions of fine art furniture a possibility, might we one day value such work much like the way the larger lexicon of artmaking has long valued the printmaker's editions? Yet for what reason did Castle's dealer show hesitation when discussing the robot with larger audiences? Amidst the opportunity of doubles or multiples may come the talk of protecting Castle's market value and preserving the more sacred qualities of each unique studio object. The importance of one-off designs for both financial and deeper, more human value must be honored.

Other questions center on the challenge of defining a reasonable stopping point in identifying tools that support without somehow damaging or violating the artisanal expectations of craft. Should the CNC's programmable nature or its past as a soldier of industry leave it outside of accepted "crafting" tools? If so, why might a chainsaw be an acceptable tool for wood craftspeople and a CNC mechanical arm (that essentially carries out a similar process as requested by its user) a potentially devalued one? How much space these developing tools are granted when it comes to evaluating and honoring craft and handwork may remain to be seen.

Castle may intuit some of the above-mentioned risk when he remarks that it is not his intention to allow the robot to *lead* him, but to merely *help* with some of the work. Such an attitude is illustrative perhaps of one of the foundations of the term *post-digital*. Such a term exposes trends in contemporary art and making that have implications for grounding the role of digital technologies as one aspect of creative work and work in general. Labaco's analysis aligns with Ingold's vision of the artist's practice as one positioned to "...join with and follow the forces and flows of material that bring the form of the work into being" [11:97]. Rather than suggesting that technology is serving the needs of the artist, we can argue that artists and their digital fabrication tools are engaged in creative entanglements where technology and human making expand and inform one another.

As the above literature shows, the space that exists between humans and the world of things is an active and productive one, giving rise to new forms of value and agency. As digital technologies remix these relationships, deeper insights about how we engage with the world of things as makers, collaborators and users of new tools emerge. Locations where traditional artistic activity is remixing with digital tools offers a rich landscape for delving deeper into such lines of inquiry.

Castle, who launched his career during the era of the "lone creative genius" working alone in the studio with his carving tools and materials, offers us a new way of looking at creative practice. His expanded creative workflow now includes processes and methods more aligned with contemporary digital art practices (or indeed, industrial manufacturing) while still honoring the material properties of organic forms and materials and human craft. This represents in some ways a break with the past, but in others a further cementing of Castle's considerable reputation as both craftsman and innovator. That Castle's emerging practice can support both evaluations simultaneously speaks to the complexity of craft transitions in a post-digital era.

CONCLUSION

As the above story makes clear, the introduction of new computational tools into longstanding and craft-based forms of creative work carry deep implications: both for the experience and organization of work and the values that surround it. It can reorganize the nature and sites of creativity, and the forms of collaborative work that give rise to it. It can call into question the basic tenets of craft, and the values assigned to these. It can point to new forms of connection and attachment between creative producers and the materials with which they engage. And it can point to new possibilities for creative work and imagination beyond these points of change.

If this analysis suggests findings relevant to the nature and organization of creative work, it also speaks to core CSCW interests in materiality and collaboration more generally. In this as in other contexts of collaborative practice, tools can rarely be isolated or reduced to their immediately functional dimensions, but are instead embedded in historically layered networks of value and meaning that can shape the nature and form of their adoption. Similarly, the built forms of tools and the material flows they engage are central to the constitution and meaning of collaborative activities, and not mere passive background to human defined and dominated fields of action. In these and other ways, places like the Castle studio and other sites of distributed creative practice may help cast important new light on core problematics of CSCW work.

ACKNOWLEDGMENTS

With great appreciation to the studio of Wendell Castle, to Samir Passi and to our anonymous CSCW reviewers for their helpful comments on an earlier draft of this paper.

REFERENCES

1. Alexenberg, M. *The Future of art in a postdigital age: from hellenistic to hebraic consciousness*. Intellect Ltd, Bristol, 2011.
2. Bayer, P. *Fine art of the furniture maker: conversations with wendell castle, artist, and penelope hunter-stiebel, curator, about selected works from the metro*. The University of Rochester, Rochester, 1981.
3. Bogost, I. *Alien phenomenology, or, what it's like to be a thing*. U of Minnesota Press, Minneapolis, 2012.
4. Castle,W. *Personal Interview,* Rochester, 2014.
5. Cramer, F. What is Post-digital? *APRJA,* Retrieved July 15, 2014 from Cornell University: http://www.aprja.net/?p=1318.
6. Crawford, M. B. *Shop class as soulcraft: an inquiry into the value of work*. Penguin Press, New York, 2009.
7. Dourish, P. and Mazmanian, M. Media as material: information representations as material foundations for organizational practice. Working paper for the *Third International Symposium on Process Organization Studies*, Corfu, Greece
8. Gordon, Alastair. Famous, again. *Design Magazine* 2011.
9. Gumbs, N. Out of hand: materializing the postdigital. *Ed. Design, Museum of Art and Design*, New York, 2014.
10. Ingold, T. The Textility of making. *Cambridge Journal of Economics* 34, 91-102.
11. Ingold, T. Towards an ecology of materials. *Annual Review of Anthropology,* 427-442.
12. Jackson, S. J., and Barbrow, S. Infrastructure and vocation: field, calling and computation in ecology. *SIGCHI Conference on Human Factors in Computing Systems*, ACM Press, 2013.
13. Jackson, S. J., and Kang, L. Breakdown, obsolescence and reuse: hci and the art of repair. *SIGCHI Conference on Human Factors in Computing Systems,* ACM Press, 2014.
14. J, Bryon, *Personal Interview,* Rochester, 2014.
15. Manfra, L. Wendell castle: shifting shapes and breaking rules. *American Craft Council,* 2008.
16. McCullough, M. *Abstracting craft: the practiced digital hand*. The MIT Press, Cambridge, 1998.
17. Morris, W. *The revival of handicraft*, Cambridge, 1888.
18. Orlikowski, W.J. Sociomaterial practices: exploring technology at work. *Organization Studies,* 28,9, 2007.
19. P, Marvin *Personal Interview*, Rochester, 2014.
20. R, Taeyoul, *Personal Interview*, Rochester, 2014.
21. Rosner, D.K, The Material practices of collaboration. *Conference on Computer Supported Collaborative Work,* ACM Press, 2012.
22. Rosner, D.K, et al. Designing with traces. *SIGCHI Conference on Human Factors in Computing Systems,* ACM Press, 2013.
23. Sennett, R. *The Craftsman*. Yale University Press, New Haven, 2008.
24. Taragin, D. S., *Furniture by wendell castle*. Hudson Hills Press Society, Manchester, 1989.
25. Tholander, J., Normark, M., Rossitto, C. Understanding agency in interaction design materials. *Proceedings of the SIGCHI Conference on Human Factors in Computing Systems,* ACM Press, 2012.
26. Wright, F. L. The Art and craft of the machine, *Brush and Pencil* (8) 1901.
27. Yates, J. Wendell castle: forms within forms. *Art and Coin* Retrieved July 15, 2014 from Cornell University, http://www.artandcointv.com/blogs/tag/forms-within-forms/.
28. Zamou, L. Art and design in the postdigital world: a conversation with ron labaco. *On Tech*, *Huffington Post* Retrieved July 15, 2014 from Cornell University, http://www.huffpost.com/us/entry/4888972.

Connected Through Crisis: Emotional Proximity and the Spread of Misinformation Online

Y. Linlin Huang, Kate Starbird, Mania Orand, Stephanie A. Stanek, Heather T. Pedersen
HCDE, DUB
University of Washington, Seattle WA, 98195
linlin@hylinlin.com, {kstarbi, orand, stanek14, htp5}@uw.edu

ABSTRACT
During crises, the ability to access relevant information is extremely important for those affected. Previous research shows that social media have become popular for rapid information exchange between members of the online community after crisis events. This study focuses on the effects of proximity to a crisis on information sharing behaviors. Using constructivist grounded theory to guide our inquiry, we conducted interviews with eleven people who used social media in the aftermath of the 2013 Boston Marathon Bombings. Salient themes emerging from this study suggest that both physical and emotional proximity to a crisis influence online information seeking and sharing behaviors. Additionally, speed of information sharing and information access renders social media especially useful during crisis and particularly susceptible to the spread of misinformation. We view the latter as a consequence of the inevitable sensemaking process that occurs as individuals attempt to make sense of incomplete information.

Author Keywords
Social computing; social media; crisis informatics; rumoring; misinformation; information-sharing; collective intelligence;

ACM Classification Keywords
H.5.3 [Information Interfaces & Presentation]: Groups & Organization Interfaces - Collaborative computing, Computer-supported cooperative work; K.4.2 Social Issues

INTRODUCTION
Widespread adoption of social media has enabled members of the public to participate in disaster events as never before. Affected individuals, emergency responders, and remote participants from all over the world are repeatedly coming together on these platforms in the wake of disaster events to exchange information, comfort and support.

Foundational research in crisis informatics suggests that these tools and the behaviors they enable have a large potential to improve crisis response [36]. However, there is also a significant fear of the downsides of public participation, including a perceived vulnerability to the spread of misinformation. Emergency response professionals continue to cite fear of misinformation as a primary reason for not integrating social media into their formal work practices [20,22], and mainstream media has repeatedly called attention to the role of social media in spreading misinformation after disaster events [19,26,28].

ACM 978-1-4503-2922-4/15/03...$15.00
http://dx.doi.org/10.1145/2675133.2675202

Rumor has always been a feature of crisis, an outgrowth of the "natural" sensemaking process that takes place after events as people try to construct meaning from often incomplete and imperfect information [2,9,41]. Researchers in social psychology have developed a thorough body of literature outlining the theory of rumor, describing the dynamics of rumor propagation and the human behaviors that factor into its transmission.

Less understood is how social media mediate, amplify or otherwise alter these dynamics. Several studies have examined the network dynamics of rumor propagation online [e.g. 39,51], and a few have attempted to look at the human behavior through the lens of existing rumor theory [4,34,44]. The vast majority of these studies focus on quantitative measures calculated using the digital traces of online activity. Indeed, preliminary research for this work relied upon digital traces of Twitter data collected after the crisis event to understand rumor propagation [46].

Complementing studies of trace data, this study relies upon qualitative methods to explore relationships between social media tools, crisis events, and rumoring behavior. We focus on public participation around the 2013 Boston Marathon bombings and the subsequent events related to the MIT shooting and manhunt through Watertown, MA. These events catalyzed massive participation online, including a great deal of misinformation [28]. Expanding upon previous research [46] examining the flow of misinformation on Twitter after the bombings, this study consists of interviews with individuals who used social media to search for and/or share information during these events.

We began with a goal to better understand the relationship between crisis events, social media, and rumoring. In particular, we were curious about the effect of situated physical proximity on the spread of misinformation online. More broadly, we were interested in evolving online information-sharing practices during crisis events and how those practices relate to rumoring behavior. From these initial questions, we used constructivist grounded theory (CGT) to shape our method of inquiry. Our findings describe a number of salient themes that emerged.

BACKGROUND: SOCIAL MEDIA, CRISIS & RUMORING

Our research began with generative questions surrounding the relationship between an individual's physical proximity to a crisis event and their social media behavior.

Social Media Use during Crisis

A growing body of research in the field of crisis informatics shows that social media use has become a consistent feature of the community response to crisis events [18,36,37,42]. These tools are being utilized by members of the affected public, professional media, and, increasingly, formal crisis responders [22,36,38], and their usage during crisis events is causing disruption to the traditional models of information transmission during such a time [23].

Rumoring Behavior during Crisis Events

Rumoring is a long-established feature of crisis events [41]. Social psychologists have posited that rumoring is a reaction to information scarcity and ambiguity [2,9], which are common characteristics of disasters; when information is scarce or ambiguous, people try to fill gaps in understanding by creating their own versions of truth. DiFonzo & Bordia define rumors as "unverified and instrumentally relevant information statements in circulation that arise in contexts of ambiguity, danger or potential threat, and that function to help people make sense and manage risk" [9, p. 13]. In these contexts, rumors serve as a method for community members to cope with uncertainty through collaboration to reach a common understanding [34, 41].

Rumors are often viewed as a negative aspect of crises, something that we should seek to minimize. Aligned with this view, Caplow [7] theorized that rumors emerge and propagate in the absence of official information, and that messages from formal channels should dampen rumoring behavior. However, others see rumor as part of the natural sensemaking process that occurs after a crisis event [41]. Proposing a more positive view of rumoring, Shibutani [41] characterizes rumor as improvised news—a collective activity to create and impart meaning. Similarly, Bordia and DiFonzo [4] describe it as collective problem solving or "social sensemaking." Sensemaking in this context is a collective activity to impose meaning on the available information and to agree on a common understanding of the situation. Rumoring can also be seen as a social coping mechanism [41] in which sharing information serves a cathartic purpose [12].

Rumoring via Social Media and Crisis Events

Several research studies have examined rumoring behavior on social media during disasters [e.g. 30,34,44]. Social media provide new opportunity to study rumoring through its digital traces [4], and may also enable new dynamics of rumor generation and propagation.

Online spaces are often viewed as particularly vulnerable to the spread of misinformation [26,28]. Some emergency responders cite misinformation as one reason for resisting the incorporation of social media into their work practices [20,22]. The negative view of social media may hold for the general public as well. In a study of source credibility after the Fukushima disaster, Thomson et al. [48] found Twitter and other social media were seen as less credible than other sources (e.g. newspapers, radio, word of mouth).

Some researchers and members of the media have contested the perceived risk of misinformation by claiming that the online crowd is naturally self-correcting [e.g. 30]. However, though researchers examining the spread of misinformation after the Boston Marathon Bombings found evidence of the online crowd identifying and correcting rumors, they also noted that the corrections had a smaller volume, and often lagged behind the misinformation [2]; therefore corrections propagated less broadly than misinformation.

The Role of Proximity in Rumor Behavior

Previous research indicates that physical proximity plays a role in information-seeking activities. For example, Thomson et al. [48] found that individuals perceived those who were proximate to a crisis event to be more credible, and Starbird & Palen [45] claimed that members of the public, especially those affected by the crisis, value local sources and locally relevant information.

For this research, we are interested in the effects of proximity on information-sharing behaviors—i.e. are those closer to a disaster more likely to share misinformation? In a study based on analysis of Twitter data, Oh et al., [34] found strong support for personal involvement in a disaster to be associated with the spread of rumors, and weak support for the feeling of anxiety to influence rumor-sharing behavior. Berger [3] demonstrated experimentally that arousal, both positive and negative, increases social transmission of information. Rosnow [40] noted that follow-up studies to the early rumor research show that personal anxiety also plays a role in rumoring behavior. Our study seeks to further explore this relationship between proximity and rumoring within the context of information-sharing via social media during a major disaster event characterized by high levels of anxiety and uncertainty.

Physical vs Emotional Proximity

Our initial research questions focused on the role of physical proximity to an event—the physical distance between an individual and the disaster event when it happened. However, our analysis revealed that emotional proximity—an emotional connection to people who were affected by a crisis or a sentimental association to the crisis location—was a significant factor as well. This distinction between physical and emotional proximity is akin to differentiations between "place" and "space."

Notions of online interactions are riddled with spatial and territorial terminology, such as "sites" and "cyberspace" [16]. These metaphors underline a distinction between the concept of *place*, the geographic location, and *space*, which provides a more functional view of situated-ness. Giddens [13] argued that place and space are also increasingly distinct concepts as technologies collapse the notion of distance. He termed this a "disembedding" of social systems, or "the 'lifting out' of social relations from local contexts of interaction and their restructuring across indefinite spans of time-space" [13, p. 21]. Extending this argument, others have described this phenomenon as the "death of distance" by noting how connective technology further expedites this disembedding [6,49].

Summarizing a variety of conceptual treatments of relationships between place and space in the context of information technology, Graham rejects the view that technologies cause social and spatial change—i.e. the notion that distance effectively "dies" or "evaporates"—as deterministic, opting instead for a relational view based on actor-network theory [16]. In this view space is neither dissolved nor transcended, but continually constructed through socio-technical interactions within virtual and physical contexts. This idea of the construction of space is important for understanding relationships between social media, physical and emotional proximity, and rumoring.

Event Background: 2013 Boston Marathon Bombings, MIT Police Shooting and Hunt for Perpetrators

This research focuses on social media behavior immediately following the April 15, 2013 bombings at the Boston Marathon and during the subsequent, related events.

The Boston Marathon occurs every year on Patriot's Day, a regional holiday in the Northeast U.S. On this day, families gather on Boylston Street to cheer on participants in the world's oldest annual marathon. For many, going to watch the Boston Marathon is a family tradition, and hundreds of volunteers sign up months ahead of time. To the Boston community, watching the Marathon is a treasured past time.

Memories of the 117th Boston Marathon are stained by the chaos and fear that ensued after two bombs were detonated at the finish line, killing three and injuring hundreds more. The bombings precipitated "100 hours of intense drama" as crisis responders and law enforcement quickly worked to simultaneously evacuate marathon athletes and spectators, conduct a criminal investigation, and protect members of the community from follow-up attacks [27].

Three days after the bombings, on the night of April 18, 2013, MIT police officer Sean Collier was shot and killed by the perpetrators of the bombing. After the shooting, a manhunt for the suspects led to a firefight in Watertown, MA, and a citywide shutdown the following day. Those in the area were instructed to stay indoors for personal safety.

The uncertainty surrounding the bombings, the police officer shooting, and the subsequent manhunt prompted massive online participation via social media. Within that discussion, several rumors developed and spread through social media and other channels. With the goal of helping law enforcement find the perpetrators, online volunteers combed through photos of the crime scene; this effort backfired when Reddit users infamously misidentified one suspect as missing Brown student Sunil Tripathi, a problem made worse when some traditional news outlets confirmed Reddit's detective work as truth [28].

METHODOLOGY

In this section, we offer a short description of how we used constructivist grounded theory to guide our methodological approach. Then, we discuss the participant recruitment process and give an overview of the data generation procedure.

Using Constructivist Grounded Theory For Social Media Research During Crisis Events

Grounded theory is a systematic qualitative research technique used to generate theories rooted in observation. Researchers who take a grounded approach allow theories to emerge from the data [15]. Several variations of grounded theory have been developed to support the array of flexibility required by researchers in diverse fields of study [11]. The constructivist approach employed here is a permutation of the classical grounded theory developed by Glaser and Strauss, and is popularized by the work of Strauss and Corbin [14,31,47].

Differences between the traditional approach and the constructivist approach appear in several aspects [8,31]. In particular, Glaser [14] of the traditional approach advocates that researchers should begin with as little previous knowledge as possible. In contrast, Strauss and Corbin of the constructivist approach argue that theories are interpretations made by researchers based on pre-existing perspectives. Following this constructivist approach, we entered the data collection and analysis phases with existing knowledge of relevant literature.

The core elements of the constructivist grounded theory offer an appropriate process to study the influence of disaster events on people's behavior on social media. The constructivist approach developed by Strauss and Corbin [47] is well documented with strategic methods of analysis that offer a high level of flexibility that befit our research requirements. Muller [32] points out that CGT is gaining popularity and usage by researchers in the CSCW and HCI communities. We chose to follow this approach for our study because we are exploring a subject area without a dominant theory, and our goal is to view the research question from various perspectives in order to gain a well-rounded understanding.

Participant Recruitment Process

To capture the richness and depth of experiences social media users encountered during the aftermath of the Boston Marathon Bombings, we adopted theoretical sampling for recruitment. To begin, we chose five Research Level 1 universities where affiliated members were likely to be varied in proximity to the crisis location yet situated in similar educational and social environments. These included MIT[1], another university in the Boston area, one in the U.S. Northeast, and two on the U.S. West Coast.

Researchers on our team are affiliated with each of these universities, which allowed us to identify opt-in email lists at each of the schools and contact the appropriate email list managers. We utilized several university-based list-servs to distribute a recruitment email with a link to a pre-interview survey instrument. We explicitly chose an email recruiting strategy rather than a social media recruiting strategy in order to avoid bias towards heavy social media users.

We received 151 responses to our screener survey, to which 57 expressed interest in a follow-up interview. After excluding survey respondents who indicated that they did not use social media to seek and share information during the event, we contacted the remaining participants to schedule an interview. Many of our follow-up inquiries were met with no response; we interviewed the eleven individuals who replied.

These interviews took place about one year after the event; thus, participants did not always remember their specific actions and thoughts concretely. To support them in remembering their own experiences, we provided facts about the event whenever the participants requested. Additionally, some participants chose to look back in their social media history as a memory aid during the interview.

Data Generation

In-depth, semi-structured remote interviews were conducted with eleven participants (five male and six female) through their preferred method of participation (one face-to-face, eight using Skype voice, and two using the phone). Participants were all affiliated with a university; most, but not all, were students. Interviews were 30-50 minutes long and were all recorded. Because the topic of discussion could be a sensitive subject for some, we gave participants the opportunity to stop the interview at anytime. We developed an efficient memoing method that captured all of the dialogue timestamps as well as contextual details that arose during the interview session. Afterwards, the interviewer transcribed critical sections using the timestamps on each interview memo from the corresponding audio recording.

ANALYSIS AND INTERPRETATION OF DATA

In analyzing the interview data, we used theoretical coding which enabled us to organize the interview transcripts and discover patterns from the data. Theoretical coding requires researchers to merge concepts into groups during the entire analysis process [11].

Stage 1: Open Coding

We began with an open card sort to collaboratively process five of the interview transcripts, placing every statement and observation from each interview onto a card, and then grouping cards together based on their similarities. Through this process, we generated a large set of individual categories. Using these initial categories as a guide, we double-coded the remaining six interview transcripts in a closed card sort, adding a small number of new codes for excerpts that did not fit into the initial categories.

Stage 2: Focused Coding

Next, we selectively combined smaller categories developed in open coding into higher-level categories, subdivided categories that were too large, and eliminated less useful categories. Through this process, we began to organize codes into larger, underlying themes. The themes salient to our research questions relate to the topics of information sharing, rumoring, and proximity to the crisis event. We present them in the next section.

FINDINGS

As often happens after crisis events [21,24], the 2013 Boston Marathon Bombings prompted a convergence of information seekers who were looking for the most up-to-date information. The interviews suggest that social media was a primary source for some of those hoping to find more information—five participants learned about the bombings through Facebook, three found out through Twitter, two through text alerts, and one through TV news.

Turning to Social Media after a Disaster Event

After a disaster event, one immediate need is information [37]. Participants in our study, both local and remote, converged onto social media to learn more about the situation, and many of those who were in the Boston area immediately after the bombing explained that the traditional news outlets did not have the updated, real-time, and locally relevant news that they were looking for.

Social Media for Real-time News

Alex (P9), who was flying into Boston on the day of the event, explained why he turned to Twitter for the real-time information he craved:

> *There wasn't a lot of news coverage because there's so much uncertainty. I remember at the Philadelphia Airport I was just sitting there trying to scrape Twitter as much as I could to get some idea of what was happening and piece together coherent narratives....I don't know if I would have had any information on the situation without that kind of stream.*

A perceived lack of information from traditional news sources after the MIT shooting also drove Emily (P6) to seek out news on social media. Emily was in her dorm room at MIT when she learned about the police shooting there:

[1] We chose not to anonymize MIT because several of the interviewees were at that university after the shooting of a police officer there, and this contextual information becomes vital for interpreting their responses.

I remember being frustrated I wasn't getting information about what was going on from the news outlets I usually go to. The first one I tried to turn to was the Times. That was when I really got frustrated. I want to know what's happening right now! I mean I know why they're doing it; it was because they had to verify all their information; but like it was really frustrating because stuff was happening now and they didn't have a story on it. So that's when I turned to Reddit for my main source of information"

Emily's comment indicates that she understands, on some level, the institutional constraints that the media face in meeting the expectations of a public now accustomed to receiving real-time news [33], but this was still a source of frustration for her at the time, and it led her to seek out information from other sources. Emily, along with another interviewee who lived near the event, eventually turned to Reddit as a source of continuously updating information.

Participants physically distant to the event—i.e. who were not in the Greater Boston area—also expressed that they found social media to be faster and more accessible than traditional news. Brianna (P3) was surprised at how quickly information about the event spread through Twitter:

...[Her friend's] friends started tweeting and I don't know how they got that information so quickly because it was maybe a minute, maybe a minute and a half after the first bomb and she was like 'wow my twitter feed is blowing up [about] the marathon' and we'd just heard something but we don't know what's happening.

Brandon (P4) who was at his office desk in Hollywood, CA at the time of the bombings shared a similar point, stating, "[Twitter] is so instantaneous, it was constantly refreshing."

Across eight of the interviews, the *speed of information transmission* emerged as a salient theme, both in the context of its benefits—in terms of using social media for real-time news—and its potential role in the spread of misinformation. We expand on this finding below.

Social Media for Locally-Relevant Information

Judy (P7), who was in D.C. when the bombs went off, had learned during a previous event that Twitter was helpful for getting crisis-related news, and turned to that site again:

I became active on Twitter probably in the last year and a half...mainly because there was something ...like we had a tornado warning or something like that and I wasn't getting the information I was looking for as far as where we lived. So I went on Twitter and I just started using search trends and that's how I found out wow this is great and responsive that I can get the information that I'm looking for really quickly and it's like a customized information just for me.

This remark underscores two interesting points regarding the use of social media during disaster events. One supports previous research suggesting that disasters can lead to new appropriations of tools that, for some, are then adopted into information practices going forward [43]. The second point suggests that timeliness is not the only factor in the heightened utility of social media during disasters. The ability to access locally relevant, "customizable" news is another perceived benefit.

This idea appeared in other interviews as well. Michelle (P10), an MIT student who was returning via train to Boston from New York when she heard about the bombing, explained that mainstream news did not have the kind of information that she needed to make decisions:

I started looking and I just googled Bomb and Boston and Copley and a bunch of news articles popped up. They didn't have that much information. I was looking for... Were [metro] trains running? Is it safe to go outside? and Could I get from Boston to MIT? I just didn't really know where to search for that.

Max (P8), who had been at the finish line hours before the bombings, also wanted more than the news sources could provide. He explained that he wanted to find out more about what was going on in the community and how local groups were helping. To Max, social media was the best place to look for efforts to help the affected community.

These responses demonstrate that speed was not the only advantage that social media had over mainstream media for interviewees, but that getting customizable, locally-relevant information was important as well.

Trusting Friends and Locals

As social media channels become more efficient at supplying timely information than traditional media, those seeking reliable information online have to develop criteria for assessing and verifying that information.

Johnny (P1) was in Seattle, WA when he found out about the bombings. Having run the Boston Marathon previously, the news came as a shock. Additionally, he had close friends running in the marathon, and was worried. He used Facebook to get in touch with friends and to find out more about the unfolding events. He remembered seeing posts from acquaintances in the area, and explained that he vetted information based on the number of corroborating sources he could find. Three other participants also expressed that they use corroboration as a method to determine the truthfulness of information seen on social media sites.

Participants also reported vetting information through friends. Alex, who was in London during the event, explained that after the MIT shooting he turned to friends who lived at the scene for news updates:

Absolutely the stuff coming out of friends, or things being shared by friends...There were a lot of secondary sources from friends or friends of friends who were saying things like 'I can look outside my office and see this is taped up' or 'I can see there's this massive amount of police cars' etc. So that was the most verifiable and the most trusted information that was coming out.

Michelle also stated that she tends to trust her friends more:

People on my Facebook, they are my friends, they are my acquaintances that I trust, and um I doubt they would post some thing like that, especially during a time when there was a bombing at the finish line at the marathon. I don't think they would joke about things like that. I also did see a lot of people posting it, so that also confirmed it.

These comments indicate that trust is in some cases related to an emotional connection between the information-seeker and information-provider. This supports research showing that social ties increase trust in online communication [5].

Max claimed that his carefully curated Twitter following list assured that "worthy" information found him. He further explained that he believed first-hand sources near the scene to be more newsworthy than the mainstream media reports:

I wasn't looking at Boston Globe I wasn't looking for Boston Fox Affiliates. I wasn't looking for that. I was looking for either photos shared by individuals who were at the scene or near the scene at the time. Or tweets of individuals and then information from groups and what groups were doing to either help or spread information.

Several participants expressed that they place the most trust on sources that are physically close to the developing situation, a finding that aligns with research assessing source credibility during disasters through digital traces [48]. Brandon was clear on this point:

I trust people that were in close proximity to the situation. I mean they were there. The news people were just getting the information from those people. Getting the news from the source I feel is more accurate.

Alex also cited a preference for "raw info" from those on the scene as opposed to commentary from people who are not there. These kinds of comments, which were shared by seven of the interview participants, demonstrate a shift in trust—at least among the young-adults in this study—from journalists and mainstream media to social media users who are either physically close to the event, or emotionally close to the information-seeker.

Feeling the Effects of Physical and Emotional Proximity

For many interviewees, the events surrounding the Boston Marathon Bombings were a source of excitement, anxiety, fear, and/or sadness. Though we did not intentionally design the interview protocol to measure emotional impact, eight interviewees explicitly mentioned being personally, emotionally affected by the event. For example, Brianna was with a neighbor in her dorm, looking out the window, trying to figure out what the loud sound was:

Her room faces Boston, and it's right on the bridge connecting Boston to Cambridge. Right after it happened she was looking outside and there were hundreds of people running across the bridge. It was pretty scary.

On the night of the manhunt, Emily was afraid for her life when the policeman was shot on her school campus:

I was [src] really freaked out...what if they come into the dorm or something...I was much more personally freaked out than when I heard about the bombings.

Michelle remembers that parents and friends of those in the Boston area were very concerned and shared information on Facebook to show sympathy and pass along warnings. She also felt a sense of solidarity within the MIT community after the police shooting and during the manhunt:

I definitely think that when it's really close...like at MIT...I felt like a real community connection more than ever at this huge school. Like everyone was sharing all this on Facebook and posting all these sites.

Even among those not located in Boston at the time, many expressed an emotional connection to the event, some because they had lived there previously. A few noted a strong connection to the marathon itself, either because they had run it before or knew what it meant to the community.

Judy: *...The last thing that I did before I left my home was going to the marathon with my family in 2010. So it's like bringing back memories of my last memories that spring before we moved to DC and just realizing that totally could have been me. 'Cause I literally was standing with my family very close to where the first bomb went off (before I left). Every year I would go to the marathon, it was like a thing you do growing up in the Boston area...So it just kind of like put it in perspective 'like wow' and then it was scary like 'OMG are any of my friends affected?' and then just trying to find information and news. So it was emotional, scary for a bit there.*

For several interviewees, the emotional connection related to having friends or family that may have been affected. For example, Johnny was worried for his friends who were running in the marathon:

I had one really close friend and another two close friends running it...saw stuff on FB pretty early on [and] I posted on her wall to say "hey Cindy let us know if you're okay."

These emotional connections may have played a role in information-seeking behaviors in general and social media use in particular. Alex explained how social media helped him cope with the emotional impact of the situation:

There was this certain sense of violation. There's this great day...there's a sense of community around Patriot's day and there's a bit of violation. The information coming from social media was just something to prevent you from feeling paralyzed or completely useless. It was just something to hold on to. I think without social media the end result wouldn't have been anything different. But at the time, it gave me a coping mechanism. Having that direct connection to friends getting that immediate response. That was new for me and just gave me a more personal connection to the events.

Not all of the participants were emotionally affected by or physically close to the crisis situation. Molly (P5) was in California when the bombings took place, and though she remembers being worried about the bombings being a terrorist attack, she was so far removed that she did not realize the MIT shooting was related to the Boston Marathon Bombings. Ajay and Mary shared similar sentiments. Often, these more distant (both physically and emotionally) participants did not remember the event details well, and explained that they were not as invested or interested in this event as they had been for other crises.

Mary explained that even though she does have friends in the Boston area, they were not affected by the bombings:

I was more interested in the outcome of that event than [the] wildfires currently going on in California because it's closer to home. But far less interested than I'd be say if let's say if it involved a personal friend, family member or was happening where I live or work now.

The Perception that Sharing Is Helping

Information about the Boston Marathon Bombings propagated quickly on social media as a result of users posting and reposting information that they thought was important. Four participants believed that sharing information would be helpful to others. Judy made this connection in a comment about her posting activity in general. Michelle remembered posting to her Facebook page telling family and friends where to find more information, indicating a motivation to help inform others. Molly expressed that the main reason she shared information was to inform her followers on Facebook:

I was mainly trying to inform the people 'cause I know I don't watch the news and I know a lot of my family members also don't watch. So I was definitely trying to reach out to them and show them the video that they probably would not have seen without the Facebook.

Max was extremely engaged with the manhunt because a close friend in Watertown was close enough to see and hear the activity. He remembers the increased flux of information on social media that he was actively passing along without worrying about being right or wrong. His main goal was to help his friend stay informed:

The night of the shootings...that was a flurry of information. It would end up being retweet this, reply about this, get new information and go back to the retweet and reply the 'no that's not right, it's this' and whatever. It was a lot of fast activity of trying to help people and help myself [and] everyone kind of get on a similar page about the information that was going on there.

Previous research examining the role of social media during live events has noted an inherent trade-off between speed and accuracy [33]. Max's comments suggest that some social media users are aware of this trade-off, even as they choose to optimize for speed.

Reflecting on Their Role in the Spread of Misinformation

As we noted in the background section, there was considerable misinformation propagating online after the 2013 Boston Marathon bombings. Previous research suggested that there were several types of rumors, including simple Internet memes like the photo of the young girl who was purportedly killed while running the race, conspiracy theories such as one about the Navy Seals carrying out the bombings as some kind of "false flag" attack, and—perhaps the most problematic—a widespread online effort to identify the suspects where the crowd drifted from digital volunteerism to digital vigilantism [46].

Initially, this study set out to examine social media behavior particularly as it related to the spread of misinformation and situated physical proximity to the crisis. Interviewees were asked specific questions about their memories of certain rumors. Few participants remembered any of the "Internet meme" rumors, and only one participant—who was not physically proximate to the event—recalled a conspiracy theory that she initially thought had some merit. A larger percentage recalled some of the activity around the search for suspects, though some had to be reminded about the incident before they recalled the details—including Johnny who later admitted to having shared rumors related to that activity via social media. Another interviewee referred to that sequence of events as a "witch hunt."

When asked to reflect on their own social media actions, some participants expressed remorse for some posts, and many offered explanations for why they might have spread misinformation. Johnny grew uncomfortable when we he began to reflect on his posts on Twitter. He said he felt guilty for contributing to the rumor that falsely accused Sunil Tripathi of being involved in the bombings:

I'm usually pretty wary with the stuff I post. I usually try to be certain about things. With this one...I even waited when I heard that...I waited till I was really sure. By the time I posted, everyone sounded sure. But it came out that it was not. But then they found out that he died right? I feel like I remember hearing that and it was really sad. I remember feeling really bad that I did that.

Max did not remember if he retweeted unconfirmed rumors, but he acknowledged that to be likely and commented on the sharing of information in a crisis event in general:

It was just the reaction ... it was just part of the process of finding out what's going on. Then I corrected myself.

After Spreading a Rumor: Retract, Delete or Let It Be

Participants disclosed different strategies for dealing with existing posts to social media after they learned that they had shared a false rumor. While Max claimed that he would go back and correct the misinformation, Molly related that she would likely just "wait for it to blow over" or delete the post without mentioning it again, "Because I don't like to be wrong. And I don't like people to know that I'm wrong."

Judy told us that she thinks she would have done the opposite, explaining that she cares about being credible. After mentioning that she did post something that she was not quite sure was true, she describes her likely actions:

> *Credibility is important to me. I would have gone back to retract it. You can't really delete it because it lives forever. That probably would've been worse than not doing anything.*

This comment suggests that Judy believes deleting a tweet is not a good approach–i.e. it is worse than doing nothing– and that she would have gone back and posted a follow up tweet correcting her earlier post.

Reflecting upon her actions, including sharing some insensitive and unconfirmed posts, Molly said that she would do things differently in a future crisis:

> *I will not pass on any more rumors that are not confirmed, and I would be a lot more cautious about that and I think that whenever I do post I will send the actual link of where I did find the information.*

These comments indicate that lessons learned about social media use during this event might lead to new social media behaviors in a future event.

DISCUSSION

This study explores the phenomena of information propagation online in the aftermath of the Boston Marathon Bombings and the subsequent manhunt for the perpetrators through interviews with eleven individuals who had used social media during those events.

Salient themes that emerged from these interviews suggest that social media sites—such as Twitter, Facebook, and Reddit—were used by some Internet users as primary sources of real-time news after the bombings and especially during the police chase after the MIT police shooting. When confronted with a 'flurry of information' online, study participants tended to trust information coming from sources who were 'on the ground' as well as from friends. Information that could be corroborated by several people was generally deemed more trustworthy. One motivation for sharing information on social media was to help others stay informed. Sometimes this resulted in passing along erroneous information; some participants experienced guilt and many chose to either retract their online posts or correct themselves to resolve their misinformed posts.

Aligned with existing theories about rumoring during disasters [e.g. 2,3,7,34], our findings suggest that the spread of misinformation on social media sites is a complex process that occurs within a short time period and is influenced by a range of social and psychological factors. This study raises concerns for understanding the nuances of how people's emotional and physical proximity to a crisis influence the spread of misinformation online and highlights areas for future research.

Emotional Proximity and (Mis)information Sharing

Though this research began with questions around physical proximity, through our CGT approach, emotional proximity emerged as a more salient theme. We define emotional proximity as a connection between a person and a disaster event. This connection can be mediated by an interpersonal connection, i.e. a close relationship with someone who is physically affected by a disaster, or through an experiential connection to the geographic location of the event. This feeling of connectedness is therefore both related to past experiences and integrated into the physical and virtual spaces where the event is unfolding.

Six interviewees shared stories indicating that they were personally affected by the bombings through a sentimental connection to the city of Boston, the annual marathon, or to a loved one who was in the area. One participant experienced heightened emotional proximity to the events surrounding the manhunt because a close friend was in the Watertown area that night. Another was shaken by the fact that he had run the marathon in a previous year—perhaps feeling, as Judy expressed, that "it could have been me."

From our study, we found that emotional proximity did not always correlate with physical proximity. Even for those who were in the Boston area, the intensity of emotional proximity varied somewhat according to sentimental connections that individuals had for the city, the marathon, and those who suffered through the traumatic event on April 15. Similarly, interviewees from within the MIT community expressed deeper emotional proximity to the MIT police shooting and manhunt (April 18–19) than those outside of that community.

This research suggests that emotional proximity affects the information seeking and sharing behaviors of social media users, and illuminates a role played by emotional proximity in the propagation of misinformation. This proposed relationship between emotional proximity and rumoring aligns with previous research that shows anxiety leads to increases in rumor sharing in general [40] and online [34], A few interview responses indicated that a heightened emotional state influenced their information sharing practices. For example, Max, whose friend was in Watertown during the manhunt, talked about the night of the shootings being a "flurry of information" where he and other members of the crowd tried to keep up, often having to correct previous information that turned out to be untrue.

Emotional proximity may also have been a motivating factor for some who wanted to help out. For interviewees in this study, helping out was often equated with passing along useful information "to make sure everyone's on the same page," as one participant reflected. These findings support previous research [12] showing altruism plays a role in interpersonal transmission of news. Unfortunately, the public record of this event shows that online "help" also took the form of a public search for suspects that turned into a "witch hunt" and spawned several false rumors [28, 46]. Thus, it is clear that well-meaning contributions online can lead to the generation and propagation of misinformation, and it is likely emotional proximity plays a role in these phenomena as well.

These findings also suggest that social media offer a virtual space for those who are feeling emotionally proximate to converge, and—aligning with theories of emotional contagion online [1,17,25]—therefore likely contribute to a sense of emotional proximity. For example Alex, who expressed a sense of violation after the MIT shooting, saw social media as a collective coping mechanism in a crisis situation as well as a way to establish both direct connection to friends on the scene and a "personal connection to the events." His comments suggest that social media allowed him to experience a heightened sense of emotional proximity.

Thus, building upon Graham's relational view of space [16], we found emotional proximity for social media users during a crisis event to be a dynamic attribute constructed through online activity, through interactions in the physical "place" of a disaster event (before, during and/or after impact), and through perceived connections with others who are physically or emotionally proximate. Critically, these spaces where emotional proximity is constructed are also interconnected, and social media plays a role within each. Our research suggests complex interactions between social media use, emotional proximity, and rumoring behavior, though more in depth research would be needed to specify these relationships. Specifically, these results lead to dual hypotheses that social media plays a role in the development of emotional proximity, and that this emotional proximity has a mediating effect on the spread of misinformation during disaster events.

Evolving Practices around Information Sharing during Disasters

For this study, we recruited individuals who had used social media during the events surrounding the 2013 Boston Marathon Bombings, and selected participants based on those who remembered sharing and finding information online about the event as well. Therefore, it is not surprising that most of these interviewees had turned to social media as their first and main source for information—i.e. they learned about the event through social media and they continued to follow it primarily through social media.

Several participants commented that they thought social media were better sources than mainstream media, citing the speed and location—the ability to follow the real-time developments of the event from first-hand sources—as two major reasons for this preference. As Palen [35] has discussed, "hyper-temporality" and "hyper-locality" are critical value attributes of crisis information. Social media seem to align well with these value attributes because they can provide information in real-time, often from those located at or near the event. This information may be imperfect, but for many interviewees it was better than nothing. Especially for those who lived near the affected areas or had friends near those areas, hyper-local and real-time information was a necessity, and misinformation was "just part of the process."

In the long view of history and the development of practices around information sharing during crisis events, social media represent a nascent information/interaction space, where norms and rules are still being negotiated. Taken as a whole, these interviews describe an environment that can be characterized by rapid change, emerging practices, trial and error, and lessons learned. When asked to reflect, some interviewees shared lessons learned and intentions to behave differently in the future. We can also consider the more spontaneous public apologies on Reddit after the actual suspects were identified, and how the incident led to changed norms and even formal rules within that site to prevent future mishaps [50]. The visible discourse around these lessons learned suggests that we, as a public, are still in the process of establishing norms around information sharing in this evolving information space.

We recognize this evolution as a multi-faceted one. Our research findings provide evidence of a shift in trust from traditional news media to a more complex array of information sources. The social media users in our study are observed making decisions about source veracity based on mixed-measures of physical and emotional proximity—emotional proximity to the source and the source's physical proximity to the event. However, complications emerge as a result of these new behaviors. Where mainstream media was seen by interviewees as too slow, some participants acknowledged that social media was moving too fast, and that the constant influx of information contributed to the spread of misinformation.

From a more positive perspective, our findings also indicate that social media users are becoming savvy about social media use; they are establishing new norms, and learning through reflection—and to some extent public reprimand.

LIMITATIONS

This study has some important limitations. A substantial amount of time passed between the event and the interviews, which means that interview responses are likely subject to misremembering. Capturing the behaviors and emotions at the moment of the event may have provided a greater level of detail and accuracy. However, as researchers have noted in the past, real-time research is exceptionally difficult in the domain of disaster response [10,29]. And, while research on digital traces may allow for examination of a disaster event as it unfolds, trace data does not necessarily convey the whole picture. For example, the post-event accounts analyzed here include informed reflections that would be absent in real-time studies.

Additionally, the participant selection process likely produced a biased sample. We tried to recruit participants from communities in different geographical locations in the United States. However, individuals who responded to the screener survey were self-selected, resulting in a set of participants who may have been more personally affected by the event. In support of this observation, our recruitment efforts from universities near Boston resulted in far more survey responses than those distributed at less proximate universities. This means that the observations here are particularly valid for those who were emotionally connected to an event, but may be less applicable individuals with limited social media engagement.

CONCLUSION

The 2013 Boston Marathon Bombings and the subsequent events surrounding the search for suspects drew widespread attention from the local community and online crowd. This research focused on recollections of eleven individuals who used social media during that event. We used constructivist grounded theory to guide our study; this enabled us to gain deeper understandings of the insights participants gained during that event, the observed social media behaviors, and the motivations behind those behaviors.

We identified emotional proximity as a key factor in online information seeking and sharing behavior. Amidst the chaos of the bombings and after the police shooting, it was likely that the spread of misinformation was a natural derivative of the fast sense-making process; information traveled quickly between social media users at a time when their main concern was to develop a coherent understanding of the situation. The interviewees reflected on the importance of real-time, locally sourced information. Even though the information on social media was often unconfirmed, it became an important channel for the wider community to cope through the crisis and to develop a shared understanding of what happened.

The record of the events discussed in this study confirms that misinformation is propagating through social media after crisis events, an issue that many have come to view as a specific danger of online interaction. However, as Max pointed out during his interview and as rumor theory has long contended, misinformation is a natural byproduct of the community sensemaking process that has always occurred after crisis events. This research shows that social media users are aware of and are concerned about the transmission of misinformation online. Furthermore, we found that many individuals are reflecting on past information sharing behaviors and continuously refining their online actions to develop better strategies for handling future crisis events.

Because information sharing practices of social media users are changing rapidly, it is important to acknowledge and respond to the increasing importance of social media as a useful tool for those affected in a crisis. Currently, some crisis responders are averse to using social media in their formal work practices due to a perception of widespread misinformation [20,22]. However, these platforms are rapidly becoming a primary venue for information-sharing and sensemaking by those who are emotionally or physically affected by the crisis event. Despite the threat of misinformation—and *because of that potential*—it may therefore be vital for crisis responders to engage in and help shape the online conversation during crisis events.

ACKNOWLEDGMENTS

This research was conducted through the emCOMP lab at UW and was partially supported by NSF Grant 1342252.

REFERENCES

1. Aaker, J., & Smith, A. (2010). *The dragonfly effect: Quick, effective, and powerful ways to use social media to drive social change*. John Wiley & Sons.
2. Allport, G. W. & Postman, L. An analysis of rumor. *Public Opinion Quarterly 10*, 4 (1946), 501-517.
3. Berger, J. Arousal increases social transmission of information. *Psychological Sci 22*, 7 (2011), 891-893.
4. Bordia, P., & DiFonzo, N. Problem solving in social interactions on the Internet: Rumor as social cognition. *Social Psychology Quarterly*, *67*, 1 (2004), 33-49.
5. Bradner, E., & Mark, G. Why distance matters: Effects on cooperation, persuasion and deception. *Proc. of CSCW 2002*, 226-235.
6. Cairncross, F. *The death of distance: How the communications revolution is changing our lives*. Harvard Business Press, 2001.
7. Caplow, T. Rumors in war. *Social Forces*, 3 (1947), 298–302.
8. Charmaz, K. (2008). Constructionism and the grounded theory method. In J. F. James A. Holstein PhD, Handbook of constructionist research (pp. 397-412). New York, The Guilford Press.
9. DiFonzo, N, & Bordia, P. *Rumor psychology: Social and organizational approaches*. American Psychological Association, 2007.
10. Drabek, T.E. Methodology of studying disasters: Past patterns and future possibilities. *American Behavioral Scientist* 13 (1970), 331-343.
11. Evans, G. L. (2014). A Novice Researcher's First Walk Through the Maze of Grounded Theory: Rationalization for Classical Grounded Theory. *Grounded Theory Review*.
12. Gantz, W., & Trenholm, S. Why people pass on news: Motivations for diffusion. *Journalism & Mass Communication Quarterly 56*, 2 (1979), 365-370.
13. Giddens, A. *The Consequences of Modernity*. Stanford University Press, Stanford, CA, 1990.

14. Glaser, B. *Basics of Grounded Theory Analysis: Emergence Vs. Forcing*. Mill Valley, California, United States: Sociology Press, 1992.

15. Glaser, B., & Strauss, A. *The Discovery of Grounded Theory: Strategies for Qualitative Research*. Piscataway, New Jersey: Aldine Transaction, 1999.

16. Graham, S. The end of geography or the explosion of place? Conceptualizing space, place and information technology. *Progress in Human Geography, 22*, 2 (1998), 165-185.

17. Hancock, J. T., Gee, K., Ciaccio, K., & Lin, J. M. H. I'm sad you're sad: Emotional contagion in CMC. *In Proc. CSCW 2008*, ACM Press (2008), 295-298.

18. Heverin, T., & Zach, L. Use of Microblogging for collective sense-making during violent crisis: A study of three campus shootings. *J. of the Amer. Society for Information Science & Technology 63*, 1 (2012), 34-47.

19. Hill, K. Hurricane Sandy, @ComfortablySmug, and the Flood of Social Media Misinformation. *Forbes.com.* (October 30, 2012). Available at: http://www.forbes .com/sites/kashmirhill/2012/10/30/hurricane-sandy-and-the-flood-of-social-media-misinformation/

20. Hiltz, S. R., Kushma, J., & Plotnick, L. Use of social Media by US public sector emergency managers: Barriers and wish lists. *Proc. of ISCRAM, 2014.*

21. Hughes, A. L., Palen, L., Sutton, J., Liu, S. B., & Vieweg, S. Sight-Seeing in Disaster: An Examination of On-Line Social Convergence. *Proc. of ISCRAM 2008.*

22. Hughes, A. L., & Palen, L. The evolving role of the public information officer: An examination of social media in emergency management. *J. of Homeland Security & Emergency Management 9*, 1 (2012), 1-20.

23. Hughes, A.L., S. Peterson & L. Palen. Social Media in Emergency Management. In *Issues in Disaster Science & Management: A Critical Dialogue Between Scientists and Emergency Managers*, (Eds) J.E. Trainor and T. Subbio. FEMA in Higher Education Program. (In press).

24. Fritz, C.E. & Mathewson, J.H. *Convergence behavior in disasters: A problem in social control.* National Academy of Sciences National Research Council, 1957.

25. Kramer, A. D., Guillory, J. E., & Hancock, J. T. Experimental evidence of massive-scale emotional contagion through social networks. *Proc. of the National Academy of Sciences, 2014.*

26. Leberecht, T. Twitter Grows Up in Aftermath of Haiti Earthquake, *CNET News*, (January 19, 2010) http://www.cnet.com/news/twitter-grows-up-in-aftermath-of-haiti-earthquake/

27. Leonard, H.B., Cole, C. M., Howitt, A. M., & Heymann, P. B. Why was Boston strong? Lessons from the Boston Marathon Bombing. Program on Crisis Leadership and Program in Criminal Justice Policy and Management, Harvard Kennedy School, April 3, 2014.

28. Madrigal, A. #BostsonBombing: The Anatomy of a Misinformation Disaster. *The Atlantic* (2013, April 19) http://www.theatlantic.com/technology/ archive/2013/04/-bostonbombing-the-anatomy-of-a-misinformation-disaster/275155/

29. Mendonca, D., & Wallace, W.A. Studying organizationally-situated improvisation in response to extreme events. *Intl J of Mass Emergencies & Disasters, 22*(2), 5-30.

30. Mendoza, M., Poblete, B., & Castillo, C. Twitter under crisis: can we trust what we RT?. *Proc. of 1st Workshop on Social Media Analytics 2010*, ACM, 71-79.

31. Mills, J., Bonner, A., & Francis, K. The Development of Constructivist Grounded Theory. *International Journal of Qualitative Methods*, 5, 1 (2006).

32. Muller, M. J., & Kogan, S. Grounded theory method in HCI and CSCW. *Cambridge: IBM Center for Social Software* (2010).

33. Newman, N. The rise of social media and its impact on mainstream journalism. *Reuters Institute for the Study of Journalism*, 8, 2 (2009), 1-5.

34. Oh, O., Agrawal , M., & Rao , H. (2013). Community Intelligence and Social Media Services: A Rumor Theoretic Analysis of Tweets During Social Crises. *MIS Quarterly, 37*, 2 (2013), 407-426.

35. Palen, L. Frontiers of Crisis Informatics. Opening Keynote at ISCRAM 2014, State College, PA.

36. Palen, L, Anderson, K.M, Mark, G, Martin, J, Sicker, D, Palmer, M., and Grunwald, D. A Vision for Technology -Mediated Support for Public Participation & Assistance in Mass Emergencies & Disasters, in *Proc. of ACM-BCS Visions of Computer Science* (2010), 1-12.

37. Palen, L., & Liu, S.B., Citizen communications in crisis: anticipating a future of ICT-supported public participation. In *Proc of CHI 2007*, ACM, 727-736.

38. Posetti, J., & Lo, P. The Twitterisation of ABC's emergency and disaster communication. *Australian Journal of Emergency Management, 27*, 1 (2012), 34.

39. Qazvinian, V., Rosengren, E., Radev, D. R., & Mei, Q. Rumor has it: Identifying misinformation in microblogs. In *Proc. of the Conference on Empirical Methods in Natural Language Processing*, (2011), 1589-1599.

40. Rosnow, R. L. Inside rumor: A personal journey. *American Psychologist 46*, 5 (1991): 484.

41. Shibutani, T. *Improvised news: A sociological study of rumor*. Ardent Media, 1966.

42. Shklovski, I., Palen, L., & Sutton, J. 2008. Finding Community Through Information and Communication Technology During Disaster Events, in *Proc of CSCW 2008*, San Diego, CA, November 8-12, pp. 127-136.

43. Shklovski, I., Burke, M., Kiesler, S., & Kraut, R. Technology adoption and use in the aftermath of Hurricane Katrina in New Orleans. *American Behavioral Scientist*, *53*, 8 (2010), 1228-1246.

44. Spiro, E. S., Fitzhugh, S., Sutton, J., Pierski, N., Greczek, M., & Butts, C. T. Rumoring during extreme events: A case study of Deepwater Horizon 2010. *Proc. of ACM Web Science Conference 2012*, ACM, 275-283.

45. Starbird, K., & Palen, L. Pass it on?: Retweeting in mass emergency. *Proc. of ISCRAM 2010.*

46. Starbird, K., Maddock, J., Orand, M., Achterman, P., & Mason, RM. Rumors, False Flags, and Digital Vigilantes: Misinformation on Twitter after the 2013 Boston Marathon Bombing. *iConference 2014*, 654-662.

47. Strauss, A., & Corbin, J. *Basics of qualitative research: Techniques and procedures for developing grounded theory (2 ed.)*. Thousand Oaks, California, United States: SAGE Publications, 1998.

48. Thomson, R., Ito, N., Suda, H., Lin, F., Liu, Y., Hayasaka, R., ... & Wang, Z. Trusting tweets: The Fukushima disaster and information source credibility on Twitter. In *Proc. ISCRAM 2012*.

49. Virilio, P. The Third Interval: A Critical Transition. In *Re-thinking Technologies*, Chapter 1. Minneapolis: University of Minnesota Press, 1993.

50. Wade, C. The Reddit Reckoning. *Slate* (April 15, 2014). http://www.slate.com/articles/technology/technology/2014/04/reddit_and_the_boston_marathon_bombings_how_the_site_reckoned_with_its_own.html

51. Zhou, J., Liu, Z., & Li, B. Influence of network structure on rumor propagation. *Physics Letters A*, *368*, 6 (2007) 458-463.

Think Local, Retweet Global: Retweeting by the Geographically-Vulnerable during Hurricane Sandy

Marina Kogan, Leysia Palen & Kenneth M. Anderson
Department of Computer Science
University of Colorado Boulder
{marina.kogan, leysia.palen, ken.anderson}@colorado.edu

ABSTRACT
Hurricane Sandy wrought $6 billion in damage, took 162 lives, and displaced 776,000 people after hitting the US Eastern seaboard on October 29, 2012. Because of its massive impact, the hurricane also spurred a flurry of social media activity, both by the population immediately affected and by the globally convergent crowd. In this paper we explore how retweeting activity by the geographically vulnerable differs (if at all) from that of the general Twitter population. We investigate whether they spread information differently, including what and whose content they chose to propagate. We investigate whether the Twitter-based relationships are preexisting or if they are newly formed because of the disaster, and if so if they persist. We find that the people in the path of the disaster favor in their retweeting locally-created tweets and those with locally-actionable information. They also form denser networks of information propagation during disaster than before or after.

Author Keywords
Crisis informatics; Disasters; Protective Decision-Making; Social Computing; Social Media; Twitter

ACM Classification Keywords
H.5.3. Groups & Organization Interfaces—collaborative computing, computer-supported cooperative work; K.4.2. Social Issues

General Terms
Human Factors

INTRODUCTION
Social media are platforms for one-to-many communication that are being used by the public during disaster response for a range of purposes. A flourishing body of research on the topic has developed in the last 5 years, with a community of researchers working apace with the socio-behavioral phenomena that are advancing in kind and number with each disaster. Some research in the *crisis informatics* space examines how formal responders use or do not use social media [6, 15, 17, 18]. Another line considers how online communication affects on-the-ground action before, during, and after disasters [30, 36, 44, 45].

However, the largest body of work is on the internal behaviors of the "Twittersphere" and other social media environments. Here again the research directions branch, with much work devoted to deriving data from existing social media logs using supervised and unsupervised machine learning (for example, [19, 42]) as well as other techniques [1, 6, 10]. The second branch of research that focuses on the social media posts as the objects of study is that which attempts to understand socio-behavioral phenomena. This includes sentiment analysis across the population represented in the streams of social media communication [7, 11]. It also includes analysis of self-organizing behaviors of groups that come together through social media to accomplish some task such as event reporting [20, 21, 22, 31] or a task they articulate as a particular need during that event [38, 44]. A third branch considers how information diffuses across social networks [4, 9, 34], particularly as the special conditions of disaster affect such diffusion [33, 37, 39].

Paper Objective & Background
This paper sits as a contribution in the space that examines online socio-behavioral phenomena, and in particular how information is diffused across a population. However, we target a line of inquiry that includes the population of people who are known to have been in the geographical area of effect of a major disaster during its height. In this case, we examine those who were under the most serious threat before and during the 2012 Hurricane Sandy, and who used Twitter to post during that time. Specifically, this is an analysis of how people who are at risk from a natural hazard with an advanced warning period—a hurricane—retweet information before, during, and after the event.

First, we investigate whether those who are geographically vulnerable spread information differently than the general public—a public that was highly active on Twitter around the world because of Hurricane Sandy's catastrophic

CSCW'15, March 14 - 18 2015, Vancouver, BC, Canada

ACM 978-1-4503-2922-4/15/03...$15.00
http://dx.doi.org/10.1145/2675133.2675218

potential and intense media attention. In addition, when the geographically vulnerable population retweets, what information do they spread, and what and whose tweets do they propagate if they do so at all? We investigate whether the Twitter-based relationships are preexisting or if they are newly formed during the disaster, and if those new relationships persist after the storm.

The objective of this line of inquiry is multi-fold. First, we want to continue to validate and deepen earlier findings by Starbird and Palen from the 2009 Red River Flood event that "locals" are more likely to retweet content that has "local utility," and that non-locals are more likely to retweet the "abstract" of the event [37]. In 2009, hardly any emergency management groups were on Twitter—but things had radically changed between 2009 and 2012 as emergency management groups tried to develop an online presence, including more police and fire departments [18]. In addition, relatively few media outlets were on Twitter in 2009, certainly as reflected in the Red River Flood data. In addition, the 2012 Sandy event had far more global attention as well as more extreme immediate consequences to a larger population than the US/Canadian Red River Flood threat of 2009—a critical event for Red River Valley locals, but incomparable to Sandy in terms of media reach. Furthermore, the number of active twitterers between 2009 and 2012 increased about seven fold (30M to 200M).[1] Finally, the act of retweeting in 2009 was only a user innovation—it was not built into the software (and therefore not into the metadata of tweets). We want to confirm, as well as elaborate, the earlier local utility versus global interest framing under these changing and far more expansive conditions.

Second, the Sandy-affected population is a desirable one to study because it is high density, where people are more likely to have enough relationships via Twitter within that geographical space to truly see what technology-abetted socio-behavioral phenomena—and particularly information diffusion—might be. The affected population also represents high variance in socio-economic status (SES) [12], though current research suggests that the affected populations in less central (and less affluent) areas might be underrepresented in the Twitter feed [35].

Such conditions, however, bring us closer to seeing if the empirical findings of geographical behavior that social science has previously revealed are echoed in the digital world. Specifically, do new relationships between people form during disasters in the online world? We expect that they do, but we do not know to what extent those relationships persist. We know from the disaster literature that in areas that experience seasonal hazards, the affiliations and connections made in prior events often (but not always) extend to subsequent events, and to the extent to which these connections can be used as a kind of "organizational memory" [2] is exactly what those who are increasingly attached to ideas of "community resilience" [14] are banking on. This research aims to provide baseline information—as well as some longitudinal information—about an important event that will undoubtedly precede similar events in the same region.

Furthermore to this point, if we find that there are retweet behaviors that are particular to the affected population, then we may be able to use those features to derive data in future disaster events more quickly, for both scientific and applied purposes, that could aid in emergency management. As Twitter volume increases, we need more sophisticated techniques beyond keyword filtering to find the people of interest—specifically those who are needing or supplying information about the impending hazard and its effects on the social and built environment [29].

Third, this research is the foundation for an important new area of research in crisis informatics: that of understanding how people who are geographically vulnerable during hazards make "protective decisions"—decisions to evacuate or to "shelter in place," which may include collecting sufficient provisions. These decisions are made as part of a "web" of sources that are available to them; they do not rely on official sources or mandates alone [13, 24, 26, 27, 47]. Because people are increasingly turning toward online sources, including social media, we must understand social media behavior as much as possible. This research is necessarily scoped to information diffusion behaviors, but it is part of a line of inquiry about "protective decision-making" by affected populations, especially as those activities vary across SES and other demographics [47].

THE 2012 HURRICANE SANDY EVENT (US LANDFALL)

Hurricane Sandy made landfall on October 29, 2012 in southern New Jersey, affecting one of the most populated regions in the US that include New Jersey, New York, and

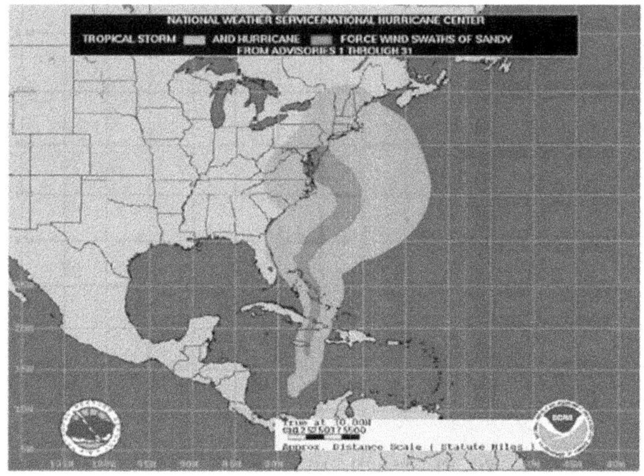

Figure 1. Path of Hurricane Sandy provided by the US National Weather Service via [12].

[1] See <http://bit.ly/1rJXKgA> and <http://bit.ly/1avywUF> for details.

Connecticut, with its impacts felt over a total of 24 States [12]. It dissipated by November 1. Prior to US landfall, it had passed through the Caribbean Sea, causing much damage to island nations before putting the entire US eastern seaboard under threat from the Gulf of Mexico and north into Canada (see Figure 1).

In the US, the number of deaths directly attributed to the storm totaled 162 [12]. It was the second costliest hurricane to hit the US; damage was estimated to be US $6 billion [5]. Approximately 776,000 people were displaced [46] and 650,000 homes were damaged or destroyed. 8.5 million people lost power as a result of the storm [5], and many were without power for weeks following.

METHODS

Data Collection Steps

Data collection is part of our ongoing and committed effort to study disaster-related Twitter data. Using a four-node Cassandra cluster, our research group collects Twitter data 24/7 in specialized software designed for high-volume Twitter data collection [3]. For the Sandy event, we started collecting data using the Streaming API on October 24 2012, using the following keywords for the first round of data collection: `frankenstorm`, `hurricane`, `hurricanesandy`, `perfectstorm`, `sandy`, `sandycam`, `stormporn`, `superstorm`. This produced the *keyword data set.* In our disaster-related data collection procedures, we mitigate against potential bias in the Streaming API sampling [28] by using carefully chosen keywords and then focusing on specific subsets of users to gather a complete set of their tweets via the REST API. In particular here, we determined which users contributed to our keyword set, and then filtered again to those who had at least one gelocated tweet that fell within the geographical area of interest (see Figure 2). We then pulled the user streams—or what we call the *contextual streams*—for each of these *geolocated users* using the Twitter REST API. The reason we collect contextual streams is because we seek the fuller semantic context before and after a tweet that contains a found keyword. A "found" tweet based on a keyword search can have a different or enhanced meaning when one examines the surrounding tweets by the same user. Even when doing non-linguistic analysis as we do here, the full contextual streams remain important because the twitterers *themselves* presume contextual continuity across their tweets as they write them such that they do not necessarily invoke a disaster-relevant keyword each time they tweet. Therefore, our thinking is that the unit of analysis should not depend on isolated keyword-found tweets [29]. Note that the REST API returns up to 3200 of a user's tweets from most recent to least; this usually allows examination of a user's behavior before the hurricane as well.

Creating the Data Sets

We next describe all the data sets used in this paper, with a summary of main sets in Tables 1 and 2. The original raw keyword search spans a long period of time. For this study we bounded the set to Oct 24-Nov 30 to constrain it to the first weeks of the recovery. We refer to this as the *Global Keyword* dataset (see Table 1). Data before October 24 preceded any reasonable predictions of where the hurricane would likely make US landfall.

Next we worked in collaboration with meteorologists, social scientists, and GIS researchers at the National Center for Atmospheric Research to define the geographic bounding box of the region most affected by Sandy. The bounded area spans a great portion of the eastern seaboard (Figure 2), and intentionally covers inland locations, to which people closer to the coastline were likely to evacuate.

Users who produced at least one geolocated tweet within the bounding box during the *global keyword* search time window (Oct 24-Nov 30) were designated as *geographically (*or *"geo") vulnerable users.* Their tweets that were part of the keyword collection yield the *Geo-Vulnerable Keyword* dataset. All tweets in the *Global Keyword* dataset produced by the geographically vulnerable users—including their non-geolocated tweets—are part of this set.

With the set of local users known, we collected their contextual streams as described above. This is called the *Geographically ("Geo") Vulnerable Contextual* dataset.

We further isolate the *Geo-Vulnerable Contextual* dataset into four distinct 5-day time slices to capture the activity of the most geo-vulnerable users *Geo-Before* (Oct 15-19), *Geo-During* (Oct 27-31), *Geo-Short-After* (Nov 8-12), and *Geo-Long-After* the event (Oct 22-26) (see Table 2). We choose these time frames based on our knowledge of socio-behavioral phenomena with respect to different phases of disaster events (drawing primarily from Powell [32]). In sum, *Geo-Before* captures the time before people in the geographical area of interest could know they would be under threat but not so far beforehand that their social

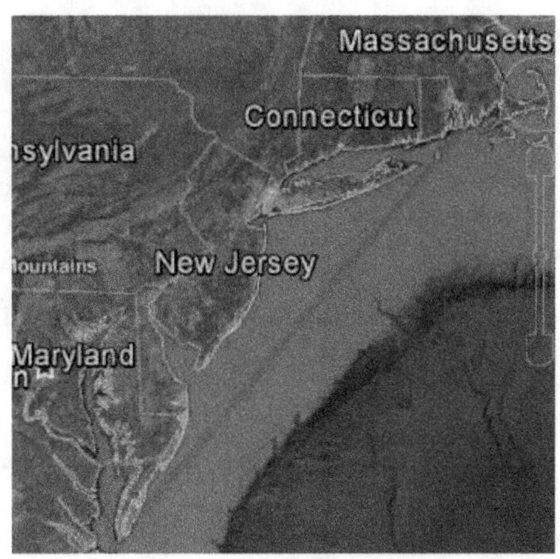

Figure 2. Bounding Box for Data Filtering. The bounding polygon is defined by the coordinates of its four corners: [-76.055416, 36.988536], [-76.416506, 39.084008], [-73.872974, 41.654353] & [-70.874853, 41.732875]).

networks would be very different simply as a function of time. This gives us a before-disaster view of their behavior. The *Geo-During* captures the intense *high warning, evacuation and storm impact periods*, when people are making "protective decisions" and then living through the storm. The *Geo-Short-After* period captures our population as they move into the second week of *recovery*: some here could return home, many others could not, and some were able to start formulating plans for repair work. In other words, they have been able to take stock and have made initial post-disaster plans. The *Geo-Long-After* represents almost a full month after the event. Even more people have stabilized at this point. Many will have returned back to normal routines, but those who lost their homes are making other arrangements.

These datasets will be used to internally compare different retweet patterns, and specifically to look at how social networks emerged in relation to the disaster and to what extent they persisted into the recovery. Because we are interested in comparing the retweeting behavior of geo-vulnerable users within these various time periods, it was necessary to *limit these four time slice sets to the unique users common to all the periods*. We did this to be able to establish a baseline comparison from which to derive heuristics about tweeting behavior without additional variables for which to account. We note that we might be losing people in the *Geo-During* period if they did not evacuate and suffered from prolonged power outages (and therefore could not tweet), but this is a limitation of the study that we opted to work around to achieve stability in the analysis elsewhere. (Future work will extend the analyses to account for differences once baseline behaviors are uncovered.) With this approach, we found 7,988 twitterers who contributed retweets to the contextual dataset in all four time periods. Limiting the time slice sets to only those overlapping users resulted in smaller sets as reported in Table 2.

Three Retweet Counts

As we are interested in retweet behavior in this analysis, we rely heavily on the retweet count metric. However, the Twitter retweet count field is not particularly useful, as for each retweet it *indicates only its current turn* in retweeting the original. For example, the tweet with a retweet count of 5 is the 5th retweet of the original source. Thus, the Twitter

DATA SET NAME & TIME SPAN	NUMBER OF TWEETS	NUMBER OF USERS
Global Keyword (Oct 24-Nov 30)	16.2M	5.9M
Geographically ("Geo") Vulnerable Keyword (Oct 24-Nov 30)	224.8K	28.5K
Geographically ("Geo") Vulnerable Contextual (Oct 13-Nov 30)	5.6M	28.5K

Table 1. Dataset Names and Descriptions.

DATA SET NAME	DATES (2012)	RETWEET VOLUME FOR IN-COMMON TWITTERS
IN-COMMON TWITTERERS ACROSS ALL TIMES SLICES: 7988		
Geo-Before	Oct 15-Oct 19	64,423
Geo-During	Oct 27-Oct 31	84,597
Geo-Short-After	Nov 8-Nov 12	55,855
Geo-Long-After	Nov 22-Nov 26	50,425

Table 2. Retweet volume for in-common Twitterers across all time slices.

metric maintains the retweet count of the original at the time of a particular retweet, and stores it associated with that retweet. We instead need to know *how many times the original tweet was propagated overall within the particular time period under study*. To compute that metric, we went through all the original tweets within a particular dataset, found all their retweets, and stored the latest/largest Twitter retweet count among those retweets as a measure of how many times the original tweets have been passed along. In the remainder of this paper, that is what we refer to as *retweet count*.

Since the technique for acquiring the retweet count requires going through all the original tweets in a dataset, these counts are necessarily timeframe- and dataset-dependent. For the retweet count distribution analysis, we were interested in the activity for the *Geo-During* time frame as it definitively includes the period when the evacuation notices were issued and the storm made landfall. We computed *three* types of retweet counts within this time frame based on the *Global Keyword* and *Geo-Vulnerable Keyword* datasets, described in Table 3. *Retweet counts* are named based on the relationship between *where the original tweet was sourced* and the *population it was retweeted by*.

ANALYSES & FINDINGS

In this section, we have opted to include the findings uncovered in each progressive step to help the general reader follow the analytic rationale and argumentation.

Geo-Vulnerable Retweet Networks for the 4 Time Slices

Time Evolution of Retweet Networks

For the four time slices with in-common users (*Geo-Before, Geo-During, Geo-Short-After, Geo-Long After)*, we collected the user ids of those who generated the retweets as well as the user ids of the authors of the original tweets that were being retweeted. Retweeting behavior can be seen to signify some kind of loosely-connected social relationship—at a minimum, the retwitterer sees value in the information or in the original twitterer. These relationships can be represented as a directed graph, with the retwitterers as source nodes and original twitterers as target nodes, and the directed edges (from source to target) representing the retweets. Thus, the four time slice datasets produce four distinct directed social networks, with the common core of overlapping retwitterers combined with the original tweet authors who are specific to the time period as nodes. These four networks are discrete time slices in the temporal evolution of the single retweet network. Next, we compare various structural aspects of the four networks to establish how the web of social relations changed during disaster in comparison to pre- and post-disaster activity.

Network Size & Density

The first difference in the four time sliced networks is the sheer size. Table 4 illustrates the size and density measures for the four networks. The *Geo-During* network is considerably larger, with more nodes and edges, than the prior and later slices. The larger size of the network corresponds to the higher volume of retweeting activity we observed during disaster, which is not so surprising considering that the underlying dataset was constructed by collecting the contextual streams of geo-vulnerable users who were found by searching on the hurricane-related keywords.

On the one hand, though the geo-vulnerable users were found through a keyword search, in this analysis we use their entire contextual tweet streams during the four time slices, which provide the most accurate measure of how much they tweeted, even when their tweets do not contain keyword terms. The higher volume of retweet activity during the hurricane suggests that the geo-vulnerable population tends to propagate social media posts more often in disaster (even if the posts do not contain event-related keywords).

The relative size of the largest connected component can serve as a proxy for how densely interconnected the network is. The largest weakly connected component of the *Geo-During* network encapsulates 92.88% of all its nodes and an impressive 96.34% of the edges—a considerably larger fraction than for the other three time periods (see Table 4). Moreover, if we construct completely comparable "internal" versions of the four networks by excluding the original tweet authors who are not also among the 7,988 overlapping users and thus retaining only the retweets between the core users, the networks show a similar trend. The "internal" version of *Geo-During* has the largest weakly connected component, with the fractional size considerably larger than the internal networks for other time slices. Therefore, we see higher density in the *During* period even in the internal networks, which allow the analysis to focus solely on the retweet dynamics among the overlapping users to avoid the varying number of external original tweet authors (though this method does not control for the underlying dynamic of varying retweet volume). The higher density suggests that the retweet activity of geo-vulnerable twitterers during the disaster connects multiple subnetworks, thereby constructing a more interconnected, dense social network.

RETWEET COUNT NAME	DESCRIPTION
1. *Global/Geo-Vulnerable*	Originating tweets come from the *Global Keyword* dataset and are retweeted within the *Geo-Vulnerable Keyword* dataset
2. *Geo-Vulnerable/Geo-Vulnerable*	Originating tweets come from the *Geo-Vulnerable Keyword* data set and are retweeted within the *Geo-Vulnerable-Keyword dataset*
3. *Global/Global*	Originating tweets come from the *Global Keyword* data set and are retweeted within the *Global Keyword* data set

Table 3. Glossary of Retweet Counts.

The reciprocity of directed links does not contribute much to the higher network density of *Geo-During*, as it is consistently low for all four networks—about 0.1%.

Degree Distributions

An even more canonical metric for measuring the difference in structure of different networks is their degree distribution. In this directed case, we are specifically interested in the out-degree, which represents the number of original authors whose tweets the in-common retwitterers have retweeted.

All the distributions in Figure 3 are long-tailed, as is common in degree distributions of real-world complex networks [8, 24]. However, some of the distributions are prone to rarer events than others. For example, the *Geo-Before* network has the highest out-degree of 181. Thus, an in-common retwitterer in this network (@BKdotNet) has retweeted tweets from 181 authors in the 5 days of interest before the event (in-degree=0). Similarly, and somewhat more impressively, a user (@LaborIrishDem) in the *Geo-During* network retweeted tweets from 192 authors during the 5 days of the event (in-degree=0). In contrast, the *Geo-Short-After* and *Geo-Long-After* networks have maximum out-degrees of 134 and 97, respectively (in-degree=0 for both). Moreover, the out-degree distributions for all the time slices are power-law-like only in the tail (out-degree>10), but not the head of the distribution. This suggests that the core users who remained active retwitterers through all the stages of the event tended to

	Geo-Before	Geo-During	Short-After	Geo-Long-After
Network size (nodes, edges)	49,413 64,423	56,527 84,597	46,040 55,855	42,829 50,425
Weakly Connected components	1,465	935	1,728	2,047
Fraction in largest component (nodes, edges)	87.61% 92.76%	92.88% 96.34%	84.10% 89.97%	81.28% 88.15%

Table 4. Network size and density. (Fraction of nodes stat. sig. with Chi-square=3304.55, p<0.0001, fraction of edges stat. sig. with Chi-square=3664.98, p<0.0001).

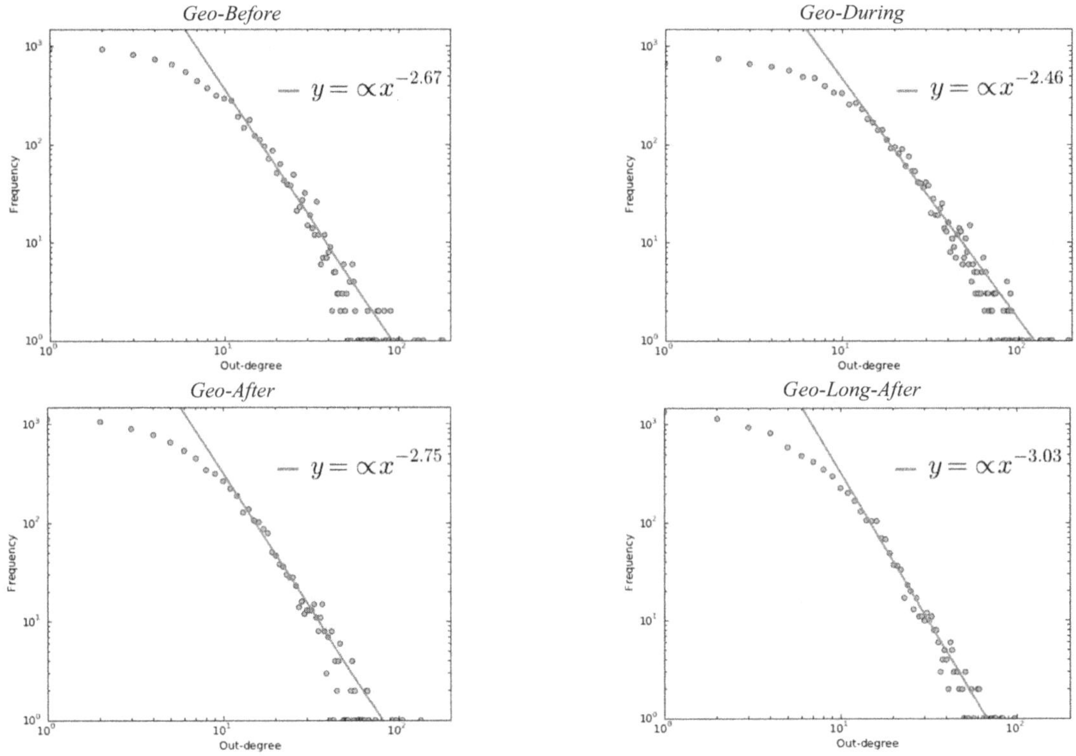

Figure 3. Loglog of out-degree distribution with linear fit to the tail (x>10).

retweet tweets of many authors. This is especially true for the *Geo-During* network, where the linear fit to the loglog distribution is the least steep of all the time slices, decreasing less rapidly and thus pushing more of the distribution's density away from the origin. Hence, the core in-common users, in aggregate, tended to retweet information from a greater variety of sources during the disaster than before or after.

The in-degree here represents how popular various original authors were in the retweet activity of the core overlapping users. For example, the *Geo-Before* network has the highest in-degree of 306. Here @BarackObama was retweeted by 306 different in-common users in the 5 days of interest before the event. This node's out-degree is zero, since we do not have the data on the retweet behavior of the original authors unless they are also one of the in-common retwitterers (see Table 6 for the intersection of the two). Similarly, but even more impressively, @MikeBloomberg —the New York city mayor at the time—was retweeted by 420 different core users during the 5 days of the event (out-degree=0). The author retweeted by the highest number of in-common users in the *Geo-Short-After* and *Geo-Long-After* networks is @XSTROLOGY (in-degree of 167 and 154, respectively; out-degree of 0 for both).

Users with high degree—many links—are often called "hubs" and are an important feature of social networks. The *Geo-During* network has more hubs based on in-degree, while the *Geo-Before, Geo-Short-After,* and *Geo-Long-After* networks have fewer of them. Figure 4 illustrates the proportion of nodes for each network that have 100 links or more, for in- and out-degree. The differences for the out-degree are less dramatic, but the *Geo-Before,* and especially *Geo-During* have more hubs than the later time networks. This suggests that among the users who appear across all datasets, there was more hub-like activity during the disaster period—retweeting from multiple sources and being retweeted by multiple retwitterers—and thus connecting many subnetworks.

Network Mixing Patterns

More insight into understanding and comparing network structure can be gleaned from "mixing patterns," which refers to what type of nodes tend to connect to each other. "Degree assortativity" is measured by a network-level coefficient quantifying the strength of the relationship between the degree of the network's nodes and degree of their neighbors. For our networks, which do not have data on the retweet activity of original authors unless they are also in-common retwitterers, we are most interested in out-in degree assortativity. This metric represents the correlation between the out-degree of a node and the average in-degree of its neighbors—tweets of how many authors the user retweeted and how many users, on average, retweeted the tweets of those original authors. The out-in degree assortativity for all the time sliced networks is low, signifying, on average, a weak relationship between each node's degree and degree of its neighbors. The out-in degree assortativity of all the networks is also weakly negative, suggesting that nodes with high out-degree are on average slightly more likely to be connected to the nodes

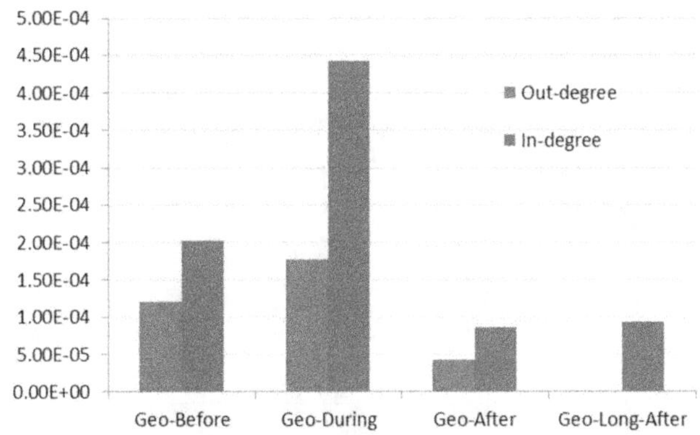

Figure 4. Hub percentage for each network. (Stat. sig. for in-degree with χ^2=19.53, p<0.001).

with low in-degree. This implies that for all four networks, when users retweet many sources, those sources are slightly more likely to be the ones that have not been retweeted very often by the in-common retwitterers. All the patterns above also hold if we remove all the nodes with an out-degree of one; we do this to verify that one-off retwitterers of popular memes (high in-degree) do not produce the observed disassortativity. This disassortative relationship is weakest for the *Geo-During* network, suggesting that during disaster, the geo-vulnerable users who retweet many different sources are slightly more likely to retweet more popular sources than before or after an event. The fact that popularity plays a role in retweet activity in disaster is somewhat intuitive, as retweeting can be seen to be about trust (in either content or here in the authority of the author as confirmed by her/his popularity), and rarely is trustworthiness more important than in disaster. We will attempt to separate the part played by content utility in this process from that of author popularity later in the paper.

We can disaggregate the concept of out-in degree assortativity by looking at the average neighbor connectivity for each node (see Figure 5). The sub-figures illustrate the average in-degree of neighbors (y-axis) for the node with out-degree *k* (x-axis).

Figure 5 shows a less pronounced negative relationship between node out-degrees and average in-degrees of their neighbors for the *Geo-During* network, supporting our assertion of slightly more frequent hub-to-hub retweeting (out-degree hub retweeting in-degree hubs). For example, @AthenasAika—the user represented by the highest point on the *Geo-During* graph—has retweeted 106 sources who on average have been retweeted 43.70 times. This user retweeted such high-degree hubs as @BarackObama, @MikeBloomberg, and other national and local authorities and media outlets.

Transitivity

A relation is transitive if when A relates to B, and B relates to C, A also relates to C. Thus transitivity captures the idea of "a friend of a friend is a friend," and specific to retweeting information, "a source of my source is also a source." In the directed case, the most meaningful network-level measure of transitivity is the proportion of transitive triples derived from the triadic census as defined by Holland and Leinhardt [16, 43]. We corrected this measure by excluding the few transitive triples in which a user retweets two authoritative sources that retweet each other. Thus, the corrected metric excludes the configurations that relate to authority-based broadcasting and retains only the transitive triple configurations associated with community-building retweeting, which is a typical understanding of transitivity. This corrected proportion, while rather low for all four time sliced networks, is the highest for the *Geo-During* network. The *Geo-After* has slightly higher corrected proportion of transitive triples than *Geo-Before* and *Geo-Long-After,* but still lower than *Geo-During.* Therefore, the higher proportion of transitive triples in *Geo-During,* suggests that when retweeting communities are likely to form, they are most likely to form during the event and persist to some degree immediately after (the difference is statistically significant with χ^2=83.29, p<0.0001).

The retweet behavior displays low transitivity because retweeting need not be limited by the boundaries of users' following networks, which are themselves low-transitivity [25] due to their directional nature and low rates of following reciprocity [23].

Important Users

We further explored the differences between the four time sliced retweet networks by establishing each network's important users, with the specific focus on the influential sources (See Table 5). PageRank—a variant of eigenvector centrality—has at its core a notion that the importance of a node can be judged by looking at the importance of nodes that link to it. Thus, this metric is especially well-suited for finding the influential nodes based on their incoming edges, like the important original tweet authors. Based on this metric, the majority of the most important nodes of the *Geo-During* network tend to be local government

Geo-Before	Geo-During
BarackObama	MikeBloomberg
MensHumor	GovChristie
XSTROLOGY	LolOhComedy
billmaher	MTAInsider
WomensHumor	NYCMayorsOffice
azizansari	ElBloombito
FillWerrell	NYGovCuomo
Geo-After	**Geo-Long-After**
XSTROLOGY	XSTROLOGY
GovChristie	UberFacts
UberFacts	HuffingtonPost
MensHumor	MensHumor
ElBloombito	BenSavage
WhatTheFFacts	SportsCenter
HuffingtonPost	WhatTheFFacts

Table 5. Nodes with the highest PageRank.

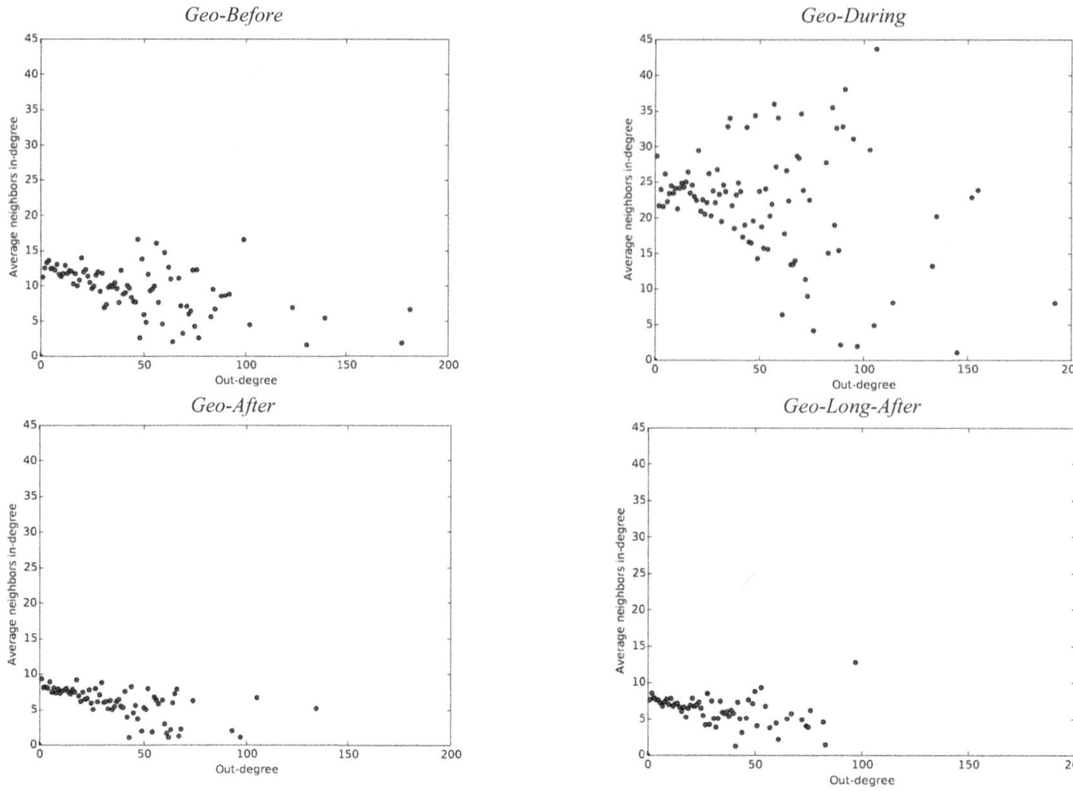

Figure 5. Average neighbor in-degree vs. node out-degree.

authorities and the media, while those accounts are much less represented in the "most important nodes" list of the other time slices.

The strong presence of local government and media sources in the list for the *Geo-During* network is consistent with our earlier observation of more in-degree hubs in this network.

Geographic Patterns of Retweet Activity

Proportion of Geo-Vulnerable Sources within the Four Time Sliced Networks

We are interested in the geographic patterns of the retweet activity. One of the ways to glean the presence of such patterns is to calculate the proportion of geo-vulnerable nodes in the time sliced networks. Remember that the in-common retwitterers around which the time slice networks were constructed are all geo-vulnerable, since we extracted them from the *Geo-Vulnerable Contextual* dataset. Thus, the only nodes with potential for different locations are the authors of the original tweets.

Table 6 indicates that for each of the time sliced networks, there is an overlap between the authors of the original tweets and the retweet authors. Thus, a small portion of the core retwitterers play both roles: authority figures whose tweets are propagated by others, and propagators of information.

All the time sliced networks also display a consistently higher proportion of geo-vulnerable original tweet authors than non-geo-vulnerable sources. Such consistency suggests that the geo-vulnerable retwitterers are more likely to propagate messages created by other geo-vulnerable users.

This is especially the case in the time of disaster. According to Table 6, the percentage of geo-vulnerable source authors is rather consistent among the *Geo-Before*, *Geo-Short-After*, and *Geo-Long-After* networks (61-62%). However, in the *Geo-During* network this percentage of geo-vulnerable source authorship goes up to 68%.

Proportion of the Geo-Vulnerable Source Tweets

Going to the tweet-level analysis of location brings some challenges. First, only a small number of tweets are geolocated (1.1% in *Global Keyword* dataset) and an even smaller portion is located within the bounding box of the event (0.4%). Moreover, our analysis indicates that retweets are never geolocated; that is, the location of the person performing the retweet is not captured. Instead, Twitter passes along the geotag (if present) of the original tweet (the tweet being retweeted). Indeed, if you attempt to load a retweet in a web browser, Twitter simply redirects you to the original tweet. These "features" make location analysis based on the retweet's coordinates impossible.

	Geo-Before	Geo-During	Geo-Short-After	Geo-Long-After
Original Twitterers	41,755	49,017	38,326	35,094
Overlap with in-common Twitterers	330	478	274	253
Geolocated Original Twitterers	1,499	1,838	1,477	1,380
Geo-Vulnerable Original Twitterers	62.58%	68.44%	62.42%	61.16%

Table 6. Source tweet author details. (Fraction of geo-vulnerable sources stat. sig. with χ^2=23.49, p<0.0001).

On the other hand, recall that we consider users to be geo-vulnerable if they produce at least one geotagged tweet within the boundary in the time frame of interest. This procedure produces many more tweets whose authors are considered geo-vulnerable than the actual tweets with geo-vulnerable geographical coordinates—and this larger set now includes retweets. Thus, in the rest of this analysis we consider tweets to be in the geographical area of interest if they were authored by a geo-vulnerable twitterer.

The geo-vulnerable twitterers in both the *Geo-Vulnerable Contextual* and *Geo-Vulnerable Keyword* dataset retweeted more tweets from geo-vulnerable authors than from non-geo-vulnerable. This is true for both overall time period of interest—Oct 13-Nov 30—and the *Geo-During* timeframe. For the *Geo-Vulnerable Keyword* dataset, the percentage remained essentially unchanged regardless of the time period (Figure 6). For *Geo-Vulnerable Contextual* dataset, however, the percentage of original tweets by geo-vulnerable authors increased noticeably during the disaster time period. This suggests that during the disaster, the Twitter conversations of geo-vulnerable authors tend to favor the local sources more strongly.

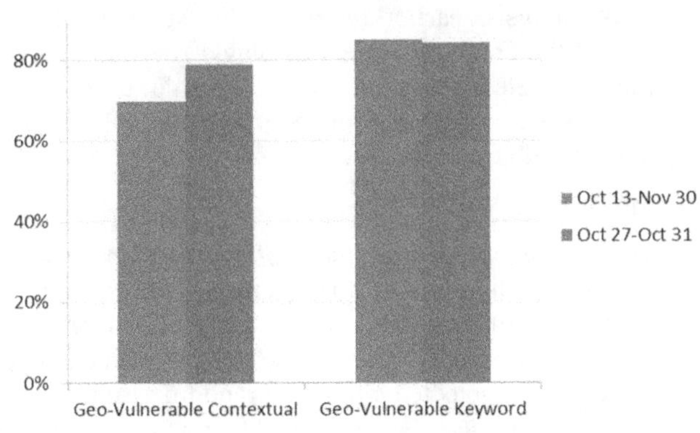

Figure 6. Percentage of source tweets in geo area of interest. (Stat. sig. with χ^2=827.11, p<0.0001)

Since *Geo-Vulnerable Contextual* dataset contains all the tweets of the geo-vulnerable users, some discussions and retweets might be unrelated to Hurricane Sandy, especially on the longer time frame. During the disaster, it is expected that more of the contextual tweets would be focused on Sandy and related local issues, making the percentage of original tweets by geo-vulnerable authors higher. The higher fraction of source tweets by the geo-vulnerable authors in the more on-topic *Geo-Vulnerable Keyword* set is consistent with the above intuition, supporting a hypothesis that the disaster-related geo-vulnerable retweet activity tends to favor the local sources more strongly.

Retweet Count Distributions of Various Populations

Now we turn to the three retweet count metrics we explained earlier, to see in another form how Global and Geo-Vulnerable populations retweet each other.

Retweet Distributions: The Geo-Vulnerable Retweeting Other Geo-Vulnerable Tweets vs Global Users Retweeting Global Tweets

The geographic patterns discussed above suggest that we might glean some insights into the retweeting behavior of the most affected geo-vulnerable twitterers by comparing their retweet count distributions to those of global twitterers. These distributions show how frequently we observe the tweets with a particular retweet count. We do not include tweets with a retweet count of 0 here, since though these tweets might be contentful, they do not contribute to the collective situational awareness because of their very limited audience, which is mostly confined to a twitterer's followers.

The distribution of *Geo-Vulnerable/Geo-Vulnerable* retweet counts on loglog scale looks significantly different from the distribution of *Global/Global* retweet count (Figure 7). The negative slope of the linear fit to the retweet frequencies of the former is less steep than that of the latter, producing a more heavy-tailed distribution with more density dispersing from the origin. The histogram inset in Figure 7 makes this

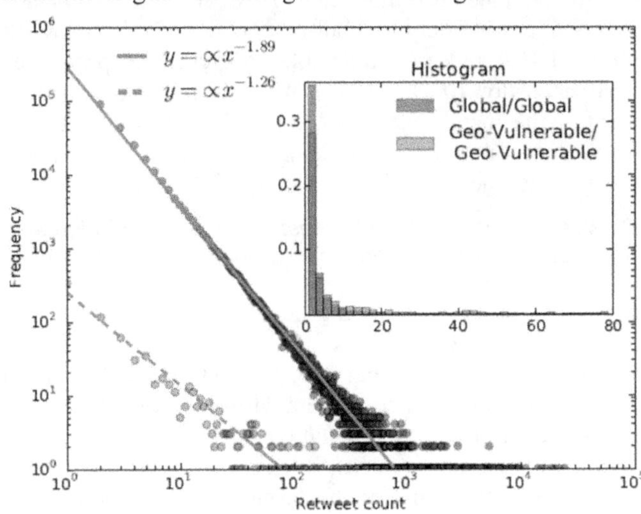

Figure 7. Retweet count distributions.

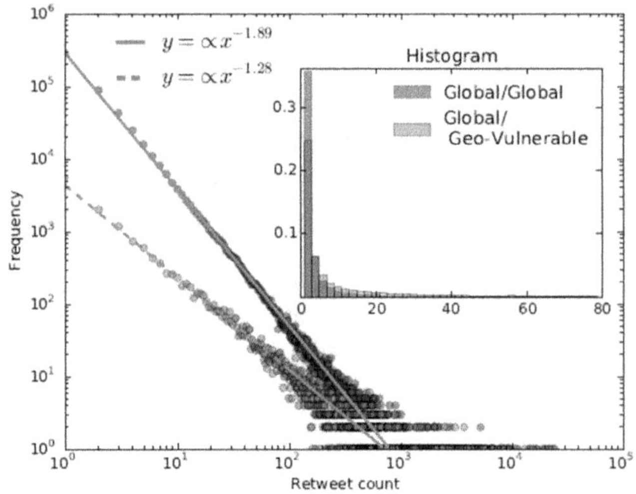

Figure 8. Retweet count distributions.

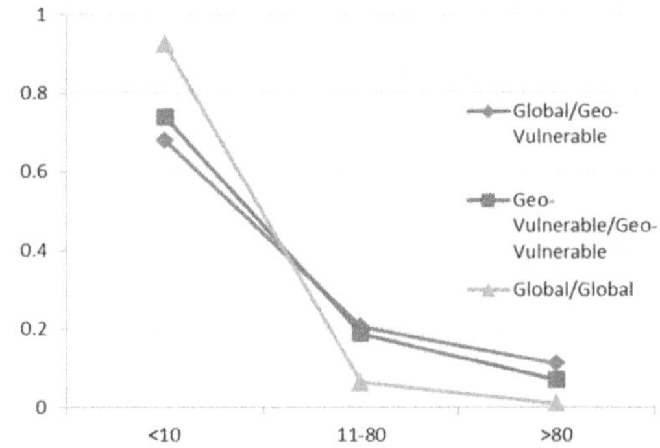

Figure 9. Fraction of tweets with 1-10, 11-80, and >80 retweets (Stat. sig, with $\chi^2 = 18876.38$, p<0.00001).

more visually apparent: the *Geo-Vulnerable/Geo-Vulnerable* distribution shows more density at retweet counts greater than 10, suggesting that the geo-vulnerable tweets get retweeted 10 or more times by the geo-vulnerable users more frequently than the global tweets get retweeted 10 or more times by all users. Specifically, we can see that the tweets with 10-80 retweets are visibly over-represented in *Geo-Vulnerable/Geo-Vulnerable* distribution, compared to the *Global/Global* histogram.

Thus, it seems that certain geo-vulnerable tweets might offer something especially useful to the discussion, making them more appealing to the geo-vulnerable users, and thus more retweeted. This makes the geo-vulnerable tweets with higher retweet counts (at 10-80 retweets) over-represented in the retweet count distributions for the geo-vulnerable users. This supports earlier findings from a smaller disaster much earlier in Twitter's life: tweets from the geo-vulnerable might be more useful for other geo-vulnerable users. Therefore, the geographic similarity might help us derive the most useful tweets. However, the geolocated tweets comprise only a small percentage of all the tweets (about 1.1%) and geo-vulnerable tweets make up an even smaller portion (0.4%). Hence it would be very helpful to identify the locally useful tweets without relying on their locality as an identifying marker, which we discuss in further detail next.

Retweet Count Distributions: The Geo-Vulnerable Retweeting Global Tweets vs Global Users Retweeting Global Tweets

To move away from using location as an identifying characteristic, we can look at the distributions of geo-vulnerable users retweeting tweets from the global keyword data set, not just the geo-vulnerable tweets. Comparing the loglog distribution of *Global/Geo-Vulnerable* retweet counts to the *Global/Global* distribution, we again observe a less steep linear fit for the former, suggesting that this distribution decreases more slowly and thus produces more rare events—tweets with larger retweet counts (Figure 8). The fact that this distribution is more heavy-tailed is more visually obvious from the inset of Figure 8, where we see the *Global/Geo-Vulnerable* histogram diffuse density away from the origin and over-represent tweets with higher retweet counts in comparison to the *Global/Global* distribution. Specifically, the tweets with 10-80 retweets are again visibly over-represented, even to the higher degree than we observed for geo-vulnerable users propagating geo-vulnerable tweets.

In summary, for all the retweet counts, the retweet patterns of the geo-vulnerable users seem to be quite different from the global users (whether the geo-vulnerable users are retweeting the geo-vulnerable or global sources). Figure 9 provides the overview of these differences.

Thus, we can conclude that the tweets that end up with the higher retweet counts and hence over-represent those counts in the distributions are propagated by the geo-vulnerable users more, not necessarily because of their locality but because of some other aspect of the tweets. There are many aspects of the tweet that might motivate geo-vulnerable users to retweet it—informational utility and social conformity are two obvious contenders, especially from the perspective of retweet as an informal recommendation system (either for content or its author) [40]. Though we cannot fully disentangle these motivations in this analysis, earlier research [37] suggests that local utility of the content is likely to play a role in these tweets being retweeted more by geo-vulnerable users than we would expect from the retweeting patterns of Twitter's general population of users.

Content

Overrepresented tweets in the Global/Geo-Vulnerable count

To test the hypothesis that certain tweets gain more retweets based on usefulness of their content to the geographically-vulnerable, we perform a content analysis of the tweets. We selected a uniform random sample of all the tweets with *Global/Geo-Vulnerable* retweet count larger than zero (17K), since the number of tweets was too large to manually code for the presence of local utility. We focused on this retweet count because the global source of

	1-10 Retweets	11-80 Retweets	>80 Retweets
Tweets	11,518	3,503	1,885
Sample	1,147	353	191
% with Local Utility	38.92%	54.83%	36.84%

Table 7. Proportion of tweets with locally useful content in Global/Geo-Vulnerable retweet samples (Fraction with local utility stat. sig. with χ^2=30.11, p<0.0001).

the tweets ensures that over-representation of certain tweets is not due to their geographic origin.

We divided the sample tweets into three groups: 10 tweets and below, 11-80 tweets, and 81 and up. We qualitatively coded the three samples with a simple binary flag indicating whether or not the tweet contains locally useful information. We considered the content to be locally useful if it provided practical information on the state of affairs, such as exact weather and path of the hurricane prediction, notification of road and school closures, public transportation announcements, declaration of state of emergency, concrete opportunities to help in the recovery and so on. We distinguished those specific and locally-applicable tweets from the general expression of fear, awe, and disbelief and from text or images that provide a large-scale overview of the event. Table 7 summarizes the findings from this content analysis.

Tweets in all three samples ranged in their content from the local utility that aids in situational awareness to the broad appeal of the bird's eye view "abstract" of the event [37], including jokes and other memes. However, the 11-80 retweet subsample included much higher proportion of the tweets with locally-useful, actionable information compared to the other two samples. Clearly, the boundary cutoffs between subsamples are somewhat arbitrary, as all the samples had a varied mixture of content with local utility and broad appeal, and would be better represented by a continuum rather than discrete thresholds. However, these thresholds we empirically obtained from the retweet count distributions offer us a reasonable starting point for finding locally-useful tweets where they are most highly concentrated.

We did not find a one-to-one direct relationship between the local utility and retweet count, as evidenced by numerous locally-useful tweets we found in 1-10 retweet category. Our basic content analysis suggests that there might be some non-textual features that impede or promote a tweet's retweetability [41]. For example, many locally-useful tweets in the 1-10 retweet sample were hard to read due to overabundance of mentions. On the other hand, the fact that retweet count distributions have considerable densities above the retweet count of 80 while the local utility decreases at this point, suggest that other factors, such as author popularity, social conformity, and imitation might be in play. The data concur: 93.58% of the original authors of tweets with more than 80 retweets are popular twitterers, as operationalized by having a thousand followers or more (a statistically significantly higher proportion than for tweets with 11-80 retweets). Qualitative analysis of over-80-retweet tweets shows that celebrities and the media have a very strong presence among authors. In future work, we plan to explore how various non-content features affect the retweet potential for the tweets with local utility, and conversely what structural features characterize the well-retweeted locally-useful and non-useful tweets.

CONCLUSION

The purpose of this research is explain how Twitter activity by those who are geographically affected by a disaster differs or not from the general global reaction. If there are differences, then we know that victims turn to social media for different reasons than the general population. To address these questions, we had to carefully manage a large set of data, comparing retweet behavior across populations and time slices, which can make written explanations difficult, but it makes results more dependable.

In summary, our major findings are that geographically vulnerable twitterers propagate more information during the disaster period than before or after. They can also be both the sources and propagators of information. In doing this, geographically vulnerable twitterers have denser interconnected retweet networks during disasters than before or after. Social network "hubs," especially those based on in-degree, are present in higher numbers during the disaster period than before or after. It also appears that during the disaster period, local government authorities and the media are the most important nodes in comparison to their presence before or after the disaster.

The geographically vulnerable are more likely to propagate tweets from other geographically vulnerable users at any time, but this is especially prominent in disaster.

In addition, the geo-vulnerable retweet quite differently than the global population of twitterers who are interested in the same event. They propagate certain tweets considerably more than the general Twitter population, creating retweet distributions where rare events are more likely. Specifically, tweets that acquire 10-80 retweets make up a higher fraction of the total retweet activity of the geo-vulnerable population, and we see from qualitative analysis of these tweets that the geo-vulnerable select from the global twitterverse and retweet more are more likely to have some kind of local utility.

Though the popularity of social media is hard to deny, some still question its impact and import during disaster response because resource allocation decisions, governance policy, and even life-or-death actions are at issue. This research shows that those who are in the geographic area of effect relate to social media content differently once a disaster strikes, and they relate to it differently from the general population that attends to the event. They tend to propagate information from other geographically-vulnerable people, and focus the bulk of their retweeting activity on the tweets containing locally-useful information.

These findings provide evidence for moving forward on practice- and policy-making initiatives that address the role of social media in disaster emergency response. Technology designers might also be influenced by the needs of geographical neighbors when we think about future social computing innovations. Finally, those who analyze social media data for basic and applied science purposes may employ some of these findings to create sampling techniques to more quickly zero in on the content and propagators in the "big data" of crisis response.

ACKNOWLEDGMENTS

This research is funded through the US NSF grants IIS-0910586 and AGS-1331490. We thank our Project EPIC colleagues for support and critique. We especially thank our reviewers for their insightful comments and assistance.

REFERENCES

1. Abel, F., Hauff, C., Houben, G. J., Stronkman, R., & Tao, K. Semantics+ filtering+ search= twitcident. exploring information in social web streams. In *Proc. of the 23rd ACM Conference on Hypertext and social media.* ACM (2012), 285-294.
2. Ackerman, M. S. Augmenting organizational memory: a field study of answer garden. *ACM Transactions on Information Systems (TOIS)*, *16*(3), (1998), 203-224.
3. Anderson, K. M., & Schram, A. Design and implementation of a data analytics infrastructure in support of crisis informatics research (NIER track). In *Proc. of the 33rd International Conference on Software Engineering.* ACM (2011), 844-847.
4. Bakshy, E., Rosenn, I., Marlow, C., & Adamic, L. The role of social networks in information diffusion. In *Proc. of WWW,* (2012), 519-528.
5. Blake, E. S., Kimberlain, T. B., Berg, R. J., Cangialosi, J. P., & Beven II, J. L. Tropical Cyclone Report: Hurricane Sandy. *National Hurricane Center*, *12*, (2013).
6. Boersma, F. K., Groenewegen, P., & Wagenaar, P. Emergency Response Rooms in Action: an ethnographic case-study in Amsterdam. In *Proc. of ISCRAM* (2009), 1-8.
7. Caragea, C., Squicciarini, A., Stehle, S., Neppalli, K., & Tapia, A. Mapping Moods: Geo-Mapped Sentiment Analysis During Hurricane Sandy. In *Proc. of ISCRAM* (2014).
8. Clauset, A., Shalizi, C. R., & Newman, M. E. Power-law distributions in empirical data. *SIAM review*, *51*(4), (2009), 661-703.
9. Coviello, L., Sohn, Y., Kramer, A. D., Marlow, C., Franceschetti, M., Christakis, N. A., & Fowler, J. H. Detecting Emotional Contagion in Massive Social Networks. *PloS one*, (2014), *9*(3), e90315.
10. Dashti, S., Palen, L., Heris, M. P., Anderson, K. M., Anderson, S., & Anderson, S. Supporting Disaster Reconnaissance with Social Media Data: A Design-Oriented Case Study of the 2013 Colorado Floods. In *Proc. of ISCRAM* (2014).
11. De Choudhury, M., Monroy-Hernandez, A., & Mark, G. Narco emotions: affect and desensitization in social media during the mexican drug war. In *Proceedings of the CHI*, (2014), 3563-3572.
12. FEMA (July 1, 2013). Hurricane Sandy FEMA After Action Report, http://www.fema.gov/media-library-data/20130726-1923-25045-7442/sandy_fema_aar.pdf
13. Gibbs, L., & Holloway, C. Hurricane Sandy After Action: Report and Recommendations to Mayor Michael R. Bloomberg. *Hurricane Sandy After Action: Report and Recommendations to Mayor Michael R. Bloomberg, The City of New York, New York, NY*, 36, (2013).
14. Goldstein, B. E. (Ed.). *Collaborative Resilience: Moving through Crisis to Opportunity.* MIT Press. (2012).
15. Hiltz, S. R., Kushma, J., & Plotnick, L. Use of Social Media by US Public Sector Emergency Managers: Barriers and Wish Lists. In *Proceedings of ISCRAM* (2014).
16. Holland, P. W., and Leinhardt, S.. "A method for detecting structure in sociometric data." *American Journal of Sociology* (1970): 492-513.
17. Hughes, A. L., & Palen, L. Twitter adoption and use in mass convergence and emergency events. *International Journal of Emergency Management*, *6*(3), (2009), 248-260.
18. Hughes, A. L., Denis, L. A. S., Palen, L., & Anderson, K. M. Online Public Communications by Police & Fire Services during the 2012 Hurricane Sandy. In *Proc.* of *CHI* (2014), 1505-1514.
19. Imran, M., Castillo, C., Lucas, J., Patrick, M., & Rogstadius, J. Coordinating human and machine intelligence to classify microblog communications in crises. *Proc. of ISCRAM* (2014).
20. Keegan, B. C. Breaking news on wikipedia: dynamics, structures, and roles in high-tempo collaboration. In *Proc. of CSCW Companion,* (2012), 315-318.
21. Keegan, B., Gergle, D., & Contractor, N. Hot off the wiki: dynamics, practices, and structures in Wikipedia's coverage of the Tōhoku catastrophes. In *Proc. of the 7th International Symposium on Wikis and Open Collaboration,* (2011), 105-113.
22. Keegan, B., Gergle, D., & Contractor, N. Staying in the loop: Structure and dynamics of Wikipedia's breaking news collaborations. In *Proc. of the 8th Annual*

International Symposium on Wikis and Open Collaboration, (2012), 1-10.

23. Kwak, H., Lee, C., Park, H., & Moon, S. What is Twitter, a social network or a news media?. In *Proc. of WWW,* (2010), 591-600.
24. Lazo, J. K., Morss, R. E., & Demuth, J. L. 300 BILLION SERVED. *Bulletin of the American Meteorological Society, 90*(6), (2009).
25. Lerman, K., & Ghosh, R. Information Contagion: An Empirical Study of the Spread of News on Digg and Twitter Social Networks. In *Proc. of ICWSM, 10,* (2010), 90-97.
26. Mileti, D. S. *Disasters by design: A reassessment of natural hazards in the United States.* National Academies Press. (1999).
27. Morss, R. E., & Hayden, M. H. Storm Surge and "Certain Death": Interviews with Texas Coastal Residents following Hurricane Ike. *Weather, Climate & Society, 2*(3), (2010), 174-189.
28. Morstatter, F., et al. "Is the Sample Good Enough? Comparing Data from Twitter's Streaming API with Twitter's Firehose." *ICWSM.* 2013.
29. Palen, L. Frontiers in Crisis Informatics. Keynote Address at *ISCRAM,* (2014).
30. Palen, L., Vieweg, S., Liu, S. B., & Hughes, A. L. Crisis in a networked world features of computer-mediated communication in the April 16, 2007, Virginia Tech Event. *Social Science Computer Review, 27*(4), (2009), 467-480.
31. Perng, S-Y., Buscher, M., Wood, L., Halvorsrud, R., Stiso, M., Ramirez, L. & Al-Akkad, A. Peripheral response: microblogging during the 22/7/2011 Norway attacks, *International Journal of Information Systems for Crisis Response and Management,* (2013), 41-57
32. Powell, J. W. An introduction to the natural history of disaster. *Univ. of Maryland: Disaster Research Project,* (1954).
33. Qu, Y., Huang, C., Zhang, P., & Zhang, J. Microblogging after a major disaster in China: a case study of the 2010 Yushu earthquake. In *Proc. of CSCW,* (2011), 25-34.
34. Romero, D. M., Meeder, B., & Kleinberg, J. Differences in the mechanics of information diffusion across topics: idioms, political hashtags, and complex contagion on twitter. In *Proc. of WWW,* (2011), 695-704.
35. Shelton, T., Poorthuis, A., Graham, M., & Zook, M."Mapping the data shadows of Hurricane Sandy: Uncovering the sociospatial dimensions of 'big data'." *Geoforum* 52 (2014): 167-179.
36. Soden, R., & Palen, L. From Crowdsourced Mapping to Community Mapping: The Post-Earthquake Work of OpenStreetMap Haiti. In *11th International Conference on the Design of Cooperative Systems (COOP),* (2014).
37. Starbird, K., & Palen, L. Pass it on?: Retweeting in mass emergency. In *Proc. of ISCRAM* (2010), 1-10.
38. Starbird, K., & Palen, L. Voluntweeters: Self-organizing by digital volunteers in times of crisis. In *Proc. of CHI,* (2011), 1071-1080.
39. Starbird, K., Maddock, J., Orand, M., & Mason, R. M. Rumors, False Flags, and Digital Vigilantes: Misinformation on Twitter after the 2013 Boston Marathon Bombing. In *Proc. of iConference,* (2014).
40. Starbird, K., Muzny, G., & Palen, L. Learning from the crowd: Collaborative filtering techniques for identifying on-the-ground Twitterers during mass disruptions. In *Proc. of ISCRAM,* (2012), 1-10.
41. Suh, B., Hong, L., Pirolli, P., & Chi, E. H. Want to be retweeted? large scale analytics on factors impacting retweet in twitter network. In *IEEE second international Conference on Social computing,* (2010), 177-184.
42. Verma, S., Vieweg, S., Corvey, W., Palen, L., Martin, J. H., Palmer, M., & Anderson, K. M. NLP to the Rescue?: Extracting "Situational Awareness" Tweets During Mass Emergency. In *Proc. of ICWSM,* (2011), 385-392.
43. Wasserman, S., and Faust, K.. "Social Network Analysis: Methods and Applications." *Cambridge University Pr*ess, (1994).
44. White, J. I., Palen, L., & Anderson, K. M. Digital Mobilization in Disaster Response: The Work & Self-Organization of On-Line Pet Advocates in Response to Hurricane Sandy. In *Proc. of CSCW,* (2014).
45. Wulf, V., Rohde, M., Pipek, V., & Stevens, G. Engaging with practices: design case studies as a research framework in CSCW. In *Proc. of CSCW,* (2011), 505-512.
46. Yonetani, M., & Morris, T. (2013). Global Estimates 2012: people displaced by disasters. IDMC.
47. Zhang, F., Morss, R. E., Sippel, J. A., Beckman, T. K., Clements, N. C., Hampshire, N. L., & Winkley, S. D. An In-Person Survey Investigating Public Perceptions of and Responses to Hurricane Rita Forecasts along the Texas Coast. *Weather & Forecasting, 22*(6), (2007), 1177-1190.

What to Expect When the Unexpected Happens: Social Media Communications Across Crises

Alexandra Olteanu
Ecole Polytechnique Federale de Lausanne
alexandra.olteanu@epfl.ch

Sarah Vieweg
Qatar Computing Research Institute
svieweg@qf.org.qa

Carlos Castillo
Qatar Computing Research Institute
chato@acm.org

ABSTRACT
The use of social media to communicate timely information during crisis situations has become a common practice in recent years. In particular, the one-to-many nature of Twitter has created an opportunity for stakeholders to disseminate crisis-relevant messages, and to access vast amounts of information they may not otherwise have. Our goal is to understand what affected populations, response agencies and other stakeholders can expect—and not expect—from these data in various types of disaster situations. Anecdotal evidence suggests that different types of crises elicit different reactions from Twitter users, but we have yet to see whether this is in fact the case. In this paper, we investigate several crises—including natural hazards and human-induced disasters—in a systematic manner and with a consistent methodology. This leads to insights about the prevalence of different information types and sources across a variety of crisis situations.

Author Keywords
Social Media; Emergency Management

ACM Classification Keywords
H.3.5 Online Information Systems; K.4.2 Social Issues

General Terms
Human Factors; Measurement

INTRODUCTION
When a disaster occurs, time is limited and safety is in question, so people need to act quickly with as much knowledge of the situation as possible. It is becoming more common for affected populations and other stakeholders to turn to Twitter to gather information about a crisis when decisions need to be made, and action taken. However, the millions of Twitter messages ("tweets") broadcast at any given time can be overwhelming and confusing, and knowing what information to look for is often difficult.

ACM 978-1-4503-2922-4/15/03...$15.00.
http://dx.doi.org/10.1145/2675133.2675242

One way to help those affected by a disaster to benefit from information on Twitter, is to provide an indication of *what* information they can expect to find. The capacity for affected populations to know what types of information they are likely to see on Twitter when particular kinds of mass emergencies occur, can potentially help them be more efficient in their information-seeking and decision-making processes.

To explore this idea, we collected tweets that were broadcast during 26 different crisis situations that took place in 2012 and 2013. For each crisis, we examine the types of information that were posted, and look at the sources of the information in each tweet. Our specific aim is to measure the prevalence of different types of messages under different types of crisis situations.

Our results suggest that some intrinsic characteristics of the crisis situations (e.g. being instantaneous or progressive) produce consistent effects on the types of information broadcast on Twitter. The results are of interest to members of the public, emergency managers, and formal response agencies, who are increasingly trying to understand how to effectively use social media as part of their information gathering processes.

Related Work
We know that tweets sent during crisis situations may contain information that contributes to situational awareness [49], and though disaster situations exhibit common features across various events [47], previous research has found that *information shared on Twitter varies substantially from one crisis to another* [26, 33, 34]. Indeed, some variability across disasters is expected. For instance, data from the United Nations Office for the Coordination of Humanitarian Affairs (UN OCHA) shows that disasters in high-income countries cause significantly more economic damage, but affect fewer people and have fewer fatal casualties, compared to disasters in countries with low or middle incomes [1].

Comparative research is an established discipline in communication studies [15], but to date, this method has not been extensively applied to the study of social media communications during crises. There is little overlap in the crises examined across research groups, and no attempt to date to apply the same methodology consistently to a large and diverse set of crises. The literature review by Fraustino et al. [17] indicates that research on social media during disasters "tends to examine one catastrophic event (...) and then imply that the findings are generalizable to other disasters."

In our attempt to fill this gap, we examine tweets that were broadcast during a broad range of different crisis situations, and systematically apply the same methodology to the analysis of each event. This methodology is based on previous work that categorizes tweets by type (including [2, 7, 24, 34, 50]) or by source (including [12, 14, 27, 29, 30, 44]).

Contributions

For decision-makers and other stakeholders to be as prepared as possible, knowing what information they are likely to gain from social media can save time and help them decide where to direct their often limited resources. When stakeholders know what types of content to expect (e.g., advice, support, damage reports), and which information sources will be prevalent (e.g. news organizations, eyewitnesses, NGOs), they do not have to sift through masses of social media posts; instead, they have a reasonable expectation of what they will find, and can then make more informed decisions regarding their situational assessment process.

Based on our goal to ease the information overload wrought by social media during crisis situations, the question we address here is: *what are the similarities and differences in Twitter communications that take place during different crisis events, according to specific characteristics of such events?* To answer this question, we study the prevalence of different information types and sources found on Twitter during different types of crises, and correlate this with some of their intrinsic characteristics.

Methodology Overview

To perform this study, we employ the following methodology:

Step 1: We determine a set of dimensions that allow us to characterize different crises: hazard type, temporal development, and geographic spread.

Step 2: We determine a set of dimensions to characterize social media messages during a crisis: informativeness, information type, and source.

Step 3: We collect Twitter data corresponding to 26 crises that took place in 2012 and 2013, using retrospective sampling on the 1% public data stream which is publicly available in the Internet Archive.[1]

Step 4: We create, run, and evaluate a series of crowdsourcing tasks to perform content annotation on approximately 1,000 messages from each of the crises.

Step 5: We perform a statistical analysis of the dependencies between types of crises and types of messages.

STEP 1: DETERMINING CRISIS DIMENSIONS

Given that our research question connects two domains: disaster studies, and social media content analysis, the framework we use is composed of two parts. We categorize the crises according to a series of dimensions that characterize them. Next, we annotate tweets from each crisis according to dimensions that characterize different types of content.

When considering how to organize our data and approach our annotation process, we turned to dimensions used in the sociology of disaster research (p. 50 in [36]). For each crisis, we consider hazard type (natural vs. human-induced), sub-type (e.g. meteorological, hydrological, etc.), temporal development (instantaneous vs. progressive), and geographic spread (focalized vs. diffused).

[1] https://archive.org/details/twitterstream

C1. Hazard type

Hazard type is the first dimension we examine that may impact the types of contents disseminated through social media. The specific hazard types we consider are based on two taxonomies used in Europe[2] and the US,[3] as well as the traditional hazard categories listed by Fischer [16].

The first distinction is between those that are *natural* and those that are *human-induced*. Sub-categories and examples of each one are listed in Table 1. All sub-categories are covered by crises analyzed in this study, with the exception of the "biological" category, which we were unable to sufficiently account for regarding Twitter communications.

Table 1. Hazard categories and sub-categories.

Category	Sub-category	Examples
Natural	• Meteorological • Hydrological • Geophysical • Climatological • *Biological (N/A)*	• tornado, hurricane • flood, landslide • earthquake, volcano • wildfire, heat/cold wave • *epidemic, infestation*
Human-Induced	• Intentional • Accidental	• shooting, bombing • derailment, building collapse

C2. Temporal Development

When considering the temporal development of crises, we classify them as *instantaneous* (e.g. an earthquake or a shooting), or *progressive* (e.g. a hurricane or a heat wave) [3, 8, 35]. As we qualitatively coded the temporal aspects of the crises, we labeled a disaster *instantaneous* if it "does not allow predisaster mobilization of workers or pre-impact evacuation of those in danger," and *progressive* if it is "preceded by a warning period" [3].

C3. Geographic Spread

We look at the geographic spread of a crisis, and specify if it is *focalized* (such as a train accident) or *diffused* (such as a large earthquake) [3, 38]. A focalized crisis affects and mobilizes response in a small area, while a diffused disaster impacts a large geographic area and/or mobilizes national or international response.

We recognize that this list of crisis dimensions is not exhaustive. In particular, linguistic and cultural differences have been shown to influence message content, and the adoption of certain conventions in Twitter, e.g. [20, 37]. We also recognize that these dimensions are not independent from one another. For instance, with the exception of war and large-scale nuclear disasters, most human-induced crises tend to be focalized, while meteorological hazards are often diffused. Additionally, the interplay between these dimensions may yield complex results in terms of the types of information included

[2] http://www.emdat.be/classification

[3] http://www.ready.gov/be-informed

in Twitter messages, and the source of that information. For example, hazard type combined with geographic spread can affect public access to firsthand information about a crisis.

STEP 2: DETERMINING CONTENT DIMENSIONS

When assessing the tweets that were broadcast during each disaster event, we turned to previous research on information broadcast via social media in disaster. We constructed a coarse-grained categorization that covers the categories of information that are highly represented in previous work (including [7, 24, 29, 49, 50] among others). Due to the large number of events and messages we consider, and the limitations of using crowdsourcing workers to perform the annotation (as opposed to experts, who would be prohibitively expensive at this scale), we formulated basic information categories broad enough to be applicable to different crisis situations. The resulting categories and the previous research represented by them, are shown in Table 2: *informativeness*, *information type*, and *source*.

M1. Informativeness

We recognize that informativeness is a subjective concept, as it depends on the person who is asking for or receiving information. In addition, as with any communication, the context in which the information exchange is taking place is critical to understanding its implications. We capture this dimension following [50], by checking whether the tweet contributes to better understanding the situation on the ground. Accordingly, we use the following annotation options:

A. Related to the crisis and informative: if it contains useful information that helps understand the crisis situation.
B. Related to the crisis, but not informative: if it refers to the crisis, but does not contain useful information that helps understand the situation.
C. Not related to the crisis.

M2. Information Type

As we closely analyzed a set of samples of messages communicated via Twitter during disasters, we found that the type of content often varies substantially across hazards; a finding corroborated by many other studies [2, 7, 24, 34, 50].

To identify a set of broad categories whose incidence (though with different degrees of occurrence) is to a large extent independent of event specificities, and to obtain a manageable coding scheme, we first identified the list of information categories used in related work studying various types of events (e.g., wildfires [50], drug wars [29], floods [6, 45], earthquake [39], nuclear power plant [46], to name a few). Then, we proceeded with merging in a bottom-up fashion those categories that overlap and/or are related. Finally, we gathered the remaining categories, typically accounting for information specific to each crisis or type of crisis (e.g., flood level, weather, wind, visibility [50]), into a "catchall" category—*other useful information*. The exact matching of information types present in the related work to each of the categories used in this paper is depicted in Table 2. The information types that we use are:

Table 2. Typologies of content used in this paper, and their relationship to some aspects mentioned in previous work

This work	Related categories from previous work
Informativeness:	
Informative	informative (direct or indirect) [24]; curating or producing content [29]; contribute to situational awareness [50]; situational information [40]; contextual information to better understand the situation [42]
Not inform.	trolling [29]; humor [28]; off-topic [34, 39, 45]; rumor [22]; humor or irrelevant/spam [42]
Information type:	
Affected individuals	medical emergency, people trapped, person news [7]; casualties (and damage), people missing, found or seen [24]; reports about self [2]; fatality, injury, missing [49]; looking for missing people [39];
Infrastruc. & utilities	(casualties and) damage [24]; reports about environment [2]; built environment [49]; damaged, closures and services [22]; collapsed structure, water shortage/sanitation, hospital/clinic services [7]; road closures and traffic conditions [48];
Donations & volunteer.	donations of money, goods or services [24]; donations or volunteering [34]; requesting help, proposing relief, relief coordination [39]; donations, relief, resources [22]; help and fundraising [6, 40]; shelter needed, food shortage/distribution [7]; volunteer information [50]; help requests [2]
Caution & advice	caution, advice [24]; warnings [2]; advice, warnings, preparation [34]; warning, advice, caution, preparation [50]; tips [28]; safety, preparation, status, protocol [22]; preparedness [51]; advice [6]; advice and instructions [40]; predicting or forecasting, instructions to handle certain situations [42];
Sympathy & emo. sup.	concerns and condolences [2]; gratitude, prayers [34]; emotion-related [39]; support [22]; thanks and gratitude, support [6, 40];
Other useful info.	fire line/emergency location, flood level, weather, wind, visibility [50]; smoke, ash [48]; adjunctive and meta-discussions [40]; other informative messages [34]; information verification, explanation of particular problems [42];
Source:	
Eyewitness	citizen reporters, members of the community [29]; eyewitnesses [6, 14, 27, 34]; local, peripheral, personally connected [45]; local individuals [43, 50]; local perspective, on the ground reports [46]; direct experience (personal narrative and eyewitness reports) [40]; direct observation, direct impact, relayed observation [48];
Government	(news organizations and) authorities [29]; government/administration [34]; police and fire services [22]; police [13]; government [6]; public institutions [46]; public service agencies, flood specific agencies [45];
NGOs	non-profit organizations [12, 46]; non-governmental organization [34]; faith-based organizations [45];
Business	commercial organizations [12]; enterprises [46]; for-profit corporation [34];
Media	news organizations (and authorities), blogs [29]; journalists, media, and bloggers [12, 14]; news organization [34]; professional news reports [28]; media [6]; traditional media (print, television, radio), alternative media, freelance journalist [46]; blogs, news-crawler bots, local, national and alternative media [45]; media sharing (news media updates, multimedia) [40];
Outsiders	sympathizers [27]; distant witness [9]; remote crowd [43]; non-locals [45, 46].

A. Affected individuals: deaths, injuries, missing, found, or displaced people, and/or personal updates.
B. Infrastructure and utilities: buildings, roads, utilities/services that are damaged, interrupted, restored or operational.
C. Donations and volunteering: needs, requests, or offers of money, blood, shelter, supplies, and/or services by volunteers or professionals.
D. Caution and advice: warnings issued or lifted, guidance and tips.
E. Sympathy and emotional support: thoughts, prayers, gratitude, sadness, etc.
F. Other useful information not covered by any of the above categories.

M3. Source

When people turn to Twitter to learn about a disaster, they are often concerned with the source of information. Hence, we focused on *content source*, which may be different from tweet author; e.g. if the Twitter account of a large media organization quotes a government official, the "source" is the government official. Sources are categorized as: *primary sources* (eyewitness accounts) or *secondary or tertiary sources* (typically mainstream media or others engaged in journalistic acts) [12, 14, 27, 29, 30, 44].

For the former, we chose to broaden the definition of an eyewitness account as originating from "a person who has seen something happen and can give a first-hand description of it"[4] to also accommodate those cases when the account does not include a direct observation, yet the user is personally impacted by the event, or it "is about a direct observation or impact of a person who is not the micro-blogger" [48]—typically relaying the observations of friends or family.

In the latter case, we can find several organizations who often aggregate information about a crisis, including business, governmental, and non-governmental sources:

A. Eyewitness: information originating from eyewitnesses of the event or of response/recovery operations, or from their family, friends, neighbors, etc.
B. Government: information originating from the local or national administration.
C. Non-governmental organization: information originating from NGOs.
D. Business: information originating from for-profit business (except news organizations).
E. Traditional and/or Internet media: information coming from sources such as TV, radio, news organizations, web blogs, or journalists.
F. Outsiders: information originating from individuals that are not personally involved/affected by the event.

STEP 3: DATA COLLECTION

List of Events

Table 3 shows our datasets, which are available for research purposes at http://crisislex.org/. They correspond to a set of 26 events during 2012 and 2013, and which spawned significant activity on Twitter. Table 3 also includes crisis dimensions of hazard type, development, and spread (we consider the Singapore haze to be partially human-induced due to intentional fires to clear land). We note that in our dataset, all human-induced crises are focalized and instantaneous, while all natural hazards are diffused, but may be instantaneous or progressive.

To obtain our list of events, we started with a set of disasters compiled mainly from Wikipedia.[5] We then filtered it by choosing events that had at least 100,000 tweets associated with them—which is reflected by at least 1,000 tweets in the 1% public data stream we used.

Floods are the most frequent type of natural hazard in our data, and also the natural hazard that affects the most people in the world. According to data from the United Nations for the 2002–2011 period, an average of 116 million people were affected by a flood every year, followed by 72 million people a year affected by drought, 40 million by storms, 9 million by extreme temperatures, and 8 million by earthquakes [1].

Data Sampling

Our data collection method is shaped by limitations to data access through Twitter, and is based on first collecting a base data sample and then retrospectively sub-sampling it. The base data sample was obtained by constantly monitoring Twitter's public stream via Twitter's Sample API, which consists of a sample of approximately 1% of all tweets[6] and it is accessible via Internet Archive[7], allowing full reproducibility of this work. In the 2012-2013 period, this collection contains on average about 132 million tweets (amounting to 38 GB of compressed data) per month. The quality of Twitter data samples acquired via the publicly available APIs that offer limited access to the full Twitter stream has been studied extensively, to understand the nature of the biases of such data samples [18, 19, 25, 31, 32]. Yet, while [32] have shown biases with respect to hashtag and topic prevalence in the Streaming API (which we do not use in this study), [31] shows that the data obtained via the Sample API closely resemble the random samples over the full Twitter stream, which corroborates the specifications of this API. Additionally, given the daily volume of tweets "the 1% endpoint would provide a representative and high resolution sample with a maximum margin of error of 0.06 at a confidence level of 99%, making the study of even relatively small subpopulations within that sample a realistic option" [18].

The sub-samples are obtained by running keyword searches over the base data—keyword searches that mimic the way in which Twitter does keyword tracking to obtain a sample of the data that one can obtain in real time.[8] An advantage of this retrospective sampling method is that one can capture the entire period of the event, which is not the case for other

[4] http://www.oxforddictionaries.com/definition/english/eyewitness

[5] From the list of significant events per month, e.g. for January 2013 we consulted http://en.wikipedia.org/wiki/January_2013

[6] https://dev.twitter.com/docs/api/1.1/get/statuses/sample

[7] https://archive.org/details/twitterstream

[8] https://dev.twitter.com/docs/streaming-apis/parameters#track

Table 3. List of crises studied, sorted by date, including the duration of the collection period for each dataset, the number of tweets collected, and several dimensions of the crises

Year	Country	Crisis Name	Days	Tweets	Hazard category	Hazard subcategory	Hazard type	Development	Spread
2012	Italy	Italy earthquakes	32	7.4K	Natural	Geophysical	Earthquake	Instantaneous	Diffused
2012	US	Colorado wildfires	31	4.2K	Natural	Climatological	Wildfire	Progressive	Diffused
2012	Philipinnes	Philipinnes floods	13	3.0K	Natural	Hydrological	Floods	Progressive	Diffused
2012	Venezuela	Venezuela refinery explosion	12	2.7K	Human-induced	Accidental	Explosion	Instantaneous	Focalized
2012	Costa Rica	Costa Rica earthquake	13	2.2K	Natural	Geophysical	Earthquake	Instantaneous	Diffused
2012	Guatemala	Guatemala earthquake	20	3.3K	Natural	Geophysical	Earthquake	Instantaneous	Diffused
2012	Phillipines	Typhoon Pablo	21	1.9K	Natural	Meteorological	Typhoon	Progressive	Diffused
2013	Brazil	Brazil nightclub fire	16	4.8K	Human-induced	Accidental	Fire	Instantaneous	Focalized
2013	Australia	Queensland floods	19	1.2K	Natural	Hydrological	Floods	Progressive	Diffused
2013	Russia	Russian meteor	19	8.4K	Natural	Others	Meteorite	Instantaneous	Focalized
2013	US	Boston bombings	60	157.5K	Human-induced	Intentional	Bombings	Instantaneous	Focalized
2013	Bangladesh	Savar building collapse	36	4.1K	Human-induced	Accidental	Collapse	Instantaneous	Focalized
2013	US	West Texas explosion	29	14.5K	Human-induced	Accidental	Explosion	Instantaneous	Focalized
2013	Canada	Alberta floods	25	5.9K	Natural	Hydrological	Floods	Progressive	Diffused
2013	Singapore	Singapore haze	19	3.6K	Mixed	Others	Haze	Progressive	Diffused
2013	Canada	Lac-Megantic train crash	14	2.3K	Human-induced	Accidental	Derailment	Instantaneous	Focalized
2013	Spain	Spain train crash	15	3.7K	Human-induced	Accidental	Derailment	Instantaneous	Focalized
2013	Phillipines	Manila floods	11	2.0K	Natural	Hydrological	Floods	Progressive	Diffused
2013	US	Colorado floods	21	1.8K	Natural	Hydrological	Floods	Progressive	Diffused
2013	Australia	Australia wildfires	21	2.0K	Natural	Climatological	Wildfire	Progressive	Diffused
2013	Phillipines	Bohol earthquake	12	2.2K	Natural	Geophysical	Earthquake	Instantaneous	Diffused
2013	UK	Glasgow helicopter crash	30	2.6K	Human-induced	Accidental	Crash	Instantaneous	Focalized
2013	US	LA Airport shootings	12	2.7K	Human-induced	Intentional	Shootings	Instantaneous	Focalized
2013	US	NYC train crash	8	1.1K	Human-induced	Accidental	Derailment	Instantaneous	Focalized
2013	Italy	Sardinia floods	13	1.1K	Natural	Hydrological	Floods	Progressive	Diffused
2013	Phillipines	Typhoon Yolanda	58	39.0K	Natural	Meteorological	Typhoon	Progressive	Diffused

collections built during the disasters, which generally lack the first minutes or hours of the event.

Keywords were selected following standard practices commonly used for this type of data collection [6, 23, 34, 46], and typically include hashtags or terms that pair the canonical name of the disaster with proper names of the affected locations (e.g., Manila floods, #newyork derailment), the proper names of the meteorological phenomena (e.g., Hurricane Sandy), or, at times, hashtags promoted by governments, response agencies, or news media. Previous work has shown that this method produces a sample of messages whose distribution of information categories closely resembles the sampling by other methods e.g. *geofencing*, which samples all tweets from users in the affected area [34].

To identify the keywords/hashtags used during each event, one of the authors used a search engine to lookup for "Hashtags ⟨Event Name⟩." The search results often included news articles discussing the social media use during the searched event,[9] resources from NGOs using social media for crisis management,[10] Internet media platforms,[11] governmental resources on social media use[12] or research papers [6, 34]. Using these resources, we built an initial list of hashtags/keywords, which we further validated and iteratively improved by manually searching for them on Twitter. In those cases in which the hashtag/keyword had been used for other purposes, we also looked for the combination of the hashtag/keyword, and the event name. When other keywords frequently appear with those already on our list, we also searched for them in Twitter. If there were at least few instances in which they appeared in relevant tweets without the other keywords, we added them to the list. The size of the resulting keywords lists vary, yet [34] suggests that keywords lists of various sizes retrieve collections which exhibit comparable representativeness with respect to a reference sample.

For the *instantaneous* hazards we start the collection from the moment when the event happen, while for the *progressive* hazards we start from the moment the hazard was detected (e.g., when a storm formed for a hurricane). The volume of tweets in each collection decreases after onset, but we continue collecting data until that volume stabilizes to a low value (specifically, when the standard deviation of the daily number of tweets becomes less than 5).

As a post-processing step, we remove very short tweets (i.e. those made up of 3 tokens or less), as they are in general hard to classify and rarely contain any useful information. We do not remove near-duplicates or re-tweets (RTs) because we are interested in the extent to which people repeat and pass along existing messages.

STEP 4: CROWDSOURCED DATA ANNOTATION

We employed crowdsource workers to perform manual annotation of our datasets in April and May 2014.[13] The workers

[9] http://mashable.com/2012/06/29/colorado-wildfire-social-media/, http://www.techinasia.com/singapore-haze-infographic/ and others.

[10] http://wiki.crisiscommons.eu/wiki/Crises, http://crisiswiki.org/

[11] http://twitchy.com/2014/07/07/earthquake-hits-southern-mexico-and-guatemala-fatalities-damage-reported-pics/, https://storify.com/ABC13Houston/plant-explosion-in-west-texas

[12] http://www.gov.ph/2013/11/09/online-efforts-for-typhoon-yolanda/

[13] We employed workers through the crowdsourcing platform *CrowdFlower: http://crowdflower.com/*

were provided with detailed instructions and examples of correctly labeled tweets, so they could successfully complete the annotation task.

Task Description

Below are the instructions given during the annotation phase to crowdsource workers. "You," in the task description refers to the crowdsourcing worker. The underlined parts, and the examples, changed for each crisis.

M1. Informativeness. The instructions used for this annotation task are shown below, and include examples for each class.

> Categorize tweets posted during the 2013 Colorado floods. Please read them carefully, following links as necessary, and categorize them as:
> A. Related to the floods and informative: if it contains useful information that helps you understand the situation:
> – "RT @NWSBoulder Significant flooding at the Justice Center in #boulderflood"
> – "Flash floods wash away homes, kill at least one near Boulder via @NBCnews"
> B. Related to the floods, but not informative: if it refers to the crisis, but does not contain useful information that helps you understand the situation:
> – "Pray for Boulder, Colorado #boulderflood"
> C. Not related to the floods:
> – "#COstorm you are a funny guy lol"
> D. Not applicable; too short; not readable; or other issues.

M2. Information Type. Instructions and examples:

> Categorize tweets posted during the 2012 Colorado wildfires. Please read them carefully, following links as necessary, and categorize as:
> A. Affected individuals: information about deaths, injuries, missing, trapped, found or displaced people, including personal updates about oneself, family, or others.
> – "Up to 100,000 people face evacuation in Colorado"
> B. Infrastructure and utilities: information about buildings, roads, utilities/services that are damaged, interrupted, restored or operational.
> – "Officials working the #HighParkFire confirmed that several roads are closed"
> C. Donations and volunteering: information about needs, requests, queries or offers of money, blood, shelter, supplies (e.g., food, water, clothing, medical supplies) and/or services by volunteers or professionals.
> – "#Offer Storage Space http://t.co/... #COwildfire"
> D. Caution and advice: information about warnings issued or lifted, guidance and tips.
> – Wildfire warnings issued for six counties Sunday - http://t.co/..."
> E. Sympathy and emotional support: thoughts, prayers, gratitude, sadness, etc.
> – "Pray for Boulder #COwildfire"
> F. Other useful information NOT covered by any of the above categories.
> – "To track fire activity in CO, check this site @inciweb Colorado Incidents http://t.co/..."
> G. Not applicable; not readable;not related to the crisis.

M3. Source. Instructions and examples:

> Categorize tweets posted during the 2013 Queensland floods (Australia). Please read them carefully, following links as necessary, and indicate the most likely source of information for them as:
> A. Eyewitness: if the information originates from eyewitnesses to the event or to response/recovery operations, or from their family, friends, neighbors, etc. :
> – "Just found out my mum is trapped at home, no water, no power, tree's down across roads out of her property near glasshouse mtns"
> – "Outside sounds like it is going to shatter my bedroom windows any sec now #bigwet #qld"
> B. Government: if the information originates from national, regional or local government agencies, police, hospitals, and/or military.
> – "PRT @theqldpremier: UPDATE SCHOOL CLOSURES: An updated school closures list is available now at http://t.co/..."
> C. Non-government: if the information originates from non-governmental and not for profit organizations such as RedCross, UN, UNICEF, etc.
> – "RT @RedCrossAU: Everyone affected by #qldfloods, let people know you're safe: http://t.co/..."
> D. Businesses: if the information originates from for-profit business or corporations such as Starbucks, Walmart, etc.
> – "RT @starbucks: With many partners impacted by OLD floods, consider making (or increasing) donations"
> E. Traditional and/or Internet news or blogs: if the information originates from television channels, radio channels, newspapers, websites or blogs such as CNN, KODA, New York Times, etc.
> – "RT @ABCNews24: #QLDfloods watch: Authorities are preparing for tornadoes in southeast Queensland."
> F. Outsiders: if the information originates from individuals that have NO acquaintances affected by the event, nor are they associate with any organization.
> – "RT @TheBushVerandah: Just heard a farmer had to shoot approx 100 sows at mundubbera ... In preference to them drowning"
> G. Not applicable; not readable; not related to the crisis.

Task Characteristics

For all annotation tasks, we provide examples both in English and the language most commonly used to communicate about the event (if there was a common language used other than English.) Regarding worker selection, the platform we used for crowdsourcing allows us to select workers by country (but not at a sub-country level), so we specified that workers must be from the country where the event took place. In few cases when there were not enough workers to perform the task, we also included workers from neighboring countries having the same official language. We selected workers in this way to ensure that they understand the tweets posted by individuals local to the event, and that they would be more likely able to understand dialects, references to regional and/or local places, and overall be versed in the culture of the area in which the event took place. Additionally, following standard guidelines from this crowdsourcing platform, 20 to 30 tweets per crisis and task were classified by the authors of this paper. We consider all workers whose assessments differ significantly from ours (less than 70% of agreement) as *untrusted*.

Workers were presented with the tweet text, including any links (which they were invited to follow), and then asked to choose a single category that best matched the content of the tweet. To avoid potential ethical concerns on behalf of Twitter users who are likely unaware that their tweets are being collected and analyzed, workers did not have access to the author username, nor the time at which the tweet was sent. In addition, we avoid possible privacy violations by not displaying the username nor the profile picture of persons affected by a given disaster. This practice follows customary procedures used for using crowdsourced annotation of text messages for both information type [4, 10, 24, 34] and information source [14, 34].

Trusted workers took from 10 to 12 seconds to label each tweet (in terms of interquartile mean, which is the figure reported by the crowdsourcing platform). We collect labels from at least 3 different trusted workers per tweet and task, and determine the final label of the tweet by simple majority.

About 15-20 trusted workers participated in each classification step (i.e. a set of 1,000 tweets from a single event and with a single question M1, M2, or M3), with the bulk of the work being done by about 10 of them in each case—with no worker labeling more than 300 items in a classification task, a limit set by us following recommendations from the crowdsourcing provider. The total amount paid to the crowdsourcing platform for the 3 classification tasks was approximately $35 (USD) per event. Payments to specific individual workers depend on how many tasks they performed and on their agreement with the test questions, following an internal procedure of the crowdsourcing provider.

Our first classification task is to identify tweets which are related to a crisis. A tweet may contain a crisis' keywords but be unrelated to it, as some keywords may be quite general, and refer to any number of topics other than the disaster situation. In addition, unscrupulous spammers sometimes exploit the popularity of a crisis hashtag to post promotional content [5]. As a result, the first labeling phase (M1) also has a data cleaning role. For each event we label a set of 1,000 tweets selected uniformly at random. We imposed a minimum threshold of 900 crisis-related tweets per crisis, and in the cases where it was necessary (9 out of 26 crises), we continued labeling tweets until passing the threshold. Next, we kept only the tweets that were related to the crisis (independently of whether they were deemed informative or not), and classified them with respect to *information types* (M2) and *sources* (M3).

Task Evaluation

Tweet classification is a subjective process, especially when performed at a large scale, and with a focus on tweet content. To evaluate to what extent subjectivity affects our results, we performed the following experiment: Two authors *independently* labeled 200 tweets sampled uniformly at random from all the crises. They classified tweets according to information types and sources, by looking at the content of the tweets as displayed in the Twitter platform, including conversations (if any), and looking at links in the tweets, and user profile information from its authors. We also note that authors had background information about each of the events.

We measure inter-assessor agreement with Cohen's Kappa, resulting in $\kappa = 0.80$ for information type (95% confidence interval CI: $[0.73, 0.87]$) and $\kappa = 0.73$ for source (95% CI: $[0.64, 0.81]$). Customarily, values in this range indicate substantial agreement.

Next, we take all tweets in which both authors agree and compare their joint label with those provided by crowdsource workers. The results are $\kappa = 0.81$ (95% CI: $[0.73, 0.88]$) for information type and $\kappa = 0.72$ for source (95% CI: $[0.62, 0.83]$). Again, these values reflect substantial agreement. The *individual* agreement of authors with workers (which includes cases in which the labels given by authors do not agree) is lower but still substantial ($\kappa = 0.69$ and $\kappa = 0.74$ for information type, $\kappa = 0.57$ and $\kappa = 0.63$ for source).

The conclusion is similar to that of previous work using crowdsourcing labeling (e.g. [14, 41]), crowdsource workers collectively provide reliable labels for social media annotation tasks, at a volume that would be very costly to achieve by other means (in our case, $26 \times 1,000 \times 3 = 78,000$ labels).

This experiment also allows us to evaluate the biases of crowdsourcing labeling. For information type, in 15% of the cases the crowdsourced label does not correspond to the one given by the authors (among the authors this discrepancy is 16%). The most common error of crowdsourcing workers is labeling "Caution and Advice" messages as either "Donations and Volunteering" or "Other Useful Information." For information source, in 17% of the cases the crowdsourced label did not agree with the one of the authors (among authors this discrepancy is 18%). The most common error was labeling "Eyewitness" as "Outsiders" or "Media." This means that in the analysis, we have to consider that "Caution and Advice" and "Eyewitness" may be underrepresented categories, while the other categories we mentioned may be overrepresented. The extent of the total underrepresentation/overrepresentation across all categories, however, is about 15%-17%, and more importantly, is not larger than the discrepancy among the two authors who performed this evaluation.

STEP 5: DATA ANALYSIS

The final step is to perform an analysis of the data annotated by the crowdsourcing workers. We begin by presenting results about the overall distribution of content types across crises, which we connect to the crisis dimensions by mining association rules. Then we consider temporal aspects, as well as the interplay between content dimensions.

Finally, we show that while substantial variability exists, similar crises tend to have a similar distribution of message types. Though we make no claims that these 26 crises are representative of every event of every type we consider, we do note patterns and consistencies in the proportion of different messages, and present potential explanations about them, to serve as foundations for future explorations.

Content Types vs. Crisis Dimensions

We first present our results regarding relationships between crisis dimensions and the prevalence of categories of information found in tweets.

Informativeness

The proportion of messages in each collection that were found to be about the crisis at hand (i.e. classified in the first two categories of M1) was on average 89% (min. 64%, max. 100%). In this case, one of the most significant factors is whether the keywords/hashtags adopted by people tweeting about the crisis are specific to the event, or were used for other purposes. For instance, `#yolandaph` was specifically used for Typhoon Yolanda, while `#dhaka` (the name of the capital of Bangladesh) was used after the Savar building collapse, but also for other purposes.

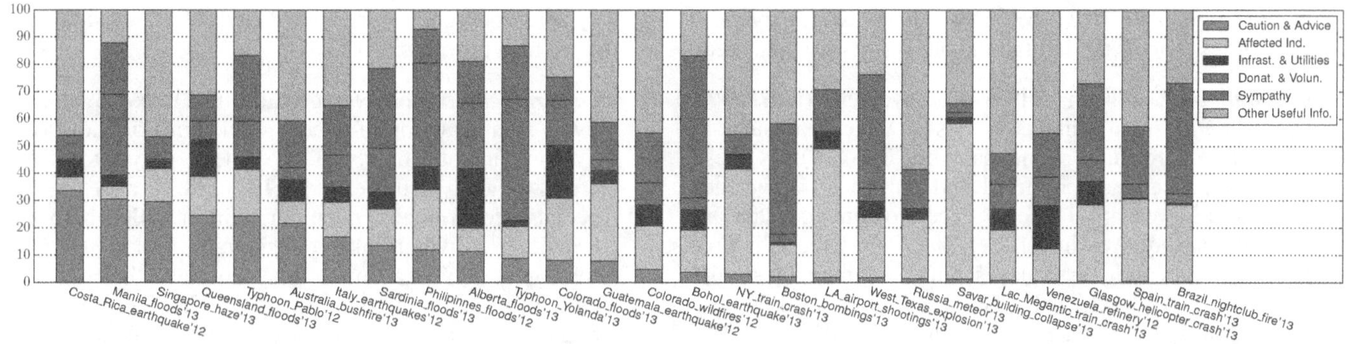

(a) Distribution of information types, sorted by descending proportion of *caution and advice* tweets.

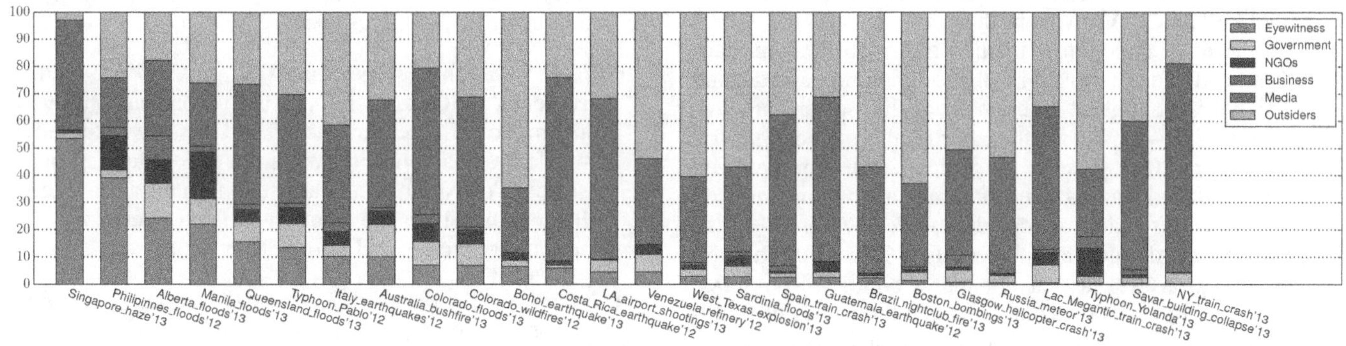

(b) Distribution of information sources, sorted by descending proportion of *eyewitness* tweets.

Figure 1. Distributions of information types and sources (best seen in color)

Among these messages, the proportion of informative messages (i.e. those in the first category of M1) was on average 69% (min. 44%, max. 92%). Most of the messages considered "not informative" contained expressions of sympathy and emotional support (e.g. "thoughts and prayers").

Information types

Figure 1(a) shows the distribution of information types found in the tweets related to each crisis. Below, we sort the categories in decreasing order of average prevalence, noting the (wide) range on the proportion of each type.

- *Other useful information*: 32% on average (min. 7%, max. 59%). This "catchall" category is the largest among the information types. An analyst interested exclusively in the remaining categories can skip these messages on the initial pass of analysis. We note that the events in which this category was the least prevalent (i.e., the other categories accounted for more than 80% of the messages) were all diffused. While we do not claim that all, or even most, diffused events will have fewer-than-average amounts of "other useful information" tweets, it is potentially useful to know that this type of tweet is not prevalent in the diffused events we studied.

The information captured by the "other useful information" category varies significantly across events. For instance, in the Boston bombings and LA Airport shootings in 2013, there are updates about the investigation and suspects; in the West Texas explosion and the Spain train crash, we find details about the accidents and the follow-up inquiry; in earthquakes, we find seismological details.

- *Sympathy and emotional support*: 20% on average (min. 3%, max. 52%). Tweets that express sympathy are present in all the events we examined. The 4 crises in which the messages in this category were more prevalent (above 40%) were all instantaneous disasters. Again, we make no hard-and-fast claims about all instantaneous disasters, but this finding leads us to conjecture that people are more likely to offer sympathy when events are not predicted, take people by surprise, and may cause additional distress due to their unforeseen occurrence.

- *Affected individuals*: 20% on average (min. 5%, max. 57%). The 5 crises with the largest proportion of this type of information (28%–57%) were human-induced, focalized, and instantaneous. These 5 events can also be viewed as particularly emotionally shocking. They resulted in casualties, but a small enough number of casualties to generate many reports regarding specific individuals who lost their lives or suffered injuries.

- *Donations and volunteering*: 10% on average (min. 0%, max. 44%). The number of tweets describing needs or offers of goods and services in each event varies greatly; some events have no mention of them, while for others, this is one of the largest information categories. In our data, tweets about donations and volunteering were more prevalent in Typhoon Yolanda in 2013 (44%) and in the floods in Sardinia, Colorado, Alberta, and Manila in 2013, and in the Philippines in 2012 (16%–38%). In contrast, they were 10% or less for all the human-induced crises we analyzed.

- *Caution and advice*: 10% on average (min. 0%, max. 34%). In instantaneous crises, there is unsurprisingly little information on this type (0%–8%), as these events are often not predicted and only post-impact advice can be present. The only exceptions in our data are the Italy earthquakes in 2012 (17%) — in which the collection covers two earthquakes plus a number of significant aftershocks which happen over an interval of less than 10 days, and Costa Rica earthquake in 2012 (34%) — when tsunami alerts were issued across Central America and parts of South America including even distant countries like Chile. Apart from these two events, the events with the most tweets that include information about caution and advice are caused by diffused natural hazards, and the 5 with the highest fraction from this set are all progressive (22%–31%). Further, baring the meteor that fell in Russia in 2013, we can see a clear separation between human-induced hazards and natural: all human induced events have less caution and advice tweets (0%–3%) than all the events due to natural hazards (4%–31%). The meteor was a rare event that felt like a bomb whose shock wave shattered windows and damaged thousands of buildings, remaining undetected before its atmospheric entry.[14]
- *Infrastructure and utilities*: 7% on average (min. 0%, max. 22%). The crises where this type of information was more than 10% were the Queensland, Alberta, and Colorado floods of 2013, and the Venezuela refinery explosion in 2012. In flood situations, it is common for electricity and water supplies to be cut, and in the case of the refinery explosion, many living in the area were suddenly without electricity due to the massive impact of the discharge.

Sources

In Figure 1(b), we see the distribution of tweet sources, and we observe the following:

- *Traditional and/or Internet media*: 42% on average (min. 18%, max. 77%). Regardless of the event, traditional and Internet media have a large presence on Twitter, in many cases more than 30% of the tweets. The 6 crises with the highest fraction of tweets coming from a media source (54%–76%) are instantaneous, which make "breaking news" in the media.
- *Outsiders*: 38% on average (min. 3%, max. 65%). Depending on the event, the number of "outsiders" can vary. This was in general about 18% or more, with the exception of the Singapore haze in 2013 that had only 3% of tweets from outsiders. The Singapore haze was an event that strongly disrupted the city, but did not result in life-threatening injuries or deaths.
- *Eyewitness accounts*: 9% on average (min. 0%, max. 54%). In general, we find a larger proportion of eyewitness accounts during diffused disasters caused by natural hazards. The 12 events with the highest percentage of eyewitness accounts are all diffused (6%–54%) and the top 6 are also progressive (13%–54%).
- *Government*: 5% on average (min. 1%, max. 13%). A relatively small fraction of tweets include information sourced by government officials and agencies—only for two of the crises we analyze this exceeds 10%. We surmise that this is because governments must verify information before they broadcast it, which takes considerable time [21]. Therefore, government accounts may not have the most up-to-date information in crisis situations. The 7 events with the highest percentage of tweets from governmental agencies are due to natural-hazards, progressive and diffused (7%-13%), which are the cases when the governments intervene to issue or lift warnings or alerts.
- *NGOs*: 4% on average (min. 0%, max. 17%). Like governments, NGOs are also careful to broadcast only verified information. In the human-induced crises we studied there is little NGO activity in Twitter ($\approx$ 4% or less). The highest levels of NGO tweets are seen in natural disasters and all those in which the fraction of such tweets was 6% or more are typhoons and floods.
- *Business*: 2% on average (min. 0%, max. 9%). For the most part, we do not see a large amount of tweet activity from businesses in the disaster situations we studied. The proportion is below 5% for all crises except the Alberta floods in 2013 with 9% of tweets. Furthermore, with only one exception—the Glasgow helicopter crash—the crises with 3% or more tweets from business were diffused.

Association Rules

To systematically search for relationships between the characteristics of crises and the messages in Twitter, we applied an association-rules mining method [11]. To err in the side of caution, we report only the automatically-discovered association rules that are valid for more than 20 out of the 26 crises. To apply this method to numerical data, each category in the information types and sources was divided into two classes: above the median, and below the median.

For information types, we found one rule that is valid for 24 out of 26 of the crises: when the geographical spread is diffused, the proportion of caution and advice tweets is above the median, and when it is focalized, the proportion of caution and advice tweets is below the median. For sources, we found one rule that is valid for 21 out of 26 of the crises: human-induced accidental events tend to have a number of eyewitness tweets below the median, in comparison with intentional and natural hazards.

Both rules are possibly related to different levels of access to the area affected by the event and to its surroundings.

Content Redundancy

We next look at content redundancy. Heuristically, we consider two tweets to be near-duplicates if their longest common subsequence was 75% or more of the length of the shortest tweet. Among the sources of information, messages originating from non-governmental organizations and government

[14]http://en.wikipedia.org/wiki/Chelyabinsk_meteor

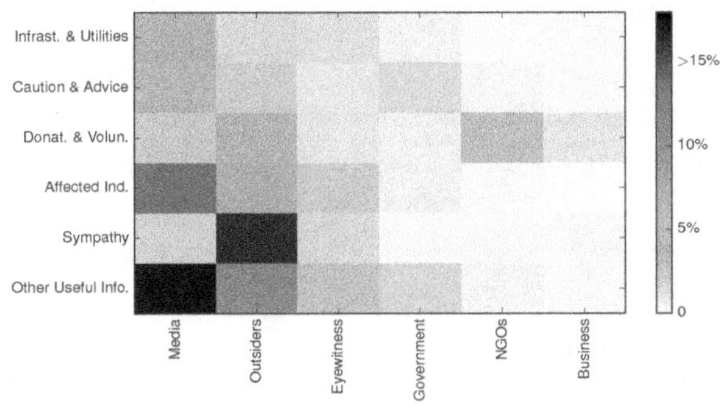

Figure 2. Average distribution of tweets across crises into combinations of information types (rows) and sources (columns). Rows and columns are sorted by total frequency, starting on the bottom-left corner. The cells in this figure add up to 100%.

sources tended to show more redundancy, with the top 3 messages (and their near-duplicates) accounting for ≈20%-22% of the tweets. Among information types, messages of caution and advice, and those containing information about infrastructure and utilities, were the most repeated ones, with the top 3 messages (and their near-duplicates) comprising ≈12-14% of the tweets.

Types and Sources

Some information types are more frequently associated with particular sources, as shown in Figure 2, in which each ⟨type, source⟩ cell depicts the probability that a tweet has that specific combination of information type and source. NGOs and business are more frequently the source of tweets related to donations and volunteering, mostly to ask for resources and request volunteer work (NGOs), or to announce free or discounted goods or services for those affected by a disaster (business).

Tweets from governments are often messages of caution and advice, such as tornado alerts; this agrees with observations in [51] where "preparedness" is the larger category used by government communications. Instead, eyewitness tweets focus on affected individuals. Both government and eyewitness tweets also frequently include a variety of messages that belong to the "other useful information" category. Outsider messages are predominantly about sympathy and support.

Finally, tweets from traditional and Internet media offer a variety of information types including information about affected individuals, and messages of caution and advice. Media are also the most prominent source of information regarding infrastructure and utilities.

Temporal Aspects

We study how the volume of different categories of messages evolves over time, as shown in Tables 5 and 6 (at the end of the paper). We separated crises according to their temporal development (instantaneous vs. progressive), depicting using "spark lines" the total volume of messages over time, and the total volume of messages in each information type and source.[15] This analysis focuses on the differences between the average timestamps of messages in different information categories.[16]

In terms of information types, the messages that arrive first are those of caution and advice, and sympathy and support, roughly in the first 12–24 hours after the peak of the crisis. This is particularly evident in instantaneous crises. Then, messages about affected individuals and infrastructure are most frequent. The last messages to appear are those related to donations and volunteering. Interestingly, this follows the progression in the stages of a crisis from emergency response to early recovery actions [47].

In terms of sources, there are differences depending on the type of temporal development. In *instantaneous* crises, outsiders, media and NGO messages appear early, with other sources following (the temporal position of eyewitness messages varies substantially depending on crisis type). On the other hand, during *progressive* crises, eyewitness and government messages appear early, mostly to warn and advice those in the affected areas, while NGO messages appear relatively late. In addition, there is an interesting temporal complementarity between messages from governments and NGOs that merits to be studied in depth in future work.

Crisis Similarity

In further seeking links between disaster characteristics and tweet content and source, we apply an unsupervised method; specifically, hierarchical agglomerative clustering. Performing this clustering uncovered groups of crises that have similar content distribution. Given that we compare probability distributions, to measure the similarity between two crisis events we use Bhattacharyya distance (for two discrete distributions p and q this is $-\ln(\sum_{c \in C} \sqrt{p(c)q(c)})$ where C is the set of all classes) which quantifies the overlap between two statistical samples. To combine clusters of crises, we used complete-linkage clustering, which merges those clusters for which the distance between their furthest elements is the smallest.

Figure 3(a) shows the resulting dendrogram when the clustering is done according to the distribution of information types. We see two large clusters: first, the cluster on the bottom is dominated by human-induced crises, while in the one on the top there are only natural hazards. This indicates that, despite the significant variations we have shown, human-induced crises are more similar to each other in terms of the types of information disseminated through Twitter than to natural hazards.

Second, events also cluster depending on how they developed. The cluster at the bottom includes instantaneous events, with one exception: the Colorado wildfires in 2012. This exception may be due to the nature of this particular fire. The combination of heat, drought conditions, and high winds

[15]Each point in the spark line corresponds to a *calendar* day, which explains why in some instantaneous crises the overall curve goes up at the beginning (when the crisis occurs at night).

[16]Peak, average, and median timestamps for each time series in Tables 5 and 6 are available in our data release.

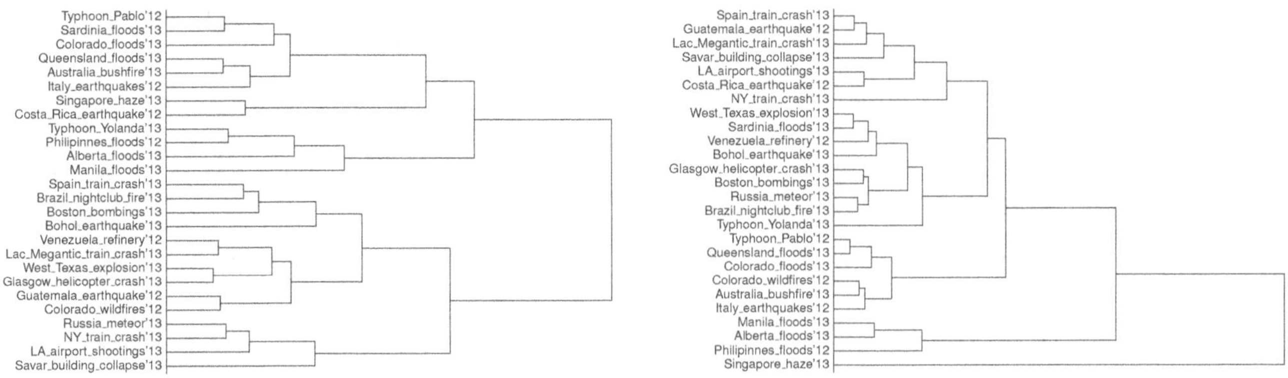

(a) Clusters by information type. (b) Clusters by source.

Figure 3. Dendrograms obtained by hierarchical agglomerative clustering of crises. The length of the branch points reflect the similarity among crises. We remark that the clusters do not reflect similar messages, but instead similarities in terms of the proportion of different information types and sources in each crisis.

caused the fire to quickly develop, and it claimed 350 houses in just over 12 hours. The cluster on the top includes progressive disasters, with two outliers: Italy earthquakes in 2012—a sequence of earthquakes and aftershocks—and the Costa Rica earthquake in 2012—during which a Caribbean-wide tsunami watch was issued, resulting in a large volume of caution and advice messages that are typically more prominent in progressive crises.

A similar picture emerges in the case of clusters by distribution of sources, shown in Figure 3(b). In this case, there is a large cluster dominated by human-induced crises (on the top), followed by two small clusters encompassing only natural hazards, and the Singapore haze 2013 as an outlier (this haze was caused by a mix of natural and human causes). Further, the large cluster on the top is dominated by instantaneous events (with two exceptions, Typhoon Yolanda and Sardinia Floods in 2013), while in the other clusters the events are progressive, excepting Italy earthquakes in 2012.

Furthermore, while the events development and type arise as the main factors impacting the clusters composition, in both Figures 3(a) and 3(b) we also notice that the clusters are being dominated by either diffused (top cluster by information type and bottom clusters by information source) or focalized events (the remaining clusters). The clusters tendency to encompass events that are similar along all these dimensions is likely explained by the dependency among the crisis dimensions (e.g., typically, the progressive events are also diffused and human-induced crises tend to be focalized).

DISCUSSION

Disasters are common events that occur regularly; the United Nations Office for Coordination of Humanitarian Affairs recorded 394 disasters caused by natural hazards in the 2002–2011 period [1]. While disasters take place often, and may be caused by similar hazards and/or human actions, each event is unique [36] (pag. 5). Regardless of their distinct nature, and of variations in individual reactions and responses, commonalities across crises exist. Sociologists of disaster point out that despite the differences among disaster agents (e.g. flood, earthquake, bomb, fire), there are actions that planning and emergency response teams must take that are independent of these differences [47].

This brings us to an interesting juxtaposition; the types and amounts of information broadcast on Twitter differ across each of the 26 specific crises we studied. This can be viewed as a display of the uniqueness of each event. In some cases the most common tweet in one crisis (e.g. eyewitness accounts in the Singapore haze crisis in 2013) was absent in another (e.g. eyewitness accounts in the Savar building collapse in 2013). Furthermore, even two events of the same type in the same country (e.g. Typhoon Yolanda in 2013 and Typhoon Pablo in 2012, both in the Philippines), may look quite different vis-à-vis the information on which people tend to focus.

Yet, when we look at the Twitter data at a meta-level, our analysis reveals commonalities among the types of information people tend to be concerned with, given the particular dimensions of the situations such as hazard category (e.g. natural, human-induced, geophysical, accidental), hazard type (e.g. earthquake, explosion), whether it is instantaneous or progressive, and whether it is focalized or diffused. For instance, caution and advice tweets from government sources are more common in progressive disasters than in instantaneous ones. The similarities do not end there. When grouping crises automatically based on similarities in the distributions of different classes of tweets, we also realize that despite the variability, human-induced crises tend to be more similar to each other than to natural hazards.

This leads us to believe that we can view Twitter as a medium through which the nuance of disaster events is highlighted or amplified; it is a tool that becomes incorporated into the social construction of the disaster event, and through which we can understand the detailed differences on a large scale when we look closely at Twitter data. At the same time, when we look at those same data at a higher level, we see commonalities and patterns.

Practitioners, including emergency managers, public information officers, and those who develop the tools used by them, should consider that the proportion of tweets that are relevant for a specific purpose will almost invariably be smaller than the proportion of the tweets that are not. For instance, if an analyst or an application focuses on content that is not present in mainstream or other Internet media sources, and wants to exclude content provided by outsiders who are not affected by the crisis, then it will have to skip through 80% of the tweets on average. The same holds for information types. If we group together the four main types we used (affected individuals, donations and volunteering, caution and advice, and infrastructure and utilities), they cover on average 47% of the tweets related to a crisis. This implies that if an application wants to focus on these information types, at least 53% of the messages will have to be discarded. These are lower bounds, as often not all of the tweets of a given type will be relevant for a particular application. *Noise* is a natural consequence of the diversity of information in this medium.

Developers should consider that emergency response includes a set of actions that have to be taken in preparation of any crisis event, plus a broad space for adaptability in response to specific events [47]. Hence, tools to process social media in disaster should consider that there are broad classes of information that are likely to be prevalent, and can be anticipated to occur. At the same time, a substantial volume of messages will depend on specificities of every event, and tools must incorporate methods to adaptively detect and process them.

CONCLUSIONS

Our systematic examination of a diverse set of crisis situations uncovered substantial variability across crises, as well as patterns and consistencies. To the best of our knowledge, this is the largest transversal study on tweets broadcast in response to various international disaster and crisis situations.

Future Work

The high-level patterns we have found lay the foundations for future studies that go into the detail of each specific crisis or each specific information category analyzed.

However, we note that we did not cover all possible crisis situations. For instance, we did not include human-induced progressive or diffused situations, which are less common than the classes we did study. The former (human-induced progressive) mostly refers to politically-driven crises, such as instability leading to demonstrations, riots, and/or civil wars. The latter (human-induced diffused) in recent years have been mostly wars affecting an entire country or region, or less-common, large-scale industrial accidents such as the oil spill in the Gulf of Mexico in 2010. Additionally, the management of a crisis is typically divided into phases: mitigation, preparedness, response and recovery [35, 47]. The work we present here is concerned mostly with the response phase and partially with the recovery phase, as these attract the bulk of social media activities [23]. Language and cultural differences could also be included as explicit crisis dimensions [20, 37], together with temporal factors. Microblogging practices are likely to evolve over the years, and our collections cover a period of just about 20 months. The study of other crisis dimensions, other types of crises and other phases, will certainly deepen our findings.

Methodologically, we asked crowdsource workers to match each tweet to one specific class. This simplifies the labeling process and makes the presentation of the results clearer. When workers associate a tweet to multiple classes, it may be possible that the distributions change. Employing professional emergency managers as annotators instead of crowdsource workers may lead to further results. Finally, assessing the quality, credibility, or veracity of the information in each tweet is relevant for most of the potential consumers of this data. However, we note that in these cases the cost of the annotation would certainly increase—or the amount of labeled data would decrease.

Data Release

The tweets used in this research, and the labels collected through the crowdsourced annotation, are available for research purposes at http://crisislex.org/

Acknowledgments

We thank Patrick Meier for his valuable advice while defining this project. We are indebted to Karl Aberer for his support. We thank the reviewers for their detailed feedback. Alexandra Olteanu was partially supported by the grant *Reconcile: Robust Online Credibility Evaluation of Web Content* from Switzerland through the Swiss Contribution to the enlarged European Union.

REFERENCES

1. World humanitarian data and trends. Tech. rep., UN OCHA, Dec. 2013.
2. Acar, A., and Muraki, Y. Twitter for crisis communication: lessons learned from Japan's tsunami disaster. *Int. J. of Web Based Communities* (2011).
3. Adams, D. S. Policies, programs, and problems of the local Red Cross disaster relief in the 1960s. Tech. rep., University of Delaware, Disaster Research Center, 1970.
4. Aramaki, E., Maskawa, S., and Morita, M. Twitter catches the flu: Detecting influenza epidemics using Twitter. In *Proc. of EMNLP* (2011).
5. Benevenuto, F., Magno, G., Rodrigues, T., and Almeida, V. Detecting spammers on Twitter. In *In Proc. of CEAS* (2010).
6. Bruns, A., Burgess, J. E., Crawford, K., and Shaw, F. #qldfloods and @qpsmedia: Crisis communication on Twitter in the 2011 South East Queensland floods. Tech. rep., ARC Centre, Queensland University of Technology, 2012.
7. Caragea, C., McNeese, N., Jaiswal, A., Traylor, G., Kim, H., Mitra, P., Wu, D., Tapia, A., Giles, L., Jansen, B. J., et al. Classifying text messages for the Haiti earthquake. In *Proc. of ISCRAM* (2011).
8. Carr, L. J. Disaster and the sequence-pattern concept of social change. *American Journal of Sociology* (1932).

9. Carvin, A. *Distant Witness*. CUNY Journalism Press, 2013.

10. Castillo, C., Mendoza, M., and Poblete, B. Information credibility on Twitter. In *Proc. of WWW* (2011).

11. Cohen, W. W. Fast effective rule induction. In *Proc. of ICML* (1995), 115–123.

12. De Choudhury, M., Diakopoulos, N., and Naaman, M. Unfolding the event landscape on Twitter: Classification and exploration of user categories. In *Proc. of CSCW* (2012).

13. Denef, S., Bayerl, P. S., and Kaptein, N. A. Social media and the police: tweeting practices of British police forces during the August 2011 riots. In *Proc. of CHI* (2013).

14. Diakopoulos, N., De Choudhury, M., and Naaman, M. Finding and assessing social media information sources in the context of journalism. In *Proc. of CHI* (2012).

15. Esser, F., and Hanitzsch, T., Eds. *The Handbook of Comparative Communication Research*. ICA Handbooks. Routledge, Apr. 2012.

16. Fischer, H. W. *Response to disaster: fact versus fiction & its perpetuation—the sociology of disaster*. University Press of America, 1998.

17. Fraustino, J. D., Liu, B., and Jin, Y. Social media use during disasters: A review of the knowledge base and gaps. Tech. rep., Science and Technology Directorate, U.S. Department of Homeland Security, 2012.

18. Gerlitz, C., and Rieder, B. Mining one percent of Twitter: collections, baselines, sampling. *M/C Journal* (2013).

19. González-Bailón, S., Wang, N., Rivero, A., Borge-Holthoefer, J., and Moreno, Y. Assessing the bias in communication networks sampled from Twitter. *Social Networks 38* (July 2014), 16–27.

20. Hong, L., Convertino, G., and Chi, E. H. Language matters in Twitter: A large scale study. In *Proc. of ICWSM* (2011).

21. Hughes, A. L. Participatory design for the social media needs of emergency public information officers. In *Proc. of ISCRAM* (2014).

22. Hughes, A. L., St. Denis, L. A., Palen, L., and Anderson, K. Online public communications by police and fire services during the 2012 hurricane Sandy. In *Proc. of CHI* (2014).

23. Imran, M., Castillo, C., Lucas, J., Patrick, M., and Rogstadius, J. Coordinating human and machine intelligence to classify microblog communications in crises. In *Proc. of ISCRAM* (2014).

24. Imran, M., Elbassuoni, S. M., Castillo, C., Diaz, F., and Meier, P. Extracting information nuggets from disaster-related messages in social media. In *Proc. of ISCRAM* (2013).

25. Joseph, K., Landwehr, P. M., and Carley, K. M. Two 1% s don't make a whole: Comparing simultaneous samples from Twitter's streaming API. In *Social Computing, Behavioral-Cultural Modeling and Prediction*. 2014.

26. Kanhabua, N., and Nejdl, W. Understanding the diversity of tweets in the time of outbreaks. In *Proc. of WOW workshop* (2013).

27. Kumar, S., Morstatter, F., Zafarani, R., and Liu, H. Whom should I follow?: Identifying relevant users during crises. In *Proc. of Hypertext* (2013).

28. Leavitt, A., and Clark, J. A. Upvoting hurricane Sandy: event-based news production processes on a social news site. In *Proc. of CHI* (2014).

29. Metaxas, P., and Mustafaraj, E. The rise and the fall of a citizen reporter. In *Proc. of WebSci* (2013).

30. Monroy-Hernández, A., boyd, d., Kiciman, E., De Choudhury, M., and Counts, S. The new war correspondents: The rise of civic media curation in urban warfare. In *Proc. of CSCW* (2013).

31. Morstatter, F., Pfeffer, J., and Liu, H. When is it biased?: assessing the representativeness of Twitter's streaming API. In *Proc. of Web Science Track at WWW* (2014).

32. Morstatter, F., Pfeffer, J., Liu, H., and Carley, K. M. Is the sample good enough? comparing data from Twitter's streaming API with Twitter's Firehose. In *Proc. of ICWSM* (2013).

33. Munro, R., and Manning, C. D. Short message communications: users, topics, and in-language processing. In *Proc. of DEV* (2012).

34. Olteanu, A., Castillo, C., Diaz, F., and Vieweg, S. CrisisLex: A lexicon for collecting and filtering microblogged communications in crises. In *Proc. of ICWSM* (2014).

35. Palen, L., and Liu, S. B. Citizen communications in crisis: anticipating a future of ICT-supported public participation. In *Proc. of CHI* (2007).

36. Perry, R. W., and Quarantelli, E. L. *What is a disaster?: New answers to old questions*. Xlibris Corporation, 2005.

37. Poblete, B., Garcia, R., Mendoza, M., and Jaimes, A. Do all birds tweet the same?: characterizing Twitter around the world. In *Proc. of CIKM* (2011).

38. Prelog, A. J. *Social Change and Disaster Annotated Bibliography*. PhD thesis, Department of Economics, Colorado State University, 2010.

39. Qu, Y., Huang, C., Zhang, P., and Zhang, J. Microblogging after a major disaster in China: a case study of the 2010 Yushu earthquake. In *Proc. of CSCW* (2011).

40. Shaw, F., Burgess, J., Crawford, K., and Bruns, A. Sharing news, making sense, saying thanks: Patterns of talk on Twitter during the Queensland floods. *Australian Journal of Communication* (2013).

41. Snow, R., O'Connor, B., Jurafsky, D., and Ng, A. Y. Cheap and fast—but is it good?: Evaluating non-expert annotations for natural language tasks. In *Proc. of EMNLP* (2008).

42. Sreenivasan, N. D., Lee, C. S., and Goh, D. H.-L. Tweet me home: exploring information use on Twitter in crisis situations. In *Online Communities and Social Computing*. 2011.

43. Starbird, K., Muzny, G., and Palen, L. Learning from the crowd: Collaborative filtering techniques for identifying on-the-ground twitterers during mass disruptions. In *Proc. of ISCRAM* (2012).

44. Starbird, K., and Palen, L. "Voluntweeters": Self-organizing by digital volunteers in times of crisis. In *Proc. of CHI* (2011).

45. Starbird, K., Palen, L., Hughes, A. L., and Vieweg, S. Chatter on the red: what hazards threat reveals about the social life of microblogged information. In *Proc. of CSCW* (2010).

46. Thomson, R., Ito, N., Suda, H., Lin, F., Liu, Y., Hayasaka, R., Isochi, R., and Wang, Z. Trusting tweets: The Fukushima disaster and information source credibility on Twitter. In *Proc. of ISCRAM* (2012).

47. Tierney, K. J. Disaster preparedness and response: Research findings and guidance from the social science literature. Tech. rep., University of Delaware, Disaster Research Center, 1993.

48. Truelove, M., Vasardani, M., and Winter, S. Towards credibility of micro-blogs: characterising witness accounts. *GeoJournal* (2014), 1–21.

49. Vieweg, S. *Situational Awareness in Mass Emergency: A Behavioral and Linguistic Analysis of Microblogged Communications*. PhD thesis, University of Colorado at Boulder, 2012.

50. Vieweg, S., Hughes, A. L., Starbird, K., and Palen, L. Microblogging during two natural hazards events: What Twitter may contribute to situational awareness. In *Proc. of CHI* (2010).

51. Wukich, C., and Mergel, I. A. Closing the Citizen-Government communication gap: Content, audience, and network analysis of government tweets. *Social Science Research Network Working Paper Series* (Aug. 2014).

APPENDIX

- Table 4 containing the list of keywords used to collect data from each crisis.
- Tables 5 and 6 depicting temporal distributions of tweets on each crisis for each type, and for each source.

Table 4. List of keywords used to collect data for each of the crises in this study.

Year	Crisis Name	Keywords	#Kw
2012	Italy earthquakes	earthquake italy; quake italy; #modena; #sanfelice; san felice; modena terremoto; modena earthquake; modena quake; #norditalia; terremoto italia; #terremoto;	11
2012	Colorado wildfires	#cofire; #boulderfire; #colorado; #wildfire; #waldocanyonfire; #waldofire; #waldocanyon; colorado springs; #highparkfire; #flagstafffire; #littlesandfire; #treasurefire; #statelinefire; #springerfire; #lastchancefire; #fourmilefire; #4milefire; #fourmilecanyonfire; #boulderfire; #bisonfire; colorado wildfire; colorado wildfires; colorado fire; colorado fires; boulder fire; boulder fires; boulder wildfires; boulder wildfires;	28
2012	Philipinnes Floods	#rescueph; #reliefph; #floodsph; #prayforthephilippine; manila flood; manila floods; philippine floods; philippine flood; #floodph; #phalert; #habagat;	11
2012	Venezuela refinery explosion	paraguana refinery; venezuela refinery; paraguaná refinery; #paraguana; #paraguaná; amuay refinery; venezuelan refinery; #amuay; paraguaná refinería; paraguana refineria; amuay refineria; amuay refinería; #falcon; #falcón; refinería venezuela; refineria venezuela; refinería paraguana;	17
2012	Costa Rica earthquake	#temblorcr; #terremotocr; #costarica; #terremoto; costa rica quake; costa rica earthquake; costa rica temblor; costa rica terremoto; #creq; costa rican quake; costa rican earthquake; #quake; #earthquake;	13
2012	Guatemala earthquake	#sismo; #guatemala; tiemblaenguate; temblorgt; terremotogt; temblor guatemala; terremoto guatemala; sismo guatemala; earthquake guatemala; quake guatemala; #sanmarcos; #terremotoguatemala; #tremorguatemala;	13
2012	Typhoon Pablo	#pabloph; #reliefph; #bopha; #typhoonpablo; #typhoonbopha; typhoon bopha; typhoon pablo; #bopha; #pablo; #typhoon; #walangpasok; #mindanao; #visayas; #hinatuan; #rescueph; #pablosafetytips; #cdo; #strongerph;	18
2013	Brazil nightclub fire	#forçasantamaria; boate kiss; #boatekiss; #santamaria; #tragédiaemsm; #tragediaemsm; #todosdesejamforçasasantamaria; #brazilfire; #brazil fire; brazil nightclub; #brasildesejaforçasasvitimasdesantamaria; #prayforsantamaria; #prayforbrazil;	13
2013	Queensland Floods	#qldflood; #bigwet; queensland flood; australia flood; #qldfloods; queensland floods; australia floods; queensland flooding; qld flood; qld floods; qld flooding; australia flooding;	12
2013	Russian Meteor	#метеорит; #meteor; #meteorite; russia meteor; russian meteor; #russianmeteor; #chelyabinsk; #челябинск;	8
2013	Boston Bombings	boston explosion; boston explosions; boston blast; boston blasts; boston tragedies; boston tragedy; prayforboston; boston attack; boston attacks; boston terrorist; boston terrorists; boston tragic; bostonmarathon; boston marathon; boston explosive; boston bomb; boston bombing; dzhokhar; tsarnaev; marathon attack; marathon explosion; marathon explosions; marathon tragedies; marathon tragedy; marathon blasts; marathon blast; marathon attacks; marathon bomb; marathon bombing; marathon explosive;	30
2013	Savar building collapse	#savar; #bangladesh; bangladesh collapse; #ranaplaza; savar bangladesh; savar collapse; rana plaza;	7
2013	West Texas Explosion	#westexplosion; west explosion; waco explosion; texas explosion; texas fertilizer; prayfortexas; prayforwest; waco tx; west tx; west texas; waco texas; #west; #waco; westexplosion; west explosion; waco explosion; tx explosion; fertilizer explosion; prayfortexas; prayforwest; westtx; wacotx; west texas; waco texas; west tx; waco tx; texas fertilizer; west fertilizer; waco fertilizer;	29
2013	Alberta Floods	alberta flood; #abflood; canada flood; alberta flooding; alberta floods; canada flooding; canada floods; #yycflood; #yycfloods; #yycflooding; calgary flood; calgary flooding; calgary floods;	13
2013	Singapore Haze	#sghaze; singapore haze; #hazyday; blamethehaze; mustbehaze; #sg #haze; singapore #hazy;	7
2013	Lac-Megantic train crash	#lacmegantic; #lacmégantic; #lacmég; #lacmeg; #tragedielacmegantic; #tragédielacmégantic; #mégantic; lac mégantic; lac megantic; quebec train explosion; quebec train derailment; quebec train crash; quebec oil train; canada train oil; canada train oil; canadian train oil;	16
2013	Spain train crash	compostela train; spain train; tren compostela; españa tren; #santiagocompostela; #accidentesantiago;	6
2013	Manila Floods	baha manila; #maringph; #rescueph; #reliefph; #floodsph; #prayforthephilippine; manila flood; manila floods; philippine floods; philippine flood; #floodph; #phalert; #safenow; #trafficph; #habagat; #maring; #maringupdates;	17
2013	Colorado Floods	#cofloodrelief; colorado floods; colorado flooding; #coloradoflood; #coflood; #opcoflood; #boulderflood; #longmont;	8
2013	Australia wildfires	#nswfires; #nswbushfire; #nswbushfires; #nswrfs; #sydneybushfire; #sydneyfire; #sydneyfires; #sydneybushfires; nsw #bushfire; #redoctober; australia #bushfire; #faulconbridge; #nswrfs; #bushfire sydney; nsw fire; #prayforaustralia; #prayfornsw; australia fire; sydney fire; nsw fires; australia fires; sydney fires; prayfornsw;	23
2013	Bohol earthquake	#phquake; #pheq; #phtrenchquake; philippines earthquake; philippines quake; ph earthquake; ph quake; #phtrenchquake; #prayforthephilippines; #rescueph; #reliefph; #tabangbohol; #tabangcebu; #bohol; #cebu; prayforvisayas; prayforbohol; #lindol;	18
2013	Glasgow helicopter crash	#prayerforglasgow; #helicopter; glasgow helicopter; #clutha; helicopter crash;	5
2013	LA Airport Shootings	lax shooting; lax shootings; lax shooter; lax suspect; #laxshooting; lax airport; #lax; airport shooting; airport shootings; #losangeles airport; lax victims;	11
2013	NYC train crash	#newyork derailment; ny derailment; nyc derailment; #metronorth derailment; #spuyten duyvil; #nyctrain; new york derailment; metro north derailment; #metronorth derailment; ny train crash; nyc train crash; newyork train crash; york train crash; #metronorth train crash; metro north crash; ny train derailed; york train derailed; nyc train derailed;	18
2013	Sardinia Floods	sardinia floods; sardinia flooding; cyclone cleopatra; #cyclonecleopatra; #sardinia; sardegna alluvione; #cleopatra alluvione; #sardegna;	8
2013	Typhoon Yolanda	#typhoonyolanda; #yolandaph; #yolanda; #haiyan; #tracingph; #floodph; #safenow; #rescueph; #reliefph; typhoon yolanda; typhoon haiyan; typhoon philippines; #typhoonhaiyan; #typhoonaid; #philippines; #typhoon; #supertyphoon; #redcrossphilippines; #yolandaactionweekend; rescue ph; typhoon ph; super typhoon;	22

Table 5. Temporal distribution of tweets across information sources (top) and types (bottom) for the progressive events we analyzed. The 3 most frequent sources, respectively, information types, per crisis are highlighted in green. The red vertical bar indicates the peak volume for all tweets related to each event. (Best seen in color.)

Name	Alberta floods'13	Australia wildfires'13	Colorado floods'13	Colorado wildfires'12	Manila floods'13	Philipinnes floods'12	Queensland floods'13	Sardinia floods'13	Singapore haze'13	Typhoon Pablo'12	Typhoon Yolanda'13
Overall											
Eyewitness											
Government											
NGOs											
Business											
Media											
Outsiders											
Affected Ind.											
Infrast. & Utilities											
Donat. & Volun.											
Caution & Advice											
Sympathy											
Other Useful Info.											

Table 6. Temporal distribution of tweets across information sources (top) and types (bottom) for the instantaneous events we analyzed. The 3 most frequent sources, respectively, information types, per crisis are highlighted in green. The red vertical bar indicates the peak volume for all tweets related to each event. (Best seen in color.)

Name	Bohol earthq.'13	Boston bombings'13	Brazil nightclub fire'13	Costa Rica earthq.'12	Glasgow helicopter crash'13	Guatemala earthq.'12	Italy earthq.'12	LA airport shootings'13	Lac-Megantic train crash'13	NYC train crash'13	Russian meteor'13	Savar building collapse'13	Spain train crash'13	Venezuela refinery explosion'12	West Texas explosion'13
Overall															
Eyewitness															
Government															
NGOs															
Business															
Media															
Outsiders															
Affected Ind.															
Infrast. & Utilities															
Donat. & Volun.															
Caution & Advice															
Sympathy															
Other Useful Info.															

Do Birds of a Feather Watch Each Other? Homophily and Social Surveillance in Location Based Social Networks

Shion Guha
Dept. of Information Science
Cornell University
Ithaca, NY 14853
sg648@cornell.edu

Stephen B Wicker
School of Electrical & Computer Engineering
Cornell University
Ithaca, NY 14853
sbw11@cornell.edu

ABSTRACT
Location sharing applications (LSA) have proliferated in recent years. Current research principally focuses on egocentric privacy issues and design but has historically not explored the impact of surveillance on location sharing behavior. In this paper, we examine homophily in friendship and surveillance networks for 65 foursquare users. Our results indicate that location surveillance networks are strongly homophilous along the lines of race and gender while friendship networks are weakly homophilous on income. Qualitatively, an analysis of comments and interviews provides support for a discourse around location surveillance, which is mainly social, collaborative, positive and participatory. We relate these findings with prior literature on surveillance, self-presentation and homophily and situate this study in existing HCI/CSCW scholarship.

Author Keywords
homophily;privacy;visibility;surveillance;vision;foursquare

ACM Classification Keywords
H.5.m.Information interfaces and Presentation (e.g., HCI): Miscellaneous.

INTRODUCTION AND MOTIVATION
Though LSAs are far from novel, in the past 10 years, the growing ubiquity of mobile phones, the proliferation of "smart" phones and the increasingly cheaper access to Wi-Fi and GPS signals have resulted in the sharp rise [47] in their development and use, particularly in mobile devices.

We define LSA's with standard social networking features such as adding friends, commenting, liking and tagging as location based social networks (LBSNs) e.g. foursquare or Jiepang. We also distinguish between these and other popular social networking sites (SNS) with geocoding features (e.g. Facebook, Twitter) by postulating that actions on LBSNs always revolve around a location or venue whereas on other SNS, locations are not the focal point. In this paper, we will concentrate on LBSNs with check-in type location sharing features because we believe that the ability to (not) disclose location is paramount when examining privacy, impressions or surveillance concerns.

There is a small, but growing body of HCI research that has looked at the patterns and practices of modern LBSN users. Lindqvist et al. [25] reports that people have multiple reasons for using foursquare. Some of these are social location sharing, personal location tracking, social gaming and location discovery. Cramer et al. [11] find emergent performative aspects around locations, linked to audience management arising from sharing location on foursquare. Guha and Birnholtz [17] discovered that users have different location sharing strategies involving deception, obfuscation etc. which, they argue is often used to manage offline social goals and enhance social signals. Patil et al. [35] found that privacy concerns have some influence on the adoption and continued usage of LBSNs. These privacy considerations may have undesired social consequences; may cause feelings of regret and grief but are also carefully balanced against economic and personal attractions i.e. a check-in might result in a discounted meal but could also have an unanticipated social cost.

However, impression management and privacy are only two of many potential perspectives to understand location disclosures. They take the point of view of the person *disclosing* the location but do not adequately inform us about the person *viewing* the location disclosures, which Trottier [44] recently theorized, can also be construed as social surveillance by network ties.

A traditional understanding of surveillance is that of a vertical, rigid structure [27] rooted in asymmetry and power politics. A contrarian position [2] maintains that in social networks, lateral surveillance – a flat, horizontal and amorphous system with opportunities for all social network ties to surveil each other is perhaps more suited for empirical explanation. In addition, two recent theoretical articles advocate for the participatory and empowering [1] and/or social and positive [28] nature of lateral surveillance.

CSCW 2015, March 14–18, 2015, Vancouver, BC, Canada.

ACM 978-1-4503-2922-4/15/03...$15.00.
http://dx.doi.org/10.1145/2675133.2675179

Homophily, or the propensity of similar users to connect together, [38] has been proposed as a theoretical framework to explain how people interact with their social network ties. Recently, homophily has also been hypothesized to contribute to self-presentation [13] on location as a natural product of [28] SNS surveillance. We asked ourselves: is this divergent from homophily friendship networks? Is there any sort of discourse around location surveillance? Towards this effort, we conceptualized a surveillance network as a weighted friendship network where edge weights represent net surveillance activity between any two pairs of connected nodes. In the paper that follows, we present a mixed methods study of 65 foursquare users, from which there are several novel findings.

First, we show that **Gender** and **Race** are significant predictors (with strong effect sizes) of homophily in surveillance networks while **Income** seems to be a significant predictor of homophily (with a weak effect size) in friendship networks. We argue that this may be driven by the engenderment and/or the racial construction of location and may be a way to carefully cultivate impressions by group affiliation. Second, we discuss participatory, social and collaborative interactions around location surveillance and debate the value of positive surveillance. Third, we pose feedback and social translucency as privacy-aware design features in supporting social surveillance in LBSNs but also advocate for recent calls against mandatory design implications in HCI based on participant design reflections.

LITERATURE REVIEW

The research reported in this paper lies at the intersection of three areas of prior work. First, we will describe existing human-centered research on LSAs focusing on behavioral patterns and practices. Second, we will illustrate current research on privacy-aware design in LSAs. Finally, we will explore relevant literature on social networks concentrating on homophily, privacy and surveillance theory.

Location Sharing: Behavioral Patterns and Practices

Systems that allow users to take advantage of location sharing or to be aware of others' location are not very new. Early systems include the Active Badge [46] in workplace settings and the Whereabouts clock [9] for family location awareness. Different groups of researchers have tried to understand the motivations and practices of LSA users. In an influential work, Consolvo et al. [10] found that users were mainly considerate of their specific audience when location was requested from them. They would acquiesce to sharing location if they felt it would be useful for that particular requester and adjust the granularity of their disclosed location accordingly. They did not find any evidence of location obfuscation strategies by their participants. Humphreys [19,20,21] conducted a study of Dodgeball and concluded that its primary use was spontaneous coordination and supporting serendipitous urban congregation. She also noted that most of her participants were not bothered by privacy concerns - perhaps because they were early adopters and heavy users.

Barkhuus et al. [4] conducted a field trial of Connecto and found that there was a gradual shift from location awareness to social interaction around collaboratively curated sets of "tagged" locations. Smith et al. [39] conducted a pilot study (n=8) of Reno and discovered that although people favored automatic location disclosure significantly more than manual location sharing there could be unexpected social costs. Location disclosure provides a context aware approach to negotiating social relations. Tang et al. [41] and found that participants (n=10) had a range of strategies for disclosing location – mainly driven by privacy and attention seeking. This latter finding gives us an intuition into location sharing - people *want to be seen* by their social networks. In a detailed questionnaire and diary study (n=10), Reilly et al. [37] studied location information need from the perspective of the viewer. They found that there is usually a negotiation of interests around location - the sharer balances her privacy concerns (and other social interests) against the receiver's need to know location and other associated information. Meanwhile, Page et al. [34] studied deception and lying in LSAs through interviews (n=20) and a large survey (n=1532) and found that deception is a relatively common tactic to negotiate online interpersonal and social boundaries but that, this may backfire and have unexpected offline social consequences.

Recently, Lindqvist et al. [25] conducted an exploratory study on foursquare and found that people use foursquare with multiple interleaving motives; foursquare could be used as a way for social location sharing and discovery, movement gamification, spontaneous coordination, as a personal diary or to take advantage of special offers and discounts. Cramer et al. [11] also studied foursquare and uncovered a shift from just location sharing to a more performative aspect around location disclosure. Guha and Birnholtz [17] reported on the results of a detailed interview study (n=30) of foursquare users. They found that users had evolved detailed strategies for managing and forming impressions to multiple audiences with multiple objectives based on the potential visibility of their check-ins. Summarizing this set of literature, it is clear that sharing location is not just a utilitarian objective but also serves as a nuanced way of managing impressions and furthering social goals. However, it is still an open question how people view and discuss the visibility of others' location disclosures.

Location Sharing: Privacy-Aware Design

Designing for privacy concerns has been a common topic in LSA research. Iachello and Hong [23] published a comprehensive survey of three decades of privacy research in HCI. In recommending future directions, they called for an expansion of research into understanding surveillance systems from a human-centered perspective. One specific example they used was the increasingly common usage of locator badges on nurses in hospitals. Iachello et al. [22] implemented Boise and suggested, among others, denial, deception and evasion as LSA design features to support privacy management and "beat" location surveillance. One system actually built with these design principles is Locaccino, which was deployed by Toch et al. [43] (n_1=28, n_2=373); they found that people shared locations frequented by larger numbers of other users; those who visited diverse locations received more location requests and over time, develop sophisticated strategies for location disclosure.

Brush et al. [8] studied location obfuscation behavior of 12 households (n=32) using always-on GPS devices. Participants mainly wanted to obfuscate places that they frequented (home, work etc.) even from their friends. Benisch et al. [6] conducted a 3-week user study (n=27) and found that more complex privacy settings were the most useful and led to more sharing but also increased the user's burden of privacy management. In a similar vein, Tang et al. [42] studied the effect of offering more disclosure choices in LSAs (n=30). They found surprisingly, that users did not mind the additional burden of adding location granularity features even when presented with several different types of privacy filters. This may lead to more sharing and less complicated privacy management rules. Wilson et al. [49] explored the impact of existing privacy profiles on location sharing with Locaccino (n=37) and concluded that (a) "the complexity and diversity of people's privacy preferences creates a major tension between privacy and usability" and (b) privacy profiles can have a substantial impact on a user's behavior. Wiese et al. [48] presented results (n=42), which indicated that stronger ties, communication frequency and commonality in current locations influence the willingness of location disclosures.

Patil et al. [35] conducted a survey (n=362) to understand privacy attitudes in LBSNs. They realized that privacy concerns in LBSNs are directly tied to future "undesired social consequences." In another study, Patil et al. [36] (n=35) advocated feedback improvement for managing location disclosures. Tsai et al. [45] used Locyotion, (n=56) to understand the impact of location surveillance feedback on future location disclosures. Their main finding was that people want to know who viewed them (but not necessarily the reverse) and they were willing to sacrifice other system features to have this functionality. Boesen et al. [7] conducted an ethnographic study on the impact of location surveillance on strong ties, specifically within households (n=14). They observed that while surveillance can support maintenance of strong tie relationships, it might also have the detrimental effect of undermining existing trust networks. Summarizing this section, we can infer that various approaches (feedback, obfuscation, transparency etc.) exist to manage privacy and surveillance concerns. Location disclosures are affected by tie strength and the nature of relationship between users. What is unknown is if these and other underlying social network factors also influence location surveillance.

Social Networks: Surveillance, Homophily and Ties

Barkhuus [5] called for reconsidering privacy as *contextual integrity*" – a term coined by Nissenbaum [31] who hypothesized that there are norms of appropriateness and norms of information flow in social networks. Privacy is the optimization of negotiating these norms. Barkhuus specifically makes a case for LSAs and writes "*It is the dual pleasure of both being able to expose ones' self and being able to 'snoop' on others' private lives that is at play here.*" She advocates against mandatory design implications, as they may not "*provide more than coarse generalizations*" for phenomena already noted in theory.

The traditional construct [27] of surveillance is hierarchical, vertical and top down with distinct classes of surveillers and the surveilled. Asymmetry and power politics are two salient characteristics of this structure. However, for social media, Andrejevic [2] and Trottier [44] have defined "*lateral surveillance*" and "*interpersonal social media surveillance*"; these are horizontal, peer-to-peer surveillance systems where everyone is equally capable of surveillance. However, they still retain the traditional connotation of negativity associated with surveillance. Albrechtslund [1] framed SNS as "*participatory surveillance*" systems. He opines that surveillance needn't always be punitive or asymmetrical but rather, can act as an empowering catalyst for social sharing. This rests on the fundamental assumption that human beings want to be seen by others and also want to see what others are "up to". Recently, Marwick [28] has also suggested the notion of "*social surveillance*" which is a similar construct but also includes a sense of collaboration, sociability, positivity and interaction around visible personal information.

Homophily and peer influence are accepted [3,24,30,38] as the main reasons behind tie formation and management. De Souza e Silva & Frith [13] propose the "presentation of location"; encapsulating how people manage impressions through location disclosure. They postulate that this might encourage homophily, bonding and trust among people. We also note that people frequently use different SNS platforms with different audiences. Thus, tie management can suffer from context collapse. For instance, partially overlapped but differing audiences on Facebook and foursquare can complicate impression management strategies. Lingel et al. discuss [26] visibility of such conflicts along with code switching strategies of users among different networks.

Summarizing this discussion, we find that there has been a shift in recent frameworks of SNS surveillance. Homophily has been proposed as one contributor towards spatial impression management. What is not clear yet, is its role on location surveillance. Moreover, we do not know yet if there are negotiations, norms and interactions around visible acts of location surveillance. We therefore ask:

RQ1: Do LBSN users view others similar to them? Is this different from homophily in their friendship networks?

RQ2: Do LBSN users interact with each other around public displays of location surveillance?

METHODS

Research Context and Terminology

We chose foursquare, a manual LBSN as our sandbox for interrogating these research questions. Our primary motivation for this choice is that foursquare is the largest and most popular LBSN [14] (as of May 2014) with over 50 million unique users and 6 billion check-ins. Moreover, the first author is a frequent user of foursquare and is deeply embedded within the foursquare user community. We deemed this an advantage for participant recruitment. A third reason for choosing foursquare is that, unlike Facebook or Twitter which also have location tracking features, foursquare is chiefly based around specific venues without much else interactivity. Finally, there are no standard privacy management features, which are usually available on other platforms such as access control lists or location granularity settings. This is ideal for studying surveillance because the primary user interaction on foursquare is to simply make the decision to (not) check-in. A detailed description [15] of foursquare features mentioned in Table 1 can be found freely online.

Our intended analytic approach was to test for homophily and compare between friendship and surveillance networks. To do this, we needed a fully connected network. In the context of our research study, this is defined as a social network where nodes represent people and ties represent their connections (via foursquare friendships). Fully connected refers to the fact that all the nodes in the network are connected to at least one other node and that, there exists at least one path from one node to every other node. Our choice of participant recruitment reflects this since we needed participants who were connected to each other to test for homophily and non-connected participants would not contribute to the homophily testing process. We followed the comparative approach described by Yuan and Gay [50] to test for homophily between two networks.

For the purpose of this work, we define two networks – a friendship network and a surveillance network. The friendship network is where the edges between the nodes are weighted by the mean of the self-reported tie strength rating. The surveillance network is where the edges between the nodes are weighted by the mean of the surveillance activity between them. The calculations of the weighting variables are defined in the "Variables and Measurements" section.

Data Collection

Data was collected along multiple dimensions. First, users were asked to complete an online consent form that included a series of basic demographic questions. Next, they had to explicitly grant the research team access to their foursquare data using a custom-built web application that communicated with the foursquare API. Unlike the APIs of many other platforms, developers need explicit permission from foursquare users to get access to their complete usage data. Users also had to download and install a simple custom-built mobile phone application (integrated with our custom foursquare data gathering application), which detected when users viewed their friends' check-ins through touch events and sent this information to our servers periodically. This was deployed because the foursquare API does not provide a summary of views for each check-in and was built for Android and iOS users. Finally, we also conducted follow-up semi-structured interviews and debriefing sessions with all our users both, in person as well as via Skype. Here, we also asked the users to rate the strength of their friendship with foursquare friends (those whose data we collected) on a scale of 1-10.

Participant Recruitment

We utilized convenience and snowball sampling using social media (such as Facebook and twitter) and personal contacts to collect data about 65 participants (34 male, 31 female). We collected their entire foursquare usage history as well as a summary of views on their friends' check-ins from May 2013 - January 2014. (9 months) Table 1 describes the overall characteristics of our participants. Our participants represent fifteen different countries including, but not limited to United States, Canada, India, Indonesia, Bangladesh, United Kingdom, Finland, Brazil and South Africa in decreasing frequency. Our participants included frequent as well as sparse users of foursquare indicated by the number of average daily check-ins.

Variables and Measurements

One of our primary challenges was to quantify surveillance activity. In the foursquare mobile application, users can visit their friends' check-ins by navigating to it within the application. This generates a touch event within the application. We use each such touch event as a proxy for a view on a check-in. For each pair of participants, μ_1 and μ_2 (when μ_1 is the focus) we calculate the total number of times μ_1 views any of μ_2's check-ins. We divide this by the total number of unique μ_2's check-ins. This gives us an overall sense of how often μ_1 looks at μ_2's location disclosures. Let us call this τ_{12}. Symmetrically, we can also derive τ_{21}. The arithmetic mean of τ_{12} and τ_{21} is the weight for the tie between μ_1 and μ_2 and gives us a sense of net surveillance activity between these two nodes.

For each pair of participants in the friendship network, μ_1 and μ_2, we calculated the arithmetic mean of their self-reported tie strengths for each other. This is the weight for the edge between μ_1 and μ_2 and represents an overall sense of the average tie strength between any two nodes. The Pearson correlation metric of tie strength between two pairs of nodes is 0.87 indicating a high level of agreement and the mean was 7.83 hinting towards perceived strong ties.

Variables	Minimum	Maximum	Mean	Std. Dev.
Check-in views	153	1012	443.8	194.13
Total check-ins	137	19435	1556.4	2782.18
Friends	1	999	89.44	193.034
Mayorships	1	189	17.02	43.734
Badges	24	225	34.1	35.96
Tips	1	133	16.15	32.22
Photos	3	761	31.15	110.21
Age	20	61	33	3.3
Income	14400	156000	67000	19342.5

Table 1: Descriptive statistics summarizing participant foursquare usage history and demographics

We selected 5 variables to test for homophily. Our primary motivation for choosing these particular categories comes from prior literature [24,30,38] on network homophily. Age and Income categories were divided into approximately equal sized buckets. We adapted Race and Occupation categories from the US Census classification. Table 2 provides a description of the different levels and categories.

Variables	Category Labels and Descriptions				
Age	18-25	26-34	35-44	45-54	55-64
Gender	Male		Female		
Race	White	African or Black	Asian (incl. Indian subcont.)	Hispanic or Latino	Mixed
Income	0-29999	30000-59999	60000-99999	100000-129999	130000+
Occupation	Unemployed	Student	White Collar	Blue Collar	Self Employed

Table 2: Description of Homophily Variables

Analysis and Results

Homophily Analysis

First, we calculated homophily measures for our network for all variables using the weighted ANOVA density variable homophily model. This is a standard model used in empirical social network analysis and was defined by Hanneman and Riddle in 2005 [18]. This model evaluates the likelihood that the weighted density of ties within each group differs significantly from ties that are not within groups. We performed this analysis by writing a customized script in R and making judicious use of the tnet package [32]. Table 3 contains the results of our analysis.

	Friendship Network		Surveillance Network	
Variables	Std.β	Effect Size (ω^2)	Std. β	Effect Size (ω^2)
Gender	0.29	0.12	0.41**	0.53
Age	0.04	0.03	0.01	0.02
Race	0.24	0.2	0.44**	0.64
Income	0.41*	0.24	0.11	0.09
Occupation	0.02	0.01	0.03	0.01
Adjusted r^2	0.43		0.56	
* p < 0.05 ** p < 0.01				

Table 3: Results of Homophily Analysis

Our results suggest that Gender and Race are significant predictors of homophily in the surveillance network. In the case of gender (β=*0.41, p<0.01*) we also noted a large effect size (ω^2=0.53). This suggests that men and women look significantly more at check-ins by their own gender. Similarly, race (β=*0.44, p<0.01*) exhibits an even larger effect size (ω^2=0.64) suggesting that location surveillance is divided strongly along racial lines.

In these types of network based ANOVA models, there is no standard agreement on post-hoc tests as the covariance matrices are assumed to be correlated with each other and the variables non-independent. In spite of this, we conducted a post hoc Tukey HSD on Race because of its conservativeness and found significant differences between [White|AfricanorBlack](Tukey$_{HSD}$=*4.86,p<0.01*),[White|Asian](Tukey$_{HSD}$=*5.13,p<0.01*)and[Asian|Hispanic](Tukey$_{HSD}$=*5.02, p<0.01*). We urge the readers to take these particular findings with a pinch of salt because of the lack of statistical unanimity. However, this could imply a further degree of difference among these racial constructs.

In the friendship network, Income (β=*0.38, p<0.05*) is the only significant predictor of homophily. However, it only demonstrated a modest effect size (ω^2=0.23) implying that while it is significant, the strength of its importance is not very high as it pertains to homophily in this case. We hypothesize that this effect is possibly because friends of the same income level initially started using foursquare together and as time progressed, they started adding other friends from other groups and "diluted" this affinity.

The main takeaway from this analysis is that, there is a significant difference between the friendship and surveillance network in terms of homophily. This highlights how latent networks reveal hidden trends about social interactions that could otherwise not be easily measurable.

Analysis of Comments and Interviews

There were a total of 4278 comments on 2856 unique check-ins. About 73.8% of these comments were made by users belonging to a similar category as that of the original user. We asked our participants questions focused on privacy concerns, surveillance, commenting patterns and location disclosure strategies. We also showed specific examples of their comments and asked them to reflect on the reasons behind their comment. The average interview length was 37 minutes and was transcribed manually by the first author. We utilized grounded theory [16] to analyze comments and interview transcripts. We iterated through the data seeking frequently occurring themes and concepts, gradually generalizing trends after discussions. We report three main themes here. All participant names are changed but reflect their ethnicity, gender and national origin.

Location Surveillance: Motivations and Strategies

Participants frequently mention that their foursquare network is different from other SNS network. This has a lot to do with perceived surveillance. For instance, Jack mentions his general "friending" strategy for foursquare:

> *"I don't accept random friend requests on foursquare like I do on Facebook. My foursquare friends ... I know all of them in real life pretty well ... I don't want random stalking from people I don't know but people, I know, that's fine."*

However, this does not mean that there are no concerns at all about privacy and surveillance but rather, they might be substantially nuanced, contextual and spatio-culturally dependent. Hao is conscious about possible conflict with his family in China:

> *"I don't want my mother or father seeing me late night checkins to a bar. They know I drink but they don't see that I also study a lot. That's not visible to them but most places* [he visits] *are fine. "*

Perceived visibility is one significant factor affecting location surveillance concerns. Frequently, participants would comment on their friends' check-ins to make this explicit. For instance, John commented:

> *"Yo ! I just saw you check-in to Teagle* [a gym] *Wassup?"*

We followed up with John who remarked that he had never seen his friend at that venue before and therefore was both surprised and curious to know he was there.

We also specifically asked participants what would motivate them to look at and/or comment on their friends' check-ins. One frequent reason was that they were curious about check-ins by friends to unexpected locations or times. For example, Megan says:

> *"Normally, I glance at all my friend's check-ins when I go to check-in myself but if I see them at some cool new venue or somewhere I wouldn't expect them to be or go to then I'll go to that check-in and at many times I'll either like it or write a comment on it as well."*

She comments on a friends' ongoing date to an expensive restaurant – something unexpected, which we learnt when we followed this comment up while interviewing her.

> *"Hows the boy? John Thomas* [the venue] *!! Good call !"*

> *"Ping me if you want a rescue call - hope he's not on foursquare to see this ! hahaha"*

Another reason is that most people were curious to see where friends with similar interests check-in. This might give them ideas for future activities other friends. For instance, George had the following to say about his friend:

> *"My friend* [name removed] *and I lift weights together and do other outdoorsy things together. I am always curious to see, especially if she is visiting someplace else if she is checking in to a new trail or outdoors store or meeting up with other friends to do fitness things. It gives me a good idea what I can expect to do if I visit this place or if I can do something similar."*

We also found evidence that participants had evolved different strategies to deal with perceived location surveillance. These were, at many times, conflated with impression management. The ability to not check-in becomes very important in these cases. Tim remarks:

> *"Sometimes, if I don't want people to know I am somewhere, I just won't check-in. ... I feel like even if it's my best friend, he doesn't need to know where I am and what I am doing at every point of time... I like my privacy sometime even though I am pretty active on foursquare and check-in a lot during the day. "*

Some participants mentioned deceptive or obfuscating strategies in "gaming" location surveillance, especially to ward off spontaneous social coordination. Sarah says:

> *"I'll check-in to a place nearby or something completely different to where I am right now sometimes if I see that a friend is nearby. I like to be alone sometimes but still want to track my location generally. I have done with this with really good friends too."*

Location Surveillance: Interaction and Collaboration

Another persistent theme from our data is how two or more foursquare friends will frequently comment, collaborate and coordinate about surveilling a *third* friend and even have conversations with the latter about their effort. For instance, Frank and Tim talk about observing the a friend.

Frank: "John went to more bars than you last night! :P"

Tim: *"Yep ! 6 bars?"*

Frank: *"Mans having fun in NYC !"*

Tim: *"I checked out the places ... pretty expensive - I can't afford that without help. :D :D"*

Frank: *"Rich gf* [girlfriend]. *:P"*

This is a very interesting example because of two reasons. First, both Frank and Tim are friends with their common friend on foursquare. One peculiar design mechanic of foursquare is that all friends can see all check-ins at all times i.e. there are no access control lists or similar types of privacy-preserving features. Therefore, potentially, their common friend can see and react to this conversation. Second, this conversation is on Tim's check-in at a local bar and while initially being sparked by the type of venue that Tim checked in to has actually little to do with it.

Playful interaction could also be mixed with more explicit and implicit announcements of surveillance and this interaction could take place across a series of check-ins. Take for instance, a set of three comments on three different and successive check-ins of a friend by Jane. The first is at an ice cream parlor; the second in a park and the third at an outdoor entertainment venue, which includes a mini golf course.

"Ice cream ! I want some right now !"

"I hate that I am working now and seeing everyone having fun. [online on foursquare]"

"BTW, I am so totally stalking you right now. :P :P "

It is evident from these comments that Jane is engaging in a sustained communication about her surveillance (and associated offline social objectives) with her friend across distinct check-ins. This one-way interactivity is often extended to multi-party conversations. In one case, Tony and Jill had interacted on a check-in to a tattoo studio.

Tony: "*heh. when this popped up i couldn't believe it ... looks like someone's getting inked !"*

Jill: "*And now you have witnesses to back this up !"*

Tony: "*Yeah ! give us monies or we will tell your boss !"*

It is clear that Tony and Jill have both observed their friends' check-in to a tattoo studio around the same time and signaled their inspection of this check-in to him. Furthermore, the tone of their banter is lighthearted and centers on making light hearted fun of their friend.

We also observed instances of similar behavior where the participants would tag the object of their conversation. There is a feature where multiple friends can be tagged in the comments section of a check-in. These friends would then get a notification regarding this tag and can then ostensibly visit that check-in. Sometimes, these friends would respond to comments and create an interactive atmosphere of lighthearted repartees. In one case, Stephanie tagged Olivia on Robert's check-in and bantered:

Stephanie: *"Running downtown are we?"*

Robert: *"grocery run + supplies!"*

Stephanie: *"you should have gone with Olivia [tagged] ... think she spends 5 hours in Wegmans* [a local grocery store]"

Robert: *"I don't want to be late like her all the time"*

Olivia: *"Who said I am late? "*

Olivia: *"PS: Stop stalking me all the time you guys! :P"*

Stephanie: *"Can't help it. You are always late!"*

Robert: *"You said it sister!"*

Olivia: *"I am not always late! Don't trust foursquare. :P"*

Stephanie: *"Yeah right ! Don't you always checkin the moment you enter a place? :P"*

Clearly, two of the three friends have been watching her activities on foursquare as well as how and when she checks in when entering a new place. This provides fodder for a fascinating conversation on her activities and even provides an opportunity for the object of surveillance to chime in and interact with her observers.

Location Surveillance: Design Reflections

We also asked participants questions about their experience with the current foursquare platform and feedback for improving their own experience. There were two general trends from this discussion. First, some participants expressed interest in some privacy management features. Anna expresses some frustration and suggests:

"I feel like foursquare is sometimes too minimalistic. Its true that random people can't stalk you like they can on facebook but sometimes you want to hide stuff from your friends as well and I think that having the ability to hide certain check-ins from some people might be cool."

Meanwhile, some participants like Tina think that knowing who watched whom or an implementation of a feedback system could be very useful for foursquare users.

"You know like Orkut had this thing where you could see which people were visiting your profile. I think that if something like that can be built here then we can have a better idea of who was visiting our profile or check-ins. This can be something very useful to foursquare users like me to know who is visiting your profile. "

However, there were a substantial number of participants who thought that the current system worked well enough for their purposes. Specifically, Mary remarked:

"I think that I am fine with how foursquare is currently. I like being able to see what my friends are upto and also I filter who I add on foursquare ... its always good friends ... I have like 800 Facebook friends but 25-ish friends on foursquare ... I don't mind them knowing where I am. If its that big a deal, I just won't checkin somewhere ... there is no point in adding too many things. I don't like Facebook for this reason."

We see that some participants want some changes to design to improve their privacy management experience whereas others seemed quite content with the present systems.

DISCUSSION

We proposed two research questions in this paper. **RQ1** focused on whether LBSN users would look at the location disclosures of others similar to them and if this would be different than the similarities in their friendship ties. **RQ2** concentrated on whether there were user interactions around overt declarations of location surveillance. The results of our study provide answers supporting both **RQ1** and **RQ2** and we discuss these in the following sections.

Homophily and Location Surveillance

It is well accepted that homophily and social influence [3,24,30,38] guide formation and maintenance of social ties. Drawing a causal arrow between these factors is intractable for most empirical studies. This is further exacerbated when dealing with tacit networks. Shalizi & Thomas [38] recommends a strategy of holistic storytelling when reporting results. In this vein, our homophily analysis constitutes one piece of the overall narrative.

Consider **RQ1**. Do people view others similar to them? Or is it their similarity that drives their surveillance? Our quantitative analysis informs us that homophily differs between friendship (income) and surveillance networks (race, gender). The dimensions themselves are quite common and have been used in a wide range [30,38] of prior work. What is curious is that they differ along two different networks constituting the same people. Here, we can make two broad inferences. First, homophily type affects surveillance. There is scholarship on the gendered nature of locations [33] as well as differential surveillance [29] on genders. We argue that perhaps it is the dissimilar participation of gender in different locations that also drives homophilic tendencies. Similarly, prior literature also points towards racially constructed spatial participation [27] as well as the unequal nature of surveillance [47] among and on races. Second, recent work [11,13,17] has alluded to the construction of self-presentation using specific acts of location disclosures. The discloser may use this to cultivate favorable impressions assuming homophilic surveillance and unintentionally resulting in a self-fulfilling prophecy.

Public Displays of Location Surveillance

Andrejevic [2] argued that asymmetry and differential power is the one of the key characteristics of surveillance. In this light, those who are being watched may not know if, when and how they are being watched. However, Albrechtshlund [1] maintains that SNS, which facilitate and enhance interactions between different people, cannot be framed from such a vertical perspective. Rather, surveillance, in this case, can be a "*mutual, empowering and subjectivity building practice*." This, supported by our qualitative results is yet another piece of the narrative.

Let us appraise **RQ2**. Consider Tony and Jill, who commented on Mike's check-in. It is evident that they noticed Mike's check in to a tattoo studio. Their playful banter reveals their tacit surveillance of Mike's activities and even playfully "threatens" to report this to his boss who may or may not be supportive of an employee getting tattoos as it is considered a social taboo in some societies. Mike, on the other hand, had no problem in revealing his location to his foursquare friends and in fact, this free revelation (that may potentially reveal an action against workplace policies) is in itself quite empowering.

Guha and Birnholtz [13] found that foursquare users are careful about accepting foursquare friends as opposed to accepting friends on other SNS such as Facebook; foursquare friends tend to be relatively stronger ties. Thus, disclosing a particular location that may imply a certain set of behaviors (in Mike's case, getting a tattoo) to stronger ties is evidence of trust, empowerment and legitimization of offline actions.

However, there may be another interpretation from these results. During interviews, participants reported that if concerned about privacy or self-presentation, they would usually make the decision to not check-in to their current location. We did not find overtly negative reactions to surveillance within comments. This may imply that self-censorship and prudent non-use is used to manage and hide potentially negative or undesired consequences from presentation of location.

Collaborative social surveillance also resonated strongly within our results. Marwick [28] defines social surveillance as "*the ongoing eavesdropping, investigation, gossip and inquiry that constitutes information gathering by people about their peers, made salient by the social digitization normalized by social media.*" Our results reinforce this definition. Take for instance, the interaction between Stephanie, Olivia and Robert around disclosing location about a grocery store, which has all the aforementioned elements of social surveillance.

However, Marwick also concludes that while the structure of social surveillance may be different from traditional surveillance and may have a few positive effects, the end result is the same - there are constantly shifting elements of power, hierarchy and reciprocity in both frameworks. We believe that her examination of twitter and Facebook - while applicable to them may not be perfectly amenable to LBSNs like foursquare. Both twitter and Facebook have audience management features embedded in their design while foursquare is minimalistic; everything is visible and there are no access control features. Guha and Birnholtz [17] found that the primary option for foursquare users to manage impressions and/or audiences is to *not* disclose their location or, for a minority, to opt for deceptive location disclosures. Thus, if foursquare activity must mean making everything visible to everyone, then everything has the potential to be seen and interacted with. As our results indicate, this makes social surveillance a symmetric, collaborative and positive process, especially for strong ties and along the homophilic tendencies of gender and race that historically have a natural tendency to cluster around specific locations.

Humphreys [19,20] found that Dodgeball users (considered the precursor of foursquare) to be generally unconcerned about privacy. She found two reasons - (a) they felt that they had no control over their personal information and to whom it was sent and (b) they believed that they were experienced Internet users with a keen sense for online friendships. Let us examine our results keeping these in mind. First, social surveillance theory [28] predicts that people want to see, be seen, interact and be interacted with online. Thus, while these location disclosures are voluntary, they are also somewhat influenced by the positivity and the participatory aspect of surveillance that we have seen in our analysis. Second, homophily theory [30] predicts that a common attribute, group membership or affiliation influences people to form ties with one another. Thus, people not only want to see and be seen online, they want to see and be seen by those with whom they closely identify and align with. This, in essence, is one of our main takeaways from this work.

Implications for Design (Or Not?)

Our results also raised two issues about privacy-aware design in LBSNs. On one hand, some of our participants wished for more support on foursquare to manage their privacy and social surveillance goals. Anna is an exemplar of a vocal minority who wishes that foursquare changes its minimalistic ways and begins to listen to the concerns of those who would want to selectively disclose locations and manage privacy concerns. Tina specifically evokes the feedback and transparency features in Orkut and hopes that similar mechanisms are also implemented on foursquare.

Prior work has shown that feedback and translucence are important design considerations in LSA's. Stuart et al. [40] distinguished between identity, content and interaction transparency. Interestingly, foursquare is unusually transparent in terms of content and interaction transparency but not for identity transparency. Incorporating user customizable functions of translucency might support the overall empowerment and positivity that social surveillance brings to LBSNs. Tsai et al. [45] and Patil et al. [36] found that feedback is extremely important in privacy management in LSAs. Currently, foursquare offers no feedback mechanisms (other than standard social networking features such as a like button and a comment space). Feedback can take many forms - understanding who or what groups are interacting with a user might go a long way towards supporting behavior that is already prevalent on foursquare while preserving privacy concerns. For instance, summarized feedback about location disclosure and surveillance might buttress existing online interaction, facilitate offline serendipitous coordination or if necessary, allow users to surveil and avoid friends from different groups at different times - thus preserving privacy. Such features can support increased or decreased sociability depending upon the user's needs while being unobtrusive and out of the way of regular usage.

Another group of our participants, illustrated by Mary's comment, wants to preserve the current status quo on foursquare. According to this faction, they are generally happy with their foursquare experience. They cite their "friending" strategies as well as the choice to not check-in to be adequate. Their main concern is that they don't want foursquare to become complicated like other oft used SNS.

Barkhuus [5] and Dourish [12] called for understanding the limits of design interventions on human-centered systems. While Dourish advocated for the removal or elimination of mandatory design implications in the reports of every HCI research study, Barkhuus discouraged the necessity of designing technological solutions, specifically mentioning LSAs. Perhaps, in our study, this makes a case for specific design interventions superfluous? Shall we fix something that is not yet broken? Or shall we preemptively design for a particular future that may not come to pass? This could be a useful theoretical consideration for future designers of privacy-aware features in LBSNs.

LIMITATIONS AND FUTURE WORK

We used a mixture of convenience and snowball sampling for participant recruitment. This was a hard constraint since people had to be willing to install our custom mobile application and grant us full access to their usage data. A sample size of 65 satisfies our statistical assumptions and is historically comparable to similar studies. We plan to scale up in a future project and tease out finer patterns and practices. In particular, we would like to delve into location deception and obfuscation strategies as well as peer influence. Another limitation was that our custom application was developed for Android and iOS platforms. We could not build for Windows platforms for a lack of resources and expertise. However, we also note that during data collection, Windows phone participants made up less than 2% of our initial survey respondents. Windows phone installations for foursquare lag behind the other platforms.

CONCLUSION

In this paper, we have explored how people view their friends' location disclosures in a LBSN through the lens of homophily through an empirical study of 65 foursquare users. We discovered that implicit surveillance in location sharing is strongly homophilous along race and gender while the friendship network displays homophily for income. Qualitatively, we find that location surveillance can be a social, collaborative and positive process rather than current theoretical frameworks that mainly focus on power and information asymmetry. We discuss both sides of the design intervention argument leaving the readers with the partially rhetorical question of whether it is appropriate to design for more privacy or more transparency if there is no compelling need for the users to change the status quo.

ACKNOWLEDGMENTS

We thank the anonymous reviewers for their constructive and detailed reviews. This project was supported by National Science Foundation Grant No.1016203.

REFERENCES

1. Albrechtslund, A. Online social networking as participatory surveillance. *First Monday*,13, 3 (2008).
2. Andrejevic, M. The discipline of watching: Detection, risk, and lateral surveillance. *Critical Studies in Media Communication*, 23,5 (2006), 391-407.
3. Backstrom, L., Huttenlocher, D., Kleinberg, J., & Lan, X. Group formation in large social networks: membership, growth, and evolution. In *Proc. SIGKDD* (2006). 44-54.
4. Barkhuus, L., Brown, B., Bell, M., Sherwood, S., Hall, M., & Chalmers, M. From awareness to repartee: sharing location within social groups. In *Proc. CHI* (2008), 497-506.
5. Barkhuus, L.The mismeasurement of privacy: using contextual integrity to reconsider privacy in HCI. In *Proc. CHI* (2012), 367-376.
6. Benisch, M., Kelley, P. G., Sadeh, N., & Cranor, L. F. Capturing location-privacy preferences: quantifying accuracy and user-burden tradeoffs. *PUC*, 15,7 (2011), 679-694.
7. Boesen, J., Rode, J. A., & Mancini, C. The domestic panopticon: location tracking in families. In *Proc. Ubicomp* (2010), 65-74.
8. Brush, A. J., Krumm, J., & Scott, J. Exploring end user preferences for location obfuscation, location-based services, and the value of location. In *Proc. Ubicomp* (2010), 95-104.
9. Brown, B., Taylor, A. S., Izadi, S., Sellen, A., Jofish'Kaye, J., & Eardley, R. Locating family values: A field trial of the Whereabouts Clock. In *Ubicomp* (2007), 354-371.
10. Consolvo, S., Smith, I. E., Matthews, T., LaMarca, A., Tabert, J., & Powledge, P. Location disclosure to social relations: why, when, & what people want to share. In *Proc. CHI* (2005), 81-90.
11. Cramer, H., Rost, M., & Holmquist, L. E. Performing a check-in: emerging practices, norms and 'conflicts' in location-sharing using foursquare. In *Proc. Mobile HCI* (2011), 57-66.
12. Dourish, P.Implications for design. In *Proc. CHI* (2006), 541-550.
13. e Silva, A. D. S., & Frith, J. *Mobile interfaces in public spaces: Locational privacy, control, and urban sociability*. Taylor & Francis, 2012.
14. foursquare. URL: https://foursquare.com/about/
15. foursquare platform feature descriptions. URL: https://support.foursquare.com/hc/en-us
16. Glaser, B., & Strauss, A. *The discovery of grounded theory*. Weidenfield & Nicolson, London, 1967.
17. Guha, S., & Birnholtz, J. Can you see me now?: location, visibility and the management of impressions on foursquare. *In Proc. Mobile HCI* (2013), 183-192.
18. Hanneman, R. A., and Riddle, M.*Introduction to social network methods*. University of California, Riverside, 2005.
19. Humphreys, L. Mobile social networks and social practice: A case study of Dodgeball. *JCMC,* 13, 1 (2007), 341-360.
20. Humphreys, L. Mobile social networks and urban public space. *New Media & Society*, 12, 5 (2010), 763-778.
21. Humphreys, L. Who's watching whom? A study of interactive technology and surveillance. *Journal of Communication*, 61, 4 (2011), 575-595.
22. Iachello, G., Smith, I., Consolvo, S., Chen, M., & Abowd, G. D.Developing privacy guidelines for social location disclosure applications and services. In *Proc. SOUPS* (2005), 65-76.
23. Iachello, G., & Hong, J. End-user privacy in human-computer interaction. *Foundations and Trends in Human-Computer Interaction*, 1, 1 (2007), 1-137.
24. Lewis, K., Gonzalez, M., & Kaufman, J. Social selection and peer influence in an online social network. *Proceedings of the National Academy of Sciences*, 109, 1 (2012), 68-72.
25. Lindqvist, J., Cranshaw, J., Wiese, J., Hong, J., & Zimmerman, J. I'm the mayor of my house: examining why people use foursquare-a social-driven location sharing application. *In Proc. CHI* (2011). 2409-2418.
26. Lingel, J., & Naaman, M. 2014. City, self, network: transnational migrants and online identity work. In *Proc. CSCW* (2014), 1502-1510.
27. Lyon, D. *Surveillance Studies: An Overview*. Polity Press, Cambridge, 2007.

28.Marwick, A. E. The Public Domain: Social Surveillance in Everyday Life. *Surveillance & Society*, 9, 4 (2012).

29.McCorkel, J. A. Embodied surveillance and the gendering of punishment. *Journal of Contemporary Ethnography*, 32, 1 (2003), 41-76.

30.McPherson, M., Smith-Lovin, L., & Cook, J. M. Birds of a feather: Homophily in social networks. *Annual Review of Sociology*, 27 (2001), 415–444.

31.Nissenbaum, H. Privacy as contextual integrity. *Wash. L. Rev.*, 79, (2004) 119.

32.Opsahl, T. Structure and Evolution of Weighted Networks. University of London (Queen Mary College), London, UK, (2009), 104-122. URL: http://toreopsahl.com/tnet/

33.Pavlovskaya, M., & Martin, K. S. Feminism and geographic information systems: From a missing object to a mapping subject. *Geography Compass*, 1, 3 (2007), 583-606.

34.Page, X., Knijnenburg, B. P., & Kobsa, A.What a tangled web we weave: lying backfires in location-sharing social media. In *Proc. CSCW* (2013), 273-284.

35.Patil, S., Norcie, G., Kapadia, A., & Lee, A. J. Reasons, rewards, regrets: privacy considerations in location sharing as an interactive practice. In *Proc. SOUPS* (2012), 5.

36.Patil, S., Schlegel, R., Kapadia, A., & Lee, A. J.Reflection or action?:how feedback and control affect location sharing decisions. In *Proc. CHI* (2014), 101-110.

37.Reilly, D., Dearman, D., Ha, V., Smith, I., & Inkpen, K. “Need to know”: examining information need in location discourse. *Pervasive Computing*, (2006), 33-49.

38.Shalizi, C. R., & Thomas, A. C. Homophily and contagion are generically confounded in observational social network studies. *Soc. Methods & Research*, 40, 2 (2011), 211-239.

39.Smith, I.Consolvo, S., Lamarca, A., Hightower, J., Scott, J., Sohn, T.,Hughes,J,Iachello,G and Abowd, G. D. Social disclosure of place: From location technology to communication practices. *Pervasive Computing*, (2005), 134-151.

40.Stuart, H. C., Dabbish, L., Kiesler, S., Kinnaird, P., & Kang, R. Social transparency in networked information exchange: a theoretical framework. In *Proc. CSCW* (2012), 451-460.

41.Tang, K. P., Lin, J., Hong, J. I., Siewiorek, D. P., & Sadeh, N. Rethinking location sharing: exploring the implications of social-driven vs. purpose-driven location sharing. *In Proc. Ubicomp* (2010), 85-94.

42.Tang, K., Hong, J., & Siewiorek, D. The implications of offering more disclosure choices for social location sharing. In *Proc. CHI* (2012), 391-394.

43.Toch, E., Cranshaw, J., Hankes-Drielsma, P., Springfield, J., Kelley, P. G., Cranor, L.,Hong,J. and Sadeh, N. Locaccino: a privacy-centric location sharing application. In *Proc. Ubicomp-Adjunct* (2010), 381-382.

44.Trottier, D. Interpersonal surveillance on social media. *Canadian Journal of Communication*, 37, 2 (2012).

45.Tsai, J. Y., Kelley, P., Drielsma, P., Cranor, L. F., Hong, J., & Sadeh, N.Who's viewed you?:the impact of feedback in a mobile location-sharing application.In *Proc. CHI* (2009),2003-2012.

46.Want, R., Hopper, A., Falcao, V., & Gibbons, J. The active badge location system. *ACM Transactions on Information Systems*, 10, 1 (1992), 91-102.

47.Wicker, S. B. *Cellular Convergence and the Death of Privacy*. Oxford University Press, 2013.

48.Wiese, J., Kelley, P. G., Cranor, L. F., Dabbish, L., Hong, J. I., & Zimmerman, J. Are you close with me? are you nearby?: investigating social groups, closeness, and willingness to share. In *Proc. Ubicomp* (2011), 197-206.

49.Wilson, S., Cranshaw, J., Sadeh, N., Acquisti, A., Cranor, L. F., Springfield, J.,Jeong, S.Y. and Balasubramanian, A. Privacy manipulation and acclimation in a location sharing application. In *Proc. Ubicomp* (2013). 549-558.

50.Yuan, Y. C. and Gay, G. Homophily of Network Ties and Bonding and Bridging Social Capital in Computer-Mediated Distributed Teams. *JCMC*, 11, 4 (2006), 1062–1084.

There's No Such Thing as the Perfect Map: Quantifying Bias in Spatial Crowd-sourcing Datasets

Giovanni Quattrone
University College London
London, UK
g.quattrone@cs.ucl.ac.uk

Licia Capra
University College London
London, UK
l.capra@cs.ucl.ac.uk

Pasquale De Meo
University of Messina
Messina, Italy
demeo@unime.it

ABSTRACT
Crowd-sourcing has become a popular form of computer mediated collaborative work and OpenStreetMap represents one of the most successful crowd-sourcing systems, where the goal of building and maintaining an accurate global map of the world is being accomplished by means of contributions made by over 1.2M citizens. However, within this apparently large crowd, a tiny group of highly active users is responsible for the mapping of almost all the content. One may thus wonder to what extent the information being mapped is biased towards the interests and agenda of this group of users. In this paper, we present a method to quantitatively measure content bias in crowd-sourced geographic information. We then apply the method to quantify content bias across a three-year period of OpenStreetMap mapping in 40 countries. We find almost no content bias in terms of what is being mapped, but significant geographic bias; furthermore, we find that bias in terms of meticulousness varies with culture.

Author Keywords
Content bias, OpenStreetMap, crowd-sourcing, volunteered geographic information, cross-cultural

ACM Classification Keywords
H.2.8 Database Management: Database Applications—*Spatial Databases and GIS*; H.5.3 Group and Organization Interfaces: Computer-Supported Cooperative Work

INTRODUCTION
Crowd-sourcing is a form of online collaborative work practice, where a task that was traditionally performed by a selected number of skilled employees is now being performed by a large, self-selected group of volunteers in answer to an open call [21]. Crowd-sourcing has been used to accomplish a variety of tasks [3]: from distributed human intelligence tasking, as exemplified by the open calls usually appearing on Amazon Mechanical Turk, to scientific (objective) problem solving; from peer-vetted (subjective) creative production, as in Threadless,[1] to knowledge discovery and management. It is the latter type of crowd-sourcing tasks we are interested in this paper, whereby a crowd is mobilised to collect and maintain large repositories of information. The most successful example of this is Wikipedia, with its online community of editors voluntarily contributing to a repository of the whole body of knowledge. A specific type of knowledge where crowd-sourcing has also been widely applied is that of volunteered geographic information, where citizens have become surveyors, with council-monitoring applications like FixMyStreet;[2] local reporters, as powered by Ushaidi's Crowdmap;[3] and cartographers, with geo-wikis like Cyclopath[4] and OpenStreetMap.[5]

Crowd-sourcing platforms for knowledge discovery and management have been subject to scrutiny by the research community over the years; one of the first issues raised was that of information accuracy, as we take a task away from skilled employees and assign it to an undefined, self-selected crowd. Several studies have revealed that the emerging crowd-editing practises result in high quality data gathering overall (e.g., [23, 18, 15, 13, 28]). However, information accuracy is not the only concern that emerges as a result of this knowledge production paradigm shift; another important issue is that of *content bias*.

Although crowd-sourcing seeks contributions from potentially anyone, in practice previous work has shown that only a tiny group of contributors (often referred to as 'power users') produces most of the content [22, 25, 32, 33, 35, 43]. For this reason, one may wonder to what extent the gathered information is biased towards the interests of this small group of highly active contributors. In this paper, we investigate this question for crowd-sourced geographic information repositories – and OpenStreetMap in particular – by quantitatively measuring the extent to which the mapping of 'power users' is *mis*aligned with respect to what done by the whole OpenStreetMap contributors' base.

If such misalignment is high, the rationale behind the very existence of OpenStreetMap might be at stake. At a time when

CSCW 2015, March 14–18, 2015, Vancouver, BC, Canada.

http://dx.doi.org/10.1145/2675133.2675235

[1] `https://www.threadless.com/`
[2] `http://www.fixmystreet.com/`
[3] `http://www.ushahidi.com/products/crowdmap`
[4] `http://cyclopath.org/`
[5] `http://www.openstreetmap.org/`

maps were in the hands of a few selected companies, and thus their content inevitably reflected private agendas (e.g., of the military, as in the case of Ordnance Survey; of commercial profit, as in Google Maps and Bing Maps), OpenStreetMap offered a radically different approach, empowering anyone to freely edit its content. As Mikel Maron, Director of the GroundTruth Initiative[6] and Board Member of OpenStreetMap Foundation states, *"We really think it's important that the people who are creating the map data, or are involved with creating the map data, are the people who are living there, and the data that's created from their communities is something they have a stake in and is something that they can fully use to improve their own situation and advantage the agenda of the community"*.[7] Although the crowd-sourcing paradigm enables this goal *in principle*, actual adoption of the paradigm sees a rather small (and also demographically-biased) community core being responsible for the vast majority of the OpenStreetMap knowledge base, thus questioning whether the map that emerges in OpenStreetMap is biased towards the interests of its 'power users'. With a growing number of companies and non-for-profit organisations worldwide relying on OpenStreetMap to deliver their own location-based services,[8] it has become important to provide a method to quantitatively answer this question.

In this paper, we propose a method to quantify *content bias*, to be interpreted here as the extent to which the interests of the power users are *mis*aligned with respect to those of the rest of the OpenStreetMap contributors' base. We consider users' *interests* as captured by what OpenStreetMap users edit in the map; we subsequently measure bias in terms of three signals that mappers implicitly leave: *what* information is being mapped, *where* the information is being mapped, and finally *how* meticulous is the information being edited. For each of these dimensions, we virtually compare two maps: one that emerges from the actions of *power users*, and one that emerges from the actions of the very long tail of *occasional contributors*. We apply the method to OpenStreetMap, as this is the most popular crowd-sourced geographic information system in existence to date. In this context, we quantify bias for 40 countries around the world, examining all contributions made in a period of three years (from 01/2010 to 12/2012).

Our findings reveal that there is almost no bias in terms of what content is being produced: the type of spatial objects that power users edit is very well aligned with the information being mapped by the very many occasional mappers. On the contrary, there is higher bias in terms of where information is being mapped: the map that emerges from power contributors is very dense around big cities and near empty anywhere else, whereas the map that emerges from occasional contributors offers a more uniform spatial coverage, albeit with lower density. Finally, we found bias in how meticulously the map is being edited to vary with culture: where power distance is low and individualism is high, the crowd performs a more accurate work than power users, and viceversa.

The remainder of the paper is structured as follows: we first position this work in the context of related literature; we then describe the dataset used in this study, and provide a definition of bias within this context. We present the method we developed to quantitatively measure the previously defined forms of bias, and analyse the results obtained when applying the method to the dataset under exam. Finally, we summarise the main contributions of this work, we reflect on the theoretical and practical implications of the proposed method, we acknowledge current limitations, and elaborate on future directions of research.

RELATED WORK

The topic of bias, interpreted as lack of neutrality, has been extensively studied in collaborative knowledge production platforms such as Wikipedia. Indeed, although Wikipedia advocates a strict 'neutral point of view' (NPOV) policy, many studies that looked into measuring the extent to which this policy is adhered to in practice have found otherwise. For example, [5, 34] examined the extent to which content and perspectives vary across *cultures*, by comparing articles about famous people in the Polish and English editions of Wikipedia, and found substantial differences between the two monolingual versions. Lam et al. [27] have studied *gender* imbalance in Wikipedia, and reported on how in some domains, such as movies, articles of particular interest to females were substantially less covered than articles of specific interest to males – a direct consequence of having very few female editors relative to male ones. The same issue of gender gap also received media attention; for example, in 2011 The New York Times reported that, according to many surveys, less than 15 percent of Wikipedia contributors are women [8].

Other studies of Wikipedia have looked into the effect that varying levels of *user engagement* have on the resulting knowledge base. Wikipedia, as many online user-generated content platforms, exhibits a highly skewed user base, with a small fraction of less than 20% of users (often called *power users*) being responsible for the creation of 80% or more of available content [33, 25, 35]. A study by Kittur et al. [25] suggests that Wikipedia was indeed initially driven by the 'power of the few' top contributors, rather than being the result of an actual 'wisdom of the crowd'; this has however been shifting over time, with a larger variety of users committing contributions in recent years. Note that varying levels of engagement do not necessarily represent a problem: as found in previous research, the top Wikipedia editors are indeed those who use the quality assurance systems [17], those who invoke community norms, and those who revise available entries [33], making them both more accurate and complete, so that their work has a positive effect, both directly (in terms of quality of the content) and indirectly (in terms of community growth).

[6] `http://groundtruth.in/` – A new media and technology consulting company specialising in community-based participatory technologies, especially mapping and citizen journalism, in poor and marginalized regions throughout the world.

[7] `http://www.wired.co.uk/news/archive/2013-08/05/slum-mapping-google-maps-cartography`

[8] `http://wiki.openstreetmap.org/wiki/List_of_OSM_based_Services`

As we shift our attention to *geographic* knowledge repositories, new and different forms of bias may emerge, as there is an intrinsic relationship between the location of a contributor and the type of knowledge they can offer (whereas, in general-knowledge repositories such as Wikipedia, it is often the case that a user can contribute to any article, regardless of where they are geographically based). Few studies exist in this domain, with a notable exception being the recent work by Hetch and Stephens [19]: they examined three of the most common sources of volunteered geographic information (VGI [14]) - that is, Twitter, Flickr, and Foursquare - and showed that all of them are strongly biased towards urban areas, at the expense of rural ones (for instance, they found that there are 24.4 times more Foursquare users per capita in urban areas than rural ones).

OpenStreetMap is probably the VGI repository most studied to date, but research has so far focused on two other questions: accuracy and coverage. The former has been found to be very high [1, 10, 13, 14, 15, 16, 28] when compared to proprietary mapping datasets, in a variety of countries across Europe. The latter has been found to sharply decrease as we move away from city centres [44], or when we move in areas with low socio-economic status [15]; for this reason, some authors have labelled user-generated geo-tagged information as geographically biased, in the sense that it does not cover with equal interest urban and rural areas [24], and neither well-off and deprived areas [15].

Geographic bias is certainly important, but it is not the only form of bias worth investigating in geographic knowledge repositories. For example, Stephens [42] found that user adoption of volunteered geographic information in OpenStreetMap and Google MapMaker is not uniform, with an abundance of men compared to women. Furthermore, similar to what observed in Wikipedia, many geo-spatial communities manifest a highly skewed user base, with a tiny fraction of users being responsible for the majority of available content [32, 22, 43]. There is thus an open opportunity here to go beyond the geographic bias, and to explore the extent to which the mapped content is representative of the interests of small groups of users only. In this paper, we propose a method to quantify different forms of content bias in geographic crowd-sourced repositories, and apply it to the case of OpenStreetMap in particular, to measure how biased the mapped information is towards the interests of a minority of very active users. In the next section, we describe the dataset under exam, and the forms of bias our method aims to measure.

We note that different forms of bias have been studied in other domains. For example, bias intended as the expression of the personal views of the editors of a community has been investigated in Foursquare [39], Pinterest [7], YouTube [6] and Yelp [9]. However, these platforms specifically call for the personal expressions of individuals' experiences. As such, their goal is fundamentally different from that of knowledge gathering platforms like Wikipedia and OpenStreetMap, that aim for a certain ideal of neutrality and objectivity.

DATASET

Before delving into a detailed description of our proposed method, we describe the crowd-sourcing datasets to which it is best applied. First, the crowd-sourced content should have a geographic component; second, the content should be semantically varied and rich, so that different geographical objects can be mapped, and with a different degree of semantic richness; finally, different users' groups should be contributing to the crowd-sourcing task, so that their actions can be compared. Many crowd-sourcing datasets meet these criteria, including WikiMapia,[9] an open-content collaborative mapping project where volunteer users mark and describe all geographical objects on Earth; Google Map Maker,[10] a service launched by Google in June 2008 designed to allow Google Map users to update and improve the map of places that matter to them; and OpenStreetMap,[11] a collaborative project to create a free editable map of the world. In this paper, we chose to apply our method to OpenStreetMap (hereafter OSM), as of all suitable geographic crowd-sourcing projects and associated datasets, this is probably the most successful one, having been running since 2004, and comprising the largest (and most geographically widespread) user and content base. Furthermore, OSM is the one that has been researched the most in the literature, so that we can relate our findings to previous studies.

The OSM dataset is freely available to download[12] and it contains the history (since 2006) of all edits (over 2 billions) performed by all users (over 1.6M) on all spatial objects. In OSM jargon, spatial objects can be one of three types: *nodes*, *ways*, and *relations*. Nodes are single geospatial points and typically represent Points-of-Interest (POIs); ways mostly represent roads (as well as streams, railway lines, and the like); finally, relations are used for grouping other objects together, based on logical (and usually local) relationships (e.g., administrative boundaries, bus routes).

In order to reduce the OSM dataset to a more manageable size, we restricted our attention to nodes that describe Points-of-Interest (POI) only. A node consists of three main attributes: a geographical position (latitude and longitude), a name, and an amenity type used to describe the category the POI belongs to; examples of categories include: 'hospital', 'place of worship', 'restaurant', and 'school'. The amenity type field is optional, and although OSM guidelines suggest a common taxonomy to use,[13] in practice users are free to use whatever vocabulary their prefer. We further restricted our attention geographically; previous research has shown that OSM presents large differences in data contributions and community development in different areas of the world [31, 37]. To capture bias in these differing contexts, we adopted a stratified sampling approach, and reduced our analysis to 40 (out of 133) countries that have OSM presence, so to in-

[9]`http://en.wikipedia.org/wiki/WikiMapia`

[10]`http://en.wikipedia.org/wiki/Google_Map_Maker`

[11]`http://www.openstreetmap.org/`

[12]`http://www.geofabrik.de/data/download.html`

[13]`http://wiki.openstreetmap.org/wiki/Map_Features#Amenity`

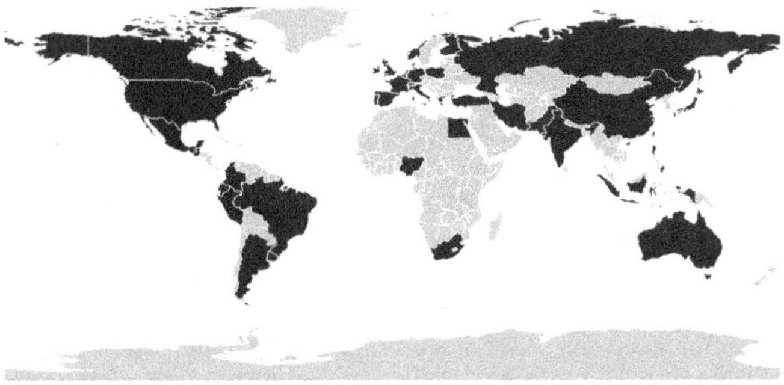

Figure 1. Map of final 40 countries under analysis (in alphabetical order: Argentina, Australia, Austria, Belgium, Brazil, Canada, China, Colombia, Denmark, Ecuador, Egypt, Finland, France, Germany, Greece, Guatemala, India, Indonesia, Iran, Ireland, Italy, Japan, Mexico, Netherlands, Nigeria, Norway, Pakistan, Peru, Philippines, Poland, Portugal, Russia, South Africa, Spain, Switzerland, Taiwan, Turkey, United Kingdom, United States, Uruguay)

	Min	*1st Qu.*	*Median*	*3rd Qu.*	*Max.*
OSM nodes	4,541	72,500	139,800	357,600	3,417,700
OSM users	161	1068	1,776	3,876	44,460
OSM nodes per km^2	0.01	0.04	0.35	1.55	9.57
OSM users per population	9.2e-07	1.3e-05	6.7e-05	2.1e-04	8.2e-04

Table 1. Summary Statistics of OSM Features in the 40 Analysed Countries

clude countries representative of different cultural values and economic status, as these will be used later in the study.

Two further pruning steps have been conducted: within the selected 40 countries, we chose to discard the very first years of OSM mapping, as only a few early-adopters were contributing at that point; the dataset would thus not have allowed us to quantify crowd (i.e., occasional workers) behaviour at that time. From 2010 onwards, all 40 countries under exam appear to have passed the cold-start phase, as an analysis of OSM users and activity showed.

Finally, from the above sample, we removed all contributions that appeared to be 'bulk imports',[14] as these are not representatives of 'human' crowd-sourcing activity, but rather of 'data donations' given to the wider OSM community by external organisations. Imports are not explicitly marked as such in the OSM dataset; we thus needed heuristics to identify them. We marked as imports those edits which came from a single user, in very large quantities (i.e., more than one thousand of edits), in a short period of time (i.e., less than one hour), and that were spread over a large geographic area (i.e., a whole city), using the same approach used in [37].

In the end, we are left with a dataset comprising nearly 120k users, who have collectively made over 13M contributions to OSM, across the 40 different countries that are highlighted in Figure 1. Summary features of this dataset are showed in Table 1.

METHOD

To understand whether the OSM map is biased towards the interests of the very active minority of 'power users', we proceed as follow. We first distinguish power users from rest of occasional mappers (which we will refer to as 'the crowd'); then we separate the OSM map in two virtual maps, one derived from the edits of power users and one derived from the edits of the the crowd; subsequently, we define which form of content bias we are interested to capture; finally, we define metrics to capture the content (mis)alignments of the virtual maps generated by power users and the crowd. We will discuss these three steps next.

[14] `http://wiki.openstreetmap.org/wiki/Import`

Power Users vs. The Crowd

The term 'power user' is used informally in online collaborative-work platforms to indicate the top contributors of the community. Many authors refer to the 80-20 rule-of-thumb (or Pareto principle) and define 'power users' those users (typically 20% or less of the whole user base) that collectively produce more than 80% of the content [4, 33, 25]. We use the same definition in this work and, for each country under exam, we consider as power users the minimum number of users required to account for 80% of the edits in that country. Interestingly, we found that these users are less than 10% of the OSM population for each country.

One may wonder to what extent the above definition of power users impacts results, and what the effect of using different thresholds would be. To investigate this, in each country under exam, we first divided OSM users into five groups (rather than just power vs. crowd), each with an exponentially increasing number of OSM contributions (from $< 10^1$ to $> 10^4$). For each group and for each country, we then computed all our bias metrics and found that, in the vast majority of cases, results for the three least active groups, and results for the two most active groups, were very similar. We found also that the activity threshold separating these two groups is, in most cases, the same emerging when distinguishing power users vs. the crowd following the 80-20 rule of thumb. We thus chose to present results comparing the two broad classes of power users and the crowd only.

Forms of Content Bias

In this work, we are interested in quantitatively measuring the extent to which the interests of the power users and the interests of the crowd are *mis*aligned. We define users' *interests* of both power users and the crowd as captured by what they edit in their own virtual maps (note that lurkers – individuals who use OSM without contributing any content – are not considered in this study, as they do not leave any quantifiable trace about their interests).

We quantify *mis*alignment according to three dimensions: *(i) what* spatial objects are being edited, *(ii) where* these objects are physically located, and *(iii) how* meticulously they are edited.

- *What is being mapped?* The fist bias dimension we measure is the extent to which the POI amenity types mapped by power users are (mis)aligned with those mapped by the rest of the OSM community. Previous qualitative studies of OSM have revealed that power editors are a niche group prevalently formed by educated, young, white male, and that evidence of this niche group dominance in OSM is also reflected in the amenities that have been mapped [42].

We thus aim to measure whether the POI amenity types that this group edits are of interest to them only, or whether the same amenity types are also being edited by the much larger crowd of occasional mappers.

- *Where is mapping taking place?* The second bias dimension we measure is the extent to which the geographic areas mapped by power users are (mis)aligned with respect to those mapped by the rest of OSM community. As power users exhibit rather peculiar demographics [42], one may wonder whether the map that emerges from their edits predominantly covers areas of interest to them (e.g., places where they live, work and mingle), and whether these areas do not align with those of interest to the much larger OSM crowd, thus leaving big holes in the emerging map.
- *How meticulous is the mapping?* The third and last bias dimension we measure is the level of accuracy that emerges from the two virtual maps. We do so as past work on Wikipedia has revealed that power editors are responsible for the high quality of Wikipedia articles, being engaged in moderating and quality control activities, such as enforcing community norms and reverting edits when they do not follow Wikipedia's policies [33]. If a similar separation of roles emerges in OSM too, then we would expect the virtual map created by power editors to signal higher accuracy than the one emerging from crowd mappers.

Metrics

Having distinguished power users from the rest of the crowd, and having defined the three forms of content bias that we want to capture, we can proceed to define metrics to measure them.

What is being edited

The first metric we define aims to measure to what extent the amenity types edited by power users are also being edited by the crowd. To do so, for each country, we compute two vectors, $\vec{a_p}$ and $\vec{a_c}$, where the i-th entry of $\vec{a_p}$ (resp., $\vec{a_c}$) indicates how many times the i-th amenity is mapped by power users (resp., the crowd). We then define our first metric *Amenity Misalignment* (AM) as:

$$AM = 1 - \theta(\vec{a_p}, \vec{a_c}) \quad (1)$$

where $\theta(\cdot,\cdot)$ is the Cosine similarity between the two vectors.[15] Since $\vec{a_p}$ and $\vec{a_p}$ cannot have negative entries, then their Cosine similarity ranges from 0 to 1 and so also AM does. Values of AM close to zero (i.e., $\theta(\vec{a_p}, \vec{a_c}) \approx 1$) indicate that power users and the crowd edit the same amenities (even if at different scale in terms of absolute number of edits), and we interpret this as an indication of very low misalignment; viceversa, values of AM close to the unit (i.e., $\theta(\vec{a_p}, \vec{a_c}) \approx 0$) signal that power users and the crowd have interest in completely different amenities (i.e., high misalignment).

[15]The Cosine similarity is a well known vector similarity measure and it is mostly used in high-dimensional positive spaces such as in Information Retrieval and Text Mining. It computes the cosine of the angle between two vectors [41], so it assumes values beloning to the real interval $[-1, 1]$ and is equal to the unit when the two vectors are perfectly aligned.

The AM metric alone is not sufficient to understand what kind of misalignment is taking place. For example, AM could be high because power users and the crowd have mapped completely different amenities; however, it could also be high because, for example, power users have mapped very few amenity types, while the crowd has mapped the same types plus many more. We thus consider, in conjunction with AM, a further metric that we call *Amenity Diversity Misalignment*, which aims to capture how *diverse* the range of amenities mapped by power users is vs. the range of those mapped by the crowd. Formally, we begin with the two vectors $\vec{a_p}$ and $\vec{a_c}$ as before; we then measure the diversity of amenities produced by power users (resp., the crowd) by computing the Shannon Diversity Index[16] on $\vec{a_p}$ (resp., $\vec{a_c}$). We refer to these quantities as $AmnDiv_p$ and $AmnDiv_c$. We then define our second metric *Amenity Diversity Misalignment* (ADM) as the relative difference between $AmnDiv_p$ and $AmnDiv_c$:

$$ADM = \frac{AmnDiv_p - AmnDiv_c}{\max(AmnDiv_p, AmnDiv_c)} \quad (2)$$

Because both $AmnDiv_p$ and $AmnDiv_c$ are equal to or greater than 0, then $ADM \in [-1, +1]$. Positive values of this metric mean that the virtual map generated by power users shows a broader set of amenities than the virtual map generated by the crowd; negative values point out the opposite behaviour; values closed to 0 mean that the virtual map generated by power users and the virtual map generated by the crowd show no misalignment in term of diversity of mapped amenities.

Where is mapping taking place

To quantify spatial misalignment, the first metric we define looks at the difference between the geographic areas mapped by power users and those mapped by the crowd. We proceeded as follow: we subdivided each country in grids of different sizes (i.e., 2km × 2km, 5km × 5km, 15km × 15km). We then computed two vectors, $\vec{g_p}$ and $\vec{g_c}$, where the i-th entry of $\vec{g_p}$ (resp., $\vec{g_c}$) indicates how many times the i-th cell of the grid has been mapped by power users (resp., the crowd). Similarly to what was done when defining Amenity Misalignment in Equation 1, we now define *Spatial Misalignment* (SM), as:

$$SM = 1 - \theta(\vec{g_p}, \vec{g_c}) \quad (3)$$

In the next section, we will report only results obtained when considering the 2km × 2km grid, as very similar results were obtained when considering the other grid sizes.

Similarly to what was done when defining Amenity Diversity Misalignment, we consider, in conjunction with SM, a further metric that we call *Spatial Diversity Misalignment*, which aims to capture how *diverse* the range of areas mapped by power users is vs. the range of those mapped by the crowd. As before, we begin with the two vectors $\vec{g_p}$ and $\vec{g_c}$; we then measure the diversity of areas mapped by power users (resp., the crowd) by computing the Shannon Diversity Index on

[16]The Shannon diversity index is a measure that reflects how many different entries there are in a data set and the value is maximised when all entries are equally high [40].

$\vec{g_p}$ (resp., $\vec{g_c}$). We refer to these quantities as $SpDiv_p$ and $SpDiv_c$. We then define the *Spatial Diversity Misalignment* (SDM) metric as the relative difference between them:

$$SDM = \frac{SpDiv_p - SpDiv_c}{\max(SpDiv_p, SpDiv_c)} \quad (4)$$

As for the SM metric, we will report results obtained on the 2km × 2km grid only, as these are consistent with those obtained when operating with other grid sizes.

How meticulous is the mapping

The previous metrics capture misalignment between the map that emerges from power users and the map that emerges from the crowd, in terms of what is being mapped and where. What is left open is to measure which of the two virtual maps is more accurate and more up to date. Previous research has shown that, in Wikipedia, high accuracy is mainly due to the actions performed by power editors [33]. We are thus interested in measuring whether a similar phenomenon is emerging also in OSM. To do so in an automatic way is extremely difficult, as we would need access to an idealistic ground truth map, against which to compare the two virtual ones emerging in OSM. As such ground truth is not ready available, we will leverage past findings to find good proxies instead.

Let us consider accuracy first. By comparing geographic information in OSM with that of proprietary mapping datasets (e.g., Ordnance Survey, Navteq, Yelp), for selected regions and for selected periods of time, past studies have found that OSM spatial data is accurate [15, 16, 30], both in terms of positioning of OSM nodes and ways, and in terms of lexicographic spelling of POI names. Furthermore, it has found that OSM nodes' accuracy (both spatial and lexicographic) is strongly correlated with the amenity type field being non-null (recall that this field is optional in OSM) [30]. We thus measure the proportion of OSM objects with a non-null amenity field and use it as proxy for accuracy. More precisely, we compute $NotNullRatio_p$ and $NotNullRatio_c$ as the ratio of edits with non-null amenity appearing in the virtual map generated by power users and in the virtual map generated by the crowd respectively. Similarly to what was done when defining Amenity Diversity Misalignment in Equation 2, we then define an *Accuracy Misalignment* (AcM) metric as the relative difference between them:

$$AcM = \frac{NotNullRatio_p - NotNullRatio_c}{\max(NotNullRatio_p, NotNullRatio_c)} \quad (5)$$

Let us now consider how to measure which of the two virtual maps is more up-to-date. As for accuracy, it is rather difficult to automatically quantify this, as we do not possess a ground truth dataset we can compare against. However, once again we can measure a plausible proxy by looking at the ratio of OSM POIs whose details have been updated at least once since first being added to the map; we consider this a signal that, for whatever reason (e.g., urbanisation of an area, migration, or unlikely natural disaster) stale information is removed as map updates are carried out. We thus compute $UpdRatio_p$ and $UpdRatio_c$ as the ratio of OSM objects that have been updated at least once in the power users' and in the crowd's virtual maps respectively. Similarly to what was done when defining Amenity Diversity Misalignment in Equation 2, we are interested to see the relative difference between the update ratio of the virtual map generated by power users and that generated by the crowd. For this reason, we define the *Update Misalignment* (UM) metric as:

$$UM = \frac{UpdRatio_p - UpdRatio_c}{\max(UpdRatio_p, UpdRatio_c)} \quad (6)$$

Dimension	*Metric*	*Min*	*1st Qu.*	*Median*	*3rd Qu.*	*Max.*
What	AM	0.01	0.03	0.05	0.08	0.15
	ADM	-0.31	-0.18	-0.01	0.07	0.24
Where	SM	0.20	0.35	0.45	0.56	0.87
	SDM	-0.84	-0.46	-0.27	-0.09	0.24
How	AcM	-0.57	-0.14	0.12	0.39	0.74
	UM	-0.38	-0.12	0.23	0.52	0.92

Table 2. Summary Statistics of Metrics

RESULTS

Quantifying Bias in the Map

We have computed the previously defined six metrics in each of the 40 countries under exam; summary statistics of the obtained values can be found in Table 2. We now elaborate on these results.

What

From the first block of rows in Table 2, we can observe that the virtual map generated by power users and the one produced by the crowd show very little misalignment in terms of what types of amenities are being mapped. In fact, AM values range between 0.01 and 0.15: that is, in all the analysed countries, the amenities mapped by power users are roughly the same (even if with different magnitude) as those mapped by the crowd. This low misalignment is further reflected in the diversity of amenities being mapped, with values of ADM in the range -0.18 to 0.24 across three quarter of the considered countries (from the first to the last quartile). These two results combined suggest that the misalignment on the 'what' dimension is low.

In order to give a graphical and intuitive visualisation of the low misalignment between the types of amenities mapped by power users and the crowd, Figure 2 plots how many times in Norway (the country with the highest AM value of 0.15) each amenity has been mapped by the crowd (x axis) and by power users (y axis). From this plot we can observe that, with the only exception of amenity type 'charging_station', that has been heavily edited by power users only, all other amenities have been commonly mapped by power users and by the crowd (albeit with different magnitude scale).

Where

From the second block of rows in Table 2, we can observe that spatial misalignment between the map generated by power users and the map generated by the crowd is higher than the 'what' dimension. In fact, SM varies between 0.35 and 0.87 in three quartiles, meaning that, in three quarter of the considered countries, the areas mapped by power users only partially overlap with those mapped by the crowd. Furthermore,

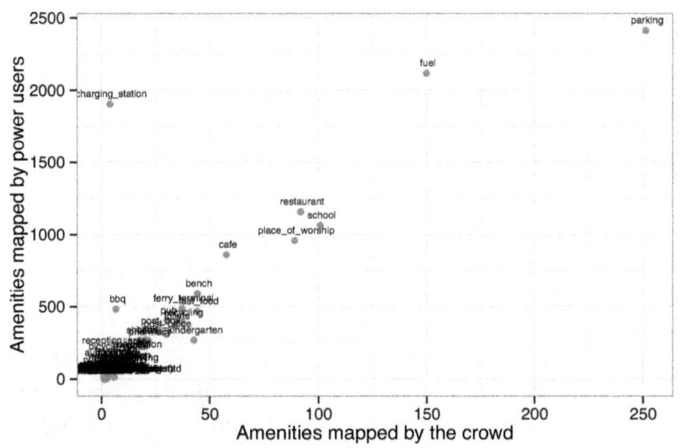

Figure 2. How many times in Norway each amenity has been mapped by the crowd (x-axis) and by power users (y-axis)

SDM is generally lower than zero, suggesting that the virtual map produced by power users concentrates on fewer areas than the one produced by the crowd. One may argue that this is simply a natural consequence of the fact that power users are much fewer than the crowd, and that, in geographic wikis, one can only map where one lives (e.g., knowledge is significantly constrained by geography, unlike what happens in Wikipedia). It is thus 'obvious' that there is high spatial misalignment between the two virtual maps of power users and the crowd. However, given how easily people adopt one map and trust its content, it is important to understand the impact of this finding.

To this end, Figure 3 overlays the two virtual maps, one generated by power users (in yellow marks) and one by the crowd (in red marks), both for the whole United Kingdom (left) and for the metropolitan city of London (right). The darker the color, the higher the relative concentration of edits. As shown, power users intensively map a very few selected areas, these being major urban areas in the UK (e.g., London, Liverpool and Manchester), and selected central areas within the city of London. Crowd mappers spread their activity over the whole country (and also over the whole city of London) much more uniformly instead. While we illustrate the case of the United Kingdom and London only, similar patterns have been observed in other countries we have examined. This signals an important problem: if power users concentrate their edits in a few, heavily urbanised areas (perhaps because that is where they live or mingle), who is going to map all the areas where there is absence of power users? And zooming in within urban areas: who is going to map areas within a city where power users do not exhibit an interest? We will elaborate on this point in the next section.

It is worth noting that, while spatial misalignment is high in three quarters of the countries examined, this is not the case for the remaining quarter, where SM is low and ranges between 0.20 and 0.35. These include Ecuador, Portugal, Philippines and South Africa, countries that have less than 1,000 OSM contributors each. It may thus be that these countries have not yet completely passed the cold start phase of OSM usage, with the user base being mainly composed of

Figure 3. Edits performed by powers users (in yellow marks) and the crowd (in red marks) in United Kingdom (left) and London (right). This figure is best viewed in color.

Metric	*Sub-Metric*	*Min*	*1st Qu.*	*Median*	*3rd Qu.*	*Max.*
AcM	$NotNullRatio_p$	0.34	0.46	0.52	0.57	0.65
	$NotNullRatio_c$	0.14	0.44	0.46	0.69	0.94
UM	$UpdRatio_p$	0.27	0.39	0.41	0.45	0.48
	$UpdRatio_c$	0.02	0.11	0.30	0.44	0.74

Table 3. Summary Statistics of Sub-Metrics from which AcM and UM are Based

homogeneous early adopters, rather than a broader and more varied crowd.

How

We now turn our attention to the third and final block of rows in Table 2. Unlike what previously found for the 'what' and 'where' dimensions, here results are not clear-cut: both the AcM metric (proxy for accuracy) and UM metrics (proxy for up-to-dateness) record high absolute values across most countries, suggesting that crowd editing behaviour is substantially different from power users editing behaviour. However, in about half the countries these values are negative (i.e., crowd workers take charge of filling in details and of updating content), while in the other half these are positives (i.e., power users take charge of these editing activities). To shed light on this, we also examined the sub-metrics from which AcM and UM are derived – that is, $NotNullRatio_p$, $NotNullRatio_c$, $UpdRatio_p$ and $UpdRatio_c$. Summary statistics of the obtained values can be found in Table 3. An important observation can be drawn from these values: while the behaviour of power users does not vary much across countries (e.g., the ratio of edits with a non-null amenity filed goes from a minimum of 0.34 to a maximum of 0.65), there is a huge variation in the behaviour of the crowd (e.g., from a minimum $NotNullRatio_c$ of 0.14 up to 0.94, and from a $UpdRatio_c$ of 0.02 up to 0.74). We thus hypothesize that culture plays a role in the way the 'how' dimension of bias manifests itself. This hypothesis is corroborated by recent studies of various online collaborative work platforms, that have revealed how the manifested users' behaviour is shaped by social norms and values that vary between countries [38, 12, 11, 34, 37]. To verify whether this hypothesis is supported, we proceeded as follow.

First, we needed to grow confidence in the fact that OSM edits in a given country are indeed performed by users who are representative of the country's culture. Though we cannot know if OSM users were 'born and bred' in any given country or if, for instance, they were migrants who only recently moved there, we can grow confidence in our analysis after performing the following steps: we inferred a 'home country' for each OSM user with more than 5 edits (while marking 'homeless' those with less than that); there was no ambiguity in this inference, as all users had over 90% of their edits (and the vast majority exactly 100%) done in a single country. We then computed, for each examined country, the ratio of edits done by home users relative to all edits done in that country; finally, we removed from our analysis countries with less than 70% of contributions made by (inferred) locals; eight countries were removed during this processing, including Canada, Libya, Nigeria, and Peru. We then proceeded with our cultural analysis, focusing on the three dimensions that previous cross-cultural studies of users' behaviour in collaborative platforms have found to be most significant [11]:

- *Power Distance Index* (PDI). This is a Hofstede's cultural dimension [20] and it represents the extent to which a nation expects power to be unequally distributed. For example, in countries where PDI is higher, decision making is accepted to be in the hands of a few powerful people, rather than a broader citizen base. Among all the countries we have included in this study, Austria, Denmark and Ireland are those with lowest PDI values; conversely, Russia, Philippines and Guatemala have the highest ones.
- *Individualism vs Collectivism* (IDV). This also is a Hofstede's cultural dimension [20] and it measures the extent to which individuals are integrated into groups: the higher the individualistic score, the higher the importance given to personal achievements and individual rights (or of those within very close circles), as opposed to wider community interest. Among all the countries we have included in this study, Guatemala, Ecuador and Colombia have the lowest IDV values; conversely, United Kingdom, Australia and United States have the highest ones.
- *Gross Domestic Product Per Capita* (GDP-pc). This index, obtained from the CIA World Factbook,[17] is often considered a good indicator of a country's standard of living. Among all the countries we have included in this study, Pakistan, Nigeria and Philippines have the lowest values of GDP-pc; conversely, United States, South Africa and Norway have the highest ones.

We then computed the Spearman Correlation coefficients between cultural/economic factors and the sub-metrics from which AcM and UM are based (i.e., $NotNullRatio_p$, $NotNullRatio_c$, $UpdRatio_p$ and $UpdRatio_c$). Table 4 shows the results.

Let us consider the first block of rows (i.e., $NotNullRatio_p$ and $NotNullRatio_c$ metrics). Results suggest three interesting findings: first, there is limited correlation between any

[17]`https://www.cia.gov/library/publications/the-world-factbook`, last access: 27/05/2013.

Metric	*Sub-Metric*	*PDI*	*IDV*	*GDP-pc*
AcM	$NotNullRatio_p$	-0.19 *	0.21 *	0.12
	$NotNullRatio_c$	-0.39 *	0.44 **	0.17 *
UM	$UpdRatio_p$	-0.18 *	0.23 *	0.16
	$UpdRatio_c$	-0.49 **	0.31 *	0.19 *

Table 4. Spearman Correlation between our metrics regarding the dimension 'how' and cultural/economic factors with p-values codes (0 '' 0.01 '*' 0.05 ' ' 1)**

cultural dimension and the behaviour of power users; indeed, Table 3 had already shown that the ratio of non-null amenities by power users did not vary much among countries. Taken together, these results suggest that OSM power users form a rather homogeneous group of contributors across the globe. Second, we find a significant correlation between the behaviour of the crowd and both power distance (-0.39) and individualism (0.44). This suggests that the virtual map emerging from crowd edits in countries with high IDV/low PDI has a higher ratio of non-null amenities (our proxy for accuracy) than the one emerging from crowd edits in countries with low IDV/high PDI; this is in line with what was found in [37], where it was showed that people from countries with high IDV/low PDI tend to edit conscientiously (lower null amenity ratio). Furthermore, this level of non-null amenities is even higher than what achieved by power editors in the same countries; this explains the negative values of AcM in Table 2. Viceversa, in countries with low IDV/high PDI, the crowd-generated map achieves lower ratio of non-null amenities than the power users-generated map, thus accounting for the positive values of AcM in Table 2. Third and last, wealth as measured by GDP-pc bears a weak correlation with the accuracy with which contributors edit the map.

If we now turn our attention to the second block of rows in Table 4 (i.e., $UpdRatio_p$ and $UpdRatio_c$ metrics), we find very similar results. That is, the behaviour of power users is only weakly correlated with the culture. On the contrary, the behaviour of the crowd is significantly correlated with power distance (-0.49): the lower the PDI, the higher the ratio of updates performed by the crowd; in high PDI countries, this ratio is even higher than the update ratio of power users, thus accounting for the negative values of UM in Table 2. This result is in line with what it was already found for Wikipedia [34], where people from countries with high power distance are less likely to modify/delete others' work, as if they did not feel to have the power or right to do so. Finally, GDP-pc plays only a weak role in the way editors update the map. We elaborate on the practical and theoretical implications of these findings next.

DISCUSSION

Main Contributions

In this paper, we have proposed a method to quantitatively measure bias in crowd-sourced geographic information repositories. The method first requires to segment the self-selected crowd-base into two groups; for the purpose of this study, we have been looking at power users versus crowd mappers in OpenStreetMap. The method then defines metrics to measure the difference between two virtual maps, each one emerging from the sole contributions of one group, in terms of: what spatial objects are being edited, where these objects are physically located, and how meticulously they are edited. We have thus quantified to what extent the emerging map in OSM is representative of the interests of the broad OSM contributors' base, despite the fact that a self-selected group of less than 20% power users is responsible for over 80% of OSM content.

Our findings reveal that the two user bases are well aligned in terms of what information is being mapped: the POIs of interest to power-users are of the same type being mapped by the crowd. However, we found strong bias in terms of the areas being mapped, with the map emerging from power users' activity being very dense around city centres, and near empty elsewhere, whereas the map constructed by the crowd covers the whole country, as well as intra-urban areas, much more uniformly. Finally, we found bias in how meticulously the map is being edited to vary with culture: where power distance is low and individualism is high, the crowd performs a more accurate work than power users (as captured by our proxies – non-null ratio and update ratio), and viceversa.

Practical Implications

Being able to quantify bias using the method presented in this paper has practical implications, to the benefit of both developers of crowd-mapping platforms (be them OSM, CrowdMap, FixMyStreet, etc.), and their potential end-users.

Developers of geographic crowd-sourcing platforms can use this method to measure the extent to which the ongoing mapping task is being representative of the broader contributors' user base. Despite the crowd-sourcing platform being open to anyone, in practice there are natural self-selection processes that cause a small subset of the user base to actually drive the majority of the mapping effort. This is not necessarily a problem: it may well be that this very active core is doing editing work that is well representative of the interests of the whole editors' base. However, up to now there has been no automatic way to measure at scale whether this was the case, and to what extent. The method we proposed offers a solution, with intuitive metrics that can reveal (mis)alignments between the two groups.

As the user base evolves over time, so does the bias they introduce. As an example, a recent study has revealed that, in 2008, power users on Amazon Mechanical Turk were primarily American, young, female, and well-educated; however, only one year after, a fundamental change had taken place, and the majority of the Turkers had then become male Indians [26]. By repeatedly applying the method we proposed over time, one can then keep track of how the mapping task is evolving, as a result of potential changes in the contributors' community.

Once bias has been made visible to developers of crowd-mapping initiatives, actions can be taken to reduce it, if deemed appropriate. What these actions might be is an open research question. For example, possible within-platform interventions include explicit cues for mapping certain types of spatial objects, and/or certain areas. At the moment, with the exception of Cyclopath, we are aware of no crowd-mapping platform that suggests what to map, where and how in any way; however, in Cyclopath, highlighting neglected areas of a map has been shown to be effective in directing mappers' work in those areas [36]. If a map happened to show 'what'/'where' forms of biases, similar visual cues could be used with the aim to drive the mapping efforts of power and occasional users alike, although research is required to see under what circumstances crowd-mappers would respond as Cyclopath users to such cues (the geographic spread of the mapping community probably being an important parameter). As evidenced by our analysis, some forms of bias vary with culture, suggesting that different interventions might be required in different countries: for example, where PDI is high, triggers that explicitly call the crowd to update possibly stale information may encourage them to conduct more map maintenance work than what they currently do; this is not necessary in countries with low PDI, as the crowd seems to already perform a more meticulous job than power users.

Being able to quantitatively measure bias in a map empowers tool developers to make it visible to map users (be them citizens, businesses and/or non-for-profit organisations): as Prof. Jerry Brottom clearly stated in a 2013 Wired article,[18] there is no such thing as a perfect map: *"No map can be perfect and there will always be gaps or lack of detail – whether it's the Scottish Island of Jura that Google somehow lost entirely, private roads in wealthy areas or informal settlements like slums. It's something that people often forget or get complacent about when they think they've found the best option though."*. While this is a basic principle that all geographers and cartographers know, people tend to forget that. If maps were to show their biases, users could make informed choices of which one to rely upon for their varying needs. The GIScience community has been actively researching methods to visualise uncertainty in geospatial data [29]; as we become capable of measuring bias too, similar lines of research open up, which may lead to the development of new and alternative approaches to map-data visualisation, and of the effects that they have on users' mapping behaviour.

Theoretical Implications

The ability to measure bias in online collaborative platforms is a powerful tool in the hands of researchers too. As online collaborative platforms have been proliferating, many large datasets have become available that afford us the ability to observe, measure and model human activity at a level of granularity unprecedented before. Indeed, a whole new research field called 'computational social science' has emerged, lying at the intersection of computer science, social science, and statistics, that claims to be able to validate old theories about human activity and relationships for the first time at scale, and possibly develop new ones.

The approach adopted by computational social scientists to understand human behaviour initially attracted criticism from traditional social scientists, who objected that the digital traces left in online collaborative platforms were not representative of the broader population, and thus their findings

[18] `http://http://www.wired.co.uk/news/archive/2013-08/05/slum-mapping-google-maps-cartography`

could not be generalised, despite being derived from much larger data samples than those used in previous social science studies [2]. Developing methods to quantify bias in online collaborative platforms offers researchers the ability to understand to what extent their findings are generalisable, and under what circumstances.

This paper makes one step in that direction: we have developed a method to quantitatively measure the bias introduced by power users versus occasional contributors in crowd-sourced maps. The comparison of power vs. occasional users has wide applications, as most online collaborative platforms exhibit the same engagement dichotomy. However, there are many other forms of bias that need quantification, including demographic bias (from gender to age to ethnicity and the like), knowledge bias (from amateur or hobbyists to professionals), and community-roles bias (from moderators to contributors to developers).

Limitations

One limitation of this work is that all results have been computed per country level. A more fine-grained study, for example at regional or city level, would be able to reveal biases emerging from more localised mapping dynamics than those we detected with this work. However, the method proposed in this paper could also be applied to more fine-grained studies of crowd-sourced geographic datasets.

Similar concerns apply to the temporal granularity of the study: here we studied the bias resulting from three years of cumulative activity; however, the group of power users may change over time, and so may their work. By selecting a more fine-grained time interval, and by repeating the same type of analysis over time, changes in bias, possibly resulting from changes in the power user base, would be captured.

It is also worth pointing out that, for scalability reasons, this work focuses on quantifying bias in OSM by looking at only one OSM data type, that is nodes. If other OSM data types were considered (e.g., ways and relations), different biases may emerge. We leave the investigation of this question to future work; however, we note that the applicability of the method proposed in this paper withstands.

We would also like to acknowledge the fact that the correlations found between the meticulousness of the emerging map and culture do not imply any causality. There might indeed exist other underlying factors that contribute to the above correlations and that our analysis does not capture. For example, map updates may take place for different reasons, such as urbanisation or migration processes, and these processes might be related to country's cultural and economic factors.

Last but not least, we are aware that the metrics we defined for the 'how' dimension are nothing but proxies; although we grounded these choices in findings from past works, there is need for further evidence that links our 'accuracy metric' and 'update metric' to what we indeed aim them to capture. Smaller scale qualitative studies could be conducted to shed light in this direction.

Finally, we would like to restate that this work focuses on quantifying bias in the *map* produced by *power users* versus that emerging from the activity of the much larger crowd of *occasional mappers*. Our method considers users' interest as captured by what OSM users edit in the map. We are aware of two main limitations of this method: first, what users map may only broadly, and not exactly, represent their interests. Second, while this method enables us to discuss how representative the emerging OSM map is of the broader OSM *contributors*' base, it does not afford us the ability to discuss its representativeness with respect to the interests of the very many lurkers that use the map without however leaving any digital trace of what their interests might be.

Future Work

As we previously hinted to, an important direction of future research is the analysis of the temporal evolution of bias in crowd-sourced geographic datasets. As time progresses, the user base keeps changing across a variety of dimensions (e.g., size, demographics, expertise); furthermore, as more and more information is being mapped, saturation effects may start to emerge, with potential impact on the user base itself (as some users may lose interest, once they see certain POI types have been completely mapped, or when they see 'sufficient' information being mapped). Developing a method that is capable of tracking users' evolution during their engagement with the crowd-mapping platform, and of measuring bias in relation to the stage of 'maturity' and 'adoption' of a crowd-sourcing platform, would offer platforms' developers a better understanding of how the community is evolving, and what types of interventions might be required and would be most effective over time.

Acknowledgment

This work was partly supported by the 3cixty EIT ICT Labs project.

REFERENCES

1. Arsanjani, J., Barron, C., Bakillah, M., and Helbich, M. Assessing the Quality of OpenStreetMap Contributors together with their Contributions. In *Proc. of AGILE* (2013).

2. Boyd, D., and Crawford, K. Critical Questions for Big Data: Provocations for a Cultural, Technological, and Scholarly Phenomenon. *Information, Communication & Society 15*, 5 (2012), 662–679.

3. Brabham, D. *Crowdsourcing*. MIT Press, 2013.

4. Bryant, S., Forte, A., and Bruckman, A. Becoming Wikipedian: Transformation of Participation in a Collaborative Online Encyclopedia. In *Proc. of GROUP*, ACM (2005), 1–10.

5. Callahan, E., and Herring, S. Cultural Bias in Wikipedia Content on Famous Persons. *Journal of the American Society for Information Science and Technology 62*, 10 (2011), 1899–1915.

6. Cha, M., Kwak, H., Rodriguez, P., Ahn, Y., and Moon, S. I Tube, You Tube, Everybody Tubes: Analyzing the

World's Largest User Generated Content Video System. In *Proc. of IMC*, ACM (2007), 1–14.

7. Chango, S., Kumar, V., Gilbert, E., and Terveen, L. Specialization, Homophily, and Gender in a Social Curation Site: Findings from Pinterest. In *Proc. of CSCW*, ACM (2014), 674–686.
8. Cohen, N. Define Gender Gap? Look Up Wikipedias Contributor List. *The New York Times* (January 2011).
9. Dai, W., Jin, G. Z., Lee, J., and Luca, M. Optimal Aggregation of Consumer Ratings: An Application to Yelp.com. Tech. rep., National Bureau of Economic Research, 2012.
10. Fana, H., Zipfa, A., Fub, Q., and Neisa, P. Quality assessment for building footprints data on OpenStreetMap. *International Journal of Geographical Information Science (IJGIS) 28*, 4 (2014), 700–719.
11. Gallagher, S., and Savage, T. Cross-cultural analysis in online community research: A literature review. *Computers in Human Behavior* (2012).
12. Garcia-Gavilanes, R., Quercia, D., and Jaimes, A. Cultural Dimensions in Twitter: Time, Individualism, and Power. In *Proc. of ICWSM* (2013).
13. Girres, J., and Touya, G. Quality assessment of the French OpenStreetMap dataset. *Transactions in GIS 14*, 4 (2010), 435–459.
14. Goodchild, M. Citizens as Sensors: the World of Volunteered Geography. *GeoJournal 69*, 4 (2007), 211–221.
15. Haklay, M. How good is volunteered geographical information? A comparative study of OpenStreetMap and Ordnance Survey datasets. *Environment and Planning B: Planning and Design 37*, 4 (2010), 682–703.
16. Haklay, M., Basiouka, S., Antoniou, V., and Ather, A. How Many Volunteers Does it Take to Map an Area Well? The Validity of Linus Law to Volunteered Geographic Information. *The Cartographic Journal 47*, 4 (2010), 315–322.
17. Halfaker, A., Geiger, R., Morgan, J., and Riedl, J. The Rise and Decline of an Open Collaboration System: How Wikipedia's reaction to sudden popularity is causing its decline. *American Behavioral Scientist 57*, 5 (2013), 664–688.
18. Halfaker, A., Kittur, A., Kraut, R., , and Riedl, J. A Jury of your Peers: Quality, Experience and Ownership in Wikipedia. In *Proc. of WikiSym*, ACM (2009).
19. Hecht, B., and Stephens, M. A Tale of Cities: Urban Biases in Volunteered Geographic Information. In *Proc. of ICWSM 2014* (2014).
20. Hofstede, G. *Culture's Consequences: Comparing Values, Behaviors, Institutions and Organizations across Nations*. SAGE Publications, 2001.
21. Howe, J. The Rise of Crowdsourcing. *Wired* (2006).
22. Hristova, D., Quattrone, G., Mashhadi, A., and Capra, L. The Life of the Party: Impact of Social Mapping in OpenStreetMap. In *Proc. of ICWSM* (2013).
23. Hu, M., Lim, E., Sun, A., Lauw, H., and Vuong, B. Measuring Article Quality in Wikipedia: Models and Evaluation. In *Proc. of CIKM*, ACM (2007).
24. Ishida, K. Geographical Bias on Social Media and Geo-local Contents System with Mobile Devices. In *Proc. of HICSS* (2012), 1790–1796.
25. Kittur, A., Chi, E., Pendleton, B., Suh, B., and Mytkowicz, T. Power of the Few vs. Wisdom of the Crowd: Wikipedia and the Rise of the Bourgeoisie. In *Proc. of WWW* (2007).
26. L., J. R., Irani, Silberman, M., Zaldivar, A., and Tomlinson, B. Who are the Crowdworkers? Shifting Demographics in Mechanical Turk. In *Proc. of CHI* (2010).
27. Lam, S. T. K., Uduwage, A., Dong, Z., Sen, S., Musicant, D. R., Terveen, L., and Riedl, J. WP:Clubhouse? An Exploration of Wikipedias Gender Imbalance. In *Proc. of WikiSym*, ACM (2011), 1–10.
28. Ludwig, I., Voss, A., and Krause-Traudes, M. A Comparison of the Street Networks of Navteq and OSM in Germany. *Advancing Geoinformation Science for a Changing World 1*, 2 (2011), 65–84.
29. Maceachren, A. M., Robinson, A., Gardner, S., Murray, R., Gahegan, M., and Hetzler, E. Visualizing Geospatial Information Uncertainty: What We Know and What We Need to Know. *Information Science 32* (2005), 160.
30. Mashhadi, A., Quattrone, G., Capra, L., and Mooney, P. On the Accuracy of Urban Crowd-Sourcing for Maintaining Large-Scale Geospatial Databases. In *Proc. of WikiSym*, ACM (2012).
31. Neis, P., Zielstra, D., and Zipf, A. Comparison of Volunteered Geographic Information Data Contributions and Community Development for Selected World Regions. *Future Internet 5*, 2 (2013), 282–300.
32. Neis, P., and Zipf, A. Analyzing the Contributor Activity of a Volunteered Geographic Information ProjectThe Case of OpenStreetMap. *ISPRS International Journal of Geo-Information 1*, 2 (2012), 146–165.
33. Panciera, K., Halfaker, A., and Terveen, L. Wikipedians Are Born, Not Made: a Study of Power Editors on Wikipedia. In *Proc. of GROUP*, ACM (2009), 51–60.
34. Pfeil, U., Zaphiris, P., and Ang, C. S. Cultural Differences in Collaborative Authoring of Wikipedia. *Journal of Computer-Mediated Communication 12*, 1 (2006), 88–113.
35. Priedhorsky, R., Lam, S., Panciera, K., Terveen, L., and Riedl, J. Creating, Destroying, and Restoring Value in Wikipedia. In *Proc. of GROUP*, ACM (2007), 259–268.

36. Priedhorsky, R., Masli, M., and Terveen, L. Eliciting and Focusing Geographic Volunteer Work. In *Proc. of CSCW*, ACM (2010), 61–70.

37. Quattrone, G., Mashhadi, A., and Capra, L. Mind the Map: The Impact of Culture and Economic Affluence on Crowd-Mapping Behaviours. In *Proc. of CSCW*, ACM (2014), 934–944.

38. Reinecke, K., Nguyen, M. K., Bernstein, A., Näf, M., and Gajos, K. Doodle Around the World: Online Scheduling Behavior Reflects Cultural Differences in Time Perception and Group Decision-Making. In *Proc. of CSCW*, ACM (2013), 45–54.

39. Rost, M., Barkhuus, L., Cramer, H., and Brown, B. Representation and Communication: Challenges in Interpreting Large Social Media Datasets. In *Proc. of CSCW*, ACM (2013), 357–362.

40. Shannon, C. A Mathematical Theory of Communication. *The Bell System Technical Journal 27* (1948), 379–423 and 623–656.

41. Singhal, A. Modern Information Retrieval: A Brief Overview. *Bulletin of the IEEE Computer Society Technical Committee on Data Engineering 24*, 4 (2001), 35–43.

42. Stephens, M. Gender and the GeoWeb: Divisions in the Production of User-Generated Cartographic Information. *GeoJournal* (2013), 1–16.

43. Vasconcelos, M., Ricci, S., Almeida, J., Benevenuto, F., and Almeida, V. Tips, Dones and ToDos: Uncovering User Profiles in FourSquare. In *Proc. of WSDM*, ACM (2012), 653–662.

44. Zielstra, D., and Zipf, A. A Comparative Study of Proprietary Geodata and Volunteered Geographic Information for Germany. In *Proc. of AGILE* (2010).

Monetizing Network Hospitality: Hospitality and Sociability in the Context of Airbnb

Tapio Ikkala[1,2]
[1] Helsinki Institute for Information Technology HIIT/Aalto University
P.O. Box 15600, 00076 Aalto
FINLAND
tapio.ikkala@helsinki.fi

Airi Lampinen[1,2]
[2] University of Helsinki
Department of Social Research
P.O. Box 54, 00014 University of Helsinki
FINLAND
airi.lampinen@iki.fi

ABSTRACT

We present a qualitative study of hospitality exchange processes that take place via the online peer-to-peer platform Airbnb. We explore 1) what motivates individuals to monetize network hospitality and 2) how the presence of money ties in with the social interaction related to network hospitality. We approach the topic from the perspective of hosts – that is, Airbnb users who participate by offering accommodation for other members in exchange for monetary compensation. We found that participants were motivated to monetize network hospitality for both financial and social reasons. Our analysis indicates that the presence of money can provide a helpful frame for network hospitality, supporting hosts in their efforts to accomplish desired sociability, select guests consistent with their preferences, and control the volume and type of demand. We conclude the paper with a critical discussion of the implications of our findings for network hospitality and, more broadly, for the so-called sharing economy.

Author Keywords

Network hospitality; sociability; hospitality exchange; money; sharing economy; collaborative consumption; Airbnb

ACM Classification Keywords

H.5.m. Information interfaces and presentation (e.g., HCI): Miscellaneous.

General Terms

Human Factors

INTRODUCTION

Peer-to-peer online platforms afford novel collaborative practices related to the sharing and exchange of both tangible and non-tangible goods and services such as space, skills, time, and money. Well-known examples of these platforms include the hospitality exchange services Couchsurfing and Airbnb. The two share several key characteristics: Firstly, users of the Couchsurfing and Airbnb sites are required to create a *profile*, through which they can make a listing, offering a free place to stay or space for rent, respectively. The profile is also needed when a user wants to request hospitality from others. Secondly, in addition to profiles trust between users is fostered, in both services, with the help of a public recommendation system wherein users are encouraged to rate and review each other after each hospitality exchange. Regardless of the similarities, there is also a crucial difference between the two: Airbnb is focused on short-term peer-to-peer rentals with a well-defined "price tag" attached to them, whereas Couchsurfing fosters hospitality that is offered with the expectation of no direct compensation, on the basis of generalized reciprocity within the community.

The social interaction and the exchange of accommodation that occur via hospitality-exchange services have been referred to as *network hospitality*. When coining the term, in the context of Couchsurfing, Germann Molz [10, p. 216] defined network hospitality as the way people "*connect to one another using online networking systems, as well as to the kinds of relationships they perform when they meet each other offline and face to face.*"

Previous studies [see e.g. 10 for an overview] have examined practices of network hospitality in the Couchsurfing community, where the hospitality exchange is, as a rule, devoid of monetary transactions. We add to the emergent body of research on network hospitality by examining hospitality-exchange processes that take place via Airbnb, a service that promotes monetizing network hospitality. We present a qualitative study that explores 1) what motivates individuals to monetize network hospitality and 2) how the presence of money ties in with the social interaction related to network hospitality in the context of Airbnb. Our study approaches the topic from the perspective of *hosts* – Airbnb users who participate in the network by offering accommodation for other members in exchange for monetary compensation.

Prior research on network hospitality [3,9,10,11] highlights that the pleasant and meaningful social encounters that hospitality exchange facilitates are an important motivation

CSCW 2015, March 14–18, 2015, Vancouver, BC, Canada.

ACM 978-1-4503-2922-4/15/03...$15.00.
http://dx.doi.org/10.1145/2675133.2675274

for participation. From an ethnographic study of Couchsurfing, Bialski [3, pp. 44–5] argues that host–guest interaction in network hospitality can be conceived of as a form of *sociability*: a form of association into which people enter for the sake of "*the sheer pleasure of the company of others*." This conceptualization originated with sociologist Georg Simmel [22, p. 255], who depicted sociability as an intrinsically rewarding "*play-form of association*" that "*has no ulterior end* [...] *but the satisfaction of the impulse to sociability*."

We found that, while the possibility of earning money is an important factor in igniting participation, the social aspects of network hospitality play a central role in sustaining hosts' motivation to keep participating. Moreover, our analysis shows that the presence of money provides hospitality exchange with a structure and formality that contributes to the hosts' sense of control and ease of participation. This is manifested in various phases of the hospitality-exchange process, from decisions about who to host to the resulting social interaction with guests.

Hosts often try to select guests who are in some way similar to them. The inclusion of money in the exchange alters the social roles of guests and hosts participating in network hospitality by moving them towards those of customer and service provider. This shift makes host–guest interaction less of an obligation, even for the host. It does not, however, exclude the possibility of sociable interaction between host and guest. Our analysis suggests that the inclusion of money in exchange relations may contribute to favorable conditions for sociable interaction since it removes a sense of obligation of intense social interaction between hosts and guests, allowing host–guest relations to develop on a more voluntary basis. We conclude by discussing the implications of these findings for further research, design, and policy efforts in the domain of network hospitality and the "sharing economy" more broadly.

RELATED WORK

Our theoretical framework draws on 1) literature on the nature and functions of hospitality, 2) Simmel's notion of sociability and his theorization on the role of money in structuring social relationships, as well as, 3) previous research regarding network hospitality.

Hospitality and Sociability

Brotheron [4] has defined hospitality in terms of exchange, emphasizing the relationship between the host and the guest, the two fundamental parties in hospitality. Hospitality is framed here as an exchange that incorporates both material and symbolic transactions, including offering accommodation, food, drink, and expressions of gratitude.

Arguing from an anthropological point of view, Selwyn [20] states that hospitality can be seen as a fundamental form of social interaction that establishes solidarity and feelings of togetherness between people. Acts of hospitality establish and consolidate links between individuals and groups; thereby, hospitality is an important social form holding societies together [20].

Importantly with respect to the topic of this paper, Morrison et al. [18] point out that hospitality can be either conditional or unconditional; that is, it can be acted out for purposes of making a profit or be offered without any expectation of compensation from the receiving party. In other words, the exchange relationship between the guest and the host may be either negotiated, in which case two individuals bargain and discuss the terms of the exchange beforehand, or generalized, in which case there is no expectation of direct reciprocity between the parties to the exchange [6].

Lashley [13] identifies three partly overlapping domains of hospitality: social, private, and commercial. The social domain of hospitality refers to the social setting in which hospitality takes place, along with the social functions of hospitality. The private domain incorporates the ways in which hospitality is acted out in domestic settings. Finally, the commercial domain has to do with the provision of hospitality as an economic activity (for example, at guest-houses and hotels). We situate the network hospitality that takes place via Airbnb at the intersection of these three domains: it is a private form of hospitality, for the hosts accommodate the guests in their homes (or at other properties that they own), in line with their own preferences and customs. Yet, because the hospitality is offered in return for financial compensation, a commercial element is present too. Finally, the hospitality exchange that Airbnb promotes is part of the emerging culture of network hospitality, a form of hospitality that takes place between individuals from around the globe and leverages online social networking tools to enable and coordinate peer-to-peer exchange.

It is notable that hospitality is often understood to go beyond its material aspects: the social interaction between the host(s) and the guest(s) is an important aspect of how hospitality plays out. It is when we view hospitality from this point of view, that Simmel's [22] idea of sociability becomes relevant. This is because we argue that ideally the host-guest interaction evolves in the frame of sociability, a stylized form of being together where sociality, often in the form of casual conversation, becomes an end in itself [22]. Sociability gains its value from interaction in its own right, rather than some ulterior motive or a practical purpose [22].

Sociability is an essentially reciprocal mode of interaction in which tact is of great importance. Participants should avoid both excessive bragging about status and excessively overt expressions of personal troubles and faults. That is, in Simmel's [22] terminology, one should not cross either the upper or the lower threshold of what is appropriate. Moreover, sociability is "homogenic interaction" in which participants are expected to act as if all interacting parties were equal and genuinely equally respected. Moreover, it is indispensable for the contents of the sociable "chat" to be interesting for all participants, in order to allow for a lively exchange of talk. As we will discuss later in the paper, these requirements explain, in part, why it can be easiest to accomplish sociable interaction with people who are similar to oneself in social standing, interests, and favored codes of interaction. This tendency to homophily is especially interesting in the context of hospitality exchange, since one could argue that the social value hospitality brings to the hosts often feeds upon the effort to cope with the uncertainty of hosting a "stranger" [5], an interesting but unfamiliar person.

Network Hospitality

As noted above, network hospitality refers to how those engaging with hospitality-exchange services connect to one another via online social networking systems, as well as, to the kinds of relationships they perform when they meet face to face [9,10]. Members of these networks can engage in hospitality exchange by hosting visitors or by staying with others as guests. The idea that hospitality exchange is not just about accommodation but also a matter of meeting people and engaging in mutually meaningful social interaction is well documented in previous research on network hospitality [3,9,10].

The concept of network hospitality has its roots in Wittel's [24] notion of network sociality. Network sociality refers to contemporary forms of association and social interaction, which, according to Wittel, increasingly consist of and are composed around flexible networks of various kinds rather than stable communities. Building on this idea, the concept of network hospitality draws attention to the interplay between hospitality and technology and to the ways in which strangers encounter one another in a mobile and networked society [10].

Network hospitality is a relatively new phenomenon [9,10], although the practice is rooted in ancient traditions of hospitality and welcoming strangers. Its more recent historical precursors include various formal and informal hospitality networks of people who would provide meals, transportation, accommodation, or other aid for traveling strangers. For example, Adler [1], in her historical analysis of "tramping," describes how trade societies established networks of homes and inns to accommodate traveling craftsmen in early nineteenth-century England.

An example of early, more institutionalized, networks of hospitality exchange is Servas International [9,10]. It was founded after the Second World War as a non-profit cooperative to promote tolerance and world peace through cultural exchange. The members' contact details were published and distributed on paper, and participants relied on telephone contact and hand-written letters to coordinate hospitality exchanges. By the late 1990s, the Internet had made pegging through printed lists obsolete as several hospitality-exchange organizations, among them Hospitality Club, Global Freeloaders, and Hospitality Exchange, appeared online [9]. As was Servas International, these networks were primarily non-profit projects guided by the belief that travel, interpersonal exchanges between people from different countries, and the generous offering of free hospitality could spread tolerance, friendship, and even world peace.

Beyond accommodation, examples of network hospitality include ride-sharing, meal-sharing, and travel-sharing wherein locals show travelers around their town [9]. All of these practices leverage online platforms to facilitate offline social interaction and the exchange of material and sociable resources [9]. In sum, networked technologies are creating new hybrid spaces of social interaction, incorporating "*complex interplay of mobility and immobility, online and offline interaction, brief but intense encounters, and local articulations of a global project*" [9, pp. 216–7].

Money and Hospitality

As said, sometimes hosts may (and are expected to) ask for compensation for their efforts. Dernoi's [7] article from the 1980s suggests that hospitality exchange wherein private individuals and families accommodate travelers in their homes for a fee was widespread, although much more scattered, already before the appearance of enterprises such as Airbnb. Moreover, in between private households and commercial hospitality businesses there are what Lynch *et al.* [15] label *commercial homes*, including small hotels, bed and breakfasts, and family accommodations. While accommodating guests often provides an essential stream of income for those running commercial homes, the practice also allows for social engagement with the guests, such as receiving gifts and hearing interesting stories of guests' home country [15]. While Airbnb does afford such professionalized hosting, none of our participants were taking advantage of this opportunity. Rather, all of them carried out hosting in (what used to be) their leisure time.

According to Simmel [21], the use of money as a means of exchange frees people from various kinds of traditional and moral constraints, thereby contributing to their personal autonomy. Simultaneously, the indifference of money has a rationalizing and homogenizing effect on the life and interactions of individuals. Simmel [21] argues that, while money affords precision and calculability in social relations, it creates indifference and increases the social distance between actors. Accordingly, it seems unlikely that monetized hospitality exchange could lead to the non-instrumental, voluntary, and enjoyable social interactions that previous research has associated with practices of non-monetary network hospitality.

However, we argue that the potential distance that money creates between actors does not exclude the possibility of meaningful, sociable interaction between individuals. On the contrary, we claim that the presence of money and the existence of a clear price for the network hospitality that is being offered may provide conditions in which sociable interaction can flourish – even more easily than it might in non-monetary network hospitality, wherein concerns over indebtedness and reciprocity may complicate interpersonal connections. Bialski [3, p. 75] has expressed a similar idea in relation to hitchhiking Web sites via which passengers pay for the ride. She reflects on how the presence of money can change the social dynamics of the situation: "*Perhaps the sociality that emerges despite the explicit nature of the reciprocity deems the conversation less instrumental, more voluntary, than the conversation and interaction in some cases during the implicit reciprocity between Couchsurfers.*"

To the best of our knowledge, no previous studies have examined network hospitality from the perspective of individuals who offer hosting via hospitality-exchange platforms that promote monetizing network hospitality. We address this gap with our analysis of what motivates people to monetize network hospitality and how money is woven into the resulting social interaction.

MATERIAL AND METHODS

We present findings from a qualitative case study comprising 11 in-depth semi-structured interviews with, all in all, 12 participants from 11 households who had listed space for short-term rental via Airbnb in the Helsinki Metropolitan Area, Finland. We will now describe in more detail our participants, as well as, present the interview and analysis procedures we applied.

Participants

We recruited the participants through the Airbnb platform. The first author created a profile on the site in order to contact potential participants. The only prerequisite for participation in the study was that the person had hosted at least one guest prior to the interview and was managing an active listing for an Airbnb rental in the Helsinki Metropolitan Area at the time of recruitment.

Participants' age varied from 22 to 58. Seven subjects were male and five female. Four of them were living alone, one shared a flat with two housemates, and seven lived with a partner (four of the latter had children, too, in their household). In one household, both adults were present for the interview. Other interviews were conducted one-on-one with the person managing the Airbnb profile. One of the households was in the city center, nine were in urban areas relatively close to the city center, and one was in a suburban area. Seven participants lived in an owner-occupied flat while the other five had a lease.

The number of guests our participants had hosted ranged from just one to over 30. Four of the participating households had hosted fewer than 10 guests, seven more than 20. The participant with the most hosting experience had listed her apartment on Airbnb in March 2012, while the most inexperienced had joined the service just a month before the interview. Eight subjects had experienced Airbnb also as guests, while the remaining four had participated solely by hosting. Two of the interviewees had experience of other hospitality-exchange networks (i.e. Couchsurfing) – one as a host and the other as a guest.

For a final characterization, we identified two primary modes of hosting through Airbnb. We use the label *remote hospitality* for hosting situations wherein the host is not physically sharing the home (or other property he or she manages) with the guest and instead lodges somewhere else during the guest's stay. Here, the interaction with the guest is typically limited to messages exchanged through the Airbnb service, e-mail, SMS contact, phone calls, and the occasional quick encounters in which the keys to the apartment are handed over and final details of the stay are discussed. Another way to perform hosting through Airbnb is by being physically present and sharing the apartment with the guest. An example of this is renting out a spare bedroom or one's living room. We refer to this mode of hosting as *on-site hospitality*. In our study, five participating households practiced remote hospitality, while the other six engaged in on-site hospitality.

Interview Procedure

The interviews were conducted the Helsinki Metropolitan Area in June–August 2013. At the time, there were, in total, around 400 Airbnb hosts in and around Helsinki; monetizing network hospitality via Airbnb was still a relatively novel phenomenon in this locale. The interviews were conducted by the first author at a location of the participant's choosing, either in their home or at a public venue such as a café. No compensation was offered for participation.

The interviews were semi-structured. The first author conducted two pilot interviews in order to test and refine the interview procedure. The pilot interviewees were acquaintances of the second author. They were active Airbnb hosts in the area at the time. On the basis of our observations from these interviews, the interview procedure was modified slightly for smooth flow, and some questions were added to make the interviews more comprehensive. The pilot interviews were used solely to improve the interview procedure. They are not included in the set of 11 interviews that forms our research material.

The interview outline was designed to elicit a holistic account of the participant's hosting experiences. The interviews started with questions addressing matters such as how the participant had first heard of Airbnb, whether he or she had used Airbnb also as a guest, whether the interviewee had experience of other hospitality-exchange networks, and how any such experiences differed from those related to Airbnb. These questions were followed by a set of questions related to the participant's motivations for Airbnb hosting. The interview then proceeded to cover the respondent's presence on the Airbnb Web site, including how he or she determined the price for the listing.

Participants were then invited to describe how they decided which inquiries to accept and how they communicated with guests before their stay. In addition, we asked questions about the hospitality exchange itself, including how stays were arranged; what kinds of things the participants felt they needed to take into consideration when hosting someone; and whether there had been any problematic, troubling, or otherwise unsuccessful exchanges. Finally, each participant was given an opportunity to bring up any topics that he or she felt had been left out or been given too little attention. Background information, such as the participant's age, level of education, and profession, along with the estimated number of guests hosted so far, was collected with a paper form at the end of the interview. The forms were left to the end of the interview since our prior interview experiences from Finland indicated that beginning with demographic inquiries does not aid in building a relaxed and comfortable atmosphere and might even be interpreted as meddlesome.

The interviews were audio-recorded and transcribed verbatim. All interviews were conducted in Finnish; with the exception of those of two participants who did not speak Finnish and so were interviewed in English, instead. Because the interviews were conducted primarily in Finnish, most interview excerpts are translations from the original Finnish transcripts. In the following, we refer to the participants pseudonymously to protect their anonymity.

Analysis

We chose a qualitative interpretative approach for the study in order to balance leveraging prior work with approaching our research material in an explorative manner. While Germann Molz's conceptualization of network hospitality and Simmel's theorizing on sociability served as the main theoretical frames for our study, the empirical analysis was grounded in the research material [23], since we wanted to foreground the participants' perspectives and approach their experiences of monetizing network hospitality in a material-driven fashion.

We began the analysis by reading through the transcripts, paying attention to any recurrent themes that could elucidate our research problem. Through this initial analysis, we identified four categories for use to frame our further analysis. The first author coded all sections of the interview transcripts that were interpreted as illustrating 1) motivations underlying the practice of monetizing network hospitality, 2) the role of money in the exchange process, 3) the resulting host–guest interaction, and 4) the ways in which hosts choose their guests. The excerpts containing descriptions of the motives for participating in Airbnb as a host were then open-coded, with a focus on the various ways in which the participants described their hosting motivations. The findings from this part of the analysis are presented in the first part of the next section of the paper. The other three categories were analyzed in detail and compared to one another. This was done to uncover themes characterizing the practice of Airbnb hosting, the resulting sociality, and the role money plays in the two. We labeled the resulting themes "sociability," "selectivity," and "control." They are presented in the latter subsection of the next section.

FINDINGS

The presentation of our findings has two parts. Firstly, we describe the intertwining of social and financial motives underlying participants' decision to monetize network hospitality. Secondly, we discuss how the presence of money plays into the emerging sociability and depict how monetary transactions and the possibility of using pricing as a tactic can help hosts to achieve desirable experiences.

Social and Financial Hosting Motivations

Our analysis shows that the financial gains Airbnb hosting can provide are an important factor driving hosts' participation. However, for most of our participants the money made through Airbnb was not an indispensable part of total income. Often, the money that was made by hosting was not used for unavoidable living expenses; rather, it was seen as a "nice extra" that could be used, for example, for travel. For example, Pia, a 25-year-old woman who practiced remote hospitality by renting out her two-room apartment via Airbnb (while she was out of town), shared the following account of how monetizing network hospitality had allowed her to fund travel with her significant other:

"*Well, yeah, the money has been nice. I have already funded a few of our trips with the money I've made this way.*" (Pia, 25)

Only one out of our 11 participants, 22-year-old Kaisa, described the financial gains made by hosting visitors via Airbnb as of significant financial importance personally. She was a host who practiced remote hospitality by renting out her room in a flat she shared with two roommates. She recounted making efforts to rent her room out for at least a few nights each month so that she could use the money she made this way to cover some of her rent.

While a commonly cited reason for engaging in the practice of monetizing network hospitality, the possibility of making a profit was typically described as supplementary to the social motives for engaging in network hospitality. These included the opportunity to meet new people from around the world and incorporating more social interaction or a new kind of interaction into one's life. For example, Ida and Sami, a couple living a busy life with three children and two full-time jobs, highly valued the novel sociality that Airbnb hosting had brought to their lives. They practiced on-site hospitality by renting out a private room in their city-center flat. For them, receiving guests through Airbnb functioned as a departure from the mundane rhythm of everyday life. Hosting visitors provided a welcome opportunity to engage in meaningful social interaction in a manageable way, meaning that they could freely limit who they would host, how frequently, and for how long:

"[...] *if we would not do this, it could be even a bit dull sometimes, you know, since our everyday life pretty much consists of just working and taking kids to their hobbies and so on. It can be quite hectic.* [...] *Since we have a family, we can't just decide with Ida to, for example, go to a salsa class to meet new people.*" (Sami, 31)

In another example case, Alfonso, a 53-year-old foreigner living and working in Helsinki, stressed the importance of the social nature of network hospitality as a reason for engaging in Airbnb hosting. For him, renting out a private room in his two-room apartment was, in essence, a way to meet new people, since his social circle in Helsinki was relatively small and at times felt insufficient to him:

"*For me, it's not that easy to meet people here in Helsinki. Of course, I could go to a bar or something, but it's not that easy for people of my age to meet people like that. But sometimes I have really nice conversations and moments with my guests, people who are total strangers to me. I think it's similar to what happens when you are traveling. You meet people on trains and airplanes, and it's just easy to connect with them.*" (Alfonso, 53)

Moreover, two participants were initially prompted to engage in Airbnb hosting by the monetary compensation for hosting but then grew to appreciate the hosting as a social practice, too, once they had accumulated more experience of network hospitality. Tomi, 33, was a remote host who rented out his investment apartment through Airbnb. Therefore, he initially had a more straightforwardly businesslike attitude to hosting than our other participants. However, Tomi too noted that one reason he had been pleased with his hosting arrangement was, indeed, the possibility for pleasant sociable interaction with the guests. Although Tomi practiced remote hospitality and did not stay with the guests, he reported that at times he might invite guests to take a little tour around the city with him:

"[...] *there is always a potential of meeting people, interesting people.* [...] *[T]here have already been quite a few guests whom I've really connected with and who have been quite similar to me or have a mindset similar to mine.*" (Tomi, 33)

Importantly, Tomi could freely choose when to initiate such interaction, and he described doing so only when he felt that he was likely to get along well with the guests and that he might enjoy their company. Thus, although Tomi was predominantly hosting for reasons other than the sociable interaction that network hospitality can entail, he was able to move away from the business-oriented mindset when he so desired and engage in social interaction with guests. Of course, whether the guests chose to take up his invitations was always up to them, but at the time of the interview Tomi's experience had been satisfying.

Mikael, a 41-year-old professor, was prompted to engage in Airbnb hosting by his wish to put the extra space he and his family had in the basement of their apartment to better use and to earn some money by doing so. His views on interaction with the guests were similar to those of Tomi. He explained how, at the start of his time as a host, he had been rather unsure of how it would feel to let a stranger into their house, what would be an appropriate amount of interaction with the guest, and what his guests would think of the hosting arrangement. However, in the course of receiving guests, it had turned out that he actually enjoyed hosting:

"*It has been nice to meet these people. I haven't talked to all of them an awful lot, but it has still been nice. This has brought, like, this new sort of sociality to my life.*" (Mikael, 41)

It is noteworthy that even some of the participants who practiced remote hospitality appreciated the social nature of the hosting. They found hosting socially enjoyable even though they did not usually spend time with their guests face to face, instead just preparing the apartment for the guest's arrival and then lodging somewhere else during the guest's stay. Despite the minimal in-person interaction embedded in their hosting arrangements, some of these hosts wanted to establish a host–guest relationship with their guests. Often, this was accomplished through small acts of hospitality such as making sure that the guests are offered a little to eat when they arrive, or giving them advice and recommendations on what to do during their stay in the city. Pia was among those with this kind of orientation towards remote hospitality:

"*I'll always try to think about how to make the guest's stay an unforgettable experience – you know, make them feel like, "Wow!"* [...]. *I'll make sure that there's some fruit or maybe some Finnish candy for the guests as they arrive, and if I have time maybe I'll leave some nice flowers on the table.*" (Pia, 25)

The hosts engaging in these acts of hospitality found it very rewarding and pleasing if the acts were recognized and acknowledged by the guests, either through the reviews posted on the host's Airbnb profile page or, considered even better, by unofficial and more personal means such as the leaving of a postcard or hand-written note for the host. Pia described this:

"*These letters and notes that people leave here are the best. Almost everyone has left a personal note or at least sent an e-mail message in addition to the official review done through the Web site.*"

In a similar vein, Pertti described the personal hand-written messages he had received from guests as one of the most rewarding aspects of hosting, creating a sense of warmth:

"*One of the most gratifying things has been the personal hand-written messages I have received from my guests. Airbnb automatically reminds people to write the reviews, but no one asks the guest to leave you a personal note. Also, the occasions when I have received, for example, a text message where the guests say that they [have] followed my hint and gone to some restaurant or event I had suggested for them are very nice. They give you a warm feeling.*" (Pertti, 33)

Interestingly, these descriptions reveal that although the terms of the exchange relation are negotiated beforehand, the hosts very much appreciate informal acknowledgment of their hospitality efforts. It thus seems that in monetized network hospitality there still exists a residue of traditional forms of hospitality exchange, as described for example in ethnographic accounts of Mauss [16] and Malinowski [17], in which exchange of material and symbolic gifts play an important role in establishing and consolidating social ties between groups and individuals.

In summary, even though the opportunity to monetize network hospitality – that is, to make a financial profit by offering hosting – was an important reason for the participants' engagement with Airbnb, the sociable interaction that has been recognized as an important driver of network hospitality in prior research was very visibly present also in the accounts of our participants. These findings complicate the narrative of how the inclusion of monetary transactions in the hospitality-exchange process affects the resulting social interactions, because they point out that, at least some Airbnb hosts are driven to monetize network hospitality not just because of the money they can make but also because they find the sociality of the practice pleasurable. In brief, the financial and social motivations that drive individuals to monetize network hospitality need not be contradictory with one another.

The Presence of Money in Network Hospitality

Our analysis indicates that the presence of money can provide a helpful frame for network hospitality. It can support hosts in their efforts to accomplish desired sociable interaction, to choose guests selectively in line with their preferences, and to control the volume and type of demand from potential visitors.

Sociability

The social interaction that practicing network hospitality spurs is an important reason for Airbnb hosting. Yet, among our participants, none of the hosts who sought social interaction with their guests talked about the sociality of network hospitality within the framework of "making new friends" or creating lasting or long-term social relationships. Instead, participants described the sociality of network hospitality more commonly in terms of enjoyable and/or inspiring moments in which one can spend time with interesting, previously unfamiliar people from around the world and engage in intriguing conversations with them. Participants reported enjoying these moments of social interaction as such, but they did not expect that the relationships with their guests would extend beyond the guests' visit. Alfonso used the following wording to describe his feelings on the topic:

"*We might have breakfast and dinner together and have interesting conversations. It's often really nice, but I haven't kept in touch with any of them.* [...] *I just haven't felt like it.*" (Alfonso, 53)

This sociality that participants sought can be understood in terms of sociability – a form of sociality that gains its value from the interaction itself. Many of the participants reported that they found the possibility of meeting interesting people with diverse cultural backgrounds intriguing and rewarding:

"*You can actually meet some nice and interesting people through hosting.* [...] *For example, I got to meet this Italian fashion designer as he stayed at my place. These kinds of things are nice, because when you think about it, how on earth could I've met this guy if he wouldn't have been my guest? You can't just go and stop people on the street and be like, 'You look interesting. Would you like to hang out?'*" (Kaisa, 22)

The hosts we interviewed often deemed the social encounters with their guests enjoyable but still stated that they had no inclination to extend those social relations beyond the one-time, short-term hospitality exchange at hand. The sociality of monetized network hospitality can, therefore, be interpreted as a form of social "play" in which participants engage for the sheer pleasure it brings, without any expectation of it leading to more serious or lasting social relationships. This echoes Simmel's notion of sociability, along with findings from prior research on non-monetary network hospitality. The difference, though, is that, alongside the value seen in sociability, there are financial profits at stake for the hosts (and presumably for the guests, too, for whom peer-to-peer accommodation is often a cheaper alternative than staying in a hotel).

Selectivity

Our participants mentioned the opportunity to engage in sociable interaction with people from around the world as a key reason for practicing Airbnb hosting. However, accomplishing the sociable interaction the hosts were hoping for was not always a foregone conclusion. Time constraints, differences in interests, or a sense of not really seeing eye to eye with one's visitors could get in the way of shared moments of sociability.

For example, Kaisa, a host who reported subletting her room via Airbnb a few times a month, expressed enthusiasm for meeting new people through her practice of monetizing network hospitality. Occasionally, she would host Couchsurfers, too. However, she felt that hosting could get tiresome if there was a mismatch in expectations between the guest and the host. She explained that this seemed to be more common in the case of non-monetary network hospitality than when the practice was monetized and hospitality came with a clear price tag:

"*The attitude is often that since you are charging these people, they think that you should somehow be in the background, whereas through Couchsurfing,* [the guests] *ask you to be their guide or boyfriend or girlfriend or whatever. It can sometimes be a bit annoying if you are not really in the mood for that or you are just busy. Usually people who come through Airbnb are a bit more independent, and they don't expect that much from you.*" (Kaisa, 22)

We can see that, while the money Kaisa could make by hosting Airbnb guests was important for her, she also felt that, at times, monetizing network hospitality was preferable because it made the hosting socially easier. Kaisa was eager to socialize with her guests, but she wanted to do it in accordance with her own preferences – that is, selectively, when she felt like it and with those guests she found interesting. This example indicates that monetary transactions can contribute to the host's sense of control, and her/his comfort with, the hospitality exchange. This may be because when hospitality exchange takes place in a *quid pro quo* fashion, it is easier for the host to withdraw if she/he feels that the social interaction with the guest is becoming burdensome. It seems that when network hospitality is monetized, the normal perceived obligation of host–guest interaction is reduced somewhat. This relaxation of a felt obligation to be sociable is echoed in the following account from Tomi, who, in addition to Airbnb hosting, had experience of being a guest through Couchsurfing:

"*I think that in Couchsurfing both the host and the guest are expected to show interest towards each other and to spend some time together. In Airbnb, the guest is paying for the accommodation, so (s)he is not expected or obliged to socialize that much with the host. So this also means that if the host wants to be more in the background, he can do that.*" (Tomi, 33)

Many respondents received various inquiries from potential guests, which often left them the opportunity to choose which guests to accept from a pool of potential candidates. In our participants' accounts, the evaluation of potential guests was based on the guests' profiles, the reviews they had received from prior exchanges, and the communication that took place prior to accepting of the accommodation request. Our participants emphasized how much they valued the fact that they knew in advance who they were going to be hosting. They felt that viewing a guest's profile gave them insight into what kind of person the guest would be, and this allowed them to be intentional in choosing which people to host:

"*The fact that you can choose who comes there is nice. I just pretty much use my intuition in choosing the guests and try to choose guests who seem nice, you know, so that I might even spend some time with them if I feel like it.*" (Tomi, 33)

Our participants made efforts to increase the likelihood of an enjoyable hospitality exchange by deliberately selecting guests they expected to be easy to host. Often this meant selecting individuals who were in some respect similar to the host him- or herself:

"*Mostly I choose to host young people, often students or people who have quite recently graduated from a university.* [...] *They are easy to get along with, and often we have something in common or are in a similar phase in our lives.*" (Sophia, 22)

"*For the most part, our guests have been highly educated and they are in interesting jobs. They are the kind of people with whom it is easy for us to find some common ground, and, therefore, the conversations have often been very interesting.*" (Sami, 31)

While these considerations are beyond the scope of this study, it is necessary to point out that the guests can, of course, make similar evaluations regarding potential hosts as they look for a place to stay. Some participants acknowledged this possibility and described how, to attract guests with interests similar to theirs, they had included a lot of information about themselves and their interests in their profiles:

"*I try to give a good picture of who I am in the profile because then the guest who is interested in staying at my place will likely be a kind of person whom I am interested in hosting. For example, I state here that I am not into drinking or smoking and that I really like to talk to people. And mostly the guests who end up at my place are quite similar to me.*" (Sophia, 22)

This tendency to look for and choose guests who are similar to the host or who share his or her interests is in line with Simmel's reflections on the circumstances in which sociable interaction is likely to occur. The similarity and equal social standing of the interacting parties is a central condition for sociable interaction. However, it is interesting to find this tendency to homophily in a practice like network hospitality, in which meeting people with different cultural backgrounds plays a central role in igniting participation in the first place.

Among our participants there were a few who openly stated that they did not wish to host people from specific countries, people of certain ethnicity, or people of a particular age. Sophia explicitly stated that, because of previous bad experiences of subletting, she chose not to host people from India or "black people". She went on to explain that she knew that this kind of selectivity is "*not a good thing*" but that she knowingly did it anyway, on account of the negative experiences of subletting her room in previous apartments:

"[These experiences] *have related to subletting my room in my previous apartments. 'Cause I am a student and I've been abroad quite a lot, I've had to sublet my room and it's annoying when you want to rent out a room and someone just causes trouble all the time.*" (Sophia, 22)

Similarly, Ida and Sami, Markku, and Pertti stated that they were "*maybe a bit more selective*" when it came to accepting Russian guests. However, they often expressed awareness that this kind of discriminatory behavior is not necessarily a good thing and that hey have tried to avoid practicing it:

"*Well, if I think about who we have declined most, they're probably Russian people. We've hosted Russian guests, but still I notice that I think twice before I accept. It's a big and diverse country, and I know I shouldn't think this way, but still...*" (Ida, 35)

These expressions of discriminatory attitudes and behaviors illustrate how, upon closer examination, the discourse of taking part in network hospitality because of the wish to engage in cosmopolitan cultural exchange by hosting people from around the world may not be the whole story. While the participants seemed to be truly motivated to meet new people, they often preferred to host people who were similar to them in some, or many, ways. As a result, the networks of social encounters that network hospitality fosters may not be as inclusive and boundary-spanning as the hype around Airbnb and other similar services might lead one to believe.

Control

Our analysis reveals that hosts do not determine the price for their hospitality solely via profit-maximizing economic thinking. Instead of always trying to find the optimal "market price," participants explained that they factor in social considerations. These consisted of the type of guests they wish to host, together with their expectations regarding whom they can attract or avoid. Also, they depended on how cheap or expensive an offering they wanted to make.

For example, Pia had priced her listing somewhat above what she believed to be the average price for the type of accommodation she was offering. She explained that she chose to do this in order to keep out "troublemakers":

"*I could sure get more guests if I would lower the price.* [...] *But I've wanted to keep the price a bit high 'cause I want to— How should I put it? Well, sort of reach a slightly higher standard. So I want especially those guests to contact me who are looking for an above-average place to stay. Because I think this flat is quite nice and then I can also go to a little extra effort of making sure that they have, for example, some food waiting here as they arrive and so forth. And maybe the higher price keeps the worst troublemakers and exploiters away.*" (Pia, 25)

Similarly, Ida and Sami noted that one reason for their guests having usually not been "regular backpackers" is that the price they had set for their room was not from the lower end of the spectrum:

"*Well, I have to admit that our place does not seem to draw the usual backpacker-type travelers who are just trying to manage with as small a budget as possible. On the contrary, actually. Our guests have, for the most part, been very educated people, bankers, architects, professors, and so forth.* [...] *This is, of course, at least partly due to the fact that the price we have set is not particularly cheap.*" (Ida, 35)

In a contrasting example of pricing with social factors in mind, some participants explained that they price their properties below "the market price" in order to achieve a situation wherein they have more options to choose from in selecting those to host. This arrangement relies on the logic that a lower price leads to larger numbers of inquiries from potential guests. Pertti, 33, described the benefits of asking for a price lower than what he could get as follows:

"*[T]he good thing in keeping the price a bit low* [...] *is that you get to choose* [the guests] [...]. *For the host, it is easier that way.*" (Pertti, 33)

These examples show how monetizing network hospitality is not a straightforward matter of maximizing profits. Our participants were using their ability to determine the price of hospitality to assert control over hosting situations. For some, this meant asking a higher price to tempt certain types of guests and discourage others, while other participants expected that offering accommodation for a lower price than they expected to be able to demand would result in a generally more enjoyable hosting experience.

Finally, the degree to which hosts could use pricing as a tactic for selecting guests and controlling demand was dependent on how established their own reputation was on the Airbnb platform. Many participants explained that they had started with a lower price in order to attract visitors early on and then hiked the price once they had accumulated a good reputation through positive reviews from their guests.

DISCUSSION

Overall, our participants were motivated to monetize network hospitality by acting as Airbnb hosts, both because of the financial gains they could make and for the social gratification they expected. Money was often the initial driver of getting started with hosting, but over time the social factors tended to gain in importance, even for some hosts who earlier had not been interested in the sociability that network hospitality can entail.

Money as a Frame for Network Hospitality

Our analysis indicates that the presence of money can provide a helpful frame for network hospitality, supporting hosts in their efforts to accomplish the desired sociability, to select guests in line with their preferences, and to control the volume and type of demand from potential visitors. The presence of clear-cut monetary transactions may contribute to hosts' sense of control by making it easier for the exchange partners to adopt a shared definition of the exchange situation. This, in turn, is helpful in the coordination of the entire exchange process.

Our findings indicate that the monetization of network hospitality is not a simple story wherein the introduction of monetary transactions leads to instrumental and calculative social interaction between hosts and guests, as Simmel's [21] theorizing would suggest. Sociability, similar to that observed in the context of non-monetary hospitality exchange, can persist. The presence of money may even contribute to the flourishing of voluntary, enjoyable interaction that entails no sense of obligation and that, in this, approaches Simmel's ideal of pure sociability as a valuable social form.

The presence of money has emerged as a central point of contention in ongoing debates over the nature and potential of the so-called sharing economy. On a higher structural level, there certainly seems to exist much to reconcile between the logics on which venture-backed peer-to-peer platforms operate and the ethos of cosmopolitan sharing. It is not the point of this paper to take a stance in that discussion beyond articulating the experiences of individuals who monetize network hospitality on a relatively small financial scale and for whom the sociability between hosts and guests is by no means a misplaced fantasy.

It is worthy of note that, in our study, even the hosts who practiced remote hospitality and, accordingly, had little in-person interaction with their guests still valued the social aspects of hosting. This indicates that the act of trusting strangers to stay in one's home, making efforts to ensure that they enjoy the stay, and receiving the occasional hand-written note that acknowledges these efforts can meaningfully contribute to a sense of connectedness and cosmopolitanism. Our interviewees' accounts point to a similar imagination being at play for guests, as well, who for their part strive for "authentic" experiences and value the opportunity to stay in a "local" home, even if they meet the hosts only in the passing. Yet, while our findings indicate that the presence of money can be not only harmless but even outright helpful for the sociable interaction and sense of connection many seek in engaging with network hospitality, this should not be taken as alleviating the need for researchers, designers, and policymakers to think critically about the implications money may have for network hospitality and about the effects that monetizing network hospitality may have on neighborhoods, cities, and societies at large.

Homophily and Discrimination in Network Hospitality

In the context of network hospitality, there is an interesting – and somewhat troubling – tension to the tendency to homophily. People participate in network hospitality in order to meet people from other cultures; they want to experience certain "strangeness". However, at the same time, they are selective of which "strangers" to engage with, often opting to host those who are in some way similar to them. From Ciborra's [5] point of view, this does not count as genuine hospitality, as for him hospitality is behavior that reveals a human effort to cope with the uncertainty and mystery of hosting a stranger.

If network hospitality continues to gain ground as a form of accommodation, homophily may become an increasingly serious and problematic source of discrimination. In some cases, our participants openly described discriminating against potential guests who were members of particular racial, ethnic, or age groups. Similarly, prior studies suggest that people tend to favor those who are in some way similar to them when making decisions on hospitality based on viewing the profiles of potential guests or hosts [3].

Some have expressed concern that social network sites in general increase this tendency to homophily. This may create an "echo chamber effect" wherein the diversity of one's social interaction decreases as he or she interacts only with similar others [2]. This has worrisome consequences for those who, for one reason or another, are seen as less desirable exchange partners. In a recent study, Edelman and Luca [8] compared the prices that black and non-black hosts charge for similar accommodations on Airbnb and concluded that non-black hosts charge approximately 12% more than black hosts. The authors suggest that this highlights the prevalence of discrimination in online marketplaces, revealing an important unintended consequence in the process of selecting exchange partners.

An open question remains as to whether the monetary transactions and the consequently lessened obligations for intense socializing that characterize Airbnb hosting can create room for increased openness to diversity in comparison to non-monetary forms of hospitality exchange that rely on indirect and implicit forms of reciprocity. It seems plausible that those practicing remote hospitality might be more willing to host strangers with whom they do not have a lot in common as long as they feel sufficiently assured of the guests' trustworthiness, while those who host on-site may be more likely to select guests with whom they expect to achieve the desired amount of sociability as comfortably as possible. Since both hosts and guests can gain meaningful social experiences from remote hospitality even when personal interaction remains minimal, monetizing network hospitality may, somewhat unexpectedly, promote experiences of connectedness that would be less likely to occur in the realm of non-monetary network hospitality that tends to entail an expectation of intense social interaction.

Limitations

There are several limitations to this study that must be acknowledged. Firstly, we make no claims of generalizability to Airbnb hosts, whether at large or within the Helsinki Metropolitan Area, where the interviews were conducted. It is important to bear in mind that Airbnb hosting can take on different social roles in different geographical and cultural settings, varying with, for instance, the population density of the area and the price of housing, both of which affect the type of space hosts are likely to have available in a given region and the type of hosting they can practice. Comparisons across such settings are beyond the scope of this paper, but we will reflect on their importance when outlining topics for future research. Secondly, we cannot control for the self-selection bias that may exist in our study: For instance, it is possible that those with especially positive experiences of Airbnb hosting were more likely to take part. However, the aim of the study was to explore hosts' motivations for monetizing network hospitality and to gain insight into how they conceive of the resulting sociality and the ways in which the presence of money ties in with it. We regard this study as an important first step in understanding aspects of network hospitality – and "the sharing economy" more broadly – in which monetary transactions are an integral and visible part of the practice.

Avenues for Future Research

We call for further research to map out the diversity of experiences related to monetizing network hospitality. These are likely to range from occasional hosting in one's primary home, as was seen with most of our participants, to more or even fully professionalized forms of making a profit by leveraging the opportunities that Airbnb and other, similar platforms provide. The volume of hosting, the importance of the income or savings involved for those engaging in the practice, and the degree of professionalism on the part of the hosts are but some of the factors that indicate the circumstances in which network hospitality is practiced. Future research should consider variations in the social role of hosting and the ways in which it is reflected in the resulting social interactions between hosts and guests, taking into account the life situations of the participants, the nature of the hosting location (urban/suburban/rural), the type of hospitality offered (remote/on-site), and cultural differences. The meanings and implications of monetizing network hospitality are likely to be diverse. This should be considered as the debate surrounding network hospitality and the "sharing economy" moves forward.

Furthermore, to complement our findings, it would be important to examine the perspective of Airbnb guests in depth to understand how they perceive the significance of monetary transactions in network hospitality and, for instance, the issues around selecting potential hosts and negotiating hospitality with them. One fruitful pathway for this would be to explore experiences of individuals who cross over between roles, acting as both guests and hosts. Moreover, some of our participants had experience of both Airbnb and Couchsurfing so that they were able to weigh the impact of monetization on network hospitality. Yet targeted, systematic comparison of exchange processes between systems of monetary and non-monetary exchange could benefit the field greatly, as could historically grounded analysis of earlier, even paper-based, forms of hospitality exchange and homestays. Also, as a part of the comparative endeavor, it would be helpful to examine the complex dynamics of how different types of reciprocation intertwine and play out in the course of hospitality-exchange processes. Finally, in drawing conclusions on the nature of network hospitality, when monetized or otherwise, we must critically and openly examine the diversity of experiences and granularity involved.

ACKNOWLEDGMENTS

We wish to thank Docent Juha Koivisto from University of Helsinki for his valuable advice and support. Moreover, we wish to acknowledge both our participants and our pilot interviewees. This study would not have been possible without their contributions. The research was funded with the support of the TEKES project FuNeSoMo, together with grants from Emil Aaltonen foundation and KAUTE foundation. Finally, we are thankful for our HIIT colleagues as well as the anonymous reviewers whose feedback helped us improve the paper significantly.

REFERENCES

1. Adler, J. (1985). Youth on the Road: Reflections on the History of Tramping. *Annals of Tourism Research 12*(3), 335–354.
2. boyd, d. (2005). Sociable Technology and Democracy. In Lebowsky J., Ratcliffe M. ed. *Extreme Democracy*. Lulu, 183–93.
3. Bialski, P. (2012). *Becoming Intimately Mobile*. Peter Lang
4. Brotheron, B. (1999). Towards a Definitive View of the Nature of Hospitality and Hospitality Management. *International Journal of Contemporary Hospitality Management 11*(4), 165–73.
5. Ciborra, C. U. (1996). Introduction: What Does Groupware Mean for the Organization Hosting It? In C. U. Ciborra (Eds.) *Groupware and Teamwork: Invisible Aid or Technical Hindrance.* Edited by John Wiley & Sons, 1–19.
6. Cropanzano R., Mitchell M. S. (2005). Social Exchange Theory: An Interdisciplinary Review. *Journal of Management 31*(6), 874-900.
7. Dernoi, L. A. (1981). Towards a New Style in North-South relations. *Tourism Management 2*(4), 253–264.
8. Edelman, B. G., Luca, M. (2014). Digital Discrimination: The Case of Airbnb.com. Working Paper. Harvard Business School.
9. Germann Molz, J. (2014). Toward a Network Hospitality. *First Monday 19*(3).
10. Germann Molz, J. (2011). CouchSurfing and Network Hospitality: 'It's Not Just about the Furniture.' *Hospitality and Society 1*(3), 215–25.

11. Germann Molz, J. (2007). Cosmopolitans on the Couch: Mobile Hospitality and the Internet. In J. Germann Molz & S. Gibson (Eds.) *Mobilizing Hospitality: The Ethics of Social Relations in a Mobile World.* Farnham, 65–80.

12. Heal, F. (1990). *Hospitality in Early Modern England.* Oxford University Press.

13. Lashley, C. (2000). Towards a Theoretical Understanding. In *In Search of Hospitality: Theoretical Perspectives and Debates.* Butterworth-Heinemann.

14. Lampinen, A. Account Sharing in the Context of Networked Hospitality Exchange. In *CSCW '14*. ACM Press (2014), 499–501.

15. Lynch P., Di Domenico M. L., Sweeney M. Resident Hosts and Mobile Strangers: Temporary Exchanges within the Topography of the Commercial Home. In J. Germann Molz & S. Gibson (Eds.) *Mobilizing Hospitality: The Ethics of Social Relations in a Mobile World.* Farnham, 122–145.

16. Mauss, M. (1923 [1990]). *The Gift: The Form and Reason for Exchange in Archaic Societies.* W.W. Norton.

17. Malinowski, B. (1992) *Argonauts of the Western Pacific.* E.P. Dutton.

18. Morrison, A. J., O'Gorman, K. D. Hospitality Studies: Liberating the Power of the Mind. In *CAUTHE 2006: To the City and Beyond*. Footscray, Vic., (2006)

19. Pyyhtinen, O. (2010). *Simmel and 'the Social.'* Palgrave Macmillan.

20. Selwyn, T. (2000). An Anthropology of Hospitality. In C. Lashley, J. Alison (Eds.) *In Search of Hospitality: Theoretical Perspectives and Debate.* Taylor & Francis.

21. Simmel, G. (1990). *The Philosophy of Money*. Routledge.

22. Simmel, G. (1949). The Sociology of Sociability. *American Journal of Sociology 55*(3), 245–61.

23. Strauss, A. and Corbin, J. (1990). *Basics of Qualitative Research*. Sage.

24. Wittel, A. (2001). Toward a Network Sociality. *Theory, Culture and Society 18*(6), 51–76.

Snack Buddy: Supporting Healthy Snacking in Low Socioeconomic Status Families

Chris Schaefbauer[1], **Danish Kahn**[1], **Amy Le**[1], **Garrett Sczechowski**[2], **Katie Siek**[3]

[1]University of Colorado Boulder
{schaefba,anle9371,danish.kahn}
@colorado.edu

[2]Purdue University
gsczecho@purdue.edu

[3]Indiana University
ksiek@indiana.edu

ABSTRACT

We conducted a 12-week comparative field trial with 20 low socioeconomic status (SES) caregivers from 10 families to explore their use of a sociotechnical mobile application designed to promote healthy snacking, Snack Buddy. Our analysis of the semi-structured interviews, pre/post-intervention instruments, and photo-elicitation interviews suggests that participants gained a greater awareness of their own snacking practices and those of their family members. Users were empowered to adjust their own practices and beliefs around healthy eating because they were more aware of their family's snacking behaviors. We describe the unique social dynamics of how families engaged with each other and the application, which includes positive social support for healthy eating. By providing insights into family interactions and experiences with the application, we identify benefits, challenges, and strategies when designing family-level sociotechnical interventions for healthy behavior.

Author Keywords

Low socioeconomic status population, family, healthy eating, mobile health, field trial

ACM Classification Keywords

H.5.2 User Interfaces: User Design

INTRODUCTION

Low socioeconomic status (SES) populations can benefit from sociotechnical interventions that promote healthy behaviors because they have increased lifestyle-based risk factors for obesity and chronic illness [2]. While there are many sociotechnnical interventions for managing dietary behaviors [35, 41], there are few that account for the lower health literacy levels and socio-cultural needs of low SES populations [13]. Research interventions for low SES populations range from interactive multimedia nutrition education programs [34] to shared experiences facilitated by mobile technology [17, 33] to mobile chronic condition management [13]. These successful interventions motivated us to consider how we could use mobile technology to empower low SES individuals to improve their eating practices.

Researchers have documented the tractable and intractable issues low SES populations face when attempting to improve their diets – including their overall sense of not being able to control their diets [25, 28]. Contrary to the perceptions faced by low SES communities, Grimes et al. showed that even in low resource areas, people can find healthier dietary alternatives [17, 33]. This work helped people find healthier alternatives, however there is a need to support people in integrating those healthier foods into their lives and previous research suggests social support plays a role in making change [41].

Although some low SES individuals were motivated to share healthy eating ideas within their community [17, 33], other researchers detailed how low SES individuals were hesitant to share dietary information with neighbors [28]. We aimed to facilitate support from a trusted social support system – the family – where individuals would feel more comfortable sharing information [24, 28]. Families are a constant dietary influence in low SES populations [25] and leveraging family dynamics can support healthier behaviors [12, 19].

We build on CSCW and HCI research in facilitating social support for healthy eating by addressing the specific needs of low SES families. We accomplished this by developing Snack Buddy, a novel Android mobile application, that provides low SES families the ability to track their snacking, receive feedback on the healthiness of snacks, and review the snack healthiness of family members through interfaces designed specifically for their family role and demographics. We scaled the problem from dietary management to snacking management because snacking is a major issue in low SES diets [25] and electronically managing one's entire diet is burdensome [13]. We deployed the application in a 12-week field trial to understand how families used the application. We used semi-structured interviews, photo-elicitation interviews (PEI) [10], and application log data to explore how participants used the application and engaged with their family members. The specific contributions of our research are:

1. An understanding of how low SES families use mobile applications for healthy eating in their everyday lives;
2. Identifying the benefits and challenges of family-level sociotechnical interventions for behavior change; and
3. Potential strategies for designing mobile applications that engage the entire family in adopting healthier behaviors.

CSCW 2015, March 14–18 2015, Vancouver, BC, Canada.

ACM 978-1-4503-2922-4/15/03 ...$15.00.
http://dx.doi.org/10.1145/2675133.2675180

RELATED WORK

Sociotechnical interventions that aim to change eating behaviors [13, 29, 35, 41] typically focus on individuals and miss key social constructs that influence behaviors. Tsai et al. developed PmEB, a dietary monitoring application on a feature phone, for individuals to improve their weight management [41]. Connelly et al. designed a mobile dietary application to assist low literacy individuals on dialysis monitor their restrictive diet [13]. Mamykina et al. designed MAHI to help people with diabetes understand the link between what they consumed and their blood glucose levels through mobile phone pictures, a glucometer, and an online website [29]. MAHI participants received feedback from an educator, but the intervention was focused on the individual. Although these interventions were mostly well received by participants and affected behavior in some instances, they did not leverage social support structures that significantly influence behavior change [8, 21]. The few sociotechnical interventions for dietary improvement that included social support structures [17, 33] were designed for sharing and reflection with the greater community and among peers. We focused on a specific, structured social unit to support behavior change by designing with and for families – a different social dynamic because parents and children are typically not considered peers within the home.

A significant body of research suggests that family-level factors are some of the most significant determinants of health behaviors. Family eating patterns, behavior modeling, and family meals all influence children's eating behaviors [39]. Parents' eating behaviors are influenced by pressure to maintain a healthy family and social support within the family [38]. The CSCW and HCI community has primarily focused on enabling communication and information sharing between family members [3, 23], however less work has been done to understand how to facilitate social support of behavior change among family members.

Grimes et al. studied how to support family reflection on health behavior, which provided insights into the design space for family support of healthy behaviors [19]. The potential of engaging the family illustrated by this work motivated our approach and informed our system design. Colineau et al. [12] designed one of the few sociotechnical interventions that influence health behaviors in the entire family. They designed a web portal to facilitate shared reflection and tracking of any healthy behavior that families wanted. Users viewed how family members performed on attaining their individual and collective health goals. Our intervention differs in that we use a mobile phone intervention as opposed to a web portal because low SES communities prefer and have greater access to these devices [25]. We also focus on a single behavior, healthy snacking, to simplify data entry, visualization, and lifestyle change focus.

HEALTH BEHAVIOR THEORIES

Researchers in the HCI and CSCW community utilize health behavior theories to enhance sociotechnical interventions for behavior change [8, 27]. These theories provide organizing frameworks for our understanding of human behavior and inform intervention design. We primarily used two theories in the development of Snack Buddy – social-cognitive theory (SCT) [4] and transportation theory [16]. SCT posits that behavior is determined by an interplay of social and cognitive factors. The key construct in SCT is self-efficacy, which is an individual's belief in her control over her actions and capability to perform a specific behavior. SCT includes other concepts and two that are relevant to our work include sociostructural factors – facilitators (factors that support behaviors) and impediments (factors that prevent behaviors) – and outcome expectations, which are beliefs about about the consequences of behaviors. Transportation Theory, the second theory that informed our design, suggests that individuals' beliefs and attitudes are affected whenever they engage in an immersive narration [16]. The decisions people make during the narrative induce behavior change after they leave it.

METHODS

We used an iterative, user-centered design process to develop an Android application for healthy snacking, *Snack Buddy*, that included two years of needs assessment studies, one year of prototyping studies, one development year, and finally one year for the pilot study; the latter we report in this paper. The intervention design was motivated by our previous research exploring the use of mobile applications to support healthy snacking in low SES communities [24, 25] and was intended to facilitate interactions among family members using the application, who were primary and secondary caregivers. Primary caregivers are typically parents who provide the majority of care for their family including cooking, cleaning, shopping, and providing income. Secondary caregivers are older teens in the family who help cook, care for their siblings, and assist with chores. Our previous research identified this family structure as prevalent within our target population [25].

Application

Based on our user needs assessment and prototyping studies, we developed Snack Buddy to provide users with the ability to enter snacks, receive healthier snack suggestions, view their personal snack history, and compare their snack healthiness with other family members. When users entered a snack, they received feedback about its healthiness based on the Fooducate database in the form of 0.5 to 5 stars [1]. Healthier snack suggestions were typically the same type of food (e.g., salty snack) and within 1 star improvement from what was input to facilitate small, manageable improvements. Participants could create a new snack if it was not in Snack Buddy. A research team member would add the snack, its image, and its healthiness rating to the server side database and push the update to all Snack Buddy users. We did not include price information in the application because our prior work suggested that low SES users do not want price information [24].

We designed the application with two different, demographic-targeted interfaces to meet the distinct design preferences of both primary and secondary caregivers. The participants could use either of these interfaces, however each interface was designed specifically for one caregiver type – the *Informational Interface* (Figure 1A and B) for primary caregivers

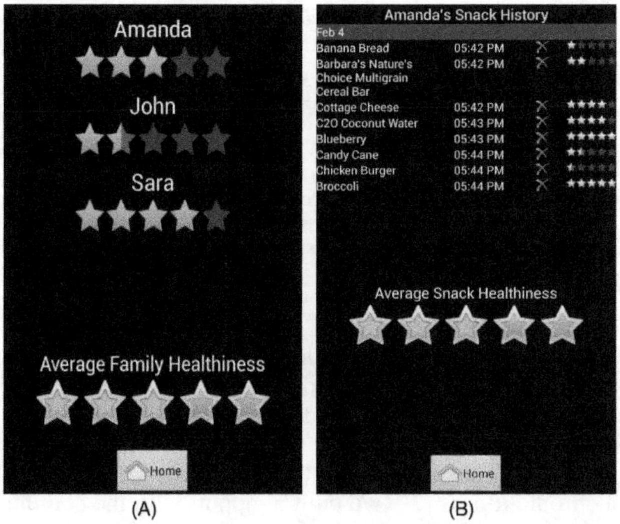

Figure 1. Interfaces for the home screen (A) and snack history screen (B) of the informational interface

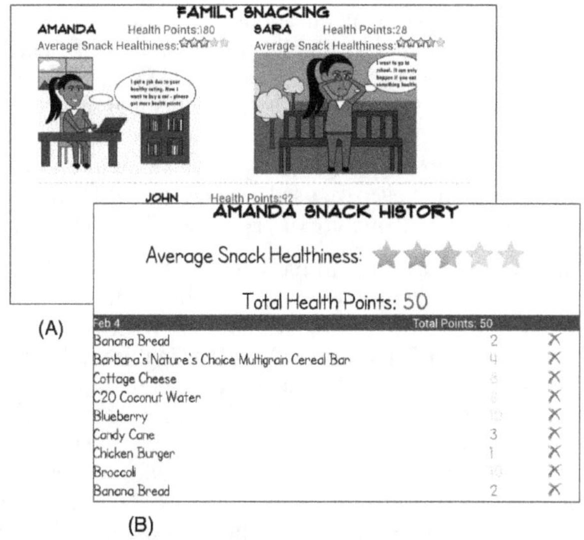

Figure 2. Interfaces for the home screen (A) and snack history screen (B) of the gaming interface

and the *Gaming Interface* (Figure 2A and B) for secondary caregivers. The informational interface was designed to support primary caregivers' management of their family snacking and prioritized simplicity in providing snack healthiness information. Primary caregivers had the ability to view the detailed snacking history of all family members, while secondary caregivers could only see the overall, average snack healthiness of their family members. We made this design decision because, in our previous research, primary caregivers suggested that they needed more information about their families' snacking behaviors to make improvements and they were concerned about altering family power dynamics if their dependents also had this data.

The gaming interface provided a narrative-based game where users could select a human avatar and progress through that characters' life goals based on their snacking healthiness. Users helped their avatar get an education, attend college, and buy a house, by getting more snack healthiness points. For example, they could eat healthy snacks to get 20 healthiness points and buy their avatar a calculator. The purchase helps the avatar earn the 65 points required to progress from primary school to college. Snacks were worth between one (e.g., Hot Cheetos) and ten (e.g., carrot) healthiness points. The narrative game was informed by informal conversations with young people in the community who regularly talked about how they wanted their lives to be different – they hoped to go to college, get a job, and own a home.

Our design of both interfaces and the underlying application was informed by SCT in that we designed features that were intended to enhance self-efficacy, socio-structural facilitation from the family, and outcome expectations. Snack Buddy was designed to increase self-efficacy through: (1) positive, vicarious experiences by providing family members with the ability to see and learn from each other's snacking progress and (2) reflection on their personal experiences via their personal snacking history. Snack Buddy also promoted self-efficacy by providing small, actionable recommendations for healthier snacks that users could deliberate and act upon. We aimed to enhance a key socio-structural facilitator, the family [12], by providing individuals with the ability to view family members' aggregate snacking healthiness. We provided users with abstract, star-based feedback on the healthiness of their snacks, which they were easily able to understand, to help them develop outcome expectations of how specific snacks would affect their health.

Transportation theory informed our creation of a long, narrative game in the gaming interface where the user develops a long-term relationship with their virtual avatar who has a relatable life, as opposed to a short, single play game such as OrderUP! [18]. The avatar's ability to progress through life was directly affected by the eating behaviors of the user, mapping the narrative to their snacking choices.

Our lab members used Snack Buddy for one-month before deployment to identify and fix interface issues. During this time we also improved the snack input mechanisms by adding voice-input and predictive type to make the process easier.

Study Design

We conducted a twelve-week field trial with twenty participants from ten families; each family had a primary and a secondary caregiver participant. Five families (10 individuals) were assigned to the intervention group and five families (10 individuals) were part of the control group, which was intended to control for behavior influences outside of the application and effects of study participation, such as interaction with researchers and data collection methods. Each participant received $120 for participating in the study – $60 Walmart gift cards were distributed during weeks six and twelve. We received human subjects research review board approval before recruitment.

The field trial, as shown in Figure 3, consisted of eight meetings over the twelve weeks. At the first meeting, individuals completed a background questionnaire, a snacking awareness survey, and a produce availability questionnaire, the latter two were informed by validated instruments [15, 26]. All participants also completed the surveys after the intervention period to assess pre/post changes. We acknowledge that it is impossible to know exactly what participants ate without invasive technologies, however we used a mixed methods approach to get a more accurate picture of participants' eating habits.

After the first meeting, all participants, those both in the intervention and control groups, were instructed to take pictures of the food that they ate for one week as part of the photo-elicitation interviews (PEI) [10]. In this study, we used PEIs as a method for gathering data on intervention and control group eating behavior. The PEIs were not a component of our intervention, though we acknowledge that using this method provided an opportunity for behavior reflection separate from the intervention components. At the end of the first week, we conducted the PEI with participants, which were semi-structured interviews where we asked questions about the pictures they took. We reviewed each picture with participants and asked them to describe the food and the context around eating it. Although the focus of the PEIs was the specific foods that they ate, broader issues around healthy eating and family influences often came up, which we captured.

After completing the PEI, participants were purposively assigned to the intervention group or control group in an attempt to balance gender and ethnicity. The intervention group was trained how to use the application and then instructed to use it to monitor their snacks for four weeks, while the control group returned to their normal activities for four weeks. The researchers were not actively part of the intervention and only interacted with participants, from both groups, to collect data by administering surveys and conducting interviews. Midway through the four-week intervention period, we met individually with all participants. We met with the intervention participants to capture their early experiences using the application while it was fresh in their minds and we met with the control group to ensure the same amount of contact for both groups.

After the four week intervention period, we met with all participants, both in the intervention and control groups. At this time we conducted another semi-structured interview with the intervention group about their experience with Snack Buddy. All participants were again instructed how to do a week-long PEI study so that we could track their eating behavior post-intervention. Following the post-intervention PEI, participants began a 6-week follow-up period where they met with researchers at 3 time points to complete 24-hour food recalls. Across the 12-week study, we conducted a 24-hour food recall at each of the eight participant meetings (see Figure 3). The 24-hour food recall is a validated food-survey method [31] used in nutrition-related research where we asked participants to identify all the foods and snacks they ate during the 24-hours before the meeting, with the goal of gaining insights into their eating behaviors [32].

Participants

We recruited participants in collaboration with the Bridge Project, a community outreach program that provides academic support to K-12 children from 500 ethnically diverse families in Denver public housing neighborhoods. In 2013, 72% of the children qualified for free and reduced lunch. We selected this population because previous research showed that 87% of the children in this community were at risk for a chronic illness [7]. We built a rapport with the community by volunteering over 100 hours tutoring children.

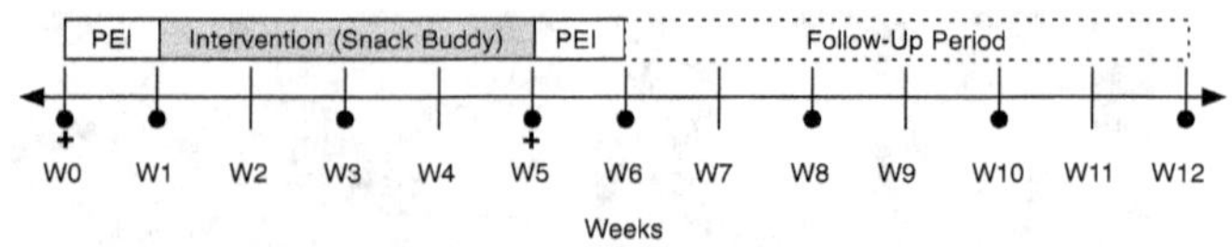

Figure 3. 12-week field trial study design: The intervention and control groups participated in the PEIs (2 total) and 8 meetings (noted with a •). Meetings included a 24-hour recall. We conducted 2 semi-structured interviews about application usage with the intervention group at W3 and W5. Meetings that included surveys are noted with a +. The intervention group used Snack Buddy in the intervention period.

Both the intervention and control group had 5 female primary caregivers and no male primary caregivers. Both groups also had 4 female and 1 male secondary caregiver. In the control group, 4 participants were Hispanic, 4 were White, and 2 were African American. In the intervention group, 6 participants were Hispanic, 2 were White, and 2 were Asian. Primary caregivers ranged from age 32 - 58 (M = 43.4) in the control group and from age 31 - 46 (M = 40.4) in the intervention group. Secondary caregivers ranged from age 12 - 18 (M = 13.8) in the control group and from age 13 - 15 (M = 14.2) in the intervention group. Four primary caregivers in the control group owned mobile phones, while all five of the primary caregivers in the intervention group owned mobile phones. Four of the secondary caregivers in the control group owned mobile phones, while two of the secondary caregivers in the intervention group owned mobile phones. There were no statistically significant differences between groups in any demographics.

Analysis

The data generated from the field trial included: (i) pictures from the pre- and post-intervention PEIs; (ii) pre- and post-snack healthiness and awareness surveys; (iii) 24-hour food recall data; (iv) intervention group participants snacking information recorded by Snack Buddy; (v) Snack Buddy usage patterns; and (vi) semi-structured interview videos. We used an inductive, qualitative analysis where the research team open-coded transcribed recordings of the PEIs and semi-structured interviews to identify emergent themes, which were then discussed and iterated on to develop key, high-level themes. We report on themes related to application use and family interaction in this paper, which primarily emerged from the semi-structured interviews with intervention group participants. On an exploratory basis, we analyzed differences between and within subjects using paired t-tests and analysis of variance (ANOVA) for snack awareness survey responses and produce availability survey responses. We controlled for baseline survey responses in our analyses.

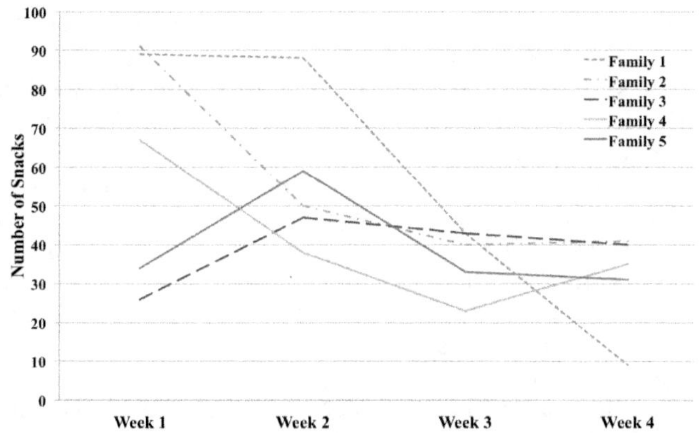

Figure 4. Average number of snacks entered per week by family. During week 4, Family 1 reported having a family emergency, accounting, in part, for the sharp decrease.

FINDINGS

In this section we report on the patterns of application usage by participants, followed by a focused exploration into how participants used specific, family-focused features, such as messaging and the demographic-targeted interfaces. This exploration provides insights into how the family members engaged with each other through the intervention. Next we examine families' health behavior awareness and interactions surrounding the application. We primarily report on the experiences of the intervention group because they were the group that used the application.

Application usage

Intervention group participants used the application consistently during the intervention period. Over the four weeks, we found that participants used Snack Buddy nearly every day – an average of 6.8 days during week one, 6.4 days during week two, 5.7 days during week three, and 6.3 days during week four. As shown in Figure 4, we found a decrease in the number of snacks entered by most families across the four week intervention, which may reflect a "Novelty Factor" [13] of using the application or a conscious decrease in snacking, as some participants reported. But even during the last week, participants still entered an average of 2.63 snacks per day. Figure 4 shows that, around week three, families converged on entering a similar number of snacks per week – between 30 and 40 snacks per week. Family 1 was an exception because they experienced a family emergency in week four.

Participants enjoyed using the application so much that PC2[1] and PC5 asked if they could have the application on their phones to continue using it. Similarly, secondary caregivers inquired if the application was on Google Play. When we asked about future Snack Buddy use, SC1 remarked, *"I would like to see this application out on mobile phones. This application was good ... I tried some other apps on Google Play, but they weren't as good as this one"* (M4).

[1]PC[#] indicates a primary caregiver and SC[#] indicates a secondary caregiver. Participants with the same number were from the same family (e.g., PC3 and SC3 are from the same family). M[#] indicates the meeting number.

Use of the demographic-targeted interfaces

We asked which Snack Buddy interface participants preferred since participants could switch between the informational and gaming interfaces. Generally, all caregivers preferred and used the interface designed for them – parents used the informational interface and teenagers used the gaming interface – even though most tried both interfaces. Participants rated the ability to switch between the two interfaces as the least useful feature in the application, suggesting that the separate interfaces appropriately met their needs.

The primary caregivers did not express interest in gaming. After using Snack Buddy for two weeks, PC4 said that she just preferred the parent interface, *"I didn't use [the gaming interface]. I did switch over and kind of looked at it, but I didn't mess with it. I preferred the [informational interface]"* (M4). PC2 also mentioned, *"I didn't use the game because I don't know how to do games. I'm lucky I know how to use the phone."* (M3). Most primary caregivers felt less confident using smartphones and perceived the gaming interface as more complicated which, in part, led to their hesitance in using that interface. Primary caregivers also stuck with the informational interface because it met their needs. PC1 explained: *"I just did the parent one. That was fine. I liked seeing the stars, and be like 'oh, okay I'm doing a good job'"* (M4).

Secondary caregivers preferred the gaming interface because it was "fun" and "cool," while the non-gaming interface was "dull" and "boring." SC4 noted that, *"I went to [the informational interface] like once ... it wasn't really as cool ... I don't know, I thought the game one was more fun"* (M4). The game engaged and motivated secondary caregivers to eat healthier foods: *"I like the game status, it shows me what I have already earned. It motivates me to keep going"* (SC5, M3). SC1 exemplified how the gaming interface engaged secondary caregivers – he entered 23 snacks in week three, beat the game, and then entered just 4 snacks the following week. A family emergency in week 4 may have compounded his decreased input.

Messaging feature use

Snack Buddy provided users with the ability to send messages within the application to their family members to support dialogue around healthy snacking. As one of the features intended to support family engagement through the application, we investigated how participants used it. In total, forty-one messages were sent by the caregivers during the four-week intervention phase. These messages generally revolved around participants' everyday lives. For example, PC2 sent to SC2: "hi did u do good at school today." They also used messaging to discuss healthy eating and remind each other to enter their snacks, for example PC4 said to SC4, "your dad text me and will be there for the kids. have a good day. Enter your snacks today."

The majority of messages – 85% – were sent during the the first week. Many participants told us that they tried the messaging feature when they first received the application, but then either forgot about it or felt like it was not useful: *"I used it a couple times, I remember like, a long time ago ... I would say how are you doing that, and like okay. I think I've had enough time with the [messaging]"* (SC3, M3). The messaging feature was not regularly utilized by participants and overall was perceived as not useful, especially when families had access to SMS text-messaging on their phones and discussed the application and food choices in person.

Family interactions and engagement

We designed Snack Buddy to engage the family as a unit in moving towards healthier eating. Family members described how their eating practices were intricately tied to their family and that they ate healthier when eating together with their family. Primary caregivers acted as the gatekeeper to much of the food and snacks that their children ate, however there was a significant amount of collaboration between family members in deciding what foods to purchase and prepare. Our findings highlight the importance of the family in healthy eating and suggest that our application engaged the family in novel and meaningful ways. Here we describe the ways that family members engaged with each other during the study and how the application played a role in those interactions.

Family Awareness

Family awareness was an important concept that participants identified in our study. We found a difference in self-reported family snack awareness between the pre- and post-questionnaire that approached significance, $t(9)=1.87$, $p=.095$. Our qualitative data supported this finding – participants reported feeling more aware of their family members' snacking behaviors and suggested that the application increased their family-level snacking awareness. Family awareness was not just an abstract concept that participants identified; it provided tangible benefits, such as helping plan meals and facilitating social comparison, which differed between primary and secondary caregivers.

For primary caregivers, increased family awareness was useful in two ways: 1) it decreased their level of concern about what their children were eating and 2) helped them plan, prepare, and purchase food. First, primary caregivers were comforted that they had the ability to track family snacking because they often did not know what their children ate throughout the day. For example, PC1 described often not knowing what SC1 ate: *"I don't always know what he is eating throughout the day. I only know what he is having when he is with me, and see in that, he is willingly putting in what he is eating. So yeah I enjoy that, I like that"* (M4). Having greater awareness decreased their uncertainty of what the secondary caregivers were eating, creating greater peace of mind. This was best exemplified by PC3, who had repeatedly described worrying about what SC3 ate at school or when she was not around. However, after using the application for four weeks, she described feeling less uncertain about SC3's eating behaviors and sense of control over the issue: *"I know she's not like, eating stuff, like if I have the non-<pause>, the less healthy stuff in the house, I know she's not eating that, she's eating stuff that I would prefer her to eat"* (M4).

Secondly, having an increased family snacking awareness prompted primary caregivers to prepare snacks ahead of time for their children and purchase healthier foods for the home. For example, PC4, who was a mother of four and worked full-time, mentioned that the awareness of her children's' eating habits motivated her to plan meals to ensure they were eating healthy: *"It is useful because then I can view my kids' snacks if they are not eating healthy at school. Or view what they are putting in because maybe then I can have something planned out where they make sure they go to school with something I know they are going to eat"* (M4). Primary caregivers discussed purchasing healthier foods, especially fruits, more often when they were at the grocery store. PC2 described how she used the suggestions from the application to purchase fruits "instead of candies or cookies". We also found an increase in the self-reported, post-intervention availability of fruits that the intervention group had in their homes compared to the control group that approached significance, $F(1,17)=3.42$, $p=.082$, suggesting that the intervention group participants either purchased more fruits or became more aware of the fruit they had in their home.

For secondary caregivers, family awareness provided three benefits: 1) it motivated them to eat healthier; 2) gave them new ideas of foods to eat; and 3) provided opportunities to compare their performance with their parents. Secondary caregivers described an increased motivation to eat healthier that came from a greater awareness of their parents' snacking behaviors. When they were aware that their parents ate healthy, they wanted to improve their own behaviors. SC4 described how seeing her mothers' healthy eating motivated her: *"I don't really eat healthy and I noticed that my mom does, so I'm like 'maybe I should eat more healthy' cus I think its better to eat healthier like now since I'm younger so it becomes a habit when I'm older"* (SC4, M3).

Secondary caregivers identified new snack ideas through an increased awareness of the primary caregivers' behaviors. Some of these ideas came directly through the application as several secondary caregivers looked at the primary caregivers' phones to see the snacks that they were eating for new snack ideas: *"Yeah, and like, I see what she's eating, and I'm like, 'hm...maybe I should have some.' But if its gross, I'm like 'no thank you'"* (SC2, M3). Other ideas came from being more aware of what the primary caregivers were eating when they were together: *"if mom were [eating] something healthy, like bananas, then I would be like, 'yeah! let's get bananas'"* (SC3, M4).

Lastly, secondary caregivers repeatedly discussed how an increased awareness of their parents' behaviors helped them compare their own behavior with their parent. This was often in the context of the game, but also outside the game: *"I see what she's doing and in mine it says she's [eating] healthier than me, so then I'm like 'oh crap' so then I really think about it and then I choose a healthy food over a fat food"* (SC4, M3). Secondary caregivers described instances of when they would compare a snack choice they made with their primary caregiver's snack healthiness to get a sense of whether the snack was more or less healthy than what their primary caregiver was eating. SC3 compared her snack choices with her mother's snack healthiness level throughout the study. When she found that her mother was eating healthier, she internalized a belief that she could eat healthier and would say to herself, *"oh wow, okay I think I can improve this"* (M4).

Although there were many benefits of increased family awareness of snacking behaviors, we also identified one example of a negative consequence. One family, PC5 and SC5, described tension that developed between them when they had a greater family awareness: *"I think I used like looking through the history and stuff because I like to see if I'm healthy or not ... and then I looked through my mom's. But her's is boring because it's all healthy stuff ... I liked to pick out her mistakes. So if she is eating something wrong and she is yelling at me for eating wrong then I would say something"* (SC5, M4). In this case, SC5 would look at PC5's phone to see the snacks that PC5 entered and used the information in a more oppositional way to defend her own behavior, however this led to dialogue around healthy eating. Both family members thought the increased dialogue was a benefit.

Honesty in reporting

Our findings highlight the importance of increasing family-level awareness through our application, which was, in part, driven by providing users with information about their family members. The utility of family behavior information, however depends on honest and consistent reporting from family members. Secondary caregivers did not raise concerns about their parents viewing the food they ate and said that they were truthful when using Snack Buddy. The only reason secondary caregivers cited for not entering a snack was because they "forgot it" (SC1, M3). We triangulated data from Snack Buddy snacking history with the 24-hour recalls to identify snack reporting accuracy. We found that only 5 out of a total of 31 snacks were not recorded in the application by secondary caregivers, but were reported on the 24-hour food recalls during M3 and M4. We did not find commonalities in the types of snacks that secondary caregivers did not report. They missed reporting both healthy and unhealthy snacks and neither type was less frequently reported. For example, SC2 recorded the cheeseburger she ate in the application, but not the healthier chicken sandwich. This suggests that secondary caregivers likely recorded the majority of their snacks in the application and did not underreport less healthy snacks. However, some primary caregivers, such as PC1 and PC5, held perceptions that the secondary caregivers may not have recorded all of their snacks: *"I don't think he has been putting in everything in either, because when I go in and look there were days he didn't put in what he was eating"* (PC1, M3). This negative perception, though inconsistent with our findings, may lead to distrust between family members or with the application.

Engaging non-users

Some participants mentioned that Snack Buddy improved family members' health habits who did not use the application, which was an unexpected finding since we focused on facilitating interaction between the two application users in each family. PC2 described this change in her grandson: *"My grandson, I didn't realize he was having unhealthy snacks either. So now we have gotten to the habit where we look at everything, like sugar content and stuff"* (M4). PC4 started cooking a new, healthy meal once a week with her son, who was not a participant, after she saw all of the different foods in Snack Buddy. Although the effects of the application spread to other family members without them using it, primary caregivers wanted to have all of their children using Snack Buddy. When we asked PC2 if she wanted to have her other children use the application, she responded, *"That would be great, because we have our own snacks"* (M4). Secondary caregivers also supported the idea of including more family members in the application. SC4 described how, as the oldest child in the family, she would model healthier behaviors to her siblings and that this would also motivate her to eat healthier: *"they copy what I eat, so if I eat something healthy then they will follow me and eat something more healthy. So [I] choose the foods that are better for you, than foods that are not"* (M3).

Family members that were not using the application supported those that were using it. For SC4, her grandmother who was not part of the study, acted as a support system for application use and helped make sure she entered snacks when they were together: *"my grandma would tell me, 'you need to put this snack in' or 'what have you eaten today? have you put it in?'"* (M4). PC2 got reminders from her youngest son about what snacks she had eaten throughout the day because she would occasionally forget what she ate. This was helpful to make sure she entered all her snacks and also engaged her son in self-monitoring and reflection. He would enter snacks for her when they were together if she was busy with something else, engaging him directly in application use.

Within-family competition

We found that our application facilitated within-family competition to maintain the highest average snack healthiness, get the most snack healthiness points, and progress through the game. Secondary caregivers expressed the greatest enthusiasm around the within-family competition, however the competition kept both primary and secondary caregivers engaged with the application, motivated them to eat healthier, and generated further dialogue.

Family members found the competition kept them using the application. Secondary caregivers found this aspect especially engaging and described how it kept them using the application and motivated them to use the application and enter their snacks: *"yeah, I use [it] a lot because ... it'll say like how many points I have and how many points she has. I'll be like - 'ooo I got more than her' and then when she has the same as me, I try to find a healthy snack to eat and then I'll eat it and I'll have more points"* (SC4, M3). Not only did the game keep them engaged, but the competition also served as a motivation to eat healthier. SC3 described how the competition motivated her to eat healthier: *"I think it helps motivate me to have more healthier snacks. Click on game mode, go to [my mom's score] and say, 'oh, dang mom, you're ahead of me'"* (M3). PC1 also felt like the competition would drive her to eat healthier, especially when her son brought it to her attention: *"the friendly competition thing where he would look at the stars and compare the stars and say, 'oh, you are not eating as healthy as I am'"* (M3).

The competition that took place in the application spilled over into participants' everyday lives and sparked further dialogue about healthy eating. PC3 and SC3 best exemplified the development of in-person dialogue around the competition and how it benefited their family. PC3 described the nature of the competition: *"It's like a competition, it seems like who's higher ... she can watch and she's like, 'you're ahead of me!' So I think it's kind of like a, a healthy competition going on"* (M3). PC3 and SC3 discussed how they would compare their snack healthiness, which created face-to-face dialogue where they would discuss their competition in person. After PC3 passed her daughter in points, SC3 asked her mother how she got ahead. PC3 provided a suggestion of a healthier snack that would help her do better in the competition: *"I told her that the almonds, she can eat as many as she wants and that those are one of the highest points"* (PC3, M3). Additionally, as a family, they showed the highest collective increase in family snacking awareness in the intervention group.

In our application, within-family competition was limited to the primary and secondary caregiver participating in each family. Both primary and secondary caregivers suggested that the competition would be even more effective with the entire family. For secondary caregivers, competing with their siblings was even more appealing than competing against their parents. When asked whether she would enjoy competing with her brother, SC5 responded, *"Yeah I think more so than with my mom"* (M4). Primary caregivers also echoed this sentiment and suggested competition within their children would be an effective strategy for healthy eating: *"It would be great, I don't know what it is with all my kids, but there is competition for everything ... I don't think it would get too intense. But I think it would probably get a lot healthier"* (PC2, M4).

Discussions about the application and healthy eating

Snack Buddy promoted discussion amongst family members about the application and healthy eating. As we previously discussed, PC3 and SC3 compared their points and healthiness stars at the end of the day when they were entering snacks. PC3 shared one of their interactions: *"I think at one point she did get ahead of me in points ... She thought it was so cool that she finally after like several weeks, finally got ahead of me"* (M4). PC4 and SC4 discussed the foods they entered into Snack Buddy and reminded each other to enter their snacks. They also reminded each other to eat healthy: *"and [mom will] remind me, oh we should eat healthier. And I'll actually be like, 'oh I need to!'"* (SC4, M3). It was also common for families to discuss their application use and remind each other to enter their snacks. PC1 and SC1 reminded each other to enter their snacks: *"I would just ask him, 'did you put in what you ate today?' or he might ask me the same question"* (PC1, M3). Discussions about entering snacks and application usage served as a launching pad for discussing what they ate and, more broadly, healthy eating.

Importance of culture in the family

In the interviews, participants discussed the importance and prevalence of foods that they associated with their ethnic culture, which differed from the dominant, white culture. PC2 described the prevalence of snacks they considered specific to their culture: *"the snacks and candies and stuff that we eat that are different ... we have Tamarindo and chili and just, [cultural] snacks"* (M4). The importance of culture came up most when participants discussed a lack of cultural snacks in the database. Although we created a large database of snacks, it was difficult to develop a fully comprehensive database. Participants noted that missing snacks was the greatest difficulty with the application and this was especially true of food from non-dominant cultures, which was problematic since we worked with a diverse population: *"there's a lot of things that, like ethnic food that's not on there. Cus like, some of our snacks are like a lot different than like a bag of chips or a cookie or something. Like, I'll grab a taco, not like a taco bell taco, but like a fresh corn tortilla, meat, fresh salsa and stuff like that. And I'll just have one and that's like my snack"* (PC2, M3). PC2's quote highlights that even the conceptualization of what constitutes a snack can differ across cultures. The idea of a snack for one vietnamese family included drinks like tea and vietnamese coffee, while the latino/a and chicano/a families considered smaller versions of meals, like tacos or menudo soup, their snacks.

Missing cultural foods was frustrating for participants and made them feel marginalized by the application; like the foods that they ate were not valid snacks. SC2 described her frustration with the lack of cultural foods: *"My mom makes menudo and it wasn't in there. We eat mexican food a lot and they didn't have them in there ... it was just kind of hard to see that because we couldn't get points for those. It was like, 'oh well, I should have ate something else'"* (M4). Other participants talked about how they would often not input a snack because it was missing from the database or would workaround the problem by entering a snack that they felt was similar in healthiness. The issue of missing cultural foods in the application was representative of the broader issue of cultural identity within the family and its interplay with our application. For participants, missing these snacks was more than an issue of not having comprehensive choices available for snack entry. They framed it as an issue of their culture and identity, reinforcing the need to consider non-dominant cultures in all aspects of our application.

DISCUSSION

Overall, participants responded enthusiastically to our application and had positive experiences. Participants appreciated the ability to receive feedback on snack healthiness, review their snack history, see family snacking information, and get reasonable snack suggestions. Although we found a decrease in the number of snacks entered over the four weeks, participants were still engaged at the end of the study – using the application almost daily. We attribute participants' positive response and continued use, in part, to providing different user experiences that met the distinct needs of primary and secondary caregivers and engaged the entire family.

The participants focused on the family aspects of the application and highlighted the importance of including the family. Researchers in the HCI-field have developed health behavior interventions targeted towards adolescents [9, 40] and adults [14, 18], however there have been few efforts to facilitate family-wide initiatives to improve health [12]. Our findings support the idea that targeting the entire family with an intervention could be a powerful strategy to support healthier behaviors. Participants described countless examples where Snack Buddy affected them at the family-level, such as PC3 and SC3 who would tease each other about their competition and encourage each other to input their snacks. These results bolster a body of research, including a recent review of strategies to create healthy eating environments by Story et al. [39], that suggests a need to develop interventions that are deployed in the home and target the family, an important factor in behavior. In the following sections we discuss benefits and challenges with developing family-level health interventions, along with strategies for designing future sociotechnical interventions for the family.

Benefits of family-level interventions

We identified five benefits of family-level interventions – 1) facilitating family support of healthy eating; 2) facilitating family support of application use; 3) increasing family awareness of behaviors; 4) restructuring the home environment; and 5) engaging the cultural and shared values of the family.

Support of healthy eating: Previous research has found that families often do not discuss health issues, especially if those dialogues cause distress about the consequences of health behaviors [6, 22], yet family social support is important in behavior change [21]. By targeting the family, our application facilitated support between family members in working towards healthier snacking. Family members encouraged each other to eat healthier snacks and had dialogue around healthy eating and snack ideas outside the application. They had conversations on topics ranging from the nutritional labels on food to what snacks were the healthiest. Participants also sent messages through the application encouraging healthy eating, though primarily at the beginning of the study. Our research suggests that family interventions can create opportunities for positive dialogue around health and prompt family members to provide social support for each other, which they may not normally do in their everyday lives [22].

Support of application use: Much like with healthy eating, we found that family members supported each other in the continued use of the application. They reminded each other to enter their snacks and use the application on a consistent basis. Reminders were provided during in-person conversations as well as through the messaging feature. They also indirectly motivated each other to use the application through their competition and positive encouragement of healthy eating. Our results suggest that family-level programs may keep users engaged with interventions for longer periods of time and to greater extents by creating environments where family members support application use. However, more work must be done to directly compare engagement in family versus individual interventions.

Increased family awareness: Previous research has identified personal awareness of behaviors as an important component in behavior change [14, 41]. In our research, we identified family awareness of health behaviors as a related and important concept. Our research revealed that family awareness was very similar to the broader concept of 'social awareness' – individuals' ability to recognize and understand the activities of others and how their own behaviors relate to others [36] – but focused on the family. This awareness of the family members' eating behaviors aided in their collaborative work towards improving their individual eating practices and the practices of the family as a whole. Similar to previous findings around awareness as a collaborative practice, family awareness allowed family members to pick up on the actions of others and adjust their own behaviors and beliefs accordingly [37]. As primary caregivers gained awareness of the secondary caregivers behaviors, they were able to adapt their own practices, such as packing healthier snacks, to continue their work towards improved family health. For secondary caregivers, family awareness helped them adopt new eating practices and also develop new beliefs and perceptions around healthy eating. Secondary caregivers described feeling more confident in their own ability to eat healthier and having a more positive attitude towards healthy eating after seeing that their parents model those behaviors. This is consistent with previous research, which highlighted family behavior modeling as an important component of family-based interventions [19, 21]. Family interventions provide the opportunity to facilitate healthy behavior modeling through increased family awareness of eating practices, not only for primary caregivers, but also for secondary caregivers, who can model healthy behaviors for their siblings and peers.

Previous CSCW research on social awareness in health has focused on creating and studying virtual spaces for people to develop an awareness of others' behaviors [8, 17]. Our findings suggest that family awareness of health behaviors is driven largely by and benefits in-person interactions, moreso than virtual interactions, because family members typically see each other daily. Features that facilitated direct virtual interactions, such as messaging, were described as not useful, whereas features that enhanced in-person interactions, like the competitive game and family snack history, generated positive feedback from families and provided them with information that they could use during in-person interactions. When working at the family-level, the focus should be on providing awareness information that empowers family members to better engage with each other in their everyday lives, outside of the application.

Restructuring the home environment: Our research also suggests that engaging the family with an intervention may support change in the home environment – a factor that has a significant effect on family behavior [39]. The home environment affects the snacks that are available, the meals that family members eat, how much they eat, and the food preferences that children develop [21]. We found that purchasing groceries was a family activity for many families, so having multiple family members advocating for healthier purchases may help increase the availability of healthier snacks, such as fruit. Increased availability of healthy foods would in turn improve the likelihood that families would eat healthier items. In addition, we found that family members noticed healthier options in their environment and brought those items with them to work and school. Conversations around healthy eating in the home meant that participants and their family members were exposed to the healthy food dialogue more often, likely increasing their preference for healthy foods [21].

Supporting culture: A final benefit that we found was engaging the culture and shared values of families. The families we worked with shared their culture within the family and identified it as a source of pride. Culture played a role in their ability to engage with the application and in their foods choices, an effect documented in previous research [30]. We did not provide a comprehensive list of culturally relevant snacks in our application, which made it more difficult for users to engage. Recognizing this limitation with our application and the effects it had on participants highlights the importance of culture and suggests inclusivity of families' cultures would be an opportunity to improve intervention engagement. Working at the family-level provides a chance to better support users' culture because it is shared among family.

Challenges with family-level interventions

Although there are benefits working at the family-level, the approach is not without significant challenges. These challenges include: 1) working with the unique dynamics of different families; 2) managing privacy and conflict within the family; 3) supporting accurate and honest reporting; and 4) engaging all family members, who are different ages and have differing family responsibilities.

Unique family dynamics: As we found in our study, families had different dynamics that manifested during application use. For some of the families, having the detailed snacking information was a major benefit and supported modeling of healthy behaviors. For other families, the family snacking information created a source of conflict and aggressive competition. Some families rarely discussed the application or healthy eating during the intervention period, while others consistently had in-person conversations about healthy eating. Families also identified with different cultures that had unique foods, traditions, and social dynamics, which, when not considered, can lead users' to feel frustrated and disenfranchised. These differences in family dynamics, and the way that they manifest through application use, make it difficult to create mobile interventions that work for every family.

Privacy and conflict: The need for users to have both transparency and privacy within their family presents a significant challenge and captures the key design tension of privacy in supporting awareness in collaborative systems [20]. Primary caregivers gained significant benefits from seeing the detailed information for their whole family, however this undermined secondary caregivers privacy and autonomy, though they did not express major concerns around this. Additionally, families identified benefits for secondary caregivers if they had more information on family behaviors, however this would limit the privacy of primary caregivers and potentially shift dynamics within the family. Care must be taken to protect family dynamics because, as we found with one family, PC5 and SC5, a lack of privacy can create conflict between family members, which could endanger engagement with the intervention and potentially cause harm to the family. Although both family members responded positively to the application and enjoyed the competition, long-term use and continual conflict may cause damage to the relationships within the family and make positive behavior change more difficult. This can be especially problematic when the information and privacy controls provided allow users to undermine their family members' autonomy or exert social control over their behaviors [42].

Schmidt poses a question when considering information transparency in social awareness systems to help address the tension with privacy – "upon what evidence does an actor rely when heeding the activities of others?" [37]. In this case, family members do not need full transparency of their eating practices to develop awareness that facilitates their desired outcomes, however they do have important awareness needs that systems must address. Understanding these needs informs the types of awareness information necessary and the extent to which privacy can be provided. For primary caregivers, there are two key needs to be addressed – 1) providing peace of mind around the kinds of foods their children eat and 2) providing actionable information that allows them to take action to improve the eating habits of their family. This could be accomplished with an approach that balances privacy and awareness. For example, P3 wanted to know that her child was not eating a significant number of unhealthy snacks, something that could be captured in an alert directing the primary caregivers attention to the fact that their child had several unhealthy snacks. Secondary caregivers had different needs that included 1) learning that healthier eating is achievable; 2) developing a positive attitude towards healthy eating, and 3) identifying what practices they can adopt to achieve those goals. Awareness systems for the family should be designed to the meet these identified needs for both types of family members with the greatest privacy possible.

Honest reporting: Another challenge is ensuring accurate and honest reporting of data. The secondary caregivers emphasized that they reliably entered their snacks, which we confirmed with the 24-hour food recalls, and did not express concerns about having primary caregivers reviewing their information. However, several primary caregivers expressed uncertainty around whether the information was accurate and suggested that they would be cautious to interpret the data. It is important, with a family intervention, to facilitate honest reporting and create confidence among family members in the integrity of self-recorded information.

Different family members: Creating components that engage and impact all family members presents another difficult task. We found that primary and secondary caregivers engaged with different features of the application and diverged in the aspects of the application that they found most valuable. Primary caregivers emphasized the importance of the family aspects of the application, specifically the ability to see what their children were eating and the overall family snack healthiness measure. They viewed the application as an opportunity to make their entire family healthier and focused on the overall healthiness of their diet. The secondary caregivers were more focused on how the application affected them as an individual and compared their own performance with the primary caregivers. They primarily focused on their progression through the game, the competition, and making specific changes to their diet.

Strategies to engage the family in healthy eating

We believe that demographic-targeted interfaces present one strategy to fill the gap to engaging the entire family towards healthy behaviors. These types of interfaces provide a single underlying framework that enables family members to collaborate, share, reflect, and compete, while displaying information in different ways that are engaging to family members of different ages and with different responsibilities. Participants used the interface that was designed for them throughout the study – primary caregivers used the informational interface and secondary caregivers used the gaming interface – even though they tried both interfaces. Secondary caregivers explicitly told us that being able to progress through the game kept them engaged and striving to eat healthier. Primary caregivers, on the other hand, preferred the informational interface and voiced a dislike of the gaming interface.

Increasing the transparency of family behaviors – allowing family members to see information about the health behaviors of others – for all members of the family would help facilitate family awareness and learning. Increasing the availability of information is important for a family-level intervention because family members can influence each other with their behaviors in a reciprocal way [21]. When secondary caregivers looked at the application on their parents' phones or had discussions about healthy eating, they described learning about specific snacks or behaviors to adopt. Our system made this sharing more difficult because secondary caregivers could not use their phone to see the primary caregiver's detailed snack history. Because the participants highlighted the value of sharing this level of detail, we believe that there is a need to allow both primary and secondary caregivers to share details about their snacking behaviors and have transparency of family behavior. However, this information can be used in a negative way, especially when it enables people to exert social control over others [42].

Our research suggests that having both 'family space' and 'private space' in family applications is one route to achieve a balance of privacy and transparency. This would provide mechanisms, as suggested by previous work [11], by which family members can have their own space within the application and control their sharing to some extent. A 'private space' would provide a safe space for users to honestly report their behaviors and allow users to personally reflect on that information [11]. The 'family space' would provide an open forum for sharing health behaviors and facilitating shared reflection and dialogue. Family members could actively decide to share certain foods or behaviors into the 'family space' that they felt comfortable sharing with the rest of their family. This, however, presents a challenge in that increasing privacy will decrease the transparency of information available to family members, likely slowing the development of family awareness [20], which we saw with the secondary caregivers who had less access to primary caregivers information. In this case, some information may be shared automatically in an abstract or aggregate way to ensure that the needs of all family members, as outlined in the privacy section above, are being met. For example, one might imagine how the 'family space' could consist of a stream of information containing highlights of family behaviors. The stream could provide a positive framing of unhealthy behaviors, such as suggesting to a primary caregiver that their child might need new ideas for healthy snacks because they ate a series of unhealthy snacks. This affords the secondary caregiver privacy around the details of what snacks they ate, while providing the primary caregiver with actionable information. However more work must be done to understand the extent to which different privacy and transparency configurations provide the desired outcomes for primary and secondary caregivers.

Within-family competition is another strategy that our research suggests is effective for engaging the family in behavior change. Although previous research suggested that families might respond poorly to within-family competition [19], we found that it was a major highlight for both primary and secondary caregivers. For secondary caregivers, this aspect of the application was the most exciting and what kept them most engaged in using the application. They also provided specific examples of how their competition with the primary caregiver led them to change their behavior such as choosing a healthier snack and increased their motivation to eat healthy snacks. Primary caregivers valued the competition, both because they enjoyed competing and also because it kept their children engaged. Because some research has suggested that some families view competition and direct comparison as negative and potential sources for discouragement [19], cooperation could be offered as an alternative mechanism to competition. Primary caregivers, as family decision-makers, could select which model of family interaction – competition, cooperation, or neither – best fit their family and the application could adapt the user experience for that mode.

The last strategy we identified for engaging the family was giving families the ability to create content in the application. In our application, giving the families the ability to not only create, but also rate the healthiness of new snacks would have helped ameliorate the problem of not having a comprehensive list of snacks. Family members could all contribute and provide feedback on proposed new snacks. Family members could also be empowered to create more content within the game to challenge themselves or others. This would help keep users, especially secondary caregivers, engaged with the application for on an on-going basis. However, more work needs to be done to develop processes and tools by which users can create and moderate family-generated content within the application.

LIMITATIONS

We recognize that we rely on self-reported eating data, which is a limitation in many eating behavior studies [5]. We triangulated several data sources – 24-hour recalls, PEIs, and snacks entered into the application – in an attempt to minimize the effect of this limitation. We also did not formally test any theory in our analysis, nor did we objectively test for effects on underlying constructs, although our application was informed by theory. We did this because our research was formative and focused on understanding how participants used the application and the family interactions surrounding the application. However, exploring mediating factors, such as socio-structural support, is essential in understanding the effects of our intervention. Our future work will involve measuring key theoretical constructs, such as self-efficacy and social support, to test for effects of Snack Buddy on those constructs. Lastly, some of our results may not be generalizable because of our small sample size. Although we found meaningful application effects and compelling interactions within families, we will confirm and build upon these findings with a larger sample in the mafuture.

CONCLUSION

In this work we used a mobile application, SnackBuddy, to explore the potential of family-level sociotechnical interventions for healthy snacking. The family plays an important role in determining health behaviors and our work highlights the potential of family-level interventions in promoting healthy eating. Our findings suggest that the concept of family awareness is distinct, but related to the broader concept of social awareness, and allowed family members to adapt their own behaviors to those of their family members, such as packing healthier snacks for someone who recently ate unhealthy snacks. Family awareness shares many of the same design tensions as social awareness – most salient in our work was the tension of greater awareness of family behaviors with the privacy and autonomy of individual family members. Strategies like public and private spaces and within-family competitive gaming can help address the challenges and design tensions that arise when working with the family, but more work needs to be done comparing the acceptability and effectiveness of different design approaches intended to bridge these tensions.

ACKNOWLEDGMENTS

We thank the Bridge Project staff for their support and our participants. Funding for this research was provided by National Science Foundation Award No IIS-0846024.

REFERENCES

1. *Fooducate*, 2014. http://www.fooducate.com.
2. Adler, N. E., and Newman, K. Socioeconomic Disparities In Health: Pathways And Policies. *Health Affairs 21*, 2 (March 2002), 60–76.
3. Ames, M., Go, J., Kaye, J., and Spasojevic, M. Making love in the network closet: the benefits and work of family videochat. In *CSCW* (2010), 145–154.
4. Bandura, A. Health promotion from the perspective of social cognitive theory. *Psychology and Health 13*, 4 (1998), 37–41.
5. Baranowski, T., Cullen, K. W., and Baranowski, J. Psychosocial correlates of dietary intake: advancing dietary intervention. *Annu. Rev. Nutr. 19* (1999), 17–40.
6. Bardach, S., Tarasenko, Y., and Schoenberg, N. The role of social support in multiple morbidity: self-management among rural residents. *J Health Care Poor Underserved 22*, 3 (2011), 756–771.
7. Barton, A. J., Gilbert, L., Baramee, J., and Granger, T. Cardiovascular risk in hispanic and non-hispanic preschoolers. *Nursing research 55*, 3 (2006), 172–179.
8. Baumer, E., Katz, S., and Freeman, J. Prescriptive persuasion and open-ended social awareness: expanding the design space of mobile health. In *CSCW '12* (2012), 475–484.
9. Byrne, S., et al. Caring for Mobile Phone-Based Virtual Pets can Influence Youth Eating Behaviors. *J of Child and Media 6*, 1 (Feb. 2012), 83–99.
10. Clark-IbáÑez, M. Framing the Social World With Photo-Elicitation Interviews. *American Behavioral Scientist 47*, 12 (2004), 1507–1527.
11. Colineau, N., and Paris, C. Family vs. individual profiles in a health portal: strengths and weaknesses. In *BCS-HCI* (2011), 321–330.
12. Colineau, N., and Paris, C. Motivating reflection about health within the family: the use of goal setting and tailored feedback. *User Model User-Adap 21*, 4-5 (Dec. 2011), 341–376.
13. Connelly, K., et al. An offline mobile nutrition monitoring intervention for varying-literacy patients receiving hemodialysis: a pilot study examining usage and usability. *J Am Med Inform Assoc 19*, 5 (2012), 705–712.
14. Consolvo, S., Everitt, K., Smith, I., and Landay, J. a. Design requirements for technologies that encourage physical activity. In *CHI '06* (2006), 457–466.
15. Eisenberg, M. E., et al. Correlations between family meals and psychosocial well-being among adolescents. *Arch Pediat Adol Med 158*, 8 (August 2004), 792–796.
16. Green, M. C., and Brock, T. C. The role of transportation in the persuasiveness of public narratives. *J Pers Soc Psychol 79*, 5 (Nov. 2000), 701–721.
17. Grimes, A., Bednar, M., Bolter, J. D., and Grinter, R. E. Eatwell: sharing nutrition-related memories in a low-income community. In *CSCW* (2008), 87–96.
18. Grimes, A., Kantroo, V., and Grinter, R. Lets Play!: Mobile Health Games for Adults. In *UbiComp* (2010), 241–250.
19. Grimes, A., Tan, D., and Morris, D. Toward technologies that support family reflections on health. In *GROUP '09* (2009), 311.
20. Gross, T. Supporting Effortless Coordination: 25 Years of Awareness Research. *Computer Supported Cooperative Work 22*, 4-6 (2013), 425–474.
21. Gruber, K., and Haldeman, L. Using the family to combat childhood and adult obesity. *Prev Chronic Dis 6*, 3 (July 2009).

22. Heitman, L. K. The influence of social support on cardiovascular health in families. *Family & community health 29*, 2 (2006), 131–42.
23. Kazakos, K., Howard, S., and Vetere, F. Revisiting the relationship between reunion and technology-mediated separation in periodically transitioning families. *CSCW* (2013), 1157–1167.
24. Khan, D., Ananthanarayan, S., Le, A., Schaefbauer, C., and Siek, K. Designing mobile snack application for low socioeconomic status families. In *PervasiveHealth 2012*, IEEE (2012), 57–64.
25. Khan, D. U., Siek, K. A., and Ananthanarayan, S. Exploring Everyday Health Routines of a Low Socioeconomic Population Through Multimedia Elicitations. *Journal of Participatory Medicine 3* (2011).
26. Larson, N. I., et al. Fruit and vegetable intake correlates during the transition to young adulthood. *Am J Prev Med 35*, 1 (2008), 33 – 37.
27. Lin, J., et al. Fish'n'Steps: Encouraging physical activity with an interactive computer game. In *UbiComp 2006* (2006), 261–278.
28. Maitland, J., Siek, K., and Chalmers, M. Persuasion not required: Obstacles faced by low-income caregiers to improve dietary behaviour. In *PervasiveHealth* (2009).
29. Mamykina, L., Mynatt, E., Davidson, P., and Greenblatt, D. MAHI: investigation of social scaffolding for reflective thinking in diabetes management. In *CHI '08* (2008), 477–486.
30. McArthur, L. H., Anguiano, R. P. V., and Nocetti, D. Maintenance and change in the diet of hispanic immigrants in eastern north carolina. *Fam Consum Sci Res J 29*, 4 (2001), 309–335.
31. McPherson, R., et al. Dietary assessment methods among school-aged children: Validity and reliability. *Preventive Medicine 31*, 2 (2000), S11 – S33.
32. Munger, R. G., et al. Dietary assessment of older iowa women with a food frequency questionnaire: Nutrient intake, reproducibility, and comparison with 24-Hour dietary recall interviews. *Am J Epidemiol 136*, 2 (July 1992), 192–200.
33. Parker, A., et al. Health promotion as activism: building community capacity to effect social change. In *CHI* (2012), 99–108.
34. Pempek, T. A., and Calvert, S. L. Tipping the balance: Use of advergames to promote consumption of nutritious foods and beverages by Low-Income african american children. *Arch Pediatr Adolesc Med 163*, 7 (2009), 633–637.
35. Pollak, J., et al. It's Time to Eat! Using Mobile Games to Promote Healthy Eating. *Pervasive Computing 9*, 3 (July 2010), 21–27.
36. Raento, M., and Oulasvirta, A. Designing for privacy and self-presentation in social awareness. *Personal and Ubiquitous Computing 12*, 7 (Apr. 2008), 527–542.
37. Schmidt, K. The Problem with Awareness. *Computer Supported Cooperative Work 11* (2002), 285–298.
38. Spruijt-Metz, D., et al. Relation between mothers' child-feeding practices and children's adiposity. *Am J Clin Nutr 75*, 3 (2002), 581–586.
39. Story, M., Kaphingst, K. M., Robinson-O'Brien, R., and Glanz, K. Creating healthy food and eating environments: policy and environmental approaches. *Annu Rev of Publ Health 29* (Jan. 2008), 253–72.
40. Toscos, T., and Faber, A. Chick Clique : Persuasive Technology to Motivate Teenage Girls to Exercise. In *CHI EA '06* (2006), 1873–1878.
41. Tsai, C. C., et al. Usability and Feasibility of PmEB: A Mobile Phone Application for Monitoring Real Time Caloric Balance. *Mobile Netw Appl 12*, 3 (2007), 173–184.
42. Veinot, T., Kim, Y.-M., and Meadowbrooke, C. Health information behavior in families: supportive or irritating? In *ASIST* (2011), 1–10.

I Would Like To..., I Shouldn't..., I Wish I...: Exploring Behavior-Change Goals for Social Networking Sites

Manya Sleeper*, Alessandro Acquisti*, Lorrie Faith Cranor*, Patrick Gage Kelley†, Sean A. Munson‡, Norman Sadeh*

*Carnegie Mellon University
{msleeper, acquisti, lorrie, sadeh}@cmu.edu

†University of New Mexico
pgk@unm.edu

‡University of Washington
smunson@uw.edu

ABSTRACT

Despite the benefits they derive from social networking sites (SNSs), members of those services are not always satisfied with their online behaviors. The investigation of desires for behavior change in SNSs both provide insight into users' perceptions of how SNSs impact their lives (positively or negatively) and can inform tools for helping users achieve desired behavior changes. We use a 604-participant online survey to explore SNS users' behavior-change goals for Facebook, Instagram, and Twitter. While some participants want to reduce site use, others want to improve their use or increase a range of behaviors. These desired changes differ by SNS, and, for Twitter, by participants' levels of site use. Participants also expect a range of benefits from these goals, including more free time, contact with others, intrinsic benefits, better security/privacy, and improved self presentation. Based on these results we provide insights both into how participants perceive different SNSs, as well as potential designs for behavior-change mechanisms to target SNS behaviors.

Author Keywords

goals; social networking sites; Facebook; Twitter; Instagram; survey

ACM Classification Keywords

H.5.m. Information Interfaces and Presentation (e.g. HCI): Miscellaneous

INTRODUCTION

Social networking sites (SNSs) provide many benefits including entertainment, information, and tools for staying in touch with others. However, as in other areas of life like health or finance, people are not always satisfied with how they use SNSs. Just as people sometimes want to eat less junk food or save more money, SNS users also sometimes want to change their behaviors on the sites. Some want to try to increase perceived benefits, while others want to avoid perceived downsides of SNS use.

CSCW 2015, March 14–18, 2015, Vancouver, BC, Canada.
ACM 978-1-4503-2922-4/15/03.
http://dx.doi.org/10.1145/2675133.2675193

We use a 604-participant online survey of SNS-behavior-change goals to examine how SNS users want to change their behaviors on Facebook, Instagram, and Twitter. Just as goals for improving health- or finance-related behaviors relate to how people see health or finance impacting their lives, looking at participants' behavior-change goals provides insights into how they view SNSs as potentially enhancing their lives or as being potentially detrimental. We also compare participant goals across Facebook, Instagram, and Twitter, and find differences in how participants view the three sites.

Different types of goals require different approaches. Thus, we look at participants' goals from the perspective of designing for behavior change, and draw on persuasive design techniques, like the Fogg Behavior Model [8], to explore how different levers could be applied to help participants achieve different types of goals.

We provide two primary contributions. We expand on prior work on perceived benefits and tradeoffs of SNSs (e.g., [11, 26, 24, 4]) by using behavior-change goals to explore how people view SNSs as impacting their lives, and by describing the range of goals participants have. We also compare perceived benefits and downsides across Facebook, Instagram, and Twitter. Additionally, we draw on the Fogg Behavior Model (FBM) to provide insight into persuasive-design levers that could be incorporated into mechanisms to help users achieve SNS-behavior-change goals. We specifically address the following research questions:

- Q1: What types of behavior-change goals do participants have for their SNS use? How do these vary by SNS? By user activity level?
- Q2: How difficult and important do participants perceive these goals to be?
- Q3: How do participants believe they could achieve these goals? What steps do they think are necessary?

Many participants view SNSs as beneficial and want to increase use or posting to obtain benefits like increased contact with others, improved self-presentation, or more attention. However, some participants see SNSs as detracting from their lives and want to use them less or better, often to free up time or reduce potential for security/privacy or self-presentation issues. We see some differences in goals described by participants for the SNSs, and for Twitter participants with different levels of site use. Participants also described barriers and facilitators, as well as steps to achieve their goals, which could inform SNS-behavior-change tools.

RELATED WORK

SNSs are an emerging part of peoples' lives and provide a range of benefits. However, user actions sometimes result in regret or other sub-optimal outcomes like unnecessary self-censorship or over-sharing. Persuasive design and goals theory provide insight into mechanisms to address behaviors users wish to change.

Uses and benefits of SNS

SNSs like Facebook, Instagram, and Twitter provide a range of uses and benefits. People use Facebook to connect and chat with others, post photos and updates, for games and apps, to look up others, to pass time, for entertainment, and for professional connections [17, 11]. They also use the site to ask for and provide social support [26].

Different motives for using Facebook predict use of different features and different actions [24], and various uses also result in different benefits. Receiving directed messages on Facebook, for example, was associated with increased bridging social capital, while passively reading the site was only associated with an increase in social capital for users with lower communication skills [4]. Similarly, on Twitter, a sense of "connection" increased with use of the site, but increased more if users tweeted [5].

We provide an expanded view on SNS uses and benefits by examining SNS-behavior-change goals. Eliciting and exploring a range of goals for SNS-behavior change allows us to explore the full range of perceived current or potential impacts of SNS-use, including perceived benefits as well as perceived downsides. We also contribute by comparing these goals across Facebook, Instagram, and Twitter, demonstrating differences in perceptions of the three SNSs.

Suboptimal behaviors on SNSs

SNS users also sometimes behave in ways they might want to change, motivating behavior-change goals. These goals may be prompted by the unique contexts and affordances–or lack thereof–presented by SNSs. For example, "context collapse," the need to communicate with different groups, and allowances for broadcast communications, can make it difficult for users to properly determine audiences, and can prompt coping behaviors [12, 15, 27]. Regret can arise when SNS users' posts are viewed by unintended audiences, from unforseen consequences, or when users violate social norms, post critical messages, post in highly emotional states, or post content that reveals too much [23, 29].

Users also sometimes employ coping strategies to try to avoid regret, which they may consider successful or suboptimal. For example, users sometimes self-censor content that they might benefit from sharing with at least some people [12, 22, 6, 27]. Similarly, some people may wish to share health struggles or successes via SNSs but choose not to do so because of a fear of boring others or appearing boastful [16]. Users also sometimes delete content after posting [1] or engage in extra profile management [21]. While these may be appropriate or desired strategies in some cases, at other times users may wish to adjust, or eliminate the need for, these behaviors. This dynamic may be reflected in behavior-change goals.

Different people may seek to avoid different types of regrets or may rely on various coping behaviors to different degrees and with different perceived levels of necessity. We examine SNS users' behavior-change goals to better understand the full range of behaviors users may wish to change.

Persuasive design for behavior change

Persuasive design, and specifically the Fogg Behavior Model (FBM) [8], provides a theoretical basis for examining behavior-change mechanisms. We draw on this model to explore potential avenues for facilitating SNS-behavior change.

In the FBM behavior requires three factors: a person is *motivated*, has the *ability* to perform the behavior, and is *triggered* to carry out the behavior. Motivation can be increased or decreased using pleasure/pain, hope/fear, and social acceptance/rejection. Ability is based on the absence or presence of time, money, physical or mental effort, compliance with social norms, and how routine the behavior is. Behavior-change designs can target these factors, can create or reduce behavior triggers, or can make triggers more or less salient [8].

The type of desired behavior can prompt additional insight. In the Behavior Grid, Fogg categorizes behaviors based on whether the behaviors require increasing, decreasing, stopping, or doing a new or familiar behavior a single time, permanently, or for a specific duration. These categories inform interventions for different types of behaviors. For example, Fogg describes how some behaviors respond to predictable "cycle" triggers, while others require unpredictable "cue" triggers [10].

We use the FBM to examine participant goals. We look at self-reported ability and motivation, as well as facilitators and barriers to achieving goals that roughly correspond to Fogg's motivation- and ability-based axes. We also draw on Fogg's Behavior Grid to examine behaviors involved in steps participants believed they could take to achieve their goals.

Our survey design was also informed by goal-setting theory. Goal-setting theory looks at the impact of goals, goal setting, and feedback on behavior change. Goal setting supports behavior change, although its efficacy is mediated by factors such as the actual and perceived difficulty of the goal and belief in the goal's importance. Work has also found that having more short term, actionable proximal goals combined with more distant, distal goals increases likelihood of success [13].

METHODS

We performed an online, Amazon Mechanical Turk (MTurk) survey with 604 SNS users. Participants were United States MTurk workers who self-reported having either a Facebook, Instagram, or Twitter account and having logged into it in the last month. Each participant answered questions about one SNS, either Facebook, Instagram, or Twitter ($n = 383, 85, 136$ respectively). If a participant reported using more than one of the SNSs, one was randomly selected. We

	Facebook			Twitter			Instagram		
	Raw alpha	Mean	Median	Raw alpha	Mean	Median	Raw alpha	Mean	Median
More time/activity	0.75	2.65	2.50	0.82	3.41	3.50	0.84	3.17	3.25
Less time/activity	0.70	2.90	3.00	0.76	2.58	2.33	0.79	2.57	2.25
Presentation of self	0.69	3.06	3.20	0.72	3.35	3.40	0.80	3.13	3.20
Hot/inebriated states	0.74	2.93	3.00	0.72	2.91	3.00	0.76	2.71	2.50
Attention	0.80	3.05	3.00	0.84	3.48	4.00	0.81	3.19	3.33
Privacy Audience	0.65	3.22	3.25						

Table 1. Average agreement ratings for combined potential-goal scales, by SNS. Full lists of questions contributing to each scale can be found in Appendix Table 4

removed an additional 29 participants who were not from the US (28) or did not answer the free response questions (1).

The survey format was loosely drawn from goal-setting theory [13]. Participants described "the one thing you would most like to change about your behavior on" the SNS, which was referred to as *their goal*. They provided open-ended responses to explain the goal, why they wanted to change their behavior, benefits of achieving it, as well as anything that currently made it easier or more difficult. They also described three concrete steps they could take toward achieving their goal. These concrete steps were intended to reflect proximal goals from goal-setting theory [13], in contrast to the more distal goal described in the initial free response. Participants also answered Likert scale questions about the difficulty and importance of achieving their goal.

Participants were then asked 23, 25, or 32 Likert scale questions, depending on the SNS. These questions were primarily potential goals that emerged from prior work on SNS regrets and behaviors [29, 23, 22], tailored to each SNS. Participants rated how much they agreed or disagreed with each (full set of Likert items listed in Appendix Table 4). They also answered questions about their SNS use, tailored to the SNS, and about their demographics. Participants were paid $0.75. The protocol was approved by the Carnegie Mellon University Institutional Review Board.

Analysis

We coded the free responses about the goals using five sets of codes (the goals themselves, reasons for the goals, benefits of the goals, steps to reach the goals, and facilitators and barriers for the goals). We iteratively developed the codes, beginning by free-coding randomly selected sets of data. For steps, facilitators, and barriers, the codes that emerged after several rounds of iterative coding resembled categories from the FBM. Thus, we then drew heavily from various aspects of the FBM for additional rounds of code development [8, 7, 9].

After codebook development, one researcher coded all the responses. A second coder coded 100 responses from each dataset to verify the codebooks. Kappa values were between 0.74-0.81, except goals/reasons, which was 0.68 (above 0.60 is considered "substantial agreement" [25]).

DEMOGRAPHICS

604 MTurk workers from the United States completed the survey. 40% of participants self-reported as male, ages ranged from 18 to 73 (average of 33), 73% of participants reported opening and viewing their accounts at least once a day, and 14% were students (12% for Facebook, 25% for Instagram, 13% for Twitter).

Gender did not significantly differ across SNSs (40% male for Facebook, 36% for Instagram, 45% for Twitter). Login frequency was significantly different: 83% of Facebook, 64% of Instagram, and 52% of Twitter participants reported opening and viewing their accounts at least once a day (Kruskal-Wallis test, $p < 0.001$). Average participant age was also significantly different across SNSs (Kruskal-Wallis test, $p < 0.001$). Instagram participants tended to be younger ($\mu = 28$) than Twitter ($\mu = 33$) or Facebook ($\mu = 34$) participants. This may reflect the relatively large and growing use of Instagram among younger users [18].

RESULTS

Participants wanted to reduce, increase, and improve SNS use to free up more time and improve contact, self presentation, and their own security/privacy. Goals varied by SNS; while participants tended to want to post more on Instagram and Twitter, they tended to want to reduce Facebook use. For Twitter, some goals also varied by participant-use levels. Participants also described a range of perceived steps toward their goals as well as factors that served as barriers and facilitators to achieving their goals.

Q1: Types of SNS behavior-change goals

Participant goals show how participants see the SNSs potentially adding to or detracting from their lives. They described the one thing they most wanted to change about their SNS behavior (*their goal*) and rated agreement with supplied goals.

Many participants (169) wanted to use the site less to be more productive. However, participants also wanted to improve how they posted (90) or used the site (72) or to increase how much they used the site (83) or posted (123) for reasons ranging from increasing contact with others to improving how they presented themselves.

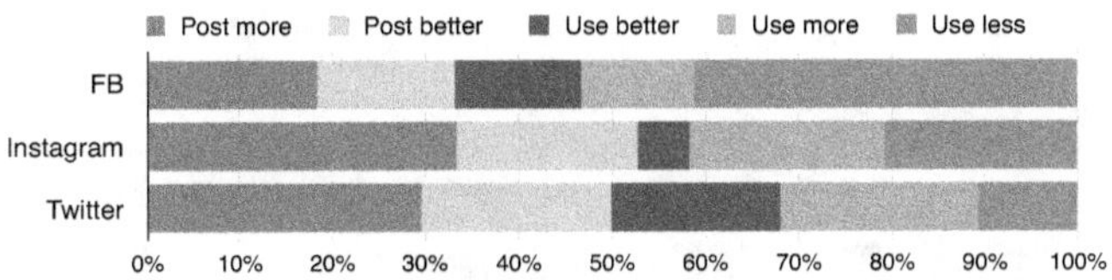

Figure 1. Percentage of participants, by SNS, with each type of goal.

Free response goals

To examine unprompted goals we asked participants to: "Think about how you typically use [the SNS]. Please describe the one thing you would most like to change about your behavior on [the SNS]" and to explain "why you would like to change your behavior in this way." We coded each set of responses into one of six goal *types* and one of nine *reasons* for wanting to achieve the goal (Table 2). Participants wanted to: post more, use the SNS more, improve their SNS use, improve their posting, and use the SNS less. We compared frequencies of goals across SNSs using ANOVA tests, with Bonferroni correction for multiple testing.

Of the participants, 540 described goals (Figure 1). We worded our question to encourage participants to volunteer a behavior-change goal based on earlier versions of the survey, in which we found that participants tended to opt out of describing a goal but then agreed with a range of provided goals. However, 27 participants indicated they didn't want to change any behaviors. We exclude these participants from our analysis. An additional 37 participants described desired changes to the SNS interface, for example an increased Twitter character limit, instead of behavior changes. Although desired interface changes may reflect underlying behavior-change goals, we focused on goals directly related to behaviors and also exclude these participants. Three participants described only desired outcomes (e.g., more followers) but not a method to achieve them. We code these three goals as having reasons, but not types, and include them in our analysis.

Post more or use more

Many participants' goals related to posting on the SNS more (*post more*), for example tweeting, commenting, or posting status updates or pictures (123/540, 23%), or increased use of other features, like reading feeds or messaging others (*use more*) (83, 15%). Frequencies of goals related to posting more were significantly different across the three SNSs (18% of Facebook participants' goals, 33% for Instagram, and 29% for Twitter; $p = 0.01$). Percent frequencies of goals related to using the sites more were not significantly different.

There were several trends in the reasons provided for wanting to post more. Facebook participants tended to want to post more for contact-related reasons (30, 48% of Facebook participants with post-more goals). They described wanting to post more to stay in touch with people they were close with, family, or friends. One participant, for example, wanted to *"post more pictures"* because *"My mom is also on Facebook, and I know she would love to see more pictures of my kids."* This may reflect trends in related work, in which Facebook was used for social support [26].

Contact– want to increase contact with others or strengthen relationships, often with family and friends	
Time– prevent lost or wasted time or spend time more productively	
Intrinsic– improve a participant's state, self, feeling, or knowledge, or an internal belief or sense of responsibility related to contributing to the SNS	
Attention– increasing likes, followers, or feedback	
Safety/security/privacy– increasing the participant's safety, privacy or security or feelings of privacy or security	
Self presentation– improving the participant's presentation of self, how they believe they are viewed by others, or how they "tell their story"	
Less bothering– reducing how much the participant bothers or annoys others	

Table 2. We used eight codes to categorize the reasons why participants wanted to complete their goals. A ninth, "Other," code is excluded from the table.

Instagram and Twitter respondents, alternatively, frequently wanted to post more for intrinsic reasons (16, 67% of Instagram and 16, 44% of Twitter participants who wanted to post more). These Instagram and Twitter participants tended to believe they should use the sites better, or would generally benefit from more posting or use, for example: *"I feel like I am not using Twitter as fully as I can."* Some participants felt a sense of responsibility to increase use or posting: *"Others follow me and I don't write anything"* or *"I might be missing important information by skipping over certain content."*

Use less

Participants also wanted to use the SNSs less (169/540, 31% overall). The prevalence of wanting to reduce use varied across SNSs (41% of Facebook, 21% of Instagram, and 10% of Twitter participants; $p < 0.001$). Participants who wanted to use Facebook less tended to want to do so for time-related reasons (104/141, 74%), describing, for example: *"I lose too many hours per day while using it."* They also sometimes wanted to reduce use for intrinsic reasons (18/141, 13%), often because Facebook evoked negative emotions. One participant explained that *"it usually just ends up pissing me off."*

Use better or post better

Some participants also wanted to *use the SNS better* (72/540, 13% overall) or *post better content* (90, 17%). Using the SNS better included changing use, for example filtering reading better or trading off use of one feature for another. Posting better included changing how or what they posted, including posting less, different, or better content, or changing their attitude about posting. There were no significant differences across the three SNSs for frequencies of wanting to post better (15% of Facebook, 19% of Instagram, and 20% of Twitter participants) or use the sites better (13% of Facebook, 6% of Instagram, and 18% of Twitter participants).

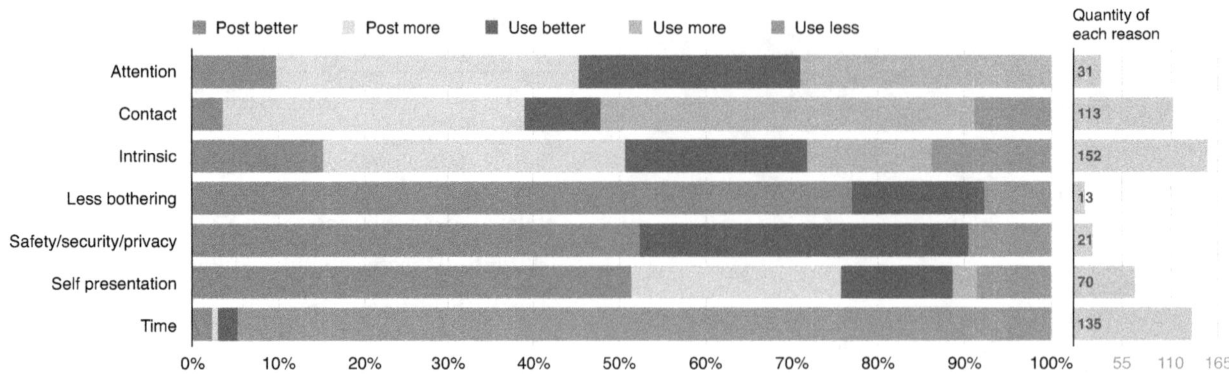

Figure 2. The reasons given, by goal type, for all three SNSs. Codes for goal reasons are defined in Table 2.

Across all three SNSs, participants (21 for Facebook, 5 for Instagram, 10 for Twitter) wanted to post better to improve self-presentation. They wanted to write more interesting or positive posts or self-censor more, for example posting less frequently while drunk or posting less profanity. Notably, some Facebook participants (14 Facebook, 2 Instagram, 3 Twitter) also wanted to improve use or posting for security or privacy reasons, often *"Not posting personal info."*

Participant-described benefits

Participants also described "any benefits you think you would get by achieving your goal." Most of the benefit codes corresponded to codes used for the reasons participants gave for their goals (Table 2). Reasons, however, were often behavioral (e.g., a time code that corresponded to *"i feel i check it too often"*), while benefits were often expected outcomes (e.g., *"more time doing other things i like"*). Participants (9) also sometimes perceived *record* creation as a potential benefit. This benefit did not also emerge as a reason, but appears as a perceived SNS benefit in prior work (e.g., Vitak et al. [27]).

For many participants potential benefits corresponded to reasons for goals (292/540, Figure 3). For example, a participant who wanted to improve their use of the site because *"I have hurt people's feelings"* felt the main benefit would be *"No one angry at me. Knowing I have not hurt anyone."* For other participants, however, potential benefits differed from their reasons (in green in Figure 3). Many participants who wanted to achieve goals for intrinsic reasons, for example, felt that the benefits would be attention- (18 participants), contact- (41), or time- (16) related. Some participants with time-related reasons felt that the benefits would be contact-related (19). These participants tended to feel they could free up time to spend with friends and family, often offline, for example: *"Having more free time with family and friends and start to get outside more."*

Potential goals from prior work

Free responses about participants' most important goals provided categories of behavior-change goals and a view of participant perceptions of the three SNSs. However, participants may want to achieve multiple goals to various degrees, and their desires to achieve these different goals may vary based on how they use the SNSs. To broaden our understanding of

Reasons \ *Benefits*	Attention	Contact	Intrinsic	Less bothering	None	Other	Record	Safety/security/privacy	Self presentation	Time
Attention	**15**	11	2			3			1	1
Contact	8	**82**	9	1	4		1	1	4	3
Intrinsic	18	41	**56**	1	2	4	5	2	8	16
Less bothering	1	2	2	**6**	1	1				
Safety/security/privacy			4					**14**	3	
Self presentation	8	10	18	5	2	2	2	1	**18**	4
Time		19	11		2	2				**101**

Figure 3. Reasons participants provided for their goals versus the benefits they felt they would attain from the goals. Green boxes indicate areas where reasons and benefits tended to differ. Reasons/benefits codes defined in Table 2.

participant goals, as well as analyze how different uses of the SNSs correlated with different goals, we also asked participants to react to goals drawn from prior work.

Participants rated their agreement with 23-32 goals drawn from prior work and tailored to the SNS. They answered on a five-point scale from "Strongly disagree" (1) to "Strongly agree" (5), with an additional "Not applicable" option. We used the Likert questions to create five (Instagram/Twitter) or six (Facebook) scales based on theory and prior work, with scores averaged for each scale (summarized in Table 1, complete questions by scale are listed in Appendix Table 4). We removed several questions, prior to creating the scales, with agreement rates of less than 15% for the SNS.

People vary in level and type of SNS use. We use logistic regressions with Bonferroni correction for multiple testing to examine associations between levels of SNS use and agreement with the different goals for each SNS. To examine different levels of use we use participants' self-reported SNS activity to create three levels of SNS interaction: *posting*, if the participant reported posting/tweeting at least weekly, *interaction*, if the participant did not post but reported applicable interactive behaviors (e.g., liking, favoriting, commenting, etc.) at least weekly, and *consumption* for the remaining participants. Because social aspects of the SNSs were often important in free responses, we also include use of SNS messaging (Facebook messenger, Twitter direct messaging, and Instagram Direct), as well as age, gender, number of friends/followers/following and use of privacy features. Questions differed by SNS, so we only perform analyses by, rather than across, SNS.

Facebook participants expressed more agreement with goals related to privacy and audience ($\mu = 3.22$), presentation of self ($\mu = 3.06$), and attention ($\mu = 3.05$), relative to other types of goals. For Facebook participants, there were no significant associations between use levels and goal types. However, rarely looking at privacy settings was positively associated with agreeing to goals related to wanting to spend more time on Facebook ($p = 0.008$) and goals related to wanting more attention ($p = 0.05$). Also, participants who used Facebook messaging weekly or more were significantly more likely to want to reduce their time on the site ($p < 0.005$).

Twitter participants also expressed relatively higher agreement with presentation of self-related goals ($\mu = 3.35$) but also tended to agree with goals related to attention ($\mu = 3.48$) and increased time or activity ($\mu = 3.41$). This was consistent with free responses in which they often gave attention or self presentation-related reasons for goals (34) and wanted to increase site use and posting (62). Twitter participants' average agreement for less time/activity-related goals was relatively lower than the other scales ($\mu = 2.58$). In the free responses Twitter participants also infrequently wanted to reduce use of the site (13/129).

Participants who tweeted regularly were less likely to agree with goals related to increasing their Twitter use ($p = 0.01$) than participants who just reported site consumption and, conversely, were significantly more likely to agree to goals related to wanting to reduce site use ($p < 0.001$).

Instagram participants also tended to have lower agreement for the scales related to spending less time on the site ($\mu = 3.5$) relative to the other scales. This was also consistent with the free responses; only 15/79 Instagram participants described wanting to use the site less. There were no significant associations between site use and goal type. However, presentation of self goals were more common for participants who regularly used Instagram's messaging feature (Instagram Direct) ($p = 0.046$). This may reflect a desire for presentation management among these users who send messages directly.

Q2: Difficulty and importance of goals

According to the FBM and goal-setting theory, goal attainment and strategies for attainment depend on perceived difficulty and importance. We asked participants how much they agreed or disagreed with "Achieving my goal is important to me" and "is difficult" on five-point Likert scales from "Strongly disagree" to "Strongly agree." 54% (294/540) agreed that their goals were important and 32% (173) that their goals were difficult.

In the FBM, behavior can be triggered when a change is considered important and the person has the ability to perform the

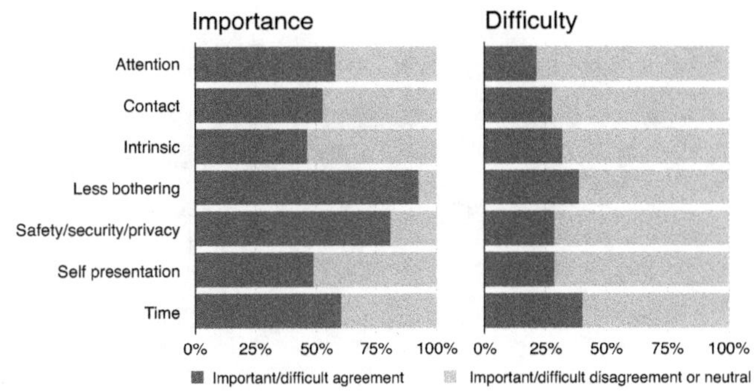

Figure 4. Perceived importance and difficulty by reasons for goals. Reason codes are defined in Table 2.

behavior (low difficulty). Identifying the perceived difficulty and perceived importance of behavior-change goals can guide designers to interventions that facilitate behavior change by enhancing ability (or perceived ability) or enhancing motivation, respectively.

33% of participants (177) considered their goals neither difficult nor important. Many of these goals related to posting more (64). Participants considered 13% (69) difficult but not important, many of which related to reducing use (35). Participants considered 35% of the goals (190) not difficult but important, many of which included using the site less (57) or posting more (41). Finally, 19% (104) of the goals were related as difficult and important, many of which included using the site less (45) or posting better (22). Figure 4 summarizes perceived difficulty and importance by the reasons given for the goals.

Q3: How could goals could be achieved

Goal attainment requires actionable near-term steps, similar to goal theory's "proximal goals." It also requires drawing on facilitating factors that may already exist as well as overcoming existing barriers. We used Fogg's Behavior Grid to examine opportunities to facilitate the steps participants believed they should take to achieve their goals. We also use ability and motivational factors drawn from the FBM as a starting point to examine factors participants perceived as *facilitators* or *barriers* to their goals.

Steps to achieve goals

After participants described their goals, we asked for "three specific steps" they could take "in the next month, toward achieving your goal." The question was free response. Some participants listed no steps and others listed less than three, resulting in 1,620 steps for 540 goals. We coded the steps based on Fogg's Behavior Grid for classifying behavior for change [7, 9]. Each was given a *time* interval, either a *one-time* action, a *permanent* or ongoing action, a *permanent cued* action, irregularly cued by events or time intervals (e.g., daily, whenever one logs onto the computer), or a *duration* event that lasted a specific amount of time. We also coded the steps for a type, either a *decrease* or *increase* in an activity or an amount (e.g., deleting friends, posting less or more), *stopping* an activity (e.g., no longer logging onto Facebook), or taking a new or familiar *action*. Figure 5 describes these steps.

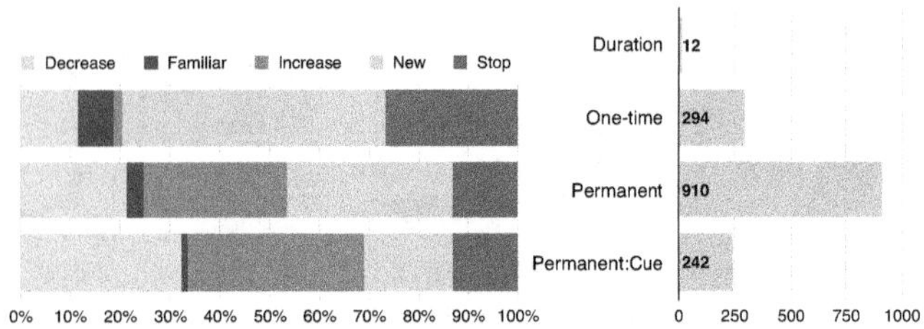

Figure 5. Frequencies of step codes (types and time intervals).

Many steps required making new or familiar actions (334/1,620) permanent. Participants described actions that would last from that point forward and were not direct increases, decreases, or cessations of existing actions. Some participants described self-monitoring strategies they thought they could take. They described adjusting their awareness level or attitude, for example, *"Exercise discipline,"* or *"not take myself too seriously."* Other prospective steps related to making it easier or harder to perform behaviors participants sought to change, for example, *"Read a book"* as an alternative to using Facebook.

Participants who wanted to improve or increase use suggested steps to proactively create better content or social connections. For example, a participant who wanted to post more varied pictures on Instagram suggested they could *"Take some pictures of scenery."* For goals related to posting more or using the SNS better or more often, steps to permanently increase an activity or quantity were common (28% of posting more, and 30% of using more, steps). These steps tended to involve increasing use of the SNS in various ways or creating more content to post on the SNS, for example: *"I could take more photos"* or *"Follow more people."*

For goals like posting better or using the SNS less or better, participants often described permanently decreasing similar activities (19% of steps for post better goals and 21% for use less). These steps tended to involve reducing general activities on the site or specific types of posts. Participants also sometimes described permanently stopping activities (7% of steps), for example, stopping certain behaviors to improve posting like: *"not Drink"* or *"Avoid very personal posts."*

Participants also suggested permanently increasing or decreasing cued behaviors, similar to Fogg's "cued" triggers [10]. These tended to be for goals related to using the site more or posting more (13% of use more goal steps and 14% of post more). Cued steps typically involved posting or using the site on a timed (e.g., daily or weekly) basis, for example, *"Post daily on Twitter."* Many participants wanted to decrease cued actions for goals related to using the SNS less (15% of use less goal steps). These steps often involved limiting use to a specific number of times per day or a specific time period, limit, or schedule.

Alternatively, some steps were one-time actions. To reduce use, this included one-time actions to limit access or use (15% of use less goal steps), such as deleting the SNS application. 10% of steps (155) were one-time new actions, like adjusting settings, installing an application, learning more about how to use the SNS, or offline actions like *"take a socializing class."*

Barriers and facilitators

Participants also described *barriers*, anything they thought "currently makes it difficult to achieve your goal" and *facilitators*, anything they thought "currently makes it easier to achieve your goal." We coded each barrier into one of eleven categories (Table 3) loosely based on ability and motivation factors from the FBM [8]. Across goal types, except using the SNS less, participants described barriers related to personality or attitude (90, 17% overall), for example, *"My stubborness"* or *"lack of self-discipline"* as well as traits like *"I'm too blunt"* or *"I am a quiet, shy reserved person by nature."* Participants also noted lack of time or general busyness as challenges, especially for goals related to increasing posting or use (41 and 33 participants respectively).

Participants also described current habits as a challenge (91, 17% overall) for reducing SNS use (43), but also for posting more (22) or better (13). They described the SNS as an *"addiction"* and how the behavior change was not part of their routine or what they currently do, for example: *"I'm too comfortable in my routine."*

For some participants (51, 9% overall), especially those who wanted to post better (14) or reduce use (29), challenges arose from pleasure in, or benefits from, behaviors they wanted to change. For example, one participant wanted to reduce use but *"I enjoy messaging my friends on Facebook, and wouldn't want to give that up."* Another participant didn't want to post when drunk but noted *"I really like beer."* Participants who wanted to use the SNSs less also described access to the site or using it frequently as challenges (29).

Participants also described factors they felt would facilitate goal achievement. We coded each facilitator into one of twelve categories (Table 3) that were again loosely based on persuasive technology work [8]. Many of these categories overlapped the barriers. The same factor can facilitate some goals while serving as a barrier to others (e.g., having free time can help a user post more but could also serve as a barrier to a user who wants to post less).

Many participants described how motivation or awareness of the goal would make it easier to achieve (101, 19% overall). This was common for participants who wanted to reduce use (46). They described, for example, *"will power."* Technology-related factors were also common, such as SNS features or general ease of use (66), or easy site access or high levels of activity (53), primarily for goals like posting or using the site more. A few participants (17), mostly those who wanted to use the site better or less, mentioned lack of access or activity as facilitators.

Some participants also described social factors that could make their goals easier (47). These included support or help from others, for example, *"Everyone I know uses Twitter, so they can encourage and remind me"* or more generally, *"Having a partner to vent to."* Participants also sometimes described more general social pressures, like comparing oneself to others, as a facilitating force.

Facilitators and Barriers	*Facilitator counts*	*Barriers counts*
Tech– generally related to technology, technical features, technological difficulties, opportunities, or ease	66	17
Tech: have access/activity– having access may make it harder to stop using or easier to use more/differently	53	31
Tech: lack access/activity– lacking access may make it harder to use more/differently or easier to stop	17	6
Time/money– availability of time/money can make it harder or easier to complete goals	29	96
Attitude/personality– a certain attitude or state of being (boredom, laziness, procrastination) makes it difficult or easier to change this behavior, also includes altered states.	35	90
Pleasure/temptation/motivation– enjoying/benefiting from the current behavior makes it hard to change or believing they will enjoy/benefit from the change in behavior is motivational	101	51
Life events– the participant's current life state (health, employment, etc.) make it easier or more difficult to complete the goal	48	19
Social– social pressure or support makes it easier or more difficult to complete the goal.	47	47
Barriers only:		
Lack motivation– doesn't want to do it, thinks it's difficult, doesn't make it a priority.	–	26
Habit/distraction– distraction prevents participants from making a change, remembering to make a change, or a change is hard to make because it is a habit or addiction.	–	91
Facilitators only:		
Take an action– making their goal easier will come through taking a concrete action, actively changing something.	92	–
Easy/fits in with life– thinking this change will easily fit into the participants life makes it easier.	3	–

Table 3. Codes used to categorize factors participants felt either facilitated or were barriers to their goals. Many codes overlapped, because a factor that could facilitate one goal could be a barrier to a different goal (or a different participant). This table excludes an "Other" category.

LIMITATIONS

We used MTurk to perform our study. While the choice of any recruitment platform introduces some biases, MTurk gave us access to a sample in a time- and cost-effective manner, has relatively known demographics, and is comparable to other online sources [19, 3]. We also used quality-control measures, including upfront open-response questions and filtering for participants who answered nonsensically, as well as requiring participants to meet a quality-control threshold.

We also chose a survey-based approach. We intended to supplement prior work that highlighted aspects of the SNS-behavior-change space (e.g., self-censorship, benefits and uses, etc.) and access a range of participants to provide a breadth of insight. To minimize biasing participants or inducing survey fatigue we limited the length of our survey and were not able to provide the rich, qualitative data that could be drawn from other formats, like interviews or fieldwork. This work is, instead, intended to provide initial insights over a wide range of dimensions, including types of participants, different SNSs, and types of goals.

We also asked participants for self-report data, allowing for a range of biases. Responses are likely biased toward more socially acceptable and recent goals, and may over-represent memorable events. We also purposefully biased participants towards responding with a goal to our free response question, based on pilot testing. This push toward identifying a goal may partially explain why several participants later said they did not think the goals they named were important. Our study results could be confirmed by future work that could include longitudinal data or observational behavior-tracking. Areas of interest should also be explored through more in-depth qualitative follow-up.

DISCUSSION

Participants described a range of behavior-change goals. These goals varied by SNS and, for Twitter participants, by site-use level. Facebook participants tended to want to reduce use, while Twitter and Instagram participants wanted to post more or improve their use. Participants envisioned steps they thought they could take to achieve their goals, many of which entailed beginning permanent new or familiar behaviors or repeating cued behaviors. Participants also described factors that could facilitate or serve as barriers to their goal achievement. These factors could inform the design of mechanisms for helping users achieve various desired behavior changes.

Perceived impact of SNSs

Participants' behavior-change goals provide a view into how SNS users perceive potential benefits they could achieve from SNSs, as well as perceived potential downsides of SNS use.

Some goals demonstrate how participants feel SNSs could positively impact their lives and changes that might help them receive these benefits more reliably. Participants described wanting to increase site use or use of specific features like posting or messaging to achieve a range of benefits including increased contact, more entertainment, or general better use of the sites.

Other goals focused on reducing potentially detrimental effects of SNSs. Some participants generally wanted to reduce time on the sites because they felt it would help with busyness, lack of productivity, or a desire for more free time. Alternatively, some participants wanted to target specific, potentially harmful behaviors. For example some participants wanted to avoid drunken posting, posting too much personal information, or posting context- or audience-inappropriate content, behaviors that have been found to cause regret or other negative outcomes [23, 29, 14].

Overall goals varied by SNS, demonstrating that participants may associate different potential benefits and negative consequences with different SNSs. For example, Facebook participants tended to want to use the site less (41%), while Instagram and Twitter participants tended to want to use the sites more (21% for each). Facebook participants also tended to want to achieve their goals for contact-related reasons.

More work is needed to explore the basis for these differences in goals across sites, but they may partially reflect differences in the affordances offered by the structures of the three sites. People tend to use Facebook for a range of content and interactions (e.g., messaging, reading, apps, etc.) primarily between "friends" (symmetric relationships). This may lead some people to feel like they waste time on the site because of large quantities of available content, and some people to feel that they should use it more for social connections because of the range of strong and weak tie relationships available. Alternatively, Twitter and Instagram provide a more limited set of content and features. The sites are also more frequently used for non-reciprocated follower/followee relationships than Facebook (e.g., to follow news sources or celebrities, or to act as a 'celebrity' and provide content to others). This may lead participants to see these sites as information sources and to aspire to increase consumption.

Twitter participants' goals also varied with different levels of site use. Compared to participants who only read content, participants who regularly tweeted tended to disagree with goals related to spending more time on the site and, conversely, agree with goals related to spending less time on the site. This may occur because users who already post regularly see the downsides of doing so (e.g., time tradeoffs), while users who do not post regularly only see the potential benefits. More research is needed to probe the factors driving these differences.

Design for behavior-change mechanisms

Beyond using participant behavior-change goals to help understand how people view SNSs, examining these goals, facilitators, and barriers allows us to explore potential mechanisms for helping users achieve desired behavior changes. Based on the range of participant goals, there are several categories of opportunities for behavior-change mechanisms. First, many goals, like reducing use, could be addressed by productivity or time-management-focused behavior-change interventions. Alternatively, other interventions could focus on helping users increase SNS use, for example, prompting use of specific features or trying to help users feel that they are making better use of the site. There is also opportunity to focus on helping users improve their posts' content, especially for self-presentation or security/privacy reasons.

Persuasive-design levers for SNS-behavior change

Participants ranged in motivation for, and ability to achieve, their goals. This demonstrates potential avenues for intervention that also are apparent in the short-term steps and perceived facilitators and barriers described by participants.

According to persuasive design, and specifically the Fogg Behavior Model, motivation is necessary for a behavior. Many participants described facilitators or barriers related to a presence or lack of motivation. Participants reported feeling motivation (or not) related to behaviors they wanted to change or achieve. Tools or mechanisms could increase or decrease these factors, for example increasing motivation by making future benefits clearer, or providing reminders of the importance of the change.

Ability to perform a task is also necessary under the FBM. Several facilitators, barriers, and near-term steps, related to ability. Participants pointed out how access to technology, time/money, habit/how well the behavior fit into the their lives, and how easy the technology was to use could facilitate or serve as a barrier to behavior change. This was also reflected in steps in which participants described seeking education or more information. Interventions could also target these areas to try to impact ability. For example, tools could help users make time for an activity through reminders or scheduling. Alternatively, a tool could help a user reduce time for an activity by helping plan alternatives.

In the FBM, a behavior also requires a trigger. Implicit triggers were reflected in many of the steps participants described. Some of these steps were cued by other behaviors or external factors; participants described taking an action every time something occurred or at regular intervals. Interventions could create more explicit triggers. For example, an alarm or reminder could help a user remember to perform an activity like posting content.

Different combinations of these levers could be included in intervention mechanisms to help users achieve different desired behavior changes.

Targeted design

Beyond insights for persuasive design levers, the range of participant goals also has implications for more general SNS-behavior-change design. Prior work focused primarily on generalized interventions; however, overly general interventions may not apply to all users. SNS-behavior-change goals, perceived facilitators and barriers, and perceived benefits vary widely. Interventions, therefore, should be personalized, targeted, or adaptable to a range of goals or needs. In some past work, for example Wang et. al. [28], all participants were provided with the same behavior-change intervention. However, goals (and motivation to achieve goals) vary, and a lever that might facilitate one goal or need (e.g., increased time for users who want to post more) might impede users with different goals or needs (e.g., increased time for users who want to post less). Future interventions should seek to match mechanisms to users' needs and goals.

Social support
Social factors may also play an important role in SNS-behavior-change design. Many participants described social support or pressure as facilitators or barriers to their goals. In SNS contexts, social connections can be powerful facilitators, especially if supported by, or included in, behavior-change mechanisms. Motivation could be boosted by enlisting others' help or by allowing the user to compare themselves to others in a network. Ability could be increased by helping the user reach out to people in their network who could help them perform relevant tasks. People in a network could also provide reminders or other triggers for behaviors.

However, designers should also be careful about drawing on social factors. For example, comparisons to other people can backfire if participants begin to perceive their current behaviors as typical of, or superior to, others [20]. Alternatively, use of social information may create tensions. It may, for example, remind users that they like the social benefits associated with using a site, even if they would, overall, prefer to decrease use so they can be more productive. Future work should examine the potential for using social factors in SNS-behavior-change interventions.

SNS context
Designers of SNS-behavior-change interventions should also consider the broader SNS context. Most SNSs have business models that rely on holding user attention. While this may be consistent with some behavior-change goals (e.g., posting more, using more), it is at least on the surface counter to others (e.g., using less, aspects of using/posting better that would reduce use). In the longer term, though, it may still be to the advantage of SNS businesses to balance support of use and non-use goals. When users feel that they are acting counter to their interests or identity, or are concerned about sub-optimal behaviors, they can fall back on coping mechanisms that can include site nonuse behaviors, ranging from content deletion, de-friending and self-censorship to account deletion [2, 12, 15, 27, 22, 6]. For longer-term user engagement, it may benefit SNSs to encourage interactions users consider beneficial.

CONCLUSION

Participants recognize a range of potential benefits from SNSs, including increased social contact, better self presentation, and more attention. In some cases they want to change behaviors to take advantage of these benefits. However, they also recognize potential downsides of the sites and sometimes want to use SNSs less or in improved ways to free up time or avoid negative self-presentation or security/privacy risks. These participant goals vary by SNS. For Facebook, participants tend to want to reduce use, while for Instagram and Twitter participants tend to want to increase use. This range of behavior-change goals and perceived benefits shows potential for different types of SNS-behavior-change interventions and, along with provided steps and facilitators/barriers, provides insight into design for SNS-behavior-change mechanisms.

ACKNOWLEDGMENTS

This material is based upon work supported by the National Science Foundation under Grants No. 0946825 and CNS-1012763 (Nudging Users Toward Privacy), as well as by Google under a Focused Research Award on Privacy Nudges, the IWT SBO Project on Security and Privacy for Online Social Networks (SPION), Microsoft Research, Facebook, and the ARCS Foundation.

REFERENCES

1. Almuhimedi, H., Wilson, S., Liu, B., Sadeh, N., and Acquisti, A. Tweets are forever: A large-scale quantitative analysis of deleted tweets. In *Proc. CSCW*, ACM (2013), 897–908.
2. Baumer, E. P., Adams, P., Khovanskaya, V. D., Liao, T. C., Smith, M. E., Schwanda Sosik, V., and Williams, K. Limiting, leaving, and (re) lapsing: An exploration of Facebook non-use practices and experiences. In *Proc. CHI*, ACM (2013), 3257–3266.
3. Buhrmester, M., Kwang, T., and Gosling, S. D. Amazon's Mechanical Turk a new source of inexpensive, yet high-quality, data? *Persp. on Psych. Sci. 6*, 1 (2011), 3–5.
4. Burke, M., Kraut, R., and Marlow, C. Social capital on Facebook: Differentiating uses and users. In *Proc. CHI*, ACM (2011), 571–580.
5. Chen, G. M. Tweet this: A uses and gratifications perspective on how active Twitter use gratifies a need to connect with others. *Comput. Hum. Behav. 27*, 2 (Mar. 2011), 755–762.
6. Das, S., and Kramer, A. Self-censorship on facebook.
7. Fogg, B. The behavior grid: 35 ways behavior can change. In *Proc. Persuasive*, ACM (2009), 42.
8. Fogg, B. A behavior model for persuasive design. In *Proc. Persuasive*, ACM (2009), 40.
9. Fogg, B. Fogg behavior grid, 2012. `http://www.behaviorgrid.org/`.
10. Fogg, B., and Hreha, J. Behavior wizard: A method for matching target behaviors with solutions. In *Persuasive technology*. Springer, 2010, 117–131.
11. Joinson, A. N. Looking at, looking up or keeping up with people?: Motives and use of Facebook. In *Proc. CHI*, ACM (New York, NY, USA, 2008), 1027–1036.
12. Lampinen, A., Tamminen, S., and Oulasvirta, A. All my people right here, right now: Management of group co-presence on a social networking site. In *Proc. GROUP*, ACM (2009), 281–290.
13. Locke, E. A., and Latham, G. P. Building a practically useful theory of goal setting and task motivation: A 35-year odyssey. *Am. psychologist 57*, 9 (2002), 705.
14. Mao, H., Shuai, X., and Kapadia, A. Loose tweets: An analysis of privacy leaks on Twitter. In *Proce. WPES*, ACM (2011), 1–12.

15. Marwick, A. E., et al. I tweet honestly, I tweet passionately: Twitter users, context collapse, and the imagined audience. *New Media & Society 13*, 1 (2011), 114–133.

16. Newman, M. W., Lauterbach, D., Munson, S. A., Resnick, P., and Morris, M. E. It's not that I don't have problems, I'm just not putting them on Facebook: Challenges and opportunities in using online social networks for health. In *Proc. CSCW*, ACM (New York, NY, USA, 2011), 341–350.

17. Papacharissi, Z., and Mendelson, A. Toward a new (er) sociability: Uses, gratifications and social capital on Facebook. *Media perspectives for the 21st century* (2010), 212.

18. Pew Internet & American Life Project. Demographics of key social networking platforms, 2013. `http://www.pewinternet.org/2013/12/30/demographics-of-key-social-networking-platforms/`.

19. Ross, J., Irani, L., Silberman, M., Zaldivar, A., and Tomlinson, B. Who are the crowdworkers?: Shifting demographics in Mechanical Turk. In *CHI EA*, ACM (2010), 2863–2872.

20. Schultz, P. W., Nolan, J. M., Cialdini, R. B., Goldstein, N. J., and Griskevicius, V. The constructive, destructive, and reconstructive power of social norms. *Psychological science 18*, 5 (2007), 429–434.

21. Silfverberg, S., Liikkanen, L. A., and Lampinen, A. I'll press play, but I won't listen: Profile work in a music-focused social network service. In *Proc. CSCW*, ACM (2011), 207–216.

22. Sleeper, M., Balebako, R., Das, S., McConahy, A. L., Wiese, J., and Cranor, L. F. The post that wasn't: Exploring self-censorship on Facebook. In *Proc. CSCW*, ACM (2013), 793–802.

23. Sleeper, M., Cranshaw, J., Kelley, P. G., Ur, B., Acquisti, A., Cranor, L. F., and Sadeh, N. I read my Twitter the next morning and was astonished: A conversational perspective on Twitter regrets. In *Proc. CHI*, ACM (2013), 3277–3286.

24. Smock, A. D., Ellison, N. B., Lampe, C., and Wohn, D. Y. Facebook as a toolkit: A uses and gratification approach to unbundling feature use. *Computers in Human Behavior 27*, 6 (2011), 2322–2329.

25. Viera, A. J., Garrett, J. M., et al. Understanding interobserver agreement: The kappa statistic. *Fam Med 37*, 5 (2005), 360–363.

26. Vitak, J., and Ellison, N. B. theres a network out there you might as well tap: Exploring the benefits of and barriers to exchanging informational and support-based resources on Facebook. *New Media & Society*.

27. Vitak, J., and Kim, J. You can't block people offline: examining how Facebook's affordances shape the disclosure process. In *Proc. CSCW*, ACM (2014), 461–474.

28. Wang, Y., Leon, P. G., Scott, K., Chen, X., Acquisti, A., and Cranor, L. F. Privacy nudges for social media: An exploratory Facebook study. In *Proc. WWW* (2013), 763–770.

29. Wang, Y., Norcie, G., Komanduri, S., Acquisti, A., Leon, P. G., and Cranor, L. F. I regretted the minute I pressed share: A qualitative study of regrets on Facebook. In *Proc. SOUPS*, ACM (2011), 10.

Facebook	*Twitter*	*Instagram*
More time/activity		
...add more friends	...follow more people	...follow more people
..."like" more content	...favorite more tweets	..."like" more photos
...spend more time on Facebook	...spend more time on Twitter	...spend more time on Instagram
...post more	...tweet more	...post more
...spend more time using game apps		–
Less time/activity		
...spend less time on Facebook	...spend less time on Twitter	...spend less time on Instagram
...post less	...tweet less	...post less
...spend less time using game apps	–	–
...remove some friends	...unfollow some people	...unfollow some people
..."like" less content	...favorite fewer tweets	..."like" fewer photos
Presentation of self		
...include fewer swear words in my posts	...include fewer swear words in my tweets	...include fewer swear words in my posts
...include more swear words in my posts	...include more swear words in my tweets	...include more swear words in my posts
...post more positive content	...tweet more positive content	...post more positive content
...post more negative content	...tweet more negative content	...post more negative content
...post less of a certain type of content	...tweet less of a certain type of content	...post less of a certain type of content
...post more of a certain type of content	...tweet more of a certain type of content	...post more of a certain type of content
...post more interesting content	...tweet more interesting content	...post more interesting content
...post less interesting content	...tweet less interesting content	...post less interesting content
Hot/inebriated states		
...post less content when I'm drunk	...tweet less content when I'm drunk	...post less content when I'm drunk
...post more content when I'm drunk	...tweet more content when I'm drunk	...post more content when I'm drunk
...post less content when I'm upset	...tweet less content when I'm upset	...post less content when I'm upset
...post more content when I'm upset	...tweet more content when I'm upset	...post more content when I'm upset
Attention		
–	...get more followers	...get more followers
...get more likes for content I post	...get more favorites for my tweets	...get more likes for photos I post
...get fewer likes for content I post	...get fewer favorites for my tweets	...get fewer likes for photos I post
...get more comments for content I post	–	...get more comments for photos I post
...get fewer comments for content I post	–	...get fewer comments for photos I post
Privacy/audience		
...make sure content I post isn't visible to certain people	–	–
...make sure content I post is visible to certain people	–	–
...make my Facebook privacy settings more restrictive	–	–
...make my Facebook privacy settings less restrictive	–	–
...spend more time checking my Facebook privacy settings	–	–
...spend less time checking my Facebook privacy settings	–	–

Table 4. Potential-goal questions asked to participants as Likert scale questions (five point scale, Strongly Disagree to Strongly Agree). The sets of Likert scale questions were collapsed into the provided scales for analysis. Questions in gray were excluded because of low levels of agreement (<%15).

Understanding the Roles and Influences of Mediators from Multiple Social Channels for Health Behavior Change

Yeoreum Lee
Department of Industrial Design,
KAIST,
Daejeon, Republic of Korea
yeoreum_lee @kaist.ac.kr

Youn-kyung Lim
Department of Industrial Design,
KAIST,
Daejeon, Republic of Korea
younlim@kaist.ac.kr

ABSTRACT

People become increasingly influenced by others in changing and maintaining health behaviors. Along with the advancement of persuasive technology and social networking technologies, the place where social interaction occurs has expanded. As a result, mediators who influence an individual's behavior change can come from diverse social channels. However, little work exists on what roles the mediators have and how differently the mediators motivate and affect the maintenance of health behavior changes of users through various social channels. To investigate this, we conducted interviews with 13 participants who use a running exercise application for maintaining their health behavior changes. This study reveals the roles of mediators from three different social channels, which are the social feature in the application, general social media, and the agent feature in the application. Mediators from the application could influence participants' health behavior change either positively or negatively according to the level of intimacy and the similarity of the physical condition. Social media mediators influence participants' social face and support their health behavior changes by keeping participants in countenance. Lastly, the agent mediator of the application provides continuous reinforcement to participants for maintaining their health behavior changes.

Author Keywords

Health behavior change; maintenance; mediator; social reinforcement; social channels; social interaction

ACM Classification Keywords

H.5.m. Information interfaces and presentation (e.g., HCI): Miscellaneous.

General Terms

Design

CSCW '15, March 14 – 18, 2015, Vancouver, BC, Canada.

ACM 978-1-4503-2922-4/15/03…$15.00.
http://dx.doi.org/10.1145/2675133.2685032

INTRODUCTION

Social reinforcement is based on the notion that rewarded behaviors are likely to be repeated. Social reinforcement has proven effective in maintaining various health behavior changes [18, 26]. Social reinforcement involves other social members who play a role as mediators and these include family members, friends, and colleagues. Such reinforcement improves the odds of sustaining healthy behavior changes because the mediators can assist the user with his or her behavior change [24] through providing advice, expressing empathy and concern, and providing direct aid from the mediator's social network [9].

According to a review of behavior change research by Hekler et al., papers that mention behavior change have significantly increased in the past five years in the HCI community [8]. This shows that the study of behavior change in interaction design is becoming more crucial nowadays. The means for promoting behavior changes have become easily accessible with technologies such as online videos and social networks [5]. The target behavior that needs to be changed can vary, and one of the areas being actively researched is an approach to promoting physical activities of the user through gamification [13]. This research encourages users to compete with each other [13], to join in collaboration [17], and to persuade users to act more with other users who also need to be physically active by using the system. However, it is hard to understand the roles and influences of mediators from diverse social channels (e.g., face-to-face, social networking services (SNSs) like Facebook, and health behavior changing applications) since current studies mainly focus on the system that they have developed.

As the use of social media, which provide different types of social channels, is woven into modern life, various social groups can interact with each other by using technology such as social networking services. While managing social media, a user tries to form self-impression on social media and makes various identities depending on his or her virtual social groups [4]. As a result, various social groups in social media can be mediators with different roles impacting reinforcement. Thus, it is necessary to explore what the roles, influences, challenges, and opportunities of mediators are in health behavior changes by understanding people's experience of using diverse social channels. To achieve this research goal, we interviewed users of mobile health applications, specifically a running exercise application, and asked about different experiences depending on the mediators from diverse social channels. After we reveal the roles and influences of diverse mediators, we suggest design implications that need to be considered in designing socially meaningful computer-supported health systems.

BACKGROUND

Reinforcement Theory

According to Skinner [22], a human learns and eventually changes his behavior through experiencing reinforcement and punishment. *Reinforcement* is one of the core methods of behavior change that increases desirable behaviors, such as studying hard and cleaning one's own room. There are two main methods of reinforcement: positive and negative. Positive reinforcement implies giving or adding a response when an individual shows desirable behavior. Negative reinforcement implies rewarding an individual by removing unpleasant and undesirable consequences when the individual shows desirable behavior (Figure 1). Skinner found that reinforcement, especially positive reinforcement, is a more effective way to persuade people to change their behavior. He claimed that reinforcement encourages people to maintain their behavior change for a longer term without other side effects such as a relapse. Health related behaviors such as exercising and having a healthy eating habit are also mentioned as effective targets for applying reinforcement [18, 26].

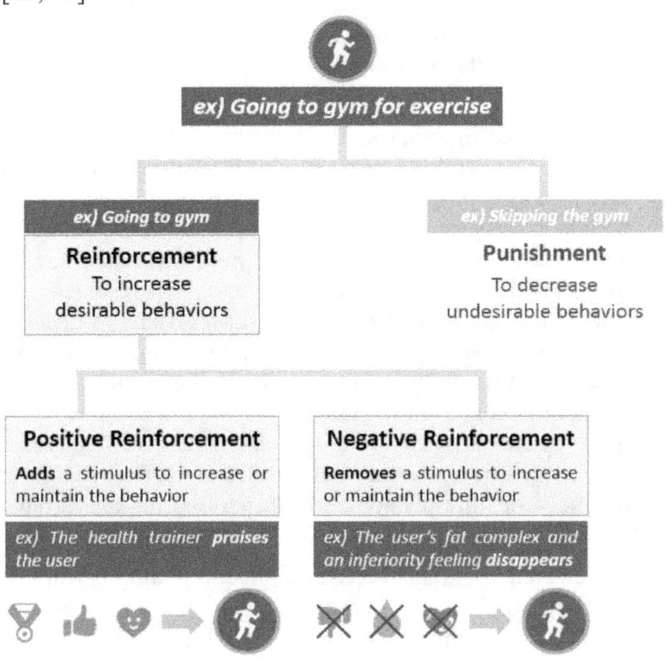

Figure 1. Two types of reinforcement and their examples in operant conditioning [22]

Social Reinforcement and Mediators

Reinforcement includes various stimuli, events, and situations that strengthen and increase a behavior. One of the representative types of reinforcement is called tangible reinforcement, with a tangible reinforcer being a tangible reward like a trophy, candy, or a toy. Other types of reinforcement, such as token reinforcement, involve awarding points, scores, or tokens for reinforcing the behavior [24] (Figure 2).

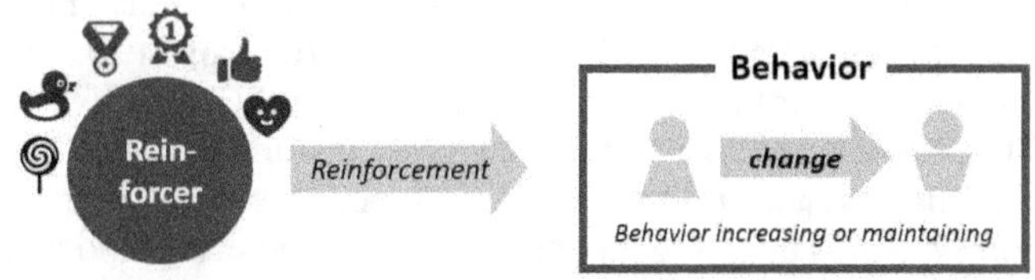

Figure 2. The process of reinforcement in behavior change

Social members, such as family members, friends, and colleagues, can provide a reinforcer to the person who tries to change his or her behavior [22]. This is called *social reinforcement*, in which rewards are delivered by another person's reaction, including social attention, affection, and reputation. These diverse rewards from another person are called social reinforcers. The person who gives a social reinforcer for behavior change is called a *mediator* [24] (Figure 3). A mediator is defined as "a social member who dispenses specific contingent consequences to a person who tries to change his or her behavior" [26, p. 242].

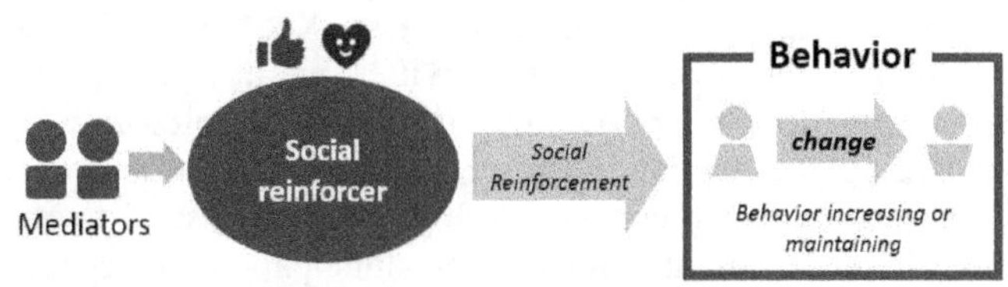

Figure 3. The process of social reinforcement

Although the effects of mediators and social reinforcement are displayed in various health issues, the roles and influences of mediators are not well defined. Existing literature mainly focuses on who the mediator is but does not distinguish which social channel through which the mediator interacts with the individual attempting to change behavior. For example, spouses appear to provide important emotional support in weight loss as mediators to each other [18]. However, we do not know how the influence pertains if the spouses were to interact with each other through the phone vs. Facebook. Thus, our goal is to explore how users perceive the influence of different mediators and the social channels through which the mediators interact.

RELATED WORKS

Persuasive Technology System for Health Behavior Change

Inducing users to change their health behaviors using persuasive technology [5] in the field of HCI has been developed rapidly in recent years [8]. Studies of health behavior changes have been conducted for various purposes from supporting patients with serious physical diseases (such as cancer [12] and mental illnesses like depression [3]) to health promotion for engaging in physical activities with people [13]. Many studies on health behavior changes have developed new systems to help users realize their goals. A messaging application, VERA (Virtual Environment for Raised Awareness), assists users with weight loss and health promotion by allowing them to share messages [1]. An exer-game, iFitQuest [13], supports adolescents' physical activities by applying gamification based on the physical location of users. However, these studies do not consider how the diverse roles of mediators and social reinforcers influence those contexts. We live in the "Connected age" [21], and products and services are multifunctional, multilayered, and connected to a huge ecosystem. Thus, we can create a synergistic effect and add value if the developed system connects to the various mediators from other diverse products and service platforms. Naturally, it is important to know about diverse roles of different mediators who are connected in a health-related ecosystem and how they differently influence each user and his or her health behavior changes.

Using Social Media for Sensing Health Behavior Change

Several studies use social media as a sensing tool of users' health behavior changes. Murnane et al. [15] find that social media, such as Twitter, can be used as a tool for an intervention system for those who are trying to quit smoking by analyzing the smoker's posts that are related to signs of relapsing in smoking cessation. Xue et al. [27] also highlights the new role of Twitter as a sensing and measuring tool for psychological stress of adolescents by analyzing the Twitter posts of teenagers. Because social media is an access channel for big data, it is useful to use social media as a database of anticipation of certain progress. However, there is another possibility of using social media as a new place for social reinforcement by utilizing diverse human resources that are connected with each other. Moreover, many mobile applications are able to link with social media, even though they have different titles and purposes. In other words, users who use different applications are able to see each other's activities if the users are connected to social media and can influence each other as mediators. In this respect, it is important to define the roles and perceptions of mediators according to the users through these diverse social channels because social media connects diverse human resources and supports many activities in various ways.

In this "Connected age" [21], getting attention for enhancing running performance can be both positive and negative, depending on who the mediators are, according to previous research on social media. For instance, a user wants to show his improvement to his or her exercising group but does not want to share it with a boss who thinks the user does not have enough time for exercise because of the heavy workload. In this way, users of social media will be affected differently according to the mediators, and these different influences will drive the maintenance of behavior change. Therefore, revealing the different influences according to different mediators with different social channels is important.

INTERVIEW

Participants and Methods

We conducted 13 semi-structured interviews (7 male and 6 female) that lasted between 40 minutes to 1 hour per participant who uses a mobile application for running exercises. The average age of the participants was 25.9 (SD=2.4, MIN=21 & MAX=31), and the average duration of using the application was 8.6 months (SD=9.4, MIN=1 & MAX=24). We recruited participants by posting a recruitment advertisement on the Facebook wall of the university students' group. We recruited the participants who use a running application for their health behavior change maintenance. We also asked these Facebook group members to share the recruitment advertisement on their individual Facebook, Twitter, and any other social media accounts. During one week, we received responses from 33 people in total. We focused on a user group in the maintenance stage of behavior change [19] regarding exercise, rather than users who are already doing exercise as a habitual behavior because social reinforcement is most effective when users are in the behavior change stage of maintenance [26]. Thus, at the recruitment process, we used an online questionnaire to ask 33 respondents if they were trying to maintain a new healthy behavior and avoid temptation like skipping exercise so that we could verify that the participants were in the maintenance state of a behavior change [19]. We finally selected 13 participants who fit to our research purpose. Participants were selected if they used a running exercise application as an additional and external aid for maintaining running exercise and if they were in the maintenance stage of behavior change based on their answers on the questionnaire.

We conducted interviews with university students who use a running exercise application. Recruiting university students was appropriate for our research goal because most of them have just started to take care of their health by themselves. Our participants are all South Korean, and we think that this is a good starting region to research this subject because South Koreans and East Asians in general, tend to be susceptive to their social group's influences. We think that this cultural characteristic helps us identify various roles and influences of mediators from diverse social channels. However, we also believe that more research will be necessary that focuses on differing cultural influences on this phenomenon in various regions around the world as a future study.

We selected running exercise applications among various types of exercise applications as a representative case for examining the impact of social reinforcement between multiple mediators. In individual sports like running, a user has to accept the full blame for any failure, and there is no social support from teammates [11]. Social reinforcement becomes more important for better performance as well as for emotional support in individual sports. Moreover, most of the running exercise applications can connect to social media for exporting users' running records. People's motivation and experience of exporting running records to social media is important in this study to see the various influences of different mediators from the application itself and social media.

Interviews were aimed at understanding each participant's experience of social reinforcement in using the application. To see the different influences of various mediators, our interviews were composed of three parts. Firstly, after a short icebreaking session, we examined the demographic information about the participants and asked them to introduce their running exercise application. We asked participants to describe the motivation of using the application, as well as the advantages and disadvantages of the application while they launched and operated the application. The first part took 10 to 15 minutes.

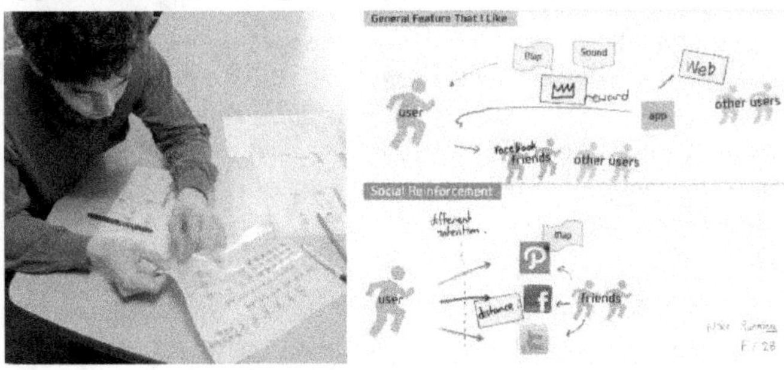

Figure 4. Creating social interaction map (left) and the map that user (P11-F-Nike + Running) created (right)

Secondly, we asked participants to create a map representing the interaction between the participant and mediators in using the application (Figure 4). The purpose of creating the map was to help participants to talk about their experiences easily [23]. We prepared a set of stickers representing a user, a mediator, and the running exercise application and other applications, including social applications, along with colored pencils and a format of the map. The format of the map had two parts: general features that users like in using the application regarding social interaction, and a social reinforcement part (Figure 5). The reason that we asked users to make two different maps is to remind users about their social interaction in the application use and to ask directly about the social reinforcement from different social channels.

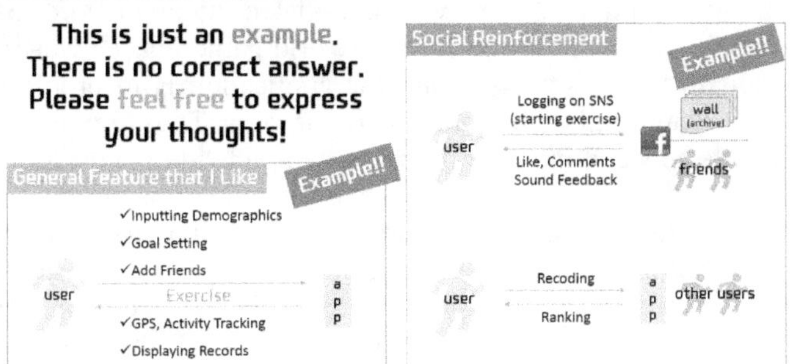

Figure 5. An example map for users that we build in advance

Thirdly, we asked participants to create a map of the interaction between them and mediators in social media (but the experience had to be relevant to the experience of using the running exercise application). Also, when participants felt difficulties in creating the map, we showed an example of the map that we made in advance to help users build their own (Figure 5). The second and third parts of the interview took 30 to 45 minutes in total.

Running Exercise Applications Used by the Participants

Eight out of the 13 participants had been using the Nike+ Running exercise application. The Nike+ Running exercise application provides all statistical results, the running history of users, and sharing through social media. Users of this application can get cheered on by a real-time crowd in social media if a user uploads the posting via social media. Two RunKeeper application users participated in this study. RunKeeper allows users to track running habits of runs, jogs, and even cycling. Similar to Nike+ Running, RunKeeper can export running data to social media. One participant had been using Endomondo, which basically allows users to track running duration, distance, and speed. Interestingly, Endomondo has several social features such as creating routes, challenging running times, and challenging friends who live in the neighborhood. Regarding the competition feature, there is the ability to see other users' times on routes and compete against users' records. One user had been using the Strava application, a riding and running support application that is similar to Endomondo. We recruited one Fitbit user. The application itself is similar to other running exercise applications, but with the Fitbit app and Fitbit wearable device, users' stats automatically sync to select smartphones wirelessly. However, the usage pattern regarding social reinforcement is not different from other running exercise applications, so we included the Fitbit case, too.

Data Analysis

Our interview data were iteratively analyzed more than five times in total with an interval of at least two days of spare time in-between the analysis sessions for enhancing validity. All interviews were audio recorded, producing 12+ hours of content. All recordings were transcribed. In this process, interesting relevant topics were noted and color-coded.

We identified 140 topics during this process, and those topics were subsequently classified with similar topics into 18 different themes. Each theme presents the positive or negative influence of mediators from different social channels for maintaining the participants' health behavior change. These themes were categorized into three different types of social channels where the participant and the mediators can interact with each other. Finally, after we classified them into these three different mediator groups from each social channels, we additionally conducted affinity diagramming to organize the topics from each mediator group based on their relationships and adjusted the level of findings. The entire process of data analysis, including interviewing, transcribing the audio recording, and iteratively using coding and affinity diagramming for finding insights, took around 60+ hours. We refer to each participant by the participant number, sex, and the name of application used (e.g., P1-F-Nike + Running).

FINDINGS

We found that mediators from the different social channels influenced the participants' experiences on health behavior change maintenance in different ways (Table 1).

#	Themes/ Positive or Negative Influences	Social channel
1	Safe feeling of being connected/ +	In-app
2	All users' competition for the 1st rank/ +, -	
3	Defeating friends in application/ -	
4	Communication with intimate friends/ +	
5	Stats of unknown in-app users/ +, -	
6	Motivated by friend's social media posting/ +	Social media
7	Reaction and encouragement from friends/ +	
8	Fragmented using of multiple social media/ +, -	
9	Gaining reputation in social media/ +, -	
10	Representing user's healthy identity/ +, -	
11	Risk of losing face and feeling pressure/ -	
12	Providing easy and smart functions/ +	Agent of the system
13	Possible to archive user's running history/ +	
14	Functional feedback for pace checking/ +	
15	Emotional supports by giving badge icon/ +	
16	Emotional supports by encouragement/ +	
17	As a coach until user get used to running/ +	
18	Real-world mediators would make synergy/ +	Etc.

Table 1. Eighteen themes in three different social channels

The first mediators are in-app users who compete for scores and share running data with each other. The second mediator group is connected via social media such as Path, Facebook, and Twitter. Several people in the first and second mediator groups can overlap if they interact with participants in both groups. The last type of a mediator group is an embedded agent of the running exercise application systems. We found that each group influences the participants' health behavior change maintenance and the roles of the mediators and influence qualities are different. We highlighted important findings from those three different mediator groups' roles and influences by investigating the experience of the participants.

In-app Mediators: Intimacy Level and Similarity of Physical Condition Matter

Within the application, users can easily find and add their friends by using the contact list in their smartphones. Although there are many friends in the application, participants classified mediators into several groups according to their intimacy level due to frequent and thoughtful interaction. In addition to the intimacy level, we also found that the similarity in physical conditions among the connected people influenced people's motivation to maintain the behavior changes. The mediators who have similar physical condition with a participant reinforce participants to maintain their health behaviors through comparing the running stats and competing with each other. The intimacy level and the physical standard are not independent but our study showed that they can be potentially important for social reinforcement. We tried to highlight the influence of these factors on the participants' experiences in social reinforcement.

Running records show user's context or become a target to defeat depending on the intimacy level of mediators

The meaning of the running records of a participant is a conversation cue that shows the context between a participant and his intimate friends in the application, rather than the statistical records for competition. All of the participants have friends who have a high level of intimacy and high frequency of interaction within the application.

"Sometimes I want to see the detailed information of my best friend who was my roommate. Well, she doesn't live here anymore, but I can see her running records in the app. A week ago, I saw that she ran for three hours! I felt that it was a bad sign showing that she may have gotten too much stress in her work, and I called her." (P6-F-Nike + Running)

Participants who have a high intimacy with a mediator share the context of living, the situation of the work, and relationship status—not only about the emotional status, but the intimate mediator group also fully understands how busy the participant is and how hard the route is that the participant ran. Interestingly, we can find strong emotional support, but it is not directly related to health behavior change maintenance. Social reinforcement between a participant and an intimate mediator in an application occurs in neither a competitive way nor a collaborative way to facilitate a health behavior change, but it becomes more like a cue for real-world interaction between them.

"It's not as easy as people think to meet together with my best friends. So we use this app for running together. Although we individually did exercise, we can see each other's records on the feed-in application. When we see the running records of all of us are accumulated in the app, we know we are not so busy. Then, we contact each other and spend hours catching up." (P9-M-Nike + Running)

As seen from the interview, accumulated running records of members become a cue for real-world gathering. However, their initial reason for using the application is to promote their health rather than for social purposes. Thus, emotional bonds between intimate friends are reflected in the usage of the application, and the sense of togetherness indirectly helped the participants to sustain their running exercise. However, when they have a low intimacy level with their acquaintances, the participants describe the relationship with the mediators as competitors. All of the running exercise applications from the interview allow users to examine the leaderboard within the system and highlight winners. This competition motivates participants to enhance their running stats, and it promotes health behavior change maintenance of participants as well.

"I was the first-ranked runner of the last month. I was a second one, but I dedicated my Friday nights for doing exercise. I was really happy to beat my friend's highest records, finally." (P8-F-Nike + Running)

Although competition may motivate a participant, competing with the explicit goal of beating other users may lead to a decrease in intrinsic motivation of users' health promotion.

"I do not say that I do it all the time, but several months ago, I wanted to really beat my friends when I was the second-ranked one with only a slightly slower running performance. So I once used cheap trick. I turned on my application and I rode my bicycle very slowly." (P7-M-Endomondo)

This shows that from time to time, participants' desire to beat their competitors is greater than the motivation of doing exercise for their health behavior change. As a result, sometimes participants forget about their initial goal of doing exercise. Although competition with the mediators who have a low intimacy level with participants can reinforce health behavior change maintenance of participants, it may lead to a change in their original motivation of using the application from maintaining health behavior changes to winning a competition.

The running stats of mediators who have similar physical conditions to those of the participants become a standard

The stats of the runners who have similar build, age, strength, and the same gender as the participants become a standard for reflecting the participants' physical ability by comparing records with them. This standard causes participants to reinforce and strive for maintaining the health-related behaviors. Also, the participants want to get better results among the runners with similar physical conditions.

"I do not know who these large numbers of people are, but I ranked a bit lower than the average for men in their 20s. So I try to change my habits a little every day." (P5-M-Fitbit)

"Actually, I feel superior when I see my running data. I am ranked higher than average among the girls in their 20s in here in my orange level (Nike+ Levels are assigned to distance-based achievements). The application does not provide this kind of comparison, so I access the website to check where I rank." (P8-F-Nike + Running)

In this case, seeing the records of other runners who have similar physical conditions to the participants can motivate the participants and help them maintain their health behavior changes. However, the competition with remarkably superior runners negatively affects participants' emotions. Eventually, it is impossible to reinforce the participants with the records of other runners who have very different physical conditions from the participants.

"He has an immovable position within the runners. At the beginning of the month, we are almost the same, but he always runs much longer and much faster. It is a bit frustrating. I just started to run, and I am female; so it is unfair to compare." (P11-F-Nike + Running)

Other runners' stats in the application become a frame for judgment of a health-related behavior. However, the influences are different, such as reinforcing participants to maintain their health behavior changes or to decrease their motivation to change, according to the similarity of the physical condition level. Interestingly, the negative influences of reinforcement that resulted in the sense of inferiority are mentioned when participants are not intimate enough with the mediators.

Social Media Mediators: Social Face Matter

All of the applications from this interview enable the sharing of participants' running data to social media. Participants are able to post route maps to social media and track their progress along them in real time. One of the interesting features in using social media is in the connection of participants' friends. It is possible for social media friends to monitor and provide encouragement in the form of virtual cheering. We found that social reinforcement from social media users affects participants, and eventually, it helps them to maintain the health behavior.

Timely and enthusiastic response to participants for gaining social face

In using most of the running exercise applications from the interview, participants can hear the sound feedback (such as a real cheering sound and just an alarm sound) when their social media friends add a "like" or comment on the participant's running data. Because of this feature, several users upload their posts through social media. The reaction of others becomes a positive social reinforcement to participants to persist in their health behavior. Participants feel proud of their running data and want to inform others about their efforts to achieve recognition.

"I feel really happy when I hear the cheering sound because someone recognizes me. Well, till high school I was a little bit chubby, and I had never ever done exercise. But I changed. Running represents the 'new me' so I want to show this to other people and want to receive cheers. When my friends 'like' my running stats, I get motivated and want to make better stats." (P4-M-Nike + Running)

"While I run, I can hear the push alarm of my friend's comments on my Facebook post. I do not know what the contents are, but I am happy with excitement and expectations." (P8-F- Nike + Running)

We can see that mediators from social media give positive influences to participants who try to maintain their behavior. From the mentioned running exercise application experiences of participants, feedback from social media friends about participants' running data at an appropriate time made participants proud. Moreover, the size of social reinforcement is a vital driving factor that encourages health behavior changes. Since social media have many features that support social encouragement in virtual space, such as clicking a "like" or a "follow" button, leaving comments, sharing posts, and tagging or mentioning participants' names, mediators from social media easily provide social reinforcement. Eventually, virtual reactions from mediators in social media reinforce participants to exercise repeatedly, and this leads to health behavior change maintenance of participants.

Risk of losing social face becomes a source of reinforcement

Social media is a feature of an activity stream, which is a list of recent activities performed by an individual, and it contains recent actions by the user's friends. Since social media allows users to access other users' individual activity streams, it is easy to recognize the absence of running posts that used to be more common.

"Once, I had not worked out for two weeks in a row. One of my Facebook friends left a post on my wall and asked me why I was not exercising. I felt kind of embarrassed at that time, and I started my running again after I got that post." (P2-M-RunKeeper)

Participants are aware that other people are looking at them, and they feel responsible for their words as a public pledge. If participants use this characteristic of social pressure in social media properly, social pressure can be a means of social reinforcement.

"Sometimes I become too lazy to run. Then the first thing I do is post a message on my Facebook wall that I will start my run. Then I have to run because everyone will see my words." (P8-F- Nike + Running)

In this case, however, it is hard to define other people in social media as mediators since the participants reinforce themselves. The apprehension of the possibility of losing face makes participants act, so it is proper to say that other social media users may have the potential to be mediators. Participants from this study emphasized the importance of the frequency of uploading running posts. If participants post continuous running-related activity streams, the reactions of other friends in social media tend to decrease. For this reason, participants adjust the number of repetitions of running data on their social media.

"I try to exercise at least two times a week, but I cannot upload all of it. If I keep uploading my running, the number of friends who like my posts will decrease. It's the matter of the value of my post among others on the newsfeed. So if I made a really good record, or I ran on a special occasion, then I upload it." (P11-F-Nike + Running)

We found an interesting phenomenon related to the fragmentation of running data. Several participants use multiple social media for uploading running data.

"I usually use Foursquare before I start my run. Whenever I get a good stat, I upload it via Facebook." (P1-M-Strava)

"I used to share my running data using Facebook at the beginning, but I realized that some of my Facebook friends may not want to see it. So I use Twitter, where I share my result with a few friends with the purpose of personal data archiving. But for bragging, I use instant messaging applications with my brother and my friends." (P13-F-Nike + Running)

Participants have two different desires for receiving social reinforcement through using social media. First, they want to share their achievements for gaining social attention. But the social attention requires participants to upload their running stats on social media, and at this moment, the second desire appears to be maintaining their social face. As a second desire, participants are worried about getting little reaction from their social media friends, and they already know such perceived indifference will lead to disappointment. Their need to care about their health by themselves and their need to get attention from others conflict, so several participants seem to negotiate those conflicting desires by using social media dispersively.

Agent Mediators: Continuous Reinforcement Matter

We found another type of social reinforcement and mediator group: reinforcement from the agent of the application system. Participants perceived the application itself, and specifically the voice feedback from the application, as a social actor [5].

"This woman (voice of the application) keeps me exercising steadily. When I finish half of my route, she cheers me on by informing me of how long I have left rather than how long I have run." (P3-M-Nike + Running)

"Once I tried to change the voice of this application from female to male. When I use a female voice, it comforts me. And, yeah, it is just a feeling, but when I change it to the male voice, it's more professional. If I buy a voice pack, then I can choose from various voice types in various languages. It may help." (P7-M-Endomondo)

All of the applications provide voice feedback and vibration feedback continuously while the participants run. However, participants perceive voice feedback as a mediator since participants hear a human voice as a notification or alarm.

DISCUSSION AND DESIGN IMPLICATIONS

In-app Mediators: Sources of Emotional Support and Better Performance

In the study of psychology, it is known that the relationship between a mediator and a person who is trying to change his or her behavior is important, and the influences of social reinforcement vary depending on the relationship [18]. From our study, intimate friends within the application were not a particularly effective mediator group for enhancing the running performance directly, but they provide emotional support to the participants. With respect to health-related issues, it becomes evident that users who share a common ground can understand each other's context and have a better chance of offering intrinsic motivation [10]. Thus, the intimate mediators can provide emotional support to participants.

However, in-app acquaintances could either positively or negatively reinforce participants' behavioral change, depending on the similarity of their physical conditions. The mediators with a similar physical condition level seem to enhance the running performance of participants and reinforce them to maintain the health behavior, although there is a risk of changed purpose due to excessive competition. Competition is defined as a situation where an individual's or a group's performance is being compared with a standard [11]. Competition and comparison are known to stimulate users to set and attain goals [11]. Since participants can access the running stats through the application without temporal and spatial limitation, it is possible to compete against users even though they may live far apart or with a time difference. However, competition has a positive impact when competitors have comparable conditions. Otherwise, competition with a no-win situation negatively affects users' emotions, with effects such as pressure, envy, and a sense of inferiority [11] when the participants were compared to remarkably superior users. Eventually, it is impossible to reinforce the participants with the records of other runners who have very different physical conditions from the participants. The running application from our study primarily focused on the competition with other competitors regardless the comparable physical conditions. However, the mediators with a similar physical ability can help in performing health-related behaviors better through practical aids.

It is necessary to redefine the concept of friends within the application by considering the different intimacy levels and similar physical conditions of the in-app users. An approach that separately provides the channels to interact with these two mediator groups, intimate friends and physically comparable friends, can be an important design implication. They are the sources of social reinforcement for health behavior change, but the balance between emotional support and practical aids is the key for providing effective health services depending on the target behavior and user's background.

Social Media Mediators: Politely Revealing the Achievement for More Effective Engagement

Timing, balance between deprivation and satiation, size, amount, type, and quality are known as factors of reinforcement, and those factors support the behavior change maintenance of users [24]. Specifically, we discovered that the timing and size of responses of reinforcement affect participants with mediators from social media. Moreover, we found that social face is importantly influence to participants' health behavior maintenance. According to Goffman [7], the face is a mask that changes depending on the audience and the variety of social interactions. Social faces are emotionally attached to people, so people try to maintain their social face and are afraid of losing it [7]. The theory is also applied in the use of social media, as people manage their reputation and disclosure process [25]. In this research, we found that social face influences users to maintain their health behavior change. Depending on the gain or loss of social face, the social reinforcement type becomes different to manage one's face.

From this study, we revealed an expanded concept of the mediator to the diverse social group in the virtual world. We found that mediators in social media positively influence participants when they provide compliments via comments and by clicking the "like" button, but the social concern about losing face hinders participants from maintaining their behavioral changes due to the lack of the social reinforcement from mediators. Interestingly, we saw that participants negotiated the ways of sharing their achievements and were careful with publicly-available information. They used a series of social media tools to avoid frequent exposure to others' activity streams. For this reason, the participants' running data became fragmented across the various social media platforms and social channels.

We found a similar phenomenon from the study of Newman et al. [16]. They found the importance of a balance between sharing health-related information and the desire to manage self-presentation by observing participants' use of an online health community for health-related information and Facebook for impression management. In Newman et al.'s study, they investigated users who tried to lose weight and/or manage Type II diabetes by using an online health community and SNS, and by sharing obese/diabetes information that may have a different level of privacy and seriousness compared to what we studied, i.e. running exercise. Although the backgrounds and situations of the participants are different from ours, the expression of a virtual identity with an ideal health state through SNS and the practical health-related behavior has a tension. For instance, if the impression management gives motivation to a participant, applying social reinforcement through social media can be effective. However, if a participant does not want to share his health-related data on social media due to privacy concerns or personal characteristics, the mediators from social media do not have a large impact on his or her health behavior change. The future research direction for this finding would be about how the tension differently affects users' health behavior changes across the diverse service platforms and backgrounds or according to the personal characteristics of users. It is difficult to demonstrate the effects of fragments of social reinforcement without further study, so such additional research is needed in order to design the feature of politely revealing participants' running data to gain social responses from social media friends. For example, by posting indirect and ambient information about improvements in running stats, shared stats via SNS can expire after a certain amount of time or selecting a certain audience group can be a possible solution. However, according to the seriousness of health-related issues, the sensitivity of health-related data to users, and the participants' individual characteristics, the effectiveness of applying social media can differ. Thus, it is important to consider the most affective and effective mediator groups for an individual's health behavior change.

Agent Mediators: Potential Mediators of Coaches and Pacemakers

The definition of a mediator is a human who delivers social reinforcement including gaining social attention, feeling affection, and building a social reputation [24]. In this perspective, the direct and real mediator is human, but it seems possible to consider even non-human agents as potential mediators from this study. Persuasive technology [5] has the potential to change attitudes or behaviors of the users through persuasion and social influence in various ways, e.g., as a tool, a form of media, or a social actor. Moreover, experimental results from human-robot interaction show that people do display social and emotional behavior toward computers when users perceive human qualities in computers, even though the computers do not actually have them [20]. The social expressions from a computer agent draw positive reactions from users; furthermore, social expressions that are offered from a robotic product are desirable as a persuasive agent [2, 14]. As a persuasive agent, users tend to accept the computer agent as an interesting counterpart, and they perceive its human qualities.

From this study, we also found a computer agent that may have the potential to influence users' behavioral change by providing social reinforcement as a mediator, such as by giving compliments and stirring up energy by playing a power song. From our study, users perceived agents as potential social mediators because the agent mediator encourages users and provide information. In general, the diversification of feedback quality, types, and characteristics from an agent is important in order to maintain users' behavior changes. Although there is advancement in the computer agent, social reinforcement from agents and from human mediators affects the participants differently. From the interview, we discovered that the reinforcement from the agent enhances running performance but only by a small amount compared with a competitor who runs with the person. However, the agent is able to give continuous and constant responses to participants and provide information relevant to the running exercise, such as notifying user of the weather conditions and running routes. For these reasons, the agent of the system influence participants as a virtual coach and pacemaker. Thus, a possible direction of enhancing the influence of social reinforcement from the agent is to design ways to support human mediators.

With respect to the study of Fritz et al. [6], they found that designers can support users' long-term use of a fitness tracker by providing at the evolved displaying of tracked activities, data sharing, and rewards. One of their finding is that designing a system that supports and engages users by using various types of rewards is important in the fitness domain. In positive reinforcement, tangible, token, social, and other types of reinforcers influence a person's behavior change. Although Fritz et al. focused on the impact and influence of tracking devices, and our study focuses on the impact and influence of different mediators, they mentioned the possibility of rich and diverse qualities of reinforcement. We see that the resources of reinforcement can be from other mediators who are not using the tracking devices. Eventually, an agent in the system becomes a channel of reinforcement from users of diverse and different service systems and social channels. In the connected services, the agent may help human mediators to lead a dialogue relevant to the health behavior change, for instance, by suggesting new routes or sharing mutual goals of participants, which will support the conversation between mediators and participants.

CONCLUSION

In this study, we sought to disclose the different influences of social reinforcement on health behavior changes, depending on the various roles of mediators from diverse social channels, specifically in applications and among social media platforms. The key factors that drive social reinforcement for maintaining healthy behavior changes for each type of mediators are as follows. Balancing between helpful emotional support and challenging users' running performance will be a key to providing positive influences to runners to sustain the desired behavior change, especially by the mediators within the application. Prompt, enthusiastic, and continuous responses and feedback from social media friends will encourage users to maintain their healthy behavior change as well. We found that the concept of mediators expands from several real-world mediators to countless virtual-world mediators. Also, the synergy of the agent from the application in the virtual world and human mediators in the real world will help users to keep their healthy habits.

As we revealed in this study, diverse mediators in different social channels influence participants' health behavior change maintenance in different ways. Developing design strategies that invite users to synergize with various mediators in the virtual and real worlds is a possible future direction of this study. Moreover, it seems important to reveal how these different roles of various mediators can interplay with each other to reinforce the maintenance of healthy behavior. As we mentioned earlier, the cultural issues on this subject will also be a very important and interesting theme to be investigated for future studies.

ACKNOWLEDGMENTS

This research was supported by "Dr. M" Project funded by KAIST (N01140095). We would like to express our sincere thanks to all the participants. We also deeply appreciate sincere and invaluable advice from Jina Huh.

REFERENCES

[1] Adams, P. et al., Staccato Social Support in Mobile Health Applications. In *Proc. CHI 2014*, ACM (2014), 653-662.

[2] Bickmore, T. & Picard, R. Establishing and maintaining long-term human-computer relationships. *Computer-Human Interaction*, 12(2) (2005), 293-327.

[3] Doherty, G., Coyle, D. & Sharry, J. Engagement with online mental health interventions: an exploratory clinical study of a treatment for depression. In *Proc. CHI 2012,* ACM (2012), 1421-1430.

[4] Farnham, S. D & Churchill, E. F. Faceted Identity, Faceted Lives: Social and Technical Issues with Being Yourself Online. In *Proc. CSCW 2011*, ACM (2011), 359-368.

[5] Fogg, B.J. A Behavior Model for Persuasive Design. In *Proc. Persuasive 2009,* ACM (2009), No. 40.

[6] Fritz, T. et al. Persuasive technology in the real world: a study of long-term use of activity sensing devices for fitness. In *Proc. CHI 2014*, ACM (2014), 487-496.

[7] Goffman, E. *The Presentation of Self in Everyday Life.* Garden City, NY: Doubleday, 1959.

[8] Hekler, E. B. et al. Mind the theoretical gap: Interpreting, using, and developing behavioral theory in HCI research. In *Proc. CHI 2013,* ACM (2013), 3307–3316.

[9] Hogan, B. E., Linden, W. & Najarian, B. Social support interventions: do they work? *Clinical Psychology Review*. Apr. 22(3) (2002), 383-442.

[10] Jeffery, R. W. et al. Monetary contracts in weight control: Effectiveness of group and individual contracts of varying size. *Journal of Consulting and Clinical Psychology*. Apr. 51(2) (1983), 242-248.

[11] Jones, G. More than just a game: Research developments and issues in competitive anxiety in sport. *British Journal of Psychology*. 86 (1995), 449–478.

[12] Kim, S. C. et al. Predictors of Online Health Information Seeking Among Women with Breast Cancer: The Role of Social Support Perception and Emotional Well-Being. *Journal of Computer-Mediated Communication*. 18 (2013), 212–232.

[13] Macvean, A & Robertson, J. Understanding exergame users' physical activity, motivation and behavior over time. In *Proc. CHI 2013,* ACM (2013), 1251-1260.

[14] Morkes, J., Kernal, H. K. & Nass, C. Humor in task-oriented computer-mediated communication and human-computer interaction. In *Proc. CHI 1998,* ACM (1998), 461-474.

[15] Murnane, E. L. & Counts, S. Unraveling Abstinence and Relapse: Smoking Cessation Reflected in Social Media. *In Proc. CHI 2014*, ACM (2014), 1345-1354.

[16] Newman, M.W. et al. It's not that I don't have problems, I'm just not putting them on Facebook: Challenges and opportunities in using online social networks for health. In *Proc. CSCW 2011*, ACM (2011), 341-350.

[17] Park, T. et al. ExerSync: interpersonal synchrony in social exergames. In *Proc. CSCW 2013*, ACM (2013), 27-30.

[18] Pasch, L. A., Bradbury, T. N., & Sullivan, K. T. *Social support in marriage: An analysis of intraindividual and interpersonal components.* Sourcebook of social support and personality. New York, Plenum, 1997.

[19] Prochaska, J.O. & Velicer, W.F. The Transtheoretical Model of health behavior change. *American Journal of Health Promotion,* 12 (1997), 38-48.

[20] Reeves, B. & Nass, C. *The Media Equation: How People Treat Computers, Television, and New Media Like Real People and Places.* Cambridge University Press, 1996.

[21] Shirky, C. *Cognitive surplus: Creativity and generosity in a connected age*. Penguin Press, New York, 2010.

[22] Skinner, B. F. *Science and human behavior*. New York: McMillan, 1953.

[23] Stappers, P. J., & Sanders, E. B. N. Generative tools for context mapping: tuning the tools. In *Proc. Design and Emotion 2004,* Taylor & Francis (2004), 77-81.

[24] Sundel, M. and Sundel, S. S. Behavior change in the human services: Behavioral and cognitive principles and applications, (5th Ed.), SAGE Publications, 2005.

[25] Vitak, J. & Kim, J. "You can't block people offline": examining how facebook's affordances shape the disclosure process. In *Proc. CSCW 2014*, ACM (2014), 461-474.

[26] Watson, D. L. and Tharp, R. G. *Self-directed behavior: Self-modification for personal adjustment*, (9th Ed.). Belmont, CA: Thomson/Wadsworth, 2005. 242-245.

[27] Xue, Y. et al. Towards a micro-blog platform for sensing and easing adolescent psychological pressures. In *Proc. UbiComp 2013*, ACM (2013), 215-218.

Is It Good to Be Like Wikipedia?: Exploring the Trade-offs of Introducing Collaborative Editing Model to Q&A Sites

Guo Li[1, 2], **Haiyi Zhu**[3], **Tun Lu**[1, 2], **Xianghua Ding**[1, 2], **Ning Gu**[1, 2]
[1]School of Computer Science, Fudan University, Shanghai, China
[2]Shanghai Key Laboratory of Data Science, Fudan University, Shanghai, China
[3]Carnegie Mellon University, Pittsburgh, PA, USA
guoli@fudan.edu.cn, haiyiz@cs.cmu.edu, {lutun, dingx, ninggu}@fudan.edu.cn

ABSTRACT

Online question and answer (Q&A) sites, which are platforms for users to post and answer questions on a wide range of topics, are becoming large repositories of valuable knowledge and important to societies. In order to sustain success, Q&A sites face the challenges of ensuring content quality and encouraging user contributions. This paper examines a particular design decision in Q&A sites—allowing Wikipedia-like collaborative editing on questions and answers, and explores its beneficial effects on content quality and potential detrimental effects on users' contributions. By examining five years' archival data of Stack Overflow, we found that the benefits of collaborative editing outweigh its risks. For example, each substantive edit from other users can increase the number of positive votes by 181% for the questions and 119% for the answers. On the other hand, each edit only decreases askers and answerers' subsequent contributions by no more than 5%. This work has implications for understanding and designing large-scale social computing systems.

Author Keywords

Collaborative Editing; Q&A Systems; Stack Overflow; Social Computing System Design.

ACM Classification Keywords

H.5.3 [Information Interfaces and Presentation]: Group and Organization Interfaces – Collaborative computing, Computer-supported cooperative work, Web-based interaction; K.4.3 [Computers and Society]: Organizational Impacts – Computer supported collaborative work.

General Terms

Experimentation; Management.

CSCW '15, March 14 – 18, 2015, Vancouver, BC, Canada.

http://dx.doi.org/10.1145/2675133.2675155

INTRODUCTION

Online question and answer (Q&A) sites are platforms for users to ask and answer questions on a wide range of topics. Successful Q&A systems include Ackerman's AnswerGarden [7, 8], Yahoo! Answers [9, 10], Stack Exchange networks [23], Quora [38], and Naver's Knowledge iN [24]. After a decade of development, Q&A sites are now large repositories of valuable knowledge and provide enduring value to societies [9, 11, 33].

One significant challenge for these Q&A sites is to ensure the quality of the content on the sites, given that users' expertise, commitment and experience are highly varied [10]. Therefore, multiple methods are used to filter out low quality content and to promote high quality content. For example, voting systems are widely used for the community to indicate which questions and answers are the most useful and appropriate. Many Q&A sites also implement mechanisms for users to report low quality content, such as spam, offensive speech or off-topic conversations.

As one effort to achieve higher quality, there is a recent trend for Q&A sites to incorporate Wikipedia-like collaborative editing function, that is, allowing questions and answers to be collaboratively edited by the whole community. For example, Stack Overflow, which features computer programming related questions and answers, claims that "*(Collaborative) Editing is important for keeping questions and answers clear, relevant, and up-to-date*" and "*This site is collaboratively edited,* ***like Wikipedia****. If you see something that needs improvement, click edit!*" [1]

Despite the benefits of improving content quality, introducing Wikipedia-like collaborative editing to Q&A sites might incur the risks of decreasing the immediate benefits of participating in the Q&A sites, and harm both the askers and answerers' motivation to contribute. Note that Q&A sites initially aim at providing useful answers to the question askers. Editors are likely to misinterpret what the original askers mean to say, leading to less useful answers for the askers and thus decreasing the askers' motivation to come to the site. Also, research has shown that people are motivated to answer the questions because it will enhance their professional identities and improve their standing in the community [29]. Therefore, answerers might feel that their expertise is challenged and their professional identities are threatened if others edit their answers and, thus, become less motivated to contribute.

For Q&A sites, is it cost-effective to be like Wikipedia? In this paper, we did an empirical study on Stack Overflow to answer this question. Stack Overflow is one of the most popular Q&A sites allowing collaborative editing. By investigating the historical data of 2 million users, 5 million questions and 10 million answers, we found that the benefits of collaborative editing significantly outweigh the risks of losing contributions. For example, we found that each additional edit from other users can increase the number of positive votes by 181% for questions and 119% for answers. On the other hand, each additional edit from other users on the question or answer body decreases the askers or answerers' subsequent contributions by no more than 5%. By allowing collaborative editing, Stack Overflow substantively increases the quality of posts without bringing in strong detrimental effects on users' motivation to contribute.

Our paper presents a quantitative case study to examine the impact of a particular design decision (i.e., allowing collaborative editing) in the Q&A sites. The implications of this research for understanding and designing large-scale social computing systems are also discussed.

RELATED WORK

Online Q&A sites are powerful tools for users to seek for help by posing questions and getting answers from peer community. The blueprint for Q&A sites was established by Ackerman's AnswerGarden [7, 8], which was designed as a tool for growing organizational memory and helped users to find expert answers inside their companies. Recent Q&A sites often operate on Internet scale and rely on the crowd people to contribute [23].

Prior research on Q&A sites falls into two main groups. The first group of research focuses on analyzing and identifying patterns from the content of the posts from Q&A sites. For example, research has been conducted to identify and understand the topics and trends of the questions [13], assess, evaluate and predict the quality of the answers [11, 21, 25, 34, 39], and identify the experts in Q&A sites [26, 27].

The second group of research treats Q&A sites as social computing systems and focuses on understanding the social dynamics in Q&A systems, such as what factors lead the Q&A sites to thrive and how people interact with each other in these sites. For example, Mamykina and her colleagues [23] investigate Stack Overflow and claim that productive competition, community credibility and feedback loop play important roles in Stack Ovewflow's initial (and continuous) fast growth. Tausczik et al. [37] identify different collaborative acts in Math Overflow (which is a Q&A site where members post and solve small novel math problems) and evaluate their influences on the quality of solutions.

Our paper takes the second approach. We believe that like most social computing systems (e.g., Wikipedia, open source projects, and social networking sites like Facebook), Q&A systems face the challenges of achieving continued success. Particularly, there are two often conflicting goals for Q&A systems: managing quality and encouraging contributions.

HYPOTHESES

Tensions between Managing Quality and Encouraging Contributions

Social computing systems need to provide high-quality content to attract users. The definitions of high quality differ widely across different systems. For example, in Q&A sites, the quality is high if the posts are informative, polite, complete, concise and useful [34, 39]. In Wikipedia, the high quality content is complete, accurate and reliable encyclopedia articles. In social networking sites, high quality content might consist of enjoyable or useful messages and interesting photos. Because users' experience, commitment and expertise are highly varied, the quality of individual contributions is often mixed [10]. To display high quality content to users, systems need to implement mechanisms to mark, change, or even delete users' low-quality contributions. Sometimes, systems have to regulate, warn, punish or even block some users if their actions harm the integrity of the whole system. In sum, quality management is inevitably associated with filtering content, regulating users' behaviors, and often limiting users' freedom.

However, the survival of social computing systems relies on users' continuing contributions. There would be no need for quality control if all the users stopped contributing. To encourage people to contribute, systems often have to treasure their efforts and respect their autonomy. If users feel that their contributions are thrown away and their behaviors are strictly controlled, they might simply leave, with fewer economic or social consequences than if they had quit a job or left a real-life social group.

A recent research on Wikipedia provides a good example to illustrate the tension. Halfaker and his colleagues found that several changes the Wikipedia community made to manage quality and consistency (e.g., the use of anti-vandalism tools), although successfully preserve the content quality, cause the decline in the number of active contributors [19]. They wrote "*we implicate Wikipedia's primary quality control mechanism, the rejection of unwanted contributions, as a strong negative predictor of the retention of high-quality newcomers*". "*Newcomers are rudely greeted by automated quality control systems... have been leaving Wikipedia in droves*".

Introducing collaborative editing to online Q&A sites might face the same dilemma. We predict that this design decision might impact the success of Q&A sites in different directions.

Effects of Collaborative Editing on Q&A Sites

Collaborative Editing Improves the Content Quality

Collaborative editing has been used in many areas (e.g., science collaboration [18, 28], software development [16]); and different kinds of tools (e.g., wikis, version control systems, and collaborative editors) are developed to promote content production. One of the most successful examples is Wikipedia.

It has been widely believed that Wikipedia's success in producing a large number of articles with quite high quality is largely attributed to the open collaboration model that allows any person in the world to participate in the editing. Particularly, having more contributors results in higher quality and less biased encyclopedia articles. According to the experiment published in 2004, the quality of scientific entries in Wikipedia is comparable to those in Britannica [17]. Furthermore, researchers investigate how factors such as coordination mechanisms and member retention affect the quality of the collaboratively edited articles [22, 30]. For example, Kittur and Kraut examined how the number of editors in Wikipedia and the coordination methods they use affect the article quality [22]. They found that adding more editors to an article is more likely to improve its quality if they use the appropriate coordination techniques.

"With enough eyeballs, all bugs are shallow" (Linus' law) [31]. By incorporating the collaborative editing feature in Q&A sites, unclear questions and inaccurate answers can be fixed. Therefore, it is reasonable to predict that incorporating the collaborative editing model will benefit the Q&A sites by improving the content quality.

Hypothesis 1. Collaborative editing will improve the content quality in Q&A sites.

Collaborative Editing Demotivates the Contributors

Even in Wikipedia, there is evidence showing that collaborative editing is associated with negative consequences on contributors' motivation. Research has shown that Wikipedia reverts (i.e., edits that revert the article back to its previous state) significantly decrease recipients' subsequent contributions. The effects are stronger for newcomers in the community [20].

We predict that the possible damage of collaborative editing would be even more severe in the context of online Q&A sites. In Wikipedia, it is wildly accepted that the content of Wikipedia is public property rather than any individual's intellectual properties [2], which might result in less resistance when people get edited by others. However, in Q&A sites, people are motivated to post questions because they need help for their specific issues. People are more likely to perceive that they "own" the questions and modification of their questions is likely to irritate them. Here is a person's comment on Meta Stack Exchange (i.e., a platform for people to discuss issues on Stack Overflow and other related sites) which clearly illustrates the point [3]:

"A wiki is an informational type of site. SO (Stack Overflow) is for people to get help for their specific issues. The person asking the question knows best about the issue and is entitled to have his question."

According to the research about motivations to participate and contribute in online Q&A sites [24, 29], the distinct motivations for people to participate in Q&A sites are personal ownership and feelings of gratitude and respect. Bringing in the collaborative editing model is very likely to devastate people's motivation and has a negative effect on the activity level of the whole site.

Hypothesis 2. Collaborative editing will demotivate the users in Q&A sites.

In the following paper, we want to test the hypotheses about the effects of combining collaborative editing in Q&A sites. Particularly, we use Stack Overflow (SO) as the study platform.

STACK OVERFLOW AS A STUDY PLATFORM

Stack Overflow [1] was selected as our study platform to conduct the analyses. It is a well-known online Q&A site which supports collaborative editing. Typical features of Stack Overflow include questioning, answering, voting, commenting, and etc. It is also very large, having more than five million questions and ten million answers; and the growth of questions, answers, and the corresponding edits is very steady (Figure 1). The large dataset provides us sufficient statistical power to test our hypotheses. Although there are other Q&A sites with the feature of collaborative editing (e.g., Quora, Wikianswers, and Math Overflow), in this study, we will present the results on Stack Overflow and leave the cross-site comparison study for future work.

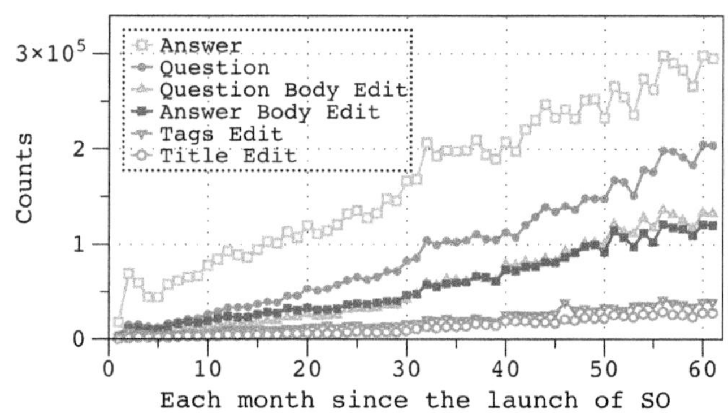

Figure 1. The numbers of questions, answers, and edits in every month since the launch of Stack Overflow.

In Stack Overflow, a question comprises a title, a body, and several tags (e.g., "Java" or "Hadoop"). The title briefly

[1] http://stackoverflow.com

describes the question's purpose; the body is used to explain the question in detail, and programing code snippets and hyperlinks are often attached to provide further information; the tags facilitate dispatching the question to the potential users who are interested in it (e.g., users interested in questions with the tag of "Java"). An answer provides solutions or related information to solve the question. Code snippets and hyperlinks are also often used in answers.

Typical user actions on Stack Overflow include: 1) posting a question to seek for help; 2) answering a question by providing a solution or relevant information; 3) casting an up-votes (positive) or down-vote (negative) to inform the quality of the question/answer; 4) commenting on a question/answer to discuss, and 5) suggesting an edit to revise an existing question/answer. There is a reputation system in Stack Overflow. By posting high quality questions and answers, and suggesting reasonable edits, users can earn points to increase their reputations. Votes are used to measure the quality of questions and answers [4].

Figure 2 shows how questions, answers, comments, and votes look like on the interface of Stack Overflow.

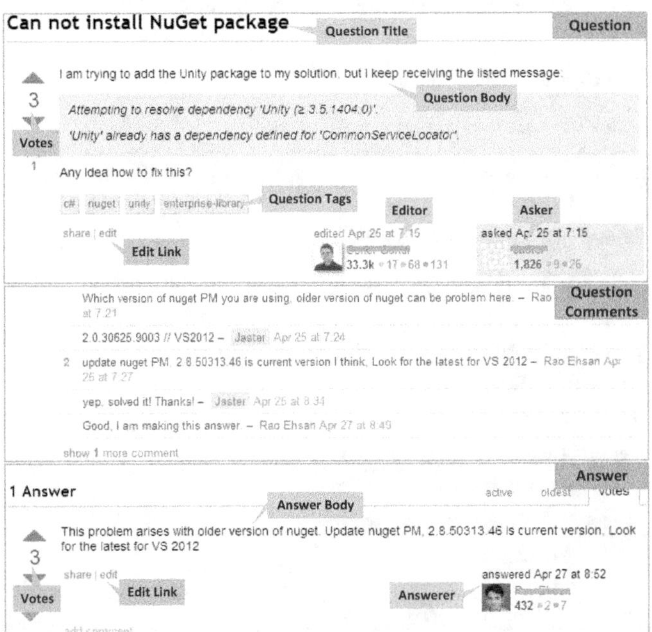

Figure 2. An example of a question and an answer in Stack Overflow.

How Collaborative Editing Works in Stack Overflow

Collaborative editing is permitted and welcomed in Stack Overflow. It is explicitly stated in the user guidelines that "*any time you see a post that needs improvement and are inclined to suggest an edit, you are welcome to do so.*" [1]

Any user can suggest edits to revise a question's title, body, and tags, or an answer's body. Suggested edits from the original askers and answerers will be applied immediately, as well as from users who have more than 2,000 reputation points (2k users). Other users' suggested edits will be reviewed by the 2k users to decide whether to be applied or not. Since unapplied edits are not visible to the community, we will only examine the applied edits in this paper.

Dataset Overview

The historical data of Stack Overflow since August 1st 2008 to September 6th 2013 was used in this paper. Stack Exchange periodically publishes the data dump of their sites, including Stack Overflow, to the public. The data dump of Stack Overflow contains all registered users' activity logs, including questions, answers, votes, edits and comments. See Table 1 for the overview of the data set.

Item	Count
Users	2,332,403
Questions	5,648,975
Answers	10,284,554
Up- and Down-Votes	36,435,956
Accepted Edits	9,059,350
Comments	22,666,468

Table 1. Dataset description.

In the following, we will first present descriptive statistics to provide an overview about the activities of collaborative editing on Stack Overflow.

23% Users Participate in Editing

About 23% distinct users (531,064) have suggested accepted edits on questions and answers. Among them, 82,762 distinct users have edited others' questions and answers. Users tend to prefer to edit question bodies and answer bodies (Table 2). As in many online communities, user editing patterns in Stack Overflow have high variability: a few users contribute most of the edits while lots of users contribute a small portion (Figure 3).

Edit Type	Distinct Contributors	Mean (Median) of Edit Count
Title Edit	124,480	6.16 (1)
Question Body Edit	417,689	8.34 (2)
Tags Edit	135,377	8.93 (1)
Answer Body Edit	221,280	15.72 (2)

Table 2. More users participate in editing question bodies and answer bodies.

24% of Answers Have Been Edited

About 23.9% answers (2,457,817) have been edited at least once. For questions, 40.2% question bodies (2,268,162) have been edited; for question titles and question tags the numbers are 12.2% and 18.2% respectively. Most of the posts (questions and answers) receive a few edits, while a small portion of posts receive lots of edits (Figure 4).

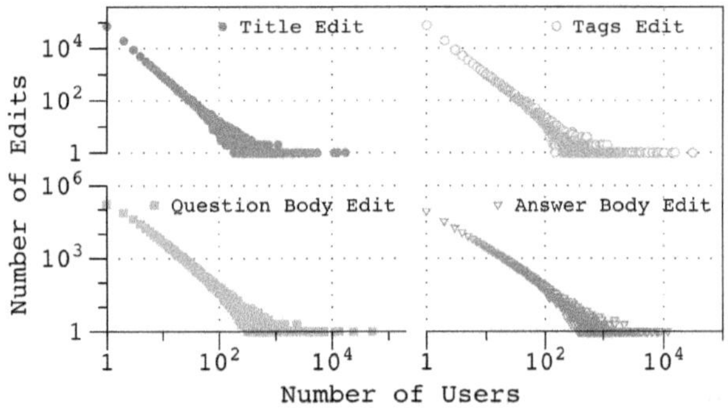

Figure 3. User editing patterns have high variability.

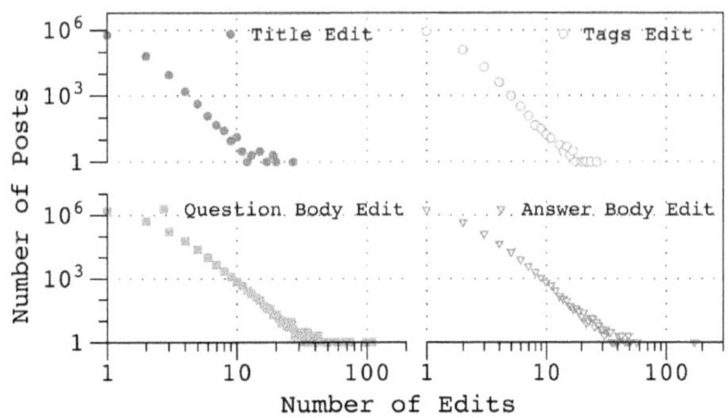

Figure 4. Questions and answers receive highly varied counts of edits.

Among all the edits, 59.4% of them come from the original askers or answers, and 38.5% of them come from others not the original askers or answers. There are 2.1% edits in the database whose author information is incomplete probably due to account deletion. We focus on the edits from other users not the originators in the following analyses, because we focus on collaborative editing rather than self-refinement.

What are the Edits about?

According to the Stack Overflow's user guidelines, there are five common types of edits: 1) fixing grammar and spelling mistakes, 2) clarifying meaning of the post, 3) including information found only in comments, 4) correcting mistakes or adding updates, and 5) adding related resources. Examples are given in Figure 5.

However, conflicts occur when people's questions and answers are edited by others, even though those editors have good intentions. By examining the Meta Stack Exchange[2] where people discuss issues they encounter in Stack Exchange networks, we found a few interesting cases. For example, a question asker said *"He (the editor) completely changed the meaning of my post. I find this to be rather unacceptable"*. Actually the editor only rephrases the original post, including changing "*users fully know that stacktrace/crash report are being sent to us*" to "*We do let our users know that we collect crash data*". And many community members believe that the edits are reasonable by making the question "*more concise and comprehensible*" [5].

Another question asker expressed strong resistance when others changed a word in his/her question. "*In my last question, someone changed 'less expensive' to 'cheaper'. I don't appreciate anyone changing my wording because they think theirs is better. 'Less expensive' is what I want to say and wanted to convey. Not 'Cheaper'. My intention was to convey that the alternatives mentioned were expensive TO ME. ... When you are in a meeting, do people talk over you to correct what you are saying or how you say it!? They don't. So why do you think it's OK to do it here? When I ask a question, it's asked for my own good. It's not a work area to exercise your English skills*" [3].

An answerer also complained when he/she found his/her correct answer was changed to a wrong one, "*Out of nowhere, a user comes in (with a reputation of 1), edits my answer which completely changes my answer(into a wrong one) and someone accepted the edit*" [6].

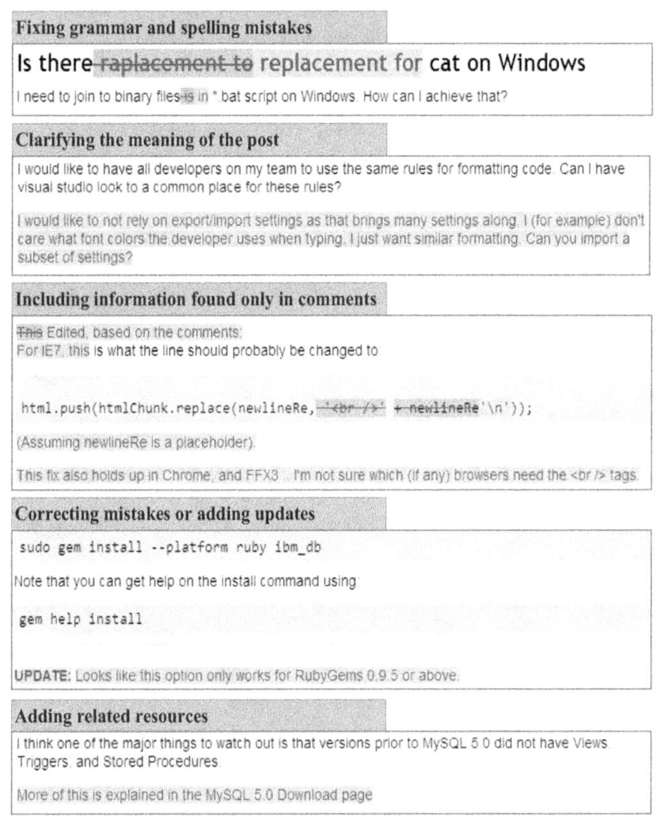

Figure 5. Stack Overflow's guidelines about proposing edits and examples.

ANALYSES AND RESULTS

In this section, we will present our main analyses, examining the effects of collaborative editing on content quality and contributors' motivation in Stack Overflow. In the first analysis, we examine the effects of collaborative editing on the quality of questions and answers by investigating how many votes the questions/answers receive,

[2] http://meta.stackexchange.com/

whether the questions have accepted answers, how many answers the questions receive, and whether the answers are chosen as accepted ones depending on how many edits were made on these questions/answers. In the second analysis, we examine the effects of collaborative editing on users' motivation by measuring the number of questions/answers subsequently posted by the users after their questions/answers got edited.

Effects on Content Quality

Measuring Quality

In order to test whether receiving edits will improve the quality of questions and answers, we need to measure the quality. The first measurement we use for content quality is the number of votes on question/answer, which is one of the most direct and commonly used measurements of content quality in Q&A communities [3] [35]. Particularly we calculated the net votes by counting the up-votes minus down-votes. Additionally, we measure the quality of questions by calculating the number of answers and whether the question has an accepted answer. For the quality of answers, we also measured whether the answer is accepted by the asker. In sum, the quality measurements include received votes (both questions and answers), the number of answers (for questions), whether the question has an accepted answer (for questions), and whether the answer is accepted (for answers).

Control for Confounding Factors

One challenge of testing the effects of collaborative editing on content quality (and user motivation as well) is to control for confounding factors. We mainly use two strategies to rule out the biases introduced by observed and unobserved confounding factors. First, we include two groups of observed variables as control variables in the analysis: poster's characteristics (such as number of the previous posts from this poster, the average score of the previous posts, poster registration date, see the complete list below) and post's characteristics (such as the post's topic, the number of page views, see the complete list below). Secondly, to control for the unobserved and unchanging characteristics of the posts (such as the popularity of the post), we use the repeated observations on each post. Repeated observations are commonly used empirical strategy to identify causal relationship from observational dataset [12]. Particularly, we test whether receiving edits in the focal week will affect the votes received in the following two weeks, controlling for the votes received the in the preceding week.

Statistics Model and Data Preparation

Negative binomial regression (nbreg) models are used to model count outcome variables with great variability [14]. We observed each post's activity in a one-month window, including the focal week, one preceding week, and two following weeks. We restricted the posts to the ones which were posted before 2013-08-01 and had complete author information. Finally, the data comprised of 5,335,456 unique questions and 9,865,021 unique answers.

Dependent Variables

- *ReceivedVotes (for questions and answers).* The newly received votes in the following two weeks.
- *AnswerNumber (for questions).* The number of new answers the question received in the following two weeks.
- *HasAcceptedAnswer (for questions).* Whether the question has an accepted answer in the following two weeks.
- *AnswerAccepted (for answers).* Whether the answer is accepted in the following two weeks.

Independent Variables

- *TitleEdits (for questions).* The number of title edits the question received excluding those from the asker in the focal week. Note that answers do not have title edits.
- *BodyEdits (for questions and answers).* The number of body edits the question/answer received excluding those from the asker/answerer in the focal week.
- *TagsEdits (for questions).* The number of tags edits the question received excluding those from the asker in the focal week. Note that answers do not have tags edits.

Control Variables

We use the following three categories of variables as control variables in the regression models.

- *Poster's Characteristics. PostCount* (the number of questions/answers from the poster before the focal week), *PostAvgScore* (the average score of the posted questions/answers from the poster before the focal week), *PosterReputation* (the reputation points of the poster), and *PosterRegDate* (the timestamp when the poster created his/her account) are a group of variables controlling for the posters' differences.
- *Post's Characteristics. Topic* (the categorical variable indicating the topic of the post[4]), *PageView* (the total number of page views of the question/answer),

[3] http://stackoverflow.com/help/why-vote.

[4] We used two methods to characterize the topics of the posts: 1) the top 10 most used tags as topics and 2) topics discovered through topic modeling [36]. We include two categorical variables indicating two different topic measurements as control variables in the regression, although they almost do not bring in any change to the results. To save the space, we do not report the *IRRs* and standard errors of these two categorical variables in Table 3 and Table 4.

	Question Quality					
	Model 1: Votes		Model 2: Answer Number		Model 3: Has Accepted Answer	
	IRR	Std. Err.	IRR	Std. Err.	IRR	Std. Err.
TitleEdits	1.39 ***	.068	1.21 ***	.058	1.12 **	.043
BodyEdits	2.81 ***	.058	2.43 ***	.048	1.41 ***	.012
TagsEdits	1.98 ***	.067	1.81 ***	.059	1.43 ***	.035
PostCount	1.00 ***	4.88e-05	1.00 ***	6.00e-05	1.00 ***	3.71e-05
PostAvgScore	1.06 ***	9.49e-04	1.03 ***	5.99e-04	1.00	4.06e-04
PosterReputation	1.00 ***	3.21e-07	1.00 ***	3.26e-07	1.00 ***	2.29e-07
PosterRegDate	1.00 ***	1.16e-10	1.00 ***	1.23e-10	1.00 ***	9.96e-11
PageView	1.00 ***	7.53e-07	1.00 ***	6.70e-07	1.00	5.13e-07
TextLength	1.00 ***	1.94e-06	1.00 ***	1.82e-06	1.00 ***	1.64e-06
HasCode	.80 ***	.006	.72 ***	.005	.850 ***	.005
HasLink	1.41 ***	.011	1.35 ***	.011	1.09 ***	.008
PostDate	1.00 ***	1.26e-10	1.00 ***	1.30e-10	1.00 ***	1.06e-10
PriorVotes	1.45 ***	.006	NA	NA	NA	NA
PriorAnswers	NA	NA	.76 ***	.002	NA	NA
PriorHasAcceptedAnswer	NA	NA	NA	NA	6.04e-10	3.39e-07
Number of Obs	5,335,456					

Table 3. Negative binomial regressions predicting the effects of collaborative editing on three question quality measurements. *** p<0.001; ** p<0.01; * p<0.05.

Note that IRR can be interpreted as the ratio change of the dependent variable when increasing an independent variable by one unit. For example, Model 1 shows that by increasing title edits by one, the questions will receive 39% more votes subsequently.

TextLength (the text length of the question/answer), *HasCode* (whether the question/answer contains programming code snippets), *HasLink* (whether the question/answer contains hyperlinks), and *PostDate* (the timestamp when the question/answer was created) are also included in the regression as control variables. Additionally, *ParentQuestionVotes* (the number of votes received by the answer's parent question) and *ArrivalOrder* (the answer's order of arrival, e.g., the 1-st answer of the parent question), which are only meaningful to answers, were included in the regression models predicting the quality of the answers.

- *PriorObservation. PriorVotes* (the number of received votes of the question/answer in the prior week), *PriorAnswers* (the number of answers the question received in the prior week), *PriorHasAcceptedAnswer* (whether the question had an accepted answer in the prior week) and *PriorAnswerAccepted* (whether the answer was accepted in the prior week) are used to control for the unobserved and unchanging characters of the posts.

Results

Table 3 presents the results of the negative binomial regression models predicting the question quality (i.e., received votes, the number of answers, and whether has an accepted answer or not). The effects are reported as incidence rate ratios (*IRR*), which can be interpreted as the ratio change of the dependent variable when increasing an independent variable by one unit.

Most of the control variables have significant effects on received votes. For example, for Model 1, the *IRR* of *PriorVotes* is significantly positive (*IRR*=1.45, $p<.001$), which indicates that when holding other variables constant, receiving one more vote in the preceding week will result in 45% more votes for the question in the following two weeks.

As revealed in Model 1 of Table 3, receiving title edits, question body edits, and tags edits in focal weeks all have significantly positive effects on number of votes the questions received subsequently. The *IRR* of *BodyEdits* is 2.81, indicating that receiving one more question body edit in the focal week will bring in 181% more votes in the following two weeks.

The effects of *TitleEdits* and *TagsEdits* can be interpreted similarly, suggesting that title edits, and tags edits also have positive effects on quality of questions with increasing the number of votes by 39% and 98%.

As revealed in Model 2 and Model 3 of Table 3, receiving edits also increase the number of answers the questions received and the likelihood that the questions will have accepted answers. *BodyEdits* still have pronounced effects: receiving one more edit on question body increases the number of answers by 143% and increase the likelihood of having an accepted answer by 41%. *TitleEdits* and *TagsEdits* also have substantial effects on question quality: receiving one more edit on title or tags significantly increases the number of answers by 21% and 81% respectively, and increases the likelihood of having accepted an answer by 12% and 43% respectively.

Table 4 presents the results of the negative binomial regression models predicting the answer quality. For the

	Answer Quality			
	Model 4: Votes		Model 5: Answer Accepted	
	IRR	Std. Err.	IRR	Std. Err.
BodyEdits	2.19 ***	.049	1.30 ***	.020
PostCount	1.00 ***	3.24e-06	1.00 ***	4.51e-06
PostAvgScore	1.07 ***	6.73e-04	1.01 ***	2.99e-04
PosterReputation	1.00 ***	5.90e-08	1.00 ***	8.85e-08
PosterRegDate	1.00	7.30e-11	1.00 ***	9.89e-11
PageView	1.00 ***	1.55e-07	1.00 ***	9.80e-07
TextLength	1.00 ***	2.29e-06	1.00 ***	1.68e-06
HasCode	.89 ***	.004	.91 ***	.006
HasLink	1.23 ***	.006	1.16 ***	.007
PostDate	1.00	7.58e-11	1.00 ***	1.09e-10
ArrivalOrder	1.00	3.91e-04	.630 ***	.002
ParentQuestionVotes	1.01 ***	9.96e-05	.994 ***	6.46e-04
PriorVotes	1.34 ***	.003	NA	NA
PriorAnswerAccepted	NA	NA	3.08e-10	1.40e-07
Number of Obs	9,865,021			

Table 4. Negative binomial regressions predicting the effects of collaborative editing on two answer quality measurements. *** p<0.001; ** p<0.01; * p<0.05.

effects of collaborative editing on the number of votes we can see that *BodyEdits* has positive effects on votes received in the following two weeks significantly (p<.001). The *IRR* 2.19 indicates that receiving one more answer body edit in the focal week will increase votes for the answer by 119% in the following two weeks. Furthermore, Model 5 of Table 4 shows that edits increase the likelihood of answers being accepted by 30% since the *IRR* of *BodyEdits* on answer accepted is 1.30.

In sum, Table 3 and Table 4 collectively show that collaboratively editing significantly and robustly improves the content quality in terms of the votes received, the number of answers received for questions, the likelihood of questions getting accepted answers, and the likelihood of answers being accepted.

Effects on Users' Motivation

Similarly to prior models testing the effects on content quality, we build negative binomial models to predict askers and answerers' contributions after receiving others' edits. Specifically, we built regression models to predict the number of questions posted by the askers and the number of answers posted by the answerers in the following two months, controlling for their prior contributions.

The independent variables are the number of edits the users received from others in two focal weeks, and the dependent variables are the numbers of questions/answers posted by the users in the following two months (so that we can test the long-term effects on user contribution). Finally, 874,369 observations are gathered to conduct the following user-level analysis. Negative binomial regression models are used in this analysis for the same reason mentioned before.

Dependent Variables

- *PostedQuestions.* The number of questions the user posted in the following two months.
- *PostedAnswers.* The number of answers the user posted in the following two months.

Independent Variables

- *TitleEdits.* The number of title edits received from others in the two focal weeks. Again, answers do not have title edits.
- *BodyEdits.* The number of question/answer body edits received from others in the two focal weeks.
- *TagsEdits.* The number of tags edits received from others in the two focal weeks. Again, answers do not have tags edits.
- *Newcomer.* This dummy variable indicates whether the user is a newcomer in Stack Overflow. A user is defined as a newcomer if he or she has registered the Stack Overflow account for no more than 180 days at the given time period. Note that we use dummy variable rather than continuous variable to describe the tenure of users for the ease of interpretation.

We also examine the interactions between editing type and user type.

Control Variables

We use three categories of variables to control the regression models.

- *PriorContributions. PriorQuestions* (the number of questions posted by the user before the focal weeks), *PriorAnswers* (the number of answers posted by the user before the focal weeks) are used in this category.
- *FocalWeeksContributions. FocalQuestions* (the number of questions posted by the user in the two focal weeks), and *FocalAnswers* (the number of answers posted by the user in the two focal weeks) are in this category.

	Model 6: Users' Subsequent Question Contributions		Model 7: Users' Subsequent Answer Contributions	
	IRR	Std. Err.	IRR	Std. Err.
TitleEdits	.98 *	.008	*NA*	*NA*
BodyEdits	1.00	.005	.95 ***	.007
TagsEdits	1.01	.006	*NA*	*NA*
NewComer	1.02 ***	.005	.60 ***	.003
TitleEdits: NewComer	1.05 ***	.012	*NA*	*NA*
BodyEdits: NewComer	.99	.006	1.18 ***	.016
TagsEdits: NewComer	1.06 ***	.009	*NA*	*NA*
PriorQuestions	1.02 ***	9.59e-05	1.00	8.32e-05
PriorAnswers	1.00 ***	2.12e-05	1.00 ***	3.39e-05
FocalQuestions	1.54 ***	.003	1.00 *	.001
FocalAnswers	1.01 ***	3.70e-04	1.19 ***	.001
Reputation	1.00 ***	3.80e-07	1.00 ***	7.37e-07
Number of Obs	874,369			

Table 5. Negative binomial regressions predicting the effects of collaborative editing on users' motivation. *** p<0.001; ** p<0.01; * p<0.05.

- *Reputation. Reputation* is the number of reputation points the user received, which is a measurement of trustiness and experience of the user in Stack Overflow. The primary way to gain reputation points is by posting highly voted questions and answers.

Results

The results of Model 6 and Model 7 are summarized in Table 5. We can see that receiving edits from others indeed significantly decreases askers and answerers' subsequent contributions (p<.05, p<.001), but the effect sizes are *much smaller* compared with the increases on the numbers of votes, the number of answers, the likelihood of having accepted answers and the likelihood of being accepted shown in Table 3 and Table 4.

For users' motivation on question contributions, we can see that receiving title edits (*TitleEdits*) from others has a negative effect on question askers' motivation with decreasing subsequent contributions by 2% (p<.05). Tags edits (*TagsEdits*) and body edits (*BodyEdits*) from others have no significant effects. Interestingly, newcomer askers are more willing to accept others' changes. Receiving title edits (*TitleEdits*) and tags edits (*TagsEdits*) actually additionally increases these newcomer askers' subsequent contributions by 5% and 6% (p<.001).

For users' motivation on answer contributions, receiving answer body edits (*BodyEdits*) has negative effects on users in general (*IRR*=.95, p<.001). However, there is a significant positive interaction effect between *BodyEdits* and *Newcomer*, indicating that newcomers are more likely to increase contributions after receiving body edits compared with experienced users.

As we know, receiving edits has small negative influences on users' subsequent question contributions and answer contributions. For comparisons, we also built models to test the effects of comments on users' motivation. Comments are considered to be a lightweight method to suggest changes or provide information, and should not directly challenge the original question askers and answerers. Table 6 lists the results of the negative binomial regression models. In these two models, receiving question comments (*Comments* in Model 8) and answer comments (*Comments* in Model 9) from others in the focal weeks are main independent variables. The outcome variables and control variables are similar to those in Model 6 and Model 7. From the results, in general, we can see that receiving comments from others has a small negative effect on users' question contributions and answer contributions (*IRR*=.99 and .96

	Model 8: Users' Subsequent Question Contributions		Model 9: Users' Subsequent Answer Contributions	
	IRR	Std. Err.	IRR	Std. Err.
Comments	.99 ***	9.06e-04	.96 ***	5.80e-04
Newcomer	1.00	.005	.54 ***	.003
Comments: Newcomer	1.02 ***	.001	1.05 ***	.001
FocalQuestions	1.54 ***	.003	1.00 *	.001
FocalAnswers	1.01 ***	3.70e-04	1.22 ***	.002
TotalQuestions	1.02 ***	9.59e-05	1.00 **	8.22e-05
TotalAnswers	1.00 ***	2.12e-05	1.00 ***	3.46e-05
Reputation	1.00 ***	3.81e-07	1.00 ***	7.34e-07
Number of Obs	874,369			

Table 6. Negative binomial regressions predicting the effects of comments on users' motivation. *** p<0.001; ** p<0.01; * p<0.05.

respectively, $p<.001$): receiving one more question comment or answer comment decreases the users' question contributions by 1% or answer contributions by 4%. The fact that the effects of collaborative editing have similar magnitude to the effects of comments on users' motivation further confirms that collaborative editing barely hurts the community.

DISCUSSION

In sum, both our hypotheses are supported by the results, although with different effect sizes.

To put the results into the context, on average each question has 1.59 votes and 2.00 answers, which means that each edit on the question body is associated with 2.88 more votes and 2.86 more answers. Tags edits and title edits have smaller but also substantial effects: each edit on question tags or question title is associated with 1.56, 0.62 more votes respectively and 1.62, 0.42 more answers respectively. On average, the likelihood of having an accepted answer for any question is 60%, and one edit on the question body increases the likelihood to 85%.

For answers, on average each answer has 2.07 votes, which means each edit on the answer body is associated with 2.46 more votes. On average, the likelihood of being chosen as accepted answer for any answer is 44%, and one edit on the answer body increases the likelihood to 57%.

For user contributions, on average each user posts 4.36 questions 10.74 answers in two months. Accordingly, receiving one edit is associated with small decrease in the number of subsequent question and answer contributions (0.09 and 0.54) in the following two months period.

Table 7 illustrates the consequences of collaborative editing by showing the gains and costs on variant quality and motivation measurements. The units of the gains and costs are not exactly the same, leaving space for decision makers

1 edit on question body	**Gain:** Receive **2.88** more votes on the question. Receive **2.86** more answers. Increase the likelihood of having an accepted answer from **60%** to **85%**.
	Cost: No effects on question posters' contributions.
1 edit on question title	**Gain:** Receive **0.62** more votes on the question. Receive **0.42** more answers. Increase the likelihood of having an accepted answer from **60%** to **67%**.
	Cost: Question poster posts **0.09** less questions in subsequent two months.
1 edit on question tags	**Gain:** Receive **1.56** more votes on the question. Receive **1.62** more answers. Increase the likelihood of having an accepted answer from **60%** to **86%**.
	Cost: No effects on question posters' contributions.
1 edit on answer body	**Gain:** Receiving **2.46** more votes on the answer. Increase the likelihood of being accepted from **44%** to **57%**.
	Cost: Answer poster posts **0.54** less answers in subsequent two months.

Table 7. Summary of the effects of each edit on content quality and user motivation in the context.

to interpret and make judgment. However, the general trend is that the gains outweigh the costs: the effects of costs are at least one magnitude smaller than the effects of gains.

The contribution of our paper is to present the trade-offs of collaborative editing on content quality (i.e., votes on questions/answers, the likelihood of getting (accepted) answers, the likelihood of being accepted, and etc.) and user motivation (i.e., the subsequent posting activities after being edited). Unlike in Tausczik et al.'s work [37], they only focus on predicting how the edits (collaborative acts in their paper) affected the number of votes the answers got, we provide a more comprehensive view of the effects of collaborative edits.

Practical Implications

Features like collaborative editing are very likely to be rejected by social computing system designers due to the concern that it might drive users away, despite its potential to boost the content quality. Current interface evaluation methods (e.g., heuristic evaluation, expert review and usability walkthrough) fail to estimate the effect sizes of the potential gains and costs of a given feature. Our analysis provides quantitative evidence showing that the Wikipedia-like collaborative editing feature in Stack Overflow substantially increases the quality of the content without unacceptably hurting users' motivation and contributions. Practitioners might want to consider incorporating the collaborative-editing feature into other Q&A sites or other content generation websites such as forums or product/book review websites.

We did an additional exploration study on Stack Overflow to further identify a few tactics to ensure the collaborative editing is effectively enforced and the potential harm is minimized. These tactics might be useful for practitioners who want to replicate the collaborative-editing features to their own environments.

First, Stack Overflow relies on the experienced users to moderate the collaborative editing activities. Note that although any user in Stack Overflow can suggest edits, only users with more than 2,000 reputation points can review and approve the suggested edits. It is important to have experienced users to judge the appropriateness of edits rather than immediately applying them, which prevents the harmful effects of spamming edits and encourages more cautious edits.

Second, Stack Overflow makes efforts to communicate their policies to the community. Stack Overflow makes the pages of "why can people edit my post" and "how does editing work" explicit in the help center: pages which are accessible and salient to every user.

Third, Stack Overflow allows users to express their opinions and presents their arguments on Meta Stack Exchange, which actually pacifics the agitated users and lessens the potential harmful effects of any system's decision. This phenomenon is called the "fair process effect" or the "voice effects" [15] in psychology literature: people would consider the procedure fair if they have control over the presentation of their arguments and there are sufficient opportunities to present their cases. This could probably explain the fact that we see complains related to collaborative editing on Meta Stack Exchange, but our empirical analysis shows little negative effects on users' actual contributions because the opportunity to complain itself might already allay their anger.

Implications for Future Research

Prior research on understanding the dynamics of social computing systems often investigates one single goal at a time (e.g., survival [20], activity level [13], motivation [29], quality [34, 39]). However, one significant challenge of building successful social computing systems is to understand, satisfy and balance different goals that the systems' owners, managers and members have. In this paper, we take a step towards untangling the complex relationships by examining the trade-offs of introducing collaborative editing to Q&A in terms of two contradicting goals - quality control and user motivation.

The overarching goal is to create the full picture of how different mechanisms (i.e., collaboration mechanisms, communication mechanisms, reward systems, transparency mechanisms, norms and policies etc.) affect the relevant but sometimes contradicting goals (e.g., content quality versus user motivation, reliability versus creativity & innovation, and efficiency versus learning) for different types of social computing systems (e.g., Q&A, social media, and peer production etc.), with the implications of guiding the conscious design of better social computing systems. We encourage more CSCW researchers to work on this area.

Limitations

Our work is also subject to limitations. First, this research is based on one in-depth analysis on Stack Overflow. We would expect our findings to apply to different Q&A systems and other knowledge creation social computing systems, but future comparative studies are needed in order to confirm the extent to which these findings are generalizable.

The second limitation is that the correlational nature of the observational data limits the causal inferences one can draw. We have tried to rule out the confounding factors by controlling for both observed factors (with control variables in the regression) and unobserved and inherent factors (with repeated measurements). However, the ultimate method of proving causal relationship is to conduct experiments with random assignments, which we will leave for future research.

Third, we present the observed trade-offs of collaborative editing in this paper, however the underlying mechanisms (i.e., how exactly the edits affect the quality and member motivation and why the effects on quality and motivation has different magnitudes) have not been deeply investigated. In the future, we will try to understand the underlying mechanisms via two approaches: 1) combining qualitative methods, including participant observation and interviews, to understand how users participate in collaborative editing, and the routes that collaborative editing affects the quality of questions, answers, and users' subsequent behavior; 2) using computational simulation (e.g., agent-based model [32]), which can combine insights from theories and empirical data, to simulate the mediating processes and dynamics of collaborative editing and provide insights about the different effect sizes.

CONCLUSION

In this paper, we examined a particular design decision in Q&A sites—allowing Wikipedia-like collaborative editing on questions and answers. Different statistics models were built with Stack Overflow's dataset to investigate the effects of collaborative editing on content quality under different quality measurements and on user question\answer contributions. The results demonstrated that the benefits of collaborative editing outweigh its risks. Each substantive edit from other users can increase the number of positive votes by 181% for the questions and 119% for the answers, increase the number of answers by 143% for the questions, increase the likelihood of having accepted answers by 41% for the questions, and increase the likelihood of being accepted by 30% for the answers. On the other hand, each edit only decreases askers and answerers' subsequent contributions by no more than 5%. Design implications for social computing systems were also discussed.

ACKNOWLEDGMENTS

We thank the reviewers for their insight suggestions to improve the paper. We thank Yla R. Tausczik, Robert E. Kraut and Aniket Kittur for their valuable feedback and suggestions on improving the paper. The work is supported by the National Natural Science Foundation of China (NSFC) under Grants No.61272533, No.61332008, No.61300201, and Shanghai Science & Technology Committee Project under Grant No.13ZR1401900.

REFERENCES

1. Why Can People Edit My Posts? How Does Editing Work? http://stackoverflow.com/help/editing.
2. Wikipedia:Copyrights. http://en.wikipedia.org/wiki/Wikipedia:Copyrights.
3. Unreasonable Editing Practices. http://meta.stackexchange.com/questions/16551/.
4. Why is Voting Important? http://stackoverflow.com/help/why-vote.
5. Can I Prevent Others From Editing My Question? http://meta.stackexchange.com/questions/28005/.
6. Problem with Wrong Edit. http://meta.stackexchange.com/questions/226293/.
7. Ackerman, M.S. and Malone, T.W. Answer Garden: A Tool for Growing Organizational Memory. *In Proc. COCS'90*, 31-39.

8. Ackerman, M.S. and McDonald, D.W. Answer Garden 2: Merging Organizational Memory with Collaborative Help. *In Proc. CSCW'96*, 97-105.
9. Adamic, L.A., Zhang, J. and Bakshy, E., et al. Knowledge Sharing and Yahoo Answers: Everyone Knows Something. *In Proc. WWW'08*, 665-674.
10. Agichtein, E., Castillo, C. and Donato, D., et al. Finding High-Quality Content in Social Media. *In Proc. WSDM'08*, 183-194.
11. Anderson, A., Huttenlocher, D. and Kleinberg, J., et al. Discovering Value from Community Activity on Focused Question Answering Sites: A Case Study of Stack Overflow. *In Proc. KDD'12*, 850-858.
12. Angrist, J.D. and Krueger, A.B. Empirical Strategies in Labor Economics. *Handbook of Labor Economics 3* (1999), 1277-1366.
13. Barua, A., Thomas, S. and Hassan, A. What are Developers Talking About? An Analysis of Topics and Trends in Stack Overflow. *Empirical Software Engineering 19*, 3 (2014), 619-654.
14. Cameron, A.C. and Trivedi, P.K. *Regression Analysis of Count Data*. Cambridge University Press, 2013.
15. Colquitt, J.A., Conlon, D.E. and Wesson, M.J., et al. Justice at the Millennium: A Meta-Analytic Review of 25 Years of Organizational Justice Research. *Journal of Applied Psychology 86*, 3 (2001), 425.
16. Dabbish, L., Stuart, C. and Tsay, J., et al. Social Coding in GitHub: Transparency and Collaboration in an Open Software Repository. *In Proc. CSCW'12*, 1277-1286.
17. Giles, J. Internet Encyclopaedias Go Head to Head. *Nature 438*, 7070 (2005), 900-901.
18. Gordon, M.D. A Critical Reassessment of Inferred Relations between Multiple Authorship, Scientific Collaboration, the Production of Papers and their Acceptance for Publication. *Scientometrics 2*, 3 (1980), 193-201.
19. Halfaker, A., Geiger, R.S. and Morgan, J.T., et al. The Rise and Decline of an Open Collaboration System How Wikipedia's Reaction to Popularity is Causing its Decline. *American Behavioral Scientist 57*, 5 (2013), 664-688.
20. Halfaker, A., Kittur, A. and Riedl, J. Don't Bite the Newbies: How Reverts Affect the Quantity and Quality of Wikipedia Work. *In Proc. WikiSym'11*, 163-172.
21. Harper, F.M., Raban, D. and Rafaeli, S., et al. Predictors of Answer Quality in Online Q&A Sites. *In Proc. CHI'08*, 865-874.
22. Kittur, A. and Kraut, R.E. Harnessing the Wisdom of Crowds in Wikipedia: Quality through Coordination. *In Proc. CSCW'08*, 37-46.
23. Mamykina, L., Manoim, B. and Mittal, M., et al. Design Lessons from the Fastest Q&A Site in the West. *In Proc. CHI'11*, 2857-2866.
24. Nam, K.K., Ackerman, M.S. and Adamic, L.A. Questions in, Knowledge in?: A Study of Naver's Question Answering Community. *In Proc. CHI'09*, 779-788.
25. Nasehi, S.M., Sillito, J. and Maurer, F., et al. What Makes a Good Code Example?: A Study of Programming Q&A in StackOverflow. *In Proc. ICSM'12*, 25-34.
26. Pal, A., Chang, S. and Konstan, J.A. Evolution of Experts in Question Answering Communities. *In Proc. ICWSM'12*.
27. Pal, A., Harper, F.M. and Konstan, J.A. Exploring Question Selection Bias to Identify Experts and Potential Experts in Community Question Answering. *ACM Trans. Inf. Syst. 30*, 2 (2012), 10-11.
28. Persson, O., Gl A Nzel, W. and Danell, R. Inflationary Bibliometric Values: The Role of Scientific Collaboration and the Need for Relative Indicators in Evaluative Studies. *Scientometrics 60*, 3 (2004), 421-432.
29. Raban, D. and Harper, F. Motivations for Answering Questions Online. *New Media and Innovative Technologies 73* (2008).
30. Ransbotham, S. and Kane, G.C. Membership Turnover and Collaboration Success in Online Communities: Explaining Rises and Falls from Grace in Wikipedia. *Mis Quarterly 35*, 3 (2011), 613-627.
31. Raymond, E. The Cathedral and the Bazaar. *Knowledge, Technology & Policy 12*, 3 (1999), 23-49.
32. Ren, Y. and Kraut, R.E. Agent-Based Modeling to Inform Online Community Design: Impact of Topical Breadth, Message Volume, and Discussion Moderation on Member Commitment and Contribution. *Hum.-Comput. Interact. 29*, 4 (2014), 351-389.
33. Sang-Hun, C. To Outdo Google, Naver Taps into Korea's Collective Wisdom. *International Herald Tribune* (2007).
34. Shah, C. and Pomerantz, J. Evaluating and Predicting Answer Quality in Community QA. *In Proc. SIGIR'10*, 411-418.
35. Singh, P. and Shadbolt, N. Linked Data in Crowdsourcing Purposive Social Network. *In Proc. WWW'13*, 913-918.
36. Steyvers, M. and Griffiths, T. Probabilistic Topic Models. *Handbook of Latent Semantic Analysis 427*, 7 (2007), 424-440.
37. Tausczik, Y.R., Kittur, A. and Kraut, R.E. Collaborative Problem Solving: A Study of MathOverflow. *In Proc. CSCW'14*, 355-367.
38. Wang, G., Gill, K. and Mohanlal, M., et al. Wisdom in the Social Crowd: An Analysis of Quora. *In Proc. WWW'13*, 1341-1352.
39. Zhu, Z., Bernhard, D. and Gurevych, I. A Multi-Dimensional Model for Assessing the Quality of Answers in Social Q&A Sites, 2009, 264-265.

Functional Roles and Career Paths in Wikipedia

Ofer Arazy
University of Alberta
University of Haifa
ofer.arazy@gmail.com

Felipe Ortega
University Rey Juan Carlos
felipe.ortega@urjc.es

Oded Nov
New York University
onov@nyu.edu

Lisa Yeo
Loyola University Maryland
mlyeo@loyola.edu

Adam Balila
University of Haifa
adambalila@hotmail.com

ABSTRACT

An understanding of participation dynamics within online production communities requires an examination of the roles assumed by participants. Recent studies have established that the organizational structure of such communities is not flat; rather, participants can take on a variety of well-defined functional roles. What is the nature of functional roles? How have they evolved? And how do participants assume these functions? Prior studies focused primarily on participants' activities, rather than functional roles. Further, extant conceptualizations of role transitions in production communities, such as the Reader to Leader framework, emphasize a single dimension: organizational power, overlooking distinctions between functions. In contrast, in this paper we empirically study the nature and structure of functional roles within Wikipedia, seeking to validate existing theoretical frameworks. The analysis sheds new light on the nature of functional roles, revealing the intricate "career paths" resulting from participants' role transitions.

Author Keywords

Peer-production; Wikipedia; organizational structure; functional roles; role transitions.

INTRODUCTION

Recent years have seen the emergence of a community-based model for the production of knowledge-based goods such as Wikipedia and open-source software [44]. As participants become more involved in their projects and gain the community's trust, they gradually move from the periphery to the community core, gaining access to more sensitive and influential decisions [1].

The problem of motivation for participation in peer production communities has attracted significant attention at the academic community, and numerous studies have discussed the various motives driving volunteers to contribute their time, effort, and expertise. Less is known, however, about how these volunteers sustain and increase their participation, take on additional responsibilities, and become involved in the project's administration. Although on the surface peer production projects may be thought to be non-hierarchical, in reality a core group of leaders usually emerges (often through formal election processes) to provide centralized coordination, manage quality control processes, mediate conflicts, and develop organizational policies [4, 16, 43].

CSCW 2015, March 14–18, 2015, Vancouver, BC, Canada.

http://dx.doi.org/10.1145/2675133.2675257

Online production communities are characterized by a core-periphery structure, where the majority of contributors are involved in few tasks and participate at the community's periphery, while a relatively small portion of contributors take on additional responsibilities and constitute the core [12, 14, 20, 24, 30]. The core-periphery conceptualization concentrates on participants' power (or authority) within the community, emphasizing lateral movements from the community's fringes to positions of responsibility and influence [56]. Prior works in the area have tried to model the process of transitioning from the community's periphery to the core. For example, the 'Reader to Leader' (R2L) framework [48] attempted to synthesize these earlier works and provide a comprehensive conceptualization on the successive steps volunteers take on their way to community leadership. According to this framework, while the main path from the periphery to the core leads through these successive stages, alternative routes are possible, including those representing attrition (i.e. transitions from the core to the periphery). Notwithstanding the importance of organizational power in characterizing the composition of online communities, this conceptualization overlooks other important dimensions, such as the functional organization of community work. Thus, extant conceptualization lack the capacity to distinguish between different functions situated at the same level of the organizational structure. Traditional organizations are characterized by a functional organization, dividing work between departments such as: Finance, Operations, Marketing, etc., and the functional organization is at the core of scholarly literature on management and organizations [40]. However, the study of functional roles has been largely absent from the literature on online communities.

Therefore, the objective of this study is to investigate the functional organization of online production communities: the nature of functional roles and the way in which these roles are traversed when participants move from the periphery to leadership positions. In part, our study could be viewed as an empirical investigation of existing conceptualizations of emergent leadership, namely the Reader-to-Leader (R2L) framework [48]. Despite the significant attention that the R2L framework has received within the research community, to date, this framework has not been empirically evaluated. In fact, Preece and Shneiderman [48] acknowledge that "Even though our [R2L] framework and discussion of its components are supported by research, the framework needs empirical testing, which is an obvious next stage of this work" (p. 24).

The setting for our study is Wikipedia, one of the most notable examples of peer production [9]. Wikipedia was able to recruit thousands of volunteers to produce millions of encyclopedic entries in 287 languages, and develop extensive policies and mechanisms for governing its collaborative authoring process. Wikipedia's success attracted the attention of scholars, who investigated Wikipedia's organizational model [4, 24, 49]. Our research methodology employs publicly available Wikipedia system logs to identify participants' access privileges. It builds on the framework from [3] to map access privileges onto organization roles, and analyzes role transition for a large sample of Wikipedia contributors. In addition, we perform a qualitative analysis of a selected subset of editors, adding depth and context to the quantitative data analysis.

Hence, the goal of this study is to address the following research questions:

RQ1: How are the functional roles of Wikipedia characterized and what activity profile is associated with each role?

RQ2: How has Wikipedia's functional composition evolved over time?

RQ3: How do contributors to Wikipedia transition between roles on the path from community's periphery to the core?

Our investigation yields important insights about the routes to leadership in peer production projects, informs extant theory in this area, and offers guidelines to designers and custodians of online communities.

SOCIAL ROLES AND ORGANIZATIONAL STRUCTURE

The concept of social role has been the subject of extensive analysis in sociology [10]. Social roles encapsulate the social context, history of actions, structures of interaction, and the attributes people bring to the interaction by providing a meaning system, which both constrains and enables action [37]. The importance of this concept lies in its utility: the classification of types of social relations and behaviors into a smaller set of roles reduces the analytic complexity of social systems and facilitates the comparative study of populations across time and settings [32]. Roles can be understood through two primary dimensions: structure and culture. The structural definition of roles pertains to commonalities in behavior patterns, while the cultural dimension refers to roles that are recognized in social (or organizational) settings and differ in terms of their accessibility (the extent to which it is easy to accept a role) and situational contingency (the contextual factors that affect action). Roles are resources that help people accomplish their goals, and tools used in the establishment of social structure [8]. Hence, social (or organizational) structure can be viewed as an ecology of roles.

Formal organizations are generally understood to be systems of coordinated and controlled activities that arise when work is embedded in complex networks of technical relations and boundary-spanning exchanges [38]. Organizational structure affects organizational action in two primary ways. First, it provides the foundation on which standard operating procedures and routines rest. Second, it determines individuals' role assignment and their access to decision-making processes. Hence, the structure determines the extent to which individuals at different organizational positions can influence the organization's actions [39].

ORGANIZATIONAL ROLES IN ONLINE COMMUNITIES

Online communities, and in particular production communities, have been investigated extensively in recent years. Relevant to our inquiry of roles and organizational structure are prior works that studied community members' roles. Previous investigations have discovered that users often follow very distinctive patterns of activity, playing roles in their online community [58]. Production communities are often described in terms of a core-periphery structure, which entails a dense, cohesive core, and a sparse, unconnected periphery [11, 13, 20, 33, 35, 45, 52]. Contributors play different roles: the majority of participants, who are not very active, are situated at the community's periphery; and a small minority, who take on additional responsibilities and privileges, constitute the community's core. For example, Long and Siau [35] found that social interaction patterns in open source projects start with a single hub, and as the project matures the configuration evolves into a core/periphery structure. Most prior studies in the area have defined participants' position on the periphery-core continuum based on the quantity and types of activities they perform [5, 30, 34]. For example, [4] categorized contributors into two primary classes: administrative- vs. content-oriented; and [57] applied a combination of interpretive and network analysis methods to identify key roles. Much less work has been devoted to studying contributors' formal duties [16]. A few prior works provide a partial description of Wikipedia's formal roles [24, 42, 55]. Building on these earlier works, a recent study [3] has analyzed access privileges in Wikipedia and developed a comprehensive description of Wikipedia's organizational structure, including twelve roles (organized in a power hierarchy: *Unregistered Users, Registered Users, Manually Registered Users, Technical Administration, Border Patrol, Quality Assurance, QA Technicians, Administrators, Security Force, Directors, Privacy Commissioner,* and *Benevolent Dictator* (see Table 1).

Level on Org. Chart	Role	Description	Access Privileges
Level 0	*Unregistered Users*	Non-community members	*
Level 1	*Registered Users*	Newly registered users	user
			autoconfirmed
	Manually Registered Users	New users who had to be manually registered to bypass some restrictions	confirmed
			IPpblock-exempt
Level 2	*Technical Administration*	Privileged users responsible for the administration of the technical aspects (e.g. user accounts, files)	filemover
			accountcreator
	Border Patrol	Users responsible for fighting vandalism by reverting malicious edits	rollback
	Quality Assurance	Privileged users responsible for patrolling Wikipedia and ensuring content quality	reviewer
			autoreviewer
	QA Technicians	Users who develop automated tools (i.e. edit filters) to assist quality assurance work	abusefilter
Level 3	*Administrators*	Highly involved users that are responsible for the social administration of the English Wikipedia community	sysop
			bureaucrat
Level 4	*Security Force*	Highly trusted users who are working to keep malicious users out and combat intentional manipulations of content	oversight
			checkuser
Level 5	*Directors*	Key users responsible for oversight of the Wikimedia organization	steward
			importer & transwiki
	Privacy Commissioner	High-ranking users who investigate complaints about violations of privacy policy	ombudsman
Level 6	*Benevolent Dictator*	Jimmy Wales; responsible for defining high-level policies and norms and for overall direction of the community	founder

Table 1: The organizational structure of Wikipedia (adapted from [3])

ROLE TRANSITIONS IN ONLINE COMMUNITIES

Traditionally, when individuals advance their careers in organizations, they move through positions that provide them with increasing degrees of responsibility, often including vertical authority over others [14]. Recently, organizational theorists have argued that traditional notions of career progression make several assumptions that no longer reflect workplace realities, such as: mobility within a single large organization, stability in the organization and its environment, and hierarchical (i.e. vertical) progression [7]. Thus, there is a need to pay more attention to lateral (or horizontal) progression that relies on expertise, identity, achievement, and community involvement, rather than on hierarchy and formal authority [27]. Such lateral movements often involve transitions between functional areas.

Online production communities are characterized by movements from the community's periphery to positions of responsibility and influence at the community's core [21, 43, 56]. Although many studies have discussed the different ways in which users participate in online communities and the various activities they take part in, no study offers an overall framework of career paths in online production communities. Prior research has concentrated on descriptions of the core members' (leaders, owners) duties and activities [15, 46], the distribution of authority among these members [20], as well as on the factors affecting a participant's promotion to a leadership role [13, 17, 18, 33]. For example, [46] showed that the nature of work differs between Wikipedians and non-Wikipedians. Others have examined promotion procedures: [13] investigated the criteria for promotion decisions (i.e. the RfA process and adminship decisions); [19] studied the relationship between editors position within the social network and promotion decisions; and [33] demonstrated that promotion depends on the candidate's relative activity levels. These studies – although rich in detail – provide a restricted and simplified conceptualization of the transitions towards leadership.

Preece and Shneiderman [48] provide an overall framework of emergent leadership in online communities by synthesizing prior works in the area. They present a nuanced classification of activities, organizing roles in successive levels of involvement, termed the "Reader to Leader" (R2L) framework. The *reader* category represents the lowest level of participation, and includes tasks such as browsing, surfing, and searching. Reading of user-generated content posted by other participants can be thought of as legitimate peripheral participation [31]; it is a necessary condition for knowledge reuse, and is a typical first step toward more active participation [47]. Next, the *contributor* category represents a gradual move towards larger and more frequent contributions as participants' confidence grows and they feel empowered and appreciated [59]. Activities in this category include: contributing comments and responses to others' postings, rating previous contributions, tagging and categorizing existing content, and making small knowledge contributions (e.g. correcting an error, adding a hyperlink). The next level of participation, *collaborator*, involves two or more contributors discussing, cooperating, and working together to create something or share information [22]. These activities allow participants to bring more from themselves and more fully express their opinions and ideas. Finally, the *leader* category represents the highest level of participation. In addition to being active contributors and collaborators, leaders (also referred to as "owners"), are responsible for social management tasks (e.g. establishing community norms and explicit policies or conflict resolution) and administration of the technology infrastructure [16]. A unique feature of the R2L framework is that it provides an intricate picture of role transitions, acknowledging both upstream and downstream transitions, as well as bypasses of intermediate stages (e.g. from *contributor* directly to *leader*, bypassing the *collaborator* stage). Notwithstanding these merits, the R2L conceptualization seems to collapse two important dimensions: organizational power and function, impeding the distinction between different functional roles that are situated at a similar point on the Reader–Leader continuum. We also note that, despite its influence in the CSCW community, the R2L framework has not yet been examined empirically. The objective of the current study is, thus, to try and fill in these gaps in the literature, empirically evaluate role transitions and assess the extent to which the R2L conceptualization captures the reality of career paths within production communities.

METHOD

Research Setting

The focus of this empirical investigation is the English Wikipedia and its community of editors. We base our data gathering and analysis on Wikipedia's system logs; harvesting these logs can reveal important insights about members' ongoing behavior in its natural setting.

Over time, the Wikipedia community has developed a comprehensive and detailed set of procedures for governing the collaborative editing process, including a well-defined scheme of roles access privileges [14]. We focus on human editors and exclude software bots [25] from this analysis. We note that in Wikipedia, anyone can contribute without registering. This results in two types of participants: anonymous (represented by the '*' tag), whose contribution is recorded and associated with an IP address, and registered users, whose contributions are associated with a user name. Since we cannot track subsequent role transitions for participants who initially contribute anonymously (it is not possible to univocally associate IP-based contributions with a user name when one starts as an anonymous contributor and later registers an account), anonymous contributors were excluded from our analysis.

Our mapping of access privileges onto organizational roles, illustrated in Table 1, was based on the earlier work of [3], employing a combination of top-down (review of relevant scholarly literature and Wikipedia's own definitions of roles and access privileges) and bottom up methods (using log data of all Wikimedia users and statistical analysis techniques). A key advantage of using the framework at [3] is that it arranges Wikipedia roles on a continuum from the community periphery to the core, thus allowing us to analyze movements up (or down) the organizational chart. Transitions between roles were defined as follows: when a participant is assigned an access privilege that is associated with a more advanced role, we designate her as being promoted to this role; and when a participant loses all privileges associated with the advanced role, we designate her as being demoted to a less advanced role.

Sample

Our sample included 2,174 Wikipedia editors who are all registered members. Since articles' topical categories may attract different types of contributors, we sought a sample of users who have contributed to a representative sample of Wikipedia articles. Therefore, our sampling procedure used a seed of 96 articles that provides a representation of Wikipedia's topical categories and which has been employed in earlier studies [4, 6]. This set of articles (created in January 2007) was selected based on randomization and a stratified sampling of Wikipedia's topics, congruent with Wikipedia's top-level classification[1] [29] (categories: culture, art, and religion; math, science, and technology; geography and places; people and self; society; and history and events). From this original set of 96 Wikipedia articles, 3 were discontinued and their edit history is no longer available, leaving us with 93 articles.

Our sample of Wikipedia participants included every editor who contributed at least one edit to any of these Wikipedia articles (prior to the 2007 cut-off). For the reasons mentioned earlier, we excluded anonymous contributors and software bots. Our procedure rendered a sample of 2,174 distinct

[1] For a list of Wikipedia top-level categories, please refer to http://en.wikipedia.org/wiki/List_of_overviews

participants. We followed these participants from the time they registered with Wikipedia until June 2012, recording every change in their Wikipedia roles during this period.

Data Collection

In order to address RQ1, we employed data harvested from Wikipedia logs. To profile the activities of the various roles, we retrieved data regarding the contributions of our user sample across all Wikipedia namespaces, including: *main article* pages (production work); *talk pages* (coordination work); *user* and *user talk* pages (communicating with others); Wikipedia and other pages (community work) [17]. For the second RQ, we gathered data regarding the evolution of roles within Wikipedia from an internal report by a senior Wikipedian[2]. Finally, for tackling RQ3 and collect data regarding role transitions, we first queried the Wikipedia API (http://en.wikipedia.org/w/api.php) to determine whether a participant is a registered user; we then used the API to receive the list of role changes for each participant in our sample, resulting in 7,563 role-change events. Organizing the role change history, we determined the participant's role at each point in time, and recorded role transitions.

In order to verify the accuracy of the user-role data, we compared it to other sources: the rights log history[3] and alternative sources archiving role transitions at the early days of Wikipedia[4]. In cases of mismatch (7% of the events), a discrepancy was flagged, and was resolved manually. Some of the more common discrepancies included software bots that were initially registered as regular users (and once identified as bots, were excluded from the sample) and administrators who lost their privileges due to inactivity (in such cases, we tracked the missing date for this event). In addition, in a few cases transitions that were recorded properly reflected a technical issue, rather than a role change (e.g. a particular privilege was added, removed a few minutes later, and then a different privilege was assigned). After a careful manual inspection of short-duration event sequences, we excluded those events that did not seem to represent an actual role transition. Once we compiled a reliable list of access privilege transitions, we mapped them onto Wikipedia roles (as specified in Table 1 above) to arrive at role transitions. Many of the access privilege transition events did not induce changes in Wikipedia roles (e.g. a 'filemover' taking on the additional privileges of an 'accountcreator'; both corresponding to the *Technical Administrator* role). We focused our attention on those access privilege transitions that entail a move between role categories.

[2]http://en.wikipedia.org/wiki/User:NoSeptember/The_NoSeptember_Admin_Project

[3]https://meta.wikimedia.org/w/index.php?title=Special%3ALog&type=rights

[4] Namely the Meta:Bureaucrat log (https://meta.wikimedia.org/wiki/Meta:Bureaucrat_log), which records privilege changes prior to 10 December 2004.

In order to provide richer context and ground the overall analysis in additional data sources and individual user cases, we identified a list of seventeen editors that capture the various role transition patterns, focusing on unique cases (e.g. editors that transition particularly quickly or slowly; extremely active editors, cases of demotions). Altogether, we investigated 17 editors with IDs: 11; 96; 20134; 29678; 44020; 82835; 124324; 126457; 274040; 889851; 1403682; 1812441; 1862829; 2164608; 2267145; 3162157; and 3138762.We gathered information about these editors from a variety of Wikipedia sources, including editors' personal pages and talk pages; requests for adminship (RFA)[5]; requests for de-adminship[6]; the logging table (e.g. checking who is operating a bot)[7]; and pages tracking dispute resolution cases. This selected set of editors captured cases to exemplify the various role-transition dimensions; in terms of *seniority*: 8 veterans (joining Wikipedia up to 2004) and 9 that joined later; *editing activity*: 7 with relatively low activity patterns across the various namespaces (no more than few thousand edits), 5 moderate (tens of thousands of edits), and 5 highly active editors (more than one-hundred-thousand edits); *rank*: 1 editor that never made a role transition, 14 that have gained Level 2 privileges, 13 Level 3 cases, and 1 editor at Level 5; *pace*: 5 that made fast transitions (less than a year), 5 that transitioned at a regular pace (one-three years), and 6 slow movers (transitioning after more than three years); and *controversial*: 5 editors that have been blocked (some only temporarily and others for prolonged periods) and 7 that have been demoted (either voluntarily or forced by the community). We used these cases to illustrate role transitions and career paths from a micro perspective.

RESULTS

Out of the 2,174 editors in our set the majority were from the community's periphery (i.e. auto and manually-registered users), relatively few were at the intermediate levels, and no instances were recorded for the top levels (namely, the 'steward', 'importer & transwiki', 'ombudsman', and 'founder' privileges)[8]. In total, we recorded 21 *Manually Registered Users* (1 confirmed and 21 IPpblock-exempt); 12 *Technical Administrators* (9 filemovers and 5 accountcreators); 127 users with *Border Patrol* (i.e. rollback) privileges; 287 at the *Quality Assurance* role (244 reviewer and 150 autoreviewer); 49 *QA Technicians* (i.e. abusefilter); 436 *Administrators* (435

[5]en.wikipedia.org/wiki/Wikipedia:Successful_requests_for_adminship

[6] en.wikipedia.org/wiki/Wikipedia:Requests_for_de-adminship

[7] For members joining Wikipedia prior to September 7, 2005, some information is missing from the logging table; in those cases we used the time of first edit as a proxy for registration date.

[8] Across the entire Wikipedia community (all languages), there are only 46 participants with the *'steward', 'importer & transwiki', 'ombudsman',* or *'founder'* access privileges. This explains why they were almost absent from our sample.

sysops and 10 bureaucrats); 11 users as *Security Force* (9 oversight and 9 checkuser); and 1 *Director* (with importer privilege).

To address RQ1 concerning the activity profile of each role, we partitioned each editor's trajectory into different temporal sections, each listing the roles held in that time period, as well as the length and activities across the various Wikipedia namespaces. Then, for each role, we aggregated the activity of all editors. In terms of overall activity, *Technical Administrators* and *QA Technicians* have the highest average daily activity, with 113 and 42 daily edits respectively. Level 2 and 3 roles make on average 11-14 edits; while those at the entry (Level 1) and top levels (Levels 4 and 5) make less than 5 daily edits. In terms of effort across the various Wikipedia namespaces, although all roles focus primarily on editing main pages, each role is characterized by a distinct activity profile, as illustrated in Figure 1. For example, *New Registered Users* focus primarily on editing main pages (74% of their edits); *Technical Administrators* and to a lesser extent *Border Patrol* are relatively inactive on main pages, but instead concentrate on coordination work (40% and 21% respectively in talk pages); *Security Force* is characterized by little production work (35% on main pages), and greater focus on pages associated with policy creation and enforcement (37% and 22% respectively on user talk and Wikipedia namespaces); and *Directors* are highly active on Wikipedia and Wikipedia talk namespaces (22% and 19% respectively). For example, editor #3162157, who joined on January 2007 and never transitioned beyond the Registered User role, made 301 edits to main pages; editor #274040, who joined on May 2005 and gained various Level 2 (*Technical Administrations, Quality Assurance, Border Patrol*) and Level 3 privileges, made roughly 30,000 edits to main pages, 3,700 in talk pages, 25,000 in user and user talk pages, and 14,000 in other namespaces; and editor #96, a Director that joined at 2001, made 4,200 edit to main pages and 1,000 edits across other namespaces.

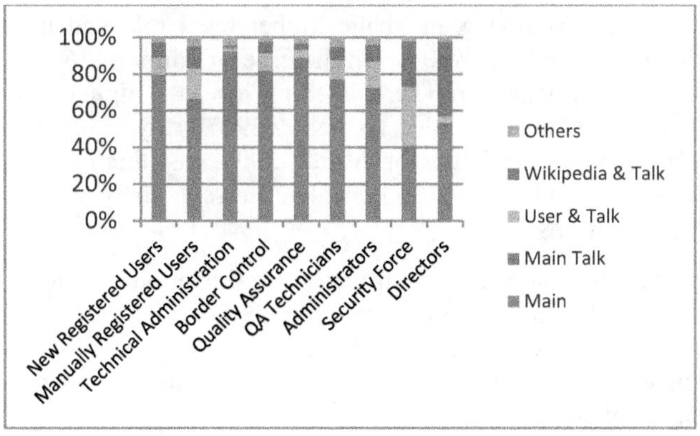

Figure 1. Activity profiles associated with functional roles (as proportion of roles overall activity).

Overall, we notice that editors at Level 3 and above consistently present a significant number of contributions to meta pages which pertain to community activity, such as talk, user, user talk, Wikipedia or Wikipedia talk pages. Level 2 roles, on the other hand, present very high levels of activity at very specific namespaces linked to their particular duties (e.g. editors in Technical Administration role spend substantially higher percentage of their work on category pages, and QA Technicians focus more on template pages).

To control for the effect of topical categories, we partitioned the sample into sub-samples (by building on the topical organization of the articles that were used to seed the editor sample), and analyzed the activity patterns of each topical sub-sample. A multivariate analysis of variance (MANOVA) revealed very similar activity patterns across topics – for all Wikipedia namespaces – suggesting that the results are independent of particular topical domains.

Our next analysis focused on the evolution of roles, addressing RQ2. Figure 2 illustrates the temporal evolution of roles within Wikipedia. As the figure shows, in the early days of Wikipedia, the entry level positions (Levels 0 and 1: unregistered and registered members) were joined by 'core' (or leadership) roles: Level 3 (sysop; 2002); Level 4 (checkuser; 2005); Level 5 (steward; granted to the founder Wales in 2002); and Level 6 (founder; 2002). In 2004 steward privileges were granted to other beyond the founder, whereas in 2006 the privileges of oversight (Level4), ombudsman, importer, and transwiki (Level 5) were introduced. Only at the next phase of Wikipedia's evolution - in 2008 and 2009 (with later additions in 2011) was the intermediate functional layer introduced and Level 2 roles emerged.

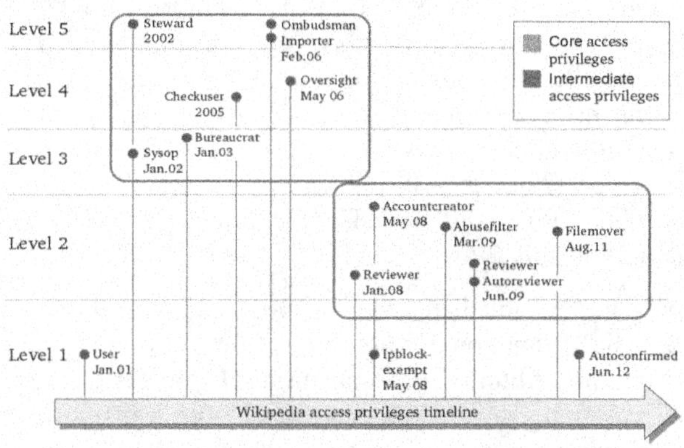

Figure 2. The Evolution of Wikipedia's access privileges

In order to understand how these various roles were populated as Wikipedia evolved, we studied the distribution of access privileges by plotting the levels reached by the users in our sample. In the early years of Wikipedia, the vast majority of users were al Level 1; by 2005, as the second phase of Wikipedia's life began, the project increasingly gained traction, and the number of new editors joining rapidly grew; realizing the need to curate the immense amounts of new content being constantly created, Level 2 functions were introduced and gradually populated. Figure 3 shows the changes in the proportion of editors (y-axis) in each of the top five levels. We can see that the proportion of Level 3 users (sysop, bureaucrat) started to represent a noticeable fraction of the total population circa April 2005, and from January 2008 it has remained quite stable. Furthermore, since the introduction of levels in the functional layer (Level 2), starting in January 2008, the proportion of users taking roles from this layer has rapidly increased, reducing the proportion of entry level users (Level 1). This finding offers evidence of the emergence of a group of intermediate level users focusing on tasks such as content curation and fighting vandalism.

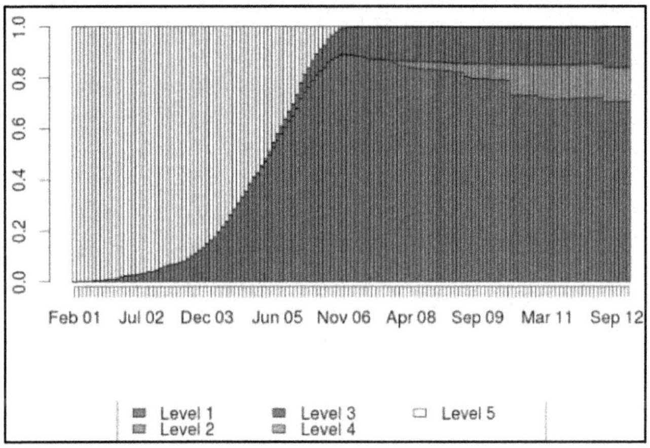

Figure 3. The proportions of role population over time.

An example from our selected subset of editors could illustrate this evolution. Consider editor #126457, a librarian who worked at Cambridge College and the British Antarctic Survey, and primarily contributes to pages covering historical figures, events, and places (in addition to his community activity). Editor #126457 became a member on October 2004, an *Administrator* (Level 3) on November 2005, and added the role of *QA Technician* (Level 2) on July 2009.

Once we established the nature and evolution of Wikipedia's functional roles, we turned our attention to investigating editors' role transitions. In order to address RQ3, we first counted the times each role transition type occurred in our sample. In total, we recorded 1,103 role transitions (see Table 2). Out of the 2,174 participants, 732 (34%) transitioned to various organizational roles, while the remainder 1,442 (66%) never moved beyond the entry levels (i.e. registered users)[9].

We observed both horizontal and vertical transitions. We note horizontal transitions at the intermediate level (Level 2), where there are transitions between the *Border Patrol* and *Quality Assurance* roles. For example, editor #20134 registered with Wikipedia in August 2003, gained the *Quality Assurance* role in June 2010, and six months later added the *Border Patrol* role. Vertical transitions from one organizational level to another include transitions such as the one from the *Registered Member* (Level 1) to *Quality Assurance* (Level 2) roles, or from *Border Patrol* (Level 2) to *Administrators* (Level 3) (for example, editor #1862829 registered on July 2006, gained the *Border Patrol* role on April 2008, and became an *Administrator* on October 2008). Overall, the majority of transitions were vertical (995 instances; 90%). For the horizontal transitions, it is interesting to note that while there are some roles with little to/from transition (e.g. *QA Technicians*), other roles are characterized by frequent horizontal movement (e.g. *Border Patrol*)[10].

For the vertical transitions, while in some cases the transition to the community's core is sequential. (e.g., 346 transitions from Level 1 to 2 and 21 transitions from Level 2 to 3), the majority of vertical transitions skip intermediate levels (e.g., 421 transitions from Level 1 to 3). Examples from our selected set of editors could illustrate the upward transition process: editors #2267145, #11, and #126457 who made the transition to administrative role (i.e. Level 3) prior to the introduction of the functional layer (at 2007, 2006, and 2005 respectively) moved directly from being *Registered Users* to administrative position, the latter two editors adding on Level 2 roles at a later time; in contrast, *editors* #1862829 and #44020 attained their administrative position later (at 2008 and 2010 respectively) and have made linear transitions: Level 1 => Level 2 => Level 3.

Despite the majority of vertical transitions are upward (792 cases), a relatively large number of transitions were downward (195 cases). In particular, we noted 81 cases where core community members (Level 3) shed their special privileges and become regular members. For downward transitions, we distinguish between cases where an editor was first granted the higher level role and later added a lower level role (as in the case of editor #126457), and cases of demotion where an editor loses the higher level privilege (for example, editor #29678, who gained *Administrator* privileges on March 2009, lost them due to inactivity on October 2011). Table 2 presents these various role transitions.

In order to represent the intricate role transition dynamics, Figure 4 illustrates promotion and demotion role transitions (for clarity, we excluded from the figure same-level transitions, as well as cases of downward transitions that do not entail demotion).

[9] Note that after becoming an *Administrator*, if one adds a series of Level 2 roles, each such addition is recorded as a transition from Level 3 to the Level 2 role.

[10] Cases where an editor played multiple Level 2 roles and lost one are not captured in our analysis.

Level	Level → To / From ↓	1: Registered Users	1: Manually Registered Users	2: Tech. Admin.	2: Border Patrol	2: Quality Assurance	2: QA Tech.	3: Administrators	4: Security Force	5: Directors
1	Registered Users		10	+2	+109	+217	+16	+420	+4	+1
	Manually Registered Users	7				+2		+1		
2	Technical Administration	-1								
	Border Patrol	-14	5	6		66		+16		
	Quality Assurance	-14	2	6	12			+4		
	QA Technicians	-2	1			1		+1		
3	Administrators	-81	6	4	8 / -7	4 / -3	40 / -2		+7	
4	Security Force						1			
5	Directors									

Table 2. Role transitions count; a plus sign ("+") represents promotions, and minus sign ("-") demotions; no sign indicates a same-level transition, or cases where higher-level roles were retained while picking up lower-level privileges.

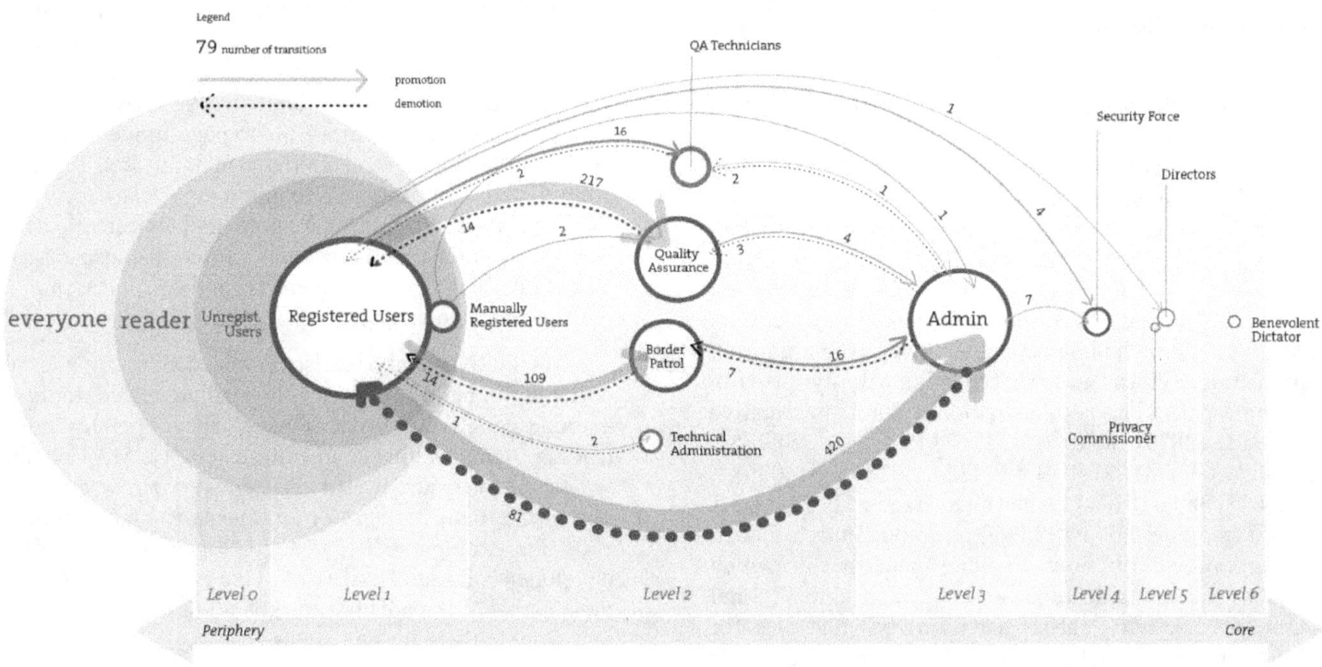

Figure 4. Promotion and demotion transitions. Circle size corresponds to the number of editors in the sample; upward solid arrows represent transition to a higher level; downward dotted arrows represent cases where editors lost higher level privileges. Width of arrows represents number of role transitions count. For clarity, same-level transitions, as well as downward transition that do not entail demotion (i.e. editors kept their higher-level privilege), are excluded from the figure.

The analyses described above highlight the importance of the mid-level strata of contributors. These contributors are characterized by functional focus and diversity and represented by Level 2 roles in Wikipedia's organizational structure. In order to fully understand how these roles are attained, we performed an analysis of incoming transitions into Level 2 roles (see Figure 5).

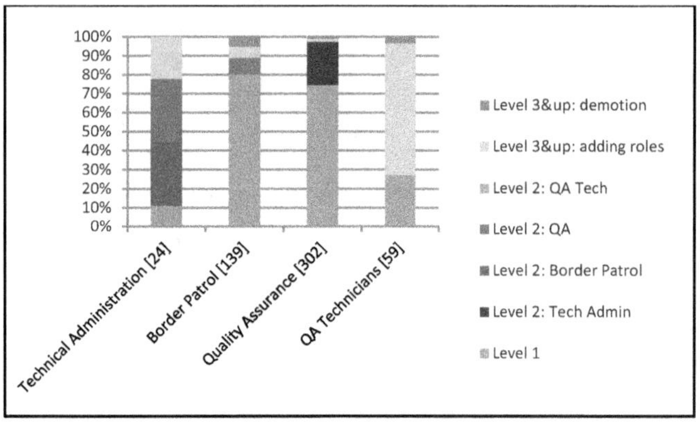

Figure 5. Sources of incoming transitions into Level 2 roles.

This analysis reveals that in addition to the differences in terms of activity profiles reported earlier, the various Level 2 roles seem to represent different career paths. For example, transitions into *Technical Administration* are primarily through other Level 2 roles (namely, *Border Patrol* and *Quality Assurance*); progression into *Border Patrol* is directly from Level 1; and the role of *QA Technicians* is often appended to *Administrators*.

In addition to the patterns emerging from our quantitative analysis (as discussed above), the qualitative analysis of the selected 17 editors revealed some interesting insights. Although we cannot validate statistically the significance of these findings, they do highlight some interesting patterns. The discussions associated with promotion decisions reveal that editing activity is a key consideration (see [13, 33]). As we have shown earlier, while all editors focus their editing activities on main pages (see Figure 1), administrators consistently present high activity levels in that namespace. The administrators in our representative set - #1862829, #44020, #2267145, #11, #889851, #126457, #29678, #274040, #124324, #82835, #1403682, #2164608, and #1812441 - had an average of 60,000 edits in main (ranging 5,000-120,000) up to our study's cutoff. In addition, contributions to other namespaces, which represent communications between editors and community activity, also seem to be relevant for promotion. For example, editor #2267145 has made over 50,000 edits to talk pages; #889851 has edited user and user Talk pages over 36,000 times; and editor #82835 made over 82,000 edits to talk pages, 38,000 to user and user talk pages, and roughly 85,000 other meta pages. This data suggests that while a significant editing activity in main pages is required for promotion to administrative position, active participation in a variety of other namespaces is also essential to achieve a promotion. Timing also seems to have influenced the promotion process, and our qualitative analysis reveals the very low volume of participation in older voting processes for *Administrator* (in contrast with the high community participation from 2007 onwards). An extreme example is editor #96, who was made an *Administrator* on Feb. 2004 with just 6 positive votes.

The in-depth examination of 17 editors also shed additional light on the process of downward transitions. As revealed through the statistical analysis, a downward transition can entail a demotion (when higher-level privileges are shed; e.g. editor #29678) or a case where a higher-level role - typically, Level 3 - adds lower-level privileges - commonly Level 2 (e.g. editor #126457). When studying the reasons for demotions, we found evidence for both community-initiated and self-demotions. Reasons for community-initiated demotions were prolonged inactivity period (as in the case of editor #29678) or abuse of Wikipedia norms (often abuse of rollback privileges). For example, editors #889851, #274040 and #124324 lost administrative privileges due to misuse of administrative tools, failing to respond to community concerns, or inappropriate off-wiki behavior. Self-demotions are often the result of continuous controversies and confrontations (e.g. editors #82835, #1403682, and #2164608). We note that demotion cases are often linked to blocking incidents, where an editor is prevented from editing activities for some period (in few cases, indefinitely). For instance, editor #274040, who was forced to give up administrative privileges, was banned 12 different times (due to page-move vandalism, blocks and violations of earlier bans). In fact, regaining administrative privileges required a clean record of 'blocks'. It is interesting to note that extremely active users who contribute across the various namespaces, are often involved in controversies and disputes, and in multiple occasions have been banned.

Our qualitative analysis also revealed that some of the users at higher ranks make use of advanced tools for automating editing tasks (that is, they operate 'bots'), leading to unusual peaks in editing activity. Most notably, we can identify the use of the AutoWikiBrowser tool as one of the main triggers for an unusually high number of edits. For example, editor #1862829 is not only one of the developers of AutoWikiBrowser, he is also one of the 20 most active Wikipedians and runs a bot to carry out tasks that would otherwise be tedious.

Our study of the selected set of editors also examined participation in additional community activity. When analyzing participation in WikiProjects – projects typically dedicated to improving articles in a particular domain – we were not able to find evidence linking WikiProject participation to any particular user profile.

DISCUSSION

Recent years have seen increasing interest in investigating organizational roles within online communities and the process by which contributors transition between roles. Conceptualizations such as the Reader-to-Leader framework [48] have received significant attention. Yet, to date, there has been no quantitative empirical evaluation of role transition processes. Our study of career paths in Wikipedia over a period of over ten years provides insights into the dynamics of transitions between the community's periphery and core. The results highlight the significance of functional roles for understanding how online production communities organize their work. In particular, our findings call into focus the functional middle organizational level (i.e. Level 2) of Wikipedia.

The findings show that formal roles determine users' actual activity patterns across a variety of editing tasks (i.e. namespaces). To date, much of the research on the organizational structure within production relied on activity counts for determining one's position on the periphery-core continuum [5, 30, 34].

A second contribution this study makes is in delineating the evolution of Wikipedia's organizational structure. Earlier studies have noted Wikipedia's increased bureaucracy [14] and have associated the growing complexity of Wikipedia's organizational structure with decreased effectiveness [26, 54]. Our findings, on the other hand, suggest that the introduction of additional functions (namely, Level 2 roles) was necessary for curating the mounting number of new contributions. This finding is in line with recent works which suggest that online production communities that fail to create such organizational structures are not sustainable [41].

We also make a contribution in describing role transition dynamics within Wikipedia. Our empirical evaluation validates prior knowledge in the area [13, 23, 35, 43] and demonstrates that the number of community members decreases as we grow closer to the core: only a relatively small number of contributors proceed to Level 3 and even fewer continue to becoming a core member (i.e. Levels 4 and higher). Level 2, because of its late introduction, is still not fully developed, but we expect that the number of contributors at this level would grow and surpass the number of administrators (Level 3). Our results (see Table 2) clearly show that not all paths are equally traversed; in fact, some paths are never traversed (at least in our sample), suggesting that – although not formally articulated – there are de-facto career paths within Wikipedia.

A key finding of our study is that the strength of paths (in terms of the frequency in which participants traverse them) does not correspond to the predictions of extant conceptualizations. In particular, against the predictions of the R2L model, which suggests a primary path to leadership characterized by a linear sequence from the periphery to the core of the community (with some additional, non-linear secondary paths that may skip a particular stage), findings from the present study suggest that these non-sequential paths are the rule rather than the exception. Namely, in most cases participants move directly from the entry levels to the community's core (skipping intermediate functional roles). This may be an artefact of the late introduction of Level 2 roles, although even after 2009 most of the Wikipedians arriving at Level 3 did so directly, bypassing Level 2 roles. The implication of this finding is that Level 2 roles must not be seen as a step towards becoming a community leader; instead, they represent functional positions that are important in their own right.

While most of the prior studies in the area emphasize upward transitions towards leadership positions, our study provides evidence for the existence of transitions from the core back to the community's periphery. In some cases this may simply reflect community regeneration, where old leadership makes way for new generations of contributors that step-up to take additional responsibilities (as has been observed in the context of open-source software development [52] and Wikipedia [49]). In fact, in mid-2011 Wikipedia developed a policy to retire inactive administrators[11]. In other cases, however, these 'downward' transitions are the result of heated confrontations between community members. For example, consider the case of editor #124324, who engaged in arguments with a few other editors, eventually became frustrated with his treatment (both directly and through the formal arbitration/incident handling process), and voluntarily gave up his administrator privileges. In the words of editor #124324:

> *"In response to the Committee's decision to declare finding ... "[#124324] ... has used his administrative tools while involved ...)", I've requested a desysopping"*

> *"anybody who cares: my self-block wasn't some kind of "tantrum" or strategy; it was a genuine attempt to get the hell away"*

In other cases, editors are forced to give up privileges, as in the case of the editor #82835, one of the most active Wikipedians. The case involves accusations of disruptive editing against the editor. The demotion decision centers around principles of collegiality and the use of automation tools. The community decided to revoke administrator privileges and ban editor #82835 for up to one year.

Interestingly, as with the upward transitions, we found that when core members (at Level 3 of the organizational chart) move down the organizational ladder they most often transition directly to become a regular member, rather than traversing through the intermediate Level 2.

[11] http://en.wikipedia.org/w/index.php?title=Wikipedia:INACTIVITY

To the best of our knowledge, demotions were not previously investigated in the context of production communities and no prior studies have investigated the departure – whether voluntary or compulsory – of key community members (aside from the well-known case of Wikipedia cofounder Sanger's exit of Wikipedia [53]). While such demotions are the exception, rather than the norm, exposing this pattern enriches our understanding of career paths within online production communities.

Another insight from our study is that the dynamics of the roles transitions are more complex and intricate than originally perceived: we found evidence for both horizontal and vertical transitions; both upward and downward movements; sequential progression through intermediate phases, as well as direct transitions that bypass intermediate levels. Preece and Shneiderman [48] have already postulated that role transition is not one-directional, and that users can move up and down the leadership ladder. However, the evidence presented here points to complex patterns of transitions, whereby participants switch between organizational roles (a pattern brought to the extreme by one editor whose career spanned six role transitions). For example, we observed repeated cases where those who directly progressed to higher-level administrative roles (i.e. Level 3) choose to later add intermediate functional roles (Level 2); a pattern not discussed in prior works. Not only do we expose previously unobserved transition patterns, our findings also offer empirically-validated weights (or probabilities) for the various role transitions.

In sum, our study builds on and extends prior knowledge in the area in several important directions. In recent years, researchers in the area have begun to recognize the need to move beyond the simplistic conceptualization of core-periphery. One line of research has focused on the process of promotion within Wikipedia. These studies tend to focus on a particular promotion decision, often to 'sysop': a single transition in the organizational chart and a single event in a user's trajectory. For example, [13, 17, 18] studied how activity patterns affect promotion to administrator position. While such studies are useful in shedding light on why and how people move to administrative positions, they tell us little about the organizational structure in its entirety; further, they do not capture contributors' full role transition trajectories. In addition, most of these studies view career path on a single dimension - promotion to position of power – not distinguishing between the functional roles played at each position. Because of the focus on promotion to higher-order positions (i.e. *Administrator*), they miss on the complex functional organization at the middle level of the organizational chart (i.e. Level 2). Another interesting line of research has been investigating the nature of leaders (and leadership) within online communities, moving beyond the single-dimension characterization of leadership (power or authority; i.e. core-periphery continuum). For example, [60] investigated editors leadership styles (transactional, person-focused, aversive, and legitimate leadership), and showed that these leadership behaviors are not restricted to those in formal administrator positions; and [61] developed a machine learning technique to automatically identify these leadership behaviors. [36] have analyzed leadership behaviors in an online community, argued that these behaviors should be distributed between many community members (as opposed to centralized leadership), and developed a tool to assist in leadership tasks. Our study extends these lines of investigation in four important ways: (a) our study focuses contributors' functional roles (as opposed to leadership behaviors), and brings into attention the intermediate "professional" level that is often absent in studies of leadership; (b) we study Wikipedia's entire functional organization (and transitions between functional roles), rather than focusing on a particular type of transition, thus enabling us to validate conceptualizations such as the Reader-to-Leader framework, and revealing unpredicted patterns (e.g. editors moving directly to administrative position and later assuming functional lower-level roles; (c) we demonstrate that despite the loose governance of Wikipedia and the fact that editing activities are open to all, the functional role seems to determine the type of activities editors engage in, such that each functional role is associated with a distinct activity profile; and (d) we shed new light on downward transitions out of the community's core, a topic that has been under-investigated.

Finally, we make a secondary methodological contribution regarding the usage of system logs as a tool for answering organizational research questions. Our experience has taught us that beyond the standard data cleaning that is necessary, there is a need to triangulate data from multiple sources to ensure its reliability. Some of the examples we have encountered include: automated bots not marked as such; incomplete registration date for early entrants; inconsistencies between two sources recording granting of access privileges; missing data on role granting in privileges logs (as evident by comments on editors' personal pages); and irrelevant privileges granting data in the logs that do not reflect role changes (i.e. a series of erroneous transactions and their corrections). We would like to offer a word of caution to researchers relying on log data in studying online communities, and to stress the importance of data triangulation.

Implications for design and management

The findings of this study have important practical implications for designers and administrators of online communities. These communities strive to sustain contributors' participation, engagement and commitment. An understanding of the paths contributors take could help to develop diverse "career paths" within the community, such that contributors with different skill sets and interests could find suitable avenues for channeling their energy. An implication would be to place more emphasis on early detection and encouragement of contributors who seem to be suitable (as indicated by their editing profiles) for particular roles. Community owners could provide more structure – through design and communication – to career paths, such that prior to advancing to core administrative duties, contributors should first serve on functional roles such as *Border Patrol* or *Quality Assurance*. Notwithstanding the recommendation above for "professional" career paths, it may be useful to create – in parallel - direct paths to leadership. Results from our study suggest that this path may be attractive to many Wikipedians (as indicated by the large number of editors who bypass Level to roles on their progression to becoming an *Administrator*). A design implication would be to develop tools that track contributors' activities and offer to them career guidance, including suggestions for roles and functions that best match their profile.

Our findings are also relevant to managers in firms who explore new collaborative production strategies. For example, some technology companies participate in open source software development [51], whereas others have adopted the practices of the open source movement for their internal software development projects [50]. In a similar vein, many companies use wiki technology as a knowledge management tool [2], and in particular for developing a Wikipedia-like organizational encyclopedia [28], adopting (at least in part) the organic processes that typify wiki-based collaboration over the Internet. Insights from this study would be valuable to such firms, help structure the community of practice, organize work more effectively, design career paths, and ensure the community's sustainability.

CONCLUSION

Taking the results of this study as a whole, we make a case for investigating the functional organization of online production communities. It is interesting to note that only now researchers of online communities are turning their attention to the functional organization of production communities, given that this topic is at the core of the organizational literature [40]. Existing conceptualizations of emergent leadership within peer production have primarily focused on the dimension of authority (i.e. proximity to the community core) and prior studies have largely relied on contributors' activity for estimating the position on the periphery-core continuum. We, however, argue than an understanding of the formal functions in the community – as well as the way in which contributors traverse these functional roles – is paramount for explaining how online production communities organize their work.

Given that this is only a first attempt to empirically analyze and quantify the process of role transition along participants' career paths in online production communities, our study has several limitations which we hope to address in future research. First, in terms of method, building on [3] we defined organizational roles within Wikipedia based on editors access privileges. This approach has advantages over the method used in earlier studies where one's position on the core-periphery continuum was determined based on a simple quantification of his activity [48][12]. Nonetheless, we propose that future studies employ a multi-method approach, determining one's role based on access privileges, activity count, and additional recognition one receives (e.g. in Wikipedia: 'barnstars'[13] , service awards[14] , and other personal awards[15] [30, 33]). Second, our analysis of Wikipedia's organizational structure has focused on human agents, whereas automated software bots, too, carry out important tasks [42]. We, thus, propose that future studies provide a more complete view of work organization by also analyzing the various tasks performed by bots. Third, we acknowledge that the role transition patterns reported in this study have been influenced by the process by which the Wikipedia community introduced access privileges. For example, in the early stages of Wikipedia development, administrators were responsible for many of the functional roles; however, after the introduction of Level 2 privileges (2008-2011) many of these functions were delegated to the *Technical Administration*, *Border Patrol*, *Quality Assurance* and *QA Technicians* roles. This implies that the nature of *Administrator* role (as well as patterns of transitions into this role) have changed over time, calling for a future research that would re-examine role transition patterns once roles stabilize. Fourth, in order to increase the generalizability of our findings, in future research we plan to expand the analysis and perform a larger-scale evaluation (more participants, longer time period). In particular, the sample we employed excluded non-member contributors and late joiners (becoming active after 2007), and we call for future research that would repeat our study on a more comprehensive sample. Lastly, in future research we plan to extend our investigation to other online communities, in particular those that differ from Wikipedia in terms of the motivational drivers, the governance structure, or the enabling IT platform. Moving the investigation beyond Wikipedia is of special importance, given that the distinct role-transition patterns we have identified – and in particular the importance of the mid-level functional layer – may be relevant to only production communities that have grown beyond a certain size. We call for future research that would explore the phase in a community's life that call for the establishment of this kind of functional layer.

---

[12] Preece and Shneiderman note that "…these metrics [employed in previous studies] only capture activity. The development of more potent measures of efficacy in achieving personal and community goals would be a big breakthrough".

[13] http://en.wikipedia.org/wiki/Wikipedia:Barnstars

[14] http://en.wikipedia.org/wiki/Wikipedia:Service_awards

[15] http://en.wikipedia.org/wiki/Wikipedia:Awards

ACKNOWLEDGMENTS

This work was partially supported by SSHRC Insight Grant 435-2013-0624, by NSF Award ACI- 1322218, and by a grant from the Spanish Ministry of Economy and Competitiveness and the European Regional Development Fund: Content & Intelligence (ref. IPT-2012-0912-430000). We thank Carlos Fiorentino for his contribution to the graphical design of figures.

REFERENCES

[1] Amrit, C. and van Hillegersberg, J., "Exploring the impact of socio-technical core-periphery structures in open source software development," *Journal of Information Technology,* 25, 216-229, 2010.

[2] Arazy, O. and Gellatly, I., "Corporate Wikis: The Effects of Owners' Motivation and Behavior on Group Members' Engagement,," *Journal of Management Information Systems,* 29, 87-116, 2013.

[3] Arazy, O., Nov, O., and Ortega, F., "The [Wikipedia] World is Not Flat: on the organizational structure of online production communities," in *The 22nd European Conference on Information Systems (ECIS'2014)*, Tel-Aviv, Israel, 2014.

[4] Arazy, O., Nov, O., Patterson, R., and Yeo, L., "Information quality in Wikipedia: The effects of group composition and task conflict," *Journal of Management Information Systems,* 27, 71 - 98, 2011.

[5] Arazy, O., Stroulia, E., Ruecker, S., Arias, C., Fiorentino, C., Ganev, V., *et al.*, "Recognizing contributions in wikis: Authorship categories, algorithms, and visualizations," *Journal of the American Society for Information Science and Technology,* 61, 1166-1179, 2010.

[6] Arazy, O., Yeo, L., and Nov, O., "Stay on the Wikipedia Task: when task-related disagreements slip into personal and procedural conflicts," *Journal of the American Society for Information Science and Technology (JASIST),* 64, 1634–1648, 2013.

[7] Arthur, M. B., "The boundaryless career," *Journal of Organizational Behavior,* 15, 295-306, 1994.

[8] Baker, W. E. and Faulkner, R. R., "Role as resource in the Hollywood film industry," *American Journal of Sociology,* 97, 279-309, 1991.

[9] Benkler, Y., *The wealth of networks: How social production transforms markets and freedom*: Yale Univ Press, 2006.

[10] Blau, J. R., Coser, R. L., and Goodman, N., *Social Roles & Social Institutions.* New Jersey, USA: Transaction Publishers, 1995.

[11] Borgatti, S. P. and Everett, M. G., "Models of core/periphery structures," *Social networks,* 21, 375-395, 2000.

[12] Bryant, S., Forte, A., and Bruckman, A., "Becoming Wikipedian: transformation of participation in a collaborative online encyclopedia," in *International ACM SIGGROUP Conference on Supporting Group Work*, 2005, 1-10.

[13] Burke, M. and Kraut, R., "Mopping up: modeling wikipedia promotion decisions," in *Proceedings of the 2008 ACM Conference on Computer Supported Cooperative Work (CSCW'08)*, San Diego, California, USA, 2008, 27-36.

[14] Butler, B., Joyce, E., and Pike, J., "Don't look now, but we've created a bureaucracy: the nature and roles of policies and rules in wikipedia," in *Proceedings of the CHI Conference on Human Factors in Computing Systems (CHI'08)*, Florence, Italy, 2008, 1101-1110.

[15] Butler, B., Sproull, L., Kiesler, S., and Kraut, R., "Community effort in online groups: Who does the work and why?," in *Leadership at a Distance: Research in Technologically-Supported Work*, Ed. Hillsdale, NJ, USA: L. Erlbaum Associates Inc., 2002, 346-362.

[16] Butler, B., Sproull, S., Kiesler, S., and Kraut, R. E., "Community effort in online communities: who does the work and why," in *Leadership at a Distance Research in Technologically-Supported Work*, S. Weisband, Ed., ed London UK: Lawrence Erlbaum Associates, 2007, 171-194.

[17] Collier, B., Burke, M., Kittur, N., and Kraut, R., "Retrospective versus prospective evidence for promotion: The case of Wikipedia," in *2008 annual meeting of the Academy of Management*, 2008.

[18] Collier, B., Burke, M., Kittur, N., and Kraut, R., "Promoting Good Management: Governance, Promotion, and Leadership in Open Collaboration Communities," presented at the *International Conference on Information Systems*, St. Louis, USA, 2010.

[19] Collier, B. and Kraut, R., "Leading the Collective: Social Capital and the Development of Leaders in Core-Periphery Organizations," presented at the *Collective Intelligence*, MIT, Boston, MA, USA, 2012.

[20] Crowston, K., Wei, K., Li, Q., and Howison, J., "Core and Periphery in Free/Libre and Open Source Software Team Communications," *Proceedings of the 39th Annual Hawaii International Conference on System Sciences (HICSS'2006).*

[21] Dahlander, L. and O'Mahony, S., "Progressing to the center: Coordinating project work," *Organization science,* 22, 961-979, 2011.

[22] Denning, P. J. and Yaholkovsky, P., "Getting to 'We': Solidarity, not software, generates collaboration," *Communications of the ACM,* 51, 19-24, 2008.

[23] Forte, A. and Lampe, C., "Defining, Understanding, and Supporting Open Collaboration: Lessons From the Literature," *American Behavioral Scientist,* 57, 535-547, 2013.

[24] Forte, A., Larco, V., and Bruckman, A., "Decentralization in Wikipedia governance," *Journal of Management Information Systems,* 26, 49-72, 2009.

[25] Geiger, R. S., "Are computers merely supporting cooperative work: towards an ethnography of bot development," in *Proceedings of the 16th Conference on Computer Supported Cooperative Work (CSCW'13)*, San Antonio, Texas, USA, 2013, 51-56.

[26] Halfaker, A., Geiger, R. S., Morgan, J. T., and Riedl, J., "The rise and decline of an open collaboration system: How Wikipedia's reaction to popularity is causing its decline," *American Behavioral Scientist,* 57(5), 664-688, 2013.

[27] Ibarra, H., *Working identity: Unconventional strategies for reinventing your career.* Harvard Business Press, 2003.

[28] Jang, S., Arazy, O., Nov, O., and Brainin, E., "'Crowding Out' in Corporate Wikis: the Effects of Job Responsibility and Motivation on Participation," in *6th Mediterranean Conference on Information Systems (MCIS'2011)*, Cyprus, 2010.

[29] Kittur, A., Suh, B., and Chi, E. H., "What's in Wikipedia? Mapping topics and conflict using socially annotated category structure," in *Proceedings of the SIGCHI Conference on Human Factors in Computing Systems (CHI'09)*, Boston, MA, 2009.

[30] Kriplean, T., Beschastnikh, I., and McDonald, D. W., "Articulations of wikiwork: uncovering valued work in wikipedia through barnstars," in *Proceedings of the 2008 ACM Conference on Computer Supported Cooperative Work (CSCW'08)*, San Diego, CA, USA, 2008, 47-56.

[31] Lave, J. and Wenger, E., *Situated Learning: Legitimate Peripheral Participation.* Cambridge, UK: Cambridge University Press, 1991.

[32] Lerner, J., "Role assignments," in *Network analysis*, U. Brandes and T. Erlebach, Eds., Springer, 2005, 216-252.

[33] Leskovec, J., Huttenlocher, D., and Kleinberg, J., "Governance in Social Media: A case study of the Wikipedia promotion process," in *AAAI International Conference on Weblogs and Social Media (ICWSM'10)*, 2010.

[34] Liu, J. and Ram, S., "Who does what: Collaboration patterns in the Wikipedia and their impact on article quality," *ACM Trans. Manage. Inf. Syst.*, 2, 1-23, 2011.

[35] Long, Y. and Siau, K., "Social network structures in open source software development teams," *Journal of Database Management,* 18, 25-40, 2007.

[36] Luther, K., Fiesler, C., and Bruckman, A., "Redistributing leadership in online creative collaboration," in *Proceedings of the 2013 ACM Conference on Computer Supported Cooperative Work (CSCW'13)*, 2013, 1007-1022.

[37] Merton, R. K., *Social theory and social structure.* New York, NY, USA: Simon and Schuster, 1968.

[38] Meyer, J. W. and Rowan, B., "Institutionalized organizations: Formal structure as myth and ceremony," *American Journal of Sociology,* 83, 340-363, 1977.

[39] Miles, R. E., Snow, C. C., Meyer, A. D., and Coleman, H. J., "Organizational strategy, structure, and process," *Academy of Management Review,* 3, 546-562, 1978.

[40] Mintzberg, H., "The structuring of organizations: A synthesis of the research," *University of Illinois at Urbana-Champaign's Academy for Entrepreneurial Leadership Historical Research Reference in Entrepreneurship,* 1979.

[41] Morell, M. F., "Governance of online creation communities: Provision of infrastructure for the building of digital commons," PhD, European University Institute, 2010.

[42] Niederer, S. and Van Dijck, J., "Wisdom of the crowd or technicity of content? Wikipedia as a sociotechnical system," *New Media & Society,* 12, 1368-1387, 2010.

[43] O'Mahony, S. and Ferraro, F., "The emergence of governance in an open source community," *Academy of Management Journal,* 50, 1079-1106, 2007.

[44] Oreg, S. and Nov, O., "Exploring motivations for contributing to open source initiatives: The roles of contribution context and personal values," *Computers in Human Behavior,* 24, 2055-2073, 2008.

[45] Ortega, F., Izquierdo-Cortazar, D., Gonzalez-Barahona, J. M., and Robles, G., "On the analysis of contributions from privileged users in virtual open communities," in *Proceedings of the 42nd Hawaii International Conference on System Sciences (HICSS'2009)* Waikoloa, Big Island, HI, USA, 2009, 1-10.

[46] Panciera, K., Halfaker, A., and Terveen, L., "Wikipedians are born, not made: A study of power editors on Wikipedia," presented at the *GROUP, 2009.*

[47] Preece, J., Nonnecke, B., and Andrews, D., "The top five reasons for lurking: improving community experiences for everyone," *Computers in human behavior,* 20, 201-223, 2004.

[48] Preece, J. and Shneiderman, B., "The Reader-to-Leader Framework: Motivating technology-mediated social participation," *AIS Transactions on Human-Computer Interaction,* 1, 13-32, 2009.

[49] Ransbotham, S. and Kane, G. C., "Membership Turnover and Collaboration Success in Online Communities," *MIS Quarterly,* 35, 613-627, 2011.

[50] Riehle, D., Ellenberger, J., Menahem, T., Mikhailovski, B., Natchetoi, Y., *et al.*, "Open collaboration within corporations using software forges," *IEEE Software,* 26, 52-58, 2009.

[51] Roberts, J., Hann, I., and Slaughter, S., "Understanding the Motivations, Participation, and Performance of Open Source Software Developers," *Managenent Science,* 52, 984-999, 2006.

[52] Robles, G., Gonzalez-Barahona, J. M., and Herraiz, I., "Evolution of the core team of developers in libre software projects," in *Proceedings of the 6th IEEE International Working Conference on Mining Software Repositories (MSR'09)*, Vancouver, BC, Canada, 2009, 167-170.

[53] Sanger, L., "The early history of Nupedia and Wikipedia: a memoir," *Open sources,* 2, 307-338, 2005.

[54] Shaw, A. and Hill, B. M., "Laboratories of Oligarchy? How the Iron Law Extends to Peer Production," *Journal of Communication,* 64, 215-238, 2014.

[55] Stvilia, B., Twidale, M., Smith, L., and Gasser, L., "Information quality work organization in Wikipedia," *Journal of the American Society for Information Science and Technology,* 59, 983-1001, 2008.

[56] Von Hippel, E. and Von Krogh, G., "Open source software and the" private-collective" innovation model," *Organization Science,* 14, 209-223, 2003.

[57] Welser, H. T., Cosley, D., Kossinets, G., Lin, A., Dokshin, F., Gay, G., *et al.*, "Finding social roles in Wikipedia," in *Proceedings of the 2011 iConference*, Seattle, WA, USA, 2011, 122-129.

[58] Welser, H. T., Gleave, E., Fisher, D., and Smith, M., "Visualizing the signatures of social roles in online discussion groups," *Journal of Social Structure,* 8, 1-32, 2007.

[59] Wenger, E., *Communities of practice: Learning, meaning, and identity.* Cambridge, UK: Cambridge university press, 1999.

[60] Zhu, H., Kraut, R., and Kittur, A., "Effectiveness of shared leadership in online communities," in *Proceedings of the 2012 ACM Conference on Computer Supported Cooperative Work (CSCW'12)* , 407-416.

[61] Zhu, H., Kraut, R. E., Wang, Y.-C., and Kittur, A., "Identifying shared leadership in Wikipedia," in *Proceedings of the SIGCHI Conference on Human Factors in Computing Systems (CHI'11)*, 3431-3434.

The Virtuous Circle of Wikipedia
Recursive Measures of Collaboration Structures

Maximilian Klein
OCLC Research
777 Mariners Island Blvd
San Mateo, CA, 94404
kleinm@oclc.org

Thomas Maillart
School of Information
University of California,
Berkeley, 102 South Hall
Berkeley, CA 94720
maillart
@ischool.berkeley.edu

John Chuang
School of Information
University of California,
Berkeley, 102 South Hall
Berkeley, CA 94720
chuang
@ischool.berkeley.edu

ABSTRACT
In open collaboration, knowledge is created and iteratively improved by a multitude of editors who freely choose what should be their contributions. The quality of knowledge artifacts (e.g. article, source code file) is deeply tied to their individual expertise, and to their ability to collaborate well. Conversely, the expertise of contributors is a function of artifacts contributed to. Building upon a large stream of literature on the measurement of article quality and contributor expertise, we propose a recursive algorithm to measure how editor expertise influences the quality of articles, and how contributions to articles influence editor expertise. This *bi-partite network random walker* metric reveals the specific structure of cooperation and how the quality of articles is achieved through coordination. We show that while the wisdom of crowds is well pulled in some categories, more editors per article can also create disvalue.

ACM Classification Keywords
H.5.3 [Information Systems]: Group and Organization Interfaces: computer-supported collaborative work

Author Keywords
open collaboration; bi-partite networks; performance; coordination

INTRODUCTION
In online open collaboration knowledge, artifacts such as open source code, Wikipedia articles, and 3D-printing designs, are usually produced and improved collectively by a multitude of contributors. Some people devote numerous hours of labor improving existing content and adding new features, while most contributors only make minor changes. Yet, in addition to the power of the few, a mass of small changes can make the difference as a form of emergent collective intelligence [25]. As the Internet has become pervasive in modern societies, open collaboration has permeated to a broad variety of social contexts and industries [4].

Despite *bottom-up* self-organization, participants in open collaboration can collectively achieve the production of high quality and reliable knowledge, as demonstrated for instance in Wikipedia [14]. This form of labor organization is called peer-production and it usually heavily relies on Internet communication systems. Peer-production is based on *task self-selection* and *peer-review* [3]: participants decide to contribute according to their skills, and in turn, skills are improved as they contribute more, and so on, following a virtuous circle.

Because open collaboration enjoys horizontal organization, the dynamics of contributions are contingent to the heterogenous motivations and incentives of participants [41], and some knowledge artifacts enjoy various attention from the community, with time localized bursts for hot topics [24]. These highly non-linear, transient and intrinsically unpredictable bursts of iterative improvements are the hallmark of successfully organized communities [42]. They can be rationalized by critical cascades of both individual contributions and interactive community-based iterative improvements [37]. *Individual* versus *interaction-based* mechanisms are hard to disentangle, and therefore, understanding the structure of collaboration remains a difficult challenge. For larger groups concentrating on precise problems (e.g., in open collaboration), interactions typically magnify coordination problems [15].

To understand the origins of cooperation structures and quality in open collaboration, we posit that the value of each knowledge artifact (e.g., source code file, article) is deeply tied to the expertise and the number of its contributors, who can witness potential mistakes or outdated information. Conversely, the expertise of contributors is a function of artifacts contributed to, and so on, recursively.

To measure how artifacts benefit from a larger number of editors with a given expertise, and how editors benefit from having contributed to more artifacts of some quality, we propose a *bi-partite network random walker* algorithm, which is a two

CSCW 2015, March 14–18, 2015, Vancouver, BC, Canada.

ACM 978-1-4503-2922-4/15/03 ...$15.00.
http://dx.doi.org/10.1145/2675133.2675286

node type extension of the recursive *pageRank* algorithm [33, 29]. We calibrate the algorithm on 12 Wikipedia categories of articles, and we show, at the level of each category, how articles do (or do not) benefit from the intervention of more editors and their expertise.

The rest of this paper is organized as follows. We first expose the reader to the large literature on Wikipedia, measuring article quality, editor expertise and their mutual interplay. We then introduce the intuition behind the *bi-partite network random walker* algorithm, as well as its implementation for the present study. Data employed and the results are then presented and discussed. We finally conclude with limitations and future research directions.

RELATED WORK

The structure and dynamics of individual and collective contributions have long since been recognized by researchers as primary factors for the achievement of high quality content, starting with scientific publications [31] and open collaboration projects [6]. In the meantime, some of these open collaboration projects have tremendously increased their size and the number of their contributors, making it hard to assess the value of each knowledge artifact, even by intensive peer-review. The Wikipedia community, as well as researchers, have tried to find ways to determine article quality and editor expertise in a systematic way. These approaches have systematically faced criticism. Many quality article metrics have been proposed from methods based on word count [5], revision history [18], general structure of articles [43], patterns of changes between article versions [45], and combinations of type and volume of edits and editor expertise [22]. Editor expertise has also been investigated by considering total number of words written, number of edits made, longevity of edits [2], time spent in edit sessions [13], and number of *barnstars* collected [30]. Other editor features that have received the attention of researchers include creative editing [19], how power editors differ from normal editors [34], and the influence of the type of contributors on the quality of articles [38].

The effort to measure article quality and editor expertise has extended to predicting the quality of contributions [12, 46], developing reputation systems for editors [1], and identifying editor candidates for promotion [7].

We believe that the general skepticism about these metrics and reputation systems is grounded in their inability to capture and make sense of coordination between contributors. Coordination, defined as an on-going process that produces other measurable outcomes, is in general hard to understand in societies [32]. CSCW researchers have been specifically concerned with coordination viewed as a feature of a community, i.e., the effect of more peers on output quality. While collaboration and additional reviews by peers are generally perceived as positive, depending on the type of tasks and their required coordination, performance can also be undermined by inadequate coordination processes [27]. On the contrary, the effects of diversity on group productivity seem to increase group productivity [9]. It was also found that editors cluster by interest, with higher coordinated efforts in densely populated clusters [20]. In particular, Wikipedia has been a heavily explored *field* for social scientists, starting with concerns on the effects of peer-review and whether single or repeated contributions by editors would help improve the quality of articles [18, 44].

As an hybrid example, the specific problem of coordination in *featured* Wikipedia articles, which are heavily contributed over short time periods, has raised concerns on implicit versus explicit coordination processes and the limited positive quality it can bring when editors are too numerous [26].

The connection between article quality and editor expertise is present in nearly all literature aiming to understand the effects of the coordination process on the value of Wikipedia articles. The typical structure of networks with edges that connect uniquely two kinds of nodes is called *bi-partite* [31]. The analysis of patterns in Wikipedia bi-partite networks, with editors being one node type and articles the other, confirmed the existence of overlapping cliques of densely connected articles and editors [20]. A more detailed analysis of medical and health-related articles on Wikipedia, showed that the position of articles in the bi-partite network of articles and editors significantly influenced its quality [21].

Recent developments in the science of bi-partite networks has shown the feasibility to rank entities of each type through a recursive algorithm called *method of reflections*.This method has been tested on the bi-partite network of countries exporting products [17, 16]. The method of reflections has been improved and complemented in more recent work, mainly to improve its robustness [39, 11, 40, 10]. Caldarelli et al. [8] have proposed an alternative method, based on biased stochastic Markov chains, which helps further understand the mutual influence between nodes in bi-partite networks.

METHOD

We present a comprehensive method to *reverse-engineer* coordination as a feature of categories in Wikipedia. We expect that categories of articles exhibit more or less coordination, which in turn can be captured by the fundamental structure of the *bi-partite* network of articles and editors. The underlying idea of our model is to account for the recursive flow of *value* circulating between editors and articles, with editors benefiting from having edited higher quality articles, and articles having been edited by more expert editors. If coordination brings "more than the sum of its parts", then articles benefit from more editors, and primarily from expert editors. Conversely, if coordination is not efficient, *disvalue* is generated by more editors editing one article, or by an editor contributing to many articles in the category. A typical example of disvalue is vandalism [13].

We now turn to explaining the formalism of the *bi-partite random walker* method, and we show how the structure of collaboration can be encapsulated and measured with a single parameter. We consider a simple input, which is a representation of the bi-partite network of editors and their contributions to articles. Namely, let us consider a matrix M_{ea} of all editors having contributed to a Wikipedia category of articles. M_{ea} takes value 1 if editor e has edited article a, and 0 otherwise. For simplicity and because mixed results have been

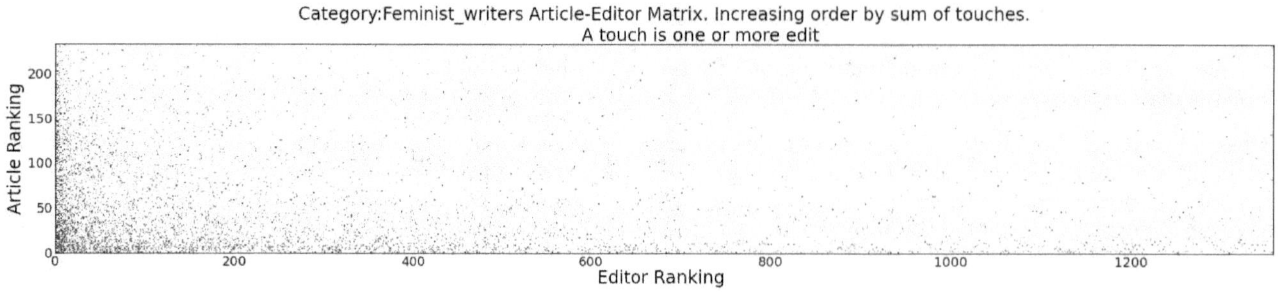

Figure 1. Typical M_{ea} matrix for a Wikipedia category (here, *Feminist Writers*) ordered on both dimensions by descending order of number of articles modified by an editor (horizontal axis) and of number editors who have modified an article (vertical axis). The structure of M_{ea} is triangular and shows that some editors have a pervasive activity over articles, while most editors edit only a few. Similarly, some articles receive widespread attention by editors, while most articles are modified only by a few editors.

previously reported in the literature [44], we consider only if editors have ever touched an article, rather than incorporating a more fine grained metric, such as the count of edits made by an editor on a specific article. As a robustness check, we show later that using edit counts reduces drastically the fitness of the method. For the category *Feminist Writers*, as presented on Figure 1, M_{ea} exhibits a triangular structure in which editors (resp. articles) are sorted (max on the bottom-left corner) by the number of articles they have touched (resp. by the number of editors who have touched each article). M_{ea} is the only input of the *bi-partite random walker* model.

Given M_{ea}, the simplest, and arguably naive, way to assess the contribution value (i.e., the *expertise* thereafter) of an editor is obtained by summing the number of articles ever edited out of all articles in a category. Similarly, a simple *quality* measure for an article is the sum of editors who have ever modified it, following the famous adage on open source development: "Given enough eyeballs, all bugs are shallow" [35]. These crude expertise and quality metrics for editors and articles, respectively given by,

$$\begin{cases} w_e^{(0)} = \sum_{a=1}^{N_a} M_{ea} \equiv k_e \\ w_a^{(0)} = \sum_{e=1}^{N_e} M_{ea} \equiv k_a \end{cases} \tag{1}$$

are the zero[th] order of our algorithm. They are the initial step of the *method of reflections* proposed by Hidalgo et al., which derives the value of producing entities (i.e., editors) from products (i.e., articles), and *vice versa* [17, 16]. To help capture the intuition behind the method of reflections for open collaboration, we walk through the first and second iterations:

- **1st order iteration,**
  - **Articles**: if an article has been edited by higher expertise editors, it is of higher quality. That is, quality is a function of expertise calculated from zero[th] iteration expertise scores.
  - **Editors**: conversely, if an editor has contributed to higher quality articles, her expertise is higher. That is, expertise is a function of quality calculated from zero[th] iteration quality scores.
- **2nd order iteration,**
  - **Articles**: if an article has been edited by higher expertise editors who have edited higher value articles, which in turn have been edited by higher expertise contributors, the article quality is higher. That is, quality is a function of expertise calculated from 1st iteration expertise scores.
  - **Editors**: conversely, if an editor has edited higher quality articles, which have been edited by better editors who have edited higher quality articles, then expertise is higher. That is, expertise is a function of quality calculated from 1st iteration quality scores.
- **And so on, recursively.**

Although interpretation is difficult past the very first iteration steps, at each iteration, the algorithm incorporates additional information on the quality of the articles and expertise of editor from the neighboring nodes in the bi-partite network. The higher order iterations can be modeled as a Markov process of random walkers on a bi-partite network, jumping with some probability from one node type to another node type [8]. A schematic representation of the random walk process on a bi-partite network is depicted in Figure 2. The intuition is the following: a random walker jumps with some probability from an editor to a given article (i.e., the editor's expertise is positively influenced by the article's quality), and with another probability from an article to a given editor (i.e. the value of the article is positively by the editor's expertise). The binary matrix M_{ea} determines whether a jump between each pair of nodes is possible: if two nodes e and a are not directly connected ($M_{ea} = 0$), the transition probability is 0. Conceptually, the *bi-partite network random walker* model is an extension of the single node type (i.e. Web pages) *Page Rank* Google search algorithm [33, 29] to two types of nodes.

We call $w_e^{(n)}$ the expertise of an editor and $w_a^{(n)}$ the quality of an article at the nth iteration, and we define the following Markov process on the bi-partite network of collaboration,

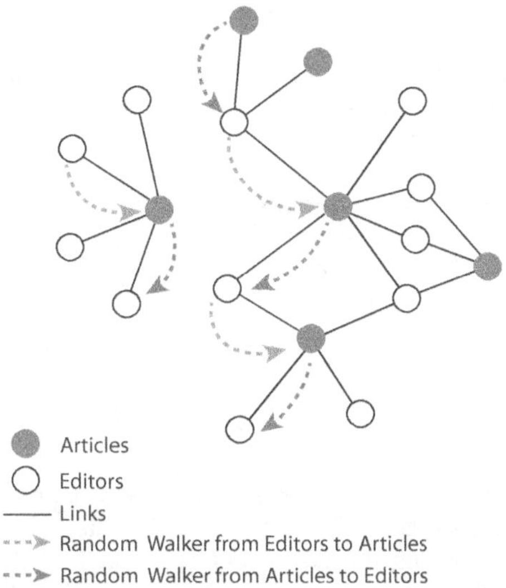

Figure 2. Representation of random walkers jumping from editors to articles (red dotted arrows) and from articles to editors (blue dotted arrows). The intuition is the following: a random walker jumps with some probability from an editor to a given article (i.e., the editor's expertise is positively influenced by the article's quality), and with another probability from an article to a given editor (i.e., the value of the article positively influences the editor's expertise).

$$\begin{cases} w_e^{(n+1)}(\alpha,\beta) = \sum_{a=1}^{N_a} G_{ea}(\beta)\, w_a^{(n)}(\alpha,\beta) \\ w_a^{(n+1)}(\alpha,\beta) = \sum_{e=1}^{N_e} G_{ae}(\alpha)\, w_e^{(n)}(\alpha,\beta) \end{cases} \tag{2}$$

with G_{ea} the probability to jump from article a to editor e in a single step, and the probability G_{ae} to jump from editor e to article a also in a single step. These transition probabilities are given by,

$$\begin{cases} G_{ea}(\beta) = \frac{M_{ea} k_e^{-\beta}}{\sum_{e'=1}^{N_e} M_{e'a} k_{e'}^{-\beta}} \\ G_{ae}(\alpha) = \frac{M_{ea} k_a^{-\alpha}}{\sum_{a'=1}^{N_a} M_{ea'} k_{a'}^{-\alpha}}. \end{cases} \tag{3}$$

The transition matrices $G_{ea}(\beta)$ and $G_{ae}(\alpha)$ depend only on the initial conditions: the binary matrix M_{ea}, as well as k_e and k_a given by (1), and are controlled only by parameters α and β. We shall therefore explain only how β influences the probability to jump from an article to an editor (i.e. the value of the article positively influences the editor's expertise). For $\beta = 0$, we recover the zeroth order iteration (1). For $\beta > 0$, the probability to jump from article a to editor e is a power law function $\sim 1/k_e^{\beta}$ of the sum of articles k_e modified by editor e. Hence, the larger k_e, the lower the probability to jump from a to e relative to other editors. On the contrary, if $\beta < 0$ the probability to jump from an article to an editor is a positive function of the sum of articles modified by the editor. For $-1 < \beta < 0$, the function is concave, while for $\beta < -1$, the function is convex, which means that the more articles have been edited by the editor, the even more the positive influence on articles. In a nutshell, β relates the amount of articles edited on the overall editor's expertise. If $\beta \gg 0$, the positive influence of the number of contributed articles on the editor's expertise decreases. If β close to 0, the number of contributed articles increases linearly the editor's expertise. The same considerations hold for α and the probability $G_{ae}(\alpha)$ to jump from an editor to an article (i.e. the expertise of the editor positively influences the quality of an article).

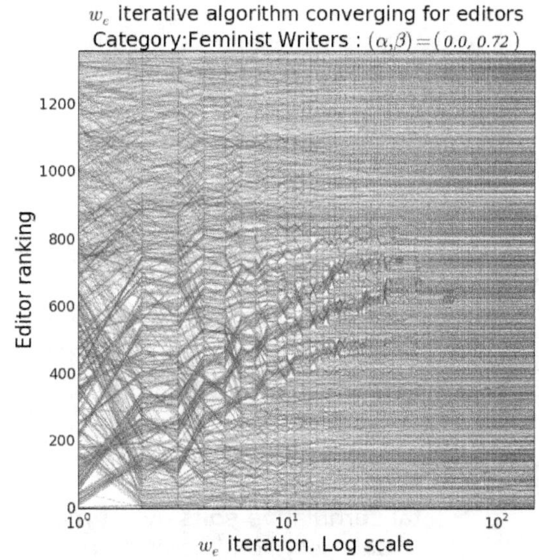

Figure 3. Convergence of the ranked expertise w_e of editors having contributed to articles in the Feminist Writers category on Wikipedia for arbitrary control parameters: $(\alpha,\beta) = (0, 0.72)$. Starting from the sum of contributed articles as the initial step, we can see how the algorithm progressively ranks editors: some editors with initial lowest rank, i.e., with few articles edited, get a higher rank as the number of iterations increases. Similarly, some initially high ranked editors, gradually drop in the ranking. In the case *Feminist Writers*, the algorithm converges after 64 iterations.

Figure 3 shows the evolution of expertise w_e ranked among editors having contributed to articles in the *Feminist Writers* category on Wikipedia for the set of control parameters $(\alpha,\beta) = (0, 0.72)$. We can see how the algorithm progressively ranks editors: some editors with initial low rank (i.e. with few articles edited), get a higher rank as more information is incorporated from neighboring nodes as the number of iterations increases. In that case ($\beta > 0$), higher ranked editors have edited and contributed to fewer, but higher quality articles (i.e. articles edited by more editors who have edited less articles). Similarly, some initially high ranked editors, gradually drop in the ranking. They have edited many, but lower quality articles.

Upon calibration of the bi-partite random walker model with ground-truth metrics of article quality and editor expertise, the parameters α and β directly inform how coordination generates value (i.e. more articles edited by more editors brings value), or on the contrary, if value is created by small clusters of highly experienced editors. This latter scenario implies less coordination among large crowds of contributors.

Category	Articles	Editors	Edits
American male novelists	2,460	9,946	224,783
2013 films	1,896	5,215	150,956
American women novelists	1,936	5,968	138,716
Nobel Peace Prize laureates	104	4,165	91,522
Sexual acts	93	2,190	45,901
Economic theories	212	1,145	28,658
Feminist writers	233	1,357	25,738
Yoga	123	730	25,315
Military history of the US	180	854	20,172
Counterculture festivals	66	578	10,515
Computability theory	92	272	7,117
Bicycle parts	70	210	4,981

Table 1. Size statistics of investigated Wikipedia categories sorted by total edits.

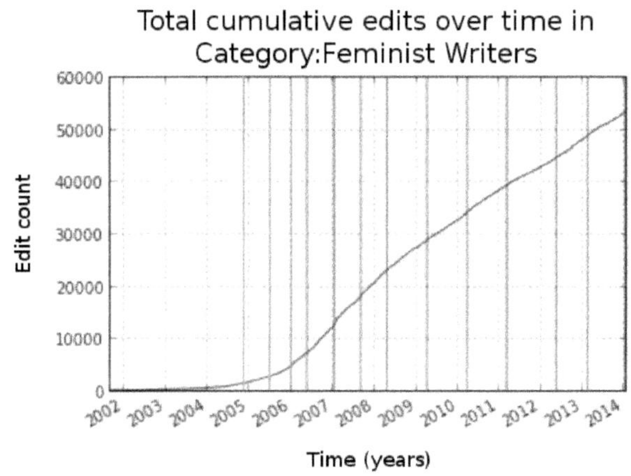

Figure 4. Cumulative edits made in Category *Feminist writers* (blue line). Vertical red lines represent the 13 snapshots taken at 2.5%, 5%, 7.5% and then, 10%, 20%, 30%, ..., 100% of edits.

DATA

To uncover the coordination features of Wikipedia categories, we seek to calibrate the bi-partite random walker model with empirical data. For that, we aim to find values of α and β, which minimize the distance between rankings, of both article quality and editor expertise, given by the model on the one hand, and on the other hand, by ground truth metrics obtained independently. We performed the model calibration for 13 snapshots (see Figure 4) for each of the 12 categories of Wikipedia articles presented in Table 1. To account as much as possible for collaboration structures, we have selected a spectrum of categories ranging from anarchy and edit-warring (e.g., *Sexual Acts*) to acknowledged high organization level (e.g., *Military history of the US*).

For each category and snapshot we have built the binary matrix M_{ea} by parsing all edit histories of all articles in the main namespace up to the snapshot time. We set $M_{ea} = 1$ for editor e having modified article a, and $M_{ea} = 0$ otherwise. We considered only editors who made 5 or more edits to any article in the category. We also discarded all software robots (i.e., *bots*) that programmatically edit Wikipedia.

To calibrate α and β, we resorted to state-of-the-art ground truth evaluations for editor expertise $\bar{w}_e$ and article quality $\bar{w}_a$. From these exogenous evaluations, we ranked editors and articles according to their expertise and quality respectively. We then performed a grid search for values of α^* and β^*, which maximize the Spearman rank-correlation ρ_e and ρ_a between rankings obtained from the bi-partite random walker model (w_e, w_a) and from exogenous metrics $(\bar{w}_e, \bar{w}_a)$. Actually, (α^*, β^*) must maximize both ρ_e and ρ_a, even though ρ_e and ρ_a might actually be different. The optimization function of (α^*, β^*) is given by,

$$\begin{cases} (\alpha^*, \beta^*) = \mathrm{argmax}_{\alpha,\beta}(\rho_e) \\ (\alpha^*, \beta^*) = \mathrm{argmax}_{\alpha,\beta}(\rho_a). \end{cases} \tag{4}$$

The set (α^*, β^*) characterizes how the structure of collaboration creates values in each Wikipedia category. To calibrate the model, we have used ground truth metrics for article quality and editor expertise.

A variety of techniques for measuring article quality have been proposed, from a collection of word-count related metrics [5] to analyzing persistent and transient contributions throughout revisions [45]. We have selected metrics used on Wikipedia [43, 28] which have also been used in the CSCW literature in different combinations [22, 23]. Our measure of actual article quality is a combination of 5 text analysis metrics: (i) ratio of mark-up to readable text, (ii) number of headings, (iii) article length, (iv) citations per article length, (v) number of outgoing intra-Wiki links. We performed principal component analysis (PCA) for each category and snapshot in order to reduce dimensionality from 5 metrics to a single one (i.e., the principal component). The variance explained by the principal component varied between 0.5 and 0.72, confirming the dominance of the axis of maximum variance. Even though these five article quality metrics do not directly incorporate information from the bi-partite network (e.g. number of contributors, number of edits), they might indirectly be related, as some editors specialize in some types of editing, such as adding citations or systematically improving the structure of articles.

Editor expertise is even more difficult to address. As each article is a blend of edits by several contributors, disentangling the value of individual contributions remains a challenge, which has occupied Wikipedia researchers long before us. Techniques ranging from parsing the revision history to measuring text survival rate [2] have been used. Although they are sophisticated, these metrics pose a variety of problems. For instance, some articles are likely to evolve not only because former editors introduced wrong statements, but simply because of new information brought to public attention.

We decided to use the *labor hours* metric proposed by Geiger and Halfaker [13], which is calculated for each editor by taking contribution history up to the snapshot point. All edits made within 1 hour of a previous edit are counted as one *edit session*. If more than one hour separates two edits, a new period of edits starts. The expertise expressed in labor hours is the sum of edit sessions. For the calculation of ground truth expertise, we only consider edits for a given category, although the same editor might have simultaneously edited other categories of Wikipedia. This metric purposefully does not tell how this time is spent in the number (resp. size) of edits actually made during a period, or whether the effort has been spent on one or multiple articles. In other words, we do not distinguish a single minded user spending 100 hours on a single article trying to get it to "feature article status" from a user making 100 stub articles for 1 hour each. However, it is clear that a highly contributing editor has more chance to touch more articles over time, but the metric does not distinguish if editors had a dispersed contribution or concentrated on a single article.

How this effort is distributed and brings quality is precisely what the *bi-partite random walker* model can say that other metrics cannot. In a nutshell, parameters α and β describe the most likely structure of collaboration given calibration of the model to ground truth quality and expertise metrics. The higher the correlation between the model and the exogenous metrics, the better the collaboration structure is captured by the model.

RESULTS

To understand how contributions by editors to articles shape the structure of collaboration in Wikipedia, we have performed a calibration of the bi-partite network random walker model on 12 Wikipedia categories (c.f., Table 1) with 13 snapshots each (Figure 4). For each category and snapshot, we found the set of parameters (α^*, β^*), which maximize the fitness of the model to ground truth metrics of article quality and editor expertise. Figure 5 shows typical optimization landscapes, which maximize the rank correlation ρ_e (upper panel) between editor expertise w_e obtained from the model and expertise obtained from ground truth measures $\bar{w}_e$. The same is done for rank correlation ρ_a between w_a and $\bar{w}_a$ (lower panel).

The maximum achievable rank-correlation with ground truth expertise and quality metrics for editors [13] and articles [43] shows that the bi-partite network random walker model accounts particularly well for both quality of articles ($0.58 < \rho_a < 0.91$) and expertise of editors ($0.46 < \rho_e < 0.75$) at the last snapshot. Actually, the model reproduces very well, and very early the ranking of editors and articles according to the ground truth metrics as shown on Figure 6. In particular, the quality of articles is very well accounted for, while the level of correlation with the ground truth of editor expertise exhibits a slightly concave, or at least linear, increase.

For the latest snapshot (i.e., the state of contributions in February 2014), we find that the best possible α^* is 0 in all circumstances, while β^* varies considerably across categories. Table 2 shows the categories ordered by β^* (and $\alpha^* = 0$ for the sake of completeness), as well as the corresponding maximum rank correlations ρ_e and ρ_a. Since there is no single optimal value for (α^*, β^*), but rather a space of optimal values for ρ_e and ρ_a separately, we have searched for a set of values that jointly maximizes both ρ_e and ρ_a. The optimal parameter $\alpha^* = 0$ means that editor expertise always benefits from contributions as a linear function of the

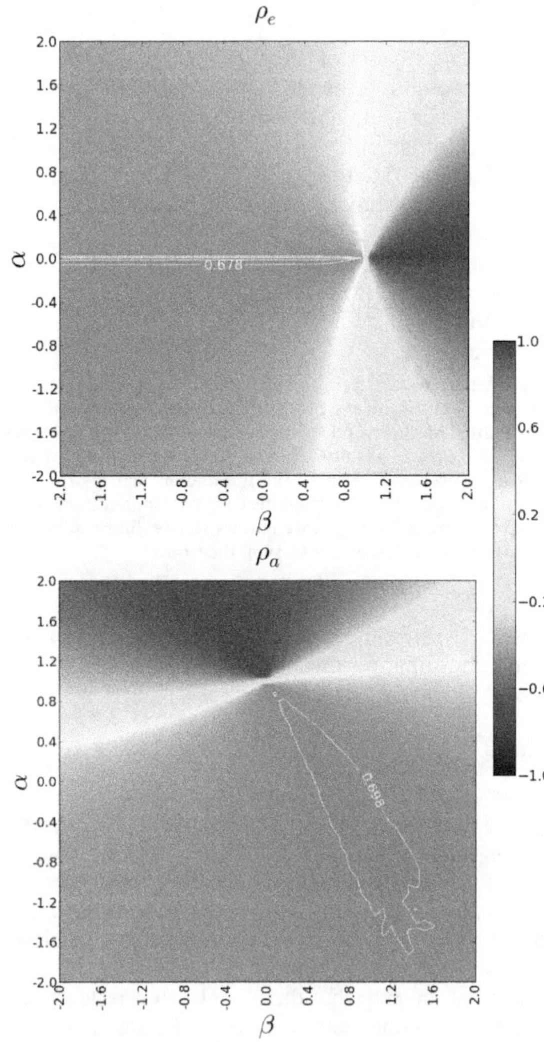

Figure 5. Typical landscape of maximum correlation as a function of α and β for articles (upper panel) and editors (lower panel). The contour line shows the 95th percentile of the rank correlation over the landscape. The category displayed here is *Feminist Writers*, for the last snapshot ending February 2014.

number of articles edited [compounded over iterations of the recursive algorithm defined by formula (2)]. However, β^* exhibits a continuum of values between 0 (*Bicycle parts* and *US Military History*) and 1.52 (*Sexual Acts*). β controls the influence of the number of editors on the quality of a given article. When $\beta \approx 0$, the quality of articles increases as a linear function of the number of editors who have modified them. For $\beta \gg 0$, the marginal gain of having more editors for a given article decreases. So, in that case, when the number of editors touching an article increases, the marginal quality improvement decreases.

The evolution of β^* over snapshots as shown on Figure 6 exhibits large variations for early snapshots corresponding to the early 10% of overall contributions per category (i.e., the 4th snapshot). While β^* exhibits a tendency to more stability afterwards, large variations within the range 0 to 1.5 can

	Category	ρ_a	ρ_e	α^*	β^*
1	Bicycle parts	0.90	0.46	0.00	0.00
2	Military history of the US	0.58	0.70	0.00	0.00
3	Computability theory	0.77	0.56	0.00	0.32
4	American male novelists	0.67	0.75	0.00	0.40
5	2013 films	0.72	0.55	0.00	0.48
6	Economic theories	0.74	0.70	0.00	0.48
7	American women novelists	0.63	0.75	0.00	0.64
8	Feminist writers	0.70	0.69	0.00	0.72
9	Yoga	0.64	0.57	0.00	1.12
10	Nobel Peace Prize laureates	0.91	0.66	0.00	1.20
11	Counterculture festivals	0.80	0.61	0.00	1.36
12	Sexual acts	0.63	0.66	0.00	1.52

Table 2. Categories ordered by increasing β^* obtained from best rank-correlation ρ_a and ρ_e of the bi-partite network random walker with the ground truth. As shown on the upper panel of Figure 5, highest rank-correlation is always obtained for $\alpha^* = 0$ suggesting that editors are experts in direct proportion to the number of articles they edit. The different values of β^* show the effect of marginal editors on a article. As β^* grows larger having more editors shows diminishing returns on article quality - "too many cooks spoil the broth".

be observed for some categories, suggesting that organization and coordination level changes can occur as categories develop.

DISCUSSION

To understand how the structure of collaboration influences article quality, we have applied and tested the *bi-partite network random walker* model for a variety of categories in Wikipedia. Our results show that the model accounts well for the quality of articles $\langle\rho_a\rangle \approx 0.64$ and for the expertise of contributors $\langle\rho_e\rangle \approx 0.72$, and overall exhibits a high degree of fitness. Moreover, ρ_a remains stable over time, while ρ_e increases, suggesting that the model better reflects editor expertise as more contributions to a broader set of articles occur, i.e., when the bi-partite network gets more densely connected. This suggests that loosely connected entities, either articles and editors, cannot be ranked accurately. From Figure 1 and from Table 1, we see that there are always significantly more editors than articles for each category. Hence, the probability for an article to get contributions early on is higher than the probability to find editors who have contributed to a lot of articles early.

To account for single-minded editors who have concentrated on only one or few articles, we have tested the *bi-partite random walker* model with a different input, namely the matrix of edit counts (instead of a binary matrix). As shown on Figure 7, the model using the *edit counts* input matrix accounts nearly as well for article quality, while it does a much worse job ranking editor expertise compared to a *binary* input matrix. Counter-intuitively, we observe a *less is more* situation: the number of articles ever touched by an editor better reflects the structure of collaboration and value creation, compared to edit counts, a much richer information input. Also, the labor-hour ground truth metric for editors is more a proxy of number of edits rather the number of articles ever touched [13]. Nevertheless, the model does not perform as well with *edit counts* as an input. This suggests that what really counts for

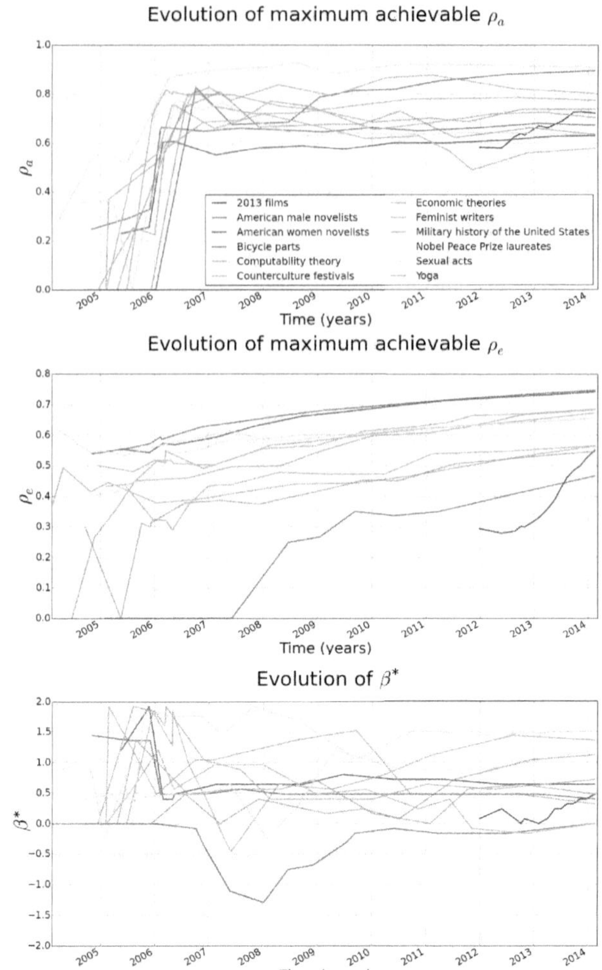

Figure 6. Evolution of Spearman ρ rank correlations between the ranking obtained from the calibrated model and the actual values for each category and for editors (upper panel) and articles (middle panel). Corresponding β^* values are also shown for interest (lower panel). The correlations are generally quite high : $0.46 < \rho_e < 0.75$ with $\langle\rho_e\rangle = 0.64$ for editors and $0.57 < \rho_a < 0.91$ with $\langle\rho_a\rangle = 0.72$. ρ_a is stable over time, which means that the quality of articles can be well captured early on by the model. However, ρ_e exhibits a convex increase over time, suggesting that it takes time (i.e., lots of edits) to capture well the expertise of editors.

assessing the expertise of an editor is the number of articles touched, rather than the number of edits per article.

We now discuss how the fitted parameters α^* and β^* inform on the structures of collaboration in Wikipedia categories. On the one hand, we have found $\alpha^* \approx 0$ for all categories, reflecting the positive influence of the number of articles edited on editor expertise. This result is compatible with previous results by Keegan et al. [23]. On the other hand, β^* varies across categories with values ranging from 0 to 1.52 at the last snapshot. β can be considered as a measure of the collaboration structure: the smaller β, the more articles benefit from more editors. On the contrary, the larger β, the more articles benefit from less editors. If we consider for instance *Sexual acts*, a category that could be considered taboo or perverse with articles being the least collaboratively edited: $\beta > 1$

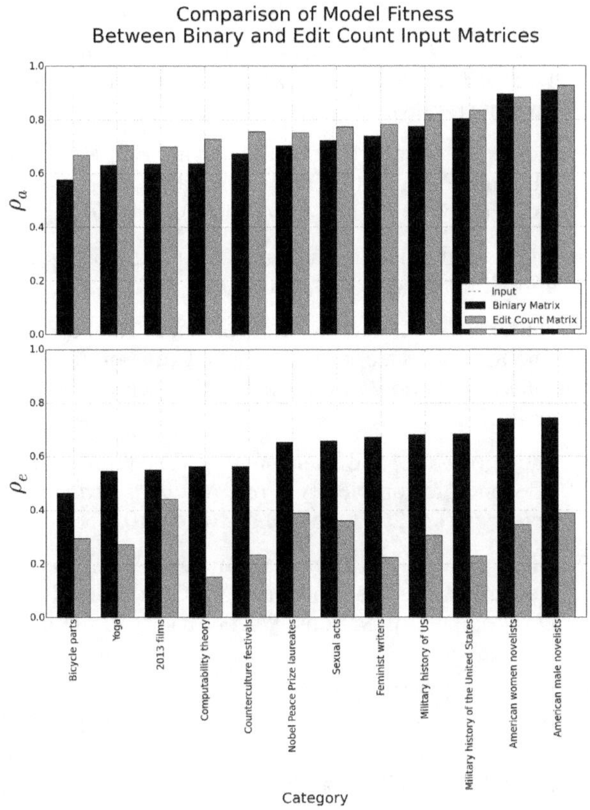

Figure 7. Comparison between ρ_a (upper panel) and ρ_e (lower panel) for two input matrices: binary (black) and edit counts (blue) for each category numbered according to Table 2. While taking edit counts as the input matrix only marginally increases ρ_a, it drastically reduces ρ_e.

reflects that an editor with edits to many articles will see her ranking drop. Indeed, it should not be taken for granted that contributions are necessarily positive. Because of their socially-sensitive nature, articles about sexual acts are particularly prone to attracting vandals or edit-warring behaviors across the whole category. Therefore, editors making the most edits are not necessarily the ones improving article quality, as we would typically expect. This result is again compatible with previous research, which has shown that, in some circumstances, most active editors exhibit deleting behaviors that lower metric-based article quality ratings [22].

Conversely, the category *Military History of the US* is famous for its self-organized task-forces. At the latest snapshot $\beta = 0$, it is the one of only a few categories we have analyzed, which exhibits β consistently negative over time. Accordingly, the marginal quality of articles is positively influenced by the number of editors touching the article. Unsurprisingly, *Military History of the US* is literally a *WikiProject* with a hierarchy of coordinators, an active IRC channel, and a mailing list. As a result of better coordination, there is less edit-warring and more efficient contributions: editors edit articles with well-defined task at hand.

LIMITATIONS AND FUTURE WORK

As a two node extension of the *pageRank* algorithm [33, 29], the *bi-partite network random walker* model is an efficient approach to recursively traverse the complex network of articles and editors in Wikipedia. Our results show that model calibration accounts well with ground-truth metrics, and can help characterize how more contributors for each article and better (resp. less) coordination create value (resp. destroy value) in open collaboration. Its very simple input (a binary matrix of contributions) makes it computationally affordable, though not cheap. While applying this algorithm to the entire Wikipedia would be a challenge, it is straightforward to use on small wikis or most open source software projects.

Our results show a first attempt to understand the structure of cooperation and how value is created with a unique model, which can be fully rationalized. The pertinence of the bi-partite network random walker for the study of open collaboration shall be confirmed by future work, to examine in a systematic way some of the results reported in this paper.

Namely, we would have expected that all categories, or at least each category, would exhibit a typical set (α^*, β^*) of explanatory parameters, which in turn would help gain better understanding of the general structure of collaboration in Wikipedia. Not only our results show that β^* varies across categories, but can also vary significantly over time for some of the categories we have analyzed. These results require further scrutiny on the evolution of contribution structures and coordination processes, in particular in these specific categories.

Future work shall also be devoted to further validation, in order to bring quantitative evidence that the model can systematically account for the influence of the coordination feature on value generated by contributions. We have only indirect evidence that coordination is efficient in some categories, like *Military History of the US*. An orthogonal way for testing the model would require measuring specifically the level of constructive (resp. destructive) interactions between editors, on articles (e.g. revert actions), and on usual communication channels used by the community of a specific category (e.g., discussion page, IRC channel, mailing list). A negative relationship between β^* and the amount of positive interactions would further demonstrate the validity of the model.

The structure of the input matrix (i.e., its dimensions and sparsity) requires further scrutiny. We aim to know the sensitivity of β^* to the total number of editors versus the total number of articles in a category. Presumably coordination problems are more likely to occur if there are more editors per article. To thoroughly perform these types of tests, we need to investigate more categories of Wikipedia.

The progressive validation process we have described will help gain trust in the model [36], and will perhaps allow meaningful out-of-sample predictions of article quality and editors experience rankings, given the structure of cooperation characterized by β^*. Conversely, the *bi-partite network random walker* model could be used in the future to set incentives for a reward system that would specifically encourage cooperation. It could also be used as a *Suggestbot*[1] to help new editors find friendly Wikipedia categories to start

[1]https://en.wikipedia.org/wiki/User:Suggestbot

their on-boarding process. This is a reverse approach from current on-boarding practices, where an interest topic is first chosen and then an edit is made in basically a random-chosen environment.

ACKNOWLEDGMENTS

This research was supported in part by the National Science Foundation under award CCF-0424422 (TRUST). One of the authors (T.M.) acknowledges support by the Swiss National Science Foundation (Grant Nr. PA00P2-145368).

REFERENCES

1. Adler, B. T., and de Alfaro, L. A Content-driven Reputation System for the Wikipedia. In *Proc. WWW '07*, ACM (New York, NY, USA, 2007), 261–270.
2. Adler, B. T., de Alfaro, L., Pye, I., and Raman, V. Measuring Author Contributions to the Wikipedia. In *Proc. WikiSym '08*, ACM (New York, NY, USA, 2008), 1–10.
3. Benkler, Y. Coase's Penguin, or, Linux and "The Nature of the Firm". *The Yale Law Journal 112*, 3 (Dec. 2002), 369+.
4. Benkler, Y. *The Penguin and the Leviathan: How Cooperation Triumphs over Self-Interest*, 1 ed. Crown Business, Aug. 2011.
5. Blumenstock, J. E. Size Matters: Word Count As a Measure of Quality on Wikipedia. In *Proc. WWW '08*, ACM (New York, NY, USA, 2008), 1095–1096.
6. Bryant, S. L., Forte, A., and Bruckman, A. Becoming Wikipedian: Transformation of Participation in a Collaborative Online Encyclopedia. In *Proc. GROUP '05*, ACM (New York, NY, USA, 2005), 1–10.
7. Burke, M., and Kraut, R. Taking up the mop: identifying future wikipedia administrators. In *CHI'08 extended abstracts on Human factors in computing systems*, ACM (2008), 3441–3446.
8. Caldarelli, G., Cristelli, M., Gabrielli, A., Pietronero, L., Scala, A., and Tacchella, A. A network analysis of countries' export flows: firm grounds for the building blocks of the economy. *PloS one 7*, 10 (2012).
9. Chen, J., Ren, Y., and Riedl, J. The Effects of Diversity on Group Productivity and Member Withdrawal in Online Volunteer Groups. In *Proc. CHI '10*, ACM (New York, NY, USA, 2010), 821–830.
10. Cristelli, M., Gabrielli, A., Tacchella, A., Caldarelli, G., and Pietronero, L. Measuring the Intangibles: A Metrics for the Economic Complexity of Countries and Products. *PloS one 8*, 8 (2013).
11. Cristelli, M., Tacchella, A., Gabrielli, A., Pietronero, L., Scala, A., and Caldarelli, G. Competitors' communities and taxonomy of products according to export fluxes. *The European Physical Journal-Special Topics 212*, 1 (2012).
12. Druck, G., Miklau, G., and McCallum, A. Learning to Predict the Quality of Contributions to Wikipedia. *Wikipedia and Artificial Intelligence: An Evolving Synergy* (2008), 7.
13. Geiger, R. S., and Halfaker, A. Using Edit Sessions to Measure Participation in Wikipedia. In *Proc. CSCW '13*, ACM (New York, NY, USA, 2013), 861–870.
14. Giles, J. Internet encyclopaedias go head to head. *Nature 438*, 7070 (Dec. 2005), 900–901.
15. Halfaker, A., Geiger, R. S., Morgan, J. T., and Riedl, J. The Rise and Decline of an Open Collaboration System. *American Behavioral Scientist 57*, 5 (May 2013), 664–688.
16. Hidalgo, C. A., and Hausmann, R. The building blocks of economic complexity. *Proc. National Academy of Sciences 106*, 26 (June 2009), 10570–10575.
17. Hidalgo, C. A., Klinger, B., Barabási, A.-L., and Hausmann, R. The Product Space Conditions the Development of Nations. *Science 317*, 5837 (July 2007), 482–487.
18. Hu, M., Lim, E. P., Sun, A., Lauw, H. W., and Vuong, B. Q. Measuring Article Quality in Wikipedia: Models and Evaluation. In *Proc. CIKM '07*, ACM (New York, NY, USA, 2007), 243–252.
19. Iba, T., Nemoto, K., Peters, B., and Gloor, P. A. Analyzing the Creative Editing Behavior of Wikipedia Editors. *Procedia - Social and Behavioral Sciences 2*, 4 (Jan. 2010), 6441–6456.
20. Jesus, R., Schwartz, M., and Lehmann, S. Bipartite Networks of Wikipedia's Articles and Authors: A Meso-level Approach. In *Proc. WikiSym '09*, ACM (New York, NY, USA, 2009), 1–10.
21. Kane, G. C. It's a Network, Not an Encyclopedia: A Social Network Perspective on Wikipedia Collaboration. *Academy of Management Proceedings 2009*, 1 (Aug. 2009), 1–6.
22. Kane, G. C. A Multimethod Study of Information Quality in Wiki Collaboration. *ACM Trans. Manage. Inf. Syst. 2*, 1 (Mar. 2011).
23. Keegan, B., Gergle, D., and Contractor, N. Do Editors or Articles Drive Collaboration?: Multilevel Statistical Network Analysis of Wikipedia Coauthorship. In *Proc. CSCW '12*, ACM (New York, NY, USA, 2012), 427–436.
24. Keegan, B., Gergle, D., and Contractor, N. Hot Off the Wiki: Structures and Dynamics of Wikipedia's Coverage of Breaking News Events. *American Behavioral Scientist* (Jan. 2013), 0002764212469367+.
25. Kittur, A., Chi, E., Pendleton, B. A., Suh, B., and Mytkowicz, T. Power of the few vs. wisdom of the crowd: Wikipedia and the rise of the bourgeoisie. *World wide web 1*, 2 (2007), 19.

26. Kittur, A., and Kraut, R. E. Harnessing the Wisdom of Crowds in Wikipedia: Quality Through Coordination. In *Proc. CSCW '08*, ACM (New York, NY, USA, 2008), 37–46.

27. Kittur, A., Lee, B., and Kraut, R. E. Coordination in Collective Intelligence: The Role of Team Structure and Task Interdependence. In *Proc. CHI '09*, ACM (New York, NY, USA, 2009), 1495–1504.

28. Klein, M. Kumusha Takes Wiki: Actionable Metrics for Uganda and Côte d'Ivoire, 2014.

29. Kleinberg, J. M. Authoritative Sources in a Hyperlinked Environment. *J. ACM 46*, 5 (Sept. 1999), 604–632.

30. Kriplean, T., Beschastnikh, I., and McDonald, D. W. Articulations of Wikiwork: Uncovering Valued Work in Wikipedia Through Barnstars. In *Proc. CSCW '08*, ACM (New York, NY, USA, 2008), 47–56.

31. Newman, M. E. J. The structure of scientific collaboration networks. *Proc. National Academy of Sciences 98*, 2 (Jan. 2001), 404–409.

32. Ostrom, E. *Governing the commons : the evolution of institutions for collective action*. Cambridge University Press, Nov. 1990.

33. Page, L., Brin, S., Motwani, R., and Winograd, T. The PageRank citation ranking: Bringing order to the web. *Technical Report* (1999).

34. Panciera, K., Halfaker, A., and Terveen, L. Wikipedians Are Born, Not Made: A Study of Power Editors on Wikipedia. In *Proc. GROUP '09*, ACM (New York, NY, USA, 2009), 51–60.

35. Raymond, E. The cathedral and the bazaar. *Knowledge, Technology & Policy 12*, 3 (Sept. 1999), 23–49.

36. Sornette, D., Davis, A. B., Ide, K., Vixie, K. R., Pisarenko, V., and Kamm, J. R. Algorithm for model validation: Theory and applications. *Proc. National Academy of Sciences 104*, 16 (Apr. 2007), 6562–6567.

37. Sornette, D., Maillart, T., and Ghezzi, G. How Much is the Whole Really More than the Sum of its Parts? 1 + 1 = 2.5: Superlinear Productivity in Collective Group Actions. *PloS ONE 9*, 8 (2014).

38. Stein, K., and Hess, C. Does It Matter Who Contributes: A Study on Featured Articles in the German Wikipedia. In *Proc. HT '07*, ACM (New York, NY, USA, 2007), 171–174.

39. Tacchella, A., Cristelli, M., Caldarelli, G., Gabrielli, A., and Pietronero, L. A new metrics for countries' fitness and products' complexity. *Scientific reports 2* (2012).

40. Tacchella, A., Cristelli, M., Caldarelli, G., Gabrielli, A., and Pietronero, L. Economic complexity: Conceptual grounding of a new metrics for global competitiveness. *Journal of Economic Dynamics and Control* (2013).

41. von Krogh, G., Haefliger, S., Spaeth, S., and Wallin, M. W. Carrots and Rainbows: Motivation and Social Practice in Open Source Software Development. *MIS Quarterly 36* (2012).

42. von Krogh, G., Maillart, T., Haefliger, S., and Sornette, D. Designing organizations for productive bursts. *in revision* (2014).

43. Wang, M. W., Cosley, D., and Riedl, J. Tell Me More: An Actionable Quality Model for Wikipedia. In *Proc. WikiSym '13*, ACM (New York, NY, USA, 2013).

44. Wilkinson, D. M., and Huberman, B. A. Cooperation and Quality in Wikipedia. In *Proc. WikiSym '07*, ACM (New York, NY, USA, 2007), 157–164.

45. Wöhner, T., and Peters, R. Assessing the Quality of Wikipedia Articles with Lifecycle Based Metrics. In *Proc. WikiSym '09*, ACM (New York, NY, USA, 2009), 1–10.

46. Zeng, H., Alhossaini, M. A., Ding, L., Fikes, R., and McGuinness, D. L. Computing Trust from Revision History. In *Proc. PST '06*, ACM (New York, NY, USA, 2006), 1.

Talkabout: Making Distance Matter with Small Groups in Massive Classes

Chinmay Kulkarni[1], Julia Cambre[1,2], Yasmine Kotturi[3], Michael S. Bernstein[1], Scott Klemmer[3]
[1]Stanford University, [2]Coursera Inc., [3]UC San Diego
{chinmay,jcambre}@cs.stanford.edu, ykotturi@ucsd.edu, msb@cs.stanford.edu, srk@ucsd.edu

ABSTRACT
Massive online classes are global and diverse. How can we harness this diversity to improve engagement and learning? Currently, though enrollments are high, students' interactions with each other are minimal: most are alone together. This isolation is particularly disappointing given that a global community is a major draw of online classes. This paper illustrates the potential of leveraging geographic diversity in massive online classes. We connect students from around the world through small-group video discussions. Our peer discussion system, Talkabout, has connected over 5,000 students in fourteen online classes. Three studies with 2,670 students from two classes found that globally diverse discussions boost student performance and engagement: the more geographically diverse the discussion group, the better the students performed on later quizzes. Through this work, we challenge the view that online classes are useful only when in-person classes are unavailable. Instead, we demonstrate how diverse online classrooms can create benefits that are largely unavailable in a traditional classroom.

AUTHOR KEYWORDS
Online education; peer learning; culture; reflection

ACM CLASSIFICATION KEYWORDS
H.5.3 [Group and Organization Interfaces]: Computer-supported cooperative work

INTRODUCTION
At their best, culturally diverse classrooms leverage students' different backgrounds to improve learning and foster cultural understanding. When students engage with peers from different cultures, they become aware of their own assumptions and how others have different perspectives [39]. This shifts students from 'automatic' thinking to more 'active, effortful, conscious' thinking, which aids learning and growth [19]. But, while physical classrooms often strive to be diverse, they remain limited by physical geography [31].

Massive online courses recruit thousands of students from over 100 countries, bringing together peers with many nationalities and experiences [44]. Instructors often advertise how many countries are represented in the class [5, 30, 44]. However, while student diversity has become a calling card of online education, this potential is currently untapped. Most online students currently see only a glimpse of their peers' global diversity, primarily in text discussion forums. This slow-motion communication is a poor fit for the open-ended dialogue characteristic of dorm hallway conversation [28], and can reinforce a one-size-fits-all, broadcast educational approach [34].

This paper illustrates the potential of leveraging diversity in online classes, and introduces the Talkabout environment and curricula for small, geographically-diverse groups in massive classes. Talkabout connects students to their global peers via guided, synchronous video discussion. Talkabout focuses on harnessing *geographic diversity*, where students connect with peers from other parts of the world. Geographic diversity enables students to access peers with different cultures [17], levels of income [16], and beliefs about learning [48].

Geographically diverse classrooms can improve educational experiences, making them deeper and more realistic. Multinational discussions create the opportunity for what one student called a 'mini United Nations', where students experience first-hand the differing concerns and beliefs of people from different countries.

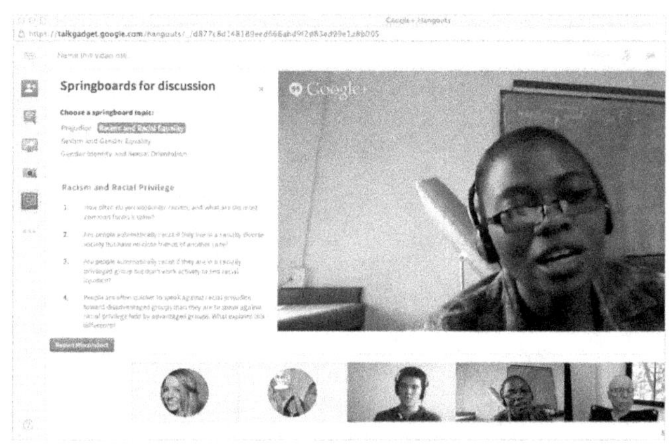

Figure 1: Talkabout provides a structured discussion agenda and enables students from around the world to discuss with each other.

CSCW 2015, March 14–18, 2015, Vancouver, BC, Canada.
ACM 978-1-4503-2922-4/15/03.
http://dx.doi.org/10.1145/2675133.2675166

Course Title	Representative Discussion topics
Critical Perspectives on Management	How do you define innovation and invention? How do manage them? Are shipping containers and labor unions innovations or inventions?
Irrational Behavior	How do you treat money as a relative rather than absolute good? Do you think that it is more painful to pay with cash than credit? How might issues of fairness vary by culture?
Organizational Analysis	Describe your experience in organizations where decisions by organized anarchy occurred. Did they solve anything? How common were they?
Social Psychology	In your country, which forms of prejudice are the most socially acceptable, and which ones are the least acceptable? Why are some forms more acceptable than others?
Think Again	Since inductive arguments are defeasible, how can it ever be reasonable to trust them? Are arguments from analogy really different from inferences to the best explanation?

Table 1: Excerpts from discussion agendas from one week in different classes. Each question below included more detailed guidance in the actual discussion

Talkabout forms groups of two to nine students from different parts of the world for a video discussion. Discussion prompts ask peers to relate course content to their local and personal experiences, encouraging students to reflect on previously unexamined assumptions about their own environments, and deepening their learning [33]. To date, more than 5,000 students from 134 countries have used Talkabout in fourteen online classes via Coursera and OpenEdX. This paper reports results from the first seven courses and 3,200 students. These classes included Social Psychology, Organizational Analysis, Behavioral Economics, and Logic and Design. Table 1 shows a sampling of topics discussed. The median discussion had six students from five countries.

Talkabout's discussion sessions improved student engagement: students randomly assigned to a Talkabout group were significantly more likely to participate in class quizzes than those placed on a wait-list for future participation (Wald $z^*=1.96$, $p=0.03$).

Geographically diverse discussions yield higher grades and engagement. A controlled experiment in two massive online classes varied the number of countries present in Talkabout discussions. Students in more geographically diverse discussions performed significantly better on subsequent quizzes and exams ($t(129)=1.78$ and $t(110)=2.03$, $p<0.05$).

Some argue that online education is only desirable when face-to-face education is unavailable [15]. This paper illustrates the benefits of inverting this proposition: global diversity enables online classrooms to create powerful, previously unavailable educational experiences and new forms of peer education at scale that go "beyond being there" [25].

RELATED WORK

A tremendous benefit of diverse classrooms is that students of differing gender, ethnicity, and ability have opportunities to interact. When people interact with similar peers, their shared background leads to automatic thinking. In contrast, interacting with diverse peers often creates a discontinuity [19] that unearths hidden assumptions—yielding more active, effortful and conscious thought [9]. This active and effortful thinking improves academic performance and makes students more inclusive and democratic [19].

Travel, and interacting with geographically diverse people, similarly induces active thinking and reflection [33]. For instance, study-abroad programs result in deeper knowledge and understanding—especially about culture and international affairs—and greater self confidence [4].

The benefits of interacting with geographically diverse peers arise from differences in experiences and thinking. Examples of these differing experiences include stark differences in population density, income and educational systems [56]. People from different parts of the world have different cultural values, reasoning, and preferred learning methods. For instance, cultures differ in their emphasis of individuality versus interdependence [22, 36] and holistic versus analytical thinking [57]. These differences impact cognition. For example, when cultures encourage people to consider objects in relation with their context, they more often apply analogical thinking. By contrast, when people consider objects in isolation, they more often apply categorical rules [57].

To maximize the benefits of diversity, prior work emphasizes two factors: the numeric representation of diverse groups *(structural diversity);* and the number of settings that students interact in (*experiential diversity*) [27]. Ideally, students must meet frequently, and with equal status, in situations where collaboration is necessary and stereotypes are disconfirmed [47], and where differing views are welcomed [23].

Informed by this research, Talkabout forms geographically diverse discussion groups, and encourages fluid roles and consensus-based decisions that emphasize equality. Furthermore, Talkabout contributes a curriculum where students can question stereotypes and compare their views to their peers.

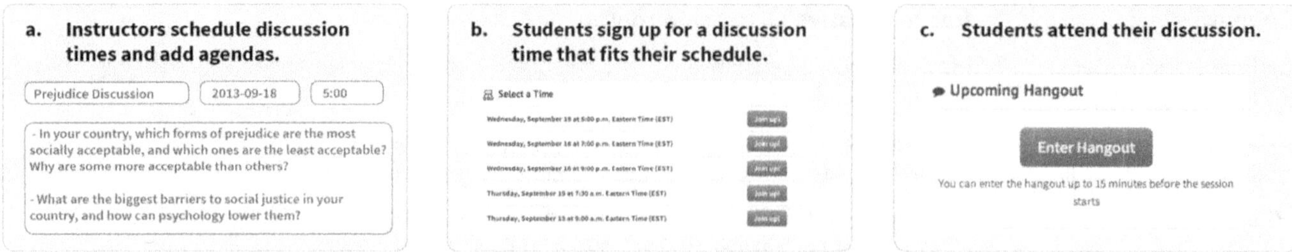

Figure 2: Talkabout discussion timeline: (a) Instructors enter a discussion agenda, and times for the discussion. (b) Students pick their preferred time. (c) When they log on to Talkabout at their selected time, Talkabout assigns them to a group, and creates a private hangout. (c) Students show up at their selected time, and enter the discussion.

In most current online classes, students' opportunities for discussions with diverse peers are limited to text-based forums. Such asynchronous text channels inhibit trust-formation [49] and open-ended discussion [52]. Synchronous channels, such as video, improve participants' sense of belonging and willingness to collaborate [50]. Channels such as video which support multimodal communication and nonverbal cues are also better suited to ambiguous discussions [11] and complex sense-making [13]. For these reasons, Talkabout leverages synchronous, small-group video discussions to encourage meaningful, open-ended dialogue.

Massive scale presents both a formidable challenge and a powerful opportunity for online education. Prior work encouraging unstructured discussion failed to find an improvement in students' sense of community or academic achievement [8]. More systematically structured approaches have enjoyed greater success. One example is the use of rater redundancy and short exercises that create micro-expertise in peer review: with this structure, peers can provide expert-quality assessment and feedback [32], and act as mentors [45]. Talkabout introduces a structured interaction and curriculum that leverages diversity.

COORDINATING GLOBAL SMALL-GROUP DISCUSSION

The Talkabout interface guides instructors through setting up their course discussions, and creating a structured discussion agenda for students (Figure 2a). This agenda is displayed throughout the discussion (Figure 1).

Students choose a discussion time from the published set (Figure 2b), up to a week in advance. As students log in at their selected time, Talkabout assigns them to groups (instructor can choose group size between 2 and 9). Talkabout has several policies for group assignment; by default it assigns arriving students to a group until it reaches its size limit; then it starts a new group. Other policies, discussed later, explicitly factor geographic location into group assignment. Discussions occur through the Google Hangouts platform for multi-person video and audio chat. For each group, Talkabout creates a discussion session exclusively for the assigned participants. Discussion groups exist only for the duration of the discussion session. If students participate in multiple discussion sessions—even in the same course and on the same topic—they are likely to have different partners, because grouping depends on students' arrival order. Consequently, students hear different ideas and experiences each time.

During discussions, the Talkabout Hangout application shows the instructor's discussion agenda on the left and the video chat on the right. An agenda typically includes suggested discussion topics or activities (Figure 1, Figure 4).

ASSIGNMENT BY ARRIVAL YIELDS DIVERSE GROUPS

To quantify the geographic diversity in discussions, we aggregate countries into eight geographical regions, and

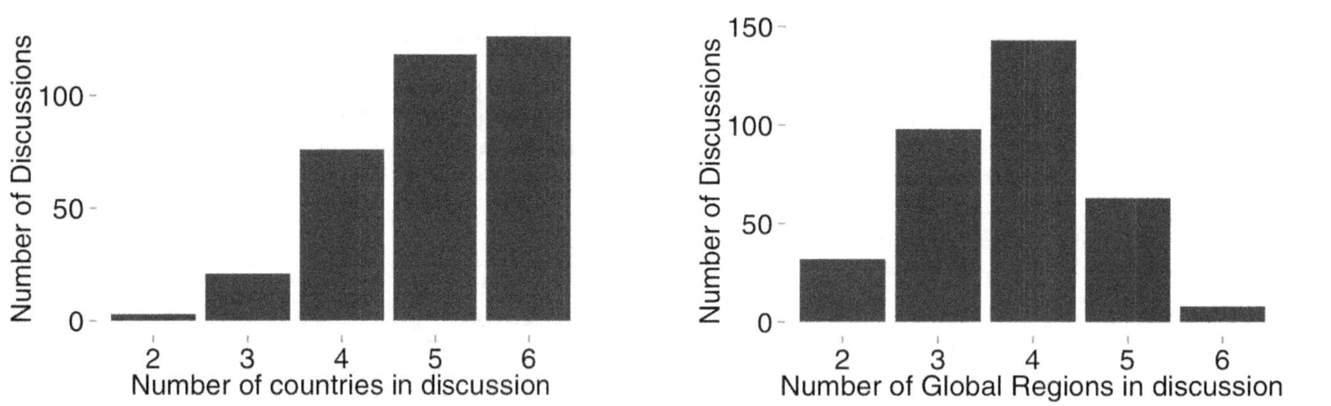

Figure 3: Across classes (a) Students from many countries participate in each six-person discussion (b) These students aren't just from neighboring countries, they are globally distributed.

count the number of regions in each discussion. Five regions are from the World Bank's classification [18]: *Eastern Europe and Central Asia* (primarily the former Soviet bloc), *East Asia and Pacific* (mainly China, Japan, Korea, and South-east Asia), *South Asia* (mainly the Indian subcontinent), *Latin America and the Caribbean* (Americas except the US and Canada), *Middle East and North Africa*, and *Sub-Saharan Africa*. The World Bank only classifies middle- and low-income countries, so we added three other regions: *North America* (US and Canada), *Western Europe*, and *South Pacific* (primarily Australia and Polynesia).

Across seven classes and the first 3,200 participants, allocating six-person groups by arrival order yielded discussions with a median of four global regions (Figure 3b), and a median of five countries (Figure 3a). The median pairwise distance between discussants was approx. 6,600km (4,100 mi): more than the distance between New York and London.

STRUCTURING TALKABOUT DISCUSSIONS

Our early experiences with Talkabout, as well as prior work, suggest that it is critical to co-design curricular strategies with educational interaction design. In particular, scripts for discussion have a major impact on student engagement and learning [42]. Talkabout succeeds best when discussions create opportunities to highlight students' diverse experiences. Based on prior work, we developed three strategies to create discussion scripts or agendas, and refined them through deployments in seven massive classes. Figure 4 shows these strategies embodied in an excerpt from an *Irrational Behavior* agenda (the complete agenda is in Supplementary Materials). We discuss each strategy in turn.

Create opportunities for self-reference

Self-reference, when students actively relate class content to their own experiences and perspectives, increases concept elaboration, memory organization, and knowledge retention [54]. Talkabout agendas that employ self-reference ask students to share personal examples that embody class concepts. Self-reference is especially effective when students feel safe in discussing personal experiences. Talkabout groups are small by design to encourage self-disclosure [40]. As each person shares with the group, it encourages peers to likewise disclose [29].

The globally distributed nature of discussions amplifies the benefits of sharing self-referential frames. After a discussion on prejudice in Social Psychology, one student wrote, "I think this may have been the first time the lady from Saudi Arabia had spoken to a Jew [referring to himself]", showing her a different viewpoint. He added, "I told her about the prejudice from Christians I experienced growing up in [US state] in the 40's and the effect of segregation on blacks," reflecting on his own experience.

Students may see different self-referential frames with different groups. For instance, even though Social Psychology had only one Talkabout discussion (with multiple slots), 454 out of 2,553 participants in the Social Psychology class voluntarily attended multiple timeslots.

Highlight viewpoint differences using boundary objects

Talkabout prompts aim to make the differences between students' perspectives salient. This encourages additional self-reference and re-evaluation of previously held theories, which in turn leads to deeper understanding [20].

To highlight differences, Talkabout discussion agendas call out boundary objects across geographical contexts. Boundary objects are objects or concepts that maintain their integrity across communities, and yet can be interpreted differently in different communities [53]. Everyday concepts, such as governments, companies/organizations or current events can serve as boundary objects. For instance, one student noted how discussing a 'recent event' yielded new perspective: "we were ... joined by [a] Syrian. She provided...insight of the situation in Syria and how the media is exaggerating it... and how the society was quite liberal on Islamic practices (such as wearing the hijab)."

Leverage students as elaborators and mediators

When a prompt says less, students sometimes say more. Rather than reviewing every relevant concept, Talkabout discussion agendas reference concepts from class without any reminders of what they mean. These underspecified references lead students who have learned these concepts to elaborate, and to act as mediators with students who would

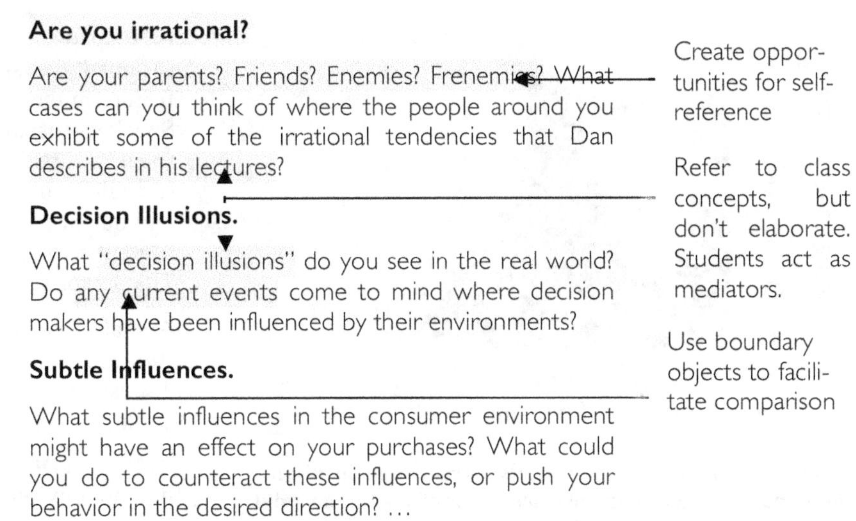

Figure 4: Excerpt from discussion agenda in an Irrational Behavior discussion, showing examples of discussion-structuring strategies (highlighted)

have otherwise not understood them. This is similar to highly effective offline strategies like jigsaw classrooms, which also rely on peer-mediated learning and contact with dissimilar peers [2].

Creating opportunities for mediation also encourages students to ask about other class concepts they haven't understood. For instance, the Organizational Analysis class used "white flight" (a large-scale migration of white Americans to suburbs in the 1950s) as an example of an organizational problem faced by cities. In one Talkabout discussion session, we observed an American student translate the key ideas in this example to a European classmate by making an analogy to intra-European migration.

THE ANATOMY OF A TALKABOUT DISCUSSION

What is the nature of a Talkabout discussion session? We observed and recorded twelve Talkabout discussion sessions in *Organizational Analysis*. An abridged transcript from an Organizational Analysis class is in Supplementary Materials. Talkabout discussion sessions followed a pattern with clear roles and norms.

Discussions follow a distinct conversational pattern

Talkabout discussion sessions usually began with introductions. Since none of the participants knew each other, introductions were fairly formal and detailed. Participants typically shared their first name, their country of residence, and a brief description of their job. Because some participants arrived late to their session, this introduction phase was often repeated.

During these introductions, an informal moderator usually emerged. Moderators often had experience with videoconferencing and a high-bandwidth connection. They exhibited leadership behaviors such as asking participants to introduce themselves, or even explicitly asking to moderate the conversation (e.g. "Shall I lead the conversation?")

After introductions, the informal moderator drew the group's attention to the instructor-provided discussion agenda. Even though agendas sometimes suggested a particular discussion order, participants did not follow it exactly. Instead, they would interpret the agenda for the major theme it embodied, and negotiate what they discussed first. Once students finished discussing a particular prompt, they returned to the agenda to decide the next topic.

While Talkabout discussion sessions were designed to last 30 minutes, the median length of the discussion was 58 minutes (Figure 5). With these longer discussions, students discussed topics that were marked optional, or chose to discuss two topics when the agenda asked only one etc. Many groups also spoke about the class in general after the assigned topics. Conversations typically ended soon after the informal moderator (or a talkative speaker) left the discussion, or when no one in the group suggested a topic to discuss next. As they left, participants often shared how they enjoyed talking to the group, or taking the class. Moderators sometimes encouraged the group to stay in touch after the discussion (e.g. "With the other hangouts, we all added each other on LinkedIn… I've already added [name]. If you'd like, feel free to add me.")

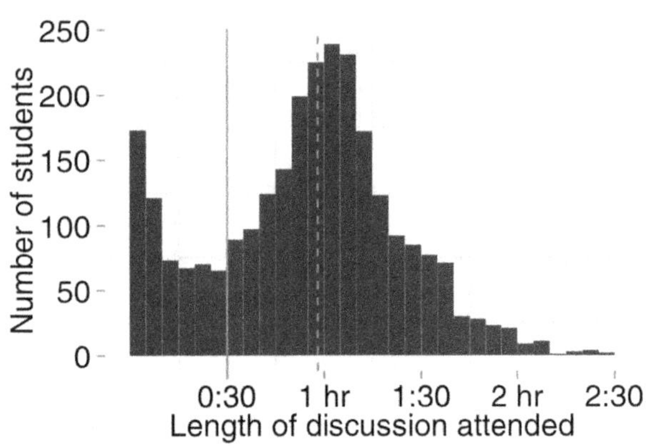

Figure 5: Across classes, students participated in discussions much longer than instructions indicated. The solid red line is the recommended duration for discussion (30 min), the dashed line is the median discussion time (58 min).

Speakers and Spectators

Students seemed to decide early on whether they primarily wanted to speak during the discussion ("speakers"), or listen to the discussion ("spectators"). Spectators often signaled their intent by muting their microphones (this showed a "mic muted" icon to others in the discussion).

Speakers tended to be native English speakers or have faster Internet connections. Their discussion was conversational, with overlapping turns similar to face-to-face conversation. Spectators spoke less frequently with longer non-overlapping turns, but were not passive participants. When spectators had trouble finding the right words (e.g., if they were non-native speakers), speakers often suggested words, or encouraged them to continue.

Participants with low-bandwidth connections generally assumed the spectator role and often used the text chat feature in the Google Hangout to "speak" in the discussion. Speakers (usually the moderator) would notice the text, and speak it aloud to the other participants. Both speakers and spectators used text-chat to demonstrate active listening without interrupting the speaker via audio (for example, a student wrote, "Working in [company] must be really cool. Thanks for sharing :)").

A shared video channel forces a single conversation. Still, students sometimes used text-chat as a way for non-discussion related talk, such as exchanging contact information or LinkedIn profiles.

STUDY 1: DO DISCUSSIONS HELP PERFORMANCE?

It is not obvious that the benefits of peer discussions [6, 46] would transfer to an online environment. In these environments, peers have vastly different backgrounds and no prior interaction with each other. Therefore, our first study measures the benefits of participation in online discussions. Later experiments measure how these benefits vary with geographic diversity in discussion groups.

With many educational practices, it is difficult to draw a causal link between participation and student learning. For instance, students may self-select to participate. To combat this bias, we use a control condition in which interested students are actively prevented from discussing. Furthermore, we use an *intention-to-treat* analysis that recognizes that some students will not participate, even when given the opportunity. Therefore, this analysis asks: after controlling for students that don't discuss given an opportunity, are discussions effective? Such analysis is common in clinical trials, where patients that are randomly assigned to a treatment group are included in the analysis even if they do not take their medication. Because intention-to-treat analyses take non-compliance into account, they result in conservative estimates of a drug's effectiveness.

Method: wait-list control

In a between-subjects experiment, we randomly assigned students in the Organizational Analysis class on Coursera to either a *Discussion* condition, or to a *Wait-list* condition. This assignment occurred when they signed up for a discussion time on Talkabout, after consenting to participate in the study.

Students in the Discussion condition were allowed to participate in discussions starting in Week 1, while those on the wait-list were not allowed to participate in discussions until Week 5. This setup results in two discussion opportunities (Week 1 and Week 3) where a subset of students was prevented from participating. Even though some participants in the Discussion condition did not attend discussion, they were included in the intention-to-treat analysis.

Hypotheses and Measures

We hypothesized that participating in a Talkabout discussion session would motivate students to engage with other course components. Prior work similarly finds that discussions motivate students to engage with in-person classes [6]. To measure engagement, we check whether the student participated in the course quiz due the day after discussion. Recall that participation in MOOCs is entirely voluntary, and several classes have battled with attrition [24]. Quizzes are a high-effort activity that most MOOC learners don't participate in: only 22.8% of students who watched a lecture video also participated in a quiz. This makes quizzes suitable as a high-effort engagement measure [8, 55].

We further hypothesized that students in the Discussion condition would do better on the quiz, aided by the self-reference, reflection and revision of class concepts.

Participants

Overall, 1,002 students were assigned to the Discussion condition, and 122 to the Wait-list condition. We used an unbalanced design to maximize the number of students who benefited from discussions. Of those in the discussion condition, 397 attended a discussion.

Results: Discussion increases class participation, marginally improves grades

Students in the Discussion condition were more likely to take the quiz. A logistic regression indicated that odds of taking the quiz were 1.46 times higher for the Discussion condition (Wald $z^*=1.97$, $p<0.05$). Students in the Discussion condition also did marginally better on the quiz ($t(1122) = 1.89$, $p=0.06$)[1]. The average improvement was 16.7%.

Thus, even accounting for students who do not follow through, discussions help students stay engaged in the course and perform better on related assessments.

While Talkabout participation improves engagement, this effect seems short-lived. Students who participate in a Talkabout one week are not more likely to participate in the quiz the following week: Wald $z^*=1.61$, $p=0.10$. We also found no significant improvement in quiz scores for the quiz due the following week.

Would participating in multiple Talkabout discussion sessions improve these short-term benefits? As is typical with online classes, many students shopped the first weeks, and only 113 students in the discussion condition attended the second discussion (397 attended the first week). Therefore, our intention-to-treat analysis lacks the statistical power to capture any benefits of participating in multiple discussions. Also, while the wait-list design can control for intent to participate, students who actually participate in discussions may still differ from those who don't (e.g. they could be more motivated). An intention-to-treat analysis estimates effects by assuming participants' distribution (e.g., for motivation) are similar in the wait-list and treatment groups due to randomized assignment, but this experiment does not verify this assumption.

The results of this study suggest that performance on class quizzes may improve even with limited participation, and that discussions improve student engagement. Do these effects depend on the participants in the discussion? Given our hypothesis that geographic diversity should help learning, our next study investigates the effect of discussants' geographic diversity on course performance.

STUDY 2: DOES DIVERSITY HELP PERFORMANCE?

Study 1 established that participating in Talkabout discussions improves class engagement. Is geographic diversity causing this effect? In a second, between-subjects experiment, Talkabout's group-assignment algorithm randomly assigned students either to a single-region group or a multi-region group. Participants regions were determined by the

[1] While only marginally significant ($p<0.10$), we include this result because it is suggests opportunities for future work.

five World Bank regions, as well as three regions to capture North America, Western Europe and the South Pacific. The *Same-region* condition grouped students with others from their region. The *Multi-region* condition grouped students from anywhere in the world. We discarded data from the South Pacific region because it had few participants.

Participants and setup

55 students in the Organizational Analysis class participated. When students logged on to the site, we recorded their IP address, found their location based on IP, and randomly assigned them to the Multi-region high-diversity or the Same-region low-diversity condition. Students were then grouped into discussion groups with a maximum of six participants.

Measures

To measure conceptual understanding, we invited students to fill out a questionnaire immediately after the discussion; 43 participated. We asked students to answer to the best of their ability, but informed them that their answer would not affect their course grade. This survey had one open-ended question which required critical thinking and an understanding of concepts discussed in the session ("Where would you want to position yourself if you wanted leverage over the flow of "information" in a social network—centrally, peripherally, or in a bridging position. Why?"). We scored this question in consultation with the teaching assistant of the course. The average score was 47% (combining both conditions). We use students' grade in a prior class quiz as a measure of prior performance (we ignore data from one participant, who did not complete the quiz). The questionnaire also asked questions about how much they liked their discussion, and how much they felt they learned from it.

Hypothesis

Students in the Multi-Region, high-diversity, condition were exposed to more contrasting viewpoints and self-reference than discussions in low-diversity groups. Thus, we hypothesized that members of more geographically diverse groups would have higher scores on the post-questionnaire.

Manipulation check

The median number of countries in the same-region condition was two (both from the same geographical region), while the median in the multiple-region condition was 4.

Does large geographical distance imply a diverse group? Some World Bank regions are large, so we examined if multi-region groups had more differing national viewpoints than same-region groups, taking into account how economic opportunities and educational experience influence everyday experience [12], as do cultural values [36].

We used each participant's country to map them onto diversity attributes used in cultural psychology and political science. We use countries as our unit of analysis because they have a consistent typology of collectivistic or individualistic culture [17], organizational attitudes such as interpersonal dependence and criteria for fulfillment [51], economic development [16] and life expectancy [37]. While each country is diverse, within-country differences are smaller than between-country differences [17], making this by-country analysis feasible.

We compared countries of participating students on three dimensions: cultural values, income, and pupil-teacher ratios in primary school. As a measure of cultural values, we used the mean overall secular values for each country from the World Values Survey [59]. Countries with lower scores have societies that emphasize religion, traditional family values, and collectivistic thinking. The average pairwise difference between participants' countries on the overall secular values scale was lower in the same-region condition than in the multi-region condition, Wilcoxon W=407.5, $p<0.05$ (*same-region* mean: 0.022, equivalent to the difference between the US and Romania, *multi-region* mean: 0.031, equivalent difference: US and Thailand).

Students' countries in the *Multi-region* condition had marginally higher differences in income levels compared to those in the *Same-region* condition (t(74)=1.81, $p=0.07$; log-transformed because income distribution is log-normal [7]). Using data from the World Bank [18], the median per-capita annual income differed on average by $8,120 (PPP) in the *same-region* condition, approximately the difference between the US and Canada. The average difference in the *multi-region* condition was $20,495 (PPP), approximately the difference between the US and Israel.

Lastly, students' countries in the multi-region condition had greater pairwise variation in educational experience, as reflected in primary school pupil-teacher ratios (t(74)=2.00, $p<0.05$). Using World Bank data [18], the median differences in the pupil-teacher ratios in the same-region condition were 2.91 (approximately the difference between schools in the US and Canada), while the median difference in the multi-group condition was 5.91 (the difference in schools between the US and Russia).

Collectively, these analyses suggest that multi-region groups brought more diverse experiences and backgrounds to their discussions.

Results: Students in diverse groups perform better

On a 7-point Likert scale question, students in the *high-diversity* condition rated their discussion as more enjoyable than those in *low-diversity* (Mann-Whitney U=140.5, $p < 0.05$). They also reported learning marginally more from their discussion partners on a different 7-point Likert scale (Mann-Whitney U=160.5, $p = 0.08$).

Based on the grades in the post-quiz, an ordinary-least-squares linear model showed that after controlling for prior performance, students in the *high-diversity* condition outperformed those in the *low-diversity* condition, (β=0.41, F(1,37)=2.31, $p<0.05$, adjusted R^2=0.11). A post-hoc comparison also found that students in discussions with more countries did better in both conditions. Using an ordinary-least-squares linear model, we found that the number of countries in the discussion was predictive of the quiz score (β=0.15, $F(1,36) = 2.57$, $p<0.01$, adjusted R^2= 0.14).

This result suggests that even countries in the same geographical region add meaningful diversity. This may be because regions are too large and diverse (e.g. the *Latin America and Caribbean* region has 35 countries). Therefore, counting countries rather than regions may provide a better measure of diversity.

However, this experiment only measures the immediate effects of diversity in a single class. Do geographically diverse discussions have a longer-term effect, and do these benefits generalize across classes? We now describe a longitudinal deployment that evaluates the effect of diverse discussions on grades in actual course tests over periods of weeks.

STUDY 3: LARGE-SCALE FIELD EXPERIMENT

In Study 3, we sought to confirm and expand upon Study 2's diversity effect across more classes and with more students. In doing so, we trade off some of Study 2's experimental control in exchange for a much larger sample. We conducted our experiment across two large online classes, Organizational Analysis and Social Psychology.

Participants

In the Social Psychology class, 2,025 students participated. In the Organizational Analysis, 397 students participated.

All students in the Organizational Analysis class who wanted to participate in discussions used Talkabout. By the instructor's request, the Social Psychology class also allowed students to choose an in-person discussion instead. In-person discussants received the same discussion agenda and directions as online discussants. 2,037 students reported participating in an in-person discussion. Except for qualitative comparisons between online and in-person discussions, we ignore their data. It is possible that online discussions attracted students who believed they would benefit more from a diverse discussion. However, the main results of this study were consistent across both classes.

Method

Similar to Study 2, Talkabout grouped students into discussions. However, students were not explicitly grouped into high- and low-diversity conditions. Instead, this study used a simpler approach where Talkabout collected participants in order of arrival. When a group had six students, Talkabout launched a new group. This setup assigns participants to diversity levels in a random fashion. Participants in both classes had no control over who their discussion partners were, and therefore had no control over the level of geographic diversity in their discussion.

The two classes implemented different schedules for their discussions. Social Psychology held discussions for one week at the end of class, two weeks before the final exam. Organizational Analysis had discussions throughout the class, starting from the first week. This variety allows us to understand the effect of Talkabout both for highly motivated students who remain active at the end of class, and for enthusiastic, but potentially uncommitted learners.

Hypotheses and Measures

We hypothesized that participating in more geographically diverse Talkabout discussions would lead to better course performance, as students became more active thinkers through conversations with diverse students. In addition, given our results in Study 1, we hypothesized that students in more diverse discussions early in the class would stay engaged with the class for longer.

To measure *geographic diversity*, we use the number of countries in a discussion as a coarse but useful metric. While students using Talkabout may be systematically different from the median resident of their country (they can afford an Internet connection), national cultures still importantly shape their thoughts and actions [21].

To measure *performance*, in Social Psychology, we used the final exam score. The final exam was a 50 multiple-choice question test (see Appendix 2 for a sample of questions). The instructor created this exam independently with no input from the research team. The Organizational Analysis class had weekly quizzes due every Sunday, which we use as a performance measure. The instructor independently created these quizzes in a previous run of the class (before Talkabout was designed), and they were used unchanged in the experimental class. The first Talkabout session was one day before the first quiz was due. We analyze the first two weeks' quizzes. The first quiz had 19 multiple-choice questions; the second had 16 (see Appendix 2). Finally, both classes invited students to participate in a post-discussion survey about their experience.

Analysis procedure

For both classes, we built an ordinary-least-square linear regression for performance based on the number of countries in the discussion. Because the number of discussants and number of countries is collinear (R^2=0.81 and 0.88 in the two classes), we only analyzed groups of six students. We controlled for each student's prior performance in class if any previous quizzes had occurred. Our model for the first week's quiz in Organizational Analysis had no measure for prior performance (model R^2=0.003). The model for the second quiz (R^2 = 0.11) used the score in the first quiz as a prior-performance metric. The model for the Social Psychology class (R^2=0.05) used a student's total grade in all assignments before the final exam as a prior-performance metric.

Results

Our analysis finds support for the first hypothesis: students perform better on tests after a more geographically diverse discussion. We find no support for our second hypothesis that diverse discussion improves retention in the long-term.

High-diversity discussions improve scores

In both classes, more diverse discussions led to higher exam grades (Table 2). In Social Psychology, on the final exam out of 50 points, each additional country adds an approximate β=1.78 points (2.4% of the final grade) to a student's final exam score (t(129)=1.78, *p=0.01*). In Organizational Analysis, on the Week 2 quiz out of 16 points, each additional country yields β=0.39 points (3.6%) to the quiz score (t(110)=2.03, *p<0.05*). However, from the model for the Week 1 quiz (without a prior-performance measure), we do not see any significant effect of diversity on score. Prior performance helps capture sufficient variation to make diversity statistically distinguishable from a null hypothesis.

Benefits of diverse discussions last roughly two weeks

In the Organizational Analysis class, while geographic diversity leads to better quiz scores one week after discussion (Week 2 quiz), we did not find any significant effects into Week 3. Similarly, we built an ordinary-least-squares linear model for predicting how many weekly quizzes a student would participate in, based on the number of countries in their first discussion. We found no significant effect (t(130) = -0.49, $R^2 < 0.001$). Similar to results from Study 2, this suggests that the benefits of a diverse discussion only persist for a short duration.

Geographic diversity leads to new perspectives

Post-discussion, a survey asked participants about the best part of their discussion. Two independent raters coded 100 responses about whether comments mentioned participant diversity: 51% mentioned it (Cohen's κ =0.7, z=7.04, *p< 0.001*). Students noted that diversity yielded different experiences and examples and perspectives, which challenged ones held by students. A Social Psychology student wrote how they learned that "...in China it is a custom for married women to keep their surnames, thus I [now] think women changing their surnames when married in other countries has something to do with sexism." An Organizational Analysis student said, "It was interesting to hear about organizations in Australia, Ukraine, Israel, Indonesia, and Canada. Similar issues appear everywhere regarding decision-making"

Organizational Analysis: Week 1 Quiz (R^2 = 0.003)	β	F	p-value
Intercept	15.7	21.51	**<0.001**
Number of Countries	0.11	0.76	0.46
Organizational Analysis: Week 2 Quiz (R^2 = 0.11)			
Intercept	8.11	4.33	**<0.001**
Week 1 grade (z-scored)	0.78	2.81	**< 0.001**
Number of countries	0.39	2.03	**0.02**
Social Psychology: Final Examination (R^2 = 0.05)			
Intercept	27.20	7.00	**<0.001**
Pre-final grade (z-scored)	0.91	1.30	0.19
Number of countries	1.78	2.34	**0.01**

Table 2: After controlling for prior performance, more countries in a discussion lead to better grades, in both Social Psychology and Organizational Analysis.

Gender representation does not influence scores

In prior work, the proportion of females participants affected collaborative group outcomes [58]. However, in our study, female participation did not affect performance after controlling for the number of countries in each group. Adding the proportion of female participants to the Organizational Analysis class model for the Week 2 quiz did not improve model fit, and the effect of gender was not significant: t(100)=1.1, *p=0.26*. The Social Psychology class shows a similar non-significant effect: t(128)=0.62, *p=0.53*.

Other non-significant factors

We test the following variables in isolation; all were non-significant with *p>0.50*. We found no significant effect of the arrival order of participants on either the diversity in their group, or the benefits of diversity on course grades. We also find no evidence that diverse discussions had larger benefits for either gender. Finally, there was no significant correlation between how early students signed up for a discussion and their benefits.

Other measures of geographic diversity

The results of our analysis were consistent when we used other measures such as the pairwise distance between participants' locations. We use the number of countries while describing results because it is more interpretable.

Limitations

This experiment included two classes, Social Psychology and Organizational Analysis. Both classes used Talkabout in discussions focused on critical thinking and sense-making. As such, evidence that geographically diverse discussions improve engagement and learning may not generalize to classes that emphasize procedural knowledge (e.g. Corporate Finance), or classes where benefits from global perspectives are smaller (e.g. physics). That said, even the most procedural topics require critical thinking and judgment, and as many instructors have found, topics like physics that seemingly don't benefit from global perspectives may still benefit from discussions [10, 38].

Geographic diversity encodes many other kinds of diversity, e.g., economic opportunities, cultural values, and education experience. Each of these dimensions may have differing benefits for online classes. Future work could build theory that differences matter when.

DISCUSSION

It can be difficult to demonstrate measurable learning effects using design interventions in online courses. For example, while it is possible to increase student involvement in forums [1], improving grades and retention has remained challenging [8, 55]. However, Talkabout increases both learning and engagement (Table 3). One reason for this improvement may be that Talkabout developed a pedagogical approach alongside the software. In pilots without meaningfully structured discussions, it fared poorly. Furthermore, Talkabout builds a social environment and an

Study 1: Discussion participation with a wait-list control
Participating in a video discussion with peers increases participation in quizzes and marginally improves performance.

Study 2: Controlled manipulation of geographic diversity
Students in high geographic diversity discussion groups perform higher.

Study 3: Large-scale study of geographic diversity
High geographic diversity discussions lead to improved short-term performance in two classes, but do not improve multi-week retention.

Table 3: Summary of experimental results

opportunity for reflection. It does this via a medium that is known to build trust [49] and is suited for open-ended discussions [52], such as those leading to sense-making [13].

Geographic diversity's direct effect is in students meeting people from other world regions. It is associated with changes in several other diversity measures (e.g., cultural values, economic opportunity, and educational experience). This paper demonstrates that geographic diversity indeed impacts these other measures. However, there may be other causal pathways involved. It is possible that students who differ in geographical location still have similar socio-economic backgrounds, and students who live very close may be very different. Future work can develop more nuanced diverse experiences.

Talkabout also points to the benefits of using video for geographically diverse discussions. Video conferencing creates a middle ground of immersion in another culture. With complete immersion in an in-person setting, the norms and views of the majority are pervasive [26, 41]. Students with a minority viewpoint in a fully-immersive experience may find themselves confronted with the choice to either embrace the majority culture (suppressing their own), or reject it and flounder [43]. On the other hand, with the minimal immersion, say, of lectures, students may ignore alternate viewpoints as a mere academic exercise. Video-conferencing may occupy an attractive middle ground: it is interactive, compelling students to engage with their diverse classmates and reflect upon their contact [33]. One student told us in an interview, "Talkabout helps bring the class together -- it makes the learning tangible and real…you are interacting with other people, who are experiencing a lot of different things."

Video-based discussions are not without their problems today. Some countries (*e.g.,* Iran) restrict access to Google Hangouts, low-bandwidth connections degrade the student experience, and installing video-conferencing software remains challenging for some students. However, these technological limitations are likely to lessen as bandwidth becomes more plentiful and software comes pre-installed.

Comparing in-person and online discussions

Recall that Social Psychology allowed students to choose to run their discussion in person instead of online. Students participating in the in-person discussions often turned to close friends and relatives. The shared context made the conversation friendlier. For instance, one participant remarked, "I really like the discussion because it was with my friends… It was really easy to start the discussion." In-person discussions also had lower geographic diversity. One student summarized, "Being from the same age group, social level and from the same community; we had very much similar views about the topics in hand." Students reported difficulties scheduling discussions and keeping them on-topic. One remarked, "We had to reschedule a couple of times [before we could meet]." And with friends, "Turning a conversation towards a scientific discipline such as social psychology was hard and a bit artificial…" Another remarked, "Members were my family... and speaking about some things is not easy!"

The design space of online peer conversations

Talkabout currently implements a particular design for online discussions. To arrive at this design, we explored a number of different decisions in this design space (Table 4).

Always-available discussions lack critical mass

Always-available and unscheduled discussions in classes may enable students to talk with a remote partner whenever they have a question or thought. To test the feasibility of this idea, we created a version of Talkabout where students could sign up for an immediate discussion. If another student indicated their availability within the next hour, Talkabout would email both to set up a discussion.

We tested this version in the Think Again philosophy and argumentation class over a three-day period. Of the 2,940 who saw the opportunity, 54 students signed up. Unfortunately, only 5 students overlapped within the one-hour window. This suggests that MOOCs attract many students, but their presence on the course site does not spontaneously overlap. Therefore, Talkabout instead adopts a *bus stop model* where discussions occur at regular time intervals, making critical mass more likely.

Students prefer to negotiate roles informally

Prior work suggests including a designated discussion facilitator to attend to group dynamics in distributed discussions [35]. Could formal facilitators improve Talkabout discussions? We conducted a between-subjects experiment with two conditions (n= 80) in the Organizational Analysis class. In the *facilitator* condition, all participants in a Hangout saw a button to volunteer to be a discussion facilitator. When a student volunteered, the system would show them facilitation tips. Other participants saw a message that the volunteer was facilitating the discussion. In the *control* condition, students were not shown the button to volunteer. Of the 40 students in the *facilitator* condition, seven volunteered. An intention-to-treat analysis showed a trend toward students in the *facilitation* condition feeling the discussion was less motivating (Mann-Whitney U = 191.5, $p=0.09$), and a trend toward less willingness to meet the same group again (U=191.5, $p=0.09$). These results suggest that fluid negotiation of moderation may work better than a formal facilitation role.

Rigidly enforced scripts lower satisfaction

Prior work in CSCL suggests that structuring collaboration between students using instructions or scripts yields improved learning [42]. What is the right degree of scripting? In a between-subjects experiment (n=82) in the Organizational Analysis class, we explored the benefit of an enforced script. In this condition, Talkabout only showed the current discussion topic, and participants needed to click a button to indicate completion and advance to the next topic. The *control* condition agenda showed all topics at once.

Design Dimension	Choices		
Same discussants every time?	Yes	No	When possible
Group size	Small		Large
Discussion guidance	None	Guidelines and prompts	Scripts
Role negotiation	Instructor specifies	Technologically mediated	Informal
Discussion scheduling	On-demand any time	Bus stop: regular intervals	Same time every week

Table 4: Talkabout's current implementation highlighted in dark blue, design choices that we found to be worse are highlighted in (light) red.

Of the 50 students in the *enforced-script* condition, only 4 clicked the "next topic" button even once. In the post-survey, students also reported they felt the discussion was less motivating (Mann-Whitney U= 193, p=0.07), and that they were less willing to meet the same group again (U = 191.5, p= 0.08). This suggests that enforcing a discussion order may undermine the social benefits of Talkabout [14].

Same-partner discussions have inadequate participation

In the in-person classroom, it is common practice to assign students to groups with fixed membership for the duration of a project or series of discussions throughout a course [6]. Repeated interactions in such groups build trust and rapport [3]. By contrast, non-persistent groups lack familiarity but expose students to different viewpoints.

In a between-subjects experiment in the Think Again class (n=522), we randomly assigned students to either a *persistent* or *control* condition. The persistent condition assigned students to the same group for every discussion. The control condition assigned them to a group when they arrived to the site, as described previously. Students in both conditions attended the same number of discussions (μ=0.46, t(522)=0.33, $p=0.73$). However, as students dropped the class, the size of discussion groups in the persistent condition kept shrinking until they were no longer viable. While 27% of the control groups had at least 5 discussants, only 2% of the persistent groups did (t(81)=4.67, $p<0.001$). Therefore, our discussion strategies structure discussions to leverage changing partners. The next step might be to forge a middle ground where Talkabout prefers familiar partners but adapts groups if previous partners drop out.

CONCLUSION

This paper suggests that the geographic diversity in online classes can be an educational asset. Instead of becoming a handicap, distance can expose students to others and to other ways of thinking. However, leveraging the diversity of online environments requires careful design. This paper describes one such approach, Talkabout, which uses video chat to create discussions between students across the world. Embracing and designing for diversity can enable other innovations. For instance, instructors could leverage students as co-creators and draw on students' local observations to showcase how course concepts arise differently around the world. Likewise, international relations or security courses might launch a global crisis simulation with each student representing their own region. These educational experiences offer a glimpse of the potential of thinking "beyond being there" [25]. They are not just leveraging geographic diversity—they would be impossible without it.

ACKNOWLEDGMENTS

We are grateful to Dan Schwartz for thought-provoking discussions and feedback with early drafts; Coursera and the OpenEdX teams for platform integration and encouraging instructors to try Talkabout; instructors of the many MOOCs who use Talkabout in their classes, and the many students who connected with their peers and shared their stories with us. This research was funded in part through NSF grants #1351131 and #1444865, the Hasso Plattner Design Thinking Program, and the Siebel Scholars Program. This research was conducted under Stanford IRB protocol #30319.

REFERENCES

1. Anderson, A. et al. Engaging with massive online courses. (2014), 687–698.
2. Aronson, E. and Bridgeman, D. Jigsaw groups and the desegregated classroom: In pursuit of common goals. In *Readings About The Social Animal*. Worth Publishers, 2004, 532.
3. Bos, N. et al. Effects of four computer-mediated communications channels on trust development. *Proc CHI: ACM conference on Human factors in computing systems*, ACM Press (2002).
4. Braskamp, L.A. et al. Assessing Progress in Global Learning and Development of Students with Education Abroad Experiences. *Frontiers: The Interdisciplinary Journal of Study Abroad 18*, (2008), 101–118.

5. Breslow, L.B. et al. Studying learning in the worldwide classroom: Research into edX's first MOOC. *Research & Practice in Assessment 8*, (2013), 13–25.
6. Brookfield, S.D. and Preskill, S. *Discussion as a Way of Teaching: Tools and Techniques for Democratic Classrooms*. John Wiley & Sons, 2012.
7. Clementi, F. and Mauro Gallegati. Econophysics of Wealth Distributions. In Chatterjee, A. et al., eds., *Econophysics of Wealth Distributions*. Springer Milan, Milano, 2005.
8. Coetzee, D. et al. Chatrooms in MOOCs: all talk and no action. *Proc. of the ACM conference on Learning @ scale*, ACM Press (2014), 127–136.
9. Coser, R.L. The Complexity of Roles as a Seedbed of Individual Autonomy. In *The Idea of Social Structure: Essays in Honor of Robert Merton*. New York, New York, USA, 1975.
10. Crouch, C.H. and Mazur, E. Peer Instruction: Ten years of experience and results. *American Journal of Physics 69*, 9 (2001), 970.
11. Daft, R.L. and Lengel, R.H. Organizational Information Requirements, Media Richness and Structural Design. *Management Science 32*, 5 (1986), 554–571.
12. Desai, M. Human development: Concepts and measurement. *European Economic Review 35*, 2-3 (1991), 350–357.
13. DeSanctis, G. et al. Learning in Online Forums. *European Management Journal 21*, 5 (2003), 565–577.
14. Dillenbourg, P. Over-scripting CSCL: The risks of blending collaborative learning with instructional design. *Three worlds of CSCL. Can we support CSCL?*, (2002), 61–91.
15. Freedman, J. MOOCs Are Usefully Middlebrow. *The Chronicle of Higher Education*. http://chronicle.com/article/MOOCs-Are-Usefully-Middlebrow/143183/.
16. Goesling, B. Changing Income Inequalities within and between Nations: New Evidence. *American Sociological Review 66*, 5 (2001), 745–761.
17. Green, E.G.T. Variation of Individualism and Collectivism within and between 20 Countries: A Typological Analysis. *Journal of Cross-Cultural Psychology 36*, 3 (2005), 321–339.
18. Group, W.B. *World Development Indicators 2012*. World Bank Publications, 2012.
19. Gurin, P. et al. Diversity and higher education: Theory and impact on educational outcomes. .
20. Guzzetti, B.J. and Others, A. Promoting Conceptual Change in Science: A Comparative Meta-Analysis of Instructional Interventions from Reading Education and Science Education. *Reading Research Quarterly 28*, 2 (1992), 116–59.
21. Hambrick, D.C. et al. When Groups Consist of Multiple Nationalities: Towards a New Understanding of the Implications. *Organization Studies 19*, 2 (1998), 181–205.
22. Heine, S.J. *Cultural Psychology*. WW Norton, 2008.
23. Hewstone, M. Intergroup contact: Panacea for prejudice? *Psychologist*, 2003, 352–355. http://www.psy.ox.ac.uk/publications/28661.
24. Ho, A.D. et al. HarvardX and MITx: The First Year of Open Online Courses, Fall 2012-Summer 2013. *SSRN Electronic Journal*, (2014).
25. Hollan, J. and Stornetta, S. Beyond being there. *Proceedings of the SIGCHI conference on Human factors in computing systems - CHI '92*, ACM Press (1992), 119–125.
26. Hurtado, S. et al. The Climate for Diversity: Key Issues for Institutional Self-Study. *New Directions for Institutional Research 1998*, 98 (1998), 53–63.
27. Hurtado, S. et al. Enacting Diverse Learning Environments: Improving the Climate for Racial/Ethnic Diversity in Higher Education. ASHE-ERIC Higher Education Report, Vol. 26, No. 8. (1998).
28. Jacobs, A.J. Grading the MOOC University. *The New York Times*, 2013.
29. Joinson, A.N. Knowing Me, Knowing You: Reciprocal Self-Disclosure in Internet-Based Surveys. *CyberPsychology & Behavior 4*, 5 (2001).
30. Konstan, J.A. et al. Teaching recommender systems at large scale. *Proc of the ACM conference on Learning @ scale conference*, ACM Press (2014).
31. Kucsera, J. and Orfield, G. *New York State's Extreme School Segregation: Inequality, Inaction and a Damaged Future*. 2014.
32. Kulkarni, C. et al. Peer and self assessment in massive online classes. *ACM Transactions on Computer-Human Interaction (TOCHI) 20*, 6 (2013), 33.
33. Lin, X. and Schwartz, D.L. Reflection at the Crossroads of Cultures. *Mind, Culture, and Activity 10*, 1 (2003).
34. Losh, E. *The War on Learning: Gaining Ground in the Digital University*. MIT Press, 2014.
35. Mark, G. et al. Meeting at the Desktop: An Empirical Study of Virtually Collocated Teams. *ECSCW*, Kluwer Academic Publishers (1999).
36. Markus, H. and Kitayama, S. Culture and the self: Implications for cognition, emotion, and motivation. *Psychological Review 98*, 2 (1991), 224–253.
37. Marmot, M. Social determinants of health inequalities. *Lancet 365*, 9464 (2005), 1099–104.
38. Mazur, E. Farewell, lecture? *Science (New York, N.Y.) 323*, 5910 (2009), 50–1.

39. Nemeth, C.J. Differential contributions of majority and minority influence. *Psychological Review 93*, 1986.

40. Nguyen, M. et al. Comparing online and offline self-disclosure: a systematic review. *Cyberpsychology, behavior and social networking 15*, 2 (2012).

41. Nora, A. and Cabrera, A.F. The Role of Perceptions in Prejudice and Discrimination and the Adjustment of Minority Students to College. *Journal of Higher Education 67*, 2 (1995), 119–48.

42. O'Donnell, A.M. and Dansereau, D.F. Scripted cooperation in student dyads: A method for analyzing and enhancing academic learning and performance. In *Interaction in cooperative groups: The theoretical anatomy of group learning*. Cambridge University Press, Cambridge, UK, 1995, 120–141.

43. Ogbu, J.U. Understanding Cultural Diversity and Learning. *Educational Researcher 21*, 8 (1992), 5–14.

44. Olds, K. Mapping Coursera's Global Footprint. *Inside Higher Ed*, 2013. http://www.insidehighered.com/blogs/globalhighered/mapping-courseras-global-footprint.

45. Papadopoulos, K. et al. Community TAs scale high-touch learning, provide student-staff brokering, and build esprit de corps. *Proceedings of the first ACM conference on Learning @ scale conference - L@S '14*, ACM Press (2014), 163–164.

46. Parker, W.C. Classroom Discussion: Models for Leading Seminars and Deliberations. *Social Education 65*, 2 (2000), 111–15.

47. Pettigrew, T.F. Intergroup contact theory. *Annual review of psychology 49*, (1998), 65–85.

48. Purdie, N. and Hattie, J. Cultural Differences in the Use of Strategies for Self-Regulated Learning. *American Educational Research Journal 33*, 4 (1996), 845–871.

49. Rocco, E. Trust breaks down in electronic contexts but can be repaired by some initial face-to-face contact. *Proc of CHI: ACM Conf on Human Factors in Computing Systems*, ACM Press (1998).

50. Saltarelli, A.J. Effects of belongingness and synchronicity on face-to-face and computer-mediated online cooperative pedagogy. (2012).

51. Shenkar, S. and Oded, R. Clustering Countries on Attitudinal Dimensions: A Review and Synthesis. *The Academy of Management Review 10*, 3 (1985), 435–454.

52. Short, J.E. et al. *The Social Psychology of Telecommunications*. Wiley, London, 1976.

53. Star, S.L. and Griesemer, J.R. Institutional Ecology, `Translations' and Boundary Objects: Amateurs and Professionals in Berkeley's Museum of Vertebrate Zoology, 1907-39. *Social Studies of Science 19*, 3 (1989), 387–420.

54. Symons, C.S. and Johnson, B.T. The self-reference effect in memory: A meta-analysis. *Psychological Bulletin 121*, 3 (1997), 371–394.

55. Tomkin, J.H. and Charlevoix, D. Do professors matter? *Proc. of the ACM conference on Learning @ scale*, ACM Press (2014), 71–78.

56. Tudge, J. *The everyday lives of young children*. Cambridge University Press, Cambridge, UK, 2008.

57. Varnum, Michael EW Grossmann, I. et al. The origin of cultural differences in cognition the social orientation hypothesis. *Current directions in psychological science 19*, 1 (2010).

58. Woolley, A.W. et al. Evidence for a collective intelligence factor in the performance of human groups. *Science (New York, N.Y.) 330*, 6004 (2010), 686–8.

59. *World Values Survey (Wave 6)*. World Values Survey Association, 2014.

Massive Open Online Proctor: Protecting the Credibility of MOOCs Certificates

Xuanchong Li Kai-min Chang Yueran Yuan Alexander Hauptmann
Language Technologies Institute, Carnegie Mellon University
5000 Forbes Ave, Pittsburgh, PA, USA
xcli@cs.cmu.edu kkchang@cs.cmu.edu yueranyuan@gmail.com alex@cs.cmu.edu

ABSTRACT
Massive Open Online Courses (MOOCs) enable everyone to receive high-quality education. However, current MOOC creators cannot provide an effective, economical, and scalable method to detect cheating on tests, which would be required for any certification. In this paper, we propose a Massive Open Online Proctoring (MOOP) framework, which combines both automatic and collaborative approaches to detect cheating behaviors in online tests. The MOOP framework consists of three major components: Automatic Cheating Detector (ACD), Peer Cheating Detector (PCD), and Final Review Committee (FRC). ACD uses webcam video or other sensors to monitor students and automatically flag suspected cheating behavior. Ambiguous cases are then sent to the PCD, where students peer-review flagged webcam video to confirm suspicious cheating behaviors. Finally, the list of suspicious cheating behaviors is sent to the FRC to make the final punishing decision. Our experiment show that ACD and PCD can detect usage of a cheat sheet with good accuracy and can reduce the overall human resources required to monitor MOOCs for cheating.

Author Keywords
Education; MOOC; Cheating Detection; Crowdsourcing; Machine Learning; Human Computer Interaction

ACM Classification Keywords
K.3.1 Computers and Education: Computer Uses in Education; H.5.m. Information Interfaces and Presentation (e.g. HCI): Miscellaneous

General Terms
Human Factors; Design; Experimentation

INTRODUCTION
Massive Open Online Courses (MOOCs) enable people from all over the world to receive high-quality education.

CSCW '15, March 14 - 18 2015, Vancouver, BC, Canada
Copyright 2015 ACM 978-1-4503-2922-4/15/03...$15.00
http://dx.doi.org/10.1145/2675133.2675245

However, current MOOC creators cannot provide an effective, economical, and scalable method to detect cheating on tests, which would be required for any certification. Although MOOC providers have not officially disclosed detailed statistical data of dishonest behaviors in MOOC, lots of cheating behaviors have been reported by both students and instructors[19][7]. Researchers have clearly shown that unproctored online testing is vulnerable to cheating behavior[14][13][12].

We introduce the Massive Open Online Proctor (MOOP) framework to proctor online exams of MOOC which tackles the test proctoring scalability problem through sensor-detection and crowd-sourcing. MOOP consists of 3 components:

- *Automatic Cheating Detector (ACD)* - an automatic, machine learning approach that utilizes different sensor technologies to detect cheating behaviors.
- *Peer Cheating Detector (PCD)* - a collaborative, crowd-sourcing approach to review ambiguous cases detected by ACD.
- *Final Review Committee (FRC)* - an authoritative committee that reviews all suspicious cheating cases detected by ACD and PCD, and make the final punishing decision.

In the following sections, we first review existing cheating detection methods. Then, we describe each MOOP component in detail. To evaluate our system, we ran a simple experiment where students are encouraged to cheat with a cheat sheet. Finally, we discuss both advantages and limitations of our proposed MOOP and suggest future directions.

EXISTING CHEATING DETECTION METHODS
The traditional solution to preventing cheating is on-site proctoring. Many standardized exams, such as SAT, GRE, etc., have adopted this solution. Students are asked take a proctored test in a specific test center and at a specific time. Since the test is administered by test center staff, the test result is credible. Nonetheless, onsite proctoring is unsuitable for large scale MOOC testing due to expense and inconveience. The cost of renting the test venue and hiring proctors translates into a test fee that is passed on to the students. Furthermore, students who are far from established test centers will need to travel great distances to take tests.

Online proctoring (a.k.a. remote proctoring) uses human proctors to monitor online exams remotely[5]. For example, ProctorU[1] enables students to take the exam remotely by assigning a human proctor to monitor the exams through a webcam. Although online proctoring increases the availability of cheating detection, scalability and cost are still issues. Because it relies largely on human judges, cost can still be relatively high. The price for a one-hour exam is $10 to $20[2], which is still too expensive for students from poor areas.

The common limitation of both on-site proctoring and online proctoring is scalability since every student action must be monitored by paid human proctors. With millions of student using MOOCs[11], hiring human proctors to detect cheating in every MOOC exam is implausible for both students and MOOC providers.

MOOP is designed to address the scability problem. By combining automated cheating detection through sensors/machine learning and a crowd-sourced verification, the number of cheating cases that must be reviewed by the central committee of hired proctors can be drastically reduced. A similar mechanism is adopted in the game industry. In *League of Legends*, the Tribunal system receives cases of possible misconduct through automatic detectors (e.g., "away from keyboard") and player reports (e.g. player harrassment, negative attitude). Players are then invited to peer-review these mal-behaviors and vote in a court-like system, before the final punishment decision is decided by the game developer. The Tribunal system has been proven effective in regulating conduct in [3].

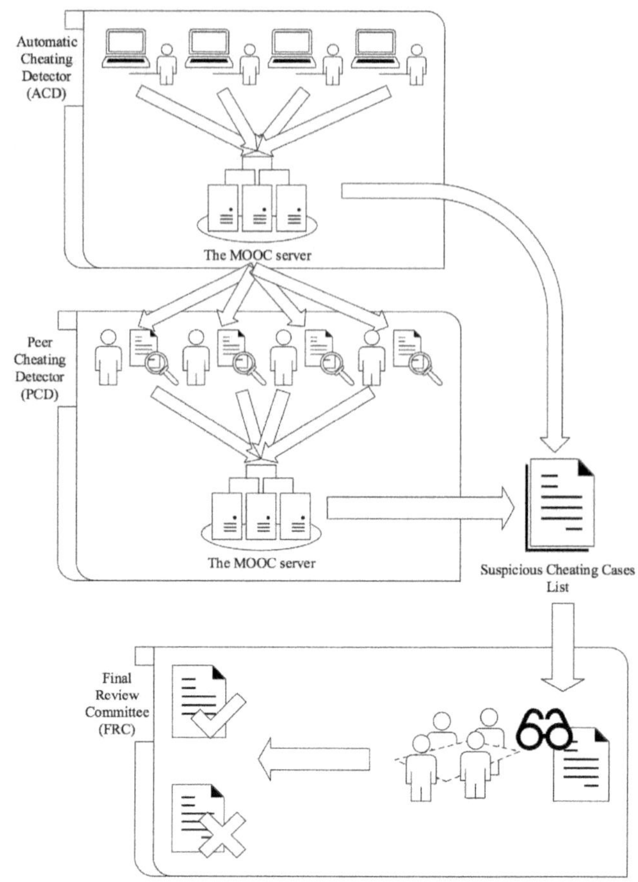

Figure 1: The MOOP framework

MASSIVE OPEN ONLINE PROCTOR

MOOP has three parts: ACD, PCD and FRC (see Figure 1).

Automatic Cheating Detector (ACD)

During the exam, students are monitored by sensors (e.g. webcam). The recorded data are then subject to automated machine learning models to flag whether students are likely to be cheating. Since ACD works completely automatically, the human resource cost is nearly zero. However, there may be an overhead cost to purchase or rent sensors if students do not already own them. In this paper, we explore two versions of ACD - a webcam-only version that seeks to reduce overhead cost and a multi-modal version which incorporates additional sensors (gaze tracker and EEG) to improve detection performance.

For the webcam-only version of ACD, we position one webcam in front of the student to capture his face, another webcam right-hand side of the student to capture his profile. Since the webcams are becoming ubiquitous and cheap, the cost of sensor will be low (or free) for many students. Students, even in poor areas, can easily set up the proctoring environment by using the low-price webcams or cameras on cellphones or laptops.

The multi-modal ACD is based on three different kinds of sensors: webcam, EEG sensor, and gaze tracker. Though EEG sensors and gaze trackers are more expensive and less available than webcams, they may be able to detect cheating in cases where webcams are insufficient. Cheating takes many forms[6] and different sensors offer complementary ability to detect different types of cheating. For example, A student who is using a mobile phone to ask a friend for answers might frequently take their gaze off the question on screen. This behavior may be captured by webcams but may be more easily captured with a gaze tracker. But a student who's been told the answers before the exam would not show the same scattered gaze, making it difficult if not impossible to detect his cheating behavior visually. In that case, EEG sensors might detect that his mental workload is too low for the problem he is supposedly working on.

In this paper, we test the ACD on one specific cheating behavior - usage of a cheat sheet. In practice, to cope with the many different ways of cheating, different ACDs should be trained to cover the wide variety of possible cheating behavior MOOCs may face. Figure 2 shows our experimental setup for evaluating ACD.

Figure 2: A user is taking an online test, proctored by multi-modal ACD. The EEG sensor mark is by blue circles, the gaze tracker is marked by green circles, and the two Kinect cameras are marked by red circles. In the right-hand picture, the user is cheating by referring to a cheat sheet.

- *Camera.* Two Microsoft Kinects are used as webcams. One Kinect is mounted above the computer monitor, monitoring the face. One Kinect is placed to the right hand side of the subject, monitoring the profile.

  Action recognition using the camera has been actively researched in past years[4]. Among the various method for action recognition, we adopt the trajectory-based approach[8][9], specifically the Dense Trajectory approach[18][17][16], which is the state-of-the-art method. We follow the typical steps of action recognition which can be roughly divided into four steps. a) extracting Dense Trajectory features (raw features) from each video or shot, b) quantizing and encoding raw features using a pre-trained k-means codebook to get the encoded feature vector for each video or shot, c) training a χ^2 kernel SVM using these encoded feature vectors and d) applying the model to test data to produce a prediction result.

- *Gaze tracker.* Gaze trackers use the relative position of the pupils and viewing area to compute the precise gaze point where someone is looking. Calibrating a gaze tracker typically requires the viewer to look at a sequence of known reference points on a computer monitor. The gaze tracker then reports subsequent gaze points in terms of computer display coordinates to translate into meaningful targets such as words in a text, items on a menu, or icons on a screen.

  Recently, portable eye-trackers have become available at a much lower cost (around $5000) than the high-end eye-trackers used in high-precision laboratory studies. In our experiment, we used the Mirametrix S2 eye-tracker because of its portability (35 cm width, 4 cm height, 3 cm depth, and 0.7 lb weight), and simple set-up (the eye-tracker simply sits below the computer screen).

  In our detector, only eyes position information from the gaze tracker is used. We trained binary K-Nearest Neighbor (KNN) classifiers to distinguish gaze data from cheating versus non-cheating. The classifier parameter K (number of nearest neighbor to consider) of KNN is set to be 8. As features for classifier we used features: average x, average y, variance of x, and variance of y, where x and y are coordinates of gazes on the screen.

- *EEG sensor.* The EEG (electroencephalogram) signal is a voltage signal that can be measured on the surface of the scalp, arising from large areas of coordinated neural activity. This neural activity varies as a function of development, mental state, and cognitive activity, and the EEG signal can measurably detect such variation.

  The recent availability of relatively inexpensive (less than $300), portable EEG monitoring devices suddenly makes it feasible to take this technology from the lab into the real world. The NeuroSky MindSet, for example, is an audio headset equipped with a single-channel EEG sensor which could be used to distinguish two fairly similar mental states (neutral and attentive) with 86% accuracy. In out experiment, the EEG sensor is placed on the forehead of the subject, measuring frontal brain activity.

  In our detector, we trained binary Gaussian Nave Bayes classifiers to distinguish EEG data from cheating vs. non-cheating. The dependent variable estimated by each classifier was the probability that a subject cheated. As features for classifier we used all available measures: NeuroSkys attention and meditation, the raw and filtered signals, and power spectrum across different frequency bands. We averaged each measure over the time interval of each stimulus, excluding times where the Mindset reported poor signal quality.

In the MOOP system, independent cheating detectors are trained for each sensor. Each sensor flags a *cheating alarm* for possible cheating behavior - the more number of alarms is flagged for a case, the more likely it is that the student has cheated. The cases which with zero or small number of cheating alarms will be dropped as non-cheating and won't go to PCD and FRC. The cases with a large number of cheating alarms are placed in the *suspicious cheating list* and reviewed by FRC directly. The cases with a moderate number of cheating alarms are placed in the *ambiguious cheating list*, which are first sent to PCD for crowdsourced peer review before it is dropped as non-cheating or sent to FRC for final review.

There are two types of detection errors from ACD - false positive (a flagged non-cheating case) and false negative (a non-flagged cheating case). On one hand, a large ratio of false positive increases the workload (and subsequently human resource cost) for PCD and FRC. On the other hand, a large ratio of false negative means that lots of cheating cases are missed. The threshold for what to send to FRC, what to send to PCD, and what to drop can be tuned depending on the resources of the MOOC provider, the size of the class, and the quality of ACD sensors used. We discuss the thresholds we use in our experiment and the limitations of higher or lower thresholds in later sections.

Peer Cheating Detector (PCD)

PCD crowdsources the preliminary verification of cheating alarms raised by the ACD by asking students to review video of their peers. After an exam, randomly selected students are shown various video clips which have been flagged by ACD. Students are asked to score each clip with a likelihood of cheating based on the criteria shown in Table 1. In addition, some "ground truth" video clips will be used to rate students' ability to peer-review. Students who were incorrect on the ground truth clips either due to malignance, apathy, or inability will be not be considered when tallying final PCD scores. All cases with an average PCD score above an adjustable threshold (3 in our experiment) would be considered as *suspicious cheating cases* and would be sent to the FRC for the final decision.

Notice that the instruction to "flag unnessary" behaviors prompts the peers to ground their ratings on evidence of cheating. These instructions are intended to give peers a "innocent-until-proven-guilty" mentality, in which they prioritize the reduction the false alarm rates over the false negative rate. By reducing the false alarm rates, the PCD which would further reduce the workload of FRC.

Score	Criterion
1	Strong non-cheating: based on the videos, you cannot find any unnecessary action by the examinee. You have no reason to believe the examinee is cheating
2	Weak non-cheating: based on the videos, although you can find some unnecessary action of the examinee, you do not believe those actions can contribute to cheating.
3	Border line: based on the videos, you saw some unnecessary action of the examinee and you are not sure whether that was related to cheating behavior.
4	Weak cheating: based on the videos, although you cannot find any clear visual proof of cheating, the examinee is taking some unnecessary actions which you believe are related to cheating behavior.
5	Strong cheating: based on the videos, you find clear visual proof of cheating.

Table 1: Score criteria for PCD

Final Review Committee(FRC)

FRC is responsible for making the final punishing decisions for suspicious cheating cases detected by ACD and PCD. It is a committee formed by staff from MOOCs provider, faculty members, and teaching assistants. Suspicious cheat cases need to be reviewed by an FRC member. We expect FRC to be comparable to online proctoring in accuracy while taking far less time and human resources than online proctoring because the ACD and PCD steps can drastically reduce the number of cases that FRC has to see.

To achieve this, we must be wary of two metrics: First, the precision of the suspicious cheating cases list generated by ACD and PCD should be high, so that FRC does not waste time judging lots of non-cheating cases; this reduction in wasted time is what gives FRC its advantage over online proctoring. Second, the recall rate of ACD and PCD should also be high so that virtually all controversial cheating cases are reviewed by the FRC; a high enough recall rate will make FRC comparable in accuracy to online proctoring.

EXPERIMENT

To validate our assumptions about ACD and PCD accuracy, we ran a controlled experiment where we induced cheating with a cheat sheet.

Experimental Setup

Exam Question Generation

We utilize an computerized test with 20 multiple choice questions. The test is implemented on the Reading Tutor platform[10], which logs and syncronizes the user's camera, gaze, EEG data with the exam questions it presents. Among the 20 questions, 10 of them are tricky questions requiring esoteric knowledge which we believe most participants will lack. The remaining 10 questions are relatively simple questions about computer science. Since most of our participants are members of the computer science department, they should not need to refer to the cheat sheet for most of the questions. Here are some examples of tricky and simple questions:

> James Bond was searching for what kind of airplane in 'Thunderball'?
> a) 707 b) Piper Cub c) Vulkan d) B-52

The answer is c) Vulkan.

> The complexity of the merge sort algorithm is
> a) $O(n)$ b) $O(\log n)$ c) $O(n^2)$ d) $O(n \log n)$

The answer is d) $O(n \log n)$.

Defining The Cheating Behavior

There are at least 53 defined forms of cheating[6] and new forms may be invented in a MOOC setting. It is therefore infeasible to include all possible cheating behavior in one experiment. In this experiment, we focus on one of the more straightforward cheating methods: using a cheat sheet. However, MOOP is designed to be a general framework to detect cheating so it can theoretically be adapted to detect other cheating methods by training new ACDs.

We provide the participants with a cheat sheet - an A4-size paper on which about 50 questions are printed along with the answers. The questions during the test are shown in random order, so the ordering of questions on the cheat sheet will be different from the test. The cheat sheet contains 30 extra questions which do not appear on the test, this is intended to simulate the searching behavior students may engage in if they were really using a cheat sheet.

Experiment Process

Our subjects are students and researchers with computer-science backgrounds. We instructed each participant to take the test to the best of their ability. The participants are only permitted to cheat with the provided cheat sheet. During the exam, the participants' gaze data, video, and EEG signals are recorded by our sensors. After the exam, the participant fills out a survey indicating which question or questions he or she cheated on. We take the survey results as ground truth.

All participants completed all 20 questions of the test. Data from 9 participants were collected successfully and analyzed to make for 180 problems in total. As Table 2 shows, students cheated on 84 out of 180 questions and answered 135 out of 180 questions correctly.

Subject	Cheating	Correct
1	11	17
2	9	20
3	8	7
4	13	10
5	8	19
6	9	16
7	2	20
8	12	10
9	12	16
All	84 (46.7%)	135 (75.0%)

Table 2: Data set collected

RESULTS AND ANALYSES

Metrics

We performed leave-one-out between-subject evaluation. For each subject, we take all other subjects' data as the training set and apply the learned machine learning model on the left-out subject's data. The major metrics used in our experiment are the recall, precision, and accuracy. Recall is the ratio of the number of true cheating cases in detected cases to the total cheating cases number in the dataset. A high recall rate means most of cheating cases in the data set are detected. Precision is the ratio of the number of true cheating cases to the number of detected cases. A high precision means most of cases, which are detected, as cheating cases are true. Accuracy is the ratio of the number of correct classification to the number of all cases. A high accuracy means most of classification results are correct.

Performance

Webcam-only ACD

Here we analyze the MOOP with the ACD purely based on webcams. Figure 3 shows that the two webcams provide similar performance. The best recall, precision and accuracy are 76.2%, 83.3% and 86.6% respectively.

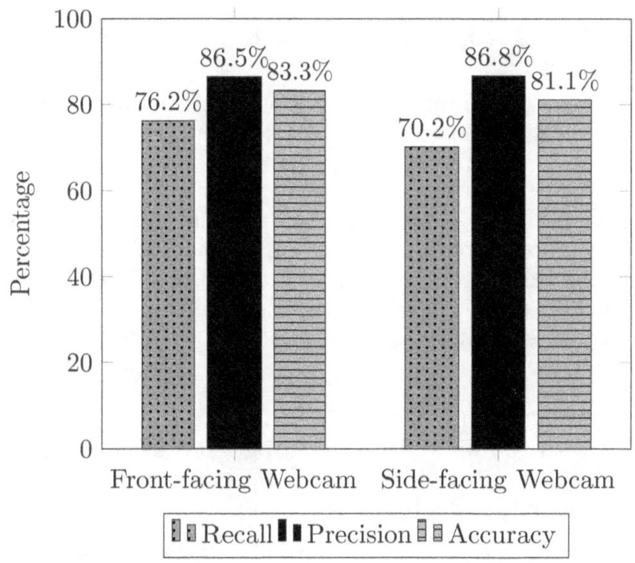

Figure 3: Recall and Precision of Webcams

We consider the number of *cheating alarms* as the indicator of whether the cases should be sent to FRC, PCD, or labled as non-cheating case directly. Figure 4 shows the relationship between the number of *cheating alarms* and the cheating cases ratio we used in our experiment. Naturally, the cases with more cheating alarms are more likely to be cheating cases. Using 1 as the threshold (i.e., cases with 1 or more cheating alarms are flagged as cheating), the recall, precision, and accuracy of the webcam-only ACD are 78.6%, 84.6% and 83.3%, respectively.

PCD

Our initial PCD consists of 2 members, who watched recorded video of the test-takers and rated whether the test-taker was cheating based on the criteria in Table 1. The front-facing video and the side-facing video are provided. Note that in order to access the PCD, we asked them to rate all 180 cases, as opposed to only those that are flagged by the ACD. As seen in Figure 5, the PCD gives clear separation between cheating and non-cheating

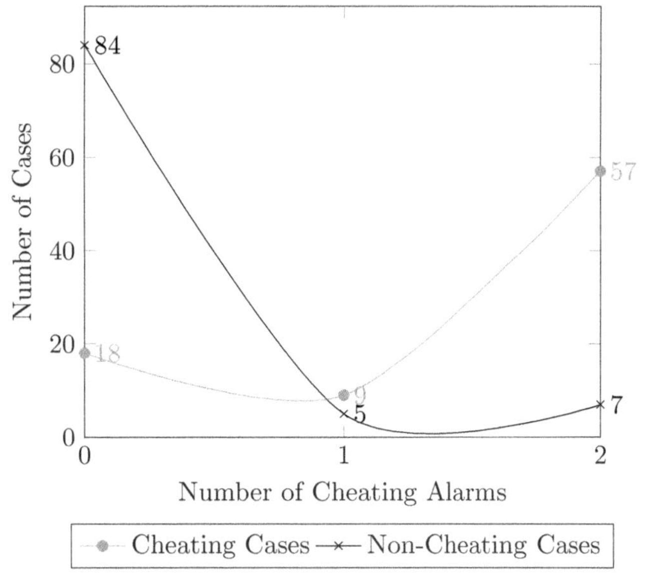

Figure 4: Number of cases with different number of cheating alarms from webcams ACD

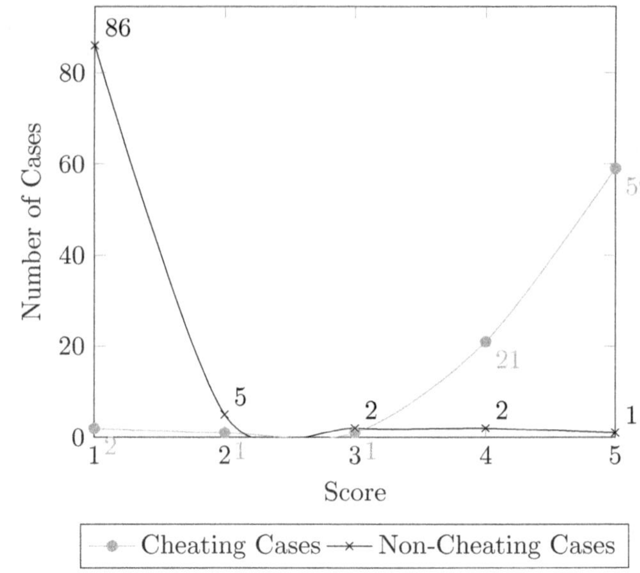

Figure 5: Human score distribution

cases. Using a score of 3 as the threshold (i.e., cases with 3 or more cheating alarms are flagged as cheating), the recall, precision, and accuracy of the PCD is 96.4%, 94.1% and 95.6%, respectively. Note that PCD is more accurate than ACD, but comes at the cost of human resource.

Combination of ACD and PCD

Due to the limited time and patience of crowdsourced labor, we only send cases to PCD which were determined to be ambiguous by ACD.

In ACD, each webcam may raise cheating alarm. According to the number of cheating alarms, we can divide the dataset into 3 subsets - cases with zero cheating alarm (likely non-cheating), one cheating alarm (ambiguous on cheating), and two cheating alarms (likely cheating). There are 102 zero-alarm cases, 14 one-alarm cases and 64 two-alarm cases. Note that the ambiguous case is the smallest subset.

Figure 6 shows a comparison of accuracy of ACD and PCD. PCD performance is good across all subsets but ACD performance varies dramatically, in particular in the one alarm ambiguous cases. By sending the ambiguous cases to PCD for verification, we can take advantage of the high accuracy in PCD while not overwhelming the students with many cases to label.

Performance of the Whole System

To summarize, in ACD, the cases that received 0 alarms are dropped by the ACD, whereas cases that received 1 alarm are verified by PCD before being dropped or sent to FRC. In PCD, cases that received a human rating of 2 or less are dropped by the PCD, whereas cases that received 3 or more are sent to FRC for the final punishing decision. Since FRC is comparable to online proctoring, we do not evaluate its performance and consider it a perfect cheating detector. Considering the whole MOOP system as a cheating detector, the recall, precision and accuracy of the whole system is 78.6%, 100% and 90.0%.

As for the human resource cost, considering there are 84 cheating cases in the dataset, traditional proctoring or online proctoring would need to manually check all of 180 cases to detect the cheating cases. In MOOP, the number of cases that needs to be manually checked in PCD and FRC are 14 and 78, respectively. Moreover, the workload of FRC can be further reduced to 14 by directly labeling the 64 two-alarm cases in ACD as the cheating cases and not sending them to FRC. In this case, the recall, precision and accuracy of the whole system is 78.6%, 90.4% and 86.1% respectively, while FRC only need to review 16.7% (14/84) of total cases. In theory, if there are 1% cheating cases as opposed to the 50% cheating cases in our experimental dataset, only 1.67‰ of total cases will be reviewed by FRC.

Multi-modal ACD and Multi-modal MOOP

We see that MOOP performs well in terms of accuracy and precision but its performance is relatively low in recall. We hypothesize that the low recall performance can be improved by including other sensor modalities. In this section, we show the experiment results of a multi-modal ACD system that utilize webcams, EEG sensor and gaze tracker.

Using the same evaluation method, we get the performance of each sensor. As can be seen in Figure 7, webcam is our best performing sensor. We believe this is at least partly due to the immaturity of EEG and gaze tracking technologies and their susceptibility to noise. For instance, EEG sensors may produce noisy data if the user performs lots of head movements. The gaze

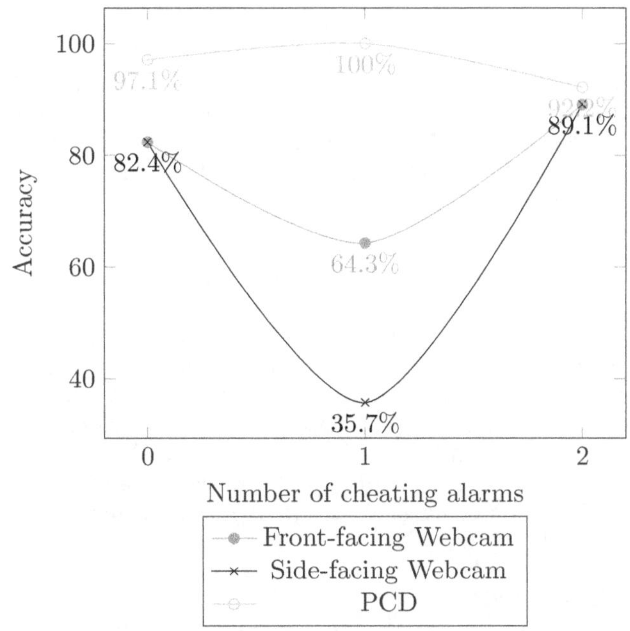

Figure 6: Comparison of PCD and ACD

tracker cannot track the users well if they are wearing glasses. We also note that automatic video processing is a more mature field than EEG and gaze processing and we used more sophisticated algorithms in processing webcam data than in EEG and gaze data.

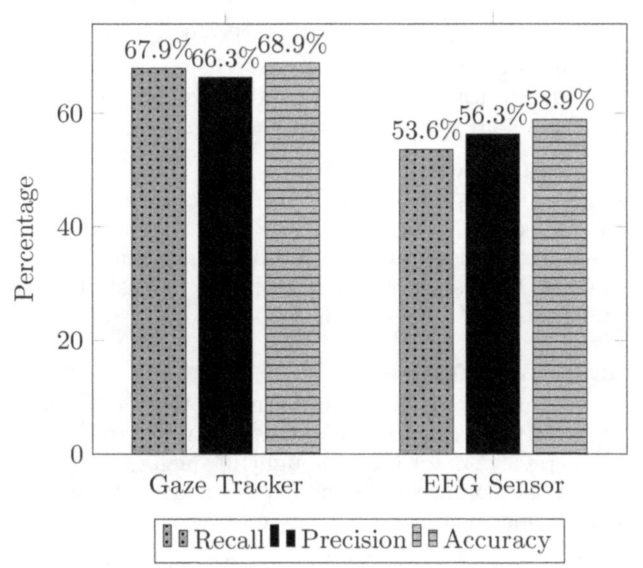

Figure 7: Performance of Gaze Tracker and EEG Sensor

Combined multi-modal ACD output can be split into 5 subsets according to the number of cheating alarms (i.e., each subsets with 0 to 4 cheating alarms). Figure 8 presents the distribution of cheating and non-cheating cases on those 5 subsets. Using a score of 2 as the threshold (i.e., cases with 2 or more cheating alarms are flagged

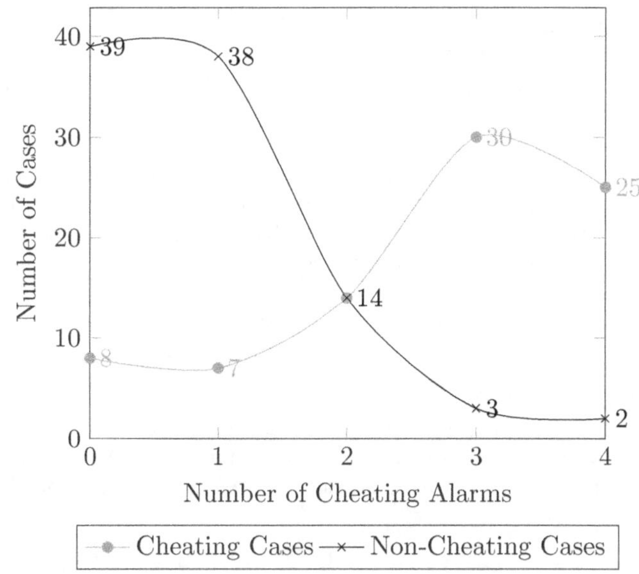

Figure 8: Number of cases with different number of cheating alarms from multi-modal ACD

as cheating), the recall, precision, and accuracy of multi-modal ACD are 82.1%, 60.0% and 81.1%, respectively. Although the recall is improved over the webcam ACD, the precision and accuracy decrease. This may be due to the added noise of gaze tracker and EEG sensor.

Combining the multi-modal ACD with PCD and FRC gives the Multi-modal MOOP. From the multi-modal ACD, we take the cases with 1 or 2 cheating alarms into the PCD. Those cases with 3 or 4 cheating alarms are directly judeged as cheating and those cases without cheating alarms are directly judged as non-cheating. Then the recall, precision and accuracy of the mutli-modal MOOP are 90.5%, 93.8%, and 92.7% respectively. It improves the performance of webcam-only MOOP, with the cost of more expensive detectors. Table 3 presents a summary of performance.

Cheating Classifier	Recall	Precision	Accuracy
Webcam-only ACD	76.6%	84.6%	83.3%
Multi-modal ACD	82.1%	60.0%	81.1%
PCD	96.4%	94.1%	95.6%
Webcam-only MOOP	78.6%	90.4%	86.1%
Multi-modal MOOP	90.5%	93.8%	92.7%

Table 3: Summary of Cheating Classifier

DISCUSSION

Automated proctoring in MOOCs is a relatively new problem and the MOOP system we present in this paper is an initial attempt with much room for improvement.

Challenges of ACD

Diversity of Cheating Behaviors

In our experiment, we trained the ACD on just one kind of cheating behavior. There are many other ways to cheat[6] and many more may be invented in the future. Thus, we consider the ACD to be an evolving component of the MOOP system and that combining complementary data streams from multiple sensors is critical to its success. In addition to the camera, gaze-tracker and EEG sensors that are already deployed, other sensors like galvanic skin response, keystroke patterns, microphone, etc. may also provide useful information.

Cost of sensors

Though additional sensors hold promise for better performance, we must beware that increasing the number and sophistication of sensors increases the cost of the ACD system.

For now, it is not realistic for MOOC students to buy an EEG sensor and gaze tracker for exams. Initially, MOOC providers can buy sensors in batch and rent them to students. As sensors become more ubiquitous in the future, it may become more feasible for students to provide their own. Webcams would not have been considered ubiquitous 10 years ago; we remain optimistic that sensor technologies like portable EEG and gaze tracking will one day become more available. In the meantime, work must be done to improve webcam-only recognition rates for various cheating behaviors.

Diversity of Test Subjects

In our experiment, we trained the ACD on a small participant pool. Future work remains to test if the ACD is generalizable across the diverse learning communities in MOOCs. More importantly, cultural and interpersonal differences in behavior, movement pattern, and brain activity may affect the ACD. For example, culutural differences in expressing attention may trigger the camera or gaze alarms; students with ADHD may trigger EEG alarms. It is not appropriate to subject non-majority cultural or non-neurotypical students to additional scrunity, especially when such status make them more prone to unfair discrimination. The ACD will have to be tuned for different participant pools.

Challenges of PCD

Quality Control

PCD is a typical crowdsourcing system. In the initial system, we suggested relying on moral incentives for students' participation in the crowd-sourcing effort. There have been a lot of previous research about how to improve the work quality of crowdsoucing tasks by using designed incentive protocols.[20] presents a reputation-based incentive proctols to optimize the work quality.[15] compares different kind of incentives, such as financial incentive, social incentive, etc., that will infere with the work quality. They are all applicable for PCD.

Another issue is avoiding the bad peer proctor who makes random decisions. Our current proposed solution is adding some known cases as the validate set into each PCD task. If the student gives wrong detection for the validate set, the weight of the student's detection is lowered. Another solution can be assigning the weight to students' detection based on their previous record. For example, a student caught cheating before should not be assigned to PCD.

Privacy

Since MOOP records the video of students in the privacy of their own home, it may record sensitive information and in some cases, that information may be sent to PCD. The first line of defense is to ask students to try to keep their video clear of private information. Students who do not allow their peers to watch the recorded video may be charged the additional fee for using the FRC instead of PCD. But the fee should still be lower than traditional online proctoring since a lot of non-cheating cases are filtered out by the ACD.

CONCLUSION

In this paper, we propose a possible solution to the MOOC proctoring problem. MOOP combines machine learning with crowdsourcing to deal with the scalability issue of MOOC proctoring.

We design and conduct an experiment to validate the MOOP based on webcams. The full MOOP system achieves 78.6% in recall, 90.4% in precision and 86.1% in accuracy. MOOP uses sensor hardware that is easy to get (e.g. webcam) and the human resource cost is greatly reduced compared to online proctoring.

We also test a multi-modal ACD which combines webcams, gaze tracker and EEG sensor. The combined system improved recall rate but lowered precision and accuracy and increased the sensor cost.

We demonstrate that MOOP has potential to be a more scalable solution to MOOC proctoring. We acknowledge that the question of MOOC proctoring is a relatively new research problem with many open questions and we believe MOOP is a promising first step in answering these questions.

ACKNOWLEDGEMENT

We thank Joseph Valeri and Anders Weinstein for helping set up the experiment. We are grateful to the anonymous reviewers for their thoughtful suggestions. We also thank the volunteers in the experiment for their participation and feedback.

This material is based upon work supported by the National Science Foundation under Grant No. IIS-12511827 and Grant No. IIS-1124240. Any opinions, findings, and conclusions or recommendations expressed in this material are those of the author(s) and do not necessarily reflect the views of the National Science Foundation.

REFERENCES

1. ProctorU. http://www.proctoru.com/.
2. ProctorU: Overview and Technology Requirements. http://www.ao.uiuc.edu/support/source/student_services/proctoru_tech.html.
3. THE TRIBUNAL. http://na.leagueoflegends.com/tribunal/.
4. Aggarwal, J., and Ryoo, M. S. Human activity analysis: A review. *ACM Computing Surveys (CSUR) 43*, 3 (2011), 16.
5. Case, R., and Cabalka, P. Remote proctoring: Results of a pilot program at western governors university. *Proceedings of the 25th Annual Conference on Distance Teaching and Learning 10* (2009), 2010.
6. Dick, M., Sheard, J., Bareiss, C., Carter, J., Joyce, D., Harding, T., and Laxer, C. Addressing student cheating: Definitions and solutions. In *Working Group Reports from ITiCSE on Innovation and Technology in Computer Science Education*, ITiCSE-WGR '02, ACM (New York, NY, USA, 2002), 172–184.
7. Eisenberg, A. Keeping an Eye on Online Test-Takers. The New York Times, 2013.
8. Jiang, Y.-G., Dai, Q., Xue, X., Liu, W., and Ngo, C.-W. Trajectory-based modeling of human actions with motion reference points. In *Computer Vision–ECCV 2012*. Springer, 2012, 425–438.
9. Matikainen, P., Hebert, M., and Sukthankar, R. Trajectons: Action recognition through the motion analysis of tracked features. In *Computer Vision Workshops (ICCV Workshops), 2009 IEEE 12th International Conference on*, IEEE (2009), 514–521.
10. Mostow, J., Chang, K.-M., and Nelson, J. Toward exploiting eeg input in a reading tutor. In *Proceedings of the 15th International Conference on Artificial Intelligence in Education*, AIED'11, Springer-Verlag (Berlin, Heidelberg, 2011), 230–237.
11. Pappano, L. The Year of the MOOC. The New York Times, 2012.
12. Prince, D. J., Fulton, R. A., and Garsombke, T. W. Comparisons of proctored versus non-proctored testing strategies in graduate distance education curriculum. *Journal of College Teaching & Learning 6*, 7 (2009).
13. Richardson, R., and North, M. Strengthening the trust in online courses: A common sense approach. *J. Comput. Sci. Coll. 28*, 5 (May 2013), 266–272.
14. Rogers, C. F. Faculty perceptions about e-cheating during online testing. *J. Comput. Sci. Coll. 22*, 2 (Dec. 2006), 206–212.
15. Shaw, A. D., Horton, J. J., and Chen, D. L. Designing incentives for inexpert human raters. In *Proceedings of the ACM 2011 Conference on Computer Supported Cooperative Work*, CSCW '11, ACM (New York, NY, USA, 2011), 275–284.
16. Wang, H., Klaser, A., Schmid, C., and Liu, C.-L. Action recognition by dense trajectories. In *Computer Vision and Pattern Recognition (CVPR), 2011 IEEE Conference on*, IEEE (2011), 3169–3176.
17. Wang, H., Kläser, A., Schmid, C., and Liu, C.-L. Dense trajectories and motion boundary descriptors for action recognition. *International journal of computer vision 103*, 1 (2013), 60–79.
18. Wang, H., Schmid, C., et al. Action recognition with improved trajectories. In *International Conference on Computer Vision* (2013).
19. Young, J. R. Dozens of Plagiarism Incidents Are Reported in Coursera's Free Online Courses. The Chronicle of Higher Education, 2012.
20. Zhang, Y., and van der Schaar, M. Reputation-based incentive protocols in crowdsourcing applications. In *INFOCOM, 2012 Proceedings IEEE* (March 2012), 2140–2148.

Structuring Interactions for Large-Scale Synchronous Peer Learning

D Coetzee‡, Seongtaek Lim†, Armando Fox‡, Björn Hartmann‡, Marti A. Hearst†‡
UC Berkeley School of Information† and EECS‡
{dcoetzee,stlim,fox,bjoern,hearst}@berkeley.edu

ABSTRACT

This research investigates how to introduce synchronous interactive peer learning into an online setting appropriate both for crowdworkers (learning new tasks) and students in massive online courses (learning course material). We present an interaction framework in which groups of learners are formed on demand and then proceed through a sequence of activities that include synchronous group discussion about learner-generated responses. Via controlled experiments with crowdworkers, we show that discussing challenging problems leads to better outcomes than working individually, and incentivizing people to help one another yields still better results. We then show that providing a *mini-lesson* in which workers consider the principles underlying the tested concept and justify their answers leads to further improvements. Combining the mini-lesson with the discussion of the multiple-choice question leads to significant improvements on that question. We also find positive subjective responses to the peer interactions, suggesting that discussions can improve morale in remote work or learning settings.

Author Keywords

Peer Learning, Group Discussion, Crowdwork

ACM Classification Keywords

H.5.m. Information Interfaces and Presentation (e.g. HCI): Miscellaneous

INTRODUCTION

Online learning should have a social component [32]; how to do that in the context of Massive Open Online Courses (MOOCs) is an open question. This research addresses the question of how to improve the online learning experience in contexts in which students do not have the opportunity to interact with the instructor directly and do not know other students. We wish to show how the positive learning results that have been found in in-person classes and Computer-Supported Collaborative Learning (CSCL) contexts can be successfully replicated and extended in a more impersonal online context.

CSCW '15, March 14-18, 2015, Vancouver, BC, Canada.
ACM 978-1-4503-2922-4/15/03.
http://dx.doi.org/10.1145/2675133.2675251

Our approach is inspired by the literature of structured peer learning [40, 51] as well as newer work by Mazur and other large-course instructors who have brought active peer learning into the classroom [10, 50, 12]. The goal of peer learning, also known as collaborative learning, cooperative learning, and in some contexts, peer instruction, is for students to work together in small groups to enhance their own and one another's learning. Peer learning in the physical classroom consists of activities in which students confer in small groups to discuss conceptual questions and to engage in problem-solving. Literally hundreds of research studies and several meta-analyses show the significant pedagogical benefits of peer learning, including improved critical thinking skills, retention of learned information, interest in subject matter, and class morale [4, 25, 34, 17, 41, 40, 51, 50, 12].

Rather than trying out untested designs on real live courses, we have prototyped and tested the approach using a crowdsourcing service, Amazon Mechanical Turk, (MTurk) [28] on a critical thinking task with multiple-choice answers. While crowd workers likely have different motivations from MOOC students, they do commonly encounter training materials when learning new tasks. In addition, the remote individual work setting without peer contact resembles today's MOOC setting where most students learn in isolation.

Our contributions consist of a method for structuring distributed synchronous peer-learning interactions; a software framework that facilitates such interactions and is positively perceived by crowd workers; and a set of experiments demonstrating that these interactions improve crowd workers' performance on a multiple-choice critical reasoning task. We have also successfully deployed these techniques in a large blended course with more than 1000 students. How applicable these results may be to MOOCs are considered in detail in the discussion.

We conducted two sets of crowd worker experiments. The first tested the effects of synchronous small-group discussions, comparing different size groups, and tested the effects of a bonus condition that rewarded cooperation. Motivated by learning sciences findings that students benefit if they have a dedicated time for generating questions about the concepts before a group discussion begins, the second set of experiments tested the effects of providing a "mini-lesson" about the underlying concepts and having workers generate concepts in advance of a discussion about those concepts. The specific findings of the experiments are:

- Small group discussion of provided multiple choice answers improved results over working alone, and
  - Incentivizing people to help one another further improved the results
  - Participating more in discussions was correlated with getting more correct answers.
- Showing people instructional material about the task and asking them to analyze the task in light of that material improves results over no instructional material.
- Discussion of the instructional material exercise is not more effective than generating responses alone to that material.
- Discussion of provided multiple choice answers after analyzing instructional materials improves results additively,
- A majority of participants enjoyed discussing the material.

These experiments inform the creation of prototype technology to bridge the gap between how peer learning is used in traditional classroom settings and how it can be adapted to a MOOC. We find that structured peer discussion produces improved results for workers in learning tasks. In addition, social interaction can be a way to improve the experience of remotely working through learning material. An advantage of this approach is the potential to go beyond what is possible in physical classrooms and determine group formation on the fly based on answers to questions, organizing students according to their current misconceptions about class materials, and pairing them with students most likely to form a good discussion.

BACKGROUND AND RELATED WORK

Empirical Support for Peer Learning

Much convincing evidence has accumulated that if students are asked to discuss the answers **with other students**, their understanding of the material increases more than if they did an active learning component on their own [25, 3], and structured group work can promote problem solving at a higher level than possible with individual effort alone [40]. As explanation, learning theorists often point to Vygotsky's writings about the interdependence between individual and social processes in learning and development [43]. For college students, Astin [1], in summarizing a longitudinal study from 139 degree-granting colleges, explains: First, students may be motivated to expend more effort if they know their work is going to be scrutinized by peers; and second, students may learn course material in greater depth if they are involved in helping teach it to fellow students [41].

Even very simple peer learning methods can be effective. For instance, Ruhl et al. [46] conducted a controlled experiment with 72 undergraduate education students comparing a standard lecture format to the simple "pause procedure" in which students formed dyads and discussed lecture material for 2 minutes three times per 45 minute lecture. Students in the pausing group performed one or two points better on after-lecture quizzes and a course-level comprehension test.

Smith [50] showed that peer discussion enhances understanding even when none of the students in the discussion group originally knows the correct answer. In an in-person introductory genetics course, 350 students answered multiple choice questions – using clickers – throughout the semester. In each case they answered first individually, and then after discussing the question with neighbors, they were allowed to change their answer. When given a second, isomorphically similar problem, despite not having been told the correct answer for the first question, the average scores for the second question of the pair were significantly higher than for the first, and gains were greatest on the hardest problems.

Applying Peer Learning

The simplest form of peer learning is the informal groups [25] or "Quick Thinks" usage [45], in which small groups of students briefly discuss material that has been presented and then decide independently how to respond to some activity, typically answering a multiple-choice question. Substantially greater learning gains have been found when peer discussion is combined with social interaction, for example, facilitated by clickers or similar technology, a result that has been replicated in a number of studies [39, 24].

Successful structured peer learning requires attainment simultaneously of *positive interdependence* and *individual accountability*. Positive interdependence requires interdependent contributions from students in the group; students must also be instructed to emphasize learning over "getting the answer." Thus, instructors must devise activities that ensure a reason for the members of the group to interact with and help one another, and both instructor direction and structure of activities must make social loafing difficult.

Students learn in part by explaining, and those who do not understand can benefit from peers' explanations. To motivate more and better understanding, in-class quizzes can be conducted using structured peer learning by first having every student take the quiz individually and then having the group take the quiz together, with both sets of answers counting toward the grade [55].

The literature provides many examples of how to both succeed and fail at introducing peer learning; many readings describe in detail mechanisms for designing successful group activities [55, 59, 40] and how to overlay other pedagogical techniques on peer learning, including Problem Based Learning (accounting) [9], the Argument-Claim-Evidence Method (Engineering) [49], and the Cognitive Tools and Intellectual Roles [43].

Fischer et al. [14] show that efficient collaborative learning is rarely achieved simply by putting learners together without some supportive instruction. While we focus on peer learning rather than collaborative learning, our work does provide such support in the form of instructional narratives and peer discussion. Fischer also cites specific mechanisms by which group co-construction of knowledge occurs during discussion, such as resolution of socio-cognitive conflicts. While our work does not focus on detecting such activity, the ease of data collection and analysis afforded by our apparatus could be beneficial for collaborative-learning researchers.

CSCL Research on Chat in Online Learning

Peer learning in an online context has been studied in the field of Computer Supported Collaborative Learning (CSCL). As Stahl and others note [52], Vygotsky argued that learning takes place in dyads or groups before it takes place by individuals, underscoring the importance of studying and enabling group cognition.

CSCL research in online collaborative learning has generally focused on asynchronous discussion, such as online discussion forums. Where synchronous interaction has been studied (such as real-time chat), most work has studied online technologies designed to be used in conjunction with in-classroom group learning [5] or has focused on interaction between a pair of students or a student and a tutor, as in [16], rather than a small group of peer learners. Recent work in chat-in-CSCL [54] acknowledges that even though this "paradigm shift" from teacher-communicated learning to discourse-based learning is widely accepted in the CSCL community, there are few theories and applications for analyzing such interaction.

Also related is the literature on online teamwork, which at times intersects with that of online learning, as in for example, Tausczik and Pennebaker [53].

Social Interaction in MOOCs

Stahl and colleagues [35] note that despite years of CSCL literature demonstrating the importance of collaborative learning for online education, neither MOOCs nor Khan Academy offer support for students to interactively explore topics themselves or with peers. Some MOOC promoters likewise feel that while peer instruction is promising, disseminating and adopting it are big challenges even in brick-and-mortar classrooms [38]. Nonetheless, there persist calls for student interaction in MOOCs [32].

Currently the main kind of social interaction supported in MOOCs are online forums; these are usually threaded discussion lists in which comments and questions are visible to everyone in the class. Forums are pervasive in MOOCs and have been characterized as "an essential ingredient of an effective online course" [36], but early investigations of MOOC forums show struggles to retain users over time. In one example, half of forum users ceased participation due to factors such as lack of forum facilitation, an overwhelming number of messages, and rude behavior of other students [36]. As an alternative form of engagement, informal groups associated with MOOC courses tend to spring up around the world. Students use social media to organize groups or decide to meet in a physical location to take the course together.

Great strides have been made in peer grading in MOOCs, where students improve their own understanding by assessing the work of others [29]. However, students in this setting do not interact with one another directly but instead review one another's work anonymously and asynchronously. Work has also been done on self-evaluation of assignments within MOOCs [60], replicating earlier results in smaller class settings showing that self-evaluation helps improve student outcomes [47]. Dow et al. [13] found that self-assessment of crowd work was just as effective as feedback from an expert judge on a consumer review writing task, although expert assessment resulted in more work activity.

Group Work in CrowdSourcing

Little research addresses how to support group work in crowdsourcing platforms. The closest is that of Zhu et al. [62] who studied how to improve productivity and quality of crowd worker output, motivated by concerns about overhead in coordinating workers (also known as process loss [42]) and the potential for groups to be swayed toward an undesirable outcome by factors relating to social influence [31, 23].

Zhu et al. [62] found that asking workers to review the work of others yielded better results on a post-test than having the workers do the work directly without any training. They also found that groups working together semi-synchronously using a shared editing tool performed better on 5 tasks (brainstorming, summarizing a paragraph, writing a product review, solving a moral dilemma, doing a mathematics problem) than individual workers, but that pooling and averaging the results of individual workers improved results still more. The one exception to the pooling result was the mathematics problem, where interactive discussion was necessary for insights to occur and workers to learn from one another. This is the kind of problem that we explore in this work, where group interaction is more likely necessary to arrive at understanding.

APPROACH

Incentivizing Collaboration

In standard peer learning, students are asked to work together to answer a question, either after reading material, hearing a lecture, watching a video, or as part of a homework assignment. Peer learning combines *individual accountability* to ensure that students work on their own with *positive interdependence* to ensure that all students in a learning group participate in group work [25, 40]. In this study, we ask MTurk workers to assume the roles of students and discuss the answers to a question posed to them.

One purpose of these experiments is to see if the design facilitates discussion of problems before introducing it into a MOOC. An important open question is whether, in the absence of the social and academic pressures of a real classroom, workers will engage in substantive discussions. Another reason to experiment is to determine how to design the user interface and answer questions including how much time to allow for individual vs group discussion, how many participants to include in a room, and what kinds of instructions should be given about proper conversational structure.

A potential drawback of using crowd workers is that they may not be motivated to have a productive conversation or try hard to get the correct answer. Therefore, in the first experiment, we manipulated a condition in which if **all** participants converged on the correct answer, they would **all** receive a bonus. This strategy is motivated by a technique from the peer learning literature in which students are incentivized to help the others in their group because their grade on a subsequent quiz will be a combination of the scores of everyone in their group

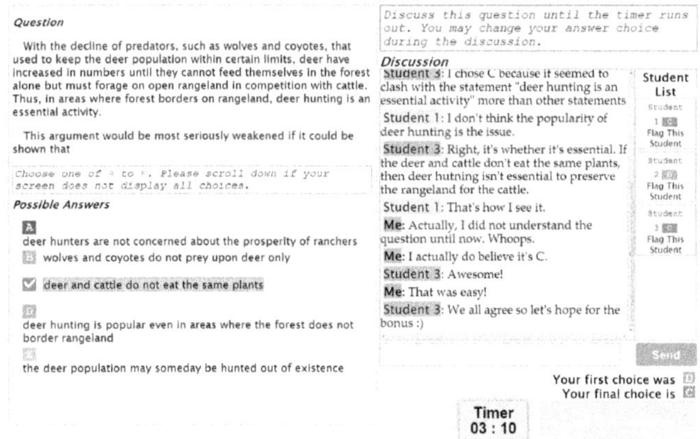

Figure 1. The chat system showed a GMAT practice question on the left while participants discussed choices on the right. In this real example, all participants selected the correct answer and received a bonus payment.

[55]. We hypothesize that this condition would better replicate the situation of earning grades in a course, by motivating the participants to try harder to figure out the right answer, and explain their reasoning to one another, which is a fundamental principle behind peer learning. To facilitate comparison we also compared the effect of offering solo workers a bonus vs. no bonus.

User Interface

We developed a custom web browser-based tool which displays a series of informational screens, many with a countdown timer, the ability to enter text strings and select among multiple choice options, and a chat room for discussion among many students or for individual reflection in the single user condition (see Figure 1).[1]

We decided on text chat rather than video for several reasons:

- Text-based interaction from students is standard in MOOCs and far more reliable than video-conferencing; many MOOC instructors wish to reach students who do not necessarily have access to high-speed internet connections required for real time video conferencing,
- Many students participating in MOOCs are non-native speakers of the instructors' language, and research shows that in some cases people in the non-dominant culture are just as or more active in text-based communication than video or face-to-face [58, 48].
- Research on the relative affordances of text chat, telephone voice communication, and video communication versus face to face communication, including Walther's Social Information Processing Theory of Computer Mediated Communication (CMC), finds that communicators deploy whatever communication cue systems they have at their disposal [56]. Walther's work has found that people can express affect and interpersonal affinity as effectively using an online

[1]The code used in these experiments was originally written using Node.js and has since been rewritten in Rails. For Experiment 2 some minor changes were made to how groups were formed using Mechanical Turk, and minor changes were made to the appearance of the user interface as compared to Experiment 1. The source code can be found at `http://github.com/stlim0730/MoocChat`

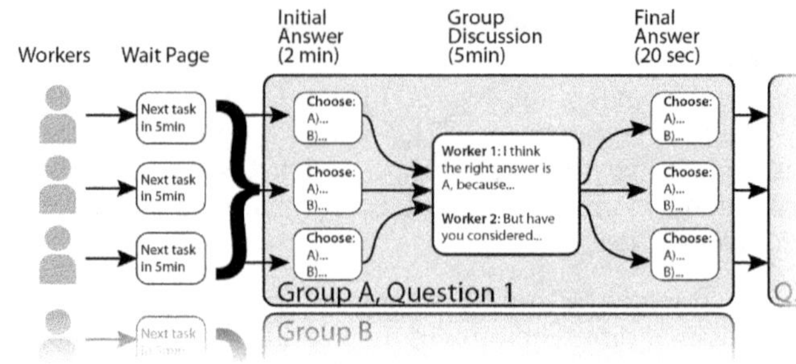

Figure 2. Illustration of worker synchronization for Experiment 1.

chat system as in a face-to-face setting, making use of the verbal cues available to them [57]. However, different studies find different outcomes, depending in part on the stated goal (trust, information exchange, etc.).

Synchronizing Workers

Mechanical Turk does not provide a mechanism to synchronize workers, but we build on earlier investigations that have shown how to assemble multiple crowd workers on online platforms to form synchronous on-demand teams [30, 2]. Our approach was to start tasks (called HITs) at fixed times, announcing them ahead of time and showing a countdown timer until those HITs began. We announced the availability every 5 minutes and had no problem filling HIT sets of size 100, looking for groups of 3. If there was an "odd person out," we placed that worker in their own solo room so their time was not wasted. In some cases, a group of 3 became a group of 2 when a crowd worker who initially accepted a HIT dropped out. This "gather-and-group" mechanism was designed for the MOOC setting, where students may arrive at any point in time; adjusting the waiting time before groups are formed allows us to configure it to suit any arrival rate, and allows students to reliably anticipate when the activity will begin so that they can focus on other tasks.

The method for synchronizing crowd workers for Experiment 1 is illustrated in Figure 2, corresponding to the workflow we call *Discuss Question* (other workflows are described below). While waiting for the timer countdown, participants were shown an information page describing upcoming steps including screenshots of sample questions and the chat room. Once the countdown completed, workers were shown the first question and given instructions to read it and choose one of the answers. The answer could be changed any number of times during this time period, while a timer visibly counted down. Once time ran out, the worker was placed into the chat room, shown the labels for the other workers (Student 1, Student 2, Student 3) and was instructed to begin discussing the question and encouraged to change their answer if appropriate. Again, a timer counted down the time. When there were only 30 seconds left, the screen showed a message in a prominent manner, instructing the worker to make their final choice of an answer. If no final answer was chosen, a null value was indicated in the logs. If more than 45 seconds went by without a message, the system sent a message to the chat room reminding participants to keep the conversation going. In the manipulated (bonus) condition, the initial message sent to the chat room reminded the workers that if all participants arrive at the same correct answer, they would receive a bonus.

In some cases a single worker was left over after random grouping. These workers went through the same steps and had the same opportunities to revise responses, but instead of engaging with others were prominently asked to explain their response. This controls for benefits due to self-explanation.

Test Materials

We sought questions that could be answered without requiring specialized knowledge, that would likely benefit from careful thought and discussion, and could not be answered by a simple web search. To this end, we obtained a private set of practice questions for the Critical Reasoning Task of the Graduate Management Admissions Test (GMAT). These tasks consist of three parts: a brief passage of text, a question, and 4 or 5 answer choices, of which only one can be selected. The questions are usually related to the construction of arguments, such as finding the evidence to support a conclusion, determining which of a set of statements weakens an argument, or determines which of a set of statements is most strongly supported by the initial paragraph. Figure 3 shows a sample essay and answer choices. Most U.S. business schools use the GMAT as an entrance exam, and more than 250,000 students take the GMAT each year.

Multiple-choice questions and to a lesser extent short-answer questions ("cued recall") are ubiquitous in MOOCs [7, 37]. Multiple-choice questions in particular are used both in quizzes that test comprehension and in assessment instruments for certificates of completion. The "testing effect" finds that frequent testing helps long-term retention [21], and recent results show that multiple choice questions can be effective at both eliciting the testing effect and increasing performance on later short-answer transfer questions [15]. Thus the testing instruments we employ are representative of MOOC tasks and conform to common peer instruction methods.

EXPERIMENT 1

The first experiment assessed if a measurable improvement would occur if workers discussed the problem in groups. It also assessed the effects of varying group sizes and tested whether or not providing an incentive to help other workers would in fact lead to better results. Because the workers do not know the correct answer, if they want to earn the bonus they should have a good incentive to try hard to understand the question well and ensure that even the most certain sounding group member is actually correct in their assumptions.

Participants

Participants were recruited on Amazon's Mechanical Turk with the qualifications of having 95% acceptance rate on 1000 tasks or more. Payment was $2 for the HIT and $2 for each bonus achieved. A given worker could do the HIT only once.

Study Design

Sessions: In a between-participants design 3x2 design, workers either worked alone (solo) or were in placed in a chatroom with a total of 2 or 3 workers and were either offered a

Essay: Tests demonstrating that the olfactory bulbs (relating to the sense of smell) of salmon will react upon exposure only to water from their spawning ground and no other water suggest the possibility that repeated exposure to a specific odorant of their spawning area during the first few weeks of life could stimulate olfactory receptor sites, increasing olfactory sensitivity to that single scent and influencing salmon migration to their spawning area.
Instructions and Possible Answers:
Which if the following, if true, would weaken the conclusion? (answer is E)
(A) Salmon have been trained, through repeated exposure, to recognize phenol and distinguish it from closely related pchlorphenol, in concentrations as small as five parts per billion.
(B) A dog can detect and distinguish the odor of a single human fingerprint for as long as six weeks, after which time the scent usually fades away.
(C) Salmon have been successfully stocked in rivers where special salmon "runs" have been constructed.
(D) Women are acutely aware of the odor of a synthetic steroid named exaltolide, which most men are unable to detect.
(E) Salmon spawned and raised in hatcheries will return to the spawning ground of their parents, and not to the source of the water (the hatcheries) in which they were spawned.

Figure 3. Sample GMAT Critical Reasoning Question (number 4).

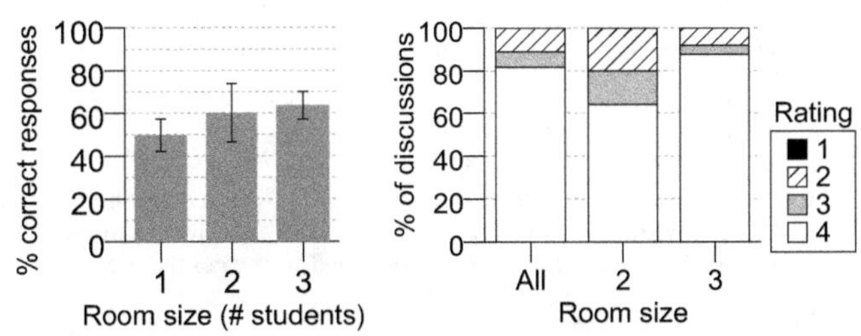

Figure 4. Left: The mean percentage of correct responses is higher in chatrooms with more than one student (Fisher's exact test, $p < 0.01$). Error bars show 95% confidence interval. Right: Most discussions were rated as substantive (4), and no discussions were rated as irrelevant (1).

bonus or not. Each session consisted of 2 questions and a followup questionnaire which asked for subjective responses to the time allocations and the quality of the discussion. Participants were also asked to optionally provide any other comments or thoughts.

Timing: We conducted initial tests in which participants were allotted 2 minutes to answer the question individually, 3 minutes for the discussion period, and then 20 seconds to make the final answer choice. After these tests, many participants indicated that they needed more time in the discussion period. The results reported here used the settings of 2 minutes for initial individual answer, 5 minutes for discussion, and 20 seconds for final answer for each question. In discussion, participants without discussion partners were permitted to continue after sending a single message of self-explanation.

Manipulated Conditions: While doing the initial individual answering of the question, participants were shown a message stating that after they chose their initial response, they would join a chat room to discuss their answer with either one or two other people. They were also told at this time if all participants in the chatroom arrived at the same answer and that answer was correct, they would receive a monetary bonus.

	Below, Student 1 initially does not have the correct choice.
Student 3	I hesitated on C
Student 2	I did as well I was trying to decide between a and c
Student 2	what other answer did you consider
Student 3	Well I was still reading and saw the timer at 1 second so I hit C.
Student 3	But
Student 1	I considered B and C
Student 1	B
Student 3	I'm going over iit again
Student 2	C seems to make the most sense as knowing whether buyers actually saw ads and were persuaded by them would help answer the question
Student 1	B won out for me because it could explain why they had more success.
Student 3	It states evaluating the argument, so I think C is correct.
Student 3	The argument is about the advertising firms success
Student 2	I can see what your thinking with B but when I really think about it I think C answers the question
Student 3	Yeah, B and C roughly address the same argument, but C supposrts it more.
Student 1	Seeing if they did actually see the ads would be good... knowing though which ads are more successful might also be good...
Student 2	I was also thinking I don't usually see car ads that contain addresses
Student 3	yeah
Student 1	c
	Below, Student 1 initially does not have the correct choice.
Student 3	I said e, and I'm sticking to it
Student 2	I also think e
Student 2	cause with bolivia they could still have 60 percent like it
Student 2	but with czech, 100 percent could hate it
Student 2	they have no way of knowing
Student 3	And in bolivia they at least had SOME data
Student 3	So they could make an informed choice
Student 2	yeah, totally
Student 1	i picked c but i can see why you guys pick e
Student 2	i think e is the easiest for me to see why it works
Student 2	i don't know if that makes sense
Student 2	it did in my head
Student 3	I have no idea if the czech have stronger money.
Student 1	true, i might change my answer then

Table 1. Two example discussions from E1, assigned the highest rating (4), each with three workers, in bonus condition, where initially two workers were correct and the third switched to the correct answer.

Results

All of the study predictions were supported. Results are reported for 267 worker sessions lasting on average 12.8 minutes (15.0 minutes excluding solo workers), with 169 solo chat sessions, 25 discussions of size 2, and 73 discussions of size 3. About 58% of the 433 attempts to answer questions were answered correctly overall (after discussion), suggesting that the questions were suitably but not too challenging.

138 workers (61%) kept their original choices unchanged on both questions, 74 (33%) changed one answer after the discussion, and 14 (6%) changed both. We found 51% of workers who changed their answers improved their score, while only 18% lowered their score; 86% of workers who changed both answers improved their score. These figures include solo and grouped workers.

We use Fisher's exact test (two-tailed) to examine the connection between independent variables and the proportion of correct answers, because it is appropriate for two-valued outcomes and because it is more conservative than the χ^2 test, particularly for small or unbalanced samples. While we are aware of sophisticated approaches such as Bayesian knowledge tracing [8] that also model whether students might get correct answers by guessing or incorrect answers by slipping, we are interested in the difference between two groups for which such effects should be similar.

Engaging in discussion leads to more correct answers. As Figure 4 (left) shows, among the 169 responses provided by solo crowd workers, 84 (50%) were correct. Among the 269 responses from crowd workers who participated in a discussion group, 169 (63%) were correct, a strongly significant difference (Fisher's exact test, $p < 0.01$).

More discussion is correlated with more correct answers. Each response is associated with a question, a participant, and a particular chatroom discussion. We examined for each response how many chat messages the crowd worker sent in the associated chatroom, and for each possible number of chat messages, determined the proportion of responses that were correct. Sending more chat messages was correlated with a higher proportion of correct answers ($r^2 = 0.53$); this was the case both with the final answers made after the discussion, and the first answers made before the discussion, suggesting correlation rather than causation.

Among workers in dyads and triads, the bonus incentive leads to more correct changed answers. In the no-bonus (control) condition, participants changed 38 out of 127 individual answers (30%); in the bonus condition they changed 47 out of 142 answers (33%). No significant difference was found (Fisher's exact test, $p = 0.60$). However, among the changed answers, 14 answers (11%) were changed from incorrect to correct in the control condition, while 31 (22%) were changed from incorrect to correct in the bonus condition, a significant difference (Fisher's exact test, $p < 0.03$). Among solo workers, changing responses was rare, occurring in only 16 or 9% of 169 solo chat sessions, and changing to the correct response occurred the same number of times (4) in both the bonus and control conditions.

The participants have substantive discussions. Three independent raters applied the following rubric to the discussions:

1. Irrelevant or no discussion: workers did not mention their answers or the question at all.
2. Merely stated answers: One or more workers mentioned their answers, and/or suggested changing answers, but gave no justification or reasoning.
3. Justified answers: One or more students justified their answers, but did not consider or address others' positions.
4. Debate: One or more students justified their answers, and one or more students did at least one of:
   - Considered and addressed positions of other students,
   - Considered and addressed other possible responses, or
   - Persuaded or attempted to persuade other students to change their choice through rational argument.

73 of 98 discussions (74%) were rated 4 by all raters, and 80 (82%) had a median rating of 4. Inter-rater reliability was moderate (Spearman's $\rho = 0.65$). Discussions with 3 participants were generally rated higher than ones with only two, as shown in Figure 4 (right). Table 1 shows two example discussions in which 2 workers begin with the correct answer and the third changes to the correct answer after the discussion.

EXPERIMENT 2

In Experiment 1, workers are asked to discuss the target essay and the five possible answers and try to determine which is the correct answer in a workflow that we call Discuss Question (see Figure 5). This takes place without provision of any kind of instructional material. Workers only choose answers and then discuss their answers with one another.

For Experiment 2, we wanted to see if additional structure would draw out further improvements or changes in the workers' behavior and scores. Our approach was motivated by pedagogy advocated by King [27, 26] which has found that students benefit by generating questions before the group discussion begins, including metacognition monitoring [18]. King's suggested stimuli (questions stems such as "What would happen if ..." and "Compare ... and ... with regard to ...") are not suitable for the GMAT-based tasks, so we designed an alternative set of study materials which we call a *Mini-Lesson*. Workers were shown instructional materials (see Figure 6) and an example critical reasoning problem and asked to identify the unstated assumption that might undermine the argument.

In the study design, we contrasted discussing just this Mini-Lesson with having a second follow-on discussion about the multiple-choice questions directly. Ideally, from a pedagogical perspective, the deeper thinking that comes from examining the assumptions helps obtain the correct answer *before* seeing the choices for the multiple choice question. If group discussion benefits understanding, those who discuss the assumptions should perform better on the multiple choice question than those who generate the assumptions working solo.

Study Design

Sessions: Building on the results of Experiment 1, all groups were of size 1 or 3 (no dyads) and all workers were offered a bonus (solo workers for getting the answer alone, triads if all 3 workers got the right answer). In a between-participants design, workers were assigned to one of three conditions (see Figure 5):

- Minimal: (solo) Read essay, select 1 of 5 answers.
- Mini-Lesson (ML): (triad or solo) Read instructional material, read GMAT essay, generate assumption, discuss assumption, select 1 of 5 answers, write a justification for the answer, view the correct answer.
- Mini-Lesson + Discuss Question (MLDQ): (triad or solo) Read instructional material, read GMAT essay, write down assumption, discuss assumption, select 1 of 5 answers, write justification for the selected answer, discuss justification and answer with group members, select final answer, view correct answer with explanation.

Each participant completed two questions in sequence in their respective condition, with the exception that the mini-lesson was only shown one time. Table 2 shows example discussions for the MLDQ workflow.

Instructions: First, workers were shown the instructional materials and the first problem essay. Then they were asked to identify "an important unstated assumption" in the essay

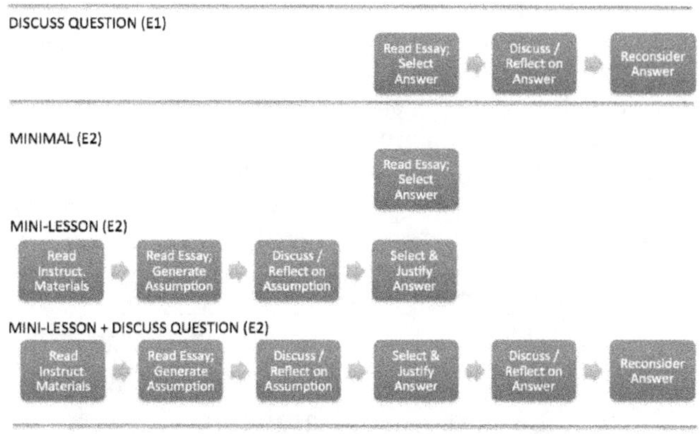

Figure 5. Workflow diagrams for Experiment 1 (E1) and 2 (E2). Not shown are the second questions in the series.

and told the response would be shared with other students on the next screen. Upon entering the discussion, workers were asked to "discuss these assumptions in order to prepare for a question shown on the next screen." Each worker in ML and MLDQ saw a second GMAT question, selected an answer, and provided justifications for responses, but did not have discussions and did not provide assumptions. They were also required to fill out a survey.

Timing: For discussion phases workers were allocated up to 300 seconds; if all members of a chat room signaled that they wanted to end the discussion, then it ended earlier. For choosing and justifying an answer, 240 seconds was allowed, but could end earlier.

Materials: The study materials were a smaller subset of the questions used in E1.

In this task, you'll learn a critical reasoning skill commonly called identifying hidden assumptions. Read the following carefully. You see arguments every day in statements by politicians, businesses, and advertisements. These arguments are a way of trying to convince you that something is true. Here is an example:
Many mobile phone companies protect their technology with patents, and mobile phones continue to become more technically advanced every year. Therefore, patents lead to strong competition in the marketplace.
This statement contains the key components of an argument: at least one premise and a conclusion. But often there are gaps in logic between the premises and the conclusion. These gaps can include assumptions, and identifying the unstated assumptions helps you spot the logical flaw in the reasoning: Premise(s) + Assumption(s) = Conclusion(s)
If the assumptions are incorrect, then the conclusion might not follow. There are several unstated or hidden assumptions in the example above which may be not actually be true:
Assumption: we have plenty of innovation in the presence of patents.
Perhaps defending against patents takes away resources from making even more innovative inventions.
Assumption: strong competition is the biggest reason for the advanced technology in the mobile phone business.
However, patents award a monopoly (exclusive rights) to the patent holder, thus reducing competition.

Figure 6. Text of Mini-Lesson given to crowd workers.

Results

This section outlines: descriptive statistics summarizing number of workers in each condition and time spent on the task, the main results regarding which conditions led to an improvement in performance on the two questions, the relationship between survey results and performance, and analyses of various metrics for discussion quality and their relationship to performance.

Condition	Total	Solo	Triad
Minimal	346	346	N/A
Mini-Lesson	409	152	257
Mini-Lesson + Discuss Question	312	122	190
Total	1067	620	447

Table 3. Number of workers in each condition and whether they participated in a discussion group of three (triad).

Condition	Min	Median	Max	IQR	Time limit
Minimal	0.3	2.2	8.8	1.5	9
Mini-Lesson	4.1	13.8	28.4	5.8	30
Mini-Lesson + Discuss Question	8.7	20.3	37.9	6.5	40

Table 4. Overall time spent by workers on the task, in minutes. After the time limit expired, workers could no longer submit.

Descriptive

Worker counts. The three experiment conditions had 346, 409, and 312 workers respectively, for a total of 1067 workers. In conditions with discussion groups, about 60% of workers participated in discussions; see Table 3 for details.

Session times. Worker time increased as stages were added: Minimal flow had a median of 2 minutes, while the Mini-Lesson flow was 14 and Mini-Lesson + Discuss Question was 20 minutes. The maximum time limit for the task was adjusted for each condition accordingly (see Table 4).

Main results

In this experiment, the dependent variables were generally two-valued (whether a response was correct or incorrect), so we rely on two main statistical tools: Fisher's exact test to determine significance, and the 95% confidence interval for the odds ratio, commonly used in medical research, to describe effect size. For example, stating that "group A was 3 to 7 times more likely to answer the question correct than group B" means that there is a 95% chance that the actual odds ratio in the population is between 3 and 7 (i.e. the confidence interval is [3,7]). Because we perform many Fisher tests below, we conservatively selected a significance threshold α using the Bonferroni correction: at least 20 tests were performed, suggesting a rough threshold value of $\alpha = 0.05/20 = 0.0025$.

Mini-Lesson instruction improves performance. We compared solo workers in either ML or MLDQ to the solo workers in the Minimal flow who received no instructional materials. Workers are 7 to 17 times more likely to answer the first question correctly on their first try given the Mini-Lesson scaffolding ($p < 0.0001$). The percentage of correct responses rose from 11% to 58%. Certain questions showed especially dramatic differences, e.g., scores on question 4 rose from 0% of 30 to 82% of 44 workers.

After completing all stages on the first question, workers in scaffolded conditions also go on to perform better independently on the second question. Solo workers in ML were 3 to 7 times more likely to answer the second GMAT question correctly than Minimal flow workers ($p < 0.0001$), with correct responses rising from 20% to 54%. Solo workers in MLDQ, who additionally received an opportunity to reflect on their response to the first question and revise it, were 4 to 9 times more likely to answer the second question correctly than Minimal flow workers ($p < 0.0001$), and correct responses rose from 20% to 60%. Question 4 again exhibits an unusual increase from 5% to 64% for ML, and 5% to 91% for MLDQ.

No significant benefit from generated assumption discussion. The mini-lesson teaches concepts by having workers formulate unstated assumptions about the problem on their own and then discuss these in groups. To justify the discussion component's inclusion, we examine whether it improves performance. We compare ML singleton workers who progressed through the stages alone to ML workers who participated in discussion triads, but found no significant difference in their responses to the first question (59.1% vs. 58.6%, $p > 0.9$ with Fisher's exact test, odds ratio 95% confidence interval $[0.7, 1.5]$) or the second question (54% vs. 56%, $p > 0.7$, $[0.7, 1.6]$). In fact, even when ML singletons are compared to grouped workers in MLDQ, which had the benefit of two discussions, no significant difference could be shown (59% vs. 64%, $p > 0.3$, $[0.8, 2.0]$).

Revising responses

Revised answers after discussion showed improvements. The MLDQ flow provides the opportunity for workers to discuss the answer choices for the first question and then revise them. This is the core feature expected to exploit the benefits of peer learning to improve performance. This process was found to be beneficial: 61% of grouped workers in ML or MLDQ answered the first question correctly on their first try, while 74% of grouped workers in MLDQ answered it correctly following discussion on their initial responses. They were 1.2 to 2.6 times more likely to answer it correctly on their second try ($p < 0.002$).

Among the 190 MLDQ workers who participated in discussions, 45 (24%) changed their response, and of these, 28 or 62.2% revised from an incorrect to a correct response. Solo workers almost never made such positive revisions to their responses: MLDQ workers not participating in groups rarely changed their response (20 of 122 or 16%) and rarely improved their response when doing so (only 4 workers).

Survey feedback

Instructors may be reluctant to deploy new instructional tools that students dislike. To investigate subjective responses to small group discussions, workers were asked to rate their experiences with the discussion. As shown in Figure 7, 401 (53%) of agreed or strongly agreed that the discussion was enjoyable, while only 81 (11%) expressed negative responses.

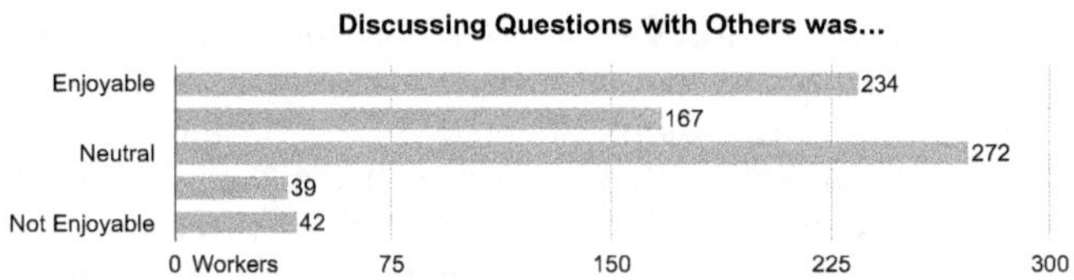

Figure 7. Enjoyment of discussion from Experiment 2 surveys. "Neutral" was chosen most, but more workers enjoyed discussion than did not enjoy it.

In an optional open-ended field for feedback, responses again reflected enjoyment of the task:

- 254 (34%) described the activity as 'interesting', 'fun', or 'enjoyable';
- 12 (1.6%) described the task as 'difficult' or 'hard' *without* also describing it as enjoyable; two of these said it was difficult because they were singletons ("there was no one to chat with");
- 4 described it as 'poor' or 'bad', in all cases because they had no one to chat with or because they thought the other workers were bots (automated responses).

Workers familiar with logical reasoning performed better. Intuitively, workers with a background in the subject area tested by the questions should perform better. The survey asked workers whether they had previously learned about the topic on which the tool provides instruction. Among all ML and MLDQ workers (no instruction was provided in the Minimal flow), 318 (44%) were familiar with the topic and 403 (56%) were not. Workers familiar with the topic were 1.4 to 2.7 times more likely to answer the first question correctly on their first try, and 1.5 to 2.8 times more likely to answer the second question correctly (odds ratio 95% confidence intervals, both $p < 0.0001$ with Fisher's exact test).

No evidence discussion helped workers unfamiliar with logical reasoning. Earlier we found no evidence that group interactions improved performance on the initial response to the first question or on the second question. However, many workers reported prior experience and experienced workers have less room to improve; so we repeat these tests considering only inexperienced workers. There is still no evidence of improvement (61% of ML flow singletons vs. 74% of MLDQ grouped workers, $p > 0.1$ with Fisher's exact test, odds ratio 95% confidence interval [0.9, 3.8]).

Better English speakers perform better. Both logical reasoning and informal discussion can be challenging for workers with limited skills with the language being used, and Turk demographics include many non-native speakers. As expected, workers who rated their English "Very Good" or better were 1.7 to 7.4 times more likely to get the first question correct on their first try than those rating their English lower ($p < 0.001$). There were 719 workers who rated their English "Very Good" or better, and they were correct in 58% of responses, whereas the 35 workers who rated their English lower were correct in only 29%.

Discussion ratings

Because discussion quality varies widely from one discussion to another, and this may influence how helpful it is, we sought to investigate how discussion quality affects performance. We asked two raters to manually label each worker according to their participation in each discussion they participated in. A score between 0 and 3 was the computed for each worker-discussion pair based on the following rubric:

- (1 point) Makes at least one substantive statement;
- (1 point) Makes at least two substantive statements;
- (1 point) Reacts in a substantive manner to a comment made by another at least once.

The subset that was rated included a prefix of the Mini-Lesson (ML) flow discussions, plus a random sample of all other discussions. Workers who were rated by only one rater received that rater's score, while workers rated by both raters received the mean of the two scores. Of the 715 rated workers, 211 were rated 2-3 and 504 were rated 0-1.

No evidence that workers with more substantive participation in discussions perform better. We might expect that workers who are more engaged with the discussion will benefit more from it. However, we found no evidence that workers with 2-3 ratings correctly answered the first question on their first try more often than workers with lower ratings (56% vs. 62%, $p > 0.1$, odds ratio 95% confidence interval $[0.6, 1.1]$). There was also no evidence they performed better on the second question (53% vs. 59%, $p > 0.1$, $[0.6, 1.1]$).

No evidence that high-quality discussions lead to better performance. Even a passive worker can benefit if their group's discussion was fruitful. To analyze this possibility, we summed the ratings of all workers in each discussion, and used this 0-9 score as a metric of overall quality of the discussion. We found no evidence that workers who participated in discussions with scores of 5-9 (29 workers) performed better on the first question on their first try than workers with scores of 0-4 (689 workers) (62% vs. 60%, $p > 0.9$, $[0.5, 2.3]$). There was also no evidence that workers in high-quality discussions performed better on the second question (66% vs. 57%, $p > 0.4$, $[0.7, 3.2]$).

Earlier we compared ML singleton workers and ML grouped workers to determine whether the peer discussion on unstated assumptions was useful. No evidence could be found, and one possible explanation is that not enough discussions were substantive enough to be helpful. Revisiting this, but restricting grouped workers to those who engaged in a discussion rated 5 or higher, we again found no evidence that grouped workers performed better on either the initial response to the first question (55% vs. 59%, $p > 0.8$, $[0.3, 2.2]$) or the second question (60% vs. 54%, $p > 0.6$, $[0.5, 3.3]$).

DISCUSSION

Comparing the Two Experiments

In both Experiments E1 and E2, workers in groups obtained better outcomes in terms of number of correct answers when discussing the actual question prompts than those working alone. However, in E2, studying the Mini-Lesson and generating a hidden assumption seemed sufficient to produce better outcomes than simply answering the question (as done in the Minimal condition) without the need for group discussion. Those discussions were not rated as highly as the discussions in E1; it may be that the work of generating the assumptions was just as effective as the group discussion in focusing the students on understanding the critical reasoning problem.

Innovating in Group Formation

Research suggests that, for in-person group problem solving, the interaction dynamics of a group can determine the success of group outcomes, independent of the capabilities of the individual group members[61]. An interesting observation from both E1 in the bonus condition and E2 in the MLDQ condition, is that that participants were more likely to move to the correct answer than to an incorrect answer, even if the majority was at the incorrect answer, so long as at least one person was right. The trend was even stronger when the room began with two workers correct.

We also noticed that when all three workers begin with the same answer, the discussion rarely moves them away from that answer even if it is incorrect. This suggests a need for intervention when the discussion group begins on the wrong track. (Other research has found that intervening in poorly performing discussions may work better than in successful ones [53].)

To address this issue, we can take this experimental platform beyond physical classrooms by "virtually" moving participants around to different discussion groups to group them with peers who have stronger understanding of the material. Students who choose an incorrect answer would be grouped with students who have chosen a correct answer to see if learning gains can be achieved. Alternatively, students who all have chosen the same incorrect answer could be given a hint by the system that their answer is incorrect and a suggestion that this guide the conversation. After the students make their next choice, the conversation room they end up in would be determined by which choice they make next in a tree-like structure. Students would continue to end up in new discussion rooms until they have arrived at the correct choice, perhaps with extensive guidance by the system or a suggestion that learning materials be revisited if they get too near the leaves of the tree.

Applicability of Results to MOOCs

Crowd Worker vs. MOOC Learner Demographics

How do the characteristics and motivations of Turkers compare to those of MOOC learners? The two cohorts are similar in many ways:

Environment: like Turkers, MOOC learners are rarely colocated in space or time and know few of their peers.

Education and Demographics: While many educators and commentators justifiably lament the fact that current MOOCs do not serve a wider audience, today's Turkers are intellectually and demographically comparable to MOOC learners. Comparing an earlier study of self-reported Turker demographics [22] and the descriptive statistics of sixteen MIT and Harvard MOOCs in 2012–2013 [19], 55% of US Turkers and about 75% of Indian Turkers had a bachelors' degree or higher, compared with 66% of MOOCers (averaged across all sixteen courses). The median age is 35–39 for US Turkers, 30–34 for Indian Turkers, and 28 for the MOOCers. On three classic critical-thinking problems, Turkers' performance was found to be statistically the same as that of a group of students recruited from a midwestern US university with respect to task completion rate and effect sizes of factors such as outcome bias, conjunction fallacy, and so on [44].

Positive Reception in a Very Large Hybrid Course

In the summer of 2014, the tool was deployed in an introductory undergraduate engineering course of more than 1000 students that is taught in a flipped-classroom style with an online component. Each week the students watched a video and read the corresponding textbook extract, then practiced with multiple choice questions on their own to gauge their level of achievement. They also participated in a two-hour hands-on workshop where they were able to engage in concept checking. A mandatory summative assessment was conducted at the end of the week; using MOOChat on one of two multiple choice questions was the first of two required tasks.

A/B comparisons were not made, but a cursory look at the chat transcripts suggests that they are similar in quality to those of the E1 crowdworker study. An optional questionnaire was administered after the MOOCChat activity containing the prompt "This activity was:" with a 5 point scale where 1 = Not Enjoyable, 3 = Neutral, and 5 = Enjoyable. 615 students responded at least one time (only first answers are reported when repeats occurred). Of these, 53% of students marked Enjoyable (4 or 5), 33% marked Neutral, and 14% marked Not Enjoyable (1 or 2).

This course differs from a MOOC in that the students were collocated in space and time. Although the large size of the class makes it unlikely that any arbitrary triad of students knows one another, it is much easier to ask a group to collaborate simultaneously than in a globally distributed MOOC, and the expectations of participation an in-person course still differ from MOOCs. Therefore, the high participation and positive reception by students in the this course may not be replicated in a standard MOOC.

Evidence of Positive Reception in a MOOC:

We surveyed sixteen learners in a programming-related MOOC [33] after an early "shake-out" deployment of the system to get subjective responses to the tool. 14 of 16 agreed or strongly agreed with the statement "I liked discussing questions in a small group and would like to do so again". Those in groups of size 2 preferred more people in the discussion, whereas those in groups of size 3 indicated that their group size was good. We therefore have reason to expect a positive reception to our approach in a real MOOC deployment.

Counter-Evidence

While we believe this evidence suggests that crowd workers are suitable stand-ins for MOOC learners for the purposes of testing this approach, there are also important differences for deployment in a real MOOC, including:

Course Context: Unlike crowd workers, MOOC learners would participate in a series of activities covering a set of related topics presented over time in the context of the course's larger narrative, rather than only a single activity. Also, such activities would be just one of several forms of knowledge construction, and the learners would presumably have multiple opportunities to demonstrate retention or transfer of any new learning acquired during the activities.

Motivation to participate: There is a question about how willing students will be to participate in small online group interaction within MOOCs. Although the hundreds of citations in the peer learning literature find that student morale, retention, and learning is increased by this form of person-to-person interaction, we do not know if it will transfer in the less personal, more distributed format of the online chat described here. MOOC students can freely select which course activities they participate in, and their motivations may not match either crowd workers or classroom students. Prior work has found that optional communication channels that expose students' comments to thousands of people such as forums [36, 20] or MOOC-wide chat [6] only attract a fraction of course students. We hypothesize that many students who are not comfortable making posts that are visible to thousands of people will nonetheless be comfortable and even take pleasure in talking in a small group of two or three fellow learners. This would be consistent with advice given to classroom instructors that "Students find it easier to speak to groups of three or four than to an entire class" [11, p. 77].

On the other hand, students in a MOOC do not have to complete all of the work to achieve a passing grade, and so we suspect that adoption will be aided if an instructor makes the use of small-group discussions integral to the running of the course in the same way that peer assessment has been used in some MOOCs [29].

Coordination of group formation: It may be more difficult to coordinate students in MOOCs than in crowd work because of the desire to align every student with a group, as opposed to grouping whichever subset of workers happens to be available at a given time. Instructors will most likely have to encourage students to arrive within pre-stated time periods and it may be necessary to modify MOOC pages to alert students to upcoming group activities.

Implications for Crowd Work

The results here have implications for crowd work. Recall from the related work section that Zhu et al. [62] found that pooling and averaging the results of individual workers improved results on the tasks they studied with the one exception being solving the mathematics problem, where (semi-synchronous) discussion led to better overall results. Thus our results find further evidence that discussion in order to solving problems, as opposed to tasks like brain storming or summarizing, may be a better approach for crowd sourcing.

Zhu et al. also found that reviewing the work of others can improve subsequent task performance. We introduce a different preparatory activity – abstract training and discussion in a mini lesson, which also helped task performance. Future work could directly compare these two approaches.

These results also build on those of Dow et al. [13] which finds that self-assessments in crowd work can lead to better quality results than no feedback; crowd workers in our study who were asked to reflect on their choices in a chat room alone achieved improvements over those who did not do so.

More generally, these results suggest that looking more deeply into the learning literature may yield additional ways to improve crowd sourcing approaches and outcomes.

CONCLUSIONS AND FUTURE WORK

We conducted two sets of experiments to bring peer learning into synchronous group work at scale. The first experiment tested unstructured discussion, compared different size groups, and tested the effects of a bonus condition. This study found evidence that discussing challenging questions in an online chat can lead to participants converging to the correct answer more often than answering the question alone. The study also found that participants were more motivated to get the correct results when an extrinsic reward was offered. These results mirror what has been found in in-person classrooms and suggests that by properly incentivizing students to participate in discussions, peer learning can be successfully introduced into MOOCs. Forming synchronous discussion groups at fixed time intervals is one way to overcome the inherent asynchrony in MOOCs though there may be alternative effective group formation methods.

The second set of experiments tested the effects of adding more structure to the interaction among students, again following the pedagogy of peer instruction, finding that adding progressively more structure and more opportunities for discussion to the learning experience led to better outcomes.

Although we do not claim that participants in this study were learning in the same way that happens in a classroom, we do think these results provides evidence that such an approach may be helpful in a MOOC to improve learning outcomes. Many crowd workers commented about enjoying the task, either in the chatroom or in the freeform section of the questionnaire. A comment made during one discussion was "wish they had these kinds of things when I was in school", and an initial very small pilot with MOOCs positive subjective reactions to the approach. This also reflects classroom findings that many students prefer the social nature of interacting with others while learning, and may bode well for improving retention in MOOCs.

Future work will include deployment in MOOCs and we are actively seeking collaborating instructors. In the coming weeks the system will be used for practice questions for an exam in an online section of an in-person course consisting of more than 1,000 students. The results of this exercise will shed additional light on the applicability of this approach to real courses.

Students individually write down unstated assumptions:	
Student 1	File sharing might be done between different people as well as different devices.
Student 2	This assumes that everyone sharing files must also be purchasing the CDs.
Student 3	That "illegal" file sharing actually helps cd.
Discussion of assumptions begins:	
Student 2	I mean, I think we're all pretty right.
Student 3	I think so too
Student 2	cuz in order to help CD sales, those illegally sharing them would have to be purchasing them to share
Student 2	but I feel like that's not what happens. I feel like one person would share and then that one would keep getting shared
Student 3	And if someone liked what they were hearing they would be open to purchasing the artist
Student 3	if they "careD"
Student 2	right, exactly
Student 2	I feel like in one way it helps broaden appreciation cuz you can get so much of it
Student 1	yeah
Student 2	then again, people at my university would just interlibrary loan CDs and then copy them to their computers.
Student 2	"the cd was bought at one point!"
Student 1	well, I would agree with that
Student 1	but I think most university students are like that
Student 3	i think that happens at every college campus
Student 2	I'm sure it does hahahaa
Student 2	that and stealing from the dining halls
Student 1	*gasp* no
Student 3	Never!
Student 2	"we already pay so much for tuition!"
Student 2	oh, entitlement
Discussion ends; students are shown 5 choices, they individually make a choice and write a justification for their answer:	
Student 1	They don't know for sure that an increase in music CD sales is due to file sharing. It could be due to any number of things (better music choices, different groups of people buying CDs than in the past, easier to purchase CDs now than before - online vs. physical store, etc.).
Student 2	Because it assumes that two things are linked just because they have to do with music, while the people sharing finals and the people who are buying CDs could be completely different people.
Student 3	Some people will never pay what they can get for free
Students 1&2 agree on the answer; Student 3 differs. Discussion of answers begins:	
Student 1	BAM
Student 2	So do we all pick D? and get $1?
Student 3	Thats essentially what it looks like
Student 1	well, we all have to get the same answer
Student 1	to get the bous
Student 2	And it has to be correct
Student 1	assuming that choice D is "correct"
Student 3	I was stuck between B, and D
Student 3	so I can swing both ways, literally
Student 2	I think it's D because it thinks that just relating to music is enough of a connection
Student 2	when the people who buy CDs may not be the ones downloading/sharing
Student 1	same here
Student 1	I think it's D
Student 2	So do we all want to stick with D
Student 3	I shall switch over to D
Student 2	cool
Student 1	aight

Table 2. Example assumptions, justifications and discussion from E2 MLDQ condition.

ACKNOWLEDGEMENTS

We thank Carl Reidsema, Grant Edwards, and Philip Long of the University of Queensland for partnering with us in the hybrid course experiment, Robert Hernandex and Steven Walentino for their work on labeling the chat sessions, and Magoosh Inc for supplying the GMAT practice questions. This material is based upon work supported by a Google Social Interactions Research Award and the National Science Foundation under Grant No. IIS 1149799 and IIS 1210836.

REFERENCES

1. Astin, A. W. *What matters in college? Four critical years revisited.* Jossey-Bass, 1993.
2. Bernstein, M. S., Brandt, J., Miller, R. C., and Karger, D. R. Crowds in two seconds: Enabling realtime crowd-powered interfaces. In *Proceedings of UIST*, ACM (New York, NY, USA, 2011), 33–42.
3. Bonwell, C. C., and Eison, J. A. *Active learning: Creating excitement in the classroom.* School of Education and Human Development, George Washington University Washington, DC, 1991.
4. Chase, J., and Okie, E. G. Combining cooperative learning and peer instruction in introductory computer science. *ACM SIGCSE Bulletin 32*, 1 (2000), 372–376.
5. Chen, W., and Looi, C.-K. Active classroom participation in a group scribbles primary science classroom. *British Journal of Educational Technology 42*, 4 (2011), 676–686.
6. Coetzee, D., Fox, A., Hearst, M. A., and Hartmann, B. Should your MOOC Forum Use a Reputation System? In *CSCW'2014* (2014).
7. Cooper, S., and Sahami, M. Reflections on Stanford's MOOCs. *Commun. ACM 56*, 2 (Feb. 2013), 28–30.
8. Corbett, A. T., and Anderson, J. R. Knowledge tracing: Modeling the acquisition of procedural knowledge. *User Modeling and User-Adapted Interaction 4*, 4 (1994), 253–278.
9. Cottell, P. Cooperative Learning in Accounting, Chapter 2. In *Cooperative Learning in Higher Education: Across the Disciplines, Across the Academy.* Stylus Publishing, LLC., 2012.
10. Crouch, C. H., and Mazur, E. Peer instruction: Ten years of experience and results. *American Journal of Physics 69*, 9 (2001), 970–977.
11. Davis, B. G. *Tools for Teaching.* Jossey-Bass, 1993.
12. Deslauriers, L., Schelew, E., and Wieman, C. Improved learning in a large-enrollment physics class. *Science 332*, 6031 (2011), 862–864.
13. Dow, S., Kulkarni, A., Klemmer, S., and Hartmann, B. Shepherding the crowd yields better work. In *Proceedings of the ACM 2012 conference on Computer Supported Cooperative Work*, ACM (2012), 1013–1022.
14. Fischer, F., Bruhn, J., Grsel, C., and Mandl, H. Fostering collaborative knowledge construction with visualization tools. *Learning and Instruction 12*, 2 (2002), 213 – 232.
15. Glass, A. L., and Sinha, N. Multiple-choice questioning is an efficient instructional methodology that may be widely implemented in academic courses to improve

exam performance. *Current Directions in Psychological Science 22* (2013), 471.

16. Gweon, G., Rosé, C. P., Carey, R., and Zaiss, Z. S. Providing support for adaptive scripting in an on-line collaborative learning environment. In *CHI 2006* (2006).
17. Hake, R. R. Interactive-engagement versus traditional methods: A six-thousand-student survey of mechanics test data for introductory physics courses. *American Journal of Physics 66* (1998), 64.
18. Haller, E. P., Child, D. A., and Walberg, H. J. Can comprehension be taught? a quantitative synthesis of metacognitive studies. *Educational researcher 17*, 9 (1988), 5–8.
19. Ho, A. D., Reich, J., Nesterko, S. O., Seaton, D. T., Mullaney, T., Waldo, J., and Chuang, I. HarvardX and MITx: The first year of open online courses, fall 2012-summer 2013. Tech. rep., Massachusetts Institute of Technology and Harvard University, Cambridge, MA, Jan 2014.
20. Huang, J., Dasgupta, A., Ghosh, A., Manning, J., and Sanders, M. Superposter behavior in mooc forums. In *Proceedings of the first ACM conference on Learning@ scale conference*, ACM (2014), 117–126.
21. III, H. L. R., and Karpicke, J. D. Test-enhanced learning: Taking memory tests improves long-term retention. *Psychological Science 17*, 3 (2006).
22. Ipeirotis, P. G. Demographics of mechanical turk. Tech. rep., New York University Stern School of Business, mar 2010.
23. Isenberg, D. J. Group polarization: A critical review and meta-analysis. *Journal of Personality and Social Psychology 50*, 6 (1986), 1141.
24. James, M. C., and Willoughby, S. Listening to student conversations during clicker questions: What you have not heard might suprise you! *American Journal of Physics 79*, 1 (Jan 2011), 123–132.
25. Johnson, D. W., Johnson, R. T., and Smith, K. A. *Active learning: Cooperation in the college classroom.* Interaction Book Company Edina, MN, 1991.
26. King, A. Improving lecture comprehension: Effects of a metacognitive strategy. *Applied Cognitive Psychology 5*, 4 (1991), 331–346.
27. King, A. Structuring peer interaction to promote high-level cognitive processing. *Theory into practice 41*, 1 (2002), 33–39.
28. Kittur, A., Chi, E. H., and Suh, B. Crowdsourcing user studies with mechanical turk. In *CHI'08* (2008), 453–456.
29. Kulkarni, C., Wei, K. P., Le, U., Chia, D., Papadopoulos, K., Cheng, J., Koller, D., and Klemmer, S. Peer and self assessment in massive online classes. *ACM Transactions of Computer-Human Interaction (TOCHI) 20*, 6 (2013).
30. Lasecki, W. S., Song, Y. C., Kautz, H., and Bigham, J. P. Real-time crowd labeling for deployable activity recognition. In *Proceedings of CSCW*, ACM (New York, NY, USA, 2013), 1203–1212.
31. Laughlin, P. R., and McGlynn, R. P. Collective induction: Mutual group and individual influence by exchange of hypotheses and evidence. *Journal of Experimental Social Psychology 22*, 6 (1986), 567–589.
32. Lieberman, M. D. Learning from others. *The Chronicle of Higher Education* (April 2014), B4–B5.
33. Lim, S., Coetzee, D., Hartmann, B., Fox, A., and Hearst, M. A. Initial experiences with small group discussions in moocs. In *Proceedings of the first ACM conference on Learning@ scale conference*, ACM (2014), 151–152.
34. Lord, T. R. 101 reasons for using cooperative learning in biology teaching. *The American Biology Teacher 63*, 1 (2001), 30–38.
35. Magee, R. M., Mascaro, C. M., and Stahl, G. Designing for group math discourse. In *2013 Conference on Computer Supported Collaborative Learning (CSCL 2013)* (2013).
36. Mak, S., Williams, R., and Mackness, J. Blogs and forums as communication and learning tools in a MOOC. In *International Conference on Networked Learning 2010* (2010), 275–285.
37. Martin, F. G. Will massive open online courses change how we teach? *Commun. ACM 55*, 8 (Aug. 2012), 26–28.
38. Martin, F. G. Will MOOCs change how we teach? *CACM 55*, 8 (aug 2012).
39. Mazur, E. *Peer Instruction: A User's Manual.* Prentice-Hall, Upper Saddle River, NJ, 1991.
40. Millis, B. *Cooperative Learning in Higher Education: Across the Disciplines, Across the Academy.* Stylus Publishing, LLC., 2012.
41. Millis, B. J., and Cottell, P. G. *Cooperative learning for higher education faculty.* Oryx Press (Phoenix, Ariz.), 1998.
42. Mullen, B., Johnson, C., and Salas, E. Productivity loss in brainstorming groups: A meta-analytic integration. *Basic and applied social psychology 12*, 1 (1991), 3–23.
43. Palinscar, A. S., and Herrenkohl, L. R. Designing collaborative contexts: Lessons from three research programs. In *Cognitive perspectives on peer learning.* Lawrence Erlbaum Associates Publishers, 1999.
44. Paolacci, G., Chandler, J., and Ipeirotis, P. G. Running experiments on amazon mechanical turk. *Judgment and Decision making 5*, 5 (2010), 411–419.

45. Robinson, P., and Cooper, J. L. The Interactive Lecture in a Research Methods and Statistics Class, Chapter 7. In *Cooperative Learning in Higher Education: Across the Disciplines, Across the Academy*. Stylus Publishing, LLC., 2012.

46. Ruhl, K. L., Hughes, C. A., and Schloss, P. J. Using the pause procedure to enhance lecture recall. *Teacher Education and Special Education: The Journal of the Teacher Education Division of the Council for Exceptional Children 10*, 1 (1987), 14–18.

47. Sadler, P. M., and Good, E. The impact of self-and peer-grading on student learning. *Educational assessment 11*, 1 (2006), 1–31.

48. Setlock, L. D., Fussell, S. R., and Neuwirth, C. Taking it out of context: collaborating within and across cultures in face-to-face settings and via instant messaging. In *Proceedings of the 2004 ACM conference on Computer supported cooperative work*, ACM (2004), 604–613.

49. Smith, K. A., Matusovich, H., Meyers, K., and Mann, L. Preparing the Next Generation of Engineering Educators and Researchers, Chapter 6. In *Cooperative Learning in Higher Education: Across the Disciplines, Across the Academy*. Stylus Publishing, LLC., 2012.

50. Smith, M. K., Wood, W. B., Adams, W. K., Wieman, C., Knight, J. K., Guild, N., and Su, T. T. Why peer discussion improves student performance on in-class concept questions. *Science 323*, 5910 (2009), 122–124.

51. Springer, L., Stanne, M. E., and Donovan, S. S. Effects of small-group learning on undergraduates in science, mathematics, engineering, and technology: A meta-analysis. *Review of Educational Research 69*, 1 (1999), 21–51.

52. Strijbos, J.-W., and Stahl, G. *Analyzing Interactions in CSCL: Methods, Approaches and Issues (Computer-Supported Collaborative Learning Series)*. Springer, 2010, ch. How to Study Group Cognition.

53. Tausczik, Y. R., and Pennebaker, J. W. Improving teamwork using real-time language feedback. In *Proceedings of the SIGCHI Conference on Human Factors in Computing Systems*, ACM (2013), 459–468.

54. Trausan-Matu, S., Dascalu, M., and Rebedea, T. PolyCAFe: Automatic support for the polyphonic analysis of CSCL chats. *International Journal of Computer Supported Collaborative Work (ijCSCL) 9*, 2 (2014).

55. Trytten, D. A. Progressing from small group work to cooperative learning: A case study from computer science*. *Journal of Engineering Education 90*, 1 (2001), 85–91.

56. Walther, J. B. Interpersonal effects in computer-mediated interaction a relational perspective. *Communication Research 19*, 1 (1992), 52–90.

57. Walther, J. B., Loh, T., and Granka, L. Let me count the ways: The interchange of verbal and nonverbal cues in computer-mediated and face-to-face affinity. *Journal of Language and Social Psychology 24*, 1 (2005), 36–65.

58. Wang, H.-C., Fussell, S. F., and Setlock, L. D. Cultural difference and adaptation of communication styles in computer-mediated group brainstorming. In *CHI'09* (2009), 669–678.

59. Webb, N. M., and Farivar, S. Developing productive group interaction in middle school mathematics. In *Cognitive perspectives on peer learning*. Lawrence Erlbaum Associates Publishers, 1999.

60. Wilkowski, J., Russell, D. M., and Deutsch, A. Self-evaluation in advanced power searching and mapping with google moocs. *ACM Learning At Scale, L@ S 2014* (2014), 04–05.

61. Woolley, A. W., Chabris, C. F., Pentland, A., Hashmi, N., and Malone, T. W. Evidence for a collective intelligence factor in the performance of human groups. *science 330*, 6004 (2010), 686–688.

62. Zhu, H., Dow, S. P., Kraut, R. E., and Kittur, A. Reviewing versus doing: Learning and performance in crowd assessment. In *CSCW'2014*, ACM (2014).

The Editor's Eye: Curation and Comment Relevance on the New York Times

Nicholas Diakopoulos
University of Maryland, College of Journalism
nad@umd.edu

ABSTRACT
The journalistic curation of social media content from platforms like Facebook and YouTube or from commenting systems is underscored by an imperative for publishing accurate and quality content. This work explores the manifestation of editorial quality criteria in comments that have been curated and selected on the New York Times website as "NYT Picks." The relationship between comment selection and comment relevance is examined through the analysis of 331,785 comments, including 12,542 editor's selections. A robust association between editorial selection and article relevance or conversational relevance was found. The results are discussed in terms of their implications for reducing journalistic curatorial work load, or scaling the ability to examine more comments for editorial selection, as well as how end-user commenting experiences might be improved.

Author Keywords
News comments; comment curation; computational journalism

ACM Classification Keywords
H.5.3 [Group and Organization Interfaces]: Computer-supported cooperative work.

General Terms
Human Factors; Design

INTRODUCTION
In a sense journalism has always incorporated an aspect of curation: selecting, organizing, and presenting information according to newsworthiness, public interest, or other editorial criteria. More recently, with the launch of services like Facebook Newswire[1], and tools like Storify, the curatorial role of journalists has expanded into the realm of social media, including everything from selecting and verifying user-generated content, to managing and moderating communities and comments on news sites [2].

A strong normative goal of providing accurate and verified information to the public underscores the curation of social media by journalists as a way to promote information quality [4,10], a desire not unlike that expressed in scientific curation communities as well [15]. Fears of comment quality in online news comment discourse [1,5] suggest a desire to improve the quality of the experience for end users both to create a safe space for civic dialogue as well as to create loyalty, host a forum for feedback and tips on news, and increase time on site for news customers [8]. Curating content is important for online communities because it helps set the tone for a site and may in turn improve the quality of subsequent comments on a site [16]. Likewise, unchecked comments that are rife with incivility expose the potential for polarizing risk perceptions [1,11]. By curating comments, journalists model and signal normative commenting behavior, thus making it more salient and visible to others in the community [9], and providing a reward for good behavior through the increased exposure and prominence of a selected comment.

In this paper, I examine the nature of comment curation on the New York Times, in particular as it relates to factors that may enable increased scale for the identification of what are termed "NYT Picks", editor's selections of the "most interesting and thoughtful" comments. While there has been some recent work on computational methods to help moderate and filter out uncivil or profane comments [14], here I instead focus on the other end of the quality spectrum: how to identify *high quality* comments that would be more likely to be selected by an editor. In comparison to related work that has examined different social voting methods for surfacing high quality contributions [18], in this work I focus on using intrinsic features of the content itself to signal quality. Could new computational tools be used to reduce the amount of time journalists need to spend doing this curatorial work, to identify worthy but overlooked contributions, or to scale their ability to consider more content?

Editorial standards for what gets filtered out, or even what constitutes a valid contribution that might be elevated and emphasized often revolve around the relevance of the comment [19]. Off topic or predictable comments have been shown to negatively affect perceptions of quality in online news comments [5].

CSCW '15, March 14 – 18, 2015, Vancouver, BC, Canada

ACM 978-1-4503-2922-4/15/03□$15.00
http://dx.doi.org/10.1145/2675133.2675160

Figure 1. The NYT commenting system, showing the NYT Picks filter and badge.

Other research has found that relevance correlates to "helpfulness" in Amazon product reviews [13], and social votes on Digg [7] and Slashdot [17]. This paper contributes a deeper look at relevance as a correlate to quality and editorial selection, including both a comment's relevance to a news article and its relevance to the broader conversation taking place in the comment thread. The findings are discussed in terms of implications for the optimization and scaling of editorial curation work in the domain of news comments.

STUDY OF NEWS COMMENTING

Platform of Study

Unlike many other online news sites, the New York Times pre-moderates all comments posted on nytimes.com, ensuring a generally high level of discourse that is largely free from obscenity, personal attacks, or other spam. Their policy states that, "most comments will be posted if they are on-topic and not abusive" [19]. The New York Times also has a feature called NYT Picks which represent a professional editorial selection of "comments that represent a range of views and are judged the most interesting and thoughtful." Like many other commenting systems users can vote up a comment by recommending it. Comments are sorted by the newest first by default, but can also be sorted by oldest first, or filtered according to "Readers' Picks" (i.e. high recommendation scores) or by the "NYT Picks". Figure 1 shows the filter interface and the additional attention-getting badge that NYT Picks receive on the site.

Data Collection

Both comment and article full text data were collected and analyzed for the New York Times website (nytimes.com). The Times' Community API[2] was first used to collect comments posted between 1/15/2014 and 4/15/2014. Data collection included full text of all comments as well as relevant metadata such whether it was an editor's selection, the recommended score, and what article the comment was directed at. The NewsCred API[3] was then used to collect full text for article content since this data was not available from the Times API directly. Within the time period, 2,815 articles had full text via the NewsCred API. In the end, 331,785 comments were collected which were directed at one of these 2,815 articles within the collection period. On average there were 118 comments per article (SD=202, Median=32) and a total of 12,542 comments that were an editor's selection.

Data Processing

Full text for the comments and articles was tokenized, normalized, stop-word filtered, and stemmed. Unigrams that occurred 10 or more times across all comments constituted a vocabulary of 22,837 terms that was then used to define a feature vector to describe each comment and article. The reason for limiting the vocabulary was to reduce the influence of spurious and infrequent terms and so to make the feature vectors more robust. Each dimension of the feature vector was then calculated as the term-frequency inverse document frequency (tf-idf) for the term, where each comment was considered a document and term frequencies reflect the stemmed version of tokens. These vectors were then normalized to unit length so that they could be used directly in cosine similarity calculations.

For each comment in the dataset two metrics of relevance were computed: (1) *article relevance*, and (2) *conversational relevance*. Article relevance was computed by taking the cosine similarity score or dot product of the respective normalized feature vectors for a comment and the article to which it is attached. The higher the cosine similarity score, the more similar the comment is to the article. The notion of conversational relevance measures how similar a comment is to other comments on the same article. Only those articles with 10 or more comments were considered in order to ensure that there was enough of a discussion to produce robust feature vectors. To measure conversational relevance, for each article's comments a centroid feature vector was created representing the text of all of the comments on the article that were posted before a given comment. This represents the terms used across the thread up to that point in time. Then, for each comment in the thread its cosine similarity to this centroid representation was calculated in order to measure the comment's conversational relevance.

Results and Analysis

The results presented here address the overriding question of whether the measures of relevance described above could help editors in the process of curating comments. Do simple measures of article or conversational relevance correlate to editor's selections? And can comments be re-ranked to make the curation process more efficient and scalable?

Let us first consider how article relevance relates to whether a comment is selected by an editor or not. The average comment to article similarity for comments selected by editors is 0.183 (SD=0.113), whereas for comments not selected by editors it is 0.125 (SD = 0.106). A t-test between the distributions is highly significant (t = 59.2, p = 0), indicating that those comments that editors do

[2] http://developer.nytimes.com/
[3] http://newscred.com/developer/docs

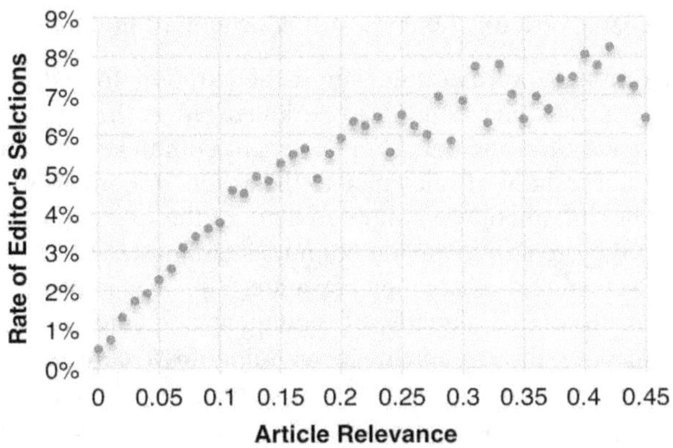

Figure 2. Article relevance score binned in 0.01 increments versus rate of editor's selections for that bin.

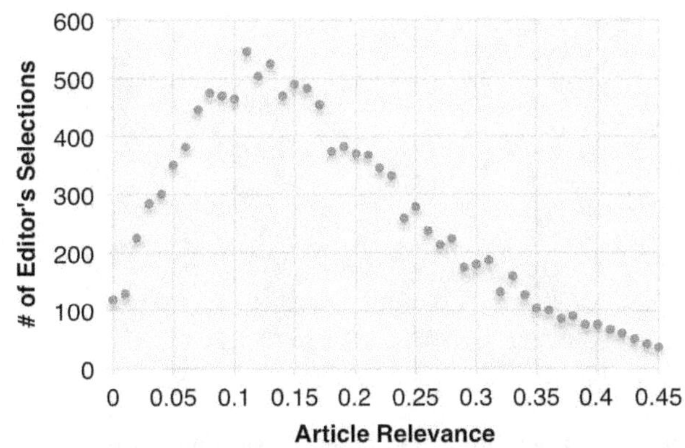

Figure 3. Article relevance score binned in 0.01 increments versus number of editor's selections in that bin.

select tend to be much more on-topic or similar and relevant to the article to which they refer.

The article relevance of the comment is positively associated with a higher chance of it being selected by an editor. Figure 2 shows that increasing levels of article relevance are correlated to higher rates of selection by editors (Pearson $r = 0.92$, $p < 0.001$). A comment with a 0.05 article relevance score has approximately a 2% chance of being selected whereas a comment with a 0.40 article relevance score has closer to an 8% chance.

Figure 3 shows a peak in the volume of editor's selections around an article relevance of about 0.125. Far fewer comments are selected with scores below 0.02. But at the same time, the total volume of comments with low article relevance is very high. Whereas only 1.98% of editor's selections have an article relevance less than 0.02, this represents 12.9% of all comments in the dataset. This suggests a clear opportunity for optimizing professional curator's time: by filtering away comments with extremely low article relevance (i.e. < 0.02) more than one eighth of the comments would not need to be read, in exchange for missing only about 2% of comments that would have been deemed worthy.

Professional editor selections also correspond to the notion of conversational relevance that was computed. The average conversational relevance for comments selected by editors is 0.315 (SD=0.130), whereas for comments not selected by editors it is 0.225 (SD = 0.133). A t-test between the distributions is highly significant ($t = 72.1$, $p = 0$), indicating that those comments that editors do select tend to be much more on-topic and relevant to the other comments in the thread. As with article relevance, there is a very strong correlation between the conversational relevance and the rate of editor's selections (Pearson $r = 0.99$, $p < 0.001$).

Previous research has found a strong correlation between when a comment was posted and how many social recommendations it receives [7], or how much moderation attention it receives [12]. A similar result was found here for editor's selections. Time was measured here as the elapsed time of a comment since the first comment on an article. This was necessary since sometimes article timestamps are updated to reflect edits and measuring time with respect to the article publication time was too noisy. There was a slight negative correlation between elapsed time and whether the comment was an editor's selection (Spearman $rho = -0.048$, $p = 0$). Thus, there are less editor's selections later in the conversation. Also there was an overall negative correlation between elapsed time and article relevance (Spearman $rho = -0.035$, $p = 0$) indicating that comments later in the conversation tend to become less relevant.

Figure 4 shows more detail on the temporal relationship between elapsed time and article relevance within the first 48 hours, when 96.1% of comments are made. Comments made in the first hour have a distinctly higher article relevance than in the immediately subsequent hours. But after about 18 hours the average article relevance begins increasing again up to hour 48 (Spearman $rho = 0.012$, $p =$

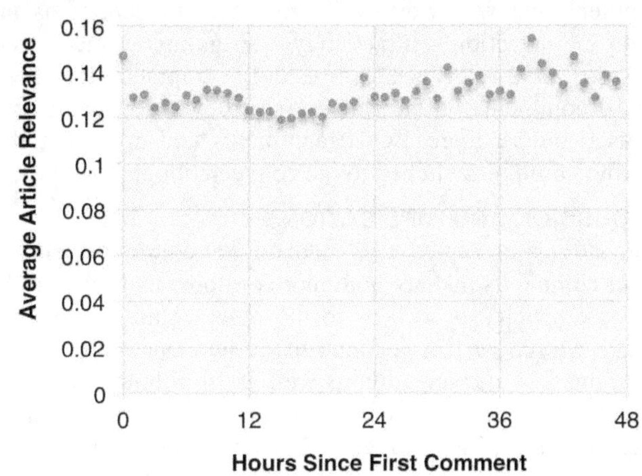

Figure 4. Average article relevance versus time binned into 1 hour increments up to 48 hours.

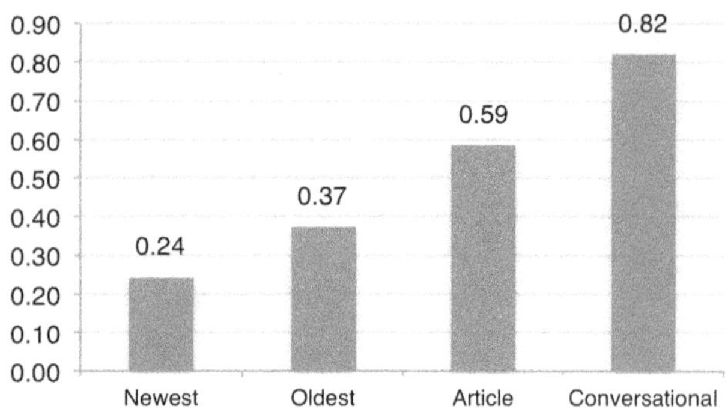

Figure 5. Average number of editor's selections in the top 10 comments when ranked by newest, oldest, article relevance, or conversational relevance.

0). However 83.5% of editors selections are for comments made in hours 2 to 18, and only 7.7% are for comments made in hours 18 to 48. So despite an overall lower likelihood for comment relevance as time progresses in the long tail, these results suggest there are interesting patterns within the first hours and days of an article. Editors might fruitfully direct attention to comments made during the first hour, or between hours 18 and 48 in order to find more relevant comments that may be worthy of editorial selection.

Finally, let us consider here how re-ranking comments by article or conversational relevance compares to the default ranking options of "newest" and "oldest" as this will help assess how other forms of ranking may boost the ability of a curator to find worthy contributions. To measure this the average number of editor's selections in the Top 10 comments was computed for rankings according to these various measures. These results are shown in Figure 5 and indicate that sorting by the newest comments surfaces the fewest editor's selections but that sorting by article relevance or conversational relevance can considerably increase the chances that a curator would quickly see a comment that was worthwhile for them to choose as an editor's selection. Practically speaking, since the conversational relevance score is only computed after there are 10 comments on an article, the article relevance could be used before there are 10 comments and after that the ranking could be switched to the conversational relevance.

DISCUSSION AND IMPLICATIONS

The findings presented here indicate that editors do tend to select comments that are both more on-topic and relevant to the base article, as well as to the other comments on the thread. Moreover it was found that comments made in the first hour in a conversation as well as from hours 18 to 48 of conversation tend to be more relevant. The results suggest that re-ranking comments by article or conversational relevance would allow editors to optimize their time in assessing comments for selection, while possibly surfacing comments in the discussion that might have been overlooked but are still deserving of highlight.

In addition to accelerating comment curation for editors, comment relevance could also be leveraged in the end-user experience of comments. For instance, comments that fall below a threshold of relevance to the article or conversation could be defaulted to a collapsed state in the user interface, so that they're still available but not as emphasized in terms of the screen real-estate they consume. This metric could be applied to entire threads of comments: if the average relevance of the comments responding to a comment is below some threshold then the whole thread could be rolled-up and condensed. Moreover, relevance scores could also be used as real-time feedback to comment authors as they are articulating their ideas as a way to signal to them if they are veering too far away from the conversation.

The goal in the above would be to guide attention and emphasis by applying the editorial criteria of relevance to comments in the interface automatically. Yet we must also consider the limitations of such an automated approach, such as the possible censorship (or at least de-emphasis) of comments that may in fact be related but not detected by the algorithm as relevant due to differences in language use. Future work should also qualitatively examine low-relevance comments including the few there *were* selected by editors in order to better understand what might be lost if such comments were automatically de-emphasized, as well as what other ranking criteria might enable editors to filter for these still-interesting yet "irrelevant" (by the metric) comments.

A further limitation of the current study is that the data available from the NYT API only reflects those comments that were approved for the site. Thus we're not able to reason about editor's judgments amongst comments that were never posted. Future work should extend the current analysis of relevance to other commenting platforms, including those that do not use pre-moderation and which might contain more incivility.

Recent research has also shown how the editorial selections of "network gatekeepers" can diverge in interesting ways from professionals [3,6], suggesting that future work in this domain also examine the differences in editor's selections from "Readers' Picks" in news comments. Understanding where professional editorial criteria diverge or are the same as those of social recommendations could enable the design of commenting systems that better take advantage of both and lead to insights that help integrate professional and user-driven curation activities [15].

REFERENCES

1. Anderson, A.A., Brossard, D., Scheufele, D.A., Xenos, M.A., and Ladwig, P. The "Nasty Effect:" Online Incivility and Risk Perceptions of Emerging Technologies. *Journal of Computer-Mediated Communication 19*, 3 (2014).

2. Bakker, P. Mr. Gates Returns: Curation, community management and other new roles for journalists. *Journalism Studies*, (2014).
3. Boczkowski, P.J. and Mitchelstein, E. *The news gap: When the information preferences of the media and the public diverge*. MIT Press, 2013.
4. Diakopoulos, N., De Choudhury, M., and Naaman, M. Finding and Assessing Social Media Information Sources in the Context of Journalism. Proc. *Conference on Human Factors in Computing Systems (CHI)*, (2012).
5. Diakopoulos, N. and Naaman, M. Toward Quality Discourse in Online News Comments. *Proc Computer Supported Cooperative Work (CSCW)*, (2011).
6. Diakopoulos, N. and Zubiaga, A. Newsworthiness and Network Gatekeeping on Twitter: The Role of Social Deviance. *International Conference on Weblogs and Social Media (ICWSM)*, (2014).
7. Hsu, C.-F., Khabiri, E., and Caverlee, J. Ranking Comments on the Social Web. *Proc. International Conference on Computational Science and Engineering*, (2009).
8. Jomini Stroud, N., Muddiman, A., Scacco, J., and Curry, A. *Journalist Involvement in comment sections*. 2013.
9. Kiesler, S., Kraut, R.E., Resnick, P., and Kittur, A. Regulating Behavior in Online Communities. In *Building Successful Online Communities*. MIT Press, 2012.
10. Kovach, B. and Rosenstiel, T. *The Elements of Journalism: What Newspeople Should Know and the Public Should Expect*. Three Rivers Press, 2007.
11. LaBarre, S. Why We're Shutting Off Our Comments. *Popular Science*, 2013. http://www.popsci.com/science/article/2013-09/why-were-shutting-our-comments.
12. Lampe, C. and Resnick, P. Slash(dot) and burn: distributed moderation in a large online conversation space. *Proc. Conference on Human Factors in Computing Systems (CHI)*, (2004).
13. Otterbacher, J. Helpfulness in online communities: a measure of message quality. *Proc. Conference on Human Factors in Computing Systems (CHI)*, (2009).
14. Owseley Sood, S., Churchill, E.F., and Antin, J. Automatic Identification of personal insults on social news sites. *Journal of the American Society for Information Science and Technology (JASIST) 63*, 2 (2012).
15. Rotman, D., Procita, K., Hansen, D., Sims Parr, C., and Preece, J. Supporting Content Curation Communities: The Case of the Encyclopedia of Life. *JASIST 63*, 6 (2012), 1092–1107.
16. Sukumaran, A. and Vezich, S. Normative Influences on Thoughtful Online Participation. *Proc. Conference on Human Factors in Computing Systems (CHI)*, (2011).
17. Wanas, N., El-Saban, M., Ashour, H., and Ammar, W. Automatic Scoring of Online Discussion Posts. *Proc WICOW*, (2008).
18. Xu, A. and Bailey, B.P. A Reference-Based Scoring Model for Increasing the Findability of Promising Ideas in Innovation Pipelines. *Proc. Conference on Computer Supported Cooperative Work (CSCW)*, (2012).
19. Help: Comments & Readers' Reviews. http://www.nytimes.com/content/help/site/usercontent/usercontent.html.

Navigating Imagined Audiences: Motivations for Participating in the Online Public Sphere

Bryan Semaan[1], Heather Faucett[2], Scott Robertson[3], Misa Maruyama[4], Sara Douglas[4]

[1]School of Information Studies
Syracuse University
Syracuse, NY, 13244
bsemaan@syr.edu

[2]Department of Informatics
University of California, Irvine
Irvine, CA, 92697
hfaucett@uci.edu

[3]Information and Computer Sciences Department
[4]Communication and Information Sciences Program
University of Hawai'i at Mānoa
{scott.robertson, misattm, sarad}@hawaii.edu

ABSTRACT
Little is known about *why* and *how* people use multiple social media platforms for political participation, or about the contexts through which social media is appropriated. This paper reports on a qualitative interview study of social media use by politically interested citizens. We interviewed 27 residents of the state of Hawaii who integrated one or more social media tools into their daily lives to participate in the online public sphere. Different social media environments offer both different affordances for action and different audiences, and we describe how media choice is driven by the match between motivations and affordances, and also by the imagined audience. We identified a number of motivations including understanding different viewpoints, formulating perspectives, engaging in positive discourse, repairing Hawaii's image, increasing political awareness and improving civic engagement. We discuss how these goals relate to both intrinsic and extrinsic motivations. Finally, we examine how social media choice and satisfaction were tied to the physical world context and people's sense of the audience within any particular medium.

Author Keywords
Public sphere, social media, audience, motivations, context

ACM Classification Keywords
K.4.3 [Computers and Society]: Organizational Impacts – Computer-Supported cooperative work.

General Terms
Human Factors.

INTRODUCTION
The evolution of the Internet into a collaborative and social medium ("Web 2.0") resulted from people's contributions of words, images, and video. As a result, an important and often asked research question is: What motivates people to contribute online? The individualized motivations of active contributors have been studied across a range of domains in a diverse set of media like Wikipedia and Facebook [e.g. 17, 27].

In the context of online political activities, certain communicative acts invite the formation of an ad-hoc public sphere—an online space where people are free to exchange political ideas and information [6, 10]. Users of social media tools like Facebook and Twitter often participate by disseminating information and opinions, or engaging in lively political discussions on a variety of topics, and the audiences present within each public sphere can vary greatly. People may be using social media to satisfy their own needs and, conversely, they may also be using media to satisfy the perceived needs of others.

Recent work has focused on whether or not online public spheres that are devoted to politics or are non-political in nature are diverse or polarized [e.g. 1, 2, 7, 8, 21, 25, 26, 30, 41]; the extent to which people are willing to expose themselves to viewpoints to which they do not agree [e.g. 25, 33]; and the degree to which sentiment patterns uncovered through the analysis of "big data", e.g. Twitter feeds, can predict potential political outcomes [e.g. 34] or determine the political attitudes of users [e.g. 21]. However, little is known about what motivates people's online political contribution behavior, especially across social media technologies.

Whereas most scholarship has focused on a single online public sphere at a time, people have access to, and can use, multiple online media that all have unique characteristics and audiences. We propose that the motivations for interacting in the public sphere, and the technological choices people make, are a reflection of the audiences present across various social media tools, as people attempt to satisfy their participatory needs, namely: the acquisition of information, the dissemination of information, discourse, and civic action.

In this paper we examine closely several individuals living in the state of Hawaii who use multiple social media tools to address audiences for varying purposes.

CSCW '15, March 14 – 18, 2015, Vancouver, BC, Canada.

http://dx.doi.org/10.1145/2675133.2675187

PARTICIPATION IN THE PUBLIC SPHERE

The notion of the "public sphere" derives from Habermas [10]. Habermas conceptualized the public sphere as a mediating space between the state and the civil society, as a democratic space where public interests, opinions, agendas and problems are formed, transformed, and exchanged by citizens' proactive participation. Critical rationality, equality, freedom of expression, reflexivity and dissemination are the necessary conditions for the proper structuring and sustainable functioning of a Habermasean public sphere.

Dahlgren [6], building on Habermas' vision, identified two forms of participation that emerge in a functioning public sphere. The first form of participation deals with how information is communicated from the media to citizens, and between citizens. Citizens not only consume information, but they also actively disseminate information and opinions to other citizens and cue calls to action. The second form of participation deals with the discursive aspect of the public sphere—the discussions that emerge between citizens.

The public sphere is integral to a functioning democracy as it facilitates the consumption of political information and opinions from diverse perspectives, the dissemination of information and opinions from diverse viewpoints, and rational discourse with people who hold varying beliefs. A variety of public spheres are available, and some might be more conducive to political learning and discussion.

MOTIVATIONS FOR PARTICIPATION IN THE ONLINE PUBLIC SPHERE

Naturally, the concept of public sphere has become prominent in the context of the Internet [1, 2, 6]. Social media, e.g. Social Networking Sites (SNSs) like Facebook and Twitter, can be viewed as a new type of public sphere [e.g. 3, 6, 7]. For example, Pew has found that today, more and more people are using the Internet to engage in a variety of political activities [30].

The affordances of social media tools support the participatory functions of the public sphere as people can connect with globally dispersed audiences in order to seek and share information and opinions, and engage in political discourse. However, it is not clear that social media are actually achieving the ideal of the public sphere [1, 29, 41]. One reason is the failure of many Internet tools to encourage exposure of individuals to a plurality of viewpoints, even as they support the expression of these viewpoints [1, 2]. Research in this area has been divided as some have found the emerging interactions to be diverse [11, 21, 26, 33, 39, 40], whereas others have found that such online spaces are leading to polarization, as users are only exchanging information and ideas with people who share the same political perspectives [1, 7, 8, 41].

Papacharissi [28] introduces a new way of thinking about the public sphere within the context of social media. Specifically, she suggests that various tools are hybrid environments that are private but also have public features. She defines the "private sphere" as an online space that provides people with the autonomy that is most associated with physical private spaces, but with the potential audience of a public act. For example, though blogging is often done as a "narcissistic" act of self- expression [28], it may still contribute to public discourse as an audience is present who may be exposed to the material being presented. The unique "hybridity" of digital media allows for different types of expression in different spaces. The proliferation of social media has thus enabled people to interact with multiple audiences in multiple expressive manners [28]—in a more private and personal manner as well as in a more public and impersonal manner. This leads to the question of how people determine which audience(s) to interact with and, importantly, what the underlying motivation is for the communicative act.

Recent work has investigated motivations for participation in online communities [e.g. 12, 17, 22, 31]. These studies have identified various motivations for participation, e.g. reputation building and entertainment. For example, Joinson [12] developed use categories for Facebook based on various affordances, finding that the different users surveyed ranked needs differently. Rafaeli et al. [31] found that contributors to Wikipedia were motivated by their need to get information, share information, and for entertainment. Building on these findings in their study of participation practices in online content generation communities, Lampe and colleagues [17] found that individual motivations to participate were based on their ability to obtain information, provide information, build reputation, develop relationships, seek entertainment and for self-discovery [17]. Importantly, they discovered that people's motivations for participation are often directed to individual users or a community at large.

Another important line of research distinguishes between intrinsic and extrinsic motivations [32]. Intrinsic motivation refers to desires to act based on intrinsic satisfaction (personal self-concept) without any external reward, for example the joy of learning something new, the increased sense of competence from seeking and assimilating information, the enhanced feeling of belongingness from joining a group or doing something with social consequence, etc. Extrinsic motivations refer to actions that are performed to achieve an outcome that has no direct intrinsic value or even goes against one's values. This includes most instrumental behaviors that are performed either to avoid something bad (losing a job) or gain something that may be perceived by others as good (get a promotion).

Researchers have since applied this framework to the study of social media [e.g. 43]. On the one hand, intrinsic motivations related to the use of social media technologies, such as Facebook, include maintaining relationships [16] and feelings of belonging [17]. On the other hand, extrinsic motivations include, for example, certain features such as Facebook's birthday reminders, which motivate people to interact on Facebook [43].

These findings suggest that people's motivations for participation can vary depending on the type of community [22]. Moore and Serva [22] describe how in open source communities contributors are often motivated by both intrinsic motivations (their desire to increase their programming skills) and extrinsic motivations (their desire to improve their reputation), whereas contributors to Wikipedia are motivated by more altruistic intentions related to improving their self-concept (intrinsic motivations). This is an important contribution as people may be making technological choices based on the community—or the audience—present within any particular social media.

Navigating Imagined Audiences

The hybridity of social media might influence the extent to which people's participatory needs are met (or not) in the online public sphere—importantly, media choice may be related to the audience present within any given online medium. Social media users are cognizant of their audiences and are often trying to control how they present themselves to others [e.g. 3]. Marwick and boyd [21] observed how Twitter users tend to collapse multiple audiences into a single context. In this view, a users' perception of their audience can influence political participation. For example, people may be unwilling to share political information from diverse perspectives, as the information may not always reflect their personal views.

There may be negative social consequences associated with the participatory activities in the public sphere. Whereas a healthy public sphere is predicated upon people's ability to share information and opinions, and engage in rational discussions, the audience can inhibit participation. People may refrain from participating freely for fear of being unfriended, unfollowed, or hidden by their audiences [36, 15]. In fact, polarizing political posts are one of the main reasons why people remove friends or hide friends' activities [30]. As such, people may choose not to participate depending on their perception of the audience within any given medium, in relation to their individual motivations. Researchers have identified various audience navigation strategies employed by social media users, e.g. self-censorship [e.g. 18, 19], selective sharing/grouping [e.g. 13, 14], and not posting [37].

Scholars have critiqued Habermas for his conception of the public sphere as it is believed to be highly utopian—ignoring the stark realities surrounding when, how and who can participate in the public sphere [e.g. 24]. It is important to consider such realities as these real world contexts can contribute to people's underlying motivations for using social media to participate in the public sphere. For example, in countries like Iran where the government limits people's ability to freely participate in the physical world political context, the online public sphere may serve as a place where people can engage in political deliberation without feeling threatened. Nevertheless, few studies have examined the interplay between offline context and motivations for participating in the online public sphere [35].

In this paper, we build on existing literature that has documented social media as an online public sphere [e.g. 2, 8, 11] and discuss specifically how the perception of "the audience" influences online tool switching and participation within specific contexts. We utilize qualitative techniques to explore *why* and *how* individuals use multiple social media to participate in the online public sphere. We argue that people use social media to satisfy their participatory needs—relative to their experiences in the physical world context—and that the technological choices they make are tied to their perception of the audience within any given online medium.

RESEARCH METHODS

The data presented in this paper is from a larger study [e.g. 33] in which we are trying to better understand how people use social media to participate in the political deliberation process. This particular component of the study is longitudinal in nature and comprises interviews, online and in-lab observations, and diary studies. For the purposes of this paper, we will be focusing on interviews supplemented by online observational data.

Participants and Recruitment

The participants of this study are United States citizens, living in Hawaii, who regularly use social media to engage in the political deliberation process. Interviews were conducted in phases and are ongoing, as we continue to follow people's use of social media across multiple election cycles. In phase one, 21 participants were interviewed beginning in May 2012 and ending in December of the same year. Eight participants were interviewed during the second phase beginning in February of 2013. In total, we conducted interviews with 29 informants. However, for the purposes of this paper, we have omitted 2 participants from our analysis, as they were not residing in Hawaii (thus limiting our analysis to 27 interviews with 13 male and 14 female informants).

Seven participants were found through fliers posted on a major university campus; 12 were enlisted through contacts made at a local news agency who disseminated an online newsletter; and finally, 8 were recruited through recruitment posts made to Facebook, Twitter and Craig's List. In order to be eligible for the study, subjects had to fulfill the following criteria: (1) they had to have some interest in politics and (2) they had to use at least one social media technology (we did not ask if they used any given technology to engage in political deliberation during the recruitment period). All subjects were given a $20 dollar Amazon gift card as remuneration for their participation in the study.

Our participants ranged from 18 to 67 years of age. We interviewed non-college graduates, as well as undergraduate and graduate students in various disciplines such as Computer Science and English. We also interviewed people who were working in various professions, e.g. professors, journalists and entrepreneurs.

Our informants all used one or more social media tools such as Facebook, Twitter, Google+ and blogs, which they described using daily to consume and/or discuss politics while at home on their personal computers, at work, and through their mobile devices while commuting.

Data Collection

The interviews, which lasted between 45-150 minutes, were semi-structured and followed an inductive approach, allowing each subject to guide us through their use of social media in a political context. In the case where participants were able, interviews were conducted face-to-face on the campus of a large US university. In the event that subjects were unable to participate in-person, interviews were conducted via telephone or Skype™.

The first phase of interviews was open-ended in nature. We asked people to situate their use of social media within the context of their daily lives by asking them historical questions as well as gathering information about their daily practices. We had our informants self-identify which technologies they used to engage in the political deliberation process. In order to better understand the different uses of each respective technology, and the underlying personal motivations for the use of each tool, we asked the same set of questions for each medium (and asked participants to provide us with relevant examples). We asked our informants to identify the activities they engaged in, how they engaged in those activities, who (if anyone) they deliberated with, what their level of participation was in the activities they described, how often and for how long they used a given tool, and the motivation(s) for using a respective technology. Informants were also asked to expand on questions by detailing which features they used to engage in activities they described and provide reasons they did or did not participate in deliberation and/or engage with others. Finally, we asked our informants to describe the reason(s), if any, which motivated their use of multiple social media.

In a second phase of interviews, we utilized our findings from the first phase to create a more focused semi-structured protocol where we sought to further validate recurring phenomenon reported in our initial interviews. Following interviews, participant permission was gathered in order for the first author to add participants to his social media accounts like Twitter, Facebook and Google+, allowing for general observations about the participants' social media activity. Twenty-six of our informants obliged, and we observed accounts so as to validate phenomenon reported during interviews.

Data Analysis

Each interview was recorded and transcribed for analysis. The coding process was initiated when interviews commenced, and continued after each respective interview was conducted and incorporated into the data corpus. Throughout the data collection and analysis, the research team met regularly to discuss trends in the observation and interview data for a period spanning over one year. One of the more dominant topics that emerged was what motivated participation in the online public sphere (which became the focus of this study).

Led by the first author, we conducted a grounded theory-based iterative and inductive analysis of our field notes and interview transcripts using coding and memoing [38]. Through this iterative process, we identified, named and categorized phenomena found in the transcripts in order to generate general themes observed in the interview data. The goal was to understand and make sense of the subjective experience (phenomenology) of the research participants and allow themes to emerge naturally. Over time, the codes were reduced, under axial coding, to the 6 themes presented in this paper.

THE CONTEXT OF HAWAI'I

In this paper we focus on United States citizens who were living in the state of Hawaii. The majority of Hawaii's population resides on the island of Oahu, in the city of Honolulu (one of the most densely populated cities in the United States). The political history of Hawaii is complex, and very significant recent historical events (Hawaii became a U.S. state in 1959) continue to have resonance in the political awareness and behavior of its residents.

The national media often paints a picture of Hawaii's residents as being apathetic towards politics [5], which is supported by the fact that Hawaii has now had the lowest voter turnout across the nation for several elections in a row [4, 5]. Some informants explained that the political apathy in Hawaii has limited their ability to participate politically as they felt the majority of people in their respective communities were not concerned with politics. As described by one informant:

Yeah, the thing about Hawaii is people just don't seem to give a damn about politics. Sometimes I feel like I'm one of the only ones who actually cares.

Other informants, however, described a much more complex political environment in Hawaii that is contributing to negative perceptions both locally and nationally. First, some participants say people living in the state are concerned with politics, but many of their concerns are specific to the region and may not be as visible outside of the state. As described by an informant:

A lot of what takes place in Hawaii [politically] isn't seen on the National stage... Just look at a publication like the New York times... you will rarely find anything having to do with the us there...

Second, whereas people are politically active and involved, their interest may not necessarily transfer to the voting booth. During national elections, for example, results are often reported before the polls close in Hawaii, thus giving local residents the impression that it is not "necessary to vote because their vote won't make a difference."

Third, the political environment in Hawaii is complex. Tensions exist between some members of the "local" community and other residents of the state—where here, the term local refers to people of Polynesian decent. For example, there are Hawaii residents who feel that the United States political system was forced upon them many years ago and choose not to participate in civic duties like voting, despite being highly enthusiastic about politics. As described by one informant:

The environment here is REALLY complicated... there are some who feel like the whole [system] was just forced upon them when the US took control of the islands and don't vote because of that, but it's much deeper than the native versus Haole[1] 'issue'... There are [also tensions] between people who recently came and those who have been here...

Finally, a large percentage of Hawaii's population is comprised of residents who are not originally from the state. Several groups are present ranging from immigrants, e.g. Micronesians, to long-standing multi-generational families from Japan and other parts of Asia, to people who have moved from the mainland United States for work and school. Seventeen of our informants, for example, were not originally from Hawaii. Some described feeling socially isolated (with respect to connecting to former political communities) as they had shifted from being geographically co-located to geographically dispersed in relation to the people with whom they typically interacted with in a political context:

I have lived all over the country because of job transfers. So I don't have a lot of personal friends here on Maui, or even in Hawaii itself... it's hard to find people here that want to discuss politics...

MOTIVATIONS FOR PARTICIPATING IN THE ONLINE PUBLIC SPHERE

Analysis of informants' accounts led to the development of several categories of motivation for participation in the online public sphere. In this section we describe these emergent categories, which include: tailoring and navigating the information environment to understand different viewpoints, moving in and out of different identities to formulate perspectives, creating spaces conducive to positive discourse, navigating audiences to repair Hawaii's image, increasing the political awareness of others, and improving civic engagement.

Navigating Audiences and Tailoring Information Spaces for Information: Diversity and Values

Hawaii has a distinct culture centered around the "`ohana"—which is the Hawaiian word for family. Members of an `ohana can be blood relatives, as well as close friends who are considered family. Native Hawaiians, who are members of the aboriginal group that comprise the State of Hawaii, have a shared set of values and traditions that they adhere to, and many feel that they are not included in the political system in the state of Hawaii. People often rely on their `ohana for support, and engage in political discussions with members of their `ohana in person. Additionally, word-of-mouth traditions are still integral to how people exchange of information.

Social media, however, enables people to transcend the confines of their local context. Nineteen of our informants purposefully appropriated social media to consume information not only within the state of Hawaii, but across the political spectrum on a national and global scale.

People were motivated by their intrinsic desire to understand alternative viewpoints and perspectives and improve their self-concept. Our informants were using social media to navigate to audiences where they could better understand *why* other people held viewpoints that conflicted with their own. By connecting with citizens and media channels that held alternative perspectives on political issues, they were able to increase their personal political awareness and understanding, and, in turn, make more well-informed political decisions.

Informants described how traditional mass media channels like the television, newspaper and radio often provided "out of context" and/or skewed interpretations of political issues, events and candidates. Similarly, they described how their friends often provided highly polarized opinions. Thus, our informants described also using social media to navigate to where they could obtain timely information "straight from the horses' mouth."

These limiting factors of traditional media outlets were seen on the local level as well. Informants described using Social Media as a means of circumventing these problems. For example, one informant, who worked for a local newspaper agency, described how she often used social media to receive information directly from local politicians. After reading articles posted by various media outlets she would, in turn, use media tools like Twitter or YouTube to receive information directly from a politician. For example, during the 2012 election, she was glued to social media as she was trying to decide on which local candidate she would vote for in the Hawaii State Senate election. As such, she added both primary candidates to her Twitter account to obtain information directly from them and their election teams. She also used YouTube to watch local candidate's political speeches and debates, so as to be able to formulate her own opinions without being misguided by skewed information that is often provided by others—which the informant described was typical of news media channels as well as people in her Facebook network.

Rather than rely solely on the interpretations of family and friends, social media enabled people to receive information directly from media personalities, event coordinators, and politicians alike, both locally and nationally. This served as a

[1] Haole is a Hawaiian term for "foreigner," also used in contemporary times as a derogatory term for Caucasians.

form of information validation, as people compared what was actually said with what was being reported, in conjunction with other people's interpretations, thus enabling them to formulate opinions. Additionally, by having both a physical and online presence, informants were able to both respect the context of their physical world environment and traditions while obtaining information that may be otherwise unavailable to them in their offline interactions.

Also, with social media, our informants described being able to tailor the information environment to more effectively consume information across the political spectrum. They curated information by creating structured information and opinion newsfeeds from media agencies, politicians and lay citizens, even when the information they were receiving did not align with their personal political beliefs. They wanted to receive timely information spanning the political spectrum in an effort to understand varied political perspectives on both a local and national level [c.f. 33].

One informant, for example, described using a Twitter aggregation tool called *Tweetdeck* to construct information feeds. Tweetdeck is a tool that enables people to structure tweet streams into tabs that can then be perused. He organized his feed by local, national and global politics, as well as by "political slant", e.g. right- or left-leaning.

Importantly, informants also created their own information spaces. Some people found that online, the way in which information was presented (or the information itself) did not adhere to their local values and interests. Thus, people constructed their own online spaces, taking into account local value systems.

One of our informants who was of Polynesian decent described how the information spaces available to the local Polynesian community did not share their values, nor report information that was relevant to their community. As such, he developed his own online information space—a converted blog—where he could report information that would be important to their community in a culturally appropriate and value-sensitive manner. Though he had a small staff, he invited members from the local community to write what they felt would be relevant to their community and context.

This new social media-enabled activity was both intrinsically and extrinsically motivated. On the one hand, our informant was creating an information space where he could learn from his community in a culturally sensitive way. On the other hand, however, the act of creating the information space was extrinsic in nature, as it made him more visible in the community.

Moving in and out of Identities: Reflexivity to Formulate Perspectives

Some of our informants reported how they felt restricted engaging in political talk, at times, in the real world. For example, one informant, who was a Hawaii transplant, reported not feeling comfortable with discussing local political issues in her every day life due to a feeling of being unwelcome as an outsider to the community. Other informants reported that having discussions with friends and family in person often led to arguments. Similarly, as described by our informants and as has been corroborated by other studies, many of those feelings migrate to the online space [30]. This is an important point to make as many social media tools, such as Facebook, are typically tied to an individuals' real world identity.

Goffman [9] discusses how people tend to create and manage impressions of themselves that they want to make publicly visible. When interacting with others our actions influence people's impression of us, and thus we conduct ourselves in a certain way in order to manage how we are perceived. Similarly, our data suggests that our informants were using the Internet to manage their impression.

To work around these restrictions, informants chose media tools like Twitter, Google+, YouTube, and blogs, so as to navigate to, and engage with, audiences that were of an impersonal nature (i.e. strangers), and/or where they could interact anonymously. The ability to move in and out of their real world identity using social media enabled them to continue to engage in the political deliberation process. For example, an informant who worked six days a week as a photographer, described how due to his busy schedule he did not have a lot of time to spend with family and friends, and when he did, political discussions rarely entered the conversion. He began using social media every evening for two or more hours to engage in political discussions:

> *...on Twitter I feel I'm able to hide my identity. On Facebook, because of the people I already have as friends, I found that I was always getting in arguments. That really bothered me because I work so much and it's hard to discuss what's going on politically outside of social media.... After complaining to a friend of mine, he suggested I use Twitter... but, you know, I still didn't want to use my real name because I wanted to be free to say whatever I wanted without people tracing it back to me. So I use an alias and I have found so many great people on Twitter that actually want to have real discussions...*

As described by Habermas [10], a key component of the public sphere is reflexivity. When people engage in the political deliberation process, they should also be re-considering and re-evaluating their perspectives in relation to the information and discussions with which they are engaged. Our informants described how, with social media, they could easily access other people's perspectives and, in turn, put themselves in other people's shoes to try and make sense of their perspectives.

Four informants used the affordances of social media—more specifically, the ability to assume alternative identities—in order to understand other people's perspectives. At times, access to these perspectives were unavailable or limited in the local setting due to feeling unwelcome in the community and/or homogenous political alignments with family or friends. They felt that the best way to reflect on their personal position on various issues was to act as if they held a variety of political positions and engage with others from each of those perspectives. In other words, people were assuming alternative identities, such as being pro-choice and pro-life, at different times, and engaging with others in discussions while roleplaying from the perspective of the identity that they were assuming at any given time. When assuming any given identity, they would navigate to audiences that would better help them understand a variety of perspectives in a space where they felt safe. As described by one informant:

Honestly, I really want to understand why people think the way they do. The only way I'm comfortable doing that is by engaging with others anonymously... I've created several dummy accounts through YouTube where each one is tied to a different political ideology or perspective, and I target the creators of videos that attempt to explain certain policies and perspectives... I like to ask them questions while roleplaying from various angles to help better understand and maybe put things into perspective for myself.

As such, our informants were motivated by their intrinsic desire to learn and better their understanding of alternative perspectives. Social media technologies gave people the freedom to assume multiple identities, as they could put themselves in other people's shoes (almost literally speaking) and try to understand the intrinsic motivations of others. This enabled people to establish new perspectives and, importantly, reflect upon and better understand themselves as individuals and political thinkers.

Navigating Diverse Audiences and Creating Spaces for Positive Discourse

Eighteen informants reported using social media to connect with and engage in discourse with other politically interested citizens. Our informants provided several reasons for why they chose to engage in discussions in the online public spheres available through social media.

Firstly, some informants described how the rigors of their day-to-day lives, e.g. work and time constraints, interfered with their ability to engage with people politically face-to-face. Secondly, some informants described feeling politically isolated after moving to Hawaii. Lastly, other informants reported that, today, their perception is that most people in their local contexts do not care about politics. Thus, people selected media based on where they could navigate to an audience that could most satisfy their need for discussion.

Six of our informants reported choosing media based on whether or not they could connect with people with whom they already had pre-existing relationships. Transplants to Hawaii face a unique form of isolation in moving to the islands in that they are not only physically isolated, but they are also often isolated by time zone differences. Being in the latest time zone in the United States, Hawaii transplants must be aware of the differences in time when contacting family and friends on the mainland where this previously may not have been as large of a concern. This can make traditional forms of communication, such as calling family on the telephone, increasingly difficult. Informants described using social media as a means of filling both the isolation and communication gap.

Informants reported how their networks consisting of family and friends (5 used Facebook and 1 used Twitter) satisfied their need for discourse in the public sphere, as they felt comfortable engaging with a more personal audience. As reported by one informant, a college student who moved from San Francisco, California, to Honolulu, Hawaii:

Before I used Facebook I was more likely to talk politics with my parents... I don't like that a lot of people here in Hawaii don't care about politics much. I really want to chat about what's going on both locally and nationally... But luckily I have Facebook, so I'm always on and discussing things with people... [t]hrough my newsfeed, through other people's newsfeeds. It doesn't matter... I can say whatever I want, everyone is my friend...

In other cases, the ability to engage with others online served as an extension of the physical world environment. One informant, who was of Micronesian decent, described how he preferred Facebook over other tools as it allowed him to interact with his family and friends, who he felt were more respectful of his opinions.

Our remaining 12 informants, however, felt that social media tools that were designed to be more personal in nature (i.e. Facebook) did not satisfy their need for discourse, as they perceived their audiences as being "easily aggravated" and "highly argumentative" [e.g. 37]. Informants described how across social media tools, oftentimes the interactions they were having in the online public spheres available through social media were negative. Online, people come together from diverse backgrounds and have diverse values. This can lead to fruitful discussion, but it can also lead to conflict as much online political discourse has been found to be negative. For example, many of the spaces devoted to political talk, e.g. politician Facebook pages, are full of messages of flaming and support [30].

With social media, people can manipulate the tool to adhere to their personal values as well as control the audience. Five informants, who felt that they could not successfully navigate to audiences where they could engage in fruitful online discussions, constructed their own online spaces through social media to satisfy this need. People created Facebook groups, blogs and other spaces where they could invite people from diverse backgrounds as well as control who was allowed to engage in discussions.

For example, an informant who was a member of a retirement community on the island of Kauai described how most of the people in her neighborhood were politically apathetic. She explained how her community was comprised of people who were "living out the rest of their lives without any interest in what was going on in the real world." As such, she adopted several social media tools ranging from Facebook to blogs, through which she could engage in political talk. To her surprise, she found that despite her best efforts, online, people were quick to "turn to irrationality when they did not agree"—this portrayal of the online audience included many of her friends and family on Facebook as well as the strangers she was meeting on Twitter. This motivated her to create a private Facebook group, where she could purposefully control the audience. She invited people from different backgrounds who held varying perspectives. Importantly, although the people she invited to join her group were diverse in political ideology, they shared what she considered to be the most important characteristic—"rationality."

Our informants who were creating spaces for rational discourse were motivated by intrinsic rewards, as they wanted to learn something new while engaging in rational discourse.

Targeting a Broader Audience: Repairing Hawaii's Image

Some of our informants felt that people in the state of Hawaii were highly enthusiastic and motivated about politics. Seven of our 17 informants who engaged in dissemination practices did so in order to navigate towards a national audience and thus increase awareness of local politics and thus reverse the image of Hawaii's residents as being apathetic about politics on a broader scale. These informants expressed how they often kept track of their impact based on the number of times their posts were "Liked", retweeted, or "favorited". One informant, for example, described how Hawaii does not receive enough attention in the mainstream media:

Hawaii news rarely ever makes it the mainland, and... if you want National news, you have to go to ABC, NBC, CBS... there is rarely anything discussed nationally about Hawaii... It's like we're living in two separate worlds.

Through their dissemination practices, people wanted to expose a national audience to news local to Hawaii as they felt the state was rarely ever in the spotlight. They chose media where they felt they could target the largest group possible. For example, one informant, who served as a member of a social media advocacy group in Honolulu, described how although she uses multiple social media tools like Facebook and Google+, she purposefully adopted Twitter to reach a national audience because the other media she used were for interacting with family and friends. It upset her that local Hawaii news "typically stays on island," and she felt that Hawaii residents were at a disadvantage having to compete with larger media centers:

It's not as much about informing people locally as it is about Hawaii gaining attention... How? Well, I'd like people to retweet my posts as much as possible... I want the information to gain traction, I want to put us on the map!

People felt compelled to alter the national perception of Hawaii's residents as being politically apathetic. They wished to, as described by one informant, "repair Hawaii's image," and thus used media where they could navigate toward and target national audiences:

The news from Hawaii rarely ever makes it to a national audience... even on Twitter, you almost never see anything from Hawaii trending to the top... I think that adds to people's perception of us as complacent... it's a... goal of mine to make people more aware of us... you think we don't care about politics?...I am trying to improve that with Twitter...[that's where]... I can reach the most people.

By aiming to gain the attention of a national audience, they were, in turn, trying to show that there is a large contingent on the islands that are politically active and motivated. These practices were both motivated by intrinsic and extrinsic rewards. On the one hand, intrinsic motivations were tied to people's desire to enact positive social consequences, where they could expose others to Hawaii politics. On the other hand, by virtue of disseminating this information, people were also motivated by the extrinsic rewards of being perceived as knowledgeable, or, as an expert. This is especially true of tools like Twitter, where users were trying to ensure that their tweets would be seen by as many people as possible—where they were keeping track of the number of times their posts were re-tweeted and "favorited".

Increasing the political awareness of others through exposure to alternative perspectives

After curating information from various channels, 17 of our informants reported disseminating information to their audiences. The information they were disseminating came from multiple media channels and lay citizens whose perspectives spanned the political spectrum. The majority of our informants had integrated several technologies like Facebook, Twitter and online news sites, into their daily news consumption and dissemination repertoires. By curating and disseminating information, they aimed to increase the political awareness of others.

Our informants employed a variety of dissemination strategies. They targeted what they considered to be the "broader audience" as well as local audiences. Informants were cognizant of their target audiences and in which media their perceived audiences resided—and made technological choices accordingly. Through our analysis of informants' accounts, people's dissemination practices were further motivated by their experiences in the physical world environment.

Our informants purposefully targeted local audiences. They described how the political environment in Hawaii was lacking in that they felt other residents were politically unmotivated. Furthermore, they had the impression that most people followed only one mainstream media network like CNN and Fox News, or local news agencies, e.g. Hawaii Star Advertiser, and were thus not aware of a variety of political perspectives and issues taking place locally, nationally and globally [c.f. 1, 41].

In order to increase the political awareness of other residents, 10 of our 17 informants who engaged in dissemination practices used media like Facebook, Twitter and Google+, to target their perceived local audiences. They wished to expose others to what was taking place locally, nationally and/or globally, and to what was not being reported by mainstream outlets. They also wished to give people a better impression of local and national politicians and policies. For example, one informant who was an intern at a newspaper outlet, described this process:

I see what people are interested in on my network just by looking at what a lot of my friends [and family] are posting on Facebook and Twitter... most people only look at CNN, Fox News, or the New York Times. You seriously think you're going to get everything you need from those channels?... I feel like [many] people [in Hawaii] don't even care about politics! I have so much information that I gather...and I post it on both Facebook and Twitter... mostly on Twitter because people understand it's a broadcast network, and I have a lot [followers].

By disseminating cross-ideological information and opinions to their local networks, our informants wished to expose other residents to diverse information that would increase their awareness of political issues and candidates, increase interest, and give people the information necessary for making well-informed political decisions.

For example, one informant, who lived and worked on Maui, described how she lived and breathed politics. Whereas she used to live in Honolulu (on the island of Oahu) and felt more people were politically active in the "big city", she felt that the other residents of Maui were just retirees or simply did not care about what was going on. As an avid social media user, she had added several local friends on Facebook. She described bombarding them with local and national political information from all sides of the political spectrum, with the intention of not only "...making them interested," but, importantly, to "give them the tools that would allow them to make better decisions."

The State of Hawaii is rare in that informants described having personally known Senate, Mayoral and Congressional candidates through their interactions in a political context. Informants also described "knowing of" candidates through family and friends. In local culture, word-of-mouth information dissemination is common practice. In Hawaii, residents often share experiences they have had either working with local politicians, or encountering them in person, e.g. at the local supermarket. The lived experiences shared amongst family and friends can serve an integral component in how people form impressions of political candidates. Social media served as a megaphone, thus enabling people to disseminate these experiences on a larger scale. As described by an informant:

Well... I've worked for [Mazie] Hirono, and I'm doing some stuff for Ed Case this time, and we all know each other, and we're all friends... you see, a lot of what people are posting about local candidates is from the Star Advertiser, or local TV... or even commercials on YouTube. I see these [candidates] everyday... I know them and I try to add to what people are saying by giving them a real picture of the candidate.

Thus, informants wanted to give others a personal perspective on candidates and issues that they may not have otherwise been exposed to, and they purposefully used social media to navigate toward where they perceived their target audiences to reside in the online public sphere. This is largely an extrinsic motivation since it involves changes in the larger community environment. Increasing awareness in this way could even work against other interests of an informant, for example by making people aware of a candidate who the informant does not like and potentially increasing interest and support of that candidate. But this tradeoff is acceptable in the larger motivational scheme.

Increasing Civic Engagement: From Online to Offline

Ten informants described how they were disseminating information online in an effort to "get people off their butts" and become civically minded. They wanted other citizens to become more civically engaged by exercising their right to vote or contact local and/or national political representatives to contest or support policies. Thus, our informants were motivated to disseminate information online so as to provide cues to action in the physical world context.

Our informants described exerting a lot of energy when thinking about *how* to present what they were sharing [c.f. 19]. Rather than post polarizing messages for or against certain candidates or policies, our informants were aware that they could potentially upset people in their networks (through previous negative experiences) [e.g. 30]. They spent considerable time thinking about how to craft their posts, many of which described using a text editor like Microsoft Word so as to ensure they were taking the time to carefully compose messages for their respective audiences.

For example, one informant, in feeling like most residents of Hawaii do not vote, used his Facebook account (where he felt the majority of his local audience was present) in order to compose messages urging people to vote:

The message I was posting was simple, but I had to write it down on a piece of paper first... I used to get carried away and just post whatever I wanted and people would get upset. But, I wrote about how... YOU should vote. I told people to go vote...but I didn't tell people who to vote for.'

Thus, people were interested in engaging others in a non-forceful way, while also providing them with relevant information that would enable them to act. As described by another informant:

I don't really go on FB or Twitter and promote any particular candidate I like. I do general things like you should vote or register to vote. For example I've been telling people that they should go vote in the upcoming election, but to be sure they know where they're supposed to go. I've been linking people to the proper place so they can figure out where they're supposed to physically vote I always have to keep in mind how I'm putting things out there... you can't upset people and expect them to listen."

Hawaii has a unique political climate in that community members often know one another. Oftentimes the respect and community associations they had with others in the physical world migrated to the online space, and people used their status in the offline world to influence the online world. For example, 6 informants were pro-active in the offline political context. They reported attending meetings with local politicians and other interested citizens. They were also part of civic groups that met on a regular basis and volunteered for campaigns. They felt it was their role to expose others to what they were learning in public meetings. Using the affordances of social media tools like Facebook and Twitter, they leveraged their status in the community and targeted specific people like "friends and family", or general local audiences, to make people more aware of what was happening in the state.

One informant described how he made an effort to attend local meetings and disseminate what he had learned via Facebook:

I try my best to attend these local [political] meetings that most people don't go to... afterwards I like to pass on what I learn to others... sometimes what I'm sending out is to everyone if it's something I think everyone needs to know. But other times I learn about something that will affect a certain area and I know people there, so I will direct my messages to them... How? Well my local group is all on Facebook so sometimes I'll use the @ symbol when I post and tag a bunch of people...

Similarly, people also used social media to inform other citizens of local gatherings, making a concerted effort to increase civic engagement.

One informant, who worked for the Department of Defense, described how he used every social media tool at his disposal like Twitter, Facebook and Google+. He believed that the majority of his local network was on Facebook, and he often let people in his Facebook network know about meetings that were taking place to discuss various political issues like sustainability and open government, so as to increase attendance and the number of "voices that would be heard."

As with the motivation of increasing political awareness, increasing civic engagement and action are also largely extrinsic motivations. This motivation seeks to change the overall nature of the public for the better, driving toward a more informed electorate and more informed and representative public sphere.

DISCUSSION

In this study we have focused on a group of highly motivated and civically engaged social media users living in the state of Hawaii. A major lesson from our observations of these people participating in the larger online public sphere is that they appropriated multiple technologies for this purpose, much of their political activities were context-sensitive, and they did so to reach different audiences. Their awareness of the different audiences afforded by different technologies was often very explicit and their behavior was influenced by this awareness.

We return to Papacharissi's [28] hypothesis about the public sphere in the age of social media, where she re-conceptualizes the public sphere as being more akin to "private spheres"—or online spaces that provide people with the autonomy that is most associated with physical private spaces, but with the potential audience of a public act. Our results show that the audience, both offline and online, plays an instrumental role in dictating how people interact in the online public sphere. In our study, people were adept at navigating audiences in various contexts depending on how they perceived their audiences in any given medium, e.g. local vs. national and personal vs. impersonal. The ways in which they navigated audiences in the online public sphere were related to their goals, and they often used media accordingly.

Intrinsic and Extrinsic Motivations for Participation

We found that people made media choices to satisfy both *individual* and *community needs*. Several categories of activity were evident when people made media choices with the intention of satisfying their own deliberation needs. Categories that were more intrinsic included: tailoring and navigating the information environment to understand different viewpoints, moving in and out of different identities to formulate perspectives, creating spaces conducive to positive discourse, and navigating audiences to repair Hawaii's image.

When people selected media with the intention of having an external effect on their audiences, they were making decisions based on the perceived needs of others. In these cases, the technological choices they made were highly tied to the audience. In this study, we saw many instances of social media users disseminating information, even information with which they disagreed, for the purpose of increasing the civic engagement of others. Participants spent considerable effort tailoring their posts in such a way that they would acceptable to others. Categories that were more extrinsic in nature included: increasing the political awareness of others through exposure to alternative perspectives, and increasing civic engagement. We note that in many cases intrinsic and extrinsic motivations were mixed.

A particularly interesting twist from this data was the finding that people sought to understand the intrinsic motivations of others by adopting alternative personas in different social media contexts. Reflexivity, or reflection one's own values and ability to understand others, is considered to be an important component of a healthy public sphere. Here we see an extreme form of reflexivity which we might refer to as the active seeking of alternative intrinsic motivations. In addition, we see participants disseminating alternative viewpoints, or "counter-intrinsics," as a way of generating diversity of opinion, and enhancing the ability of the community to understand others.

The process of internalization is the movement from extrinsic motivation to intrinsic motivation by adopting the values of others, a process that is desirable in the context of political discourse and afforded by social media. It remains a research question to what extent these attempts to diversify the community information environment are effective in instilling intrinsic motivations to participate in the civic life of the community.

Concluding Remarks

We studied a very specific population as they used social media for civic purposes. All of our informants were Hawaii residents (the majority transplanted from the mainland) who were proactive social media users with an interest in politics. Although this limits generalizability to some extent, we offer that our results are characteristic of people of several ages and both genders with diverse educational and professional backgrounds. We note that people located in other US cities and in other parts of the world may also feel social isolation and a lack of political engagement in their daily lives.

In our study, whereas various limitations to political participation existed in the offline world and the online world, people were navigating to and between different online audiences, re-appropriating tools, and creating their own spaces through which they could maintain civic agency.

A major contribution of our research is to show that social media technologies have a materiality to them—they are malleable. We found that people tailor the online public sphere to their liking so as to satisfy their desire for civic engagement. For example, although Facebook served as a space through which some informants could participate by engaging in rational discourse, others found that people in their Facebook networks did not share their values and were irrational. Thus, they sought discussants that shared similar values (i.e. rationality) through other media like Twitter. Similarly, they took it upon themselves to construct the spaces through which they could engage in rational discourse, by creating Facebook groups that were more conducive to positive discussions. In the most extreme cases, people were even re-appropriating media to serve their personal and local community needs by constructing spaces that aligned with local values.

The public sphere is not confined to any single tool and thus it exists, as Dahlgren [6] asserts, as a "sprawling" public sphere. Civically engaged users are keenly aware of the sprawling nature of the online public sphere and see it as an opportunity to take advantage of the different audiences it affords. By conducting in-depth interviews, in contrast to analyzing posts alone, we are able to show how these users view different audiences and navigate them for a variety of intrinsic goals related to being informative and effective and extrinsic goals related to raising community awareness and political participation. Thus, designers should begin envisioning technologies that can help people view and understand their audiences better and satisfy their needs across multiple social media contexts. Sociotechnical theorists and researchers should recognize the limitations inherent in studying a single technology environment and embrace the sprawling public sphere as the appropriate level of analysis for studies of technologically-mediated civic participation.

ACKNOWLEDGMENTS

This research was funded by NSF award No. IIS-1064852. Any opinions, findings and conclusions or recommendations expressed in this material are those of the authors and do not necessarily reflect the views of the National Science Foundation. We are grateful to our participants who graciously gave us their time so that we could conduct our investigation.

REFERENCES

1. Agre, P. E. (2002). Real-time politics: The Internet and the political process. *Inf. Society*, 18(5), 311-331.
2. Bimber, B., and Davis, R. (2003). *Campaigning online: The internet in U.S. elections.* Oxford University Press, Oxford.
3. Boyd, D., and Ellison, N. (2007). Social Network Sites: Definition, History, and Scholarship. *Journal of Computer-Mediated Communication*, 13, 1, 210-230.
4. http://www.civilbeat.com/articles/2012/11/07/17582-hawaii-voter-turnout-drops-even-lower/
5. http://www.cnn.com/2012/10/21/opinion/why-hawaii-doesnt-vote
6. Dahlgren, P. (2005). The Internet, public spheres, and political communication: Dispersion and deliberation. *Political Communication*, 22, 2, 147-162.
7. Foot, K.A., and Schneider, S.M. (2006). *Web campaigning*, MIT Press, Cambridge, MA.
8. Gilbert, E., Bergstrom, T., and Karahalios, K. (2009). Blogs are echo chambers: Blogs are echo chambers. *Proc. of HICSS-44,* 1-10.
9. Goffman, E. (1959). *The Presentation of Self in Everyday Life*. Doubleday, Carden City, NY
10. Habermas, J. (1991). The public sphere. In Mukerji, C. and Schudson, M. eds. *Rethinking popular culture: Contemporary perspectives in cultural studies*. Berkeley: University of California Press, pp. 398-404.
11. Horrigan, J., Garrett, K., and Resnick, P. (2004). The internet and democratic debate. *Pew Internet and American Life Project.*

12. Joinson, A.N., (2008). Looking at, looking up or keeping up with people?: Motives and use of facebook. *Proc. of CHI'08*, 1027-1036.
13. Kairam, S., Brzozowski, M., Huffaker, D. and Chi, E. (2012). Talking in circles: selective sharing in Google+. *Proc. of CHI '12*, 1065–1074.
14. Karr-Wisniewski, P., Wilson, D., and Richter-Lipford, H. (2011). A new social order: mechanisms for social network site boundary regulation. *Proc. of AMCIS'11*.
15. Kwak et al. (2011). "Fragile online relationship: a First look at unfollow dynamics in Twitter," *Proc. of CHI'11*.
16. Lampe, C., Ellison, N., and Steinfield, C. (2006). A face (book) in the crowd: Social searching vs. social browsing. *Proc. of CSCW'06*, 167-170.
17. Lampe, C., Wash, R., Velasquez, A., and Ozkaya, E. (2010). Motivations to participate in online communities. *Proc. of CHI'10*,1927-1936.
18. Lampinen, A., Lehtinen, V., Lehmuskallio, A., and Tamminen, S. (2011). We're in it together: interpersonal management of disclosure in social network services. *Proc. of CHI '11*, 3217–3226.
19. Lampinen, A., Tamminen, S.,and Oulasvirta, A. "All my people right here, right now": management of group co-presence on a social networking site. *Proc. of GROUP '09*, 281–290.
20. Madden, M., & Zickuhr, K. (2011). 65% of online adults use social networking sites. *Pew Internet and American Life Project*.
21. Marwick, A. E., and boyd, D. I tweet honestly, I tweet passionately: Twitter users, context collapse, and the imagined audience. *New Media & Society*, 13(1), 114–133, 2010.
22. Moore, T. D., and Serva, M. A. (2007). Understanding member motivation for contributing to different types of virtual communities: A proposed framework. In Proc. SIGMIS-CPR, 153–158.
23. Morgan, J.S., Shafiq, M.Z., and Lampe, C. (2013). Is News Sharing on Twitter Ideoligically Based? *Proc. of CSCW'13*.
24. Mouffe, C. (1999). Deliberative democracy or agonistic pluralism?.
25. Munson, S., and Resnick, P. (2010). Presenting diverse political opinions: how and how much, *Proc. of CHI'10*, 1457-1466.
26. Munson, S., and Resnick, P. (2011). The prevalence of political discourse in non-political blogs. *Proc. of WSM*.
27. Nardi, B., Schiano, D., and Gumbrecht, M. (2006). Blogging as Social Activity, or, Would You Let 900 Million People Read Your Diary? *Proc. of CSCW'04*, 222-231.
28. Papacharissi, Z. (2010). *A private sphere: Democracy in a digital age*. Polity Press, Malden, MA.
29. Papacharissi, Z. (2001). The virtual public sphere. The Internet as a public sphere. *New Media and Society*, 4(1), 9-27.
30. Raine, L., and Smith, A. (2012). Politics on social networking sites. *Pew Internet and American Life Project*.
31. Rafaeli, S., Hayat, T. and Y., A. (2009). Knowledge Building and Motivations in Wikipedia: Participation as "Ba". in Ricardo, F.J. ed. *Cyberculture and New Media*, Rodopi, New York, 52-69.
32. Ryan, R.M., & Deci, E.L. (2000). Intrinsic and extrinsic motivations: Classic definitions and new directions. *Contemporary Educational Psychology*, 25, 54–67.
33. Semaan, B., Robertson, S., Douglas, S., Maruyama, M. (2014). Social Media Supporting Political Deliberation Across Multiple Public Spheres: Towards Depolarization. *Proc. of CSCW'14*.
34. Shamma, D., Kennedy, L., and Churchill, E.F. (2009): Tweet the debates: understanding community annotation of uncollected sources. *Proc. of the first SIGMM workshop on Social media*, 3-10.
35. Shklovski, I. and Valtysson, B. (2012). Secretly Political: Civic Engagement in Online Publics in Kazakhstan. *Journal of Broadcasting & Electronic Media*, 56(3), 417–433.
36. Sibona, C. and Walczak, S. (2011). "Unfriending on Facebook: Friend Request and Online/Offline Behavior Analysis." *Proc. of HICSS-46*.
37. Sleeper, M., Balebako, R., Das, S., McConahy, A., Wiese, J., Cranor, L. (2013). The Post that Wasn't: Exploring Self-Censorship on Facebook. *Proc. of CSCW'13*.
38. Strauss, A. L. and Corbin, J. M. (1998). *Basics of Qualitative Research: Techniques and Procedures for Developing Grounded Theory*. Sage, CA.
39. Stromer-Galley, J. (2003). Diversity of political conversation on the Internet: Users' perspectives. *Journal of Computer-Mediated Communication*, 8, 3.
40. Stroud, N. J. (2007). Media effects, selective exposure, and Fahrenheit 9/11. *Political Communication*, 24(4), 415–432.
41. Sunstein, C.R. (2007). *Republic.com 2.0*. Princeton University Press, MA.
42. Weick, K. E. (1993). The collapse of sensemaking in organizations: The Mann Gulch disaster. *Administrative Science Quarterly*, 38(4), 628-652.
43. Wilson, R. E., Gosling, S. D., and Graham, L. T. (2012). A review of facebook research in the social sciences. *Perspectives on Psych. Sci.*, 7(3), 203–220.

Content, Context, and Critique: Commenting on a Data Visualization Blog

Jessica Hullman[1], Nicholas Diakopoulos[2], Elaheh Momeni[3], Eytan Adar[4]
[1]University of Washington, Seattle, WA, USA. jhullman@uw.edu
[2]University of Maryland, College Park, MD, USA. nad@umd.edu
[3]University of Vienna, Vienna, Austria. elaheh.momeni.roochi@univie.ac.at
[4]University of Michigan, Ann Arbor, MI USA. eadar@umich.edu

ABSTRACT
Online data journalism, including visualizations and other manifestations of data stories, has seen a recent surge of interest. User comments add a dynamic, social layer to interpretation, enabling users to learn from others' observations and social interact around news issues. We present the results of a qualitative study of commenting around visualizations published on a mainstream news outlet, The Economist's Graphic Detail blog. We find that surprisingly, only 42% of the comments discuss the visualization and/or article content. Over 60% of comments discuss matters of context, including how the issue is framed and the relation to outside data. Further, over one third of total comments provide direct critical feedback on the content of presented visualizations and text articles as well as on contextual aspects of the presentation. Our findings suggest using critical social feedback from comments in the design process, and motivate the development of more sophisticated commenting interfaces that distinguish comments by reference.

Author Keywords
Information visualization; commenting; data journalism.

ACM Classification Keywords
H.5.2 [Information Interfaces and Presentation].

General Terms
Human Factors; Design; Measurement.

INTRODUCTION
With the launch of sites like Nate Silver's FiveThirtyEight [17] and the New York Times' The Upshot [15], data journalism has become a mainstream means of presenting news to the public. These sites, along with data blogs published by the Guardian [6] and The Economist [3], present the news using a data-driven approach to storytelling. Information visualization techniques are frequently used to make the data accessible to large public audiences. We seek to understand how audiences of online data-driven news outlets comment on data visualization-based posts.

ACM 978-1-4503-2922-4/15/03…$15.00.
http://dx.doi.org/10.1145/2675133.2675207

We analyze the commenting discourse that emerges on The Economist's Graphic Detail (GD) blog. GD posts integrate visualizations and commenting within an online news ecosystem with an active community of users who are intrinsically motivated to reason about the content [13] (Figure 1). Related research has looked more generally at commenting in online news ecosystems [2, 12, 21] or on blogs [5, 14] but is limited to users commenting on text-only articles. Visualization commenting, on the other hand, has been investigated primarily through laboratory studies or smaller-scale deployments of research systems [1, 8, 19, 23]. These studies characterize commenting as a means for individuals to better understand a data presentation by sharing observations, hypotheses, and other insights derived from presented data, as well as to socially interact through jokes and affirmations of one another's findings [8, 20, 22].

We contribute findings from a qualitative analysis of over 1,100 manually-coded comments on GD posts. Our results provide evidence of several forms of visualization-based commenting behavior that emerge when sensemaking occurs "in the wild" of a mainstream data journalism outlet. While our findings reinforce prior observations that comments support collaborative sensemaking around *content* such as the visualized data and article, surveying GD comments overall indicates an even stronger preoccupation among commenters with matters of *context,* such as how the presentation can be reconciled with non-present yet related data or how the issue was framed by the author.

Additionally, we find that over half of content-oriented comments and over one third of context-oriented comments offer explicit *criticism* of the presentation. Commenters use such comments to reference or "point" to perceived obstructions to interpretation presumed to stem from issues with the design of representations or framing of the issue. Our work contributes a coding scheme that can be used to distinguish content-oriented versus context-oriented and critical versus non-critical foci in subsequent studies of visualization-based commenting. We also provide detailed examples of subclasses of content, context, and critical comments, and describe how properties of the commenters themselves relate to the content-context distinction.

By deepening understanding around commenting behavior in such sites, we aim to identify new uses for numerous comments that arise in data journalism environments, and

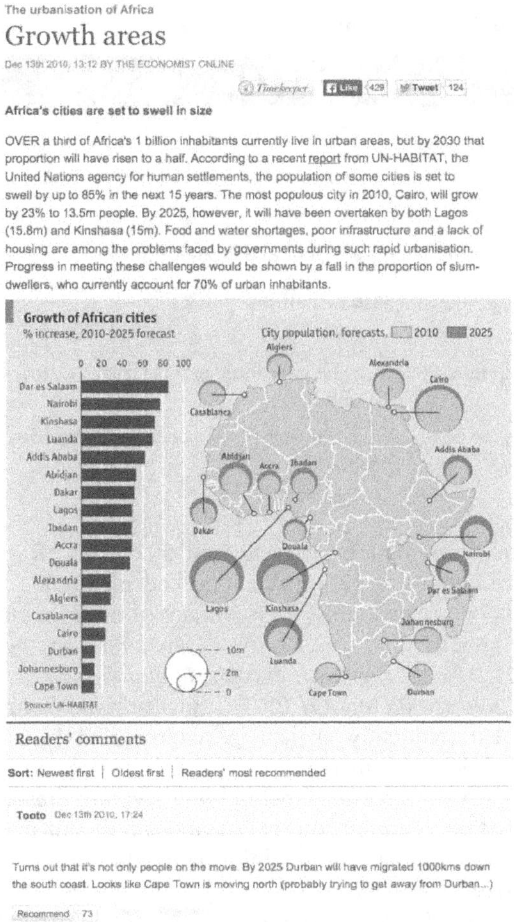

Figure 1: A post from the Economist's Graphic Detail about urbanization in Africa.

new design features to enhance the user's experience. We conclude with a discussion of directions for future research aimed at incorporating comments in the content design process and for enhancing the user's experience via new design features in commenting platforms.

STUDY DESIGN: COMMENTING ON THE GD

We provide a general characterization of the GD context and describe the dataset and methods.

General Characterization of GD

GD is a publicly accessible blog that is part of The Economist online. GD (originally the "Daily Chart") has been published since August 2010. Each workday the blog publishes "charts, maps and infographics", which are mostly static but sometimes include interactive visualizations. Posts also include a one or two paragraph text article contextualizing the graphic. In line with "a belief that what is written is more important than who writes it," post authorship on GD is left anonymous. User comments are pseudo-anonymous, and appear below the visualization in paged blocks of twenty. Comments are sorted in reverse chronological order by default, but can be sorted chronologically or by recommendation score. Threading (added in late 2011) allows users to respond directly to another comment.

Data Collection and Coding Methodology

In April 2011 we collected all comments from 168 posts on GD resulting in a dataset of 4,468 comments across 118 posts containing one or more comments. We randomly sampled the posts to arrive at a more manageable set of 38 posts with one or more comments each and a total of 1,103 comments across the sample. Statistics reported in our findings below refer to this manually coded sample unless the full sample of 4,468 comments is noted. For each post we noted the format of its visualization. We observed a variety of chart types (10+ distinct types); eight of the posts (21%) contained interactivity. The mean GD article was 167 words and 29 comments (median=20). We observed 764 unique users (mean=1.4 comments/user). Across the full sample, most users (72.5%) only commented once.

We analyzed comments through iterative qualitative coding, affinity diagramming, typologizing, and memoing [11]. Comments were analyzed in the context of the original webpage (including the article, visualization, and comments). Two of the authors analyzed one half of the comments to build the codebook and obtain ground truth. We resolved differences to arrive at elemental categories.

During the coding process, we observed various *anchors,* aspects of the presentation that a comment could use as a basis for interpretation. Anchors included the visualization and/or data, the article, related information external to the GD presentation, and the issue itself (e.g., obesity), including how it was framed (e.g., as an epidemic). We explain these categories in detail in the next section. Anchors were not mutually exclusive, as a single comment could address multiple aspects.

We also observed in coding that some comments (spanning all anchor types) directly criticized the presentation. We coded a mutually exclusive "critical" class for all comments. A subsequent coding of the 1,103 comment sample sought to distinguish frequencies and patterns of anchor usage. Fifty of the 1,103 comment sample were sampled and coded independently by each coder, with Cohen's kappa computed for each category of reference to which comments were directed: the Visualization/Data 0.80, Article: 0.91; Critical Visualization, Data, or Article: 0.78, Related Data: .92; or Issue Framing: .92, Critical Related Data or Issue Framing: 0.72. The coders split the remainder of the 1,103 sample and recoded anchor usage.

FINDINGS

Summary: Comments Debate Content & Context

A general lens for understanding the sensemaking activity we observed on GD is that of *critical interpretation of content and context.* At the highest level, our analysis revealed two dimensions along which comments could be meaningfully distinguished that have not surfaced in prior visualization commenting work.

Firstly, we observed a distinction between comments that focused on the *content* that was explicitly available (the

Table 1: Prevalence of types (percentage of manually coded comments, N=1,103).

Description	Prevalence	Examples	
Content-oriented comments	42.2%		
Non-critical	20.9%	Question asking/answering, data-based observations.	
Critical	21.4%	Discuss data exclusion or obfuscation, critique aggregation, question definitions.	
Context-oriented comments	62.1%	**Related Data** (39.7%)	**Issue Framing** (28.3%)
Non-critical	38.9%	Relate issue to personal knowledge; link to potentially related sources.	Suggest solutions, expose hopes or fears around issue.
Critical	23.2%	Add related data for comparison, expose overlooked conditions.	Question metric of success or significance of problem.

visualization, data, or article that was presented) or comments that reflected on matters of *context*: broadly speaking, how the issue is located with a broader set of knowledge and conditions. References to the *content* of the visualization, data, and/or article appeared in 42.2% of comments. An example is this reference to an edge in a visualized telephone network: "*That big connection between Glasgow and London is probably about 50% my mum.*" References to matters of *context* appeared in 62.1% of comments. We observed two main forms of context-oriented comments. Related Data context-oriented comments (39.7% of sample) discussed how the presentation would be impacted by considering other variables and conditions external to the presented data. For example, a comment on a post about youth unemployment suggested that "*another factor is that young people, prior to having children, are the most likely to 'rock the boat', and least likely to lay back and take bad treatment by management, etc.*" On the other hand, issue-framing context-oriented comments (28.3% of sample) debated how the information was framed, including the ultimate significance, possible solutions to, or moral implications of the issue being discussed. This comment on a post about obesity reflect on the ostensible awareness of the issue: "*Obesity is a puzzling condition. Even without any study, nearly everybody seems to know exactly what causes it and what the solutions are.*"

As stated above these categories are not mutually exclusive: 35.5% of comments were associated with two or more foci including Visualization, Data, or Article; Related Data; or Issue Framing. However, a relatively small proportion (15.4%) of comments referenced both content *and* context matters, suggesting that these orientations tend to be distinct. An analysis of commenter-based statistics (see "Who Comments on What") shows that the distinction between content- and context-oriented comments may result from a difference in commenters' levels of engagement with GD.

A second meaningful dimension of commenting behavior, we observed that a significant proportion of comments (38.3%) directly *criticized* aspects of the news presentation. A critical orientation characterized 50.6% of all content-oriented comments (21.4% of total coded sample), including this one questioning the accuracy of a statement in an article about China's economy: "*How could any economy have 6 - 9 % GDP growth in a phase of deflation, as shown for Q3 and Q4 08 and Q1 09?*" Context-oriented comments were also frequently critical in nature (37.4%), albeit in more subtle ways that often implied a goal to understand the rhetorical intentions behind the overall presentation, such as this comment on a post about political prisoners, which implies that certain information has been wrongly overlooked: "*Is it the Human Rights Watch or the Economist that can't see the reality? Where is the "selection of political prisoners" held in Russia?*

Below, we detail the main distinctions between these types of comment feedback, including statistics and examples.

Content Orientation (Visualization, Data, Article)

We describe sensemaking activities in GD comments that reinforce the results of prior commenting studies. We then provide examples of the many comments that focus instead on criticizing the design of content like the visualization.

Non-Critical Sensemaking in Content-Oriented Comments

Among the 49.3% of content-oriented comments that did not explicitly critique the representations (20.9% of total coded sample), we observed categories of sensemaking activity that have been described in prior studies on visualization commenting [8, 18, 22]. These included sharing of hypotheses and observations based on the visual (e.g., "*The data clearly show that it takes three quarters of declining growth rate to cap inflation (Q1-Q3 of 2007)*"), and posing of questions ("*Is there any relation between the number of delegates and 'value' they can offer to solve the global warming problem?*"). The article text served as another form of reference. Direct quoting of the article occurred in 1.3% of the 4,468 comment sample (e.g., as "*The Economist asks: 'So why did China's central bank raise reserve requirements for six banks ...?' It sure caught the world, particularly the West and the Economist by surprise.*")

Critical Content-Oriented Comments

Among the half of content-oriented comments that criticized the visualization or article, topics discussed included barriers to comparative operations, such as using inconsistent baselines, depicting normalized (e.g. percentage) values instead of absolute, or comparing apples to oranges. Other noted barriers include dynamic axis labeling, the validity of a data transformation such as a rank ordering, and the appropriateness of mappings to visual attributes. For instance, this comment was made in response to a chart depicting relative city population forecasts using circles, "*I have trouble discerning that, for example, the projected circle for Dar es Salaam is almost twice the area for 2010. To me, it looks about 1/4 bigger... If I note that the diameter is about 40% larger and the area is squared, then I get to about two times. But that is not intuitive which is what a good graphical presentation should be.*"

Some content-oriented comments (3.7%) were directed at the data aggregation, indicating an awareness of how aggregation can skew distributions. Most often this was expressed as a desire to disaggregate the visualized data. For instance, commenters indicated a desire to disaggregate continents into countries, and countries into states or regions. Comments also suggested that an aggregate might be disproportionally inflated by certain observations.

Other comments that explicitly critiqued the visualization focused more on the limitations of the selected data. For instance, 8.9% of coded comments referenced the exclusion, inclusion, or obfuscation of specific values of a variable shown in the visualization (e.g. "*I notice that the inclusion of the United States excluded the land mass of Alaska, which is material*").

Critiques oriented at the visualization were sometimes directed at its anonymous *creator*, as is the prior comment. 3.6% of coded comments explicitly addressed both the visualization and the creator. Other comments directed at the creator indicate that commenters perceived traces of the designer's intentions in the visualization. For example, one commenter suggested "*This graphic is imaginative but I think too much effort went into making it clever rather than accurate.*" Others reflect on the point that is intended by the creators (e.g., "*what G.D. is trying to say*").

Critiques of the definition or choice of words or labels (3.0% of coded comments) could be anchored both on the visual as well as the article text, including critiques of graph annotations, labels, or the article title. Assessments of how a measure or label is defined sometimes also indicated a desire to understand the designer's intentions: "*Your headline refers to waist lines, so the Waist to Hip Ratio would be a better measure than BMI. BMI does not adjust for muscularity.*" Comments relating to definitions (3.0%) often pointed out nuances in terminology (such as measure labels like "entitlements" or "economic wealth") that could influence interpretations of the content.

Among those critiques oriented toward the content of the accompanying article, we observed comments criticizing specific claims in the articles, questioning or disagreeing with them, adding clarifications, suggesting corrections, or adding a caveat to a claim.

Context Orientation (Related Data and Issue Framing)

We describe two forms of context-oriented discussion—concerning Related Data and Issue Framing—that we observed in the 62.1% of comments that focused on matters of context, then detail how critical feedback manifested in context-oriented comments.

Two Varieties of Context-Oriented Comments

Related Data comments contribute information from external sources, data, and personal experiences that may be useful for interpreting the presentation. One obvious form is direct linking using URLs to external sources (e.g. blog posts, news articles, visualizations, or other data), which occurred in 5.9% of comments (full sample), and are often used to support one's arguments or explanations.

Another 4.9% of Related Data comments drew on personal knowledge, opinions, experiences, or narratives to add context or argue. The following comment on a post about youth employment illustrates how these comments add context by bringing in personal storytelling, "*I'm 25 in China and thank goodness I have found a nice job. And as well as many of my classmates. We'll graduate next July. However, a good job is still hard to get for those who don't has [sic] a relatively high and famous degree.*"

Other distinguishable subsets of Related Data comments including adding related data in order to point out comparisons that impact interpretation (20.9%); or to explicate conditions surrounding the sources of data used in the graph (20.4%). An example of the former case includes citing statistics so that others could compare them with the presented data. For instance, one comment introduced population statistics correlated with the visualized data. Examples of commenters' interests in conditions surrounding the data sources includes a comment characterizing the agenda of the sources responsible for the data (e.g. "*The Bertelsmann Foundation is surely no leftish organization. It's a liberal/neocon [sic] think tank...*").

Issue Framing comments are a second form of context-oriented comments (28.3% of total comments) focused on the *framing of the issue*. Subsets of these comments interpreted causality, reflected on the moral considerations associated with an issue, and suggested solutions for the issue, touching on many established facets of media frames [3]. Other issue framing comments put the presented issue in perspective against another (ostensibly relevant) issues that it might impact, such as a comment on a post about food prices that introduced the issue of obesity. Such comments can be distinguished from Related Data comments in that the former direct the focus from the current issue (food

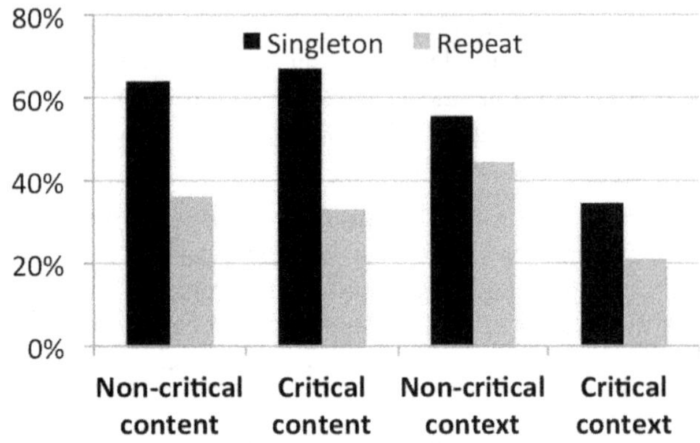

Figure 2: Percentage of comments of varying types contributed by singleton versus repeat commenters. Singletons are more likely than repeat commenters to provide comments on content.

prices) to a related issue (obesity), rather than surfacing factors to improve understanding of the current issue.

Critical Context-Oriented Comments

We observed directly critical feedback occurring in 37.4% of all context-oriented comments. Critical Related Data comments implied that incorporating the information the commenter was adding would improve the accuracy of the presentation. Others asked pointed questions implying overlooked factors in the analysis: "*The approach to compare the current ratio of house prices to rents seems overly simplistic... How is rent control taken into account for apartments?*" Suggestions of other variables to include in analysis were the most common form of Related Data critique. These comments differ from critical content-oriented comments around data exclusion in that Related Data comments focused on the overlooking of entire factors or variables rather than a single datum.

Critical issue framing comments often questioned the significance of a "problem," as in this comment on a post about the upcoming World Economic Forum "*Hey, a way more game changing event is taking place in Egypt. Forget Davos.*" Such comments indicated sensitivity among commenters to how media frames select and emphasize different perspectives or ways of thinking about an issue.

Other critical issue framing comments provided "meta-insights:" realizations that seek to understand not just the single presentation, but the nature of the domain from which the data comes. For example, one commenter concluded that a conventional approach to describing economic relationships was not appropriately complex or dynamic: "*social justice has always been-and always will be a fuzzy term with no meaning... instead of making and publishing indexes of social justice, separate indexes on poverty, education, and so on should be made.*"

Who Comments on What

Previous research finds that high "facticity" (i.e. reporting on concrete actions or events) attracts fewer average comments per user on political news articles [21]. Here, we pose a similar question: do aspects of the presentation that are most obviously factual and concrete (the content such as the data and visualization) attract more singleton or repeat commenters? Our of 764 unique commenters across the 4,468 comment set, 602 of these commenters commented once (singletons), implying that 87% of comments were written by the other 21% of users (repeat). This aligns with observed content generation dynamics where a few core users contribute the majority of content [15].

Figure 2 compares the percentage of the four subclasses based on the content- vs. context and non-critical versus critical distinctions that are contributed by singletons versus repeat commenters. The biggest disparity is for content anchors. Singletons provide the majority of non-critical comments about content (64%) and the majority of critical comments about content (67%). Repeat commenters more frequently focus on matters of context (67.2% of all comments from repeat commenters discuss context critical or not critically). These results suggest that the lower average comments per user on high facticity posts found in [21] is due to an attraction of singletons to high facticity content.

DISCUSSION AND FUTURE WORK

Our results show several interesting differences compared to prior work in visualization commenting. Prior studies emphasize the focused, analytical nature of comments posted when interacting with research-based systems [8,19,22], such as how comments represent hypotheses and observations around a dataset. Subsets of the content and context categories we observe fit these characterizations. However, matters of context were more frequently discussed in our sample. Discussions ranged from listing "overlooked" variables to questioning the moral significance of an issue.

Additionally, a considerable proportion of the comments we observed showed a preoccupation with *removing perceived obstructions* to allow for accurate interpretations. Commenters on the GD seem to naturally engage in what has been termed "visualization criticism" [9]: a practice in which the shortcomings of visualization designs are discussed with reference to aesthetic criteria. In this case, however, the most common criteria appeared to be an expected journalistic ethic. Commenting behavior diverged from prior study results in that commenters frequently alluded to decisions made in framing the data, visual, and other content [9] including facets of media frames like problem definition, causality, moral significance, etc. [3].

The content-context dichotomy and prevalence of criticism may result from novel aspects of GD compared to laboratory studies or research prototypes. The potential for a text article to paint an issue in broad strokes may compel commenters to similarly consider the broader context surrounding the issue as opposed to the content alone. Awareness of the media source of the presentation may cue a critical mindset among commenters wary of the power of media frames to persuade. Future research should continue to explore how these aspects impact commenting activity.

Design Implications

The frequent direct criticism in comments motivates using comments in the design process, as a mean of incorporating a mutually beneficial "social feedback loop." As an audience considers a designer's decisions in light of their expectations, their comments uncover specific design choices that may have led to misunderstandings, misinterpretations, or strong criticism. Content critiques provide designers with direct advice for adjusting the design of a visualization or article to improve its accuracy or interpretability. Future work should explore developing interfaces that automatically categorize content critiques for easier integration into the designer's process.

Critiques discussing related data could similarly be consulted to make a presentation more comprehensive or "complete" in its representation of an issue, such as through adding textual qualifications to explain the reasoning behind omissions. The prevalence of Related Data comments suggests that platforms incorporate features that allow commenters' to more directly link related yet external evidence with aspects of a presentation. Finally, interfaces that make the anchor schema visible, such as by enabling commenters to link their comments to the appropriate part of the presentation, could simplify the sensemaking process of subsequent commenters.

CONCLUSION

We presented a study of collaborative visual analysis via comments in a naturalistic data journalism setting. We report rich observations and quantitative measures describing how commenters direct their attention to matters of content but more frequently, context. We describe how this content versus context distinction is related to whether commenters are singletons or repeat commenters. Our results also indicate that over one third of comments provide explicit critical advice for how to improve the presentation. We observe a sensitivity to framing choices in particular that has not been surfaced in prior work. We contribute a novel coding scheme for differentiating content versus context-oriented and critical versus non-critical comments in studying comments around data presentations. Our results motivate new users for comments as social feedback that is potentially useful in the design process, and also suggest new features for commenting platforms.

REFERENCES

1. Chen, Y., Yang, J. & Ribarsky, W. Toward Effective Insight Management in Visual Analytics Systems. *IEEE Pacific Vis. '09*, 49–56.
2. N. Diakopoulos, N. & Naaman, M. Towards Quality Discourse in Online News Comments. *CSCW '11,* 133–142.
3. The Economist. Graphic Detail (blog), http://www.economist.com/blogs/graphicdetail.
4. Entman, R. Framing: Towards Clarification of a Fractured Paradigm. *J. of Communication 43* (4), 51-58, 1993.
5. Gilbert, E., Bergstrom, T., & Karahalios, K. Blogs are echo chambers: Blogs are echo chambers. *HICSS'09.*
6. The Guardian. Data Blog (blog), http://www.theguardian.com/news/datablog.
7. Heer, J. & Agrawala, M. Design Considerations for Collaborative Visual Analytics. *Info.Visualization 7,* 49–62, 2008.
8. Heer, J. Viégas, F., & Wattenberg, M. Voyagers and Voyeurs: Supporting Asynchronous Collaborative Information Visualization. *CHI '07,* 1029–1038.
9. Hullman, J. & Diakopoulos, N. Visualization Rhetoric: Framing Effects in Narrative Visualization. *InfoVis '11,* 2231–2240.
10. Kosara, R., Drury, F., Holmquist, L., & Laidlaw, D. Visualization Criticism. *IEEE CG&A Visualization Viewpoints 28* (3), 13-15. 2008.
11. Lofland, J. & Lofland, L. Analyzing social Settings: a Guide to Qualitative Observation and Analysis. Wadsworth, 2005.
12. Manosevitch, E. & Walker, D. Reader comments to online opinion journalism: A space of public deliberation," *Int'l Symp. on Online Journalism,* 2009.
13. Mercier, H. & Sperber, D. Why do humans reason? Arguments for an argumentative theory, *SSRN*, 2013.
14. Mishne, G. & Glance, N. Leave a Reply: An analysis of weblog comments. *Weblogging Ecosystem Wkshp.,* 2006.
15. The New York Times, The Upshot (blog), http://www.nytimes.com/upshot/.
16. Ochoa, X. & Duval, E. Quantitative analysis of user-generated content on the web. *Webevolve'08 Workshop, WWW '08.*
17. Silver, N. FiveThirtyEight (blog), fivethirtyeight.com.
18. Viégas, F., Wattenberg, M., McKeon, M, van Ham, F., & Kriss, J. Harry Potter and the meat-filled freezer: A case study of spontaneous usage of visualization tools. *HICSS '08.*
19. Viégas, F., Wattenberg, M., van Ham, F., Kriss, J., & McKeon, M. Manyeyes: A site for visualization at internet scale. *IEEE InfoVis '07,* 1121–1128.
20. Wattenberg, M. Baby Names, visualization, and social data analysis. *IEEE InfoVis '05*, 1-7.
21. Weber, P. Discussions in the comments section: Factors influencing participation and interactivity in online newspapers' reader comments. *New Media & Society* 2013.
22. Willett, W., Heer, J., & Agrawala, M. Strategies for crowdsourcing social data analysis. *CHI '12,* 227-236.
23. Willett, W., Heer, J., Hellerstein, J., & Agrawala, M, CommentSpace: Structured support for collaborative visual analysis. *CHI '11,* 3131-3140.

Disclosure, Stress, and Support During Gender Transition on Facebook

Oliver L. Haimson, Jed R. Brubaker, Lynn Dombrowski, Gillian R. Hayes
Department of Informatics
University of California, Irvine
Irvine, CA, USA
{ohaimson, jed.brubaker, ldombrow, hayesg}@uci.edu

ABSTRACT
Social computing technologies, such as social networking sites (SNSs), often privilege people who fit within expected, static categories. Thus, users embarking on major identity changes, such as gender transition, often encounter stress when using SNSs to interact with their online social networks. To address this problem and reflect on the design of SNSs and other social computing systems, we present the results of a comprehensive online survey of transgender and gender non-conforming SNS users. Our findings indicate that although Facebook can be a stressful place for gender transition due to difficulties of transition disclosure, support from one's Facebook network can help to mitigate some of this stress. We examine Facebook both as a site of stress and as a site of support. Better understanding the relationships between stress, disclosure, and support on SNSs for these particular users can inform technology design that will benefit people who struggle with navigating a wide range of major identity changes online.

Author Keywords
Social networking sites; identity transitions; life transitions; transgender; LGBTQ; online identity; stress; support.

ACM Classification Keywords
H.5.3. Information interfaces and presentation (*e.g.*, HCI): Group and Organization Interfaces: Collaborative computing, Computer-supported cooperative work, Web-based interaction.

INTRODUCTION
Many people struggle with online self-presentation during periods of life transition. Announcing and representing changes on social networking sites (SNS) can cause stress and uncertainty. The pervasive nature of social media adds additional challenges and opportunities to a wide range of identity transitions, particularly those that involve potential disapproval or estrangement from others in one's network (*e.g.*, changes in relationship status, job termination, coming out as gay or lesbian, child birth, gender transition). The complexities that arise during identity transitions on SNSs warrant specific analysis of issues including disclosure concerns and the role of one's online social network in transition support.

ACM 978-1-4503-2922-4/15/03···$15.00
http://dx.doi.org/10.1145/2675133.2675152

Taking gender transition as a case study of identity transition more broadly, what particular SNS practices add to or diminish stress as individuals change gender on SNSs? Gender transitions have already been shown to be stressful offline [29]. In this work, we demonstrate that they are also stressful online. However, simply knowing that something is stressful is not enough. We must understand how and why these transitions are stressful to effectively design technology and SNSs that counter stress while leveraging one's online social network for transition support. Designing such systems with considerations for life transition support can reduce stress for transgender people and others during periods of identity transition.

In what follows, we describe ways in which gender transition on Facebook can be uniquely stressful, beyond the stress experienced from gender transition in general. We describe what kinds of Facebook account management activities are related to self-reported online transition stress. In particular, transition disclosure and concerns around how others will respond to this disclosure are major stressors. However, we also find that transition-related support from one's Facebook network may reduce this stress. Our analyses investigate Facebook both as a site of stress and as a site of support during gender transition.

In this work, we determine that navigating the parts of Facebook's user interface and infrastructure that relate to disclosure predict additional stress for this group of users, while support from one's Facebook network predict reduced stress. Additionally, Facebook's new gender options, a "fix" for some of the classification problems that the system has with transgender and gender non-conforming users, have not actually reduced transition-related stress for this group of users, likely due to problems of disclosure. These results give insight into the ways that sociotechnical systems can improve disclosure options and use social network support to reduce stress for those changing identities online.

CSCW has a rich history of scholarship critiquing the uneven politics of classification and categorization (*e.g.*, [5, 42]). Classification of gender and its relation to self-presentation is a secondary theme of this paper and an important area for continued research. However, our findings show that addressing categorization issues alone is not enough. Disclosure of personal information about identity transitions on Facebook is a more fundamental concern for participants in this work. Therefore, in this paper, we focus primarily on five research questions related to differential identity disclosure, as outlined here:

Stress. How stressful is gender transition on Facebook, and how does this compare with stress experienced during gender transition in other settings?

Account management strategies and disclosure. In what account management activities do people engage during gender transition on Facebook, and how are these activities related to disclosure and associated with stress?

Network transition support. During gender transition, how supportive are peoples' Facebook networks, how does this compare with support received from other networks, and how is this support associated with stress experienced?

Custom gender options and disclosure. How do Facebook's new custom gender options relate to gender transition-related disclosure and stress?

Demographics. Are demographic variables such as race, gender, or socioeconomic status associated with higher levels of stress during gender transition on Facebook?

The remainder of this paper is organized as follows. First, we provide some background on transgender issues and identity transitions. Next, we discuss related research, followed by a description of our methods. We then present empirical findings based on analysis of data from our online survey. We close with a discussion of design implications and a summary of our findings.

BACKGROUND

This section provides background by first defining transgender, then situating it among other life transitions and identity changes. We then discuss the recent history of gender representation on Facebook.

Gender Transition as Identity and Life Transition

Transgender is an umbrella term that can broadly be defined as including "those who transition from one gender to another…and those who may not, including genderqueer people, cross-dressers, the androgynous, and those whose gender non-conformity is part of their identity" [27:12]. Importantly, a person's relationship to their gender is what matters here, not necessarily physical characteristics or changes. Following [29], we use "trans" for the remainder of this paper to refer to the broad transgender population, except when designating between different facets of the transgender community.

Little is known about how trans people navigate gender transition online. Studying this community of SNS users and their information practices as an extreme case of identity transition can lead to better understandings of the sources of stress during life transitions more broadly, particularly those that involve substantial changes to identity. This work also provides insight into identity transition-related constraints within SNSs and their corresponding information infrastructures and user interfaces. These insights inform our knowledge of how stress and constraints encountered on SNSs more generally affect those embarking on major identity changes.

Although many major life changes cause people to change their identities substantially, gender transition is unique because numerous complex identity changes are coupled with risks of discrimination, harassment, and rejection [22, 27, 29]. Gender transition often leads to severe marginalization as well as rejection and disapproval from friends, family members, and networks at work and school [22, 29]. All of these factors contribute to stress for trans people [29], making transition especially difficult. At the same time, gender transition is one of the only life changes so drastic that a person often becomes literally unrecognizable to their friends, family, and online social networks. For example, during transition, a person's SNS profile will often change in three substantial ways: name, gender, and physical appearance in profile photo. These changes can occur months or even years apart from each other. If such changes are made without announcement, or if the announcement of gender change is not displayed or noticed by some members of the trans person's online social network, a person who was once a "friend" now appears as a stranger. Thus, gender transition requires many complicated decisions around disclosure. Facing discrimination, violence, and rejection, while at the same time managing complex disclosure decisions, may make a trans person feel uncomfortable and unfamiliar within their online social network, thus causing stress, frustration, and disengagement with the SNS.

Because few other life transitions encompass such potentially drastic, numerous, and complex identity changes, gender transition allows insight into SNS practices in a way that other major life changes do not. Previous research found that students changing gender allowed university information systems administrators to uncover structural holes in databases [12, 30]. Likewise, studying the experiences of trans SNS users gives us a unique view into the potentially problematic nature of SNSs during identity transitions, which we will examine in the remainder of this paper.

Gender Representation on Facebook

Recently, the needs of trans people have received popular attention with Facebook's introduction of custom gender

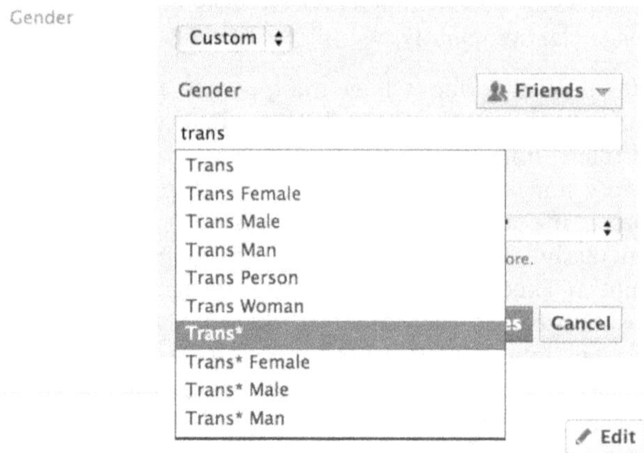

Figure 1. Custom gender option selection on Facebook [screenshot taken May 26, 2014].

options. On February 13, 2014, Facebook activated its new "Custom" gender options. Instead of only two gender options, users could now choose from 58 terms to describe their gender. Additionally, users could choose from three rather than two pronoun options. However, behind the user interface, Facebook's database continues to store gender in simplified ways, effectively categorizing many of its 56 custom gender options into more prominent gender codes [4]. This simplified classification system results in instances in which Facebook's underlying categories, which can be problematic for the trans user, bleed through into the various places in the system in which gendered language is used (*e.g.*, the pronouns attached to an individual's activity) [4]. Inputting a custom gender is also problematic for some trans users, because the system imposes constraints on gender representation. While the interface includes what appears to be a freeform text box, the user is actually limited to a pre-set list of options that become visible as the user attempts to type in their preferred gender term (see Figure 1).

The recent implementation of additional gender options on Facebook is a laudable step in supporting the trans community. However, features that allow trans people to control the display of their gender identities cannot mitigate the much broader set of stressors of which self-presentation is only a part. In fact, in some cases, as we describe in this paper, the availability of additional options may create additional stress. In this work, we describe a broad range of account management activities, including those related to disclosure and representation, in terms of their potential to both create and diminish stress related to gender transition on Facebook.

RELATED WORK

Researching the trans population provides a unique contribution to existing CSCW literature on major life changes. With the exception of [4] and [31], no work has focused specifically on trans people's use of SNSs, and no empirical research has been conducted in this area. Thus, we present a review of related work about stress, support, and disclosure on SNSs during life transitions more broadly.

Social computing systems, such as SNSs, allow users unique ways to express identity online during major life changes and can be major sources of social support [11] and helpful information for adapting to changes [41]. Studies show that online social networks and support groups benefit a wide range of transitional communities, such as new parents [20], those who have recently lost a job [11], adults transitioning to old age [37], and students entering college [19, 39, 41, 43]. In the absence of socialization that allows people to gain the skills necessary to smoothly navigate life transitions [25], some of these skills are learned via SNS networks. Networks on SNSs are an important source of support for people facing major life changes.

However, SNSs can also be potentially harmful spaces during life transitions. The public, open nature of SNSs can place users at risk of harassment, which can complicate and even impede life transitions online [16, 36]. Communication with one's Facebook network can cause added stress during life transitions when friends offer unhelpful advice, and passive consumption of news feed content can decrease social support [11]. Additionally, SNSs open up a whole new set of "digital possessions," such as photographs, messages, and even SNS profiles themselves, many of which must be sorted through and changed during a life transition [38]. By further examining the potentially negative aspects of using SNSs during life transitions, we seek to understand how to best support transition processes online, including ways to preserve privacy and allow for optimal network support.

In particular, SNSs complicate life transitions due to complexities around disclosure of transition-related information and self-presentation online. People carefully curate their self-presentation depending on their intended audience [26]. Impression management [26] has always been an important topic in SNS research [7], but is particularly relevant when considering complex and multiple identities that emerge during major life changes. On SNSs, people commonly present different information depending on the audience [6, 15, 23, 34, 35]. Maintaining multiple SNS profiles is a common practice, but is a burden and comes with the risk of unintended "leakage" between accounts [15]. Particularly for marginalized groups, having incompatible faceted identities may cause people to worry more about posting on Facebook, thus leading them to use email, a private platform, more often [23]. However, even with email, people maintain multiple accounts for use in different settings [28]. People use both mental strategies and account management behaviors on Facebook to "divide the platform into separate spaces" in order to manage disclosures among different groups of friends [32:288]. Customizing privacy settings, for instance creating lists of friends, is a common account management technique for disclosure, and has been shown to increase the amount of content shared on Facebook [40]. However, many Facebook users misinterpret privacy settings [1], which can lead to information being shared with unintended audiences [34, 47]. Although users employ many strategies to manage disclosure on SNSs during life transitions, in this work we show that some of these behaviors are associated with increased transition-related stress.

Stress associated with life transitions [25, 41] can carry over to, or even be exacerbated by, SNSs. Our contribution to CSCW lies in understanding which Facebook account management behaviors relate to increased stress during transition, and how support from one's network may diminish this stress. In turn, by documenting the conditions under which the stress and support occurs, this work sheds light on how SNS designers can help reduce transition-related stress and promote network support.

METHODS

We developed an online survey aimed at trans people who had experienced gender transition on SNSs. Due to the nature of the research questions, the survey excluded people who had transitioned prior to establishing a profile on a SNS, because they would not have experienced gender transition on a SNS. Participants were recruited and asked to complete the survey via several methods. The authors shared recruitment materials on their social media profiles and encouraged our networks to share the link. Recruitment materials were emailed to several email lists targeted at the transgender and LGBTQ communities, and shared on LGBTQ and transgender-focused groups or forums on Facebook and other SNSs. We also distributed recruitment materials to our contacts at several health centers specializing in trans healthcare. Participation was incentivized by entering survey participants into a drawing for a $500 Visa gift card. The survey was active April 15 – May 31, 2014

Most of the questions provided Likert-style response options (N = 51) or yes/no with other possible response options (N = 16), while others provided lists of possible SNS practices with an "Other (please specify)" option that included a write-in answer box (N = 8). Other optional questions were more qualitative in nature and provided free-form write-in answer fields (N = 15). Many questions were shown to some participants but hidden to others depending on answers to previous questions. All survey questions relevant to the results presented in this paper are included in an Appendix at the end of the paper.

While our survey included questions about a variety of SNS platforms, the data and findings we report in this paper are specific to questions about Facebook (Q3-18). Because Facebook is the dominant SNS in the U.S., used by 71% of online adults [18] and by 98.90% of participants in our study, we focused on Facebook specifically to collect a large sample of data about one platform. This allowed us to analyze participants' gender transition practices and challenges on Facebook in more depth. Facebook is also particularly interesting, because the platform recently implemented custom gender options, which we analyze in relation to self-reported transition stress.

The first part of the survey (Q3-14) focused on Facebook use. Those who had previously maintained a Facebook profile but did not currently use Facebook were asked to reflect on "the time when you were last active on Facebook." Questions about Facebook touched on common practices regarding online transition account management activities in general (Q7) and management of one's "friends" list (Q8). Participants were then asked about how stressful it was to transition on Facebook (Q9a) and how many people in their Facebook network they perceived were supportive of their transition (Q10). These questions were followed by open-ended questions (Q11-14) such as "What parts of transitioning on Facebook were especially difficult? Why were they difficult?" and "What do you think would improve the online gender transition experience on Facebook?"

Next, respondents were asked about their thoughts and practices regarding Facebook's new custom gender options (Q15-18). Those who were not aware of the new custom gender options skipped this section of the survey. Questions then turned to stress experienced in particular offline settings (Q19-20) and self-perceived transition support received offline from friends, family, and co-workers (Q21-24). Finally, demographic information was collected from participants (Q25-31).

Because a validated scale does not exist for measuring stress or support during gender transition, or even for measuring such variables during a previous time period, our stress and support variables instead measure self-perceived stress and support experienced during transition. We evaluated several validated stress and social support scales for possible use (*e.g.*, [13, 33]), but none were appropriate for evaluating stress and support experienced around a particular past event. Additionally, we were concerned that adding multi-question scales to an already lengthy survey would lower survey completion rates. However, our survey instruments exhibit face validity. To test the face validity of our stress variable, two of the authors qualitatively coded levels of stress represented in 35 randomly-selected participants' responses to open-ended questions. The average of the two coders' measures of qualitative stress was highly correlated with participants' Likert scale response to Q9a, $r(33) = .63$, $p < .001$, indicating face validity of Q9a as a measure of stress. Inter-rater reliability between the two coders was high at $r(33) = .86$, $p < .001$. Face validity was also demonstrated by positive feedback from a pilot group of survey participants.

Each section of the survey included optional questions for any additional information that participants wished to share (*e.g.*, "Is there anything else you would like to tell us about your transition experience on Facebook?"). Answers to these and the aforementioned open-ended questions allowed us to qualitatively support our quantitative results using open coding of free-form response data. On average, for each of the open-ended questions about gender transition on Facebook, 55.81% of participants opted to spend the extra time to include a write-in response.

Data

Our sample included 371 participants who completed the online survey. 615 participants started the survey but some did not finish, either being disqualified due to not meeting the study's criteria, or opting not to finish for other reasons. The first author manually cleaned the data, removing responses from participants whose answers appeared illogical or insincere, or who completed the survey despite not qualifying. Data from 62 participants was not used because they either were not a Facebook user or had not transitioned on Facebook. Our final model included data from 242 participants after removing participants with missing data for any of the relevant variables. All of these participants had experienced a gender transition of some sort on Facebook, whether from male to female, female to male, or from a binary gender to a non-binary gender such as genderqueer, agender, or gender non-conforming.

Participants were allowed to choose multiple gender and race/ethnicity options (for instance, a person may identify both as transfemale and as genderqueer, or as both white/Caucasian and Hispanic/Latino). As such, percentages add up to greater than 100%. When asked their current gender, 46.30% of participants identified as female/ transfemale/transwoman/MTF, 39.18% as male/transmale/ transman/FTM, and 25.48% as genderqueer, agender, gender non-conforming, or a different gender. Our sample was not racially diverse: 90.68% were white/Caucasian, 5.21% were Asian/Pacific Islander, 5.48% were Hispanic/Latino, 3.01% were American Indian/Native American, and 1.92% were black/African-American. The lack of racial diversity may be a result of our networks used to recruit participants, and is a limitation of this research. The mean age was 28.93 (SD = 8.84, range: 18-66).

Participants reported a median of approximately 201-500 Facebook friends and a median daily Facebook usage of approximately 1-2 hours. On average, participants began their transition on Facebook 2.41 years prior to taking the survey (SD = 2.07, range: 0-10) and began their transition overall 3.97 years prior to taking the survey (SD = 4.60, range: 0-45).

We cannot claim that our sample is representative of the trans population overall. It is not currently possible to obtain a random sample of trans people [27], however, the most comprehensive and representative survey of trans people to date is Grant *et al.*'s National Transgender Discrimination Survey [27]. Our sample is comparable to Grant *et al.*'s [27] in terms of gender identity when categorizing participants as male, female, or other, $X^2(2, N = 371) = 3.39$, $p = .18$. However, significant racial differences exist between our sample and Grant *et al.*'s [26], $X^2(4, N = 371) = 20.41$, $p < .001$. Specifically, our sample includes significantly fewer blacks/African-Americans (standardized residual = -3.32), fewer American Indians/Native Americans (standardized residual = -2.24), and more Whites/Caucasians (standardized residual = 2.71) than Grant *et al.*'s [27], a limitation of our study.

Data Analysis

Quantitative data were analyzed using descriptive statistics and statistical modeling to explore relationships between stress, support, and account management activities, the variables of interest in this work. Stress around transition disclosure also emerged as a common theme in qualitative open-coding of short-answer responses by two of the authors.

To understand which disclosure-related activities (see Table 1) most contributed to and reduced stress, we used regression models to explore the relationships between account management activities and self-reported transition stress. We first ran 11 separate regressions, one for each account management activity in Table 1, with self-reported stress as the outcome variable and the account management activity as an independent variable along with control variables. Then, only those account management activities that predicted increased stress of transition on Facebook were used as independent variables in a final standardized linear regression model (see Table 2). This model included self-reported stress as the outcome variable, and self-reported transition practices on Facebook and level of support from one's Facebook network as independent variables. Control variables included gender, age, years since transition, race/ethnicity, socioeconomic status indicators, amount of time spent on Facebook daily, and number of Facebook friends.

Limitations

Because our analysis is based on survey data, we present correlational results without causal claims. Our model includes control variables to eliminate potential confounds. This allows us to argue that real relationships exist between disclosure-related Facebook behavior, self-reported support and self-reported stress. Additionally, as described in the methods section, using non-validated survey instruments to measure stress and support is a potential limitation of this work. However, the face validity of our survey questions gives us confidence that our survey captured participants' self-perceived levels of stress and support during gender transition. Self-reported data is also a limitation because participants transitioned on average several years prior to taking the survey, leading to potential difficulties in recalling transition experiences. Next, as noted in the Data section, our sample may not be representative of the overall trans population, thus limiting the generalizability of our results. A final limitation is that peoples' lived experiences are more complex than can be captured by the online/offline binary that some of our survey questions assume.

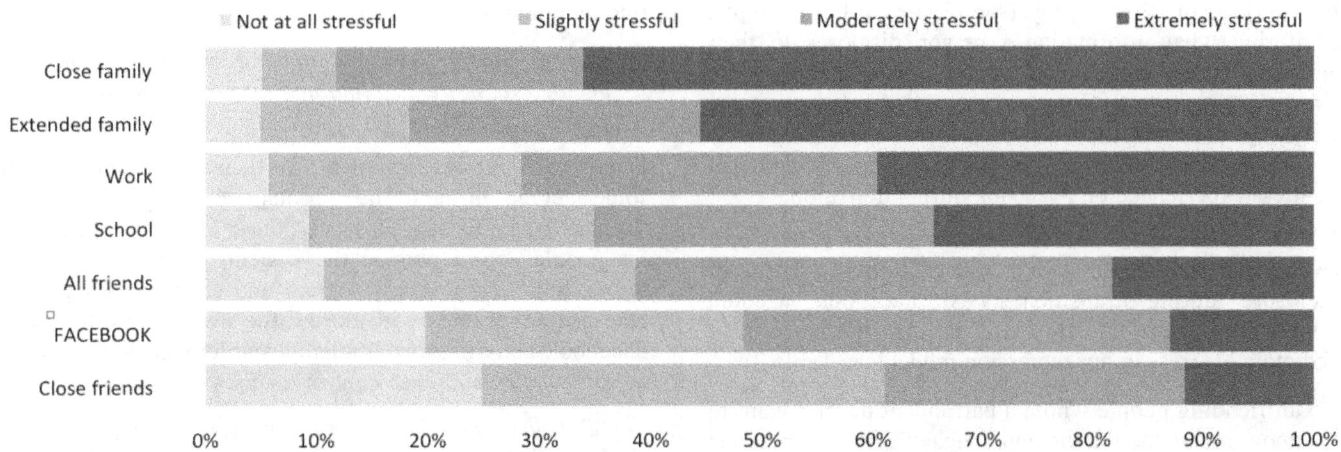

Figure 2. How stressful was it to transition in each of these environments? (Ordered from most stressful to least stressful)

RESULTS

The results of our work offer insight into the self-reported stress experienced by trans Facebook users and provide a statistical model examining relationships between stress and transition-related Facebook account management activities. These results also illuminate participants' perceived transition-related support among different networks, and how this relates to transition stress on Facebook in general and in light of Facebook's custom gender options. We also analyze demographic variables and transition-related stress.

Stress

How stressful is gender transition on Facebook?

During gender transition, trans people experience substantial stress while using Facebook. When asked how stressful it was to transition on Facebook (Q9a), 51.70% of participants responded that it was "extremely stressful" or "moderately stressful", while only 19.73% described it as "not at all stressful" (see Figure 2).

How does this compare with stress experienced during gender transition in other settings?

Interactions on Facebook (Q9a) were reported to be significantly less stressful (M = 2.45, SD = .95) than interactions in most non-SNS transition settings (see Figure 2), such as among close family (Q19c) (M = 3.49, SD = .85), $t(282) = -16.95$, $p < .001$; among extended family (Q19d) (M = 3.34, SD = .89), $t(261) = -13.10$, $p < .001$; at work (Q19e) (M = 3.04, SD = .92), $t(234) = -7.93$, $p < .001$; at school (Q19f) (M = 2.85, SD = 1.00), $t(178) = -5.00$, $p < .001$; and among all friends (Q19b) (M = 2.69, SD = .89), $t(290) = -4.21$, $p < .01$. However, transitioning on Facebook was significantly more stressful than transitioning among close friends (Q19a) (M = 2.24, SD = .95), $t(292) = 3.38$, $p < .01$. Although other transition settings cause people to experience more stress during gender transition, Facebook is unique because one's Facebook network often includes people from all of the categories considered most stressful – close family, extended family, co-workers, classmates, and friends. During gender transition, an individual may want to present their identity differently to different social groups, thus complicating disclosure of transition-related information.

Account Management Strategies and Disclosure

In what account management activities do people engage during gender transition on Facebook, and how are these activities related to disclosure?

Participants engaged in many account management activities aimed at controlling disclosure, such as creating "lists" to share content with only certain friends, unfriending, switching to a new profile/account, and/or maintaining multiple profiles/accounts (see Table 1). Lists allow profile owners to disclose certain information only to particular groups of people. For example, separate lists can be maintained for family members, co-workers, and close friends. When posting a status update, the privacy setting can be toggled to restrict the audience of that post to only people appearing on particular lists. The ability to use lists to control disclosure may make transition on Facebook less

Activity	Percentage who engaged in activity
Announced transition	48.77%
Changed the gender listed on profile	68.49%
Changed the name displayed on profile	59.73%
Changed my profile picture	62.74%
Deleted profile/account	10.96%
Created new profile	18.90%
Maintained multiple accounts	14.79%
Unfriended or blocked people who may not be supportive	41.64%
Unfriended or blocked people I did not want to know about transition	20.00%
Made some posts visible only to some people in network	30.96%
Created lists or groups to make posts visible to only certain groups of people	19.18%

Table 1. Disclosure-related activities on Facebook.

stressful than in other settings (see Figure 2). For example, monitoring what information a person discloses to their transphobic uncle on Facebook is much easier than doing so at a family gathering. However, the act of monitoring the audience of transition-related content and regularly scrutinizing friends lists may in fact contribute to some of the stress experienced on Facebook during transition.

How are these activities associated with stress?

Several important findings highlight the stressful nature of disclosure during transition. Two Facebook account management practices emerged as significant positive predictors of stress in our regression model (see Table 2):

- unfriending people whom a participant did not want to know about their transition (engaging in this practice predicted a 0.30 standard deviation increase in stress)
- creating lists or groups to make posts visible to only certain groups of people (engaging in this practice predicted a 0.40 standard deviation increase in stress)

Both of these practices directly relate to disclosure on Facebook. These associations between disclosure practices and stress highlight how complex management practices may actually increase stress, as we argue here. They may also, however, indicate that people experiencing more stress are more likely to engage in complex management practices in attempts to reduce stress. Many participants expressed concern with certain portions of their Facebook networks finding out about their transition:

> *"[The] hardest part was making sure that what I decided to share ... remained only viewable to that group." (P268)*

	Self-Reported Stress of Transition on Facebook	
Variable	Coefficient	Standard error
Unfriended people I didn't want to know about my transition	**0.30***	**(0.14)**
Created lists or groups to make posts visible to only certain groups of people	**0.40****	**(0.15)**
Perceived support from Facebook network	**-0.21*****	**(0.06)**
Female	-0.04	(0.15)
Non-binary gender	-0.18	(0.19)
Age	-0.16	(0.09)
Years since transition	-0.18*	(0.08)
American Indian/Native American	-0.05	(0.31)
Asian/Pacific Islander	-0.03	(0.27)
Black/African American	0.15	(0.43)
Hispanic/Latino	0.01	(0.24)
Highest degree	0.14	(0.07)
Income	0.10	(0.07)
Time spent on Facebook	-0.04	(0.06)
Size of Facebook network	0.05	(0.07)
Intercept	-0.15	(0.11)
Adjusted R^2 = 0.14, N = 242		

* p < .05; ** p < .01; *** p < .001

Table 2. Results of standardized linear regression model examining factors associated with self-reported stress of transition on Facebook.

People can control the audience of their online transition to some degree through the various technological features supplied by Facebook. However, these tools do not account for people acting outside the system, such as by taking screenshots of Facebook content and sharing with people who are not friends with the profile owner, or other non-Facebook activities. Additionally, participants struggled to use or trust the audience control features provided:

> *"Because of Facebook's privacy settings, it's basically impossible to transition incrementally. (I imagine it's *technically* possible – but I don't know anyone who's actually understood the FB privacy setup well enough to pull it off.) So I had to be thoroughly closeted on FB until I was ready to post a completely public announcement." (P131)*

> *"Because Facebook doesn't have an easy way of systematically sharing to/excluding circles of friends (like managing circles on G+ [Google+]), coming out or being myself with people on Facebook especially in the early stages of transition is really hard, or not worth the effort." (P143)*

Understandably, the creation of a second account was a common pattern for *"preventing 'leakage' between online personae" (P276)*. Although such practices did not significantly affect stress in regression models, almost 19% of participants reported creating a new Facebook account during their gender transition, and almost 15% maintained multiple Facebook accounts, perhaps due to the complexities of disclosure activities.

Engaging in account management practices allows trans Facebook users control over their transition disclosure, but in our model these practices also predicted increased stress. Severing ties to parts of one's network and keeping secrets from others is clearly stressful, and the social and public nature of Facebook requires trans users to actively manage friends lists throughout their transition. Additionally, the difficulty of navigating some account management activities may add to the stress of online transition.

Network Transition Support

During gender transition, how supportive are peoples' Facebook networks?

Facebook networks can also help reduce a trans person's stress during transition. Participants' networks on Facebook were generally perceived to be supportive (Q10), with 73.36% of participants reporting that they perceived that all, almost all, or most of the people in their Facebook network were supportive of their transition (see Figure 3). Only 11.84% perceived that few, almost none, or none of the people in their Facebook network were supportive.

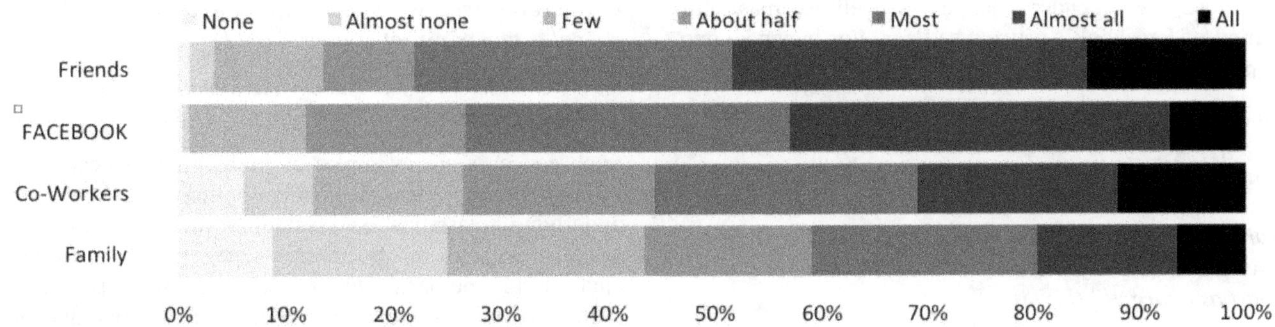

Figure 3. Roughly how many people in this network do you perceive were supportive of your transition online? (Ordered from most supportive to least supportive)

How does support on Facebook compare with support received from other networks during gender transition?

Compared to other networks (see Figure 3), participants' Facebook networks (Q10) were marginally less supportive ($M = 5.11$, $SD = 1.16$) than their friends in offline settings (Q21) ($M = 5.24$, $SD = 1.32$), $U = 50821$, $p = 0.05$; but significantly more supportive than their co-workers (Q23) ($M = 4.54$, $SD = 1.66$), $U = 50607.5$, $p < .001$; or family members (Q22) ($M = 3.90$, $SD = 1.72$), $U = 78327$, $p < .001$ in offline settings.

How is transition-related support from one's Facebook network associated with stress during gender transition on Facebook?

The more supportive a respondent perceived their Facebook network to be of their transition, the less stressful they reported transition being on Facebook. From our model in Table 2, one standard deviation increase of support predicted a 0.21 standard deviation decrease in stress. Support from offline networks, such as family and coworkers, did not have a significant relationship with stress on Facebook, while one's offline friends network has a significant association with stress only before controlling for support from one's Facebook network.

A participant with a particularly supportive Facebook network described the ways that some friends expressed support in ways that may not have been possible offline:

> *"I came out in a letter I wrote to my friends list. All the people that commented on it had nothing but support to show me, and even some people sent me messages telling me that they could not publicly support me, but were happily supporting me behind closed doors." (P287)*

Facebook can also provide access to new networks that have the unique ability to offer support for online transition:

> *"The social circles of supporters and fellow trans people I've made on Facebook have provided substantial and vital support during my coming-out process." (P92)*

Because those with more supportive Facebook networks experienced less stress, we can see the potential for Facebook network support to mitigate the stressful nature of managing transition-related information disclosure.

Custom Gender Options and Disclosure

How do Facebook's new custom gender options relate to gender transition-related disclosure and stress?

Facebook has recently made efforts to support trans people on its site by increasing options available for representing gender identity [21]. Notably, the new custom gender options, as described in the Background section above, provide numerous options for gender self-presentation. In its initial announcement about the new gender options, Facebook's Diversity team stated that its new custom gender options were introduced to help users to "feel comfortable being your true, authentic self" [21]. Among LGBT organizations [24] and in our survey responses, people praised Facebook for the usefulness of the new gender options. However, reported use of custom gender option(s) (Q15) has no statistical association with stress experienced by survey respondents during transition on Facebook. Those who used the custom gender options ($M = 2.50$, $SD = .97$) and those who did not ($M = 2.42$, $SD = .92$) experienced similar levels of stress, $t(269) = -.65, p = .52$.

Using Facebook's custom gender options is a complex process of disclosure. Although the options are appealing in many ways, this complexity may in and of itself contribute to increased stress on Facebook. In particular, although being able to more accurately represent their gender on Facebook may reduce stress for some, this is counterbalanced by the stress of disclosing one's transgender or non-binary gender to one's social network.

Changing one's gender option to the opposite gender or to a non-binary identity is akin to disclosing one's transgender or non-binary status to one's entire network, or selected parts of one's network (by allowing only certain lists of people to see one's gender option). In our statistical model, we found that disclosure activities such as unfriending people and creating lists to control the audience for one's Facebook content are related to increased stress. Thus, it follows that trans people would be hesitant about or unwilling to change their gender option on Facebook. Changing one's gender option involves considerable contemplation about the audience to which one will disclose their gender change, as well as masterful navigation of Facebook's privacy settings. For instance, one participant stated:

> *"It actually worries me, to be honest. I think that outing yourself as clearly transgender/gender non confirming/etc – and having it visible by EVERYONE – is dangerous. There are people out there that target trans/gn-c [gender non-conforming] people, and having that publicly listed on your profile can set you apart as a target." (P295)*

Facebook privacy settings do allow individuals to control what audiences are able to see gender choices, but regardless, people often do not have a good understanding of who can view their profile content. Our qualitative data show that the challenges of maintaining privacy settings and understanding one's disclosure that has been noted elsewhere [1, 46] are particularly poignant in the case of gender transition.

Although most respondents appreciated Facebook's custom gender options (80.00% said that they agreed or strongly agreed that these options improve the online gender transition experience in Q17a), only 39.18% actually reported using the new gender options (Q15) at the time of data collection (roughly two months after the custom gender options were implemented). Custom gender options are used significantly more often by those trans people who identify outside of the male/female binary, such as genderqueer and agender people ($M = .70$, $SD = .46$), than those trans people identifying with more binary genders ($M = .29$, $SD = .45$), $t(363) = -7.54$, $p < .001$, and can indeed be a powerful way for some users to express their gender identity online:

> *"They're great for people who identify as genderqueer, agender, bigender or one of the other identities that falls outside the male/female binary." (P310)*

> *"I'm so happy that there are more gender options, it was hard just seeing male. I feel that two-spirit/trans/genderqueer represent me most accurately." (P239)*

Calling gender options "custom" suggests that individuals have the ability to tailor their disclosure based on the gender terms that they choose. However, at the time of this writing, gender options on Facebook are in fact not fully customizable. As noted in the Background section, Facebook gives the illusion of freeform text entry, but only allows users to select from a pre-set list (see Figure 1). When asked if they tried to enter a custom gender option that was not recognized by Facebook (Q16), 29.37% of those using custom gender options reported that they had. Many participants expressed desires for truly customizable gender:

> *"I know that data collection is a primary focus of facebook. But damn it, custom gender should mean custom. A person should be able to gender themselves however they wish to, instead of choosing from a collection of preset options." (P11)*

> *"The thing I've heard everyone lament (and I agree), is that there is no write-in option." (P137)*

Such concerns are examples of problems that occur due to rigidity of the custom gender options and Facebook's underlying classification system. Since custom gender options map to much broader categories in Facebook's database [4], perhaps allowing users to truly customize the terms used to describe their gender could improve disclosure experiences while adding little overhead.

The combination of disclosure-related stress and the constraints that still exist around Facebook's custom gender options highlights the fact that simply giving people more gender options is not enough. To avoid privileging static identities, design of SNSs like Facebook should specifically address support for major identity changes.

Demographics

Are demographic variables such as race, gender, or socioeconomic status associated with higher levels of stress during gender transition on Facebook?

Gender transition on Facebook is stressful regardless of demographic factors. Demographic variables such as gender (*i.e.*, sub-categories within the trans population) (Q25-26), race/ethnicity (Q27), and socioeconomic status (Q30-31) had no significant association with stress of gender transition online, although the non-randomness of our sample may have influenced these results. We found no significant difference between stress experienced by transgender men, transgender women, and those of non-binary genders such as genderqueer and agender. Similarly, race/ethnicity did not significantly affect online transition stress. Socioeconomic status was measured in two ways: income and highest degree obtained, both of which had no significant association with transition stress on Facebook. Because gender transition on Facebook is equally stressful on average for those of different genders, races/ethnicities, and socioeconomic statuses, this points to a widespread need for technology to support transition for a broad array of the trans population.

Summary of Results

In summary, our results demonstrate that although Facebook can be a stressful place for gender transition due to difficulties of transition disclosure, support from one's Facebook network can help to mitigate some of this stress. Taken together, these results highlight the duality of Facebook as both a site of stress and a site of support. Given this, SNSs like Facebook as well as other platforms could be designed to reduce some of the existing disclosure-related stressors and simultaneously build on the positive nature of support during gender transition.

DISCUSSION

During identity transitions on SNSs, many users are challenged with how and when to disclose content related to these changing identities. Identity is both multifaceted and fluid [6, 15, 26, 35], and our results indicate that this is particularly true during major life transitions. The crude support currently offered for complex, changing identities confirms the ways that SNSs often privilege normative self-presentations [35, 45] and deem non-static concepts of self as problematic. In response to the ways that Facebook privileges those with static identities, trans users and others facing identity transitions adopt multiple accounts or actively manage disclosure practices as a way of negotiating technical constraints and social demands. However, our results indicate that such account management activities lead to stress.

The expectation of static identities on SNSs presumes that individuals come to SNSs to represent an already established identity, rather than to discover, invent, and reinvent themselves. However, in contrast to the authenticity that is now expected [35], online spaces were historically lauded for allowing people a space to explore and experiment with identities [10, 17, 44]. On SNSs, people are "not simply representing but constructing themselves" [45:426], a process that is highly influenced by SNS site design and policy that privileges certain identities while problematizing others [45].

Although we argue that the association between disclosure activities and stress highlights the difficulties and complexities of account management activities on Facebook, it is also useful to briefly explore the possibility of causality in the opposite direction. Perhaps increased stress of gender transition on Facebook causes people to use disclosure-related account management practices. Our qualitative data leads us to believe that stress is increased by navigation of complex account management activities, and not the other way around. However, further research is needed to fully understand the relationships between account management activities and stress, and in particular, whether those who use disclosure features in an attempt to reduce stress actually experience a reduction in stress after using these features.

Difficulties around identity transitions on Facebook extend beyond the user interface and into the database and system infrastructure. As we have demonstrated, Facebook's account management features for selective disclosure of transition-related content can be confusing and stressful. Similarly, Facebook's accommodation of non-binary genders via a list of pre-set gender options constrains gender presentation, causing frustration for some. Both point to larger issues about how Facebook operationalizes "identity" as a set of static attributes with distinct values [9].

Identity transitions are not as simple as pressing a button or flipping a switch – a person is not one day male, the next female. SNSs' emphasis on discrete states, and frequent inability to design for users that move between static categories, is consistent with emerging critiques in a growing body of work on use and non-use [2, 3, 8]. Existing systems often assume a binary – a person either uses a technology or doesn't [2], is married or isn't, is male or is female – when use practices and users themselves are instead much more complex The experience of using SNSs during identity transitions, gender transition on Facebook in particular, can in part be described as a kind of *torque,* the "twisting" that results from a mismatch between a person's identity and a classification system [5]. However, as shown by the lack of impact Facebook's new custom gender options had on stress, the design challenge is greater than just creating more categories. There remains a need for design that addresses torque and improves user experience for trans people and others who, during identity transitions, do not fit neatly into or move effortlessly between existing categories.

Many opportunities for enhanced system and SNS design arise regarding collaborative and social ways to support gender transitions on SNSs. Drawing from our finding that those with Facebook networks more supportive of their transition experience less stress during transition on Facebook, CSCW systems can help to encourage collaborative ways to support online transition. For instance, a system could enable members of a trans person's online social network to help their friend by providing support throughout the transition process in specific ways. Trusted friends could help by monitoring and/or removing digital artifacts that are non-representative and potentially harmful in light of a gender change (*e.g.*, a photograph of a person prior to transition). Systems could include features to facilitate digital artifact management as collaborative work in support of life transitions. SNSs could also incorporate new ways for users to communicate support and empathy to those in their network who are facing a life transition. For instance, a SNS could allow people to publicly denote themselves as "trans friendly," thus alleviating from trans users some of the burden of identifying which friends to disclose transition-related information. Each of these SNS design enhancements, described here with respect to gender transition, could easily be modified to address other major identity changes.

Additionally, while we found a strong association between support from one's Facebook network and decreased stress around transition, not all Facebook users have a supportive network in place. Innovative methods could offer support resources to those who lack a social network of support. For instance, machine learning techniques could be employed to analyze profile text and network activity to determine users who may be facing transitions without network support. Such users could be targeted with transition-related and stress-reduction resources, and/or given supportive volunteers as "suggested friends." Additionally, a system could provide resources (such as relevant support groups, healthcare providers, and legal consultants) that may be helpful during transition. However, due to the sensitive nature of identity transitions and particularly gender transitions, great care should be taken to preserve user privacy and maintain ethical practices when employing such methods.

Finally, because users experience considerable stress around disclosure of gender change and gender identity, designers must consider the granularity [5] of gender options provided. As an example, Facebook's massive list of gender options, many of which are redundant, incorporates far too much granularity. A more appropriate approach would involve less granularity but more control over disclosure. For example, a simple but elegant solution would lump gender options into three categories – male, female, and other/undisclosed – and would allow a free-form write-in box for the third option, as suggested for use in a healthcare context [14]. Such a design would also allow users to control which people or lists of people in their network can see the new gender option, and would display the user's gender as "undisclosed" to others in their network. This design would empower users to choose their own terms to represent their identities, as well as their own level of disclosure. For example, a trans person may simultaneously feel strongly about not identifying within the male/female binary and about not disclosing their trans identity to some in their online social network. A less granular infrastructure with more user control would allow such a person to identify outside of the binary without necessarily disclosing their trans status.

CONCLUSION

We present results from a comprehensive online survey targeted at trans SNS users examining stress, disclosure, and support throughout the gender transition process online. The results of this study demonstrate that specific Facebook account management activities impact stress during gender transition both positively and negatively. In particular, we argue that although practices around disclosure on Facebook are particularly stressful, online network support can mitigate some of this stress. Thus, technology and SNSs can be designed with a focus on disclosure and support in order to reduce the stress that accompanies online transition.

This work contributes to research on disclosure and social computing within the CSCW literature. In particular, lessons learned around disclosure, stress, and support during gender transition are likely to apply to those experiencing other "face threat" identity changes. Like those embarking on gender transition, these people likely also experience stress when interacting with user interfaces like Facebook's to limit the audience of certain content regarding their identity change. CSCW systems can help to leverage online social network support to reduce the stress around transition disclosure.

ACKNOWLEDGEMENTS

We thank our participants for sharing their experiences with us. Thank you to Karen Cheng, Rena Bivens, Anne Bowser, Ellie Harmon, members of STAR and LUCI, and our anonymous reviewers for their generous help and support with this paper. This work was funded in part by a UC Irvine Eugene Cota-Robles Fellowship.

REFERENCES

1. Acquisti, A. and Gross, R. Imagined communities: Awareness, information sharing, and privacy on the Facebook. In *Privacy Enhancing Technologies*. Springer, 2006, 36–58.
2. Baumer, E.P.S., Adams, P., Khovanskaya, V.D., *et al.* Limiting, leaving, and (re)lapsing: An exploration of Facebook non-use practices and experiences. *Proceedings of CHI* (2013).
3. Baumer, E.P.S., Ames, M.G., Brubaker, J.R., Burrell, J., and Dourish, P. Refusing, limiting, departing: Why we should study technology non-use. *Proceedings of CHI Extended Abstracts* (2014).
4. Bivens, R. *The Gender Binary Will Not Be Deprogrammed: Ten Years of Coding Gender on Facebook*. Social Science Research Network, 2014.
5. Bowker, G.C. and Star, S.L. *Sorting Things Out: Classification and Its Consequences*. MIT Press, 1999.
6. boyd, d.m. Friendster and publicly articulated social networking. *Proceedings of CHI* (2004).
7. boyd, d.m. and Ellison, N.B. Social network sites: Definition, history, and scholarship. *J of Computer-Mediated Communication 13*, 1 (2007), 210–230.
8. Brubaker, J.R., Ananny, M., and Crawford, K. Departing glances: A sociotechnical account of 'leaving' Grindr. *New Media & Society*, (2014).
9. Brubaker, J.R. and Hayes, G.R. Select * from user: Infrastructure and socio-technical representation. *Proceedings of CSCW* (2011).
10. Bruckman, A.S. Gender swapping on the Internet. *Proceedings of INET* (1993).
11. Burke, M. and Kraut, R. Using Facebook after losing a job: Differential benefits of strong and weak ties. *Proceedings of CSCW* (2013).
12. Clarkson, N. "A Letter From Your Surgeon": Negotiating State Authority in University Administration. Cultural Studies Assoc. Conf. (2013).
13. Cohen, S., Kamarck, T., and Mermelstein, R. A global measure of perceived stress. *Journal of Health and Social Behavior 24*, 4 (1983), 385–396.
14. Deutsch, M.B., Green, J., Keatley, J., Mayer, G., Hastings, J., and Hall, A.M. Electronic medical records and the transgender patient: Recommendations from the World Professional Association for Transgender Health EMR Working Group. *J of the American Medical Informatics Assoc. 20*, 4 (2013), 700–703.
15. DiMicco, J.M. and Millen, D.R. Identity management: Multiple presentations of self in Facebook. *Proceedings of GROUP* (2007).
16. Dimond, J.P., Fiesler, C., and Bruckman, A.S. Domestic violence and information communication technologies. *Interacting with Computers 23*, 5 (2011), 413–421.
17. Donath, J.S. Identity and Deception in the Virtual Community. In *Communities in Cyberspace*. Routledge, 1998.
18. Duggan, M. and Smith, A. Social Media Update 2013. *Pew Research Center's Internet & Amer. Life Project*.

www.pewinternet.org/2013/12/30/social-media-update-2013/.

19. Ellison, N.B., Steinfield, C., and Lampe, C. The benefits of Facebook "friends:" Social capital and college students' use of online social network sites. *J of Computer-Mediated Comm. 12*, 4 (2007), 1143–1168.
20. Evans, M., Donelle, L., and Hume-Loveland, L. Social support and online postpartum depression discussion groups: A content analysis. *Patient Education and Counseling 87*, 3 (2012), 405–410.
21. Facebook Diversity. *Facebook.com*, 2014. www.facebook.com/photo.php?fbid=567587973337709.
22. Factor, R.J. and Rothblum, E.D. A study of transgender adults and their non-transgender siblings on demographic characteristics, social support, and experiences of violence. *Journal of LGBT Health Research 3*, 3 (2008), 11–30.
23. Farnham, S.D. and Churchill, E.F. Faceted identity, faceted lives: Social and technical issues with being yourself online. *Proceedings of CSCW* (2011).
24. Ferraro, R. Facebook introduces custom gender field to allow users to more accurately reflect who they are. *GLAAD*, 2014. http://www.glaad.org/blog/facebook-introduces-custom-gender-field-allow-users-more-accurately-reflect-who-they-are.
25. George, L.K. Sociological perspectives on life transitions. *Annual Review of Sociology 19*, 1 (1993), 353–373.
26. Goffman, E. *Presentation of Self in Everyday Life*. Doubleday Anchor Books, New York, NY, 1959.
27. Grant, J.M., Mottet, L.A., Tanis, J.D., Harrison, J., Herman, J.L., and Kiesling, M. *Injustice at Every Turn: A Report of the National Transgender Discrimination Survey*. National Center for Transgender Equality and National Gay and Lesbian Task Force, 2011.
28. Gross, B.M. and Churchill, E.F. Addressing constraints: Multiple usernames task spillage and notions of identity. *Proc. CHI Ext. Abstracts* (2007).
29. Hendricks, M.L. and Testa, R.J. A conceptual framework for clinical work with transgender and gender nonconforming clients: An adaptation of the Minority Stress Model. *Professional Psychology: Research and Practice 43*, 5 (2012), 460–467.
30. Jankovic, C. and Haimson, O.L. Transdisciplining the Problem: Addressing Administrative Violence in University Information Systems. Cultural Studies Association Conference (2013).
31. Kannabiran, G. Themself: Critical analysis of gender in Facebook. CHI workshop paper (2011).
32. Lampinen, A., Tamminen, S., and Oulasvirta, A. All my people right here, right now: Management of group co-presence on a social networking site. *Proceedings of GROUP* (2009).
33. Lovibond, S.H. and Lovibond, P.F. *Manual for the Depression Anxiety Stress Scales* (2nd ed.). Psychology Foundation, 1995.
34. Marwick, A.E. and boyd, d.m. I tweet honestly, I tweet passionately: Twitter users, context collapse, and the imagined audience. *New Media & Society 13*, 1 (2011), 114–133.
35. Marwick, A.E. I'm more than just a Friendster profile: Identity, authenticity, and power in social networking services. Association for Internet Researchers (2005).
36. Massimi, M., Dimond, J.P., and Le Dantec, C.A. Finding a new normal: The role of technology in life disruptions. *Proceedings of CSCW* (2012).
37. Norval, C., Arnott, J.L., Hine, N.A., and Hanson, V.L. Purposeful social media as support platform: Communication frameworks for older adults requiring care. *Proceedings of PervasiveHealth* (2011).
38. Sas, C. and Whittaker, S. Design for forgetting: Disposing of digital possessions after a breakup. *Proceedings of CHI* (2013).
39. Smith, M.E., Nguyen, D.T., Lai, C., Leshed, G., and Baumer, E.P.S. Going to college and staying connected: Communication between college freshmen and their parents. *Proceedings of CSCW* (2012).
40. Stutzman, F., Capra, R., and Thompson, J. Factors mediating disclosure in social network sites. *Computers in Human Behavior 27*, 1 (2011), 590–598.
41. Stutzman, F.D. Networked Information Behavior in Life Transition. 2011. http://gradworks.umi.com/34/56/3456300.html.
42. Suchman, L. Do categories have politics? *Computer Supported Cooperative Work (CSCW) 2*, 3 (1993), 177–190.
43. Tamir, M., John, O.P., Srivastava, S., and Gross, J.J. Implicit theories of emotion: Affective and social outcomes across a major life transition. *J of Personality and Social Psychology 92*, 4 (2007), 731–744.
44. Turkle, S. Cyberspace and Identity. *Contemporary Sociology 28*, 6 (1999), 643–648.
45. Van House, N.A. Feminist HCI meets Facebook: Performativity and social networking sites. *Interacting with Computers 23*, 5 (2011), 422–429.
46. Wang, Y., Leon, P.G., Acquisti, A., Cranor, L.F., Forget, A., and Sadeh, N. A field trial of privacy nudges for Facebook. *Proceedings of CHI* (2014).
47. Wang, Y., Norcie, G., Komanduri, S., Acquisti, A., Leon, P.G., and Cranor, L.F. "I regretted the minute I pressed share": A qualitative study of regrets on Facebook. *Proceedings of SOUPS* (2011).

APPENDIX. ONLINE SURVEY

	Question	Response options
1.	**Do you consider yourself to be transgender and/or gender non-conforming in any way?**	Yes; No
2.	**Did you have a social network site profile prior to transitioning?**	Yes; No
	[If participant answered No to question 1 or 2, they were disqualified and exited the survey.]	
3.	**Do you use Facebook?**	Yes; No
	[If participant answered No to question 3, they skipped the questions about Facebook and answered questions instead about the SNS that they used most frequently.]	
4.	**In a typical day, about how much time do you spend using Facebook?**	10 minutes or less 10 – 30 minutes 31 – 60 minutes 1 – 2 hours 2 – 3 hours 3 or more hours
5.	**About how many "friends" or connections do you have on Facebook? If you are not sure, please give your best guess.**	0–10 11–25 26–50 51–100 101 – 200 201 – 500 501 – 750 751 – 1000 1001 – 1500 More than 1500
6.	**In what year did you begin your gender transition on Facebook? Although it may be difficult to pinpoint a particular year, please estimate the year in which you first began to change your name, gender, and/or profile picture appearance on Facebook.**	[List of years 2004 – 2014]
7.	**Which of the following have you done in order to transition on Facebook?** *[Multiple options possible]*	Announced transition (e.g., a status update) Changed the gender listed on my profile Changed the name displayed on my profile Changed my profile picture Deleted my profile or account Created a new profile Other (please specify)
8.	**Which of the following have you done with your friends list on Facebook during your gender transition?** *[Multiple options possible]*	"Unfriended" or blocked people who may not be supportive "Unfriended" or blocked people who I didn't want to know about my transition Made some posts visible only to some people in my network Created groups or "circles" to make posts visible to only certain groups of people (*e.g.* to share gender transition information with only those people) Other (please specify)
9.	**How stressful was it to transition in each of these environments?** **a. Facebook**	1-Not at all stressful 2-Slightly stressful 3-Moderately stressful 4-Extremely stressful N/A
	[Other environments included in survey but not relevant for this paper]	
10.	**Roughly how many people in your Facebook network were supportive of your transition online?**	1-None 2-Almost none

	3-Few 4-About half 5-Most 6-Almost all 7-All
11. What parts of transitioning on Facebook were especially difficult? Why were they difficult?	[Open-ended response]
12. What do you think would improve the online gender transition experience on Facebook?	[Open-ended response]
13. What would you change about Facebook to make it more friendly to transgender / gender non-conforming people?	[Open-ended response]
14. Is there anything else you would like to tell us about your transition experience on Facebook?	[Open-ended response]
15. Did you change your gender to a Custom gender option on Facebook?	Yes; No
16. Did you try to enter a Custom gender option that was not recognized by Facebook?	Yes; No
17. To what extent do you agree with the following statements: **a. Facebook's Custom gender options improve the online gender transition experience.**	1-Strongly Disagree 2-Disagree 3-Undecided 4-Agree 5-Strongly Agree
[Other statements included in survey but not relevant for this paper]	
18. Is there anything else you would like to tell us about your thoughts about and experience with Facebook's Custom gender options and/or Neutral pronoun options?	[Open-ended response]
19. How stressful was it to transition in each of these environments? **a. Among close friends** **b. Among all friends** **c. Among close family (*e.g.* parents, children)** **d. Among extended family (*e.g.* grandparents, aunts, uncles, cousins, nieces, nephews, etc.)** **e. At work** **f. At school**	1-Not at all stressful 2-Slightly stressful 3-Moderately stressful 4-Extremely stressful N/A
20. Is there anything else you would like to tell us about any stress that you may have experienced as part of your transition offline and/or online?	[Open-ended response]
21. Roughly how many of your friends were supportive of your transition offline (*e.g.* in- person, on the phone, etc.)?	1-None 2-Almost none 3-Few 4-About half 5-Most 6-Almost all 7-All
22. Roughly how many of your family members were supportive of your transition offline (*e.g.* in-person, on the phone, etc.)?	1-None 2-Almost none 3-Few 4-About half 5-Most 6-Almost all 7-All
23. Roughly how many of your co-workers were supportive of your transition offline (*e.g.* in-person, on the phone, etc.)?	1-None 2-Almost none 3-Few 4-About half

Question	Response options
	5-Most 6-Almost all 7-All N/A
24. Is there anything else you would like to tell us about the support that you received during your transition?	[Open-ended response]
25. What is your current gender identity? *[Multiple options possible]*	Male Female Transmale/transman/FTM Transfemale/transwoman/MTF Genderqueer/gender-non-conforming Different identity (please state)
26. What is your sex assigned at birth?	Male Female Other
27. With which racial or ethnic group(s) do you *most* identify? *[Multiple options possible]*	American Indian/Native American Asian/Pacific Islander Black/African American Hispanic/Latino White/Caucasian
28. In what year were you born?	[List of years]
29. In what year did you begin your gender transition? Although it may be difficult to pinpoint a particular year, please estimate the year in which you first began to change your physical appearance, name, and/or pronoun.	[List of years]
30. What is the highest degree or level of school you have completed?	No schooling completed Elementary school to 8th grade Some high school, but did not finish High school graduate, diploma or the equivalent (for example: GED) Some college, but did not finish Trade/technical/vocational training Associate degree Bachelor's degree Master's degree or professional degree Doctorate degree
31. What is your annual household income, before taxes?	Under $10,000 $10,000 – $19,999 $20,000 – $29,999 $30,000 – $39,999 $40,000 – $49,999 $50,000 – $74,999 $75,000 – $99,999 $100,000 – $124,999 $125,000 – $149,999 Over $150,000 Prefer not to disclose Not sure

Simulating Marriage: Gender Roles and Emerging Intimacy in an Online Game

Guo Freeman
Indiana University
Bloomington, IN
guozhang@indiana.edu

Jeffrey Bardzell
Indiana University
Bloomington, IN
jbardzel@indiana.edu

Shaowen Bardzell
Indiana University
Bloomington, IN
selu@indiana.edu

Susan C. Herring
Indiana University
Bloomington, IN
herring@indiana.edu

ABSTRACT
Virtual marriage is a complex social activity in virtual worlds, yet it has received relatively little research attention. What happens when an important relationship such as marriage is transformed into gameplay? In this paper we present an empirical study of how players perceive, experience, and interpret their in-game marriages, especially with regard to representations of gender and sexuality, in an online game (*Audition*) where a ludological simulation of marriage is centrally embedded in gameplay. Findings reveal that marriage-as-ludic-rule-system and marriage-as-significant-sociocultural-institution provide a double set of gameplay/social/psychosexual resources that players collaboratively learn and perform, and that this negotiation is a source of pleasure, frustration, and meaning in the game. These findings can contribute to understanding the specificity and heterogeneity of players' gender representation in virtual worlds and inform the design of mixed reality games that simulate important life events for learning.

Author Keywords
Intimacy, intimate interaction, gender, sexuality, in-game marriage, emergence, free-to-play monetization

ACM Classification Keywords
H.1.2 [User/Machine Systems]: Human factors

General Terms
Human Factors; Design

INTRODUCTION
Virtual marriage is an interesting but often overlooked topic in research on collaborative systems. Many popular online games that have been routinely studied throughout the history of massively multiplayer games have explicitly incorporated virtual marriage into their broader game systems (e.g., *Final Fantasy*, *Star Wars Galaxies*, *Everquest*), or they at least allow add-ons for role-playing wedding ceremonies and crafting wedding rings (e.g., *World of Warcraft*). Yet in-game marriage, as a social activity intertwined with gender, sexuality, intimacy, sociability and game culture itself, has received relatively little research attention. The juxtaposition of the social meanings of marriage with the implementation of marriage as a game mechanic (inscribed with its own ideologies) raises interesting questions about players' experiences of in-game marriage.

CSCW '15, March 14 - 18, 2015, Vancouver, BC, Canada.

http://dx.doi.org/10.1145/2675133.2675192

In this paper we explore how players perceive, experience, and interpret their in-game marriages, especially with regard to representations of gender and sexuality, in an online game where traditional gender roles are deeply embedded in a ludological simulation of marriage ("ludological" ties back to [10]'s concept of *ludus*, which "captures playing structured by rules and competitive strife toward goals." [13], p.11). Specifically, we use *Audition*, a dance battle Multiplayer Online Game (MOG), and its implementation of marriage as our study site. *Audition* was chosen for this study for two reasons. First, it is a prominent example of a MOG in which in-game marriage is centrally embedded in gameplay. "Marriage" in *Audition* is a simulated game feature that is rule-bound and goal-oriented within the broader system of the game. Whereas marriage in other MOGs does not necessitate leveling-up, in *Audition* marriage is tied directly to progress or achievements in the game, allowing it to seamlessly meld (or confuse) gameplay for utility and gameplay for intimacy. Second, because *Audition* is a non-fantasy/sci-fi, non-adventure based role-playing game, its addition to the empirical research on MOGs can contribute to a more inclusive understanding of player experiences.

Methodologically, we draw on players' self-reports on public forums, interviews, and in-game observations to study their in-game marriage experiences. Inspired by phenomenology and using a Grounded Theory approach [17], we sought out first-person, subjective, narrative accounts of players' intimacy/marriage experiences and coded them thematically. To support and contextualize our in-depth qualitative analysis of user data, we also interpret *Audition's* implementation of marriage using players' own accounts, especially with regard to gender roles.

We argue that it is important to study the dense social meanings of in-game marriage and players' reflections on them, not only for game designers, but for all researchers concerned with digital sociability. First, as [14] notes, "while online games are significantly different from more traditional, offline environments, there are still ways to draw interesting parallels between the two provided one carefully considers the diverse factors contributing to the observed behaviors" (pp. 143-144). The key to design mixed-reality games is simulation: Traditional goal directed, structured play experiences are not fully contained by virtual or physical worlds, but mixed reality MOGs can transform existing technologies, relationships, and places into platforms for gameplay [7]. What happens, then, when a traditionally gendered relationship such as marriage is transformed into gameplay, especially as a ludological simulation in a game world? Our study addresses this question.

Second, since social norms of gender and sexuality are deeply embedded in marriage, this study contributes to a growing social scientific literature in HCI and CSCW on gender and sexuality representation in virtual worlds, including [14][21][24][27][30][31]. Digital environments such as MOGs allow players to choose and customize their digital representation of gendered selves by creating one or more avatars [26][30]. Marriage between avatars, as a simulation of a culturally dense real-life institution and set of rituals that embodies values regarding gender and sexuality, provides a novel lens through which to explore the players' gender representations -- as both *chosen* by players and *shaped* by their sociocultural background and *constrained* by the affordances of the specific game environment.

In a broader sense, this study continues and builds on earlier CSCW research by studying interpersonal dynamics forged around technological objects in digital environments. It contributes to the core research question of "how people really work and live in groups, organizations, communities, and other forms of collective life" ([1], p. 199), by shedding light on how ordinary people find emotional fulfillment in online social spaces, and what the relationships are between technology and "some of the deepest and most meaningful dimensions of human experience ([5], p. 11).

GENDER AND SEXUALITY IN GAMEPLAY

It is impossible to study in-game marriage without taking gender and sexuality in gameplay into consideration. In MOGs, gender becomes a choice, as a player can "choose" to create a female or male avatar when he or she enters the game. Players can adopt different strategies of femininity and of masculinity in virtual worlds based on their own beliefs of gender and sexuality. [30] found that gender differences were socially constructed, and that gender is reproduced in MOGs such as *WoW*. MOGs also allow for gender performance and cross-gender play. [18] reported that homosexual *EverQuest* players gender swapped (i.e., a difference between the offline gender reported by the player and the gender of the player's main character in the game) more often than straight players in gameplay. [14] found that *WoW* female players can (re)create themselves as gendered and sexual beings in the virtual world by creation of an avatar and ideological negotiation with the game rules. Focusing on lesbian, gay, bisexual, and transgender perspectives (LGBT), [9] found that male sexual dominance and female sexual passivity are effectively propagated as the "natural" state of sexual difference in *Second Life*, and LGBT users comply with the heteronormative demand to keep their practices private, even in the virtual world.

These previous studies looked at avatar choice in relation to gender, as one aspect of player behavior. They found that players take advantage of the freedom in virtual worlds to (re)create their gendered and sexualized identities and explore human relationships mediated via these sociotechnical systems. One of our goals is to investigate the deeper socio-cultural contexts in which gender and sexuality representation may occur, in the simulation of a real life sociocultural practice – marriage – in a game world.

MARRIAGE ONLINE AND OFFLINE

Marriage in everyday life is "a long-term mating arrangement that is socially sanctioned and that typically involves economic, social and reproductive cooperation between the partners" ([23], p. 181). Marriage is supposed to be a legitimated commitment (involving a legal license, a ceremony, and vows) to a stable and responsible intimate relationship (involving faith, trust, and care). This definition includes the intimacy and commitment components in [25]'s triangle model of love, but the passion component (love and affection) is optional.

Only a few studies have investigated marriage in virtual spaces; these show that online marriage takes on various meanings. An archaic example of in-game marriage is text-based cyber marriage in MUDs (Multi-User Dungeons/Domains). [12] found that couples usually first met in the MUD and then started a real-life relationship, even though they might be geographically distant. In-game marriage is also characterized by some researchers as part of a "playful" game experience, since games can be designed to encourage in-game marriage and may offer special benefits to married couples. For example, in a study of in-game marriage in Chinese fantasy based MOGs, [29] found that most players listed "having fun" as a main reason to get married in games. Among all types of "fun," one of the most important aspects is gender performance involving "switched gender" in the words of [20], which "shake [up] binary gender roles" ([29], p. 87).

This small body of prior work does not provide a homogenous picture of online marriage. Not only do players interpret the significance and implied commitments of online marriage in diverse ways [3], the research also shows that the meaning of online marriage varies by platform. Moreover, marriage is optional to players in the environments studied. In *Audition*, in contrast, marriage is central to gameplay.

MARRIAGE IN *AUDITION*: AN OVERVIEW

Audition was released in South Korea in 2004, launched in the U.S. in 2008, and now attracts more than 300 million players worldwide. *Audition* is a non-violent, non-fantasy

MOG with a popular marriage system that mediates and facilitates couple-related collaborative behaviors (e.g., dancing as a couple to compete with other couples). An online poll posted to the official forum for *Audition* in the U.S. shows that more than 80% of players have gotten married at least once in the game. *Audition* has a balanced gender distribution among its players. According to Redbana.com (the company that runs, maintains, and manages *Audition* in North America), 48.6% of *Audition* players are female, while 48.1% are male and 3.3% are unknown.

The in-game marriage system in *Audition* is a simulation of offline marriage: marriage is a one-to-one relationship between two players. If a married player wants to marry another player, he or she has to "divorce" his or her current partner first. In *Audition*, players can form an ad hoc couple when they join a "couple mode" battle in the "room." However, to pursue long-term collaborative relationships, players tend to use the marriage system. This includes using matching cards to search for potential "dance partners," a date planner to schedule and accomplish missions with partners everyday, and a wedding party to officially become a couple with a love license and a ring.

Once an in-game couple decides to commit to a marriage, they find that the game simulates key aspects of offline marriage. The wedding party, as a virtual wedding ritual, and the love license, as a virtual marriage certificate, constitute an analog of how marital commitments are socially legitimated in everyday life. For example, the couples-to-be usually announce their weddings on public forums and invite guests and friends to witness their wedding dance and to attend a "reception," so as to celebrate their marriage. This routine, as a public affirmation [11], is very similar to how new couples publicize their marriage in the offline world.

The *Audition* marriage system is also a sophisticated and strict rule-based system. In order to get married, players must follow well-defined "quantified" rules, including time investment, in-game skills, and purchases with real-life money. The latter is key, because *Audition* is a free-to-play online game whose business model depends on players making micro-transactions to improve their game experience. The dynamic of the *Audition* marriage system is designed such that once players identify a dance partner, they can both go to the lobby of the Dancing Hall and send each other "kisses." They are only allowed to send one kiss per day, however. Once they get five kisses, they are eligible to purchase a wedding ticket that costs 5600 Bana cash ($1USD=1000 Bana cash). With this ticket, there is an option to create a wedding room. In this room, the couple will have three chances to accomplish the dance task in a wedding party. All wedding party dance tasks use the same song: *Audition - Wedding Day* (130 beats per minute) in Couple Dance mode. The two players have to coordinate with each other in pressing keys to get at least 12 Perfects, 3 Synchro Perfects, and a score of 160,000, which is a very difficult task. The couple may need to spend more time practicing together and may need to purchase more than one wedding ticket (more than three tries) to accomplish the task. Once they accomplish the wedding party dance task, they will officially be married and will get a love license and a ring.

Audition thus uses explicitly designed, ludic rules to simulate and signify offline qualities of marriage: a couple's compatibility and commitment to one another are quantified as point-based couple levels and ring levels in *Audition.* Designers intentionally divide the 60 couple levels into 14 relationship phases, and assign each phase a suggestive name indicating increasing degrees of intimacy. For example, Level 1 to 5 is "Puppy Love" while Level 46 to 50 is "True Love." Designers also add a semiotic layer (i.e., virtual rings) to represent degrees of intimacy. The higher the couple level, the more attractive the ring is. The highest level of rings is "Max ring." Thus the quantification of intimacy is explicit: dancing coordination, game levels, and ring levels are calibrated together to assert that the higher couple level and ring level a couple achieves, the stronger the connection they will have.

RESEARCH APPROACH

Data Collection

We collected data in three ways. First, we collected online documents from the two most active public English-language forums for *Audition*: the *Redbana* Forum (forums.redbana.com), which is the official forum for *Audition* in the U.S.; and Tgforums (http://forums.jordantrudgett.com), a popular gaming community started in January 2013 by gamers. Documents available online that we consulted include the guides and manuals for *Audition* provided by the company, which describe the design, technical, and system features of the game and its marriage system, as well as players' self-reports regarding their game-related communication and behavior.

In addition to these publicly available data, the first author interviewed 35 *Audition* players. In January 2014, she posted a message on the above-mentioned two forums to recruit *Audition* players who had used the marriage system and were willing to be interviewed. Whether they had been in romantically intimate relationships with their in-game marriage partner was not a criterion for recruitment. Semi-structured in-depth interviews were conducted via text chat in Skype (which participants preferred over voice or video chat) in order to investigate the implicit psychological and social reasons for players to get married in *Audition.* Interview questions include players' backgrounds and daily lives (e.g., school, family, friendship) to get a context of their gameplay and other open-ended questions such as "What does your *Audition* marriage mean to you?" (no definition of marriage was provided so as to encourage participants to describe their feelings, attitudes, and emotions of *Audition* marriage in their own way).

All *Audition* players who responded to the recruitment post by February 2014 were interviewed – 35 players in total (25 females, 10 males). Of these, 16 were aged 14-17 (46%), and 19 were aged 18-22 (54%); the average age was 17.5 (SD = 1.9). The age distribution of our interviewees is consistent with the general age distribution information provided by Redbana (13-17: 42.4%; 18-24: 46.2%). In terms of race, participants encompassed four different ethnicities (white, Asian, black, and mixed), but our findings did not focus on a particular ethnicity. Five interviewees (14%) identified themselves as homosexual or bisexual. Most of them (N=31) were located in North America (U.S. and Canada). Regarding their gaming experience, 49% of all interviewees (N=17) had played *Audition* for 6 to 8 years, 46% (N=16) had played for 3 to 5 years, while only 6% (N=2) had played for 1 to 2 years. We concluded that the interviewees were serious, veteran players of *Audition*. The interviews lasted for 90 minutes on average, with a median word count of 3822.4 words (Max. = 12773 words).

Three limitations of the interview data should be noted. First, the interview participant pool is predominantly female (71%), suggesting that male players' view of "marriage" may be underrepresented. Second, according to the interviewees' preferences, interviews were conducted using text chat. Although interviewees used many emoticons in the chat logs to express their feelings, text-chat-only interviews did not account for the non-verbal cues (e.g., body language and tone of voice) when participants described their in-game marriage experience. In addition, all interviewees were volunteers recruited from online forums. There is a potential bias in a self-selected convenience sample. At the same time, despite these limitations, the interview population represents demographic diversity and experience with the game and can provide valuable insights.

Additionally, the first author is an experienced *Audition* player, with more than five years experience playing *Audition* in Mandarin on an East Asian server. As a supplement, she also logged into *Audition* from a North American server. In several months during the data collection phase of this study, she observed and video recorded game behavior as well as players' chat logs that were visible on the public chat channel in different dancing rooms at different times every day for one hour, in order to collect data from a larger and more diverse player population.

Analytical Procedures

Our analysis involved two levels. First, we identified the gender and sexual ideologies that the marriage system implies, by reading through the game guides, manuals, and players' self-reports on online forums, and by experiencing the game world directly. We drew on quotes from players' own accounts to support our interpretations.

Inspired by phenomenology and using a Grounded Theory approach [17], for the second level of analysis we sought first-person, subjective, narrative accounts of players' intimacy/marriage experiences in the interviews and the forum self-reports, and we coded them thematically. We focused on what players actually make of the marriage system, including a deep qualitative interpretation of their own accounts.

The coding and interpretation procedures followed for the second level of analysis were: 1) All authors closely read through players' narratives (as derived from forum threads, transcripts of interviews, and chat logs from observations); 2) All authors examined the thematic topics in a text, identified a set of narrative themes emerging in *Audition* players' in-game marriage; 3) All authors collaborated in an iterative coding process to discuss, combine, and refine themes to generate a rich description, then synthesized these themes to summarize the fundamental aspects of players' in-game marriage experiences.

FROM MARRIAGE RULE SYSTEM TO INTIMACY EXPERIENCES

Using quotes from players' own accounts, in this section we present our interpretation of the cultural gender roles that the *Audition* marriage system implies, along with an in-depth investigation of how *Audition* players use, interpret, and experience the in-game marriage system.

Marriage in *Audition*: A Traditionalist Ideology

Researchers often claim that cyberspace offers a "liberatory perspective" which grants Internet users agency to explore and refigure gender norms and sexual roles [9]. This optimistic picture is countered by the regressive gender and sexual norms in many games, including *Audition*. The *Audition* marriage system legislates binary gender options, a hetero-normative view of marriage, and masculine dominance, all of which are mainstream social values especially in East Asia, where the game originated, but among conservatives in the West as well.

After logging into *Audition*, players can create their avatars. They can choose basic attributes including nickname, gender, and skin color (as an implication of ethnicity). Thus gender is a choice in this game, but only a binary one: male or female. Moreover, after creating an avatar, players cannot change the basic attributes of the avatar, so they will have a consistent gendered identity throughout the game. A forum moderator (Redbana employee, Female, Asian, age unknown) explains the game designers' perspective: "*You chose to be what you chose. It's not like you didn't have a choice like in real life. You just have to stick with the choices you've made from the start.*"

Some *Audition* players are unhappy with the binary gender choices and feel "locked" into a gender. One player (female, black, age unknown) initiated a discussion about a gender change option on the *Redbana* forum:

Wouldn't it be nice if you could change your gender for x amount of cash? O_O I'm sure it could be done and I'm sure people would like to change their gender from time to time.

Many players supported this idea: "*I really don't see what's wrong with this. It's just something silly like changing your skin color, and it will bring in more income (in theory).*" For these players, gender in *Audition* is a performance ("*like changing your skin color*"), a fluid attribute ("*would like to change their gender from time to time*"), and a playful feature ("*silly*"). The players' understanding of gender fluidity diverges from the original establishment of a conventional heterosexual game world that is divided up into male and female.

This divergence is more obvious when the in-game marriage system also forces players to enact hetero-normative marriages: marriage can only happen between a male avatar and a female avatar. This reflects a traditional ideology of marriage and rejects more contemporary notions that are open to, for example, gay marriage. LGBT players strongly reject the heterosexual marriage norm in the game because it conflicts with their own sexual experiences. We found many threads on the forums requesting same-gender marriage, which players considered a sign of freedom and equality. One player (male, black, age unknown) posted:

To those of you saying that "This is a bad idea" or "OMG No You're teaching little kids how to be gay and that is not right", I say that it's not doing anything bad. Since when was freedom of expression banned? If I want to couple a guy I'll couple a guy.

He received many supportive replies such as, "*I'm standing up for the gay community and requesting gay marriage on Audition. On the forum it even states equality, why not equality in game as well?*" For these players, same-gender marriage in the virtual world has the same political resonances as in the offline society ("*freedom of expression*" and "*equality*"), and they protested against the inequality like the LGBT community would do offline: "*How in any way is a homosexual relationship any less than a heterosexual relationship? That's just ridiculous. Have you yet to hear, love is love? Where is the equality among all sexualities when it comes to marriage?*"

Moreover, male avatars have more power in *Audition*. In spite of the game's traditionally feminine features (e.g., colorful background, cute avatars, pop music), one player observes, "*Music, rhythm and dressing up in cool clothing do not make the game girly. It still follows all those guys' rules*" (Female, Asian, age unknown). In *Audition*, male avatars take the lead in almost all couple-related activities. Only male avatars can buy wedding tickets and create a wedding room so a couple can officially get married; only males can buy love party tickets so a couple can upgrade their rings and love licenses. The only capability a female avatar has is to write some words on the love license. If a female player chooses a gender-consistent avatar, she is completely dependent on her male partner's moves in marriage-related activities. A female player (Asian, 17) posted on the forum to express how women's value is limited ("*Women are inferior to men*"), how their autonomy is weakened in *Audition* marriage ("*Women must depend on men*"), and how ideologically dangerous it is that this biased norm has become a natural part of the game world ("*brainwashing the younger generation*"):

I find this offensive because seriously, what does this say about society's view on females and gender roles? Women must depend on men? Women are inferior to men? And because this is just a 'game,' it sadden[s me] to know how it's viewed as the 'normal' way of life in addition to brainwashing the younger generation. Just because something is viewed as normal, doesn't make it normal. The normal could be crazy, and the crazy can be normal.

For a game that caters to female players, and given the importance of in-game marriage in achieving certain ludic goals, the regressive ideology of the marriage system creates a set of both practical and ideological tensions that players have to negotiate.

Marriage as a Gendered Avatar-Mediated Experience

In response to the ludic-ideological tensions that *Audition* stages, players' in-game marriage is a gendered experience. For some, this involves cross-gender play and account sharing, which are closely related to the players' in-game goal-oriented behaviors and gendered self-expression. Though gender representation (especially cross-gender play) and account sharing are not new in gameplay, *Audition*, being a non-fantasy, non-science fiction, non-adventure based role-playing space, demands of its players different suspensions of disbelief – with different implications for gendered self-representation, compared to fantasy games such as *WoW*, *EverQuest* and *Guild Wars* [14][18][24][27][28][30]. In addition, as we will show, *Audition* players' cross-gender play and account sharing are often highly instrumental strategies to cope with the specificities of in-game marriage as a rule system (and have, in many situations, little to no intended role play aspect).

Cross-gender Play

In *Audition* marriage, cross-gender play allows players to work around the game's strict rules of one-time binary gender choice. Different player groups show different patterns of cross-gender play: Some players create multiple secondary accounts to be able to play as both genders, while others create an opposite gender avatar at the outset. Their purposes also vary: Some players express aesthetic preferences through gender selection, while others take advantage of the rules that favor masculine dominance, and still others reflectively explore their sexual identities.

Most of the straight players (both male and female) we encountered in this study show the first pattern. They chose a same-gender avatar as their main account simply because they considered themselves female or male in the offline world. Then they played both a main account and an "alternative" account of the opposite gender as a compromise. For these players, cross-gender play is usually not an attempt to reconstruct their gender identity but rather an experimental way to seek novel and fun experiences from the opposite gender's perspective.

For example, I9 (male, Asian, 15) said, "*I've only had two accounts, my main guy account, and my secondary girl account. I used it because girl clothes were cute and I'm curious to try them, but never went further than that.*" Similarly, I11 (female, Asian, 15) wrote, "*It's fun playing guy account because I get to look at guy stuffs, and dress as a guy with my own style. Many guys have terrible tastes for clothes,*" and I24 (female, Asian, 19) wrote, "*I tend to like guy pixels over girl pixels.*" These players had no problem making an "either-or" gender choice when they entered the game world, since it did not conflict with their offline gender. But they used cross-gender play to satisfy their curiosity about the opposite gender ("*I'm curious to try them*") and express their fashion sensibilities ("*dress as a guy with my own style*") and aesthetics ("*girl clothes were cute,*" "*many guys have terrible tastes for clothes*"). For these players, playing an opposite gender avatar is a way to appreciate the "beauty" or "cuteness" of the opposite gender.

Some other straight female players used cross-gender play to subvert masculine dominance in *Audition*. For these players, playing a male avatar has nothing to do with sexuality but is rather a way to seek equality and power, which contributes to the "fun" gaming experience. I18 (female, Asian, 18) said, "*I created a guy account before to dick around with the benefits of being a dude. I always notice guys get better treatment and have more power than girls [in Audition]. It feels good to enjoy guys' power as a girl.*" Similarly, I10 (female, Asian, 18) said, "*It's def[initely] fun when I pretend to be a guy and play jokes/troll around a bit. Sometimes I feel I'm a 'troller/prankster' but I think people are more tolerant of a guy troller than a girl troller. Anyway it can be fun playing a guy, but it's just as fun playing a girl.*" Both female players used same-gender avatars as their main accounts and had no intention of sticking to their alternative male accounts ("*it's just as fun playing a girl*"). But they were well aware of male avatars' privileges ("*get better treatment and have more power,*" "*people are more tolerant of guy troller*") in the seemingly female-player-friendly game environment, and used gender swapping to "*enjoy guys' power as a girl.*" In so doing, they experienced fun by temporarily role-playing a guy, and they resisted the traditional gender stereotypes built into the game.

Players of all sexual orientations used cross-gender play to subvert the game's implied hetero-normative view of marriage. Some straight female players created secondary male accounts in order to marry their friends, who were also straight female players using female avatars as their main accounts. I22 (female, 19, Asian) said, "*I have a guy account that I made to marry my friend on it because she didn't want to find a couple.*" She had no emotional or identity-related connections to her male avatar. For her, playing as a male was just an instrumental strategy to allow two straight female players to get married in the game and enjoy its couple-related features and benefits.

LGBT players expressed an ideology-related and identity-related connection to their avatar choices. If they wanted to do cross-gender play, gay players usually created main avatars of the opposite gender at the very beginning. A gay teenager (I33, male, Asian/white, 15) told us, "*I play a girl account as my main. I just feel I want to be a girl, not a guy. Also I can marry guys in this way.*" In a deeper sense, cross-gender play is not merely a compromise to allow same-gender marriage in *Audition,* but it is also a vehicle and a tool to experiment and explore one's real-life sexual identity at no risk. A lesbian player (I34, female, black, 16) said,

In all my Audi marriages, it was me who created and played the male account. Most of my Audi-playing career, I've enjoyed playing as male than as a female. On a male account, I felt free to be whoever I wanted to be and say whatever I wanted to say. I'm more confident to be myself than before.

For both I33 and I34, performing as an opposite gender avatar liberated them from the mismatched expectations the game placed on their gender identity *("I want to be a girl, not a guy;"* "*I felt free to be whoever I wanted to be*"). This performance helps clarify their beliefs about gender and facilitates the construction of self-identities *("I'm more confident to be myself than before"*).

Interestingly, the *Audition* marriage system, although it prohibits same-gender marriage, offers an unexpected way for LGBT players to explore and construct their sexual identities. Some players who did not want to play opposite gender avatars would buy clothes and hair in the in-game mall to dress up their avatars as transgendered. This is not so much a feature of the game design as users creatively co-opting the resources of the designed world to express non-traditional and non-binary gender identities.

Account Sharing

Audition designers usually consider account sharing to be a rule-breaking behavior. A forum moderator (Redbana employee, Female, Asian, age unknown) posted, "*Account sharing is extremely bad and has extremely destructive effects. Our community should stop this behavior.*" But for many female players, account sharing is an effective way to reject the masculine dominance built into the game.

Account sharing is especially common among straight female players who use female avatars and want to marry male avatars. An interesting thread on the forum describes how a female player (Asian, age unknown) who wanted to propose in the game finally worked through the obstacles the game placed in her path. Her original post asked for help:

I am a female and my couple is a male (obviously). However, I'm the only one out of the two of us who can buy bana cash. We want to get married but I can't gift him a wedding ticket, and only the guy can start the wedding. Is there a way to get around this? I'd think it really lame if we can't get married because I, a female, cannot propose to him, a male.

From her post, she was very familiar with masculine dominance in *Audition ("only the guy can start the wedding")* and tried to solve this marriage issue in a normal way ("*gift him a wedding ticket*"), although the game did not allow it. The rule that "only men can propose" undercut her gaming experience ("*really lame*"). She was actually the more financially powerful party in the couple *(I'm the only one out of the two of us who can buy bana cash")*, and her male partner depended on her for any marriage-related activities. When responding to her post, many players suggested account sharing, such as "*Just log into his account and buy some bana cash for your baby.*" Later she accepted this suggestion and posted an invitation to her wedding party.

In this example, it was still her male partner who proposed in the game, but she took the dominant role from the very beginning: She wanted to marry him, sought help on the forum, got access to his account and login password, paid for the wedding tickets, and posted the wedding invitation. The male partner was quiet and was characterized in the thread by other players as being in a powerless and submissive role ("*your baby*"). For these female players, account sharing is not a destructive behavior but a practical way to take the lead in marriage-related activities.

Although it is unusual, players also share accounts to marry themselves, e.g., because they do not want to be controlled by the coupling rules. For example, I18 (Female, 18, Asian) revealed, "*You are forced to be nice to your partner even he turned out to be a jerk, in order to keep a stable ring. When I marry myself, I always have a stable ring and I'm not forced to do anything.*" Marrying oneself is impossible and even absurd in the real world, but it is appealing in the *Audition*, since couple and ring levels communicate a player's reputation in the game. The higher the couple level and ring level a player can achieve, the more successful he or she is perceived to be, and the more respect he or she receives from other players. Players who want to enjoy reputation and respect without being "forced" to marry someone usually create two avatars. When they need to get married, or to upgrade couple and ring levels, they share one account with a friend in order to complete couple-related tasks. As I1 (female, white, 17) explained, "*Right now I'm technically just married to myself. I asked a friend to help me. And I'm cool with that. I can control the whole thing. Isn't this great?*" Using account sharing, these players can enjoy couple-related features, reputation, and respect, and at the same time feel self-governing ("*I can control the whole thing*") and self-sufficient ("*have a stable ring*").

Marriage as Emerging Intimacy

As we have described, in-game marriage in *Audition* is a ludological construct, a straightforward scoring mechanism designed to attract more players, keep them playing longer, and encourage them to spend more money in the game by making micro-transactions. The designers' goals presumably did not include fostering genuine intimate relationships. Many players, however, establish strong emotional connections to their partners over time, and as they do so, their attitude changes from viewing *Audition* merely as a game and *Audition* marriage merely as a feature of the game, to viewing *Audition* as a platform for sociable intimacy. These players interpret their in-game marriages as opportunities to learn from others, grow, and gain friendships, emotional support, and someone to talk to – in general, to satisfy their social and emotional needs. Interviewees often referred to their re-interpretation as an emergent process. For example:

Honestly, I didn't really take game marriage seriously since it was just a game. But after meeting my current partner, I began to take it seriously because our relationship isn't just about rings. We do other things together besides audition as a couple and have emotional attachment like lovers do. (I4, female, Asian, 17)

I did not expect a relationship from online marriage. It was just a fun game. But the feeling just came naturally. (I20, female, Asian, 20)

It just happened. I never used the game as a form of finding romance. I just chill in game and end up finding someone who shares the same interests as I do. And one thing leads to another. (I21, male, Latino/white, 19)

Seeking emotionally significant connections was not a pre-existing goal for these *Audition* players. An instrumental goal of acquiring pretty rings and leveling up may have been the driving motivation for coupling, but their subjective experiences gradually diverged from the original motivations as they grew close to another, and "*the feeling just came naturally.*" They started to reflect on their gameplay experience and redefine what in-game marriage meant for them, associating *Audition* marriage with deeper social meanings such as intimacy, warmth, and love ("*have emotional attachment like lovers do*"). The players themselves were surprised at this gradual change and how genuine connections emerged, as this typical love story shows:

Just like all of you, we don't expect to meet our someone on Audition. At least for us we didn't. We started off as friends during winter break of 2011 and we coupled only as friends. We are on the opposite sides of the United States so we definitely didn't want a long distance relationship. We became best friends, partners in crime, then lovers. We've had a lot of struggles as the days go by, but we still love each other. (*posted on the Redbana forum by two Asian players who developed their in-game marriage into a serious relationship offline, age unknown*)

Especially for some ethnic minority players (e.g., Asians) who were first or second generation immigrants in the U.S., *Audition* marriage helped them get through difficult moments in the offline world. For example:

I use it [Audition marriage] all the time [to seek romance] because my family overprotects me and doesn't let me talk to boys until just a year ago actually. You know, very typical Asian parents. It [Audition marriage] helped me through all the difficulties in my life that my family has caused. I had a really tough childhood coz I couldn't make any friends. White kids did not understand my family or me. (I12, female, Asian, 17)

I moved to the U.S. from Vietnam 5 years ago. He is the first [Audition] partner I met in real life. I don't have family in the U.S., so I was alone by myself. Life was so hard, language, culture, everything. So when I came to visit him, his family asked me to stay. And we have been living together for 6 months. (I20, female, Asian, 21)

These examples show that some ethnic minority players struggle to balance different cultures in their offline lives. I12's parents raised her with traditional Asian values, such as academic excellence, modesty, obedience, and chastity ("*overprotect*," "*doesn't let me talk to boys*"), while her non-Asian American peers appeared to enjoy a more independent and liberal culture. She was in an awkward situation, trying to satisfy both cultures, which led to exhaustion ("*really tough childhood*") and isolation ("*couldn't make any friends*"). As an adult immigrant, I20 suffered cultural conflicts in a new environment ("*life was so hard*"), which made her crave emotional support. In-game marriage in *Audition* offers these players an opportunity to meet other first or second generation Asian immigrants in the U.S. who have similar lifeworld experiences, thus affording a specific kind of *Audition*-enabled intimacy. As I20 noted, such intimacy can even develop into offline support ("*we have been living together for 6 months*").

Another intriguing finding is how players re-interpret *Audition* marriage as a learning process in which they experienced life lessons. I7 (male, Asian, 19) said, "*I'm learning about other people, realizing their routines in life, the society they are exposed to and how they are different from mine. They are actual people that are divided from a screen. It has allowed me in a way to seek romance and learn each time a heart is broken.*" Similarly, I15 (Male, white, 19) described his experience as follows:

You learn so much through so many experiences about relationships. I learn from the bad times, rather than mourn over them. If I didn't have these experiences I wouldn't be who I am today. The thing about Audition is through every avatar, there is a person behind that monitor. These are all real people with real emotions. When two people begin to like each other, it's real. It doesn't matter if it's on a game because it's 2 individual people. From my experience, I've learned many things through the relationships I've had with people through this game, and it's real as it gets. The things I've learned about relationships through the women I've been with online can easily be applied to real life. And that's why it [Audition marriage] is not a game.

Both I7 and I15 told us that they had multiple serious relationships in *Audition*, but they all ended badly. For them, *Audition* marriage is not about rings, scores, or levels but all about people – how to know them ("*their routines in life*"), how to appreciate their differences ("*the society they are exposed to and how they are different from mine*"), how to learn from both good and bad relationships ("*learn each time a heart is broken,*" "*learn from the bad times*"), how to grow from such experiences ("*I wouldn't be who I am today*"), and how to use such experiences to improve offline lives ("*can easily be applied to real life*"). For these players, the importance of *Audition* marriage is not in experiencing the game mechanics, but rather in learning and experiencing what genuine emotional connections are, knowledge that they bring back to the offline world.

Most *Audition* players we encountered in this study considered their *Audition* marriage experiences to be "positive." But their evaluations have nothing to do with the marriage system as a game mechanism. Players had positive experiences because their attitudes towards the marriage system changed and they experienced real emotional benefits, including trust ("*My partner reminds me why I play Audition, and also knows that at least one person in the game appreciates who I am and how I act.*" I6, female, Asian, 16); learning ("*It had taught me a lot about life, and opened my heart to what may have been the truth of love.*" I9, male, Asian, 15); closeness ("*I have someone close to me mentally and emotionally.*" I14, female, 19, Asian); support ("*Parents are proud of me and happy for me that I found someone who they can trust to be with me and to interact with.*" I27, male, Asian, 18); and courage ("*Honestly, because of an incident a few years back, I stopped loving. She's the one who brought me back into this world. She is the one who made me brave.*" I30, male, Asian, 16).

In sum, although marriage is implemented in *Audition* as a rule-based system constrained by traditional gender roles and designed to encourage continued play and in-game purchases, players worked around that constraints of the system to meet their needs for less conventional gender expression, and reinterpreted *Audition* marriage as not merely game mechanics but rather as a means to achieve genuine intimacy.

DISCUSSION

As [14] (pp. 143-144) points out, "[online games] are societies in their own right, capable of evolving their own norms and cultures. Some (but not all) of this indigenous culture will be influenced by the way the software is architected, which permits certain actions and prevents others." In this study our goal was not to offer a design assessment of *Audition's* marriage system, nor to offer an ideological critique of its embedded gender and sexuality norms. Instead, we have argued that marriage-as-ludic-rule-system and marriage-as-significant-sociocultural-institution provide a double set of gameplay/social/psychosexual resources that players collaboratively learn and perform, and that this negotiation is a source of pleasure, frustration, and meaning in the game, and hence an important part of the collaborative experience. Thus, even if we might offer reasons why a given design choice in the game is bad from a ludic or ideological perspective, it is clear nonetheless that the game supports—perhaps even in spite of its design—meaningful intimacy.

Why did this happen? To offer an interpretation it is necessary to take into account the broader socio-cultural context in which the game is developed, played, and interpreted. A game is a cultural object that involves semiotic systems – "material and perceptual qualities as well as [...] broader situatedness in visual languages and culture" ([4], p. 604). It can embody political, socio-cultural, and ethical values [16] which players perceive and adopt, and which shape the play of the game [6]. Moreover, similar to other cultural artifacts, a game represents designers' struggles "between their own values, those of users and other stakeholders, and those of the surrounding culture" ([16], p. 751). *Audition* represents multiple sets of values: cultural gender roles, marriage as a micro-transaction-business-model, and players' beliefs of gender, sexuality, and intimacy. How players negotiate and balance these sets of values leads to their interpretation of in-game marriage and the ways in which they incorporate "marriage" into their gendered and intimate experience.

Our findings also highlight the component of "collaborative learning" that takes place through players' gender representation, especially "learning" how to develop gender/sexuality identity and seek intimacy. Besides negotiating the marriage system, *Audition* users, who are often teenage females, are also negotiating values of teenhood – an awkward period "between childhood and adulthood, dependence and independence" ([8], p. 17). Players mentioned that they loved their parents but that they wanted to escape from their "boring" family lives; they craved friendships but struggled to find "true friends" in school; they looked forward to love and romance but were afraid of responsibilities; they expected to grow up but were scared of the "cold" adult world. All these struggles are reflected in how they represent their gendered selves and experience the in-game marriage system. For them, in-game marriage is "learning," a workshop in which they test, construct, and (re)define their realistic or unrealistic expectations regarding gender, sexuality, friendship, and love. Experiencing intimacy in the game thus becomes part of these players' transition from teenhood into adulthood.

This learning process suggests a new research frontier for open, mixed-reality game based learning [2]. MOGs are creative playgrounds that blur "the boundaries between real and virtual, everyday life and imagination, work and play" ([22], p. 6). Intimate experiences and relationships have penetrated and mediate virtual worlds. It follows that online-game-simulated cultural institutions (e.g., birth, adolescent development, courtship, weddings, breakups, funerals) could be used to teach players, especially teenagers, useful life lessons. These institutions and rituals represent important serious moments and phases in the human experience, which are critical for people's psychological well-being. How players interpret and experience the simulations of these solemn institutions and rituals in games, and to what degree they apply social experiences from games to their offline lives, suggest further avenues of research in HCI and CSCW to explore mundane human experience through games.

CONCLUSIONS

We have presented an empirical study of *Audition* players' gendered and intimate experiences that occur in the ludological simulation of a culturally dense real-life institution, marriage. Our study finds that many members of the player community changed their perceptions and interpretation of in-game marriage by resisting and subverting the traditional gender roles inscribed in the game, and through this, experiences that players themselves characterize as "intimate" were able to emerge. Thus, players experience their in-game marriage via a complex navigation among an enterprise business model (e.g., free to play with in-game micro-transactions), cultural gender roles (e.g., male-dominated marriage assumptions in East Asian culture; and the male-dominated game enterprise that designed a game targeted primarily at females), life stage (e.g., teenhood), sociocultural rituals and institutions (e.g., courtship and marriage), and, of course, online gamer culture itself. In addition, culturally regulated gender roles can blend with ludic rules, which means that who is allowed to marry and under what circumstances a marriage is recognized as legitimate intertwine with the sequence in which events must happen in order to get married in-game. This blend happens in both the game system itself, that is, rules stating that marriage can only be between one man and one woman, and in the phenomenologically felt experience of the game -- in the case where the game system is felt to be patriarchal, unjust, and oppressive and therefore a site of public resistance.

ACKNOWLEDGMENTS

We thank the anonymous reviewers for their useful suggestions. We also thank Redbana for providing user information.

REFERENCES

1. Ackerman, M. S. (2000). The intellectual challenge of CSCW: the gap between social requirements and technical feasibility. *Human–Computer Interaction, 15*(2-3), 179-203.

2. Asbell-Clarke, J., Rowe, E., & Sylvan, E. (2013). Assessment design for emergent game-based learning. In *Proc. of CHI'13.* New York: ACM, 679-684.

3. Bardzell, J., Bardzell, S., Zhang, G., & Pace, T. (2014). The lonely raccoon at the ball: Designing for intimacy, sociability, and selfhood. In *Proc. CHI'14*. New York: ACM, 3943-3952.

4. Bardzell, J. (2011). Interaction criticism: An introduction to the practice. *Interacting with Computers*, *23*(6), 604-621.

5. Bardzell, J., & Bardzell, S. (2008). Intimate interactions: Online representation and software of the self. *Interactions*, *15*(5), 11-15.

6. Barr, P., Noble, J., & Biddle, R. (2007). Video game values: Human-computer interaction and games. *Interacting with Computers*, *19*(2), 180-195.

7. Bonsignore, E. M., Hansen, D. L., Toups, Z. O., Nacke, L. E., Salter, A., & Lutters, W. (2012). Mixed reality games. In *Proc. of CSCW'12.* New York: ACM, 7-8.

8. boyd, D. (2014). *It's complicated: The social lives of networked teens*. New Haven, CT: Yale University Press

9. Brookey, R. A., & Cannon, K. L. (2009). Sex lives in second life. *Critical Studies in Media Communication*, *26*(2), 145-164.

10. Caillois, R. (2001). *Man, play, and games*. Chicago: University of Illinois Press.

11. Cott, N. F. (2009). *Public vows: A history of marriage and the nation*. Cambridge, MA: Harvard University Press.

12. Curtis, P. (1997). Mudding: Social phenomena in text-based virtual realities. In S. Kiesler (Ed.), *Culture of the Internet* (pp. 121-142). Mahwah, NJ: Lawrence Erlbaum.

13. Deterding, S., Dixon, D., Khaled, R., & Nacke, L. (2011). From game design elements to gamefulness: defining gamification. In *Proc. of MindTrek*. New York: ACM, 9-15.

14. Ducheneaut, N. (2010). Massively multiplayer online games as living laboratories: Opportunities and pitfalls. In *Online worlds: Convergence of the real and the virtual* (pp. 135-145). London: Springer.

15. Eklund, L. (2011). Doing gender in cyberspace: The performance of gender by female World of Warcraft players. *Convergence*, *17*(3), 323-342.

16. Flanagan, M., Howe, D. C., & Nissenbaum, H. (2005). Values at play: Design tradeoffs in socially-oriented game design. In *Proc. of CHI'05,* ACM: New York, 751-760.

17. Glaser, B.G., & Strauss, A.L. (1967). *The discovery of grounded theory: Strategies for qualitative research.* Chicago, IL: Aldine.

18. Huh, S., & Williams, D. (2010). Dude looks like a lady: Gender swapping in an online game. In *Online worlds: Convergence of the real and the virtual* (pp. 161-174). London: Springer.

19. Hussain, Z., & Griffiths, M. D. (2008). Gender swapping and socializing in cyberspace: An exploratory study. *CyberPsychology & Behavior*, *11*(1), 47-53.

20. Li, N., Jackson, M., & Trees, A. (2008). Managing dialectical contradictions in massively multiplayer online role-playing game relationships. *Games and Culture*, *3*(1), 76–97.

21. Nardi, B., & Harris, J. (2006). Strangers and friends: Collaborative play in World of Warcraft. In *Proc. CSCW'06*. New York: ACM, 149-158.

22. Pearce, C., Boellstorff, T., & Nardi, B. A. (2011). *Communities of play: Emergent cultures in multiplayer games and virtual worlds*. MIT Press.

23. Regan, P. (2003). *The mating game: A primer on love, sex, and marriage*. London: Sage.

24. Rosier, K., & Pearce, C. (2011). Doing gender versus playing gender in online worlds: Masculinity and femininity in Second Life and Guild Wars. *Journal of Gaming & Virtual Worlds*, *3*(2), 125-144.

25. Sternberg, R. J. (1986). A triangular theory of love. *Psychological Review*, *93*(2), 119-135.

26. Taylor, T. L. (2009). *Play between worlds*. MIT Press.

27. Taylor, T. L. (2003). Multiple pleasures women and online gaming. *Convergence*, *9*(1), 21-46.

28. Wong, N., Tang, A., Livingston, I., Gutwin, C., & Mandryk, R. (2009). Character sharing in World of Warcraft. In *ECSCW'09*. London: Springer, 343-362.

29. Wu, W., Fore, S., Wang, X., & Ho, P. S. Y. (2007). Beyond virtual carnival and masquerade in-game marriage on the Chinese Internet. *Games and Culture*, *2*(1), 59-89.

30. Yee, N., Ducheneaut, N., Yao, M., & Nelson, L. (2011). Do men heal more when in drag?: Conflicting identity cues between user and avatar. In *Proc. CHI'11*. New York: ACM, 773-776.

31. Yee, N., Bailenson, J. N., Urbanek, M., Chang, F., & Merget, D. (2007). The unbearable likeness of being digital: The persistence of nonverbal social norms in online virtual environments. *CyberPsychology & Behavior*, *10*(1), 115-121.

32. Yee, N. (2006). The demographics, motivations, and derived experiences of users of massively multi-user online graphical environments. *Presence: Teleoperators and Virtual Environments*, *15*(3), 309-329.

Outnumbered But Well-Spoken: Female Commenters in the New York Times

Emma Pierson
Department of Statistics, Oxford University
Oxford, United Kingdom
emma.pierson@st-annes.ox.ac.uk

ABSTRACT

Using eight months of online comments on *New York Times* articles, we find that only 28% of commenters of identifiable gender are female, but that their comments receive more recommendations from other readers. Comments from women are more common on forums about parenting, fashion, and health, and on articles written by women. The number of recommendations comments from women receive is positively correlated with the percentage of men on a forum, and the number of recommendations men receive is *negatively* correlated with the percentage of men on a forum. Female commenters are more likely to remain anonymous and anonymous commenters receive fewer recommendations. Male and female commenters differ in their choice of topics to emphasize, backgrounds, and language; we find three specific examples in responses to articles about sexual assault, contraception, and farm subsidies. We discuss the implications of these gender differences for democratic discourse and suggest ways to increase gender parity.

Author Keywords

Gender; computer-mediated communication; online commenting.

ACM Classification Keywords

H.5.3. Group and Organization Interfaces: Asynchronous interaction

INTRODUCTION

Newspapers have long been male-dominated. 67% of newspaper reporters are men, as are 76% of people featured in newspaper stories [17]. These two disparities are probably entwined: stories by female reporters are more likely to feature female subjects and to challenge gender stereotypes [17, 63]. Among all categories of people featured in the news, only homemakers and students are majority female [17]. Women outnumber men worldwide [17], so it is somewhat troubling that the news is primarily written by and about men.

The rise of the internet has added a new dimension to this dynamic: newspapers are increasingly accessed online [21], allowing readers to comment on articles and providing forums for discussion and argument. Previous researchers have considered the ways in which these forums interact with gender [28, 46, 27]. On the one hand, they may make it easier for women to participate, by allowing authors to choose anonymity and thus overcome social stereotypes, find like-minded individuals and potentially facilitate activism, and use a purely textual medium which may avoid many of the stereotypes which may bias face-to-face communication [28, 46]. On the other hand, the forums do not always fulfill this potential: men still post more and longer comments and are more likely to assert opinions strongly, begin and close discussions, and persist when their comments receive no response [28]. Women also are more likely to face harassment [46, 42], and perhaps as a consequence are more likely to worry about privacy [28, 46, 27].

Here we explore the gender dynamics of online comments on newspapers using 892,999 comments on *New York Times* articles made from June 2013 to January 2014. We infer the gender of the commenter from their name for 413,072 comments, yielding 9,809 unique female commenters and 25,607 unique male commenters. Using the URL of the article, we are also able to derive the article's forum (for example, "parenting.blogs.nytimes.com", or "sports/olympics") and its title. In total, our dataset contains 13,429 articles posted on 144 forums.

This dataset is of interest for two reasons. First, the *New York Times* is one of the most widely read and influential newspapers in the world: it has the largest digital readership (1.1 million) of any newspaper in the United States [21], and its website ranks second among all online newspapers in terms of daily visitors [50]. This dataset thus offers an opportunity to study an institution with large social influence. Second, *New York Times* comments are moderated: every comment is read by a Times staffer prior to publication and comments are rejected if they are obscene, insulting, or inappropriate. (On average, 17 articles, and all blog posts, are opened for comments every day, and articles are left open for comments for 24 hours [62].) This modera-

http://dx.doi.org/10.1145/2675133.2675134

tion, more stringent than that of other news sites like CNN, is of interest for two reasons. First, previous research has found that women may comment more actively if forums are moderated and insulting comments are prohibited [28]; one might expect the *New York Times* comment pages to show greater participation. (It is worth noting that this moderation itself exhibits interesting gender dynamics, because some studies suggest that most moderators are female [69]. Data on the *New York Times* moderators is not public, but we confirmed with staff at the *New York Times* that most moderators were female.) Second, as a result of the moderation, comments are more coherent and linguistically sophisticated than those on unmoderated forums like YouTube, offering a richer dataset for analysis. We are making the full dataset available at `http://cs.stanford.edu/~emmapl/data/nytimes/`. We also provide an interactive visualization online at `http://outnumberedbutwellspoken.herokuapp.com/`.

DATA AND FRAMEWORK

Data Collection and Inference of Commenter Gender

Comments on articles were collected using the *New York Times* Community API. Authors of articles were collected using the Article Search API [14]. We determined gender from commenter first name, a commonly used methodology [61, 22, 43, 51], by comparing the first name to a list containing 40,000 first names which were classified by native speakers [48]. To ensure clean data, we only assigned a commenter a gender if their name was exclusively used for men or women, and discarded commenters with names that could be used for both men and women (e.g., "Pat"), commenters who identified themselves with words that were not names (e.g., "A Reader"), and commenters who used only initials (e.g., "AJ"). We were able to infer the gender of the commenter for 46% of comments. To confirm the performance of this method on our dataset, we hand-classified 300 randomly selected commenter names and compared these classifications to the classifications of our algorithm. When the algorithm assigned a definite gender to a commenter, it agreed with our hand classifications 96% of the time. We were thus confident that when our algorithm classified gender, it did so correctly. We also confirmed that our algorithm was not better at identifying men's or women's names, which might produce illusory gender disparities: the algorithm identified as women's names 67% of the names human labelers identified as women's names, and identified as male 69% of the names human labelers identified as men's names. The roughly equal percentages indicate a lack of bias. (The algorithm failed to identify all the names humans could identify either because, to ensure a clean dataset, it classified names as androgynous if there was any uncertainty, or because some names contained gender cues – e.g., "FemaleLawyerOf2Boys" which were not recognizable as names.) As a final confirmation, this algorithm was also used in a previous analysis of online education [51], in which its outputs were compared to students' self-identified genders; the algorithm was not found to be better at identifying men's or women's names.

Throughout this paper, we refer to commenter "gender" as opposed to commenter "sex". This follows previous work which has drawn inferences based on first name [61, 22, 43], and is motivated by the fact that a name is a socially chosen attribute and therefore part of gender, not sex. (Sex is based on biological characteristics, while gender is fluid, socially constructed and refers to the cultural and behavioral characteristics which society attributes to the sexes [15].) When we use "male" and "female", we refer only to gender, not sex, inferred from name; thus, "male" includes both cisgender and transgender men, and "female" includes both cisgender and transgender women. We note, as an important caveat, that this approach does not account for commenters whose gender does not fit a binary description or does not match that implied by their name.

Gender in online discourse

Many paradigms for considering gender within human computer interaction exist [54]. We follow previous authors [10] in using the *gender as a variable* approach, which posits that gender is a variable that may be relevant to analysis. This perspective is well-substantiated by the previous literature, which details the myriad ways in which men and women approach the world differently: offline, in policy preferences, political behavior, moral reasoning, and language use [58, 24, 25, 64, 31]; online, in their behavior on forums like MySpace [63] and Twitter [13]; and, most saliently for our purposes, in their comments on online forums [28, 46, 27].

We briefly review previous theoretical and empirical research on gender in online discourse to provide context for our results. When online forums first became popular, there was hope that they would increase gender equality by allowing authors to choose anonymity and thus overcome social stereotypes or use a purely textual medium which might avoid many of the stereotypes which bias face-to-face communication [28, 46, 39, 70, 29]. Unfortunately, this ideal has not been achieved for several reasons. First, women initially had lesser access to the internet [29]. But even in situations where women have achieved equal access, gender equality has sometimes remained elusive. Women are often driven away from forums by aggressive tactics or harassment [29, 46, 42]. Even when they are not, gender norms often persist online: women tend to be more polite, to assert opinions less strongly, and to "like" products which are consistent with gender stereotypes [27, 29]. Consequently, online forums often end up reproducing the same power imbalances observed in offline interactions. One study of an online forum for the Linguistic Society of America found that women were underrepresented relative to their membership in the society, posted shorter messages, and received fewer replies [28, 26]. Another study found that men and high-status individuals continued to dominate online forums even when participants were given the option to conceal gender [57]. Overall, while online forums offer promise for increasing gender equality, gender differences can persist and these differences often work to the disadvantage of women [16, 29]. Our study provides a large-scale analysis of the extent to which early hopes for increased gender equality have been realized.

Reader demographics

Readers of the *New York Times* are 56% male, 63% younger than 50, and 80% at least partially college-educated [9].

These statistics are for all *New York Times* readers, not just readers of the digital edition: in general, readers of the digital editions of newspapers are 5% more likely to be male than readers of the print edition, and they are also younger and less wealthy [32]. An analysis of the political affiliations of online news readers found that 45% of online *New York Times* readers described themselves as liberal, 25% as moderate, and 30% as conservative [23].

RESEARCH QUESTIONS

Among commenters whose gender we could identify (whom we refer to henceforth as "gender-identified" commenters), only 27.7% were women. The average woman also made fewer comments than the average man (10.4 versus 12.1), so in total women made 24.8% of comments. This is considerably lower than the fraction of *New York Times* readers who are women (44%) even accounting for the fact that readers of the digital version of a newspaper tend to be slightly more male than readers overall [32, 9]. To better understand the disparities between male and female commenters, we investigated gender differences in four areas. First, for each comment, our dataset included the number of recommendations the comment received from other readers, and whether the comment was chosen as a "Times pick" by *New York Times* staffers (indicating particularly noteworthy comments).

RQ1: Is there a difference in how positively comments by male and female commenters are received (both by other readers and by *New York Times* staffers) and does this vary by forum or article?

Second, previous researchers have found that men and women are interested in news in different areas: women report greater interest in news relating to lifestyle topics, education, and health, while men report greater interest in sports and international issues [32]. We searched for evidence of this in the *New York Times* dataset.

RQ2: Do male and female commenters comment on different forums, and are there other factors which affect the gender distribution on an forum?

Third, 54% of comments were made by commenters who chose anonymous pseudonyms with no identifiable gender (we refer to these commenters as "anonymous commenters"). To provide a more complete view of our dataset, we sought to identify the gender distribution of these anonymous commenters. Women face a greater threat of harassment on the internet and display greater concern for privacy than do men; they are, for example, less likely to display their phone numbers and addresses online [46, 42, 20, 3]. Nonetheless, we might expect the moderation of the *New York Times* comment pages to mitigate this effect.

RQ3: Can we detect gender differences in the extent to which commenters choose to remain anonymous?

Finally, the underrepresentation of women is of potential concern because comments on online forums can play an important role in democratic deliberation [67, 20]. If men and women express different views, as substantial previous research indicates that they do [58, 24, 25, 64, 31], discourse will not contain an equal representation of all views, to the detriment of representative democracy.

RQ4: Do male and female commenters express different views on the same article?

RQ1: WOMEN RECEIVE MORE RECOMMENDATIONS

Women's comments received significantly more recommendations from other readers ($M = 13.0, SD = 41.4$) than did men's ($M = 11.3, SD = 37.1$), $t(413,011) = 12.6$, $p < 10^{-5}$. (The large standard deviations occur because the number of recommendations comments receive is right-skewed, suggesting that analysis of the logarithm of the number of recommendations may be appropriate. We confirmed that we observed the results in this section regardless of whether or not we took the logarithm of the number of recommendations.) However, women's comments no more likely to be selected by *New York Times* editors as "Times picks" (2.62% vs. 2.59%, $p > .05$). Consequently, we examined the hypothesis that women were not actually making comments that appealed more to other readers, but were merely commenting more than men on more popular forums and articles. We found two signs, however, that this was not the case. First, when we regressed the number of recommendations a comment received on the gender of the commenter and the number of comments on the article (as a way of controlling for article popularity) the coefficient for gender remained highly significant ($p < 10^{-5}$) with women receiving 1.9 more recommendations than men on average (Table 1). Second, women received more recommendations than men on individual forums and articles. Women's comments received more recommendations than men's on 67/100 forums with more than 100 comments (67%, 2-tailed binomial $p = 8.7 \cdot 10^{-4}$) and 636/1153 articles with more than 100 comments (55%, 2-tailed binomial $p = 5.1 \cdot 10^{-4}$).

Variable	Coefficient	p
Commenter Female	1.9 ± 0.1	$< 10^{-5}$
Comments on Article	0.0071 ± 0.0002	$< 10^{-5}$

Table 1. Regression of the number of recommendations a comment received on the gender of the commenter and the number of comments made on the article. $N = 413,011$

Women's comments received more recommendations on more male forums; men's comments received *fewer* recommendations. For each comment made by women, we regressed the number of recommendations the comment received on the female fraction of the forum (the percentage of comments on that forum made by women). The lower the female fraction, the more recommendations women's comments received ($p < 10^{-5}$). This was not because forums with few women tended to give more recommendations to *everyone*. On the contrary, we found a highly significant relationship for men in the opposite direction ($p < 10^{-5}$): the lower the female fraction of the forum, the *fewer* recommendations men's comments received. These correlations endured when we looked at the female fraction of an article as opposed to the female fraction of a forum. As a final check, we ran a regression on both genders controlling for article popularity as described above; the interaction between gender and the female fraction of an article was significant ($p < 10^{-5}$; Table 2). For male commenters, a 10% increase in the female fraction of an article corresponded to 1.1 more recommendations on average; for female commenters, a 10% increase in the female fraction of an article corresponded to 1.0 fewer recommendations. In short, the less frequently a gender commented on a forum or article, the more positively their comments were received when they did.

Variable	Coefficient	p
Commenter Female	7.7 ± 0.3	$< 10^{-5}$
Article Female Fraction	11.4 ± 0.5	$< 10^{-5}$
Commenter Female * Article Female Fraction	-20.9 ± 0.8	$< 10^{-5}$
Comments on Article	0.0067 ± 0.0002	$< 10^{-5}$

Table 2. Regression of the number of recommendations a comment received on the gender of the commenter, the female fraction of the article, the interaction between the two, and the number of comments made on the article. The interaction term is negative and highly significant: as the female fraction of the article increases, men receive more recommendations, and women receive fewer recommendations. $N = 413,011$

Frequent commenters receive more recommendations

Male commenters on average made 12.1 comments; female commenters made 10.4 comments. But most commenters fell below this average: 49% of men, and 54% of women, made only one comment during the eight months we examined, and 86% of men and 87% of women made fewer than 10. Commenters who made more comments received more recommendations per comment (Figure 1), and this effect was particularly pronounced for female commenters. Comments made by women who made only one comment averaged only .7 more recommendations than comments made by men who made only one comment; comments made by women who made more than 100 comments averaged 2.6 more than those by men who made more than 100 comments. We confirmed that the difference in effect sizes was statistically significant by regressing the number of recommendations a comment received on the gender of the commenter, the number of comments the commenter made, and the number of comments the article received (Table 3). There was a significant interaction term between the commenter being female and the number of comments the commenter made, indicating that the number of comments a commenter made had a greater effect on recommendations for women. (We filtered out commenters who made more than 100 comments to avoid unduly weighting the dataset, but confirmed that the interaction remained significant – $p < 10^{-5}$ – when we did not.) We note that including the number of comments the commenter made and the interaction term with gender makes the coefficient for gender much smaller: this does not imply that gender is not significant, but that the greater number of recommendations that women receive is due primarily to women who make many comments.

Variable	Coefficient	p
Commenter Female	0.31 ± 0.26	0.23
Comments Made by Commenter	0.02 ± 0.003	$< 10^{-5}$
Comments Made by Commenter * Commenter Female	0.02 ± 0.006	0.002
Comments on Article	0.01 ± 0.001	$< 10^{-5}$

Table 3. Regression of the number of recommendations a comment received on the gender of the commenter, the number of total comments the commenter made, the interaction, and the number of comments made on the article. The significant positive interaction indicates that, for female commenters, making more comments correlated with a greater increase in recommendations. $N = 182,237$**. The smaller** N **occurs because we filter out commenters who made more than 100 comments to avoid unduly weighting the dataset.**

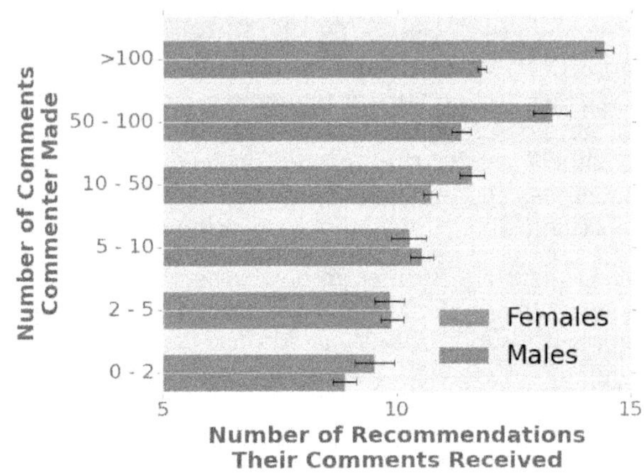

Figure 1. Commenters who make more comments receive more recommendations on average, and this effect is especially pronounced for female commenters.

RQ2: MEN AND WOMEN FAVOR DIFFERENT FORUMS

In Tables 4 and 5, we provide the articles and forums with the highest percentages of comments made by men and women (filtering out articles and forums with fewer than 100 comments). Women constituted the majority in only 5 of the 144 forums. Topics relating to sports and science tended to be dominated by men; topics relating to parenting, fashion, and health tended to be dominated by women.

Three of the ten most male-dominated articles related to global warming, all of them posted on Andrew Revkin's Dot Earth blog. This is curious given that previous research has found that if anything, women have more knowledge and concern about global warming and the environment than do men [41, 44]. This discrepancy may be partially due to a small number of men who returned to the forum frequently and dominated the discussion. (As one irritated commenter wrote to the blog's author, "Have you noticed what an utter disaster your blog threads have become? Basically, you have the same 5 cranks authoring thousands and thousands of repetitive words"). The Dot Earth blog was one of the forums with the largest number of comments per user (7.4

comments, 4th out of 101 forums with more than 100 comments). To more systematically explore this "power user" effect, we compared the fraction of women among the 20 "power users" who commented most frequently on each forum to the fraction of women on the forum overall. On most forums, women were less represented among the power users than they were among users overall (68% of forums, 2-tailed binomial $p = 3 \cdot 10^{-4}$). However, the power users also tended to be more gender-skewed than the users on the forum overall: on the most female forums, power users tended to be more female than the users on the forum overall, and on the most male forums, they tended to be more male ($p = .006$, logistic regression).

To examine connections between forums, we computed the forum-commenter matrix F, where $F_{ij} = 1$ if commenter j commented on forum i and $F_{ij} = 0$ otherwise. We then computed C, the correlation matrix of F, where C_{ij} was the correlation between forums i and j (in other words, two forums were correlated if commenters on one tended to comment on the other). We clustered this matrix using spectral clustering [49], dividing forums into ten groups. We provide an interactive visualization online at `http://outnumberedbutwellspoken.herokuapp.com/` and a screenshot in Figure 2. Several specific-interest clusters were apparent: a cluster of sports-related forums (basketball, football, olympics, etc); a cluster related to arts and music; an international-events consisting of news pages (world, world/asia, world/middleeast), and so on. Notably, all five forums in which women constituted the majority occurred in the same cluster: in addition to these forums, the cluster contained forums related to travel, real estate, gardening, health, dining, and arts.

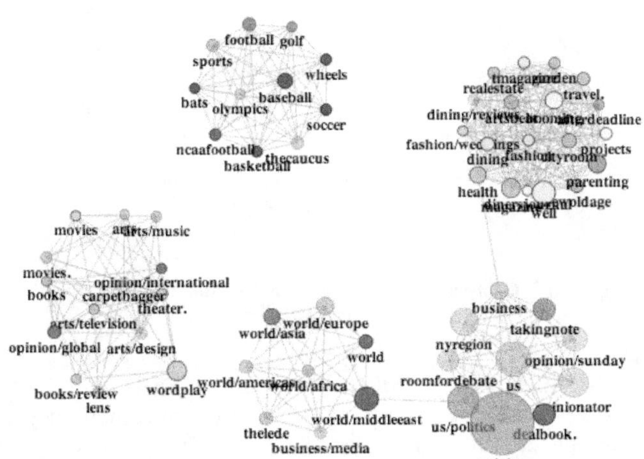

Figure 2. Five of the clusters of forums portrayed in our online visualization. Blue clusters are majority male; red clusters are majority female. All five majority female forums occur in the top right cluster.

Most Male Articles	Most Female Articles
Can We Respond To Problems Like Global Warming Where There's No Simple Villain? (0.0%)	How Much Would You Pay To Have A Baby? (90.6%)
An Update On Risks Of Abrupt Jolts From Global Warming (0.0%)	Fertility Diary: I'm Old (85.8%)
That Unskewed Feeling (1.8%)	When The Bully Is A Sibling (81.5%)
Milton Friedman, Unperson (1.8%)	A Balanced School Needs A Balance Of Volunteers (81.2%)
A Nuclear Submariner Challenges A Pro Nuclear Film (1.9%)	"Maxed Out" Author Thought Readers Would Critique Her Ideas. Instead, They Judged Her Choices. (80.8%)
A Radio Chat On Cold Snaps And Global Warming (2.0%)	My Half-Jewish Child Wants Christmas. I Don't, Anymore (80.4%)
On The Symmetry Between Microsoft And Apple (2.5%)	Bounced From Hospice (77.2%)
A Closer Look At Tornadoes And Global Warming (2.7%)	Widening Ripples Of Grief In Adoptee's Death (76.4%)
Iran Nuclear Talks – Unfinished, But Alive (3.6%)	"Mixed Kids Are Always So Beautiful" (76.1%)
What Janet Yellen And Everyone Else Got Wrong (3.9%)	Blaming The Patient, Then Asking Forgiveness (70.4%)

Table 4. The article titles with the highest percentage of comments made by men (two left columns) and women (two right columns). All articles have at least 100 gender-identified comments.

Most Male Forums	Female	Most Female Forums	Female
soccer	5.4%	parenting	79.3%
bats.blogs	6.9%	newoldage	70.0%
basketball	7.2%	weddings	62.6%
wheels	8.0%	dinersjournal	53.0%
baseball	8.1%	projects	51.8%
dotearth	9.6%	booming	47.6%
keller	10.4%	well	46.7%
energy-environment	10.6%	tmagazine	45.3%
krugman.blogs	10.9%	dining	44.6%
science/space	13.4%	india	44.4%

Table 5. The forums with the highest percentage of comments made by men (two left columns) and women (two right columns). All forums have at least 100 gender-identified comments

Women comment more on articles written by women

Women wrote only 34% of all articles, but the articles they wrote had a higher percentage of female commenters. 32% of commenters on articles by women were female, as opposed to only 21% on articles by men. This is at least partially because female authors and commenters frequented the same forums:

85% of articles on the Parenting blog, for example, were written by women. But we found the relationship endured when we controlled for this by including the forum on which the article was written as a categorical variable: an article written by a woman will tend to have more female commenters than an article *on the same forum* by a man.

RQ3: WOMEN ARE MORE PRONE TO ANONYMITY

To provide a more complete view of the dataset, we sought to infer the gender distribution of the anonymous commenters. Since this is obviously a somewhat difficult task, we used two different estimation methods which yielded the same conclusion: women are disproportionately likely to remain anonymous.

As a first method of estimating the relative strength of preferences for anonymity, we looked at the relative probability that commenters we could identify as male or female from their first names would also include their last names. Male commenters were more likely to use their full names (78% of male commenters versus 63% of female commenters; $p < 10^{-5}$, logistic regression). One explanation for this is the greater threat of harassment that women face online [46, 42]; one might expect this threat to both reduce someone's probability of using their full name, and to reduce their probability of even using their first name.

As a second method, we examined anonymous commenters who identified themselves only by first initial (e.g., "W. Bostock" or "CG") and examined the proportion of names beginning with each letter (ignoring "A" and "I" which frequently corresponded to spurious names like "A Reader"). We then compared this distribution p_{anon} to the distribution of female commenter names beginning with each letter p_f, and the distribution of male commenter names beginning with each letter p_m by fitting the following model:

$$p_{anon} = \beta_f p_f + \beta_m p_m + (1 - \beta_m - \beta_f) p_{uniform}$$

where $p_{uniform}$ was the uniform probability vector and β_f and β_m were the coefficients of the model ($\beta_m, \beta_f \geq 0$, $\beta_m + \beta_f \leq 1$). Essentially, this model says that anonymous commenters arise from a mixture of three possibilities: women abbreviating their names, men abbreviating their names, and commenters who choose their anonymous pseudonym via some other process (for which we use the uniform prior $p_{uniform}$). We fit this model using maximum likelihood; the fit to the data was very good ($r = .97$, Figure 3) with $\beta_f = .312, \beta_m = .494, \beta_{uniform} = 1 - \beta_m - \beta_f = .194$. Taking the ratio $\frac{\beta_f}{\beta_m + \beta_f}$ yields an estimate of the proportion of anonymous commenters who are female: 39%, considerably higher than the 28% for non-anonymous commenters. (We confirmed that our model better fit the data than did the models with only female commenters, only male commenters, or only female and male commenters with no uniform term; $p < 10^{-5}$ for all comparisons, likelihood ratio test. The model with only female and male commenters yielded a similar estimate of the proportion of women: 41%).

Anonymous comments received fewer recommendations than gender-identified comments even when we controlled for article popularity (Table 6). They were also less likely to be chosen as editors' selections (2.2% versus 2.6%; $p < 10^{-5}$, t-test). Similarly, comments made by authors who used their full name as opposed to just their first name received 2.8 more recommendations when we controlled for gender and article popularity (Table 7). (The effect remained significant when we did not control for gender).

Variable	Coefficient	p
Commenter Anonymous	-1.4 ± 0.1	$< 10^{-5}$
Comments on Article	0.002 ± 0.0001	$< 10^{-5}$

Table 6. Anonymous commenters get fewer recommendations when controlling for article popularity. $N = 892,548$

Variable	Coefficient	p
Commenter Uses Full Name	2.8 ± 0.1	$< 10^{-5}$
Commenter Female	2.3 ± 0.1	$< 10^{-5}$
Comments on Article	0.007 ± 0.0002	$< 10^{-5}$

Table 7. Commenters who use their full name get more recommendations when controlling for author gender and article popularity. $N = 413,011$

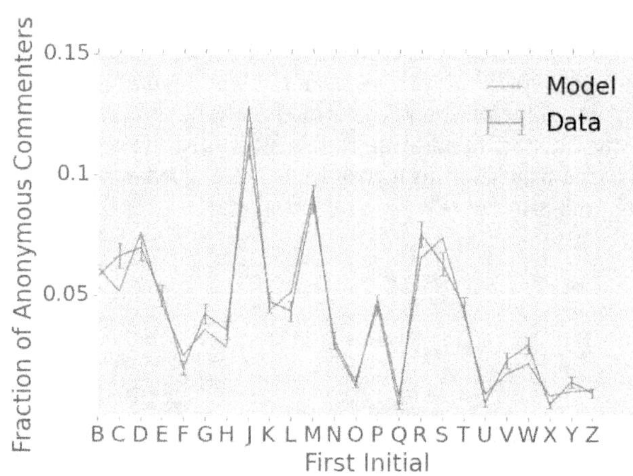

Figure 3. Comparison between modeled and actual proportions of anonymous usernames beginning with each letter.

RQ4: MEN AND WOMEN EXPRESS DIFFERENT VIEWS

These gender skews would be of less concern if men and women said the same things; however, this is not, of course, the case, as numerous previous authors have found [58, 24, 25, 64, 31]. We searched for evidence of this in the *New York Times* comments. We initially explored standard natural language techniques like sentiment analysis [60] and topic modeling [5] but found, by comparing the results of these algorithms with hand-coded results for a small subset of comments, that the comments were too linguistically complex for the algorithms to yield reliable results. Nonetheless, we found clear evidence that men and women differed in terms of their choice of topics to emphasize, backgrounds, and language.

We began by analyzing the frequencies with which men and women used different words. Men and women use different words, of course, simply because they comment on different types of articles – but this is less interesting than gender differences in reactions to the *same* article. To isolate the latter effect, we looked for words that men used more frequently than women (or vice versa) in commenting on the same article as follows. For each article, we computed the word count vectors for both men and women (sampling the same number of comments for both men and women to avoid frequency effects). Then, for each word, we computed the fraction of articles in which men used the word more frequently in responding to the article. We report the single words and 2-grams whose fractions showed the largest discrepancies from one half in Table 9, after filtering out stop words and words that appeared fewer than 10 times in the dataset as a whole. (For conciseness, we also filtered out phrases that are semantically uninteresting: for example, we filtered out "my husband", which is the 2-gram that indicates most strongly that a commenter is a woman, and "my wife", which indicates most strongly that a commenter is a man).

As this analysis makes clear, men and women tended to emphasize different things and use different language *even in responding to the same articles*. Women were more likely to use female-specific words and phrases ("breast", "misogyny", "pregnancy", "woman", "female", "rights [for/of] women") as well as phrases relating to issues which disproportionately affect women ("birth control", "domestic violence"). They were more likely to use words related to family ("daughter", "babies", "children", "sister", "mother", "son","parents", "family"). (Note that "father" does not appear on the list.) They were also more likely to use phrases related to education ("critical thinking", "my students", "public schools"), healthcare ("health issues", "existing condition", "cancer", "nurse", "my doctor", "mental health", "blood pressure"), and labor ("time jobs", "poor working", "living wage").

Men, on the other hand, were more likely to use numerical words: "trillion", "billion", "zero". They were also more likely to use words related to economics – "currency", "economic growth", "wealth" – and government – "liberals", "constitutional", "federal government ", "administration". The fact that men and women used different words in responding to the same articles may indicate that they found different topics worth emphasizing even when reading the same article.

In addition to emphasizing different topics, men and women also used different language. Women were more likely to use positive phrases like "thank [you so] much". (47% of 7770 "thank you"s came from female commenters, as opposed to 28% of comments overall). This is consistent with prior findings that women on online forums tend to be more polite [46, 27]. Men and women also differed in how they referred to Barack Obama: men preferred "Barack Obama", "Mr. Obama", or "Obama administration", while women preferred "Pres[.] Obama". The arguably more positive and less formal female epithet may be due in part to the fact that Barack Obama has enjoyed higher approval ratings among women than men [52]. Women were also more likely to use the more respectful "affordable care act" or "ACA" rather than "Obamacare" (70% of comments from women versus 63% of comments from men, $p < 10^{-5}$).

To explore whether male and female commenters came from different backgrounds, we looked at discrepancies in commenter self-descriptions by examining phrases following "I am a" or "I'm a" (Table 8). While most commenters did not provide detailed self-descriptions, we did find phrases which showed significant gender skews: all 13 mathematicians, for example, were men, while 14/15 feminists were women.

Self-Description	Female commenters/ Total
canadian	0% (0/14)
gay	0% (0/15)
libertarian	0% (0/14)
mathematician	0% (0/13)
conservative	6% (2/35)
republican	6% (2/34)
gun	10% (3/29)
scientist	11% (3/28)
fan	24% (53/220)
teacher	53% (49/93)
school	62% (21/34)
single	64% (21/33)
family	67% (12/18)
working	68% (17/25)
therapist	73% (8/11)
read	75% (9/12)
trained	75% (9/12)
child	76% (13/17)
public school	80% (8/10)
social worker	83% (10/12)
nurse	90% (26/29)
feminist	93% (14/15)

Table 8. Self-description words and phrases that showed the most pronounced gender skews; 37% of self-descriptions came from female commenters overall. All gender skews are significant (binomial p) after multiple hypothesis correction for number of n-grams (false discovery rate $< .05$).

We supplemented this automated analysis by using human coding to find specific articles on which men and women expressed different views. One of the most commented-on articles was an open letter from Dylan Farrow [18] which accused Woody Allen of sexual abuse. In the first 48 hours after the letter was posted, more than 3,000 comments were made, and of those with identifiable author gender, 53% were from women. Based on previous findings that women exhibit greater sympathy towards victims of sexual assault [47], we investigated whether there was a significant difference in how sympathetic men and women were to Farrow's allegations. We used both two methods to quantify sympathy. First, we marked comments that included a link to a widely read rebuttal entitled "The Woody Allen Allegations: Not So Fast" [68], which cast doubt on Dylan Farrow's claims. Women were much less likely to cite this rebuttal than men: only 38% of those citing the rebuttal were women, as opposed to 53% overall, a statistically significant discrepancy (odds ratio = .52, $p = .046$, logistic regression). Because few comments cited this rebuttal, however, we supplemented this automated analysis with human-aided coding. A randomly selected, gender-balanced subset of comments ($n = 200$) were coded by a researcher blinded as to the gender of the commenter as to whether they expressed support for Dylan Farrow, expressed opposition to Dylan Farrow, or provided no definite view. Men were far more likely to express opposition: 37% of men expressed opposition, as opposed to 11% of women ($p < 10^{-5}, \chi^2$). (38% of men expressed support, as opposed to 71% of women; the remainder took no definite position.)

Since analyzing every article in this depth would have introduced multiple-hypothesis problems, we filtered for articles on which men and women seemed likely to express different views by sorting all articles by the cosine distance between the word frequency vector for comments from men and the word frequency vector for comments from women. Among the most divergent articles, we selected ones where the divergences appeared to be semantically significant based on the title of the article or the words that showed divergence (for example, an article in which the divergence was primarily due to the word "probable" was less interesting than one in which it was due to "contraception"). A gender-balanced subset of comments was then classified by a researcher blinded as to the gender of the commenter based on a pre-specified criterion. (We note a potential confound: while researchers were not aware of the true gender of the commenter, they might be biased in their coding by expectations about the commenter's gender. The effect of this bias is likely small, however, because the criteria for coding were unequivocal in the vast majority of cases. We also confirmed that the coding done by researchers was consistent with that done by a volunteer who was not involved in the study.) We examined three divergent articles: "Your Submissions for Most Neglected Topic", "Trouble for the Contraception Mandate", and "The Insanity of Our Food Policy" . The latter two showed statistically significant gender differences; the first did not.

"Your Submissions for Most Neglected Topic" invited readers to submit topics they believed had not received sufficient coverage. Based on the high proportion of male commenters on the global warming articles discussed above, we hypothesized that men might be more likely to submit topics related to global warming; however, we found no statistically significant discrepancy. This may reinforce the idea, discussed above, that female commenters may not actually be less interested in global warming, but are rare on the Dot Earth blog for other reasons.

"Trouble For The Contraception Mandate" argued that employers should not be granted religious exemptions to the Affordable Care Act's contraception mandate. We hypothesized that female commenters would be more likely than male commenters to support this view, based on previous findings that women are more likely to express support for mandated coverage of birth control medication [45]. Comments were rated by a gender-blinded researcher on whether they expressed support for employer-provided contraception, expressed opposition to employer-provided contraception, or expressed no definite view ($n = 73$; the small n is due to the smaller number of comments on the article). Comments made by women were significantly more likely than comments made by men to support employer-provided contraception: 0% of comments made by women opposed employer-provided contraception, as opposed to 26% of comments made by men (70% of comments by women, and 53% of comments by men, supported contraception; $p = .01, \chi^2$).

"The Insanity of Our Food Policy" argued against giving large farm subsidies to wealthy commercial operations while many Americans struggled to survive on food stamps. This was a long and complex article that commenters reacted to in a variety of ways: some discussed the economic details of subsidies, some focused on the details of providing food to people. Women were more likely to use food-related words like "corn" and "food"; based on this, comments were classified based on whether they focused on food (healthy diets, good or bad eating habits, specific foods, or nutritional information). Comments from women were significantly more likely to be food-related (30% of comments from women as opposed to 6% of comments from men; $p = .006, \chi^2$).

DISCUSSION

These results are troubling. Identifiably female commenters are rare, and the effects of this gender skew are exacerbated by the fact that men and women comment on different forums: the average man will see that only 21% of other comments are made by women (the average woman will see 36%). While it is possible that this gender skew is purely the product of individual volition, we find two lines of evidence that it is not. The first is that women can be rare even on forums discussing topics in which external evidence indicates they have as much interest as men, the Dot Earth blog being a representative example. The second is that women are disproportionately likely to favor anonymity – to not include their last name, or to use only initials. This may indicate lesser comfort on the forums: either with being identified as women, or with having their full identity known. We also found that anonymous commenters received fewer recommendations from other readers. Anonymity may offer benefits to women: the equalization hypothesis predicts that minorities with less power in traditional forums may use anonymity to free themselves from social stereotypes and express unpopular views. Some previous research has indicated that anonymity can increase equalization [59], although other studies have challenged this view [44, 53]. Women may favor anonymity to a greater degree than men in order to increase their influence [19].

Strikingly, we also find that women receive more recommendations from other readers, as do people commenting on forums dominated by the opposite gender. It is somewhat remarkable that in spite of societal prejudices against women offering opinions about football, and men offering opinions about parenting, women who comment on both football forums (sports/football and sports/ncaafootball) do in fact receive more recommendations than do men, and men who comment on the Parenting Blog receive more recommendations than do women. There are at least two possible explanations for this. One is that men and women might not comment on issues usually dominated by the other gender unless they have something unusually substantive to say. A second might be that when they do choose to comment, they offer a novel perspective which is attractive to other readers.

Our results imply that those with the most to offer to other readers (as measured by their recommendations) are those most often silenced. We see this in two ways: women comment infrequently, though their comments are more positively received, and commenters rarely venture to forums dominated by the opposite gender, though their comments are also more positively received. So views that would be valued go unvoiced, to the detriment of democratic discourse.

Further, the discourse that does occur is not equally representative of all views. As we illustrate both with automated and human-aided analysis, men and women differ in their choice of topics to emphasize, their backgrounds, their language, and their opinions on sexual assault, food policy, and contraception. Given the richness of our dataset, we suspect we have only scratched the surface of the ways in which male and female commenters differ, and that the evolution of natural language techniques will only bring them into sharper focus. The fact that commenters on the *New York Times* are predominantly liberal [23] may make the gender gap smaller in views smaller than it would be on a more diverse forum.

These gender discrepancies in views, combined with our finding that men are overrepresented on the forums, have a simple implication: the views that are heard do not fairly reflect the views that are held. This has profound implications for a democratic society [67], which strives for fair representation of all opinions. For example, the overrepresentation of men has direct consequences for the level of sympathy expressed towards sexual assault victims; this in turn makes it less likely that victims of sexual assault will speak out [1]. Since people are influenced by reading online comments [30, 37], these discrepancies may propagate throughout society. Readers of comments about intimate partner violence, for example, were influenced by the views expressed in those comments [8]. Worse, these discrepancies may be exacerbated because if people falsely believe their own views are unpopular, they may be persuaded not to express them at all, creating a "spiral of silence" [66].

Four things ought to be kept in mind in interpreting our results. First, while the *New York Times* is a large and influential newspaper, it is only a single newspaper. Future analyses should test our findings on other newspapers or online forums to determine how broadly they apply. Any discrepancies are themselves interesting grounds for future study. Second, online discourse is full of complexities and nuances which quantitative analysis may not always capture. For example, our regression models accounted for only a small fraction of the variance ($r^2 < .1$) in the number of recommendations a comment received, indicating that, while our results are highly statistically significant, there are many factors which determine how people react to a comment which are not captured in our analysis. We have supplemented our quantitative methods with qualitative hand-coding of the comments in order to better capture the nuances in our dataset.

Third, one might question to what extent our results on gender-identified commenters extend to the anonymous commenters. This is certainly a question worthy of future study, but we believe our results about gender-identified commenters are of interest for three reasons. The first is that, while anonymity can certainly influence behavior [44], gender norms run deep enough that it seems likely that what is learned about gender dynamics under non-anonymous conditions extends at least partially to anonymous ones. (The persistence of gender norms explains, for example, why some studies have failed to find that anonymity exerts an equalizing effect [44, 53].) Second, comments made by gender-identified commenters will impact societal gender stereotypes as comments by anonymous commenters cannot: a woman who anonymously makes an insightful comment on an article with mostly male commenters, for example, will not increase the perception that women can offer insight on this topic, but an identifiably female commenter may. Third, many forums do not easily allow anonymity – writing for the *New York Times* rather than reading it, using Facebook, running for political office – and for these forums our results on non-anonymous commenters may be especially salient.

Finally and most importantly, while our quantitative analysis reveals important gender gaps, it cannot always explain the reasons these gaps occur. For example, we do not know if women comment more on articles by women because they are influenced by the author's gender, or because women are interested in writing and reading about similar topics. In particular, the importance of social forces in producing gender gaps must be kept in mind. For example, our findings that women are more likely to comment on articles related to parenting, and to use words related to family, should not be taken to indicate that women have a greater inherent interest in these topics. Women spend far more time on child care, and do so in part because traditional gender ideologies define child care as feminine; this dynamic is often influenced by government policies that influence how child rearing tasks are allocated [33]. Similarly, our finding that women rarely comment on sports-related articles, while consistent with previous findings [32], must be considered in light of the stigma that confronts women who are interested in sports [55, 6]. Our findings that women are rare in general should be considered in light of the factors which encourage women to stay silent. Men tend to be more confident [36, 38], especially in areas perceived as masculine [4], and are therefore more eager to offer opinions [34]. This may occur in part because women who behave assertively fear social backlash [65, 2]. Previous literature on online discourse makes it clear that social forces that create inequality offline persist online as well [29, 27].

The importance of social forces can be viewed positively, because it means the gender gaps we observe may not be immutable. While the roots of these problems run deep, we offer three potential solutions:

- *Increase the number of female authors.* We find that women are more likely to comment on articles written by women even when we control for the forum on which the article is posted. It is unclear if this is a causal effect of the author's gender, or whether female authors simply choose topics (or favor writing styles) that appeal to female readers. A simple means of discriminating between the hypotheses would be to run an AB test varying whether the gender of an author was displayed on an article, and to examine whether the gender composition of the readership was affected. But even if commenters do not care at all about the author's gender and are responding only to the topic of the article, getting more women to write articles might increase the number of articles written on topics of interest to women, and thereby the number of women who comment. Previous authors have found that female journalists are more likely to feature women in their stories and to challenge gender stereotypes [17, 63].
- *Increase awareness.* Making people aware of the gender skew in forums they read might increase the extent to which they visit forums favored by the opposite gender. This idea has been investigated in other online forums: for example, a project from the MIT Media Lab seeks to decrease gender bias on Twitter by making people aware of the gender split of those they follow [40]. One might also encourage comments from women, and people on opposite-gender forums, by making them aware of the fact that their comments tend to be better-received. This may be especially important for women given our finding that there is a stronger correlation for women between the number of recommendations they receive and how many comments they make, and in light of previous findings that women are more deterred when their comments receive no response [28].
- *Limit collaborative filtering.* The *New York Times*, like many other websites, recommends new content based on what its readers have already consumed. Many websites do this using collaborative filtering algorithms [56], where readers are directed to articles that other "similar" readers have consumed. While this often produces good recommendations, it also reinforces gender segregation, because women are referred to articles that many other women read, and similarly for men. While it seems extreme to discard collaborative filtering entirely, one might experiment with interventions where people were occasionally referred to articles primarily read by the opposite gender.

CONCLUSION

Our analysis indicates that there is still much work to be done to realize the early hopes that online forums would allow gender equity [27, 29]. Yet there is cause for hope: the finding that women's comments receive more recommendations, particularly on more male forums, is not one we expected, and speaks to the possibility of greater gender equity.

Further, the timing of our analysis is serendipitous: even as we completed our study, we learned that the *New York Times* was going to build a new platform for its comments pages [35], in collaboration with Mozilla and the Knight Foundation. We shared the conclusions in this paper with the team at the *New York Times* in charge of the comments pages and found that they shared our interest in drawing out women's voices. For example, the team has experimented in the past with allowing readers to separate comments by gender to see how men and women offer different perspectives [7]. We hope that some combination of the measures we have discussed, along with continued study, will decrease the polarization of discourse and draw out the silenced who, as the data indicate, have something to say.

ACKNOWLEDGMENTS

We thank Suzanna Fritzberg, Nathan Matias, Nat Roth, and Jacob Steinhardt for helpful contributions, and the staff at the *New York Times* for their cooperation and guidance.

Male Words	Female	Female Words	Female
hoover	13.2%	huffingtonpost	83.1%
phenomena	19.3%	tariffs	78.5%
embraced	23.0%	breast	78.5%
currency	24.7%	horrified	77.8%
trillion	25.8%	misogyny	77.4%
substantially	26.5%	pregnancy	72.6%
roughly	27.5%	grateful	71.5%
worlds	28.3%	disgusted	71.4%
generate	30.5%	nurse	70.2%
liberals	32.0%	daughter	69.7%
principle	32.7%	thank	69.6%
constitutional	33.4%	woman	69.3%
academic	33.5%	lovely	68.3%
establishment	33.7%	scary	68.1%
virtually	34.2%	babies	67.8%
competitive	34.5%	children	67.4%
collapse	35.0%	sister	67.0%
conflict	35.3%	mom	66.9%
measure	35.9%	female	66.7%
billion	35.9%	struggling	64.7%
rational	37.2%	child	63.9%
zero	37.3%	son	63.6%
failure	37.3%	feel	63.2%
reduce	37.5%	beautiful	63.0%
central	37.6%	kids	63.0%
federal	38.0%	cancer	62.9%
political	38.4%	loved	62.2%
administration	38.4%	parents	61.6%
solution	38.6%	think	61.4%
usa	38.7%	school	61.0%
market	39.4%	tired	61.0%
society	39.5%	family	60.6%
wealth	39.7%	home	60.4%

Male 2-grams	Female	Female 2-grams	Female
mr krugman	23.6%	existing condition	78.4%
government run	25.4%	big corporations	74.2%
american exceptionalism	25.5%	public transportation	73.7%
century ago	25.9%	poor working	73.4%
bill rights	28.3%	critical thinking	72.3%
create new	28.3%	rights women	71.9%
national debt	28.8%	oh please	71.9%
tax cuts	29.0%	my doctor	71.9%
election day	29.4%	free trade	70.5%
welfare state	29.4%	pres obama	70.4%
developed countries	30.9%	thank much	70.2%
us constitution	31.6%	time jobs	70.0%
nuclear weapons	31.9%	self employed	69.8%
richard nixon	32.2%	hard earned	69.8%
economic growth	33.3%	living wage	69.6%
executive branch	33.3%	big oil	69.5%
second amendment	34.4%	blood pressure	68.6%
mr obama	35.5%	public schools	68.3%
great depression	35.9%	my heart	68.3%
obama administration	36.8%	domestic violence	67.9%
global warming	37.7%	china india	67.9%
gun control	37.7%	my students	67.9%
barack obama	38.2%	health issues	67.7%
federal government	39.3%	big business	67.1%
		bernie sanders	66.7%
		support family	66.7%
		campaign finance	66.7%
		birth control	66.0%
		chris christie	65.8%
		big pharma	64.7%
		mental health	63.4%

Table 9. A selection of the words and 2-grams used more often by men and women. Percentages are the percent of articles on which women use the word more frequently than men. All percentages are statistically significantly different from 50% (binomial p) after multiple hypothesis correction (false discovery rate $< .05$)

REFERENCES

1. Ahrens, C. E. Being silenced: The impact of negative social reactions on the disclosure of rape. *American Journal of Community Psychology 38*, 3-4 (2006), 263–274.
2. Amanatullah, E. T., and Morris, M. W. Negotiating gender roles: Gender differences in assertive negotiating are mediated by women's fear of backlash and attenuated when negotiating on behalf of others. *Journal of Personality and Social Psychology 98*, 2 (2010), 256.
3. Bartel Sheehan, K. An investigation of gender differences in on-line privacy concerns and resultant behaviors. *Journal of Interactive Marketing 13*, 4 (1999), 24–38.
4. Beyer, S., and Bowden, E. M. Gender differences in self-perceptions: Convergent evidence from three measures of accuracy and bias. *Personality and Social Psychology Bulletin 23*, 2 (1997), 157–172.
5. Blei, D. M., Ng, A. Y., and Jordan, M. I. Latent Dirichlet Allocation. *The Journal of Machine Learning Research 3* (2003), 993–1022.
6. Blinde, E. M., and Taub, D. E. Women athletes as falsely accused deviants: Managing the lesbian stigma. *The Sociological Quarterly 33*, 4 (1992), 521–533.
7. Board, T. E. Who Says Math Has To Be Boring? *The New York Times* (2014).
8. Brossoie, N., Roberto, K. A., and Barrow, K. M. Making sense of intimate partner violence in late life: comments from online news readers. *The Gerontologist 52*, 6 (2012), 792–801.
9. Pew Research Center. Demographics and Political Views of News Audiences, 2012.
10. Chang, S., Kumar, V., Gilbert, E., and Terveen, L. Specialization, homophily, and gender in a social curation site: Findings from Pinterest. *CSCW 2014* (2014).

11. Chesney, T., and Su, D. K. The impact of anonymity on weblog credibility. *International Journal of Human-Computer Studies 68*, 10 (2010), 710–718.

12. Christopherson, K. M. The positive and negative implications of anonymity in Internet social interactions: "On The Internet, Nobody Knows You're a Dog". *Computers in Human Behavior 23*, 6 (2007), 3038–3056.

13. Cunha, E., Magno, G., Almeida, V., Gonçalves, M. A., and Benevenuto, F. A gender based study of tagging behavior in Twitter. In *Proceedings of the 23rd ACM conference on Hypertext and social media*, ACM (2012), 323–324.

14. New York Times Developers. APIs. Available online: `http://developer.nytimes.com/docs` (2014).

15. Esplen, E., and Jolly, S. Gender and sex: A sample of definitions. *Bridge (December 2006) 10* (2010).

16. Ess, C. A plea for understanding–beyond false dilemmas on the net. *Philosophical Perspectives on Free Speech and CMC* (1996).

17. Gallagher, M, et al. Who Makes the News? *Global Media Monitoring Project* (2010).

18. Farrow, D. An open letter from Dylan Farrow. *The New York Times* (2014).

19. Flanagin, A. J., Tiyaamornwong, V., O'Connor, J., and Seibold, D. R. Computer-mediated group work: The interaction of sex and anonymity. *Communication Research 29*, 1 (2002), 66–93.

20. Fogel, J., and Nehmad, E. Internet social network communities: Risk taking, trust, and privacy concerns. *Computers in Human Behavior 25*, 1 (2009), 153–160.

21. Alliance for Audited Media. Top 25 US Newspapers for March 2013 (2013).

22. Garcia, D., Weber, I., and Garimella, V. R. K. Gender asymmetries in reality and fiction: The Bechdel test of social media. *arXiv preprint arXiv:1404.0163* (2014).

23. Gentzkow, M., and Shapiro, J. M. Ideological segregation online and offline. *The Quarterly Journal of Economics 126*, 4 (2011), 1799–1839.

24. Gidengil, E., Blais, A., Nadeau, R., and Nevitte, N. *Women to the Left?: Gender Differences in Political Beliefs and Policy Preferences*. Université de Montréal, 2001.

25. Gilligan, C., and Attanucci, J. Two moral orientations: Gender differences and similarities. *Merrill-Palmer Quarterly* (1988), 223–237.

26. Herring, S. C. Gender and participation in computer-mediated linguistic discourse. *ERIC* (1992).

27. Herring, S. C. Gender differences in CMC: Findings and implications. *Computer Professionals for Social Responsibility Journal 18*, 1 (2000).

28. Herring, S. C. *The Handbook of Language and Gender: Chapter 9, Gender and Power in Online Communication*. John Wiley and Sons, 2008.

29. Herring, S. C., and Stoerger, S. Gender and (a) nonymity in computer-mediated communication. *The Handbook of Language, Gender, and Sexuality* (2013), 567–586.

30. Houston, J. B., Hansen, G. J., and Nisbett, G. S. Influence of user comments on perceptions of media bias and third-person effect in online news. *Electronic News 5*, 2 (2011), 79–92.

31. Huffaker, D. A., and Calvert, S. L. Gender, identity, and language use in teenage blogs. *Journal of Computer-Mediated Communication 10*, 2 (2005).

32. American Press Institute. Social and Demographic Differences in News Habits and Attitudes (2014).

33. Kan, M. Y., Sullivan, O., and Gershuny, J. Gender convergence in domestic work: Discerning the effects of interactional and institutional barriers from large-scale data. *Sociology 45*, 2 (2011), 234–251.

34. Kantor, J. Harvard Business School Case Study: Gender Equity. *The New York Times* (2013).

35. Kaufman, L. Mozilla to Develop Comments Platform with New York Times and Washington Post. *New York Times* (2014).

36. Kay, K., and Shipman, C. The Confidence Gap. *The Atlantic* (2014).

37. Lee, E.-J., and Jang, Y. J. What do others' reactions to news on internet portal sites tell us? Effects of presentation format and readers' need for cognition on reality perception. *Communication Research 37*, 6 (2010), 825–846.

38. Lenney, E. Women's self-confidence in achievement settings. *Psychological Bulletin 84*, 1 (1977), 1.

39. Li, Q. Computer-mediated communication and gender difference: A meta-analysis. Presented at the Annual Meeting of AERA (2005).

40. Matias, N., and Szalavitz, S. Followbias. Available online: `http://followbias.com/` (2014).

41. McCright, A. M. The effects of gender on climate change knowledge and concern in the American public. *Population and Environment 32*, 1 (2010), 66–87.

42. Meyer, R., and Cukier, M. Assessing the attack threat due to IRC channels. In *International Conference on Dependable Systems and Networks, 2006*, IEEE (2006), 467–472.

43. Mislove, A., Lehmann, S., Ahn, Y.-Y., Onnela, J.-P., and Rosenquist, J. N. Understanding the demographics of Twitter users. *ICWSM 11* (2011), 5th.

44. Mohai, P. Gender differences in the perception of most important environmental problems. *Race, Gender & Class* (1997), 153–169.

45. Moniz, M. H., Davis, M. M., and Chang, T. Attitudes about mandated coverage of birth control medication and other health benefits in a US national sample. *JAMA* (2014).

46. Morahan-Martin, J. Women and the internet: Promise and perils. *Cyber Psychology & Behavior 3*, 5 (2000), 683–691.

47. Mori, L., Bernat, J. A., Glenn, P. A., Selle, L. L., and Zarate, M. G. Attitudes toward rape: Gender and ethnic differences across Asian and Caucasian college students. *Sex Roles 32*, 7-8 (1995), 457–467.

48. Muller, B. A Python library to determine gender based on first name. Available online: `https://pypi.python.org/pypi/SexMachine/` (2014).

49. Ng, A. Y., Jordan, M. I., Weiss, Y., et al. On spectral clustering: Analysis and an algorithm. *Advances in Neural Information Processing Systems 2* (2002), 849–856.

50. Pew Research Center, State of the News Media. Top 10 Online Newspapers Worldwide, (2012).

51. Pierson, E., and Do, C. What About the Women? Available online: `http://blog.coursera.org/post/79073490420/what-about-the-women` (2014).

52. Gallup Politics. Gender Gap in Obama Approval Constant Since Term Began (2012).

53. Postmes, T., and Spears, R. Behavior online: Does anonymous computer communication reduce gender inequality? *Personality and Social Psychology Bulletin 28*, 8 (2002), 1073–1083.

54. Rode, J. A. A theoretical agenda for feminist HCI. *Interacting with Computers 23*, 5 (2011), 393–400.

55. Sartore, M. L., and Cunningham, G. B. The lesbian stigma in the sport context: Implications for women of every sexual orientation. *Quest 61*, 3 (2009), 289–305.

56. Sarwar, B., Karypis, G., Konstan, J., and Riedl, J. Item-based collaborative filtering recommendation algorithms. In *Proceedings of the 10th International Conference on World Wide Web*, ACM (2001), 285–295.

57. Selfe, C. L., and Meyer, P. R. Testing claims for online conferences. *Written Communication 8*, 2 (1991), 163–192.

58. Shapiro, R. Y., and Mahajan, H. Gender differences in policy preferences: A summary of trends from the 1960s to the 1980s. *Public Opinion Quarterly 50*, 1 (1986), 42–61.

59. Siegel, J., Dubrovsky, V., Kiesler, S., and McGuire, T. W. Group processes in computer-mediated communication. *Organizational Behavior and Human Decision Processes 37*, 2 (1986), 157–187.

60. Socher, R., Perelygin, A., Wu, J. Y., Chuang, J., Manning, C. D., Ng, A. Y., and Potts, C. Recursive deep models for semantic compositionality over a sentiment treebank. In *Proceedings of the Conference on Empirical Methods in Natural Language Processing (EMNLP)* (2013), 1631–1642.

61. Larivier, V., Ni, C., Gingras, Y., Cronin, B., Sugimoto, C. Bibliometrics: Global Gender Disparities in Science. *Nature 504*, (2013), 211 – 213.

62. Sullivan, M. Questions and Answers On How The Times Handles Online Comments From Readers. *The New York Times* (2012).

63. Thelwall, M. Social networks, gender, and friending: An analysis of Myspace member profiles. *Journal of the American Society for Information Science and Technology 59*, 8 (2008), 1321–1330.

64. Thomson, R., and Murachver, T. Predicting gender from electronic discourse. *British Journal of Social Psychology 40*, 2 (2001), 193–208.

65. Tinsley, C. H., Cheldelin, S. I., Schneider, A. K., and Amanatullah, E. T. Women at the bargaining table: Pitfalls and prospects. *Negotiation Journal 25*, 2 (2009), 233–248.

66. Walther, J. B., and Jang, J.-w. Communication processes in participatory websites. *Journal of Computer-Mediated Communication 18*, 1 (2012), 2–15.

67. Weber, P. Discussions in the comments section: Factors influencing participation and interactivity in online newspapers' reader comments. *New Media & Society* (2013).

68. Weide, R. B. The Woody Allen Allegations: Not So Fast. *The Daily Beast* (2014).

69. Wilson, J. Hate Sinks. *The New Inquiry* (2014).

70. Yates, S. J. Gender, identity and CMC. *Journal of Computer Assisted Learning 13*, 4 (1997), 281–290.

Predicting a Community's Flu Dynamics with Mobile Phone Data

Katayoun Farrahi
Goldsmiths, University of London
Department of Computing
London, United Kingdom

Rémi Emonet
Jean Monnet University
Hubert Curien Laboratory
Saint Étienne, France

Manuel Cebrian
NICTA
University of Melbourne
Melbourne, Australia

ABSTRACT
Human interactions that are sensed ubiquitously by mobile phones can improve a significant number of public health problems, particularly helping to track the spread of disease. In this paper, we evaluate multiple avenues for the integration of high-resolution face to face Bluetooth-sensed interaction networks into standard epidemic models. Our goal is to evaluate the capacity of the different avenues of integration to track the spread of seasonal influenza on a real-world community of 72 individuals over a period of 17 weeks. The dataset considered contains real-time tracking of individual flu symptoms over the whole observation period, providing a concrete individualized source for evaluation. We obtain an error of less than 2 infected people on average for predicting the total number of individuals affected by the flu and precision of approximately 30% when predicting exactly which individual will become infected at a given time. To the best of our knowledge, this is the first study considering mobile phone Bluetooth-sensed interaction data for dynamic infectious disease simulation that is evaluated against real human influenza occurrence. Our remarkable results indicate that high-resolution mobile phone data can increase the predictive power of even the simplest of epidemic models.

Author Keywords
Health; Mobile sensing; Social interactions; Social computing; Epidemic models;

General Terms
Human Factors; Theory

INTRODUCTION
Traditionally, the field of epidemiology has faced two major challenges. The first regards the quality and granularity of data for epidemiological modeling (how much we know about an individual's health status, and how often we obtain updates of such health status). The second relates to the complexity of an epidemiological scenario (how epidemics are affected by seasonal effects, individual's health history, demographics, past and undergoing vaccination campaigns, and general cultural factors regarding hygiene and social interactions) [22]. Recent advances in face to face interaction sensing, for example sociometric badges [10], and wearable devices in general, are ground-breaking tools for epidemic research, and can significantly help address the challenges of data quality. In a number of studies [9, 11, 12, 20, 23], different communities were equipped with devices for fine-grained sensing of interaction dynamics for disease transmission modeling. However, these studies require individuals to wear such devices (normally around their necks) consistently during the study period. Given that the devices have no use other than helping the experimenters gather data, participants may forget to wear them, charge their battery, or activate them at the beginning of the day rendering them more suitable for small, experimental studies both in terms of the number of participants and the duration of time for which the face to face interactions are monitored.

Mobile phone Bluetooth sensors can complement such research by providing longitudinal dynamics of human interaction networks, with the major advantage of not requiring participants to use any additional sensors. Because most of the population carries mobile phones ubiquitously, this can potentially be a powerful tool for global research in health and disease transmission. While Bluetooth sensors can prove to be a much larger scale tool for understanding and modeling interactions, they also have some drawbacks. People may not turn their Bluetooth on; Bluetooth is available for devices other than phones (e.g. headsets, laptops), which can create spurious face to face interactions; Bluetooth signals may also be sensed across walls, creating even more spurious interactions; and of course, people may not always carry their phones with them, even though that seems to be a decreasing problem in recent times. However, given the value of Bluetooth as a global, cross-cultural interaction sensor, these drawbacks can be addressed potentially in the future by mobile phone's sheer volume of usage. This paper is a preliminary step towards evaluating Bluetooth sensors for simulating the spread of flu within a community. This is important as only limited number of previous studies have presented research in epidemiology simulated over mobile phone data at the individual level [5].

More generally, behavior inferred by mobile sensing has recently been shown to bear a relationship with changes in weather [19], political opinions [15, 4], and personality traits [3]. These promising advances in modeling human be-

CSCW 2015, March 14–18, 2015, Vancouver, BC, Canada.

http://dx.doi.org/10.1145/2675133.2675237

havior reveal that mobile sensing may be a tool which could eventually address challenges currently facing epidemiology research, in term of both data quality as well as scenario complexity.

In this paper, we consider the interaction dynamics of a community of 72 participants obtained by mobile phone Bluetooth sensors, over a period of 17 weeks. The real mobile sensed interaction dynamics of the community are integrated and simulated in different epidemic models, in particular different Susceptible Infected Recovered (SIR) epidemic scenarios. SIR is the basic compartmental model used in epidemiology to model a group of individuals that can transmit a disease to others when they interact. Individuals in the SIR model can have one of three possible states: susceptible, infected, or recovered. The model details are covered in the section titled "The SIR Model". We consider two different classes of dynamic models simulated using the real interaction dynamics of a community obtained entirely by their mobile phone sensors. The interaction dynamics are considered to be aggregated on two different levels: on a weekly basis, and on a daily basis. We also consider a homogeneous interaction model, in which the amount of interaction between users (the weights of the edges in their interaction graph) are disregarded. We compare this to a heterogeneous scenario, where the pairwise interaction strengths between individuals are taken into account in the epidemic model. These multiple simulated scenarios are evaluated against participant real influenza occurrence, as reconstructed from survey questionnaires collected at the same time as the mobile phone data.

The general motivation of this paper is to determine whether mobile phones and the interaction information obtained from Bluetooth sensors, are suitable for modeling the spread of disease. In particular, we are interested in determining how much of the flu transmission in a community can be traced, and predicted using standard epidemic models. To the best of our knowledge, this is the first study considering mobile phone Bluetooth interaction data for dynamic infectious disease simulation that is evaluated against real human influenza occurrence – particularly over the long period of time we are able to obtain individual-level data data. Our longitudinal access to individual flu incidence of participants whose interactions are sensed makes the dataset and epidemiological scenario particularly unique and novel.

The data used in the present paper has previously been analyzed in studies involving public health [13]. However the focus in this previous study was to determine correlations between mobile phone usage patterns and individual well-being, not exploiting the structure of the interaction network for epidemiological studies. The focus of this work is to investigate the use of mobile phone interaction data for research in standard epidemiology. Our goal is to quantify the accuracy of incorporating mobile phone interaction data into dynamic epidemic models for infectious disease prediction.

Overall we find that Bluetooth sensors are a promising tool for obtaining large-scale continuous face to face interaction patterns in order to simulate disease spread. Furthermore, we find that it is possible to predict which particular individuals will become infected. The most accurate predictions result from the daily Bluetooth data, as the weekly data overestimates the infection rates. We also find a homogeneous model outperforms a heterogeneous one in predicting the infection rates and targeting which individuals become infected at a given time. This suggests that the important factor for epidemiological purposes is wether or not two individuals interacted, not necessarily the duration or intensity of their interaction. Taken together, these results provide robust support for the use of mobile phones as valuable tools for research in epidemiology, particularly since daily dynamics can be sensed for realistic epidemic simulations.

The contributions of this paper are as follows:

1. We propose two methods to incorporate real face to face interaction data into the SIR epidemic model. These methods are referred to as homogeneous and heterogeneous interaction models and encompass how the face to face interactions are incorporated (or weighted) into the SIR model. Note the methods proposed here are extensions of Stehlé et al. [23] which were presented over SEIR models (which is an extension of the SIR model to include a fourth state, exposed (E), that is not consider in the present work).

2. We simulate an epidemic over 17 weeks of real data-driven human interactions obtained by mobile phone data. This is the longest duration over which such a simulation has taken place. Previous studies presented results with real interaction data on the order of days.

3. We validate our results over these 17 weeks with actual participant infection ground truth, obtained simultaneously to the interaction data collection. Validation of the disease spread model to participant ground truth over a 17 week interval is novel, as are the evaluation measures obtained which can be used as a benchmark for future work.

4. This paper reports predictions of which particular individuals are infected over time, providing the first such performance results on a real dataset.

METHODOLOGY

Mobile Phone Data

The mobile phone data considered here has been collected at an undergraduate student dormitory at MIT [14], and has been made publicly available [18]. Please refer to Madan et al. [14, 18] for complete details about the dataset.

Our main dataset of interest is made of the physical proximity interactions obtained by mobile phone Bluetooth sensors. The data considered here are for 72 subjects over a 9 month period, between October 2008 to June 2009. The simulation results and results in the figures are presented based on weeks 15 to 31 of the study. This corresponds to the same period for which the influenza survey data was collected. This time period can be seen in figure 2. We consider each Bluetooth event sensed, not its duration, and we consider such Bluetooth dyadic interaction events as undirected. Whenever there is a Bluetooth interaction between individual A and individual B, we consider that both A interacted with B and B interacted with A (interaction data is symmetrized). Bluetooth events are only considered between known devices (i.e. the 72 participants in the study). The distribution of the number of person to person interactions (averaged per day) is presented in figure 1. The top figure excludes $x = 0$ due to a large number of pairs of users never having interacted with anyone on a given day, on average. The bottom figure presented on a log-log scale includes $x = 0$. We can see that the majority of users have few daily interactions with each other, though several pairs of users interact regularly with a maximum of 55.3 average daily Bluetooth events sensed.

Though Bluetooth sensing by mobile phones contains many sources of noise, the distribution of the interactions over time presents a similar exponential distribution to that obtained by the RFID sensors by Stehlé et al. [23] (figure 1, bottom). In Stehlé et al.'s work, the distribution of the RFID interactions is presented over the duration in seconds, with a mean of 49 seconds. The average number of Bluetooth events sensed per day in this community is 1.1 and is presented in even counts.

Survey Data

Influenza-specific participant symptom data was collected using a daily survey designed by an experienced epidemiologist [13]. The survey consisted of 6 questions with Yes/No responses. In the present work we consider the following subset of four questions: (1) Do you have a sore throat or cough? (2) Do you have a runny nose, congestion or sneezing? (3) Do you have a fever? (4) Have you had any vomiting, nausea, or diarrhoea? Please refer to Madan et al. [13] for further details about the design of the questionnaire.

The number of participant self-reported symptoms, flu (vomiting, nausea, diarrhoea), fever, runny nose (including congestion or sneezing), and sore throat are plot in figure 2. For simulation results, we consider the number of unique participants who reported at least one symptom over time. This overall participant symptom data is presented over time in the results presented, and labeled as ground truth.

The SIR Model

The stochastic process based on the susceptible-infected-removed (SIR) epidemic model is used for cases where individuals recover after an infection of a particular strain of influenza. The SIR model is a compartmental model, meaning the population is divided into three different non-overlapping compartments: those individual who are susceptible to get the flu, $S(t)$; those infected with the flu, $I(t)$; and those removed (hospitalised) or recovered from the disease, $R(t)$. The standard model is given by the differential equations (1)-(3), describing the dynamics of the SIR process [1]:

$$\frac{dS}{dt} = -\beta SI \quad (1)$$

$$\frac{dI}{dt} = \beta SI - \gamma I \quad (2)$$

$$\frac{dR}{dt} = \gamma I \quad (3)$$

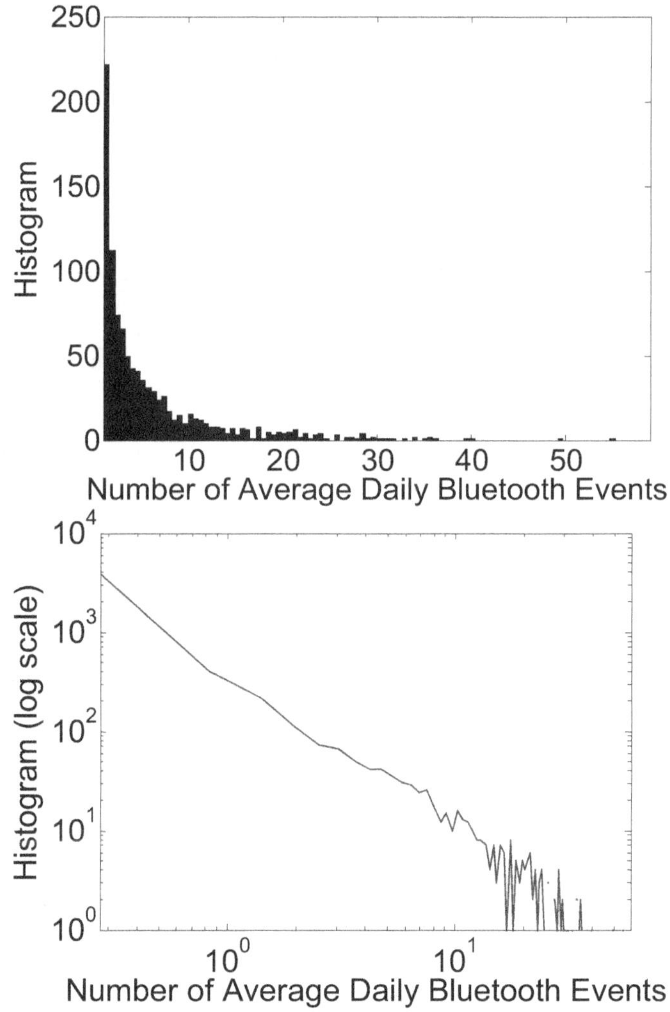

Figure 1. Distribution of the average daily individual Bluetooth interactions in the dataset. The top figure is for a number of events larger than 0, and the bottom figure — presented on a log log scale — includes the number of times individuals had 0 daily interactions. We can see a large number of users have no average daily interactions with any other individual, though several pairs of users have on average 10 or more (maximum 55.3) interactions per day.

where β is the rate of transmission of infection (the larger the rate, the higher the probability of the flu passing from an infected individual onto another upon interaction); γ is the recovery rate (the probability of an infected individual recovering spontaneously from the flu). In this paper, we assume there are no births or deaths as there are no new or lost users in the dataset, and thus $N = S + I + R$ is the total population size. We vary the values of β and γ in the results presented to evaluate a wide variety of epidemiological scenarios.

The SIR model, defined by equations (1)-(3), is not defined for network data. Therefore, here we adopt the methodology by Stehlé [22] to incorporate the interaction dynamics, and apply them them to the SIR process.

Stochastic Process

The stochastic process is simulated using a continuous time implementation of the SIR model. A continuous time ap-

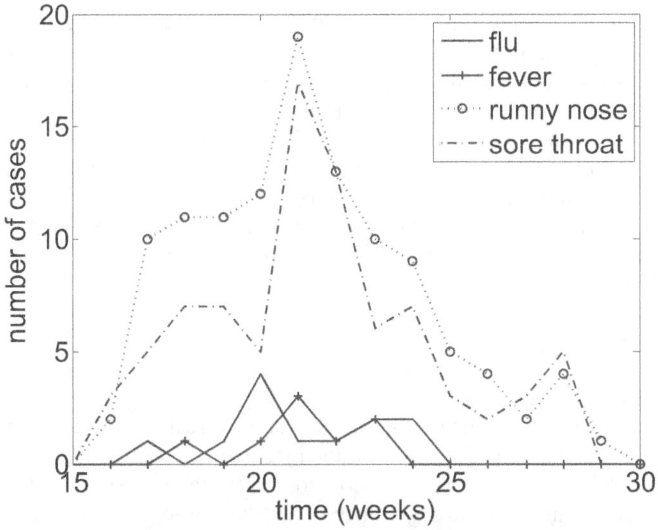

Figure 2. Distribution of participant self-reported symptoms, including flu (vomiting, nausea, diarrhoea), fever, runny nose (including congestion or sneezing), over time.

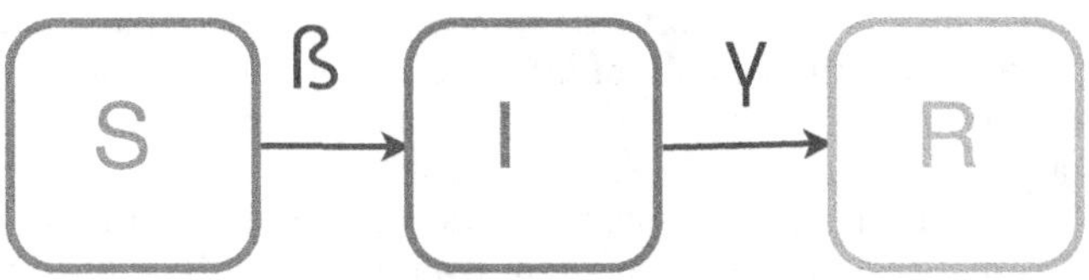

Figure 3. SIR model.

proach entails sampling the next time at which an individual will change his or her health state. We assume the probability of transitioning between health states is sampled from a geometric distribution with mean $\frac{1}{C}$ (from Susceptible to Infected) and $\frac{1}{D}$ (for Infected to Recovered) as follows.

$$p_{S\to I}(t) = Ce^{-Ct}, \quad C = k\beta \tag{4}$$

$$p_{I\to T}(t) = De^{-Dt}, \quad D = \gamma \tag{5}$$

At time t, for each susceptible individual n, we sample the next time of infection from equation (4). Note that k is the number of infected individuals in proximity to susceptible node n. We assume the time increment is $dt = 10 \times 10^{-6}$. Similarly, for each infected node, we sample the next time at which recovery will occur from equation (5). For each simulation result, we run $1,000$ random trials of the epidemic model.

For the initial infectious individuals, we consider two different scenarios. On the first experimental set, we assume one initial infectious individual, selected randomly from the whole population. On the second, for the results presented in figure 9, we use the actual initial infected individuals, as we are trying to predict which individuals are infected and not the overall number of infected individuals.

We consider dynamic models in which the interaction dynamics between the individuals simulated vary over time. This is in contrast to a static epidemiological model, which would

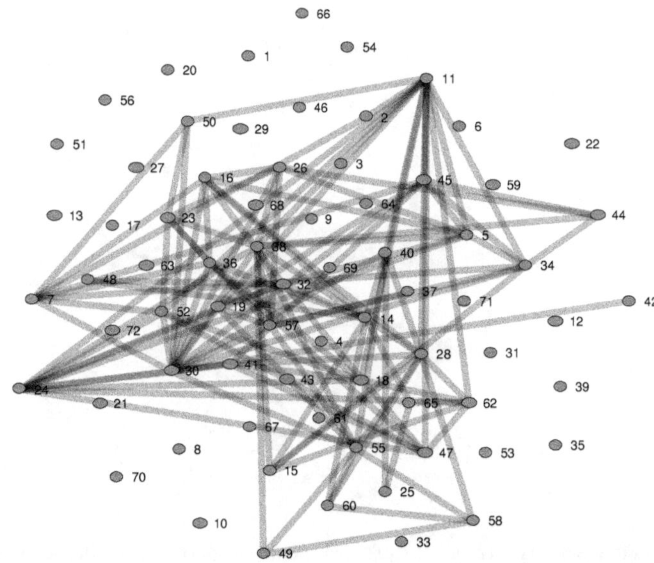

Figure 4. Homogeneous network model of participant interactions. This network is for day 10 of the dataset considered. The nodes are the participants and the edges represent interactions sensed by Bluetooth. Note that the edges are not weighed by the amount of interaction time for the homogeneous model.

assume that the interactions across individuals are constant over time (they either exist or they do not). Finally, we consider two dynamic network cases, a homogeneous model and a heterogeneous interaction model, which we explain next.

Dynamic Homogeneous Model

In the homogeneous case, the real interaction network is used to determine which pairs of individuals interact; however, the probability of disease transmission (the weight) is equivalent for each pair. This can be seen in figure 4, where the edges between nodes are all of equivalent weight and are simply present if at least one person-to-person interaction is sensed within the time interval x. The time interval x is either one week or one day depending on whether the simulation scenario is weekly or daily.

Dynamic Heterogeneous Model

The dynamic heterogeneous model extends the dynamic homogeneous model by considering network weights over time, as seen in figure 5. The greater the number of interactions between two individuals, the greater the weight and the more likely the infection will transmit between these two individuals. Again, this model considers the amount of contact between pairs of individuals in two scenarios of time-aggregation: a weekly or daily basis. The infection rate is weighed such that, $\beta W_{i,j}/\hat{W}$, where $W_{i,j}$ is the given week's (or day's) total number of interactions between nodes i and j, and $\hat{W}$ is the overall average interaction weight of the network.

RELATED WORK

Many applications which currently use individual interaction data sensed by social media can greatly benefit from the use of face to face interaction data sensed by mobile phone Bluetooth, particularly in the CSCW community. Applications

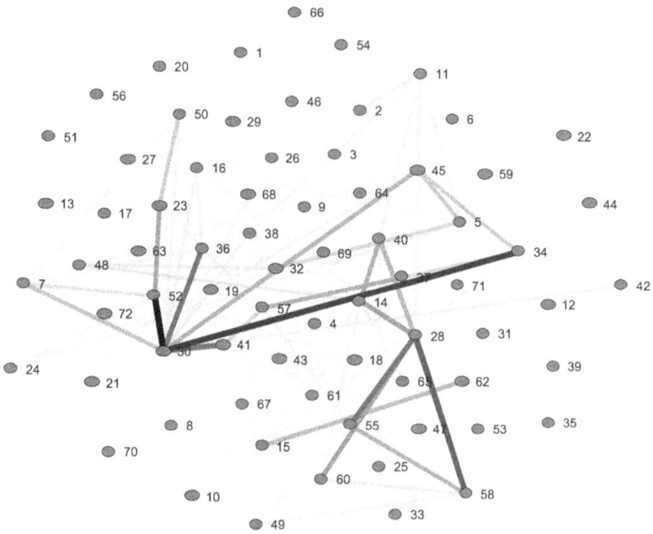

Figure 5. Heterogeneous network model of participant interactions. Network of interactions on day 10 of the dataset. The edges representing interactions are weighed in this network configuration, resulting in the appearance of far fewer interacting pairs in comparison to the homogeneous model of figure 4.

range from understanding information diffusion across social networks [21, 6], cross cultural studies [25], and collaboration [16], just to name a few. Some specific examples which have previously used face to face interaction data, beyond the health domain, include the inference of social relationships [17], mapping workplace behavior and understanding cultural differences [2].

As mentioned above, physical proximity interactions have recently been sensed using wearable badges for improved epidemic modeling. Stehlé et al. [23] consider a network of real-life human interaction patterns obtained by RFID devices. The authors simulate the spread of epidemics considering an SEIR model (SEIR is an extension of the SIR model which includes a fourth state, E for exposed). The 405 participants were attendees of a conference that lasted 2 days (3-4 June, 2009). The focus of the work is on varying timescales (20 second versus daily resolution) and network structures to determine the level of detail needed to correctly inform computational models for real epidemic management. Due to the lack of longitudinal data, the authors present different procedures to longitudinally extend their data.

Another closely related, motivating work is by Salathé et al. [20], where 788 participants' close proximity interactions (CPIs) are sensed on a school day to determine the high resolution dynamics of disease transmission considering an SEIR model. The authors' results suggest that contact network data is required for more effective immunization strategies. Isella et al. [8] use wearable RFID badges to monitor the dynamics of disease transmission in a hospital setting. In the study, 119 subjects are monitored over a one week period for monitoring the spread of respiratory infections; their goals are critical pattern discovery and tailored prevention strategies.

These recent studies reveal the importance of new data-driven approaches to epidemiology. In particular, high resolution human interaction network data have much to offer in the domain of public health (see [24] for a review). However, previous work has used real life human interaction data on the order of days. Bluetooth interaction data has much to offer in this respect, particularly due to its longitudinal nature (weeks to months to years). Even though Bluetooth interaction data may suffer from noise, it offers a *nearly high-resolution* human interaction network, comparable in quality to RFIDs, yet on orders of magnitude longer of duration and larger population samples.

RESULTS

Data Only

First we consider the likelihood of an infected individual being in proximity with another infected individual (figure 6). An infected individual is considered to have reported at least one symptom on a given day for the survey given. Figure 6 shows how often an infected individual was in proximity with another infected individual, considering a time window of up to 8 days (time presented on the x-axis). As the time window increases, there is a higher probability of an infected individual to have interacted with another infected individual. In this community, 30% of infected individuals did not have a Bluetooth interaction with another infected individual within a 8 day window (i.e. 7 days previous to the onset of infection reported). This result gives an indication of the best range of results we can expect to obtain from this experiment. Given a time window of 7 previous days, only 30% of infected individuals were not in physical proximity to another individual sensed by Bluetooth. This means that the 30% of infected individuals were likely either infected from an outside source or their interaction was not sensed by Bluetooth (if they were infected from someone within this population). Note that for the flu, we can never be certain who an individual is infected by based on interactions alone, but we can develop models which can make predictions about potential avenues for such infection.

Dynamic SIR Models

The simulation results of the homogeneous model are presented in figure 7. Our initial finding is that, considering weekly intervals for the interaction network, time aggregation tends to overestimate the actual number of infected cases. We observe that the daily time-aggregation gives more accurate counts (weekly is denoted by (W) and daily by (D) in figure 7). This is likely due to the network being much more dense when aggregated on a weekly basis, resulting in more predicted infection transmissions than really occur. This overestimation of weekly aggregates also holds for the heterogeneous model, presented in figure 8. We further evaluate the difference between the homogeneous and heterogeneous models below.

In figure 9 we consider the error over all combinations of parameters γ and β for all model cases. The error is the absolute difference in the real number of infectious cases and those predicted using the models run on the mobile phone data. The error is calculated as the absolute value of the average error determined for each week over the 17 week period.The results

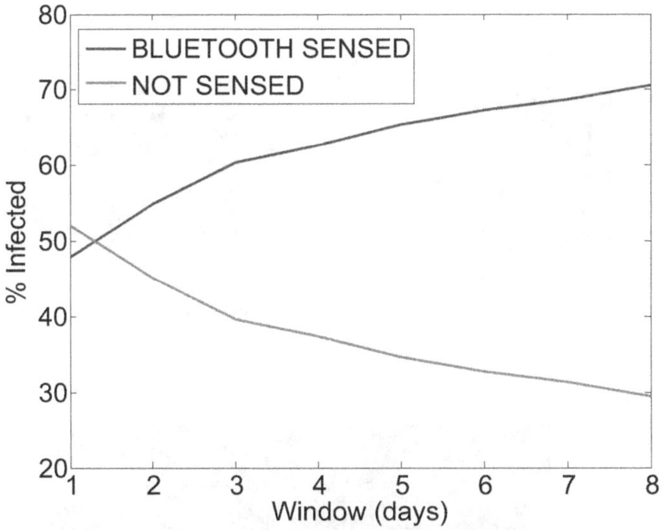

Figure 6. Percentage of infected individuals sensed (blue) / not sensed (red) in proximity to another infected individual with Bluetooth. The time window is given for the number of previous days up to infection (including the current day). Note, the "not sensed" cases are based on individuals with reported symptom data but without having been traced with Bluetooth as being in proximity with another infected individual.

re-confirm that the models perform better when we consider the data on a daily basis as opposed to a weekly basis. The minimum overall error occurs for the homogenous daily case, with an error of 1.89 (for $\beta = 0.2$ and $\gamma = 0.3$). The minimum error for the heterogenous daily experiments is 2.18 for $\beta = 0.1$ and $\gamma = 0.3$. The best performing model was able to predict with an overall average error of 1.89, which is the error in the number of infected individuals predicted. This means that, in theory, we could predict the number of infected individuals with an error of just under 2 people given this population of 72 people.

When optimizing the epidemic model parameters using only real data-driven interactions obtained by the mobile phones, we obtain the lowest errors for model parameters of β and γ which are in close agreement to parameters used in epidemiology research [7]. These results can be considered an indirect validation of our model and data.

We further consider the difference between the homogeneous and heterogeneous experiments on a daily scale for the optimal cases in figure 10, given that these parameter settings displayed the lowest errors. While the heterogenous model may be able to capture some of the 'jumps' in infectious cases over time, the homogeneous model provides better estimates for the number of infected cases over time. The reason for the better performance with the homogeneous model is likely the imbalance in weighting. With the current heterogenous model, if a few pair of individuals have a large number of interactions they will greatly outweigh the other interactions which may have occurred only once or twice (as can be seen by the difference between figures 4 and 5). However, the results indicate these interactions that may occur only a few times are important to weigh equivalently in order to better capture the spread of disease in this community.

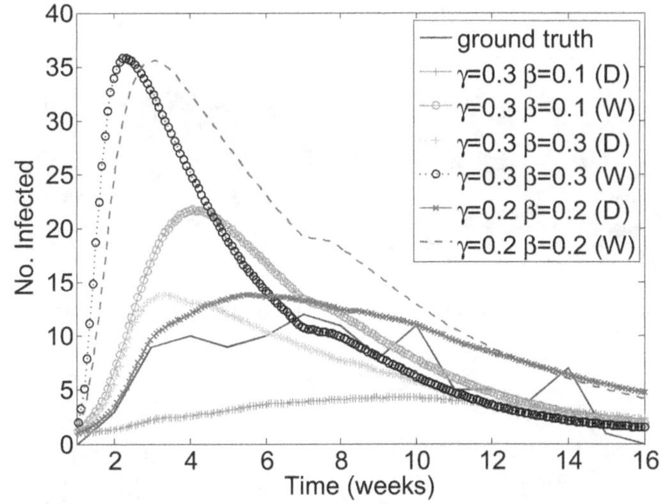

Figure 7. Simulation results for the dynamic homogeneous cases over varying model parameters. The real weekly (W) and daily (D) interactions are presented with the same colour for a given set of model parameters.

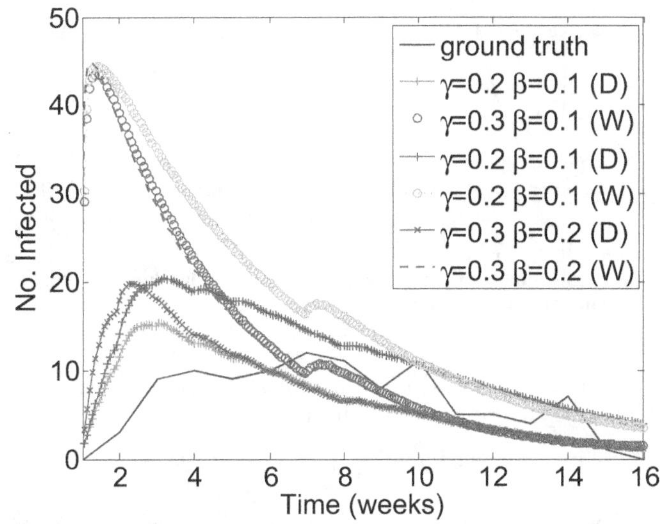

Figure 8. Simulation results for the dynamic heterogeneous cases over varying model parameters.

We further consider how well the homogeneous daily model can predict which particular individuals will become infected by looking at precision values next. In figure 11, the average precision is plot for a wide range of γ and β considering 1000 runs. Precision is the fraction of particular infected individuals correctly predicted by the model (note that this is not the aggregated number of infected individuals, but which particular individuals are correctly predicted to get the flu). In this case, the initial infections in the homogeneous daily model correspond to the actual infections in the dataset as opposed to initial infections chosen randomly as in previous experiments. Because increasing γ continuously improves the precision of the model, this reflects the model artefact that if takes longer and longer for infected individuals to recover, this artificially increases the likelihood of correctly identify-

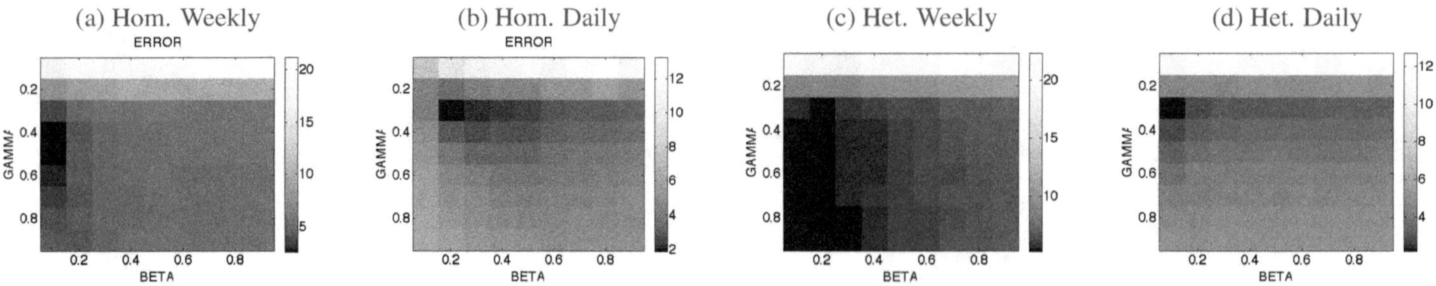

Figure 9. The overall average absolute error between the (a),(b) homogeneous and (c),(d) heterogenous models considering weekly and daily time frames.

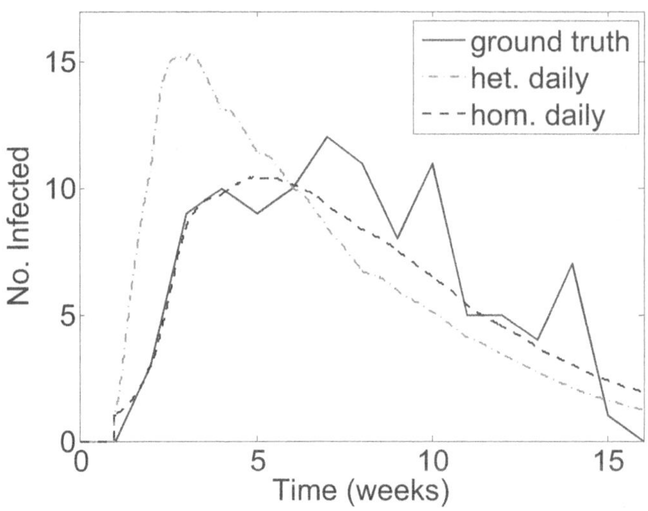

Figure 10. The best performing homogeneous (hom) and heterogeneous (het) daily models in comparison to the real data. For hom $\gamma = 0.3, \beta = 0.2$ and for het $\gamma = 0.3, \beta = 0.1$.

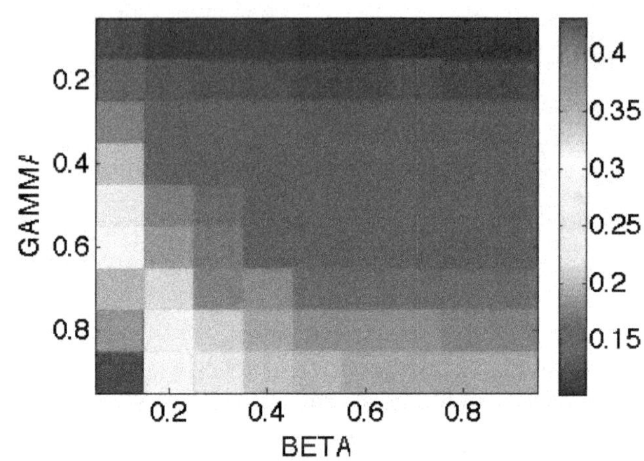

Figure 11. The average precision of the daily homogeneous model run over 1000 random trials. The epidemic was initialized with the actual infected cases. Precision here shows the fraction of infected individuals correctly predicted by the model.

ing them over time. This is an important insight to avoid mistakes when modeling with this type of data.

Looking at the more realistic parameter range of $\gamma = 0.1-0.5$ and $\beta = 0.1 - 0.5$, the homogeneous daily model can achieve a precision of nearly 30% over the entire 17 weeks simulated. Note, this implies that over the 17 weeks, 3 out 10 individuals were correctly pin-pointed as being infected. These results were averaged over 1000 random trials, and the results varied greatly over trials. However, in general, the precision is very high near the beginning of the experiment, and drops down to zero as time progresses, lowering the overall precision results presented here. This is expected since the errors in identifying infected individuals propagate given the nature of the models.

CONCLUSION

We incorporate an individual-level dataset obtained from mobile sensing (Bluetooth) into a classical epidemiological scenario and study how such new data can improve infectious disease prediction. By simulating weekly and daily Susceptible Infected Recovered (SIR) models for influenza transmission — i.e. models that incorporate mobile sensed interactions at a weekly and daily time scales — we find that daily sensed interactions provide improved prediction performance over weekly sensed interactions. Given a daily homogeneous model – using equal interaction weights for those pairs of individuals that interact at least once – we are able to achieve an error of less than 2 people out of 72 subjects when predicting the number of infected cases over a 17 week interval. Given the same homogeneous model, we can predict with 30% precision the actual individuals which will become infected within the 17 week period evaluated. This remarkable predictive power by such a standard epidemiological model indicates that high resolution mobile phone data can increase the predictive capacity of even the simplest epidemic models.

Extensions of this work include replicating the evaluation of our results with other Bluetooth interaction data collections in similar epidemiological scenarios where both the Bluetooth interactions and the health symptoms are obtained. Improved infection prediction based on mobile sensing could be further validated by considering other types of infectious diseases, as well as other existing epidemiological compartmental models.

ACKNOWLEDGEMENTS

The authors would like to thank Anmol Madan and Alex (Sandy) Pentland for collecting, processing and providing the empirical dataset. Thank you to Shirin Farrahi for proof reading the paper.

REFERENCES

1. L. J. S. Allen. An introduction to stochastic epidemic models mathematical epidemiology. volume 1945 of *Lecture Notes in Mathematics*, chapter 3, pages 81–130. Springer Berlin / Heidelberg, Berlin, Heidelberg, 2008.
2. C. Brown, C. Efstratiou, I. Leontiadis, D. Quercia, and C. Mascolo. Tracking serendipitous interactions: how individual cultures shape the office. In *CSCW*, pages 1072–1081. ACM, 2014.
3. G. Chittaranjan, J. Blom, and D. Gatica-Perez. Mining large-scale smartphone data for personality studies. *Personal Ubiquitous Comput.*, 17(3):433–450, Mar. 2013.
4. K. Farrahi. *A Probabilistic Approach to Socio-Geographic Reality Mining*. PhD thesis, EPFL, Lausanne, 2011.
5. K. Farrahi, R. Emonet, and M. Cebrian. Epidemic contact tracing via communication traces. *PloS one*, 9(5):e95133, 2014.
6. M. Garcia-Herranz, E. Moro, M. Cebrian, N. A. Christakis, and J. H. Fowler. Using friends as sensors to detect global-scale contagious outbreaks. *PloS one*, 9(4):e92413, 2014.
7. R. Huerta and L. S. Tsimring. Contact tracing and epidemics control in social networks. *Physical Review E*, 66(5):056115, 2002.
8. L. Isella, M. Romano, A. Barrat, C. Cattuto, V. Colizza, W. Van den Broeck, F. Gesualdo, E. Pandolfi, L. Rav, C. Rizzo, and A. E. Tozzi. Close encounters in a pediatric ward: Measuring face-to-face proximity and mixing patterns with wearable sensors. *PLOS ONE*, 6(2):e17144, 02 2011.
9. L. Isella, J. Stehlé, A. Barrat, C. Cattuto, J. Pinton, and W. Van den Broeck. What's in a crowd? analysis of face-to-face behavioral networks. *Journal of Theoretical Biology*, 271(1):166–180, 2011.
10. T. Kim, A. Chang, L. Holland, and A. S. Pentland. Meeting mediator: enhancing group collaborationusing sociometric feedback. In *CSCW*, pages 457–466. ACM, 2008.
11. S. Lee, L. E. Rocha, F. Liljeros, and P. Holme. Exploiting temporal network structures of human interaction to effectively immunize populations. *PloS one*, 7(5):e36439, 2012.
12. A. Machens, F. Gesualdo, C. Rizzo, A. E. Tozzi, A. Barrat, and C. Cattuto. An infectious disease model on empirical networks of human contact: bridging the gap between dynamic network data and contact matrices. *BMC infectious diseases*, 13(1):185, 2013.
13. A. Madan, M. Cebrián, D. Lazer, and A. Pentland. Social sensing for epidemiological behavior change. In *Ubicomp*, pages 291–300, New York, NY, USA, 2010. ACM.
14. A. Madan, M. Cebrián, S. T. Moturu, K. Farrahi, and A. Pentland. Sensing the "health state" of a community. *IEEE Pervasive Computing*, 11(4):36–45, 2012.
15. A. Madan, K. Farrahi, D. Gatica-Perez, and A. Pentland. Pervasive sensing to model political opinions in face-to-face networks. In *Pervasive*, pages 214–231, Berlin, Heidelberg, 2011. Springer-Verlag.
16. R. C. Miller, H. Zhang, E. Gilbert, and E. Gerber. Pair research: matching people for collaboration, learning, and productivity. In *CSCW*, pages 1043–1048. ACM, 2014.
17. J.-K. Min, J. Wiese, J. I. Hong, and J. Zimmerman. Mining smartphone data to classify life-facets of social relationships. In *CSCW*, pages 285–294. ACM, 2013.
18. MIT Human Dynamics Lab. Social evolution dataset. http:realitycommons.media.mit.edu/socialevolution.html.
19. S. Phithakkitnukoon, T. W. Leong, Z. Smoreda, and P. Olivier. Weather effects on mobile social interactions: A case study of mobile phone users in lisbon, portugal. *PLoS ONE*, 7(10):e45745, 10 2012.
20. M. Salathé, M. Kazandjieva, J. W. Lee, P. Levis, M. W. Feldman, and J. H. Jones. A high-resolution human contact network for infectious disease transmission. *PNAS*, 107(51):22020–22025, Dec. 2010.
21. K. Starbird and L. Palen. (how) will the revolution be retweeted?: information diffusion and the 2011 egyptian uprising. In *CSCW*, pages 7–16. ACM, 2012.
22. J. Stehlé. *Human proximity networks: analysis, modeling and dynamical phenomena*. PhD thesis, Aix-Marseille Universit, 2012.
23. J. Stehlé, N. Voirin, A. Barrat, C. Cattuto, V. Colizza, L. Isella, C. Regis, J. Pinton, N. Khanafer, W. Van den Broeck, and P. Vanhems. Simulation of an seir infectious disease model on the dynamic contact network of conference attendees. *BMC Medicine*, 9(87), July 2011.
24. L. Sun, K. W. Axhausen, D.-H. Lee, and M. Cebrian. Efficient detection of contagious outbreaks in massive metropolitan encounter networks. *Scientific Reports*, 4, 2014.
25. S. P. Wyche and R. E. Grinter. This is how we do it in my country: a study of computer-mediated family communication among kenyan migrants in the united states. In *CSCW*, pages 87–96. ACM, 2012.

Spending Time with Money: From Shared Values to Social Connectivity

Jennifer Ferreira
Brunel University London,
Middlesex UB8 3PH, UK
jennifer.ferreira@brunel.ac.uk

Mark Perry
Brunel University London,
Middlesex UB8 3PH, UK
mark.perry@brunel.ac.uk

Sriram Subramanian
University of Bristol,
Bristol, BS8 1TH, UK
sriram@cs.bris.ac.uk

ABSTRACT
There is a rapidly growing momentum driving the development of mobile payment systems for co-present interactions, using near-field communication on smartphones and contactless payment systems. The design (and marketing) imperative for this is to enable faster, simpler, effortless and secure transactions, yet our evidence shows that this focus on reducing transactional friction may ignore other important features around making payments. We draw from empirical data to consider user interactions around financial exchanges made on mobile phones. Our findings examine how the practices around making payments support people in making connections, to other people, to their communities, to the places they move through, to their environment, and to what they consume. While these social and community bonds shape the kinds of interactions that become possible, they also shape how users feel about, and act on, the values that they hold with their co-users. We draw implications for future payment systems that make use of community connections, build trust, leverage transactional latency, and generate opportunities for rich social interactions.

Author Keywords
Ubiquitous computing; digital money; mobile payment; trust; community; prosocial computing, social practices.

ACM Classification Keywords
H.5. Information interfaces and presentation (e.g., HCI)

INTRODUCTION
Money has a highly complex role in modern society and plays a critical role in a huge range of our activities. As users of money, we are perhaps most familiar with it as a form of exchange for goods and services, an area that is rapidly undergoing change through the introduction of digital payments over the internet and, more recently, on mobile devices. This paper presents a study of how users make payments through one such mobile technology, and how this impacts on their activities, understandings and social interactions. In our analysis, we explore how user practices contrast against the rhetoric of the computer industry in automation, and of the ways that the banking and financial services industry have positioned payment technologies as a route to enabling 'frictionless' consumption.

CSCW '15, March 14-18, 2015, Vancouver, BC, Canada.
ACM 978-1-4503-2922-4/15/03.
http://dx.doi.org/10.1145/2675133.2675230

In this regard, the role of technology is often presented as a means of automating complex, difficult, dangerous, time-consuming or otherwise unpleasant activities. Take for example, speed: it is a broadly held, if implicit, assumption that computers, and our interactions with them, should be fast and effortless. Chip designers appear to be highly concerned with faster processing, network engineers with data transmission speeds, and within the HCI literature, numerous papers report on methods and techniques to optimize interfaces to support rapid task completion. Yet, faster interactions are not always better interactions, and this is especially so where device interactions operate at a pace that is not well matched to their users' abilities to make sense of, and react to this. This bringing together of fast digital processing, network connectivity and methods of interaction has also been applied to financial systems. Industry leader Visa's payWave card system promotes itself as "*fast, convenient and secure and means you can wave goodbye to cash... Payments are completed in less than a second ... and means no more fumbling for the right notes or coins or waiting for change – just quick, hassle-free transactions*" [46]. A variety of mobile payment systems make similar claims, operating over a variety of technical protocols, transactional systems and devices with claims that they are rapid and trustworthy (usually described as 'secure', 'safe' and 'encrypted'): features that lie at the core of any credible financial system, let alone a digital one.

The move towards speed and ease of payment has been a slow progression, and has had to be balanced against the trustworthiness of such transactions to manage the exchange of goods, from like-for-like in barter, to shells, tusks and beads, precious metals, bullion coinage, tokens, IOUs, banknotes and electronic payments (amongst others). Each media or technological development of exchange has been associated with material and social practices that shape and are shaped by them, but as transactions become faster and requiring of less inspection for credibility, there are fewer opportunities to engage in these practices. Indeed, cumbersome and slow interactions have been recognized to have been involved in the failure of previous mobile payments systems [37], and when payment systems provide clumsy solutions, they can cut across *'the physical environment and the behaviors associated with payments in local stores. Consumers have deeply ingrained habits to pay in certain ways with associated physical behaviors'* [ibid, pp. 9-10]. What then is lost as digital transactions remove opportunities for social and material exchange, and how might mobile technologies be designed to reconnect any such lost opportunities?

In this work we consider these questions in the context of digital transactions of the Bristol Pound payment system. We first frame the current research with respect to related work on digital currency, mobile money and the user experience in relation to time. We then present the Bristol Pound payment system, and our mixed method approach to studying it. Our findings detail the social practices around transactions and how users describe their interactions with the payment system, we extend these to develop implications for design.

RELATED WORK

There has been a great deal of research examining interaction and collaboration around mobile money in developing countries. In particular, M-Pesa, a mobile phone payment system, has been studied in detail (e.g. [33]) with attention to key themes such as trustworthiness and security [34], and how the system addresses the specific financial needs of developing economies [9]. While we similarly draw on an ethnographic approach to research mobile money, our study resides not in a developing economy, but a developed one, is not targeted at the unbanked, and is not tied to a particular mobile network operator in the way that M-Pesa is tied to Safaricom/Vodafone through its business model and technology platform. Our own study of mobile money in the relatively wealthy 'developed' world is very different to this work which forms the core of the literature on the use of mobile money.

Our particular interests in mobile money here lie in the value, use and interpretation of mobile money, and in this respect, the sociological and anthropological literatures around monetary practices are especially enlightening (for an excellent introduction, see Maurer [29]). There are broadly two competing schools of thought, the first building on standard economic models in which money allows depersonalised (cf. [4]) and asocial quantified value transfers [28, 41, 48], and the other, in which money is both produced through and shapes our social relations (traditionally seen through the lens of rank and prestige). Within economic anthropology, there is a long history and debate about how money operates as a medium of exchange and a store of value, and how the practices forming around this impact on social and cultural institutions. Granovetter [15], for example, explores how the embeddedness of rational economic choices is woven into on-going systems of social relations, so for example, the cultivation of personal relationships can, in some instances, assume equal or greater importance than the economic transactions themselves. On a similar theme, Zelizer's extensive work examines social practices around money and the circumstances that shape those practices, with an orientation to shared understandings and interpersonal relationships. Related to our own work on local currencies, Bohannan [5] introduced the concept of *general-purpose* and *special-purpose* money, with the (now disputed, see for e.g. [17]) idea that special-purpose money (e.g. wampum and cowries) was restricted to particular forms of use, and could only circulate within restricted 'spheres of exchange'. The increasing availability of general-purpose money circumvents these spheres of exchange, causing social disruption. It is interesting to consider that modern local currencies that restrict 'spheres of exchange' are often paradoxically created to promote social harmony.

Our work extends the utilitarian view of money as *capital* to explore the 'extraeconomic, social basis of money' [50]. Following Zelizer [50], we approach the study of mobile money and its exchange as necessarily a study of how meaning and value are assigned by those who use it, and recognise that it lies at the intersection of technological design, culture, and economic exchange. Studies in the HCI literature have investigated people's values, practices and everyday concerns when conducting financial transactions, including the circumstances in which they do so (e.g. [24, 45]). Some have focused particularly on digital money use across different countries and applications, connecting cultural aspects with the design of software. Mainwaring et al.'s ethnographic study of digital money use in Japan shows how cultural aspects can be leveraged to design mobile payment systems that fit with the context of its users [26]. Illustrating this point, the paper opens a discussion on how to minimize commotion during digital transactions while also upholding "aesthetic pleasure". By studying how online gamers in China perceive, obtain and spend virtual currency, Wang and Mainwaring explore how the gaming experience is shaped, heightening its realness, trust, and fairness [47]. Yang et al.'s [49] study shows how reflecting Chinese cultural practice successfully in the design of the virtual currency of an online community allowed that community to express that practice ('guanxi') and subsequently thrive. Community is a recurrent theme that shows up in the literature on financial practices, with time-banking being explicitly set up to benefit community relationships; Bellotti et al. [3], for example, explore how time-dollars are earned and spent, developing design implications which recognise that relationships are formed and maintained through transactions.

Virtual currencies in gameworlds (e.g. Linden Dollars in SecondLife or 'gold' in World of Warcraft) hold the strange character of being purchasable for real money, but only holding practical value within the game. Greengard [16] suggests that behaviours with virtual currency have implications beyond the gameworld, affecting the course of tax legislation. Similarly, Bitcoin is a digital currency that has gained considerable media attention through the debates in the international community regarding its legislative status–as money [43] or as a commodity [40]. One feature of Bitcoin transactions is the time it takes for the transaction to be verified, and therefore, completed. Karame et al. [23] have investigated the times involved in payment verification, and concluded that Bitcoins are not a good fit for fast payments, i.e., exchanges where payment for goods and receiving them takes a "few seconds." Their investigation describes how delayed payment makes the system prone to double-spending when accepting immediate payments, but they reveal little about how these delays shape the user experience.

Time experienced during interactions with technology has been demonstrated to hold implications for the user experience (e.g. [25, 35]). Of special interest to us here is how the speed of an interaction can support experiences of reflection and pleasurable anticipation around interactions, changing perceptions of value and meaning around digital media. Further, how long or short waiting time is, or how slow or fast response times are, hold meaning for those participating in the interaction, such that Sundar et al. [44] propose guidelines for designing mobile interfaces based on users' expectations around time. Harmon & Mazmanian's [20] study of the use of smartphones mentions the temporal aspects of mobile interactions, exploring response speed as it relates to perceptions of togetherness and community, but time is not considered as a main object of study. Other designers have attempted to take conscious control of time around interactions. Games designed by Hong et al. [21] are instances of designers specifically harnessing the intervals in slow interactions usually spent waiting; in this case the time spent waiting at a printer. Designers have also deliberately slowed interactions down, introducing the concept of "slow technology" to counter the trend in striving for better productivity and efficiency with technology [19].

RESEARCH CASE

The Bristol Pound

The Bristol Pound (£B) is a local complementary currency in use in Bristol, England (Population: 432,500; the 6th largest city in England). It was launched by the Bristol Pound CIC (Community Interest Company) in September 2012 and as of July 2014, there are approximately £B620,000 in circulation with over 650 businesses listed in their directory as members. The currency is both paper-based and digital. Transactions occur in printed notes (in denominations of £B1, £B5, £B10 and £B20), SMS on any mobile phone, or online via an electronic account similar to a bank account. Printed notes are accessed from a number of businesses at various locations in the city (known as cash points). Anyone can exchange sterling for £B notes free of charge, but once sterling has been exchanged for £B notes, the notes cannot be exchanged back into sterling. Payments by SMS and online differ from this access model in that they require an electronic £B account. Eligibility to open an electronic account is granted by the Bristol Pound CIC, subject to certain rules based on membership type. Exchanging electronic £B for sterling is possible–by withdrawing £B from an account as sterling – but this incurs charges. £1 sterling is equivalent to £B1 and businesses in the city trade in £B on a voluntary basis.

The Bristol Pound CIC

The Bristol Pound Community Interest Company (CIC) is a not-for-profit company incorporated on 16 August 2010 that administers the £B. The CIC have registered physical premises in the centre of Bristol from where a team of individuals conducts the day-to-day tasks of running the currency. At the time of our study the core team of the Bristol Pound CIC consisted of four directors, one communications and events manager, one trader manager, one accounts and office manager, one technical director, one project coordinator, one project manager and one poet-in-residence. There were also six assistants on the team. All roles on the team were working on a volunteer basis. From this point on we will refer to the team administering the currency as the £B team.

Bristol Pound Membership Types

Membership of the scheme falls into two categories: *Individual* and *Trader*. Businesses can become trader members, and hence maintain a £B account, if they are locally owned and operated. Individuals may become members and granted accounts if they reside or work in Bristol. From this point on we will refer to individual members and traders members as either 'users' or 'members' as required by the context.

Txt2Pay

Txt2Pay (T2P) is the platform that enables business and individual Bristol Pound members to conduct transactions via SMS. It is implemented on the Cyclos platform (cyclos.org), which is widely used for mobile and online banking by commercial banks internationally, as well as social enterprises such as the Bristol and Brixton pounds, T2P is a type of mobile money transfer in which business members and individual members can exchange electronic £B, irrespective of their mobile network operator. There is one mobile phone number to which all SMS payments are sent. When a member pays another member by sending an SMS text message, the payer transfers the amount in electronic £B from their account to the payee's £B account. SMS texts are charged by mobile network operators at their standard rates and the payee incurs charges when receiving electronic £B via T2P. In the next section we describe a typical T2P transaction to set the scene for our more detailed examination of interactional features in our discussion that follows.

Vignette: a typical SMS Transaction

Andy is hungry and visits the small café near his office that sells his favourite coffee. It is lunchtime and the ordinarily empty café is bustling with people. He grabs a sandwich, falls into the queue and almost immediately two more people fall in behind him. While he checks his phone for new text messages, he glimpses his latest £B balance request and remembers that he has about £B10 in his account. The text confirms a balance of £B9.85 and he decides to use £B to pay. When it is his turn, Jo, the café owner greets him by name and takes his order. While the coffee is being made, Andy tells Jo that he would like to use Txt2Pay. Jo smiles and reaches for the mobile phone lying on a shelf directly below the cash register. Andy composes a text message on his phone and sends it. A few moments pass, and they chat about the building work in the street outside, holding their phones within eyesight. 30 seconds later, Jo's phone beeps, and she confirms that the payment has gone through. Andy waits for the confirmation text message to appear on his phone. As it arrives, Andy's coffee is poured into a cup. Andy thanks Jo, who says, "See you tomorrow, Andy!"

Figure 1: Demonstrating Txt2Pay use from instructional video provided by the Bristol Pound CIC. Source: bristolpound.org.

This scenario, drawn from our observations and interview data, is typical of many T2P transactions, and while there is variation in the detail of the transactions, it illustrates aspects of interactions that we will return to in our analysis. Fig. 1 depicts the typical arrangement of the transactors during the T2P transaction. T2P usually involves transactions when both parties are collocated (although this is not a requirement), and with merchants or service providers that are independently owned or run. Most member businesses operate within a specified geographical region (in this case, within 50 miles of the Bristol area).

METHODS

The aims of the study were to examine the values and needs of the community of £B users, including traders that accept £B and the currency administrators, and explore the implications for designers to reflect and support these patterns of use, practices and values in digitally augmented media. We report on findings from a survey and fieldwork conducted in Bristol (UK), presented in separate sections that address quantitative and qualitative dimensions. Although the primary focus of this paper is on the experiences of users and their practices around the use of the £B, quantitative data allows us to examine the proportion and frequency of use in spending, their length of experience with it, spending characteristics, and user demographics to illustrate the breadth of its use, and the penetration of the currency into people's everyday lives.

Bristol Pound Member Survey

The online survey was run with Bristol Pound members in conjunction with the £B team who helped promote and publicise it. The number of respondents who attempted the survey was 197, of which 152 completed it. The 45 partial survey responses are included in the analysis. Respondents were not paid for participation. As well as quantitative data, the survey included open questions enquiring about respondents' reasons for joining the £B, its value to them, reasons for using or not using the printed and T2P versions of the £B, and its problems and effects on them personally. For the quantitative data, SPSS was used to obtain summary statistics from the responses.

Membership and demographics: At the time of the survey, 34.5% of respondents had been Bristol Pound members for the 12 months that the Bristol Pound CIC had been in existence for, with 26.4% of respondents as members for 6 months or less (N=197). Of the total respondents, 68 indicated that they were female and 83 male. Respondents ranged from 20 to 72 years old with a median of 44 years (N=149). Respondents included 128 (84.2%) employed, 6 students (3.9%) and 10 retirees (N=152). Those employed reported to be in professional occupations (57.7%), managers (19%), while the remaining included technicians, administrative support workers, one craft worker, labourers or helpers, service workers, voluntary workers and homemakers (N=142). All respondents lived, worked and/or studied within a 10-mile radius of the centre of Bristol. We anticipate that the majority of these members have basic competence in using computers: among the respondents, most applications for Bristol Pound membership were lodged online (52.3%, N=197).

Frequency and values of spending: Of all respondents answering this question (N=156), only 1 reported spending £B several times a day, 7 respondents spent them every day, while the spending frequency for the remaining respondents were a few times a week or less. The largest group of respondents reported spending them less than once a month (32.1%, N=156). Average use of £B was reported to be 14.1% of weekly spend (N=150 ranging between 0% to 80%. The largest proportion of respondents (56.8%, N=155) reported an average spend of 0 - 20 electronic £B per week from their accounts. The next largest proportion (18.1%, N=155) reported an average spend of 21-40 electronic £B per week. This is spending either online or using T2P. Only 3.9% of respondents (N=155) reported to spend more than £B60 per week from their account.

We recognise that any survey conducted online is open to sampling bias in the sense that those individuals who choose to respond online may have different characteristics to those who choose not to respond. This has to be taken into account when interpreting the results of the Bristol Pound member survey. It is possible that some members may not have access to the Internet. However, this is a low probability in a developed, well-connected city such as

Bristol, UK, and also because members who use T2P are required to join an online account in order to make or receive payments.

Qualitative data and analysis

Interviews and ethnographic observations were conducted over a 3 month period to explore the behaviour, patterns and practices around £B use in context. Participants include individual members and traders (trader is the term used by the £B team to denote both sellers of goods and services, as well the business members of the Bristol Pound), as well as the £B team administering the currency. The qualitative findings are based on the authors' personal shopping experiences using £B, participant observation through involvement with the £B team at their premises, and formal and ad hoc interviews with individual and trader members. The authors used the (printed) £B while shopping with trader members and observed T2P payments in at least three different locations in Bristol (including a café, a market stall and a road side food stall). Ad hoc informal interviews were conducted at these times. Formal interviews were conducted with 18 participants. Of these, 17 participants were contacted on the basis that they agreed to be formally interviewed as part of the survey, and one member from the £B team, the trader manager, was formally interviewed. Table 1 shows the demographics of interview participants. Using the survey data reported, we categorised respondents into higher (>10% of spend) or lower spenders (<5% of spend) in £B, approximately split evenly across both groups. In addition, participants were deliberately selected from a range of backgrounds, ages and income groups, and split evenly across gender, allowing us to get a broad range of views and patterns of £B use. Interviews were either face to face in a café setting, their workplaces or via Skype (two). The interviews, of approximately 30 minutes duration, were audio recorded and transcribed for analysis. Interviews were semi-structured and open-ended allowing the interviewer to follow topical trajectories.

Age	
Median	46
Youngest	25
Oldest	69
Gender	
Male	9
Female	9
Spender type	
High	9
Low	9
Membership type	
Individual	14
Trader	2
Both (individual and trader)	1
£B team	1

Table 1: Demographics of the 18 interview participants.

Working through specific examples of their recent spending, we focused on themes around interviewees intentions in using the £B, how they used T2P and its problems, differences in their use and understanding of paper and T2P transactions, and the ways that they understood, used and distinguished between £B and sterling in transactions.

Our analytic approach was data-driven such that the themes that emerged from our iterative scrutinising of the data were grounded in examples from our interviews, field notes and survey responses. The data was scrutinised for descriptions of behaviours in relation to the T2P system. Patterns in the data were identified and named according to the process described by Braun and Clarke [7]. In the findings that follow, we do not attempt to quantify the qualitative data, but rather examine *how* and *why* these concerns are of relevance to our analysis: verbatim quotes from interviews here are used not as evidence or proof, but as illustrations of reported events and to enable the participants' 'voice' to come through. Where individual instances of data that are of sufficient interest to report are discussed in the analysis, this is noted. In the analysis below of this qualitative material, we also include material from both the open questions in the survey and the interviews. Participant quotes are labelled [*xyz*] where *x* is either 's' indicating that the quote is taken from the survey open questions, or 'i' indicating that the quote is taken from an interview; *y* indicates the participant's Bristol Pound membership type and can be either 'i' for individual members, 't' for traders or 'a' for £B team; *z* is a number assigned to each participant and is unique within the categories of interview participants and survey participants. Thus participant 6 in the survey who was also a trader would be labelled as 'st06' and participant 6 who was an interview participant and an individual member would be labelled as 'ii06'. These would not necessarily be the same individual as not all survey respondents identified themselves by name. In the sections that follow, we describe how the participants in our study described their use of the T2P system and interactions around T2P transactions.

TRANSACTIONAL CONCERNS

Our interest in the role of time in making £B payments was initially identified in the qualitative reports from the survey results. Several respondents explicitly reported that T2P mobile payments were too slow and cumbersome. The response *"Transaction takes too long, is too fiddly" [si011]* is typical of these, and points to a recognition that the temporal and interactional demands on making payments is high. Compared to payment in the form of *handing over cash* or *waving* a plastic card, payment by T2P introduces more points in the transaction where interactional variations can occur. Transactions using T2P may be slowed down for several reasons and for variable amounts of time. Users may wish to verbally confirm with the trader that payment by SMS is possible, for example, counter staff may not know how to use the equipment, or their mobile phone or fixed terminal may not be working. Prior to making the transaction, payment details have to be manually typed in on occasionally awkward keypads (function phone keypads often being especially slow to use, and T9 variants making non-standard text strings error-prone). These payment details must then be checked to ensure that the correct recipient details and sum are included in the text, and this may only be possible to determine after the cost of several items are totalled up. Where mobile phone coverage is poor, the payer may need to check that their mobile phone has a signal before sending, and the trader has to receive the SMS payment confirmation to ensure that the transaction has been processed. Several of these factors may come together to produce complex and extended sequences of interaction.

While the some of the sentiments of the survey respondents align with trends in more efficient, faster and secure interaction, the data presents a complementary account, i.e., one in which these transactions offer rich social interactions through which individuals are able to express themselves as members of their community. Pulling out data in which participants reported on their £B transactions, we identify three analytic features that offered opportunities for users to engage in: (1) pleasure and play, (2) conversation and sociability, (3) mindful reflections on purchases and patterns of spending, and (4) trust judgements. We present each of these topics in turn below.

PLEASURABLE TRANSACTIONS

Opportunities for playfulness

As we have seen, T2P payments could vary in their interpersonal demands, while at the same time requiring different forms of device interactions and providing different forms of feedback to cash or card-based payments. Building on top of these differences provided unexpected and occasionally interesting outcomes:

"For me it was like, wow, this is really cool and really fun." [ii12]

The relatively slow, and in particular, the unpredictable speed of the transaction allowed its users opportunities to fill this time with ludic, or playful interactions (cf. [14, 22]). Such opportunities were shaped around the social interactions and spaces that the transactions were situated in. This opportunity for playfulness occurred not so much with the technology (which has a rigid interactional format), but with the way that the digital payment interactions were formatted and temporally paced to match the unfolding purchasing transactions. In a quote from one informant, we see an element of fun and competition where the buyer and seller are both waiting for a confirmation text. Although this appears to be a random process, the participant describes the arrival of the first text as winning a kind of informal 'bingo' game with the name of the other participant being used here as a 'winning' call out that completes the interaction:

"Txt2Pay's more fun because you can't do that with normal money. You can't do that with a card...You're both standing there with your phones waiting for the first one to beep. And someone says "Oh is your name John" and I say "Yeah" and it's quite nice." [ii05]

The informant makes a clear distinction between traditional 'normal' forms of money, which afford different, and less informative, social interactions; it brings together elements of anticipation, a quantifiable (chance) result, completion and tension relief, alongside the pleasant social nicety of being introduced to someone by name. While these are not elemental or necessary requirements of gameplay, the informant reflects on these features as being both competitive and sociable. The nature of paying using T2P and the 'special' (cf. [51]) status of this form of money is described here as involving a kind of 'fun', and something very different than can be achieved with other forms of payment. We cannot discount the fact that this may be due to the novelty or infrequency of its use, but the way that it is usually the individual's personal phone being used, personal details exchanged, and the fact that both users are aware that they share membership of an unusual 'club' or scheme, that makes this experience notably and qualitatively different from paying with other forms of money.

Pleasure in Spatial Exploration

The playfulness with this special money extends beyond the T2P transaction itself to the activity of finding a place to use T2P. As we have already identified, while many places in Bristol do accept £B, many more – indeed, the vast majority – do not. The £B team provides a searchable map (via the Google Maps API) of the approximately 600 retailers that accept £B (electronically or as cash) on their website, and this is also reported as being used in playful games of searching out new places to visit and go shopping:

"Using the online directory on the £B website. I look on the map, who's near me, where can I spend my money?" [it04]

That people may experience fun (e.g. [1]) and pleasure (e.g. [31]) from shopping is hardly a novel finding, but the implementation of the interactive map (often accessed on the same smartphones that are used in making payments) provides an opportunity and motivation to explore new areas of the city. In some ways, this is similar to user practices around geocaching (e.g. [36]), in providing a new way to explore and experience our spatial environment, building on different motivations and perspectives than simply heading off into unknown locations.

Extending this finding of goal-based spatial exploration, participants also reported that they enjoyed the experience of being the first to spend £B with traders:

"There's a veg shop up in Wells Road and I was the first one to spend £B there." [ii06]

There is currently no technical way to identify a first-to-spend with a trader, so this was evidently notable enough for some verbal discussion to have taken place between the trader and customer, and worthy of report to have brought up, unprompted, in an interview. This was not just visible in our interview data collection: social media was actively deployed to do this in a somewhat similar way to "checks-ins" and claiming badges on FourSquare.com [12]. A typical example drawn from the @BristolPound Twitter feed of this kind of behaviour can be seen in fig. 2, in which a Twitter user records their first-to-spend status, with a linked photo of a cup of coffee to evidence their purchase, and an encouraging comment linked back to the trader's twitter account:

Figure 2: Tweet claiming first to spend with T2P

This 'checking in' can be likened to a form of playful activity in 'winning' a game or race in doing so, while simultaneously using these episodes as vehicles for promoting a representation of themselves via their digital personas as ethically-minded.

SOCIABILITY

Transaction As Conversation

Speech is more than an instrumental way of getting things done (e.g. [27]), allowing us to build rapport and social bonds. Buying things in shops or in service transactions can offer opportunities for these kinds of sociable interactions, especially where these are in local communities. Placencia [39] describes the ways in which transactors in neighbourhood corner shops try to engage in social interaction that is personal, for example through greetings and goodbyes, respectfulness and wit, rather than simply fulfilling the institutional roles of shopkeeper and customer. The kinds of shops and services that have been allowed to become trader members of the Bristol Pound have a close fit with Placencia's neighbourhood corner shops, and performing payment via SMS was reported as a welcomed opportunity for phatic conversation:

"It is very rare that you have a Bristol Pound transaction where it is just routine, where you don't really speak beyond the kind of set phrases." [ii08]

This is an area of interaction that is directly challenged by the recent industry move towards faster forms of digital payment. With rapid, anonymous transactions comes the potential for losing this sociable interaction and the loosening of social bonds between local buyers and sellers, and consequent weakening of community connections.

This anticipated loosening of bonds seems to be in direct contrast with what we have ourselves observed and had reported in the use of £B. In part, this is due to the technical demands of making a T2P transaction, which provides users with an opportunity to make conversation with one another. Compared to other traditional forms of payment, the relatively slow pace of the technology in the transaction itself opens up interactional space for a degree of conversational engagement, and the relative complexity of the mechanics of entering and checking the payment text message requires the participants to engage in conversation:

"It has been quite fun, since normally the trader wont [sic] have had many payments that way so we get to chat a bit about whether it will work or not etc, [sic] so its been a bit more social than just handing over some cash." [si029]

Coupled to the technological features of the T2P transaction leading to the necessity of verbal interaction, other social factors also provided openings for more enjoyable forms of communication between transactors. Both the relative unusualness of such payments is an immediate opening for conversation:

"I think you spend more time talking to the cashiers which is quite nice. Because it's a novelty, you start joking about it." [ii01]

This increased time spent interacting is not just a direct consequence of technical latency, but of an engagement that develops around common interests between transactors.

Shared Values and Interests

One of the reasons that these reported sociable and relaxed interactions could occur is a plausible assumption held between parties that both buyer and seller subscribe to common collective ethical concerns:

"What I'm using it [£B] for at the moment is an indicator of what kind of place a trader is. I take it as somehow an indicator of their values." [ii08]

These social and technical factors come together to provide a resource for conversation; it is not that both participants *need* to have an engaged conversation, but this situation provides an accountable way in which they can begin to engage with one another and build relationships from this:

"It's still a novelty to use your phone and use the currency, more importantly, and that sparks a conversation with the people. You build a relationship with the business owners." [ii01]

While these conversations were opportunities for exchanging first names and reinforcing common values, these discussions also opened up possibilities to new ways of using the T2P system to get access to printed £B:

"In my local cafe where I live I now am on first name terms with the manager, George. I say "George, if I pay you £B80 in Txt2Pay will you give me 60 pounds in cash?" [ii11]

Here, the informant is not talking about withdrawing notes in pounds sterling, but £B. This access to the physical notes was something of a difficult issue for many £B users, as at the time of the study, there were few places to withdraw £B in printed form, and most of these were not conveniently located from where most users lived. Access by the informant to £B60 in cash is also a significant amount of money, and falls outside the contractual expectations on £B account-holding traders to provide a service to their customers. It also imposes a small additional cost on the trader (who pays a percentage fee on T2P transactions; see below), so this is a very personal service for a valued customer, and also requires a degree of trust in the credibility of the payment being non-fraudulent. Without the social interactions formed through regular conversations and a first-name relationship that has been built up over time, this kind of interaction would seem unlikely.

MINDFUL TRANSACTIONS

As participants conducted their T2P transactions, they reported that this type of payment itself, and the interactional demands that it imposes on them provides an opportunity to think about their purchasing practices and the broader impacts of their own patterns of consumption.

The real costs of spending

For a variety of reasons that spill out of their use of T2P payments, participants reported becoming more aware of how much they spend, the real and environmental costs of their spending, as well as the implications of using SMS as a medium for payment. Users considered the £B in all of its forms *"a more ethical way to spend money" [si024]*, and the very act of spending it, rather than cards or sterling:

"... makes you think about money in a broader sense than picking up a tomato in a supermarket and paying for it. You start to think about the supply chain, how you value it and what little effort you can do by buying it at a independent trader translates to a larger effect." [si052]

The speed and manual entry of payments on their own devices when making T2P transactions also confronted users with considering payment in ways that they would not usually have to do when they pay with plastic in shops, as one participant described it:

"It's about seeing it on your screen and seeing the amount that you're typing in as well. I think that helps. Because usually if you go into a shop and you're paying by card, they've already entered the amount and you're just looking at accepting it and pressing go. Whereas if you have to enter the amount you need to send it's like taking money out of your pocket as well. With me it's right in your face, the number. That has a big impact." [ii01]

Choosing considerate payments

The comparison of T2P with payment by plastic also goes beyond spending on goods to users' mindfulness around the transaction costs imposed on users (traders and their customers) of using these financial services. In this case, both bank cards and the £B typically incur costs. In the case of bank cards these fall purely on traders, but for £B users, these fees can fall on both parties, costing traders 2% (or minimum of 10p) and may cost customers any SMS charges levied by the mobile network operator (in practice, this often works out free). Problematically, T2P (and credit cards) renders transaction charges (and notably charges that *others* will incur) invisible through the interactional format of the transaction. Indeed, it is clear that these T2P costs to traders were not always recognised by customers, and in their attempts to act in a socially responsible way, some actively chose to use T2P in making payments because they thought traders would therefore avoid these costs: *"[I used] the 'Text to pay' service, to avoid credit/debit card fees in local shops," [si005]* and that they *"Don't want the local trader to have the extra cost of paying commission fees." [si180]*

While these attempts did not ultimately have the intended result, the survey exposes these users' intentions to be considerate and responsible customers. What we are primarily concerned with here is not an interactional failure causing a misunderstanding about transaction costs (although this is interesting), but the fact that users are consciously mindful of the impact of their payment media on traders, and *actively choosing* to use one payment method over another because of their beliefs about the financial costs that they are imposing on others.

FOSTERING TRUST, THROUGH SOCIAL CONNECTIONS

As with any form of financial transaction, there are potential risks in using T2P, from fraud to outright theft. We therefore need to closely inspect the ways in which people make these trust-dependent value judgements.

Managing conditions of uncertainty

Risk and uncertainty can be experienced in various ways with the T2P system, for example, the uncertainty associated with a transactor receiving no confirmation text message about whether the amount has been deducted from or added to their account, in which case sellers risk giving away goods for free. Participants experienced this sense of uncertainty seemingly on a regular basis, as seen in this typical quote:

"I always have that nervousness. Whenever I do it, I think it's never going to come through on their phone and then the payment's going to come out of my account, and the same the other way around." [it04]

No credible financial system can work without some form of trust, rendered through social or technical protocols. While fiat payment systems rely on users' sense of institutional trust, i.e., trust in the banking system, the T2P system operates outside those institutions and therefore cannot rely on that same sense of trust. In using T2P, users need to overcome inherent uncertainties to form a sufficient degree of trust in the transactions, the devices, the organisations involved, the individuals involved, and the various networked components that make up the T2P system. As a starting point, a sense of trust may be imported from users' understanding of *who* is involved. One participant talks about a credible outside institution, such as the city council, being a part of the scheme:

"It's great that Bristol Council supports it and it's

wonderful that the staff are starting to take their salaries that way and the mayor is taking his salary in Bristol Pounds." [ii11]

However, unless that initial trust is validated, the use of the T2P system is unlikely to be sustained. The system would simply not function without a sufficient number of users making a value judgement around the potential costs to them of *not* making a purchase, as one participant explained:

"Well if people hold back because they're not sure if it's going to work or not, it's not going to work." [ii09]

Current levels of use would suggest that the system is working, and that a form of critical mass has been achieved, to the extent that its use is reasonably high and increasing, rather than fading away.

Interactional trouble and judgement calls

The implementation of T2P on the SMS platform lends itself to a degree of trust in the technology. The high penetration of SMS text messaging in the UK means that users are familiar with the technology and have expectations around its transmission speed and likelihood of failure. This means that delays in the system or where there are problems in receiving confirmation of payment are normally tolerated, and may be simply ignored:

"Where they've had a problem with their phone, where they've not charged it or they can't find it. But I'll just show them my confirmation text and that's been fine as well." [ii12]

This apparent trust in the platform has to be balanced against the low value of the majority of transactions discussed here, and consequent low risk of a fraudulent behaviour having a major financial impact. At the same time, these decisions to trust the SMS platform or the device's display text is not made independently of the social and contextual fabric against which the transaction occurs: these are not fast-paced, anonymous transactions taking place in the absence of rich social cues.

While the carrier technology and its limitations is largely understood, the lack of established protocols in making transactions using T2P means that how a transaction unfolds is negotiated on-the-fly. Our data show that this is highly locally contingent on factors as diverse as the users' experience of network coverage in payment locations, judgements made around users' clothing and attitude, previous encounters between them, or even balanced against the potential of trouble that failing to accept the £B might cause with the till operator's employer if they did not take the T2P payment:

"On one occasion where it was taking a rather long time they were in a debate with a colleague about whether it would be ok to just go by my text or if that was going to give them problems." [ii12]

When making normal transactions, payment must be seen to have been made in order to consider an exchange successful. With bank notes this is a simple matter, and with a card this is bound into the interactional process with an approval message on the display of the point-of-sale device and printing of a confirmation receipt. However, proof of payment is not always required when using T2P:

"In a number of shops they didn't really seem that bothered [waiting for a confirmation text]. They just wrote on their till receipt the amount in £B and they file it." [ii12]

In a similar example of non-payment, another £B member reported being allowed to walk away before the trader's confirmation of payment had been received, contradicting previous notions of "walking away as a means of 'closing' a mobile interaction [8]:

"I literally had to walk away from the building in order to get a phone signal to send a text message. It was [successful]." [ii06]

This seems extraordinary; as there are few normal occasions in which people can buy something, say that they have paid, and that this be accepted. It would be plausible that the payer might not have a £B account, or have an account but have no funds in it to pay for their purchases, yet this was ignored for the purposes of finalising this particular transaction.

Building and leveraging social connections

As we have seen, interactional troubles were usually delicately negotiated through talk and the other situational features that surround the physical interaction. While these can take time to resolve, they also help build lasting connections between traders and their customers, fostering longer term networks of community and trust. One participant explained that, as a trader, her close and temporally extended relationships with customers affected her attitudes and actions around T2P difficulties resulting in non-payment, likening these technical problems to difficulties with other forms of payment:

[interviewer: Would you make them wait there?] "No I wouldn't. I'm in a position where I know my customers. But I think if you were in the shop that would be a bit awkward. I have people I hope I'm going to see again. I've had people who've forgotten their purse and that's fine." [it04]

Here, instead of requiring the customer to wait until she was sure that their payment had been received, she was comfortable knowing that because of the social relationship they have built up, payment problems were solvable in other ways. The fact that this was not likely to be a one-off, impersonal interaction impacted on her expectations. In doing this, participant 'it04' reports drawing from the same social protocols that she used when customers forgot other means of paying (e.g. a purse). It seems that despite T2P being implemented on a different technical platform, the same kinds of social connections and methods provide resolution to these difficulties. In this sense, social and community relationships provide a bond in which trust allows for flexibility in managing payment problems. For these small-scale shopping experiences, it appears that users trust the business to better gauge whether personal contact with the customer is acceptable:

"[interviewer: Is it weird that your name is given?] No not at all. I wouldn't like it if it was in Tesco's but it's a local experience anyway so it's just part of where I live. It's a small little shop they're going to say "So you're Liz would you mind if I send you regular texts?" It's just the benefit of small interactions." [ii05]

Thus while it is considered acceptable for local independent businesses to know a customer's personal information, it would appear that this is not the case for large chain supermarkets (such as Tesco) to collect and use this information in the same way.

DISCUSSION AND IMPLICATIONS FOR DESIGN

Our analysis of the use and interactions around the T2P system provides an account in which these digitally mediated transactions offer opportunities for rich social interactions through which individuals are able to express themselves as members of their community and make lasting connections based on trust.

As we know from the literature, the concept of trust is complex and dynamic, in that it is built up over time under certain conditions [30, 32]. Boyd [6] connects trust with community, stating that "trust is based in the construct of community." In our work, participants' belief that T2P is a credible service is evident in the conversations, gamifications and reinforcements of each other's values. The special nature of T2P transactions gives space for users to build rapport and to consider any reasons for transactional problems that might arise. In particular, there are features of this trust-based transaction that demonstrate how participants' confidence in the T2P system is inextricably linked with their concept of community: it is negotiated on the fly, embedded in proximal social relations (c.f. [13]) and enables reciprocation of common concerns. We argue that this is centrally linked to the characteristics of the transaction process: the effort and time required for interaction and inspection does double work here, in that it also allows users to assess the probability of deceit by the person they are transacting with.

Although T2P was not designed specifically to complicate or slow down interactions between transactors, among alternative payment systems, unpredictability and slowness is not uncommon. In the case of Bitcoin, the exchange between goods and payment can be even slower. Validating transactions can last tens of minutes, exposing parties that choose to make fast payments to the risks of double spending, and making payments of large amounts undesirable [42]. One might extrapolate from our own data that recipients of Bitcoin payments would likely be similarly nervous until payment was verified, although this could be somewhat ameliorated where social connections could be leveraged to mitigate this. Supported by our data, the utilisation of local and social connections may support small co-present interactions more than remote purchases (where the majority of Bitcoin transactions currently take place). Remote purchases with Bitcoin (or other systems requiring prolonged algorithmic verification) may benefit from being linked to users' online social networks or recommender-style systems may offer an additional means of limiting risk. Interestingly, there appear to have been no reports from the Bitcoin community of the serendipitous outcomes highlighted in our investigations that connect slow transactions with community cohesion and trust. Designers who have deliberately designed for slowness, such as Odom's [35] study of the Photobox, have demonstrated new experiences that are possible when time is manipulated in interactions with technology. The reflection and anticipation that the Photobox evokes in its users can also be observed in the ways that T2P evoked playfulness, conversations and mindfulness in our own participants. While Photobox helped users to reflect on the role of technology in their everyday lives, T2P (perhaps more unintentionally) helped the £B users to build connections, to other people, to their communities, to the places they move through, to their environment, and to what they consume.

While we have pointed to several advantages that build from protracted social and technical interactions around T2P, we are not making a case that this slowness and complexity in making payments comes without costs. It is worth noting at this point that being in a position to use the T2P system takes effort: besides the effort of joining the scheme and signing up for an account there are other implicit costs. Members need to have sufficient £B in their accounts, which means they have to remember to top up their accounts. It becomes clear that in the face of so many competing demands on their time, users are making a conscious choice to engage with a cumbersome method of payment rather than waving a credit card, for example. What this trade-off illustrates is how users are making astute calculations regarding their payment options in balancing the non-trivial effort required to make use of T2P against the value they gain from it. The value in this case seems to be intertwined with the friction in the interaction thus making the cumbersome interaction a desirable option.

To think about how we could conceive of and design payment systems in light of the findings of this study, we propose a framing of transactions as *co-productions* at the *seams*. We examine these in turn below.

Co-production: As both payer and payee negotiate issues of trust, effort and value around the transactions they conduct, they are effectively participating in what can be called a *co-production* relation. Ostrom [38] explains co-production using the example of Chicago street crime where the community and police officers work together to co-create a safe environment. In co-production, power and responsibility is shared between parties to achieve a collective goal. This has been carried forward in the literature on Timebanking (see for e.g. [10]) where members synchronously provide and benefit from social services in the community. Applied to our studies of £B use, at the level of the transaction, the co-produced achievement that arises from the collaboration of both payer and payee is not only that particular successful exchange of £B for a good or service, but also (as shown by our findings) the social bonding and community engagement that arises from the personal interaction. The quote from participant 'ii11' illustrates this concept: *"In my local cafe where I live I now am on first name terms with the manager, George. I say "George, if I pay you £B80 in Txt2Pay will you give me 60 pounds in cash?"* In this example, participant 'ii11' needs printed £B and the special businesses where printed £B can be withdrawn are not accessible to him. Instead, he makes use of his local café, a Bristol Pound member business. He is willing to offer £B80 in digital form in exchange for the service and the printed £B60. Negotiating the T2P transaction to make this exchange possible participant 'ii11' and the local café manager achieve emergent social goals that would otherwise not have been possible. It is important to recognise that a community in which co-production is on-going – indeed £B are designed for circulation – other members can benefit from its effects. In our example, as a result of the T2P transaction the café manager now has £B80 in digital form to re-spend with other member businesses, allowing new emergent social needs to be addressed in other parts of the community, and so on – in effect sustaining community relationships. Casting the transaction as an instance of co-production exposes where design challenges lie: *How can we preserve and design for the benefits of the co-produced transaction (community cohesion and trust) in a more predictable way?* Addressing this question requires articulating the collective goals that co-producing entities achieve and then providing support that allow those goals to be achieved in a collaborative manner, without unnecessary encumbrance.

Seamfulness: Monetary transactions, as an interweaving of digital technology with social spheres are a type of activity that requires moving across the *seams* discussed by Chalmers and Galani [11]. Seamful design aims to expose and transform limitations and breakdowns in systems design into opportunities to engage, convey information and be useful [18]. This concept has been taken up in mobile location-based games, with one example (Feeding Yoshi) deliberately exposing WiFi coverage and security to drive gameplay in a multiplayer game, with different WiFi conditions leading to differing game elements [2]. The T2P transaction seen here requires users to shift focus between mobile devices and the unfolding social protocol of a monetary exchange. The creative ways in which users of the T2P system filled in the temporal pauses, negotiated failed payment verifications, or dealt with network blackspots, were the ways in which these individuals collaboratively enriched the transaction. Applying the concept of seamful design to slow or unpredictable payment systems, the challenge becomes: *How can we take advantage of the seams in payment systems to enable co-production of desirable outcomes?* This is not to say that we recommend slow, complex or ambiguous payment, but recognise that these interactional 'failures' also present positive opportunities for action, and should not simply be regarded as flaws that demand rectification. Moreover, these seams can potentially offer practically useful interactional outcomes (for social, community, or payment verification purposes) through the design decisions made: considering these seams as opportunities is a practical and useful solution to what may be a technically insurmountable problem.

CONCLUSION

In this paper we have discussed our findings relating to the opportunities for social and material exchange afforded by the T2P transaction process. T2P may not be the most fluid or robust of payment mechanisms, yet our findings show that by choosing to use T2P users engage in a rich set of behaviours and interactions that bring useful implications for the design of future payment systems. Transactions experienced as playful, as conversations, and as opportunities to be mindful show how T2P supports people in making connections to other people, to their communities, to the places they move through, to their environment, and to what they consume. While these social and community bonds shape the kinds of interactions that become possible, feelings of trust also shape how users feel about the social and community bonds that they hold with their co-users. We have to recognise that this is a detailed study of a small number of users, interacting with a unique technical system, and acting within a relatively small and spatially bound location: generalising the results beyond this group should be approached with care. Nevertheless, our analysis shows a number of highly relevant practices, concerns and implications that have relevancies for future payment systems that would appear to extend beyond these limits. We propose a framing of transactions as *co-productions* at the *seams*, thereby challenging designers of payment systems to view monetary transactions as achievements between collaborating agents and as opportunities for rich social interactions.

ACKNOWLEDGMENTS

We thank our interviewees, questionnaire respondents and the Bristol Pound CIC staff. This research was funded by the Digital Economies programme (EPSRC EP/K012304/1).

REFERENCES

[1] Arnold, M., & Reynolds, K. (2003). Hedonic shopping motivations. *Jnl. Of Retailing, 79* (2), 77-95.

[2] Bell, M., Chalmers, M., Barkhuus, L., Hall, M.,

Sherwood, S., Brown, B., et al. (2006). Interweaving mobile games with everyday life. In Proc. ACM CHI'06 (pp. 417-426).

[3] Bellotti, V., Cambridge, S., Hoy, K., Shih, P., Handalian, L., et al. (2014). Towards community-centered support for peer-to-peer service exchange: rethinking the timebanking metaphor. In Proc. ACM CHI'14 (pp. 2975-2984).

[4] Bloch, M., & Parry, J. (1989). Introduction: money and the morality of exchange. In B. &. Bloch (Ed.), In Money and the Morality of Exchange (pp. 1-32). Cambridge, UK: CUP.

[5] Bohannan, P. (1959). The impact of money on an African subsistence economy. *J. Econ. Hist., 19,* 491–503.

[6] Boyd, J. (2006). *In Community We Trust: Online Security Communication at eBay*. Retrieved April 13, 2014, from http://onlinelibrary.wiley.com/doi/10.1111/j.1083-6101.2002.tb00147.x/full.

[7] Braun, V., & Clarke, V. (2006). Using thematic analysis in psychology. *Qual. Res. in Psychology, 3*(2), 77-101.

[8] Broth, M., & Mondada, L. (2013). Walking Away. The embodied achievement of activity closings in mobile interaction. *Journal of Pragmatics, 47*, 41-58.

[9] Buku, M., & Meredith, M. (2013). Safaricom and M-Pesa in Kenya: financial inclusion and financial integrity. *Washington Jnl of Tech. & Arts, 8* (375).

[10] Carroll, J. (2013). Co-production Scenarios for Mobile Time Banking. Proc. 4th International Symposium, IS-EUD 2013, (pp. 137-152). Copenhagen, Denmark: Springer.

[11] Chalmers, M., & Galani, A. (2004). Seamful interweaving: heterogeneity in the theory and design of interactive systems. In Proc. ACM DIS '04. (pp. 243-252).

[12] Cramer, H., Rost, M., & Holmquist, L. (2011). Performing a check-in: emerging practices, norms and 'conflicts' in location-sharing using Foursquare. In Proc. MobileHCI 2011 (pp. 57-66). ACM Press.

[13] Dissaux, T. (2014). Endogenous development and complementary currencies in Africa. Retrieved April 13, 2014, from www.veblen-institute.org.

[14] Gaver, W. (2002, June). Designing for Homo Ludens. *I3 Magazine*.

[15] Granovetter, M. (1985). Economic Action and Social Structure: The Problem of Embeddedness. American *Journal of Sociology, 91*(3), 481-510.

[16] Greengard, S. (2011). Social games, virtual goods. *Commun. ACM, 54*(4), 19-22.

[17] Guyer, J. I. (2004). Marginal Gains: Monetary Transactions in Atlantic Africa. University of Chicago Press.

[18] Höök, K., & Löwgren, J. (2012). Strong concepts: Intermediate-level knowledge in interaction design research. *ACM Trans. Comput.-Hum. Interact., 19*(3, Article 23).

[19] Hallnäs, L., & Redström, J. (2001). Slow technology – designing for reflection. *Pers. Ubiq. Comput., 5*(3), 201-212.

[20] Harmon, E., & Mazmanian, M. (2013). Stories of the Smartphone in everyday discourse: conflict, tension & instability. In Proc. ACM CHI '13 (pp. 1051-1060).

[21] Hong, J., Price, M., Schilit, B., & Golovchinsky, G. (1999). Printertainment: printing with interactive cover sheets. In Ext. Abstracts ACM CHI'99 (pp. 240-241).

[22] Huizinga, J. (1955). Homo Ludens: a study of the play-element in culture. Boston: Beacon Press.

[23] Karame, G., Androulaki, E., & Capkun, S. (2012). Double-spending fast payments in Bitcoin. In Proc. Computer and communications security (pp. 906-917). ACM.

[24] Kaye, J., McCuistion, M., Gulotta, R., & Shamma, D. A. (2014). Money talks: tracking personal finances. In Proc. ACM CHI'14 (pp. 521-530).

[25] Lenz, E., Diefenbach, S., & Hassenzahl, M. (2013). Exploring relationships between interaction attributes and experience. In Proc. 6th Int. Conf. on Designing Pleasurable Products and Interfaces (DPPI '13) (pp. 126-135). ACM.

[26] Mainwaring, S., March, W., & Maurer, B. (2008). From meiwaku to tokushita!: lessons for digital money design from Japan. In Proc. ACM CHI '08 (pp. 21-24).

[27] Malinowski, B. (1923,1972). Phatic communion. In Hutcheson, & Laver (Eds.), Communication in face-to-face interaction. Middlesex, UK: Penguin.

[28] Marx, K. (1977 [1844]). Economic and philosophic manuscripts. In D. McLellan (Ed.), Karl Marx, Selected Writings (pp. 75–112). Oxford, UK: Oxford Univ. Press.

[29] Maurer, B. (2006). The Anthropology of Money. *Annual Review of Anthropology, 35,* 5-36.

[30] McKnight, D., & Chervany, N. (1996). The Meanings of Trust. Technical Report, University of Minnesota, Management Information Systems Research Center.

[31] Menon, S., & Kahn, B. (2002). Cross-category effects of induced arousal and pleasure on the internet shopping experience. *J. Retail, 78*(1), 31.

[32] Meyerson, D., Weick, K., & Kramer, R. (1996). Swift trust and temporary groups. In R. Kramer, & R. Tyler (Eds.), Trust in organizations: Frontiers of theory and research (pp. 166–195). Thousand Oaks, CA: Sage.

[33] Morawczynski, O. (2010). Examining the adoption, usage and outcomes of mobile money services the case of M-PESA in Kenya. PhD Thesis, Edinburgh Uni.

[34] Morawczynski, O., & Miscione, G. (2010). Trustworthy mobile transactions: a longitudinal study on M-PESA in Kenya. In Latusek, & Gerbasi (Eds.), Trust and Technology (pp. 160-173). Hershey, PA: IGI Global.

[35] Odom, W., Sellen, A., Banks, R., Kirk, D., Regan, T., Selby, M., et al. (2014). Designing for slowness, anticipation and re-visitation: a long term field study of the photobox. Proc. ACM CHI '14 (pp. 1961-1970).

[36] O'Hara, K. (2008). Understanding geocaching practices and motivations. In Proc. ACM CHI'08 (pp. 1177-1186.).

[37] Ondrus, J., Lyytinen, K., & Pigneur, Y. (2009). Why mobile payments fail? Towards a dynamic and multi-perspective explanation. In Proc. IEEE HICSS, January 5–8 (pp. 1-10).

[38] Ostrom, E. (1996). Crossing the great divide: Co-production, synergy, and development. *World Development, 24*(6), 1073-1087.

[39] Placencia, M. (2004). Rapport-building activities in corner shop interactions. *Journal of Sociolinguistics, 8*, 215-245.

[40] Pohjanpalo, K. (2014). Bitcoin Judged Commodity in Finland After Failing Money Test. Retrieved June 4, 2014, from http://www.bloomberg.com/news/2014-01-19/bitcoin-becomes-commodity-in-finland-after-failing-currency-test.html.

[41] Simmel, G. (1990 [1907]). Philosophy of Money. London: Routledge.

[42] Singh, P., Chandavarkar, B., Arora, S., & Agrawal, N. (2013). Performance Comparison of Executing Fast Transactions in Bitcoin Network Using Verifiable Code Execution. In Proc. IEEE ADCONS '13 (pp. 193 - 198).

[43] Sparshot, J. (2013). Web Money Gets Laundering Rule. Retrieved June 4, 2014, from http://online.wsj.com/news/articles/SB100014241278873243732045783746113511252O2.

[44] Sundar, S., Dou, X., & Lee, S. (2013). Communicating in a ubicomp world: interaction rules for guiding design of mobile interfaces. In Proc. INTERACT 2013, Part II, LNCS 8118 (pp. 730–747). Springer.

[45] Vines, J., Dunphy, P., & Monk, A. (2014). Pay or Delay: The Role of Technology When Managing a Low Income. In Proc. ACM CHI'14 (pp. 501-510).

[46] Visa (2014). Retrieved June 4, 2014, from Visa: http://www.visaeurope.com/en/cardholders/visa_paywave.aspx.

[47] Wang, Y., & Mainwaring, S. (2008). Human-Currency Interaction: learning from virtual currency use in China. In Proc. ACM CHI '08 (pp. 25-28).

[48] Weber, M. (2011). The Protestant ethic and the spirit of capitalism. (S. Kalberg, Trans.) NY: OUP.

[49] Yang, J., Ackerman, M., & Adamic, L. (2011). Virtual gifts and guanxi: supporting social exchange in a chinese online community. In Proc. ACM CSCW '11 (pp. 45-54).

[50] Zelizer, V. (2011). Economic Lives. Princeton: Princeton University Press.

[51] Zelizer, V. (1989). The Social Meaning of Money: "Special Monies". *American Journal of Sociology, 95*(2), 342-377.

NUGU: A Group-based Intervention App for Improving Self-Regulation of Limiting Smartphone Use

Minsam Ko, Subin Yang, Joonwon Lee, Christian Heizmann[†], Jinyoung Jeong, Uichin Lee, Daehee Shin, Koji Yatani[‡], Junehwa Song, Kyong-Mee Chung[§]

KAIST, [†]Hochschule Furtwangen University, [‡]University of Tokyo, [§]Yonsei University

{msko, subin.yang, joonwonlee, jinyjung, uclee, daehee.shin, junesong}@kaist.ac.kr

[†]c.heizmann@hs-furtwangen.de, [‡]yatani@ee.t.u-tokyo.ac.jp, [§]kmchung@yonsei.ac.kr

ABSTRACT

Our preliminary study reveals that individuals use various management strategies for limiting smartphone use, ranging from keeping smartphones out of reach to removing apps. However, we also found that users often had difficulties in maintaining their chosen management strategies due to lack of self-regulation. In this paper, we present NUGU, a group-based intervention app for improving self-regulation of limiting smartphone use through leveraging social support: groups of people limit their use together by sharing their limiting information. NUGU is designed based on *social cognitive theory*, and it has been developed iteratively through two pilot tests. Our three-week user study ($n = 62$) demonstrated that compared with its non-social counterpart, the NUGU users' usage amount significantly decreased and their perceived level of managing disturbances improved. Furthermore, our exit interview confirmed that NUGU's design elements are effective for achieving limiting goals.

Author Keywords

Social Support; Group-based Intervention; Smartphone Use

ACM Classification Keywords

H.5.m. Information Interfaces and Presentation (e.g. HCI): Miscellaneous

INTRODUCTION

As smartphones have become an integral part of our daily lives, negative aspects of smartphone use have emerged. For example, habitual checking/multitasking disrupts study, work, and social interactions [1, 18, 24], and consuming stimulating online content (e.g., social media, news) may lead to excessively long usage [16]. However, we still lack a holistic understanding of the interfering usage behavior/contexts, and the common management strategies and their effectiveness. This knowledge is critical for designing a software tool that can help users self-regulate their smartphone usage; this is the primary focus of this work.

Our survey results ($n = 114$) showed that diverse interfering contexts exist, and a majority of participants wanted to change their usage habits (60.2%). We identified several common management strategies for limiting usage such as physical separation, deleting/turning off apps, and limiting services (e.g., usage monitoring, notification setting, and blocking apps [20]). However, we also found that users often had difficulties in maintaining their chosen management strategies due to a lack of self-regulation.

In this paper, we propose a new approach for improving self-regulation in limiting smartphone usage that leverages social support; that is, a group of friends limit their smartphone use together and share their limiting information with one another. Our approach is based on *social cognitive theory* (SCT) proposed by Bandura [2]. From the SCT perspective, learning occurs in a social context and much of what is learned is gained through observation. Through social learning, people can have better awareness of normative behaviors and can also be motivated to self-regulate.

Based on our approach, we designed NUGU (when No Use is Good Use), which is a group-based intervention app that improves self-regulation of limiting smartphone use. It consists of three components: (1) self-monitoring, (2) goal-setting, and (3) social learning and competition. Each component is designed to support three sub-processes of self-regulation from the SCT perspective [2], i.e., self-monitoring, self-judgment, and self-reaction. Deficient self-regulation is attributed to a lack of personal/social awareness and attention to usage/limiting behaviors, and to failures of self-controlling usage. NUGU confronts these issues through visualizing objective usage/limiting behaviors, setting limiting goals, sharing limiting practices, and reinforcing desirable behaviors. We followed an iterative prototyping process; two working prototypes were developed and tested in field trials ($n = 10$, $n = 20$) to design the final version of NUGU.

In order to evaluate the performance of NUGU, we conducted a user study ($n = 62$) for three weeks. In this study, we analyzed the changes in the participants' smartphone usage and experiences after using our group-based intervention app. Also, for comparison, we implemented an individual-based intervention app and analyzed differences in the intervention effects by social support. The results demonstrated that the social support was critical in assisting the participants to limit their smartphone use (e.g., lowering usage hours/frequency and managing disturbance). Through the exit interview, we confirmed that our design elements were helpful in achieving the users' limiting goals.

CSCW 2015, March 14–18, 2015, Vancouver, BC, Canada.

ACM 978-1-4503-2922-4/15/03 ...$15.00.
http://dx.doi.org/10.1145/2675133.2675244

BACKGROUND AND RELATED WORK

Problematic Use of Smartphones

Many smartphone users have experienced interference in their lives that resulted from their smartphone use [8]. Ames [1] observed that the constant availability often demands multitasking that interferes with the current task such as study/work and social relationships. Levine et al. [18] found that mobile phone usage disrupts driving, pedestrian activity, and study/work. Oulasvirta et al. [24] and Bohmer et al. [4] presented the source of multitasking: the user's habit of checking updates involves brief and frequent content consumption (e.g., checking emails and SNS). Lee et al. [16] found that consuming stimulating online content (e.g., SNS, news) might lead to excessive smartphone usage.

Prior studies also have demonstrated that typical users wanted to manage the smartphone interference in their daily lives. For example, Shin and Dey [27] found that study participants who had normal usage patterns self-reported that sometimes they used smartphones too much and had concerns about their usage. The participants in Lundquist et al.'s work [21] also agreed that they needed to limit some of their smartphone use, but there was a lack of consensus on how to solve this issue. In this work, we investigate how users perceive usage interferences and what the current strategies are for interference management. We demonstrate that a lack of self-regulation causes the existing strategies to be less effective, and we propose a group-based intervention method.

Technology Non-Use

While HCI literature mostly regards non-users as potential users who have not yet adopted the technology, increasing attention has been drawn to non-users in recent years, and researchers explored the sociocultural, socioeconomic, demographic, and other issues related to non-use [3, 9, 25, 29]. Earlier studies attempted to categorize the diverse forms of non-use, which also significantly deepened our understanding about (non)users [25, 29]. Recently, Baumer et al. [3] demonstrated that Facebook exhibited more complicated non-use patterns, e.g., resisting (never using it), leaving (deactivating or deleting an account), relapsing (leaving it but subsequently returning), and limiting (e.g., filtering status-update emails).

Our work is along with the line of non-use research in the field of HCI. Compared with the other technology non-use cases, we believe that smartphone non-use is more complicated due to its accessibility and functionality. Smartphones are always carried by users and typically serve as gateways for numerous services ready at hand (e.g., information seeking and social networking). Discarding smartphones can be done at the significant expense of losing *in situ* digital assistance and instant social connectivity as clearly identified in prior work [1, 8]. Given that it is difficult to strictly practice non-use when compared with other technologies [3, 9], our study demonstrates that people tend to choose to limit its use via temporary non-use in which people actively regulate its use under various situation as a part of active resistance [17]. Therefore, it is necessary to more carefully consider in what specific contexts people do (and do not) want to use it and how to effectively support such behaviors. Our work complements earlier studies in that we deepen understandings of non-use of smartphones and explore design spaces in order to systematically support these behaviors.

Persuasive Systems

Fogg [7] defined *persuasive technology* as interactive technology designed to change users' attitudes or behaviors. Our work fits within the literature on persuasive technology because we aim to change smartphone users' problematic usage. Oinas-Kukkonen et al. [23] summarized the key principles of persuasive system design: primary task support, dialogue support, system credibility, and social support. First, the primary task support is about helping users conduct their tasks, e.g., by reducing the effort required for a target behavior, or by providing visual feedback to support self-monitoring. Second, the dialogue support is related to helping users continue to move towards their goal or target behavior via verbal information such as praise and rewards. Third, the system credibility describes the principles of designing more credible services such as displaying information in order to verify authority. Finally, the social support describes how to motivate users through leveraging social influences (e.g., comparison and competition).

Existing persuasive systems have leveraged information technologies primarily for health [5] and sustainable behavior [10]. We consider mobile apps that assist in changing problematic smartphone usage, as reported in recent studies [15, 20]. While our design can be considered as a synthesis of the key principles of persuasive system design (e.g., self-monitoring [14], social support [5]), the key contribution of this work lies in its integration into a new problem space based on a theoretical framework, i.e., social cognitive theory of self-regulation [2]. Toward this goal, we first characterized the limiting practices and demonstrated that the existing strategies often failed due to a lack of self-regulation. In order to overcome this problem, we design a system to harness social learning and comparison to help people learn from one another and to make sustained efforts to limit usage.

Smartphone Overuse Intervention Apps

We surveyed 41 smartphone intervention apps from the Google Play (using the keyword 'smartphone addiction') and the related literature [15, 20]. We classified the apps into four categories based on their purpose: (1) diagnosing smartphone addiction based on the smartphone addiction scales (e.g., All's), (2) intervening in smartphone overuse (e.g., Momo, BreakFree, SAMS [15], and AppDetox [20]), (3) supervising children's smartphone use/overuse through remote control, monitoring, and chatting (e.g., Net Nanny, Qustodio), and (4) assisting in focusing on the task at hand (e.g., StayOnTask, StudyLocker). There are various persuasive and intervention mechanisms for mediating smartphone overuse, such as locking apps/screens, self-monitoring (e.g., usage hours/frequency), using alarms, and repeatedly encouraging (e.g., "Show me your will power" in Smart Self Coach).

The dominant mechanisms for intervening in smartphone overuse belong to the primary task support principle; We identified that 70.7% used locking and 68.2% supported self-monitoring. The only app that utilizes social support at the time of the survey was WatchApp, where group members determine apps to limit for a given period of time, and they are ranked based on usage time of the selected apps. The approach of WatchApp is similar to NUGU in terms of using social support to assist in regulating smartphone usage, but the method of implementing the social support is different. First, the competition in WatchApp is based on the amount of usage time (i.e., the user who uses their smartphone less wins), so contextual factors were not considered. Our study shows that most smartphone users perceive their problematic usage when their daily activities are disrupted. This indicates the necessity of encouraging users to practice temporary non-use when a primary activity begins. Even though a user limits their usage time to two hours per day, their usage could still disturb their daily activities, e.g., playing games in a classroom. On the contrary, NUGU allows users to share limiting time and contexts (activities), thereby facilitating the positive effects of social learning within and between groups.

SURVEY STUDY OF LIMITING SMARTPHONE USE

We investigated the usage habits that interfere with everyday life activities through analyzing the characteristics and consequences of these usage habits. Then, we classified the common management strategies and their effectiveness in limiting smartphone use. From our results, we drew several key design directions in order to develop an effective method for limiting smartphone usage. In the study, we adopted an online survey method because our focus is primarily on exploring representative contexts and general behaviors of people rather than understanding specific cases in depth. However, because the typical survey methods are often limited to shallow data, we designed the survey items to capture more detailed responses through several open-ended questions as well as five-point Likert scale questions. Our survey content consisted of three parts: usage habits, management strategies, and demographics. We posted this survey in large online communities. There were 114 participants (60 males and 54 females), and their ages ranged from 18 and 32 years ($M = 24.8$, $SD = 5.0$). Most participants were students: high school (6.1%), college (57.0%), and graduate students (20.2%), but office workers also participated (16.7%). We conducted open coding for the responses of the open-ended questions.

Usage Habits: Characteristics and Consequences

Many participants reported that they felt overusing their smartphones (64.0%; $M = 3.69$, $SD = 0.91$) and wanted to change their usage habits (60.2%; $M = 3.49$, $SD = 1.00$). The open-coding results illustrated that the usage that people wanted to change could be classified into two categories: (1) frequent short usage and (2) occasional long usage.

First, the frequent short usage was largely triggered by app notifications (e.g., instant messages, social media, and social games). One participant said, *"I belong to several group chat rooms because my business is in my mobile instant messenger, and notifications come very regularly"* (P40). Frequent checking of these notifications often disrupts the user's tasks, such as work and offline social activities. One participant said, *"When I receive a notification during work, I lose concentration easily"* (P18). When socializing, many participants had negative experiences with smartphone usage. For example, one participant commented, *"I wanted to search for information while I was meeting my friend. So I did it, but she got really annoyed with that"* (P1). Our participants also acknowledged that after a short checking session, they often spent time using a series of other apps. One participant commented, *"When I study, I often use a web browser to search. But, I get easily tempted to check the news whenever I open my browser"* (P27).

Methods	%	Examples
Physical Separation	31.5%	*"I just left my phone at home."* *"I put my phone out of reach."*
Turning Off	27.2%	*"I put it into the airplane mode."* *"I muted all notifications."*
Deleting	17.5%	*"I deleted Facebook, some games, and browsers."* *"I moved addictive applications into one folder."*
Limiting Apps	9.6%	*"I installed a monitoring app and checked my overall usage"* *"I used a study app that blocks app usage."*
Others	14.0%	*"I changed my data plans to a smaller data size."* *"I consciously tried not to use smartphone."*

Table 1. Common limiting strategies.

Another problematic usage type was the occasional long usage, which sometimes led to excessive usage. Interestingly, the participants concurred that excessive usage often involved web browsing and mobile gaming. When browsing web pages, the participants kept following hyperlinks and checking new content, which often led to excessive usage. One participant complained as follows: *"One day, I came across one interesting webtoon and read only one episode. But soon I found myself reading every episode and I could not do my work"* (P28). Many participants stated that they started playing social games for fun for a while, but as the competition become more intense, they were not able to stop playing the games. Consequently, they often spent 2 to 3 hours playing the game in order to win. This type of excessive usage was typically observed at night (e.g., in bed), during breaks between daily activities, or while commuting. Such usage primarily occurred when users were alone. Many participants were sleep deprived due to smartphone use; for example, they habitually used their smartphones to check updates while in bed, but this often led to excessive usage.

Management Strategies and Their Effectiveness

In our survey, 63.6% of participants attempted to limit their smartphone use. In Table 1, physical separation from smartphones was the most popular strategy that the participants had used (31.5%). This is because the physical separation is the simplest approach that participants could take. Some participants used different degrees of turning off strategies ranging from disabling notifications to disconnecting from mobile networks (airplane mode) and to turning the smartphone off completely (27.2%). Deleting addictive applications or making the applications less easily accessible was another direct method for limiting (17.5%). Limiting apps that help overcome overuse were also used (9.6%). The participants used various tools for limiting, such as self-monitoring of usage, notification management, and blocking apps during specified times. The remainder of the specified management strategies included mindful efforts to avoid using the smartphone, downgrading to feature phones or changing data plans, removing the batteries or not charging phones, and focusing on alternative activities (e.g., reading books).

Then, we asked the participants about the effectiveness of these strategies. While some participants reported the usefulness of such approaches, they concurred that these strategies often failed and did not last long. The significant reason for this is related to these strategies relying on the user's self-control. However, the participants demonstrated that real situations were complex, and simple limiting strategies tended to be overridden by the urge to use the smartphones. One participant commented, *"I've tried to not spend time in useless online communities, so I deleted every bookmark. But the funny thing was that later I just entered the URLs myself. Taking the time to enter the URLs does not bother me at all"* (P43). Another reason is related to the social expectation of constant connection [1]. While the participants sometimes disabled the sound/vibration-based notifications, due to the social expectation of constant connection, they constantly checked whether new messages had arrived. One participant said, *"I adjusted the notification setting to mute in order to concentrate on my work. But the feeling that I might have received messages kept me checking my smartphone"* (P13).

Design Implications

Our results provide useful design insights. First, it is important to design a mechanism that can help protect daily activities from problematic smartphone use. According to our survey, people tended to perceive their problematic use when their primary activity was disturbed (e.g., working). The results address the necessity of considering usage contexts (activities) as well as daily usage amounts in order to help users' limiting behaviors. Using only the usage amounts could overlook different contexts. For example, even though users limit their usage time per day to two hours, this could still disturb their activities, e.g., playing games in a classroom. Therefore, instead of simply limiting the usage time per day, our design should allow users to activate a limiting goal that they limit the usage for some times (e.g., 10 minutes, 2 hours) whenever focus on an activity is required.

Second, the participants preferred to use less restrictive management strategies (e.g., muting, airplane mode) than downgrading to feature phones or changing data plans because they wanted to use their smartphones when really necessary (e.g., information seeking and urgent messaging). Therefore, flexible intervention should be employed such that limiting can be cancelled whenever users need to use phones. For this flexibility, the intervention app should be designed to let users pull back their limiting goal when really necessary, but it may need to have a procedure that can make it difficult to stop the limiting usage, e.g., by introducing reinforcing mechanisms including a point system or encouragement.

Finally, it is highly recommended to employ other mechanisms to boost individuals' self-regulation of smartphone usage. Our results indicate that relying on an individual's self-control to limit their smartphone usage is not much effective. In order to overcome this limitation, we can utilize social support functionalities specifically designed to limit usage, e.g., users share their limiting times and contexts to help them learn from one another about when no use is good use and to encourage continued usage moderation.

DESIGN OF THE GROUP-BASED INTERVENTION APP

We propose a new approach of improving self-regulation of limiting smartphone usage through leveraging social support, i.e., a group of friends limit their smartphone use together and share their limiting information with one another (for learning and supporting). Our approach is based on the theoretical background of social cognitive theory (SCT) proposed by Bandura [2]. From the SCT perspective, learning occurs in social contexts and much of what is learned is gained through observations. Through social learning, people can have better awareness of normative behaviors, and they can be also motivated to self-regulate.

SCT perspective of self-regulation emphasizes three sub-processes [2]: self-observation, self-judgment, and self-reaction. First, self-observation indicates an individual's ability to monitor or track their own behaviors and their outcomes. Second, self-judgment is a process where individuals evaluate their actions based on personal, social, and collective norms. Finally, self-reaction occurs when they respond to the evaluations that they have made in order to revise their behaviors if their behavior falls short of their standards. Lack of self-regulation (or deficient self-regulation) is attributed to deficient self-monitoring/judgment (i.e., lack of awareness and attention to the behavior) and deficient self-reaction (i.e., failures of self-control) [13].

Based on our approach, we designed NUGU (when No Use is Good Use), which is a group-based intervention app that improves self-regulation of limiting smartphone use. The key features of the NUGU are to support the sub-processes of self-regulation in the SCT view, i.e., (1) self-monitoring to visualize objective usage/limiting behaviors, (2) setting goals and limiting usage, and (3) social learning and competition from sharing limiting practices with others. Our design encourages users to set limiting goals and sharing limiting information with one another (thereby improving self-monitoring/judgment), by assisting in limiting usage (e.g., locking apps), and by reinforcing desirable behavior with rewards (e.g., praise, points) and social support (thereby improving self-reaction).

Iterative Design Process

We performed rapid iterative prototyping: two working prototypes were developed in series, followed by a week-long field trial for each. This process occurred over a period of four months. We rapidly prototyped a working app that implemented the key features. In the first pilot test, we hired two groups of college students (five participants per group) who were interested in changing their usage habits with their friends. For the second pilot test, we recruited four groups of college students (five participants per group). The second test was also conducted for one week and focus group interviews were conducted afterward. In each pilot, after the par-

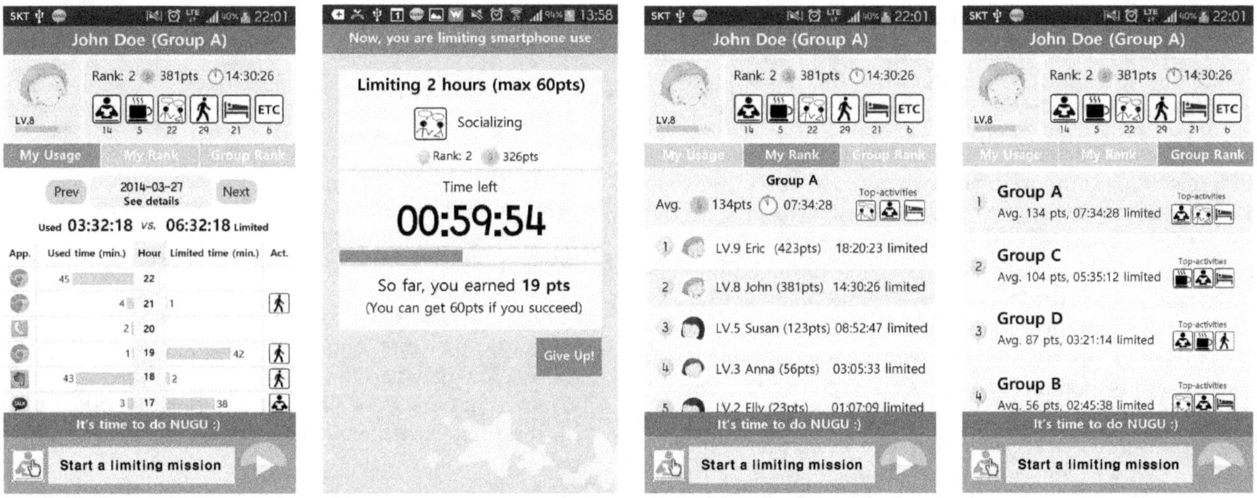

(a) Self-monitoring (b) Goal setting and limiting (c) Individual ranking (d) Group ranking

Figure 1. User interfaces of NUGU.

ticipants had used NUGU for one week, we invited them to focus group interviews. In these interviews, the participants were asked to discuss the advantages and limitations of the prototype. The interview data were transcribed and coded into a list of requests. Next, we prioritized the requests and implemented the most important ones.

NUGU Application Description

Figure 1 presents the three features of NUGU: *self-monitoring of usage behavior*, *setting goals and limiting usage*, and *social learning and competition.*

Self-monitoring of Usage Behavior

The first part is self-monitoring (see Figure 1(a)). This main screen displays a user's profile (screen name, level, points, weekly usage time, activity statistics of the week), which allows users to understand the overall status of usage/limiting behavior. It also has a comparative view of usage information (i.e., hourly usage time and the apps used in that hour) and limiting information (i.e., the amount of usage limiting time and the representative activity that a user performed while limiting usage). This comparative view helps users easily compare their usage and limiting behavior in recent hours. If a user clicks a date, the detailed usage information (ranked based on daily usage time per app) can be viewed.

The first pilot results demonstrated that the participants wanted to know more detailed usage and limiting information because they hoped to better understand their usage (e.g., app names) and limiting patterns (e.g., related activities when limiting usage). In the second prototype, we designed the following screens: mission history with related activities, daily usage hour graph (a bar graph for readability), activity frequency ranking, and app usage ranking (daily app usage and frequency). However, the participants in the second pilot used the information on these screens less and complained that navigating multiple screens was difficult. Thus, we carefully selected the minimal information that was required and aggregated the information related to self-monitoring into a single screen. This revised one-page view shows the hourly usage amount and limiting time with representative app and activity icons.

Setting Goals & Limiting Usage

The second part is goal-setting in Figure 1(b). This screen helps users set a limiting goal (called a limiting mission) through the start button at the bottom of Figure 1(a). A user can set a goal of limiting usage with information including the duration (ranging from ten minutes to two hours) and the current activity (e.g., work/study, socializing). When the mission is started, the app's mode is switched to the *goal-mode* that forbids the execution of any apps (except receiving incoming calls) and puts the smartphone into silent mode (see Figure 1(b)). In the following, we explain the detailed design of beginning a mission (or setting a goal), managing the current goal in progress, and the reinforcing mechanisms for continued participation.

Beginning a mission: From the field trials, we found that the participants wanted to begin their usage limiting as quickly as possible because they were in the process of starting a new activity (e.g., studying). Our final design attempted to minimize the cost of goal setting through trading the amount of freedom for simplicity. From the log data analysis, we found that the most popular time options were 10 m, 30 m, 1 h, and 2 h. Likewise, we coded the most frequent activities that the participants entered and reached the following activity categories: studying/working, resting, socializing/eating, getting up/going to bed, moving/commuting, and other.

Mission in progress: In the first prototype, when users unlock their smartphone, the NUGU app considered the action to be a mission failure. The participants had many mission failures due to their checking habits, and they wanted to be reminded that a mission was in progress. For this reason, we introduced the goal-mode screen that displays the current progress of a mission (e.g., remaining time, user's points/rank) with a give-up button. After unlocking, the goal-mode became the foreground activity because it always overrode all other apps, except checking the notification drawer (in order to allow users to make an informed decision about giving-up) and receiving incoming calls. If smartphone usage is a real necessity, the users can give up on a mission by clicking the give-up button; the points are earned in proportion to the elapsed time of usage limiting.

Reinforcing mechanisms: In the first prototype, once a user failed a mission, points were not awarded. However, after the field trials, the participants strongly wanted to receive partial points particularly when they had failures near the end of executing a long mission, e.g., two hours. We assumed that enabling partial points would make users more likely to give up, thereby lowering mission completion rate. Therefore, in order to solve this issue, we decided to introduce bonus points when they successfully completed a mission. Another reinforcing mechanism that we introduced after the second trial was to include a praise/encouragement message when users finished a mission ("Wow! Congratulations! You accomplished your mission.") and an encouraging message when they were about to give up ("Do you really want to give up? Please be more patient.")

Social Learning and Competition

The social learning and competition aspects of NUGU have critical functions. One key function is to allow users to learn from each other (e.g., how much usage limiting a user should do or under which everyday life activities usage limiting should be undertaken). Another key function is to motivate users to continually participate. We designed two screens: the individual ranking (within-group) and the group ranking (between-group) screens, as displayed in Figure 1(c) and Figure 1(d), respectively. In the individual ranking screen, each group has a scoreboard where group members are ranked based on each member's weekly points. A group member can check other members' limiting activities (i.e., a list of limiting activities with frequency counts) when the user ID is touched. Furthermore, NUGU also supports between-group competitions with a scoreboard for groups; for a given group, the average weekly points earned per user is used for ranking; the average weekly limiting hours per user and the top three activities are displayed along with the group's score.

Initially, we provided the individual and global ranking (global ranking is a scoreboard of all participants). Our field trials revealed two findings. First, there were some highly motivated participants who always tried to achieve high scores. The highly motivated participants dominated the ranking, which discouraged participation from the lower ranked users. Second, there were cases where all participants were weakly motivated and did not make much effort. This behavior may form a group norm of low performance. In this group, while the top ranker may boast about their performance, their level could be much lower when compared with other users. We expected that the global ranking screen could have this function for relative comparison, but it transpired that the participants generally did not consider the global ranking because they were less concerned about strangers.

In order to overcome these limitations, in our final design, we replaced the global ranking with the group ranking where each group's rank was determined based on the group's aggregated weekly points. Like the individual ranking screen, a group's limiting hours and top activities are displayed. Here, we expected that the group naming and ranking would facilitate group cohesiveness (i.e., friendship-based bonds, group identity) such that both participants who have strong/weak motivation had certain roles in the group ranking, and the group members were likely to establish a collective norm of limiting usage, which would greatly encourage user participation.

		Within-subjects	
		Pre-intervention period	**Post-intervention period**
Between-subjects	**NUGU-Group**	NUGU-Group (pre-intervention)	NUGU-Group (post-intervention)
	NUGU-Alone	NUGU-Alone (pre-intervention)	NUGU-Alone (post-intervention)

Figure 2. 2×2 quasi-experimental design: NUGU-Group and NUGU-Alone (without individual/group ranking screens).

EVALUATION

We set up a 2×2 quasi-experiment as depicted in Figure 2. Two variants of NUGU were considered: one with a group-based intervention (NUGU-Group), and the other with individual-based intervention where social support were not considered (NUGU-Alone). For NUGU-Group, we assumed that a group of friends participated in order to facilitate social learning and support. This assumption made it difficult to conduct randomized experiments.

Using online advertisements in a large Korean university, we recruited participants who were interested in improving their smartphone usage. For NUGU-Group, we hired 35 participants (total of eight groups: each group consists of 3–6 people); for the NUGU-Alone, we hired 27 participants. The NUGU-Group participants primarily consisted of close friends from the same department, laboratory, or academic club. In addition, there was a family group that included one brother and two sisters, and a group of acquaintances who met each other at church every week. The participants were 20 females and 42 males (age: $M = 25.74$, $SD = 0.53$). We found no significant difference in the demographics between the two groups (age: $p = .440$ and gender: $p = .876$). In the latter analyses, we conducted the standard t-tests in order to compare the group means on various dependent variables, ranging from survey data to usage data. Note that differences in the variances of the two groups cause the standard t-tests to be problematic, particularly when the sample sizes of the two groups were not equal [22]. F-tests did not find significant differences between the variances of the dependent variables from our two groups, and this indicates that standard t-test analyses can be conducted in our samples [22].

The experiments were conducted for three weeks: one week for the pre-intervention period and two weeks for the post-intervention period. First, we collected the participants' usage data by installing a usage logging app that collects the usage data about the start-up time of an app, its name, and its use duration. Before the pre-intervention period began, the participants had 2–3 days for an adaptation period, as recommended by an earlier measurement study [16]. The usage data collection continued during the entire experiment. At the end of the pre-intervention period, we asked the participants

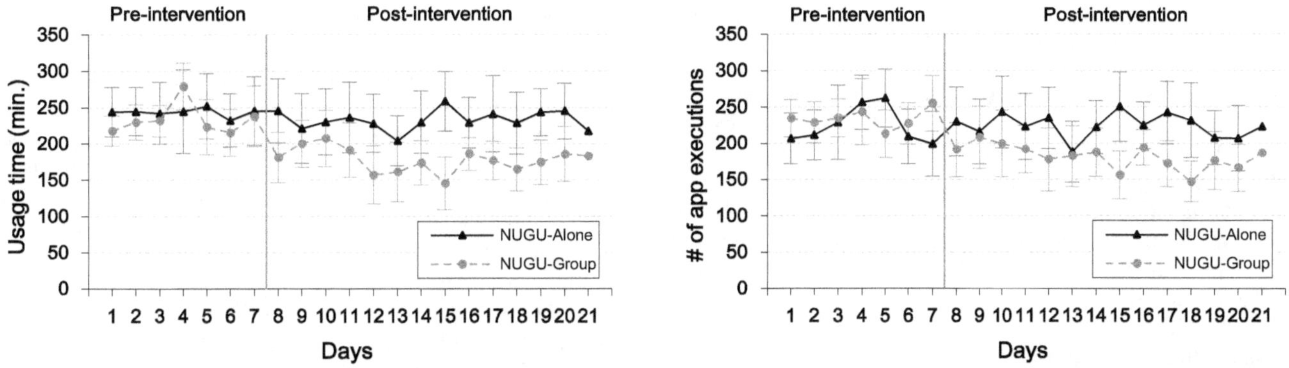

(a) Daily usage time

(b) Daily usage frequency

Figure 3. Changes in smartphone usage over the duration of the study (Pre-intervention period: 1∼7 and post-intervention period: 8∼21).

	Within-groups						Between-groups	
	NUGU-Group			NUGU-Alone			Pre	Post
	Pre	Post	*p(d)*	Pre	Post	*p(d)*	*p(d)*	*p(d)*
Usage time (min.)	234.00 (67.12)	177.07 (68.13)	**.000 (0.99)**	242.97 (84.72)	232.34 (91.46)	.320 (0.20)	.654 (0.12)	**.012 (0.69)**
# of app executions	233.81 (100.00)	180.98 (84.64)	**.000 (1.14)**	224.89 (92.79)	228.42 (95.21)	.529 (0.13)	.719 (0.09)	**.046 (0.53)**
Total SAS	3.02 (0.49)	2.49 (0.70)	**.000 (0.94)**	3.24 (0.69)	2.87 (0.67)	**.000 (0.99)**	.168 (0.38)	**.038 (0.54)**
Daily-life disturbance	4.05 (0.85)	2.73 (1.08)	**.000 (1.02)**	4.04 (0.88)	3.55 (0.99)	**.000 (0.93)**	1.000 (0.02)	**.017 (0.79)**
Positive anticipation	2.13 (0.67)	2.01 (0.77)	1.000 (0.17)	2.60 (0.93)	2.31 (0.99)	**.000 (0.87)**	.191 (0.59)	1.000 (0.35)
Withdrawal	3.10 (0.82)	2.69 (0.96)	**.012 (0.57)**	3.45 (0.94)	2.98 (0.80)	**.000 (0.87)**	.715 (0.41)	1.000 (0.33)
Cyberspace -oriented r.	2.45 (0.67)	2.16 (0.79)	**.005 (0.62)**	2.51 (0.92)	2.13 (0.83)	**.013 (0.66)**	1.000 (0.08)	1.000 (0.04)
Overuse	4.16 (0.85)	3.30 (0.89)	**.000 (0.84)**	4.33 (0.95)	3.98 (1.04)	.112 (0.45)	1.000 (0.19)	.054 (0.71)
Tolerance	3.32 (1.04)	2.70 (0.91)	**.002 (0.57)**	3.43 (1.13)	3.21 (0.96)	.186 (0.45)	1.000 (0.10)	.242 (0.54)
Self-efficacy	26.49 (5.32)	29.43 (4.45)	**.002 (0.57)**	26.56 (5.72)	28.11 (5.68)	**.012 (0.52)**	.961 (0.01)	.326 (0.26)

Table 2. Two-tailed *t*-tests on NUGU-Group and NUGU-Alone.

to complete two surveys (see below for details). The post-intervention period started with an orientation in which the participants learned about how to install and use the intervention app. After the orientation, the participants used NUGU for two weeks at their own discretion and further usage mediation like mindfulness training [19] was not conducted. After the post-intervention, we asked the participants to complete the same surveys and we conducted exit interviews. The interviews were semi-structured: we prepared questions about how they used NUGU and what features were effective (or not) for each step of limiting their smartphone use using the app, i.e., starting to limit, setting a limiting goal, and achieving the goal. The participants were compensated with USD 50–60 depending on their participation in the exit interview.

Metrics

First, we measured the smartphone usage amount, which is an objective outcome of smartphone usage behaviors; they included the total usage time and the number of app executions. Second, we measured the level of problematic smartphone usage using the *Smartphone Addiction Scale* (SAS) [12], which is an established scale for problematic smartphone usage. The scale comprises 33 six-point Likert scale questions. The higher the SAS score is, the more addicted the user is to their smartphone. The items in the SAS can be grouped into six sub-factors: *daily-life disturbance*, *positive anticipation*, *withdrawal*, *cyberspace-oriented relationship*, *overuse*, and *tolerance*. Third, we measured the users' self-efficacy of self-regulation of smartphone use in order to verify whether the self-efficacy had changed. Here, self-efficacy refers to the strength of belief in one's ability to complete tasks and reach goals. It has been reported that self-efficacy is associated with behavior changes [28]. In order to measure self-efficacy, we customized the Korean version of the *General Self-Efficacy Scale* (GSE) [26] to our context of self-regulation of smartphone use; the customized GSE consisted of 10 items using a four-point Likert scale. Examples include 'I am confident that I can efficiently manage unexpected disruptions due to the smartphone' and 'I can limit my smartphone use if I invest the necessary effort'.

Quantitative Results

Smartphone Usage Amount: Figure 3 presents the daily usage time and number of daily app executions. NUGU-Group's mean usage time tended to decrease after the intervention began while NUGU-Alone's mean usage time did not. Further analyses also revealed significant reductions in the NUGU-Group users' usage amount. First, we conducted two-tailed paired *t*-tests on the usage time/frequency between the pre-intervention period and post-intervention period of each group. Table 2 presents the results of these tests. The NUGU-Group users' usage time and number of app executions decreased significantly as they started to use the intervention app. However, we did not find significant differences in the NUGU-Alone users' usage amounts even though their usage time slightly decreased after the intervention.

Next, we conducted two independent samples *t*-tests in order to analyze the differences between the NUGU-Group and NUGU-Alone users in the usage time and number of app executions. Our analysis did not find significant differences between the groups during the pre-intervention period, but did in the post-intervention period: after the intervention began, NUGU-Group's usage amount reduced significantly compared to that of the NUGU-Alone'.

SAS and Self-Efficacy Changes: Before the interventions, no significant differences were found in the SAS scores between NUGU-Group and NUGU-Alone (see Table 2); the scores were normalized by dividing them by the number of items, and multiple tests were adjusted using the Bonferroni correction. Similarly, we found no significant differences in the groups' sub-factors during the pre-intervention period. Among the sub-factors, *daily-life disturbance* and *overuse* tended to be higher, which indicates that these were important factors for the participants. In contrast, the scores on *positive anticipation* and *cyberspace-oriented relationship* were lower than the borderline (i.e., less than three points).

After the intervention, both groups' SAS scores changed, albeit differently. In common, their total scores and most sub-factors were significantly decreased after using the intervention apps. However, we also found sub-factors that did not change significantly. NUGU-Group did not exhibit significant decreases in *positive anticipation* probably because their score was already sufficiently low in the first survey. However, NUGU-Alone did not exhibit significant decreases in *overuse* and *tolerance* neither. When comparing the two groups, we found that NUGU-Group's decreases in their total SAS scores were significantly greater than those of NUGU-Alone's. This is related to *daily-life disturbance*; in the post-intervention period, NUGU-Group's scores on *daily-life disturbance* were significantly lower than NUGU-Alone's.

Then, no significant differences were found in the self-efficacy scores before the interventions between NUGU-Group and NUGU-Alone (see Table 2). When comparing each group's scores between the pre-intervention period and post-intervention period, we found significant decreases in self-efficacy scores in both groups. Contrary to expectations, no significant differences were observed in the self-efficacy improvements between two groups. Our further investigation using the exit interviews aided in understanding the results. Some NUGU-Group users reported that they realized they had difficulty with self-regulation through knowing their quantified usage amounts and comparing their limiting efforts with others. One participant stated, *"At first, I really thought that I could do very well. But, I found myself often giving up due to an instant message, while others appeared to be doing well. So, I think I lost my confidence"* (P24).

Qualitative Results

The interview results demonstrated that the NUGU-Group users perceived that limiting usage during various daily activities and for a long time is good for them through observing the top rankers' behaviors, unlike NUGU-Alone users who maintained their original limiting behaviors (i.e., a few of limiting contexts and short time limiting). Also, the social support offered by NUGU-Group was effective in strongly motivating the participants to limit their smartphone use. Finally, we confirmed that NUGU components were helpful to achieve limiting goals; the participants succeeded in completing goals at a high rate.

Limiting usage by learning when no use is good use

For the participants in both groups, the contexts of no use is good use were primarily when they wanted to concentrate on an activity and when they perceived their problematic usage. We asked the participants about the contexts in which they usually set a limiting goal. First, most participants stated that they usually set a goal when they wanted to concentrate on an activity such as studying, working, and sleeping. One answered, *"When I wanted to do something such as studying, meeting someone, or commuting; whenever I need to focus on something"* (P32). Another significant context was when they realized their problematic use, e.g., when they perceived their overuse or frequent checking use. Furthermore, some NUGU-Group users responded that the competition with friends encouraged them to limit their use; one response was *"When my friends were catching up with me in the ranking screen"* (P20).

However, we found differences between the two groups' limiting behaviors and contexts; the NUGU-Group users tended to set limiting goals in diverse contexts (selecting diverse daily activities for a goal) and they tried more challenging goals (i.e., long time limiting). According to the interview analysis, these differences are explained by the effects of social learning from top rankers' limiting behaviors. NUGU-Group users could share their limiting efforts (e.g., activities and times); in particular, the top rankers' behaviors (diverse contexts and long time limiting) tended to be a good reference for other users. However, NUGU-Alone users could not see others' behaviors, and each user tended to rely on their own original behavior (skewed limiting contexts and short time limiting). The details of the analysis results are as follows.

First, the NUGU-Group and NUGU-Alone groups exhibited a significantly different tendency for selecting activities (limiting contexts) while limiting use ($\chi^2 = 48.20$, $p < .001$, $df = 5$). Both groups preferred to select *studying and working* the most. This resulted from participants spending most of their daily time studying or working. However, the NUGU-Group users selected more diverse types of activities from *socializing* to *resting* while the NUGU-Alone users' selections were highly skewed toward studying and working. NUGU-Alone's entropy values of the activity selection ($M = 0.37$, $SD = 0.06$) were significantly lower than NUGU-Group's ($M = 0.70$, $SD = 0.03$; $p < .001$, $d = 1.51$). This could be an effect of social learning. NUGU-Group users stated, *"I often checked how others had selected activities. It made me try to use NUGU for other activities"* (P5) and *"I wondered how the top rankers limited their use. I tried to follow their behavior through referencing the activities they selected"* (P32).

Second, the NUGU-Group users tended to set a limiting goal with a longer time than the NUGU-Alone users ($\chi^2 = 139.72$, $p < .001$, $df = 3$). For the NUGU-Group, 66.1% of their goals set were more than 30 minutes as opposed to 47.0% for the NUGU-Alone users. The NUGU-Group users stated that they became familiar with long use limiting and understood its usefulness through learning from the others that attempted goals with a longer time. One user stated, *"At first, I preferred a short time for a goal because I thought I would need my smartphone soon. But, after knowing that setting a longer time helps me concentrate on studying more, I often started to set a goal for two hours"* (P15). In contrast, many NUGU-Alone users regarded limiting for longer times as a difficult task. They stated, *"I liked to set 10 minutes to deal with urgent messages"* (P45).

Motivating limiting behaviors with social support

The NUGU usage logs show a significant difference in the number of setting limiting goals between the groups (NUGU-Group: 5.6 goals per day *vs.* NUGU-Alone: 1.3 goals per day, $p < .001$, $d = 1.87$). In order to better understand this, our next question focused on the effectiveness of NUGU's features for motivating users. Almost every NUGU-Group user answered that the social comparison of usage limiting durations from the scoreboard was the strongest motivator. Some noted its helpfulness for evaluating their own actions, by saying, *"I was surprised by others' limiting efforts and I became motivated to catch them"* (P34). In contrast, many NUGU-Alone users were less satisfied with the app because they felt that it did not help them take actions to limit their usage. One participant asked for recommended usage amount, by saying *"I want to be alarmed when I use it too much. Then, I may start to set goals"* (P40).

In particular, the degree of motivation by the competition appeared to differ depending on the social interactions among the group members. We found several interesting interactions among the group members. For example, one group offered a small reward that members buy some snacks for the top ranker, and another group's members called the top ranker by a funny nickname, 'king of limiting'; the top ranker was proud of the nickname and was motivated to keep the position. Also, most group members reported that they often talked about NUGU and their current rankings whenever they met. Furthermore, we also found that the family group had direct and strong interactions to motivate others. One of the family members stated, *"In the first stage, my younger brother told me that my limiting efforts were less than the others, so I started to do more"* (P3).

Interestingly, it appears that such interactions between group members were somewhat related to their interpersonal relationships. More frequent and stronger interactions were reported by close friends and family members, and their performances tended to be better. However, we found that the group of acquaintances, who only had social interactions once per week, exhibited relatively low performance. One group member explained, *"The members in other groups appeared to have frequent interactions. I think I could do more if I were in that situation."* (P10). Furthermore, one of the friend group members reported that she really wanted to push members who did not limit the usage actively because she worried about her team ranking. However, she could not point out their problem in the end because she thought that the relationship with them was not sufficiently close.

According to the interviews, the main function of self-monitoring was primarily to enable users to understand their problematic usage behavior rather than to motivate them to take action. The participants expressed, *"I learned that I spent too much time using my phone in the early hours of the day"* (P31). In addition, some participants mentioned the app's usefulness for tracking the outcomes of their use limiting efforts saying, *"I wanted to check whether my usage time is really reduced or not. I wanted to manage my time"* (P21). However, the users also noted the limitations of self-monitoring in maintaining their motivation. Once they became familiar with their usage and perceived their problems, they tended to neglect the self-monitoring screen. Furthermore, taking action was different to perceiving their problems. One NUGU-Alone user, who answered that the self-monitoring was useful, stated, *"I often forgot to limit my use. Maybe a push notification could be helpful for me"* (P39).

Achieving and abandoning goals

Our analysis demonstrates that the participants succeeded in completing goals at a high rate (success rate: 76.5%). We did not find significant differences in the rates of NUGU-Group (76.2%) and NUGU-Alone (77.5%) A slightly higher success rate in NUGU-Alone resulted from tendency to select goals with a short time. As a result of the interviews, the proposed design elements for helping users achieve their limiting goals contributed to the high success rate. In particular, the participants described four helpful elements: the goal-mode screen, the give-up button with a reconsideration popup, the remaining time for the goal achievement, and the incentive point system.

First, the goal-mode screen encouraged users not to play with their smartphone; one said, *"I liked the functions that lock the screen and turn it to the silent mode. These helped me not play with my smartphone"* (P6). Second, the give-up button with the confirmation popup allowed users to reconsider their choice to give up. One stated, *"The popup made me hesitate on giving up"* (P8). Finally, the remaining time and incentive points helped users manage their current goal and encouraged them to think *"I could think like that 'ah. . . I can succeed in my goal if I just bear with it. Then, I can get more points and the bonus points'"* (P33).

Furthermore, we investigated when the participants gave up and why they did. Their answers were primarily related to the need to use apps related to their productivity (e.g., dictionaries) and their need to do something urgently (e.g., call someone, search for information). Some participants stated, *"Sometimes, I gave up because I needed to write a memo"* (P34). Furthermore, almost half of the give up actions occurred within the first 10 minutes (47.5%). This is related to the opportunity cost. One participant stated, *"If I did not give up within the first 30 minutes, I thought I could succeed in the goal for two hours easily because I didn't want to lose the bonus points"* (P29). The results imply that it is necessary to support users, particularly in the first stage or first ten minutes, in order to help them succeed with their goal.

DISCUSSION

NUGU design aimed to assist in improving self-regulation of limiting smartphone usage through visualizing usage/limiting behaviors, sharing usage/limiting information, encouraging user participation with social competition, and helping limiting use by locking apps and muting notifications. This work contributed to the body of knowledge in the related fields of CSCW, HCI, and Ubicomp as follows. Our design can be considered as the first example of socially translucent system design for systematically supporting temporary non-use [17, 25]. A socially translucent system makes user activities visible to support awareness, thereby encouraging accountable user behavior according to the social norms [6]. In NUGU, one of the key design choices was how to represent use limiting (or temporary non-use) activities for awareness support. Instead of sharing detailed information, for privacy reasons, NUGU shared an individual' summary statistics among group members (e.g., aggregated limiting time and activity counts), and a group's summary statistics among different groups. Our results confirmed that this level of disclosure was sufficient for achieving desirable outcomes while preserving user/group privacy. Our work also contributed to the scholarship of non-use [3, 9, 17, 25, 29] as we detailed the needs of temporary non-use of smartphones and demonstrated a tool for supporting temporary non-use. Furthermore, NUGU design leveraged the key features of persuasive systems design, namely self-monitoring and social support [23]. When designing systems for assisting in limiting smartphone use, we showed that social support was more critical than self-monitoring. Existing usage intervention mechanisms for mitigating smartphone overuse [15, 20] can be significantly extended through implementing social learning and competition features.

Then, we discussed several practical design implications based on our findings and the limitation of this work. NUGU allows users to share usage/limiting information, but it does not provide other social interaction mechanisms. In our experiment, we found that a group with high cohesion (e.g., a family group) is more likely to have frequent on/offline social interactions, which helped them to encourage one another for continued participation. Likewise, we expect that enabling social interactions through NUGU, such as exchanging short messages and emoticons, might further encourage user participation, thereby successfully self-regulating usage behavior.

We designed NUGU to allow users to start missions through specifying the limiting time and activity to do while limiting. While performing a limiting mission, users cannot execute any apps unless they decide to give up. The participants generally liked this design choice. However, some users stated that fine-grained limiting control (i.e., app-level usage) needs to be supported. For example, they mentioned that some apps related to the productivity, as notes and dictionaries, should not be disabled. There is a trade-off between fine-grained limiting control and support for usage limiting. Because smartphone usage is often contextual (e.g., using dictionaries while studying), the designers (or a group of users) can specify a list of allowable apps for a given context/activity.

Users can benefit from contextual alarms for limiting smartphone use. In NUGU, users should decide when to limit their use. We demonstrated that users' willingness for limiting could be improved through social support. However, due to high accessibility of smartphones, users must pay attention to their smartphone usage throughout the day, which is a challenging task. For example, one group-based intervention participant commented,*"The most difficult thing is to recognize that I should decide to limit use for a given context. I know it is good for me if I do not use a smartphone when I get up. However, I often found myself using it when I woke up. I need some kind of an alarm for usage limiting to better manage my habitual usage"* (P9). One solution is to allow users to schedule reminders for limiting smartphone use, e.g., while taking regular classes or having weekly meetings. In addition, an intervention app can recommend users to limit smartphone use, if it can automatically identify problematic usage (based on the previous usage history) [16, 27].

The validity of our experiment may be limited because the number of participants was small ($n = 62$) and the experiment was conducted over a short time of three weeks. A longitudinal, large-scale experiment should be performed in order to improve the validity of this work. Due to the design constraints of social support, we could not use randomized participant assignment; the statistical analysis partly affirmed the internal validity in that between these groups, and we did not find significant differences in the pre-intervention period results regarding the demographics, usage patterns (time, frequency), and measurement scales (SAS, self-efficacy). Our work closely followed the guidelines [11] through conducting a tailored evaluation on the social support. Besides the quantitative data comparison, we also performed qualitative data analysis in order to present how and why participants used our software and to draw practical design implications.

CONCLUSION

We designed and implemented NUGU (No Use is Good Use), which is a group-based intervention app to support self-regulation on smartphone use. Our three-week user study ($n = 62$) demonstrated that compared with its non-social counterpart, NUGU-Group users' usage decreased significantly, and their perceived level of managing interruptions was improved significantly. We are transitioning into a society of ubiquitous technologies, ranging from smartphones and quantified-self gadgets to the Internet of things, that promise to make our lives easier and more convenient. However, such technologies sometimes cause diverse side effects, such as technology overuse and abuse. We believe that it will become increasingly important for designers and researchers to investigate how to help people be in harmony with these new ubiquitous technologies through managing the side effects beyond simply focusing on technology diffusion.

ACKNOWLEDGEMENTS

This work was supported in part by ICT R&D program of MSIP/IITP [10041313, UX-oriented Mobile SW Platform], by Basic Science Research Program through the National Research Foundation of Korea (NRF) funded by the Ministry of Science, ICT & Future Planning (NRF-2012R1A1A1008858), and by the MSIP and Microsoft Research, under IT/SW Creative research program supervised by the NIPA (National IT Industry Promotion Agency) (NIPA-2013-ITAH0503130110270001000100100). U. Lee is the corresponding author.

REFERENCES

1. Ames, M. G. Managing Mobile Multitasking: The Culture of iPhones on Stanford Campus. In *Proc. ACM CSCW* (2013), 1487–1498.
2. Bandura, A. Social Cognitive Theory of Self-Regulation. *Organizational Behavior and Human Decision Processes 50*, 2 (1991), 248–287.
3. Baumer, E. P. S., Adams, P., Khovanskaya, V. D., Liao, T. C., Smith, M. E., Sosik, V. S., and Williams, K. Limiting, Leaving, and (re)Lapsing: An Exploration of Facebook Non-Use Practices and Experiences. In *Proc. ACM CHI* (2013), 3257–3266.
4. Böhmer, M., Hecht, B., Schöning, J., Krüger, A., and Bauer, G. Falling Asleep with Angry Birds, Facebook and Kindle: a large scale study on mobile application usage. In *Proc. ACM MobileHCI* (2011), 47–56.
5. Consolvo, S., Everitt, K., Smith, I., and Landay, J. A. Design Requirements for Technologies that Encourage Physical Activity. In *Proc. ACM CHI* (2006), 457–466.
6. Erickson, T., and Kellogg, W. A. Social Translucence: An Approach to Designing Systems that Support Social Processes. *ACM TOCHI 7*, 1 (2000), 59–83.
7. Fogg, B. *Persuasive Technology: Using Computers to Change What We Think and Do*. Morgan Kaufmann Publishers, 2003.
8. Harmon, E., and Mazmanian, M. Stories of the Smartphone in Everyday Discourse: Conflict, Tension & Instability. In *Proc. ACM CHI* (2013), 1051–1060.
9. Helsper, E. J., and Reisdorf, B. C. A Quantitative Examination of Explanations for Reasons for Internet Nonuse. *Cyberpsychology, Behavior, and Social Networking 16*, 2 (2013), 94–99.
10. Kjeldskov, J., Skov, M. B., Paay, J., and Pathmanathan, R. Using Mobile Phones to Support Sustainability: A Field Study of Residential Electricity Consumption. In *Proc. ACM CHI* (2012), 2347–2356.
11. Klasnja, P., Consolvo, S., and Pratt, W. How to Evaluate Technologies for Health Behavior Change in HCI Research. In *Proc. ACM CHI* (2011), 3063–3072.
12. Kwon, M., Lee, J.-Y., Won, W.-Y., Park, J.-W., Min, J.-A., Hahn, C., Gu, X., Choi, J.-H., and Kim, D.-J. Development and Validation of a Smartphone Addiction Scale (SAS). *PLoS ONE 8*, 12 (2013).
13. LaRose, R. Use and Gratification of Internet Addiction. In *Internet Addiction: A Handbook and Guide to Evaluation and Treatment*, John Wiley & Sons, Inc. (2012), 55–72.
14. Lee, G., Tsai, C., Griswold, W. G., Raab, F., and Patrick, K. PmEB: A Mobile Phone Application for Monitoring Caloric Balance. In *Proc. ACM CHI* (2006), 1013–1018.
15. Lee, H., Ahn, H., Choi, S., and Choi, W. The SAMS: Smartphone Addiction Management System and Verification. *Journal of Medical Systems 38*, 1 (2014).
16. Lee, U., Lee, J., Ko, M., Lee, C., Kim, Y., Yang, S., Yatani, K., Gweon, G., Chung, K.-M., and Song, J. Hooked on Smartphones: An Exploratory Study on Smartphone Overuse among College Students. In *Proc. ACM CHI* (2014), 2327–2336.
17. Lee, U., Yang, S., Ko, M., and Lee, J. Supporting Temporary Non-Use of Smartphones. In *CHI'14 Workshop: Refusing, Limitng, Departing: Why We Should Study Technology Non-Use Workshop* (2014).
18. Levine, L. E., Waite, B. M., and Bowman, L. L. Mobile Media Use, Multitasking and Distractibility. *International Journal of Cyber Behavior, Psychology and Learning 2*, 3 (2012), 15–29.
19. Levy, D. M., Wobbrock, J. O., Kaszniak, A. W., and Ostergren, M. The Effects of Mindfulness Meditation Training on Multitasking in a High-Stress Information Environment. In *Proc. GI* (2002), 45–52.
20. Löchtefeld, M., Böhmer, M., and Ganev, L. AppDetox: Helping Users with Mobile App Addiction. In *Proc. ACM MUM* (2013).
21. Lundquist, A. R., Lefebvre, E. J., and Garramone, S. J. Smartphones: Fulfilling the Need for Immediacy in Everyday Life, but at What Cost? . *International Journal of Humanities and Social Science 4*, 2 (2014), 80–89.
22. Moser, B. K., and Stevens, G. R. Homogeneity of Variance in the Two-Sample Means Test. *The American Statistician 46*, 1 (1992), 19–21.
23. Oinas-Kukkonen, H., and Harjumaa, M. Persuasive Systems Design: Key Issues, Process Model, and System Features. *Communications of the Association for Information Systems 24*, 28 (2009), 485–500.
24. Oulasvirta, A., Rattenbury, T., Ma, L., and Raita, E. Habits Make Smartphone Use More Pervasive. *Personal and Ubiquitous Computing 16*, 1 (2012), 105–114.
25. Satchell, C., and Dourish, P. Beyond the Users: Use and Non-Use in HCI. In *Proc. ACM OZCHI* (2009), 9–16.
26. Schwarzer, R., Born, A., Iwawaki, S., Lee, Y.-M., Saito, E., and Yue, X. The Assessment of Optimistic Self-Beliefs: Comparison of the Chinese, Indonesian, Japanese, and Korean Versions of the General Self-Efficacy Scale. *Psychologia: An International Journal of Psychology in the Orient 40*, 1 (1997), 1–13.
27. Shin, C., and Dey, A. K. Automatically Detecting Problematic Use of Smartphones. In *Proc. ACM UbiComp* (2013), 335–344.
28. Strecher, V. J., Devellis, B. M., Becker, M. H., and Rosenstock, I. M. The Role of Self-Efficacy in Achieving Health Behavior Change. *Health Education Quarterly 13*, 1 (1986), 73–91.
29. Wyatt, S. Non-Users Also Matter: The Construction of Users and Non-Users of the Internet. In *Nelly Oudshoorn and Trevor Pinch's How Users Matter: The Co-Construction of Users and Technologies*, The MIT Press (2005).

Studying and Modeling the Connection between People's Preferences and Content Sharing

Amit Sharma
Dept. of Computer Science
Cornell University
Ithaca, NY 14853 USA
asharma@cs.cornell.edu

Dan Cosley
Information Science
Cornell University
Ithaca, NY 14853 USA
danco@cs.cornell.edu

ABSTRACT
People regularly share items using online social media. However, people's decisions around sharing—who shares what to whom and why—are not well understood. We present a user study involving 87 pairs of Facebook users to understand how people make their sharing decisions. We find that even when sharing to a specific individual, people's own preference for an item (individuation) dominates over the recipient's preferences (altruism). People's open-ended responses about how they share, however, indicate that they do try to personalize shares based on the recipient. To explain these contrasting results, we propose a novel process model of sharing that takes into account people's preferences and the salience of an item. We also present encouraging results for a sharing prediction model that incorporates both the senders' and the recipients' preferences. These results suggest improvements to both algorithms that support sharing in social media and to information diffusion models.

Author Keywords
Directed sharing; Information diffusion; Sharing process; User preferences

ACM Classification Keywords
H.1.2 Models and Principles: User/machine Systems—*Human Factors*; H.3.3 Information Storage and Retrieval: Information Search and Retrieval—*Information filtering*

General Terms
Human Factors; Experimentation

INTRODUCTION
Many people get recommendations for movies, music, articles, and products through their social connections both online and off. Online, we often think of sharing primarily as a public broadcast through tweets, status updates, and the like. Much online sharing, however, is narrower, targeted at specific audiences (as with Google+ circles or Pinterest boards) or *directed* [5] at specific individuals through email, chat, and person-to-person messages (e.g. suggesting movies on Netflix [17]). Recent studies show that sharing content through email is still popular [5, 1], surpassing social media in certain product categories [24].

http://dx.doi.org/10.1145/2675133.2675151

Such sharing is a surprisingly complex process affected by a number of considerations, as illustrated by a study participant:

> *"I tend to share ... when I understand something about the other person and I think that a certain movie, book, song, etc., might interest that person, whether it be to challenge what someone is saying or feeling, or to reinforce and reaffirm what someone is thinking or feeling. Sure, with close friends, with whom you maintain a close relationship, you might just say, 'hey I liked this movie. check it out.' But I think we do that because we already know the person and the person already knows us. There's a certain level of mutual understanding and respect already established. I say I don't recommend 'all willy-nilly' and I mean that I don't run up to strangers and recommend they read George Orwell, because I don't know anything about that person or how they feel. Unfortunately, to some extent, we do do just that, we all do that sometimes, when we recommend in order to show off our own interests, to show how cool we are, to show how much we know, to show how diversified our interests are, to show how much niche-specific music we listen to. You know, when we're self-interested assholes."* (P23)

Untangling this complexity is important for understanding how information diffuses online.

Recommender systems within social networks will also benefit from better models of sharing decisions. These models can be used to support sharing online by suggesting which items to share and who to share them with [5, 33]. However, while there is extensive research on understanding people's rating behavior and predicting their preferences for items [29], little is known about people's online sharing behavior and its predictability.

From past research on word-of-mouth product sharing and information sharing on the web, we know that people share items for many reasons: enhancement of personal image, personal interest in the item, helping others, a desire to help or harm the item's producer, seeking advice, and so on [30, 11, 15]. On balance, these motivations can be seen as special cases of two primary drivers of sharing proposed by Ho and

Dempsey: *individuation*, the need to establish a distinct identity for oneself, and *altruism*, the desire to help others [16].

Based on the primary motivations of individuation and altruism, we can expect people to share content that is some balance of their own and others' interests. What that balance is, and how it comes to be so, however, is an open question and our main focus in this paper. A recent study on Twitter suggests that the balance is tilted toward the self: around 80% of people primarily share content about their activities and opinions, while only 20% share informational content more likely to be useful to others [23]. However, this may be because of the broadcast nature of sharing on Twitter where in the absence of a specific audience, sharing becomes an expression of one's thoughts and ideas [36]. When people share to specific recipients, they may be more likely to think about usefulness for the recipient (and thus be more altruistic) than when they share to larger groups [4, 5].

Present Work. To study the relative effects of individuation and altruism, we conducted an empirical study where pairs of friends were independently shown the same set of movies and asked to rate those movies and/or share them with their friend. Ratings for movies by the sharer can be considered as a proxy for her preference in movies, which in turn is expected to reflect her self-image (individuation). Similarly, we regard sharing movies that align with the recipient's preferences as other-oriented altruistic behavior. 87 pairs of Facebook friends took part in the study, providing rating and sharing data along with answers to open-ended questions about their sharing behavior.

Our results provide several concrete findings about person-to-person sharing. First, individuation is the dominant factor for sharing items. Shared items are rated significantly higher by senders than items that aren't shared. Further, senders' ratings are significantly higher than recipients' ratings for shared items.

Second, participants describe customizing their recommendations based on the recipient, consistent with results from earlier studies [4, 5]. We argue that these two seemingly contrary results—people claiming to personalize but still sharing items that they themselves like—can be best explained by the following decision process: people choose items to share based on their preferences and context, then decide to share or not depending on the recipient. We formalize this process as the *preference-salience* model of sharing and provide some evidence for it.

Third, we show that we can (noisily) predict which items a person might share. A model using sharers' and recipients' preferences for movies along with sharers' promiscuity can predict shares by study participants with more than 75% precision. We also find that item characteristics such as average rating and popularity play little role in predicting sharing decisions compared to people's own preferences for an item.

RELATED WORK

Our goal of better understanding of sharing behavior is situated between existing work around word-of-mouth sharing, recommender systems, and diffusion in social media. We discuss each in turn, along with a key question related to that body of work.

Word-of-mouth sharing

When communicating with others, people customize their message based on their estimation of the audience's knowledge or attitudes [19]. At the same time, much word-of-mouth sharing is driven by people's desire to share items that closely align with or enhance their self-image [31, 9]. Our first question addreses how people balance customization with self-expression.

This dual motivation between *self* and *other* has also been found to drive sharing activities in online contexts. Research in online word-of-mouth referrals has shown individuation and altruism as two dominant motivations for sharing [16, 15, 30]. Studies of knowledge sharing in online professional communities reveal a similar pattern: people share knowledge to enhance their professional reputation or when they enjoy helping others [34].

When sharing items such as movies, these two motivations of individuation and altruism can be mapped to sharing based on one's own interests or the audience's. These, in turn, can be estimated from the rich preference data available online, then used to study the relative influence of these factors.

RQ1: To what extent do people tend to share items that they like themselves (individuation) versus those that they perceive to be relevant for the recipient (altruism)?

Directed recommendation

Studying sharing behavior also allows us to ask how well people can recommend content for others; such directed suggestions can provide a useful complement to algorithmically-generated recommendations [5]. Most studies in this space have focused on the question of influence, using recipients' acceptance of recommendations as a proxy for how influential the sender is. For example, network influence [12, 18], the relationship with the sender [6, 3], the explanation accompanying the content [27, 32, 21], and the susceptibility of an individual towards shared items [2] have all been shown to affect people's likelihood of accepting suggestions.

However, little is known about whether people make suggestions that receivers would actually like. The study most related to this question compared people's ability to predict a stranger's movie ratings based on part of that person's rating profile to predictions from a standard collaborative filtering algorithm [20]. On balance, people were not as accurate—and, interestingly, got worse as the profile became more similar to their own.

In this paper, we study how well people's suggestions match the recipient's interests when they share items with known friends and compare their results with algorithmic recommendations. Instead of making inferences from profile information [20], people rely on their own knowledge about a friend to choose which items to share, which we see as a more natural recommendation scenario. For consistency in terminology, we use recommendations to refer to algorithmic recommendations and shares to refer to human-generated directed recommendations in the rest of the paper.

RQ2: Do people share items to friends that are well-liked compared to recommendations?

Diffusion models

In computer science, sharing is most commonly studied as a component of information diffusion models [35, 18, 3, 14, 8]. These models simulate the spread of items in a network, where people adopt an item through either probabilistic transfer between connected people or based on a threshold number of adoptions in a person's neighborhood. However, these models don't actually explain most adoption in social media [13] because the viral analogy breaks down. Sharing is a *voluntary* process shaped by social forces such as people's willingness to diffuse [22], attention to targets' needs [5], and relations between sharer and target including tie strength [7] and homophily.

The present work aims to build models of sharing that account for this voluntary decision-making. If successful, these models can explain how people weigh their own and recipients' preferences when sharing items and present a computational framework for predicting future shares. This model can be used to estimate sharing probabilities for different recipients and items; diffusion models can leverage these probabilities to better account for these influences and make more accurate predictions around diffusion.

RQ3: How well can we predict whether an item is shared using readily available information about people's preferences and properties of people and items?

DESCRIPTION OF THE USER STUDY

To tackle the above questions, we conducted an experiment that asked pairs of friends on Facebook to rate and share items. We chose movies as the item domain for several reasons. Movies are a common domain in recommender systems research and an important cultural item that people often share and discuss, making them a natural domain for studying sharing. They are also fairly popular to Like on Facebook [26] (among our participants, $\mu = 18.2, \sigma = 31.8$), allowing us build reasonable user profiles for making recommendations.

Study logistics. Figure 1 shows an overview of the experiment, which proceeded in three main stages. In the first stage, a participant (A) signs up for the study and invites one of her Facebook friends as a partner (B) through email sent by our system. When Person B accepts the invitation, the second stage starts. Person B is shown a set of movie recommendations which he is asked to rate and/or share with Person A, followed by a questionnaire that asks about B's relationship with A and his practices around sharing items in general. Person A then gets a notification and, in the third stage, performs the same tasks on the same items, then answers the same questions as Person B.

Showing both partners the same items allows us to get overlapping sharing and rating data to address the research question. The asynchronous design allows partners to participate independently, making the study easier to complete. To minimize explicit social influence that might affect sharing and rating behaviors [27], participants do not see information about their partner's ratings or shares.

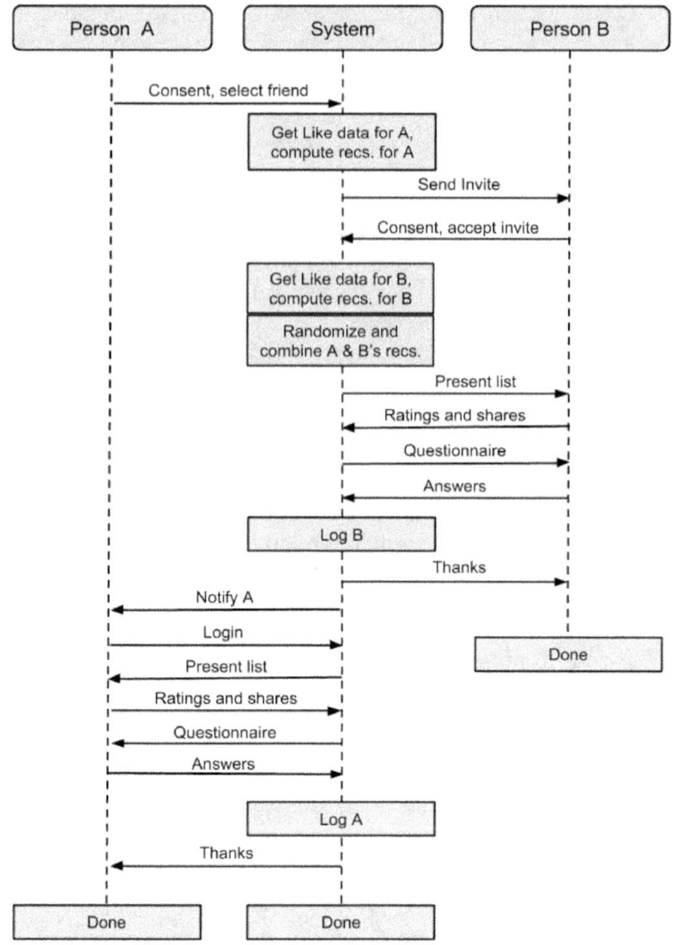

Figure 1. The flow of the experiment. Person A invites a Facebook friend (B) to take part in the study. Once B accepts, B rates and shares recommendations computed from both A and B's past movie Likes. Finally, person A logs into the study again and rates and shares an identical set of recommendations. To reduce effects of social influence, there is no direct communication between A and B and the system presents no information about the other person's decisions.

Figure 2 shows a screenshot of the interface, designed to broadly resemble other systems that recommend lists of items. Participants were free to choose the movies to rate or share among the movies shown. All ratings are on a Likert scale from 0.5-5, with half ratings allowed. Movies are shared by clicking on the Recommend button and providing a short message explaining the recommendation. The system showed the study partner as the default choice for sharing; all but four shares were to their partner so we removed those four shares from the dataset.

After the rating and sharing task, participants completed a short questionnaire asking how close they were to their study partner, as well as open-ended questions about how and why

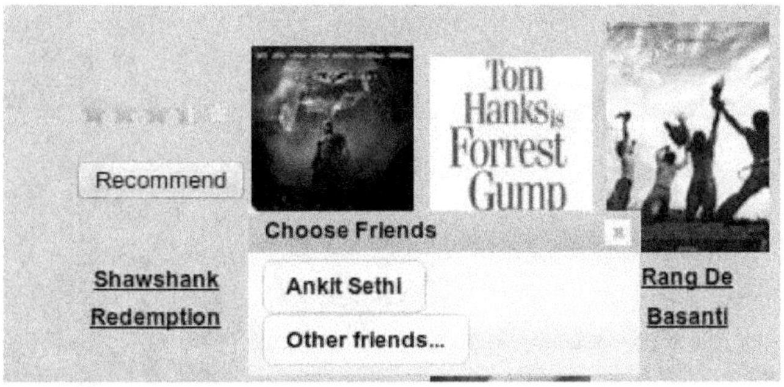

Figure 2. A screenshot of the interface. A maximum of 20 movies was shown; participants rate and/or share as many movies as they wish. The study partner was shown as the default recipient.

they suggest items, and how and when they receive suggestions from others.

Computing recommendations. For each user, we computed recommendations based on Likes within their ego network. We first selected the user's $k = 20$ most similar friends based on Jaccard similarity of their Likes with the user. We then computed a score for each movie based on its similarity-weighted popularity among the k friends:

$$Score(item_i, u) = \frac{\sum_{j=1}^{k} JSim(u, f_j) Likes(f_j, item_i)}{\sum_{j=1}^{k} JSim(u, f_j)}$$

where $Likes$ is 1 if friend f_j likes $item_i$ and 0 otherwise. This algorithm gives comparable results to using data from thousands of Facebook users using a generic k-nearest neighbors algorithm [28].

The ten highest scoring movies for each user that were not already liked by her were chosen as recommendations. Some users may have less than 10 recommendations because they do not have enough friends or enough Likes in their profile to compute recommendations. Further, Facebook API errors and rate limits prevented some users' Likes from being fetched. Thus, participants saw between 0 and 20 movies; we pruned those who saw less than 10.

Recommendations for both partners were computed and stored in the second stage, ensuring that both saw the same set. Each pair's recommendations were combined and presented in a randomized order to minimize presentation order effects.

Participation. We recruited participants through two sources, a pool of participants at a large northeastern U.S. university and Amazon Mechanical Turk. The university pool consists of students and staff who elect to take part in user studies. We conducted a drawing with a 1/3 chance of winning \$10 gift cards to motivate participation inside the university and paid Mechanical Turk users a flat \$2.50. There were no significant differences in terms of the number of shares, ratings, or Facebook Likes between the groups so we treat them as a composite sample (Table 1).

After pruning people who saw fewer than ten recommendations, a total of 87 pairs took part, 59% female. Due to turnover between the three stages, only 142 participants saw

Participants' statistics	MTurk	Univ	All
Rated at least once	36	82	118
Shared at least once	28	58	86
Total ratings	246	720	966
Total shares	97	217	314
Num. ratings/person	6.83	8.81	8.18
Mean rating/person	3.82	3.87	3.85
Num. shares/person	2.69	2.64	2.66
Num. likes/person	16.2	19.1	18.2

Table 1. Aggregate statistics for participants recruited from Amazon Mechanical Turk and the university. About a third of the participants were recruited through Mechanical Turk. There was no significant difference in study activity between the two populations.

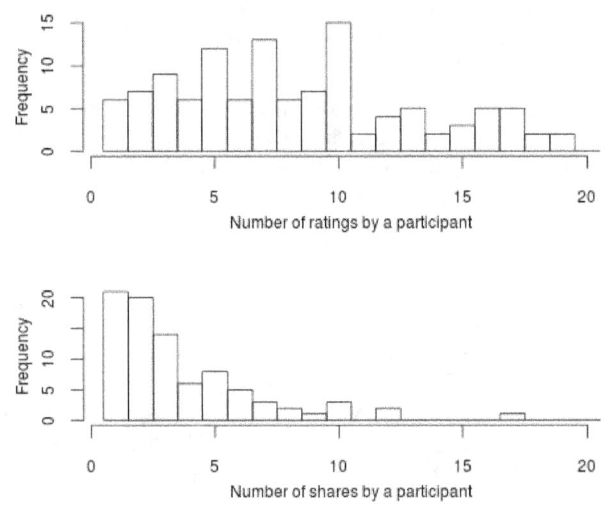

Figure 3. Distribution of ratings and shares per participant. On average, people rated about three times more items than they shared.

recommendations. Figure 3 shows the distribution of number of ratings and shares by the participants. 118 participants rated at least one movie and 86 shared at least one movie for a total of 966 ratings and 314 shares to their partner; each session took 11 minutes on average. These are the data that we consider for our analysis.

We expected pairs to know each other (and their preferences) well since people chose their own partners. When asked to evaluate the statement "We are very close to each other", 83% of participants answered "Agree" or "Completely Agree", indicating that most pairs were close ties.

Participants were divided into three groups based on the recommendations they saw during the experiment.

- *Both-Shown*: All participants who saw more than 10 movies belong to this group. Since our algorithm computes a maximum of 10 recommendations for each user, this means they saw movies recommended based on both their own profile and their partner's. The least number of movies shown is 14 for this group.
- *Own-Shown*: These participants saw 10 movies that were recommended based on their own profile.

Condition	No. of Users	Ratings	Shares
Both-Shown	60	609	141
Own-Shown	29	179	96
Other-Shown	29	178	77
All users	118	966	314

Table 2. Aggregate rating and sharing statistics for users in the three groups. *Both-Shown* participants saw a mix of recommendations for themselves and their partner, *Own-Shown* participants saw only recommendations made for themselves, and *Other-Shown* only saw recommendations made for their partners.

- *Other-Shown*: These participants saw 10 movies that were recommended based on their partner's profile. Since both participants in a pair see the same movies, this means that partners of participants in *Own-Shown* are in *Other-Shown* and vice versa.

Table 2 shows the breakdown of participants between the three groups. Note that these groups are not randomly assigned; Liking behavior and API errors in data fetching affected the recommendations any participant saw and thus which group they are in.

Before we discuss factors affecting sharing, a couple of sanity checks for our study design are in order. The first concerns the efficacy of our recommendation algorithm. The average rating of items recommended using a participant's own Likes is significantly higher than those recommended for her partner ($\mu = 3.93, \sigma = 1.00, N = 515$; $\mu = 3.76, \sigma = 1.17, N = 451$; $t(887) = 2.37, p = 0.02; d = 0.2$[1]). This indicates that the algorithm does capture users' preferences to some extent.

Second, while we designed the study so that participants do not have an incentive to tell their partners about their shares (compensation was for completing the study, not getting the ratings right), nothing prevents participant B from disclosing her shares to A before A logs on to the study again (especially if they are close to each other). To check whether our study results may have been impacted by such information exchange, we compared the average ratings for received movies (i.e., those that were shared by their partner) between participants who completed the experiment first and those that completed the experiment after their partner. A t-test revealed no significant difference ($\mu_A = 3.87$, $\mu_B = 3.89$), which makes us believe that such disclosure between A and B was not prevalent.

THE ROLE OF OWN PREFERENCES IN SHARING

We start with **RQ1**, examining the extent to which people share items they like themselves versus those they perceive to be relevant for the recipient. We use both people's sharing data and their open-ended answers to the question: "How/why do you suggest items to people?"

Senders' own preference matters

We first analyze whether senders tend to share movies they like by comparing their ratings for shared and non-shared movies. The overall distribution of ratings for shared and

[1]We report Cohen's-d [10] as a measure of effect size throughout.

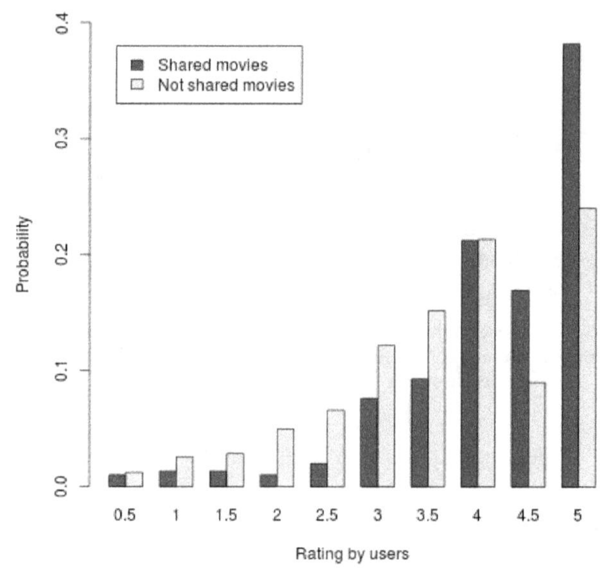

Figure 4. Probability of different sharer ratings for shared and non-shared items. Highly rated items are more likely to be shared than lower-rated items.

non-shared movies is shown in Figure 4. On average, shared movies are rated higher. Further, highly rated movies are more likely to be shared: 77% of the shared movies are rated 4 or above.

Table 3 shows that for all three groups of participants, shared movies are rated significantly higher than those that are not shared[2]. The effect size is biggest for the *Other-Shown* group. This is because the mean rating for shared movies ($\mu = 4.18$) is as high as for other groups, but the mean rating for non-shared movies is lower since the recommendations were generated for the sharer's partner rather than the sharer.

Item characteristics are not informative

One possible explanation for shared movies having higher ratings is that sharers may only share high quality or popular movies. To check this, we collected average rating and popularity data from the popular movie reviewing website IMDB[3]. For each movie, IMDB reports an average rating on a scale of 1-10 (*IMDB rating*) and the number of people who have rated that movie (*IMDB popularity*).

We find that there is no significant difference between shared and non-shared movies for either IMDB rating ($\mu = 7.64, \sigma = 1.23; \mu = 7.48, \sigma = 1.20$) or IMDB popularity ($\mu = 11.2M, \sigma = 9.68M; \mu = 13.1M, \sigma = 10M$). This indicates that aggregate opinions about items such as average rating or popularity did not matter much when sharing

[2]Ratings are not strictly normal and independent, which are assumptions for conducting a t-test. There is a skew towards higher ratings and ratings for the same movie or by the same user may be interdependent. Thus, we also considered a linear mixed-effects model to account for sender and item variability as a random effect with sharing as a fixed effect. The results were similar and are described in the Appendix.

[3]Internet Movie Database www.imdb.com, accessed Feb. 2014.

	Shared			Non-Shared				
Group	N	μ	σ	N	μ	σ	Significance	Effect Size
Both-Shown	140	4.20	0.93	469	3.81	1.07	$t(258) = 4.20; p < 0.0001$	0.4
Own-Shown	90	4.16	0.87	89	3.56	1.05	$t(170) = 4.14; p < 0.0001$	0.6
Other-Shown	71	4.18	1.08	107	3.31	1.24	$t(164) = 4.92; p < 0.0001$	0.7
All users	301	4.18	0.95	665	3.70	1.11	$t(671) = 6.98; p < 0.0001$	0.5

Table 3. Comparison of sender ratings for shared and non-shared movies, along with results of an unpaired t-test and Cohen's-d effect size measure. In all three groups, shared movies are significantly higher rated than non-shared movies.

movies. These results align well with the motivation of individuation, which suggests that people will share items that help establish a distinct identity for themselves.

Participants' responses support individuation

These results are supported by participants' accounts of how they select items to share. For more than half of the participants, liking the item themselves is the most important factor in sharing an item with someone.

> *"Usually when I suggest, it depends on the item, not the target individual, because I want to share what I enjoyed."* (P8)

Sharing items that one likes may also signal expertise [34].

> *"I suggest items to people because in my case, I've usually seen more movies than they have and I have a better relative perspective of what is considered good or bad."* (P61)

It can also be a useful way to have shared experiences and discussions around items.

> *"I suggest because I like something and I want to see if other people feel the same way about an item. When I suggest items to my friends we are able to talk and laugh about the certain item."* (P91)

All of the above can be connected to individuation as the guiding motivation for sharing.

Differences in sharing promiscuity among participants

While participants tended to share movies that matched their preferences, we saw great variability in how much people shared, or their sharing *promiscuity*. Among the users who shared movies, the minimum number of movies shared was 1 and the maximum was 17 ($\mu = 3.65, \sigma = 3.05$), as shown in Figure 3.

For many people, sharing is reserved only for *"something I really, really enjoy"* in part because sharing too frequently *"tends to water down my stamp of approval."* (P16)

Selective sharing is also connected to the common problem of managing one's image in social media [31].

> *"Sometimes I'm paranoid that if I suggest items to someone I don't know very well, they will change their perception of me."* (P15)

A likely hypothesis connected to sharing promiscuity is that people tend to select items for sharing in decreasing preference order. This suggests that sharing more items should lead to lower average ratings by both senders and recipients; in fact, there is a negative correlation between the number of items shared and both average sender ($corr = -0.31$) and recipient ($corr = -0.36$) ratings.

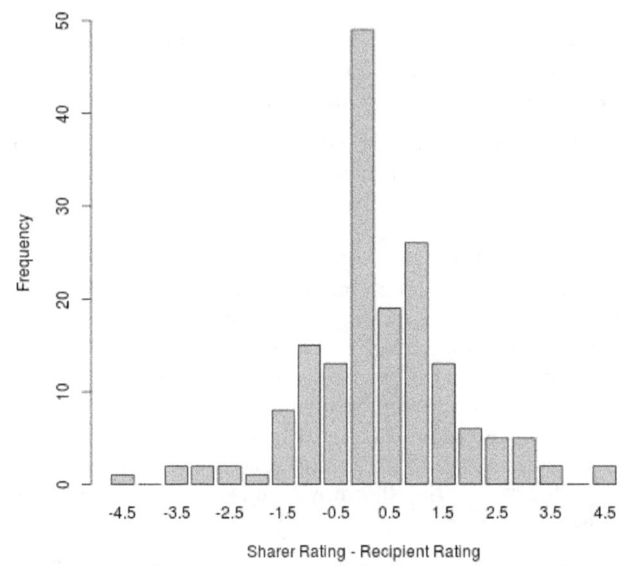

Figure 5. Comparison of sender and recipient ratings for shared movies. The x-axis represents the difference between the sender and recipient rating; on average, sender ratings are higher than recipient ratings.

HOW USEFUL ARE SHARES FOR THE RECIPIENT?

Analysis of recipients' ratings for shared items reveals more about the relative effects of individuation and altruism (**RQ1**).

Senders rate shared items higher than recipients

A total of 171 shares were rated by both sharers and recipients. Figure 5 shows the difference between their ratings. About half of the shares have a higher sender rating and a quarter have equal ratings. A paired t-test for these shares shows that senders' ratings are significantly higher than recipients' ($\mu = 4.19, \mu = 3.88; t(170) = 2.90; p = 0.002$).

Although recipients' ratings for shared items are lower than senders', many participants claimed that they consider the recipient's preferences before sharing an item.

	Sender Rating			Recipient Rating				
Group	N	μ	σ	N	μ	σ	Significance	Effect Size
Both-Shown	81	4.12	0.95	81	3.80	1.05	$t(80) = 2.19; p = 0.01$	0.3
–Own Algorithm	38	4.14	0.94	38	3.71	1.27	$t(37) = 1.93; p = 0.03$	0.4
–Other Algorithm	43	4.10	0.97	43	3.88	0.81	$t(42) = 1.14; p = 0.13$	0.2
Own-Shown	49	4.40	0.75	49	3.67	1.34	$t(48) = 3.52; p < 0.001$	0.7
Other-Shown	41	4.06	1.09	41	4.28	0.70	$t(40) = 1.10; p = 0.14$	0.2
All users	171	4.19	0.94	171	3.88	1.09	$t(170) = 2.90; p = 0.002$	0.3

Table 4. Comparison of sender and receiver ratings for shared movies using a paired t-test. Across all groups, shared movies have a significantly higher rating from the sender than the recipient when the sender shares from a list close to her movie preferences. The difference is not significant when a sender shares from a list close to the recipient's movie preferences; still, sender ratings in this case are high ($\mu > 4$).

> *"I make suggestions to people if I think they might gain enjoyment. Obviously it really depends on their personality and their likes/dislikes."* (P22)

This disconnect between people's self-reports and actual sharing behavior is surprising; we will consider likely explanations for it in the discussion.

Recipients' ratings depend on the item set shown

When senders saw recommendations from both algorithms (*Both-Shown* group), sender rating is significantly higher than the recipient rating for a shared item (Table 4). However, when we break up the shares in the *Both-Shown* condition by algorithm, a more complex picture emerges. Although participants shared movies about equally from both sets of recommendations, the difference in sender and receiver ratings is significant only for the movies selected by sender's *Own Algorithm*.

We see a similar pattern when we compare the *Own-Shown* and *Other-Shown* groups. As shown in Table 4, participants in the *Own-Shown* group had significantly higher ratings than the recipient, but not those in the *Other-Shown* group. In fact, recipients' ratings were higher than senders' ratings for shares in the *Other-Shown* group.

It is not surprising that recipient ratings are higher when shares come from movies recommended by *Other Algorithm* because those recommendations are based on the recipient's past Likes. Still, senders' rating for shares is high across groups and algorithms. These findings, coupled with higher ratings by senders for shares versus non-shares, lead us to conclude that one's own preferences (and thus individuation) are the dominant criterion when choosing movies to share.

Shares are comparable to algorithmic recommendation

We saw that when restricted to the movies recommended for recipients, people share movies that are more aligned with recipient's preferences. We now turn to **RQ2**, about how those shares compare to the recommendations generated by the algorithm for the study.

We use data from the two groups (*Both-Shown* and *Own-Shown*) where recipients saw recommendations based on their own Likes and compare these recommendations with shares. For the *Both-Shown* group, about half of the movies shown were recommended based on the recipient's preferences. A t-test shows that the recipients' average rating of shared movies is not significantly different than their average rating for algorithmically recommended movies (see Table 5). This indicates that shares are comparable to a recommender algorithm in terms of recipient liking.

For recipients in the *Own-Shown* group, whose partner shared movies from a set of recommendations tuned for the recipient, the average rating for shared movies is significantly higher than for algorithmically recommended ones. Thus, items deemed relevant by the recommendation model attain higher ratings if they are also shared by a person's friend.

Shares have higher overall quality than recommendations

However, shared items do differ from recommended items in terms of overall quality. We again use IMDB rating and IMDB popularity as measures of movie quality and popularity. Among all movies (with or without participant ratings), shared movies are of higher average IMDB rating than recommended movies ($\mu = 7.83, \sigma = 1.03$; $\mu = 7.54, \sigma = 1.15$; $t(317) = 3.02, p = 0.0026$; $d = 0.3$), but there is no significant difference in popularity ($median = 9.65M$, $median = 9.52M$). This indicates that on average people select higher quality movies to share compared to the baseline recommender.

PREDICTING SHARES

From the last two sections, it seems that senders' own preferences for movies matter more than the recipients' in sharing decisions, although they are still at least as well-liked by recipients as recommendation. We now examine how well we can predict these sharing decisions (**RQ3**) using information about senders, recipients, and items. We build a series of models—starting from simple ones that use a single feature—to predict shares.

Data and method. We have 279 shares for movies that also have IMDB rating and popularity data. We use these shares to create 10 balanced datasets by randomly sampling sets of 279 non-shares. For each model, we perform 10 cross-fold validation in each dataset and average the results. For ease of interpretability, we use a decision tree classifier[4].

Computing features. Based on our results earlier, we consider a sharer's own preferences for an item, her sharing promiscuity, and the recipient's preferences for the item as

[4]We also tried random forests, logistic regression, and support vector machines. Results were qualitatively similar.

	Shared			Recommended				
Group	N	μ	σ	N	μ	σ	Significance	Effect Size
Both-Shown	81	3.80	1.05	119	3.81	0.97	$t(164) = 0.05; p = 0.95$	0.04
Own-Shown	42	4.28	0.70	109	3.86	1.01	$t(103) = 2.75; p < 0.01$	0.5
Combined	123	3.96	0.96	228	3.84	0.97	$t(250) = 1.07; p = 0.28$	0.1

Table 5. Comparison of recipients' ratings for shared and recommended movies. Shared movies are rated significantly higher when senders were shown only movies tailored for the recipient, not when they were shown mixed recommendations. Recipients in the *Other-Shown* group did not see recommendations tailored for them, so we excluded them from the comparison.

Features	Precision	Recall	Accuracy
Item-based			
Average IMDB Rating	49.5	61.9	50.1
Popularity	51.8	60.6	51.1
Both	51.8	62.1	50.9
Recipient-based			
Recipient-Item Similarity	64.0	38.5	58.7
Sender-Recipient Similarity	64.8	41.2	58.7
Both	62.9	54.1	60.5
Sender-based			
Sender-Item Similarity	66.3	**79.2**	68.4
Sharing Promiscuity	69.0	72.1	69.1
Both	72.3	74.9	72.7
Sender+Recipient	**78.4**	70.8	**75.7**

Table 6. Precision, recall, and accuracy for predicting whether an item is shared. Bold numbers are per-metric maximums. Item features such as popularity and average rating do little better than random guesses. Recipient-based features improve precision, but the most predictive features are connected to the sharer.

features for prediction. We also add preference similarity between the sharer and recipient to examine effects of homophily, along with IMDB rating and IMDB popularity to examine effects of item characteristics.

Sharing promiscuity is the number of shares by a user in our training dataset.

The sharer's and recipient's rating are not available for every item, so we estimate their preference for a movie through a method similar to item-based collaborative filtering [25]. We convert ratings in the study to a unary scale by denoting each rating 4 or above as a Like and combine those with the Likes we collected during the study, giving a total of 43K users and 785K likes on all movies. We represent each movie as a set of users who Liked the movie and compute Jaccard similarity between each pair of movies.

To estimate a user's preference for a movie, we compute the average similarity between the given movie and the movies that a user had Liked. We use this similarity score between a user and a movie as a feature denoting their preference for the movie, computing both the sender's and recipient's preference for each movie.

Finally, we compute the sender-recipient similarity feature as the Jaccard similarity between sets representing each user's movie Likes as defined above.

Prediction performance. Table 6 shows each model's precision, recall, and accuracy, common metrics for evaluating such models. Accuracy is the overall fraction of correct predictions of whether an item is shared or not. Sometimes it makes sense to focus only on predicted or actual shares; to do this, we also compute precision and recall. Precision is the fraction of correct predictions among all the items predicted as shares and recall is the fraction of true shares that were correctly predicted.

Item-based features of movies such as quality or popularity have little predictive power, with accuracy close to the 50% that a random predictor would achieve on a balanced dataset.

Using only recipients' similarity with a movie gives a precision of 64%, but the recall is low (38%). This is because a high recipient rating is a better than random predictor of a share but does not cover many other shares that have lower recipient ratings. The similarity between Likes of the sharer and the recipient gives comparable precision and recall to using recipients' similarity.

Sender-based features are more useful. A sender's similarity with a movie is able to predict whether a movie is shared or not with 66% precision and 79% recall, higher than recipient-based features. These results are consistent with the results around individuation described earlier.

Sharing promiscuity of a sender is also important; shares can be predicted with 69% precision based only on promiscuity. The model, though, is trivial, predicting that users above a certain threshold of promiscuity would share all movies shown to them while those below the threshold will share none.

The model that includes both promiscuity and similarity (the sender-both line in the table) is more interesting. Precision increases to 72% compared to either alone; a fitted decision tree is shown below. Similar movies above a threshold are shared depending on the sharer's promiscuity, but not those below it.

```
sharer_sim <= 0.0101: Non-shared
sharer_sim > 0.0101
| sharer_prom <= 1: Non-shared
| sharer_prom > 1: Shared
```

Finally, combining sender-based and recipient-based features achieves an accuracy of 76% and precision of 78%. Knowledge about preference similarity between the sender and the recipient helps; however, the decision tree ignores a recipient's similarity to the item.

```
sharer_sim <= 0.0107: Non-shared
sharer_sim > 0.0107
| sharer_prom <= 3
| | sharer_prom <=1: Non-shared
| | sharer_prom > 1
| | | sharer_recip_sim <= 0.0754
| | | | sharer_sim <= 0.0601: Non-shared
| | | | sharer_sim > 0.0601: Shared
| | | sharer_recip_sim > 0.0754: Shared
| sharer_prom > 3: Shared
```

Although our experiment design restricted the set of movies that can be shared and we used a modified, balanced dataset of shares and non-shares, these results demonstrate the potential of predicting sharing decisions using people's preferences.

DISCUSSION

When broadcasting as on Twitter, past research shows that most people post messages about themselves rather than sharing useful information [23]. Based on results in communication around tuning messages for the audience [19] and recent work showing that people think more about usefulness for the recipient as the audience size decreases [4], we expected people would weigh recipients' preferences more when sharing to an individual. However, both people's sharing data and their self-reports underscore the importance of their own preferences. For **RQ1**, the answer is clearly that sharing is more driven by people's own preferences than recipients'.

Yet people claimed to customize their shares for the recipient. Comparing shares with recommendations (**RQ2**) suggests that the items shown to a person affected their sharing behavior. When restricted to a set of items recommended for the recipient, people share items that are on average better liked than the recommendations, but not when they are shown their own recommendations or a mix of both.

Further, much of the sharing in the experiment could be predicted using people's preferences (**RQ3**). In particular, sharer-based features such as similarity with the item and promiscuity are important and can predict shares with over 70% precision. Recipient-based features are useful but not as discriminating, while item-based features reveal little.

To explain these findings, we propose a model for sharing and discuss the implications of that model for improving both information diffusion models and practices of online sharing.

A preference-salience sharing process

One way of explaining the disconnect between people's data and descriptions of how they personalize shares for recipients is that people do not really try to balance individuation and altruism when they share items. Rather, they share based on their preference for items and what is salient to them at the moment. Here salience denotes the particular items and recipient that the sharer is thinking of.

> *"I try to assess if the individual that I am recommending to would like the movie that I am suggesting. Otherwise, I do not tell them about the movie, and may think of someone else who would like the movie."* (P5)

In addition to their own preferences, people's selection of a candidate item for sharing also depends on the context that makes a certain item salient. When asked "When do you suggest items to others?", participants responded that they share just after consuming an item, during conversations when a relevant topic comes up, or when asked explicitly.

> *"I usually suggest either after I see the content or if something related comes up in conversation."* (P82)

Thus, a likely process for sharing can be described as follows. People's own preferences determine shareable items. Among these candidates, some items become salient based on the context and then are shared or not depending on whether the sharer thinks they are suitable for the recipient[5].

This process can explain how participants shared items that they like, yet claim to be personalizing for the recipient. Out of the movies shown, participants considered the movies that they like for sharing, and then decided to share or not in part based on their perception of their partner's preferences. The increase in recommendation quality for shares when selecting from items tuned to recipients underscores the saliency aspect: showing items appropriate for the sharing task led to shares that recipients rated higher.

We believe our preference-salience model presents a reasonable abstraction of people's sharing decisions that has more empirical support than two other models we considered:

- *High Quality Model.* It is possible that people simply share higher quality items which are likely to be liked by all. This is supported by the fact that shares are rated highly by the senders, are comparable to recommended items in matching recipients' preferences, and are significantly higher-rated on IMDB than recommendations. However, there is no difference between overall IMDB ratings for shared and non-shared movies, which led us to reject this model.

- *Misguided Altruism Model.* It could also be that people do try to customize shares to recipients but fail because of imperfect knowledge [19]. This is supported by participants' accounts of how they personalize for recipients and the fact that shared items are not rated as highly by recipients as they are by sharers. However, across all groups of participants, senders' own ratings are significantly higher for shares than for non-shares, which indicates that even if people do try to personalize for the recipient, their own preferences still play an important role.

Still, a simplification of a complex process

While we propose the preference-salience model as a likely explanation of our observations, our binarization of motivations into individuation and altruism is a simplification that

[5]This is somewhat the dual of the FeedMe system's making possible recipients for an item salient by recommending them as targets [5].

does not account for other motivations (e.g., to dissuade people from trying an item) or factors (e.g., relationships between people) that affect sharing behavior.

In particular, the closeness of ties between most of our participants might have played a role in people's decisions. Knowing a recipient well increases people's chances of knowing his preferences and customizing their suggestions.

> *"I'll only recommend a movie to a close friend or relative because I know them well enough to know what they would like in a movie."* (P54)

Close ties may also allow people to be more open about their preferences.

> *"With my close friend I feel like I can share anything, but with an acquaintance, I will feel less open to sharing my interests."* (P71)

Finally, people don't just share good items; sharing may also warn others about bad items.

> *"if i really liked something i want others to experience it too...if i hated it i want to help them avoid it."* (P34)

Applications of the preference-salience sharing process

We now discuss how the preference-salience process of sharing can be used to improve diffusion models and online sharing practices.

Directed sharing in diffusion models

By demonstrating the effect of people's preferences on directed sharing, our work joins other recent work in questioning the broadcast assumption used for modeling diffusion in social networks [13, 24]. One way to improve these models is to acknowledge that not all sharing is broadcast; as described in the introduction, much sharing takes place to individuals and small audiences (@-mentions in Twitter, Google+ circles, small subsets of friends in Facebook).

The preference-salience model lends itself well to incorporating sharing decisions in a diffusion model. Instead of assuming that items are shared to each friend with a fixed probability, the model posits that salient items that match senders' preferences are more likely to be shared, and (to a lesser extent) only to recipients who are more likely to like it. Salience, preferences, and similarity could be measured and used to set sharing probabilities tuned for each sharer, recipient, and item, which we expect would lead to more accurate diffusion models.

Accounting for sharing promiscuity of individuals is also important, as demonstrated in a recent study on diffusion within blog networks [22]. Although we did not consider promiscuity in our preference-salience process model, it can be readily included. Our process model essentially defines which items are good candidates for sharing. Promiscuity can be thought of as a cutoff for sharing: people with low promiscuity would have a higher barrier for actually sharing one of the candidate items. We can estimate promiscuity by considering the number of shares made by a user, either absolute or relative to others, as we did for our sharing prediction model.

Supporting effective sharing

Our work also has implications for improving sharing behaviors in social networks. We found that higher promiscuity is correlated with lesser liked shares by both senders and recipients. Systems might help people consider this by providing feedback about their promiscuity relative to others. Similarly, showing information about the outcomes of their shares such as the average liking by recipients might help people reflect on how their shares are being received.

The model suggests that making the right items salient may also improve sharing outcomes. In personal consumption contexts, systems should still focus on recommending items that align with the user's interests. In contexts where people are likely to share items with friends or consume them together, however, our results suggest that showing recommendations tailored to the friends rather than the user might lead to better outcomes.

Limitations

It is important to keep in mind the limitations of our study while interpreting the above results. First, although we broadened our sample by recruiting from two different participant pools in the U.S., differences in demographics and culture may affect people's decisions around sharing.

The design of our experiment may also have affected people's sharing behavior. We allow participants to invite their own partners so they can choose people with whom they feel comfortable sharing and whose preferences they would be more likely to know. This led to high tie strength for most of the participant pairs; understanding more about sharing between weaker ties would be an interesting area to study.

We also restricted the set of items in order to get ratings from both members of a pair. Many real contexts also make subsets of an item domain salient, such as in recommendation lists and filtered activity feeds, and we expect our results apply best there. Studying scenarios where items are not made explicitly salient (e.g., searching for an item and sharing) would tell us more the relative effects of salience and personal preferences.

Finally, we studied movies as a specific domain. Though a reasonable choice, sharing decisions in other domains such as news or photos might be different because of differences in cost of consuming an item or ease of sharing items. Our results may also less readily apply to knowledge sharing scenarios where goals may be more strategic and individual preference may be expected to be less discriminating (such as sharing job information or advice).

CONCLUSION

Our results demonstrate connections between people's preferences and their sharing behavior that pave the way for better models of sharing in online social networks. Individual preferences of senders appear to dominate, despite the fact that altruism (and other considerations such as the nature of the relationship and identity management) are both theoretically and self-reportedly present. The preference-salience model serves to explain why this may be so. We posit that people select an item to share based on a combination of their preference for it and what is salient at the moment and show that this information can help to predict sharing decisions.

Our work also points to the need for learning more about the motivations for directed sharing and how they might be modeled. Future work addressing how preferences, salience of items and recipients, and other social forces impact sharing decisions will shed more light on people's sharing processes and lead to diffusion models well-suited for online social networks.

ACKNOWLEDGMENTS

This work was supported by the National Science Foundation under grants IIS 0845351, 0910664, and 1422484.

REFERENCES

1. K. Abrahamson. Pinterest surpasses email for sharing online and beats Facebook growth in 2013. *Retrieved from* `http://www.sharethis.com/blog/2014/01/16/pinterest-surpasses-email-sharing-online-beats-facebook-growth-2013`, January 2014.
2. S. Aral and D. Walker. Identifying influential and susceptible members of social networks. *Science*, 2012.
3. E. Bakshy, I. Rosenn, C. Marlow, and L. Adamic. The role of social networks in information diffusion. In *Proc. WWW*, 2012.
4. A. Barasch and J. Berger. Broadcasting and narrowcasting: How audience size impacts what people share. *Journal of Marketing Research*, 2014.
5. M. S. Bernstein, A. Marcus, D. R. Karger, and R. C. Miller. Enhancing directed content sharing on the web. In *Proc. CHI*, 2010.
6. R. M. Bond, C. J. Fariss, J. J. Jones, A. D. Kramer, C. Marlow, J. E. Settle, and J. H. Fowler. A 61-million-person experiment in social influence and political mobilization. *Nature*, 2012.
7. J. J. Brown and P. H. Reingen. Social ties and word-of-mouth referral behavior. *Journal of Consumer Research*, pages 350–362, 1987.
8. M. Cha, A. Mislove, and K. P. Gummadi. A measurement-driven analysis of information propagation in the flickr social network. In *Proc. WWW*, 2009.
9. C. M. Chung and P. R. Darke. The consumer as advocate: self-relevance, culture, and word-of-mouth. *Marketing Letters*, 17(4):269–279, 2006.
10. J. Cohen. A power primer. *Psychological bulletin*, 1992.
11. E. Dichter. How word-of-mouth advertising works. *Harvard Business Review*, 44(6):147–160, 1966.
12. P. Domingos and M. Richardson. Mining the network value of customers. In *Proc. KDD*. ACM, 2001.
13. S. Goel, D. J. Watts, and D. G. Goldstein. The structure of online diffusion networks. In *Proc. ACM Electron. Commerce*, EC '12, 2012.
14. D. Gruhl, R. Guha, D. Liben-Nowell, and A. Tomkins. Information diffusion through blogspace. In *Proc. WWW*, 2004.
15. T. Hennig-Thurau and G. Walsh. Electronic word-of-mouth: Motives for and consequences of reading customer articulations on the internet. *Int. J. Electron. Commerce*, 8(2), Dec. 2003.
16. J. Y. Ho and M. Dempsey. Viral marketing: Motivations to forward online content. *J. of Business Research*, 2010.
17. C. Johnson. Got any good recommendations? *Retrieved from* `http://blog.netflix.com/2014/09/got-any-good-recommendations.html`, September 2014.
18. D. Kempe, J. Kleinberg, and É. Tardos. Maximizing the spread of influence through a social network. In *Proc. KDD*, 2003.
19. R. M. Krauss and S. R. Fussell. Perspective-taking in communication: Representations of others' knowledge in reference. *Social Cognition*, 9(1), 1991.
20. V. Krishnan, P. K. Narayanashetty, M. Nathan, R. T. Davies, and J. A. Konstan. Who predicts better?: results from an online study comparing humans and an online recommender system. In *Proc. RecSys*, 2008.
21. C. Kulkarni and E. Chi. All the news that's fit to read: a study of social annotations for news reading. In *Proc. CHI*, 2013.
22. C. Lagnier, L. Denoyer, E. Gaussier, and P. Gallinari. Predicting information diffusion in social networks using content and users profiles. In *Advances in Information Retrieval*. Springer Berlin Heidelberg, 2013.
23. M. Naaman, J. Boase, and C.-H. Lai. Is it really about me? Message content in social awareness streams. In *Proc. CSCW*, 2010.
24. J. Neff. Email beats social networks for online offer sharing: Study. *Retrieved from* `http://adage.com/article/digital/socialtwist-sharing-e-mail-facebook-twitter/244397/`, October 2013.
25. B. Sarwar, G. Karypis, J. Konstan, and J. Riedl. Item-based collaborative filtering recommendation algorithms. In *Proc. WWW*, 2001.
26. A. Sharma and D. Cosley. Network-centric recommendation: Personalization with and in social networks. In *Proc. IEEE SocialCom*, 2011.
27. A. Sharma and D. Cosley. Do social explanations work? Studying and modeling the effects of social explanations in recommender systems. In *Proc. WWW*, 2013.
28. A. Sharma, M. Gemici, and D. Cosley. Friends, strangers, and the value of ego networks for recommendation. In *Proc. ICWSM*, 2013.
29. X. Su and T. M. Khoshgoftaar. A survey of collaborative filtering techniques. *Adv. in Artif. Intell.*, 2009.

30. D. S. Sundaram, K. Mitra, and C. Webster. Word-of-mouth communications: a motivational analysis. *Advances in consumer research*, 1998.

31. D. G. Taylor, D. Strutton, and K. Thompson. Self-enhancement as a motivation for sharing online advertising. *Journal of Interactive Advertising*, 2012.

32. S. J. Taylor, E. Bakshy, and S. Aral. Selection effects in online sharing: Consequences for peer adoption. In *Proc. ACM Electron. Commerce*, EC '13, 2013.

33. B. Wang, C. Wang, J. Bu, C. Chen, W. V. Zhang, D. Cai, and X. He. Whom to mention: Expand the diffusion of tweets by @ recommendation on micro-blogging systems. In *Proc. WWW*, 2013.

34. M. M. Wasko and S. Faraj. Why should i share? examining social capital and knowledge contribution in electronic networks of practice. *MIS Quarterly*, 2005.

35. D. J. Watts. A simple model of global cascades on random networks. *Proc. PNAS*, 99(9), 2002.

36. D. Zhao and M. B. Rosson. How and why people twitter: The role that micro-blogging plays in informal communication at work. In *Proc. GROUP*, 2009.

APPENDIX

Effects of people and items on observed ratings

In earlier sections, we presented t-tests for comparing ratings by participants for ease of exposition. However, two empirical observations for our data violate the assumptions for a t-test. First, the distribution of participants' ratings is not normal. Second, ratings by the same user, or for the same item, may not be independent of each other. Thus, we now present a linear mixed-effects analysis to account for non-normality and interdependence in the data.

Mixed-effects analysis (or hierarchical regression) accounts for the interdependence in data by identifying the fixed and random effects on the dependent variable (in our case, people's ratings). We can encode the dependence between ratings by the same user or for the same item as random effects due to user and item, and consider our specific experimental manipulation as the fixed effect. Being a form of regression, the specific assumptions made are that the residual errors have expectation zero, are independent, and have equal variances.

Senders' ratings for shared and non-shared movies

When comparing ratings given by senders for shared and non-shared movies as in Table 3, whether a movie was shared or not can be considered as a fixed effect on the rating. The sender and the movie are random effects on the rating, which leads us to the following model:

$$rating \sim shared\_or\_not + (1|participant) + (1|movie) + \epsilon$$

where ϵ denotes the random error. Using this formulation, we compare this model against a null model which does not incorporate the sharing variable.

$$rating \sim (1|participant) + (1|movie) + \epsilon$$

We analyze the significance of whether a movie was shared or not by comparing the likelihood of the observed data given our model and the null model. Table 7 shows the results, using *lme4* in R (`http://CRAN.R-project.org/package=lme4`), including by-participant and by-movie random slopes for the effect of sharing. As before, shared movies are rated significantly higher than non-shared ones in all three groups.

Group	N	$\chi^2(1)$	p-value
Both-Shown	609	6.6	< 0.01
Own-Shown	179	5.4	0.02
Other-Shown	178	13.6	< 0.001
All users	966	23.5	< 0.001

Table 7. Significance tests using a linear mixed-effects analysis for comparing senders' ratings of shared and non-shared movies. Across all groups, shared movies are rated significantly higher.

Group	N	$\chi^2(1)$	p-value
Both-Shown	200	0.63	0.4
Own-Shown	151	5.1	0.02
Combined	351	1.4	0.2

Table 8. Significance tests using a linear mixed-effects analysis for comparing recipients' ratings for shared and recommended movies. As we saw before, ratings for shared items are significantly higher than algorithmic recommendations only when senders shared from movies recommended for the recipient.

Recipients' ratings for shared and recommended movies

We can use a similar analysis for comparing recipients' rating for shared and recommended movies. Our null model would be the same as before.

$$rating \sim (1|participant) + (1|movie) + \epsilon$$

The full model would include information about whether the movie was shared or recommended.

$$rating \sim shared\_or\_rec + (1|participant) + (1|movie) + \epsilon$$

Table 8 shows the comparison between the two models above. The difference between the two models is significant for *Own-Shown* but not for *Both-Shown*, similar to our earlier statistical analysis using t-tests.

Using Groups of Items for Preference Elicitation in Recommender Systems

Shuo Chang, F. Maxwell Harper, Loren Terveen

GroupLens Research
University of Minnesota
{schang, harper, terveen}@cs.umn.edu

ABSTRACT

To achieve high quality initial personalization, recommender systems must provide an efficient and effective process for new users to express their preferences. We propose that this goal is best served not by the classical method where users begin by expressing preferences for individual items - this process is an inefficient way to convert a user's effort into improved personalization. Rather, we propose that new users can begin by expressing their preferences for *groups* of items. We test this idea by designing and evaluating an interactive process where users express preferences across groups of items that are automatically generated by clustering algorithms. We contribute a strategy for recommending items based on these preferences that is generalizable to any collaborative filtering-based system. We evaluate our process with both offline simulation methods and an online user experiment. We find that, as compared with a baseline rate-15-items interface, (a) users are able to complete the preference elicitation process in less than half the time, and (b) users are more satisfied with the resulting recommended items. Our evaluation reveals several advantages and other trade-offs involved in moving from item-based preference elicitation to group-based preference elicitation.

Author Keywords

Recommender System; Cold Start Problem; Interaction Design

ACM Classification Keywords

H.1.2. User/Machine Systems

INTRODUCTION

Collaborative filtering-based recommender systems [26] are among the most successful social computing applications. They automate "word-of-mouth" recommendations by first learning about the preferences of users, then matching these preferences against those of all other users of the system to provide personalized recommendations. From recommending videos on YouTube to suggesting people to connect with on Facebook, collaborative filtering is widely applied in various popular online platforms.

Despite the popularity of collaborative filtering (CF), there are some open problems, one of which is *cold start problem*. There are three types of cold start problem. In the *user cold start* problem, new users enter into a recommender system with only existing preference data about other users. In the *item cold start* problem, new items are added to a system with no preference data on them. The combination of the two is the *system cold start* problem, which occurs when a system is first released. [25] In particular, for *user cold start problem*, the system cannot provide personalized recommendations until it collects enough preference information from users. In practice, there are two common approaches to addressing this problem. In the first approach, users are admitted directly into a system with no requirements, leading to an initial experience that is non-personalized. In the second approach, users are asked to complete a *preference elicitation process* before gaining access to a personalized view of the site. In this work, we are primarily concerned with the second approach, as we focus our attention on systems where the core features are built around personalization.

There are two critical challenges in designing a new user bootstrapping process in a personalization-oriented system: providing an *efficient and easy* mechanism for eliciting preferences, and delivering *high quality recommendations* based on relatively little data. Systems with difficult or slow preference elicitation processes may waste user time and effort, and may see decreased activity. For example, in the movie recommendation website MovieLens[1], new users are required to provide ratings on at least 15 movies as part of the sign-up process. Our analysis of MovieLens data shows that users take an average of 6.8 minutes to complete this process, and 12.6% of these users fail to complete the process and never even get to the front page! But on the other hand, systems that do not learn user preferences will deliver poorer

[1] www.movielens.org

CSCW 2015, March 14–18, 2015, Vancouver, BC, Canada.

http://dx.doi.org/10.1145/2675133.2675210

recommendations, may not gain users' trust, and therefore may receive less use. As evidence, an analysis of MovieLens shows that users who receive bad recommendations initially are less active than other users.

There has been substantial research interest in improving these aspects of the user cold start problem [8,12,13,24,25]. These studies generally focus on algorithmic solutions that maximize the information gained about new users from item ratings. Though further optimizing the selection of items for rating remains an open problem, we posit that larger advances may be possible by re-thinking the user interaction model.

We are motivated by a simple intuition that runs contrary to the assumptions in these studies: perhaps the process of rating items to bootstrap user profiles is inherently inefficient. An obvious alternative to rating individual items is to rate groups of items. We hypothesize that if we can derive groups of items that are understandable, recognizable, and that span the preference space, then perhaps we can improve upon the classical methods for new user preference elicitation. Such a system would ask relatively few questions to minimize the time required, but would be able to turn the answers to those questions into a valuable source of information for bootstrapping personalization.

In this paper, we evaluate the potential of a new user preference elicitation process that combines automatic clustering algorithms with interfaces for capturing preferences about groups of items. We hypothesize that this type of system will allow users to accurately express their preferences, and quickly give them high quality personalization. Specifically, we evaluate our group-based process with two research questions:

RQ1-Minimal user effort. Is group-based preference elicitation efficient, flexible, and easy for users to understand ?

RQ2-High quality recommendation. Does group-based preference elicitation lead to an accurate model of user preferences and therefore high-quality personalized recommendations?

We study these research questions using multiple methods. To determine the theoretical feasibility of our algorithmic approach, we run an offline simulation analysis based on data from MovieLens, our research platform. To better evaluate the real-world characteristics of our system, we follow this with a user experiment with MovieLens users where we compare our process to a baseline process that has been in production for over ten years.

This paper is structured as follows. We first survey related work and situate our contribution. Then, we describe the design challenges related to generating high-quality groups of items, eliciting preferences for those items, and turning those preferences into recommendations. We follow this by describing the methods and results of two related experiments: a simulation-based feasibility study, and an online user experiment. We conclude with a discussion of the lessons learned from these experiments and the advantages and trade-offs we perceive in using a group-oriented preference elicitation process.

RELATED WORK

Most existing work on preference elicitation for new users in recommender systems focuses on algorithmic solutions that maximize the information gained about new users. However, recent work has called attention to the need for research on user experience that includes both interaction design and algorithm development to address this problem [17].

Designing for New Users

Dealing with newcomers in online communities has been an active research area [18]. Prior work looked at various interventions that can improve user retention. For example, authors in [6] conducted a field experiment in MovieLens. They found that fewer users completed the sign-up process when they were required to do additional work. However, they found that the users who finished the sign-up process contributed more value to the community.

More recently, research in [33] studied "social bootstrapping", a common method whereby users import their social connections from other social networking sites. For example, users signing up for Pinterest are asked to import their network from Facebook. Authors in [2] point out that importing social connections is not necessarily effective in personalizing content. They suggest that this might be improved by asking users' preferences on existing topics in Pinterest by clustering content as part of sign up process.

This work. Inspired by [6], we seek to strike a balance between the effort required from new users and participation of users over the long term. And similar to the suggestion in [2], we study a preference elicitation process on group of items that is based on automatically clustering content.

Preference Elicitation in Recommender System

Research on bringing new users into recommender systems has traditionally been focused on effective algorithms for optimizing the process of collecting high-quality preference information from users. Further, prior research in CF recommender systems focuses on methods to elicit users' preferences on individual items or pairs of items.

Collaborative filtering algorithms can provide personalized recommendations based only on user-item rating data and are therefore unable to make recommendations for new users until they have rated some number of items. To collect these ratings, most CF recommender systems ask new users to go through a preference elicitation process. The first batch of research on this type of process [8,24,25] framed the problem as finding the optimal item sequence for new users to rate, so that users

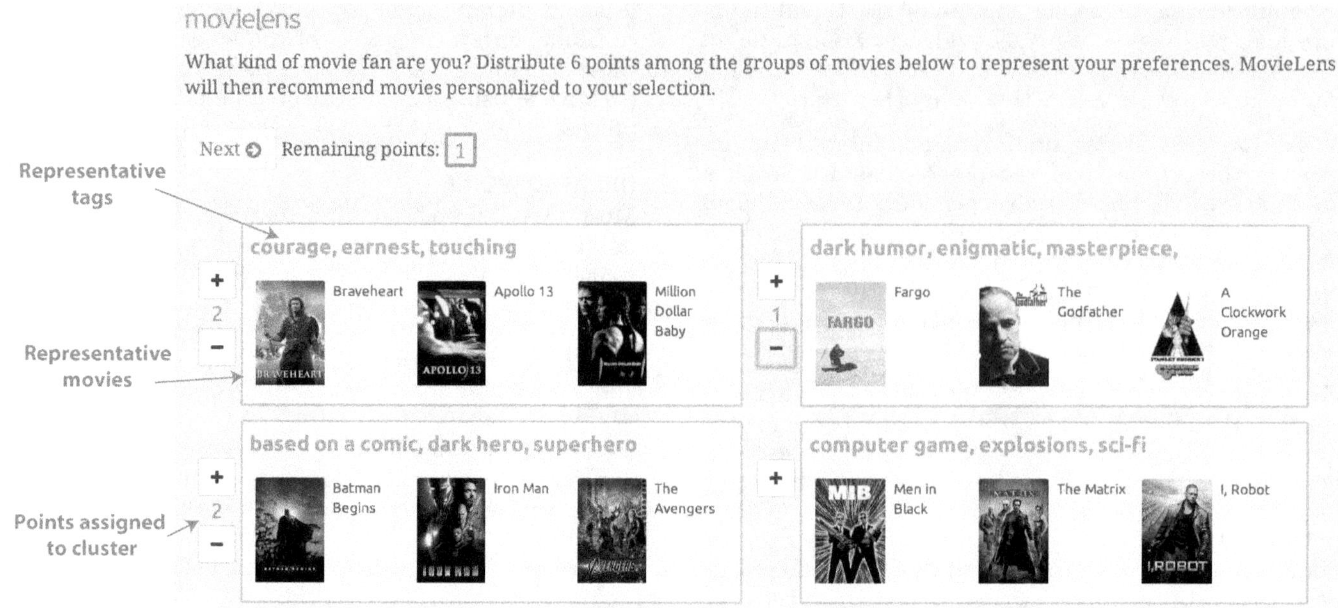

Figure 1. Screen shot of the interface for 14 movie groups, 4 of which are visible, and 6 preference points to allocate.

spend the least effort finishing the required number of ratings, and so that the system can optimize the resulting prediction accuracy. Authors in [24,25] showed that ranking movies based either on popularity or a combination of popularity and entropy of ratings led to good performance in both offline simulation and in a user experiment. Another study [8] used a different simulation method and more comprehensive evaluation metrics to shed light on the performance of the above two ranking strategies and further proposed ranking strategies based on highest predicted rating and lowest predicted rating.

Commercial systems have introduced a variety of user experiences for new user preference elicitation. Some systems use explicit ratings data. For example, Netflix asks users to step through a variety of pages where they rate genres and movies. Other systems use implicit feedback to infer users' preferences for recommendation: Youtube and Netflix use viewing history, Amazon uses clicking and purchasing history, and Facebook uses user activities on news feed items. However, implicit feedback is not as useful for systems that wish to allow users to control the personalization. Content-based recommender systems can directly elicit preferences on content features. For example, both Facebook Paper and Pinterest ask new users about the categories they are interested in before recommending content. However, similar content features are not necessarily available in other application domains, and these features may not offer the flexibility to control the granularity of users' stated preferences.

Under the same problem definition, other research has recently developed decision tree-based preference elicitation methods [12,13,30], whereby the recommender system repeatedly asks new users to pick their preference from a pair of movies. According to the user's previous choice, the system adaptively generates movie pairs for comparison. In the end, the system categorizes users into a user group with similar taste and then uses an average of the group's taste for generating recommendations.

However, algorithmic approaches have limitations in real-world applications. There is little transparency and limited control for users in the process of rating movies from a list or comparing a series of movie pairs. As is shown in [20], less control results in more perceived effort even though users spend less time. And in the case of decision tree-based methods, there is a high probability that users will be asked for movie pairs that they have not seen, because the algorithm is optimized only to pick movie pairs to best divide user groups.

Recently, some research has focused more on interaction in recommender systems [1,14,19]. SmallWorlds [14] provides interactive graph visualization for social recommendation on Facebook. Through a user study, authors find that users think the system is transparent and are satisfied with the system. TasteWeights [1], an interactive music recommender, allows users to control their recommendations by choosing their preferred artists or by leveraging the preferences found in their social network.

The most directly relevant work to this paper [19] studied a choice-based preference elicitation process. Similar to decision tree-based methods, the system iteratively asks users to compare two groups of movies before making any recommendations. In contrast with decision tree-based methods, movies are picked to represent two opposite values of a latent factor, which is computed from a matrix factorization collaborative filtering algorithm. In picking movies to present, they consider both the algorithmic latent space and the transparency to users. Through a user study, they showed that the system has advantages on 15 parameters over both a manual system where users search for items and an automatic recommender system with no interaction.

This work. Similar to [19], we propose an interactive preference elicitation process that strikes a balance between user effort and quality of recommendation by asking users to rate groups of items. Compared to [19], we provide a different presentation of movie tastes with tag-labeled movie clusters. Moreover, our approach is generalizable to any collaborative filtering recommender system, while [19] is constrained to matrix factorization-based systems. And, similar to decision tree-based methods [12,13,30], we represent users' tastes as the average preference of users who are similar.

DESIGN SPACE ANALYSIS

In this section, we describe the design space surrounding our preference elicitation process, guided by our two research questions. As part of this analysis, we articulate several design challenges related to the creation and display of groups of items, ways of allowing users to express preferences for those items, and how we might turn these preferences into item recommendations. Specifically, we target our analysis on the design of a new user process for MovieLens, a CF-based movie recommender system that recommends movies based on movie ratings.

Design space

Designing a preference elicitation process involves making a choice along a spectrum of user effort, and a correlated spectrum of personalization. On the one hand, a system may require a demanding process that asks users for lots of information - such as ratings or survey responses - in exchange for high-quality personalization. On the other hand, a system might admit users directly, making the process fast and easy at the cost of foregoing the opportunity for personalized recommendations. In this research, we are interested in developing a part of the design space that is both low-effort and high-personalization.

The standard preference elicitation process for CF systems extracts preferences from the most basic unit - ratings on individual items. However, some ratings contain highly overlapping information. For example, if a user has rated "Toy Story", it may be the case that rating "The Lion King" does not add much additional information for the purposes of personalization, since they both reflect a preference for children's animation. Research on active learning in recommender system [28] explores a similar idea that ratings on similar items represent correlated information about user preference. Therefore, we believe that asking users for preferences on *groups* of similar movies is more efficient at the cost of some information loss. Higher quality clusters, where movies in the same cluster are more similar, will result in less information loss. One obvious way to group items in the movie domain is to use existing categorization such as genres. However, categorization is not necessarily available in other item domains and existing categorization has no flexibility to control the granularity of groupings. Therefore, we propose a preference elicitation method based on groups of items. The item groups (or item *clusters* for the rest of this paper) are identified by automatic clustering algorithm.

Design challenges

To accomplish our goal of achieving a new user preference elicitation process that is both minimal effort and leads to high quality recommendations, we must address several design challenges. In this section, we detail the following challenges (shown in Figure 2), along with our proposed solutions:

- DC1: Generating groups,
- DC2: Describing groups,
- DC3: Eliciting preferences,
- DC4: Recommending based on preferences.

DC1: Generating groups

We use an unsupervised clustering method to identify non-overlapping groups of item. In MovieLens, the items are movies. As mentioned above, the quality of clusters is critical to the effectiveness of preference elicitation: good clustering puts similar movies in the same cluster, dissimilar movies in different clusters, and covers the whole preference space.

Selecting data for clustering. We use only the MovieLens user-item rating matrix for clustering movies. Because rating information is available for all CF-based recommender systems (attributes of items are not always available), this method is generalizable. However, ratings matrices in CF systems are sparse, because both ratings from users and ratings on items follow a long tail distribution. We can get data with higher quality on movies with more ratings from seasoned users who have rated more movies, resulting in better movie clusters. Based on this intuition, we extract a dense ratings matrix to serve as the input to the clustering algorithm. To build this dense matrix, we pick the 200 most frequently-rated movies in MovieLens, and those users who have rated more than 75% of those movies. These numbers are chosen according to the size of the dataset and sparsity of the ratings. Our intuition is confirmed by manual inspection of clustering results using dense rating matrix and the full matrix.

We further experimented with data transformation techniques such as normalizing ratings and dimension reduction on the rating matrix. Based on extensive offline simulation, we chose to use mean subtracting normalization as our technique [5].

Clustering algorithm. After selecting data for the clustering, we compute pairwise cosine similarities [26]

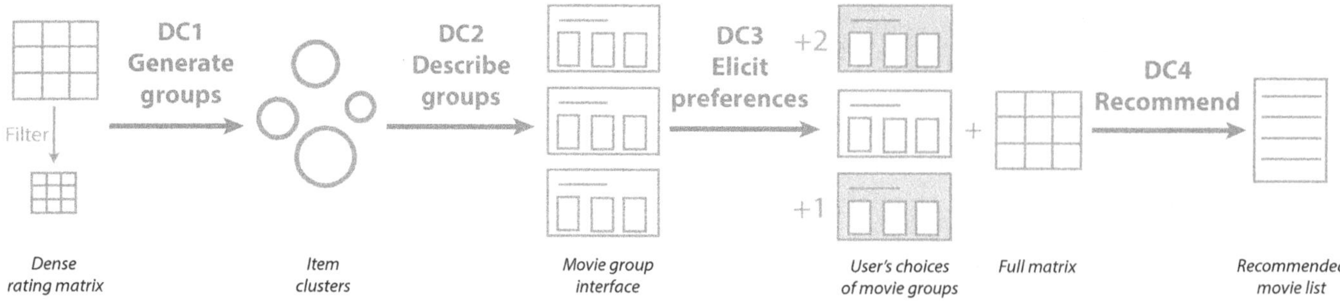

Figure 2. An overview of the design challenges in our group-based preference elicitation process.

between all movie vectors, and run the Spectral Clustering algorithm [23] to partition movies into clusters. Spectral Clustering is a standard graph-based clustering technique commonly applied to similar domains such as document clustering and community detection [3,9]. Again, we evaluate the performance of Spectral Clustering by manual inspection of clustering result and find it to generate more sensible clusters in comparison to Affinity Propagation [10], another popular graph-based clustering algorithm.

DC2: Describing groups

To help users better understand the preference elicitation process, we need to present the movie groups in a comprehensible way. In our implementation, we use both movies and tags to represent movie groups in the user interface (see Figure 1). Tags, which are created and applied to movies by users in MovieLens, provide high quality descriptions for the movie groups. However, they can be replaced by manual labeling for a system that does not have tags.

For picking representative movies and tags, there are two options: (1) select representative movies then find the most descriptive tags, and (2) pick representative tags then find the most relevant movies. We decide to use the latter because it results in more comprehensible representations of groups in our informal analysis.

For each movie group, we first pick the top-three tags that both *uniquely describe* and are *highly relevant* to the group. Therefore, we define the measure of tag uniqueness as Equation 1 and tag relevance as Equation 2. We pick the three tags with the highest multiplication of uniqueness and relevance. (Multiplication is used to handle different scales of the two metrics.)

$$unique(t,c) = \frac{rel(t,c)}{\sum_{c_i \in C} rel(t,c_i)} \quad (1)$$

$$relevance(t,c) = \frac{rel(t,c)}{\sum_{t_i \in T_c} rel(t_i,c)} \quad (2)$$

where t denotes one of the tags T_c that appears in cluster c, and C denotes all the clusters. Note that $rel(t,c)$ is the aggregated relevance of tags t to all movies in cluster c. In our implementation, we use relevance between a tag and a movie generated from the Tag Genome [31], but other systems could replace this data with a count of applications of the tag to the movie.

DC3: Eliciting preferences

There are many possible user interfaces that support the design goal of eliciting user preferences for movie groups. For example, users might rank the movie groups, or they might provide 5-star ratings for each group. In this work, our goal is to minimize effort while achieving high personalization. Therefore, we start with a very simple interface: users choose one favorite group.

Intuitively, one movie group may not be sufficient to represent movie taste, e.g., a user might enjoy both horror movies and sci-fi movies, which are likely to be in different groups. To give users more control of how they express their preferences for movie groups, we further propose experimenting with an interaction technique that asks users to allocate a fixed number of points across one or more movie groups.

We use a data-driven approach to decide on the appropriate number of points to give users to allocate. Again, we analyze ratings from users in the dense matrix and check how many groups their top-rated movies[2] fall into. As a result of this analysis, we are able to pick the number of points that covers all the top-rated movies for 80% of the users for any number of groups. The results of this analysis inform the design of our user experiment (described in the user experiment section below) where we examine the impact of point allocation versus an interface where users simply pick their favorite movie group.

DC4: Recommending based on preferences

The next step, given a user's chosen preference for one or more movie groups, is to generate personalized recommendations from the full item space. One important feature of our recommendation process is that it can be generalized to any standard collaborative filtering algorithm.

Our algorithm, summarized in Algorithm 1, represents the preferences of a new user as the average rating from users in the dense matrix who share a similar taste.

[2] movies rated ≥ 4 on a 5 star rating scale

To recommend based on one "favorite" cluster, we find users from the dense matrix who have the highest ratings for movies in that cluster and generate a *pseudo rating profile* by taking the average ratings of those users. Though this technique builds the pseudo rating profile from data in the dense matrix, it is able to generate recommendations and predicted ratings that cover the full item space using standarad collaborative filtering.

Let r_{um} be the dense rating matrix, where $u \in U$ denotes user and $m \in M$ denotes movie. Assume there are K clusters of movies $C_k, k \leq K$. The new user u_0 has distributed p_k on each cluster k. Picking one favorite cluster is the special case where only one $p_k = 1$ is non zero.

Step 1: Compute average rating vectors
foreach *cluster* C_k **do**
  1. Find the set of users U_k where average rating $\bar{r}_{um}, m \in C_k$ is the highest
  2. Compute $\vec{r}_{U_k}$, which is the average rating for $u \in U_k$ on all movies $m \in M$
end
Step 2: Make recommendations
foreach *cluster k where* $p_k > 0$ **do**
  Make recommendation Rec_k for the pseudo user rating profile $\vec{r}_{U_k}$ using a standard CF algorithm
end
Step 3: Aggregate recommendations Rec_k using weights p_k

Algorithm 1: Algorithm for the recommendation process

To aggregate recommendations in the case where users allocate multiple points across clusters, there are two types of recommendation results to combine: predicted ratings and a top-N list. For predicted ratings, we compute a simple weighted average of multiple predicted ratings, based on different pseudo rating profiles. For generating a top-N list, we aggregate multiple ranked item lists by assigning scores $(N - rank + 1)$ to items based their rank in the list, then computing weighted averages of the scores, and finally ranking items accordingly. An example is shown in Table 1.

FEASIBILITY STUDY

To evaluate the effectiveness of group-based preference elicitation, we conduct an offline simulation study. We focus on an evaluation of *RQ2-High quality recommendation* using prediction accuracy and top-N recommendation accuracy [29], and leave *RQ1-Minimal user effort* for the user experiment. We also evaluate the trade-offs inherent in increasing the number of clusters through an analysis of resulting recommendation quality and of clustering quality metrics.

Table 1. Example of weighted aggregation of ranked item lists. List 1 has 2 points and list 2 has 1 point. We assign scores to items in the lists based on ranking. We re-rank items based on the weighted average of item scores in two lists and take top 3.

	List1(2 points)		**List2**(1 point)		**Combined list**	
Rank	**movie**	**score**	**movie**	**score**	**movie**	**score**
1	A	3	D	3	A	2.33
2	B	2	B	2	B	2
3	C	1	A	1	D	1

Data

We construct a data set of 2.2M ratings from 5,018 users on 22,115 movies from the MovieLens database. We select users who have provided at least 50 ratings and who have rated at least one movie since June 1, 2013. We choose users based on their ratings behavior because we can more accurately simulate user preferences and evaluate quality-based metrics for users with many ratings.

Method

Our simulation study has two parts: first, we build item groups and simulate user group choices; second, we use those simulated group choices to evaluate the quality of the resulting recommendations. To fairly evaluate the results, we conduct a 5-fold cross validation on the data set, where 80% of the users (and their ratings) are used to build the item groups, and the remaining 20% are used to simulate group choices and evaluate recommendation quality. Further, for each user in the test set, we randomly select 80% of their ratings to guide the simulated group choices, while the remaining 20% are left for evaluating recommendation quality. We simulate users picking one favorite movie group. We assume that users will choose the movie group for which they have the highest average rating across items in that group. Because this assumption is a crude approximation of actual user behaviour, we also include an oracle strategy that assumes users will always pick the group that has the best prediction accuracy, so as to approximate the theoretically optimal performance. Then, we make recommendations using a standard CF algorithm.

Baseline

We compare group-based preference elicitation to the standard method used in MovieLens for the last 10 years - asking users to rate 15 movies from a long list of movies generated by an algorithm. We analyzed our data set to compare various movie sorting algorithms [25] as well as several state of the art CF algorithms - item-item [5] and FunkSVD [11] - with respect to their resulting recommendation quality after 15 ratings. Item-item CF has the best recommendation quality in combination with popularity-based sorting. [3] Therefore, we will use item-item CF both to serve as our rate-15 baseline recommender, and to recommend movies based on users' choices of movie groups.

Evaluation

For prediction accuracy, we measure RMSE [16] of predictions on ratings from the set of test users. Lower

[3] All evaluations are carried out in Lenskit [7] and the scripts with details of the algorithm configurations will be shared online.

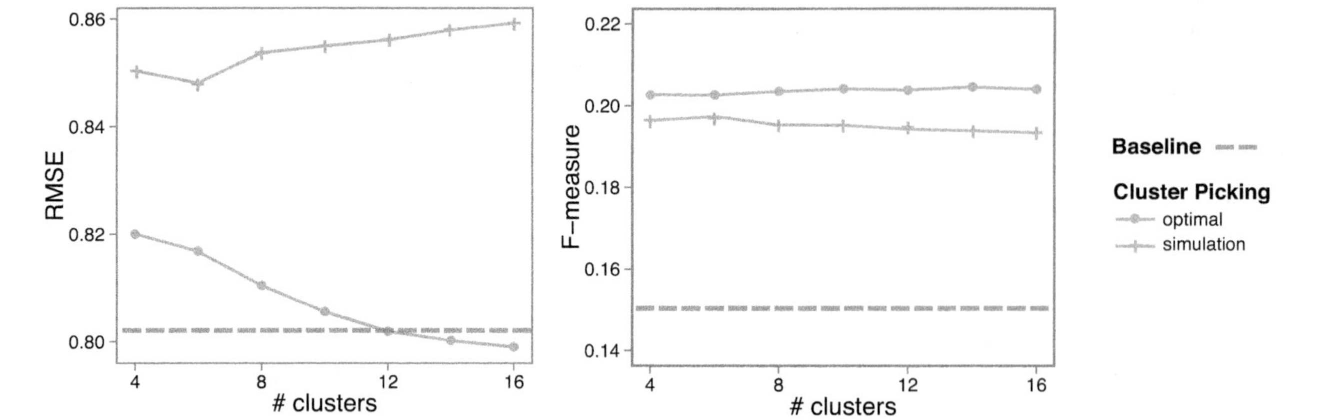

Figure 3. Results of simulated group-based preference elicitation compared to a baseline. "Baseline" shows the performance of the rate 15 movies process. The two simulated cluster-picking strategies are "simulation", where users pick the cluster with movies they've rated the highest, and "optimal", where users pick the cluster that results in the best predictions. Lower RMSE scores are better and higher F-measure scores are better. The chart on the left shows that prediction accuracy is slightly worse than the baseline in most cases while the chart on the right shows that recommendation accuracy is significantly improved compared with the baseline.

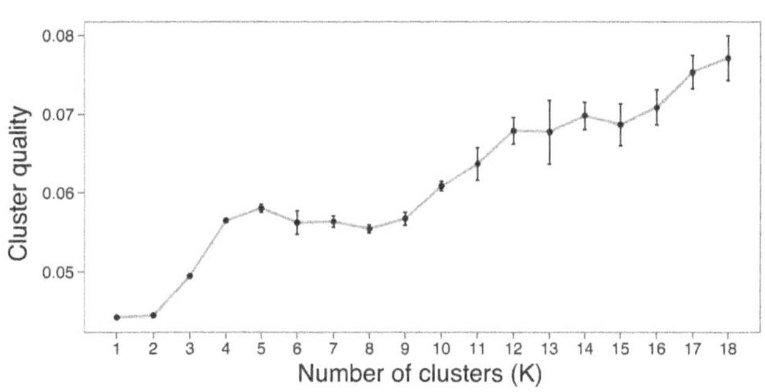

Figure 4. Cluster quality measured by Silhouette Coefficient vs. number of clusters. For each cluster number, we run the clustering algorithm 10 times and plot the standard deviation with error bars. This figure shows two local maxima around 5 and 14 clusters.

RMSE scores are better. For top-N recommendation accuracy, we follow the methodology of [4]. For easy interpretation, we report F-measure scores[4] to combine precision and recall. Higher F-measure scores are better.

Results

The results of the simulation is summarized in Figure 3.

RQ2-Quality of recommendation.

Group-based preference elicitation has better average top N recommendation accuracy (in aggregate, $F > 0.19$ for both optimal and simulation conditions) than the baseline (in aggregate, $F = 0.15$). In other words, the top N recommendation list generated from our group-based process contains more movies that users may be interested in.

We find that the optimal prediction accuracy of group-based preference elicitation varies with the number of clusters, but in general is close to the baseline (in aggregate, $RMSE = 0.804$ for the baseline condition, and $RMSE = 0.801$ for the group-based process when the number of clusters is 12). However, the actual prediction accuracy is likely to be worse than baseline. E.g., the RMSE is 0.856 when simulating 12 clusters. This is as expected, because 15 ratings provide information about user rating patterns, such as the tendency to rate higher or lower on average than other users; cluster-based preference elicitation doesn't provide such information.

Our simulation gives us evidence that the group-based method will provide better top N recommendation accuracy but slightly worse prediction accuracy. This tells us that our method is feasible, especially considering prior research [15, 21] that argues prediction accuracy is less relevant to the end user experience than recommendation accuracy.

Number of clusters.

One goal of this simulation is to inform our design choices concerning the best number of groups to display to users. As shown in Figure 3, the theoretical bound for prediction accuracy improves with the number of clusters. This is intuitive because as the number of clusters increases, the groups of items become smaller and more homogeneous - these smaller groups may better capture user preferences.

However, we see two potential downsides to increasing the number of clusters. First, this improvement is likely gained at the cost of increasing user effort: the act of picking one movie group from sixteen choices is intuitively harder than picking one movie group from four choices. Second, when we simulate cluster-picking behaviour using highest average ratings rather than the optimal method, we find that RMSE increases slightly with the number of clusters. This indicates the possibil-

[4] $F - measure = \frac{Precision * Recall}{Precision + Recall}$

ity that in a real-world system, increasing the number of choices will decrease the chances of users picking the best cluster in terms of the resulting prediction accuracy.

We also measure the quality of clusters using the Silhouette coefficient [27]. Silhouette coefficient values range from -1 for poor clustering to 1 for good clustering. We plot the Silhouette coefficient for a varying number of clusters (K) in Figure 4. This figure shows a general trend of increasing cluster quality as K increases, and the presence of two local maxima around 5 and 14 clusters.

Combining these results, we find that there is a trade-off in increasing the number of groups for our preference elicitation process: we can have high quality groups and the best prediction accuracy with many groups, or we can minimize user effort with few groups. We investigate this trade-off in our user experiment (below).

USER EXPERIMENT

We conduct an online user experiment to evaluate both *RQ1-Minimal user effort* and *RQ2-Quality of recommendation* with real users. We invite MovieLens users to participate in this experiment, comparing the performance of our group-based process with a baseline process that is currently used in MovieLens. In addition to the offline simulation work discussed above, this user experiment can shed light on user effort and subjective perception of recommendation quality.

Method.

We invite recently active MovieLens users to participate, using the same selection criteria as the feasibility study (see above). We send emails to 2.8K users and receive 342 responses between May 18 and May 23, 2014. This group of users is already familiar with the MovieLens recommender system.

We ask users to complete two tasks, using an experimental interface designed for this evaluation.[5] First, users pick one or more groups (see experimental conditions below) from our prototype interface, shown in Figure 1. Users then answer survey questions about the process of picking among the groups, and evaluate a top 10 list of recommended movies that is generated based on their group choices. Second, users evaluate a top 10 movie list generated based on their historical first 15 ratings after signing up for MovieLens. The order of the above two tasks is randomized. Users are not aware of how the recommendation lists are generated. We can evaluate *RQ2-Quality of recommendation* based on survey responses about the two recommendation lists, and we can evaluate *RQ1-User effort* by measuring the time users take picking groups and based on survey responses about perceived ease-of-use.

[5]The experimental interface was available by invitation only on a members-only preview version of Movielens (http://beta.movielens.org) that was not publicly available at the time of writing.

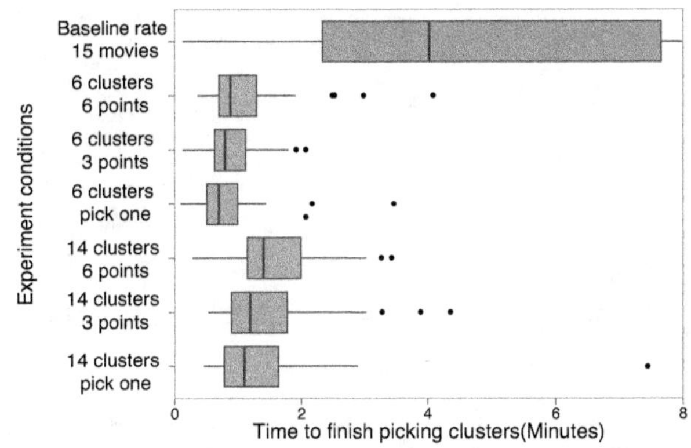

Figure 5. Time to finish preference elicitation process. Time is measured in minutes. The group-based approach takes less than half as long as the baseline, on average.

For the group-based process, we have a 2x2x3 between-subjects design with the following three factors:

1. *Order.* The order in which the user evaluates the two top-10 movie lists. We include this condition to make sure that there is no order effect.
2. *Number of groups.* The number of movie groups to display to the user. We experiment with 6 groups and 14 groups, based on our findings and open questions from the quantitative analysis discussed above. Further, considering UI design, we pick an even number of groups to better organize them in the interface.
3. *Group-picking interface.* The interface given to users for picking groups. We experiment with three conditions: picking one favorite movie group, and distributing either 3 or 6 points across movie groups (multiple points may be given to a single group). These values are chosen based on the design space analysis discussed above.

Users are randomly assigned to one of the twelve experimental conditions. All survey questions have likert scale answers ranging from strongly disagree to strongly agree.

Results

RQ1 - Minimal user effort.

Time. We examine the time spent by subjects picking movie groups as an objective metric measuring user effort. We compare the time required in the new process to the time required by the baseline rate 15 process, as measured by a historical analysis of 27,226 new users who signed up to MovieLens between Jan. 1, 2008 and Dec. 31, 2010. We show a summary of the results in Figure 5. Users spend more time as the interface becomes more expressive (more groups or more points). However, even for the most time-consuming task - distributing 6 points across 14 groups - the median time is only 1.5 minutes. This is less than half of the median time (4 minutes) that users have historically spent in the rate 15 baseline process!

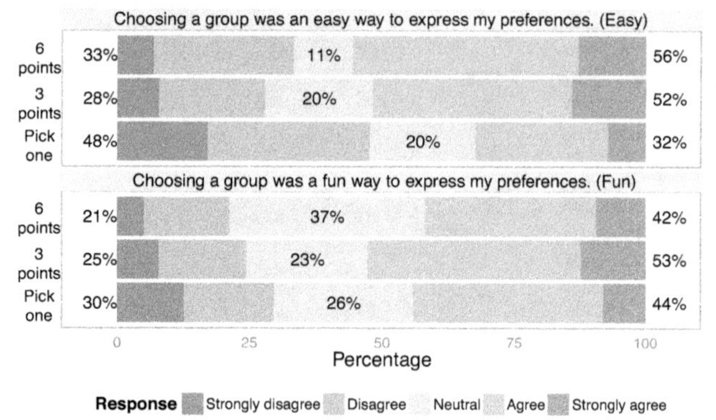

Figure 6. Survey results about the easiness and fun of our group-picking process. We compare picking one group with distributing 3 or 6 points across groups. The percentages summarize the responses after combining disagree/strongly disagree, and agree/strongly agree. Respondents think point allocation is easier and more fun than picking a single favorite.

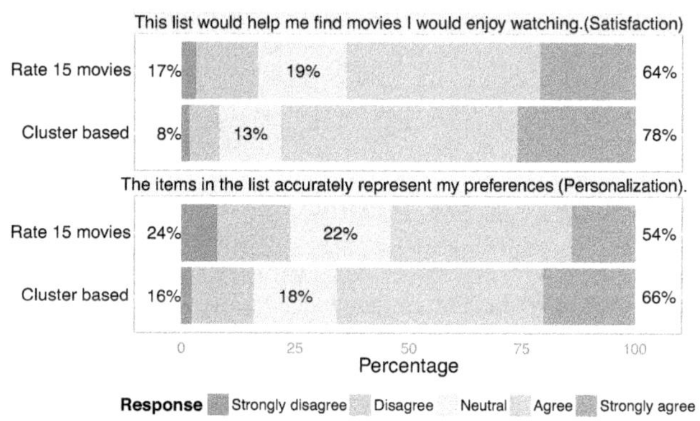

Figure 7. Survey results about recommendation quality, comparing our group-based process with the baseline rate 15 process. The percentages summarize the responses after combining disagree/strongly disagree, and agree/strongly agree. Respondents answer more positively concerning the group-based recommendations.

Subjective feedback. To evaluate whether the group-picking interface is easy and fun, we asked users two likert scale questions about the process. We did not find statistically significant differences in user responses when comparing users in the 6 and 14 group conditions. However, we did find that varying the group-picking interface had an effect on perceived ease of use. Interestingly, although picking one group is the task that takes the least time to finish (Figure 5), users think that this is the hardest task (p value < 0.001, Wilcoxon test [32]). In fact, we received an email from one user speaking to this point:

"I'm finding that my movie preferences cannot be accurately described by selecting just one group of three movies."

Point allocation gives more flexibility and more control to users in expressing their preferences.

Table 2. User-expressed familiarity with recommended movies and prediction accuracy. Familiarity is represented by the average number of movies (out of 10) that users had heard of or seen. Prediction accuracy is measured by average RMSE.

Method	Heard of	Seen	RMSE
Rate 15 movies baseline	8.5	6.7	0.784
Group-based	9.0	7.4	0.797

RQ2 - Quality of recommendation.

Top N recommendation accuracy. To evaluate the resulting recommendation accuracy of the group-based process, we ask users to evaluate two lists of recommendations in randomized order. One of these lists is generated based on the user's group choice(s), and the other is generated based on their initial 15 ratings in MovieLens. Based on these data, we can perform a within-subjects comparison of user perceptions of recommendation quality. Figure 7 shows the responses to two questions related to this goal - one about general satisfaction and another about personalization. Users rate both factors higher for the group-based method (p values ~ 0, paired Wilcoxon test). Specifically, users felt that lists from the group-based recommender would better help them "find movies I would enjoy watching" and "accurately represent my preferences". These results echo the earlier findings from our offline simulation of top N recommendation accuracy. Note that satisfaction and personalization are both rated higher on average by users in the point allocation conditions (as compared with the pick one condition), but these differences are not statistically significant.

We also ask users to count the number of movies that they have heard of or seen from the list of recommended movies. Results are shown in Table 2. The group-based method recommends movies that users are more familiar with.

Prediction accuracy. We also evaluate the prediction accuracy of the group-based method. For each user, we make predictions on all movies except their first 15 rated movies. These prediction are either based on their group choices or their historical first 15 ratings. The average RMSEs are summarized in Table 2. Consistent with findings from the offline simulation study, the group-based method has slightly worse prediction accuracy (0.797 vs. 0.784). It is, however, unclear if this small difference in accuracy would be perceptible to users.

To summarize, the group-based method reduces user effort and improves top N recommendation quality, while potentially losing some prediction accuracy. Most importantly, users are more satisfied and get better personalization from the resulting top N recommendations, which is the fundamental goal of most recommender systems.

DISCUSSION

In this research, we develop a new process for preference elicitation in recommender systems based on the idea that recommender systems may bootstrap new users more effectively by having them express preferences for groups of items rather than individual items. We evaluate this process with the dual goals of *minimal user effort* and *high quality recommendation*. A user experiment showed that our method succeeded. Compared to a baseline condition where users rate 15 movies - mirroring a process that has been in production on movielens.org for over a decade - the new process is much faster and leads to more highly-evaluated recommendation lists.

We claim that the process described here is generalizable to any collaborative filtering recommender system. Implementers must create groups of ratable entities, and then present those groups to users in an understandable fashion to collect their expressions of preference. Once users have expressed their preferences for those item groups, our algorithm for building a pseudo-ratings profile can be used to bootstrap personalization.

Our process depends on high-quality methods for grouping ratable entities. In this work, we apply a Spectral Clustering algorithm. In addition to the evaluation already presented, we asked subjects in our experiment to evaluate the scrutability of the movie groups. Figure 8 summarizes their responses. 80% of subjects understood the types of movies in each group, giving us confidence that our clustering algorithm resulted in good separation. Additionally, most subjects agreed that displaying three movies (89%) and three tags (74%) helped them to understand the movie groups. In other questions, we learned that subjects felt that three tags was about the right number to display, while showing one or two additional movies for each group might be better. Future work might explore these or other interface-oriented questions in more depth. By extension, as noted in the design challenges section, there are many possible interfaces for the display and collection of preference data on groups of items - future work might explore different alternatives such as ratings- or ranking-based interfaces.

Why was our group-based method highly evaluated by users? One explanation is that our method resulted in more familiar recommendations (see Table 2) - recent work [22] found that too much novelty in top-N recommendation lists harms user perceptions of those lists. It is possible that this increased familiarity would be lead to lower evaluations over time; however, in the context of new user recommendations, we are more interested in maximizing first impressions to establish trust in the system. A second explanation is that our method was perceived by users to be more transparent because of its group-oriented interaction design. We are not sure how users perceive the inner workings of these types of algorithms; future work might investigate how users perceive the relationship between their expressions of preferences and algorithmic "decision making". A third explanation is that by clustering on dense rating matrix from active users, we achieve high quality representation of the movie space. Asking new users to express their preference on the movie groups is more efficient than eliciting ratings on individual movies. It is worth pointing out that we can not decouple these possible reasons for better user satisfaction, because our experiment is only one exploration in the design space of preference elicitation process. We need controlled experiment over these factors to understand the keys to a successful design.

LIMITATIONS AND FUTURE WORK

One limitation of our cluster-based process is that users exit the preference elicitation process with no ratings data. Therefore, a user's initial experience is semi-personalized, based on a weighted combination of pseudo-profiles. To achieve fully ratings-based personalization, users still must express their preferences about items directly. This leads to a practical question: how should the system transition users away from this semi-personalized profile to a ratings-based profile? One approach would be to simply cut over to a user model based on ratings data at a discrete cutoff point (e.g., 20 ratings). Alternatively, the system could use some weighted combination of the outputs of the group-based and ratings-based models until users hit the cutoff point. This question of how to transition gracefully from one recommendation model to another as a user adds data is contextually broader than other questions we have addressed in this paper (i.e., it applies to all recommender systems, not just ratings-based ones) and is an interesting direction for future work.

There are several limitations of the methods employed in this research. Most importantly, we studied experienced users of MovieLens rather than new users as they entered the system. This granted us more confidence in subjects' abilities to evaluate items and recommendation lists, but did not allow us to directly compare their evaluation of user experience between the rate-15 process and our new process. In addition, we chose to perform our evaluation in the movie domain, which is different from other domains. Although we suspect our fundamental idea of picking favorite groups of items is generalizable, we have no evidence of that. Finally, it is important to note that we only compare top-10 recommendation lists - we have not examined whether system recommendations are better or worse as users venture deeper into lists of recommended items.

Future work might extend the ideas presented here more broadly to a variety of social computing systems. Many existing systems already ask users to import their contacts from other social networking platforms such as Facebook or Twitter. It is an interesting question whether this social network-based approach to bootstrapping personalization results in recommendations that are as high quality as those that would result from choosing among groups of content. For example, the social curation site Pinterest asks new users to choose among a set of predefined categories to specify their

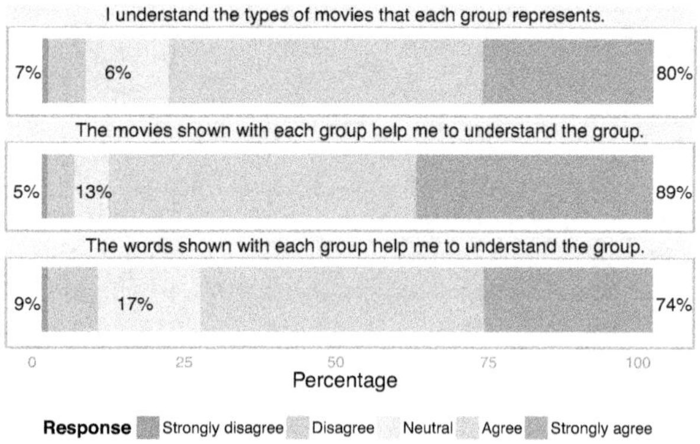

Figure 8. Survey response regarding the whether the groups are comprehensible. The percentages summarize the responses after combining disagree/strongly disagree, and agree/strongly agree. The movie groups presented to users were scrutable; both the example movies and the example tags contributed to this outcome.

interests, and to import their social network from Facebook. Could this process be improved though the use of automated clustering algorithms? What are the most effective ways of combining users' social networking information with the results of the content-based preference elicitation process to form a coherent user profile?

CONCLUSION

Research in bootstrapping new users in personalized systems has to date been largely dominated by algorithmic work seeking to optimize interfaces that elicit item ratings. In this work, we advance the idea that this classical interface design does not necessarily lead to the best user experience, nor the best personalization outcomes. Clearly, the process introduced in this paper is simply one of many possible improvements, and we expect that our process will be improved upon. Further exploratory work is needed to find interaction designs that make the new user experience more efficient (and fun!) while contributing rich information towards user profiles.

ACKNOWLEDGEMENT

We thank anonymous reviewers for providing valuable feedback to our paper. We also acknowledge the thoughtful discussions and helpful feedback from Daniel Kluver, Michael Ekstrand, and other members of GroupLens Research. Finally, we thank National Science Foundation for funding this research with awards IIS-1212338 and IIS-1210863.

REFERENCES

1. S. Bostandjiev, J. O'Donovan, and T. Höllerer. TasteWeights. In *RecSys*, New York, New York, USA, 2012.
2. S. Chang, V. Kumar, E. Gilbert, and L. Terveen. Specialization, homophily, and gender in a social curation site: Findings from pinterest. In *CSCW*, 2014.
3. S. Chang and A. Pal. Routing questions for collaborative answering in community question answering. ASONAM, Niagara, Ontario, Canada, 2013. ACM.
4. P. Cremonesi, Y. Koren, and R. Turrin. Performance of recommender algorithms on top-n recommendation tasks. In *RecSys*, Barcelona, Spain, 2010. ACM.
5. C. Desrosiers and G. Karypis. A comprehensive survey of neighborhood-based recommendation methods. In F. Ricci, L. Rokach, B. Shapira, and P. B. Kantor, editors, *Recommender Systems Handbook*, pages 107–144. Springer US, 2011.
6. S. Drenner, S. Sen, and L. Terveen. Crafting the initial user experience to achieve community goals. In *RecSys*. ACM Press, 2008.
7. M. D. Ekstrand, M. Ludwig, J. A. Konstan, and J. T. Riedl. Rethinking the recommender research ecosystem: Reproducibility, openness, and lenskit. RecSys, Chicago, Illinois, USA, 2011. ACM.
8. M. Elahi, F. Ricci, and N. Rubens. Active learning strategies for rating elicitation in collaborative filtering. *ACM Transactions on Intelligent Systems and Technology*, 5(1):1–33, 2013.
9. S. Fortunato. Community detection in graphs. *Physics Reports*, 486(3–5):75 – 174, 2010.
10. B. J. Frey and D. Dueck. Clustering by passing messages between data points. *Science*, 315(5814):972–976.
11. S. Funk. Netflix update: Try this at home. *http://sifter.org/ simon/journal/20061211.html*, 2006.
12. N. Golbandi, Y. Koren, and R. Lempel. On bootstrapping recommender systems. In *CIKM*, New York, New York, USA, 2010.
13. N. Golbandi, Y. Koren, and R. Lempel. Adaptive bootstrapping of recommender systems using decision trees. *WSDM*, 2011.
14. B. Gretarsson, J. O'Donovan, S. Bostandjiev, C. Hall, and T. Höllerer. SmallWorlds: Visualizing Social Recommendations. *Computer Graphics Forum*, 29(3):833–842, 2010.
15. A. Gunawardana and G. Shani. A survey of accuracy evaluation metrics of recommendation tasks. *J. Mach. Learn. Res.*, 10:2935–2962, Dec. 2009.
16. J. L. Herlocker, J. A. Konstan, L. G. Terveen, John, and T. Riedl. Evaluating collaborative filtering recommender systems. *ACM Transactions on Information Systems*, 22:5–53, 2004.
17. J. Konstan and J. Riedl. Recommender systems: from algorithms to user experience. *User Modeling and User-Adapted Interaction*, 22(1-2):101–123, 2012.

18. R. Kraut, M. Burke, and J. Riedl. Dealing with newcomers.
19. B. Loepp, T. Hussein, and J. Ziegler. Choice-based preference elicitation for collaborative filtering recommender systems. In *CHI*, pages 3085–3094, New York, New York, USA, 2014.
20. S. M. McNee, S. K. Lam, J. A. Konstan, and J. Riedl. Interfaces for eliciting new user preferences in recommender systems. pages 178–187, 2003.
21. S. M. McNee, J. Riedl, and J. A. Konstan. Being accurate is not enough: How accuracy metrics have hurt recommender systems. In *CHI Extended Abstracts*. ACM, 2006.
22. M. W. Michael Ekstrand, F. Maxwell Harper and J. Konstan. User perception of differences in movie recommendation algorithms. In *Recsys*, 2014.
23. A. Y. Ng, M. I. Jordan, and Y. Weiss. On spectral clustering: Analysis and an algorithm. In *NIPS*, pages 849–856. MIT Press, 2001.
24. A. Rashid, I. Albert, and D. Cosley. Getting to know you: learning new user preferences in recommender systems. *IUI*, 2002.
25. A. Rashid, G. Karypis, and J. Riedl. Learning preferences of new users in recommender systems: an information theoretic approach. *ACM SIGKDD Explorations Newsletter*, 2008.
26. P. Resnick, N. Iacovou, M. Suchak, P. Bergstrom, and J. Riedl. GroupLens: an open architecture for collaborative filtering of netnews. In *CSCW*, 1994.
27. P. J. Rousseeuw. Silhouettes: A graphical aid to the interpretation and validation of cluster analysis. *Journal of Computational and Applied Mathematics*, 20(0):53 – 65, 1987.
28. N. Rubens, D. Kaplan, and M. Sugiyama. Active learning in recommender systems. In F. Ricci, L. Rokach, B. Shapira, and P. B. Kantor, editors, *Recommender Systems Handbook*, pages 735–767. Springer US, 2011.
29. G. Shani and A. Gunawardana. Evaluating recommendation systems. In *Recommender Systems Handbook*, pages 257–297. Springer US, 2011.
30. M. Sun, F. Li, J. Lee, and K. Zhou. Learning multiple-question decision trees for cold-start recommendation. *WSDM*, 2013.
31. J. Vig, S. Sen, and J. Riedl. The Tag Genome. *ACM Transactions on Interactive Intelligent Systems*, 2(3):1–44, 2012.
32. F. Wilcoxon. Individual comparisons by ranking methods. In S. Kotz and N. Johnson, editors, *Breakthroughs in Statistics*, Springer Series in Statistics, pages 196–202. Springer New York, 1992.
33. C. Zhong, M. Salehi, S. Shah, M. Cobzarenco, N. Sastry, and M. Cha. Social bootstrapping: how pinterest and last. fm social communities benefit by borrowing links from facebook. In *WWW*, 2014.

Understanding Online Reviews: Funny, Cool or Useful?

Saeideh Bakhshi
Yahoo Labs
San Fransisco, CA
sbakhshi@yahoo-inc.com

Partha Kanuparthy
Yahoo Labs
Sunnyvale, CA
parthak@yahoo-inc.com

David A. Shamma
Yahoo Labs
San Fransisco, CA
aymans@acm.org

ABSTRACT
Increasingly online reviews are relied upon to make choices about the purchases and services we use daily. Businesses, on the other hand, depend on online review sites to find new customers and understand people's perception of them. In order for an online review community to be effective to both users and businesses, it is important to understand what constitutes a high quality review as perceived by people, and how to maximize quality of reviews in the community. In this paper, we study Yelp to answer these questions. We analyze about 230,000 reviews and member interaction ("votes") with these reviews. We find that active and regular members are the highest contributors to good quality reviews and longer reviews have higher chances of being popular in the community. We find that reviews voted "useful" tend to be the early ones for a specific business. Our findings have implications on enabling high quality member contributions and community effectiveness. We discuss the implications to design of social systems with diverse feedback signals.

Author Keywords
Yelp; Online Reviews; Social Signals; Votes; Social Feedback; Zero Inflated Negative Binomial Regression; Funny, Cool, Useful Votes

ACM Classification Keywords
H.4 Information Systems Applications: Miscellaneous; D.2.8 Software Engineering: Metrics—*complexity measures, performance measures*

INTRODUCTION
Online review sites such as Yelp are important and widely-used resources that enable members to share their experiences with products, services and activities in the form of reviews and ratings at scale—which may otherwise be difficult to ascertain before receipt of the service or product. Over 139 million unique users visited Yelp in the mid 2014 and had over 67 million reviews [1]. Research has shown that consumers perceive online review sites as unbiased sources of information when compared with business websites [11].

CSCW '15, March 14 - 18 2015, Vancouver, BC, Canada.

http://dx.doi.org/10.1145/2675133.2675275

Online review sites are only as good as the content their users provide. It is critical for an online community to provide mechanisms that encourage contributions from members, and at the same time, and perhaps even more important, to have *high quality* contributions that engage users. Unfortunately, the abundance of user-generated content comes at a price: for every interesting opinion or helpful review, there are content and opinions that are unhelpful, subjective or misleading. Sifting through large quantities of reviews to identify high quality and useful information is a tedious and error-prone process. Online review sites typically use crowd-sourced methods to rank reviews. An example of such a social evaluation mechanism is the Yelp *review votes*, that enable members to flag a review as *funny*, *cool* and/or *useful*. Understanding social evaluation of reviews can aid review sites design mechanisms to improve the quality of contributions.

Yelp is an online community where people review and rate businesses. Users of Yelp can search for businesses using keywords. Yelp allows users to *interact* with each other by voting others' reviews, and by following activity of their friends. In this work, we ask three research questions: *(i)* What are the factors behind engaging reviews? *(ii)* What is the nature of reviews voted funny, cool or useful (social feedback)? and *(iii)* How do these votes relate to user ratings of establishing quality?

We use a large dataset from Yelp from the Greater Phoenix metropolitan area in the USA. We study 43,873 reviewers and their 229,907 reviews of 11,537 businesses, spanning 2005 to 2013. While our data and analysis is specific to Yelp, the implications and research questions we answer are general and may apply to online review communities in general.

We find that members who are active for longer periods of time tend to be more significant contributors of quality reviews. We find that reviews that members find funny tend to be negative in tone. We also find that there is a direct relationship between social evaluation and individual evaluation: funny reviews tend to have low contributor ratings, while cool reviews tend to have high ratings. Our results also suggest that readers tend to like long and objective reviews.

Our study highlights insights on online review communities, and brings implications for design of recommendation communities to promote high quality contributions by members. We show mechanisms that can encourage longer reviews, provide incentives for new members to contribute and review new businesses, and significantly improve quality of contributions. Further, our findings on Yelp's social feedback system inspires design of distinct signals in other social platforms.

RELATED WORK

General aspects of online user engagement have been discussed in detail in prior work [19, 27]. One common way to study user engagement is through peer evaluation. For a user, feedback from fellow members could lead to future participatory behavior. Theories of reciprocity [9, 14], reinforcement [22], and the need to belong [5] suggest that feedback from other users should predict long term participation on the part of the users. For example, users of the online news community Slashdot whose first comments received positive numeric ratings returned significantly faster to the site to post a second comment, and when their first comment received a reply, they also tended to return more quickly [18]. Controlled experiments also show that social approval in the form of messaging increases a user's number of contributions [8].

To encourage both creators of content and the readers to engage with the site, many online communities provide users with a feedback system. Facebook likes, Twitter's favorites or retweets, Amazon's helpful votes on reviews and Yelp's useful, cool and funny votes are all examples of such systems. Prior research suggests that perceived attributes of the review text, reviewer and social context may all shape consumer response to reviews [2, 20]. It has been shown that even exogenous factors such as weather and demographics of users might impact the ratings and reviews [3].

There is a body of work on analyzing product reviews and postings in forums. Lu et al. use a latent topic approach to extract rated quality aspects from comments in Ebay [20]. Another work looked at the temporal development of product ratings and their helpfulness and dependencies on factors such as the number of reviews or effort required (writing review vs. just assigning a rating) [26]. A 2008 work looked at the helpfulness of answers on the Yahoo Answers site and the influence of variables such as required type of answer and the topic domain of the question [15]. A study on Amazon reviews looked at the helpfulness scores and found that the helpfulness scores are not only dependent on the content of the review but also on other reviews posted for the product [10]. More recently, we ran a study on Yelp, to indetify whether the social signals of a review are indicative of review's rating and sentiment [4]. While there have been studies on understanding and predicting helpful votes, we do not know much about what factors shape the other social signals such as cool and funny votes on Yelp.

DATA

We use a publicly released dataset from Yelp to answer our research questions[1]. Yelp is a large online review community that is also a member-maintained business and service directory. The Yelp dataset consists of a sample of Yelp data from the Greater Phoenix Arizona metropolitan area. It includes 11,537 businesses, 43,873 reviewers and 229,907 reviews. The data spans 2005 to 2013.

Businesses listed on Yelp have three prominent review attributes that a user sees: an average "stars" rating (scale of one to five), the number of reviews and the reviews themselves (along with ratings). We process the review timestamps for a business to measure the *active period*, defined as the duration between the first and last reviews written on Yelp for that business. We use active period to account for time when a business was not operational (e.g., if it was established after our dataset started, or ended before the dataset finished).

Variable	μ	σ	$\tilde{x}$	Max
cool votes	0.85	1.93	0	117
funny votes	0.85	1.82	0	70
useful votes	1.38	2.28	1	120
all votes	2.91	5.56	1	237

Table 1. Distributions of dependent variables used in this paper as the mean (μ), standard deviation (σ), median ($\tilde{x}$), and maximum of the distributions.

As in any online review community, Yelp members contribute reviews for businesses. A review consists of a stars rating and a review text. In order to understand the effect of review text, we process the text for each review to quantify the *subjectivity* (between 0 and 1) and *polarity* (between -1 and 1) of the text using the Pattern Toolkit [23]. We have used the number of words in the review as a measure of the length of the review. Yelp users can vote a review as one or more of *cool*, *funny* and *useful*. We use these vote counts, along with total number of votes, as a measure of review social feedback.

We quantify reviewer activity on the site by looking at the number of reviews the reviewer writes, and the votes (*cool*, *funny* and *useful*) those reviews get from other Yelp users. We also consider the average stars the reviewer uses in her reviews. We process a user profile to compute two metrics: *(i)* activity duration, defined as the duration between the first and last review written on Yelp and *(ii)* activity rate, defined as the number of reviews written divided by the activity duration. For example an activity rate of 0.2 implies that on an average, the reviewer wrote one review every five days during the active period.

We expect that demographics in the location of a business can have an impact on reviews and ratings of a business [3]. All businesses in our data are from the same metropolitan area; however, they are located in different neighborhoods (qualified by latitude-longitude), each with its own demographics. We analyze the effect of user diversity by including demographic factors in the neighborhood of the business. For each business, we collect two dimensions of demographics at the business location (latitude-longitude or neighborhood). First, We collect the *median income* for residents in the location. Second, we collect the *education level* for that location, defined as the fraction of residents who have a bachelors degree or higher. This was collected from the US National Broadband Map for demographics data[2].

[1]`https://www.yelp.com/dataset_challenge`

[2]`http://www.broadbandmap.gov`

Type	Variable	Quality count model β	$Pr(>\|z\|)$	Funny count model β	$Pr(>\|z\|)$	Cool count model β	$Pr(>\|z\|)$	Useful count model β	$Pr(>\|z\|)$
	(Intercept)	0.82	$< 10^{-15}$	−0.70	$< 10^{-15}$	−0.46	$< 10^{-15}$	0.14	$< 10^{-15}$
	Log(theta)	−0.13	$< 10^{-15}$	−0.50	$< 2^{-15}$	−0.03	$< 10^{-3}$	0.52	$< 10^{-15}$
Business	business stars	0.00	$< 10^{-9}$	0.00	$< 10^{-3}$	0.02	$< 10^{-4}$	0.03	$< 10^{-15}$
	business active days	−0.01	$< 10^{-5}$	0.03	$< 10^{-5}$	0.02	$< 10^{-4}$	−0.04	$< 10^{-15}$
	business review count	0.07	$< 10^{-15}$	0.08	$< 10^{-15}$	0.08	$< 10^{-15}$	0.07	$< 10^{-15}$
	median Income	−0.04	$< 10^{-15}$	−0.03	$< 10^{-8}$	−0.02	$< 10^{-7}$	−0.02	$< 10^{-7}$
	education Bachelor+	−0.04	$< 10^{-15}$	−0.05	$< 10^{-15}$	−0.06	$< 10^{-15}$	−0.04	$< 10^{-15}$
Review	review stars	0.02	$< 10^{-5}$	−0.04	$< 10^{-7}$	*0.18*	$< 10^{-15}$	−0.01	$< 10^{-4}$
	polarity	*−0.12*	$< 10^{-15}$	*−0.24*	$< 10^{-15}$	*−0.13*	$< 10^{-15}$	−0.09	$< 10^{-15}$
	subjectivity	−0.01	$< 10^{-4}$	−0.03	$< 10^{-6}$	−0.01	$< 10^{-3}$	−0.02	$< 10^{-5}$
	review words	*0.30*	$< 10^{-15}$	*0.29*	$< 10^{-15}$	*0.27*	$< 10^{-15}$	*0.27*	$< 10^{-15}$
Reviewer	reviewer average stars	0.05	$< 10^{-15}$	0.04	$< 10^{-6}$	*0.16*	$< 10^{-15}$	−0.04	$< 10^{-15}$
	reviewer review count	*0.41*	$< 10^{-15}$	*0.54*	$< 10^{-15}$	*0.53*	$< 10^{-15}$	*0.33*	$< 10^{-15}$
	active days	*0.22*	$< 10^{-15}$	*0.23*	$< 10^{-15}$	*0.24*	$< 10^{-15}$	*0.18*	$< 10^{-15}$

Table 2. The results of zero inflated negative binomial regression for four different models with the dependent variables being the total votes, *funny*, *cool*, and *useful* votes. While the variables effects are all significant ($p < 10^{-3}$) the magnitude and sign of the β coefficient are representative of the variable's effect. For example, the business variables have a very small effect across all the models while the word count of the review (review words) has a larger effect. In the cool count model, the review stars are of consequence but have little effect towards the other models. Effects ≥ 0.10 are marked in *italics*.

FACTORS SHAPING SOCIAL FEEDBACK

There are multiple ways to study the social feedback system on Yelp. These feedback signals provide three different utilities for users: *funny*, *useful*, and *cool* signals. We utilize statistical methods to understand the relationship between review, user and business attributes with these signals; this allows us to understand the relationship between votes given by users to reviews and the reviews themselves. If votes are distributed randomly by people on site, then there would be no consistent relationships. If we find systematic relationships, this suggests votes are used and can be used to evaluate reviews.

We use regression models that take the number of votes (total number of votes as well as *cool*, *funny* and *useful* votes) as their dependent variables; and consider business, review and reviewer features as independent variables. The number of votes is an overdispersed, distributed count variable (See table 1) with a probability function for a zero-inflated negative binomial regression model [7]. We study two types of independent variables: the variables describing the attributes of the review and the variables describing the attributes of the reviewer writing the review. We also consider variables related to the business being reviewed to control for the factors such as business active days and demographics around the business. Table 2 shows the coefficients of our zero-inflated negative binomial regression model for the count model. We consider the count model and effect on reviews with non-zero votes. The regression coefficients allow us to understand the effect of an independent variable on the number of votes (note that to be able to compare coefficients, we z-score all numerical variables before regression).

We use the Chi-square Test to find the statistical significance of our regression models, by computing the reduction in deviance from a *null model*. For our model for the total number of votes, we found the reduction in deviance χ^2 of $(447.1 \times 10^3 - 390.9 \times 10^3)$, or 13%, for 27 degrees of freedom. The test rejected the null hypothesis of a null model ($p < 10^{-15}$); hence, the regression model is well-suited to characterize the effects of the independent variables. We test coefficients of all independent variables for the null hypothesis of a zero-valued coefficient (two-sided) and found that the test rejects the null hypothesis ($p < 10^{-3}$) in all cases.

Active reviewers are more likely to write high quality reviews.

The regression model shows that the activity level of a Yelp user has a significant relationship with the review quality (Table 2). Activity can be quantified as either the number of reviews the reviewer has written (coefficient $\beta = 0.41$, $p < 10^{-15}$) or the duration the user has been reviewing on Yelp ($\beta = 0.22$, $p < 10^{-15}$). We can explain this relationship through the knowledge and experience an active user gains from the Yelp community: active users have the advantage of gaining knowledge about the community and its interests. Such knowledge may reflect on the quality of reviews experienced members write. Prior studies have shown that one of the reasons people join online communities is to access information and gain knowledge [17, 25].

We see that the average number of stars a reviewer tends to give in her reviews has a small positive coefficient for the number of votes ($\beta = 0.05$, $p < 10^{-15}$). In other words, a user who rates businesses higher might have a slight advantage in receiving votes compared to a reviewer who rates lower. Moreover, activity level of a user is also related to the number of votes the user's reviews receive. One way to explain this relationship is through theories of social identity [12, 16, 24], according to which people form a social identity of values, attitudes and behavioral intentions from the perceived membership in social groups. On the other hand, one could argue that the feedback system might be the encouraging factor to more participation. We know from previous work that theories of reciprocity [9, 14], reinforcement [22], and the need to belong [5] suggest that feedback from other users predicts long term participation on the part of the users.

Longer and objective reviews are the main identifiers of high quality reviews.

The content of a review and how much information it provides can be one of the reasons why reviews get more votes. Indeed, our model shows that the length (number of words) of a review plays a significant role in the number of votes that the review gets ($\beta = 0.3, p < 10^{-15}$). This may be explained by the hypothesis that longer reviews are likely to contain more information about the business, and such reviews are likely written by more dedicated reviewers. In the next section, we show that longer reviews get higher number of useful, cool and funny votes. Our observation on longer reviews also shows that Yelp users tend to prefer to read longer reviews.

Interestingly, certain features of the review text have a negative effect on the number of reviews. Our sentiment analysis shows that sentiment polarity of the review text has a strong negative relationship with the number of votes ($\beta = -0.12$, $p < 10^{-15}$). We also find that subjectivity of the review text has a small but negative relationship with the number of votes ($\beta = -0.01$, $p < 10^{-4}$). These observations show that users perceive objective and less polarized reviews as higher quality than subjective and more polar ones. The coefficient for user rating is positive but small compared to other review features ($\beta = 0.02$, $p < 10^{-5}$).

COOL, FUNNY, USEFUL VOTES

In the previous section, we modeled the total number of votes a review gets and studied the factors shaping review quality. In this section, we try to understand how users perceive (vote) a review. Specifically, what are some differences among funny, cool and useful reviews?

We construct zero-inflated negative binomial regression models for funny, cool and useful votes of a review as a function of reviewer, review and business-related features. The independent variables in our models are similar to those used in the previous section for modeling total number of votes. For all models, we test statistical significance using a Chi-squared Test on reduction of deviance. We find that all tests reject the null hypothesis of a null model ($p < 10^{-15}$). Hence, the models are well suited to characterize the effects of the independent variables. We test coefficients of independent variables for the null hypothesis of a zero-valued coefficient (two-sided) and find that the test rejects the null hypothesis ($p < 10^{-3}$) for all variables.

Funny, cool, and useful votes are correlated with the reviewer's activity and average stars.

We find that the number of reviews a user writes has a strong relationship with all three types of votes that the user's review gets ($\beta_{\text{cool}} = 0.53$, $\beta_{\text{funny}} = 0.54$, $\beta_{\text{useful}} = 0.33$). In addition, we see that a regular Yelp reviewer has higher chances of writing funny or cool-voted reviews; however, the chances of getting useful votes are lower. This suggests that the reviewer's experience has a smaller impact on writing useful reviews compared to writing funny or cool reviews (as perceived by other users). Another explanation could be that while useful votes are given to informative reviews for the wider set of Yelp readers, cool and funny votes are more community oriented as hence are more likely to be given to *Elite* users with higher number of reviews.

The reviewer activity duration has a similar relationship with different types of votes as the number of reviews ($\beta_{\text{cool}} = 0.25$, $\beta_{\text{funny}} = 0.23$, $\beta_{\text{useful}} = 0.18$). This can probably be explained using the hypothesis that older users in the community understand the community and the notions of cool, funny and useful better than new users.

We also find that the average stars a reviewer gives in her ratings is positively correlated with the number of cool, funny and useful votes that her review gets ($\beta_{\text{cool}} = 0.16$, $\beta_{\text{funny}} = 0.04$, $\beta_{\text{useful}} = 0.04$). Further, we find that this correlation is stronger with cool votes compared to funny and useful votes. This suggests that reviewers who rate businesses higher have higher chances of writing reviews that are perceived cool. This could be explained by more positive expectations from cool reviews than from funny ones, given our findings that funny reviews tend to a more negative tone.

Early reviews are usually the most useful ones.

We see that highly reviewed businnesses are more likely to receive funny, cool and useful votes. ($\beta_{\text{funny}} = 0.08$, $\beta_{\text{useful}} = 0.07$, $\beta_{\text{cool}} = 0.09$). This effect is intuitive, we expect that the restaurants with higher number of reviews are more popular, and so more visitors check out their profiles and reviews on Yelp. As a result, the average number of votes on those businesses are expected to be higher than the less reviewed businesses. We also find a small but positive effect of business review stars ($\beta_{\text{cool}} = 0.02$, $\beta_{\text{funny}} < 10^{-2}$, $\beta_{\text{useful}} = 0.03$).

The active duration for a business has a positive effect on funny and cool votes ($\beta_{\text{funny}} = 0.03$, $\beta_{\text{cool}} = 0.02$) but a negative effect on useful votes ($\beta_{\text{useful}} = -0.04$). This observation suggests that the businesses that have been on Yelp for a long time are not likely to receive useful votes, but could receive funny and cool votes. This is a possible indicator of *maturity* of an online community and we find it an interesting observation for a successful community such as Yelp. In a recent work, Gilbert asked a related question [13]: why do reviewers write reviews when there are already enough useful reviews? He found that an overwhelming number of reviewers who write *deja* reviews look for individual status in the online community.

Funny reviews are more negative in tone.

We find that the length (number of words) of a review has a strong correlation with the number of funny, cool and useful votes it gets ($\beta_{\text{cool}} = 0.27$, $\beta_{\text{funny}} = 0.29$, $\beta_{\text{useful}} = 0.27$). This can be explained by considering that longer reviews are likely to have higher information content about the business.

We find a disparity in the coefficients of review stars (ratings) on the different types of votes the review gets. Review stars has a small negative relationship with the funny and useful votes ($\beta_{\text{funny}} = -0.04$, $\beta_{\text{useful}} = -0.01$). However, the relationship of stars is positive and much higher in magnitude with cool votes ($\beta_{\text{cool}} = 0.18$). In other words, higher rated reviews are likely to get cool votes, but are unlikely to get useful or funny votes.

We find that review text is related to all three types of votes. We see that both polarity ($\beta_{\text{cool}} = 0.16$, $\beta_{\text{funny}} = 0.04$, $\beta_{\text{useful}} = 0.04$) and subjectivity ($\beta_{\text{cool}} = 0.16$, $\beta_{\text{funny}} = 0.04$, $\beta_{\text{useful}} = 0.04$) of a review have negative impact on funny, cool and useful votes that the review gets. In addition, polarity has a strong negative relationship with funny votes, showing that polarized and subjective reviews are not likely to be perceived as funny by users. This can be explained in two ways. First, it might be that the general audience on the review sites such as Yelp enjoy reading reviews with "sarcastic" tone or those reviews that criticize the business or service with humor. The second hypothesis could be that users find the lower rated reviews and those with negative tone more funny or humorous. Either way, the observation that higher funny votes are related to the lower rated reviews illustrates an artifact of the what the Yelp user considers funny. Additionally, one could argue that funny votes are used as a negative signal to express *dislike* on the review—since the other voting signals on Yelp have positive connotations, users may have utilized the funny signal to express negative emotions. Unlike the perceptions of funny and useful on the reviews, we also found that reviews that are perceived as cool are more likely to be highly rated. This suggests that the cool perception is usually tied with the higher rated reviews. The lower rated reviews are less likely to be perceived as cool.

IMPLICATIONS AND FUTURE WORK

On Yelp, *funny*, *cool*, and *useful* votes are not random or whimsical signals to attract click engagement, but are actually good measures of quality—quality that is expressed in different ways. Online review communities can rely on member contributions to index and serve recommendations to their users. It is critical to maximize the articulation and the quality of these contributions.

Most social networking sites use *like*, *favorite* or *upvote* signals to capture users interest in a piece of content. Product sites like Amazon allow users to vote reviews as "helpful". Similar to social networking sites, online review communities have adopted various signals to improve user engagement and crowdsource quality control. However, these signals can carry different meanings within themselves. For example, someone can like a photo on Facebook because she likes the person in the photo, or because the photo captures a beautiful scene. Yelp, on the other hand distinguishes the votes by dividing them into three different signals. Each of these signals carry different meanings beyond their specific labels.

Our findings suggest that there are deeper meanings and interaction forms than the generic measure of votes. The Yelp community, for example, judges and communicates meaning through its own interpretation of the signal labels, which is similar to findings in the multimedia community [21]. Future work can elaborate on the use of these labels and their corresponding social perceptions in other communities. For example, what do *likes* on Facebook mean in different contexts and by different people? Is it some form of social confirmation? Do users support the content of the post? How does it relate to Yelp's *cool* and *funny* signals?

Deeper understanding of forms of user feedback can enable designing better recommendation and social networks. For example, mechanisms for users to search for useful reviews or cool reviews or providing them with ranking options based on the number of votes. On the other hand, in social networks with more broad content types, new feedback signals might enable users to interact with the content in a more meaningful way.

Based on our findings, sections of active members can be leveraged to improve contributions by other members. For example, old timers who are active in the community tend to be the people who write the most reviews and get the most votes for their reviews. This is an important finding, since such users are popular in the community, and social mechanisms can be designed to encourage interaction with newer members and as a consequence, quality contributions by newer members.

We showed that longer reviews get more user votes. Community mechanisms to encourage review length or reward reviewers who write longer reviews may help improve review quality. At the same time, such mechanisms should be carefully designed so that they do not discourage reviewers who have a tendency to write short (but useful) reviews from not writing reviews.

New businesses added to an online review community can benefit from initial opinions, especially from old timers, to help gather "review momentum". We found that new businesses have the highest chances of receiving useful reviews in the initial period of their appearance on Yelp. To improve the quality of reviews for such businesses, the community can include incentives for old timers and experienced reviewers to write reviews for new businesses. Such users are influential and can set a trend for better quality reviews for new businesses in the community.

Finally, design of social feedback signals such as Yelp funny, useful and cool votes can encourage conversations around a piece of content. As Brown [6] suggests in his work, review sites are beyond search and recommendation, and can be starting points to conversations around local businesses. By voting a review as useful, the reader conveys that she likes to see more of such reviews. While this can be used in personalizing search and recommendation, it can also start a new conversation between the voter and the reviewer.

CONCLUSION

Online review communities such as Yelp enable people to find right businesses and services, and enable businesses to find new customers and improve profit margins. Hence, it is critical for such communities to maximize high quality member contributions. In this paper, we studied member interaction, reviews and businesses in the Yelp online recommendation community. We found that active and older members tend to contribute significant content. We found several factors that contribute to recommendations that are perceived as *useful*, *cool* or *funny*. For example, we found that reviewers who give higher ratings in their reviews tend to be perceived as writing cool reviews. We found that longer reviews are perceived as *useful*, *cool* and *funny*. We saw that reviews that are negative in tone are more likely to be seen by users as funny. We showed that early businesses listed on Yelp tend to get reviews that are perceived as useful. Our findings have implications on online review community design for improving quality of member contributions.

REFERENCES

1. 10 things you should know about yelp. `http://www.yelp.com/about`, April 2013.
2. Archak, N., Ghose, A., and Ipeirotis, P. G. Show me the money!: deriving the pricing power of product features by mining consumer reviews. In *Proceedings of the 13th ACM SIGKDD international conference on Knowledge discovery and data mining* (2007), 56–65.
3. Bakhshi, S., Kanuparthy, P., and Gilbert, E. Demographics, weather and online reviews: a study of restaurant recommendations. In *Proceedings of the 23rd international conference on World wide web* (2014), 443–454.
4. Bakhshi, S., Kanuparthy, P., and Shamma, D. A. If it is funny, it is mean: Understanding social perceptions of yelp online reviews. In *Proceedings of the international ACM SIGGROUP conference on Supporting group work*, ACM (2014).
5. Baumeister, R. F., and Leary, M. R. The need to belong: desire for interpersonal attachments as a fundamental human motivation. *Psychological bulletin 117*, 3 (1995), 497.
6. Brown, B. Beyond recommendations: Local review web sites and their impact. *ACM Transactions on Computer-Human Interaction (TOCHI) 19*, 4 (2012), 27.
7. Cameron, C. A., and Trivedi, P. K. *Regression Analysis of Count Data (Econometric Society Monographs)*. Cambridge University Press, Sept. 1998.
8. Cheshire, C. Selective incentives and generalized information exchange. *Social Psychology Quarterly 70*, 1 (2007), 82–100.
9. Cialdini, R. B. *Influence (rev): The Psychology of Persuasion*. HarperCollins, 1993.
10. Danescu-Niculescu-Mizil, C., Kossinets, G., Kleinberg, J., and Lee, L. How opinions are received by online communities: a case study on amazon. com helpfulness votes. In *Proceedings of the 18th international conference on World wide web* (2009), 141–150.
11. Dellarocas, C. The digitization of word of mouth: Promise and challenges of online feedback mechanisms. *Management science 49*, 10 (2003), 1407–1424.
12. Ellemers, N., Kortekaas, P., and Ouwerkerk, J. W. Self-categorisation, commitment to the group and group self-esteem as related but distinct aspects of social identity. *European journal of social psychology 29*, 2-3 (1999), 371–389.
13. Gilbert, E., and Karahalios, K. Understanding deja reviewers. In *Proceedings of ACM conference on Computer supported cooperative work* (2010), 225–228.
14. Gouldner, A. W. The norm of reciprocity: A preliminary statement. *American sociological review* (1960), 161–178.
15. Harper, F. M., Raban, D., Rafaeli, S., and Konstan, J. A. Predictors of answer quality in online q&a sites. In *Proceedings of the SIGCHI Conference on Human Factors in Computing Systems* (2008), 865–874.
16. Hogg, M. A. Intragroup processes, group structure and social identity. *Social groups and identities: Developing the legacy of Henri Tajfel 65* (1996), 93.
17. Jones, Q. Virtual-communities, virtual settlements & cyber-archaeology: A theoretical outline. *Journal of Computer-Mediated Communication 3*, 3 (1997), 0–0.
18. Lampe, C., and Johnston, E. Follow the (slash) dot: effects of feedback on new members in an online community. In *Proceedings of the 2005 international ACM SIGGROUP conference on Supporting group work*, ACM (2005), 11–20.
19. Lehmann, J., Lalmas, M., Yom-Tov, E., and Dupret, G. Models of user engagement. In *User Modeling, Adaptation, and Personalization*. Springer, 2012, 164–175.
20. Lu, Y., Zhai, C., and Sundaresan, N. Rated aspect summarization of short comments. In *Proceedings of the 18th international conference on World wide web* (2009), 131–140.
21. Shamma, D. A., Shaw, R., Shafton, P. L., and Liu, Y. Watch what I watch: using community activity to understand content. In *Proceedings of the international workshop on Workshop on multimedia information retrieval*, ACM (2007), 275–284.
22. Skinner, B. F., Ferster, C., and Ferster, C. B. *Schedules of reinforcement*. Copley Publishing Group, 1997.
23. Smedt, D., Daelemans, W., et al. Pattern for python.
24. Tajfel, H. *Social identity and intergroup relations*, vol. 7. Cambridge University Press, 2010.

25. Wellman, B. For a social network analysis of computer networks: a sociological perspective on collaborative work and virtual community. In *Proceedings of the 1996 ACM SIGCPR/SIGMIS conference on Computer personnel research*, ACM (1996), 1–11.

26. Wu, F., and Huberman, B. How public opinion forms. *Internet and Network Economics* (2008), 334–341.

27. Yom-Tov, E., Lalmas, M., Baeza-Yates, R., Dupret, G., Lehmann, J., and Donmez, P. Measuring inter-site engagement. *IEEE International Conference on Big Data* (2013).

Shared Calendars for Home Health Management

Jordan Eschler[1]
jeschler@uw.edu

Logan Kendall[1]
kendall5@uw.edu

Katie O'Leary[1]
katieole@gmail.com

Lisa M. Vizer[1]
lmvizer@gmail.com

Paula Lozano[2]
lozano.p@ghc.org

Jennifer B. McClure[2]
mcclure.j@ghc.org

Wanda Pratt[1]
wpratt@uw.edu

James D. Ralston[2]
ralston.j@ghc.org

[1]Universty of Washington, Seattle, WA

[2]Group Health Research Institute, Seattle, WA

ABSTRACT
What is the role of shared calendars for home health management? Utilizing a maximum variation sampling method, we interviewed 20 adult individuals with diabetes and 20 mothers of children with asthma to understand calendar use in the context of chronic disease home health management. In comparing the experiences of these two groups, we explore participants' use of tools for organizing tasks and appointments, their strategies for capturing health and non-health events in the family calendar system, the ecology of artifacts that intersect with their scheduling tools, and the failures they experienced while managing their calendar systems. Through this work, we offer a context-specific perspective of schedule management strategies for individuals and families who must integrate their handling of chronic illnesses with everyday living.

Author Keywords
Medical and health support; Home/family/intimacy support; Empirical Methods, Qualitative; Workflow management

ACM Classification Keywords
H.5.3 Group and Organization Interfaces

INTRODUCTION
Calendars are crucial to managing daily life in the home [22]. Household calendars depict complex interactions among individual schedules of family members and can convey meaning and values behind the priorities of scheduling [14]. With the importance of the household calendar in mind, we investigate the use of calendars in the home among families who have one or more individuals living with a chronic illness (pediatric asthma or diabetes).

ACM 978-1-4503-2922-4/15/03…$15.00.
http://dx.doi.org/10.1145/2675133.2675168

Individuals living with a chronic illness must perform a large number of daily self-care activities to ensure the best health outcomes [1, 2]. Management of diabetes can include regular activities such as home blood pressure measurements as well as clinical tests to assess blood glucose control [12, 19, 26]. For children with asthma, symptoms are monitored through clinic outpatient visits [10] and caregivers must monitor symptom control and often administer medications on a daily schedule [18]. For individuals with diabetes and asthma, these extra disease management activities take place in addition to the everyday schedule management typical of all families. Thus, we investigate calendar management in this context and explore the strategies that patients with diabetes and caregivers of children with asthma use to meet their health goals and coordinate with clinicians.

Given that our participants must make decisions about prioritizing regular self-care activities, and integrate medical care with their schedule management practices, we explore complicated behaviors in interactions with healthcare information systems and personal calendar tools. Through a user-centered approach we consider the unique context of chronic disease management and build upon previous work in the design space for shared calendar systems in the home. In this paper, we focus on describing the day-to-day routines of patients and caregivers, as well as current patient engagement with provider healthcare information systems. The descriptive work reported here is an initial investigation that provides contextual information to inform future design of user-centered reminder systems in the healthcare and home health management settings.

RELATED WORK
Research in the shared calendar space—of which family calendars are one example—started in the domain of workplace groupware, where electronic calendars were used initially in the workplace context [23]. As adoption in the workplace increased, usage of personal digital assistants and mobile phones blurred the boundaries of calendar management between work and home [9] and led to in-

creased research in personal life and family unit domains. We review the history of investigation of the shared calendar space as well as the limited work on the use of calendars in home health management to build upon and update research in this area.

Groupware calendar use in the workplace context

Payne's [24] investigation of electronic calendar use among professionals revealed that, despite access to a range of software tools for schedule and to-do list management, interviewees continued to use supplementary paper calendars. Calendar tools of any type were critical to "prospective remembering"—that is, remembering to do things and forming intentions for future actions. Payne also found that calendars were valuable for eliciting information about users' intentions and priorities in their lives.

More recent investigations of groupware calendars in the workplace have incorporated the shifting boundaries of work and home calendars, particularly with the adoption of personal digital assistants and mobile phones. Sellen et al. [27] deployed a short survey to working parents and found one highly-ranked concern about the ability to coordinate tasks in real time among family members. Grimes and Brush [9] researched parents who used Microsoft Outlook professionally to explore the overlap between work and personal schedule management through calendar tool use. Parents described failures in being able to share Outlook calendars and coordinate with spouses working in other organizations, but parents also feared judgment from coworkers for entering personal appointments on the shared work calendar. As a result of this study, Grimes and Brush argued for more finely tuned controls over calendar information, with the ability to share or not share event information at the appointment level, rather than the calendar preference level. Mariani et al. [15] also identified user privacy through access controls of event information as an important design feature in electronic calendars.

Sell and Walden [28] found that mobile calendars used among knowledge workers were valuable for managing self-described "hectic" and "volatile" personal schedules. Participants in the study valued certain design features of digital calendars over those of paper calendars, including: the inability to inadvertently double-book time slots; reminder functions that "free up" the brain from remembering upcoming commitments; the backward archive of previous commitments for personal records; and the always-available nature of electronic calendars.

Shared calendar use in personal and intrafamily context

Investigating calendar use in the family context introduces different challenges to the coordination of schedules. The adoption of electronic calendars, personal digital assistants, and mobile phones in the workplace and then in the home has encouraged greater exploration of personal schedule management integrated within the family environment.

Crabtree and Rodden [7] observed that the domestic unit (its inhabited structure, individual actors, and involved technology and coordinating habits) is not strictly analogous to an organizational unit of work, but treating the domestic unit as a discrete subject of interest has thus far yielded valuable ethnographic insights to the "routines" of everyday life therein. Through direct observation of home life, Crabtree and Rodden used physical and locational mapping of family homes to highlight ecologies, activity centers, and coordinating displays of domestic habitat. Further research into calendar management in the home context has identified more complex calendar use among working parents [6], as well as the importance of informal information management practices that supplement calendar management. Informal management of schedules in families identified in Brush and Turner's [6] survey included face to face or email interactions, which enabled coordination between partner parents.

To gather descriptive information around tool use, Brush and Inkpen [5] interviewed 15 families and found linkages between device type and ownership types. For example, mobile phones and iPods were generally individually owned, whereas shared computers in shared areas did not have such individual ownership ties. Ownership of calendar content was explored by Neustaeder et al. [22], who articulated a taxonomy of three calendar content ownership types: monocentric families relied on a sole primary scheduler to maintain the calendar, pericentric families had a primary scheduler, with an occasional secondary scheduler assisting in recording or maintaining calendar content, and polycentric families maintained calendars among multiple schedulers, who would add and edit content as needed. The concepts of device or content ownership in these two studies are valuable in articulating the access and control needs for managing a calendar across family members.

Design-based research into family calendar management includes participatory design with mothers [20] and a pilot field test of the resulting tablet PC-based system, LINC, in four family homes [21]. Using existing knowledge about high-traffic areas in the family home and opportunities for family calendar collaboration, families were encouraged to place the calendar where it could be accessed by all members. In both studies, along with Tungare and Perez-Quinones [31], researchers found a preference for always-on access to shared family calendars among interviewees, meaning that the family members could walk up and immediately access calendar information with minimal start-up time when a digital device tool was used.

Importantly, Bødker and Grönvall [3] moved their scope of family calendar investigation to that of shared goal spaces, which may involve people or organizations outside of the family. The authors presented two case studies of shared-work space calendars designed to aid 1) elder care tasks involving family members, paid caregivers, and clinicians, and 2) parental leave scheduling in a Danish municipality.

This work is unique in its support of family-based goals, with an application of a calendar tool as an artifact of negotiation and coordination among family members and people outside of the family. In this sense, Bødker and Grönvall's research resembles our exploration into current use of calendar artifacts in families to coordinate the "work" of chronic disease management with outside organizations (e.g., the healthcare system) and people (e.g., individual clinicians or specialists involved in family care).

Calendar use in home health management

Other researchers have investigated personal health information management practices in the home and identified calendars as a component of patients' health information management strategy. In one of the first studies of personal health information management in the home, Moen and Brennan identified a variety of strategies—just in time, just because, just at hand, just in case—that people used to remind themselves of health tasks [17]. Although they note calendars as one of many tools used to support those strategies, they did not describe any details for how or why calendars were used. In Klasnja et al.'s [13] study of breast cancer patients, they also noted calendars as an artifact that patients frequently used to help them manage health information while they were out and about. Based on their fieldwork, they also used calendars as a core component in the design of their personal health information management system—HealthWeaver—in linking information to their mobile calendar [14] as well as in coordinating help among patients' social network [29]. Based on their fieldwork of elderly home health management, Bossen et al. also chose to use a calendar system as the main artifact to support care coordination for elderly patients [4]. Thus, several researchers have noted use of calendars in personal health information management, but none have thoroughly documented its role of the calendar in personal or home health information management.

Current study contributions

Previous work in the shared calendar area has investigated calendar groupware use in organizations, user-designated ownership of calendars and content, management of tools between home and work (particularly among working parents), and calendar features that enhance sharing opportunities and user coordination. In this study, we explore calendar use in a specific context: among families who manage chronic health conditions in the home, and face complexities in schedule management related to daily health management activities. By focusing on calendar tool use within a maximum variation sample, we are able to reflect on a range of schedule management behaviors in support of goals for health outcomes and describe perceptions about multiple modalities of calendar control (e.g., paper and electronic calendars) from a holistic, user-centered point of view. We probed successful and unsuccessful strategies for calendar management in this context, with the goal of updating work on taxonomies of shared calendar management, as well as identifying design opportunities for shared calendar and reminder systems that will assist patients and clinicians in managing chronic diseases.

METHODS

Participants were recruited from 18 clinics within an integrated healthcare delivery system in the northwestern United States. Over 300,000 members receive care from these facilities from over 1,000 physicians. This healthcare system has offered patient access to online health services since 2003, including: secure messaging with primary and specialty healthcare providers; ordering medication refills; scheduling in person appointments; viewing summaries of care; viewing results of medical tests; and viewing lists of immunizations, allergies and health conditions. As of May 2014, 74% of those enrolled in the integrated delivery system were registered for these online services [25].

Sample

Adults with Type 2 diabetes (n=20) and mothers of children with asthma (n=20) were recruited using a purposeful sampling framework. Inclusion of these two distinct groups, each managing different aspects of chronic illness, allowed us to maximize the variation in the elicited responses regarding home health care and calendar management. Since both asthma and diabetes require ongoing self-management as well as communication with healthcare providers, we also anticipated that some calendaring and other reminding strategies may be shared across the groups. Our intention was not to compare asthma and diabetes cohort responses, but to gather the widest range of calendar management behaviors for chronic disease management. By collecting the perspectives and needs of a diverse population of chronic disease users we can improve our approach to future design work that incorporates user strategies around both paper and electronic calendars.

All participants were recruited by telephone. Interviews were conducted in the home and ranged from 45 to 90 minutes, including a supplemental home tour during which participants demonstrated where and how they manage their calendars and other relevant home health care. Participants were asked to share information about their health care priorities, day-to-day health care routines, calendar management, frequency and modality of clinical contact, and perceptions about interactions with their healthcare system, specifically how they schedule medical appointments, manage appointment reminders, and utilize patient information artifacts such as after-visit summaries. Each participant was paid $50 for his or her participation.

Interviewees included 10 men (patients with diabetes) and 30 women (10 patients with diabetes and 20 mothers of children with asthma). The median sample age was 54.5, but varied within each sub-sample, with mothers being younger on average than the patients with diabetes. We intentionally oversampled racial and ethnic minorities and sought to recruit a sample with an educational level representative of the United States population. Finally, we sought a mixture of those using and not using the online patient portal services, to reflect growing patient engagement in the electronic health record. Sample characteristics are presented in Table 1.

ANALYSIS

All 40 interviews were transcribed and then imported into qualitative analysis software (Atlas.ti). Four independent coders worked on three coding schema iterations to identify significant themes related to schedule management behaviors, calendaring strategies and artifacts, and home health management. The group of coders used "brainstorming the data" [30] individually as an approach to identify themes during the open coding period. The group then met periodically to review and revise codes to develop consensus around code definitions and their use within the transcripts. To organize the emerging codes and consolidate similar themes, we then used affinity grouping and refinement of code definitions to agree on a final set of codes [16].

Table 1: Sample Cohort Demographics

	Total	Asthma		Diabetes	
	N	N	%	N	%
	40	20	100	20	100
Median Age (Years)	54.5	37.0		64.0	
Mean Age (Years)	54.4	37.5		64.5	
Race & ethnicity					
Asian	2	0	0	2	10
Black	12	6	30	6	30
Hawaiian	1	1	5	0	0
Indian	0	0	0	0	0
Mixed	1	0	0	1	5
Other	2	1	5	1	5
Unknown	2	2	10	0	0
White	20	10	50	10	50
*Hispanic**	2	1	5	1	5
Online health portal use					
User	27	17	85	10	50
Non-user	13	3	15	10	50
Education					
>High school	28	16	80	12	60
High school or less	12	4	20	8	40

*Hispanic ethnicity designation overlapped with other designations of race; total is > 100%

Descriptive overview

Twenty-eight of the 40 total participants indicated that they used a calendar (N=15) or a mobile phone (N=13) as their primary tool to manage the household schedule. However, each cohort demonstrated different primary calendar tool use; participants were asked to indicate which calendar tool they used daily or considered to be the go-to information source for schedule management. Diabetes cohort participants reported wall calendars as a primary tool (N=11, or 55%) more often than mothers (N=4, or 20%), while a greater proportion of mothers used mobile phones (N=11) as a primary tool than diabetes cohort interviewees (N=2).

In addition to the differences in primary tool use, the behavior around sharing calendar information related to tools differed. Shared tools were those that were displayed intentionally in the household (in the case of paper tools) or opened access controls for multiple users (in the case of electronic tools, such as a Google calendar). Tools were shared for the benefit of multiple individuals or for frequent reference. Unshared tools were intentionally private, due to concerns about privacy, preferences for information sharing, or perceived difficulty in managing technology features, such as with mobile calendars. Wall calendars were generally indicated as shared primary tools, whereas mobile phone calendars were largely used as private calendar aids. In Table 2, we summarize the primary schedule management tools used by the study participants. A more detailed overview of tool use is available in Appendix A.

RESULTS

Given the differences in calendar tool use profiles between the participant cohorts, we were interested in investigating themes that reflected the diverse strategies participants used to integrate their health management needs within their regular daily schedules. Using affinity diagramming and iterative coding practices, we identified four major thematic groups: (1) the participant's rationale for particular scheduling tool use; (2) their strategies for capturing events in the family calendar system; (3) their integration of reminder systems into their calendar tools; and (4) the challenges and failure points that they experienced in family calendar and schedule-keeping strategies.

Table 2: Primary tool use reported by each study participant, by cohort

	# reporting **unshared** primary tool	# reporting **shared** primary tool
Asthma moms cohort (N=20)		
paper reference*		1
phone	9	2
tablet		1
wall calendar (paper)		4
whiteboard		2
e-calendar		1
Diabetes cohort (N=20)		
desk calendar	1	1
phone	2	
planner	1	
tablet	1	
wall calendar (paper)	1	10
whiteboard		1
e-calendar	1	1

*Participant primarily used a basket of mail to manage her schedule

Rationale for particular tool use

Throughout the interviews, participants described their reasoning for using a particular calendar tool based on the tool's visibility, accessibility, trust, and ease of use. These qualities strongly influenced whether a participant used a paper-based or electronic system in different situations. When coordination with other family members was paramount, often a simple wall calendar system was used to keep family members informed about the schedule. The paper wall calendars were one of the most widely used tools across our participants and often placed in prominent, high traffic areas to maximize schedule visibility and sharing.

[The calendar is] probably more for [my husband] so that he knows that I have a doctor's appointment that day or something. It's that communication between the two of us more than anything. I probably wouldn't - I might, but I probably wouldn't be as tempted to do it if it were just me alone. (D20)

The participants valued the highly visible tool because it encouraged regular dialogue about upcoming activities and helped avoid last minute coordination. However, although the wall calendars were easily accessible in the home, some participants favored a shared e-calendar for making it easier for multiple family members to manage content regardless of their location. A13 and her family describe how, "We just couldn't keep [our family wall calendar] up to date because we're in so many different places...so we do it online now." The family's polycentric scheduling model was supported best through shared input online by multiple members of the family. In this type of environment, electronic calendars helped to organize and streamline information by reducing the amount of paper clutter (A20).

Despite the growing use of electronic tools, some study participants disliked maintaining schedules in a virtual environment. They highlighted the issue of already spending too much time in front of a mobile phone or other computing device. In addition, the participants who resisted adoption of electronic calendars expressed anxiety about losing data, running out of battery, or lacking technical skills to troubleshoot the tool.

Figure 1: Examples of home calendar systems. Clockwise from top left: A) Whiteboard calendar with paper artifacts attached; B) Shared electronic calendar accessed through tablet computer; C) Dual paper planner and mobile phone calendar system that requires manual information transfer; D) Paper-based system using artifacts from healthcare system and "basket" of related health care items

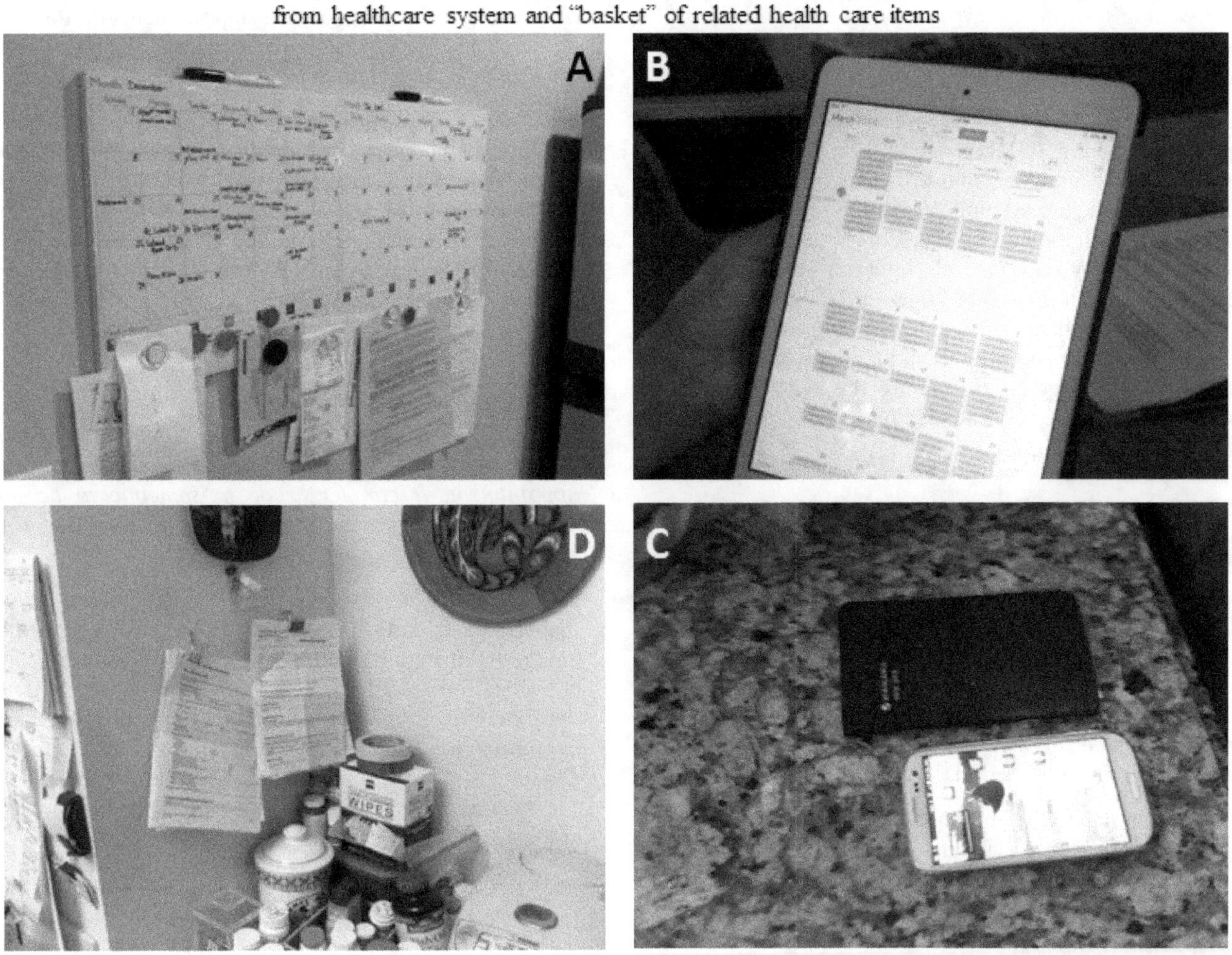

[I] write it on a piece of paper and then I usually put it on the planner because that's what I look at really, that's what I depend on. I don't depend on my phone to have everything in it. Until I get to that point, I just don't see how, I mean what if you need to look at it and there's no more juice in it? (D01)

Regardless of which primary tool a participant used, they often incorporated additional artifacts that supported their schedule management. These artifacts included pre-printed school calendars, appointment cards from a dentist or doctor, letters in the mail, temporary post-it notes, and secondary calendar tools. In most cases, the artifacts served as workarounds to compensate for periodic shortcomings in accessibility to the primary calendar system (e.g. being outside the home). One mother described using the "notes" feature of her mobile phone calendar to temporarily record data when out of cellular range in the workplace (A15). Others found it easier to place a temporary artifact such as an appointment card or soccer schedule in a visible location rather than enter it into the calendar.

I don't know, I feel like I still appreciate both [written and electronic]. Like the dentist office, they'll still hand out the little, it looks like a business card and it shows the date and time. I just throw it in my wallet and I feel like whenever I'm reaching for other stuff in my own wallet, basically it lives there for about six months and I see it once in a while and it just reminds me. (A06)

Some participants that had a secondary calendar system appreciated having different aspects of their lives (work, home, health) segmented into different systems, felt more secure with a backup system of upcoming events, or did not want to deal with the burden of transferring everything over into their primary tool. Overall, interviewees characterized their use of additional scheduling artifacts based on the accessibility of their primary tool, enhanced schedule awareness created through redundant streams of information, and the ease of integrating the event information from multiple sources. Examples of tools used by participants are shown in Figure 1.

Strategies for capturing events

The bulk of calendar information participants reported was manually input; this information included both health and personal events. Transferring information from artifacts such as external calendars (e.g., those provided by the school district for mothers) or appointment cards (e.g., from hair salons, doctors, or dentists) often helped participants remember upcoming events more effectively: as one participant stated, "When you write it down, it tends to stay in my memory a lot better" (D10).

Behavior in manually entering calendar content changed depending on whether planning for events was taking place in the short or long term time horizon. Participants were more likely to skip entering an event on the calendar if it was to take place the same day, such as an urgent care appointment for a child, since the engagement occurs relatively quickly thereafter and is likely a priority. The exception to this theme included situations of sharing information about a same-day appointment with a partner or spouse; one mother stated, "I'll put it in the calendar so my husband knows where we're at" (A19).

Participants recorded more information about their upcoming appointments, such as the clinic location, when they had a greater number of clinicians involved in their own or their child's care. Other purposes for recording information outside of the doctor's name and the time of the appointment included visiting a new location for the first time (A03, A09), preparing transportation for future appointments (D15, D18), or adding geolocation data through an electronic calendar application for future navigation in the car on the way to the appointment (A06, A12).

The act of adding content to calendars was described as highly situational by the majority of participants. Participants noted that it was important to capture details about a new event as soon as possible to make sure the content was captured successfully. Event details were most likely to end up on the desired calendar tool if the participant was physically near the tool while discussing the event or making appointments. In one case, a participant described putting off making follow-up doctor's appointments until she could go home and look at her paper calendar: "I don't think I've ever made an appointment at the [doctor's] office. I think I always come home and call them back" (D13).

Capturing content in a timely manner was not only reported as an issue with paper calendars, however. Mobile phone calendar users reported problems with making appointments while using their mobile phones and the calendar application at the same time. One mother described her necessary, but seemingly impolite, work-around:

If I'm on the phone with someone, I will put them on speaker and change modes so I'll look at the calendar while I'm talking to them, because often if I rely on my brain, even if we just hung up three minutes later, I might not remember what day it is, especially if we go over multiple dates for an appointment. It can feel rude to someone to be put on speaker, but if we want this on my calendar, I have to do that. (A09)

Both mothers of children with asthma and adults with diabetes had strong personal preferences for calendar content. Some participants preferred to maintain separate calendars for specific purposes; diabetes cohort participants described keeping one calendar specifically for medical appointments, avoiding extra clutter from personal engagements (D15, D12). Separate calendars were also used for synchronizing appointment information, a different strategy by which the act of transferring information from one calendar to another was itself a memory aid:

If I get an appointment, then I write it down...I go in [the patient website], because it shows upcoming appointments so then I'll print off the deal and go in there and check my calendar, so it's a backup type, so I got a system, my checks and balances. (D05)

In addition to adding content to calendars manually, participants provided a number of examples in their personal lives where electronic calendar invites simplified schedule management. Participants were generally receptive toward receiving calendar invitations for special events, which saved them the trouble of manually updating the calendar:

My older son's soccer team, his coach was a Microsoft guy so he was very tech savvy. He sent out basically like a Google calendar invite so he had all our games and all our practices basically preloaded for us. All we had to do was accept the invite and then automatically it showed up on my calendar. It's like magic. (A06)

Helpful external aids for calendaring events were not limited to electronic users; paper calendar users also pointed to helpful tools, as one mom explained:

This is kind of a neat thing the school does. The school does these preprinted stickers so that we get all the events for the whole year on [the wall calendar]. (A18)

For participants who used mobile phone calendar applications, several also reported automatic syncing between social media applications and their personal calendars, such as for birthdays from Facebook.

Integration of reminder systems

Another important theme was habits of engagement with calendar tools that users developed to help them remember activities that they had captured in their calendars. We refer to these habits of engagement as reminder systems. Reminder systems were important behaviors associated with calendar use, because as one interviewee explained, "It's not the system failing me, it's me not engaging with the system sometimes, if I think I know something" (A09). Examples of reminder systems include alarms that participants set on their phones or e-calendars to remember an appointment, actively scanning paper calendars to review the day's activities at a routine time in the morning, or even having informal discussions with family members to coordinate on details of upcoming events.

Based on our participants' reports of using reminder systems, we identified two facets of preferred reminder characteristics: active vs. passive and push vs. pull. In the first facet of reminder systems, we found that reminders could be active or passive. *Active reminders* were those that the participant had to initiate, where the individual described interacting with the system to record the reminder and determine its characteristics (such as an alarm on the phone, or a post-it note on the front door). *Passive reminders* were those in which the individual did not explicitly interact with their system to create a reminder, and rather relied on receiving an outside prompt—such as a reminder phone call from their clinic—to remember about an upcoming obligation or event.

The second facet of reminder systems was push versus pull information acquisition. In a *push* information acquisition, the participant expressed a need to have her attention drawn to an upcoming obligation or event—essentially, an interruption helped the individual to remember. This strategy could incorporate reminders set on a mobile phone, for instance, and make a particular sound to alert the participant to look at the event details.

Alternatively, a *pull* information acquisition involved encountering or scanning information—although an individual could choose to stop and read a dentist's appointment card found at the bottom of a purse, it could also be ignored, and lacked the same disruptive quality of a push reminder. By using the two facets of reminder management associated with calendar tool use, we are able to discern a structure in participant preferences for how they maintained awareness about their health appointments (see Figure 2).

Finally, patterns in preferences and behavior around reminders were found to be tool agnostic. Participants using mobile phone calendars described using pull-type reminders in the same way as wall calendar users did, particularly when push reminders were troublesome to set or inappropriately disruptive at the participant's place of work.

Challenges and failure points in schedule management

In addition to probing strategies and habits related to calendar management and sharing, we also inquired about negative events in scheduling behaviors that led to participant-perceived failures. Participants discussed failures related to tool access, user entry errors, and missed appointments or events due to scheduling mistakes or forgetfulness. Using the body of narratives we collected about failures in calendar management, we identified multiple points of potential failure in the processes for setting an appointment or scheduling an event and remembering to attend the appointment as scheduled.

Initial opportunities for failure in calendar management can occur at the time event details are added. Sufficient details of the event must be added to the calendar to remind the user of the upcoming events successfully. For this event-entry stage, we identified three distinct types of failures: uncaptured events, events captured incorrectly, or events not synchronized to multiple tools. In all types of failures, participants described experiencing a negative event that was unavoidable without outside intervention or unless the calendar owner reviewed the tool or tools to verify information.

Subsequent to capturing an event or appointment, the next major point of potential failure in calendar management occurs at the reminder stage. Both paper and electronic calendar users reported failures in scanning calendar content as a cue for reminding about upcoming events. As one participant stated, “If I don’t look at the calendar, I may forget” (D04).

Participants who used electronic calendars as their primary tool also reported failures in push reminders associated with events, a problem paper calendar users did not encounter. Failures at the reminder stage could be caused by ineffective reminder settings, or by dismissal of or distraction from the reminder that reduces its effectiveness.

[Microsoft] Outlook for sure can be really frustrating if you don’t set it for enough notification time. I’m really good at setting it, it’s got a default for 15 minutes. Well, 15 minutes is not enough time if you forget...That’s probably the biggest one is Outlook for me, because if I don’t reset that default, then I miss things or forget about things at the last minute. (A04)

I guess the one thing I changed after [the missed doctor’s appointment] is I’ve set reminders on my phone - or thought I set reminders on my phone and I never actually activated the alarm and that has made me miss appointments. (A03)

Incorporating participant narratives about failures in our analysis helped us to understand vulnerabilities in the different stages of schedule management and provided a richer understanding of the challenges patients can face in attempting to achieve their health goals.

DISCUSSION

Participants spoke about knowing which tactics could successfully engage their prospective memory as often as they discussed the devices and artifacts of calendars and reminders. Discussing calendars and schedules revealed participants’ priorities for their lives, as described previously by Payne [24] and Mariani et al. [15]. Participants’

Figure 2: Reminder systems can be classified by facets such as push or pull information acquisition, and the type of user engagement (passive, active): examples of each classification are shown here

User Engagement		Information Acquisition: Push	Information Acquisition: Pull
Active		*Definition:* The user engages with their calendar system to input information about a future health appointment, employing a push mechanism in the system to actively remind (such as a mobile phone alarm).	*Definition:* The user engages with their calendar system to input information about a future health appointment, then scans the system regularly to pull information about upcoming health appointments.
		Example: "Two hours is always my go-to on my first reminder. My second reminder, if it's further, it'll be an hour reminder instead of 30 minutes. So that way if I do an hour reminder and it only takes me 30 minutes, I still have 30 minutes to say okay, this is where we're wrapping it up and we're getting out of the house." (A07)	*Example:* "I go in for blood tests every so often so I do keep that on my calendar, to remind me to go in this week at some point. Even though it's not a schedule thing, as far as you have to be here on this day at this time, it helps remind me." (A15)
Passive		*Definition:* The user does not engage with their calendar system to input information about the upcoming health appointment, and depends on notifications from outside the system, such as reminder calls.	*Definition:* The user does not engage with their calendar system to input information about the upcoming health appointment, but instead seeks information from outside the system to stay current about upcoming health appointments.
		Example: "I like to use the calendar but obviously I haven't put a lot of appointments on there...I'm dependent kind of on [the doctor's office] or whomever to call me back and be like, you know, you have an appointment tomorrow. " (A10)	*Example:* "Sometimes I forget [about an appointment] and I have to call the next morning and say do I have an appointment? And they say no or yes." (D18)

accounts of intentions and priorities in managing daily schedules led to more in-depth discussions about personal importance of activities such as doctor's visits and self-care routines. One mother described the events that migrated to her calendar as things that "make me money and keep [my daughter] healthy." A caregiver for an adult with advanced diabetes referred to the act of keeping the household schedule as "what's keeping [her partner] alive." The importance of the calendar systems, and the involvement of calendar and scheduling activities in health-related activities, proved to offer rich interrelated themes.

Our investigation also revealed that the majority of the households we visited employed an "ecology" of calendar, scheduling, and reminder tools. The interaction between multiple tools created an even more complicated meta-system of information fragmentation, information transfer, redundancies, and information dissemination among family members, and is supported by previous work examining home health management strategies [17]. This complexity of home information management observed in this study underlines the importance of considering the wide range of preferences and needs of users and how they rely on and integrate healthcare information systems as part of their schedule management ecologies.

As previous studies have found through the years [6, 24], paper systems in these ecologies have not disappeared, and are often a critical part of the calendar and schedule system in the household, even when the primary calendar tool is a mobile phone—9 (69%) of 13 participants who used mobile phone calendars primarily used at least one secondary paper system. Participants in the diabetes cohort were more likely to use paper-based primary tools, whereas the asthma cohort reported using mostly digital calendars as their main tool; each cohort contained notable exceptions (e.g., enthusiastic technophiles in the diabetes cohort and reluctant technology users in the asthma cohort), but the preference for paper versus digital appeared to adhere to generational preferences, with the younger asthma moms using digital tools and diabetes patients preferring paper calendars. Although each participant had a primary calendar tool, it was unusual for an individual (diabetes patient or mother-caregiver) to rely on just one tool; diabetes participants reported an average of two calendar tools in use, and asthma mothers used an average of 3.4 tools each. This is consistent with the finding from Brush and Turner [6] that people who have children in the household use more tools than people without children. Additionally, participants in the diabetes cohort reported fewer needs to display shared information, and often consolidated calendar information to one artifact, resulting in fewer paper systems per household.

Redundancy in the ecosystem of household calendar management was often cited as a mechanism that helped participants avoid failure. Participants cited a variety of backup tools – including those outside of their own systems or generated by users who shared the systems – that reduced the effects of calendar failures. Backup mechanisms outside of the internal family system tended to include reminder calls, emails and texts from medical or service providers. Participants also confirmed calendar information by checking in with other sources, such as by calling the doctor's office or checking the patient portal for appointment information. We described such strategies as methods for increasing reliability of calendar systems in a previous analysis of calendar system failures [11], categorizing such adaptations by calendar users as redundancy, diversity of systems used, and active monitoring behavior.

Informal reminders from partners or spouses who shared a calendar tool served to reduce failures in schedule management; these informal methods were also identified as a major element of schedule management in previous studies [6, 21]. Participants reported that keeping external artifacts, such as appointment cards from doctors or dentists, also served as a dual, backup reminder system. Paper proved to be an essential part of the ecosystem and its redundancy surrounding primary calendar tools. In particular, participants in the asthma cohort often reported multiple paper supplementary systems in their system used to share information with others, such as tacked up paper reminders to notify partners or children who could read about upcoming events (please see Appendix A).

We also elicited information from participants about their use of external systems that interacted with participants' calendar management strategies, such as electronic calendar invites and preprinted stickers sent home from school, which aided paper calendar users in transferring important information to the home system. As we move forward in seeking design opportunities for individual calendar and reminder systems and healthcare information systems, we will be able to address approaches for integrating external healthcare information systems with patients' home calendar ecologies and better support home health management.

Finally, we observed how the heath-care system touched the day-to-day routines and calendar management of chronically ill patients and their caregivers through multiple modalities. Our participants still relied on paper-based artifacts, such as appointment cards and letters, but increasingly used the patient portal for activities such as referring to appointment calendars and communicating with providers. Patient perceptions of the timeliness and effectiveness of different types of healthcare reminders also highlighted the importance of tailoring these reminders to the home calendaring practices and capabilities of patients and caregivers.

For designers, this work sheds light on the importance of user engagement as a feature of calendar systems that support home health management. We found that the highly situational and time-sensitive nature of health information influenced user's habits of engagement in ways not anticipated by current information system designs, despite the different affordances digital and paper tools have for push/pull and active/passive engagement. Future work will explore opportunities for enhancing user engagement, especially with redundant and external systems that reduce failure opportunities and reinforce user discretion and competence in managing health information.

LIMITATIONS

This study is limited in its generalizability due to its qualitative nature and purposive sampling, meant to mimic the demographics of the United States. However, the inquiry is intended to give a broad set of information about calendar use in the home in the chronic disease management context through maximum variation between the two sample cohorts. By gathering participant experience that is both typical and divergent, we construct a rich set of findings about participant context and use of calendar tools. In this study, we are more concerned with "a full array of multiple realities" than statistical significance [8], and we hope to build upon the rich contextual descriptions with further design work (see below), but we cannot claim to make generalizable findings to a wider population.

CONCLUSIONS

This paper describes our exploration of calendar management strategies among patients, caregivers, and families coping with chronic disease. We approached the topic of calendar management in the context of chronic disease management to update and enrich the knowledge around shared calendars among users whose day-to-day routines often are complicated by home health care activities. Information about calendar management was elicited from a holistic point of view, allowing us to discuss calendar ecosystems – including interactions among users of shared tools, multiple tool modalities, and system failures – rather than focus on individual tools. We found that calendar ecosystems overwhelmingly included multiple tools in each household, and paper systems continue to back up electronic device use. Integration of reminder systems into their calendar tools included both active and passive reminders as well as those that relied on push and pull approaches.

By studying shared calendar use and the range of behaviors described by our participants, we are able to show diverse user needs and a complex ecosystem of paper and electronic tools. Improvements to healthcare information systems must consider this complexity to integrate and support home health management successfully. This work provides valuable contextual information for design opportunities in calendar management systems for supporting individuals and families living day-to-day with chronic illness.

References and Citations

1. Bodenheimer, T., Lorig, K., Holman, H., & Grumbach, K. Patient self-management of chronic disease in primary care. *JAMA* 288, 19 (2002a), 2469-2475.
2. Bodenheimer, T., Wagner, E. H., & Grumbach, K. Improving primary care for patients with chronic illness: the chronic care model, Part 2. *JAMA* 288, 15 (2002b), 1909-1914.
3. Bødker, S., & Grönvall, E. Calendars: time coordination and overview in families and beyond. In *ECSCW 2013: Proceedings of the 13th European Conference on Computer Supported Cooperative Work* (2013), 63-81.
4. Bossen, Claus, et al. CareCoor: Augmenting the coordination of cooperative home care work. *International journal of medical informatics,* 82, 5 (2013), e189-e199.
5. Brush, A. J., & Inkpen, K. M. Yours, Mine and Ours? Sharing and Use of Technology in Domestic Environments. In *UbiComp 2007: Ubiquitous Computing* (2007), 109-126.
6. Brush, A.J. & Turner, T.C. A Survey of Personal and Household Scheduling Practices: Implications for Digital Family Calendars. MSR-TR-2007-23 (2007). http://research.microsoft.com/pubs/70417/tr-2007-28.pdf 2007.
7. Crabtree, A., & Rodden, T. Domestic routines and design for the home. *Computer Supported Cooperative Work (CSCW)*, 13, 2 (2004), 191-220.
8. Erlandson, D. A. (Ed.). *Doing naturalistic inquiry: A guide to methods.* (1993). Sage.
9. Grimes, A., & Brush, A. J. Life scheduling to support multiple social roles. In *Proceedings of the SIGCHI Conference on Human Factors in Computing Systems*, (2008), 821-824.
10. Halterman, J. S., Yoos, H. L., Sidora, K., Kitzman, H., & McMullen, A. Medication use and health care contacts among symptomatic children with asthma. *Ambulatory Pediatrics, 1,* 5 (2001), 275-279.
11. [redacted for anonymity]
12. Kirkman, M.S., Briscoe,V.J., Clark, N., Florez, H., Haas, L.B., Halter, J.B., Huang, E.S. et al. Diabetes in older adults: a consensus report. *Journal of the American Geriatrics Society* 60, 12 (2012): 2342-2356.
13. Klasnja, P., Civan Hartzler, A., Unruh, K. T., & Pratt, W. Blowing in the wind: unanchored patient information work during cancer care. In *Proceedings of the SIGCHI Conference on Human Factors in Computing Systems,* (2010), 193-202.

14. Klasnja, P., Hartzler, A., Powell, C., & Pratt, W. Supporting cancer patients' unanchored health information management with mobile technology. In *AMIA Annual Symposium Proceedings*, (2011), 732.

15. Mariani, J.A., Crabtree, A., Hemmings, T., & Rodden, T. Informing the design of calendar systems for domestic use. In *Proc of the Eighth European Conference on Computer-Supported Cooperative Work*, (2003).

16. Miles, M. B., & Huberman, A. M. *Qualitative data analysis: An expanded sourcebook.* (1994). Chicago: Sage.

17. Moen, A., & Brennan, P. F. Health@ Home: the work of health information management in the household (HIMH): implications for consumer health informatics (CHI) innovations. *Journal of the American Medical Informatics Association*, 12, 6 (2005), 648-656.

18. National Heart, Lung and Blood Institute. *Expert Panel Report III: Guidelines for the diagnosis and management of asthma.* (2007). Bethesda: NIH.

19. Neumiller, J.J. & Setter, S.M. Pharmacologic management of the older patient with type 2 diabetes mellitus. *The American journal of geriatric pharmacotherapy*, 7, 6 (2009), 324-342.

20. Neustaedter, C. & Brush, A.J. "LINC-ing" the family: the participatory design of an inkable family calendar. In *Proceedings of the SIGCHI Conference on Human Factors in Computing Systems*, (2006), 141-150.

21. Neustaedter, C., Brush, A.J., & Greenberg, S. A digital family calendar in the home: lessons from field trials of LINC. In *Proceedings of Graphics Interface*, (2007), 199-20.

22. Neustaedter, C., Brush, A.J., & Greenberg, S. The calendar is crucial: Coordination and awareness through the family calendar. *ACM Transactions on Computer-Human Interaction (TOCHI)*, 16, 1 (2009), 1–48.

23. Palen, L., & Grudin, J. Discretionary adoption of group support software: Lessons from calendar applications. In *Implementing collaboration technologies in industry*, (2003), 159-180. London: Springer.

24. Payne, S. J. Understanding calendar use. *Human-Computer Interaction*, *8*, 2 (1993), 83-100.

25. Ralston, J.D., Carrell, D., Reid, R., Anderson, M., Moran, M., & Hereford, J. Patient web services integrated with a shared medical record: patient use and satisfaction. *Journal of the American Medical Informatics Association* 14, 6 (2007), 798-806.

26. Saudek, C.D., Derr, R.L., & Kalyani, R.R. Assessing glycemia in diabetes using self-monitoring blood glucose and hemoglobin A1c. *JAMA*, 295, 14 (2006), 1688-1697.

27. Sellen, A. J., Hyams, J., & Eardley, R. The everyday problems of working parents: Implications for new technologies. *Hewlett-Packard Labs Technical Report HPL-2004-37*, (2004).

28. Sell, A., & Walden, P. Mobile digital calendars: an interview study. In *System Sciences, 2006. HICSS'06. Proceedings of the 39th Annual Hawaii International Conference on System Sciences*, (2006).

29. Skeels, M. M., Unruh, K. T., Powell, C., & Pratt, W. Catalyzing social support for breast cancer patients. In *Proceedings of the SIGCHI Conference on Human Factors in Computing Systems*, (2010), 173-182.

30. Strauss, A. L., & Corbin, J. *Basics of qualitative research (Vol. 15)*. (1990). Newbury Park, CA: Sage.

31. Tungare, M., & Pérez-Quiñones, M. An exploratory study of personal calendar use. Technical report, Computing Research Repository (CoRR), (2008).

Appendix A: Shared and Unshared Calendar Tool (Detailed)

■ = 1 tool observed

		Private Tools								Shared/Public Tools								
		<--analog							digital-->	<--analog							digital-->	
	Participant ID	wall calendar (paper)	paper reference	white board	desk calendar	planner	tablet	e-calendar	phone	wall calendar (paper)	paper reference	white board	desk calendar	planner	tablet	e-calendar	phone	Total tools used
Asthma cohort	01							■	■■			■						4
	02									■	■							2
	03		■			■			■■	■								5
	04							■	■	■	■							4
	05								■	■	■■							4
	06							■	■■									3
	07								■	■	■■							4
	08								■			■						2
	09								■■	■								3
	10								■	■	■							3
	11								■		■	■						3
	12								■	■	■■■					■		6
	13							■								■	■	3
	14					■		■	■									3
	15														■			1
	16		■							■	■■							4
	17								■	■	■					■	■	5
	18									■	■					■		3
	19															■■		2
	20							■	■			■						3
Diabetes Cohort	01					■		■	■									3
	02	■	■		■					■								4
	03										■	■						2
	04							■										1
	05		■		■			■										3
	06									■	■							2
	07						■		■									2
	08								■	■								2
	09							■		■								2
	10									■								1
	11									■	■							2
	12		■							■	■							3
	13		■							■								2
	14									■								1
	15												■					1
	16								■	■						■		3
	17									■	■							2
	18									■								1
	19								■									1
	20							■		■								2

Collaboration in-between: The Care Hotel and Designing for Flexible Use

Claus Bossen
Aarhus University
Helsingforsgade 14
8200 Aarhus, Denmark
imvcb@dac.au.dk

Erik Grönvall
IT University of Copenhagen
Rued Langgaards Vej 7
2300 Copenhagen, Denmark
erig@itu.dk

ABSTRACT
In this paper, we analyse the challenges of working between organizations and established information infrastructures. The Care Hotel is a municipal healthcare facility where persons, typically following a hospital stay, undergo rehabilitation to enable them to live independently at home. Admission, stay, and discharge from the Care Hotel entail numerous coordination activities with a variety of frequent and sporadic, heterogeneous, external collaborators, including general practitioners, relatives, and hospitals, some of which are already part of large information infrastructures, whereas others are too small or shifting to allow for stable arrangements. Hence, work at the Care Hotel may be characterized as 'collaboration in-between'. We propose a design solution for flexible use to further stimulate reflection on design implications, and how to meet the challenges of collaboration in-between. As large infrastructures continue to develop, we posit that many 'in-between settings' will encounter similar challenges to collaboration. Healthcare providers in contexts of fragmented healthcare are also likely to face such challenges.

Author Keywords
Cross-organizational work; collaboration in-between; older adults; transitional care; flexible use; rehabilitation.

ACM Classification Keywords
H.5.3 Group and Organization Interfaces – Computer supported cooperative work.

General Terms
Human Factors; Design; Theory.

INTRODUCTION
In this paper we describe the challenges of 'collaboration in-between'. By this term, we intend a work setting where collaborative work is dependent on coordination and communication among a heterogeneous array of external actors whose commitments lie elsewhere, and some of which are already part of large information infrastructures.

Our case study focuses on the Care Hotel, which provides rehabilitative care, primarily to senior citizens, to enable them to live independently at home. To the staff at the Care Hotel, care and treatment of each rehabilitee entails a challenge, because these activities must be coordinated with hospitals, general practitioners, the municipality, and other external collaborators upon whom the Care Hotel depends for information and activities. The involvement of these external actors is required, but often only intermittently. Also, the work goals of the external actors differ from, and overlap only partially, those of the Care Hotel, and hence they prioritize tasks differently. The Care Hotel is an 'in-between facility' in at least two senses: The senior citizens staying at the Care Hotel (the rehabilitees) are temporary visitors transitioning between hospital and home, and bring along a shifting set of relatives, general practitioners, and other actors. Also, the recently-launched Care Hotel exists between powerful organizations and professions with large, established infrastructures, and therefore is in no position to enforce standards of communication, nor is it economically or temporally realistic to build a shared IT system.

The characteristics of collaborative work at the Care Hotel entail design considerations that go against CSCW's preference for 'localized studies' that establish an opposition between internal and external demands on work, and see the latter as detrimental: work should be supported according to its 'internal' needs and requirements (e.g. [5]. For a general critique, see [27]). In our case, design of IT support for the local work arrangement must be premised on recognizing the character of the external collaborators. This does not entail adoption of external standards, as these collaborators are too transient and heterogeneous to make this meaningful. The Care Hotel's coordination challenges resemble those of transitional care, recovery rooms, and emergency wards, which also treat transitional patients. However, the variety of collaborators and their involvement is greater and routinizing collaboration more difficult. Also, ad hoc actions are numerous, owing to inherent contingencies in the rehabilitation efforts.

CSCW '15, March 14 - 18, 2015, Vancouver, BC, Canada.
Copyright 2015 ACM 978-1-4503-2922-4/15/03…$15.00.
http://dx.doi.org/10.1145/2675133.2675243

This paper analyses and discusses the particular challenges of cooperation and of building infrastructures at an 'in-between place' such as the Care Hotel. We suggest that in this case, the design challenge is to develop a system that supports and fits internal work arrangements, *and* is flexible enough to allow for coordination and communication with external collaborators. In particular, we propose a move towards an open-ended design that supports adaptation and ad hoc integration of diverse systems. The point is to design for flexible use, inspired by design-for-future-use and design-for-appropriation [4, 13].

In the following, we review related work, and establish our theoretical framework. In section three, we present the case study, including the methods applied and the setting. In section four, we analyse the cooperative work and its challenges at the Care Hotel, and in section five, we discuss findings and theoretical implications. In section six, we discuss design implications, and present a design proposal as a way to further reflection upon, and investigate our case. Section seven concludes the paper.

RELATED WORK AND THEORY

Healthcare IT and collaboration have been of continued interest to CSCW (For overviews, see [16] and [18]). However, there are few studies of the collaborative challenges of working across organizational settings.

An early contribution to CSCW was made by Symon et al. [37], who analysed interdepartmental cooperation and conflicts surrounding booking, and note the importance of differences in status, goals, and the different uses of information among organizations. Kane and Luz [25] describe how different professions work together to reach diagnoses by consensus, and note the importance of feedback, good communication, and adequate technologies for reaching agreement and avoiding errors. Lee et al. [26] describe the challenges faced by multi-disciplinary care teams in emergency departments, and argue for role-based communication and informative interruptions as facilitative mechanisms for that work. Finally, Abraham and Reddy [2] analyse the challenges posed by negative interactions between intra- and inter-organizational activities related to patient transfers. They detail the re-coordinative activities surrounding goal and resource alignment, which emerge from such cross-boundary breakdowns. A common theme throughout these CSCW studies is the need for (improved) communication, establishment of common goals, and support technologies. However, in these studies collaboration occurs within the shared framework of healthcare with (mostly) well-defined roles, goals, functions, and responsibilities. In part, this also pertains to the Care Hotel, but staff also collaborate with actors outside this framework (e.g. taxis and the municipality).

Broadly, studies of transitional care are also relevant to our case. Transitional care is defined as the 'set of actions designed to ensure the coordination and continuity of healthcare as patients transfer between different locations or different levels of care in the same location' [10, pp. 533]. With an aging population, and an increasing number of people with co-morbidity or chronic diseases, people are more likely to move into and out of various care facilities (e.g. from hospital to nursing home), and successful transitions between these are crucial for attaining desired healthcare outcomes. However, prescription errors and incomplete information on diagnoses and functional status are recurrent problems [10]. Improving transitional care is challenging, according to these studies, because institutions function in isolation, the issues are under-recognized, and economic incentives are lacking. Proposed solutions include goal alignment among various actors, standardized transfer protocols, and tackling differing information needs of multiple disciplines [39]. Again, in these studies, as those in CSCW, the focus is on collaboration within healthcare. Furthermore, transfers between units or organizations (usually) imply a clear transfer of responsibility, which, at the Care Hotel, is divided (e.g. responsibility for prescriptions is the general practitioner's, dispensing medicine, the Care Hotel's).

Discussions of care coordination across settings in the USA are also relevant. The Care Hotel's challenges stem from their existing between universal, nationally organized primary and secondary healthcare infrastructures in a Northern European context. In comparison, US healthcare is more fragmented, which poses its own set of care coordination issues for patients and healthcare professionals [23, 24]. Central challenges in the US include identifying, contacting, and collaborating with other healthcare providers, and the call is to establish a common Health Information Exchange infrastructure, nationwide National Provider Identification number register, standard care coordination plans, and support for a- and synchronous communication [30]. Indeed, the care coordination functions for the newly established model of Patient Centered Medical Homes (http://pcmh.ahrq.gov/) are close to those of the Care Hotel [38]. While many of the proposed solutions are already in place at the Care Hotel, the challenges of existing between large infrastructures, and establishing better tools for a- and synchronous communication are the similar. The challenges faced by the Care Hotel are in many respects similar to those outlined within the above studies within CSCW, on transitional care and in the US with regards to collaboration across various healthcare entities. However, they are accentuated by the fact that the Care Hotel's collaborators are more transient and come from without the healthcare sector.

Long ago, Bowker and Star remarked '...one person's infrastructure may be another's barrier' [6, p. 34]. However, few studies analyse how to support actors working between infrastructures. Ellingsen and Monteiro address the issue head-on, but argue that aiming for integrated information relies on unwarranted purifications [14]. Instead, redundant, fragmented, and ambiguous information has a productive role that outweighs its drawbacks. In a similar study, they conclude that integration merely redistributes, rather than eliminates disorganized information [15].

Theory

The theory of symbolic interaction, as developed by Strauss and others, and based on healthcare studies, is particularly relevant to our case: it highlights the work necessary to establish and stabilize cooperation [35]. Rather than assuming that collaborating actors share goals and aims, and merely follow routines and plans, cooperation and its outcomes are seen as achievements that require effort.

Actors must align their actions in ways that contribute to the goal of the collaboration, leading to efforts at *articulation work*: agreeing on goals, when which tasks should be executed, by which means, according to which standard, and so on. Articulation work may be reduced by establishing routines or standard operating procedures (SOP), and in this way temporarily stabilized *work arrangements* may be *worked out*. By subsequently inscribing these in schemes of classification, standards, and procedures of technologies, such as intranet, e-mail, electronic patient records, work arrangements are further routinized and stabilized. The accumulation of multiple, aligned artefacts and standardized practices may be regarded as an 'ordering system' [32]. However, articulation work is never eliminated completely, because actors must continuously monitor the progression of others' work to align it with their own, and because unanticipated contingencies and feedback effects arise during the unfolding of work processes [36]. Within this framework, booking systems or patient records, for example, whether paper-based or electronic, may be seen as ordering systems that stabilize the cooperative work at hospitals through inscribed routines and work arrangements [42].

Collaboration is not assumed to be based on consensus and equality. Each actor has his or her own *stance*, that is, perspective, interests, and interpretation of a situation. Working out arrangements, routines, SOP, and such is a process that may include persuasion, enticement, trickery, and force, as well as deliberate consensus [36]. For example, whereas relatives of the elderly receiving home healthcare might like immediate access to, and close relations with home healthcare workers, the latter may adopt a professional, detached attitude, to protect themselves from interruptions and excessive emotional involvement. Hence, agreeing on a shared information system may be controversial [8] (e.g. Symon et al. [37]).

A basic cooperative challenge relevant to this case is that cooperating actors must have a sufficient understanding of the ways in which their own actions interrelate with, and depend on the actions of other actors. They must have a sufficient, though not necessarily complete, understanding of the common *field of work*: actors must take the interdependences for granted, and assume that their co-actors do the same. Communicatively, *common ground* is essential: if actors do not share understandings and frameworks of interpretation, coordination becomes troubled, and delays, misunderstandings, and absent, duplicated, or conflicting collaborative efforts are the result [9]. Working face to face, actors can draw on a range of communicative resources to establish common ground and fields of work. However, these are often unavailable in distributed, non-collocated cooperative settings, which, in CSCW, has led to a continued interest in how to develop IT systems that support *context awareness* [20].

Integrated, IT-based ordering systems are inherently difficult to establish, as the difficulties of developing electronic patient records for hospitals testify (e.g. [14, 15]). If a one-size-fits-all solution is not possible, it is either 'let a hundred flowers blossom', or go for interfaces and standards that may link across infrastructures, according to Bowker and Star [34]: 'Infrastructures subtend complex ecologies: their design process should always be tentative, flexible and open' [34, p. 242]. Flexible and open design seems even more pertinent in cases where various heterogeneous and transitional actors collaborate across different settings, and make it difficult to develop a common IT system. Here, an infrastructuring approach, as defined within the design community, may be helpful. This approach aims to allow for future innovations for situations that could not be envisioned when the system was initially designed. Star and Ruhleder originally introduced infrastructuring as an analytical shift from *what* (to design) to *when* (to design) [33]. Following this, infrastructuring as a design approach is an ongoing process, rather than limited to the early project phases [4]. This entails moving from design-for-use to design-for-future-use. The approach may be described as 'the work of creating socio-technical resources that intentionally enable adoption and appropriation beyond the initial scope of the design, a process that might include participants not present during the initial design' [12, p. 247].

Based on the foregoing framework for conceptualizing cooperative work and approaching design implications in an infrastructuring way, below we analyse the challenges of collaboration in-between at the Care Hotel, the design implications that emerge, and propose a solution.

THE CASE STUDY: THE CARE HOTEL

As hospital stays are expensive, in Denmark and other countries efforts are made to decrease the duration of hospital stays. Hence, while the elderly population that requires more healthcare increases, the available hospital beds decrease, and patients are discharged earlier in their recovery process.

Senior citizens, in particular, may still need treatment and care following discharge, to improve their level of functioning to an extent that enables them to live in their own homes. This task has been taken over by the municipalities, which monitor and evaluate the functional levels and needs of discharged patients. If necessary, support services or a rehabilitative stay (e.g. at the Care Hotel) may be provided. Some years ago, these persons would have been admitted to a nursing home. However, institutional care is more resource-intensive than home-based care [19], therefore government efforts are directed at enabling senior citizens to live in their own homes. Notably, senior citizens generally also prefer to remain in their own homes, as this is perceived as providing greater independence and a better quality of life [11].

The Care Hotel opened in 2011, and is the first of its kind in the municipality. This study is the result of a project aimed at understanding the nature of collaborative work at the Care Hotel, and how IT could support this.

Methods

The project lasted for five months, and included a range of qualitative methods of which workshops were the most important, and structured the overall project activity.

Field studies and interviews

About 60 hours of fieldwork were conducted by the first author and an employee from a software firm. External entities (e.g. the municipal referral centre) were also interviewed. These interviews were semi-structured, and took place at the interviewees' offices. Each such field trip lasted about two hours, and furnished examples of how external entities collaborated with the Care Hotel. Ad hoc interviews with staff were also conducted during the field studies, when clarification or additional information was needed to understand fieldwork observations or workshop results. To avoid increasing staff workload, questions were asked during periods of less work, or during breaks. As a result, these interviews were rather short, and either unstructured or semi-structured. As different healthcare workers were available at different times, many were asked questions. In all, 10 staff members (healthcare assistants, team leader and nurse) were interviewed and these interviews lasted between 5 and 20 minutes. The interviews were recorded or documented in situ.

Workshops

The project included five two-hours workshops, which involved healthcare workers, their team leader, and the director of the facility. Between five and ten healthcare workers participated in each workshop, with a core of three to four staff members participating in most of the workshops. The workshops were designed to, a) elicit the nature and specifics of collaborative work at the Care Hotel, and b) to provide initial design ideas for a future collaborative system (see Figure 1). There were two to three weeks between each workshop. The workshops became occasions to better understand aspects of collaboration observed during the fieldwork, and to discuss and confirm temporary findings with the healthcare workers.

Based on the initial fieldwork, the first workshop (WS1) required the healthcare workers to write down as many coordination tasks as they could think of. They then indicated where these tasks were performed, and the tools used such, as telephone, search engines, fax, and e-mail. Guided by this initial step, the healthcare workers were asked to write down experienced scenarios of collaboration. The scenarios should present two perspectives: a) a situation where everything went well, and b) the same situation but when things were more complicated.

Figure 1. Pictures from the workshops.

At the second workshop, the healthcare workers took the activities listed in WS 1, and drew a timeline of when the different cooperative activities occurred in relation to a rehabilitee's stay. For example, which activities occur before and during admission, what activities occur during a stay, and what tasks are performed upon discharge? The duration of each task was also indicated, when possible.

The third and fourth workshops elaborated on the same theme. However, before the third workshop, a large poster presenting all the tasks identified in WS2 was put in a common area at the Care Hotel. The staff were requested to annotate the poster with information regarding which stakeholders were involved in performing these tasks. At WS3 and WS4, the staff produced flow charts to document the order in which sub-tasks were executed while performing each task. They also indicated the stakeholders involved, and how they became involved. The staff drew flow charts of 'template' activities and more (real-life) complex versions of the same activities.

The fifth workshop encouraged the staff to draft potential solutions for the collaborative challenges identified in the preceding workshops, and during fieldwork. WS5 applied creative design methods, such as Inspiration cards [21] and Attribute listing [22]. These methods support out-of-the-box thinking by highlighting less-obvious aspects of relevant themes (e.g. collaboration). The ideas for the design proposal outlined below came from WS5.

Diaries

Twelve Care Hotel staff members were given dedicated diaries in which to make two sets of entries: a) descriptions of their work roles, what they enjoyed and disliked about their work, and their perceptions of the general challenges and possibilities of cross-organizational cooperative care; b) a table listing daily activities involving the rehabilitees directly (e.g. providing care) or indirectly (e.g. calling a general practitioner regarding a rehabilitee's stay at the Care Hotel). The diaries complemented the in-situ fieldwork and the workshops, revealing daily activities, with a focus on staff coordination tasks and interactions with each rehabilitee. Eight (of twelve) of these diaries (used one to eight days [average: five days]) were returned to the researchers after two weeks. The diary entries varied in number and extent, included between one and fourteen activities (average: nine). In total, 68 activities were reported, comprising 51 unique activities, such as contacting a rehabilitee's general practitioner, serving meals, communicating with a hospital, coordinating meetings with relatives, and arranging transportation. The activities reported in the compiled diaries were largely similar to, or represented sub-divisions of, the activities reported during the workshops.

Video recordings

Activity in the office space, the main location for cross-organizational communication and coordination, was recorded on video for five hours. Recording took place on two randomly selected mornings, and started just before 07:00, when the day shift starts and the healthcare workers have their daily meetings, and most cross-organizational, collaborative activities occur. The video material was annotated using the video annotation software, ELAN. The recordings identified collaborative situations and how the office space was used. Follow-up discussions with staff revealed, for example, situations where staff overheard a telephone conversation, and as a consequence, could contribute useful information, or how different staff members enter and leave ongoing conversations, to orientate themselves within a situation, or to assist in solving problems.

Steering committee meetings: ongoing evaluation

During the project, a steering committee of representatives from all project partners regularly met to evaluate the data and findings obtained. Hence, throughout the project, data was collectively assessed and analysed, so that upcoming project activities and foci could be directed towards the overarching goal: investigating collaborative work and designing IT support for the Care Hotel. These meetings and the workshops also functioned as occasions for the ongoing collaborative validation of data, and central findings and themes. For the purpose of this paper, the first author has gone over the material again, to assess findings and themes and the adequacy of the theoretical framework.

Exclusion of rehabilitees

The initial idea was to actively include the Care Hotel rehabilitees and relatives in the project. A resourceful rehabilitee whom the healthcare workers perceived as capable of participating in project activities was selected as a first test-participant. However, compiling a project diary was too demanding for this person, even with assistance from the healthcare workers. As a consequence, the project group decided to not involve rehabilitees, as they were considered to lack the resources to participate, and had to focus on their rehabilitation work. As a side-note, involving therapeutic patients in design work does raise ethical issues [3]. The exclusion of rehabilitees from this study focuses attention on staff, which is a study limitation. Still, the design proposal at the conclusion of this paper also invites informal care-providers to participate and benefit from this collaborative work.

The Setting

The Care Hotel has three floors, each with dining and office spaces, and 22 'mini apartments' for the rehabilitees. There is a café, a small library, and common areas for social activities. Rehabilitation facilities are provided in the basement, but rehabilitees also train in their apartments and shared spaces, since the aim is for them to function in home environments.

Day staff consists of a nurse, one or two therapists, healthcare assistants, a team leader, and other affiliated personnel, such as kitchen and front desk staff. The healthcare providers' office is situated in the middle of the floor, and is used for daily morning meetings and informal coordination (see Figure 2). Here, healthcare providers read records, document care, and contact people outside the Care Hotel. All rehabilitees are listed on a whiteboard, including his or her current status (e.g. upcoming meetings, temporary hospital admittance). Computers and telephones are few, and staff often must wait before they can input or access data, or make a phone call. A healthcare worker stated: '... it is completely crazy. Often, you cannot document [in the computer], you cannot call the general practitioners...' (Healthcare worker, 22-11-2011). In the interim, they may execute other tasks, which generate new data, and temporary notes are important to their work practices. Outside the office, the staff use small notebooks or Post-it® notes to document and remember important information. To deal with the limited number of computers and the somewhat cumbersome ways of finding relevant data, all rehabilitees' records are printed and placed in binders stacked on shelves in the healthcare providers' office. The binders are used throughout the day, since they contain frequently used information, such as the rehabilitees' healthcare plans, contact information for relatives, their general practitioners, and key persons at the last ward to which they were admitted. The municipality has a computerized healthcare record system, which is accessible to the Care Hotel, and the municipality's home healthcare service and referral centre. The Care Hotel staff use this to document care and rehabilitation activities, and as an information database about each rehabilitee. However, neither hospitals nor general practitioners can access it, as they are not part of the municipal organization. Instead, each system has its own record system, which does not communicate with the municipality's and which the

Care Hotel therefore cannot access. Instead, information is exchanged among these entities by post, telephone, fax, and e-mail. Sometimes, written notes are given to a transferring rehabilitee to pass along to other healthcare staff.

Figure 2. The Care Hotel's office space.

A rehabilitee's stay typically lasts four to six weeks, depending on their needs. Rehabilitees are evaluated daily to provide optimal, personal, and holistic treatment and rehabilitation. The entire patient journey from private home, to the Care Hotel and home again is illustrated below (Figure 3): a person is referred to the Care Hotel either after a period of hospitalization, to *return* to his or her home, or to be able to *continue* living independently at home.

Figure 3. A person's progression through the Care Hotel.

COOPERATION AT THE CARE HOTEL

Although the daily activities and focus of work at the Care Hotel relate to rehabilitation, collaboration with a number of actors outside the facility itself is required. This predicament of 'being in-between' presents a number of collaborative challenges, which we describe below.

Daily coordination of work at the Care Hotel

As a rehabilitee moves through the rehabilitation process – admission, the actual stay, discharge and the return home – a number of isolated and collaborative activities occur. For example, in parallel with providing individualized rehabilitation, the Care Hotel also takes over the care normally done by home healthcare workers (e.g. medication). However, medical decisions remain the responsibility of, and must therefore be coordinated with, the rehabilitee's general practitioner.

At the Care Hotel, the daily rhythms of the rehabilitees are tightly coupled with those of the healthcare providers. Most coordination work occurs during the day shift, which starts at 07:00. While the rehabilitees breakfast, the healthcare providers telephone external stakeholders, such as hospital wards and rehabilitees' general practitioners, who typically have telephone consultation hours between 08:00 and 10:00. Later, more work is focused on registration and documentation. During evening and night shifts, most work concerns care, rather than rehabilitative activities.

Healthcare workers spend much time seeking, gathering, and using information to support their daily activities. Data is mostly managed in the office, but generated elsewhere, for example with the rehabilitees in their apartments, or in the gym. At morning staff meetings in the office, each rehabilitee is discussed with respect to progress, challenges, planned activities for the current day, and other upcoming activities that must be coordinated. These meetings establish the basis for a common ground and shared understanding of the field of work. Apart from the hand-over between the day and evening shifts, there are no other formal daily information exchanges.

Work processes are supported by less-formal information exchanges. For example, as observed during the field studies and from video recordings, conversations and questions are often clearly audible in the healthcare providers' office, where the computers and telephones are located. Ongoing, unintended 'eavesdropping' is the result, and therefore healthcare providers can have a constantly updated overview, that is, context awareness, of what happens at the Care Hotel. During the day, no one seems to have a 'complete picture'; instead, each healthcare provider has one piece of the puzzle, and they collectively construct an adequate understanding of the field of work, including the location and availability of staff, and rehabilitees' current functional states. However, a negative aspect of these overheard conversations is added noise, and the resulting risks. A healthcare worker explained: '...previously, we dispensed [each individual patient's] medication up in the ward, but there were too many distractions, and that may lead to more errors...' (Healthcare worker, 22-11-2011). As a result, the Care Hotel has allocated a room as dispensary.

The Rehabilitation process and its contingencies

Each rehabilitee's rehabilitation process is precariously dependent on various collaborators and cross-organizational work. From an upper-level perspective, most Care Hotel rehabilitees share a template-style process (Table 1). For healthcare staff, this standard operating procedure (SOP) represents a baseline for what activities should occur, and when. However, a more fine-grained analysis reveals significant vast individual variation, and not all standard activities apply to each rehabilitation process. Also, although a standard activity may be simple in one case, it may be complicated and challenging in another, requiring numerous additional tasks. Therefore, the template for executing 'standard' activities must be adapted to each specific situation. Hence, SOPs and work arrangements are often inadequate, and instead new efforts of articulation work must be made. The variety of adjustments in many activities is such that, during WS3 and WS4, when the healthcare providers were asked to illustrate the tasks in the previously identified activities, they had difficulty relating to these as 'standard' or 'mappable'. They found it difficult hard to define exactly what occurred within a particular activity, as to a great extent, this varied from one occasion to the next, and from rehabilitee to rehabilitee. Eventually, they drew and presented a number of alternative solutions or ways of executing the tasks, based on various internal and external contingencies.

	TYPE OF ACTIVITY
BEFORE ARRIVAL	ARRIVAL COORDINATION
	TRANSPORT TO THE CARE HOTEL
WEEK 1	MEDICINE LIST MANAGMENT
	RECEIVE AND WELCOME THE REHABILITEE
	GOAL DISCUSSION
	CONTACT WITH HOSPITAL
	COORDINATION WITH NEXT OF KIN
	CONTACT WITH REFERRAL OFFICE
WEEK 2	CONTACT WITH THERAPISTS AT LOCAL CENTRE
WEEK 3	*CONTACT TO REFERRAL CENTRE IF REHABILITEE DO NOT BENEFIT*
WEEK 4	CONTACT TO REFERRAL CENTRE ABOUT REHABILITEE'S FUTURE
WEEK 5	CONTACT TO REHABILITEE'S LOCAL CENTRE
	CONTACT WITH NEXT OF KIN – REHABILITEE RETURNING HOME
	BOOKING AND MANAGING HOME-TRANSPORTATION
WEEK 6	CONTACT FROM REHABILITEE'S LOCAL CENTRE OR NEXT OF KIN
	FORWARDING NEWSPAPERS AND MAIL
	COORDINATE WHO MAKE THE PACKING FOR THE TRIP HOME
AFTER DISCHARGE	CONTACT TO NEXT OF KIN, PICK UP FORGOTTEN ITEMS
	FOLLOW-UP MEETING WITH REHABILITEE IN HIS/HER OWN HOME

Table 1. The general, template-style rehabilitation process.

The variation in the template-style steps of the rehabilitation process may be illustrated by two examples. Receiving a new rehabilitee at the Care Hotel ('Receive and welcome the rehabilitee', Table 1) may include between one and seven different organizational partners, and depend on up to twelve different interactions or communication flows amongst these actors. According to the healthcare providers, coordinating the arrival of a new rehabilitee takes about seven work hours to complete, distributed over one week. However, the personnel also rate this activity as highly dynamic and not 'template'-based (rated 4 on a 1 to 5 scale, where 1 equals a very stable routine, and 5 a very instable activity). Also, as described by a healthcare care worker, the staff must manually check their electronic system several times a day, if new rehabilitees are to be admitted; 'We should go in and check this several times a day, or we risk...that unexpectedly, the next day a new rehabilitee arrives' (healthcare worker, 22-11-2011). Another rather complicated coordinative and communicative task is validating a rehabilitee's medication plan: In the best situation, the hospital sends a fax to the Care Hotel with the arriving rehabilitee's prescribed medication, which the Care Hotel forwards to the general practitioner, who validates the list, and subsequently, the Care Hotel can administer medication based on the plan. Two faxes and two telephone calls are required. However, at the workshops it became clear that the pharmacy and relatives may also be involved in the medication list verification process: they may be aware of medication not previously registered, or confuse validation efforts by providing incorrect information. A healthcare worker provided the following example:

...they are seven children [to the rehabilitee], and hence the information is fragmented, and it's not the same information we receive. And they [the children] do not really like to have us involved at all... ...they are a bit special and spiritual ... and hence they think that we have nothing to do with the medicine... ... but we must administer the medicine, so we must know... And the cardiac heart outpatient clinic says that they have never given the medicine. That they [the children] give her a German remedy that we do not know about on the side, that she gets when they are here visiting. And we are not so happy about that... ... But now they [the cardiac outpatient clinic] will fax the medication list to me, so I can show the children that it [the German remedy] is not prescribed by them [the outpatient clinic]... ...and then I fax the medication plan to the [rehabilitee's] general practitioner, so she is updated on what is happening... so that she does not prescribe other medication that may not work with the current ones. (Healthcare worker, 24-11-2011).

The healthcare worker then concluded that the task required three communication activities: with the hospital, the relatives, and the general practitioner. All in all, validating a medication plan may take between one hour of one day, to eight hours distributed over four days. Typically, this task takes three hours of work, distributed over three days.

In addition to the foregoing contingencies, there are difficulties in contacting persons, people not reporting back as promised, telephone queues, and even finding the right contact information within the existing information system. To illustrate, during fieldwork the following conversation between a healthcare worker at a computer (CW1) and an assisting colleague (CW2) was recorded:

CW1: I cannot find him [the general practitioner]... I cannot find his communication, but we have received it.
CW2: You will have to try some different [search criteria]...try the telephone number.
CW1: ...but I have tried it all...
CW2: Maybe you should delete some of it [content in search fields] and just use one thing. Try the telephone number only, and not the outpatient clinic name.
CW1: Only the telephone number?
CW2: ...yes, for example, sometimes it [the system] responds when you just use one thing [search criterion]...
CW1 (locates the correct information): I thought I had tried first with the telephone number... (Observation 24-11-2011).

The internal contingencies of the rehabilitation process are predominantly caused by day-to-day changes in rehabilitees' conditions. They have good and bad days, and do not always have the resources to participate in scheduled activities. This may also be due to common illnesses, alcoholism, or periodic confusion. Such problems may require altering, postponing, or cancelling planned activities, or even terminating a rehabilitee's stay at the Care Hotel. Hence, ad hoc changes in individual rehabilitation plans and the healthcare providers' schedules are frequent, and may affect the relevance of various external collaborative partners. The contingencies require

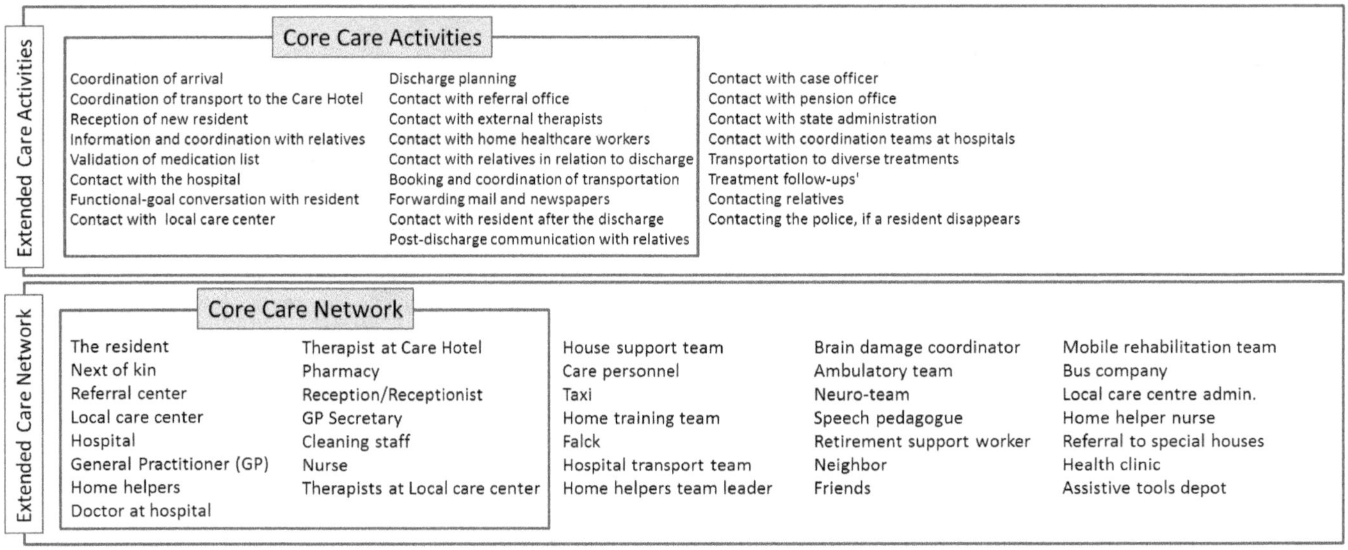

Figure 4. Care activities and actors involved in care.

additional articulation work, and work to re-establish work arrangements, which in turn affects other actions.

External contingencies are often caused by missing or incorrect information from external partners. This includes failure to communicate the correct date and time of a new rehabilitee's arrival, or special conditions related to a particular rehabilitee. A healthcare worker stated: 'Once they [the hospital] sent us someone who weighed 130 kg… [without a lifting aid]… they had to return [to the hospital]′ (healthcare worker, 22-11-2011). The hospital's discharge summary which usually arrives with the rehabilitee does not always include information on hospital-initiated rehabilitation and progress, because the physiotherapists at the hospital have their own documentation system. Then, the Care Hotel must contact the hospital (phone or e-mail) to obtain information on rehabilitees' functional levels, or even re-assess this with new tests.

Shifting and heterogeneous external collaborators

Situated at the margin of its external collaborators' core foci, coordinating and maintaining steady rehabilitation processes is challenging for the Care Hotel. Even locating relevant staff at the other organizations is difficult, and there is rarely any way to know when the relevant hospital nurse or physician is available, and has the time to talk. All external collaborators have limited time to invest in the cross-organizational work related to the rehabilitees, for which the Care Hotel is the primary responsible unit.

To obtain an overview of activities and collaborators, lists of both were generated with the staff at workshops. At these workshops, staff identified seventeen collaborative activities, almost always part of a rehabilitee's process as core care activities, and an additional sixteen collaborative activities were identified as periodically occurring (i.e., part of the extended set of care activities) during a rehabilitee's stay or on an as-needed basis (see Figure 4, Top).

At the workshops, Care Hotel staff also identified fifteen different partners (excluding Care Hotel staff) as collaborators who participate regularly or 'in most cases' in the above-mentioned activities. Another twenty-one partners were identified, that participate occasionally, depending on the rehabilitee and particular situations. We call these two subsets of partners the 'core care network' and the 'extended care network'. In Figure 4 (bottom), the partners are listed in descending order of the frequency with which they participate in the diverse collaborative care activities. Ideally, from the Care Hotel's perspective, only the core care network is needed to accomplish all patient activities. But this is rarely the case; as activities become complex and involve more partners, the centrality of actors may change. Figure 4 illustrates the difficulties the Care Hotel encounters when working out stable rehabilitation processes. Although this is possible with regard to the core activities and core care network, it is cumbersome with the extended care activities and actors. Working out a lasting work arrangement with these is an investment that does not clearly pay off by reducing the amount of articulation work. Instead, the healthcare providers spend time on ad hoc management and coordination of rehabilitees' rehabilitation and everyday lives. Similarly, the external collaborators belong to various organizations and professions, and often have limited or no understanding of the field of work at the Care Hotel. Therefore, the Care Hotel staff must invest effort to establish a shared understanding of, and overlapping stances towards the situation. For example, they must repeatedly explain to taxi companies the special transport requirements of rehabilitees (space for a wheel chair, high seats, etc.).

Many collaborative settings share similar challenges of aligning stances, establishing overlapping understandings of the field of work, and determining routines. However, in cases of interdepartmental cooperation or telemedicine for patients with chronic diseases, these are established over time by the actors involved. Long-term collaborators exist, such as a few hospital wards that discharge many patients to the Care Hotel. But there are also many temporary collaborators with whom constant effort must be made to support each individual rehabilitation process.

DISCUSSION

The Care Hotel's activities are 'in-between', as they a pivot around temporary rehabilitees, and b) depend extensively on external collaborators, c) whose composition varies, and d) who have different goals. This 'in-betweenness' presents specific challenges for the Care Hotel, as it must obtain, validate, and distribute information; coordinate both core and extended tasks; and achieve collaboration among the heterogeneous partners.

As outlined in 'Related Work', the cooperative challenges at the Care hotel are similar to those found with unit hand-overs, transitional care, and inter-departmental or organizational transfers, and care coordination across settings [1, 26, 29, 30, 37]: lack of overview, integrated care, and follow-ups; incomplete information; ad hoc, multi-disciplinary collaboration; negotiating agreements between organizational entities and actors with different goals and interests. The recommended solutions calls for common infrastructures (such as Health Information Exchange, or EPRs), standardized transfer protocols or care coordination agreements that address the different information needs of the various actors, align goals and delineate responsibilities. However, these settings typically have the advantage of existing within the general framework of the healthcare sector, with the resources of existing or developing standards, shared infrastructures, and well-defined roles, functions, and responsibilities that this entails. The Care Hotel must work across and beyond the healthcare sector, and standard protocols and common infrastructures are resource-intensive solutions that presently do not seem economically viable or achievable within a reasonable time, owing to the heterogeneity and mix of stable and temporary collaborators. For example, general practitioners may have different EPRs, which makes integration with the Care Hotel's systems cumbersome. Also, when directly asked whether they wanted direct access to the hospitals' EPR, staff promptly replied 'No': it is not designed for them, and they would require assistance to filter and interpret the EPR data.

In certain respects, the case of the Care Hotel is also similar and relevant to settings within a more fragmented healthcare system, such as that in the USA. It shares with these the challenges of identifying, contacting, monitoring, and collaborating [30]. Here, healthcare providers and Patient Centered Medical Homes would seem to share the predicament of being in-between, as long as common infrastructures are unavailable, or they are situated between them. Fruitful comparative analyses may be made between these settings and the Care Hotel.

Collaboration in-between, based on the Care Hotel case, entails work arrangements that are brittle, semi-opaque, and partial: brittle, because internal and external contingencies constantly require articulation work to stabilize the work arrangement (e.g. family members that administer non-prescribed medication); semi-opaque, since the fleetingly involved collaborators' understanding of the respective fields of work is limited (e.g. taxi-drivers and various general practitioners); partial, since the arrangements include only the core collaborators involved (e.g. the municipal referral office). Maintaining the brittle work arrangements and keeping rehabilitation processes on track requires continuous articulation work and effort. Such effort may yield various outcomes: lack of effort, as when someone fails to fulfil a necessary task (e.g. a general practitioner fails to validate a medication plan); duplicated efforts, as when requests or information must be forwarded several times (e.g. multiple calls to a general practitioner for drug validation); or conflicting efforts (e.g. relatives and pharmacy provide contradictory information, or relatives administer drugs owing to or misunderstandings).

Under these circumstances, establishing understandings of the common fields of work raises difficulties that may be framed in terms of social, action, and activity awareness [7]. Social awareness concerns knowing who is available: For example, the staff at the Care Hotel have a good sense of what their colleagues are doing and whether they can help, whereas the availability of general or hospital physicians is opaque. The healthcare workers state that they spend hours each day on internal communication, although it is rare that a general practitioner is aware of, or understands the day-to-day activities at the Care Hotel, and his or her impact on these activities. Action awareness concerns the status of tasks to be conducted: Care Hotel staff achieves this by working and interacting collocatedly, and sharing the same collaborative resources (records, notebooks, calendars, and Post-its®), whereas the task status of non-collocated actors requires information exchange effort. However, activity awareness is often a challenge: the shared understanding of the common field of work, including the overall objectives, interdependencies, and roles. Between core collaborators such an understanding is achievable, but is much more challenging and effort-intensive with fleeting and peripheral collaborators (compare [26] and [29]). Work arrangements often remain partial, since only for core collaborators does establishing an arrangement pay off in terms of less articulation work. The result is the need to establish ad hoc collaboration.

The last point accords with the general thrust of our theoretical framework of symbolic interactionism, which takes pains to emphasize the ongoing effort needed to achieve collaboration and order (by aligning stances, articulation work, working-out, etc.) [36]. Simultaneously, this approach tends to emphasize a shift towards arrangements, and regarding these as stable and stabilizing interactions: arrangements become embedded in artefacts as protocols stipulating action, and reduce articulation work and ad hoc coordination (e.g. [31]). Hence, proposed solutions often incline towards establishing standards and protocols for collaboration, as reflected in the studies in CSCW, transitional care, and care coordination noted above (see 'Related Work'). Furthermore, discussions focus on whether the embedded protocols should stipulate collaboration weakly (as a map) or strongly (as a script) (ibid). In contrast, our case highlights a constant state of having to continuously establish collaboration, and a failure to reach stable arrangements with embedded protocols. For example, Care Hotel staff found it difficult to identify standard ways of conducting activities, and many of these were rated as highly dynamic. Also, collaborators, such as various hospital wards, taxi drivers, general practitioners, and relatives may be involved only temporarily, and therefore represent a diversity that challenges stable work arrangements. The challenges are less about weak or strong stipulations of action, and more about having channels of communication and coordination. Instead of a map or script, a protocol embedded in an arrangement or IT system should be an open 'canvas' establishing coordination with almost no stipulations.

DESIGNING FOR FLEXIBLE USE

The Care Hotel's challenges of collaboration in-between may be summarized as follows: stabilizing brittle work arrangements; making collaborators' fields of work more transparent to others; contributing to a comprehensive, rather than a partial overview of collaborators; supporting ad hoc collaboration and articulation work.

Given that these challenges arise from the heterogeneous set of collaborators and contingency of work activities, building a platform for collaboration includes (as a minimum) the following design challenges: a) establishing a shared platform of communication, that b) is flexible enough to enable standard and ad hoc communication and coordination, c) enables a comprehensive overview of required information and establishes shared understandings of information among collaborators, and d) enables articulation work among both stable and more fleeting collaborative partners, which may not share work rhythms, roles, and goals. Since one common infrastructure is out of reach, the first issue involves the combination of media that might be feasibly integrated and used.

We suggest two complementary solutions. First, a person-based strategy is to enhance activity awareness (overall aims, rationales, work arrangements, shared field of work) by enhancing mutual organizational transparency. Core collaborators should be invited to the Care Hotel to meet its rehabilitees and staff, and learn about its work processes, and vice versa. The invitation should include temporary collaborators, but information via pamphlets and web pages should be readily available. Second, since work arrangements are brittle and healthcare workers must constantly establish ad hoc collaboration and reworking arrangements, we propose a design for flexible use, to actively support continuously (re-)establishing collaboration among various, and partly shifting actors. The system and shared protocols or standards should be open and flexible, like a canvas. This aligns neatly with the infrastructuring approach, and the ideal of flexible use previously outlined.

Next, we present an explorative design proposal to address the collaborative challenges at the Care Hotel. The design proposal is intended to bridge the gap between 'design implications' and actually designing, and also aims to stimulate further reflection on the challenges related to 'in-between' places.

Infrastructuring for the Care Hotel

The proposal presented below is inspired by four technologies: whiteboards, timelines, activity and message notifications, and loosely coupled web architectures. First, whiteboards are widely used, and are central coordinative devices in healthcare [40]. Large displays support complex, contingent planning of surgeries, by providing overviews and updatable information, on- or off-line [41]. Whiteboards have also been suggested as a way to overcome the challenges of hand-overs, and to support continuous care by increasing the visibility of information [28]. At the Care Hotel, a whiteboard is already used to visualize and share information: information may easily be changed, everyone present can see it, and entering information requires only the ability to write. Second and third, activity and message notifications combined with visualized timelines have been shown to be useful in virtual organizations. Notifications support information exchange and action awareness, and visualized timelines provide overviews, reviewability, and an understanding of the overarching collaborative arrangement [7]. Fourth, a flexible and loosely coupled web architecture (e.g. REST [17]) allows for distributed, ad hoc access to data objects.

To support the Care Hotel staff in both their local, day-to-day activities and their (current and future) collaborations with heterogeneous yet undefined actors, we suggest designing a flexible system. We envision a flexible interface, accessible in the Care Hotel's staff office via a large, electronic whiteboard, and via the healthcare workers' computers. The displays would allow staff to add each rehabilitee, and their past, present, and planned activities on a timeline that acts as a backdrop to their work (Figure 5 provides a simplified illustration of the interface). The interface is divided into four areas: the objects pane (top), the main work area or canvas (middle), and the timeline elements pane (bottom). To the left, there is a rehabilitee selection pane. Timeline elements may be selected or created from the bottom pane and dragged and dropped onto the main work area. Similarly, objects from the top pane may be attached to a specific rehabilitee's timeline. To support flexible use, 'objects' are openly defined, and may be placed anywhere on a rehabilitee's timeline (compare [13]). New objects may also be created to respond to future use situations and innovations.

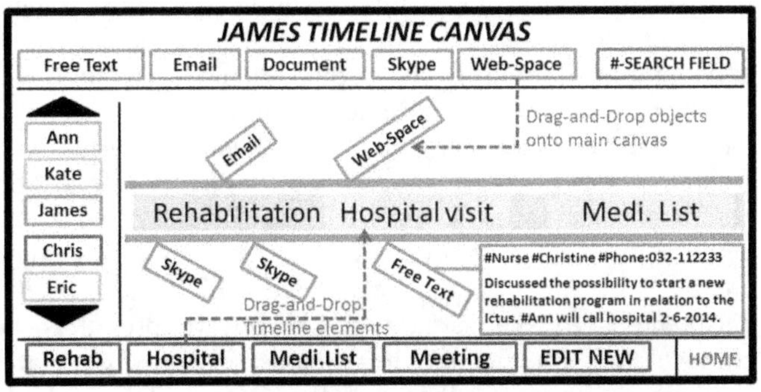

Figure 5. Simplified view of the flexible collaborative system.

However, since *some* activities recur and templates exist, an initial set of objects may be preformatted: 1) a *free text* object that creates a simple text box, allowing any textual information to be inserted; 2) an *E-mail* object that enables and saves an e-mail conversation with an external partner; 3) A *Document* object that may hold an image, or .pdf file, Word document, or similar; 4) a *Skype conversation object* that enables and saves a combined text and video/audio dialogue; 5) a *Shared Web-space* object that sends a web link to a partner by e-mail (e.g. a nurse at a hospital ward, a taxi company, or a general practitioner responsible for a specific rehabilitee's medication list). The web link allows the collaborative partner to access a shared web space from his or her own computer, where text, images, and other data may be inserted and shared with the Care Hotel (e.g. data from the hospital EPR). Each instantiated object is tagged with the rehabilitee's ID, time, and date associated with the object's location on the timeline, and the date and time of its creation. Each object may also be tagged with user-defined hash tags. Hash tags allow for searching and filtering of information (e.g. all conversations made with a specific nurse regarding one rehabilitee) and for the visualization of activities and touch points across rehabilitees. Hash tags allow staff to flexibly define relations and assign meaning to data and may develop into a vocabulary that makes sense to staff and its work practice.

The whiteboard is physically situated at the Care hotel, but through objects such as *E-mail* and *Shared Web-space*, it becomes a flexible, distributed, collaborative tool. It allows for both collaboration and privacy through the healthcare workers' control of whom to invite and what information to share. Some information on standard tasks and core collaborators may be formatted, and automatically imported into the whiteboard interface through dedicated objects, for example from the municipality's healthcare records and the hospital EPR, or from frequent collaborative partners, where the investment of determining a work arrangement in the form of a particular module may pay off. However, these standardized objects are supplemented by open-ended objects for non-routine tasks and temporary collaborators, for example, simple 'free text' or .pdf repository 'containers'. The whiteboard at the office provides staff with an overview of each rehabilitee's programme and associated tasks, and makes ongoing coordination and negotiation visible, accessible, and retrievable. Online access through collaborative objects situated on a rehabilitee's timeline provides information and an overview to external collaborators, enabling awareness among collaborators while protecting the rehabilitees' privacy by filtering information or access control.

The proposed solution does not eliminate communication and negotiation via telephone, nor the risk of absent, double, or conflicting efforts. However, it supports current activities and may reduce the amount of articulation work and re-forming arrangements, and helps to establish common fields of work among the Care Hotel collaborators. Also, perceiving the whiteboard as a 'repository' for 'information and collaborative objects', rather than a predefined system, facilitates flexible use and infrastructuring, rather than tight integrations and a one-system-fits-all solution.

The day-to-day use of the infrastructuring proposal

A healthcare worker may select a rehabilitee from the left pane to visualize the corresponding timeline on the main work area (Figure 5). The healthcare worker may then add timeline elements (e.g. mid-point evaluation, hospital visit, medication list approval) to the rehabilitee's timeline by dragging these from the bottom pane up to the 'canvas'. Also, the healthcare worker may add activity and collaborative objects from the top pane to the timeline. To add a telephone number and other contact details for a specific hospital nurse who is the contact person when a rehabilitee temporarily visits the hospital, he or she may enter this data as a *Free text* object associated with the timeline element, 'hospital stay'.

Communication and collaborative objects, such as an *E-mail* object may be used by staff to communicate with a rehabilitee's general practitioner about the medication list. A photograph of a specific rehabilitation aid, or video instruction may also be added to a specific rehabilitee's timeline as a *Document* object. Furthermore, an object may be flagged as 'ongoing' or 'completed'. This functionality allows staff to track negotiations and ongoing collaborative activities. The online functionality provided by diverse collaborative objects using the REST-based service architecture creates a loosely coupled system where external collaborators may interact directly with relevant data in a privacy-ensuring view of the timeline, via an Internet browser, without accessing other, sensitive information. By seeing their own activities in relation to the timeline (and in relation to upcoming, planned activities at the Care Hotel), external collaborators may improve their awareness of the situation at the Care Hotel, and of the need for their timely response. In turn, the above-outlined functionality may support an increased transparency of collaborators' fields of work. Healthcare workers must telephone to initially contact a new actor, but once contact has been established, the collaborative objects, such as the *E-mail* or *Shared Web-space* objects, enable asynchronous communication and automatic documentation between the external actors and the Care Hotel. All the functionalities should help stabilize brittle work arrangements between the Care Hotel and its collaborators. The loosely coupled web architecture allows partners to seamlessly enter and leave the system and collaborations. In turn, this supports the establishment of ad hoc collaboration. Hash tags (automatically created or manually added) allow healthcare workers to search and filter objects and information.

The timeline approach aims to provide an overview of each rehabilitee's progress, and the current status of coordination and negotiations, in contrast to the piecemeal fashion in which information is currently received and documented. This may not change the character of the initial contact with external collaborative partners, but helps systematize the information needed from and by them. The *Shared Web-space* object and other collaborative objects support loosely coupled, and both opportunistic and scheduled collaboration among heterogeneous partners, each with their own work rhythms and trajectories. By providing overviews and detailed, revisable information, the solution supports collaborative actors' understanding of one another's fields of work.

CONCLUSION

In this paper, we have analysed the collaborative challenges of the Care Hotel, and argue that these have specific characteristics, owing to the Care Hotel's position: between existing infrastructures, and among shifting and heterogeneous collaborators. The challenges of working in-between include stabilizing brittle work arrangements, achieving a comprehensive, rather than a partial overview of collaborators, making collaborators' fields of work transparent to one another, and ad hoc efforts to align stances, coordinate tasks, and reach agreements. Hence, the study highlights the ongoing and repeated effort needed to establish collaboration, and the necessity of developing 'open' agreements and standards that enable establishment of channels of communication with flexible stipulations of actions (shared canvases, rather than maps or scripts).

As one way to address the foregoing challenges, and of spurring further reflection, we propose an infrastructuring approach, designing for flexible use and redesign; generic 'empty' objects may be flexibly used and redesigned, but also preformatted, whenever stable work patterns occur, whether these pertain to standard activities, stable collaborators, or reoccurring modes of communication. The 'objects' and the 'canvas' on which they are placed may be shared via a local, public whiteboard, and on a web browser, to enable rapid communication and coordination.

As governments and corporations in Europe and North America continue to invest heavily in building integrated IT infrastructures for healthcare, we suspect that more in-between places will emerge. Large infrastructures come with standards that often conflict with local settings, which must either adjust, or opt out of use and future collaborations. Similarly, as hospitals focus increasingly on treatment, and shift aftercare into private homes, municipalities, and such, more in-between facilities will emerge, which must coordinate with a range of heterogeneous partners. In such translocations of care, neither universal standardization, nor endless localization are options, and often the challenge will be that of in-betweeness. At the same time, healthcare providers in contexts of fragmented healthcare sectors may face challenges similar to those of the Care Hotel. In both settings, imaginative solutions to the challenges of working in-between are required.

ACKNOWLEDGEMENTS

We would like to thank all involved project partners and especially the healthcare workers at the Care Hotel.

REFERENCES

1. Abraham, J. and Reddy, M.C. Moving patients around: a field study of coordination between clinical and non-clinical staff in hospitals. In *Proc. CSCW 2008*, ACM Press (2008), p. 225-228.
2. Abraham, J. and Reddy, M.C. Re-coordinating activities: an investigation of articulation work in patient transfers. In *Proc. CSCW 2013*, ACM Press (2013).
3. Bertelsen, O. Suffering Beyond Negotiation: Towards a Biographic Perspective on Cooperative Design for Therapy. In *Proc. COOP 2014,* Springer (2014).
4. Björgvinsson, E., Ehn, P., and Hillgren, P.-A. Participatory design and "democratizing innovation". In *Proc. PDC 2010*, ACM Press (2010), p. 41-50.
5. Bowers, J., Button, G., and Sharrock, W. Workflow From Within and Without: Technology and Cooperative Work on the Print Industry Shopfloor. In *Proc. ECSCW '95*, Springer (1995), p. 51-66.
6. Bowker, G.C. and Star, S.L. Sorting things out: Classification and its consequences. 1999.
7. Carroll, J.M., Neale, D.C., Isenhour, P.L., Rosson, M.B., and McCrickard, D.S. Notification and awareness: synchronizing task-oriented collaborative activity. *International Journal of Human-Computer Studies*, 2003, **58**(5), p. 605-632.
8. Christensen, L.R. and Grönvall, E. Challenges and Opportunities for Collaborative Technologies for Home Care Work. In *Proc. ECSCW 2011*, Springer (2011).
9. Clark, H.H. and Brennan, S.E. Grounding in communication. *Perspectives on socially shared cognition*, 1991, **13**(1991), p. 127-149.
10. Coleman, E.A. and Berenson, R.A. Lost in Transition: Challenges and Opportunities for Improving the Quality of Transitional Care. *Annals of Internal Medicine*, 2004, **141**(7), p. 533-536.

11. Coley, C., Li, Y., Medsger, A., Marrie, T., Fine, M., Kapoor, W., Lave, J., Detsky, A., Weinstein, M., and Singer, D. Preferences for home vs hospital care among low-risk patients with community-acquired pneumonia. *Archives of Internal Medicine*, 1996, **156**(14), p. 1565.
12. Dantec, C.L. and DiSalvo, C. Infrastructuring and the Formation of Publics in Participatory Design. *Social Studies of Science*, 2013.
13. Dix, A. Designing for appropriation. In *Proc. BCS-HCI 2007*, ACM Press (2007), p. 27-30.
14. Ellingsen, G. and Monteiro, E. A Patchwork Planet Integration and Cooperation in Hospitals. *Computer Supported Cooperative Work (CSCW)*, 2003, **12**(1).
15. Ellingsen, G. and Monteiro, E. Seamless Integration: Standardisation across Multiple Local Settings. *Computer Supported Cooperative Work (CSCW)*, 2006, **15**(5-6), p. 443-466.
16. Ellingsen, G., Monteiro, E., and Røed, K. Integration as interdependent workaround. *International Journal of Medical Informatics*, 2013, **82**(5), p. e161-e169.
17. Fielding, R.T. and Taylor, R.N. Principled design of the modern Web architecture. *ACM Trans. Internet Technol.*, 2002, **2**(2), p. 115-150.
18. Fitzpatrick, G. and Ellingsen, G. A Review of 25 Years of CSCW Research in Healthcare: Contributions, Challenges and Future Agendas. *Computer Supported Cooperative Work (CSCW)*, 2012, p. 1-57.
19. Gesano, G., Heins, F., and Naldini, A. Regional Challenges in the perspective of 2020, *Regional desparities and future challenges*, 2009, ISMERI Europa.
20. Gross, T. Supporting Effortless Coordination: 25 Years of Awareness Research. *Computer Supported Cooperative Work (CSCW)*, 2013, **22**(4-6), p. 425-474.
21. Halskov, K., Dalsg, P., #229, and rd. Inspiration card workshops. In *Proc. DIS 2006*, ACM Press (2006).
22. InnoSuTra. Tools for Developing Innovative Solutions-Attribute Listing. 2008; Available from: http://www.innosupport.net/uploads/media/4_5_Attribute_Listing.pdf.
23. Jeffs, L., Lyons, R., Merkley, J., and Bell, C. Clinicians' views on improving inter-organizational care transitions. *BMC Health Services Research*, 2013, **13**(1), p. 289.
24. Jeffs, L., Kitto, S., Merkley, J., Lyons, R.F., and Bell, C.M. Safety threats and opportunities to improve interfacility care transitions: insights from patients and family members. *Patient Prefer Adherence*, 2012, **6**.
25. Kane, B. and Luz, S. Achieving Diagnosis by Consensus. *Computer Supported Cooperative Work (CSCW)*, 2009, **18**(4), p. 357-392.
26. Lee, S., Tang, C., Park, S.Y., and Chen, Y. Loosely formed patient care teams: communication challenges and technology design. In *Proc. CSCW 2012*, ACM Press (2012), p. 867-876.
27. Monteiro, E., Pollock, N., Hanseth, O., and Williams, R. From Artefacts to Infrastructures. *Computer Supported Cooperative Work (CSCW)*, 2013, **22**(4-6), p. 575-607.
28. Randell, R., Wilson, S., Woodward, P., and Galliers, J. Beyond handover: supporting awareness for continuous coverage. *Cognition, Technology & Work*, 2010, **12**(4).
29. Ren, Y., Kiesler, S., and Fussell, S.R. Multiple group coordination in complex and dynamic task environments: Interruptions, coping mechanisms, and technology recommendations. *Journal of Management Information Systems*, 2008, **25**(1), p. 105-130.
30. Rudin, R.S. and Bates, D.W. Let the left hand know what the right is doing: a vision for care coordination and electronic health records. *Journal of the American Medical Informatics Association*, 2014, **21**(1), p. 13-16.
31. Schmidt, K. and Simone, C. Coordination mechanisms: Towards a conceptual foundation of CSCW systems design. *Computer Supported Cooperative Work (CSCW)*, 1996, **5**(2-3), p. 155-200.
32. Schmidt, K. and Wagner, I. Ordering systems: Coordinative practices and artifacts in architectural design and planning. *Computer Supported Cooperative Work (CSCW)*, 2004, **13**(5-6), p. 349-408.
33. Star, S.L. and Ruhleder, K. Steps toward an ecology of infrastructure: Design and access for large information spaces. *Information systems research*, 1996, **7**(1).
34. Star, S.L. and Bowker, G.C. How to infrastructure. *Handbook of new media: Social shaping and social consequences of ICTs*, 2006, p. 230-245.
35. Strauss, A., Fagerhaugh, S., Suczek, B., and Wiener, C. *Social Organization of Medical Work*. 1985.
36. Strauss, A.L. Continual permutations of action. 1993.
37. Symon, G., Long, K., and Ellis, J. The coordination of work activities: Cooperation and conflict in a hospital context. *Computer Supported Cooperative Work (CSCW)*, 1996, **5**(1), p. 1-31.
38. Taylor, E.F., Lake, T., Nysenbaum, J., Peterson, G., and Meyers, D. Coordinating Care in the Medical Neighborhood: Critical Components and Available Mechanisms. *Mathematica Policy Research Rep.*, 2011.
39. Thraen, I., Bair, B., Mullin, S., and Weir, C.R. Characterizing "information transfer" by using a Joint Cognitive Systems model to improve continuity of care in the aged. *International Journal of Medical Informatics*, 2012, **81**(7).
40. Wears, R., Perry, S., Wilson, S., Galliers, J., and Fone, J. Emergency department status boards: user-evolved artefacts for inter- and intra-group coordination. *Cognition, Technology & Work*, 2007, **9**(3), p. 163-170.
41. Xiao, Y., Hu, P., Moss, J., de Winter, J., Venekamp, D., Mackenzie, C., Seagull, F., and Perkins, S. Opportunities and challenges in improving surgical work flow. *Cognition, Technology & Work*, 2008, **10**(4).
42. Østerlund, C. Documents in Place: Demarcating Places for Collaboration in Healthcare Settings. *Computer Supported Cooperative Work (CSCW)*, 2008, **17**(2-3).

The Modern Day Baby Book: Enacting Good Mothering and Stewarding Privacy on Facebook

Priya Kumar, Sarita Schoenebeck
School of Information
University of Michigan
{priyaku,yardi}@umich.edu

ABSTRACT

The practice of sharing family photographs is as old as the camera itself. Many mothers now share baby photos online, yet little is known about what kinds of baby photos they share and their motivations for doing so. Drawing on semi-structured interviews with 22 new mothers, we find that they share cute, funny, milestone, and family and friend photos but refrain from sharing crying and naked photos. While some mothers harbor concerns about controlling information, oversharing, and digital footprints, the benefits of receiving validation outweigh their concerns. Sharing baby photos on Facebook helps new mothers enact and receive validation of "good mothering." However, mothers are charged with the responsibility of stewarding their children's privacy and identities online. We introduce the concept of *privacy stewardship* to describe the responsibility parents take on when deciding what is appropriate to share about their children online *and* ensuring that family and friends respect and maintain the integrity of those rules. As a result, mothers must exchange benefits of sharing baby photos with risks of creating digital footprints for their child.

Author Keywords

Motherhood; photo sharing; babies; Facebook; social media.

ACM Classification Keywords

H.5.m. Information interfaces and presentation (e.g., HCI): Miscellaneous.

INTRODUCTION

In the Fall of 2013, Amy Webb wrote a column in Slate explaining how she refused to post photos of her daughter online. Doing so, she said, would create a trove of data that college admissions counselors and future homecoming dates could scour [3]. She argued that posting photos online prevented her daughter from having any future hope of anonymity. Webb's behaviors were extreme—she even chose her daughter's name based on Gmail availability—but her narrative was shared heavily by mainstream media sources. The story highlighted a tension between new parents' desire to share baby photos online and the risks that might arise through this sharing. Though we originally conceived of this research as a study of privacy violations of sharing baby photos on Facebook, our analysis of interview transcripts revealed a complex set of decisions new mothers made about the nuanced tradeoffs and benefits available through sharing baby photos.

Taking and sharing family photos is a common practice. Pregnancy and childbirth are periods of "snapshot significance," where the expectant mother and then the newborn are primary "on-camera participant[s]" [10]. Family photography increases when couples have children [10,16,45] and first-time parents are particularly prolific photographers [10,16]. Evidence suggests similar patterns are playing out online. Among Facebook users, 98% of new mothers upload pictures to the site [5]. Mothers tend to post more multimedia content after having a child and mothers who use Facebook report posting baby pictures more often than baby-related status updates [34]. We focus on mothers because women tend to be more active social network site users, mothers are the fastest growing demographic of social media users, and mothers post to Facebook more than fathers do [5,29,34]. Though roles are changing, women are often still the primary child caregivers [22].

The transition to motherhood can be rewarding but can also be demanding, and can cause women to feel isolated and alone [4]. Sharing online offers a variety of possible benefits to new mothers, including information and social support, which can help to alleviate stress and increase wellbeing [5,14,34,46]. However, these benefits have been documented primarily in text-based communication platforms like blogs, forums, and social networking sites. Our research questions were: 1) What baby pictures do new mothers share on Facebook? and 2) What factors do new mothers consider when sharing baby pictures on Facebook? To investigate these questions, we conducted semi-structured interviews with 22 new mothers about how they share baby photos on Facebook. This study reveals mothers' decision-making processes about sharing baby photos online and puts forth the argument that sharing baby photos online allows mothers to enact and receive validation of "good mothering." We introduce the concept of *privacy stewardship* to describe the responsibility

CSCW 2015, March 14–18, 2015, Vancouver, BC, Canada.

ACM 978-1-4503-2922-4/15/03...$15.00.
http://dx.doi.org/10.1145/2675133.2675149.

mothers take on as they consider what kinds of baby photos are appropriate to share and the implications for their children's digital footprint. Results also extend literature on family photo sharing as a small group activity and reconsider it in the context of broadcasting to a large and diverse online audience.

RELATED WORK

Family Photography

The widespread adoption of inexpensive cameras throughout the twentieth century gave rise to what Chalfen (1987) called "Kodak culture," referring to the taking, organizing, and sharing of family pictures [10]. These pictures are types of "home mode" communication, which Chalfen defined as "a pattern of interpersonal and small group communication centered around the home" [10]. Pictures of children are a staple of family photography [10,16,48,51], and the birth of a child has been among the most common reasons for families to buy a camera [10]. People share pictures with family members and friends to foster connection and maintain relationships [13,19,33,45,48]. Family members particularly enjoy seeing pictures of young children [2,13,45,48], though parents may feel "pressure from extended families to keep a steady stream of images coming" [2]. Though family photograph collections may contain many pictures, certain types of pictures are more prevalent: births more than deaths, young children more than older children, and firstborn children more than their younger siblings [10,50].

Pictures of "firsts" begin soon after the birth and continue as documentation of major milestones: going home, meeting family, eating, sleeping, playing, smiling, bathing, crawling, or walking. Such pictures "tug on people's emotions" [51], transport viewers into another place and time, and play significant roles in memory and storytelling [10,16,43]. Certain facets of a child's early life do not appear in pictures, such as crying, distressed facial expressions, breastfeeding, dirty diapers, rashes, or health problems [10]. Thus, family pictures portray limited, structured depictions of the way people want their lives to appear [10]. Families "strive to construct and present idealised images of the family, both through careful selection of occasions and rigorous staging of events [39]. These self-presentation considerations also occur with digital photography. People typically delete low-quality or unattractive pictures [23,54]. Affordances of social networking sites, such as the ability to untag or delete pictures, further enable users to modify the way they present themselves to their audience [32].

Audience, Information Disclosure, and Privacy

Privacy and photography are deeply intertwined. Early concern over the dissemination of pictures prompted Warren and Brandeis (1890) to call for a right to privacy:

> "Instantaneous photographs and newspaper enterprise have invaded the sacred precincts of private and domestic life; and numerous mechanical devices threaten to make good the prediction that `what is whispered in the closet shall be proclaimed from the house-tops.' For years there has been a feeling that the law must afford some remedy for the unauthorized circulation of portraits of private persons" [53].

The right to privacy debate is magnified online. While physically displaying a photo reflects a person's decision that the time, place, and audience are suitable for photo sharing, online audiences are often unknown, forcing people to consider an "imagined audience" [6,26,30]. For example, Facebook users underestimate their audience size by a factor of three [6]. Vitak and Kim present six self-disclosure goals on Facebook: social approval, social control, intimacy, identity clarification, relief of distress, and personal record [52]. They also describe how participants manage self-disclosure risks, including regulating their Friend networks, targeting messages, or censoring themselves [52]. These types of strategies help Facebook users to manage multiple groups ("group co-presence") and navigate multiple audiences ("context collapse") [24,30]. Hogan suggests that people envision a lowest common denominator, only posting content that would be appropriate for any Facebook Friend to see [15].

Privacy scholars have emphasized the need for privacy to be contextual and proportional, where technical designs are appropriate to the social settings and risks a user might experience [12,18,37]. Communication Privacy Management (CPM) offers a lens for understanding how people manage privacy boundaries and disclose private information through five principles: ownership, control, privacy rules, shared ownership, and boundary turbulence [40]. Petronio argues that people take on the responsibility of guarding other people's private information when it is put into their trust, which can lead to betrayal, errors in judgment, deception, gossip, and privacy dilemmas [40]. Photo owners can experience boundary turbulence when the desired level of privacy or exposure is inconsistent with that of those who gain shared ownership, creating a need for "discursive practice" in how privacy is framed. In American culture, "infants and babies tend not to be accorded much privacy… because they are not cognitively aware of such privacy needs" [40]. Nonetheless, people are protective of how pictures of children can be shared. Parents typically express concern over sharing pictures of children or information that reveals the location of children online [1,2,33]. Privacy concerns are expanded with the introduction of new ways of interacting with pictures online, such as tagging [7], challenging parents to incorporate an increasingly complex and vast set of considerations about how they share content online.

Motherhood, Identity, and Internet Use

The transition to motherhood can be a challenging experience (e.g. [4,25,41,47]). This adjustment may be complicated by social factors like "unrealistic expectations, and cultural stereotypes of motherhood as easy, natural, and fulfilling, and of the mother-child relationship as immediately and unambiguously positive" [25]. As a result, mothers face social pressures to enact and perform good mothering [11]. One way of doing this is to present themselves to others using their children as "props" and showcasing their children's manners, clothes, and activities as reflections of their mothering [11]. Online, mothers can present a constructed view of themselves via photos of their children that they choose to share. Among new parents who use Facebook, 98% of new mothers had posted pictures of their children to Facebook, compared to 83% of fathers [5]. Pictures can be powerful tools to help women navigate their transition to motherhood [44]. Photo sharing on Facebook can highlight relationships and foster social connection [32,38]. Mothers may prefer sharing photos online because it is easier and faster than telling a story [21]. Both Morris and Bartholomew et al.'s survey studies find that over 95% of mothers on Facebook have shared photos of their children on Facebook and these posts attract more attention [5,34]; but neither investigates motivations for sharing and perceived benefits, risks, and implications, a gap addressed in the current research.

Mothers use the Internet to seek information, advice, and support [14,34,42,46]. Sharing information about one's children online provides social capital benefits [20]. Women who participate in "mommy blogging" enjoy validation and solidarity [28], develop a sense of community with others [35], and may experience greater wellbeing and increased feelings of connectedness [31]. Almost 40% of Facebook users have a parent or child relationship on their profile, and parent-child communication is common, including parent-grandparent discussions about grandchildren [9]. However, Gibson and Hanson suggest that new mothers preferred not to use Facebook as a "baby diary" but rather as a place to share information about themselves, revealing a desire to "preserve their identity as a person in their own right" [14]. Self-presentation and impression management on Facebook are well-documented (e.g., [5,11,52]); our study extends this work to show how identity performance allows mothers to enact—and receive validation of—good mothering, both important processes for the wellbeing of new parents. It further focuses on privacy considerations new mothers take on when sharing photos of their children online.

METHODS

We conducted an interview study with 22 new mothers to gather their narratives and experiences about sharing baby photos on Facebook. To recruit participants, we posted paper fliers to local daycare centers and wellness centers, and posted online recruitment text to Meetup.com, a local Yahoo! group for parents, and a local university graduate student group. We also used snowball recruiting among personal networks. Most participants were first time mothers (n=19) with at least 1 child ages 0-2 (n=21). All participants either lived in the United States (n=20) or had lived in the United States in the past (n=2). Participants ranged in age from mid-20s to late-30s. All were married to men and lived with their husbands and children. Seven participants were stay-at-home mothers and 15 worked out of the home. The 26 children ranged in age from three months to five years. Eighteen children were male and 8 were female. All participants had Facebook accounts.

We conducted interviews in the Fall of 2013 and the Winter of 2014. Interviews lasted about one hour, and ranged from 50 to 80 minutes. We conducted interviews until we reached data saturation in the stories we were hearing from participants. Nine interviews were conducted face-to-face, 11 over the phone, and two on Skype. Three in-person interviews were in their home and six outside of their home. Babies were present at four of the face-to-face interviews. After walking through the consent process, participants logged into their Facebook profile to refer to it during the interview. We looked at participants' Facebook profiles during the interview either in-person or remotely but did not have access to them outside of the interview period. We chose not to collect pictures to protect participants' privacy.

We began with warm-up demographics questions to build rapport with participants. We then asked participants to tell us about how they used Facebook and their experiences seeing baby-related content on Facebook. We asked them about experiences with photos they had taken, shared, or removed (e.g., did they share an ultrasound image online; had they ever taken down a baby picture they shared online; had anyone else ever posted a picture of their child online). We also asked them to share their attitudes and opinions about sharing baby photos of Facebook (e.g., while they were pregnant, did they think they would share photos of their babies on Facebook once they became a mother; did they envision one day showing their child the pictures they shared of the child online?). We asked participants about their opinions of Facebook, Inc. as a company. We also asked them about other sites they shared baby photos on and why. Because of our original focus on privacy, we did not use the term "privacy" in the recruitment materials, consent form, or interview questions to avoid priming their responses. If they introduced the term in the course of the interview, we used it subsequently in the context of how they framed it.

We transcribed the interviews and used an inductive approach to develop codes [49]. In a first pass, we hand-wrote codes while reading through the interviews. In a second pass, we created a more detailed list of codes. We discussed the codes as a research team then used NVivo to code transcripts. Drawing on codes and related literature, we organized our results around categories of pictures that participants did or did not share, why they shared them or not, and factors that influenced these decision-making processes. We use the term "picture" to refer to the objects and "photography" to refer to the act of taking a picture.

Mother*	Child*	Child Age	Work**
Ella	Neil	7 mos	SAHM
Clara	Ryan	1 yr	SAHM
Emily	Randall	6 mos	SAHM
Karen	Brooke, Brendan	5 yrs, 13 mos	SAHM
Christine	Oliver	2 yrs, 2 mos	WOHM
Rebecca	Louise	1 year	GS
Sabrina	Owen	2 years	SAHM
Jimena	Andres	4 years	GS
Lee Ann	Hunter	16 mos	WOHM
Judy	Quinn	14 mos	WOHM
Brianna	Abigail	4 mos	WOHM
Marina	Cooper	10 mos	WOHM
Jessica	Matthew	5 mos	WOHM
Shelby	Finn	8 mos	SAHM
Lindsey	Charlotte	16 mos	GS
Rita	Ava, Michael	2.5 yrs, 9 mos	WOHM
Melissa	Connor, Thomas	2.5 yrs, 3 mos	WOHM
Cara	Ye-jun	2 yrs	WOHM
Carrie	Gabriel, Grace	1 yr, 1 yr	WOHM
Wendy	Ashley	4 mos	SAHM
Isabel	Emiliano	1 yr	WOHM
Zainab	Nailah	8 mos	WOHM

Table 1. *Pseudonyms. **WOHM=Work out of Home, SAHM=Stay at Home, GS=Grad Student.

We use "posting" when focusing on participants' actions and "sharing" when focusing on their motivation.

Limitations
This study's sample primarily included educated, married, heterosexual white women in the United States or who had lived in the United States at some point. Participants' ages ranged from mid-twenties to late-thirties. This study does not address the role of fathers—an important gap to address. Although we viewed participants' Facebook profiles during the interview and took care to uncover impression management behaviors they may have been engaging with us as researchers, we relied on participants' self-reports and perceptions of their own behavior. We did not interview Facebook non-users or Facebook resistors; their attitudes are likely to be different than those reported here. Our recruitment process is likely to have yielded mothers who have had generally positive experiences on Facebook. A downside of not mentioning privacy in the recruitment is that we may have omitted a demographic of mothers who are reluctant Facebook users or have had negative privacy experiences.

RESULTS
Results are organized into four sections. The first two sections set the stage by describing what types of baby photos mothers choose to share. The third and fourth sections describe benefits and risks perceived from sharing baby photos and strategies for managing those tradeoffs.

Types of Baby Photos Shared on Facebook
Participants typically shared four types of photographs: cute, funny, with family or friends, and milestones. Most participants shared pictures directly from their mobile phones. Nearly all (21) participants felt at least somewhat comfortable sharing pictures online; one voiced strong reservations despite having shared a few pictures on Facebook. Another five participants felt comfortable sharing online but expressed some hesitation at sharing on Facebook.

Cute: All but one participant offered the word "cute" to describe the kinds of baby pictures they had shared online. Participants shared a variety of stories, such as "chubby-cheeked and open-mouthed while watching Sesame Street," "wearing adult glasses with wind blowing his hair around his face," or "wrapped in a towel and sitting in a swing." Several participants shared pictures of their children asleep as "cute" photos. They also shared pictures of their baby with the family dog, with other family members, or placed side-by-side with pictures of themselves as babies. Food and clothing featured prominently in cute photos.

Funny: Many participants said they posted "funny" pictures, such as of their children blowing bubbles, putting crayons in their mouth, eating dirt, crawling into cupboards, and expressions of confusion while being weighed at the doctor's office or chewing on their fingers after their teeth started coming in. Food and clothing also featured prominently in funny photos. Participants posted pictures of their children with Cheerios, chocolate, and other food on their faces and spaghetti on their head. Some participants shared pictures of their children wearing outfits such as a bear suit, a fedora, a superhero cape, and Elmo pajamas.

With and for Family or Friends: Participants posted pictures of their babies with family or friends in a variety of settings, such as at the beach, during a winter walk, in Halloween costumes, and in matching sports gear. Many pictures of spontaneous moments occurred when children were relaxing or napping with a family member. Several participants also shared pictures of their children with the children of friends, especially over reunions, holidays, and group outings. All participants described sharing pictures as a way to connect with family and friends, especially when family lived far away. This helped them to maintain a sense of community and enable their family to watch their baby grow up. Participants also used Facebook photos to publicly thank someone for a gift by tagging the gift-giver in the photo with the baby wearing or playing with the gift.

Milestones: More than half of participants took and shared pictures of developmental milestones and other "firsts." This included children making different facial expressions, getting teeth, and learning new skills (e.g., holding head up, sitting up, clapping, saying bye, crawling, walking). Nearly half of participants shared their ultrasound images on Facebook. Most participants posted pictures online shortly after the birth of their child, depicting the newborn wrapped in a blanket, sometimes in the mother or father's arms. Additional milestone pictures included children meeting new people, experiencing new activities (e.g., swimming, meeting Santa), and participating in events (e.g., Christmas). Several participants took "progress pictures" on the day their children turned another month older, typically in the same place each time and with a sign displaying the month. As their children got older, especially after the one-year mark, milestone pictures started to decline.

Types of Baby Photos Not Shared on Facebook

Participants were reluctant to share three types of pictures: pictures that were low quality or blurry, that exposed the child, or that portrayed negativity.

Low Quality: Participants did not share low quality pictures that were blurry and unfocused or hard to see. For example, Judy did not share pictures where her son was "not smiling or his eyes aren't bright or he doesn't look like he's paying attention." Lindsey only shared pictures that were in focus and her daughter was looking at the camera. Emily deleted unflattering pictures entirely, because she would never be using them for anything. Participants typically took several pictures at a time and shared the best one online.

Exposing the Baby and Mother: Most participants took pictures of their babies naked, but felt these were not appropriate for an online audience. Some shared them if babies' private areas were obscured, such as in the bath. Appropriateness of sharing also decreased as the baby became a toddler. A few participants surfaced concerns about what unknown audiences might do with those photos. Sabrina referenced that her Facebook profile was public and "there are a lot of creepers on the Internet, so I don't need people creeping naked pictures of my baby." Participants also avoided sharing photos of the birth process (e.g., during labor, in pain, or immediately after delivery), which typically exposed both the mother and baby in intimate and vulnerable contexts. They also refrained from sharing pictures of the umbilical cord, the placenta, or the newborn baby immediately after delivery.

Negativity: Participants generally did not share pictures that portrayed their children or themselves in a humiliating light or that revealed health concerns. Participants refrained from sharing pictures of children crying or throwing tantrums. Rita referred to these as "private moments," where what children need at that moment is for "somebody to make you feel better, not for somebody to document it for posterity." Their desire to protect their children's dignity influenced how they shared pictures of their children's birth. Clara's son had to be ventilated immediately after birth, and Melissa's son was born three months premature. Neither shared the first picture they took of their sons online, but instead shared ones that showed their children as healthy. After posting an ultrasound to Facebook while in the doctor's office, Shelby learned something might be wrong with the fetus and immediately regretted posting. When she learned the baby would be okay, she updated Facebook to share the good news.

Benefits of Sharing Baby Photos on Facebook

Archiving Childhood: Participants found themselves beginning to use Facebook as an archive because it was an easy way to store and share photos.

> Marina: "I have a modern day baby book. I can go back to my Facebook profile and tell you the exact day that Cooper took his first step... If I asked my mom for pictures of me the first time I took a step, she would laugh in my face."

Clara had not planned to post pictures of her baby online before he was born. She later shared them and created a montage of his Facebook pictures for his first birthday.

> Clara: "[The montage] was so emotional to me…You think it's silly to weigh that against what you're conceding with your privacy, but if I lost that stuff, I don't know what I would do."

Participants felt it was important that this online archive would be available if anything were to happen to them. Online photo archiving displaced physical albums, but did not entirely replace them. About half of participants created physical photo albums for themselves or to give to family members. Participants who created physical photo albums valued having a tangible representation of their child's life, and planned to show those albums to their children as their children grew older.

Identifying as a Mother: Participants considered how pictures they posted would reflect them and their parenting skills and styles. Participants told us they shared pictures to portray their children or themselves in a certain light. Christine posted a picture of her husband and son at a museum because she wanted to show her Facebook Friends that they did cultural activities. She described posting pictures on Facebook as a "display" where people "intentionally pick and choose" what they show of themselves, a sentiment echoed by Isabel:

> Isabel: "I think Facebook in general has a lot to do with showing off and showcasing, like, who you are and the life you lead and however...self-absorbed that it is, I think it's just kind of the culture and the generation we live in right now."

At the time of the interviews, nine participants' profile photos contained them with their child and six contained only the child (the remaining seven had a photo of the mother). Five participants' cover photos contained them with their child and eight contained only the child (the remaining nine had other content in their photos). For Isabel, whose profile picture showed only her son's face, being a mother became "a central focus for my identity."

> Isabel: "I like showcasing that...He represents me right now. You know, he represents what makes me the happiest, what my daily life is all about."

Marina called herself, "that mom that if my profile picture isn't of my baby, I have to have him up, him up somewhere. Or else I feel like a failure." Marina shared a picture of her son sitting on the ground eating dirt because she wanted to show people that she was the type of mother who liked that her son was playing in dirt. Marina chose not to post pictures of her son crying because she wanted him "to be seen as a happy-go-lucky kid." Lee Ann did not plan to share photos online while she was pregnant, but after having her child she realized it was too difficult to leave her role as a mother off of Facebook.

However, not all participants shared this view. Some participants told us they felt irritated when they saw a baby picture as a profile picture. Melissa and Christine perceived that showing only the child in the profile picture indicated that the child had taken over the mother's entire life. Brianna similarly felt that Facebook was a space to document her life, not her daughter's.

> Brianna: "It's not her Facebook. It's my Facebook. Yes, she's a big part of my life, obviously. But, I think that my Facebook should be about me."

Rebecca, who also felt her Facebook profile should reflect information about her, was critical of Facebook content that solely focuses on the child's behavior instead of the mother. Emily felt frustrated when she saw Facebook Friends post only about their children, saying it felt like "you're hiding behind your kid and their accomplishments." Though all participants identified with their role as a mother, the extent to which they felt it was appropriate to express their identity as a mother on Facebook varied widely.

Receiving Validation of Motherhood: Participants received many likes and comments on the baby photos they shared on Facebook, generally far more than they would receive on other photos and statuses that they posted.

> Judy: "It was rare before Quinn for a random picture to get 97 likes unless it was, like, our wedding picture. I mean, this is a kid eating breakfast."

The photos of Melissa's son Thomas, who was born three months premature, were among the most liked and commented pictures she had ever posted. She felt gratified to receive messages of support on Facebook and through private messages. Isabel's picture of her new family in the hospital room received nearly 140 likes and 30 comments. She took a screenshot of the picture with the feedback to show Emiliano "how many people knew when he entered the world." Christine similarly received "hundreds" of comments on the photo she posted after giving birth, an arduous process that involved several trips to the hospital. She had not heard from some of those people in years but appreciated the feedback, saying "the warmth... it's so artificial, but it's kind of not." Both Clara and Carrie highlighted that seeing other people's baby photos and receiving feedback on her own felt validating, as if they were a part of a community:

> Carrie: "You know that you're doing a good job, but it feels better when somebody else confirms that...I don't post to feel validated, but I do after I post."

Participants sometimes wondered whether they were posting too many pictures, but they received so many positive responses in the form of likes and comments that they continued to post. They also wanted to save these instances for their children to receive in the future. The tangible and immediate benefits of receiving positive support and feedback outweighed concerns about sharing on Facebook for almost all participants. Participants worried about what might happen to their data but told us that they "tried not to dwell on it" and took steps to share baby photos in ways that aligned with their privacy views.

Risks of Sharing Baby Photos on Facebook

Controlling Information: More than half of participants received requests from family or friends to see baby pictures, especially from their children's grandparents. Participants who preferred not to share baby pictures online felt pressured by the constant requests for pictures. Brianna originally intended to keep her daughter Abigail off social media entirely, saying she "felt more private about her than I've ever felt about anything else in my life." Brianna wanted the only people who saw Abigail's face to be the people who actually see her face every day. However, to satisfy her family's requests, she created a private Facebook group and posted an album of ten pictures of Abigail.

> Brianna: "It highlighted for me the inevitability of the fact that [Abigail] was going to be on Facebook. And so that's when I really started thinking about, well how can I control this as much as possible... Privacy is having control over who has information relevant to me and my life. When I realized I could make that closed group...I said, fine, I'll just put some pictures up even though I'm still uncomfortable with it."

Participants engaged in strategies to control how information about their babies was shared. Judy and Rebecca sent emails to family and friends announcing the birth and asking them to keep their child's name and pictures, respectively, off of Facebook. Wendy asked her mother to change her privacy settings after strangers from her mothers' online games commented on photos of Wendy's baby. Though Clara did not like the naked photo her mother shared on Facebook of her son's first bath, she decided to not to ask her mother to remove it to honor her mother's decision. Christine found that her baby was on her babysitter's cover photo, but similarly decided not to say anything because they appreciated that the nanny loved and cared for their child and she did not want to disrupt that harmony.

Most participants said they set their Facebook profile to Friends only, though some set them to Friends-of-Friends and Public. One participant believed her profile was set to Friends-only and discovered during the interview that it was Public. Many participants perceived Facebook's privacy settings and group management features to be difficult to use and felt frustrated by Facebook's evolving privacy settings. Lee Ann had not realized that people who were not her Friend could see which Facebook groups she had joined, "which ended up basically being identifying information because, you know, I'm part of the [town name] Kids group, the [town name] Moms group."

Participants took steps to manage their and their child's privacy by creating private groups, changing visibility of individual posts that contained sensitive information, or created limited groups who could see baby content. Some participants mentioned concern about losing technical control via location-tracking, advertising, or facial recognition. Three participants turned off location-tracking on their phones and five more expressed caution about revealing real-time location information, their baby's names, or their baby's facial features in the content they shared. Some planned to share photos less as their children got older when their faces might be more permanently identifiable by facial recognition technology. Ella and Brianna, who were generally the most concerned about privacy, used privacy preserving strategies such as obscuring the child's face and allowing group photos but not individual photos.

Limiting Oversharing: Thirteen participants were concerned about oversharing, or posting too many pictures of their children online. They used vivid metaphors to describe this activity, saying they did not want to "overwhelm," "inundate," "barrage," "saturate," "bombard," or "blow up" Facebook with pictures. Participants typically said they could not help but post pictures of their children, especially in the first few weeks of their child's life. Clara told us she "went nuts" posting baby pictures during her son's first few weeks. Melissa had planned to give herself six months "to just go full-bore and then I was going to try and get it under control." Participants adopted rules for managing the frequency of their own sharing behaviors. Karen and Shelby tried to gauge what would annoy people.

> Karen: "I feel like there has to be some sort of a reason or some sort of special thing that it's marking... I don't need to put something on every day of just her sitting there."

> Shelby: "People are not going to want to be your Friend if you post every picture of your child."

Participants were sensitive that people in their friend networks might be struggling to conceive. Seeing an abundance of Facebook posts and pictures about pregnancies and babies was "really painful" for Emily, who had been trying to have children for several years and had suffered interrupted adoptions. She stopped using Facebook for 10 months, saying that was better than "getting bitter about something I can't control." Carrie had had difficulty conceiving, and she endured a miscarriage before becoming pregnant with twins. Before she had children, she also found it, "extremely painful to watch everybody else post about their baby" and recognized that seeing these photos might be difficult for others. However, she posted pictures of her children to make people smile and also to honor her own personal growth.

> Carrie: "So many people were with me through the struggle of conceiving...And then my pregnancy was rough. So then I feel like, if you stuck with me through that, you should reap the benefits of seeing how cute these babies are... I've finally [gotten] to that place where I can be the people I was so jealous of, and now I'm not apologizing for that."

Participants also turned to other forms of communication to limit oversharing on Facebook. Some participants used Instagram and a small number used Google+, Dropbox, WhatsApp, or Snapfish to share photos. Zainab and Lindsay shared photos on Instagram where their friend networks were smaller. Ella, Rita, and Emily posted pictures to Google+ for the same reason. Karen sent photos by email in addition to Facebook because "sometimes I'll get shit if something's on Facebook and my mom doesn't see it but her sister does."

Managing Children's Digital Footprints: Participants expressed hesitation and uncertainty about how their photo-sharing behavior now might impact their child's online identity later. Clara recognized that by posting pictures on Facebook, she was making a decision for her son Ryan that could not be easily reversed and wondered if she was making the right decisions for him. Brianna and Shelby felt they had a responsibility to "protect" their children, and many participants felt their children had rights to privacy themselves.

> Emily: "I feel like I'm kind of stewarding his privacy, and he doesn't have a chance yet to say, 'Hey Mom, could you not put that on Facebook?'"

Like many participants, Wendy avoided posting pictures that might humiliate her daughter.

> Wendy: "I don't post pictures of like, poop explosions... I mean, I'm not going to embarrass her on Facebook."

Melissa did not share early photos of her son, born three months premature, because she wanted to "preserve [his] dignity a little bit." The first picture she shared on

Facebook was when he was one month old, fully clothed and with healthy coloring. He still had a feeding tube in his nose but a viewer could not see how small he was.

> Melissa: "I more wanted people to see him and not all the equipment... I didn't want a pity party; I wanted joy that he was doing so well."

Cara's son Ye-jun had his own Facebook profile with over 320 friends. She did not post naked pictures, but she posted pictures and videos that showed different facets of his personality, such as laying down in a cardboard box to throw a temper tantrum. It was important to Cara that Ye-jun grew up learning how to navigate himself in a public world both offline and online:

> Cara: "He's going to be sweet, and he's going to be a little turd sometimes. And so I post that.... I want him to know that everything he does, regardless if he posts it on Facebook, people will know about."

Participants who were more reserved about sharing photos on Facebook expressed concern about how their children would feel about their information being online. Brianna explained, "It's not my right to make the decision about what of hers goes online." Ella echoed this sentiment, saying her son had the right to decide what information about himself he wanted to be online. If he decided he wanted to post aspects of his life online, she would have the records to give him. However, Brianna and Ella's sentiments were the minority among our participants; most were thoughtful about their children's perspectives but did not heavily constrain their photo-sharing based on their child's future rights.

DISCUSSION

We find that mothers share certain types of baby photos to present themselves as a particular type of mother to their online audience. Furthermore, they reap benefits from this online audience that can offer validation of their roles as mothers. Finally, mothers face a complex decision-making process that involves considering privacy, identity, and children's rights both at the current moment as well as 10-20 years in the future when children are old enough to look back on their own online footprints.

Enacting Good Mothering through Baby Photos

Echoing prior work [17,52], mothers viewed Facebook as a place to share positive or happy information. Through sharing photos of their babies, mothers portrayed their identities as good mothers, conveying attractive children, embracing humor, and showing evidence of milestones—all indicators of a healthy and happy family. Sharing photos helped participants accomplish several self-disclosure goals described by Vitak and Kim [52]. Participants shared baby pictures as a way to gain social approval (i.e., share information they thought Friends would find interesting), increase intimacy (i.e., maintain a connection with people important to them) and create a personal archive. Participants also surfaced different kinds of self-disclosure risks than identified by Vitak and Kim [52], perhaps because they were making decisions on behalf of their babies rather than themselves. Though mothers self-censored what kinds of photos to share, as documented in [52], these behaviors were guided by a complex combination of self-presentation goals and projections about what was appropriate to share about their babies. Parents were especially cognizant of security and identity concerns [1], but they could not easily anticipate how sharing baby photos now would affect their children's online identity later, an open question for future work.

Our work contrasts Gibson and Hanson, who found that new mothers wanted to use technology to be more than "just" a mother [14]. However, both studies find validation of good motherhood is critical, echoing other work [4,25,41,41,47]. Neither our work nor Gibson and Hanson's addressed the role of online audiences and what they want to see online. In particular, online audiences may feel obligated to "like" a baby photo because they want to identify as the kind of person who likes babies. As a result, the inflated audience experienced by new mothers might come at the cost of the audience's experience, with some people potentially giving positive feedback grudgingly. A smarter news feed would 1) show baby photos to receptive audiences and minimize baby photos for audiences who prefer to see fewer or none of them; and 2) provide clearer signals to mothers about what kinds of content their audience actually wants to see.

Unanticipated Benefits of Imagined Audiences

Though imagined audiences have often been portrayed as presenting a challenge for people trying to craft a message for these multiple or unknown audiences [30], these audiences appear to offer unintended benefits to new mothers. Participants were motivated to share photos with family and close friends; however, Facebook's news feed promotes sharing with a wider audience of online friends. As a result, several participants said they received more feedback, typically in the form of likes or comments, on baby pictures compared to other types of content they posted online, confirming recent quantitative results [34]. Chalfen's "home mode" communication theory [10] described family photo sharing among interpersonal small groups in the home. Our results suggest new theories are needed to explain the expanded nature of family photo-sharing on social networking sites. The act of broadcasting a baby picture online for an audience of hundreds or more moves that communication beyond the realm of small groups into a broad, "imagined audience" [26,30].

Participants reporting feeling validated by the numerous likes and comments they received from their Facebook networks, even when they came from weak ties (e.g. high school acquaintances) who were not part of participants' originally intended audience. Furthermore, even though participants knew that receiving "likes" was a weak signal that required little effort to perform, they still felt positive about receiving validation from this broad audience. These results suggest that over time, weak ties like high school acquaintances may in fact continue to offer some benefit in a Facebook network. Women will typically be the same age as their high school acquaintances, and thus share the same (broad) range of child-bearing years, perhaps offering a forum for reintroduction of shared experiences.

Privacy Stewardship

How will this generation of young children feel when they become old enough to find out that their digital footprint has been shaped since before their birth? From a privacy perspective, we might fear that pictures will not disappear, but from an archival perspective, we worry that they will. Many participants described using Facebook as a digital archive, taking comfort in knowing that Facebook was storing their "modern-day shoebox." But what would happen if Facebook disappeared? For mothers who valued the archive of support from their geographically dispersed online community, losing records could be devastating. Thus, parents face an almost impossible tension between the expectation that they will document and archive their children's social lives, while simultaneously ensuring that their child's privacy is protected and identity is carefully stewarded. Brubaker et al. introduce the concept of stewardship to explain the responsibility for managing a digital legacy that is taken on when a family member passes away [8]. New mothers take on a similar responsibility of stewarding their children's digital footprint before their children are able to say, as Emily articulated: 'Hey Mom, could you not put that on Facebook?'

We introduce the concept of *privacy stewardship* to describe the responsibility parents take on when deciding what is appropriate to share about their children online *and* ensuring that family and friends respect and maintain the integrity of those rules. Among our participants, extended family members and caregivers violated parents' desires, resulting in uncomfortable tensions about whether to address the violation or not. This complements other privacy frameworks like contextual integrity [37] and proportionality [18] which look to determine appropriate privacy levels within social and technical contexts. Here, parents must determine appropriate privacy behaviors on behalf of their children; a daunting task when risks are unknown and where impact extends years into the future.

Surprisingly, participants had little to say about how Facebook, Inc., the company, managed its data. They were instead focused on broad audiences, unknown audiences, and lack of control about what these audiences might do with their children's content, echoing CPM's five privacy dimensions [40]. Perhaps ironically, some mothers switched to platforms like Google+ and Instagram (which is owned by Facebook), not because the privacy policies were necessarily better, but because audiences were smaller and more easily controlled. Similar to Ames et al's findings [2], none of our participants described experiencing direct harm from posting baby pictures online, but they experienced boundary turbulence. Privacy is not a binary [27,52] and participants considered a range of self-disclosure risks and strategies before deciding what kinds of baby photos to share. Individual privacy concerns (i.e., making sure only people who are supposed to see content see it) are critically important, and are something that Facebook itself is working to address [36]; however, shared ownership and corresponding privacy concerns (i.e., making sure people who are supposed to see content maintain the integrity of the original owners' privacy preferences) remains unaddressed. This challenge becomes even more pronounced when considering the global Facebook network; for example, childhood nudity tends to be more acceptable in some cultures than in others, a difference that is collapsed online [30].

CONCLUSION

Participants shared cute, funny, and milestone photos with family and friends but refrained from showing pictures that portray negativity or nakedness. Mothers were able to enact "good mothering" through their photo-sharing behaviors, to indicate a happy and healthy family. However, the responsibility of stewarding children's privacy presents new challenges for parents to maintain their children's privacy at the time the photo is shared and to anticipate how children will feel about their identity being formed online without their consent. Facebook and other online social platforms offer a new and promising platform for new mothers to enact and receive validation of good mothering, both critical processes in the early months of new motherhood; however, future research will need to explore the long-term privacy and archival implications for families.

REFERENCES

[1] Ahern, S., Eckles, D., Good, N.S., King, S., Naaman, M., and Nair, R. Over-exposed?: Privacy Patterns and Considerations in Online and Mobile Photo Sharing. In *Proc. CHI, ACM* (2007), 357–366.

[2] Ames, M., Eckles, D., Naaman, M., Spasojevic, M., and House, N.V. Requirements for mobile photoware. *Personal and Ubiquitous Comp. 14*, 2 (2010), 95–109.

[3] Amy Webb. We Post Nothing About Our Daughter Online. *Slate*, 2013.

[4] Barclay, L., Everitt, L., Rogan, F., Schmied, V., and Wyllie, A. Becoming a mother — an analysis of women's experience of early motherhood. *Journal of Advanced Nursing 25*, 4 (1997), 719–728.

[5] Bartholomew, M.K., Schoppe-Sullivan, S.J., Glassman, M., Kamp Dush, C.M., and Sullivan, J.M. New Parents' Facebook Use at the Transition to Parenthood. *Family Relations 61*, 3 (2012), 455–469.

[6] Bernstein, M.S., Bakshy, E., Burke, M., and Karrer, B. Quantifying the Invisible Audience in Social Networks. In *Proc. CHI, ACM* (2013), 21–30.

[7] Besmer, A. and Richter Lipford, H. Moving Beyond Untagging: Photo Privacy in a Tagged World. In *Proc. CHI, ACM* (2010), 1563–1572.

[8] Brubaker, J.R., Dombrowski, L.S., Gilbert, A.M., Kusumakaulika, N., and Hayes, G.R. Stewarding a Legacy: Responsibilities and Relationships in the Management of Post-mortem Data. In *Proc. CHI, ACM* (2014), 4157–4166.

[9] Burke, Moira, Lada A. Adamic, and Karyn Marciniak. Families on Facebook. ICWSM 2013, *AAAI Press*.

[10] Chalfen, Richard. *Snapshot Versions of Life*. The Popular Press, Bowling Green, OH, 1987.

[11] Collett, J.L. What Kind of Mother Am I? Impression Management and the Social Construction of Motherhood. *Symbolic Interaction 28*, 3 (2005), 327–347.

[12] Dourish, P. and Anderson, K. Collective Information Practice: Emploring Privacy and Security As Social and Cultural Phenomena. Hum.-Comput. Interact. 21, 3 (2006), 319–342.

[13] Frohlich, D., Kuchinsky, A., Pering, C., Don, A., and Ariss, S. Requirements for Photoware. In *Proc. CSCW, ACM* (2002), 166–175.

[14] Gibson, L. and Hanson, V.L. Digital motherhood: how does technology help new mothers? In *Proc. CHI, ACM* (2013), 313–322.

[15] Hogan, B. The presentation of self in the age of social media: Distinguishing performances and exhibitions online. *Bulletin of Science, Technology & Society 30*, 6 (2010), 377–386.

[16] Holland, P. History, memory and the family album. *Family snaps: The meanings of domestic photography* 3, (1991).

[17] Hutto, C.J., Yardi, S., and Gilbert, E. A longitudinal study of follow predictors on twitter. In *Proc. CHI*, ACM (2013), 821–830.

[18] Iachello, G. and Abowd, G.D. Privacy and proportionality: adapting legal evaluation techniques to inform design in ubiquitous computing. In *Proc. CHI*, ACM (2005), 91-100.

[19] Jacobs, D. Domestic Snapshots: Toward a Grammar of Motives. *J. of American Culture 4*, 1 (1981), 93–105.

[20] Jang, J. and Dworkin, J. 2004. Does social network site use matter for mothers? Implications for bonding and bridging capital. *Computers in Human Behavior, 35*, 489-495.

[21] N. Jomhari, V. M. Gonzalez, and S. H. Kurniawan. 2009. See the apple of my eye: baby storytelling in social space. In *Proc. British HCI*, (2009), 238-243.

[22] Parker, K. and Wang, W. *Modern Parenthood*. Pew Research Social & Demographic Trends, 2013 .

[23] Kirk, D., Sellen, A., Rother, C., and Wood, K. Understanding Photowork. In *Proc. CHI, ACM* (2006), 761–770.

[24] Lampinen, A., Tamminen, S., and Oulasvirta, A. "All my people right here, right now": Management of group co-presence on a social networking site. In *Proc. of GROUP '09*, (2009), 281–290.

[25] Lee, C. Social context, depression, and the transition to motherhood. *British Journal of Health Psychology 2*, 2 (1997), 93–108.

[26] Litt, E. and Hargittai, E. Smile, snap, and share? A nuanced approach to privacy and online photo-sharing. *Poetics 42*, (2014), 1–21.

[27] Litt, E. Knock, Knock. Who's There? The Imagined Audience. *Journal of Broadcasting & Electronic Media 56*, 3 (2012), 330–345.

[28] Lopez, L.K. The radical act of 'mommy blogging': redefining motherhood through the blogosphere. *New Media & Society 11*, 5 (2009), 729–747.

[29] Maeve Duggan and Joanna Brenner. The Demographics of Social Media Users — 2012. *Pew Internet*, 2013.

[30] Marwick, A.E. and boyd, d. I tweet honestly, I tweet passionately: Twitter users, context collapse, and the imagined audience. *New Media & Society 13*, 1 (2010), 114–133.

[31] McDaniel, B.T., Coyne, S.M., and Holmes, E.K. New Mothers and Media Use: Associations Between Blogging, Social Networking, and Maternal Well-Being. *Maternal and Child Health Journal 16*, 7 (2012), 1509–1517.

[32] Mendelson, A. and Papacharissi, Z. *A Networked Self: Identity, Community, and Culture on Social Network Sites*. Routledge, 2010.

[33] Miller, A.D. and Edwards, W.K. Give and Take: A Study of Consumer Photo-sharing Culture and Practice. In *Proc. CHI, ACM*, ACM (2007), 347–356.

[34] Morris, M.R. Social Networking Site Use by Mothers of Young Children. In *Proc. CSCW*, ACM (2014), 1272-1282.

[35] Morrison, A. "Suffused by Feeling and Affect": The Intimate Public of Personal Mommy Blogging. *Biography 34*, 1 (2011), 37–55.

[36] Munson, L. The 'Privacy Dinosaur' urges Facebook users to check their privacy settings. *naked security*, 2014.

[37] Nissenbaum, H. *Privacy in Context: Technology, Policy, and the Integrity of Social Life*. Stanford University Press, 2009.

[38] Oeldorf-Hirsch, A. and Sundar, S.S. Online photo sharing as mediated communication. Paper presented at ICA (2010).

[39] Pauwels, L. A private visual practice going public? Social functions and sociological research opportunities of Web-based family photography. *Visual Studies 23*, 1 (2008), 34–49.

[40] Petronio, S. *Boundaries of Privacy: Dialectics of Disclosure*. SUNY Press, 2002.

[41] Phoenix, A. and Woollett, A. Motherhood: Social construction, politics and psychology. In A. Phoenix, A. Woollett and E. Lloyd, eds., *Motherhood: Meanings, practices and ideologies*. Sage Publications, Inc, Thousand Oaks, CA, US, 1991, 13–27.

[42] Plantin, L. and Daneback, K. Parenthood, information and support on the internet. A literature review of research on parents and professionals online. *BMC Family Practice 10*, 1 (2009), 34.

[43] Rose, G. Family photographs and domestic spacings: a case study. *Transactions of the Institute of British Geographers 28*, 1 (2003), 5–18.

[44] Rose, G. 'Everyone's cuddled up and it just looks really nice': an emotional geography of some mums and their family photos. *Social & Cultural Geography 5*, 4 (2004), 549–564.

[45] Rose, P.G. *Doing Family Photography: The Domestic, The Public and The Politics of Sentiment*. Ashgate Publishing, Ltd., 2012.

[46] Schoenebeck, S.Y. The Secret Life of Online Moms: Anonymity and Disinhibition on YouBeMom.com. In *Proc. ICWSM*, AAAI Press, (2013).

[47] Tardy, R.W. "But I Am a Good Mom" The Social Construction of Motherhood through Health-Care Conversations. *Journal of Contemporary Ethnography 29*, 4 (2000), 433–473.

[48] Tee, K., Brush, A.J.B., and Inkpen, K.M. Exploring communication and sharing between extended families. *Int. J. Hum.-Comput. Stud. 67*, 2 (2009), 128–138.

[49] Thomas, D.R. A General Inductive Approach for Analyzing Qualitative Evaluation Data. *American Journal of Evaluation 27*, 2 (2006), 237–246.

[50] Titus, S.L. Family Photographs and Transition to Parenthood. *Journal of Marriage and the Family 38*, 3 (1976), 525.

[51] Van House, N. Collocated photo sharing, story-telling, and the performance of self. International *Journal of Human-Computer Studies 67*, 12 (2009), 1073–1086.

[52] Vitak, J. and Kim, J. "You Can't Block People Offline": Examining How Facebook's Affordances Shape the Disclosure Process. In *Proc. CSCW, ACM* (2014), 461–474.

[53] Warren, S.D. and Brandeis, L.D. The Right to Privacy. *Harvard Law Review 4*, 5 (1890), 193–220.

[54] Whittaker, S., Bergman, O., and Clough, P. Easy on That Trigger Dad: A Study of Long Term Family Photo Retrieval. *Personal Ubiquitous Computing 14*, 1 (2010), 31–43.

Computer Support for Financial Advisors and Their Clients: Co-creating an Investment Plan

Susanna Heyman
KTH Royal Institute of Technology
SE-100 44 Stockholm, Sweden
susanna.heyman@abe.kth.se

Henrik Artman
KTH Royal Institute of Technology
SE-100 44 Stockholm, Sweden
artman@kth.se

ABSTRACT

This paper is a workplace study of how financial advisors use their computer systems in advisory meetings with clients, with special focus on the collaborative decision-making. Observations and interviews show that the financial advisors in the study were not much helped by their computer system in visualizing and explaining financial concepts to their clients, and that not all of them trusted the system's decision support feature. Furthermore, client meetings can involve more than one client, which has further implications for the design of financial decision support.

Author Keywords

Advisory scenario; Workplace studies

ACM Classification Keywords

H.5.2 [Information Interfaces and Presentation]: Group and Organization Interfaces - Computer-supported cooperative work

INTRODUCTION

In today's society, it is becoming increasingly important to make the "right" financial choices in order to have a secure future. For example, the Swedish retirement system has moved some of the responsibility for managing pension funds from the government to individual citizens [6]. At the same time, studies show low levels of financial literacy among the general population [1], few people make any active choices regarding their retirement investments, and those who do make choices tend to get worse results than people who make no choice at all [6].

This creates a demand for help with financial decision-making, which is met by professional financial advisors employed by banks. Although independent freelance advisors exist, many people who have regular meetings with financial advisors choose one who works at the bank at which they are customers. This creates a somewhat conflicting incentive structure for the advisors, who may find themselves in a situation where they are expected to give their clients unbiased advice, but at the same time earn a profit for their employer [20, 24].

In order to prevent negligent advice, increasingly detailed laws and regulations at both the national and the European level control the practices of Swedish financial advisors [9, 14]. Law dictates that financial advice must be carefully suited to the individual client's circumstances, goals, and willingness to accept risk. This means that the advisor must learn relevant information about the client before being allowed to provide advice. They must also be able to prove after the client meeting that such assessment did in fact take place before any advice was given. If documentation from the meeting is missing, the client's version of events is regarded as true in case of a dispute.

The strict requirements for documentation and traceability create an incentive for financial service providers to standardize their advisory process. To this end, the bank in this study has developed a computer application which is mandatory for advisors to use at client meetings. The application logs events for the purpose of documentation and provides advisors with decision support based on the bank's centrally managed outlook on financial markets. The application's decision algorithm matches clients with a suggested investment portfolio. It is common for financial service institutions to have a selection of standard portfolios that are categorized according to their level of risk, for example "conservative", "moderate" or "aggressive" [15]. In such cases, the advisor's is job to categorize the client as risk-averse, risk-neutral or risk-willing. Even when the bank does not apply such discrete categorization, some similar process could be expected to occur.

The implications and problems with categorization have been discussed extensively in CSCW literature [4, 27, 29]. For example, Bjørn and Balka [4] described problems with using a computer application to categorize patients in healthcare. This paper builds upon this tradition and examines how scripted financial advisory systems are used in financial advisory meetings. While financial advising might be less stressful than categorization of patients in emergency situations, the situations are similar in that they both necessitate a discrete and one-dimensional categorization of

CSCW '15, March 14 - 18, 2015, Vancouver, BC, Canada.
Copyright 2015 ACM 978-1-4503-2922-4/15/03...$15.00.
http://dx.doi.org/10.1145/2675133.2675191

rather complex and vague characteristics; urgency of need for medical attention, or financial risk tolerance.

The aim of this workplace study was to find answers to the following: How do financial advisors use their computer systems, particularly the decision support? What influence does the advisor's use of tools have on the interaction between the advisor and the client? And how does the advisor assess the client's attitude to financial risk?

RELATED RESEARCH

Most traditional systems are designed for a primary individual user or for collaborative task management in teams where several users have access to the data. However, as Alsos and Svanæs [2] have pointed out, there is often a secondary user who is directly or indirectly affected by the primary user's use of computer systems. The financial advisory meeting is one such case, where the primary user, the financial advisor, has access to a computer system for information retrieval or decision support which has direct impact on the decisions and possibly the future well-being of the secondary user, the client. Alsos and Svanæs [2] found that the user experience of the secondary user (in their case a patient seeing a physician) would have been helped by tailored language and representation. Furthermore, they concluded that when designing such systems, the designer needs to deal with conflicting needs and goals between the primary and secondary user.

Decision Support in CSCW

It is widely agreed in the CSCW community that no process instructions based on rational, context-free rules can ever capture all nuances or possibilities of real work practice [4, 23]. Hence, decision aids should not be blindly followed but need to be monitored by human judgment. Bjørn and Balka [4] showed that a system for categorizing patients according to urgency of needs undermined nurses' professional judgment in categorizing patients based on their experience. They describe the role of professional judgment in skilled work; a novice worker will tend to follow context-free rules, in the style of "If A, do B," while an expert will quickly assess a situation and immediately know what to do, based on long experience and processing of information on a subconscious level. However, the expert will not necessarily be good at articulating how they arrived at their decision, but the decision will nevertheless usually turn out to be correct [4]. It is assumed in this paper that this also applies to skill acquisition in finance. CSCW literature generally has high respect for the intuitive judgment of experts, and recommends designers to allow proficient users great flexibility instead of having the scripted systems dictate exactly what to do and how to do it. Indeed, Bjørn and Balka found that experienced nurses disliked the patient categorizing system, while novice nurses accepted it since they tended to base their decisions on general rules-of-thumb the same way the system did. However, Bjørn and Balka warn that novice nurses who are trained to use the computerized categorizing system may never learn to do their job without it; hence the system hampers the development of independent judgment and professional skill.

Financial Advisory in CSCW

Financial advisory meetings have been studied in CSCW as well as in other fields [7, 8, 25, 26]. "Mystery shopping" studies, where researchers pose as clients and visit banks to ask for financial advice, have been conducted in Switzerland, Austria and Germany [16, 19]. Results showed that advisors, particularly older ones, did not use their computer systems at client meetings because they were afraid of looking incompetent if there were any technical problems, and because they were skeptical that the system could add any value [16]. Clients however wanted more visualizations and simulations of portfolio scenarios [16].

Nussbaumer et al. [19] showed that the information that advisors communicated at meetings was rarely tailored to the client's needs and capacity, and that clients were critical of their advisors; advisors were perceived as "passive, inexperienced, lacking an in-depth understanding of the product and showing a tendency to take advantage of an uninformed customer." In contrast, Swedish clients seem to trust their banks, their advisors, and the advice they get [8].

Schmidt-Rauch and Nussbaumer [24] identified a number of problems in financial advisory meetings, many of which are related to information asymmetry between the client and advisor; for example, the client and the advisor may speak different "languages" and fail to understand each other's views, the client may be unable to express their needs, and the client and advisor have different goals. Mogacito et al [16] showed that clients were aware of this information asymmetry, and that it lowered their trust in their advisors.

In Schmidt-Rauch and Nussbaumer [24] and in a later article by Nussbaumer, Matter, and Schwabe [18], increased transparency for the client is proposed as a solution to this problem. Nussbaumer et al [17, 18] tested a prototype designed to increase process transparency as well as information transparency. By "process transparency," they referred to a better explanation to the client of what will happen during the meeting and the purpose of the different discussion points. This was visualized in their prototype through a map of the different activities that were to take place during the meeting. However, this feature was not liked by clients and advisors, who felt restricted by it. "Information transparency," on the other hand, referred to the client having access to all the information that the advisor had; particularly information about the client themselves and what impact that information had on recommendations. Nussbaumer et al [18] managed to increase information transparency by improving the software interface and by using a screen that laid flat on the table, so that the client could see everything that the advisor saw. Additionally, Schmidt-Rauch and Nussbaumer [24] suggested that the client should control the keyboard when filling out the system's forms and questionnaires, in order to "engage interaction with the system."

Heinrich et al [13] focused on the interpersonal contact between client and advisor. In a first version of their prototype, advisors tended to focus more on the computer interface than the client, which made clients feel ignored. In a second iteration, Heinrich et al managed to alleviate the problems by introducing a session of small-talk before the advisory meeting and by having advisors take notes on pen and paper and only turn to the computer when discussing some information or visualization on the screen. Additionally, they made some changes to the physical layout of the meeting space and to the GUI of the prototype. These results are important for supporting collaborative meetings; the collaboration will not go well if the client is alienated. However, it could be noted that not all clients want more personal contact with their financial advisor; some clients are in fact put off by too much intimacy [7].

RESEARCH SETTING AND METHOD

The first author spent one working week at two branch offices of a bank in Sweden. The purpose of the visit was to observe as many client meetings and interview as many advisors as possible. The bank did not permit audio or video recording due to privacy concerns on behalf of clients, so all data was recorded in the form of hand-written notes which were transcribed as soon as possible after meetings. The aim was to write down verbatim quotes as far as possible. However, in quotes containing personal details, such details have been altered to protect the confidentiality of clients.

At the end of the week, four client meetings had been observed. Meeting agendas included home equity loans, new mortgages, inheritance, and financial planning. Advisors were also observed and interviewed before and after meetings. Interview questions included how they prepared, what they considered to be a good meeting, what their goals were for the upcoming meeting, and how they thought the observed meetings went. They were asked to demonstrate their tools and talk about them. The advisors who were interviewed but not observed with clients were asked the same questions and they also demonstrated their tools. Interviews and observations took roughly 1.5-2 hours each. Notes were also taken and transcribed after informal lunch discussions and morning meetings. Some weeks later, an additional financial advisor was interviewed who was employed by the same bank, but at a third branch office.

Some advisors were quite eager to talk about perceived flaws with the computer system. They initiated a meeting (the "Focus group" in Table 1) where they criticized the system and showed their own workarounds.

ID	Role	Gender	Age	Method
1	Advisor	F	30-40	Observation, interview
2	Advisor	F	50-60	Observation, interview
3	Manager	M	40-50	Interview
4	Premium advisor	M	40-50	Interview
5	Advisor	F	50-60	Interview
6	Premium advisor	M	40-50	Focus group, interview
7	Advisor	F	40-50	Focus group
8	Advisor	F	30-40	Focus group
9	Premium advisor	M	30-40	Observation, focus group, interview
10	Premium advisor	M	30-40	Interview

Table 1. Respondents

Empirical Setting

The bank in this study offers different service agreements at different prices. The basic package gives access to meetings with a financial advisor at the client's request. The premium packages include more frequent, scheduled advisory meetings. Hence, advisors for the premium segments see their clients more often and have fewer clients. This makes it easier for premium advisors to ensure that decisions made at meetings are followed up. Premium advisors typically hold more advanced practice licenses and can be specialists in for example securities trading. They are allowed, even expected, to go outside the bank's centrally administered investment recommendations and exercise their own judgment when making recommendations to individual clients. All advisors can however call each other or a helpdesk if they have any questions about something outside their own area of expertise.

Swedish financial advisors are required to document what happens during each client meeting. The documentation must be signed by the client to confirm that the documentation represents what actually happened at the meeting, and the bank is required to print a copy of the documentation for the client to take home. This means that the advisor must continuously enter data into the system while talking to the client, so that the documentation is ready for printing at the end of the meeting.

One crucial factor that must be documented is the level of financial risk suitable for the client. To prove that they have made a proper investigation of the client's risk tolerance, the advisors at this bank must fill out an electronic questionnaire regarding the client's personal preference for risk and the time horizon of their investment. Based on the answers provided to this questionnaire, the system can generate a suggested investment portfolio that the client and advisor can choose to accept, reject or modify. However, the system flags when modifications were made to the suggested portfolio, and the advisor is expected to note in the system why they made those modifications.

At this bank, client and advisor sit at opposite sides of a desk. The desk features a computer with a traditional PC monitor, not the horizontal type of screen recommended by [18, 21]. The advisor controls the orientation of the computer screen and can turn it towards or away from the client to selectively choose when they want to share what goes on in the system. This lowers information transparency for the client, which can hamper the client's trust and comprehension [18], but it is a common practice due to the existence of sensitive information in the system that is meant for the advisor's eyes only.

RESULTS

Process Visualization

In contrast to previous research, the advisors in this study did not say anything negative about the process visualization provided by the system. In fact, those advisors who mentioned the system's structure did so because they found it useful.

- The system is good because it gives me a red thread to follow. [R2]

- If you use the advisory application, you will usually find something to talk [to the client] about. [R5]

Thus, some advisors think the system supports their conversations with clients. The support is both structural (making sure that all topics are covered) and conversational (avoiding pauses and awkward silences). However, the structure is only apparent to the advisor, and not to the client, since the advisor controls the screen.

Assessing the Client's Risk Preference

One of the most central parts of this bank's advisory application is the risk questionnaire that categorizes the client's risk preferences. The questionnaire is meant to be answered by the client, and as mentioned earlier, Schmidt-Rauch and Nussbaumer [24] suggested that the client should also be the one to do the manual input. However, most of the respondents in the present study considered it the advisor's professional responsibility to find the appropriate risk level for the client. This was due to a perceived low knowledge level on the part of the client.

- The problem with the risk questionnaire is that clients don't really understand what they are answering. [R6]

- The biggest problem is that clients' risk preferences change with time. When the stock market is doing well they want high risk, when it's doing poorly they want low risk. [Focus group]

The two above quotes show advisors' experience with clients' misunderstandings of financial risk. The advisors in the focus group did not consider answers based on ignorance to be a good foundation for eliciting clients' "true" preferences. It could be noted that the advisors' observation that people accept more risk in a strong market has wide support from research [22].

*- Almost all clients choose the medium option [in the questionnaire]. I think it's because that one is worded in such a way that anyone would agree with it. I usually decide what risk **I** think the client should take and make the selection for them, and then I inform them of my choice. Sometimes I only read them the highest risk option and the lowest risk option in order to force them to make a choice. If they hesitate, I classify them as medium risk. [R10]*

Respondent 10 did not trust his clients' responses to the risk questionnaire to be a valid representation of their preferences. He believed the wording of the questionnaire to be misleading, and perhaps he thought that he as a professional advisor was better suited than the client to determine the proper risk level with regards to the client's financial situation. Independently of respondent 10, respondent 5 too said that clients tend to pick the middle option when they do not know how to answer.

*- One must keep in mind that the result of the risk questionnaire is a recommendation that **might** [or might not] suit the client. [Focus group]*

The risk questionnaire is not an exact measuring instrument like a thermometer. It measures human attitudes, which are notoriously unreliable and difficult to measure. There might also be unforeseen factors in the client's life that the questionnaire designers did not account for, but that are relevant to the client's financial risk. Considering this, the advisors in the focus group thought they were in a better position to decide what risk was appropriate for the client than the questionnaire. They were still legally obligated to complete the questionnaire with the client, but they thought of it more as documentation than decision support.

- How do you assess the client's proper risk level? [Researcher]
- If you look at the client's assets, their behavioral patterns, and their plans for the future, you know when not to recommend them to invest in stocks. [R9]
- Does the risk questionnaire help? [Researcher]
- In 9 cases out of 10, I already know the client's appropriate risk level before filling out the questionnaire. [R9]

The above quote tells something about how respondent 9 went about assessing his clients' proper risk level; the procedure he described lies completely outside of the system's risk questionnaire.

- The bank will often suggest a larger portion of stocks than I would, and that's because the bank believes in the stock market right now, but... when you are the one who will face the client, you know that they will not be happy when the stocks have lost value, even when you have agreed that this is a long-term investment. Clients tend to be a bit myopic. [R9]

Thus, respondent 9 also (cf. R10) hinted that he did not trust clients' own assertions of their risk preferences, as his experience had shown him that clients change their mind once they are exposed to the downside of risk. Therefore, he acted as a moderating filter on clients who were about to invest a large share of their capital in stocks. It could be noted that respondent 9 was generally conservative and tended to go for low-risk recommendations.

As another strategy to elicit the client's proper risk level, respondents said casual small talk was an invaluable source of information. Some described how they prepared for client meetings by looking up family members and the client's recent transaction history in order to form a picture of the client's lifestyle. This made it easier to think of topics for casual conversation, and provided the advisor with clues to possible developments in the client's future.

- [When assessing the client's situation and risk tolerance] social small talk is extremely important. That's when you find out the most important things about the client. The client tells you that they will be travelling somewhere, that they are becoming a father or a grandfather, or something like that. That's where you catch things you can use. I spend a lot of time there. Also [when assessing the client's risk preference and expectations], social small talk is important. That part consists of the risk questionnaire and social small talk taken together. [R6]

- The system gets a bit mechanical. When you talk to the client, you get a completely different picture of what the client wants. [R9]

No advisor followed the system's assessment of the client's risk profile slavishly, though there were variations in how much freedom they took. One advisor seemed slightly more passive when it came to making her own independent assessment of the client's risk profile, as when asked about how she made her assessment she answered by pointing to features in the application. When asked about whether she ever made any modifications to the system's recommendations, she answered that she made modifications when clients asked for something specific.

Thus, most respondents expressed a need for the system's algorithm-based risk assessments and recommendations to be checked and modified by a human advisor. The advisors had more of an intuitive, experience-based understanding of what financial risk would suit each client, similar to the professional skill of nurses described in [4].

It could be noted that the above discussion presumes a single individual client, while in fact many decisions are made at the household level. The laws on financial advice [9, 14] do not specifically address this fact.

- It's difficult to do risk assessment with couples. They can have different risk preferences but share the same capital. In those cases you have to do individual risk assessments with them both and then average the results. [R10]

The above dilemma has no optimal solution, regardless of IT support. The best the advisor can do is probably to try to discuss with both clients until some consensus is reached. Out of the four observed meetings, two included more than one client. One meeting involved a middle-aged couple, who seemed equally informed and active, and the other meeting involved a client in their early twenties and the client's parent, where the parent seemed more controlling even though the meeting mostly concerned the client's affairs. In this setting, the notion of who is "secondary user" becomes more complex. For example, information seemed less transparent to the client (who was less experienced with finance terminology than their parent), yet decisions were made where the parent and the advisor agreed but the client seemed more hesitant. In the below quote, the client was about to take out a large mortgage to buy their first apartment. The parent paid the down payment and acted as guarantor for the mortgage, and seemed to be of the opinion that it was time for the client to learn to live on their own.

- I still want to use any money I have left to amortize the mortgage. [Client]
- It's good to keep some emergency savings, especially when you have never lived on your own before and don't know how much things will cost. [Advisor]
- But it doesn't feel good to have a 1.9 million SEK mortgage. [Client]
- In Stockholm, that's normal. [Advisor]
- How many 20 year olds have 400,000 to put on a down payment? [Parent]
- Well, but... How many people with a monthly income of 22,000 have a 1.9 million mortgage? [Client]

As this transcript shows, the conversation is not solely between the client and the advisor, but also involves the client's parent. The different communication activities involve all parties and in this case the parent is actively taking part in the advisory conversation. This changes the social dynamic of the meeting; one party may feel pressured into making a certain decision or not to dwell on details for too long.

Making Investment Choices

After the mandatory risk level questionnaire is completed, the system generates a suggested investment portfolio for the client. If the client already has some capital invested with the bank, the system shows what changes need to be made (i.e. what to buy and sell) to obtain the suggested portfolio. The system-generated portfolio is explicitly said to be a suggestion and not an imperative, but advisors still had quite mixed reactions to the suggestions.

- The advisory application is a bit messy—if you have a client with both retirement savings and other types of investments, the system will generate so many suggested changes that it gets difficult to explain all the changes to the client. You almost want to blame it on how 'the computer thinks so', or 'the bank thinks so'. [R3]

- There are mutual funds that the experienced [advisors] choose, but then you must be able to vouch for them personally, if you are to dare go outside the bank's recommendation. I'm not that experienced. [R5]

The above quotes illustrate how some advisors shift responsibility for the advice provided to the client between themselves and the computer. Respondent 3 finds himself in a situation where he is tasked with explaining something that he does not quite feel capable of explaining—perhaps because the contents of the recommendation was not of his own design, and he cannot know the full reasoning behind it. Respondent 5 describes how she feels more personally accountable should she stray outside the institutionally sanctioned portfolio recommendation, which exposes her to greater personal risk of liability.

Some advisors were quite comfortable recommending the system-generated suggestions to clients, and hence only made changes if the client asked for something specific. Others wanted to personally stand behind everything they recommended, and some felt uneasy when the system recommended complicated or unfamiliar products.

The advisors had different strategies for dealing with this situation. Respondent 10 said that he always had a "practice session" before the actual meetings, to see what the system would recommend so that he would not be caught in surprise at what the system suggested, since the system's recommendations are continuously updated according to the bank's market outlook. A group of advisors at another branch office had made their own "application" in the form of a spreadsheet, where they kept track of investment products that they had personally or collaboratively scrutinized and felt that they could recommend to clients (those were the funds that respondent 5 talked about in the above quote). When asked how they explained to clients why they chose not to follow the computer's recommendations, several answered that they simply turn the screen away from the client so that the client never knows that there was any discrepancy.

While advisors are quite free to choose what particular investment products to recommend, they were still careful not to stray from the system-generated recommendations regarding allocation between stocks and bonds, and the allocation between regional markets. Even when they made their own custom portfolios in spreadsheets, they made sure not to add a larger share of stocks or stock market derived products to it than the system recommended. This is because the proportion of stocks in a portfolio is considered the most important factor determining the portfolio's risk level. If the advisor recommends a larger share of stocks than the system does, they are expected to have a very good reason for doing so.

- What are the advantages to the risk questionnaire? [Researcher]
*- I would say that it's a confirmation that you have done your job. If the Swedish financial supervisory authority comes, you can show them that the bank is behind this [advice to the client]. And if you can show them that you gave the client **lower** risk than recommended [by the system], they won't say anything. All the disputes have been about clients who got too **high** risk and lost money. [R9]*

In this case, the computer system acted as a form of protection for the advisor, against regulatory authorities and against litigatious clients.

- Do you usually follow the bank's recommendation or make your own suggestions? [Researcher]
- I usually tell the client that [the system-generated portfolio] is the bank's suggestion, but that they can choose whichever funds they want. And many of the clients that I have are not that informed, so they usually go with the bank's suggestion. [R5]

As respondent 5 was a less experienced advisor, she took less initiative in making her own recommendations to clients, which meant that her clients were more exposed to the "raw" system-generated recommendations with no advisor modifying—or explaining—the system's recommendations.

Few observations were made in this study where the client took a very active part in the value co-creation, although such clients definitely exist. The client has the final say in what gets done, and critical clients have every chance (theoretically) to defy the advisor's recommendations.

Explaining and Educating Clients

The inherent complexity of finance theory and portfolio selection is mirrored in the system, which provides very little support for advising or explaining to the client. This creates a need and an opportunity for the advisor to put their own personal touch on the information from the system by assuming a teaching role.

- This client wasn't ready for more advanced suggestions. It would have been too much for her if I started discussing asset allocations. [R2]

In the above quote, respondent 2 shows that she tries to sense the client's maturity level regarding financial decisions, and adapt her presentation accordingly. She acts as a filter that "protects" the client from information overload. Respondent 2 said the above after her first meeting with this client, where many practical matters regarding a decedent estate needed to be dealt with, and presumably she was planning to get to the discussion of asset allocation at a later meeting.

The bank's proprietary application could potentially be used for visualizing concepts and scenarios such as accumulated return at different risk levels, mortgage payments at different interest rates, and so on. However, as in [16], this opportunity seems underutilized. Respondent 3 (the office manager) said that such calculators and simulators can probably be found online, but that that leaves it up to individual advisors to search for them.

Some advisors go to great lengths to explain the basics of personal finance to clients before making any investment decisions with them. In this study, all the advisors who were observed to do so or talked about doing it in the interview [R4, R6, R10] happened to belong to the premium segment. The advisor would typically turn away from the computer completely, sit down with a notepad and a pen, and draw lines and charts in front of the client while explaining step by step. The details of the drawings differed between advisors, but what they had in common was that they took into account how much money the client needs for monthly expenses and for emergency funds, and not just for investing. They all attempted to paint a broader picture than simply the allocations between stocks and bonds. All of them also tried to explain *why* a certain type of investment is considered risky. Respondent 4 even made his sketch "interactive" by simulating movements with a pencil and eraser. When asked whether it was important to him to draw by hand, rather than have a ready-made picture in the computer, he agreed strongly.

The advisors who drew these sketches said that the clients usually asked to take the hand-drawn sketches home with them rather than the official documents from the bank, which only show a list of recommended investment products. Respondent 4 added with pride that his clients had adopted his terminology when they called him for advice.

The sketch in figure 1 describes an investment portfolio with a certain allocation between stocks and bonds, which changes with time as the market changes. All respondents who hand-drew sketches made some variant of this chart. Interestingly, a similar chart already exists in the advisory application, as one of few visual graphics. Advisors liked the chart in the application as it showed clients' real data and real exposure to the stock market, but some still seemed to prefer to draw by hand when explaining general principles.

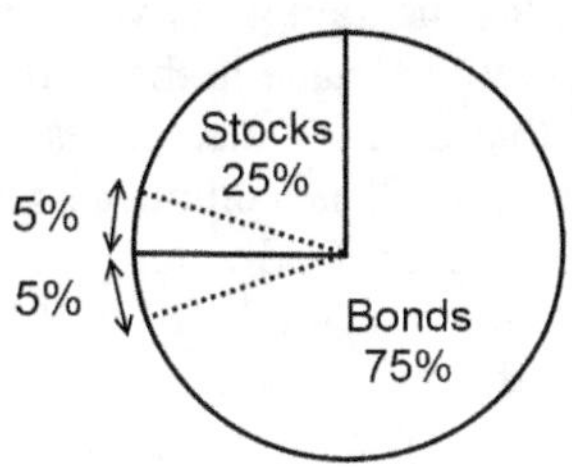

Figure 1 Stylized example of hand-drawn chart.

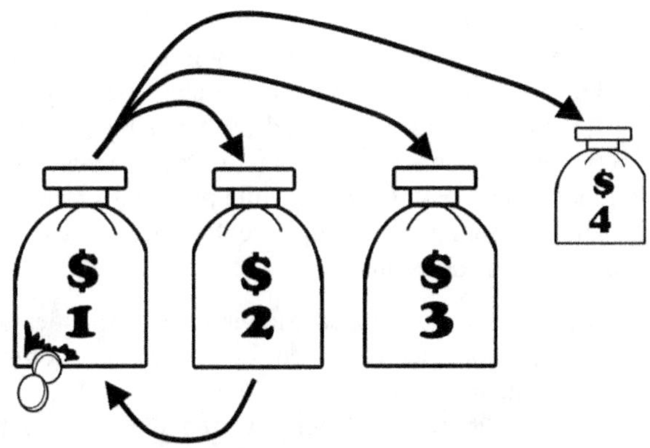

Figure 1. Stylized example of sketch explaining budgeting.

The sketch in figure 2 shows four bags of money, which represent different parts of the client's personal finances. The first bag is for monthly expenses, and it is constantly "leaking." The second bag is emergency savings, which will sometimes need to be used to refill the bag for monthly expenses. After the first two bags are in order, the client can start considering a third bag—long-term savings and investments. For some clients, a fourth bag can be suitable; it represents retirement savings that go under special tax rules in Sweden.

- It's important that the client feels that they can come back to ask questions. Humans work that way; they understand something now, but then they forget and need to hear the explanation again. And when you tell them, they go 'oh yes, that's right'. You just have to be responsive, then there is no problem. [R6]

Respondent 6 expresses an empathic view of clients' lack of finance expertise. Respondent 6 was also one of the advisors who drew their own sketches and took the time to explain how financial markets work. The system provided surprisingly little support for the kind of educational work that advisors like respondent 6 perform.

DISCUSSION

This research was conducted at two branch offices in a Swedish retail bank. The purpose was to study how financial advisors use their computer tools and how well said tools support the client meeting. The computer system aided the advisor in terms of structuring the discussion but demanded too much of the advisor's attention. Several advisors supplemented the discussion with clients with tailored sketches explaining financial reasoning. Some advisors wanted more interactive visualizations to aid in discussions with the client about different scenarios and potential outcomes. It is possible that this would empower clients to make more informed choices and thereby help alleviate the information asymmetry. Some experiments with visualizing financial concepts have shown promising effects on clients' comprehension (see e.g. [12, 28]). However, creating charts that project e.g. expected returns over a certain time period will necessarily involve design choices that cannot be neutral; some studies show that clients will take more risk the longer the time period displayed in the chart (see e.g. [28], see [3] for a dissenting result), and by choosing the default time period the designers will tend to steer clients toward taking more or less risk. As such, while potentially beneficial on the whole, visualizations will have "politics" in the same way that categorizations do.

In contrast to Nussbaumer and Matter [17], respondents in this study did not feel restricted by having an advisory application with a menu structure to follow. Contrariwise, they seemed to appreciate having a "red thread" in cases where they felt unsure of what talk about next. The explanation for this discrepancy is probably that Nussbaumer's and Matter's prototype was more rigid than this bank's advisory application, which has grown organically and does not require that steps be taken in any fixed order. Another explanation could be that the Swedish advisors were used to using the advisory application in their work, as it has been a requirement for a long time, while the advisors in the Swiss study may have been less used to including computers in their client meetings, even though they classified themselves as proficient IT users [17].

However, the advisory application did not offer much in ways of process transparency for the client; advisors were completely in control of what was discussed and in what order. Advisors could turn the screen away from the client if they wanted to, and there was no way for the client to know what parts existed in the system and what might be overlooked. Clearly, the application is designed for advisors and not for clients, which maintains the information asymmetry between knowledgeable professional and layman client. However, no client at any of the observed meetings seemed to object to this, and the focus on increasing process transparency in [17] did not seem to have any beneficial effects on client satisfaction, which was also confirmed in [13]. It is therefore debatable whether process transparency is an important concept for financial advisory meetings.

Regarding information transparency, advisors took an active role in "filtering" information to the client, for example by introducing difficult concepts and discussions (such as asset allocation) at a pace they deemed suitable for the client's knowledge level. They also sometimes altered the information from the client to the system, by actively expressing their own views on what risk level the client should choose. Hence, it could be said that the advisors provided a layer of personalization and tailoring of information between the system and the client; a personalization capability that the system itself lacks. On the one hand, it is likely that a human advisor is better at providing such personalization than a system, simply by being human and possessing qualities such as empathy and social skills. On the other hand, it introduces a risk of less stream-lined and uniform recommendations within the bank; the same client might get different recommendations from different advisors. From the bank's perspective, this might be problematic if the bank wishes to promote certain products across large client segments, or if the bank has a very rigid idea of how investment decisions should be made and documented. From the client's perspective, perhaps this is less of an issue. Hearing different recommendations from different advisors could potentially be confusing, but it might also enrich the client's understanding of the complexity of financial markets; there is no universally agreed-upon "best" risk attitude or investment strategy—not even the one that the bank has currently decided to endorse.

However, some respondents hesitated to make any modifications to the system-generated recommendations, because they felt that doing so would increase their own personal accountability for the advice given. This is both in relation to the client, who they will have to meet again in the future to tell them how their investments have performed, and in relation to the bank and to regulatory authorities who expect that advisors be able to explain why they have made the recommendations they made. By simply following the centrally administered recommendations, advisors are provided with an "easy way out" —they can always point to the system and say that they were simply following the rules. Additionally, as Bjørn and Balka have pointed out [4], experts can have trouble expressing the exact reasons behind their judgment calls, which can make them reluctant to modify the default suggestion when the system requires them to explain and modify every such modification that they make.

As cautioned by Bjørn and Balka [4] and others [9], having access to decision aids can make users (advisors) overly reliant on them. A novice advisor who is only trained in operating the system, and not in making their own independent judgment of where the market is going and what type of investment would suit which client, may never develop that skill set. If advisors become unable to spot errors in the computer-provided advice, the whole system will be potentially more error-prone.

Two unexpected findings came out of this study. The first is that while previous research, consumer protection laws, and system design principles, all assume that a meeting involves one client and one advisor, it was actually fairly common for meetings to involve more than one client. This is of course not a statistical claim as the sample is very small and non-random, but the observations made in the study were enough to question the idea that a client meeting is a conversation between two people only. This complicates the idea of a primary and a secondary user. Traditionally, the primary user is thought of as being in control of the interface and having access to most of the information, while the secondary user is affected by the system but not in direct control of it. Thus, designing "for" the secondary user might mean trying to be more inclusive toward the secondary user and give them more control and access to more information—but how does that work when there are two clients who might have different ideas and different knowledge levels? Should the advisor just listen to the dominant client or also try to elicit responses from the less dominant client? Is it enough if only one of the clients is able to follow the discussion and understand the terminology?

The other unexpected finding was advisors' accounts of their clients' low knowledge levels of basic personal finance concepts. Clients needed, and wanted, explanations of how to structure their budget, of how financial markets work, and of what "financial risk" really means. This means that recommendations for asset allocations that are simply provided by a computer system and passed on to clients risk going over many clients' heads. Currently, it might not make financial sense for banks to spend time explaining basic personal finance to clients, as the law does not specifically require it and it is not directly linked to the sale of products. On the other hand, there is potential that clients would become more satisfied with their advisors and their banks, and that they would be better suited to make investment decisions that they are less likely to regret and try to dispute later.

Some respondents were very skilled in explaining basic personal finance to clients. Typically, those respondents had extensive job experience and were extremely interested in finance even in their spare time. For them, turning away from the computer and drawing on paper had an intrinsic value; it provided for a more personal, intimate moment with the client and perhaps there was also an element of pride; they got to show off how well they knew financial concepts by heart, which impressed clients and increased client trust. Such skilled advisors should be allowed the freedom to keep explaining and talking to clients in the way that suits them best. Additionally, they could be studied as an inspiring source of educational ideas and concepts to include in a financial advisory application, to support less experienced advisors. That way, more clients could get access to examples and sketches provided by advisors with a life-time of experience in how to explain finance concepts to clients.

We believe the intention behind the risk questionnaire is good and that there is good reason to maintain some level of standardization of the method used to determine the client's risk level, though admittedly the construction of a good and valid risk questionnaire is a challenge. The details of how such a questionnaire should be designed is an ongoing debate, however slightly outside the scope of this paper (se e.g. [5, 11, 15]). The advisors did not always trust the system's categorization of clients, and would sometimes claim to have better judgment. It is difficult for a researcher as an outside observer to determine who is really more accurate—the advisor or the system. However, the tradition within CSCW is to trust that the professional with their background and experience is best suited to be the ultimate judge. Nevertheless, the question of how much subjectivity is appropriate in advisory meetings is interesting and important, though we recognize that the system's categorization by no means represents any "objective" standard.

CONCLUSIONS

Our results suggest that there is room for improvement in the process of categorizing clients' risk preferences as low, medium, or high. An interesting area for future research would be to try to make the discussion more concrete for the client and explain the foundations behind financial theories and concepts, so that the client can give better answers.

One suggested way to do this could be to start the meeting with a discussion of more basic personal finance concepts such as budget keeping. The application could show clients how much they spend each month and how much is left for saving. The advisor could then help the client allocate savings between an emergency fund for unexpected expenses (the size of which would depend on the client's circumstances, such as whether they own a house that could suddenly need repair) and long-term savings goals such as retirement, children, or a large purchase. Talking about long term savings in terms of goals would presumably make it easier for clients to express whether they are willing to take any risk with the money saved for that particular goal, and the advisor can determine the level of risk necessary to allow the growth that is needed to reach the goal on time.

The application should support the more complex situation when more than one client is present at the meeting. In fact, even when only one client is present, we believe the client would benefit from seeing and being able to switch between an individual-level view and a household-level view of their personal finances. The difficult problem of determining what risk to take with capital that is shared within the household needs to be studied more in depth.

For experienced advisors who prefer to recommend products that they have personally scrutinized, the application could allow them to save their favorite products of different risk levels, and have the system compose a portfolio that is based on the system-recommended allocation between stocks and bonds, but contains the advisor's favorite products instead of the ones that the system recommends by default. This could potentially conflict with any sales goals that the bank might have, but on the other hand, advisors already have the discretion to recommend whichever products they find suitable and this would simply be a way of simplifying their jobs while also helping them make sure that they keep to the recommended allocation between stocks and bonds.

As today's society increasingly relies more on individual financial choices, and such financial decisions are often done in cooperation with financial advisors it is of utmost importance that supporting systems are designed in a way that helps both the client and the advisor make informed, traceable decisions.

ACKNOWLEDGEMENTS

We thank VINNOVA for funding this research through project 2013-05083. We also thank the anonymous reviewers who gave constructive criticism which improved the paper.

REFERENCES

1. Almenberg, J., and Säve-Söderbergh, J. Financial Literacy and Retirement Planning in Sweden. *Journal of Pension Economics and Finance 10,* 4 (2011), 585.
2. Alsos, O. and Svanæs, D. Designing for the Secondary User Experience. In *Proc. Interact 2011*, Springer Berlin Heidelberg (2011), 84-91.
3. Bateman, H., Eckert, C., Geweke, J., Louviere, J. J., Satchell, S. E., and Thorp, S. *Investment Risk Framing and Individual Preference Consistency*. UNSW Australian School of Business Research Paper, (2011).
4. Bjørn, P., and Balka, E. Health Care Categories Have Politics Too: Unpacking the Managerial Agendas of Electronic Triage Systems. *In Proc.10th European Conference on Computer Supported Cooperative Work,* Springer London (2007), 371-390.
5. Callan, V. J. and Johnson, M. Some Guidelines for Financial Planners in Measuring and Advising Clients about Their Levels of Risk Tolerance. *Journal of Personal Finance 1,* 1 (2002), 31-44.
6. Cronqvist, H. and Thaler, R. Design Choices in Privatized Social-Security Systems: Learning from the Swedish Experience. *American Economic Review,* (2004), 424-428.
7. Eriksson, K., and Söderberg, I.L. Customers' Ways of Making Sense of a Financial Service Relationship through Intersubjective Mirroring of Others. *Journal of Financial Services Marketing 15*, 2 (2010), 99-111.
8. Eriksson, K., Persson, A. and Söderberg, I.L. *Bankrådgivningsrelationen och rådgivningslagen* (2009).
9. Financial Advice to Consumers Act (SFS, 2003:862). http://www.government.se/sb/d/2016/a/31099
10. Glover, S., Prawitt, D. and Spilker, B. The Influence of Decision Aids on User Behavior: Implications for Knowledge Acquisition and Inappropriate Reliance. *Organizational Behavior and Human Decision Processes 72*, 2 (1997), 232-255.
11. Guillemette, M. A., Finke, M. S., and Gilliam, J. *Which Types of Risk Tolerance Questions Should Be Used When Determining a Client's Portfolio Allocation Preference?,* (2012). Available at SSRN 2009419.
12. Haisley, E., Kaufmann, C. and Weber, M. *How Much Risk Can I Handle?: The Role of Experience Sampling and Graphical Displays on One's Investment Risk Appetite and Comprehension.* Lehrstuhl für Allgemeine Betriebswirtschaftslehre, Finanzwirtschaft, insbesondere Bankbetriebslehre, Universität Mannheim (2010).
13. Heinrich, P., Kilic, M., Aschoff, F. and Schwabe, G. Enabling Relationship Building in Tabletop-Supported Advisory Settings. *In Proc. 17th ACM Conference on Computer Supported Cooperative Work & Social Computing*, ACM Press (2014), 171-183.
14. Markets in Financial Services Directive. http://ec.europa.eu/internal_market/securities/isd/index_en.html
15. McCrae, M. Profiling the Risk Attitudes of Clients by Financial Advisors: The Effects of Framing on Response Validity. *Faculty of Commerce-Accounting & Finance Working Papers 36,* (2006).
16. Mogacito, R., Schwabe, G., Nussbaumer, P., Stehli, E., and Eberhard, M. *Beratungsqualität in Banken.* Solution Providers AG (2009).
17. Nussbaumer, P., and Matter, I. What You See Is What You (Can) Get? Designing for Process Transparency in Financial Advisory Encounters. In *Proc. Interact 2011*, Springer Berlin Heidelberg (2011), 277-294.
18. Nussbaumer, P., Matter, I. and Schwabe, G. "Enforced" vs. "Casual" Transparency--Findings from IT-Supported Advisory Encounters. *ACM Transactions on Management Information Systems 3*, 2 (2012), 11.
19. Nussbaumer, P., Slembek, I., Lueag, C., Mogacito, R. and Schwabe, G. Understanding Information Seeking Behaviour in Financial Advisory. In *ISI: Internationales Symposium für Informationswissenschaft,* (2009).
20. Oehler, A. and Kohlert, D. Financial Advice Giving and Taking--Where Are the Market's Self-Healing Powers and a Functioning Legal Framework When We Need Them? *Journal of Consumer Policy 32*, 2 (2009), 91-116.
21. Rogers, Y. and Lindley, S. Collaborating around Vertical and Horizontal Large Interactive Displays: Which Way is Best? *Interacting with Computers 16*, 6 (2004), 1133-1152.
22. Roszkowski, M. J. and Davey, G. Risk Perception and Risk Tolerance Changes Attributable to the 2008 Economic Crisis: A Subtle but Critical Difference. *Journal of Financial Service Professionals 64*, 4 (2010).
23. Schmidt, K. Of Maps and Scripts: The Status of Formal Constructs in Cooperative Work. *Information and software technology 4,* 6 (1999). 319-329.
24. Schmidt-Rauch, S., and Nussbaumer, P. Putting Value Co-Creation into Practice: A Case for Advisory Support. In *Proc. ECIS: European Conference on Information Systems,* (2011), 138.
25. Söderberg, I.L. *Financial Advisory Services: Exploring Relationships Between Consumers and Financial Advisors.* Ph.D. thesis, KTH Royal Institute of Technology, (2013).

26. Söderberg, I.L., Sallis, J. and Eriksson, K. The Dark Side of Trust and the Light Side of Working Alliances in Financial Services. *Journal of Consumer Research* (2013).

27. Suchman, L. Do Categories Have Politics? The Language/Action Perspective Reconsidered. *In Proc. 3rd European Conference on Computer-Supported Cooperative Work,* Springer Netherlands (1993), 1-14.

28. Sundali, J. A., and Guerrero, F. Managing a 401 (k) Account: An Experiment on Asset Allocation. *Journal of Behavioral Finance 10,* 2 (2009), 108-124.

29. Winograd, T. Categories, Disciplines, and Social Coordination. *Computer Supported Cooperative Work (CSCW) 2,* 3 (1993). 191-197.

Coercing into Completeness in Financial Advisory Service Encounters

Mehmet Kilic
University of Zurich
Binzmühlestr. 14
8050 Zürich, Switzerland
kilic@ifi.uzh.ch

Peter Heinrich
University of Zurich
Binzmühlestr. 14
8050 Zürich, Switzerland
heinrich@ifi.uzh.ch

Gerhard Schwabe
University of Zurich
Binzmühlestr. 14
8050 Zürich, Switzerland
schwabe@ifi.uzh.ch

ABSTRACT
In this article, we report on design insights found during the evaluation of an innovative IT-artifact to support financial service encounters. Relating to previous work in this field, we carefully designed the artifact to omit any visualization and enforcement of rigid process structures, as those had turned out to be harmful. Our main design element was a mind-map-like content hierarchy to capture the client's situation. Surprisingly, we noticed that both clients and advisors talked about every information item visible on the screen just for the sake of completeness. They also followed a sequential process apparently inferred from the content hierarchy. We call this phenomenon "coercing into completeness". This phenomenon negatively influences the conversation between client and advisor inducing shorter discussion units and sudden, incomprehensible topic shifts. This article contributes an exploration of this phenomenon and its effects on the collaborative setting.

Author Keywords
financial advisory service; needs elicitation; completeness; exploratory research; design research

ACM Classification Keywords
H.5.3 [Group and Organization Interfaces]

INTRODUCTION
Performing tasks completely can be an important factor for qualitative work. In medicine, for example, a physician is required to carefully carry out an anamnesis in order to obtain a sound diagnosis. Engineers have to analyze requirements completely in order to design a purposeful solution to the given problem. Factory workers need to perform all steps completely to assemble products. In all those cases a standardization of the workflow can help guiding the ongoing work towards an expected outcome. It can also help to assess the level of work-completion by comparing its status to the workflow's definition. However, if processes are defined in too fine-grained manner, this may lead to acceptance problems, as this restricts process participants in an undesired and unnecessary way [14]. Therefore, the level of detail has to be well balanced between optimal guidance and reasonable levels of restriction.

Collaborative settings are even harder to manage, especially if the participants have different opinions on the level of completeness. Financial advisory services, for example, are loaded with different perceptions of completeness. On the one hand, the clients might be primarily interested in having their individual situation and their goals considered completely in order to obtain the best matching financial product. On the other hand, the financial advisor might have his own incentives, and thus his targeted level of completeness might be restricted by the minimum information required to make an offer. In the worst case, the advisor also limits the range of products according to his personal sales goals in order to receive an extra bonus at the year's end. An inherent conflict of interest between the parties is often referred to as "principal-agent-conflict" [6, 16] and implies an associated asymmetry of information [23, 24]. Executives from the bank still might be interested in another level of completeness. They might prefer complete standardization of the advisory process in order to deliver constant service quality and to comply with normative regulations. In general, these different levels of completeness are never explicated and only implicitly communicated among subgroups of the participants.

Scholars and practitioners have tried to support those encounters with IT-based tools in order to dampen the information asymmetry by making the process itself and the information processed transparent to all stakeholders [17]. However, it has been shown that those supportive tools have to be designed with great care, as they might otherwise endanger the social setting [11]. An explicit visualization and enforced guidance through a rigid process "was perceived to be authoritative and deterministic, imposing its process structure upon the users and restricting the user's control of the process" [18]. An implicit process guidance is far superior and even leads to higher levels of perceived process transparency, process control, and higher overall satisfaction with the service encounter [19].

CSCW '15, March 14 - 18 2015, Vancouver, BC, Canada

ACM 978-1-4503-2922-4/15/03...$15.00
http://dx.doi.org/10.1145/2675133.2675289

We set out to design an IT-tool to support the first and arguably most crucial phase of financial advisory services — namely, the client's needs elicitation. In this initial phase, the current situation of the client is captured as well as his attitudes, preferences, and goals. We designed an advisory-support tool to support this phase. Our main intention was explicitly not to impose any process onto the participants, because we were aware of the different demands of the various stakeholders (clients, advisors, and executives). Based on literature and prior experience with those settings, we opted for a mind-map-like interface to provide maximum freedom with respect to both the process as well as the content used within a service-encounter.

Besides the obvious benefits that our solution has from a management perspective, some participants felt coerced by the tool to adapt the visualized content as process structures and as notion of completeness. We call this phenomenon "coercing into completeness".

In this paper, we introduce the phenomenon of "coercing into completeness" (1) by describing one exemplary context in which it occurs, (2) by describing its manifestation in the particular collaborative setting from the perspectives of the clients and the advisors, and (3) by making conjectures on the reasons why the phenomenon occurs.

Hence, our research questions are:

RQ1: How does coercing into completeness affect the service encounter?

RQ2: Why does coercing into completeness still occur in the absence of any explicit process and progress visualizations within the IT artifact?

The paper ends with a detailed discussion of the phenomenon as well as implications of our findings for the future design of advisory support systems.

RELATED WORK

Coercing into completeness in single user contexts

Many companies like Google, LinkedIn, and Dropbox provide a feature called "completeness meter". These kinds of progress indicators give the user feedback on how far he or she is while completing a task. These meters are mostly used to motivate new users to add personal information or to complete activities. Myers has shown that people prefer to have progress indicators [15]. Completing a task is intrinsically rewarding. The discrete task completion hypothesis by Skinner states that a completed task is a conditioned reinforcer [25]. Zeigarnik [32] has shown that people have a tendency to remember incomplete tasks better than completed tasks. Uncompleted tasks are kept in memory until they are completed. These open tasks cause an uncomfortable feeling or even tensions and stress. People want to resolve this tension. This is called negative reinforcement in operant conditioning [7]. People want to remove something distasteful. For example, this effect is used in many mobile operating systems with the annoying persistent badge to motivate us to update our apps or to give attention to new messages. We will usually update our apps because we want those annoying numbers to disappear (negative stimulus). In summary, a progress bar bears both effects at the same time: It is possible to achieve something (positive reinforcement) and to complete an undone task (negative reinforcement).

Coercing into completeness in dyadic advisory contexts

Financial advisory services are predominantly delivered in a dyadic setting and can be divided into three phases [20]: "information collection phase", "information phase", and "recommendation phase". During the encounter, the problem space of the client (information collection) has to be mapped with the solution space (recommendation phase) to identify matching solutions [16]. For this paper, we focus on the first phase, the information collection phase. At the beginning of the advisory session, an information asymmetry is inherently given because the advisor has insufficient knowledge of the current client's situation. During this first phase of the service encounter, this information asymmetry shall be lowered.

In the information collection phase a notion of completeness depends on the desired modus of advice-giving. Literature describes this as a continuum between two extreme positions: either the "Informed Decision Making model" or the "Perfect Agent Model" [8]. In the "Informed Decision Making model", the clients make all decisions by themselves, in contrast to the other model, where the advisor makes all decisions. For the first model, the client needs profound knowledge about the solution space, whereas in the other model, the advisor needs substantial knowledge of the client's problem space [8]. Neither model can be established in practice, as knowledge transfer in either direction is difficult. Transferring all relevant knowledge about the solution space, i.e. financial products, is considered unrealistic for practical settings due to the missing levels of expertise on client's side and the large amount of required information [13]. The transfer of the client's personal situation, needs, and desires without showing the client concrete solutions options is also difficult [16], and is referred to as the "sticky information" problem [28]. Therefore, in practice there will be a mixture of informed decision-making and perfect agent models with missing information on both sides and practically reachable levels of completeness below the theoretical maximum. Of course, the goal is to minimize the amount of information lacking needed to foster informed decision. Based on the limited shared knowledge, we argue that, on the one hand, in traditional advisory settings a sufficient level of completion is mutually perceived, when the clients have told everything they considered to be important for an advisor to develop a purposeful solution. And on the other hand, this sufficient level of completion is also achieved when the advisors have asked everything they perceive relevant in order to give advice (and sell the appropriate products of course). Besides these situational levels of completeness, there also exist extrinsic motivations to gain information from the clients that go partially beyond the perceived needs of the participants within the service encounter. Normative regulations like the WpHG (German law on trading bonds) [31] put banks under pressure to establish standards to ensure a minimum of information acquisition with the aim to protect the client from buying unsuited products. Moreover, additional information items gained during personal interactions can be beneficial to the financial institutions for profiling and cross-/up-selling opportunities [27]. During a traditional face-to-face interaction, these additional drivers for completeness can only be transported through the advisor, as the client is unaware of them.

Coercing into completeness in the presence of structures

Coercing into completeness is a phenomenon that can be analyzed in the context of the role of structures in the appropriation of technology. In his seminal "structuration theory", Giddens [9] pointed out that structures may have unintended consequences and that it is necessary to understand the intentions of the creators and users of the structures to understand the effects of structures. Building on Giddens' work, DeSanctis and Poole [4] developed the Adaptive Structuration Theory. Among other things, it stresses the importance of the "spirit" of an application and proposes different styles of appropriation ranging from direct use to direct negation.

There has been an intensive discourse on the role of structures in collaborative technologies. Researchers from the traditional CSCW disciplines (most prominently represented by Lucy Suchman in the famous dispute on the coordinator-mail system [26]) tend to warn that pre-structuring sensitive processes such as communication or collaboration may conflict human cognition or established social norms. Researchers with a more business-oriented perspective (in the case of the coordinator dispute Terry Winograd [30]) tend to stress the organizational benefits of prescribing structures ranging from less misunderstanding to higher productivity. There is even an emerging research stream on "collaboration engineering" [1,5] coercing to prescribe structured collaboration routines to organizational users. While we see more failures than successes with rigid structures in the domain of collaborative technologies, the widespread adoption of ERP systems in organizations indicates that the organizational benefits of information systems can be so important that users adopt the system and the structured work practices even though many dislike them.

The conflict between organizational interests on the one hand and cognition and social norms on the other hand play an important role in pre-structuring financial advisory service encounters. Struggling with principal-agent conflicts [6,16], quality problems, and regulatory requirements [31], banks push hard to establish structured advisory processes. In a straightforward implementation, they are interested in enforcing the process by the required use of a process-oriented software. Nussbaumer et al. [19] have shown that an explicitly visible pre-defined structure of the advisory process (e.g. "information collection phase", "information phase", and "recommendation phase") will incentivize both the advisors and clients to follow this process. Nevertheless, all participants in such a highly structured process were dissatisfied with the whole service encounters because they felt part of a machinery [19], and the interpersonal relationship-building between advisors and clients suffers [11] in an unacceptable manner. Providing the process structure implicitly (hidden) instead of explicitly (visible), and thus leaving the process to the users instead of the information system, proved to be a superior solution [17,19].

Designing IT artifacts to support implicit completeness

Supporting advisory encounters with appropriately designed IT-artifacts can be beneficial in many ways. Besides the obvious features of process documentation and integration of other information systems, they can also help to make the whole process more transparent to the clients [19] through the use of shared artifacts between client and advisor [16]. But with respect to the information collection phase, IT-artifacts can be used as a way to commonly objectify [11,29] the discussed information items.

IT-artifacts have to be designed carefully so that they do not interfere with the fragile social setting, which is given in any dyadic service encounter. As stated before, it has been demonstrated that enforced process guidance has strong negative effects on the acceptance of such solutions [18]. However, visualizations and interaction models without fixed structures like "loose widgets" and the "zoom and filter" metaphor have been evaluated to be far more successful than "PowerPoint-like" step-by-step metaphors of process guidance [19]. Such representations deliberately omit a notion of beginning, completion, or progress of the current task or process. Hence, negotiating on completeness should still happen between the participants as within traditional pen and paper-based encounters.

This stream of research leaves open the following issue: Why did the advisor and the client in our setting strive for completeness, although the software did not explicitly visualize or enforce it?

RESEARCH FRAMEWORK

The methodology used for the research project can be conceptualized as exploratory research [2], emerging from design science research [12] (DSR) activities. Thus, this paper generally follows a structure typical for DSR-related publications [10] and describes all of the six typical DSR activities [21]: *(1) problem identification, (2) objectives of a solution, (3) design and development, (4) demonstration, (5) evaluation, and (6) communication*. The introduction covers (1) and (2), whereas the artifact description covers (3) and (4). However, the paper focuses especially on the evaluation (5). In contrast to "confirmatory research" [2], where the fulfillment of the solution objectives is demonstrated, we use the evaluation as a vehicle to explore why the observed phenomenon emerged and how it manifested itself. Therefore, this paper has an in-depth results and discussion section, where we reason about the factors that lead to coercing into completeness. The last activity (6) — namely, the communication of the results — is the purpose of this paper.

According to Briggs [2], the core contribution of exploratory design research is the description of new phenomena and/or its emergence in new contexts. In this paper, we identify and describe the "phenomenon of coercing into completeness" in the context of dyadic advisory service encounters, in which it occurred and started the discussion on possible explanations and factors that lead to the occurrence of this phenomenon.

INITIAL IMPLEMENTATION OF THE ARTIFACT

Following the DSR methodology [22], we have specified, designed, implemented, and evaluated an IT-prototype. In that research project, we worked in close cooperation with a major Swiss retail bank.

The *main design rationale* was to support advisors and clients during the needs elicitation process. Therefore, we intended to support the collaboration with technology to enhance the understanding of the client's situation. Together, advisors and clients should create a "picture" of the client's situation and needs. The advisor should have a means to externalize, organize, and discuss the client's information and to summarize the client's themes using this picture. The client should observe that the data was collected transparently and have the opportunity to make immediate corrections, if necessary. In consequence, the advisors' understanding of the clients' situation should be externalized and be verifiable for the client. Furthermore, to overcome the sticky information needs problem, the client should be stimulated to talk about additional topics, which were visualized on the display serving as prompts but not asking for information directly. From an organizational point of view, the bank is interested in collecting information in a holistic manner and to analyze this data. The bank wants to know its clients to unhide up- or cross-selling potentials and use them for marketing actions. Therefore, the data should be structured and digitalized. If this data is seized electronically, it is possible to transfer it into a customer relationship management (CRM) system for further analysis.

To guide the design of our artifact, we choose the metaphor of a mind-map to support the information collection phase, as it fulfills the aforementioned demands of providing a flexible and adaptive content structure. Computer supported mind-maps have been shown to be applicable in collaborative settings and have also proven to be beneficial to collaboration in terms of leveling the amount of contribution between the collaborating participants [3].

Artifact design

The IT-prototype ("Needs Map") was designed with a mind-map analogy displaying the text "me" and the name of the client in the middle and six connected branches as a start: work, residence, family, leisure, finance, and assistance. Stimulating information items, which could be attached to the existing structure, were displayed adaptively with respect to the currently selected item within a large list on the sidebar: selecting one item within the map showed information items related to this branch on the right sidebar. For example, by selecting the branch "work" the items "job", "part time job", "study", and "career" were shown (see Figure 1).

There are three kinds of information items available: information regarding the current situation (such as the current job), concrete goals (such as buying a car), and wishes (for example, goals in future such as buying a family home). The interaction to assign an information item to a branch or another item is realized by dragging and dropping an item on the touchscreen from the right side near to the selected branch or item. There was no limit on the amount and level of items, which could be attached to a branch or another item. It is also possible to add one-time or monthly income and expense information to every information item. The six initial branches (see Figure 1) provided an opportunity to structure the discussed information. The additional information items were provided to stimulate the participants during the needs elicitation phase.

It was intended that clients tell about their current situation, needs, and goals, and that the advisors organize this information in the map in an appropriate branch. We also expected that advisors would use the inherent features of a mind-map, especially the possibility to extend the given structure according to the conversation. In doing so, the client has the opportunity to see transparently how the information is recorded and to correct wrong information.

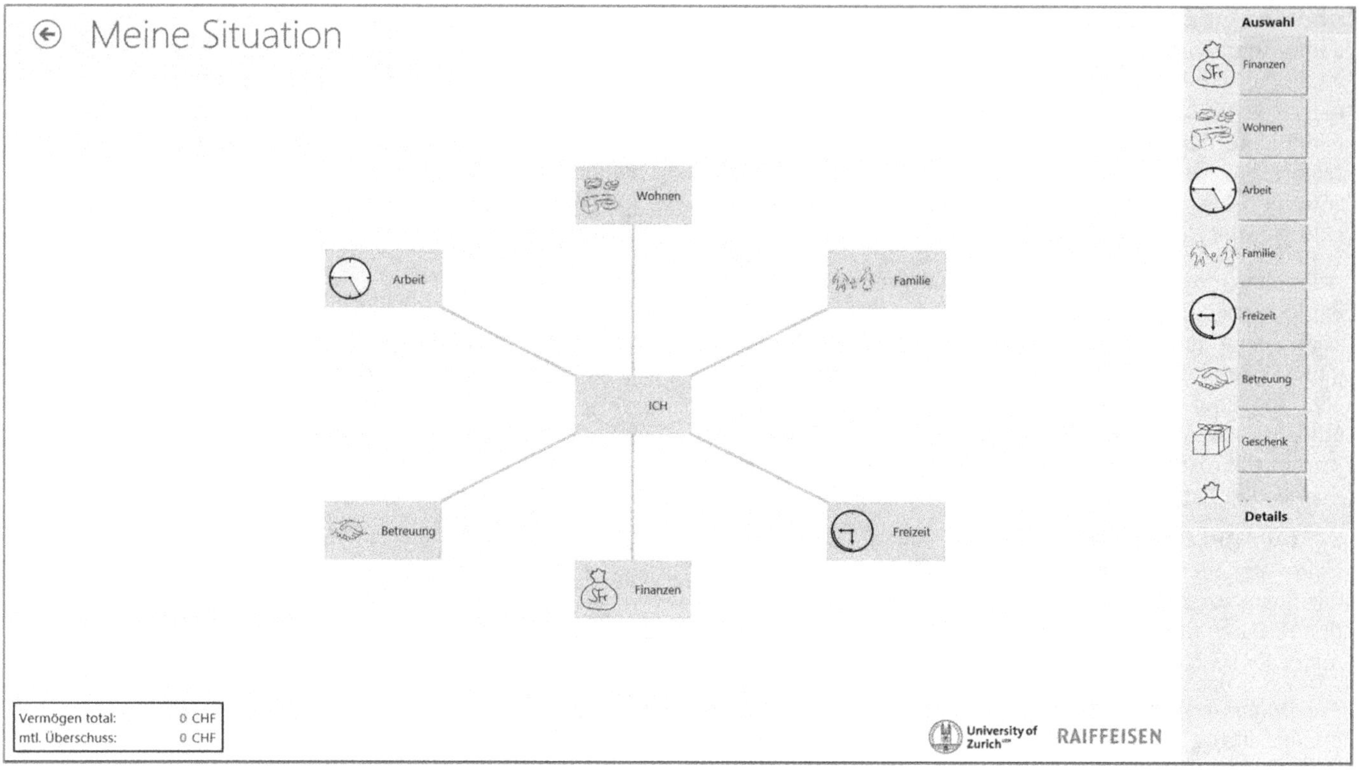

Figure 1. Start screen with empty mind-map. Translation from German: Meine Situation – my situation, Arbeit – work, Wohnen – residence, Familie – family, Freizeit – leisure, Finanzen – finance, Betreuung – assistance

EVALUATION

Data collection

The evaluation of the IT-prototype was accomplished with 16 experienced financial advisors and 48 potential clients (bachelor students from a business informatics course) in a realistic setting. During the advisory service encounter, the participants worked with our IT-prototype. The software was executed on a tabletop computer (a 27-inch touchscreen). The physical environment was designed to enable both participants to interact with the system. The evaluation was conducted as a within-subject design. Thus, every client took part in two advisory service encounter treatments: one traditional pen and paper encounter and one supported by the IT-artifact. The evaluation was carried out over eight days. On every day, two advisors were present onsite and each of them conducted six advisory sessions (three traditional, three IT-supported). Preceding the evaluation, the advisors were first trained one week prior through video explanations and written training material. On the day of the evaluation, each advisor received 60 minutes of personal hands-on training with the artifact.

After the clients had received their two treatments, they were interviewed. Advisors were interviewed at the end of each test day. The interviews were conducted in the form of a semi-structured interview of approximately 30 minutes duration for the clients and approximately 45 minutes for the advisors on average. Video-recordings were taken of the encounters. Screencasts were also recorded for the IT-artifact supported encounters.

Results

To broadly elicit data about the phenomenon, we studied the resulting mind-maps from the sessions, the conversations, and interactions between clients and advisors and how the participants perceived the encounter. The mind-maps were extracted from the screencasts, the conversations were analyzed through the video recordings, and the perceptions of the participants were mainly extracted from the interview data as well as from comments made during the video-recordings. Within each following section, we briefly describe how the data sources were analyzed before presenting the results.

Manifestation of coercing into completeness in the resulting mind-maps

We assessed the result of the mind-maps by capturing the state of the map after the last interaction with it.

In almost all advisory sessions the participants filled out at least five of the provided six branches with personal information of the client (see Figures 2 and 3). Additionally, in most sessions they also talked about the branches that were not filled, but there was either no information to fill out or they decided to leave the branches empty. For example, when the clients were not married or in a partnership they decided not to record this in the family branch (see Figure 3). One advisor of 16 did not really use the mind-map; she filled only the "finance" branch with minimal information.

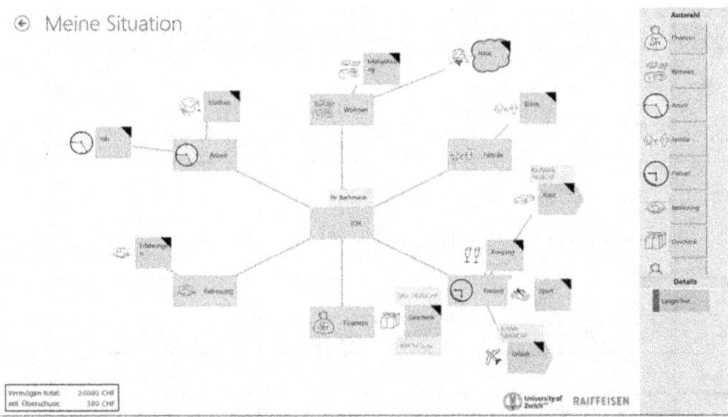

Figure 2. Example of completely filled mind-map

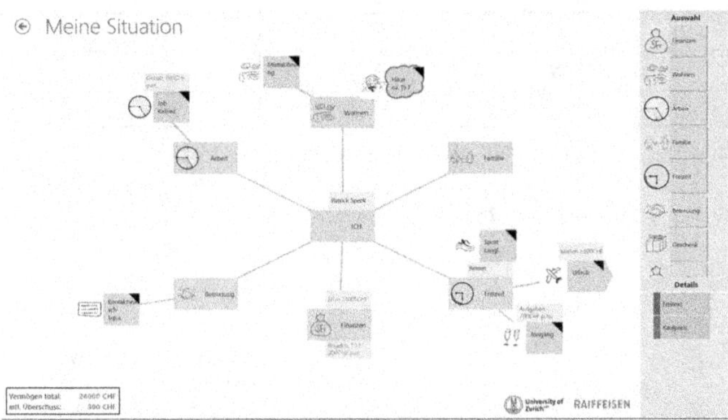

Figure 3: Example of mind-map with empty family branch.

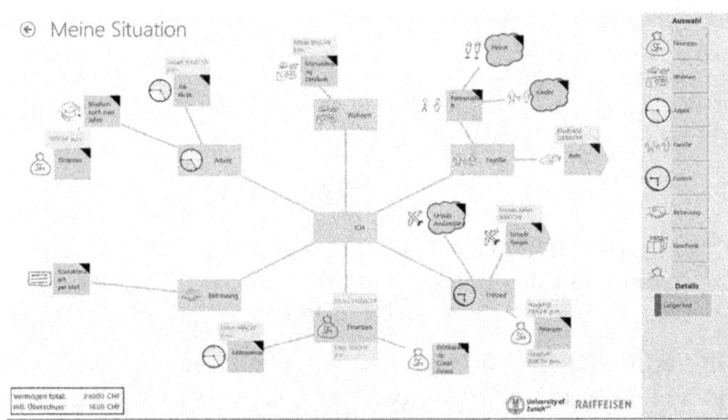

Figure 4: Example of filled mind-map with two levels.

Examples of resulting mind-maps are shown in Figures 2, 3, and 4. Figure 2 shows a mind-map where at least one information item is attached to a branch, so they have talked about the topic of each branch and recorded the corresponding information. In Figure 3, a mind-map is shown where the family branch is left empty. The mind-maps were mostly filled out in a broad and rather superficial manner. The participants only used one level of depth. From all 48 advisory sessions, only in one session did the participants create items on the second level (see Figure 4). In the remaining 47 sessions the information items were directly attached to a branch.

Manifestation of coercing into completeness in the conversation

By analyzing the screencast alongside the video recordings, we can assess the structure and flow of conversation. In this section, we present a two-step approach analyzing the structure of the conversation. (1) We analyze in which order the topics were discussed within the IT-supported setting. (2) Then, we analyze the transitions between the discussed topics to shed light on the question of how the presence of the artifact changed the discussion behavior of the participants.

In the first step, we analyzed 16 video-recorded sessions and traced the sequence of the discussion topics (see Table 1). For this analysis, we included each advisor's last IT-supported session in the sample. We argue that in the last session the advisors showed the most proficient use of the IT-artifact and were well accustomed to the setting.

Seven advisors start with the branch "work" and talk about the topics in a clockwise direction. Four advisors start with another branch (2 x finance, 1 x residence, and 1 x leisure), go to "work", and then go further in a clockwise direction. In summary, 11 advisors start with "work" as the first or second topic and then follow a clockwise structure. When all paths are visualized together, (Figure 5) a pattern emerges and reveals that most advisors follow an identical path. Four advisors do not follow an identifiable pattern. One advisor does not make use of the mind-map at all. Those five were omitted in the visualization for clarity.

In the second step, we took another sample. As we assume that the conversation behavior is strongly related to the individual advisor's personality, we only select advisors with comparable customer satisfaction ratings in the traditional encounter. We analyzed the pairwise recordings from 8 advisors and 8 clients, including 8 traditional encounters and 8 IT-supported ones. Thus, there were 16 sessions in total.

An analysis of how many conversation sequences are present within the information collection phase reveals that significantly more sequences are present within the IT-supported encounter compared to the traditional one. For the analysis, we have transcribed the participant's utterances and identified conversation sequences. One conversation sequence is characterized by the amount of adjacency pairs, i.e. pairs where the question of the advisor is related to the ongoing discussion or answer of the client. Every time the advisor asks a question not related to the ongoing discussion, a new sequence starts.

In the IT-supported encounter the conversations consisted on average of 7.9 (sd=2.17) sequences, while the traditional ones only had 4.5 (sd=2.07) sequences. A two-sided paired-sample T-test reveals this difference to be significant ($T(7)=4.473$, $p<=0.005$). However, the numerous sequences of IT-supported encounters seem to be shorter.

	Work	Reside	Family	Leisure	Finance	Assistance
Adivsor01	1. N	2. N	3. D	4. N	5. N	6. N
Advisor02	1. N	2. N	3. D	4. N	5. N	6. D
Advisor03	4. N	1. N	2. A	3. N	5. N	-
Advisor04	3. N	4. N	5. N	2. N	1. N	-
Advisor05	2. N	3. N	4. N	5. N	1. N	6. N
Advisor06	2. N	1. N	3. N	4. D	5. N	6. N
Advisor07	1. N	2. N	3. N	4. N	5. N	6. N
Advisor08	2. N	3. N	-	4. N	1. N	5. N
Advisor09	3. D	2. D	-	4. A	1. N	5. N
Advisor10	1. N	2. N	3. D	4. N	5. N	6. N
Advisor11	1. N	2. N	3. D	4. A	5. N	6. D
Advisor12	1. N	2. N	3. A	4. N	5. N	-
Advisor13	4. N	1. N	2. N	3. N	5. N	6. N
Advisor14	1. N	2. N	3. N	4. N	5. N	-
Advisor15	3. N	2. N	6. D	1. N	4. N	5. N
Advisor16	2. N	3. N	4. N	1. N	5. N	6. N

Table 1: Summary of the topic order discussed in the last IT-session of each advisor. N: discussed and noted information in the mind-map, D: discussed information but not noted in the mind-map, A: asked about, but no information provided, - : not discussed at all. The numbers represent the sequential order of occurrence in the conversation.

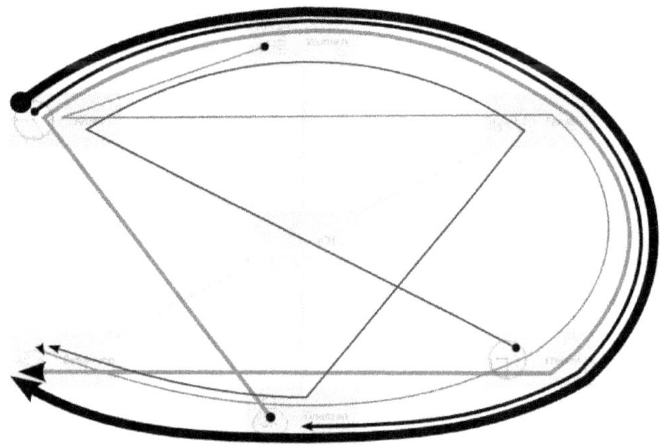

Figure 5: Visualized path of 11 clockwise conversation patterns. Thick lines visualize several occurrences of the same path. Patterns from the other 5 advisors were omitted.

The length of the sequences is determined by the number of continuous turn-takings while relating to the previous given answers. A sequence ends when the advisor switches to another topic without relating it to the previous content. An example could be an ongoing discussion about the employment situation terminated by the advisor by asking the client to provide details on his leisure time. Figure 7 shows that in IT-supported encounters more than half of the sequences are only of length one or two. This means that those sequences consist of a single question-answer pair with or without a following single turn-taking of asking and answering details.

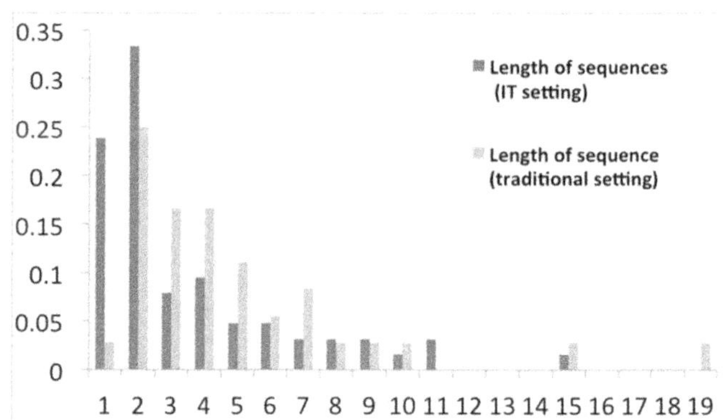

Figure 6: Relative distribution of length of conversation sequences (histogram) for traditional and IT-supported service encounter

In traditional encounters, however, the sequences tend to be longer. It has to be noted that one advisor had a completely different conversation style than the other 7 advisors that we analyzed. This particular advisor used pen and paper together with the IT-system. When discussing a topic, he made short notes on paper, and after a sequence was finished, he entered the data into the IT-system. This resulted in a conversation comparable to a traditional one with only 5 sequences of which two of them were exceptionally long, containing 10 and 15 turns. Removing this case from the sample, a Related Sample Wilcoxon Signed Rank Test supports the impression of the samples being longer within traditional encounter settings ($p<=0.05$) in pairwise comparison.

Regarding the discussion strategy within the IT setting, two groups of advisors are identifiable. The main difference between these groups is the appropriation of the mind-map to guide the conversation and the usage of the wording from the mind-map. Many conversation sequences begin with an explication of an inferred process in the IT setting. Typical statements at the beginning are "Then, we go to the next topic which is family" or "Next to residence". Analyzing the last sample, more than 39% of all sequences were motivated like that. Of those sequences, more than 77% had only one or two adjacent pairs (question-answer pairs) (cf. Figure 7) — a style we barely observed in traditional settings.

The other sequences resemble discussions with the client about his situation without any observable influence originating from the mind-map's structure. Parallel to the conversation, they fill out the provided information in the mind-map. This group asks more open questions like "Where do you live?" instead of "Let's go to the topic of residence", or "Have you already had experience with investments?" instead of "The last topic is assistance".

In some sessions, even clients expressed an adaption of a process structure. An exemplary statement is "*Should I begin with work?*" while pointing onto the touchscreen. Another participant asked, "*Should I follow the pattern?*" (while gesturing a path around the map). In some cases the clients pointed out that they, for example, have not yet talked about the family situation. When recognizing other information items relevant in their situation (like part time job, travel, or marriage), some of the clients mention them without being asked, such as having a plan to marry.

Manifestation of coercing into completeness in interviews

We have transcribed the audio-recorded interviews and analyzed them to find statements from advisors and clients regarding the phenomenon of coercing into completeness. Almost every advisor (13 of 16) reports on a strict process or a perceived obligation to fill out the mind-map completely or at least to talk about every topic. One advisor says, "*For most young advisors it could be a benefit having to talk about all topics that would otherwise not be addressed*". Another advisor declared, "*For me it is too rigid; everything is predetermined*". A third advisor talks about a "*given schema*" which guides the conversation. Yet another advisor compares the mind-map with a checklist: "*With a checklist you ask the client how much he earns, you fill it out, and it is done. The mind-map has the same principle. You go through every branch, starting with one than the other. You are filling out each of them*". One more statement supports this felt obligation: "*You know exactly that you have to go through family and everything*". One advisor also had the perception that he can follow the given process without having to think about it: "*You do not have to think; everything is given*". These statements show a strong perceived obligation to talk about every provided branch and the cognition of the mind-map as a checklist.

Besides some advisors, a substantial number of clients (15 of 48) also report in the interviews to have negative opinions concerning the mind-map design and stated that they would still prefer a traditional setting. Some statements from the clients are "*The traditional advisory was more personal, maybe because the process was not so obvious*", and "*You go structurally through everything*". Thus, some clients have the feeling of only filling out something without understanding why this should be necessary: "*You only have to fill out something in a tool*", "*it was just a matter of filling out numbers and list the expenses*", and "*With the IT tool, some information was gathered that was not necessary. Not all of those questions were necessary to get to know each other*". One client expresses that he has the feeling of being restricted while acting with the mind-map and that "one is restricted to the topics on the mind-map".

Reasons for coercing into completeness in interviews

In our interviews, we have identified statements from advisors which partly explain the phenomenon of coercing into completeness.

First, advisors do not want to **forget to ask something important**. Some advisors say that with the tool they ask for information that they otherwise would forget to ask. For example: "*There are certainly three or four things I usually do not think about. I have been reminded*". Another advisor reports that he is filling out everything because it reduces the risks of forgetting something: "*You can fill out everything. What is in it is there. Then you cannot forget it*". Interestingly, in the traditional advisory sessions the advisors do not act in the same manner. In the conventional, pen and paper-based session, it seems to be acceptable for the advisor not to ask for information, but in the IT-supported session they do not want to forget something, and therefore fill out the mind-map in a perfect manner.

Secondly, advisors report that it is **much easier to retrieve information** from the client. They report from reduced obstacles in the IT-supported setting: "*The IT-tool is helpful to talk about certain topics and to analyze the situation without hesitation*", and, "*One dares to ask more directly to get an answer. In the traditional setting you are quicker satisfied if someone is shirking away. With IT I have to fill it out*". Another advisor points out that the clients are willing to tell more in the IT-supported sessions: "*The client is talking quicker about his family and leisure activities. I think he is more open because he sees: 'I also have to complete this field'*". One more statement regarding this aspect was mentioned: "*I consider that one is asking the client with the IT-solution more precisely; you are expecting much more detailed answers*".

The third reason, which we identified, is that many advisors have the perception that the **client is expecting** the advisor to talk about the topics: "*It is not acceptable that I do not talk about some topics. I think this would be strange for the client*". Other advisors identify the visual aspect of the mind-map as a reason for the perceived client expectation: "*The client is seeing all topics of the mind-map and* *comments them on its own*", and, "*Because the field is represented there. The client said on its own that we still have to talk about the topic of family*". Another statement, which stresses this perception, is the following: "*If family is shown there, the client is asking himself: why does he not talk about this?*" Moreover, the statement "*The client can estimate what is expected of him*" also hints into this direction for interpretation.

Fourth, one advisor has the perception of **being monitored** by the bank: "*My supervisor would ask, 'Why have you not talked about his topic?' So it is possible to monitor me and see the missing topics*".

DISCUSSION

Based on the rich data we gathered from the video analysis, interview statements, and observations presented in the results section, we make conjectures on the mechanisms that lead to the "coercing into completeness" phenomenon. By discussing the relevant findings and relating them to the existing literature, we aim to answer our two research questions: (1.) how the service encounter was affected through the phenomenon and (2.) why the phenomenon could still occur although the problem of rigid process visualization and enforcement is known in literature and was deliberately avoided in artifact construction. Finding explanations for this phenomenon is important, because IT-supported service encounters as such can bring great benefits to all stakeholders but must not interfere with the social setting at the same time, thereby deteriorating the otherwise successful collaboration. Financial advisory services need to be flexible to the clients' situation and their desires and goals.

According to our data, advisors liked our artifact and most of them appreciated the guidance from the system. However, a substantial amount of our clients still preferred the traditional setting and were concerned about the way their information was collected. Many of them stated that they perceived several discussed information items as unnecessary for the ongoing service. In general, we could not demonstrate in our data that the information provided by the client was any different between those settings. However, the way that information was retrieved turned out to be substantially different: While in the traditional settings we generally see a small number of long conversation sequences (where any further question to the advisor is highly related to the previous discussion within those sequences), in the IT-supported counterpart the conversation is much more fragmented. This style of conversation is characterized by a large number of very short question-answer pairs. As those sequences are not well related to each other, this style of conversation resembles the discourse structure based upon a structured questionnaire. As the artifact does not enforce (or even visualize) any representation of a process but the IT-supported conversation is heavily related to the content presented within the tool, our main conjecture is that those content structures are the cause of the observed phenomenon.

Content structures coerce for completeness.

Traditional service encounters are typically executed in an isolated environment. Only the client and the advisor are present. The information and topics that were discussed stay private, except for a written documentation of the advisory encounter prepared by the advisor afterwards, which is filed in the bank's CRM system. Therefore, the quality of the service encounter itself can only be directly controlled through the participants. However, we generally assume that the client only has a vague and limited idea of what a good advisory service should consist of. Thus, the appraisal of the service quality strongly relies on the role of the advisor and his skills.

When technology is introduced in such service encounters, different mechanisms may emerge. With our IT-artifact of an advisory support system we did not only support the activities of clients and advisors but also injected a content structure into the setting. Initially, we intended this structure to serve as a help to organize the objectified topics of a discussion. But actually, we thereby unintentionally fostered a coercing into completeness as expressed by the interview statements from the participants: Both clients and advisors inferred a notion of completeness from that given structure and even more worrying a notion of service quality. Some clients and advisors seemed to agree that a good service needs to cover all items from the given structure. We attribute this to the perception that the advisory service is no longer delivered in a private dyadic setting but is rather directly connected with the institutional quality standards through the IT-artifact. And since the design of the artifact is also influenced by the institution, its norms and values ("spirit" of the design) are embedded within the artifact itself. Hence, we can understand the perception that any given element within a structure is included for a reason and — being visible to the client and advisor simultaneously — might be perceived as equally stimulating and important. We found at least two driving forces within the interviews and observations that help to explain the phenomenon of coercing into completeness from this perspective, which we will present in the following sections.

First of all, in the IT-supported sessions, some advisors had the perception that it is easier for the bank to control if they are doing their jobs correctly. One advisor explicitly feared that her performance could be measured along the structure by their principals later on; she feared that she might need to explain why she omitted to discuss some items on the structure. From a client perspective it also seems unreasonable to omit items in a given structure. As we could observe during the evaluation, some clients explicitly asked the advisor why an object was omitted and demanded an explanation for what it was intended for. Thus, both participants seem to treat the given content structure as the gold-standard for quality. We call this the **"invisible third participant"**, who influences the course of the advisory service through the spirit embedded in the artifact and provokes the phenomenon of coercing into completeness.

Content structures promote a process to reach "completeness"

In traditional financial service encounters, the order of the topics to be discussed is highly individual and dynamic. None of the participants can prepare a definitive script as the course of the discussion emerges on-the-go, driven by events (like one party mentioning an interesting aspect) that sparks the motivation to follow this topic in the succeeding discussion. It remains a challenge and is the responsibility of the advisor to keep the discussion coherent and logically structured.

Content structures that manifest through the artifact seem to be willingly adapted by the advisors to implicitly guide the whole process and help them to retain a common thread. In our experiments, there were statements from the advisors directed to the clients that clearly back up this claim. We observed that the majority of the advisors, guided by the mind-map, followed the given structure item-by-item, and they even verbally marked the switch from one item to another. Thus, the process is not event-driven anymore and does not adapt to verbal statements made by the client. Therefore the process is much more fixed. An unhindered flow with natural conversational sequences - where given answers spark new questions - is hardly noticeable. With the tool we see processes where advisors ask the clients to tell them all relevant issues to a specific topic before switching abruptly to the next one. This "game" ends when there are no more items that need to be covered. Again, we attribute this observation to the dyad's participant's striving for completeness, albeit they bear different motivations.

Even worse, the mind-map's default structure with the six branches could be interpreted as a progress indicator with six sub-tasks. Like other progress indicators, a minimum and maximum ("no topics discussed" and "all topics discussed") are visualized at any time during the interaction, and therefore implicitly provide a notion of completeness and progress although never intended as such. Filling out nothing and leaving the map empty explicates the minimum state. Discussing about one branch or filling it out brings the participants one step further to task completion. Just talking about the topic of a branch or even filling it out with at least one information-item contributes to the participant's perception that this sub-task has been finished. It has to be noted that the discussion is far richer than the information entered into the system. However, this might also be solely explainable by the effort of entering data into the system and potential usability problems. As discussed in the related work section, progress indicators can have a positive influence on the motivation to complete tasks in a single user context. But in dyadic settings, this effect can negatively influence the collaboration. As previous design activities [,18,19] have demonstrated, the negative effect of explicit process representation (visible) can be dampened by implicit representations (hidden). However, the given content structure in our design led our participants to develop an unintended perception of having a process indicator visualized. The appropriation of this content structure as a process indicator representation can be explained by the adaptive structuration theory [4]. This effect was certainly not intended during the artifact's construction. We call this driving force **"parasitic process and progress visualization"**.

Content structures fixate the level of details

In traditional financial service encounters, the level of detail on which items are discussed and written down on paper is based on a subjective perception of their relevance. Topics that are perceived more relevant than others are covered in greater levels of detail. A notion of completion is either implied by the perceived level of saturation on a given topic or the discussion is deliberately aborted due to time constraints.

Given the driving forces of the "invisible third participant" and the "parasitic process and progress visualization", a pattern emerges which causes concerns: Instead of adapting the level of detail to the relevance of the topics, we observed a uniformly low level of detail for all topics discussed. Referring to the related work, the information items are considered "sticky" [28] and thus hard to express for the client. It was our intention to facilitate the process of their explication by providing graphical stimulating icons in order to unhide and identify this sticky information. This should have been also happening by refining the map's content incrementally. But instead, most advisors added to each category only one or two items without adding more levels of hierarchy to the map.

In the light of a realistic model of financial advice giving and taking [13], this practice can be judged twofold: (a) it could serve as a help for unskilled advisors reminding them to elicit and capture the most basic information items; (b) but it constitute at the same time a threat to the performance of skilled advisors because they might be able to capture more information items within a convenient conversation in the traditional pen and paper setting and subsequent manual written documentation.

Judging on the low levels of actual information content recorded within the mind-map, we also assume that the average advisor performance with respect to captured information quality might be lesser compared to the traditional encounters and their subsequent manual documentation. However, this is subject to further research, as we do not have sufficient data from this evaluation. We call this **"dilution"**.

CONCLUSION

In this article, we report on the phenomenon of coercing into completeness. The phenomenon emerged in the context of IT-supported financial service encounters. A carefully designed IT-artifact could successfully support the first phase of financial service encounters (information collection phase) but negatively influenced the participant's collaboration as they tended to strive for reaching completeness. We identified content structure as the cause for the observed three effects. This conclusion is also based on the results of our evaluation and the literature. In collaborative situations, content structures can induce severe and unintended effects, such as (a) the identified invisible third participant, (b) the parasitic process and progress visualization, and (c) possibly lead to a decrease in information quality. Therefore, a central design implication for future systems is that any form of predefined structures has the potential to be interpreted as rigid process structures. Thus, care has to be taken when presenting predefined content structures within those artifacts. This finding extends the current research, as non-sequential process visualizations have been thought to be unproblematic within those settings in general. Nevertheless, we could demonstrate one case where this conjecture does not hold. Even worse, a hierarchical structure, which never was intended as a process representation has been perceived as such. Through this evaluation, we have also shown how difficult it can be to construct non-trivial artifacts while maintaining the quality of collaboration in socially sensitive settings.

We also respect the necessity to provide structures in some way within the artifact to enhance transparency and thus diminish information asymmetry and the principal-agent conflict [19]. We conclude that there will be a tradeoff in the design between the provision of structures for desired outcomes and the endangerment of social interactions. When predefined structures cannot be avoided, proper and special training of the advisors seems to be crucial for dealing with these problems on an organizational level. We assume this because we observed a few advisors neglecting the structure as guidance completely and using their usual discourse practices from traditional pen and paper encounters. They interpreted the spirit in another way and used the structure only to fill in the gathered information like using a notebook. Also, due to the fact that none of the advisors recognized this disruptive style of conversation by themselves, we do not assume that the problem vanishes by itself solely due to rising work experience with the artifact.

We assume our findings are generalizable to other advisory service encounters as well (like physicians, assurances, travel agencies, etc.) whenever technological artifacts are to be designed. With our contributions, we extend the current state of knowledge on how design aspects of such artifacts and how those artifacts can influence the behavior of the encounter's participants. More specifically, we shed light on the harmful role of content structuring in advisory encounters.

LIMITATIONS

The external validity of this research is limited by the fact that the evaluation was carried out in a laboratory setting. Apart from that, the evaluation was carried out realistically with real and experienced advisors and potential customers. Also, during the design of the artifact the management of the bank was involved. Statements from the advisors suggest that they behaved as if they were still in their organizational context. Although it was an experiment, the setting was close to reality. We are aware of the fact that the clients from this experimental evaluation were undergraduate students, and thus a relatively homogenous group compared to average bank clients. For example, in this group it is unlikely that clients have children, but the advisor still felt obligated to cover this topic. Due to the experimental environment one could argue that the advisors might have felt to be urged to use the artifact completely. However, this seems unlikely, as the advisors provided numerous reasons why they coerced for completeness but no single one attributed it to the experimental setting.

REFERENCES

1. Briggs, R.O., De Vreede, G.-J., and Nunamaker Jr, J. Collaboration engineering with ThinkLets to pursue sustained success with group support systems. *J. of Management Information Systems 19*, 4 (2003), 31–64.
2. Briggs, R. and Schwabe, G. On expanding the scope of design science in IS research. *Service-Oriented Perspectives in Design Science Research*, (2011), 92–106.
3. Buisine, S., Besacier, G., Najm, M., Aoussat, A., and Vernier, F. Computer-supported creativity: Evaluation of a tabletop mind-map application. In *Engineering Psychology and Cognitive Ergonomics*. Springer Berlin Heidelberg, (2007), 22–31.
4. DeSanctis, G. and Poole, M.S. Capturing the complexity in advanced technology use: Adaptive structuration theory. *Organization Science*, 5.2 (1994), 121–147.
5. De Vreede, G. and Briggs, R.O. Collaboration engineering: Designing repeatable processes for high-value collaborative tasks. *System Sciences, 2005. HICSS'05. Proceedings of the 38th Annual Hawaii International Conference on*, IEEE (2005), 17c–17c.
6. Eisenhardt, K.M. Agency theory: An assessment and review. *Academy of Management Review*, 14.1 (1989), 57–74.
7. Ferster, C.B., Skinner, B.F., Harvard University, United States, and Office of Naval Research. *Schedules of reinforcement, by C. B. Ferster and B. F. Skinner.* Appleton-Century-Crofts, New York, (1957).
8. Gafni, A., Charles, C., and Whelan, T. The physician-patient encounter: The physician as a perfect agent for the patient versus the informed treatment decision-making model. *Social Science & Medicine*, (1998).

9. Giddens, A. *The constitution of society: Outline of the theory of structuration.* University of California Press, Berkeley, (1984).

10. Gregor, S. and Hevner, A. Positioning and presenting design science research for maximum impact. *Management Information Systems Quarterly 37*, 2 (2013), 337–355.

11. Heinrich, P., Kilic, M., Aschoff, F.-R., and Schwabe, G. Enabling relationship building in tabletop-supported advisory settings. *Proceedings of the 17th ACM Conference on Computer Supported Cooperative Work & Social Computing*, ACM (2014), 171–183.

12. Hevner, A.R., March, S.T., Park, J., and Ram, S. Design science in information systems research. *MIS Quarterly 28*, 1 (2004), 75–105.

13. Jungermann, H. Advice giving and taking. *Proceedings of the 32nd Annual Hawaii International Conference on System Sciences, 1999. HICSS-32*, IEEE (1999).

14. Littler, C.R. Understanding Taylorism. *The British Journal of Sociology 29*, 2 (1978), 185.

15. Myers, B.A. The importance of percent-done progress indicators for computer-human interfaces. *Proceedings of the SIGCHI Conference on Human Factors in Computing Systems*, ACM (1985), 11–17.

16. Novak, J. Mine, yours... ours?: Designing for principal-agent collaboration in interactive value creation. *Wirtschaftsinformatik 2009, Vienna, Austria, 25 February 2009 - 27*, (2009).

17. Nussbaumer, P. Essays on Transparent IT Support for Asymmetric Client-advisor Encounters: The Case of Swiss Investment Advisory Services. *Doctoral dissertation*, (2012).

18. Nussbaumer, P. and Matter, I.S. What you see is what you (can) get?: Designing for process transparency in financial advisory encounters. *Interact 2011*, (2011).

19. Nussbaumer, P., Matter, I., and Schwabe, G. "Enforced" vs."casual" transparency: Findings from IT-supported financial advisory encounters. *ACM Transactions on Management Information Systems (TMIS) 3*, 2 (2012), 11.

20. Oehler, A. and Kohlert, D. Financial advice giving and taking: Where are the market's self-healing powers and a functioning legal framework when we need them? *Journal of Consumer Policy 32*, 2 (2009), 91–116.

21. Peffers, K., Tuunanen, T., Gengler, C.E., et al. The design science research process: A model for producing and presenting information systems research. *Proceedings of the First International Conference on Design Science Research in Information Systems and Technology (DESRIST 2006)*, (2006), 83–106.

22. Peffers, K., Tuunanen, T., Rothenberger, M.A., and Chatterjee, S. A design science research methodology for information systems research. *Journal of Management Information Systems 24*, 3 (2008), 45–77.

23. Prahalad, C.K. and Ramaswamy, V. Co-creation experiences: The next practice in value creation. *Journal of Interactive Marketing 18*, 3 (2004), 5–14.

24. Schmidt-Rauch, S. and Nussbaumer, P. Putting value co-creation into practice: A case for advisory support, *ECIS 2011 Proceedings. Paper 138.* (2011).

25. Skinner, C.H. An empirical analysis of interspersal research: Evidence, implications, and applications of the discrete task completion hypothesis. *Journal of School Psychology 40*, 4 (2002), 347–368.

26. Suchman, L. Do categories have politics? *Computer Supported Cooperative Work (CSCW) 2*, 3 (1993), 177–190.

27. Tallon, P.P. A service science perspective on strategic choice, IT, and performance in U.S. banking. *Journal of Management Information Systems 26*, 4 (2010), 219–252.

28. Von Hippel, E. "Sticky information" and the locus of problem solving: Implications for innovation. *Management science*, (1994), 429–439.

29. Weber, W.G. Organizational conditions fostering prosocial work orientations in teams. *Innovative Theories, Tools, and Practices in Work and Organizational Psychology. Seattle, WA: Hogrefe and Huber*, (2000), 75–96.

30. Winograd, T. Categories, disciplines, and social coordination. *Computer Supported Cooperative Work (CSCW) 2*, 3 (1993), 191–197.

31. WpHG. Wertpapierhandelsgesetz in der Fassung der Bekanntmachung vom 9. September 1998 (BGBl. I S. 2708), das zuletzt durch Artikel 2 Absatz 44 des Gesetzes vom 22. Dezember 2011 (BGBl. I S. 3044) geändert worden ist. 2011.

32. Zeigarnik, B. On finished and unfinished tasks. In *A Source Book of Gestalt Psychology*, (1938) ed. WD Ellis, pp. 300–314. New York: Harcourt, Brace & World (Reprinted and condensed from Psychol. Forsch. 9:1–85).

On Becoming a Counsellor: Challenges and Opportunities To Support Interpersonal Skills Training

Petr Slovák[1], Anja Thieme[2], Paul Tennent[3], Patrick Olivier[2], Geraldine Fitzpatrick[1]
[1]Human Computer Interaction Group, Vienna University of Technology, Austria
[2]Culture Lab, Newcastle University, UK
[3]Mixed Reality Laboratory, University of Nottingham, UK

ABSTRACT
Well-developed interpersonal skills are crucial for all social interactions. However, understanding how interpersonal skills are taught or learned, and how technology can play a part in this, is yet an under-researched area in CSCW and HCI research. To start addressing this gap, our research explores the learning processes of counselling students, for whom developing interpersonal skills forms a fundamental part of their university education. We followed an iterative process to gain an in-depth understanding of a specific counselling program in the UK, combining interviews and low-fidelity technology prompts. Overall, 26 participants comprising tutors, students and expert counsellors took part. Our findings first provide insights into the highly collaborative and social learning process of the students. We highlight the complexity of interpersonal reflection as a crucial process for developing counselling skills, and identify the challenges to learning that students face. Second, we build on this understanding to draw out empirically grounded design considerations around opportunities for technology innovation in this setting.

AUTHOR KEYWORDS
Relational Skills; Empathy; Education; Healthcare; Counselling Training; Reflective Design.

ACM CLASSIFICATION KEYWORDS
H.5.m. [Information interfaces and presentation]: Miscellaneous.

INTRODUCTION
The importance of interpersonal skills in our everyday lives has been widely acknowledged [8, 36, 12, 16, 35]. Interpersonal skills are particularly important for mental health professionals such as counsellors and psychotherapists. Indeed, it is the counsellors' interpersonal skill and competence—gained through education, training, and experience—that is considered one of the critical elements for the positive effects of counselling interventions [11, p.29]. However, thus far, no research has yet explored how digital technology could support counselling education, and the interpersonal skills training of students.

As a first step in this direction, this paper focuses on counselling students, for whom interpersonal skills development forms a crucial part of their university education and who have access to established training programs to support them in the learning of such skills. Our research aims to reach a deep understanding of the processes and challenges of how interpersonal skills are taught and learned in counselling; to outline opportunities for technology support for students' learning; and to offer specific examples of how some of these may translate into technology design. In this paper, we report on a study with students and tutors of an under- and postgraduate counselling program at a leading university in the UK over a period of 14 months. We use an iterative process based on a series of interviews and observations (see Table 1 for an overview), with the later phases including low-fidelity prototypes that were employed to deepen discussions with participants and to enhance both their and our understanding of opportunities for technology design in this setting.

We begin with a review of related work and describe how technology has been previously employed for supporting interpersonal skills learning in other settings. Following a description of our iterative research and design process, our findings are then presented in three parts. The first provides insights as to how counselling skills are learnt by the students, and how the learning is facilitated by professional counsellors as tutors. We particularly focus on the use of experiential and non-directive learning, and the importance of *interpersonal reflection* in the learning process, drawing out the *key challenges to learning* in this context. The second part then draws on this understanding to identify a set of four *design considerations* to support the development of counselling students' skills using technology. These include opportunities for (i) non-directively promoting students' reflection processes; (ii) helping in the co-construction of interpersonal interpretation; (iii) scaffolding constructive feedback; and (iv) facilitating iterative, multi-phase reflection over time. In part three, we build on these considerations to guide the development of a design prompt used to further explore and deepen our understanding of some of the identified challenges as well as possible design directions. In particular, the design prompt aims to support a core aspect of counselling students' training—

CSCW 2015, March 14–18, 2015, Vancouver, BC, Canada.

ACM 978-1-4503-2922-4/15/03 ...$15.00.
http://dx.doi.org/10.1145/2675133.2675190

'practice counselling sessions' by role-play with peers—by providing them tools that support students' reflection on this activity. We conclude by highlighting the complementarity of the interpersonal reflection process with previous works on reflection within CSCW and HCI communities.

This paper makes two important contributions. First, we provide a nuanced understanding of how interpersonal skills are taught in this particular counselling setting and outline the related challenges learners face. Second, we provide empirically driven design considerations for systems aiming to address some of these challenges, and support the learning of interpersonal skills more generally. In doing so, this paper introduces a novel context for technology design targeted at supporting the learning of interpersonal skills, arguing that this is an important but so far under-researched area in CSCW, with wider implications for other contexts in which social and emotional skills learning is relevant.

BACKGROUND

Counselling skills and education

Counselling is part of the psychotherapy profession, with several competing schools of thought that differ in the approach to client and philosophical background (cf. [10]). Interpersonal skills such as the abilities to deeply understand the other, give attention, reflect, listen, or paraphrase, are however at the core of counsellors' training, regardless of the chosen school or training model. In addition, humanistically oriented training such as the counselling program that was the focus of our research, emphasizes the Rogers' three core conditions of a therapist [30], which include (1) *deep empathic understanding*, when the therapist is 'so much inside the private world of the other that he or she can clarify not only the meanings of which the client is aware but even those just below the level of awareness'; (2) *unconditional positive regard*, during which the therapist experiences a 'positive, acceptant attitude toward whatever the client is at that moment', i.e, accepts the client without judgment or conditions; and (3) *congruence*, which points to a 'close matching between what is being experienced at the gut level, what is present in counsellor's awareness, and what is expressed to the client', i.e., full authenticity of the counsellor in the interaction [ibid, p. 115].

Approaches to the training of interpersonal skills in counselling have a long history, with a number of manualized training programs that are widely used in practice – such as the Human Relation Training [7], Micro-Counselling [21], Interpersonal Process Recall [23], or the Skilled Helper Model [13]. A large body of literature in psychology has also shown the effectiveness of each of these to promote skill acquisition over the last 30 years – see for example [16] for a recent summary and narrative meta-review.

However, there is a clear gap in the counselling literature around how students actually experience the learning process and which aspects they find most challenging to learn [6, 17]. Similarly, very little is known about how technology solutions could be mobilized to support students' learning in this regard.

	Research Phase	Methods	Participants and activities	Length Demographics	Participants' IDs
UNDERSTANDING THE LEARNING PROCESSES	Phase 1	Semi-structured interview	**Participants:** 5 counselling students **Activities:** • Discussed the main issues students encounter as part of learning • Identified areas to explore in next stages -- practice counselling sessions, and facilitating feedback **Aims:** Design inspiration; understand the basics of the learning process and the key challenges	4 females 1 male Length 45 min	S1-S5
	Phase 2	Observation	**Participants:** 4 expert counsellors, 8 counselling students **Activities:** • Observed practice counselling sessions led by expert counsellor • Observed (and recorded) reflection practices of both student client and expert therapist after the session **Aims:** Design inspiration; understand the practice counselling sessions, and students' reflective abilities	10 females 2 males Length 60 min	E1-E4 S4, S6 - S12
	Phase 3	Semi-structured interview Design prompts	**Participants:** 3 members of staff, 3 counselling students **Activities:** • Discussed how learning is scaffolded in class, particularly around practice counselling sessions • Followed by design prompts to envision potential of novel sensing and feedback support technologies **Aims:** Refine design considerations.	5 females 1 male Length 60 min	T1-T3 S11, S13 - S14
	Development of the design prompt for Phase 4				
DESIGN EXPLORATION	Phase 4 part 1	Practice counselling session Semi-structured interview	**Participants:** 6 students (3 pairs), each participating in both parts **Activities:** • Practice counselling sessions -- each student took part once as the client and once as the counsellor. • Observe and explore students' reflection practices on recorded counselling session. • Review and critique of the design concept presented through WoZ **Aims:** Confirm identified challenges and design confiderations	5 females 1 male Length 90 + 90 min	S13, S15 - S19
	Phase 4 part 2	Wizard of Oz Semi-structured interview			

Table 1. Outline of the iterative design approach – methods and activities for each phase

Technology and interpersonal training in other settings

A large body of work in CSCW and HCI has recently focused on technology support for social skills training for disadvantaged populations. Most of this work has supported people with autism spectrum disorders (see review by Kientz et. al. [25]), and in particular on children with autism with a view to promoting basic collaboration (e.g., [28]), core interpersonal acts such as eye-contact or turn taking (e.g., MOSOCO [14]), or self-reliance (e.g., [18]). Outside of the autism domain, researchers have looked at using Virtual Reality systems to support the training of people with anxieties such as Social Phobia (e.g., [26]), or video-based training of interpersonal skills for parents of children with behavior problems [36].

In contrast, design and research on the teaching and learning of interpersonal skills for non-challenged populations has so far received only limited attention. Existing work includes, for example, the early exploration of opportunities offered by virtual agents to augment the training of communication skills for medical students [22], inter-cultural communication training for US Army soldiers [9], and automated system to improve non-verbal behavior during work interviews [19].

However, none of these systems embrace the full complexity and mastery of interpersonal skills—such as picking up on subtle feelings and thoughts that might be hidden to the client[1] himself—that are needed and developed within counselling settings.

APPROACH (METHOD & PROCEDURE)

This paper presents findings from a series of interviews and observations that form part of an ongoing collaboration with a counselling degree program in the UK. We intended to better understand how interpersonal skills were taught and scaffolded in counselling training, and the challenges that this may entail generally and for technology design more specifically. To this end, we took an iterative, four phase research approach, with each of the stages being analyzed and informing the next (see Table 1 and below for more details). Overall, 3 teaching staff, 4 expert counsellors and 19 counselling students took part in the various research activities. Altogether 22 females and 4 males participated. This reflects the ratio of females to males in the course. Generally, each participant took part in a single Phase only; with the exception of three students participating in two Phases each (S4, S11, S13). We also drew on our multi-disciplinary research team, comprising a counsellor, interaction designer, psychologist and computer scientists.

Phases 1-3: Understanding the design context

In the first phase, we conducted 5 semi-structured, 45 min long interviews with 5 counselling students. We explored how students experience their skills training with a particular focus on what they find difficult. Based on these interviews, we identified that so called 'practice counselling sessions' formed an integral, but also the most challenging part in their learning process. The second phase aimed to gain insights into some of the practical issues that surround 'practice counselling sessions', and to increase our understanding as to how expert counsellors and students reflect on these sessions afterwards. We observed a set of eight practice counselling sessions that involved overall eight students and four expert counsellors (approx. 20 min for each session and 40 min for reflection). Our analysis of these initial two phases led to first ideas for a potential technology design. This centered on the development of an online tool to provide students with a wide range of opportunities to reflect, annotate, and receive peer feedback on practice counselling sessions.

The third phase aimed to elicit critique and comments on our initial ideas, and to gain a better understanding of how such a technology solution would fit into existing learning practices. We conducted semi-structured individual interviews (60 min) with three teaching staff and three master students. Each interview was divided into two parts: During the first, we asked participants to describe their experiences of how counselling skills are taught and practiced, focusing specifically on how students work with recordings of their practice counselling sessions, and their previous experiences of technology use as part of this process. During the second, we then presented our interviewees with a series of design prompts in the form of post cards that visualized different ideas for potential sources of *feedback* (e.g. by tutor vs. other students; opportunities for video annotations; ideas for automatically generated feedback on the interaction dynamic between conversation partners); and offered examples of certain *modalities* for capturing such information (e.g. 1st or 3rd person camera perspective for video recordings; use of a smartphone app vs. physical buttons for providing feedback; use of sensor devices).

[1] In mental health contexts, patients with mental health problems are referred to as clients.

Phase 4: Translating identified challenges into design

Our findings from Phase 3 enabled the refinement of some of our considerations for the design, leading to the development of low-fidelity design prompts for Phase 4. This fourth phase consisted of interviews exploring the ways in which students reflected on their skills practice in greater depth, and also provided an initial, Wizard of Oz- style testing of our low fidelity prototype. Three pairs of students joined discussion with the researchers, each on two separate days. During the first meeting (90 min), we asked each pair to run two practice counselling sessions with their partner (so that each student took once the role of the client and once of the counsellor) and then interviewed them separately. As part of the interview, we invited the students to use the video recording of their session to talk us through their usual reflective processes. This led to a set of 6 interviews and 6 practice counselling sessions. For the second meeting (90 min), each student would individually be invited to discuss their experiences with our design prompts and to share their ideas for technology design aimed at supporting their learning process. This phase is described in more detail in the Design Led Exploration section on p. 7.

Analysis

All collected data from Phases 1 to 4 underwent a two-stage analysis process, whereby the data of each phase was at first analysed individually (to inform preparations for subsequent phases), and then revisited as a whole once the data collection was completed. Our final data set therefore encompasses all audio-recorded interviews, which were carefully transcribed and then included into a systematical thematic analysis following the approach by [5]. To this end, two of the researchers closely familiarized themselves with the data to identify and systematically search for (reoccurring) themes. Identified themes were then coded and higher-level categories developed. Our findings present the key themes that evolved through this analysis. To protect anonymity, participants are referred to by using an abbreviation of their role such as a T for teaching staff or S for student, followed by a participant number.

PART 1: UNDERSTANDING THE LEARNING PROCESSES

This section presents our findings and understanding of the current teaching processes that mediate learning of interpersonal skills for student counsellors, building mainly on the data gained from Phases 1-3. These findings complement the existing literature in two important ways. Firstly, they provide a nuanced understanding of the fundamental approaches shaping counsellors' learning in the setting of this course. Secondly, the interviews highlight how students' learning is based on a set of social reflection practices around the practice counselling sessions with peers.

Fundamental learning practices

Our interviews with staff and students emphasise several fundamental learning practices that were used throughout their learning and underplayed all interactions within the course.

Experiential, non-directive learning

In agreement with the literature [30, 16, 17], both students and tutors understand the learning process as (a) fundamentally based on tutors' on-going modelling of counselling skills (e.g. being empathic, congruent, respectful to other's experiences) in all their interactions with the students; and (b) strongly shaped by person-centered counselling values of *non-directiveness*, *experiential learning*, and a *focus on the 'here and now'*. In particular, both students and tutors referred to the non-directive approach, describing its evolution from a core belief that people learn best if they feel they are understood and that their perspectives are valued by others; rather than simply being told what to do. As such, the learning processes were described by teaching staff as designed to help students directly experience what they learn about, and to deeply engage with and reach new insights about themselves through reflection – helping them to *"push the edge of their awareness"* (T1).

Discomfort as a cue for learning

In addition, teaching staff regarded experiential learning to only happen when students are *"willing to come out of their comfort zone"* (T2). This is particularly important due to their belief that, if one is to learn, *"there needs to be a dynamic moment of feeling off-balance, like a waking up moment"* (T2), during which students learn. This highlights the need for enabling, at least to a certain extent, uncomfortable experiences to invite important processes of reflection and thereby the development of interpersonal skills. However, the teaching staff as well as the students frequently emphasized how such interactions had to be facilitated within a 'safe space', where confidence and trust could develop among the students. This need for a safe space and mutual respect was also manifested in a 'learning contract' that all students and tutors agreed to, and breach of which would be severely reprimanded.

Learning in stages

Similarly to the other counselling training programs (e.g., [13, 23]), the tutors frequently described in the interviews how they structure activities across the study program to stage the learning of counselling skills. Their goal entailed that students started their training by developing deep self-awareness and reflection abilities, scaffolded for example through sessions that aimed to support students to re-live strong feelings (e.g., shame, loneliness, loss). This was followed by rehearsing core interpersonal skills such as attentive listening, understanding or paraphrasing the other. These skills are deliberately practiced in 'isolation', without being connected to other aspects of the interaction. Only then the students would move onto the key part of the training—practice counselling sessions—where the interpersonal aspects of counselling skills were developed, tried out, and fine-tuned before the students were able to embark on interactions with real clients as part of post-training placement (see Figure 1).

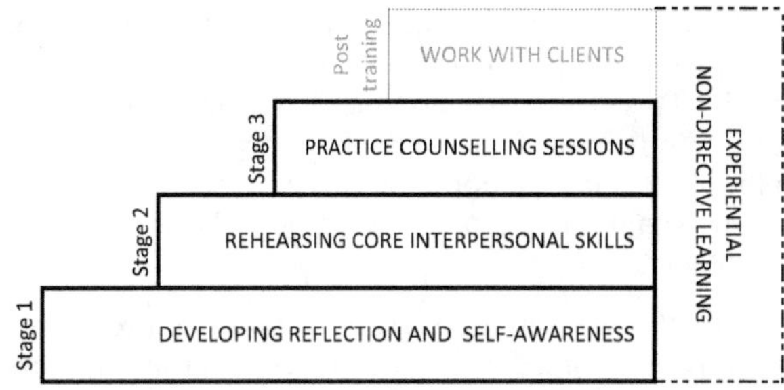

Figure 1. A diagram of the stages in student counsellors' training

Practice counselling sessions

Practice counselling sessions were described as the crucial stage where interpersonal counselling skills are taught in context. Such sessions took place in a 'triad', where three students took on the role of either a 'client', 'counsellor' or 'observer'. During the practice sessions, the student in the role of the 'client' was encouraged to talk about an existing issue they face, and the 'counsellor' would attempt to counsel him or her. The 'clients' were expected to choose something that felt important to them, but was not overly sensitive. Frequently however, students reported how 'clients' would bring quite intimate topics to these sessions, such as substance abuse in the family or serious marital and relationship issues. In the rest of the paper, we will continue to use the word 'client' as a shorthand for 'student in the role of client' unless explicitly stated otherwise; and will also use the analogous shorthand meaning for the words 'counsellor' and the 'observer'.

Participants explained how such practice sessions would be scheduled regularly (e.g., weekly) and that the sessions lasted between 5-20 minutes, with the duration increasing over time as students' experience with the activity develops. Each session is usually followed by a feedback phase (10 minutes in duration), where the observer, and at times also the client or counsellor, would share what they had observed during the interaction. Occasionally, the tutors would join the triad as additional observers and providers of feedback. Moreover, the students commonly rotated in the roles they were taking, enabling each to practice their counselling skills in turn. Some of these triad sessions were further reported to have been video recorded (e.g. 3-4 sessions a year) but there were no other reported uses of technology. The key part of the learning for the counselling student was however described to occur *after* the practice session had finished, when the student would 'process' and reflect on their experiences.

Learning through interpersonal reflection

Reflection on practice sessions is vital for student counsellors' learning. Our interviews point to the reflection process as a complex, inherently social activity. The students aim to deeply understand how their own actions have affected the client's thoughts and feelings, although these are generally not directly observable and need to be collaboratively established. This leads to a complex interplay between several types of reflection that combine a deep, personal reflection on the student counsellor's own experiences with the need for 'interpersonal reflection', drawing on a shared sense-making with others.

In particular, we saw three ways of how such reflection was currently scaffolded around practice counselling sessions: (i) students received *external cues* provided directly after the triad session; (ii) such feedback was then employed to support *self-cued reflection*, when the student reflected on their session repeatedly over time, often at home and alone; and (iii) reflection on selected sessions could be guided through *Interpersonal Process Recall*, which is a structured process to facilitate deep self-awareness of the counsellor.

In the remainder of this section, we draw out the benefits and issues with each of the three reflection practices, preparing the ground for a set of design considerations to support students' interpersonal reflection through digital technology. Overall, our analysis suggests that the existing scaffolding of students' reflection is geared to mainly support internal self-reflection of the student-counsellors, only marginally facilitating the sharing of important interpersonal perspectives that could be offered for example by the client student and the observer student or tutor, or that would focus on the dynamics of the counselling session itself.

External cues for counsellors' reflection

Students in the counsellor role highly valued hearing about the client's and observers' experiences of the practice sessions, even if these conflicted with their own perspective. Such external feedback then served as a valuable cue for their reflection. However, students also described how the current processes could be improved by facilitating a more detailed interaction with the client and observers after the sessions; as well as the need to further improve the quality of feedback provided by their peers.

Both tutors and students described how the 'observers'—i.e., peers and/or tutors watching the practice session—provide most after-session feedback. Observers are expected to give a specific kind of comments that are tightly bound to what was directly *"observed and seen in the practice session"* (T1). Tutor 3 has eloquently described it as 'noticing', saying *"I don't want them to make a judgement about whether it's right, wrong, helpful, unhelpful, but just noticing."* Both tutors and students emphasised how providing *constructive feedback* from the observers' position is a difficult skill to learn; and that the students frequently struggle with providing such concrete, non-judgemental, yet constructive feedback. The tutors considered the ability to give good, constructive feedback as an important part of students learning, as well as a method of assessing their development.

In contrast, clients' feedback was rarely elicited, despite the fact that it is felt by students as even more relevant than feedback from observers. This is understandable as counselling is *"all about the relationship with the client"* (S17) and, especially when *"you're not experienced, you don't know what the client's experience [was]"* (S3). However, even if client's did share their experiences, it was mostly only a very high-level overview summary of the session, not detailed enough to fully support more nuanced reflection on the counselling performance of the student in the role of the counsellor.

Finally, participants highlighted the qualitative difference between feedback from the tutors and peers. The students were often not satisfied with the feedback quality they receive from their peers; but also with the quality of feedback they are able to provide themselves when in the observer's role. The tutors were described as being more capable to help students pin-point areas for future development—an example of constructive feedback—as opposed to students comments being often described as much less specific. Some students particularly highlighted the lack of critical but constructive comments they would receive from peers. For example, students disliked the overly positive comments that are often shared among the group as *"even if it is genuine, I still hate it because I am not getting anything out of it"* (S13).

Self-cued reflection

Self-cued reflection is also an important part of the learning process, during which students repeatedly analyse their practice sessions by themselves. This mostly happened at home, especially if the practice session was video recorded. Both students and tutors saw the usefulness of such repeated, deep immersion into the session via video. This helps students unpick their session in detail and learn from both mistakes as well as accomplishments. While the students saw it as an opportunity to *"work deeply when you see the tape again and again by yourself"* (S6), they also described how there is a very limited support for further interaction with the client and observers during or after the self-cued reflection, although the inferences about the others' thoughts and feelings are crucial for students' reflective processes in this stage. This makes it very difficult for them to check whether their own assumptions about the client and observers' experiences are correct.

The following quotes provide an example of the level of detail in which students would reflect on their session and highlight the various aspects students generally paid most attention to.

> *(S15): "I noticed she said, 'That's a really amazing achievement', and there was just like a pause and the slight forcing of her saying she'd had an amazing achievement. [...] I found a pause and was able to say, 'I noticed that you did this. I just wanted to know if you noticed anything?' Then she thought about it and talked it though, and it turned out that she had some difficulty accepting that she'd had an achievement, because of various things that were to do with the support of her husband and stuff. [...] It gave her the option to change the flow of what she was talking about, to get a little bit deeper into acknowledging her own feelings, which is really important.*

> *(S17): [Watching the session is] all about concentrating on not what was said, but what I was doing, my reactions, what were the client's reactions, facial expressions. I thought they are very, very interesting to*

watch because a smile in the right place, or a frown, or a 'Mmm, mmm.' If the client goes, 'Mmm,' does that mean they are not quite understanding what I am asking, or saying?"

Both quotes illustrate how students generally paid attention to several interrelated aspects. First, we see a very detailed focus on their own and the client's non-verbal behaviour. While non-verbal behaviour is important also during the session, students often picked up on cues they have not noticed before revisiting the video.

Second, the focus on non-verbals was then combined with attempts to go beyond of what the client has said, and create a deeper understanding/interpretation of why they did what they did. For example, S15 has picked up on his client's subtle hesitations around accepting an achievement and used this to uncover a deeper issue they then spend the session talking about. Similarly, most of the students were using the video to continuously analyse and double-check if they had understood their clients well enough during the session; or if they had missed something crucial. Students always viewed their interpretations as tentative accounts of clients' experience that need to be verified. Such verification is however not a part of the current training processes.

Third, although noticing new aspects can be perceived as validation/clarification with advanced students when they watch the video (e.g., S15 or S17), it can also raise self-critical attitudes. This was particularly common for early students, as the video highlighted things they believed they had missed, or their own responses they thought they could improve. For example, speaking about the bachelor students, Tutor 3 said *"[T]hey always choose the worst bits and then beat themselves up. They never choose the bits that they do really well and show you that."* Balancing such self-critical attitudes seemed to be another important challenge for the students.

Fourth, counsellors often explored alternative ways of responding to a situation in their minds, especially after identifying a situation they were not happy with. Again, these required them to work with complex assumptions about the clients' possible responses and thoughts, but could not be sense-checked with the client later.

'Interpersonal Process Recall' (IPR) – guided reflection

Students are also taught a structured way of reflection, called Interpersonal Process Recall (IPR), as part of their normal learning process. IPR is a traditional technique developed by Kagan [24] in the 1970s, aiming to facilitate counsellors' deep reflection on, and awareness of, their own feelings and thoughts during counselling sessions – i.e., the focus is on their own self-awareness and experience of the sessions, not on the dynamic of the interaction as such. A brief description of the IPR process is below, see [23] for more detail. IPR draws on repeated viewing of a video recording of the session. The student in the role of a counsellor can stop the video at any time of their choice, often when they believe something important has happened. Another student or a tutor then asks the 'counsellor' a question from a list compiled by Kagan. The 'counsellor' then uses this to reflect aloud on what was going on for them at that time. If done according to the guidelines, this is a very long process – e.g., 8 hours of IPR for 1 hour of the videotaped session.

As this protocol was originally designed for analysing real-world counselling sessions, the client's view is not supposed to be shared, nor can the clients stop the video at moments they would like to discuss, although they might be present at the IPR session. However, the students saw this as overly restrictive to their learning and told us that for most of the sessions they facilitated (i.e., without the tutor present), the comments would be eventually shared by all involved. The tutors were aware and accepted that such adaptations of the IPR protocol happen, and indicated that they would be open to modify IPR such that it would also involve the client to a larger extent.

Effects of video-recording on reflection practices

The inclusion of the video recording markedly changed the perception of the practice sessions for the students. Tutors and students described how having the video was useful as it provided more opportunities to explore and reflect on their own practice in detail, regardless whether it was to support external cues, the students' own reflection at home, or IPR. Video is understood as providing 'evidence' and specificity to reflection. In other words, by having the option to stop and point out particular moments, it was perceived as providing specific, non-judgemental grounds for deep reflection on the part of the student counsellor.

While the students saw the video as beneficial for their learning process, students also told us that they initially felt conscious, vulnerable, and very uncomfortable about the video recording, although they eventually got used to it. Tutors were aware of these challenges for students, but believed that this was an important part of the learning process, and that the benefits outweigh any uncomfortableness whilst engaging in this process. For example, after giving an example of her own experience with video-recorded skills practice (as a student), Tutor 2 told us: *"As soon as you start to get the feedback and you begin to see, 'Oh my God, this is powerful. I'm really learning a lot about myself here', the equipment becomes an aid not an enemy".*

PART 2: CHALLENGES TO LEARNING AND DESIGN

While the practices around the teaching and learning of counseling skills are effective, to the extent that students graduate as counselors, the previous section also outlined a number of challenges that suggest a potential for technology support.

Design considerations to support counselling training

Each of the three key reflective practices highlights particular facets that are crucial for interpersonal reflection, but each is, for pragmatic reasons, used independently in the current learning process. This points to opportunities for technology to combine and support all of these aspects of interpersonal reflection together, as well as to address some of the key challenges present.

In particular, the importance of external cues highlighted the need to include the client and observers in the interpersonal reflection process of the student-counsellor. Self-cued reflection highlights how counselling students process and learn from their practice sessions over longer periods of time, and thus do so mostly outside of formal learning settings (e.g., at home). The IPR then suggests the benefits of scaffolding reflection non-directively, for example by providing a structure for reflection while keeping the student-counsellor in charge to decide what to focus on and when; and also pointing to the importance of specificity and 'evidence' that a video recording can facilitate. We now outline four design considerations for systems aiming to support the learning of students' counselling skills.

(C1) Non-directive facilitation of the reflection process: We already brought attention to the limited scaffolding for interpersonal reflection processes, especially for the counsellors' self-cued reflection outside of the lessons. Technology supporting such reflection should empower students to reflect and make personal choices, rather than directively restrict their experience. Furthermore, designs should aim to facilitate localised reflection, i.e., tying the reflection and feedback to particular moments of the session to provide specificity and 'evidence'.

(C2) Support co-constructing of interpretation with the client: We saw the need for processes or technologies that facilitate a better access to clients' experiences for the student in the role of the counsellor during their reflection process. In particular, technology should facilitate interactions with clients (and observers) to allow counsellors to verify and sense-check the intricate assumptions they may make about their client's feelings, thoughts or behaviours. Further facilitation would be useful to support students in making their reflection work or felt experience more tangible, and thus more accessible for discussion.

(C3) Scaffold constructive feedback from observers: Providing constructive feedback from the role of an observer (or client) is understood as an important but difficult skill that students need to learn but tend to struggle with. In particular, students find it difficult to be concrete enough and link their comments to specific observations; or to provide constructive criticism instead of praise. Technology should aim to facilitate such localised, constructive (i.e., not only positive), yet non-shaming feedback from the observers, as well as support the observer's learning whilst giving feedback by presenting it for example as a valuable self-reflection exercise.

(C4) Support for iterative, multi-phase reflection: Our data suggests that interpersonal reflection requires a long-term process, combining periods of deep individual sense-making and reflection (including creating assumptions about others' experiences and states), with periods of interactions where such thoughts are shared, checked and discussed. Technology should aim to scaffold such a series of in-depth engagements between the client, the counsellor and the observers, including enough time for deep reflection in between. It is also important to respect and design for the limited time available for the students (as opposed to a full IPR process).

PART 3: DESIGN-LED EXPLORATION

In response to these identified design challenges, we developed a series of low-fidelity design prompts for Phase 4 of our research. These were designed to be used by students in conjunction with the video recordings of their training session, which we recognized as a valuable source for reflection. Our aim was to explore and triangulate the design considerations in more depth, and to invite further thoughts and input on the potential design functionalities from the students.

Each of the design prompts explored specific ways of supporting one or more of the design considerations. For example, to probe the possibilities to promote constructive feedback (C3), we presented the students with draft interface designs that would allow the observers to indicate the moments they 'notice' in real-time when observing the session (e.g., through a simple mobile phone application time-synced with the video-recording), also scaffolding the type of feedback observers can then provide to the counsellor (e.g. by suggesting pre-formulated sentence starters such as "*I felt ____ when I saw ____ happening.*"). Other prompts explored how students could use the system to send and request feedback on specific parts of the video from each other (e.g. choosing and commenting on a particular video segment).

In the scope of this paper, we only focus on one of the design prompts—the AffectSlider—in detail. We chose to highlight the AffectSlider as it explores possible design directions to most of our design considerations (C1, C2, C4) in a single tool, and embodies many of the key design mechanisms that can support interpersonal reflection in this space.

Developing a design prompt: The AffectSlider

Drawing on the difficulties students indicated with the existing practices around reflection, such as the cognitive overload when reflecting and the time inefficiency of IPR process, we started exploring other mechanisms to indicate and track certain emotional responses that may support students' understanding of the interaction during the training. The design of the AffectSlider was inspired by our conversations with students and tutors in Phase 3, in which we explored different modalities as to how feedback on a training session could be provided or received, including examples of physical as well as digital push-buttons, dials and sliders. We were also inspired by literature in cognitive psychology using physical dials to indicate the positive and negative affect felt by experimental participants [31].

The final version of the AffectSlider, as presented to the students, was an interactive mock-up prototype that takes the form of a virtual 'slider' on a single line with two poles, where poles can represent any concept that students wish to explore, e.g., from non-empathic to empathic (see Fig. 2). The student can indicate their in-the-moment experience while they watch a video-recording of their session, by manipulating the slider position moving their PC mouse. The sequence of such slider position changes is recorded and time-stamped to tie the changes to the respective time in the video, and can be thus later presented as an overview graph (see Fig. 3).

Figure 2. Indicating in-the-moment experience with the AffectSlider.

Figure 3. Visualisation of the AffectSlider traces, connected with the video, as presented during the Wizard of Oz (Phase 4).

Our design envisioned that such a form factor would support novel reflection practices for the students in several ways. First, asking students to choose a specific concept to analyse could help them prioritise and make conscious decisions about which aspects of their counselling skills they want to specifically focus on, reducing the cognitive overload. Moreover, we expected AffectSlider to promote sustained attention, as the slider position is to be continuously changed according to felt experience. Visualisation of the resulting trace once it has been indicated could further support localised reflection, as it is tied to the video-recording. Altogether, AffectSlider was therefore expected to non-directively promote focussed reflection (C1).

Second, we thought that use of the AffectSlider could directly promote students' perspective taking and help explore the differences in experiences between client and counsellor. For example, the student can decide to use AffectSlider to indicate not their own experience, but their assumptions about how another person feels – e.g., we asked the students in the role of the counsellor to indicate how they believe their client felt as part of Phase 4. Moreover, once such an AffectSlider trace is created, it can easily be presented to the client for comments, or compared with the client's own AffectSlider trace of the same concept, making it a tangible visualisation of the reflective process. Finally, the time required to provide feedback with AffectSlider equals only to the time needed to watch the part of the session to be rated. This is quite time efficient, especially when compared to IPR or similar procedures, and could allow for iterative engagements. As such, we hoped that interaction with the AffectSlider would promote co-construction of interpretation through sharing and discussion of felt experiences with the client (C2), and do so by facilitating an iterative, multi-phase engagement with the recorded data (C4).

Exploration of AffectSlider with students

For the exploration of the AffectSlider functionalitites we prepared a specific sequence of interactions for students to perform, designed to test our assumptions about the effects the use of the AffectSlider could have on students' reflection. In particular, we aimed to explore the combination of explicit perspective taking (i.e., counsellor indicating their assumptions about client's experience) and facilitated sharing of experience between the student-client and counsellor via the AffectSlider trace.

Specifically we asked the counsellor at first to decide on a concept they would like to ask their client to feedback on using the AffectSlider (e.g., how anxious the client felt). The counsellor also chose a 5-10 minute long fragment from the session they've just finished, to specify which part of the session the client was asked to watch and give feedback on. We then passed this information to the client, who was in a different room, and who used the AffectSlider to indicate their experiences regarding the chosen concept on that video fragment. Independently, the counsellor rated the same fragment and concept, but *from the perspective of the client*, e.g., indicating how anxious he/she thinks the client was at moment. The two traces were thus recorded independently, but when brought together, this allowed the counsellor to compare the AffectSlider trace visualising their own assumptions of how, e.g., anxious the client was, with the trace indicating the felt anxiety directly by the client.

We then presented the counsellor with the overview of both AffectSlider traces and let the counsellor explore and compare these. The traces were connected to the video recording and counsellors could easily move to and review moments in the session they found interesting (see Fig 1). We recorded such interaction with the AffectSlider for each of the six practice counselling sessions in Phase 4. The following presents the findings from this process.

Students' responses to the AffectSlider

All six students found the slider interaction understandable, and were able to choose a concept they would like their client to feedback on. The concepts ranged from selecting one of the core Rogers' conditions such as felt empathy or congruence, to more specific concepts such as 'positively to negatively challenged' or 'helpful to unhelpful facilitation'.

Students shared with us that—by limiting their attention to a single facet of the experience and continuous manipulation with the slider—the interaction with the AffectSlider often facilitated a state of heightened awareness just for behaviours around the selected concept (without distraction by other aspects). This was described as a novel and pleasant experience for many students. For example, S15, who was indicating 'challenging responses', explained: *"I'm not really focussing on any of that [other aspects], I'm just focussing on the flow into whether I'm going to challenge or not and when there's a right pause, or whether I've missed it. That's quite interesting, just to go through that experience and be so focussed."* A downside to this extremely focussed attention was that the choice of the concept became crucial, and some students found it difficult to decide which of the many complex concepts they are potentially interested in should be chosen for detailed analysis. This suggests that the AffectSlider would require (but thus also promote) repeated passes through the video. Moreover, students reported that despite the sustained focus, other interesting aspects of the interaction could, momentarily, come to their attention. Students then wanted to have the option of leaving a marker in the video (e.g. by double clicking the mouse) to be able to easily come back to that point of the video once the AffectSlider exercise was completed.

Importantly, comparing their own and the client's trace helped students identify very specific moments they wanted to explore further. These were particularly moments where the two traces did not match (e.g., the client indicated a sharp position change of the slider while the counsellor did not) and thus the counsellor felt to may have misunderstood the client. Once the students returned to such moments (by re-watching the relevant part of the video), we saw them often re-frame their previous understanding of the situation. For example, S18 asked to revisit a particular fragment where her client indicated a drop in perceived helpfulness, but S18 did not. After revisiting the video, she shared: *"I think what happened there is [that] all I did then in my response was just copy, paraphrase of what she said, but that's it; I didn't do anything with it, I just reflected it. I think [she] needed a little bit more of something from me. [...] If I'd just watched that back, I wouldn't have picked that up."*

In other cases, for example when the traces did match remarkably, this served our students as a useful validation, i.e., that the assumptions they had were consistent with what the client experienced – which is something the students said they didn't have access to before. Similarly, the overview mode at times highlighted particular moments to look at for the counsellors even before seeing client's data, i.e., the overview showed some aspects they were not aware of when doing the reflection-in-the-moment.

However, relying entirely on the AffectSlider data could bring the risk of mis-interpretation of the mismatch or similarity of the traces. Acknowledging such a risk, students also often suggested that such pinpointed moments and the re-framing they made are something they would have liked to take further and discuss with their client face-to-face, as the next step of the learning process. On a similar note, students highlighted concerns related to potentially hurting the feelings of the counsellor after the feedback is exchanged, e.g., if the client was to indicate they perceived no empathy in a particular moment. While no such occasion arose during the six interactions we recorded, there is a clear need to ensure mechanisms are in place to safeguard practice; such as the opportunity to discuss the indicated traces in person soon after exchanging and/or opportunity to provide more detailed written explanations for parts that might perceived as hurtful.

DISCUSSION

Learning how to develop sophisticated interpersonal skills is a critical but challenging part of studying to be a counselor. Participants in our studies painted a nuanced picture of their learning processes, and the importance of interpersonal reflection practices to learn counselling skills. In this section, we discuss how these findings might inform the design of systems to support learning of interpersonal skills in counselling settings.

Specifics of 'interpersonal reflection' in counselling

Our findings show how learning of interpersonal skills in counselling is an inherently social endeavour, building on a complex interplay of interpersonal reflection processes around practice counselling sessions, and involving multiple actors. In other words, we saw that although the student in the role of a counsellor might do most of the reflection work, the reflection process cannot be fully completed by any one participant alone. The client and possibly observer(s) need to partake and share their perspectives to jointly co-construct the interpretation of the session, and this is needed for the learning to take place. As such, the focus on the 'interpersonal' comes in several variants – the activity itself, the skills that are learned and thus reflected on, and the interactions between the counsellor, the client, and observers in the processing stage after the practice session. As highlighted by the suggested design considerations, systems aiming to facilitate counselling learning will need to take into account, and provide support for, all these aspects of interpersonal reflection.

This presents an interesting reflection case that is complementary to existing reflection research in CSCW and HCI. The majority of such work aims to cue or facilitate reflection on individuals' reflection (e.g., [32, 34, 20]) supporting people to become more thoughtful about their everyday experiences. In contrast, the understanding of reflective processes as a collaborative or shared social activity is relatively rare [15, 29, 37], and is arguably an area ripe for more detailed study [2]. Further exploration of the interpersonal reflection processes, which we saw as crucial for counsellors' learning, could thus contribute to this increasing interest to explore technology support for social reflection, as a relevant part of learning and sense-making in other social situations.

Returning to the design consideration

Building on our experiences across the Phases 1-3 of this research project, we drew out four design considerations to support interpersonal reflection, which were then further triangulated in Phase 4 through a series of design prompts. We now return to these considerations to discuss the broader implications and opportunities for technology, using the experiences with AffectSlider to ground our analysis.

Non-directive facilitation of the reflection process

One promising option to non-directive facilitation is to support the learner in focusing their attention to specific aspects of the interaction. For example, the structure 'enforced' by AffectSlider—i.e., the need to choose and focus on a single concept while watching the video—led to very deep and focused reflection, while keeping control over the content in the hands of the counsellor. Similarly, the ability of technology to allow for easy re-structuring and novel viewpoints on data, such as the real-time indication combined with a post-hoc overview, can further support a focused reflection process. Moreover, prior HCI work (e.g., [27, 34]) suggest the possibility of using sensor or video-based data to provide people with novel cues for reflection and learning. Such cue-based support could again help to focus attention and empower students to explore novel interpretations of their and others' experiences. In particular, the recent advances in detecting relevant social signals such as non-verbal mimicry [3, 38] could be a promising avenue to explore in future work.

Support co-constructing of interpretation with the client

We saw that understanding of others' perspectives and feelings is a core aspect of counsellors' learning, but that the counsellor is unable to reach that understanding without including the others into the reflection process; this is an endeavour that often requires large commitments from all involved. As one possible approach, by helping make participants' reflection work or felt experience more tangible, technology could support counsellors in identifying, challenging, and testing their own assumptions about the other's experiences. For example, the perspective taking exercise with the AffectSlider not only provided a visible trace of a particular facet of the client's lived experience, but also allowed the counsellor to visualise and directly compare her own understanding of what the client could have been feeling with the clients own indication as to how they were feeling in, or experiencing, the interaction. While such a single slider trace cannot encompass the full complexity of the counselling interaction (a problem likely shared by any technology tool in this space), it showed potential for the counselling student to either 'validate' their understanding or pinpoint specific moments where misunderstandings were more likely to occur. Once such specific moments were found, we have observed during phase 4 how the students used these to improve their understanding of the interaction. Moreover, the students explained how such moments could provide good grounding for further discussion, and thus help the counsellor and their client to jointly re-frame their interpretation and understanding of the interaction.

Scaffold constructive feedback from observers

We suggest that technology can help scaffold the 'noticing' process for the observers, supporting them in providing more specific and non-judgemental feedback, but also facilitate the learning of their feedback-giving skills. For example, mobile or wearable technology could be used to help student observers ground their observations to specific moments within the session on-the-fly, such as allowing them to 'mark' or 'label' situations they would like to comment on while observing the session. Not only would this be a useful, grounded feedback for the counsellor, but also the act of indicating such situations could provide material for reflection and learning on the part of the observer.

Moreover, the distancing nature of technology, especially when used to provide feedback remotely, could be utilised to facilitate more 'honest', constructively critical interaction. For example, we would expect observer feedback given through AffectSlider to work this way, as it: (i) asks the observer or client to non-verbally indicate their own personal experience, and as such it is not felt directly as a judgement of the counsellor; and (ii) the act of requesting such information alone includes an implicit 'permission giving', as the counsellor is the one to select the concept in question as well as the part of the session to be looked at. Nevertheless, designs using such mechanisms need to put safeguards in place (e.g., allowing the counsellor to give 'feedback on feedback' back to the observer) to ensure that the interaction stays constructive, and that any misunderstanding or hard feelings are promptly talked about and resolved.

Support for iterative, multi-phase reflection

Asynchronous interaction, such as various forms of focussed 'requests for feedback' sent by the counsellor to the client, could prove particularly useful to support the long-term, multi-phase interpersonal reflection process. Such asynchronicity allows the individual students to engage with the sessions at the time of their choice, and provides an opportunity for the counsellor to carefully select the parts of the session they are particularly interested to focus on. We envision that such a series of asynchronous, iterative interactions would help identify a set of key discussion points, leading to a more in-depth and focussed face-to-face engagement to jointly interpret and discuss differences in viewpoints. This is again exemplified in the interaction we staged as a part of such a process with the AffectSlider, where the counsellor first reflected to select both the concept they were interested in as well as the part of the session to be looked at by the client. Once the request had been fulfilled (a relatively easy and quick activity for the client), the counsellor received useful data to further guide their own reflection, often leading to a focussed set of points they would like to discuss with the client in more detail at a face-to-face meeting.

Broader implications – social skills learning

The lessons from the counselling context can also inform and inspire a broader agenda looking at social and emotional skills learning in other settings, such as training for medical staff [1, 35], leadership [4], and increasingly also school education [12]. These are all areas where development of interpersonal skills is also crucial, and where similar sets of learning approaches are being used, including experiential learning and the need for interpersonal reflection [40]. As specific examples, curricula aiming to teaching skills such as empathy, awareness of own and other's emotions, or perspective taking are increasingly rolled out across primary and secondary schools within the US [12, 39]. Similarly, there is an established need in the medical community for an increase in support for training communication skills and empathic interaction for medical staff across all roles [1, 33, 35] – including students, practicing doctors, and nurses. As all these programs use very limited technology so far, this opens questions if and how CSCW and HCI could support the social and emotional learning in these settings, and whether the findings around the opportunities to support counsellors' learning here could serve as a good starting point.

Potential Limitations

The study described in this paper presents exploratory research aimed at gaining a nuanced understanding of existing counselling practices and to then inform technology design in an area novel to CSCW. To this end, our research activities involved counselling students and tutors from one particular degree program in multiple phases of research that built on each other, rather than attempting to provide a overview of practices across many such programs. We believe that this continued and more in-depth involvement with our participants enabled us to gain rich insights into the particularities of this design context and the associated challenges, which can inspire and translate to similar design contexts (e.g., as per the previous section). We further acknowledge that the majority of our participants were women, which might suggest possible gender bias in the interview data. While this cannot be disregarded, this ratio also reflects the approximate gender distribution of students in the counselling program we worked with. Moreover, we did not observe any difference in the responses to the interviews or design probes that could be directly linked to gender alone.

CONCLUSIONS

This work presents a first exploration into the role digital technology could play in supporting the learning of interpersonal counselling skills. We present a nuanced understanding into how such skills are taught as part of a humanistically oriented counselling degree program, highlighting the challenges to learning students currently face. These revolve mainly around the need to better support interpersonal reflection processes, which are crucial for the student learners. Drawing on our interviews, observations and the design prompt, we offer four design considerations for systems aiming to mediate such challenges. Overall, our findings point to the potential for technology to enhance and support the learning of interpersonal skills in counselling training, and possibly also other settings, and provide an important first step for future research in this direction.

ACKNOWLEDGEMENTS

We thank our participants for their time, support, and the deep engagement with which they took part in the design process. We are particularly grateful to Dr. David Murphy for his ongoing support and facilitation of this research at School of Education at Nottingham University. We would also like to thank Pengfei Zhang for his support with AffectSlider development; and Eva Ganglbauer and Francisco Nunes for their valuable comments on earlier drafts of this paper. Petr Slovák has been supported in this work by the Austrian Academy Sciences under the DOC Fellowship.

REFERENCES

1. J. Barth and P. Lannen. Efficacy of communication skills training courses in oncology: a systematic review and meta-analysis. *Annals of oncology*, 22(5):1030–40, May 2011.
2. E. P. S. Baumer, V. Khovanskaya, M. Matthews, L. Reynolds, S. Sosik, and G. K. Gay. Reviewing Reflection : On the Use of Reflection in Interactive System Design. In *DIS'14*, 2014.
3. S. Bilakhia, S. Petridis, and M. Pantic. Audiovisual detection of behavioural mimicry. In *ACII'13*, 2013.
4. J. E. Bono, R. K. Purvanova, A. J. Towler, and D. B. Peterson. Survey of Executive Coaching Practices. *Personnel Psychology*, 62(2):361–404, June 2009.
5. V. Braun and V. Clarke. Using thematic analysis in psychology. *Qualitative research in psychology*, (February 2013):37–41, 2006.
6. H. Bulpitt. Learning about reflection from the student. *Active Learning in Higher Education*, 6(3):207–217, Nov. 2005.
7. R. R. Carkhuff. *The art of helping*. Human Resource Development, 1972.
8. J. Cohen. Social, emotional, ethical, and academic education: Creating a climate for learning, participation in democracy, and well-being. *Harvard educational Review*, 76(2):201–237, 2006.
9. M. Core, D. Traum, H. C. Lane, W. Swartout, J. Gratch, M. van Lent, and S. Marsella. Teaching Negotiation Skills through Practice and Reflection with Virtual Humans. *SIMULATION*, 82(11):685–701, Nov. 2006.
10. D. Coyle, G. Doherty, M. Matthews, and J. Sharry. Computers in talk-based mental health interventions. *Interacting with Computers*, 19(4):545–562, July 2007.
11. B. Duncan, S. Miller, B. Wampold, and M. Hubble. *The heart and soul of change: Delivering what works in therapy* . 2nd edition, 2010.
12. J. A. Durlak, R. P. Weissberg, A. B. Dymnicki, R. D. Taylor, and K. B. Schellinger. The impact of enhancing students' social and emotional learning: a meta-analysis of school-based universal interventions. *Child development*, 82(1):405–32, 2011.
13. G. Egan. *The skilled helper: A problem-management and opportunity-development approach to helping*. Cengage Learning, 10th edition, 2013.
14. L. Escobedo, D. H. Nguyen, L. Boyd, S. Hirano, A. Rangel, D. Garcia-Rosas, M. Tentori, and G. Hayes. MOSOCO: a mobile assistive tool to support children with autism practicing social skills in real-life situations. In *CHI '12*, page 2589, New York, New York, USA, May 2012. ACM Press.
15. R. Fleck. Rating reflection on experience: A case study of teachers and tutors reflection around images. *Interacting with Computers*, 24(6):439–449, Nov. 2012.

16. C. E. Hill and R. W. Lent. A narrative and meta-analytic review of helping skills training: Time to revive a dormant area of inquiry. *Psychotherapy (Chicago, Ill.)*, 43(2):154–72, Jan. 2006.

17. C. E. Hill, C. Sullivan, S. Knox, and L. Z. Schlosser. Becoming psychotherapists: Experiences of novice trainees in a beginning graduate class. *Psychotherapy (Chicago, Ill.)*, 44(4):434–49, Dec. 2007.

18. H. Hong, J. G. Kim, G. D. Abowd, and R. I. Arriaga. Designing a social network to support the independence of young adults with autism. In *CSCW '12*, page 627, New York, New York, USA, Feb. 2012. ACM Press.

19. M. E. Hoque, M. Courgeon, J.-C. Martin, B. Mutlu, and R. W. Picard. MACH: My Automatic Conversation Coach. In *Proceedings of the 2013 ACM international joint conference on Pervasive and ubiquitous computing - UbiComp '13*, page 697, New York, New York, USA, Sept. 2013. ACM Press.

20. E. Isaacs, A. Konrad, A. Walendowski, T. Lennig, V. Hollis, and S. Whittaker. Echoes from the past: how technology mediated reflection improves well-being. In *CHI '13*, pages 1071–1080, New York, New York, USA, 2013. ACM Press.

21. A. E. Ivey. *Microcounseling: Innovations in interviewing training.* Charles C Thomas, 1971.

22. K. Johnsen, A. Raij, A. Stevens, D. S. Lind, and B. Lok. The validity of a virtual human experience for interpersonal skills education. In *Proceedings of the SIGCHI conference on Human factors in computing systems - CHI '07*, page 1049, New York, New York, USA, Apr. 2007. ACM Press.

23. N. Kagan. Interpersonal process recall: Basic methods and recent research. *Teaching psychological skills: Models for giving psychology away*, pages 229–244, 1984.

24. N. Kagan, P. Schauble, A. Resnikoff, S. J. Danish, and D. R. Krathwohl. Interpersonal process recall. *The Journal of nervous and mental disease*, 148(4):365–374, 1969.

25. J. A. Kientz, M. S. Goodwin, G. R. Hayes, and G. D. Abowd. Interactive Technologies for Autism. *Synthesis Lectures on Assistive, Rehabilitative, and Health-Preserving Technologies*, 2(2):1–177, 2013.

26. E. Klinger, S. Bouchard, P. Légeron, S. Roy, F. Lauer, I. Chemin, and P. Nugues. Virtual reality therapy versus cognitive behavior therapy for social phobia: A preliminary controlled study. *Cyberpsychology & behavior*, 8(1):76–88, 2005.

27. D. McDuff, A. Karlson, A. Kapoor, A. Roseway, and M. Czerwinski. AffectAura: an intelligent system for emotional memory. In *CHI '12*, page 849, 2012.

28. A. M. Piper, E. O'Brien, M. R. Morris, and T. Winograd. SIDES: a cooperative tabletop computer game for social skills development. In *CSCW '06*, page 1, New York, New York, USA, Nov. 2006. ACM Press.

29. M. Prilla and K. Knipfer. Computer support for collaborative reflection on captured teamwork data. In *ECSCW'13*, number 257617, pages 56–61, 2012.

30. C. R. Rogers. *A way of being*. Houghton Mifflin Harcourt, 1980.

31. A. M. Ruef and R. W. Levenson. Continuous measurement of emotion. *Handbook of emotion elicitation and assessment*, pages 286–297, 2007.

32. C. Sas and A. Dix. Designing for reflection on personal experience. *International Journal of Human-Computer Studies*, 69(5):281–282, 2011.

33. J. M. Satterfield and E. Hughes. Emotion skills training for medical students: a systematic review. *Medical education*, 41(10):935–41, Oct. 2007.

34. A. Stahl, K. Höök, M. Svensson, A. S. Taylor, and M. Combetto. Experiencing the Affective Diary. *Personal and Ubiquitous Computing*, 13(5):365–378, June 2008.

35. K. A. Stepien and A. Baernstein. Educating for empathy. A review. *Journal of general internal medicine*, 21(5):524–30, May 2006.

36. S. Strathie, P. Forsyth, H. Kennedy, M. Landor, and L. Todd. *Video Interaction Guidance: A relationship-based intervention to promote attunement, empathy and wellbeing*. Jessica Kingsley Publishers, 2011.

37. A. Thieme, J. Wallace, J. Thomas, K. Le Chen, N. Krämer, and P. Olivier. Lovers' box: Designing for reflection within romantic relationships. *International Journal of Human-Computer Studies*, 69(5):283–297, May 2011.

38. A. Vinciarelli and M. Pantic. Bridging the gap between social animal and unsocial machine: A survey of social signal processing. *IEEE Transactions on Affective Computing*, 3(1):69–87, Jan. 2012.

39. K. Weare and M. Nind. Mental health promotion and problem prevention in schools: what does the evidence say? *Health Promotion International*, 26(S1):i29–i69, Nov. 2011.

40. J. E. Zins and M. J. Elias. Social and Emotional Learning: Promoting the Development of All Students. *Journal of Educational and Psychological Consultation*, 17(2-3):233–255, July 2007.

Strangers at the Gate: Gaining Access, Building Rapport, and Co-Constructing Community-Based Research

Christopher A. Le Dantec
School of Literature, Media, & Communication
Georgia Institute of Technology
ledantec@gatech.edu

Sarah Fox
Human Centered Design & Engineering
University of Washington
sefox@uw.edu

ABSTRACT

This paper is about the work we do to create productive partnerships in community settings: developing relationships, demonstrating commitments, and overcoming personal and institutional barriers to community-based design research. Through an ethnographic account of the elements of community-based research normally elided from reports of design process, we explore how the impact of institutional histories and personal relationships went beyond simply identifying potential partners, but fundamentally guided the research questions and approach. We examine the different roles researchers play—researcher, confidant, advocate, interloper, invader, and collaborator—and how those roles create particular relations in the field. The contribution of this work is the development of a reflective account of the research in order to evaluate knowledge production, rigor, and advance methods for engaging in community-based research.

Author Keywords

Community Informatics, Participatory Design, Qualitative Methods, Reflective Practice

ACM Classification Keywords

H.5.m Information Interfaces and Presentation: Miscellaneous.

INTRODUCTION

"*In many respects, the legendary—if too frequently over-hyped—ethnographic sympathy and empathy often comes from the experience of taking close to the same shit others take day-in and day-out...*" [46:152]

Community-based research can be difficult. It places demands on the researcher that go beyond the work of structured inquiry. It places demands on the community members to accept unknown individuals and unknown outcomes into their lives. It is bound to relationships and requires balancing contributions to community with contributions to research.

Design research in computing has made impressive moves in the last decade to develop community-based research agendas with an aim to create strong participatory practices in order to meet communities on their own terms (*e.g.* [12, 13, 29]. These efforts have under taken considered strategies to understanding the impact of community-based approaches on research [11, 26], they have examined the implications of computing on a wide variety of communities (*e.g.*, [16, 32, 39]), and they have begun to sketch out a set of shared theoretical boundaries for productively engaging with community contexts (*e.g.*, [4, 19, 33]).

A common thread through this body of work is an agenda that seeks to elevate and engage with the perspectives of those within these sites of research and design. They are, whether situated in familiar cultures or not, sites Taylor has described as "out there" [43], where the social order and community structures are made exotic and privileged through careful deference to community perspectives and voice. To take Taylor seriously, however, we need to attend to the perspectives and voice of the researchers in order to articulate how research and design in communities together constructs the complexities "right there."

The challenge for CSCW is that as we endeavor to seek out and engage with perspectives in non-workplace settings, where attending to authority and power differentials entail explicit elevation of the voice of the disempowered, we need to attend to the consequences of privileging the voice of the research subject at the expense of revealing the concomitant influences of the researchers themselves. While it is often necessary to place our focus on research products that inform technology design, rather than on the process by which those products came to be, we often paint the researcher out of the picture, resulting in accounts that omit a substantial component of community-based research: the co-production of knowledge through exchange between researcher and subject [31].

Our aim here is to develop an account of how our endeavors in a community-based project were guided by the interactions with the community; to bring into our research account the challenges, day-in and day-out, that shaped the research and our analysis. We aim to reintroduce the mess

CSCW '15, March 14 - 18 2015, Vancouver, BC, Canada

ACM 978-1-4503-2922-4/15/03...$15.00
http://dx.doi.org/10.1145/2675133.2675147

into accounts of community-based research in order develop an account that acknowledges the many sites of knowledge production and the method assemblages that relate and enact those different sites of knowledge production [31, 46]. This paper is about the work that occurs before the work: developing relationships, demonstrating commitments, and overcoming personal and institutional barriers. Each of these shaped and guided our research and influenced our analysis and interpretation of what happened "right there." They are the often invisible elements of community-based research elided from accounts of design process, of technology development, of interventionist outcomes; however, the invisible work of becoming of the community no less shapes these outcomes than the choices made through design on which technology to develop, or which kinds of interactions to explore.

COMMUNITY-BASED DESIGN RESEARCH

In talking about "community-based" research, we are working from a specific but broad definition of community, one that Carroll has called "proximate community" [11]. Proximate communities are the settings where individuals share a common geography, a need to negotiate access to shared resources, and which determine membership through moral and behavioral norms [11]. Just as spaces become places through social construction [25, 44], the kinds of communities we are concerned with here build upon shared geographies but emerge from social relations.

Like Carroll, we agree that the use of "community" in the CSCW literature results from a turn toward engaging in socially meaningful sites of work—where the work comprises the numerous means of mediating membership, brokering influence, fulfilling individual and collective needs, and established shared affective connections [37]. While many of these elements also rightly apply to on-line or virtual communities (*e.g.*, [9, 40]), our intent here is to develop perspectives that are grounded in the shared corporeal and social experience of place—neighborhoods, civic groups, and public associations. By attending to the shared histories that are not solely mediated by technology, we can begin to trace the physical and social and moral encounters of individuals and institutions [47]; the enactment of heritage via the departure and return of diaspora [8]; and the means for negotiating and contending with shared issues and social conditions [32].

The consequence of our perspective on community is the enmeshing of "practical dependencies of living in proximity with commitments to shared purposes and meanings" [11:308]. It gives us purchase from which to examine the social mechanisms that lead to moral or normative communities and the material and psychological conditions that are involved in both [11, 37]. Furthermore, proximate communities provide local settings from which to understand institutional relationships and the implications, limitations, and affordances for technology-mediated democratic discourse [45].

Within this broad context, we are concerned with the relationship between qualitative methods and design research that seek to explicate a community setting. Two points in particular drive our turn of attention: the need to make explicit the ways in which the field site is constructed through the *in vivo* negotiations and interactions with community members; and the need to engage with the multi-sitedness of community-based design and research where the plurality of community comes in contact with the need for structure and constraint. By turning our attention to how we entered a community, we are developing an account that both provides insight into the social dynamics of different kinds of communities and provides an opportunity for critically reflecting on social and technical experimentation through design.

Reflexivity and Constructing the Field Site

Blomberg and Karasti point out that in ethnographic reports within CSCW, "the more subtle ways in which the field site is continuously constructed remain implicit and unarticulated" [5:390]. One of the consequences of not engaging with how we construct field sites is that binaries of work/non-work remain unexamined [5]. A more relevant consequence here, is that in the absence of a single organizing principle—*e.g.*, a workplace and professionalization—the boundaries of the field site are less readily apparent and are more easily contested.

If, for example, we ask questions about office workers—wanting to understand hierarchical and procedural work settings (*e.g.*, [2, 27])—the office and the professional work provide pragmatic affordances for bounding the site of inquiry. On the other hand, if we venture away from professional practices (*e.g.*, [6, 41]) then questions about who and what compose the site, what kind of work, and the means for accomplishing it no longer have ready-to-hand answers. In both cases the boundaries can be interrogated, our contention here, however, is that in community settings, we need to pay particular attention to how we construct our field sites because there is no simple way to signal via organization or work practice what those bounds might be.

One tactic for examining how field sites are constructed is to turn to reflexive accounts of the research in order to engage with the role of authorial voice and subjectivity when conducting and reporting ethnographic work [17, 42]. What these accounts provide is a map of how the research developed, the ways the field site was constructed, and a more explicit sense of how such work may be carried out that neither relies on prescriptive descriptions of method nor on the frank exposé of serendipity and good luck [24].

An important, but often omitted part of ethnographic work is what Harper calls "initiation rituals" [24]. These rituals have much in common with the what McMillan and Chavis describe as part of gaining community membership [37]: they both draw on the affective and moral connections necessary in order to become an insider in a field site or, more broadly, a community. Harper is less concerned with the way these rituals shape the research site—arguing that while an important and often interesting piece of the research, the question of whether or not to "go native" is a moral and not an empirical question [24]. We would disagree on this point, as the work of gaining access to a community shapes the empirical work in pervasive and important ways. It is not just that being initiated and building rapport lend moral authority to speak about the site, the process determines, to a greater degree, what will be spoken about.

The larger point here is that the choices researchers make when interacting with a research site are integral to the method and its outcomes. Exposing these elements positions the researcher within the social hierarchy of the context, providing a better understanding of the site and the researcher's influence over the events that comprise the ethnographic report. Doing so also contributes to a shared understanding of how the research developed over time and contextualizes the establishment or deterioration of relationships between researcher and subject. With few notable exceptions [15, 30, 50], such reflexive discussions are often completely absent and are rarely pivotal to how we discuss our research.

Omitting reflexive accounts can be viewed as a way to establish the interpretive omnipotence that enables a representational authority. It also obscures process-oriented insights that could be gleaned by researchers not involved in the reported study. As we embark on research in community settings, articulating the intellectual and political commitments of the researchers are important to its reportage because these commitments often serve as a kind of infrastructure for the work. Moreover, the lack of reflexive accounts impedes progress in terms of evaluating knowledge production, gauging rigor, and advancing method as we continue to expand the contexts of inquiry and the multidisciplinarity of our research [5, 10].

Before and After Method

By taking seriously questions of how our field sites are constructed, and the consequences that construction has on both the process of our research and on the subject of it as well, we begin to engage with what Law has called the multi-sitedness of research where the many different professional and cultural practices of different stakeholders become entangled [31]. Through this entanglement, we are confronted with a complex set of locations where analysis and knowledge are made material—through the creation of field notes and other records, the development of technical artifacts, scholarly analysis, and the multiple practices of writing up. Law described these multiple locations as distinct along particular lay, professional, or disciplinary practices—*e.g.*, in one of the case studies Law presents, the production of atherosclerosis is enacted over many sites: "the clinic (which can be divided between the patients' complaints and the physical examination); the pathology laboratory; the radiology department; duplex [the use of ultrasound to detect blood-flow]; and the operating theatre" [31:50].

Design researchers in community settings similarly occupy multiple sites, serially and in parallel, as a matter of course in conducting their research. It is the negotiations across these sites that shape the interpretive act as researchers navigate the course of conceiving, developing, and running community-based research programs.

The issues we are contending with here have been present in different disciplinary discourses for some time, though their integration into computing research has only occurred more recently. Taylor, bringing Law's argument to the HCI literature, makes a compelling case for attending to how the dominant metaphors of relation, and our subjective position as researchers with commitments to viewing the technical in the social, shape our discursive scholarship on context, culture, and communication [43].

The challenge for research in community-contexts is to productively engage with the mess, recognizing and explicitly embracing the view that "methods [no longer] *discover* and depict realities... they participate in the *enactment* of those realities" [31:45]. To extend the points made above, researchers do not just construct *a* field site, but *many* field sites as they participate in the selection, connection, and bounding of a particular context [5]. Building out from this perspective, we can point more specifically to the multiple subjectivities that are enacted through community-based research. These subjectivities not only shape the research agenda, guiding the formation of questions and contextualizing those questions in ways that bear relevance for both researcher and community, they demand the researcher occupy different subjective perspectives throughout the process: researcher, confidant, advocate, interloper, invader, and collaborator.

It is within this frame of presenting a reflexive account to explore how a field site was constructed that we turn to our concern with design research and community-based participatory design. Introducing a reflective and critical account of how we developed a field site is an important part of acting on our commitment to co-construct the research agenda, and not just the research product, and to support a radical position of community empowerment and democratization [4, 13, 20].

COMMUNITY AS RESEARCH SITE

Our research agenda at the outset was to examine the role of, and co-produce systems to support community and civic engagement. We chose to engage a community close to our university to begin developing a new university-community partnership as part of a larger university-wide effort modeled after the Netter Center at the University of Pennsylvania to more constructively partner with neighboring communities to address economic and social disparities [23]. There were two additional factors that guided our choice of research site: first, we wanted to engage with a community with rich historical and cultural legacies in our city; second, our research was, and continues to be, guided by principled commitments to social justice and considering the role of technology in supporting participation in *all* communities, regardless of socio-economic status.

Moving forward with our three considerations, we began our work in a distressed, predominantly African-American neighborhood that abutted our university. The neighborhood was close to Atlanta's urban core, was adjacent to multiple culturally and historically diverse universities (in addition to our own), and was bordered by several international corporate headquarters along with the city's downtown. The substantial economic, social, and cultural activity occurring around the neighborhood stood in contrast to the conditions within the neighborhood: more than 50% of properties in the neighborhood were vacant; public infrastructure was inadequate or failing; a large portion of the community lived at or below the poverty line; and the attendant socials ills of drug dealing and use, prostitution, and petty and violent crime were common and conducted in the full light of day.

Despite the current state of decline in the neighborhood, its history was rich and deeply connected to both local and national social movement for racial equality that occurred through the end of the previous century. Several prominent leaders of the Civil Rights Movement lived in the community and organized in the neighborhood during the 1950s and 1960s. Many of the local marches and events that took place during that time were planned and staged in the community. There were also two racially-motivated bombings in the community: one at a home and another at an elementary school. Once desegregation was enshrined in law, there was a dramatic demographic shift as white-flight took hold, and a community that had been previously majority Caucasian became majority African American: by 1970, over 99% of residents identified as African American [7].

Over the following decades, several confounding events contributed to the erosion of the community. Immediately following desegregation, institutions like the neighborhood's Carnegie Library and an anchoring elementary school saw their use rapidly decline and were eventually closed. Economic growth was eventually stifled after the completion of a large conference center and professional football stadium. The new complex severed roads that provided east-west access to downtown and resulted in the isolation of the community. Contemporary issues include chronic problems with failing city infrastructure—particularly storm drainage and water issues—high vacancy rates and abandoned buildings, illegal dumping, and unaddressed requests for the paving of dirt roads.

The current situation bore the signs of a disenfranchised community; largely invisible to local government, residents were not politically engaged and apathy had been cultivated over time because local activism rarely resulted in desired outcomes within the neighborhood. A great deal of distrust and a prevailing suspicion of outsiders was also present—the motivations of outsiders were questioned in light of decades of broken promises and failed projects. This distrust was particularly acute for individuals from our university with whom the community's experience had alternately been as research subject (objectified and studied from afar) or as undesirable neighbor (a drug and crime and prostitution problem the university wanted fixed).

These factors informed our efforts to build robust relationships with community partners, and more crucially, they informed the re-framing and calibration of our goals and our understanding of what a successful outcome would look like for all parties involved. The research we were undertaking was not just about the issues of exploring digital tools for civic and community engagement, it bore the weight of institutional and racial legacy: we were upper-middle class caucasian researchers from a wealthy (and paternalistic) neighboring university confronting realities of the systematic disenfranchisement of a poor, African-American community. What became clear very quickly was that our goals of working with the community to cultivate shared identity and raise the voices of individual experiences was secondary to the issue of *how* we intended to work with the community to reach those goals. Moreover, that how—the procedures and protocols, the design work and technology building—had to be determined by the community and not simply imposed by our research agenda.

Context & Method

The following account developed over the course of two years of ethnographic fieldwork in the community. Our field work comprised participant observation, semi-structured interviews, and design workshops; these activities were carried out in a diverse range of settings, including neighborhood association meetings, public street events and festivals, non-profit organization meetings, and private homes.

We were involved with institutional and organizational settings within the community including: the neighborhood association which met monthly to discuss present issues and activities in the neighborhood—reports on public safety and development projects were the primary focus of these meetings; the Neighborhood Planning Unit which was one of a formalized citizen advisory board for all planning decisions in the city, including development, zoning, and land-use; finally, we entered a partnership with a local cultural arts non-profit with whom we developed and ran the design workshops focused on documenting and reflecting on community identity [20]. In addition to the design workshops, we participated in multiple community events to showcase artifacts from the workshops as well as to demonstrate good faith and solidarity as a conscientious neighbor.

Our field documentation included audio recording and carefully compiled hand-written notes along with artifacts and documents developed as a result of the planning and running of the design workshops. These materials collectively form the basis for our ethnographic account, motivating our reflection on the multiple roles we inhabited as we developed a set of relations—research-based and personal—in the community.

A JOURNEY OF A THOUSAND MILES

When we began our engagement, residents were skeptical of our motives, interpreting our presence as another instance of objectification and exploitation. It was only through a slow and fitful process that we were able to overcome the institutional momentum of "mining" the community as a research site and develop a discourse of what partnership could and should look like between our university and the residents, organizations, and institutions of the community.

While we entered the scene with ideas of supporting community and civic engagement, we did not know what form that might take nor what particular issues the community was contending with. We had notions of what kinds of issues the area was facing based on the apparent physical conditions and our understanding of how it had been represented in the media as a place to be cleaned up. Despite these apparent problems, we began our enterprise with a commitment to focusing on issue formation [33, 36], allowing for the individuals and institutions we encountered to frame what was, and was not, important.

Our measured approach to entering the community began with attending monthly neighborhood association meetings. The neighborhood association formally included our university due to a shared and overlapping geography, however, the university's presence in the neighborhood was perceived as a paternalistic institution rather than community partner. As such, when we began attending the neighborhood association meetings, we were immediately identified as being from the university—there was no blending in or "hanging out" to quietly build rapport as our affiliation with the university defined our identity and ascribed a legacy of motivations.

Establishing Presence

As highly visible outsiders, we attended the neighborhood association meetings to begin building familiarity. Familiarity for the residents of the community so they could gradually get to know us, as well as familiarity for ourselves as we began to pay close attention to the social and authority dynamics within the neighborhood. Through the first few months, we learned a lot about the organizations of the neighborhood and the concerns and issues that were habitually raised by elected members of the association as well as members at large.

We learned that public safety issues were important and always brought up during the meetings; however, they were generally tacked on to the end of the meeting and given little time. Incidents, concerns, problem locations were quickly listed, but there were no detailed discussions about how to address the problem or action the police or other authorities might take. The facts of drug dealing and the associated violence were not an outrage to those attending the neighborhood association, instead they were a part of daily life in the community. Moreover, as one resident expressed early on, the drug dealers, gang members, and prostitutes were often the sons, daughters, nieces, nephews, or grandchildren of the very residents at the meeting, and while no one could condone their actions, they needed to be met with love and support as one would offer a troubled member of the family.

We also learned of visceral tensions within the community around the use and distribution of resources. At the first meeting we attended, a member-at-large continually confronted the then-president of the association of fraud and embezzlement. The issue stemmed from an employment contract for event support where the individuals who worked the event had not been paid (or not paid according to their expectations, the details remained clouded). The contract had been negotiated and executed by the association president and there was an apparent history of distrust from some quarters of the community that he had long been using his position, both as association president and as church leader, to enrich himself.

The rift over accusations of fraud split the meeting largely along lines of members-at-large uncertain about the veracity of the association president's claims, and other community leaders, including a State Representative, stepping in to vigorously defend the association president.

As outsiders, the events and discussions that occurred during these neighborhood association meetings pointed toward opportunities for exploring the tools we might build to support the community. There was an apparent need for ways of documenting physical conditions to enable the community to catalogue and contend with the problems like illegal dumping, absentee property owners, and public safety. At the same time, issues of transparency and accountability seemed like more contentious points of entry to explore ways of building stronger ties within the community. Beyond any specific project direction, however, our initial observations merely helped us begin to build a vocabulary for speaking about the current conditions in the neighborhood.

Choosing a Partner

After three months of attending community meetings, we began a series of interviews and project-scoping meetings with the director of the neighborhood association. The director had a distinct role from the president of the association in that he was paid a modest stipend and was meant to be the stable functionary who ran the volunteer efforts and who attended planning and zoning meetings in order to act in a limited fashion on behalf of the neighborhood association.

Our meetings with the director were to explain our broad research goals of running a participatory design project to explore and cultivate local forms of community engagement. Based on our time at the neighborhood association meetings, we suggested issues of public safety and city infrastructure as specific areas that seemed of concern to the community and outlined strategies for exploring them through participatory design with the dual goal of creating a more specific dialog with the community about particular issues and producing new tools and skills for contending with those issues.

It took several meetings with the director to explain our approach and to understand his perspective on how community-centered projects should be run. It became immediately clear that he was more familiar with public health research that was commonly conducted in the community. As such, he had expectations around participant compensation and the kinds of financial support that might be forthcoming; for example, a public health project run out of another local university had supported community liaisons with a substantial annual stipend along with per-participant compensation. Additionally, the director persistently asked that we commit to establishing scholarships for students from the neighborhood; that we commit the university to hiring people from the neighborhood; and that we commit to writing grants that included community staff positions and stipends like the one he was currently collecting as the director of the neighborhood association.

At the onset of the project, we did not have access to resources that would allow us to provide compensation at the level that was being suggested by the director. We were not opposed to pursuing funding opportunities to do so—such tactics have proved successful in other venues [3, 48]—but wanted to first develop a working relationship with a community partner in part to more clearly define how such support could be productively sewn back into the community. In the mean time, we outlined our commitments to working *with* the community, building design encounters that would eventually result in working systems supporting community goals and engagement. In support of our position, we offered up examples from our previous work to show how the design process worked and that real, working systems resulted and would be provided to the community.

After a series of meetings with the director, he agreed to give us time at the following neighborhood association meeting to explain the project and solicit volunteers who would be interested in working with us. Even though we did not have complete resolution for many of the financial requests that came from the director, we agreed that we would begin the project and continue to look for creative ways to build in more direct support in the future.

What Does Not Kill The Project...

When we presented the project at the neighborhood association meeting, we provided a brief overview of our desire to work with individuals in the community to explore ways to support and broaden community engagement. The initial pitch was aimed at recruiting community members for a short photo elicitation activity for documenting the kinds of neighborhood problems we had heard discussed in prior meetings—issues of property, infrastructure, and public safety—and which would form the basis for future participatory design sessions. Immediately, we fielded questions and concerns from the residents at the meeting: questions about who would participate and how that participation was related in any official way with the neighborhood association; concerns about the intent of the work derived from past experience with photo-based public health work; skepticism of its potential value to the community because the final system or artifact was not something we could clearly articulate as its form and function would ultimately result from the project.

We responded to the questions and concerns by explaining anyone could participate and that our connection to the neighborhood association was an informal collaboration and venue for reaching out to residents; that our intent in working with the community grew out of our own commitments to working with low income communities who have traditionally been marginalized by standing institutions and re-development efforts; that the value to the community would come through both the participatory design process and the system or artifact that we created together.

The reaction to this short, and to our mind straight-forward clarification of the project, was swift and certain. Two community leaders in attendance—one of whom was the State Representative we encountered earlier in our fieldwork, the second the chairperson of the Neighborhood Planning Unit, an Atlanta-specific civic structure for citizen oversight on issues of land-use—took issue with our presence at the meeting, our vocabulary in speaking broadly about "low-income" and "marginalized" communities, and the lack of specific details on how the community would benefit. The result was a motion raised, seconded, and unanimously voted for in-favor that the association not support our research project (including strong language discouraging individual participation), that no further discussion move forward until they had a meeting with the university president that resulted in a master agreement, "institution to institution," between the neighborhood association and the university, and that these conditions be delivered in written form to university administration.

Earlier successful community projects had conditioned us that a reasonable approach to starting a project included providing a broad-strokes outline of our approach and letting curiosity and a benefit of the doubt (perhaps conferred by the association with our university) fill in the initial gaps. However, in this instance, we were faced with a legacy of particular kinds of community relations enacted by our university that had foreclosed the very notion that mutually beneficial collaboration was possible. The community had been the object of study for so long, and the faculty and students had entered the community only to carry off the riches of research and knowledge production for so long, that there was no benefit-of-the-doubt to be found. Our arrival, and attempt to try something we thought would be new and genuine was dismissed and then parlayed into a larger set of issues in how the university related to and supported the community.

The issues of scholarships, employment, and institutional relationships were far more pressing than this small project, and our presence became an opportunity for those issues to be made visible. Our relationship to the community had gone from innocuous outsider during initial observational fieldwork, to interloper once we attempted to build a working collaboration. The strategies we had thought to deploy in order to build a mutually productive collaboration were legitimately called into question and placed within the historic context of the community's experience with research. And while our overarching goal was a participatory design project, it was still interventionist and positioned the participation only with respect to the design of technology systems and not with respect to the design of the research program itself.

Being Chosen as a Partner

Following the neighborhood association meeting, the technical assistant from a community cultural arts organization asked that we contact contact her to further discuss the project. Despite her expressed skepticism during the association meeting, she told us she recognized the potential for the work to contribute to her organization's agenda of empowering the community through culture and the arts.

Her invitation lead to a new set of meetings that took place over a period of about eight weeks. During those weeks, we met at her home to discuss a potential partnership, the theoretical basis of our research, and our commitment to community partnership. We were asked about our religious beliefs—not as a moral test, but to establish clear language by which to communicate. She identified herself as a former Marxist and a liberation theologist who had been trained as a nurse. We openly discussed issues of race and privilege and she suggested that we read the *Pedagogy of the Oppressed* and *The Wretched of the Earth* in order to help frame and motivate our work with community members. Our meetings together were kept confidential because our presence in the neighborhood remained contentious. And during this time, it was also made clear that our discussions were person-to-person and that she was not yet acting on behalf of the cultural arts organization she advised.

These meetings formed the basis of a new collaboration, one that grew out of a set of shared commitments to community and human development, and one that was based first in a ground-up desire to try something new, rather than a top-down attempt to secure resources. It was only after we had developed genuine rapport did she agree to present the collaboration to the board members of the cultural arts organization. Unlike our previous experience at the neighborhood association meeting, we were not directly involved in this process. Instead, she advocated for the project to her organization's leadership.

Presenting the project to the board in our absence meant we had developed a shared understanding of the project and the intended goals. As researchers and academics, it also meant ceding considerable control over a situation that might again turn against our proceeding with the project. The board voted in support of the collaboration and we began in earnest to do two things to cement the collaboration. First, we co-authored a Memorandum of Understanding (MoU) with the president of the board; second, we began the work of co-developing the research plan.

The MoU established an official relationship between us and the organization and summarized the obligations we had to each other in the project. It also outlined foreseeable benefits that might arise from the collaboration and clearly articulated how we would return benefits to the participants and the community at large (whether through on-going funding, or local opportunities to present the work). The cultural arts organization agreed to manage volunteer recruitment and development and to provide space in the community for design workshops and future meetings. We committed to providing all technology resources and training necessary to conduct or participate in the workshops and to lead grant proposal development and management. The MoU formalized a commitment to each other and to plotting the course for a new kind of collaboration between our institution and a local organization in this particular community.

More important than the MoU, however, was the collective turn to co-developing the research plan for our project. Our broad goals were still in place—we wanted to work through the challenges and opportunities for co-designing and deploying community-focused technologies to support local engagement and different forms of civic action—but instead of beginning the participatory process at system design, we shifted and began the participatory process at research design.

One of the more productive tensions grew out of a mismatch between our expectations about how the project would develop and our collaborators' expectations of how community members would benefit from working with us. We were accustomed to environments where the benefits of research were realized over time through analysis and reflection; our community partners wanted to ensure that participation resulted in an immediate benefit for community members—if we asked someone to spend two hours with us, then we needed to articulate what they would gain from those two hours, and not just what our goals for the workshop were. This pushed us to co-design the workshops with a focus on benefit through design process, rather than from a resulting design artifact or our analysis.

Working through how to match our research interests with the concerns of our collaborators meant adjusting how we developed our research agenda. Not only were we co-designing the workshops with our collaborators in order to provide a worthwhile experience for individuals participating in the workshops, but we also had to re-imagine the temporal aspects of our planned research and be concrete about how each workshop would be conductive both to our desire to contribute to particular research communities and attend to the immediate desire for benefits—specifically, benefits that could be connected to forms of empowerment—for community members involved.

Ultimately, we shifted the focus of our research aim from documenting issues we had identified, to developing a series of workshops to explore individual experiences in the neighborhoods and to connect those experiences to the history and heritage of the community. Each workshop had concrete outcomes for the participants along with outcomes that we wanted to achieve; we developed a plan that included public presentations of the work as a way to build toward a larger participant-centered goal of raising their voice within the community; "participants" became "Community Historians" to make clear a relationship that was not subjecting the community to research, but building a project around individual and collective agency. Most importantly, research that initially conceived of civic engagement through the lens of institutional relationships, public services, and specific kinds of collective action was reshaped with the guidance of our community partners to understand engagement through the creation and enactment of community identity—through the responsibilities and accountabilities focused within, rather than those directed toward external agencies and authorities.

Keeping the Faith and Continuing the Work

Having worked over the course of months to build rapport with our community partners, to develop our research plans and then to begin holding workshops, we had accomplished something substantial. But beyond the work done to build trust and rapport with our community partners, there was a need to constantly maintain that relationship as the project progressed over the next 18 months. During that time, community historians often questioned us about things like our professional affiliation, our age, home address, hometown, as well as questions about personal or private information like our parents' names, their jobs, and whether we were given cars when we turned 16. Being asked to disclose things about ourselves that we would not typically share made us feel unusually vulnerable. However, these questions and the vulnerability they elicited enabled us to move from a position outside the community to one within the community and ultimately were an important part of the shared commitment to the project: we were meeting in the home of the cultural arts organization's technical assistant, we were asking the Community Historians personal questions about current and past experiences in the area, and we were probing issues of socio-economic status, authority, and power relations. On reflection, it was only natural that we would be asked to share similarly personal experiences.

The reason such questions stood out to us at the time, however, was due to our expectations and experiences of entering field-sites developed through largely professional settings. Becoming an insider in ethnographic work in the workplace occurs under the professional boundaries of workplace etiquette; becoming an insider in a community context requires different kinds of etiquette and operates within different boundaries. Our community partners, like other community members, continued to question our presence in the neighborhood, even at later stages of the project. These questions were often as much about clarifying a particular technical point about the workshop as they were about reaffirming the shared commitments that formed the basis of the partnership. Ultimately, the personal connections we formed were the most important part of the work; the collaboration was built on an understanding of traveling a journey together, and both sides occasionally needed reminders of what "together" meant.

The journey to becoming an insider and developing a rich community partnership was not just about gaining trust and building rapport: it shaped the research from the questions we finally set out to understand to the ways in which we went about developing that understanding; it exposed our own assumptions about what it meant to be in a community and act civicly; and it gave us the opportunity to confront the realities of community-based research where the success or failure of the project with respect to the community is often orthogonal to the success or failure of the project with respect to the research.

DISCUSSION

By articulating an account of how our community partnership developed, we aim to shine a light on the mess in community-based research and design and connect that mess to a productive discourse for how to further develop disciplinary and practice-based approaches to conducting community-sited design research. As we have set this paper up as a reflective ethnographic account meant to better understand the research site, we now want to turn more explicitly to the challenges and opportunities of relating such an understanding to modes of design.

Participatory Design in Community Settings

Community settings are explicitly plural and a mix of motivations, histories, and goals which bring different individuals and organizations together in complex ways. This plurality is the primary practical difference between community-based participatory design and participatory design in the workplace where work and commercial enterprise organizes constituencies around clear authority relations, incentives, and obligations. Within community settings, Carroll points to the absence of similarly explicit authority dynamics as a defining difference between participatory design in the workplace versus in the community noting that, "an important contrast between workplace and community informatics is the absence of 'us' and 'them.' No one is 'boss' in a community" [13:249]. We agree that community-based research necessarily needs to engage with a ground-up effort to build capacity and support local initiative, however, we would contend that community settings may be more productively described as multiples of "us'es and thems," where the single narrative of authority and power found in the workplace is replaced by multiple and overlapping domains of influence and conflict. Given these complexities, the work to develop a field site and research project is largely about navigating those connections in order to create productive collaborations.

More than simply finding the right community partner, however, we want to point to the explicit need to develop research plans together. There is a strong case to be made for participatory design's place in developing rich community-based interventions [4, 13]; there is a compelling legacy upon which to draw for engaging in political and emancipatory practices [1, 18, 35]; there are clear examples of how such work can succeed in developing novel design approaches and working systems (*e.g.*, [14, 20, 34]; and there are accounts of how participatory design can be evolved to contend with alternate power and authority differentials in global settings [38, 49]. Each of these point to clear ways communities can be productive locations for research, and more importantly how that research can be productive for the community. What is less visible is how that work came to be, the negotiations through collaboration, and the co-creation not just of the final technical artifact, but of enacted method and analytic lens [31].

Locating and Translating Contribution

In the process of building a community partnership, we had to make an important conceptual reversal. When we began the project, we had sought to frame community contributions in terms of the kinds of advances we might make through the research. The tension this created was not so much about whether the research would be of value in the community, but that it perpetuated several prevailing and negative perspectives on the community. By starting with research contribution, our attention was inadvertently drawn to particular kinds of issues, and to particular kinds of relationships with respect to what it meant to be engaged in the community.

Our method had continued to enact certain realities in the community [31], realities that we had in fact set out to challenge through our commitment to developing tools for community and civic engagement. What we missed in seeking acute or instrumental problems against which to pitch design and technology was that membership in the community could not be defined by as a "singular loyalty, identity and belonging," but had to consider the "new 'sites', 'scales' and 'acts' through which 'actors' claim[ed] to transform themselves... into citizens" [28]. It was this complex relationship between the individuals with whom we were working and the alternate enactments of community identity that both caused us to stumble as we began the project, but which would become a very productive avenue for building a community partnership and coordinating design activities [20].

The reversal that enabled us to develop a working community partnership was the move to situate our contribution in terms of the local community instead of the research community. Even to the point of whether to pay community members or not, our partners pointed out that volunteering was an important kind of engagement, one that reflects commitment to the community. It was around this set of priorities, to cultivate commitments to the community, that we came to focus on the workshops themselves as a form of engagement: an end, rather than a means. This point is important because it puts into relief the many ways engagement might be enacted. Treating community-based research projects as a means to engagement—by producing artifacts and systems that ostensibly support community goals—is only one way such relations can be created. As alternate visibilities of engagement came into focus, our responses to the work shifted.

Ultimately, this reconfigures method, where ethnography and design workshops are typically deployed to shape the design of an interventionist artifact, here those activities were the artifact, revealing and creating the boundaries of the community and the means for being engaged. Much of what we encountered illustrates Blomberg and Karasti's point:

> "Researchers and designers are finding themselves in new terrains and unaccustomed positions with respect to the 'subjects' of study and to the design of the socio-technical systems in focus. This argues for increased flexibility (at times interchangeability) in roles vis-à-vis the dual ambitions of 'theorizing' about the organization, including the structuring of cooperative activity and 'participating' in shaping future (design) possibilities" [5:406].

Oscillating between theorizing and participating allowed us to see where our assumptions had created blinders with respect to community identity and engagement, and pushed us to develop a dialog and vocabulary within the community that enabled translation between the goals of community engagement from a perspective on the ground, to the goals of community engagement as a topic of research. The challenge for us became translating the community contribution into research instead of translating the research into community contribution.

A Productive Mess

Our intent in sharing a more discursive and reflective account of our fieldwork is not simply to recount a tale of personal struggle when working in a challenging research setting, but to bring to the discourse the realities of what such work entails. The familiar subjectivities we occupy as researcher, those that we impose on participants, and our comfortable reliance on technology are left far behind when embarking on work in community settings. It has become an aphorism for recent research that lo, we have left the workplace and *things are different*. This is an incantation we have been guilty of ourselves; however, the differences are not simply confined to the social context, or the kinds of technologies we might encounter, nor to the methods we might use to mediate our understanding of context and technology. They are expansive and include the relationships we inhabit as researchers in these settings. We are variably researcher, confidant, advocate, interloper, invader, and collaborator. Moving between these roles is difficult and rending work that is necessary for community-based research to succeed, but is rarely part of how we talk about that research. Even while we include details of participants or research site, we do not tend to frame our findings with our own personal accounts so as to give depth to our insights, or add length to the shadows of our forecasts.

Taylor, in pointing to the default positions taken up by studying contexts and communities "out there" raises important points about how the work we do in social-science informed computing research is often that of othering, of making strange mundane practices in order to gain some incremental insight into the totality of global relations to our familiar technologies [43]. The flip side to this, of course, is how we are positioned as "the other" by community members with whom we work. The point of community based research, called variously participatory or action or value centered research [4, 21, 26], is in part a move to embrace the subjectivity as researcher so as to be aware of the assumptions and perspectives such a subject position imposes within a given social context. And to a greater extent, the appropriation of social-science methods in computing has managed to create an ongoing discussion about how we account for our own perspectives in technology-driven research.

What is less well discussed, less well understood and incorporated into how we operate as a discipline, is how we account for the subjectivities to which we are assigned, not by ourselves as researcher or collaborator, but by the communities in which we work. We are often continually balancing scales of institutional authority with personal connection, where we may be setting aside principled philosophical differences in the service of access, and where each of these inform what we attend to and what we ignore; what we note as remarkable, and what we dismiss as unimportant; what we see as positive change, and what is disappointingly admitted as not having made a difference.

As computing matures in its use of social-science methods, and as it embraces the mess that is encountered out there (and in here, and right there) [31, 43], we need to have ways to to account for the multiple narratives we tell about our research. As we continue our encounters in non-technocentric contexts, where the focus of research might shift from building a thing and making it usable to questing whether to build the thing at all, we need a vocabulary for talking about these challenges. Much as design research has grappled with how to disclose and discuss design failure as a rich source of learning and insight [22, 32], we need to similarly grapple with how to make visible the work before the work, and the work to keep the work going, so its role in shaping the research and the outcomes of research are made more accessible.

ACKNOWLEDGEMENTS

We extend a heartfelt thanks to HWCAC, Mother Moore and Sister Tracy for their patience, energy, and mentorship—the work presented here would not be possible without their willingness to work with us. This research was supported by the Intel Science and Technology Center for Social Computing.

REFERENCES

1. Beck, E.E. P for Political: Participation is Not Enough. *Scandinavian Journal of Information Systems 14*, 1 (2002), 77–92.
2. Bentley, R., Hughes, J.A., Randall, D., Rodden, T., Sawyer, P., Shapiro, D., and Sommerville, I. Ethnographically-informed systems design for air traffic control. *CSCW '92: Proc of CSCW*, ACM (1992), 123–129.
3. Bidwell, N.J., Reitmaier, T., Marsden, G., and Hansen, S. Designing with Mobile Digital Storytelling in Rural Africa. *CHI '10: Proc. of CHI*, ACM (2010), 1593–1602.
4. Björgvinsson, E., Ehn, P., and Hillgren, P.-A. Participatory design and "democratizing innovation." *PDC '10: Proc. of PDC*, ACM (2010), 41–50.
5. Blomberg, J. and Karasti, H. Reflections on 25 years of ethnography in CSCW. *Computer Supported Cooperative Work* 22, (2013), 373–423.
6. Blythe, M. and Monk, A. The Enigmatics of Affect. *DIS '02: Proc. of DIS*, ACM (2002), 87–98.
7. Brandon, B., Causby, S.W., Delahanty, A.R., Jacobs, B., Kulinski, E., Larsen, M., Lawrence, J.D., Mikalonous, C., McCarey, H., McClendon, R.B., Simms, S.C., Wearing, B., and Etienne, H.E. *English Avenue Redevelopment Plan*. Georgia Institute of Technology, (2008).
8. Brewer, J. and Dourish, P. Storied spaces: Cultural accounts of mobility, technology, and environmental knowing. *International Journal of Human-Computer Studies 66*, 12 (2008), 963–976.
9. Bruckman, A.S. A new perspective on "community" and its implications for computer-mediated communication systems. *CHI '06: Proc. of CHI*, ACM (2006), 616–621.
10. Button, G. The ethnographic tradition and design. *Design Studies 21*, 4 (2000), 319–332.
11. Carroll, J.M. Community computing as human-computer interaction. *Behaviour & Information Technology 20*, (2001), 307–314.
12. Carroll, J.M. and Rosson, M.B. A Trajectory for Community Networks. *The Information Society 19*, 5 (2003), 381–393.
13. Carroll, J.M. and Rosson, M.B. Participatory Design in Community Informatics. *Design Studies 28*, 3 (2007), 244–261.
14. DePaula, R. Lost in Translation: A Critical Analysis of Actors, Artifacts, Agendas, and Arenas in Participatory Design. *PDC 04: Proc. of PDC*, ACM (2004), 162–172.
15. Dimond, J.P., Dye, M., Larose, D., and Bruckman, A.S. Hollaback!: the role of storytelling online in a social movement organization. *CSCW '13: Proc. of CSCW*, ACM (2013), 477–486.
16. DiSalvo, C.F., Clement, A., and Pipek, V. Communities: Participatory design for, with and by communities. In J. Simonsen and T. Robertson, eds., *Routledge International Handbook of Participatory Design*. Routledge, New York, 2013, 182–209.
17. Dourish, P. Implications for design. *CHI '06: Proc. of CHI*, ACM (2006), 541–550.
18. Ehn, P. *Work-Oriented Design of Computer Artifacts*. Arbetslivscentrum, Stockholm, 1988.
19. Ehn, P. Participation in design things. *PDC '08: Proc. of PDC*, Indiana University (2008), 92–101.
20. Fox, S. and Le Dantec, C.A. Community historians: scaffolding community engagement through culture and heritage. *DIS '14: Proc. of DIS*, ACM (2014), 785–794.
21. Friedman, B., Kahn, P.H., Jr, and Borning, A. Value sensitive design and information systems. In P. Zhang and D. Galletta, eds., *Human-Computer Interaction in Management Information Systems Foundations*.

Human-Computer Interaction in Management Information Systems: Foundations, 2006, 348–375.

22. Gaver, W.W., Bowers, J., Kerridge, T., Boucher, A., and Jarvis, N. Anatomy of a failure: how we knew when our design went wrong, and what we learned from it. *CHI '09: Proc. of CHI*, ACM (2009), 2213–2222.

23. Harkavy, I. The role of universities in advancing citizenship and social justice in the 21st century. *Education, Citizenship and Social Justice 1*, 1 (2006), 5–37.

24. Harper, R.H.R. The Organisation in Ethnography: A Discussion of Ethnographic Fieldwork Programs in CSCW. *Computer Supported Cooperative Work 9*, 2 (2000), 239-264.

25. Harrison, S.R. and Dourish, P. Re-place-ing space. *CSCW '96: Proc. of CSCW*, ACM (1996), 67–76.

26. Hayes, G.R. The relationship of action research to human-computer interaction. *Transactions on Computer-Human Interaction 18*, 3 (2011), 15:1–15:20.

27. Heath, C. and Luff, P. Collaborative Activity and Technological Design: Task Coordination in London Underground Control Rooms. *ECSCW'91: Proc. of ECSCW*, (1991), 65–80.

28. Isin, E.F. Citizenship in flux: The figure of the activist citizen. *Subjectivity 29*, 1 (2009), 367–388.

29. Jackson, L.A., Barbatis, G., Biocca, F., Zhao, Y., Eye, von, A., and Fitzgerald, H.E. HomeNetToo: Home Internet Use in Low-Income Families: Is Access to the Internet Enough? In E.P. Bucy and J.E. Newhagen, eds., *Media Access: Social and Psychological Dimensions of New Technology Use*. Mahwah, NJ, 2004.

30. Johnson, R., Rogers, Y., van der Linden, J., and Bianchi-Berthouze, N. Being in the thick of in-the-wild studies: the challenges and insights of researcher participation. *CHI '12: Proc. of CHI*, ACM (2012), 1135–1144.

31. Law, J. *After Method: Mess in Social Science Research*. Routledge, 2004.

32. Le Dantec, C.A. Participation and Publics: Supporting Community Engagement. *CHI '12: Proc. of CHI*, ACM (2012), 1351–1360.

33. Le Dantec, C.A. and DiSalvo, C.F. Infrastructuring and the Formation of Publics in Participatory Design. *Social Studies of Science 43*, 2 (2013), 241–264.

34. Le Dantec, C.A., Farrell, R.G., Christensen, J.E., Bailey, M., Ellis, J.B., Kellogg, W.A., and Edwards, W.K. Publics in practice: ubiquitous computing at a shelter for homeless mothers. *CHI '11: Proc. of CHI*, ACM (2011), 1687–1696.

35. Luke, R., Clement, A., and Bortolussi, D. The promise and perils of a participatory approach to developing an open source community learning network. *PDC ' 04: Proc. of PDC, ACM (2004), 11–19*.

36. Marres, N. The Issues Deserve More Credit: Pragmatist Contributions to the Study of Public Involvement in Controversy. *Social Studies of Science 37*, 5 (2007), 759–780.

37. McMillan, D.W. and Chavis, D.M. Sense of community: A definition and theory. *Journal of Community Psychology 14*, (1996), 6–23.

38. Merritt, S. and Stolterman, E. Cultural hybridity in participatory design. *PDC '12: Proc. of PDC*, ACM (2012), 73–82.

39. Parker, A., Kantroo, V., Lee, H.R., Osornio, M., Sharma, M., and Grinter, R.E. Health promotion as activism: building community capacity to effect social change. *CHI '12: Proc. of CHI*, ACM (2012), 99–108.

40. Reingold, H. T*he Virtual Community: Homesteading on the Electronic Frontier*. MIT Press, 1993.

41. Rode, J.A. The roles that make the domestic work. *CSCW '10: Proc. of CSCW*, ACM (2010), 381–390.

42. Rode, J.A. Reflexivity in digital anthropology. *CHI '11: Proc. of CHI*, ACM (2011), 123–132.

43. Taylor, A. Out there. *CHI '11: Proc. of CHI*, ACM (2011), 685–694.

44. Tuan, Y.-F. *Space and Place: The Perspective of Experience*. University of Minnesota Press, Minneapolis, MN., 1977.

45. van Dijk, J. Models of Democracy and Concepts of Communication. In K.L. Hacker and J. van Dijk, eds., *Digital Democracy: Issues of Theory and Practice*. SAGE Publications Ltd, 2000, 30–53.

46. Van Maanen, J. *Tales of the Field: On Writing Ethnography*. University Of Chicago Press, 2011.

47. Voida, A., Dombrowski, L., Hayes, G.R., and Mazmanian, M. Shared values/conflicting logics: working around e-government systems. *CHI '14: Proc. of CHI*, ACM (2014), 3583–3592.

48. Winschiers-Theophilus, H., Bidwell, N.J., and Blake, E. Community Consensus: Design Beyond Participation. *Design Issues 28*, 3 (2012), 89–100.

49. Winschiers-Theophilus, H., Chivuno-Kuria, S., Kapuire, G.K., Bidwell, N.J., and Blake, E. Being participated: a community approach. *PDC '10: Proc. of PDC*, ACM (2010), 1–10.

50. Wyche, S.P. and Grinter, R.E. "This is how we do it in my country": a study of computer-mediated family communication among kenyan migrants in the united states. *CSCW '12: Proc. of CSCW*, ACM (2012), 87–96.

Increasing the Reach of Snowball Sampling: The Impact of Fixed versus Lottery Incentives

Aditya Vashistha
University of Washington
adityav@cs.washington.edu

Edward Cutrell
Microsoft Research India
cutrell@microsoft.com

William Thies
Microsoft Research India
thies@microsoft.com

ABSTRACT
Though many researchers have studied how to incentivize people to respond to surveys, little is known about how these incentives impact respondents' willingness to recruit others to participate as well. In this paper, we show that the incentives offered for individual survey responses can have a dramatic impact on the overall reach of a survey through a network of peers. In a field experiment in India, we made a survey accessible via mobile phones and offered respondents either a fixed incentive (guaranteed payment of about $0.17) or a lottery incentive (1% chance of winning $17). When asked to choose, a significant fraction of respondents preferred the lottery incentive. However, when encouraged to spread the survey, the fixed incentive spread over 100 times further, reaching about 800 people in a day. We interpret this surprising result and discuss the implications for HCI.

Author Keywords
Snowball sampling; survey response; crowdsourcing

ACM Classification Keywords
H.5.m. Information interfaces and presentation (e.g., HCI): Miscellaneous.

INTRODUCTION
To reach out to inaccessible, excluded, or hidden populations, researchers often recruit participants based on chains of personal referrals, a process known as snowball sampling [1,5,11,20]. Snowball sampling suffers from the obvious limitation that participants are not selected randomly from the population, thereby limiting the statistical validity and generalizability of study findings. Nonetheless, snowball sampling is often embraced as the only way to approach hidden or marginalized populations, such as drug users [17], prostitutes [19], pickpockets [15], and low-income respondents in the developing world [13,18,22,23,26]. Researchers have also championed the use of snowball sampling in social computing research, where a global directory of all users is usually unavailable and snowball sampling can be viewed as a form of convenience sample [4].

CSCW '15, March 14 - 18, 2015, Vancouver, BC, Canada.
Copyright 2015 ACM 978-1-4503-2922-4/15/03...$15.00.
http://dx.doi.org/10.1145/2675133.2675148

For snowball sampling to be successful, each participant needs to recruit a sufficient number of other people to join the sample. While many researchers have studied incentives for increasing participation in surveys [10], prior work focuses almost exclusively on improving the *response rate*. In the context of snowball sampling, the response rate is only half of the equation; it is equally or more important to know whether someone will *spread* the survey opportunity to others. One way to promote spread is to use referral bonuses that explicitly reward participants for recommending others. However, this approach requires a means of tracking the chain of referrers and can be difficult to implement in practice, especially in low-income communities that have limited access to technology. As an alternative approach, can one design the incentives for survey response so as to make the survey as appealing as possible to spread to others? We are not aware of prior work that considers this question.

In this paper, we demonstrate that the incentives offered for survey response can have an enormous influence on the eventual spread of a survey. We consider two of the most common incentives used in HCI research: a fixed incentive, in which each respondent receives a small reward, and a lottery incentive, in which respondents have a chance of winning a larger prize [27]. There is a large literature that debates the relative merits of these incentives (e.g., [7,12]). In the context of survey response, some studies favor lottery incentives (e.g., [6,14]) while others favor fixed incentives (e.g., [24,25]). However, nothing is known about which of these incentives promotes spreading the survey to others, increasing the overall reach of snowball sampling.

Via a field experiment in India, we show that a mobile survey with fixed payment to respondents spread to about 100 times more people (in a single day) than surveys using a lottery. At the same time, individuals who were given a choice between fixed and lottery incentives preferred the lottery incentives by a significant margin. In other words, what people choose for themselves is different than what they spread to others.

We attribute this surprising result to the immediate gratification afforded by a fixed incentive, as well as the guaranteed social capital that participants accrue by passing this earning opportunity to their friends. While our primary contribution is to the methodology of peer recruitment and snowball sampling, we also discuss the broader implications for HCI, including incentives for crowdsourcing and behavior change.

RELATED WORK

Increasing the spread of a survey is related to viral marketing. However, "viral" spread is characterized by a long chain of referral events, which is sufficient but not necessary for obtaining a large response to a snowball sample. In a recent book, Berger summarizes years of evidence-based research and points to six factors influencing virality: social currency, triggers, emotion, public visibility, practicality, and narrative [3] . Of these, social currency, emotion, and practicality are linked to the spread that we observe in our experiment.

There is also a wealth of research in behavioral economics that examines decision making under risk. For example, Prospect Theory predicts that people give too much weight to small probabilities [16], consistent with individuals' preference for lottery incentives over fixed incentives. However, we are unaware of any prior work that links probabilistic incentives to the eventual spread of a survey.

Crowd mobilization challenges such as the DARPA Network Challenge [21] have demonstrated the power of hierarchical incentive schemes to recruit participants. Our study is different because we do not offer financial rewards for making referrals, which can be difficult to track in practice. Instead we show that differences in task payment alone are sufficient to spur large variations in the reach of a survey.

HYPOTHESES

In prior work on mobile crowdsourcing [13] and phone-based surveys [8], we observed that a small but guaranteed earning opportunity led to rapid referral of new participants via word of mouth. We hypothesized that this rapid spread was caused by the gratification and trust engendered by the guaranteed payout: as soon as participants received payment, they knew the benefit was real and eagerly enrolled their friends. Our intuition was that participants did not have any *a priori* preference for a fixed payment; if asked to choose in advance of performing the task, participants might find it more enticing to have a chance of winning a large prize.

Based on this experience, we formulated more precise hypotheses. Consider a *fixed incentive*[1] that guarantees an immediate micropayment P to each respondent, and a *lottery incentive* that offers each respondent a small chance (1/100) of immediately winning a large payment (100P). In expectation, these alternatives offer the same amount of compensation, and a risk-neutral actor may not prefer one over the other. However, our hypotheses are as follows:

H1: Individuals who have not yet completed the task prefer the lottery incentive over the fixed incentive.

H2: In a group where some people have completed the task, the fixed incentive survey spreads to a greater number of total respondents than the lottery incentive survey.

Taken together, these hypotheses imply that participants' personal preference in advance of the task is *different* than what actually spreads in a real-world environment.

EXPERIMENTAL METHODOLOGY

To test our hypotheses, we designed a study that also served as a useful survey for a social enterprise in Bangalore, India. Our partner is Babajob, a mobile and web-based jobs portal for workers in the informal labor sector, such as cooks, maids, drivers, etc. Babajob sought to know whether current and potential job-seekers on its platform own a government-issued ID, such as a passport, driver's license, ration card, etc. For the benefit of the organization, we gathered this information using a phone survey, seeded with registered users and spread to potential users. At the same time, we tested our hypotheses by offering different incentives for users to respond to and spread the survey.

The seed group of participants were all drivers, who were registered as potential job seekers on Babajob's platform. The company supplied us with a list of about 300 drivers, half from Mumbai and half from Delhi. While we did not collect demographic information on these participants, they were likely very similar to those described in a prior paper [8], which surveyed drivers registered with Babajob in a different Indian city (Kolkata). Those drivers were found to be exclusively male and about 31 years old. The majority had received 10 years or fewer of education, and their average individual income was Rs. 8,300 (USD 140) per month. The majority owned a feature phone, or otherwise a basic phone; only one person in 20 owned a smart phone.

Our protocol used a between-subjects design with three conditions (see Table 1). In all of the conditions, we cold-called participants who were already enrolled as drivers in the company database. We introduced ourselves as an associate of the company, and we explained the purpose of the call: to assess whether the user has a government-issued ID. The arms of the study differed by the specific information solicited, and the incentive offered to participants.

To test H1, we conducted a single arm, the BASELINE. In this arm, we assessed whether participants owned a government ID by way of a verbal question and response. We described two alternate payments for the participants' response: a guaranteed payment of Rs. 10 (USD 0.17), or a 1-in-100 chance of winning Rs. 1,000 (USD 17), both delivered as mobile airtime credit ("top-up"). To collect users' preferred payment, we sent them an SMS that re-iterated the options and included two phone numbers on which to reply (see Table 1). Participants indicated their choice of payment by giving a missed call on one of the numbers. (A *missed call*, common in India, is one that rings but hangs up before it is answered, thereby incurring no expense to the caller). Upon receiving the missed call, we

[1] This term has two aspects: guaranteed (non-zero) payment, and constant amount of payment. We use the term "fixed" to align with prior literature, but it may be that the guarantee of payment is the more important part. A guaranteed but variable payment (with the same expected value as our fixed payment) would be interesting to explore in future work.

Table 1: SMS's used in the study.

Condition	SMS (Translated from Hindi)
BASELINE	Greetings from Babajob. If you want to get a guaranteed recharge of 10 Rs then give a missed call on <number1>. If you want to try to win 1000 Rs lottery recharge, then give a missed call on <number2>. Please note that only 1 in 100 people will win the lottery. You can choose only one of the two options. This offer is valid for only 1 hour. Thanks!
FIXED	Do you have a government ID? If your answer is Yes, give a missed call on <number1>. If your answer is No, give a missed call on <number2>. As soon as you give a missed call on any one of the two numbers, **we will recharge your mobile with 10 Rs. Everyone who gives a missed call will get a 10 Rs top-up.** This offer is valid only until <date>, 7PM. Please tell your friends as well.
LOTTERY	*Same as fixed incentive, except bold text is as follows:* **... you will be eligible to win a lottery of 1000 Rs mobile recharge. Please note that only 1 person in 100 people will win 1000 Rs mobile recharge ...**

issued payment within 15 minutes using an online portal, easymobilerecharge.com. The reasons that we used an SMS to solicit the user's response (as opposed to asking for it in the phone call) are two-fold: (i) to minimize the response bias inherent in verbal interviews [9], and (ii) to avoid a selection bias relative to other arms, which require participants to understand SMS. The order of options in the phone conversation and the SMS was randomized and balanced across participants. In this baseline condition, we told participants not to spread the survey to anyone else.

To test H2, we conducted two additional arms: FIXED and LOTTERY. In both arms, we called the participants as before. However, instead of soliciting their ownership of a government ID over the phone, we asked them to submit this information by sending a missed call on one of the two numbers (one for `yes' and another for `no'). In the fixed incentive arm, we offered Rs. 10 (USD 0.17) for their reply, while in the lottery incentive arm, we offered a 1-in-100 chance of a Rs. 1,000 (USD 17) payment for their reply. After explaining this offer over the phone, we sent users an SMS that restated the survey question and provided the phone numbers on which to reply (see Table 1). Unlike the baseline condition, we encouraged users to spread this survey question (and earning opportunity) to as many people as possible, up until 7:00pm on the day of the experiment. Because the survey was summarized in a single SMS, users could easily forward the message to others.

Whenever we conducted a lottery, we determined the payment to each participant using a random number generator that was evaluated only at the time of payment. This lent credibility to the experimenter, who could offer each participant an honest 1-in-100 chance of winning. However, it also implied that very few participants (in fact, zero) actually won the Rs. 1,000 payment. In order to study the effect of winning on the spread of the survey, we also conducted another variation of the experiment ("lucky incentive") where the first 5 participants won Rs. 1,000 each.

Table 2: Details of the experiments.

Condition	Date	City	Received our call	Received our call & replied
Baseline	May 10	Mumbai	34	20
	May 17	Delhi	28	20
Fixed Incentive	May 16	Mumbai	15	12
Lottery Incentive	May 13	Mumbai	15	13
	May 20	Delhi	24	14
	May 21	Delhi	15	14
Lucky Incentive	May 22	Delhi	10	6

In the fixed incentive arm, we contacted 15 drivers via phone; 12 of them replied with a missed call. In the lottery incentive arm, we contacted drivers until at least as many of them (12) replied with a missed call. In the lucky incentive arm, we contacted participants until five of them replied; each won Rs. 1,000 (we would have made more awards if not for budget constraints). We ran each study from about 10:30am to 7:00pm. While each arm restricted attention to a specific location (Mumbai or Delhi), drivers within a given location were selected for the experiments at random. We checked that the phone numbers of participants were not repeated across any two of the experiments.

To improve our confidence in the results, we replicated the baseline and lottery arms of the study multiple times (with different participants each time). The lucky and fixed incentive arms were too costly for us to replicate. A summary of the dates and size of each experiment appears in Table 2.

Phone calls were conducted in Hindi by a native Hindi speaker (male, age 27). For participants who won Rs. 1000, we also conducted follow-up interviews the day after the experiment. While we did not record the conversations, we took detailed notes that form the basis for our reporting.

QUANTITATIVE RESULTS

The baseline experiment encompassed 20 respondents from Mumbai and 20 respondents from Delhi. Results were identical in both locations: 13 drivers preferred the lottery incentive, while 7 preferred the fixed incentive. We tested H1 using a one-tailed binomial test (if drivers had an equal 50/50 preference for the lottery and fixed incentive, what is the chance that we would observe at least 26 of 40 responses in favor of the lottery?) The result ($p=0.04$) supports H1.

Results of the lottery experiments appear in Figure 1. The lottery survey did not spread very far at all. Across three trials, it spread to 6 people, 6 people, and 1 person. Similarly, the experiment with the `lucky' incentive, where the first five people won Rs. 1000, spread to only 6 people (see Figure 2).

Results of the fixed-incentive experiment appear in Figure 3. In contrast to the survey with lottery incentives, the fixed-incentive survey spread rapidly, logging 800 respondents by the announced closure time (7:00pm). Even after payments stopped, it spread to an additional 532 people overnight. We received missed calls from 11 states in India. 62% of calls were from Mumbai (where we seeded the experiment), 8% from other cities in the same state (Maharashtra), 13% from

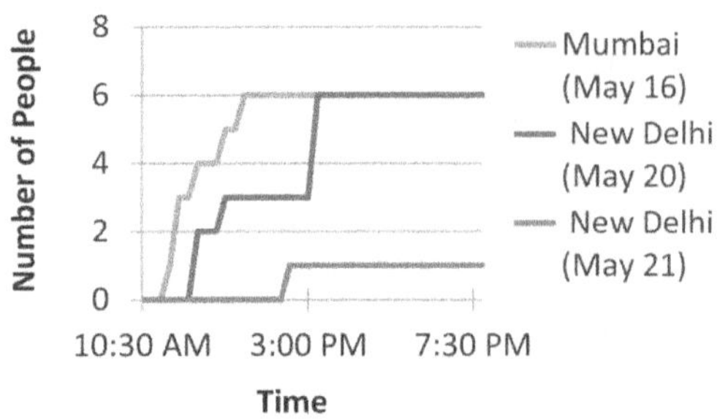

Figure 1: Spread of lottery incentive.

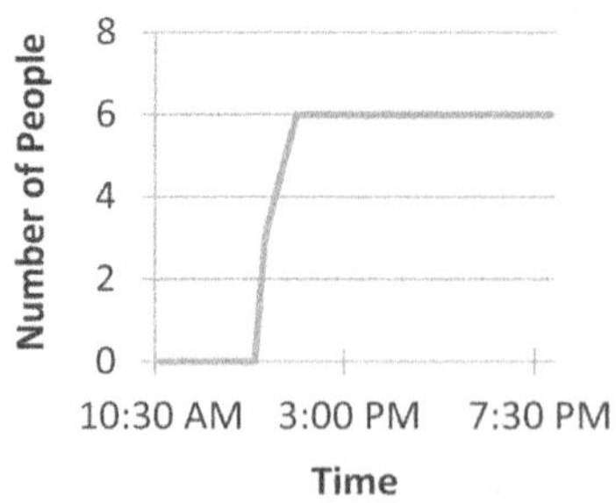

Figure 2: Spread of lucky incentive.

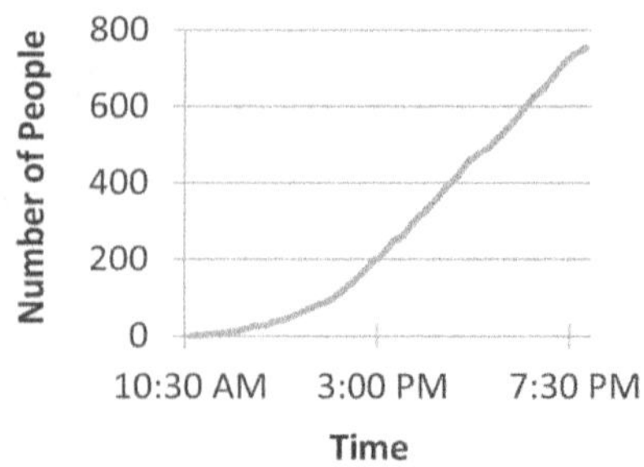

Figure 3: Spread of fixed incentive.

the state of Bihar and rest were spread across 9 other states. The rate of spread was approximately constant during the day. The spread might have been faster if the mobile recharge was automatic; we processed all payments manually, which added a delay of up to 15 minutes. In combination with the results of the lottery surveys, these results confirm H2.

QUALITATIVE RESULTS

To further understand the lack of spread in the lottery case, we conducted interviews with the five participants who were awarded Rs. 1000. As described previously, these awards happened only in the last (`lucky') trial, as an experiment to understand how winners would spread the survey to others. Our interviews confirmed that all of these participants received the Rs. 1000 top-up, and each of them told some of their friends. However, they did not tell many friends; usually they told 2-3 people, and at most 7 people.

Why didn't the Rs. 1000 winners tell more of their friends about the survey? Three themes emerged out of our interviews. First, their friends usually thought that the award was a joke or scam; they had to see the SMS payment confirmation in order to believe that Rs. 1000 was paid out. As one participant said (quotes translated from Hindi):

> When I first told them, they said it is fake, it is a lie and it is a trick to lure me. After that, I showed them the SMS. I also showed them congratulations SMS and after seeing that they somewhat believed me. Otherwise, it is hard to believe.

In a similar vein, the winners did not want to risk their own credibility and social capital by convincing friends to enter a lottery that they would not win. As one respondent said:

> When three friends gave a missed call and received the message 'Sorry you did not win', then I didn't tell anyone else. Because I thought that people I tell will think I am playing a prank on them.

The third theme emerging from the interviews is that winning participants did not want to share the survey too broadly out of a desire to maintain exclusivity. By winning the prize, they had become `special' and desired to maintain that distinction in the eyes of their friends. One person said:

> The profit I have earned, why should others get it? That is why I will tell it only to some special people.

DISCUSSION

Why did the fixed incentive spread faster than the lottery incentive? We offer three explanations. First, the fixed incentive offers immediate gratification, leading to a high state of arousal that can increase sharing behavior [2]. Second, immediate payment proves to participants that the offer is legitimate, boosting their confidence that they will gain social capital by spreading the news to friends [3]. Third, even winners of the lottery are unlikely to spread the survey widely, because the large prize gives them a sense of exclusivity. A small, guaranteed incentive may be "just right" to share with a large number of people.

Why, then, might people prefer the lottery incentive to the fixed incentive when given a choice? It could be that the lure of Rs. 1000 (almost four times their daily wage) is very enticing, or that people overestimate their personal odds of winning. It's possible that Rs. 10 is simply too small to interest some respondents. Finally, the chance of a large incentive may feel more like a game, making the process exciting even if the endpoint is unlikely to be profitable.

Our study has some limitations that will be important to address in future work. Our users were limited to low-income drivers in India, and generalizability to other contexts remains untested. Evaluating other incentives, such as a 50/50 chance of payment, a guaranteed base payment with variable bonus, or longer delays between response and payment, will be important to understand the full space of parameters and their influence on sharing behavior.

CONCLUSIONS

We conducted a field experiment that compares the effects of fixed incentives and lottery incentives on the total response volume of a snowball sample. While participants prefer the lottery incentive for themselves, they are much more likely to spread the fixed incentive to others.

While this study contributes most directly to the domain of snowball sampling, there could also be broader implications for HCI. Completing a survey is only one of many tasks that might be beneficial to spread via social networks. While crowd mobilization challenges such as the DARPA Network Challenge [21] have explored incentives for the spread of tasks, there was only a single winner. Thus, the strategies explored are variants of a lottery rather than a fixed payment. Our results suggest that a fixed payment to each participant may be able to mobilize an even larger crowd in a disaster scenario, something that is worthy of follow-up study.

Our results may also have implications for approaches to behavioral change. If an intervention offers small benefits with high probability, it might spread further (and thus impact more people) than an intervention which offers large benefits with low probability. By the same reasoning, the jobs portal in our study is considering changing its marketing strategy: rather than promote the chance of getting a new job (a big but unlikely prize), they could advertise a small but assured benefit (e.g., direct payment for creating a profile). To control costs, payment can be done on a first-come first-served basis, up to some maximum number of respondents.

ACKNOWLEDGMENTS

We are grateful to Sean Blagsvedt and Maya Chandrasekaran of Babajob for their assistance with the study. We also thank the anonymous reviewers for their helpful comments.

REFERENCES

1. Atkinson, R. and Flint, J. Accessing hidden and hard-to-reach populations: Snowball research strategies. *Social Research Update 33*, (2001).
2. Berger, J. Arousal increases social transmission of information. *Psychological science 22*, 7 (2011).
3. Berger, J. *Contagious: Why Things Catch On*. Simon & Schuster, 2013.
4. Bernstein, M.S., Ackerman, M.S., Chi, E.H., and Miller, R.C. The trouble with social computing systems research. *CHI EA*, (2011).
5. Biernacki, P. and Waldorf, D. Snowball Sampling: Problems and Techniques of Chain Referral Sampling. *Sociological Methods Research 10*, 2 (1981), 141–163.
6. Bosnjak, M. Prepaid and Promised Incentives in Web Surveys. *Social Science Computer Review*, (2003).
7. Brown, J., Schonfeld, T., and Gordon, B. "You May Have Already Won...": An Examination of the Use of Lottery Payments in Research. *IRB: Ethics and Human Research*, (2006).
8. Chakraborty, D., Medhi, I., Cutrell, E., and Thies, W. Man versus machine: evaluating IVR versus a live operator for phone surveys in India. *DEV*, (2013).
9. Dell, N., Vaidyanathan, V., Medhi, I., Cutrell, E., and Thies, W. "Yours is better!" Participant Response Bias in HCI. *CHI*, (2012).
10. Edwards, P., Roberts, I., Clarke, M., et al. Methods to increase response to postal and electronic questionnaires. *Cochrane Database of Systematic Reviews*, (2009).
11. Faugier, J. and Sargeant, M. Sampling hard to reach populations. *Journal of Advanced Nursing 26*, 4 (1997), 790–797.
12. Gajic, A., Cameron, D., and Hurley, J. The cost-effectiveness of cash versus lottery incentives for a web-based, stated-preference community survey. *European Journal of Health Economics,* (2012).
13. Gupta, A., Thies, W., Cutrell, E., and Balakrishnan, R. mClerk: Enabling Mobile Crowdsourcing in Developing Regions. *CHI*, (2012).
14. Haisley, E., Volpp, K., Pellathy, T., and Loewenstein, G. The Impact of Alternative Incentive Schemes on Completion of Health Risk Assessments. *American Journal of Health Promotion*, (2012).
15. Inciardi, J.A. In search of the class canon: a field study of professional pickpockets. In R.S. Weppner, ed., *Street Ethnography: Selected Studies of Crime and Drug Use in Natural Settings*. Sage, 1977.
16. Kahneman, D. and Tversky, A. Prospect theory: An analysis of decision under risk. *Econometrica*, (1979).
17. Kaplan, C.D., Korf, D., and Sterk, C. Temporal and social contexts of heroin-using populations. An illustration of the snowball sampling technique. *The Journal of nervous and mental disease 175*, 9 (1987).
18. Kumar, N. and Parikh, T.S. Mobiles, music, and materiality. *CHI*, (2013).
19. McNamara, R.P. *The Times Square Hustler: Male Prostitution in New York City*. Praeger, 1994.
20. Penrod, J., Preston, D.B., Cain, R.E., and Starks, M.T. A Discussion of Chain Referral As a Method of Sampling Hard-to-Reach Populations. *Journal of Transcultural Nursing 14*, 2 (2003), 100–107.
21. Pickard, G., Pan, W., Rahwan, I., et al. Time-Critical Social Mobilization. *Science*, (2011).
22. Sambasivan, N., Cutrell, E., and Toyama, K. ViralVCD: Tracing information-diffusion paths with low cost media in developing communities. *CHI*, (2010).
23. Shroff, G. and Kam, M. Towards a design model for women's empowerment in the developing world. *CHI*, ACM Press (2011).
24. Ulrich, C., Danis, M., Koziol, D., Garrett-Mayer, E., Hubbard, R., and Grady, C. Does It Pay to Pay? *Nursing Research*, (2005).
25. Warriner, K., Goyder, J., Gjertsen, H., Hohner, P., and Mcspurren, K. Charities, no; Lotteries, no; Cash, yes. *Public Opinion Quarterly*, (1996).
26. Wyche, S.P., Smyth, T.N., Chetty, M., Aoki, P.M., and Grinter, R.E. Deliberate interactions: characterizing technology use in Nairobi, Kenya. *CHI*, (2010).
27. Zangeneh, Z., Barmaki, R., Gibson-Wood, H., Levitan, M., Romeo, R., and Bottoms, J. Research Compensation and Lottery: An Online Empirical Pilot Study. *Int J Ment Health Addiction*, (2008).

LabintheWild: Conducting Large-Scale Online Experiments With Uncompensated Samples

Katharina Reinecke
University of Michigan
Ann Arbor, MI 48109, USA
reinecke@umich.edu

Krzysztof Z. Gajos
Harvard School of Engineering and Applied Sciences
33 Oxford St., Cambridge, MA, USA
kgajos@eecs.harvard.edu

ABSTRACT
Web-based experimentation with uncompensated and unsupervised samples has the potential to support the replication, verification, extension and generation of new results with larger and more diverse sample populations than previously seen. We introduce the experimental online platform LabintheWild, which provides participants with personalized feedback in exchange for participation in behavioral studies. In comparison to conventional in-lab studies, LabintheWild enables the recruitment of participants at larger scale and from more diverse demographic and geographic backgrounds. We analyze Google Analytics data, participants' comments, and tweets to discuss how participants hear about the platform, and why they might choose to participate. Analyzing three example experiments, we additionally show that these experiments replicate previous in-lab study results with comparable data quality.

Author Keywords
Online experimentation; crowdsourcing; replication; social comparison; uncompensated samples; WEIRD

ACM Classification Keywords
H.5.m. Information Interfaces and Presentation (e.g. HCI): Miscellaneous

INTRODUCTION
An estimated 95% of research findings in psychology, behavioral economics, and related fields are based on studies with student samples from Western and industrialized countries [1]. As a consequence, some of the knowledge derived from these usually small and locally-recruited student sample populations has been found to be non-generalizable [1, 17] — a finding that led researchers to call these participant samples "WEIRD", an acronym for Western, Educated, Industrialized, Rich, and Democratic [17].

The fact that WEIRD participants are not always representative of the broader population also affects the generalizability of findings in human-computer interaction (HCI). For instance, research has found that age and education level influence visual preferences for websites [32], and that groups in Western societies, such as in the US, are less likely to reach consensus in online scheduling systems than groups in Eastern societies, such as in China and Japan [33].

Figure 1. LabintheWild enables participants to compare themselves to others in exchange for study participation. By making experiments short, intrinsically motivating, and easy to access, LabintheWild has attracted nearly 750,000 participants from more than 200 countries.

Ideally, we would therefore routinely study diverse populations to analyze the generalizability of results and uncover demographics-related differences in users' behaviors. However, studying and comparing diverse groups in laboratory settings requires access to these populations and a means to bringing them into a lab, which is not always feasible within time, geographic and financial constraints. Conducting web-based experiments through online labor markets such as Amazon's Mechanical Turk has enabled researchers to reach larger and more diverse samples than what was previously possible in laboratory studies (e.g., [16, 18, 23, 26]), but the plurality of participants in these experiments are from two countries [30], and participation is restricted to those who have signed up to use the service.

To expand the range of available research methods, we show that online experiments with unsupervised and uncompensated samples (i.e., participants who complete experiments without a direct contact with the researcher and who do not receive financial compensation) have the potential to attract larger and more diverse participant pools than previously feasible in laboratory studies without compromising the data quality. More specifically, this paper introduces our online experiment platform LabintheWild, which enables participants to compare themselves to others in exchange for study participation. Synthesizing the major design decisions we made in the course of deploying LabintheWild, we reflect

CSCW 2015, March 14–18, 2015, Vancouver, BC, Canada.

http://dx.doi.org/10.1145/2675133.2675246

on their impact on recruitment, participant behavior, and data quality. We show our progress toward three core objectives that guided the design of LabintheWild:

1. Larger scale: LabintheWild reaches more participants than what is feasible in typical laboratory studies. In less than two years of its existence, LabintheWild was visited more than 2 million times, and nearly 750,000 visitors completed an experiment (an average of about 1,000 participants/day). Using Google Analytics data, participants' comments, and tweets, we discuss our main sources of traffic, how people hear about LabintheWild, as well as their motivation and perceived benefit of participating.

2. Less WEIRD: In contrast to laboratory studies, LabintheWild participants report a larger age range, more diverse educational backgrounds, and — coming from more than 200 countries and six continents — a wider geographic dispersion. This data shows that LabintheWild enables comparative studies between a large number of geographic regions and a variety of demographic groups.

3. Equal data quality: We report on the results of three prior laboratory studies that we replicated on LabintheWild. Our results match those obtained in laboratory settings despite the different incentive structure on LabintheWild and despite the fact that our participants complete the tests without direct supervision. We discuss participants' role in reporting distractions, identifying untruthfully provided information, and sharing useful context.

We continue this paper with a brief overview of previous innovations for conducting experiments, before providing details about LabintheWild. The article is structured following our three core objectives as stated above, starting with an analysis of the scale, followed by an overview of how LabintheWild participants are less WEIRD, and concluding with an evaluation of the data quality in three replication experiments. We finish with an overall discussion and an overview of future work.

RELATED WORK

The importance of conducting behavioral experiments across a variety of demographic groups was perhaps most prominently raised by Henrich and colleagues, who concluded that WEIRD samples "are among the least representative populations one could find for generalizing about humans" [17, p. 1]. For certain kinds of research, online experiments provide a feasible mechanism for studying more representative populations. Mason et al. [26], for instance, suggested that crowdsourcing experiments using Amazon's online market platform Mechanical Turk can broaden the subject population and increase generalizability. Workers on Mechanical Turk, the so-called "Turkers", have been found to be more diverse and more representative of the US population than conventional student samples [19, 3].

Mechanical Turk also provides the infrastructure for recruiting large numbers of subjects at low cost (Turkers receive an average of $4.80 per hour [20]). The site has therefore become increasingly popular in various fields such as political science [3], economics [18], and psychology [4]. However, the financial incentive might also mean that some Turkers attempt to maximize their return while investing minimal effort and time into the tasks [10]. In particular, researchers worry that Turkers might not sufficiently read and focus on study instructions and materials, which could potentially compromise the data quality [28]. Much research has since shown that the data quality is indeed affected by some Turkers investing minimal effort [22, 28, 21, 10, 15]. It was also found that when including precautions in the design and analysis of experiments, such as mechanisms to detect satisficing, effective training procedures, outlier removal techniques, as well as incorporating contextual factors (e.g., hardware, demographics) in the statistical analyses, the data quality and statistical power can be comparable to that of in-lab studies [16, 18, 23, 28, 30, 31, 38]. Research that requires collection of truthful subjective responses, however, remains challenging on Mechanical Turk [22, 28, 34].

While Mechanical Turk has a rapidly growing user population, its user base is insufficiently diverse to conduct studies spanning many countries (the plurality of Turkers come from the United States and India [30, 11, 11, 26]). Eriksson and Simpson reported that of 984 Turkers who participated in their study, no other country beside the US and India reached more than 5% of the overall sample [11].

Mechanical Turk's subject pool is additionally restricted to those who have signed up as Turkers, creating a barrier to participation. Removing this sign-up barrier, Germine et al. [13] developed TestMyBrain.org to make several cognitive and perceptual studies available online for anyone to participate in exchange for personalized performance feedback. Their analysis comparing data from online and in-lab participants in four distinct experiments showed no significant differences between results obtained in the two settings [13]. Our results corroborate these findings and extend them to a broader range of types of experiments.

ABOUT LABINTHEWILD

LabintheWild (www.labinthewild.org) is an online experiment platform for conducting behavioral research studies with self-selected, uncompensated web samples. When developing LabintheWild, we had three goals in mind:

1. Larger scale: The platform had to attract sufficiently large numbers of participants to enable rapid iteration of design prototypes at low cost, and to detect effects that cannot be reliably observed in small-scale experiments. This meant that we had to rethink recruitment strategies and participant compensation.

2. Less WEIRD: Our goal was to make it possible to reach participants from diverse geographic and demographic backgrounds in sufficient numbers to reason about the generalizability of findings and compare specific populations.

3. Equal data quality: We wanted the quality of the data collected on LabintheWild to match that of conventional methods. This required mechanisms that ensured participants' engagement and truthfulness, as well as mechanisms to detect if the quality of the data was compromised.

Major Design Decisions

Unrestricted Online Access

Developing LabintheWild as an online platform was central to meeting the goals of engaging larger and less WEIRD populations as easy online access lowers the barrier to participation compared to studies conducted in physical labs. LabintheWild studies are conducted without experimenter supervision, which provides the benefit of allowing participation in large numbers and around the clock independent of location and time zones.

LabintheWild experiments are open to anyone to participate. This has several consequences: First, even if the scientific objective of an experiment is to study a specific population (e.g., people who speak two or more languages fluently), we design studies such that all can have a rewarding experience participating in a study, which sometimes requires designing multiple tracks through an experiment. Second, we carefully design studies to be appropriate for minors and other vulnerable populations.

Finally, to make participation as easy as possible, we decided that people should not be required to sign up. This decision was further reinforced by a request from our Institutional Review Boards that we do not track our participants in any way. While these decisions lower the barrier to participation and protect participants' privacy, the current design of LabintheWild precludes longitudinal studies, combining a participant's results from multiple studies, or automatically detecting participants taking the same test more than once. This last limitation is particularly important because many experiments have prominent learning effects. To maintain integrity of our data, the first question we ask in all our questionnaires is whether a participant has taken the test before. Participants who answer this question in the affirmative are typically excluded from the analysis.

Participant Incentives and Compensation

One of the major design decisions that we made was that LabintheWild should work without providing financial compensation for study participation. Paying participants would limit both the size and the diversity of the participant pool because our financial resources are limited and because only some participants have the ability to receive online payments or are interested in spending their money online (e.g., Mechanical Turk workers can receive their payments only in U.S. dollars, Indian Rupees, or as Amazon.com store credit [26]). The necessary registration would also pose a hurdle. Instead, we leverage the human urge to learn about themselves and to compare themselves to others [12]: After participating in an experiment, participants are shown a personalized results page, which explains how they did and how their performance or preferences compare to others. For each experiment, we produce a short slogan that advertises the type of feedback participants would receive (e.g., "Can we guess your age?", "Are you more Eastern or Western?", "Test your social intelligence!"). We use these slogans to advertise each experiment on LabintheWild's front page and for sharing the experiments via social media.

The personalized feedback is designed to be either value-neutral or performance-based, but always compares the participant to others. In most cases, the feedback corresponds to our own research questions. For example, in a study that compares aesthetic preferences across cultures, participants' website preferences are shown in comparison to people from the same or other countries. However, if research questions and the corresponding experiments are not inherently interesting to participants, we find an aspect of the results that might be of higher interest. For example, for a Fitts' Law experiment that required participants to click on a number of dots on a screen for a duration of around five minutes—a task that can be extremely tedious and boring—we implemented a regression model to predict a person's age from their mouse movements. This experiment's slogan was "Can we guess your age?" (rather than the more obvious "What is you pointing ability?"). Our primary research interest was clearly revealed in the informed consent form and again on the personalized results page. But participants' main incentive was to see whether we could, indeed, guess their age.

Recruitment

Designing experiments to be intrinsically motivating and providing personalized feedback plays a major role in the recruitment of participants. LabintheWild supports a self-perpetuating recruitment mechanism by enabling sharing through online social networks. LabintheWild's pages, including the first and last page of each experiment, are equipped with social sharing buttons via Facebook, Twitter, Google+, Tumblr, and email.

When we launched LabintheWild in July 2012, we first advertised three studies through our personal social networks on Facebook, Twitter, and Google+. As more and more participants took part in our experiments, we observed an increase in mentions of LabintheWild in social shares, on blog posts, and in online newspaper articles: Participants and other interested people write about and link to LabintheWild, which attracts others to the site. To further leverage the word-of-mouth and to enable users to hear about new experiments and research results, we added a Facebook page and the possibility to "like" LabintheWild in April 2013, as well as an option to sign up for email notifications in July 2013.

When an experiment is ready to go online, we initially advertise it on our own online social networks. This limited deployment gives us a chance to uncover any remaining implementation bugs and design flaws. Next, we advertise the experiment on our Facebook page and add it to the homepage of LabintheWild. We do not otherwise actively advertise or recruit participants.

Because some experiments are naturally more intrinsically motivating than others, we employ a special recruitment strategy among participants who just completed a study. Below their personalized results, we suggest two other LabintheWild experiments. Consequently, our most popular experiments end up generating traffic for those that are less popular.

In our recruitment, we focused on encouraging participants to advertise LabintheWild to their friends. We also offer participants the option of following LabintheWild's Facebook page or signing up for email announcements, but we made these opportunities less prominent. Our decision was motivated by the fact that new studies appear on LabintheWild every two months on average, which provides little opportunity for nurturing frequent return visitors.

Study design

To ensure that participation does not become tedious or exhausting, we design our experiments to take 5–15 minutes. Although it might be feasible to conduct longer studies, a duration of around 15 minutes has proven to successfully engage participants on TestMyBrain.org [13]. We also clearly communicate progress through the experiment, use friendly, casual language, and occasionally include humorous interludes.

To ensure honest answers to our demographic questions, we chose to make the questions optional wherever possible. We also provide easy and non-judgmental mechanisms for reporting situations that might have compromised the data quality at the end of each experiment. Specific questions depend on the experiment, but we frequently ask participants if they experienced technical difficulties or distractions and whether they cheated in any way. As we discuss later, participants often provide an informative explanation of how they were distracted or how they cheated.

Choice of studies

Our decision to limit the length of our studies imposes constraints on the experiment design. Studies that require showing large numbers of stimuli are shortened by presenting participants with different randomized subsamples of the full set of stimuli, and we account for the resulting differences in sample frequencies in the analyses.

The unsupervised online environment and the social recruitment mechanism additionally limit the type of studies that can be feasibly run on LabintheWild. For example, we have not attempted to run studies that require participants to be in specific environments or use specific devices. Studies that require deception (i.e., to avoid that demand characteristics [29] influence participants' behavior) could also impact the results in the longer term, because the debriefing content at the end of the study might be shared with others.

LARGE SCALE

Conducting experiments with uncompensated and self-selected online samples at large scale naturally requires a self-sustaining recruitment mechanism. This section first reports on the current scale of LabintheWild, that is, its visitor and participant numbers, before describing how people hear about LabintheWild and why they participate. Information about visits to LabintheWild is based on data from Google Analytics, while the participation data is based on data logged on LabintheWild.

Visitors and Participant Numbers on LabintheWild

Between launching LabintheWild in July 2012 and April 2014, the platform has been visited 2,072,384 times, 11.6% of which were return visits. Visitors came from 219 countries and regions, with the plurality of them coming from the United States (36.66%, see Table 1 for a list of countries).

Country	# visitors	% of total	Country	# visitors	% of total
United States	759,663	36.66	Israel	9,459	0.46
United Kingdom	312,135	15.06	Italy	9,026	0.44
Hungary	159,431	7.69	Spain	7,902	0.38
Canada	96,446	4.65	Switzerland	7,461	0.36
Romania	87,074	4.20	Mexico	7,337	0.35
Lithuania	78,349	3.78	Denmark	6,696	0.32
Australia	45,107	2.18	Poland	6,364	0.31
Germany	43,358	2.09	Greece	6,236	0.30
Norway	36,168	1.75	Malaysia	6,090	0.29
Singapore	28,940	1.40	Philippines	4,753	0.23
China	28,938	1.40	Hong Kong	4,436	0.21
Netherlands	28,424	1.37	Bosnia and Herzegovina	4,154	0.20
Macedonia (FYROM)	25,072	1.21	Russia	3,591	0.17
Finland	23,944	1.16	Turkey	3,430	0.17
Chile	19,082	0.92	Argentina	3,373	0.16
India	16,108	0.78	South Africa	3,239	0.16
Austria	14,544	0.70	South Korea	3,234	0.16
France	14,466	0.70	Slovakia	3,107	0.15
Sweden	13,387	0.65	Bulgaria	2,897	0.14
Ireland	13,282	0.64	Pakistan	2,742	0.13
Japan	12,279	0.59	Portugal	2,681	0.13
New Zealand	11,544	0.56	United Arab Emirates	2,580	0.12
Belgium	11,533	0.56	Thailand	2,576	0.12
Serbia	11,293	0.54	Taiwan	2,545	0.12
Brazil	10,132	0.49	Vietnam	2,317	0.11

Table 1. The top 50 countries (of more than 200) with the largest numbers of visitors on LabintheWild between June 2012 and April 2014.

Referral source	# visitors	% of total	Referral source	# visitors	% of total
facebook.com	408,162	19.70	mokslas.delfi.lt	8,364	0.40
m.facebook.com	142,343	6.87	gizmodo.co.uk	8,349	0.40
huffingtonpost.co.uk	114,424	5.52	krone.at	7,367	0.36
dailymail.co.uk	83,460	4.03	neogaf.com	6,556	0.32
eduline.hu	77,120	3.72	komando.com	5,602	0.27
t.co	57,555	2.78	yoda.ro	5,019	0.24
realitatea.net	45,089	2.18	rtv.net	4,838	0.23
tumblr.com	24,347	1.17	wowbiz.ro	4,649	0.22
hvg.hu	20,467	0.99	plus.url.google.com	4,470	0.22
origo.hu	19,223	0.93	boards.4chan.org	4,210	0.20
reddit.com	18,792	0.91	laikas.lt	3,632	0.18
alfa.lt	15,123	0.73	updateordie.com	3,491	0.17
szeretlekmagyarorszag.hu	14,800	0.71	taringa.net	3,482	0.17
forum.bodybuilding.com	14,110	0.68	telegraf.rs	3,376	0.16
technologijos.lt	13,782	0.67	h2w.iask.cn	3,137	0.15
weibo.com	13,007	0.63	i-am-bored.com	3,136	0.15
crnobelo.com	11,011	0.53	tigerdroppings.com	3,129	0.15
side3.no	10,932	0.53	smallbusiness.yahoo.com	2,995	0.14
faculteti.mk	10,390	0.50	quo.mx	2,269	0.11
sociedad.biobiochile.cl	9,552	0.46	pcwelt.de	2,048	0.10

Table 2. List of predominant referral sources to the site between June 2012 and April 2014.

During the July 2012 – April 2014 period eleven distinct experiments were available on LabintheWild at some point. Visitors completed 744,739 experimental sessions. This number only includes those participants who have finished the whole length of an experiment and did not report to have taken the same experiment before. Because we do not track participants across experiments, we do not know how many unique participants completed experiments on the site. An analysis of visitor flow suggests that very few participants completed more than two experiments in a single visit.

How People Hear About LabintheWild

Table 2 lists the predominant referral sources to LabintheWild over the past two years. Although Facebook is the primary source of traffic, more than 5,000 websites currently mention LabintheWild or one of its experiments and lead visitors to the site.[1] The fact that people link to the site is also no-

[1]This data reports on statistics provided by Google Analytics and reports on visitors, not participants.

ticeable in that even after removal of an experiment from the LabintheWild front page, many people still access the experiment directly. The diversity of referral sources additionally conveys that LabintheWild attracts people with a variety of interests.

To find out why people invite others to participate, we analyzed the 200 most recent tweets that included LabintheWild's URL or referred to the site name. Following the thematic analysis method [14], we first added codes to the tweets that described the reasoning behind encouraging others to visit LabintheWild. These codes were then iteratively clustered into themes. We saw two patterns emerge: First, people appear to share their interest in science for altruistic reasons, such as exemplified with these tweets:

> *Participate in these #studies because #science is cool! And it's an interesting insight into yourself.*

> *Intriguing research trying to quantify difficult-to-quantify things. Add to their data.*

> *LabintheWild.org Help advance the design of all sorts of cool things. Older people especially welcome.*

The last tweet referred to a request that we added at the end of an experiment to tell not just "your friends" to participate, but especially people over 50. After adding this sentence, the average age of participants noticeably increased.

A second reason for sharing the experiments is to communicate the discovery of something that could potentially be exciting for others:

> *Savvy web users - do you think you can spot an untrustworthy website? Take this test*

> *take these tests and learn that you're older and more japanese than you ever knew: LabintheWild.org*

> *Check out LabintheWild.org for some pretty neat cultural / perception experiments [...]*

> *These tests have been amusing: LabintheWild.org , particularly the social intelligence one. Let me know if you try any of them!*

> *take some fun tests! one of them will guess your age by how you click on the red dot.*

The tweets demonstrate the role that online social media users play in recruiting others and spreading the word.

Why People Come to LabintheWild

To explore the reasons for participation, we again analyzed tweets that contained references to LabintheWild. In addition, we also included comments that participants provided at the end of four experiments that represented a diverse set of study and feedback designs. The resulting set contained nearly 30,000 comments. We first excluded one-word comments (e.g., "interesting", "fascinating", "boring", "no") that did not contain any reasoning. We then thematically analyzed the data [14] by labeling the remaining comments and tweets with keywords, and clustering them until no more additional categories emerged.

The analysis indicates that people come to LabintheWild for diverse reasons, but that the main categories are (1) an urge to compare themselves to others, (2) a general curiosity about themselves, (3) a fascination with the idea that their own characteristics could be predicted, and (4) the desire for improving particular skills. In the following, comments (but not tweets) will be reported along with the test and participant number that they refer to.

Consistent with the social comparison theory [12], many tweets sent after participation showed that people enjoyed the comparative feedback that LabintheWild experiments provide. For example, some Twitter users wrote

> *I got 31/36 (above average).... not bad for a confirmed social nincompoop! RT Test your social intelligence*

> *Uh oh. Only 3% of people (roughly 0 / 10) from United Kingdom share your visual preferences!*

> *I challenge you all to beat my score of 35 out of 36! Post your results here.*

Sharing results online seems to be a way of differentiating oneself from others and showing off these differences.

Other tweets suggest that participants appreciate discovering something new about themselves:

> *Fascinating. Apparently I'm better at perceiving the background. Psychology tests are awesome.*

> *LabintheWild.org I love this ..according to this I'm more Japanese than American..& I'm 30!! Yipee!!*

Similarly, participants' comments describe that the studies made them aware of their own preferences:

> *love the test. It makes you think about design trends, simplicity in web design and color usage. I rated some websites lower just because I didn't like the color combination!* [P42367, aesthetics test]

> *Roughly around the break it started to become clear to me that I like quite simple pages. At least when it comes to colors. But even more important than that seemed to be the layout of the page. If the main thing was big and clear, maybe accompanied with a calm picture, it appealed to me more than the over simplistic ones or the ones that were just simply too full of <beep>.* [P459, aesthetics test]

Some tweets show that participants were surprised about the accuracy of results, and fascinated that the studies could produce unexpected predictions about themselves.

> *So, er, LabintheWild.org guessed my age exactly! Science is cool.*

> *My score: Low Colorfulness, High Complexity, Medium Color Sat.: Visual Preferences Test - yes, I like neutral colors.*

> *okay this is sort of spooky. It makes me a little more afraid of smart people :) It guessed me at 29 (i'm 30)...*

Comments additionally suggest that for some participants improving particular skills is the main motivation for participating:

> *Very interesting! It would be nice to have the results after the test, I'd be curious to know if I rated the designs consistently, and also to take a better look at which ones I've rated high or low* [aesthetics test, P43024]

> *It would be great [...] to see which eyes we guessed wrong. I personally took the test hoping to practice or improve my skills; but as it stands I really don't take anything out of it.* [P872, social intelligence test]

> *Thanks! I hope to use this to improve my business skills.* [P15464, social intelligence test]

In some cases, revealing the correct answers so that participants can see what exactly they got wrong risks the validity of the experiment if the answers get shared or discussed between participants. Hence, we only offer a summary of an individual's results, but provide the full answer key whenever participants ask us for it via email.

Discussion

The previous analyses demonstrate the feasibility of conducting uncompensated online experiments with large numbers of participants (an average of a thousand participants a day), allowing us to study more participants at lower cost than possible in lab. People's comments and tweets show that LabintheWild participants play an essential role in enabling this scale by recruiting others.

A noteworthy aspect of LabintheWild is that 88.4% of its visitors are new to the site. Hence, in contrast to Mechanical Turk, LabintheWild largely taps into new participant pools rather than a stable base of returning participants. There are two reasons for this: First, LabintheWild does not require visitors to sign up before engaging with the content, and thus, lowers the barrier for testing it out. The second, and more important, reason is that LabintheWild does not offer new content at the same frequency as Mechanical Turk. Because it takes us two months on average to add a new experiment to LabintheWild, we made little effort to encourage participants to return other than giving them the opportunity to follow the LabintheWild Facebook page where we announce new experiments. However, we do encourage the recruitment of others by including social network sharing buttons in the results pages of our experiments.

LESS WEIRD

In contrast to the convenience samples of many in-lab experiments (most often North American undergraduate students [17]), one of LabintheWild's core goals is to conduct experiments with less WEIRD participants. In particular, our aim is to reach a broader range of age groups, countries, and education levels.

Table 3 shows participants' self-reported demographics for nine of our previous experiments. These experiments were on the LabintheWild front page for varying lengths in time (usually, LabintheWild features five experiments at the same time), but most of them remained accessible through the study link and had ongoing, albeit lower, traffic afterwards. The number of participants includes only those who did not report to have participated in the study before. The percentage of US participants represents people who are currently living in the US, but are not necessarily originally from the US.

Across experiments, approximately 49% of all participants are female. This is slightly more balanced than the 55% females found in Mechanical Turk samples [26], and shows that females as much as males are attracted to participate in LabintheWild experiments.

LabintheWild participants have a mean age of 29 years (median 26, range 5-99), which is older than the average age in laboratory studies, but younger than the mean age of 32 years (median 30) that has been reported for Turkers (see e.g., [26]). LabintheWild reaches a larger age range of people than Mechanical Turk does ([26] report an age range of 18 to approximately 75), mainly due to the fact that Turkers are required to be at least 18 years before being able to sign up.

About 73% of LabintheWild participants report to be currently enrolled in college or have a college degree or higher, which suggests that our participant samples are not representative of the general population. The higher education level is consistent with that of the Mechanical Turk population [30]. In fact, Paoloacci et al. suggest that the higher education level of Turkers could be typical among early adopters of technology [30]. Importantly, roughly 27% of our participants have a lower education level than the traditional student samples recruited for in-lab experiments.

Participants self-reported to be from more than 200 countries and regions on six continents, which is in line with the Google Analytics report for LabintheWild visitors (see also Table 1). Moreover, approximately 66% of participants across all experiments (the majority in all except one of our previous studies) comes from countries other than the US. In contrast, Mechanical Turk surveys suggest that Turkers come from 190 countries, but 81% of them are from India and the US [30]. This makes the overall LabintheWild sample less WEIRD than the typical Western convenience samples in lab experiments, and it also demonstrates that LabintheWild enables us to reach more geographically diverse participants in higher numbers than currently possible using Mechanical Turk. We expect this diversity of LabintheWild to increase after the site and experiments are offered in languages other than English.

Discussion

The previous analysis of demographics demonstrates that LabintheWild participants are arguably less WEIRD than common convenience samples of laboratory studies (see, e.g., [3, 17]). LabintheWild is also more diverse than Mechanical Turk in terms of a larger age range, and a larger number of countries that contribute substantial numbers of participants. This opens up new possibilities for cross-country comparisons and cross-cultural research. Likewise, more diverse populations within countries enable comparisons between several demographic groups. In the past, the diversity among LabintheWild participants has allowed us to empiri-

Experiment	Abbreviation	# months on front page	# participants	% female	age range	mean age (median)	stdev age	# countries	% US participants	% college or above	# of native languages	% native English speakers
What is your website aesthetic? (Experiment 1)	aesthetics	21	42,171	52.7	6-99	32 (29)	12.83	190	41.4	73.5	38	62.6
How fast is your memory? (Experiment 2)	memory	4	1,121	N/A	13-99	26 (23)	11.53	81	28.8	62.2	36	49.6
Test your social intelligence! (Experiment 3)	social intelligence	10	125,570	48.5	12-98	30 (26)	12.24	227	46.9	N/A	N/A	N/A
What do you perceive as colorful?	colorfulness	3	8,600	56.9	7-99	29 (26)	12.37	140	40.6	72.5	38	57.4
Are you more Eastern or Western?	frame-line	21	7,623	57.7	6-99	27 (24)	11.58	148	47.3	74.1	37	70.7
How do you predict changes in future trends?	graph prediction	5	1,216	45.3	6-99	26 (23)	12.95	86	40.8	73.1	37	59.3
What do you perceive as complex?	complexity	1	176	46.6	12-70	33 (30)	12.19	32	65.9	90.3	23	61.9
Trust us. You will love this test!	trust	7	1,944	56.9	6-99	27 (23)	12.63	97	43.4	69.5	35	66.4
Can we guess your age?	age guessing	4	556,330	39	5-99	32 (29)	12.09	139	30.7	N/A	N/A	66.4

Table 3. Demographic composition of participant samples from nine LabintheWild experiments. Two further experiments are not shown here, because they were only online for brief periods of time. The first three experiments are presented in this paper as part of the data quality analyses.

cally demonstrate differences between the visual preferences of people from more than 40 countries and various demographic groups [32].

The finding that 73% of LabintheWild participants have received or are currently pursuing a college degree or higher is not surprising given our recruitment methods with our own social networks as a starting point. We believe that a key to increasing the diversity will be to further explore how exactly different segments of the population hear about LabintheWild, and what motivates them to take part.

EQUAL DATA QUALITY

The third and perhaps most important goal of LabintheWild was to maintain the data quality on par with traditional in-lab experiments with controlled conditions and experimenter supervision. To evaluate this, the following sections report on LabintheWild replications of three experiments from the literature, and show how participants play an important role in detecting issues that could compromise the data quality.

Experiment Replications

We implemented online versions of the following three experiments from the literature:

1. An experiment on subjective ratings on appeal [25].
2. A study of working memory processing speed [35].
3. A test assessing social intelligence, originally called "Reading the mind in the eyes" [2].

In the first experiment, participants are asked to provide subjective ratings of the aesthetic appeal of websites. They rate each website twice, which enables an analysis of reliability. We include this test because soliciting truthful and reliable subjective responses is still considered challenging in unsupervised online studies [22, 28, 34] making this test a particularly sensitive probe of the truthfulness of data reported by LabintheWild participants: are they reporting their actual subjective reactions at least as reliably as in-lab participants or are they prone to "spamming" as some participants on Amazon Mechanical Turk? The successful completion of this study also requires careful attention as stimuli are presented for only 500ms each, giving us insights into whether LabintheWild participants get distracted substantially more than in-lab participants.

The second experiment on working memory processing speed involves working under considerable cognitive load. Hence, this test provides an insight into whether or not LabintheWild participants are willing to put in substantial mental effort into completing experiments.

In some experiments, as in the test measuring the working memory processing speed, the overall phenomenon is reproducible across laboratories, but the exact values of the measurements differ substantially across experimental settings. We included a third test, the "Reading the mind in the eyes" study, because its measurements should be exactly replicable *independent* of the experimental setting. The scores obtained in this experiment depend on both actual ability and effort. If LabintheWild participants achieved scores similar to those obtained by supervised in-lab participants, it would provide evidence that they exerted as much effort.

Experiment 1: Website Aesthetics

The first experiment that we replicated was originally presented by Lindgaard and colleagues in 2006 [25]. The authors established that people are able to make reliable judgments on the visual appeal of websites after a short stimulus exposure time of 500ms.

The experiment was divided into two blocks, in which participants were shown the same set of websites (in different randomized order) for 500ms each. After each website, they were asked to rate the visual appeal of the site on a single-item 9-point Likert scale. The results showed that the ratings of the same websites in the two phases are significantly correlated, suggesting a high intra-participant reliability.

In our replication, we used the intra-participant reliability to verify the effort and truthfulness of participants' subjective visual preference ratings. If participants give the study their undivided attention and provide ratings that truly correspond to their visual preferences, the ratings between the two phases should be highly correlated.

Main Results From Prior Studies

In the original study [25], the authors tested the intra-participant reliability of 20 participants using Pearson correlations for each participant's rating in the first and the second phase. All correlations were significant at a $\alpha < .05$ level and all correlation coefficients were above r=.60 (see Table 4).

We closely followed the design of the third experiment presented in [25], replicating the condition in which participants were shown website stimuli with a 500ms exposure time. Participants were first presented with an informed consent form, a demographics questionnaire, as well as a screen containing instructions on the task. The instructions also emphasized the short stimulus exposure time, which would require extra attention. Participants were then asked to rate websites on visual appeal on a single-item 9-point Likert scale. Website stimuli were pre-loaded in the background to ensure that the exposure time was unaffected by varying Internet connection speeds. The experiment was divided into three parts, starting with a practice session, and two main experiment parts, which included the same website screenshots in (differently) randomized order.

To keep the experiment under 10 minutes, we used 5 practice website screenshots (as opposed to 20 in the original study), and 30 websites per test phase (as opposed to 50). We added text and a picture between the two test phases to divert participants' attention from the main purpose of the test and encourage them to take a break. The study ended with personalized feedback about a participant's visual preferences in comparison to other people from their country of current residence.

Analysis

Following the procedure described in [25], we conducted separate Pearson product-moment correlations for each participant. Lindgaard and colleagues only provided an aggregation of their correlation coefficients, and so we did not perform a comparative statistical analysis of the distributions.

Participants

For an overview of participant demographics see Table 3. Because the original laboratory study was conducted at a North American university and required participants to speak English as their first language, we only included 10,976 LabintheWild participants who had always lived in Canada or the US, and who reported English as their native language. The demographic composition changed only slightly: Participants had a mean age of 33 (stdev = 13.24, median 29), and 59% were female. The education level increased to 79% who reported pursuing college or above.

Adjustments of Data

We excluded 166 participants for whom our system reported that the stimulus was not displayed for 500ms, and 75 participants who reported having experienced technical difficulties, and/or having cheated. Together this accounted for 2.2% of the 10,976 participants, resulting in a data set of 10,735 participants.

Correlation coefficient	Laboratory study (N=20)		LabintheWild, 18-24 years old (N=199)		LabintheWild, all (N=10,735)	
	N	%	N	%	N	%
.0-.09					3	0.03
.10-.19					9	0.08
.20-.29					21	0.20
.30-.39			1	0.5	67	0.62
.40.49			1	0.5	212	1.97
.50-.59			4	2.01	539	5.02
.60-.69	1	5	6	3.02	1338	12.46
.70-.79	4	20	16	8.04	3055	28.46
.80-.89	15	75	97	48.74	4469	41.63
.90-.99			74	37.19	1022	9.52

Table 4. Overview of the distribution of correlation coefficients comparing the results of the laboratory study to the one conducted on LabintheWild. LabintheWild participants were only included if they were from North-America and reported being a native English speaker.

Main Findings

Table 4 provides an overview of the correlation coefficients from the in-lab study and those from LabintheWild. Because participants in the original laboratory study were students at a Canadian university (participants' age was not reported in [25]), we first analyzed how the results of LabintheWild participants aged 18-24 years (N=199) compared against the in-lab results. All correlations on LabintheWild were significant at a $\alpha < .05$ level. In comparison to Lindgaard et al.'s study, a higher percentage of participants (85.93% versus 75% in the laboratory study) achieved correlation coefficients above $r = .80$. This suggests that LabintheWild participants at comparable age to the in-lab study participants were at least as consistent in their responses than those in the lab study.

When including all LabintheWild participants (i.e., those from the US and Canada who reported speaking English as their first language), we see a wider distribution of coefficients. We found that 84 correlations (0.78% of the total) were not significant at a $\alpha < .05$ level, indicating that a small percentage of LabintheWild participants might have been distracted or randomly rated the websites. The remaining 99.22% of correlations were significant, and 92.07% of correlations were above $r = .60$; the vast majority of LabintheWild participants were as or even more consistent in their responses as participants in lab.

We performed an additional analysis across the entire data set of 42,171 participants from 190 countries, again excluding participants with technical difficulties and/or those who reported having cheated. The excluded data accounted for 2.3%, resulting in 41,201 participants. We observed no substantial relationship between country of origin and the results, indicating that the phenomenon of people forming lasting impressions of aesthetic appeal based on brief exposure is universal across the sample population of our dataset.

In summary, our overall results match Lindgaard et al.'s finding that participants are able to form consistent impressions of a website's appeal after seeing it for only 500ms. Moreover, our results indicate that this phenomenon generalizes across a variety of demographic and geographic groups.

Experiment 2: Working Memory Processing Speed

In 1966, Saul Sternberg published results of an experiment demonstrating that the time needed to retrieve an item from working memory was linearly proportional to the number of items stored there [35].

Tasks

This study has been replicated and extended by numerous researchers (e.g., [6, 7, 8, 9, 36, 37]). All variants of this study have a common basic structure: In each experimental block, participants are first presented with a sequence of several (typically 1–6) symbols to memorize (Figure 2 left). After that, they are presented with one symbol at a time (a probe) and asked whether the symbol was present in the original set (Figure 2 right).

We based our main design decisions on the original study [35] (some of the details were not revealed in the original paper,

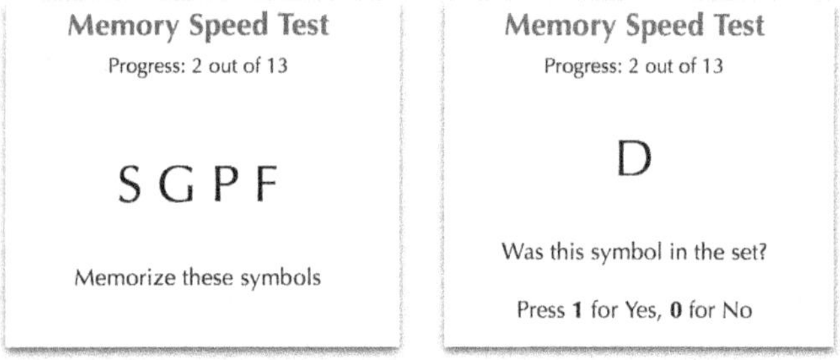

Figure 2. An example task in the Working Memory Processing Speed experiment.

but were made apparent in a later publication [37]). Each experimental block presented participants with a set of 1–6 randomly chosen symbols and 11 probes. Three of the probes (i.e., 27%) were positive (that is, contained a symbol from the original set) and 8 were negative. The order of the positive and negative probes was random and so was the selection of the specific symbols to display.

Unlike in the original study, we used the combined set of digits and uppercase English alphabet letters (rather than just digits). The choice of symbol does not affect the main outcome of the study [5]. We removed digit-letter pairs that could be visually confused for each other (i.e., 1-I, 0-O). The resulting set contained 32 distinct symbols.

Main Results From Prior Studies
The linear relationship between the size of the symbol set and the reaction time has been reliably confirmed and researchers repeatedly reported r^2 values of .99 and higher [35, 8]. This is the primary finding that we aimed to replicate.

Another prominent property of this task is that the marginal response time per item does not change with practice: That is, the absolute response time tends to improve as participants gain practice with the task, but the *slope* of the line of fit, which captures how much additional time is needed as the size of the set held in working memory increases by one item, does not change with practice [24, 27]. This is the second finding we aimed to replicate.

Detecting the relationship between set size and the response time rests on the assumption that participants actually make the effort to memorize the items and to respond correctly. All replications of this experiment exclude participants whose overall accuracy fails to meet an accuracy criterion (typically a number over 95%). A recent article provided the distribution of participant accuracies prior to any exclusions showing that lab-based participants accurately recalled items as often as 98% on average when there was only one item to be remembered and 90% on average when they had to memorize six items [8]. We compare these results to the accuracies of LabintheWild participants.

Procedure
The first three screens of the study presented participants with the basic information about the study, the informed consent form, and a short demographic questionnaire, which also asked whether participants had taken the study before. All questions were optional. Next, participants were presented with brief instructions followed by a single practice block of 11 trials. During the practice block participants were given feedback about the correctness of their responses immediately after each trial. No such feedback was provided during the subsequent blocks. The main experiment consisted of 12 blocks (2 for each set size between 1 and 6), each with 11 trials. Participants could take breaks between blocks.

The feedback page showed each participant their mean accuracy (what percentage of the probes they gave correct responses to) and their mean response time in comparison to previous study participants.

Measures and Analysis
We first conducted a least squares linear regression with *set size* [1–6 items] as the only factor and the *response time* as the response variable. As in the original study, we first averaged response times over all non-excluded blocks separately for each set size.

Next, we conducted an analysis of variance meant to uncover learning effects. This was a between-subjects analysis with the following factors and levels:

- *set size* [1–6 items] (modeled as a continuous variable)
- *prior exposure* {first time, repeat} (modeled as a categorical variable)
- *age bin* {10–14, 15–19, 20–24, 25–29, 30–39, 40–49, 50+} (modeled as an ordinal variable)

The *response time* measured participants' reaction time.

To analyze participant accuracies, we computed the mean percentage of correct responses for each of the six set sizes. Because the results in prior work were only reported graphically (i.e., they were summarized visually in a chart, but neither mean values nor variances were explicitly stated in the article), we did not attempt a statistical comparison.

Participants
The experiment was completed 1,319 times (198 repeat participants). The demographics of 1,121 participants who took this test for the first time can be seen in Table 3.

Adjustments of Data
We removed 100 experiment instances, in which participants reported having experienced technical difficulties, and/or cheated. These exclusions accounted for 7.6% of the 1,319 completed experiments leaving 1,219.

As in the original experiment, we removed experimental instances in which accuracy (i.e., the fraction of trials in which participants correctly recalled whether a probe was in the original set) did not meet the requirement. In the original study, three out of eleven participants (27%) were excluded and the mean accuracy of the participants retained for analysis was 98%. The accuracy threshold for exclusion was not reported. We excluded experimental sessions in which accuracy was lower than 94% (N=103, or 8.4%). We found that setting the threshold any higher did not impact the results. We

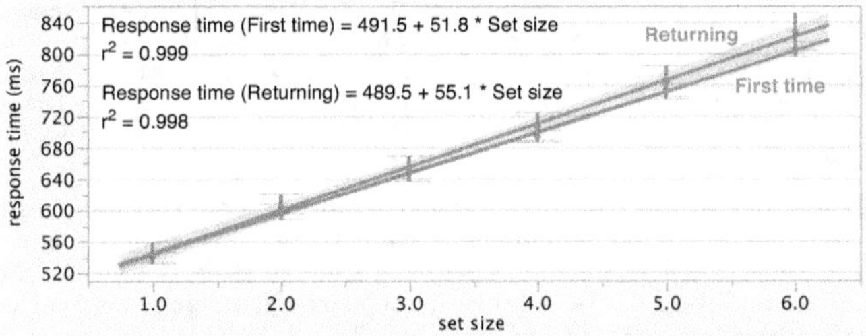

Figure 3. Main results for the Working Memory Processing Speed test: Results show a strong linear relationship between the number of items held in working memory and response time. Error bars show 95% confidence intervals. There is no significant difference in slope between first time and returning participants.

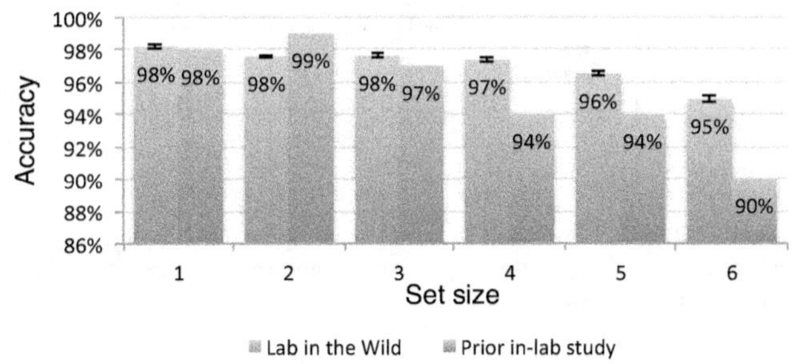

Figure 4. Accuracy comparison between LabintheWild and a prior laboratory study with 36 university students. Participants on LabintheWild were as likely to correctly recall what symbols were shown to them as participants in a traditional laboratory experiment. Error bars show the standard errors (available for LabintheWild participants only).

thus retained 1116 completed experimental sessions for analysis, 951 of which were completed by first time participants and 165 by returning participants.

In the original study, the first three trials in each block were excluded. We only removed the first trial because we found no substantial differences in mean or standard deviation in the response times for any of the subsequent probes.

To identify participants who might have gotten distracted during the test, we looked for extreme outliers in response time. Specifically, we computed the median and interquartile range (IQR) for the response times for set size of 6 (the condition with the slowest response times and largest variance). Similarly to prior studies with unsupervised online participants [23], we computed median + 3×IQR (2028ms) as the cut-off. 1.7% of the trials were thus identified as extreme outliers. Some took as long as 1.5 minutes indicating a major distraction. Because such a distraction was likely to have caused the participants to forget the symbols they were meant to memorize, we excluded entire blocks that contained at least one extreme outlier trial. This resulted in 15.2% of the blocks being excluded from analysis.

Main Findings

The main results are summarized in Figure 3. For first time participants, we observed a linear relationship between the number of items held in working memory and the response time: the response time increased by 51.8ms (±2.0ms, 95% confidence interval) for each additional item stored in working memory. This value is consistent with prior work and the model fit ($r^2 = 0.998$) matched or exceeded fits observed in prior work.

For people who reported having taken the test before, the results were similar: their response time increased by 55.2 (±2.2)ms for each additional item stored in working memory. The model fit is similar as for first time participants: $r^2 = 0.998$.

Comparing performance of first time participants to the returning ones, we observed no significant main effect of prior exposure to the experiment ($F_{1,9667} = 0.01, n.s.$). There was also no significant interaction between prior exposure and set size ($F_{1,9667} = 0.60, n.s.$). This last result indicates that—consistent with prior results—we observe no learning effect on the rate with which response time changes with the number of items held in working memory.

Accuracy

Figure 4 illustrates the performance of all first time LabintheWild participants (only excluding those who reported technical difficulties or cheating) compared to the accuracy of 36 students participating in a recent laboratory replication of this study [8]. Because of a lack of information about variance in the prior study, we did not test the significance of these differences, but the comparison does suggest that the unsupervised LabintheWild participants are attending to the task at least as well as in-lab participants.

In summary, we have reproduced two prominent results associated with this experimental paradigm: a strong linear relationship between set size and the response time and lack of significant learning effects. Our results also suggest that participants on LabintheWild are at least as accurate in recalling the items as participants from a conventional in-lab study.

Experiment 3: Reading the Mind in the Eyes

Our third experiment replicates the "Reading the mind in the eyes" test [2]. Participants were presented with 36 images (plus one practice image), each showing a portion of a person's face that included the eyes, but not the nose or the mouth. For each such image, participants were shown four words describing emotions and asked to choose one that was most likely being expressed by the person in the image. We used identical images in the same order as the original study [2].

The test was initially developed in the context of the study of Autism and the results demonstrated that, on average, people on the Autism spectrum are less likely to recognize a person's emotion just by looking at their eyes than controls drawn from the general population [2]. Later investigations in the area of collective intelligence demonstrated that the average performance of group members on this test was a better predictor of the group's success on a difficult problem solving task than the group's mean IQ [39]. Because of this association, we advertised it as a test of social intelligence on LabintheWild.

The original publication [2] included results for British students and for the general British population. For both popu-

	Original study						Lab in the Wild				
			Age (years)		Gender (%)			Age (years)		Gender (%)	
	N	age data available for	Mean	Stdev	Female	Male	N	Mean	Stdev	Female	Male
General British Population	122	88	46.5	16.9	55%	45%	1973	46.3	8.0	59%	41%
British student-aged participants	103	103	20.8	0.8	49%	51%	1519	20.4	1.1	30%	70%

Table 5. Reading the Mind in the Eyes study (social intelligence): Participants from the original study and a matching subset of participants from LabintheWild.

		Original study			Lab in the Wild			F-test		t-test	
		N	Score	Stdev	N	Score	Stdev	F	p	t	p
General British population	male	55	26.0	4.2	817	27.2	3.8	0.83	ns	2.31	ns
	female	67	26.4	3.2	1156	27.6	3.8	1.42	ns	2.48	ns
British student-aged participants	male	53	27.3	3.7	1064	27.3	3.9	1.14	ns	0.08	ns
	female	50	28.6	3.2	455	27.6	3.8	1.39	ns	-1.77	ns

Table 6. Results from the "Reading the mind in the eyes" study. Scores were computed as the number of trials for which the correct answer was given. There were no significant differences in the mean scores or variances in scores between in-lab participants and the matching LabintheWild participants.

lations, results were reported separately for men and women. Arguably, the performance on this test is dependent on both ability and effort. Equal or higher performance for matching populations on LabintheWild would provide evidence that LabintheWild participants exerted as much effort as participants who performed the study in lab.

Procedure

The first three pages of the study presented participants with a brief description of the study and its duration, an informed consent page, and instructions on the task. They were given one practice trial for which they received feedback about the correctness of their response. Participants then performed 36 experimental trials. No feedback about the correctness of those responses was provided until the very end of the study.

After completing the experimental trials, participants were presented with a voluntary demographic questionnaire, which also asked them if they were native speakers of English, and, if not, whether they had any difficulty understanding the words describing the emotions.

Participants were then presented with the feedback page showing their own score (i.e., the number of correct answers) in comparison to the average score of 26 as reported for the adult population reported in the original study [2].

Participants

The experiment was completed by 131,785 first-time participants. To match the populations used in the original study (British students and general British adult population), we selected participants who reported currently living in the United Kingdom and being native speakers of English, and excluded participants who reported having an impairment affecting their ability to use a computer. To match the age distribution of the student population, we selected participants aged 19–22 and to match the general adult population we selected participants aged 36 through 75. Table 5 summarizes the demographics of the participants in both the original study and in our analysis.

Measures and Analysis

The main dependent variable was the score, computed as the number of images for which a correct emotion was given. For each sub-population included in the study, we first used an F-test to test for significant differences in variance in scores. Because no such differences were found, we compared mean scores using a t-test for independent samples with equal variances. For both analyses, we applied Bonferroni correction to account for multiple hypotheses being tested.

Results

Table 6 contrasts results from the original study with those obtained on LabintheWild. While adult British participants had slightly higher scores on LabintheWild than in lab and while British student-aged female participants had slightly higher scores in lab than on LabintheWild, none of these differences were statistically significant. There were also no statistically significant differences in the variances across the two experimental settings for any of the four populations. In summary, the results suggest that LabintheWild participants put in as much effort as those in the laboratory study.

We conducted an additional analysis of variance for all participants who reported being native speakers of English, who were at least 11 years old, who provided gender information, and who were currently living in the same country in which they grew up. We excluded participants from countries for which fewer than 100 such participants were available. In the end, 59,934 participants from 10 countries were included in this analysis. After controlling for age and gender, we observed a significant effect of country ($F_{9,59917} = 8.9, p < 0.0001$). Post hoc Tukey HSD test revealed that this effect can be explained by scores from India and Malaysia being significantly lower than those from Australia, Singapore, New Zealand, United States, United Kingdom and Canada. Given these results, we find it likely that the test is sensitive to participants' prior cultural exposure (the way emotions are communicated in media and in person; exposure to facial features of a particular ethnic group) and that it may not be robust for comparing participants from substantially different cultures.

In summary, our results showed no significant differences in mean scores or score variance between the participants from the original in-lab experiment and the equivalent sample of LabintheWild participants. However, an analysis of a broader sample of native English speakers indicated a significant effect of country, suggesting that the design of this test may be culture specific.

Participants' Role in Ensuring Data Quality

The results of the three experiment replications show that the data obtained in online studies with uncompensated study participants can be as reliable as data collected in lab. However, the uncontrolled environment online means that participants might have technical difficulties, they might get distracted, or they might deliberately try to "cheat" to get a better result. We found that an essential part of LabintheWild studies is asking participants to leave open-ended comments at the end of an experiment to report on possible distractions, technical difficulties, or cheating. About 5% of participants (depending on the experiment) leave feedback in these comment boxes. We learned from the comments that participants are taking the tests in various situations and locations, and that this often leads to distractions or interruptions by other humans or even pets:

> *My daughter came in and I missed one picture.* [P42515, aesthetics test]

> *cat sat briefly on keyboard.* [P36211, aesthetics test]

Participants' comments also made us aware of potential distractions resulting from the lack of control over other software running on their computers and disrupting the participant while taking a test:

> *I had a software update popup during one of the slides, which prevented me from viewing the image, and so I may have given an average rating, when I might have rated it otherwise.* [P4958, aesthetics test]

> *my friend spoke to me in a voice chat client halfway through.* [P933, memory test].

The diversity of LabintheWild participants also means that participants can be more systematically distracted or unable to perform the test at their best due to temporary or long-term conditions:

> *I suddenly lost hearing in my right ear during the first set of images. As a result I was a bit disoriented and confused for a little while and this may have affected my ability to accurately appraise.* [P35721, aesthetics test]

> *epilepsy* [P27753, aesthetics test]

> *I was really, REALLY drunk when I did this... and I don't in any way believe it is reflective of my true memory capacity.* [P1545, memory test]

Some comments additionally provide more context explaining why their data might not be good for inclusion:

> *Not sure if I am a good subject. I do UX professionally, and was distracted by what I perceived as usable or unusable design.* [P35395, aesthetics test]

> *I'm in a bit of a mood and probably rated a few things one or two lower than i normally would, but all of the ones i put as ones were pretty solid.* [P12134, aesthetics test]

> *Difficult to press no with my right hand. I'm right-handed and it just felt the wrong way around.* [P1212, memory test]

> *Please note that I have my screen set to Black & White, which is how I normally view the internet.* [P36395, aesthetics test]

Participants also reveal strategies that they apply to improve their performance. In response to the experiment testing the working memory processing speed, participants revealed how they supported their memory:

> *I felt it didn't test my memory so much as my ability to arrange the characters quickly into a memorable string (I put them in alphabetical then numerical order, e.g. AUVW67). Then I could just chant the string to myself constantly. Oh dear, was that cheating?* [P2257, memory test]

> *I don't know if this is cheating, but I would repeat it out loud to myself.* [P1515, memory test].

Apparently, these participants were unsure whether a particular strategy is "allowed", suggesting that instructions need to precisely address expectations on participants' behavior while taking part in an online experiment.

Participants also commented that they knowingly cheated or provided untruthful information. For example, in our aesthetics experiment with short stimulus exposure times, two participants reported employing strategies to work around the short timing:

> *You can click and hold the image, and put it into a new tab to view the image for a longer amount of time.* [P801, aesthetics test]

> *USED A PRINTSCREEN :)) FOR COUPLE OF PIC...* [P28434, aesthetics test]

Such strategies — even if not revealed by the participants — can be efficiently caught by recording the time it takes participants to provide answers and removing outliers before analysis. However, there is no straightforward way to deal with dishonest responses to demographic questions, except to rely on participants' comments. In fact, we found that even when demographic questions are voluntary, participants sometimes admit to having provided wrong information:

> *I shaved a few years from my actual age - still same decade.* [P40989, aesthetics test]

> *I said I was 99.* [P8508, memory test]

While participants' corrections are essential for us, we currently do not know how many participants provide wrong information or cheat without revealing it later.

Discussion

Replicating three experiments from the literature on LabintheWild, the previous sections confirm that the data collected in an unsupervised online environment without compensating participants can replicate in-lab study results. Our findings suggest that this setting enables reliable data quality for both subjective and performance-based experiments.

We also showed how providing participants with the option to leave comments leads around 5% of them to report untruthful behavior, distractions, or unusual settings and situations that might have compromised the quality of the data. Many of these comments show that participants are distracted by other humans, pets, a TV, or computer software that diverts their attention. Participants also report on health conditions that impact their performance. These comments can inform necessary changes of instructions, the experiment design, or the feedback pages, and therefore provide essential support for iteratively improving experiments.

GENERAL DISCUSSION

One of the first questions we ask ourselves before designing an experiment for LabintheWild is "What can participants learn from this?". By offering participants personalized feedback on their performance, we have been able to conduct a variety of studies that, at first, might seem to have little intrinsic appeal. For example, our study of cross-cultural differences in aesthetic appeal involved rating 60 websites, which can be a tedious and exhausting task. Yet this study attracted more than 42,000 participants who provided as reliable ratings as participants in lab. Performing a series of Fitt's law tasks (clicking on a number of dots on the screen) for five minutes, as in our study of age-related differences in motor performance, is usually perceived as monotonous and tiring, yet the experiment was completed by more than 550,000 participants. In some cases, the measurement we report back to the participants is close to the one we are interested in. For example, in the study of cross-cultural differences in aesthetic appeal, participants were able to compare their own preferences to those of other people in their country. If the measurement related to our research interest might not be exciting for participants, we find another facet of the results that might be more suitable. In the case of the study on age-related differences in motor performance, we did not compare participants' motor performance to others, but instead "guessed" participants' age based on their mouse movements and pointing behavior.

The feedback provided by the experiments also appears to be the feature that most influences people's decision to share the studies with others. Participants share their experience in their online social networks, in blog posts, or newspaper articles, with the result that LabintheWild receives traffic from more than 5,000 referral sources.

Although LabintheWild is currently only available in English, previous experiments have already attracted participant samples that are more diverse than those of conventional laboratory studies and even those on Mechanical Turk. In particular, LabintheWild participants have a wider age range and come from a larger number of countries across six continents. This has enabled us to conduct comparisons of factors influencing subjective perception of aesthetic appeal between more than 40 countries and various demographic groups in the past [32], suggesting that LabintheWild is a feasible tool for conducting cross-cultural studies.

However, LabintheWild's participant sample is still far from being perfectly representative of the broader population. Because people hear about LabintheWild through social media channels and web pages, the sample is almost certainly biased towards people who frequently use the Internet, and are most likely more WEIRD (in particular, more educated, more industrialized, and richer) than the actual world population. The comparison-based incentives might additionally attract particular kinds of participants. As the demographics data across nine experiments (Table 3) show, even different experiments on LabintheWild attract slightly different populations. Understanding why varying demographic groups are drawn to certain experiments will be part of our immediate next steps. Much of our future work will therefore focus on attracting even more diverse samples: Apart from translating the content into a variety of languages, we are also in the process of making experiments available for use on touchpads and smartphones in the hope of reaching different kinds of populations.

All LabintheWild experiments are currently 5–15 minutes long on the assumption that participants would be unlikely to choose to participate in a longer study. Researching the influence of the length of studies on participant recruitment, engagement, and data quality will be one of our immediate next steps. Study duration is one aspect where Mechanical Turk compares favorably to LabintheWild: While recruiting participants on Mechanical Turk for studies that last 30 minutes or more is a matter of increasing the financial compensation, we currently do not know whether the social comparison feedback on LabintheWild will be sufficient for recruiting and engaging similarly large numbers of participants.

In addition, many LabintheWild visitors arrive with the intention of participating in a specific study. It typically takes a few weeks for a new study to receive as much traffic as the established ones. Even though most LabintheWild studies eventually attract thousands of participants, recruiting participants via online labor markets is still a more effective recruitment mechanism when immediate participation is required.

It is important to note that the goal of LabintheWild is not to replace laboratory studies or experiments on Mechanical Turk. LabintheWild is intended to complement existing methods by enabling large scale replications of previous results, the extension of results with more diverse subject populations, and the generation of new results with studies that do not require specialized hardware or direct supervision of participants. In-lab studies will remain the best option for conducting experiments that require controlled settings, close observation of participant behavior, or specific devices. Mechanical Turk is arguably the best option for fast recruitment of participants and it is effective for recruiting participants for studies longer than 15 minutes. It might also be a better option for experiments that cannot be packaged into intrinsically motivating stories.

CONCLUSION

This research has addressed the issue that most research findings in HCI, psychology, behavioral economics, and related fields are based on studies with WEIRD (i.e., Western, Educated, Industrialized, Rich and Democratic) participants, and thus, might not generalize to other populations [1, 17]. Our goal was to find a way to conduct experiments with larger sample sizes including participants from non-WEIRD populations, and without compromising the data quality.

Reporting on almost two years of experience with our online experiment platform LabintheWild, we showed that online experiments that provide interesting personalized feedback (but no money) in exchange for study participation can fulfil this goal: LabintheWild attracts more than 1,000 participants on an average day, the sample population is significantly more diverse in terms of geographic dispersion and demographic composition than what is common in laboratory studies, and LabintheWild experiments accurately replicate the results of in-lab studies.

We additionally analyzed statistics derived from Google Analytics, tweets that mention LabintheWild, and participants' qualitative feedback to explain who the participants are, how they hear about LabintheWild, why they participate, and how they contribute to ensuring the reliability of data.

Our findings emphasize the power of social comparison: In their tweets and comments, participants repeatedly refer to the personalized feedback that enables them to compare themselves to others. This is the main factor in motivating participants to recruit others, generating a self-perpetuating recruitment mechanism that spreads around the world. After less than two years, LabintheWild participants now come from 200 countries on six continents and have a variety of demographic backgrounds.

Our experience with LabintheWild demonstrates that many people are willing to contribute. Over the course of almost two years, we not only saw large numbers of participants volunteer the time, but we also received an overwhelming number of comments and emails containing feedback on technical issues, experiment design, suggestions for improvements, people offering help with the recruitment, sending us translations of our studies, or even offering the donation of bitcoins. We believe that one of our main future tasks should be to give back, perhaps by creating more ways for participants and researchers to interact, and by providing meaningful learning opportunities. Exploring participants' role in recruiting others, designing and debugging experiments, and analyzing and interpreting the data will be exciting avenues in the future.

DATA SETS

The data sets used for the analyses of the three replication experiments can be accessed at www.labinthewild.org/data.

ACKNOWLEDGMENTS

We thank the members of the Test My Brain project: Ken Nakayama, Laura Germine, and Sam Anthony for sharing expertise and code. Ofra Amir, Sarita Yardi Schoenebeck, and Trevor Croxson provided valuable feedback on the earlier drafts of this manuscript. Yuechen Zhao, Dianna Hu, Jonathan Taratuta-Titus, Rishav Mukherji, and William Xiao contributed to the implementation of LabintheWild. We also thank the Intelligent Interactive Systems Group at Harvard, and in particular Kenneth Arnold, for brainstorming the name for the platform, as well as experiment incentives and slogans. This work was funded in part by a research fellowship from the Alfred P. Sloan foundation, by a grant from the Harvard Mind Brain and Behavior Initiative, and by the Swiss National Science Foundation.

REFERENCES

1. Arnett, J. The neglected 95%: Why American psychology needs to become less American. *American Psychologist 63(7)* (2008), 602–14.
2. Baron-Cohen, S., Wheelwright, S., Hill, J., Raste, Y., and Plumb, I. The "Reading the Mind in the Eyes" Test revised version: A study with normal adults, and adults with Asperger syndrome or high-functioning autism. *Journal of child psychology and psychiatry, and allied disciplines 42*, 2 (Feb. 2001), 241–251.
3. Berinsky, A. J., Huber, G. A., and Lenz, G. S. Using Mechanical Turk as a subject recruitment tool for experimental research. *Political Analysis 20* (2012), 351–68.
4. Buhrmester, M., Kwang, T., and Gosling, S. D. Amazon's Mechanical Turk: A new source of inexpensive, yet high-quality, data? *Perspectives on Psychological Science 6*, 1 (2011), 3–5.
5. Cavanagh, J. P. Relation between the immediate memory span and the memory search rate. *Psychological Review 79*, 6 (1972), 525–530.
6. Cavanagh, J. P., and Chase, W. G. The equivalence of target and nontarget processing in visual search. *Perception & Psychophysics 9*, 6 (Nov. 1971), 493–495.
7. Chase, W. G., and Calfee, R. C. Modality and similarity effects in short-term recognition memory. *J Exp Psychol 81*, 3 (1969), 510–514.
8. Corbin, L., and Marquer, J. Effect of a simple experimental control: The recall constraint in Sternberg's memory scanning task. *European Journal of Cognitive Psychology 20*, 5 (Sept. 2008), 913–935.
9. Cruse, D., and Clifton, Jr, C. Recoding strategies and the retrieval of information from memory. *Cognitive Psychology 4*, 2 (1973), 157–193.
10. Downs, J. S., Holbrook, M. B., Sheng, S., and Cranor, L. F. Are your participants gaming the system?: Screening Mechanical Turk workers. In *Proc. CHI'10*, ACM (2010), 2399–2402.
11. Eriksson, K., and Simpson, B. Emotional reactions to losing explain gender differences in entering a risky lottery. *Judgment and Decision Making 5*, 3 (2010), 159–163.
12. Festinger, L. A theory of social comparison processes. *Human relations 7(2)* (1954), 117–140.
13. Germine, L., Nakayama, K., Duchaine, B. C., Chabris, C. F., Chatterjee, G., and Wilmer, J. B. Is the web as good as the lab? comparable performance from web and lab in cognitive/perceptual experiments. *Psychonomic bulletin & review 19*, 5 (2012), 847–857.
14. Glaser, B. G., and Strauss, A. L. *The discovery of grounded theory: Strategies for qualitative research.* Transaction Publishers, 2009.
15. Goodman, J. K., Cryder, C. E., and Cheema, A. Data collection in a flat world: The strengths and weaknesses of mechanical turk samples. *Journal of Behavioral Decision Making 26*, 3 (2013), 213–224.
16. Heer, J., and Bostock, M. Crowdsourcing graphical perception: Using Mechanical Turk to assess visualization design. In *Proc. CHI'10* (2010), 203–212.

17. Henrich, J., Heine, S. J., and Norenzayan, A. The weirdest people in the world. *Behavioral and Brain Sciences 33* (2010), 61–83.

18. Horton, J. J., Rand, D. G., and Zeckhauser, R. J. The online laboratory: Conducting experiments in a real labor market. *Experimental Economics* (2011).

19. Ipeirotis, P. Demographics of Mechanical Turk. NYU Working Paper No. CEDER-10-01, March 2010.

20. Ipeirotis, P. G. Analyzing the Amazon Mechanical Turk marketplace. *XRDS: Crossroads, The ACM Magazine for Students 17*, 2 (2010), 16–21.

21. Kapelner, A., and Chandler, D. Preventing satisficing in online surveys. In *Proceedings of CrowdConf* (2010).

22. Kittur, A., Chi, E. H., and Suh, B. Crowdsourcing user studies with Mechanical Turk. In *Proc. CHI'08*, ACM (2008), 453–456.

23. Komarov, S., Reinecke, K., and Gajos, K. Z. Crowdsourcing performance evaluations of user interfaces. In *Proc. CHI'13* (2013), 207–216.

24. Kristofferson, M. W. Effects of practice on character-classification performance. *Canadian Journal of Psychology/Revue canadienne de psychologie 26*, 1 (1972), 54–60.

25. Lindgaard, G., Fernandes, G., Dudek, C., and Brown, J. Attention web designers: You have 50 milliseconds to make a good first impression! *Behaviour & Information Technology 25*, 2 (2006), 115–126.

26. Mason, W., and Suri, S. Conducting behavioral research on Amazon's Mechanical Turk. *Behavior research methods 44*, 1 (2012), 1–23.

27. Nickerson, R. S. Response times with a memory-dependent decision task. *J Exp Psychol 72*, 5 (Nov. 1966), 761–769.

28. Oppenheimer, D., Meyvis, T., and Davidenko, N. Instructional manipulation checks: Detecting satisficing to increase statistical power. *Journal of Experimental Social Psychology 45*, 4 (2009), 867–872.

29. Orne, M. T. Demand characteristics and the concept of quasi-controls. In *Artifacts in Behavioral Research*, R. Rosenthal and R. L. Rosnow, Eds. Oxford University Press, July 2009, ch. 5.

30. Paolacci, G., Chandler, J., and Ipeirotis, P. G. Running experiments on Amazon Mechanical Turk. *Judgment and Decision making 5*, 5 (2010), 411–419.

31. Rand, D. G. The promise of Mechanical Turk: How online labor markets can help theorists run behavioral experiments. *Journal of theoretical biology* (2012).

32. Reinecke, K., and Gajos, K. Z. Quantifying visual preferences around the world. In *Proc. CHI'14*, ACM (2014), 11–20.

33. Reinecke, K., Nguyen, M. K., Bernstein, A., Näf, M., and Gajos, K. Z. Doodle around the world: Online scheduling behavior reflects cultural differences in time perception and group decision-making. In *Proc. CSCW'13*, ACM (2013), 45–54.

34. Shaw, A. D., Horton, J. J., and Chen, D. L. Designing incentives for inexpert human raters. In *Proc. CSCW'11*, ACM (2011), 275–284.

35. Sternberg, S. High-speed scanning in human memory. *Science 153*, 3736 (Aug. 1966), 652–654.

36. Sternberg, S. Two operations in character recognition: Some evidence from reaction-time measurements. *Perception & Psychophysics 2*, 2 (1967), 45–53.

37. Sternberg, S. Memory scanning: New findings and current controversies. *The Quarterly journal of experimental psychology 27*, 1 (1975), 1–32.

38. Suri, S., and Watts, D. Cooperation and contagion in networked public goods experiments. *Arxiv preprint arXiv10081276* (2010).

39. Woolley, A. W., Chabris, C. F., Pentland, A., Hashmi, N., and Malone, T. W. Evidence for a collective intelligence factor in the performance of human groups. *science 330*, 6004 (2010), 686–688.

Social Barriers Faced by Newcomers Placing Their First Contribution in Open Source Software Projects

Igor Steinmacher
Department of Computing
Federal University of Technology – Paraná
igorfs@utfpr.edu.br

Tayana Uchôa Conte
Institute of Computing
Federal University of Amazonas
tayana@icomp.ufam.edu.br

Marco Aurélio Gerosa
Institute of Mathematics and Statistics
University of São Paulo
gerosa@ime.usp.br

David F. Redmiles
Department of Informatics
University of California, Irvine
redmiles@ics.uci.edu

ABSTRACT
Newcomers' seamless onboarding is important for online communities that depend upon leveraging the contribution of outsiders. Previous studies investigated aspects of the joining process and motivation in open collaboration communities, but few have focused on identifying and understanding the critical barriers newcomers face when placing their first contribution, a period that frequently leads to dropout. This is important for Open Source Software (OSS) projects, which receive contributions from many one-time contributors. Focusing on OSS, our study qualitatively analyzed social barriers that hindered newcomers' first contributions. We defined a conceptual model composed of 58 barriers including 13 social barriers. The barriers were identified from a qualitative data analysis considering different sources: a systematic literature review; open question responses gathered from OSS projects' contributors; students contributing to OSS projects; and semi-structured interviews with 36 developers from 14 different projects. This paper focuses on social barriers and its contributions include gathering empirical evidence of the barriers faced by newcomers, organizing and better understanding these barriers, surveying the literature from the perspective of the barriers, and identifying new potential research streams.

Author Keywords
Onboarding; barriers; joining; open source software; newcomers; social barriers; entry; new contributor; barriers; socialization; qualitative study; open collaboration; online communities

ACM Classification Keywords
D.2.9 [Management]: Programming teams, K.4.3 [Organizational Impacts]

General Terms
Human Factors

INTRODUCTION
Open collaboration communities leverage and depend on new contributors [23]. According to Qureshi and Fang [60], motivating, engaging, and retaining new contributors promotes a sustainable community. Kraut et al. [45] claim that newcomers are a source of innovation, new ideas, and work procedures.

According to Forte and Lampe [23], open collaboration relies on an online environment that presents a low barrier to entry. However, during the onboarding period, newcomers may be susceptible to several barriers such as expectation breakdowns, reception problems, setup misconfiguration, and learning curve. Each of these may have varying levels of importance to and impact on the overall joining process.

To better support newcomers' onboarding, barriers must be identified and understood. Focusing on open source software (OSS) development communities,, in which newcomers are usually left to learn on their own [64], the qualitative study described in this paper aimed to identify, understand, and organize the barriers faced by newcomers. Since OSS communities require developers with specific skills, and delivering a task to an OSS project is usually a long, multi-step process, some newcomers may lose motivation and even give up contributing if there are too many barriers to overcome during this process. As Karl Fogel [22] states, *"if a project doesn't make a good first impression", newcomers may wait a long time before giving it a second chance."*

Previous research related to newcomers' joining process examined the dynamics driving OSS contributors, mostly focusing on the motivations for becoming a member, roadmaps to becoming a core developer, or indicators of potential long-term commitment [29,35,65,83,85]. An understudied aspect of the OSS joining process is what happens during the period after a newcomer decides to participate and before their first code contribution is accepted and included in the shared repository. This period is particularly relevant to OSS projects, as many newcomers do not want to join or remain at the project, only to post a single contribution (e.g., a bug correction or a new feature). What happens in this period affects, for example, students in computer courses whose assignments include OSS project contribution, and professional developers who find a bug or wish to customize a particular software product. With a more in-depth understanding of the barriers, researchers and community can invest their efforts in building or improving tools and processes, ultimately gaining more contributions, such as '*drive-by commits*' [57], which are small changes made by developers who are only casually or briefly interested in a project and do not intend to have a prolonged engagement.

CSCW '15, March 14 - 18 2015, Vancouver, BC, Canada

ACM 978-1-4503-2922-4/15/03...$15.00
http://dx.doi.org/10.1145/2675133.2675215

In this study, we qualitatively analyzed four different sources: (i) a systematic literature review (SLR) aimed at identifying the literature's empirically evidenced barriers; (ii) feedback from 9 students after they contributed to OSS projects; (iii) 24 open-question responses from 9 OSS projects; and (iv) semi-structured interviews with 36 developers from 14 different projects, including newcomers, dropouts, and experienced members. To analyze this data, we used Grounded Theory procedures [76]. We found 58 barriers, which we organized into 6 main categories comprising technical and social barriers. The 45 technical barriers primarily relate to running or developing environments' domain technologies and concepts, documentation, and source-code; the remaining 13 social barriers, which were similar across different projects and are the focus of this paper, relate to issues that arose from the relationship between the newcomers and the established community.

The contributions of this paper include: (i) providing detailed empirical evidence of the social barriers faced by newcomers to OSS projects, which was drawn from data obtained from 69 practitioners contributing to 19 different projects; (ii) relating this empirical evidence to results from 21 studies identified in a systematic literature review, as well as to related studies on open collaboration communities; (iii) organizing the barriers into a single model; and (iv) providing a discussion of the social barriers (and possible mitigation strategies) in the context of CSCW and related literature. We hope that OSS communities and researchers will take advantage of this paper to better understand the barriers in their context and design strategies to deal with them.

This paper is organized as follows: related work; data collection and analysis method, resulting conceptual model; some discussion; and conclusions.

RELATED WORK

Many barriers influence open communities newcomer behavior and permanence. In the following subsection, we present significant findings related to social barriers in several online communities, such as Wikipedia, Reddit, MovieLens, Facebook, and Q&A communities. Afterwards, we delve into the literature on OSS projects, this paper's focus.

Newcomers in Various Open Collaboration Communities

Perhaps due to its new contributors decline [26], Wikipedia has been the subject of several studies, including Zhu et al.'s [87], which identified that received feedback influences newcomers' engagement. In addition, Halfaker et al. [27] and Suh et al. [77] found that newcomers are negatively impacted by how many edit reverts they suffer. From a more positive angle, Choi et al. [13] found that welcome messages, technical assistance, and constructive criticism over time retarded the natural decline in newcomers' editing. Similarly, Faulkner et al. [21] found that modifying first time warnings prompted additional newcomer contribution. Offering a sentiment that seems to undergird each of these studies' implications, Halfaker et al. [26] concluded that *"Wikipedia has changed from the encyclopedia that anyone can edit to the encyclopedia that anyone who understands the norms, socializes himself or herself, dodges the impersonal wall of semi-automated rejection, and still wants to voluntarily contribute his or her time and energy can edit."*

Recent studies have also focused on other online communities, including social media, support, and discussion networks. Burke et al. [8] analyzed Facebook newcomers and found that when newcomers learn by example and receive proper feedback, one can more easily predict their future contributions. Wang et al. [81] investigated an online health support group, finding that participants exposed to both emotional and informational support demonstrated lower dropout rates. Lampe and Johnston [49] analysis of Slashdot newcomers revealed that new, un-moderated commenters were less likely to post a second comment. Similar conclusions were drawn by Joyce and Kraut [39], who analyzed Usenet group newcomers.

Newcomers to Open Source Software Projects

Developer motivation and project attractiveness are well-explored OSS research topics [52,63,68,83], and many studies also investigate how newcomers join projects and become core project members [18,19,47,51,54]. Motivation and project attractiveness entice outsiders and bring them into the joining process. However, contribution barriers can impede developers from completing the joining process. These barriers comprise technical and social impediments, including steep learning curve, lack of community support, and difficulties finding out how to start. Furthermore, these barriers influence both developers who are willing to make a single contribution and those who are willing to progress and become a project member. Given their importance, remarkably little is known about these barriers.

Many papers in the literature focus on the joining process by defining stages and activities in the path to becoming core members or long-term contributors. For instance, the Onion Model [54,83] was presented as a general layered structure to organize OSS project member roles as well as the process a developer needs to follow in order to contribute. Jergensen et al. [35] studied whether this model still held true in large project ecosystems, finding little evidence that individuals migrate from the edges of a project to the core through a gradual socialization process. Herraiz et al. [31] found that at least 52.5% of developers commit before sending a message to the mailing list, thereby contradicting the onion model. They also found two groups with clearly different joining patterns: volunteer and hired developers. Whereas volunteers tend to follow a systematic joining process, hired developers usually experience a quick integration. In addition to the Onion Model, other studies mapping the OSS project joining process include Von Krogh et al. [47], which proposed the concept of a joining script. Ducheneaut [18] similarly analyzed mailing list archives, offering an in-depth look at a successful newcomer's socialization history. Based on this individual, the author identified a set of socialization activities that contributed to his success.

Other parts of the literature focus on the forces of motivation and attractiveness that drive newcomers toward projects. Lakhani and Wolf [48], for example, found that extrinsic benefits (e.g.; better jobs, career advancement) primarily motivate new contributors, together with enjoyment, challenges derived from writing code, and improved programming skills. Hars and Ou [29] reported that internal motivation plays a role, but note that external factors, such as building human capital and personal software solution needs, are more influential. Shah [68] distinguished between two different contributors: need-driven and hobbyists. Hertel et al. [32] identified seven factors as distinct motivational sources. Several other studies dealt with motivation in OSS [4,16,38,40,46,56,62]. Moreover, motivation is generally extensively studied in software engineering [2,24,25,69,84]. Attractiveness is also a force influenced by several characteristics, such as license [63], source code attributes [50,52], and code base [12].

Regarding newcomers' retention and long-term contribution, Qureshi and Fang [60] quantitatively identified four distinct classes of newcomer retention behavior, considering their initial amount of interactions with core members and the growth of these interactions. Fang and Neufeld [19] qualitatively revealed that initial participation conditions do not effectively predict long-term participation, but that situated learning and identity-construction behaviors were positively linked to sustained participation. Other research revealed that retention is influenced by the familiarity with the project's coordination practices [65] and individual's attitude [85].

While the current literature focuses on motivation and forces that lead developers to the project's core, studies neglect those newcomers who do not envision a long-term engagement as well as those who want to place a single contribution. Counterexamples include Hannebaun et al. [28] and Steinmacher et al. [74], which explicitly focus on barriers that influence newcomers' first contribution. Some other studies proposed ways to help newcomers' first contributions. Wolff-Marting et al. [82], for example, proposed two patterns to support newcomers in overcoming contribution barriers. Also aiming to support newcomers, Cubranic et al. [14] presented Hipikat, a tool that builds a group memory comprising source code, email discussions, and bug trackers. The tool enables newcomers to request recommendations based on existent artifacts. With a similar goal in mind, Wang and Sarma [79] presented a tool to enable newcomers to identify bugs of interest and resources related to that bug, as well as to visually and interactively explore the bug's appropriate socio-technical dependencies. Canfora et al. [9] proposed and evaluated an approach to identifying and recommending mentors for open source project newcomers by mining data from mailing lists and source code versioning systems.

As opposed to the traditional focus on motivation, attractiveness, and retention in OSS projects, our study focused specifically on the initial contribution barriers. Other studies cite barriers that influence newcomers' overall experiences, however do not provide an in-depth understanding of the barriers, their relations, and their relevance in multiple projects. Thus, knowledge about contribution barriers is spread thin across the literature, and there is little exploration of the barriers faced by newcomers who ultimately stop contributing or do not become members.

Additionally, we observed that the majority of the related research on specific barrier effects in open collaboration communities (including OSS) predominantly relied on quantitative evidence. Those that qualitatively uncovered barriers [6,18,19,20,47,78] missed research questions or objectives related to the identification of first contribution barriers faced by newcomers.

In this paper, we systematically review the OSS literature and discuss it in the context of the evidenced data from practitioners and from the literature of open collaboration communities. Our study aims to provide this neglected in-depth understanding of the initial contribution barriers and to add to the dominant quantitative-based research on newcomers' joining process.

METHOD

Our study aimed to identify and understand the barriers that hinder newcomers from posting their first contribution to an OSS project. We chose a qualitative approach [17] because this phenomena occurs in a complex, social environment, in which the context of its occurrence is important. Moreover, a qualitative view complements the existing literature, which relies mostly on quantitative evidence.

Our study relied on four different sources: a systematic literature review; feedback from students after having them attempt to contribute to OSS projects; responses to an open-ended question sent to OSS communities; and interviews with both newcomers and experienced OSS project members. Three models emerged from these studies, and we compiled these models to generate a broad model of barriers for newcomers to OSS.

Figure 1 depicts the method followed. The first data set was collected from students who contributed to OSS projects. From their feedback, we noticed that there were recurrently reported barriers. Motivated by the students' reports, we conducted a systematic literature review to identify the available research related to these barriers. From the literature review, we built a model reporting what was already published in OSS domain. To gather more understanding about the phenomena, and to check how the practice was related to the literature, we surveyed a small set of OSS developers. We analyzed the data from these practitioners alongside the data from the students to conceive a preliminary model of barriers. The results of this preliminary model were used as input for an in-depth investigation. This investigation was made by means of semi-structured interviews conducted with both experienced members and newcomers in order to identify and explore the barriers from different perspectives. By analyzing data from different sources and perspectives, we aimed for a broad understanding of the barriers.

In the following, we detail the methods used to conduct the systematic review and the practitioner interviews.

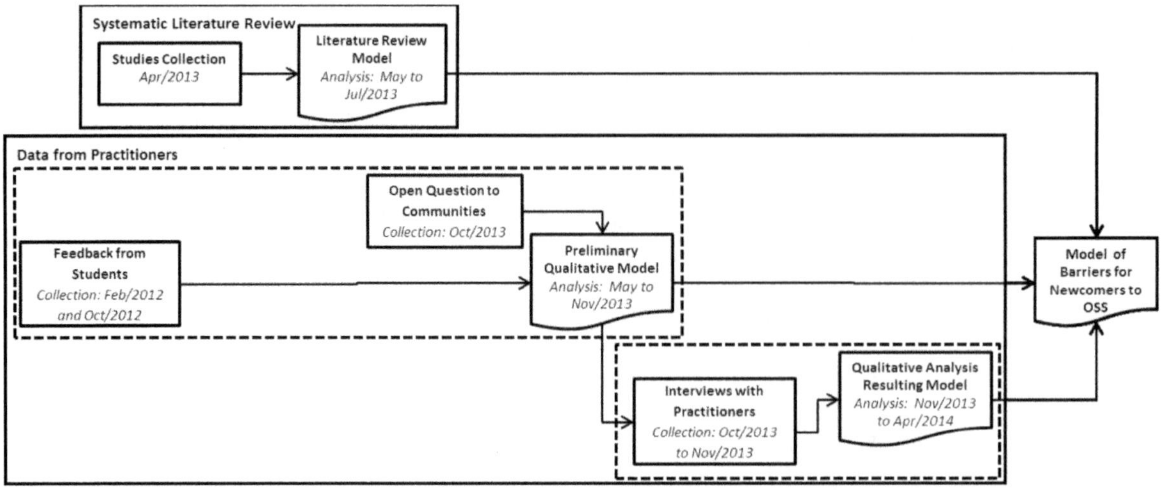

Figure 1: Research Method

Systematic Literature Review

We conducted a systematic literature review to identify the empirically evidenced and reported barriers [73]. The goal was to generate a list of the barriers newcomers encounter that can influence their first project contributions. We then aggregated the barriers evidenced by the different studies in a single model. Since we were interested in comparing the empirical data collected from the practitioners, we restricted the systematic review to the OSS domain.

This study has been undertaken as a systematic literature review (SLR) based upon guidelines established by Kitchenham et al. [41,42]. The following question guided our SLR: *What are the barriers that influence newcomers' onboarding to OSS projects?*

After some iterative refining, the following query was used to retrieve the studies from the ACM, IEEE, Scopus, and Springer Link digital libraries. These libraries were selected because they index relevant venues for this study, support searches using Boolean expression, and provide access to complete texts. The search was performed in April 2013.

```
("OSS" OR "Open Source" OR "Free Software" OR FLOSS OR
FOSS) AND (newcomer OR "joining process" OR newbie OR
"new developer" OR "new member" OR "new contributor" OR
novice OR beginner OR "potential participant" OR
retention OR joiner OR onboarding OR "new committer")
```

We considered for selection papers that were available for download, written in English, dealt with newcomers' OSS project onboarding, presented empirical results, and were published in peer-reviewed journals or event proceedings. We excluded studies that analyzed only newcomers' motivation for joining a project. We focused on the issues newcomers face after deciding to contribute.

For each selected paper, we conducted snowball sampling [33], checking if the authors of the selected studies published other relevant studies not retrieved from the digital libraries. We checked their profiles in ACM, IEEE, DBLP, and personal homepages (when available).

After running the query on the digital libraries systems, our resulting sample comprised 291 candidate papers. For each paper, two independent researchers analyzed title, abstract, and keywords. In a consensus meeting, we agreed on 33 papers. We checked other papers published by the authors of these 33 candidate studies, finding 20 other candidate papers. After analyzing these papers, we selected nine relevant papers, resulting in 42 candidate papers. After further analysis, 21 papers were deemed relevant and were considered for data extraction. Next, we applied Grounded Theory procedures [76] (open and axial coding) to classify the barriers reported in the selected studies [73].

Data from practitioners

This subsection presents the method for the qualitative practitioner study. We gathered this data from: (i) students that contributed to OSS projects; (ii) answers to an open question sent to OSS projects; and (iii) semi-structured interviews with newcomers to and members of OSS projects.

The first source comprised feedback received from four PhD candidates and five undergraduate students who contributed to OSS projects as part of a course assignment. All the students were newcomers to the projects they were contributing to. The PhD candidates were all males, experienced developers, and 30 years old or older. The undergraduate students, including four males and one female ranging between 21 and 24 years old, were attending the last semester of the Internet Systems course and therefore were preparing to join the software development industry. The students received an assignment to contribute to an OSS project.

The students contributed to JabRef (2 graduate/1 undergraduate), LibreOffice (3 undergraduate), and Mozilla Firefox (3 graduate) projects. After the conclusion of the assignment, their feedback was collected by means of an open-ended questionnaire. The open questions enabled students to debrief and explain the problems they faced while trying to place their first code contribution. The data was collected at the end of the course (February 2012 for the graduate students and October 2012 for the undergraduate students).

The second data source comprised answers to a questionnaire sent to OSS project developers. The data was obtained from 24 answers to an open question sent to OSS project mailing lists and forums. The messages were posted and the answers received during October 2013. We sent messages to nine projects from different domains: Apache OpenOffice, aTunes, Audacity, LibreOffice, emacs, FreePlane, jEdit, Mozilla Firefox, and OpenVPN. None of these projects delivers development frameworks or scaffolding technologies, which are generally more complex, demanding a higher degree of specific skills and knowledge. These characteristics could hide some possible barriers encountered by newcomers, since they could face complex problems related to the inherent project technology and domain.

The questionnaire delivered to the community members comprised two questions designed to profile the contributor (project and contribution time) as well as an open question: "*In your opinion, what are the main difficulties faced by newcomers when they want to start contributing to this project? (Consider technical and non-technical issues).*" We received 24 complete answers to the questionnaire, as detailed in Table 1.

Table 1. Project to which participants mainly contribute (left) and Period of contribution for questionnaire respondents (right)

Project	Count
LibreOffice	6
OpenOffice	3
aTunes	3
Mozilla Firefox	3
Audacity	2
jEdit	1
OpenVPN	1
FreePlane	1
Emacs	1
Did not inform	3

Time contributing to the project	Count
Less than 6 months	7
Between 6 months and 1 year	3
Between 1 year and 3 years	6
More than 3 years	8

The final data collection entailed semi-structured interviews with practitioners. Semi-structured interviews include a mixture of open-ended and specific questions, which are designed to elicit foreseen and unexpected information types [67]. We conducted interviews in order to complement the findings gathered from sources 1 and 2, thereby deepening and broadening our understanding of the newcomers' barriers. We recruited subjects belonging to four different groups: *Experienced Members* (project owners, managers, or developers that commit code directly to the software repository), *Successful Newcomers* (participants that started to contribute to the project less than one year before the interview), *Dropout Newcomers* (volunteers that tried to contribute to the project, but gave up), and *Onboarding Newcomers* (volunteers trying to place their first contribution).

The participants were recruited primarily through mailing list and forums from 15 different projects. In addition, we also directly invited different types of newcomers, identifying them by mining and following projects' mailing lists and issue trackers. Only adults older than 18 were eligible to participate in this study; but we made no distinction related to gender, nationality, or other identity categories. Participants were expected to have software development experience, primarily because we were interested in the barriers to contribute to a project and not to learn how to program. The interviews were conducted in English from October 2013 to March 2014.

We interviewed 36 participants from 14 different projects (Pardus, TextMate, zxing, Gephi, Hadoop, jEdit, Moodle, Integrade, Noosfero, Apache OpenOffice, cogroo, etherpad, JabRef, and LibreOffice), including 11 experienced members, 16 newcomers that succeeded, 6 dropout newcomers, and 3 newcomers that were still trying to place their first contributions.

Table 2 shows some profiling information of the students and interviewees. The participants received an ID, shown in the first column. The first character of the ID represents the profile of the participant: "S" for student, "E" for Experienced member, "N" for Successful newcomer, "D" for Dropout newcomer, and "O" for Onboarding Newcomer.

Table 2. Profile of the participants (H = Hours per week in OSS; F = First Project?; C = Country; Y = Years in the project)

ID	H	F	Project	C	Y	ID	H	F	Project	C	Y
E1	< 5	N	JabRef	FR	8	N13	10-20	N	LibreOffice	BR	1
E2	05-10	Y	Etherpad	DE	3	N14	05-10	Y	LibreOffice	BR	1
E3	10-20	N	JabRef	DE	3	N15	N/I	Y	Etherpad	FR	0
E4	05-10	N	jEdit	CA	10	N16	05-10	N	JabRef	DE	0
E5	05-10	N	LibreOffice	DE	15	D1	05-10	N	Hadoop	US	0
E6	> 20	N	LibreOffice	HU	10	D2	< 5	Y	Hadoop	IN	0
E7	> 20	N	Moodle	AU	5	D3	< 5	N	JabRef	DE	0
E8	> 20	N	Noosfero	BR	5	D4	< 5	Y	OpenOffice	BR	0
E9	> 20	N	Pardus	TR	8	D5	< 5	Y	LibreOffice	IN	0
E10	05-10	N	Cogroo	BR	5	D6	< 5	Y	OpenOffice	IN	0
E11	< 5	N	Noosfero	BR	7	O1	< 5	N	OpenOffice	IN	0
N1	< 5	Y	JabRef	DE	0	O2	10-20	Y	LibreOffice	CN	0
N2	< 5	Y	Gephi	BR	0	O3	< 5	Y	OpenOffice	GR	0
N3	05-10	Y	Gephi	IN	1	S1	N/I	N	Mozilla	BR	0
N4	05-10	Y	Moodle	IN	0	S2	N/I	Y	LibreOffice	BR	0
N5	< 5	Y	JabRef	DE	0	S3	N/I	Y	LibreOffice	BR	0
N6	< 5	Y	jEdit	US	0	S4	N/I	Y	Firefox	BR	0
N7	< 5	Y	TextMate	US	0	S5	N/I	Y	Jabref	BR	0
N8	> 20	Y	Zxing	GR	0	S6	N/I	Y	Firefox	BR	0
N9	< 5	Y	Cogroo	BR	0	S7	N/I	N	Jabref	BR	0
N10	< 5	Y	Integrade	BR	0	S8	N/I	N	Jabref	BR	0
N11	< 5	Y	Cogroo	BR	0	S9	N/I	Y	LibreOffice	BR	0
N12	N/I	N	Etherpad	UK	0						

We used a semi-structured format in which a script (interview guide) supported the interviewing process. We started with pilot interviews with five developers involved in Open Source Software Development to adjust the script. After that, we recruited the subjects and conducted the interviews. All interviews were conducted using text-based chat tools, like Google Talk, because the participants used this means of communication in their work, and because it facilitates data collection and interview scheduling.

Each interview was individually conducted and the data was saved on a local computer. Interviews began with a short explanation of the research, followed by some questions to profile the interviewees regarding their technical experience and main occupation. The questions in the interview script guided the interview, but were not necessarily directly asked.

Data Analysis

We qualitatively analyzed the data using procedures of Grounded Theory (GT) [76]. We selectively applied open coding, whereby concepts are identified and their properties and dimensions are discovered, and axial coding, whereby connections among codes are identified and grouped according to their properties to represent categories.

We split our analysis into two steps. The first (preliminary) step consisted of analyzing the data obtained from the students' feedback and the open questions sent to communities. In the second step, the codes and categories found in the preliminary study were used as seeds for the interview coding. During open coding, we assigned codes to sentences, paragraphs, or revisions. This procedure overlapped the axial coding, in which we identified connections between categories. We executed open and axial coding several times to refine the emerging codes and categories.

In the first step, open coding was conducted in parallel by three researchers. Each researcher independently quoted and coded the documents. After coding, the researchers discussed the quotes and codes until they came to a consensus for the entire document set. This was done to mitigate the bias caused by a single researcher and to reach a common understanding about the nomenclature and criteria. After the discussion, we began axial coding iterations, followed by discussions and changes in codes and categories. The result of this study was a Preliminary Qualitative Model of the barriers faced by newcomers to OSS.

For the second step, we analyzed the data obtained from the interviews. The analysis process was similar to the one applied in the first step, however, we used the codes and categories identified in the first step as seeds to the open coding. This time, a single researcher conducted open and axial coding and discussed with the other two the doubts and proposed new or merged categories.

After obtaining the model from the interview analysis, we iteratively reanalyzed the models obtained from all studies, relying on their respective data. The goal of this reanalysis was to combine the findings to create a single model accommodating all the barriers evidenced. Once again, we merged some barriers and reorganized the categories.

In the next section, we present our model. As our focus is on social barriers, we will only discuss the 13 barriers related to the relationship between newcomers and established open collaboration community.

RESULTING BARRIERS MODEL

The resulting model (Figure 2) aggregates all the barriers evidenced in the intermediate models. It comprises 58 barriers, organized in 6 categories and in several subcategories. In the following subsections, we focus on the 13 social barriers, supported by empirical evidence and related to the open collaboration communities literature.

Whenever we introduce a social barrier, we present the amount of times (different documents) that the barrier was identified per data source. The numbers represent, in order: number of studies from the SLR that evidenced the barrier (out of 21); number of students that reported the barrier in their feedback (out of 9); number of mentions in the open questions (out of 24); and number of interviewees that reported the barrier (out of 36). We also provided the number of projects in which the barriers were evidenced, considering only the data from practitioners.

Reception Issues

We identified four barriers related to reception issues, as presented in Table 3. This table presents the sources in which the barrier was evidenced and the number of times it was reported per source and per profile. Reception issues were evidenced in all sources, and were reported by both newcomers and experienced members.

Not receiving an answer (5-1-0-1, 1 project) was found to be a problem. During the feedback sessions, students reported that their forum post was never answered and they ended up working on an incorrect issue: "*They never answered our forum post. We spent a lot of effort in something that was already being done…*" [S5] In the interviews, an experienced member highlighted: "*In my opinion, the first [barrier] is not getting any reply*" [E1].

We also identified studies focusing on the reception barrier in our SLR [47,70,74,75]. Analyzing the Freenet project, von Krogh et al. [47] found that "*… only 29 (10.5%) participants did not receive any reply to their initial posting and subsequently did not appear on the developer list again.*" Singh [70] reported a similar behavior: "*non returning newcomers can be attributed to not receiving a response…*"

CSCW research similarly studies this particular barrier, and the results reported are in accordance to those in the OSS literature and evidenced in our qualitative analysis. Joyce and Kraut [39] analyzed newcomers' posts to Usenet and found that newcomers who got a reply to their first posts were 12% more likely to post to the community again. Analyzing newcomers to Slashdot, Lampe and Johnston [49] evidenced similar results.

Compounding the lack of answers, we also found delayed answers (2-1-0-3, 3 projects) to be a contribution barrier affecting newcomers' motivation: "*[a problem was] a huge delay to receive an answer. It was necessary to send more than one email to receive an answer after a week. Demotivating. I was about to give up*" [S6] It also bothered a newcomer to the Zxing project: "*The biggest 'bottleneck' would have probably been the slow pace in communication… if you have a deadline a few days every now and then it can be quite bothersome*" [N8].

Table 3. Evidences of Reception Issues per Source

Barriers	Literature	Students Feedback	Open Question: Less than 6 months	Open Question: 6 months to 3 years	Open Question: More than 3 years	Interviews: Dropouts	Interviews: Newcomers	Interviews: Experienced
Not receiving an answer	• (5)	• (1)						• (1)
Delayed answers	• (2)	• (1)					• (1)	• (2)
Impolite answers	• (2)	• (1)					• (1)	• (2)
Receiving answers with too advanced/ complex contents			• (1)				• (1)	• (1)

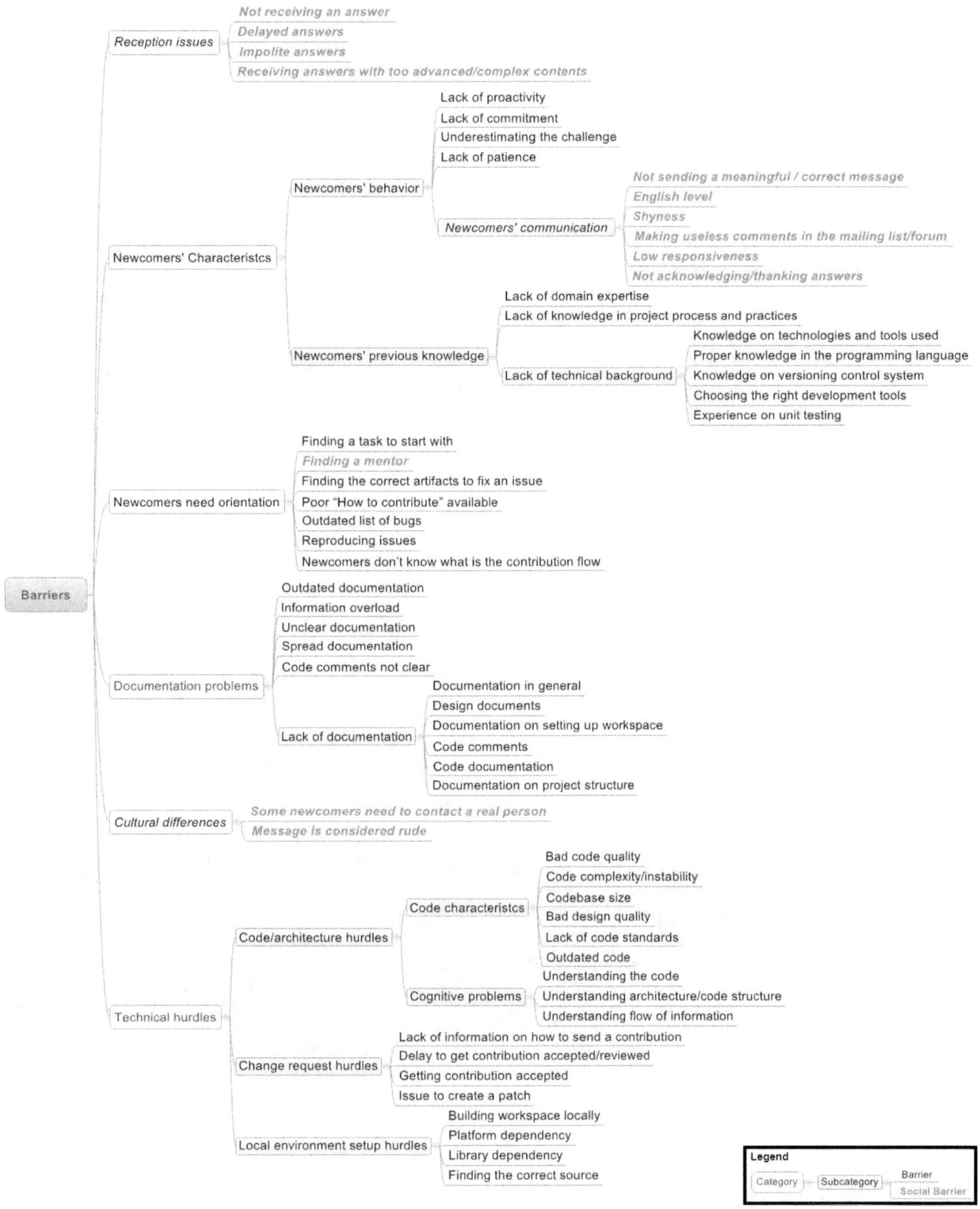

Figure 2. Model of barriers for newcomers to OSS

In the SLR, we identified evidence of this barrier in two studies [34,85]. Jensen et al. [34] analyzed the mailing lists of four OSS projects and found that "*None of the newbies who failed to receive a reply within 24 hours of posting their first question were still posting to the mailing lists beyond the study period.*" However, we could not find any specific evidence of delayed or late reply in the complementary CSCW literature analyzed for this study. Additional study may be necessary to verify whether this is an issue in other domains.

Impolite answers (2-1-0-3, 4 projects) also appeared in the students' feedback and in the interviews. For example, an experienced member reported: "*...and of course one more thing is the developers' attitude. Some developers may not be suitable for receiving newcomers, they may get angry pretty quickly and kill the interest of the newcomers. Very few of the newcomers know how to behave against this kind of tough developers*" [E9].

CSCW literature, including the studies related to OSS, confirms this barrier. One of the OSS studies [70] reported that non-returning newcomers can be attributed to receiving a condescending response. In the context of Wikipedia, Farzan and Kraut [20] reported demotivated newcomers due to experienced editors' hostile behavior. Some students complained of reversions and deletions that occurred without proper/polite explanation. Zhu et al. [86], Suh et al. [77], and Halfaker et al. [27] found that negative feedback reduced motivation in Wikipedia. And Suh et al. [77] reported that the excessive number of newcomer reverts evidence the growing resistance from the Wikipedia community to new content, especially from occasional and new editors.

Receiving answers with too advanced/complex contents (0-0-1-2, 3 projects) was another barrier evidenced in our data obtained from practitioners. In some cases, newcomers receive answers that required in-depth knowledge about the project and technologies. For example, a newcomer reported: "*The reason I didn't find the reply helpful is due to they talk a little bit out of my understanding of the project*" [O2]. Another newcomer reported a similar problem: "*I found it awesome to get a quick and nice reaction, but the suggestions I could do seemed a bit far fetched to give to a beginner*" [N8]. We could not find any literature reporting or supporting this specific finding.

From the analysis of these 4 barriers, we noticed that reception could result in a smaller number of returning newcomers. Open collaboration communities therefore ought to be attentive to newcomer reception. Indeed, welcome messages, assistance, and constructive criticism increase the retention of newcomers [13]. The literature presented automated strategies that can be used to soften reception issues [21,26], which were mainly focused on automated answer/feedback to newcomers' contributions. We are not aware of any approach like this in OSS communities, but this strategy's applicability and effectiveness in these settings should be explored and assessed.

Newcomers' Communication Behavior

Newcomers' characteristics may be barriers to project contribution. Newcomers are expected to possess a minimum requirement of previous technical background to perform a development task. In addition, the community also expects newcomers to have certain social skills. We could evidence 6 barriers under this category as presented in Table 4. Notably, only experienced members reported these barriers, whereas the newcomers did not mention their own communication behavior as possible problems.

Three experienced members reported not sending a correct / meaningful message (2-0-0-3, 2 projects) as a barrier. Community members may not answer a message if they do not understand it: "*in general I answer the questions that are well written ... some people post things that... I don't know how to answer. So, I wait until someone else makes an attempt and see if the original poster will make a better effort the second time to post something that I can understand*" [E4].

Singh [70] studied this problem in OSS forums. She demonstrated that the community responds better to informative subject lines, comprehensible posts, and correct messages, which is also studied in other CSCW domains. Burke et al. [7], for example, analyzed Usenet communities, finding that self-introductions can double the odds of receiving answers. Arguello et al. [1] also analyzed Q&A history and found that on-topic messages and use of vernacular language increased reply likelihood. Joyce and Kraut [39] also analyzed Usenet communities and reported that newcomers were more likely to receive a response if they asked a question or wrote a longer post.

A more specific and related barrier regards English level (0-0-0-4, 3 projects). English is adopted in most OSS projects. After reporting problems with incorrect messages, E4 amended: "*for some people it is due to English as a second language, I understand that but still...*" Other participant reinforced this issue: "*Having a decent English is needed*" [E1]. It is difficult to address this issue, but providing guidelines or asking for clarification may help. For larger communities, matching a newcomer to a member that speaks the same language might be helpful.

Table 4. Evidences of Newcomers' Communication Behavior per Source

Barriers	Literature	Students Feedback	Open Question			Interviews		
			Less than 6 months	6 months to 3 years	More than 3 years	Dropouts	Newcomers	Experienced
Not sending a meaningful/correct message	• (2)							• (3)
English level								• (4)
Shyness								• (2)
Making useless comments in the mailing list/forum								• (1)
Low responsiveness								• (1)
Not acknowledging/thanking answers received								• (1)

Shyness (0-0-0-2, 2 projects) was also reported as a problem. An experienced member reported that once he gave up contributing because he was shy to ask the community: *"I was trying to solve a bug... by myself. I was kind of shy to ask for help"* [E11]. Preece et al. [58] analyzed the MSN bulletin board and found that 28.3% of the lurkers gave shyness as a reason for not posting. A possible approach to deal with this issue would be "breaking the ice." As soon as newcomers subscribe, a member could approach them; automatic greetings could also be used.

For this category of barriers, we found that CSCW literature mainly studies and provides evidence on how, in order to be well received, newcomers should behave when sending their first messages. The evidence found relies on studies conducted with historical data of Q&A communities. For the other barriers, we could not find any evidence in the literature.

Finding a mentor

In accordance with Dagenais et al.'s [15] work on software projects, we found that newcomers often face unfamiliar and rugged landscapes when starting to contribute to an OSS project. Consequently, they need proper orientation to find their way into the project and to contribute correctly.

Finding a mentor (3-3-2-5, 7 projects) was identified as a social barrier for newcomers to OSS. This was evidenced in all the sources we examined, and was reported both by newcomers and experienced members, as presented in Figure 2. One newcomer gave up because of the difficulty of finding a mentor: *"... basically, see, I was not active contributor at that time ... if some meaningful direction could be provided then I would have started. This direction I didn't get ... someone with my profile ... who want to do some stuff with open source project probably some basic handholding would have helped."* [D2]

Ease in locating an expert or a mentor was also evidenced in the systematic review. Cubranic et al. [14] reported, *"It can be difficult for newcomers to join such groups [OSS projects] because it is hard to obtain effective mentoring."* To alleviate this problem, Canfora et al. [9] proposed a tool that recommends mentors to newcomers. They evaluated the tool by surveying project members, finding that mentoring is important to newcomers. There are also some mentorship-related studies in open collaboration communities. For instance, Musicant et al. [53] qualitatively analyzed data from Wikipedia's program Adopt-a-user and found that several key mentor functions are missing or not consistently fulfilled. Most adopters focus on establishing their legitimacy rather than proactively guiding, protecting, and supporting the long-term growth of adoptees. Choi et al. [13] analyzed Wikipedia socialization tactics and found that they rarely assign new members a mentor or provide clear guidance about how to behave in a project.

We observed that newcomers look for mentorship when placing their first contributions. However, as reported by Musicant et al. [53], the goal of experienced members seems to be self-promotion rather than coaching and supporting. Discovering what motivates experienced members to properly mentor newcomers is therefore likely a fruitful future research area.

Cultural Differences

Differences related to individuals' cultural backgrounds are a known problem in distributed software development [72], including OSS development [31]. Cultural differences exist in open collaboration; volunteers have diverse national, organizational, and professional backgrounds, resulting in different values, perceptions, and work behaviors. According to Herbsleb and Moitra [30], this can lead to serious misunderstandings and conflicts. In our study, barriers from this category appeared only during the interviews, as reported by two experienced members and one newcomer.

Some newcomers may consider a message rude (0-0-0-2, 2 projects) due to cultural interpretation: *"All the community is very nice. Of course, there are some 'German' guys. One time, a guy was rude with me, but, you know, we Brazilians are not used to the 'German way to talk directly'"* [N13]. In the OSS scenario, projects rely only on textual communication and often involve people who do not want to spend time writing careful messages. In addition, there are strong egos involved.

Another kind of barrier evidenced concerns for the need of a personal contact (0-0-0-2, 2 projects) to create a bridge, or a stronger connection, to the project. One experienced member reported the specific case of his compatriots: "*...people behave more emotionally in our country, I mean, newcomers need some special attention. Maybe since we are Mediterranean people, I don't know, but I think this is not the case in many projects in the world."* [E9]. An experienced member from another project also reports the same issue in a more general context: *"Although it may be a cultural aspect of open source that people prefer to make initial contact with a real person, so I don't have a problem with that*" [E7].

Although the literature underscores cultural differences among participants as an important aspect [36,44,55,59], the systematic review conducted by Steinmacher et al. showed that few studies investigated or dealt with cultural issues in distributed software development [72]. This category of barriers could be another fruitful research topic.

DISCUSSION

For purposes of clarity, we present most of our results discussion alongside each of the barriers in the previous section. In this section, we highlight some of the findings and present some higher-level discussion.

In general, this study discovered empirical evidence of the barriers faced by newcomers to OSS projects when placing their first contribution. This empirical evidence is important as many studies are motivated by or deal with anecdotal evidence. This paper brings evidence from reality, which is rarely precisely documented.

The model presented in Figure 2 groups social and non-social barriers into six categories, illustrating the high number of technical barriers compared to social barriers. This imbalance can be explained by the characteristics of OSS communities, which demand contributors and tasks with specific technical skills and knowledge requirements.

In the previous section, we related our findings to those reported in the literature on other open collaboration communities, mainly Wikipedia. We observed that the social barriers identified are fairly similar to those evidenced in other domains. Thus, some of the solutions and mitigation strategies used in those contexts could be tried on OSS communities and vice versa.

Some barriers are well reported and analyzed by the literature; the most explored barriers are those related to reception issues. For example, not receiving an answer is well evidenced quantitatively in both OSS and Q&A literature, and these results were in line with our results. Receiving impolite answers was also largely studied in the CSCW literature, mainly on the analysis of reverts in Wikipedia. The proposed strategies of automated answers and feedback used in Wikipedia can be adapted and then evaluated in OSS context.

On the other hand, some barriers identified by our study are neglected in the literature. One of them is receiving answers with too advanced/complex contents. We could not identify any study dealing with this barrier. There are opportunities to investigate this kind of barrier in different domains, and provide a deeper understanding of this issue.

The barriers related to newcomers' communication behavior are also under-studied. These barriers were evidenced by the community members' perspective, which is rarely investigated. Sometimes, the newcomers themselves are creating the barriers when they post useless comments or do not acknowledge an answer, which heightens the need to better understand what the community expects from the newcomers, and how these expectations affect or impact the newcomers' reception issues.

Cultural differences also deserve to be highlighted here. There are some possibilities related to this barrier that can be followed up in different CSCW domains. For example, how do collaborators observe cultural differences? Do they consider such differences when dealing with their peers? Do these barriers cause issues related to trust, misunderstandings, etc.?

In general, having substantiated and characterized the barriers faced by newcomers in a particular domain, we believe that the CSCW community can benefit from our research. Future research ought to focus on searching for commonalities and differences among barriers faced in different domains in order to build models and theories about joining processes in open collaboration communities.

OSS researchers can benefit from these results by using them to conceive strategies for newcomer support. By including the context of the CSCW and related research literature, we provide a starting point to conceive such support. To achieve this, it would be necessary to put more effort on specific research topics, such as understanding (and creating ways to measure) the influence of the barriers in newcomers' experience, identifying and creating different strategies to lower each barrier, and proposing metrics to grade the support offered for each barrier.

OSS practitioners can take advantage of adapting the existing strategies used in other domains to design their own tool-based support. Assuming that, as stated by Dagenais et al. [15], "newcomers are explorers who must orient themselves within an unfamiliar landscape," the model of barriers can be used by open collaboration communities to place the proper signs and maps to help newcomers orient themselves, and alert them about the obstacles that they might face.

Are the barriers always a problem?

Although we considered the barriers as a negative aspect of onboarding, some barriers can be used as filters. Findings from some studies [18,26] revealed some of these entry barriers led to improved contributions in the future. Moreover, research conducted in the OSS domain demonstrated that socialization barriers are useful for maintaining community integration and the quality of the community's product.

Since our focus was on newcomers placing their first contribution, regardless of their intention to become a community member, we were not concerned about overall socialization issues or future contributions, thus distinguishing our study from the existing literature. However, a clear direction for future work is to explore how the communities perceive these barriers and how they impact the quality of contributions from newcomers.

Are newcomers good?

Even knowing that a continual influx of newcomers is often related to the OSS project success [3,11,60,71], there are some downsides. These negative aspects revolve around the two main premises that underlie the Brooks' Law: productivity (the *ramp up* problem) and communication/ coordination overhead [5].

In the context of this research, we do not consider the *ramp up* to reach high productivity as a threat. We understand that most newcomers do not want to become core developers. Regarding coordination overhead, we believe that by providing the right support to newcomers this overhead can be reduced. Besides, Eric Raymond, in his well-known paper "The Cathedral and Bazaar" [61], claims that the effects of Brooks' Law regarding communication/coordination overhead does not apply as the more peripheral developers work on *separable parallel subtasks and interact with each other very little.* Therefore, coordination overhead has its effects mainly within the core group [10,37,43,66].

LIMITATIONS

Although we analyzed data from a variety of sources and from different projects, we likely did not discover all possible barriers or provide full explanations of the barriers. We are aware that each project has its singularities and that the OSS universe is huge, meaning the level of support and the barriers can differ according to the project or the ecosystem. Our strategy to consider different projects and different developer profiles aimed to alleviate this issue, identifying recurrent mentions of barriers from multiple perspectives.

In our systematic literature review, we considered any study that empirically evidenced barriers faced by newcomers during their joining process. We did not constrained our search to those papers that focused on the very first contribution of newcomers. Therefore, there could be studies focusing on different phases of joining process.

Another threat to the results' validity is the data classifications' subjectivity. We used Grounded Theory procedures to mitigate this threat, given that Grounded Theory requires the entire analysis to be grounded in the data collected. Additionally, we discussed the analysis process along with two other researchers to encourage a better validation of the interpretations through mutual agreement.

During interviews, experienced members were asked to answer questions regarding barriers faced by newcomers when they were seeking to place their first contribution, but due to memory effects they may have referred to the whole joining process. To avoid this kind of situation, we reinforced the focus of the research and verified some answers.

Since we sent open invitations to a mailing list, sampling bias affects our interviewees and open question respondents, namely self-selection bias and social desirability bias. However, we tried to counteract this effect by seeking out different sources and analyzing the answers in context to identify specifics.

CONCLUSION

Numerous communities are maintained by volunteers, who can easily drop out [8]. Explicit effort is necessary to mitigate obstacles and problems in these communities [80]. In this study, we identified, organized, and discussed social barriers that hinder newcomers' first contribution to OSS projects. The barriers emerged from a literature review on OSS newcomers, as well as from interviews conducted with, and questionnaires answered by, developers in different stages of the OSS community joining process. This study differs from the existing literature by focusing on the barriers newcomers face when trying to place their first contribution to a project, rather than focusing on the entire joining process. Additionally, our study followed a qualitative approach based on practitioner feedback. The qualitative view complements the existing dominant quantitative-based research on newcomers' joining process [26,27,34,81,85,86].

This study's results provides insights for communities that want to smooth newcomer onboarding and lays a foundation for building better onboarding support tools. In addition, researchers can use the model to plan further qualitative and quantitative studies to investigate specific barriers, their interplay, and their in-practice implications. In particular, some barriers, such as cultural differences, receiving answers with too advanced/complex contents, and newcomers' shyness, were evidenced by the practitioners, but not found in the systematic literature review. These barriers certainly warrant further investigations.

Identifying and understanding the initial barriers was a first step towards better orienting newcomers' first steps. OSS projects can benefit from additional contributions if they offer the right support to newcomers who are trying to contribute to the project for the first time. A smooth first contribution may increase the total number of successful contributions made by single contributors and, hopefully, the number of long-term contributors.

More details and information about this study, including results of further steps of this research can be found at http://lappesc.ime.usp.br/newcomersOSS

ACKNOWLEDGEMENTS

The authors would like to thank Fundação Araucária, CNPq (proc. 477831/2013-3), NAPSoL-PRP-USP, NAWEB, FAPESP, UTFPR and FAPEAM (proc. 062.00146/2012; 062.00600/2014; 062.00578/2014; and 01135/2011), for their financial support. Igor Steinmacher received grants from CAPES (BEX 2038-13-7).

REFERENCES

1. Arguello, J., Butler, B.S., Joyce, E., et al. Talk to Me: Foundations for Successful Individual-group Interactions in Online Communities. *Proceedings of the SIGCHI Conference on Human Factors in Computing Systems*, ACM (2006), 959–968.
2. Beecham, S., Baddoo, N., Hall, T., Robinson, H., and Sharp, H. Motivation in Software Engineering: A systematic literature review. *Information & Software Technology 50*, 9-10 (2008), 860–878.
3. Bird, C., Gourley, A., Devanbu, P., Swaminathan, A., and Hsu, G. Open Borders? Immigration in Open Source Projects. *ICSE Workshops MSR '07. Fourth International Workshop on Mining Software Repositories, 2007*, (2007), 6–6.
4. Bonaccorsi, A. and Rossi, C. Altruistic individuals, selfish firms? The structure of motivation in Open Source software. *First Monday 9*, 1 (2004).
5. Brooks, F.P. *The Mythical Man-Month: Essays on Software Engineering*. Addison-Wesley Professional, 1995.
6. Bryant, S.L., Forte, A., and Bruckman, A. Becoming Wikipedian: Transformation of Participation in a Collaborative Online Encyclopedia. *Proceedings of the 2005 International ACM SIGGROUP Conference on Supporting Group Work*, ACM (2005), 1–10.
7. Burke, M., Joyce, E., Kim, T., Anand, V., and Kraut, R. Introductions and Requests: Rhetorical Strategies That Elicit Response in Online Communities. In C. Steinfield, B. Pentland, M. Ackerman and N. Contractor, eds., *Communities and Technologies 2007*. Springer London, 2007, 21–39.
8. Burke, M., Marlow, C., and Lento, T. Feed Me: Motivating Newcomer Contribution in Social Network Sites. *Proceedings of the SIGCHI Conference on Human Factors in Computing Systems*, ACM (2009), 945–954.
9. Canfora, G., Di Penta, M., Oliveto, R., and Panichella, S. Who is Going to Mentor Newcomers in Open Source Projects? *Proceedings of the ACM SIGSOFT 20th International Symposium on the Foundations of Software Engineering*, ACM (2012), 44:1–44:11.
10. Capiluppi, A. and Adams, P. Reassessing Brooks' Law for the Free Software Community. In *Open Source*

Ecosystems: Diverse Communities Interacting. Springer Berlin Heidelberg, 2009, 274–283.

11. Capiluppi, A. and Michlmayr, M. From the Cathedral to the Bazaar: An Empirical Study of the Lifecycle of Volunteer Community Projects. In J. Feller, B. Fitzgerald, W. Scacchi and A. Sillitti, eds., *Open Source Development, Adoption and Innovation*. Springer Boston, 2007, 31–44.
12. Chengalur-Smith, I.N., Sidorova, A., and Daniel, S.L. Sustainability of Free/Libre Open Source Projects: A Longitudinal Study. *Journal of the Association for Information Systems 11*, 11 (2010).
13. Choi, B., Alexander, K., Kraut, R.E., and Levine, J.M. Socialization Tactics in Wikipedia and Their Effects. *Proceedings of the 2010 ACM Conference on Computer Supported Cooperative Work*, ACM (2010), 107–116.
14. Cubranic, D., Murphy, G.C., Singer, J., and Booth, K.S. Hipikat: a project memory for software development. *IEEE Transactions on Software Engineering 31*, 6 (2005), 446–465.
15. Dagenais, B., Ossher, H., Bellamy, R.K.E., Robillard, M.P., and Vries, J.P. de. Moving into a new software project landscape. *32nd International Conference on Software Engineering*, (2010), 275–284.
16. David, P.A. and Shapiro, J.S. Community-based production of open-source software: What do we know about the developers who participate? *Information Economics and Policy 20*, 4 (2008), 364–398.
17. Dittrich, Y., John, M., Singer, J., and Tessem, B. Editorial: For the Special Issue on Qualitative Software Engineering Research. *Inf. Softw. Technol. 49*, 6 (2007), 531–539.
18. Ducheneaut, N. Socialization in an Open Source Software Community: A Socio-Technical Analysis. *Computer Supported Cooperative Work (CSCW) 14*, 4 (2005), 323–368.
19. Fang, Y. and Neufeld, D. Understanding Sustained Participation in Open Source Software Projects. *J. Manage. Inf. Syst. 25*, 4 (2009), 9–50.
20. Farzan, R. and Kraut, R.E. Wikipedia Classroom Experiment: Bidirectional Benefits of Students' Engagement in Online Production Communities. *Proceedings of the SIGCHI Conference on Human Factors in Computing Systems*, ACM (2013), 783–792.
21. Faulkner, R., Walling, S., and Pinchuk, M. Etiquette in Wikipedia: Weening New Editors into Productive Ones. *Proceedings of the Eighth Annual International Symposium on Wikis and Open Collaboration*, ACM (2012), 5:1–5:4.
22. Fogel, K. *Producing Open Source Software: How to Run a Successful Free Software Project*. O'Reilly Media, 2013.
23. Forte, A. and Lampe, C. Defining, Understanding, and Supporting Open Collaboration: Lessons From the Literature. *American Behavioral Scientist 57*, 5 (2013), 535–547.
24. Franca, A.C.C., Gouveia, T.B., Santos, P.C.F., Santana, C.A., and Silva, F.Q.B. da. Motivation in software engineering: A systematic review update. *Evaluation Assessment in Software Engineering (EASE 2011), 15th Annual Conference on*, (2011), 154–163.
25. França, A.C.C., Silva, F.Q.B. da, L. C. Felix, A. de, and Carneiro, D.E.S. Motivation in software engineering industrial practice: A cross-case analysis of two software organisations. *Information & Software Technology 56*, 1 (2014), 79–101.
26. Halfaker, A., Geiger, R.S., Morgan, J., and Riedl, J. The Rise and Decline of an Open Collaboration System: How Wikipedia's reaction to sudden popularity is causing its decline. *American Behavioral Scientist 57*, (2013).
27. Halfaker, A., Kittur, A., and Riedl, J. Don't Bite the Newbies: How Reverts Affect the Quantity and Quality of Wikipedia Work. *7th Intl. Symposium on Wikis and Open Collaboration*, ACM (2011), 163–172.
28. Hannebauer, C., Book, M., and Gruhn, V. An Exploratory Study of Contribution Barriers Experienced by Newcomers to Open Source Software Projects. *Proceedings of the 1st International Workshop on CrowdSourcing in Software Engineering*, ACM (2014), 11–14.
29. Hars, A. and Ou, S. Working for free? Motivations of participating in open source projects. *34th Annual Hawaii Intl. Conference on System Sciences*, (2001), 9 pp.
30. Herbsleb, J.D. and Moitra, D. Global software development. *Software, IEEE 18*, 2 (2001), 16–20.
31. Herraiz, I., Robles, G., Amor, J.J., Romera, T., Barahona, J.M.G., and Carlos, J. The processes of joining in global distributed software projects. *2006 International Workshop on Global Software Development for the Practitioners*, (2006), 27–33.
32. Hertel, G., Niedner, S., and Herrmann, S. Motivation of software developers in Open Source projects: an Internet-based survey of contributors to the Linux kernel. *Research Policy 32*, 7 (2003), 1159–1177.
33. Jalali, S. and Wohlin, C. Systematic Literature Studies: Database Searches vs. Backward Snowballing. *Proceedings of the ACM-IEEE International Symposium on Empirical Software Engineering and Measurement*, ACM (2012), 29–38.
34. Jensen, C., King, S., and Kuechler, V. Joining Free/Open Source Software Communities: An Analysis of Newbies' First Interactions on Project Mailing Lists. *System Sciences (HICSS), 2011 44th Hawaii International Conference on*, (2011), 1–10.
35. Jergensen, C., Sarma, A., and Wagstrom, P. The Onion Patch: Migration in Open Source Ecosystems. *19th ACM SIGSOFT Symposium and the 13th European Conf. on Foundations of Software Engineering*, ACM (2011), 70–80.
36. Ji, Y.G., Hwangbo, H., Yi, J.S., Rau, P.L.P., Fang, X., and Ling, C. The Influence of Cultural Differences on

the Use of Social Network Services and the Formation of Social Capital. *International Journal of Human-Computer Interaction 26*, 11-12 (2010), 1100–1121.

37. Johnson, J.P. Economics of Open Source Software. *Unpublished paper*, (2001).
38. Jørgensen, N. Developer autonomy in the FreeBSD open source project. *Journal of Management & Governance 11*, 2 (2007), 119–128.
39. Joyce, E. and Kraut, R.E. Predicting Continued Participation In Newsgroups. *Journal of Computer-Mediated Communication 11*, (2006), 2006.
40. Ke, W. and Zhang, P. The Effects of Extrinsic Motivations and Satisfaction in Open Source Software Development. *J. AIS 11*, 12 (2010).
41. Kitchenham, B. and Brereton, P. A systematic review of systematic review process research in software engineering. *Information and Software Technology 55*, 12 (2013), 2049–2075.
42. Kitchenham, B. and Charters, S. *Guidelines for performing Systematic Literature Reviews in Software Engineering*. Keele University and Durham University, 2007.
43. Koch, S. Profiling an Open Source Project Ecology and Its Programmers. *Electronic Markets 14*, 2 (2004), 77–88.
44. Koh, J., Kim, Y.-G., Butler, B., and Bock, G.-W. Encouraging Participation in Virtual Communities. *Commun. ACM 50*, 2 (2007), 68–73.
45. Kraut, R.E., Burke, M., Riedl, J., and Resnick, P. The Challenges of Dealing with Newcomers. In MIT Press, 2012, 179–230.
46. Krogh, G. von, Haefliger, S., Spaeth, S., and Wallin, M.W. Carrots and Rainbows: Motivation and Social Practice in Open Source Software Development. *MIS Quarterly 36*, 2 (2012), 649–676.
47. Von Krogh, G., Spaeth, S., and Lakhani, K.R. Community, joining, and specialization in open source software innovation: A case study. *Research Policy 32*, 7 (2003), 1217–1241.
48. Lakhani, K.R. and Wolf, R.G. Why Hackers Do What They Do: Understanding Motivation and Effort in Free/Open Source Software Projects. In *Perspectives on Free and Open Source Software*. MIT Press, Cambridge, Mass., 2005.
49. Lampe, C. and Johnston, E. Follow the (Slash) Dot: Effects of Feedback on New Members in an Online Community. *Proceedings of the 2005 International ACM SIGGROUP Conference on Supporting Group Work*, ACM (2005), 11–20.
50. Maalej, W., Happel, H.-J., and Rashid, A. When users become collaborators: towards continuous and context-aware user input. *Proceeding of the 24th ACM SIGPLAN conference companion on Object oriented programming systems languages and applications*, ACM (2009), 981–990.
51. Marlow, J., Dabbish, L., and Herbsleb, J. Impression Formation in Online Peer Production: Activity Traces and Personal Profiles in Github. *Proceedings of the 2013 Conference on Computer Supported Cooperative Work*, ACM (2013), 117–128.
52. Meirelles, P., Santos, C., Miranda, J., Kon, F., Terceiro, A., and Chavez, C. A study of the relationships between source code metrics and attractiveness in free software projects. *2010 Brazilian Symposium on Software Engineering (SBES),*, IEEE (2010), 11–20.
53. Musicant, D.R., Ren, Y., Johnson, J.A., and Riedl, J. Mentoring in Wikipedia: A Clash of Cultures. *Proceedings of the 7th International Symposium on Wikis and Open Collaboration*, ACM (2011), 173–182.
54. Nakakoji, K., Yamamoto, Y., Nishinaka, Y., Kishida, K., and Ye, Y. Evolution Patterns of Open-source Software Systems and Communities. *Proceedings of the International Workshop on Principles of Software Evolution*, ACM (2002), 76–85.
55. Nguyen, D.T. and Fussell, S.R. Effect of Message Content on Communication Processes in Intercultural and Same-culture Instant Messaging Conversations. *Proceedings of the 2013 Conference on Computer Supported Cooperative Work*, ACM (2013), 19–32.
56. Oreg, S. and Nov, O. Exploring motivations for contributing to open source initiatives: The roles of contribution context and personal values. *Computers in Human Behavior 24*, 5 (2008), 2055–2073.
57. Pham, R., Singer, L., Liskin, O., Figueira Filho, F., and Schneider, K. Creating a Shared Understanding of Testing Culture on a Social Coding Site. *Proceedings of the 2013 International Conference on Software Engineering*, IEEE Press (2013), 112–121.
58. Preece, J., Nonnecke, B., and Andrews, D. The top five reasons for lurking: improving community experiences for everyone. *Computers in Human Behavior 20*, 2 (2004), 201–223.
59. Preece, J. Sociability and usability in online communities: Determining and measuring success. *Behaviour & Information Technology 20*, 5 (2001), 347–356.
60. Qureshi, I. and Fang, Y. Socialization in Open Source Software Projects: A Growth Mixture Modeling Approach. *Org. Res. Methods 14*, 1 (2011), 208–238.
61. Raymond, E.S. *The Cathedral and the Bazaar*. O'Reilly & Associates, Inc., Sebastopol, CA, USA, 1999.
62. Roberts, J.A., Hann, I.-H., and Slaughter, S.A. Understanding the Motivations, Participation, and Performance of Open Source Software Developers: A Longitudinal Study of the Apache Projects. *Manage. Sci. 52*, 7 (2006), 984–999.
63. Santos, C., Kuk, G., Kon, F., and Pearson, J. The Attraction of Contributors in Free and Open Source Software Projects. *J. Strateg. Inf. Syst. 22*, 1 (2013), 26–45.
64. Scacchi, W. Understanding the requirements for developing open source software systems. *IEE Proceedings Software 149*, 1 (2002), 24–39.

65. Schilling, A., Laumer, S., and Weitzel, T. Who Will Remain? An Evaluation of Actual Person-Job and Person-Team Fit to Predict Developer Retention in FLOSS Projects. *Proceedings of the 2012 45th Hawaii International Conference on System Sciences*, IEEE Computer Society (2012), 3446–3455.
66. Schweik, C.M., English, R.C., Kitsing, M., and Haire, S. Brooks' Versus Linus' Law: An Empirical Test of Open Source Projects. *Proceedings of the 2008 International Conference on Digital Government Research*, Digital Government Society of North America (2008), 423–424.
67. Seaman, C.B. Qualitative methods in empirical studies of software engineering. *Software Engineering, IEEE Transactions on 25*, 4 (1999), 557–572.
68. Shah, S.K. Motivation, Governance, and the Viability of Hybrid Forms in Open Source Software Development. *Manage. Sci. 52*, 7 (2006), 1000–1014.
69. Sharp, H., Baddoo, N., Beecham, S., Hall, T., and Robinson, H. Models of motivation in software engineering. *Information & Software Technology 51*, 1 (2009), 219–233.
70. Singh, V. Newcomer integration and learning in technical support communities for open source software. *Proceedings of the 17th ACM international conference on Supporting group work*, ACM (2012), 65–74.
71. Sinha, V.S., Mani, S., and Sinha, S. Entering the circle of trust: developer initiation as committers in open-source projects. *Proceedings of the 8th Working Conference on Mining Software Repositories*, ACM (2011), 133–142.
72. Steinmacher, I., Chaves, A., and Gerosa, M. Awareness Support in Distributed Software Development: A Systematic Review and Mapping of the Literature. *Computer Supported Cooperative Work (CSCW) 22*, 2-3 (2013), 113–158.
73. Steinmacher, I., Silva, M.A.G., and Gerosa, M.A. Systematic review on problems faced by newcomers to open source projects. *10th International Conference on Open Source Software*, (2014), 10pp.
74. Steinmacher, I., Wiese, I., Chaves, A.P., and Gerosa, M.A. Why do newcomers abandon open source software projects? *International Workshop on Cooperative and Human Aspects of Software Engineering (CHASE)*, (2013), 25–32.
75. Steinmacher, I., Wiese, I.S., and Gerosa, M.A. Recommending mentors to software project newcomers. *Third International Workshop on Recommendation Systems for Software Engineering (RSSE)*, IEEE Computer Society (2012), 63–67.
76. Strauss, A. and Corbin, J.M. *Basics of Qualitative Research : Techniques and Procedures for Developing Grounded Theory*. SAGE Publications, 1998.
77. Suh, B., Convertino, G., Chi, E.H., and Pirolli, P. The Singularity is Not Near: Slowing Growth of Wikipedia. *Proceedings of the 5th International Symposium on Wikis and Open Collaboration*, ACM (2009), 8:1–8:10.
78. Vora, P., Komura, N., and Team, S.U. The n00b Wikipedia Editing Experience. *6th Intl. Symposium on Wikis and Open Collaboration*, ACM (2010), 36:1–36:3.
79. Wang, J. and Sarma, A. Which bug should I fix: helping new developers onboard a new project. *Proceedings of the 4th International Workshop on Cooperative and Human Aspects of Software Engineering*, ACM (2011), 76–79.
80. Wang, L.S., Chen, J., Ren, Y., and Riedl, J. Searching for the Goldilocks Zone: Trade-offs in Managing Online Volunteer Groups. *Proceedings of the ACM 2012 Conference on Computer Supported Cooperative Work*, ACM (2012), 989–998.
81. Wang, Y.-C., Kraut, R., and Levine, J.M. To Stay or Leave?: The Relationship of Emotional and Informational Support to Commitment in Online Health Support Groups. *Proceedings of the ACM 2012 Conference on Computer Supported Cooperative Work*, ACM (2012), 833–842.
82. Wolff-Marting, V., Hannebauer, C., and Gruhn, V. Patterns for tearing down contribution barriers to FLOSS projects. *12th Intl. Conf. on Intelligent Software Methodologies, Tools and Techniques*, (2013), 9–14.
83. Ye, Y. and Kishida, K. Toward an Understanding of the Motivation Open Source Software Developers. *Proceedings of the 25th International Conference on Software Engineering*, IEEE Computer Society (2003), 419–429.
84. Yu, S. and Ming, W. Research on individual motivation model of software engineering. *Journal of Communication and Computer 6*, 11 (2009), 12.
85. Zhou, M. and Mockus, A. What make long term contributors: Willingness and opportunity in OSS community. *Software Engineering (ICSE), 2012 34th International Conference on*, (2012), 518–528.
86. Zhu, H., Kraut, R., and Kittur, A. Effectiveness of Shared Leadership in Online Communities. *Proceedings of the ACM 2012 Conference on Computer Supported Cooperative Work*, ACM (2012), 407–416.
87. Zhu, H., Zhang, A., He, J., Kraut, R.E., and Kittur, A. Effects of Peer Feedback on Contribution: A Field Experiment in Wikipedia. *Proceedings of the SIGCHI Conference on Human Factors in Computing Systems*, ACM (2013), 2253–2262.

Mudslinging and Manners: Unpacking Conflict in Free and Open Source Software

Anna Filippova, Hichang Cho
Communications and New Media
National University of Singapore, Singapore
{annaf, hichang_cho}@nus.edu.sg

ABSTRACT

As the nature of virtual work changes, so must our understanding of important processes such as conflict. The present study examines conflict in ongoing virtual teams by situating itself in the context of Free and Open Source Software (FOSS) development. A series of semi-structured interviews with diverse representatives of the FOSS community highlight differences in the way conflict occurs. Specifically, a transformation of conflict types is observed together with a form of conflict previously unidentified in work on virtual teams. Findings suggest that the changing structure of ongoing virtual teams has important consequences for team processes like conflict.

Author Keywords

Virtual Teams; Free and Open Source Software; Conflict; Ongoing teams; Peer-Production; Computer-Supported Work; Computer-Mediated Communication.

ACM Classification Keywords

K.4.3 [Computers and Society]: Organizational Impacts---Computer-Supported Collaborative Work.

General Terms

Human Factors; Management.

INTRODUCTION

Virtual work is continuing to evolve, and so must our understanding of the foundational processes that underpin on-line collaboration. Teams are increasingly shifting away from fixed membership towards dynamic composition [37,38]. Team boundaries are becoming more fluid, while team members are more likely to be assigned to multiple teams [37]. At the same time, virtual teams are now increasingly less likely to experience life cycles with distinct start and end points [35]. Given that team age and structure significantly affect group processes and outcomes in virtual teams [21], these changes have important consequences for our understanding of virtual work.

CSCW '15, March 14–18, 2015, Vancouver, BC, Canada.
Copyright 2014 ACM 978-1-4503-2922-4/15/03…$15.00
http://dx.doi.org/10.1145/2675133.2675254

Conflict is an important team process that has received a lot of attention from literature on temporary virtual teams: teams with fixed membership structures that experience short and finite life cycles [19,21,26]. However relatively less attention has been given to conflict in ongoing virtual teams: teams with dynamic membership composition that can progress for several years [11,14,35].

Free and Open Source Software (FOSS) development represents a unique opportunity to examine conflict in ongoing distributed teams in a natural setting. Due to the largely voluntary nature of participation, FOSS teams have fluid team boundaries, with team members frequently belonging to several projects [15]. Additionally, FOSS teams rarely have fixed end points, with notable projects continuing for many years [8].

Despite the potential for informing virtual team research, there is a lack of existing empirical work on conflict in FOSS [8]. The limited studies performed to date have been largely descriptive, focusing on a few case studies of well-established projects with strong free software ideals [12,13]. The present study therefore aims to build a more complete understanding of conflict in FOSS as an example of ongoing virtual teams. We do this by examining the process more generally in diverse representatives of FOSS communities with different ideologies, age and success rates.

While some important work has been done on conflict in Wikipedia [6,24,25], FOSS teams differ in several significant ways that may affect how conflict occurs. Aside from differences in the nature of output produced, FOSS teams can also be relatively more hierarchical than Wikipedia [33], with disagreements arising from authority issues [29]. In addition, while the Wikipedia community values maintaining a "Neutral Point of View" [27], conflict in FOSS teams is not only their defining feature [23], it is considered an art form [5].

Through an exploratory study of FOSS teams, this paper seeks to understand how the unique structure of ongoing teams affects team processes such as conflict. We propose the following research question:

RQ1: How do ongoing virtual teams such as FOSS development teams experience conflict?

Ongoing virtual teams must tackle process, structural and other socio-technical issues that evolve over time, whereas temporary virtual teams tend to focus primarily on the task at hand [35]. As such, conflict in ongoing virtual teams is more complex [14]. The anticipation of working together again may make it necessary for ongoing virtual teams to surface issues that temporary teams are able to suppress [35]. Additionally, unresolved conflicts may evolve and transform over time [34]. Yet these processes have not been well tested. To the best of our knowledge, only one study to-date has examined the transformation of conflict types in Wikipedia [1]. Crucially, the few initial studies focused on FOSS conflict, while not examining conflict sources directly, allude to disagreements arising from sources that do not fit neatly into the classical conflict taxonomy proposed by literature thus far [12,13]. We expand on these in the following section.

Taken together, the literature suggests that more research is needed to uncover how hybrid and new types of conflict manifest and transform in ongoing virtual teams like FOSS. However, most related findings are rather preliminary or based on observations of qualitatively different Wiki communities. Hence we aim to advance this line of research further by asking the following research questions:

RQ2: Do conflict types transform over time in ongoing virtual teams such as FOSS development teams?

RQ3: Do ongoing virtual teams such as FOSS development teams experience other sources of conflict beyond the traditional model?

The following section will briefly summarize the existing understanding of conflict in temporary virtual teams. We will also explore theory and related work that help to predict how conflict may occur differently in ongoing virtual teams such as FOSS development teams.

CONFLICT IN SHORT-TERM VIRTUAL TEAMS

Research on conflict in temporary virtual teams has typically separated this process into three distinct types: task, relationship and process conflict [19].

Task conflict in virtual work involves disagreements about the content of the task at hand, that is, about what needs to be done [20]. Task conflict arises out of a different interpretation of the team's goal or aim. Task conflict has the potential to generate a greater diversity of opinions and improve team function [21]. However, empirical research on virtual teams has found mixed results for the effectiveness of task conflict in improving team outcomes [18,28]. Task conflict has been found to frequently co-occur with other conflict types, in which case a reduction in its positive effects on team development is observed [3,11].

Relationship (or "affective") conflict involves interpersonal incompatibilities, and occasionally feelings of annoyance, frustration, and irritation with teammates [20]. Relationship conflict has been traditionally conceptualized as having negative effects on team function [19,28]. This effect is amplified when relationship conflict occurs together with process conflict [3,11].

Process conflict evolves out of differences regarding how the team's goal should be accomplished, and involves disagreements regarding resource and duty delegation [20]. Research in virtual work has found mixed support for the effects of process conflict on outcomes, because it overlaps conceptually with task conflict [3] and co-occurs with other conflict types [11].

CONFLICT IN ONGOING VIRTUAL TEAMS

Ongoing virtual teams have qualitatively distinct features from temporary teams, and therefore are likely to experience the process of conflict differently. Ongoing teams have a greater long-term orientation of working together in the future, a "shadow of the future" [35], and thus evolve unique intragroup processes [10]. For instance, trust operates differently in ongoing virtual teams [16]. Ongoing teams are also more likely to accumulate common knowledge to aid in more adaptive coordination [4].

While several studies examine ongoing virtual teams, they do not address in great depth the issue of long-term team dynamics, such as conflict. Furthermore, some studies conceptualize ongoing teams as either management teams [39] or simply teams having longer time frames for tasks with fixed end points assembled on an as-need basis [32]. This differs from the emerging teams without fixed end points and fluid, voluntary membership structures that we describe here. Below we elaborate on the two main differences we may find in conflict within ongoing virtual teams.

Transforming Conflict

The above findings on virtual teams suggest that different conflict types may occur at the same time and interdependently influence group outcomes [11]. In ongoing teams, conflict also has the potential to transform from one type into another [14]. Because ongoing virtual teams do not have fixed end points, they have more time and potential to evolve. Thus, if conflicts are not resolved initially, due to the longer time frames involved, conflicts may transform [34]. Additionally, the constant flux of members in ongoing teams who join at different times leads to different perspectives and interpretations of the same conflict. We expect to see not just co-occurrence but an evolution of conflict types in ongoing virtual teams. We refer to such hybrid conflict types as transforming conflict.

Rahim [34] has theorized two variations of transforming conflict: relationship conflict that may evolve into task conflict when team members indirectly express their negative affect through disagreements about the task; and task conflict that can transform into relationship conflict, especially if the conflict is unresolved, or when frustrations are already running high in the group. Work on ongoing virtual teams has yet to examine these variations empirically.

One exception is recent work on Wikipedia that shows initial support for transformative conflict [1]. Arazy, Yeo and Nov [1] have found that task conflict can evolve into both relationship or process conflict, and that this transformation leads to a reduction in team performance. We need to extend this line of research further to better understand the different transitions conflict types can take. Do these findings hold for ongoing virtual teams such as FOSS teams? Do other kinds of transitions occur? When does one conflict type evolve into another?

Normative Conflict

Because ongoing teams have more time to evolve than temporary virtual teams, they are more likely to develop distinct group norms [35]. In fact, Ke and Zhang [22] found that FOSS teams develop their own community norms, and that these can vary significantly from project to project. Additionally, FOSS teams are a recursive public [23]: they are able to not only view and modify the source code to their software, but also reflect on and adapt their own practices and conditions of production.

As a result, ongoing teams such as FOSS development teams may experience normative conflict, that is disagreements about the norms of the group itself [30]. Normative conflict arises from a dissonance between the descriptive norms in a group, or observed behavior, and prescriptive norms, or expected group behavior [31]. In other words, when a group member observes the behavior of the group is no longer in line with team expectations, they may express dissent leading to conflict within the group.

Normative conflict is conceptually distinct from task, relationship and process conflicts because it is one level of abstraction higher. For example, rather than disagreeing about what task to perform, or how to perform the task of writing software, normative conflict may involve disagreements about project policy, direction, or ideology. This is a logical practice for ongoing teams that hope to survive for longer periods of time, because the group needs to be able to recursively adjust its own norms and procedures in response to critical events [35].

Several studies on FOSS teams, though not examining conflict sources directly, provide initial evidence that normative conflict may occur. For instance, Elliot and Scacchi [13] documented a disagreement that emerged in BOS because the descriptive norms of the community in using proprietary software were not in line with the prescriptive norm of using only Free Software. In a later study, Elliot and Scacchi [12] observed similar conflict patterns in the GNUe project as well. Both case studies involve well-established FOSS projects with a strong normative drive towards using only Free Software in all aspects of the projects' function. Though these studies provide initial hints of different conflict sources, we need to empirically examine conflict process in FOSS in greater detail among projects of different size, age and with ideological assumptions.

The next section will outline the methodology used in this study to explore how conflict manifests in FOSS teams as examples of ongoing virtual teams.

METHOD

To address our research aims, we conducted 16 semi-structured interviews with software developers who have contributed code to a FOSS project or released code under a FOSS license. Interviews were chosen as methodology for this exploratory study to allow for categories of conflict to emerge that would be given by, and meaningful to, the community being studied.

As the aim of this research was to explore conflict patterns among different types of FOSS projects, we placed emphasis on sampling a diverse set of participants. Developers were selected to represent a variety of positions in the community, level of experience, location and the type of problems their projects solve. Participants were invited to participate face-to-face at technology events and meet-ups, or by e-mail. Participants also recommended other members of the community, who were then selected for participation based on the same criteria, to avoid sampling homogenous clusters of developers.

We used GitHub profiles and filtering interview questions to assess levels of experience of our participants both in terms of length of time spent contributing to the project as well as volume of contributions made. Based on the hierarchical, or onion-like, model of FOSS organization [9], we also interviewed developers at different levels: committers, maintainers, core contributors, project founders (of both simple and complex projects) and community advisors.

4 women and 12 men participated in this project. Women currently make up about 11% of FOSS developers according to a recent survey [2]. Given the small number of participants in our study, for better gender representation, we oversampled and interviewed 4 women.

The final sample represented 7 countries: Australia, China, India, Malaysia, the Netherlands, Singapore, and the United States, and 14 projects. Projects included libraries: BitcoinJS, libXML, PrawnPDF; languages, tools and frameworks: Git, Grok, Node.JS, Python, Ruby on Rails, Zope; and end-user applications: Debian, Mozilla Firefox and Thunderbird, Plone, ScrollBack and Ubuntu. Though varying in size and stage of development, all the above projects are active and at least one year old, with a majority spanning several years. They therefore represent examples of ongoing virtual teams that have had a chance to evolve.

To avoid priming interviewees about conflict, participants were asked to discuss their experiences in contributing to FOSS more generally, such as motivations, decision making in the team and memorable instances of disagreement. Additionally, participants were not limited to current conflict episodes - conflicts across different aspects of the project lifespan were discussed. Interviews lasted approximately one hour and were transcribed verbatim for further analysis. Participants were encouraged to share additional materials after the interviews, such as news articles. These materials supported the analysis process.

We applied a grounded approach to examine the common patterns of conflict in different FOSS projects [17]. First, all anonymised transcripts were open coded to identify conflict sources and their trajectories. In the second stage, we compared each instance to other examples across all the interview transcripts, identifying conceptually similar groups. We iterated this process until conceptual saturation, that is, until no new behaviors and inferences were being captured by the emerging categories.

RESULTS

This study explores how conflict occurs in ongoing virtual teams through the unique context of FOSS development. Our findings suggest that firstly, FOSS teams experience conflicts arising from constraints such as time zones and communication overload, as well as dependencies on other software projects. Second, due to their ongoing nature, FOSS teams experience transformation of conflict sources. Finally, due to their long-term orientation, FOSS teams experience conflict types previously unobserved by literature, such as normative conflict. These conflict sources are summarized in Table 1.

Socio-technical nature of conflict

RQ1 explores how conflict manifests in FOSS teams as examples of ongoing virtual teams. To address this, we begin by describing conflict sources that emerge from the specific conditions of work in FOSS. We identify structural limitations such as time zone and communication channels that affect conflict, as well as technical features of software production such as version clashes and dependencies on other software projects that give rise to conflicts about competing technologies.

Structural Sources

Though FOSS developers occasionally meet face-to-face to encourage community building, most important decisions are made on archived mailing lists or internet relay chat (IRC) meetings to allow the whole distributed team to participate [7]. In practice, this presents some challenges. Several participants have reported conflicts arising from communication issues such as different time zones, having too many communication sources to monitor, information overload, and difficulties being heard (P2, P8, P13, P4, P5, P12).

Several participants have noted that they have to stay up late at night in order to interact with team members in Europe and North America (P4, P5, P13). For many projects IRC, a synchronous communication tool, is used to co-ordinate important issues such as obtaining feedback on a proposed feature before making a formal pull request (P8) or to ask more experienced contributors questions (P4, P5). Some participants express frustration that developers from Asia and Australia need to conform to North American time zones (P4, P5, P13).

Developers also report conflicts arising from communication overload and problems being heard (P13, P8). For instance, particularly in larger projects, a steady flow of communication comes through the mailing lists every day as subsequent time zones come online:

"[You] can't subscribe to everything these days, [and] can't read everything subscribed. [By] the time you're done a whole bunch of other e-mails come in. [It's] a whole global thing [...] people go to sleep, the next time zone wakes up and starts replying." (P13)

Additionally, projects may use multiple communication channels for decisions that are not always well publicized, resulting in an impression that decisions happen "behind closed doors" (P2). For P13, the inability to follow all possible communication channels has left the packager out of an important decision regarding their project:

"There was a decision that happened at some random IRC session that I didn't know about. [...] One day I just woke up [and] I read on some Ubuntu blog somewhere, "Banshee is no longer default". I'm like, "Huh?"" (P13)

P13 was unable to weigh in on the decision to select the default Ubuntu media player, thus another package was chosen instead. P13 raised the issue on IRC, linking notes from the missed meeting. Conflict erupted when other Banshee supporters expressed their solidarity by "spamming [flaming] the whole meeting notes upside down" (P13).

Some developers have reported issues being heard even when they submit pull requests (P8, P1):

"One thing I do disagree with is [people] who just don't respond. [...] Thank you for letting me use your tool for free, [but] I went to effort to umn contribute that thing back, umn it would be nice if you could at least just respond to say no. [I've] accidentally done that to a few people. And I feel like an asshole every time". (P8)

Because it is relatively easy to create an issue or give feedback on a platform like GitHub or Launchpad, developers find that many users open "dumb issues" and as a result their contributions "get lost in the noise" (P8).

Conflict Source	Conflict Type	Examples
Structural	Procedural and Relational	Time zone differences, difficulties keeping up with multiple communication channels, information overload, noise in communication channels
Competing Technologies	Task	Version conflicts due to backward-compatibility issues, multiple alternative libraries/software dependencies
Transforming	Task–Relationship	Disagreements with authority figures, frustrations due to lack of task progress
	Task–Process	Emergence of procedural errors during task conflict discussions
	Process–Relational	Disagreements among project leaders about important procedures that become personal, personal attribution of blame following procedural mistakes
Norms	Normative	Disagreements regarding project policies, governance issues, ideological clashes arising from community interaction rather than the task at hand.

Table 1. Summary of conflict sources and types

Finally, the amount of conflict experienced in a team varies with the level of interdependency in the project. P8 points out that Node.JS has a modular codebase, and therefore, "if you disagree with someone's choice, you can [just] replace the piece". "In Node, there is less need for people to all agree on something." (P8) On the other hand, the NPM project is more centralized in it's code architecture design, and:

[It] has all of the same problems as [you would] expect [...] a whole bunch of people who have different uh concerns, different priorities and different needs out of a piece of software [...] They're all like vying to get NPM to suit their needs. (P8)

Thus, because a project's technical structure is more interdependent, their social structure also experiences greater friction.

Taken together, the above findings highlight that just like temporary teams, larger ongoing teams experience difficulties with information overload [18]. Similarly, teams that rely on synchronous communication also suffer from issues of distance and time. Finally, the amount of friction in a team can vary with the level of code base interdependence. That is the social processes within a group change depending on the technical conditions

Competing technologies

A second source of conflicts that arise during FOSS development involve competing ideas about the appropriate technology to use to solve a problem, or competing versions of the same technology. A number of the surveyed developers reported such conflicts (P13, P10, P9, P8). For instance, in the Banshee example presented in the previous section, difficulties of communication have compounded an existing conflict between supporters of two competing technologies, Banshee and Rhythmbox:

"There was a lot of mudslinging [flaming] going around as well by people who wanted Rhythmbox as the default. [...] I think a lot of the perception was that, "Oh no, it's because Banshee uses MONO that's why it's slow" and all that. It's mostly the same stigma that happens with Java. Except with Java it's true." (P13)

Disagreements between supporters of different projects are common, and often turn into flames. This observation is consistent with previous work by Coleman [5] who highlighted that disagreements among FOSS developers about different technologies can occur for sport, that is, be an end in themselves.

However, our findings show that beyond their autotelic function, conflicts about competing technologies are also able to influence the social dynamics of a project. For example, P10 recalls having to negotiate different contributors' suggestions for libraries to include in the project:

"So this person jumped in, and be like, 'Hey, I have a library. Use mine!' And then the other person, who has commit rights, and he jumped in, he was like, 'I also have a library'" (P10)

Such disagreements occur at an intersection of competing priorities and agendas, as contributors may prefer to include their own libraries to enhance their reputation in the community or due to familiarity with the code base.

Because FOSS projects depend on the efforts of volunteers, the maintainer is challenged to weigh these suggestions against other approaches and come up with a solution that satisfies both the volunteers and projects' aim:

[...] and then there's also a big number library, which is written by someone else, which is more popular than both of their libraries combined, so I'm like, "How about, I don't know, let's use the standard?" (P10)

Negotiating conflicting opinions on project dependencies is difficult not only because choosing a side means rejecting the suggestion of some team members. Software dependencies also have their own teams behind them. Thus, choosing to include an outside project also means choosing to depend on the project's community for parts of your own project function.

Additionally, more mature projects sometimes find themselves in conflict between old and new versions of the same software. While version upgrades are commonplace, breaking compatibility with earlier versions is sometimes required in order to make substantial improvements to the project and "fix early mistakes" (P8). This can create faultlines in the community because rewriting old code to conform to the new version is too time consuming:

"Yeah that's all very nice but I have a lot of code written in Python 2 and what's gonna happen right? What's gonna happen, not just to this code, but to the community where some people will write like Python 3 code, some people will write Python 2 code" (P9)

These faultlines can generate community-wide friction and conflict between supporters of the opposing versions (P9).

Taken together, the above examples highlight that disagreements between developers about conflicting versions or competing software projects significantly impact community function. They not only advance technical decisions about the project, they also become critical junctures that influence the social structure of the team going forward.

Transformative conflict

The majority of conflicts reported above can be classified into conflict sources based on Jehn's taxonomy [20]. Task conflict is expected in any teams that have a certain degree of interdependence of task, and as we have seen above, FOSS teams frequently need to negotiate code commits as well as issues related to procedure and personal disagreements. However, more interestingly, the conflict episodes uncovered in this study have a tendency to evolve into different conflict types over time. Thus to address RQ2, the next section will present examples of such transformations, and discuss their significance with relation to the changing nature of ongoing teams.

Task-Relational conflict

Firstly, out findings highlight the transformation of task into relational conflicts (P9, P1, P8). Often, the relational conflicts described were the result of already mounting frustrations with a task, or involved a power imbalance between disagreeing parties.

For example, the lead of the Zope project approached one of his maintainers after a conference and chastised him personally instead of the team for not being more careful when making changes to the code base (P9). P9 suggested that this task conflict turned personal because of already mounting frustrations during the conference about the lack of progress in the project in general:

"And in part it was a reaction to my negative sort of attitude, [and] all this frustration behind me already to get this small progress. [...] So we had this sort of discussion and we had been friends [for] years by then [and] that was the last time actually I met him in real life". (P9)

Interestingly, participants often reported relational conflicts emerging from task conflicts with authority figures (P9, P1). P1 suggests this may be because project maintainers and leads have greater demands on their time, and are also in a position of authority that allows them to get away with being more offensive.

One respondent suggested that this transformation into relationship conflict could be avoided if contributors choose not to make the issue personal (P1). Some have also suggested that it is not worth arguing with a maintainer even if they may be right because the maintainers have control over what features may be accepted:

"You want to keep those people who are in charge of okaying or not okaying, keep them on your side. But if you [...] throw a tantrum when they don't accept your feature, they are less likely to take you seriously" (P8).

Taken together these findings indicate that in FOSS teams, task conflicts can evolve a relational dimension over time due to the ongoing nature of the teams, as frustrations about a lack of progress build up over time. Interestingly, task conflicts can also evolve into relational conflicts due to power imbalance and harsh communication style of some authority figures. Given the long-term focus of the projects, developers recognize that it is better for the overall health of the team and their relationships with authority figures to accommodate the individuals in charge.

Task-Process conflict

Some FOSS projects have a 'way' of doing things within the group that may be unwritten, such as a style of writing code (P10, P2, P1) or accepted practices for division of labor (P8, P2, P9, P3). Disagreements about a task can evolve into procedural conflicts when developers are not aware of this style, or have a strong opinion about doing things differently.

For instance, P1 recalls another contributor having very poor success getting his contributions into the Git project due to disagreements on the style the code should be written in:

"What he is doing, adding a new feature, [is] something that Git cannot do, it's just the way [...] the code is doing it, they prefer it to be done in another manner but he doesn't agree" (P1)

In the above example, discussion about process took over the discussion about task because the contributor refused to adjust to the project's coding style.

In another example, a maintainer for the Zope project sparked a conflict when he removed a list of dependencies without discussing the decision with his teammates (P9). The other maintainers disagreed with his decision to remove the dependency list, resulting in a task conflict. However, when it emerged that procedure wasn't followed, and this change wasn't discussed with other members who may still depend on this list, the conflict became procedural. Interestingly, when P9 attempted to revert this change, in essence fixing the task element of the conflict, he also faced backlash from the community for going against procedure.

Taken together, the above examples highlight a prioritization of conflict occurring in ongoing virtual teams. When disagreements about the task at hand begin to overlap with conflict on how the task should be performed, procedural issues appear to be given more weight than task related ones. This may be because procedural issues are relatively more important for ongoing teams to address and resolve to improve coordination and ensure project longevity [29]. Thus some projects would rather reject a significant code contribution if it does not fit in with the project coding style, and suspend activities on task related disagreements until a procedural issue is resolved.

Process-Relational conflict

Our findings have also uncovered a combination of conflict types theorized by previous literature [34], but not yet well-documented by research on ongoing virtual teams [1]. Specifically, participants have reported a number of examples of procedural issues that evolve into relational conflict.

For example, following a prominent incident in which the Linux kernel was hacked, a disagreement emerged between two leaders, Linus Torvalds, and Shawn Pierce, about implementing tighter contribution security in their software version control system. (P1). Though the task at hand to improve security was clear, the leaders disagreed on the procedure to accomplish this. The conflict escalated to a relational one, when Shawn suggested an alternative solution to the one Linus proposed, and

"Linus said 'No, totally wrong'. Except he didn't use those words, he used something worse". (P1)

According to P1, Linus Torvalds' harsh tone had transformed a procedural issue into a relational one, just like in some of the task-relational conflicts above. Though Linus is known for his specific communication style, the previous sections have documented some other examples of project leaders exhibiting similar patterns due to their positions of authority. This suggests that in projects with more pronounced hierarchies, there is a greater tendency for conflicts to take on a relational dimension when they involve project leaders.

We also observe situations in which process conflict can become relational among regular committers and maintainers.

For instance, when Debian developers with commit access wish to modify code they are not themselves responsible for, they are expected to follow an unwritten rule (P13). Committers need to submit their Non-Maintainer Upload with a delay (7 days) to allow the maintainer of this code to review and accept the changes. A Debian maintainer points out that other maintainers get "very angry" if code is uploaded without adhering to this convention (P13).

Debian has evolved the above community norm to avoid procedural conflict transforming into relational conflict. This once again highlights the long-term focus of ongoing virtual teams, who have time to recursively adopt social norms that help them prevent disagreements experienced in the past.

In general, the above section has shown that ongoing virtual teams such as FOSS development teams exhibit strong tendencies for conflict types to transform and evolve over time. In addition, more combinations of conflict transformations have been observed than those documented in previous work [1]. In particular, conflicts involving project leaders or an imbalance of power appear to frequently take on a relational dimension. At the same time, procedural conflicts appear to be given higher priority when they emerge from other conflict types. This suggests that while ongoing virtual teams evolve hierarchies and procedures to help them manage their community growth [29], this introduces new tensions in the project. However, the long-term orientation of on-going virtual teams allows them to iteratively adjust their behavior when moving forward.

Normative conflict

The previous section dealt with conflict that emerged due to misunderstandings about the coding task to be performed, project styles and procedures or interpersonal friction. Addressing RQ3, this section deals with conflicts that do not fit into this classification. We refer to them here as normative conflicts, as they involve a dissonance between the stated aims of the group, or prescriptive norms, and its practices, or descriptive norms [30]. Normative conflicts are thus distinct from procedural conflicts and issues of authority, because they occur at a level of abstraction higher. Instead of disagreeing about how a task should be performed, or by whom, normative conflict involves disagreements about issues like project policies, governance structures, and project ideology.

For instance, following an incident where a few users were banned after being "quite abusive" (P13), Debian developers debated the practice of banning users on the project mailing list:

"There was a bit of a debate about [the] trigger happy banning behavior of some people. Some people were concerned that freedom of speech was being obstructed" (P13)

The Debian community was not only debating its own policies with respect to banning of users when referring to the obstruction of free speech. Developers were also concerned that the community was no longer living up to their own beliefs. The descriptive norms of banning individuals were thus misaligned with prescriptive norms of free speech in the community, causing a conflict.

Similarly, in a high profile incident within the Ruby on Rails project, a community member resorted to hacking the project to demonstrate a dissonance between the community norms and practices. The Rails community has strong opinions on how the programming framework should work and be used (P2, P8):

"Rails is opinionated software. It makes the assumption that there is the 'best' way to do things, and it's designed to encourage that way." [40].

The "Rails way" is the group's ideological construct that helps to align the efforts of contributors towards the same goal. However, this belief of the 'best way to do things' came into conflict with actual group practices when a developer uncovered a critical security flaw in Rails, but received little support in addressing the issue from the core team:

"He [Homakov] was pretty much ignored and put down because the core team thought it was a non-issue and that things just weren't done that way because it's not the Rails way" (P2)

To illustrate the severity of the security flaw, Homakov exploited the vulnerability to make unauthorized commits to the Rails project on GitHub. He also spoofed comments by prominent members of the Rails team, such as dhh, the project lead.

"Perhaps if he didn't feel that his point was worth proving we would be dealing with an insecure by default framework just because the core maintainers or a majority of them don't think that's 'the way' to do so". (P2)

Through this hack, Homakov pointed out that the prescriptive norms of Rails as the "best way" to write software were at odds with their actual practices because they overlooked the severity of a security flaw in the framework. By spoofing comments of prominent team members and essentially speaking for them, Homakov was also drawing attention to the fact that his attempts at improving the project were ignored.

Though Homakov was initially banned from GitHub for this incident, his account was reinstated shortly thereafter and the security flaw was fixed in the next version of Rails (P2), showing an indirect acknowledgement that Homakov made an improvement to the "Rails way".

Normative conflicts therefore have powerful implications for the team as a whole, as when they erupt they force the group to iteratively evaluate their collective goals and purpose, and if necessary, make changes so that group practices continue to be in line with their aims.

To conclude this section of the paper, we will present one final example illustrating that normative conflict is not immutable and can interact with other conflict types. The following conflict episode was independently discussed by a number of participants (P9, P1, P2, P8, P13, P16), and simultaneously involves procedural, relational and normative dimensions.

In late 2013, a developer submitted a pull request to libuv, a sub-project of Node.JS, replacing a gendered pronoun inside a line of documentation with a gender-neutral alternative (P9). Ben Noordhuis, the project maintainer, rejected the pull request for being "too trivial to bother" (P8). While for Ben the source of the disagreement was procedural, an issue of time management, the community saw this as sexist, a personal issue, and "went a bit crazy at him about it" (P8).

The conflict took on an additional procedural dimension when Isaac Schlueter stepped in. Isaac created one of the other foundational Node.JS programs, NPM, and has since left the project but maintained his upload access. Isaac accepted the pull request without any discussion, thus undermining Ben's authority as maintainer (P9). Ben, in turn, reverted Isaac's commit (P8):

"He [Ben] didn't revert it because he disagreed with it, he reverted it because [they] have procedures for getting stuff into libuv. And although Isaac has commit rights, he shouldn't [...] get around the process." (P8)

Isaac, on the other hand, argued that he was upholding the norms of the project, to be "inclusive of non-male people and that our language should reflect this explicit inclusion" [36]. The conflict gained a normative dimension in highlighting this disconnect between upholding the prescriptive norms of inclusivity and the way the norms were put into practice through documentation language.

As the above example demonstrates, it is possible for localized conflicts, such as about group processes, to bring to light higher order issues in the project that cause fundamental faultlines in the group. In the case of Node.JS, this conflict allowed the community to clarify several community norms, such as inclusivity and when it is appropriate to revert others' commits.

Taken together, the above normative conflict examples highlight its power in driving forward team development in ongoing virtual teams that recursively evaluate and adjust their techno-social structures. Normative conflict therefore has potential to be generative to community health and function.

DISCUSSION

The present study aimed to explore the relatively understudied occurrence of conflict in Free and Open Source Software (FOSS) development teams as a special example of ongoing virtual teams. Ongoing virtual teams are characterized by changes such as more fluid membership structures and no fixed end points [35], which we expected to lead to changes in the experience of social processes like conflict.

Through an exploratory study of FOSS development teams we aimed to uncover how the process of conflict manifests (RQ1), transforms (RQ2) and differs (RQ3) in ongoing virtual teams. Our findings contribute several important insights.

Firstly, we find that conflicts can arise directly out of the technical constraints and features of FOSS development teams, such as communicating across time zones via multiple communication channels. This is consistent with literature on temporary virtual teams [18] and is likely to vary with team size. An interesting question is whether large Wiki communities experience similar frictions. This may not be the case because FOSS teams have a greater expectation for and reliance on synchronous communication through channels, like IRC.

Additionally, we find that conflicts can arise from incompatible software versions, and create faultlines in the social fabric of the group. Similarly, because FOSS teams produce software that frequently depends in some part on other FOSS projects, they are also likely to experience conflicts about competing technologies. Thus because FOSS teams are socio-technical systems, decisions they make about the technologies they build and borrow affect their social processes, like conflict.

Second, our findings highlight that conflict types occurring in ongoing teams frequently evolve. Consistent with earlier work on Wikipedia [1], this study observes task conflicts transforming into relational and process conflicts. Our study further highlights that process conflicts may also evolve into relational conflicts, suggesting that the transformations we observe may not be limited to only the types previously identified.

We find that issues of authority or imbalance of power appear to be significant factors contributing to this transformation. When conflicts evolve, projects prioritize addressing certain types of conflict over others. Ongoing virtual teams try to focus their attention on conflict types that are more significant to the long-term viability of the group. Some projects are even willing to reject a significant code contribution if it is not in line with the norms or processes of the group.

It would be interesting for future research to explore what other factors contribute to each of these transitions, and whether the way transitions are handled has an impact on team outcomes. Our findings also have implications for research interested in examining outcomes in ongoing virtual teams. Our results suggest that research designs should be carefully crafted to ensure that when a conflict episode is studied, it is measured in its entirety in relation to team outcomes, because viewing the conflict in cross section at different times may lead to inconsistent and possibly contradictory findings.

Finally, in addition to task, relationship, process and transformative conflicts, our results show that ongoing teams also experience normative conflict. Normative conflict deals with distinctly different kinds of intra-group disagreements, and involves a dissonance between the stated aims of a group and its practices [30]. In our findings we have seen normative conflict arising when the norms of free speech clashed with the practice of banning users, as well as when the norms of providing the "best way" to write software conflicted with an oversight of a major security flaw. Normative conflict can also evolve from other conflict types: when a procedural issue about contributing documentation occurred, it highlighted how existing practices were not reflecting the community aims to be gender inclusive.

We argue it is natural to find normative conflict in ongoing teams such as FOSS teams because they are recursive publics [23]. Recursive publics modify their own social and technical conditions, and thus they are not only able to reflect and adjust their technological foundations, but they also reflexively adjust their social foundations. Normative conflict is a channel that drives this process forward, and if handled well, allows ongoing virtual teams greater long-term sustainability.

To the best of our knowledge, ours is the first study to examine normative conflict in virtual teams. Work on normative conflict in collocated groups has only featured a handful of experimental studies thus far [31]. Thus this is a fruitful avenue for future research into ongoing teams, in particular in examining what effects normative conflict may have on group outcomes like performance, satisfaction and member attrition in a team.

Limitations and future work

The present study is not without limitations. Though all efforts were made to select participants such that there were no homogenous clusters of developers, the size and nature of the sample strategy may limit generalizability of the above findings. It would be interesting for future research to examine these patterns in a broader survey of the FOSS community. Additionally, self-reporting conflict episodes may have a dimension of social desirability – other research methods that do not rely on self-reports, such as a textual analysis of richly available mailing list archives, could serve to further validate these findings.

Our study focuses on the intragroup level of analysis. There may be different patterns of conflict at the intergroup level. In particular, since FOSS projects have complex interdependencies between communities this may introduce additional complexity into their social processes. This is an interesting question for further research – how do different teams interact and coordinate with one another given the differences they may have in norms and ideology?

Finally, this paper does not look closely at the way organizational sponsorship of FOSS projects might affect their social dynamics, such as conflict. This is another potential avenue for future research to explore, as we know that a significant proportion of FOSS developers are paid to contribute to projects [15].

CONCLUSION

The present study set out to examine the way conflict occurs in ongoing virtual teams. We found that conflict types can evolve over time, while group norms recursively become a source of conflict for ongoing teams. At the same time, due to their long-term orientation, ongoing teams prioritize certain conflicts over others to ensure their resolution and sustainability. Our results inform research on virtual work, and suggest further research is needed to explore the way ongoing teams are changing our understanding of virtual team processes.

ACKNOWLEDGMENTS

We gratefully acknowledge our anonymous reviewers, whose insightful comments have helped to make significant improvements to this manuscript.

REFERENCES

1. Arazy, O., Yeo, L., and Nov, O. Stay on the Wikipedia task: When task-related disagreements slip into personal and procedural conflicts. *JASIST 64*, 8 (2013), 1634–1648.
2. Arjona-Reina, L., Robles, G., and Dueñas, S., *The FLOSS2013 Free/Libre/Open Source Survey.* (2014)
3. Behfar, K.J., Mannix, E.A., Peterson, R.S., and Trochim, W.M. Conflict in Small Groups: The Meaning and Consequences of Process Conflict. *Small Group Research 42*, 2 (2011), 127–176.
4. Caya, O., Bassellier, G., and Pinsonneault, A. Virtual Team Common Knowledge: Construct Specification and Effect on Knowledge Integration Effectiveness. *ICIS 2008 Proc.*, (2008), 14.
5. Coleman, E.G. *Coding Freedom: The ethics and aesthetics of hacking.* Princeton University Press, (2013).
6. Collier, B. and Bear, J. Conflict, criticism, or confidence: an empirical examination of the gender gap in Wikipedia contributions. *CSCW'12*, ACM (2011), 383–392.
7. Crowston, K., Howison, J., Masango, C., and Eseryel, U.Y. The role of face-to-face meetings in technology-supported self-organizing distributed teams. *IEEE Transactions on Professional Communication 50*, 3 (2007), 185–203.
8. Crowston, K., Wei, K., Howison, J., and Wiggins, A. Free/Libre Open-Source Software Development: What we know and what we do not know. *Computing Surveys 44*, 2 (2012), 1–35.
9. Crowston, K., Wei, K., Li, Q., and Howison, J. Core and Periphery in Free/Libre and Open Source Software Team Communications. *Institute for Software Research.* (2006) Paper 489.
10. de Jong, B.A. and Elfring, T. How does trust affect the performance of ongoing teams? The mediating role of reflexivity, monitoring, and effort. *Academy of Management Journal 53*, 3 (2010), 535–549.
11. de Wit, F.R.C., Greer, L.L., and Jehn, K.A. The paradox of intragroup conflict: A meta-analysis. *Journal of Applied Psychology 97*, 2 (2012), 360–390.
12. Elliott, M. and Scacchi, W. Communicating and mitigating conflict in open source software development projects. *Projects & Profits,* (2002), 25–41.
13. Elliott, M.S. and Scacchi, W. Free Software Development: cooperation and conflict in a virtual organizational culture. *Free/Open Source Software Development,* IGI Global, (2005), 152–173.
14. Filippova, A and Cho, H. Below boiling point: negotiating conflict thresholds in distributed work. *IR'15 Proc.*, AoIR (2014).
15. Ghosh, R.A., Glott, R., Krieger, B., and Robles, G. Free/Libre and Open Source Software: Survey and study, *Working Paper,* International Institute of Infonomics, University of Maastricht (2002).
16. Gibson, C.B. and Manuel, J.A. Building trust. *Virtual teams that work*, (2003), 59–86.
17. Glaser, B.G. and Strauss, A.L. *The discovery of grounded theory: Strategies for qualitative research.* Aldine Transaction (2009).
18. Griffith, T.L., Mannix, E.A., and Neale, M.A. Conflict and Virtual Teams. In E.M. Turner, ed., *Groups at Work: Theory and Research*. Lawrence Erlbaum, Mahwah, NJ, (2001), 445–470.

19. Hinds, P.J. and Bailey, D.E. Out of sight, out of sync: Understanding conflict in distributed teams. *Organization Science 14*, 6 (2003), 615–632.

20. Jehn, K.A. and Mannix, E.A. The dynamic nature of conflict: A longitudinal study of intragroup conflict and group performance. *The Academy of Management Journal,* (2001), 238–251.

21. Kankanhalli, A., Tan, B.C.Y., and Wei, K.-K. Conflict and Performance in Global Virtual Teams. *JMIS 23*, 3 (2006), 237–274.

22. Ke, W. and Zhang, P. Motivation, Social Identity and Ideology Conviction in OSS Communities: The Mediating Role of Effort Intensity and Goal Commitment, *International Journal of Electronic Commerce 13,* 4 (2007), 39–66.

23. Kelty, C.M. *Two Bits: The Cultural Significance of Free Software.* Duke University Press, (2008).

24. Kittur, A. and Kraut, R.E. Beyond Wikipedia: coordination and conflict in online production groups. *CSCW'10*, ACM (2009), 215–224.

25. Kittur, A., Suh, B., Pendleton, B.A., and Chi, E.H. He says, she says: conflict and coordination in Wikipedia, *CHI 2007,* ACM (2007), 453–462.

26. Martinez-Moreno, E., Gonzalez-Navarro, P., Zornoza, A., and Ripoll, P. Relationship, task and process conflicts on team performance: The moderating role of communication media. *International Journal of Conflict Management 20*, 3 (2009), 251–268.

27. Matei, S.A. and Dobrescu, C. Wikipedia's 'Neutral Point of View': Settling Conflict through Ambiguity. *Information Society 27*, 1 (2011), 40–51.

28. Mortensen, M. and Hinds, P.J. Conflict and shared identity in geographically distributed teams. *IJCMA 12*, 3 (2001), 212–238.

29. O'Mahony, S. and Ferraro, F. The emergence of governance in an open source community. *Academy of Management Journal* 50, 5 (2007), 1079–1106.

30. Packer, D.J. On being both with us and against us: a normative conflict model of dissent in social groups. *Personality and Social Psychology Review 12*, 1 (2008), 50–72.

31. Packer, D.J. and Chasteen, A.L. Loyal deviance: testing the normative conflict model of dissent in social groups. *Personality and Social Psychology Bulletin 36*, 1 (2010), 5–18.

32. Powell, A., Piccoli, G., and Ives, B. Virtual Teams: A Review of Current Literature and Directions for Future Research. *SIGMIS Database 35*, 1 (2004), 6–36.

33. Prasarnphanich, P. and Wagner, C. The role of Wiki technology and altruism in collaborative knowledge creation. *JCIS 49*, 4 (2009), 33–41.

34. Rahim, M.A. *Managing Conflict in Organizations*. Transaction Publishers, New Brunswick, NJ, (2011).

35. Saunders, C.S. and Ahuja, M.K. Are All Distributed Teams the Same? Differentiating Between Temporary and Ongoing Distributed Teams. *Small Group Research 37*, 6 (2006), 662–700.

36. Schlueter, I., ed. *Comment on "The Next Phase of Node.JS."* [Retrieved 1/5/2014 from https://news.ycombinator.com/item?id=7064470]

37. Tannenbaum, S.I., Mathieu, J.E., Salas, E., and Cohen, D. Teams Are Changing: Are Research and Practice Evolving Fast Enough? *Industrial and Organizational Psychology-Perspectives on Science and Practice 5*, 1 (2012), 2–24.

38. Wageman, R., Gardner, H., and Mortensen, M. The changing ecology of teams: New directions for teams research. *Journal of Organizational Behavior 33*, 3 (2012), 301–315.

39. Zack, M.H. and McKenney, J.L. Social context and interaction in ongoing computer-supported management groups. *Organization Science 6*, 4 (1995), 394–422.

40. Anonymous. *Rails Guides* [Retrieved 25/7/2014 from http://guides.rubyonrails.org/getting_started.html]

Towards Understanding Relational Orientation: Attachment Theory and Facebook Activities

Bumsoo Kang
KAIST
Republic of Korea
steve.kang@kaist.ac.kr

Sujin Lee
KAIST
Republic of Korea
sujinlee@kaist.ac.kr

Alice Oh
KAIST
Republic of Korea
alice.oh@kaist.ac.kr

Seungwoo Kang*
KAIST
Republic of Korea
sngwoo@kaist.ac.kr

Inseok Hwang
IBM Research - Austin
USA
ihwang@us.ibm.com

Junehwa Song
KAIST
Republic of Korea
junesong@nclab.kaist.ac.kr

ABSTRACT
Knowing individuals' relational orientation is imperative for effective offline, as well as online, interactions and collaborations. We use attachment theory to examine the link between Facebook users' relational orientation (in terms of attachment styles: anxiety and avoidance) and their relational activities. Our research examines whether and how the two key relational processes identified in offline social relationships (self-expression and responsiveness) are manifested on online social networks and related to attachment styles. We describe our dataset of 640 Facebook users, their attachment scale survey results, and their 525,334 posts. We define four features that map onto relational activities on Facebook: status updates and status updates with emotional words (self-expression); comments and likes (responsiveness). We find significant relationships between the users' attachment styles and their self-expression and responsiveness activities on Facebook. A key takeaway of our research is that without relying on self-reported surveys, a computational analysis of a Facebook user's self-expressing and responding activities alone can reveal the user's underlying relational orientation (i.e., attachment style).

Author Keywords
Relational orientation; interpersonal relationship; personality; attachment theory; social network behavior

ACM Classification Keywords
H.5.3. Information Interfaces and Presentation [Information Interfaces]: Group and Organization Interfaces–Web-based interaction, Computer-supported cooperative work; J.4. Social and Behavioral Sciences: Psychology

* A corresponding author.

CSCW 2015, March 14–18, 2015, Vancouver, BC, Canada.

http://dx.doi.org/10.1145/2675133.2675211

INTRODUCTION
The ever-increasing ubiquity of online social media is transforming the way we connect and interact with others. We work, learn, entertain, and engage in business activities with a wide variety of people, some of whom we have little or no interactions in an offline setting. For example, we collaborate with previously unfamiliar people on an open-source project; we take massive open online courses (MOOCs) and discuss lectures together; we join online communities around interests and hobbies; we crowdsource tasks requiring large-scale human intelligence; and the list goes on.

Unlike connections based on offline interactions, most of the online-only connections face challenges in understanding one another in terms of relational orientation, that is, how an individual views and behaves toward partners in interpersonal communication. There are individual differences in such relational orientations, and those differences contribute to concrete behavioral differences in emotional expressiveness, confirmation of affection, physical proximity, and many other communicative traits. In face-to-face interactions, most people can quickly grasp the relational orientation of the partner to tune their interactional behaviors and avoid misunderstandings. With a lack of non-verbal cues, as well as shared context, this is much harder to do in an online setting, and thus, a computational technology can be a solution to analyze and present the relational orientation of the online interactional partners. Such technology has the potential to help manage the large number of online connections. For example, we may be able to recruit people with certain relational orientation rather than randomly selecting people from the crowd to carry on socially intensive tasks such as online emotional support [39]. In remote collaboration, we may strategize for effective interaction depending on the relational orientation of interactional partners.

Individuals' relational orientations have received much attention in offline relationship research [36, 44] to understand how they react to social relationships and communicate with others. Such an understanding is complex and delicate; many factors are collectively considered such as personality, reputation, education, culture, family, social position, etc. It has been a main theme of exploration in diverse disciplines of humanities and social sciences. However, most of the efforts try to understand a person through background information, observation, and interviews, which basically requires significant amounts of time and human efforts.

In this paper, we explore the possibility to develop a computational method to help understand the relational orientation of people. To this end, we utilize already obtainable and rich data on the Internet such as online social network service (SNS) data. While there have been many attempts to analyze personal characteristics based on SNS data, most of them focus on understanding the users' personality traits [4] based on personality analyses (e.g., the Big Five or the MBTI). The relational orientation, a key aspect affecting the interpersonal behaviors of people, remains underexplored in the online social setting.

As an initial step, we propose a new model of interpersonal behaviors of SNS users. We build the model based on *attachment theory* which is one of the leading theories of interpersonal relationships in developmental and social psychology [35, 43, 44]. Attachment refers to an individual's psychological ties to specific relationship partners [24, 35]. Individuals' attachment style explains their relational cognition, emotion, motivation, and behavior across an entire life span and in multiple relational settings [7, 35, 43], such as infant-mother attachment [1], adult romantic attachment [24], and work colleague attachment [31]. The attachment style is conceptualized by two continuous dimensions: *attachment anxiety* and *attachment avoidance* [10]. These anxiety and avoidance dimensions of attachment shape individuals' mental model of self (i.e., their belief or expectation about their own worthiness) and model of others (i.e., their belief or expectation about others' benevolence or trustworthiness). These models of self and others serve as mediating mechanisms for interpersonal behavior [5, 7].

To build and test the model, we target Facebook users and examine the link between users' attachment styles and their Facebook activities. Our investigation focuses on answering the following questions:

- Is Facebook users' attachment style related to their Facebook activities? Can we predict Facebook users' relational orientations by looking at their Facebook activities?
- Do people behave similarly or differently in offline and online interactions? Are attachment theory-based predictions replicated in online relationships?

To analyze relational activities on Facebook in terms of attachment style, we use two key relational processes identified by previous research on attachment theory: self-expression and responsiveness [43]. We select and classify Facebook activities into two sets of features to represent self-expression and responsiveness. While self-expression is related to the Facebook activities that a user initiated, e.g., status updates and emotional expression, responsiveness is associated with passive or active responses to others' posts (those initiated by others), e.g., liking and commenting. Through regression analysis, we examine the link between the features and the two continuous dimensions of attachment anxiety and avoidance. We collect the data via a Facebook application we developed, called KnowYourself, which obtains users' consent for a survey of attachment style and their Facebook activities. In total, we analyzed 640 Facebook users and their 525,334 posts. We find a significant link between the users' attachment styles and their self-expression and responsiveness activities on Facebook.

Our main contributions are as follows:

- We integrate attachment theory, a leading theory of interpersonal relationships, with Facebook activities and identify four features that represent relational processes online.
- We show that attachment theory-based predictions, which have long been examined in offline social interaction, are applicable to online social interactions, even though the relational environments are different.
- We present how Facebook activities can be used to predict users' relational orientations (attachment anxiety and avoidance).

The rest of this paper is organized as follows. We first describe attachment theory, the details of our data, and the features we propose to link attachment styles and Facebook activities. Next, we present the regression results analyzing attachment anxiety and avoidance as continuous values. Then we classify users' attachment styles based on the proposed features. We conclude by discussing ideas for future research.

ATTACHMENT THEORY AND RESEARCH

The recent increase in popularity of SNS for interpersonal communication has opened new opportunities to observe and analyze naturally occurring interpersonal behavioral patterns at an unprecedented scale. Attachment theory is one of the leading theories of interpersonal relationships [35, 43, 44] with which we can explain SNS users' behaviors. The theory states that an individual's relational qualities with respect to a specific relationship partner affect a large variety of cognitive and psychological processes [8], such as styles of loving [12], interpersonal communication [3], interpersonal distance [28], and cognitive processes [6].

Attachment Dimensions: Anxiety and Avoidance

The anxiety dimension of attachment refers to the degree of concern over others' evaluation, and the avoidance dimension reflects the degree of comfort with closeness and intimacy. Combining the two dimensions, people can be roughly categorized into four attachment types. People high on the anxiety dimension and low on the avoidance dimension are *anxiously* attached. They have a negative model of self, viewing themselves negatively, and are highly concerned about others' approval, but they have a positive model of others, generally liking others and desiring to build close relationships. Anxiously attached people attempt to increase closeness with others. People low on anxiety dimension and high on avoidance dimension are *avoidantly* attached. They have a positive model of self, thinking highly of themselves, but a negative model of others, mistrusting them. Thus, avoidantly attached people attempt to increase distance from others and dismiss intimacy. Those high on both dimensions are *fearfully* attached. Their models of self and other are both negative. They think negatively about themselves and believe that

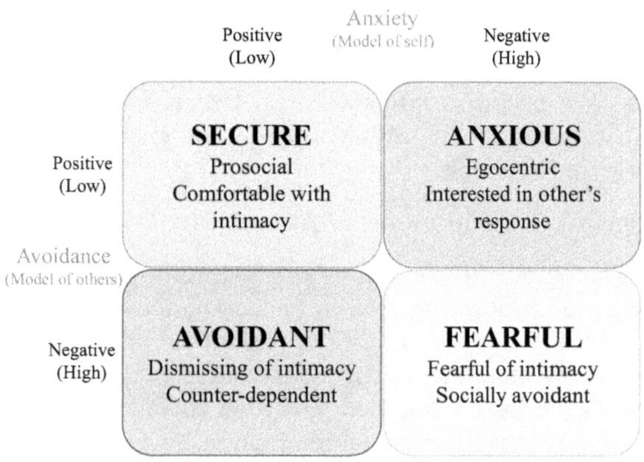

Figure 1. Four attachment types based on the two dimensions, anxiety and avoidance.

others are unresponsive or rejecting. In contrast, people low on both dimensions are *securely* attached. Their models of self and other are positive. They think positively about themselves and believe that others are benevolent and trustworthy [35].

Figure 1 shows the four attachment types. Although people can be categorized into the four types based on their levels of anxiety and avoidance, the attachment literature views anxiety and avoidance as two continuous dimensions, allowing each survey participant to be placed anywhere along the two axes.

Self-report survey is the typical method of measuring individuals' attachment [10]. The Experiences in Close Relationships-Revised (ECR-R) is a well-constructed survey for measuring individuals' attachment through two subscales of 18 items: anxiety and avoidance [21, 45, 19]. It has 36 items such as "I prefer not to show my significant other how I feel deep down," "I feel comfortable opening up to my significant other," and "I often worry that my significant other will not want to stay with me." In this survey, participants are asked to indicate their relationship qualities with respect to their significant other (e.g., spouse, romantic partner, family, or friends). The survey results generate two scores of anxiety and avoidance for each participant. An individual can be high or low on either or both dimensions.

Attachment Theory and SNS Behavior

Previous studies examined the relationship between attachment styles of individuals and their technology-mediated behaviors. Jin and Pena studied mobile phone usage by college students in romantic relationships and its association with relational uncertainty, love and commitment, and attachment styles [27]. Their results regarding attachment styles have shown that the higher the avoidance scores were, the smaller voice call frequency and the shorter call time. Drouin and Landgraff focused on texting and sexting behaviors and their association with attachment styles of college students in romantic relationships [17]. Weisskirch and Delevi studied the association between the use of technology such as text message, instant message, and email in relationship dissolution and attachment style [50]. Gentzler et al. focused on the college students' use of technology-mediated communication with parents and examined its links to loneliness, attachment, and relationship quality [22]. Unlike these studies, we focus on studying the association between attachment styles of Facebook (a popular SNS) users and their activities on Facebook. In addition, our study is based on a computational analysis with a large amount of data generated from Facebook activities of users, quite different from the studies based on self-report surveys about technology use.

Similar to our study, several studies have explored SNS behaviors and their relationship with attachment style. Oldmeadow et al. examined data collected with a self-report questionnaire that measures attachment style, social skills, and Facebook use and experience [41]. They found that individuals with high anxiety showed more frequent Facebook use, while ones with high avoidance showed less Facebook use. Andangsari et al. conducted a similar study for Indonesian young adults [2]. Their study also showed that people with high anxiety would be more active in using Facebook. Jenkins-Guarnieri et al. investigated how attachment style, personality traits, and self-esteem were related to perceptions of Facebook use and interpersonal competency [26]. These studies were also based on self-report surveys about Facebook use, e.g., the frequency of log in, the frequency of status updates, time spent on Facebook, whereas we collected a large amount of actual Facebook data from users and investigated detailed activities including status updates, photo uploads, comments to others, and likes received, associated with individuals' attachment style. In this research, we examine whether we can link specific Facebook activities to attachment styles, much in the same way that attachment researchers have predicted relational behavior in offline social interactions. We map offline relational processes identified in prior research to user behavior on Facebook.

Prior research on attachment and relationship-building in social psychology categorizes two key processes involved in real-life (as opposed to online) relationship-building: self-expression and responsiveness [43]. These are purposeful behaviors intended to increase or decrease intimacy. Although Facebook has a different relational context in that many of the interactions are through text, images, and clicks, compared to face-to-face interactions in the offline setting, Facebook users may have a similar underlying motivation, that of building and strengthening friendships. Thus, we borrow the same classification of relational processes (self-expression and responsiveness) to analyze the relational activities on Facebook. Specifically, in our research, self-expression includes Facebook activities that are clearly initiated by self: status updates and emotional expression. Responsiveness includes commenting or pushing a like button to posts generated by others. We propose that the models of self and others associated with attachment styles will affect Facebook users' self-expression and responsiveness. More specifically, attachment anxiety is related to negative model of the self (viewing the self negatively) and positive model of others (viewing others positively). In contrast, attachment avoidance is associated with positive model of the self (viewing the self positively) and negative model of others (viewing others negatively) [5, 10]. We propose that the model of the self influences Facebook users' self-expression activities, whereas the model of others affects their responsiveness activities.

DATA AND PROPOSED FEATURES

This section describes how we collected Facebook users' attachment styles and detailed Facebook activity data and transformed specific Facebook actions to key relational features that are used to link with attachment styles.

Participants

We collected data from two different cultures: the United States and the Republic of Korea. These two countries are quite disparate in language and culture, but both have a big number of Facebook users. Using data from two countries ensures that our findings are indeed driven by the relationship between Facebook activities and attachment styles, not particularly biased by a specific cultural setting in which the social network service is operating. Initially, 1,060 Facebook users were recruited for the study. Participants in the United States (N = 497, 54% female) were recruited through Amazon Mechanical Turk (MTurk). MTurk users with more than three consecutive months of Facebook usage were allowed to participate. They were rewarded with $0.50 each. Since MTurk was not available in Korea, Korean participants (N = 563, 31% female) were recruited through an advertisement on Facebook groups and online communities of universities in Korea. After the completion of the study, 50 of them were randomly selected and rewarded with gift certificates worth about $3.50. Note that different recruiting and rewarding methods for American and Korean participants might motivate people to participate in the study differently. The collected Facebook activities of the participants, however, were not affected by the different recruiting methods because they were done before the users' participation. Moreover, we ruled out untrustworthy participants to ensure the quality of the collected data as explained below.

The recruitment and data collection were performed during the period between September 6, 2012 and March 29, 2013. For data collection, we developed an application on Facebook, *KnowYourself*. It asked for participants' permission for us to access their Facebook data. When the user granted permission, the app showed the attachment survey questionnaire and gathered answers from the user. Facebook data were automatically collected and anonymized while the user took the survey. Note that we explicitly announced on the front page of the survey that user data would be collected. We also informed them that the data would be used only for academic research and automatically anonymized. In addition, we allowed the participants to drop out of the survey at any time. The number of participants who dropped out was 138.

We ruled out participants who gave untrustworthy answers to survey questionnaires or had too few Facebook activities. First, we designed and added dummy questions that were the same as the original questions with slightly different wording, so that we could check for the similarity of the answers. We also measured the time taken by each user in completing the

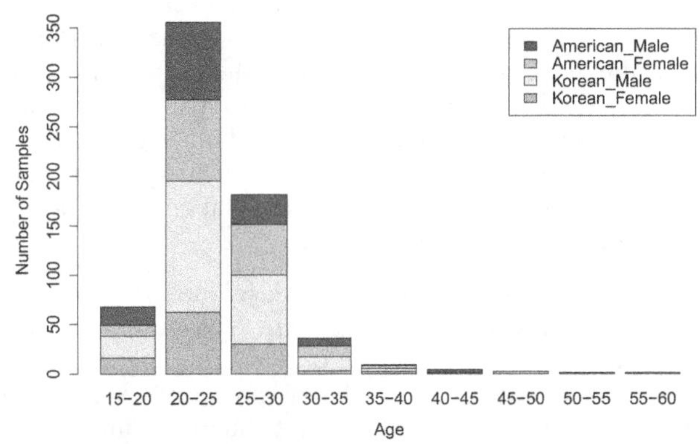

Figure 2. Summary of collected data. Most samples are concentrated in the range of 20 to 30 years old.

survey to filter out those who completed the survey within 30 seconds. As for the Facebook data, we excluded participants who had less than six months of Facebook usage prior to the beginning of recruitment. We also examined the amount of Facebook usage and excluded those who had fewer than five photo uploads or 10 status updates. In total, 282 participants were ruled out (inconsistent answers to questions: 28, survey completed in less than 30 seconds: 100, less than 6 months: 42, not enough Facebook activities: 112).

The final dataset for analysis is 640 users, 42% female. The cultural and gender makeup of the users is: 136 U.S. men, 159 U.S. women, 236 Korean men, and 109 Korean women. Figure 2 summarizes the detailed statistics of the participants.

Data

Attachment style survey data were collected with the shortened version of ECR-R which is an attachment scale questionnaire widely used in the attachment literature. 7-scale responses (ranging from "Not at all" to "Very much") are used for rating each question. We were cautious that participants might correctly guess the purpose of our research (i.e., the link between their significant-other relationship with their Facebook behavior). To ameliorate this concern, we shortened the number of items on the attachment questionnaire by randomly selecting four items of attachment avoidance and four items of attachment anxiety from the original version of ECR-R Form (See the Appendix for shortened version of ECR-R). We also tested the reliability of shortened version of ECR-R by Cronbach's Alpha (avoidance: $\alpha = 0.685$, anxiety: $\alpha = 0.848$). To the extent that both anxiety and avoidance items were randomly selected, the anxiety's high reliability signals that the avoidance's relatively low reliability was not driven by our random selection of the items. Instead, it appears associated with SNS context, in which there would be more anxious users (seeking social interaction) than avoidant users (shunning it).

Attachment avoidance and attachment anxiety are measured by four relevant questions, respectively: questions 1, 2, 3, 7 for attachment avoidance and questions 4, 5, 6, 8 for attachment anxiety. Each of attachment scores is obtained by taking an average of the answers to the relevant questions. Note that scores about questions 2 and 7 are given reverse-coded. Since the score 4 is the middle score (cut-off value), each attachment dimension is defined as *Low* if the score is lower than 4; otherwise, it is defined as *High*. Participants responded to the attachment questionnaire while thinking about their broad significant other (including spouse, romantic partner, family, or friend). We expect the general attachment styles to influence Facebook friend relationships.

The ECR-R Form was originally developed in English and there is no official Korean version. Thus, for our Korean participants, we translated the original English version into Korean using the back-translation procedure [11]. Back-translation is usually accepted as a valid procedure for cross-cultural research. Following [11], one bilingual research assistant, who is fluent in English and Korean, translated the original English version into Korean. Then, another English-Korean bilingual research assistant back-translated the Korean version into English. Then one of the authors of this research confirmed the equivalence of the original English version and the back-translated English version. Any discrepancy was resolved by discussion.

We collected the participants' Facebook data that can be accessed via user data permissions and extended permissions of Facebook. This includes the users' basic profile, status updates, photos, shared posts, tagged posts, comments/likes received, comments/likes to other posts, liked pages and friend lists. The basic profile includes only a public profile such as ID, name, gender, age range, and locale. Other data include ones shown to public as well as ones to friends only. The time durations of Facebook use by participants were different from each other. Thus, among the collected data, we used data updated during the six-month period prior to the beginning of recruitment and data collection (from March 6, 2012 to September 6, 2012) to control the effects of the variability in the period of Facebook use. A total of 525,334 posts were collected.

For our analysis, we used 10 features from the collected data: the number of status updates, photos, shared posts, tagged posts, comments received, likes received, comments to other posts, likes to other posts, liked pages, and friends. Besides, we incorporated two additional features derived from the collected Facebook data. There are previous studies showing that attachment style affects people's emotional disclosure [36], as well as their responding characteristics to others' behavior [5]. There are several ways to examine such emotional disclosures and responding characteristics. As one way for examining them from our collected dataset, we added two features, i.e., the number of status updates containing emotional keywords and the average time taken to respond to other's comments on user's posts (we calculated the time difference between other's first comment on a user's post and user's comment on the post after others have commented).

Proposed Features for Self-Expression

We propose that the two attachment dimensions will be related to how individuals disclose themselves on Facebook. There are at least two motivations underlying self-expression. First, self-expression is a strategic action aimed at achieving one's social goals [37]. It is an individual's desire to enhance a relationship that promotes self-expression [43]. In detail, observers infer expressers' feeling or traits from the self-expressed materials and get useful information for relationship-building. Thus, self-expression initiates a potential relationship: Unless an individual self-discloses, a relational process does not follow [43]. Second, an anticipated response is an important determinant of self-expression. People expecting others to respond supportively disclose themselves more than those expecting a discouraging or no response [13, 43].

We predict that due to these motivations, the users' activity to express themselves on Facebook will be positively associated with attachment anxiety, but negatively related to attachment avoidance. As briefed, the social goal of anxiously attached people is to enhance close relationships [35], and they have a positive model of others, anticipating responsive and encouraging others. These motivations should lead people with high anxiety to self-disclose frequently on Facebook. In contrast, the goal of avoidantly attached people is to increase their distance from others and maintain self-sufficiency [35]. Their negative model of others should lead them to expect an unfriendly or no reactions from others. Thus, people who have high avoidance are less likely to self-express on Facebook. In support of our prediction, prior research has demonstrated that attachment avoidance is related to less self-expression in offline social interaction [34].

We consider the status update to be the typical and the most direct way of self-expression because Facebook users express their current activity and/or thought via the status update. Although there is an option for a user to limit the disclosure of the status updates from only him/herself all the way to everyone, the main purpose of the status update is for the user to disclose him/herself to others.

H1. Status updates will be positively associated with attachment anxiety.

H2. Status updates will be negatively associated with attachment avoidance.

Emotion also plays an important role in self-disclosure [42], and it is closely related to attachment [7]. Thus, as a self-disclosure medium, emotional expression on Facebook likely varies by attachment dimensions. Specifically, people with high anxiety draw others' attention by expressing negative emotion, such as anger, hostility, or contempt [16, 40]. Desiring to build a relationship and expecting others to respond to their emotions, people who have high anxiety are likely to engage in frequent emotional expression on Facebook. In contrast, attachment avoidance is generally characterized by the lack of emotional expression. People with high avoidance defensively inhibit painful memories of past rejection and separation and thus prevent those emotions from becoming conscious [33]. Because they are likely to expect others to be unresponsive or unfriendly to their emotional disclosure, emotional expression will be negatively associated to attachment avoidance.

Anger (9)	Fear (9)	Sadness (31)	Disgust (16)	Joy (27)
angry	afraid	alone	ashamed	amazing
frustrated	helpless	bad	awful	awesome
jealous	naked	broken	bored	beautiful
mad	scared	confused	disgusting	best
mean	stressed	crappy	gross	fine
upset	trapped	depressed	pathetic	happier
pissed	vulnerable	drained	wasted	loved

Table 1. Sample emotional keywords of five primary emotions defined in "We Feel Fine."

While emotional expression can be shown in a range of ways, we take a simple keyword-based approach to capture the emotional expression. Facebook users might reveal their emotion via photos that they take. Another user might share photos or postings that he/she sympathizes with. Also, status updates written by users might have different degrees of emotional expression. Analyzing such diverse channels could provide a more comprehensive view to understand emotional expression, but it is highly difficult. In the current study, we considered the proportion of status updates containing emotion keywords as a key feature to measure emotional expression. To identify emotion keywords in postings, we used the list of emotion words in the We Feel Fine project [29], which were collected from Web blog posts and manually placed into emotion categories. We focused on the five emotions: anger, fear, sadness, disgust, and happiness, as they were identified as the primary emotions in social psychology [18]. Table 1 contains the list of keywords for those five primary emotions. To analyze Korean postings, each English keyword is manually translated to relevant Korean word(s) based on the English-Korean dictionary. We also considered applying LIWC, a computerized text analysis tool that can calculate the degree of positive and negative emotion words used in text. However, the limitation of applying LIWC for our study is that LIWC does not support Korean. Moreover, keywords from We Feel Fine are based on blog posts, which tend to be more similar to Facebook posts than the general lexicon used in LIWC. For both English and Korean, we simply counted the number of status updates containing the emotion keywords. Note that we also examined the use of emoticons as a part of emotional expression. We counted the number of status updates containing emoticons from the Wikipedia list[1] as of September 2012. However, the absolute number of emoticon uses was very small (*Median = 0, Mean = 0.2, Std.Dev. = 0.63*, across 640 Facebook users), so we did not include it for our analysis.

H3. Status updates containing emotional keywords will be positively associated with attachment anxiety.

H4. Status updates containing emotional keywords will be negatively associated with attachment avoidance.

Proposed Features for Responsiveness

We propose that attachment dimensions will be related to how Facebook users respond to others. We predict that responsiveness will be significantly associated with attachment anxiety. Relational process is reciprocal: Person A's response generates Person B's response. That is, showing responsiveness is a strategic way to elicit more responses and thus build a relationship [43]. People with high anxiety are likely to fulfill their desire to build close relationships by showing responses actively. Research in the caregiving literature has documented that individuals who have high anxiety tend to be over-involved and impulsive in caring for others, because they need greater interdependence [13, 20]. The responsiveness of people who have high anxiety may be motivated by a desire to meet strategic goals (e.g., closeness) and an impulsive desire to avoid negative consequences (e.g., rejection) [20] that can result from their not responding. Thus, we think that people who have high anxiety are likely to respond to others more actively.

People with high avoidance show inconsistent relational behaviors. On one hand, they are disinterested or unresponsive in social relationships. Because their primary goal is to maintain self-sufficiency, they are uninvolved in relationship-building [35]). Individuals who do not want to build a relationship are unlikely to reciprocate [43]. Also, people who have high avoidance are egoistically oriented and lack a sense of interdependence [13, 20, 36]. Thus, they may show less responsiveness. On the other hand, other research suggests that because all human beings have the fundamental need to belong [6], high-avoidance individuals value relationships at a preconscious level [33]. Thus they might show responsiveness on Facebook as a defensive means to counteract the indifference and rejection they perceive in past relationships. We expect these conflicting motivations to nullify the link between responsiveness on Facebook and attachment avoidance.

Facebook users can show their responses to others by adding comments or pushing a "like" button to others' posts. We considered comments to other posts as a relatively active response compared to likes; commenting implies that the user saw the posts and engaged in them actively. In contrast, likes to other posts can be considered as a response that may be shown by people who do not want to express their opinions or thoughts.

H5. Comments to other posts will be positively associated with attachment anxiety (and will not be associated with attachment avoidance).

H6: Likes to other posts will be negatively associated with attachment anxiety (and will not be associated with attachment avoidance).

REGRESSION ANALYSIS

We selected four Facebook features that are closely related to attachment dimensions in terms of self-expression and responsiveness. We further consider other Facebook features that also might prove significant to the attachment dimensions. For this, we tested our hypotheses by hierarchical regression for each attachment dimension with all Facebook features. We considered 12 variables, shown in Table 2, including the 10 Facebook features and two derived ones.

[1] http://en.wikipedia.org/wiki/List of emoticons

Attachment dimensions	Median	Mean	Std. Dev.
Attachment anxiety	4	3.87	1.56
Attachment avoidance	3.25	3.29	1.23

Facebook features	Median	Mean	Std. Dev.
Self-expression			
Status updates	4	42.16	90.62
Status updates with emotional words	1	14.12	35.98
Responsiveness			
Comments to others	56	87.03	128.73
Likes to others	30	174.89	254.80
Other Facebook features			
Number of friends	278	339.3	273.51
Comments received	218	235.18	173.99
Likes received	187	240.05	222.48
Photos	35	97.39	133.72
Liked pages	5.61	5.49	1.96
Tagging	2	2.66	1.84
Sharing	2	2.82	2.24
Response time (hour)	52.48	55.34	36.51
Number of observations: 640			

Table 2. Descriptive statistics for participants' activities across six months. All behavioral variables except number of Liked pages follow heavy-tailed distributions and have variances larger than their means.

Predictor	β for Anxiety Model 1	Model 2
Controls		
Age	−0.16**	−0.13*
Gender	0.05	0.03
Culture	−0.21**	−0.16*
Self-expression		
Status updates		0.18*
Status updates with emotional words		−0.12*
Responsiveness		
Comments		0.07
Likes		−0.18***
Other Facebook features		
Number of friends		−0.07
Comments received		0.08
Likes received		−0.04
Photos		0.16*
Liked pages		0.04
Tagging		−0.17*
Sharing		−0.17*
Response time (hour)		−0.06*
F-statistic	9.587	4.458
(df)	(3, 360)	(15, 348)
Adjusted R^2	0.07	0.13
F change	–	3.015***

significance codes: '***' 0.001 '**' 0.01 '*' 0.05
Gender *(1 = male, 2 = female)*, Culture *(1 = United States, 2 = Korea)*
Number of observations: 640

Table 3. The results of hierarchical regression for attachment anxiety.

All Facebook features (independent variables) except the number of Liked pages follow heavy-tailed distributions, and their variances were larger than their means (see Table 2). To control for skew, all dependent variables except Liked pages were standardized after log-transformation (i.e., log-transformed with base 2 after adding 1, and then converted to z-scores). The number of Liked pages was standardized without log-transformation. Attachment dimensions (dependent variables) are also standardized.

Additionally, we entered three demographics-related control variables in regression analysis. Our U.S. samples were MTukers, whereas the Korean samples were mostly college students. Due to the difference in demographics, we controlled for age and gender (*1 = male, 2 = female*). We also controlled for culture (*1 = United States, 2 = Korea*). The attachment literature has documented mixed results on the relationship between culture and attachment. On one hand, prior research demonstrated culturally universal effects of attachment [1, 23, 48]. On the other hand, there is evidence that attachment effect varies by culture [14, 38, 49]. Because there is no evidence on *a priori* effect of culture interacting with SNS users' attachment styles, we entered culture as a control variable, rather than hypothesizing how culture moderates the link between Facebook activities and attachment styles.

To examine the relationships between attachment dimensions and Facebook features, we applied hierarchical regression with the first model including control variables (3 variables) and the second model including all Facebook features (12 variables). Table 3 and Table 4 show the result of regression analysis for attachment anxiety and that for attachment avoidance, respectively.

In Table 3, in the control variables, the age and culture show a significant relationship with attachment anxiety (age: $\beta = -0.13, p = 0.02$, culture: $\beta = -0.16, p = 0.02$). The status updates and the emotional statuses, representing self-expression, show a significant relationship with attachment anxiety (status updates: $\beta = 0.18, p = 0.02$, emotional statuses: $\beta = -0.12, p = 0.03$). However, for attachment responsiveness, the number of comments does not show a significant relationship with attachment anxiety, while the number of likes does (comments: $\beta = 0.07, p = 0.70$, likes: $\beta = -0.18, p < 0.001$). As for other features, the number of photos is associated with a significant increase in attachment anxiety ($\beta = 0.16, p = 0.05$), while the number of tagged posts and the number of shared posts are associated with a significant decrease in attachment anxiety (tagging: $\beta = -0.17, p = 0.04$, sharing: $\beta = -0.17, p = 0.03$).

As for attachment avoidance (see Table 4), in the control variables, the culture shows a significant relationship with attachment avoidance ($\beta = -0.26, p < 0.001$). The status updates and emotional statuses are associated with a significant decrease in attachment avoidance (status updates: $\beta = -0.09, p = 0.01$, emotional statuses: $\beta = -0.10, p = 0.002$). The number of friends and the response time are associated with a significant decrease in the attachment avoidance (number of friends: $\beta = -0.17, p = 0.006$, response time: $\beta = -0.14, p = 0.009$), while the number of liked pages is associated with significant increase ($\beta = 0.13, p = 0.05$).

As for self-expression, the number of status updates is associated with a significant increase in attachment anxiety, while the number of those containing emotional keywords is associated with a significant decrease in attachment anxiety. On the other hand, in Table 4, status updates and those with emotional keywords are associated with a significant decrease in attachment avoidance. Thus, *H1, H2, and H4* – which were developed based on offline interaction research that used at-

Predictor	β for Avoidance Model 1	Model 2
Controls		
Age	0.03	−0.02
Gender	−0.02	0.01
Culture	−0.36**	−0.26***
Self-expression		
Status updates		−0.09*
Status updates with emotional words		−0.09**
Responsiveness		
Comments		−0.07
Likes		0.08
Other Facebook features		
Number of friends		−0.17**
Comments received		−0.01
Likes received		−0.14
Photos		0.11
Liked pages		0.13*
Tagging		−0.03
Sharing		−0.05
Response time (hour)		−0.14**
F-statistic	4.285	3.894
(df)	(3, 360)	(15, 348)
Adjusted R^2	0.03	0.11
F change	–	3.700***

significance codes: '***' 0.001 '**' 0.01 '*' 0.05
Gender *(1 = male, 2 = female)*, Culture *(1 = United States, 2 = Korea)*
Number of observations: 640

Table 4. The results of hierarchical regression for attachment avoidance.

tachment theory – are supported in online interaction as well, however, *H3* is not supported.

H1, H2, and H4 are supported.

H3 is not supported.

As for responsiveness, the number of comments does not have a significant relationship with attachment anxiety, while the number of likes is associated with a significant decrease (Table 3). However, in Table 4, comments and likes are not significantly associated with attachment avoidance. Thus, *H5* is not confirmed and *H6* is confirmed. Like self-expression activities, Facebook features related to responsiveness, not comments but likes, followed offline interpersonal behavior predicted by the attachment theory.

H5 is not supported.

H6 is supported.

In summary, the regression results showed that the attachment theory usefully predicts both offline and online relational behaviors. Self-expression activities on Facebook can predict both attachment anxiety and attachment avoidance. In contrast, responsiveness activities on Facebook (the number of likes) can predict attachment anxiety only.

It is not appropriate to directly characterize individual attachment types from the above regression analysis. However, it would be somewhat meaningful to compare different attachment styles. For example, anxious and fearful types are both high in anxiety; however, the former would potentially show more self-expression since it is lower in avoidance. Similarly, comparing the secure and anxious types both with low avoidance, the latter would show more self-expression via status update; however, less with emotional words, and would probably respond more with comments but less with likes. As for avoidant and fearful types, the fearful would be more active in status update, but less with emotional terms, and would respond more with comments and less with likes.

Anxiety	Avoidance
Tagging	**Likes**
Photos	**Status updates**
Likes	**Emotional statuses**
Response time	Photos
Status updates	Like received
Emotional statuses	Comments received
Comments	**Comments**
Likes received	Tagging
Comments received	Response time
Liked pages	Liked pages
Number of friends	Number of friends
Sharing	Sharing

Table 5. Features sorted by information gain. Selected four features (bold-faced) are relatively highly ranked.

ATTACHMENT CLASSIFICATION

In this section, we present a classification experiment of attachment styles into two classes, high and low, for each of the two attachment dimensions. We show that using Facebook features with the Support Vector Machine (SVM) [15] can automatically classify attachment styles with accuracy much better than a baseline.

We start by computing information gain[2] to measure the degree of the discriminatory power of each Facebook feature. Table 5 shows the features sorted by the information gain metric. The bold-faced ones are the four selected features in the previous sections, and they are relatively highly ranked.

Among other features, *tagging* (i.e., the number of events a user is tagged in) and *response time* (i.e., the time spent on responding to others' posts) have high information gain for attachment anxiety, but relatively low information gain for attachment avoidance, which implies that they may not be effective when classifying for both attachment anxiety and attachment avoidance. Similarly, *like received* and *comment received* have high information gain for attachment avoidance, indicating that received Facebook activities are good indicators in classifying the level of attachment avoidance, but not for attachment anxiety.

[2]Information gain is defined as $H(X) - H(X|Y)$, where $H(X)$ is the entropy of a random variable X, i.e., $H(X) = -\sum_i^n P(X{=}x_i)\log P(X{=}x_i)$, given that $P(X{=}x_i)$ is the probability of $X{=}x_i$, and $H(X|Y)$ is the conditional entropy of X given another random variable Y, i.e., $H(X|Y) = \sum_i^n P(Y{=}y_i)H(X|Y{=}y_i)$.
In the context of this paper, it is used as a metric to measure the impact of a feature from a set of features (i.e. independent variables) in classifying the class of each attachment dimension (i.e. dependent variable). It does not make any prior assumption on the nature of relationship between the variables (e.g., monotonic relationship, linearity in the relationship).

	ALL	Selected-4	Random-4	Base Line
Anxiety	87.44%	83.26%	64.26%	58%
Avoidance	89.46%	84.65%	65.64%	52%

Table 6. The results of classification accuracy. They imply that the four selected features are representative features for binary classification of each attachment dimension.

Class (*# of participants*)	Precision	Recall	F-measure
High Anxiety (*368*)	0.796	0.954	0.868
Low Anxiety (*272*)	0.915	0.668	0.772

Table 7. The performance results of binary classification for attachment anxiety.

We then perform and compare binary classification using all of the features (labeled as *All* in Table 6), the four selected features (labeled as *Selected-4*), and four random features (labeled as *Random-4*). We evaluate the classification accuracy using 10-fold cross-validation with SVM. For *Random-4*, we take the average of 20 repeated evaluations. Table 6 presents the classification accuracy of attachment anxiety and attachment avoidance.

Binary Classification

The accuracy of *All*, i.e., with all available features, is the highest that we can get. The accuracy of *Selected-4* is almost identical to that of *All* and higher than that of *Random-4*. The baselines of anxiety and avoidance are 58% and 52%, respectively (the case of every participants is classified as one class).

The difference between *All* and *Selected-4* is larger for avoidance than for anxiety classification. We conjecture that this is consistent with the results in Table 6, in which responsiveness-related features, i.e., comments and likes, do not show a significant relationship with avoidance.

Table 7 shows the classification performance with the four selected features on attachment anxiety. Since the number of people with low anxiety is smaller than the number with high anxiety, the recall of low anxiety is small and the baseline is 58% (the case of every user is classified as high anxiety). We think this is natural since previous work states that people with high attachment anxiety and low attachment avoidance tend to use SNS more [41].

Table 8 shows the classification performance with the four selected features on attachment avoidance. The baseline is 52% (the number of people who have low avoidance is larger than the number of people who have high avoidance), which shows more people in low avoidance use Facebook.

Multi Class Classification

Binary classification can be used to determine users' attachment level of each attachment dimension. For more practical use, we further examined multi-class classification for the four types of attachment styles.

Class (*# of participants*)	Precision	Recall	F-measure
High Avoidance (*308*)	0.904	0.761	0.827
Low Avoidance (*332*)	0.807	0.925	0.862

Table 8. The performance results of binary classification for attachment avoidance.

Class (*# of participants*)	Precision	Recall	F-measure
Secure (*156*)	0.838	0.790	0.813
Anxious (*177*)	0.710	0.921	0.802
Avoidant (*116*)	1	0.444	0.615
Fearful (*191*)	0.757	0.839	0.796

Table 9. The performance results of multiclass classification.

Table 9 shows the classification performance of multi-class classification. The baseline is 29.8% (the case of every user is classified as fearful). Overall accuracy was 77.83%. Since the number of the avoidant type is much smaller than the other types, the F-measure shows the lowest performance (0.615) even when the precision shows 1.

DISCUSSIONS

This research examined the relationship between Facebook users' online behavioral patterns and their relational orientation based on the attachment theory. Our results show that Facebook users' attachment style is significantly related to their self-expression and responsiveness activities on Facebook. There may be many reasons for Facebook users liking, commenting, and posting, etc. Our research shows that one reason, their relational orientation, can be inferred by looking at their self-expressing/responding activities on Facebook. Our research demonstrates that the attachment theory is useful in predicting not only offline but also online social interaction. Our findings will be informative for both social scientists who study the implications of attachment style and social media practitioners who could use this information to design customized social media.

Our research opens multiple new inquiries of social computing research. For example, there are many issues in online behavioral analysis, such as the inter-attachment activities. The communication between two anxious users may be different from the communication between an anxious user and an avoidant user. Analyzing such inter-attachment activities and their implications would be an interesting future study issue. Another issue is to incorporate the analysis of the topic of the users' posts. People of different attachment styles might have different topics in their posts. For instance, avoidant users may usually talk about a non-relational, task-oriented topic to decrease intimacy, whereas anxious users may often post about their emotional feelings to increase intimacy. Thus, looking into the topics would also be helpful to analyzing the user's attachment style.

Future research might examine whether our findings are generalizable to other types of social media or specific to Facebook. Twitter is another social media form seen as a combination of both social networking and microblogging [30]. However, there exist multiple differences between Facebook and Twitter. For example, Facebook allows reciprocal interaction between users: Facebook users post comments on each other's pages and form virtual groups based on common interests. In contrast, Twitter is less reciprocal: Twitter is a platform where people usually argue or debate on various topics, e.g., political debate [46] and its message is targeted for general audience [9]. Moreover, Facebook is used more by people who are gregarious in their nature, whereas Twitter is preferred by those who seek cognition or utilitarian values [25]. Due to the less relational characteristic of Twitter usage, Twitter might not reflect the users' attachment styles. Facebook may be a more appropriate social media to examine interpersonal online relationship. The characteristic of Facebook, which does not support anonymity, seems to make Facebook activities possible to reflect the same attachment styles of offline research. Further study might extend our Facebook-based analysis to other social network services.

The current research analyzed Facebook features only from the perspective of the user him/herself, i.e., how the user expresses and responses to others. However, SNS user behavior involves essentially dynamic and reciprocal interaction, such that Person A's expression influences Person B's responses, which then affects Person A's response to Person B. It is an important topic to explore this feedback process and extend our understanding of SNS user behavior. For example, how will others respond to status updates and emotional communication expressed by users who have high anxiety? Will others' reactions to users who have high anxiety differ from the anxious users' responses to others? These questions await future research.

Because culture's effect on attachment has generated mixed results [1, 14, 23, 38, 48, 49], we entered culture as a control variable and did not systematically compare the impact of culture on Facebook activities/attachment across the U.S. and Korean samples. Moreover, attachment research has demonstrated that intra-cultural attachment variance is much bigger than inter-cultural attachment variance [47, 32]. An important follow-up would be to investigate more thoroughly how culture moderates the relationship between Facebook users' attachment styles and online behavior. While this paper addressed an initial study on the coherence of users' relational orientations in online and offline interactions, we are planning the following important steps including user studies and pilot application design across cultures.

Our model included three demographic-related control variables. However, it is likely that many other variables could also potentially contribute to the attachment styles, and the current model is limited to that extent.

CONCLUSION

Social interaction in a popular online social network, Facebook, reflects people's relational orientation. There are several models to figure out human personality, such as the Big Five or MBTI. These models focus on individual personal traits, although an online social network is a relational context and major activities in online social network involve interpersonal communication. Therefore, our study focused on attachment theory, a leading theory of interpersonal relationships. We crawled users' Facebook data and surveyed attachment styles using a Facebook application, KnowYourself. We summarized behavioral differences of two attachment dimensions (anxiety and avoidance) and four attachment types and identified four features that significantly affect each attachment dimension, by exploring the two key relational processes (self-expression and responsiveness) on Facebook. We used regression analysis and found relationships between two attachment dimensions (anxiety and avoidance) and Facebook activities. The results present classifications for attachment dimensions that can successfully determine users' attachment style.

APPENDIX

Attachment Style Questionnaires

To shorten the survey's length, we randomly selected four items of attachment avoidance ($\alpha = 0.685$) and four items of attachment anxiety ($\alpha = 0.848$) from the ECR-R [21, 45, 19]. This questionnaire uses a 7-point scale ranging from "Not at all" to "Very much."

1. I prefer not to show my significant other how I feel deep down.

2. I feel comfortable sharing my private thoughts and feelings with my significant other.

3. I find it difficult to allow myself to depend on my significant other.

4. I often worry that my significant other will not want to stay with me.

5. I worry a lot about my relationships with significant other.

6. I often wish that my significant other's feelings for me were as strong as my feelings for him or her.

7. I feel comfortable opening up to my significant other.

8. I worry that my significant other won't care about me as much as I care about him or her.

Attachment avoidance and attachment anxiety are measured by taking an average of relevant questions as follows.

- Avoidance: 1, 2 *(reverse-coded)*, 3, 7 *(reverse-coded)*
- Anxiety: 4, 5, 6, 8

ACKNOWLEDGMENTS

The authors thank the anonymous reviewers for their valuable comments and our shepherd, Professor Susan Fussell, for her support and insightful comments to improve the quality of our paper. This work was partly supported by National Research Foundation of Korea (NRF) grant (No. 2011-0018120) and by Next-Generation Information Computing Development Program through NRF (No. 2010-0020729), both funded by the Korea government (MSIP).

REFERENCES

1. Ainsworth, M. D. S., Blehar, M. C., Waters, E., and Wall, S. *Patterns of attachment: A psychological study of the strange situation*. 1978.
2. Andangsari, E. W., Gumilar, I., and Godwin, R. Social networking sites use and psychological attachment need among indonesian young adults population. *International Journal of Social Science Studies 1*, 2 (2013), 133–138.
3. Anders, S. L., and Tucker, J. S. Adult attachment style, interpersonal communication competence, and social support. *Personal Relationships 7*, 4 (2000), 379–389.
4. Back, M., Stopfer, J., Vazire, S., Gaddis, S., Schmukle, S., Egloff, B., and Gosling, S. Facebook profiles reflect actual personality, not self-idealization. *Psychological Science 21*, 3 (2010), 372–374.
5. Bartholomew, K., and Horowitz, L. Attachment styles among young adults: a test of a four-category model. *Journal of Personality and Social Psychology 61*, 2 (1991), 226.
6. Baumeister, R. F., and Leary, M. R. The need to belong: desire for interpersonal attachments as a fundamental human motivation. *Psychological Bulletin 117*, 3 (1995), 497.
7. Bowlby, J. *Attachment and loss*. 1969.
8. Bowlby, J. The making and breaking of affectional bonds. *The British Journal of Psychiatry 130*, 3 (1977), 201–210.
9. Boyd, D., Golder, S., and Lotan, G. Tweet, tweet, retweet: Conversational aspects of retweeting on twitter. In *System Sciences (HICSS), 2010 43rd Hawaii International Conference on* (2010), 1–10.
10. Brennan, K. A., Clark, C. L., and Shaver, P. R. Self-report measurement of adult attachment. *Attachment theory and close relationships* (1998), 46–76.
11. Brislin, R. W. Back-translation for cross-cultural research. *Journal of cross-cultural psychology 1*, 3 (1970), 185–216.
12. Collins, N. L., and Read, S. J. Adult attachment, working models, and relationship quality in dating couples. *Journal of personality and social psychology 58*, 4 (1990), 644.
13. Collins, N. L., and Read, S. J. Cognitive representations of attachment: The structure and function of working models. *Advances in personal relationships 5* (1994), 53–90.
14. Cooper, M. L., Shaver, P. R., and Collins, N. L. Attachment styles, emotion regulation, and adjustment in adolescence. *Journal of personality and social psychology 74*, 5 (1998), 1380.
15. Cortes, C., and Vapnik, V. Support-vector networks. *Machine learning 20*, 3 (1995), 273–297.
16. Crowell, J. A., Treboux, D., Gao, Y., Fyffe, C., Pan, H., and Waters, E. Assessing secure base behavior in adulthood: Development of a measure, links to adult attachment representations and relations to couples' communication and reports of relationships. *Developmental Psychology 38*, 5 (2002), 679.
17. Drouin, M., and Landgraff, C. Texting, sexting, and attachment in college students' romantic relationships. *Computers in Human Behavior 28*, 2 (2012), 444–449.
18. Ekman, P., and Friesen, W. V. Unmasking the face: A guide to recognizing emotions from facial cues, 1975.
19. Fairchild, A. J., and Finney, S. J. Investigating validity evidence for the experiences in close relationships–revised questionnaire. *Educational and Psychological Measurement 66*, 1 (2006), 116–135.
20. Feeney, B. C., and Collins, N. L. Motivations for caregiving in adult intimate relationships: Influences on caregiving behavior and relationship functioning. *Personality and Social Psychology Bulletin 29*, 8 (2003), 950–968.
21. Fraley, R. C., Waller, N. G., and Brennan, K. A. An item response theory analysis of self-report measures of adult attachment. *Journal of personality and social psychology 78*, 2 (2000), 350.
22. Gentzler, A. L., Oberhauser, A. M., Westerman, D., and Nadorff, D. K. College students' use of electronic communication with parents: Links to loneliness, attachment, and relationship quality. *Cyberpsychology, Behavior, and Social Networking 14*, 1-2 (2011), 71–74.
23. Grossmann, K. E., Grossmann, K., Huber, F., and Wartner, U. German children's behavior towards their mothers at 12 months and their fathers at 18 months in ainsworth's strange situation. *International Journal of Behavioral Development 4*, 2 (1981), 157–181.
24. Hazan, C., and Shaver, P. Romantic love conceptualized as an attachment process. *Journal of personality and social psychology 52*, 3 (1987), 511.
25. Hughes, D., Rowe, M., Batey, M., and Lee, A. A tale of two sites: Twitter vs. facebook and the personality predictors of social media usage. *Computers in Human Behavior* (2011).
26. Jenkins-Guarnieri, M. A., Wright, S. L., and Hudiburgh, L. M. The relationships among attachment style, personality traits, interpersonal competency, and facebook use. *Journal of Applied Developmental Psychology 33*, 6 (2012), 294–301.
27. Jin, B., and Pena, J. F. Mobile communication in romantic relationships: Mobile phone use, relational uncertainty, love, commitment, and attachment styles. *Communication Reports 23*, 1 (2010), 39–51.
28. Kaitz, M., Bar-Haim, Y., Lehrer, M., and Grossman, E. Adult attachment style and interpersonal distance. *Attachment & human development 6*, 3 (2004), 285–304.

29. Kamvar, S., and Harris, J. We feel fine and searching the emotional web. In *Proceedings of ICWSM* (2011).

30. Kwak, H., Lee, C., Park, H., and Moon, S. What is twitter, a social network or a news media? In *Proceedings of WWW* (2010).

31. Lee, S., and Thompson, L. Do agents negotiate for the best (or worst) interest of principals? secure, anxious and avoidant principal–agent attachment. *Journal of Experimental Social Psychology 47*, 3 (2011), 681–684.

32. McLeod, S. A. Cultural differences in attachment. Retrieved from `http://www.simplypsychology.org/culture-attachment.html`, 2014.

33. Mikulincer, M., Gillath, O., and Shaver, P. R. Activation of the attachment system in adulthood: Threat-related primes increase the accessibility of mental representations of attachment figures. *Journal of Personality and Social Psychology 83*, 4 (2002), 881.

34. Mikulincer, M., and Nachshon, O. Attachment styles and patterns of self-disclosure. *Journal of Personality and Social Psychology 61*, 2 (1991), 321.

35. Mikulincer, M., and Shaver, P. R. Boosting attachment security to promote mental health, prosocial values, and inter-group tolerance. *Psychological Inquiry 18*, 3 (2007), 139–156.

36. Mikulincer, M., Shaver, P. R., Gillath, O., Nitzberg, R. A., et al. Attachment, caregiving, and altruism: Boosting attachment security increases compassion and helping. *Journal of personality and social psychology 89*, 5 (2005), 817.

37. Miller, L. C., and Read, S. J. Why am i telling you this?: Self-disclosure in a goal-based model of personality. *Self-disclosure: Theory, research, and therapy* (1987), 35–58.

38. Moore, R. L. Love and limerence with chinese characteristics: Student romance in the prc. *Romantic love and sexual behavior: Perspectives from the social sciences*, 251–283.

39. Morris, R. R., and Picard, R. Crowdsourcing collective emotional intelligence. In *Proceedings of Collective Intelligence* (2012).

40. Moss, E., and St-Laurent, D. Attachment at school age and academic performance. *Developmental Psychology 37*, 6 (2001), 863.

41. Oldmeadow, J. A., Quinn, S., and Kowert, R. Attachment style, social skills, and facebook use amongst adults. *Computers in Human Behavior 29*, 3 (2013), 1142–1149.

42. Pennebaker, J. W. *Opening up: The healing power of confiding in others*. 1990.

43. Reis, H. T., and Patrick, B. C. Attachment and intimacy: Component processes. *Social psychology: Handbook of basic principles* (1996), 523–563.

44. Shaver, P. R., and Hazan, C. Adult romantic attachment: Theory and evidence. *Advances in personal relationships* (1993), 29–70.

45. Sibley, C. G., Fischer, R., and Liu, J. H. Reliability and validity of the revised experiences in close relationships (ecr-r) self-report measure of adult romantic attachment. *Personality and Social Psychology Bulletin 31*, 11 (2005), 1524–1536.

46. Tumasjan, A., Sprenger, T. O., Sandner, P. G., and Welpe, I. M. Predicting elections with twitter: What 140 characters reveal about political sentiment. *ICWSM 10* (2010), 178–185.

47. Van Ijzendoorn, M. H., and Kroonenberg, P. M. Cross-cultural patterns of attachment: A meta-analysis of the strange situation. *Child Development* (1988), 147–156.

48. Van Ijzendoorn, M. H., and Sagi-Schwartz, A. Cross-cultural patterns of attachment: Universal and contextual dimensions. *Handbook of attachment: Theory, research, and clinical applications* (2008), 880–905.

49. Wang, C.-C. D., and Mallinckrodt, B. S. Differences between taiwanese and us cultural beliefs about ideal adult attachment. *Journal of Counseling Psychology 53*, 2 (2006), 192.

50. Weisskirch, R. S., and Delevi, R. Attachment style and conflict resolution skills predicting technology use in relationship dissolution. *Computers in Human Behavior 29*, 6 (2013), 2530–2534.

The Role of Social Influence In Security Feature Adoption

Sauvik Das
Carnegie Mellon University
sauvik@cmu.edu

Adam D.I. Kramer
Facebook, Inc.
akramer@fb.com

Laura A. Dabbish
Carnegie Mellon University
dabbish@cmu.edu

Jason I. Hong
Carnegie Mellon University
jasonh@cs.cmu.edu

ABSTRACT

Social influence is key in technology adoption, but its role in security-feature adoption is unique and remains unclear. Here, we analyzed how three Facebook security features—Login Approvals, Login Notifications, and Trusted Contacts—diffused through the social networks of 1.5 million people. Our results suggest that social influence affects one's likelihood to adopt a security feature, but its effect varies based on the observability of the feature, the current feature adoption rate among a potential adopter's friends, and the number of distinct social circles from which those feature-adopting friends originate. Curiously, there may be a threshold higher than which having more security-feature adopting friends predicts for higher adoption likelihood, but below which having more feature-adopting friends predicts for lower adoption likelihood. Furthermore, the magnitude of this threshold is modulated by the attributes of a feature—features that are more noticeable (Login Approvals, Trusted Contacts) have lower thresholds.

Author Keywords

Social Cybersecurity; Social Influence; Facebook; Security; Security Adoption

ACM Classification Keywords

H.1.2 **[MODELS AND PRINCIPLES]:** User/Machine Systems—*Human factors*

INTRODUCTION

In early 2013, the Associated Press's Twitter account was compromised through a password phishing scheme, and erroneously tweeted that President Obama was injured in a bombing [30]. In response, stock prices plummeted [19], adversely affecting thousands. Moreover, this incident could have been easily prevented with the use of two-factor authentication—a security feature, available at that time, that requires entry of a random code generated on one's phone in addition to a password when authenticating [16].

CSCW'15, March 14 - 18 2015, Vancouver, BC, Canada

ACM 978-1-4503-2922-4/15/03...$15.00
http://dx.doi.org/10.1145/2675133.2675225

This incident is just one example of how the underutilization of available security features remains a large, outstanding problem. Indeed, in our age of increasing connectivity, it is critically important for widespread awareness of and appropriate use of security features.

Recent work suggests that one promising approach to widespread security feature awareness and uptake is by understanding the social diffusion of security feature adoption, or how the feature propagates from person-to-person through a social network. Indeed, a recent retrospective interview study [11] outlines that security behavior changes are often the result of a social diffusion process. Many participants of this study reported adopting security features solely because their friends also used those features—in other words, their behavior was driven by *social proof* [10] (e.g., other people like me use this feature, so I should too). However, there is also evidence that social processes can work *against* security related behavior change (e.g., only paranoid people use complex security features, and I'm not paranoid) [11, 13].

Thus, while the idea that social influence affects security feature adoption is interesting, what little we know suggests that *social influence may uniquely affect security technology* because security features are preventative, intrusive, and can be associated with paranoia [11,13]. Indeed, if only 'experts' or people who are perceived as paranoid initially use a security feature, lay people might develop an illusory correlation [9] between using a security feature and paranoia that makes them avoid using the feature. Conversely, *social proof* can also be an effective motivator for security driven behavior change [11], especially when people can *observe* others like them behaving securely. In other words, social influence can be both a helpful and harmful force in security-feature adoption, but we do not yet fully understand the parameters under which it is helpful or harmful.

To address this gap in the literature, we analyzed whether and how three Facebook security features—Login Approvals, Login Notifications and Trusted Contacts—diffused through the social networks of 1.5 million people who use Facebook. Our results confirm that social influence does indeed play a role in security-feature adoption, but that the direction and strength of its effect seems to be moderated by the overall adoption of the feature among a potential adopter's friends, the number of distinct social circles from which those feature-adopting friends originate, and the individual attributes of the security feature.

BACKGROUND

Social Diffusion and Friend Diversity

Earlier work suggests that exposure to novel information on social networking sites increases information diffusion through social channels [3], but that these diffusion chains are most effective when the seed information is shared by many different sources [3,27], especially when the information is intended to enact behavior change [6,7]. Ugander and colleagues [29] extended this result, finding that people who were invited to join Facebook through e-mail recommendations from their friends were more likely to join if the recommenders were from distinct social contexts—i.e., receiving an invitation from a school friend and a family member was more convincing than receiving invitations from two different family members. Romero and colleagues [22] found that the "persistence" of the information being spread—or, the marginal likelihood that content will be re-shared after one more exposure—is also important in determining whether content will be diffused. Specifically, controversial topics—like information about security, say—require repeated exposure from many sources before they are diffused.

***H1:** People with exposure to feature-adopting friends from many distinct social contexts will be more likely to use that feature than others with exposure to the same number of feature-adopting friends from fewer distinct social contexts.*

Social Diffusion and Observability

It is well established that not all behavior diffuses equally [6,7], and the adoption of technology is no different. Thus, efforts have been made to model the factors that influence the adoption of technology. Rogers [21], in his seminal work on the diffusion of innovations, argued that new technology gets widely adopted through a process by which it is communicated through members of a social network. Rogers argues that primarily subjective perceptions get communicated through social channels, and that these perceptions are key to the success of an innovation. He further outlines that preventative innovations—or innovations, like security features, that prevent undesirable outcomes from happening—typically have low adoption rates, in part because of their low *observability*, or the invisibility of their use and benefits. More recently, Das and colleagues [11] confirmed that the *observability* of security tools and behaviors was a key factor in driving the adoption of security tools. In fact, they found that of all social catalysts for behavior change, observing others use security tools was the most prevalent.

***H2:** More observable security features will more effectively diffuse through social channels than less observable security features.*

Diffusing Behavior via Social Influence

Social influence, of course, affects not only our knowledge but our behavior as well. Christakis and Fowler [12] argue that our social connections can influence our health and weight, whereas Bond and colleagues [5] found that awareness of friends' voting activity was significantly effective at getting people who use Facebook to vote in the 2010 U.S. congressional elections. Kramer [17] found that emotions are contagious on Facebook as well: friends of those who shared emotional content were themselves more likely to share similar emotions. Furthermore, in the context of security, prior work suggests that we do learn about security from each other [20], though communication about security remains relatively rare [11].

Others have looked at the psychological mechanisms underlying social influence. Indeed, most of the previously mentioned work addresses the concept of *social proof*, or our tendency to look to others for examples of what to do when we are uncertain [10]. Milgram, Bickman, and Berkowitz [18] demonstrated the social proof principle when they showed that simply getting a small crowd of people—the more, the better—to look up at the sky on a busy sidewalk caused others to do the same. Other work has shown how social interventions can be powerfully effective at eliciting behavior change: for example, at reducing household energy consumption by informing people about their neighbors' reduced energy consumption [25], reducing hotel guests' wasteful use of towels by telling them previous patrons chose to be less wasteful [14], and even in eliminating young children's phobia of dogs by showing them film clips of other children playing with dogs [4].

Taken together, it appears that the social diffusion of behavior and technology adoption is often driven by *social proof* [10]—or evidence of what to use and how to behave based on the actions of others. Furthermore, this social proof becomes more compelling as one finds *more* examples of others acting similarly, especially examples of others similar to oneself [8,10,18].

The Unique Effect of Social Influence on Security

Prior work in the psychology and application of social influence implies, thus, that if many of one's friends and acquaintances use a security feature, one should be more likely to use that security feature herself. Yet, we see some counter examples of this implication in the usable security literature. Indeed, Gaw and colleagues [13] found that many non-experts perceived others who used e-mail encryption as "paranoid", a perception that inhibited their own use of e-mail encryption. Das and colleagues [11] found that their non-expert participants were similarly aversive towards using security tools, and spoke of their security-expert friends as being "nutty" or going "above and beyond".

Thus, it appears that social proof does not always have the expected effect on security feature adoption. We believe, in fact, that *the use of security features may be uniquely affected by social proof* given that security feature usage is often invisible, rarely communicated, and generally undesired [15,24]. Indeed, prior work in usable privacy and security suggests that many security features remain unused because stringent security measures are often antagonistic towards the specific goal of the end user at any given

Variable	Description
Demographic Variables	
Age	Age of the individual.
Gender	Self-reported gender: male or female.
Friend count	Count of the individuals number of friends with Facebook accounts.
Account length	Days that have passed since the individual activated his account.
Days active in last 30	Days the individual was active on Facebook in the past 30 days.
Social Network Variables	
Mean friend age	Average age of the individual's Facebook friends.
Friend age entropy	Shannon entropy of the individual's Facebook friends' ages.
Percent male friends	Percentage of the individual friends that are male.
Mean friends' account length	Average number of days an individual's Facebook friends have used Facebook.
Friend country entropy	Shannon entropy of countries from which the user has friends.
Mean number of friends among friends	Average number of Facebook friends among an individual's Facebook friends.
Behavioral Variables (all aggregated across the week prior to data collection)	
Posts Created	Number of posts created.
Posts Deleted	Number of posts deleted.
Comments Created	Number of comments created.
Comments Deleted	Number of comments deleted.
Likes	Number of likes given.
Friends Added	Number of friends added.
Friends Removed	Number of friends removed.
Photos Added	Number of photos added.
Videos Added	Number of videos added.
Social Proof Variables	
Percent of friends who use Login Approvals	Percent of friends who use the Login Approvals security feature.
Percent of friends who use Login Notifications	Percent of friends who use the Login Notifications security feature.
Percent of friends who use Trusted Contacts	Percent of friends who use the Trusted Contacts security feature.
Number of diverse social contexts	Number of social contexts from which friends who use security features originate.

Table 1. Collected feature descriptions and distributions. These variables were all collected or computed at an individual level.

moment [24]. For example, while a user might want to check her e-mail, a complex password that usually requires three attempts to get right *prevents* her from checking her e-mail. Thus, people often reject security features when they expect or experience them to be weighty [1].

Consequently, typically only people who are especially dedicated to protecting their information use interruptive security features, and we know from prior work that non-experts may perceive these early adopters as "paranoid" [13]. More formally, because early adopters of security features are likely to be perceived by others as behaviorally *different* (e.g., either paranoid, or in possession of expert knowledge), non-experts may perceive an illusory correlation [9], or an exaggerated relationship, between security feature usage and this behavioral difference. In turn, as non-experts consider themselves different from those who use security features, they may reject the use of security features. Moreover, this illusory correlation should only *strengthen* as more of these security-enthusiast early adopters use the feature because of the "availability heuristic"—a mental shortcut that biases people's judgments towards what is more frequently recalled [28].

The upshot is that the subjective perceptions of a security feature that propagates through social channels may be tainted into working *against* its adoption, at least until enough of a potential adopter's behaviorally similar friends start using the feature so that its use becomes normative.

In other words, there may be a non-linear relationship between one's exposure to feature-adopting friends and one's likelihood to adopt a security feature. Specifically, if a potential adopter is only exposed to *few*, early-adopter friends who use a security feature, it is possible that he might find social proof that a security feature should *not* be used (because of an illusory correlation), and the strength of this *negative* social proof should increase with the number of these feature-adopting friends (because of the availability heuristic). On the other hand, once a potential adopter is exposed to *many* feature-adopting friends, especially those that are similar to himself, he might find social proof that a security feature *should* be used (because of the positive effects of homophilous networks on technology adoption [8]), and the strength of this *positive* social proof should increase with the number of his feature-adopting friends.

H3: *When a potential adopter is exposed to many feature-adopting friends, he will be more likely to adopt a security feature than those with fewer feature-adopting friends.*

H4: *When a potential adopter is exposed to few feature-adopting friends, he will be less likely to adopt a security feature than those with even fewer feature-adopting friends.*

METHODOLOGY

To test our hypotheses, we monitored security feature adoptions for the following three Facebook security features: (1) **Login Approvals**—A feature that requires adopters to enter a separate code, usually generated on or sent to the adopter's smartphone, in addition to their password when they attempt to authenticate; (2) **Login Notifications**—A feature that notifies adopters, via e-mail or SMS, when their account is accessed from previously unseen browsers and devices; and, (3) **Trusted Contacts**—A feature that allows an adopter to specify three to five friends who can verify her identity if she forgot her password and cannot access her e-mail. We investigated multiple security features to avoid drawing conclusions specific to any one feature, especially because the individual attributes of a security feature may play a role in its diffusion [21]. Furthermore, we chose these three features because of their diversity and colocation within the "security settings" page on Facebook.

For 12 days in late 2013, we collected data from a random subset of people who use Facebook and newly adopted one of the aforementioned security features: Login Approvals, Login Notifications, or Trusted Contacts. In total, we collected data from n=250,000 people per feature (750,000 adopters overall)—the positive examples of feature adopters in our dataset. Then, for each day and feature, we also obtained a random sample of an equal number of people who had not adopted that feature up to that day—negative examples of feature adopters. In total, we had n=1,500,000 people across all twelve days, three features (Login Approvals, Login Notifications, Trusted Contacts), and two feature usage states (i.e., uses or doesn't use).

For all people in our sample, we also collected a set of variables that we believed could have affected one's decision to adopt a security feature. These variables fell under four categories: *demographic variables* that described individual characteristics such as age and gender; *behavioral variables* that described activity on Facebook, such as posts shared and deleted; *network variables* that described one's social network, such as friends' average age and gender diversity; and, *social proof variables* that described how many and which of a person's friends had adopted any of the aforementioned security features up to the day during which the data was collected. In Table 1, we provide a full list of variables included in our analysis. All data was de-identified prior to our analysis.

We selected people who newly adopted security features because security feature adoptions were not time-stamped in our data, so it would be otherwise impossible to know who, between two people, adopted a security feature first. For someone who newly adopted a security feature on a given day, however, we knew that all friends of their friends who used that feature adopted it before that day.

Notably, we could not measure *how* security feature adoptions diffused—i.e., we did not alter the observability of security feature usage and initiation. Rather, we simply control for other factors that also affect security feature adoption, such that we can compare the feature adoption rate of two sub-populations that differ primarily in their exposure to friends who have adopted a security feature. We do not believe this limitation to be stifling—understanding the channels through which social diffusion occurs is separate from our goal of understanding its ultimate effect on security feature adoption.

Finally, all data collection complied with Facebook's terms of use and data use policy and was performed in aggregate so that we were not privy to any individual's information. Furthermore, as our data was observational, we believe our analysis constituted minimal risk to those in our sample.

REGRESSION ANALYSIS

To test **H1**—that people with security-feature adopting friends from many distinct social circles should be more likely to adopt a security feature than those with the same number of feature-adopting friends from few distinct social circles—we estimated a logistic regression model for each security feature. These regressions modeled the strength of the relationship between a person's likelihood to adopt a security feature and the number of distinct social contexts from which his feature-adopting friends originated. Note that we define a "distinct social context" as a distinct connected component in one's friend graph, following similar definitions used in prior work [29].

As linear regression analysis assumes independence in the response variable (in our case, whether or not someone in our sample adopted a security feature), we only included a balanced subset of our full sample into the regressions after eliminating people in our sample who happened to be Facebook friends with one another. This reduced sample consisted of n=65,000 positive and negative examples of feature adopters for each of our three features, resulting in n=130,000 people for each regression, all of whom were not friends with one another.

In running these regressions, we controlled for the demographic, social network and behavioral variables described in Table 1. In addition, we also controlled for the *number* of one's feature-adopting friends, so that the coefficient for the *number of distinct social contexts* variable can be interpreted after controlling for a potential adopter's number of feature using friends.

Results

The coefficient for the *number of distinct social contexts* variable for each logistic regression is shown in Figure 1, while the full regression table is shown in Appendix A. These coefficients represent a change in "log-odds", or $ln\frac{P}{1-P}$, where P represents the probability that an individual adopted the security feature. A positive coefficient implies that the log-odds ratio increases, or that an increase in the variable increases the likelihood that a person adopts the feature, P. A negative coefficient implies the opposite. Furthermore, each variable was centered and scaled, such that its coefficient represents the expected change in log-odds that a person uses a feature given a one standard deviation increase in the predictor variable, holding all other numerical variables at their means and categorical variables at their baselines. Additionally, larger absolute

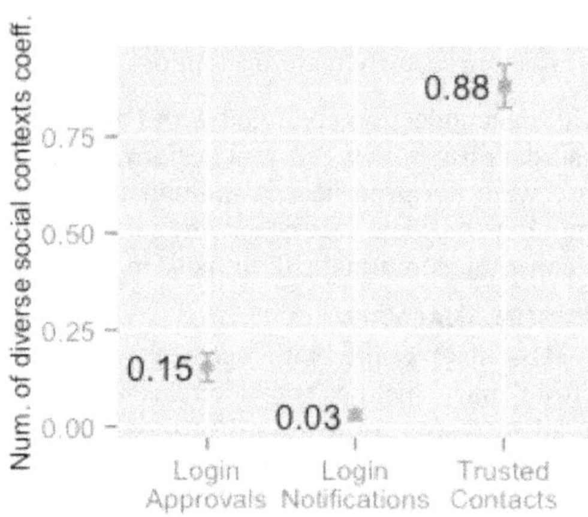

Figure 1. Coefficients for the three logistic regressions relating the number of diverse social contexts variable to use of each security feature, with 95% confidence intervals. All coefficients significant, p < 2e-16.

coefficient values imply a stronger relationship between the independent and dependent variables.

Thus, from Figure 1, we can see that the *number of diverse social contexts* variable positively correlated with the adoption of *every* security feature (b_{LA}=+0.15, p<2e-16; b_{LN}=+0.03, p<2e-16; b_{TC}=+0.88, p<2e-16). This finding offers support for **H1**—people with friends from more diverse social contexts (e.g., high school friends, college friends, family) who use a security feature should be more likely to adopt that feature themselves than those with feature-adopting friends from fewer distinct social contexts. In other words, it is not just the *number* of one's friends who use a security feature that matters in influencing one to adopt the feature himself; these friends should be independent of one another for the effect to be strongest.

In addition, the discrepancy of effect size across features offers some support for **H2**—that more observable security features will be more effectively diffused through social channels. Indeed, the absolute effect size of the *number of diverse social contexts* variable is largest, by far, for Trusted Contacts (the most observable feature, b_{TC}=+0.88), then for Login Approvals (the next most observable, b_{LA}=+0.15) and finally lowest for Login Notifications (the least observable feature, b_{LN}=+0.03).

Indeed, Login Notifications are private messages that are not very observable, and are thus difficult to passively diffuse via social channels. Thus, while having many different friends use Login Notifications may make for a more convincing case for a potential adopter to use the feature, the case is unlikely to be made. Login Approvals are more observable than Login Notifications in that friends who are collocated with an adopter will see the additional authentication step it requires, which in turn may passively provide these friends with social proof to use Login Approvals [11]. This modest increase in observability appears to correlate with a modest increase in the effect size of the *number of diverse social contexts* variable. Finally, the Trusted Contacts feature sends out a notification to each of one's friends who was specified as a Trusted Contact, thus substantially increasing its visibility in a direct way and, in turn, correlating with a substantial increase in effect size. It is also possible that the social nature of the feature—in enlisting friends to help recover one's account—lends itself to amplified social diffusion.

In summary, our regression analysis provides us with support for **H1** and limited support for **H2**, but we have yet to test **H3** and **H4**—that the feature-adoption rate of one's current set of friends will moderate whether the effect of social proof will be positive or negative on one's own likelihood to adopt that security feature. Unfortunately, linear regression analysis is limited in that it does not consider this form of non-linearity in the relationship between predictor and response. Furthermore, regression analysis confounds homophily-based diffusion with social-influence based diffusion [2,26]. In other words, because similar people cluster together as friends, we cannot tell if co-adoption of a feature is due to one friend influencing another or because both friends share an interest. Thus, to test **H3** and **H4**, we ran an adapted version of *matched propensity sampling* [2].

MATCHED PROPENSITY SAMPLING ANALYSIS

Matched propensity sampling is a form of causal inference that helps us differentiate feature adoption due to homophily from feature adoption due to social influence. It distinguishes between homophily and social influence by comparing the feature adoption rates of two sets of people who are *equally likely* to have a fixed proportion of friends who have adopted a security feature, where one set *actually does* have the fixed proportion of friends who have adopted this feature and the other set does not. People in the former set are "exposed" to their feature-adopting friends at this fixed rate, while those in the latter set are "unexposed."

Exposed and unexposed individuals are matched, in pairs, based on a "propensity score" computed from a set of covariates Z that are theorized to represent homophily-based diffusion [23]. We used a logistic regression to calculate the propensity score as suggested by prior work [2], and the covariates included in the model were the demographic, behavioral, and social network variables listed in Table 1. As we are not concerned about estimating exact coefficients and their variances with the logistic regressions in this analysis, we are able to break the independence assumption and include the full set of 1.5 million users in our sample.

Unfortunately, as we could not capture the security expertise of those in our sample, there remains some form of "latent homophily" for which we do not control. However, the demographic, behavioral, and social network variables for which we control likely predict security expertise, so we believe this limitation to be minimal.

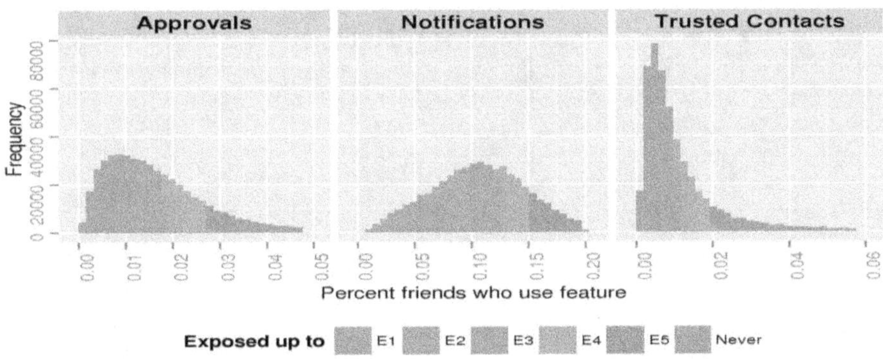

Figure 2. Histogram of percent of friends who use login approvals (left), login notifications (middle) and trusted contacts (right). Colors represent up to what exposed conditions users with x% of feature-adopting friends would be considered "exposed" in the matched propensity sampling analysis.

	Percentile	Approvals	Notifications	Trusted Contacts
E1	1st	0.2%	2.0%	0.1%
E2	21st	0.8%	7.3%	0.4%
E3	41st	1.3%	10.0%	0.7%
E4	61st	1.8%	12.3%	1.1%
E5	81st	2.7%	15.1%	2.0%

Table 2. Exposed condition prerequisites for each security feature. For example, if a user is "exposed" at E3 for login approvals, at least 1.3% of her friends must have adopted login approvals at the time of data collection.

By matching exposed and unexposed individuals who have the same likelihood of being exposed, we can take the difference in feature adoption rates between the exposed and the unexposed as evidence of the effect of social influence. Indeed, after the propensity matching process, the only theoretical difference between these two sets of people are that the exposed set has a certain proportion of friends who use a security feature and those in the unexposed set do not. If social influence has no effect, we should see the *same* rate of adoption for the exposed and unexposed, whereas if social influence has a positive or negative effect, we should see that exposed individuals adopt the feature at a *higher* or *lower* rate, respectively.

We specified five empirical exposure conditions for each security feature—Login Approvals, Login Notifications, and Trusted Contacts—with each exposure condition representing whether or not the user was at least in the 1st percentile, the 21st percentile, the 41st percentile, the 61st percentile, or the 81st percentile in the *percent of friends who use feature* variable, or the total percentage of their friends who used a security feature at the day of data collection. Notably, a potential adopter could count as "exposed" at some levels but not others.

Figure 2 depicts the values of the *percent of friends who use feature* variable that qualified for "exposure" under E1 through E5, with actualized values for these conditions shown in Table 2. Concretely, an individual is exposed in *E1* for Login Approvals if at least 0.2% of her friends adopted the feature, because that puts her at least at the 1st percentile of people whose friends have adopted the feature. Likewise, she is exposed in *E5* for Login Approvals if at least 2.7% of her friends adopted the feature.

We chose five exposure conditions uniformly spaced across the distribution of the *percent of friends who use feature* variable to get a detailed map of the relationship between exposure to friends who have adopted a security feature and one's own likelihood to adopt that feature at different levels of exposure. This map will help us evaluate both **H3** and **H4**—specifically, **H3** predicts a higher adoption rate for the *exposed* relative to the unexposed at high exposure conditions because of positive social proof, whereas **H4** predicts a higher adoption rate for the *unexposed* at low exposure conditions because of negative social proof.

Results

Figure 3 shows the rate of feature adoption for exposed and unexposed individuals for all three features across all five exposures. In interpreting the results of the matched propensity analysis in Figure 3, we note the following: (i) If social influence has *any* effect on the adoption of a security feature at a particular level of exposure, we should see a significant difference in the adoption rates of exposed and unexposed individuals; (ii) If social influence has a *positive* effect on the adoption of a security feature at a particular level of exposure, then we should see that exposed individuals have a significantly *higher* adoption rate than the unexposed; and, (iii) If social influence has a *negative* effect on the adoption of a security feature at a particular level of exposure, we should see that exposed individuals have a significantly *lower* adoption rate than the unexposed.

First, as we show in Table 4, *all* of the differences in adoption rate between the exposed and unexposed were significant, suggesting that irrespective of the security feature and level of exposure to friends who use that feature, social influence appears to have a significant effect on one's likelihood to adopt a security feature. This finding empirically supports some recent, smaller-scale qualitative results that surfaced social influence as a key factor in the adoption of security features [11].

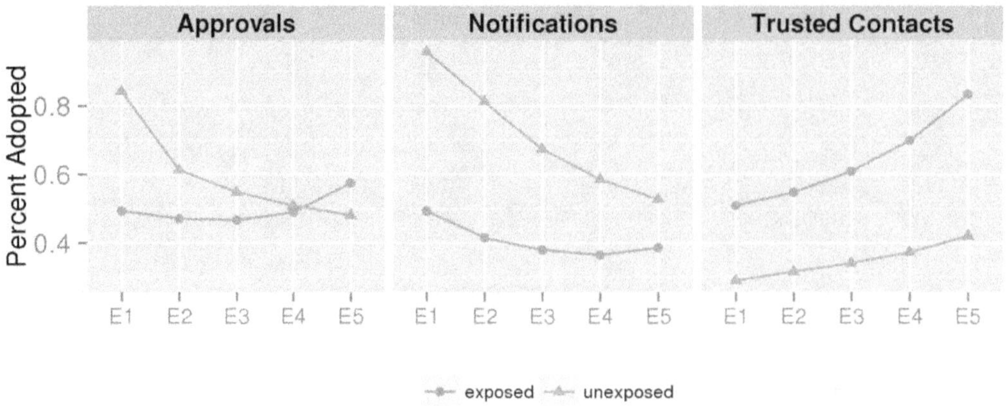

Figure 3. Feature adoption rates, plotted for each security feature for each exposure condition, for both exposed and unexposed individuals. Exposed feature adoption rates are plotted as red circles, and unexposed feature adoption rates are plotted as blue triangles. Every difference between the exposed and unexposed for all features was statistically significant.

	Approvals		Notifications		Trusted Contacts	
	N	χ^2, df=1	N	χ^2, df=1	N	χ^2, df=1
E1	5852	1553	25061	13743	4995	491
E2	122765	4994	518907	172603	105156	11742
E3	240061	3104	1014159	174619	205541	29775
E4	228905	140	963824	93771	196397	42022
E5	111092	1976	468147	18828	95393	34665

Table 3. Chi square significance tests for the difference in adoption rate between exposed and unexposed individuals across all exposure conditions and all security features. All differences significant, p < 2e-16.

For Login Notifications, we see that people who are *exposed* to a certain proportion of feature-using friends appear to be *less* likely to adopt those features than people who are *unexposed* for all levels of exposure we tested. Thus, in our sample, even people with a higher-than-average proportion of feature-adopting friends (i.e., those exposed at E4-E5 who are at least at the 61st percentile) were themselves *less* likely to use Login Notifications than people who had fewer friends who used those features. It appears, therefore, that exposure to friends who use Login Notifications *stifles* the adoption of Login Notifications, a finding that supports **H4**—that social influence will have a negative effect on feature adoption at low exposure levels—but conflicts with **H3**—that social influence will have a positive effect on feature adoption at high exposure levels.

We see just the opposite trend for Trusted Contacts, however: even at E1, the lowest level of exposure, exposed individuals are significantly *more* likely to adopt Trusted Contacts than the unexposed. In other words, it seems that *any* exposure to friends who use Trusted Contacts subsantially increases one's own likelihood to adopt that feature, a finding that supports **H3** but contradicts **H4**.

Finally, for Login Approvals, we see exactly the nuanced, thresholded relationship we predicted. At lower levels of exposure, unexposed individuals are more likely than the exposed to adopt the feature, but at the highest level of exposure, exposed individuals are more likely to adopt the feature—a finding that supports *both* **H3** and **H4**.

Thus, we have three security features for which adoption is significantly affected by social influence, but for which the effect of social influence appears to manifest differently. For Login Notifications, it appears that social influence is a categorically negative force on its adoption, for Trusted Contacts it is a categorically positive force, and for Login Approvals, the direction of its effect is based on a threshold level of exposure a potential adopter has to friends who already use that feature. What could explain the differences in the effect of social influence across these features?

Theoretical vs. Empirical Exposure Threshold

The matched propensity sampling analysis only reflects the effect of social influence on the adoption of a feature at its rate of adoption *at the time of data collection*. Indeed, our exposure conditions were based on an *empirical* division of the *percent of friends who use feature* variable; therefore, it is possible that there is a theoretical exposure *greater* than E5 where social influence could have a positive effect on the adoption of Login Notifications. Indeed, for Login Notifications, exposure at E5—at which about 15% of one's friends use Login Notifications—may not yet be at the threshold where **H3** predicts social influence should have a positive effect on its adoption.

To test this possibility, we must observe how the *adoption rate difference* between the exposed and unexposed varies across exposure conditions. We plot these differences in Figure 4, by subtracting the unexposed adoption rate from the exposed adoption rate. From this plot, we can understand the *marginal* effect of social influence on adoption at higher exposure conditions. In interpreting Figure 4, we note the following: (i) If unexposed individuals are more likely than the exposed to adopt a feature at a certain level of exposure, then the value of the difference will be negative, whereas it will be positive if exposed individuals are more likely to adopt the feature than the unexposed; and, (ii) If the value of the difference increases (moves up) at higher exposure conditions, then the marginal effect of having more friends who use a

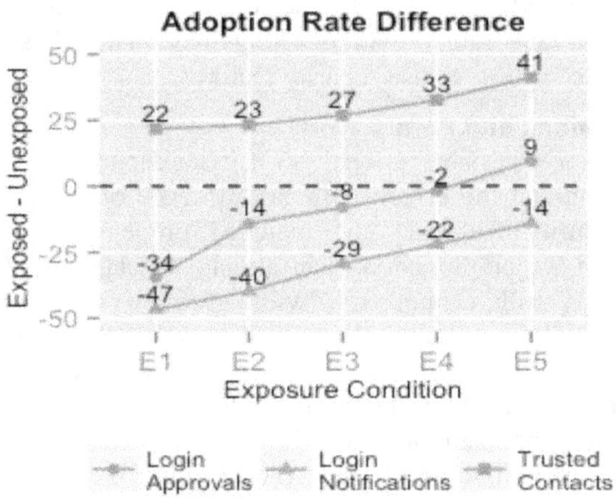

Figure 4. Differences in adoption rate between the exposed and unexposed for all three features across all exposure conditions. Values above the dashed horizontal line signify that those who were exposed had a higher adoption rate than the unexposed. All differences significant, $p < 2e\text{-}16$ (Table 4).

security feature on that feature's adoption is positive, whereas if the value of the difference decreases (moves down), then the marginal effect is negative.

From Figure 4, we see that the value of the difference between exposed and unexposed adoption rates *increases* (moves up) constantly, for all three features, from E1 to E5. For Login Notifications and Login Approvals, the initial adoption rate advantage of unexposed individuals gradually diminishes at higher levels of exposure. In fact, the advantage is ultimately in favor of exposed individuals for Login Approvals at E5, when the difference shifts from negative to positive. For Trusted Contacts, the advantage starts with exposed individuals and simply gets larger at higher levels of exposure. Thus, at higher levels of exposure, the likelihood for exposed individuals to adopt any of the security features grows at a rate faster than the unexposed. It seems likely, therefore, that there *is* a theoretical exposure higher than E5 where exposed individuals are more likely to adopt Login Notifications than the unexposed—as would be predicted by **H3**. Unfortunately, we did not have a large enough number of people at a high enough exposure to empirically confirm this prediction from the data in our random sample.

It is tempting to also apply this logic to entertain a theoretical exposure lower than E1 at which the effect of social influence is negative for Trusted Contacts. However, as the exposure threshold for E1 for Trusted Contacts is just 0.1%, the theoretical and empirical exposure lower bounds are essentially the same—i.e., having at least one friend who uses the feature. Thus, while it seems like **H3** may be true even for Login Notifications, it seems likely that **H4** may not be true for some features—social influence does not *have* to be a negative force at low exposure conditions.

Individual Feature Attributes

Another consideration in interpreting the differences in the effect of social influence across security features is the individual attributes of each feature. Specifically, as **H2** suggests, more *observable* security features should be more positively affected by social influence.

The threshold beyond which the effect of social influence toggles from negative to positive appears to be inversely proportional to the observability of the feature, lending further support for **H2**. Indeed, the threshold is "lowest" for Trusted Contacts in that the threshold seems to be at its theoretical lowest possible value of having just *one* friend who uses the feature. The threshold is next lowest for Login Approvals at E5—or when approximately 2.7% of ones friends use the security feature. Finally, the threshold is highest for Login Notifications at a level of exposure higher than E5, if such a threshold exists at all.

It makes intuitive sense that the threshold of friends required for *negative* social proof to be overcome by *positive* social proof should be lower for more observable features. If our reasoning for **H4** is correct, *negative* social proof is the result of stereotypes and generalizations that may be overcome if potential adopters can see, concretely, that security feature usage is not necessarily limited to those who they may consider "paranoid" or who have an unachievable level of specialized knowledge about security.

Summary

In summary, the results from our matched propensity sampling analysis lends additional support to **H2** and conditional support to **H3** and **H4**. Specifically, the prediction, of **H3** and **H4,** that the direction of the effect of social influence on a potential adopter's likelihood to adopt a security feature will shift at a threshold appears to be true for Login Approvals and is likely true for Login Notifications. For Trusted Contacts, however, it appears that social influence has a positive effect on its adoption, regardless of the level of exposure. Furthermore, the *observability* of a security feature appears to at least partially moderate the presence and value of this threshold.

DISCUSSION

We analyzed whether and how security feature adoptions diffused through the social networks of 1.5 million people who use Facebook. Our results provide large-scale empirical evidence that social processes do, indeed, affect the uptake of security features—for better *and* for worse. For Login Approvals, when a potential adopter is exposed to few feature-adopting friends, social proof appears to reduce her own likelihood of adopting the feature. But, when she is exposed to many feature-adopting friends, social proof appears to increase her own likelihood of adopting the feature. The same is likely true for Login Notifications, but we did not find conclusive evidence that social proof can have a positive effect on its adoption at a high enough level of exposure. For Trusted Contacts, though, social proof appears to increase a potential adopter's likelihood of adopting a security feature with even just one feature-adopting friend. These results, taken together, provide us with conditional support for **H3** and **H4**—depending on the feature, social proof can be either helpful or harmful to security feature adoption, and there may be a threshold of exposure to feature-using friends at which the effect transitions from harmful to helpful.

In addition, if a potential adopter is exposed to feature-adopting friends from many, independent social contexts—for example, a tennis friend and a travel buddy as opposed to two tennis friends—she is more likely to adopt each of the three security features, a finding that supports **H1**.

Finally, the strength of these effects varied across the features we tested—features that are more observable more effectively spread through social networks, a finding that supports **H2**. Indeed, we found that the effect of the *percentage of friends who use a security feature* and the *number of distinct social contexts* from which those friends originated were highest for Trusted Contacts (the most observable), followed by Login Approvals (the next most observable), and then Login Notifications.

Practical Implications

Prior work has outlined the positive potential of social influence in driving security feature adoption [11]. While we agree that this approach shows potential, our results suggest that social proof can also have a negative effect on the adoption of some security features for people with low exposure to feature-adopting friends. These findings should be taken into consideration before attempting to leverage social proof to drive the adoption of security features.

Nevertheless, social proof *can* drive the adoption of security features once those features come into use by more than just early-adopters. Indeed, our findings indicate that people with exposure to many friends who use Trusted Contacts and Login Approvals are more likely to use those features themselves, even after controlling for co-adoption due to homophily. Furthermore, our results suggest that the same may be true for Login Notifications, but at overall adoption rates higher than they are presently. Thus, the question remains: how do we increase the adoption of security features to reach the point where social influence has a positive effect on their spread?

Our results suggest that having friends from many social circles that use a security feature is strong social proof that a security feature should be used. Thus, one method to maximize the social spread of security features may be to target people from distinct social contexts and offer them personalized incentives to try security features.

It also appears that individual attributes of a security feature can affect its spread. Therefore, security feature designers should be mindful of the fact that use of a security feature can have social consequences. If, as prior work suggests, use of security features can be seen as a sign of paranoia, then designing security features like Trusted Contacts that draw friends in, can be seen, and feel trusting and collaborative rather than isolating may make it easier to convince people to use security features.

Limitations and Future Work

Our data was observational, so it is harder to make causal claims about the effect of social influence on the adoption of security features. The matched propensity sampling method we employed was an attempt at causal inference, but we still cannot say with absolute certainty that individuals exposed to feature-adopting friends adopted a security feature *because* of their friends. There may be some forms of latent homophily [26] for which we did not control—for example, a user's technical proficiency—that might explain some of the variance in our data. Thus, one rich opportunity for future work is to experimentally test, with consent, whether higher security feature observability does indeed yield greater diffusion of security features.

Future work should also explore how *other* feature attributes affect a feature's diffusion through a social network. While *observability* appears to be important, it alone likely does not account for *all* of the differences in effect size we observed across the three security features. The *diffusion of innovations* [21] literature suggests four additional attributes of a security feature that may be fruitful to test: its (1) *relative advantage*, or how much of an advantage the innovation provides over what it is replacing; (2) *complexity*, or how difficult it is to use the innovation; (3) *compatibility*, or how well the innovation matches a user's needs, experiences and values; and, (4) *trialability*, or how easily the user can try the innovation before making a final decision about whether to adopt it.

CONCLUSION

Through an observational analysis of whether and how security features diffused through the social networks of 1.5 million people who use Facebook, we illuminated the unique effects of social influence on security feature adoption. Social influence appears to drive security feature adoption when people have examples of feature-adopting friends from multiple social circles—for example, a high school friend *and* a family member as opposed to just two high school friends. However, the relationship between the number of one's feature-adopting friends and her own likelihood to use the feature is more nuanced. Indeed, when one is exposed to many security feature-adopting friends, she is likely to find positive social proof that increases her own likelihood to adopt a security feature. Conversely, when one is exposed to just a few feature-adopting friends, she might find negative social proof that stifles her adoption of the security feature. Furthermore, these effects may vary substantially across security features. Specifically, security features that are more *observable*—i.e., features for which the use and benefits are easily noticeable—seem to be more effectively spread via social channels.

ACKNOWLEDGEMENTS
This work was generously supported, in part, by NSF Award #1347186 and the NDSEG Fellowship. We would also like to thank Tiffany Hyun-Jin Kim, Stuart Schechter, Sofus Macskássy and Lada Adamic for providing helpful feedback on this and related projects.

REFERENCES
1. Adams, A. and Sasse, M.A. Users are not the enemy. *CACM 42*, 12 (1999), 40–46.
2. Aral, S., Muchnik, L., and Sundararajan, A. Distinguishing influence-based contagion from homophily-driven diffusion in dynamic networks. *PNAS 106*, 51 (2009), 21544–9.
3. Bakshy, E., Rosenn, I., Marlow, C., and Adamic, L. The role of social networks in information diffusion. *Proc. WWW '12*, ACM Press (2012), 519–528.
4. Bandura, A., Grusec, J.E., and Menlove, F.L. Vicarious Extinction of Avoidance Behavior. *Journal of Personality and Social Psychology 5*, 1 (1967), 16–23.
5. Bond, R.M., Fariss, C.J., Jones, J.J., et al. A 61-million-person experiment in social influence and political mobilization. *Nature 489*, 7415 (2012), 295–8.
6. Centola, D., Macy, M., and Macy, M. Complex Contagion and the Weakness of Long Ties. *American journal of Sociology 113*, 3 (2014), 702–734.
7. Centola, D. The spread of behavior in an online social network experiment. *Science (New York, N.Y.) 329*, 5996 (2010), 1194–7.
8. Centola, D. An experimental study of homophily in the adoption of health behavior. *Science 334*, 6060 (2011).
9. Chapman, L.J. Illusory correlation in observational report. *Journal of Verbal Learning and Verbal Behavior 6*, 1 (1967), 151–155.
10. Cialdini, R.B. *Influence*. Harper Collins, 2009.
11. Das, S., Kim, H.J., Dabbish, L.A., and Hong, J.I. The Effect of Social Influence on Security Sensitivity. *Proc. SOUPS'14*, (2014).
12. Fowler, J.H. and Christakis, N. a. Cooperative behavior cascades in human social networks. *PNAS 107*, 12 (2010), 5334–8.
13. Gaw, S., Felten, E.W., and Fernandez-Kelly, P. Secrecy, flagging, and paranoia. *Proc. CHI '06*, ACM Press (2006), 591–600.
14. Goldstein, N.J., Cialdini, R.B., and Griskevicius, V. A Room with a Viewpoint: Using Social Norms to Motivate Environmental Conservation in Hotels. *Journal of Consumer Research 35*, 3 (2008), 472–482.
15. Herley, C. So long, and no thanks for the externalities. *Proc. NSPW '09*, ACM Press (2009), 133–144.
16. Johnson, R.C. Cyber security solutions underused. *EE Times*, 2013. http://www.eetimes.com/author.asp?section_id=36&doc_id=1287251&page_number=1.
17. Kramer, A.D.I. The spread of emotion via facebook. *Proc. CHI '12*, ACM Press (2012), 767–770.
18. Milgram, S., Bickman, L., and Berkowitz, L. Note on the drawing power of crowds of different size. *JPSP 13*, 2 (1969), 79–82.
19. Moore, H. and Roberts, D. AP Twitter hack causes panic on Wall Street and sends Dow plunging. *The Guardian*, 2013. http://www.theguardian.com/business/2013/apr/23/ap-tweet-hack-wall-street-freefall.
20. Rader, E., Wash, R., and Brooks, B. Stories as informal lessons about security. *Proc. SOUPS '12*, ACM Press.
21. Rogers, E.M. *Diffusion of Innovations*. Free Press, 2003.
22. Romero, D.M., Meeder, B., and Kleinberg, J. Differences in the mechanics of information diffusion across topics. *Proc. WWW '11*, ACM Press (2011).
23. Rosenbaum, P.R. and Rubin, D.B. The Central Role of the Propensity Score in Observational Studies for Causal Effects. *Biometrika 70*, 1 (1983), 41–55.
24. Sasse, M.A. Computer security: Anatomy of a Usability Disaster, and a Plan for Recovery. *Proc. CHI '03 Wkshp on HCI and Security Systems*.
25. Schultz, P.W., Nolan, J.M., Cialdini, R.B., Goldstein, N.J., and Griskevicius, V. The constructive, destructive, and reconstructive power of social norms. *Psychological science 18*, 5 (2007), 429–34.
26. Shalizi, C.R. and Thomas, A.C. Homophily and Contagion Are Generically Confounded in Observational Social Network Studies. *Sociological Methods and Research 40*, 2 (2011), 211–239.
27. Sun, E., Rosenn, I., Marlow, C.A., and Lento, T.M. Gesundheit! Modeling Contagion through Facebook News Feed. *Proc. ICWSM '09*, (2009).
28. Tversky, A. and Kahneman, D. Availability : A Heuristic for Judging Frequency. *Cog. Psych. 5*, 2 (1973), 207–232.
29. Ugander, J., Backstrom, L., Marlow, C., and Kleinberg, J. Structural diversity in social contagion. *PNAS 109*, 16 (2012), 5962–6.
30. Wyler, G. AP Twitter Hacked, Claims Barack Obama Injured In White House Explosions. *Business Insider*, 2013. http://www.businessinsider.com/ap-hacked-obama-injured-white-house-explosions-2013-4.

APPENDIX A

Variable Name	Login Approvals		Login Notifications		Trusted Contacts	
Intercept	0.28	***	0.12	***	0.31	***
Age	-0.06	***	0.08	***	-0.01	
Gender: male (relative to female)	0.05	***	-0.06	***	-0.10	***
Days with active account	-0.04	**	-0.26	***	0.02	
Friend count	-0.07	***	-0.11	***	-0.03	***
Days active in past 30	0.62	***	0.58	***	0.50	***
Mean friend age	-0.47	***	-0.21	***	-0.49	***
Friend age entropy	-0.16	***	-0.36	***	-0.07	***
Percent male friends	0.36	***	0.34	***	0.43	***
Mean friends' days with active account	-0.84	***	-1.00	***	-1.04	***
Friend country entropy	0.32	***	0.21	***	0.29	***
Mean number of friends of friends	-0.08	***	-0.02	**	-0.14	***
Posts created	-0.20	***	0.19	***	-0.17	***
Posts deleted	0.27	***	0.20	***	0.15	***
Comments created	0.10	***	0.06	***	0.18	***
Comments deleted	0.18	***	0.17	***	0.16	***
Likes given	-0.07	***	-0.09	***	-0.01	
Friends added	1.81	***	2.37	***	1.36	***
Friends removed	0.57	***	0.49	***	0.50	***
Photos added	0.10	***	0.14	***	0.26	***
Videos added	-0.01	***	-0.02	**	-0.02	**
Percent of friends who use feature	**0.13**	***	**-0.12**	***	**0.29**	***
Number of diverse social contexts	**0.15**	***	**0.03**	***	**0.88**	***

Table A1. Coefficients for the three logistic regressions relating social proof variables (bolded, at the bottom), to use of login approvals (left), login notifications (middle) and trusted contacts (right). All coefficients are normalized.

*** $p < 2e\text{-}16$, ** $p < 0.001$

Give Social Network Users the Privacy They Want

Pamela Wisniewski[*] **A.K.M. Najmul Islam**[†‡] **Bart P. Knijnenburg**[♯] **Sameer Patil**[†§ϕ]
[*]College of Information Sciences and Technology, Pennsylvania State University
University Park PA 16802, USA
[†]Helsinki Institute for Information Technology HIIT / Aalto University
P O Box 15600, 00076 Aalto, Finland
[‡]Information Systems Science, University of Turku, 20500 Turku, Finland
[♯]Department of Informatics, University of California, Irvine, Irvine CA 92697, USA
[§]Department of Information Systems and New Media, University of Siegen, 57068 Siegen, Germany
[ϕ]Yahoo Labs, 701 First Avenue, Sunnyvale, CA 94089, USA
puw16@psu.edu, najmul.islam@utu.fi, bart.k@uci.edu, sameerpatil@yahoo-inc.com

ABSTRACT
Social Network Sites (SNS) are often characterized as a trade-off where users must give up privacy to gain social benefits. We investigated the alternative viewpoint that users gain the most benefits when SNSs give them the privacy they desire. Applying structural equation modeling to questionnaire data of 303 Facebook users, we examined the complex relationship between privacy and SNS benefits. We found that SNS users whose privacy desires were met reported higher levels of social connectedness (i.e., perceived relational closeness with others) than those who achieved less privacy than they desired. Social connectedness, in turn, played a pivotal role in building social capital (i.e., the benefits derived from relationships with others). These findings suggest that more openness may not always be better; SNSs should aim to achieve 'Privacy Fit' with user needs to enhance user experience and ensure sustained use.

Author Keywords
Privacy; Facebook; social capital; social connectedness; Social Network Sites; SNS.

ACM Classification Keywords
H.5.2. Information Interfaces and Presentation (e.g. HCI): User Inferfaces

INTRODUCTION
In recent years, Social Network Sites (SNSs) have become an integral part of people's everyday online activities. Interpersonal interactions through SNSs have been shown to have a positive impact on a host of factors, including social capital, social connectedness, self-esteem, and personal well-being [5, 9, 10, 24]. At the same time, there is increasing concern about the negative impact of SNSs on personal privacy [30]. Technology related issues that raise privacy concern range from deliberate abuses to inadvertent violations [4]. SNS users may regret past disclosures and face negative social and professional consequences as a result of SNS interactions [49]. Inadequate privacy support has often led to user protests and has been shown to impact user participation negatively, e.g., through self-censorship or temporary or even full abandonment of SNSs [2, 39, 52, 53]. Thus, there seems to be a considerable rift between the primary SNS goal of promoting social engagement and the secondary goal of protecting users' personal privacy [29].

CSCW 2015, March 14–18, 2015, Vancouver, BC, Canada.

http://dx.doi.org/10.1145/2675133.2675256

Privacy researchers have historically conceptualized privacy as a *trade-off* between risks and benefits [27]. The argument that one must make a trade-off between personal privacy and the interactional benefits of technology-mediated sociality has been a prevailing paradigm also within the CSCW research community: "There is a tacitly held assumption in CSCW and social psychology that some degree of privacy risk is the inevitable cost of social life" [4]. In light of this trade-off, popular SNSs typically downplay the importance of privacy preservation in favor of facilitating social connection. For instance, Facebook CEO Mark Zuckerberg has frequently asserted that SNS users are no longer concerned about their personal privacy because sharing has become the new social norm: *"People have really gotten comfortable not only sharing more information and different kinds, but more openly and with more people. That social norm is just something that has evolved over time,"* Zuckerberg explained [31].

Yet, not all SNS users share Zuckerberg's belief. While some SNS users have become more open, others continue to value their privacy [30]. Does this mean that only users who are unconcerned about their privacy are able to derive benefits from SNS use? Or can SNS users maintain a level of privacy they desire *and simultaneously* benefit from SNS engagement?

Several privacy scholars have already challenged the assumption that users must give up personal privacy in order to benefit from technology use and have explored the opportunities of simultaneously enhancing privacy and benefits [4, 18, 26, 36]. Our study extends this approach specifically to the context of SNSs. We follow the suggestion of these contemporary theorists to move beyond a definition of privacy in absolute terms (i.e., as the opposite of being "public"). Specifically, we take a user centered approach to SNS privacy, which defines privacy in relative terms based on the unique privacy preferences of individual users (cf., Altman's definition of privacy [1]). Additionally, we take an *evaluative* approach (i.e., examining the effect of a match between preferred and achieved levels of privacy on socialization benefits in an existing SNS) rather than a generative approach (i.e., offering design principles). Our goal is to provide empirical weight to the argument that helping users attain an optimal level of privacy can increase their perceived benefits of using SNSs. Specifically, we hypothesized that meeting SNS users' privacy needs is a crucial aspect of supporting social benefits and proposed that if a user gives up more personal privacy than he or she desires, it can actually be detrimental to fostering effective and meaningful social connections. In this way, we further unpack the complex relationship between privacy and sociality and extend the existing SNS privacy literature by empirically examining the relationship between user based privacy preferences, achieved privacy outcomes, and SNS benefits.

To this end, we administered a Web based questionnaire to Facebook users (N=303) and applied structural equation modeling (SEM) to study the effects of the match between users' desired privacy level and the privacy level they actually achieved. We labeled this match as *Privacy Fit*. Privacy Fit occurs when a user has either a low level of desired privacy and achieves it, or alternatively, when a user has a high desire for privacy and achieves it. Conversely, *Privacy Mismatch* occurs when a user's desired privacy level is not sufficiently met. Our results indicate that Facebook users who achieved Privacy Fit (regardless of high or low desired level of privacy) reported higher levels of Social Connectedness than those who achieved less privacy than desired. Higher levels of Social Connectedness were in turn associated with increased Bridging and Bonding Social Capital. Additionally, we found that Privacy Fit was associated with higher levels of Facebook Usage Intensity and that the positive effect of Privacy Fit on Social Connectedness was moderated by Facebook Usage Intensity (i.e., Privacy Mismatch negatively impacted casual Facebook users more strongly than avid users).

Our work provides empirical weight to Boyle and Greenberg's claim that catering to users' privacy desires can increase the perceived benefits of using a system [4]. This highlights the need to re-examine the assumed dichotomy between privacy and socialization. Consequently, we argue that SNS providers could maximize the benefits of their service by promoting user tailored privacy, rather than simply urging users to share as much as possible. Specifically, our work makes the following contributions to SNS privacy research:

- Operationalizes and statistically validates a broader conceptualization of privacy in the form of a *measurement instrument* that captures users' desired versus achieved privacy levels across 10 different aspects of SNS privacy,

- Examines privacy relative to SNS users' individual privacy preferences, as opposed to viewing privacy in absolute terms,

- Empirically confirms that Privacy Fit affords more social benefits than Privacy Mismatch, thereby challenging the assumption that SNS users must share more and give up personal privacy in order to benefit from SNS use,

- Uncovers additional relationships between Privacy Fit, Facebook Use, Social Connectedness, and Social Capital, and

- Advocates for designing user tailored SNS privacy mechanisms that optimize the fit between users' desire for privacy and their actual privacy experiences.

In the next section we summarize related work on SNS privacy and explain our contribution beyond extant literature. We then lay out the theoretical groundwork leading to structural models of hypothesized relationships among Privacy Fit, Facebook Use, Social Connectedness, and Social Capital. Next, we operationalize our constructs, test our models, and present the results of our analyses. We conclude with a discussion of how our findings provide theoretical, methodological, and design implications for SNS privacy.

RELATED WORK

Empirical SNS privacy research typically frames privacy as "the ability of individuals to control when, to what extent, and how information about the self is communicated to others" [11], thus narrowing SNS privacy specifically to examining the regulation of private versus public disclosures [25]. By framing SNS privacy in such absolute terms, privacy management is often presented as a trade-off or balancing act, where giving up privacy through information disclosures is necessary for connecting with others [29]. For example, Stutzman et al. [44] found that Facebook users who disclosed more personal information reported higher levels of Social Capital but also higher privacy concerns.

In contrast, contemporary privacy theorists have attempted broader conceptualizations of privacy issues. For example, Langheinrich [26] and Iachello and Abowd [18] offered principles for design of ubiquitous computing systems based on application of the legal principles of Fair Information Practices and the Principle of Proportionality, respectively. In the domain of technology mediated interpersonal interactions, Palen and Dourish [36] described how Altman's work on interpersonal boundary regulation in physical interactions [1] could be applied to interactions mediated by technology. Using the example of video media spaces, Boyle and Greenberg [4] further linked the conceptual insight of Palen and Dourish with operational design guidance for effective privacy management support. In particular, Boyle and Greenberg explored the opportunities of simultaneously enhancing privacy and utility in the design of video conferencing systems [4]. We aim to promote a similar broadening of the discourse on privacy and design in the SNS context by challenging the assumption that users must give up privacy in order to benefit from SNS use. We thus extend existing SNS privacy literature by unpacking the complex relationships between expressed privacy preferences, achieved privacy outcomes, and social benefits of SNS.

Boundary Type	Dimensions	Definition
Disclosure	Self Disclosure (SELF)	Regulating what personal information one discloses within one's network
	Confidant Disclosure (CONF)	Regulating how co-owned personal information is disclosed within one's network
Relationship	Connection (CONN)	Regulating whom to let into one's social network
	Context (CONT)	Regulating appropriate interpersonal interactions given the type of relationship
Territorial	Inward Facing (IN)	Regulating incoming content for personal consumption
	Outward Facing (OUT)	Regulating semi-public content available through interactional spaces
Network	Discovery (DISC)	Regulating access others have to one's network connections
	Intersection (INTER)	Regulating social interactions between connections or groups of connections
Interactional	Disabling (DIS)	Regulating potential interaction through turning on/off interface features
	Blocking (BLOCK)	Regulating overall access of oneself to specific individuals outside of one's network

Table 1. SNS interpersonal privacy boundary types.

We frame SNS privacy using Altman's work on interpersonal boundary regulation [1]. Altman defined privacy as "an interpersonal boundary process by which a person or group regulates interaction with others" by altering the degree of openness of the self to others [1]. Boundary regulation is an interactive process where two or more individuals collaborate in order to negotiate an acceptable level of social interaction [1, 37]. The process is dialectic, balancing both the restriction and seeking of social interaction based on an individual's changing privacy needs. Altman proposes that meeting one's privacy needs through this process of interpersonal boundary regulation is the key to effective social interactions. Ineffective boundary regulation can lead to sub-optimal outcomes, such as a state of *social crowding* or *social isolation*, experiencing much more or much less social interaction than one desires, respectively [1].

Several SNS privacy researchers have adopted Altman's definition of privacy as a boundary regulation process [25,35,36, 43,45]. However, these works primarily focused on boundaries related to information disclosure, not considering Altman's broader framing of privacy as any 'interpersonal event' that serves to optimally regulate one's social interactions [1]. In this sense, interpersonal boundaries help us define who we are, as well as with whom, how, and when we interact. Part of the problem may be that Altman's boundary control mechanisms — coping behaviors, verbal, paraverbal, nonverbal, personal space, and territorial behaviors — were originally identified in the *physical realm* and are difficult to translate to analogous online behaviors [4].

Previous qualitative work by Karr-Wisniewski et al. [19, 52, 54] extended Altman's broader conceptualization of privacy as an interpersonal boundary regulation process specifically to the realm of SNSs. This prior work provided better understanding of the unique coping behaviors [52] and other mechanisms SNS users employ to regulate various aspects of interpersonal privacy [19, 54]. In addition to *disclosure* boundaries, SNS users were found to negotiate *relationship*, *network*, *territorial*, and *interactional* boundaries to regulate their privacy levels. For instance, hiding annoying posts from a friend's game application helps regulate *inward facing territorial* boundaries (such as one's News Feed), but this is orthogonal to whether the information is considered private [19]. Table 1 summarizes the taxonomy of the different SNS boundary types proposed by Karr-Wisniewski et al. We operationalized this taxonomy by developing a measurement scale that quantifies SNS users' desired and achieved privacy levels according to each of these privacy dimensions. Our examination of SNS privacy, therefore, considers privacy from this broader perspective rather than limiting our scope to public versus private disclosures.

HYPOTHESIZED STRUCTURAL MODEL

Figure 1 summarizes our research framework with hypothesized relationships between Privacy Fit, Facebook Usage Intensity, Social Connectedness, and Social Capital. Below, we introduce our theoretical constructs and provide justification for our hypotheses.

Social Capital

Social Capital refers to the benefits afforded through social networking that are derived from the development and maintenance of relationships with others [24, 50]. It is one of the most prevalent dependent variables examined in SNS research [9–11,24,46,47,50]. Williams [50] developed an 'Internet Social Capital Scale' (ISCS) through an in-depth review of the literature coupled with statistical validation of the emergent dimensions of Social Capital. He found that Social Capital varies along two dimensions: *Bridging Social*

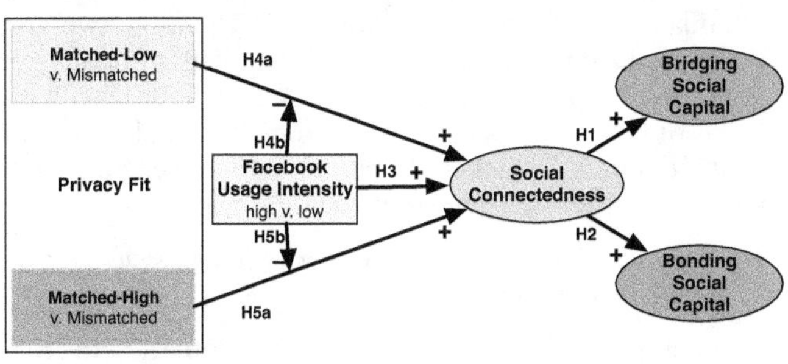

Figure 1. Structural model combining all hypotheses. This model was tested for each of the 10 boundary types.

Capital refers to the resources gained through connections with weak ties (e.g., acquaintances) whereas *Bonding Social Capital* deals with the benefits derived through more intimate relationships, such as those between close friends and family. Benefits of Bridging Social Capital include a sense of community, an increased curiosity for the world-at-large, and a desire to try new things while benefits of Bonding Social Capital include emotional support and the ability to mobilize resources, such as obtaining a reference, borrowing money, or receiving advice [9, 50].

Social Connectedness

Koroleva et al. [24] differentiated between the sources and benefits of Social Capital. They suggested that *Social Connectedness* is a cognitive dimension of perceived relational closeness, which is necessary to activate connections between individuals and realize the benefits of social capital. Social Connectedness involves staying in touch with and connecting with other individuals. In this way, Social Connectedness acts as a *source* of and/or prerequisite for obtaining the *benefits* of Social Capital [24]. Therefore, we hypothesized that:

H1: *Social Connectedness is positively associated with Bridging Social Capital.*

H2: *Social Connectedness is positively associated with Bonding Social Capital.*

Facebook Usage Intensity

We define *Facebook Usage Intensity* as the degree to which users are emotionally connected to Facebook and the extent to which Facebook is integrated in their daily activities [9]. Facebook has become a pervasive means of social interaction and communication among adults. Prior research found Facebook usage linked to positive social outcomes, such as greater social capital, increased self-esteem, and enhanced well-being [9]. In early SNS research, Facebook Usage Intensity showed positive relationships with both Bonding and Bridging Social Capital, with the latter being stronger, while general Internet usage did not influence social capital [9]. Later research clarified that the generation of social capital was driven by social information-seeking behaviors, not by the initiation of new relationships or the maintenance of existing relationships on Facebook [10]. Further, the increase in social capital was attributed to active content contribution rather than passive information consumption [10]. These findings indicate that the relationship between Facebook Usage Intensity and Social Capital is driven by the type and the quality of connections with others. Therefore, we argue that Social Connectedness *mediates* the relationship between Facebook Usage Intensity and Social Capital; those with high levels of Facebook Usage Intensity remain socially connected to their friends, which in turns helps them generate Social Capital. We thus hypothesized that:

H3: *Facebook Usage Intensity is positively associated with Social Connectedness.*

In conjunction with H1 and H2, this hypothesis effectively links Facebook Usage Intensity to Bridging and Bonding Social Capital through its relationship to Social Connectedness. In the remainder of this paper, we refer to those with high levels of Facebook Usage Intensity as *avid* Facebook users and those with low levels of Facebook Usage Intensity as *casual* Facebook users.

Privacy Fit

According to Altman, individuals try to reach their *desired privacy level* in order to achieve an optimal level of social interaction [1]. In optimal cases, boundary negotiation results in boundary coordination. We labeled this optimum as *Privacy Fit*. Failure to achieve Privacy Fit results in what has been termed 'boundary turbulence' [37] or boundary violation [1, 20]. We characterized this lack of Privacy Fit as *Privacy Mismatch*. Two types of mismatches can occur: *social crowding* refers to over-stimulation by undesirably high levels of social interaction (i.e., less privacy than needed); inversely, *social isolation* leads to less social interaction than desired (i.e., more privacy than intended) [1]. Both crowding and isolation are sub-optimal and may result in a variety of negative outcomes, including physical, physiological, and psychological stress, vulnerability, illness, anxiety, embarrassment, bewilderment, discomfort, flight reactions, and anger [1]. For example, older adults living in assisted living facilities were found to be prone to feeling more crowded than those living independently and this social crowding was associated with lower levels of adjustment to the living environment [21]. Another study found that students living in family housing felt more attached to their living arrangements if they felt that the space afforded them adequate means to adjust privacy boundaries [17].

Recent work suggests that the findings from these studies conducted in the physical world [17, 21] may also apply to SNSs. For instance, Ellison et al. [11] found that the use of advanced privacy settings on Facebook was *positively* associated with the number of Facebook friends and perceived social capital. This finding provides some empirical indication that effective interpersonal boundary regulation within SNSs may afford enhanced social benefits. However, little research has explored the relationship between SNS privacy and benefits. We attempt to fill this gap with structural models that link the match or mismatch between desired and actual privacy levels to the social benefits of SNS use (i.e., Social Capital and Social Connectedness). Specifically, we argue that Privacy Fit leads to more beneficial SNS interactions than Privacy Mismatch. Consequently, users who attain Privacy Fit will have better SNS interactions *regardless of whether they desire and attain low (Matched-Low) or high (Matched-High) levels of privacy*. Given that enhanced social interactions foster greater Social Connectedness, we hypothesized that:

H4a: *Facebook users who report a Matched-Low Privacy Fit perceive greater Social Connectedness than those who experience a Privacy Mismatch.*

H5a: *Facebook users who report a Matched-High Privacy Fit perceive greater Social Connectedness than those who experience a Privacy Mismatch.*

However, we acknowledge that the relationship between Privacy Fit and Social Connectedness (Hypotheses H4a and

H5a) may be influenced by Facebook Usage Intensity. Based on cognitive dissonance theory [14], avid Facebook users are likely to engage in dissonance reduction to achieve uniformity between their privacy cognition and their high Facebook Usage Intensity. As a result, these individuals may justify their avid usage by ascribing lower importance to Privacy Fit. Moreover, avid users may experience habituation in their Facebook usage. Automatic and habitual behaviors require little (if any) conscious attention and only minimal mental effort [28]. Therefore, Privacy Mismatch is less likely to reduce the ability of these users to maintain social connections. This led us to the following two moderating hypotheses:

H4b: *The difference in Social Connectedness between those who achieve Matched-Low Privacy Fit and those who experience a Privacy Mismatch is smaller for avid Facebook users than for casual Facebook users.*

H5b: *The difference in Social Connectedness between those who achieve Matched-High Privacy Fit and those who experience a Privacy Mismatch is smaller for avid Facebook users than for casual Facebook users.*

We combined the above hypotheses into the theoretical structural model shown in Figure 1. Since we examine the contrasting outcomes between Privacy Fit (Matched-Low and Matched-High) and Privacy Mismatch, we chose to represent Privacy Mismatch as the baseline condition. We compared the two types of Privacy Fit — low and high — against this baseline. We tested 10 separate instances of the model, one for each of the 10 privacy boundary types defined in Table 1.

METHOD

To test our 10 hypothesized models, we operationalized and measured relevant constructs in the form of a questionnaire.

Construct Operationalization

We utilized pre-validated measures for Bridging and Bonding Social Capital [9, 50], Social Connectedness [24], and Facebook Usage Intensity [9]. We created our own measures for desired and actual SNS privacy levels across the 10 privacy boundary types described in Table 1. The Appendix provides the individual items for these measures along with associated psychometric properties. Prior to data collection, we confirmed the face validity of these measures using card sorting techniques [32, 42].

Data Collection

We obtained a random sample of 10,000 email addresses of students, faculty, and staff from the registrar of the University of North Carolina at Charlotte.[1] These individuals were invited to fill out a Web based questionnaire between February and April 2012. Only those over 18 years of age with an active Facebook account qualified for participation. The questionnaire could be completed in about 20–25 minutes. At the end, respondents could enter a random drawing for one of two $100 Amazon gift certificates. Respondents were encouraged to refer others to the study and were offered an additional entry in the drawing for each referral who completed the questionnaire, up to a maximum of 25. The questionnaire instrument and recruitment procedures were approved by the university's Institutional Review Board (IRB).

[1]The study was conducted while the first author was a doctoral student at the University of North Carolina at Charlotte.

Respondents

A total of 331 respondents filled out the questionnaire. We excluded 3 respondents who did not maintain an active Facebook account, 24 respondents who did not answer all questions, and 1 respondent who was a multivariate outlier due to choosing the first option for each answer over 45% of the time. The analyses that follow are based on the remaining 303 responses. Most respondents (96%) reported having an active Facebook account for more than a year. We asked respondents to report how many minutes per day on average they spent on Facebook in the preceding week. 33.6% of respondents reported spending one to more than 3 hours, 45.2% spent 10 minutes to an hour, and 20.5% spent fewer than 10 minutes on Facebook each day. Respondents had an average of 385 Facebook friends with a standard deviation of 333 and median of 300. Respondents covered a broad age range from 18 to 66 years (median: 27), with 74% females and 27% students. The majority of respondents were Caucasian (78%); 8% were African American, 4% Hispanic, and 6% Asian. Most respondents (96%) had attended college, with nearly 80% holding Bachelor's or advanced degrees. Reported occupations included stay-at-home mother, student, teacher, manager, consultant, etc. Some respondents were unemployed.

FINDINGS

We first ascertained the validity of our constructs. Next, we grouped respondents according to Privacy Fit and employed Partial Least Squares (PLS) based Structural Equation Modeling (SEM) using WarpPLS to test our hypothesized models [23]. We tested 10 separate models, one for each privacy boundary type.

Validity of Constructs

We evaluated construct validity by carrying out a confirmatory factor analysis and examining convergent validity, discriminant validity, and internal consistency of our measures [7]. The measures are included in the Appendix along with corresponding questionnaire items and factor analysis results. All constructs exceeded the recommended convergent validity cutoff values for Composite Reliability (CR) and Average Variance Extracted (AVE) of 0.7 and 0.5, respectively [15, 33]. To verify discriminant validity, we confirmed that the square root of the AVE was larger for each construct than the correlation between the construct and any other construct [6]. For internal consistency, prior research has recommended that loadings of individual items in factor analysis be at least 0.7 [33]. This criterion was met for all except two items: "I want to be able to choose what to share and what to hold back on Facebook." *(desired Self Disclosure)* and "My friends keep personal information they know about me between us." *(actual Confidant Disclosure)*. However, we decided to retain these two items since the corresponding constructs met the requirements of CR and AVE. Given adequate construct validity of all measures, this analysis provided additional confirmation of the validity of the measurement scales we created for the 10 privacy boundary types.

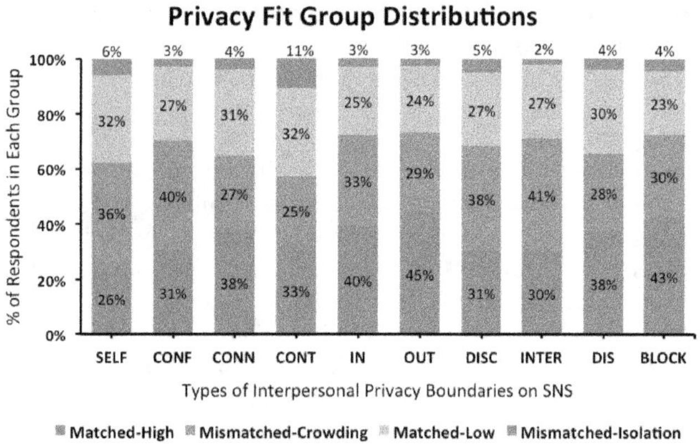

Figure 2. Distribution of respondents across the four Privacy Fit profiles for the 10 types of interpersonal privacy boundaries on SNS.

Distribution of Privacy Fit

To assess Privacy Fit, we first created separate scales for desired and actual privacy by summing the responses to the individual scale items of each boundary type. These scales were then compared with the overall mean across all respondents for the corresponding boundary type. Scores lower than or equal to the mean were classified as 'low,' while those higher than the mean were marked as 'high.' Based on this classification for each of the 10 privacy boundary types, respondents were assigned to one of four groups indicating different Privacy Fit profiles: Mismatched-Crowding (high desired privacy, low actual privacy), Mismatched-Isolation (low desired privacy, high actual privacy), Matched-High (high desired privacy, high actual privacy), and Matched-Low (low desired privacy, low actual privacy). The Mismatched-Crowding and Mismatched-Isolation groups correspond to Altmans conceptualization of social crowding and social isolation, respectively [1]. Note that this classification was done per boundary type; i.e. a given respondent could be classified differently for each of the 10 privacy boundaries.

Figure 2 shows the distribution of respondents across the four Privacy Fit profiles for each of the 10 boundary types. The purple segments show that the Mismatched-Isolation groups were consistently much smaller than the other three groups. We chose to exclude the Mismatched-Isolation groups from further analyses since the small proportions of respondents (3% to 11%) in these groups did not provide sufficient power for meaningful statistical analysis.

Verification of Structural Models

After removing the Mismatched-Isolation group, three Privacy Fit groups remained: Mismatched-Crowding, Matched-High, and Matched-Low. Therefore, the Mismatched-Crowding group was used as the baseline for the structural models in Figure 1. For testing our moderating hypotheses, we employed a mean split to dichotomize Facebook Usage Intensity between casual and avid users. The final structural models for each of the 10 boundary types explained between 44–45% of the variance in Bridging Social Capital, 27–30% in Bonding Social Capital, and 27–31% in Social Connectedness. The explanatory power for the dependent variables in

Boundary Type	H1 Connectedness → Bonding SC	H2 Connectedness → Bridging SC	H3 FBuse → Connectedness
SELF	0·54***	0·55***	1·20***
CONF	0·55***	0·52***	1·20***
CONN	0·55***	0·53***	1·24***
CONT	0·55***	0·54***	1·12***
IN	0·56***	0·53***	1·10***
OUT	0·53***	0·53***	1·39***
DISC	0·55***	0·53***	1·18***
INTER	0·55***	0·54***	1·10***
DIS	0·58***	0·55***	1·55***
BLOCK	0·56***	0·55***	1·06***

*** $p < 0.001$

Table 2. Model verification results: H1–H3.

our models is comparable to that found in prior work (e.g., Ellison et al. [11] explained 44% of the variance in Bridging Social Capital and 23% in Bonding Social Capital, while Krasnova et al. [24] explained 26–35% of the variance in Social Connectedness) and is well beyond the recommended threshold of 10% as an indication of substantive explanatory power in the social sciences [12].

Facebook Use, Social Connectedness, and Social Capital

Hypotheses 1, 2, and 3 were supported for all 10 privacy boundary types. Table 2 provides corresponding path coefficients and p-values for the 10 structural models. The path coefficients are based on standardized factor scores. The values of path coefficients in Table 2 indicate that 1.00 standard deviation difference in Social Connectedness is related to a 0.53–0.58 standard deviation difference in Bridging Social Capital and 0.53–0.55 standard deviation difference in Bonding Social Capital. Further, there is a 1.06–1.39 standard deviation difference in Social Connectedness between casual and avid users. These results show that avid Facebook users reported higher levels of Social Connectedness (H3), and in turn, Social Connectedness helped them generate Bridging and Bonding Social Capital (H1 & H2).

Privacy Fit, Facebook Use, and Social Connectedness

Next, we tested the main effects of Privacy Fit on Social Connectedness (H4a & H5a) along with interaction effects between Privacy Fit and Facebook Usage Intensity (H4b & H5b). To understand the true nature of the relationship between Privacy Fit and Social Connectedness, main and interaction effects should be interpreted together. Table 3 provides corresponding path coefficients and p-values for each of the 10 privacy boundary types. Statistically significant path coefficients for H4a and H5a indicate a main effect of Privacy Fit on Social Connectedness such that Privacy Fit is associated with higher levels of Social Connectedness than Privacy Mismatch, independent of Facebook Usage Intensity. As Table 3 shows, our hypotheses were supported for all but two of the privacy boundary types (Inward Facing Territorial and Outward Facing Territorial) for the Matched-Low group and for all but three of the privacy boundary types (Self Disclosure, Confidant Disclosure, and Network Discovery) for the Matched-High group. However, taking interaction effects into account, the only cases when a Privacy Fit did not equate to significantly higher levels of Social Connectedness at ei-

Boundary Type	H4a Matched-Low → Social Connectedness	H4b Matched-Low x FBUse → Social Connectedness	H5a Matched-High → Social Connectedness	H5b Matched-High x FBuse → Social Connectedness
SELF	0·83***	−0·63***	0·09	0·06
CONF	0·80***	−0·76***	0·15	−0·05
CONN	0·43***	−0·31**	0·18*	−0·36**
CONT	0·23*	−0·48***	0·33***	0·18
IN	0·18	−0·38**	0·50***	−0·33***
OUT	0·01	−0·61***	0·38***	−0·49***
DISC	0·36***	−0·40***	0·09	−0·25*
INTER	0·33**	−0·23*	0·20*	−0·05
DIS	0·91***	−0·90***	0·71***	0·63***
BLOCK	0·23*	−0·34**	0·30**	0·07

*** $p < 0.001$, ** $p < 0.01$, * $p < 0.05$

Table 3. Model verification results: H4ab - H5ab.

ther level of Facebook Usage Intensity were for the Matched-High group across the two Disclosure boundaries, i.e., Self Disclosure and Confidant Disclosure.

Table 3 also shows that H4b was consistently confirmed across all 10 boundary types: the difference in Social Connectedness between Matched-Low versus Mismatched-Crowding was larger for casual users than for avid users. However, H5b was confirmed for only half of the privacy boundary types (Relationship Connection, Inward Facing Territorial, Outward Facing Territorial, Network Discovery, and Interactional Disabling). Arguably, matching high desired levels of privacy for some of the other boundary types is beneficial for both casual and avid Facebook users because these boundaries regulate the flow of information; avid users benefit from this regulation as well, since it increases the effectiveness of their Facebook usage.

Since interaction effects can be hard to interpret using only the coefficients in Table 3, we include graphs of the interaction effects for the 10 privacy boundary types in Figure 3). As Social Connectedness is a latent factor, we set its value to zero for casual Facebook users in the Mismatched-Crowding group across all graphs. The graphs show the differences (in standard deviation terms) in Social Connectedness between the Mismatched-Crowding (blue), Matched-High (red), Matched-Low (green) groups, stratified by casual versus avid Facebook Usage Intensity. We provide tests of the effect of Privacy Fit separately for casual and avid users. In the graphs, an asterisk (*) over a bar signifies that a Privacy Fit (either Matched-High or Matched-Low) resulted in statistically significantly higher Social Connectedness than the Mismatched-Crowding group. Since we did not hypothesize any differences between the two Matched groups, we refrained from testing these differences, thus avoiding the need for post-hoc Bonferroni corrections.

The graphs in Figure 3 show that Matched-Low was consistently associated with greater Social Connectedness than Mismatched-Crowding for casual users (for whom the result was statistically significant for all privacy boundary types). For avid users, the corresponding association was statistically significant for only 2 out of the 10 boundary types (Relationship Connection and Interactional Disabling). Matched-High was also associated with higher Social Connectedness than Mismatched-Crowding for 7 out of 10 boundary types for casual users (Relationship Connection, Relationship Context, Inward Facing Territorial, Outward Facing Territorial, Network Discovery, Interactional Disabling, and Interactional Blocking) and 4 out of 10 boundary types for avid users (Relationship Context, Inward Facing Territorial, Interactional Disabling, and Interactional Blocking). In other words, for all boundary types, Matched-Low was associated with higher Social Connectedness than Mismatched-Crowding, but primarily for casual users, and Matched-High was associated with higher Social Connectedness for a subset of the boundary types for both casual and avid users.

DISCUSSION

Our results point to a number of insights important for characterizing the SNS privacy discourse.

Contemporary SNSs May Encourage Oversharing

Our focus on Privacy Fit versus Privacy Mismatch led to the notable finding that very few of our participants experienced *social isolation*, (i.e., Mismatched-Isolation or more privacy than they desired). Figure 2 shows that this finding was consistent across the 10 privacy boundary types with only 3-11% of participants achieving higher levels of privacy than desired. This finding, combined with the predominance of people who attained low levels of privacy (i.e., Mismatched-Crowding or Matched-Low), confirms the common belief that SNSs tend to urge their users to share as much as possible [38]. This tactic may be based on the belief that social connectedness and social capital can be increased only via pervasive sharing. Our results show that this belief is mistaken. A practical implication of our findings, therefore, would be the importance of questioning the social norms, values, motivations, and assumptions that currently drive SNS interface design.

Privacy May Enhance, Not Hinder Social Connection

If plentiful and strong social connections required unbounded openness and sharing, then one would expect the highest levels of Social Connectedness from avid Facebook users who desired and achieved low levels of privacy (Matched-Low). However, Figure 3 indicates that such a relationship is unequivocally true for only Relationship Connection, not for

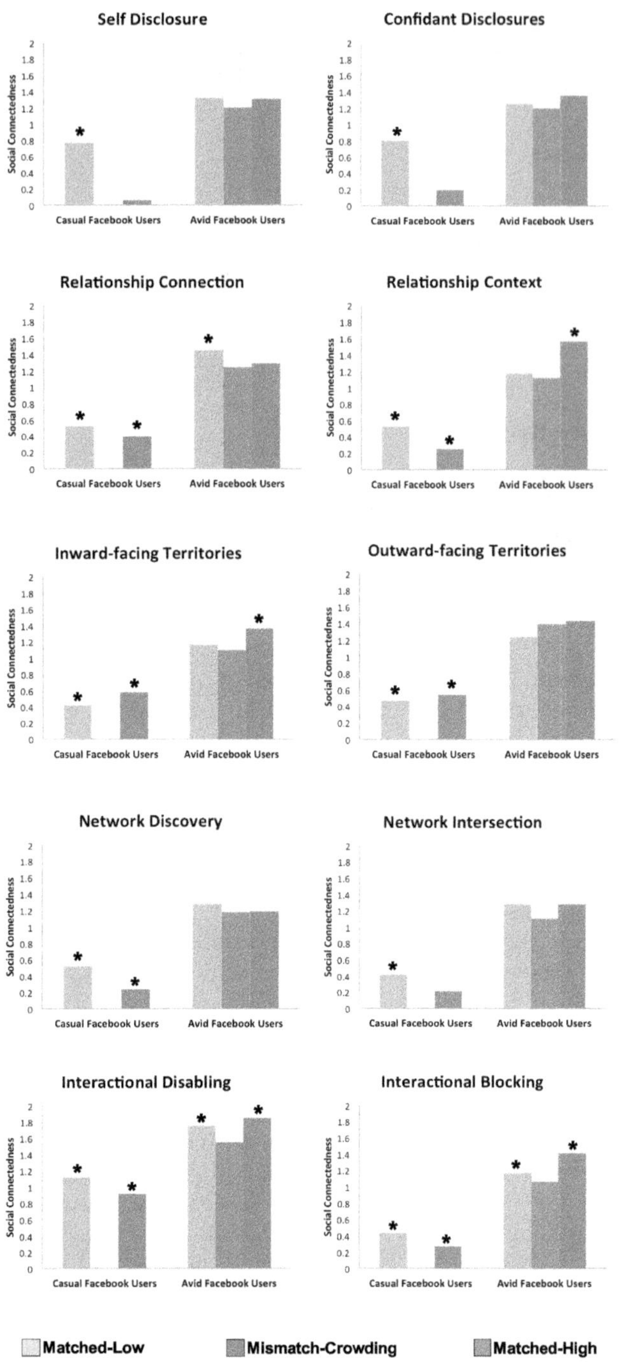

Figure 3. Interaction effects between Privacy Fit and Facebook Usage Intensity for each privacy boundary type.

any other privacy boundary types. This finding suggests that when users desire and acquire a large and open network of friends, family, acquaintances, and strangers, they tend to have higher levels of Social Connectedness. Yet, Figure 3 also shows that avid Facebook users who desired and achieved high levels of privacy (Matched-High) perceived the highest level of Social Connectedness for 3 of the 10 boundary types (Relationship Context, Inward Facing Territorial, Interactional Blocking). Further, the positive effect of Privacy Fit at high privacy levels is even more prominent for casual Facebook users. Indeed, casual Facebook users in the Matched-High group perceived higher levels of Social Connectedness across 7 of the 10 privacy boundary types (note that in these cases the Matched-Low group often perceived even higher levels of Social Connectedness).

Overall, these findings suggest that supporting certain privacy boundaries may actually aid in building intimate social connections instead of hindering them, especially at casual usage levels. For example, both casual and avid users who wish and believe that they can closely manage their Inward Facing Territorial boundaries, such as filtering the Facebook News Feed in order to see only the content from friends that matter the most to them, also reported the highest levels of Social Connectedness.

Social Connectedness as a Mediator

H1 and H2 confirmed a positive relationship between Social Connectedness and Bridging and Bonding Social Capital. Consequently, Social Connectedness *mediates* the effects of Privacy Fit and Facebook Usage Intensity on the two types of Social Capital. We tested whether this mediation is a *full mediation* with saturated models [16] which included six additional paths that examined direct effects of Facebook Usage Intensity and Privacy Fit on Bridging and Bonding Social Capital. All statistically significant path coefficients in the original hypothesized models remained statistically significant in the saturated models. Moreover, only one of the additional paths in the saturated models was statistically significant: the direct path from Facebook Usage Intensity to Bridging Social Capital, which is consistent with the strong relationship between the two shown by past research [9]. The analysis of the saturated models implies that Social Connectedness fully mediates the relationship between Facebook Usage Intensity and Bonding Social Capital and partially mediates the relationship between Facebook Usage Intensity and Bridging Social Capital. The effect of Privacy Fit and its interaction with Facebook Usage Intensity on the two types of social capital is also fully mediated by Social Connectedness. The fully mediated relationships suggest that Social Connectedness is an important factor that should be taken into account in future studies that address social capital generation and maintenance via SNSs.

Privacy Fit Matters Most for Casual SNS Users

The effect of Privacy Fit was most prominent for casual Facebook users. For these users, Privacy Fit was almost always associated with higher levels of Social Connectedness than Privacy Mismatch. Arguably, due to the lower levels of Facebook Usage Intensity, casual SNS users need to 'make every interaction count.' Therefore, fulfillment of privacy expectations might have a stronger influence on their overall perception of online connections. In contrast, avid users, who use Facebook frequently, to the point where it is highly enmeshed in their daily lives, likely derive Social Connectedness as a natural side-effect of active participation. As a result, they may become less attentive to Privacy Mismatch due to habituation. Alternatively, they may downplay any Privacy

Mismatch as a means to achieve uniformity between their privacy cognition and their high levels of Facebook Use (i.e., to reduce cognitive dissonance).

To further explore the interplay between Privacy Fit and Facebook Usage Intensity, we tested the direct path from Privacy Fit to Facebook Usage Intensity. We found a statistically significant positive relationship (for either Matched-Low or Matched-High) for 7 out of the 10 the boundary types. Compared to Privacy Mismatch, Privacy Fit was associated with higher Facebook Usage Intensity about 40% of the time; users whose privacy desires were satisfied used Facebook more intensely than those with unmet privacy needs. Privacy Fit thus creates a virtuous cycle, leading casual users to feel more socially connected as well as increase their Facebook Usage Intensity, thereby further increasing Social Connectedness. We must also point out that a subset of casual Facebook users in our sample may have been relatively new to Facebook and, as a result, yet to achieve avid usage. Therefore, our findings suggest that early achievement of Privacy Fit may be crucial to ensuring that such users increase participation and achieve greater connectedness over time. A longitudinal study could provide important insight regarding this potential accelerating effect of Privacy Fit on the evolution of SNS practices.

Privacy Is More Complex than Information Disclosure

SNS users manage their social interactions in a number of ways, including but not limited to information disclosure. Our findings were consistent with past research that suggested the necessity for some trade-off between privacy and social benefits when it comes to information disclosure on SNSs [44]; only users who desired and achieved low levels of disclosure privacy reported significantly higher levels of social connectedness (see the results for the Self Disclosure and Confidant Disclosure boundaries in Table 3 and Figure 3). However, treating privacy only in terms of information disclosure provides an incomplete picture. Among the 10 privacy boundary types in our models, the information disclosure privacy boundaries (Self Disclosure and Confidant Disclosure) were in fact the least affected by Privacy Mismatch. When privacy boundaries other than information disclosure were considered, we found that Privacy Fit could lead to more Social Connectedness, even when users desired and achieved high levels of privacy.

The psychometric properties of our models confirmed the discriminant validity of the 10 different privacy boundary types, emphasizing the need to broaden the conceptualization of privacy in future research. Our validated scales can be used and/or modified for future SNS privacy studies to help broaden privacy measures beyond private versus public information disclosure. The consistency of our results across the 10 boundary types confirms the robustness of these scales. At the same time, the interaction graphs (Figure 3) illustrate unique and nuanced differences between the 10 boundary types that enrich our overall understanding of privacy.

IMPLICATIONS FOR DESIGN

To our knowledge, our models are the first to assess the effects Privacy Fit — the match between desired and achieved levels of privacy — on Social Connectedness and Social Capital within the context of SNSs. We first point to a potentially fruitful design direction focusing on Privacy Fit, followed by ethical considerations when pursuing this direction.

A Call for User-Tailored Privacy Design

Overall, we found strong support that Privacy Fit is associated with higher levels of Social Connectedness than Privacy Mismatch, especially for casual users. Yet, the large proportion of users who experienced a lack of Privacy Fit — i.e., social crowding (see Figure 2) — confirms reports that SNS users have a hard time translating their desired privacy level into concrete interface actions [30]. As our study illustrates, users have the complex task of maintaining no less than 10 types of interpersonal privacy boundaries; attaining Privacy Fit across all these boundaries is a formidable task. Our results show that SNS providers seeking to maximize the benefits of their service should opt to *help their users attain Privacy Fit*, rather than urge them to share as much as possible. However, as SNS users vary wildly in their desired level of privacy [34], this is not simply a matter of urging them to share less (e.g., using *privacy nudging*, cf. [48]), because that could force some users from the Matched-Low group into the Mismatched-Isolation group.

The best solution, then, may be to move beyond the one-size-fits-all approach to privacy towards 'user tailored' [22] privacy design that personalizes the conceptualization and operationalization of privacy to fit the unique needs of each user. Existing work on user tailored privacy shows that users' privacy preferences can be predicted with a reasonable level of accuracy [3, 13, 40, 41]. Given the large amount of personal user data SNSs collect (implicitly via interaction traces as well as explicitly via user input), they may already be equipped with the resources necessary to explore such personalization. Alternatively, 'privacy profiles' can be created to characterize SNS users based on the strategies they employ for attaining their privacy needs [51]. In sum, the work on privacy personalization shows that it is *possible* to predict SNS users' personal privacy preferences and then help them meet these desires. Our work further motivates existing work on privacy personalization within SNSs by empirically demonstrating the importance and benefits of leveraging these user tailored approaches to help users attain Privacy Fit.

Ethical Considerations

Some argue that the interests of SNS providers are inherently in conflict with privacy needs of SNS users, thus leading providers to promote and normalize openness and sharing with little regard to privacy [31]. Our Privacy Fit profile distributions (Figure 2) lend some credence to this claim by showing that it is rare for Facebook users to achieve high privacy levels unless driven by a strong personal desire for privacy; few users in our sample achieved high levels of privacy despite desires for low levels.

Our findings support an alternative design approach that helps users be more effective in attaining the level of privacy they desire: "Give SNS users the privacy they want," whether this is a lot of privacy, little privacy, or no privacy at all. Our work demonstrates the *doubly beneficial* effect of Privacy Fit — enhancing Privacy Fit may not only reduce privacy concerns for the users themselves, but may also enrich SNS interactions and encourage greater participation from casual users, which is typically in the interest of the SNS provider. Thus, such an approach has the potential to enhance the interactional benefits derived by SNS users and would likely serve the commercial interests of SNS providers and affiliated advertisers. Yet, as designers and privacy researchers, we must also raise the ethical question of whether striving to meet users' privacy desires is always the right course of action. Instead, it may sometimes be necessary to influence a *change* in these desires (e.g., by nudging users toward choices that provide more privacy [48] or educating them about potential consequences of reduced privacy). While this ethical debate is beyond the scope of this paper, we mention it here to emphasize that user tailored privacy design may involve more than simply giving users what they want.

LIMITATIONS AND FUTURE RESEARCH

While our structural models imply causal directions, it must be kept in mind that such models cannot confirm or disprove causality. When we report that a match between desired and actual privacy levels is associated with higher Social Connectedness, we essentially confirm that the two are correlated. The hypothesized causal direction (Privacy Fit $\rightarrow$ Social Connectedness) is based on Altman's theory, not on explicit confirmation by our analyses. It is possible that higher Social Connectedness leads users to feel that their privacy needs are being met rather than vice versa. Given that prior research has found it challenging to resolve the apparent conflict between privacy and social networking benefits, the positive association is noteworthy regardless of causal direction.

Further, we examined only one type of mismatch between desired and actual privacy, i.e., social crowding. Although research within social psychology makes a theoretical distinction between social crowding and social isolation [1], analysis of the latter (i.e., Mismatched-Isolation) was statistically infeasible due to the dearth of participants in this category. Therefore, our findings and implications regarding Privacy Mismatch apply only when SNS users achieve less privacy than they desire. Additionally, our sample has an inherent self-selection bias and is therefore skewed toward Facebook users who are well-educated, Caucasian, and female adults from the US. Further research is needed to ascertain generalizability to the populations of the US and other countries.

Our work motivates a number of directions for future research. For example, past studies that examined SNS outcomes in terms of information disclosure may benefit from replication to confirm whether their findings remain stable across our broader conceptualization of SNS privacy as interactional boundary regulation. Follow up studies may also examine how SNS users' privacy management strategies influence their subsequent perception of Privacy Fit. Additionally, longitudinal investigations are needed to examine how our current findings hold up as the interactive capabilities and privacy interfaces of SNSs undergo changes, as SNS users gain experience, and as social norms related to SNS usage evolve.

CONCLUSION

The interactive benefits of using SNSs are often described as being in conflict with people's desire for personal privacy. Therefore, proponents of online social networking often advocate for open and 'frictionless' sharing with little regard for privacy [8, 31]. However, disregarding users' privacy concerns may either encourage SNS users to overshare [49] or, alternatively, to curtail or even cease their SNS usage altogether [2, 52, 53], limiting the potential social benefits of SNSs. Social psychologists remind us that sharing too much and too soon can be just as detrimental as social isolation [1,37]. Therefore, the key to optimizing the interactional benefits of SNS use may be to tailor privacy to fit the unique needs of each individual user. Indeed, our findings show that SNS users can fulfill their desires for privacy without sacrificing social benefits. In fact, doing so may actually enhance their social interactions with others. Moreover, our results suggest that enabling users to meet their privacy needs could serve the interests SNS providers as well. Thus, we believe that promoting a fit between users' desired and achieved SNS privacy is a step toward reconciling the tension between the goals of privacy and online social networking.

ACKNOWLEDGMENTS

We thank the participants of the study. We acknowledge anonymous reviewers for insightful comments that helped us revise and refine the paper. Thanks are also due to Sara E. Justinger for editorial comments on draft versions of this paper. This research was supported in part by the Helsinki Institute for Information Technology (HIIT) project on Future Networks, Society and Modeling (FuNeSoMo) funded by Tekes - the Finnish Funding Agency for Innovation.

REFERENCES

1. Altman, I. *The environment and social behavior: Privacy, personal space, territory, crowding*. Brooks/Cole Publishing Company, Monterey, CA, USA, 1975.

2. Baumer, E. P., Adams, P., Khovanskaya, V. D., Liao, T. C., Smith, M. E., Schwanda Sosik, V., and Williams, K. Limiting, leaving, and (re)lapsing: An exploration of facebook non-use practices and experiences. In *Proceedings of the SIGCHI Conference on Human Factors in Computing Systems*, CHI '13, ACM (New York, NY, USA, 2013), 3257–3266.

3. Bilogrevic, I., Huguenin, K., Agir, B., Jadliwala, M., and Hubaux, J.-P. Adaptive information-sharing for privacy-aware mobile social networks. In *Proceedings of the 2013 ACM International Joint Conference on Pervasive and Ubiquitous Computing*, UbiComp '13, ACM (New York, NY, USA, 2013), 657–666.

4. Boyle, M., and Greenberg, S. The language of privacy: Learning from video media space analysis and design. *ACM Trans. Comput.-Hum. Interact. 12*, 2 (June 2005), 328–370.

5. Burke, M., Marlow, C., and Lento, T. Social network activity and social well-being. In *Proceedings of the SIGCHI Conference on Human Factors in Computing Systems*, CHI '10, ACM (New York, NY, USA, 2010), 1909–1912.
6. Campbell, D. T., and Fiske, D. W. Convergent and discriminant validation by the multitrait-multimethod matrix. *Psychological bulletin 56*, 2 (1959), 81.
7. Cook, T. D., Campbell, D. T., and Day, A. *Quasi-experimentation: Design & analysis issues for field settings*. Houghton Mifflin, Boston, MA, USA., 1979.
8. Eler, A. Top trends of 2011: Frictionless sharing, December 2011. `http://readwrite.com/2011/12/14/top_trends_of_2011_frictionless_sharing`.
9. Ellison, N. B., Steinfield, C., and Lampe, C. The benefits of Facebook "friends:" Social capital and college students' use of online social network sites. *Journal of Computer-Mediated Communication 12*, 4 (2007), 1143–1168.
10. Ellison, N. B., Steinfield, C., and Lampe, C. Connection strategies: Social capital implications of Facebook-enabled communication practices. *New Media & Society 13*, 6 (2011), 873–892.
11. Ellison, N. B., Vitak, J., Steinfield, C., Gray, R., and Lampe, C. Negotiating privacy concerns and social capital needs in a social media environment. In *Privacy Online*, S. Trepte and L. Reinecke, Eds. Springer Berlin Heidelberg, 2011, 19–32.
12. Falk, R. F., and Miller, N. B. *A primer for soft modeling*. University of Akron Press, Akron, OH, USA, 1992.
13. Fang, L., and LeFevre, K. Privacy wizards for social networking sites. In *Proceedings of the 19th International Conference on World Wide Web*, WWW '10, ACM (New York, NY, USA, 2010), 351–360.
14. Festinger, L. *A theory of cognitive dissonance*, vol. 2. Stanford University Press, Palo Alto, CA, USA, 1962.
15. Fornell, C., and Larcker, D. F. Evaluating structural equation models with unobservable variables and measurement error. *Journal of Marketing Research 18*, 1 (February 1981), 39–50.
16. Gefen, D., Straub, W. D., and Rigdon, E. An update and extension to SEM guidelines for administrative and social science research. *MIS Quarterly 35*, 2 (2011), iii–xiv.
17. Harris, P. B., Brown, B. B., and Werner, C. M. Privacy regulation and place attachment: Predicting attachments to a student family housing facility. *Journal of Environmental Psychology 16*, 4 (1996), 287–301.
18. Iachello, G., and Abowd, G. D. Privacy and proportionality: Adapting legal evaluation techniques to inform design in ubiquitous computing. In *Proceedings of the SIGCHI Conference on Human Factors in Computing Systems*, CHI '05, ACM (New York, NY, USA, 2005), 91–100.
19. Karr-Wisniewski, P., Wilson, D., and Richter-Lipford, H. A new social order: Mechanisms for social network site boundary regulation. In *Americas Conference on Information Systems*, AMCIS 2011 (2011).
20. Katherine, A. *Boundaries Where You End and I Begin: How to Recognize and Set Healthy Boundaries*. Hazelden Publishing, 1994.
21. Kaya, N., Webb, J. D., and Miller, N. G. Adjustment to congregate living environments: Older adults and privacy regulation. *Journal of Interior Design 31*, 1 (2005), 14–24.
22. Knijnenburg, B. P. Simplifying privacy decisions: Towards interactive and adaptive solutions. In *Workshop on Human Decision Making in Recommender Systems*, Decisions@ RecSys '13 (2013), 40–41.
23. Kock, N. WarpPLS 4.0 user manual, 2010. `http://scriptwarp.com/warppls/UserManual_v_4_0.pdf`.
24. Koroleva, K., Krasnova, H., Veltri, N., and Günther, O. It's all about networking! Empirical investigation of social capital formation on social network sites. In *International Conference on Information Systems*, ICIS 2011 (2011).
25. Lampinen, A., Lehtinen, V., Lehmuskallio, A., and Tamminen, S. We're in it together: Interpersonal management of disclosure in social network services. In *Proceedings of the SIGCHI Conference on Human Factors in Computing Systems*, CHI '11, ACM (New York, NY, USA, 2011), 3217–3226.
26. Langheinrich, M. Privacy by design — principles of privacy-aware ubiquitous systems. In *Proceedings of the Third International Conference on Ubiquitous Computing*, UbiComp '01, Springer-Verlag, Springer-Verlag (London, UK, 2001), 273–291.
27. Laufer, R. S., and Wolfe, M. Privacy as a concept and a social issue: A multidimensional developmental theory. *Journal of Social Issues 33*, 3 (1977), 22–42.
28. Limayem, M., Hirt, S. G., and Cheung, C. M. How habit limits the predictive power of intention: The case of information systems continuance. *MIS Quarterly 31*, 4 (2007), 705–737.
29. Lipford, H. R., Wisniewski, P. J., Lampe, C., Kisselburgh, L., and Caine, K. Reconciling privacy with social media. In *Proceedings of the ACM 2012 Conference on Computer Supported Cooperative Work Companion*, CSCW '12, ACM (New York, NY, USA, 2012), 19–20.
30. Madden, M. Privacy management on social media sites. Tech. rep., Pew Research Center's Internet & American Life Project, Washington, DC, USA, February 2012. `http://www.pewinternet.org/files/old-media/Files/Reports/2012/PIP_Privacy_management_on_social_media_sites_022412.pdf`.

31. Matyszczyk, C. Zuckerberg: I know that people don't want privacy, February 2010. `http://news.cnet.com/8301-17852_3-10431741-71.html`.

32. Moore, G. C., and Benbasat, I. Development of an instrument to measure the perceptions of adopting an information technology innovation. *Information systems research 2*, 3 (1991), 192–222.

33. Nunnally, J. C. *Psychometric Theory*, 2nd ed. McGraw-Hill, New York, NY, USA, 1978.

34. Olson, J. S., Grudin, J., and Horvitz, E. A study of preferences for sharing and privacy. In *CHI '05 Extended Abstracts on Human Factors in Computing Systems*, CHI EA '05, ACM (New York, NY, USA, 2005), 1985–1988.

35. Page, X., Kobsa, A., and Knijnenburg, B. P. Don't disturb my circles! Boundary preservation is at the center of location-sharing concerns. In *The Sixth International AAAI Conference on Weblogs and Social Media*, ICWSM 2012 (2012).

36. Palen, L., and Dourish, P. Unpacking "privacy" for a networked world. In *Proceedings of the SIGCHI Conference on Human Factors in Computing Systems*, CHI '03, ACM (New York, NY, USA, 2003), 129–136.

37. Petronio, S. *Boundaries of privacy: Dialectics of disclosure*. State University of New York Press, Albany, NY, USA, 2002.

38. Rainie, L., Kiesler, S., Kang, R., and Madden, M. Anonymity, privacy, and security online. Tech. rep., Pew Research Center's Internet & American Life Project, Washington, DC, USA, Sept. 2013. `http://www.pewinternet.org/files/old-media//Files/Reports/2013/PIP_AnonymityOnline_090513.pdf`.

39. Rainie, L., Smith, A., and Duggan, M. Coming and going on Facebook. Tech. rep., Pew Research Center's Internet & American Life Project, Washington, DC, USA, February 2013. `http://www.pewinternet.org/files/old-media//Files/Reports/2013/PIP_Coming_and_going_on_facebook.pdf`.

40. Ravichandran, R., Benisch, M., Kelley, P. G., and Sadeh, N. M. Capturing social networking privacy preferences: Can default policies help alleviate tradeoffs between expressiveness and user burden. In *Proceedings of the 9th International Symposium on Privacy Enhancing Technologies*, PETS '09, Springer-Verlag (Berlin, Heidelberg, 2009), 1–18.

41. Sadeh, N., Hong, J., Cranor, L., Fette, I., Kelley, P., Prabaker, M., and Rao, J. Understanding and capturing people's privacy policies in a mobile social networking application. *Personal and Ubiquitous Computing 13*, 6 (2009), 401–412.

42. Straub, D., Boudreau, M.-C., and Gefen, D. Validation guidelines for IS positivist research. *Communications of the Association for Information Systems 13*, 1 (2004), 380–427.

43. Stutzman, F., and Hartzog, W. Boundary regulation in social media. In *Proceedings of the ACM 2012 Conference on Computer Supported Cooperative Work*, CSCW '12, ACM (New York, NY, USA, 2012), 769–778.

44. Stutzman, F., Vitak, J., Ellison, N. B., Gray, R., and Lampe, C. Privacy in interaction: Exploring disclosure and social capital in Facebook. In *The Sixth International AAAI Conference on Weblogs and Social Media*, ICWSM 2012 (2012).

45. Tufekci, Z. Can you see me now? Audience and disclosure regulation in online social network sites. *Bulletin of Science, Technology & Society 28*, 1 (2008), 20–36.

46. Valenzuela, S., Park, N., and Kee, K. F. Lessons from Facebook: The effect of social network sites on college students' social capital. In *9th International Symposium on Online Journalism* (2008).

47. Valenzuela, S., Park, N., and Kee, K. F. Is there social capital in a social network site?: Facebook use and college students' life satisfaction, trust, and participation. *Journal of Computer-Mediated Communication 14*, 4 (2009), 875–901.

48. Wang, Y., Leon, P. G., Acquisti, A., Cranor, L. F., Forget, A., and Sadeh, N. A field trial of privacy nudges for facebook. In *Proceedings of the SIGCHI Conference on Human Factors in Computing Systems*, CHI '14, ACM (New York, NY, USA, 2014), 2367–2376.

49. Wang, Y., Norcie, G., Komanduri, S., Acquisti, A., Leon, P. G., and Cranor, L. F. "I regretted the minute I pressed share": A qualitative study of regrets on Facebook. In *Proceedings of the Seventh Symposium on Usable Privacy and Security*, SOUPS '11, ACM (New York, NY, USA, 2011), 10:1–10:16.

50. Williams, D. On and off the 'Net: Scales for social capital in an online era. *Journal of Computer-Mediated Communication 11*, 2 (2006), 593–628.

51. Wisniewski, P., Knijnenburg, B. P., and Richter Lipford, H. Profiling facebook users' privacy behaviors. In *SOUPS 2014 Workshop on Privacy Personas and Segmentation* (2014).

52. Wisniewski, P., Lipford, H., and Wilson, D. Fighting for my space: Coping mechanisms for SNS boundary regulation. In *Proceedings of the SIGCHI Conference on Human Factors in Computing Systems*, CHI '12, ACM (New York, NY, USA, 2012), 609–618.

53. Wisniewski, P., Xu, H., and Chen, Y. Understanding user adaptation strategies for the launching of facebook timeline. In *Proceedings of the SIGCHI Conference on Human Factors in Computing Systems*, CHI '14, ACM (Toronto, Canada, 2014), 2421–2430.

54. Wisniewski, P. J. *Understanding and Designing for Interactional Privacy Needs Within Social Networking Sites*. PhD thesis, University of North Carolina at Charlotte, Charlotte, NC, USA, 2012. AAI3527994.

APPENDIX

The Tables below provide the items used for operationalizing our constructs in the questionnaire.

Facebook Usage Intensity $(CR = 0.92, AVE = 0.67)$	**Loading**
Facebook is part of my everyday activity.	0·86
I am proud to tell people I'm on Facebook.	0·75
Facebook has become part of my daily routine.	0·88
I feel out of touch when I haven't logged onto Facebook for a while.	0·81
I feel I am part of the Facebook community.	0·84
I would be sorry if Facebook shut down.	0·77

Table 4. Facebook Usage Intensity items.

Social Connectedness $(CR = 0.89, AVE = 0.58)$	**Loading**
On Facebook, I feel close to the people in my friend list.	0·76
On Facebook, I have a feeling of being connected to others.	0·79
On Facebook, I am updated about my friends.	0·64
On Facebook, I stay in touch with my friends.	0·81
On Facebook, I keep in contact with the people in my friend list.	0·80
Now that I use Facebook, I interact with my friends more.	0·74

Table 5. Social Connectedness items.

Bridging Social Capital $(CR = 0.95, AVE = 0.65)$	**Loading**
Talking with people on Facebook makes me curious about other places in the world.	0·79
Interacting with people on Facebook makes me feel like a part of a larger community.	0·85
Interacting with people on Facebook reminds me that everyone in the world is connected.	0·78
Interacting with people on Facebook makes me want to try new things.	0·83
Interacting with people on Facebook gives me new people to talk to.	0·79
I am willing to spend time to support general Facebook community activities.	0·76
On Facebook, I come into contact with new people all the time.	0·72
Interacting with people on Facebook makes me interested in things that happen outside of my town.	0·87
Interacting with people on Facebook makes me interested in what people unlike me are thinking.	0·80
Interacting with people on Facebook makes me feel connected to the bigger picture.	0·86

Table 6. Bridging Social Capital items.

Bonding Social Capital $(CR = 0.91, AVE = 0.63)$	**Loading**
There are several people on Facebook I trust to solve my problems.	0·82
The people I interact with on Facebook would help me fight an injustice.	0·79
There is someone on Facebook I can turn to for advice about making very important decisions.	0·85
The people I interact with on Facebook would put their reputation on the line for me.	0·82
When I feel lonely, there are several people on Facebook I can talk to.	0·75
If I needed an emergency loan of $500, I know someone on Facebook I can turn to.	0·73

Table 7. Bonding Social Capital items.

Desired Privacy		Actual Privacy	
Self Disclosure ($CR = 0.80, AVE = 0.57$)	**Loading**	**Self Disclosure** ($CR = 0.91, AVE = 0.78$)	**Loading**
I do not want to post very intimate things about myself on Facebook.	0·78	I post very intimate things about myself on Facebook.	0·89
I want to share only minimal information about myself on Facebook.	0·82	I share only minimal information about myself on Facebook.	0·88
I want to be able to choose what to share and what to hold back on Facebook.	0·65	I choose what to share and what to hold back on Facebook.	0·88
Confidant Disclosure ($CR = 0.82, AVE = 0.60$)	**Loading**	**Confidant Disclosure** ($CR = 0.75, AVE = 0.51$)	**Loading**
I do not want my friends to tag me in photos or posts without my permission.	0·77	My friends do not tag me in photos or posts without my permission.	0·75
I want to limit what personal information my friends share about me on Facebook.	0·81	I limit what personal information my friends share about me on Facebook.	0·81
I want my Facebook friends to keep personal information they know about me between us.	0·75	My friends keep personal information they know about me between us.	0·55
Relationship Connection ($CR = 0.85, AVE = 0.66$)	**Loading**	**Relationship Connection** ($CR = 0.84, AVE = 0.64$)	**Loading**
I only want people in my Facebook social network who I associate with on a regular basis in real life.	0·82	I only have people in my Facebook social network who I associate with on a regular basis in real life.	0·79
I do not want to have Facebook friends who are no longer real friends.	0·80	I do not have Facebook friends who are no longer real friends.	0·77
I only want to accept intimate friends and family members as Facebook friends.	0·82	I only accept intimate friends and family members as Facebook friends.	0·83
Relationship Context ($CR = 0.83, AVE = 0.62$)	**Loading**	**Relationship Context** ($CR = 0.82, AVE = 0.57$)	**Loading**
I want to make a distinction between my friends based on the type of relationship I have with them. For example, family, friends, co-workers, etc.	0·78	I make a distinction between my friends based on the type of relationship I have with them. For example, family, friends, co-workers, etc.	0·70
I want my interactions on Facebook to be different between me and a close friend than they would be with an acquaintance.	0·82	My interactions on Facebook are different between me and a close friend than they would be with an acquaintance.	0·79
I want my one-on-one interactions on Facebook to be appropriate and unique based on my relationship with that specific person.	0·76	My one-to-one interactions on Facebook are appropriate and unique based on my relationship with that specific person.	0·78
Inward Facing Territorial ($CR = 0.83, AVE = 0.62$)	**Loading**	**Inward Facing Territorial** ($CR = 0.89, AVE = 0.73$)	**Loading**
I want to pick and choose what kinds of updates show up in my News Feed.	0·81	I pick and choose what kinds of updates show up in my News Feed.	0·84
I want to decide whose updates show up in my News Feed.	0·80	I decide whose updates show up in my News Feed.	0·88
I want to hide News Feed updates from others that I would rather not see.	0·76	I hide News Feed updates from others that I would rather not see.	0·84

Continued on next page...

... continued from previous page.

Desired Privacy		Actual Privacy	
Outward Facing Territorial ($CR = 0.79, AVE = 0.56$)	**Loading**	**Outward Facing Territorial** ($CR = 0.84, AVE = 0.64$)	**Loading**
I want to remove any content I do not want from my Timeline/Wall.	0·70	I remove any content I do not want from my Timeline/Wall.	0·79
I want to manage everything that shows up on my Timeline/Wall for others to see.	0·83	I manage everything that shows up on my Timeline/Wall for others to see.	0·85
I want to approve all content before it is posted to my Facebook Timeline/Wall	0·72	I approve all content before it is posted to my Facebook Timeline/Wall.	0·75
Network Discovery ($CR = 0.82, AVE = 0.59$)	**Loading**	**Network Discovery** ($CR = 0.89, AVE = 0.74$)	**Loading**
I do not want others to have access to my friends through my Facebook friend list.	0·71	Others do not have access to my friends through my Facebook friend list.	0·92
I want to restrict others in my network from being able to see who I am and am not friends with on Facebook.	0·83	I restrict others in my network from being able to see who I am and am not friends with on Facebook.	0·86
I want to hide my friend list so that others cannot browse my Facebook friends.	0·77	I hide my friend list so that others cannot browse my Facebook friends.	0·89
Network Intersection ($CR = 0.86, AVE = 0.68$)	**Loading**	**Network Intersection** ($CR = 0.90, AVE = 0.74$)	**Loading**
I want to avoid letting specific groups of friends interact with each other on Facebook.	0·80	I avoid letting specific groups of friends interact with each other on Facebook.	0·87
I want to keep my different social circles separate from each other on Facebook.	0·86	I keep my different social circles separate from each other on Facebook.	0·84
I want to moderate how my different groups of friends interact with one another on my Facebook page.	0·81	I moderate how my different groups of friends interact with one another on my Facebook page.	0·88
Interactional Disabling ($CR = 0.82, AVE = 0.60$)	**Loading**	**Interactional Disabling** ($CR = 0.90, AVE = 0.76$)	**Loading**
I want to be able to turn off chat, my Wall, or other Facebook features that allow others to interact with me anytime they want to.	0·72	I turn off chat, my Wall, or other Facebook features that allow others to interact with me anytime they want to.	0·91
I want to disable the ability for my friends to contact me on Facebook when I want to be left alone.	0·82	I disable the ability for my friends to contact me on Facebook when I want to be left alone.	0·82
I want to limit the different ways my friends can communicate with me via Facebook.	0·79	I limit the different ways my friends can communicate with me via Facebook.	0·88
Interactional Blocking ($CR = 0.83, AVE = 0.63$)	**Loading**	**Interactional Blocking** ($CR = 0.86, AVE = 0.68$)	**Loading**
I want to prevent some people on Facebook from having any access to me what-so-ever.	0·78	I prevent some people on Facebook from having any access to me what-so-ever.	0·82
When I do not want to interact with someone anymore, I want to be able to sever all contact with them on Facebook.	0·74	When I do not want to interact with someone anymore, I sever all contact with them on Facebook.	0·78
I want to block certain people from finding me or knowing what I am up to on Facebook.	0·85	I block certain people from finding me or knowing what I am up to on Facebook.	0·87

Table 8. Items for measuring *desired* and *achieved* privacy across the 10 interpersonal boundary types on SNS.

Making Time

Siân Lindley
Microsoft Research
21 Station Road, Cambridge, CB1 2FB, UK
sianl@microsoft.com

ABSTRACT

This paper draws on research on time and technology, with a view to examining the notion that technology is implicated in the speeding up of everyday life. We begin by looking at research that shows how the adoption of the clock and of 'clock time' was framed by more general shifts in ways of conceptualising and using time. Likewise, we suggest that the ways in which digital technologies are said to shape experiences of time need to be understood in the context of the fractured routines of the modern Western world. We argue that 'redesigning' these experiences necessitates a broader way of dealing with the temporal structures of social life. Technology may play various roles here, for instance by shaping temporal infrastructures and highlighting reified temporal patterns. However, complex challenges also need to be addressed, central to which are recent accounts that position time as collective and entangled.

Author Keywords

Temporality; clock time; digital time; plastic time; socio-temporal pattern; rhythm; routine; temporal experience.

ACM Classification Keywords

H.5.m. Information interfaces and presentation (e.g., HCI): Miscellaneous.

INTRODUCTION

Time is a topic that is pervasive in HCI, yet it is also one that is hard to unpack. Unlike concepts such as 'space' and 'place', which have been the subject of careful enquiry and definition [17, 11], time is considered sporadically and in rather heterogeneous ways (see, for example, topics covered in various HCI workshops held over the years [18, 26, 52]). Recently, though, it seems that particular attention is being paid to how digital technologies intersect with the experience of time. In his book *Present Shock*, media theorist and commentator Douglas Rushkoff [40] argues that we are losing sight of what 'organic' time is through our relationship with digital technologies and the related need to be always-on and always-connected. This general theme can also be seen in Bell's [4] critique of the lack of opportunity to experience boredom, said to be exacerbated by the always-availability of digital technologies, and in Pang's [36] book *The Distraction Addiction*, in which he addresses the question: 'Can we reclaim our lives in an age that feels busier and more distracting by the day?' Pang's book is aimed at a general audience (its tagline is 'Getting the information you need and the communication you want, without enraging your family, annoying your colleagues, and destroying your soul'), but perhaps the strongest evidence that these concerns have become part of the zeitgeist is that the phrase 'digital detox' was entered into the Oxford English Dictionary in 2013.

CSCW '15, March 14 - 18 2015, Vancouver, BC, Canada
Copyright 2015 ACM 978-1-4503-2922-4/15/03...$15.00
http://dx.doi.org/10.1145/2675133.2675157

The motivation in writing this paper is to examine some of these ideas about time and technology. The notion that digital technologies in themselves have a temporal quality that is problematic is questionable. Yardi Schoenebeck [58] has recently pointed to the moral panics that may drive users to give up or take breaks from social media when the technology may in fact be harmless or even beneficial, and propositions that the pace of life is speeding up, this being compounded through our relationships with technologies, are not new. The steamship, railway and telegraph led to the phrase "the annihilation of time and space" becoming commonplace in the 19th century [47], and arguments that position the introduction of technologies as responsible for shifts in the ways in which people understand and experience time have been critiqued as technological determinism [e.g. 12].

In this paper, we take a careful look at research that indicates how technology is bound up with experiences of time. We begin with a classic example of this: the adoption of the clock and of 'clock time', by considering research that shows how the introduction of the clock was framed by broader sociocultural shifts in ways of thinking about and using time. We then consider ways in which the experience of 'digital' time is linked to the fractured routines of the modern Western world, with digital technologies having evolved alongside increased flexibility of personal schedules and variance of leisure and work rhythms. This leads us to argue that 'redesigning' the experience of time as mediated by technologies necessitates a broader way of dealing with the rhythms and routines that frame their use. We consider what role technology might play in this, through shaping temporal infrastructures and shifting reified temporal patterns. We conclude by noting the considerable challenges that this entails, especially in view of recent accounts that position time as collective and entangled.

CLOCK TIME

Clocks are associated with a historical shift in the way that time is understood, with clock time often being described as abstract, generic and interchangeable. Yet, to suggest that clock time simply came along with the invention of the clock is, of course, simplistic. In this section, we first look to research that highlights how underlying sociocultural shifts in the ways in which time was conceptualised and used in the Western world framed the clock's invention and acceptance. We then detail a position outlined by Glennie and Thrift [12], in which clock time is described as a series of practices rather than a concept created by new timekeeping technologies.

We begin with work by the historian Alfred Crosby [9], who argues that the development and acceptance of the clock was preceded by a shift in thinking about the nature of time, and of reality more broadly. Prior to this, numbers were not neutral ways of quantifying, but were "dramatic, even melodramatic, and teleological" [p. 47]. They had religious and spiritual connotations; for instance, the number 7 signified perfection, 11 sin, and 12 judgment. He writes,

"The old Europeans preferred broad focus and settled for imprecision in the hope of including as much as possible of what might be important. Often they were reaching not for a handle on material reality, but for a clue as to what lay beyond the scrim of reality. They were as poetic about numbers as about words." [pp. 46-47]

The move to interpreting numbers as a way of measuring things of continuous quality, and the conceptualization of time as something that could be understood in this way, was significant. Crosby links these changes to advances in a range of areas, including music, painting and book-keeping. For example, he argues that music was essential to the development of "[f]aith in absolute time, which the musicians who invented Western mensural notation were among the first to think about seriously [...] Such a faith altered perception of reality and promoted a reordering of the ways to understand it" [p. 157]. These broader shifts, and the different ways of thinking about time that they were bound up with, were essential to innovations in mechanical clocks.

Glennie and Thrift [12] have also noted how music, alongside dance and even the etiquette of turn-taking, were part of a 'culture of the interval' that prefigured and strengthened the hold of clock times in general society. They avoid asserting causality, but see clocks as being integrated into existing time-based practices that drew on 'unequal' hours (divisions of the sunlit day, which vary with the season and were indicated using technologies such as sundials) and other temporal indicators:

"the spread of clocks, the use of clocks to keep equal hour time, and the use of time markers to structure daily life were all intertwined. We cannot see one of these as determining the others, whichever way we point the causal arrow. Although equal hour clock time became used for very many purposes, it was often taking over existing – and essentially similar – functions of unequal hour time." [p. 26]

Glennie and Thrift suggest that the grounding of new practices around clocks depended, quite simply, on "whether they 'worked' on an everyday basis" [p. 410]. Indeed, central to their argument is the position that there was (and is) no singular concept of clock time. For them, clock time is best understood as sets of practices, which are bound up with time-reckoning and time-keeping technologies, but which vary and are shaped by different times, places and communities.

This view of clock time is quite different to that often depicted in the literature, where it is positioned as abstract and mechanistic. For example, in his classic analysis of the history of the machine, Lewis Mumford [30] notes that,

"Abstract time became the new medium of existence. Organic functions themselves were regulated by it: one ate, not upon feeling hungry, but when prompted by the clock: one slept, not when one was tired, but when the clock sanctioned it." [p. 17]

Similarly, E. P. Thompson [53], in his paper on time discipline and industrial capitalism, suggests that a view of time as an interchangeable commodity came to replace what had been a more task-oriented approach to time use. Glennie and Thrift argue against this conceptualisation of clock time. They acknowledge that people's consciousness of time was disrupted by the clock, but disagree with a notion of clock time that is "inauthentic, unnatural, omnipotent" [p. 50], that follows the metaphor of the production line, or that adopts a narrative of a world that is intensifying and speeding up. Instead, technologies and the uses made of them are positioned as coevolving, with new temporal knowledges being gradually accumulated and integrated into the practices of everyday life.

As noted in the Introduction, a narrative of a world that is intensifying and speeding up is increasingly associated with digital technologies and the experiences they offer. Yet, as is the case for clocks, a careful treatment of the topic should consider how technologies, practices, and broader shifts in time use have coevolved. In the following section, we look at how 'digital time' has been described by both media commentators and scholars, before considering research that demonstrates its links with certain features of modern Western time use. We then consider what this might mean when it comes to developing technologies with the aim of designing for certain temporal experiences.

DIGITAL TIME

We begin this section by considering what is actually meant by 'digital time'. Rushkoff's [40] writing on the topic summarises how technology is often described in the media in terms of its relationship with temporality. He notes that computers are disconnected from the personal and collective rhythms of everyday life, be these "natural and emergent" [p. 98], reflecting solar and lunar cycles, or the rhythms of those around us (whether biological or social; for example, group members are known to pace themselves against each other). Rushkoff argues that technologies provide people with the means "to ride roughshod over all these nooks and crannies of time [...] what we often forget is that our bodies are not quite as programmable as our schedules" [p. 92]. Furthermore, and differentiating digital time from clock time, he suggests that a lack of adherence to chronological time is compounded by the fact that digital technologies connect with a flow of information that is always and instantly available. He argues that continual change, which is bound up with web services such as social network sites, blogs and the news, is central to the experienced need for constant connectivity.

A related, but richer, argument is made by the sociologist John Tomlinson [55], in his account of the 'condition of immediacy'. Tomlinson argues that speed is central to modern cultural practices, experiences and values, and he focuses on immediacy in particular because it has three connotations. One of these is a play on the word media: the condition of im*media*cy is bound up specifically with electronic media, which convey a notion of speed that is effortless. Secondly, immediacy is chosen because it indicates the notion of a "culture of instantaneity – a culture accustomed to rapid delivery, ubiquitous availability and the instant gratification of desires" [p. 74]. Finally, immediacy expresses a sense of directness and an increasing sense of connectedness with others. In contrast to mechanical speed, which "displayed the will, the force and the effort involved in the overcoming of distance" [p. 91], the culture of immediacy has at its core the notion that the gap is already closed:

"in one way or another, electronic media try to hide their mediation. Far from advertising it, they obscure the artifice of their practice and present their product or their access to communication as pristine, untouched, immediate. " [p. 99]

Research in HCI has illustrated how this notion of immediacy is upheld through the social conventions associated with technologies, as well as through their design. For example, Harper *et al.* [16] have described the lived experience (or *durée*, following Bergson [6]) of Facebook as being located firmly in the now, and have noted that this necessitates a particular approach to the performance of identity on the site by its users. They observe that interactions privilege the present and underpin an impression of events unfolding as they happen (even if this is not the case in terms of spatial time, or Bergson's *temps*). Because of this, the performance of identity is one of the moment: users reported feeling it inappropriate to post old content, and were similarly aggrieved when others uploaded photos that surfaced 'out of time'. Research by narrative theorist Ruth Page [35] (a co-author on the above paper) considers further how Facebook users learn to interpret social media posts when reading the newsfeed. While the series of snippets of 'breaking news' posted by a variety of members of one's social network do not offer a typical narrative, readers nevertheless draw their own story-like experience, using their knowledge of those posting content to build a backstory, whilst imagining what may happen next. They create what Adam [1] calls the 'expanded present', by creating a relevant past and future that serves to enrich the moment.

This research suggests that the impression of nowness associated with social media is upheld partly through the interface and partly through social conventions. The temporal experience is as much a product of the ways in which the technologies are used as it is a feature of their design. This points to how, just as has been argued for the case of clocks, digital technologies and practices have coevolved to underpin particular experiences of time. However, social media is obviously a rather narrow example of this. Accordingly, and in the interests of exploring how broader shifts in time use have may coevolved with digital technologies, we now look to work by Rattenbury *et al.* [37], which relates the always-on quality of digital technologies to more general shifts in the organization of everyday life. These are changes that have resulted in a temporal experience that they describe as plastic, a temporal experience that is both shaped by and shapes the use of digital technologies.

Plastic Time

Rattenbury *et al.* [37] observe that while the amount of leisure time available to those in the United States went up during the 20th century (citing Aguiar and Hurst [2], who looked at surveys from 1965 to 2003), the occurrence of sustained moments of free time is decreasingly likely in modern life, especially for women (here they draw on Bittman and Wacjman [7] and Deem [10]). With this as their starting point, Rattenbury *et al.* conducted a large-scale study of mobile personal computer use (in this case, of notebooks), to explore how daily life rhythms are made manifest through use of technology. They argue that the usage patterns their participants exhibited suggest a particular temporal experience, that which they refer to as plastic time. Plastic time is described as unanticipated, un-reflexive and fluid, as the "experience of temporal 'scraps', of gaps in the schedule", and as "the negative space of busyness" [p. 233]. Plastic time flies under the radar, being unplanned and non-immersive, and associated with neither productivity nor leisure. It is interruptible, but can also expand until some other activity presents itself.

Rattenbury *et al.* argue that Internet use is a perfect filler for plastic time. For their participants, this was an activity that could easily be interrupted, could always be resumed, and was not seen as a priority. Interestingly, the lack of rhythm that is sometimes bemoaned of technology is crucial here: "As much as the Internet evokes notions of instantaneity and 'real-time' information, the heart of the matter was the asynchronicity – the fact that it did not *dictate* or even set the pace of interaction." [37, p. 237, original italics]. Computer use becomes fractional through its dependence on a lack of other, higher priority, events; it falls into a 'temporal remainder' category. Yet at the same time, it creates a sense of fluidity in daily temporal rhythms; it fits into people's practices by resonating with the ways in which time is used.

While Rattenbury *et al.* highlight web browsing as the perfect plastic activity, the concept has also been applied to television watching by Irani *et al.* [20]. They observe that by choosing particular kinds of programs and utilizing features such as rewinding, skipping and watching on-demand, television can become temporally flexible. It can be used ad hoc to fill unplanned segments of time, it can be shrunk through actions such as fast-forwarding commercials, and it can be expanded by switching to a broadcast channel, which will fill the time available. Furthermore, and like web browsing, television watching can fly under the radar. Irani *et al.*'s participants were sometimes surprised when shown representations of their own viewing patterns; their memories of watching had already faded.

In these analyses of plasticity we see how, like clock time, digital time is not simply a property of technologies, nor does it straightforwardly emerge as a sociotechnical convention associated with their use. Rather, it has coevolved with broader shifts in the temporality of everyday life, such as the emergence of fractured rhythms, and the associated need to fill the gaps between them.

This underlines the necessity of taking a holistic view of technologies in use when attempting to design for particular temporal experiences. HCI researchers have, on occasion, adopted this approach when building technologies that aim to support particular experiences of time [e.g. 28]. More frequently however, they look to 'organic' or 'human' time as points of inspiration, or build on the ideology of the slow movement, itself a reaction to the concept of speed-up. In the following sections, we look to examples of these approaches, before considering how we could draw on broader, and multiple, temporalities in designing for temporal experience.

DESIGN AND TEMPORAL EXPERIENCE

The slow technology design agenda, first presented by Hallnäs and Redström [15], builds on the idea that as technologies become more ubiquitous they must do more than prioritise the efficiency and productivity associated with task-completion. In contrast to *fast* technologies that *save* time, the aim with slow technologies is to *produce* time, by serving as an incitement for reflection. Their approach has proved inspirational (see [33] for a brief overview), but for the purposes of this paper we limit ourselves to three examples of work in the area. These indicate how slow technologies are experienced over long durations of time, how they are understood differently when they include organic components, and how they are perceived as better suited to some parts of everyday life than others.

The first study we wish to consider entailed a 14 month deployment of a prototype called *Photobox* by Odom *et al.* [32]. Photobox is a wooden box that prints photos from the user's Flickr collection randomly and infrequently, so that the user is unaware of what (if anything) they will find when they open it. The intention behind this is to support reflection on and reminiscence about the past, to challenge the "always-on-and-accessible qualities of many contemporary consumer devices" [p. 1693], and to see how attachment to a device that does this would change over time. Odom *et al.* report how their participants expressed initial experiences of frustration, confusion, and attempts to work out what the technology, and study, was 'really' trying to accomplish, before they came to accept and eventually appreciate the device. They conclude by highlighting design for anticipation as well as for re-visitation and reflection in the context of slower-paced technologies.

One can juxtapose the confusion Odom *et al.*'s participants initially experienced with reactions to a technology that incorporates organic processes. Kuznetsov *et al.* [24] built a system to visualise bacterial activity inside Winogradsky columns (used for cultivating microorganisms), which were filled with different soil samples and deployed with members of a gardening community. Like the Photobox, and in line with the slow technology design philosophy, it might be more accurate to say that the columns are not so much used in the traditional sense as simply experienced; they demand neither attention nor input. However, participants in this study did not see the system as slow; instead it was viewed as simply reflecting the speed of "real life". This interpretation is different again to those expressed in a third study by Grosse-Hering *et al.* [14], in which reactions to a juicer developed in line with slow design principles were explored. Here, participants saw slowness as connected with laziness and a lack of productivity, appropriate at weekends but not suitable for weekdays. Grosse-Hering *et al.* conclude by highlighting the importance of balancing slowness with convenience; there are, of course, times when efficiency is important.

Given the acceptance of slowness when bound up with organic processes, and the distinction drawn between the speed of 'real life' and that of technology, it is perhaps not surprising that researchers have looked to organic rhythms and embodied experiences in their efforts to design for temporality. Studies in this area include Höök's [19] reflections on her sense of being in (and out of) time with a horse when learning to ride, and Kosmack Vaara's [22] exploration of temporality as an embodied experience that emerges during sourdough baking. Here, rhythm and tempo are bound up with living microorganisms and chemical processes. Temporality is inherent in the materials and the movements of the baker, the tempo altering with the changing characteristics of the material. In both pieces of work, the non-digital is looked to as inspiration for what experiential qualities might be supported through technology, with *timing* being emphasised over time per se.

This emphasis on timing is taken further by Martin and Holtzman [28], in their endeavour to design for a more "human experience of time" [p. 1977]. They developed and deployed an automatic scheduling system called *Kairoscope*, which draws on Ancient Greek notions of time and in particular on the notion of *Kairos*. Kairos relates to the idea of timing, or the opportune moment, and is contrasted with *Chronos*, which represents sequential time and is typically at the core of scheduling systems. Rather than using Chronos, Kairoscope emphasises malleability, and positions time as relative to the present. It was motivated as a means of addressing the busyness that is inherent to modern life; accordingly, it assigns precise times to appointments only as they approach, and alerts users to advancing events through an interface that looks like a pie-chart, which gradually changes from green to red. The aim is to remove the need for the user to think about *when* things will happen, so that they may instead simply rest assured that they *will*, and focus on the present. Additionally, the system optimises for social interaction. When used by multiple people, it aims to bring them together serendipitously.

Notably, Martin and Holtzman's attempt to manage the multiple temporalities that frame everyday life stands alone here. Efforts to design for experiences of temporality tend to focus on the felt experience of the individual: Can technology offer a slow experience? How might technology align with a sense of temporality that is embodied? Yet, Grosse-Hering *et al.*'s findings make clear the need to address multiple temporalities, and prior research in CSCW has emphasised how understanding the ways in which different temporal structures intersect is essential to designing for the felt experience of time. In the following section, we outline research that shows how this is so, before highlighting in particular the concept of quality time in relation to intersecting temporalities.

INTERSECTING TEMPORALITIES

We begin by considering prior work by Reddy *et al.* [38], which indicates how the interplay between temporal structures frames not only the organization of action but also how it is experienced. Reddy *et al.*'s study of information-seeking in medical work led them to identify three temporal structures: rhythms, trajectories and horizons. The temporal sequence of events pertaining to an individual patient (described as an illness trajectory) interplays with the rhythms of the workplace, so as to provide a context for medical workers in seeking, providing and managing information, and in planning, organizing and coordinating activities. Trajectories and rhythms frame temporal horizons, described as knowledge of likely future activities that are drawn upon in the organization of current work. The three together bring orderliness to the working day, with the nature of temporal horizons dictating how flexibly work can be organised, and the urgency with which it needs to be carried out.

The idea that temporal experiences (in this case, urgency) are underpinned by the ways in which temporal structures intersect can also be seen in a rather different analysis of time; one that draws on time diaries and looks to unpack the concept of quality time. Many readers of this paper may understand quality time as that dedicated to being spent with others, although the term itself is relatively new. In his analysis of the concept, Southerton [45] identifies quality time as a contemporary concern, and uses it alongside an analysis of diaries written in 1937 and 2000 to examine the impression that everyday life is speeding up. His findings lead him to argue that the feeling of time pressure that seems inherent to modern life is due to difficulties in coordinating practices, rather than the sheer density of events that need to be accomplished. Of the participants from the year 2000, he writes,

"Respondents described their daily lives as a roller-coaster ride with moments of harriedness and calm, of 'hot' and 'cold spots' of temporal activity [...] The challenge as described by respondents was to coordinate within their networks so that cold spots, which were variously described as 'quality time' and 'family time', were aligned." [p. 53]

Southerton suggests that these moments of quality time need to be "re-instituted" due to the flexibility of personal schedules and the variance in leisure and work rhythms; coordinating devices become necessary due to the lack of centralised coordination in modern life. This is in contrast to daily life in 1937, when fixed institutional events such as meal and work times meant that coordination was embedded in the routine of daily life. Rush was of course a part of life, but it was a rush to keep within collective rhythms, rather than to pull into alignment individual routines.

Southerton's account implies that it is the nature of rush rather than its existence per se that has shifted over the years and so, what comes to be valued is positioned as time with others rather than time 'off' in itself. A similar view is expressed by Urry [56], who notes how the desynchronisation of "the time-space paths of individuals" [p. 139] has led to efforts to underpin time spent together, such as through short breaks or long weekends away. If we accept that so-called free time is increasing but is also increasingly fractured, then we can see why quality is ascribed to sustained moments of time that can be spent with others.

When considered in light of this research, it is interesting to ask what it would be like to live with a system like Kairoscope, where temporal structures and their interplay are managed by computers and hidden from view. Visions for technologies like this have little to say about how a sense of urgency might be underpinned, or the rhythms of collaborative work established. Furthermore, automated systems reduce the expression of choice in relation to how time is spent. As noted by Zerubavel, "[t]ime is definitely one of the principles that can best allow us to establish and organise priority in our lives as well as to symbolically display it" [59, p. 53]. Put simply, quality time takes some of its value by dint of being time dedicated by one person to another. A situation where time spent together is engineered by a system could resonate with a past in which time spent with others was produced by institutionalised routines, and so was taken for granted.

This does, however, raise the question of how one might design for quality time. Southerton's argument brings us back to the idea of temporality and value, and puts some of the critiques outlined in the Introduction into context. The fractional and distracting experiences that technology is associated with are opposite to how quality time is conceptualised. Designing for an alternative temporal experience means understanding the ways in which multiple temporalities intersect, whether these frame a person's working day, or allow a family to spend time together. While scheduling technologies do of course have a role to play here [see e.g. 31], many of the temporal structures that frame everyday life are not so much scheduled as unfold in a way that is unremarkable [54], or are so firmly established that they are no longer seen as alterable. In the following two sections, we consider two challenges associated with designing for temporal experiences by manipulating temporal structures. The first lies in supporting the recognition that temporal structures, which are seen as immovable, are in fact malleable. The second lies in dealing with the complexity of temporal structures that are collective and entangled.

THE SOCIOTEMPORAL AS REIFIED AND MALLEABLE

Zerubavel [59] has argued that sociotemporal patterns, or the established temporal structure of social life, tends to be seen as rigid. Sociotemporal patterns are neither recognised nor treated as the product of human behaviour, yet this is precisely what they are. He asks, "Given its considerable temporal regularity, cannot social life in itself function as a clock or a calendar which is as reliable as any natural clock or calendar?" [p. 14], and points out that sociotemporal cycles, while being "based, to a large extent, on purely arbitrary social convention" are "usually perceived by people as given, inevitable, and unalterable" [p. 42]. Orlikowski and Yates [34], working in the field of organization studies, build on this point. They argue that time is plural; it can be experienced as objective, quantitative and independent of humankind, but also as subjective, situated and socially constructed. In their view, time is both independent of and dependent on behaviour: temporal structures are produced and reproduced through everyday action, and these in turn shape the rhythm and form of ongoing practices. Existing temporal structures become taken for granted and appear to be unbending, but time is also treated as malleable in that temporal structures can be changed and new ones established. The objective/subjective dichotomy is not inherent to the nature of time, but is a property of the particular temporal structures being enacted at a particular moment. They call for a focus on examining how temporal structures become established for a particular activity, and how they are sustained, reinforced or modified in practice.

This is a theme that has been picked up in anthropology more broadly as well as specifically within CSCW. Wilk [57] has considered how routines come to be cultivated, observing that every day we are presented with opportunities to "naturalize something new", and turn events into the "precedents" of new routines [p. 151]. He argues that the decisions that surround the adoption of these routines are part of the process of their cultivation, in which unconscious habits are brought forward into consciousness, reflection and discourse. Cultivation can be active or passive (routines may be actively initiated, or forced upon us), and is governed by "tacit rules" that reveal "how often things must be discussed before they can be done without discussion, how often things have to be repeated by agreement or with supervision before they can become an accepted part of shared daily routine" [p. 151]. A shared context is implicit here, but the ways in which rhythms that bind people are shaped has been pulled into sharper focus by Jackson *et al.* [21]. Picking up on Orlikowski and Yates' position, they argue that "distributed collective practices not only have rhythms, but in some fundamental sense are rhythms" [p. 247]. Rhythms shape collective action but are also shaped by it, and efforts to build them and to bring them into alignment are an essential part of collaborative work.

Jackson *et al.*'s efforts to study the shaping of rhythms at work, alongside Reddy *et al.*'s [38] account of the different temporal structures that frame the ways in which it is organised and experienced, underline the relevance of this line of research to CSCW. Yet, what might we say more specifically about the role of technology in shaping and bringing into alignment the rhythms of everyday life? Firstly, we might consider the role of technologies in framing everyday rhythms. A classic, although outdated, example of this is presented by Silverstone [44], who argues that television provided a structure of "public time" that also served as a framework for managing "private time". His 1993 analysis demonstrates how media can underpin "times grabbed and privileged by women at home who use a favourite soap opera or radio program in the middle of the day to free themselves from their mundane and monotonous domestic duties" [p. 303], as well as serving as a focus for families to congregate. Ten years later, Taylor and Harper's [50] descriptions of television use show how television continued to facilitate different means of spending time, from "switching on to switch off" when returning home from work, to engaged viewing later in the evening.

Even Irani *et al.*'s [20] most recent positioning of television as plastic indicates the existence of temporal windows that anchor collective rhythms: people coordinate around digital television as well as broadcast television. The flexibility that the medium now supports suggests that technologies might be used to enable the building of personalised temporal infrastructures. Through time-shifting, television can become the focus of collective rhythms, produced by viewers who coordinate watching to enable synchronous viewing with household members, or to keep to a schedule with friends and family members who are engaging with the same content separately. By viewing content within particular temporal windows, shared experiences, conversation, and perhaps even quality time can be underpinned. The plasticity of time-shifting produces new rhythms, built upon tacit and explicit coordination.

Of course, this only has relevance where temporal structures clearly involve technology (as in the case of media consumption). A second role for technology in shaping and bringing into alignment the rhythms of everyday life entails using it to modify the naturalised routines that are unthinkingly performed. This is a much more difficult challenge, but there are avenues for research and design here too. One possibility draws on evidence that has shown how making routines visible, and presenting them back to the user in a way that makes them abstract or defamiliarised, could support what Orlikowski and Yates term *temporal reflexivity*, or the recognition that reified temporal patterns are flexible and changeable.

Prior work by Ståhl *et al.* [46], in relation to the *Affective Diary*, and by Lindley *et al.* [27] in relation to *SenseCam*, has shown how simple depictions of daily routine can lead to reflection on behaviour and sometimes to change. In the former, sensor data is captured and represented as abstract visualisations of one's movements and levels of arousal; in the latter, a wearable camera captures images every 20 seconds or so, which can be watched back as a time-lapse stream. Studies of SenseCam [27] in particular have indicated how providing a sense of how time is spent can lead to the realisation that changes can be made. When presented in a more abstract form, people can recognise that those routines that appear to be fixed and outside of their control are in fact flexible. Relatedly, technologies could play a role in highlighting routines that are in the process of becoming cultivated. For example, tracking and monitoring technologies such as *Time of My Life* [51] provide a means to reflect upon how time has been spent. Returning to the idea of intersecting temporalities and quality time, research within CSCW that has focused on how visualizations of work rhythms can be used to support coordination [3] could have a role to play in bringing everyday rhythms into alignment. This is complex, as it requires a consideration of the meta-routines that are based on the interdependencies across people, but Kairoscope [28] provides a good example of what bold thinking in this space could underpin.

To recap the argument so far, we have suggested that design for temporal experience might be supported by efforts to reshape the temporal patterns that form the backdrop of everyday life, with an especial focus on how these intersect. We have noted that while sociotemporal patterns tend to be reified, they are malleable. Technologies can play a role in highlighting this malleability and in supporting their alignment. However, while we have primarily looked at intersections with a view to supporting togetherness, or quality time, a fuller treatment of the topic requires a consideration of other ways in which temporalities are linked. In the final section, we consider this challenge, building on recent accounts that position time as collective and entangled.

TIME AS COLLECTIVE AND ENTANGLED

To provide some background here, we begin by highlighting what Zerubavel [59] has described as a "temporal division of labor". He notes that in modern Western life, "group members participate in one and the same temporal order, yet differently from one another" [p. 69]. Action is complementary, coordinated, but it is not collocated. Here we consider what it means to position time in this way, as something that is collective and entangled. We will show that doing so raises a different set of implications for what it means to 'slow down', or otherwise design for different experiences of temporality.

In considering time as collective, we look first to Mazmanian and Erickson [29], who recently pointed to a temporal division of labour as a possible means for managing an appearance of availability in the workplace. They observe that there is an increasing need for people at work to maintain an impression of being 'always-on', and suggest that by positioning time as collective rather than individual, a front stage [cf. 13] that conveys availability could be sustained, while back stage, individual workers could disconnect.

Pushing this further, Sharma [43] argues for a need to view time as collective not just for workforces, but across society, insofar as the management of personal time is intertwined with the temporalities of those at work. In her recent book *In the Meantime*, she argues that discussion about speed-up ignores the fact that time is experienced differently by different populations, and indeed can be cast as a justification for the exploitation of some by others:

> *"Whether it is theories of speed or cultural responses to speed, articulating the contemporary moment as one of all-consuming speed adds an element of novelty and urgent necessity to the demand and desire to exert more time control over one's quickly passing life "in these sped-up times". Too often, the belief that we are living in a dangerously sped-up culture makes the demand for the labor of others justifiable as a systemic need "in these fast-paced times" rather than the structurally excessive privilege that it is."* [p. 19]

She exemplifies this through accounts of the intersection of the routines of business persons, taxi drivers, office-based yoga instructors, and slow restaurants, noting that taxi drivers are part of a temporal architecture that supports the fast-paced business person, but that in itself can involve long periods of waiting, and often requires the adoption of a temporal ordering that sets them against the conventional nine-to-five working day. Yoga instructors are part of this architecture too, positioned as playing a supportive role in the office, which maintains and normalises elevated time practices, while "[s]low living is mandated as correct yet reserved only for those who have time to make time" [p.

128]. Sharma describes the slow movement as a consumer choice, and observes that "the return to nature via natural rhythms of the body and eating seasonal fruits and vegetables will not change the fact that the largest group of low-wage workers in the world is farmworkers" [p. 121]. When time is problematized in this way, not as an individual but as a collective problem, it becomes clear that slowing down does not present a solution: "Slowing down does not necessarily change (and certainly does not ameliorate) the ways in which individuals and social groups are tangled together in time" [p. 111].

Of course, Sharma's argument is political, stated explicitly as a call for a "temporal politics grounded in an understanding of how social experiences of time are multiple and uneven" [p. 149]. But her point that time is differential, relational, and tangled raises a challenge for CSCW and for HCI more generally, one that picks up on Mazmanian and Erickson's question too. How can we design for time as collective and interdependent, rather than individualised on the one hand, or explicitly scheduled on the other? What does it mean to position collective time not as something that is achieved when people come together, but as a set of relationships through which they are connected? Both Sharma and Mazmanian and Erickson raise this challenge while highlighting the difficulty in addressing it; neither offer a solution. In the Discussion, we draw on the arguments made in this paper to consider what we have learnt about designing for experiences of time, before offering some tentative suggestions with regards to what this would mean when time is positioned as collective and entangled.

DISCUSSION

The temporality of modern life is often cast as overloaded, fast-paced and distracted, yet statistics also indicate that we have increasingly more free time. The work we have considered in this paper indicates that it is the nature of rush that has shifted rather than the amount of things to do: routines become fractured; coordination entails a temporal division of labour; and time spent with others becomes something that is striven for rather than embedded in the sociotemporal patterns that frame everyday life. This is compounded by a sense that it is important to be busy, at least in cultures such as that of the USA. Where there is free time, there is a compulsion to fill it [25].

We began this paper by looking at clock time, noting in particular Glennie and Thrift's [12] position that clock time can be understood as sets of practices that coevolved with timekeeping technologies. We have suggested the value of a similar treatment for so-called digital time: the sense of 'nowness' experienced through social network sites is upheld by social conventions; the Internet has been described as underpinning practices that are perfectly suited to plastic time [37]; and more broadly, sociotemporal structures are enacted through human behaviour. Consequently, efforts to design for temporal experience must do more than simply build desirable temporal models into technologies. Just as an experience of time as mechanical and quantifiable did not simply come along with the clock, neither will a reconnection with organic time be supported through the undertaking of a digital detox. A more fundamental shift would be required; one that is bound up with addressing the broader practices of which these technologies are part [42].

Notably, a practice-oriented treatment of digital time does open up avenues for research and design, one that resonates with Kuutti and Bannon's [23] recent account of a practice perspective forming a new paradigm for HCI. They propose that a central issue in a practice-based research agenda is the need to develop the capability to transform practices through technology. Essential to this is understanding the role of computer artefacts in the emergence and transformation of practices, and the possibilities for influencing these by changing the artefacts themselves.

In this paper we have highlighted various ways in which technologies might play a role in shaping practices that are bound up with the experience of time. Technology can, at times, give shape to the ways in which time is organised. We have seen how television, for instance, can be appropriated to support plastic viewing practices, but that it can also frame broader rhythms and routines. Alternatively, technology can underpin temporal reflexivity by encouraging reflection on existing practices. The provision of abstract visualisations of sociotemporal patterns, and of how these intersect both within and across individual schedules, may encourage attempts to shape how these unfold and fit together. Finally, technologies may encourage particular ways of thinking about time, which then influence how they are used. While it is simplistic to argue that technologies can project an idea or experience of time onto human behaviour, we have seen how, in social media for example, the immediacy of the technology alongside coevolving social conventions can come to frame temporal experience.

Importantly, a practice-oriented treatment of digital time also requires a unit of analysis that goes beyond the individual. Kuutti and Bannon posit that practices are a shared resource amongst a community of people. However, design that takes into account and potentially disrupts the ways in which practices are intertwined is challenging. Research in CSCW has indicated how the coordination of rhythms in the workplace demonstrates power relationships, with regards to which rhythms are prioritised and who is brought into alignment with whom [21, 48]. So questions regarding how change can be effected across individuals necessitates a consideration of how alignment work can be supported, not only within organisations such as workplaces, but outside of them as well.

This point ties into the conceptualisation of time as collective [29] and entangled [43]. The infrastructure that supports a 24/7 society is one that relies on people as well as technologies, the conventional nine-to-five work rhythm, for example, being underpinned by people working shifts outside of these hours. Grappling with these broader temporal infrastructures necessitates a close inspection of the multiple temporalities that exist within cities and neighbourhoods, and the ways in which they are interwoven and cross-dependent. Initial approaches to research and design in this space could include making these infrastructures visible and facilitating possibilities for connection across the temporal boundaries that are inherent to them. Sharma highlights the difficulties that workers who keep to temporal orders outside of the norm experience in terms of integration with local communities; some had never met their neighbours. There is a long history of work within CSCW that might be adapted to this problem, ranging from an understanding of how to support awareness [e.g. 41] to community [e.g. 8] to communication across time zones [e.g. 49]. Even technologies such as timebanks could be reimagined with an interpretation of time as collective, by maintaining an idea of community and giving [5], while explicitly recognizing that some people have more time to spare than others, or that some people's time is more fractured.

It is worth noting too, that the above approach could be critiqued as upholding rather than disrupting existing temporal experiences. In her analysis of office-based yoga, Sharma suggests that this is one means through which the elevated temporal practices of office workers are maintained. This viewpoint brings questions of agency and power back into the frame; shifting the problem of how to design for temporality to the question of how to seriously disrupt the rhythms that form the backdrop to everyday life. Taking a holistic approach, whereby technology is seen as part of a broader system, one that might support an emerging social process in which time is positioned as 'our time' rather than 'my time', is a central challenge here.

Limitations

Before concluding, it is worth acknowledging some limitations of this paper. In writing it, we have focused primarily on Western metaphors for, and accounts of, time. Extending the analysis presented here to reflect additional ways of thinking about time presents a promising direction for future work, and one that is obviously essential if designing for users with different cultural interpretations of time. Recent work by Reinecke *et al.* [39] is one example of how culture affects the ways in which people organise themselves around time, and Adam [1] provides a useful account of different cultural metaphors of time, contrasting, for instance, timelines, which emphasise linear, directional movement, with cyclic representations, which represent rhythm and stability.

CONCLUSION

In this paper we have drawn on existing research to suggest that digital time is a reflection of as much as it underpins the fractured rhythms of everyday life and the sense that it is speeding up. Building on this view, we have suggested that rather than designing more 'human' models of time into technology, what is needed is a recognition that everyday temporalities are multiple, and that it is through understanding and influencing how these intersect that different temporal experiences might be enabled. We have suggested that while technologies have a role to play in shaping the temporal infrastructures of which they are part (television being an exemplar here), richer but more challenging possibilities for CSCW research and design lie in addressing questions such as how broader temporal infrastructures can be made visible, and how temporal reflexivity and agency can be supported. We have highlighted this as especially challenging when time is considered as collective and entangled. Yet it will be essential, if we are to better understand the ways in which experiences of time are not only underpinned by the technologies that we use, but also by the rhythms and routines of the people with whom our lives are intertwined.

ACKNOLWEDGEMENTS

Thanks to Richard Harper and to the reviewers of this paper for their thought-provoking comments. The ideas in this paper were also shaped through a workshop on Temporal Design, organised by Michelle Bastian, Larissa Pschetz and Chris Speed.

REFERENCES

1. Adam, B. *Time*. Polity Press, Cambridge, 2004.
2. Aguiar, M. and Hurst, E. Measuring trends in leisure. *Quarterly Journal of Economics 11*, 3 (2007), 969-1006.
3. Begole, J. "B.", Tang, J. C., Smith, R. B. and Yankelovich, N. Work rhythms: analyzing visualizations of awareness histories of distributed groups. In *Proc. CSCW 2002*, ACM Press (2002), 334-343.
4. Bell, G. Will we ever be bored again? And why it might matter. Presented at *TED[x]Portland*, April 2011. http://tedxtalks.ted.com/video/TEDxPortland-Genevieve-Bell/ Accessed 16 May 2014.
5. Bellotti, V., Cambridge, S., Hoy, K., Shih, P. C., Renery Handalian, L., Han, K. and Carroll, J. M. Towards community-centred support for peer-to-peer service exchange: rethinking the timebanking metaphor. In *Proc. CHI 2014*, ACM Press (2014), 2975-2984.
6. Bergson, H. *Time and Free Will*. Swan Sonnesnschein, London, 2010.
7. Bittman, M. and Wacjman, J. The rush hour: character of leisure time and gender. *Social Forces 79*, 1 (2000), 165-189.
8. Carroll, J. M. and Rosson, M. B. Wild at home: the neighborhood as a living laboratory for HCI. *ACM Trans. Comput.-Hum. Interact. 20*, 3 (July 2013), Article 16.
9. Crosby, A. W. *The Measure of Reality: Quantification and Western Society, 1250-1600.* Cambridge University Press, Cambridge, 1997.

10. Deem, R. No time for a rest? an exploration of women's work, engendered leisure, and holidays. *Time and Society 5*, 1 (1996), 5-25.
11. Dourish, P. Re-space-ing place: "place" and "space" ten years on. In *Proc. CSCW 2006*, ACM Press (2006), 299-308.
12. Glennie, P. and Thrift, N. *Shaping the Day: A History of Timekeeping in England and Wales 1300-1800.* Oxford University Press, Oxford, 2009.
13. Goffman, E. *The Presentation of Self in Everyday Life.* Anchor Books, Doubleday, New York, 1959.
14. Grosse-Hering, B., Mason, J., Aliakseyeu, D., Bakker, C. and Desmet, P. Slow design for meaningful interactions. In *Proc. CHI 2013*, ACM Press (2013), 3431-3440.
15. Hallnäs, L. and Redström, J. Slow Technology – Designing for reflection. *Personal Ubiquitous Comput. 5*, 3 (January 2001), 201-212.
16. Harper, R., Whitworth, E. and Page, R. Fixity: identity, time and durée on Facebook. *IR 13.0* (2012). http://spir.aoir.org/index.php/spir/article/view/8/ Accessed 16 May 2014.
17. Harrison, S. and Dourish, P. Re-place-ing space: the roles of place and space in collaborative systems. In *Proc. CSCW 1996*, ACM Press (1996), 67-76.
18. Hildebrandt, M., Dix, A. and Meyer, H. A. Time design. In *Ext. Abstracts CHI 2004*, ACM Press (2004), 1737-1738.
19. Höök, K. Transferring qualities from horseback riding to design. In *Proc. NordiCHI 2010*, ACM Press (2010), 226-235.
20. Irani, L., Jeffries, R. and Knight, A. Rhythms and plasticity: television temporality at home. *Personal Ubiquitous Comput. 14*, 7 (October 2010), 621-632.
21. Jackson, S. J., Ribes, D., Buyuktur, A. and Bowker, G. C. Collaborative rhythm: temporal dissonance and alignment in collaborative scientific work. In *Proc. CSCW 2011*, ACM Press (2011), 245-254.
22. Kosmack Vaara, E. Kneading time: exploring sensuous dimensions of temporality. Presented at *IxD13*, Toronto, January 27-31 2013.
23. Kuutti, K. and Bannon, L. J. The turn to practice in HCI: towards a research agenda. In *Proc. CHI 2013*, ACM Press (2013), 2543-2552.
24. Kuznetsov, S., Harrigan-Anderson, W., Faste, H., Hudson, S. E. and Paulos, E. Community engagements with living sensing systems. In *Proc. C&C 2013*, ACM Press (2013), 213-222.
25. Leshed, G. and Sengers, P. "I lie to myself that I have freedom in my own schedule": productivity tools and experiences of busyness. In *Proc. CHI 2011*, ACM Press (2011), 905-914.
26. Lindley, S., Corish, R., Kosmack Vaara, E., Ferreira, P. and Simbelis, V. Changing perspectives of time in HCI. In *Ext. Abstracts CHI 2013*, ACM Press (2013), 3211-3214.
27. Lindley, S. E., Glancy, M., Harper, R., Randall, D. and Smyth, N. "Oh and how things just don't change, the more things stay the same": Reflections on SenseCam images 18 months after capture. *Int. J. Hum.-Comput. Stud. 69*, 5 (May 2011), 311-323.
28. Martin, R. and Holtzman, H. Kairoscope: managing time perception and scheduling through social event coordination. In *Proc. CHI 2011*, ACM Press (2011), 1969-1978.
29. Mazmanian, M. and Erickson, I. The product of availability: understanding the economic underpinnings of constant connectivity. In *Proc. CHI 2014*, ACM Press (2014), 763-772.
30. Mumford, L. *Technics & Civilization*. University of Chicago Press 2010 edition, Chicago, 1934.
31. Neustaedter, C., Bernheim Brush, A. J. and Greenberg, S. The calendar is crucial: coordination and awareness through the family calendar. *ACM Trans. Comput.-Hum. Interact. 16*, 1 (April 2009), Article 6.
32. Odom, W., Sellen, A., Banks, R., Kirk, D., Regan, T., Selby, M. *et al.* Designing for slowness, anticipation and re-visitation: a long term field study of the Photobox. In *Proc. CHI 2014*, ACM Press (2014), 1961-1970.
33. Odom, W., Banks, R., Durrant, A., Kirk, D. and Pierce, J. Slow technology: critical reflection and future directions. In *Proc. DIS 2012*, ACM Press (2012), 816-817.
34. Orlikowski, W. J. and Yates, J. It's about time: an enacted view of time in organizations. Presented at the *58th Annual Meeting of the Academy of Management*, San Diego, CA, August, 1998.
35. Page, R. Re-examining narrativity: small stories in status updates. *Text & Talk 30*, 4 (2010), 423-444.
36. Pang, A. S. K. *The Distraction Addiction: Getting the Information You Need and the Communication You Want, Without Enraging Your Family, Annoying Your Colleagues, and Destroying Your Soul*. Hachette Digital, Inc., 2013.
37. Rattenbury, T., Nafus, D. and Anderson, K. Plastic: a metaphor for integrated technologies. In *Proc. UbiComp 2008*, ACM Press (2008), 232-241.
38. Reddy, M. C., Dourish, P. and Pratt. W. Temporality in medical work: time also matters. *Comput. Supported Coop. Work 15*, 1 (February 2006), 29-53.
39. Reinecke, K., Nguyen, M. K., Bernstein, A., Näf, M. and Gajos, K. Z. Doodle around the world: online scheduling behaviour reflects cultural differences in time perception and group decision-making. In *Proc. CSCW 2013*, ACM Press (2013), 45-54.

40. Rushkoff, D. *Present Shock: When Everything Happens Now.* Penguin Press, 2013.
41. Schmidt, K. The problem with 'awareness': introductory remarks on 'awareness in CSCW'. *Computer Supported Cooperative Work 11*, (2002), 285-298.
42. Sengers, P. What I learned on Change Islands: reflections on IT and pace of life. *interactions 18*, 2 (March 2011), 40-48.
43. Sharma, S. *In the Meantime: Temporality and Cultural Politics.* Duke University Press, 2014.
44. Silverstone, R. Time, information and communication technologies. *Time & Society 2*, 3 (1993), 283-311.
45. Southerton, D. Re-ordering temporal rhythms: coordinating daily practices in the UK in 1937 and 2000. In *Time, Consumption and Everyday Life*, E. Shove, F. Trentmann and R. Wilk (Eds), pp. 49-63. Berg, Oxford, 2009.
46. Ståhl, A., Höök, K., Svensson, M., Taylor, A. S. and Combetto, M. Experiencing the Affective Diary. *Personal Ubiquitous Comput. 13*, 5 (June 2009), 365-378.
47. Stein, J. Reflections on time, time-space compression and technology in the nineteenth century. In *Timespace*, J. May and N. Thrift (Eds), pp. 106-119. Routledge, Oxon, 2001.
48. Steinhardt, S. B. and Jackson, S. J. Reconciling rhythms: plans and temporal alignment in collaborative scientific work. In *Proc. CSCW 2014*, ACM Press (2014), 134-145.
49. Tang, J., Zhao, C., Cao, X. and Inkpen, K. Your time zone or mine? a study of globally time zone-shifted collaboration. In *Proc. CSCW 2011*, ACM Press (2011), 235-244.
50. Taylor, A. and Harper, R. Switching on to switch off. In *Inside the Smart Home*, R. Harper (Ed), pp. 115-126. Springer-Verlag, London, 2003.
51. Time of My Life. http://www.windowsphone.com/en-us/store/app/time-of-my-life/3ad82b05-ac06-4fe2-b2d6-04d47007566e/ Accessed 16 May 2014.
52. Thomas, J. C., Pan, Y., Erickson, T., Blevis, E., Letondal, C. and Tabard, A. Avec le temps!: time, tempo, and turns in human-computer interaction. In *Ext. Abstracts CHI 2013*, ACM Press (2013), 3303-3306.
53. Thompson, E. P. Time, work-discipline, and industrial capitalism. *Past and Present 38*, (1967), 56-97.
54. Tolmie, P., Pycock, J., Diggins, T., MacLean, A. and Karsenty, A. Unremarkable computing. In *Proc. CHI 2002*, ACM Press (2002), 399-406.
55. Tomlinson, J. *The Culture of Speed: The Coming of Immediacy.* Sage, London, 2007.
56. Urry, J. Time, leisure and social identity. *Time & Society 3*, 2 (1992), 131-149.
57. Wilk, R. The edge of agency: routines, habits and volition. In *Time, Consumption and Everyday Life*, E. Shove, F. Trentmann and R. Wilk (Eds), pp. 143-154. Berg, Oxford, 2009.
58. Yardi Schoenebeck, S. Giving up Twitter for Lent: how and why we take breaks from social media. In *Proc. CHI 2014*, ACM Press (2014), 773-782.
59. Zerubavel, E. *Hidden Rhythms.* University of California Press, Berkeley, 1981.

Circumscribed Time and Porous Time: Logics as a Way of Studying Temporality

Melissa Mazmanian
Department of Informatics
University of California, Irvine
m.mazmanian@uci.edu

Ingrid Erickson
School of Communication &
Information Rutgers University
ingrid.erickson@rutgers.edu

Ellie Harmon
Department of Informatics
University of California, Irvine
ellie.harmon@uci.edu

ABSTRACT
In this paper, we introduce the notion of a *temporal logic* to characterize sets of organizing principles that perpetuate particular orientations to the lived experience of time. We identify a dominant temporal logic, *circumscribed time*, which has legitimated time as *chunkable, single-purpose, linear,* and *ownable.* We juxtapose this logic with the temporal experiences of participants in three ethnographic datasets to identify a set of alternative understandings of time – that it is also *spectral, mosaic, rhythmic,* and *obligated.* We call this understanding *porous time*. We posit porous time as an expansion of circumscribed time in order to provoke reflection on how temporal logics underpin the ways that people orient to each other, research and design technologies, and normalize visions of success in contemporary life.

Author Keywords
Temporality; Rhythm; Social Norms; Logics; Ethnography; Close Reading

ACM Classification Keywords
H.5.m. Information Interfaces and Presentation (e.g. HCI): Miscellaneous

INTRODUCTION
Rodger, a 43 year-old director of sales describes his plan for the following day: "Up at 2:50[am], 10 min to stumble around, in the pool by 3:15[am] … [and so on, until] … crashing at 9:30pm." Albeit somewhat extreme, Rodger's approach to scheduling is not unusual. Like many Americans, he feels compelled to quantify the temporal resources of his day. In attempting to do it all, he looks to precision scheduling to measure, circumscribe, and conquer the demands in his life: *"It has to work like clockwork or I'm screwed."*

Time animates the ways that technologies are used in professional and social situations, and has been a longstanding topic of interest within CSCW [13, 14, 18, 20, 24, 38]. Cooperation and collaboration, both core activities within this domain, require attention to temporal patterns almost by definition, whether it be in the sequential ordering of interdependent tasks or the particular rhythms of subgroups. Despite this core focus, Steinhardt and Jackson [53] suggest that time continues to be a fertile topic to explore within the field of CSCW. A richer understanding of the ways that time animates the multiple overlapping domains of contemporary professional and social—and now highly mobile—lives is needed. We respond to this call by returning to our field's legacy of interrogating the design, use and resistance to temporal technologies such as calendars and scheduling software to showcase how certain logics of time pervade everyday sociotechnical practices, both inside the office and out.

In this paper we articulate the concept of a *temporal logic* – a particular orientation to time that manifests in time-related social norms, moral judgments, daily practices, and technologies for scheduling and coordination. We use this frame first to delineate a dominant temporal logic that we refer to herein as '*circumscribed time.*' This logic, which is embedded in many popular tools, current scholarship, and especially in the discourse of time management, is characterized by assumptions that time is *chunk-able* (i.e. unitized and measurable), oriented to a *single purpose*, experienced *linearly*, and *owned* by individuals. We then draw on ethnographic data and prior research to juxtapose the core tenets of a circumscribed temporal logic against lived temporal experiences. We find and name an emergent set of temporal elements – *spectral, mosaic, rhythmic* and *obligated* time – which implicitly challenge the assumptions of the dominant logic. We call this collective set *'porous time.'*

The temporal logic of circumscribed time falls short of describing, let alone organizing, the complex temporalities that govern American lives today. As an expansion of the dominant logic, porous time aims to provide a more nuanced account of how temporality shapes interactions among people, technologies, and the self. In articulating a conception of porous time, we aim to emphasize the ways that individuals can and do understand and adapt to the fluidities of time even when the organizations and institutions that they live and work within – be they technical, social, or political – do not. When pressured for time, we find individuals like Rodger struggling to get in 'control' of their time by adhering ever more strenuously to society's dominant logic of circumscribed time. Success appears immanent by breaking a day into single-purpose temporal

CSCW '15, March 14 – 18, 2015, Vancouver, BC, Canada.

http://dx.doi.org/10.1145/2675133.2675231

chunks of time, which can be optimally gridded. Embedded in social and institutional norms, as well as promoted by task management techniques and calendaring tools, this logic perpetuates a promise that an autonomous individual can control the spontaneity and unpredictability of a life that inevitably involves other people and plans [18].

In this paper, we challenge ourselves, and the CSCW community more broadly, to be more reflexive about the temporal constructs we assume as givens when we conduct our work. In addition, we seek to engender a conversation about the multi-faceted nature of temporality. Thus, our goal is less to specify the particularities of a preferred typology or conceptualization, but to provide a vocabulary to galvanize continuing research and design in this area.

RELATED WORK

CSCW has been investigating the relationship of time and work practically from its inception as a scholarly field [12, 13, 20, 39]. Not surprisingly, calendars, particularly Groupware Calendaring Systems (GCS) and their use within organizational contexts, have been well studied in this area (e.g., [20, 24, 38]). Grudin and Palen, for example, showed that usage patterns related to calendar access and visibility differed markedly among organizations [20]. Palen [38, 39] further contributed a set of core constructs regarding 'calendar work', showing how calendars are used variably for temporal orientation, scheduling, tracking, reminding, recording and archiving, and retrieval and recall [38: 19]. Later work by CSCW researchers has documented the wide spectrum of roles that calendars play for individuals [58, 59], the role of calendaring within family contexts [34, 35], and the potential of predicting attendance at events from calendrical patterns [33]. This focus on calendars and "calendar work" instantiates and reinforces the understanding that time can be positively managed, whether for personal, professional or familial ends.

Building on organizational scholarship about the formation and routinization of temporal regularities in organizations [25, 41, 42, 63], CSCW scholars have also introduced the concept of *rhythms* to describe various temporal experiences. Much of this work has pointed to the multiplicity of rhythms in workplace environments and the significant effort required to bring them into alignment [4, 22, 36, 45, 52]. Drawing from Zerubavel [67, 68], Reddy and Dourish detail large-scale and fine-grained *temporal rhythms* within a hospital that reflect repeated tasks or procedures within the organization [45]. In parallel, they present the idea of a *temporal trajectory*, or temporal path a patient takes during his/her stay in the hospital.

Egger and Wagner [11], a decade prior, also underscored the organizational nature of time in their research on "the problems of temporal ordering" [11:250], outlining the notions of *temporal ambiguity* and *temporal dependences* to describe situations that arise when tasks are loosely coupled but temporal synchronization is necessary. Bardram [1] articulated the notion of *temporal coordination*—"the temporal aspect of coordinating cooperative work" [1:158]—to form the basis for his 'Patient Scheduler' system design, a tool for synchronizing distributed work within a hospital. Bardram, like Palen, linked successful temporal coordination to artifacts, noting "...a temporal artefact, such as the clock or the calendar, can be turned into a temporal coordination artefact, mediating the temporal coordination, when shared within a collaborating community of practice" [1:164]. Notably, the ability for an artifact to manifest as a coordination tool requires a shared sense of temporality, or rhythm, among a group of workers.

Rhythms have also been noted at the individual level such as "bored Mondays" or "focused afternoons" [28], and the presence of multiple event horizons – those of plans-in-the-making versus plans-in-action – are rhythmic patterns that have been shown to implicate coordination and collaboration [53]. Relatedly, Ubicomp researchers have developed tools to aid individuals in aligning their lives to one temporal rhythm at the expense of others [3, 58, 59].

The proliferation of mobile and networked communication technologies over the last decade has also inspired scholars to focus on multi-tasking and interruptions (e.g., [14, 15, 36, 47]). While some of this research has been aimed at building technologies to better support multi-tasking, other research has been critical, pointing out the negative consequences of distraction and task-switching [29]. A parallel line of thinking, called 'presence bleed' [16], articulates the way that multi-tasking and extended temporal boundaries blur individuals' professional and personal identities as work bleeds into and throughout multiple spheres of life. This research emphasizes that temporal experience is rarely singular, rather more often layered in complex ways.

Finally, scholars from a variety of disciplines have drawn attention to the moralities and politics of time management. Leshed and Sengers [26] argue that American professionals struggle to construct identities around a positive moral value of 'busyness' while also experiencing the tensions of multiple and conflicting commitments. Sengers continues to develop this line of work in an emerging project on the moral orders of time [49]. Gregg draws attention to the relationship between technology and broader societal patterns arguing that, "apparently individual choices add up to a structural shift in work practices that is exacerbated by online technology's extensive reach" [17:123-24]. Sharma [51] raises the political and ethical question of how certain people's temporal rhythms are implicated in or subject to the times of others. For her, temporality is not just an individual experience; time is a site of impingement and the negotiation of social and institutional power relations rather than a site of personal agency. Mazmanian and Erickson [32] echo this refrain with the suggestion that time has become de-commoditized within the global capitalist superstructure that promotes '24/7' competition and within which, marketing the total availability of employees is a competitive advantage.

Taken together, ideas such as temporal ordering, patterns, rhythms and politics confirm the situated, cultural and socially constructed nature of time. As Palen writes,

"...clocks and calendrical systems make time tangible and meaningful by imposing both natural and artificial boundaries on it – minutes, hours, days, weeks, months, years. In this sense, calendrical systems (like the Gregorian calendar) are themselves artifacts. Paper and electronic calendars contain these time system representations, which allow for the manipulation of time, exchanging one meeting hour for another, allotting time for a task, splicing events in between others. It is time-as-artifact that, in part, makes calendars useful." [38:20].

It is precisely this organization and experience of time-as-artifact, and the ways that it is then enacted in observable cultural patterns, that prompts our reflections herein.

THEORETICAL FRAMING

The notion of time-as-artifact [38] reflects and embodies a common understanding of time that is shared among the members of a society. We call a common understanding a *temporal logic.* We adapt this concept from institutional theory and its theorization of 'institutional logics' [6, 43, 60]. As defined by [48], an institutional logic comprises "the belief systems and related practices that predominate in an organizational field." These logics "provide the 'organizing principles' that furnish guidelines to field participants as to how they are to carry out the work" [5].

In particular, by *temporal logic* we mean the socially legitimated, shared assumptions about time that are embedded in institutional and societal norms, discourses, material and technological processes, and shared ideologies. A temporal logic defines what is rational, normal and expected, and imbues a society with a definition of *what time is* that directs individuals in *how they should operate in and through time.* It provides an understanding of time that becomes so embedded that it seems to define reality.

In previous temporalities research, scholars have drawn productively on Zerubavel's similar concept of a *sociotemporal order* – an orientation to time that is shared amongst a social group and thusly produces coordinated rhythms and temporal alignments [15, 53]. While many have built on this concept in a way that suggests multiple orders or the practices of ordering, Zerubavel himself defines the term as analogous to "the 'physiotemporal order' which regulates the motions of celestial bodies and to the 'biotemporal order' which regulates the lives of organisms" [68]. His perspective attends to the ways that a particular orientation to time manifests in the routines of day-to-day activities and technologies of planning, scheduling and coordination. However, it also implies that a single sociotemporal order regulates activities or technologies in a stable and unified way.

By contrast, we find that a temporal logic approach centers less on universal rules and more on the social construction of norms and practices related to time [5]. In Western society, the dominant temporal logic reflects a tradition of professionalized time commodification with correlate linear and quantifiable qualities. According to Egger and Wagner, this orientation, which we refer to as circumscribed time, holds that "time is homogeneous, objective, measurable, and infinitely divisible" [11:249]. It is this conceptualization of time—and its implications—that we analyze, critique, and try to reframe in this paper.

METHODOLOGY

Our analytical approach adopts the infrastructure studies concept of an 'infrastructural inversion' [8]. We conduct a 'temporal inversion' here – moving time from its usual position in the background up into the foreground of this research. This temporal inversion unfolds in two parts.

First, we provide a close reading of a recent commercial for Microsoft Outlook. Research in the CHI and CSCW community has been enriched by recent engagements with humanistic and critical methodologies [2]. Though close reading is less common in HCI (see [21] for exception), it comes from a disciplinary tradition similar to that of discourse analysis, used to analyze constant connectivity [21], e-government systems [60], and video game play [55]. We take particular guidance from the HCI-adjacent field of video game studies, which has used close reading to simultaneously "[lay] bare the faults and inconsistencies of a media artifact" while also "[celebrating] the many ways in which a text can create meaning" [7: 1]. Our reading of the advertisement provides an analytical artifact that we use as an exemplar of the enactment of the dominant temporal logic, circumscribed time. Our production of this artifact is merely functional; we ascribe no valuation to the example of technology in use presented.

Second, we compare this analytical artifact to a subset of qualitative data culled from fieldwork on knowledge professionals in Boston, families of professionals in southern California, and long distance hikers on the Pacific Crest Trail (PCT). These collective data detail how a variety of people negotiate work and everyday activities, outline personal and professional relationships, and struggle to define a sense of self in alignment with prevalent norms around time, connectivity, work, and productivity. All data were collected by the first and third author cumulatively over the last ten years using traditional qualitative interview and observation techniques (see [31, 32] for more details). While the data that inform this work are not derivative of a single study, collectively they provide a broad picture of normative understandings of time within different social and occupational communities.

The comparison between our close reading and our field data followed the spirit, if not the exact letter, of grounded theory [10, 54], including iterative rounds of verbal coding and theorizing. This analytical work was carried out collectively among the three authors, both in person and via a series of video conferences in the spring of 2014.

OUTLINING A DOMINANT TEMPORAL LOGIC

A temporal logic operates at multiple levels. It is perpetuated in social and cultural discourse; is embedded in institutional expectations and policies; drives the design and implementation of technologies; establishes resilient social norms; and provides a cache of normative, rational examples to draw on when individuals need to make sense of their everyday engagements with time. When a tool like Microsoft Outlook is designed, presented, and justified in a marketing campaign it is both reflecting and perpetuating a temporal logic.

In 2010, Microsoft ran a commercial for its Outlook email and calendar program called "Yoga Quest." According to the company's promotional copy, the advertisement shows, "…how one busy woman uses Outlook to manage what matters – from play dates, to work meetings, to emails, to a much needed, but seemingly unattainable, yoga session. See how Microsoft Outlook 2010 can help you balance all aspects of your work *and* personal life by integrating multiple calendars and email accounts into one, easy-to-manage place." [66]. This commercial provides rich, detailed examples of this technology as it might be used and an idealized picture of how one should act on and through time via the help of a calendaring system. This promotion is thus marketing not only a product but also a normative way of living. It is precisely for its popular cultural resonance that we chose to analyze this advertisement.

Yoga Quest

The Microsoft Outlook video commercial begins with a close up of an arrow clicking to open the Outlook application to its weekly calendar view, accompanied by sitar music. The first calendar item is 'Yoga,' scheduled for 7:00am. The frame of reference shifts to the perspective of a woman beginning a yoga move – a downward dog asana. The angle of the camera reflects the view of the protagonist, pulling the commercial's viewer into her body. A chirping interruption from the mobile phone at the edge of the yoga mat prompts a hand to reach out to pick up the device and view a message soliciting a replacement for a sick parent in the neighborhood carpool. Our protagonist selects the 'Yoga' event in the calendar and moves it to 12:00pm.

The scene shifts to a car dashboard, a crossing guard, and the inferred suggestion of a task accomplished. After waving goodbye to a young child (revealing the cuffs of a blue jersey sweatshirt), we are returned to Outlook, this time on a computer display at the end of a kitchen counter. To a new upbeat soundtrack, reminiscent of an industrious scene from *Snow White and the Seven Dwarves*, the video quickly moves to a view of the calendar's task list and its direction to "Complete Contoso logo design." We see a PowerPoint presentation being edited, and then fingers toggle between a Work calendar and Home calendar – it is time to take the car in for an oil change. Immediately we are driving into a mechanic's garage. While waiting in the car, the protagonist's hands take out a dual laptop-tablet computer that is already open to Outlook's calendar view. Fingers tap off the three completed tasks from a longer list and linger for a moment over the next one: Yoga.

The shot cuts to Outlook's email view where our protagonist receives a tweet-like recommendation for a new local restaurant, Lou's. She also sees a message about the logo presentation, "Scheduling conflict tomorrow. Reschedule for today?" We see a response typed out: "No problem. I'll take him to Lou's." This necessitates another rescheduling of yoga. The video cuts to a coffee shop landscape, a handshake (the protagonist's sleeves now suggesting a black suit jacket and cuffed collared shirt), a computer hand off (when our protagonist's laptop proves to be out of power), and the presentation of the Contoso logo design via cloud-based file access.

That job accomplished, we are back with our protagonist on the yoga mat just as scheduled in the calendar (though the exact time of day has become unclear). She stretches out bare arms (no longer wearing long sleeves) onto the mat, beginning the downward dog pose once again. The music returns, briefly, to the sitar.

Just as before, the smartphone on the corner of the mat chirps; this time the Outlook app reveals an "urgent" message. The elementary school needs a book reader at 2pm; and so yoga is delayed again. The music changes back to an upbeat melody and we are transported to a classroom of kids and a shot of hands (no sleeves visible) flipping through a colorful picture book. This image bleeds into a scene of a home play-date with kids running around a living room. Meanwhile, our protagonist uses her smartphone to scroll up and down through the things on her 'agenda' with no empty time slots left. Up next: a PTA meeting at 5pm.

We see our protagonist sneak a bite out of a box of donuts, presumably at the meeting. Then the scene jumps back to the computer monitor at the end of the kitchen counter. Coffee cup in hand and weekly calendar view in sight, we watch as yoga is dragged downward through the day, but see that there is no empty slot in which to drop it.

We see a shared calendar labeled "Michael" open (presumably belonging to her husband), and a new event, "Pick up Caroline," is added to his strikingly empty schedule. Included in message-event are the location of the soccer field and a note to "Bring dinner!" This shifting of responsibility opens up time, finally, for yoga. The video closes with our protagonist in lotus pose, sitar music again in the background. The message '*How do you achieve balance*?' flashes on the screen immediately followed by the icon for Microsoft Outlook.

Circumscribed Time

The "Yoga Quest" video embeds a number of assumptions about the nature of time that reflect a dominant temporal logic – specifically that time is *chunkable*, *single-purpose*, *linear* and *ownable*. While this is not a comprehensive or exhaustive list of dimensions, we provide this proto-typology as a way of stimulating discussion among scholars interested in further theorizing the nature and implications of temporal logics beyond our particular perspective.

Time is chunk-able

The expectation that time is chunk-able is conditioned by an understanding that **time exists in units (a second, a minute, a year) and that temporal units are equal** – that can be swapped and exchanged with relative ease. The yoga video exemplifies this understanding with its vision of seamless temporal shifting and manipulation. Calendaring systems like Outlook usually default to 30 or 60 minute chunks that can be dragged across various slots with ease.

As our protagonist continually drags her coveted yoga activity from one time slot to the next, the implication is not only that she can manipulate time like a Tetris game, eliminating any open spaces, but that each chunk of time is equal. According to this logic, doing yoga at 6:30pm after an incredibly long day is the same experience as doing it at 7:00am. Her constant rescheduling of activities underscores her and others' expectation that one time slot is as good as another for any particular activity.

Understanding time as chunk-able is the basis for what has been referred to elsewhere as 'gridded' or 'clock' time, which holds that time is unitized and measurable. This temporal orientation emerged in the 17th-19th centuries alongside the adoption of clocks, watches, and railroads [55, 61]. Chunking time into measurable units is now so normalized in most institutions and policies that it appears unremarkable – the hourly wage, the measurement of sick days, the scheduling of a doctor's appointment. Time chunks open up the possibility for future-oriented temporal manipulation and valuation; they assume that we are able to know, in advance, the duration of tasks and experiences.

Further, gridded calendaring systems rarely suggest that we account for unanticipated activity when planning time, (i.e., the client running late, traffic jams, etc.). By rendering time into apparently equal measurable units, such systems encourage an assumption that activities form to the shape of temporal units rather than vice versa. In addition such applications also perpetuate a sense that time is malleable and responsive; a single swipe of a finger can transform a 2pm appointment to a 3pm appointment with no regard for the possible domino effect of such a move.

Time is allocated for a single-purpose

Aligned with chunk-able time is the assumption that **each chunk of time, or its particular gridded arrangement, is allocated to a single purpose**. The clear delineation between the protagonist's 'home' and 'work' calendar in the video suggests an underlying assumption that any one chunk of gridded time is inhabited solely by 'home' or 'work' activities. This understanding is held constant even though we see our protagonist engaged in the Contoso presentation while getting her car fixed. She is layering 'home' and 'work' activities in practice, but the calendar's representation does not accommodate this complexity.

The common rhetoric of 'family time,' 'work time,' and 'me time' suggests that certain activities are appropriate only in certain social spheres. These practices are all the more noticeable in a culture both fascinated and fearful of the promise of multi-tasking, wherein people maintain a taken-for-granted correspondence between certain 'types' of time and the tasks, ways of being, and social roles that (rationally and normatively) inhabit temporal 'buckets.'

Time is linear

The dominant temporal logic also conceptualizes time as linear. In other words, **one chunk of time leads to another in a straight progression**. While chunks of time can be manipulated and reordered in the course of a day (or week, or month), each chunk of time has a limited duration and each activity has a beginning and an end. An hour is an hour is an hour, and in the course of a day (or a lifetime) hours stack up like a vector, moving one forward in a straightforward progression. While we only see one day in the life of our 'yoga quest' protagonist, her day nevertheless unfolds in a straightforward progression even as this overarching linearity is achieved through micro-manipulations of temporal units within a given day.

The various ways in which we account for historical evolution in terms of timelines or display visions of the future as straight trajectories perpetuate a notion of linear progress. Timelines, calendars, course syllabi, 10-day forecasts, etc. all underscore the temporal logic that time moves forward at a standard rate.

Time is owned (ownable) by the individual

Finally, **time is understood as a resource that is owned by an individual and thus needs to be managed and apportioned by that individual.** Like personal income, time is a resource that the individual has both the burden and responsibility to manage well. This vision of time reflects an assumption there are 'better' or 'worse' ways to use, spend and save time and it is up to the individual to engage in practices of temporal ownership. Controlling time does not suggest that an individual can speed up or slow down time, but rather, suggests that time can be personally configured to meet individual aims or goals.

The protagonist in our video appears to be fully in charge of her life as a parent, homemaker, and professional. Her ability to respond to last minute requests and manipulate her schedule at will suggests that she is in complete control of her own time. Her movement of tasks between time slots – and between calendars when she assigns her husband to 'pick up Caroline' – showcases both her perceived agency and authority over time. She is portrayed as a skilled master, controlling the ordering of time with intentionality and playful rigor.

These four aspects of time illustrate a temporal logic that is embedded in American norms, discourses, institutions, and technologies. While we have focused on the advertisement as a way of unpacking this dominant logic, this is simply an illuminating device. This logic is not tied to this one advertisement or only to calendaring technologies. Logics about time seep throughout institutions, bureaucracies, and everyday social norms. For example, some U.S. academics are expected to sign paperwork that states that when funded by federal grants during the summer months, one will spend their full work-week on the funded research. Course planning or other university work must happen in addition to this 'normal work week.' Furthermore, the 'normal' week is not defined in hours, but rather the 'typical' amount of time one works during the academic year. So if one is working a 70 hour week because of teaching and research during the school year, this is the 'normal' work week that should be devoted only to research in the summer.[1]

We call this prevailing temporal logic 'circumscribed time.' We use this label to highlight the underlying orientation to time as a resource that can, and should, be mastered. A circumscribed temporal logic infers that time should be harnessed into 'productive' capacity by approaching it as something that can be chunked, allocated to a single use, experienced linearly, and owned. In turn, the norms of society place the burden on individuals to manage and 'balance' time as a steward, optimizing this precious resource by way of control and active manipulation.

TEMPORAL LOGIC TENSIONS

One of the ways that a temporal logic becomes visible for analysis and critique is through the tensions that emerge when its assumptions and norms do not align with daily experience. In our collective fieldwork we have observed multiple examples of mundane daily practices coming into conflict with the logic that time is, or should be, chunk-able, singular purpose, linear, and/or owned. These tensions help bring to the fore the extent of the dominant temporal logic and showcase the inadequacy of this narrow set of assumptions to fully describe temporal experiences.

Conceptions of time as porous

In witnessing how people struggle to orient to the dominant temporal logic, we find it is insufficient to encapsulate temporal experiences. Thus, we now theorize a set of expanded notions, an initial typology that we call 'porous time'. Notably, these terms do not reflect emic articulations from our participants, but are our own labels. To date, we have found that our subjects have a minimal ability, and almost no language, to discuss the vagaries of time. In general, people attempt to negotiate their subjective experiences of time through the assumptions of the dominant temporal logic outlined above. In outlining the logic of 'porous time' we aim to provide a vocabulary for expanding the discussion and research about how temporal logics interweave throughout American life.

Time is spectral

Our data reveal that not every temporal experience is easily articulated, planned for, measurable or able to be rendered into a schedule. We call these temporal experiences *spectral time,* to capture how time trails or ghosts in ways that cannot always be expected, planned, or accounted for. Spectral time references moments that do not lend themselves to scheduling (i.e. chunking), either because the act seems too mundane to justify articulation (i.e., getting dressed), because it is difficult to assess (i.e., travel time) or simply because it cannot be anticipated (i.e., creative phases). In alignment with Reddy and Dourish's concept of temporal trajectory [45], spectral time suggests that temporal experience is more than a grid of accountable blocks; multiple temporalities create flows that often defy both logical rendering and seamless manipulation.

We see an example of how spectral time relates to gridded time in the excerpt from the schedule left by Olivia, a mother of two and small business owner, for her daughter's caregivers when she took a weeklong trip (Table 1).

	Wednesday
Father AM	Drop Tessa off at school & then Opal & Nora before 8:45am for late start, or coordinate with Neighbor for her to drop older girls
Father PM	Pickup Tessa from swim at 7pm
Grand-father AM	Pick up Nora & Opal from School at 1:55pm and drop them both off at our house.
Grand-father PM	Take Opal to Swimming at 4pm & come back to our house
Grand-father PM	Drop off Tessa at Mathnasium at 4:45pm. Make sure Tessa takes all swimming stuff with her in the car.
Grand-father PM	Pick up Tessa from Mathnasium at 5:45pm & drop off at swimming by 6:00pm. Wait for Opal and pick her up from swimming at 6pm.
Neighbor PM	Pick up Ishan and Tessa from school at 1:15pm & 1:30pm and take them to Art Class from 2-4pm.

Table 1. Excerpt from caregiver's spreadsheet

Olivia's attempts to articulate the requisite temporal coordination provides a gridded view of how she imagines the week will proceed. Yet tightly fitted as it is, this schedule does not reflect how Olivia would actually navigate these activities as observed during fieldwork. Picking her daughter up from school at 1:55pm actually means leaving the house at 1:43pm. The time between Mathnasium and swimming can vary up to 6 minutes depending on streetlights. It is also not uncommon for Olivia to pull over to the side of the road to scribble notes during a work-related call while performing these activities.

Although the grid tried to align everyone to regularized temporal patterns, it could not reflect the temporal reality of

[1] We would like to thank one of the anonymous reviewers for this excellent example of how, "the dominant temporal logic is a logic that becomes quantifiable, and then mathematical, and completely ignores the rhythms of the year."

the week, which included many fits and starts and much waiting. The spectrality of time, whether experienced by a habituated parent like Olivia or a neighbor filling in on childcare duty, shines through in the details and impromptu workarounds that pad every cell of this temporal grid.

We find another example of the spectrality of time in our fieldwork with PCT thru-hikers. Like many other hikers, Seth created an Excel spreadsheet to serve as a mailing plan for his mom who would be sending him resupply packages. Knowing that his predictions would be imperfect, before beginning his hike, he showed her how to tweak the digital version of the schedule as he hiked. He used a spreadsheet to link together the dependencies of each event such that the time of the hike could expand or contract in response to what happened in reality. In contrast, Seth gave a paper copy of his schedule to his girlfriend, whom he planned to meet a few months into his hike. This printed copy was not only inflexible, but approximate:

I just dropped in averages. I didn't know how far [I would actually hike]. ... It wasn't figuring in off days and that kind of stuff. So, when [my girlfriend] saw, 'Okay, he should be here then.' It was like 'No no no no no!'

Like an optimistic Outlook user who schedules back-to-back meetings with no room for running long, Seth's original plan proved unrealistic and the un-walked miles started to accumulate in the way that items on a to-do list accrue toward the end of a day or week. The spectrality of time asserted itself as Seth's pace aligned to a different rhythm than his original schedule. Notably, this lack of predictability had large social, rather than individual, implications—a finding that strongly echoes prior CSCW research [1, 4, 13, 15, 20, 22, 34, 35, 36, 38, 45, 46, 59].

Time is a mosaic

In contradiction to the assumption that time is allocated for a single purpose, our fieldwork reveals that people occupy time less as a discrete whole and more as a mosaic of interactions each tied to roles, identities, and social spheres. By *mosaic*, we mean that time is often simultaneously inhabited by multiple types of interaction that are forced to form a coherent whole. Unlike concepts like *multi-tasking* (doing multiple tasks 'at once') or *polychronicity* (a reported preference for doing multiple tasks at once) [44], mosaic time refers to the negotiated merging of multiple social spheres into a layered or fitted set of simultaneous interactions. Successful inhabitation of mosaic time occurs, if at all, when these multiple pieces of temporal life appear coherent, like a mosaic.

Mosaic time questions the assumption that time can or should be accorded a singular purpose. For example, does being with family eating dinner equal 'family time' when the mother is checking work-related email under the table? Is going for a run with a smart phone considered 'me time' when one's wife is concurrently texting with a shopping list? As we find repeatedly in our data, a multiplicity of identities and activities inhabit any individual time chunk.

Fiona, the wife of a senior consultant and mother of three young children, provides one example of this mosaic aspect of time. She expresses frustration when her husband invites a partner in his firm, visiting from out of town, for a last minute dinner:

Fiona is half-laughing, describing the dinner as a "disaster." She says something like, "I'm sure we horrified him. The kids were being their usual crazy selves and David was trying to have adult conversation with the Partner and I was like, are you serious?" According to Fiona the kids were tired and having a rough night. Melody broke down and Brandon was throwing food. She, "just wanted to scream" at David and say something like, "Can't you just be a dad?"

This is mosaic time at its most obvious—when the boundaries and borders between activities are highly evident. With effort, this family manages to mash together identities, social worlds, temporal rhythms, etc., and to experience them, at least somewhat, as a temporal whole.

We also observed a more seamless mosaic, where tasks, worlds and identities seemed more integrated; tiles of the picture less obvious. Chad moves in and out of his role as father of two and the demands of being a corporate executive with apparent ease – merging worlds and identities rather holistically. When one of his daughters suggested playing the board game *Clue* on a Sunday afternoon, we all (mother, father, older daughter, younger daughter, and ethnographer) gathered around the board, moving our pawns, bantering, and deducting the details of the murder. Between each round of the game, when others were clearing the pieces and rearranging the cards, Chad typed on his iPhone until it became clear that it was time to begin the next game. Chad was able to keep track of the progress of the game and merge his work into this scene harmoniously. No one around him appeared to be frustrated and Chad was actively engaged with his family. When asked later what he was doing, Chad listed various substantive emails that he wrote during this time. In his words, it was "real work."

Thinking about time as mosaic raises numerous questions about: when the mosaic is and is not obvious; what forms of interaction (or tiles) are given priority in any one moment; what skills are needed to engage in mosaic time with more or less effort; and what the effects of mosaic time are on concentration, stress, and affect. Mosaic time appears most successful when people engage in attention switching in order to enact multiple social roles at once. Yet, it is not without its moments of charged, circumstantial dynamics – priorities, power relations, and complex 'choices' are key parts of when and how people experience mosaic time.

Time is rhythmic

In contrast to the assumption of time as linear, with ordered chunks progressing in a straightforward manner, people often negotiate time rhythmically, arranging time in patterns and tempos that do not always co-exist harmoniously. In line with earlier CSCW findings [e.g., 4, 9, 45, 46], we term this *rhythmic time*, which acknowledges both the rhythmic nature of temporal experience as well a potential disorderliness or 'dissonance' when temporal rhythms conflict. Like mosaic time, bringing dissonant rhythms into semi-alignment requires adaptation, work, and patience.

For example, Lisa attempts to navigate the multiple sports teams and activities that her three children are engaged in. Snorting with laughter at an incoming text message (see Figure 1), she explains to the researcher,

Danielle has soccer tryouts for school next week and it is going to go into her club soccer practice so I'm writing the coach to warn him. And I'm totally kissing his ass. Because last time this happened he was an ass about it. Yeah, he took it out on Danielle and there's nothing these girls can do about it.

Rhythmic temporal dissonance in Lisa's life forces her to think ahead about misalignments in schedules and undertake the social work of mollifying egos to help her children navigate the overlap between activities.

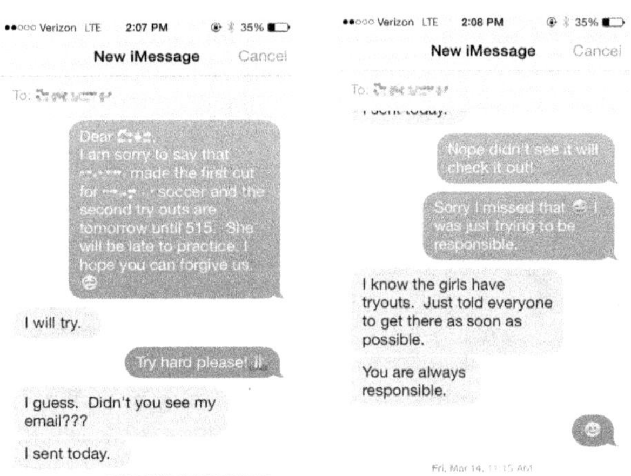

Figure 1. SMS exchange between mom and soccer coach

We also see dissonance in a more protracted timeframe. Nancy, a single mother of two and director for a hotel management firm, finds herself stressed, overwhelmed, and with a chronic headache every fall. Starting in August her company engages in an intensive budgeting process that requires extra time and attention. This is the same time of the year that her son starts a new grade in school. His annual transition to a new teacher and classroom environment, as demanded by the calendaring and grade-level-based organization of the education system, is anxiety producing for both of them. This autumnal rhythm of stress and emotional and physical exhaustion is what Nancy experiences rather than contemporaneous chunks of intensified tasks at work and at home. Moreover, the tempo of budgeting is sped up during this period, and the pattern of school-day normalcy is slowed down as her son adjusts to his new surroundings. Nancy succeeds in making these dissonant rhythms livable by persistent accommodation, and by telling herself everything will balance out come January when the budget is complete and her son is more adjusted.

Time is obligated

Finally, our data reveal how much we exist in social worlds – professional, personal, family, etc. – in which time is experienced in relation to others. This social state *obligates* individuals to navigate a temporal web of moral and professional expectations, and accountabilities to others. These temporal obligations affect temporal agency. Obligations emerge from numerous origins: workplace policy might delineate proper response times for emails and people feel normative pressure to 'be there' for colleagues, to push forward the work and to show themselves as dedicated and responsible colleagues; parents express an unqualified obligation to be available to their children; and people often assume certain friends 'deserve' their time in ways that perpetuate trust and gratitude. A close look at the ways that people continually navigate the expectations and rhythms of those around them reveals how much the rhetoric of time management and control, built on the assumption that one is a solo temporal agent, is a fiction. To be considered a success in various social arenas (either via internal assessment or external validation) means that individuals often cannot choose whether or not to attend to certain temporal obligations.

These social arenas have evident hierarchies. This is particularly vivid in the case of Matt, a corporate attorney, who describes how his elite position in the firm (partner) does not excuse him from a sense of needing to be available to those structurally below him,

Where I sit now, there are many kind of pyramids. And I'm at the top of each pyramid. So, people, they're not going to make a move without checking with you. So, you become, whether you like it or not, a kind of a bottleneck in the process. So, this [holds up his smartphone] is a way to clear the bottleneck.

Matt's words reveal how social roles and information and communication technologies are often tightly coupled. Tools like smartphones appear to appease the pressures of social obligation, but at the same time they also perpetuate new expectations of availability. This paradox is evident in the case of George, a private criminal defense attorney, who believes that by being available to work via his iPhone every Wednesday afternoon, he can come home early to spend time with his son, often attending a Little League baseball game. Yet, the promise of social control afforded by information and communication technologies belies the inadequacy of the dominant temporal logic. The possibility of working remotely, of taking the office to the baseball game, becomes an obligation to take advantage of the technology for his family's benefit. Yet, George cannot control when his clients call; their positions within the US legal system demand immediate attention. Thus, he cannot inhabit his time at his son's baseball game with singular purpose. He is simultaneously obligated to his family and his clients; he must enact time's porousness in each of his actions – an incredibly difficult challenge. Both George and his wife express frustration at not being able to focus on their child's game because they are receiving emails and phone calls. Yet, they also value the mobility that they credit with making it possible for him to even attend the game at all. Each of these moments of obligation invokes questions of power, economies of attention, time valuation, and the invisible work that goes into managing obligated time alongside spectral trails, dissonant rhythms, and time's mosaic qualities.

Taken together, an orientation to time as *spectral, mosaic, rhythmic (dissonant),* and *obligated* suggests a possible alternate understanding of what time is and how it can work. An initial typology of porous time honors the fluidity of time and its unexpected shifts; it also acknowledges novel integrations of time in everyday practice. Addressing these alternate temporal realities allows us to build on CSCW's legacy of related research to question the reach and scope of the dominant temporal logic. Our rendering of porous time imagines a new perspective on time, in which the dominant temporal logic expands beyond ideals of control and mastery to include navigation (with or without conscious attention) of that which cannot be gridded or managed: the temporal trails, multiple interests, misaligned rhythms and expectations of others.

DISCUSSION

In the spirit of Wajcman's call for theorists of temporality to incorporate long-standing STS theorizations of "the technical as part of the constitution of the social" [62], this paper presents a vocabulary to re-inspire the discussion of time in CSCW. Comparing the logic of temporal circumscription with the experiences of daily temporal struggles surfaces a nascent set of alternate—*porous*—ways of orienting to time that are *spectral, mosaic, rhythmic (dissonant),* and *obligated.* Like a pool spilling out and absorbing into concrete, the logic of porous time avers that lived time contains unpredictable directions, patterns, integrations, and negotiations that seep out beyond gridded boundaries to create an unstable temporal landscape.

The idea of porous time acknowledges the inadequacy of a temporal logic centered on 'managing' time and suggests an expansion of the dominant temporal logic to include more improvisational and fluid relationships to time. Such a reframing provokes us to reassess what 'normative' engagements with time should or could look like. It creates a space to reimagine these 'successful' temporal practices.

Temporal Experience, Success and Power

Interrogating the temporal logic of circumscribed time raises three related sociotemporal concerns particularly relevant to CSCW: *lived experience*, *visions of success*, and *power relations*. We address each concern in relation to key theoretical works to show how the insights presented here both point to the limitations of the dominant temporal logic of circumscribed time and demand expanding this logic to include those orientations suggested by porous time.

Lived Experience: The Disparity of Time

The temporal logic of circumscribed time portends that temporal units are neutral. This resource-based view orients time as a set of equal units that can be regulated and managed, reflecting the earliest use of the clock in Benedictine monasteries. Well entrenched in American society [15, 52, 65], this logic begets calendaring tools representing all the days in a month – or hours in a day – in a visually similar way: a regular grid. The apparent equivalency of these time chunks mask the affective experiences and emotional intensities of lived temporality – that practicing yoga at 6:30pm is a different subjective experience than at 7:00am. It perpetuates guilt and frustration in those who find themselves unable to live up to the expectations of time management and control implicit in circumscribed time [26].

In addition to these moral and political concerns, the disconnect between lived experience and tools for coordination is particularly salient for CSCW. For example, as readers of this paper are likely familiar, some people prefer to write in the mornings, and others in the evenings. When co-authoring a paper, taking such rhythms into account can be a critical aspect of a successful collaboration. When creating tools for scheduling and coordination, it is crucial to provide ways for people to take into account not just the multiplicity of (potentially dissonant) *rhythms* [22, 46], but also the differential affective experiences of time rendered by such rhythms.

In the context of collaboration, we are reminded that temporal units also differ along a dimension of *obligation.* An hour of work at 7am might set up another person's work at 8am. Dragging that hour of work down through the day and rescheduling it for 7pm is not the autonomous task that appears on a calendar screen. In many ways, one 'chunk' of time is not equivalent to any other 'chunk.'

Visions of Success: Balance, Busyness, & Temporal Control

The temporal logic of circumscribed time tacitly defines a 'good' day as a 'full' day – a day in which there are no unchecked boxes and no empty slots in the calendar. This valuation underscores both a sense of success (getting it all done) and a sense of identity (busyness is perceived as 'good' [26]); both of which harken back to the virtuosity of industriousness espoused by the Protestant Work Ethic [52, 64, 66]. Leshed and Sengers's research reminds us that calendars are not just tools for the management of time, but are also sites of identity work where people can project to themselves and others the density of their days and apparent 'success' at doing it all [26]. These seemingly innocuous artifacts can thus perpetuate deeper normative logics about busyness and productivity that compete directly with values of presence, focus, or prioritizing leisure time.

A social vision of success influenced by these Protestant tenets is well aligned with the idea of achieving 'balance' by adding more (and more) to each side of an imaginary scale. The Yoga Quest protagonist schedules a business meeting directly after an oil change, with no time to change clothes or drive between locations. How efficient! How virtuous! In reality, we encounter a much messier scene. Time trails in *spectral* ways and the innumerable tasks and activities that 'get in the way' of perfect efficiency often leave people feeling constantly bereft of time and failing at any attempt at mastery.

The goal of balance implicitly suggests that individuals can allocate chunks of time to a single purpose, add them, and compare them. However, our research participants describe Saturday mornings as 'personal time' even as they read work emails or review documents in advance of a Monday meeting. How do we understand such *mosaic* time in terms of striving for balance? Temporal units are rarely single-purpose and their boundaries and dependencies are often implicit. What sociotemporal values should we be honoring? How can we account for time that fits on neither side of a scale? How might scholarship rethink balance or efficiency with different forms of accounting, with attention to institutions as well as individuals?

Temporality, Values, and Power

Finally we draw our attention to the ways that temporality is inherently political and power-laden at interpersonal and societal levels.

Our fieldwork examples draw into relief the ways that people's relationships to time are differential, especially in the context of dissonant temporal *rhythms*. Our participant, Nancy, has no choice but to accommodate other aspects of her life to the institutional requirements of budgeting season. Her time is that which must flex to accommodate the temporal demands of the workplace. Far from being individually controlled, her time is multiply *obligated* – tethered to her children, her co-workers, her subordinates, her superiors, her friends, and her family.

As Sharma describes temporality, it is "uncompromisingly tethered and collective" [51]. In our observations of parent-workers trying to negotiate such multiple social roles, questions of power and value often rise to the surface, not only in negotiations of obligation, but in related negotiations of *single-purpos*e versus *mosaic* time as well. People are constantly faced with choices about where to 'spend' their time, with who, and how much attention they should direct to an interpersonal interaction, business meeting, or family dinner. Each of these choices reflect power dynamics and conflicting tensions. Desires for 'presence' or singular focus often conflict with obligations to be responsive and integrate 'work' and 'life' [21].

A focus on temporality also calls to the fore theoretical work on the relation between temporal regulation and the development of industrial capitalism [64]. Scholars have long argued that the regularity and mastery of time is a necessary condition for capitalism, because it requires a mechanism for exchanging labor for a wage. This conceptual premise has reified and institutionalized a functional understanding of time as chunkable, single purpose, linear, and ownable. The valuation of busyness or density of time use corresponds directly to a system that thrives on continuous effort and perpetually unsatisfied need. Recent scholarship on time and structures of power have emphasized the political and moral implications of such a temporal logic [51, 63]. We, too, call for continued work to build an understanding of "how differential relationships to time organize and perpetuate inequalities" [51:137]. What would it look like to more explicitly acknowledge power dynamics in information and communication technologies? In the tradition of critical and reflective design [50], how might CSCW scholarship think about designing technologies that 'protect' users from temporal obligations and render messiness and disorganization a possible way of engaging with time?

Inspiration for Change

By making the dimensions of circumscribed and porous temporal logics explicit and visible, we hope to inspire the CSCW community to embrace new ways of thinking about, orienting to, and designing for (and with) time. By introducing the concept of temporal logic and teasing apart the limitations of the dominant logic, we provide a generative framework and vocabulary that invites future discussion, scholarship, and elaboration on the fundamental concept of time. In moving forward, we recognize that additional conceptions of time and/or temporal practices exist and we assume that other temporal logics will surface as scholars continue to examine and debate the ways that people orient to time in the context of institutions, organizations, families, social circles, and daily life. We hope that future work continues to make visible the power of temporal logics in shaping our most basic orientations to daily activity and perpetuate new ideas about how to navigate, rather than control the unpredictability of life.

ACKNOWLEDGMENTS

This work has been supported by the Intel Science and Technology Center for Social Computing and the Center for Organizational Research at the University of California, Irvine. We owe particular thanks to our ethnographic collaborator, Christine Beckman; our many study participants over the years; our colleagues Phoebe Sengers, Steve Jackson, Judy Wajcman, and Melissa Gregg for their ongoing work on the multi-faceted relations between temporality, technology, and morality. Amy Voida, and Oliver Haimson provided valuable feedback on early drafts. The anonymous reviewers gave commentary that was detailed, generous, challenging and much appreciated.

REFERENCES

[1] Bardram, J. Temporal Coordination: On Time and Coordination of Collaborative Activities at a Surgical Department. *Computer Supported Cooperative Work*, (9) 157-187, 2000.

[2] Bardzell, J., Bardzell, S., DiSalvo, C., Gaver, W. and Sengers, P. *The humanities and/in HCI*. City, 2012.

[3] Bauer, J. S., Consolvo, S., Greenstein, B., Schooler, J., Wu, E., Watson, N. F. and Kientz, J. ShutEye: encouraging awareness of healthy sleep recommendations with a mobile, peripheral display. In *Proceedings of the SIGCHI*, 2012.

[4] Begole, J. B., Tang, J. C., Smith, R. B. and Yankelovich, N. *Work Rhythms: Analyzing Visualizations of Awareness Histories of Distributed Groups*. City, 2002.

[5] Berger, P. L. and Luckman, T. *The Social Construction of Reality: A treatise in the sociology of knowledge*. Anchor Books, New York, NY, 1966.

[6] Besharov, M. L. and Smith, W. K. Multiple institutional logics in organizations: Explaining their varied nature and implications. *Academy of Management Review (*In press).

[7] Bizzochi, J. and Tanenbaum, J. *Well Read: Applying Close Reading Techniques to Gameplay Experiences*. ETC Press, City, 2011.

[8] Bowker, G. C. *Science on the run: Information management and industrial geophysics at schlumberger: 1920–1940*. MIT Press Cambridge, MA, 1994.

[9] Brdiczka, O., Su, N. M. and Begole, B. Using Temporal Patterns (T-patterns) to Derive Stress Factors of Routine Tasks. *CHI Extended Abstracts*, 2009.

[10] Charmaz, K. *Constructing Grounded Theory: A Practical Guide Through Qualitative Analysis*. Sage, London, 2006.

[11] Egger, E., Wagner, I. TIME-MANAGEMENT: A Case for CSCW. *CSCW Proceedings*, 249-256, 1992.

[12] Edwards, K., Mynatt, E. Timewarp: Techniques for Autonomous Collaboration, *Proceedings of CHI*, 1997.

[13] Fisher, D. and Dourish, P. *Social and Temporal Structures in Everyday Collaboration. Proceedings of CHI*, 551-558, 2004.

[14] Gonzalez, V. M. and Mark, G. *Constant, Constant, Multi-tasking Craziness: Managing Multiple Working Spheres. Proccedings of CHI,* 113-120, 2004.

[15] Gonzalez, V. M. and Mark, G. *Managing currents of work: multi-tasking among multiple collaborations*. Springer-Verlag New York, Inc., City, 2005.

[16] Gregg, M. *Work's Intimacy*. Polity, Malden, MA, 2011.

[17] Gregg, M. *Presence Bleed: Performing Professionalism Online*. In Mark Banks, Rosalind Gill and Stephanie Taylor (eds) Theorizing Cultural Work: Labour, Continuity and Change in the Creative Industries. Routledge, City, 2013.

[18] Gregg, Melissa. Getting Things Done: Productivity, self-management and the order of things in *Networked Affect*, Ken Hillis, Susanna Paasonen and Michael Petit (eds) Cambridge: MIT Press, forthcoming 2014.

[19] Grudin, J. A Case Study of Calendar Use in an Organization, SIGOIS Bulletin, Vol. 17, No 3., 49-51, 1996.

[20] Grudin, J., Palen, L. Emerging Groupware Successes in Major Corporations: Studies of Adoption and Adaptation. In *Proceedings of WWCA*, 1997.

[21] Harmon, E. and Mazmanian, M. Stories of the Smartphone in Everyday Discourse: Conflict, Tension & Instability. In *Proceedings of CHI,* 2013.

[22] Jackson, S. J., Ribes, D., Buyuktur, A. G. and Bowker, G. C. Collaborative Rhythm: Temporal Dissonance and Alignment in Collaborative Scientific Work. *Proceedings of CSCW*, 2011.

[23] Knouf, N. A. HCI for the real world. *Extended Abstracts CHI,* 2009.

[24] Lee, H. Your time and my time: a temporal approach to groupware calendar systems. *Information & Management*, 40, 159-164, 2003.

[25] Lee, H., Sawyer, S. Conceptualizing time, space and computing for work and organizing. *Time and Society*, 19(3), 293-217, 2010.

[26] Leshed, G. and Sengers, P. *"I Lie to Myself that I Have Freedom in My Own Schedule": Productivity Tools and Experiences of Busyness*. ACM, City, 2011.

[27] Lounsbury, M. A tale of two cities: Competing logics and practice variation in the professionalizing of mutual funds. *Academy of Management Journal*, 50(3), 289-307, 2007.

[28] Mark, G., Iqbal, S. T., Czerwinski, M. and Johns, P. *Bored Mondays and Focused Afternoons: The Rhythm of Attention and Online Activity in the Workplace*. City, 2014.

[29] Mark, G., Voida, S. and Cardello, A. "A Pace Not Dictated by Electrons": An Empirical Study of Work Without Email. In *Proceedings of CHI* (2012).

[30] Marcus, G. E. Ethnography in/of the world system: The emergence of multi-sited ethnography. *Annual Review of Anthropology*, 24, 95-117, 1995.

[31] Mazmanian, M. Avoiding the trap of constant connectivity: When congruent frames allow for heterogeneous practices. *Academy of Management Journal*, 56(5), 1225–1250, 2013.

[32] Mazmanian, M. and Erickson, I. The Product of Availability: Understanding the Economic Underpinnings of Constant Connectivity. In *Proceedings of CHI* (2014).

[33] Mynatt, E., Trullio, J. Inferring Calendar Event Attendance. Proceedings of IUI '01, 121-128, 2001.

[34] Neustaedter, C., Brush, A.J.B., Greenberg, S. The Calendar is Crucial: Coordination and Awareness through the Family Calendar. ACM Transactions on Computer-Human Interaction, 16(1), 2009.

[35] Neustaedter, C., Brush, A.J.B. "LINC-ing" the Family: The Participatory Design of an Inkable Family Calendar. *Proceedings of CHI' 2006,* 141-150, 2006.

[36] Nilsson, M. and Hertzum, M. Negotiated rhythms of mobile work: time, place, and work schedules. *GROUP*, 2005.

[37] Nowotny, H. *Time: The Modern and Postmodern Experience*. Polity Press, 1994.

[38] Palen, L. Social, Individual and Technological Issues for Groupware Calendar Systems, *Proceedings of CHI,* 17-24, 1999.

[39] Palen, L. a. G., J. *Discretionary Adoption of Group Support Software: Lessons from Calendar Applications. in Implementing collaboration technologies in industry.* City, 2003.

[40] Perry, M., O'Hara, K., Sellen, A., Brown, B., & Harper, R. Dealing with Mobility: Understanding Access Anytime, Anywhere. ACM Trans. Computer-Human Interaction, 8(4), 323-347, 2001.

[41] Perlow, L. Boundary Control: The Social Ordering of Work and Family Time in a High-Tech Corporation. *Administrative Science Quarterly*, 43(2), 328-357, 1998.

[42] Perlow, L. The Time Famine: Toward a Sociology of Work Time. *Administrative Science Quarterly*, 44 (57), 57-81, 1999.

[43] Pine, K. and Mazmanian, M. Institutional Logics of the EMR and the Problem of 'Perfect' but Inaccurate Accounts. In *Proceedings of CSCW,* 2014.

[44] Poposki, E. M. and Oswald, F. L. The Multitasking Preference Inventory: Toward an Improved Measure of Individual Differences in Polychronicity. *Human Performance*, 23, 247–264, 2010.

[45] Reddy, M., Dourish, P. A Finger on the Pulse: Temporal Rhythms and Information Seeking in Medical Work. *Proceedings of CSCW,* 344-353, 2002.

[46] Reddy, M. C., Dourish, P. and Pratt, W. Temporality in Medical Work: Time also Matters. *Proceedings of CSCW*, 15, 29-53, 2006.

[47] Rouncefield, M. Hughes, J., Rodden, T., Viller, S. Working With "Constant Interruption": CSCW and the Small Office. *CSCW Proceedings*, 275-286, 1994.

[48] Scott, W. R. *Institutions and Organizations: Ideas, Interests, and Identities*, Thousand Oaks, CA: Sage Publications, 2014.

[49] Sengers, P. A Moral Order of Time. *Intel Science & Technology Center for Social Computing: All Hands Meeting* (Atlanta, Georgia, 2014).

[50] Sengers, P., McCarthy, J. and Dourish, P. Reflective HCI: articulating an agenda for critical practice. In *Proceedings of the CHI: Extended Abstracts* (2006).

[51] Sharma, S. *In the Meantime: Temporality and Cultural Politics*. Duke University Press, Durham, NC, 2014.

[52] Snyder, B. H. From Vigilance to Busyness: A Neo-Weberian Approach to Clock Time. *Sociological Theory*, 31(3), 243–266, 2013.

[53] Steinhardt, S. and Jackson, S. Reconciling Rhythms; Plans and Temporal Alignment in Collaborative Scientific Work. In *Proceedings of the CSCW*, 2014.

[54] Strauss, A. and Corbin, J. M. *Basics of Qualitative Reserach: Techniques and Procedures for Developing Grounded Theory*. Sage Publications Inc., 1998.

[55] Su, N. M. S. *Street Fighter IV: braggadocio off and on-line*. City, 2010.

[56] Thompson, E. P. Time, Work-Discipline, and Industrial Capitalism. *Past and Present*, 38 (December, 1967), 56-97.

[57] Thornton, P. H., Ocasio, W. and Lounsbury, M. *The institutional logics perspective: A new approach to culture, structure, and process*. Oxford University Press, 2012.

[58] Tomitsch, M., Grechenig, T., Wascher, P. Personal and Private Calendar Interfaces support Private Patterns: Diaries, Relations, Emotional Expressions. NordiCHI 2006, 401-404.

[59] Tullio, J., Goecks, J., Mynatt, E., Nguyen, D. Augmenting Shared Personal Calendars. UIST'02 Proceedings, 4(2), 11-20, 2002.

[60] Voida, A., Dombrowski, L., Hayes, G. R. and Mazmanian, M. Shared Values/Conflicting Logics: Working Around E-Government Systems. In *Proceedings of CHI*, 2014.

[61] Voida, A., Olson, J. S. and Olson, G. M. Turbulence in the Clouds: Challenges of Cloud-Based Information Work. In *Proceedings of CHI*, 2013.

[62] Wajcman, J. Life in the fast lane? Towards a sociology of technology and time *The British Journal of Sociology*, 59(1), 59-77, 2008.

[63] Wajcman, J., Rose, E. Constant Connectivity: Rethinking Interruptions at Work. *Organization Studies*, (32) 941-961, 2011.

[64] Weeks, K. *The Problem with Work: Feminism, Marxism, Antiwork Politics, and Postwork Imaginaries*. Duke University Press, 2011.

[65] Weber, M. *The Protestant Ethic and the Spirit of Capitalism*. Routledge Classics, 1930 (2001).

[66] *Yoga Quest: Microsoft Outlook 2010*. https://www.youtube.com/watch?v=HFD-agsuBAI.

[67] Zerubavel, E. The Benedictine Ethic and the Modern Spirit of Scheduling: on Schedules and Social Organization. *Sociological Inquiry*, 50(2), 157-169, 1980.

[68] Zerubavel, E. The Standardization of Time: A Sociohistorical Perspective. *The American Journal of Sociology*, 88(1), 1-23, 1982.

Designing for Temporal Awareness: The Role of Temporality in Time-Critical Medical Teamwork

Diana S. Kusunoki and Aleksandra Sarcevic
College of Computing and Informatics
Drexel University
Philadelphia, PA 19104
{dsk38, aleksarc}@drexel.edu

ABSTRACT
This paper describes the role of temporal information in emergency medical teamwork and how time-based features can be designed to support the temporal awareness of clinicians in this fast-paced and dynamic environment. Engagement in iterative design activities with clinicians over the course of two years revealed a strong need for time-based features and mechanisms, including timestamps for tasks based on absolute time and automatic stopclocks measuring time by counting *up* since task performance. We describe in detail the aspects of temporal awareness central to clinicians' awareness needs and then provide examples of how we addressed these needs through the design of a shared information display. As an outcome of this process, we define four types of time representation techniques to facilitate the design of time-based features: (1) timestamps based on absolute time, (2) timestamps relative to the process start time, (3) time since task performance, and (4) time until the next required task.

Author Keywords
Temporality; time; awareness; information displays; trauma resuscitation; participatory design; emergency medicine.

ACM Classification Keywords
H.5.0 **[Information Interfaces and Presentation]:** General.

INTRODUCTION
Temporal information provides clinicians with awareness about the timing of past, present, and future activities [5], and is critical in prioritizing tasks, especially in time- and safety-critical settings such as trauma resuscitation—a rapid evaluation and management of critically injured patients. Medical personnel in general often use time as a frame of reference to evaluate team performance, gauging and adjusting their actions accordingly [3]. Such use of temporal information is particularly evident in an emergency. The first hour after trauma injury—the Golden Hour—is a critical period that is indicative of patient outcomes [24]. Trauma resuscitation lasts 20-30 minutes on average and must take place within this hour to increase the chances of patient survival. It is therefore critical that the total time spent on diagnosis, treatment, and patient monitoring is kept as short as possible [24]. While training and low-tech interventions, such as clocks and stopclocks, have been used for improving team coordination, errors and inefficiencies are still observed even among experienced teams. Computer-based coordination mechanisms can provide a degree of visibility and flexibility to their analog counterparts [23], but their design first requires an understanding of how time is perceived and managed in actual work.

In this paper, we present the findings from a study of temporal awareness in time-critical medical teamwork that emerged through the iterative design process of an information display to support situation awareness during trauma resuscitation. We examined how trauma resuscitation teams (a) experience and perceive time, (b) construct their own time-keeping mechanisms, (c) communicate temporal information, and (d) respond to different presentations of temporal information. To gain this understanding, we conducted a series of participatory design workshops, video review sessions with interviews, and simulated resuscitations. Because this study was part of a larger effort to design an information display, we experimented with different presentations of temporality in a simulation setting. As an outcome of this process, we defined four types of time representation techniques to facilitate the design of time-based features in a time-critical, collocated teamwork: (1) timestamps based on absolute time, (2) timestamps relative to the process start time, (3) time since task performance, and (4) time until the next required task. Our work has three contributions to CSCW:

- Four time representation techniques separated into static and dynamic categories of temporal information features.
- Description of how clinicians perceive, communicate and manage time within an emergency medical context.
- Implications for designing information displays to support temporal awareness in time-critical, collocated contexts.

CSCW '15, March 14 - 18, 2015, Vancouver, BC, Canada.
Copyright 2015 ACM 978-1-4503 2922-4/15/03...$15.00.
http://dx.doi.org/10.1145/2675133.2675279

RELATED WORK: TEMPORALITY IN CSCW

The nature of temporality in cooperative work has been of interest to CSCW since its beginnings. Early CSCW work defined "coordination mechanisms" as the different temporal artifacts that have been used for coordinative purposes in cooperative settings for centuries: timetables, schedules, checklists, routing schemes, catalogues, and classification systems in large repositories [23]. Seminal studies of time-critical work settings described other coordination mechanisms designed to reduce the time it takes to perform recurring tasks, such as flight strips that provide the controllers with dynamic representations of each flight [6], or timetables to coordinate traffic flow in the underground lines service [13]. While these studies offer important design principles for coordination, they are based on a scale both temporally and spatially larger than the fast-paced, collocated medical resuscitation context.

CSCW Studies of Temporality in Medical Teamwork

Several CSCW studies of medical work have looked closely at temporality [2,3,5,7,11,18,20]. We roughly divide this body of work into studies of temporal coordination and scheduling, and studies of temporal rhythms.

Coordination and Scheduling

CSCW studies of coordination in medical work describe activities occurring over several hours, days, weeks, or even months. Bardram and colleagues discussed temporal coordination for scheduling patient care, synchronizing actions, and time allocation [2,5]. Bardram and Hansen emphasized the importance of work articulation around scheduling in surgery called "situated planning" [3]. Egger and Wagner examined the social and cultural complexity of time management and creating schedules for surgeries due to the different work routines of clinicians [11]. They discussed the inherent problems of collaborative time management in complex organizations: temporal ambiguity, conflicting temporal interests and requirements, and scarcity of temporal resources. To address those problems, they developed a prototype, called "operation book," which resembles the document used in a clinic's daily planning sessions. The spatial and temporal scale of the medical work contexts described in these studies, however, is larger than that of trauma resuscitation. The activities described are being coordinated across a department, rather than within a collocated team. We build on this work by discussing the role of temporality in coordinating highly time-sensitive tasks among a team of clinicians within the scale of minutes. In addition, scheduling and coordination in trauma resuscitation are not a primary concern because teams are collocated (though task coordination is still required) and their formation is *ad hoc*.

Temporal Rhythms

There are several studies of temporal rhythms in clinical and emergency medical contexts. A classic study by Zerubavel described the rhythmic structures of social organization in hospital life as characterized by five major social cycles: the year, the rotation, the week, the day, and the "duty period" [27]. Reddy and Dourish focused on the role of rhythms and temporal patterns in information seeking of clinicians in an intensive care unit (ICU) [18,20]. They found that temporal rhythms orient members of the ICU towards likely future activities and information needs, forming patterns that characterize the work in the unit, such as large-scale rhythms (e.g., nursing shifts, rounds) and finer-grained rhythms (e.g., lab results, medication administration). Some medications are ordered based on urgency and circumstances, like they are in trauma resuscitation, but because medications in the ICU are given on a known schedule, nurses can arrange their activities around this schedule. Temporal awareness has also been considered as an essential dimension of "achieving overview" in medical work, especially when achieving a shared overview of the patient status that requires convergence of multiple schedules [7]. Through our study, we identified a different set of temporal awareness issues that are unique to collocated, time-critical collaboration: perceptions of time are skewed; clinicians often lose track of time, which makes it challenging to maintain temporal awareness during time-sensitive procedures; and, the short time period and too recent information make continuous monitoring for trends in the data difficult.

The CSCW studies reviewed in this section differ from the studies of temporality and temporal artifacts in the medical sciences due to their greater focus on teamwork and coordination. In medical research, there is more emphasis on (1) the importance of time to measuring clinical performance [24,25]; (2) the completeness and accuracy of documentation for medical records, research, and cross-referencing events between different units [12]; and (3) the accuracy and synchronization of timepieces, especially pre-hospital and across hospital departments [10,12]. Although not focused on the design of time-based features for medical work, these studies point to the importance of time and the need for considering temporality in systems design.

RESEARCH DOMAIN: TRAUMA RESUSCITATION

Based on our prior fieldwork, long-term engagement with the domain, and review of medical and CSCW literature, we uncovered a number of factors that can complicate clinicians' ability to maintain temporal and situation awareness during trauma resuscitation. The resuscitation process is fast-paced and requires the focused, collocated effort of seven to 20 specialists from various disciplines. Clinicians start with a rapid evaluation of major physiological systems to identify life-threatening injuries, followed by a thorough head-to-toe evaluation for other injuries. Teams are formed *ad hoc* upon receiving patient arrival notification, with members called from different departments, making their prior acquaintance with each other less likely [17,22]. A typical trauma team consists of surgical attending physicians or fellows (team leaders),

Figure 1. Display and temporal artifacts setup in the resuscitation room during simulation sessions: (1) our information display, (2) auxiliary display for vital signs or overhead view, (a) absolute time, (b) time since patient arrived (starts when data is inputted on the back end interface of the display), (c) time since patient arrived (manual start). Room stopclock (c) was not synchronized with our display stopclock (b) due to the technical constraints of our prototype and room stopclock hardware.

emergency medicine physicians (co-leaders), surgical residents (bedside physicians), bedside nurses, an anesthesiologist, a respiratory therapist, a scribe nurse (for documenting the process), and critical care technicians.

Resuscitation rooms are generally noisy because of the frequent communication to coordinate complex tasks distributed among team members. To complete their work, teams need to detect patterns and changes in patient status, as well as filter out irrelevant data [1]. Clinicians often miss important clinical events due to increased noise levels, resulting in repeated requests for information and interruptions [1,21]. Any inefficiency in communication and task completion can contribute to adverse outcomes.

To be efficient in treating severely injured patients, teams must also use directives that communicate priority, urgency, and time frame expectations, which is based on the timing of previous activities. Clearly indicating the speed and urgency of the requested task in turn allows for proper timing [9]. Priorities in trauma resuscitation, however, change dynamically and may not always be the same across all team members at all times [14]. It is important to ensure that priorities are articulated and frequently updated to support team situation awareness.

Although *information-rich* with constantly changing vital signs, bedside reports of patient status, and multiple treatments being ordered and given at different times, resuscitation settings are also *information-poor* in that they have few information technologies for synthesizing patient information and monitoring team activities. Resuscitation room instruments, such as the vital signs monitor, provide data about patient status but do not track work processes or communication. Monitoring of instruments is visual (e.g., looking at the monitors) or aural (e.g., listening for the tone of the pulse oximeter). Patient data are recorded manually even when digital devices are used for data acquisition.

Clocks, Timers and Stopclocks as Temporal Artifacts

Because time is a major factor in high-risk, safety-critical patient management, most resuscitation settings are equipped with several types of temporal artifacts. First, there are *clocks* presenting the *absolute time* (Figure 1(a)), which is important for coordinating work not only within the room, but also with other hospital departments. Scribe nurses rely on the clock to manually document the timestamps for procedures and trends in vital signs on paper flowsheets. Second, there are *timers* that *count down from a specified amount of time* to automatically read blood pressure every five minutes and remind clinicians to check vital signs. When time permits, the bedside nurse setting up the vital signs monitor will configure the amount of time between reminder alerts to suit their work style preference (typically between 3-5 minutes). Finally, there are *stopclocks* mounted to the wall that show the *resuscitation time* (time since the resuscitation started), an important feature for presenting the temporal context of the resuscitation (Figure 1(c)). Teams are instructed to have a team member manually turn on the stopclock by pressing a button on the stopclock upon patient arrival and turn it off upon patient discharge.

These temporal artifacts are essential for team efficacy, yet little is known about how clinicians perceive and manage time during high-risk, safety-critical patient care. To design time-based features that will enhance their work, it is necessary to first understand the current work practices surrounding clinicians' use of the existing temporal artifacts and their perceptions of time. Peripheral information displays can serve as a useful mechanism for presenting temporal information and reducing the amount of missed or forgotten information that is easily lost [5].

METHODS

This two-year study is part of a larger research effort to develop a shared information display to support situation awareness of trauma resuscitation teams that has involved several years of fieldwork and user-centered development activities. Through this fieldwork, we gained a better understanding of teamwork practices and issues in the trauma resuscitation domain, and found significant clinician emphasis on temporality that we further explore through this study. The data presented in this paper focus on describing the nature of temporality in a time-critical medical setting and how best to support temporal awareness in such domains through the development of time-based design features for a shared information display.

Research Site

Research activities were conducted at a pediatric teaching hospital with a Level I (highest) trauma center in the U.S. Mid-Atlantic region. Each year, the center admits about 1,000 children with trauma and burn injuries. Patients are treated in two adjoining resuscitation rooms in the emergency department by dedicated specialists in trauma and burn care. The main room has three large wall-mounted monitors installed for augmenting vital sign information and showing the overhead view of the patient. During our simulation studies, two of the displays at the front and back of the room presented our design (front display shown in Figure 1(1)). An auxiliary display to the right of our display was used to show the overhead view of the patient (Figure 1(2)). Vital sign data were presented on a separate vital signs monitor. Both resuscitation rooms have two temporal artifacts installed—a clock and stopclock (Figure 1(a,c))—currently the only mechanisms for time management.

Participants

A total of 43 clinicians that typically serve on trauma resuscitation teams at our site were recruited to participate in our research activities (Table 1). For group-based participatory design workshops and simulated resuscitations, participants were recruited to represent an entire resuscitation team. Several clinicians participated multiple times throughout the study. One of the main benefits of continued participation was that we received feedback from those who saw the evolution of the design in addition to those seeing it for the first time.

Roles	Participants (N=43)
Anesthesiologist	5
Bedside nurse*	9
Emergency medical physician	5
Bedside physician	7
Respiratory therapist	6
Scribe*	3
Surgical team leader	8

Table 1. Participant count. *Some bedside nurses also served as scribes, but were only counted once as bedside nurses.

Figure 2: Data collection sessions and number of participants (includes participants that participated multiple times).

Data Collection

We conducted three types of data collection activities between November 2012 and April 2014 that elicited discussions about temporal awareness: participatory design workshops (PDW), video review sessions with interviews (VRS), and simulated resuscitations (SIM) (Figure 2). Coupled with fieldwork, these activities provided a holistic approach to conceptualizing, designing, and evaluating the information display and its time-based features.

Participatory Design Workshops

Participatory design workshops brought clinicians together to determine and discuss the requirements of the information display. Each participant was asked to sketch an individual display to support the information needs of their particular role. Clinicians then worked together as a group to create a shared display design that combined and prioritized the information needs of the team. During these design activities, clinicians were asked to discuss their work challenges, information needs, time management, and the features they believed would support their work.

Video Review Sessions with Interviews

Video review sessions involved individual clinicians narrating a 10-minute video of a simulated resuscitation. Clinicians were asked to comment on things they found unusual or important as they observed the resuscitation and teamwork. Examples included what they thought about the performed tasks, the information that emerged, what the team did well or what needed improvement, and team awareness of what other team members were doing. During each session, we asked clinicians how they adjust and manage their awareness in different situations (e.g., when arriving late to a resuscitation).

Simulated Resuscitations

High-fidelity simulations were developed to engage clinicians in realistic and challenging clinical scenarios to evaluate the usefulness and effectiveness of our display. Simulations were conducted in the main resuscitation room of the emergency department using a high-fidelity simulation mannequin and the existing wall monitors (Figure 1). A physician researcher acted as a "Wizard of Oz" and entered display information using a computer interface. Following each scenario, we asked clinicians to discuss their experiences using the display within the context of work. We also asked questions specific to the time-based features of the display to elicit targeted feedback about temporal awareness support.

Data Analysis

We conducted a thematic analysis [8] of discussions to identify patterns in how clinicians perceive temporal aspects of their work and the ways in which they need temporal awareness support. Each transcript was first reviewed for the context and flow of the discussion. In subsequent passes of each transcript, we identified parts that focused on temporal aspects of work and time-related design features. Relevant quotes were extracted and analyzed for themes across discussions. The following aspects of the statements were considered during analysis: type of the statement (e.g., if it was about a perception, experience, or design suggestion), timing of the statement in the design process, role making the statement, and the nature of what was being discussed about time.

RESULTS: TEMPORALITY IN TRAUMA RESUSCITATION

Teams must understand and maintain awareness of information according to various time dimensions. Time dimensions range from individual task duration to overall resuscitation duration. In this section, we describe how clinicians perceive and manage their work in relation to time. We present our results in two parts. First, we describe the perceptions and experiences of time discussed in participatory design workshops and video review sessions. Second, we describe how these perceptions and experiences materialized during simulations when clinicians used the display and time features within the context of their work. Using this mix of clinicians' input, we were able to validate data across different data collection activities, as well as to ensure a holistic approach to design while minimizing methodological biases tied to each of the approaches.

Part 1: Experiencing and Communicating Time

A major theme that emerged from analyzing discussions, particularly from participatory design workshops and video review sessions, was how clinicians experience and communicate time during resuscitations. In this subsection, we illustrate three important aspects of maintaining temporal awareness in trauma resuscitation: (1) perceiving and representing time, (2) monitoring continuously to identify trends, and (3) conveying speed and urgency.

Perceiving and Representing Time

Clinicians' perceptions of time during these high intensity situations are often skewed. Each person's experience of time passing is different—whether they experience time as being shorter or longer than actual may depend on the tasks they are performing. It is therefore important that teams have time presented accurately and intuitively so they can pace themselves accordingly. A respiratory therapist (RT) commented in one of the workshops about how perceptions of time can be warped during the event:

> *Three minutes can feel like five seconds, or three minutes can feel like three hours just depending on the situation that you're in. (RT, PDW #1)*

Most clinicians agreed that the existing stopclock showing the resuscitation time is useful for their overall temporal awareness because it helps them gauge the progress of the resuscitation. An emergency medicine (EM) physician highlighted the importance of having the stopclock in the room (Figure 1(c)):

> *Just starting a zero clock is important. [...] So it's like a stopwatch. (EM Physician, PDW #1)*

A respiratory therapist also noted the value of the stopclock in helping teams maintain temporal awareness:

> *Honestly if you tell me he showed up at 6:10, I don't remember what time I came downstairs. I'd rather just know for the minute, like when the patient arrives, click, and now there's a running stopwatch saying we've been running for ten minutes. (RT, PDW #1)*

These comments also imply that resuscitation time can be used as a feedback mechanism for assessing team performance. An entire resuscitation should generally be completed within 20-30 minutes, with the initial evaluation completed within the first 7-10 minutes [24]. The amount of time to complete an intervention or perform the initial survey can give the team a sense for how they are performing, so they can adjust their pace as necessary. All resuscitations are unique, and the actions that take place require unique judgments about patient response and team performance according to the particular scenario. Awareness of resuscitation time can help teams interpret their actions and progress regardless of the way they individually experience time.

While teams are instructed to manually start the existing stopclock upon patient arrival (Figure 1(c)), participants suggested integrating this feature into the display (Figure 1(b)). This was a plausible suggestion because team members often forget to start the manual stopclock and no specific role is assigned to this task, making this approach somewhat unreliable. Implementing a stopclock that starts automatically would help teams by reducing the cognitive load of remembering to turn on the stopclock.

Time was also discussed in the context of time-sensitive, multi-step tasks, when team members must keep track of how much time has passed since the last step so they can proceed with the next step. Administering the medication epinephrine (an emergency drug for treating cardiac arrest) was a useful example for discussing these types of tasks because it needs to be performed every three minutes until the patient's status improves. A bedside nurse commented that supporting awareness of time since epinephrine (epi) has been administered would be helpful because they often lose track of time due to the hectic nature of the process:

> *What does need to be on the screen is the fact that it's been three minutes since [epi], or this is the time you are aside. Because the time is so skewed in the midst of all of this, you lose track. (Bedside Nurse, PDW #2)*

Monitoring Continuously to Identify Trends

Trends in patient data can also provide clinicians with feedback on the effectiveness of their treatments and the big picture of what has occurred during the event. Maintaining awareness of the status of the patient, such as monitoring vital signs is important, but subtle changes over time can be easily missed if a lot of information is presented and if the information is too recent. A bedside nurse described:

> *I think the trending is important. [...] The most recent, of course, [...] and then the initial maybe always needs to be up there, because we don't notice trends if they're casual. [...] If I'm taking a heart rate every minute, I'm only going to have room for like five sets [on the trauma flowsheet], so I'm not going to see a trend. I'm just going to see an increase of five, whereas maybe an increase actually of 40 from when they got here, that would be important. (Bedside Nurse, PDW #1)*

Presenting trends from a short period (i.e., 20-30 minutes) in a form useful for supporting awareness is challenging. Scribes document vital signs data onto a paper flowsheet, but this information is not visible to other team members. A scribe noted that they are often responsible for alerting the team when there are noticeable changes in patient status:

> *I mean we rely so much on whoever is documenting to notice all the trends and to notice when it's three minutes from medication [epi]. But I think that other people need to also be aware. (Scribe, PDW #2)*

There are already built-in alerts and functions in the vital signs monitor to help teams continuously track vital signs. These alerts and functions, however, need to be set manually for individual patients and are rarely activated due to the lack of time. Instead, scribes and bedside nurses monitor trends in vital signs and indicate to the team when there is a change. A scribe participating in a video review session commented:

> *If you have a really good [bedside nurse], they're really keeping track because they're either hitting the button or they're the one that has set it up for 'cue 5.' [...] The good ones will keep an eye on the vital signs. Every five minutes, like blood pressures and all. (Scribe, VRS #5)*

Bedside nurses will set timers to automatically run the blood pressure cuff, which also function as reminders for the team to review vital signs. These reminders present important temporal information for promoting awareness.

Conveying Speed and Urgency

Conveying expectations for speed and a sense of urgency—and communicating in general—is challenging in the resuscitation context due to the increased pace, noise, and intensity. A bedside nurse described the nature of communication during severe trauma cases as follows:

> *Communication tends to be very good when kids aren't sick. They just seem to stay quiet, and then you can move slower. [...] It's when something, a rare event happens. Somebody needs a chest tube. Even intubating, that will throw a wrench. But the more rare opportunities hit, the more panic the room gets, the less communication happens, and the more the occasion tends to fall apart a little bit. (Bedside Nurse, PDW #1)*

Managing tasks that are similar in urgency and priority is difficult for teams, especially when more complicated procedures such as endotracheal intubation to treat an obstructed airway dominate the team's focus, as described by an anesthesiologist during a video review session:

> *The other thing is [they're] so focused on the airway now. [...] I would be looking up at the blood pressure making sure my fluids were hung. [...] He [the leader] doesn't need to wait until after intubation to hang fluids. They're not going to risk the intubation by just hooking up an IV. [...] Blood pressure was dropping, so I would've expected one of these nurses already to be hanging fluids instead of feeling for pulses and finishing taping up the IV. (Anesthesiologist, VRS #1)*

Urgency of tasks can also be lost, especially when there are competing tasks that require immediate attention. Expectations of speed can vary greatly depending on different people's perception of time and urgency, as well as training background and work style. The need for clinicians to clearly specify the necessary speed of tasks to the team became apparent during a video review session when a participant described how the team leader in the video managed competing demands:

> *The team leader is asking for fluids to go in as fast as possible. Well something I think he could do better would be how he wants those fluids to go in. What that means. There's a couple of ways to get fluids in fast. One is a pressure bag. But in what seems like probably a 20-kilo kid, you probably want to do a push-pull method. To be able to specify that would be better because you get [fluids] in faster that way. [...] Just to kind of up the ante too by "let's get fluid going through both IVs." (EM Physician, VRS #4)*

It is therefore important for clinicians to specify what they mean by "fast" such as the rate at which fluids should be administered or indicate a specific time frame during which a task should be completed. Knowing how long fluids have been running and at what rate can help clinicians gauge whether the treatment is effective by monitoring the trends in blood pressure. If the blood pressure does not increase within a certain time frame, they may choose to increase the fluid administration rate, or start another bag of fluids if the patient shows no sign of improvement after the first bag.

Having learned these important aspects of experiencing and communicating time that clinicians described, we iteratively designed and evaluated the time-based features for our information display to better support temporal awareness during trauma resuscitation, as described next.

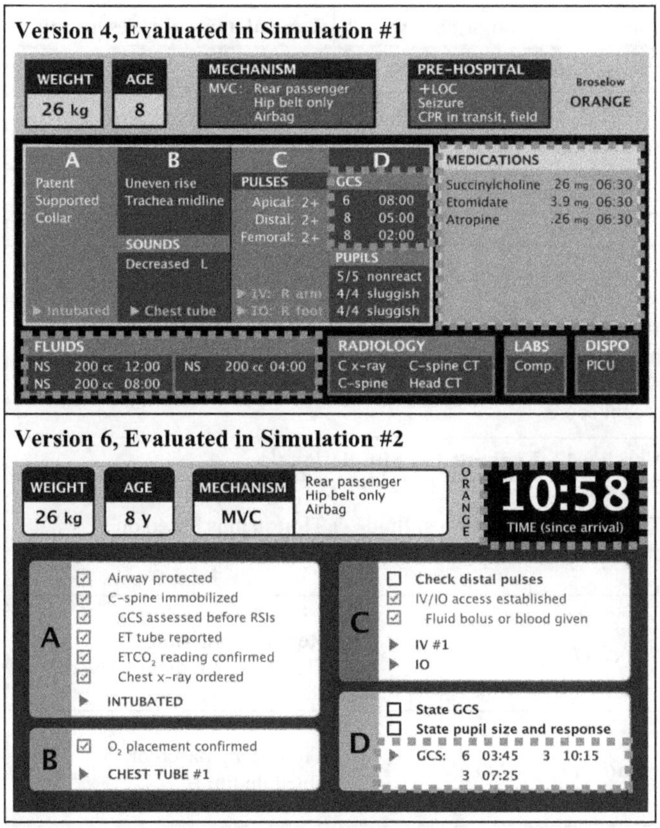

Figure 3. Time-based design features on display versions # 4 and 6. Timestamps (outlined by dashed red boxes) indicate time reported or administered relative to resuscitation time.

Part 2: Supporting Temporal Awareness

We now describe how the design of the time-based features evolved during the iterative design and evaluation of our information display to support temporal awareness in the high intensity, fast-paced environment of trauma resuscitation. To illustrate this process, we show five designs (out of 14 iterations) that were evaluated in a simulation setting (Figure 3 and Figure 4).

In the early stages of the design, the emphasis of discussions was mainly on determining which information features to include on the display. Participants in general responded positively to the inclusion of initial time-based features such as administration times for medications and fluids (Figure 3, v.4 and v.6). As the design progressed through testing in a simulated resuscitation environment, clinicians were able to see how different time presentations function within the context of their work, allowing us to focus on fine-tuning specific temporal awareness support features. We experimented with three different methods of presenting temporal information: (1) timestamps based on resuscitation time, (2) timestamps based on absolute time, and (3) time since critical tasks or treatments.

Timestamps Based on Resuscitation vs. Absolute Time

Indicating treatments according to resuscitation or absolute time was debated throughout the design process. In participatory design workshops, clinicians discussed their individual display designs in terms of timestamps for treatments, such as medications and fluids, relative to patient arrival time or absolute time (i.e., exact time administered). The first nine of 14 display designs incorporated temporal representations using timestamps for treatments based on resuscitation time (Figure 3, v.4 and v.6; Figure 4, v.10). The stopclock on the display prototypes started automatically when the physician researcher began entering patient information into the display input interface upon patient arrival. Treatment timestamps for display design versions #1 through 9 were automatically recorded when the physician researcher began inputting information about a treatment, which they tended to do when the treatment was first ordered.

Although participants did not express dissatisfaction with timestamps being relative to resuscitation time in the first two simulations, conflicting views on presenting temporal information about treatments started to emerge through discussions from simulation session #3 onward. It was confusing for clinicians to calculate how much time has passed since a particular task was completed when looking at the timestamps while also considering the overall stopclock for resuscitation time as a reference. If they have to calculate time, clinicians prefer to do it in terms of absolute rather than relative time, because they are used to working with absolute time (e.g., documentation is in absolute time). A bedside nurse noted:

> *Knowing if it's been more than three minutes, you have to do some subtraction too, right, so you have to say that it has been four minutes since the last epi, you can't just tell how long ago it was (Bedside Nurse, SIM #5)*

Scribe nurses generally preferred absolute time because it is the standard format for recording time information on the paper flowsheet ("*Should be just time it was given 'cause that's when I am documenting*" *SIM 3*), even though they also keep the team aware of time since the last task for time-sensitive treatments. An emergency medicine physician agreed:

> *Yeah, so the absolute time is your reference time… whatever time you walked through the door, because if you go back and try to review, you could learn the times it was given, not how long it would take to give it. (EM Physician, SIM #3)*

Representing events according to absolute time then seemed to be the most straightforward way to present temporal information for tasks and treatments. We therefore experimented by using absolute time for timestamps in simulation session #4 (Figure 4, v.13).

Time Since Critical Tasks or Treatments

While some clinicians continued to value information as a log of time-stamped tasks based on absolute time, the majority of participants in simulation session #4 found it

<table>
<tr><th>Design Version</th><th>Time-based Design Feature</th><th>Type of Time Representation</th></tr>
<tr><td rowspan="4">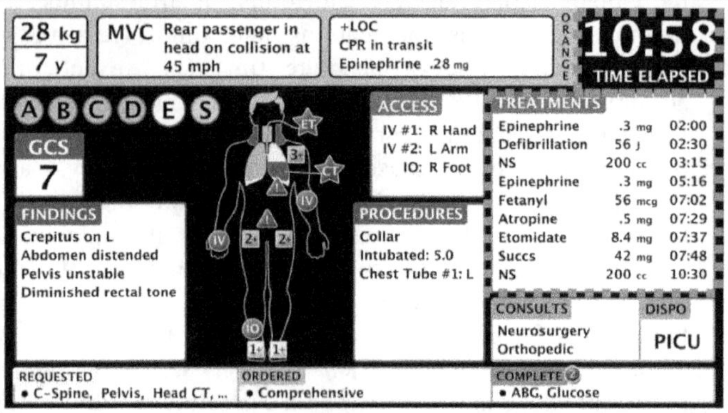
</td><td colspan="2">Version 10, Evaluated in Simulation #3</td></tr>
<tr><td>Treatments (medications, fluids, cardiac treatments)</td><td>Timestamps based on resuscitation time</td></tr>
<tr><td>Stopclock</td><td>Resuscitation time
(Time since patient arrived)</td></tr>
<tr><td colspan="2">+ Medications & fluids
+ Cardiac treatments (defibrillation & cardioversion)
– Time from Glasgow Coma Score (GCS) assessment, which indicates the level of cognitive function. GCS is assessed several times during a resuscitation. Display now shows only the most recent score.</td></tr>
<tr><td rowspan="4">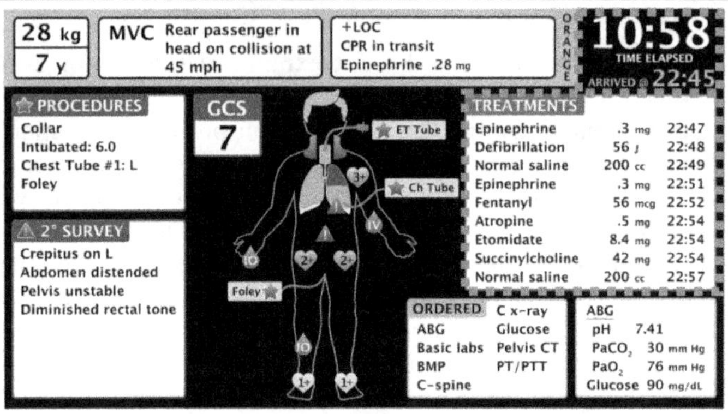
</td><td colspan="2">Version 13, Evaluated in Simulation #4</td></tr>
<tr><td>Treatments (medications, fluids, cardiac treatments)</td><td>Timestamps based on absolute time</td></tr>
<tr><td>Stopclock</td><td>Resuscitation time
(Time since patient arrived)</td></tr>
<tr><td>+ Patient arrival time</td><td>Timestamp based on absolute time</td></tr>
<tr><td rowspan="6">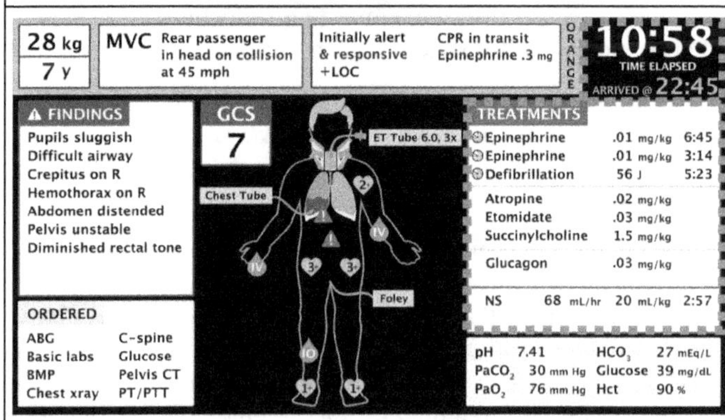
</td><td colspan="2">Version 14, Evaluated in Simulation #5</td></tr>
<tr><td>Treatments (medications, fluids, cardiac treatments)</td><td>Time since treatment was last administered (only for fluids & time-sensitive treatments)</td></tr>
<tr><td>Stopclock</td><td>Resuscitation time
(Time since patient arrived)</td></tr>
<tr><td>Patient arrival time</td><td>Timestamp in absolute time</td></tr>
<tr><td>+ Rate of fluid administration</td><td>mL per hour</td></tr>
<tr><td colspan="2">Separated treatments: time-sensitive, intubation related, fluids</td></tr>
</table>

Figure 4. Time-based design features (outlined by dashed red boxes) on display versions #10, 13, and 14. Plus and minus signs ('+' and '–') indicate the features added to or removed from each display design version.

more important to have awareness of time since the last task. For time-sensitive treatments in particular, clinicians preferred to interpret time according to the amount of time since the treatment was completed, not as a timestamp given in absolute or resuscitation time. Participants noted that the amount of time since treatment administration would be most accurate if it is based on when treatments are actually administered, rather than automatically recorded when the physician researcher begins inputting the treatments as they are ordered. In display design versions #10 through 14, selecting an "administered" checkbox on the input interface triggered the treatment administration times. As we learned through further discussion, clinicians currently calculate time since treatments based on absolute time, but would prefer a stopclock feature that shows the interval since the last treatment to avoid calculation:

> *Even when we do epi we don't say at minute five epi was given. We say epi was given two minutes ago based on the actual time (Bedside Nurse, SIM #3)*

Some time-sensitive medications turned out not to be critical for displaying with "time since administered" because their effectiveness wears off quickly (within a minute or so). Displaying "time since" for medications that were not time-sensitive was also unnecessary because the need for additional doses is more apparent based on the patient's response to the treatment. Using this feedback, we implemented stopclocks for presenting temporal information (Figure 4, v.14) and tested them in simulation

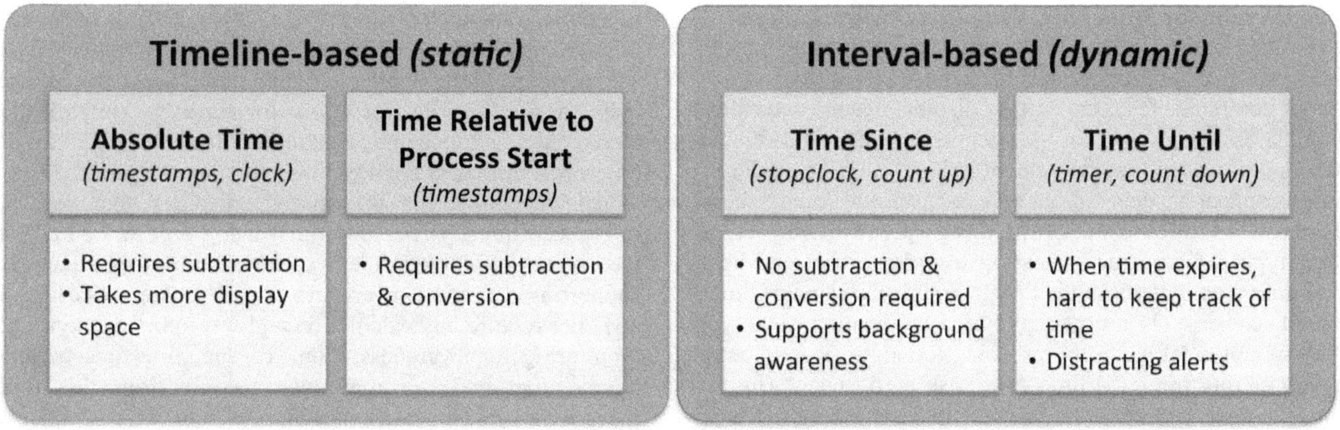

Figure 5. Four different types of time representation techniques for time-critical, collocated teamwork.

session #5, the final simulation. Participants overall responded positively to using a stopclock feature instead of absolute timestamps to convey time since the last treatment. Showing time in this dynamic form (i.e., time is actively counting up) proved to be an important mechanism for coordinating future tasks. As participants commented, awareness of time since the last treatment assists in managing the complexity of tasks and remembering to check if the patient needs more medication or additional time-sensitive treatments.

We also found that having a log of all the times for repeated treatments was not necessary for planning or remembering future treatments. Given the number of treatments administered in a typical resuscitation, the list would become long and it would take longer to find the last treatment given. Most participants suggested that only the recent instance of time-sensitive treatments was the most important to display. A respiratory therapist commented:

> *Is there any way you can roll it from the last epi instead of 'having done'...when you give the next one, the other one moves off? It rolls off so then you won't have so many. (RT, SIM #5)*

Participants noted that this presentation would be enough to understand what the team has done and make decisions about the next step. In a future iteration, we plan to modify the display to present the count of times the same treatment was previously performed. The decision about when to administer the next dose is based on the time since the most recent dose was administered. Furthermore, the dosages are likely to be the same because they are weight-based, so there is no need to show all instances for each treatment.

Getting the Terminology for Temporal Features Right

We did not notice until simulation sessions #4 and #5 that the terminology for time features may not have been clear to participants and even among our own research team members. When discussing how to program the functionality of the display within our team, there was confusion about whether the time representation for treatments (e.g., fluids and medications), would be a "stopclock" measuring time by counting *up* from zero or a "timer" measuring time by counting *down* from a specified amount of time (e.g., 3:00, 2:59...0:01, 0:00). In some cases, the term "timer" was used to describe both the functionalities of a timer and a stopclock, which was discovered after reviewing transcripts, even in the initial participatory design sessions:

> *See like for me, I think of it more of a time of arrival or a timer. [...] I'd rather just know for the minute, like when the patient arrives, click, and now there's a running stopwatch saying we've been running for ten minutes, we've been running for fifteen. I like the timer idea versus time of arrival. (RT, PDW #1)*

This participant described the functionality of a stopclock and used the term "timer" and "stopwatch." Clinicians were familiar with the idea of the stopclock at the top right of our display because it assumed the metaphor of the physical stopclock already in use.

DISCUSSION: DESIGNING FOR TEMPORAL AWARENESS IN DYNAMIC AND FAST-PACED EVENTS

Presenting temporal information is challenging when designing for highly dynamic and time-critical events. In these environments, perception of time is skewed, priorities change rapidly [14], information is easily lost in the shuffle [5], and it is difficult to identify trends as time passes. It is thus important to carefully decide which time-based features should be used to support temporal awareness. Experimenting with time-based features in trauma resuscitation has allowed us to understand the fundamental differences between these features as *static* and *dynamic* time representation techniques. Below we discuss four time time-based features falling into these two categories (Figure 5). These insights have implications for the design of information systems in domains where time plays a critical role in collocated collaboration.

Implications for Presenting Temporal Design Features

We found that using and explaining specific terminology is important for facilitating accurate and focused discussions about temporal features during display design activities. Confusion and lack of awareness about time-related terminology, such as the use of "timer" and "stopclock" interchangeably, delayed our progress on developing these features. As an outcome of the design process, we present four types of time representation techniques that can help designers facilitate both the design and discussions of time-based features: (1) timestamps based on absolute time, (2) timestamps relative to the process start time (in our case, resuscitation time), (3) time since task performance (in our case, completed treatment or evaluation step), and (4) time until the next required task (Figure 5). These techniques can then be separated into static and dynamic categories of temporal representations.

Static Temporal Representations

The first two techniques, *timestamps based on absolute time (wall clock)* and *timestamps relative to the process start time*, can be considered as static techniques where temporal representations are based on unchanging timestamps to indicate a fixed point on the timeline of a process. These techniques require users to calculate the amount of time that has passed (by subtracting the time when a task was performed from the present time) when deciding what future tasks are necessary and at what speed, which makes it difficult to quickly interpret, analyze, and use the information on the display [15]. *Timestamps based on absolute time* take more screen real estate because it is necessary to include the hour even when the whole process is completed within an hour. Screen real estate is even more limited when trying to present information about tasks on peripheral displays in contexts spanning longer periods. *Timestamps relative to the process start time* were confusing because they not only require subtraction, but also conversion to the same time axis because the present time is shown in relative time units and the record about the task performance time is kept in absolute time units. It is important to note that clinicians in our domain still found it helpful to see the absolute time of the patient's arrival to situate their temporal awareness within the larger temporal context and rhythms of their workday [18,20].

Dynamic Temporal Representations

The second two techniques, *time since task performance (stopclock)* and *time until the next required task (timer)*, can be considered as more dynamic time representation techniques where time is shown as ticking and temporal information is based on intervals between tasks (or steps). These techniques remove the requirement for users to calculate how much time has passed since the last task in comparison to the static techniques. *Time until the next required task* is less preferable because when the time reaches zero, it stops counting, making it difficult to keep track of how much time has passed since it stopped. This could mean the difference between a few seconds or several minutes past the expiration time. A common remedy is to use periodic alerts indicating that timer has expired, but even these alerts do not allow for time tracking. Active alerts can also become distracting or overlooked in an environment that is already noisy, hectic, and intense [26]. When designing for information displays that can be referenced quickly, we found that using *time since tasks* is the most effective time representation technique for supporting temporal awareness in our context because it does not require any calculation and it supports background monitoring for awareness. Contexts spanning time periods longer than an hour may also benefit from this time representation technique because it can help condense information.

The accuracy and reliability of all four temporal representation techniques depend on the mechanism for setting the reference points (i.e., patient arrival and task completion) by which times are calculated. Although automatic methods such as recording patient arrival time upon the start of documentation seem advantageous, there is a higher possibility that they will be inaccurate in emergency medical work. While the exact time of patient arrival is not as difficult to determine, a few minutes passing between the start and end of a task can make a significant difference in temporal awareness, especially for time-critical tasks. Clinical expertise is still required due to variability and subjectivity in determining the actual task completion. A manually selected mechanism (e.g., checkbox, button) for indicating task completion appears most feasible.

Implications for Peripheral Information Displays

The information display we designed is meant to be a quick reference for busy medical teams. Clinicians in the trauma resuscitation environment generally allocate their visual attention to information sources (e.g., the vital signs monitor) for approximately 1-3 seconds [16]. The information on the supplemental displays, especially for updating temporal awareness, therefore needs to be accessible and absorbable at a glance. Too much detail about tasks would require clinicians to spend time looking and analyzing the display to gain situation awareness, which can be hazardous to patient safety [4].

Because many tasks and treatments are repeated throughout the process, it is important to not only provide a sense for what has been completed, but also what is the current status of the patient and the resuscitation, all within a limited amount of space. An overview of critical tasks to remind clinicians of what was recently completed turned out to be more useful than a detailed log of events, as also concluded by Bardram and Hansen [4]. In our case, however, we found that the time since a completed task is still helpful, but only for select tasks—time-sensitive treatments. Through trial and error, we were able to identify "time since task performance" as the suitable time-based feature for our problem domain. We also found it was more useful to present temporal information of iterative tasks by showing the most recent task iteration, but then also by indicating the number of times the task has been performed. This presentation method not only saves space on the display, but also time when searching through a task list.

CONCLUSION

In this paper, we examined the temporal awareness of clinicians in a regional trauma center. We conducted participatory design workshops, video review sessions with interviews, and simulated resuscitations to understand how clinicians experience and perceive time, communicate temporal information, and respond to different presentations of temporal information. Analysis of the discussions revealed the aspects of maintaining temporal awareness that clinicians perceived as important in trauma resuscitation. These findings then contributed to the design of time-based features that evolved during the iterative design of an information display to support the temporal awareness of clinicians. Using the insights from the design process, we discussed four different types of time representation techniques and offered guidelines for deciding which time-based features should be used when designing information systems to support temporal awareness in time-critical, collocated teamwork.

ACKNOWLEDGMENTS

This work is supported by the National Library of Medicine of the National Institutes of Health under Award Number R21LM011320-01A1 and partially by the National Science Foundation Award No. 1253285. Special thanks to our research team members for their contributions throughout the project: Randall S. Burd, Nadir Weibel, Zhan Zhang, Genevieve Tuveson, Ivan Marsic, and Nicole Ferraro. We would also like to thank the medical staff at the research site for participating in this study.

REFERENCES

1. Barach, P. and Weinger, M. B. Trauma team performance. In Wilson, W. C., Grande, C. M., and Hoyt, D. B. (Eds.), *Trauma: Emergency Resuscitation Perioperative Anesthesia, Surgical Management*. CRC Press, 2013, 101-114.
2. Bardram, J. E. Temporal coordination—on time and coordination of collaborative activities at a surgical department. *Computer Supported Cooperative Work 9,* 2 (2000), 157-187.
3. Bardram, J. E. and Hansen, T. R. Why the plan doesn't hold – a study of situated planning, articulation and coordination work in a surgical ward. In *Proc. CSCW 2010*, ACM Press (2010), 331-340.
4. Bardram, J. E. and Hansen, T. R. Context-based workplace awareness. *Computer Supported Cooperative Work 19*, 2 (2010), 105-138.
5. Bardram, J. E., Hansen, T. R., and Soegaard, M. AwareMedia: a shared interactive display supporting social, temporal, and spatial awareness in surgery. In *Proc. CSCW 2006*, ACM Press (2006), 109-118.
6. Berndtsson, J. and Normark, M. The coordinative functions of flight strips: Air traffic control revisited. In *Proc. GROUP 1999*, ACM Press (1999), 101-110.
7. Bossen, C. and Jensen, L. G. How physicians 'achieve overview': A case-based study in a hospital ward. In *Proc. CSCW 2014*, ACM Press (2014), 257–68.
8. Braun, V. and Clarke, V. Using thematic analysis in psychology. *Qualitative Research in Psychology 3*, 2 (2006), 77-101.
9. Cabitza, F., Simone, C., and Sarini, M. Leveraging coordinative conventions to promote collaboration awareness. *Computer Supported Cooperative Work 18*, 4 (2009), 301-330.
10. Cordell, W. H., Olinger, M. L., Kozak, P. A., and Nyhuis, A. W. Does anybody really know what time it is? Does anybody really care? *Annals of Emergency Medicine 23*, 5 (1994), 1032–1036.
11. Egger, E. and Wagner, I. Time management: A case for CSCW. In *Proc. CSCW 1992*, ACM Press (1992), 249-256.
12. Ferguson, E. A., Bayer, C. R., Fronzeo, S., Tuckerman, C., Hutchins, L., Roberts, K., Verger, J., Nadkarni, V., and Lin, R. Time out! Is timepiece variability a factor in critical care? *American Journal of Critical Care 14*, 2 (2005), 113–120.
13. Heath, C., and Luff, P. Collaboration and control: Crisis management and multimedia technology in London underground line control rooms. *Computer Supported Cooperative Work 11*, 1-2 (1992), 69-95.
14. Hertz, D. and Ezer, Y. B. Pitfalls in trauma teamwork. *Australian Emergency Nursing Journal 1*, 2 (1997), 30-31.
15. Hutchins, E. *Cognition in the Wild.* Cambridge, MA: The MIT Press, 1995.
16. Kusunoki, D., Sarcevic, A., Zhang, Z., and Burd, R. Understanding visual attention of teams in dynamic medical settings through vital signs monitor use. In *Proc. CSCW 2013*, ACM Press (2013), 527-540.
17. Lee, S., Tang, C., Park S. Y., and Chen, Y. Loosely formed patient care teams: Communication challenges and technology design. In *Proc. CSCW 2012*, ACM Press (2012), 867-876.
18. Matthews, T., Rattenbury, T., and Carter, S. Defining, designing, and evaluating peripheral displays: An analysis using activity theory. *Human-Computer Interaction 22*, (2007), 221-261.
19. Reddy, M. C. and Dourish, P. A finger on the pulse: Temporal rhythms and information seeking in medical

work. In *Proc. CSCW 2002*, ACM Press (2002), 344-353.

20. Reddy, M. C., Dourish, P., and Pratt, W. Temporality in medical work: Time also matters. *Computer Supported Cooperative Work 15*, 1 (2006), 29-53.

21. Sarcevic, A., Marsic, I., Lesk, M. E. and Burd, R. S. Transactive memory in trauma resuscitation. In *Proc. CSCW 2008*, ACM Press (2008), 215-224.

22. Sarcevic, A., Palen, L.A., and Burd, R.S. Coordinating time-critical work with role-tagging. In *Proc. CSCW 2011*, ACM Press (2011), 465-474

23. Schmidt, K. and Simone C. Coordination mechanisms: Towards a conceptual foundation of CSCW systems design. *Computer Supported Cooperative Work 5*, 2 (1996), 155-200.

24. Spanjersberg, W. R., Bergs, E.A., Mushkudiani, N., Klimek, M., and Schipper, I. B. Protocol compliance and time management in blunt trauma resuscitation. *Emergency Medicine Journal 26*, 1 (2009), 23-27.

25. van Olden, G. D. J., van Vugt, A. B., Biert, J., Gorbis, R. J. A. Trauma resuscitation time. *Injury 34*, 3 (2003), 191-195.

26. Xiao, Y., Seagull, F. J., Nieves-Khuow, F., Barczak, N., and Perkins, S. Organizational-historical analysis of the "failure to respond to alarm" problems. *IEEE Transactions on Systems, Man and Cybernetics 34*, 6 (2004), 772-778.

27. Zerubavel, E. *Patterns of Time in Hospital Life*. University of Chicago Press, Chicago, IL, USA, 1979.

Friendship Maintenance in the Digital Age: Applying a Relational Lens to Online Social Interaction

Irina Shklovski
IT University of Copenhagen
Copenhagen, Denmark
irsh@itu.dk

Louise Barkhuus
Stockholm University
Kista, Sweden
barkhuus@dsv.su.se

Nis Bornoe
Aalborg University
Aalborg Ø, DK
nis@cs.aau.dk

Joseph 'Jofish' Kaye
Yahoo Labs
Sunnyvale CA, USA
jofish@yahoo-inc.com

ABSTRACT
HCI research has explored mobile technologies to support social activity and to support greater feelings of connectedness. Much of this has focused on different mobile devices, individual preferences and modes of use. Yet social activity and connectedness are about ongoing enactments of relationships *across* technologies. We propose the relational lens as a way to include a notion of relational tension in addition to individual preferences in the design and analysis of mobile communication technologies. We discuss three strategies people use to manage tensions in their relationships: *selection, segmentation* and *integration*. Our data show that use of social technologies can at times destabilize social relations and occasion relational tensions, forcing users to renegotiate how they enact these relationships.

Author Keywords
Social network sites; mobile communication; personal relationships; information sharing.

ACM Classification Keywords
H5.m. Information interfaces and presentation (e.g., HCI): Miscellaneous.

INTRODUCTION
Investigations of computational support for connectedness in everyday life have been extensive in HCI and CSCW research [2, 18, 19, 27, 30, 44]. As devices, people, and practices increasingly intermesh, researchers are faced with compounded technical and social challenges. Understanding what connectedness means socially and how people manage technologies that strive to support or even increase connectedness remains crucial. Online social media offer increased possibilities to maintain constant contact. Yet interpersonal interactions continue to be guided by situated strategies that people employ to manage friendships and these strategies often contain conflicting goals and desires [5, 47]. For example, the desire to feel connected to others and yet to maintain a level of autonomy is a common relational tension that people negotiate – a tension that is often challenged by technologies designed for sociability [23, 47].

CSCW '15, March 14 – 18, 2015, Vancouver, BC, Canada.

ACM 978-1-4503-2922-4/15/03...$15.00.
http://dx.doi.org/10.1145/2675133.2675294

Another common contradiction is the tension between the desire to disclose information and to keep it private. What people share, how and with whom, has been an ongoing question of interest in CSCW. Studies of self-disclosure in social media suggest that perceptions of intimacy are affected by how public or private these disclosures are perceived [8]. Research on mobile technologies has considered perceptions of recording or information sharing technologies [34], and assessed when and how users may be willing to share different types of information [43] or to engage their social ties [18]. While research on individual preferences is important, when it comes to social technologies we also need to consider the personal relationships those technologies support as well as the strategies for maintaining those relationships. Research on online relational management mostly focuses on social capital [22], perceptions of disclosure [8] and tensions between sociability and privacy on SNSs [13]. The question remains, what strategies might be used to maintain and negotiate relationships online?

In this paper we use a relational approach based on theories of relational dialectics and relational maintenance [4, 16] to analyze data from a study of Facebook as an empirical case. We focus on how college students engaged with their social ties on Facebook via mobile phones and personal computers in their daily lives. Previous work has explored how students negotiate off-line socializing through online social media [3] and how management of information disclosure can include collaborative as well as individual strategies [31]. Some studies have also utilized aspects of the relational framework but focused on very specific relational types, such as romantic relationships [47] or considered narrow concerns such as privacy [31, 41, 42]. In our work, we expand on these efforts to identify and describe the way college students use Facebook to negotiate, build, groom and maintain friendship. We look at the dynamics of social media use among this group in order to illustrate how a relational lens can be productively used to make sense of online social network use practices.

BACKGROUND
Social media allow people to be connected to one another in new ways and smartphones have made this experience mobile [23]. The ability to bring social ties with us has also meant that remote connections may be able to share in some

aspects of our embodied experiences through the content we share [18]. HCI researchers have stressed that information sharing on social media is not just about accomplishing coordination and collaborative work tasks, but also about enhancing feelings of connectedness and supporting sociability. They have provided new tools to support such social practices, from sharing awareness cues within a couple [2, 27] to producing systems that enhance connectedness through a sense of remote presence among friends and family [19]. Across these approaches, researchers have designed technologies to enhance both peripheral awareness of remote others and direct sharing of experiences with them.

The majority of these technologies rely on the user's willingness to share information about themselves with others. What information people are willing to share, with whom and under what conditions has emerged as a productive area of inquiry in HCI research such as for example identifying purpose-driven and socially-driven practices around location sharing [43]. Several studies have explicitly considered that information sharing preferences might hinge on more than individual desires and concerns and include the role of personal relationships, focusing on role-relationships [10] or relational characteristics such as closeness and frequency of communication [45]. Studies that considered both senders and receivers of communication suggest that the mutual sense of awareness was often achieved through observing others' activities as well as contributing personal information [3, 20]. In fact, users are far more likely to consume information about others than to share their own [37].

Much of the research on information disclosure that takes both sender and recipient into account has focused on information ownership and boundary management practices based on Irwin Altman's privacy regulation theory [1, 41, 42]. Building on the notion that privacy regulation "is a dynamic response to circumstances" [36] this work has explored boundary management as a collaborative process primarily based on interdependent strategies and rules that people develop as a form of relational maintenance [31]. Zhao and colleagues went further, exploring how negotiation of boundary rules happens in a relational context of romantic connections, noting the way participants had to navigate conflicting goals and desires [47].

Understanding what people might share, when and with who hinges on investigations of why people share. Studies of boundary regulation practices have revealed a range of motives for both sharing and boundary regulation but these remain at the level of individual preferences, such as propriety or utility [41]. A wealth of research on self-disclosure on Facebook has utilized Goffman's dramaturgical perspective using concepts of presentation of self, impression management and performance as explanatory tools [20, 46]. This work goes beyond personal preferences, paying attention to the social context of self-disclosure. Hogan [25] questions whether online content can be considered a performance, noting that there is a temporal dimension to online communication on Facebook, which makes it more akin to an exhibit than a performance. Zhao [46] develops this point further highlighting spatial and temporal tensions that people have to negotiate when posting on Facebook. Both impression management and curation are interaction-centered rather than individual-centered approaches, paying attention to the social construction of interaction by both actor and audience as a transactional process.

This recent turn towards considering aspects of the social context of social media use in HCI is important but will remain limited unless we consider relational practice as central to decision-making implicated in online information sharing. Whether or not individuals might feel that particular content may contribute to their definition of self, their decision-making around posting it online for their personal network to consume will also include considerations of the effect this content may have on their relationships. In this paper we present a relational perspective that builds on and expands beyond notions of self-presentation and privacy in relational practice. We show how several basic relational strategies [4, 5, 7] can be productively used to analyze and interpret information-sharing practices on Facebook.

THE RELATIONAL PERSPECTIVE

Social relationships can be construed as stable but never static [24]. Some scholars argue that it is more useful to frame relationships as ongoing dynamic processes where meaning is constructed through communication as people manage tensions and contradictions that arise in everyday relational practice [4]. We refer to processes that involve negotiation of ongoing contradictions and resolutions as *dialectic* [1, 5]. By this, we mean that the aim is not to settle on a single resolution for an issue, but rather to remain in dynamic tension along a given axis, moving back and forth in reaction to situations as these emerge. Baxter and colleagues [4, 5, 7, 14] articulated and developed this idea, originally proposed by Altman [1], by specifying dialectic tensions inherent in relational practice, and identifying specific strategies people use to manage these [4].

Relational dialectics theory is predicated on the idea that relationships are developed and managed through acts of self-disclosure [1,4]. This is a relationship-centered theory where contradiction is a core concept, meaning a dynamic interplay between unified oppositions – two tendencies or forces that are interdependent and mutually negate each other. There is no finite list of contradictions (or dialectical tensions) but researchers seem to consistently agree on three: autonomy-connectedness, novelty-predictability and openness-closedness [4, 5, 33]. Relational partners respond to these contradictions through different strategies. Here we consider three strategies that are commonly identified in the literature: *selection, segmentation* and *integration* [4, 33].

Selection describes instances when people select or prioritize one aspect of the contradiction over the other. For example, people can choose to disclose information (openness), even if they fear or even expect rejection and want to protect themselves (closedness). *Segmentation* refers to instances when people acknowledge and respect activity or content domains that they see as mutually exclusive, such as taking the time to post information about a high school reunion only to the set of friends to whom it is relevant. Finally, *integration* is an attempt to respond simultaneously to both opposing tendencies by neutralizing the content of communication: avoiding the need for *segmentation*, via ambiguity or reduced emotional content of communication.

Baxter's theory of relational dialectics has typically been applied to the study of relational practice at the level of dialogue by analyzing the content of communication and identifying dialectic tensions and coping strategies as these emerge through dialogic interaction [5, 6, 33]. Yet relational practice does not only exist in the moment of communication, but relies on a range of interactive and non-interactive actions that serve to maintain relational continuity [16, 39]. The contribution we make in this paper is in presenting a relational lens, that is rooted in the ideas of relational dialectics, but takes a broader view, paying attention to what people say (post on Facebook) as well as what they describe (their motives sand actions) as they enact relationships.

As people appropriate communication technologies into their daily lives, these technologies often exacerbate or highlight relational tensions [17, 28, 33]. Consider the following example. CoupleVibe [2] was designed for couples as an implicit messaging channel to inform each other about their whereabouts. A partners' location-information was automatically pushed to mobile phones via vibrotactile cues in order to notify unobtrusively when a partner has arrived home. The application supported the couple's desire to feel connected through the sharing of implicit but very intimate information. Bales *et al.* [2] found that long-distance couples indeed experienced feelings of greater connectedness through learning of their partner's activity. However, couples were willing to experience only so much connectedness as an increase in information sharing would have encroached too much on their autonomy. Despite the success of the application, users also expressed discomfort with sharing detailed information with their partners or sharing this information with other close ties. The introduction of Couple-Vibe changed the balance in the connectedness-autonomy dialectic, forcing couples to address an increase in connectedness. The same technology also exacerbated the openness-closedness dialectic. Couples that lived in different time zones turned off the application to allow their partner to sleep in peace. Here participants used *selection* to artfully manage both tensions, utilizing technology in ways that facilitated their partner's autonomy and offered moments of autonomy and closedness to the user.

Relational dialectics proposes that all relationships come into being through "the interplay of conflicting and interconnected forces" which arises from the partners themselves and from the contextual environment where relationships are enacted [4, 33]. In other words, relational tensions are present in all relationships, but the extent of these tensions and the practices for managing them differ [5]. Though not unique, the CoupleVibe example demonstrates how in order to manage relational tensions, people not only negotiate regulation of their personal boundaries, at times being sociable or even dependent on each other and at other times being independent and inaccessible, but also express respect for their partner's boundaries through action [33].

Facebook and the work of relationship maintenance

A social connection expressed on a social networking site can be evidence of a connection that extends beyond the site. Yet, it says nothing about the nature of that connection and the relational work necessary to sustain it. Early studies of Facebook suggested that time spent on the site and attitudes toward it were reasonable predictors of positive social outcomes [21]. Later work by the same authors acknowledged that relational maintenance practices evident on the site are much more complex [22]. Similarly, others have shown that Facebook users experience considerable social tension in the course of their social activity on the site [11].

Relationships are organized through social structures and norms, but they are enacted and continuously renegotiated through actions and interaction that signal commitment and support relational continuity [39]. As relationships develop they can become comfortable and predictable, sustained with infusions of contact and attention, able to withstand substantial upheavals. Yet even in the most stable relationships people generate meaning through interaction and constantly navigate tensions inherent in any relational construct [4]. The process of maintaining relationships relies on interactive as well as non-interactive behaviors [16]. Examples of interactive maintenance may include making a phone call or leaving a comment on a photograph a friend posted online. Browsing the newly uploaded photos, on the other hand, is a form of non-interactive maintenance. Following this logic, we can reframe Facebook use as a range of interactive and non-interactive relational acts. For example, sending a private message or posting on someone's wall is an example of interactive behavior while spending the time to catch up on what your friends post on Facebook can be seen as a non-interactive relationship maintenance behavior.

While there is evidence that people use Facebook for relational maintenance [21, 26], only a few studies have considered what this means in practice [12, 28]. SNSs and an increasing number of mobile social applications enable people to broadcast communication to many social ties at once. People engage in self-disclosure, personal information sharing and exchanges of support that target or at least become visible not just to specific individuals but also to their social networks as a whole [20]. Thus individuals do not just navigate tensions within relationships but also must balance the way each communicative action may become relationally meaningful to all of their social ties simultaneously.

Boyd and Marwick illustrated that teenagers manage a range of relationships on Facebook simultaneously through "social steganography" where the true meaning of a status update or a wall post is "visible" to a limited audience [12]. This is possible because such posts are intentionally obscure and can be interpreted in more than one way. The intended recipients, however, are expected to properly interpret the obscure meanings. Self-disclosure is a necessary part of relational practice, implicated in relational growth and closeness [5, 33]. SNSs and mobile phones could potentially make relational maintenance more efficient and pervasive. At the same time increasing connectedness and accessibility could exacerbate the tensions inherently present within relationships and across increasingly mutually visible networks of connected but disparate relational partners.

In what follows we use an interpretive lens that relies on a combination of theories of relational dialectics and relational maintenance for an analysis of college student's Facebook use practices. We highlight how a relational lens can provide insights into characteristics of electronically mediated friendship. We close with a discussion of what these findings suggest for future designs of social technologies.

METHOD

Although relational dialectic theory was originally developed for analysis of dyadic relationships, it has also been used for research on group interaction [40] and social network maintenance [7, 47]. This theoretical lens can also be productively applied to data collected through more common study designs where each respondent describes a range of their relational practices [28].

The data presented here were collected in the spring and fall of 2010 at a large public university in the Midwest of the US. Although, this might seem to represent 'old' data, for such rapidly changing area as online media, we argue that this specific time was particularly appropriate for such study as ours with college student participants: Facebook was the default and omnipresent social network for college students and a very large proportion of them were active on Facebook [22]. One of our participants admitted that "*sometimes I am so busy that I will not check Facebook for eight hours*", emphasizing the ubiquity of Facebook in these participants' everyday lives. Similarly, the use of college students was deliberate: This particular population lives highly social but also nomadic lives leading to a need and desire for communication technology on the go [3]. Thus college students were a relevant group to investigate, as we wanted to investigate a group that blends social media into their everyday lives, rather than use it sporadically,

One of the authors conducted 48 semi-structured interviews with students at a large public university in the Midwest of the US. None of the authors were affiliated with this university. Instead we chose this site because it was more representative of public universities in the US than our own. We were able to gain access to the site by approaching colleagues at the university and ensuring compliance with their IRB protocols. Participants were recruited using snowball sampling via a range of means including word of mouth, flyers, mailing lists, and Facebook. All participants taking part in an interview received a small monetary compensation in the amount of $10 for their time.

Interview structure

We deliberately selected college students who were frequent users of both mobile phones and Facebook in order to access a group of technically and socially savvy individuals who blended Facebook into their everyday nomadic lives [3]. The semi-structured interviews were conducted in-person and primarily focused on the use of Facebook across platforms (computers and mobile phones) along with more general questions about recent use of Facebook. On average, interviews lasted about 40 minutes.

During the interviews, we asked participants to show us their last ten status updates on their Facebook profiles, and allowed them to show however many they wished. For each status update they explained why they had posted that update and in what context. Browsing the profile during the interview also allowed the participants to show us other aspects of their Facebook use that they found salient. This approach ensured that during the interview we always discussed specific examples aiding memory and recall. All interviews were videotaped. We did not collect or analyze comments on these profiles, as our consent form covered only content produced by the participants themselves, and we felt it would have been unethical to include content produced by individuals who did not participate in our study.

Participants

Of the 48 students in our sample 17 were males and 31 were females, aged between 18 and 29 (mean: 21, SD: 2.3). Most were undergraduates with two at the graduate level. We ensured diversity in our sample by recruiting respondents from a variety of majors including computer science, biology, business, journalism and psychology. All participants used mobile phones to connect to Facebook. Eighteen respondents used mobile access extensively while three interacted with Facebook exclusively through text messaging eschewing other functions. Participants had between 187 and 2939 friends on Facebook (mean: 860, SD: 523). During the interviews, we asked participants to show us at least 10 status updates, but allowed them to show however many they wished. As a result we collected a total of 598 status updates, receiving between 1 and 22 updates from each participant (mean: 12.4, SD: 4.2, median: 11.5).

Analysis

The themes presented in this paper are based on findings that initially emerged through a series of analysis workshops where the research team iteratively stepped through and discussed video-recorded face-to-face interviews. We then narrowed and refined these themes based on data analyzed from extensive field-notes, transcriptions of interview videos and status updates that our respondents chose to share with us. The initial goal of the project was to explore potential differences in how our participants used Facebook from computers and mobile phones. However, our early analysis of the interviews highlighted the way Facebook use seemed to underscore how our participants managed relational tensions across both mobiles and computers, sometimes through the use of the site and sometimes because of its use.

We conducted a content analysis on all collected status updates. Although status updates are not directed and have previously been interpreted as primarily self-oriented [29] more recent work showed both self-presentational and relational aspects present [9]. Two authors conducted an open coding on a sub-sample of 100 status updates separately as a way to develop initial categories. This sub-sample was selected using systematic sampling by randomly selecting status updates, while ensuring the sample contained at least one status update form each respondent. Authors refined the resulting codes through an iterative process of extensive discussion before explicitly defining coding rules. In the course of this discussion, the two authors identified three initial major theoretical categories: forms of relational work (37% i.e. exchanges of support or relational announcements), self-disclosure (53% i.e. posting about completed, ongoing or upcoming activities, expressing feelings or opinions) and media sharing (16%), all of which can be conceptualized as critical components of communicative relational practice. In addition, we noted two more categories: locally relevant (21% i.e. a sorority event or a college party) and obscure (12% i.e. updates with meaning that was not immediately obvious to all or part of the participant's network). About 10% of the updates were announcements or reminders for big local events (i.e. a marathon, a football game), which were coded as a separate category. Upon completion of this initial exercise, one author coded all of the status updates, using the videos of the interviews as a guide to interpretation of the meaning of each status update.

When we coded status updates, we paid close attention to potential differences in the kind of updates our participants might post while mobile and thus potentially more engaged socially. After all, sharing on the go is likely to demand more complex forms of relationship management. We compared the frequency and breadth of content posted from mobile phones and computers, using the Wilcoxon signed rank test to compare the code-frequencies. Although our participants tended to post similar things from both platforms, we noted that a significantly higher proportion of updates from the mobile phone included photos ($z=2.66$, $p<0.01$), while from the computer media sharing was primarily links and videos. Overall, more than 50% of updates were related to disclosing information about the self and engaging in relational work. However, participants posted significantly more about upcoming activities from the computer ($z=-2.01$, $p<0.05$) and about current activities (what I am doing right now) from the mobile phone ($z=2.32$, $p<0.05$). Our analysis, including a Wilcoxon sign test, revealed no gender differences in these patterns. However, our sample size was quite small and it is entirely possible that subtle gender differences would be present in larger populations.

We report here on the major themes using data excerpts to illustrate points, which are reproduced exactly as spoken or written by respondents. Data are denoted by [I] for interview and [S] for status update; participants are anonymized.

FINDINGS

In line with previous work [15], we divide the discussion of Facebook use into content consumption and production.

Consumption of Facebook content

Similar to prior research, [37] our participants spent more time consuming content than posting updates or sharing pictures. One way we could study the reasons behind Facebook usage is to ask 'why' these students used Facebook. Many of our participants commented that the act of consumption of social content was a less important activity, often described as "*empty calories*." Schoenebeck notes that the use of social technologies can carry a stigma of "empty calories" due to media driven moral panics despite potential or real benefits of use [38]. Our data suggest that the practice of filling idle moments with consumption of Facebook content indeed had an underlying *relational* function, explaining in part a consistent pattern of enthusiastic usage.

Facebook feed as entertainment

Social life has high entertainment value especially when this is the social life of friends and acquaintances; there is clearly some explanatory power in understanding Facebook use as entertainment. Mobile use of Facebook was often filling up the spare moments of the day. Our participants called the site "*time filler*" because the social information available for perusal was boundless. Many emphasized appreciation for the quirky humor of people in their feed and the range of information they could stumble upon just by scrolling through. Here, entertainment happened through the experiences, views, and facts shared by one's social ties: "*...it's for the same reason that people find celebrities entertaining and so many gossips [sic]. It's like reading about other people's life, especially when you know them, it's just really entertaining but also if there is a sports game and you missed it or something you know everyone is posting about the scores and stuff so its just good to stay updated on my world*" (JB, 20, [I]).

While many referred to browsing through the news feed as a form of entertainment, the quote above highlights another important point. Along with enjoying the social minutiae of the feed, JB used it to get caught up on the important social and cultural events she may have missed as well as to keep track of the activities of her network. She also demonstrated a kind of contradiction when she equated her feed to something similar to a "*celebrity watch*" while pointing out that this was a way "*to stay updated on my world*".

Browsing the feed as a way to maintain friendships

While browsing the feed may have been described as a time filler and entertainment, it seemed to often function as a non-interactive relational maintenance strategy. Our participants voraciously consumed the social information available in their feed or got lost in friends' photos. Yet they were also aware that this was important for their relationships: "*It is sort of having a conversation with one of your friends except not really right, but if you just want to talk to somebody and you can't the next best thing I suppose you can do is read a message from someone and when you are reading Facebook that is essentially what you are doing. Reading these little snippets of people, you know, things they want to share with whoever you know and you read it*" (JP, 27, [I].) This evocative quote illustrates the relational value of perusing the feed. Whereas reading the feed was entertaining, posting to the feed was a much more considered act of self-disclosure. Self-disclosure is a necessary part of relational practice, implicated in relational growth and closeness [16]. Yet the very act of self-disclosure is predicated on the fact that information is disclosed to someone who is interested in it. By "*reading the little snippets of people*" our participants were validating acts of self-disclosure performed by their contacts.

Reading the feed then was relational work to stay updated on what other people are doing, engaging what they wanted to share and at times acknowledging it. For college students, being in the know was vitally important and reading the feed was the necessary background work for relational maintenance: "*...what is everybody else doing that might affect me [...] what are the guys I hangout with doing... if they are going to the game... can I... should I?*" (SA, 21, [I]). This is an example of how non-interactive maintenance strategies can become crucial for managing the connectedness-autonomy dialectic and navigating desires and necessities of sociability. It seems apparent that this *need* to know is not well characterized by mere entertainment but rather it is part of a deeper sense of ongoing and valuable relationships. Not only did the feed serve as a source of relevant social information, it could also provide important lubrication for interactive relational maintenance activities in the future: "*Newsfeed works as a sort of small talk starter, see what he or she did*" (SP, 27, [I].) Knowing a little bit in advance could make further discovery of another person a simpler task, but knowing too much could get creepy highlighting the use of *selection* to manage a novelty-predictability dialectic in relational practice. Thus what happened on Facebook was a kind of strategic sharing of social information and users built up expectations that their content would be read and understood as part of their relational maintenance practices.

Posting content on Facebook

Along with Facebook content consumption, our participants also posted a substantial amount of content from both computers and mobile phones. In this section, we focus primarily on the tendency to share the current experience (the now) as the most relevant example of relational practice.

Sharing the now

Our respondents shared future plans from the computer, but preferred sharing their current ongoing experiences from their mobile phones. Mobile phone status updates tended to be grounded in the now, defined by the present time or moment. Many referred to mundane experiences of eating out, school activities, made commentaries on the weather or annoyance with fire alarms: "*Eating at Eddie George's Grille in* [city]. *(photo)*" (SA, 21, [S]); "*this weather is amazing!*" (NC, 19, [S]);

As the majority of photos were posted from the mobile phones, we examined these closely, noting that most were of little anomalies – things just slightly out of the mundane and ordinary that people encountered while traversing physical places, such as commenting on a badly dressed individual with "*What a GEETUS!*[1] [photo]" (NC, 19, [S].) These little anomalies, shared with the Facebook network through text and pictures, were contextually situated, often requiring some relevant local knowledge and awareness of the local context to be correctly interpreted. At the same time they could be evocative and of interest to distant contacts.

At times, mobile updates were examples of sharing personal experiences as well as inclusions of friends in the pictures, links and text. "*Maggie & I at the homecoming game* [photo]" (CS, 21, [S].) Some updates were telling a shared history that could target parts of or the entire network. "*It looks like Jack-Leeeeen's birthday!!* [picture of refrigerator]" (NC, 19, [S].) Several updates were posted precisely because they somehow connected the current experience with some portion of the remote audience, bringing those far away into the conversation: "*Hey jess??? No it's just your twin from behind... creepy* [photo tagged]" (HB, 19, [S].) As this participant explained that while at a cafe with her college friends, she saw a woman that looked "*identical to my friend from back home, so I took a picture and tagged my friend from home and all my friends were all like oh my gosh it is totally her!*" (HB, 19, [I].)

Although these students rarely interacted in person with the vast majority of their Facebook connections many of their connections were local to the university. The "now" status updates illustrated strategies for maintaining remote connectedness by posting "*little snippets of people*" (JP, 27 [I]) while retaining autonomy by limiting this sharing to activity with very few instances of disclosure of location (just 3 of the 164 updates were explicitly named locations). Several students commented that they would not disclose their location in such updates because "*I would be afraid of who would show up*" (AE, 21 [I]) nor would they meet people based on location disclosed in a status update because "*that would be way too creepy*" (AK, 19 [I]). This differed significantly from postings made from computers, which often included announcements for large upcoming events or entreaties to participate in various college activities.

Controlled Spontaneity

Mobile phones enabled sharing of spontaneous expressions of wonder and emotion, highlights of mundane details, notifi-

---

[1] According to the Urban Dictionary "geetus" is a slang word that refers to "a stupid, dorky person. Usually someone you know who repeatedly displays this behavior." http://www.urbandictionary.com/define.php?term=geetus

cations of being someplace or attending an event and sharing the experience with others: "*More immediate responses. I can write statuses as soon as I can, I do that a lot more. More spontaneous*" (SX, 20, [I].) Much of this activity was spontaneous in the sense that sharing these moments wasn't planned far in advance. At the same time, there was much thought and deliberateness behind every post: "*Anything that I post, I am careful about that*" (HL, 21, [I].) Participants thought deeply about what to share, when and how – a practice we termed *controlled spontaneity.* At times this deliberateness stemmed from efforts of impression management: "*I put a lot of thought into everything that I put on my profile because I want people to look at it and see the me that I want them to see*" (SL, 21, [I].) Yet this practice was also critiqued: "*Posting pictures on Facebook, especially Mobile Uploads are like a caption contest in on itself. Who won on your News Feed today? :)*" (KW, 25, [S].)

It is tempting to interpret behavior on Facebook exclusively from the point of view of self-presentation, vanity or kinds of exhibits of the self [25]. Our study participants spoke of their Facebook use in similar terms where self-presentation and deliberate performance are underscored in seeing pictures on Facebook as a "*caption contest.*" Yet online self-presentation itself is a kind of relational practice [35]. These students put a lot of thought into information that they shared, because they were also managing the level of openness of their relationships that were represented on Facebook: "*Don't put things in status like that, more serious things because I want to keep in contact with acquaintances, like people from High School*" (SX, 20, [I].). Our participants were so thoughtful about online content production because they were managing simultaneous dialectics of openness-closedness and connectedness-autonomy in deciding whether, what and how to share with their Facebook networks. They performed *selection* where acts of sharing prioritized openness and connectedness over closedness and autonomy. This selective self-disclosure served to groom their relationships, not just to present themselves in a particular fashion. This suggests that regardless of connectivity or having the right filter settings each act of sharing is also about managing relational tensions.

Sharing just the right amount

Could sharing the now be simply a "look how cool I am" kind of activity? Most participants deliberately disclosed only the information they found suitable for the entire network. When considering what to post they explained that they relied on 'commonsense' so as not to 'overshare': "*it is sort of a way to share part of your life yet not too much because that is a little creepy*" (SA, 21, [I]) Sometimes, however, a different part of life impinged on information sharing practices forcing changes in posting routines. For example, one participant got actively involved in geocaching but by posting many status updates related to that activity she had broken the unwritten rule of posting too much content irrelevant to most of her network: "*I noticed that I post about geocaching and 4-H* [youth volunteer organization] *a lot and so I lose friends because they don't want to be hearing about these things*" (JF, 25, [I].) Note that she spoke of literally "*losing*" her friends, a far more serious concern than just getting complaints. To manage this emergent dialectic of openness-closedness she used *segmentation* by posting through different networks: "*Most of my status updates I actually customize who they are going out to so this one is only going out to 4-H people [...] I usually try to make sure that when I am sending out any message that they are audience specific*" (JF, 25, [I]). Yet such explicit *segmentation* was rare among our participants who often simply limited how much content they shared.

Snippets of conversations

Mobile status updates shared one other quality that caught our attention. A subset of statuses we coded as "obscure", as these required significant discussion with the participants to decipher meaning. These were obscure statements, obscure references to local landmarks, strings of numbers, single words, passionate expressions, inside jokes, random smartphone pictures, questions, requests and complaints:

"*1 year...lovin it. :)*" (KH, 21, [S]), she and her boyfriend had their one-year anniversary. "*yayy new baby turtles :)*" (SO, 20, [S]), a reference to a crop of new sorority recruits. "*26.2 26.2 26.2 26.2*" (HL, 21 [S]), expressing excitement about an upcoming marathon.

These status updates required context and explanation because they did not represent accessible communication to the full social network. Instead these updates were deeply meaningful to the interlocutors, but potentially taken out of context and perhaps even boring or nonsense to the rest of the network. By posting a status that was intelligible and interesting to a subset of the network, our participants reinforced their relationships with that subset. At the same time, they risked alienating the subset of the network for who the status was unintelligible, much as our participant JF did with geocaching. By using vague and obscure statements our participants actively negotiated the level of openness through messages that appeared cryptic. Even when the post was deliberately intended as an inside joke many of our participants tried to "*post things that more than one person will get*" (AE, 21, [I]) in order to involve as many contacts as possible and to avoid accidentally "*losing*" them.

Similar to the behavior described by Ding *et al.* [20], students crafted messages for different audiences at the same time. Yet some of these updates seemed to follow the logical progression of conversations started in some other context and medium. Consider this status update as an example: "*J.* [...], *Y.* [...] *was this what/who you guys saw that's blue? (photo Mobile Uploads)*" (KW, 25, [S].) Here the status update was a direct question to recent conversation partners. What we encountered here were multimodal conversations, continued over a period of time, with thoughts, emotions and ideas transmitted via whatever most convenient medium at hand. Increased connectedness via social media meant that colocation was no longer required for continuing a conversation. Greater connectedness then in some ways facilitated greater autonomy while managing the openness-closedness dialectic and illustrating a curious form of *integration*. At times a turn or two of these conversations would surface as an update on Facebook, as if allowing the rest of the network to overhear friends talking and perhaps even to join in. Such snippets of conversations had short-lived meaningful lives. Even just a few days later, when coming back to these updates during interviews, participants reflected how inside jokes, funny "*at the time*", were not really funny anymore and bereft of context.

At times, status updates with unclear messages remained obscure to the entire network. For example, one participant posted "*something is missing :/*" (BP, 20 [S]) that, as she explained, was not clear to anyone in her network, but was posted "*just to see people's reactions*" (BP, 20 [I]). She had felt sad that she didn't have a boyfriend after watching a romantic movie alone. Her status update elicited a lot of commentary that, as she explained was "just really funny" as a kind of friendly banter. This is an example of *integration* dealing with the openness-closedness dialectic, a kind of social sharing without needing to explain herself in detail to anyone. Here the tension between disclosure of potentially embarrassing information (crying when watching a romantic movie) and the desire for companionship and comfort were managed through neutralizing the shared information and using ambiguous statements to elicit response while leaving the cause open to discussion.

The 'now' was deeply meaningful and relevant when shared, but it was often only meaningful in the moment and could loose its color and flavor over time. While there were postings that were regarded as memories to hang on to, much of the action on Facebook, especially the content posted from mobile phones, seemed to be about sharing in the immediacy of experiencing, engaging and relating, relevant only at that moment but always carefully constructed to manage relational tensions inherent in Facebook use. Some of our participants even went so far as to remove old status updates from their wall because, as they explained in interviews, these were no longer relevant to their current experience. These participants enacted a kind of ephemerality to their Facebook interactions – in some ways antithetical to the very design of the SNS – in order to produce an ongoing rather than an archival set of practices.

DISCUSSION

As our world becomes more interconnected, it is important to understand how people are appropriating communication technologies. We show that social interactions can continue across communication platforms as people engage in different tasks with different technologies throughout the day, rather than being neatly contained in a particular piece of software on a specific platform. This sort of interleaving of technology and conversations will likely become more common and more complex. The mobile phone is an addition and an extension of social platforms, and it offered students in our study an easy and often irresistible way to check Facebook during micro-breaks or unexpected moments of idleness. Keeping up with the experience that their friends had chosen to share was both entertainment and a kind of social grooming.

Applying a relational lens to online communication

By utilizing the concept of relational dialectics we propose that apparent contradictions in human behavior are a feature and not a bug and treat these contradictions as necessary, dynamic and omnipresent parts of life. People may say they want one thing and behave in ways that accomplish an opposite result. They may consider two things incompatible and then find a way to reframe these into a complimentary match. The relational approach underscores that when people adopt new technologies offering new ways to interact or connect, these technologies necessarily alter the pre-existing practices of managing relational tensions. The identified dialectics of openness-closedness, connection-autonomy and novelty-predictability can be managed through the strategies of *integration, selection and segmentation* and these suggest ways to support and mitigate the subsequent renegotiation of relational contradictions. For example, when building for connectedness, it is important to remember that the desire for connectedness is but one part of an attendant dialectic inherent in relationships, and we need to also support the attendant desire for autonomy.

Baxter's three strategies for managing dialectic tensions [4, 5, 7, 14] allowed us to articulate and make sense of the ways our participants shared the "now" with their Facebook audiences. For example, a geocaching enthusiast used *segmentation* as a strategy to manage sharing content with different parts of the network, selecting via Facebook's controls which of her contacts could see particular status updates. SNS developers have put a considerable amount of effort into solutions to deal with such a problem. Google's 'circles' or Facebook's 'lists' support explicit *segmentation*. Prior studies have found that people increasingly use segmentation tools as they become better designed and easy to configure [32]. Admittedly at the time of our study this functionality was less developed on Facebook. However, recent studies show that the lists and circles still receive limited use and the vast majority of content is posted to the "lowest common denominator" of audience [8]. Our participant felt she was forced to resort to this strategy because she had started "losing" friends, which is a pretty extreme perception of the situation. Yet the types of status updates that needed to be posted for a select group of people were simple to identify–anything that had to do with geocaching. The audience, too, was easy to segment–geocaching friends. Such clear lines of separation are rarely present in most everyday cases and *segmentation* then requires significant cognitive effort. Putting the onus of *segmentation* on the users is clearly a useful feature for some but only in very specific situations. Instead, most participants relied on *integration*–such as using obscure language–or *selection*–often achieved through self-censorship of posted content.

As our participants interacted with their friends they at times interleaved different modalities into ongoing conversations. Their Facebook use reflected this with status updates and other forms of information sharing shifting between content oriented toward the whole network and content that was directed at specific people. This was more prevalent in the mobile phone updates perhaps because the content here tended to arise from selected moments of the ongoing embodied experience. This was an artful way to manage the connectedness-autonomy and openness-closedness dialectics through *selection* and *integration*. This kind of occasional drawing in of proximal and remote friends into casual conversation on the site rather than in an SMS or in an in-person conversation provides an explanation for the irresistible draw of Facebook that makes relational sense and suggests potential avenues for design.

Designing with relationships in mind

As our digital networks grow more diverse and interconnected, the balancing act of relational dialectics becomes ever more challenging. The relational lens suggests that in designing social software we must keep in mind that shifts and destabilizations in existing contradictions are unavoidable, but there are ways to support managing these contradictions through provision of tools or capabilities that offer at least one of the three types of coping approaches described here. For example the recently deployed stand-alone Facebook messenger app has location disclosure turned on by default – a detail that may problematize the strategy of *integration* through steganography. The assumption that users would want to broadcast their physical location because they are engaging with Facebook via the mobile phone is at odds with the connectedness-autonomy dialectic. This suggests that location disclosure must be made clear at the point of composing the status update, offering ways to manage granularity of such disclosure.

Despite the pervasive impression of Facebook use as "empty calories" and entertainment, perpetuated by the media, our participants also acknowledged its importance in "staying updated" on their social worlds. Yet the current design of many SNSs privileges the entertainment and "popularity contest" factor of content which may interfere with relational practice by deprioritizing less popular status updates and thus rendering them less visible. Relational dialectics suggests the need to manage openness-closedness from both sides: I may be annoyed by too much self-disclosure from my contacts in my feed just as much as I worry about annoying them with my own update frequency. While getting too much information about someone may be creepy, not seeing updates from friends at all is an even worse social faux pas. So perhaps a mode of browsing social media can be developed to accommodate the desire for an "update on your social world" by showing the latest or most popular recent update from each friend with an option to see more updates from the more prolific friends in situ.

LIMITATIONS

As an inductive qualitative project, we were not concerned with universal generalizability of our results. Rather, our goal was to show how a relational lens could be applied to data on students' use of Facebook, from their point of view, through detailed descriptions of their actions and thoughts. While the use of college students in research has a long (and varied) history in research, we remain cautious about generalization of particulars outside of a similar sample. Facebook's user base has expanded vastly since the completion of data collection for this study, as has the use of SNS on mobile phones. Future research would need to consider diverse samples of participants to identify whether and how Facebook and other social media use may be implicated in relational practices further. College students in this sample represent a population in a life stage when social relationships are in a considerable flux. Decades of prior research on relational practices among adults of a range of ages suggest that while Baxter's dialectic tensions are commonly present throughout life span, people's strategies for managing these tensions may manifest differently. Although applications of the relational lens to more diverse samples in future research is imperative, we feel that even with such a limited sample our study successfully demonstrates the importance and utility of this approach.

CONCLUSIONS

Communication technologies continue to develop toward support of seamless connectivity in people's daily lives. Yet the very idea of connectedness relies on people having relationships. After all, in order to be connected we need people with whom to connect. Connectedness itself is about ongoing enactments and performances of relating and relationships. It follows then that in order to design technologies that support connectedness it is crucial to consider designing for both individuals *and* relationships, which means recognizing the carefully crafted ways in which people actively negotiate the relational tensions in their multiple and overlapping social networks.

We apply the relational lens to the analysis of a study on Facebook use. When our study participants shared the "moments of now" with their Facebook friends, they were also performing a kind of public broadcasting of their point of view of ongoing events in their immediate physical space. This type of sharing could strain existing relational tensions within their social networks and they employed *selection, integration* and *segmentation* as self-disclosure strategies designed to address emergent dialectics.

Some might say we are making an artificial distinction between designing for individuals and designing for relationships, bringing as an example of the former features such as individual differences in psychological makeup or personal preferences. However, personal preferences are precisely geared towards relational management. After all, managing one's online presence is an important aspect of modulating one's social relationships as everything we do that has an interface to the outer world does have social valence. The question then is whether the relational perspective that we present is substantially different from the more individual perspective expressed in previous work, and if so, how might this be reflected in the design of social technologies?

Our answer is that the management of relational tensions is based on individual decisions before it is mediated by technology, and much of this management is rooted in meanings and connections, which are contextually grounded in and emerge through interaction. Relational dialectics is rooted in the idea that relationships are constituted through communication because it is in the instances of interaction where relational partners negotiate the nature of their relationships. Individuals (including their preferences, presence, etc.) do remain, so to speak, the bottleneck and the primary focus of social modulation. Yet why individuals make certain decisions and engage in particular relational acts is best understood when the form and content of relational practice is taken into account. We believe our findings can be used to identify opportunities that would better support individuals in their relational work through social media.

Our approach demonstrates that connectedness is about negotiating a need for autonomy, managing awkwardness, and exploiting "in the moment" sharing to speak to many audiences at once without overstepping boundaries. Current HCI research is deeply concerned with users and their needs. Domain analysis often looks at individual preferences resulting in limited options that cover potential use scenarios. In this paper we have introduced a set of self-disclosure strategies, but in the context of relationship maintenance. We have shown that social networking technologies can destabilize social relations and cause tensions forcing users to renegotiate how they enact these relationships. Paying attention to the relational work users must do as they adapt the new technologies in their relational practice would enable HCI researchers to develop new sets of requirements for iterating on their designs. The relational context underscores the idea that where there is a desire for connectedness and openness there is also simultaneously a desire for autonomy and closedness. For example, technologies that privilege information sharing necessarily tip the balance forcing people to develop new ways of managing autonomy and closedness which could range from non-use to joint efforts at renegotiation the meaning of disclosure.

As we design for social connectedness through device interconnectivity, we perhaps should consider that every interactional or non-interactional communicative act not only influences sociability in the moment but also affects the nature of future interactions. The relational view forces us to conceive of social relationships not as static constructs with predictable features, but as an ongoing dynamic process that involves nuanced management of relational tensions.

Relational dialectics brings to the fore the pushes and pulls implicated in online communication and offers an alternative to the perplexing conundrum of differences between stated preferences and subsequent action. If we accept G. H. Mead's idea that "selves can only exist in defined relationship to other selves" [c.f. 20] then understanding of social action necessarily requires a more holistic view, which can be better achieved through the use of a relational lens.

ACKNOWLEDGMENTS

This research was funded by Nokia Research and NSF grant IIS-0917401. We are indebted to all of our respondents for their generous participation in our study. We thank anonymous reviewers for extensive and constructive feedback that helped us improve this paper considerably.

REFERENCES

1. Altman, I. (1975) *The environment and social behavior: Privacy, personal space, territory, crowding.* Brooks/Cole, Monterey, CA.
2. Bales, E., Li, K. & Griwsold, W. CoupleVIBE: mobile implicit communication to improve awareness for (long-distance) couples. In *Proceedings of CSCW* (Hangzhou, China, 2011). ACM
3. Barkhuus, L. & Tashiro, J. Student socialization in the age of facebook. In *Proceedings of CHI* (Atlanta, Georgia, 2010). ACM
4. Baxter, L. (1988) A dialectical perspective on communication strategies in relationship development. In S. Duck (Ed). *Handbook of personal relationships: Theory, research, & interventions.* Wiley, New York.
5. Baxter, L. (1990) Dialectical Contradictions in Relationship Development. *Journal of Social and Personal Relationships*, 7, 1, 69-88.
6. Baxter, L. (2004) Relationships as dialogues. *Personal Relationships*, 11, 1, 1-22.
7. Baxter, L. & Widenmann, S. (1993) Revealing & Not Revealing Status of Romantic Relationships to Social Networks. *Jou. of Soc. & Pers. Rels*, 10, 3, 321-337.
8. Bazarova, N. Contents and contexts: disclosure perceptions on facebook. In *Proceedings of CSCW* (Seattle, Washington, 2012). ACM
9. Bazarova, N., Taft, J., Choi, Y. & Cosley, D. (2013) Managing Impressions and Relationships on Facebook: Self-Presentational and Relational Concerns Revealed Through the Analysis of Language Style. *Journal of Language and Social Psychology*, 32, 2, 121-141.
10. Biehl, J., Rieffel, E. & Lee, A. (2012) When privacy and utility are in harmony: towards better design of presence technologies. *Personal and Ubiquitous Comput.*, 1-16.
11. Binder, J., Howes, A. & Sutcliffe, A. The problem of conflicting social spheres: Effects of network structure on experienced tension in social network sites. In *Proceedings of CHI* (Boston, MA, 2009). ACM
12. boyd, d. & Marwick, A. Social Privacy in Networked Publics: Teens' Attitudes, Practices, and Strategies. A *Decade in Internet Time* (Oxford, UK, 2011)
13. Brandtzæg, P., Luders, M. & Skjetne, J. (2010) Too Many Facebook "Friends"? Content Sharing & Sociability Versus the Need for Privacy in Social Network Sites. *Internat. Jour. of HCIs*, 26, 11-12, 1006-1030.

14. Bridge, K. & Baxter, L. (1992) Blended relationships: Friends as work associates. *Western Journal of Communication*, 56, 3, 200-225.
15. Burke, M., Kraut, R. & Marlow, C. Social capital on facebook: differentiating uses and users. In *Proceedings of CHI* (Vancouver, BC, Canada, 2011).
16. Canary, D. & Stafford, L. (1994) Maintaining relationships through strategic & routine interaction. In D. Canary & L. Stafford (Ed). *Communication & rela-tional maintenance*. Academic Press, San Diego, CA.
17. Choi, B., Jiang, Z. & Yap, E. Information Sharing in Online Dyadic Exchange: A Relational Dialectic Perspective. In *Proceedings of HICSS* (2012). IEEE
18. Consolvo, S., Smith, I., Matthews, T., Lamarca, A., Tabert, J. & Powledge, P. Location disclosure to social relations: why, when, & what people want to share. In *Proceedings of CHI* (2005). ACM
19. Dey, A. & Guzman, E. From awareness to connectedness: the design and deployment of presence displays. In *Proceedings of CHI* (Montreal, Quebec, Canada, 2006).
20. Ding, X., Erickson, T., Kellogg, W. & Patterson, D. (2012) Informing and performing: investigating how mediated sociality becomes visible. *Personal Ubiquitous Comput.*, 16, 8, 1095-1117.
21. Ellison, N., Steinfield, C. & Lampe, C. (2007) The benefits of Facebook "friends:" Social capital & college students' use of online social network sites. *Journal of Computer-Mediated Communication*, 12, 4, 1143-1168.
22. Ellison, N., Steinfield, C. & Lampe, C. (2011) Connection strategies: Social capital implications of Facebook-enabled communication practices. *New Media & Society*, 13, 6, 873-892.
23. Harper, R. (2010) *Texture: Human expression in the age of communications overload*. MIT, Cambridge, MA.
24. Hays, R. B. (1988) Friendship. In S. Duck (Ed). *Handbook of personal relationships: Theory, research, and interventions*. Wiley, New York.
25. Hogan, B. (2010) The Presentation of Self in the Age of Social Media: Distinguishing Performances and Exhibitions Online. *Bulletin of Science,Technology & Society*, 30, 6, 377-386.
26. Joinson, A. Looking at, looking up or keeping up with people?: motives and use of facebook. *In Proceedings of CHI* (Florence, Italy, 2008). ACM
27. Kaye, J. J. I just clicked to say I love you: rich evaluations of minimal communication. In *CHI '06 extended abstracts*. ACM
28. Kim, K.-H. & Yun, H. (2007) Cying for Me, Cying for Us: Relational Dialectics in a Korean Social Network Site. *Jour. of Comp.-Mediated Comm.*, 13, 1, 298-318.
29. Kramer, A. & Chung, C. Dimensions of Self-Expression in Facebook Status Updates. *In pro. of ICWSM* (2011)
30. Kranz, M., Holleis, P. & Schmidt, A. (2010) Embedded Interaction: Interacting with the Internet of Things. *Internet Computing, IEEE*, 14, 2, 46-53.
31. Lampinen, A., Lehtinen, V., Lehmuskallio, A. & Tamminen, S. We're in it together: interpersonal management of disclosure in social network services. In *Proceedings of CHI* (Vancouver, Canada, 2011).
32. Lindtner, S., Chen, J., Hayes, G. & Dourish, P. (2011) Towards a framework of publics: Re-encountering media sharing and its user. *ACM Trans. Comput.-Hum. Interact.*, 18, 2, 1-23.
33. Montgomery, B. (1993) Relationship Maintenance versus Relationship Change: A Dialectical Dilemma. *Journal of Social & Personal Relationships*, 10, 2, 205-223.
34. Nguyen, D. & Hayes, G. (2010) Information privacy in institutional and end-user tracking and recording technologies. *Personal & Ubiquitous Comp.*, 14, 1, 53-72.
35. O'Sullivan, B. (2000) What you don't know won't hurt me. *Human Communication Research*, 26, 3, 403-431.
36. Palen, L. & Dourish, P. Unpacking "privacy" for a networked world. In *Proceedings of CHI* (Ft. Lauderdale, Florida, USA, 2003). ACM
37. Pempek, T., Yermolayeva, Y. & Calvert, S. (2009) College students' social networking experiences on Facebook. *Jour. of App. Dev. Psych.*, 30, 3, 227-238.
38. Schoenebeck, S. Y. Giving up Twitter for Lent: how and why we take breaks from social media. In *Proceedings of CHI* (Toronto, Canada, 2014). ACM
39. Sigman, S. (1991) Handling discontinuous aspects of continuing social relationships: Toward research on the persistence of social forms. *Comm. Theory*, 1, 106-127.
40. Smith, K. K. & Berg, D. N. (1987) *Paradoxes of group life: Understanding conflict, paralysis, and movement in group dynamics*. Jossey-Bass, San Francisco.
41. Stutzman, F. & Hartzog, W. Boundary regulation in social media. In *Proceedings of CSCW* (Seattle, Washington, 2012). ACM
42. Stutzman, F. & Kramer-Duffield, J. Friends only: examining a privacy-enhancing behavior in facebook. In *Proceedings of CHI* (Atlanta, Georgia, 2010). ACM
43. Tang, K., Lin, J., Hong, J., Siewiorek, D. & Sadeh, N. Rethinking location sharing: exploring the implications of social-driven vs. purpose-driven location sharing. In *Proceedings of Ubicomp* (Copenhagen, DK, 2010).
44. Tollmar, K., Sandor, O. & Schömer, A. Supporting social awareness @ work design and experience. In *Proceedings of CSCW* (Boston, MA, 1996). ACM
45. Wiese, J., Kelley, P., Cranor, L., Dabbish, L., Hong, J. & Zimmerman, J. Are you close with me? are you nearby?: investigating social groups, closeness, and willingness to share. In *Proceedings of Ubicomp* (Beijing, China, 2011). ACM
46. Zhao, X., Salehi, N., Naranjit, S., Alwaalan, S., Voida, S. & Cosley, D. The many faces of facebook: experiencing social media as performance, exhibition, and personal archive. In *Proceedings of CHI* (Paris, France, 2013). ACM
47. Zhao, X., Sosik, V. & Cosley, D. It's complicated: how romantic partners use facebook. In *Proceedings of CHI* (Austin, Texas, USA, 2012). ACM

Clinical Questions in Online Health Communities: The Case of "See your doctor" Threads

Jina Huh
Department of Media and Information
Michigan State University
jinahuh@msu.edu

ABSTRACT
Online health communities are known to provide psychosocial support. However, concerns for misinformation being shared around clinical information persist. An existing practice addressing this concern includes monitoring and, as needed, discouraging asking clinical questions in the community. In this paper, I examine such practice where moderators redirected patients to see their health care providers instead of consulting the community. I observed that, contrary to common beliefs, community members provided constructive tips and persuaded the patients to see doctors rather than attempting to make a diagnosis or give medical advice. Moderators' posts on redirecting patients to see their providers were highly associated with no more follow up replies, potentially hindering active community dynamic. The findings showed what is previously thought of as a solution—quality control through moderation—might not be best and that the community, in coordination with moderators, can provide critical help in addressing clinical questions and building constructive information sharing community environment.

Author Keywords
Online health communities; moderators

ACM Classification Keywords
H.5.2 User Interfaces, J.3 Life and Medical Sciences, Medical information systems

General Terms
Design

INTRODUCTION
The canonical role of online health communities discussed in the literature includes providing psychosocial support, where peer patients exchange emotional, informational, and appraisal support [23,24,28]. Websites' policies generally discourage the sharing of clinical advice [40,41,42] due to liability issues. Although medical professionals agree with psychosocial benefits of online health communities, they are still concerned with potential misinformation being shared among patients [20].

CSCW '15, March 14 - 18 ,2015, Vancouver, BC, Canada.
Copyright 2014 ACM 978-1-4503-2922-4/15/03…$15.00.
http://dx.doi.org/10.1145/2675133.2675259

This perception against potential misinformation around clinical questions is also reflected in moderators' roles in online health communities. In addition to moderators' positive, facilitating roles for building online communities, moderators also shy people away from asking for uncensored medical advice from the community by redirecting patients to see their providers instead of consulting the community [17]. Such response might discourage further participation by community members on the thread because the moderator has declared clinical questions, such as those requiring diagnosis or prescription of medications, are not something the community should answer. The possible assumption embedded in this practice is that patients have not consulted their providers when they ask clinical questions; patients want easy and quick diagnosis from the Internet; and peer patients might respond with health information they are not equipped to provide.

However, moderators might not know that patients already have seen or are planning to see their providers about the issue. Patients might want to talk to peer patients and receive additional information beyond just a diagnosis, empowering themselves as informed patients. Community's peer-knowledge has a great potential to provide such information, including patients' experiential knowledge largely unavailable in traditional clinical settings offered by health care providers.

In this paper, I challenge the widespread notion that online health communities are not an appropriate place to receive clinical help. I studied cases of online health community conversation threads where moderators redirected patients to see their providers instead of talking to the community. By studying these threads, I was able to investigate the context of the patients' clinical questions and how these questions are handled in the community by the moderators and peer patients. Furthermore, I learned how to better manage patients' clinical questions in online communities by observing what worked and did not work.

My overall goal is to examine how peer patients' and moderators' roles should be in addressing clinical questions in online health communities. To get to this goal, I examine current practice around threads where moderators redirect patients' clinical questions. My specific research questions are as follows: (1) In what contexts do moderators redirect patients to see their providers? (2) How do other community members work with moderators in this context? (3) How does the moderator redirecting patients to see providers relate to the patients' and other community members' participation with the community? The results will contribute to the state of clinical information sharing in online health communities from a quality control standpoint. Further, the findings will shed light on online health community development, specifically in defining the roles of moderators and the community members in providing help to patients' clinical questions.

BACKGROUND

The role of community members in online health communities has been discussed as researchers presented social and clinical effectiveness of online health communities. Maloney-Krichmar and Preece [25] found strong group norms and reciprocity, membership, and strong sub-groups as critical elements in building sustainable community that positively influences members' offline lives. Frost and Massagli [12] studied patientslikeme.com and found that members who shared similar health conditions benefited from each other through questions and answers. The authors further emphasized the importance of patients' sharing health information, which worked as a catalyst for peer patient support in their case. Hartzler et al [14] have been investigating mechanisms to match peer-mentors who can provide well-coordinated support among peers. Peers' emotional support has been shown to satisfy cancer patients' questions regardless of their purpose and content [36] and further prolong community participation compared to information support [38].

Select online health communities use moderators—an external governance, such as health professionals and staff moderators who moderate community discussions. Literature shows mixed perspectives toward the role of online health community moderators. Maloney-Krichmar and Preece [25] found that strong group norms made externally driven governance, such as moderators, unnecessary, further illustrating the importance of community members' roles over moderators. A randomized controlled trial showed that peer mentors were significantly more effective than nurse mentors in improving diabetes [16].

Other researchers, however, found moderator roles as helpful for online health community dynamic. Resnick et al. [31] found staff moderators facilitating online health forum to be crucial in moving lurkers into posters and bootstrapping an active community. Through a meta-analysis, Eysenbach [9] found that most studies of online health communities showing clinical effectiveness involved health professionals—the external moderators—making it difficult to tease out the effectiveness of "pure" peer to peer support on the outcomes. Huh et al. [17] studied moderators' roles in WebMD online health communities and found that moderators went beyond purely moderating the community content and attempted to build rapport and supply useful resources to the patient members. At the same time, moderators redirected patients to see their doctors instead of consulting the community. Such moderators' acts contrast with other kinds of moderating practices, because these acts could drive members away from the community.

According to the literature so far, the role of community members has been heavily focused on psychosocial support [2,27,32], whereas the role of moderators has been focused on dealing with misinformation and community management in general [8,25,39]. Such dichotomous roles between community members and moderators place moderators as those who should play the "policing" roles, where moderators have to prune discussions that potentially produce misinformation. The canonical policing situation occurs when patients ask for medical advice or diagnosis, which could potentially result in misinformation if answered by non-health professionals. However, I do not know how such moderation impacts the constructive sharing of health information in online health communities and the dynamic among the community members. How other community members—who are known to focus in socially supportive roles—work with such situation is also unknown.

In this paper, I address such gap in the literature around dichotomous roles of peer patients and moderators around clinical questions. I challenge the notion that peer patients' help is only beneficial in the case of psychosocial support. To do this, I examine the threads handling clinical questions that the moderator evaluates as something the community could not immediately answer. I will then study how clinical questions can be handled both by moderators and peer patients, maximizing the benefit of peer patients in online health communities.

RESEARCH SITE SELECTION, SAMPLING, AND ANALYSIS

Only a few online health communities have used moderators due to various resource limitations [18], but more online communities are adopting moderators as part of their growth. Moderators can help with answering questions that are not replied to, welcoming new comers, and providing useful information and resources [3]. WebMD.com is one of the few online health communities that offer moderated forums. Thus, studying WebMD will help us to understand the role of moderators in the large number of communities that will begin to use them.

I chose the WebMD diabetes community as a research site for this study. The moderators as well as patients at the WebMD diabetes community are more active—regarding total posts and update frequency—than other disease communities under WebMD. Managing diabetes is about changing lifestyle. Accordingly, the peers' discourse around diabetes as illness revolves around accepting the disease as part of daily routine and examining various aspects of everyday life as opposed to involvement in activities of serious problem solving and medical decision making like cancer. Such characteristic of a diabetes community might have influenced a study finding that the topic of diabetes allowed diverse moderator responses to be shared with patients, such as sharing clinical expertise, building rapport, and urging to see providers [17]. Because I was studying situations where moderators redirected patients to see providers compared to other moderating situations, having access to enough diverse moderator posts was important.

In February of 2014, I scraped publicly available forum data of the WebMD diabetes community dating from its beginning, which was June of 2007 to a secure MySQL database. The Institutional Review Board at my institution determined my project as unregulated by the review board. The community had 5,196 unique posters and 15 moderators (only two of them were actively posting hundreds of messages, which is common for all WebMD communities), and 711,777 total posts under 9,576 conversation threads.

Identifying "see your doctor" posts

From this big corpus, I had to find reasonable ways to identify the relevant conversation threads connected to my study purpose, which is to examine threads that clinical questions are being asked and moderators redirect patients to go see their doctors instead. The following are representative examples of moderator responses that tell patients to "See your doctor" after patients ask clinical questions:

"Talk to your doctor and pharmacist about it." (Moderator, WebMD diabetes community)

"You should call your doctor. No one here can tell you how to adjust your insulin or whether you need to go to the ER to have it brought down in a safe, monitored, setting." (Moderator, WebMD diabetes community)

In these posts, the common languages used included "see your doctor," "call your doctor," and "talk to your doctor." Other ways of conveying similar content include "consult your provider" or "Have you seen your diabetes educator?" However, I learned from querying various keywords within the database that these variations do not return as many results as the first three phrases mentioned. Querying "your doctor" returned too many results that included unrelated posts outside the scope of this study to be useful.

Our main goal was to qualitatively study in-depth situations where moderators and community members managed threads when moderators urge patients to see their providers because the community cannot help them. Thus, extracting a few, representative cases was more important than identifying all possible relevant cases. Accordingly, within moderators' first replies (first occurring reply from a moderator in a thread) to the initiator[1] of the thread, I queried from the database the exact match of the three phrases: "see your doctor," "call your doctor," and "talk to your doctor." Out of 1,700 threads that had replies from 12 unique moderators, the query resulted in 109 total threads that contained replies from the two most active moderators.

Further identifying "see your doctor"

The phrase, "See your doctor," can mean many things. It could mean that moderators ask patients to see their doctors because the problem noted seems to be urgent needing immediate help from the health care providers, which is not within the scope of my study.

To identify the relevant threads pertaining to my goal, a coder (myself), performed an open coding analysis [35] of the moderators' posts of the query results (109 threads). From this analysis, this coder generated a codebook for identifying various situations of what "see your doctor" phrase could mean. The coder then discussed the codebook with a second student coder to revise the codebook using 10 moderator post examples. The second coder then used the revised codebook to code a randomly selected half of the moderators' posts in those 109 threads excluding the examples used in the codebook discussion. Cohen's kappa between the coders was 0.6. Main disagreements occurred in distinguishing posts about moderators telling posters to go see their doctors because "the community cannot help" versus "the poster should see the doctor right away." For the results that the coders disagreed with, the two coders discussed and collaboratively revised the analysis to what both coders can agree. The agreement for the problem in distinguishing "See your doctor because we cannot help" versus "See your doctor because the problem you state is dangerous," the coders decided to find explanations in the Seedoc posts for why the problem is dangerous enough to see a doctor to code the post as the latter case.

The rest of the posts were coded by the first coder based on the discussion. As a result, the coders identified 39 threads out of 109 threads as relevant to this study—threads that involved clinical questions and moderators redirected patients to go see their doctors instead of consulting with the community. These threads contained in total of 186 messages. For qualitative studies, 186 often provides reaching saturation point [26]. Only one moderator was present in the 39 threads. This moderator was the most active moderator in the diabetes community, meaning the moderator had posted most messages in the community.

From exploring other WebMD disease communities, the coders found "See your doctor" posts come from other moderators as well, showing that the "See your doctor" posts are not unique to this one moderator on the WebMD diabetes community. However, due to each disease having

[1] Initiator: A person who started the conversation thread

unique cultural norm built around patients' relationships with peer patients as well as care providers and other helpers, the findings should not be interpreted as such that requires generalization. The goal should be to deeply understand community dynamic around the practice of "See your doctor" posts by moderators, particularly in the WebMD diabetes community. The applicability of the findings to other communities should be tested through reexamination of other communities as future work.

From now, I will call these 39 threads, ***SeeDoc threads***. I will use ***SeeDoc posts*** for the moderator's replies that ask the thread initiators to see their doctors because the community cannot help.

In the remaining 70 threads, the coders found three other ways in which the phrase "See your doctor" was used. 37 cases showed moderators urging initiators to see their providers because the medical problem was a serious one to be checked out immediately. 26 cases showed moderators explaining initiators how to communicate with their providers. 7 cases showed moderators informing when initiators should call their providers. Compared to SeeDoc posts, these other cases were more inviting for the initiators and encouraged the community to provide useful information around the clinical question.

Research questions and analysis methods

Using inductive coding [35], the coders qualitatively examined the whole thread of those 39 SeeDoc threads, including the thread initiating posts and replies to the thread, 186 posts in total. My goal was to answer three research questions: (1) In what contexts do moderators redirect initiators by asking clinical questions to see their providers? (2) How do other community members work with moderators and initiators in this context? (3) How do moderators redirecting initiators to see providers relate to the initiators' and other community members' participation with the community?

In addition to (1) and (2) requiring qualitative analysis, I added (3) to gain objective measure of community participation related to Seedoc threads as a supplement to my main questions of (1) and (2). To further understand (3), I quantitatively examined: (a) how often initiators replied back to the thread; (b) how many replies followed after the moderator's SeeDoc post; and (c) how often initiators returned to the community after receiving the SeeDoc posts. I descriptively compared (a), (b) and (c) with the rest of the cases where initiators received moderators' first replies in general using Wilcoxon Rank Sum test because the data were not normally distributed.

Next, I will talk about what sorts of problems initiators brought to the community in the case of SeeDoc threads. As I introduce initiators' posts, I will give context around how the community and the moderator responded to the post. I will then examine more in depth the kinds of help that the community provided before and after the moderator's SeeDoc post and how the initiators interacted with them. Lastly, I will quantitatively examine what potential relationship there might be between SeeDoc threads and initiators and other community members' participation with the community.

INITIATORS' POSTS: WHEN DID INITIATORS GET THE "SEE YOUR DOCTOR" RESPONSES?

In this section, I will describe the kinds of questions SeeDoc thread initiators asked in the community and the context of how they were followed up by the moderator and the community members.

Initiators asked for clinical expertise

Initiators did ask specific questions that needed someone with clinical expertise to respond to. Initiators asked whether the symptoms they were experiencing were related to the medications they were taking, whether the symptoms they were experiencing was something they should be worried about, which medications to take, and what should be done for the severe medical problem they were having at the moment.

For instance, one initiator asked whether the pain on the side of his torso and vomiting episode was related to Byetta he started taking:

I was diagnosed with type 2 diabetes approx. 3 years ago. I am currently taking byetta 10mg 2x day & 2000 mg of metformin. In the last week I have noticed a hard area on my right side as well as vomiting and diarrhea. Could this be complications from the byetta.

To this post, the moderator responded with a typical SeeDoc post:

There is no way for us to diagnose over the Internet. You need to see your doctor.

And then another community member responded with more detail what the problem could be while emphasizing why the initiator should go see his doctor:

This could be a complication of BOTH byetta and metformin. HOWEVER... you need to report this to your doctor and see what he says about it. But the hard area I don't believe is one of the side effects of either unless you are talking about injection sites... If it is the injection site that you are talking about.. make sure you alternate where you inject. But you really should be seen by your doc.

This community member's post nicely assisted the moderator's SeeDoc post with why the problem is something that the community cannot answer—that we do not know the answer to the symptom unless the initiator gets checked out by a medical professional. More importantly, the member was giving tips for insulin injection sites that could avoid potential hardening of skin, which might have been the cause of pain.

In two other instances, initiators replied to the thread to report they saw the doctor after getting the response to go see the doctor. Here, the SeeDoc posts indeed motivated some initiators to see their providers. From their providers, the initiators received answers to their medical problems or they were able to change the dosage of the medication to solve the problem they were having.

In most cases, however, the initiators already had seen or were planning on seeing their providers by the time they initiated the thread. Even though initiators did not explicitly say they have seen their providers in the initiating post, when I examined the returning replies of the initiators (which was only 11 out of 39 threads), 9 of the 11 clarified they already had seen the doctor or have doctor's appointment.

Initiators' providers confirmed they do not have medical problems, but initiators wanted more knowledge.
Initiators either did not feel it was an "ER call," which refers to calling an emergency room, or their doctors have already told them that there were no problems with their health. For both of these cases, the initiators were not diagnosed with diabetes, but they have been having symptoms that were unusual, such as feeling "woozy" after eating food, have "low blood sugar occasionally," or their fasting blood sugar was high. This initiator who monitored blood sugar only started to do so because he had a strong family history of diabetes. A few months ago, his doctor had confirmed he did not have diabetes. Thus, this initiator needed more information than his status with diabetes—why he has been having such symptoms and blood sugar levels even though he did not have diabetes. To his post, the moderator replied and told him to see a doctor because the community cannot make any diagnosis:

It sounds like time to see your doctor. We are here to support you, but no one can diagnose over the Internet. This article contains more information on Diagnosis of Diabetes and Pre-Diabetes.

To this standard moderator's SeeDoc post, the initiator responded again clarifying that he was not looking for a diagnosis but was seeking knowledge, which he expressed as his understanding of the purpose of WebMD:

Obviously I didn't make my question clear.... First and foremost, I am NOT looking for a diagnosis, I am simply seeking knowledge and that is what I understand to be the purpose of WebMD. I'll rephrase my question as follows: Is it unusual for fasting levels to be elevated, yet to see otherwise normally acceptable levels throughout the day.

To this reply, the moderator again responded with more detailed information on what factors could lead to high fasting blood sugar and again stressed that he should see his doctor. The initiator did not respond again, but three other community members shared their personal experiences around how to measure fasting blood sugar correctly and when they tend to have unusually high reading of fasting blood sugar according to their own experiences.

This thread shows a typical problem that SeeDoc posts might have in online health communities. At least in this thread, the initiator responded back to the moderator and clarified the purpose of his post—not wanting a diagnosis but peer-knowledge—and ended up getting informative responses from both the moderator and other community members. However, if the initiator did not clarify, the thread could have been left with the moderator defining the initiator's post as a diagnosis question and potentially ended without further helpful responses from the community.

Initiators already have a doctors' appointment scheduled but need somebody to talk with them about it
Initiators knew they needed to see a doctor and had an appointment set up in the upcoming few weeks. However, they either wanted to get more community feedback on the problems they were concerned with or they asked how sick should they be before they call the emergency room instead of waiting for the appointment.

For instance, one initiator wanted to know why he was having certain symptoms, such as shaky hands, feeling light-headed, or always feeling hungry. He had an appointment scheduled in a few weeks with an endocrinologist. He described his health history and symptoms at length and what food makes the symptoms worse or better. However, he did not receive any replies for three days and received only one response from the moderator:

Your symptoms [can come from] a number of health conditions. The best way to find the reason is to see your doctor. Unfortunately, it is impossible for any of us to diagnose over the internet. Even your own doctor could not tell what the problem is without lab work. The Symptom Checker might help you organize your thoughts for your doctor. You also may want to keep a food/symptom journal until your appointment. Let us know what your doctor has to say.

The thread ended this way without any further responses.

The problem was beyond setting up a doctor's appointment
The problem was not whether initiators should see their providers or are attempting to get a diagnosis, but they wanted to get second opinions about the solution they received from their providers.

For instance, an initiator replied and clarified that she was concerned whether she will be "ok" until the appointment and wanted further information on what to prepare for the appointment:

Have an appointment scheduled all the way on the 20th of next month. Hopefully I'll be ok in that time? I have to fast for the test right?

When the initiators responded back to their own threads, a prevalent response was that they already talked or will talk to their providers. The initiators had intentions that were beyond getting answers to their medical problems—such as preparing for their appointment, getting second opinions about what their doctors have told them, or wondering whether to see a specialist since they were not satisfied with what their doctors have told them. One initiator had symptoms similar to heart palpitations but the initiator's doctor had told him it was stress related. The initiator came back from the appointment without any diagnosis or treatment while still having the worrisome symptoms. Thus, the initiator posted to get more help from the community. Instead, the initiator only received the SeeDoc post and no other community members chimed in.

Initiators wanted other patients' personal experience and second opinion

Other initiators explicitly asked for personal experience and opinions from the community members about their medical problems. Still, the moderator responded with a SeeDoc post.

For instance, an initiator was recently told by her doctor that her body started rejecting her insulin due to many complications she had. She wanted to hear whether others had similar problems who could share any second opinions. She also asked whether she would be qualified for social security disability benefits:

... THE DRS ARE NOW THINKING THAT SINCE I HAVE HAD HCV AND CELIAC SPRUE THAT MY BODY TENDS TO REJECT THE INSULIN DUE TO AUTOIMMUNE. DOES ANYONE ELSE HAVE THIS PROBLEM? ALSO SINCE OBVIOSLY I CANT WORK LIKE THIS WOULD I QUALIFY FOR ssd? [sic]

To this post, the moderator responded and told the initiator to talk to her doctor and lawyer about the qualification of the benefits. Two other community members replied afterwards to inform the initiator to talk to an endocrinologist to change the dosage of the insulin or consult changing medications. It was unclear whether the advice of the community members came from those who also have HCV and Celiac sprue, and the initiator ended up not getting a second opinion on her issue. It would also have been helpful if somebody with the disability benefit responded and gave her tips for what process is involved in talking to lawyers or doctors about being qualified for the disability benefits. However, such interaction did not happen in this thread either.

Initiators had concerns in seeing the doctors

Initiators had reasons for not wanting to call their doctors. One initiator asked for help because he was afraid seeing the doctor would "end up in either an appointment or buying meds [costing extra money that I do not have]" and another 13-year old teenager said he was "afraid of needles." In both cases, after the moderator told the initiators to see their doctors instead, other community members gave the initiators convincing explanations for why their concerns are not something to be worried about.

For instance, the first initiator lost a sliding scale for his insulin, which helps him determine how much insulin to take depending on the food he eats. The initiator was afraid that calling his doctor will cost him money to set up an appointment or had to buy another medication. To this post, the moderator responded that the community cannot help with how much insulin he should take but he should call his doctor to get the sliding scale again. Another community member clarified that there will not be any additional charges for getting a new sliding scale and explained how to talk to the clinic about it.

This case showed how other community members can add helpful clarifications to why seeing the doctor makes sense to the initiators, when the moderator's SeeDoc posts on its own cannot fully clarify the initiators about their concerns.

Summary: The initiators needed something more than "See your doctor"

The topics of initiators' posts mostly included clinically related questions that the initiators should get answers from their providers instead. However, the findings showed various reasons initiators wanted to talk to the community instead of their own providers. The initiators already had seen their providers about the problem or had a doctor's appointment set up unlike what the moderator had assumed. The initiators needed more information, such as what the community members were giving to the initiators. Still, moderators responded with SeeDoc posts to these initiator posts. Some were because the moderators did not have a full understanding of the initiators' context.

THE COMMUNITY'S WORK AROUND "SEE YOUR DOCTOR"

In this section, I will further examine the posts that were posted before and after the moderator's SeeDoc posts to understand how other community members interacted with the initiators and the moderator.

On average, the moderator's first replies in SeeDoc threads were positioned 1.9th (Median: 1st) out of 3.8 replies (Median: 2.0 replies). There were 1.6 other unique members replying per thread on average (Median: 1 member), where 1.9 unique members (Median: 1 member) on average replied after the moderator's SeeDoc post among those threads that had replies following the moderator's SeeDoc post (54% of the SeeDoc threads). Below I describe what these 1.6 unique community members said in the thread before and after the SeeDoc posts.

Encouraged initiators to see their doctors

Medical professionals fear misinformation being shared among community members [20]. Contrary to their worries, even before the moderator told the initiators to see their doctors, the community members clarified with the initiators that "none of us can diagnose this" and urged the initiators to see their providers just "for the peace of mind." Also, the members provided their own experiences around similar medical problems where visiting a doctor prevented what could have been a severe problem.

Similarly, after the moderator's SeeDoc posts, community members supported the moderator and encouraged the initiators to see their doctors by explaining that it will help the initiators let go of their concerns:

A very simple blood test will confirm or dispel any thoughts that you have about this. Go to your doctor.

Some missed the initiator's reply that the initiator has set up a doctor's appointment thanks to the community and continued to urge the initiator to see his doctor because "we care about your health and life":

Stacy, are you just funin' us? Or maybe you are just playing a game of "yeah but" YEAH you hear us BUT you aren't intending to pay any attention. This is not a game. We really care about you and your health and life and the life of your unborn baby. Do you care enough about yourself to make that doctor's appointment?

Discussed medical information

Community members discussed possible phenomenon or symptoms that the initiators might be experiencing, which the initiators could clarify with their doctors. For instance, a member explained what the initiator could potentially be experiencing, called Dawn Phenomenon, which the initiator could ask his doctor about:

There is something called the Dawn Phenomenon which is stronger in some people than in others. Your body (through the liver) releases glucose early in the morning to help your body prepare for the stresses of the day. This is possibly what is happening. If your A1C and post prandial levels are ok and you maintain contact with your physician...

Similar to this member, I saw that the community members emphasized initiators should continue to communicate with their providers about the issue.

Supplemented discussion with personal experience and tips

The strength of online health communities that a clinical environment cannot provide is peer-patients' similar experiences and their everyday coping strategies in various aspects of managing illness. Examples range from saving money to finding ways to communicate with their providers. Community members added after SeeDoc posts what they personally experienced around a similar issue and provided useful tips, making the SeeDoc thread useful.

For instance, community members added to the moderator's SeeDoc posts how to talk to the providers. One community member explained how to talk with a doctor who is a "one-word answerer" and what kinds of doctors to choose:

Hi, [Jim], When you ask your doctor about this, make sure you ask him why this warning is on the package. It may be that using both insulin & Januvia might cause lows in some people but make sure he explains it to you thoroughly. My first doctor was a "one--word answerer" & that wasn't any help at all so I changed doctors. My new doctor spent one hour talking & answering my questions in detail before any lab work. That's the type of doctor you want—not one who can't wait to get you out of his office.

Summary: Community members' active roles in medical questions

Community members attempted to actively help with topics sensitive to medical liability issues when they can. The members rarely attempted to share uncensored medical advice. Perhaps the moderator explicitly attempting to prevent any medical advice sharing might have been why other community members were not providing what could have been misinformation. However, the members provided distinct support compared with the moderator in the cases of SeeDoc threads—to help initiators communicate better with their providers, give convincing reasons for why talking to providers can be helpful, and share similar experiences that can help initiators to not feel alone.

QUANTITATIVE ANALYSIS: "SEE YOUR DOCTOR" POSTS AND COMMUNITY PARTICIPATION

In this section, I will examine how the moderator's SeeDoc posts can potentially be associated with initiators' and community members' participation with the community. To do this, I examined three things: the rate of initiators returning to the thread, the number of following replies after the SeeDoc post, and the rate of initiators returning to the community in general after having experienced the SeeDoc threads.

In examining these three phenomena, I compared SeeDoc threads' results with those of ***Other threads***, meaning all of patient initiated threads from the community where moderators have replied to the initiators, excluding the SeeDoc threads. A ***moderator's first post*** refers to the first moderator post per thread. All SeeDoc posts were moderators' first posts.

How often initiators replied back to the thread?

Our findings showed that initiators tended not to reply back to threads in general, not just in SeeDoc threads. In SeeDoc threads, initiators on average replied 0.5 times back to their own threads (including before the SeeDoc posts), where only 11 out of 39 (28%) initiators replied after the moderator's SeeDoc post. For Other threads, on average initiators replied back to their own threads 1.4 times, where 631 out of 1591 (40%) replied after a moderator's first reply. Using Wilcoxon Rank Sum test, the difference between SeeDoc and Other threads on the initiators' rates of replying back to the thread after moderators' first reply was not significant ($W = 27470.5$, $p = 0.1482$).

Did conversations end after the SeeDoc post?

I found that SeeDoc posts tended to stop conversations compared to moderators' other first posts in general. On average, 18 out of 39 (46%) SeeDoc threads ended right after the moderator's SeeDoc post. 450 out of 1591 (28%) Other threads ended right after a moderator's first post. The difference in the number of following replies after moderators' posts was significant between SeeDoc and Other threads when tested using Wilcoxon Rank Sum test ($W = 21192$, $p < 0.001$). I note that this result should not be interpreted as SeeDoc post cutting conversations, since the topic matter of the thread involved in SeeDoc threads versus Other threads might matter more than the SeeDoc post itself. Still, there is a strong association between SeeDoc posts and the number of replies that follow.

How much initiators return to the community after receiving the SeeDoc posts?

I found that initiators tended not to come back to the community in general (by the time the data collection ended, which was February 2014), not just in SeeDoc threads. 82% of the initiators in the SeeDoc threads (31 out of 38 unique initiators) did not post again in the community after receiving the moderator's SeeDoc post. Among the eight returning initiators, two initiators have already been active before they received the "See your doctor" post, and they continued to post 496 and 58 posts after experiencing the SeeDoc thread. Half of the returning initiators posted only once after the SeeDoc thread experience. The remaining two initiators posted two and three times after the SeeDoc thread.

Similarly, 76% initiators in Other threads (601 out of 793 unique initiators) did not post again in the community after receiving moderators' first replies. 9% of the returning initiators from Other threads participated once after receiving moderators' first replies. The Wilcoxon Rank Sum test showed no significant differences between the initiators who experienced SeeDoc threads and moderators' general responses in how often they participated in the community afterwards ($W = 15679$, $p = 0.5724$).

When looking at the general activity of the community, out of 5,213 total users, 3,290 users (63%) did not return after their first post in the community. 16% (853 users) of those who returned posted only once more.

This last finding further highlighted the prevalence of the lack of continuous participation throughout the community, following the typical long-tail distribution of community participation and the challenges of patients' sustained participation with online health communities.

In summary, SeeDoc posts were strongly associated with ceased community conversations, and patient participation with community was generally unsustainable.

DISCUSSION

I first discuss how my work connects back to the previous literature on online health communities, particularly around the roles of peer patients and moderators in dealing with clinical questions. I then turn to how findings translate to practical implications for the CSCW community.

What is really harmful in managing clinical questions in online health communities

Despite the increasing evidence that online health communities help with managing illness psychosocially [5,13,16,33], concerns toward misinformation being shared among peer-patients are common [20]. To emphasize the importance of peer-patient interaction, previous work illustrated what distinctive expertise patients can provide [15] compared to the medical expertise that health professionals provide to patients.

Studies emphasizing the importance of peer patient expertise, however, focused on non-clinical information that patients share. On the other hand, in this study, I focused on investigating how clinically oriented problems, not just psychosocial problems, were being moderated in an online community setting, and, more importantly, how peer patients helped with those clinically oriented problems. Peer patients helped to supplement information closely linked to their daily experiences and coping strategies and advised peers how to communicate with providers and motivated each other to talk to the providers as necessary.

Our results aligned closely with a survey result on online diagnosers [10]. The respondents in the survey stated that they did not visit a clinician to get a professional opinion (35%), medical professionals confirmed their diagnosis performed online (41%), or the respondents could not agree with the clinicians' suggestion (18%). Although my analysis showed that the primary purpose of the initiators was not online diagnosis, my results uncovered the process by which online diagnosers could potentially get help from others in online community settings.

Still, I should not be concerned with the phenomenon that people look for clinical answers from online communities. My findings directly challenge the prevalent position of the medical community on what is considered harmful and helpful. My findings challenged the notion that clinical information shared by peer patients can be harmful and that peer patient help should be confined to non-clinical information. This finding is in line with Smithson et al [34]'s work where self-harm community members reciprocally provided "mundane" advice to go see health professionals and sought support with one another, reverting assumptions that online communities would promote self-harm. Also, my findings challenged the current practice of online communities, which relies on content moderation for quality control. Moderators posted Seedoc posts with good intentions, but it could lead to harmful results, hindering healthy community dynamic, as shown from the number of follow up replies in Seedoc threads. Liao et al [22]'s work supports this finding, where they showed, depending on the community culture, the tightness of governance should be adjusted.

No literature has looked specifically at how moderators and community members work together to address clinical questions. I showed how community members supplemented with information that moderators overlooked to share with patients. Accordingly, patients were able to get the benefits of both sides—information coming from patients and moderators.

Below, I discuss how the CSCW community can help patients and moderators take roles in online health communities in addressing clinical questions.

Moderators should focus on the inviting role rather than the governing role

When people schedule an appointment due to concerns with their health, there are no other options to talk to their providers than to wait until the appointment, which usually takes from a few days to a few weeks. During that time, people can feel anxious and want to gain as much information as possible. The community was an outlet for them to fulfill this need. However, moderators' SeeDoc posts can potentially hinder this process of getting help and support from peers by making a conclusion to the thread that the only solution to the problem is to see their doctors.

Rather than a governing role, moderators should play an inviting role, even in circumstances where patients might be asking for answers that the community cannot answer. Moderators should respond to clinical questions as I observed in other cases of where "See your doctor" phrases occurred, such as helping patients to communicate with providers and informing them about when to call an emergency room. Furthermore, calling out other members who have similar experiences to share how they worked with their providers or what the process was like—any additional information regarding similar situation—can help initiators to feel welcome and not alone and direct them to make better decisions.

Depending on the culture of the community and the purpose of each thread, however, strict governance might be necessary. Liao et al [22] explained how properties of communities determine how tight governance should be. Content-centric communities, such as Flickr, tend to impose tighter management control, whereas social networking sites emphasize social transparency and self-governance to accommodate members' goals in community participation. In the case of Seedoc threads, I observed a mix of both content-centric culture (sharing resources around clinical questions) and social networking purpose (sharing social support among community members). While the quality of information they collect is critical and might need strict regulation, I saw collectively gathering socially supportive comments as effective in getting a message across. An example includes the case of community members being more successful than the moderator in convincing the asker to go see the doctor. Accordingly, some mix of appropriate governing and inviting roles should help, depending on how content-centric the community is.

The real value of online health communities that providers cannot provide

The literature discussed community members' roles as focusing on psychosocial support, primarily in response to non-clinical questions. Community members' participation with SeeDoc threads demonstrated value in what peer-patients from the community could offer even in the cases of patients asking for clinical information, not just in non-clinical domains. Community members did not try to diagnose or give medical consultation. The initiators did not expect the community to answer their questions as their doctors would. Rather, the initiators wanted to see whether others had similar experiences and what they did to overcome the situation.

On the other hand, I did see cases where the initiator came back to the thread after talking with their doctors, asking questions that could have been consulted with their doctors. Literature shows the lack of communication between patients and providers. On average, patients in the U.S. spend 20 minutes with their providers [4], but depending on the purpose, it could last as short as 5 minutes [7]. During that time, it is difficult to remember all the questions they had and ask follow up questions [21], and even though they have questions later on, the process by which they get the answer is tedious, such as a long wait on the phone or waiting to get a call back. Studies demonstrated that the majority of online health information seekers benefited in changing their health behavior, learning something new that was useful, and their search has affected the way they decide treatments and care [11,30].

The community should not be an alternative place to get clinical expertise, but it can be a place where community members can help each other learn how to manage communicating with their providers and motivate positive behavioral change towards better health. Research shows the strong persuasiveness of self-referencing, involving communicators' personal experiences [19,29]. Peer patients' advice and suggestions coupled with personal experiences can have a big impact on patients. The initiators needed peers' similar experiences around the clinical problem and how they coped with the problem.

Supporting the gray space between online diagnosis and community help

A gray space exists between what the community cannot do and what the community is supposed do. The former being diagnoses or prescribing dosage of medication, which only providers are legally allowed to do. The latter—what the community is supposed do—refers to the canonical role of online communities known in the literature—social support, including emotional, informational, tangible, and companionship support [6]. However, I saw that communities can offer help around clinically oriented problems coupled with personal experience and coping strategies. Moderators should be facilitating that process, instead of building boundaries for what an online community could or could not do.

Here are some implications for the CSCW community in supporting online communities to address this gray space:

- The challenges emerge when the community attempts to directly answer questions such as "Do I have diabetes?" Such questions should be considered as a starting point of discussion instead of responding based on the assumption that the forum is a Q&A site. For instance, the moderators or system features can highlight the topic being mentioned in the question. The community can talk further about what they experienced around the symptoms and share personalized knowledge around them.
- It is hard to know what initiators' status in communicating with their providers is. We can help initiators share status with their providers, either through members' follow up questions or the system pushing cascades of questions to reveal patients' context.
- Showing guidelines in the new post submission screen for how to get supportive answers depending on the initiator's purpose would help initiators better formulate initiating posts.
- SeeDoc posts can be portrayed as template responses. A system can help moderators include individualized advice or questions based on the context the initiator has provided. A system providing moderators with Webpage links or past conversations among peers related to keywords mentioned in the initiators' posts can help moderators provide further helpful information.
- The persistent challenge of online communities in general is dealing with unanswered questions and lack of discussions. Notify community members with similar interests based on past posts to engage with the thread and facilitate sharing second opinions.

CONCLUSION

Our study contributes to the online health community and CSCW literature in three ways: I challenged the existing notion of peer patients' non-existent role around clinical questions; I demonstrated how shared roles among community members and moderators can provide benefits to discussing clinical questions; and finally I provided practical implications that the CSCW community can take away to help moderated online health communities better address clinical questions.

The quantitative analysis in this work was limited to descriptive, small-scale data. Compared to the overall size of the community, the proportion in which Seedoc threads occur is minimal. Thus, how important the effect that Seedoc threads have for the entire community is still unknown. However, the influence moderators have for the community could be bigger than that of regular members. For instance, moderator responded threads are weighted higher in featured threads. Also, in the case of WebMD, users see which threads were moderated, making users consider moderated threads as more special than unmoderated threads. Future work should address other factors, such as topic and similarity of posts together with Seedoc posting practices to see how these factors influence community dynamic. Furthermore, larger scale data beyond Seedoc threads can be harnessed through machine learning techniques, identifying moderators' posts that attempt to control conversations. Other disease communities should be examined to see how my findings theoretically generalize to other communities' cultures. I was not able to get in touch with the WebMD moderators to further understand what training they were given. I was informally aware of the fact that practices around Seedoc threads were similar across varying moderators. However, I did not systematically study all moderators' Seedoc threads. Future work should address how prevalent the Seedoc threads practices that I described in this paper exist in online health communities. The WebMD editing staff policy, however, states the following, illustrating that the moderator's Seedoc post practice I described in this paper is derived from the site-wide policy:

Be aware, however, that information on WebMD or any other web site should not be used as a substitute for professional healthcare. You should always seek the advice of your physician or other qualified health provider with any questions you may have regarding a medical condition [42].

The challenge here is how we can maneuver between medical liability and practical help. How do we facilitate peer patients to continue sharing content around unmet needs from their healthcare providers that peer patients could fulfill, such as how to choose care providers or how to communicate with physicians?

The preconception towards clinical advice sharing online should shift away from laymen discussing clinical materials as a taboo. We should rethink sharing medical information as something that a community together can actively help support one another.

Such paradigm shift applies to other domains where the validity of laymen knowledge becomes debatable, such as citizen science [1], fine arts [37], and education [39]. As social media provide large-scale platforms in which any lay person can participate and share knowledge, the constant battle for what is a valid information will continue to be present. How to manage content quality and to maximize benefits that communities of practice can offer will continue to be a reoccurring challenge for the CSCW community.

ACKNOWLEDGMENTS

This work has been in part funded by NIH 1K01LM011980-01. I would like to thank the iCARE Lab and the BitLab, especially Katie Hoban, for their continuing support. I also thank Wanda Pratt, David McDonald, and Andrea Hartzler, who have been providing immense insights for this problem around moderator-patient relationships in online health communities.

REFERENCES

[1] Bäckstrand, K. Civic science for sustainability: reframing the role of experts, policy-makers and citizens in environmental governance. *Global Environmental Politics 3*, 4 (2003), 24–41.

[2] Bacon, E.S., Condon, E.H., and Fernsler, J.I. Young widows' experience with an Internet self-help group. *Journal of psychosocial nursing and mental health services 38*, 7 (2000), 24.

[3] Berge, Z.L. and Collins, M.P. Perceptions of e-moderators about their roles and functions in moderating electronic mailing lists. *Distance Education 21*, 1 (2000), 81–100.

[4] Camasso, M.J. and Camasso, A.E. Practitioner productivity and the product content of medical care in publicly supported health centers. *Social science & medicine (1982) 38*, 5 (1994), 733–48.

[5] Campbell, H., Phaneuf, M., and Deane, K. Cancer peer support programs-do they work? *Patient Educ Couns 55*, 1 (2004), 3–15.

[6] Cohen, S., Gottlieb, B., and Underwood, L. Social relationships and health. In S. Cohen, L. Underwood and B. Gottlieb, eds., *Measuring and intervening in social support*. New York: Oxford University Press, 2000, 3–25.

[7] Dugdale, D.C., Epstein, R., and Pantilat, S.Z. Time and the patient-physician relationship. *Journal of General Internal Medicine 14*, S1 (1999), S34–S40.

[8] Edwards, L.L., Reis, J.S., and Weber, K.M. Facilitators and Barriers to Discussing HIV Prevention With Adolescents: Perspectives of HIV-Infected Parents. *American journal of public health 103*, 8 (2013), 1468–1475.

[9] Eysenbach, G., Powell, J., Englesakis, M., Rizo, C., and Stern, A. Health related virtual communities and electronic support groups: systematic review of the effects of online peer to peer interactions. *BMJ (Clinical research ed.) 328*, 7449 (2004), 1166.

[10] Fox, S. and Duggan, M. *Health Online.* Pew Internet & American Life Project, Jan 15, *2013.* http://www.pewinternet.org/files/old-media/Files/Reports/PIP_HealthOnline.pdf. Accessed on December 10, 2013.

[11] Fox, S., Rainie, L., Horrigan, J., Lenhart, A., Spooner, T., and Burke M. *The online health care revolution: how the Web helps Americans take better care of themselves*. Nov 26, 2000. http://www.pewinternet.org/2000/11/26/the-online-health-care-revolution/. Accessed on December 10, 2014

[12] Frost, J. and Massagli, M. PatientsLikeMe the case for a data-centered patient community and how ALS patients use the community to inform treatment decisions and manage pulmonary health. *Chron. Respir. Dis. 6*, 4 (2009), 225–9.

[13] Giese-Davis, J., Bliss-Isberg, C., Carson, K., et al. The effect of peer counseling on quality of life following diagnosis of breast carcinoma: An observational study. *Psycho-Oncology 15*, 11 (2006), 1014–1022.

[14] Hartzler, A., McDonald, D., Pratt, W., Park, A., and Huh, J. Facilitating Mentoring in peer health communities through social matching: Detecting mentorship characteristics from community data. *American Medical Informatics Association Extended Abstracts.* (2012).

[15] Hartzler, A. and Pratt, W. Managing the Personal Side of Health: How Patient Expertise Differs from the Expertise of Clinicians. *J Med Internet Res 13*, 3 (2011), e62.

[16] Heisler, M., Vijan, S., Makki, F., and Piette, J.D. Diabetes control with reciprocal peer support versus nurse care management: a randomized trial. *Ann Intern Med 153*, 8 (2010), 507–15.

[17] Huh, J., Mcdonald, D.W., Hartzler, A., and Pratt, W. Patient Moderator Interaction in Online Health Communities. *Proceedings of American Medical Informatics Association* (2013), 627–636.

[18] Huh, J., Patel, R., and Pratt, W. Tackling Dilemmas in Supporting 'The Whole Person' in Online Patient Communities. *In Proceedings of the 2012 ACM annual conference on Human Factors in Computing Systems (CHI '12)*, ACM (2012), 923–926.

[19] Johnson, B.T. Effects of outcome-relevant involvement and prior information on persuasion. *Journal of Experimental Social Psychology 30*, 6 (1994), 556–579.

[20] Johnson, G.J. and Ambrose, P.J. Neo-Tribes: The Power and Potential of Online Communities in Health Care. *Communications of the ACM 49*, 1 (2006), 107–113.

[21] Klasnja, P., Hartzler, A., Powell, C., and Pratt, W. Supporting cancer patients' unanchored health information management with mobile technology. *AMIA Annual Symposium Proceedings*, (2011), 732.

[22] Liao, Qinying, Yingxin Pan, Michelle X. Zhou, and Fei Ma. Chinese online communities: balancing managementcontrol and individual autonomy. *In Proceedings of the SIGCHI Conference on Human Factors in Computing Systems*, pp. 2193-2202. ACM, 2010.

[23] Liess, A., Simon, W., Yutsis, M., et al. Detecting emotional expression in face-to-face and online breast cancer support groups. *Journal of consulting and clinical psychology 76*, 3 (2008), 517–23.

[24] Malik, S.H. and Coulson, N.S. A comparison of lurkers and posters within infertility online support groups.

Computers, informatics, nursing : CIN 29, 10 (2011), 564–73.

[25] Maloney-Krichmar, D. and Preece, J. A multilevel analysis of sociability, usability, and community dynamics in an online health community. *ACM Transactions on Computer-Human Interaction (TOCHI) 12*, 2 (2005), 201–232.

[26] Mason, M. Sample Size and Saturation in PhD Studies Using Qualitative Interviews. *Forum Qualitative Sozialforschung / Forum: Qualitative Social Research 11*, 3 (2010).

[27] Namkoong, K., Dubenske, L.L., Shaw, B.R., et al. Creating a Bond Between Caregivers Online: Effect on Caregivers' Coping Strategies. *Journal of health communication*, (2011) 17, 2 (2012): 125-140.

[28] Orizio, G., Schulz, P., Gasparotti, C., Caimi, L., and Gelatti, U. The world of e-patients: A content analysis of online social networks focusing on diseases. *Telemedicine journal and e-health : the official journal of the American Telemedicine Association 16*, 10 (2010), 1060–6.

[29] Petty, R.E., Cacioppo, J.T., and Goldman, R. Personal involvement as a determinant of argument-based persuasion. *Journal of personality and social psychology 41*, 5 (1981), 847.

[30] Pourmand, A. and Sikka, N. Online health information impacts patients' decisions to seek emergency department care. *The western journal of emergency medicine 12*, 2 (2011), 174–7.

[31] Resnick, P.J., Janney, A.W., Buis, L.R., and Richardson, C.R. Adding an online community to an internet-mediated walking program. Part 2: strategies for encouraging community participation. *Journal of medical Internet research 12*, 4 (2010), e72.

[32] Roberts, L., Salem, D., Rappaport, J., Toro, P., Luke, D., and Seidman, E. Giving and receiving help: Interpersonal transactions in mutual-help meetings and psychosocial adjustment of members. *Am J Community Psychol 27*, 6 (1999), 841–68.

[33] Setoyama, Y., Yamazaki, Y., and Namayama, K. Benefits of peer support in online Japanese breast cancer communities: differences between lurkers and posters. *Journal of medical Internet research 13*, 4 (2011), e122.

[34] Smithson, J., Sharkey, S., Hewis, E., et al. Problem presentation and responses on an online forum for young people who self-harm. *Discourse Studies 13*, 4 (2011), 487–501.

[35] Strauss, A.L. and Corbin, J. *Basics of qualitative research: Grounded theory procedures and techniques.* Sage, Newbury Park, CA, 1990.

[36] Vlahovic, T.A., Wang, Y.-C., Kraut, R.E., and Levine, J.M. Support matching and satisfaction in an online breast cancer support community. *Proceedings of the 32nd annual ACM conference on Human factors in computing systems - CHI '14*, ACM Press (2014), 1625–1634.

[37] Walsh, P. The Web and the unassailable voice. *Archives and Museum Informatics 11*, 2 (1997), 77–85.

[38] Wang, Y.-C., Kraut, R.E., and Levine, J.M. To Stay or Leave? The Relationship of Emotional and Informational Support to Commitment in Online Health Support Groups. *CSCW*, (2012), 833–842.

[39] Zibit, M. What online facilitators say is difficult-experiences from Mathemagica online professional development. *World Conference on E-Learning in Corporate, Government, Healthcare, and Higher Education*, (2003), 843–844.

[40] dLife forum guidelines. http://www.dlife.com/policy/forum_guidelines.

[41] diabeticconnect.com terms of use. http://www.diabeticconnect.com/terms-of-use#disclaimer.

[42] webmd policies. http://www.webmd.com/about-webmd-policies/additional-info?ss=ftr.

Creating Value Together: The Emerging Design Space of Peer-to-Peer Currency and Exchange

John M. Carroll
College of Information Sciences and Technology
The Pennsylvania State University
University Park, PA 16802 USA
jcarroll@ist.psu.edu

Victoria Bellotti
Palo Alto Research Center
3333 Coyote Hill Road
Palo Alto, CA, 94304 USA
bellotti@parc.com

ABSTRACT
Paradigms for the collaborative creation of value through trade and exchange have developed over millennia. Thus, coins emerged in response to a set of challenges in barter and gift exchange. The development of paradigms for trade and exchange continues today, and is accelerating due both to crises in the mainstream global economy, and to new possibilities enabled by information technology. In this discussion paper, we consider alternative and complementary currency and exchange innovations, including local/community currencies, timebanks, crypto-currencies, and person-to-person collaborative economy microenterprises, as a technology design space for currency and exchange. We consider the consequences and trajectories of the rapidly evolving currency ecosystem, particularly with respect to research and development opportunities for CSCW.

Author Keywords
Currency; Exchange; Local/community currencies; Timebanks; Crypto-currency; Collaborative economy microenterprises; P2PX

ACM Classification Keywords
H.5.2 [Information Interfaces and Presentation]: User Interfaces - Interaction styles.

General Terms
Human Factors; Design

INTRODUCTION
Exchange of services and commodities is a defining activity among humans, with a long history and diverse consequences [7,8,38]. Trade has facilitated divisions of labor, and eventually mass production, as well as the organization of alliance networks and markets, and the identification and cultivation of comparative advantage in production of tradable commodities [37].

CSCW 2015, March 14–18, 2015, Vancouver, BC, Canada.

ACM 978-1-4503-2922-4/15/03…$15.00.
http://dx.doi.org/10.1145/2675133.2675270

The social and economic arrangements through which humans create value together, for example, incentivizing and recognizing one another, have developed over millennia. Thus, coins and money are a technology invented and adopted to address challenges in economic interactions. New frameworks and supporting technologies for economic interactions are developing today, indeed, the sustained crisis in the mainstream global economy and new possibilities enabled by information technology have accelerated and diversified contemporary developments in currency and exchange.

In this paper, we analyze the historical innovations of barter and gift exchange and of money to characterize a design space for currency and exchange interactions. We then use this analysis to understand contemporary innovations in systems and technologies, including local/community currencies, timebanks, crypto-currencies, and person-to-person collaborative economy microenterprises. Finally, we speculate on the consequences and trajectories of this currency ecosystem, particularly with respect to research and development opportunities for computer-supported cooperative work. With financial markets in turmoil and increasing anger about the ongoing concentration of wealth and power in the hands of a small minority, intense public discourse about what systems might help us better and more fairly manage economies is erupting (e.g. [22,35]. Our paper seeks to focus the attention of the CSCW community on economic innovations that may hold the seeds for positive change with implications for the design of novel technology solutions to support them.

BARTER AND GIFT EXCHANGE
The simplest paradigm for trade is barter, the direct exchange of goods and services. Barter depends on coincidence of wants, and negotiation of relative value between participants. These practical limitations motivated the adoption of commodity money with more generally convertible valuations, such as grains, livestock, and precious metals, which better facilitated the emergence of markets. And commodity money, in turn, eventually led to the minting of standard coins.

Non-market based economies do not necessarily rely exclusively on barter. Indeed, anthropological studies of non-market societies that survived into the modern period have identified complex trading protocols, including trading spheres and gift exchange, which co-occur with barter frameworks. Trading spheres are categories of commodities regarded exchangeable; items in different spheres are normally never exchanged. Trading spheres are seen as a social mechanism that prevents hegemony with respect to subsistence goods. Thus, if goods in the subsistence sphere (for example, vegetables, grains, hand tools, small animals) can only be traded for other goods in that sphere, if it is considered immoral to trade high prestige items for subsistence goods, then individuals who control a disproportionate share of wealth objects nonetheless cannot exert undue influence, for example, by creating artificial scarcities [42].

Gift exchange protocols in non-market societies are community-oriented and political as well as economic [27]. In these contexts, giving is a community service obligation that enhances one's prestige generally, and with respect to the recipient; receiving creates indebtedness, and places one's prestige in jeopardy [17]. If the recipient has relatively low social standing, repayment may be unnecessary. However, among persons with similar social standing, it is typical that even full repayment does not restore balance; the only way forward for reputation and prestige is to continue the relationship, and give more. Ironically, while terms of exchange are normally not explicitly negotiated, and immediate reciprocity is not expected, gifting is an ongoing, and somewhat competitive relationship, maintained by continued gifting. The protocols of spheres of exchange and gift exchange exemplify the evolved sociality of trading interactions in non-market societies.

In social exchange theory [7], traditional gifting is a paradigmatic example of *generalized exchange,* networks of voluntary and non-dyadic exchange that strengthen groups; barter bargaining is a paradigmatic example of dyadic *negotiated exchange*, in which uncertainties about the value of what is exchanged evoke the development of partner trust and norms of fairness, strengthening relational ties.

MONEY

The first manufactured coins came into use independently between 700 and 500 BC in India, China and the Mediterranean, though commodity money, such as cattle, grains, salt and precious metals, had been in use for more than a thousand years before that in Mesopotamia [13]. One motivation for coinage was to mitigate some of the complications and inefficiencies of barter's coincidence of wants, the cumbersome need to identify particular trading partners who currently had extra quantities of goods one wanted, who wanted goods for which one had current extra quantities, with whom one could successfully negotiate a trade, and to and from whom one could physically transfer traded goods in a timely fashion. Coins also mitigated logistic complications of commodity money, such as securing and assaying metals, feeding cattle, preserving grains, and storage and transport in general. Graeber [13] emphasizes the alternate, or possibly coextensive factor of providing better quantification of obligations in gift exchange, that is, going from "I owe you a gift" to "I owe you some number of units of something".

Money enables new possibilities for exchange. Providing a universal scale for valuing all services and commodities encourages the development of markets. Exchanges are simplified logistically and procedurally. Market-based pricing reduces the need for case-by-case negotiation and for the development of dyadic trust relationships. Obligations to others, including charity, can also be placed on the universal scale of value. Money commodifies trade itself; coincidence of wants is not an issue when trade is mediated by money. In a market economy, everyone always wants money.

Beyond the immediate context of trade, money facilitates the formation and leveraging of capital, permitting the preservation and aggregation of value obtained in exchanges to an extent not feasible in barter or commodity currency frameworks. This in turn expands useful practices such as borrowing, lending, investment, and taxation [43]. Indeed, money enables concentration of capital resources for projects unimaginably ambitious from the perspective of barter and commodity currency; for example, early corporations such as the British East India Company colonized large areas of the world during the 17th century as vast commercial enterprises. These early corporations were the models for modern corporate entities.

Money enables a variety of currency-oriented abstractions and secondary markets including specialty markets, speculation in futures, short selling, and derivative repackaging of investments. It creates the possibility and the ultimately the need to frame and manage monetary policy, nationally and globally, through adjustments to (central bank) interest rates and money supply intended to maintain economic growth and stability [10]. In modern society some job roles involve managing money and abstractions of money, but not with respect to trade or exchange of goods or services per se. Money is no longer merely a medium or measure used in trade; it is as well itself a primary commodity of trade.

The objectification of exchange through money has social and psychological consequences beyond the mechanics of trade. For example, simplifying exchange interactions reduces the need for trading partners to create and strengthen particular social ties and trust relationships, perhaps generalizing identification and trust to the overall economic system [33]. Quantifying debt and obligation also simplifies economic life by clarifying terms of satisfaction. These are both examples of efficiencies within the scope of

	Barter Bargaining	Pre-negotiated Money Exchange
Pre-conditions of exchange	Requires coincidence of wants	Universal exchange motivator; everyone can use money
	Requires participant trust as to what will be exchanged	Pre-negotiated money reduces the need to trust given trading partners
		Money must be earned in advance of exchange
		Money can become an end in itself
Exchange interaction dynamics	Exchanges are concrete social interactions that create and strengthen ties	Exchanges can be efficient, relatively scripted interactions
	Value of goods and exchange terms must be negotiated case by case	Universal scale for valuing, setting reference commodity prices
	Logistics payment involves storage and transport, maintaining animals and grains, assaying metals, etc.	Logistics of payment is simplified to handing over coins
		Exchange interactions create and strengthen social ties less
Consequences of exchange	People feel interdependent	People feel autonomous and self-sufficient [46]
	Cultivates division of labor and bilateral co-dependency relationships	Undermines social sensitivity, reliance on/collaboration with other people; increases social isolation [46]
Disparity and support	Exchange spheres ensure access to subsistence goods	Concentration of capital and thus power marginalizes the poor
	Gifts to persons of low standing are not expected to be reciprocated	Concentration of control in exchange marginalizes smaller enterprises
Reciprocity	Competitive gift exchange regulates prestige and standing through community-based reciprocity	Quantified obligations have clear terms for satisfaction, and rely less on (vague) mores of reciprocity
	Decay of goods encourages dynamism in exchanges	Supports scaling and abstractions for a coordinated global system of systems
Market System	Not scalable	Non-decay of money encourages hoarding
	Key **Positive** **Neutral** **Negative**	Complexity and invisibility of system elements allows market manipulations and profiteering

Table 1: Tradeoff analysis of barter and pre-negotiated money as exchange paradigms, summarizing discussion in the text.

exchange interactions that could nonetheless undermine the formation of social capital through society: Case-by-case negotiation and other trading interactions, and elaborate but underspecified gifting protocols to regulate social standing and prestige are rich social relationships that expand and strengthen social ties [7]. Graeber [13] argued that modern charity and alms emerged in concert with coinage as a way to preserve sociality in money transactions.

A benefit of money is that it provides a universal motivator and scale of value. Thus, where we might naively see two people engaged and working productively, money valuation emphasizes to us that one is receiving twice as much, or perhaps 400 times as much, for his or her efforts. That is, it objectifies the people and their activity as positions on a linear scale of money valuation. Such disparity can be a motivator for people to acquire more valuable skills by working harder, that is, a person can clearly calibrate how she/he is doing (e.g., in dollars per minute) and set concrete goals. However, if the perceived magnitude or immutability of the disparity are too great it could also demoralize and marginalize. Indeed, the introduction of money into non-market economies can disrupt social protocols such as exchange spheres, and thereby reduce access to subsistence goods [42].

The universality of money also entrains downsides. For example, Gesell [11] argued that money ceases to be an effective instrument of exchange whenever it becomes preferable to the goods and services it can purchase. Indeed, coins and notes ineluctably cause such a preference imbalance by being easy to handle relative to goods that can decay and rot, and must be stored and transported. Gesell suggested the remedy of depreciating currency, proposing that money be continuously discounted enough to ensure a poorer return from hoarding and collecting interest than from investing or otherwise circulating money [9].

Money has powerful psychological consequences. Vohs et al. [46] showed that priming the concept of money can cause people to feel self-confident and autonomous, and to be self-focused and relatively insensitive to others. In a series of experiments, participants were incidentally reminded of the concept of large amounts of money while performing various difficult tasks in contrived social situations. Money priming caused people to resist asking for or providing help. Indeed, Vohs et al. found that money priming caused people to pick up fewer pencils after a staged accident in which a box of pencils was spilled, to position their chairs further from interlocutors in a staged discussion, to express a survey preference for individually oriented leisure activities, and even to prefer working alone over working with a partner when working with another person would have allowed them to share workload. In summary, the mere idea of money evokes a sense that one is self-sufficient and that other people ought to be self-sufficient as well.

However, non-market mechanisms like spheres of exchange and gift exchange manifest in market societies in ritualized protocols that sustain and reproduce family structures, such as weddings and birthdays.

Barter and coinage, though ancient systems, are human designs that facilitate specialization, collaboration and economic growth. Analysis of implicit tradeoffs in the barter and money paradigms, as designs for exchange, as presented in Table 1, can help us to understand subsequent and contemporary innovations in currency and exchange, as well as to identify a design agenda for future innovations. But need and opportunity continue to energize design efforts with respect to currency and exchange.

ALTERNATIVE AND COMPLEMENTARY CURRENCIES

Barter and money are conceptual and historical anchors for understanding paradigms for trade and exchange, but are also themselves diverse and evolving. They can help to frame alternative and complementary currency paradigms that have emerged in the past several decades, and that have become impactful in the past decade.

The past three decades have seen an explosion in currencies other than government-backed currencies. The term "alternative currency" is widely employed, but few if any non-government backed currencies actually aspire to provide an alternative. Most currency innovations are complementary currencies, intended to augment the currency ecology with respect to particular needs or possibilities, though it is possible that a truly alternative currency could emerge at some point.

Most complementary currencies address critical analyses of national money, and embody new currency designs that remedy or meliorate identified issues [24]. For example, one critical analysis of national money is that by providing a universal framework for value and exchange, money undermines the sociality and intimacy of exchange interactions. As reviewed above, the universal framework of money may indeed be so powerful as to undermine perceptions of the self as part of a social world. A strong design theme in complementary currencies is the goal of better evoking and strengthening locality and community through transactions. Local/community currencies [23,31] are an example of this sort of design.

Another critique of universal money is that it is socially inertial. People with more money have disproportionately more access to generating money than do people with less money. Over time, this causes income and possession distributions to skew: the rich become the super-rich, but many others are left behind, marginalized in society; they are left ever further behind. This pattern is characteristic of money-based market economies [35]. Another strong design theme in complementary currencies is the goal of enabling marginalized persons to contribute to society, to participate for their own good and for the good of society. A goal of complementary currencies is to facilitate the economic rehabilitation of marginalized people by enabling economic interactions that do not depend on already having accumulated some degree of wealth. Designing interactions for economic co-production is an example of this [4].

Contemporary national currencies are in no sense commodity money; no one is guaranteed conversion of dollars into anything else. Market dynamics set the value of dollars. A third critical analysis of national currencies is that they are grounded ultimately in the confidence citizens have in government. Monetary policies and currency management strategies of central banks mediate this ultimate grounding, and are intended to enhance confidence by regulating swings of inflation and deflation. A complementary design strategy is to ground currencies in something beyond confidence in national government. Time-based currencies and crypto-currencies are an example of this sort of strategy [4,34].

A fourth critique of national money is that the monetary system has become unnecessarily complex, permitting subtle manipulations by incumbents like large banks to effectively tax currency transactions through collection of various fees or unfair high-speed trading that the average investor cannot compete with [27]. As we write this paper, the bank Credit Suisse has just pled guilty to felony conspiracy in tax evasion [36]. Even when banking practices are legal, it is argued, they are not productive except for the very few privileged entities that are able to manipulate the system to their advantage [22]. A strong design theme in complementary currencies is the streamlining of the monetary system, generally through more sophisticated and transparent use of information technology, which would diminish the role of banks, including national central banks. Crypto currencies like Bitcoin are example of this sort of design.

A fifth, related and longstanding critique, one identified as a threat to the United States by President Abraham Lincoln, is that money centralizes and concentrates power and control of exchange relationships in the hands of corporations [25]. In the past this was justified in enabling human projects of unprecedented complexity. However, the case for such concentrated control is weaker in contemporary economics where close collaboration and coordination of means and goals can be enabled by sophisticated information technology, including peer-to-peer endeavors [4] and crowd finance [44]. Collaborative economy microenterprises still depend on the exchange of money, but, unlike crowd financing, they are implemented through direct reciprocal exchange, person-to-person, emphasizing the sociality of exchange.

LOCAL/COMMUNITY CURRENCIES

Local/community currencies are intended to strengthen local economic activity by facilitating exchanges of goods and services within the community. One rationale for local currency is that it increases the money supply; circulating additional currency in a locale increases the amount of potential local economic activity. A second rationale is that because the local currency is only accepted by local merchants and used by local citizens, the economic activity produced tends to stay centered in the locale, encouraging community members to engage in transactions with one another. Sometimes additional rationales are incorporated, as in the example of the Austrian town of Wörgl; in 1932, the town issued negative interest local scrip in an effort to restart its damaged economy, producing a (successful) test of Gesell's [11] theory that economic recovery can be stimulated by the introduction of 'free money' [9,23].

Contemporary local/community currencies typically bind the value of the local currency to a national currency, but incentivize adoption and use in various ways. For example, BerkShares (www.berkshares.org), in the Bershire region of Massachusetts, offer purchase price discounts. They can be purchased for $US 0.95, but redeemed at parity with the US dollar. OakShares (www.oaklandgrown.org), in Oakland, California, operate like rewards points. They are generated by local purchases made with the Oakland Grown card. Local currencies also employ distinctive graphical designs that vividly evoke the local area, for example, the local scenes and portraits on Salt Spring Island dollars in Canada (www.saltspringdollars.com), or the elaborately witty designs and proud slogan (Our city. Our Money.) of the Bristol Pound in the United Kingdom (bristolpound.org; cf. [26]).

Currently, there are several thousand community currencies; more than a thousand of these are associated with the *transition towns* movement, framing local/community currency as a component of a broader effort to develop community resilience in the context of global economic and ecological crises [31].

TIMEBANKS

Timebanks regulate service exchanges purely on the basis of the time required to perform the services. Everyone has time, and ipso facto can participate in time-based exchange, moreover, valuing services only by the time required to provide them is absolutely equitable; a laborer's time has the same value basis as a boss's time. Timebanks afford new possibilities for social innovation. Thus, time-based exchange helps to integrate economically marginalized members of society, valuing their participation as equal to the most advantaged and central members [40].

Timebanks often coordinate with or are embedded in existing social service institutions (hospitals, schools, churches, food banks, elderly support groups), integrating social service provision, exchange interactions, and opportunities for human development. In the United Kingdom, for example, National Health Service doctors and other healthcare professionals can refer their patients to a timebank as part of treatment for mood disorders. Thus, in the Rushley Green timebank in London, the patients provide services such as accompanying elderly members who are shopping, visiting elderly people in their homes, etc., helping the elderly to live on their own [39]. This innovatively conflates the traditional roles of *recipient* and *provider* in health care services: the participants in these exchange interactions are helped by helping others.

Service exchange interactions in which the roles of provider and recipient are conflated, are called co-productions [19,32]. Co-production interactions are a key mechanism for bringing marginalized persons into the broader economy: Providing services affirms one's ability to contribute something of value. At the same time, it provides an opportunity to learn from working with and helping others. And in a timebank, it also generates time credits, a concrete manifestation of one's contribution [5,12,29].

Timebanks are not a universal framework for exchange; they are better suited to regulating service exchanges than commodity exchanges. For example, it is not obvious how to extend principles of accessibility and equity to valuing a sandwich, a lawnmower, or your house in units of time, nor does the principle of voluntary exchange seem compelling for exchanges involving commodities. Even within the realm of service exchanges, timebanking raises valuation issues; for example, could the equity principle impede exchanges that are inherently inequitable, removing valuable services (e.g., dentistry, software development) from timebanking systems? And the "banking" metaphor is somewhat misleading in implicitly emphasizing the financial economic framing of accretion [2].

Timebanking can be seen as an innovation in generalized exchange [7]. From this standpoint, the uncertainties inherent in its principles of equitable value, voluntary participation, and co-production are social resources that potentially strengthen commitment and trust throughout communities. Because contributions are valued purely on the basis of time, and because the exchanges are voluntary, timebank activity has been granted tax exemption in the United States and in many other countries [4,23]. Timebanks transparently address issues of currency supply and inflation/deflation; members can always generate more or fewer hours, and time is literally a physical constant.

VIRTUAL/DIGITAL/CRYPTO-CURRENCY

Where community currencies and timebanks are examples of currency and exchange innovations that now incorporate information technology, such as database systems, innovation has also flowed the other way round, from new ideas about digital currency applications and infrastructures toward appropriation by society.

	Community Currency Systems (e.g., BerkShares)	**Timebanks** (e.g., Rushley Green timebank)	**Crypto-currency Systems** (e.g., Bitcoin)	**Collaborative Microenterprises** (e.g., an airbnb host)
Pre-conditions of exchange	Encourages local exchange interactions	Everyone always has time to exchange Requires trust among participants	Universal exchange motivator; everyone can use Low need for trust among partners Must be earned in advance of exchange	Enables utilization of resources that might otherwise go unused Requires trust among participants Money must be earned in advance of exchange
Exchange interaction dynamics	Exchanges are social interactions that create and strengthen ties and community identity Can only be used within the local community	Exchanges are social interactions that create and strengthen ties and community identity Everyone's time is valued equally Time is a universal scale valuing services Service exchanges often co-productions Can only be used within the timebank	Exchanges are socially direct but private and encrypted Transactions and logistics are simple and efficient Universal scale for valuing Adoption is not universal	Exchanges are social interactions that introduce people Leverages money economy
Consequences of exchange	Participants feel locally interdependent Resources/capacities are developed and invested locally	Participants feel interdependent; that every member can contribute, and knows this Uncertainties of generalized exchange build social capital	Participants feel autonomous and self-sufficient	Participants feel interdependent, and more able to benefit from interdependence
Disparity and support	Exchange spheres ensure access to subsistence goods Gifts to persons of low standing are not expected to be reciprocated	Concentration of capital and thus power marginalizes the poor Concentration of control in exchange marginalizes smaller enterprises	Direct peer-to-peer exchange undermines central concentration and control of capital	Direct peer-to-peer exchange undermines central concentration and control of capital
Reciprocity	Integrate quantified terms for satisfaction with community-based reciprocity	Integrate quantified terms for satisfaction with community-based reciprocity	Integrate quantified terms for satisfaction with public reciprocity	Integrate quantified terms for satisfaction with direct social interaction
Market System	Backed by the value of the community itself Comprehensiveness and potential for growth limited by locality of exchange	Equitable/voluntary time-based exchanges can be tax exempt Robust with respect to inflation/deflation; intrinsically adjust "money-supply" (hours exchanged) Applies much better to services than commodities	Supports scaling for a coordinated global system Bitcoin supply limitations encourages hoarding Complexity and novelty may limit adoption	Enterprises can be very narrow Federated exchange can be comprehensive
Key	**Positive**	**Neutral**	**Negative**	

Table 2: Tradeoff analysis of alternate/complementary currency and exchange paradigms, summarizing discussion in text.

Much has been made of currency that is used within virtual worlds, such as Second Life's Linden and World of Warcraft's Bloody Coin. Originally designed to facilitate exchange between players in these worlds, the currencies quickly came to achieve real world value in that some individuals were willing to buy the currency in exchange for national currency. This has led to problems with 'farming' in which organizations, often in China, employ or force players to earn currency through their game efforts in order to be able to buy real currency with their earnings [18]. Another issue is that personal gains can be very high in some cases, raising the problem of how to tax virtual currency income [28].

During the 1990s, many initiatives explored digital currency concepts, including secure cash distributions from banks to personal electronic devices, anonymous crowdfunding for assassinations, voluntary online economies that could defy taxation, and solving cryptographic equations to generate digital coins [34]. An imperative that emerged from this early work was to protect privacy and minimize transaction costs through peer-to-peer exchange, that is, to eliminate central mediation of transactions by banks and other financial institutions, but at the same time, to ensure the integrity of currency exchanges, specifically to prohibit double-spending.

Bitcoin, the first successful crypto-currency, was defined in 2008 [30]. Many others exist (310 are listed on coinmarketcap.com at the time of writing) but we will focus our discussion on Bitcoin, which is currently worth more than all the rest combined. Peer-to-peer Bitcoin transactions are verified by public-key encryption, in effect, carried out in public without revealing personal identities. Transactions are bundled and then encrypted, by Bitcoin miners, who compete to provide cryptographic hash equations in order to earn Bitcoin. The bundled and encrypted transactions are then added to the block chain of time-stamped/digitally signed Bitcoin transactions.

Bitcoin has attracted attention as a serious alternative to contemporary national fiat money. It is important to note that the underlying computational mechanisms for a crypto-currency need to be sound, and need to be regarded as sound, but do not need to be explicitly understood or directly used by individuals. Indeed, user testimonials often refer specifically to reduced transaction costs, created by eliminating the role of banks and credit card companies, and reduced risks, entrained by the security and real time finality of transactions [34].

Bitcoin's reputation has been undermined somewhat from its reported appropriation by criminal enterprises, security breaches of Bitcoin online exchanges, such as Mt. Gox, and the great volatility in its valuation One concept that accelerated the early adoption of Bitcoin was the limitation to create no more than 21 million Bitcoins. Not surprisingly, this policy has led to hoarding [21], which has occasionally caused the value of Bitcoin to soar, but more generally undermined it as an effective currency (recall [11]).

COLLABORATIVE ECONOMY MICROENTERPRISES

Collaborative consumption [3], also called the sharing economy [16], has emerged and grown meteorically through the past couple years. It consists of person-to-person exchanges of commodities and services, for example, a meal (cookening.com), the loan of a garden tool (yerdle.com), use of a parking space (parkatmyhouse.com), a ride to work (carpooling.com), a place to sleep (airbnb.com), and so forth. There are hundreds of such services catered to by investment funds, professional associations and networking and advocacy groups (e.g., collaborativefund.com, ouishare.net, shareable.net, peers.org).

In general, collaborative consumption exchanges are arranged through social media interactions, and are executed through face-to-face interactions. They utilize money, but, similar to crypto-currency, they eliminate the institutional mediation entailed in the standard economic paradigm (usually in the form of companies that provide products and services). We call these service exchanges collaborative economy *microenterprises* because the providers operate as tiny independent businesses; they use social websites, like Airbnb, to identify themselves to potential service recipients, for which they pay a fee.

Collaborative economy entrepreneurs provide access to resources (lawnmowers, cars, parking spaces, beds) and experiences (yachts, beach houses, gourmet food) that people might otherwise not be able to arrange or afford, and which otherwise might go unused, and, in that sense, be wasted. Reciprocally, these transactions are opportunities for the entrepreneur to earn money and make social contacts. Collaborative economy microenterprises tend to be quite narrow with respect to the services and commodities exchanged; each is somewhat of a boutique. However, the spectrum of the new microenterprises is quite broad; thus, in aggregate they seem more like a paradigm change.

Collaborative economy microenterprises use national money as currency, thus one has to have money in order to obtain any resource or service at all. The role of money may thereby entrain social isolation [46], diminished connection to others, and reinforce seeing money as end in itself. Of course, the microenterprises also inherit the upsides of money, such as its universal exchange utility. Moreover, this paradigm confronts some downsides of money-based exchange, such as concentration of capital, power, and control of economic activity in small elites (Table 1).

Like the other emerging currency and exchange paradigms, the microenterprises replace hegemonic scale with direct peer-to-peer responsiveness. All of the paradigms rest upon direct peer-to-peer interactions among people, and diminish or eliminate the role of large institutional mediators such as national and global corporations and banks. Thus, as crypto-currency attenuates bank-based transaction costs, collaborative economy microenterprises reduce corporate overheads.

All of the complementary currency and exchange paradigms create new opportunities for people to generate value through working together, and thereby forge social ties that enable greater access to a variety of resources [14]. All of the new paradigms increase the range of economic opportunities available to individuals, and thus to some extent address the inertial incumbency challenge of the conventional money economy that the rich get richer and the poor get marginalized. In various ways, they restore sociality to economic exchange.

DISCUSSION

The history of trade and exchange is not a simple matter of innovation and improvement. For example, the spice trade between Europe and Asia initially entrained unprecedented interaction among civilizations, but eventually led to the colonization and domination of much of the world by European powers. Indeed, contemporary geo-politics includes many debates about trade policy. The present and future of exchange is likewise not a simple matter, and is of course susceptible also to untoward consequence.

Nevertheless, the innovations currently underway can change, and perhaps are now changing paradigms for currency and exchange in contemporary society.

The history of currency and exchange can be viewed as evolutionary design. In a social context without even barter, direct exchange, negotiated case by case, is incredibly innovative. But in leveraging the dynamics of comparative advantage and divisions of labor, barter also helps to manifest its own downsides, for example, the coincidence of wants and unscalably cumbersome negotiations and logistics. Standard exchange values and commodity currencies entrain coins, relieving problems of case-by-case negotiation and logistics, and raising many new affordances for lending/borrowing, taxation, and a wide range of investment paradigms. But money-based exchange also raises new challenges such as objectifying people and activity on an over-simple scale of value, complicating transactions, over-concentrating wealth and economic activity, creating diverse and arcane opportunities for criminal activity, and more generally evoking social isolation and undermining trust and empathy [7,46].

We suggest that the downsides of money are addressed by emerging alternate/complementary currency and exchange paradigms of community currencies, timebanks, crypto-currency, and collaborative economy microenterprises. Indeed, the core rationales for these newer designs address salient features of the money economy that the designers regarded as problematic: community currencies anchor exchange interactions and benefits in local communities; timebanks facilitate equity in access to currency and exchange, and thereby in opportunities to contribute, learn and benefit; crypto-currency increases individual privacy and control, and eliminates the supervision of governments and banks through direct peer-to-peer transactions; collaborative economy microenterprises reduce mediation and transaction costs, while enhancing the direct social consequences of exchange interactions.

The variety of complementary currencies can be analyzed as an emerging ecosystem, that is, as more than a collection of reactions to hegemonic money. This currency ecosystem can be seen as embodying design propositions about future trajectories of economic exchange. Thus, all four examples we discussed favor direct peer-to-peer exchanges over exchanges mediated by national and global institutions. More specifically, these paradigms protect individual privacy relative to centrally-supervised trade and exchange (local/community currencies, timebanks, crypto-currencies), strengthen and encourage strongly social trade and exchange relationships, that is relationships among people who live and/or work in proximity (community currencies, timebanks, many collaborative economy microenterprises), and indeed, between them ensure that every member of society can always participate equitably in at least some economic interactions (timebanks). The trading spheres for the four paradigms are complementary, raising the potential for future integration in a peer-to-peer economy.

Perhaps most importantly, the emerging design space of peer-to-peer currency and exchange is still emerging; each of the four paradigms we analyzed is a work-in-progress. They are developing and changing. We are also aware of ongoing innovations that do not fit well into our four types, for example, modern barter schemes, like www.u-exchange.com, use the web to vastly expand the sphere of users transaction possibilities and credits to overcome the coincidence of wants problem, gift exchanges, like yerdle.com, use the web to expand the sphere of possible transactions. These further examples do fit well into our overall analysis of contemporary peer-to-peer currency and exchange innovations as less centrally supervised and more social and equitable than the long-running paradigm of national money.

IMPLICATIONS FOR DESIGN

Our review and conceptual analysis of contemporary complementary currency and exchange innovations suggests many further design directions. The notion that socio-technologists should or can redesign systems and technologies for currency and exchange may seem over-ambitious, if one focuses on redesigning established systems like the US Federal Reserve. But the alternative and complementary paradigms we have reviewed and analyzed are still emerging, and are relatively plastic with respect to their ability to incorporate new ideas. They are still developing and rapidly growing.

Crypto-currency is a good example for information technologists, as it is literally a data exchange protocol. The Bitcoin experience has evoked many ideas and directions for successive crypto-currencies. Krugman [21] noted that Bitcoin's design, which incorporated a money supply cap of 21 million Bitcoin, encourages speculative hoarding, which, in turn, has limited the impact of Bitcoin. As discussed earlier, hoarding is common whenever financial incumbents believe they can earn more from holding money than they can from investing it. This problem is not likely to ever be directly addressed by national banks, indeed the few (successful) historical cases of implementing Gesell's [11] concept of negative interest (or a tax on wealth, not just income) were stopped by national banks [9]. Crypto-currencies easily afford implementation of negative interest in their underlying algorithms. This is a case where implications for design seem obvious and the consequences could be dramatic.

Negative interest could also be incorporated into timebank designs. It is known that timebanks also evoke hoarding behaviors [40]. The issue is not the same one Gesell identified, since time-based currencies do not accrue interest, and cannot be invested, though they can be shared. The reluctance to circulate time credits appears to be due to preference on the part of some participants for contributing time over consuming services [40]. Still, the negative interest mechanism might serve to loosen inhibitions about requesting services, and in any event, would diminish hoarded time balances and renew motivation to earn time credits.

We described the co-production principle above, the notion that many exchanges depend upon strongly reciprocal interactions in which the roles of provider and recipient are conflated. Thus, when a patient provides a timebank service as part of treatment for a mood disorder, all parties to the exchange are *both* providers and recipients of services [4,12]. Although co-production is cited as a core value and practice of timebanking [4,40] no timebanking software explicitly supports crediting co-production [6]. Instead, co-production is recognized in timebank communities through work-arounds, such as sending messages, awarding ad hoc time credits, and under-reporting (and various other improvisations). It could be that recognizing co-production non-explicitly is a feature, not a bug, in timebanking. Or, it could be that allowing co-production interactions to remain invisible depresses the extent to which co-production exchanges occur. This could be investigated directly through supporting and studying recognition mechanisms such as recommendations, badges, testimonials, and reciprocal donations of time [2,6].

A key goal of local/community currencies is to strengthen local economic activity by encouraging trade and exchange among local community members. Standard approaches of implementing community currencies through commodity money or local currency involve the logistical overheads of managing, or even producing, physical money. Recently, Knowles et al. [20] proposed integrating local sensing technologies into a community currency system; in this design, people employ national currencies, but allow their located transactions to be sensed or declared as they occur, and thus participate transparently in a community currency through their meta-data. This concept has not yet been empirically evaluated. An even more transparent implementation would be to include location information in the profiles and/or transactions of crypto-currency users, thus allowing everyone in the world to participate in a community currency without physical/logistical overheads.

A further implication of using context awareness is that it should be possible to recommend exchange possibilities to potential participants, based on context. Context could be relatively static information such as someone's interests, social connections and history of activities or it could be highly dynamic such as current location, availability or ongoing activity. For example, if a timebank knew that a person enjoys working with the elderly and discussing local politics, and that the person was currently located near an elderly person interested in local politics, the timebank could push a suggestion for a service exchange, instead of merely managing a database of manually submitted service offers and requests [2].

Pushing the use of context-awareness even further, a more sophisticated system might be able to recommend transactions based on personal goals or societal ideals. For example, a person who wants to but isn't getting much exercise (as sensed by a personal mobile device) might receive a recommendation to walk a neighbor's dog each morning. Or a youngster interested in learning about citrus growing, might receive a recommendation to help out on a nearby local fruit farm at harvest time. In a situation where rifts exist in a community (for example in Oakland, California, African American and Spanish-speaking populations that live side-by-side are not well integrated and experience a high degree of inter-racial tension) a system could detect the lack of social connections and interactions between two such groups. It could then recommend transactions between community leaders on each side of the cultural divide who are highly connected in their respective networks and have common interests. In discovering common interests, such individuals are likely to form bonds and help to bring their communities closer together.

Context awareness and automated transaction partner matching offer intriguing design possibilities for increasing the timeliness, convenience, attractiveness and benefits of peer-to-peer exchanges across all four emerging currency paradigms. The collaborative economy microenterprise TaskRabbit has already made a first move in this direction, announcing their use of a matching algorithm in the past few weeks at the time of writing, albeit their algorithm is not yet context-aware.

Alternative currency designs emphasize possibilities for social and economic exchange that mitigate downsides of the established paradigm of pre-negotiated money-based exchange. Especially in the past decade, relatively simple and robust empirical methods, such as the money priming method used by Vohs et al. [46], have been widely applied in psychological studies of the meaning and behavioral impacts of money. These methods could be directly extended to investigate *differences* between the established concept of money and emerging complementary currency concepts, such as those we discussed above.

Alternate/complementary currency and exchange paradigms are growing rapidly. This makes them a natural laboratory for relatively large-scale investigation. For example, the timebank collective hOurWorld (www.hourworld.org) has over 20,000 members and a very high rate of growth for a non-profit, more than doubling in the last two years, according to its website; the collaborative economy enterprise airbnb.com, grew more than tenfold, in guest nights booked, between June 2010 and June 2012, when they reported 10 million rooms booked. Indeed bitcoin and timebanks are great examples of why CSCW research and design innovation is needed; people designing radical p2p technology without economic and collaboration theories may have gotten it wrong (or at least only partially right).

CONCLUSION

The observation that global banking and finance is in crisis has become a worrying commonplace. As we finish this paper, major new economic powers like Brazil, China and Russia are in crisis, while the old economic powers of Europe and North America are barely recovering from the economic crisis of 2007. Engaging and addressing the challenges of creating value together, and of how new designs and technology can better support human economic endeavors is rich and relevant opportunity for CSCW.

A more diverse ecosystem of currency and exchange, including alternate and complementary currencies, could contribute to greater economic equity and stability [24]. A planning document created as part of the, United Nations Millennium Declaration process [45], called for national governments: "To make serious commitments to restructure the global financial architecture based on principles of equity, transparency, accountability and democracy, and to balance, with the participation of civil society organizations, the monetary means to favour human endeavour and ecology, such as an alternative time-based currency." This statement was not included in the final UN Declaration, and eight years later Western economies collapsed. The statement was recently deleted from the UN website.

Technologists understand well that change occurs at the edges of incumbent paradigms, eventually undermining less effective paradigms [1]. Similarly perhaps, the global financial architecture is unlikely to be reformed significantly through top-down initiatives of the UN. Incumbents do not give up power, rather they lose it to innovation and disruption. The opportunity for CSCW is to help reform global financial systems through design.

ACKNOWLEDGMENTS

We thank our collaborators in our timebanking and peer-to-peer exchange projects. This work was supported by the U.S. National Science Foundation (IIS 1218544, 1406858).

REFERENCES

1. Basalla, G. 1988. *The evolution of technology.* Cambridge: Cambridge University Press.
2. Bellotti, V., Cambridge, S., Hoy, K., Shih, P.C., Handalian, L.R., Han, K. & Carroll, J.M. 2014. Towards community-centered support for peer-to-peer service exchange: rethinking the timebanking metaphor. In *Proceedings of the SIGCHI Conference on Human Factors in Computing Systems (CHI '14).* ACM, New York, NY, USA, 2975-2984.
3. Botsman, R., & Rogers, R. 2010. *What's mine is yours: The rise of collaborative consumption.* HarperBusiness.
4. Cahn, E.S. 2000. *No More Throw-Away People: The Co-Production Imperative.* Essential Books, Washington, D.C., USA.
5. Cahn, E.S. & Rowe J. 2000. *Time Dollars: The New Currency that Enables Americans to Turn Their Hidden Resource – Time – Into Personal Security and Community Renewal.* Rodale Press, Emmaus, PA, USA.
6. Carroll, J.M. 2013. Co-production scenarios for mobile timebanking. In *End-User Development.* Springer Berlin Heidelberg, pp. 137-152.
7. Cook, K.S., Cheshire, C., Rice, E.R.W. & Nakagawa, S. 2013. Social exchange theory. In J. DeLamater & A. Ward (Eds.), *Handbook of social psychology.* Dordrecht: Springer, pp. 61-88.
8. Diamond, J. 1999. *Guns, Germs, and Steel: The Fates of Human Societies.* W. W. Norton & Company.
9. Eisenstein, C. 2011. *Sacred economics: Money, gift, and society in the age of transition.* Evolver Editions.
10. Ferguson, N. 2008. *The Ascent of Money: A Financial History of the World.* The Penguin Press.
11. Gesell, S. 1906. *The natural economic order.* Trans. by P. Pye. Berlin: NEO-Verlag.
12. Glynos, J. & Speed, E. 2012. Varieties of co-production in public services: Timebanks in a UK health policy context. *Critical Policy Studies, 6,* 4, 402-433.
13. Graeber, D. 2011. *Debt: The first 5,000 years.* New York: Melville House.
14. Granovetter, M. 1973. The strength of weak ties. *American Journal of Sociology, 78(6),* 1.
15. Greco, T.H. Jr. 2001. *Money. Understanding and creating alternatives to legal tender.* White River Junction, VT: Chelsea Green Publishing.
16. Hamari, J., Sjöklint, M. & Ukkonen, A. 2013. The Sharing Economy: Why People Participate in Collaborative Consumption (May 30). Available at SSRN: http://ssrn.com/abstract=2271971
17. Hann, C. & Hart, K. 2011. *Economic Anthropology: History, Ethnography, Critique.* Cambridge: Polity Press.
18. Heeks, R. Understanding "Gold Farming" and Real-Money Trading as the Intersection of Real and Virtual Economies. *Journal of Virtual Worlds Research, 2*,4.
19. Jacobs, J. 1961. *The death and life and great American cities.* New York: Random House.
20. Knowles, B., Lochrie, M., Coulton, P & Whittle, J. 2014. *BARTER – Promoting local spending behavior.* CHI 2014 Extending Abstracts.
21. Krugman, P. 2013. Bitcoin is evil. *The New York Times,* Opinion Pages, December 28.
22. Lewis, M. 2014 *Flash Boys: A Wall Street Revolt.* W. W. Norton & Company.
23. Lietaer, B.A. 2000. *The Future of Money: Creating New Wealth, Work and a Wiser World.* Random House, London, UK.

24. Lietaer, B.A. & Dunne, J. 2013. *Rethinking Money: How New Currencies Turn Scarcity into Economic Prosperity.* Berrett Koehler Publishers, Inc.

25. Lincoln, A. 1864 Nov. 21, Letter to Col. William F. Elkins. In Shaw, A.H., 1950, *The Lincoln Encyclopedia*, Macmillan, NY.

26. Mainwaring, S., March, W. & Maurer, B. 2008. From meiwaku to tokushita!: Lessons for digital money design from Japan. In *Proceedings of the SIGCHI Conference on Human Factors in Computing Systems (CHI '08).* ACM, New York, NY, USA, 21-24.

27. Mauss, M. 1954. The Gift: *The Form and Reason for Exchange in Archaic Societies.* Re-published by W. W. Norton & Company, August 17, 2000.

28. Mennecke, B.E., Terando, E.E., Janvrin, D.J., & Dilla, W.N. 2007. It's just a game or is it? Real money, real income and real taxes in virtual worlds. *Communications of the Association for Information Systems, 20,* 134-141.

29. Moffett, M & Brat, I. 2012. For Spain's jobless, time equals money. *The Wall Street Journal,* August 27, page A1.

30. Nakamoto, S. 2008. Bitcoin: A Peer-to-Peer Electronic Cash System. Accessed May 17, 2014 at https://bitcoin.org/bitcoin.pdf

31. North, P. 2010. *Local money: How to make it happen in your community.* Cambridge, UK: Green Books.

32. Ostrom, E. 1996. Crossing the great divide: Co-production, synergy, and development. *World Development, 24(6),* 1073-1087.

33. Parry, J. & M. Bloch 1989. *Money and the Morality of Exchange.* Cambridge: Cambridge University Press. Pp. 28–30.

34. Peck, M.E. 2012. Bitcoin: The cryptoanarchists' answer to cash. *IEEE Spectrum, 49(6),* 50-56.

35. Picketty, T. 2014. *Capital in the Twenty-First Century.* Belknap Press.

36. Reuters 2014. Credit Suisse pleads guilty to U.S. criminal charge in tax probe. *Reuters*, May 19, 2014.

37. Ricardo, D. On the Principles of Political Economy and Taxation. London, 1817. Re-published by Dover Publications, June 11, 2004.

38. Ridley, M. 2010. *The Rational Optimist: How Prosperity Evolves.* Fourth Estate.

39. Ryan-Collins, J., Stephens, L., & Coote, A. 2008. The new wealth of time: How time banking helps people build better public services. London: New Economics Foundation.

40. Seyfang, G. 2009. *The New economics of sustainable consumption: Seeds of change.* Palgrave Macmillan, New York, NY.

41. Seyfang, G. & Longhurst, N. Growing green money? Mapping community currencies for sustainable development. *Ecological Economics* 86 (2013), 65-77.

42. Sillitoe, P. (2006) Why spheres of exchange? *Ethnology 45(1),* 1-23,

43. Smith, A. 1776. *An Inquiry into the Nature and Causes of the Wealth of Nations.* London Printed for W. Strahan; and T. Cadell. Re-published by Thrifty Books, October 27, 2009.

44. Spirer, G. 2013. *Crowdfunding: The Next Big Thing.* CreateSpace Independent Publishing Platform.

45. United Nations. 2000. United Nations Millennium Declaration. Adopted 8 September. See especially Articles 13 and 14. Accessed 4 June 2014 at http://www.un.org/millennium/declaration/ares552e.htm A description the of Millennium Declaration process is at http://www.onecountry.org/story/un-civil-society-representatives-gather-millennium-forum

46. Vohs, K. D., Mead, N. L., & Goode, M. R. 2006. The psychological consequences of money. *Science, 314(5802),* 1154-1156.

Forum77: An Analysis of an Online Health Forum Dedicated to Addiction Recovery

Diana MacLean[1], Sonal Gupta[1], Anna Lembke[2], Christopher Manning[1] and Jeffrey Heer[3]
[1] Computer Science Department. Stanford University. Stanford, CA 94305 USA.
[2] Psychiatry & Behavioral Sciences Department. Stanford University. Stanford, CA 94305 USA.
[3] Computer Science & Engineering Department. University of Washington. Seattle, WA 98195 USA.
{malcdi, alembke, cmanning}@stanford.edu, sonal@cs.stanford.edu, jheer@uw.edu

ABSTRACT
Prescription drug abuse is a pressing public health issue, and people who misuse prescription drugs are turning to online forums for help. Are such forums effective? We analyze the process of opioid withdrawal, recovery and relapse on Forum77, MedHelp.org's online health forum for substance abuse recovery. Applying Prochashka's Transtheoretical Model for behavior change, we develop a taxonomy describing phases of addiction expressed by Forum77 members. We examine activity and linguistic features across the phases USING, WITHDRAWING and RECOVERING. We train statistical classifiers to identify addiction phase, relapse and whether a user was RECOVERING at the time of her last post. Applying our classifiers to 2,848 users, we find that while almost 50% relapse, the prognosis for ending in RECOVERING is favorable. Supplementing our results with users' own accounts of their experiences, we discuss Forum77's efficacy and shortcomings, and implications for future technologies.

Author Keywords
Substance abuse; addiction; cessation; online health forums

ACM Classification Keywords
H.5.3 Information Interfaces and Presentation: Group and Organization Interfaces

INTRODUCTION
Drug and alcohol use disorders, in particular the escalating misuse of prescription drugs, present one of the most pressing public health issues of the day. Addiction affects 16% of Americans ages 12 or older (about 40 million people), far exceeding the number of people afflicted with heart disease (27 million), diabetes (26 million), or cancer (19 million) [4]. In 2008, more than 36,000 deaths were due to drug overdoses; of these, opioid pain reliever (OPR) overdoses accounted for more than heroin and cocaine combined [3, 56].

CSCW 2015, March 14–18, 2015, Vancouver, BC, Canada.

http://dx.doi.org/10.1145/2675133.2675146

One traditional and well-accepted addiction management strategy is joining and participating in a mutual help group, such as Alcoholics Anonymous (AA) or Narcotics Anonymous (NA). However, a large and increasing number of people are going online for medical information and advice [20], and those with substance abuse problems are no exception. Several of the largest online health community websites, like MedHelp (`www.medhelp.org`), PatientsLikeMe (`www.patientslikeme.org`), and Daily Strength (`www.dailystrength.org`) include forums dedicated to the topic of addiction. It is telling that Forum77, MedHelp's substance abuse and addiction community, is the largest community on MedHelp, comprising some 740,045 posts in 80,528 discussion threads authored by 51,152 unique users.

Online mutual help groups for recovery are uniquely positioned to offer novel insight into the process of prescription drug abuse cessation for two reasons. First, prescription drug abuse is severely stigmatized, even within the medical community [44, 40]. Prior work shows that people affected by stigmatized conditions are more likely to seek help from peers [10] and to seek help online [8]. Second, patients may be unwilling to discuss issues of prescription opioid misuse with their health care providers, who may be the source of the drugs [56].

Despite the prevalence of online health forums for substance use disorders, and despite the unique role that they could play in the process of cessation, such groups are understudied. Little is known about when, in the cycle of abuse, such groups are most useful to users, what they help with, and whether they aid progression towards recovery. In this paper, we make the following contributions:

A *quantified taxonomy of phases of addiction* as expressed by users on Forum77. Our taxonomy, developed in concert with an addiction specialist, is based on Prochaska's Transtheoretical Model (TTM) of behavior change [49], and serves both as a labeling rubric for mapping text to phases of addiction, as well as a quantified summary of phase-based activity on Forum77. We use the taxonomy to manually label initiating post sequences from 191 Forum77 users (2,266 posts total) with the labels USING, WITHDRAWING or RECOVERING.

An *analysis of activity and linguistic features* across the phases of addiction. We identify features that are characteristic of each phase, and leverage them to train a Conditional Random Field (CRF) model to automatically label users' phases of addiction over their tenure on Forum77. Our CRF achieves an F1-score of 67.6% against a baseline F1-score of 20%. Using CRF-labeled sequences, we are able to identify (1) whether a user relapsed at some point during their tenure, and (2) whether a user was RECOVERING at the time of her final initiating post, with F1-scores of 78% and 82%, respectively. We make our CRF classifier freely available for download at `vis.stanford.edu/projects/forum77`.

An *analysis of transition, relapse and recovery* based on the CRF-labeled phase sequences of 2,848 Forum77 users (32,345 posts). We find that overall, progressive transitions are more prevalent than regressive transitions. Moreover, despite the fact that relapse is common (almost half of users relapse at some point during their tenure), the chances of a user RECOVERING by her final post are favorable. Finally, we observe a significant correlation between high forum engagement (both frequency of participation and volume of response posts authored) during a user's phases of USING and WITHDRAWING and the probability that she is RECOVERING when she leaves Forum77.

BACKGROUND

To our knowledge, our work is the first to investigate the topic of prescription drug abuse cessation in social media. Given the secretive and stigmatized nature of this condition [44], our contribution provides a unique and often overlooked perspective on prescription drug abuse: that of patients themselves. In this section, we provide an overview of prescription drug abuse as well as the traditional, in-person mutual help groups Alcoholics Anonymous (AA) and Narcotics Anonymous (NA). Next, we discuss work evaluating the efficacy of online health communities in general. Finally, we present work which, like ours, attempts to infer a person's health state from her social media contributions.

Prescription Drug Abuse

Prescription drug abuse (or "nonmedical use") is defined as "the use of a medication without a prescription, in a way other than prescribed, or for the experience or feelings elicited" [56]. Opioid pain relievers, such as hydrocodone, oxycodone, morphine and codeine, are the most frequently abused prescription medications [5]. In 2010, some 5.1 million Americans reported misusing prescription pain relievers in the last month, followed by sedatives (2.6 million) and stimulants (1.1 million) [5].

Recent medical research argues that drug dependence is a chronic, relapsing and remitting disorder that behaves like other chronic illnesses with a behavioral component, such as Type II Diabetes Mellitus [38]. Despite this, prescription opioid abuse is a highly stigmatized condition: the viewpoint that opioid misuse is a flaw of a person's moral character, rather than a legitimate medical condition, is common [44, 40]. The stigma is compounded by the fact that the most effective treatments for opioid use disorders are methadone or buprenorphine-assisted replacement therapies [44]. Finally, as pain treatment is often the starting point of a longer addiction to prescription opioids, it is common for people with prescription drug use disorders to acquire their drug of choice via a doctor's prescription [53, 56, 34]. In a survey of 571 individuals at an opioid detoxification clinic, Sproule et al. [53] report that 37% acquired their prescription opioids via prescription, 21% on "the street", and 25% through a combination of both.

Withdrawal

Withdrawal (or detoxification) is a painful process that is frequently compared to having a bad case of flu [6, 17]. Common withdrawal symptoms include agitation, anxiety, muscle aches, insomnia, sweating, abdominal cramping, diarrhea, goose bumps, nausea and vomiting [6]. Typically, symptom onset aligns with the first missed dose in the case of a "cold turkey" approach, or within a few days of dose reduction in the case of a taper [17]. Symptom severity peaks within a few days of final exposure, and gradually reduces as the user's physical dependence on the drug weakens [17]. Withdrawal duration, which depends on biological factors, drug, dosage levels, and withdrawal method, ranges broadly from 7-10 days (cold turkey) [21] to 20-35 days (methadone-assisted taper) [17].

Research on easing the withdrawal process focuses primarily on medication-assisted detoxification overseen by a medical professional. However, Green et al. [23] showed that informing patients in full as to the nature and severity of withdrawal symptoms that they were likely to experience resulted both in lower self-reported symptom severity scores as well as an increased probability of completing the detoxification process. Patient-reported strategies for effectively completing withdrawal include distraction and avoidance, especially in the form of physical activity [21].

Self-Detoxification

Almost no research focuses on the subject of self-detoxification. We found two studies in which attendees of the same London methadone treatment facility were interviewed about prior self-detoxification attempts. In both studies, most patients had attempted self-detoxification, and many had made multiple attempts [21, 43]. The short-term success rate per episode (24 hours of abstinence) was 41% [43], while the medium-term success rate per episode (10 days abstinence) was 24% [21]. The design of these studies naturally exclude patients who successfully maintain abstinence. When asked why their attempts had failed, subjects pointed to lack of support during detoxification [21], as well as easy access to drugs and severity of withdrawal symptoms [21, 43].

Relapse & Recovery

Relapse rates for opioid use are high. Reported reuse statistics for individuals having gone through detoxification programs range from 81–91% [22, 52]. However, long-term prognoses are more favorable, with evidence suggesting that 45–51% of patients may achieve sustained abstinence, and that sustained abstinence is a gradual process [22].

"Recovery" is a hotly contested term in drug use disorder communities. Many align with the Alcoholics Anonymous viewpoint that addiction is an uncurable disease and, as such, an individual never fully "recovers" from addiction [2].

Rather, users who reach sustained sobriety are referred to as being "in recovery". In this work, we refer to users who have overcome physical withdrawal as RECOVERING.

In-Person Mutual Help Groups

Alcoholics Anonymous (AA), founded in the 1930s [1], is one of the most utilized services for substance use disorders in the world, with over 4 million members across 100 different societies [28]. It has also given rise to other peer recovery groups for addiction, like Narcotics Anonymous (NA) and Gamblers Anonymous (GA). AA and NA are almost entirely based on mutual support, even condemning the giving of medical advice as outside the expertise of the group, instead encouraging members to see a doctor if medical or psychiatric problems arise [28].

Three decades of accumulated evidence demonstrates that active participation in such groups for addiction improves outcomes [35], although success rates are ill-defined and vary across studies [7]. A high participation level in AA is reported to be one of the strongest predictors for abstinence [45, 51]. For example, Pagano et al. [45] found that users who actively helped other AA members had a relapse rate of 55%, while those who did not relapsed at a rate of 75%. Correspondingly, many of the benefits of AA are thought to stem from the social network that it provides its members, who afford each other support, role modeling and experiential advice [30]. Kelly et al. [31] find that through their interactions with other AA members, users experience increased abstinence self-efficacy, increased spirituality/religiosity and reduced negative affect. Having a sponsor (an informal mentor) is also thought to help newcomers avoid relapse [54].

Online Health Communities

Studies of cancer-oriented online support groups show that participation assists effective disease management [27, 32], as they serve as information conduits for lifestyle management and coping [32, 41] as well as arenas for personal empowerment through narrative [18, 27]. Additional user-perceived benefits for sharing health data included suggestions for symptom management and treatment, improved understanding of one's condition, and enhanced confidence in doctors' evaluations [59]. Patients report that information provided by peers is both valuable and distinct from that given by clinicians [24]. Mankoff et al. [36] find that online peer interaction facilitates a positive shift in users' perspective about their condition, and that over time participants' roles evolve towards supporting and helping others. In concert, prior work supports the notion that people struggling with addiction may benefit from online health community participation.

Inferring Health State from Social Media

The idea that social media users' health states will be somehow reflected in the content that they contribute, and that it may be possible to predict health state from these data, has captured the interest of several researchers. De Choudhury et al. [11, 12, 13] analyze how postpartum depression (PPD) might be reflected on both Twitter and Facebook. Using their findings, they leverage activity and linguistic features to build models that predict the onset of PPD from Facebook data [13]. In other social media studies, both activity features, such as social engagement and connectivity, and linguistic features, such as affect and writing style, have been shown to be useful indicators of depression [14, 26, 50, 46], neuroticism [50] and post-traumatic stress disorder [9].

A related challenge is to identify a user's current *phase* within a specific medical condition. Jha and Elhadad [29] found that a combination of linguistic and activity features are helpful for identifying cancer stages I–IV. Murnane and Counts [42] conducted an analysis of smoking cessation as reflected on Twitter. They find that linguistic features of positive and negative sentiment, as well as social interaction variables, were significant differentiators between users who relapsed and users who ceased their smoking behavior during the time of the study. Finally, Wen and Rosê use logistic regression and flexible pattern matching over posts from an online cancer community to extract pre-defined events onto a timeline [57].

THE FORUM77 DATASET

Forum77 is an online health forum dedicated to addiction recovery. It is the largest of several topic-specific, online health forums that comprise MedHelp (`www.medhelp.org`), the world's largest online health community. In keeping with most of MedHelp's forums, Forum77 is peer moderated. We acquired our Forum77 dataset through a research agreement with MedHelp, who anonymized the data prior to sharing.

Our dataset comprises roughly 7 years of discussions on Forum77 (Jan 2007 to Apr 2014). During this time 51,153 unique users authored some 740,046 posts (80,529 threads). Figure 1 shows summary plots describing Forum77 content and user volume, average user tenure and posting rates, and thread length distribution. While most users have a tenure shorter than one month, thousands of users participate for several years. Note that we have neither demographic data (age, geographic location etc.) describing Forum77 users nor page view data describing lurking (reading without posting). As such, we restrict our analyses to Forum77 discussion content.

Discussions on Forum77 follow a simple thread structure: a user starts a discussion with an *initiating post*, along with a descriptive title. Responses are displayed below the initiating post in the order in which they are received. Features for sub-discussions (nested responses) as well as for selecting a reply as the "best response" exist, but are infrequently used.

Typically, users present *their own* substance use situation (e.g., drugs used and number of days clean) in initiating posts. In contrast, in response posts users are liable to discuss a wide range of substance abuse situations. Accordingly, we restrict our analysis of users' addiction phases to initiating posts.

EXPLORING & MODELING PHASES OF ADDICTION

To systematically analyze phases of substance abuse in Forum77, we require both a valid taxonomy of phases and a rubric mapping post text to these phases. Towards this aim, we use a set of phase labels derived from the Transtheoretical Model (TTM) of behavior change.

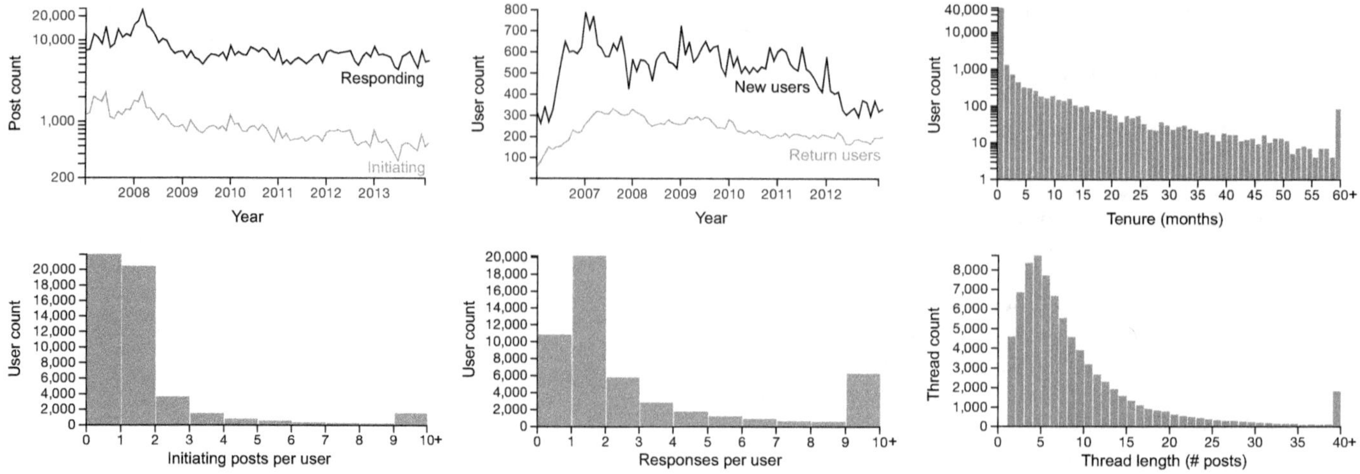

Figure 1: Summary statistics of Forum77 variables: post volume by month (top left), user volume by month (top middle), user tenure distribution (top right), user initiating post distribution (bottom left), user response post distribution (bottom middle), and thread length distribution (bottom right)

Transtheoretical Model for Behavior Change

The Transtheoretical Model (TTM) is a framework that describes six *stages of change* that a person traverses in order to manifest permanent behavior change. Established in 1997 by Prochaska & Velicer [49], the TTM has been applied to a range of behaviors, from smoking cessation [15, 42, 55] and substance abuse [39], to sustainable energy usage [25]. The intuitiveness and universal applicability of the TTM make it a useful descriptive tool; however, care should be taken before utilizing it to inform treatment or intervention [39, 58].

According to the TTM, prior to considering behavior change, a person is in the stage of **pre-contemplation**. After **contemplation**, she moves on to **preparation**, in which she makes any preparations necessary to initiate a behavior change. The person then moves on to **action**, a concerted and deliberate attempt to affect short-term behavior change. If successful, the person enters a period of **maintenance**, in which she tries to sustain the behavior change in the long term. If successful, she eventually enters the stage of **termination** [49]. As there is considerable debate over whether addiction is a terminable condition [2], we omit this stage for our purposes.

Rubric Development

In order to match Forum77 posts to TTM stages, we randomly sampled 1,000 initiating posts. Two authors mapped these posts to stages in the TTM, assigning descriptive labels to emergent sub-categories specific to the topic of addiction (e.g., *tapering* and *cold turkey* are both part of the TTM stage *Action*). We repeated this process several times, reviewing the rubric with an addiction specialist prior to finalization.

A Taxonomy of the Phases of Addiction

Table 1 describes our resulting phase taxonomy, along with example posts (synthesized from genuine posts to preserve user privacy) and the prevalence of each label in our final 1,000 initiating post sample. Although descriptively interesting, several of the labels in the taxonomy (e.g., *intent to quit* and *about to quit*) are rare. For parsimony, and to aid subsequent classification accuracy, we collapse labels into three categories: USING, WITHDRAWING and RECOVERING.

Labeling People, not Posts

Moving forward, we want to analyze addiction phases at the level of individual *people*. Two factors that emerged in our taxonomy development (see Table 1) convinced us that labeling randomly sampled posts would be insufficient for such analyses, and that we should instead label users' entire post *sequences*. The first was the high prevalence (9.8%) of *n/a* labels. These posts are often social in nature and, taken independently, are impossible to assign a class. However, when read in the context of the author's previous and following posts, the label is usually obvious. The second factor was the low prevalence of *relapse* labels. While we noticed that many users relapse, few announce the fact directly. Rather, most users will mention a relapse when they are already committed to another cessation attempt (e.g., *about to quit* or even *quitting* again). However, a relapse can still be observed in a regressive sequence (e.g., WITHDRAWING $\rightarrow$ USING). Based on these observations, in the rest of this paper we label *sequences* of posts.

CHARACTERIZING THE PHASES OF ADDICTION

Phases of addiction coincide with distinct psychological and physiological states. In this section, we analyze activity and linguistic features that might characterize an author's phase on an *initiating-day*. We define an initiating day to be any day on which the user initiated a thread on Forum77. If the author initiated multiple posts, we combine them for analysis. Our goal is two-fold: (1) to characterize phases of addiction as they are expressed on Forum77, and (2) to identify discriminative features that might be used for classification.

Sample & Labeling

To study how addiction phase changes over time, we restrict our analysis to users who have initiated at least 5 threads on

Table 1: Addiction Phase Taxonomy

Final Category	TTM phase	Label	Description	Synthesized Example	%
USING	Pre-contemplation	Using	Subject is using substances and demonstrates no intention to quit.	it has been forever since I've been here and not much has changed. I am still using the prescribed amount of oxycodone for neck pain.	3.1
		Addicted	Subject is using substances and indicates that she is addicted, but demonstrates no intent to quit.	my girlfriend and i r both addicted to percs but she is taking way more than me and keeps getting chest painonce every other week.	7.4
		Relapse	Subject has used substances again after an attempt to quit.	I just messed up majorly. I was 6 days clean, doing OK-ish, when my mother stopped by with 10 Vics "incase I needed them". Of course, being the WEAK person I am, I took them all right there.	1.3
	Contemplation	Intent to quit	Subject expresses desire to stop abusing a substance in the future.	I want off roxies. is methadone the answer. I need to work daily. I cannot do withdrawls. PLEASE HELP!	9.3
	Preparation	About to quit	Subject notes time and/or plan (e.g., tapering schedule) to quit.	i was planning to quit the first week of March. True to form addict fashion I'm out of both money and pills. So I'm about to go ct now instead of next week when I'd planned.	2.5
WITHDRAWING	Action	Quitting	Subject is in withdrawal; method unspecified.	Today is my 5th day of FREEDOM! I havent experienced any w/ds yet. So much energy.	39.1
		Tapering	Subject is in withdrawal; detoxification method is a taper.	Have some Vics I am taking. I am down to 6 a day. I plan to go down to 3 a day then 1 a day until I am done!	6.4
		Cold Turkey	Subject is in withdrawal; detoxification method is cold turkey.	I am on day 6 of CT from 150mg+ a day of oxycodone. I'm doing fine just some overall anxiousness	3.3
RECOVERING	Maintenance	In recovery	Subject has finished detoxing; no physical withdrawal symptoms expressed	Just an update to tell you that I have 67 clean days today. I feel amazing. I sleep well now and feel good! I've had a lot of discussions about aftercare.	17.8
		n/a	Impossible to determine status based on post	I've been away for few days and everything seems different. Anyway I hope everyone is doing great.	9.8

Forum77 (n=2,848 out of 29,196 users who initiated at least one post). Of these, we randomly sampled 200 users ($\sim$7% of the full 2,848) and all of their initiating posts. We discarded 9 users from the sample: two who had authored more than 100 posts, one account that belonged to MedHelp, and six accounts for which there was no clear ownership (several different people appeared to be using the same MedHelp account). The resulting sample contains 2,266 initiating posts (average 11.9 posts per user) and comprises $\sim$5.5% of the full 41,387 initiating posts authored by the 2,848 users.

Two authors categorized each initiating post in the sample using the taxonomy presented in Table 1. We labeled each user's data in chronological order so as to transfer context learned from prior labels. Disagreements (which were rare) were relabeled based on a consensus reached after discussion.

Activity Characteristics

We identify 15 activity characteristics that describe an initiator's *global* activity over time, her *local* activity 5 days prior to the initiating-day in question, and both initiator's and respondents' activity on the *initiating-day*. Table 3 describes each feature as well as feature distributions across each class.

Linguistic & Content Characteristics

Differences in word use and linguistic style are believed to reveal a range of information about people, from psychological state to social identity [48]. The Linguistic Inquiry and Word Count (LIWC) [47] software calculates 80 linguistic variables over text. In prior work, LIWC has been used to characterize and distinguish women suffering from Post-Partum Depression (PPD) [13], individuals at risk for depression [14] and smokers on Twitter who are at risk for relapse [42]. We calculate all 80 LIWC variables over initiating post text as well as any responses received on the initiating-day, then examine differences in these variables across the phases of substance abuse recovery. Due to the large number of LIWC variables, we include Tables 7 & 8 at the end of the paper.

In addition to the LIWC features, we calculate three additional variables over initiating post text. Users frequently mention how long they have been clean at the time of posting. We extract *days clean* automatically by using hand written patterns, such as "clean X days" and "X weeks off", where X represents a number. We convert X to days if necessary. We also use a more relaxed version of this feature, called *days mentioned*, in which we do not require the user to explicitly mention terms like "clean" or "off". Finally, we count the number of questions asked by identifying sentences that start with a question word and/or end with a question mark. This feature has proved helpful in prior work [13]. In subsequent experiences, we find that including these features improves classifier performance by $\sim$2.2%.

Finally, we count how many phase-specific words occur in both initiating post text as well as response text. To deter-

Table 2: Example terms typical of USING, WITHDRAWING and RECOVERING posts and their responses.

	Initiating Post	Responses
U	withdrawls, wants, hate, addicted, scared, tried, stop	situation, willing, treatment, withdrawl, option, advise, rehab, counseling
W	rls, hot, restless, aches, slept, arms, legs, headache, wd, worst, stomach, tramadol	potassium, heating, fluids, baths, pad, showers, legs, melatonin, hot, slept, bananas
R	craving, recovery, lately, sober, fight, truly, clean, cravings, true, worth	inspiration, accomplishment, congratulations, sharing, thank, miss, proud, paws

mine whether a term t is particularly descriptive of a phase p, we calculate its frequency-based odds ratio. If $f_p(t)$ is the number of posts of phase p that contain t, then:

$$OR(t,p) = \frac{f_p(t) * f_{\bar{p}}(\bar{t})}{f_p(\bar{t}) * f_{\bar{p}}(t)}$$

The odds ratio is a measure of strength of association. We calculate the odds ratio for each term across each phase, and retain terms with an odds ratio > 2. Table 2 shows sample terms for both initiating and response posts.

Results: Activity and Linguistic Features

Our feature analysis indicates that both users' activity and users' content and linguistic characteristics differ measurably across addiction phases. We present activity features in Table 3, linguistic features over initiating posts in Table 7, and linguistic features over response posts in Table 8. Unless otherwise mentioned, we use Kruskal-Wallis tests to assess statistical significance. A non-parametric test is appropriate for data that are not expected to follow a normal distribution (such as ours), and Kruskal-Wallis tests whether any pair in a trio of distributions is significantly different.

USING

This phase is characterized by long absences from the forum and, correspondingly, low levels of recent activity. Users who are USING have, on average, been absent from forum participation in all capacities for more than twice as long as users who are WITHDRAWING or RECOVERING (40 vs. ~18 *days since last activity*). A longer absence from the forum may partially explain why USING posts are, on average, longer (208 vs. ~180 words): users must account for lost time and bring their audience back up to speed.

Both *days clean* and *days mentioned* vary widely in USING posts, and have surprisingly high median values. Examining the underlying data provides an explanation: users who are USING often mention how long they had been clean prior to relapse in statements such as, "I was clean for 4 months before...", or, "I would have had 717 days clean today".

Finally, USING posts offer the lowest levels of positive affect (16% less than WITHDRAWING and 32% less than RECOVERING), and the highest levels of discussion around the topic of health (16% more than WITHDRAWING and 36% more than RECOVERING); characteristics that are mirrored in responses to USING posts. The lack of positivity resonates with the fact that users who are USING have either relapsed or failed to progress towards recovery.

WITHDRAWING

In recent activity, users who are WITHDRAWING issue more initiating posts and self responses than those who are USING or RECOVERING. In addition, they have the smallest average number of *days since last initiating post* (21 vs. 31 RECOVERING and 50 USING) and *days since last self-response* (29 vs. 42 RECOVERING and 66 USING).

As we might expect, WITHDRAWING users express the lowest numbers of *days clean* and *days mentioned*. In addition there is a great deal more language about feeling, biological processes and the body (Table 7). These observations align with the fact that detoxification is an uncomfortable physical process from which people constantly seek relief [17].

Responses to WITHDRAWING posts are not particularly distinctive. Aside from expressing slightly more anxiety, and containing more content about feeling and the body, other linguistic variables tend to take on a value somewhere in between those of responses to USING and RECOVERING. This may reflect that respondents try to influence users from one side of the spectrum to the other, modifying their language according to the user's progress.

RECOVERING

These users are highly active, especially in the area of responding to *other* peoples' posts. In recent activity, they issue, on average, 15.2 responses to other peoples' threads, compared to 5.5 by users who are WITHDRAWING and 1.9 by users who are USING. Moreover, unlike WITHDRAWING and USING users, their $\frac{\text{\# initiating posts}}{\text{\# responses authored}}$ tend to be < 1.

Linguistic features also suggest that RECOVERING users tend to focus on others. The pronoun *you* is used almost 100% more while the *I* pronoun is used less, and language is more social. Moreover, users express significantly more positive affect (25% more than WITHDRAWING, 48% more than USING) and less anxiety (18% less than WITHDRAWING, 16% less than USING). The evident outward focus of initiating posts from RECOVERING users resonates with the 12th step in traditional twelve-step programs such as AA, which encourage people to strengthen their sobriety by using their experiences to help others achieve it [2].

Responses to RECOVERING posts are distinct in that they express substantially more positive affect (27% more than responses to WITHDRAWING, 57% more than responses to USING). They also tend to host a notable quantity of exclamation marks (100% more than WITHDRAWING, 350% more than USING). Inspection reveals that this is an expression of excitement and encouragement in response to good news, for example, "ooooooorrrraaaahhhhh!!!!!!!!!" and "I am so PROUD of YOU!!!!!".

Table 3: Activity and content-based features for the three classes in the labeled dataset. Statistical significance is determined using Kruskal-Wallis tests (* $p < 0.05$; ** $p < 0.005$; *** $p < 0.001$) after Bonferroni corrections to adjust for family-wise error rate across all 184 variables (includes 160 LIWC variables). Column c denotes (○) if the feature is used in our CRF classifier.

		c	p	USING Mean	USING Med	USING IQR	USING MAD	WITHDRAWING Mean	WITHDRAWING Med	WITHDRAWING IQR	WITHDRAWING MAD	RECOVERING Mean	RECOVERING Med	RECOVERING IQR	RECOVERING MAD
Activity Characteristics															
All time	# initiating posts authored		***	8.84	5.00	10.00	5.93	8.78	5.00	8.00	4.45	20.73	14.00	22.00	13.34
	# self responses authored		***	13.93	5.00	18.00	7.41	13.80	8.00	15.00	8.90	33.26	23.00	36.25	23.72
	# responses authored		***	26.90	6.00	21.00	8.90	23.61	8.00	21.00	10.38	178.69	67.00	159.25	83.77
	# initiating posts / # responses authored	○	***	1.36	1.00	1.31	1.02	1.28	0.82	1.26	0.85	0.53	0.22	0.35	0.21
	Days since last init. post	○	***	50.94	5.00	24.00	5.93	21.04	2.00	5.00	1.48	31.04	4.00	12.00	4.45
	Days since last self resp.	○	***	66.34	9.00	43.50	11.86	29.94	2.00	8.00	1.48	42.05	6.00	17.00	7.41
	Days since last response	○	***	73.37	5.00	27.00	5.93	33.51	2.00	6.00	1.48	28.68	2.00	5.00	1.48
	Days since last activity		***	39.56	3.00	13.00	2.97	16.66	1.00	2.00	0.00	17.76	1.00	4.00	0.00
Last 5 days	# initiating posts authored	○	***	0.93	0.00	1.00	0.00	2.01	1.00	3.00	1.48	1.81	1.00	3.00	1.48
	# self responses authored	○	***	1.37	0.00	2.00	0.00	3.32	1.00	4.00	1.48	2.89	0.00	4.00	0.00
	# responses authored	○	***	1.87	0.00	2.00	0.00	5.48	1.00	6.00	1.48	15.20	5.00	16.00	7.41
	# initiating posts / # responses authored	○	***	1.02	1.00	0.00	0.00	1.06	1.00	0.58	0.64	0.58	0.33	0.87	0.42
Today	# replies received		.	5.15	4.00	5.00	2.97	5.52	4.00	5.00	2.97	6.09	4.00	6.00	4.45
	# respondants		.	3.82	3.00	3.00	2.97	4.05	3.00	3.00	2.97	4.68	3.00	4.00	2.97
	# self responses		**	1.57	1.00	2.00	1.48	1.89	1.00	3.00	1.48	1.53	1.00	2.00	1.48
Post and Response Content Characteristics															
Initiating	Days clean	○	***	421.15	14.00	175.00	17.79	47.50	5.00	7.00	4.45	125.97	45.00	74.00	43.00
	Days mentioned	○	***	52.10	10.00	38.25	11.86	19.08	5.00	7.00	4.45	57.03	27.00	48.00	28.17
	# questions	○	**	2.94	2.00	3.00	1.48	2.35	2.00	2.00	1.48	2.60	2.00	2.00	1.48
	# USING terms	○	***	0.73	0.00	1.00	0.00	0.35	0.00	1.00	0.00	0.25	0.00	0.00	0.00
	# WITHDRAWING terms	○	***	0.50	0.00	1.00	0.00	1.11	1.00	2.00	1.48	0.44	0.00	1.00	0.00
	# RECOVERING terms	○	***	0.38	0.00	1.00	0.00	0.39	0.00	1.00	0.00	0.94	1.00	1.00	1.48
Responses	# USING terms	○	**	0.31	0.00	0.00	0.00	0.19	0.00	0.00	0.00	0.18	0.00	0.00	0.00
	# WITHDRAWING terms	○	***	0.86	0.00	1.00	0.00	1.18	1.00	2.00	1.48	0.76	0.00	1.00	0.00
	# RECOVERING terms	○	***	0.53	0.00	1.00	0.00	0.53	0.00	1.00	0.00	0.78	0.00	1.00	0.00

STATISTICAL CLASSIFICATION OF ADDICTION PHASE

Informed by our feature analysis, we next train a statistical classifier to automatically annotate sequences of Forum77 initiating posts with the labels USING, WITHDRAWING or RECOVERING. Analyses of phase sequences can give insight into events such as relapse and recovery. Our classifier allows us to scale such analyses to the entire Forum77 dataset. Below, we describe our classifier and report its performance. We discuss relapse and recovery in the next section.

Model & Features

A user's path through addiction phases forms a natural sequence. A Conditional Random Field (CRF) [33] is a probabilistic graphical model that performs inference over sequences, rather than individual data points. By taking into account prior and subsequent data items in a sequence, CRFs are *context sensitive*. For example, unlike a CRF, a non-sequence-based classifier might have difficulty classifying a post like, "I've been away for a few days and everything seems different. Anyway I hope everyone is doing great...", even if it was sandwiched between two posts that were obviously USING, as the post itself contains no clues as to the user's phase.

Accordingly, we train a 3-class CRF to annotate a user's sequence of initiating-days with the labels USING, WITHDRAWING or RECOVERING. We use an adapted a version of the Stanford Named Entity Recognizer package, a trainable, Java implementation of a CRF classifier, (`http://nlp.stanford.edu/software/CRF-NER.shtml`) that analyzes sequences of documents (default unit of analysis is a token). Tables 3, 7 and 8 indicate the subset of features that we used for classifier training. We selected features based on apparent discriminability, and iterative evaluation through 10-fold cross validation. In order to improve robustness and model potentially non-linear responses, we binned numeric features into octiles: ranks that divide the data evenly into 8 groups. While using quartiles is arguably more common in standard practice, we found that using octiles improved classifier performance.

Table 4: CRF performance scores aggregated over 10 runs of 10-fold cross validation, with randomly shuffled input sets.

Label	Precision	Recall	F1-score	Accuracy
Combined	**68.3**	**68.0**	**67.6**	**69.8**
USING	62.4	61.7	61.4	
WITHDRAWING	70.6	71.9	70.9	
RECOVERING	72.1	71.2	70.9	
Baseline	14.0	33.0	20.0	43.0

Performance

Table 4 shows Precision, F1 and Recall scores for the CRF classifier. Our classifier achieves an F1-score of 67.6%

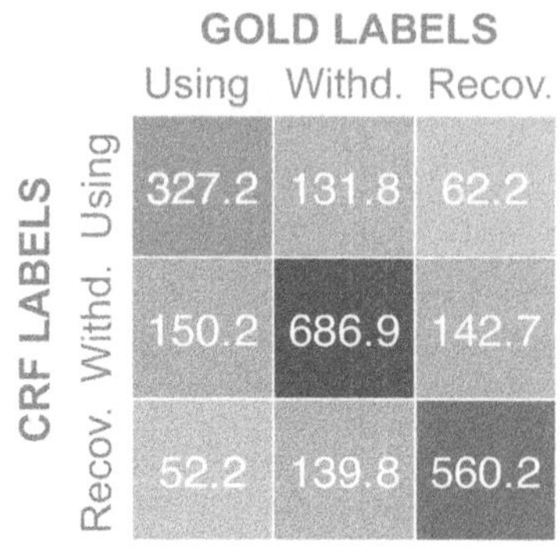

Figure 2: Confusion matrix for our CRF classifier aggregated across 10 randomized runs of 10-fold cross validation.

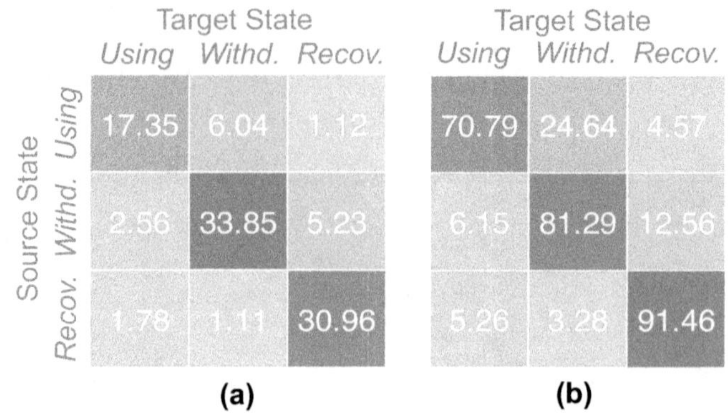

Figure 3: **(a)** Normalized transition frequencies between addiction phases (e.g., RECOVERING → USING edges comprise 1.78% of the total transitions in the CRF-labeled data) and **(b)** conditional transition probabilities (e.g., the probability of a user moving from USING to RECOVERING is 4.57%.)

against a baseline F1-score of 20.0%, acquired by labeling each instance with the majority class, WITHDRAWING.

It is useful to know which labels the CRF is likely to confuse. Figure 2 shows the CRF classifier's confusion matrix. Diagonal entries indicate counts of correctly-classified instances. The strong diagonal indicates a relatively high level of accuracy. Most classification errors occur between adjacent phases: confusing USING and WITHDRAWING, and confusing WITHDRAWING and RECOVERING is common, but confusing USING and RECOVERING less so. This resonates with a point prevalent in the addiction literature: stages of recovery are not black and white but rather fall on a spectrum [16, 37].

Results

We analyze the result of applying our CRF classifier to the entirety of the Forum77 membership base who have initiated > 5 posts (2,848 users, 32,345 initiating posts). Our results give us insight into common transitions between addiction phases, enabling us to answer questions such as, "If a user is WITHDRAWING today, how likely is it that she will be RECOVERING on her next initiating-day?" and "what is the most frequent phase change observed on Forum77?"

Figure 3(a) shows the normalized transition frequency matrix for USING, WITHDRAWING and RECOVERING. The most common transitions lie along the diagonal, indicating that users typically initiate consecutive posts in any one phase. Self-transitions aside, the *progressive* edges between consecutive stages (USING → WITHDRAWING and WITHDRAWING → RECOVERING) are the most common, accounting for approximately 6% and 5.2% of total transitions, respectively. In contrast, *regressive* edges between consecutive stages (WITHDRAWING → USING and RECOVERING → WITHDRAWING) are less common, accounting for 2.6% and 1.1% of total transitions, respectively.

Figure 3(b) shows transition probabilities across states. The likelihood of a same-state transition increases with the progressiveness of the state. For example, there is a 91% chance that a RECOVERING user will be RECOVERING in their next initiating post, but a 71% chance that a user in a USING state will be USING in their next initiating post.

Figure 4 shows the distributions of phase length in days for each phase. We calculate phase length as the number of days between the first and last post in a contiguous sequence. The typical WITHDRAWING phase lengths align well with those reported in the literature on addiction, which suggests a 7–35 day duration depending on the detoxification method used, as well as other factors [21, 17].

CLASSIFYING RELAPSE AND RECOVERY

Relapse and recovery are critical events in the process of addiction that are often viewed as "failure" or "success". Prior work in the addiction literature suggests that recovery is a long, iterative process of which relapse is a part [22]. Leveraging our CRF classifier, we present methods for identifying (1) if a user has relapsed during her tenure on the forum, and (2) if a user is RECOVERING on her last initiating-day on Forum77. We then investigate if relapse adversely correlates with a user's chance of RECOVERING. Finally, we identify activity features during USING and WITHDRAWING phases that discriminate users who last post in a state of RECOVERING.

Identifying Relapse

To identify a relapse incident, we codify three transition patterns that relate to relapse:

RECOVERING → { **WITHDRAWING, USING** }
WITHDRAWING → **USING**
WITHDRAWING → (45+ days absent) → **WITHDRAWING**

This last pattern is based on the observation that a general window for withdrawal duration is 7 - 35 days [17, 22]. As such, if a user was absent for more than 45 days, and then returned in a state of WITHDRAWING, it is likely that they failed in their initial attempt and have restarted. While it is possible that this pattern will capture individuals on a slow taper, in our experience it is unlikely that such users would be inactive for a full 45 days.

We identify whether a user relapsed or not during her tenure on Forum77 by testing whether any of the above patterns exist in her sequence of phase transitions. To evaluate the efficacy

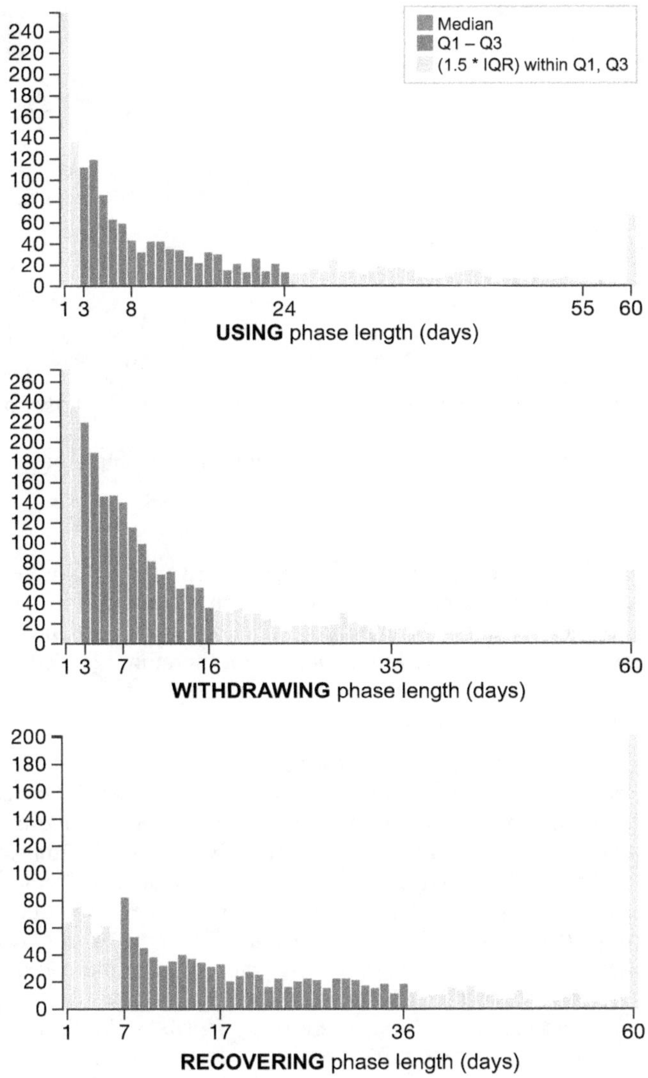

Figure 4: Distributions of phase lengths. Each red bar highlights the median value, while the dark blue region indicates the middle spread. The light blue region indicates values that fall within 1.5 $*$ the interquartile range of the middle spread.

of this approach, we apply it to both the *gold label sequences* as well as the *CRF-labeled sequences* in our labeled sample dataset. Using this technique, we achieve an F1-score of 78% and accuracy of 78% in identifying *Relapse* and *No relapse*, compared to baseline scores of 33.9% and 51.3% if we labeled each user with *No relapse*, the majority class (Table 5).

Identifying Recovery

To identify whether a user was RECOVERING when she last initiated a post on Forum77, we simply examine the final phase label in her transition sequence. Using the CRF-labeled sequences, we classify a user's last post as RECOVERING or ¬RECOVERING with an F1-score of 81.5% and accuracy of 81.6%; the comparative baselines are 34.9% and 53.4%, in which all last posts are labeled as ¬RECOVERING (Table 5).

Table 5: Performance for identifying relapse events (top) and whether a user's final state is RECOVERING (bottom).

Identifying a relapse event

Label	Precision	Recall	F1-score	Accuracy
Combined	**79.92**	**78.18**	**78.04**	**78.42**
Relapse	86.11	66.67	75.15	
No relapse	73.73	89.69	80.93	
Baseline	25.65	50.00	33.91	51.30

Identifying final initiating post phase

Label	Precision	Recall	F1-score	Accuracy
Combined	**81.47**	**81.52**	**81.49**	**81.57**
RECOVERING	79.78	80.68	80.23	
¬RECOVERING	83.17	82.35	82.76	
Baseline	26.84	50.00	34.93	53.40

Results

Using the methods described above, we identify users who are RECOVERING at the time of their last initiating post on Forum77, as well as users who have relapsed at least once during their tenure on Forum77. We apply this analysis to the entirety of the Forum77 membership base who have initiated more than 5 posts (2,848 users, 32,345 initiating posts).

Do users tend to recover on Forum77?

Overall, users progress towards recovery during their tenure. Figure 5 shows the distribution over start state, relapse, and end state for the 2,848 users described above. Most users first initiate contact on the forum when they are USING (48%), followed by WITHDRAWING (44%). In contrast, only 17% of users are USING by the time of their last post, while 37% are WITHDRAWING and 46% are RECOVERING.

Does relapsing hurt recovery likelihood?

Roughly half of users experience a relapse during their tenure. Users who experience *no relapse* are significantly more likely to end in RECOVERING than users who *relapse* (53.4% vs. 44.4% end in RECOVERING, $\chi^2_1 = 55.1, p < 0.001$). Despite this, RECOVERING is still the most likely end state for Forum77 users who relapse.

Are relapses associated with longer tenure?

Given the documented prevalence of relapse [22, 52], the observation that more than half of the users in our dataset experience *no relapse* is surprising. Analyzing tenure values reveals that the average tenure of *no relapse* users is 128 days, compared to 418 days for users who *relapse*. One hypothesis is that users who experience *no relapse* do relapse after leaving the forum and do not return.

What differentiates users who are ultimately RECOVERING*?*

We define a user as *active* if she initiated a post on the forum in the last 45 days of our dataset, and remove these.

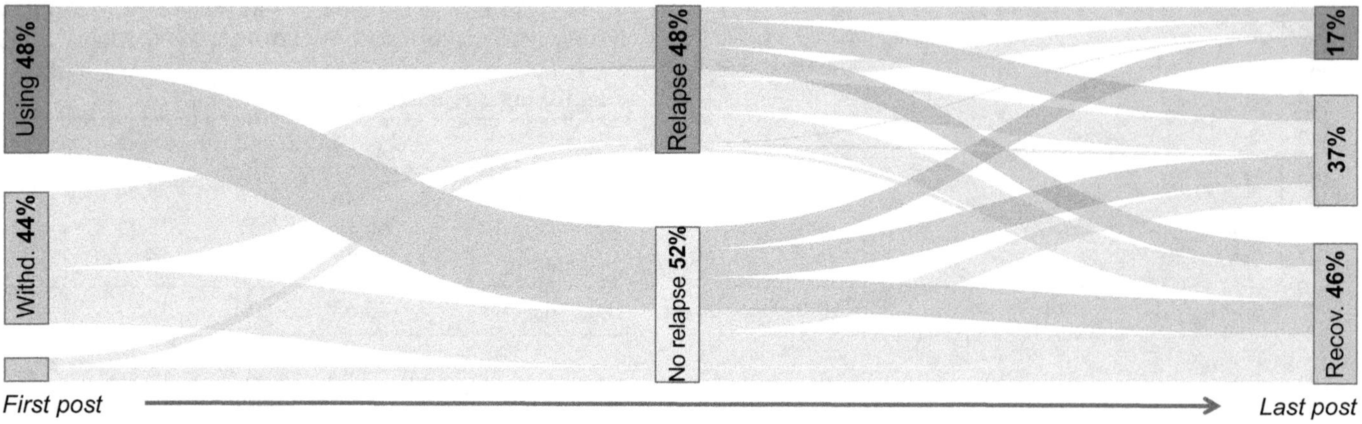

Figure 5: Aggregated user transitions from start to end state. Bar widths denote population proportion. For example, 48% of users in our sample relapsed during their tenure on Forum77.

We then analyze users' global activity characteristics (Table 3) aggregated over their USING and WITHDRAWING posts (RECOVERING posts are omitted as this is the phenomenon that we are studying). Table 6 shows the results.

Users who leave the forum in a state of RECOVERING are significantly more engaged in forum activity, even when they are USING and WITHDRAWING. The average time lapse between any form of activity (initiation, self-response and response) is about 30% shorter for those who are RECOVERING when they leave. Moreover, their activity is focused outwardly on other community members: users who are RECOVERING author, on average, 50% more responses than those who are ¬RECOVERING (average 45.6 vs. 33.8), but author slightly fewer initiating posts (average 9.0 vs. 9.9). These results resonate strongly with prior work on AA that finds that both active participation in AA and explicitly focusing on helping other members correlates with sustained abstinence [51, 45].

DISCUSSION

Use and Efficacy of Forum77

Our motivating goals were to study phases of addiction as seen on Forum77 and to analyze the forum's effectiveness in promoting recovery. In this section, we discuss Forum77's efficacy as a tool for supporting users through withdrawal, relapse and sustained recovery, drawing on post excerpts to contextualize our findings.

Supporting Withdrawal

Our results suggest that Forum77 is an effective tool for helping users through opioid withdrawals and physical detoxification. In general, users *progress* more often than they *regress* (Figure 3), and these local progressions translate into a global trend of many users reaching a state of RECOVERING during their tenure. When first initiating a post, 48% of users are USING, 44% WITHDRAWING and 8% RECOVERING; in their most recent initiating post, however, only 17% of users are USING, 37% are WITHDRAWING and 46% are RECOVERING, despite the fact that almost half of the population experiences a relapse (Figure 5). If we interpret our results as a 46% success rate on users' final detoxification attempt before leaving the forum, this is an improvement over self-detoxification success rates reported in the addiction literature [21, 43]. We must be cautious here, however, as we are comparing across differing study designs.

Forum77's efficacy at supporting detoxification may be attributable, in part, to both the strong social support and the detailed information on withdrawal that members receive from each other. Both of these factors have been shown to improve withdrawal outcomes [21, 23, 43], and qualitative remarks from users suggest that Forum77 meets the mark on both. *"I have tried to cope by myself for too long. Its so hard to deal with something like addiction by your self"*, wrote one user. *"[T]here is so much support and advice on getting through this and addiction I am living proof it works!!!!!!"*, and *"i was on here once before and was able to achieve 9 months of sobriety due to the support i had here and from meetings."* remarked others. In other cases, simply discovering a supportive community might galvanize a cessation attempt: *"up until 3 weeks ago, I had no intentions of quitting, i was just looking to find some stuff on addiction...and i just happened to run across this forum..."*.

Relapse and Shame

Despite the favorable prognosis that users are more likely to reach a state of RECOVERING during their tenure (Figure 5), we do not know whether they maintain this state upon leaving. It is possible that the same strong support network that helps users through detoxification deters them from wanting to admit a relapse. Quantitatively, although almost half of our sample relapsed (Figure 5), we rarely observed posts in which users reported a relapse immediately after the fact (Table 1).

The hypothesis that users are too ashamed to admit relapse until they implement a renewed attempt to quit is qualitatively well supported. Statements such as *"I suck!! I am so sorry, I've been too embarrased too admit I fell off the proverbial wagon around Christmas."* are common. Others, such as *"haven't posted in a few weeks because, of course, i slipped*

Table 6: Comparison of activity features for users who are RECOVERING and ¬RECOVERING in their last initiating post. Per-user values are aggregated over USING and WITHDRAWING posts. Statistical significance was determined using Kruskal-Wallis tests (* $p < 0.05$; ** $p < 0.005$; *** $p < 0.001$) after Bonferroni corrections to adjust for family-wise error rate across all 11 variables.

		RECOVERING				¬RECOVERING			
Activity Characteristic	p	**Mean**	**Med.**	**IQR**	**MAD**	**Mean**	**Med.**	**IQR**	**MAD**
# initiating posts authored	***	8.99	5	8	4.44	9.89	6	6	2.96
# self responses authored	***	19.56	8	16	10.37	17.04	9	16	8.89
# responses authored	***	45.56	9	31	13.34	33.81	8	24	10.37
$\frac{\text{\# initiating posts}}{\text{\# responses authored}}$	***	0.73	0.50	0.76	0.44	1.04	0.67	0.83	0.49
Days since last init.	***	16.39	3.33	12.41	3.95	27.05	8.30	28.36	10.53
Days since last self-response	***	17.47	3.00	13.38	3.95	29.53	8.29	31.45	10.81
Days since last response	***	15.92	1.66	7.32	2.47	25.30	4.37	21.75	5.99
Days since last activity	***	14.11	1.80	6.09	1.90	20.94	4.80	20.09	5.79
# self responses	***	1.93	1.50	1.64	1.19	1.83	1.50	1.50	1.11
# replies received	***	5.63	5.00	3.40	2.37	5.56	4.83	3.30	2.29
# respondents	***	4.09	3.83	2.00	1.60	4.01	3.70	2.03	1.42

up and am ashamed. but now i am back on track with the sub" and *"Im in day 3 of detox, i was too embarassed to post the first 3 days..."* echo these sentiments.

Supporting Sustained Recovery

Without observing users' behavior outside the forum, we cannot quantify Forum77's effectiveness at supporting long term recovery. Qualitatively, however, some users feel that this is something that Forum77 could improve upon. One user summarizes: *"I wonder if there is not a need for a forum community for long-term support. This community is great, but is skewed towards the short-term wd symptoms and getting through the initial physical pain of wd."*. Also prevalent are observations that the forum does not sufficiently prepare users to handle post-acute withdrawal syndrome (PAWS): *"I wish people would warn others about this PAWS thing"*, wrote one user. *"i was doing so good i made it to about 100 days sober ... the PAWS really got me"*, expressed another. Moreover, users who return to Forum77 after some time may find that their support network has moved on. One user who was struggling not to relapse asked *"Where are all of the friends i made here that I no longer see?!?"*.

Other users, however, give qualitative evidence in support of Forum77's efficacy at aiding sustained recovery. *"I have not posted much lately but continue to log on and read ppls posts and I believe that is a key aspect in my recovery"*, states one user. Another wrote *"when I get a craving I come here and read, even if I read it before, it helps me think of what I went through what I'm going through and how others cope"*. We found that higher engagement, in the form of activity levels and volumes of responses contributed, correlated with the chances of a user being in a phase of RECOVERING by her final initiating post. Extending this idea, one possibility is that remaining engaged with the forum (even in the form of "lurking") after reaching a state of RECOVERING helps to prevent relapses, in a similar way that continued participation in AA correlates with longer periods of sobriety [45, 51]. A deeper analysis into the mechanisms through which Forum77 does and does not support long-term recovery is an important topic for future work.

Implications for Forum Design

Our computational tools for automatically identifying addiction phases, relapses, and whether a user's tenure ends in RECOVERING could prove valuable to communities like Forum77. One question commonly asked by users is what to expect when they quit their drug of choice, and having access to this information has been shown to improve the chances of a successful cessation attempt [23]. Using phase sequence data labeled by our CRF classifier, users could set realistic expectations by exploring patterns based on thousands of users' prior experiences. Having a realistic perspective on the process of relapse and recovery may also reduce the number of instances in which users feel too embarrassed or ashamed to return to Forum77 after relapsing. Finally, exposing such data could help people find others who exhibit similar patterns to their own. Finding "people like me" is one of the primary stated reasons for user participation in online health communities [19].

While Forum77 appears to promote detoxification effectively, we observed that users have mixed feelings about how well it supports sustained recovery. It is possible that this could be addressed via altering community dynamics. For example, as we suggested above, continued participation in Forum77 post RECOVERING might help users achieve sustained recovery. Efforts focused on decreasing user churn and increasing member retention could support this. Alternatively, in a similar vein to AA's sponsorship program, which is thought to promote sustained recovery [54], we might consider automatically matching newcomers with long-term members who would act as formal mentors (or sponsors). Finally, it is possible that the community dynamics that support detoxification are different from those that would support sustained recovery. In this case, a forward reference to a different community might help RECOVERING Forum77 users plan what to do next.

Implications for Addiction Treatment

Forum77 accrues, at scale, information that is difficult to acquire through formal medical channels. First, abusing prescription drugs usually entails deceiving one's doctor. Second, addiction research data are typically acquired at point-of-care facilities (e.g., emergency rooms) or surveys at high schools or colleges. Although the ethics and privacy of such analyses must be carefully considered, it is possible that data extracted from sites like Forum77 (e.g., CRF-based transition frequencies, recovery trends, etc.) could help medical professionals and policy makers better understand patients' experiences with drug abuse. For example, insight into the day to day difficulties of opioid-assisted withdrawal might inform policy for improving the management of this popular treatment down the road. It is also possible that research like ours could illuminate poorly understood aspects of addiction: to our knowledge, ours is the first attempt to quantify the cycle of addiction.

Limitations

One limitation of this work is the selection bias of our subjects: users who come to Forum77 are likely already open to (or at least, considering) the possibility of quitting. This problem is well known to those hoping to analyze the efficacy of Alcoholics Anonymous [7]. As such, care should be taken in applying our results to a more general population who misuse prescription medication. We cannot assume, for example, that a random sample of people who misuse prescription medication would similarly progress towards recovery if they were asked to participate in Forum77. We also cannot draw epidemiological conclusions that apply to the population as a whole from these data. However, the size of Forum77, the prevalence of the opioid epidemic, and the increasing popularity of online health communities alone make the forum worth studying.

Another limitation is the acceptable—but still improvable—accuracy of our CRF classifier. While we were able to use CRF-based sequences to identify relapse and whether a final post was RECOVERING with high accuracy, improving our underlying classifier accuracy would open up more nuanced analyses. Finally, having page view data would allow us to incorporate measures of passive participation ("lurking") into our analyses, which would add a new dimension to our study. We hope to address such opportunities in future work.

CONCLUSION

We analyze the process of opioid withdrawal, recovery and relapse on Forum77, MedHelp's Addiction and Substance Abuse community. Using Prochashka's Transtheoretical Model for behavior change, we develop a taxonomy of phases of addiction that comprises three main categories: USING, WITHDRAWING and RECOVERING. The majority of initiating posts are authored when users are WITHDRAWING. Next, we analyze linguistic and behavioral features across the USING, WITHDRAWING and RECOVERING phases. Several significant differences characterize each phase, and we leverage the results of our feature analysis to train a CRF model to automatically annotate users' phase sequences. We can identify relapse events, and whether a user was RECOVERING when she authored her final post, with high accuracy from our CRF-annotated sequences.

Applying our classifier to 2,848 users reveals that progressive transitions towards RECOVERING are much more prevalent than regressive transitions. Moreover, despite the fact that almost 50% of users relapse during their tenure, leaving Forum77 in a state of RECOVERING is the most probable outcome for all users. Finally, we find that increased participation in the community correlates with a user RECOVERING by the end of her tenure: users who are RECOVERING by their final initiating post are significantly more engaged with the community when they are USING and WITHDRAWING than users who are ¬RECOVERING by their final initiating post.

To our knowledge, ours is the first work to investigate the efficacy of online mutual help groups for prescription drug abuse. Our results, which help to illuminate a previously poorly understood resource, suggest that Forum77 is an effective detoxification aid. Based on our findings, we also highlight several ways in which Forum77 might be enhanced to better support its users, such as exposing aggregate user data describing the cycle of addiction, or matching newcomers with sponsors. Finally, as the type of information shared on Forum77 is difficult to acquire at scale through traditional channels, we note that the tools and insights presented here may be of use to the addiction research community.

ACKNOWLEDGMENTS

We thank MedHelp.org for sharing their forum data. This work was supported by NSF grant number 0964173.

REFERENCES

1. Alcoholics Anonymous: Over 70 years of growth. *Alcoholics Anonymous*. [Online: `www.aa.org/aatimeline/`, accessed 15-Sept-2013].
2. The Big Book. *Alcoholics Anonymous*. [Online: `http://www.aa.org/bigbookonline`, accessed 5/20/2014].
3. Vital signs: Overdoses of prescription opioid pain relievers united states, 1999-2008. *Center for Disease Control. Morbidity and Mortality Weekly Report.* (2011). Online: `http://www.cdc.gov/mmwr/preview/mmwrhtml/mm6043a4.htm`. Accessed 93/4/2014.
4. Addiction medicine, closing the gap between science and practice. *CASAColumbia* (2012). Online: `http://www.casacolumbia.org/download/file/fid/1177`, accessed 4/5/2014.
5. Commonly abused prescription drugs. *National Institute on Drug Abuse* (2012). [Online: `http://www.drugabuse.gov/sites/default/files/rx_drugs_placemat_508c_10052011.pdf`, accessed 5/28/2014].

6. Opiate withdrawal. *MedlinePlus - U.S. National Library of Medicine* (2012). [Online: `http://www.nlm.nih.gov/medlineplus/ency/article/000949.htm`, accessed 28-May-2014].

7. Bebbington, P. E. The efficacy of alcoholics anonymous: the elusiveness of hard data. *British Journal of Psychiatry 128*, 6 (1976), 572–580.

8. Berger, M., Wagner, T. H., and Baker, L. C. Internet use and stigmatized illness. *Social Science & Medicine 61*, 8 (2005), 1821–1827.

9. Coppersmith, G., Harman, C., and Dredze, M. Measuring post traumatic stress disorder in twitter. In *Proc. ICWSM 2014*, AAAI (2014), 579–582.

10. Davison, K. P., Pennebaker, J. W., and Dickerson, S. S. Who talks? the social psychology of illness support groups. *American Psychologist 55*, 2 (2000), 205.

11. De Choudhury, M., Counts, S., and Horvitz, E. Major life changes and behavioral markers in social media: case of childbirth. In *Proc. CSCW 2013*, ACM (2013), 1431–1442.

12. De Choudhury, M., Counts, S., and Horvitz, E. Predicting postpartum changes in emotion and behavior via social media. In *Proc. CHI 2013*, ACM (2013), 3267–3276.

13. De Choudhury, M., Counts, S., Horvitz, E. J., and Hoff, A. Characterizing and predicting postpartum depression from shared facebook data. In *Proc. CSCW 2014*, ACM (2014), 626–638.

14. De Choudhury, M., Gamon, M., Counts, S., and Horvitz, E. Predicting depression via social media. In *Proc. ICWSM 2013*, AAAI (2013), 128–137.

15. DiClemente, C. C., Prochaska, J. O., Fairhurst, S. K., Velicer, W. F., Velasquez, M. M., and Rossi, J. S. The process of smoking cessation: an analysis of precontemplation, contemplation, and preparation stages of change. *Journal of Consulting and Clinical Psychology 59*, 2 (1991), 295.

16. DuPont, R. L., McLellan, A. T., White, W. L., Merlo, L. J., and Gold, M. S. Setting the standard for recovery: Physicians' health programs. *Journal of Substance Abuse Treatment 36*, 2 (2009), 159–171.

17. Farrell, M. Opiate withdrawal. *Addiction 89*, 11 (1994), 1471–1475.

18. Finfgeld, D. L. Therapeutic groups online: the good, the bad, and the unknown. *Issues in Mental Health Nursing 21*, 3 (2000), 241–255.

19. Fox, S. Peer-to-peer health care. *Pew Internet & American Life Project* (2011). [Online: `http://pewinternet.org/Reports/2011/P2PHealthcare/Summary-of-Findings.aspx`, accessed 6-January-2014].

20. Fox, S., and Duggan, M. Health online. *Pew Internet & American Life Project* (2013). [Online: `http://pewinternet.org/Reports/2013/Health-online/Summary-of-Findings.aspx`, accessed 2-April-2013].

21. Gossop, M., Battersby, M., and Strang, J. Self-detoxification by opiate addicts. a preliminary investigation. *British Journal of Psychiatry 159*, 2 (1991), 208–212.

22. Gossop, M., Green, L., Phillips, G., and Bradley, B. Lapse, relapse and survival among opiate addicts after treatment. a prospective follow-up study. *British Journal of Psychiatry 154*, 3 (1989), 348–353.

23. Green, L., and Gossop, M. Effects of information on the opiate withdrawal syndrome. *British Journal of Addiction 83*, 3 (1988), 305–309.

24. Hartzler, A., and Pratt, W. Managing the personal side of health: how patient expertise differs from the expertise of clinicians. *Journal of Medical Internet research 13*, 3 (2011).

25. He, H. A., Greenberg, S., and Huang, E. M. One size does not fit all: applying the transtheoretical model to energy feedback technology design. In *Proc. CHI 2010*, ACM (2010), 927–936.

26. Homan, C. M., Lu, N., Tu, X., Lytle, M. C., and Silenzio, V. Social structure and depression in trevorspace. In *Proc. CSCW 2014*, ACM (2014), 615–625.

27. Høybye, M. T., Johansen, C., and Tjørnhøj-Thomsen, T. Online interaction. effects of storytelling in an internet breast cancer support group. *Psycho-Oncology 14*, 3 (2005), 211–220.

28. Humphreys, K. *Circles of recovery: Self-help organizations for addictions*. Cambridge Univ. Press, 2004.

29. Jha, M., and Elhadad, N. Cancer stage prediction based on patient online discourse. In *Proc. BIO-NLP 2010*, ACL (2010), 64–71.

30. Kaskutas, L. A., Bond, J., and Humphreys, K. Social networks as mediators of the effect of alcoholics anonymous. *Addiction 97*, 7 (2002), 891–900.

31. Kelly, J. F., Hoeppner, B., Stout, R. L., and Pagano, M. Determining the relative importance of the mechanisms of behavior change within alcoholics anonymous: a multiple mediator analysis. *Addiction 107*, 2 (2012), 289–299.

32. Klemm, P., Bunnell, D., Cullen, M., Soneji, R., Gibbons, P., and Holecek, A. Online cancer support groups: a review of the research literature. *Computers Informatics Nursing 21*, 3 (2003), 136–142.

33. Lafferty, J., McCallum, A., and Pereira, F. C. Conditional random fields: Probabilistic models for segmenting and labeling sequence data.

34. Lembke, A. Why doctors prescribe opioids to known opioid abusers. *New England Journal of Medicine 367*, 17 (2012), 1580–1581.

35. Lembke, A. Humphreys, K. *Self-Help Organizations for Substance Use Disorders*. Oxford Univ. Press, 2009.

36. Mankoff, J., Kuksenok, K., Kiesler, S., Rode, J. A., and Waldman, K. Competing online viewpoints and models of chronic illness. In *Proc. CHI 2011*, ACM (2011), 589–598.

37. McLellan, A. T. What is recovery? Revisiting the Betty Ford Institute consensus panel definition. *Journal of Social Work Practice in the Addictions* (2010), 109–113.

38. McLellan, A. T., Lewis, D. C., O'Brien, C. P., and Kleber, H. D. Drug dependence, a chronic medical illness: implications for treatment, insurance, and outcomes evaluation. *JAMA 284*, 13 (2000), 1689–1695.

39. Migneault, J. P., Migneault, J. P., Adams, T. B., Migneault, J. P., Adams, T. B., Read, J. P., Migneault, J. P., Adams, T. B., and Read, J. P. Application of the transtheoretical model to substance abuse: historical development and future directions. *Drug and alcohol review 24*, 5 (2005), 437–448.

40. Miller, N. S., Sheppard, L. M., Colenda, C. C., and Magen, J. Why physicians are unprepared to treat patients who have alcohol-and drug-related disorders. *Academic Medicine 76*, 5 (2001), 410–418.

41. Mulveen, R., and Hepworth, J. An interpretative phenomenological analysis of participation in a pro-anorexia internet site and its relationship with disordered eating. *Journal of health psychology 11*, 2 (2006), 283–296.

42. Murnane, E. L., and Counts, S. Unraveling abstinence and relapse: smoking cessation reflected in social media. In *Proc. CHI 2014*, ACM (2014), 1345–1354.

43. Noble, A., Best, D., Man, L.-H., Gossop, M., and Strang, J. Self-detoxification attempts among methadone maintenance patients: what methods and what success? *Addictive Behaviors 27*, 4 (2002), 575–584.

44. Olsen, Y., and Sharfstein, J. M. Confronting the stigma of opioid use disorderand its treatment. *JAMA 311*, 14 (2014), 1393–1394.

45. Pagano, M. E., Friend, K. B., Tonigan, J. S., and Stout, R. L. Helping other alcoholics in Alcoholics Anonymous and drinking outcomes: Findings from Project MATCH. *Journal of Studies on Alcohol 65*, 6 (2004), 766.

46. Park, S., Lee, S. W., Kwak, J., Cha, M., and Jeong, B. Activities on facebook reveal the depressive state of users. *Journal of Medical Internet Research 15*, 10 (2013).

47. Pennebaker, J. W., Francis, M. E., and Booth, R. J. Linguistic inquiry and word count: Liwc 2001. *Mahway: Lawrence Erlbaum Associates 71* (2001), 2001.

48. Pennebaker, J. W., Mehl, M. R., and Niederhoffer, K. G. Psychological aspects of natural language use: Our words, our selves. *Annual Review of Psychology 54*, 1 (2003), 547–577.

49. Prochaska, J. O., and Velicer, W. F. The transtheoretical model of health behavior change. *American Journal of Health Promotion 12*, 1 (1997), 38–48.

50. Resnik, P., Garron, A., and Resnik, R. Using topic modeling to improve prediction of neuroticism and depression. In *Proceedings of the 2013 Conference on Empirical Methods in Natural*, Association for Computational Linguistics (2013), 1348–1353.

51. Sheeren, M. The relationship between relapse and involvement in alcoholics anonymous. *Journal of Studies on Alcohol and Drugs 49*, 01 (1988), 104.

52. Smyth, B., Barry, J., Keenan, E., and Ducray, K. Lapse and relapse following inpatient treatment of opiate dependence. Online: `http://www.lenus.ie/hse/bitstream/10147/110022/1/Article5260.pdf`, accessed on 4/5/2014.

53. Sproule, B., Brands, B., Li, S., and Catz-Biro, L. Changing patterns in opioid addiction characterizing users of oxycodone and other opioids. *Canadian Family Physician 55*, 1 (2009), 68–69.

54. Tonigan, J. S., and Rice, S. L. Is it beneficial to have an alcoholics anonymous sponsor? *Psychology of Addictive Behaviors 24*, 3 (2010), 397.

55. Velicer, W. F., Prochaska, J. O., Fava, J. L., Norman, G. J., and Redding, C. A. Smoking cessation and stress management: Applications of the transtheoretical model of behavior change. *Homeostasis in Health and Disease*, 5-6 (1998), 216–233.

56. Volkow, N. D. Prescription drug abuse. *National Institute on Drug Abuse Research Report Series* (2005). Online: `http://www.drugabuse.gov/sites/default/files/rxreportfinalprint.pdf`, Accessed 6/3/2014.

57. Wen, M., and Rosé, C. P. Understanding participant behavior trajectories in online health support groups using automatic extraction methods. In *Proc. GROUP 2012*, ACM (2012), 179–188.

58. West, R. Time for a change: putting the transtheoretical (stages of change) model to rest. *Addiction 100*, 8 (2005), 1036–1039.

59. Wicks, P., Massagli, M., Frost, J., Brownstein, C., Okun, S., Vaughan, T., Bradley, R., and Heywood, J. Sharing health data for better outcomes on PatientsLikeMe. *Journal of Medical Internet Research* (2010).

Table 7: LIWC features for the three classes in the labeled dataset over initiating posts. Only statistically significant variables are shown. Statistical significance is determined using Kruskal-Wallis tests (* $p < 0.05$; ** $p < 0.005$; *** $p < 0.001$) after Bonferroni corrections to adjust for family-wise error rate across all 184 variables (includes activity features). Column c denotes (∘) if the feature is used in our CRF classifier.

Initiating Post Linguistic Features

			USING			WITHDRAWING			RECOVERING		
	c	p	Mean	Median	SD	Mean	Median	SD	Mean	Median	SD
Word count	∘	*	208.20	151	211.06	178.92	127.00	168.81	183.23	124.50	209.24
Dic	∘	***	89.26	90.17	4.89	88.10	88.89	6.26	89.38	90.54	6.59
Numerals	∘	***	1.28	0.89	1.51	1.75	1.33	1.97	1.32	0.83	2.04
Function words	∘	***	60.50	60.92	5.31	58.40	59.28	6.45	59.74	60.48	7.07
Pronoun		***	18.51	18.68	4.32	16.99	17.17	4.70	17.97	18.16	5.28
Personal pronoun	∘	***	12.83	13.05	3.83	11.49	11.54	4.19	11.88	11.86	4.60
Pronoun: I	∘	***	9.72	9.97	3.60	9.02	9.14	3.76	7.89	8.18	4.31
Pronoun: you		***	0.98	0.41	1.70	1.02	0.13	2.04	2.05	0.99	2.89
Pronoun: he/she	∘	***	1.14	0	2.08	0.74	0	1.82	1	0	2.46
Pronoun: they	∘	***	0.65	0.20	1.05	0.47	0	1.12	0.54	0	1.03
Pronoun: impersonal		*	5.68	5.33	2.82	5.49	5.26	2.81	6.09	5.76	3.35
Verb	∘	**	18.54	18.69	3.76	17.64	17.59	4.20	18.13	17.96	4.91
Present tense	∘	***	12.56	12.55	3.90	11.53	11.24	4.09	11.95	11.63	4.45
Numbers	∘	**	0.71	0.48	0.93	0.75	0.37	1.12	0.54	0	0.89
Social	∘	***	7.60	6.59	4.79	6.38	5.26	5.18	8.85	7.89	5.90
Humans	∘	*	0.49	0	0.76	0.40	0	0.79	0.57	0	1.04
Affect	∘	***	5.30	5.00	2.76	5.76	5.54	3.09	6.41	6.11	3.52
Affect: positive	∘	***	2.80	2.45	1.99	3.33	2.86	2.85	4.14	3.50	3.16
Affect: anxiety	∘	**	0.61	0.25	0.88	0.55	0	0.98	0.45	0	0.90
Cognitive Mechanisms	∘	*	17.27	16.98	4.50	17.14	17.09	4.95	17.93	17.96	5.11
Certain	∘	*	1.21	1.03	1.22	1.41	1.21	1.41	1.57	1.36	1.53
Inhibition	∘	*	0.50	0.23	0.70	0.41	0	0.74	0.43	0	0.76
See	∘	*	0.34	0	0.65	0.30	0	0.80	0.50	0	1.14
Feel	∘	***	0.73	0.45	1.10	1.18	0.83	1.50	0.85	0.50	1.23
Biological	∘	***	3.87	3.46	2.63	4.01	3.70	2.90	3.31	2.89	2.72
Body	∘	***	0.58	0	1	1.13	0.63	1.53	0.68	0	1.12
Health	∘	***	3.00	2.63	2.29	2.58	2.13	2.36	2.20	1.72	2.25
Relative	∘	***	13.46	13.39	4.65	15.04	14.75	5.25	13.72	13.61	5.23
Time	∘	***	7.24	6.86	3.46	8.51	7.87	4.21	7.33	7.02	4.23
Home	∘	***	0.30	0	0.54	0.40	0	0.77	0.68	0.14	1.18
Comma	∘	**	3.01	2.17	3.36	2.75	1.94	3.27	2.19	1.63	2.43
QMark	∘	*	1.35	0.52	2.87	1.34	0.40	2.58	1.50	0	4.92
Other Punctuation	∘	***	0.81	0	1.77	0.89	0	1.91	0.62	0	2.05

Table 8: LIWC features for the three classes in the labeled dataset over response posts. Only statistically significant variables are shown. Statistical significance is determined using Kruskal-Wallis tests (* $p < 0.05$; ** $p < 0.005$; *** $p < 0.001$) after Bonferroni corrections to adjust for family-wise error rate across all 184 variables (includes activity features). Column c denotes (○) if the feature is used in our CRF classifier.

Response Post Linguistic Features

			USING			WITHDRAWING			RECOVERING		
	c	p	Mean	Median	SD	Mean	Median	SD	Mean	Median	SD
Word count		***	494.69	347.00	506.67	427.38	284.00	487.46	356.29	210.50	439.75
Words per sentence		***	19.21	15.40	18.60	17.04	14.09	14.73	14.98	12.99	14.25
Numerals	○	*	0.75	0.43	1.02	0.95	0.68	1.12	0.95	0.56	1.49
Function words		***	59.01	59.85	4.56	56.95	57.69	5.41	55.82	57.06	7.17
Personal Pronouns		***	10.86	11.36	3.99	10.21	10.53	3.81	10.86	11.58	4.71
Pronoun: she/he		**	0.68	0	1.35	0.44	0	1.16	0.64	0	1.63
Pronoun: they		***	0.66	0.41	0.91	0.49	0.27	0.66	0.49	0.13	0.90
Pronoun: impersonal		**	5.48	5.67	2.20	5.57	5.78	2.36	5.10	5.32	2.75
Article		***	4.91	4.98	2.06	4.75	4.96	2.02	4.20	4.41	2.23
Verb		**	17.26	18.15	4.94	17.13	17.82	4.88	16.09	17.23	5.78
Aux. verb		***	10.67	11.11	3.51	10.37	10.68	3.44	9.66	10.33	3.96
Future		***	1.50	1.44	1.07	1.50	1.43	1.13	1.10	1.01	1.03
Preposition		***	11.63	12.27	3.57	11.19	11.66	3.38	10.61	11.51	4.14
Conjunction		***	6.39	6.76	2.33	6.18	6.58	2.46	5.72	6.13	2.69
Quantitative		***	3.00	2.99	1.52	2.94	2.88	1.64	2.50	2.58	1.67
Social	○	***	10.26	10.11	4.77	8.83	8.75	4.23	9.78	9.81	5.45
Affect	○	***	5.73	5.76	2.68	6.55	6.34	3.25	7.54	7.33	4.31
Affect: positive	○	***	3.72	3.53	2.43	4.61	4.10	3.17	5.84	5.13	4.36
Affect: negative	○	***	1.96	1.92	1.34	1.90	1.87	1.33	1.67	1.50	1.51
Affect: anxiety	○	***	0.36	0.24	0.47	0.40	0.23	0.55	0.32	0	0.61
Cognitive Processes		***	19.37	17.81	7.77	18.71	17.43	7.83	18.77	16.80	10
Discrepancy		***	2.32	2.32	1.31	1.92	1.88	1.33	1.63	1.60	1.30
Tentative		***	3.35	3.25	1.79	3.12	3.09	1.77	2.55	2.45	1.96
Exclusive		***	3.35	3.40	1.62	3.07	3.18	1.66	2.56	2.60	1.83
Perceptual processes		***	1.52	1.48	1.07	1.90	1.81	1.34	1.87	1.68	1.55
Feel		***	0.64	0.53	0.70	0.91	0.76	0.85	0.65	0.45	0.76
Biological		***	3.46	3.20	2.17	3.42	3.22	2.46	2.71	2.41	2.39
Body		***	0.52	0.28	0.78	0.78	0.45	1.08	0.52	0.19	0.90
Health	○	***	2.68	2.45	1.85	2.24	1.95	1.90	1.70	1.32	1.76
Sexual		***	0.15	0	0.35	0.14	0	0.36	0.30	0	0.89
Ingetion		*	0.17	0	0.39	0.30	0	0.66	0.25	0	0.71
Relativity		**	11.46	11.82	4.39	12.36	12.68	4.70	11.90	12.50	5.37
Time		**	5.29	5.10	2.90	5.88	6.06	3.12	5.66	5.69	3.33
Money		*	0.32	0.13	0.55	0.28	0	0.56	0.23	0	0.42
Assent	○	***	0.27	0.07	0.50	0.40	0.18	0.81	0.62	0.27	2.01
Colon		**	0.09	0	0.20	0.15	0	0.42	0.27	0	0.84
Exclamation	○	***	1.02	0.34	1.79	2.25	0.82	5.08	4.52	1.68	8.40
Dash		**	0.79	0.28	2.08	0.82	0	2.20	0.62	0	1.64
Other punctuation	○	***	3.41	2.84	2.55	4.29	3.53	3.22	5.64	4.29	6.35
All punctuation	○	***	22.07	21.51	9.71	25.75	23.69	14.52	29.69	26.82	19.27

"I'm Not Like My Friends": Understanding How Children with a Chronic Illness Use Technology to Maintain Normalcy

Leslie S. Liu
Microsoft Research
Biomedical & Health Informatics
University of Washington
lsliu@uw.edu

Kori Inkpen
Microsoft Research
One Microsoft Way
Redmond, WA USA
kori@microsoft.com

Wanda Pratt
The Information School
Biomedical & Health Informatics
University of Washington
wpratt@uw.edu

ABSTRACT
Children diagnosed with a chronic illness, such as cancer, experience a vastly different childhood than their healthy counterparts. They may struggle with accepting that they are no longer seen as "normal". We surveyed 10 children who have a chronic illness and interviewed 15 healthcare professionals and 7 parents of chronically ill children to understand their communication practices and challenges of how these patients stay connected with their peers. We found that due to the nature of their illness and constant hospitalization, pediatric patients often use various communication technologies to stay in touch with friends and try to maintain normalcy in their lives. Some patients also had to create a "new normal" that balanced life before and after being diagnosed. Based on these results, we suggest opportunities for technology to help patients connect to others and retain a sense of normalcy or to encourage them to embrace their "new normal".

Author Keywords
Children; health; chronic illness; communication; video; normalcy; asynchronous technologies; synchronous technologies.

ACM Classification Keywords
J.3. Life and Medical Sciences (Health)

General Terms
Human Factors.

INTRODUCTION
For children who are diagnosed with a chronic illness, growing up can be harder than their healthy peers. These patients face numerous challenges in staying connected with their social circle. Regardless of whether the patient is confined to a hospital room or is simply missing a few days a week from school to receive treatments, they may feel isolated because of their temporary removal from familiarity. They may also feel as if they are no longer who they used to be because of changes in their physical appearance.

With the ubiquity of technology, patients are likely to use some communication technology to keep in touch with their friends while they are in the hospital or at home. The prevalence of technology can be particularly high with children. In a 2013 report on teenagers and technology, the Pew Research Center found that 78% of teenagers in the United States have their own cell phone [23]. Studies have focused on healthy children and how they use various ways of communicating, such as teenagers and video chat [5] or looking at how children communicate with remote family members [2]. Few studies have examined how children with chronic illnesses communicate with healthy peers.

In our work, we conducted a small-scale survey (n=10) with children who have a chronic illness, followed by a qualitative study that consisted of 22 interviews among 15 healthcare professionals and 7 parents of pediatric patients with a chronic illness. We found that due to the uncommon nature of having a chronic illness, patients use a wide variety of technologies in an attempt to maintain normalcy with their peers. At the same time, patients recognize that they are not the same as their healthy peers and try to meld their "new normal" with their previous identity. Although numerous studies have found that pediatric patients seek to be seen as normal by their friends and peers during their illness, our study focuses on *the role of technology* in their endeavor for maintaining normalcy. Pediatric patients may have vastly different needs and experiences when using a communication technology than their healthy counterparts. We found that along with using different technologies to maintain normalcy, patients also appropriated the technology to fit their current needs and feelings of having an illness (for example, using Skype as a way to still participate in a special event). Based on these results, we suggest opportunities for appropriate technologies to help patients connect to others and thus, to feel a sense of normalcy in their lives.

CSCW '15, March 14 - 18, 2015, Vancouver, BC, Canada.
Copyright 2015 ACM 978-1-4503-2922-4/15/03...$15.00.
http://dx.doi.org/10.1145/2675133.2675201

RELATED WORK

Normalcy in Health and HCI

Children with a chronic illness, regardless of age, often express a desire to feel normal and fit in with their healthy peers. For example, Williams *et al.* found that there were two types of normality for cystic fibrosis (CF) patients: self-referential (defined by themselves) and socially derived (defined by their peers) [26]. Though the CF patients saw themselves as "normal", they recognized that they tried to do things so that their peers would also think they were normal. For children whose illness caused physical changes, they struggled even more to feel normal. Children with liver disease tried to hide their physical changes or even the presence of their disease because they had a desire to fit in with their peers [27]. In another example, Aamodt *et al.* found that some young pediatric patients equated losing hair with losing friends [1]. Teenagers with a chronic illness can be especially susceptible to feeling the need to fit in with their peers [20]. Larouche and Chin-Peuckert interviewed 5 teenage cancer patients where all interviewees stated that they would do as much as they could to try and minimize their physical changes and to dress as "normally" as possible [13]. Woodgate found that adolescent cancer patients wanted their friends and family to treat them normally, rather than as a sick patient. Patients talked about wanting their friends to act the same as before their diagnosis. Such acts of normalcy made patients feel that they had a life outside of one with cancer. [28].

Despite normalcy being a common theme in the chronic health literature, little work has focused on how technology could play a role in maintaining normalcy. Much of the work that has been done in HCI has focused on adults. For example, Mamykina *et al.* found that participants with diabetes maintained certain practices and traditions that reminded them of their lives before diagnosis, helping to reestablish normalcy [15]. Similarly, Massimi *et al.* suggests that technology could help those who have had a life disruption (*e.g.*, homelessness) transition towards a new lifestyle with new routines [16]. Another study found that new mothers used different types of technologies such as Facebook or their smartphones as a way to return to normalcy after the birth of their child and connect back to their social world [10]. Lee and Dey developed a lifelogging system that helped participants with episodic memory impairment regain a sense of normalcy by helping them recollect significant experiences [14]. However, these studies tend to focus more on readjusting the affected person's sense of normalcy, rather than on how they maintain normalcy in the eyes of others. Most importantly, none of these studies examined normalcy in the lives of children.

Pediatric Patients and Technology

There have been numerous studies that have focused broadly on pediatric patients and the use of technology. Studies have examined how technology—such as a telepresence system or a BlackBerry phone [8]—can connect hospitalized children with their classroom or classmates. Weiss *et al.*'s study on a remote telepresence system called PEBBLES found that not only did the system help a hemodialysis patient feel more included in the classroom, but helped her classmates become more aware and sensitive to people who are in difficult situations (such as someone with a chronic illness) [25]. The increased sensitivity by the classmates helped create a smooth transition when the patient was able to physically attend school again [9]. Fels *et al.* looked at the use of a BlackBerry for children and young people in a hospital. The researchers noted that having an immediate connection to their school through the BlackBerry could cause positive health and well-being outcomes [8]. These studies looked mainly at how a pediatric patient might maintain a connection with the classroom as a student attending class, but they did not examine the role of technology in supporting social connections among friends.

Other studies have focused on helping pediatric patients share their story with others. For example, Bers *et al.* suggest technological "play kits" that help hospitalized pediatric patients leave a trace and signature in the world. They found that others appreciating and recognizing the patient's creations made them feel empowered [3]. Building on that work, Chin and Tsuei created a narrative sharing system for peer patients that allowed patients to "express their idealized self" through selecting a user name and avatar [6]. Another system, "Coping Cart", allows patients to watch videos of other patients in similar situations, draw or write stories about their experiences, and play with toy stethoscopes and surgical tools. They found that this mobile multimedia system was useful for patients to see how other patients cope with similar illnesses. Sharing their story through videos and comic books also helped patients develop a sense of mastery over their illness [18]. Using a virtual community for pediatric patients undergoing kidney dialysis, patients reported feeling closer to other patients after using the system. Patients said that although they knew and recognized other patients when they would see them, they didn't actually know their fellow patients, and that the system helped in getting to know their peer patients [4]. Plaisant *et al.* also suggested that using a storytelling robot might help patients meet a therapy goal in rehabilitation [19]. Although these studies looked at how patients might share their experiences with other peer patients, they did not look at how chronically ill pediatric patients stayed connected with their existing friends.

Besides looking at how patients might share experiences with other peer patients, studies have also looked at the interactions between pediatric patients and adults (*e.g.*, clinicians or caregivers). For example, Hourcade *et al.* explored a Draw-and-Tell Conversation system on a tablet to encourage children to provide clinicians with more information on their headaches. The system was able to augment the face-to-face communication between patients and their clinicians [11]. Farnham *et al.* developed a novel virtual community for cancer patients (18+ years old) and caregivers to interact with one another and find social support. They found that users particularly liked the ability to broadcast their health updates to friends and families [7]. Mokashi *et al.* studied video chat use for children with autism and caregivers and suggest that video-mediated communication could be used between the children and trusted caregivers, such as teachers [17].

Most closely related to our work is van der Velden and El Emam's work on examining the usage of social media, such as Facebook, by teenagers with a chronic illness. However, their study focuses on the privacy implications of sharing health information through social media. For example, the authors found that patients often used Facebook as a way to stay updated with their friends, but at the same time, patients would also consciously refrain from sharing anything regarding their health as a way of protecting their privacy with friends who were only acquaintances [24].

In contrast to these previous studies, our study explicitly examines how patients use different communication technologies as a way to regain a sense of normalcy during their illness. Our study found that patients often use different communication technologies in specific ways to help maintain normalcy in their lives.

METHODS

To understand how chronically ill pediatric patients are staying connected with their peers, we first conducted a small-scale survey with 10 children who have a chronic illness. The age range of participants was from 6 to 18 years old. We recruited participants through online forums and Facebook groups. Because of human subjects concern and forum policies, we could only post on forums that provided permission from moderators, and that were meant for parents of children with chronic illnesses. For example, we did not recruit in teenager forums, such as Starbright World[1]. Because our participants were minors, parental consent was collected for all participants before they took the survey. These factors could have influenced the population of respondents who filled out our survey. Survey participants had a range of chronic illnesses including cancer (4), type 1 diabetes (3), Friedreich's Ataxia (1), and both type 1 diabetes and asthma (1). Our survey targeted a wider range of chronic illnesses and included illnesses that may not have a significant lifestyle change for patients. The communication needs for a patient who has a chronic illness but does not need constant hospitalization for treatment likely differs vastly from a patient who does require hospitalization. However, we did not distinguish between types of chronic illnesses because we wanted to gain a comprehensive view of how connected children with any chronic illness felt about their friends. Survey questions included how children felt when they were away from their friends due to their chronic illnesses, what types of technologies they used to stay in touch with friends, and what thoughts they had about connecting with friends. Survey participants reported ratings on a 5-point Likert scale with 1 being "strongly disagree" and 5 being "strongly agree".

For the next phase of our research, we sampled only parents and clinicians of children with a chronic illness who might be physically away from home or school for a long period of time, such as those with cancer or those who need kidney transplants. This allowed us to obtain a more in-depth perspective on how these patients stayed connected with their friends. We conducted semi-structured interviews with 22 participants from hematology/oncology, nephrology, and general pediatrics departments after receiving IRB approval from our university. Fifteen of these participants were healthcare professionals including physicians (4), registered nurses (6), clinical social workers (3), and a Child Life Specialist (1). These were healthcare professionals at large Children's Hospitals and interacted with an average of 30 patients per week. Interview questions and topics included methods that pediatric patients use to stay connected to their friends during hospitalization, challenges for patients to stay connected with their friends, and thoughts about connecting patients to peer patients. Interviews lasted 30 to 60 minutes. We chose to interview healthcare professionals because they see a large number of children with a chronic illness and can reflect upon patterns that they have observed with a variety of pediatric patients.

The remaining 7 participants were parents of chronically ill pediatric patients. We chose to interview parents because they are able to articulate, reflect upon, and generalize on their child's experiences more easily than young children. These parents felt confident that they had a good understanding of how their child felt during treatment and the types of technologies their child used. Because we wanted to reduce the burden for sick children we only had children participate using the survey and did not have them participate in the interviews. Due to the sensitive situations that these children are going through, we felt it was important to gain an understanding of the key issues before interacting directly with the children. Our future work will involve more interactions with children in the design of the communication technologies.

Parents were from the United States (6) and the United Kingdom (1). Out of the 7 parents, 6 were parents of children with various types of cancer (Acute Lymphoblastic Leukemia, Non-Hodgkin's Lymphoma, and osteosarcoma) and one was a parent of a child with a blood disorder (aplastic anemia) that required constant blood transfusions. Patients ranged from 5 to 17 years old. Interview questions included ways that their child stayed in touch with friends, positive and negative experiences related to staying in touch

[1] http://www.starbrightworld.org/

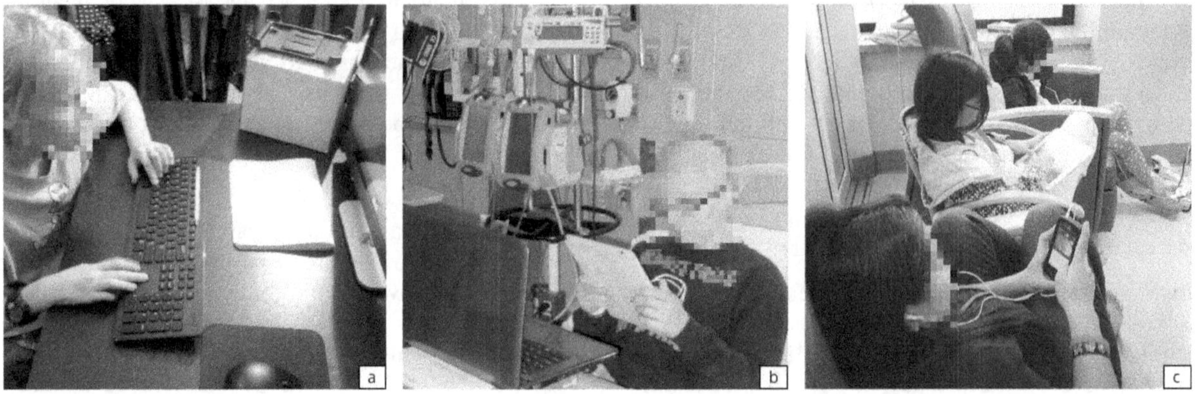

Figure 1. (a) Cancer patient playing games; (b) Cancer patient Skyping on a laptop while using Facebook on her iPad; (c) Aplastic anemia patient (rightmost) listening to her iPod while friends are visiting. (All images were approved by their parents)

with friends, and thoughts about connecting their child with peer patients. Interviews lasted 45 to 60 minutes.

We coded our transcribed interviews looking for emergent themes, following a grounded theory approach [22] by using axial and open coding, affinity diagrams, and stopping upon data saturation when themes no longer presented new theories. We did not ask specifically about normalcy in the interviews. Instead, it was a theme that we saw come up repeatedly during analysis. The most widely used codes in our analysis were ones such as "methods: technology: [different kinds of technology]", "social isolation", "life: normalizing their 'sick' life", and "fitting in".

RESULTS

In this section we describe a key theme that emerged from our interviews and survey—how pediatric patients utilize different technologies in an attempt to maintain normalcy by staying in touch with their peers (Figure 1). We also discuss ways that patients begin creating a "new normal" that integrates their prediagnosis lives with their lives after diagnosis. We present data from both the survey and the interviews combined when discussing the observed themes.

In describing our results, we refer to healthcare professionals with the label "hcp", parents with the label "pcg", and children who participated in the survey with the label "sch". All names are pseudonyms.

Interfering with Normalcy

While undergoing treatment, pediatric patients must deal with numerous hurdles that challenge the normalcy of their lives. Based on reports from the survey as well as the healthcare providers and parents we interviewed, we outline various obstacles that can cause patients to feel different than their healthy friends.

Struggling with Health Aspects

At a time when children and teenagers are constantly developing, chronically ill patients often have to deal with the extra burden of physical changes from their illness. For example, medications can cause many side effects—such as acne, a bloated face, or weight gain. Having surgery may leave scars, and chemotherapy often causes patients to lose their hair. Many patients are forced to realize that their appearance is no longer what it was prior to their diagnosis. Not only are patients aware of changes in their appearance, but it may be equally obvious to strangers as well. Having a recognizable physical change (*e.g.*, baldness) essentially advertises their illness to the rest of the world.

Besides physical changes, patients sometimes have other issues related to their illness that contributes to a lack of normalcy. Side effects from having the illness or going through treatments often hinders patients' lives, leaving them unable to participate in certain events or causing them to become self-conscious about things out of their control. Physical limitations could also hinder their ability to use certain technology, thus potentially limiting their capacity to stay connected with friends. One patient said, "*I have trouble using phones with buttons…my parents are looking for an inexpensive touch-screen phone for me*" (sch4). Medications or treatments could leave patients feeling exhausted. Many clinicians and parents mentioned that during certain treatment times (*e.g.*, chemotherapy), patients would be so tired that they would sleep for a week, not want to see any friends or family, and not talk to anyone (hcp1, hcp2, hcp3, hcp6, hcp7, hcp8, hcp13, pcg1, pcg6).

Missing Out

As expected, patients often miss out on activities due to the health aspects of their chronic illness. For example, they miss out on special events, such as birthday parties, graduations, or weddings. Some also stop attending school regularly and miss out on school events. When asked whether patients felt connected with their friends even if they were too sick to be with them, using a 5-point Likert scale with 1 being "strongly disagree" and 5 being "strongly agree", patients reported that while they did not feel strongly disconnected to their friends, on average these children did not feel connected either (*mean=2.8; SD=1.47*).

Besides not participating in events, patients also miss out on social interactions with friends. Many of their social interactions prior to being diagnosed happened during school. However, without being in that environment, patients miss out on building and growing their relationships with friends. Healthcare professionals and parents both stated that friends would often move on and form new friendships, especially the younger children. One patient agreed with this sentiment, stating that *"it's important to have friends and stay in contact with them because as I get older, I may have more and more trouble seeing them in person"* (sch4).

Fitting In

Because of the diagnosis and treatment that patients have to go through, they often have to balance their old identity before being diagnosed with their new identity after being diagnosed. For many, this balance is challenging because they feel they are now outsiders of their previous social circles. For example, one oncology nurse explained how there was a patient who was very studious, but because chemotherapy can cause issues in memory, the patient felt she was no longer as smart as her friends (hcp9). Healthcare professionals and parents alike also spoke about how patients tried to keep up with the news of their sports teams, but that it was difficult for them knowing that they could no longer participate (hcp9, pcg3, pcg6).

Patients often had to adjust to being recognized as "the sick kid". When patients were well enough to return to school, many students immediately recognized the patients. One parent said that her seven-year-old daughter became shyer after being diagnosed with cancer. This shyness resulted from everyone, including people that she did not know, recognizing her (pcg5). Additionally, sometimes being recognized as "the sick kid" caused jealous peers to post negative comments about patients. A 17-year old patient being treated for cancer had the opportunity to meet an NFL player. Her peers wrote negative comments directed to her on Twitter. For example, *"'Maybe you're doing this for attention' and 'oh, this is all I need to do to get to meet [NFL player]', and things like that..."* (pcg7). Her mother recognized that these were most likely not her daughter's friends, but rather classmates who seemed ignorant about having such an illness.

Although this struggle in balancing an identity seemed to be less of an issue for younger children who had been in treatment since they were very young (before really forming a previous identity), they still had to eventually deal with the realization that they were different than their healthy friends. Many of them assumed that the hospitalizations, procedures, and medications were all part of a normal routine that everyone had to go through.

The mother of Jeffrey, a five-year old patient who had been in treatment since he was two years old, spoke about when Jeffrey began realizing that he was different:

> *We go fortnightly to his hospital to have chemotherapy administered, and he got in the car the other day, cried and said, "All my friends have popsicles and a DVD to watch this afternoon as a treat. But I have to miss out. I'm not like my friends. I'm different to everybody." He's realizing he misses treats and fun things at school and parties. It's starting to really bug him.* (pcg1)

After Jeffrey started interacting with healthy peers at school, he began realizing that his friends did not have to go through the same things that he did and that he was actually missing out on things his friends were doing. His mother explained how the older he became, the more difficult it was to get him to adhere to medications because he began to correlate the side effects of taking the medication to missing out on events with his friends.

One healthcare professional explained that younger children who have not had a chance to form a previous identity prior to being "the sick kid" might have trouble developing the appropriate coping mechanisms:

> *As you grow up and you start to determine how different you are from society, that is isolating. And some kids...have a hard time learning the coping skills that they need to establish friendships and relationships, see themselves as normal, and worthy of friendships.* (hcp8)

Feeling Rejected

Aside from the lack of normalcy that the illness creates, patients also have to deal with a fear of rejection where they fear that if they miss school or events, their friends will eventually forget them and leave them out. A cancer nurse explained that even children as young as preschoolers and kindergarteners *"talk a lot about their friends, about being missed, about being left out. They talk about, 'Does anyone know I'm not showing up for school?'"* (hcp2)

These fears were not limited to young children. Even adolescent patients expressed similar fears. The same cancer nurse said that there was another adolescent patient who had friends who were going back to school who said:

> *"Now I'm going to have to do this on my own." And I [nurse] said, "Well, you will still stay in touch with them." And she said, "Yeah, but they'll be in school and they'll be working. And they'll have their own lives, and they're going to leave me behind."* (hcp2)

Although the healthcare professional said that she had met the patient's friends and did not believe that the friends would leave the patient behind, the patient feared the possibility of that happening.

Beyond the fear of rejection, patients also had a perception of rejection where they believed that their friends no longer cared about them. One healthcare professional stated that for some patients, *"I think they feel that when they're not there, their friends forget about them"* (hcp2). It is difficult for patients to understand that there might be external factors inhibiting their friends from contacting or visiting them, such as their friends worrying that a visit would be a burden. A Child Life Specialist talked about how sometimes patients have friends who fall off their support system *"which makes them sad because they realize, 'Oh, I thought this person was a better friend'"* (hcp1).

In addition, some patients agonize over rejection when friends do not respond or reach out for long periods of time. One patient mentioned that sometimes technology made it "*too easy for others, then they don't visit*" (sch2). For her, various technologies made it easy for friends to stay connected virtually, but she also wanted her friends to physically visit as well. One healthcare professional described a situation in which an acute myeloid leukemia patient had been in the hospital for months and no friends had visited her or texted her. The healthcare professional said:

> *Her mom actually came to me...and was like, "This is a really hard day. It has been months that no one's returning her Facebook thing she sent out." She had posted something on YouTube...and no one had really responded.* (hcp7)

Although her friends did not explicitly make it clear that they were leaving her out, the fact that they did not make an effort to respond to her made the patient feel like her friends had abandoned her. A cancer nurse explained potential reasons as to why friends may no longer reach out to patients:

> *The cancer makes it really difficult because [patients] can't go do things...They can't participate in things, so then the friends often stop calling them, and they don't reach out because they're a little shy...But now, because they cannot accept invitations to things as often and because they're not going to school as often, they – people just move on.* (hcp9)

Lacking Control

Patients have to surrender to the fact that having a chronic illness means that many of the things that happen to them are out of their control. For example, if a patient has low blood counts, they may have to stay overnight at the hospital even if they are feeling fine. One nurse described the patient's lack of control as, *"Sometimes the body's just not functioning the way it should be. So they're feeling well, but they have to be stuck there"* (hcp12).

Patients were aware of their lack of control in these situations, which caused even more annoyance and frustration. One father explained how his daughter would feel unhappy and frustrated about the situation and *"sometimes she'll verbalize it. You know, 'I didn't choose to have this cancer' is a term that she'll use"* (pcg6).

Some patients took this lack of control and tried to turn it around. A social worker described a situation where the patient's friends were not reaching out and *"this one patient, she pushed people away. And so in some ways, it looks like the peers held back first, but really, she became bristly because...you know, taking control of the situation by becoming bristly"* (hcp13). In this case, the patient took control by making it seem like she had chosen not to interact with her friends rather than the other way around.

Maintaining Normalcy

Patients were extremely cognizant that they were not the same as their healthy peers. In this section, we discuss various methods that patients used to try and maintain normalcy in their lives.

Staying Connected

Not surprisingly, patients stayed connected with their friends through a variety of technologies. All of the healthcare professionals and parents mentioned some kind of communication technology that the patients used. Most of them recognized that texting and social networking sites—such as Facebook and Twitter—were the most prevalent ways of staying connected. Technology also allowed rapid response times from friends and allowed multiple conversations simultaneously (sch7). One patient mentioned that she liked "*Instagram and FaceTime because it gets me in instant contact with my friends"* (sch4). According to most healthcare professionals and parents, email was not a very popular tool because it was seen as a more formal way for communicating with relatives or for school purposes. The survey supported this conclusion—only one out of the ten patients said that they used email to stay in touch with their friends (sch10).

Typical communication methods—such as texting, email, and social networking sites—are beneficial because they are prevalent for the general population. Patients can use these tools and easily correspond with their healthy friends because they are already using them.

At times, which friends stay connected to patients depends on which have access to that technology (hcp11). For example, one 12-year old patient explained that, *"Not all of [my friends] have a phone or Facebook, so [I] can't talk to them"* (sch1). Another parent echoed this sentiment, saying *"some kids have better resources to technology...So who she's just communicating with may just be who has FaceTime or has all the things that she has. You just talk to who's there sometimes"* (pcg3).

Although many technologies helped patients stay connected with their friends, using a 5-point Likert scale with 1 being "strongly disagree" and 5 being "strongly agree", patients still reported that they wanted to be able to talk more with their friends (*mean=3.8; SD=1.13*), play more with their friends (*mean=3.9; SD=1.19*), and have better ways of talking with their friends if they could not be there physically with them (*mean=3.8; SD=1.31*).

Feeling Present without Being Present

Because of their hospitalization or their compromised immune systems, patients are not always able to be physically present. At times, patients simply want to be with their friends and do everyday activities—such as playing games. Other times, patients have to miss out on special or momentous events. In these situations, they often take advantage of various technologies, such as the rich affordances of video chat.

One parent recounted how her daughter was able to work around the limitations of Minecraft, a game that she would often play with her friend. The patient would FaceTime her friend while they were playing, but they would not spend most of the time speaking directly to each other. The patient left her iPod in her peripheral view so that she could still see her friend while playing her game (pcg4). The parent explained that:

> *They can both be in the same place in Minecraft, but they can't hear each other, so if they're on FaceTime, they can talk, "Hey, I'm in this part of the castle" or..."Come here and get something." There's no voice part, so they do that part on FaceTime.* (pcg4)

In one case, a patient had to miss her sister's wedding. Although she was only able to participate in part of the wedding through Skype, the patient acknowledged the hard work and effort of the healthcare professionals who had set it up for her. The patient told them that it was better than not being able to see or participate in anything (hcp1). One patient also suggested having an "*in-school cam for classroom to participate if [I'm] feeling ok or a mobile one, so friends can take [me] to sports I miss*" (sch9).

Another patient had to miss out on her eighth grade graduation because she was hospitalized. The school put a laptop that was running Skype on a chair. The patient was able to watch and listen to the ceremony and speeches. Her father said, *"It was like she attended the ceremony...and then after, people were coming up to the laptop saying 'Hi Elizabeth,' and talking to her, and her talking back"* (pcg6).

Even times when patients would video chat to participate virtually in an event, they would still dress up as if they were physically attending. For example, Elizabeth's father was very surprised that she had dressed up when Skyping into the eighth grade graduation ceremony (pcg6). Another patient was involved in a school club, but since she wasn't able to attend to school, it was very difficult for her to be part of the club election. Instead, she dressed up and Skyped her election speech to the club (hcp1).

Another patient would Skype into her classroom any time she could. The healthcare professional said:

> *It was just like she was there. She would get up in the morning, shower, brush her teeth, and brush her hair and put on nice clothes 'cause she knew she was going to be Skyping just like she would go to school...it wasn't like, "Oh, I'm not going to school and I'm just staying home, so it doesn't really matter. I can stay in sweats on the couch all day." She actually felt like she had to get up and get ready to go to school.* (hcp2)

Not only did keeping this routine gave the patient structure, mimicking her daily routine at home, it allowed for an easier transition when she began to attend school again, and brought back a sense of normalcy where she felt like she was actually attending school.

Conversation Topics

When talking with their friends, patients often talked about topics that did not revolve around their illness such as typical life topics, depending on the age of the patient.

Younger patients usually do not sit and simply talk to friends, but instead conduct show-and-tells or play. For example, the mother of a five-year-old patient explained how the patient showed his friend things over video chat:

> *They like to show each other stuff, and he'll go get things...They showed each other their baby brothers...It encourages him to get up and move around...or go and get things to show his friends...Toys and books and DVDs – things that he's been bought...* (pcg1)

The affordances of video and the mobility of many devices allows younger patients to feel as if they are face-to-face with their friends. One nurse explained that she would see young patients use video chat to play Barbies with their friends and family (hcp12). This follows work that has shown that younger children enjoy showing things through video chat while they play [29].

Other patients talk about various games, such as Minecraft (pcg4) or building LEGOs online (pcg2). As patients got older, conversations shifted towards adolescent topics and staying updated with what was going on in their social circles outside of the hospital. Patients would discuss school, celebrities, bands, and sports (pcg4, pcg5, pcg6, sch2-4, sch7-10). They would also talk about parties that were happening (hcp14), who was dating who (hcp8, pcg6), other friends (sch2, sch3, sch4, sch7) and prom (hcp14).

Although patients would talk to their friends about typical life topics, as well as staying updated with the current gossip, some of them were cautious to create a balance between staying in the loop without knowing too much in fear that they would feel left out. As one mother explained:

> *For the most part, she'll ask them questions like, "What's happening with soccer? Has soccer started yet?"...She still has an interest in what's happening, but she's very careful to not ask too much to where she*

> *starts to feel sad because she's missing it. So it's a fine line of keeping communication yet staying at a distance because it's hard to be away.* (pcg3)

Patients would also take advantage of the asynchronous properties of various technologies such as text or Facebook. This allows patients to step back if they begin feeling sad about missing out on things without feeling pressured to constantly stay engaged in the conversation.

Validating Feelings

Patients often express fears about their illness. Sometimes they articulate to healthcare professionals and their parents how awful they feel or that perhaps having this illness was of their own doing. Healthcare professionals and their healthy friends were able to validate patients' feelings as well as ensure that although this was something they had to go through, this was not by their own choice. However, patients had to deal with the paradox of wanting to be seen as normal by their peers but needing the social support and validation that only a peer group can provide.

One patient, who needed a kidney transplant, actively chose to isolate himself from his family and friends. He told the hospital staff that he wanted to be alone and that nobody understood what he was going through. However, a surgeon, who he held in high esteem talked with him:

> *Yes, [the patient] needed a transplant - but he didn't get to choose if he got a transplant; it was done to him. We had the surgeon come back and sit down with him and just hear him out. He was a totally different kid after that point.* (hcp8)

Having someone that the patient held in high esteem listen to him, assure him, and validate that what he was going through was not his fault and that it was normal to have these feelings made the patient open up again. He was then able to interact with his friends and family without feeling like he needed to pretend to be strong and upbeat.

A cancer social worker explained that when patients share their fears, healthcare professionals normalize those feelings. They *"validate where they're coming from and how they can overcome it: 'You're not your cancer. Your cancer is part of your experience, but that doesn't define who you are. You're still the person that you are'"* (hcp15).

A general pediatrician recounted when an eight-year-old cystic fibrosis patient would wait by the door every day for visitors, but because she was on contact precaution, it was difficult for visitors to come by. She eventually broke down, thinking that she was very different. The healthcare professional explained:

> *We try to make it very clear to her that "this doesn't make you a worse person. This isn't your fault." It's making her realize that [her friends] are not here not because they don't like [her], but because they can't. It's just hard to [physically] come to [her].* (hcp14)

At the same time, it can be difficult for patients to accept validation from healthcare professionals or their parents. One mother of a patient who lost her hair explained that her daughter felt better when her friends or strangers validated her, even if her parents or her healthcare team said the same thing:

> *To lose [her hair] that she was always guaranteed to get a compliment on really devastated her. She was like, "Forget about cancer. I'm going to go bald?" – I can tell her a million times that she's beautiful. Her dad, the doctors, the nurses [but she won't believe it] until [her] peers and even people that didn't have to stop for a second to say something nice do.* (pcg3)

Some patients might have felt that it was part of a parent's or a healthcare team's job to compliment or validate them. However, when the validation came from others who did not "need" to do so, the patient would begin to believe those compliments. Patients also utilized social media, such as Facebook, Twitter, and Instagram for validation. Posting a picture or a status update generated many positive and encouraging comments from acquaintances that might have otherwise never contacted them (pcg3).

Creating a New Normal

Although patients strived for normalcy, they also knew that they still had an illness and therefore, by the nature of having it, could not lead the same lives as their healthy peers. In this section, we talk about various methods that many patients go through to "create a new normal".

Connecting to Peer Patients

Although patients were often stuck at home, in clinic, or in the hospital, they had the opportunity to meet others who were going through similar situations. One physician explained how being treated for similar illnesses can create strong bonds, even resulting in a case where two patients on the same ward got married to each other. He explained the reason behind such a strong connection is because:

> *[Patients] understand each other, they can empathize with each other and there's no secrets because they know all the ins and outs of what it means to be a chronically ill patient. They've found someone who can look past the tubes and the hoses and embarrassing things that happen.* (hcp3)

While their healthy friends might not be able to fully comprehend or know exactly what it's like to go through treatment, other patients do. The common ground that the experiences provide is something that patients would not be able to have with anyone who wasn't chronically ill.

Being able to connect with those who already went through what they are currently going through was very valuable for patients. In many cases, older patients were able to calm younger patients down and show them that it was not as bad as they thought. For example, one mother explained that her daughter, Anna, had a mentor who she met while in the hospital, and she helped Anna learn to take medication.

> *When it was time to learn how to take medication and she couldn't learn how to swallow pills...we'd FaceTime [her mentor] and she was able to give Anna some ideas on how to take the pill so that she wouldn't have to taste this yucky medicine. It didn't matter what Mom and Dad said, but having it come from another kid was pretty instrumental for her.* (pcg5)

Patients were not only able to learn from other patients but help those who are not as far along in the treatment process. While, at times, patients can provide support to other patients, those experiences can also be a double-edged sword. Some patients would rather not associate with peer patients simply because doing so reminds them of their illness and that they are different than their healthy friends. Healthcare professionals sometimes recommend that patients attend a cancer camp, where many pediatric cancer patients can gather to connect with one another, over the summer. However, one cancer nurse said:

> *I've had some kids go, "Why would I want to go to Cancer Camp? I got cancer enough. I want to go to school. I want to go to my Boy Scout Camp."* (hcp2)

In these cases, the patients have no desire to create a new normal, but instead, attempt to maintain their previous life. These patients do not want to be reminded of their illness – something that is too often present in their daily experiences.

It wasn't just the patients who had apprehensions about interacting with peer patients. Parents were also concerned about the constant reminder to their child. One mother explicitly stated that she would prefer her daughter not talk about her illness with other peer patients because *"I don't really want her to talk about her sickness 'cause I just want her to be a normal kid. I'll deal with that medical part. She just needs to be a kid"* (pcg4).

Educating Healthy Peers

Often, healthy peers do not understand the gravity of a patient's illness – they just know that the patient cannot attend certain events or that they look different. One social worker explained that it had been very helpful for patients to do some kind of education within their school to say *"'Hey this is what I've got, this is why I've got it, this is what it looks like for me'...it may not be the whole 7th grade, but these twenty kids know a little bit better what she's experiencing"* (hcp13).

Another nurse explained that another form of education is to have their friends physically visit them at the hospital. She said that, *"then their friend sees what a hospital looks like; what a clinic looks like; what it means to have a port access and get chemotherapy"* (hcp9).

Although healthcare professionals encourage this type of education between patients and their healthy peers, none of the parents mentioned their child explaining more to their friends. There could be multiple reasons for this such as patients wanting to maintain normalcy with their friends and to not remind their friends that they were not well or because it can be difficult for patients' friends to come to the hospital.

Managing Reactions

Patients had to balance other people's expectations of how they saw them, particularly because their physical appearances often changed vastly from before they were diagnosed. Instead of showing up one day at school looking very different than before, patients sometimes managed those reactions by using certain technologies.

For instance, Lucy, a 15-year old osteosarcoma patient who had long, dark red hair, was very self-conscious about losing her hair. Every time they drove home, if she didn't have her wig, she would begin panicking. She would run into the house and put on her makeup and wig because *"she wanted the world to still see her as her"* (pcg3). However, she slowly started posting pictures of herself with less makeup on Facebook. Her mother explained that:

> *I think, just slowly putting pictures of herself...putting that out there, and then getting some really positive feedback to now. Like yesterday, she finally just put a full collage of herself on Facebook, which is just of her doing different things, all without her wig and without makeup and getting feedback from people like, "You're really brave for that."* (pcg3)

Some patients used Facebook as a way to asynchronously manage real-time reactions. Lucy was able to acclimate others to her new appearance. Once she was ready to go back to school or go home, she wouldn't have to deal with other people's shock of her drastic change in appearance. Not only did Facebook help in mediating reactions asynchronously, it also allowed others to validate and commend Lucy for her strength in dealing with cancer. The positive comments that Lucy received encouraged her to post even more pictures, thus constantly readjusting her appearance in other's minds.

However, there were also other patients who feared what their friends would think, so they chose not to share their appearance with their friends. In one instance, there was a cancer patient who had to have both her legs amputated because of an infection. Every time she'd go home, she would say that she saw her relatives, but that she did not want her friends to see her without her legs. The nurse expressed that going home will be very difficult for her:

> *The little bit of connection that she's done [in the past 14 months she's been in the hospital] has been texting, and so [her friends] have not seen her and they've not*

When the patient…	*Text*	*Video*	*SNS*
does not feel well enough to engage in the conversation	X		X
does not have enough energy to update individuals			X
wants to be "there" with friends		X	
wants to play games with friends	X	X	X
wants support and validation from peers	X	X	X
is worried about other's reactions	X		X
wants to educate healthy peers		X	X
wants to find and meet peer patients			X
wants to connect with peer patients they have already met	X	X	X

Table 1. Technologies that can help maintain normalcy.

> *had to deal with the fact that she's in a wheelchair and doesn't have legs...* (hcp2)

Although texting is beneficial because it requires minimal effort on the patient's side and provides asynchronous access, in many cases it is still primarily a one-to-one interaction. Therefore, if patients use text to share their appearance, they may have to deal with multiple conversations and multiple reactions, which is different from Lucy's case where she just posted it on Facebook.

BENEFITS & DRAWBACKS OF TECHNOLOGIES

Patients try to maintain normalcy by doing things they would normally do—including communicating with friends using whatever technology their friends use. When designing for this population it is important to remember that it might be difficult to gain critical mass if it is a novel system that their friends do not have easy access to. However, novel applications can be built on top of existing platforms that are already being used (*e.g.*, Facebook). Systems can also be adapted to better support a blend of asynchronous and synchronous communication, thereby helping reduce the rigidity of current technologies.

In this section, we will outline how and when existing technologies might be leveraged to assist chronically ill patients. Based on our analysis, we examined the various needs as well as challenges for patients and identified benefits and drawbacks of existing technologies to support children with chronic illnesses (summarized in Table 1).

Health Limitations

When the patient does not feel well enough to engage in conversation (*e.g.*, those who are going through intensive treatment), texting and social networking sites can be a good solution. For example, from our results, many clinicians and parents mentioned times where because of the treatment, patients felt "crappy" and did not want to talk to their friends in their tired state. These asynchronous technologies allow patients to control when they want to interact with their friends, without feeling pressured to be connected constantly. It allows the patient to remain connected and up-to-date with what their friends are doing, but on the patient's own schedule. In contrast, synchronous technologies, such as phone or video calls, might not work as well because patients might feel obligated to engage in the conversation, even if they do not feel well enough to do so.

When the patient does not have enough energy to update individuals, social networking sites (*e.g.*, Facebook or Twitter) allow the patient to update everyone at once, relieving the burden of many individual conversations. We found that many patients were not only feeling bad after their treatment, but were also so completely exhausted that they would often go for a week without talking with their friends. Social networking systems also allow others to comment on the patient's status updates, which can engage others in keeping the patient's social network informed [21]. Social networking apps, such as Instagram or Snapchat, that focus on sharing photos to a large audience can allow patients to share richer contexts through photos, rather than textual status updates. However, this type of interaction can be difficult for younger patients who do not necessarily have access to social networking sites. Parents could also be concerned about privacy or safety with social networking sites that have more public postings (*e.g.*, Twitter). However, blogs like CaringBridge that are meant for parents and caregivers can help with safety and privacy issues. These sites can provide status updates to the public, taking away some of the responsibility of keeping everyone updated from the patient. In contrast to social networking sites, texting and many synchronous technologies are more likely to be one-on-one interactions, requiring patients to update friends individually.

Being Present

When the patient wants to be "there" during an event or activity, they could take advantage of a rich medium, such as synchronous video, that can help patients to feel as if they are interacting with their friends face-to-face. Patients can see friends' faces, reactions, and gestures that do not come across well in other technologies. For example, one parent described how his daughter utilized Skype to be part of her graduation ceremony, even though she wasn't able to physically attend. Similarly, patients can use video to virtually attend classes, enabling them to continue daily social interactions with classmates. Other synchronous technologies may also be useful but less valuable for patients to feel "present" if the communication is through text.

Although video is a rich communication medium, it is still limited in how well it can support some activities. Currently, most of these systems have been designed to support conversations (*i.e.,* a talking head format where both sides just show the person's head) and the mobility of these systems can also create barriers. For patients who really want to have a strong sense of "being there" it will be important to explore systems that can better support shared experiences so patients feel like they are actually participating [12]. Asynchronous technologies, such as texting or Facebook, can give quick updates to patients in the moment, but are not as immersive as video communication, potentially making the patient feel more like a bystander than being present.

Integrating Peers

When the patient wants to play games with friends, especially synchronous games, using technologies such as text (mainly, synchronous texting systems such as instant messaging) or video can help patients play games with friends even when they are physically separated. For example, one patient from our findings used FaceTime as a way to see and talk to her friend while playing a game that did not support talking. She appropriated a video communication technology to help her feel as if she was sitting next to her friend, playing the game. Other parents mentioned that it would be great if applications such as Skype supported different games while still being able to see the other person. This type of synchronous video communication would work well for patients who are not self-conscious about their appearance and who would like to feel as if they were present with their friends. For patients who might be less willing to share their appearance or simply do not feel like it, using synchronous texting systems such as instant messaging may work well. Alternatively, patients and their friends could play a wide variety of asynchronous games. For example, Facebook supports different social games, such as Words with Friends, Candy Crush Saga, or Farmville. These games do not require both players to be playing at the same time. This type of game can work well for patients who do not want to feel pressured to play games with their friends when they don't have enough energy to play.

When the patient wants to receive support and validation from peers, depending on the individual, potentially any type of communication tool could work well, however, social networking sites like Facebook, Twitter, YouTube, and Instagram have the ability to reach a wide audience. Patients can receive support and validation as well as generate positive feedback from acquaintances or people who are not comfortable enough to reach out directly. However, because social networking sites can produce fleeting interactions, patients might feel that the support and validation they receive from this medium is superficial. Similar to the example of the patient who received jealous comments directed to her through Twitter, these social networking sites can sometimes be public, potentially garnering negative feedback from strangers, which can be detrimental to a patient.

Synchronous technologies can also work well for receiving support and validation from close friends. With synchronous technologies, like videoconferencing tools, friends can actually see how the patient is doing or what the patient is going through. This can create a type of sincerity that might not always be present in the interactions from social networking sites.

When the patient is worried about other's reactions to their different appearance, video communication could accentuate these concerns. Patients who have lost their hair or have gained weight may feel self-conscious about communicating through this medium.

In contrast, asynchronous or non-video tools can be useful for patients who are worried about other people's reactions. For patients who are not ready to show their friends their physical changes (*e.g.*, losing their hair), texting or sending audio messages can be a good way to stay connected with friends while still maintaining some control over what type of information is being shared. Additionally, social networking sites have the potential to encourage patients to put themselves out there, such as posting a photo without any hair, without the awkwardness that might come with a synchronous interaction. Social networking sites can also generate a lot of positive feedback that can help the patient come to terms with these changes. In our results, one parent described how her daughter received positive reactions after posting a picture of herself without hair, which encouraged her to continue posting such pictures.

When the patient wants to educate friends and classmates, various technologies can help others see what the patient has to go through. For example, asynchronous technologies such as websites, blogs, video blogs (vlogs), and social networking sites can allow for in-depth explanations on the illness or the procedures and treatments that a patient is undergoing. Videoconferencing tools can also be a way to educate others to see what it is really like. For example, many clinicians suggested ideas where patients can "bring" his or her whole class to the hospital via video and educate them on what it's like to be hospitalized and the different treatments that the patient has to go through.

Peer Patients

When the patient wants to find and meet distant peer patients, social networking sites can be very helpful. Social networking sites, such as Facebook, have many groups where patients with similar illnesses converge to share their experiences with one another. Many of our survey respondents were members or had parents who were members of various Facebook groups. Patients can find other peer patients through other sites such as Twitter or Instagram by using various hashtags. Using other types of technologies, such as synchronous technologies or other asynchronous technologies like texting, seems to be too personal for patients who want to first establish a relationship with other peer patients.

When the patient wants to connect with peer patients they have already met, although any type of technology can connect patients, certain technologies could encourage a common ground when establishing their friendship. For example, many parents and healthcare professionals commented that it was difficult for some patients to connect with other peer patients in the same clinic because they did not know if they shared any of the same interests and were often too shy to find out. By utilizing social networking sites, patients might be able to discover things they have in common with other patients, aside from their illness.

LIMITATIONS AND FUTURE WORK

In this section, we discuss the limitations of our study as well as opportunities for future work.

Limitations

The age of the survey respondents and the age of the children of the parents we interviewed spanned a large range (5-18 years old), which may have influenced some of the responses that we received. Similarly, it is important to note that the responses we received may have been varied due to the age range and the differences in how children at different ages use technology. In this first stage of research we gathered data from multiple sources, including children with chronic illnesses, parents of children with chronic illnesses, and healthcare professionals. However, we only collected survey data from the pediatric patients because we were concerned about the sensitivity of the topic, and the potential burden an interview may pose. Parents however felt confident that they were aware of most of their child's interactions online.

Future Work

Now that we have gathered preliminary insights, we plan to include children in future studies focusing on the child's perspective which may give us more insight into what the child is going through during this difficult time. Other future research can also explore the asymmetry and dynamics in the relationship between patients and their healthy counterparts. For example, are there any tension or negative feelings that come from the healthy peer such as feeling guilty that they are healthy? Other research studies might explore the significance of patients' interactions with their friends (*e.g.*, do patients feel the conversations they have with friends are superficial?). At each age range, technology may play a very different role in patients' attempt to maintain normalcy. Future studies should look at how these may differ in each age range, particularly since younger children have less access to social media.

CONCLUSION

Children with a chronic illness lead very different lives than their healthy friends. Treatments, side effects, changes in appearance can all cause chronically ill pediatric patients to feel different. Yet, little work has examined the role of technology as a method for maintaining normalcy in a chronically ill child's life.

The results from our work show that children with a chronic illness utilize various technologies to maintain normalcy in a life that can be very different than their life before diagnosis. At the same time, these patients must also balance integrating a new type of "normal" with their previous before-diagnosis identity. We present opportunities for technology to help patients connect with others and feel a sense of normalcy, as well as point out considerations to take into account when designing for this population. Although chronically ill patients might not always feel "normal", communication tools could help them maintain a sense of normalcy while embracing their "new normal".

ACKNOWLEDGEMENTS

This work was supported in part by Microsoft Research and the NIH NLM training grant (2T15LM007442). We thank all of the participants for their time. Ari Pollack and Abby Rosenberg helped with recruitment. We also thank Norman Makoto Su and the iMed research group for their helpful feedback.

REFERENCES

1. Aamodt, A., Grassl-Herwehe, S., Farrell, F., and Hutter, J. The child's view of chemically induced alopecia. In *Care: The Essence of Nursing and Health*, M. Leininger, Ed. Slack, Thorofare, NJ, 1984, 217-231.
2. Ames, M.G., Go, J., Kaye, J.J., and Spasojevic, M. Making love in the network closet: the benefits and work of family video chat. In *Proc. CSCW'10*, 145-154.
3. Bers, M.U., Ackermann, E., Cassell, J., Donegan, B., Gonzalez-Heydrich, J., DeMaso, D.R., Strohecker, C., Lualdi, S., Bromley, D., and Karlin, J. Interactive storytelling environments: coping with cardiac illness at Boston's Children's Hospital. In *Proc. CHI'98*, 603-610.
4. Bers, M.U., Gonzalez-Heydrich, J., and DeMaso, D.R. Identity Construction Environments: Supporting a Virtual Therapeutic Community of Pediatric Patients Undergoing Dialysis. In *Proc. CHI'01*, 380-387.
5. Buhler, T., Neustaedter, C., and Hillman, S. How and why teenagers use video chat. In *Proc. CSCW'13*, 759-768.
6. Chin, J. and Tsuei, M. Multi-user Narrative Sharing System for Children with Chronic Illness. In *Proc. Advanced Learning Technologies 2009*, 479-481.
7. Farnham, S., Cheng, L., Stone, L., Zaner-Godsey, M., Hibbeln, C., Syrjala, K., Clark, A.M., and Abrams, J. HutchWorld: clinical study of computer-mediated social support for cancer patients and their caregivers. In *Proc. CHI'02*, 375-283.

8. Fels, D.I., Samers, P.J., and Robertson, M. Use of the asynchronous BlackBerry technology in a large children's hospital to connect sick kids to school. In *Proc. Int. Conf. on Computers in Education 2003*, 1-6.
9. Fels, D.I. and Weiss, P.L. Video-mediated communication in the classroom to support sick children: a case study. *International Journal of Industrial Ergonomics 28*,5 (2001), 251-263.
10. Gibson, L. and Hanson, V.L. Digital Motherhood: How Does Technology Help New Mothers? In *Proc. CHI'13*, 313-322.
11. Hourcade, J.P., Driessnack, M., and Huebner, K.E. Support Face-to-Face Communication Between Clinicians and Children with Chronic Headaches Through a Zoomable Multi-Touch App. In Proc. *CHI'12*, 2609-2618.
12. Inkpen, K., Taylor, B., Junuzovic, S., Tang, J., and Venolia, G. Experiences2Go: Sharing Kids' Activities Outside the Home with Remote Family Members. In *Proc. CSCW'13*, 1329-1340.
13. Larouche, S.S. and Chin-Peuckert, L. Changes in body image experienced by adolescents with cancer. *Journal of Pediatric Oncology Nursing 23*,4 (2006), 200-209.
14. Lee, M.L. and Dey, A.K. Lifelogging memory appliance for people with episodic memory impairment. In *Proc. UbiComp'08*, 44-53.
15. Mamykina, L., Miller, A.D., Mynatt, E.D., and Greenblatt, D. Constructing Identities through Storytelling in Diabetes Management. In *Proc. CHI'10*, 1203-1212.
16. Massimi, M., Dimond, J.P., and Le Dantec, C.A. Finding a New Normal: The Role of Technology in Life Disruptions. In *Proc. CSCW'12*, 719-728.
17. Mokashi, S., Yarosh, S., and Abowd, G.D. Exploration of Videochat for Children with Autism. In *Proc. IDC'13*, 320-323.
18. Novotney, A. Lights, camera, action! *Monitor on Psychology 41*, 7 (2010), 58.
19. Plaisant, C., Druin, A., Lathan, C., Dakhane, K., Edwards, K., Vice, J.M., and Montemayor, J. A Storytelling Robot for Pediatric Rehabilitation. In *Proc. ASSETS'00*, 50-55.
20. Shama, W. and Lucchetta, S. Psychosocial Issues of the Adolescent Cancer Patient and the Development of the Teenage Outreach Program (TOP). *Journal of Psychosocial Oncology 25*,3 (2007), 99-112.
21. Skeels, M., Unruh, K.T., Powell, C., and Pratt, W. Catalyzing Social Support for Breast Cancer Patients. In *Proc. CHI'10*, 173-182.
22. Strauss, A. and Corbin, J. *Grounded theory methodology: An overview.* Handbook of Qualitative Research. Sage, Thousand Oaks, CA, 1994.
23. Teens and Technology 2013. http://www.pewinternet.org /Reports/2013/Teens-and-Tech.aspx.
24. van der Velden, M. and El Emam, K. "Not All My Friends Need To Know": A Qualitative Study of Teenage Patients, Privacy, and Social Media. *Journal of the American Medical Informatics Association 20*,1 (2013), 16-24.
25. Weiss, P.L., Whiteley, C.P., Treviranus, J., and Fels, D.I.. *Personal and Ubiquitous Computing 5*,3 (2001), 157-168.
26. Williams, B., Corlett, J., Dowell, J.S., Coyle, J., and Mukhopadhyay, S. "I've Never Not Had it So I Don't Really Know What it's Like Not to": Nondifference and Biographical Disruption Among Children and Young People With Cystic Fibrosis. *Qualitative Health Research 19*,10 (2009), 1443-1455.
27. Wise, B.V. In their Own Words: The Lived Experience of Pediatric Liver Transplantation. *Qualitative Health Research 12*,1 (2002), 74-90.
28. Woodgate, R.L. The Importance of Being There: Perspectives of Social Support by Adolescents with Cancer. *Journal of Pediatric Oncology Nursing 23*,3 (2006), 122-134.
29. Yarosh, S., Inkpen, K.M. and Bernheim Brush, A.J. Video Playdate: Toward Free Play Across Distance. In *Proc. CHI'10*, 1251-1260.

Individual and Social Recognition: Challenges and Opportunities in Migraine Management

Sun Young Park
Donald Bren School of Information and Computer Science
University of California, Irvine
sunyp1@uci.edu

Yunan Chen
Donald Bren School of Information and Computer Science
University of California, Irvine
yunanc@ics.uci.edu

ABSTRACT

This study investigates how people manage chronic migraine – an illness characterized by unpredictable, intermittent breakouts in everyday life. Participants in our study must self-identify migraine symptoms, triggers, and effective coping mechanisms while also seeking social recognition and assistance from a social network during migraine attacks. We argue that the challenges in identifying and managing migraine as well as in communicating with clinicians and social networks arise in response to the patients' need to deal with the unpredictability and intermittency of the disease. We suggest technologies that, unlike current chronic care systems, enable patients with migraine and similar diseases to track a wide range of life events across intermittent time stamps and help make sense of subjective information. We argue that technologies should also help patients gain social recognition and assistance during breakouts. This work contributes to the growing body of knowledge in personal informatics and quantified-self research.

Author Keywords

Migraine management; migraine; chronic disease; self-care; self-management; health; personal informatics

ACM Classification Keywords

H.5.m. Information interfaces and presentation (e.g., HCI): Miscellaneous.

INTRODUCTION

In recent years, technologies for chronic diseases such as cancer [28], diabetes [11, 17, 24], and asthma [39], have attracted significant attention in the HCI and CSCW communities. Given the prolonged duration and significant health impact of chronic diseases, a majority of systems have been designed to engage patients in monitoring, reflecting, and learning about long-term disease management [24, 39, 35] and to minimize the potential negative impacts of the illness on people's everyday lives [11].

CSCW 2015, March 14–18, 2015, Vancouver, BC, Canada.

http://dx.doi.org/10.1145/2675133.2675248

Despite the growing interest in chronic illness management practices, past research in the HCI and CSCW communities has focused mostly on the management of a few high-profile and well-known chronic diseases such as cancer and diabetes where the impacts and symptoms of the disease are constantly present [11, 17, 24, 28, 31]. In contrast, in this paper we aim to examine migraine – a distinctly different chronic illness characterized with unpredictable and intermittent breakouts. Such characteristics make the management of migraines and the consequent system requirements different from other diseases.

A migraine is a primary headache disorder. It involves an abnormal sensitivity of arteries in the brain to various triggers resulting in rapid changes in the artery size due to spasm (constriction) [3, 4, 38]. Although there is little consensus on whether to consider migraine a disease, recent medical research points out that migraine should be conceptualized as a chronic-episodic and sometimes chronic progressive disorder [22]. According to the WHO [38], while 15-18% of women and 6-8% of men suffer from migraine each year, nearly 90% migraine sufferers do not even know their specific condition, and more than a half have never consulted a clinician about migraine [15]. Additionally, migraine symptoms can cause lasting debilitation, forcing many patients to wait until symptoms disappear to resume their normal activities. For this reason, migraine is one of the leading causes of loss of productive time at work [32].

One unique challenge of migraine management lies in the difficulties of diagnosing and treating it. Unlike many other chronic diseases that have constant impacts on patients' everyday lives, migraine patients have to face intermittent, but extremely painful short-term breakouts caused by a wide variety of unknown triggers, either internal to patients themselves, or residing in their external environments. Thus, the goal of migraine care mostly consists of alleviating pain and reducing the duration of pain after breakouts. Migraine management therefore differs greatly from many other chronic diseases. Even though migraine has been studied in medical literature, it has not yet been reported in the field of HCI and CSCW, and it presents new challenges for designing chronic care management systems.

As previous research shows [27], it is crucial to understand the behaviors in users' daily life in order to design health technologies; in this study we take a similar approach to obtain an in-depth understanding of migraine sufferers' daily practices. We intend to understand the challenges migraine sufferers face in the process of migraine management, and to explore opportunities for designing better technologies for assisting migraine patients. Our study identifies the critical need for both self-recognition and social recognition in migraine management: first, migraine sufferers have to perform a series of individual tasks to discover and identify their own triggers, and find effective coping mechanisms. At the same time, they also need to obtain social recognition and help during migraine attacks. These needs arise in response to the challenges of dealing with the unpredictable and intermittent nature of migraine attacks. Based on these findings, we suggest that future migraine management systems help patients perform extensive sense-making across a wide range of life events, occurring at different times. We also suggest that future migraine management systems should help patients to communicate and obtain support from social circles and to gain social recognition during migraine attacks. We believe this study provides new understandings of chronic disease management dealing with unpredictability and intermittency, and contributes to the growing field of personal informatics and quantified-self research.

RELATED WORK

A large body of HCI studies focuses on the use of technologies to mitigate the challenges of chronic care management [16, 19, 24, 29, 39]. Many studies focus on monitoring and collecting personal health information to support crucial aspects of chronic care management, such as tracking disease progress [24; 5] and sharing collected information with clinical providers [39]; others have also studied how technologies should be designed to fit the special needs of home healthcare activities [1]. Previous studies have investigated the role of online health communities and social networking sites in promoting social support for patients. In particular, online communities can empower patients, as they learn from each other [16], borrow individualized coping strategies from peer patients [17] and provide social-emotional support to patients who may not be able to obtain such support in real life [29]. As a result, patients with chronic illnesses such as cancer and diabetes were found to be more satisfied in their everyday lives after becoming connected to online communities [14,17].

Unlike many chronic diseases that have specific diagnostic criteria and measurements, migraine lacks an established physiological basis and a medical diagnostic measurement. Due to this unique challenge, the diagnosis and treatment processes for migraine are largely guided by patients' own descriptions of their symptoms. In addition, due to the invisibility of symptoms, a sufferer's life may appear to be normal in front of others, yet at the same time, a sufferer may be experiencing severe pain. During migraine attacks, patients must deal with their daily work, family and social responsibilities while also suffering from extreme pain.

Existing migraine management research is comprised mostly of clinical studies focusing on diagnosis and symptoms. For instance, it is often difficult to distinguish whether a symptom has resulted from migraine, another disease, or a side effect of a medication [9]. This lack of understanding migraine at the point of care often prevents clinicians from selecting the most effective medications, leading them to prescribe preventive medications only in most cases [13]. The challenges in diagnosing and treating migraine can lead to frustration and dissatisfaction among patients, often resulting in a choice to discontinue clinical consultations [21]. To effectively manage migraines, most clinicians recommend avoiding triggers – provoking factors that induce headache attacks alone or in combination [10]. Successful migraine management therefore relies primarily on the engagement of the patients themselves instead of healthcare providers. However, the wide range of triggers, from food intake to environmental factors, often keeps patients from recognizing them effectively. Blau and Thavapalan [10] noted, "*everything can produce a migraine*." This makes preventive self-care particularly challenging for patients.

It is noteworthy that although migraine management has been studied extensively in medical literature, very few studies have explored the use of technology for migraine. The existing technologies are mostly commercial mobile applications [1] designed for patients to track migraine characteristics, such as triggers, symptoms, attack durations and frequencies of the attacks. A medical study has evaluated web-based programs, reporting the usefulness of electronic diaries over traditional paper-and-pencil methods in monitoring the efficacy of over-the-counter analgesics [37]. Another study examined the impact on clinician-patient communication of online training programs before clinical visits [30]. Although these online systems are designed for tracking migraine-related events and improving the quality of clinical consultations, they often fail to consider the importance of interactions within a pool of patients or between patients and their social circles.

The challenges migraine patients face raises an important question as to how technologies can be designed to help patients better manage their migraine and to diminish migraine's possible impact in their lives. Thus, it is essential to first obtain a thorough understanding of the patient behaviors and needs exhibited within real-life migraine management processes. To do so, we conducted a qualitative study to understand migraine patients' daily disease

[1] *iHeadache,* (http://www.iheadache.com), *iMangeMigraine* (http://itunes.apple.com/us/app/imanage-migraine/id340537912?mt=8), and *Headache Relief Diary* (http://itunes.apple.com/us/app/headache-relief-diary/id331098973?mt=8)

management practices as well as their attendant challenges, concerns and needs.

METHOD

To understand current migraine management practices, we conducted an exploratory study using contextual interviews with 12 participants suffering from migraine and interviewed two clinicians over the phone.

Contextual interviews [8] were conducted with 12 participants to understand how patients manage migraine in their everyday lives. To recruit participants, we disseminated the study announcement via fliers on campus or nearby coffee shops. We also recruited participants through the snowball sampling method – meaning people could refer friends and family members suffering migraine to us. Interviews were conducted at participants' homes, where most migraine management activities occur. Contextual interviews allowed us to gain a better understanding of how participants manage migraine attacks and to observe various artifacts that aided the migraine management process, e.g. migraine diaries. In general, interviews lasted about 1 hour and were audio-recorded. Photos were taken when participants showed their migraine-related activities or aid items. Study participants were adults ranging in age from 22 to 75, and all verbally consented following the university institute review board (IRB) requirements. All participants were clinically diagnosed and most believed that they could distinguish between a migraine and tension-type headache. Of the 12 participants, nine are female and the other three are males. This number is correspondent with the fact that females are more likely to have migraine than males.

We conducted semi-structured interviews using a brief interview protocol inquiring about possible triggers, medication/treatment, and tool use in managing migraines. The data collection and analysis followed a grounded theory approach, in which the first few interviews were discussed by a team of four researchers as soon as an interview was finished. The discussion helped us identify important questions and issues that were not explored initially, such as coping strategies, and allowed us to follow up on these critical issues in following data collection processes.

Since study participants' migraine symptoms differed in frequency, duration and severity, we divided them into three categories: patients with severe symptoms (five participants), intermediate symptoms (three participants), and mild symptoms (four participants). We grouped participants into these three types since the treatment strategies, needs and impact on a sufferer's everyday life were radically different depending on the severity of his or her migraines. For example, the frequency and duration of migraine attacks differed widely, with duration ranging from about 1-4 hours (mild), 1-3 days (intermediate) to 1-2 weeks (severe), and with frequency ranging from once or few times a year (mild-intermediate) to 5-6 times per week (severe). Participants were considered severe migraine patients when they met one of the severe categories of either duration or frequency.

In addition, to understand clinicians' attitudes about migraine management, we also performed brief phone interviews with two primary care physicians (one male, and one female). We studied primary care physicians because patients often visit them as their first step in treating migraine. Each phone interview took about 40 minutes. Clinicians were asked questions including how often they consult with migraine patients; how they diagnose migraines; common clinical treatments they use; difficulties they encounter when consulting with patients in migraine management; and what general advice they offer for managing migraine.

Besides the preliminary data analysis carried out during the data collection process, after all the interviews were finished, we further analyzed collected data using an affinity diagram [8]. The affinity diagram helped us to gain initial understanding of factors such as similarities in migraine management practice (i.e. treating symptoms, seeking information) across all the interviews. Then, we performed another round of data analysis by randomly selecting three interview transcripts from the 12 interviewees. Sample data were analyzed independently by three researchers using detailed line-by-line analysis techniques [34]. First, open coding [34] was used by each researcher to look for salient concepts and their properties (i.e. characteristics). Once these core categories were identified, axial coding was then conducted to systematically explore the properties and dimensions of the category. This led to the formation of subcategories, i.e. the three themes of coping strategies. The themes produced by each researcher were compared, discussed and revised through a series of iterations until agreement was reached among all researchers. Through this analysis, we were able to reveal how migraine patients manage their disease, cope with their symptoms, apply different treatments, communicate with clinicians, and deal with social issues.

FINDINGS

Numerous resources are available for people with migraine, such as a list of common symptoms and triggers in medical guidelines, as well as professional assistance from health providers. However, our study participants reveal that they face major challenges utilizing these resources in their everyday lives. In this section, we first describe why it is so difficult to utilize external resources in migraine management; then we report how our study participants were forced to undertake a process of self-discovery and self-trial in understanding their migraine and coping with the attacks. Lastly, we report on the implicit social recognition and assistance needed by individuals dealing with migraine attacks.

Do I Have Migraine?

A unique behavior shared among our study participants was an uncertainty about the disease – do I have migraine, and what are my symptoms? Unlike many other diseases that have clear diagnostic criteria and identifiable symptoms, migraine has considerable diversity in terms of its onset, attack occurrence, duration, and symptom attributes. Although the most obvious symptom is headache, many other symptoms co-exist that are less known and differ from person to person. In addition, the intermittent and unpredictable nature of migraine also presents a great obstacle for people to recognize their disease. For instance, people may not associate occasional headaches with migraine, but instead interpret them as other medical problems. Recognizing the disease and understanding symptoms, therefore, is the first challenge involved in migraine management.

In our study, most interviewees began to experience symptoms in their teenage years; one participant had even suffered migraines since childhood. Similar to what has been reported in prior medical studies [13, 21], we found that migraine symptoms differ significantly among individuals. For instance, one participant described her symptoms starting with blurred vision, followed by vomiting within 2-3 hours with stomach pains; another participant described his pain as a belt tightened around his head. For the duration of symptoms, participants indicated periods ranging from 1 hour to 2 weeks. Moreover, symptoms may change over the course of a single migraine or resume after a long absence. In our study, one participant did not realize she had migraine for 40 years and never consulted a health professional until her daughter was diagnosed with the same conditions, indicating the challenges of recognizing symptoms among participants.

In the study, we found that the individualized and subjective nature of migraine symptoms not only made it difficult for participants to recognize their own symptoms, but also caused significant barriers in seeking professional help. In our study, even though participants had consulted clinicians previously, only 4 of them (1 with intermediate and 3 with severe symptoms) continued with clinical treatment after the initial visit.

Because of the intermittent and subjective nature of symptoms, the diagnosis of migraine depends on verbal communication between a patient and a clinician. However, our study showed that many participants believed it was not easy to communicate effectively with clinicians about what they experienced. As one study participant stated: *"It is difficult consulting with physicians about specifics because I don't know what details are relevant. A lot of the information, the clinician can't do much with...* [P1: Alicia*, mild migraine]*."* For patients, the difficulty lies in the subjective nature of the disease and their insufficient understanding of different types of headache symptoms. They often struggle over what to report to their doctors and how much detail to supply. Eventually this communication barrier led many participants in our study to believe that their doctors did not have enough knowledge to treat them, leaving them to figure out the question of "what are my migraine symptoms" on their own.

The challenges in communicating with clinicians differed based on the severity of the disease. Participants with severe symptoms were often good at communicating with their doctors because they had frequent breakouts and spent more time finding triggers; accordingly, they were more satisfied with their clinical consultations in general. On the other hand, participants with mild and intermediate symptoms were often unable to describe their symptoms and triggers and often had lower satisfaction and expectations regarding professional assistance.

We also found that participants with severe symptoms tended to have a better understanding of their symptoms since, in addition to more frequent migraine attacks, they also had more severe, distinctive symptoms, such as vomiting, auras and pain in one side of the head, with prolonged periods of discomfort. In contrast, participants with mild and intermediate symptoms were often unable to distinguish migraine symptoms from ordinary headache (i.e. headaches with lesser frequency, duration, and intensity, without distinctive symptoms like aura or vomiting, and often relieved by over-the-counter medication). This lack of understanding of migraine among mild and intermediate symptoms participants influenced their decisions about obtaining clinical diagnosis and treatment, as seen in this quote from an interviewee with intermediate migraine symptoms:

"I think it may be something kind of serious but since it has only happened twice I don't want to go to the doctor and get no results... With my migraines with vertigo I never had the symptoms when I was at the doctor and it took them over a year to figure out that that was what it may be...after many tests that told them nothing."– P11: Gina (intermediate migraine)

Likewise, while all participants with severe symptoms found it relatively easier to quickly obtain clinical diagnoses, only half of the participants with mild and intermediate symptoms had visited a doctor for a migraine consultation in years or even decades after their first migraine breakout.

What Triggers My Migraine?

After identifying their illness as migraine, the next question for most participants is to determine what led to their migraine symptoms. For them, identifying triggers is critical in understanding and predicting the onset of migraine attacks. Triggers are 'provoking factors that, alone or in combination, induce headache attacks [10].' Migraine patients are advised to identify a causal relationship between triggers and symptoms, since avoiding or minimizing exposure to avoidable triggers can diminish the severity and frequency of their migraine attacks [10]. Not surprisingly, participants had a wide range of idiosyncratic triggers. For instance, coffee helps reduce migraine for one of our participants, whereas it often triggers migraine for many others. Even though many

*All the participant names used in the paper have been changed, i.e. the patients are anonymous.

triggers are listed in various medical brochures, participants still had to rely on their own observation to discover their own triggers.

	Disease presentation
Triggers	fatigue, stress, allergies, menstruation, specific foods/ingredients, upset stomach, hunger, heat, air quality, alcohol, sleep pattern, weather, fluorescent lights, driving, and dehydration.
Symptoms	nausea, vomiting, photophobia (sensitivity to light), auras, sensitivity to sound, pulsing pain or sharp pain in distinct areas (in one side; behind eye; near ear; around head like a belt), tight neck muscles, blurry vision, numbness

Table 1: Diversity of migraine triggers and symptoms reported by our study participants

However, identifying triggers is a task that relies heavily on individuals' ability to make sense of numerous of daily activities occurring in their lives. As showed in table 1, our participants reported to us a diverse range of triggers that are all quite subjective and subtle to identify. For instance, not all weather changes will trigger migraines and have to do with the intensity of heat or cold (e.g. one participant's migraine started whenever the temperature was over 90 degree outside) or the kind of weather (another participant reported migraine on rainy days or very windy days) or sometime even simply a change in the weather (one participant reported his migraines appeared whenever the weather switched from hot to cold, or from dry to wet).

In addition, triggers can be a combination of two or more factors, such as stress and hot weather. It is therefore difficult for people to know exactly what caused their migraine. In the study, only half the participants (6 out of 12) knew their possible migraine triggers; five of them had between two and 14 triggers, and one participant was not sure about what his triggers were. Possible triggers ranged from personal factors like diet, sleep patterns and stress, to environmental factors like weather changes and light. This wide range of potential triggers makes it particularly challenging for participants to distinguish genuine triggers from other uninvolved factors that co-exist in everyday life. One interviewee described his experience in finding triggers:

"I really don't know [my triggers]. It's hard to tell because they happen at such odd times. For instance, I had one – I was actually Skyping, doing an interview with a class and then all of the sudden I could feel, 'Oh, my vision is getting blurry,' and I started to get nauseous. I'm like, 'Oh, God,' you know? Another one I had was when I was asleep. I was completely fine going to sleep and then it woke me up and then I went to the bathroom and threw up. It was awful. So, there's no way for me to know, they are so unpredictable." – P6: Jason (mild migraine)

For Jason, the apparently random occurrence of migraines made it almost impossible for him to track down all possible life events that may constitute triggers. Also, the timing of his attacks, as described in the quotation, highlights other challenging aspects of trigger identification, since participants may not always remember to track relevant factors at a given time.

In our study, participants and clinicians demonstrated opposing viewpoints regarding identifying migraine triggers. The doctors participating in our study believed finding triggers was fairly easy for patients. One doctor stated, *"I usually tell [patients] to just write in their own notebook and then I tell them the main issue for them is to track, try to figure out the trigger...if they pay more attention to it (the triggers), then most likely they will figure it out [D01]."* In contrast, participants felt that finding migraine triggers was not as easy as simply writing things down. Instead, they perceived it as a labor-intensive process, in which they had to first determine all possible causes, then compare each different factor or different combinations of possible factors over and over again in order to make sense of a large amount of daily information. To identify triggers, participants had to recall events occurring immediately before or 1-2 days before migraine attacks, form hypotheses about which ones might be possible triggers, and experiment with them one by one. As described below, Rachael, a participant with severe migraine symptoms, used a headache diary to find out her triggers:

"For example, if I got a migraine today, I'm like, 'Did I eat chocolate today?' And I would write it in my calendar, 'milk chocolate.' And then if I got a migraine the next week, 'Did I eat pizza today?' And I would put 'pizza,' and then I'd get a migraine next week, I'm like, 'Okay, my boss yelled at me today.'... So it would be, 'pizza, boss.' Then, I was able to at least eliminate, 'Okay, so it wasn't pizza, it wasn't processed food, it wasn't this, it wasn't that.' So, then I would find a pattern eventually over six months, eight months. I just notice over time it was... 'Okay, it's definitely stress. I didn't keep it consistent, but I kept it over years enough to know that... I've kept them from the time I was 18 because it really affected my lifestyle."- P4: Rachael (severe migraine)

In Rachael's case, her migraine was not triggered by a factor such as food or exercise, but by her mental state, stress; her trigger identification process lasted years and required her to track a broad range of activities systematically over long period of time. By noting activities occurring near the time of each attack, Rachael was able to test hypotheses regarding what did or did not cause her migraine, using a trial and error process. After careful reviews, she was able to eliminate irrelevant factors. In her case, using a written diary was helpful in discovering her trigger; however, she also needed to constantly make sense of the diary by forming new hypotheses and eliminating unrelated factors. Especially for subjective triggers such as stress, mood and sleep quality, this hypothetical-deductive process had to be performed thoroughly and contextualized with other information – when, where, and what she was doing. In our study, we found that only participants with frequent and severe migraines were motivated to do such extensive trigger identification work.

Thus, even with a list of common migraine triggers, identifying one's own triggers is still a daunting task, and several participants with severe symptoms even consulted online forums in hopes of finding better and quicker methods to assist their trigger discovery process.

How Should I Cope With Migraine?

To cope with migraine symptoms, many participants developed a variety of strategies that worked for them. In this section, we describe these strategies according to their goals: *(i) alleviating symptoms, (ii) preventing symptoms from happening, and (iii) preparing for breakouts and migraine-related activities.*

The most common coping method among participants was using various medications and alternative solutions to alleviate the symptoms (See Table 2). Our findings in the study suggest that this coping mechanism was highly individualized for each person. Although all the participants had to take over-the-counter (OTC) drugs or prescribed medications, the effectiveness of these medications varied based on the severity of each person's condition, symptoms, or response to medications, such as side-effects. In addition to medications, participants also relied on alternative solutions to alleviate their symptoms, such as lying down in a dark room or listening to music. The efficacy of alternative treatments was also dependent on symptoms, triggers and personal preferences. For instance, one participant listened to soothing music to relieve her pain, while another interviewee mentioned he had to use earplugs to block out all sounds in order to alleviate the headaches.

Preventing symptoms from happening was another method many participants actively deployed, mostly through lifestyle changes, avoiding known triggers and the use of preventive drugs (See Table 2). Some participants adopted preventative strategies suggested by media sources or other patients. For example, Sean (P9) had tried *Bikram yoga* at a private studio, instead of typical exercise at the gym, based on a recommendation from a friend who also had migraine. Sean later developed his own body-stretching exercises at home that he believed to be most effective for his situation. Sean tried to perform these stretches daily or as soon as he sensed the onset of migraine [Figure 1]. Also, a few participants with severe symptoms took daily preventive medication prescribed by their doctors as a way to control migraine symptoms on a daily basis.

Participants often needed effective and timely strategies to prepare for potential breakouts. Based on their own disease management experiences, most participants had developed their own way of being prepared for with migraine attacks. Several participants carried aid items with them at all times, such as a Ziploc bag for vomiting or water for taking medication, in case they had an attack; others kept aid items ready at home for quick use, such as ice packs in the fridge or a certain tea available in the cupboard.

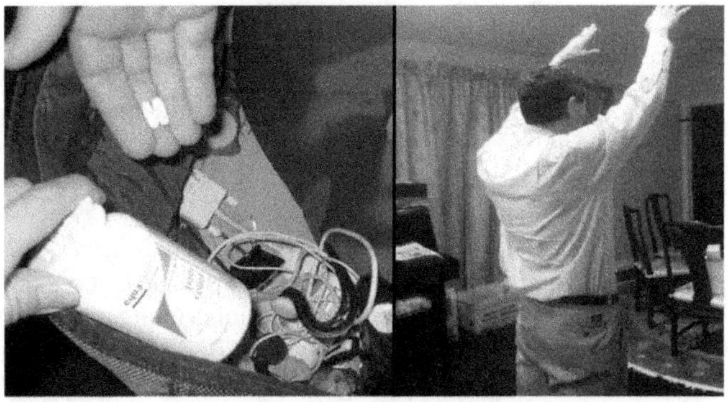

Figure 1. Individualized strategies – OTC medication in the bag for urgent triage for attacks (left) and body stretching method for preventive purposes (right)

Moreover, participants in our study used different reminder methods, including paper or online calendars or iPhone applications, to remember and coordinate migraine-related activities or to-do lists. These tools were used to keep track of medication intake (preventive drugs in particular) and activities participants had to reschedule due to migraine attacks, such as preparing others to pick up children or rearranging meetings and other daily responsibilities.

Treating migraine pain	OTC medications, Prescribed medication such as Topamax[2], Triptans, Imitrex, Caffergot, Vitamin B12, Botox injections, drinking water, wearing earplugs, using ice pack, lying down in dark room, listening to music
Preventing symptoms from happening	Preventive drugs such as Depakote, Botox injections, Diet (e.g. baking own bread, making fresh food, drinking coffee every morning), regular life schedule, exercise (e.g. developing daily stretching methods), and stress management.
Preparing for migraine breakouts and migraine activities	Carrying aid items such as a Ziploc bag for vomiting, OTC medication in a bag or traveling bag, and water for taking medication. Setting reminders for migraine related activities using a paper calendar and iPhone calendar.

Table 2: Participants' various individualized strategies for managing migraine

In the study, we noticed that although these methods were useful, only participants with severe symptoms had concrete management strategies. Since the impact of migraine was so intense and frequent, they found solutions proactively on their own. In contrast, participants with mild and intermediate symptoms were not motivated enough to

[2] All strategies, including drug names, in table 2 were directly extracted from interview transcripts and reflect what the participants reported to us.

take similar proactive steps to develop their own individualized strategies. As a participant with intermediate migraine commented, *"I don't know if there really is a treatment since I can't really identify the trigger, it's hard to know how to prevent or how to treat. So, but, I mean, it is interesting. I have tried to figure out why they occur, but I don't get any sense of – there's no consensus presented in the information [available resources including information online], there's no regular story offered as to why these things occur. There's just a list of symptoms and some theories about why people get them."* Thus, the real challenge for inexperienced participants with mild and intermediate symptoms was *not* to find generalizable knowledge on migraine management/treatment, but to find meaningful self-knowledge that was relevant to their individual illness.

Beyond Individual Management

Despite the individual nature of migraine management described earlier, we found the management of migraine also comprises a social aspect that often involves and impacts other people in a patient's social circle, such as co-workers, family members, and friends. In our study, participants constantly reported their desire for more social recognition and social assistance for migraine, largely because of the unpredictable nature of migraine attacks.

Most participants in the study mentioned that some sort of physical help is needed during migraine attacks, either to cope with the pain, or to attend to responsibilities abandoned by them due to sudden migraine breakouts. When seeking assistance, participants relied on close networks such as family members, friends, or certain coworkers. An interviewee told us how she trained her family members as first line helpers for sudden attacks.

"It was difficult...I taught them [her children] all... a meal they could make by the time they were about four years old... if I was down in bed... they took turns and alternated and made their dinner for the family and I'd sleep it (the migraine) off in the bedroom..." – P5: Gwen (severe migraine)

In Gwen's case, even her 5 and 7 year old children have to be prepared for her sudden migraine breakouts, since the pain and other symptoms would prevent her from doing her daily chores. Having a list of helpers readily available who understand the difficulties a patient experiences during migraine attacks appears critical in managing the disease.

In addition to a close social circle, many participants also needed to obtain help from peripheral networks outside their close circle, such as coworkers or less intimate friends. Nevertheless, many participants in the study commented that, unless it is really necessary, they were often reluctant to share their migraine conditions with people in the peripheral network and often only shared their symptoms with close friends and family members. One interviewee with intermediate symptoms explained how he tried to deal with sudden migraine attacks at work:

"How do people really know that I'm having a migraine? I don't necessarily say, 'I'm canceling the meeting because I have a migraine.' I just said, 'I'm sick.'... I think that I don't tell people necessarily why. I just say I'm sick because I think that some people think that if, "Well, if you just have a headache, take some aspirin and get over it," whereas it's like, 'No, this is a special kind of headache.' ...So, I tend not to tell people I'm going home just because I have a headache." – P7: David (intermediate migraine)

During attacks, David did not reveal his disease to his colleagues, even though he was in a difficult situation where he had to call off meetings. Yet, since most his co-workers had never had migraine, David was afraid they might not understand the disease and associated symptoms. The lack of wide acknowledgement of migraine becomes a barrier for participants to communicate and share their situations with other non-patients, especially when the attacks happen periodically, and cannot be observed externally. Like David, many other participants chose to not share their migraine information, either coping with it alone, or claiming they were sick without revealing any details. For instance, Sarah, a participant with mild migraine symptoms, said: "*if you talk to somebody who hasn't had a bad, severe headache, then their attitude is more like, 'Why are you bothering me with this information?' But if you talk to somebody who has gone through it they're like, 'Oh, I know.'*" Clearly as these quotes indicate, although migraine participants suffer from extreme pain during attacks, there is not always sufficient social recognition from their social circles. Especially at times when many participants are unable to perform their daily activities, and had to rest immediately, others may not understand the urgency of such needs, and many employers even complain about patients for not completing their tasks on time. Patients' low expectations of others and difficulties in communicating their subjective, individualized pain led them to choose to simply say they were sick, rather than saying they were suffering from a migraine.

For this reason, although nearly all participants were good at sharing their migraine information within a close network of family and friends, many chose not to share it with people in their peripheral network. The severe-symptom participants tended to be more open in talking about their illness during attacks, because they experienced more frequent attacks, and expect higher-level social recognition from others.

"[Migraine] makes me slow... If I am doing something – reading, designing application, I cannot... it affects my work... I say oh I need two hours off and they [his colleagues] say ok. I'm not that shy about these things. If you are shy, it's bad, you know. You cannot work, but people think that you are not working so that is bad... If I have headache or I need help, I will just give a call over there and somebody, a friend, or co-worker, just bring me home." – P12: Michael (severe migraine)

As shown in the quote, when migraine occurred, Michael actively sought two different types of help: requesting a ride home and asking coworkers to cover some work in his absence. His more frequent attacks made co-workers more aware of Michael's situation, and more apt to grant social acceptance his sudden absence from work due to the migraine breakouts.

In contrast, participants with mild and intermediate symptoms tended to stay passive and did not want to share their symptoms beyond their closest network because they were afraid of being misunderstood as invoking migraine as an excuse. As such, lesser frequency of attacks resulted in lack of social recognition and led mild migraine participants to be even more passive during attacks. Like David and Sarah, most participants with mild symptoms preferred to keep their illness private from external networks, despite often needing help from them, especially when their first line helpers were not available. Two participants in our study mentioned they never asked anyone for help and never expected proper understanding or emotional support from others. Therefore, it is worth considering how to help patients with mild and intermediate symptoms obtain social acknowledgment and assistance. We also wish to note that social recognition can go beyond simply providing help; it can involve showing understanding and acknowledging patients' difficult, stressful situations.

DISCUSSION AND DESIGN SUGGESTIONS

Our study uncovers the multi-faceted challenges, both from individual and social aspects, faced by people with migraine in the management of their everyday lives. In this section, we first discuss the need for sufferers to make sense of days, weeks and possibly years, of life events in order to understand their condition, as well as coping with unpredictable and intermittent migraine attacks. Then, we consider migraine's nature as an under-recognized disease, which makes it difficult to obtain appropriate recognition from others. We also discuss the need to engage patients with mild symptoms, who are currently underserved.

Making Sense of a Whole Spectrum of Life Events

As our study has shown, due the individual differences of migraine presentation, patients are often unable to easily identify their own triggers and symptoms using available medical resources. Instead, the management of migraine requires them to engage in a series of activities including recognizing migraine related symptoms, tracking down possible triggers from numerous of life events, and finding appropriate ways to cope with sudden breakouts.

Tracking and making sense of personal health data has been advocated broadly in recent personal informatics [18, 20, 24], and qualified-self initiatives [26]. As a result, many mobile apps and tracking systems have been developed to facilitate ways for individuals to understand their personal behaviors, such as apps that track exercises, diet and glucoses in diabetes management and sleep patterns [18, 20, 24]. Nevertheless, the current systems often emphasizes tracking and counting limited and often pre-determined measurements, instead of supporting the sense making of more subjective, and wide range, of possible life events. A recent study [12] has examined extreme users who have used existing self-tracking technologies and indicated that while most technologies focused on tracking symptoms and health outcomes, they often failed to capture and track *triggers* of the health problem, and the *context* in which the health symptoms occurred. This common pitfall makes it difficult for these systems to facilitate self-refection and self-recognition – a critical step identified in our study.

What we have found with migraine patients suggests that identifying triggers and effective treatments actually requires more extensive information tracking and sense-making efforts since what relates to migraine reaches far beyond diet, exercises and a few physiological factors. The triggers and coping mechanisms reported by our participants cover a wide variety of factors embedded in people's everyday lives. In particular, many of them are related to patients' subjective and situational feelings. For instance, whether a person feels hot or cold can depend on his/her physical condition at the time, and a person's stress level during the same task can be more or less depending on mood and the ability to perform the task. In addition, since many potential triggers are subjective factors that can hardly be defined using numerical scales, having a 1 to 5 scale may not be effective for patients to track them. Because of these challenges, we suggest a migraine management system should allow users to create their own tracking features from the spectrum of life events, and define the ways in which they want to track them. Doing so can provide people a chance to track life events beyond a few pre-defined triggers, and enable them to track these events in a way they prefer and feel comfortable with. For example, in such systems users can add stress as a tracker and define a tracking scale based on their own subjective perceptions. For instance, a weekly project meeting with the board can be categorized on a scale such as 'no stress, just regular stress, pretty bad, awful, and getting a headache right afterwards'. Migraine sufferers can also add temperature as a tracker based on their own experiences; 'hot weather' can be a serious trigger for some people, although it will not lead to any discomfort among others. This approach can allow users to personalize tracking features and to cover a broader range of activities. It also helps capture the contextual information that is relevant to the events being noted, similarly to what has been advocated recently [12]. Contextual information can be critical in understanding and making connections across several life events, especially when the trigger is a combination of multiple factors, e.g. hot weather and stress.

Having personalized trackers beyond conventional diet and exercise activities creates a more user-friendly way to engage patients and promote the use of personal informatics tools, as they will be more applicable to one's own preference and situation. Beyond migraine, this personal defined tracking mechanism may work for many other chronic conditions. For instance, mood has been suggested as an important, interesting factor in general chronic care management including physical performance [20, 26]. However, mood is also a subjective measure, and having a 1 to 5 scale may not be an appealing way to engage users and have them enter data in the system on a daily basis.

Coping with Unpredictability and Intermittency

Compared to other well-studied chronic diseases where the influences of the ailment are constantly present, migraine represents another range of health conditions that are characterized by unpredictable and intermittent breakouts, e.g. asthma, and chronic pain. Such characteristics make the management of these diseases and the consequent system requirements different from other chronic conditions.

First of all, recognizing intermittent and diverse forms of symptoms makes the disease management more challenging to undertake. In this sense, patients have to learn to recognize the periodically occurrence of migraine symptoms, and to identify possible commonalties between different migraine attacks that may be separated by days, weeks, month or even years. Intermittency requires patients to engage more with the "diagnostic work" since it prevents others, even medical professionals, from easily being involved in the diagnosis process. Thus, in managing migraine, patients often take on a leading role and serve as "*diagnostic agents*" [25] to understand, and learn about the disease themselves. Oudshoorn [25] believes patients can take on this role since they "*have to perform all manner of articulation work required to make ... new healthcare services work.*" As a diagnostic agent, a patient with migraine has to track and link each migraine incident happened in the past in order discover the specific associations between contextual factors and their migraine symptoms. This explains why most of our study participants believed that seeing a doctor was not useful in helping them with migraine treatment.

The intermittency makes the daily activity tracking and information sense-making more critical for patients, especially when the sense-making may not be centered on information recorded continuously, but happen across different time periods when migraine attacks appeared. For instance, a severe migraine triggered by hot weather may have to be linked with past attacks in the previous summer or even earlier. This is certainly a difficult endeavor since these events are so temporally separated, and it may not occur to patients to consider them together. In this sense, a chronic care management system for diseases of an intermittent nature has to help patients connect these temporally disconnected episodes. To cope with unpredictability and intermittency in migraine management, we suggest that the system should not only track, but sustainably associate different types of migraine symptoms and life events in patients' past trajectories, and even enable suggestions for users. For example, the system might tell a user that past tracking information has shown severe migraine attack co-presented with high consumption of chocolate. Thus, chocolate might be a potential trigger. Or when a person cannot figure out why there was a severe migraine attack, the system can either retrieve information on past breakouts occurring in similar situations, e.g. in summer heat, or after a stressful project due date, to remind the user of possible triggers in these chronologically separate events. In addition, the system could even make suggestions to avoid certain triggers when possible or prepare coping materials – e.g., when the weather is going to be extremely hot the next day, the system can remind the user to stay inside, or bring more water and medication.

Second, the unpredictable nature of migraine attacks leads to difficulties among migraine patients, especially for patients with severe symptoms who have to rest and may even need immediate help in performing their current tasks. As our findings show, during attacks, migraine sufferers wished people in their social circles understood the nature of their migraine so that people could provide physical help. The study identifies two levels of help for patients: helping the patient cope with pain (e.g. taking them home, delivering medications), and taking care of various responsibilities patients were unable to perform, such as covering work, daily chores like cooking, etc. This collaborative aspect of migraine management is not sufficiently acknowledged in current systems, and most system designs assume coping with migraine as an individual task, neglecting the needs in obtaining physical help during migraine attacks. Nevertheless, since the breakouts are often unpredictable, it is difficult for patients to arrange social help in advance. In our study, we have seen participants who have prepared and trained people in their close social circles to be first line helpers who can take on tasks immediately.

However, the approach of obtaining and coordinating help may not always be effective when severe breakouts serve as a barrier to communicate these needs with others, and locate the available helpers in a timely manner. For instance, calling friends one by one may take some time, but a system to facilitate the sharing of a migraine status to all the first line helpers can be more effective. By communicating the migraine status to a sharable network, the patient can share his/her needs with all helpers at once, and to allow them sign up for tasks they are able to take on at the moment. Second, the system should also reach out to more peripheral people when first line helpers are not available. This can be seen as a similar suggestion made in a previous study [31] in terms of a connect platform that helps create help request, informing social networks, and coordinating helping activities. However, migraine patients cannot anticipate what kinds of help request they want and who to ask in advance, since it all depends on when an attacks occur, how severe it is, and how long it lasts. Thus, they have to perform this coordinating work of getting help the after migraine occurs. Additionally, since the degree of the disclosure of the migraine status and consequent needs may vary depending on the patient's situation, the system should allow patients to choose specific networks or to create predefined networks to share their migraine status information.

In particular, based on the study findings, we suggest that the system should consider people's preferences, as well as privacy issues pertaining to the sharing of migraine-related information. For instance, instead of sharing information with all co-workers, users can pre-select a small set of co-workers who they believe can understand the migraine situations and are likely to help. This subset of co-workers will be alerted as their front line helpers at work. When severe attacks occur, they can select the level of migraine, and the types of help they need to share with people they are comfortable with. The rest of their co-workers will only see an "unavailable" indicator or away from work message but will not receive other details. Similarly, when a person needs physical help, the request can be sent only to those who are physically nearby, so that relatives and friends who live remotely will not get such messages. Those on the receiving end can also define how they would like to receive such messages; for instance, a husband might want to know his wife's situation at once so he can arrange to help her or pick up children, but other friends may wish to limit disruptions to their own life or to be available only when they are not otherwise engaged. Allowing both migraine sufferers and their social network to define how the messages are delivered, the degree of detail desired, and the delivery method is critical in maintaining the balance between getting sufficient assistance and protecting privacy. Such "status delivery" systems could potentially benefit patients with similar health conditions, such as chronic pain, which is also intermittent and unpredictable in nature [7].

In addition, since the severity and duration of migraine attacks varies, the system design can also allow users to indicate the level of symptom severity as well as their specific needs. Based on the level of severity and duration, the system can provide the patient with a means of sending group notices to all those involved, and to tailor the message. The system can be integrated with the patient's daily schedule, so a migraine status sent at a given time could reach recipients involved in the patient's current activity for both work and home, and help can be sought from people who are located nearby at the time of the attack. Doing so could ease the stress and the coordination of workload for migraine patients during sudden breakouts.

Obtaining Social Recognition

Despite much of the emphasis in migraine management on the role of self-recognition, in the study we find that recognizing migraine socially is also critical in the management of migraine. The unpredictable and invisible nature of attacks makes it difficult for people in patients' social circles to understand and acknowledge it. First of all, unlike those managing other chronic illnesses, migraine patients experience sudden, unpredictable disease breakouts that disrupt their everyday lives, yet function like healthy people at most other times. Second, migraine is invisible to others since most symptoms are subjective feelings that cannot be measured, such as pain. Unless patients vomit or feel nausea, their migraine attacks can hardly be noticed by others. Just as a patient mentioned in the study – unless someone has experienced extreme pain previously, he/she may not understand how difficult it is during a migraine attack. Therefore, it is hard but critical for patients to obtain appropriate social recognition, as this may be the first step in seeking social support during migraine attacks.

When social recognition is lacking, we find that patients often strategize how they can communicate migraine information, and how much detail to share with others. Especially when dealing with pain and seeking help from peripheral networks, patients often experience a dilemma over whether to reveal their specific health status or to share only vague information to others (i.e. just being sick), because they are uncertain about how the disease will be perceived by others, and worry about whether misperception would occur. Because of this, many sufferers carefully conceal their symptoms from their external network to avoid being labeled as lazy or unwillingness in taking on some tasks, thus making the migraine attack at work or social events surprising to others who did not know the patient well.

Though social recognition for migraine patients is particularly lacking, it is also absent in many other diseases, and worth emphasizing in general. For instance, cancer patients may not share their chemotherapy appointments with co-workers but to ask for sick leave using general sick requests [28]. However, comparing cancer treatments that are often pre-scheduled in advance and can be hidden under regular sick leave, the sudden breakouts of migraine certainly present a greater level of challenges in obtaining social recognition, and proper understanding. In this research, we note the importance of obtaining social recognition, especially when the consequences of migraine breakouts influence and impact others, such as being suddenly absence from social events, canceling meetings or delaying task completions. We believe subtle ways of gradually building social recognition may help for both patients and their peripheral social members. With a simple micro-blogging feature, a patient could post and share brief text statuses through Twitter and Facebook updates, or he/she may display an icon or status indication of having migraine on their chat (mobile) messenger/window, which can also show education material by mouse-over or click. This would help increase an awareness in others about a patient's status at that point and their interest in learning more about migraine by exposing migraine related materials, and would eventually help gain social recognition from those who do not experience migraine. We note that this is still based on a patient's personal decision to disclose their real situation, but we have seen nearly all study participants express their wish to have others' understanding, acknowledgement, and empathy.

Engaging "Underwater" Patients

In studying migraine patients, we notice a clear dichotomy between patients with severe symptoms and those with mild symptoms. Just like 90% of an iceberg is underwater and invisible to the outside world, the practices of migraine patients, especially those with mild symptoms, have not been studied sufficiently. Medical study has shown that 90% of migraine sufferers do not know their specific condition and do not know the best approach to alleviate their pain; almost half of sufferers have never received a formal diagnosis [21], and even fewer have received consistent treatment [32]. It is therefore worth investigating how to engage and assist migraine patients with mild symptoms more effectively.

As our study has shown, the uncertainty of the disease has caused more difficulties and complexities for patients with mild symptom to manage migraine, both individually and socially. Patients often experience less frequent and irregular attacks, unclear triggers, and vague symptoms, which result in inefficient diagnostic work, and lead to the lack of social recognition from others. This group also faces more difficulties regarding clinical diagnosis, with the result that they are apt to ignore medical advice or to stop seeing doctors. However, the severity of migraine often increases over time [13], and it is important to consider this "under-the-water" group of patients and prevent their symptoms from deteriorating earlier. It is important for system design to take into account the need to engage and support this under-recognized migraine population.

In addition, our study shows that public recognition of migraine, unlike that of other chronic diseases [23], suffers from abundant misconceptions, and this makes migraine management even more challenging for patients with mild symptoms. The fact that most people experience ordinary and usually mild headaches creates a misperception of migraine, as non-sufferers may believe migraine is an ailment that can be resolved with a single dose of painkillers, or causes trivial discomfort that should not stop a person from working normally. Because of this, many migraine patients treat their symptoms privately and do not want to disclose them to others. There is an urgent need to create proper social understanding to support the under-recognized majority of migraine patients.

To better support this large group of "under-the-water" migraine patients, we believe that providing further motivation can help engaging patients with mild symptoms. Motivating patients to engage in health behavioral changes has been widely studied in HCI community recently [6, 24]; however, the key need with migraine patients lies in the self-identification process. As such, facilitating triggers, and coping mechanism discovery and the trial-and-error activities are needed in system design. For example, instead of starting from nowhere, a patient can receive a list of suggested triggers, e.g. banana, white chocolate, and wine, from a pool of known trigger list or peer patients' who have similar symptoms or types of attacks. In addition, by inviting patients to conduct data reflection sessions in the form of a game or quiz, the system could offer appealing ways to engage these underserved users and help them make sense of their migraine triggers. It would be useful to encourage patients to connect with other sufferers in a similar situation in order to help them gain a better understanding of migraine and benefit from the experiential knowledge of experienced patients, whose input could eventually help patients solve their own "puzzle" more easily.

CONCLUSION

Through our analysis of migraine sufferers' migraine management practices, we discover that patients face great challenges, both when they attempt to understand the individual manifestations of their illness and when they manage its social aspects by communicating about their condition and soliciting help. We argue that these challenges arise in response to the patients' needs to deal with the unpredictability and intermittency of the disease. We also argue that external resources and current systems are not appropriately suited for patients dealing with subjective symptoms, unknown triggers and treatments, as well as a lack of social recognition and help from others. Future systems should facilitate patients' extensive sense-making process of life events, help patients request support from social circles, and support the patients' gain of social recognition and acknowledgement. Finally, system design should also consider targeting patients with mild symptoms, the majority of the migraine population. We believe this work can contribute to prior chronic illness studies by offering insights into a previously under-studied disease, as well as its potential applicability to other similar illnesses.

REFERENCES

1. Aarhus, R., & Ballegaard, S. A. (2010). Negotiating boundaries: managing disease at home. In *Proc. CHI*. pp. 1223-1232
2. Abowd, G.D., Hayes, G.R., Kientz, J.A., Mamykina, L., and Mynatt, E.D. Challenges and opportunities for collaboration technologies for chronic care management. In *Proc. HCIC 2006*.
3. American Medical Association, http://www.ama-assn.org/ama/pub/education-careers/continuing-medical-education/cme-credit-offerings/therapeutic-insights/management-migraine-adults.page.
4. American Association of Neurologists. Migraine, http://patients.aan.com/disorders/?event=view&disorder_id=987.
5. Bardram, J. E., Frost, M., Szántó, K., Faurholt-Jepsen, M., Vinberg, M., & Kessing, L. V. Designing mobile health technology for bipolar disorder: A field trial of the MONARCA system. In *Proc of CHI*. pp. 2627-2636
6. Baumer, E. P., Khovanskaya, V., Matthews, M., Reynolds, L., Sosik, V. S., & Gay, G. K. (2014). Reviewing Reflection: On the Use of Reflection in Interactive System Design. In *Proc of DIS*.
7. Benjamin, A., Birnholtz, J., Baecker, R., Gromala, D., & Furlan, A. Impression management work: How seniors with chronic pain address disruptions in their interactions. In *Proc of CSCW*. pp. 799-808.
8. Beyer, H. and Holtzblatt, K. *Contextual Design: Defining Customer-Centered Systems*. Morgan Kaufmann Publishers Inc., CA, USA, 1997.

9. Bigal, M.E. and Lipton, R.B. Obesity is a risk factor for transformed migraine but not chronic tension-type headache. *Neurology*, 67, 2 (2006), 252–257.
10. Blau, J.N. and Thavapalan, M. Preventing Migraine: A Study of Precipitating Factors. *Headache: The Journal of Head and Face Pain*, 28, 7 (1988), 481–483.
11. Chen, Y. Take it personally: accounting for individual difference in designing diabetes management systems. In *Proc. DIS 2010*, 252–261.
12. Choe, E. K., Lee, N. B., Lee, B., Pratt, W., & Kientz, J. A. (2014). Understanding quantified-selfers' practices in collecting and exploring personal data. In *Proc of CHI*. pp. 1143-1152.
13. Diamond, S. and Wenzel, R. Practical approaches to migraine management. *CNS Drugs*, 16, 2002, 385–403.
14. Farnham, S., Cheng, L., Stone, L., et al. HutchWorld: clinical study of computer-mediated social support for cancer patients and their caregivers. In *Proc. CHI 2002*.
15. Graves, G. Stop that splitting headache. *Health Magazine*. Retrieved September 18, 2012.
16. Hartzler, A. and Pratt, W. Managing the Personal Side of Health: How Patient Expertise Differs from the Expertise of Clinicians. *J Med Internet Res*, 13, 3, 2011.
17. Huh, J. and Ackerman, M.S. Collaborative help in chronic disease management: supporting individualized problems. In *Proc. CSCW* 2012. 853–862.
18. Kay, M. et al. (2012). Lullaby: a capture & access system for understanding the sleep environment. *UbiComp '12* , 226–34.
19. Klasnja, P., Civan Hartzler, A., Unruh, K. T., & Pratt, W. (2010). Blowing in the wind: unanchored patient information work during cancer care. In *Proc. CHI.*
20. Li, I., Dey, A., & Forlizzi, J. (2010). A stage-based model of personal informatics systems. In *Proc. CHI*. pp. 557-566.
21. Lipton, R.B., Stewart, W.F., and Simon, D. Medical Consultation for Migraine: Results From the American Migraine Study. *Headache: The Journal of Head and Face Pain*, 38, 2 (1998), 87–96.
22. Lipton, R. B., & Pan, J. (2004). Is migraine a progressive brain disease?. *Jama, 291*(4), 493-494.
23. Lonardi, C. The passing dilemma in socially invisible diseases: Narratives on chronic headache. *Social Science & Medicine 65*, 8 (2007), 1619–1629.
24. Mamykina, L., Mynatt, E., Davidson, P., and Greenblatt, D. (2008). MAHI: investigation of social scaffolding for reflective thinking in diabetes management. In *Proc. CHI*, 477-486.
25. Oudshoorn, N. Diagnosis at a distance: the invisible work of patients and healthcare professionals in cardiac telemonitoring technology. *Sociology of Health & Illness*, 30, 2 (2008), 272–288.
26. Personal Data for the Public Good: New Opportunities to Enrich Understanding of Individual and Population Health. March 2014. Health Data Exploration Project. *Robert Wood Johnson Foundation.*
27. Pols, J. (2012). Care at a Distance.
28. Pratt, W., Unruh, K., Civan, A., and Skeels, M.M. Personal health information management. *Commun. ACM*, 49, 1 (2006), 51–55.
29. Preece, J. Empathic communities: reaching out across the Web. *Interactions*, 5, 2 (1998), 32–43.
30. Sciamanna, C.N., Nicholson, R.A., Lofland, J.H., Manocchia, M., Mui, S., and Hartman, C.W. Effects of a Website Designed to Improve the Management of Migraines. *Headache: The Journal of Head and Face Pain*, 46, 1 (2006), 92–100.
31. Skeels, M. M., Unruh, K. T., Powell, C., & Pratt, W. (2010). Catalyzing social support for breast cancer patients. In *Proc. CHI*. pp. 173-182.
32. Solomon, G. D., & Price, K. L. (1997). Burden of migraine. *Pharmacoeconomics*, *11*(1), 1-10.
33. Star, S.L. and Strauss, A. Layers of Silence, Arenas of Voice: The Ecology of Visible and Invisible Work. In *Proc. CSCW*, 8, 1 (1999), 9–30.
34. Strauss, A. L., and Corbin, J. *Basics of Qualitative Research: Techniques and Procedures for Developing Grounded Theory (2nd ed.)*, Sage, USA, 1998.
35. Storni, C. (2011). Complexity in an uncertain and cosmopolitan world. Rethinking personal health technology in diabetes with the Tag-it-Yourself. *PsychNology Journal*, *9*(2), 165-185.
36. Unruh, K. T., and Pratt, W. The Invisible Work of Being a Patient and Implications for Health Care:"[the doctor is] my business partner in the most important business in my life, staying alive." In *Proc EPIC,* 2008, pp. 40-50.
37. Van Gerven, J.M.A., Schoemaker, R.C., Jacobs, L.D. Self-medication of a single headache episode with ketoprofen, ibuprofen or placebo, home-monitored with an electronic patient diary. *British Journal of Clinical Pharmacology*, 42, 4 (1996), 475–481.
38. WHO. Headache disorders. http://www.who.int/mediacentre/factsheets/fs277/en/.
39. Yun, T.-J., Jeong, H.Y., Hill, T.D., et al. Using SMS to provide continuous assessment and improve health outcomes for children with asthma. In *Proc. IHIS 2012*.

A Framework for Understanding and Designing Telepresence

Irene Rae[1,2], Gina Venolia[1], John C. Tang[1], David Molnar[1]

[1] Microsoft Research
One Microsoft Way
Redmond, WA 98008
{ginav | johntang | dmolnar} @microsoft.com

[2] University of Wisconsin—Madison
1210 West Dayton Street
Madison, WI 53706 USA
irene@cs.wisc.edu

ABSTRACT

As a field, telepresence has grown to include a wide range of systems, from multi-view videoconferencing units to humanlike androids. However, the diversity of systems and research makes it difficult to form a holistic understanding of where the field stands. We propose a framework consisting of seven design dimensions for understanding telepresence, iteratively developed from previous literature, a series of three surveys, the construction of two design probes, and a field study. These design dimensions uniquely categorize 17 telepresence scenarios. In this work, we explain our development process, describe our design dimensions—initiation, physical environment, mobility, vision, social environment, communication, and independence—as well as our scenarios, and demonstrate the use of our framework as a tool to (1) highlight opportunities for future work, (2) identify generalizable findings from research, and (3) facilitate communication in the telepresence community.

Author Keywords

Telepresence; video-mediated communication; CSCW.

ACM Classification Keywords

H.5.3. Group and Organization Interfaces

INTRODUCTION

"The biggest challenge to developing telepresence is achieving that sense of 'being there.' Can telepresence be a true substitute for the real thing?" – Marvin Minsky [39]

When Marvin Minsky coined the term "telepresence," he envisioned technologies where remote users' experiences would be so similar to actually being there that there would be no noticeable difference [39]. Since then, innovation and research within the realm of telepresence has encompassed a vast range of technologies aimed at achieving this vision. From work on the use of these systems in specific domains, such as medical [31,64], education [67,68], or office settings [49,58,63,69], to the development of novel systems such as flying telepresence blimps [46] or three dimensional embodiments of the remote user [40,42], the diversity of approaches has not only allowed exploring many different avenues of research, but has also informed our understanding of how these systems mediate our communications.

However, as the field of telepresence has matured, this diversity has caused the relationship between disparate studies to become increasingly complicated, making it difficult to understand how each piece is situated within the greater whole. This lack of cohesive structure can obscure opportunities for new research and can mean that designers start from scratch each time a new technology is introduced. As a result, researchers and designers are often faced with reinventing solutions, reproducing results, or struggling to identify whether their findings are novel.

To address this, we propose a framework for the telepresence research space which enables designers and researchers to:

- Identify opportunities for future research.
- Reflect on past and future work to determine potentially generalizable findings.
- Share a structure and language for reporting research to facilitate interaction within the telepresence community.

To develop this framework, we engaged in a multi-stage iterative process. This process involved examining previous literature and conducting a series of exploratory surveys. We used these surveys to identify the contexts in which telepresence technologies might be used and the unique design dimensions which distinguish them. Based on this initial framework, we created two design probes—developed to match the needs of disparate scenarios—and field tested

Figure 1. Participants in our field study share a meal (left) or a visit to the local art museum (right) with a remote user.

CSCW '15, March 14–18, 2015, Vancouver, BC, Canada.

ACM 978-1-4503-2922-4/15/03...$15.00.
http://dx.doi.org/10.1145/2675133.2675141

them as a proof of concept. Last, we used the insights gained from these field tests to further refine our framework.

RELATED WORK

As various human-computer interaction domains have matured, each has grappled with finding a structure to organize their growing bodies of work. Examples in CSCW include Gutwin et al.'s framework for workspace awareness [19], Neale et al.'s model for evaluating computer-supported cooperative work [41], Benford et al.'s review of spatial approaches [3], and the work of Ellis et al. and Grudin [13,18] in groupware. With over 1800 papers and journal articles classified as telepresence work by 2007 [34], telepresence is reaching a point where the need for such an organizational structure is becoming critical.

For example, what is considered telepresence has varied across disciplines and has become more confounded as the term has become ubiquitous. Draper et al. divided the prevalent telepresence methods into three main categories: (1) *simple telepresence*, the ability to operate in a computer-mediated environment; (2) *cybernetic telepresence*, the efficiency or quality of the human-machine interface; and (3) *experiential telepresence*, the state where the user feels physically present within the mediated environment [12].

Other literature has organized specific telepresence subdomains. For example, Kristoffersson et al. created a comprehensive survey of past literature and available systems in the realm of mobile telepresence robots [28], Haans et al. developed a framework for understanding embodiment in telepresence [20], Draper et al. surveyed overarching theories of telepresence [12], and multiple papers have proposed robotic telepresence design requirements [10,11,52].

While their approaches have differed, these works have largely focused on creating an organizational structure as a tool, rather than delivering an exhaustive taxonomy of their fields. We have taken an analogous approach by synthesizing previous work and extending it into a conceptual framework. We therefore introduce further related work within the description of each design dimension or scenario later in the paper to provide a contextualized understanding for how it has informed our development process.

FRAMEWORK DEVELOPMENT

We next describe each stage of our development process, beginning with a series of three surveys. We designed these surveys to explore how people envision using telepresence technologies in the future unbound by current technical constraints and to augment prior theories in face-to-face interactions [15,26,59]. We then discuss the development of two design probes, and end by detailing the process and results of our field study.

Survey 1

Our first survey was designed to extend techniques in scenario-based design [7,55], providing an exploratory venue to understand the breadth of experiences that people could envision using a technology to attend remotely.

We asked participants three open-ended questions about how they might envision using a telepresence technology ("Imagine that there was a technology that allowed you to appear in a different place, just as if you were actually there, without having to travel. What would you use this technology to do?")

Participants. A total of 44 adults anonymously participated in our survey via SurveyGizmo, recruited through Cint (http://www.cint.com).

Analysis & Results. We used open-coding and affinity diagramming to systematically identify trends in responses. We grouped these trends into 26 categories of scenarios.

Next, we examined prior theoretical literature and work describing design requirements for various telepresence systems. Informed by this research, we identified nine potential design dimensions which might vary in priority between scenarios.

Survey 2

Our second survey focused on validating our categories of scenarios by asking about participants' interest in using a technology to remotely attend each one. Participants rated their interest on a five-point Likert scale (1=not at all interested, 5=extremely interested). We also asked two open ended questions to refine our design dimensions and scenario categories ("What do you think would be challenging about using this technology?" "Please tell us about other things that you would want to use this technology for.").

Shared Experience Scenarios (shared socially)	
Physically interactive activities *(dance, play basketball)*	Visiting a new place *(museum, new apartment)*
Object-centered activities *(play cards, fish)*	Sharing a meal *(lunch dates, family dinners)*
Movement-based activities *(hike, ski)*	Talking socially *(hang out, share news)*
Giving or receiving help *(fix a bike, give shopping input)*	Mingling *(parties, conferences)*
Goal-based collaboration *(work meetings, craft projects)*	Mingling and viewing *(weddings, graduations)*
Shared viewing *(movies, ballgames, new purchases)*	
Solo Experience Scenarios (on your own)	
Self-improvement *(take a class, train)*	Obligations of Presence *(jury duty, wait in line)*
Monitoring *(check on house, watch kids)*	Performance *(act, conduct a choir)*
Exploring on your own *(solo tour, cultural site)*	Hazardous environments *(first response, military)*

Table 1. Surveys yielded 17 categories of scenarios.

Participants. We recruited a total of 174 adult participants (75 male, 99 female) through Cint, administered through SurveyGizmo, and Instant.ly. Ages were distributed thusly: ages 18-24: 17, ages 25-34: 35, ages 35-54: 75, age 55+: 47.

Analysis & Results. We calculated the average and standard deviations of how much interest participants showed in each scenario. We used these averages to create a ranked list of scenarios to choose the design contexts for our field study.

We also used open-coding and affinity diagramming on the responses to the open-ended questions, resulting in a re-categorization and refinement of our previous scenarios—from 26 types down to 17. These naturally divided into two major groups, *shared experiences*, where social interaction with others was the primary goal, and *solo experiences*, where the focus was on a specific activity and social interactions were secondary, as shown in Table 1.

Additionally, we revisited our original nine design dimensions in the context of these 17 scenarios to test whether these dimensions sufficiently encompassed the characteristics unique to each scenario. Based on these criteria, we further refined our initial nine design dimensions down to seven:

1. ***Initiation.*** How a telepresence interaction is started.
2. ***Physical Environment.*** The physical environment that the system will be used in.
3. ***Mobility.*** The obstacles and amount of movement the remote user will engage in while using the system.
4. ***Vision.*** What users see and how they adjust their visual focus of attention.
5. ***Social environment.*** Relationships among all the *stakeholders*—those involved both directly and indirectly in the interaction.
6. ***Communication.*** How users communicate or interact.
7. ***Independence.*** The level of autonomy that users have.

Next, we provide a brief description of each design dimension and the previous work related to it.

Initiation. The initiation dimension encompasses the factors that influence how interaction begins between local and remote users via a telepresence system.

Theories in the context of telephone interactions discuss the concept of *caller hegemony*—the power disparity between the caller and the answerer [22]. Later work in the context of cellphones elaborated on this concept by exploring how changes to the technology, such as the addition of caller id, disrupts hegemony power dynamics [23].

In the context of telepresence robots, which further shifts the power dynamics in caller hegemony, previous field research has investigated the instigation of interactions when remote users, or *remotes*, have been present via an embodied telepresence system. These studies showed that when a remote user is connected via a telepresence robot, there is an increase in informal and spontaneous interactions initiated by users local to the system, or *locals* [32,63]. Other work focused on user concerns about the etiquette of starting a call and apprehensions about privacy [1,10]. Last, participants in our surveys brought up concerns about the potential setup costs and the overhead of learning to use a new technology.

Items in this design dimension therefore seek to answer such questions as: Who has the ability to begin the interaction? What is the etiquette surrounding initiating the interaction? What options does the non-initiating party have for controlling the other person's access? What is the amount of planning required for the interaction to take place and are there any additional setup costs?

Physical Environment. Although physical environments may vary, successful operation within a setting is a common challenge in designing telepresence systems. When examining obstacles to movement, research has explored a number of approaches, from telepresence blimps [46] to wheeled vehicles that can traverse hazardous terrains [38] to wearable companions [40]. Beyond transportation modes, other aspects of the physical environment have been highlighted in prior work, such as spatial formations in co-present interactions [26], ambient noise levels in real-world scenarios [24,60,61] or the need to interact with or share items to enhance feelings of presence in remote meals [66].

Questions within the scope of the physical environment include: Where will interactions take place (e.g., indoors, outdoors, or both)? What will the ambient noise level be? What spatial configurations might users need to interact within? Where will users manipulate items or interact with a workspace? What properties might the workspace have?

Mobility. As emphasized in the literature, different contexts may present very different obstacles to mobility [5,24]. Prior research has highlighted contrasts—such as terrain, number and type of obstacles, and range of motion—between movement in business settings and movement in non-workplace environments [5,24].

Additionally, while providing mobility for the remote user may increase their feelings of presence, it may not immediately contribute to task outcomes due to other factors, such as cognitive load [50]. While not every obstacle can be predicted, anticipating the needs and constraints for the target scenario and prioritizing based on the context may reduce breakdowns and improve user experiences.

Examples of key elements to consider within this design dimension are: How large is the area that the system is expected to navigate within? What barriers exist to the system's mobility (e.g., stairs, elevators that can also block network connectivity)? How might the design of the system restrict the local user's or bystander's freedom of movement?

Vision. When viewing the environment, the remote user's ability to focus on objects at a variety of ranges [24] and to understand how they are situated in the local's environment

[21] can be critical to their enjoyment and ability to complete tasks. In collaborative work scenarios, the amount of visual data from the shared workspace that is communicated to both parties has been shown to facilitate the success of their outcomes [15,19,58]. In Draper et al.'s attentional model of telepresence, visual information is particularly critical as a focus of attentional resources for remote users, which they argue is the central component in telepresence [12].

Prior work has found that the ability to see the other person improves collaborative outcomes [4]. Research has also shown that the visibility of the remote user's upper body—beyond just their face—improved empathy between users and increased interaction fluency [44]. In addition to examining the amount of visual information shared, telepresence systems have also explored the preservation of spatial positioning [43,57] and eye gaze [40].

Although numerous ways may be found to supplement visual information for both the local and the remote users, different scenarios may have different needs. In the dimension of vision, designers and researchers may seek answers to questions such as: What will the primary *focus of attention* during the interaction be (e.g., other people, shared workspace, the environment)? How far do we expect the primary focus of attention to be from the viewer? Will the ability to perceive referential gestures be important? What kind of visual feedback will be provided about the system and the state of the users?

Social Environment. Research has begun to explore the relationship between theoretical work in face-to-face interactions and how it may translate to remote interactions. For example, within the context of Actor-Network theory, research on cellphone usage has examined remote users as actor-nodes [23,30]. Within the context of public places, theories on normative behaviors and social landscapes have been extended to examine how cellphone usage disrupts the status of being with another person—shifting those who are not engaged in the call into the status of being alone [16,23].

Informed by these theoretical contributions, we further categorized the people that might be affected by the use of a telepresence system into six types of *stakeholders*—those involved in the interaction directly as well as those involved peripherally, or indirectly.

Remote users: The user or users in a remote location who are managing the connection as the main actors. For example, the mother holding most of the conversation with her son, who is the local user.

Remote party members: People in the remote location who are peripherally involved in the interaction. For example, the father who may occasionally come into view to answer a question but who is doing other things in his environment.

Remote bystanders: People who are not part of the interaction, but are in the remote environment and affected by what occurs. For example, the daughter who is in the same room as the parents but is involved in her own activities.

Local users: The user or users who are local to the telepresence system who are participating in the interaction as main actors. For example, the son who is interacting with his remotely connected mother.

Local party members: People in the local environment who are peripherally involved in the interaction. For example, the son's friends who may occasionally join the conversation.

Local bystanders: People who are not part of the interaction, but are in the local environment of the system and are affected by what occurs. For example, if the interaction is taking place at a restaurant, other customers in the restaurant.

Previous work primarily focused on two stakeholders, the local and the remote users. These studies have largely focused on either: (1) examining the effects that telepresence technologies have on the relationship between the users; or (2) defining the mediating effects that these technologies have on user perceptions.

Studies on the effects of telepresence technologies on user relationships explored how systems might be used differently between work and leisure contexts [5] and how they might support the formation of common ground—a common base of shared knowledge and vocabulary [9,45]. Related research also raised questions about what etiquette should exist or how the privacy (or lack of it) afforded by telepresence systems may strain users' ties [1,10,11,37].

When seeking to define the mediating effects that telepresence technologies may have on user perceptions, literature has shown that instant messaging or videoconferencing may equalize user relationships [27] and that in videoconferencing, the amount of user multitasking may be reduced [5,65]. Research has also begun to explore how the appearance of telepresence technologies might shape user perceptions. Examples include manipulating the remote user's level of embodiment to increase the development of trust between users [48], altering the height of a robotic telepresence system to support or undermine the remote user's authority [46,49], and creating a more human-like embodiment to increase the local user's perceptions of the remote user's presence [54]. Additional studies have also discussed leveraging the appearance of the system's embodiment to aid in identifying remote users [32,49,63].

Informed by this previous work and our surveys, questions that fit within the realm of the social environment include: How private is the setting expected to be? Do the users have pre-existing relationships? How might pre-existing relationships shape the way in which the system is used? In what ways might the embodiment or presentation of the system influence perceptions of the local or remote users?

Communication. The ability to communicate with others verbally, through gesture, and through language has been shown to be a core component in face-to-face interactions [15,59]. As a result, most telepresence systems integrate aural and visual information as a matter of course. Despite these commonalities, many questions arise about how large the visual field should be [10,11,24], what constitutes critical visual information (e.g., the ability to see referential gestures, posture of users, spatial positioning of users) [4,21,29,52], at what fidelity this information should be available [10,11], and how to measure communicative performance [61].

In addition to aural and visual information, different modalities for promoting communication between users have been explored, such as indicators for when a telepresence system is occupied [60], signaling other people's meal status in shared dining scenarios [17], allowing people to send messages via a tablecloth and printed on food [66], or integrating deictic gestures using a laser pointer [36].

In considering factors for the dimension of communication, questions should fit the scope of the scenario. For example: What verbal and non-verbal cues will be critical in this context? How much time might be spent listening vs. speaking? What gestures may need to be supported in this context? Is physical contact common in these scenarios?

Independence. Prior work on cellular phones highlights the power disparity between caller and answerer, particularly in light of social norms, and how the addition of various supportive technologies may shift that dynamic [1,22,23]. As advances in navigation and visual identification systems have enabled remote or autonomous control, particularly in robotic telepresence systems [8,35,60], new insights and theories may be constructed about how greater independence may affect user relationships, such as in building trust [48].

Items in this design dimension seek to answer questions such as: Should the users be able to act independently of each other? Will any of the users be reliant on others for direction or to act? Will design choices, such as those affecting situational awareness or cognitive load, empower users? Will users feel in control? Are there points of enforced dependency due to design choices?

Survey 3

We constructed our third online questionnaire to examine each of the 17 scenarios that we identified earlier in the context of our seven design dimensions. Our goal was to augment the theoretical work on understanding face-to-face interactions with what people felt to be crucial in the context of their own public and private experiences. By combining our survey responses in each of these scenarios with prior theory, we sought to create a blueprint for how these design dimensions are prioritized in different contexts.

To accomplish this, we asked participants to choose three of the scenarios that they had experienced, in-person, in the past. We asked them to recall these face-to-face experiences and to answer a combination of open-ended, multiple choice, percentage, rating, and yes or no questions about them. Examples of responses to these questions are in Table 2.

Participants. A total of 121 adults (45 male, 76 female), recruited through Cint, responded to our survey resulting in descriptions of 342 face-to-face experiences. Ages were distributed as follows: ages 18-24: 24, ages 25-34: 25, ages 35-44: 23, ages 45-54: 24, and age 55+: 25.

Analysis & Results. We examined each scenario separately, calculating the average, standard deviation, or percentage responding positively, for every question. We then compared these scores across scenarios. From this comparison, we identified the elements in each design dimension that had the highest contrast between scenarios, as illustrated in Table 2.

Our goal in collecting responses about people's face-to-face experiences was to uncover how these scenarios differed in interactions unmediated by technology in both public and private contexts. Revealing these distinctions might help predict when and where interactions within these scenarios would differ when using a telepresence technology.

These insights can also aid us in:

- Predicting and prioritizing what functionalities should be implemented in future systems.
- Understanding and predicting where results from research may generalize across scenarios, or where perceptions, attitudes, and outcomes may differ.
- Highlighting that a one-size-fits-all approach to telepresence is unlikely to meet the needs of all scenarios.

However, these potential benefits are based on the theory that needs and constraints vary across scenarios and that our framework of design dimensions can help differentiate them.

Design Probes

To validate our framework, we chose two scenarios that had large contrasts along our design dimensions, as shown in Table 2. Due to the many differences between scenarios identified in our third survey, we further narrowed the scope of our testing by prioritizing the most popular scenarios from our second survey. These criteria resulted in our choosing two scenarios to test: remotely sharing a meal together and remotely visiting a new place with someone. Using the needs found along our design dimensions from our third survey as a guide, we constructed two design probes: a "freestanding" probe and a "wearable" probe.

Freestanding Device: Sharing a Meal

We designed a freestanding device, shown in Figure 2a, for sharing a meal with a remote person. Similar in design to previous systems [63,69] our freestanding probe consisted of a Windows tablet with an 11.6 inch 1080p screen, an external battery, a web camera, a speaker system, and a microphone, mounted on a laser cut plastic frame on a metal stand. Skype v6.6 in full screen mode was used for videoconferencing.

Below, we list the key choices made in each design dimension and match them to the results from our third survey, shown in Table 2.

- Initiation: Setup time for the freestanding device was high, requiring installation of additional software for the remote user, and positioning/transport of the device for the local user, as we chose to deprioritize this dimension.

▪ Physical Environment: We worked to accommodate long periods of time where the local's hands would be occupied and minimized the amount of dynamic adjustment that locals had to do by providing the remote user with software to control the positioning of the camera. To handle variable levels of background noise, we used a Jawbone Jambox with a CAD U7 USB Desktop Condenser microphone. The height of the system was adjustable to match the dining surface—30–66 inches to the center of the screen—so that no changes would be needed after setup.

▪ Mobility: We traded mobility for stability in our design, constructing our probe with a triangular metal stand, two wheels, and a portable battery pack that was secured to the base. In total, the freestanding probe weighed 6.5kg.

▪ Vision: We provided remote users with control over a Logitech BCC950 1080p webcam with pan, tilt, and zoom capability to accommodate visual switching at close to middle distances (e.g., other diners, food on the table).

▪ Social Environment: We leveraged expected existing relationships between remote and local users and gave the

		Physically interactive activities	Object-centered activities	Movement-based activities	Visiting a new place	Sharing a meal	Talking socially
Initiation	Initiator	Self: 36% Others: 36%	Self: 45% Other: 27%	Self: 53% Other: 33%	Self: 47% Other: 37%	Self: 34% Other: 41%	Self: 50% Other: 29%
	Pre-planning	Planned: 47% Semi-planned: 37% Spontaneous: 37%	Planned: 9% Semi-planned: 36% Spontaneous: 55%	Planned: 60% Semi-planned: 40% Spontaneous: 0%	Planned: 42% Semi-planned: 32% Spontaneous: 26%	Planned: 38% Semi-planned: 34% Spontaneous: 29%	Planned: 25% Semi-planned: 29% Spontaneous: 50%
Physical Environment	Location	Indoor: 47% Outdoor: 53%	Indoor: 64% Outdoor: 36%	Indoor: 33% Outdoor: 67%	Indoor: 32% Outdoor: 89%	Indoor: 95% Outdoor: 13%	Indoor: 61% Outdoor: 43%
	Ambient noise	5.4/10	5.4/10	3.9/10	5.2/10	3.9/10	5.4/10
	Manipulated objects	71%	85%	60%	45%	72%	45%
Mobility	Movement	None: 10% Location-based: 32% Room-wide: 21% Floor-wide: 11% Building-wide: 11% Area-wide: 21%	None: 18% Location-based: 18% Room-wide: 45% Floor-wide: 18% Building-wide: 0% Area-wide: 0%	None: 0% Location-based: 0% Room-wide: 7% Floor-wide: 20% Building-wide: 0% Area-wide: 73%	None: 5% Location-based: 11% Room-wide: 0% Floor-wide: 5% Building-wide: 10% Area-wide: 68%	None: 29% Location-based: 32% Room-wide: 21% Floor-wide: 16% Building-wide: 0% Area-wide: 2%	None: 25% Location-based: 36% Room-wide: 11% Floor-wide: 14% Building-wide: 0% Area-wide: 19%
Vision	Visual distance	Arms-length: 52% Across room: 30% Far distant: 18%	Arms-length: 36% Across room: 53% Far distant: 11%	Arms-length: 38% Across room: 25% Far distant: 37%	Arms-length: 37% Across room: 37% Far distant: 23%	Arms-length: 62% Across room: 32% Far distant: 6%	Arms-length: 59% Across room: 34% Far distant: 7%
	Focus of attention	People: 56% Object: 26% Screen: 3% Environment: 16%	People: 25% Object: 20% Screen: 41% Environment: 14%	People: 15% Object: 26% Screen: 2% Environment: 57%	People: 24% Object: 19% Screen: 3% Environment: 54%	People: 57% Object: 13% Screen: 13% Environment: 16%	People: 56% Object: 13% Screen: 7% Environment: 25%
Social Environment	Privacy	Public: 63% Private: 37%	Public: 18% Private: 82%	Public: 73% Private: 27%	Public: 89% Private: 21%	Public: 43% Private: 59%	Public: 36% Private: 64%
	Group size	Alone: 0% Two people: 42% Small (3-5): 32% Medium (6-10): 5% Large (10+): 26%	Alone: 0% Two people: 73% Small (3-5): 27% Medium (6-10): 0% Large (10+): 0%	Alone: 0% Two people: 67% Small (3-5): 20% Medium (6-10): 13% Large (10+): 0%	Alone: 0% Two people: 53% Small (3-5): 32% Medium (6-10): 11% Large (10+): 5%	Alone: 0% Two people: 48% Small (3-5): 41% Medium (6-10): 3% Large (10+): 7%	Alone: 7% Two people: 39% Small (3-5): 42% Medium (6-10): 36% Large (10+): 11%
	Relationship	Close: 80% Acquaintance: 0% Coworker: 5% Stranger: 5% N/A: 0%	Close: 100% Acquaintance: 0% Coworker: 0% Stranger: 0% N/A: 0%	Close: 93% Acquaintance: 7% Coworker: 0% Stranger: 0% N/A: 0%	Close: 100% Acquaintance: 0% Coworker: 0% Stranger: 0% N/A: 0%	Close: 94% Acquaintance: 2% Coworker: 4% Stranger: 0% N/A: 0%	Close: 78% Acquaintance: 4% Coworker: 7% Stranger: 11% N/A: 0%
Communication	Speaking/listening	Speaking: 43% Listening: 40% No talking: 17%	Speaking: 50% Listening: 43% No talking: 7%	Speaking: 53% Listening: 39% No talking: %8	Speaking: 42% Listening: 42% No talking: 16%	Speaking: 51% Listening: 44% No talking: 15%	Speaking: 52% Listening: 43% No talking: 5%
	Gestures used	51%	76%	8%	57%	27%	31%
	Physical contact	Impersonal: 74% Personal: 47%	Impersonal: 73% Personal: 82%	Impersonal: 47% Personal: 20%	Impersonal: 63% Personal: 68%	Impersonal: 43% Personal: 59%	Impersonal: <1% Personal: <1%
Independence	Direction	They directed: 18% I directed: 32% Equal direction: 23% No direction: 22%	They directed: 10% I directed: 20% Equal direction: 35% No direction: 35%	They directed: 16% I directed: 11% Equal direction: 49% No direction: 25%	They directed: 15% I directed: 15% Equal direction: 35% No direction: 35%	They directed: 10% I directed: 11% Equal direction: 20% No direction: 58%	N/A
	Dependence	I depended: 5% They depended: 5% Equal: 84% None: 11%	I depended: 0% They depended: 9% Equal: 82% None: 9%	I depended: 7% They depended: 7% Equal: 60% None: 27%	I depended: 0% They depended: 0% Equal: 74% None: 26%	I depended: 0% They depended: 5% Equal: 71% None: 23%	I depended: 14% They depended: 4% Equal: 54% None: 32%

Table 2. Examples of responses from six scenarios along the seven dimensions in the framework.

locals responsibility for handling the probe.

- Communication: We did not prioritize any methods of communication beyond audio and video in the shared meal probe because our third survey did not show a strong need for referential gestures or physical contact.
- Independence: While the initial setup of the freestanding probe required aid from the local users, we increased the remote user's independence by providing them with the ability to control their camera and point of view.

Wearable Device: Visiting a New Place Together

We created a wearable device, shown in Figure 2b, as a design probe to match the needs for visiting a new place with a remote person. Similar in concept to other wearable telepresence systems [40,47], our system consisted of a Nokia Lumia 920 Windows Phone with a 4.5 inch screen, a wide-angle lens, an external speaker system or earbuds, and an external battery, mounted on a wearable cross-body bag. Videoconferencing was accomplished via Skype v4.9, installed as an application on the phone.

We next list the key decisions made in each design dimension, matching them to the results shown in Table 2.

- Initiation: Although there was no setup cost for the remote user in our wearable probe, the local user was required to put the carrier on, adjust the straps, and connect the earbuds (if desired); this was due to the low priority placed on minimizing setup time.
- Physical Environment: The wearable system used a SuperTooth Crystal Portable Speakerphone or earbuds with a microphone (the local user's choice) to address the expected variability of ambient noise levels.
- Mobility: We designed the wearable probe to leverage the local's ability to navigate and maneuver through a large area with multiple obstacles in the physical environment. We minimized the weight of the probe, limiting it to 1kg, and designed it to closely conform to the local's body.
- Vision: We affixed a wide angle Camkix lens to the wearable probe's built-in front camera to increase the remote user's range of view, accommodating mid-to-distant visual ranges.
- Social Environment: We leveraged the expected close relationships between locals and remotes to provide greater mobility for the probe, having the local wear the device.
- Communication: To allow users to not only share audio and video information, but also gestures made by the local user, we used a modified iOttie car mount holder with a quick-release mechanism, allowing locals to swap between wearing and holding the phone as needed. The positioning of the mount on the chest helped remote users to see and to follow deictic (pointing) gestures made by the local user, from the local's perspective.
- Independence: Remote users were not provided with a way to control the camera on the wearable device so that we could minimize the weight of the system.

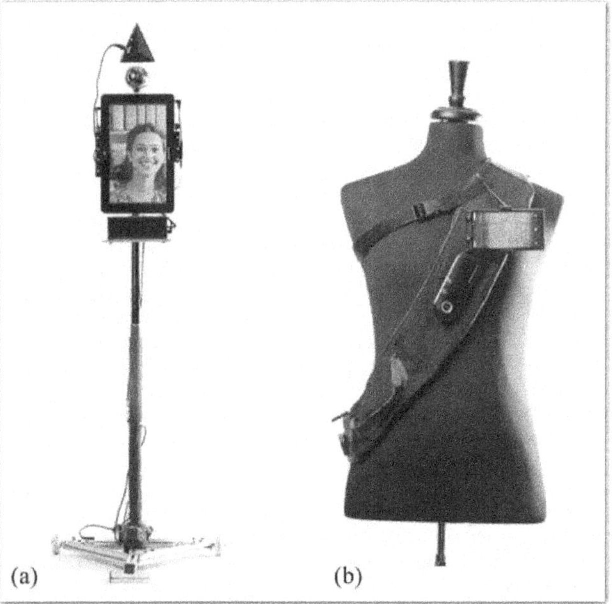

Figure 2. Telepresence design probes built for our field study: (a) the freestanding device on the left, and (b) the wearable device, shown on a mannequin, on the right. (Probes are not accurately scaled relative to each other.)

Applying Our Framework: Scoring the Probes

We used our framework to evaluate the expected performance of the probes in our two targeted scenarios. We used extensive pilot testing to assign performance weights to each probe for the elements in each design dimension. Positive weights indicated higher performance and negative weights indicated lower performance. For example, because the freestanding probe is stable and wheeled but unwieldy to move, we gave it a weight of 0.5 for mobility "Within a room," but -0.5 for "Between rooms on a floor." Weights were multiplied by scores in each dimension from the third survey and summed to yield a final score for each probe in the two scenarios. Table 3 shows examples of these weights along two of our dimensions, vision and physical environment, as well as final scores. Our framework predicted that the freestanding probe would be a better fit for the "Shared Meal" scenario, while the wearable probe would be a better fit for the "Visiting a New Place" scenario.

Field Study

We conducted a two (museum vs. restaurant between-subjects) by two (freestanding vs. wearable within-subjects) mixed-design field study to evaluate our framework's predictions and explore design issues. We chose the field study setting to evoke realistic responses to our design probes in natural settings among users with pre-existing relationships, as our surveys indicated that these were highly likely use cases for telepresence systems.

	% reported Meal	Place	Question	Weights Free.	Wear.
Vision	62	39	Close (within arm's length)	1	0.5
	33	39	Middle (up to across a room)	1	1
	6	23	Far distance (> room length)	-0.5	-1
Physical Environment	95	32	Indoors	1	1
	13	90	Outdoors	-1	1
	2	68	Area beyond a building	-1	1
	0	11	Between floors in a building	-1	1
	16	5	Between rooms on a floor	-0.5	1
	21	0	Within a room	0.5	0.5
	32	11	Localized around an object	1	-0.5
	29	5	No movement	1	-1
			...		

	Device	Shared meal	Visit a place
Scores	Freestanding	473	142
	Wearable	299	407

Table 3. Example of percentage responses along two design dimensions for target scenarios. Assigned weights for each probe are listed on the right, total scores at the bottom are the sum of the weighted percentage of performance along all elements in the design dimension.

Shared Meal Setting: Restaurant

The restaurant used as the setting for sharing a meal had two floors, with high ceilings and an open floor plan. Participants were seated at a booth near the windows on the first floor and the experimenter sat at a table within view of the participant. The booth was near a bar area and during some meals, sunlight reduced the visibility of the device screens. Ambient noise levels ranged between relatively quiet to extremely loud during busy mealtimes. The post-study interview took place at the participant's booth, after completing the meal. An example of a participant in this environment is shown in Figure 3.

Visiting a Place Together Setting: Museum

The museum used as a setting for visiting a new place together was located in a downtown area and had three floors connected via escalators containing 16 galleries. Tickets and admission took place on the first floor, with exhibits on the second and third floors. The floor plan was open without any enforced order to the artwork and participants were permitted to explore anything in the general collection. The post-study interview took place in a children's play room provided by the museum on the second floor, after participants indicated that they had completed their visit.

Procedure. Local participants were greeted by the experimenter once they were seated at the restaurant or had arrived in the lobby of the museum. After completing a consent form, the local users were trained on the first device by the experimenter. Ordering of the devices was counter-balanced. After the locals were comfortable with operating the device, the experimenter connected the remote user to the device and the participants began their restaurant or museum experience. Throughout the experience, the experimenter was on hand at a discreet distance to handle any technical difficulties that arose such as connection issues and dropped calls. After approximately 30 minutes, the experimenter approached the participants and asked the remote to log out of the first device. The experimenter instructed the locals on the second device, and once they indicated their readiness, reconnected the remote. The experimenter then retreated from view as they continued their shared experience. Approximately 30 minutes later, the experimenter returned and asked the participants which device they would like to complete their experience on, switching the devices, if necessary. During the session the experimenter took photographs and field notes on the interaction.

Survey and Interviews. Following the shared experience, we administered a survey to measure individual impressions of using each system. Participants rated their agreement with 15 statements, designed to measure difficulties along each design dimension (e.g., "Everyone in my party was comfortable with the remote person/me being there on the device") on a five-point Likert scale (1=Strongly Disagree, 5=Strongly Agree).

Upon completing the questionnaire, we engaged participants in a semi-structured, audio-recorded group interview with remote and local users, as well as any party members, of about 20 minutes. The interview was designed to elicit feedback on breakdowns that occurred and to provoke reflections on the social dynamics surrounding the interaction. We asked users to contrast their experiences with the different devices and for potential improvements. Additionally, participants were asked to consider other contexts that might suggest using one device over the other.

Participants. We recruited 7 groups for each condition, comprising 45 people (28 females, 17 males) to participate in the study. In each group, one person acted as the remote user and participated from a location of their choice, one person acted as the local user and was responsible for handling the device, and any other people present were part of the local or remote user's party. Participant groups ranged in size from 1 to 4 people on the local side, usually friends or family, and 1

Figure 3. Father and son sharing a meal with a remote family friend using the wearable device.

to 2 people on the remote side, generally friends or family members of the local user. Participant ages ranged between 17 to 52 years old, $M = 30.1$, $SD = 10.4$, and all participants had pre-existing social ties or shared a relationship with one of the users (e.g., the local user invited the people he was working with to share the meal with his remote mother, whom he introduced during the interaction).

Data Analysis. For our field notes and interviews, we transcribed our audio recordings and organized responses into groups as trends emerged. We then extracted insights from these trends and used them to expand our framework.

Although our survey was not the focus of our study, we followed a process of testing for covariates, doing a confirmatory factor analysis on our questionnaire items, and analyzing our results using a mixed-measures analysis of variance (ANOVA). Due to the group sample size of our data set, we treated each survey as independent.

In testing for covariates, we found that there were no significant effects of device order and participant role. For our questionnaire items, our confirmatory factor analysis found a good fit for our questions regarding the independence of the remote user, two items ($\alpha = .82$), and for our questions regarding communication, two items ($\alpha = .87$). The alpha values for the remaining questionnaire items were below .70, indicating that they did not fit together to measure the other five design dimensions, so we analyzed those questions individually to understand subjective trends.

Results. We organize the results of our field study into two parts: (1) the emergent themes extracted from our field observations and interviews; and (2) the quantitative results from our post-experience survey.

Emergent Themes

Our field study yielded six key insights beyond those found in our surveys or in previous research for elements within the design dimensions of vision, social environment, communication, and independence.

In highlighting these insights, we refer to participants by condition and role—D for dinner, M for museum, L for local, R for remote, and P for members of the local's party—followed by a number indicating the group. For example, DR1 would stand for the remote user in the shared dinner experience from the first group of participants.

Insight 1: Differences in feedback requirements for shared perspectives in telepresence (Vision)

> *"I tried to direct him how to move so I could see* [with the wearable device], *but that became very confusing, because I would say, 'To my left,' and he would say, 'Well, which left?'"* (DR2)

In face-to-face communications, attentional focus is signaled by several factors, such as the direction of the eyes, the head, or the positioning of the body [14]. However, when using both of our devices, participants frequently voiced uncertainty about what other users were looking at.

When using the wearable device, these breakdowns manifested when the local user was unable to see the screen or had no feedback on what their camera was showing. With the freestanding device, failures occurred when the remote's ability to control the camera made it difficult for the local to track where the remote was looking: "[In response to what they liked about the wearable device] *Basically that we both could see the same thing, so look at a painting and be like, 'Oh, look at this. This is cool,' and it's like, yeah, I'm looking at the exact same thing – with the rotating one* [the freestanding device], *I can be looking off in a random different direction."* (MR4).

Prior work on spatial perspective-taking in face-to-face conversation has shown that speakers use more *egocentric perspectives*—referring to the speaker's point of view—when speaking to a partner [56]. However, in interactions mediated by a telepresence technology the relationship between remote and local perspectives is not always clear. Users may experience incorrect mental models of what is visible to the other user and the remote user's perspective may change suddenly (e.g., as when being flipped around or moved in the local user's hand), making it difficult to maintain an accurate perception of the addressee's relative position. In addition to the way that users share spatial perspectives, previous literature has highlighted the need to support gaze cues to aid in a shared understanding of attentional focus [11,40].

While this literature may serve to inform the design of future telepresence systems, more work must be done to understand how telepresence features, particularly those that grant abilities beyond those found in face-to-face interactions (e.g., the ability to see 360° or to directly see the speaking person's perspective), support interactions across scenarios and integrate with previous theoretical work.

Insight 2: Bystander responses to the remote's varying levels of embodiment (Social Environment)

> *"...I think some people looked at me kind of funny and thought I was awkward."* (MR3)

In face-to-face interactions, participant presence is self-apparent and their appearance is similar to others in the environment. When using our telepresence probes, however, remote and local users were extremely sensitive to how differences in the remote user's appearance affected bystander behavior.

Some users enjoyed the attention drawn by the higher visibility of the freestanding system's embodiment: "*So many people stopped. They were like, 'Who is that? Who are you talking to?' I feel like it was more interactive with other people. I had more fun with* [it]." (ML2)

However, others revealed discomfort with the level of disruption that they were causing with the freestanding device that they did not feel with the wearable device in the same environment: *"I think more just not wanting to draw attention and stuff. People are there to look at art."* (MR7).

These examples illustrate how the appearance of the remote user might shape not just the local user's or local party member's perceptions, but also the impact that it might have on bystander perceptions and how this may be shaped by the expectations within a given context.

Recent work has examined emergent social norms and themes in cellphone usage and how these relate to concepts in human communication literature, such as by disrupting existing physically collocated interactions [1,23,25]. However, this prior body of work presumes a consistent physical appearance of the other person's (e.g., as a human or a cellphone). With various telepresence systems available—between wearable and freestanding in our field study—our insight illustrates the need for telepresence research to follow the evolution of social norms and expectations as new form factors emerge [53].

Insight 3: User concerns about negative responses to technology use (Social Environment)

> *"...I kinda felt like the stigma of having the phone* [on the wearable device] *had more of a stigma than the other one* [the freestanding device]*"* (MR6)

People voiced differing concerns about how the two devices might be perceived by bystanders. Some users compared the wearable device to cellphone use because of the removable phone, as shown in the quote above. Others felt that the overt nature of the video on the freestanding device created concerns among bystanders of being recorded: "[With the freestanding device] *I have the ability to start recording anything...but I don't know if people across the table, if they would feel comfortable with me being here and just staring at them eating.*" (DR7). Others compared the visibility of the freestanding device to an accessibility aid, citing greater acceptance as it bore some similarities to pushing someone in a wheelchair.

This insight highlights the importance of understanding how the social connotations of previous technologies may shape perceptions of new systems, particularly when designing telepresence technologies to fit within a given context. For example, more embodied and visible systems may invoke concerns about being recorded, who has control, and access to the system [37], while more phone-like form factors may prompt excluding local party members [23]. In contrast, scenarios that are not socially motivated, such as remotely attending a class, might be less vulnerable to concerns about negative social stigmas or reactions from bystanders. As telepresence technologies explore new interfaces, there is an opportunity to develop a process to predict how user perceptions will be affected by previous media and how transfer of knowledge and experience may tie in to theories such as the Technology Acceptance Model [62].

Insight 4: The implicit debt of remote users (Social Environment)

> *"I felt like I was the device on the second one* [the wearable device]*, which did not feel good. I felt used. I was the tripod."* (ML2)

An unexpected emergent theme was the sense from users that by logging in, the remote user was implicitly incurring a social debt to the local user. Some locals felt responsible for making the experience enjoyable for the remote: *"Yeah, she didn't really ask for me to focus on other things. I just personally took it on my own..."* (DL3). However, this occasionally led to perceptions that the local was obligated to sacrifice his or her own experience in favor of the remote user's, leading to feelings of resentment and unhappiness, as shown in the first quote by ML2.

Conversely, others reacted by prioritizing their enjoyment over that of the remote user's: *"He did mention that it* [the freestanding device] *was, like, pointed at the ground, 'cause the best, most comfortable way I found to carry it was definitely at a pretty extreme angle...but I don't really care what he thinks, so I just kept it the way that was comfortable for me."* (ML4).

Both of these views accentuate that the implicit social debt incurred by the remote user is a unique factor for telepresence systems. When compared to prior literature on caller hegemony [22], this implicit social debt adds a new dimension to the power dynamic between local and remote users. While some prior literature has focused on users who are already familiar with each other [24,32,63], understanding how this debt might be reduced, the dynamics by which this debt is incurred, and how this debt may play out among users who have no prior relationship, are all areas that offer rich opportunities for future research.

Insight 5: Visibility of the technology and lack of awareness leading to self-regulation (Communication)

> *"I wasn't sure who was around or if I was gonna offend someone or anything like that..."* (MR4)

Throughout the interactions in our field study, one of the more pervasive themes was a sensitivity exhibited by users about the visibility of the conversation to bystanders, sometimes leading to self-censorship. In person, people have the ability to gauge bystander awareness and to adapt their communication modalities accordingly (e.g., speaking more softly, turning away, or using gestures). However, in a majority of mediated communications, users are at the mercy of the technology or of local users.

While the ability to self-regulate volume for remote users has been emphasized in previous work [11,32,60,67] and the literature has examined the theme of the "lack of control over one's accessibility accelerating the erosion of the public-private distinction" [25], our observations were that volume, visibility, and self-consciousness about the use of technology all played a role in affecting user interactions. In fact, due to its potential for more visible embodiments and capabilities

Question	Freestanding	Wearable	F	*p*
Planning required	3.11 (1.19)	1.94 (1.00)	5.20	.029
Ease of maneuvering	3.22 (1.31)	4.28 (0.75)	10.35	.005
Remote's independence	3.66 (1.21)	2.90 (1.10)	10.44	.003
Ability to see each other	4.03 (1.36)	3.05 (1.02)	8.97	.005
Ability to see museum	3.05 (1.33)	3.89 (0.96)	5.08	.030
Meal bystander comfort	3.67 (0.86)	3.00 (0.97)	5.20	.028
Museum ease of use	4.28 (0.76)	3.23 (1.31)	9.13	.004
Meal ease of use	3.64 (1.05)	3.09 (1.19)	5.01	.036

Table 4. Field study survey results. * = p < .05, ** = p < .005, standard deviations are shown in parentheses next to means.

"beyond being there," we believe that telepresence technologies may offer new and unique ways of allowing users to control their communications, increasing the options that users have in allowing the regulation of their interactions.

Insight 6: Contrasting reactions of remote users to enforced feelings of helplessness (Independence)

> *"...it felt like I was in a wheelchair like I was being moved differently...because I have had an experience of being in a wheelchair recently, it didn't feel like I wanted to be in a wheelchair..."* (MR2)

During interviews, we observed contrasting reactions to how remote users felt about their independence through the probes. Some users felt helpless and compared the experience to being in a wheelchair, emphasizing the unpleasantness of having to rely on local users for assistance. Others liked how the system constrained their actions. For example: "[on the freestanding device] *I'm more curious about pressing buttons and scrolling around and intruding on other people's privacy. With the cell phone* [the wearable device], *because I can't control anything, once he sets it up it's like, 'Okay, I'm just talking with him.'*" (DR7)

These contrasting views on the constraints that our probes enforced on the remote user illustrated how perceptions may differ across users and across scenarios. Although little work has been done to explore what might affect these perceptions thus far, these insights serve to enhance our understanding of telepresence-specific factors that may need to be considered when developing and researching these systems.

Survey Results

Results from our questionnaire largely supported our predictions of each probe's scenario performance, based on our framework. These results are summarized in Table 4.

DISCUSSION

We developed a framework for telepresence consisting of seven design dimensions and 17 categories of scenarios that was informed by prior research and a series of surveys. We used our framework to develop two contrasting design probes and tested them in a real-world field study. Our study not only demonstrated how our framework might be used to prioritize design choices amongst different contexts, but also identified insights into interactional nuances unique to telepresence. Incorporating these insights into our framework, we summarize our final design dimensions in Table 5.

In developing a framework for designing and understanding telepresence, our goal was to a create tool that would help designers and researchers to:

- Identify opportunities for future research.
- Reflect on past and future work to determine potentially generalizable findings.
- Share a structure and language for reporting research and facilitating communication within the telepresence community.

Next, we demonstrate how our framework may be used as a tool to accomplish each of these tasks.

Design Dimension	Dimension Characteristics
Initiation	Person initiating interaction Options for refusing access Amount of planning Setup costs
Physical Environment	Indoors, outdoors, or both Ambient noise levels Material workspace properties Manual manipulation required
Mobility	Size of movement area Barriers or obstacles Movement restrictions
Vision	Primary focus of attention Distance to focus of attention Ability to see non-verbal cues Feedback of other user views
Social Environment	Privacy of setting Stakeholder relationships Negotiations of social capital Bystander perceptions of users Pre-existing views of technology used Implicit debt incurred by remote users
Communication	Impersonal touch Personal touch Referential gestures Non-verbal cues Speaking & listening time Technology mediating content
Independence	Ability to act without aid or direction Control of the system Effects on user confidence

Table 5. Table of the seven design dimensions and corresponding characteristics.

Identify unexplored areas for future research

Situating prior research within our framework highlights that a number of studies have examined how the remote user's appearance affects local users [32,46,49,49,63]. However, our identification of potential stakeholders within the design dimension of the social environment and the insights revealed by our field study showcase that the remote user's appearance may also affect bystander perceptions. While some prior work identifies bystanders as stakeholders [11,24], little work has been done to conduct an in-depth study of the interplay between users, bystanders, and the system's appearance, in real-world settings.

Reflect on the generalizability of prior and future work

In the context of previous work, we might establish that the informal conversations that occur in the workplace [32,63] and the natural exchanges that take place in the home [1] share similarities in how the interaction is initiated. Both scenarios involve spontaneous and opportunistic interactions with little to no planning among people who already know each other. Additionally, both types of interactions commonly occur in social settings where users have comparable means of managing their availability.

Having used our framework to identify the similarities between these scenarios, we may expect that some findings about the initiation of interactions in business settings may be similar in home settings. For example, increases in spontaneous or opportunistic interactions in business settings due to remote user presence via the system may be similarly increased by remote user presence in home settings, despite the differences within other design dimensions.

By using our design dimensions in this way to identify the similarities and differences between scenarios, designers and researchers may distinguish between results which should generalize between contexts, and those which require further investigation or differing design solutions.

Facilitate communication within the community

As the community working under the auspices of telepresence has grown, telepresence research has become increasingly divided in the terminologies used [28] and even in making decisions about what should be categorized as telepresence [34]. One example of how our framework may be used to unify the terminology from prior literature lies in examining multiple sources which present design requirements for robotic telepresence systems.

Cohen et al. suggested 10 requirements for robotic telepresence systems [10]: (1) visitor (remote user) perceptions of presence, (2) local perceptions of visitors, (3) mobility of visitors, (4) physical interaction, (5) fidelity of human expression, (6) visitor environment, (7) virtual content, (8) session management, (9) security and privacy, and (10) acceptance.

Riek proposed a set of seven candidate requirements for designing telepresence robots [52]: (1) video, (2) camera, (3) control, (4) latency, (5) gaze and appearance, (6) audio, and (7) gesture.

And Desai et al. enumerated 20 essential features for telepresence robots [11]: (1) dynamic video profile, (2) stationary video profile, (3) video resolution, (4) graceful degradation, (5) audio quality, (6) volume control, (7) UI type, (8) sensor information, (9) feedback, (10) integrated map, (11) robot height, (12) robot speed, (13) multiple cameras, (14) wide field of view, (15) independent head/torso, (16) access point switching, (17) assisted navigation, (18) human-speed navigation behaviors, (19) adjustable autonomy, and (20) appropriate occupancy awareness.

Each of these three previous works has segmented what robotic telepresence systems should support in different ways, making it difficult to understand how they relate. By using our framework of design dimensions and scenarios as a tool, we can begin to make sense of how the findings of each study interact. For example, Riek's work examines design requirements in the context of a classroom, which might fit in our self-improvement scenario if done alone, or a shared viewing scenario if socially motivated. Desai et al.'s perspective is from an office setting, where experiences may be more focused on goal-based collaboration. Lastly, Cohen et al.'s work does not clearly define the setting that they are examining. These differences in scenarios may help to explain why each of these works seems to prioritize or highlight different features.

In delving into the reported design requirements, we might define the question that each requirement attempts to resolve and use this to identify the framework dimension that it fits under. For example, Cohen et al.'s "fidelity of human expression" encompasses the transference of body language, head movements, eye gaze, facial expressions, and arm and finger movements, which would fit under our dimension of *communication.* Items in Riek's categories which would similarly be included in the framework dimension of *communication* include the "gaze and appearance," which indicates that systems should preserve gaze and portray clear facial appearance and expression, and the category of "gesture," which specifies the need for a minimum of two degree-of-freedom mechanisms for deictic gestures. Lastly, in Desai et al.'s work, items in the domain of the *communication* dimension are included not under the headings of the video profiles, but under "independent head/torso" where they indicate the support of these features for the purpose of providing social cues.

Organizing these requirements under the design dimensions and scenarios of our framework allows those in the telepresence community to understand why past literature may differ in categorizing and prioritizing these guidelines. Furthermore, by considering this work through the lens of our framework, researchers and designers can more easily make comparisons and combine these insights into a cohesive whole.

By creating a framework for telepresence, our goal is to provide a tool by which researchers and designers can communicate across domains, terminologies, and disciplines, to share discoveries and solutions. To do this, we have identified seven design dimensions which uniquely categorize 17 scenarios as a starting point. By using these design dimensions to pinpoint similarities between contexts, terminologies, or concepts, researchers from different domains may begin to form a common ground with which they can share findings.

CONCLUSION

It has been over 30 years since Marvin Minsky first proposed the term telepresence to describe the sensation of "being there" via a facilitating or mediating technology. Since that time, the telepresence field has grown by leaps and bounds. However, this expansion has not been without its growing pains. Motivated by technological advances which continue to offer new approaches to developing telepresence systems and with the field as a whole reaching maturity, a tool is needed to aid in understanding how the previously disparate approaches fit together into a cohesive whole.

In this paper, we described our process for creating a framework for telepresence. First, we iterated through a series of surveys and used prior literature to create a framework of design dimensions and potential telepresence scenarios. Our framework was predicated on the theory that these design dimensions can be used to differentiate between the needs of each scenario, and that these needs and constraints vary across contexts.

To test this, we validated our framework by developing design probes for two contrasting scenarios and tested them in real world settings through a field study. Our field study provided a proof of concept, demonstrating the utility of our framework as a tool for design and research. Additionally, our observations and interviews revealed six key insights, providing a more nuanced view of elements that are unique to telepresence in our design dimensions.

Last, we discussed how our framework could be used to (1) identify unexplored areas for future research, (2) reflect on the generalizability of prior and future work, and (3) facilitate communication within the telepresence community.

We hope that developing this framework for understanding and designing telepresence will encourage a greater dissemination of findings, discoveries, and solutions. By being able to share and place past and future research, we hope that work in telepresence can continue to evolve and to thrive, until being "here" is no different from "being there."

ACKNOWLEDGMENTS

We thank Wild Ginger in Bellevue and the Seattle Art Museum for their support. We also acknowledge our colleagues Asta Roseway, Patrick Therien, Chris O'Dowd, Tom Blank, Sasa Junuzovic, and Kori Inkpen, who helped with this project. We thank our anonymous participants for recruiting their remote partners and allowing us to observe their activity.

REFERENCES

1. Ames, M. G. (2013, February). Managing Mobile Multitasking: the Culture of iPhones on Stanford Campus. In *Proc. CSCW 2013*, ACM Press (2013), 1487-1498.
2. Beer, J. and Takayama, L. Mobile remote presence systems for older adults: acceptance, benefits, and concerns. In *Proc. HRI 2011*, ACM Press (2011), 19-26.
3. Benford, S., Greenhalgh, C., Reynard, G., Brown, C., and Koleva, B. *Understanding and constructing shared spaces with mixed-reality boundaries.* In *ACM TOCHI 1998*, *5*(3), 185-223.
4. Boyle, E.A., Anderson, A.H., and Newlands, A. The effects of visibility on dialogue and performance in a cooperative problem solving task. In *Language and speech 37*, 1 (1994), 1-20.
5. Brubaker, J., Venolia, G., and Tang, J. Focusing on shared experiences: moving beyond the camera in video communication. In *Proc. DIS 2012*, ACM Press (2012), 96-105.
6. Brush, A.J., Meyers, B.R., Scott, J., and Venolia, G. Exploring awareness needs and information display preferences between coworkers. In *Proc. CHI 2009*, ACM Press (2009), 2091-2094.
7. Carroll, J. M. *Making use: scenario-based design of human-computer interactions*. MIT press (2000).
8. Cesta, A., Cortellessa, G., Orlandini, A., and Tiberio, L. Evaluating Telepresence Robots in the Field. In *Agents and Artificial Intelligence*, Springer Berlin Heidelberg (2013), 433-448.
9. Clark, H. H., and Brennan, S. E. Grounding in communication. *Perspectives on socially shared cognition* (1991), *13*, 127-149.
10. Cohen, B., Lanir, J., Stone, R., and Gurevich, P. Requirements and design considerations for a fully immersive robotic telepresence system. In *Proc. HRI 2011 Workshop on Social Robotic Telepresence*, ACM Press (2011), 16-22.
11. Desai, M., Tsui, K. M., Yanco, H. A., and Uhlik, C. Essential features of telepresence robots. In *Proc. TePRA 2011*, IEEE Press (2011), 15-20.
12. Draper, J. V., Kaber, D. B., and Usher, J. M. Telepresence. In *Human Factors: The Journal of the Human Factors and Ergonomics Society 1998*, *40*(3), 354-375.est
13. Ellis, C.A., Gibbs, S.J., and Rein, G. Groupware: some issues and experiences. In *CACM, 34*, 1 (1991), 39-58.
14. Frischen, A., Bayliss, A.P., and Tipper, S.P. Gaze cueing of attention: visual attention, social cognition, and individual differences. In *Psychological bulletin 133*, 4 (2007), 694-724.

15. Gergle, D., Kraut, R. E., and Fussell, S. R. Language efficiency and visual technology minimizing collaborative effort with visual information. *Journal of Language and Social Psychology (2004), 23*(4), 491-517.

16. Goffman, E. Behavior in public spaces. *Notes on the Social Organization of Gatherings.* The Free Press, NY (1963).

17. Grevet, C., Tang, A., and Mynatt, E. Eating alone together: new forms of commensality. In *Proc. GROUP 2012*, ACM Press (2012), 103-106.

18. Grudin, J. Groupware and social dynamics: eight challenges for developers. In *CACM, 37*, 1 (1994), 92-105.

19. Gutwin, C. and Greenberg, S. A Descriptive Framework of Workspace Awareness for Real-Time Groupware. In *Proc. CSCW 2002*, Kluwer Academic Publishers (2002), 411-446.

20. Haans, A., and IJsselsteijn, W. A. Embodiment and Telepresence: Toward a Comprehensive Theoretical Framework. *Interacting with Computers 2012*, 24(4), 211-218.

21. Heath, C. and Luff, P. Disembodied conduct: communication through video in a multi-media office environment. In *Proc. CHI 1991*, ACM Press (1991), 99-103.

22. Hopper, R. *Telephone conversation*. Indiana University Press (1992), 724.

23. Humphreys, L. Cellphones in public: social interactions in a wireless era. *New media & society 2005*, *7*(6), 810-833.

24. Inkpen, K., Taylor, B., Junuzovic, S., Tang, J., and Venolia, G. Experiences2Go: sharing kids' activities outside the home with remote family members. In *Proc. CSCW 2013*, ACM Press (2013), 1329-1340.

25. Katz, J. E., and Aakhus, M. *Perpetual contact: Mobile communication, private talk, public performance.* Cambridge University Press (2002).

26. Kendon, A. *Conducting interaction: Patterns of behavior in focused encounters.* CUP Archive (1990), 7.

27. Kiesler, S., Siegel, J., and McGuire, T.W. Social psychological aspects of computer-mediated communication. In *American psychologist 39*, 10 (1984), 1123.

28. Kristoffersson, A., Coradeschi, S., and Loutfi, A. A review of mobile robotic telepresence. In *Advances in Human-Computer Interaction 2013*, 3.

29. Kristoffersson, A., Eklundh, K. S., and Loutfi, A. Measuring the quality of interaction in mobile robotic telepresence: a pilot's perspective. *International Journal of Social Robotics 2013*, *5*(1), 89-101.

30. Latour, B. Reassembling the social-an introduction to actor-network-theory. *Reassembling the Social-An Introduction to Actor-Network-Theory,* Oxford University Press (2005).

31. Latifi, R., R. S. Weinstein, J. M. Porter, M. Ziemba, D. Judkins, D. Ridings, R. Nassi, T. Valenzuela, M. Holcomb, and F. Leyva. Telemedicine and telepresence for trauma and emergency care management. In *Scandinavian journal of surgery: SJS: official organ for the Finnish Surgical Society and the Scandinavian Surgical Society*, 96, 4 (2006), 281-289.

32. Lee, M. and Takayama, L. Now I have a body: uses and social norms for mobile remote presence in the workplace. In *Proc. CHI 2011*, ACM Press (2011), 33-42.

33. Leigh, J., Rawlings, M., Girado, J., Dawe, G., Fang, R., Verlo, A., et al. AccessBot: an Enabling Technology for Telepresence. In *Proc. INET 2000.*

34. Lombard, M., and Jones, M. T. Identifying the (Tele) Presence Literature. In *PsychNology Journal 2007*, *5*(2), 197-206.

35. Macharet, D. G., and Florencio, D. A. (2012, October). A collaborative control system for telepresence robots. In *Proc. IROS 2012*, IEEE press (2012), 5105-5111.

36. MantaroBot TelePresence Robots.*MantaroBot.* Retrieved August 1, 2014, from http://www.mantarobot.com/products/teleme.

37. Massimi, M., Truong, K. N., Dearman, D., and Hayes, G. R. Understanding recording technologies in everyday life. *Pervasive Computing, IEEE* (2010), *9*(3), 64-71.

38. McGovern, D.E. Experiences in teleoperation of lan d vehicles. *No. SAND-87-1980C; CONF-8708156-1*, Sandia National Labs, Albuquerque, NM.

39. Minsky, M. Telepresence. *Omni 1980*, 45-51.

40. Misawa, K., Ishiguro, Y., and Rekimoto, J. Ma petite cherie: what are you looking at?: a small telepresence system to support remote collaborative work for intimate communication. In *Proceedings of the 3rd Augmented Human International Conference 2012*, ACM Press (2012), 17.

41. Neale, D., Carroll, J.M., and Rosson, M.B. Evaluating computer-supported cooperative work: models and frameworks. In *Proc. CSCW 2004*, ACM Press (2004), 112-121.

42. Nishio, S., Ishiguro, H. and Hagita, N. Geminoid: Teleoperated android of an existing person. In *Humanoid robots-new developments, I-Tech*, 14 (2007).

43. Nguyen, D. T. and Canny, J. Multiview: improving trust in group video conferencing through spatial faithfulness. In *Proc. CHI 2007*, ACM Press (2007), 1465-1474.

44. Nguyen, D. T. and Canny, J. More than face-to-face: empathy effects of video framing. In *Proc. CHI 2009*, ACM Press (2009), 423-432.

45. Olson, G. M. and Olson, J. S. Distance Matters. *Human-Computer Interaction 15*, 2 (2000), 139-178.

46. Paulos, E. and Canny, J. PRoP: personal roving presence. In *Proc. CHI 1998*, ACM Press (1998), 296-303.
47. Procyk, J., Neustaedter, C., Pang, C., Tang, A., and Judge, T. K. (2014). Exploring Video Streaming in Public Settings: Shared Geocaching Over Distance Using Mobile Video Chat. In *Proc. CHI 2014*
48. Rae, I., Takayama, L., and Mutlu, B. In-body experiences: embodiment, control, and trust in robot-mediated communication. In *Proc. CHI 2013*, ACM Press (2013), 1921-1930.
49. Rae, I., Takayama, L., and Mutlu, B. The influence of height in robot-mediated communication. In *Proc. HRI 2013*, ACM Press (2013), 1-8.
50. Rae, I., Takayama, L., and Mutlu, B. One of the gang: supporting in-group behavior for embodied-mediated communication. In *Proc. CHI 2012*, ACM Press (2012), 3091-3100.
51. Rae, I., Mutlu, B., and Takayama, L. Bodies in Motion: Mobility, Presence, and Task Awareness in Telepresence. In *Proc. CHI 2014*, ACM Press (2014), 2153-2162.
52. Riek, L. D. Realizing Hinokio: candidate requirements for physical avatar aystems. In *Proceedings of the ACM/IEEE international conference on Human-robot interaction 2007*, ACM Press (2007), 303-308.
53. Šabanović, S., Bennett, C. C., and Lee, H. R.. Towards Culturally Robust Robots: A Critical Social Perspective on Robotics and Culture. In *Proc. HRI Workshop on Culture-Aware Robotics 2014*, ACM Press (2014).
54. Sakamoto, D., Kanda, T., Ono, T., Ishiguro, H., and Hagita, N. Android as a telecommunication medium with a human-like presence. In *Proc. HRI 2007*, IEEE Press (2007), 193-200.
55. Schwartz, P. *The art of the long view: paths to strategic insight for yourself and your company*. Random House LLC (1996).
56. Schober, M. F. (1993). Spatial perspective-taking in conversation. *Cognition* (1993), *47*(1), 1-24.
57. Sellen, A., Buxton, B., and Arnott, J. Using spatial cues to improve videoconferencing. In *Proc. CHI 1992*, ACM Press (1992), 651-652.
58. Tang, J.C., Xiao, R., Hoff, A., Venolia, G., Therien, P., and Roseway, A. HomeProxy: exploring a physical proxy for video communication in the home. In *Proc. CHI 2013*, ACM Press (2013), 1339-1342.
59. Tomasello, M. *Origins of human communication*. MIT press, Cambridge (2008).
60. Tsui, K., Desai, M., Yanco, H., and Uhlik, C. Telepresence robots roam the halls of my office building. In *HRI 2011 Workshop*, 58.
61. Tsui, K. M., Desai, M., and Yanco, H. A. Towards measuring the quality of interaction: communication through telepresence robots. In *Proceedings of the Workshop on Performance Metrics for Intelligent Systems*, ACM Press (2012), 101-108.
62. Venkatesh, V., and Davis, F. D. *A theoretical extension of the technology acceptance model: four longitudinal field studies*. Management science (2000), *46*(2), 186-204.
63. Venolia, G., Tang, J., Cervantes, R., Bly, S., Robertson, G., Lee, B., and Inkpen, K. Embodied social proxy: mediating interpersonal connection in hub-and-satellite teams. In *Proc. CHI 2010*, ACM Press (2010), 1049-1058.
64. Vespa, P. M., Miller, C., Hu, X., Nenov, V., Buxey, F., and Martin, N. A. Intensive care unit robotic telepresence facilitates rapid physician response to unstable patients and decreased cost in neurointensive care. In *Surgical neurology 2007*, *67*(4), 331-337.
65. Weeks, G.D. and Chapanais, A. Cooperative versus conflictive problem solving in three telecommunication modes. *Perceptual and motor skills, 42*, 3 (1976), 879-917.
66. Wei, J., Wang, X., Peiris, R.L., Choi, Y., Martinez, X.R., Tache, R., Koh, J.T.K., Halupka, V., and Cheok, A. CoDine: an interactive multi-sensory system for remote dining. In *Proc. UbiComp 2011,* ACM Press (2011), 21-30.
67. Weiss, P. L. T., Whiteley, C. P., Treviranus, J., and Fels, D. I. PEBBLES: a personal technology for meeting educational, social and emotional needs of hospitalised children. In *Personal and Ubiquitous Computing* 5, 3 (2001), 157-168.
68. Wesselink, M. Videoconferencing as an educational intervention for children with autism (Master's thesis). Retrieved from *http://webteach.org*, ID: 0638210, 2012.
69. Yankelovich, N., Simpson, N., Kaplan, J., and Provino, J. Porta-person: Telepresence for the connected conference room. In *Proc. CHI'07 extended abstracts on Human factors in computing systems*, ACM Press (2007), 2789-2794.

Not Really There: Understanding Embodied Communication Affordances in Team Perception and Participation

Jacob T. Biehl, Daniel Avrahami, Anthony Dunnigan
FX Palo Alto Laboratory, Inc.
3174 Porter Drive
Palo Alto, CA, USA
{biehl, daniel, tonyd}@fxpal.com

ABSTRACT
We conducted a study that compared basic video conferencing, emergent kinetic video-conferencing techniques, and face-to-face meetings. Remote and co-located participants worked together in groups of three. We show, in agreement with prior literature, the strong adverse impact of being remote on participation levels. We also show that local and remote participants perceived differently their own contributions and others'. Local participants exhibited significantly more overlapping talk with remote participants who used an embodied proxy, than with remote participants in basic-video conferencing (and at a rate similar to overlapping speech for co-located groups). We describe differences in how the technologies were used to follow conversation. Our findings indicate that while the kinetic embodied technology increased local participants' perceived presence of remote teammates, it did not enhance remote participants' own sense of telepresence. We discuss our findings in the context of theories of agency and presence, and discuss how these findings extend our understanding of the promise and limitations of embodied video-conferencing solutions.

Author Keywords
Telepresence, Video Conferencing, Embodied Proxies

ACM Classification Keywords
H.5.3 [Group and Organization Interfaces]: Computer-supported cooperative work.

INTRODUCTION
Advances in processing hardware, encoding techniques, and broadband networks are driving a rise in the adoption of video-based communication technologies, especially in the workplace. These technologies have been shown to increase the frequency of communication between co-workers and, in some cases, improve productivity [32]. A recent industry survey of human-resource executives illustrates the disruptive nature of this technology and boldly postulates that video-based communication tools will be preferred over email in the workplace by 2016 [25]. Although world travel has been steadily growing [13], recent reports on corporate travel budgets show a 17% overall decline [41] and an increase in travel-related costs of 3-9% [16]. This suggests an economic driving force for adoption of video-based communication.

Despite the benefits of video-based communication, limitations still exist. Past work in this community has shown that remote users still face a disadvantage when compared to their co-located colleagues. Remote collaborators participate less in conversations, take less dominant roles in groups, and feel less connected to distant coworkers. A new class of technologies has emerged that seeks to mitigate the social disadvantages of video-based communication by providing remote users with a local embodiment. These technologies range from fully mobile robots, to smaller devices that sit on a meeting room table.

Studies of these embodied telepresence devices show that they provide distributed teams with an increased sense of their remote colleagues' presence in the local environment and a reciprocal sense of "being there" for that remote worker. Studies have also shown that using these devices can change collaborative behavior. For example, [35] found that their use led to more opportunistic interactions among distant workers.

While the impact of introducing these technologies has been explored at a group level, few studies have investigated how they impact an actual collaborative engagement (e.g. a workplace meeting). Further, there is need to extend classic work (e.g. [28]), to account for the capabilities introduced by modern embodied devices.

In this paper, we present a lab study that compares the use of an embodied telepresence device, a traditional video-conferencing configuration, and fully co-located baseline to complete a specific, collaborative task. In agreement with

CSCW '15, March 14 – 18, 2015, Vancouver, BC, Canada.

ACM 978-1-4503-2922-4/15/03...$15.00
http://dx.doi.org/10.1145/2675133.2675220

prior work, we first show the adverse effect of being remote on actual and perceived contributions. We then describe qualitative and quantitative shifts in group interaction and attitudes related to the use of embodied technology. In particular, our results show that local participants interact with a remote person in a fashion more similar to face-to-face when using an embodied technology – potentially as a result of increased perceived agency of the remote person. Our results also highlight the difficulty providing participants a sense of agency in the remote space.

We believe the results and insights from our work strengthen the findings of past studies, while providing a comparative baseline across technologies. Using our comparative result, we also offer design insight for improving the current state-of-the-art embodied telepresence devices.

RELATED WORK

Studies of group work have shown the importance of providing access, presence, and a sense belonging across members of distributed teams [10, 39].

Pioneering work, like PARC's Portholes, which shared photo snapshots of colleagues' in their offices, found that this type of sharing improved awareness and a "sense of community" with the team [6]. Erickson and Kellogg [7] describe the phenomenon as Social Translucence and argue its importance in the design of computer mediated communication tools.

Fostering stronger connections in distributed teams has been the focus of many research systems. These include physical presence tools (e.g. [9, 18, 34]), as well as those that attempt to facilitate interaction explicitly. Cruiser [8], for example, presents users with short, symmetric glimpses into co-workers offices to simulate the effect of walking down a hall of open office doors. Tools like MyUnity [40] combine physical presence with structured messaging to facilitate interactions that are thought to be context and location ideal.

A large body of research exists aimed at improving video collaboration. The Hydra system, for example, used "video surrogates" to represent individuals in a 4-way video conference [28] and compared its use to a traditional video conferencing setup and to face-to-face collaboration. More recently, the Embodied Social Proxies (ESP) work [35] presented a video conferencing cart that can be moved and reconfigured in a workspace. This embodied device was deployed for several months within distributed teams. ESP was found to have a profound impact on the remote worker's membership and participation with the team. Particularly, local team members developed stronger affinity towards, and gave more attention to remote workers. A key finding was that "improved interpersonal social connections" were established through the proxy's continuous physical presence.

Figure 1. A group discussion in the Kinetic condition, with two co-located participants and a single remote participant using the Jarvis embodied device.

Indeed, embodied presence through physical movement has surged in both commercial and research landscapes. These include small devices, such as the AnyBot [2], Kubi [15], MeBot [1], and Porta-Person [42] and fully mobile robots like the Beam [3], VGo [36], and PRoP [19]. The smaller devices are typically intended to be placed on a table in a conference room to provide a fixed proxy for a remote person or location. The fully mobile devices can be maneuvered around an office environment and have even greater physical presence in the local environment.

Many of the affordances of embodied devices relate back to core psychological and psychophysical principles of presence and agency [13, 19, 29]. Sheridan [29] noted that the perception of presence is guided not only by the quality of the representation (e.g. video quality), but also how that representation exists within time and space. Work in the virtual reality community noted that agency, defined as non-human entities acting with intelligence, can improve an overall sense of feeling present in a remote space [19].

Agency also plays a role in the perception and use of embodied telepresence devices, specifically in how these devices exist as machines and representations of remote individuals. The impact of these principles on collaboration is important area of research. For instance, in [23], Rae *et al.* showed that physical presence impacted the group dynamics in 1:1 tasks. In [24] researchers compared the use of embodied (telepresence robot) and non-embodied (tablet) tele-mediated collaboration in support of 1:1 tasks. Embodiment and the ability for the local person to control view were found to foster trust between the users. Recently, [22] examined the use of a mobile embodied device to allow remote participants to assist a local person (a confederate) with tasks of varied mobility. Their findings showed that remote users had a greater sense of presence with the local participant when performing a high-mobility task, but highlighted the burden of maneuvering the device.

a. F2F b. Static c. Kinetic

Figure 2. Study setup with a presenter and three participants. In the Static (b) and Kinetic (c) conditions, one participant is remote.

Closely related to our work, [30] created a kinetic videoconferencing proxy that allows a remote user to pan the remote display. In a controlled study, they examined the influence of different motion control schemas (in which the controller was a confederate) on group participation and attitudes. They showed higher engagement in conversation, higher user rankings, and improved attention awareness with the kinetic version.

While these past studies provide evidence that embodied devices may assist in breaking down known barriers in distributed collaboration (e.g. member isolation [4], local sub teams [38]), many questions still remain. In this paper, we extend the exploration of these new technologies for group meetings, compared to traditional forms of non-embodied, video-based communication as well as to face-to-face collaboration. Using a between-subject study, we explore group dynamics in co-located and distributed settings. This allowed us to examine the effect of kinetic embodied devices (similar to [30]), while keeping participants unaware of the mediation manipulation. As such, our work creates a relevant, much needed link between the classic comparative work on video and face-to-face collaboration, and recent explorations into kinetic embodied devices.

STUDY

To capture group communication and task engagement, we conducted a between-subject group-collaboration study in which some participants were co-located and others remote. Similar to [22, 30], our study employed a confederate. In our study, groups of three participants evaluated a junior sales trainee (the confederate) on a short sales presentation.

Task

The groups' task – evaluating a junior sales trainee – consisted of three phases: *Presentation*, *Discussion*, and *Feedback*.

In the *Presentation* phase, the sales trainee gave a short sales presentation about a specific multifunction printer for home and small-office use. (We chose printers because they are one of the product categories made by our company.) In order to keep the task consistent across all groups and conditions, we hired a professionally trained actor to play the role of the trainee. The actor was instructed to "play the same character" in all sessions, including consistently performing the same non-verbal behaviors, body posture, and vocal delivery. Scripted content and behaviors gave the appearance of a young, naïve sales trainee who had many faults and struggles in her presentation.

After the presentation was done and the presenter excused from the room, a *Discussion* phase began, in which participants privately discussed the presenter's performance (see Figure 1). Finally, the presenter was brought back into the room for the *Feedback* phase, and participants provided her with feedback.

Conditions

Our study consisted of three group-level conditions used to understand how groups performed an authentic task where group communication was mediated through different technologies: a baseline condition (*F2F*), with all 3 participants co-located, and two conditions (*Static* and *Kinetic*) where one participant was "remote" and the other two in the same room. This is similar to the *hub-and-satellite* meeting paradigm used in [30].

In the *F2F* condition, which served as baseline, all 3 participants (say, participants A, B, and C) were co-located and sat around a medium-sized meeting table (see Figure 2a). In the *Static* and *Kinetic* conditions, however, participant C was in a different room (as a "*Remote*" participant), and communicated via a two-party video call.

In the *Static* condition, which represents current practices for business video conferencing, participant C was in a different room, and communicated with the group via a two-party video call. A large, 30" display was placed on the meeting table in the approximate position of participant C in the F2F condition (Figure 2b). A camera was positioned at the top of the display.

In the *Kinetic* condition (Figure 2c), participant C communicated with the group using a prototype desktop telepresence device called *Jarvis* (see Figure 3). The Jarvis device was chosen as it faithfully represents the emerging class of embodied telepresence devices, which include commercial devices like the Kubi [15] and previously investigated research prototypes (e.g. [1, 31, 35, 42]). Jarvis uses a large, portrait-oriented 18" tablet to display the

Figure 3. Jarvis: A desktop pan & tilt telepresence robot equipped with an 18" screen and HD video camera.

remote participant. This larger display represents the remote participant at "human scale" and proportional to how remote participants were represented in the Static condition. A camera is mounted to the top of the device, creating a direct mapping between display orientation and remote view direction and angle. Jarvis enables the remote participant to pan and tilt the display by clicking on the remote video, which re-centered the camera view at the click point. Similar to the Static condition, Jarvis was placed on the meeting table in the approximate position of participant C in the F2F condition.

Video and audio transmission was handled using custom software built on top of the Vidyo API [37]. All of the clients and infrastructure (including the Vidyo router) were installed on our gigabit local network. Video was captured and streamed from both locations using a Logitech C920 camera running at 960x540 resolution, 30 frames per second, and at an average bit rate of 1200 Kbps. Remote video that appeared on Jarvis was cropped to fit the aspect ratio of the device's screen. In both conditions, the audio channel was open (i.e. no "push-to-talk" interaction was needed).

Procedure

Upon arriving at our lab, participants were shown to a meeting room. For the Kinetic and Static conditions, the first participant to arrive at the lab was whisked to a separate room and assigned the role of *Remote* participant. They all completed informed consent, demographic, and pre-study questionnaires.

Participants were told that their task was to evaluate a junior sales trainee who, as part of her training, had to make a short sales pitch in front of a live audience. The three phases of the task were described and the presenter was brought to the room.

After a short introduction, the confederate began her presentation, following a script that covered the features, functionality, and characteristics of the printer. Participants were allowed to interrupt and ask questions, but the actress was instructed to keep to and return to her script as much as possible. The presenter was then excused from the room and the group began their private discussion. Participants were told that they are allowed to move around the table or reposition the display if they so wished and that they could take as much time as they needed. When participants informed the researcher that they were done, the presenter was brought back and the group provided feedback.

Participants were then taken to separate rooms to complete post-study questionnaires where they rated the performance of the presenter, as well as their own and fellow evaluators' performance. Finally, we asked remote participants to comment on the challenges of working as a group through mediated communication.

Participants

We recruited participants via fliers and postings to community bulletin boards (e.g. Craigslist). The call indicated that participants would be given an Amazon gift card in return for an hour of their time to evaluate a sales presentation. 27 participants were recruited (11 women), with an average age of 44 (SD=13.8).

A pre-study questionnaire was administered to determine all participants' familiarity and experience using video communication tools (e.g. video chat). Responses varied from no experience to daily use. Most users reported using video chat at a frequency of 1-3 times per month across a variety of work and personal uses. No meaningful differences in frequency or type of use were seen across conditions.

Participants were randomly assigned to one of the three Group conditions, with three groups per condition. Participants did not know each other.

Measures

We collected a variety of subjective and objective measures, which included:

- *Performance questionnaire*. Participants rated the quality of the trainee's presentation across several dimensions. They also rated their own performance as evaluators, as well as the performance of fellow evaluators. The questions were modeled after existing shared identity, reciprocity, and group efficacy questionnaires [5, 11, 21].
- *Video analysis*. We recorded each session using multiple cameras (local and remote, when applicable) and coded for gestures and manipulation of artifacts and devices (including display and robot).
- *Turn-taking and Overlapping Talk*. We hand-coded video and audio recordings for start and end of speech segments ("turns"). Additionally, we coded turns that began when another participant was already talking as "Overlapping

Talk" and noted the role (*remote* or *local*) of the already-speaking participant.

- *Open-ended post-study questions*. We examined comments from participants in the Static and Kinetic conditions on the challenges of working as a group through mediated communication.

RESULTS

A total of 4.5 hours of video were recorded (30 minutes per group, on average). The average length, in minutes, for Discussion and Feedback were 9:47 (SD=5.2) and 10:26 (SD=7.6), respectively. Length varied across groups because we allowed participants to take as long as they wished for their discussion and the feedback.

We now report observations from the performance questionnaires, analysis of the videos, and the post-study interviews. We compare the behavior and attitudes of remote and co-located participants then report some surprising behavioral differences between our conditions. Finally, we examine whether (and how) participants took advantage of the ability to adjust the point-of-view (POV).

Participation and Perceived Performance

We examined if being a remote participant affected participation and perception, and looked for differences between the Kinetic and Static conditions. As highlighted by [38] and other work, remote participants are often at risk of becoming isolates. Indeed, we found that participation levels of remote participants were significantly lower than their co-located counterparts. Remote participants took the floor 22% of the time, on average, compared to 37% for local participants ($t(25)=2.184$; $p=0.039$). We saw no significant difference in floor time between the Kinetic and Static conditions (although differences in turn length and overlapping talk are reported later).

The reduced participation (or perceived ability to contribute) was further reflected in participants' responses in the performance questionnaire; Remote participants rated their own contribution (out of 7) significantly lower than local participants did (4.3 vs. 6.1; $F(1,5)=11.41$, $p=0.02$, with Group as a random factor). Additionally, looking at how local participants in the Kinetic and Static conditions rated the contribution of teammates showed a marginally significant effect with remote teammates receiving lower ratings than co-located (5.1 vs 6.25; $t(5)=1.99$, $p=.052$). However, no significant differences were found between the Kinetic and Static conditions. Finally, when asked to rank order the group from most contributing member (1) to least contributing member (3), not a single remote participant ranked themselves as most helpful, while 62% of local participants did. (In fact, 83% of remote participants ranked themselves as least helpful.)

Interestingly, remote participants in both Kinetic and Static conditions rated the sales presentation significantly less favorably than local participants did (2.3 vs. 3.4; $F(1,5)=12.3$, $p=0.017$, with Group as a random factor). Asked to rate whether they thought the trainee will be a successful sales professional, remote participants gave significantly lower rating than co-located participants (M=3.0 vs. 5.1; $F(1,5)=12.00$, $p=0.018$, with Group as a random factor). In their post-study interview, a remote participants in the *Static* condition stated *"I was able to observe more objectively maybe, listen to what they're saying."* We saw no significant difference in ratings of the presentation and presenter between the remote conditions and there was no significant difference between remote participants in the Kinetic and Static conditions.

Talk and Overlapping Talk

Next, we wanted to explore whether the use of the embodied device would produce communication style more similar to face-to-face communication. We used recorded video and audio to code the start and end times of participants' speech. We also coded for overlapping talk (i.e., whether a participant started speaking over a participant that was already speaking [26]). To investigate group turn-taking and overlapping talk absent the presenter's (confederate) influence, we focus our analysis on the Discussion phase (during which, the presenter was not in the room).

Turn-Taking

Analysis of turns taken per minute showed no significant difference across conditions (Kinetic M=1.65, SD=0.93, Static M=1.51, SD=0.76, and F2F M=2.11, SD=1.04). Turn *length* showed a marginal difference across conditions; turn length was greater on average in the Static condition (15.5s, SD=19.41) compared to F2F (11.8s, SD=11.78) and Kinetic conditions (11.7s, SD=14.10; $F(2,410)=2.693$, p=0.07). Comparing length of turns taken by *remote* participants showed only a marginally significant difference between conditions (Bonferroni correction, with $\alpha=0.017$), with Kinetic participants taking shorter turns than Static participants (8.5s vs. 20.2s; $t(50)=2.078$, $p=0.043$).

Overlapping Talk

Overlapping talk—when *"more persons than one talk at once"*—is a natural component of turn-taking in conversation [26, 27]. Prior literature found overlapping

	Static	Kinetic	F2F	*p*
Turns per minute	1.51	1.65	2.11	.367
Turn length	15.5s	11.7s	11.8s	.07
Turn length (by remote participants)	20.2s	8.5s		.043*
Overlapping talk	40.3%	48.3%	52.9%	.638
Overlapping talk (local over remote)	18.4%	50.0%		.017**
Overlapping talk (remote over local)	13.5%	7.5%		.625

Table 1. Rates of Talk and Overlapping Talk (α=0.017)

talk in natural face-to-face conversations in over 40% of turns (*c.f.* [11, 16, 30]). Computer-mediated meetings have been shown to contain less overlapping talk than collocated meetings [28].

In our data, the rate of overlapping talk was high (47.8%, SD=13.8) and there was no main effect of condition. However, looking specifically at the involvement of remote participants in overlapping talk uncovered interesting results: local participants were *three times more likely* to interrupt a remote participant in the Kinetic condition (at 50%, similar to the rate of overlapping talk in the F2F condition) than to interrupt a remote participant in the Static condition (where only 18% of turns were interrupted by a local participant). This difference, with Bonferroni connection, is significant ($t(4)$=7.47, p=0.017).

On the other hand, there was no significant difference when the remote participant was the one interrupting (7.5% and 13.5% for the Kinetic and Static conditions, respectively; t(4)=1.573, p=0.625).

Manipulating the Remote View

The ability of a remote participant to adjust their point-of-view (POV) was a key difference between the Kinetic and Static conditions. Unlike in [30], where a confederate operated the embodied proxy, our study allowed participants to use this capability as their own discretion.

Thus, we felt it was interesting to look at when this ability was used and for what purpose. Further we wanted to understand if there was contrasting behavior the Static condition when the capability was unavailable.

Through examination of recorded video, we saw that remote participants exhibited varying degrees of use. While one remote participant changed their POV only twice: at the beginning of the Discussion phase, and at the beginning of the Feedback phase, another remote participant adjusted their POV 22 times in a 40-minute session. (The remaining remote participant changed their POV 6 times in that group's 30-minute session.)

As expected, a large portion (43%) of all changes in POV were made to be able to see the person(s) speaking (since co-located participants rarely moved, orienting the POV to the person speaking was relatively easy). Another trigger to change the POV was when the focus of attention of the co-located participants has shifted. This included non-verbal shift – e.g., when co-located participants look towards the presenter who's returned to the room for the Feedback session – or when the subject of the conversation was out of view – e.g., when features of the printer were discussed. Finally, in two cases, changing POV was also used to visually track a local participant moving around the room (e.g., to inspect the printer).

At the end of the Presentation phase, participants were told that they should feel free to move around or turn the screen around. However, unlike the Kinetic condition, remote participants in the Static condition could not adjust their POV. As stated by one of the participants "*they can hear me, they can see me, but I could only see [one of the local participants]* ***or*** *[the presenter].*" Thus, these participants had to rely on co-located group members to change their POV. Through examination of recorded video we observed that in all groups in the Static condition, co-located users manually adjusted the display and camera of the remote participant to afford them a better view of the participants (Discussion phase) or presenter (Feedback phase). In fact, one of the Static groups deliberately asked the presenter to sit at a seat at the opposite end from the remote participant for the Feedback phase, such that participants and presenter could be in view. These observations are important as they highlight the groups' need for adjusting the remote person's POV as meeting circumstances change. This supports findings from [35], that local participants moved the embodied remote participant to foster inclusion in the group. Interestingly, manually adjusting a remote person's POV was sometimes accompanied with a statement such as "*We're going to move you now*" (local participant to remote participant).

DISCUSSION

Our study compared an embodied technology against both a non-embodied technology *and* a baseline face-to-face, all co-located group configuration. Our results highlight a likely understood, but not often discussed assessment of the state-of-the-art; despite many advantages, embodied technologies still exhibit many of the known negative effects introduced by a mediated communication channel. Remote participants (in both conditions) contributed less, rated the experience poorer, and generally felt less connected than their co-located peers. Further, these negative findings were not significantly different between the two remote conditions. This suggests that the affordances of the kinetic embodiment are unable to fully overcome the negative impacts of the mediated channel.

In [30] a confederate was used as the operator of a proxy when studying the impact of different forms of kinetic motion, while in [22] a confederate was used as the local participant. In contrast, our study used both local and remote participants. Our observations suggest that, when the use of the kinetic capability is left up to a participant, one will observe a wide range of usages of the medium.

Prior work (e.g. [35]) showed that in addition to improved group collaborations, embodied technologies facilitated social integration and team building over time. Our study, by contrast, used participants who did not know one another, and yielded several different findings. While work team members in the real world are likely to be familiar with one another, the difference in findings suggests that embodied technologies may not directly impact group collaboration, but the stronger social connections fostered by the technology are what direct impacts collaboration quality. This consideration certainly needs further exploration. However, if true, it has strong implications for the use of these technologies. Specifically, loosely affiliated or one time groups (e.g. a product evaluation panel demonstrated in our study) may not be the ideal user population of embodied technologies.

While we did not find many differences between the Kinetic and Static conditions with respect to perceptions of group performance, we did find several interesting nuanced differences. It was particularly interesting to examine how and why the remote participant adjusted their point of view (POV), contrasted with reliance on local participants in the Static condition. Kinetic remote participants used and appreciated the capability – it assisted in focusing conversation and conveyance of visual attention. Local participants appreciated the impact on group dynamic as well. One local participant noted, *"to use this [referring to the embodied device] in a group setting, for meetings like this, that's great that he can, you know, move around and see everyone."* In comparison, the Static condition placed a burden on local participants, and as local participants explained, the *"[she] was so far away"* and *"[he] only had one point of view."* In contrast to prior findings [24], the differences in behavior and perception we observed suggests that for larger, unbalanced teams relying on local teammates to adjust the POV might not support equitable group interaction.

A particularly interesting difference was found in turn-taking behavior between Kinetic and Static remote participants. Kinetic remote participants' turn-taking behavior more closely matched that of their co-located counterparts. A difference was also found in the frequency of overlapping talk. Particularly, the rate of interruptions of remote participants by local participants in the Kinetic condition was similar to rates of interruption between participants in the co-located condition. This is in contrast to the Static condition where interruptions were far fewer.

These results suggest that the increased agency in the Kinetic condition led participants to interact with the remote person in a fashion more similar to their interaction with co-located participants - that is, interrupt them in the same way they would interrupt a person at the same table. Thus, Kinetic embodiments may have meaningful value in business and other professional meetings where participation equality is important to preserve. It is interesting to consider that the amount of overlapping talk generated by the remote participants themselves did not differ significantly between the Static and Kinetic conditions.

Finally, qualitative feedback in the post-study interviews also indicated a subtle shift in how the disadvantages of the mediated channel were perceived by local participants. In the Static condition, local participants were sympathetic to the remote participants. As one local participant put it, *"We could adjust to the situation. We can just jump in. He [remote participant] can't."* Another stated *"it's harder for the person on that end [remote participant] to get a good idea of what's really going on."*

This was in contrast to the Kinetic condition, where participants' feedback did not directly discount the affordances of the remote participant. For instance, one participant stated he *"...recognized there were three people here, he [remote participant] wasn't more or less included."* Another participant stated *"every time he [remote participant] had a question we would address him without any problem."* Some participants even attributed the reduced remote participation to the personality of the remote participant – *"he [remote participant] was more non talkative than he should have been. Which, of course, this would affect you interacting with anyone. So I don't think that this was the technology, just the person who is using it."* These observations may be early evidence of the embodied device's ability to support stronger social integration and team bonding that was previously discovered by [35].

Taken as a whole, our findings may provide broader insights into how embodied telepresence devices impact collaborators' *sense of presence* and ability to achieve *agency*. For instance, the shift in communication behavior that resembled the F2F teams could suggest that local participants perceived an increased sense of presence with remote participant. In contrast, our results also show that, despite an ability to adjust their point-of-view, remote participants in the Kinetic condition did not exhibit detectable behavior shifts, nor provide any qualitative feedback that would point to a change in presence or agency. Findings by Tang et al. [33], may explain that remote users' inability to view their own physical remote representation inhibited their sense of agency in the remote space. Indeed, the environment through which remote participants in both conditions experienced the remote space were nearly identical –as a video on the screen. We feel these findings push forward our understanding of the value and use of embodied telepresence devices, while also outlining the need for much deeper investigations. Based on the current results, we are particularly compelled to explore ways to provide a remote team member with a proper representation of their remote physical manifestation.

CONCLUSIONS AND FUTURE WORK

In this work, we compared basic video conferencing, emergent kinetic video-conferencing techniques, and face-to-face meetings. Our findings build upon previous research, showing the adverse impact of being remote on participation levels and perception of contribution. We also showed an interesting difference in overlapping speech between the conditions. We then showed the potential of kinetic embodied proxies to impact behaviors exhibited by local participants in video conferencing meetings.

Still, a better understanding is needed of the work tasks that benefit (or suffer) from use of kinetic telepresence, and the types of work teams for whom such proxies are most appropriate. As such, we plan to investigate the use of a proxy similar to Jarvis in across a variety of tasks and settings using methodology similar to ESP [35].

Lastly, a key limitation of telepresence proxies, such as the one used in this study and others (e.g., [1, 22, 30]) is that, while they create an embodiment of the remote person in the local space, the remote person still experiences the space the same way – as a video on the screen (albeit with an ability to adjust their POV). This is supported in part by our results that show difference in turn-taking behavior for local participants with an embodied device present, without a parallel effect on the remote participants.

In future work, we plan to explore mechanisms (such as a 3rd person view of their proxy) to provide the remote person a sense of their representation in the local space, and examine its effect on their sense of presence.

ACKNOWLEDGMENTS

We thank the talented and versatile Katherine Goldman, the actress who was the confederate used in our study. We also thank the FXPAL admins, Barbara Tanada and Yasuko Nishimoto, for assisting in scheduling and routing study participants.

REFERENCES

1. Adalgeirsson, S. O., & Breazeal, C. MeBot: a robotic platform for socially embodied presence. *In Proc. HRI 2010*. IEEE Press (2010), 15-22.
2. AnyBots. http://www.anybots.com.
3. Beam. https://www.suitabletech.com/beam/
4. Bos, N., Shami, N. S., Olson, J. S., Cheshin, A., and Nan, N. In-group/out-group effects in distributed teams: an experimental simulation. *In Proc. CHI 2004*. ACM Press (2004), 429-436.
5. Carroll, J., Rosson, M.B. and Zhou, J. Collective efficacy as a measure of community. *In Proc. CHI 2005*. ACM Press (2005), 1–10.
6. Dourish, P., and Bly, S. Portholes: Supporting Awareness in a Distributed Group. *In Proc. CHI 1992*, ACM Press (1992), 541-547.
7. Erickson, T., and Kellogg, W.A. Social Translucence: An approach to designing a system that supports social processes. *ACM TOCHI*, 7,1 (2000), 59-83.
8. Fish, R., Kraut, R., Root, R., and Rice, R. Evaluating video as a technology for informal communication. *In Proc. CHI 1992*, ACM Press (1992), 37-48.
9. Fogarty, J., Lai, J., and Christensen, J. Presence versus availability: the design and evaluation of a context-aware communication client. *IJHCS*, 61 (2004), 299-317.
10. Fussell, S.R. Kraut, R.E. and Siegel, J. Coordination of communication: effects of shared visual context on collaborative work. *In Proc. CSCW 2000*. ACM Press (2000), 21-30.
11. Heldner, M., & Edlund, J. Pauses, gaps and overlaps in conversations. *Phonetics*, 38(4), (2010), 555-568.
12. Henry, K.B., Arrow, H. and Carini, B. (1999) A tripartite model of group identity. *Small Group Research*, 30, 5 (1999), 558–581.
13. Herrera, G., Jordan, R., & Vera, L. Agency and presence: a common dependence on subjectivity?. *Presence*, 15(5), (2006), 539-552.
14. ITB Library. *ITB world trends report 2013*. http://www.itb-berlin.de/media/itbk/itbk_media/itbk_pdf/WTTR_Report_2013_web.pdf (2013).
15. Kubi. http://www.kubi.me.
16. Kurtić, E., Brown, G. J., & Wells, B. Resources for turn competition in overlapping talk. *Speech Communication*, 55(5), (2013), 721-743.
17. Kwoh, L, and Kornat, M. *CEOs fly coach? Business travel turns frugal*. http://online.wsj.com/news/articles/SB10001424127887323511804578300181289786570 (2013).
18. McEwan, G., and Greenberg, S. Supporting social worlds with the community bar. *In Proc. GROUP* 2005, ACM Press (2005), 21-30.
19. Nowak, K. L., & Biocca, F. The effect of the agency and anthropomorphism on users' sense of telepresence, copresence, and social presence in virtual environments. *Presence: Teleoperators and Virtual Environments*, 12(5), (2003), 481-494.
20. Paulos, E., and Canny, J. PRoP: personal roving presence. *In Proc. CHI 1998*. ACM Press (1998), 296-303.
21. Perugini, N., Gallucci, M., Presaghi, F., and Ercolani, A.P. The personal norm of reciprocity. *European Journal of Personality*, 17, 4 (2002), 251–283.
22. Rae, I., Mutlu, B., and Takayama, L. Bodies in Motion: Mobility, presence, and task awareness in telepresence. *In Proc. CHI 2014*. ACM Press (2014), 2153-2162.
23. Rae, I., Takayama, L., and Mutlu, B. One of the gang: Supporting in-group behavior for embodied mediated communication. *In Proc. CHI 2012*. ACM Press (2012), 3091-3100.
24. Rae, I., Takayama, L. and Mutlu, B. In-body experiences: Embodiment, control, and trust in robot-mediated communication. *In Proc. CHI 2013*. ACM Press (2013), 1921-1930.
25. Redshift Research. *Global View: Business Video Conferencing Usage and Trends*. (2014) http://www.polycom.com/company/news/press-releases/2014/20140318.html
26. Sacks, H., Schegloff, E. A., & Jefferson, G. A simplest systematics for the organization of turn-taking for conversation. *Language*, 50(4), (1974), 696-735.
27. Schegloff, E.A., Overlapping talk and the organization of turn-taking for conversation. *Language in Society*, 29, Cambridge Press (2000), 1-63.
28. Sellen, A. J. Speech patterns in video-mediated conversations. *In Proc. CHI 1992*. ACM Press (1992), 49-59.

29. Sheridan, T. B. Further musings on the psychophysics of presence. In *Proc. IEEE Systems, Man, and Cybernetics*. (1994), 1073-1077.
30. Shriberg, E., Stolcke, A., & Baron, D. Observations on overlap: findings and implications for automatic processing of multi-party conversation. In *Proc. INTERSPEECH 2001*, IFIP (2001), 1359-1362.
31. Sirkin, D., Venolia, G. Tang, J.C., Robertson, G.G., Kim, T., Inkpen, K., Sedlins, M., Lee, B., and Sinclair, M. Motion and attention in a kinetic videoconferencing proxy. *In Proc. INTERACT 2011*. IFIP (2011), 162-180.
32. Stofega, W. *Seeing is believing: The value of video collaboration.* Technical Report, International Data Corporation (2007).
33. Tang, A., Biocca, F., & Lim, L. Comparing differences in presence during social interaction in augmented reality versus virtual reality environments: An exploratory study. *In Proc. Presence 2004*, (2004), 204-208.
34. Tang, J., Yankelovich, N., Begole, J., Kleek, M., Li, F., and Bhalodia, J. ConNexus to awarenex: extending awareness to mobile users. *In Proc. CHI 2001*, ACM Press (2001), 221-228.
35. Venolia, G., Tang, J., Cervantes, R., Bly, S., Robertson, G., Lee, B., and Inkpen, K. Embodied social proxy: mediated interpersonal connection in hub-and-satellite teams. *In Proc. CHI 2010*, ACM Press (2010), 1049-1058.
36. VGo. http://www.vgocom.com.
37. Vidyo. http://www.vidyo.com.
38. Voida, A., Bos, N.D., Olson, J.S., Olson, G.M. and Dunning, L. Cross-cutting faultlines of location and shared identity in the intergroup cooperation of partially distributed groups. *In Proc. CHI 2012*. ACM Press (2012), 3101-3110.
39. Whittaker, S., Frohlich, D., and Daly-Jones, O. Informal communication: what is it like and how might we support it? *In Proc. CHI 1994*, ACM Press (1994), 130-137.
40. Wiese, J., Biehl, J.T., Turner, T., van Melle, W., and Girgensohn, A. Beyond 'yesterday's tomorrow': towards the design of awareness technologies for the contemporary worker. *In Proc. MobileHCI 2011*. ACM Press (2011), 455-464.
41. Winston, A. *Will video conferencing kill business class travel?* http://blogs.hbr.org/2009/08/will-video-conferencing-kill-bisiness-class/ (2009).
42. Yankelovich, N., Simpson, N., Kaplan, J. and Provino, J. Porta-person: telepresence for the connected conference room. *Ext. Abstracts CHI 2007*, ACM Press (2007), 2789-2794.

Making Decisions From a Distance: The Impact of Technological Mediation on Riskiness and Dehumanization

Min Kyung Lee[1], Nathaniel Fruchter[1], Laura Dabbish[1,2]
[1]Human-Computer Interaction Institute, [2]Heinz College
Carnegie Mellon University
{mklee, fruchter, dabbish}@cmu.edu

ABSTRACT
Telepresence means business people can make deals in other countries, doctors can give remote medical advice, and soldiers can rescue someone from thousands of miles away. When interaction is mediated, people are removed from and lack context about the person they are making decisions about. In this paper, we explore the impact of technological mediation on risk and dehumanization in decision-making. We conducted a laboratory experiment involving medical treatment decisions. The results suggest that technological mediation influences decision making, but its influence depends on an individual's self-construal: participants who saw themselves as defined through their relationships (interdependent self-construal) recommended riskier and more painful treatments in video conferencing than when face-to-face. We discuss implications of our results for theory and future research.

Author Keywords
Computer-mediated decision making; Teledecision; Risk-taking; Risk-preference; Dehumanization; Telemedicine; Telepresence; Decontextualized decision making.

ACM Classification Keywords
H.5.2 [Information Interfaces and Presentation]: User Interfaces - Interaction styles.

General Terms
Human Factors; Design.

INTRODUCTION
In many domains, people now use technology to work with remote others and make decisions about remote people or events. Physicians use telepresence systems to diagnose patients 3,000 miles away from their office [36]; soldiers use drones to rescue victims [67]; managers oversee remote workplaces using mobile telepresence robots [44]; surgeons use robotic surgical tools to operate on remote patients [36]; and a suite of experts provide advice to their clients over video [33]. How does technological mediation influence perceptions of, and decision-making about a remote target? Are people risk-seeking and more dehumanizing at a distance? Are certain people more risk seeking and dehumanizing at a distance than others?

While telepresence technologies support sharing and collaboration across geographical and temporal boundaries, decision makers are now decontextualized from their decision targets. Research in social psychology and decision science suggests that this mediation and de-contextualization could create distance in how decision makers construe, feel toward, and engage with remote people and events [45]. This perceived distance may be exacerbated by intrinsic differences among cultural dimensions, such as styles of self-construal [10] as previous work has shown that culture changes the nature of mediated communication [68, 77]. The change in perceived distance should ultimately impact the quality of the decision outcomes, yet their impacts are largely unknown.

Some researchers have begun to raise such concerns about the effects of mediation in areas as diverse as humanitarian work [21], medicine [30], and drone warfare [65]. Despite this attention, mediated and decontextualized decision-making on a remote decision target has not been a focus of previous studies in computer-supported collaborative work (CSCW), computer-mediated communication (CMC), and telepresence.

Research on CSCW and CMC has investigated the impact of mediating technologies on collaboration: interpersonal communication [40], impression formation [23, 72, 55], collaborative group decision-making [39, 49], collaborative work [52], knowledge sharing [15], distributed team collaboration [56] and awareness [18, 29], physical collaboration [24], and trust [8]. Research on telepresence has explored ways to measure [79] and improve [51] social presence of a remote person or situation, and improve teleoperators' navigation and control of the telepresence systems [61]. However, to our knowledge, little research has looked at how the quality of decisions about a remote person or event change through mediating technologies, with the exception of a study on job interviews and the hiring decision [70].

Our research takes a first step towards systematically understanding the impact of mediating technology on decision-making about remote decision targets. Although

CSCW '15, March 14 - 18 2015, Vancouver, BC, Canada

ACM 978-1-4503-2922-4/15/03...$15.00
http://dx.doi.org/10.1145/2675133.2675288

there is a wide range of possible remote decision tasks and there are many types of decisions that can be made through mediating technology, we first focus on risk and dehumanization in medical decision-making. The area of medical decision-making is especially relevant as it is one of the most prominent areas where mediating technologies are starting to be implemented and used widely [36]. Additionally, medical decision tasks are often used to test the decision-making behaviors of both everyday people and medical experts [62]. We conducted a laboratory experiment where a participant made treatment recommendations to another participant (a confederate), either face-to-face or through video conferencing. We examined the influence of mediation on risk and dehumanization in the decisions made.

In this paper, we make three contributions. First, we offer a theoretical framework explaining how technological mediation may influence decision-making. Our framework draws from the social psychology, decision science, CSCW, and CMC literature. Second, we experimentally demonstrate that technological mediation can significantly influence important decision-making outcomes, and that this influence is dependent on one's cultural self-construal. Finally, we consider implications of our results and research insights to help frame future work in this critical, yet unexplored area.

MEDIATION, DISTANCE & DECISION-MAKING

We investigate the following research question about the impact of technological mediation on decision-making:

- How does technological mediation influence different types of distances and decisions?

Drawing from the literature in social psychology, decision science, CSCW and CMC, we elucidate three interconnected ways that mediating technologies increase distance between decision-makers and decision targets. We explain how this distance can influence the riskiness and dehumanization inherent in a decision context (Figure 1). We then consider how an individual's self-construal could moderate technology's influence on decision-making.

Among different qualities of decision outcomes, we first focus on risk preferences and the dehumanizing tendencies of decision-making. Risk preference, or a decision maker's willingness to accept risk for a certain decision outcome, is a classic concept in decision science with relevance to many tasks and lines of work [46]. Dehumanization, the perception or representation of others as "animal-like" or "less human", is a similarly important concept in the realm of social psychology. Dehumanization occurs when out-group members are perceived as fundamentally different and even inferior to a perceiver's in-group [31].

Construal Level Distance

An event, person, or object is said to be psychologically distant when it is not present in one's direct experience [45]. A framework grounded in psychological distance, construal-level theory suggests a decision maker's distance from a decision target – whether it is spatial, temporal, or social – leads to a higher, more abstract construal level representation of the decision target (for a review, see [73]). Psychological distance research has shown that greater distance can influence many different facets of decision-making such as self-control, willpower, negotiation behavior, and ethical decision-making.

We posit that mediating technologies could increase the psychological distance of decision makers from remote decision targets. Geographical distance, inherent in working through technology with someone in a different place, can influence decision-makers to construe another person more abstractly. In fact, a study by Bradner and Mark demonstrated that increasing perceived distance of a collaborator decreased cooperation and trust [9]. In addition, mediating technologies reduce contextual information and social cues about the remote decision target [15], which in turn may lead to less concrete mental representations of a decision target.

Promotion Focus and Risk-Taking

If mediating technologies increase decision makers' psychological distance from a remote decision target, they can influence decision-makers to make riskier decisions. Research has shown that psychological distance – either temporal [58] or social [59] – influences regulatory focus: a promotion focus that involves sensitivity to *positive* outcomes (i.e., a half-filled glass) or a prevention focus that involves sensitivity to *negative* outcomes (i.e., a half-empty glass).

Greater psychological distance elicits abstract representations of an event (such as a goal or desirability) whereas lesser distance elicits more concrete, task-specific representations (such as a method or feasibility). For example, in a study by Sagristano et al., people made riskier gambling decisions when gameplay was to take place two months later instead of at the time of the choice [66]. They explain that with greater temporal distance, the "desirability" (higher payoff) of the choice is highlighted over the "feasibility" (low probability) of the choice. According to construal-level theory, which suggests that temporal and spatial distance could work interchangeably, we posit that decision-makers may make a risker treatment decision about the remote decision target when video conferencing, as compared to face-to-face.

Psychological Distance and Dehumanization

Increased psychological distance may also lead to dehumanized decision-making. Previous research suggests that people tend to dehumanize others when they have greater social distance, such as out-group members [32]. For example, Lammers demonstrated that people who imagined themselves in more powerful positions (e.g., senior surgeon) became less sensitive to others' pain and recommended more painful and effective treatments, compared to those who imagined themselves in less powerful positions (e.g., nurse) [42]. This research suggests that decision-makers may make a more dehumanizing decision via video conferencing, compared to face-to-face.

Experiential Level Distance

In addition to their influence on mental representations of the decision target, mediating technologies could also create experiential distance from a remote decision target – that is, how immersed and engaged decision makers are in the experience of communicating with another person. Previous research suggests that mediated communication is inherently less engaging, physically, cognitively, and emotionally than face-to-face communication [57]. The previous work in the following sections suggests that this increased experiential distance can elicit both more or less risky and dehumanizing decisions.

Salience Change of Decision Attributes

Mediating technologies can impact what attributes of a remote decision target become salient to decision-makers. In mediated communication, information that conveys social presence – social cues and non-verbal gestures – is significantly limited whereas the delivery of factual information is less impacted [12, 56]. This difference in information quality might make factual information more salient than social presence in mediated communication. Along with increased salience of factual information, reduced social presence may influence people to make riskier and more dehumanizing decisions for others.

Research on the role of affect in decision-making (e.g., Lowenstein's "risk as feelings" [46]) suggests that risk preferences and tendencies towards loss aversion can depend on individual perceptions of risk. The relative salience of factual information in mediated communication may reduce the vividness of the decision target's feeling toward the risk, thus eliciting a riskier decision. In the same way, people may put more weight on factual, quantitative information and put less weight on social considerations (such as pain that the decision target would experience) in mediated communication. In fact, it has been shown that people make more rational choices when making a decision for others as, when thinking about others, perceived risk can be less vivid than the feelings of risk evoked when making decisions for one's self [37, 81].

We posit that in mediated communication, people will put more weight on factual, probability-based information and put less weight on social consideration, whereas when face-to-face, they will put similar weight on both risk neutrality and how their decision target would feel about the risk.

Stress

According to Porcelli [60], when people are under stress, they make more conservative betting choices for gains. Stress interferes with people's rational, deliberate thought processes resulting in more intuitive and automatic thought processes that are susceptible to loss-aversion biases [38]. Previous research suggests that face-to-face communication can be more cognitively taxing [57], thereby increasing stress and leading people to minimize risk in their decisions.

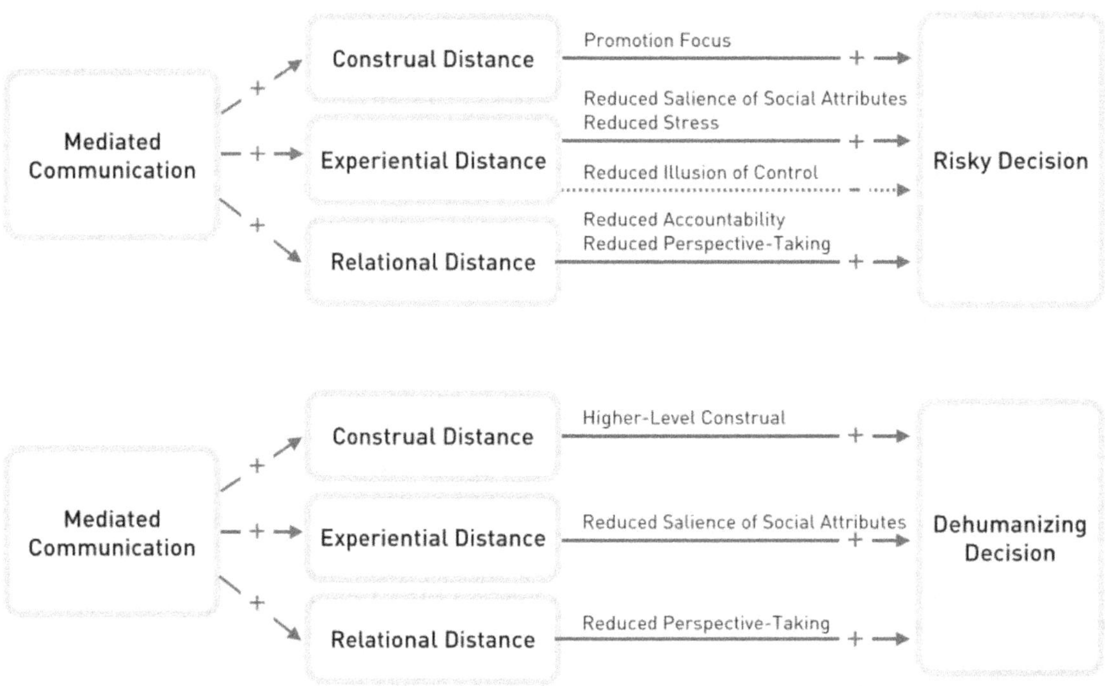

Figure 1. A conceptual model that shows how mediated communication may influence three types of distances, and in turn yield different types of risky and dehumanizing decisions.

Reduced Illusion of Control

On the other hand, mediating technologies may lead to a less risky decision. Previous research suggests that people feel "the illusion of control" [43] over objects or events when they are co-located. Similarly, being co-located with another person is correlated with greater interpersonal control (e.g., greater persuasion and cooperation) compared to talking via voice or another medium [50]. This suggests that people may make a riskier choice when talking face-to-face than when video conferencing, as they feel that they have greater control over the co-located person or situation, and perceive the risky choice's chance of success as higher. In fact, Goh et al.'s study shows that people gave higher bets on a physical roulette wheel when in the room with it compared to when they saw the wheel over video conference [25].

Relational Level Distance

The reduced bandwidth of mediating technologies may also decrease the relational connection that decision-makers feel towards the remote decision target. Previous research on CMC suggests that during their first encounter, people communicating face-to-face form more positive impressions about their conversational partners than those video conferencing [55, 23]. This reduced relational closeness could also influence the decision-maker to make a riskier and dehumanized decision about the decision target.

Reduced Accountability

Reduced closeness may influence decision makers to feel less accountable about their decisions. Previous research investigating decision making differences in a self-other paradigm suggests that people make less risky financial and monetary decisions for others, as they feel more responsible for the decision that they make [76, 63]. This suggests that a potential decrease in accountability can lead to riskier decisions.

Less Perspective Taking

Reduced closeness can also result in less effort in perspective taking [11]. That is, decision-makers may make a riskier decision as they base their decision on their own perspective (self) rather than their decision targets' perspectives (others). Reduced relational closeness may also induce more mechanistic dehumanization (i.e., perceiving other people as devoid of the capability of feeling emotion), which can result in a more dehumanized decision.

Interdependent and Independent Self-Construals

We posit that whether mediating technologies increase distance may depend on an individual's cultural self-construal, or the way they perceive and define their identity as interdependent or independent (Figure 2). People with more interdependent self-construals define themselves through their relationships with others, while people with independent self-construals define themselves through their individual achievements and personal attributes [10, 48]. Research on social cognition and psychology suggests that this self-construal influences cognitive and social information processing. People with interdependent self-construals are more sensitive to others' emotions, social cues and social presence, and base their judgment both on these social cues and their internal states. On the other hand, people with independent self-construals are less sensitive to others' emotion and put more weight on their internal states in making decisions [10, 48]. This suggests individuals with interdependent self-construal may be more sensitive to reduced social cues caused by technological mediation.

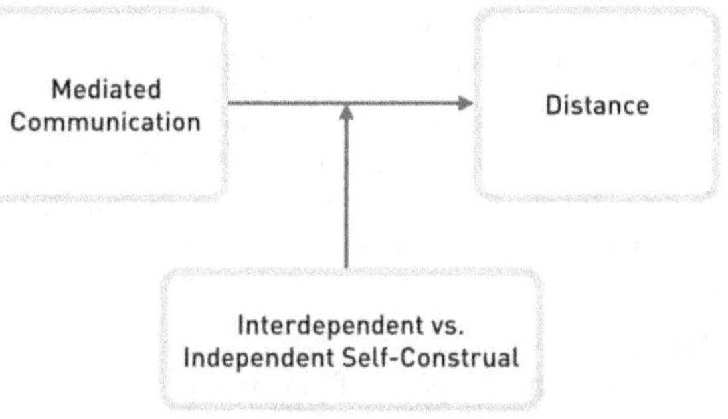

Figure 2. Interdependent versus independent self-construal may influence whether mediating technology creates distance from a remote decision target.

A growing body of research on cultural differences in the use of CMC also lends support for this prediction. For example, Wang, Fussell & Setlock found that Chinese participants, associated with highly interdependent self-construals, were significantly less engaged (i.e., made fewer attempts to understand the other) when using text-based chat when compared to face-to-face communication. However, American participants' engagement did not differ across mediums [68]. There is evidence that people with interdependent self-construals rely more on contextual information during communication than people with independent self-construals [77].

No Increase in Distance with Technological Mediation

Despite the above-mentioned reasons why mediating technologies may increase decision makers' distance from a decision target, recent mediating technologies with high communication bandwidth such as video-conferencing or telepresence robots may not influence distance from the decision target and qualities of decision-making. Even though the decision targets are geographically distant from the decision-makers, a high quality live video-feed of the decision target may create experiences realistic enough that decision-makers may feel like *being there*.

Most research on psychological distance has been conducted using textual scenarios (e.g., asking people to think about a person in the same city versus in a distant city). Recent research, however, suggests that an engaging experience can compensate for physical distance. In a study conducted by Ebert & Myvis, when a description of a temporally distant event was very engaging, the engagement eliminated the effect of temporal distance, making people construe the story in a low-level, concrete way [20]. Similar phenomena may be at work when interacting through higher-bandwidth communication media, possibly cancelling out any psychological distance caused by differences in location.

In order to better understand these variables, we empirically investigate the impact of mediating technology on the decision makers' distance from the decision targets, and its impact on the riskiness and dehumanization of their decision-making.

METHODS

To measure the impact of mediating technologies on decision-making, we conducted a between-subjects laboratory experiment where a participant was asked to give advice to another participant (confederate) on health issues. Participants were told that the aim of the study was to learn how people give advice to other people to inform the design of a virtual health advisor. The participants were randomly assigned to talk with another participant either face-to-face or through video conferencing (Figure 3). The experiment was approved by the Institutional Review Board in the university where this research was conducted.

Decision Tasks

In order to measure risk preferences and dehumanization, we adopted two medical decision-making tasks used in previous psychology and decision science research about the decision-making behaviors of lay people without medical expertise. One decision task involved a risky decision (deciding whether to add a medication with an 85% chance of success and 15% chance of failure) (see [62]) and the other involved a 'tough' decision with a pain-efficacy tradeoff (choosing between a painful, effective treatment and a painless, less effective treatment), as a lack of sensitivity to others' emotions is one indicator of dehumanization (see [42]).

Both tasks were presented as hypothetical, textual scenarios in previous research, so we adopted them to be conversational and suitable for our confederate's age. The confederate stated that she was encouraged to seek advice from others by their doctor and the experimenter emphasized that there were no right or wrong answers. The order of the tasks was counterbalanced. One confederate, an Indian American female in her early 20s, played the advisee role for all of the experiment's sessions.

Scenario Text

Introduction Ok. I've been dealing with many health issues lately, and have some tough decisions I need to make. My doctor told me that there's no right or wrong answer, so he recommended that I talk to many people for a second opinion. When I found about this study online, I thought that it would be a really good opportunity to do so. I was hoping you would give me some advice and help me make the decision. So I guess I'll just get started.

Abdominal Treatment Choice (adapted from [62]) Last month, I was diagnosed with an abnormality in my abdominal wall, and my doctor told me that this will cause problems in the long run even though I don't have any symptoms now. There are two different treatments available. The first treatment is painless but the abnormality has a chance of recurrence like 20-25%, so I may need another treatment if this happens. The second treatment is tougher and has almost 0 chance of recurrence, but the disadvantage is that anesthesia is impossible. So I would experience a lot of distress and pain. Which treatment would you recommend I choose?

Allergy Treatment Choice (adapted from [42]) Another question that I have is about a medication for my allergy. I developed a rare and serious allergy, which gave me painful headaches all the time. This made it really hard for me to study and sometimes I couldn't even carry out daily tasks. I started a treatment last month, and it worked, so I can have a normal life again. With this treatment, I am expected to not have any symptoms for the next 5 to 10 years. What is unknown about this treatment is whether the same treatment would work again after this first one loses its effect after 5 to 10 years. This means that there might not be anything that I can do at that point, and I would experience the symptoms again. My doctor told me that there is a medication that can be added to my treatment, which has been shown to work overall, although sometimes it makes things worse. With this medication, there is an 85% chance that I will gain 2 more symptom-free years, and a 15% chance that I will lose 2 symptom free-years. What do you think? Should I take this medication or not?

Participants

We recruited participants who resided in an east coast American city. Participants were recruited through a participant recruitment website managed by the university and through flyers posted on campus and around the city. Starting with 74 participants, we omitted those who reported being suspicious about the other participant (confederate) during the debriefing session and who responded incorrectly to our attention check. This left 46 participants (M age = 29.8 years, SD = 8.8, 52% female).

Participants had diverse ethnicities: there were 18 Caucasians, 18 Asians, 6 African Americans, 1 Pacific Islander, and 3 with mixed ethnicities. Participants' ethnicities and genders were equally distributed across categories of self-construal and conditions. 29 were native English speakers, and the remaining 17 non-native English speakers were fluent, having lived in the US for 10 years (SD = 16.9) on average. The participants reported using video conferencing once a month on average (M = 2.7, SD = 1.4; "Less than a month" = 2, "1-3 times a month" = 3).

Figure 3. Face-to-face condition (a) versus video conferencing condition (b).

Procedures

Participants were randomly assigned to either the face-to-face or video conferencing conditions. The procedure was adapted for each condition as described below to maintain realism.

Introduction and Cover Story

Following arrival at the lab space, participants were told that they were waiting on a second participant (the confederate) in order to enhance realism. In the face-to-face condition the other "participant" (the confederate) arrived in the lab a couple of minutes after the participant arrived. In the video conferencing condition, the experimenter called the confederate in front of the participant in order to "confirm their availability for participation."

In the face-to-face condition, participants were then seated across from each other at a table. In the video conferencing condition participants were seated in front of a computer with active video conferencing software. In the latter condition, the confederate was seated in front of a backdrop made to look like a house or dormitory room, as opposed to an academic building (see Figure 3). Additionally, both webcams were angled to show the participants' upper torsos.

After reviewing the consent form, participants were given a brief explanation of the study, expanding on the cover story of a "human conversation study." Participants were told that the other participant was recruited from local medical community boards by soliciting those who wanted to get health advice from non-experts. They were told that both participants were there to help with the creation of a "virtual conversational system with collective intelligence" and that the experimenters were "collecting types of health issues that people will ask other people about and the types of advice that people give."

Participants were then informed (or reminded, in the case of the confederate) of their roles in the experimental task. Real participants always took the role of *advisor* and the confederate was always the *advisee*. The experimenter explained that the advisee had been contacted prior to the experiment and told to "think about what they wanted to ask." To further reinforce this cover story, the confederate took out notes and was reminded to review them and make sure their options were presented in a two-choice format.

Experimental Task

Participants were given a "decision sheet" to record their answers to the advisee's questions and were told to note down several things: the advisee's question, the two choices the advisee offered, which choice the participant recommended, and any notes or follow-up questions they had for the advisee. (It was explained to both the advisor and advisee that follow-up questions needed to be limited and that responses should be recorded on the decision sheet as the dialogues needed to be "structured" for computer simulation.)

After explanation of the task concluded, participants were reminded that their interaction would be recorded and that they had ten minutes to complete the task. Participants were then told to find the experimenter in the lab waiting room when they finished the task or if they had questions.

Survey and Debrief

Once participants finished conversing, the experimenter re-entered the room. The advisor and advisee were then asked to complete the survey portion of the study (see *Measures*). In the face-to-face condition, advisors completed the survey on a computer in the same lab space and advisees were told to follow the experimenter out of the room to another computer. In the video conferencing condition, advisees were told that a survey link would be emailed to them. Advisees then disconnected from the videoconference and advisors completed the survey on the same computer they had used for videoconferencing. After completing the survey, advisees were asked for their opinions on the confederate and study, debriefed about the study goal study and the use of confederate, and compensated.

Participants in both conditions filled out the same survey. The video conferencing condition had two questions about where they thought the other participant was located during the videoconference, and in which city they thought the other participant lived. The survey included questions that measured participants' construal-level, experiential-level, and relational-level distances from the other participant (confederate), dehumanization of the other participant, individual differences, and demographics. One attention check was also included. All questions were presented using seven-point scales.

Interaction Recordings

We recorded participants' conversation using a digital camcorder set up in the room in both conditions. Screen recording software was used to record video-conferencing.

Measures

We used both behavioral and subjective measures to evaluate the influence of technological mediation.

Risky and Dehumanizing Decisions

To measure riskiness and dehumanizing aspects of decisions, we calculated the percentage of the participants who recommended the risky treatment (i.e., adding the risky medication) and the percentage of the participants who recommended the dehumanizing treatment (i.e., effective but painful treatment). As a subjective measure of dehumanization, the survey asked participants to rate how well a set of adjectives would describe the other participant they interacted with. Eight adjectives (e.g., ambitious, jealous) were used to measure "infrahumanization", or the denial of "uniquely human" qualities to out-groups [32, 14]. An additional four adjectives (cold, superficial, responsive, and sensitive) were used to measure "mechanistic dehumanization", the tendency to attribute cold, object-like characteristics to others [31].

Construal Level Distance
We adopted three measures to assess participants' construal level distance from their advisee, which have been commonly used in psychological distance research. People have been shown to describe another person more abstractly when they have greater psychological distance from them [22, 75]. Thus, four behavior identification questions from [22] asked participants to choose which activity description – abstract (e.g., getting organized) versus concrete (e.g., writing things down) – better described an imagined task being done by the advisee. Each abstract response was coded as 1 (versus 0), and responses were summed to calculate a score.

Greater psychological distance deemphasizes individual particularities and reinforces the belief that the individual will follow the average behavior of a group that the individual belongs to. Three questions adapted from Henderson et al. [34] asked participants to estimate the likelihood that their advisee will exhibit typical behaviors (e.g., "the likelihood that [the advisee] will spend more than 3.8 hours online when the average student spends 4.6 hours per day"), and the answers were averaged. Participants were also asked to describe the advisee. We analyzed the answers to count the prevalence of linguistic categories (such as the use of past tense, as well as more concrete and less tentative language) that suggest low-level construal using the LIWC software [71].

To check whether participants felt spatial distance with their advisee, we also asked how far the other participant seemed to the participant and how much geographical space there seemed to be between the participants and their advisee [34].

Relational Level Distance
We measured participants' relational level distance from their advisee using constructs such as liking, closeness, similarity, enjoyment, empathy, and care. The survey included questions about how much participants liked, identified with, and felt close and similar to their advisee, and a self-other inclusion question [4]. We used a 5-item empathy scale from Batson [5] to measure how participants felt while interacting with their advisee (α=0.86). We also asked how much they enjoyed the interaction overall. As a measure of care, we asked whether participants would share their email address with their advisees for a potential follow-up, and how willing they were to check on their advisee regarding the situation that she talked about.

We posited that relational level distance would influence how much the participants took the perspectives of their advisee and how accountable they felt about their advice. To this end, we included 2 items about perspective taking from [15] as well as a perceived accountability question.

Experiential Level Distance
To measure how engaged and immersed participants were in interacting with their advisee, we included four questions that assessed four aspects of engagement (e.g., "the interaction was very engaging") [47].

We theorized that stress felt during the interaction and perceived control over the advisee could influence decision-making. Thus, we asked how tense or relaxed and how comfortable participants felt during the interaction. To measure perceived control, we also asked how much influence participants felt like they had on the opinion of their advisee, and how likely it was that their advisee would follow their advice.

To check whether any differences in decision-making were due to cognitive effort as opposed to distance, we asked participants how much they concentrated on their advisee, how much effort they put into evaluating their situation, and how important they thought the situation was to their advisee.

Interdependent and Independent Self-Construal
The survey also measured individual differences in self-construal. To measure cultural self-construal, we included three items from the interdependent self-representation scale (e.g., "My happiness depends very much on the happiness of those around me"; α=0.70) and three items from independent self-representation scale ("I enjoy being unique and different from others in many ways"; α=0.76) [10]. We performed a median split on the independent self-representation scale such that half of the participants were coded as having a high independent self-construal and the remaining half were coded as having a low independent self-construal.

Individual Differences and Control Variables
We used scales from the International Personality Item Pool [26] to measure extroversion (α=0.81). We also included 5 items on dispositional empathy from Davis [15] in the survey (e.g., "I often have tender, concerned feelings for people less fortunate than me"; α=0.73). Finally, we asked whether the participants had personally encountered any of the situations that their advisee discussed.

Conversation and Eye-Gaze Analysis
We transcribed participants' speech to understand reasons the participants gave to support their treatment recommendations. The effectiveness and increased odds of success were given in support of risky and dehumanizing decisions. Less risky and dehumanizing decisions were supported with "wait and see" approaches. We also annotated video recordings using ELAN behavioral analysis software. Participants' head direction and eye direction were marked to understand how much time they spent looking at the other participant, the decision form, and other places in the room.

RESULTS
To analyze the impact of mediating technologies on decisions and cultural self-construal, we built a multi-level regression model. We included dispositional empathy traits and participants' presence of similar experience as control variables since low empathy (p = 0.05) and presence of similar experiences (p = 0.1) was correlated with higher levels of risk taking.

Effects of Mediation on Risky Decision Making

There were no main effects of communication medium on decision-making. Self-construal had a significant main effect (p = .03), and the interaction between self-construal and communication medium was also significant (F(5, 36) = 3.2, p = .02, interaction p=.03). Participants with interdependent self-construals were significantly more risky, with 100% recommending adding the risky medication when they consulted their advisee through video conferencing while only 66% recommended the risky medication face-to-face (F(1, 31) = 4.8, p = .04) (Figure 4). Participants with independent self-construal did not make different recommendations when face-to-face versus video conferencing (Independent face-to-face = 66%, Independent Video = 47%; F(1, 31) = 1, p = .3).

Effects of Mediation on Dehumanizing Decision Making

There were no main effects of communication medium or cultural self-construal on dehumanization, but the interaction effect was significant. Less than half of the participants with interdependent self-construal (44%) recommended the painful, effective treatment in face-to-face whereas most of them (91%) recommended the more dehumanizing painful, effective treatment in video conferencing (F(1, 34) = 5.6, p = .02). Most participants with independent self-construals recommended the painful, but more effective treatment regardless of the communication medium (Independent Face-to-face = 91%, Independent Video = 84%; F(1, 34) = 0.13, p = .7).

This difference in sensitivity to pain was not observed in dehumanization measures in the survey. While empathy strongly negatively correlated with all dehumanization measures, there were no difference in our measures of infrahumanization and mechanistic dehumanization.

Effects of Technological Mediation on Distance

The analysis of the survey measures suggests that the differences in the treatment choices of the participants with interdependent self-construals were driven by differences in experiential level distance.

Construal Level Distance

There were no effects of communication medium and cultural self-construal on the three measures of psychological distance in the survey: behavioral identification questions, predictability of behavior questions, and analysis of participant descriptions.

The analysis of perceived spatial distance questions suggests that technological mediation did not create substantial distance from the advisee. Participants in the video condition reported having equal geographical distance and feeling equally spatially close to their advisee as the participants in the face-to-face condition. As indicated in the survey responses, participants did not think that their advisee was far away as both were located in the same city. On the other hand, cultural self-construal had an impact on perceived spatial distance – participants with independent self-construal felt that there was less geographical distance (Independent M = 3.5, SE = .26; Interdependent M = 4.3, SE = .3; "A little space" = 3, "Some space" = 4; F(1, 40) = 4.79, p = .03), consistent with cultural differences in relational level distance which will be reported in the later part of the paper. There was no interaction effect of the medium and culture.

Experiential Level Distance

There were no main effects of communication medium or cultural self-construal on participants' engagement measures. However, there was a significant interaction between the two. Participants with interdependent self-construals reported less feelings and emotions for the advisee in video conferencing (M = 5, SE = .43) than in face-to-face (M = 6.48, SE = .5; F(1, 37) = 5.51, p = .02). Participants with independent self-construals reported similar feelings and emotions in both face-to-face (M = 6, SE = .43) and videoconferencing (M = 6.67, SE = .41).

This reduced social presence suggests that video conferencing attenuated the salience of social attributes of the decision for people with interdependent self-construals.

While participants felt that videoconferencing (M = 5.76, SE = .26) was marginally more relaxed than face-to-face (M =

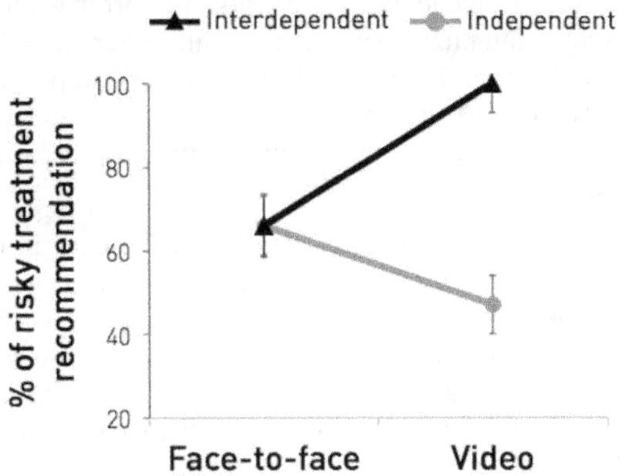

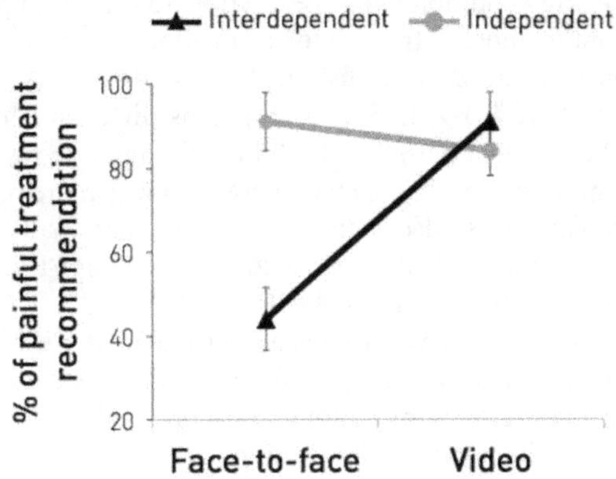

Figure 4. Participants with interdependent self-construal recommended riskier treatments in videoconferencing than face-to-face (a) and recommended less painful treatments in face-to-face than in videoconferencing (b).

5.18, SE = .29; F(1, 40) = 2.4, p = .1), and participants with independent self-construal felt the interaction was more comfortable (M = 6.3, SE = .24) than those with interdependent self-construal (M = 5.5, SE = .27; F(1, 40) = 5.7, p = .02), there was no interaction effect between the two. There were also no effects of communication medium or cultural self-construal on perceived control.

Relational Level Distance

There were no significant effects of communication medium and no interaction effect, but cultural self-construal had a significant main effect on most relational distance measures. Participants with independent self-construals were more likely to share their email address for a follow-up (Independent M = 1, SE = .06; Interdependent M = 0.8, SE = .07; F(1, 40) = 5.4, p = .03) and were marginally more willing to check on their advisee in the future (Independent M = 5.9, SE = .23; Interdependent M = 5.3, SE = .3; F(1, 40) = 3.2, p = .08). They also identified with (Independent M = 4.55, SE = .26; Interdependent M = 3.75, SE = .3; F(1, 40) = 4.2, p = .05) and liked their advisee more (Independent M = 5.57, SE = .2; Interdependent M = 4.9, SE = .23; F(1, 37) = 5.1, p = .03) and enjoyed the interaction marginally more (Independent M = 5.4, SE = .25; Interdependent M = 4.8, SE = 2.9; F(1, 40) = 2.75, p = .1). This result is consistent with previous research that suggests people with interdependent culture exhibit more hostile attitudes to out-group members and strangers [28].

Relational distance, however, did not influence how accountable they felt for their advice and how much they took the perspectives of their advisee. There were no significant main and interaction effects of communication medium or cultural self-construal on perceived accountability and perspective taking.

Cognitive Effort

Another factor that might have contributed to differences in people's treatment choices may be that people put less effort in making decisions about the remote advisee, which would result in cursory decisions. However, survey responses do not support this idea. In fact, participants in the video conferencing condition (M = 5.91, SE = .13) reported putting significantly more effort into evaluating their advisee's situation than those in the face to face condition (M = 5.51, SE = .15; F(1, 40) = 4.15, p = .05). This difference may be due to the fact that participants had more cognitive resources free for problem solving, as the interaction was more relaxed. The problem was also perceived to be marginally more important to the advisee over video conferencing (Face M = 5.92, SE = .2; Video M = 6.4, SE = .17; F(1, 37) = 3.49, p = .07), which may have influenced participants in the video-conferencing condition to put more effort. However, there were no main effects of cultural self-construal on cognitive effort and no interaction with medium.

Gaze Behavior

One reason why the participants with independent self-construal might have felt less emotion from the interaction might be the lack of gaze at their advisee. On average, participants interacted with their advisee for 7.7 minutes (SD = 2.3), looking at their advisee 55% of the time (SD = 17.8%) and looking at the decision form 43% of the time (SD = 18.3%). However, we found no significant differences in the percentage of time that participants spent looking at their advisee (either in person or on screen) or at their decision form, which suggests that the reduced engagement was not due to differences in gaze behavior.

DISCUSSION

This study examined the impact of mediating technologies and decision makers' cultural self-construals on riskiness and dehumanization in decision-making. Results suggest that participants with interdependent self-construals were influenced by technological mediation, recommending riskier and more painful treatments when video conferencing. On the other hand, participants with independent self-construals were not influenced by the medium. Our survey results suggest that experiential-level distance in mediated communication contributes to these differences. In the following section, we revisit the framework presented at the beginning of this paper to consider explanations for our results.

Effects of Mediation on Experiential Level Distance

Our results are best explained by the *salience change in decision attributes* hypothesis, with its interaction with cultural self-construal. This hypothesis suggests that the reduced bandwidth of mediating technologies influences the relative weights given to social and factual attributes of decisions, and this process is dependent on cultural self-construal.

Consistent with research on the differences in social-cognitive processing styles and types of self-construal, participants with interdependent self-construals were sensitive to the reduced bandwidth of mediating technologies. Despite spending equal amounts of time looking at their advisees and reporting equal (compared to participants with independent self-construal in the video conferencing condition) or more (compared to participants in the face-to-face condition) amounts of effort in evaluating the advisee's situation, participants with interdependent self-construals found interaction less engaging and perceived less emotion from their advisee when video conferencing. This suggests a decreased social and emotional presence of their advisee.

The attenuation of the advisee's social presence in the video conferencing condition may have influenced participants with interdependent self-construals to put more weight on factual information rather than social attributes of the decision. This reasoning supports the pattern of increased risk and dehumanization in treatment decisions made over video conferencing.

On the other hand, people with independent self-construals were not sensitive to the reduced bandwidth of mediating technologies and put equal weights on both social and factual attributes of decisions. A lack of difference in relational distance suggests that this process may be subconscious, and not the result of a judgment (e.g., a conscious dislike of the advisee.)

This result suggests that mediating technologies can influence the mindset or orientation people have when approaching and assessing situations and problems, leading people to differentially engage in social or utilitarian decision processes [6, 13, 19].

No Changes in Stress & Perceived Control

In our study, technological mediation did not influence decision makers' stress levels in interactions or perceived control of their decision target. This may be because our task involved low levels of stress and advice giving. Mediation may influence decisions differently in a higher-stress context because of associated stress-induced changes in perception and cognition. Results may vary in contexts involving physical objects, where illusion of control may be more of a factor.

No Effects of Mediation on Construal Level Distance

We did not observe any relationship between mediation and construal level distance between participants and their advisee. There are two possible explanations for this lack of relationship. First, as mentioned earlier, the vivid, interactive representation of a remote decision target in video conferencing may have overridden any changes in construal level distance, which occurs when people take an abstract view of their decision target.

Second, the location of our remote decision target may have been too close geographically to change construal level distance. Survey responses indicate that participants did not feel that they were farther away from their advisee in the video conferencing condition than in the face-to-face condition. We deliberately chose to tell our participants that the advisee was located in the same city as them in order to separate the effects of technological mediation from ones of spatial distance. On the other hand, most previous research on psychological distance has manipulated distance so that the decision target is in a distant location (e.g., a city 1,000 miles away), if not in another country. This suggests that, for a geographically distant decision target, the effects of distance may intensify as both experiential and conceptual level distance may be created. In other words, mediating technologies could lead decision makers to be more risk seeking and dehumanizing, regardless of decision makers' self-construal.

No Effects of Mediation on Relational Level Distance

In our study, mediating technologies did not increase relational distance between participants and the advisee. This is seemingly contrary to previous research where video conferencing led to poorer impressions of another party [23, 55]. We believe this discrepancy could be due to differences in experimental tasks.

Tasks in previous research on impression formation were primarily social – either getting to know each other [55] or playing a game without performance evaluation [23] – whereas the task in our study was more utilitarian and goal-directed. This suggests that in decision tasks where social interaction plays a greater role, differences could be accentuated, depending on the medium through which the decision is made.

LIMITATIONS

Like any study, the present study has several limitations. This was a laboratory study with a confederate and structured conversations. This format allowed us to study people's decision making in a systematic way with decision tasks used in previous research; however, further research in the real world, either with field studies or archival data is needed to examine whether the same bias occurs when people can converse freely. We also had a small set of participants, and the main effect of media may be present with a larger set of participants. Further research with a large-scale experiment or archival data analysis will shed more insights. Additionally, follow-up research should examine the effects of expertise. Expert knowledge and training may influence decision makers to behave differently, even if some experts like physicians are subject to cognitive and psychological biases in making treatment decisions [74]. Because we used a controlled experiment we investigated a limited set of variables. Our study only used one operationalization of risky and dehumanizing treatments, and did not explicitly evaluate the impact of other individual differences such as gender [17], race [3], or dyad demographics [80] that could have influenced the results. The influence of these and other individual differences are worth exploring in future research.

IMPLICATIONS

This study is one of the first that investigates how mediation influences decision making at a distance. It opens up new areas of research in CSCW and HCI, and offers implications for theory and future research.

Implications for Theory

Our study demonstrates that mediating technologies can influence people to make riskier and more dehumanizing decisions because they change the salience of decision attributes. This is particularly true for decision makers with interdependent self-construals. This finding contributes to the literature on CSCW, CMC, and intercultural studies.

The present study offers opportunities to expand existing theories of trust, awareness and collaboration in CSCW and CMC to new tasks and contexts. In our task, the relationship between two parties—decision maker and decision target—was asymmetric, involving different roles, statuses and levels of power. The majority of collaboration studies in CSCW investigate symmetric relationships. Our results suggest that mediation may influence well-studied aspects of interaction in unexpected ways during asymmetric relationships. In particular decision makers may take social information into account less at a distance, and this may be true particularly for individuals with interdependent self-construals. As asymmetric relationships and interactions become more common we will need to update our existing theories of social outcomes such as trust development or awareness at a distance.

Our study offers initial evidence that mediating technologies may influence the mindset, schema or orientation that people bring to the table when making decisions. The mindset concept has been applied in CSCW in a limited way. Previous research has shown that mindsets or schemas have profound impacts on how people behave and interpret situations [1, 19].

Finally, this study provides evidence that culture can significantly influence the nature and effectiveness of mediated decision-making, adding to the growing literature on intercultural studies in CSCW and CMC. Additionally, our results highlight the importance of examining individual-level cultural differences, in addition to more commonly studied nationality-based cultural differences. Individual-level cultural differences offer a complementary analytic lens as previous research suggests that individual and nationality-based cultural differences are not always correlated.

Future Research Directions

Further research can untangle what aspects of reduced social cues influence the sensitivity of people with interdependent self-construal in their perception of social presence. Investigating other mediating technologies with varying communication bandwidth – such as text, voice, video, telepresence robots, and VR glass – can also help us unpack the impact of technology on risky and dehumanizing decision-making.

More broadly, the present research points to a critical, yet unexplored area of mediated decision-making on remote decision targets. Our study covers just one dimension, one task, and one stakeholder in this area. There are many other important decision dimensions such as liability, accountability, ethics, morality, as well as the effects of biases documented in the decision science and psychology literature. In addition to making decisions for others, people also enact or make judgments about remote objects, persons, and events through mediating technologies. Empirically investigating how mediation changes (or does not change) these decisions and actions is a very important line of research. We believe the frameworks explained in this paper can help devise hypotheses for these areas.

Another important line of research is the design of interventions that optimize mediated decision contexts for various problems and situations. For example, how can we design novel telepresence systems to elicit the right combination of weights on social versus factual attributes to yield an optimal decision outcome? Simply zooming in on the face of a remote person could increase their social presence for people with interdependent self-construals. On the other hand, presenting information about the decision (such as a medical chart or interaction history) next to a video conferencing screen may reinforce people to put more weight on factual information. Systematically investigating this design space is an important area for future research.

CONCLUSIONS

Mediating technologies support sharing and collaboration in many important sectors such as business, healthcare, policy, defense, education and manufacturing, removing decision makers from the person and event that they are making decisions about. Drawing from the literature on social psychology, decision-making, and CSCW, we provide an early theoretical framework that explains how distance created by mediating technologies can influence decision makers to make riskier or more dehumanizing decisions on remote decision targets. To test our model, we conducted a laboratory experiment where participants recommended risky and dehumanizing treatment decisions to an advisee, either face-to-face or via video conferencing. Results suggest that participants with interdependent self-construals made riskier and more painful treatment decisions when videoconferencing. They were less engaged and felt less emotion from their advisee, which may have influenced them to put more weight on factual, probability-based information while video conferencing. Our results begin to illuminate a critical, but unexplored research area of mediated decision-making. We hope that this research can inform future designs in order to improve decisions and decision outcomes.

ACKNOLWEDGEMENTS

This research was supported by NSF grants CNS-1205539 and ACI-1322278. We thank Sonal Chakrasali, Justina Eng, and Susanna Park for helping us conduct the experiments and George Loewenstein for pointing us to the paper [62].

REFERENCES

1. Abelson, R. P. (1981). Psychological status of the script concept. *American Psychologist, 36*(7), 715.
2. Ackerman, M. S. (1998). Augmenting organizational memory: A field study of answer garden. *ACM Transactions on Information Systems (TOIS)*, *16*(3), 203–224.
3. Ainscough, T. L., & Motley, C. M. (2000). Will you help me please? The effects of race, gender and manner of dress on retail service. *Marketing Letters, 11*(2), 129-136.
4. Aron, A., Aron, E. N., & Smollan, D. (1992). Inclusion of other in the self scale and the structure of interpersonal closeness. *Journal of Personality and Social Psychology*, *63*(4), 596-612.
5. Batson, C. D., Polycarpou, M. P., Harmon-Jones, E., Imhoff, H. J., Mitchener, E. C., Bednar, L. L., Klein, T. R., & Highberger, L. (1997). Empathy and attitudes: Can feeling for a member of a stigmatized group improve feelings toward the group. *Journal of Personality and Social Psychology*, *72*(1), 105–118.

6. Bhanji, J. P., & Beer, J. S. (2012). Taking a different perspective: Mindset influences neural regions that represent value and choice. *Social Cognitive and Affective Neuroscience, 7*(7), 782-793.
7. Blais, A., & Weber, E. U. (2006). A domain-specific risk-taking (DOSPERT) scale for adult populations. *Judgment and Decision Making*, *1*(1), 33–47.
8. Bos, N., Olson, J., Gergle, D., Olson, G., & Wright, Z. (2002). Effects of four computer-mediated communications channels on trust development. In *Proc. of CHI'02,* 135–140.
9. Bradner, E., & Mark, G. (2002). Why distance matters: Effects on cooperation, persuasion and deception. In *Proc. of CSCW'02*, 226–235.
10. Brewer, M. B., & Chen, Y. R. (2007). Where (who) are collectives in collectivism? Toward conceptual clarification of individualism and collectivism. *Psychological Review*, *114*(1), 133-151.
11. Cialdini, R. B., Brown, S. L., Lewis, B. P., Luce, C., & Neuberg, S. L. (1997). Reinterpreting the empathy–altruism relationship: When one into one equals oneness. *Journal of Personality and Social Psychology*, *73*(3), 481-494.
12. Clark, H. H., & Brennan, S. E. (1991). Grounding in communication. *Perspectives on socially shared cognition, 13*, 127-149.
13. Costa, A., Foucart, A., Hayakawa, S., Aparici, M., Apesteguia, J., Heafner, J., & Keysar, B. (2014). Your morals depend on language. *PloS one, 9*(4), e94842.
14. Costello, K., & Hodson, G. (2010). Exploring the roots of dehumanization: The role of animal—human similarity in promoting immigrant humanization. *Group Processes & Intergroup Relations*, *13*(1), 3-22.
15. Cramton, C. D. (2001). The mutual knowledge problem and its consequences for dispersed collaboration. *Organization Science*, *12*(3), 346–371.
16. Davis, M. H. (1983). Measuring individual differences in empathy: Evidence for a multidimensional approach. *Journal of Personality and Social Psychology*, *44*(1), 113–126.
17. Dennis, A. R., Kinney, S. T., & Hung, Y. T. C. (1999). Gender differences in the effects of media richness. *Small Group Research, 30*(4), 405-437.
18. Dourish, P., & Bellotti, V. (1992). Awareness and coordination in shared workspaces. In *Proc. of CSCW'92,* 107–114.
19. Dweck, C. (2006). *Mindset: The new psychology of success*. Random House LLC.
20. Ebert, J., & Meyvis, T. (2014). Reading fictional stories and winning delayed prizes: The surprising emotional impact of distant events. Social Science Research Network, ID No. 1654673. http://papers.ssrn.com/abstract=1654673
21. Federman, M. (2006). On the media effects of immigration and refugee board hearings via videoconference. *Journal of Refugee Studies*, *19*(4), 433–452.
22. Fujita, K., Henderson, M. D., Eng, J., Trope, Y., & Liberman, N. (2006). Spatial distance and mental construal of social events. *Psychological Science*, *17*(4), 278–282.
23. Fullwood, C. (2007). The effect of mediation on impression formation: A comparison of face-to-face and video-mediated conditions. *Applied Ergonomics*, *38*(3), 267–273.
24. Fussell, S. R., Setlock, L. D., & Kraut, R. E. (2003). Effects of head-mounted and scene-oriented video systems on remote collaboration on physical tasks. In *Proc. Of CHI'03*, 513-520.
25. Goh, L. Y. Q., Phillips, J. G., & Blaszczynski, A. (2011). Computer-mediated communication and risk-taking behaviour. *Computers in Human Behavior*, *27*(5), 1794–1799.
26. Goldberg, L. R., Johnson, J. A., Eber, H. W., Hogan, R., Ashton, M. C., Cloninger, C. R., & Gough, H. G. (2006). The international personality item pool and the future of public-domain personality measures. *Journal of Research in Personality*, *40*(1), 84–96.
27. Grudin, J. (1988). Why CSCW applications fail: Problems in the design and evaluation of organizational interfaces. In *Proc. of CSCW'88*, 85-93.
28. Gudykunst, W. B., Yoon, Y., & Nishida, T. (1987). The influence of individualism□collectivism on perceptions of communication in ingroup and outgroup relationships. *Communication Monographs*, *54*(3), 295–306.
29. Gutwin, C., & Greenberg, S. (2002). A descriptive framework of workspace awareness for real-time groupware. *Computer Supported Cooperative Work (CSCW), 11*(3-4), 411-446.
30. Haque, O. S., & Waytz, A. (2012). Dehumanization in medicine causes, solutions, and functions. *Perspectives on Psychological Science*, *7*(2), 176–186.
31. Haslam, N. (2006). Dehumanization: An integrative review. *Personality and Social Psychology Review*, *10*(3), 252–264.
32. Haslam, N., Bain, P., Douge, L., Lee, M., & Bastian, B. (2005). More human than you: Attributing humanness to self and others. *Journal of Personality and Social Psychology*, *89*(6), 937–950.
33. Google Inc. June 4, 2014. Helpouts by Google. https://helpouts.google.com/.
34. Henderson, M. D., Fujita, K., Trope, Y., & Liberman, N. (2006). Transcending the "here": The effect of spatial distance on social judgment. *Journal of Personality and Social Psychology*, *91*(5), 845–856.

35. Henderson, M. D., & Wakslak, C. J. (2010). Psychological distance and priming: When do semantic primes impact social evaluations? *Personality and Social Psychology Bulletin*, *36*(7) 975–985.
36. Hersh, W. R., Hickam, D. H., Severance, S. M., Dana, T. L., Krages, K. P., & Helfand, M. (2006). Diagnosis, access and outcomes: Update of a systematic review of telemedicine services. *Journal of Telemedicine and Telecare*, *12*(s2), 3–31.
37. Hsee, C. K., & Weber, E. U. (1997). A fundamental prediction error: Self–others discrepancies in risk preference. *Journal of Experimental Psychology: General*, *126*(1), 45–53.
38. Kahneman, D., & Tversky, A. (1979). Prospect theory: An analysis of decision under risk. *Econometrica: Journal of the Econometric Society*, 263–291.
39. Kane, B., & Luz, S. (2009). Assimilating information and offering a medical opinion in remote and co-located meetings. In *Proc. of CBMS'09*, 1-6.
40. Kiesler, S., Siegel, J., & McGuire, T. W. (1984). Social psychological aspects of computer-mediated communication. *American Psychologist*, *39*(10), 1123-1134.
41. Kray, L. J. (2000). Contingent weighting in self-other decision making. *Organizational Behavior and Human Decision Processes*, *83*(1), 82–106.
42. Lammers, J., & Stapel, D. A. (2011). Power increases dehumanization. *Group Processes & Intergroup Relations*, *14*(1), 113–126.
43. Langer, E. J. (1975). The illusion of control. *Journal of Personality and Social Psychology*, *32*(2), 311-328.
44. Lee, M. K., & Takayama, L. (2011, May). Now, I have a body: Uses and social norms for mobile remote presence in the workplace. In *Proc. of CHI'11*, 33-42.
45. Liberman, N., Trope, Y., & Stephan, E. (2007). Psychological distance. In A. W. Kruglanski & E. T. Higgins (Eds.), *Social Psychology: Handbook of Basic Principles* (353-385). Guilford Press, New York, NY
46. Loewenstein, G. F., Weber, E. U., Hsee, C. K., & Welch, N. (2001). Risk as feelings. *Psychological Bulletin*, *127*(2), 267–286.
47. Lombard, M., Ditton, T. B., Crane, D., Davis, B., Gil-Egui, G., Horvath, K., Rossman, J., Park, S. (2000). Measuring presence: A literature-based approach to the development of a standardized paper-and-pencil instrument. In *The third international workshop on presence*. Delft, The Netherlands.
48. Markus, H. R., & Kitayama, S. (1991). Culture and the self: Implications for cognition, emotion, and motivation. *Psychological Review, 98*(2), 224-253.
49. McGuire, T. W., Kiesler, S., & Siegel, J. (1987). Group and computer-mediated discussion effects in risk decision making. *Journal of Personality and Social Psychology*, *52*(5), 917–930.
50. Milgram, S. (1965). Some conditions of obedience and disobedience to authority. *Human Relations*, *18*(1), 57–76.
51. Nakanishi, H., Kato, K., & Ishiguro, H. (2011). Zoom cameras and movable displays enhance social telepresence. In *Proc. CHI'11,* 63–72.
52. Nardi, B. A., Whittaker, S., & Bradner, E. (n.d.). Interaction and outeraction: Instant messaging in action. In *Proc. CSCW'00, 79-88.*
53. Nisan, M., & Minkowich, A. (1973). The effect of expected temporal distance on risk taking. *Journal of Personality and Social Psychology*, *25*(3) 375–380.
54. O'Conaill, B., Whittaker, S., & Wilbur, S. (1993). Conversations over video conferences: An evaluation of the spoken aspects of video-mediated communication. *Human-Computer Interaction*, *8*(1), 389–428.
55. Okdie, B. M., Guadagno, R. E., Bernieri, F. J., Geers, A. L., & Mclarney-Vesotski, A. R. (2011). Getting to know you: Face-to-face versus online interactions. *Computers in Human Behavior*, *27*(1), 153–159.
56. Olson, G. M., & Olson, J. S. (2000). Distance matters. *Human-Computer Interaction*, *15*(1), 139–178.
57. Patterson, M. (1991). A functional approach to nonverbal exchange. In R. S. Feldman (Ed.), *Fundamentals of Nonverbal Behavior* (458-513). Location: Cambridge University Press, Cambridge, MA.
58. Pennington, G. L., & Roese, N. J. (2003). Regulatory focus and temporal distance. *Journal of Experimental Social Psychology*, *39*(6), 563–576.
59. Polman, E. (2012). Effects of self–other decision making on regulatory focus and choice overload. *Journal of Personality and Social Psychology*, *102*(5), 980–993.
60. Porcelli, A. J., & Delgado, M. R. (2009). Acute stress modulates risk taking in financial decision making. *Psychological Science*, *20*(3), 278–283.
61. Psotka, J., Lewis, S. A., & King, D. (1998). Effects of field of view on judgments of self-location: Distortions in distance estimations even when the image geometry exactly fits the field of view. *Presence: Teleoperators and Virtual Environments*, *7*(4), 352–369.
62. Redelmeier, D. A., & Tversky, A. (1990). Discrepancy between medical decisions for individual patients and for groups. *New England Journal of Medicine*, *322*(16), 1162–1164.
63. Reynolds, D. B., Joseph, J., & Sherwood, R. (2011). Risky shift versus cautious shift: Determining differences in risk taking between private and public management decision-making. *Journal of Business & Economics Research*, *7*(1), 63-78.
64. Rim, S., Uleman, J. S., & Trope, Y. (2009). Spontaneous trait inference and construal level theory: Psychological

distance increases nonconscious trait thinking. *Journal of Experimental Social Psychology*, *45*(5), 1088–1097.

65. Royakkers, L., & Van Est, R. (2010). The cubicle warrior: The marionette of digitalized warfare. *Ethics and Information Technology*, *12*(3), 289–296.
66. Sagristano, M. D., Trope, Y., & Liberman, N. (2002). Time-dependent gambling: Odds now, money later. *Journal of Experimental Psychology: General*, *131*(2), 364.
67. Why are search-and-rescue drones grounded? http://spectrum.ieee.org/automaton/robotics/aerial-robots/search-and-rescue-drones-grounded.
68. Setlock, L. D., Fussell, S. R., & Neuwirth, C. (2004). Taking it out of context: Collaborating within and across cultures in face-to-face settings and via instant messaging. In *Proc. CSCW'04,* 604-613.
69. Stone, E. R., Yates, A. J., & Caruthers, A. S. (2002). Risk taking in decision making for others versus the self. *Journal of Applied Social Psychology*, *32*(9), 1797–1824.
70. Straus, S. G., Miles, J. A., & Levesque, L. L. (2001). The effects of videoconference, telephone, and face-to-face media on interviewer and applicant judgments in employment interviews. *Journal of Management*, *27*(3), 363–381.
71. Tausczik, Y. R., & Pennebaker, J. W. (2010). The psychological meaning of words: LIWC and computerized text analysis methods. *Journal of Language and Social Psychology*, *29*(1), 24–54.
72. Tidwell, L. C., & Walther, J. B. (2002). Computer□ mediated communication effects on disclosure, impressions, and interpersonal evaluations: Getting to know one another a bit at a time. *Human Communication Research*, *28*(3), 317–348.
73. Trope, Y., & Liberman, N. (2010). Construal-level theory of psychological distance. *Psychological Review*, *117*(2), 440–463.
74. Ubel, P. A., Angott, A. M., & Zikmund-Fisher, B. J. (2011). Physicians recommend different treatments for patients than they would choose for themselves. *Archives of Internal Medicine*, *171*(7), 630–634.
75. Vallacher, R. R., & Wegner, D. M. (1989). Levels of personal agency: Individual variation in action identification. *Journal of Personality and Social Psychology, 57*(4), 660.
76. Wallach, M. A., Kogan, N., & Bem, D. J. (1964). Diffusion of responsibility and level of risk taking in groups. *The Journal of Abnormal and Social Psychology*, *68*(3), 263-274.
77. Wang, H. C., Fussell, S. F., & Setlock, L. D. (2009). Cultural difference and adaptation of communication styles in computer-mediated group brainstorming. In *Proc. of CHI'09,* 669-678.
78. Williams, E. (1977). Experimental comparisons of face-to-face and mediated communication: A review. *Psychological Bulletin*, *84*(5), 963–976.
79. Witmer, B. G., & Singer, M. J. (1998). Measuring presence in virtual environments: A presence questionnaire. *Presence: Teleoperators and Virtual Environments*, *7*(3), 225–240.
80. Zanbaka, C., Goolkasian, P., & Hodges, L. (2006). Can a virtual cat persuade you? The role of gender and realism in speaker persuasiveness. In *Proc. of CHI'06*, 1153-1162.
81. Zikmund-Fisher, B. J., Sarr, B., Fagerlin, A., & Ubel, P. A. (2006). A matter of perspective: Choosing for others differs from choosing for yourself in making treatment decisions. *Journal of General Internal Medicine*, *21*(6), 618–622.

Engaging Around Neighborhood Issues: How Online Communication Affects Offline Behavior

Sheena L. Erete
College of Computing and Digital Media
DePaul University
Chicago, IL 60604
serete@cdm.depaul.edu

ABSTRACT

This paper describes how online conversations amongst local residents about crime impact offline behavior. We conducted a three-year study in five middle to low-income geographically-bound communities (defined as police beats), where we observed community meetings for two years, interviewed 45 residents, and performed qualitative content analysis on over 7,000 online messages on community-based email lists and web forums. Interviewees reported that community-based online communication influenced how they 1) protect themselves and their property to avoid victimization and 2) participate and engage in local in-person civic engagement initiatives. This paper provides insights into the relationship between online and offline behavior and implications for designing community-based ICTs that effectively address local issues.

Author Keywords

Online and offline behavior; neighborhoods; place-based communities; crime; computer-mediated communication

ACM Classification Keywords

H.5.m. Information Interfaces and Presentation (e.g. HCI): Miscellaneous

INTRODUCTION

For the past two decades, human computer interaction (HCI) researchers have considered neighborhoods to be a rich context to understand how people use information and communication technologies (ICTs) [7]. Much of place-based research (i.e., studies that focus on users in a geographically-bound area) has been viewed as an opportunity to examine relationship building and social networks in a local context [6, 20, 26, 38, 39, 54] as well as an opportunity to examine how people feel about local places and spaces [3, 14, 25].

CSCW 2015, March 14–18, 2015, Vancouver, BC, Canada.

ACM 978-1-4503-2922-4/15/03…$15.00.
http://dx.doi.org/10.1145/2675133.2675182

Though much of the work in HCI has focused on online relationships and behaviors, it is essential to understand if and how online communication (i.e., digitally mediated conversations) amongst local residents affect offline behavior and in-person interactions. Such in-person behaviors can influence how citizens engage around social issues such as crime [3, 30], volunteerism [53], sustainability [13], health [35], and local activism [10, 32]. Thus, we pose the research question: *How does online communication about crime affect local residents' offline behavior?* We focus on crime to examine the role that technology plays in influencing in-person actions and civic engagement around a topic of shared concern that is essential to neighborhood outcomes [33].

In this paper, we present common themes that emerge across three of five middle to low-income geographically-bound communities regarding how residents engage and interact online and in-person around a local issue, crime. Based on data from observations of in-person community meetings for over two years, 45 interviews with residents, and community-created web forums and email lists, community-based online communication seemed to influence 1) how residents protect themselves and their property to avoid victimization and 2) residents' participation and engagement in local in-person civic engagement initiatives.

This paper makes several contributions. It provides insight into how behavior can be influenced by online communication in a local context, which adds to the growing literature in CSCW that focuses on the relationship between online and offline interactions [19, 24, 25]. Furthermore, it provides insight into how neighborhoods with varying demographics (income, education, race) use technologies to address social issues rather than focusing on a single type of neighborhood. Lastly, it provides implications for designing technologies that focus on civic engagement, building on prior studies about digital activism and volunteerism [10, 32, 53].

RELATED WORK

Neighborhoods play a critical role in shaping the social and economic outcomes of their residents [1, 15, 33]. ICTs have the ability to strengthen neighborhoods by supporting residents' collective responses to social issues that may plague communities. In the following sections, we discuss the role and context of neighborhoods and present prior research that focuses on location-based ICTs that support collective action.

ICTs in Neighborhoods

Neighborhoods have been linked to numerous factors essential to the success and well-being of residents. Issues such as mortality [15], economic mobility [55], health [1, 34], and crime [33, 40] have all been linked to 'neighborhood effects,' meaning that neighborhood characteristics are confounded with these social issues. The effects of neighborhood characteristics are particularly important in lower income areas, where lack of political capital and collective efficacy tend to make these neighborhoods susceptible to continual decline [40, 41, 44].

HCI scholars have recognized the importance of neighborhoods and have shown enthusiasm in understanding the role of ICTs in improving health, education, job opportunities, and civic engagement in the local context [7, 12, 20, 30]. In the 1990s, Carroll and colleagues studied Blacksburg Electronic Village [6, 25, 26] and later Moosburg, which provided "real-time, situated interaction and a place-based model for community information" [8]. Hampton and Wellman [20] explored social capital in local neighborhoods in Netville, a suburban neighborhood wired with high-speed internet. Blom and colleagues created Comfortzone, a shared mapping system that allowed individuals to tag different locations in a city to indicate areas where they did not feel safe [3]. These studies provide us with a foundation regarding technology use in neighborhoods that are not low-income.

There has also been recent focus in HCI to study low-income communities and marginalized populations in the US [12, 27, 56, 57]. In sustainability, for example, Dillahunt et al. found that low-income households are interested in sustainable living practices regardless of the financial benefits [11] and created Community Monitor, an application that allows low-income residents to view their energy consumption in comparison to their neighbors [13]. In health, Community Mosaic, a system that allows local residents to share healthy eating practices, focuses on improving dietary habits in neighborhoods that are disproportionally affected by negative health outcomes. Our paper extends these studies by contributing implications for designing community-based technologies that support local collective action in low income communities around the topic of crime and safety.

Digitally-Enabled Collective Action

Collective action is essential to neighborhood vitality [40]. Despite concerns that people are less civically engaged [37], over a quarter of U.S citizens volunteered over 15 billion hours in 2011, an estimated worth of $296 billion [2]. These hours of service and engagement are not only beneficial to the organization and society, but also to the citizens who participated [37]. Participating in community crime prevention, for instance, decreases fear and anxiety of becoming victimized [28] while also reducing crime and increasing public confidence in the police [45]. Such examples indicate the importance of civic engagement and collective action to address local issues.

Citizens have used ICTs to inform, organize, and mobilize others in local collective action initiatives [36]. Dialup Radio, for example, is a telephone-based information distribution system created for citizens and human rights workers in Zimbabwe to share information outside of the government's tightly controlled media outlets [23]. Smyth and colleagues created MOSES, a mobile kiosk that allows Liberian citizens to record and watch video messages [47]. Other related work has focused on the use of technology in volunteerism [53] and collective digital intelligence and action during crises [48].

Taken together, prior literature suggests that neighborhoods are an ideal research setting to understand how to best design ICTs to support local collective action. While there has been much work done on digitally supported collective action, few have focused on how online communication about crime affects offline behavior, interactions, and collective action, specifically in low income communities. In this paper, we address this gap.

STUDY DESIGN

To understand how online communication influences offline behavior, we took a triangulated approach to the study design using observations, interviews, and qualitative content analysis. We observed two years of community-police (CP) meetings in five geographically-bound areas in Chicago, Illinois, USA. These meetings were sponsored by the city of Chicago and held once a month with local residents and the police. Additionally, we interviewed 45 residents from five communities. We also conducted qualitative content analysis on over 7,000 online messages sent amongst local residents in three of the five areas through grassroots community-created web forums or email lists. The following sections describe the five communities, their technologies, and how the data was collected and analyzed.

The Communities

We studied five communities. We define the geographic boundaries of a "community" as police beat, which is a relatively small geographic area (typically 30 to 40 square blocks) containing roughly 20,000 residents (sometimes fewer in less densely populated areas of the city). We selected beats as the geographic boundaries because 1) in preliminary observations, we found that residents often used the terms "beat" and "community" interchangeably in their online and offline language and 2) when appropriating ICTs for community use, residents typically described the tools as being for those who live in certain police beats. Beats may have been heavily used by residents, because it may be easier to have conversations about crime if the targeted boundaries are mapped onto police beats. We do not refer to the areas as neighborhoods, because in Chicago, the term "neighborhood" is typically referred to as a much larger geographic region that was named in the 1920s, with populations up to 98,000 residents (with a median of approximately 31,000). As many as 9 beats could make up one neighborhood in Chicago. In this paper, we use the term "community" to refer specifically to the beats studied and "neighborhood" to refer to a more general definition open to interpretation by a broader audience outside of Chicago. We acknowledge that the use of police beats may be an area of concern as there is much debate amongst scholars about the geographic boundaries that define community.

Table 1. Demographic information of the communities based on data from Census and the American Community Survey

	Population	Income Level	% White	% Black	% Latino	Index Crime Rate
Community 1	24,200	Middle	54%	12%	17%	1528
Community 2	10,300	Middle-Low	28%	29%	34%	2889
Community 3	22,000	Low	2%	70%	25%	6339
Community 4	23,643	Low	3%	38%	58%	6962
Community 5	17,260	Low	2%	78%	19%	3048

The Index Crime Rate is the number of serious crimes (e.g., 1st and 2nd degree murder, rape, robbery) per 100,000 residents from August 2012 - August 2013.

The five communities were selected using purposive sampling, accounting for crime rates and racial compositions. Crime rate was important to consider, because citizens' behaviors, reactions, and attitudes towards civic participation may be affected by the amount of local crime in their neighborhood [46]; therefore, we selected communities with varying crime rates. Additionally, we considered the racial composition of the communities so the results from this study could be compared to prior crime studies, most of which consider race [43, 52]. Similar to prior studies [33, 43], crime rates and racial compositions were confounded with SES levels. By considering race and socioeconomic status, our study builds on prior work in HCI that provides insights into designing for groups who have traditionally been marginalized [27, 35, 56, 57].

To select the communities, we ordered the city's beats by crime rate, then by the three most prominent racial[1] groups in Chicago: Caucasian (or white), African American (or black), and Latino. We then randomly selected a beat from the 10 highest crime areas representing each racial group. Table 1 displays demographic details about each community. The end result was one majority white, one majority black, one majority Latino, and one community where the racial groups are evenly distributed. We added a second majority black beat (Community 5), because the one initially selected lacked a strong online presence.

Based on Census data, two communities were classified as middle income based on the median income levels per household. The other three communities were classified as low income, with poverty and unemployment rates greater than 21% and 15%, respectively. Index crime are calculated per capita, with the lower income communities reporting higher criminal activities than the middle income communities.

Data Collection

To understand how technology is appropriated to support community crime prevention efforts, we conducted a study that combines observations, interviews, and online qualitative content analysis.

Observations

We observed monthly meetings between the police and community in each of the five communities for roughly two years (2011-2013). The meetings were held at local churches, libraries, schools, and community centers. There was an average of 22 citizens and 4 police officers in attendance at the community-police meetings; there was at least one community facilitator (i.e., a resident who volunteered to be the liaison between the community and police) present. In addition to the monthly community-police meetings, we attended other community events, such as community walks, block parties, and block club meetings. In total, we collected over 400 pages of ethnographic notes from attending over 60 meetings.

Semi-structured Interviews

In addition, we formally interviewed 45 local residents (roughly 9 from each beat) during July - September 2012. We recruited 21 interviewees at the community-police meetings and 12 from invitations sent on the community-based online discussion tools. We recruited 12 interviewees from public places such as local libraries or by word-of-mouth to gather insight from those who live in the community but do not attend the community-police meetings or use the online discussion tools.

Each interview was transcribed in its entirety. Interviewees' ages ranged from 23 to 82, with the median age being 57. Twenty-eight of the 45 participants were women. Sixty-four percent of the interviewees were homeowners. The education level varied as follows: 16% of participants did not complete high school, 16% had high school diplomas or equivalent, 33% had some college or vocational training, and 35% completed college with a bachelors degree or higher. Race varied as well; 53% identified as being black, 38% white, and 7% Latino. Table 2 provides details about the interviewees by community.

Interviews lasted an average of 45 minutes. During semi-structured interviews, we asked residents about:

- their attendance at in-person community meetings and/or participation in online discussions with their neighbors about crime;
- their online and in-person participation and the factors that influence their decision to select either medium;
- their satisfaction with community-police meetings and trust level of the police;
- their use of technology in any other capacity to address crime (e.g., if they send text messages or emails about crime outside of the community-based web forums);

[1]The US Census bureau defines Latino as an ethnicity, not race. For simplicity, this study refers to race based on self-identification as Latino, regardless of race (e.g., White Latino, Black Latino).

Table 2. Demographic information about the interviewees by community

	# of Interviewees	Avg. Age	% Female	Race			% Homeowners	% > High School Diploma
				% White	% Black	% Latino		
Community 1	7	60	43%	100%	0%	0%	86%	100%
Community 2	9	41	56%	67%	22%	0%	33%	100%
Community 3	10	53	80%	30%	60%	10%	50%	60%
Community 4	8	52	63%	0%	88%	13%	50%	25%
Community 5	11	61	64%	9%	82%	9%	27%	36%

- their style of online participation, specifically whether they actively participate (i.e., post messages to the discussion board) or passively participate (i.e., read the forum posts but do not contribute).

Online Qualitative Content

Lastly, we gathered online conversations from "grassroots" community-based ICTs (i.e., created by residents not by the police or other government agencies). We identified such ICTs by asking residents to describe if and how they engage in online discussions about local issues. Based on our in-person conversations with residents, three of the five communities (Communities 1, 2, & 5) had a main method of online communication to facilitate local discussions and share information outside of police-created technologies. We were unable to identify ICTs that were widely used in Communities 3 and 4; however, residents in Community 3 sporadically used Everyblock, an online tool that, at the time of this study, was freely available to discuss local issues. We thereby focus much of our discussion on the three communities that more widely used technology, because we were unable to draw definitive conclusions about the effect of online communication in Communities 3 & 4.

Community 1. Community 1's main method of online communication was a Yahoo! Group that was created in April 2004. Roughly 250 users signed up using their real names, email addresses, and home addresses. Though there was no official affiliation with community-police meetings, citizens promoted the website at the community-police meetings (i.e., encouraged citizens to sign up).

Community 2. From January 2008 - March 2011, Community 2 used an open discussion board, where anyone could send a message to all the members. The posts to the discussion board were publicly accessible, because logins were not required to read messages. To post to the board, real names and home addresses were required. As of March 2011, over 350 residents primarily used a private email list instead of the message board, where members could not see others' email addresses. Like Community 1, the private email list was not officially affiliated with the police but meeting attendees were encouraged to sign up with the mailing list moderator at the community-police meetings.

Community 5. Since May 2011, residents in Community 5 used a private email list to distribute information related to crime. All emails were sent out "blind copy" from the moderator so no information about who was on the email list was shared. People signed up at the community-police meetings, ward (i.e., alderman's) meetings, or by contacting the moderator directly, who reported over 300 emails on the list.

We then developed a web crawler using Python that retrieved information (i.e., forum post, date, subject, author) from the community-based ICTs (e.g., web forums). Using this method, we collected 5,425 messages from Community 1's Yahoo! Group, 1,054 messages from Community 2's public message board and private email list, and 665 from Community 5's private email list. The message dates ranged from April 2004 - June 2013. Below is an example of an online forum post written by a local resident: *"Saw drug dealing on Saturday afternoon @ 2:30 while having late lunch on my front porch. I can identify the car and will look for it now that I know....here's the info: A reddish-marroon Buick (at least 10 yrs old) did a strange move at the stop sign as it was heading south[...] As the Buick went by me there were 3-4 young men sitting - I could not take the license number, but can identify the car again - very shiny!!"*

Though the community-based ICTs in this study were web forums and email lists, we also searched for discussions on using search engines and social media websites (e.g., Facebook, Twitter). While we found announcements about local meetings and resources on social media websites, we did not find ongoing conversations amongst residents. Interviewees stated that they didn't use social media to have conversations with neighbors, because either they did not use social media regularly, or they did not view social media as a tool to have open conversations about the neighborhood. The former could be attributed to age and generational differences in technology use amongst the interviewees (median age was 57). The latter could be related to differences in technology use and skill [21, 22] or fear of retaliation [29, 45]. Our study was conducted prior to the popularity of websites like Nextdoor.com, a private local social networking tool [31]. Future work could examine the extent to which neighborhood characteristics influence the type of technologies citizens use and the structure of information sharing [17].

Analysis

We (the author and a paid research assistant) analyzed the data described above using inductive qualitative analysis [49]. We began by reading each line of the observations, interviews, and the online content; then using TAMSAnalyzer, a qualitative analysis tool, we created codes that described various phenomena. We iteratively applied these codes to phrases in the observation notes, interview transcripts, and the online content (i.e., the forum posts). As additional codes emerged, we reanalyzed the data, applying the new codes. The codes were then grouped into higher level categories until overarching themes emerged. Interrater reliability was calculated using intra-class correlation coefficient using a two-way mixed model and absolute agreement, which resulted in 81% reliability. In the following section, we present two major themes that emerged based on our analysis along with quotes from participants that illustrate the themes. Quotes are verbatim, with little alteration except to protect the identity of participants.

RESULTS

Twenty-four of the 45 interviewees regularly used a technology to discuss local crime and disorder (e.g., community email list, Everyblock, CLEARpath). Of the 24, 17 (71%) said that the technology influenced how they protect themselves and their property to avoid victimization. Sixteen of the 24 (67%) stated that the online communication affected their attendance and engagement at the community-police meetings and other civic activities.

Behavior Change to Avoid Victimization

Online communication influenced how people protect themselves and their property as well as their interactions with strangers. Seventeen interviewees reported that they changed their behavior in hopes of avoiding victimization against themselves, their family, and/or their personal property. Twelve of the seventeen (71%) interviewees stated that after receiving the online communication, they changed their behavior to avoid being personally assaulted, and 15 of the 17 (88%) changed their behavior to protect their personal property. Furthermore, 11 of the 17 (65%) residents stated that the technology changed their awareness and consequently their behavior as a result of receiving information directly from other residents about scams and crime that they had encountered.

Prompts Change in Self Protection

During the interviews, residents stated that they changed their behavior to better protect themselves from being victimized based on the online communication from the prominent community technologies. One woman in Community 5, for example, described how she changed her behavior after getting an email from the moderator about his daughter's near attack while exiting her garage. The woman described the email and how she subsequently changed her behavior, saying,

> *"It changed how I come into the garage. [Now] I let someone know when I am coming into the garage and ask my daughter to let me know when she's coming into the garage, because I remember [the moderator] sending out this email. [His daughter] was coming home at night [..] So the person that was over the fence, waiting on her to come out the garage. She opened the door and so she had [her] child in front of her. [..] The child screamed [..] So she just shut the door and as she was shutting the door, he was putting a gun in the door, but she was able to shut the door [..] [The moderator] was saying that he had told his daughter to always alert them when she's coming in, so they can just watch out. So when I'm coming in [now] I always call my daughter and say, I'm coming in if it's dark. She will call me if she's coming in. [We] let the garage down. Before [we used to] turn the car in, and [now] we back in. [..] You know, you watch, you make sure nobody runs in with you."*

In this example, the woman vividly remembered details of the email about the attempted attack of the moderator's daughter, which was sent over eight months prior to the interview. The woman stated earlier that she read an average of 30 emails per day. Her detail and accuracy in describing the incident demonstrates the effect that the message had on her. Additionally, she encouraged her daughter to change her behavior.

Other residents also stated that they received online messages that impacted their behavior. For example, another woman from Community 5 said, *"[The moderator] sent me an email one time about when you are in the parking lot, you know and you're next to a van, you know. How if my car is parked here, and I am going to get in here, you know, the person that's in the van can grab me easy, you know. So [now I] enter through the other side."* In this instance, the woman described how she became more aware of large vehicles that are parked near her car because of a message received from the email list. Others stated similar changes in how they protect themselves.

Residents also stated that online communication impacted how they encouraged their family to behave. A man from Community 2, for example, described how he asked his wife to change her behavior, saying *"If something comes up, I'll reference it. Like I say 'People have been doing snatch and grab robberies. Make sure you carrying your mace when you walk the dogs.'"* This demonstrates how online communication may also influence individuals to warn family members about their safety habits, implying the importance of family in crime prevention [28].

Prompts Change in Protection of Personal Property

In addition to personal safety, results suggest that citizens also reported that they sometimes modified their behavior to better protect their homes and personal property based on others' experiences shared online. One woman from Community 1 said that after hearing someone describe how they were burglarized, she learned *"don't leave the windows open when you leave if no one else is home. It prompted me to call my landlord about some broken windows, yeah, definitely. There's an overall feeling of 'I don't want that to happen to me' or 'Let's buckle down to prevent that from happening again in the community.'"* This woman stated previously that she had lived in the same place and had problems with the windows for years but reading about others' experiences prompted her to take action to better protect her home.

Others also stated that they protected home differently based on what they read online. A man from Community 1 said, *"The big thing that I learned on that site, I always keep my doors locked you know because before I would like go out the back of the door, and I would leave it unlocked just to walk the dog down the block or whatever. Now I don't take that chance anymore. My door is [now] locked."* Another man from Community 5 said, *"[The moderator] sent out one about people going around taking stuff out of yards and I have my grill out there and I have a wrought iron table. So now that made me put it in the garage because if they're going in people yards taking stuff, I don't want my stuff taken."* These statements illustrate how residents changed how they protect their home and personal property based on their neighbors' experiences. These grassroots technologies afford residents an opportunity to share their experiences with a vast amount of people, which subsequently impacts people's behavior.

Influences In-Person Interactions

At least nine residents (i.e., 20% of all interviews and more than half of those who reported offline behavior change) stated that receiving the online messages from other community members impacted the way they interacted with strangers. Interviewees reported this was due to people online sending messages to "alert" residents of certain burglary or robbery scams. One woman from Community 1, for example, described how she became aware of a burglary scam after reading a message on the community mailing list and how as a result, she changed her behavior based on other residents' experiences being victimized, saying *"So I also have gotten information from other people, that are on the emails, telling us of what they experienced. Like there was somebody going around selling this new electricity stuff and we're like, 'Oh, good to know.'"* She continues to say how that made her more cautious when answering the door. She says that after receiving that email, she operates under a new rule. She said if she doesn't *"know who is on the other side of that door, [I] do not open it. They could punch you in the face and they could be in the house."* In this example, the woman described the impact the message had on how she answered the door of her home. Similarly, a woman from Community 2 described a burglary scam that her neighbors posted online: *"Another thing that was big was [..] people ringing doorbells and soliciting or saying that they were from the gas company and they might not be. I don't open my door anymore."* A man from Community 2 said, *"I am probably more aware of certain specific things. Like for instance if someone [online] says there is a guy in a dark blue jacket walking around and is asking people for, you know like, the guy who was asking people for money for an inhaler. I was more attentive to people in blue jackets."* These residents described how the online conversations influenced their in-person interactions with strangers.

Four of the interviewees stated that what they read online changed how they interact with their neighbors. One woman from Community 1 stated that after receiving information that her neighbors were using drugs, she changed her behavior when interacting with them. She said that someone posted online that *"we have got some neighbors who are into drug use, so that concerns me. And so I am always leery around them and pay attention and I probably wouldn't walk, walk past them if it was late at night and they were all hanging out."* Thus, technology may not only influence users' behavior towards strangers but may also affect how they interact with people that they have met in-person. This may be a lesser effect considering evidence of perception change of neighbors were only mentioned by 4 out of 24 interviewees that used the community-based crime prevention technology. However, future work should investigate the degree to which technology influences the perceptions of strangers as well as acquaintances.

Our results suggest that the source of the information is important. More specifically, the information was from neighbor-to-neighbor, which may be extremely effective in influencing behavior, because recipients may view the source more credible or reliable since they live on the same block or street. If one's next door neighbor is assaulted, one may be more likely to identify with the victim; after all, they may walk down the same street during their commute, leading them to feel like "If it happened to them, it could happen to me." Most stated that they changed their behavior to avoid victimization after hearing about another neighbor being victimized. We asked interviewees if they used other sources to receive information about their community. At least half stated that they watch the news or read local newspapers; however, less than 10% of those that receive information about their neighborhood from TV news and/or newspapers stated that it affected their behavior. This suggests that the source matters regarding if and how online communication influences offline behavior. Describing how information from neighbors affects his interaction with strangers, a man from Community 1 said, *"I feel like even if I just keep reading the emails, it's a free society that is able to say, 'Dude there's somebody on a street corner pretending to be a guy who fixes screens. Don't let him in. He's not real,' or 'Dude, there's a guy on the street corner with a clipboard and he actually is a screen fixer. Believe me, he's fine. Dude, let him in.' If I know these people over time, even if it's 'cyber-know-them,' then when that person comes to the door, I'm going to be like, 'I actually do have a screen that needs fixing and I heard you were cool.'"* This statement demonstrates the effect that online messages may have, even when the messages are received from neighbors who have never met in-person. This may be due to the relationships and trust developed online.

Effects on Civic Participation and Local Engagement

Our findings suggest that online communication affects citizens' attendance at community meetings and other forms of civic engagement. Specifically, six interviewees stated that the online messages impacted their participation in community-organized activities such as community walks, vigils, etc. Eight interviewees said they attended community-police meetings as a result of the online communication. Furthermore, the observations and interview data suggest that online communication affects what residents ask and how they participate during community-police meetings. Residents asked questions about what was said online, which led to a more community-driven agenda.

Heightens Participation in Community-Organized Activities

Residents stated that they became more involved in grassroots community crime prevention strategies such as local walks and efforts to curb disorder as a result of reading messages from the community-based ICTs. They stated that the technologies provided additional details about the community events that they may not have otherwise known. Additionally, technology sometimes made it easier to organize community-created activities. For example, residents in Community 1 identified a deleterious business (a drugstore) and attempted to organize action to address the disorder. During an interview, a woman from Community 1 described that situation, saying that the online messages *"changed how I perceived the [drugstore] on [street name] and [street name] because it was reported that there was violence in that park so makes me think twice about going to the [drug store]."* She continued to say that due to the reports there, she helped organize online to try to stop the drugstore from being able to sell alcohol, saying *"actually, I was part of the group of people who encouraged the [drug store] to not sell liquor because there was already a weird vibe going on around there. They did not stop but they didn't sell it like packaged goods. I think not as broadly but no they did not stop. Man, I think we made a big stink and that's good enough."* This exhibits how residents used the website to not only identify disorder, but also engage in offline activities to address the disorder. In this particular situation, the store did not completely stop selling alcohol but residents were happy that their efforts encourage the store to limit the type of alcohol sold (e.g., no single beers). The woman later said that she would not have otherwise known about the in-person protest without the discussion board. Residents from Communities 2 and 5 described similar situations.

When we asked citizens why did they participate in more locally organized activities, the most frequent response was that they were motivated after hearing about others' participation though online discussions and photos posted. A woman from Community 2, for instance, said, *"I guess it has changed my feeling that there are a lot of people who are watching, who are watching out that you know. We don't just go into our houses and shut the door, that people are paying attention, and that there's a common want to improve."* Online participation influenced people's perception of what was happening in the community, because they virtually witnessed neighbors organizing walks, clean-ups, etc. Other said that they participated more because of the reminders of when and where local activities were occurring.

Increases Community Meeting Attendance

Over 80% of the residents who stated that the technology affected the community-police meetings believed that attendance increased because of the technology. A woman from Community 5 stated, *"A lot of people have gotten on the email [list] plus giving out the information - like I said, we gave out the information that picks other people's interest - so they come [to the in-person meetings] and they listen. And a lot of times, they have not even experienced the problem, but they heard about it or read it on the email so they want to talk about it."* The community facilitator from Community 5 agreed, saying, *"[Messages from the email list] makes them come. What happens is, everyone gets - everyone is hungry for information, they just don't get it. So when you don't get it, you say, 'Man, nothing going on. If nothing's going on, why do I need to go to the [community-police] meeting for? So if you haven't done anything to bring me to the [community-police] meeting, to make me want to come, then why should I come?' "* All of the interviewees who reported that the technology increased attendance were from Communities 2 and 5. No one from Community 1, a low crime area, stated that they felt the same. In fact, attendance at most of Community 1's community-police meetings were low (a median of 15 citizens in attendance) in comparison to the other communities studied. Given the low crime rate in the area, perhaps residents did not feel as compelled to attend the community-police meetings as the other communities. Yet, many residents in Community 1 still wanted to be informed about local crime and disorder.

Catalyzes a Community-Driven Agenda at Local Meetings

Results suggest that the technology allows citizens to actively engage in community-police meetings (i.e., introduce topics, direct the agenda) as opposed to being passive recipients of information from the police (i.e., only asking about issues that the police introduce). At the meetings, citizens asked the police questions about incidents that were mentioned in online discussions or emails. Residents introduced at least one topic from the online website in over 85% of Community 1's community-police meetings and 70% and 75% in Communities 2 and 5, respectively. Citizens said that they had a greater influence on the community-police meeting agenda, because residents would ask questions about the information they read online as opposed to simply responding to the topics introduced by the police.

Though the police have traditionally dictated the community-police meeting agendas [43], some residents stated that the meetings seemed to be more community-driven as a result of online communication. A woman from Community 1, who attended community-police meetings for at least 10 years, described how technology use has impacted her approach to the community-police meetings: *"Well you know it all works hand in hand because when you know you've read it online and then you go [to the community-police meetings] prepared. It may be discussed or it already has happened and it's resolved. Or you may have more questions like, 'What happened with that thing? Did they ever catch the guy?'"* Her statement suggests that the online information affected the questions that residents asked. Another resident in Community 2 said that what he read on the community email list or discussion board *"has driven questions I might ask [at the community-police meetings] about general stuff in the neighborhood."* Similarly, a community facilitator from Community 5 agreed that the technology leads to more "community-driven" discussions, saying, *"They get all this information [online] and then they want to talk about it at the meeting."* His statement referred to those who asked the police at the community-police meetings about incidents that they heard about online.

At times, the person who posted the message online raises the topic at the meeting. The community facilitator from Community 1 said, *"Sometimes it's the people that sent the original [online message] that bring it up to make sure that it actually was recognized and that may be some preliminary work had been done [by the police] and [they] might have an answer."* Thus, people sometimes discuss their concerns online but then follow up their comments by coming to the meetings to seek answers from the police. Another male from Community 1 agreed, saying, *"At most of our beat meetings, we usually have a collection of things that come in over the websites that may or may not have been part of the information collected by the police [..] There are things that happen, which we don't know if the cops know about or not. But [community facilitators] will discuss it or it will be brought up by the people [at the meetings]."* These statements suggest that the citizens questioned the police about issues and concerns discussed online.

In the two communities that did not have a strong online presence (Communities 3 and 4), citizens discussed issues that they witnessed in-person (e.g., "I heard gunshots last Sunday") or that they heard about via word-of-mouth. Also, more meeting time was spent on the police-led agenda. With most community-police meetings lasting one hour, an average of 35 minutes were spent on police agenda items in the communities that did not use community-based ICTs while only an average of 20 minutes were spent in the communities with the community-based ICTs. The online discussions seemed to provide people with a vast amount of information about what was happening, which became a focal point during the community-police meetings.

Furthermore, some felt that by receiving information about the previous meeting (through the meeting minutes), they were able to more confidently request information from the police and city services about their actions. One woman from Community 5 explained, *"[the moderator] goes and gets those ordinances and [..] when you come back to the next [meeting], you can say 'Well, the city says such and such a thing, but this isn't happening. The police is supposed do such and such thing, but this isn't happening.'"* This woman felt that the emails allowed citizens to hold the police more accountable for their actions. We observed citizens holding the police accountable most often in Community 5, where citizens reported having the least trust for the police and satisfaction with the community-police meetings in comparison to the other communities.

Four interviewees (two each from Communities 1 and 2) felt that the police were more prepared to answer residents' questions at the community-police meetings as a result of the community-based crime prevention ICTs. One man from Community 1 said, *"It used to seem to me that when I would go to the [community-police] meetings that [a police officer] was monitoring [..] the [community discussion] site, because things that we would post on there [..] would be discussed in the meetings [..] The police, then I think, were more prepared for what was, you know, going to be discussed or what people were kind of up in arms about or concerned about."* Though the police never responded online, Community 2's police sergeant said she did regularly check the community message boards but did not respond because of liability concerns from police headquarters.

Overall, most residents felt that the online communication improved the community-police meetings. One man from Community 2 reflected on times before the community-based online discussions were created: *"[The meetings] are a lot better now than it used to be. Everyone knows more. Everyone has more information to everything now and we're all connected a lot tighter than we used to be. Yeah, I mean [the community email list] was really grassroots when we started. We didn't have cell phones. Imagine that? We couldn't even talk to each other. Most, not even just some, most people didn't even have email. They didn't have computers. They weren't online. So there was none of that communication going on [..] So it was a lot harder to communicate."* This suggests that community-based ICTs can be beneficial to local in-person meetings.

DISCUSSION

Towards understanding the influence of community-based ICTs on in-person behavior, this section describes 1) the importance of topic and source, 2) the ICTs' role as supplements to in-person interactions, and 3) the drawbacks of online communication.

Topic and Source Matter

The topic of crime and safety is important as evidenced by the amount of attention it has received in HCI [3, 4, 16, 30, 51]. Given that discussing crime elicits emotions such as fear, anxiety, and anger [18, 29, 50], the topic itself may induce behavior change. Most people instinctively avoid hurt or harm; therefore, discussions about crime may lead to natural reactions of internalizing others' experiences in order to avoid victimization. Community-based ICTs targeted at other social issues (e.g., health, sustainability) may elicit different in-person responses. The differences in emotional responses to these topics should be further explored, as they may trigger in-person behavior changes. By understanding the emotions tied to other topics, systems may be designed to more effectively encourage civic engagement.

Similarly, results suggest that the source of information may be important in influencing behavior. In our study, residents stated that they were influenced by comments from people who resided in the same area. Thus, the geographical proximity, or physical closeness, may be important in influencing behavior change. Also, a community-based ICT may prompt a different response than a government or privately funded ICT. For example, residents may be more likely to trust information coming from a neighbor who lives a few doors away than statistics from the police. Furthermore, online comments from the neighbor a few doors down who experienced a break in may elicit empathy and self-reflection (i.e., if it happened to them, it could happen to me). This aligns with prior studies that suggest the importance of trust when designing community ICTs for crime prevention [3, 5]. Thus, avenues for future exploration include investigating the effects of the origin of information on offline behavior and the impact that trust has on information sharing and receiving. Additionally, by exploring questions like "Should community-based ICTs be designed for a select few blocks or a larger area?," we can begin to understand the potency of proximity on issues like trust. Also, researchers could examine how online communication affects the behavior of indirect stakeholders, which are those whom the technologies were not designed for (e.g., potential offenders). While preliminary work suggests that burglars rarely use online tools to determine if they will commit a burglary [16], we should continue to explore the consequences of using community-based crime prevention technology by various users (e.g., citizens, potential offenders, city officials).

ICTs Are Supplements, Not Replacements

During this study, we witnessed the complex relationship between in-person community meetings and online communication. Our results suggest that the two are very much intertwined where residents gained information from online discussions and shared it during the meetings (and vice versa). This demonstrates the importance of the in-person meetings as well as the ability for residents to communicate online, which can increase social capital and collective efficacy [25]. Such issues are particularly important in low income communities that tend to have higher crime rates and less collective efficacy [33]. Kavanaugh et al. [25] suggest that communities plagued with less education (typically low socioeconomic communities) may not experience the benefits of community-based ICTs such as social capital and collective action. However, by designing community-based ICTs that allow residents in low income areas to have positive interactions with city officials, social capital and collective efficacy may increase, leading to more collective action.

> "Populations with low socioeconomic status can develop higher levels of efficacy through positive experiences and reinforcement. These positive experiences tend to be external, such as local government's concern and active recruitment of feedback and from underrepresented groups over sustained periods of time...While such responses from community organizations tend to be the exception rather than the rule, they are demonstrated to be effective in raising collective efficacy and fostering optimism in targeted populations" [25].

We observed residents in Community 5, a low income community, hold the police and other city officials accountable, such that the police began asking for residents' input in identifying and solving local problems. This suggests an opportunity for technologists to design experiences, rather than features aimed at increasing collective action online. Our study is an example of how technologies can supplement established in-person meetings, not replace them. Future work could explore if this is a possibility and how we can begin to design technologies that support positive in-person interactions at in-person meetings.

Concerns About Online Communication Regarding Crime

While there are benefits of online communication amongst residents, there are also concerns such as increased fear and negative stereotyping. Residents may feel increased fear and anxiety as a result of reading about neighbors being victimized. Fear caused by online communication is concerning because some react individually to feelings of fear and anxiety by trying to protect themselves using tactics that cause isolation (e.g., not going out, buying guns and locks) [9]. Individual responses to crime ultimately increase fear and distrust [9] and decrease feelings of community and safety [42]. This leads to additional questions about technology design, specifically how to support discussion while also limiting exposure to information that users are uncomfortable with receiving.

Online communication could also lead to stereotyping or having biases towards certain people based on their outward appearance. In our study, residents reported that online communication influenced their interaction with strangers. Future research could begin to unpack how online conversations influence perceptions of others, positively or negatively. For example, all three of the communities that heavily used technology posted pictures of alleged offenders. Of the photos posted, over 90% were of black males. Community 1 sent out the most pictures (over 100 photos on the site), and Community 2 sent out significantly less (roughly 30). Community 5 sent out less than 10 photos, all within local newspaper articles. For Community 1, which is a less racially diverse community, online communication could perpetuate the stereotype that black males are criminals, leading to racial profiling. These photos are an example how the technology may assist citizens in redefining the community's "norms" of outsiders.

Potential negative consequences, such as racial profiling, underscores the importance of design implications that address issues such as group think and stereotyping. Designing more democratic online systems (e.g., people vote on inflammatory remarks anonymously) may result in more users feeling comfortable enough to share their diverging opinions online, which could alter the formation of negative "norms." Moreover, a democratic system may help reduce marginalizing a large group of people who may not have Internet access. Future work should consider those who do not use the community-based ICTs and the effect that online norms (which may differ from a community's in-person social norms) has on non-users. Designing community-based ICTs that do not marginalize those that lack online access or people who are viewed as "undesirable" (e.g., technologies that avoid an 'us' versus 'them' situation in gentrifying neighborhoods) can lead to more effective and inclusive design solutions that encourage building relationships and social capital in neighborhoods.

LIMITATIONS

There are limitations to this study. First, residents self-reported behavior change during the interviews after reflection. Self-reported behavior change may not be as accurate as observed behavior change. Assuming that there was indeed a change in behavior, it may be caused by a combination of receiving online information as well as attending community-police meetings, news media, and/or even word-of-mouth communication. We acknowledge that both of these issues are concerns based on self-reported data. Future work has an opportunity to address such concerns by conducting a study that extends beyond self-reports.

Second, this paper specifically focuses on digital communication about crime, which may have a major effect on the type and rate at which behavior change occurs. Online conversations with neighbors about other topics may have a very different outcome. Similarly, conversations amongst residents at different geographic levels (e.g., block, beat, ward, city) may have very different effects on in-person and online behavior. We used beats, because it aligned with how residents set up their online communication tools and with the community-police meetings in Chicago, but this may differ in other cities. In addition, the type of people interviewed were those who purposefully signed up for digital communication related to local crime. This raises questions for future exploration regarding those who are not so civically engaged and what effect (if any) would online conversations with neighbors have on their in-person behavior.

Lastly, though more than half of our observations of topics emerging from online conversation were blatantly stated, some were inferences that were made (i.e., We compared the online data to the topics from the community-police meetings). Such an assertion may negatively affect the data analysis. These limitations are opportunities for future studies to conduct a more controlled study to understand the extent to which online communication influences behavior at the community-police meetings.

CONCLUSION

In this paper, we describe how online conversations about crime amongst local residents impact offline behavior. Interviewees reported that online communication influences their behavior to avoid victimization and the interactions that happen during in-person community meetings. Community-based technologies aimed at addressing local social issues should be designed to support online discussions and lead to positive experiences during in-person meetings with city officials.

ACKNOWLEDGMENTS

Thanks to the wonderful participants that welcomed me into their community. Thanks to Jennifer Burrell, Lynette Kvasny, Dan A. Lewis, Elizabeth Lenaghan, and anonymous reviewers for their comments on previous versions of this paper. This work was supported by the NSF Graduate Research Fellowship.

REFERENCES

1. Bilger, M., and Carrieri, V. Health in the cities: When the neighborhood matters more than income. *Journal of Health Economics 32*, 1 (2013), 1 – 11.
2. Blackwood, A., Roeger, K., and Pettijohn, S. The nonprofit sector in brief: Public charities, giving and volunteering, 2012. Tech. rep., The Urban Institute, Washington DC, 2012.
3. Blom, J., Viswanathan, D., Spasojevic, M., Go, J., Acharya, K., and Ahonius, R. Fear and the city: role of mobile services in harnessing safety and security in urban use contexts. In *Proc. of CHI*, ACM (2010), 1841–1850.
4. Blythe, M. A., Wright, P. C., and Monk, A. F. Little brother: could and should wearable computing technologies be applied to reducing older people's fear of crime? *Personal and Ubiquitous Computing 8* (2004), 402–415.
5. Brush, A. B., Jung, J., Mahajan, R., and Martinez, F. Digital neighborhood watch: Investigating the sharing of camera data amongst neighbors. In *Proc. of CSCW* (2013), 693–700.
6. Carroll, J. M., and Rosson, M. B. Developing the blacksburg electronic village. *Commun. ACM 39* (1996), 69–74.
7. Carroll, J. M., and Rosson, M. B. Wild at home: The neighborhood as a living laboratory for hci. *ACM Trans. Comput.-Hum. Interact. 20*, 3 (July 2013), 16:1–16:28.
8. Carroll, J. M., Rosson, M. B., Isenhour, P., Ganoe, C., Dunlap, D., Fogarty, J., Schafer, W., and Metre, C. V. Designing our town: {MOOsburg}. *International Journal of Human-Computer Studies 54*, 5 (2001), 725 – 751.
9. Conklin, J. *The impact of crime*. Macmillan New York, NY, 1975.
10. De Choudhury, M., Monroy-Hernández, A., and Mark, G. "narco" emotions: Affect and desensitization in social media during the mexican drug war. In *Proc. of CHI* (2014), 3563–3572.
11. Dillahunt, T., Mankoff, J., Paulos, E., and Fussell, S. It's not all about "green": Energy use in low-income communities. In *Proc. of Ubi Comp* (2009), 255–264.
12. Dillahunt, T. R. Fostering social capital in economically distressed communities. In *Proc. of CHI* (2014), 531–540.
13. Dillahunt, T. R., and Mankoff, J. Understanding factors of successful engagement around energy consumption between and among households. In *Proc. of CSCW* (2014), 1246–1257.
14. Dourish, P. Re-space-ing place: "place" and "space" ten years on. In *Proc. of CSCW* (2006), 299–308.
15. Ellen, I. G., Mijanovich, T., and Dillman, K.-N. Neighborhood effects on health: Exploring the links and assessing the evidence. *Journal of Urban Affairs 23*, 3-4 (2001), 391–408.
16. Erete, S. L. Protecting the home: exploring the roles of technology and citizen activism from a burglar's perspective. In *Proc. of CHI* (2013), 2507–2516.
17. Erete, S. L., Miller, R., and Lewis, D. A. Differences in technology use to support community crime prevention. In *Proc. of CSCW* (2014), 153–156.
18. Franzini, L., Caughy, M., Spears, W., and Eugenia Fernandez Esquer, M. Neighborhood economic conditions, social processes, and self-rated health in low-income neighborhoods in texas: A multilevel latent variables model. *Social Science & Medicine 61*, 6 (2005), 1135–1150.
19. Ganglbauer, E., Fitzpatrick, G., Subasi, O., and Güldenpfennig, F. Think globally, act locally: A case study of a free food sharing community and social networking. In *Proc. of CSCW* (2014), 911–921.

20. Hampton, K., and Wellman, B. Neighboring in netville: How the internet supports community and social capital in a wired suburb. *City & Community 2*, 4 (2003), 277–311.

21. Hargittai, E. Beyond logs and surveys: In-depth measures of people's web use skills. *Journal of the American Society for Information Science and Technology 53*, 14 (2002), 1239–1244.

22. Hargittai, E. Digital na(t)ives? variation in internet skills and uses among members of the ?net generation?*. *Sociological Inquiry 80*, 1 (2010), 92–113.

23. Hirsch, T. Communities real and imagined: designing a communication system for zimbabwean activists. In *Proc. of C&T* (2009), 71–76.

24. Huang, A.-J., Wang, H.-C., and Yuan, C. W. De-virtualizing social events: Understanding the gap between online and offline participation for event invitations. In *Proc. of CSCW*, CSCW '14 (2014), 436–448.

25. Kavanaugh, A., Carroll, J. M., Rosson, M. B., Zin, T. T., and Reese, D. D. Community networks: Where offline communities meet online. *Journal of Computer-Mediated Communication 10*, 4 (2005).

26. Kavanaugh, A. L., Reese, D. D., Carroll, J. M., and Rosson, M. B. Weak ties in networked communities. *The Information Society 21*, 2 (2005), 119–131.

27. Le Dantec, C. A., and Edwards, W. K. Designs on dignity: Perceptions of technology among the homeless. In *Proc. of CHI*, CHI '08 (2008), 627–636.

28. Lewis, D. A., and Salem, G. Community crime prevention: An analysis of a developing strategy. *Crime & Delinquency 27*, 3 (1981), 405–421.

29. Lewis, D. A., and Salem, G. *Fear of crime: Incivility and the production of a social problem*. Transaction Publishers, 1986.

30. Lewis, S., and Lewis, D. A. Examining technology that supports community policing. In *Proc. of CHI* (2012), 1371–1380.

31. Masden, C. A., Grevet, C., Grinter, R. E., Gilbert, E., and Edwards, W. K. Tensions in scaling-up community social media: A multi-neighborhood study of nextdoor. In *Proc. of CHI* (2014), 3239–3248.

32. Monroy-Hernández, A., boyd, d., Kiciman, E., De Choudhury, M., and Counts, S. The new war correspondents: The rise of civic media curation in urban warfare. In *Proceedings of the 2013 Conference on Computer Supported Cooperative Work*, CSCW '13, ACM (New York, NY, USA, 2013), 1443–1452.

33. Morenoff, J., Sampson, R., and Raudenbush, S. Neighborhood inequality, collective efficacy, and the spatial dynamics of urban violence*. *Criminology 39*, 3 (2001), 517–558.

34. Morenoff, J. D., House, J. S., Hansen, B. B., Williams, D. R., Kaplan, G. A., and Hunte, H. E. Understanding social disparities in hypertension prevalence, awareness, treatment, and control: The role of neighborhood context. *Social Science & Medicine 65*, 9 (2007), 1853 – 1866. Placing Health in Context.

35. Parker, A., Kantroo, V., Lee, H. R., Osornio, M., Sharma, M., and Grinter, R. Health promotion as activism: building community capacity to effect social change. In *Proc. of CHI*, ACM (2012), 99–108.

36. Pirolli, P., Preece, J., and Shneiderman, B. Cyberinfrastructure for social action on national priorities. *Computer 43*, 11 (2010), 20–21.

37. Putnam, R. Bowling alone: America's declining social capital. *Journal of democracy 6* (1995), 65–78.

38. Redhead, F., and Brereton, M. A qualitative analysis of local community communications. In *Proc. of OZCHI*, ACM (2006), 361–364.

39. Redhead, F., and Brereton, M. Designing interaction for local communications: An urban screen study. In *Proc. INTERACT*, Springer-Verlag (2009), 457–460.

40. Sampson, R. J. *Great American city: Chicago and the Enduring Neighborhood Effect*. University of Chicago Press, 2012.

41. Sampson, R. J., and Morenoff, J. D. Durable inequality: Spatial dynamics, social processes, and the persistence of poverty in chicago neighborhoods. In *Poverty Traps*, K. H. Samuel Bowles, Steven N. Durlauf, Ed. Princeton University Press, Princeton, 2006, 176–203.

42. Schwab-Stone, M., Ayers, T., Kasprow, W., Voyce, C., Barone, C., Shriver, T., and Weissberg, R. No safe haven: A study of violence exposure in an urban community. *Journal of the American Academy of Child & Adolescent Psychiatry 34* (1995), 1343–1352.

43. Skogan, W. G. *Police and Community in Chicago: A Tale of Three Cities*. Oxford University Press, 2006.

44. Skogan, W. G. Collective action, structural disadvantage, and crime. *Tides and Currents in Police Theories: Journal of Police Studies*, 25 (2012), 135–152.

45. Skogan, W. G., and Hartnett, S. *Community Policing, Chicago style*. Oxford University Press, 1997.

46. Skogan, W. G., Lewis, D. A., Podolefsky, A., DuBow, F., Gordon, M., Maxfield, A. H. . M., and Salem, G. The reactions to crime project. Tech. rep., U.S. Department of Justice-National Institute of Justice, Washington DC, 1982.

47. Smyth, T. N., Etherton, J., and Best, M. L. Moses: Exploring new ground in media and post-conflict reconciliation. In *Proc. of CHI*, ACM (New York, NY, USA, 2010), 1059–1068.

48. Starbird, K. Delivering patients to sacre coeur: Collective intelligence in digital volunteer communities. In *Proc. of CHI* (2013), 801–810.

49. Strauss, A., and Corbin, J. *Basics of qualitative research: Grounded theory procedures and techniques.* Sage Publications, Inc, 1990.

50. Taylor, R. B., Gottfredson, S. D., and Brower, S. Block Crime and Fear: Defensible Space, Local Social Ties, and Territorial Functioning. *Journal of Research in Crime and Delinquency 21*, 4 (1984), 303–331.

51. Tullio, J., Huang, E., Wheatley, D., Zhang, H., Guerrero, C., and Tamdoo, A. Experience, adjustment, and engagement: the role of video in law enforcement. In *Proc. of CHI*, ACM (2010), 1505–1514.

52. Tyler, T. R. Policing in black and white: Ethnic group differences in trust and confidence in the police. *Police Quarterly 8*, 3 (2005), 322–342.

53. Voida, A., Harmon, E., and Al-Ani, B. Bridging between organizations and the public: Volunteer coordinators' uneasy relationship with social computing. In *Proc. of CHI* (2012), 1967–1976.

54. Wellman, B., Haase, A., Witte, J., and Hampton, K. Does the internet increase, decrease, or supplement social capital. *American behavioral scientist 45*, 3 (2001), 436–455.

55. Wilson, W. J. *The truly disadvantaged: The inner city, the underclass, and public policy*. University of Chicago Press, 1987.

56. Woelfer, J. P., Iverson, A., Hendry, D. G., Friedman, B., and Gill, B. T. Improving the safety of homeless young people with mobile phones: values, form and function. In *Proc. of CHI*, ACM (2011), 1707–1716.

57. Yardi, S., and Bruckman, A. Income, race, and class: Exploring socioeconomic differences in family technology use. In *Proc. of CHI* (2012), 3041–3050.

The Group Context Framework: An Extensible Toolkit for Opportunistic Grouping and Collaboration

Adrian A. de Freitas and Anind K. Dey
Human Computer Interaction Institute, Carnegie Mellon University
Pittsburgh PA, 15213
{adefreit, anind}@cs.cmu.edu

ABSTRACT
In this paper, we present the Group Context Framework (GCF), a general-purpose toolkit that allows mobile devices to opportunistically share contextual information. GCF provides a standardized way for developers to request contextual data for their applications. The framework then intelligently groups with other devices to satisfy these requirements. Through two prototypes, we demonstrate how GCF can be used to support a broad range of collaborative and cooperative tasks. We then show how our framework's architecture allows devices to opportunistically detect and collaborate with one another, even when running different applications. Finally, we present two real-world domains that show how GCF's ability to form groups increases users' access to relevant and timely information, and discuss possible incentives and safeguards to context sharing from a user standpoint.

Author Keywords
Context-sharing; middleware; ubiquitous computing; mobile computing

ACM Classification Keywords
D.3.3 [Language Constructs and Features]: Frameworks

INTRODUCTION

Forming and working in groups is an integral part of the human experience. In addition to satisfying our innate need to interact and belong to a community [17], there are several practical benefits of working in groups, including 1) improved situational awareness [8], 2) increased opportunities for communication and collaboration [11], and 3) the ability to tackle and solve much larger problems and tasks than we can on our own [24].

In recent years, the rapid proliferation of mobile devices and Internet connectivity has dramatically increased our ability to form and work in groups. Applications such as Twitter and Facebook have established themselves as our *de facto* applications for discovering, managing, and keeping in touch with our social circles. Meanwhile, researchers have experimented with context-aware chat clients [11,18], virtual workspaces [7], and location monitoring systems [16] in order to provide distributed group members with increased situational awareness and improved productivity, regardless of their physical location.

All of this work demonstrates how we can preserve, enhance, and even create new group experiences through technology. We believe, however, that there are still significant opportunities to improve upon and expand our range of group interactions. To date, technology has primarily been used to assist with groupings that are well defined or predictable. We link Facebook accounts with close friends or share work calendars with colleagues because the opportunities for interaction are expected to be frequent and long-lived. However, there are many types of group interactions that occur without warning. We will ask a stranger for directions, or offer one time advice to an acquaintance without planning these exchanges in advance. These types of *opportunistic* interactions are natural to us and allow us to connect as a community, but our devices currently lack an equivalent means of interacting and sharing information with one another unless they are explicitly told to do so. This is because the cost of creating and participating in a group using computer mediation has traditionally been non-trivial. As a result, there is an entire range of applications that our devices have difficulty supporting, and this prevents them from being able to provide us with the right information at the right time.

In this paper, we aim to make mobile devices more human-like by improving their ability to serendipitously work together. To achieve this, we have developed the Group Context Framework (GCF), a novel programming toolkit that allows mobile devices to autonomously form groups and share information. While GCF supports a broad range of use cases, we focus on sharing context in this work because it is both time and situational dependent, making it a perfect example of a category of information that is worth sharing between devices, regardless as to whether they have ever met before or will meet again. Through GCF, applications broadcast requests for contextual information. Neighboring devices can then review these requests, and determine how they can best assist one another.

While prior work has demonstrated how opportunistic groupings of mobile devices can be used to conserve power

CSCW '15, March 14 - 18, 2015, Vancouver, BC, Canada.
Copyright 2015 ACM 978-1-4503-2922-4/15/03…$15.00.
http://dx.doi.org/10.1145/2675133.2675205

and share resources [10,12,13], GCF offers two novel contributions. First, by abstracting the process by which applications request and receive contextual information into a mobile middleware, we dramatically increase the opportunities for serendipitous group formation. In GCF, context is produced and shared through a series of *context providers*. Context providers provide a critical abstraction that allows devices to share information in an application agnostic manner. This allows GCF-enabled devices to 1) gain access to information that they could not obtain or produce on their own, 2) conserve and share resources when they are in the presence of other devices that can produce the same context, and 3) serendipitously work together, even if they are performing different tasks.

Secondly, GCF is extremely flexible. While there are several middleware solutions that support opportunistic device groupings, they tend to be optimized for a specific task (*e.g.*, conserving power, discovering members with common interests [1]) or group type. As part of our design process, we have developed a conceptual model that describes the various situations in which one might form an opportunistic group, and looked at systems that have been proposed or developed over the years to support these *ad-hoc* exchanges. We then build upon this literature by providing a framework that supports the full range of group interactions. Using GCF, developers can choose to opportunistically interact with a specific device, or with any devices that satisfy a set of conditions. More importantly, developers can use our framework to define their own group selection strategy or criteria, thus allowing it to accommodate an even wider range of use cases.

This paper is structured as follows. In the next section, we provide a survey of related work. We then describe GCF's architecture, and present a series of prototypes that demonstrate its utility and flexibility. Afterwards, we suggest further domains that could benefit from GCF's grouping support, discuss the implications of context sharing on user privacy, and provide a roadmap for future work.

RELATED WORK

Grouping is commonly used in context-aware applications to facilitate information sharing. While the exact reasons to form a group vary from case to case, the motivation to group can be expressed as a cross-section of 1) the tasks members are performing, and 2) the information they need to perform that task. We have combined these factors in Table 1, resulting in a conceptual model that describes the most common scenarios that lead to group formation.

The most recognizable form of grouping occurs when members' tasks and information requirements directly align (Table 1, Quadrant I). There are a number of systems that have supported these *collaborative* groupings at both the user and device level. TeamSpace is a virtual office environment that allows geographically separated co-workers to share documents with each other, allowing them to view, discuss, and modify documents in real-time [7]. Similarly, in [21], researchers experimented with sharing real-time computer screenshots between distributed group members to allow them to talk and point to objects on a shared display as if they were collocated. In the E2A2 system [10], devices were configured to share GPS coordinates when navigating in physical proximity of one another, thus allowing them to conserve power without any noticeable reduction in accuracy. Similarly, in [12], researchers showed how sensor sharing can be used to optimize individual activity recognition tasks by allowing body-worn sensors to borrow readings from nearby users that are likely performing the same activity.

	Same Data	**Different Data**
Same Task	I. Collaboration	II. Cooperation
Different Task	III. Convenient Collaboration	IV. In-Situ

Table 1. Commonly encountered grouping scenarios.

Another common form of grouping occurs when members perform the same task but require access to different sets of data (Quadrant II). This type of group is *cooperative* since each member contributes to the same task by providing different data or capabilities. In Smart Party [6], cooperative groups were used to generate a music playlist by combining the individual libraries of each group member. Similarly, the Active Map [16] and GroupChat [24] systems combined information about individual users' locations and status, respectively, in order to provide users with greater situational awareness and improve their ability to identify opportunities for communication. Frameworks such as Mobile Gaia [2] supported cooperative groupings of devices, which can share different capabilities with each other in order to perform a common task.

A third form of grouping is *convenient collaboration* (Quadrant III), which occurs when members are performing different tasks that utilize the same data. Microsoft's SenseWeb [9] supports convenient collaboration by providing a database that collects and shares mobile sensor data with applications that have similar data requirements. More recently, researchers have developed an architecture that enables first-responders to share tasks and location information with each other and an incident commander, increasing the latter's situational awareness by taking advantage of a common need for the same information [14].

The final quadrant describes groupings where members' tasks and information requirements completely differ from one another (Quadrant IV). From an end-user perspective, this scenario is not conducive to grouping as there is a complete disconnect between users. From a device perspective, however, this scenario allows for the creation of *in-situ* groups. Several research efforts have examined the idea of dynamically forming groups for the purposes of sharing computing resources. In mobile *ad-hoc* networks, numerous algorithms have been proposed to facilitate service discovery and provisioning [4,5,15], but these approaches mainly focus on the technical challenges associated with discovering and accessing resources in a constantly changing environment. In ErdOS [23] and CoMon [13], researchers developed a series of operating system and middleware techniques to support spontaneous context sharing, but only focused on long-lasting groupings (lasting at least 5 minutes) for the purposes of improving battery efficiency. Finally, systems like MobiShare [22] and Anonysense [20] allow devices to dynamically group and share context, but require a centralized server or assume that group members are known beforehand, respectively.

While our discussion thus far has covered the most common scenarios that lead to grouping, it is important to note that opportunistic groups are not limited to a single quadrant. On the contrary, supporting opportunistic groups is challenging precisely because they are unpredictable in terms of the situations in which they occur and their duration. Although prior work has shown that it is possible to form groups of devices across a wide range of scenarios, there is no single solution that is designed to operate across our entire model. Thus, there is a need for a truly generalizable framework for grouping and context sharing that supports a wide range of group types while simultaneously minimizing the need for user intervention and therefore the cost of forming an opportunistic group. We aim to address this need through GCF.

FRAMEWORK DESIGN

Our primary aim with GCF is to create a toolkit that allows devices to autonomously form groups and share context. To achieve this, we have identified four key design principles:

- **Ease of Use.** Developers are more likely to use a toolkit if it can be easily used. Our framework supports this by standardizing the process by which devices request and receive contextual information.
- **Extensibility.** As noted in the previous section, many frameworks that support context sharing are designed with a single type of group (*i.e.*, collaborative, cooperative, *etc.*) in mind. In contrast, GCF is designed to support a wide range of groups, and can be extended to support additional (or special case) groupings as needed.
- **Automated Grouping.** GCF abstracts the process by which devices discover and collaborate with one another. Developers only need to define which context(s) their application requires, and the framework will automatically search for and form the appropriate group structures to satisfy these requirements.
- **Dynamic Group Management.** Due to the transient nature of mobile devices, a device may need to group with several devices in order to achieve a consistent quality of service. GCF addresses this problem by periodically monitoring the state of the environment and modifying its group membership as needed.

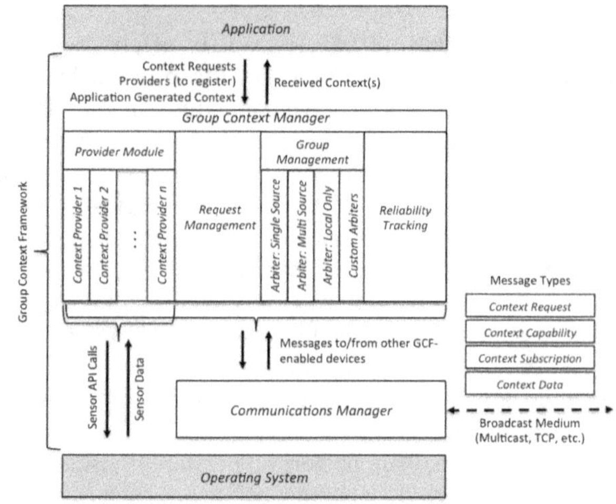

Figure 1. GCF High Level Architecture

We envision GCF as a foundation rather than a feature complete solution. While our framework contains the abstractions necessary to support a wide range of use cases, we acknowledge that there are various aspects of opportunistic grouping and context sharing that cannot be predicted in advance. To address this, we have embedded hooks to allow the framework to be extended as needed.

Framework Components

GCF's high-level architectural diagram is provided in Figure 1. The main components of our framework are:

- A *communications manager* that facilitates message passing between devices and applications.
- A series of *context providers* that collect, process, and disseminate contextual information.
- A *group context manager* that tracks an application's contextual requests and forms groups as needed.

Communications Manager

The communications manager is responsible for passing messages between GCF-enabled devices. It allows the framework to broadcast requests for context, receive advertisements, and subscribe/unsubscribe to context providers. GCF uses four types of messages:

- **Context Requests** express an application's desire for contextual information. They contain the unique identifier of the device making the request, as well as the type of context being requested (*e.g.*, location, accelerometer), and the desired refresh rate. Additionally, each request contains a *type* value to let the framework know how it should be processed. For *single-source* type requests, the framework will examine all nearby devices and group with the best device that can satisfy the requirement. For *multi-source* requests, the framework will group with all devices in range. Finally, for *local* requests, the framework will try to generate the requested context on the local device.
- **Context Capability** messages advertise a device's willingness to provide contextual information. They contain a description of the type of context being offered,

as well as the rate at which the requester must send keep-alive messages in order to keep receiving information. By default, GCF requires devices to include information concerning their available battery life, whether or not they are already providing the context, and the quality of context produced by this device. The message, however, also contains an optional field that allows developers to insert other types of performance metrics as needed.

- **Context Subscription** messages are sent by a device in order to either establish or dissolve a group relationship. They contain the unique identifiers of the context requester and provider, as well as the type of context that is to be provided by the latter.
- **Context data** messages contain contextual information. These messages provide a description of the information being shared, the identifier of the device providing the data, and the data itself.

The communications manager can operate over any broadcast network technology. We specifically focus on TCP broadcast and UDP multicast in our work, as both protocols are widely used, support a large number of simultaneous users, and allow for unrestricted communication across a subnet (typically limited to a single building or floor). Alternatively, GCF can also communicate through a dedicated socket server in order to share context across arbitrary distances and/or mobile network providers. However, this approach is less opportunistic, as it limits the framework's ability to group to only those devices that are on the same server.

Context Providers

Context providers are tasked with producing, storing, and distributing contextual information. Each provider produces a specific type of context, and a GCF-enabled device may have zero or more context providers depending upon what contexts it is able to produce and what it is willing to share.

Context providers perform two main tasks. Their primary responsibility is to convert raw data into usable context. The means by which this is accomplished varies depending upon the provider. For example, a *Location Provider* may utilize GPS and network sensors to pinpoint the user's location. A *Shopping List* provider, on the other hand, may not use any sensors, but instead simply store a list of items provided by a user through a mobile shopping application.

The second job of a context provider is to keep track of active subscriptions. When a device subscribes to a provider, its identifier is stored. The provider then listens for periodic heartbeat messages from the requesting device and automatically cancels the subscription if it does not receive a heartbeat within a set period of time. This allows a provider to keep track of which devices are still nearby, and automatically conserve resources when it is not in use.

As part of our initial release, GCF already includes a library of providers for commonly used contexts (*e.g.,* GPS, compass, temperature). However, we also allow developers

```
public class ExampleProvider extends ContextProvider
{
 // Constructor
 public void ExampleProvider()
 {
  // Registers the Provider's Globally Recognized Name
  super("EXAMPLE");
 }

 // Code to initialize the provider
 public void start() { }

 // Code to halt the provider
 public void stop() { }

 // Return TRUE if provider should respond to a request
 public boolean sendCapability(ContextRequest msg) { }

 // Calculates the "Quality" of this Provider
 public double getFitness() { }

 // Sends Context to all Subscribers
 public void sendContext()
 {
  commManager.sendContext(new ContextData(…));
 }
}
```

Figure 2. Sample Java Implementation of a Context Provider

to create *custom* providers as needed. As shown in Figure 2, creating a new context provider involves inheriting from our base class and implementing the following methods:

- In the constructor method (*i.e., ExampleProvider*), developers assign their provider a unique string value that is associated with a particular context (*e.g.,* Location = "LOC", Bluetooth = "BT"). This value needs to be globally associated with this context, as it is what allows our framework to link context requests to individual providers across applications/devices.
- The *start* and *stop* methods are automatically called by the framework when the first device subscribes to it, or when the last device unsubscribes, respectfully. It gives the provider an opportunity to activate/deactivate sensors, and to perform initialization or cleanup tasks.
- The *sendCapability* method allows developers to decide whether or not the provider should respond to a request for context. By default, providers will always respond to requests from the local device, and will only stop responding to external requests once the device's battery reaches a predefined threshold (*e.g.,* 20%). However, developers can override this method to prevent a provider from responding in special cases, such as when 1) it does not have any information to share, or 2) when the request is considered to be unreasonable.
- The *getFitness* method allows a context provider to report the quality of information that it produces. Since the notion of quality is context-specific, we require each provider to define its own quality metric. For example, a location context provider might use the accuracy of coordinates returned, measured in meters. Likewise, for a camera sensor, one possible metric might be its image fidelity (in megapixels). GCF assumes that higher fitness values correspond to higher quality, and that this metric is standardized across all providers of the same type.
- Finally, the *sendContext* method gives providers the ability to control how context is delivered to all subscribed devices. The framework automatically calls this method whenever context is requested, and allows

developers to transmit the same context to all devices, or to deliver a specific context value to each one.

Context providers are the primary means by which applications group and collaborate in GCF. They provide a standardized, application independent interface for collecting and distributing contextual information. Developers can use the default providers available in our toolkit (location, light intensity, compass, temperature, barometric pressure, Bluetooth proximity, accelerometer, and audio magnitude), and/or create additional providers as needed. This allows us to maximize code reuse while still increasing our opportunities to obtain and share context.

Group Context Manager

The group context manager (GCM) is the controller for the entire framework. It is created at startup, and is responsible for monitoring an application's requests for context, searching for device groupings that best satisfy these needs, and delivering context to the application as it arrives.

The GCM consists of four components (Figure 1, middle). The *request management module* is responsible for tracking a device's active context requests. It broadcasts requests, periodically contacts providers so that they continue to provide data, and disconnects from providers in the event that the application no longer needs information or in the event of a communications timeout.

The *provider module* is responsible for managing an application's context providers. At instantiation, the GCM does not contain any context providers. Instead, providers are created and registered to the GCM so that developers and/or end users can explicitly specify which contexts they are willing to produce and share. When a request arrives, the GCM queries the provider module in order to determine if a provider with the matching context type is both registered and willing to satisfy the request. If both conditions are satisfied, a capability advertisement is then created and sent back to the requester.

The *group management module* is responsible for evaluating and subscribing to devices that contain the desired context. It accomplishes this through a series of *arbiters* that examines each context capability message and selects the best one(s) depending upon a predefined grouping strategy (more details on arbiters is provided in the following section).

The last module in the GCM is the *reliability monitor*. This component maintains a log of communication timeouts for all previously encountered devices. This information is used to discourage the framework from grouping with unreliable devices in the near future.

Selecting Context Provider(s)

A key feature of GCF is its ability to automatically discover and form groups. For example, in order to receive location information from a single device once every five seconds, a developer only has to write the following line of code:

```
gcm.sendRequest("LOC", SINGLE_SOURCE, 5000);
```

In order to form a grouping that best satisfies this request, the GCM transmits a context request message to all devices in communications range and collects the context capability messages sent in response. An *arbiter* then processes these capabilities to determine which device(s) to group with. GCF includes three arbiters: a single-source arbiter, a multi-source arbiter, and a local arbiter. These arbiters match to a corresponding request type, and form groups according to a predefined strategy, as discussed below.

Single Source Arbitration

A single source context request is useful in situations when a device requires contextual information, but is not concerned about where it comes from. This strategy takes advantage of the fact that there are many types of context (*e.g.,* location, temperature) that are not device specific, and can be reliably reported by any device that is nearby.

In single source arbitration, the arbiter examines the context capability messages provided by each device and selects the "best" one. To calculate the best device, GCF considers the following criteria:

- **Battery Life (*b*):** To maximize the lifespan of all participating devices, the arbiter will favor devices with the largest remaining battery life. To compensate for variances in battery size and drain rates between mobile devices, each device reports its battery life in estimated minutes remaining.
- **Context Quality (*q*):** It is not possible to have a universal metric to measure quality. Instead, as previously discussed, context providers must define their own quality metric. The arbiter then compares each provider by this metric and favors those that are of higher quality.
- **Communication Overhead (*c*):** To ensure that a device is in range, GCF allows context providers to specify a heartbeat interval. Requesting devices must then send a message at least once per interval in order to keep receiving information. The single source arbiter favors context providers with longer heartbeat intervals, as this minimizes overhead for the requesting device.
- **Duplicate Effort (*d*):** To increase efficiency, the arbiter will try to group with devices that are already providing the requested context to other users. This metric takes advantage of GCF's reliance on broadcast technologies, as it allows a device to provide context to multiple devices without increasing energy consumption.
- **Reliability (*r*):** GCF uses a reliability value in order to estimate a device's ability to dependably provide context. When GCF first encounters a device, it assumes that is reliable and assigns it an r of 1.0. Then, after each disconnect or timeout, this value is halved. By decreasing the value of r and incrementing it slowly over time, the framework is able to favor context providers that have been reliable in the past, while still giving providers the chance to be reconsidered after enough time has passed.

Each of the above factors are normalized to a 0.0 – 1.0 numeric range. A composite fitness value is then calculated for each responding device using the following equation:

$$\text{Fitness} = (w_1 * b) + (w_2 * q) + (w_3 * c) + (w_4 * d) + (w_5 * r)$$
$$w_1 + w_2 + w_3 + w_4 + w_5 = 1.0$$

where w_1 through w_5 are weights that correspond to each of the five criteria listed above.

By setting w_1 through w_5, developers get to specify which criteria matter most for their specific application. When using the standard form of *sendRequest*, GCF uses a set of default weights that we have found to yield good overall performance. However, if developers favor some criteria over others, they can modify these values as they see fit. For example, if sensor quality is especially important for a particular application, developers can assign a higher value to w_2 by using an overloaded version of the *sendRequest* command, as shown below:

```
gcm.sendRequest("LOC", SINGLE_SOURCE, 5000,
        0.0, 1.0, 0.0, 0.0, 0.0);
```

After calculating the fitness values, the device with the highest fitness score is selected, and GCF automatically transmits a context subscription message to it. In the event of a tie, the first device to respond is selected.

Multi-Source Arbitration

Multi-source arbitration is intended for situations when a device requires information from all of its neighbors simultaneously. This method of group formation is useful for applications where each device provides a unique and equally valuable context, (*e.g.*, a map application displaying everyone's positions using their individual GPS receivers).

Unlike single-source arbitration, the multi-source arbiter greedily subscribes to all devices in range. In this fashion, the arbiter is able to create an *ad-hoc* sensor network, and gather context data across a wider geographic area.

Local Arbitration

Local arbitration is intended for situations when a device requires information that can only be produced internally. An example of this is a compass application, as information from both the accelerometer and magnetometer must both be obtained from the local device in order to provide the user with an accurate heading. The local arbiter uses a simplified fitness function that only takes a context provider's context quality (q) into account. Other factors (*i.e.*, battery life, reliability, *etc.*) are not considered as their values will be the same across all advertisements.

Proximity Detection

There are many situations where devices must be physically near one another in order to effectively share context. For example, sharing location data to conserve battery life is best accomplished by grouping with a nearby device as opposed to one that is far away but network accessible. For these cases, GCF provides an alternative version of the *sendRequest* method called *sendProximityRequest*. When used, the framework uses the device's Bluetooth sensor to determine which devices are nearby. Arbiters will then only consider these devices when forming groups.

While proximity requests give developers finer control over which devices are considered during the group selection process, this approach has a limitation: it requires GCF devices to keep Bluetooth discoverable at all times, regardless as to whether or not devices are making use of the proximity feature. From our experience, the drain on battery caused by this is small but noticeable, and we plan on addressing this in future work.

Periodic Refresh

GCF repeats the request and selection process after a specified amount of time has elapsed, or when the current context provider stops providing context information or moves out of range. This allows devices to continually scan the environment and automatically switch between context providers in order to offer a consistent or higher quality of service. When this process is repeated on multiple devices, it allows devices to dynamically reassign context collection tasks in order to efficiently meet the group's needs.

We have implemented GCF in Java. Our implementation communicates over TCP or UDP, and all messages are transmitted using Javascript Serialized Object Notation (JSON). The framework was originally optimized for Android devices, and utilizes the AWARE framework [26] to access and store raw sensor data. Additionally, we have also ported the framework to Mac and Windows platforms in order to increase the range of possible device groupings and use cases that can be explored.

VALIDATION

In order to showcase GCF's support for multiple group types, we have created two mobile phone applications. The first application, GROUPMAP, satisfies quadrants I and III of our model by allowing devices to share and broadcast location information, respectively. The second application, GROUPHIKE, satisfies quadrants I and II by allowing devices to both *share* location information, and *combine* accelerometer data in order to gather information about an unknown environment. When used concurrently, our prototypes also demonstrate the potential of *in-situ* groupings (Quadrant IV) by showing how GCF-enabled applications can serendipitously work together. Despite being simple, these prototypes highlight the benefits of forming groups by demonstrating how devices running different applications can work together.

GroupMap

GROUPMAP is a mapping tool that allows users to track their location. Figure 3 shows a screenshot of the application and its two modes of operation. When users start GROUPMAP, they are provided with an adjustable map that is centered on their current location. Users can either view their own location, or the location of any other nearby users simultaneously.

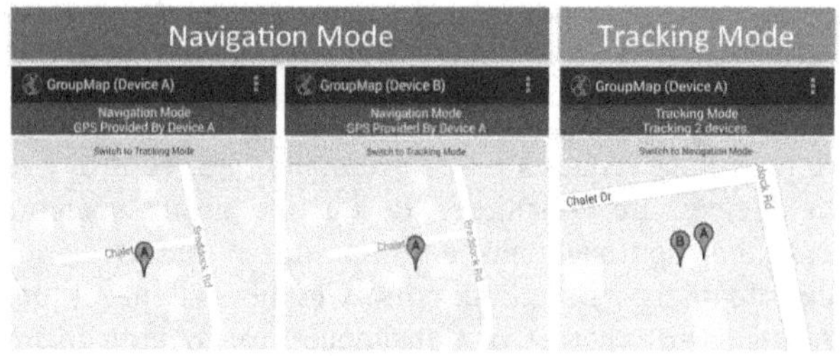

(a) (b) (c)

Figure 3. GROUPMAP screenshots. Through the application, Devices A (a) and B (b) can either share GPS coordinates in Navigation Mode (a and b), or see all users in range in Tracking Mode (c).

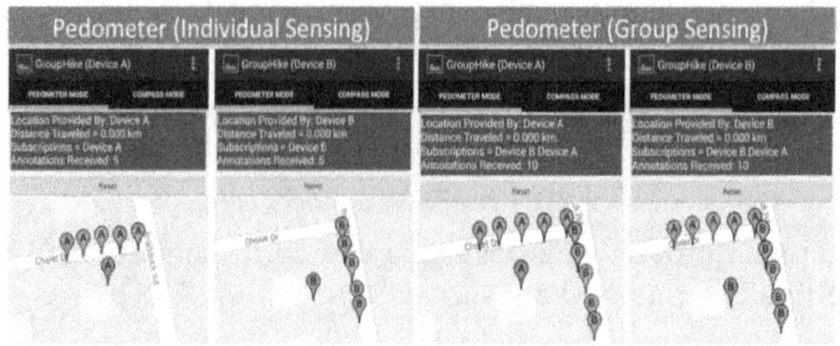

(a) (b) (c) (d)

Figure 4. GROUPHIKE screenshots. Devices A and B collect terrain data individually (a and b), and share it with each other when in range (c and d). Icons show the device's location (blue) and terrain difficulty (green, orange, red).

GROUPMAP utilizes a *location provider* that uses either the phone's GPS or network sensors to determine the user's location. When the application starts, it immediately broadcasts a single-source request for location information. If a compatible device is nearby (as determined by Bluetooth) and is willing to share, the application subscribes to it and begins pulling location data (Figure 3b); else, it uses its own location provider.

GROUPMAP is primarily a collaboration tool (Quadrant I), as it allows users to share information when they are performing the same task (*i.e.*, navigation/exploration) and require access to the same information (*i.e.*, location data). However, the application can also support convenient collaborations (Quadrant III). By switching to *tracking mode* (Figure 3c), the application begins subscribing to *all* location context providers in broadcast range. This supports two distinct groups of users at the same time: those who only want to know their own location and those who want to know everyone's location.

While GROUPMAP utilizes grouping for different purposes depending upon the currently selected mode, GCF abstracts the process by which these groups are formed. From a developer standpoint, switching between modes is accomplished by changing the location request type from *single* to *multiple source*. The framework then finds the best group for providing context, and delivers data as it arrives.

GroupHike

GROUPHIKE is a pedometer application designed to monitor a user's hiking experience (Figure 4). The application has two modes of operation. In *pedometer mode* (Figure 4a and 4b), GROUPHIKE monitors the path that the user is traveling along and creates an annotation whenever the user has a sudden change in instantaneous velocity (as the result of *e.g.*, a hole, a steep step). This information is shared with other users and used to gauge the "difficulty" of traveling along a stretch of terrain (Figure 4c and 4d). GROUPHIKE also has a *compass mode* (Figure 5, right side) where it uses a combination of magnetometer and accelerometer readings to provide the user with his or her current heading.

GROUPHIKE uses three context providers: 1) a *location provider*, identical to the one used in GROUPMAP, 2) a *compass provider,* which tracks orientation data, and 3) a customized *annotations provider* that stores locations where the user experiences a sudden change in acceleration. When operating in pedometer mode, the application sends a single-source request for location data in order to estimate the user's current position, and a multi-source request for annotations data in order to provide the user with real time terrain information from other users. In compass mode, the application sends a local request for compass data since a user's heading is device specific, and cannot be derived from other nearby devices.

Similar to GROUPMAP, GROUPHIKE's pedometer mode allows users to share location data to conserve battery (Quadrant I). It also supports cooperative grouping (Quadrant II) by allowing devices to share their own annotation data in order to accomplish the same task (*i.e.*, gauging the difficulty of a particular stretch of trail). By grouping with all devices in communications range and obtaining their individualized annotations, GROUPHIKE builds a comprehensive map of the environment without requiring users to explore it on their own.

Sharing Context Across Applications

Together, GROUPMAP and GROUPHIKE demonstrate how GCF supports Quadrants I, II, and III of our model. Yet the most novel feature of our framework is its ability to support *in-situ* interactions between devices (Quadrant IV).

In the real world, the chance of encountering another device that has the same exact application installed and running is relatively low. As a result, many developers only design their applications to work with other devices when it is absolutely necessary. GCF addresses this problem by allowing devices to group and share context *across* applications. This eliminates a significant hurdle to grouping, and allows devices to assist each other, even when performing logically separate tasks.

Figure 5 shows an example of *in-situ* grouping. In this demonstration, Device A (left) is running GROUPMAP in tracking mode, while Device B (right) is running GROUPHIKE in compass mode. In their current configuration, Device A is utilizing its location provider while Device B is only utilizing its compass provider. Yet

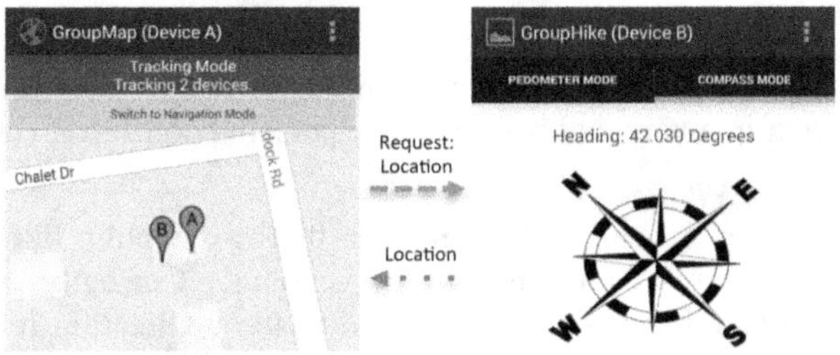

Figure 5. Demonstration of *in-situ* grouping. In this example, Device A's request for location data from nearby devices (red) is answered by Device B's location provider (blue). By using GCF, the two applications can share context with each other.

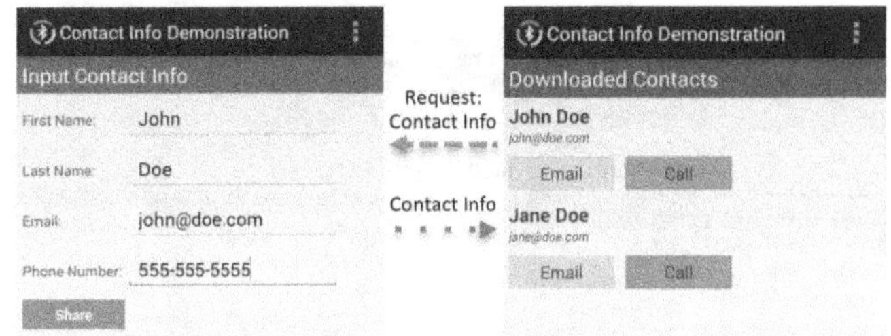

Figure 6. Sample first responder application using GCF. Citizens enter their contact info using a custom application (left). Responders can then request this information and view it on their mobile phone (right).

because Device B also has a location provider, it is able to respond to Device A's multi-source request for location data. This allows GROUPMAP to benefit from the information provided by GROUPHIKE, despite the fact that the two devices are performing two distinct tasks (*i.e.*, monitoring user locations vs. monitoring a user's direction), and using different sets of data (*i.e.*, location vs. compass).

Through the GROUPMAP and GROUPHIKE prototypes, we have demonstrated how GCF can support grouping across all four quadrants of our model. Initially, we expect developers to adopt our framework because it simplifies the process of requesting and receiving contextual information. As more applications use GCF, however, the chances of opportunistic groupings increase, and developers can take advantage of the benefits of these groupings without having to alter their code or coordinate with others. This "value added" strategy distinguishes GCF from other systems, and provides a compelling reason to adopt our framework.

Applying GCF to More Realistic Problem Domains

While GROUPMAP and GROUPHIKE are useful as pedagogical examples, they only represent a starting point. In this section, we highlight two problem domains that stand to benefit from opportunistic groups, and show how GCF's functionality can be utilized to increase users' access to timely and relevant information.

First-Responders

First responders (*e.g.*, police, fire, medical, military) are regularly tasked with operating in unfamiliar or unpredictable environments. Consequently, this population stands to greatly benefit from the ability to gather information from nearby devices (*e.g.*, of other first responders or civilians) without having to coordinate these exchanges in advance.

As part of our ongoing work, we have conducted a series of interviews with police officers from local and state authorities. One insight gained from these discussions is that responders spend a significant amount of time identifying witnesses and manually recording contact information. In incidents where there are a large number of witnesses, this process can become tedious, prone to error, and can even interfere with the investigative process. In Figure 6, we provide a sample GCF application that allows police officers to automatically obtain contact information from nearby individuals. In this prototype, users voluntarily

Figure 7. Demonstration of intelligent signage. Users add an appointment in a GCF-enabled calendar application (left). GCF signs can then guide the user to his/her destination.

download an application and input their contact information (e.g., name, email, phone number). This information is then stored in a custom-built *identity provider*, and can be retrieved by an officer through a multi-source context request and stored for later use. Currently, we are looking into incorporating this feature in our institution's dedicated emergency response application. In the future, however, we envision that this functionality could be an optional service of a phone's operating system. This would allow responders to quickly and reliably obtain contact information from good Samaritans without infringing on others' privacy.

Intelligent Signage

Many environments now contain a wide assortment of digital signs and displays. Yet while these devices have the capability to alter their content at will, they have traditionally lacked the means of determining what information should be presented at any given moment. GCF's ability to request context from multiple devices provides a potentially elegant solution to this problem. In Figure 7, we show an example of an indoor sign that can vary its contents depending upon the needs of nearby users. We created a *calendar provider* that can access a user's schedule and store the location of the user's next appointment (Figure 7a). Digital signs can then request this information *via* GCF, and change their contents to direct users to their destination. Similarly, we are testing a system in our library that allows users to specify one or more books that they would like to read (similar to *e.g.*, GoodReads app). That information is then stored in a *book provider*, which is then shared with signs when the device enters Bluetooth proximity, allowing them to direct users to the aisle where the book is located. In both cases, the ability to

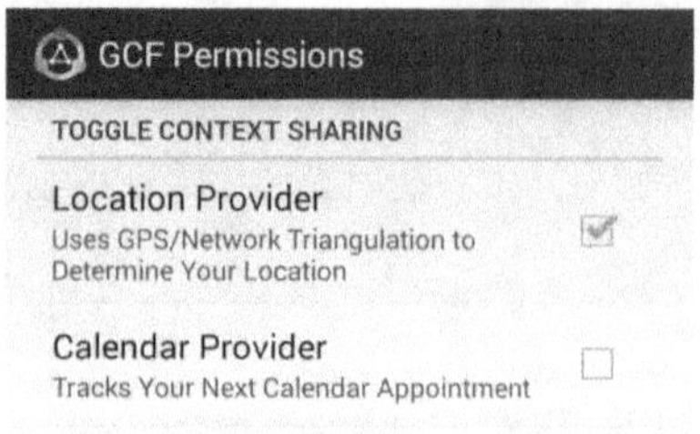

Figure 8. Sample context provider permissions screen. Users can configure GCF to share some, all, or no context with other users from within specific applications.

share context allows signs to provide users with the right information at the right time. More importantly, since all of this data sharing is occurring in the background, users will spend less time trying to get needed information, and more time using it as it arrives.

User Privacy and Incentives

One of the main goals of GCF is to enable devices to interact and share context with one another, even if they have never met. Yet while the above examples demonstrate GCF's usefulness, users have become increasingly concerned about what information is being posted online or shared with others [25]. Consequently, while GCF provides the *means* to opportunistically share context, the bigger question is whether or not users will *want* to use it.

We believe that the answer to this question is "yes." From a context-consumer's standpoint, GCF's benefits are obvious, as it allows users to gain access to information that they might not otherwise be able to obtain, as well as conserve resources in situations when other devices can provide the same context for "free." Yet even from a context-provider's perspective, there is an incentive to use our framework. Since GCF fairly distributes computing tasks between devices, users will, on average, be able to obtain services as much as they provide them to others. In this sense, GCF allows users to participate in a *community of devices* whereby they offer services with the understanding that they will receive them later when they need it. More importantly, by sharing context, users benefit from being able to take advantage of services that they might not otherwise have known existed. Our intelligent sign demonstration (Figure 7) is just one example of how sharing a small amount of context (*i.e.,* a book title) can be beneficial. As more developers adopt our toolkit, these types of opportunities will become more frequent, and we believe that users will be more willing to persistently share *some* of their context in order to take advantage of them.

Ultimately, though, we believe that users must have the option to explicitly opt in or out of context sharing. To support this, GCF provides users with a permissions screen that allows users to toggle context sharing on a per-application basis (Figure 8). GCF automatically generates this interface, and allows users to see 1) which context providers are sharing information, and 2) determine which ones, if any, are allowed to respond to external requests. This maximizes user choice, and allows users to share context in a way that best fits their personal comfort levels.

FUTURE WORK

There are several enhancements that we would like to introduce to GCF in future versions. Currently, the framework is designed to be used at the application level. While this makes GCF simple to use, it also creates unnecessary overhead when multiple GCF-enabled applications run simultaneously on the same device. If GCF were implemented as a service, a single instance could be shared among these applications, reducing some overhead.

Second, in addition to exploring the application domains described earlier where context can be shared, we see GCF as a platform for sharing computation. Previous work in cloudlets has shown how devices can leverage the computational power of nearby devices in order to perform intensive tasks [19], and GCF can build upon this by allowing devices to distribute computational tasks.

Third, we will conduct an in-depth investigation to see if users' concerns about sharing context can be alleviated once the benefits of opportunistic grouping (*i.e.*, value-added services, increased battery life) are made apparent.

Finally, while GCF is specifically designed for mobile devices, it is still limited to communications with devices that are on the same network. One possible solution to this problem is to have each device store its IP address and port in its Bluetooth name. This approach was already used in [3] as a way to send remote commands to a public display, and would allow devices to connect and communicate without the need for explicit pairing.

CONCLUSION

In this paper, we presented the Group Context Framework, a programming toolkit that allows mobile devices to effortlessly form groups and share information. Through an extensive literature review, we developed a model that identifies four conditions that commonly lead to groups. We then described the features of our toolkit, and present two applications, GROUPMAP and GROUPHIKE, that demonstrate how our toolkit supports grouping across our entire model. Through a proof-of-concept demonstration, we showed how GCF allows devices to form groups and work together across applications, thus providing developers with a practical way to take advantage of grouping in real-world situations. We then described two problem domains where using GCF is beneficial, and examined the implications of our framework from a privacy standpoint. This work represents a first step in our long-term goal to show how technology can be used to support new and frictionless collaborations between users and devices. In future work, we will continue work on GCF and show how it can expand our ability to work in groups.

ACKNOWLEDGMENTS

This work is supported by NSF grant CHS-1404698 and the Software Engineering Institute, Carnegie Mellon University.

REFERENCES

1. Boix, E.G., Carreton, A.L., Scholliers, C., Van Cutsem, T., De Meuter, W., and D'Hondt, T. Flocks: Enabling Dynamic Group Interactions in Mobile Social Networking Applications. *Symposium on Applied Computing*, ACM (2011), 425–432.
2. Chetan, S., Al-Muhtadi, J., Campbell, R., and Mickunas, M.D. Mobile Gaia: A Middleware for Ad-Hoc Pervasive Computing. *CCNC '05,* (2005), 223–228.
3. Davies, N., Friday, A., Newman, P., Rutlidge, S., and Storz, O. Using bluetooth device names to support interaction in smart environments. *Mobisys '09*, ACM Press (2009), 151-164.
4. Doulkeridis, C., Valavanis, E., and Vazirgiannis, M. Towards a Context-Aware Service Directory. In B. Benatallah and M.-C. Shan, eds., *Technologies for E-Services*, (2003), 54–65.
5. Doulkeridis, C. and Vazirgiannis, M. Querying and Updating a Context-Aware Service Directory in Mobile Environments. *Int'l Conference on Web Intelligence*, IEEE Computer Society (2004), 562–565.
6. Eustice, K., Ramakrishna, V., Nguyen, N., and Reiher, P. The Smart Party: A Personalized Location-Aware Multimedia Experience. *Consumer Communications and Networking Conference*, (2008), 873-877.
7. Ferscha, A. Workspace awareness in mobile virtual teams. *WETICE '00, (2000),* 272–277.
8. Flentge, F., Weber, S.G., and Ziegert, T. Designing Context-Aware HCI for Collaborative Emergency Management. *Int'l Workshop on HCI for Emergencies in Conjunction with CHI*, (2008).
9. Grosky, W.I., Kansal, A., Nath, S., Liu, J., and Zhao, F. SenseWeb: An Infrastructure for Shared Sensing. *MultiMedia, IEEE 14*, 4 (2007), 8–13.
10. Huang, Y., Tomasic, A., An, Y., Garrod, C., and Steinfeld, A. Energy Efficient and Accuracy Aware (E2A2) Location Services via Crowdsourcing. *Int'l Conference on Wireless and Mobile Computing, Networking and Communications,* (2013), 436–443.
11. Isaacs, E., Walendowski, A., and Ranganthan, D. Hubbub: A Sound-Enhanced Mobile Instant Messenger that Supports Awareness and Opportunistic Interactions. *CHI '02*, (2002), 179–186.
12. Keally, M., Zhou, G., Xing, G., and Wu, J. Remora: Sensing Resource Sharing Among Smartphone-Based Body Sensor Networks. *Int'l Symposium on Quality of Service,* (2013), 1–10.
13. Lee, Y., Ju, Y., Min, C., Kang, S., Hwang, I., and Song, J. CoMon: Cooperative Ambience Monitoring Platform with Continuity and Benefit Awareness. *MobiSys '12*, ACM Press (2012), 43-56.
14. Lewis, G., Novakouski, M., and Sánchez, E. A Reference Architecture for Group-Context-Aware Mobile Applications. *Mobile Computing, Applications, and Services*, (2013), 44–63.
15. Liu, J., Sacchetti, D., Sailhan, F., and Issarny, V. Group Management for Mobile Ad Hoc Networks: Design, Implementation and Experiment. *IEEE MDM '05*, (2005), 192–199.
16. McCarthy, J.F. and Meidel, E.S. Active Map: A Visualization Tool for Location Awareness to Support Informal Interactions. *HUC '99,* (1999), 158–170.
17. McMillan, D.W. and Chavis, D.M. Sense of Community: A Definition and Theory. *Journal of Community Psychology 14*, 1 (1986), 6–23.
18. Ranganathan, A., Campbell, R.H., Ravi, A., and Mahajan, A. ConChat: A Context-Aware Chat Program. *IEEE Pervasive Computing 1*, 3 (2002), 51–57.
19. Satyanarayanan, M., Bahl, P., Caceres, R., and Davies, N. The Case for VM-Based Cloudlets in Mobile Computing. *IEEE Pervasive Computing 8*, 4 (2009), 14–23.
20. Shin, M., Cornelius, C., Peebles, D., Kapadia, A., Kotz, D., and Triandopoulos, N. AnonySense: A system for anonymous opportunistic sensing. *Pervasive and Mobile Computing 7*, 1 (2011), 16–30.
21. Tee, K., Greenberg, S., and Gutwin, C. Providing Artifact Awareness to a Distributed Group Through Screen Sharing. *CSCW 2006*, (2006), 99–108.
22. Valavanis, E., Ververidis, C., Vazirgianis, M., Polyzos, G.C., and Norvag, K. MobiShare: Sharing Context-Dependent Data & Services from Mobile Sources. *Int'l Conference on Web Intelligence*, (2003), 263–270.
23. Vallina-Rodriguez, N., Efstratiou, C., Xie, G., and Crowcroft, J. Enabling Opportunistic Resources Sharing on Mobile Operating Systems. *Workshop on Wireless of the Students, by the Students, for the Students - S3 '11*, ACM Press (2011), 29.
24. Wang, B., Bodily, J., and Gupta, S.K.S. Supporting Persistent Social Groups in Ubiquitous Computing Environments Using Context-Aware Ephemeral Group Service. *PerCom 2004*, (2004), 287–296.
25. Wiese, J., Kelley, P.G., Cranor, L.F., Dabbish, L., Hong, J.I., and Zimmerman, J. Are You Close with Me? Are You Nearby?: Investigating Social Groups, Closeness, and Willingness to Share. *Ubicomp '11*, (2011), 197–206.
26. AWARE | Android Mobile Context Instrumentation Framework. http://www.awareframework.com/home/.

Using Multiple Contexts to Detect and Form Opportunistic Groups

Adrian A. de Freitas and Anind K. Dey
Human Computer Interaction Institute, Carnegie Mellon University
Pittsburgh PA, 15213
{adefreit, anind}@cs.cmu.edu

ABSTRACT

We present a new technique that allows mobile devices to opportunistically group with one another, thus improving their ability to facilitate one-time or spontaneous exchanges of information. In our approach, devices share context with each other, and form groups when these readings are found to be similar to one another. Through a formative study, we examine the limitations of using a single type of context to form groups, and show how leveraging multiple contexts improves our ability to detect and form relevant groupings. We then present DIDJA, a robust software toolkit that automatically collects and analyzes contextual information in order to find and form groups. Through two prototypes, we demonstrate how DIDJA enhances existing user experiences, and show how developers can use our toolkit to easily facilitate frictionless collaborations between users and their environment. We then perform an extended experiment and show how DIDJA is able to accurately form groups under realistic conditions.

Author Keywords

Context sharing; middleware; mobile computing

ACM Classification Keywords

D.3.3 [Language Constructs and Features]: Frameworks

INTRODUCTION

In recent years, there has been a significant increase in the availability of mobile and Internet-connected devices. This trend has led to a fundamental shift in the way we value our computing devices, causing us to place less emphasis on hardware specifications, and more emphasis on their ability to facilitate meaningful exchanges of information.

Ironically, the proliferation of network-connected devices has led to an interesting problem: given that most devices *can* group and share information with one another, which groupings actually matter? Two issues exacerbate this problem. First, determining what constitutes a meaningful group largely depends on the task being performed; some tasks (*e.g.,* determining one's location) can be accomplished by sharing GPS with virtually any nearby device, whereas other tasks (*e.g.,* sharing contact information) require much more nuanced control over group membership. Secondly, many of our interactions with others are unplanned and can occur without warning. Since there is only a short duration in which it makes sense to group in these situations, devices need to be able to detect and capitalize on these opportunities without having to wait for users to give permission.

CSCW '15, March 14 - 18, 2015, Vancouver, BC, Canada.
Copyright 2015 ACM 978-1-4503-2922-4/15/03...$15.00.
http://dx.doi.org/10.1145/2675133.2675213

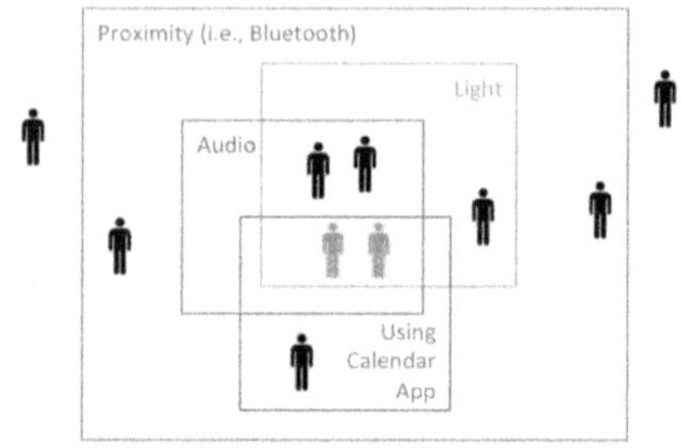

Figure 1. DIDJA examines the context of all nearby devices. It then looks for similarities, and forms groups with users that match in multiple modalities (green, in the center).

In spite of these challenges, we envision a future where opportunistic groupings of devices will enable a wide range of instantaneous interactions with users and/or their environment. To illustrate the potential benefits of such groupings, consider the following scenarios:

Scenario 1: Jack is riding a GPS-equipped bus and tracking his location on his smartphone. The phone discovers that it is on the bus, and uses the bus' GPS data in order to conserve its own battery life.

Scenario 2: Alice and Bob are engaged in a conversation in a common area. The microphones on both devices detect the shared conversation and form a temporary group. At the end of their discussion, Alice and Bob look at their calendars to schedule a future meeting, and their phones, having already linked, provide temporary access to each other's schedules.

In both scenarios, the decision to group and share information is predicated by the discovery of shared context. In the first case, Jack's phone is able to capitalize on the bus' GPS data because they are temporarily co-located. In the second case, it is the shared, sustained conversation between Alice and Bob that allows their devices to anticipate their need to share information in the near future.

While prior research has used context comparison as a means of forming associations between devices, they have typically focused on a single modality (*e.g.*, accelerometers [7], Bluetooth [5], or vision [9]) in order to conserve resources and/or battery life. This strategy works well for simple use cases, but also suffers from a single point of failure. For example, it is technically possible for Jack's phone to discover the bus *via* Bluetooth alone. However, Bluetooth will also detect devices from nearby vehicles, thus preventing it from being able to differentiate between groupings that will improve battery life (*i.e.*, the bus), and more intermittent groupings that will rapidly deplete it (*i.e.*, GPS sources that continuously move in and out of range). Similarly, while an audio sensor might be sufficient to tell if Alice and Bob are participating in the same conversation, it is not discerning enough to exclude others who are within earshot.

In this paper, we describe a new generalizable technique for finding and forming opportunistic groups. It is flexible enough to be applied to a wide variety of use cases, while still allowing for precise determination of group membership. Our work is motivated by the realization that there is no single context that works well in all conditions. Instead, we examine multiple modalities at once, thus overcoming any one context's limitations while simultaneously allowing us to make more precise and reliable determinations of group membership (Figure 1). A key benefit of our approach is that it only relies on context that can be produced on a mobile device. This allows it to operate in environments that have not been instrumented or engineered in any way.

To demonstrate the effectiveness of our approach, we created DIDJA, a general-purpose software toolkit that allows devices to autonomously share context and form groups in real-time. DIDJA's rule-based architecture provides a generalizable approach for comparing context and forming groups, regardless as to where the devices are located or what sensors are used. However, in this paper, we use it to detect and form groupings of users/devices that are too close to be distinguished *via* Bluetooth, but far enough that they are not physically touching one another. This "sweet spot" represents an interesting area of study from a CSCW perspective, as the opportunities for opportunistic interaction dramatically increase when users are within a short distance from one another. Our solution not only provides a way to infer these types of situations, but also allows devices to take advantage of them without requiring assistance or needing to ask for permission.

The rest of this paper is organized as follows. In the following section, we provide a discussion of related work. This is followed by a preliminary study that shows the advantages of using multiple modalities to find and form groups. We then present DIDJA's design, and showcase two prototypes that demonstrate how the toolkit can be used to facilitate meaningful collaborations between users and/or devices. We then evaluate our approach's accuracy, examine the implications of our toolkit from a usability and privacy perspective, and discuss areas for future work.

RELATED WORK

Context comparison has long been used as a mechanism for allowing users and devices to discover and group with one another. In this section, we discuss notable efforts at using context comparison as a grouping mechanism, and show how our approach builds upon this literature.

The earliest systems that utilized context-comparison contained no internal group-making intelligence, but instead focused on providing users with information so that they could identify grouping opportunities on their own. In Active Map [11], office workers wore an infrared badge that allowed their location to be constantly tracked *via* a series of overhead sensors. This information was then conveyed on a digital map, which allowed users to identify momentary opportunities to initiate informal, face-to-face interactions with their co-workers. A similar approach focused on sharing images of users' computer desktop environments instead of their location [15], and allowed co-workers and colleagues to determine the best time to converse with one another. Numerous chat applications have also been augmented with contextual information in order to enhance group awareness. In ConChat [12] and GroupChat [18], multiple streams of context were fused in order to create a unified display that showed the locations and activities of their colleagues. This information could then be used to identify opportunities to communicate and send group-specific messages.

While early work improved our ability to identify and form groups, the need for constant human involvement imposed a significant burden on the user. To address this concern, later systems focused on finding and forming groups autonomously. One of the earliest examples of automated grouping is Smart-Its Friends [6], where mobile sensor platforms paired with one another when shaken simultaneously. Since then, a number of research efforts have demonstrated the value of being able to directly compare sensor data across devices. Accelerometer data was used to detect when two or more devices were being carried by a single person [7], or by a group of individuals walking near one another [19], respectively. Accelerometer data was also used in Shake Well Before Use [10] to generate a shared cryptographic key, and in Rhythm Link [8] to pair multiple devices when tapped on in the same fashion. In [13], Near Field Communications (NFC) was used to detect and establish a secure communications channel between two nearby devices. Radio Frequency Identification (RFID) was also used in Find & Connect as a way of automatically tracking user locations and forming group recommendations based on their shared research interests [2]. In Amigo [17], Wi-Fi radio signal strengths were compared across multiple devices to determine if two devices are in proximity of one another. In Ubisound, devices securely paired with one another when they determined that they were hearing the same audio [3]. Lastly, in [4], imagery from multiple back facing cameras were combined to determine 1) if two devices are looking at the same physical area, and 2) the relative

Modality	Example(s)	Strength(s)	Weakness(s)
Outdoor Location	GPS	Standard on most mobile devices; provides accurate and precise location	Does not work indoors
Indoor Location	Wi-Fi / Cellular Triangulation	Provides reasonable estimate of location; can be used to find devices within a general area	Cannot reliably determine if two or more devices are located in the same room, hallway, etc.
Proximity	Near Field Communications (NFC), Bluetooth, RFID	Works in both indoor and outdoor environments; can determine if two devices are nearby	NFC requires extremely close contact (i.e., touching). Bluetooth lacks sub-room precision.
Temperature	Thermometer	Can detect changes in temperature between rooms with their own climate control systems.	Works poorly in environments that have the same temperature throughout.
Light Intensity	Light Sensor	Can detect variances in lighting in a single room. Many areas have unique light profiles.	Works poorly in environments that have uniform lighting, such as an office building.
Audio	Microphone	Can detect unique conversations in a room	Produces false positives in quiet areas. Does not work well if the microphone is covered.
Motion / Movement	Accelerometer	Commonly available sensor. Can detect even slight changes in movement.	Cannot differentiate when devices are still (such as lying on a table)
User Heading	Magnetometer, Accelerometer	Can distinguish between two devices that are moving in the same direction or facing each other	Requires *a priori* knowledge to know if similarities/differences are informative.
Vision	Camera	Can determine if devices are looking at the same direction, and determine their relative orientation	Computationally expensive to analyze. Does not work when camera lens is blocked

Table 1. A summarization of the strengths and weaknesses of mobile device sensors when used to detect and form groups.

orientation of these devices, and this information was used to opportunistically group devices and share information.

In each of these examples, group detection is accomplished through a single modality. While this approach works under carefully controlled conditions, each modality has its own inherent limitations. Using general knowledge about mobile sensors, we summarize the types of sensors used in previous studies, and describe the conditions that stop each from providing useful information (Table 1). For example, accelerometer data is reliable when devices are in motion, but produces false positive readings when the majority of devices are stationary. Likewise, camera imagery is useful if each device is being held, but is ineffective once the camera is obscured or placed in a dark room or pocket.

From Table 1, it becomes apparent that there is no single modality that works well in all situations. Yet by combining multiple contexts, we are able to capitalize on their strengths while simultaneously overcoming their individual shortcomings. To date, there has been surprisingly little research that has looked into how multiple contexts can be leveraged to detect and form groups in a mobile setting, because doing so is generally regarded to be wasteful from a resource and power consumption standpoint. In [14], researchers installed a series of light and motion sensors throughout an environment, and tracked how these sensors were triggered throughout the course of several days. Then, through an offline process, they formed groupings of devices by learning which sensors were triggered in tandem. In GroupTogether, a combination of Kinect sensors and accelerometer data was combined to determine the locations and orientation of users in an instrumented environment [9]. This information was used to facilitate a number of real-time interactions between user devices. Our approach is similar in that we hope to discover groupings of devices by comparing multiple sensor modalities. However, our approach focuses on sensors commonly found on smartphones. Consequently, our approach operates in environments where devices may be constantly changing position, and does not depend on the environment being instrumented or engineered beforehand.

Our work also draws inspiration from the Flocks framework [1]. In Flocks, users enter their grouping preferences and interests (*e.g.*, "Likes Badminton") *via* a GUI interface. That information is then used to find nearby members with complementary interests. Again, our approach is similar in that we believe that the inclusion of multiple contexts will improve our ability to form precise and accurate groups. However, we differ from Flocks in two significant ways. First, our system focuses on comparing system-generated contexts rather than human-input values, as these values can be obtained without the need for human intervention. Secondly, whereas the groups in Flocks are intended to be persistent, the groups generated by our approach are more spontaneous, and, as such, facilitate interactions that are only meaningful for a short period of time.

PRELIMINARY STUDY

To evaluate the viability of using multiple modalities for group detection, we performed an experiment in our lab (Figure 2). While it may seem biased to use our work area, our lab has several features that make it reasonable to study:

1. There are few walls, allowing sound to easily travel.
2. Students oftentimes bring in their own lamps, creating unique lighting conditions throughout the room.
3. It contains two common meeting areas as well as a

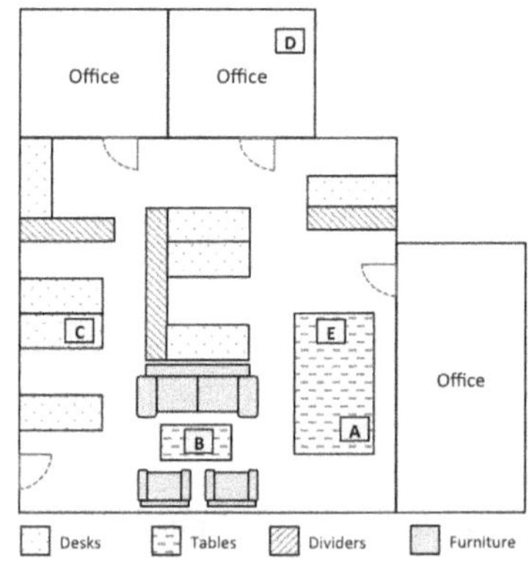

Figure 2. Overhead floor plan of our lab. Lettered locations indicate areas where smartphones were placed.

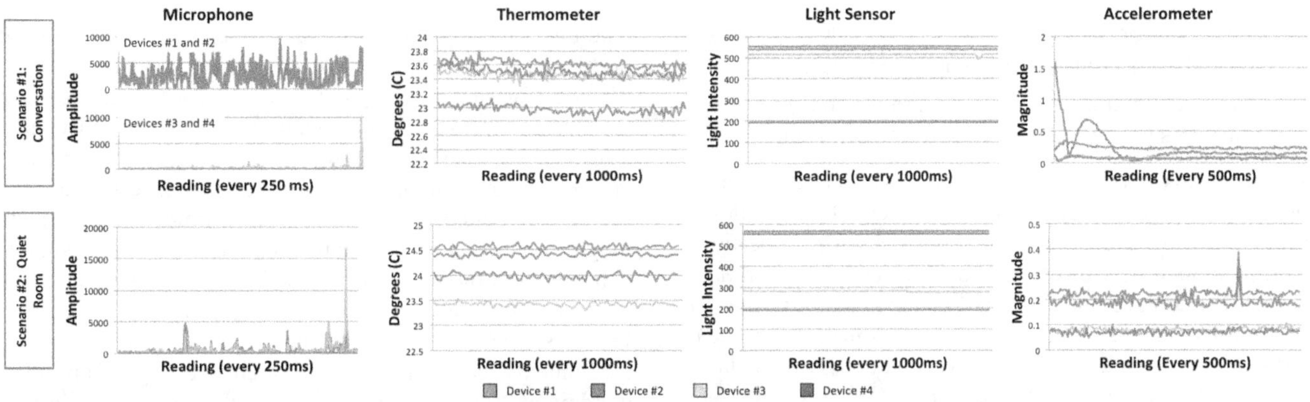

Figure 3. Results from two exploratory trials. In scenario 1 (top row), devices 1 and 2 were placed near a conversation. In scenario 2, devices recorded the room when it was silent. Bluetooth readings are omitted since all devices were able to sense one another.

private office, allowing it to host multiple meetings/conversations simultaneously.

For our initial exploration, we positioned four Samsung Galaxy S IV smartphones throughout the environment and analyzed their sensor readings to see if we could determine which devices were near one another. Two phones (devices 1 and 2, location A) were used to represent an opportunistic grouping between two people, and were positioned near one another. A third device (device 3, location B) was placed nearby, and represented an innocent bystander. Finally, device 4 was placed in a separate but adjacent room (location D), and served as an obvious outsider.

Although modern smartphones can detect a wide range of contexts, we only focused on a few for this initial exploration. For example, we avoid using GPS because our lab is in a closed indoor environment. Similarly, while NFC provides highly accurate proximity data, we use Bluetooth because it provides a balance of range and accuracy. The Galaxy S IV's microphone is highly sensitive, but we only examined audio amplitude to preserve user privacy. Finally, while most smartphones have a camera and compass, we did not use them because we observed that users rarely oriented their devices the same way, even when working together.

Figure 3 summarizes the sensor readings obtained from the microphone, thermometer, light, and accelerometer sensors during two separate trials. In the first trial, devices 1 and 2 recorded a conversation between two lab members. From the resulting audio waveforms, we discovered that devices 1, 2, and 3 appeared to be experiencing the same changes in amplitude at the same time. We then calculated the Pearson correlation coefficient, and found that there was a positive correlation between the audio readings of devices 1 and 2 ($r = 0.726$, $n = 426$, $p < 0.0001$), and a weaker correlation between devices 1 and 3 ($r = 0.235$). This result illustrates the increased precision that can be obtained through audio analysis. All four devices detected each other *via* Bluetooth, but Bluetooth alone could not differentiate between devices that were nearby and those in adjacent rooms. Yet through audio, we were able to distinguish devices 1 and 2 *from* 3, despite the latter being less than three meters away.

Other sensors were less adept at determining that devices 1 and 2 were grouped. While temperature varied between rooms, we found the onboard thermometer took several minutes to detect these changes. When looking at accelerometer data, we found no significant difference in reported values as they were all placed on flat surfaces. Finally, while light sensor readings were able to tell that device 4 was in a separate room (with separate lighting), it was unable to distinguish between devices 1-3. This is because all three phones were exposed to the same lighting fixture, and, as such, reported similar intensity levels.

While our initial results suggest that audio is a powerful group discriminator, we suspected that this is not always the case. In a second trial, we recorded sensor data during a period of silence. During this experiment, we moved Device 3 to a desk on the opposite side of the room (location C). We then waited until the room was mostly quiet before recording. Although we still observed several small audio peaks that occurred due to ambient noise, all three waveforms were positively correlated to each other. This time, however, we were able to use the light sensors to detect subtle shadows created by overhead lamps and office dividing furniture. This allowed us to distinguish device 3 from devices 1 and 2.

Overall, our initial exploration provided us with three key findings. First, we discovered that phones of the same model can detect slightly different contexts, even when exposed to the same set of conditions. Secondly, we discovered that sensor noise is a significant distractor, and that sensor data needs to be filtered to determine if observed trends between two sensor streams are real or random. Finally, our findings demonstrate the potential of using multiple modalities in order to find and detect opportunistic groups. Throughout our trials, we did not find a single sensor that could consistently determine that devices 1 and 2 were part of a group. Yet by examining multiple contexts, we are able to find the group of interest with a higher rate of success, and with a lower false positive rate than if we had relied on Bluetooth alone.

DIDJA – A TOOLKIT FOR IDENTIFYING GROUPS

Based on the results of our pilot study, we sought to create a software solution that *automatically* allows devices to easily detect and form opportunistic groups for a wide range of use cases. Our efforts have resulted in an extensible software toolkit that we call DIDJA. DIDJA allows devices to gather multiple streams of context and locally analyze them in near real-time. When these streams are similar to one another,

```
<Rule Context="Light" Threshold="0.7" Window="10" />
<Rule Context="Temp" Threshold="0.95" Window="5" />
```

Figure 4. Sample Group Membership Rules

DIDJA then automatically forms a group and creates a communications channel (*i.e.,* socket) for sharing data.

DIDJA performs two main tasks. First, it detects and shares contextual information between devices. Our toolkit allows devices to broadcast context over a local network connection. In lieu of explicit peer discovery, each device sends a *request message* that contains the type(s) of contexts that it wishes to receive and a desired refresh rate (typically once per second). Nearby devices then detect this request and deliver the data.

Second, DIDJA analyzes context according to a set of application-configurable rules. Our toolkit uses a sliding window to store the most recent readings for each device. When new context arrives, it is added to the window and evaluated by a *context comparator* using a pre-specified evaluation metric (*e.g.,* statistical correlation, proportional analysis). These results are then used to determine whether or not the two devices are experiencing the same context

A significant challenge in finding and forming opportunistic groups is that the conditions for grouping are oftentimes application specific depending upon the size and type of group that is trying to be detected. For this reason, our work with DIDJA focuses on providing a systematic and automated way of analyzing context that is both easy to use, while still being robust across a wide variety of use cases. We now examine the components of our toolkit, and show how it can be customized to accommodate a range of applications.

Rules

DIDJA utilizes rules to define the criteria for group membership. For each application, developers provide DIDJA with a list of context(s) that they are interested in examining. These rules are then used by the toolkit to request context from other devices and perform comparisons.

A set of example rules is provided in Figure 4. Each DIDJA rule consists of three parameters: context type, threshold value and window size. The *context type* is a unique identifier that is used to represent a particular sensor or family of sensors. This identifier is agreed upon in advance by all devices, and allows devices to talk about the same context (*i.e.,* "location") regardless of how that context is actually being produced (*e.g.,* GPS, cellular triangulation).

The *threshold value* represents how similar two context streams need to be before they are considered to be matching. Each time a context is received, it is analyzed using a predefined metric. The result of this comparison is a numeric value that determines how similar two streams are to one another. The threshold value compensates for individual sensor differences by allowing applications to specify when two context values are considered to be "close enough" to be considered a match.

The *window size* specifies the number of sensor readings that are to be used during the comparison process. Since sensor readings can significantly vary due to noise, they are problematic to compare. Instead, DIDJA records the last *n* readings for each device, and uses all of these values during comparison. There is a noticeable tradeoff between window size and accuracy. Larger windows are less influenced by erratic sensor readings and provide better estimations of group membership, but require more time to fill and take longer to forget problematic readings. Shorter windows consume less memory and allow for faster determinations of group membership, but are more susceptible to sensor noise. From experience, we found that a window of 10 works well for contexts that do not change often (*e.g.,* light), and that a window of 30 works well for sensors that do (*e.g.,* audio).

Techniques for Context Comparison

Comparing two contexts to one another is a nontrivial task, as there is no single comparison method that works for all contexts. For this reason, we have designed DIDJA to compare sensor streams using three techniques: *proportional comparison*, *correlational comparison*, and *exact match.*

Proportional comparison is used to compare numeric sensor values that do not change dramatically over time. Many sensors report the same (or very similar) value (*e.g.,* those that measure light intensity, barometric pressure and temperature) if run repeatedly. For these types of context, a reasonable measure of similarity can be obtained by dividing the average value of each device's sensor readings. To account for individual sensor differences, we also define a noise range for each sensor type. If two sensor values are within this range, we return a similarity of 1.0.

$$similarity = \begin{cases} \frac{\min(a_{avg}, b_{avg})}{\max(a_{avg}, b_{avg})}, |a_{avg} - b_{avg}| > noise \\ 1.0, otherwise \end{cases}$$

While proportional comparison is applicable to a wide range of sensor types, it assumes that any sudden change in a sensor's reported value is caused by noise. As a result, proportional analysis works reliably when the environment is static, but takes longer to detect sudden, intentional changes (*e.g.,* turning off the lights in a room).

The second type of comparison, correlational comparison, is used to compare contexts that significantly vary over time. During our initial trials, we found that audio amplitude readings can significantly vary over the course of a few seconds, especially when users are listening to music or participating in a conversation. For these types of sensors, similarity can be measured by computing the correlation coefficient (*e.g.,* Pearson's R) between the host device and all other devices.

The last type of comparison, exact match, is designed for contexts that are represented as strings or nominal values. Google's Activity Recognition Toolkit [20], for example, reports the user's activity as nominal values (*i.e.,* "in_vehicle," "on_foot", *etc.*) Bluetooth also reports the discovery of nearby devices by listing their IDs. Exact match is the simplest form of comparison. It simply performs a strict string comparison, and returns a value of 1.0 if the values match, and 0.0 otherwise.

We have preconfigured DIDJA to select an appropriate context comparison method for a wide range of commonly used contexts. However, developers can also direct the toolkit to use a specific comparator, or insert their own comparators as the need arises. Through these alternatives, DIDJA is infinitely extensible, and can be used on a wider range of contexts than what is directly covered in this paper.

Group Formation Strategies

DIDJA's rule-based architecture provides a straightforward and efficient way to define group membership criteria. However, precisely defining the exact conditions that will lead to a group is extremely difficult when groupings are spontaneous and/or unpredictable. Developers may have a general sense of how their application should form groups (*e.g.,* "group with everyone in the same room") but it can be challenging to translate these vague notions into a robust rule set. Likewise, users may want to define their own custom groups, but lack either the capacity or patience to express these groupings as a set of structured rules.

To mitigate these issues, we have created several developer and user level settings that allow DIDJA to specify its group formation strategy. While our toolkit still uses rules in order to define the criteria for grouping, the toolkit can interpret or modify these rules depending upon the currently selected policy. DIDJA supports four grouping strategies:

Match All Rules. In this mode, DIDJA only forms a group with devices that satisfy *all* rules. This mode is the strictest, and provides the tightest control over the exact conditions that must be met in order to form a group.

Match N. Rather than require devices to satisfy *all* rules, *Match N* allows DIDJA to form a group as long as at least *N* rules have been met. While a higher N value will reduce the chance of false positive matches, we allow programmers to specify the value of N to fit their particular application.

Max N. There are many situations where a user or developer wants to form an opportunistic group, but cannot define the exact conditions that will result in a grouping. *Max N* attempts to address this problem by searching for a grouping of devices that satisfies the *most* rules at once.

Manual. Some opportunistic groupings are so personalized that they simply cannot be described by rules beforehand. For these situations, DIDJA offers users the ability to build a custom rule set by manually selecting members, and using their sensor readings in order to derive reasonable group threshold values (Figure 5). Users can save these rules for later use, allowing them to create customized "grouping profiles" that complement their daily routine.

Scalability

One of the key challenges in designing DIDJA is finding an effective balance between speed and scalability. While the current toolkit is technically capable of allowing devices to share a wide range of contexts simultaneously, the overhead required to do so and process the results can be significant.

Figure 5 Manual grouping using DIDJA. In this example, a user selects a device that is known to be part of the group (left). DIDJA then modifies its rules to include other devices that have similar characteristics (right).

From a processing standpoint, there are limits to the number of simultaneous sensor feeds that can be analyzed by a single device. DIDJA provides two mechanisms to mitigate this problem. By default, the toolkit uses Bluetooth to determine if two devices are nearby before any context is shared. Since DIDJA uses TCP/UDP for communications, this optimization significantly reduces overhead traffic, as the number of devices in the same space is small compared to the total number of devices in a broadcast domain. Secondly, DIDJA can be configured to ask for context in stages instead of all at once. In this mode, the toolkit will obtain a single context from each device and evaluate it for similarity. The toolkit then only asks for additional streams from those devices that have satisfied the previous rule, thus limiting sensor data from devices that have a low probability of being part of the group.

We have implemented DIDJA as a library for the Android operating system. While we tuned the toolkit to provide reasonable performance across a wide range of use cases, we also allow developers to programmatically specify group membership rules, choose context comparators, and select grouping strategies. This makes DIDJA easy to use, while still giving developers the flexibility they need.

VALIDATION

We evaluate DIDJA through a two-step process. In the following section, we present two real-world prototypes that use DIDJA (Figure 6). We then run DIDJA for a sustained period of time, and evaluate its ability to find and form groups when devices are either stationary or moving.

Prototypes

We have deployed two Android prototypes that use DIDJA's grouping functionality. Despite their simplicity, they highlight the breadth of user experiences that are possible once devices are able to autonomously group with each other.

CalendarSync

CALENDARSYNC is a scheduling tool that allows users to temporarily share calendar information with one another. When users first turn on the application, they only see their own schedule. When two or more CALENDARSYNC users are near one another, however, the applications form an

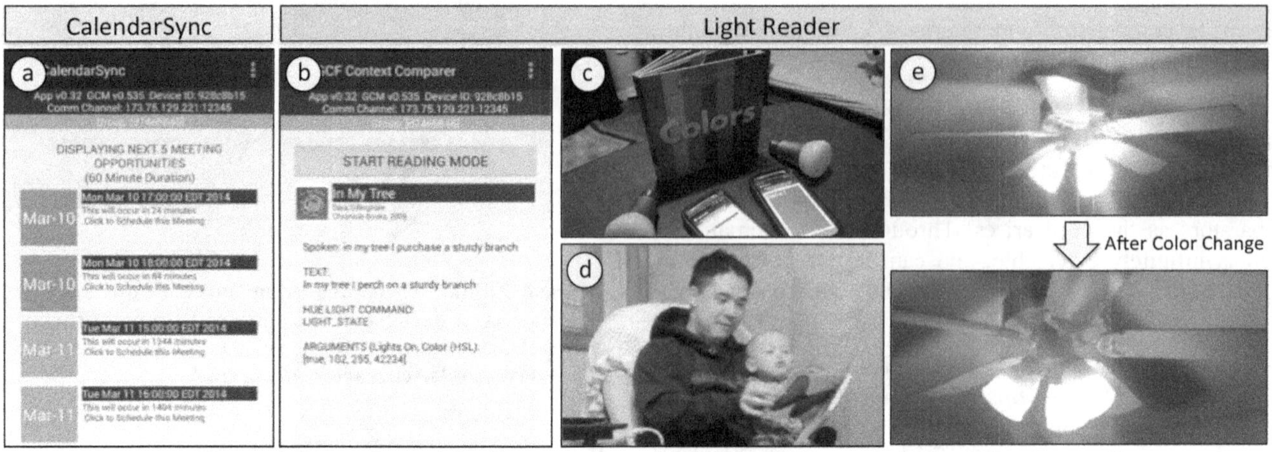

Figure 6. Screenshots of the CALENDARSYNC (a) and LIGHT READER (b-e) applications.

opportunistic group and automatically share calendar information. The application then presents users with a list of times when they are available to meet again (Figure 6a).

CALENDARSYNC demonstrates how opportunistic grouping increases the usability of existing calendar systems. While there are numerous tools that allow users to share their schedules with one another, they require users to manually grant permissions to others before they can see it. Furthermore, these systems tend to share an *entire* calendar with users, which can lead to privacy issues. Because of these drawbacks, traditional calendar sharing is only used in cases where the need to share calendars is either so great and/or frequent that it outweighs the inconvenience. CALENDARSYNC eliminates the need for access lists in many cases by granting users access to each other's calendars on a "need-to-know" basis. Users only see each other's calendars when they are grouped, and lose access when they are no longer grouped. Through this approach, CALENDARSYNC provides a capability that is missing in comparable applications, and allows users to easily share schedules, even if they are meeting for the first time.

CALENDARSYNC was designed to facilitate information sharing between two or more acquaintances when they meet in a common area (*e.g.,* a water cooler). To support this type of opportunistic group, we configured DIDJA so that it only groups with devices that are 1) in close proximity (as determined by Bluetooth), 2) displaying the user's calendar, and 3) hearing the same audio (correlation $\geq$ 0.5). Given the limited numbers of users that currently have access to CALENDARSYNC, examining three types of context may seem counterintuitive when Bluetooth alone can technically suffice. However, this functionality is needed when multiple CALENDARSYNC instances are in Bluetooth range, as it reduces our system's likelihood of producing false positives.

Light Reader

Whereas CALENDARSYNC is designed to form groups with users, our second prototype, LIGHT READER, shows how DIDJA can be used to form groups *with the environment.* Inspired by the authors' own experiences reading books to their children, the LIGHT READER system consists of three components (Figure 6c): 1) a set of Wi-Fi controllable light bulbs, 2) a series of sensors (*i.e.*, smartphones) that are installed in each room and control a different set of light bulbs, and 3) a mobile application, which is built using DIDJA. When a user turns on LIGHT READER (Figure 6b), the application compares sensor readings from each room-based computer and forms an opportunistic group. Then, as the user reads out loud (Figure 6d), the application uses a speech-to-text converter to cross-reference what the user is saying against a database of known titles. When a match is found, the application retrieves the light configuration settings for that particular book/passage and transmits them to the room-based computer, altering the lights accordingly (Figure 6e).

LIGHT READER is similar to Disney's StoryLight [21], in that it allows users to dynamically adjust the lighting of a room based on the contents of a story. However, our system's ability to form opportunistic groups improves upon the former from a usability standpoint. While StoryLight only works with a dedicated light bulb in one room, our system's ability to form opportunistic groups allows it to control lighting of whatever room the user is location. In preliminary deployments, this feature was found to be especially valuable, as parents oftentimes do not want to go to a specific part of the house in order to read a book to their children. Additionally, since our system is able to continuously monitor context and adjust group membership as needed, our system also allows parents to move about the house while reading a story. This allows them to start a story in one part of the house, and seamlessly carry that experience to another room. In order to take advantage of these features, our current implementation assumes that a house contains sensors and Wi-Fi controllable lights. However, such products are already commercially available, and should become more commonplace with time.

Since LIGHT READER is designed to complement the traditional experience of reading a storybook, we have configured DIDJA so that it forms a group with devices that 1) are in proximity of one another, 2) hear the same audio (correlation $\geq$ 0.5), and 3) experience the same lighting conditions (light intensity $\geq$ 0.8). As was the case with CALENDARSYNC, the use of multiple contexts allows for higher degrees of accuracy when determining which devices are part of the group. From our experience, the rate of false positives using either audio or light readings alone can be quite high, as bedrooms are typically grouped together, and can cause audio sensors to hear the same thing (especially if doors are open), and the use of similar overhead lighting fixtures (*e.g.*, fans, lamps) can confuse light sensors. By using both, we significantly reduce the chance of error.

Accuracy Evaluation

In addition to the above prototypes, we conducted two experiments to evaluate DIDJA's accuracy in identifying opportunistic groups. Similar to our pilot study, these evaluations were performed in our lab using four smartphones (Figure 2) during normal (busy) business hours. For the first test, two devices represented an opportunistic group, and were placed on a conference table (location E). A third device was placed nearby on a coffee table (location B), and a fourth was placed in an empty office (location D). We then instructed the toolkit to request and compare contexts according to the rules in Table 2, which we derived empirically from our pilot study.

Although our focus is on quick and spontaneous groupings of devices, we allowed DIDJA to analyze sensor data for one hour in order to see how well the toolkit performs under extended use. During this first experiment, devices were not touched or moved, and remained within Bluetooth range.

Over the course of the first evaluation, DIDJA performed 12,000 sensor comparisons. Table 3 provides a summary of DIDJA's grouping performance as seen from the perspective of device 1. We define a *correct group* as one that only includes device 2. Additionally, we define a *false negative* as a group that does not include device 2, and a *false positive* as a group that includes either device 3 or device 4.

Similar to our initial set of experiments, we found that using a single sensor works with varying degrees of success. The light sensor was by far the best in terms of accuracy, matching with device 2 over 99% of the time, and with devices 3 and 4 less than 0.5% of the time. Meanwhile, thermometer and accelerometer readings were the least discerning, and matched with all three devices regardless of their location. When comparing audio data, device 1 frequently matched with device 2 (75.9%), and occasionally matched with devices 3 (52.2%) and 4 (23.1%). These results were not surprising, however. While we were recording, we observed several sidebar conversations that occurred either at the back of the room (between devices 1, 2, and 4) or at the opposite corner (between devices 1, 2, and 3). Additionally, there were several periods of extended silence, which, as we have shown previously, can trick the audio sensor into believing that it should match with other devices when there is no associated group.

After each sensor comparison, we had DIDJA analyze its group membership using the *Match All Rules, Match N Rules*, and *Max N* strategies. The groups formed by these strategies are shown in Table 3. As expected, Match All Rules proved to be the strictest, and allowed device 1 to only group with device 2. However, this was accomplished at the cost of increased false negatives, thus making this strategy useful in situations where the penalty of forming an incorrect grouping is significant. Match N Rules, on the other hand, minimizes the rate of false negatives, but at the cost of dramatically increasing the rate of false positives. This makes this strategy useful in applications where precision is useful, but not necessarily required. Interestingly, Max N offered a mix of accuracy and precision. By allowing N to fluctuate at each time step, device 1 is able to consistently group with device 2 while keeping false positives and false negatives low.

Sensor	Update Rate	Compare Method	Window Size	Threshold
Light	1000ms	Proportion	10	0.8
Thermometer	1000ms	Proportion	10	0.95
Accelerometer	500ms	Proportion	10	0.95
Microphone	250ms	Correlation	30	0.5

Table 2. Grouping rules used during our system evaluation.

At first glance, these results appear to negate the need for DIDJA, as they suggest that highly accurate groups can be formed using a single sensor. Yet while the light sensor proved to be highly discerning, it is important to remember that this is only the case for *this particular arrangement* of devices. For our second evaluation, we positioned devices 2, 3, and 4 at locations B, C, and E, respectively. We then moved device 1 between these locations every five minutes for an hour. This setup allows us to test DIDJA's ability to form opportunistic groups, as device 1's group constantly changes as it moves between locations.

The results from our second experiment are provided in Table 4. Since device 1's group is constantly changing, we simply report the amount of time that it found the correct group, whether that is with device 2, 3, or 4. Similar to the previous experiment, we found that DIDJA is able to accurately and reliably form precise groupings. Although the toolkit does perform slightly worse than in our first trial, most of the inaccuracies occurred as the device was moved from one location to another. More importantly, we also found that using a single sensor to form groups was less effective in this scenario. While the light sensor again proves to be the best single sensor, its accuracy dips to 84% with a 15% false positive rate. Max N outperforms the sensor on both metrics, thus showing how our approach provides an accurate *and* consistent way to form groups.

DISCUSSION

In this section, we evaluate DIDJA's overall usability, to include its responsiveness, reliability, impact on battery life, and impact on user privacy.

Responsiveness

Didja cannot find groups instantaneously. Our toolkit requires devices to receive a full sliding window's worth of context before it is able to calculate its group membership. As a result, there is a noticeable delay from the moment that a user starts an application (and starts receiving context) to the moment the group is formed.

Strategy	Grouped w/Device 2	Grouped w/Device 3	Grouped w/Device 4	% False Negative	% False Positive
Match All Rules	75.6%	0%	0%	**24.4%**	**0%**
Match N Rules (N≥1)	100%	100%	100%	**0%**	**100%**
Match N Rules (N≥2)	100%	99.9%	100%	**0%**	**100%**
Match N Rules (N≥3)	99.6%	52.4%	23.3%	**0.4%**	**57.1%**
Find Best (Max N)	100%	8.9%	2.7%	**0%**	**10.4%**

Table 3. Comparison of grouping strategies from device 1's perspective (all devices stationary). Errors are bolded.

While using CALENDARSYNC and LIGHT READER, we found that it took Didja approximately 10 seconds to find and form a group. In preliminary demonstrations, users commented that this delay did not detract from the usability of either application. If necessary, however, developers can shorten this by 1) decreasing the window size, 2) increasing the refresh rate, or 3) by allowing devices to continuously record context so that they can transmit the entire window's worth at once. Each option comes with its own set of drawbacks (*e.g.*, susceptibility to noise, power consumption) and it is up to developers to determine which tradeoffs work best for their particular application.

Reliability (*i.e.*, the "Pocket Problem")

While our prototypes and evaluation demonstrate DIDJA's effectiveness, they assume that the devices being grouped are in the user's hands or on a table when the decision to group is made. However, there are many situations where it is reasonable to assume that at least some users' phones will be in a pocket when DIDJA is activated. In these situations, certain sensors (*e.g.*, light, sound) become distorted, and prevent the toolkit from providing accurate results.

There is not a simple solution to this problem. Instead, developers need to be conscientious of these factors when creating their applications. For example, when we created LIGHT READER, we took advantage of the fact that most users know to keep their phone unobstructed when using voice recognition. Similarly, when creating CALENDARSYNC, we observed a large number of meetings, and concluded that users would have their phones in hand while scheduling an appointment.

Another possible solution this problem is to consider context generated from non-smartphone devices. Wearable technologies such as Google Glass and smart watches are becoming commonplace, and have sensors that are directly exposed to the environment at all times. By leveraging these additional sources of contexts, DIDJA would be able to form groups under a wider range of circumstances.

Battery Consumption

Although we did not specifically focus on power consumption during our evaluation, it is an important aspect of usability and overall user acceptance. In our experiments, we found that DIDJA consumed approximately 20% of the device's battery life *per hour* on the device that was

Strategy	Found Exact Group	False Negative	False Positive
Match All Rules	70.4%	**29.1%**	**1.7%**
Match N Rules (N≥1)	0%	**0.5%**	**100%**
Match N Rules (N≥2)	0.6%	**2.5%**	**99.3%**
Match N Rules (N≥3)	55.5%	**7.2%**	**39.4%**
Find Best (Max N)	88.2%	**3.8%**	**11.8%**

Table 4. Comparison of grouping strategies from device 1's perspective (device 1 moves every 5 min). Errors are bolded.

performing context comparison (*i.e.,* the context consumer). The overall impact on battery life was slightly less for devices providing context, but still noticeable.

Given these results, it becomes clear that it is not practical to run DIDJA for long periods of time. Fortunately, opportunistic encounters tend to be short-lived. For example, in our sample demonstrations of CALENDARSYNC, the average use case session lasted less than two minutes, which was just long enough for users to turn on the app, detect the group, and schedule an appointment. Likewise, while the sensors in LIGHT READER are designed to provide context continuously, the mobile phone app only ran for as long as it took to read a story, which in most cases, only took a few minutes. In both cases, the observed impact on battery life was negligible, leading us to believe that our experimental results are a worst-case assessment.

User Privacy

In order for DIDJA to work, devices must be willing to share context with one another. However, this introduces several usability and privacy concerns. Users may not be willing to have their devices automatically turn on sensors or transmit context, especially if their battery is low or if the information being transmitted is potentially sensitive. More importantly, users may not be comfortable with the idea of sharing context with strangers or neighbors, even if doing so increases their access to timely and relevant information.

Work by Trevor *et al.* has demonstrated that users are keenly sensitive of the types of information that they share with others, and has demonstrated the importance of mechanisms that maximize users' ability to choose what information is being shared [16]. Consequently, DIDJA offers two safeguards to try to preserve user privacy. First, we intentionally focus on comparing low-level contexts such as Bluetooth proximity, audio *amplitude*, and light readings. In comparison to contexts such as the camera, this type of information is less intrusive, as it is indicative of the environment as opposed to a specific individual. Secondly, users can review which contexts DIDJA is sharing and can turn off sharing of individual contexts. While this may reduce their opportunities to take part in groups, this approach maximizes user choice, and ensures that users only share what they are comfortable with sharing.

CONCLUSION

In this paper, we demonstrate how multiple streams of context can be used to find and form opportunistic groups.

Through a proof-of-concept experiment, we show the limitations of using a single type of context to find and form groups, and show how using multiple modalities allows us to more accurately and reliably determine if two devices are likely experiencing the same context. We then presented DIDJA, a software toolkit that automatically finds and forms opportunistic groups, and describe two prototypes that show how it can be used to improve users' access to timely and relevant services/information. Finally, we presented a discussion of DIDJA's usability along multiple dimensions.

DIDJA represents an important first step in our effort to create new opportunities for users and devices to collaborate and share information. An obvious extension of our work is to consider contexts that are not purely captured by sensors. As mentioned previously, there are several toolkits that can infer the user's current activity/state by combining the results of multiple modalities, and this higher-level knowledge would allow DIDJA to make more nuanced predictions of the user's grouping intentions and respond accordingly.

Additionally, while we have primarily focused on groupings of nearby devices, we also acknowledge that this is not the only way to form an opportunistic group. Specifically, we believe that it is also possible to form groups of individuals across both distance (*e.g.*, group with everyone in that is looking at a particular website) and time (*e.g.*, group with anyone who has ever taken a photograph at a tourist location). Our technique is extensible to these potential grouping opportunities, and we are extremely interested in exploring applications that use them in a compelling way.

ACKNOWLEDGMENTS

This work was supported by NSF grant CHS-1404698 and the Software Engineering Institute, Carnegie Mellon University.

REFERENCES

1. Boix, E.G., Carreton, A.L., Scholliers, C., Van Cutsem, T., De Meuter, W., and D'Hondt, T. Flocks: Enabling Dynamic Group Interactions in Mobile Social Networking Applications. *SAC '11*, (2011), 425–432.
2. Chin, A., Xu, B., Yin, F., et al. Using Proximity and Homophily to Connect Conference Attendees in a Mobile Social Network. *Int'l Conference on Distributed Computing Systems Workshops*, (2012), 79–87.
3. Clay, W.R. and Shin, D. Secure Device Pairing Using Audio. *ICCST '09*, (2009), 77–84.
4. Dearman, D., Guy, R., and Truong, K. Determining the Orientation of Proximate Mobile Devices Using their Back Facing Camera. *CHI '12*, (2012), 2231-2234.
5. Eagle, N. and Pentland, A. Social Serendipity: Mobilizing Social Software. *IEEE Pervasive Computing 4*, 2 (2005), 28–34.
6. Holmquist, L., Mattern, F., Schiele, B., Alahuhta, P., Beigl, M., and Gellersen, H.-W. Smart-Its Friends: A Technique for Users to Easily Establish Connections between Smart Artefacts. *Ubicomp '01*, (2001), 116–122.
7. Lester, J., Hannaford, B., and Gaetano, B. "Are You with Me?" – Using Accelerometers to Determine if Two Devices are Carried by the Same Person. *PerCom '04*, (2004), 33–50.
8. Lin, F.X., Ashbrook, D., and White, S. RhythmLink. *UIST '11*, (2011), 263.
9. Marquardt, N., Hinckley, K., and Greenberg, S. Cross-Device Interaction via Micro-Mobility and F-Formations. *UIST '12*, (2012), 13-22.
10. Mayrhofer, R. and Gellersen, H. Shake Well Before Use: Intuitive and Secure Pairing of Mobile Devices. *IEEE Transactions on Mobile Computing 8*, 6 (2009), 792–806.
11. McCarthy, J.F. and Meidel, E.S. Active Map: A Visualization Tool for Location Awareness to Support Informal Interactions. *HUC '99*, (1999), 158–170.
12. Ranganathan, A., Campbell, R.H., Ravi, A., and Mahajan, A. ConChat: A Context-Aware Chat Program. *Pervasive Computing, IEEE 1*, 3 (2002), 51–57.
13. Rekimoto, J., Ayatsuka, Y., Kohno, M., and Oba, H. Proximal interactions: A Direct Manipulation Technique for Wireless Networking. *Interact 3*, (2003), 511–518.
14. Takada, T., Kurihara, S., Hirotsu, T., and Sugawara, T. Proximity Mining: Finding Proximity Using Sensor Data History. *DARPA Information Survivability Conference and Exposition*, (2003), 129–138.
15. Tee, K., Greenberg, S., and Gutwin, C. Providing Artifact Awareness to a Distributed Group Through Screen Sharing. *CSCW '06*, (2006), 99–108.
16. Trevor, J., Hilbert, D.M., and Schilit, B.N. Issues in Personalizing Shared Ubiquitous Devices. *Ubicomp '02*, (2002), 56–72.
17. Varshavsky, A., Scannell, A., LaMarca, A., and De Lara, E. Amigo: Proximity-Based Authentication of Mobile Devices. *Ubicomp '07*, (2007), 253–270.
18. Wang, B., Bodily, J., and Gupta, S.K.S. Supporting Persistent Social Groups in Ubiquitous Computing Environments Using Context-Aware Ephemeral Group Service. *PerCom '04*, (2004), 287–296.
19. Wirz, M., Roggen, D., and Troster, G. Decentralized Detection of Group Formations from Wearable Acceleration Sensors. *Int'l Conference on Computational Science and Engineering*, IEEE (2009), 952–959.
20. Recognizing the User's Current Activity | Android Developers. http://developer.android.com/training/location/activity-recognition.html.
21. Disney StoryLight. http://www.usa.philips.com/c-p/719945548/disney.

From "nobody cares" to "way to go!": A Design Framework for Social Sharing in Personal Informatics

Daniel A. Epstein[1], Bradley H. Jacobson[2], Elizabeth Bales[1,2], David W. McDonald[2], Sean A. Munson[2]
[1]Computer Science & Engineering, [2]Human Centered Design & Engineering
DUB Group, University of Washington
{depstein, lizbales}@cs.washington.edu, {bhjacobs, dwmc, smunson}@uw.edu

ABSTRACT
Many research applications and popular commercial applications include features for sharing personally collected data with others in social awareness streams. Prior work has identified several barriers to use as well as discrepancies between designer goals and how these features are used in practice. We develop a framework for designing and evaluating these features based on an extensive review of prior literature. We demonstrate the value of this framework by analyzing physical activity sharing on Twitter, coding 4,771 tweets and their responses and gathering 444 reactions from 97 potential tweet recipients, learning that specific user-generated content leads to more responses and is better received by the post audience. We conclude by extending our findings to other sharing problems and discussing the value of our design framework.

Author Keywords
Personal Informatics; Social Sharing; Self-Tracking; Health; Social Network Sites; Social Awareness Streams

ACM Classification Keywords
H.5.m. Information interfaces and presentation (e.g., HCI).

INTRODUCTION
Technological devices and applications for tracking personal data have become increasingly ubiquitous. The motivations for tracking vary by application and person, from curiosity and fascination with data [32] to having a record [19,33,36] to motivating behavior change [19,42] to engaging with others [3,24,46].

Many applications, both research (e.g. [11,15,27,35]) and commercial (e.g., *FitBit*, *Spotify*, *FourSquare*), have integrated features for sharing this data with others. Considerable research attention has been paid to sharing with others who have similar goals or who are in the same situation (referred to in this paper as *peer support networks*). In particular, research has considered online support communities [26,51] and in-application comparison features [11,56], and has identified several best practices [47]. This form of sharing specifically articulates a set of friends who will share data with each other. Within the group, known individuals directly share information with each other.

CSCW 2014, March 14–18, 2015, Vancouver, BC, Canada.
Copyright © 2014 ACM 978-1-4503-2922-4/15/03...$15.00.
http://dx.doi.org/10.1145/2675133.2675135

A second form of sharing – sharing through social awareness streams (SAS) such as timelines and newsfeeds in Twitter or Facebook – is also commonly used in practice. The use of SAS is a more indirect form of sharing amongst individuals who may or may not be known to each other. Sharing personal informatics data (defined by Li et al. as personal information collected for self-reflection [32]) through SAS can help people reach friends, family, acquaintances, coworkers and others with whom they wish to stay connected. People who collect and post personal informatics data (referred to in this paper as *sharers*) often hope to gain emotional support or communicate their identity as someone engaged in these activities [20,24,44,55]. This form of sharing can also help identify potential activity partners [18,42], create sources of accountability and motivation [43,44], and elicit advice from people who know them and their context [44,51].

Despite reported interest in and a prevalence of features supporting sharing personal data through SAS, these features often find limited or problematic use. While usage data from commercial systems is hard to obtain, the record from research literature is clear: most study participants ignore social sharing features, have concerns that prevent their use, or are disappointed by the reactions they receive when they are used [35,37,42,56]. Prior work (e.g., [11,35,42]) has identified several barriers to their use, including not wanting to share a trivial accomplishment and feeling uncomfortable sharing with an unfamiliar audience. Other work has pointed out the importance of finding an appropriate audience [21] or that the responsibility of choosing to ignore or engage with shared content is left to the recipient [55].

In this paper, we reconcile the gap between social sharers' aspirations and their actual behaviors and outcomes. We develop a descriptive framework of social sharing research, consolidating findings in this space and identifying underexplored design alternatives. We demonstrate the value of this framework by using a subset of the dimensions to analyze how and why people use one popular application to share physical activity information on Twitter and how the details of the sharing affect responses. We consider perspectives of both sharers and their audiences, conducting two studies to learn what sharers post to SAS and how the audience views these posts. This combined analysis allows us to make design recommendations for sharing physical activity information on Twitter and broader recommendations for sharing personal informatics data, including how the design framework we developed can be used in future studies.

Specifically, we address the following questions:

RQ1: What design space of social sharing has been explored by prior research and practice in personal informatics and what conclusions can be drawn from this body of work?

RQ2: How do self-trackers presently share physical activity data in SAS, and how do recipients respond to seeing posts with this content?

RQ3: How do potential recipients feel about seeing this data in SAS, and what content features elicit replies or other positive reactions?

In the remainder of this paper, we review motivations and benefits associated with social sharing, the ways in which systems support this form of sharing, and how well these features support sharers' goals and how they break down. To support our discussion, we draw on prior work on people who socially share personal informatics data and an analysis of tweets from the popular fitness application *RunKeeper*. We conclude by discussing possible implications of these findings for other sharing domains within personal informatics.

SOCIALLY SHARING PERSONAL INFORMATICS DATA

While the majority of personal informatics research focuses on helping individuals improve themselves by reducing barriers to collecting and making sense of data, research and commercial applications have included features to share collected data with others. In this paper, we consider the sharing of self-tracked data to online social networks with a target audience of friends and family.

Many systems support symmetric sharing among groups [4,26,51] or pairs [40] in peer support networks. With peer groups, people can receive and offer experience-based advice, identify mentors and other motivators, and have a sense of shared experience. The audience – other members of the group – has personal experience with the sort the data shared. This helps people share it without needing to provide much additional context about the data. Sharing with peer strangers, on the other hand, may mean that they have to provide additional context about themselves.

Sharing personal informatics data through SAS creates opportunities not possible in peer support networks, such as reaching an audience of people whose opinions matter for emotional support. However, this space has challenges distinct from those in peer support networks, such as how to frame data for an audience potentially unfamiliar with the domain or goals. We continue to compare sharing personal informatics data through SAS to peer support networks throughout this paper, but focus on design issues and opportunities for SAS.

Why people share

People have many reasons for sharing their personal informatics data with peers and with their support networks of friends, family, and colleagues [41]. In many domains, such as health, social support is an important factor in behavior change [31,51]. In this section, we review the reasons for social sharing in personal informatics identified in prior work, including sharing intended to support behavior change and other uses of the data.

Request for information

Many people share their data and experiences to receive some form of information from their audience. People turn to their social networks for recommendations, advice on how to improve, or for something new to try [39,44,51]. This is a common practice in – and often the expressed goal of – peer support networks, as the audience has a shared experience to draw upon and offer recommendations from [26,51].

Desire for emotional support

Sharers also seek emotional support, both from peers going through a similar experience and from caring friends and family [44,51]. For example, the HeartLink system enabled a social network to cheer on participants running a race, which participants found motivating [15]. In controlled studies, participants enjoyed receiving and felt motivated by encouraging messages sent from others in the study [11,56].

Seeking motivation or accountability from audience

Sharers may seek motivation and accountability by making commitments public, identifying potential activity partners, or creating competitions [42,44]. Collaborating in a shared activity can create a source of accountability [40]. Some people post their plans and goals to Twitter to create a commitment mechanism that helps motivate them to remain active and achieve their goals [55].

Motivating or informing the sharing audience

Some people also strive to motivate or inform their audience by sharing their experiences collecting personal data [10]. People also share records of activities and goals, such as eating healthy or exercising, to motivate others to act similarly [7]. In location-sharing applications, people may broadcast their location to recommend a cool place they found or to potentially meet up with nearby friends [36].

Impression management

People use social sharing to communicate an identity to their social networks and achieve impression management goals [20,44], but this also leads to curation and concerns about self-presentation [44,58]. Posts about runs or workouts can communicate that the sharer is an active, fit individual; feeds of music can communicate one's tastes. This also creates challenges; for example, people may curate their music listening histories to remove guilty pleasures [50].

DEVELOPING A DESIGN FRAMEWORK

While substantial prior work has explored social sharing within personal informatics, it remains disparate and unorganized. Systems share data in a multitude of ways, but system evaluations often lack integration with other prior work because each evaluation focuses on a single approach to data sharing. We develop a design framework by looking across many different studies, integrating and synthesizing results.

The framework can facilitate analysis of new sharing features by isolating a single design choice to vary in evaluation. We describe these different design choices along several *dimensions*, discussing factors of social sharing across one dimension. The six dimensions developed and discussed are:

- **Data Domain**: the type of data collected and shared
- **Preprocessing**: transformations applied prior to sharing
- **Sharing Trigger**: what causes the data to be shared
- **Persistence**: how long the share is visible
- **Post Content**: what information is shared
- **Audience**: who receives the post

We summarize these dimensions and a selection of prior work representing them in Table 1. These dimensions were created though a bottom-up consideration of related literature; three members of the research team categorized and named identified dimensions. While the literature surveyed is not exhaustive, it represents some of the most seminal and influential work on this topic in the CSCW and HCI communities. We believe that other prior work and future work on shared personal informatics data can be categorized according to these dimensions.

Data Domain

Self-tracking occurs in a wide variety of domains as people look to quantify various aspects of their lives. Many systems have been built to examine physical activity [11,35,38,56], bioinformatics data such as heart rate and ECG data [15,16,40,49], location [6,27,54], ecologically friendly activities [22,37], and music [20,50]. These domains are tracked for a variety of reasons, including to make healthier decisions or track health factors [8,38,41,55] or simply to know thyself [19,32,33].

Others have studied the use of commercial applications across these domains as well. Location sharing has been studied in FourSquare [14,36] and Google Latitude [46], now integrated into Google+. Teodoro and Naaman report on the use of Twitter to share physical activity [55] while Fritz et al. [21] and Rooksby et al. [48] consider other sharing networks. Last.fm has been studied for how people share music listening practices [20,50].

When deciding what is appropriate to share, designers should consider the norms attached to that type of data. For example, biometric data is perhaps more personal than someone's music listening history, and thus is more influenced by other dimensions. Sharing hourly data about music listening might be acceptable, while this might be an invasion of privacy for biometric data.

Preprocessing

Personal informatics data can go through a series of transformations prior to sharing, such as filtering or aggregating by time. Some systems immediately share raw data as it is collected [7,15,18,20,40,46], while others share aggregate daily totals [7,11,18,35,42,56]. Other times, shares communicate achievement of a specific goal or milestone [42]. Sharing high level syntheses from the raw data has been considered, such as a sentence describing a trend in activity [19] or a story drawn from collected data [23].

Preprocessing of data occurs for a variety of reasons. One is to maintain privacy, as aggregation can hide potentially private events, such as specific purchases. Social sharing has considered transforming raw data prior to sharing [18,29,30]. Designers of other systems have discussed electing not to disclose potentially sensitive events [37] or sharing less specific information (e.g. a generic place like "Grocery Store" or city-level information) [3,12,54].

Preprocessing data can also prevent inundating recipients with large amounts of data or frequent posts. Prior work on physical activity tracking has recommended that designers avoid sharing mechanisms that overwh the recipient [18,21]. It is common for people to self-censor in these networks [52] or post something that they later regretted [53].

Sharing Trigger

Another important dimension to consider is what triggers a share. Many applications stream data constantly, viewable in a profile or on a webpage. This streaming data may be collected and updated in the background as long as the application is enabled (e.g. steps [18], location [46]) or may be limited to during a specific activity (e.g. while running [15,40], while listening to music [20]). Other applications share when a self-tracker arrives at a designated location [3,5] or arrives near another self-tracker [34]. In other applications, shares are triggered automatically once a day [11,35,56].

All of the above systems implement automatic sharing of activity, but another class of features enable the self-tracker to trigger sharing on their own [14,36,42]. Other systems enable recipients to solicit data from the sharer, giving the sharer the choice to respond [11,27].

In applications that share automatically, the sharer can become disconnected from their data and lose the opportunity to explain its significance. By requiring the self-tracker to share manually, they are required to both reflect upon the data collected and decide whether the post is worth making. However, when sharing is automatic, self-trackers may share more and thus receive more benefits from sharing. For example, automatic sharing may be particularly important for creating accountability. To our knowledge, researchers have not systematically studied the tradeoffs

Dimension	Definition	Points Within Dimensions	Prior Work
Data Domain	Type of data collected and shared	Physical activity	[2,10,11,18,19,21,35,38,40,42,48,55,56]
		Biometrics	[10,15,16,40,49]
		Location	[3,5,6,9,12,14,17,19,23,24,27,28,29,30,34,36,45,46,54]
		Pictures	[7,13,23,25]
		Other, including environment, food, and music	[7,10,20,22,37,50,51]
Preprocessing	Transformations applied prior to sharing	Raw data	[7,10,12,15,18,19,20,23,24,25,36,46,49,50]
		Aggregate daily totals	[2,10,11,18,35,56]
		Goal achievement	[2,11,21,35,42,56]
		Summarization into trends	[10,19]
		Automatic or manual naming of data	[3,5,9,12,27,54]
Sharing Trigger	What causes the data to be shared	Always-on passively streaming	[5,9,18,20,28,46,50]
		Streaming during a special activity or event	[15,16,40,49]
		Arrival at or departure from a location	[3,6,34]
		Once per day	[18,21,56]
		Determined by the self-tracker	[2,7,11,13,14,17,21,23,24,25,27,36,37,42,54,55,56]
		Request by the sharing audience	[12,27]
Persistence	How long the share is visible	Transient	[3,5,11,12,13,27,40,49]
		For the lifetime of the system	[7,9,35,56]
		For the lifetime of the social network	[14,15,16,18,20,42,46,50,55]
		Self-tracker can delete content	[18,20,25,50,55]
Post Content	What information is shared	System-generated text	[2,5,11,12,19,42]
		Numerical summaries	[2,11,15,16,35,37,42,56]
		User-generated text	[2,9,11,38,54,55,56]
		Graphs or other visualizations	[2,10,15,16,19,23,37,42,49]
		Passive notification (noise, vibration)	[3,34]
Audience	Who is receiving the post	Broader social network	[15,16,18,19,21,28,37,42,55]
		Dedicated social network	[14,20,21,24,36,46,50]
		Strangers involved in a study	[7,35]
		Friends involved in a study	[2,5,6,11,12,13,27,34,38,40,56]
		Family or significant others involved in a study	[3,9,38]

Table 1. We develop a design dimension framework for sharing personal informatics data by extensively considering prior work and the points explored within the space.

between encouraging automatic posts and self-tracker initiated posts.

Persistence

Applications can also vary how long shared data is available. CoupleVibe automatically shared messages about a remote partner's location using short vibrations. If the recipient did not notice when it occurred, the old location was lost forever [3]. This approach is especially applicable for other time-dependent systems, where the relevant data to share is occurring at the current moment.

Other research applications, including Chick Clique and Fish'N'Steps, implement shares persisting for the life of the system [35,56]. Posts of personal informatics data made to a social network (versus a research prototype), including from [36,42,55], exist for as long as the network is relevant. Both groups of systems preserve a record of previous shares for browsing or searching. These systems may also enable the self-tracker to delete a prior share [55].

People sometimes post data to social network sites to create a private record of events in their lives [58]. This, combined with being aware of and finding patterns in their activity [8,19], demonstrates the value of sharing to a persistent social network even when another record does not exist. Enabling the deletion of shares is important for impression management, and deletion is a common strategy for managing regretful posts to social networks [53].

Post Content

Application designers have explored different types of share content. Systems have supported sharing personally collected data through numerical summaries [11,35], maps [36,46], and graphs [15,18,37]. These have varied in level of detail, ranging from a vague statement that an activity has been completed to a detailed post, including, for example, distance, route, time, and location of a run, as well as heart rate and mood [38, RunKeeper]. People have also expressed an interest in having the details hosted outside of the SAS and posting only a link. Apart from providing more detail than possible in a SAS post, people rarely use these features because they lead to uninteresting posts [38].

Some applications encourage users to annotate the tracked data with information about its significance, provide more details, or photos [13,23]. This content conveys more context, but also requires user time and effort to generate.

Prior work has not explored the importance of post content. It is unclear when it is necessary for the self-tracker to provide self-generated content versus system-generated content to receive feedback. Furthermore, what self-generated content posters should add has not been studied; we explore this later in this paper, considering both how self-trackers currently curate their posts, as well as how the audience views these posts.

Audience

Sharers and system designers must also decide who will receive posts. Systems have connected sharers with a variety of audiences, including pre-organized teams of random co-workers at a large corporation [35] to people who are friends or otherwise already know each other [11,27,56] to family and significant others [3,9]. In each of these systems and evaluations, all users were also participating in the activity. Thus, they saw each other as peers with similar goals and shared experiences [42].

Other systems and studies explored posting to a broader social network, such as Facebook [42] and Twitter [55]. GoalPost participants could share physical activity goals and journals to Facebook, but many worried about posting accomplishments that would seem trivial to others. Participants were also underwhelmed and discouraged when their posts received few responses [42]. Teodoro and Naaman found people posted to Twitter to feel accountable to their audience and did not express concern about their audience's opinion on their posts [55].

One way of negotiating post audience is to use a popular social network site to distribute the posts, but to restrict its distribution to a subset of the network. Prior work has limited the audience on these social network sites by building apps on the platform [37] or restricting post visibility to a list of supportive friends identified by the user [42]. Groups also self-organize on these networks, such as by creating Facebook groups with shared step goals or utilizing the same Twitter hashtag.

Post audience in prior work has varied from other study participants (both friends and strangers) to social networks (both specific to the data being tracked and broad). The norms of each of these audiences vary. In self-contained studies where the audience is a part of the study, the audience can relate with the sharer through their joint experience [44].

Despite hopes for using social network sites to share personal informatics data [43,55], there remain many challenges and best practices are not yet well understood [42]. Some social networks include features to help both sharers and their audience navigate sharing challenges. For example, Facebook and some Twitter clients enable hiding posts originating from a certain application or with a certain hashtag.

Individual preferences and comfort with different sharing audiences are heterogeneous. For example, some people are comfortable sharing their fine-grained physical activity with their entire social network, while others were only willing to share with close friends, or no one at all [18]. In the GoalPost study, some participants configured a "support group" of Facebook friends who could view their posts. Some included no one in their support group – making their posts a private record for themselves – and others shared with supportive friends, partners, or teammates; many other participants just chose to share with their entire Facebook network [42].

APPLYING THE DESIGN FRAMEWORK DIMENSIONS

To demonstrate the value of using these sharing dimensions as an analytical framework, we apply the dimensions to a case study of physical activity shares from the RunKeeper application posted on Twitter. RunKeeper is a commercial smartphone physical activity tracker with 25 million users, with runners logging over 2 million miles per day through the application at the time of this publication.

RunKeeper automatically records distance, time, and route, and enables posting to Twitter either automatically or manually after each exercise session. The user can add personalized text or a picture to each tweet. The app also enables sharing of runs, walks, or bike rides in real time.

This analysis focuses on unpacking the dimension of **Post Content** to answer the question: *How does the content of a RunKeeper post to Twitter influence follower impressions and responses*? The results of our analysis are generalized to the other sharing dimensions of our design framework in the discussion section below.

The combination of application (RunKeeper) and social awareness stream (Twitter) constrain the remaining dimensions:

- **Data Domain:** physical activity, specifically RunKeeper
- **Preprocessing:** minimal, configurable text around activity, pace, distance, and cumulative time
- **Sharing Trigger:** posted at the conclusion of an activity, either automatically or manually triggered by the user. Live events are shared at the beginning of the activity with a link to follow activity progress
- **Persistent:** exist as long as the social network does or until the poster deletes it
- **Audience:** followers on Twitter social network and anyone following the "#RunKeeper" hashtag

Focusing on the content dimension and fixing the other dimensions in this way facilitated a more tractable analysis.

Framework evaluation methods

We conducted two evaluations of tweets made through RunKeeper, supported by a formative survey on sharer goals and desired reactions. We first learn about the posts people make by analyzing recent tweets made via RunKeeper, characterizing the types of posts people make as well as what posts generate responses (referred to as the Collected Tweets, or CT study). We then evaluated audience reactions to similar tweets by generating a set of tweets representing a variety of commonly shared content and then conducting a survey to elicit audience feedback (referred to as the Generated Tweets, or GT study).

Formative survey: sharer goals and desired reactions

To identify desirable reactions to sharing, we conducted a formative survey about self-tracker's experiences sharing physical activity on a social network. 32 respondents recruited from University mailing lists and self-tracking forums (26 female, 6 male; average age 35.3, median 31, min

21, max 63) described their best and worst sharing experiences. Likes, comments, and in-person conversations were mentioned important characteristics of their best experiences sharing personal informatics data by 14, 14, and 2 respondents, respectively. Twelve respondents described their worst experience sharing their physical activity; the remainder either stated that they had not had a negative experience or left the question blank. Eight respondents mentioned receiving no feedback (e.g. likes or comments) as part of what made the experience their worst.

From this survey, we learn that self-trackers positively correlate comments or likes to how positive of an experience they had making the post. R39 mentions how feedback on their physical activity made them feel: "*likes and encouraging comments make me feel good about what I did*." R19 strongly stated his feelings when his posts did not receive feedback: "*If a tweet falls in a timeline and nobody's there to hear it... No feedback is the worst feedback!*" These results, and their consistency with prior work [42,43], encouraged us to use SAS feedback mechanisms (e.g., likes or favorites, comments or replies) as measures for how positively a sharer evaluates the success of their posts.

Collected Tweets (CT) study

We began our CT study analysis by randomly sampling 5,000 tweets from all public tweets posted with the hashtag "#RunKeeper" between late-December 2013 and mid-April 2014. Approximately 652,000 public tweets were posted with this hashtag during this span, so our initial sample represents 0.77% of all tweets posted in this span with the hashtag "#RunKeeper".

We coded each tweet for 10 features, described in Table 2. These features were selected to characterize the variability in the post content, highlighting common trends when posting to Twitter from RunKeeper. We additionally coded for the number of replies, favorites, and retweets.

Two researchers coded each tweet. When the assigned codes differed, a third researcher coded the tweet and the dispute was resolved by majority vote. 4,256 of the 5,000 tweets had agreement across all codes after two coders. 19 of the remaining 744 tweets still had disagreement after three coders (each of these disagreements occurred as a result of the dimension having more than two levels), and were resolved through group discussion by five coders.

Eight people coded unequal portions of the tweets. To measure the agreement among the coders, each person coded a set of 100 tweets presented in a random order. We used Fleiss' Kappa to assess inter-coder reliability among our 10 subjective, nominal codes. We received high agreement for "live event", "not an activity share", "activity type", "broken", and "zero minutes ran" (1.00, 1.00, 0.97, 0.96, 0.87) and moderate agreement for "post type", "non-English tweet content", "negative emotion", and "positive emotion" (0.79, 0.76, 0.64, 0.56). Mentions of another user did not occur in the set sampled for inter-coder reliability.

Tweet Feature	Coding
1. Tweet content type	Any combination of: default text, user-generated text, user-generated picture
2. Activity type	Walk, run, bike, other
3. Tweet contains a positive emotion	Yes or No
4. Tweet contains a negative emotion	
5. Tweet link still exists	
6. Tweet contains non-english text	
7. Activity lasts for 0 minutes, 0 seconds	
8. Tweet @mentions another user	
9. Tweet is not an activity share	
10. Tweet is a live event	

Table 2. Coding scheme for tweet features in the CT study.

We excluded a portion of these tweets from analysis. Tweets were captured in real-time, so if the tweeter changed their profile settings to make their tweets private or deleted their account or the specific tweets, the tweet became no longer publically accessible. We removed 189 tweets not publically accessible as of mid-May 2014. We additionally removed 13 tweets where the tweeter had no followers, as these tweets were unlikely to receive responses. Finally, we removed 27 tweets not posted by the RunKeeper application (such as recommendations to friends to install RunKeeper or links to news articles mentioning RunKeeper). These tweets differed content and goals from posts made using the RunKeeper app.

Removing all tweets with these characteristics reduced our sample to 4,771 tweets, and our remaining analysis considers only these tweets.

Statistical methods in the CT study

We used regression analyses to characterize the correlations between different tweet attributes and responses. We used a Poisson model for the number favorites and retweets because each favorite or retweet came from one unique user. For replies, however, we used a negative binomial model for if a tweet received replies or not: many tweets received a high number of replies but involved only a small number of users or quickly went off topic, and so additional replies rarely offered further support. In all models, we used log(followers) as an offset (exposure) variable, because one's follower count limited their potential for replies.

To differentiate between excess zeros caused by attributes of the user's account and zeros caused by attributes of the tweet, we used zero inflated model in all three analyses, due to the fact that 4,362 of the 4,771 tweets (91.4%) did not receive any response from Twitter users. We used the presence of the default image and the log of the user's tweet frequency to predict the excess zeros.

For the regression analysis, we removed an additional 432 tweets containing non-English text because we were not confident in our ability to code emotion in these tweets. A robustness check – including these tweets and repeating our analysis – does not alter the results.

Descriptive findings of the CT study

From our analysis of these tweets, a few common trends emerged. Most (74.0%) of the tweets included only system-

Figure 1. Tweets generated for the GT study varied on several dimensions, allowing us to separately evaluate the role of each of these features.

generated content. Of the tweets that included user-generated text, 22.0% contained positive or negative emotion. We also observed tweets containing descriptions of the weather, asking for advice or support, and additional information such as heart rate or run intervals. 299 runners added pictures in their tweets, which were typically landscapes, pictures of their shoes, or selfies.

Prior work has studied the sharer perspective for generating such posts [11,38,42,56]. Because sharers in prior work and in our survey of goals and desired responses emphasize the importance of audience responses for feeling that they have achieved their posting goals, we focus on audience reactions and opinions. We analyzed these tweets for audience response, including replies, favorites, and retweets.

Analysis of tweets in this study, however, only takes into account the observable responses. It cannot measure unobservable actions or audience members' opinions and reactions that did not result in a favorite, reply, or retweet. That is, from the CT study we can learn *what* tweets get replies, favorites, or retweets by not *why* or any other ways in which people may have reacted.

Generated Tweets (GT) study

With the limitations of the CT study in mind, we conducted a second study to better understand how a post about physical activity to a SAS would be interpreted by potential consumers or readers. We used the descriptive findings from the CT study to generate parameters for a system to randomly generate tweets similar to those we coded in the CT study. Three tweets generated by our system appear in Figure 1.

We varied nine parameters when generating tweets. Tweets could contain a milestone event (half marathon, return from surgery, or a long-term goal), one of four types of requests to the audience (asking for a recommendation, support, accountability, or an activity partner), or details about the sharer's run. The details about the run included positive emotion (e.g., "felt good", "best run in a while"), negative emotion (e.g., "that sucked", "knee hurt"), and/or information about the weather (e.g., "weather is great", "a little chilly"). The distance of the run was random between 2 and 15 miles, and could be either live or have already taken place. Finally, the post could include a photo of either a runner's shoes or a landscape depicting the run's location. For the posts that did not include a photo, RunKeeper's default Twitter card was displayed with statistics about pace (an 8:30 per mile pace regardless of distance) and calorie consumption (calculated using the American College of Sports Medicine metabolic consumption rate formula [1] for a person weighing 150 pounds).

Some parameters affected what we displayed for other parameters. For example, if the tweet communicated poor weather and a picture was to be shown, the picture changed to a rainy park or wet shoes. We additionally removed certain combinations of parameters that did not make sense, such as displaying distance or calorie information for a tweet announcing the beginning of a live run. To ensure short, realistic-sounding tweets, specific information was not combined with life event information or audience requests; otherwise generated tweets could exceed 140 characters. We sought to preserve grammar, with tenses corrected for live tweets (e.g., "great run" for a previously-occurring tweet versus "excited to run" for a live tweet) and appropriate use of conjunctions (e.g., "that sucked, but happy I did it" for a tweet containing a positive and negative emotion).

Varying all of these parameters resulted in 102 possible styles of tweets, plus additional variation in exact wording, content ordering, and run distance. We used a factorial study design to obtain responses to these tweets, surveying 97 respondents recruited from Twitter, Facebook, and University mailing lists; respondents were entered into a raffle for one $50 or two $25 Amazon gift cards. Each respondent saw five tweets. Each tweet contained a randomly-ordered gender-neutral name (Alex, Jamie, Cameron, Kendall, and Taylor), a randomly composed Twitter username (supplementing the name with letters or numbers), and a random profile picture (a landscape). These three parameters had no statistically significant effects on our responses, and we exclude them from further analysis.

The five tweets that each respondent saw were selected to overlap on four or fewer parameters to avoid the feeling that respondents were seeing the same tweets multiple times. Finally, our survey enforced that no two tweets among the five generated for an individual contained the same picture. As a result, tweets containing RunKeeper Twitter cards were oversampled in our analysis.

a) Tweet received replies (Negative Binomial)

Variable	Estimate	Std. Error	p
Count Model Coefficients			
(Intercept)	-8.789	1.092	<0.001***
Default text	0.063	1.073	0.953
User text	1.147	0.248	<0.001***
User picture	-0.533	0.407	0.190
Positive	-0.116	0.409	0.777
Negative	0.326	0.604	0.590
Tweet is live	-13.851	671.103	0.984
@mentions	0.070	0.600	0.907
0:00	-0.346	0.629	0.582
Zero-inflation model coefficients			
(Intercept)	-0.011	0.392	0.979
Egg image	13.456	877.604	0.988
log(tweet frequency)	0.440	0.114	<0.001***

b) Favorites (Poisson)

Variable	Estimate	Std. Error	p
Count Model Coefficients			
(Intercept)	-7.811	0.801	<0.001***
Default text	0.098	0.788	0.901
User text	0.806	0.154	<0.001***
User picture	-0.170	0.208	0.413
Positive	-0.153	0.200	0.442
Negative	0.496	0.375	0.187
Tweet is live	-0.093	0.466	0.841
@mentions	-0.403	0.289	0.163
0:00	-1.483	0.787	0.060
Zero-inflation model coefficients			
(Intercept)	-0.351	0.205	0.088
Egg image	-2.095	9.624	0.828
log(tweet frequency)	0.473	0.076	<0.001***

c) Retweets (Poisson)

Variable	Estimate	Std. Error	p
Count Model Coefficients			
(Intercept)	-6.860	0.828	<0.001***
Default text	-2.056	0.787	0.009**
User text	0.283	0.543	0.601
User picture	-0.053	0.641	0.934
Positive	0.833	0.650	0.200
Negative	-13.250	895.397	0.988
Tweet is live	0.383	1.163	0.742
@mentions	1.586	0.832	0.057
0:00	0.440	1.180	0.709
Zero-inflation model coefficients			
(Intercept)	1.552	0.581	0.008***
Egg image	-14.428	434.771	0.974
log(tweet frequency)	0.141	0.135	0.294

*** p<0.001 ** p<0.01 * p< 0.05

Table 3. Results from regression models on a) whether a Tweet received replies, b) the number of favorites received, and c) the number of retweets received.

For each tweet, we asked respondents to select from a list of reasons why they believed the poster shared. This list was motivated by prior work [44,55]. Reasons included to receive emotional support, to be held more accountable, and to boast or show off. Respondents were asked to describe their initial reaction to the tweet in a freeform text box. They were additionally asked to indicate on four 5-item Likert-scales whether they agreed with being happy or annoyed that their friend made the post and whether they found the post interesting or boring. Finally, they were asked whether they would reply to the post, and to describe how they would reply or why they would not reply using an open-ended text box.

97 people responded to at least one tweet in the survey; 83 responded to all five they were presented (mean: 4.58, stdev: 1.06), resulting in 444 total responses to the tweets. Sixty-two respondents identified as female, thirty-four male, and one did not provide a response. Respondent average age was 28.49 (stdev: 7.79, median: 26, min: 18, max: 63). 45 stated they ran regularly, and 14 of these respondents regularly posted their runs to social media. 18 respondents had used RunKeeper to track their runs before, and 56 used Twitter.

Seven researchers used affinity diagramming to categorize respondent reactions and reply descriptions into similar themes. Two researchers further refined these initial groups, and the qualitative results from this refinement are presented in the results section.

Statistical methods in the GT study

We used similar regression analyses to the CT study to characterize the correlations between different tweet attributes and audience reactions. We used Ordinal Logistic Regression on responses to the 5-item Likert questions about whether respondents found the tweet interesting or boring, or whether they would be happy or annoyed if a friend made the tweet. We perform multilevel modeling by respondent to control for intrinsic respondent opinions.

Limitations

Even with two studies, there remain some limitations in our analysis. Because we only analyzed tweets that were publically available in mid-May 2014 in the CT study, we did not analyze any that a sharer removed after receiving no response or a negative response, an impression management strategy identified in prior work [53]. We additionally did not collect any replies, favorites, or retweets occurring after that point, though we anticipate that there were very few, as all tweets had been shared for at least 30 days before we collected the reply data. Since followers can change at any time, the audience count we use may differ somewhat from their count at the time they shared. We also noticed some of the tweeters had been followed, favorited, and/or retweeted by bots, and these are included in our analysis even though they may not result in the same feelings of support as reactions from real people.

The tweets in the GT study were all hypothetical, so respondents' actual behavior may differ from what they described in the survey and respondents may or may not actually respond to the tweets posed if they were presented in context. Given the frank nature of the responses, we believe respondent reactions to tweets seen in the study were authentic. As discussed later, many respondents indicated their response would depend on their relationship with the tweeter. Neither our study of actual tweets nor our survey measured the influence of these factors.

RESULTS

We triangulate the results from CT and GT studies to create a more complete understanding of how people post and respond to posts from RunKeeper to Twitter. Results from the regressions analyses of the CT and GT study data appear in tables 3 and 4, respectively.

System-generated content

Analysis of tweets from our CT study shows that tweets with user-generated text receive more replies ($Z = 4.63, p < 0.001$, 95% CI: 1.94-5.12 more replies) and how many favorites a

	Annoyed	Bored	Happy	Interesting
User picture	$F_{2,356} = 0.53$	$F_{2,358} = 8.50$***	$F_{2,358} = 2.58$	$F_{2,358} = 4.58$*
Positive	$F_{1,360} = 0.19$	$F_{1,362} = 1.74$	$F_{1,362} = 1.68$	$F_{1,363} = 0.17$
Negative	$F_{1,356} = 0.84$	$F_{1,358} = 0.55$	$F_{1,357} = 0.04$	$F_{1,358} = 3.17$
Tweet is live	$F_{1,372} = 0.58$	$F_{1,376} = 0.11$	$F_{1,375} = 2.79$	$F_{1,377} = 0.99$
Distance	$F_{1,374} = 0.73$	$F_{1,378} = 0.77$	$F_{1,377} = 1.43$	$F_{1,378} = 0.04$
Weather	$F_{2,353} = 2.13$	$F_{2,355} = 0.11$	$F_{2,354} = 1.30$	$F_{2,355} = 1.54$
Specific	$F_{1,363} = 15.84$***	$F_{1,365} = 10.35$**	$F_{1,365} = 15.09$***	$F_{1,366} = 6.47$*
Contains ask	$F_{1,362} = 5.58$*	$F_{1,364} = 7.05$**	$F_{1,364} = 2.06$	$F_{1,365} = 4.67$*
Number seen	$F_{1,347} = 3.83$	$F_{1,348} = 8.08$**	$F_{1,348} = 0.003$	$F_{1,348} = 6.89$**

*** p<0.001 ** p<0.01 * p< 0.05

Table 4. Results from regression model on how tweet characteristics impacted respondent opinions.

tweet receives ($Z = 5.25, p < 0.001$, 95% CI: 0.51-1.11 more favorites), while tweets containing any system-generated text receive fewer retweets ($Z = -2.61, p < 0.01$, 95% CI: 0.51-3.60 fewer retweets) than those that do not. This suggests that adding content to a tweet, even when combined with system-generated content from an application, is more likely to generate responses.

The factorial design in the GT study resulted in only 13 respondents viewing a tweet containing only system-generated content. Three of these respondents said such tweets felt automatic: "*there's no comment attached to this - just an automatic posting*" (GT80). GT49 reacted negatively to the tweet as a result, saying, "*this looks more canned, like maybe the app shot it off without Cameron knowing about it... very impersonal.*"

Even when a tweet contained user-generated content, some GT study respondents reacted negatively to the system-generated content. GT2 saw a tweet containing a request for a running buddy, and reacted, "*I wouldn't take the 'run with me next time' thing seriously. It feels impersonal mostly because it's not some kind of direct message to me, but also because it's part of a canned tweet. Even if they really mean it, I don't believe they do.*"

We conducted a secondary analysis on the 27 tweets in the CT study made with the RunKeeper hashtag not containing any system-generated text, which were previously excluded. These tweets were more likely to receive responses (χ^2 (1, N = 4798) = 28.14, $p < 0.001$), favorites (χ^2 (1, N = 4798) = 15.63, $p < 0.001$), and retweets (χ^2 (1, N = 4798) = 65.75, $p < 0.001$) than tweets posted through RunKeeper. However, this is dependent on a small proportion of tweets without any system-generated text.

Details about activity are well-received

Many tweeters in the CT study included additional details about the weather in their tweets, such as CT4756: "*Just completed a 10.26 mi run - A cold wind and lovely sunshine*" and CT2912: "*Just completed a 7.49 km run - 6°C, WC: 2°C, 20km/h WSW, 81%*". Others supplemented their posts with additional statistics about their run, such as biometrics or how they were training in CT1843: "*Just completed a 2.24 mi run - 6x400, pace 09:34 /mile, max HR 169*".

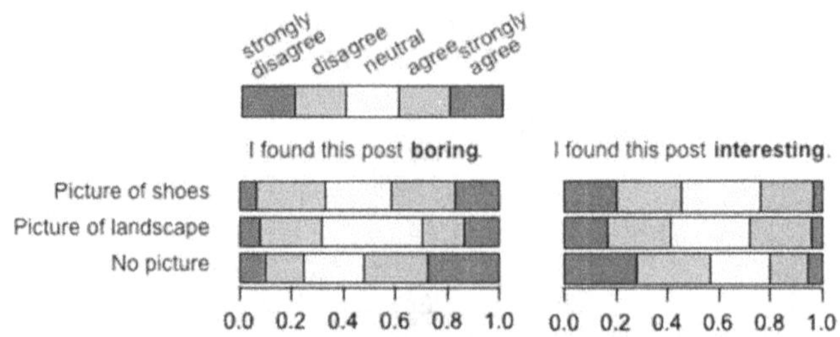

Figure 2. Respondents agreed that both posts lacking pictures and posts with pictures of shoes were more boring than pictures of landscapes.

RunKeeper includes distance as part of the system-generated content in the tweets. Twitter users occasionally responded to this distance, such as in CT2250, which received the response "*only 2.71? ... And you were giving me grief for 4 ;p*". Twelve GT study respondents explicitly reacted to the distance of a run. Most were impressed by the tweeter, including GT67: "*Holy shit he ran 9 miles?*" Other respondents acknowledged the significance of the event in their response, such as GT23 who wrote "*4 miles for a first run sounds impressive.*"

The content of the tweet influenced GT study respondents' opinions of the tweet. When a post included a specific reason for the run, respondents found the post less annoying ($F_{1,363}$ = 15.84, $p < 0.001$), less boring ($F_{1,365}$ = 10.35, $p < 0.01$), and more interesting ($F_{1,366} = 6.47, p < 0.05$), and were happier to see it ($F_{1,365} = 15.09, p < 0.001$). Consistent with suggestions from prior work [42,44], when a post contains a request of the audience, respondents found the post less annoying ($F_{1,362}$ = 5.57, $p < 0.05$), less boring ($F_{1,364} = 7.05, p < 0.01$), and more interesting ($F_{1,365} = 4.67$, $p < 0.05$).

Pictures in posts are seen as valuable

In the CT study, we did not find a significant effect of pictures on whether a tweet receives replies ($Z = -1.31$, *n.s.*) or how many favorites ($Z = -0.82$, *n.s.*) or retweets (Z = -0.08, *n.s.*) a post receives. The GT study identified a significant effect of picture on whether a post was boring ($F_{2,355}$ = 8.50, $p < 0.001$) and interesting ($F_{2,356}$ = 4.58, $p < 0.05$), displayed in Figure 2. While a picture may not trigger more feedback, the tweet audience still values posts with photos more.

The content of the picture also affected audience responses. We used a Wilcoxon signed rank test to compare the impressions of the 54 audience respondents who saw both a landscape and a shoe picture. Shoe pictures were more boring ($Z = 2.36, p < 0.01$, 95% CI: 0.25-4 on a 5-item Likert scale) than pictures of landscapes. However, there was no difference in how interesting participants found these two types of pictures (Z = -0.49, *n.s.*). Both received primarily positive reactions from the audience, with respondents reacting to the "*nice shoes*" (GT50; sentiment shared by GT57, 64, 76), "*liking the setting that is pictured*" (GT14; shared by GT5, 41, 50, 56, 57, 64, 65, 74, 88), and even

"*Makes me want to go walk the same location*" (GT55). Others wondered, "*Why are you showing me a picture of your shoes?*" (GT93).

Live events do not receive feedback

Live tweets were not more likely to receive responses (Z = −0.02, *n.s.*) or influence the number of favorites (Z=−0.20, *n.s.*) or retweets (Z = 0.33, *n.s.*); none of the 123 live tweets in the CT set received replies. Eight of the ninety-four GT study respondents who saw a live tweet stated they would follow the link to watch their friend run live. Seven others did not see value in watching someone else run, such as GT96: "*I have better things to do than watch someone's run online*".

Positive outcomes from sharing

Both the CT and GT study found positive experiences that could result from sharing, for both the tweeter and the audience.

Positive impressions of the tweeter

GT study respondents were "*happy for*" the tweeter (GT8, 9, 10, 14, 32, 79). GT66 elaborated more on this sentiment, being "*glad that my friend is making a commitment to be active.*" Providing context for a run tended to support these feelings: "*Good to see them back on their feet*" (GT62, a sentiment shared by GT24, 45) and "*Oh good, they're running a half marathon. I hope they do well.*" (GT74, a sentiment shared by GT80, who stated "*I am grinning just looking at this*"). While these respondents may not reply or interact with the tweeter within the social network, these positive impressions indicate a potential for in-person conversations about running that might not have occurred without the share. We do not evaluate impressions generated from the CT set, as this would not be feasible.

Favoriting

Favoriting a tweet requires little effort from followers but provides an easy way to provide emotional support or motivate the poster without taking as much effort as a reply. Six GT study respondents said that they would favorite a tweet, with GT18 noting the lower threshold: "*just a favorite. I don't reply to anything often.*"

User-generated text in a tweet seemed to give followers more to respond to. This could be a positive sentiment: CT4204 received four favorites for stating a run was "*Easy Peasy Lemon Squeezy*", a negative sentiment: one favorite for adding "*#dying #turtlesrunfaster*" (CT4678), or simply what the runner was thinking: one favorite for "*Push it to the limits*" (CT508).

Replying

Twenty-seven GT study respondents indicated they would reply to at least one of the tweets that they saw. These replies fell into three general categories. Congratulating the runner was a common type of support with "*good job!*" (GT1, 8, 10, 31, 42, 67, 85, 97; replies to CT1221, 1661, 2311, 3570, 4419), "*congrats!*" (GT15, 81, replies to CT2160, 3755), "*great work!*" (replies to CT563, 1607, 4170, 4454, 4533, 4832) or simply "*yay!*" (GT11, reply to CT4382) or "*wow!*" (replies to CT1128, T4423, T4907). Others encouraged the runner, with "*come on!*" (GT1, 10), "*you can do it!*" (reply to CT1121) or "*keep at it!*" (GT8, 85). Finally, GT study respondents responded expressing care for the runner: "*be careful*" (GT1, 59 in response to runners who were injured or recovering for injury).

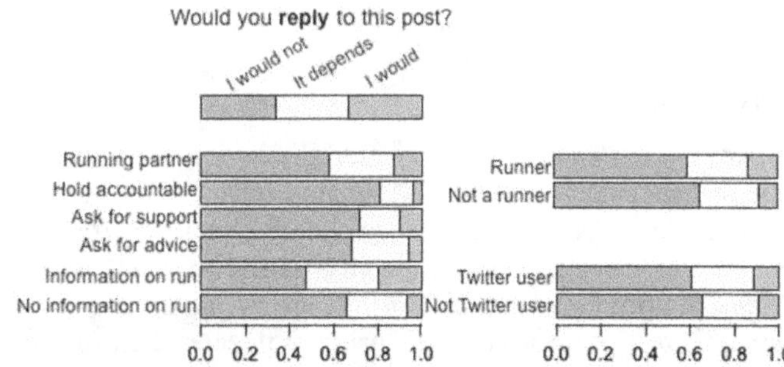

Figure 3. Respondents indicated that they were more likely to respond to posts that included information about a run, a request for a running partner, a request for support, or if they were a runner or a Twitter user.

Forty-three tweets in our CT set received more than two replies. These posts show conversations occurring over Twitter as a result of the post. These conversations were often follow-ups about how the runner was feeling, such as "*How's the hammy?*" (reply to CT1779) and "*How are you feeling now?*" (reply to CT4170). GT study respondents similarly replied with questions for the tweeter, such as "*Where are you running?*" (GT85). These questions serve as an effective way to engage the runner and can provide useful advice for other followers.

GT study respondents said they would offer or solicit advice in response to several hypothetical tweets. GT8, 35, and 71 offered recommendations on routes, with GT35 saying, "*I might think of my favorite running routes and suggest one to them*", and GT7 indicated they might reply "*if I wanted advice on getting a better time*". The original tweeter of CT4423 offered advice to one of their followers who stopped running: "*joining the running club & #parkrun have got me back into it, I'm loving it!*"

Figure 3 presents how characteristics of the tweet and of the respondent vary GT study respondents' likelihood of responding. Runners are slightly more likely to respond to tweets than non-runners (χ^2 (1, N = 444)=2.34, $p < 0.1$), but Twitter users were no more likely to respond than non-Twitter users (χ^2 (1, N = 444)=0.15, *n.s.*). Sharing the interest or experience increases a follower's likelihood of reply, and responses may increase with an audience who can better relate to the post content.

Responding beyond Twitter

Nine GT study respondents indicated that they would want to run with the tweeter in the future, some in direct response to a request for a running buddy "*Let me join next time?*" (GT45, similar replies by GT1, 35, 47, 77), or following up from an injury recovery "*Oh cool, he's back from surgery, let's go on a run together*" (GT24). CT3969 received a response asking to run together: "*nice run, up for 15 [miles] this Sunday?*"

Finally, posts sometimes motivated their audience to go run themselves, such as GT88, "*I wanna go for a run*". Others posted concerns about their own running habits. A reply to CT763 expressed concerns about starting to run: "*wish I could get myself motivated and off my ass to start running mate. Can't get started.*" The original tweeter then offered encouragement back to the replier.

Connecting with the tweeter

When tweets made an audience member think of their own experiences, the audience member felt more connected with the tweeter and was more inclined to respond. GT80 reminisced about her own running experiences: "*I remember when I was in that place, posting short runs with pictures and training for my first half!*", and indicated she would want to reply with saying "*I empathize with this situation and I'd want to encourage this person to keep working toward their goal.*"

Other GT study respondents discussed relating to or commiserating with the tweeter. GT19 commented "*Seeing as I have knee pain from time to time, I'd be pretty sympathetic to this individual.*" GT92 similarly related to the runner, commenting, "*I would commiserate, as I also rarely look forward to runs.*"

The CT set also contained several examples of shared experiences between tweeters and an audience member. People encouraged their teammates and people who they ran with, such as CT4705 "*motor on teammate!!!*" and CT469 "*great, we have to keep the momentum.*" Some tweeters added text to indicate who they were with, e.g., "*With Dave & Matty*" (CT123) and "*Walking with Vinny*" (CT3922) or @mentioning the others, including: "*Thanks @[removed] for getting me out of bed!!*" (CT4074).

Undesired consequences to sharing

A large portion of GT study respondents reacted negatively to some or all of the tweets they saw. In this section, we describe negative repercussions of sharing and how some audience members react to seeing these posts.

Our CT study analysis is unable to capture many of the potential negative reactions: we were unable to observe reactions such as unfollowing a person, hiding posts from the RunKeeper app, feeling bored, or forming a more negative impression about the sharer. Thus, to characterize potential negative reactions, we use data from the GT study.

Tweets are ignored by the audience

Thirteen out of the ninety-seven GT study respondents indicated they would ignore at least one the tweets, with eight others reacting to a tweet with "*meh.*" Seventy-three of the respondents agreed or strongly agreed with the statement "I found this post boring" for at least one tweet, suggesting survey respondents did not care for this content. GT52 wondered why this content appeared on Twitter: "*I scoff because why do they need to tweet this.*" GT74 and GT93 wondered, "*why would I want to watch you run?*"

Fifty-five respondents agreed or strongly agreed with the statement "I would be annoyed if a friend shared this" to at least one tweet. In the free response section, sixteen respondents described being annoyed by at least one tweet, with eleven reacting "*ugh*". GT16 reacted "*annoyed, don't care*" and "*I don't want to encourage posts like this.*" GT70 commented, "*Really, bro, no one cares.*" Four respondents said they would unfollow the poster or try to hide the post.

This sentiment did not come through in our CT study, likely because Twitter followers did not want to post negative replies publically. GT62 stated, "*I dislike this post and would want to keep that negativity off their account.*" GT2 felt similarly: "*I wouldn't reply because if I did it'd be something really rude so it's better to just keep it to myself. Or maybe it's better to unfollow the person.*"

An audience member ignoring or being annoyed by a tweet often has the same outcome to the tweeter: they do not respond. Given that people generally correlate responses with positive sharing experiences, a large audience ignoring these tweets is counter to people's goals for posting. A lack of response also makes it difficult for the tweeter to learn how to regulate their posting habits. Learning that followers are annoyed by certain posts may lead to changes in tweeting behavior, but this sentiment is rarely publically expressed.

In our CT study analysis, we observed that some tweeters created separate accounts for posting only their physical activity. This can complicates the process of following people on Twitter – how do you learn a Twitter user has a separate physical activity feed – but it also gives audience members more control because they can choose whether to follow such accounts and receive physical activity tweets.

Negative impressions of the tweeter

Some GT study respondents also expressed negative opinions of the tweeter because of the tweet. Some respondents believed that the tweeter was posting to brag about their success. GT48 reacted, "*someone likely wants attention,*" with GT49 stating, "*it looks like he's just showing off.*" GT35 and GT74 thought that the tweeter was "*fishing for compliments*".

DISCUSSION

In our analysis of the CT and GT studies, we identified both successes in sharing and problems with many shares. In this section, we describe some potential causes for the disparity, offer design recommendations, and relate our findings to social sharing in personal informatics more broadly.

System vs. Sharer-generated content

GT study respondents reacted negatively to tweets they believed RunKeeper had automatically generated. GT66 was "*annoyed that they didn't customize their automatic tweets*", with GT22 and GT44 suggesting that the tweet "*looks like an advertisement*". Respondents also appeared to fatigue after seeing multiple tweets, reporting later tweets seen as more boring and less interesting. We believe respondents got bored seeing the same or similar content repeatedly, a byproduct of the prevalence of automatically generated content.

GT study respondents desired more information about the importance of the run when deciding whether to reply, and often responded positively when this information was provided. GT45 decided to root for a runner "*because it's her first run back from surgery.*" GT46 contemplated replying, stating "*If they were working towards a goal, I'd be more likely to reply.*" GT92 reports both extremes in their response: "*I don't give a shit about watching people's live runs unless they're in an important race or they're doing an event in which they need support.*"

We note that posts were better received in the GT study when they contained a request of the audience or the context of why a run was significant. While not every run can be a personal best or major milestone, we believe that describing the importance of a run will lead to more positive responses and support.

Design recommendation: Together, these findings demonstrate the importance of supplementing the details of a run with sharer-generated content or possibly carefully crafted automatically-generated context (such as reporting a personal best). A system can encourage this by prompting the runner to take a picture or answer a question prior to sharing, and including this content in the post. Facebook recently took steps toward this. They noticed that people are more likely to engage with posts shared explicitly rather than automatically from within apps, and encourage application developers to share more personal content [57].

GT study respondents wanted to know the context of a run to determine whether to reply. GT43 reacted, "*It needs more context. Was this related to an event? Or was it a major training run? There is nothing really personal about it. It's just a robot post.*" A sharing application could easily prompt the user with, "why did you run today?" as part of the sharing process.

Audience and post frequency

Twitter is broad social network where followers range from close friends to total strangers. We expect that it is difficult to frame a post about physical activity to match the expectations of everyone in this audience.

In the GT study, thirty-three respondents said that their willingness to reply depended on how well they knew them. This ranged from "*If I know the person or not*" (GT14) to "*Only if it's a close friend*" (GT23). On a whole, our audience seemed more willing to respond to posts made by close friends or family members.

Five GT study respondents emphasized the importance of "*how often they post content like this*" (GT62, sentiment shared by GT10). After seeing multiple posts, GT97 notes, "*the sense of novelty is wearing off,*" and was left less enthusiastic about posting support. Audience fatigue may play a role, especially if this genre of posts appears frequently in a Twitter feed. A highly motivated audience, such as one of close friend or one that can relate to the poster's challenges, might suffer from less poster fatigue.

Design recommendation: Despite – or *because* of – the ability to reach a wide audience, Twitter may not be the best venue for regularly sharing everyday physical activity or other personal informatics information. One potentially improved system would enable sharing physical activity with a smaller audience of close friends or family members through lists within a broader social network, though previous work has found that many users do not want to spend the effort to configure such lists [42]. Another approach would be to share only to people interested in running, either through a dedicated social network, lists of a subset of friends or followers, or dedicated accounts.

The responses to our GT study indicate that people are willing to offer support to a close friend even if they are not self-trackers themselves. Routing messages to close, supportive friends and to people who have an interest in running or self-tracking may result in a better experience for sharers and their SAS audiences.

Twitter may still be an appropriate venue for sharing significant achievements, such as returning from injury or running a race. An application could recommend sharing these activities to Twitter while dissuading others, changing the interaction from automatically generating tweets to one that recommends tweeting if the content supports this.

Mismatch between sharer goal and audience interpretation

Sharers have a variety of goals for posting their personal informatics data to a social networking site, but these reasons are not always apparent to the post audience. Followers are often left wondering "*why would someone post this?*" (GT57) or believing that there is "*nothing to say*" in reply (GT72, sentiment expressed by GT32, 65) and thus elect not to provide any feedback.

GT90 alludes to another problem: even when a poster does not desire specific replies to meet their goal, their post may have harmful side effects, such as causing them to be seen as a braggart, especially when the post is not clear about why about the sharer's goals.

> *I think it's great when people share this kind of stuff because it helps hold them accountable (accountability is the positive byproduct). However, most people are probably posting this because they want to brag about their physical activity and the sweet views they get while running, but that's not a bad thing either if it motivates other people to hit the streets, too.*

For each tweet, respondents were asked to speculate why the tweet was posted from a list of reasons. Respondents marked 55.0% of tweets as posted "to receive emotional support" and 50.9% as posted "to boast/show off", (25.3% were perceived as motivated by both goals). This shows two different audience interpretations, which have conflicting sentiments about the tweeter. Bragging might be accepted and even encouraged in peer support communities, which GT21 implies: "*I kind of just ignore [posts] unless on [MyFitnessPal] because it is FOR bragging about exercise ;)*", but less well-received on general-purpose SAS.

Design recommendation: Personal informatics applications should encourage sharers to be more explicit about what feedback they are looking for when they decide to share. Prior to sharing, sharers could be asked to answer "why are you making this post?" Posting this answer along with the original post could give the post audience enough context to provide meaningful feedback for the sharer.

While we focus our analysis on audience reactions in the form of replies, favorites, and retweets, some goals may not be better achieved through more replies. For example, someone seeking advice may need just one or two informative replies, rather than a variety of less accurate replies. Furthermore, for some goals, no specific reply may be necessary. Posts made to foster an impression of oneself as an active, athletic individual might not need replies to achieve their goal. People also post physical activity and other goals to social networks to feel more accountable to those goals. If posting alone is sufficient for people to feel more committed to their goal, they may not require feedback from their audience.

Extending beyond RunKeeper and Twitter

We believe that many of the design recommendations we developed for sharing RunKeeper data on Twitter apply for other domains in which people self-track data and for other SAS. For example, GT study respondents felt that that many posts were made to brag or show off. We expect this occurs regularly when sharing personal informatics data, such as when someone shares that they consumed fewer calories, lost weight, or cut unnecessary spending habits. However, this might not be true for all domains. Some types of data, such as personal finances or health results, may be seen as more private, but in some cases some members of the audience may have a greater desire to see regular updates, such as when someone has had an ongoing struggle to manage a chronic illness [44]. Future work should more fully explore heterogeneity between different domains of shared data.

Regardless of the data presented, we believe automatic posts from self-tracking applications are likely to receive negative reactions from audience members. While perhaps some types of personal data are less annoying or more interesting in a SAS – something future work should assess – we anticipate that adverse reactions to automatically generated posts will still be common.

Audience reactions to personal informatics posts may correlate to how frequently these posts appear. Current commercial self-tracking applications including Strava, Last.fm, FourSquare and RunKeeper, encourage self-trackers to post to SAS regularly. We believe changes to the design of these applications to encourage fewer, more meaningful posts and descriptions of the post's importance or what sharers hope to gain from posting, will result in better sharing experiences for both sharers and their audiences.

It not always correct to design personal informatics sharing features to maximize post audience. Applications should help sharers route frequent posts to the right audience. These posts should target people who will respond positively to the content and can offer reactions the sharers need, be tolerant or even desiring of seeing it more frequently, and have sufficient context to understand it. For more significant events, they might encourage posters to share more broadly and to provide sufficient context so the audience will understand why they are sharing.

Use of the design dimension framework

In this paper, we describe a framework for evaluating sharing features in personal informatics studies. Use of this framework can help designers consider each design choice they make when creating a sharing feature for a personal informatics application.

We demonstrate the value of our design framework with a relatively simple and constrained sharing problem, varying only a single dimension (shared content) in our experiments. Thorough, empirical evaluation of a range of design options can inform the design of such features. This level of evaluation may not always scale to investigating to less explored, less constrained design questions. In those situations, we believe that our framework and corresponding review of previous literature can guide designers to select and evaluate a smaller number of options.

CONCLUSION

This paper presents a sharing dimension framework that characterizes different design choices for features that support socially sharing personal informatics data. Designers can use this framework determine the impact of a single factor to best share personal informatics data, and researchers can use it to identify unanswered questions and guide future study designs. We characterize prior work into these dimensions and summarize findings made in each dimension. We offer design recommendations for improving sharing of physical activity on Twitter through two studies of RunKeeper, and extend these findings to other domains.

ACKNOWLEDGMENTS

Lindsey Brockish, Danni Hu, Sara Jennings, Chuck Johnston, Rahul Mehan, An Ping, Sreedev Sidharthan, and Melinda Yang contributed to this work through coding tweets, affinity diagramming, and thoughtful discussion. We also thank Felicia Cordeiro, James Fogarty, and Nicole Lee for their feedback throughout this project. We also thank the University of Washington Statistical Consulting Program for advice on the statistical methods. Finally, we thank participants in the CHI 2014 Workshop on Beyond Quantified Self for their feedback on an early version of this project, and Andrew Miller for several helpful suggestions. This work is sponsored in part by the Intel Science and Technology Center for Pervasive Computing, Microsoft, Facebook, and the National Science Foundation under awards OAI-1028195 and SCH-1344613.

REFERENCES

1. ACSM and Pescatello, L.S. *ACSM's Guidelines for Exercise Testing and Prescription*. Lippincott Williams & Wilkins, 2014.
2. Al Ayubi, S.U., Parmanto, B., Branch, R., and Ding, D. A Persuasive and Social mHealth Application for Physical Activity: A Usability and Feasibility Study. *JMIR 2*, 2 (2014), e25.
3. Bales, E., Li, K.A., and Griswold, W. CoupleVIBE: Mobile implicit communication to improve awareness for (long-distance) couples. *CSCW 2011*, 65–74.
4. Bales, E. Supporting Implicit Mobile Communication: Harnessing Ubiquitous Sensors for Context and Content to Support Social Connection. 2013, 127–136.
5. Barkhuus, L., Brown, B., Bell, M., Hall, M., Sherwood, S., and Chalmers, M. From Awareness to Repartee: Sharing Location within Social Groups. *CHI 2008*, 497–506.
6. Barkhuus, L. and Dey, A. Location-Based Services for Mobile Telephony: A Study of Users' Privacy Concerns. *Interact 2003*, 207–212.
7. Baumer, E.P., Katz, S.J., Freeman, J.E., Adams, P., Gonzales, A.L., Pollak, J.P., Retelny, D., Niederdeppe, J., Olson, C.M., Gay, G.K., and Ave, C. Prescriptive persuasion and open-ended social awareness: Expanding the design space of mobile health. *CSCW 2012*, 475–484.
8. Bentley, F., Tollmar, K., Stephenson, P., Levy, L., Jones, B., Robertson, S., Price, E., Catrambone, R., and Wilson, J. Health Mashups : Presenting statistical patterns between wellbeing data and context in natural language to promote behavior change. *TOCHI 20*, 5 (2013), 1–27.
9. Brown, B., Taylor, A.S., Izadi, S., Sellen, A., Kaye, J., and Eardley, R. Locating family values: A field trial of the Whereabouts Clock. *UbiComp 2007*, 354–371.
10. Choe, E.K., Lee, N.B., Lee, B., Pratt, W., and Kientz, J.A. Understanding Quantified-Selfers' Practices in Collecting and Exploring Personal Data. *CHI 2014*, 1143–1152.
11. Consolvo, S., Everitt, K., Smith, I., and Landay, J.A. Design Requirements for Technologies that Encourage Physical Activity. *CHI 2006*, 457–466.
12. Consolvo, S., Smith, I.E., Matthews, T., LaMarca, A., and Tabert, J. Location Disclosure to Social Relations: Why, When, & What People Want to Share. *CHI 2005*, 81–90.
13. Cowan, L., Griswold, W.G., Barkhuus, L., and Hollan, J.D. Engaging the Periphery for Visual Communication on Mobile Phones. *HICSS 2010*, 1–10.
14. Cramer, H., Rost, M., and Holmquist, L.E. Performing a Check-in : Emerging Practices, Norms and 'Conflicts' in Location-Sharing Using Foursquare. *MobileHCI 2011*, 57–66.
15. Curmi, F., Ferrario, M.A., Southern, J., and Whittle, J. HeartLink : Open Broadcast of Live Biometric Data to Social Networks. *CHI 2013*, 1749–1758.
16. Curmi, F., Ferrario, M.A., and Whittle, J. Sharing Real-Time Biometric Data Across Social Networks: Requirements for Research Experiments. *DIS 2014*, 657–666.
17. Elhamshary, M. and Youssef, M. CheckInside : A Fine-grained Indoor Location-based Social Network. *UbiComp 2014*, 607–618.
18. Epstein, D.A., Borning, A., and Fogarty, J. Fine-Grained Sharing of Sensed Physical Activity: A Value Sensitive Approach. *UbiComp 2013*, 489–498.
19. Epstein, D.A., Cordeiro, F., Bales, E., Fogarty, J., and Munson, S.A. Taming Data Complexity in Lifelogs: Exploring Visual Cuts of Personal Informatics Data. *DIS 2014*, 667–676.
20. Fitzpatrick, C. Scrobbling Identity: Impression Management on Last.fm. *Technomusicology: a Sandbox Journal 1*, 2 (2008).
21. Fritz, T., Huang, E.M., Murphy, G.C., and Zimmermann, T. Persuasive Technology in the Real World : A Study of Long-Term Use of Activity Sensing Devices for Fitness. *CHI 2014*, 487–496.
22. Froehlich, J., Dillahunt, T., Klasnja, P., Mankoff, J., Consolvo, S., Harrison, B., and Landay, J.A. UbiGreen: Investigating a Mobile Tool for Tracking and Supporting Green Transportation Habits. *CHI 2009*, 1043–1052.
23. Gemmell, J., Aris, A., and Lueder, R. Telling Stories with Mylifebits. *2005 IEEE International Conference on Multimedia and Expo*, (2005), 1536–1539.
24. Guha, S. and Birnholtz, J. Can You See Me Now? Location, Visibility and the Management of Impressions on foursquare. *MobileHCI 2013*, 183–192.
25. Hoyle, R., Templeman, R., Armes, S., Anthony, D., Crandall, D., and Kapadia, A. Privacy Behaviors of Lifeloggers using Wearable Cameras. *UbiComp 2014*, 571–582.
26. Hwang, K.O., Ottenbacher, A.J., Green, A.P., Cannon-Diehl, M.R., Richardson, O., Bernstam, E. V, and Thomas, E.J. Social Support in an Internet Weight Loss Community. *International Journal of Medical Informatics 79*, 1 (2010), 5–13.
27. Iachello, G., Smith, I., Consolvo, S., Abowd, G.D., Howard, J., Potter, F., Scott, J., Sohn, T., Hightower, J., and LaMarca, A. Control, Deception, and Communication: Evaluating the Deployment of a Location-Enhanced Messaging Service. *UbiComp 2005*, 213–231.
28. Kostakos, V., Venkatanathan, J., Reynold, B., Sadeh, N., Toch, E., Shaikh, S.A., and Jones, S. Who's Your Best Friend? Targeted Privacy Attacks In Location-Sharing Social Networks. *UbiComp 2011*, 177–186.
29. Krumm, J. Inference Attacks on Location Tracks. *Pervasive 2007*, 127–143.

30. Krumm, J. A Survey of Computational Location Privacy. *Personal and Ubiquitous Computing 13*, 6 (2008), 391–399.
31. Leahy-Warren, P. *Theories Guiding Nursing Research and Practice: Making Nursing Knowledge Development Explicit.* Springer, 2014.
32. Li, I., Dey, A., and Forlizzi, J. A Stage-Based Model of Personal Informatics Systems. *CHI 2010*, 557–566.
33. Li, I., Dey, A.K.A., and Forlizzi, J. Understanding my data, myself: supporting self-reflection with ubicomp technologies. *UbiComp 2011*, 405–414.
34. Li, K.A., Sohn, T.Y., Huang, S., and Griswold, W.G. PeopleTones: A System for the Detection and Notification of Buddy Proximity on Mobile Phones. *MobiSys 2008*, 160–173.
35. Lin, J.J., Mamykina, L., Lindtner, S., Delajoux, G., and Strub, H.B. Fish'n'Steps: Encouraging Physical Activity with an Interactive Computer Game. *UbiComp 2006*, 261–278.
36. Lindqvist, J., Cranshaw, J., Wiese, J., Hong, J., and Zimmerman, J. I'm the Mayor of My House: Examining Why People Use foursquare-a Social-Driven Location Sharing Application. *CHI 2011*, 2409–2418.
37. Mankoff, J., Fussell, S.R., Dillahunt, T., Glaves, R., Grevet, C., Johnson, M., Matthews, D., Matthews, H.S., Mcguire, R., Thompson, R., Shick, A., and Setlock, L. StepGreen.org: Increasing Energy Saving Behaviors via Social Networks. *ICWSM 2010*, 106–113.
38. Miller, A.D. and Mynatt, E.D. StepStream: A School-based Pervasive Social Fitness System for Everyday Adolescent Health. *CHI 2014*, 2823–2832.
39. Morris, M.R., Teevan, J., and Panovich, K. What Do People Ask Their Social Networks, and Why? A Survey Study of Status Message Q&A Behavior. *CHI 2010*, 1739–1748.
40. Mueller, F., Vetere, F., Gibbs, M.R., Edge, D., Agamanolis, S., and Sheridan, J.G. Jogging over a distance between Europe and Australia. *UIST 2010*, 189–198.
41. Munson, S.A., Cavusoglu, H., Frisch, L., and Fels, S. Sociotechnical challenges and progress in using social media for health. *JMIR 15*, 10 (2013), e226.
42. Munson, S.A. and Consolvo, S. Exploring Goal-Setting, Rewards, Self-Monitoring, and Sharing to Motivate Physical Activity. *PervasiveHealth 2012*, 25–32.
43. Munson, S.A., Lauterbach, D., Newman, M., and Resnick, P. Happier Together: Integrating a Wellness Application into a Social Network Site. *Persuasive Technology*, (2010), 27–39.
44. Newman, M., Lauterbach, D., Munson, S.A., Resnick, P., and Morris, M.E. It's not that I don't have problems, I'm just not putting them on Facebook: Challenges and Opportunities in Using Online Social Networks for Health. *CSCW 2011*, 341–350.
45. Page, X., Knijnenburg, B., and Kobsa, A. What a Tangled Web We Weave: Lying Backfires in Location-Sharing Social Media. *CSCW 2013*, 273–284.
46. Page, X. and Kobsa, A. Navigating the Social Terrain with Google Latitude. *iConference 2010*.
47. Resnick, P.J., Janney, A.W., Buis, L.R., and Richardson, C.R. Adding an Online Community to an Internet-Mediated Walking Program. Part 2: Strategies for Encouraging Community Participation. *JMIR 12*, 4 (2010), e72.
48. Rooksby, J., Rost, M., Morrison, A., and Chalmers, M. Personal Tracking as Lived Informatics. *CHI 2014*, 1163–1172.
49. Schnädelbach, H., Egglestone, S.R., Reeves, S., Benford, S., Walker, B., and Wright, M. Performing thrill: designing telemetry systems and spectator interfaces for amusement rides. *CHI 2008*, 1167–1176.
50. Silfverberg, S., Liikkanen, L.A., Lampinen, A., and Hall, S. "I'll press Play, but I won't listen": Profile Work in a Music-focused Social Network Service. *CSCW 2011*, 207–216.
51. Skeels, M.M., Unruh, K.T., Powell, C., and Pratt, W. Catalyzing Social Support for Breast Cancer Patients. *CHI 2010*, 173–182.
52. Sleeper, M., Balebako, R., Das, S., Mcconahy, A.L., Wiese, J., and Cranor, L.F. The post that wasn't: exploring self-censorship on facebook. *CSCW 2013*, 793–802.
53. Sleeper, M., Cranshaw, J., Kelley, P.G., Ur, B., Acquisti, A., Cranor, L.F., and Sadeh, N. "I read my Twitter the next morning and was astonished": A Conversational Perspective on Twitter Regrets. *CHI 2013*, 3277–3286.
54. Tang, K.P., Lin, J., Hong, J.I., Siewiorek, D.P., and Sadeh, N. Rethinking Location Sharing: Exploring the Implications of Social-Driven vs. Purpose-Driven Location Sharing. *UbiComp 2010*, 85–94.
55. Teodoro, R. and Naaman, M. Fitter with Twitter: Understanding Personal Health and Fitness Activity in Social Media. *ICWSM 2013*, 611–620.
56. Toscos, T., Faber, A., Connelly, K., and Upoma, A.M. Encouraging Physical Activity in Teens: Can Technology Help Reduce Barriers to Physical Activity in Adolescent Girls? *PervasiveHealth 2008*, 218–221.
57. Yang, P. Giving people more control over when they share from apps. *Facebook Developers Blog*, 2014. https://developers.facebook.com/blog/post/2014/05/27/more-control-with-sharing/.
58. Zhao, X., Salehi, N., Naranjit, S., Alwaalan, S., Voida, S., and Cosley, D. The Many Faces of Facebook: Experiencing Social Media as Performance, Exhibition, and Personal Archive. *CHI 2013*, 1–10.

A Classroom Study of Using Crowd Feedback in the Iterative Design Process

Anbang Xu[1], Huaming Rao[2], Steven P. Dow[3], Brian P. Bailey[4]
[1] IBM Research - Almaden, San Jose, CA, USA, anbangxu@us.ibm.com
[2] Nanjing University of Science and Technology, Nanjing, China, huaming.rao@gmail.com
[3] Carnegie Mellon University, Pittsburgh, PA, USA, spdow@cs.cmu.edu
[4] University of Illinois, Urbana, IL, USA, bpbailey@illinois.edu

ABSTRACT
Crowd feedback systems offer designers an emerging approach for improving their designs, but there is little empirical evidence of the benefit of these systems. This paper reports the results of a study of using a crowd feedback system to iterate on visual designs. Users in an introductory visual design course created initial designs satisfying a design brief and received crowd feedback on the designs. Users revised the designs and the system was used to generate feedback again. This format enabled us to detect the changes between the initial and revised designs and how the feedback related to those changes. Further, we analyzed the value of crowd feedback by comparing it with expert evaluation and feedback generated via free-form prompts. Results showed that the crowd feedback system prompted deep and cosmetic changes and led to improved designs, the crowd recognized the design improvements, and structured workflows generated more interpretative, diverse and critical feedback than free-form prompts.

Author Keywords
Crowd feedback; crowdsourcing; design iteration; visual design; creativity.

ACM Classification Keywords
H.5.3 [Information Interface and Presentation]: Group and Organization Interfaces – Collaborative computing.

INTRODUCTION
Feedback is essential for the iterative design process because it reveals gaps between what is intended by the designer and how an audience interprets the design [15]. Knowing such gaps can help the designer iterate toward an outcome that better connects with its target audience.

However, receiving quality feedback can be hard. Face-to-face critiques are the gold standard [13] but impose an organizational burden. Peer requests are quick and simple but burn social capital and the feedback may be biased by friendship or competition [30]. Online communities provide another outlet but the quantity and quality of feedback typically falls below users' expectations [33, 35].

To overcome these issues, researchers have been exploring how *crowd feedback systems* can leverage online crowds as a simulated audience to provide feedback on designs. Researchers have used online crowds to collect preferences on design alternatives [2, 11] and to generate structured feedback on individual designs [23, 36]. Crowd-based usability sites [39, 40, 42] can be also utilized to conduct surveys and task-oriented tests of Web designs.

Although this class of system shows promise, there is little empirical knowledge of the effectiveness of these systems for iterative design. Prior work has shown that crowd feedback helps users discover problems with their designs [36], but this finding was based on user perceptions of the feedback and did not study changes to the designs. Other studies have shown the validity of using online crowds to test interfaces based on task performance [21] and for conducting A-B tests of design alternatives [11]. However, none of these studies investigated how crowd feedback prompts changes to a design, the validity of the feedback relative to expert evaluation, or how structuring the feedback generation process affects feedback content.

To fill this empirical gap, we conducted a study of how crowd feedback affects visual design. Crowd feedback was generated with a research prototype called Voyant [36]. Voyant generates five types of feedback on a visual design (e.g., first impressions, adherence to design guidelines, etc.) by decomposing the generation process into micro-tasks that can be executed by crowd workers without design expertise. The study was conducted in context of a two-week project in an introductory visual design course. Users (N = 10) created initial designs satisfying a challenging design brief prepared by the instructor. Crowd feedback was generated on the designs and given to the users. The users then revised the designs for their final deliverable. After the deadline, crowd feedback was once again generated so that we could examine changes between the initial and revised designs and how the feedback affected those changes. We also compared the feedback content to expert evaluation and feedback generated via open-ended

CSCW '15, March 14 - 18 2015, Vancouver, BC, Canada
Copyright 2014 ACM 978-1-4503-2922-4/15/03…$15.00
http://dx.doi.org/10.1145/2675133.2675140

prompts (e.g., what do you think of this design?). The main findings are:

- Crowd feedback was able to prompt a variety of changes in the iterative design process. A majority of the changes reported for the designs were deep changes relating to the theme and layout of a design. Cosmetic changes were also reported relating to the colors and fonts used in a design.
- The non-expert crowd was able to reliably evaluate design improvements based on design guidelines, as compared against expert ratings. However, the non-expert crowd and domain experts did not agree on how well a design achieved its communicative goals.
- The discourse in the structured feedback generated with the system, which poses specific prompts to the crowd, was more diverse and detailed than the discourse in the free-form feedback generated without such prompts. The most common category of critique discourse in the structured feedback was *interpretation* whereas the most common category in free-form feedback was *judgment*. These differences, along with the results from linguistic style analysis, show that structured workflows can help crowd workers think more critically about a design.

These outcomes provide initial evidence that can increase the design community's confidence in and knowledge of using crowd feedback systems in the iterative design process. The outcomes also provide insights into workflow patterns for improving the generation of crowd feedback.

RELATED WORK

We describe how our work contributes to the class of crowd feedback systems and situate our work within prior studies of design feedback and crowdsourcing in design.

Crowd Feedback Systems

The purpose of crowd feedback systems is to enable users to receive helpful, timely, and affordable feedback on their designs. For example, FeedbackArmy [39] is a commercial system that enables a user to pose open-ended questions about a design and the site returns free-form responses collected from an online crowd. Similar sites include Usabilla [42], Fivesecondtest [40], and UITests [41]. In research, Voyant is a crowd feedback system that generates five types of feedback by posing specific prompts to the crowd [36]. The rationale for the feedback types was based on a need finding study conducted with designers at various skill levels. CrowdCrit is similar, but uses learning theory to scaffold worker responses for feedback generation [23].

As these technologies emerge, it is important to assess their benefits and limits for design. Prior studies have shown that crowd feedback helps users discover problems with their designs [36] and is an enjoyable part of the process [11]. However, prior work has not investigated how crowd feedback prompts changes in the iterative design process.

Our work addresses this gap. From a classroom study, we report the types and depth of changes prompted by crowd feedback for visual design and how this feedback compares to expert evaluation. We also compare the content of the structured crowd feedback, which uses specific prompts, to free-form feedback collected from the same online crowd.

Prior crowdsourcing studies showed that directing worker attention with prompts and using examples improves the responses from the crowd for data analysis [20, 33]. Our works extends a similar concept for visual design and compares it to crowd feedback elicited holistically.

Studies of Design Feedback

Studies show that feedback from designers' peers and instructors improves their ability to create effective designs and understand how to better assess creative work [16, 27]. Designers who receive feedback during iterative design produce higher quality outcomes than those who do not [12, 13]. Peer feedback can also foster effective communication and collaboration among designers [9, 22]. Moreover, researchers have developed a typology of critique discourse generated by design novices and experts [8]. Feedback from experts was more collaborative and interpretative and less directive than feedback from novices.

Another body of work has investigated the effects of audience feedback in the design process. The feedback helped designers iterate toward design solutions that better connect with the intended audience [15, 32]. For example, to better design a computer-based system, designers often present their designs to a target audience and perform qualitative studies such as walkthroughs with a small group of individuals to collect feedback on the design [5].

Crowd feedback systems purportedly allow designers to receive similar feedback, acquired from a larger and more diverse audience, faster, and with lower cost. But how does a designer react to the feedback delivered from an online crowd, how does an online crowd react to the changes made by the designer, and how does crowd feedback compare to expert evaluation and typologies of critique discourse? Our work studies these questions for one crowd feedback system in context of visual design.

Crowdsourcing in Design

Researchers have investigated many directions for how a non-expert crowd can aid design activities. For example, Yu et al. showed how crowds can be integrated with genetic algorithms [38] and analogical transfer [37] to generate creative ideas. For example, a crowd can generate better ideas when given appropriate analogical schemas. In the CvC design method, the crowd works with the designer to form a team as part of an open design competition [25]. The designer can leverage these team members to brainstorm design solutions. In our work, we are leveraging online crowds for the purpose of providing feedback on visual designs and studying how it affects the design process.

(a) Initial Designs

(b) Revised Designs

Figure 1. The designs created during the study. (a) Initial Designs: preliminary designs completed by participants in the first week. (b) Revised Designs: after receiving crowd feedback, participants spent one week revising their initial designs. Each column represents the initial / revised pair of designs for a participant.

Participant	P1	P2	P3	P4	P5	P6	P7	P8	P9	P10
Theme			●			●		●		
Layout	●	●			●	●	●	●		●
Typeface		●	●		●			●		●
Color		●	●	●	●	●	●			

Table 1. The distribution of the four types of changes made by participants according to crowd feedback.

VOYANT: THE CROWD FEEDBACK SYSTEM USED

Voyant is a system that engages an online crowd as a simulated audience to collect, aggregate, and present their interpretation of a design [34, 36]. To use the system, a user uploads a design, configures the audience (age, gender, geography), and submits the design for feedback generation.

The system generates five types of feedback: *Elements* are the individual elements visible or otherwise perceived in the design including colors, shapes, objects, and activities. *First Notice* is the self-reported order in which elements are seen in the design. *Impressions* are the first perceptions formed in one's mind upon viewing the design. *Guidelines* refer to how well the design is perceived to meet guidelines in the domain using a seven point scale. The guidelines currently include proximity, alignment, repetition and contrast, which are commonly taught in visual design. *Goals* is how well the design is perceived to meet its communicative goals on a seven point scale. If this type of feedback is selected, the user is prompted to briefly describe each of her goals.

The feedback generation process is decomposed into a set of micro-tasks doable by crowd workers without design expertise. The micro-tasks relate to a description and interpretation phase. The first phase enumerates what elements can be "seen" in a design. The second phase is to interpret the design related to the visual hierarchy, first impressions, guidelines, and communicative goals entered by the user. In each phase, a micro-task focuses worker attention on a specific aspect of a design related to the feedback type rather than soliciting holistic judgments. For each task, a worker reacts to a prompt (e.g. what is your first impression?), annotates the design to indicate the regions associated with her reaction, and enters brief rationale. Using the coordinates of the annotation, the system also provides up to three elements (e.g. colors, shapes, or objects) identified by prior workers as examples to aid the rationale. The responses from each worker are then aggregated. The micro-tasks are submitted to Amazon Mechanical Turk, a popular online labor market. To reduce latency and costs, the system does not currently use explicit quality controls such as peer-assessment. It also allows a worker to perform multiple micro-tasks. The full set of feedback requires about $10 and several hours to generate.

Once complete, each feedback type is presented as a visual summary of the crowd's reactions and annotations. The system also provides interactions for exploring details of the feedback from the perspective of either the reactions or annotations on the design. We chose Voyant for our study

Figure 2. The *Impression* feedback on the initial and revised designs for the participant [P3]. (a) The impression word "hard to read" on the initial design prompted the participant to change the image treatment. The revision (b) was no longer perceived as "hard to read" by the crowd.

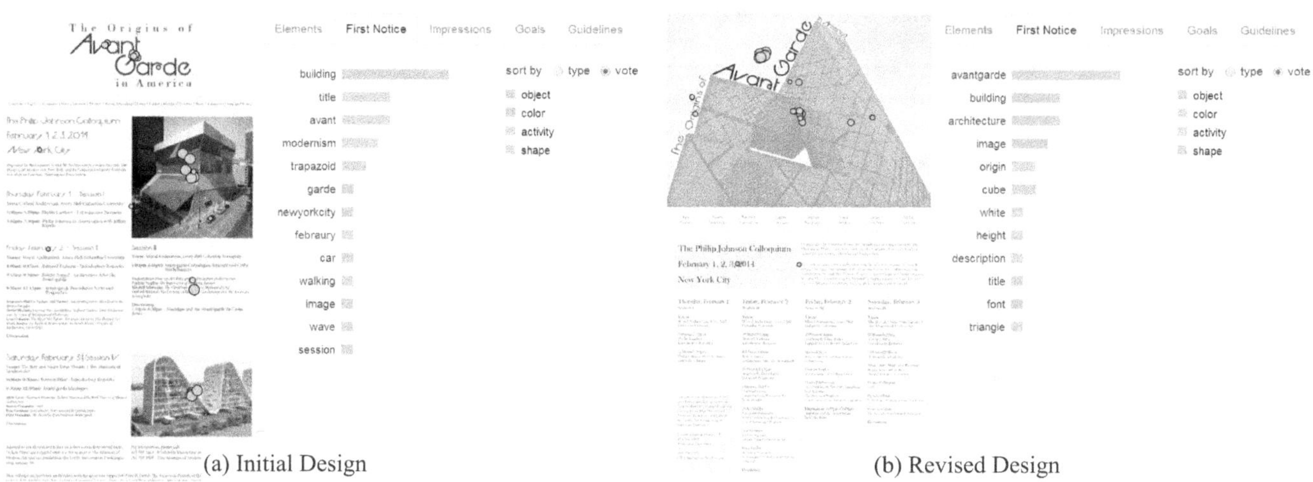

Figure 3. In (a), the first noticed element by the crowd is "building." In the revision (b), the first noticed element is the event. The feedback helped the participant [P8] understand how to utilize an image to attract people's attention more effectively.

because it is representative of the class of crowd feedback systems for visual design.

RESEARCH QUESTIONS

The purpose of the study was to understand how the use of crowd feedback affects the iterative design process. As a first step, the study addressed three related research questions:

RQ1: How is crowd feedback leveraged by users to iterate on a visual design? What types of changes are prompted by the feedback? What is the depth of the changes?

RQ2: Once users iterate on a design, how effectively does the crowd recognize the changes made to the design? What is the validity of the crowd feedback, e.g. how do the crowd's ratings compare to the ratings of experts for guidelines and goals?

RQ3: How is crowd feedback affected by structuring the generation process with prompts? What are the differences and overlaps between structured and free-form feedback?

These questions are not exhaustive, but do provide a starting point for understanding the effects of crowd feedback in the context of iterative design and identifying opportunities for improving this class of system.

METHOD

To answer the research questions, we deployed the crowd feedback system in an entry-level visual design course at a large private university in the United States.

Participants

Ten students volunteered to participate in the study out of the fifteen students enrolled in the course. Students came from various disciplines including engineering, computer science, and information technology and they were trying to gain experience with visual design. The third author was a co-instructor of the course and only invited participation during the study to minimize conflicts of interest.

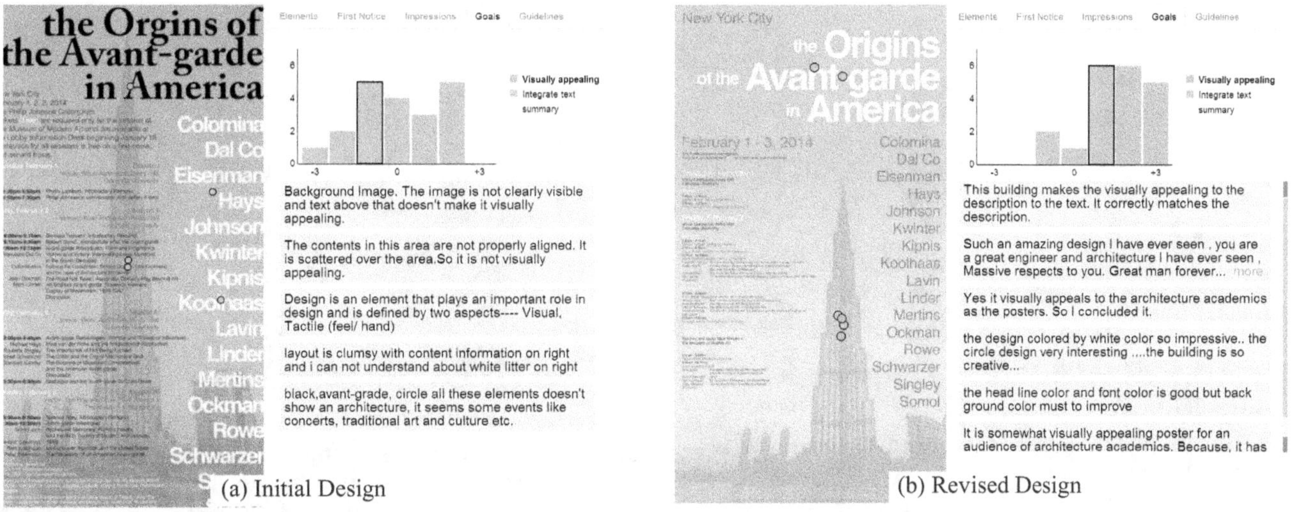

(a) Initial Design (b) Revised Design

Figure 4. In (a), the design goal "visually appealing" is not well supported. After the participant [P5] changed the layout and typeface, the average rating on the design goal in (b) was improved from 0.05 (σ = 1.5) to 1.5 (σ = 1.2). The range of the rating scale shown is -3 (low) to 3 (high).

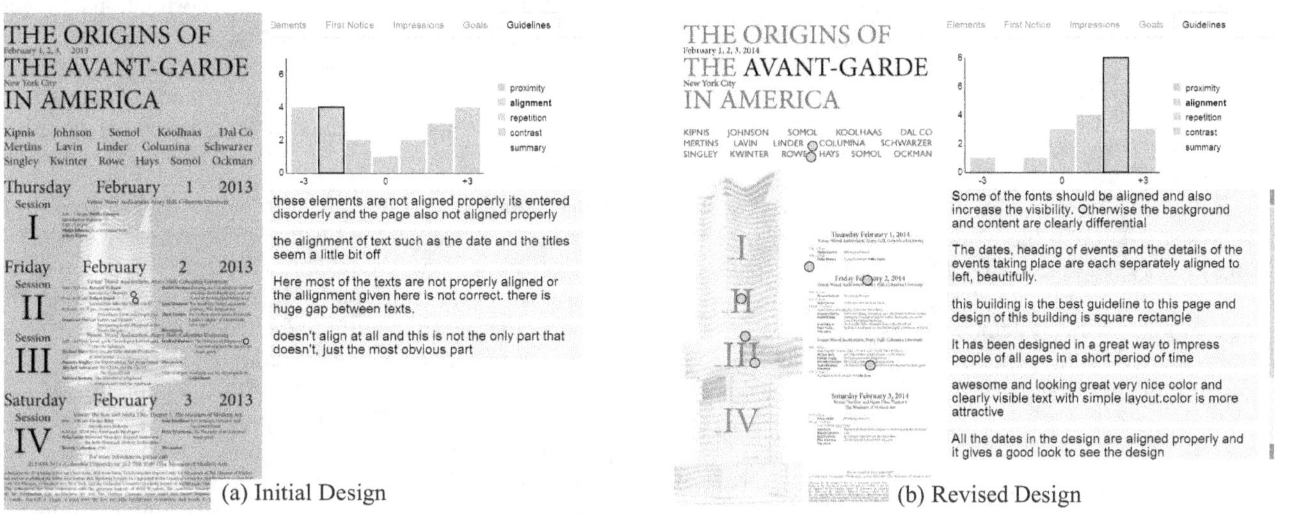

(a) Initial Design (b) Revised Design

Figure 5. The *Guidelines* feedback on the participant's designs [P7]. Based on the feedback, the participant changed the layout and color in (a). The average rating on the guideline *alignment* in (b) was improved from -1.0 (σ = 2.3) to 1.3 (σ = 1.4).

Design Project

The course contained a two-week project where the students needed to design an event poster for an architecture conference named "Origins of the Avant-garde in America." All students enrolled in the course were assigned the project and produced an initial and revised design. However, only those students who participated in the study received crowd feedback from our system and only their designs were included in any of the analyses.

Procedure

Our study was conducted in context of the two-week project. In the first week, each participant created an initial design of a poster for the event (*Initial Design*, see Figure 1a). Participants electronically sent their designs to the research team along with a description of their communicative goals for the poster. Since participants were assigned the same project, most of the stated goals were the same – to attract the audience's attention and provide details of the event. Other goals were more specific (e.g. "*Lay out the Thursday-Saturday events in a pleasant way*", "*Integrate text and image smoothly…*"). The research team generated the complete set of crowd feedback on the designs and notified the participants that the feedback was available. Participants then had one more week to revise their designs (*Revised Design*, see Figure 1b) and submit it. Feedback was generated on the revised designs in order to compare it to the feedback on the initial designs. After submitting the Revised Designs, participants completed a survey (see Measures) for which they received a $3 gift card.

The system recruited workers from Mechanical Turk. Workers were paid five cents (US) per task. The costs were

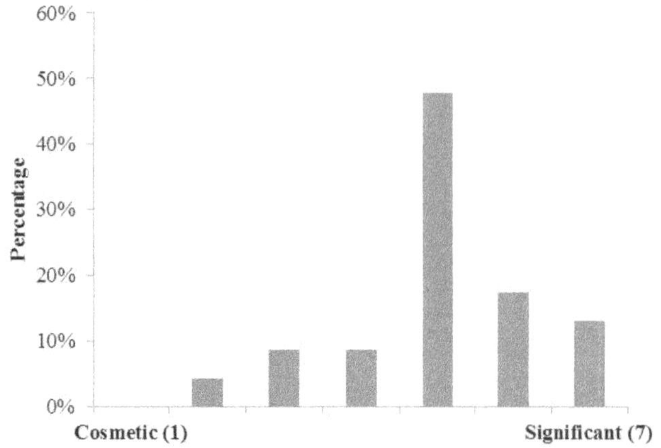

Figure 6. Distribution of ratings of the depth of changes made on the Initial Designs (n = 22).

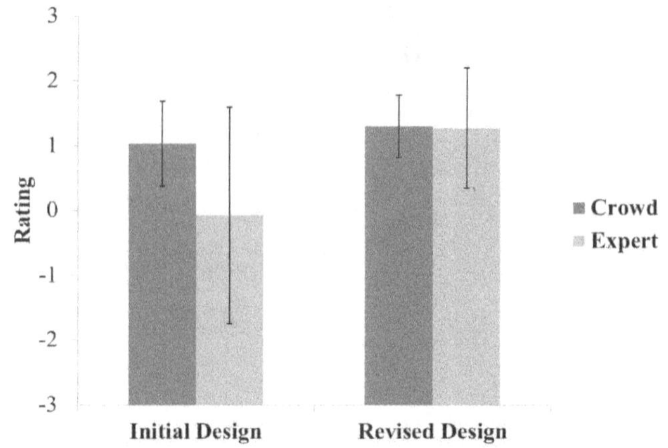

Figure 7. Overall ratings of the designs from the non-expert crowd and experts on the Initial and Revised designs.

paid by the research team. The feedback was generated by about 500 workers within 24 hours. We note that about 67% of workers performed two or more micro-tasks for feedback generation while about 14% of the workers provided feedback on both the Initial and Revised Designs.

After the two-week project ended, we collected free-form feedback from crowd workers on the same designs in order to compare it against the structured feedback. The free-form feedback was not shared with the participants. The payment for a task in the free-form condition was the same as for a task in the system. Though the workloads may differ, prior work shows the payment affects wait time, not the response quality [17, 24]. In contrast to the structured (prompted) feedback generated by the system, workers in the free-form condition responded to a general, open-ended question: "What do you think about the design and why do you think that is?"

Measures

In addition to the designs and the crowd feedback collected on those designs, the study collected four sets of measures:

Survey responses. On the survey, a participant described each notable change made to her design based on the crowd feedback and estimated the depth of the change on a seven-point scale ranging from "Cosmetic"(1) to "Significant" (7). Each participant also rated to what degree the feedback impacted their revision overall and how helpful each feedback type was on a seven-point scale. The survey responses were used to answer our first research question.

Expert evaluations. Three experts in visual design were recruited to evaluate the collected designs based on the same criterion used by crowd workers. In the crowd feedback system used, twenty crowd workers rated how well a design adheres to each of the four guidelines (proximity, alignment, repetition, and contrast) and each of the goals described by participants on a seven-point scale. Similarly, the experts rated how well the designs met each of the guidelines and goals on the same scale. The designs were presented in a random order. The *overall rating* of a design was calculated as the mean of the ratings on the guidelines and goals from the experts. Inter-rater reliability was measured by the correlation coefficients between the ratings provided by the experts. The correlations ranged from 0.61 to 0.72, with an average correlation of 0.67. Comparing the ratings between experts and non-experts would allow us to assess the validity of feedback generated by a non-expert crowd, which was our second research question.

Content analysis. For the structured and free-form feedback, we measured the feedback genres, topic diversity, and linguistic styles. For feedback genres, we adopted the categories of critique discourse developed in prior work [8] and coded a large sample of the feedback to identify what is discussed. For topic diversity, we applied a standard topic modeling method – the latent Dirichlet allocation (LDA) to extract the topics [4]. For linguistic styles, the Linguistic Inquiry Word Count (LIWC) program was used to extract psycholinguistic features from the content. Results of the analysis were used to answer our third research question.

TYPES OF CHANGES (RQ1)

Following qualitative analysis methods [29], the changes on the Initial Designs described in the survey were coded using a bottom-up approach. The descriptions of the changes were first segmented into the smallest logical units. A first pass was then performed to assign categories to the units and subsequent passes were made to revise and aggregate the categories. We found that there were four types of design changes (see Table 1):

- **Theme**. Change the visual theme or main image in a design.
- **Layout**. Reorganize visual elements in a design.
- **Typeface**. Change font style and size in a design.
- **Color**. Change the color scheme in a design.

We found that significant changes were often related to the theme and layout of a design, while cosmetic changes were often related to the color and font in a design. Note that the

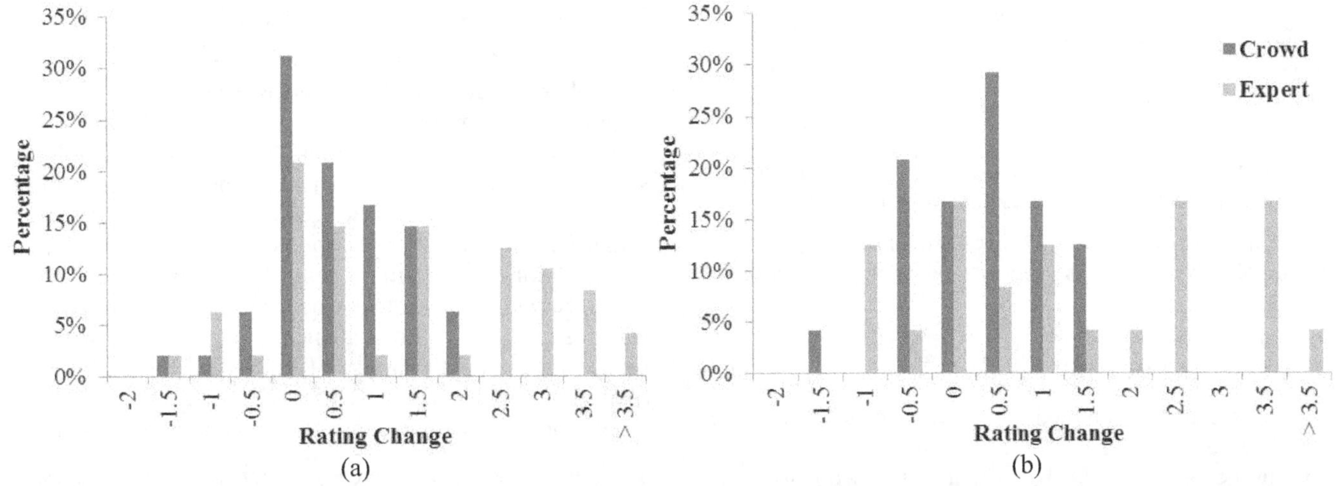

Figure 8. (a) Distribution of the changes in crowd and expert ratings on *Guidelines* across all designs; (b) Distribution of the changes in crowd and expert ratings on *Goals* across all designs.

changes listed in Table 1 only include the changes made based on crowd feedback. Participants may have made additional changes which were driven by their own reflections or the feedback from their peers and instructors. For example, the participant [P9] reported that he did not change the design according to the feedback. However, the color scheme was changed in the revision (see Figure 1).

Theme

Three participants reported creating new visual themes to accommodate crowd responses by adopting different manipulations or choices of an image for the revisions. This type of change often led to other consequential changes. As a result, these participants "*pretty much redid the entire poster*". For example, as shown in Figure 2a, one participant [P3] brightened the main image of the design because her initial design yielded unintended impressions such as "*hard to read*" and "*dark*". After revising, these impressions were no longer present in the feedback (see Figure 2b).

Similarly, the crowd feedback caused another participant [P8] to reconsider the choice and treatment of the images:

> *"The two pictures make the article not too attractive, should put them on another spot or [use] other pictures ..."*

> *"The pictures that grab the eye the most are just plastered on like you found them on the internet and pasted them onto a white board with glue, they aren't integrated into the design."*

To address these problems identified from the feedback, the participant decided to replace the images in the poster and reported that the feedback helped him understand how to utilize an image to attract people's attention appropriately:

> *"The emphasis section [First Notice Feedback] helped get a sense of what was attracting the viewers' attention, and some comments helped in getting a better sense of the overall visibility of the information or lack there of."* [P8].

The feedback also helped the participant reconsider the treatment of the images and reorganize visual elements. The feedback on the revision indicates that the first noticed element in the design was successfully changed from the building images to the event (see Figure 3).

Layout

A majority of participants (n = 7) revised the layout of their designs based on crowd feedback, such as "*used different grid layout for displaying the text blocks/Sections*" [P8] and "*reorganized the bottom half and simplified the design*" [P2].

One participant [P5] learned that visual elements in the design were overwhelming and caused visual clutter (see Figure 4a). In the revision, the participant repositioned the design content to reduce the visual clutter (see Figure 4b):

> *"Making the poster much less cluttered because, again, a lot of people mentioned that... The goals section [Goals Feedback] is really helpful because it lets me know if I'm doing a good job getting my point across."* [P5]

Another participant [P10] reported that the feedback helped him understand the effects of visual elements and the relationships among them in the design:

> *"I knew which elements worked well with a majority of reviewers, and what elements to specifically keep"*. [P10]

As a result, the feedback helped the participant reorganize elements. For instance, she decided to *"change the organization of my speakers and their [information]"*.

Typeface

Many participants (n = 6) customized the typeface styles and sizes guided by crowd feedback such as *"the font was too slanted"* [P8] and *"people didn't like the color change of my fonts."* [P6]. As a consequence, participants manipulated their typefaces to address these types of problems:

> *"Changed the type of the texts to make the title standing-out and obvious... It [feedback] helps me to understand which part of my poster stands out the most, and how should I keep making such eye-capturing features in my future works."* [P2]

"I changed the spacing of a lot of my text. There were many comments in the impressions section about how cluttered and messy it was, so I took those into consideration when updating my design." [P10]

Color

According to the survey, participants (n = 6) attempted to better match colors to the impressions they intended:

"I changed the background color, removing the gray (see Figure 5). People said it was overpowering and looked dreary."[P7]

"I changed the color and gradient effect to make it more natural and realistic." [P4]

Also, the feedback prompted one participant to change the color scheme of the design in order to increase the contrast between the text and the background. Consequently, the readability of the content was improved:

"They find some sections hard to read against a gradient background. So I kept it consistent to one color."[P6]

DEPTH OF CHANGES (RQ1)

In total, twenty-two changes were described in the surveys and a majority of the changes were on the "significant" side (see Figure 6). The average rating of change depth is 5.2 (σ = 1.1). Most participants (n = 9) reported that they changed their designs based on the feedback, and a majority (n = 6) agreed the feedback helped them make substantive changes. Participant [P8] anticipated that the first noticed element in the design is the "Avant Garde" event; however, the participant found that the element first noticed by the crowd was the building instead of the event (see Figure 3a). To address this problem, the participant substantively revised the design using different thematic images and reorganized the visual elements. After the changes, the event Avant Garde became the first noticed element in the design (see Figure 3b).

The participants' ratings of their overall depth of changes to a design prompted by crowd feedback positively correlated with the changes in overall rating from the initial to revised designs ($r = 0.56, p < 0.05$). Recall that the overall rating of a design was the mean of the ratings on the guidelines and goals given by the experts for that design (see "Measures"). The overall ratings decreased from the initial to the revised designs for only two participants (P1 and P9), and they made few or no changes based on the crowd feedback. This result indicates that leveraging crowd feedback to iterate on a visual design can lead to improved design outcomes, as measured by the overall rating in our study.

Additionally, all of the feedback types were perceived as helpful to improve designs ($\mu > 4$). For instance, consistent with prior work [36], the *Impressions* feedback was perceived as the most helpful feedback type for participants to improve their designs (μ = 5.5, σ = 1.0). The *Guidelines* feedback was the second most helpful type (μ = 5.4, σ = 1.2), which was more favorable than in a prior study [36]. This difference is likely due to the emphasis on the teaching and practice of design principles in this particular course.

VALIDITY OF CROWD FEEDBACK (RQ2)

Figure 7 summarizes the non-expert (crowd) and expert overall ratings on the Initial and Revised designs. Table 2 shows the same data, but grouped by the guidelines and the two most commonly stated goals. Non-experts rated the Initial Designs higher than experts (F (1, 244) = 22.04, $p <$ 0.001). Non-experts may have lower expectations and therefore were less critical when rating the designs. There was also a small, but statistically significant difference between the crowd's ratings of Initial and Revised designs (paired t-test, $p < 0.01$). This indicates that a non-expert crowd can effectively react to changes made to a design.

To examine how the crowd's reactions compare to experts, we tested the correlation between the rating changes by the crowd and the experts. Several steps were taken to compute the correlation. First, for each design guideline and goal, we computed the average of the ratings for that guideline or goal. For instance, if twenty crowd workers rate how well a design adheres to the *contrast* guideline, then the crowd's *average rating* for this guideline is the average of these twenty ratings. The experts' *average rating* for a guideline is the average of the ratings from the three experts. Second, a *rating change* on a guideline or goal was calculated by subtracting the *average rating* on an initial design from the *average rating* on the revised design for that guideline or goal. The distribution of the rating changes for *Guidelines* and *Goals* are shown in Figures 8a and 8b respectively.

There was a moderate positive correlation between changes in *Guidelines* ratings from the crowd and experts (r = 0.45, $p < 0.01$). This indicates that the aggregation of the ratings from non-experts offer a reasonably valid assessment of

	Initial Designs		Revised Designs	
	Crowd	Experts	Crowd	Experts
Guidelines (all)	0.88 (0.63)	0.07 (1.68)	1.18 (0.48)	1.41 (0.75)
Proximity	1.07 (0.86)	0.50 (1.88)	1.2 (0.48)	1.75 (0.62)
Alignment	0.81 (0.57)	0.33 (1.66)	1.37 (0.44)	1.58 (0.67)
Repetition	1.03 (0.40)	-0.25 (1.56)	1.19 (0.50)	1.25 (0.81)
Contrast	0.60 (0.57)	-0.29 (1.68)	0.98 (0.46)	1.04 (0.75)
Common goals (all)	1.36 (0.60)	-0.38 (1.67)	1.46 (0.45)	1.00 (1.12)
Grab Attention	1.24 (0.74)	-0.17 (1.81)	1.35 (0.59)	0.88 (1.15)
Provide Details	1.48 (0.40)	-0.58 (1.56)	1.58 (0.23)	1.13 (1.13)

Table 2. The means and (standard deviations) of the crowd and expert ratings of the guidelines and the two most commonly stated goals for the initial and revised designs. The scale of the ratings was from -3 (Worst) to +3 (Best).

Free-from Feedback	Structured Feedback
"Design is excellent looking grand. The font is very nice. I feel pleasant. Very nice"	*"The darker green text on the green. This green instantly made me think of the Statue of Liberty."*
"It is pretty one. The design is marvelous one. The shape of the building is very nice."	*"The words are not aligned properly and also the fonts are very small. The content is not clearly seen"*
"This looks really nice ...and also color combination of black and white color so nice ... and it contains total sessions and date details."	*"Details for each date are clearly below the date and session number, all names/details are grouped together well."*
"This design looks good.it highlights the name of the event, place where it is held, and the dates of the event."	*"It's very colorful and cleat font style. I like this page and this advertisement design also look too good."*
"Design is ok. It should be in light orange and the text should be in navy blue color, small text should be made readable."	*"Light beam is in the background. America is the world in the bounded box... All these elements are perfectly aligned."*

Table 3. A sample of responses from the free-form and structured feedback conditions (n = 1000 in each condition).

improvement in a design based on standard guidelines. We also computed the correlation for each individual guideline. The *contrast* guideline had the highest correlation value ($r = 0.59$, $p < 0.05$), while the *alignment* guideline had the lowest ($r = 0.28$, $p = 0.4$). Consistent with a prior study of crowd feedback [34], non-experts may have experienced different levels of difficulty when applying the different guidelines. A potential solution is to explore scaffolding techniques such as task instructions or examples that can help workers apply the guidelines more effectively [33, 35].

However, there was no statistically significant correlation ($r = 0.37$, $p = 0.07$) between changes in the ratings for *Goals* given by the crowd and experts. The experts thought a revised design better satisfied its goal while the crowd did not agree. The disagreement may be due to different perceptions of how well a goal is satisfied due to different interpretations of the goal or understanding of the context.

The rating changes from the experts were more pronounced than those from the crowd. Figure 8 shows that a large proportion of experts' rating changes was more than 2 units; while most of crowd' rating changes were less than 1. This reflects the fact that experts have higher discriminating ability [14] and thus are more likely to react to changes in a design. Also, a majority of experts' ratings were increased. This result confirms that designers were able to improve their designs in a design iteration based on feedback [12].

CONTENT ANALYSIS (RQ3)

Our final research question was to compare how generating structured feedback compares to generating free-form

	Free-form Feedback			Structured Feedback		
Judgment	Positive	86%	**46%**	Positive	78%	**32%**
	Negative	14%		Negative	22%	
Interpretation	Individual	69%	**42%**	Individual	40%	**64%**
	Relation	31%		Relation	60%	
Suggestion	**12%**			**4%**		

Table 4. Frequencies of the categories of critique discourse found in each form of feedback (n = 100 in each condition).

feedback on the same twenty designs shown in Figure 1. For each design, we randomly sampled 50 responses generated by the crowd in the free-form and structured feedback conditions (see Table 3). The data set therefore includes 1,000 worker responses in each condition. Each response had on average 22 words ($\sigma = 7.8$). There are no significant differences between free-form and structured conditions with regard to the length of the feedback.

Feedback Genres

Because five types of feedback were specifically generated in the structured condition, we first examined whether free-form feedback spontaneously produces these same types. A random sample of 100 responses from the free-form feedback was coded based on the definition of the feedback types described in [36]. We found only 4 responses that described elements first noticed in a design; 6 responses that commented on design guidelines; and only 8 responses that discussed the intention of a design. Though these types of feedback are known to be desired from non-experts, the free-form condition yielded little content in these areas. Having specific prompts in feedback generation is therefore important for generating the feedback desired by designers.

In order to assess the category differences in free-form and structured feedback, the collected feedback was coded using the nine categories of critique discourse derived in prior work [8]. 100 responses were randomly sampled from both the free-form and structured conditions. The responses were independently coded by two coders (kappa = 0.80) and disagreements were resolved through discussion. Table 4 shows the frequency of occurrence of each category. Several categories of discourse such as *comparison*, *identity invoking*, and *process oriented* did not occur in the collected feedback. One explanation is that these categories were derived from expert feedback [8] and therefore non-experts may not be able to provide this type of insight into users' design approaches and contemporary trends.

Judgment was the most commonly applied feedback category ($\chi^2 = 15.7$, $p < 0.001$; see Table 4). Judgments occurred more often in the free-form feedback (46%) than in the structured feedback (32%). Workers in the free-form condition offered many simplistic judgments, especially related to positive reactions such as "I like it". This result corroborates previous findings that a majority of online feedback does not go beyond simplistic judgments [33, 35].

Feedback coded as *interpretation* occurred when crowd workers tried to make sense of a design and explain their perceptions of it. Interpretation was the most common category in the structured feedback (64%). The structured feedback had higher frequency of interpretation than free-form feedback (χ^2 = 5.8, $p < 0.05$). In the structured feedback condition, workers first provide their overall reaction to a design (e.g. a rating or impression) and *then* explain this reaction. This task separation could help workers pay more attention to the interpretation process.

During the interpretation process, crowd workers in the structured condition more often associated their reactions with elements in a design than workers did in the free-form condition (see Table 4). A worker in the free-form condition attempted to associate his perception with an individual element: *"The tall building gives you the idea of a skyscraper"*. In contrast, a worker in the structured condition was more likely to relate several elements in a design: *"Having the text on the building helps establish a spatial relationship in an attractive manner."* One explanation is that workers in the structured condition are exposed to multiple design elements (e.g. design elements offered by the system to help a worker explain the rationale). These specific examples may facilitate the interpretation process and help workers consider the relation among elements in a design.

The *suggestion* category was also significant (χ^2 = 7.4, $p <$ 0.01). Free-form feedback offered more suggestions for improvement than the structured feedback (see Table 4). Although crowd workers were not rewarded for offering suggestions in either condition, workers in the free-form condition provided more suggestions. The suggestions were apparently given because there was no constraint imposed by providing a specific prompt. However, the quality of these suggestions needs further investigation.

Topic Diversity

We used LDA to extract the topics from the free-form and structured feedback [4]. LDA is a standard topic modeling method that is often used to discover topics in documents and the words associated with each topic. The method excels at analyzing large amounts of unlabeled documents by clustering words that frequently co-occur. We built LDA topic models from the free-from and structured feedback respectively, treating each response as a document. Since the number of topics affects the interpretability of the extracted topics, we set the number of topics the same in the free-form and structured feedback in order to make a fair comparison. The number of topics was varied between five and twenty, and the differences between the free-form and structured feedback were observed consistently.

Cosine similarity between topic words derived from LDA is used to measure the similarity between topics [1]. We computed the cosine similarity between each pair of topics in the free-form and structured conditions respectively. The similarity values were higher in the free-form condition than in the structured condition (Student's t-test, $p < 0.01$). We observed that many topics in the free-form feedback shared the words such as "design" and "like". It appears that the structured feedback offered a wider range of topics. This indicates that the topics represented in the structured feedback were more diverse than in the free-form feedback. This observation may be best explained by the use of various prompts when generating the structured feedback.

Linguistic Styles

LIWC was adopted to measure linguistic styles for each response received in the free-form and structured feedback conditions. Specifically, each response in the feedback data is measured by percentages of the total words belonging to specific categories. A series of t-test comparisons were carried out between the free-form and structured feedback in terms of the LIWC generated language-use categories. Our null hypothesis is that the free-form and structured feedback are equal in the LIWC features. All 70 categories in LIWC were considered. Due to these 70 simultaneous tests, we allow for a *Bonferroni* correction which adjusts the significance threshold by the total number of statistical tests performed (e.g. $\alpha = 0.05/70 = 0.00014$) [3].

Significant differences were found for affective processes ($p < 0.01$). Crowd workers in the free-form condition used more emotional words than did workers in the structured condition. In many domains, better emotion regulation is a trait of expertise [7, 10]. As described previously, workers in the free-form and structured conditions were unlikely to have design knowledge. Therefore, when non-experts are asked to provide spontaneous judgments of a design, they may rely on affective processes and analyze a design more from an emotional perspective. However, the use of specific prompts and examples in the structured feedback condition may have enabled workers to analyze the design rationally rather than relying solely on affective processes.

The structured feedback had more words per sentence, and long words consisting of six or more letters ($p < 0.01$). A higher ratio of words per sentence and long words is often used as an indicator for better domain-specific working knowledge [18, 19]. One interpretation is that structured workflows facilitate non-experts' ability to interpret a design and communicate their perceptions of it, whereas open-ended prompts do not facilitate non-experts' potential to develop thoughtful responses for creative work.

We found that words related to certainty (e.g. 'always' and 'never') were more common in the structured feedback ($p <$ 0.01). Increasing the use of certainty words is an indicator of improved critical thinking [6]. The structured feedback also had a higher rate of articles ($p < 0.01$). Prior work shows that people using articles at a higher rate tend to be more concrete in their thinking [18]. In contrast, free-form feedback was characterized by more spoken categories including more filter and assent words. This result indicates that the free-form feedback was less formal and deliberate.

DISCUSSION AND FUTURE WORK

Our study found that crowd feedback prompted deep changes to the theme and layout of visual designs, and that these and other cosmetic changes led to improved designs as rated by domain experts. The changes were prompted by synthesizing the feedback on *impressions*, *first notice*, *guidelines*, and *goals* generated by the system used in the study. It is hard to tease apart precisely which feedback type or comment prompted each change since design is a reflective and emergent process [28], but each type of feedback was perceived as helpful by the participants.

Though crowd feedback prompted changes that led to improved designs, generating crowd feedback should be considered as a supplement to expert evaluation rather than a replacement. Expert evaluation yields a range and depth of feedback that cannot yet be matched by crowd systems, e.g., analysis of trends, precedents, and design strategies. Our experience to date indicates that crowd feedback is most appropriate when designers need to deliver a clear message to a target audience or need feedback quickly. Future work is needed to explore how to broaden the feedback that can be generated by non-expert crowds.

By comparing non-experts (crowd)' ratings with experts' ratings, we found that non-experts and experts reached better consensus on design guidelines than communicative goals. The result reflects the nature of design feedback, which can be conceived either as a measured judgment governed by universal principles or personal tastes and perceptions [31]. The use of design principles offer a firmer basis for evaluating designs and it is therefore easier to reach agreement. How well a design meets its intended goals is more subjective and varied and therefore more difficult for external evaluators to agree.

The analysis of feedback content in the structured and free-form conditions showed that crowd workers suggest more solutions when prompted to enter free-form feedback. Note that workers were not asked to propose solutions in either condition. Using structured workflows appears to cause workers to respond only as instructed in the task and thus did not propose solutions. We also found many content and stylistic differences between the structured and free-form feedback from the non-expert crowd. In addition to non-experts, it would be interesting to compare how experts perform in both the free-from and structured feedback conditions. Moreover, future work needs to examine how design outcomes are affected by the feedback generated using different formats or crowds with different expertise.

Our study was conducted in context of an entry-level course on visual design. Results from the study point to a benefit of integrating the use of crowd feedback systems into design education. For example, this class of system could be useful in large online courses where students may be unable to obtain sufficient or timely feedback from peers or instructors. In other design courses, crowd feedback may provide a useful supplement to in-class critiques. However, the results of our study may not apply to expert designers since they may have different considerations in their work. For example, experts spend more time evaluating their goals and strategies while novices spend more time being aware of and monitoring design guidelines [26]. Future work is needed to examine how design expertise mediates the use and perception of different types of crowd feedback.

Our study examined how crowd feedback affected a single iteration on a design, but reaching an effective solution often requires multiple iterations. Future work is needed to observe how crowd feedback is utilized throughout an entire design project. Such a study could reveal how crowd feedback benefits different phases of the process. Also, our study focused on one form of visual design, a poster, which is a popular form of visual communication. Our findings should generalize to other forms of visual design such as Web pages, logos, and illustrations. However, an interesting avenue for future work is to determine the types of visual designs for which crowd feedback is most desirable and how often the feedback is requested for these types of designs during the process. It would also be interesting to examine and compare how crowd feedback affects design outcomes in other domains such as architecture.

An assumption of our work is that designers want to utilize crowd feedback to improve their designs. However, there could be unintended uses of crowd feedback. For example, in design education, students may attempt to use favorable crowd feedback to argue for higher scores or to counter the recommendations provided by the instructor or peers. Another consequence is that crowd feedback systems could unintentionally limit creativity in design by shifting too much attention to audience interpretations and suggestions rather than pursuing new and creative directions.

CONCLUSION

Crowd feedback systems offer a new approach for helping designers iterate on their designs, but there has been little research on the effects of these systems. From an empirical study of crowd feedback for visual design, our work has contributed several findings addressing this gap. First, we found that crowd feedback prompted users to make both deep and cosmetic changes to their designs, which led to improved designs. Deep changes related to the theme and layout of a design, while cosmetic changes related to the colors and fonts in a design. Second, we found that a non-expert crowd was able to recognize design improvements based on the use of design guidelines. However, the crowd had lower agreement with experts on the improvements related to communicative goals. Finally, as compared with free-form feedback, the structured feedback produced more interpretative, diverse and critical discourse. Our work shows that crowd feedback systems can be leveraged to help users iterate toward more effective solutions.

REFERENCES

1. Baeza-Yates, R. and Ribeiro-Neto, B. *Modern Information Retrieval*. ACM press, 1999.
2. Bernstein, M.S., Brandt, J., Miller, R.C., & Karger, D.R., Crowds in Two Seconds: Enabling Realtime Crowd-Powered Interfaces. In *UIST*, (2011), 33-42.
3. Bland, J.M., and Douglas G. Altman Multiple Significance Tests: The Bonferroni Method. *British Medical Journal*, *310*, 6973, (1995).
4. Blei, D.M., Ng, A.Y., & Jordan, M.I. Latent Dirichlet Allocation. *Journal of machine Learning research*, *3*, (2003), 993-1022.
5. Blomberg, J.L. and Henderson, A., Reflections on Participatory Design: Lessons from the Trillium Experience. In *CHI*, (1990), 353-360.
6. Carroll, D.W. Patterns of Student Writing in a Critical Thinking Course: A Quantitative Analysis. *Assessing Writing*, *12*, 3, (2007), 213-227.
7. Chaffin, R. and Imreh, G. Practicing Perfection: Piano Performance as Expert Memory. *Psychological Science*, *13*, 4, (2002), 342-349.
8. Dannels, D.P. and Martin, K.N. Critiquing Critiques: A Genre Analysis of Feedback across Novice to Expert Design Studios. *Journal of Business and Technical Communication*, *22*, 2, (2008), 135-159.
9. Dave, B. and Danahy, J. Virtual Study Abroad and Exchange Studio. *Automation in Construction*, *9*, 1, (2000), 57-71.
10. De Groot, A.D. and Groot, A.D.d. *Thought and Choice in Chess*. Walter de Gruyter, 1978.
11. Dow, S.P., Gerber, E., & Wong, A., A Preliminary Study of Using Crowds in the Classroom. In *CHI*, (2013), 227-236.
12. Dow, S.P., Glassco, A., Kass, J., Schwarz, M., Schwartz, D.L., & Klemmer, S.R. Parallel Prototyping Leads to Better Design Results, More Divergence, and Increased Self-Efficacy. *ACM Transactions on Computer-Human Interaction (TOCHI)*, *17*, 4, (2010).
13. Dutton, T.A. Design and Studio Pedagogy. *Journal of Architectural Education*, *41*, 1, (1987), 16-25.
14. Einhorn, H.J. Expert Judgment: Some Necessary Conditions and an Example. *Journal of Applied Psychology*, *59*, 6, (1974), 562–571.
15. Elkins, J. *Art Critiques: A Guide*. New Academia Publishing, Washington DC, 2012.
16. Feldman, E.B. *Varieties of Visual Experience; Art as Image and Idea*. H.N. Abrams, New York, 1971.
17. Heer, J. and Bostock, M., Crowdsourcing Graphical Perception: Using Mechanical. Turk to Assess Visualization Design. In *CHI*, (2010), 203-212.
18. Kamhi, A.G. and Catts, H.W. *Language and Reading Disabilities*, 2012.
19. Kim, K., Bae, J., Nho, M.-W., & Lee, C.H. How Do Experts and Novices Differ? Relation Versus Attribute and Thinking Versus Feeling in Language Use. *Psychology of Aesthetics, Creativity, and the Arts*, *5*, 4, (2011).
20. Kittur, A., Nickerson, J.V., Bernstein, M.S., Gerber, E.M., Shaw, A., Zimmerman, J., Lease, M., & Horton, J.J., The Future of Crowd Work. In *CSCW*, (2013), 1301-1318.
21. Komarov, S., Reinecke, K., & Gajos, K.Z., Crowdsourcing Performance Evaluations of User Interfaces. In *CHI*, (2013), 207-216.
22. Kulkarni, C. and Klemmer, S. Learning Design Wisdom by Augmenting Physical Studio Critique with Online Self-Assessment. *Stanford University technical report*, (2012).
23. Luther, K., Pavel, A., Wu, W., Tolentino, J.-l., Agrawala, M., Hartmann, B., & Dow., S.P., Crowdcrit: Crowdsourcing and Aggregating Visual Design Critique. In *CSCW*, (2014), 21-24.
24. Mason, W. and Watts, D.J. Financial Incentives and the Performance of Crowds. *SigKDD Explorations Newsletter*, *11*, 2, (2010), 100-108.
25. Park, C.H., Son, K., Lee, J.H., & Bae, S.-H., Crowd Vs. Crowd: Large-Scale Cooperative Design through Open Team Competition. In *CSCW*, (2013), 1275-1284.
26. Perez, R.S. and Emery, C.D. Designer Thinking: How Novices and Experts Think About Instructional Design. *Performance Improvement Quarterly*, *8*, 3, (1995), 80-95.
27. Risatti, H. Art Criticism in Discipline-Based Art Education. *Journal of Aesthetic Education*, *21*, 2, (1987), 217-225.
28. Schön, D.A. *Educating the Reflective Practitioner*. Jossey-Bass, San Francisco, 1987.
29. Strauss, A.L. *Qualitative Analysis for Social Scientists*. Cambridge University Press, 1987.
30. Tohidi, M., Buxton, W., Baecker, R., & Sellen, A., Getting the Right Design and the Design Right. In *CHI*, (2006), 1243-1252.
31. Venturi, L. and Marriott, C. *History of Art Criticism*. Dutton, New York, 1964.
32. Vredenburg, K., Mao, J.-Y., Smith, P.W., & Carey., T., A Survey of User-Centered Design Practice. In *CHI*, (2002), 471-478.
33. Willett, W., Heer, J., & Agrawala, M., Strategies for Crowdsourcing Social Data Analysis. In *CHI*, (2012), 227-236.
34. Xu, A. Designing with Crowds. *University of Illinois at Urbana-Champaign, PhD diss.*, (2014).
35. Xu, A. and Bailey, B.P., What Do You Think? A Case Study of Benefit, Expectation, and Interaction in a Large Online Critique Community. In *CSCW*, (2012), 295-304.
36. Xu, A., Huang, S.-W., & Bailey, B.P., Voyant: Generating Structured Feedback on Visual Designs Using a Crowd of Non-Experts. In *CSCW*, (2014), 1433-1444.
37. Yu, L., Kittur, A., & Kraut, R.E., Distributed Analogical Idea Generation: Inventing with Crowds. In *CHI*, (2014), 1245-1254.
38. Yu, L. and Nickerson, J.V., Cooks or Cobblers? Crowd Creativity through Combination. In *CHI*, (2011), 1393-1402.
39. Feedbackarmy. http://www.feedbackarmy.com.
40. Fivesecondtest. http://fivesecondtest.com.
41. UITests. http://www.uitests.com.
42. Usabilla. http://www.usabilla.com.

From Awareness to Empowerment: Using Design Fiction to Explore Paths towards a Sustainable Energy Future

Sebastian Prost[1], Elke Mattheiss[1], Manfred Tscheligi[1,2]

[1]AIT Austrian Institute of Technology
Vienna, Austria
firstname.lastname@ait.ac.at

[2]ICT&S Center, University of Salzburg
Salzburg, Austria
manfred.tscheligi@sbg.ac.at

ABSTRACT

This paper presents a novel application of participatory design fiction for sustainable domestic energy consumption. In our study we examine how social practices relate to a newly developed energy management system introduced to households. We explore how design fiction can be used to identify current design limitations and to showcase future design directions to overcome these limitations. In particular, we investigated how energy consumption feedback is leaving users in a state of 'helplessness' despite raising awareness of their environmental impact. Through participatory fictional future story-writing workshops we identified five levels of empowerment that design for sustainability practitioners can engage with. Our proposal is to use those levels of empowerment to reframe sustainable design by shifting from behaviour to social practices and from awareness to empowerment.

Author Keywords

Sustainability; social practices; empowerment; activism; design fiction; energy management; grounded theory;

ACM Classification Keywords

H.5.m [Information interfaces and presentation (e.g., HCI)]: Miscellaneous;

INTRODUCTION

To limit climate change and resource exploitation is a global challenge. Sustainable HCI seeks to contribute by supporting people in reducing their environmental impact through technology. One of the major areas these efforts are focused on is domestic energy use [4,34]. Energy consumption feedback systems aim at raising awareness and persuade users to change their consumption behaviour accordingly [15]. However, as several evaluations of such systems show, behavioural change is rather limited and the overall global impact of such efforts remains questionable [4,34], if not negligible [24,28].

CSCW '15, March 14–18, 2015, Vancouver, BC, Canada.

ACM 978-1-4503-2922-4/15/03...$15.00.
http://dx.doi.org/10.1145/2675133.2675281

This paper argues that there are two interrelated issues that need to be addressed in order to overcome this limitation of current research and design approaches. As others have criticised, sustainable HCI is focusing too heavily on individual behaviour, and thus ignoring social and cultural dimensions that are beyond an individual's immediate influence [4,11,24,34]. As we will demonstrate, this issue results in a second shortcoming, a state of 'helplessness', in which users are left alone with the awareness of their unsustainable practices. Drawing on practice theory [36] and design fiction [3,18], we will argue that energy consumption behaviour is embedded in social practices and thus connected to a larger cultural system. We will outline a process of empowerment for larger cultural change to avoid people ending up in frustration or neglect [20].

We used participatory design fiction to uncover social implications that need to be addressed by a sustainable CSCW. To this end, we will first introduce related research, which we are building our work upon. Following this, we will introduce the energy feedback system and the study methodology. We will then present the findings of the study, followed by a discussion. Finally, we will draw practical implications for sustainable design and wrap up with conclusions and future work.

RELATED WORK

This work relates first to sustainable HCI and domestic energy consumption. We use the term sustainable CSCW to refer to research particularly addressing social aspects. Second, we will relate to participatory design fiction to tackle open issues of energy management systems.

Eco-Feedback and Energy Monitoring

A wealth of research in the field of sustainable HCI is related to energy consumption in private homes [4,15,25,34]. So far, energy-related HCI research strongly focused on energy conservation motivated by eco-feedback [25,34]. Feedback is commonly provided via In-Home Displays (IHDs) (e.g. [43]). The aim of such feedback is to raise awareness of one's own energy consumption and consequently trigger a change in behaviour.

Theories of Behaviour and Practice

Behaviour models are commonly used to explain pro-environmental behaviour and consequently inform and influence the design of eco-feedback systems. Most eco-feedback designs correspond to one of two different theoretical models: the economic rational choice or the sociological norm-activation model [15]. Rational-choice models assume that the behaviour is driven by self-interest, whereas norm-activation models focus on pro-social motives.

A third theory, which takes up the long tradition in CSCW to look at practices [48], is the culturalistic *practice theory*. Wakkary et al. [47] have argued with Reckwitz [36] to frame sustainability through green practices and not rational choice or social order, thus dismissing the former two models. The practice-theoretical view understands practices as the unit of analysis of social phenomena [48]. All practices are social as they are grounded in shared knowledge that defines desires and norms and reproduces social order. In our analysis we use this approach of practices as a lens to *not* look at energy consumption *behaviour*, but to look at the *practices* such behaviour is embedded in. Moving beyond analysis, practices have also been positioned as a valuable unit of design [26].

Beyond Individual Consumption Feedback

Eco-feedback applications usually not only present pure consumption data, but also include information about the environmental consequences of the consumption or social aspects. A reason for that is to increase the effectiveness, as pure consumption information is often not able to induce medium and long-term behaviour change [4,20] especially for highly habitual behaviour [6].

Sustainable CSCW has researched various forms of social engagement to encourage energy conservation, e.g. neighbourhood comparisons, competitions, or message boards [12,14,33]. However, results regarding the impact of these techniques are mixed, with various factors affecting the success of social energy applications. For example in [8] the influence of the built environment, context knowledge of community members, and accountability and adherence to social norms is discussed. Looking at the family or household context, the importance of social accessibility of a system for all members and mutual accountability [1], as well as periodic re-engagement or pseudo-ambient displays [12] have been pointed out.

A further approach beyond energy consumption feedback is to focus on using energy differently instead of just using less energy. One common strategy for this is load-shifting or demand-response, which promotes consumers to shift energy consumption from times of high demand (peak) to times of low demand (off-peak) [34]. The system evaluated in the present study included such recommendations to shift energy consumption.

Impact of Domestic Energy Reduction Measures

Reviews of studies with IHDs [7,13] revealed that those users, who actively use the displays, can reduce their consumption of electricity by about 5 to 15 percent. Despite these effects, as argued by Mankoff [28], reductions in domestic energy waste might only have a .6 % share of global energy consumption. In this light it is understandable that energy-monitoring approaches have been criticised for adopting reformist approaches with 'quick-fixes' and low impact [4, 25]. The alternative proposal for sustainable HCI is to tackle the hard problems, such as 'How can we design for the 3-tonne carbon lifestyle?' [25]. In order to achieve this, a design for empowerment and political activism has been proposed to support users (or citizens for that matter) to both understand power relations that maintain an unsustainable system and enhance social movements for political change [24, 32].

To better understand what empowerment and political activism can mean in the context of energy consumption, we turn to participatory design fiction.

Design Fiction

HCI research and science fiction have a common history and share common ground, as both are grounded in the present but envisioning desirable or undesirable futures enabled by technological developments [10,37]. Design fictions are, however, more realistic than science fictions as they are not 'too far away from our concerns' [41, 18]. More precisely, they present 'possible worlds' that have specific accessibility criteria [29]. Thus, they can be easier translated into design implications. Therefore, design fictions recently became popular in HCI [18,27,45].

Like collaboration personas and scenarios, design fictions provide social context and address ethical dimensions [30,35]. Design fictions are, however, less task-oriented and thus wider in scope [3]. They allow exploration of implications of a technology that only become apparent when the technology is put in a future or alternative world [1,23]. In sustainable CSCW, Wakkary et al. [47] illustrated how design fictions can be a valuable approach to translate analysis of sustainable practices into design for sustainability.

Given the importance of social practices for sustainability research, this paper argues that design fiction as a research method is useful on three levels: First, in its participatory form, it allows users to express concerns and aspirations related to the researched technology, but independent of a present usage context. Second, it allows channelling radical visions into design implications by extrapolating and thus accentuating current trends into the future. Third, it inherently includes social, political and cultural dimensions that are important to pay attention to by sustainable design.

STUDY CONTEXT

The study presented in this paper is part of an ongoing one-year field trial taking part in a newly built apartment building complex in Salzburg, Austria. The complex, named 'Rosa Zukunft', consists of 130 apartments and row houses and is intended as a space for communal and cross-generational living. The concept is based on bilateral support between young families and older adults.

85 of the homes agreed to participate in the study and 34 of them are equipped with technology aiming at facilitating energy conservation behaviour (the so-called 'monitoring homes'). The remaining homes form the control group. The workshops described in this paper were conducted after one month of a trial investigating long-term energy conservation behaviour.

The energy management technology installed in the 34 monitoring homes consists of three components: Main element is the so-called FORE-Watch [38], an application installed on an Android tablet. It provides the users with a forecast about energy demand in the power grid of the next 12 hours. Using a colour-coded ring (red, yellow and green) it suggests the most grid-friendly phases to use energy (Figure 1 left). Each colour is also associated with a different electricity tariff. Furthermore, users can access statistics of how much energy they have consumed in each phase (Figure 1 right). The second component is the commercially available ambient feedback device 'Wattson' (Figure 2). It shows the current energy usage numerically in kilowatt-hours and changes its colour according to the comparison of current with average past consumption. The third element of the system is a so-called 'eco button'. It allows the users to deactivate several specially marked power outlets and lower the room temperature by 1° Celsius with a simple button press. The button is placed next to the main door and looks similar to a standard light switch.

Research Questions

The main research question guiding the present study was: *How do social practices within and between households relate to the energy management technologies put in their homes?* Placing these technologies in people's homes created a unique social space of energy consumption. We wanted to investigate this space on three levels:

1. While we did not prescribe users where to put the devices, we encouraged them to place them in locations where they are visible. Thus, the first level is: *How does the presence of the technology at a communal location and its (proposed) joint use spark reflection and discussion about energy consumption and its relation to their daily practices among household members?*
2. The second level is formulated in respect to the communal and generational setting of the housing complex: *What forms of interactions between neighbours related to the use of the technology and energy consumption in general emerges?*
3. Finally, on the third level the FORE-Watch is inherently a social application, as it represents energy demand by other participants in the grid: *In which way do users relate their own energy consumption practices with those of others via a demand-response system? How do participants reflect on their environmental impact through engaging with the FORE-Watch?*

The following section will outline the methodology we deployed to answer those questions.

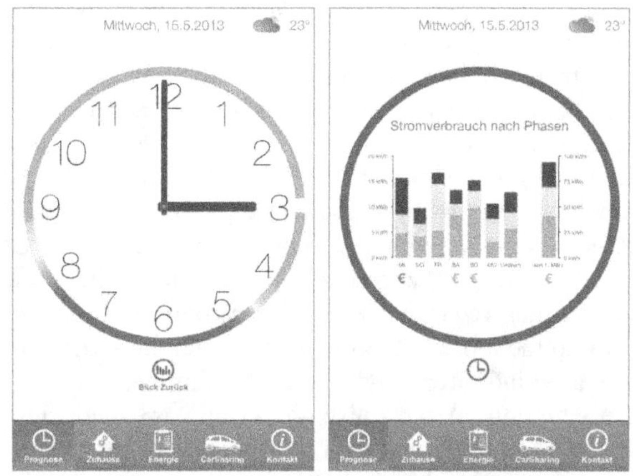

Figure 1: The FORE-Watch showing a forecast of energy demand (left) and past energy consumption (right); image courtesy of Salzburg AG.

Figure 2: Ambient feedback device Wattson in a user's home; own photograph.

STUDY METHOD

We invited all residents of the group of 34 apartments with eco-feedback technology installed to take part in the workshops, of which 18 were able to come. We conducted two workshops, with 9 participants each.

Participants

The 18 participants (nine male, nine female) were aged between 25 and 81 years (mean age = 55.00, standard deviation = 15.77). Educational levels ranged from compulsory school to university education. Eight of the participants were retired, six worked full-time, three part-time and one was currently on parental leave. Seven participants lived alone, seven with their partner, three were single mothers, and one lived with a partner and children. Participants got a tablet as compensation for their participation in the one-year field trial.

Procedure

The first part of the workshop consisted of a focus group-style discussion of the participants' experiences with the eco-feedback technologies, the role it has in their daily routines, interactions with others, and situations where behaviour was changed and not changed. Attention was paid to allow the discussion to be based on the topics brought up by the participants during an initial individual brainstorming phase.

In the second part we used the participatory design fiction format to collaboratively create future domestic energy visions. First, participants brainstormed to identify topics of domestic energy consumption, which will, according to their personal believe, be relevant in the year 2039, i.e. in 25 years. Subsequently, participants formed subgroups of three and chose one topic of interest that would be central to the fiction they were about to write together. A few story parameters were given to the participants: They should all imagine a family named 'Gruber' living in 2039. Using fictional stories, they should illustrate how the family's daily routines regarding energy consumption look like in relation to the topic of their choice. Participants were free to invent all kind of details about the family structure and living situation. After finishing writing up their fictions, each subgroup presented their story to the whole group. The workshop concluded with discussions regarding plausibility of each vision and, depending how 'positive' or 'negative' the story was, how to enable or prevent such a future.

Data Analysis

Both workshops were video recorded. Afterwards, the recordings were transcribed and analysed using a grounded theory approach based on Strauss & Corbin [42]. In a first step of open coding, codes were assigned to units of meaning (ranging from fragments of sentences to short paragraphs). Following this, codes were clustered and put into relationships using axial coding. Based on the coding scheme proposed by Strauss & Corbin we aligned categories of codes based on how they link or crosscut. Five categories were used: *phenomenon*, *causes*, *context*, *strategies*, and *consequences*. For illustrative purposes, a graphical representation of this scheme is given in Figure 3.

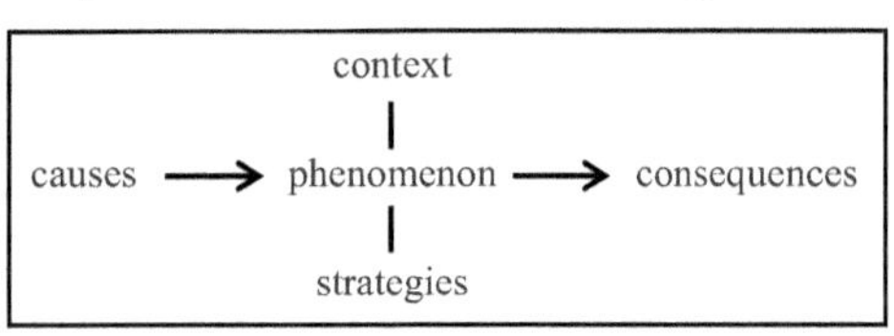

Figure 3: Axial coding scheme based on [42]

In a final step, a core concept was derived from the coding scheme. Since discussions during the first and second half of the workshops concerned different topics, the coding scheme was applied independently to both parts.

The following section presents the emerged codes, their relationships and the core concept they correspond to. The subsequent discussion section then explores how the two core concepts interrelate and intersect.

FINDINGS

Using Strauss and Corbin's coding scheme outlined above we will now discuss the two core concepts developed through analysis of the two workshop parts. The first concept is called the participants' *perceived inability to act* and the second their *lack of empowerment*. Workshop participants are numbered, with a leading 'M' or 'F' to indicate their gender. The workshop the respective participant has attended is indicated as W1 or W2.

Concept 1: Perceived Inability to Act

The Phenomenon: Awareness

Central theme regarding the intervention in the participating households was raised awareness. Users recognised the connection between use of certain appliances and the immediate feedback they got on the Wattson or the daily phase consumption feedback on the FORE-Watch. As one participant puts it: "I got sensitised, I did not use to really pay attention to my electricity consumption, but now I am" (F7W2). Not only consumption as such, but also time of consumption was suddenly paid attention to:

> I think for the first time in my life about dealing more consciously with electricity. I would have never thought of washing the laundry at night. (F8W1)

The Cause: Visibility

The primary cause for such increased awareness was a heightened knowledge about energy consumption. Users generally treated the devices as social, placing both Wattson and the tablet in central locations that can be accessed by the whole household, such as next to the telephone, in the kitchen, in the living room, or next to the TV, "so that I can always observe it and have it always in sight" (M1W1). Interestingly, the position of the devices in some cases reflected task distribution among genders in the household. For example, in one case the participant placed the Wattson in the kitchen, "so that my wife has it in sight, because she spends most of her time there" (M4W1).

The Context: Practices, Location, and Time

Increased awareness is not simply the result of deploying energy-related technology in participants' home. Instead, it is moderated by location and time and the social practices associated with them, such as using the telephone, watching TV or cooking. Visibility and consecutive awareness is connected to (and depending on) the practices carried out at a location. For example, one user reported he put the tablet in his office, but due to an accident he is hardly ever there and thus has not paid much attention to it (M2W1).

A trend from use to non-use was reported by several participants. They used the Wattson to find out the consumption of specific appliances, but now that they know they do not really look at it anymore or have even turned it off. For example the system was not integrated into some users' practice of cooking: "At some point you get it under control and know that letting a goulash cook for three hours is consuming a lot of energy" (F7W2).

The Strategies: Exploration and Learning

One of the most common activities participants have reported is that they started to explore and learn about their energy consumption. "The Wattson really helped. I went through the apartment and checked out what is consuming how much" (F8W2). Discoveries include how energy intensive some appliances are, such as an electric kettle, stove, or conventional light bulbs. This exploration could cause some initial surprise: "In the beginning it was quite a shock when the Wattson jumped to 2000 Watts [when using the electric kettle]" (F9W2).

However, the value of these learning effects is questionable. Neither lighting nor appliances that are only used for a very short time, such as an electric kettle, are major contributors to the overall energy consumption in a household. Inhabitants might therefore pay attention to the wrong areas for conversation. As pointed out by other research, this can be attributed to heightened visibility of lighting [17] or to the design of the eco-feedback technology itself [43]. In our case, the design of the Wattson with its real-time feedback encouraged paying attention to short-term spikes instead of identifying long-term energy drainers.

The Consequences: Changes and Doubts

The consequences that result for participants are two-fold: On one hand, there are certain behavioural changes. Changes can be one-time efforts or continuous adjustments of daily routines. For example, several users reported they switched to LED lamps. One user even removed all power draining devices since he has been using the Wattson (M4W2). Additionally, several users said they are following the recommendations of the FORE-Watch and try to laundry during green phases, in particular if they had programmable devices. Also people started to include the eco button in their daily routines: "I turn it on every time before going to bed, it's like turning off the TV" (F8W1).

On the other hand, we found three main types of barriers to behavioural change, which can be circumscribed as *personal*, *social*, and *cultural*. Personal barriers prevent users to follow recommendations because they do *not want* for reasons of personal values: "I cook when I want. You should not enslave yourself" (M9W1). Also, an existing practice of sustainability can conflict with a desired one. F9W2 reported that she never throws things away, so she continues using conventional light bulbs until they brake. Similarly, other participants have already bought switchable power strips, and now refrain from using the eco button.

Additionally, there was considerable discussion about the return of investment on energy-efficient appliances and the overall savings effect in general:

> I don't think anyone [who is buying LED lights] has ever calculated that. If I buy a 100 Watt bulb today, that costs, let's say 20 cents, and the other one [...] costs 10 Euros, how long does the 10 Euro bulb have to run so that it pays off? And if it's hanging in the corridor, where it's on for just 10 minutes per day, this will never amortise. (M5W2)

Moreover, the same participant argued that, even if the reduction in energy consumption is substantial, the savings are minimal in comparison to total household costs.

On a social level, users *negotiate* practices with other household members, visitors, and other residents. M2W1 reports that he is in discussion with his wife to do the laundry at night, but he has not yet convinced her. Again, technology here makes gender distributions in the household visible. Visitors are also a source of reflection on energy consumption habits, as they did for example question the effectiveness (M4W1). Other residents, especially neighbours, make limitations of one's freedom to adjust daily practices visible: "I haven't dared to wash at night. I am afraid it is too loud for the neighbours" (F5W1).

Finally, on a cultural level, participants report practices they *cannot* change, even if they wanted to. Stable cultural arrangements, such as eating habits, represent circumstances they cannot influence: "I always cook during the red phase. I have a small child, and thus cannot change [the eating times]" (F8W1). One participant puts it straight:

> I don't think anyone who is sitting here is using electricity in the red phase purposefully. But if you don't have a *choice*, then you *have to* consume in the yellow or red phase. (M4W1, emphasis added)

This notion of lack of choice has been identified in other research and labelled as non-negotiable practices [43]. They manifest themselves when participants got confronted with consumption recommendations that clash with their daily routines: "You can't do anything anyway. Things that are important you have to do" (F3W2). It might be possible to change a few things, but to have "a *real* influence is more difficult" (M6W2, emphasis added). Also, the question of the 'whole picture' was raised:

> People only look at a small part of the story. [...] If I really care about the environment, I have to look at the whole picture. What does production cost? How many resources are used for production? (M5W2).

Summarising, the following themes emerged from this initial discussion: First, the technology introduced in people's homes did lead to an increased awareness of one's energy consumption. Second, visibility of usually mostly invisible energy is key to this awareness. Third, visibility is structured by spatial and temporal arrangements. Specific practices can remove visibility and can lead to non-use of technology over time. Forth, while the technology encourages exploration and learning, it might put the wrong issues front and distract from the 'real' problems. Fifth, there was some positive response to the implicit or explicit recommendations given by the system. However, this also caused both reflections on what can *really* be done and considerable doubts about the *actual* positive impact of one's energy saving measures. The core concept we derived from this analysis is termed as a *perceived inability to act*. In the second part of the workshops we extrapolated on this issue by exploring possible futures using design fiction.

Concept 2: Lack of Empowerment

The stories all feature different instances of family Gruber and are numbered as S1 to S6. The first three were developed during the first workshop, the latter three during the second workshop.

The phenomenon: Regulations and Social Inequality

The most obvious commonality of all six stories is that they are all dystopian. This aspect reflects the state of dystopias as the dominant type of future visions in contemporary culture [40]. There are three elements that make our users' futures dystopian: First, family Gruber will live under conditions of scarce energy resources. Second, there will be some form of strict access regulation by the state and/or high market prices to manage access to energy. Third, all this will lead to increased social inequality, where only the rich can maintain the current standard of living.

While several stories include state regulations of scarce resources, a worst-case scenario is outlined in S6:

> Due to energy shortage the government has to respond with an energy emergency programme that looks as follows: Every family of two, like the Grubers, may only cook for one hour per day anymore, wash one load of laundry, and may only shower – taking a bath is forbidden by the authorities. Showering is restricted to five minutes per day per person. Drinking or cooking water is restricted to two litres per day. Electricity is turned off at 10 P.M. Blow-drying is also forbidden. (S6)

High energy prices and restrictions will, in most stories, mainly affect low-income households:

> Mr. and Mrs Gruber and their three kids live in a small apartment and have to cut spending drastically. They only use the washing machine once or twice a week, even though they are five people […]. They don't have a tumble drier, because it is too expensive. Even in winter they heat reduced. They cover themselves with blankets and cuddle, because they have to save money. (S4)

There is a fear of increasing social inequality among the participants, as the rich will use their financial resources to be independent of state control: "Rich people can afford private solar panels. The poor part of the population, however, has to comply with the state rules" (S6).

The Cause: Radical Changes

The main driver for the futures is, across all fictions, a speculated depletion of fossil energy sources. Even though most futures include alternative forms of energy, it appears there is disbelief that solar and wind can fully substitute fossil energy sources, thus leading to high prices and state regulation:

> There can be wars, there will be wars. Diseases will break out. If you consider history, then this will repeat itself again and again, as long as humanity does not rethink. (M5W2, discussing S5)

The Context: Technology and Power

Three out of six stories mention explicitly advancements in technological development, leading to alternative fuel sources and more efficient household appliances. These developments come, however, out of a necessity: "So, a lot has happened to save electricity, because there is no way around it anymore; because there is nothing left" (M2W1).

This technological change is accompanied by a struggle for power and control over the energy market. Participants expressed their concern that an energy shortage will be exploited by private industries:

> The corporations define the future, they define our lives, and we won't get rid of that. And then there are the vassals in politics, who do not dare to say anything, because they are depending on them. (M2W1)

However, among our participants there is both a fear of excessive state control (as outlined above) *and* in failing market mechanisms:

> Since months Oskar and Shiva are trying hard to find their own water in the well they dug themselves in their village, in order to become independent of the state's despotism (that turns off the water for days or hours frequently) and not to have to pay the horrific prices anymore that get them in dire financial straits every month. (S2)

The Strategies: Adapt and Accept

Under all this political and economic pressure, the Grubers have to adapt their lifestyle. In two futures the family is developing some do-it-yourself (DIY) strategies: S2 talks about the aforementioned well the family is trying to dig and in S3 the family relies on wood-fired water heating as a replacement for gas and electricity. However, the Grubers are not necessarily discontent with the little they have: "People now ride more bicycles. Children are now more outside and in nature instead of in front of the TV and the computer. Less is more" (S4). The appreciation of simple living is contrasted with dissatisfaction with contemporary excessive consumerism:

> To the contrary, I think it's good, because in today's society there are so many people, who really have a lot, but are still unhappy. […] You have to appreciate the little you have. (F9W2)

However there is also a notion of nostalgia. S3 starts as follows: "2039. Where have the good old times gone? The time, when electricity and water were not yet restricted". State regulations can, however, not only be seen as an act of despotism. It can be seen as a *necessary* measure taken to survive as a society: "[Energy consumption] just has to be regulated externally, if individuals do not regulate it themselves. […] There is no other way" (F8W1).

The Consequences: Awareness and Responsibility

"We all now woke up from a bad dream. We are still in Austria and live on the 'island of the blessed'. For now!" (S2). This final sentence of S2 exemplifies a certain fear of the future outlined. Participants agreed that *something* has to change, otherwise we *will* end up like in their dark fictions: "If we do not manage to do this, then even in our 'holy land' [...], with mountains, water, glaciers [...] we will have to turn off water for three hours at some point" (M9W1).

Interestingly, for the participants, spreading awareness is uniformly the key to stopping such dystopian futures from happening. They do, however, differentiate between two types of awareness: First, it is necessary to develop *individual awareness for costs*. This includes awareness of how high one's energy bill will be and additionally, on a more general level, awareness or appreciation of the value energy has. Second, participants stress the importance of awareness for an individual's responsibility towards others and future generations:

> As long as everyone says, well, you save a lot of water anyway, so I don't have to do it, [nothing will change]. To raise this awareness in some way [...] is one of the most important starting points. (M9W1)

Education is named as crucial for raising awareness. Participants highlighted the point that it is also up to each individual to be a role model:

> There is the chance that if a few understand, more and more will understand. [...] Everyone can lead the way. You just have to start yourself [...] and don't just float with the current. Floating with the current is of course easy (M5W2).

Summarising, the design fictions brought up a number of relevant concepts that were not addressed in the first half of the workshops. First, there is the notion of both necessary and at the same time unfair and excessive regulation that is seen as way to come by with energy scarcity. Second, for the better or the worse, participants believe that radical changes will be necessary. Third, they are clearly aware that use of technology is interrelated with a system of power and that those who have power will take the necessary measures to keep it, no matter the (social) costs. However, especially during times of transition, there is the potential to shift power relations. Forth, there is an, admittedly vague, idea of a bottom-up DIY movement, where people will re-learn to appreciate simple living once (forcefully) freed from excessive consumerism. Fifth, participants call to appeal to universalistic values when citing education for responsibility for future generations as key for a successful prevention of climate change. The core concept based on this analysis is a *lack of empowerment*, which will, along the current state of *perceived inability to act*, be discussed in the following section.

DISCUSSION

The two core concepts derived from qualitative analysis of the workshop discussions are tightly interrelated. It can be argued that the first one, *perceived inability to act*, is (potentially unknowingly) the result of an unsuccessful realisation of the latter one, *lack of empowerment*. While awareness of the problem is arguably necessary for empowerment, it fails to achieve anything more than minor changes. This has several implications for a sustainable CSCW.

From Use to Non-Use

As has been argued, current energy monitoring systems focus heavily on raising awareness. As we have seen in the present study, visibility and engagement with the system is depending on social practices, location, and time. Simply putting a display into people's living rooms will not automatically result in its adoption. As Pantzar [31] argues, technology is only then successfully 'domesticated' when it becomes rooted in our daily lifestyle. Several other studies have reported a decline in interaction with feedback technology [1,12,20,33,39].

Awareness of What?

The type of information (and thus the type of awareness that is created) needs to be carefully considered. As we have discussed, the design of the feedback technology might lead participants to misinterpret information and draw the wrong conclusions with regard to how to act [43]. While changing some light bulbs and stop using the kettle might seem engaging at first, minuscule monetary rewards can lead to harsh rejection [20]. Sustainable CSCW should therefore look at how this information is translated and embedded in everyday practices. This is to look at the sociality of energy feedback technology.

Furthermore, awareness alone is not enough. When designing energy-related technology, it is crucial to understand sustainability holistically, meaning its reality as (un)sustainable social practices. The topic of research for sustainable CSCW is thus not energy consumption; it is social practices that include the use of energy-consuming devices. To change those practices, design for sustainability has to go beyond the individual consumer and think of social practices not only as units of analysis, but as units of design [26]. Otherwise the perceived inability to act may even destroy the little pro-environmental gains in the long run due to frustration.

On the other hand, awareness that teaches environmental responsibility for future generations and an appreciation for the value of energy can be a first step towards real change. In the case of our design fictions this came along with a certain fear of constraints and restrictions that would be enforced. It is certainly a challenging task to tackle this issue. S4 hinted on one possible way, namely to frame consuming less energy not as a restriction but a gain. Here, sustainable CSCW can pick up on promising trends in HCI looking at green practices, such as simple living families [19], repair cultures [22] and DIY communities [47].

A Change in Culture

The apparent belief among our participants that *something* has to change and that this something has to be *radical* opens up various design opportunities. Instead of designing for incremental change [24], our designs might be well off questioning the established lines of thinking in modernist terms [4]. Empowerment in its literary sense then means to become powerful to act in society. Technology-enhanced empowerment therefore means designing for a change in culture. This lies at the very heart of what we envision what sustainable CSCW can be: Facilitating a cultural change that includes a shift of power. Those who do not have power, the citizens, engage in more equal terms in political action with those who have, i.e. the political establishment.

Design Fiction: New Questions and New Perspectives

Applying the design fiction approach to this end has real merit in two dimensions. First, it helped us to question the existing world [18] and think of radical change as something that might well become a reality soon. As we discussed, during the first half of the workshops awareness in terms of monetary costs was prevalent. This can at least partially be attributed to the design of the system itself, whose feedback mechanisms are focused on consumption and not environmental impact. However, deploying the method of design fiction to extrapolate from *current*, mainly economic issues (i.e. saving money), to *future* issues [18,27,47] immediately turned the discussion towards social issues (i.e. saving humanity). Exempt from the constraints of the immediate present, i.e. living with this specific technology at home, it allowed participants to collaboratively build upon the notion of perceived inability to act and extrapolate it into the future. This process opened exploration space [2,45] and revealed the question of lack of empowerment. Consequently, design fiction allowed us as researchers to turn this new structure of relevance into implications for a design for empowerment, which we will discuss in the next section.

The second benefit is the shift away from technological solutions. In fact, none of the stories included an energy management system. In other words, people don't necessarily need such technology to live a sustainable lifestyle. This way, non-use of a technology is not an issue. Of course this is true of any energy management system, as it is never an end in itself. What counts is not application usage time but environmental impact. Maybe because real impact is so hard to measure, evaluation studies, however, do tend to look on factors like system interactions [20,33] and engagement of users [8,12]. We do not, however, want to design for Resource Man [44], whose sole concern is to rationally manage his energy consumption, ignoring the practices it is originating from. We want to design for the empowered man and woman.

The power of the design fiction approach is to allow translating insights into practical design implications. The next section will thus outline how sustainable CSCW can approach the endeavour of empowerment in the future.

IMPLICATIONS FOR SUSTAINABLE DESIGN

Based on the findings of the present study, we propose to design for supporting the following five levels of empowerment:

First-level empowerment: Awareness for one's responsibility is a first step towards sustainable practices. This can start in one's personal environment, but has an inherent social dimension that needs to be addressed. Design needs to teach these values to current and future generations. This includes a shift from monetary, purely environmentally, or resource-oriented systems to systems that communicate social responsibilities.

Second-level empowerment refers to the potential to take action by knowing about one's own behaviour and its consequences. Such empowerment did lead to some behaviour changes in our study. However, consequences must not be reduced to abstract visualisations of environmental and economic effects, but must be thought along broader lines to include personal, social, and cultural impacts.

Third-level empowerment means to shift perspectives when exploring radical changes in future energy consumption, such as regulations or even war. The aim could be to alter the collective representation of what a 'good' life defines. This has been attempted for example in the context of life in an 'online world' [46], but is lacking for life in a 'sustainable world'. By introducing alternative measures to economic growth, as the examples of green cultures do, one can shed off the fears of an (economically) doomed future.

Forth-level empowerment aims at overcoming the perceived inability to act. To break this attitude, a holistic picture of environmental impact has to be outlined and communicated to people, including production and distribution costs and rebound effects. A holistic model of sustainability also includes the power structure that is involved, thus pointing out directions for change. This is again a social and collaborative endeavour. One household alone cannot change much, but collective actions can, for example, be coordinated through social networks.

Finally, *fifth level-empowerment* enables citizens to reach out to political or economic stakeholders involved in energy generation, distribution, and regulation. Reaching-out here has to include the ability to build up pressure to influence decision makers. This, however, remains an understudied field of HCI, despite several suggestions to embrace activism for reframing what sustainable HCI is about [5,11,16, 21]. We believe that it is also the responsibility of CSCW to actively seek out decision makers and promote ideas of collaboration and participation between stakeholders, where traditionally stark power differences exist between them, such as citizens and governments or corporations.

This list of levels of empowerment is not a cookbook recipe. To design is to deal with wicked problems that cannot be solved with ready-made building blocks. This list *can* be, however, a mind-set and a guiding direction for sustainable CSCW practitioners. It is our hope that, by looking at people's practices with the goal of empowering them to do change with technological support, designers might not only do things right, but also do the right thing. Using practices not only as a unit of research, but also as a unit of design can allow the designer to embed technology in practices [39] or to disrupt them [26]. We believe both approaches can work in conjunction. The former can serve as an entry point in terms of technology domestication, the latter as the trigger for political action.

Others in HCI also have pointed out ways forward. Examples include Knowles et al.'s 'alternative Plan A' for sustainable HCI [24], Ganglbauer et al.'s 'activist lens' for sustainability [16] or Brynjarsdottir and Håkansson's reframing of persuasion [4]. We hope we have contributed to this paradigmatic shift in HCI and CSCW.

CONCLUSION AND FUTURE WORK

This paper presented a qualitative analysis of household practices related to energy consumption. One contribution is an empirical grounding of the limitations of current energy monitoring systems. While they are successful in raising awareness and achieve limited behaviour change, they do not address social practices appropriately and leave users with a perceived helplessness or inability to act. To better illustrate this and also to go beyond in a constructive manner, we have turned to participatory design fiction to extrapolate current (largely implicit) concerns regarding energy consumption and the environment. Based on the participants' visions of *future* life, we constructed five levels of empowerment to be addressed by CSCW.

We argue that this allows a more differentiated look at how technology can support and enhance empowerment. By addressing each of the proposed levels, we believe designers can create technology that respects the practices it is embedded in and at the same time allow users change them through engaging in broader cultural transitions. Design fiction can serve as a valuable approach to shift focus from technology to practices and use practices both as a unit of analysis and a unit of design. Furthermore, design fiction allows envisioning radical solutions to strive for fifth-level empowerment instead of small incremental changes with only little impact. Obviously, HCI can only be a small contributor, but it is our responsibility as researchers to use our means to participate in moving this world towards a more sustainable future.

ACKNOWLEDGMENTS

This work has been partly funded by the Klima- & Energiefonds project HiT Begleit-F&E (FFG #834676) as part of the "Neue Energien 2020" programme and is part of the Smart Grids Model Region Salzburg. We thank our project partners Salzburg AG, Salzburg Wohnbau, and Siemens AG for their collaboration.

REFERENCES

1. Barreto, M., Karapanos, E., and Nunes, N. Why don't families get along with eco-feedback technologies? Proc. CHItaly '13, ACM Press (2013), 1–4.
2. Blythe, M.A. Research through design fiction. Proc. CHI '14, ACM Press (2014), 703–712.
3. Blythe, M.A. and Wright, P.C. Pastiche scenarios: Fiction as a resource for user centred design. Interacting with Computers 18, 5 (2006), 1139–1164.
4. Brynjarsdottir, H. and Håkansson, M. Sustainably unpersuaded: How persuasion narrows our vision of sustainability. Proc. CHI '12, (2012), 947–956.
5. Busse, D.K., Borning, A., Mann, S., et al. CHI at the barricades. Proc. CHI EA '13, ACM Press (2013), 2407.
6. Cowan, B.R., Bowers, C.P., Beale, R., and Pinder, C. The Stroppy Kettle: An Intervention to Break Energy Consumption Habits. Proc. CHI EA '13, ACM (2013).
7. Darby, S. The effectiveness of feedback on energy consumption. A Review of Defra of the literature on metering, billing and direct displays. Environmental Change Institute, University of Oxford, 2006.
8. Dillahunt, T.R. and Mankoff, J. Understanding factors of successful engagement around energy consumption between and among households. Proc. CSCW '14, ACM Press (2014), 1246–1257.
9. DiSalvo, C., Light, A., and Hirsch, T. HCI, communities and politics. Proc. CHI '10 EA, (2010).
10. Dourish, P. and Bell, G. "Resistance is futile": reading science fiction alongside ubiquitous computing. Personal and Ubiquitous Computing 18, 4 (2013), 769–778.
11. Dourish, P. HCI and environmental sustainability: the politics of design and the design of politics. Proc. DIS '10, (2010), 1–10.
12. Erickson, T., Podlaseck, M., Sahu, S., Dai, J.D., Chao, T., and Naphade, M. The dubuque water portal. Proc. CHI '12, ACM Press (2012), 675–684.
13. Faruqui, A., Sergici, S., and Sharif, A. The impact of informational feedback on energy consumption—A survey of the experimental evidence. *Energy 35*, 4 (2010), 1598–1608.
14. Foster, D., Lawson, S., Blythe, M., and Cairns, P. Wattsup?: Motivating Reductions in Domestic Energy Consumption Using Social Networks. Proc. NordiCHI '10, ACM (2010), 178–187.

15. Froehlich, J., Findlater, L., and Landay, J. The Design of Eco-Feedback Technology. Proc. CHI '10, ACM (2010), 1999–2008.
16. Ganglbauer, E., Reitberger, W., and Fitzpatrick, G. An activist lens for sustainability: from changing individuals to changing the environment. Proc. Persuasive '13, (2013), 63–68.
17. Gram-Hanssen, K. Consuming technologies – developing routines. Cleaner Production 16, 11 (2008).
18. Grand, S. and Wiedmer, M. Design Fiction: A Method Toolbox for Design Research in a Complex World. Proc. DRS '10, (2010).
19. Håkansson, M., Leshed, G., Blevis, E., Nathan, L., and Mann, S. Simple, sustainable living. Proc. CHI EA '12, ACM Press (2012), 2795.
20. Hargreaves, T., Nye, M., and Burgess, J. Keeping energy visible? Exploring how householders interact with feedback from smart energy monitors in the longer term. Energy Policy 52, (2013), 126–134.
21. Hirsch, T. Learning from activists: lessons for designers. interactions 16, 3 (2009), 31–33.
22. Jackson, S.J., Pompe, A., and Krieshok, G. Repair worlds. Proc. CSCW '12, ACM Press (2012), 107.
23. Kirman, B., Linehan, C., Lawson, S., and O'Hara, D. CHI and the future robot enslavement of humankind. Proc. CHI EA '13, ACM Press (2013), 2199.
24. Knowles, B., Blair, L., Coulton, P., and Lochrie, M. Rethinking plan A for sustainable HCI. Proc. CHI '14, (2014), 3593–3596.
25. Knowles, B., Blair, L., Hazas, M., and Walker, S. Exploring sustainability research in computing. Proc. UbiComp '13, ACM Press (2013), 305.
26. Kuijer, L., Jong, A., and Eijk, D. Practices as a unit of design: An exploration of theoretical guidelines in a study on bathing. ToCHI 20, 4 (2013).
27. Linehan, C., Kirman, B.J., Reeves, S., et al. Alternate endings: using fiction to explore design futures. Proc. CHI EA '14, ACM Press (2014), 45–48.
28. Mankoff, J. HCI and sustainability: a tale of two motivations. interactions 19, 3 (2012), 16.
29. Markussen, T. and Knutz, E. The poetics of design fiction. Proc. DPPI '13, ACM Press (2013), 231.
30. Matthews, T., Whittaker, S., Moran, T., and Yuen, S. Collaboration personas. Proc. CHI '11, ACM Press (2011), 2247–2256.
31. Pantzar, M. Domestication of Everyday Life Technology: Dynamic Views on the Social Histories of Artifacts. Design Issues 13, 3 (1997), 52–65.
32. Paulos, E., Foth, M., Satchell, C., and Kim, Y. Ubiquitous Sustainablity: Citizen Science and Activism. Proc. UbiComp '08, (2008).
33. Petkov, P., Köbler, F., Foth, M., Medland, R., and Krcmar, H. Engaging energy saving through motivation-specific social comparison. Proc. CHI EA '11, ACM Press (2011), 1945.
34. Pierce, J. and Paulos, E. Beyond energy monitors: interaction, energy, and emerging energy systems. Proc. CHI '12, (2012), 665–674.
35. Pinelle, D., Gutwin, C., and Greenberg, S. Task analysis for groupware usability evaluation. ToCHI 10, 4 (2003), 281–311.
36. Reckwitz, a. Toward a Theory of Social Practices: A Development in Culturalist Theorizing. European Journal of Social Theory 5, 2 (2002), 243–263.
37. Schmitz, M., Endres, C., and Butz, A. A survey of human-computer interaction design in science fiction movies. Proc. INTETAIN '08, (2008).
38. Schrammel, J., Gerdenitsch, C., and Weiss, A. FORE-Watch–the clock that tells you when to use: persuading users to align their energy consumption with green power availability. Proc. AmI '11, (2011).
39. Schwartz, T., Stevens, G., Jakobi, T., et al. What People Do with Consumption Feedback: A Long-Term Living Lab Study of a Home Energy Management System. Interacting with Computers, February (2014).
40. Slaughter, R.A. Futures Beyond Dystopia: Creating Social Foresight. Routledge, London, 2003.
41. Sterling, B., Wild, L., and Lunenfeld, P. Shaping things. MIT Press, Cambridge, MA, 2005.
42. Strauss, A. and Corbin, J. Basics of qualitative research: Techniques and procedures for developing grounded theory. Sage, Thousand Oaks, CA, 1998.
43. Strengers, Y. Designing eco-feedback systems for everyday life. Proc. CHI '11, (2011), 2135.
44. Strengers, Y. Smart energy in everyday life. interactions 21, 4 (2014), 24–31.
45. Tanenbaum, J., Tanenbaum, K., and Wakkary, R. Design fictions. Proc. TEI '12, ACM Press (2012), 347.
46. The Online Initiative. The Online Manifesto: Being Human in a Hyperconnected Era. European Commission, 2013. http://ec.europa.eu/digital-agenda/futurium/sites/futurium/files/Manifesto.pdf. Accessed 2014-09-15.
47. Wakkary, R., Desjardins, A., Hauser, S., and Maestri, L. A sustainable design fiction: Green practices. ToCHI 20, 4 (2013), 23.
48. Wulf, V., Rohde, M., Pipek, V., and Stevens, G. Engaging with Practices: Design Case Studies as a Research Framework in CSCW. Proc. CSCW '11, ACM Press (2011), 505.

Paper-Digital Workflows in Global Development Organizations

Nicola Dell† Trevor Perrier† Neha Kumar† Mitchell Lee† Rachel Powers‡ Gaetano Borriello†

†Computer Science and Engineering, University of Washington
{nixdell,tperrier,neha,mitchl2,gaetano}@cs.washington.edu

‡VillageReach
rachel.powers@villagereach.org

ABSTRACT

Global development organizations rely on the essential affordances provided by both paper and digital materials to navigate hurdles posed by poor infrastructure, low connectivity, linguistic differences, and other socioeconomic constraints that render communication and collaboration challenging. This paper examines the collaborative practices around paper-digital workflows within global development organizations operating in low-resource environments. We use a mixed methods approach to gather data from 23 organizations in 16 countries. Our findings show the tensions that arise between the ubiquitousness of paper and the desirability of digitized data, and highlight the challenges associated with transitioning information several times between paper and digital materials. We also reveal design opportunities for new tools to bridge the gap between paper-based and digital information in low-resource settings. Finally, we contribute a nuanced understanding of the cross-cultural and infrastructural challenges that influence the paper-digital lifecycle. Our findings will be useful for researchers and practitioners interested in understanding or participating in the workflows that drive global development.

Author Keywords

Paper; digital; paper forms; data entry; affordances; global development; ODK Scan; ICTD; DEV; HCI4D.

ACM Classification Keywords

H.5.m. Information Interfaces and Presentation (e.g. HCI): Miscellaneous

General Terms

Design; Human Factors; Measurement.

INTRODUCTION

Global development organizations, big and small, have gradually but steadily evolved into an established presence across the world, particularly in low- and middle-income countries. Teams within these organizations are frequently present in multiple countries at once, engendering complex and collaborative work environments that require an ever-present awareness of temporal, spatial, and cultural divides. Individuals with different backgrounds, perspectives and responsibilities work together on the design, deployment, and evaluation of initiatives that aim to examine and/or improve the lives of socioeconomically disadvantaged populations around the world. At the same time, these initiatives may require them to collaborate with various partner, donor, and government organizations to perform large-scale data collection in the communities they target. For the relevance and success of these development initiatives, collecting this data becomes an essential endeavor.

The task of gathering accurate and timely data from people living in low-resource environments is not without its challenges. In regions constrained by poor infrastructure and limited resources, where the availability of technology is limited and digital literacy is slowly rising, data must often be collected using paper - not digital - materials. People trust and are familiar with paper. Paper is tangible, portable and does not require batteries. These material affordances make it easy to use and almost universally accessible. As a result, paper documents have always provided essential support for organizational work processes, particularly in low-resource settings, and will remain an integral and critical component of global development workflows for years to come.

However, although paper has been used to collect data for hundreds of years, the onset of digital data has transformed the organizational workflow. Data in digital formats, particularly 'big' data, is easier to navigate, process, manage, and store than paper-based data, and many of the complex analyses and visualizations that now routinely help people to make sense of collected data are only feasible if the data is in communicable, searchable and mutable digital formats. Our research examines the tensions between the ubiquitousness of paper and the desirability of digitized data as we uncover the collaborative practices surrounding paper-digital workflows in global development organizations. We use a mixed methods approach to study the paper-digital lifecycle from the perspective of the researchers and practitioners that drive development initiatives, organizing our findings in relation to the different stages of the data lifecycle as it is sought, collected, digitized, and analyzed.

The CSCW community has long interested itself in the tension between paper and digital materials [3] [30] [32]. We introduce a novel dimension to this conversation by examining paper and digital artifacts in low-resource settings,

ACM 978-1-4503-2922-4/15/03...$15.00
http://dx.doi.org/10.1145/2675133.2675145

where infrastructural challenges play a significant role. We also contribute to the rich body of prior work that is concerned with understanding organizational workflows and exploring how individual activities are organized to achieve collective ends [31]. Although there has been a growing interest in CSCW research that focuses on disadvantaged communities [21] [29] and geographically distributed teams [18], very little research thus far has examined the workflows of global development organizations. These organizations often operate in low-resource settings where they must navigate hurdles posed by poor infrastructure, low connectivity, cultural differences, and other socioeconomic constraints.

We contribute an in-depth analysis of the complex organizational workflows that drive global development, focusing on the perspectives and understandings of the researchers and practitioners who design field studies to collect data from target communities. We show that workers within these organizations spend considerable time and effort transitioning data between paper and digital materials, while attempting to preserve the correctness and completeness of the data. In addition, we highlight workers' frustrations with the software tools that they use to collect, communicate and synchronize data between remote offices, and present design opportunities for new tools to better support their workflows. Finally, we reveal the impact of infrastructural, cultural and socioeconomic challenges on the paper-digital lifecycle in the context of global development work, many of which can only be understood, not eliminated. Taken together, our findings will be useful for survey designers, researchers and practitioners interested in understanding and participating in the complex workflows that drive global development.

BACKGROUND AND RELATED WORK

Paper and Digital Materials in Low-Resource Settings

Paper has long played a central role in the collection and communication of information within governments and other organizations. Gupta [14] and Hull [19] note that, by moving through a bureaucracy as documents, physical materials such as health registers, government notices, or written complaints gain status and trigger actions by officials. Veeraraghavan [36] describes how digitizating paper records can reduce corruption. Singh et al. [33] analyze the use of paper in non-governmental organizations (NGOs) and show that workers prefer numeric and multiple-choice surveys since they can fill them more quickly and accurately than text-based surveys.

A variety of technical interventions have been proposed to bridge the gap between paper and digital worlds in low-resource settings. CAM [26] was among the first to propose the use of a camera-enabled mobile phone for assisted data entry from paper surveys. ODK Scan [7], a smartphone-based system that uses computer vision to interpret data from paper, recently showed that transforming field data into machine-readable documents is a challenging task [8]. Shreddr [6] (now Captricity [5]) takes a novel approach to digitization, segmenting paper surveys and assigning them as images for transcription by crowd-sourced workers. Ratan et al. [28] combined physical paper with a digital slate device that provided electronic feedback. Although this performed well in usability studies, the purchase and maintenance of specialized slate devices hindered its scalability and sustainability [25]. The PartoPen [35] uses a digital pen-and-paper solution for monitoring women in labor. The system provides real-time reminders for health workers, but extracting data from the pens and integrating it with patient medical records or other data collection tools remains a challenge. In addition, a smart pen is needed for each worker, rendering the system less scalable for low-cost.

Although many of these interventions aim to bridge the gap between paper and digital materials in low-resource settings, they focus mainly on evaluating the usability of new technologies with end users. Our work examines the collaborative practices surrounding paper-digital workflows at multiple organizations, focusing on key moments at which data is transitioned between paper and digital materials.

Bridging the Gap Between Paper and Digital Materials

According to Harper and Sellen, *"Observation of any organizational setting only serves to confirm that the most pervasive, ubiquitous artifact in support of collaborative work is paper"* [16]. The fact that paper and digital materials are both widely used suggests that each medium provides essential affordances that the other does not [3][32]. Paper is cheap and has inherent material properties that make it easy to use and access in almost any environment. Digital documents are easy to store, search, link and analyze. However, coordinating information across paper and digital materials has proven challenging, and a large body of prior work examines and aims to bridge this paper-digital divide.

Proposed technical solutions focus on personal document management and new ways of integrating the affordances of paper and digital materials. Several solutions use camera- and projector-based systems to enhance paper with digital resources [20] [34] [37] or augment computers with paper affordances [9] [13] [17]. Other systems use digital pen technologies to link physical locations on paper to digital content [15] [23] [27]. Although these studies repeatedly emphasize the importance of paper for a diverse array of work processes, they focus mainly on the management of personal documents for greater individual productivity. By contrast, we consider how *organizations* collect and transition information between paper and digital formats. In this context, Luff et al. [22] examined the relevance of paper in collaborative workflows in an architectural practice, a medical center and a London Underground control room. Harper and Sellen used ethnographic methods to assess the role of paper in an air traffic control room, a police station and the International Monetary Fund [16]. Other studies examine the use of paper and digital media in healthcare [11], particularly with respect to medical records [10] and information flow [4]. These studies emphasize that, despite efforts to replace paper with digital alternatives, paper remains an integral component of any work environment.

The above studies focus, however, on the work practices of organizations situated in infrastructure-rich settings. Our research focuses on paper-digital workflows within global development organizations that span multiple cultures and geographies, including low-resource environments, and must frequently struggle with infrastructural hurdles such as poor electricity and Internet connectivity. Through an in-depth consideration of these constraints, we identify factors that could influence the design of future technologies that aim to support global development workflows.

METHODOLOGY

Our study contributes an in-depth understanding of paper-digital workflows within the global development context by examining the work practices of our target organizations, particularly as they relate to the use of paper and the move towards digitization. The methods we use to arrive at this understanding include an online survey, a design probe, and a set of interviews. We describe these in detail below.

Online Survey

Our online survey consisted of 50 questions that sought information regarding the demographic background of the participants and their organizations, their survey design and approvals processes, data collection and entry, and collaborative work practices. Our 48 participants from 23 organizations (of varying sizes) were situated in 16 countries and have been active in a variety of domains, including health, education, agriculture, finance, and logistics. Their responses gave us a preliminary and global perspective on the relevance of paper and the importance of digitization in these domains.

Design Probe

Based on our survey responses, we prototyped a new survey design tool to expand our understanding of the design process within our target organizations. The tool was designed with the single objective of ease of digitization and allows participants to create a variety of question formats that are optimized for machine-readability (see Figure 1). Participants can move and reformat individual questions, and import content from a variety of other sources, including from existing images or Microsoft Word. The tool is freely available online, and paper surveys that are generated using the tool can be automatically digitized using the ODK Scan application [7]. Our goal was to use the tool as a probe [12] to elicit survey designers' views on the process of converting research questions into material paper surveys and the value of optimizing for digitization and machine-readability.

Interviews

Participants

We recruited nine participants from three global development organizations[1]. All participants were female, aged between 27 and 37 years, and selected based on (1) having participated in our online survey; (2) being actively engaged in designing paper-based surveys for global development initiatives; and (3) being willing and able to participate in our study. We interviewed both researchers and practitioners, since both play vital roles in global development workflows but are somewhat differently motivated. Participants who identified themselves as practitioners were usually employed by NGOs primarily concerned with applying existing knowledge and technologies to improve the quality of life of people in resource-poor settings. By contrast, participants who described themselves as researchers usually worked for academic institutions and were motivated by high-level research questions that they hope will be answered through field studies in low-resource settings. These participants were concerned about ensuring the validity of the study, enrolling well-defined samples of specific target populations and controlling for external variables. Having both kinds of participants afforded us a more nuanced understanding of the workflows involved in global development initiatives.

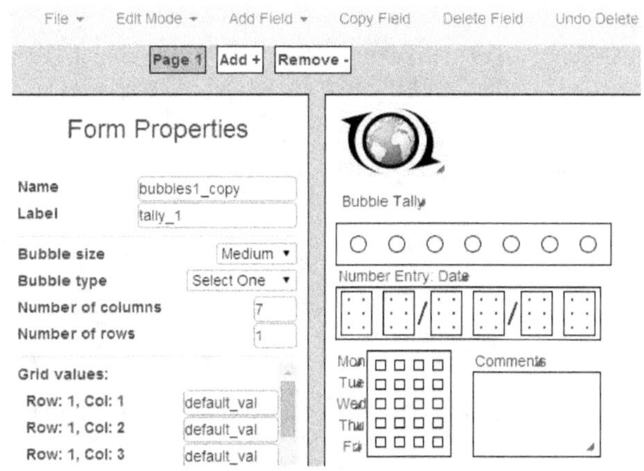

Figure 1. Screenshot showing how our prototype design probe generates a variety of machine-readable question types and incorporates content generated by other tools (such as images).

Finally, all our participants are survey designers who work with diverse and geographically dispersed teams, but who are themselves primarily based in the US. Our findings therefore document the priorities and perspectives of these survey designers with regard to the paper-digital lifecycle within their organizations. Exploring the perspectives of the other stakeholders will be the subject of future research.

Procedure

Participants were introduced to our prototype design tool by watching a 20-minute sequence of tutorial videos that described the tool's features. After watching the videos, we asked participants to use the tool to create a previously designed paper survey of their choice and observed as they completed this process on their own computers. This phase of the study took approximately 30 minutes and we encouraged participants to articulate their thought processes by requesting them to follow the think-aloud protocol.

We also conducted in-depth 60-minute interviews with the same nine participants. The interviews began with a short design exercise. Participants were provided with a research question and used a paper and pen to design a survey that would collect the data required to answer the question. The research questions were selected at random from the World Health Survey[2] conducted by the World Health Organization. This phase of the interview lasted approximately 15 minutes and allowed us to observe the participants' design process

[1]Organization names have been anonymized for review.

[2]Available at http://www.who.int/healthinfo/survey/en/

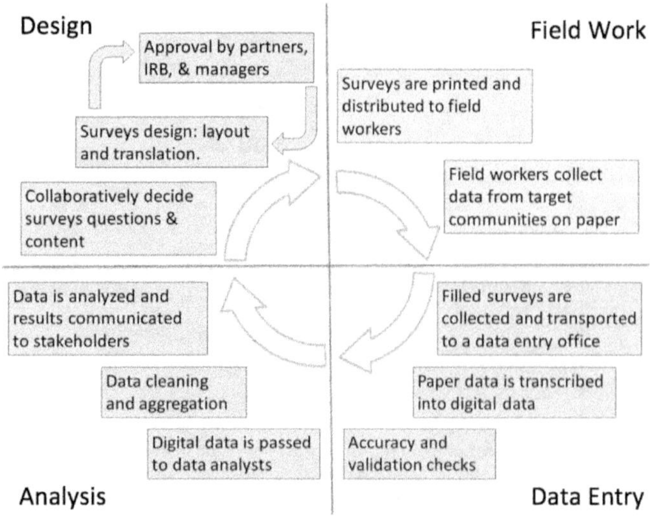

Figure 2. The four phases of the paper-digital lifecycle in the context of global development work: design, field work, data entry, analysis.

and how they prioritized data digitization. The next phase of the interview lasted approximately 45 minutes and consisted of an in-depth discussion of the participants' current work practices, their backgrounds, work responsibilities, current survey design tools and processes, the workflows surrounding the use of paper surveys in the field, and the data entry processes employed by their organization.

Analysis

To analyze our data, we went through our survey results and interview transcripts and organized them using the *"design"*, *"field work"*, *"data entry"*, and *"analysis"* codes to determine which findings were relevant for the distinct phases of the workflows that we examine. For each of these codes, we conducted iterative analyses to ascertain and organize our prominent findings that we present below.

FINDINGS

We study paper-digital workflows from the perspective of researchers and practitioners responsible for driving global development initiatives. The success of these initiatives depends upon effective collaboration across four phases of work between remotely located workers, as depicted in Figure 2. In the design phase, researchers and practitioners use digital tools to create surveys. In the data collection phase, workers in the field convert these surveys to paper and use them to collect data. In the data entry phase, workers transcribe data from paper into digital formats. Finally, in the analysis phase, researchers and practitioners process the digitized data to address research or program objectives.

At a high-level, we identify several layers of issues that affect paper-digital workflows in global development organizations, including (1) issues that relate to the material affordances and limitations of paper and digital media; (2) issues that relate to the low-resource nature of the work environments; and (3) issues that relate to the cross-cultural and geographically distributed nature of global development work. In presenting our findings, we limit our focus to how these issues affect the four phases of the paper-digital lifecycle, although we note that each category is worthy of additional study.

1. Design: Creating Paper Materials with Digital Tools

Our analysis reveals that survey design is a highly collaborative process involving multiple stakeholders, although effective collaboration is challenging for geographically dispersed teams that may speak different languages. Survey designers must also manage a number of trade-offs regarding the quantity of data collected from target communities, the layout and complexity of surveys, and the amount of work required to complete the survey. To make them easy to fill, surveys are typically highly structured documents that designers struggle to create using currently available software tools. However, the structured nature of the surveys means that, for the most part, they are already optimized for machine-readability, despite not currently being digitized by a machine.

1a: Collaborative survey design is challenging for geographically dispersed teams that may speak different languages

The process that determines the content to be included on new surveys is collaborative and involves multiple stakeholders, often remotely located, *e.g.*, office staff in the US, field staff in target countries, Ministry officials, and funding agencies. In many cases, time differences between stakeholders in different countries introduce additional complexity to the collaboration, with one of our participants describing how it took her *"four months to go from the idea to the survey."* Potential delays and constraints for meeting times must be factored in, as must holidays. Feedback from staff in target countries takes at least a day, while feedback from Ministry officials can often take a few weeks. In addition, obtaining the necessary approvals for survey designs can take anywhere from a few days to many months.

Moreover, surveys designed by English-speaking researchers and practitioners must be translated into local languages if they are to be understood by all interested parties. However, communicating the goals of a survey across languages can be challenging and potentially lossy, particularly if the translator is not a native speaker of both. This could introduce subtle differences between the meanings intended by the designers, and the meanings on the translated survey. In addition, as the survey design evolves, these differences could become compounded by iterative design, editing and translating. Furthermore, the translation can affect the appearance and layout of content on the survey, which may complicate the work processes of both the designers and the translators:

> *"For most English-Portuguese translations, the stuff that takes three words in English takes seven in Portuguese. So we really have to think about how we fit it all in."*

1b: Survey designers manage several trade-offs regarding the content, layout and complexity of surveys

Survey designers face a number of challenges deciding the content, layout and complexity of new surveys. Many participants described how they strive to design surveys that collect only the data necessary to answer specific research questions and nothing more, explaining how trying to collect too much data would both complicate their analyses and increase the likelihood of error. However,

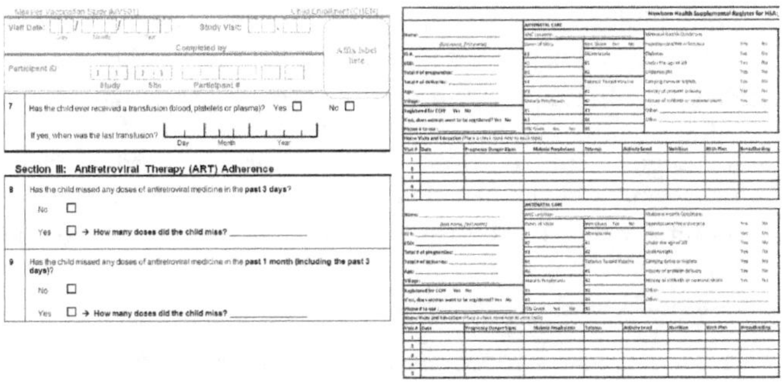

Figure 3. Two surveys that highlight how some of our participants optimize for clarity (left) and others optimize for density (right). Note that we do not intend for readers to read the questions on these surveys, rather, we are illustrating their high-level layout characteristics.

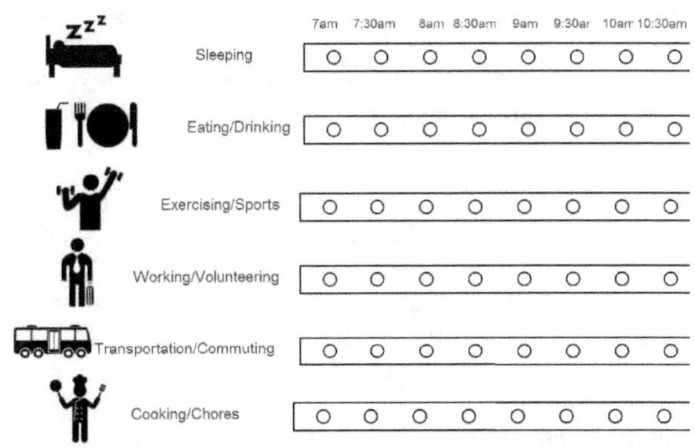

Figure 4. Part of a survey created for use by rural farmers in Tanzania.

since collecting data from target communities in low-resource settings requires organizations to invest large amounts of time and effort, it often also makes sense to collect additional data that could be used to answer future research questions:

> *"It's always a push-pull of collecting enough information to be useful in the future, even for questions we haven't thought of yet. I mean there's stuff in here that I'm not using at all, there's a lot of redundant data. Looking back on this, it could be a little more streamlined. But there's a lot of data here that isn't used yet."*

Many participants were also concerned about how field workers would perceive the amount of work required to fill in a survey and they devised strategies to make surveys appear easy to complete. Some participants prioritized density (see Figure 3, right), packing large amounts of information onto a single page to keep the survey as short as possible:

> *"We don't want them carrying around too many sheets of paper, so we try to get as much information as possible on one page. And that's also because of cost."*

Other participants prioritized for clarity and compromised on space (see Figure 3, left). Then, they broke each question into multiple parts so that it appeared as if the entire survey consisted of only a small number of questions:

> *"You can see that there's question 3a, 3b, 3c. We have stupid numbers of subquestions. And that was specifically asked for by the team, because psychologically if we're on question 7 in section 1, that's much nicer than question 23 of 49."*

In either case, the designer's expectation and understanding of who will use the survey in the field heavily influenced the complexity of the survey. For example, one participant designed two surveys to collect data regarding how rural farmers in Tanzania spend their time. The first is a household survey designed to be filled by trained field workers employed by the organization. Since the designer expected that these workers would be relatively well educated, the survey consists of many pages and includes complex features like conditional branching. By contrast, the second survey is a diary that will be filled out by rural farmers. The designer does not know the characteristics of these farmers, whether they will be literate, or their willingness to engage in the work. As a result, the survey is a single page that consists of images showing common household activities with a simple grid of bubbles for farmers to fill in (see Figure 4).

Since the consequences of misjudging the field workers' abilities may substantially reduce the quality of the data collected, designers use a variety of strategies to increase the likelihood that field workers and target populations will understand the questions. One common strategy is to copy question formats from pre-existing, tried and tested surveys:

> *"We are trying to write as little original content as possible and use past surveys that have already piloted these questions in a similar context."*

Another popular content layout strategy involved mimicking the format of government registers whose contents were to be transferred onto the survey. Keeping the structure of the two surveys identical may make it easier for field workers to simply copy the content from the register onto the survey.

1c: Designers struggle to create surveys using currently available tools and are willing to try new tools that optimize surveys for digitization and machine-readability

One goal in our study was to probe participants' reactions to the idea of optimizing their surveys for machine-readability and digitization. Although machine-readable surveys exist (such as Scantron[3]), none of the tools that our participants use currently support machine-readability. Instead, almost all of our survey participants reported using Microsoft Word as their primary survey design tool.

However, despite its prevalence, a large number of our interviewees were vocal about how challenging and frustrating they found the process of designing their highly structured surveys in Word. One participant who tried to switch from Word to Adobe InDesign shared that it had taken her several months to learn the new software but *"there is a startup cost to learning any new tool,"* and InDesign allowed her to *"create surveys that look very pretty"*. However, she also found the cost of purchasing the software to be significant (InDesign currently costs US $240 per year) and,

[3]Available at www.scantron.com

since designing surveys is typically collaborative, her team members would also need to purchase the software to edit the survey. Thus, despite her (time and financial) investment in the new software, and a personal preference for InDesign, she returned to using Word.

Although it is clearly challenging to incorporate new software into their workflows, all of our participants were eager to learn about viable alternative design tools. Moreover, they welcomed the idea of designing surveys that were optimized for machine-readability, with several assuming that automated digitization would be more accurate than human data entry. When participants used our prototype tool to create their surveys, all of the question types that they needed could be represented using features that the tool offered. In addition, almost all data fields used for analysis are already structured as numeric, bubble or checkbox fields, which could be automatically interpreted. Text, which cannot be automatically converted, must be saved in image format and/or manually transcribed by a person. However, several of our participants' surveys contained no text-based data, while some contained a single text field for the person's name, which was typically not used for analysis:

> *"Nobody ever looks back at the name. I don't see how the name field would be relevant, except maybe if you needed to contact the person later."*

These findings suggest that, for the most part, our participants' surveys are *already* optimized for machine-readability. They simply need to be created using software that enables a machine to digitize the data. Participants also claimed that they would be willing to spend substantial amounts of extra time designing the survey if it meant that the survey would be machine-readable and ease the data entry process, particularly for large scale surveys:

> *"There would be 1200 of these. 10 hours upfront definitely outweighs typing in 1200 paper surveys. I think the time trade-off is in favor of [the tool]."*

They also argued,

> *"Using [the tool] might not take longer than doing it in Word, because creating, resizing, moving and aligning so many boxes in Word can be very challenging."*

Finally, we noticed that participants' thought processes were frequently shaped by the software that they use. For example, participants told us, *"I would do this as a table in Word"* or *"I use boxes because creating bubbles in Word is a nightmare."* When asked to design a survey using our prototype, they again thought in terms of the tool's features, *"Yesterday I would have said to use a handwritten number. Now, I would use bubble tallies."* Participants' experiences using our tool suggest that using software that encourages them to think in terms of digitization could change survey designers' perspectives and increase their awareness of digitization.

2. Field work: Collecting Data from Target Communities

In the second phase of the paper-digital lifecycle, paper surveys are used by field workers to collect data from target communities. Our findings highlight both the benefits and challenges of paper-based data collection. Although paper does not require power or Internet connectivity, field workers who use paper still face a variety of social and infrastructural challenges. In addition, despite working hard to design understandable surveys that are appropriate for use by field workers, many participants admitted that they do not fully understand the complexities of conducting field work in low-resource settings.

2a: Field workers conducting surveys in low-resource settings face infrastructural and social challenges

One of the primary benefits of using paper surveys to collect data in low-resource settings is that recording data on paper does not require electricity or Internet connectivity. However, the printed paper surveys still need be transported to target communities, and limited transportation infrastructure means that field workers frequently travel on foot, which can make it difficult for them to carry a large number of paper surveys:

> *"Our clinic assistant takes these binders, puts them in a suitcase and rolls them to our office. And then if something is missing she has to take them back. And they go back and forth. It's terrible. This poor girl...it's an enormous suitcase full of binders."*

In addition, field workers may also face social challenges operating within target communities. Participants reported that field workers would sometimes feel unwelcome or uncomfortable asking questions of a personally sensitive nature, and they expressed sympathy for the field workers:

> *"They are out in the field, having people slam doors in their face and telling them to go away. If they are interacting with somebody who is getting fidgety or bored, I imagine they would want to skip questions or rush through questions that have lots of options."*

However, although the physical properties of paper do make it feasible for field workers to skip questions or sections of the survey, this behavior is not desirable from the perspective of the researchers and practitioners since it would result in incomplete or missing data. Moreover, several participants told us that field workers frequently repurpose parts of the physical paper as they see fit. In one case, a field worker crossed out a particular question, wrote in a different question, and then recorded an answer to the new, handwritten question (see Figure 5). Again, although modifications like these are relatively easy to make on paper, they have not been intended or approved by the survey designer, and almost certainly complicate the data entry, since the value recorded on the paper no longer corresponds to the value expected by the digital entry form. To resolve these kinds of issues, participants expressed that it would be preferable to digitize the data in the field so that they could ask field workers clarifying questions if necessary.

2b: Survey designers may not fully understand the complexities of field work in low-resource settings

Although our participants spend substantial amounts of time thinking about the work performed in the field, several acknowledged that they had never met the field workers and

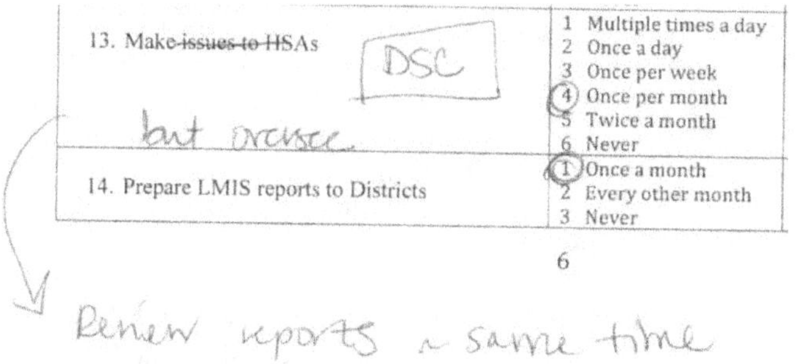

Figure 5. Part of a survey that shows how field workers can take advantage of paper's flexibility, which may make data entry challenging. In this case, a field worker repurposed part of the survey to record something new that the data entry worker may not be able to transcribe.

did not fully understand their backgrounds or perspectives. This lack of understanding sometimes leads to a mismatch between the expectations of the researcher/practitioner and the capabilities of the field workers. For example, when we asked one participant if field workers had trouble filling out her complex survey, she told us, *"They're used to filling out complex registers,"* although she later revealed that *"60% of [the field workers] couldn't do it after two days of training."* In addition, several participants were concerned about the quality of their field workers and the potential for fraudulent data [1] and many expressed a desire to monitor field workers and track their progress as the data is collected.

Finally, participants described how there are frequently events that occur in the field that cannot be anticipated or predicted. Since our study focuses on analyzing paper-digital workflows from the perspective of the survey designers, additional research is necessary to comprehensively analyze the complexities of field work in low-resource settings.

3. Data Entry: Transcribing Data from Paper Surveys

All of our participants hire data entry workers to manually transcribe paper-based data into digital formats and identified data entry as a major bottleneck in their workflows. Participants described how intermittent power and unreliable connectivity complicate data entry and communication. However, despite these challenges, data entry workers receive less attention and training than field workers. Instead, researchers and practitioners attempt to control the data entry process by constraining the values that may be entered and by employing time intensive quality control techniques.

3a: Unreliable electricity and intermittent connectivity complicate the process of entering and communicating data

Many participants explained how unreliable electricity and intermittent Internet connectivity can complicate the process of transcribing data into digital formats:

> *"There is limited electricity and Internet in the data entry offices. They mostly use desktops, so when the power is out, they can't do data entry, and when the Internet is down, they can't enter data using REDCap."*

Our participants predominantly use two software tools to store their entered data: Microsoft Access and REDCap[4]. The benefit of using REDCap is that data is entered directly into an online database. This simplifies the synchronization of digitized data between offices in different locations, and allows stakeholders in other countries to view or analyze the data as soon as it has been entered. However, entering data into REDCap requires continuous access to the Internet, which means that if there is no connectivity, data entry workers are unable to enter any data. By contrast, Access is often chosen because it is capable of running locally on the data entry worker's computer, which means that (s)he can still enter data in the absence of an Internet connection. However, using Access complicates the process of synchronizing and communicating the data to remote researchers and practitioners:

> *"After entering the data, [the data entry worker] zips the database and uploads it to Google docs. It's awful. I wrote out step by step how to zip it. A real issue for us is figuring out how to get data back in a secure way."*

This finding illustrates how even digital information can be difficult to store and communicate in low-resource settings. In addition, in some situations, organizations do not have sufficient resources to perform data entry in the target country. Instead, several participants described how they outsource the data entry to external companies, which may introduce additional challenges:

> *"I know that for a paper survey that we worked on in Mexico, we ended up scanning all the surveys to somewhere in Thailand, and these Thai workers were inputting Spanish into their computers."*

3b: Survey designers may not fully appreciate the challenges of performing data entry in low-resource settings

Our findings reveal a mismatch between the expectations of the survey designers and the constraints experienced by data entry workers. Many survey designers assume that data entry is a relatively simple task that should happen seamlessly, with one participant describing the data entry worker as *"the comfy data person, sitting in an office, sipping a beverage."* However, in contrast to the assumption that data entry workers simply sit in front of a computer all day, we discovered that in fact data entry workers are often responsible for an array of additional tasks, such as preparing surveys for field workers, collecting and transporting completed surveys to the data entry office, communicating with field workers to resolve discrepancies, filing surveys for safekeeping, and preparing reports.

Moreover, all of our participants prioritized the needs of the field workers over the needs of the data entry workers, with most reporting that their field workers are usually well-trained and informed about the project's objectives so that they are motivated to collect good quality data:

> *"We try to set up the environment with high standards. Having a passion for the data they are collecting will help ensure the quality of data is high."*

[4]REDCap is an open-source cloud-based tool designed for research.

By contrast, when we asked if data entry workers understood the project's objectives, several participants told us that *"there really isn't any need for them to know about the goals of the project."* In addition, several participants admitted that they were unaware of how long it takes workers to enter data:

> *"I don't know how long it takes them to enter one of these forms. At one point I heard some number that was a little bit frightening."*

Given the lack of attention afforded the data entry workers, it is perhaps not surprising that the organizations in our study find it difficult to recruit and retain good data entry workers:

> *"We've had high turnover with data entry people. Data entry is a tedious job, it is boring, and so it's tough to get someone who wants to do it and wants to do it well."*

3c: Survey designers try to ensure data accuracy by constraining the values that may be entered and by employing time intensive quality control techniques.

Maximizing the accuracy of entered data is a priority for our participants and they described a variety of strategies that they use to ensure entered data is complete and correct. For example, many participants spend a large amount of time designing the data entry interface to look as much like the paper survey as possible. This allows data entry workers to more easily find the correct digital entry box for each value that they see on the paper, although it complicates the process of creating the digital data entry forms:

> *"After this paper survey was already designed, it took me about four months to recreate the survey in Microsoft Access. It took forever. It's a huge process."*

Moreover, many participants constrain the values that can be input into the database using pre-populated dropdown menus and complex validation rules:

> *"We have data validation, so when she's typing something in, if she says someone is 200 years old, it won't let her move on. But [setting up this validation] takes incredible amounts of work."*

However, despite constraining the values that may be entered by data entry workers, many participants still experience significant issues with the accuracy of entered data. To reduce these issues, data entry workers also spend substantial amounts of time and energy doing quality control. Some organizations use double data entry, which requires that each survey be transcribed twice. Alternatively, some participants described using a technique called *"line-listing,"* which involves holding the paper next to the screen and visually scanning the paper and digital data for discrepancies. One participant said that this process can add weeks of delay and that, in general, quality control is another major bottleneck.

Finally, in addition to transcribing data from paper surveys, data entry workers are often also responsible for finding and correcting data collection errors that have been made by the field workers. In some cases, this can be relatively simple, such as correcting spelling mistakes, while in others, the data entry worker is required to locate and communicate with the field worker in question before they can proceed with the data entry. Several participants also described the data entry workers as being *"at the mercy"* of the field workers. Illegible handwriting results in additional challenges for the data entry workers who have to decipher what has been written on the paper. Deciding the best way to resolve these issues is subjective and may result in additional stress for the designers and/or data entry workers.

4. Analysis and Storage: Making Sense of the Data

The reason for investing so much time and effort to gather data from target communities is so that researchers and practitioners can perform analyses to understand their impact, answer research questions and generate reports for stakeholders. Our analysis of this phase of the workflow highlights that it is challenging for organizations to quickly communicate digitized data to geographically dispersed team members for analysis and visualization. In addition, organizations often expend valuable resources to securely store paper surveys even after the data has been digitized.

4a: Communicating digitized data to geographically dispersed stakeholders is challenging

Our findings reveal several challenges that affect the synchronization and communication of digitized data between workers located in different countries. Many participants described that slow or unreliable Internet connectivity frequently delays the transmission of data from field offices in target countries to US-based offices where the analysis is performed. One participant shared that her organization uses software from Tableau to analyze data and create reports for stakeholders. However, since Tableau is relatively expensive, her organization purchased only a single license for the software, and, since the license is located in their Seattle office, the data must be communicated from the Mozambique office to the Seattle office before it can be analyzed. In addition, the paper surveys from which the data has been digitized are in Portuguese, and the Seattle-based worker who performs the analysis does not speak or understand Portuguese. However, she described,

> *"As it stands, you have the Portuguese version that they do data entry in, but the background code is in English. So then when we extract it, we have set up Tableau so that it feeds into the right worksheets in Tableau. So I see only numbers, and because the code is in English, I see that, oh, they have entered this into the tetanus field."*

Finally, after completing the analysis in Tableau, the Seattle-based worker emails a pdf of the results to her colleagues in Mozambique once a month.

4b: It is difficult for organizations to securely store large quantities of paper-based surveys

Many organizations keep all their paper materials for reference and/or safekeeping and, although the materiality of paper makes it easy to use in the field, it is unarguably more challenging to store than digital data:

> *"There are literally rooms where it's just stacked ceiling to floor with old study surveys. And we have to get grants to get new space to store all the old surveys. It's tough. But that's what we do. This is a lot of very personal data.*

I have to spend hours blacking out people's names and personal identifiers. These are kids with HIV."

DISCUSSION

Having presented a close look at paper-digital workflows across the four stages of design, field work, digitization, and analysis, we now synthesize our findings to offer the following takeaways. First, we show that *both* paper and digital materials play vital roles in global development workflows and are necessary if these organizations are to operate effectively in target communities. Second, we show that, in the workflows we examine, the challenges of transitioning data between paper and digital materials reveal opportunities to design new tools to ease the burden of digitization. Third, we aim to increase awareness of the disconnectedness in global development workflows that largely results from geographical, cultural and socioeconomic differences that can only be understood, not eliminated. Finally, we argue that our findings are relevant for development initiatives across domains.

Paper and Computer Supported Cooperative Work

We find that global development work relies on essential affordances provided by both paper and digital materials, and argue that the two *must* coexist if these organizations are to successfully navigate the hurdles posed by poor infrastructure, low connectivity, cultural differences, and other socioeconomic constraints. Paper is cheap, easy to use in almost any environment, and provides stakeholders with visible and material evidence of data collected. However, in contrast to digital data, which can be stored in vast quantities with relative ease, paper materials must be transported by people and stored in warehouses. It is difficult to imagine how any organization would go about storing and navigating tera- or even gigabytes of paper-based data. In reality, many of the complex analyses and visualizations that help organizations to make sense of the data they collect are only feasible if it is in communicable, searchable and mutable digital formats.

However, our findings also show that global development organizations must pay attention to the material properties of digital data, since *"bits cannot escape the material constraints of the physical devices that manipulate, store and exchange them"* [2]. Organizations must purchase and maintain digital devices for their workers, which may introduce additional challenges. Several of our participants had previously tried providing field workers with laptops or tablets to collect data in digital formats. However, in many socioeconomically disadvantaged communities, possessing an expensive digital device could have social implications for field workers' relationships with local communities that may be unfamiliar or suspicious of new technologies. The material value of digital devices also makes them a target for theft, as described (in all seriousness) by one participant:

"In a previous survey that I worked on, it was not safe to send field workers out with tablets. It would be like, "please have them - steal them - I'm taking them around your village, I don't care about them." We couldn't send [field workers] out with technology."

Finally, infrastructural challenges also affect organizations' abilities to communicate and synchronize digital materials. According to Blanchette, people in resource-rich environments may assume that *"digital information can be reproduced and distributed at negligible cost and high speed, and thus, is immune to the economics and logistics of analog media"* [2]. We find that this is certainly not the case for global development organizations in low-resource environments, where intermittent electricity, poor Internet connectivity and costly data transmission may make the communication of digital materials expensive, slow and unreliable.

In summary, the reliance on both paper and digital materials, and the challenges of effectively coordinating the paper-digital lifecycle, suggest a need for further research that explores how to better support the complex and highly collaborative workflows that drive global development.

Opportunities for Design

One goal of our work was to probe participants' reactions to the idea of optimizing surveys for machine-readability and digitization. In particular, we wanted to investigate if survey designers at the top of the workflow may be willing to change their design practices, and potentially perform more work, to simplify the data entry process further down the workflow.

Researchers and practitioners currently view the process of transitioning information from paper surveys to digital formats as a major bottleneck in their workflow. They also expressed frustration with the tools that they currently use to design surveys and are willing to try new alternatives, even if they take time to learn or disrupt their existing workflows (several participants have already spent months searching for viable alternatives to Word). This suggests an opportunity to design new tools that ease the pain of converting digital to paper, and paper to digital. In the context of global development organizations, we found that survey design tools need to be affordable, provide creative control over the appearance of surveys, and be easily accessible by team members in multiple countries. Our prototype design probe (see Figure 1) appears to meet these criteria and provides a starting point on which to base the design of a new tool for creating surveys. In fact, shortly after we completed our study, we discovered that one of our participants had independently used the tool (which is freely available online) to design several surveys for an ongoing project in Tanzania.

Optimizing surveys for machine-readability would undoubtedly impact the entire paper-digital workflow. In the design phase, since designers think in terms of the software they are using, a tool that encourages them to optimize for digitization could shape their thought processes and increase their awareness of the digitization process. In the field work phase, filling in machine-readable surveys could create additional work, since field workers may need to complete surveys more neatly to ensure they are accurately interpreted by software. This, in combination with the visual appearance of the survey, could also make field workers more aware that collected data needs to be digitized. In the data entry phase, the majority of workers' time would no longer be spent typing data from paper into a computer. Instead, workers would be responsible for scanning the surveys, double-checking the interpretation of critical fields, and transcribing the few data items that are not machine-readable. Several participants also suggested that they would teach the data entry workers to perform simple, immediate analyses on the data so that they could monitor the field workers and identify problems. Thus, optimizing surveys for machine-readability could improve the digitization bottleneck in two ways: first, by automatically interpreting machine-readable data, and second, by making *all* workers more aware of the digitization process.

Cross-Cultural Cooperative Work

Successfully coordinating work processes across multiple geographies and cultures poses several challenges for global development organizations. In particular, the four distinct phases of the paper-digital lifecycle that we examined suggest that these workflows are somewhat disconnected. Remote locations, infrastructural challenges, cultural differences and changing time zones all exacerbate this problem. Field workers are trained to understand the importance of collecting data from target communities, but not the challenges associated with digitizing the collected data. Data entry workers are expected to seamlessly digitize large numbers of paper surveys without understanding the broader implications of their work. Survey designers often do not understand the perspectives of the field and data entry workers, and may have misplaced expectations or not fully appreciate the constraints experienced by their remote colleagues.

We also find that the nature of workers' roles within global, cross-cultural workflows are, to borrow from Massey, subject to *"a highly complex social differentiation. There are differences in the degree of movement and communication, but also in the degree of control and initiation"* [24]. Researchers and practitioners have a higher degree of control than field workers, who have a higher degree of control than data entry workers. This hierarchical structure impacts the resulting attitudes of and relationships between workers in a variety of ways. For example, our findings reveal disparities between the realities of data entry work and the desires and expectations of researchers and practitioners. Our participants frequently expected the data entry process to be seamless, and expressed frustration and confusion as to why data entry workers found it difficult when *"all they have to do is type this stuff in."* They frequently attributed delays in data entry to the workers' backgrounds and attitudes, rather than the challenging nature of the work, with one commenting that *"it turns out data entry in Malawi is not super-accurate."* Another participant commented that when she performed data entry, she would *"turn on techno and move through it."* Though this tactic may work for her, it may not necessarily help data entry workers operating in remote locations, who may be struggling with computer safety issues, intermittent electricity, and poor Internet connectivity.

Although we have limited our analysis of cross-cultural issues to those that specifically affect the paper-digital workflow, our findings highlight rich opportunities for future research that focuses on more fully understanding the impact of culture in global development work. In addition, the differences in backgrounds, experiences and attitudes of culturally diverse workers suggest that it may be beneficial to increase workers' awareness of their cultural and social differences. Although it may not be possible to entirely overcome these differences, our paper contributes to a greater awareness of such challenges, in the belief that a greater awareness can strengthen work processes and practices.

Limitations and Generalizability

Our paper provides a close look at the challenges presented by the relevance of paper and the desirability of digitization in the context of global development workflows. Since our participants were all engaged in development work but drawn from a wide range of organizations and a variety of domains, we argue that our findings are domain-independent, and researchers and practitioners engaged in multi-country, cross-cultural research in any aspect of development could benefit from our work. In addition, by offering a comprehensive examination of the various abstract types of survey questions and how they can be optimized for digitization, we aim to be of help to survey designers as well.

Some of our findings may also hold for collaborative work outside the field of development. Commenting on these, however, lies outside the scope of our paper. We do stress that the workflow challenges that accompany global, cross-cultural research in general are exacerbated when low-resource environments are involved. For example, linguistic barriers can impact non-development work as well. However, when they are additionally accompanied by low literacy and awareness, the situation is much worsened. Finally, we study paper-digital workflows from the perspective of researchers and practitioners responsible for driving global development initiatives. On-going research is exploring additional issues from the perspective of other stakeholders.

CONCLUSION

This paper presents a study of the collaborative practices surrounding paper-digital workflows as enacted by organizations engaged in global development initiatives. We used a mixed methods approach to examine these workflows that span cultures and geographies, organizing our findings according to the different stages of data as it is sought, collected, digitized, and analyzed. We highlight the tensions that arise between the ubiquitousness of paper and the desirability of digitized data, also discussing the inherent affordances of paper and digital materials, and contribute a nuanced understanding of the accompanying challenges and tradeoffs. Taken together, our findings could influence the design of new tools that aim to bridge the gap between paper and digital materials in the context of global development. In addition, our findings will be useful for survey designers, researchers and practitioners interested in global, cross-cultural research and practice.

ACKNOWLEDGEMENTS

This work was funded by NSF Grant 1111433 and a Facebook Graduate Fellowship. We thank all our participants and the anonymous reviewers for their valuable feedback.

REFERENCES

1. Birnbaum, B., Borriello, G., Flaxman, A. D., DeRenzi, B., and Karlin, A. R. Using behavioral data to identify interviewer fabrication in surveys. In *SIGCHI Conference on Human Factors in Computing Systems*, CHI '13 (2013), 2911–2920.
2. Blanchette, J.-F. A material history of bits. *J. Am. Soc. Inf. Sci. Technol. 62*, 6 (June 2011), 1042–1057.
3. Bondarenko, O., and Janssen, R. Documents at hand: Learning from paper to improve digital technologies. In *SIGCHI Conference on Human Factors in Computing Systems*, CHI '05 (2005), 121–130.
4. Bossen, C., and Jensen, L. G. How physicians 'achieve overview': A case-based study in a hospital ward. In *ACM Conference on Computer Supported Cooperative Work & Social Computing*, CSCW '14 (2014), 257–268.
5. Captricity. http://captricity.com/.
6. Chen, K., Kannan, A., Yano, Y., Hellerstein, J., and Parikh, T. Shreddr: pipelined paper digitization for low-resource organizations. In *ACM Conference on Computing for Development* (2012).
7. Dell, N., Breit, N., Chaluco, T., Crawford, J., and Borriello, G. Digitizing paper forms with mobile imaging technologies. In *ACM Conference on Computing for Development* (2012).
8. Dell, N., Crawford, J., Breit, N., Chaluco, T., Coelho, A., McCord, J., and Borriello, G. Integrating ODK Scan into the Community Health Worker Supply Chain in Mozambique. In *International Conference on Information and Communication Technologies and Development*, ICTD '13 (2013), 228–237.
9. Dymetman, M., and Copperman, M. Intelligent paper. *Electronic Publishing, Artistic Imaging, and Digital Typography* (1998), 392–406.
10. Fitzpatrick, G. Integrated care and the working record. *Health Informatics Journal 10*, 4 (2004), 291–302.
11. Fitzpatrick, G., and Ellingsen, G. A review of 25 years of cscw research in healthcare: Contributions, challenges and future agendas. *Computer Supported Cooperative Work (CSCW) 22*, 4-6 (2013), 609–665.
12. Gaver, B., Dunne, T., and Pacenti, E. Design: Cultural probes. *interactions 6*, 1 (Jan. 1999), 21–29.
13. Guimbretière, F. Paper augmented digital documents. In *ACM Symposium on User Interface Software and Technology (UIST)* (2003), 51–60.
14. Gupta, A. *Red Tape: Bureaucracy, Structural Violence, and Poverty in India*. Duke University Press, Durham, NC, 2012.
15. Haller, M., Leitner, J., Seifried, T., Wallace, J. R., Scott, S. D., Richter, C., Brandl, P., Gokcezade, A., and Hunter, S. The nice discussion room: Integrating paper and digital media to support co-located group meetings. In *SIGCHI Conference on Human Factors in Computing Systems*, CHI '10 (2010), 609–618.
16. Harper, R., and Sellen, A. Paper-supported collaborative work. *Rank Xerox Research Centre, Cambridge Laboratory* (1995).
17. Heiner, J. M., Hudson, S. E., and Tanaka, K. Linking and messaging from real paper in the paper pda. In *ACM Symposium on User Interface Software and Technology (UIST)* (1999), 179–186.
18. Hinds, P., and McGrath, C. Structures that work: Social structure, work structure and coordination ease in geographically distributed teams. In *ACM Conference on Computer Supported Cooperative Work*, CSCW '06 (2006), 343–352.
19. Hull, M. Documents and Bureaucracy. *Annual Review of Anthropology 41* (2012), 251–267.
20. Johnson, W., Jellinek, H., Leigh Klotz, J., Rao, R., and Card, S. Bridging the paper and electronic worlds: the paper user interface. In *ACM SIGCHI Conference on Human factors in computing systems* (1993), 507–512.
21. Kolko, B. E., Hope, A., Brunette, W., Saville, K., Gerard, W., Kawooya, M., and Nathan, R. Adapting collaborative radiological practice to low-resource environments. In *ACM Conference on Computer Supported Cooperative Work*, CSCW '12 (2012), 97–106.
22. Luff, P., Heath, C., and Greatbatch, D. Tasks-in-interaction: Paper and screen based documentation in collaborative activity. In *ACM Conference on Computer-supported Cooperative Work*, CSCW '92 (1992), 163–170.
23. Luff, P., Heath, C., Norrie, M., Signer, B., and Herdman, P. Only touching the surface: Creating affinities between digital content and paper. In *ACM Conference on Computer Supported Cooperative Work*, CSCW '04 (2004), 523–532.
24. Massey, D. A global sense of place. *Marxism today 35*, 6 (1991), 24–29.
25. Medhi, I., Tewari, A., Jain, M., and Cutrell, E. The Fate of a Digital Slate: Unexpected Issues with Deployment in Rural India. *User Experience Magazine 11*, 2 (2012).
26. Parikh, T., Javid, P., Sasikumar, K., Dhosh, K., and Toyama, K. Mobile Phones and Paper Documents: Evaluating a New Approach for Capturing Microfinance Data in Rural India. In *ACM SIGCHI Conference on Human factors in computing systems* (2006), 551–560.
27. Piper, A. M., Weibel, N., and Hollan, J. D. Introducing multimodal paper-digital interfaces for speech-language therapy. In *ACM SIGACCESS Conference on Computers and Accessibility*, ASSETS '10 (2010), 203–210.
28. Ratan, A., Chakraborty, S., Chitnis, P., Toyama, K., Ooi, K., Phiong, M., and Koenig, M. Managing Microfinance with Paper, Pen and Digital Slate. In *International Conference on Information and Communication Technologies and Development (ICTD)* (2010).
29. Rosner, D., and Ames, M. Designing for repair?: Infrastructures and materialities of breakdown. In *ACM Conference on Computer Supported Cooperative Work and Social Computing*, CSCW '14 (2014), 319–331.
30. Rosner, D. K. The material practices of collaboration. In *ACM Conference on Computer Supported Cooperative Work*, CSCW '12 (2012), 1155–1164.
31. Schmidt, K. The critical role of workplace studies in cscw. In *Workplace Studies: Recovering Work Practice and Informing System Design*, University Press (2000), 141–149.
32. Sellen, A. J., and Harper, R. H. *The Myth of the Paperless Office*. MIT Press, Cambridge, MA, USA, 2003.
33. Singh, G., Findlater, L., Toyama, K., Helmer, S., Gandhi, R., and Balakrishnan, R. Numeric Paper Forms for NGOs. In *International Conference on Information and Communication Technologies and Development (ICTD)* (2009).
34. Tabard, A., Mackay, W. E., and Eastmond, E. From individual to collaborative: The evolution of prism, a hybrid laboratory notebook. In *ACM Conference on Computer Supported Cooperative Work*, CSCW '08 (2008), 569–578.
35. Underwood, H., Sterling, R., and Bennett, J. The Design and Implementation of the PartoPen Maternal Health Monitoring System. In *ACM Conference on Computing for Development* (2013).
36. Veeraraghavan, R. Dealing with the digital panopticon: The use and subversion of ict in an indian bureaucracy. In *International Conference on Information and Communication Technologies and Development*, ICTD '13 (2013), 248–255.
37. Wellner, P. Interacting with paper on the DigitalDesk. *Communications of the ACM 36* (1993), 87–96.

KrishiPustak: A Social Networking System for Low-Literate Farmers

Indrani Medhi-Thies[1], Pedro Ferreira[2], Nakull Gupta[1], Jacki O'Neill[1], Edward Cutrell[1]

[1]Microsoft Research, Bangalore, India
{indranim, t-nakgup, jacki.oneill, cutrell}@microsoft.com

[2]Mobile Life @ KTH, Kista, Sweden
i@pedropaf.com

ABSTRACT

With the wide penetration of mobile internet, social networking (SN) systems are becoming increasingly popular in the developing world. However, most SN sites are text heavy, and are therefore unusable by low-literate populations. Here we ask what would an SN application for low-literate users look like and how would it be used? We designed and deployed *KrishiPustak*, an audio-visual SN mobile application for low-literate farming populations in rural India. Over a four month deployment, 306 farmers registered through the phones of eight agricultural mediators making 514 posts and 180 replies. We conducted interviews with farmers and mediators and analyzed the content to understand system usage and to drive iterative design. The context of mediated use and agricultural framing had a powerful impact on system understanding (what it was for) and usage. Overall, *KrishiPustak* was useful and usable, but none-the-less we identify a number of design recommendations for similar SN systems.

Author Keywords

Social media; ICTD; low-literate; HCI4D; India

ACM Classification Keywords

H.5.m. Information interfaces and presentation (e.g., HCI):

INTRODUCTION

As of 2014 there were 6.9 billion mobile phone accounts in the world and 78% of the subscribers lived in developing countries [18]. Beyond facilitating communication, mobile phones have transformed the way we send money, manage our health, check market prices, engage with government, manage emergency response, and many other things. Along with the wide penetration of mobile phones, mobile internet is becoming increasingly affordable. For example in India, Aircel's 'pocket internet' offers 25 Megabytes for USD 0.083, valid for one day [2]. Studies conducted among low-income youth in slum communities in India found that they were accessing social networking (SN) sites such as

CSCW '15, March 14–18 2015, Vancouver, BC, Canada
Copyright 2014 ACM 978-1-4503-2922-4/15/03…$15.00
http://dx.doi.org/10.1145/2675133.2675224

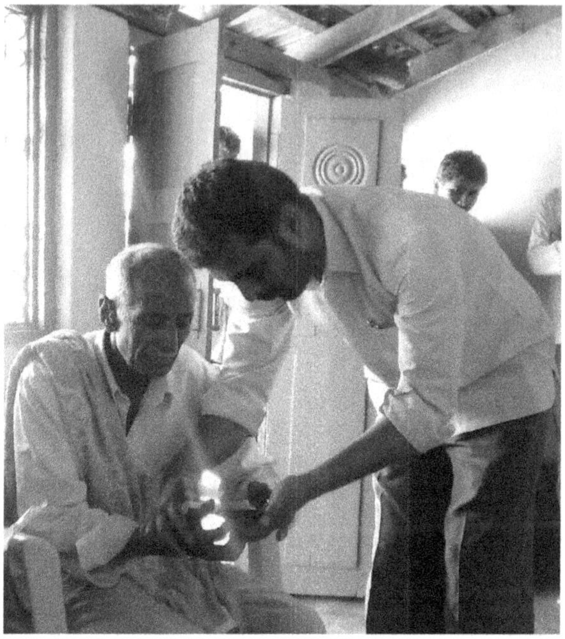

Figure 1: Farmer using *KrishiPustak* with the help of a mediator

Facebook and Orkut within the first month of mobile internet usage [47].

Currently there are a number of popular SN sites that offer users an online presence: Facebook, Twitter, Orkut, Google+, Pinterest, Instagram, etc. However, most of these sites rely heavily on text, and are therefore unusable by low-literate populations. This led us to ask: Is it possible to have a social networking system for low-literate users? Is the notion useful or interesting? What would the application look like? How would it be used? How would content be shared and viewed?

Other obstacles to the use of SN systems by low-income populations include the cost of devices and network activity, and digital literacy. While the cost of mobile devices and connectivity is decreasing, smartphones capable of running non-textual apps usable by low-literate communities are still out of the reach of most very low-income people. To meet constraints in literacy and the availability of devices, a common work-around we see is for non-literate or poor members of a community to seek help from someone who has access to technology and is more digitally-literate [52] (see Fig. 1). This mediated use of technology can amplify its use to many people in the community who would otherwise not be able to use it. So, in addition to the above questions related to the design of an SN application for low-literacy, we wanted to know if we could design the system to work through a human mediator.

To answer these questions, we designed, deployed, and evaluated *KrishiPustak*, an audio-visual SN mobile application that we distributed to low-literate farming communities in a rural area near Mysore, India. We followed a multistage process that included: design and deployment, user testing and discussion, redesign and deployment, and follow-up user testing. *KrishiPustak* was deployed on Nokia Lumia 820 phones via eight agriculture extension workers serving as mediators. Over a period of four months, mediators registered 306 farmers who made 514 posts and 180 replies. We conducted two rounds of user evaluations, including interviews with mediators and farmers as well as an analysis of the content of posts. In this paper, we describe the design and evolution of the system, as well as how *KrishiPustak* was used by farmers. In particular, we found that the context of mediated use within the agricultural setting strongly influenced how farmers described and used the system. Many posts had a professional theme, including pictures of cows and agricultural fields. Other posts related to families, local grievances, and aspirational content, but since usage of the device was gated by a mediator who was affiliated with an agricultural organization, the propensity for farming related posts is perhaps unsurprising. Results also suggest that the system could be enhanced by the addition of third party content, and UI features for encouraging and maintaining conversations.

Overall, there are two main contributions of our paper. First, we design and develop *KrishiPustak*, an audio-visual SN mobile application, and demonstrate through a four months pilot deployment that the interface worked for our target users. Low-literate farmers were able to post and comment on the application through mediated use. Secondly, our study shows potential use cases and demand for SN systems for low-literate users in rural settings.

RELATED WORK

There are three areas of related literature that are particularly relevant for our purposes: UX for social networking, UIs for low-literate users, and intermediated technology use in low-income contexts.

Social networking user experience

With some notable exceptions [12, 58, 59], most research in the use of SN systems is with populations in North America and Europe. Previous work in this area attempted to find a formal definition, describing SN systems as networked communication platforms in which participants 1) have uniquely identifiable profiles that consist of user-supplied content, content provided by other users, and/or system-provided data; 2) can publicly articulate connections that can be viewed and traversed by others; and 3) can consume, produce, and/or interact with streams of user generated content provided by their connections on the site [9].

A number of related studies have investigated why people use SN sites like MySpace and Facebook (e.g. [5] [25] [56]). Research suggests that Facebook use is motivated by two primary needs: (1) the need to belong and (2) the need for self-presentation [35]. People get on to and use social networking sites for social connection, shared identities, content, social investigation, SN surfing, and status updating [19]. Users' motivations, use and perceptions may change over time [24]. Research into social media use, particularly MySpace, in rural life found differences between rural and urban users. Rural users had far fewer friends online, and those friends lived much closer to home. Rural users also have substantially different gender distributions and use privacy features more heavily [12]. Other research focuses specifically on SN systems on the mobile phone [e.g. 13]. Of relevance here is the research developing Facebook clients to enable offline access by prefetching content [60].

SN systems have also been used in a more instrumental way to achieve some particular end. For example, food sharing communities to prevent food wastage [11], organizing political demonstrations in Palestine [57] or as rich educational aids in Nepal [43].

Research in the use of SN within developing countries is still sparse, mainly examining how existing social networks are used. Two studies of low-income youth in slum communities in India found that within the first month of mobile internet usage, these youth get onto SN sites such as Facebook and Orkut. They argue that SN sites are instrumental in helping young people to transgress social identity and expand social connections and life chances [47, 48]. Another study discusses the usage of Facebook in Kenya where social media participation is growing, but describes how limits in technical infrastructure and uneven access put constraints on use. They show that high costs associated with using the internet, limited access to computers and smartphones, and unreliable electricity hinder online participation [59]. In another study, researchers found that to overcome the costs associated with internet use, young adults in informal settlements in Kenya consolidated diverse online activities to support income generation, e.g., looking for employment, marketing themselves, and seeking remittances from friends and family abroad [58].

To our knowledge, our study is the first to design, develop, deploy and evaluate a new (prototype) SN system for low-literate, resource constrained users in the developing world.

UIs for low-literate users

Research in the design of UIs for users with little or no education is a growing body of work. Early work in this area recognized the value of imagery and advocated the extensive use of graphics to overcome users' inability to read text [14, 17, 29, 36]. Work in "Text-Free UIs" established that static, hand-drawn representations are better understood than photographs or abstract iconography. But with deeper interaction and an increase in the specificity of information represented, more photorealism can be helpful [32]. Among other features, some authors note that numbers can be acceptable as many low-literate people can read and understand numerical digits. Researchers have also recognized the value of combining voice feedback with graphical imagery [29, 36, 37, 44]. Krishi Mitra [50] is a prototype UI for low-literate rural farmers to access market information without having to go through a middle man. Like our system, it is virtually text-free, with audio-visual cues for navigation. As it is an information access system, however, it has a rather different purpose and functionality, e.g. it does not enable content creation and sharing between farmers.

Beyond navigation and content consumption, one interaction issue for UI's for low literate users is how to manage access. Various studies have investigated how passwords might be implemented for such users. Relevant to our work, previous research shows that both pictorial and numeric passwords can be difficult for low-literate users [22, 45]. Indeed, to our knowledge an optimal solution has not yet been found, and this remains an important area of research.

One body of research on interfaces for low literate users looks at voice as an interaction modality because it is a natural means of expression well-suited to input, and avoids some of the issues related to non-literacy. [1, 8, 23, 34, 40, 49, 53]. Particularly relevant for our context are a Q&A forum for small-scale farmers [40] and a citizen journalism portal for rural users [34]. Researchers have examined the tradeoffs between IVRs (spoken menu output with DTMF/keypad input navigation) and spoken dialogue systems (SDS) (spoken menu output with speech input navigation) and have reached varying conclusions regarding the benefits of typed versus spoken inputs [15,54]. There is also research that identifies design principles for voice-based virtual communities [38]. However, speech input is technically challenging to implement [33] and challenges in voice UIs include threading content, indexing, searching, and browsing. To overcome some of these difficulties, the VideoKheti system combined speech input, graphics, audio output, and touch to address farmers' information needs. However, the addition of speech input did not provide much assistance over a graphical touch system with audio output for low-literate farmers [6].

Finally there is work that explores the suitability of menu-based navigation for low-literate users [20, 21]. Researchers have compared linear, hierarchical and cross-linked navigation [4], and linear, and hierarchical navigation with varying depths [30, 31] and have found that users perform better with linear structures where items are listed as a flat array on one or more pages.

Research in the area of UIs for low-literate users have spanned multiple application domains, including agriculture, citizen journalism, health data collection and dissemination, job information, video search, mobile banking, microfinance, map navigation, video communication and so on. However, to our knowledge there has been no previous work in SN for low-literate users.

Technology and intermediation in low-income contexts

As noted in the introduction, *intermediation* is a common work-around in low-income areas to meet constraints in literacy and the availability of technology. Non-literate or poor members of a community will seek help from individuals in the community who either have access to technology (e.g., ownership) or are more digitally-literate (e.g., a friend or relative who can read or knows how to use a device) [52]. In their study of technology usage and mobile media sharing in low-income communities in India, Sambasivan and Smyth analyze shared social norms and practices, flows of information and materials, and the creative processes that underlie existing information access through a human infrastructure. They argue that technological interventions will be more effective if they take into consideration the underlying infrastructures such as intermediation that are embedded in communities [51].

Some notable projects which rely heavily on human infrastructure include: DakNet (human transport networks - busses, motorcycles, ox carts) [42]; MOSES (Groups of kiosk users) [55]; Digital Green (farmers and villagers in close-knit communities) [10]; data entry accuracy using forms, SMS, and voice (Human data entry operations) [41]; and rural mobile health (community health workers and patients) [27, 46].

BACKGROUND, CONTEXT AND TIMELINE

We partnered with two non-profit organizations to deploy *KrishiPustak*: Digital Green (DG) and Bharatiya Agri Industries Foundation (BAIF). DG shares agriculture extension information with small and marginal farmers across villages in India, Ethiopia and Ghana. DG screens videos of farmers demonstrating best practices in farming and animal husbandry relevant for the local context and in the local dialect of that region. Videos typically feature a local progressive farmer explaining and demonstrating an agriculture-related technique. Videos are screened to groups of 15-20 rural farmers by a local mediator [7, 10]. DG primarily works with other organizations to meet the specific needs of farmers in a given area, and BAIF is one of these [3]. BAIF focuses on development intervention programs in animal husbandry and agriculture with 4.5 million poor families and has field operations across 60,000 villages in India. We chose their operations in Mysore district, Karnataka, as the location for our pilot because of close proximity to where we are based and a long partnership with DG. This operation employs field extension staff who work closely with the target farming communities, including the screening of DG videos. All the field extension staff are male. Eight field extension officers from BAIF (henceforth known as 'mediators') at Hunsur in Mysore participated in our study as technology aides to the low-literate farming population. They were pre-selected by BAIF to participate in our study as reliable mediators who had been with the organization for some time. Each of the mediators was given a Nokia Lumia 820 mobile phone with the *KrishiPustak* application installed. They were to register low-literate farmers and help them use the application throughout the pilot study. The villages that mediators worked with were all within about 100 km of Hunsur.

Target Communities

The eight mediators in our study were on-call para-veterinary workers who conducted artificial insemination of domestic cattle. They lived in the same or neighboring villages as the farmer families they worked with. All mediators were male, 23-33 years old, and their education level was between Grade 10 and 12. Household expenditure per year was between USD 500 – 3300. Fluent in local languages such as Kannada and Tamil, they did not speak English, but could understand and read short phrases and used the English alphabet for transliteration of local languages. Each of them used a Nokia X201/202 phone given to them by BAIF for coordinating activities in the field. They used the phones for receiving and making calls, texting in transliterated Kannada, taking pictures, listening to music, watching videos (purchased offline at local mobile shops) and using Facebook. Of the eight mediators, six had Facebook accounts. Most of them had opened their accounts on the PC at the BAIF office, with the help of office staff, thereafter they used Facebook on their mobiles. Most posts and comments to Facebook were made in transliterated Kannada.

The role of the (literate) mediators was to provide technology intermediation – that is access to the technology, support, encouragement and on-the-spot training - to the low-literate farmers who were the end-users of *KrishiPustak*. The eight mediators were asked to register end users who met the following criteria: a) Low levels of

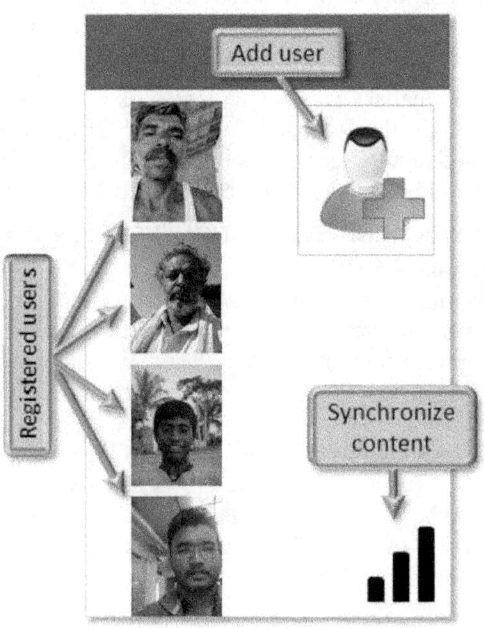

Figure 2: Start page for mediators to select or add users and synchronize content.

formal education (less than Grade 5); b) Little or no experience with mobile phone uses beyond voice calls; and c) No existing SN accounts. For their facilitation of the project, mediators received remuneration in the form of phone talk time. We viewed this as essential as we were asking them to spend time and effort on our project. End users (farmers) did not receive any remuneration; we were explicitly interested in understanding whether farmers would understand the value proposition and take to the use of the system without any economic incentive.

Design constraints

A number of user and system constraints had to be taken into account to design an SN system for low-literate farmers in rural India. 1) End use was mediated. 2) The system was designed for use in settings with intermittent and low-bandwidth internet connectivity. While video content might have provided the system with greater richness, bandwidth limitations made this difficult so only audio and static images were shared. 3) Since the user group was low-literate, audio-visual rather than textual content was used. 4) We wanted to keep the barriers for use low, so we chose to have no password for login. 5) To encourage broader use and critical mass, there were no 'friends'; instead everyone on the network would be connected to everyone else. While this mirrors village life (where everyone knows everyone else), this is an important difference with other popular SN systems where users can publicly articulate connections [9].

Timeline

We followed a multistage design process which consisted of the design and development of a first version of the prototype application. This was deployed for two months from December 2013 to February 2014. This was followed by a round of user testing and interviews in mid-February, which led to the design of prototype version 2. After another four weeks of deployment another round of user testing and interviews were conducted.

PROTOTYPE DESIGN (VERSION 1)

User Interface

We drew inspiration from guidelines for 'Text-Free UIs' [26, 28, 29] and designed an audio-visual application to allow multiple users to create photo or audio posts through their own accounts on a shared smartphone. Users could reply to posts using photos or audio as well. There was no text in the UI, though numerals were used to denote the number of replies to a post. Since there were no 'friends,' anybody who registered on the system could view content from and reply on the posts of all other users. Below we provide some detail of the first version of the *KrishiPustak* application.

Start page

The *KrishiPustak* start page was intended to be used primarily by mediators for managing the accounts of farmers they were working with (see Fig. 2). It comprised a list of user accounts registered on that phone, a button to add a new user ('+' symbol on the top right corner), and an option to synchronize the content on the phone with the

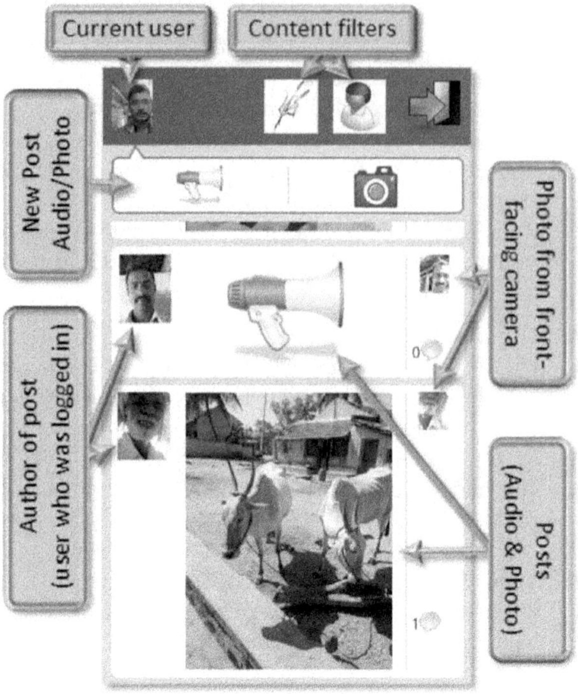

Figure 3: Version 1 consolidated posts page (home page).

server. User accounts were displayed as a list of their profile photographs - clicking on any photo would 'log in' as that user with no authentication. When a mediator wanted to add a new user, they would be sent to a page to record a brief audio message and create a profile photo. The vertical bars on the bottom right corner were used by mediators to synchronize content with the server when internet connectivity was available.

Consolidated posts page

This was the primary "home page" for farmers, where they could view all the posts made on the system (see Fig. 3). The page was divided into three components: a header, a row to make new posts, and a content pane for existing posts. The header consisted of four images: left-most was the user who was currently logged in; on the far right was a 'log out' button; and in between were images of an *agriculture* filter and a *personal* filter. Tapping on these filter buttons would filter posts in the content pane for these categories.

The row to make new posts had a *loudspeaker* button to record an audio post and a *camera* button to make a photo post. Tapping either button directed the user to a page for creating the new post. Before confirming the photo or audio post, the user had to pick a filter: *agriculture* or *personal*. Selecting a category at the time of posting helped other users to filter relevant content on the consolidated posts page.

Similar to other popular SN sites, synchronized posts were displayed on an infinite scroll page and were temporally ordered with the most recent at the top. Each individual post contained three pieces of information. 1) A picture of the author of the post. Tapping on this picture navigated the user to a profile page where he/she could view all the posts made by that author and listen to the recording that they made when they signed up. 2) The actual post content—a rendered photo or an image of a loudspeaker for an audio post. Clicking on the loudspeaker/picture post would send the user to a detailed post view. 3) On the right of the post content was an image of the person who actually made the post, taken from the front-facing camera upon posting. We included this image for two reasons: First, we were interested in how often posts were actually made by mediators (on behalf of users) vs. farmers themselves. Second, because we had no authentication it was relatively easy to accidentally make a post from someone else's account. In this case, the image of the poster would be different from the 'logged-in' user.

Detailed post view page

When users selected a post of interest by tapping on it, they were taken to a page dedicated to that post. This page included the posts' contents (a photo or loudspeaker image played by tapping), all the related replies in an infinite scroll layout, and buttons (*camera* and *loudspeaker*) for posting a reply to that post. Individual replies had the same structure as posts in the consolidated posts page (with some indentation between the post and its replies), including a photo of the reply author taken by the front-facing camera.

System backend

Due to intermittent connectivity and limited bandwidth in rural India, we designed our application to enable seamless offline interactions. Whenever any new content was created during user registration, posting, or replying, an entry was created into a local database and the associated files (audio clips/images) were stored locally. Then, a background process polled for internet connectivity and incrementally synchronized the local content with a database in the cloud. The background process alternated between uploading and downloading content, each in small atomic units to maximize usage of short bursts of connectivity. In addition, in case of problems with the background process there was also a manual option to synchronize content on the start page.

The cloud database was implemented as an Azure Mobile Service, while the local database used SQLite. The actual images and audio recordings were stored outside of the database and hosted on a server using PHP.

DEPLOYMENT AND EVALUATION (VERSION 1)

Training session 1

The deployment of *KrishiPustak* was initiated by a one-day training session attended by eight mediators, one researcher and a Kannada translator. *KrishiPustak* was introduced as a way by which low-literate farmers could connect with each other, similar to Facebook but using photos and audio. The Facebook analogy was used because six of the eight mediators had Facebook accounts, and the others had heard of, but not used, Facebook. The training included a three-hour demonstration of *KrishiPustak* in groups of four mediators, followed by individual practice for one hour each. The translator called each mediator twice a week for the first eight weeks after the training session to encourage them to use the system.

Data collection

We conducted face-to-face interviews with all eight mediators and eleven farmers after two months of deployment. Criteria for recruiting the eleven farmers was they should have used the *KrishiPustak* application at least once and were representative of the *KrishiPustak* user pool across age and gender. Eight of the farmers were male and three female (in keeping with the ratio of male/female clientele of the mediators). They were between 21-71 years of age. The mean age was 44.6 yrs and median was 43 yrs. The mean years of schooling was 1.5. Verbal informed consent was collected before recording the interviews. Respondents could refuse to be interviewed but no one did. All mediator and farmer interviews were conducted in Kannada. They were asked about their experiences while using *KrishiPustak*. All interviews were transcribed and translated into English for analysis; mediator and farmer comments are denoted by M* and F* respectively in the results. To complement the interview data, we also analyzed the content posted on the system.

User testing, version 1

During the almost two months of deployment of version 1, eight mediators registered a total of 256 farmers. We did not collect user metadata or demographics (e.g., age and gender) beyond that required to join the system (photo and introductory statement). Farmers made 374 new posts and 97 replies on the *KrishiPustak* application during the two months. Whilst *KrishiPustak* received a fair amount of use, user testing identified a number of design problems that significantly impacted how the system was used.

Photo information was not enough

To conserve bandwidth, any new post was either a photo or an audio recording. However, it became clear that stand-alone photo posts were not enough to explain what people wanted to share. For example, two of the interviewed farmers had posted pictures of roads they wanted the local government to repair. They wished to say something along with the photo about the inconvenience caused to them due to the road condition, so they created a reply to that effect. Indeed, 40% of 'replies' to posts were created by the authors of the post, and many of these were audio supplements or descriptions of a photo. For instance a farmer had taken a photograph of some boys doing stretching exercises outside a hut. The same farmer had added an audio reply saying "There is a college here. So they do exercises. They do it well."

Difficulty in threading

Users could not reply to a post from the home page. Rather, they had to click on the post to open the detailed post view and reply to it from there. We found this was not intuitive: in testing, when asked to reply to a post, nine of the eleven farmers and six of the eight mediators made a new post instead. This was borne out in our data analysis which showed that many *new* audio posts seemed to be replies to prior photo posts, though it was not always clear which ones. For example, all the following were new audio posts that clearly referred to *some* photo on the page: "Shankar, *this* cow is now pregnant. Give her good food and rear it well. Safeguard it so that it yields lot of milk."; "*This* sheep is very nice."; "*That* man is not looking nice in the photo". This could well be why the total number of replies was so much lower than new posts (97 replies to 374 posts).

PROTOTYPE DESIGN (VERSION 2)

User Interface revisions

Based on the findings from version 1, we made a number of changes to the prototype ranging from small visual revisions to basic changes in how users replied to posts. Some of these changes can be seen in the revised consolidated posts page in Figure 4.

Annotating photos and improving replies

Since users wanted to annotate their photo posts with an audio explanation, we added the option to record an audio message along with new photo posts.

We also improved the reply mechanism, enabling users to reply to a post directly from the consolidated page without going to the detailed post view. For photo posts, we provided an overlay including *camera* and *microphone* icons for replies (see Fig. 4). For audio posts, these icons were provided below the *loudspeaker* icon. This design scheme was kept consistent on the detailed post view page.

Adding an animal husbandry tag

Our server data revealed that a large number of posts (~44%) were related to cattle. A number of farmers also wanted to see more posts of livestock and some wanted them prioritized (to appear at the top). Based on this, we

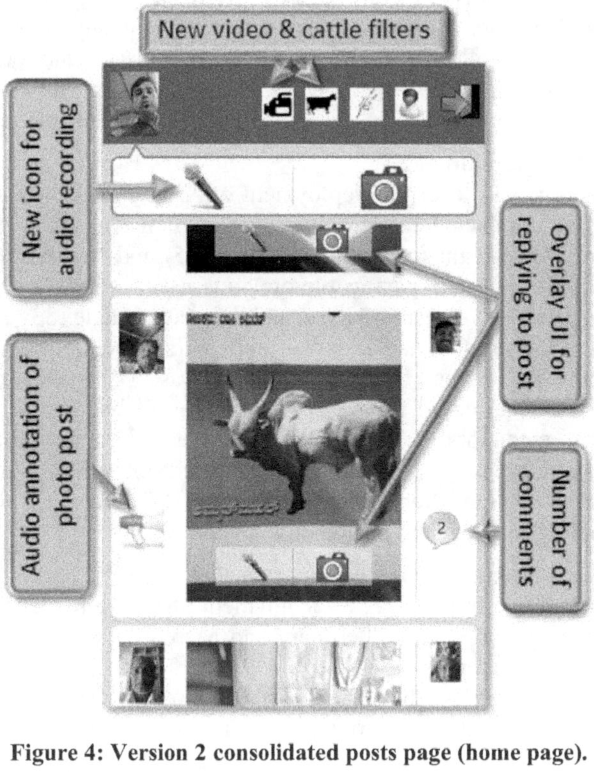

Figure 4: Version 2 consolidated posts page (home page).

added a new filter—an animal husbandry tag—to help segregate relevant content. The icon used was a cow - the most frequently posted animal. When making new posts, users now chose from three filters instead of two.

Seeding curated external content

As discussed below, our interviews indicated that there was a desire for content beyond user-generated material. While a wide range of content was mentioned (from images of Gods to music), many users were keen to see more agricultural information, particularly related to animal husbandry. Since one of the goals of our partner organizations was to improve information sharing among farmers, we wanted to explore how people would perceive external, curated content.

While it would have been nice to allow users to download a variety of videos, bandwidth constraints made this very difficult. Therefore, to gauge users' reception of external content, we embedded a single Digital Green video into the application. Among 26 DG videos for the state of Karnataka, we picked one related to cattle mulching and included it on all of the mediators' phones. To provide easy access to the video from the consolidated page, we added a video tag on the title bar. Tapping on it directed users to the video page. Here they could play the video and reply to it just like they could for any other post.

DEPLOYMENT AND EVALUATION (VERSION 2)

Training session 2

The deployment of version 2 was initiated by a one-day training session. Eight mediators, one researcher, and a Kannada translator attended the session. The training included a thirty-minute individual session with the new version of *KrishiPustak* (the mediators were given the phones so they could explore the revised application without any prompts from us), followed by a group demo with all the eight mediators and a one-hour practice session in groups of two so the mediators could help each other with the new version.

Data collection

Three weeks after the deployment of *KrishiPustak* version 2, we conducted face-to-face interviews in Kannada with two of the eight mediators (M1 and M5) and two farmers who did not take part in the previous user testing. One of the farmers was male (35 yrs) and the other female (33 yrs). Both the farmers had less than two years of schooling. As before, informed verbal consent was collected and respondents could refuse to be interviewed but none did. The mediators and farmers were asked about their experiences using *KrishiPustak* and all interviews were transcribed and translated into English. As before we also analyzed the content posted on the system.

User testing, version 2

During the three weeks of deployment of prototype version 2 between the end of February and March 25th, 2014, the eight mediators registered a total of 50 additional farmers. We observed 140 posts and 83 replies on the *KrishiPustak* application. Overall, from a combination of the interview data and data coming from direct systems use, we found that the revisions to the application appeared to be beneficial to mediators and farmers.

Video page receives traffic

The DG video that we introduced received 22 replies from farmers. These included audio replies as well as picture replies (such as photographs of cows). Interviews with F1, F2 and M5 revealed that they found having the video both interesting and relevant for their needs. M5 and F2 requested that more videos be added to the system. However, according to M1, three farmers he had registered said that the dialect of the video needed to be more localized (the video was produced in a different region in Karnataka). M5's farmers had questions about whether they could avail loans to practice what was shown in the video.

Replying to posts becomes easier

During the training the mediators reported that the new reply design was much easier to use because it allowed direct association with the post a user was replying to and would save time as it could be done from the consolidated page. This was borne out by our data which showed that the ratio of replies to posts increased by 127%.

FINDINGS RELATED TO THE OVERALL SYSTEM

In this section we discuss more general findings related to the overall implementation and deployment of *KrishiPustak* across both versions.

Number and topics of posts

Over a period of four months, mediators registered 306 farmers who made 514 posts and 180 replies. Approximately 70% of all posts were picture posts and 30% audio posts. About 30% of the posts were tagged as *agriculture* and 70% as *personal*. However, in browsing the photos, it was clear that many of the photos tagged as *personal* were related to farming and cattle rearing. We tried to classify the content of a random subset of photos tagged as *personal* and found that about 50% of them were of livestock or other agriculture. This may suggest a misunderstanding of what the tags were for or were intended to represent, or it may just indicate the pervasive nature of agriculture in farmers' lives.

We did a further analysis of the subjects of all photo posts. We found that 44% of the photo posts were pictures of cows and other livestock, 18% were of fields and countryside, 14% were of village fairs, 13% were people, and 11% were of home exteriors. Of the audio posts, 26% were self-introductions, 16% were songs, and 14% were about local grievances that local authorities needed to fix. The remaining 44% of the posts were unclassifiable; they were unclear, repeated or blank recordings.

Posting from others' accounts

By examining the photos taken from the front-facing camera when posts were made, we found that 30% of the posts were made by someone other than the person who was logged in. Of these posts, about 30% show that the mediator was the one physically making the post (i.e., about 10% of all posts actually have the mediator captured from the front camera while making the post). It's not clear who made the remainder of these—it is possible these were other users who were incorrectly logged-in, or just unidentifiable camera shots. This is one of the consequences of not having passwords for log-in (and mediated use, where many users were accessing the system from the same device). However, it did not seem to be too consequential for our system, since we have the photo which showed who had actually posted. It is an open question as to whether passwords might need to be implemented at a later date.

Reasons and rationales for use

The mediation by trusted agriculture workers was a major factor in uptake and usage of the system and it was clearly influential in how users understood what the system was for. There was an overwhelming proportion of agricultural or farming related posts, rather than what might typically be considered 'social' posts. This is perhaps unsurprising, given that the users were farmers and the mediators para-veterinaries who interacted with the farmers for professional purposes. We take up this point below, but first examine how mediators and users understood the system.

The mediators

Mediators largely ascribed professional rationales for the use of *KrishiPustak*—typically information sharing from one farmer to another on farming best practice. For example, M4 said "I do put together people with the same problems and show the posts, e.g., a cow that had miscarriages. I show the posts mutually. I tell them listen to the information from the man himself." This was a recurrent theme, likely to have arisen because the researchers were initially introduced to them by their association with DG. For M4 this even extended to his rationale for who he signed up to the system "a good farmer […] one who can answer well, not one who digresses from the question." Only one mediator described the system as being like Facebook for low-literate users, despite that being how it was presented in the training. However, at least three other mediators, described features which might be considered SN features: to find friends or to see posts from other people whilst "sitting in this place only". Interestingly, one of the mediators, who had actually registered 35 end users admitted that he could not tell the farmers what the system was for as he did not know himself. That end users were willing to sign up to the system even so demonstrates just how important the mediators were in the uptake of the system.

The end users

Farmers were asked about their reasons for joining and their understanding of what the system was for. Reasons for joining often included direct reference to the mediator, for example, "[M3] called me and said let's do this and I agreed" (F6); "This is good for you. People like you will help. [M2] said so" (F4), "[M1] said that it is good for me, he did the account for me, it must be good" (F8). Three of the farmers described the system as being for sharing farming information with others. For example, one farmer described the system as being "To show other people. The cows were given such facilities, my cow's photo has reached others", another as "You take these and show to people in other countries and tell about how to tend cows." This is consistent with the mediators' accounts of the value of the system being for sharing farming best practice.

A couple of farmers had trouble articulating what the system was for. A number of users gave accounts which included the idea that using the system would confer some benefit on them, as illustrated by F4 and F8 above. Given this idea of some sort of good, the famers typically constructed rationales about the system according to the concerns which impact their lives. For example, F8 said "others like officials can see only through such phones. It is good if a few people see. Officials may take action about our difficulties"; (F2) "[the photo] goes to a bank because I want to take a loan" "My house is broken, can I post my house? I want a house for my cow". Two of the female farmers we interviewed had posted pictures of the poor condition of the road near their house, in the hope that officials would see it and fix it.

What users post and why

We were initially surprised by how few obviously personal posts there were (e.g., photos of family and social events). When asked why they did not post family pictures, it was clear that users' perceptions of what the system was for played a part. Whilst 13% of posts were family or friends, most users said they did not know they could make such posts. On being told this option was open to them, some farmers specifically said they would not want to as they are concerned about privacy or misuse of the pictures. However, others were keen to do so: F2 said he would like to put up family photos and F9 said "I do not know that I can post [pictures of family] henceforth I shall do if the phone is given to me". This last comment, "if the phone is given to me" hints at how the mediated nature of use has a practical impact on what is and isn't posted. That is, since the mediators visit the farmers for work purposes, it is not clear how easy it would be to take photos of family during these visits or if the family would be doing something 'post-worthy' at that time.

The strong farming theme underlying *KrishiPustak* use was also seen when farmers were asked what else they would like to post or see from others. Comments included "Coconut tree, tomato, all good crops so that others see and follow the same what we have done" (F5); F8, a land owning farmer, said "I am interested in posting crops like turmeric, coconut because I grow them"; and F7, an agricultural day labourer interviewed at the same time, agreed "I am also interested in doing these but I do not have land of my own." However, some farmers could see a more social side to the system. F5 said he "would like to post our temple fair, our village play" and F9 could envisage social benefits to the system: as well as wanting to post family pictures, he said, "I joined the system as I have not travelled. Maybe I will come to know about other places". Other users said they would like to see pictures of Hindu Gods and Goddesses (this was common), film stars, peacocks, rivers, or listen to religious songs.

Incentivization of mediators crucial

The mediators said that they had different motivations for joining the system, such as ownership of an expensive phone, respect within the community, helping broadcast information from one farmer to another and finding ways to help the farmers. However, the remuneration we provided with talk-time was an important driving force for their activity. From the time we deployed the system up until the first round of interviews, we charged the mediators' personal phones (Nokia X201/202) with currency once every 2-3 weeks. We ranked mediators in order of number of farmers registered and number of posts and replies received and then distributed talk time in a decreasing rank order. The person with the most activity received the highest amount of talk time while the person with the least activity received the lowest. During the interviews, five of the eight mediators asked for talk time recharges to be done once a week. In fact, whenever the translator called the mediators to encourage use during the deployment, mediators enquired about the next talk-time recharge and whether it could be done early.

Robustness of the System and Hardware

Despite being a prototype, the system was robust and worked well throughout the deployment with no major crashes or issues. However, some minor issues started surfacing when the amount of content increased substantially. From the mediators' perspective, there were some concerns about the robustness of the hardware in the field; one speaker broke, one screen cracked and M4 was afraid of losing or dropping the handset.

DISCUSSION AND RECOMMENDATIONS

When we deployed *KrishiPustak*, our aim was to provide low-literate users with the richness of a modern SN system. In this section we examine how this played out in practice, covering three key topics: the preponderance of professional posts, social relations on the system and the limitations of user-created content.

Context of use: mediation

The notion of mediation is central to our system. This design was based on earlier findings about technology use by low-literate users [10, 27, 46]. Trust in, and respect for the mediators was central to farmers' decision to sign up. However, mediation had both practical and conceptual impacts on system use.

Practically the system was not *to-hand* for the users. It was only available to them when they saw the mediator, typically during professional visits. Indeed, based on analyzing the authors of the posts we also found that around 10% of the posts were actually made by the mediators from the farmer's accounts. Naturally, this impacted what kinds of content users posted—for example, personal and social photos were less likely, simply because of when and where the farmers have access to the technology. It would be interesting to examine if using different people as mediators, for example people at the center of a social hub such as a village shop, might impact use differently.

To compound this, the mediators largely ascribed professional rationales to the usage of the system typically for information sharing to spread good practice. It is likely that this stems from the context of the study: they are para-vets, largely interacting with their end users on professional business. Furthermore, the association of the researchers with a farming information dissemination project (DG) is likely to have influenced the mediators' understandings of the systems. This would have had an influence on how the system was explained to and used by the farmers.

Context of use: Farming communities

Technology use is always situated, that is, influenced by and embedded in a wider ecosystem. In this case, that of small subsistence farming communities. This is reflected in the kinds of posts that were made and desired (here a strong agricultural theme) and in the rationales which were constructed as to what *KrishiPustak* was.

In the light of limited information on what the system might actually be, the farmers constructed accounts of what it could be for. There was a repeated idea that some good would come (to them) from using the system, often related to problems they actually faced—whether a loan was required or a road needed fixing. Their accounts were typically *practical*, that is the system must be *for something*, i.e., have some practical use, even if they did not always articulate what that might be. If we can take a step back from our own grounded understanding of social and professional networking systems, the *idea* of a SN system, is a pretty nebulous one (indeed the extensive research into *why* people use SN system might remind us of this [5, 25]). Furthermore, as discussed in the literature, it is not uncommon for SN systems to be put to practical use, so it is perhaps not surprising to that farmers ascribe such uses to the technology.

Having said this, in their actual and desired use of the system, we can see many of the regular features of an SN system, albeit with a strong agricultural bias. Indeed, given the overwhelming proportion of apparently agricultural and animal posts, one might ask whether *KrishiPustak* was in practice used as a *social* networking system, or might it be better conceived of as a *professional* networking system? Both farmers and mediators describe the system as being useful for spreading information on farming best practice and their wish list of posts included many agricultural themes. Nonetheless, the social side of the system still shows through in existing usage. Some posts were visibly (or audibly) social—village fairs, people posts, and songs. In addition, whilst farmers did want to see more farming-related content, they also expressed a desire to see more village events, religious imagery, film stars, and so on.

Around 70% of the posts were tagged as personal, although to our (non-farmer) eyes more than half of these were pictures of farming or cattle rearing. It is quite possible that for these farmers, the distinction between "personal" and "agriculture" is simply irrelevant because agricultural concerns pervade their lives. Whilst there are clearly professional elements to the system use (such as sharing farming best practices), these users are predominantly from agricultural communities and clearly have a passion for their work; they are interested in posts related to agriculture and nature more generally. To illustrate, favorite posts included animals they admired (well fed, well-tended), a nature scene (good perspective), and a fruit tree (small but with many fruits).

Social relationships

To try and understand how much *KrishiPustak* could be said to be a social *network*, we analyzed the cross-replying network graph of users [16]. The graph was made on the basis of replies made by people. A directed edge was drawn between the person replying and the person whose post he/she was replying to. A dense graph would have shown a lot of cross activity, and a large number of bi-directional edges would have pointed to developing relations between people. However, our graph was quite sparse, with little evidence of individual relationships (see Fig. 5). Of all the replies there was only one instance when two users had replied on each other's (separate) posts. However, the picture is more nuanced than that, as many people did comment on other users' posts (whether using the 'reply' channel which occurred more in version 2 or by creating new posts in version 1). Furthermore there were a number of 'conversations,' where multiple people interacted around a post. That is, they posted audio replies comprising a conversation. For instance, in an audio reply to a photo post of a cow, two people converse: "1st person: What is your name? 2nd person: Subramanya 1st: How many cows do you have? 2nd: – 4 1st: How much milk do you supply to the diary? 2nd: 2 litres." Such instances for replies as well as

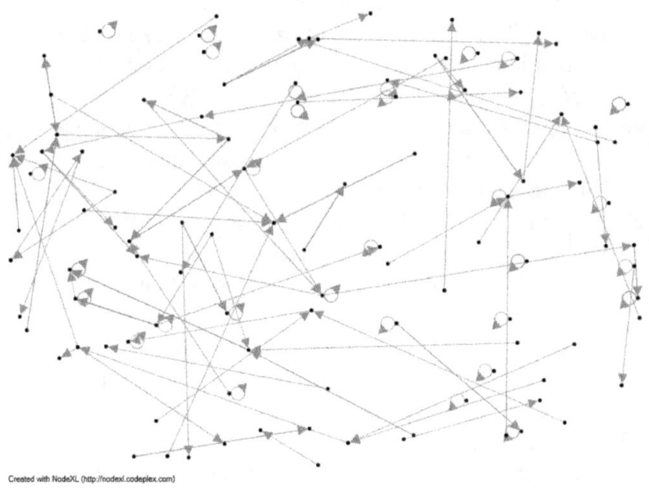

Figure 5: Graph analyzing cross-replying among users (represented as nodes). A directed edge represents one user commenting on another (or the same) post. Note that there are no bidirectional edges.

posts are common: almost 9% of the total posts and replies are conversations. Whilst these are not bidirectional relationships in the conventional sense, i.e., two people who reply to each other's posts, they definitely point to community interactions while using the application.

External or third-party content

User-created content is only one part of what users share on SN systems like Facebook; users frequently share content available on the Web, such as videos, music, political commentaries, etc. Indeed, a study of users in Indian slums showed that one way to manage language barriers (such as limited literacy in English) was to post content containing English slogans or text [47]. Whilst we are not suggesting our users would want to post content in English, this research, combined with the ready acceptance of the DG video and farmers' desire to see pictures of Gods and film stars and so on, does suggest that the system might be enhanced by the addition of third party content. How this could be best done is an interesting question given the constraints we must design for: the mediated nature of the interaction (users only have access to the phone for limited time, typically during a visit for other work-related purposes); the users' low-literacy (how would they search for and identify relevant content); and the limited internet access in the villages. However, it is not impossible. One could imagine banks of content that could be created (perhaps with local language verbal tagging, etc.). Then, mediators or other curators might seed this content, and a well-designed speech-based search could be used to locate resources where internet is present and so on. However it is done, third party content is likely to be an important part of any SN system for low-literate users.

CONCLUSIONS AND FUTURE WORK

In this research we designed, developed, deployed and evaluated *KrishiPustak*, an SN system for low-literate farmers in rural India. The system was deployed on Nokia Lumia 820 phones that were provided to eight agriculture extension workers of a non-profit organization. These workers acted as human mediators to provide access and help farmers use the system. *KrishiPustak* allowed farmers to make posts and replies using audio-visual content. Over a period of four months, 306 farmers registered on the system and made 514 posts and 180 replies. We conducted interviews with farmers and mediators and performed an analysis of posts to understand how the system was used and to drive iterative design. We found that the context of mediated use and the agricultural framing had a powerful impact on how the system was used. Mediators largely described the system as being for sharing agricultural information and farming best practices, and most posts reflected this. However, despite a strong professional bent, other uses also showed through, with posts related to families, local grievances, and aspirational content. This suggests that even if the concept of SN is not immediately obvious to such an audience, there is real potential for such uses to come through.

As the application scales up, we may want to investigate other ways that users can manage posts that they view. In our version there was no friends' lists, but this might be something to explore in the future. For example, everyone in the village might be automatically connected, but then users may be able manage their connections by adding or removing them. With scale, we may also want to experiment with user-friendly graphical or numerical passwords, to help manage privacy.

In future work it would be interesting to see how an audio-visual SN system plays out in other low-literate contexts, particularly if it expanded beyond the confines of single usage to see whether and how more social uses might emerge. For example, mediators might be local shop owners, health workers or others who have substantial contact with people from the area. Another interesting line of work could be to explore non-mediated use: what does usage of *KrishiPustak* look like when farmers use their own devices?

ACKNOWLEDGMENTS

We thank Digital Green and BAIF for all their support in this project. Thanks to Vyshak Jain, Nandish K. N. and Prathiba G. for help with the video, Kamala Anilkumar, Manjunath Patil, Deepti Desai for field work. We thank Bill Thies for the many useful suggestions throughout the project.

REFERENCES

1. Agarwal. , S., Jain, A., Kumar, A., Nanavati, A. A., Rajput, N. The Spoken Web: A Web for the Underprivileged *ACM SIGWEB Newsletter, 2010.*
2. Aircel Pocket Internet. http://www.aircel.com/AircelWar/appmanager/aircel/ap?_nfpb=true&_pageLabel=VAS_aircelPocketInternet_page. Retrieved on 30th April,2014
3. BAIF http://www.baif.org.in/ Retrieved on May 5, 2014.
4. Chaudry, B.M., Connelly, K.H., Siek, K.A., Welch, J.L. Mobile interface design for low-literacy populations. *2nd ACM SIGHIT International Health Informatics Symposium Pages 91-100*
5. Cheung, C., Chio, P., and Lee, M. "Online social networks: Why do students use Facebook ?" *CHI, 2011*
6. Cuendet, S., Medhi, I., Bali, K., Cutrell, E. VideoKheti: Making video content accessible to low-literate and novice users. *CHI, 2013.*
7. Digital Green http://www.digitalgreen.org Retrieved on May 25, 2014.
8. Duggirala, M.M., Kummamuru, K., Srivastava, S., White, J.S. Designing a Voice-Based Employment Exchange for Rural India. *ICT4D 2012, ICM DEV, 2011.*
9. Ellison, N. and Boyd, D. (2013). "Sociality through Social Network Sites." In Dutton, W.H. *The Oxford Handbook of Internet Studies*, Oxford University Press.
10. Gandhi, R., Veeraraghavan, R., Toyama, K., and Ramprasad, V. Digital Green: Participatory video for agricultural extension. *ICTD, 2007*
11. Ganglbauer, E. Think globally, act locally: a case study of a free food sharing community and social networking. *CSCW,2014*
12. Gilbert, E., Karahalios, K. and Sandvig, C. The Network in the Garden: An Empirical Analysis of Social Media in Rural Life. *CHI, 2008*
13. Gou, L., Kim, J. Chen, H., Collins, J., Goodman, M., Zhang, X. and Giles, C.L. MobiSNA: a mobile video social network application. *MobiDE, 2009*
14. Grisedale, S., Graves, M., And Grunsteidl, A. Designing a graphical user interface for healthcare workers in rural India. *CHI, 1997.*
15. Grover, A. S., Plauch´e, M., Barnard, E., and Kuun. C. HIV health information access using spoken dialogue systems: touchtone vs. speech. *ICTD, 2009.*
16. Hansen, D., Shneiderman, B. and Smith, M. "Analyzing Social Media Networks with NodeXL". *C & T, 2009.*
17. Huenerfauth, M. Developing design recommendations for computer interfaces accessible to illiterate users. *Master's thesis, University College Dublin, 2002.*
18. ITU. 2014. The World in 2014 : ICT Facts and Figures
19. Joinson, A.N. "Looking at, looking up or keeping up with people? : motives and use of Facebook." *CHI, 2008.*
20. Jones, M. and Marsden, G. *"Mobile Interaction Design"* John Wiley & Sons, 2005.
21. Jones, M., Buchanan, G., Thimbleby, H., & Marsden, G. User interfaces for mobile web devices. *[www9 mobile workshop position paper]. World Wide Web Conference, 2000.*
22. Katre, D. Using mnemonic techniques as part of pictorial interface for self-identification of illiterate villagers. *CHI, 2004.*
23. Koradia, Z., Aggarwal, P., Seth, A., and Luthra, G. Gurgaon idol: a singing competition over community radio and IVRS. *DEV, 2013*
24. Lampe, C., Ellison, N. and Steinfield, C. Changes in Participation and Perception of Facebook. *CSCW, 2008.*
25. Lampe, C., Wash, R., Velasquez, A., and Ozkaya, E. Motivations to Participate in Online Communities. *CHI, 2010.*
26. Medhi I., Gautama S.N.N., and Toyama, K. A Comparison of Mobile Money-Transfer UIs for Non-Literate and Semi-Literate Users. *CHI, 2009.*
27. Medhi I., Jain, M., Tewari, A., Bhavsar, M., Matheke-Fischer, M. and Cutrell, E. Combating Rural Child Malnutrition through Inexpensive Mobile Phones. *NordiCHI, 2012.*
28. Medhi I., Patnaik, S., Brunskill, E., Gautama, S.N.N., Thies, W. and Toyama,K. Designing Mobile Interfaces for Novice and Low-Literacy Users. *CHI, 2011.*
29. Medhi I., Sagar, M. and Toyama, K. Text-free User Interfaces for Illiterate and Semi-literate users. *ITID, 2007.*
30. Medhi I., Toyama, K., Joshi, A., Athavankar, U. and Cutrell, E. A comparison of list vs. hierarchical UIs on

mobile phones for non-literate users, *Interact. 14th IFIP TC13 Conference on Human-Computer Interaction, 2013.*

31. Medhi, I., Lakshmanan, M., Toyama, K. and Cutrell, E. Some Evidence for Impact of Limited Education on Hierarchical User Interface Navigation. *CHI, 2013.*
32. Medhi, I., Prasad, A., and Toyama, K. Optimal audio-visual representations for illiterate users. *International World Wide Web Conference, 2007.*
33. Moore, R. K. A comparison of the data requirements of automatic speech recognition systems and human listeners. *Eurospeech, 2003.*
34. Mudliar, P., Donner, J. and Thies, W. Emergent Practices Around CGNet Swara, A Voice Forum for Citizen Journalism in Rural India. *ICTD, 2012.*
35. Nadkarni, A. and Hofmann, S.G. "Why do people use Facebook?" *Personality and individual differences, 2012.*
36. Parikh, T., Ghosh, K., and Chavan, A. Design considerations for a financial management system for rural, semi-literate users. *CHI, 2003.*
37. Parikh, T., Ghosh, K., and Chavan, A. Design studies for a financial management system for micro-credit groups in rural India. *ACM Conference on Universal Usability, 2003.*
38. Patel, N. Designing and evaluating voice-based virtual communities. *CHI Extended Abstracts, 2010.*
39. Patel, N., Agarwal, S., Rajput, N., Nanavati, A., Dave, P., and Parikh, T. S. A comparative study of speech and dialed input voice interfaces in rural India. *CHI, 2009.*
40. Patel, N., Chittamuru, D., Jain, A., Dave, P., Parikh, T.S. Avaaj Otalo - A Field Study of an Interactive Voice Forum for Small Farmers in Rural India". *CHI, 2010.*
41. Patniak, S., Brunskill, E., and Thies, W. Evaluating the Accuracy of Data Collection on Mobile Phones: A Study of Forms, SMS, and Voice. *ICTD, 2009.*
42. Pentland, A., Fletcher, R., and Hasson, A. Daknet: Rethinking connectivity in developing nations. IEEE *Computer, 2004.*
43. Pimmer, C., Linxen, S. and Gröhbiel. U. "Facebook as a learning tool? A case study on the appropriation of social network sites from mobile phones in developing countries." *British Journal of Educational Technology, 2012.*
44. Plauche′, M. and Prabaker, M. Tamil market: A spoken dialog system for rural India. *CHI, 2006.*
45. Prasad A., Medhi I., Toyama, K. and Balakrishnan, R. Exploring the feasibility of video mail for illiterate users. *Working conference on Advanced visual interfaces, 2008.*
46. Ramachandran, D., Canny, J., Das, P.D., and Cutrell, E. Mobile-izing Health Workers in Rural India. *CHI, 2009.*
47. Rangaswamy, N and Cutrell, E., 'Anthropology, Development and ICTs: Slums, Youth and the Mobile Internet in Urban India'. *ICTD, 2012.*
48. Rangaswamy, N., Challugulla, G., Young, M. & Cutrell, E. Local Pocket Internet and Global Social Media. Bridging the Digital Gap: Facebook and Youth Sub-Stratum in Urban India. *International Conference on Social Implications of Computers in Developing Countries, 2013.*
49. Raza, A., Haq, F.U., Tariq, Z., Pervaiz, M., Razaq, S., Saif, U. and Rosenfeld, R. Job Opportunities through Entertainment: Virally Spread Speech-Based Services for Low-Literate Users, *CHI, 2013.*
50. Rege, R. and Nagarkar, S. Krishi-Mitra: case study of a user-centric ICT solution for semi-literate and illiterate farmers in India. *IHCI, 2010*
51. Sambasivan, N. and Smyth, T. The human infrastructure in ICTD. *ICTD, 2010.*
52. Sambasivan, N., Cutrell, E., Toyama, K. and Nardi, B. Intermediated Technology Use in Developing Communities. *CHI, 2010.*
53. Sherwani, J., Ali, Mirza, S., Fatma, A., Memon, Y., Karim, M., Tongia, R., and Rosenfeld. R. (2007). HealthLine: Speech-based Access to Health Information by Low-literate Users. *ICTD, 2007.*
54. Sherwani, J., Palijo, S., Mirza, S., Ahmed, T., Ali, N. and Rosenfeld. R. Speech vs. Touch-tone: Telephony Interfaces for Information Access by Low Literate Users. *ICTD, 2009.*
55. Smyth, T.N., Etherton, J., and Best, M.L. MOSES: Exploring New Ground in Media and Post-Conflict Reconciliation. *CHI, 2010.*
56. Urista, M. A., Dong, Q. and Day, K.D. "Explaining why young adults use MySpace and Facebook through uses and gratifications theory." *Human Communication, 2009.*
57. Wulf, V., et al. "Fighting against the wall: Social media use by political activists in a Palestinian village." *CHI, 2013.*
58. Wyche, S. and Murphy, L. Powering the cellphone revolution: findings from mobile phone charging trials in off-grid Kenya. *CHI, 2013.*
59. Wyche, S., Schoenebeck, S.Y. and Forte, A. "Facebook is a Luxury": An Exploratory Study of Social Media Use in Rural Kenya. *CSCW, 2013.*
60. Zhao, Y., Do, N., Wang, S., Hsu, C. and Venkatasubramanian, N. Enabling offline access to Facebook streams on mobile devices. *MiddlewareDPT, 2013.*

Accessible Crowdwork? Understanding the Value in and Challenge of Microtask Employment for People with Disabilities

Kathryn Zyskowski[1,2], Meredith Ringel Morris[1], Jeffrey P. Bigham[3], Mary L. Gray[1], Shaun K. Kane[4]
[1]Microsoft Research
[2]University of Washington, Department of Anthropology, Seattle, WA
[3]Carnegie Mellon University, Human Computer Interaction Institute, Pittsburgh, PA
[4]University of Colorado Boulder, Department of Computer Science, Boulder, CO
kcz@uw.edu, {merrie, mlg}@microsoft.com, jbigham@cmu.edu, shaun.kane@colorado.edu

ABSTRACT
We present the first formal study of crowdworkers who have disabilities via in-depth open-ended interviews of 17 people (disabled crowdworkers and job coaches for people with disabilities) and a survey of 631 adults with disabilities. Our findings establish that people with a variety of disabilities currently participate in the crowd labor marketplace, despite challenges such as crowdsourcing workflow designs that inadvertently prohibit participation by, and may negatively affect the worker reputations of, people with disabilities. Despite such challenges, we find that crowdwork potentially offers different opportunities for people with disabilities relative to the normative office environment, such as job flexibility and lack of a need to rely on public transit. We close by identifying several ways in which crowd labor platform operators and/or individual task requestors could improve the accessibility of this increasingly important form of employment.

Author Keywords
Crowdsourcing; accessibility; Mechanical Turk; employment

ACM Classification Keywords
H.5.3 [Group and Organization Interfaces]

INTRODUCTION
Crowdsourcing often involves doing microtasks—short jobs online for small payments. Crowdsourced microtasks have become integral to the information services economy, from matching images and product descriptions listed on commercial websites to transcribing a doctor's recorded notes. At the same time, microtasks offer a new way to organize labor, much like the technological innovation of the assembly line did at the turn of the Industrial Revolution. Job requesters dismantle a single job into many microtasks that are completed by workers drawn from a group (crowd) via an open call. As such, crowdwork, designed with economic and technological efficiencies as well as human needs in mind, could transform digital labor, and more generally, the future of work.

CSCW '15, March 14-18, 2015, Vancouver, BC, Canada.

ACM 978-1-4503-2922-4/15/03…$15.00 .
http://dx.doi.org/10.1145/2675133.2675158

Crowdsourcing platforms are often based on a simple model: requesters post tasks to be completed by workers online. Some of the major crowdsourcing sites for microtasks are Amazon Mechanical Turk (mTurk), CrowdFlower, and MobileWorks. Some of the most common types of microtasks that workers complete fall under the categories of transcription, translation, image tagging and classification, data collection, content generation (e.g., product reviews), and usability testing of websites [[18]]. While there are crowdsourcing sites that offer mobile jobs in the real world (e.g., TaskRabbit) [[31]] and some that offer larger, more skilled work opportunities (e.g., Freelancer.com, oDesk, 99designs), in this paper we are primarily concerned with microtasking sites.

Crowdwork may offer a unique proposition for people with disabilities, due to features such as the ability to work from home, avoid the frustrations of navigating inaccessible transportation, vary the pace of individual or multiple tasks, set a flexible work schedule, determine whether or not to reveal one's disability status, and use their personal adaptive technologies. In this paper, we explore whether or not people with disabilities are currently doing crowdwork, what motivates them to do so, and whether they are able to effectively and fully participate in this new form of labor.

This paper contributes the first research into crowdwork from the perspective of disabled workers. Disability status was self-identified by participants, and encompassed a range of short-term or permanent physical, cognitive, and/or socio-emotional challenges; as a first exploration into the participation of people with disabilities in crowdwork, we felt it was important to include a variety of perspectives and experiences. However, we acknowledge that the breadth of the generic "disability" label has drawbacks, such as the risk of missing out on key needs of specific subpopulations by focusing on commonalities among a larger group [[7]] – future work that focuses on experiences specific to particular disability subpopulations (or compares and contrasts the experiences of crowdworkers with different types of disabilities) would be a valuable next step beyond the scope of the current article.

Using grounded theory, this paper follows an iterative data collection and analysis methodology to analyze the experiences of people with disabilities learning about and doing crowdwork. Following the grounded theory approach, we both discuss the implications of this at the macro level of disability rights and employment, and on the micro level by offering a range of different contextualized experiences and attendant implications for design. Drawing on critical theory [[9]], we argue that the discourse on digital accessibility is currently too narrow, and suggest that accessibility to digital technologies expand to include accessibility to employment and social experiences in computer-mediated environments.

RELATED WORK

We review the previous literature in the areas of disability and employment, crowdworker demographics, and crowdsourced accessibility applications. This literature review explains the theoretical framework of this paper and its interdisciplinary nature.

Disability and Employment

History of Legal Policies around Disability and Employment

During the 20th century people with disabilities repeatedly fought for legal protection against discrimination in employment opportunities. The landmark legal act for people with disabilities was the Americans with Disabilities Act (ADA). The ADA, enacted in 1990, made discrimination on the basis of disability to any employment, public or private services, accommodation, telecommunications, or transportation illegal. Although a landmark for disability civil rights, ongoing debates about the ADA's protective measures circulate on both the legal definition of disability as well as how to adapt the ADA to changes in the labor force and telecommunications sectors [[28]]. Though the ADA clearly prohibits discrimination in the areas of employment and telecommunications, we are unaware of prior research inquiring about the accessibility of digital labor or the experiences of those who self-identify as disabled who are doing crowdsourcing work.

Some of the primary ADA Title 1 goals are "ending employer discrimination, encouraging workplace accommodations, and making workplaces accessible" [[20]]. In 2011, researchers at Rutgers University and the National Bureau of Economic Research projected potential future work opportunities for people with disabilities. One major concern of their study was that people with disabilities would not be equally represented in the fastest-growing occupations; however, the study also noted that in the fastest growing occupations, not many required specific abilities (and therefore could be opportunities for people with disabilities) [[20]]. The researchers found that the increase of home-based work will be important for people with disabilities, enabling people to work regardless of transportation or medical issues necessitating people to stay at home [[20]].

The history of the struggle for equality in employment opportunities for people with disabilities is important in understanding how crowdsourcing can potentially offer a form of employment for people with disabilities. Furthermore, understanding the importance of accessibility to employment opportunities helps us understand how making crowdwork accessible means not only making sure the primary UI is accessible, but also the full experience of doing online paid work. Crowdsourcing offers a type of employment that, if designed with awareness of the challenges and diversity inherent in employing workers with disabilities, could offer people with disabilities an equal opportunity in the era of digital employment.

CDS and the Social Construction of Disability

Critical Disability Studies (CDS) is an interdisciplinary field of research questioning the history, current state of, and future of the full societal inclusion of people with disabilities. CDS explores disability studies drawing from the disciplines of anthropology, law, gender studies, social work, history, and others [[6]] [[9]] [[22]]. CDS also draws on critical theory, a school of thought originating with the Frankfurt school of philosophers from the 1930s, who argued for a critical look at societal practices and historical contextualization of current societal norms. Drawing on this, CDS scholarship challenges assumptions about the "able" body, and views the construction of disability as a cultural phenomenon [[25]].

From a framework of the social construction of disability, attaining employment is a critical part of participating fully in society for people with disabilities [[20]]. These perspectives see disability "as resulting from society's failure to adapt to the needs of impaired people" [[1]]. Recent scholarship coming out of CDS looks at the cultural construction of disability in the digital age [[13], arguing that the design of technology is complicit in upholding a narrative of the normative, or "abled," person.

The idea of disability as a social construction is important to bring to the discussion on creating accessible technologies. It shows that there is a historical precedent to how disability is commonly talked about, understood, and experienced in both the accessibility of everyday devices as well as employment experiences. Furthermore, understanding how important employment can be to one's self-understanding as a social participant in society helps frame crowdsourcing work as an activity beyond an economic exchange.

The Demographics of Crowdworkers

While much of the literature on crowdsourcing focuses on the employer's perspective, in recent years scholars have begun to look at the demographics of people who perform crowdwork. Ross et al. [[27]] argue that the demographics of Amazon Mechanical Turk (mTurk) have been shifting from moderate-income U.S. citizens to an increasing amount of international workers, especially young educated workers in India. Looking at this longitudinal change in demographics via a survey embedded as a HIT ("Human Intelligence Task," i.e., a single unit of microwork) on mTurk, Ross et al. argue that it may signify a shift from crowdwork as part-time to crowdwork as a full-time job. Ipeirotis [[17]] has also looked at the demographics of crowdworkers, focusing primarily on gender, income levels, and educational background; his work concluded that crowdworkers on mTurk largely mirrored Internet users in the U.S., with some biases (e.g. slightly younger, more females, slightly lower income, smaller families). He also found that for many workers in India mTurk work was a primary source of income, in comparison to workers in the U.S. where it usually served as complementary to other sources of income [[17]]. Both U.S. and Indian workers also shared secondary, non-economic motivations for performing crowdsourcing work, including entertainment and education. Our work builds on this literature by investigating a new demographic trait, disability status, which was not reported on in prior crowdworker demographies.

Martin et al. [[23]] analyzed posts on Turker Nation, one of the online web forums for mTurk workers. Their study went beyond looking only at primary motivations for doing crowdwork, also focusing on the "practical, emotional and moral aspects" of crowdsourcing – they found that earning a living wage was a key concern among forum posters. Our work builds on this by investigating whether wages are the key concern of disabled crowdworkers, as well, or whether other motivations may be more prevalent in this group, such as social interaction, entertainment, and/or education.

In the paper "The Future of Crowdwork," Kittur et al. ask whether they can imagine a crowd labor market in which they would want their children to work [[19]]. The authors outline the major challenges in crowdwork becoming a desirable work option for the middle class. Our work builds on Kittur et al.'s work by trying to understand the role of crowdwork as a potential meaningful source of employment to a group that is often relegated to low-status jobs in the non-digital world, and to understand how to make sure that digital labor for people with disabilities is not only accessible, but also fulfilling, fair, and respected.

Accessibility and Crowdsourcing

There is a large body of research on accessible technology, including studies of barriers to use with status quo technologies, interface design guidelines for more universal usability, and creation of novel software and hardware to facilitate usability for people with varying abilities. Beyond the research community, standards bodies like the World Wide Web consortium maintain accessibility guidelines (in this case, for websites: www.w3c.org). However, as our findings reveal, such standards do not adequately cover emerging online experiences, e.g. crowdsourcing workflows.

Recently, a number of researchers have studied how people with disabilities can be consumers (rather than producers) of crowdwork. The ESP game enticed workers to add descriptive tags to images (for fun, rather than for money); though the primary purpose of such tags was to enhance web search, they also held potential for making images more accessible to people with visual impairments [[32]]. Bigham et al.'s VizWiz application demonstrated that paid workers on mTurk could answer questions about photos for blind requesters in near real-time [[3]]. Brady et al. extended this work to examine whether members of a blind person's social network could provide a free source of this crowd labor [[5]]. Burton et al. examined the possibilities of using crowd workers to provide fashion advice to people with visual impairments [[8]]. Lasecki et al.'s Scribe system demonstrated that crowdsourced captioning for people with hearing impairments was cheaper and faster than professional captioning [[21]]. Hara et al. have explored using crowd workers to examine Google Street View images to identify features of a city that might impact a disabled person's navigation, such as whether sidewalks contain obstacles or how bus stops are laid out [[14]] [[15]]. Hong et al. have explored how people with autism can use crowdsourcing to receive advice about actions to take in particular social situations [[16]]. These projects have all examined how crowd labor can be used to improve quality of life for people with disabilities by doing tasks on their behalf – in contrast, our research considers whether participating in crowd labor as a worker, rather than a beneficiary of such work, is a valued and accessible experience for people with disabilities.

METHODOLOGY

For this project we used a mixed-methods approach to better understand the extent to which people who self-identify as disabled are doing crowdwork, their experiences with this work, and if their disability status interfered with task completion. Our method combined in-depth interviews (17) with broader surveys (631).

We used a grounded theory process to code transcribed interviews and qualitative survey responses [[34]]. We analyzed these data through open coding [[11]]. In contrast to quantitative coding, where interviews are arranged around themes connected to a theory that a researcher is interested in, open coding categories are not determined until after the interviews are finished: "qualitative coding is a way of opening up avenues of inquiry: the researcher identifies and develops concepts and analytic insights through close examination and reflection" [[11]]. The important methodological difference of analyzing interviews and qualitative survey answers by qualitative coding is that it allows for emergent themes, perspectives that the researchers may not have set out to find. It is a way of identifying significant experiences and observations. In this way, qualitative data analysis is iterative: what may have been important themes at the beginning may not make it into the final analysis.

The main author first performed open coding on the interview transcripts by labeling phenomena as they come to mind. From the collated list of phenomena, we created categories and cut-and-pasted related sections of interviews and qualitative survey data under the different categories. In grounded theory, analysis is an iterative process, and the labels of concepts and categories shifted through ongoing conversations between all of the authors. After we organized data under categories we did axial coding, which is a process of organizing categories and their sub-categories of data "to form more precise and complete explanations of their data" [[34], p.124]. Some categories were split into subcategories, while others became less important as the paper evolved. The themes from these analysis are organized in the "Findings" section, and create the foundation for the thematic issues discussed in this paper.

Interviews

Interviews included eight people with disabilities and nine job coaches working at organizations that help people with disabilities find employment who are not disabled themselves. Interviews took place between December 2013 and February 2014, and were conducted in person when possible, or else via Skype. Interviews were recorded and transcribed for analysis. Interviewees were compensated $50 for their time.

The method of anthropological semi-structured interviewing values the unexpected themes that emerge throughout interviews, and prioritizes understanding the world from another's particular experiences and perspective. For this reason, interviews have a protocol, but every interview may not get to exactly the same questions. Particular peoples' experiences are important because they often complicate general ways of understanding an experience or phenomena. However, qualitative ethnographers are also always paying close attention to emergent patterns that are evidenced through shared narratives among groups of people.

Job Coaches

We initially reached out to job coaches in order understand the current ways in which people with disabilities navigate finding employment, the options for employment, and what job coaches look for in potential employment for clients who identify as having a disability. We identified job coaches by reaching out to local organizations that work with disabled populations, and by referrals ("snowball sampling") from job coaches whom we had already interviewed.

The job coaches we interviewed are full-time workers who match people with disabilities with jobs. Job coaching includes services such as job skills training, interview practice, resume building, and computer classes. These job coach interviews were a formative part of the research project in gaining an understanding of the history and current daily experiences of training people and placing people with disabilities in employment. The interviews aimed to learn about the current role of mediation by job coaching centers and training programs for people with disabilities, to learn about the requirements for job placement for people with disabilities, and to learn about how organizations who have worked with different disability populations for decades incorporate technology and view the role of computer-mediated work for disability employment in the near future. Some of the questions asked in job coach interviews included: *Have you ever heard of crowdwork? Do you have any clients who do crowdwork? Would you recommend this to future clients? How can you see crowdsourcing being a part of a job (i.e., educationally, transitional work)?* Of the job coaches, one had a client who did crowdsourcing work and one job coach had experimented with mTurk as a component of a computer skills class with a client; the other seven coaches were not familiar with crowdwork until we explained the concept.

There are many people who self-identify as disabled who hold steady employment, and many of these people never seek out help to find employment. However, in the U.S. job coaching organizations often work closely with government departments and programs, and hence are mindful of workplace accessibility and play an integral part of the social services offered to people with disabilities. Initially we thought that through contact with job coaches we could reach interviewees who had tried crowdwork. However, confidentiality kept the job coaches from directly putting us in contact with clients for interviews.

A related part of our methodology consisted of site visits to local job coaching organizations. We visited three job coaching offices in Seattle and were able to meet with employees and clients to gain an understanding of the workplace environment. The purpose of meeting job coaches in their environment was to gain a depth of understanding about the day-to-day environment for job coaches working in this sector as well as to understand the population of people who work at or attend job coaching centers. Of the three organizations we visited, one focused specifically on the blind population, and the two other organizations worked exclusively with people who self-identify as disabled, which included a range of cognitive disabilities, social anxieties, hearing difficulties, physical disabilities, and motor impairments.

Workers with Disabilities

We also interviewed eight people with disabilities who had experience with crowdsourcing work. There were six men and two women. The interviewees lived in five different U.S. states, including the west coast, east coast, midwest, and southwest United States. Two were between 18 and 24 years old, three in their forties, one in their fifties, and one in their sixties. These interviewees identified as having the following disabilities: blindness (3), Autism (1), other disability (1), severe social anxiety (1), serious health condition (1), combined type ADHD (1).

We recruited interview participants by advertising our study via a variety of media, including postings on online forums related to various disability interest groups, emails to distribution lists for various disability interest groups, and social media posts from our organizations Twitter account that used the hashtag #a11y (a hashtag followed by many with interests in accessibility). We also made use of referrals ("snowball sampling") from other interviewees.

Interviews took 45 minutes and asked about the research participant's background, employment experiences, educational experiences, ideal work, general accessibility issues with technology, and experiences with crowdwork.

Survey

The in-depth interviews allowed us to gather rich qualitative feedback from a small sample of crowdworkers with disabilities. The emergent themes from the interviews then enabled us to create an online survey designed to complement our interview approach by gathering perspectives from a larger group of people.

We created an accessible online survey using SurveyGizmo's accessible template. The survey consisted of 30 closed- and open-format questions to gather both quantitative and qualitative data. Questions asked participants to identify their disability(ies) and any assistive technologies they used. Respondents were asked about their familiarity with crowdsourcing, and to indicate which (if any) popular crowdwork sites they had worked through. Respondents were also asked whether they had experienced accessibility-related challenges in performing crowdwork, and to describe any such incidents. Finally, participants were asked several questions about employment more generally, including their own employment history and their attitudes toward and goals regarding work.

The survey was administered over a two-week period in February 2014. We used the Cint service to recruit a panel of 500 U.S.-based respondents who self-identified as disabled (after manually identifying "spam" responses, 486 valid surveys remained for analysis). Respondents were paid a small gratuity to complete the survey. Note that respondents were recruited only on the basis of disability status, and did not need to know anything about crowdsourcing in order to take the survey.

Because respondents were completing an online survey, and because they were registered with an online recruiting service (Cint), they may be more tech-savvy and/or more likely to engage in online activities (such as crowd labor) than typical. To mitigate this possible selection bias, we also advertised the survey to several email lists, forums, and social media aliases relating to particular disabilities, resulting in an additional 145 eligible survey completions. Additionally, we placed a HIT on Mechanical Turk to attempt to recruit Turkers who self-identify as disabled; 83 Turkers completed the survey through this route. The trends among all three recruitment sources were similar (though the group recruited from mTurk was obviously familiar with crowdwork, unlike the other two groups), so our quantitative analysis of the closed-form survey questions focuses on the 486 respondents recruited by Cint, who represent a broader variety of disabilities than those recruited through email lists (which ended up drawing heavily from people with visual impairments, due to some of the authors' previous work with visually-impaired communities). Though relatively diverse, we do not anticipate that the Cint survey respondents are a statistically representative sample of disabled people in the U.S.; however, this relatively informal sample can provide insight into high-level questions about the challenges in and value of crowdwork for people with disabilities.

FINDINGS

We first provide an overview summarizing the backgrounds and interests of interviewees and survey respondents, followed by more in-depth, qualitative analysis of the interview responses and survey free-response questions.

Quantitative Summaries from Interviews

Of the nine job coaches, one had a client who did crowdwork, and one had a client who used crowdwork in a computer class. All of the job coaches were very interested in crowdwork, but none felt that right now they could recommend crowdwork to clients as employment. Rather, all of the job coaches indicated they would suggest crowdwork as an educational tool to clients, both for learning how to use technologies and for learning how to maintain a good working relationship with an employer.

Of the eight disabled crowdworkers we interviewed, four do crowdwork multiple times a week, three do crowdwork sporadically, and one tried it once. The four who regularly perform crowdwork use Amazon Mechanical Turk the most and do a variety of tasks. Some of the task examples given were image recognition, French translation, research surveys from universities, and tasks related to music.

Quantitative Summaries from Surveys

Disability: The types of disabilities represented among survey respondents are shown in Table 1. Many write-in descriptions in the "other disability" and "serious health condition" categories overlapped; sample common responses included arthritis, schizophrenia, and PTSD.

Disability	Respondents
Cognitive impairment	5.0%
Dyslexia/reading disability	7.9%
Blindness/low vision	12.7%
Motor/dexterity challenge	16.4%
Autism spectrum	4.4%
Deafness/hard-of-hearing	18.4%
Other disability	41.2%
Serious health condition	35.5%

Table 1. Self-identified disabilities of 486 survey respondents recruited through Cint. All participants had at least one disability, and some had multiple disabilities, so numbers total to greater than 100%.

Geography: 100% of participants currently live in the United States. Participants represented almost every state in the U.S., with the exclusion of Vermont, Delaware, and Alaska. California residents represented 7.5% of the survey respondents, or 38 people. Florida closely followed with 37 respondents, or 7.3%.

Age: Table 2 shows the distribution of respondent ages; participants skewed older, which is not surprising given that many disabilities are acquired with advanced age.

Age	Respondents
14-17	1.4%
18-29	13.8%
30-39	11.7%
40-49	18.4%
50-59	28.1%
60+	26.5%

Table 2. Age distribution of 486 Cint survey respondents.

Gender: Female 57.4%, Male 42.2%, Transgender 0.2%, and prefer not to answer 0.2%.

Education: Participants represented a wide range of educational backgrounds, summarized in Table 3.

Education Level	Respondents
High school or less	5.0%
Some college/associate's degree	41.8%
Bachelor's degree	24.0%
Graduate degree	8.9%

Table 3. Highest level of education completed by the 486 Cint survey respondents.

Employment: Table 4 summarizes respondents' employment status. Unsurprisingly, a large proportion of respondents were not currently employed – Table 4 distinguishes between those who reported being unable to work due to their disability versus those whose unemployment was a more transitory state.

Employment Status	Respondents
Salaried Job	13.0%
Hourly Job	7.5%
Self-Employed	7.9%
Student	7.5%
Homemaker	9.3%
Retired	22.2%
Unable to work	32.8%
Unemployed (seeking work)	12.9%

Table 4. Employment status of the 486 Cint respondents.

Technology: 39.2% of respondents regularly use a device or feature on their computer or mobile phone to increase accessibility. These include speech recognition input, software or features to increase the contrast of the screen, screen reader software, keyboard accessibility features (e.g. Sticky Keys), and alternative pointing devices. 94.9% regularly use the Internet at home.

Employment considerations: 31% of respondents felt like they had been treated differently at a job because of their disability. Respondents ranked their top considerations for employment: 70.4% said that "loving what you do" was the most important aspect of a job, with salary (52.3%), flexible work time and place (45.1%) and health insurance (38.2%) following. 58.4% of people were interested in having a job search site specifically for people with disabilities.

Crowdwork: 12.4% of respondents had completed work on a crowdsourcing site. Among those who had experience doing crowdwork, the most commonly used platforms were Amazon Mechanical Turk (25 people), Clickwork (13 people), and MobileWorks (15 people). 18.8% of respondents who had tried crowdwork reported declining a crowdsourcing task in the last three months because they thought their disability would make it difficult to complete, and 28.1% reported facing a challenge completing a HIT due to their disability in the last three months.

Qualitative Findings

Using the qualitative open-coding methods described earlier, we identified several themes common in both the interview sessions and the open-ended survey responses (which asked survey respondents to describe any occasions when they had trouble completing crowdwork due to their disability and for thoughts on ways to improve crowdworking). However, we also indicate specific points of view that disrupt generalized ways of understanding an experience or commonly held belief. The main categories concern the accessibility of crowdwork and the tradeoffs inherent in performing at-home digital work.

We present the qualitative findings organized chronologically according to stages of the crowdwork process – learning about crowdwork, selecting tasks, performing tasks, completing tasks, and career prospects.

Learning about Crowdwork

One of the questions asked both in the surveys and interviews was how people learned about crowdwork. Many participants expressed excitement about the possibility of at-home work, and then disappointment with the real possibilities for crowdwork as a long-term employment option.

Participants shared a general feeling of satisfaction in finding real work online. In contrast to innumerable sites that offer points or an entrance into a survey drawing, participants found crowdsourcing sites unique for the quick and efficient payment. Other participants were generally excited about the idea of crowdwork and enjoyed it for aspects other than payment.

"I was laying around ... or sitting around because I've made myself sit up. I don't let myself lay back anymore. I sit in the chair and I click, click, click all day, and I was playing video games is all I was doing. One day, I thought, 'You know, I've got to be able to make money somehow,'

and so I put into a search engine, 'making money from home,' and just started going through, step-by-step, all of these different websites. mTurk is one of the ones that I found that you actually can make a little money. It's not big money, but it keeps me in ... gas money for the car and the few little things." P4

"I heard about it from a friend of mine who's blind and who uses a thing called VizWiz. He was talking about and not the first time he talked about it, but the second time we did it and I just thought it was great. Obviously a real need, obviously something that was technologically fine, and that was sustainable somehow if you imagine some way of funding it. I just followed up. I just took a look at it. My *French is one of the few things from my childhood that I can hold onto, at least my French text translation so I do a lot of that. Whenever I see a French to English translation I jump on it no matter what the rate is."* P6

These quotes share a positive reaction to crowdwork both as a source of payment but also as a means to participate in new activities, or to continue a previous hobby.

Most participants felt as though crowdwork marketplaces (where workers search for jobs) were generally accessible. That is, the UI of the crowdsourcing sites worked well for the most part. However, a subset of workers (particularly those with visual impairments) did encounter accessibility issues with the homepages of the crowdsourcing sites. Getting past CAPTCHAs to create accounts was a common challenge for visually impaired workers accessing the site via screen readers (a well-known accessibility problem not unique to crowdwork platforms) [[4]].

"Actually, a friend of mine and I were talking about different types of jobs and she was also thinking about some sort of transcription job...All I can remember it was through Amazon, so I typed something like Amazon transcription job into Google and after a plummet seeing around for a couple of minutes I found it, The Mechanical Turk. I thought, 'This is an interesting concept.' So I immediately went to sign up and ran into one of those CAPTCHAs" P1

One worker reflects on running into an accessibility issue with her screen reader while signing up to work on Amazon Mechanical Turk. She reached out to customer service, and was happy with the response. However, the step of reaching out to customer service may be prohibitive for the participation of some individuals who may be immediately frustrated by the lack of accessibility:

"And I said, 'Oh crap, I'm stuck.' But I took a gamble and I emailed them and I said, 'I'm blind and I really want to work with you, but I can't do the CAPTCHA.' They actually broadcast it [the CAPTCHA] *for me which was the first time anybody has been willing to do that, so they got me in and I've been off and running ever since then. It was kind of neat."* P1

Selecting tasks

Identifying tasks that were a good match for their abilities was a challenge for our participants.

Even when a crowdwork platform itself was accessible (or a participant had become accustomed to how to navigate it sufficiently), tasks linked to third-party sites with varying interfaces and levels of accessibility:

"Even if you did put in like a little formatting [on a crowdsourcing UI] *maybe that site will be accessible, you can't guarantee in that third party.."* P3

Many tasks sounded achievable from their initial descriptions, but then partway through would involve an unanticipated component not suited to a participant's abilities. Multiple people expressed frustration with not being able to effectively filter HITs for accessibility. Participants started a task and halfway, or two-thirds of the way through, were unable to complete the task:

"There's one that's been happening where the whole thing works just fine until you get to the end and it's a set of demographics: enter your age, what was your education, that stuff and for some reason, it won't accept the selections. You'll make two choices and click next and it just get stuck and there is nothing you can do. Interestingly enough, they're the ones that have a link at the top that say, 'For an optimized version for screen readers, click here,' but it seems to be now that if I don't choose that option, I don't have that problem. I'm not sure what happened there but that's been the biggest and then of course some of the surveys will require you to look at a picture without giving you any description. It's like, 'Oh crap. I can't do that.' That's frustrating." P1

Workers were not only frustrated by the lack of compensation for their time on such "abandoned" tasks, but also concerned about the effects of quitting a task partway through, after accepting, for their reputations (reputation on mTurk influences a user's future task opportunities).

Performing Tasks

The issue of socializing (or not) while working was a key theme that emerged in discussions of performing crowdwork. One concern is that for specific disability sub-populations the social aspect of a workplace is critical for personal development. On the other hand, for people with social anxiety, at-home work became a space not dominated by social interactions, while at the same time social interaction over the internet remained possible.

While job coaches were generally concerned about the lack of socialization of workers with disabilities, participants who had worked in traditional settings did not share this worry. Some people disagreed with the assumption that digital socialization is not a form of socialization; they shared that crowdwork actually enabled them to feel connected to a broader national and global community.

For some people with social anxieties, a workplace exacerbates issues and the result is that people end up out of work. Crowdwork offers a compelling alternative, allowing people to participate in employment without the person-to-person factor. One job coach described a client who has experience working in the customer support industry, but has a delay in voice communication that makes telephone support or interoffice communication difficult. The job coach expressed that the ideal job for the client is an at-home job of providing customer support in the form of text, either email or instant messenger. Another job coach talked about a client for whom working in a social environment is extremely stressful:

"*I don't know if we've found her a job yet, but she has social anxiety, and I think this crowdsourcing, would be perfect for someone who wants to work, is okay interfacing over phone or computer, but not okay going out of her home.*" P8

However, some coaches expressed concern that avoiding challenging situations might not be the best way for a client to grow their skills:

"*Mechanical Turk or other crowdsourcing opportunities might be good in those situations where students with autism and who have a social disability and it's really hard for them to get past those barriers, they wouldn't have to have that necessary contact that you would working in an office but at the same time a negative impact would be learning those skills and trying to teach those skills while learning on Mechanical Turk. I mean it doesn't offer too many face-to-face interactions so it wouldn't help us, as job coaches, to teach that social aspect of a job skill.*" P46

This following interviewee, who is visually impaired, shares the positive feelings towards digital anonymity as he reflects on respect while taking courses, or working, online. He currently crowdworks, but in this quote he draws on the comparison of taking college courses in person or online:

"*The nice thing is the people that I work with in the class itself, the other students, the fellow students, had no idea that I even had a disability. They didn't even know that I was blind because everything is done online. My posts looked just like the next guy's posts. As long as you get your work done then nobody cares. That concept was really awesome because it was just neat – I was just another student just like everybody else. Of course, I'm working differently but I'm getting it done and who cares if I use a mouse or if I don't. I'm getting the work done. It was a really cool concept that way.*" P2

This theme of removing social tension by having a worker's disability status not be apparent to co-workers was echoed by another participant who was pleased that when microtasking the pace of his work would not be visible to other workers:

"*Working online would be more comfortable than working in a public place due to the fact I am slower than other people*" P10

Completing Tasks

In our surveys and interviews we asked: "Did you ever have a time where you started a task, and were unable to complete the task due to a disability?" Answers to this question revealed that working within a timed task was an issue across multiple types of disabilities:

"*I was chosen to place a review in the time allotted to me but the words were too small and the machine I was using didn't have a magnifier so I kept getting sick and couldn't finish on time.*" P30

"*I was working on a very long transcription job that I was allowed 12 hours to complete when I developed a high pressure headache (something you get with BIH) and I didn't think I was going to complete it in time because of the pain level.*" N33

A job coach tried crowdwork with a client as a way to practice computer skills. However, she felt that the frustration of almost completing tasks, and then running out of time, negatively affected her client's self-confidence and has since stopped trying to incorporate crowdwork:

"*I think she did a business card one as well. Trying to do it in the time limit even though it seems like it might be a long time for her it really wasn't so she would get almost done and then it would time out and then she wouldn't be able to submit it so that got really frustrating for her.*" P46

Other participants, who couldn't complete tasks within the designated time limits due to a variety of disabilities, offered suggestions for changes in the design of the workflow to address this issue:

"*To be able to accept 'chunks' of jobs that would not expire so fast.*" P40

"*I would have more flexible time limits*" P36

One interviewee sent an email weeks after her interview. The excerpt below expresses a continued frustration with task completion and concerns about this issue's impact on her reputation as a worker:

"*In cases where a HIT has to be returned because of an accessibility issue I wish there was somewhere to be able to indicate that. I've had to return a bunch of HITs this week because halfway through there would be images I couldn't deal with or the survey would time out because sometimes it takes a little longer to make choices with a screen reader. I feel like that makes someone look bad as a worker when he or she has to return so many HITs which skews task completion statistics. I would like to be able to explain why or maybe have a second chance to try and complete the task. That probably is not possible to implement, but I thought I'd throw it out there for you.*" P1

On the other hand, one interviewee with a psychological disability expressed a history of getting severe anxiety regarding long-term work expectations. One thing that he liked about crowdwork is the ability to stop mid-task with no consequences:

"*They're intermittent and they're short and like no harm no foul if you stop. If you stop you just stop, you don't have to explain yourself. This is what I was saying about expectations. It's really clear and it's very permissive. You jump in, you try it, and you finish it and that's it or you don't finish it and nobody comes screaming down the hallway at you. I don't think I looked at something and said, 'Oh this looks like trouble. I'm feeling anxious just looking at this task.' That's never happened to me. But...Yeah. There are times when I've just had a little tantrum or something and stopped.*" P6

Career Prospects

In this section we reflect on the economic and career prospects of crowdwork noted by people with disabilities. The ability to perform work at home, without the need to navigate transportation challenges, is a big plus in favor of crowdwork for this population, as is the ability to work part-time as a supplement to government disability benefits. However, job coaches described many of the key factors they look for when placing workers with disabilities in positions (such as health insurance benefits), which might limit the potential of crowdwork as a career.

Many workers expressed that the ability to do crowdwork work from home far outweighs the benefits of working in an office. The primary theme here is the stress of transportation to and from work. A job coach emphasized that transit was a key problem with placing people with disabilities with employment:

"*Transportation, transportation, transportation. That is, I think, one of the biggest barriers is getting folks to where they need to be. If they can ride the typical bus and then that's usually not an issue. If they have to rely on specialized transportation and it gets you there either 45 minutes before your shift or 45 minutes after your shift, and picks you up 45 minutes early or doesn't pick you. That, I think, is a big issue.*" P8

People with disabilities who are covered by U.S. government disability payments expressed a range of emotions toward their motivations to do crowdwork. While many said it provided a valued supplement to their government payments, others said that they do crowdwork for fun and do not need the money. While no interviewees mentioned this, there is the risk that if people make too much money performing crowdwork they may become ineligible for disability assistance. Some people voiced frustration over the system of getting disability payments and others wished that stable at-home work opportunities existed so that they would not have to rely on government payments:

"*[I would like to work at-home] to find out if there might be something I could do to earn a wage and supplement my social security disability.*" P19

All of the job coaches said that they would not, at this point, encourage crowdwork as a real career option for clients because they had guidelines for viable work opportunities which included providing health insurance. In the next quote, a worker who needs medical assistance to fix an injury talks about the frustration of trying to make ends meet through crowdwork and social services. While the lack of health insurance for those successfully on disability may be a non-issue, for people who are in-between and due to a physical injury cannot work, the lack of health insurance offered by crowdwork is particularly problematic:

"*I don't even want to be on disability. I just need the insurance so that I can get fixed so that I can get back out into the workforce and be a productive citizen again. So, it's been highly frustrating ... very frustrating. Meanwhile, I can't do a lot of things, but I can lay back on the bed, prop myself up [coughs], excuse me, prop myself up with pillows and get my arms settled just right, and I can go click, click, click on the mouse with one finger. It doesn't hurt. That's what got me started into crowdsourcing.*" P1

We asked job coaches how they match clients with jobs and what standards they have for a job for their clients. Our interest here was to understand how job coaching currently works for people with disabilities and whether crowdwork may be a future potential employment opportunity:

"*They have to be permanent positions. They have to be a certain number of hours. We like to aim for 20 but we'd like to go with more if we can. They have to be an established organization and they can't be just in someone's home. It has to be actually a business. We like to involve people with inclusion in a workplace where they can have natural supports, a place where they can have a supportive manager, a place that's going to help work on their social skills, that's not going to stick them in the back, in a dark room somewhere.*" P45

DISCUSSION

This study was the first to look at the intersection of people with disabilities and crowdwork. Our findings illustrate that some people with disabilities are already participating in crowd labor markets as workers, that they participate for nuanced reasons that go beyond simple economic exchange, and that they face some challenges with respect to this participation. These findings lead us to re-interpret the meaning of "accessibility" with respect to crowd labor, to suggest design improvements for enhancing the accessibility of crowdwork platforms, and to suggest key directions for further research.

Unpacking Accessibility

Our interviews and surveys revealed that understanding the accessibility of crowdwork for people with disabilities was more nuanced than merely the accessibility of the UI of any particular piece of software they were using. Rather, accessibility seemed to operate at three different levels of abstraction.

The first level was what typically comes to mind when discussing accessible technologies – the basic usability of crowdwork software. In the case of crowdwork, this included not only having the crowdwork platform itself having an accessible website, but also involved dependencies on all the third-party sites, software, and tools that were often embedded within requesters' tasks. For instance, on mTurk, Amazon only controls the interface used for tasks created with its frameworks – requesters are free to point workers to web pages that they have designed themselves, which may have their own accessibility issues.

The second level concerned the accessibility of the workflow of microtasking. Workflow-related accessibility challenges included identifying which tasks of those available would be most appropriate to a workers' abilities, managing multi-tasking and switching among several different apps and UIs, and dealing with inflexible time limits on tasks.

The third level regarded the accessibility of the new job experiences enabled by crowdwork. This involved challenges like learning about the availability of such work. In their book on "Employment and Work," Bruyere and Barrington [[7]] note the need for education programs for people with disabilities to impart skills needed for modern job opportunities; our findings build on theirs by revealing that meta-education (about the *types* of opportunities available, e.g., crowdwork) is also necessary, in addition to education related to specific skills. Job coaches seemed to view crowdwork more negatively than people with disabilities, suggesting a possible bottleneck on disseminating information about the opportunity of this new class of work. For people who do learn about crowdwork opportunities, do current reputation structures allow them to participate fully and engage with the most challenging and rewarding work? Our findings suggest that challenges with the workflow might negatively impact the reputation ratings of people with disabilities in a way that limits their ability to advance up the crowdwork ladder.

Implications for Design

Our findings reveal several concrete steps that platform designers and/or individual requesters could take to enhance the participation of people with disabilities in crowdwork. These suggestions could benefit platform operators and task requesters by increasing the efficiency of crowd labor markets (e.g., better matching of users with tasks, fewer abandoned tasks), and by enhancing their reputation as communicative employers willing to recognize the needs of a diverse pool of workers. Many of these changes would benefit all workers, not only those with disabilities, as is often the case with improving technology's accessibility. However, it is unclear whether such motivations alone, without platform or legislative policies to compel compliance, would be sufficient to motivate any actions that require extra work or changes in working style by individual task requesters.

Platform operators could improve the experience of finding tasks by introducing metadata fields that indicate what types of abilities a task requires (e.g., ability to work under time pressure, ability to view images, ability to hear audio, etc.); alternatively, another set of crowdworkers could be employed to add such labeling to existing tasks, or, to some extent, this may be fully automatable (e.g., identifying which tasks contain captionless imagery, or which contain audio files). Recommender algorithms could be developed to identify tasks that require similar abilities to those already successfully completed by a given worker. Individual requesters could also take more care in providing descriptions of specific tasks to include ability-related details.

Adding the ability for a worker to easily "sub-contract" a component of a task to a different worker mid-task might be a solution for workers with disabilities who discover partway through a task that they cannot complete a particular aspect. Unfortunately, many microtasks cannot be further decomposed.

Platform operators could also provide an adjudication process through which workers with disabilities could seek to remove negative reputation points that have accrued due to disability issues, such as inability to complete a task due to improper description of required abilities or inadequate time allotments.

If platforms allowed people to optionally identify disabilities as part of their worker profile, such information could be used to automatically provide certain accommodations, such as extending time limits on tasks with flexible "due dates," supporting built-in microbreaks [[29]], filtering out inaccessible tasks, etc. Such profiles could also be useful for matching workers with particular disabilities to potential new crowdwork task types – if there is a significant presence of disabled crowdworkers, then software companies might be able to use such sites for crowdsourced accessibility testing of websites and services. However, evidence shows that people with disabilities have concerns about disclosing this information in other employment situations, and are unlikely to do so [[2]], which may limit the effectiveness of a self-disclosure based approach.

Developing an online community for crowdworkers with different disabilities could be valuable to this community. While not all workers are interested in identifying themselves publicly as disabled or interacting with others with disabilities, a substantial percentage of our survey respondents indicated interest in employment websites targeted to people with disabilities. Such a forum could help with disseminating information about available opportunities, curating reputation of requesters and platforms with regard to their accessibility, organizing for policy and lobbying purposes, and providing a space for a different kind of social interaction surrounding the work experience.

It is unclear, both legally and ethically, to what extent crowdsourcing platform operators versus individual task requesters should be responsible for ensuring the accessibility of tasks. For example, should platforms require compliance with certain standards before allowing a requester to post a task, or should they modify their APIs in a way that makes it easier to create accessible HITs and harder to create inaccessible ones, or perhaps create clear instructions and guidelines for requesters about accessible task design? Even though current U.S. law does not require this, it may be something crowdwork platforms ought to consider for ethical reasons, to broaden their potential participant base, to enhance their task completion rates, and/or to stave off potential future legal actions.

Future Directions

Our findings suggest several areas that warrant further investigation. An important avenue for future research is about understanding the level of representation of people with disabilities—in general and for specific disabilities—in this category of employment as compared to people without disabilities. This would involve more representative sampling than was done in this initial study, and would help answer questions about whether people with disabilities are adequately, under- or over-represented in this type of work.

Our research focused on people with disabilities participating in microtasking. An important avenue for future research would be to investigate the level of representation in higher-skilled crowdsourcing work such as oDesk and Freelancer. Such research may elucidate whether or not similar accessibility issues exist for the contract work population, as well. Throughout our research we met some people with disabilities who worked on higher-skilled contract sites, but we did not focus on collecting data on contracting crowdsourcing work.

Another possible avenue for research is to understand how crowdworkers with disabilities are currently interacting together and helping one another. A related direction is a comparative project on the accessibility of different crowdwork forums. Such a research direction would facilitate understanding whether accessibility to crowdwork is a platform-specific issue or whether it is a more systemic issue. In particular, it seems that platforms that allow for greater flexibility in task design by allowing requesters to point workers to their own web pages may also be at greatest risk for high variability in the experienced accessibility of the platform.

Our research found that people of all ages with a range of disabilities are performing crowdwork. Different disability sub-populations faced different challenges in crowdwork. Future research looking at how specific disability sub-populations are using crowdwork – such as the elderly, people on the autism spectrum, etc. – will be important in understanding changing crowdworker demographics. One promising aspect of crowdwork for the disability population is the possibility to work from home, set one's work hours, and manage social interactions. We share Kittur et al.'s suggestions for future research looking at how to build a) a career ladder, b) continuing education, and c) stability into future crowdwork UIs. Such research will be critical in order to make crowdwork a viable long-term option.

CONCLUSION

This research offered a first look into the participation of people with disabilities in an emerging form of digital labor – microtasking on crowdsourcing platforms. Through interviews and surveys, we demonstrated that people with disabilities are already participating in this new labor system, and identified some of the advantages and challenges they encounter through this type of employment. We reflected on how accessibility of digital work involves more nuance than the mere accessibility of a particular crowdsourcing website, and on design steps that employers can take to address the challenges identified by our participants. Full access to participate in emerging forms of labor is important not only as an economic opportunity for people with disabilities, but as a social recognition of their full participation in all aspects of society; our work has highlighted important considerations for platform operators, job requesters, and policy makers to consider as a next step along the path to making this full access a reality.

ACKNOWLEDGMENTS

We thank all those who wrote and provided helpful comments on previous versions of this document. In addition, we thank those who gave feedback on in-person presentations of this research material. We would also like to thank all participants in the research study.

REFERENCES

[1] Abberley, P. (1999). The significance of work for the citizenship of disabled people. University College Dublin.

[2] Allen, S. M. M., & Carlson, G. M. (2003). To conceal or disclose a disabling condition? A dilemma of employment transition. *Journal of Vocational Rehabilitation*, *10*, 19–30.

[3] Bigham, J.P., Jayant, C., Ji, H., Little, G., Miller, A., Miller, R.C., Miller, R., Tatarowicz, A., White, B., White, S., and Yeh, T. VizWiz: Nearly Real-Time Answers to Visual Questions. *Proceedings of UIST 2010.*

[4] Bigham, J.P. and Cavender, A.C. Evaluating Existing Audio CAPTCHAs and an Interface Optimized for Non-Visual Use. *Proceedings of CHI 2009.*

[5] Brady, E. L., Zhong, Y., Morris, M. R., & Bigham, J. P. Investigating the appropriateness of social network question asking as a resource for blind users. *Proceedings of CSCW 2013.*

[6] Breckenridge, C. A., & Vogler, C. A. (2001). The critical limits of embodiment: reflections on disability criticism. Durham, N.C.: Duke University Press.

[7] Bruyere, S.M. and Barringtron, L. (2012) "Employment and Work." In *Disability: Key Issues*

and Future Directions (G.L. Albrecht, ed.). SAGE Publications, Inc.

[8] Burton, M. A., Brady, E., Brewer, R., Neylan, C., Bigham, J. P., & Hurst, A. Crowdsourcing subjective fashion advice using VizWiz: challenges and opportunities. *Proceedings of ASSETS 2012.*

[9] Devlin, R. F., & Pothier, D. (2006). Critical disability theory essays in philosophy, politics, policy, and law. Vancouver, B.C.: UBC Press.

[10] Diament, M. (2014, March 25). Feds Move Forward with Disability Hiring Mandate - Disability Scoop. Retrieved from http://www.disabilityscoop.com/2014/03/25/feds-disability-hiring-mandate/19222/

[11] Emerson, R. M., Fretz, R. I., & Shaw, L. L. (2011). Writing ethnographic fieldnotes. Chicago: The University of Chicago Press.

[12] Folbre, N. The Unregulated Work of Mechanical Turk. (2013). Economix Blog, *New York Times.*

[13] Goggin, G., & Newell, C. (2003). Digital disability: the social construction of disability in new media. Lanham [Md.]: Rowman & Littlefield.

[14] Hara, K., Azenkot, S., Campbell, M., Bennett, C., Le, V., Panella, S., Moore, R., Minckler, K.,Ng, R., and Froehlich, J. Improving Public Transit Accessibility for Blind Riders by Crowdsourcing Bus Stop Landmark Locations with Google Street View. *Proceedings of ASSETS 2013.*

[15] Hara, K., Le, V., and Froehlich, J. Combining Crowdsourcing and Google Street View to Identify Street-level Accessibility Problems. *Proceedings of CHI 2013.*

[16] Hong, H., Yarosh, S., Kim, J.G., Abowd, G.D., and Arriaga, R.I. Investigating the Use of Circles in Social Networks to Support Independence of Individuals with Autism. *Proceedings of CHI 2013.*

[17] Ipeirotis, P. G. (2010). *Demographics of Mechanical Turk* (Working Paper). New York, NY, USA. Retrieved from http://archive.nyu.edu/handle/2451/29585

[18] Ipeirotis, P.G. Analyzing the Amazon Mechanical Turk Marketplace. *ACM XRDS*, Winter 2010.

[19] Kittur, A., Nickerson, J.V., Bernstein, M.S., Gerber, E.M., Shaw, A., Zimmerman, J., Lease, M., and Horton, J.J. The Future of Crowd Work. *Proceedings of CSCW 2013.*

[20] Kruse, D., Schur, L., & Ali, M. (2010, March 2). Projecting Potential Demand for Workers with Disabilities. *Monthly Labor Review.*

[21] Lasecki, W.S., Miller, C.D., Sadilek, A., Abumoussa, A., Borrello, D., Kushalnagar, R., and Bigham, J.P. Real-Time Captioning by Groups of Non-Experts. *Proceedings of UIST 2013.*

[22] Mankoff, J., Hayes, G. R., & Kasnitz, D. Disability Studies as a Source of Critical Inquiry for the Field of Assistive Technology. *Proceedings of ASSETS 2010.*

[23] Martin, D., Hanrahan, B. V., O'Neill, J., & Gupta, N. Being A Turker. *Proceedings of CSCW 2014.*

[24] Marvit, M. Z. (2014, February 4). How Crowdworkers Became the Ghosts in the Digital Machine. *The Nation.*

[25] McDermott, R., & Varenne, H. (1995). Culture as Disability. Anthropology & Education Quarterly, 26(3), 324–348.

[26] Notte, J. (2013, June 21). Goodwill pays disabled workers pennies an hour. *Msn.com.*

[27] Ross, J., Irani, L., Silberman, M. S., Zaldivar, A., & Tomlinson, B. Who Are the Crowdworkers?: Shifting Demographics in Mechanical Turk. *Extended Abstracts of CHI 2010.*

[28] Rush, C. L. (2012). Amending the Americans with Disabilities Act Shifting Equal Employment Opportunity Obligations in Public Human Resource Management. *Review of Public Personnel Administration*, 32(1), 75–86.

[29] Rzeszotarski, J. M., Chi, E., Paritosh, P., & Dai, P.. Inserting Micro-Breaks into Crowdsourcing Workflows. *Proceedings of HCOMP 2013.*

[30] Suzanne, L (2014). Some companies see opportunity in autism. CBS News. Retrieved May 10, 2014, from http://www.cbsnews.com/news/some-companies-see-opportunity-in-autism/.

[31] Teodoro, R., Ozturk, P., Naaman, M., Mason, W., & Lindqvist, J.. The Motivations and Experiences of the On-demand Mobile Workforce. *Proceedings of CSCW 2014.*

[32] von Ahn, L. and Dabbish, L. Labeling images with a computer game. *Proceedings of CHI 2004.*

[33] Weiss, R. S. (1995). Learning from strangers: the art and method of qualitative interview studies. New York: Free Press.

[34] Strauss, A. L., & Corbin, J. M. (1998). *Basics of qualitative research: techniques and procedures for developing grounded theory* (2nd ed.). Thousand Oaks: Sage Publications.

Illegitimate Civic Participation: Supporting Community Activists on the Ground

Mariam Asad **Christopher A. Le Dantec**

School of Literature, Media, & Communication
Georgia Institute of Technology
Atlanta, GA 30332 USA
{missasad, ledantec}@gatech.edu

ABSTRACT

In this paper we examine the way Information and Communications Technologies (ICTs) support forms of community activism that operate outside formal political and institutional channels. We have done fieldwork with local housing justice activists in order to gain insight into the way ICTs play a role in complementing forms of civic engagement that challenge, rather than work with, institutional authority. We argue that ICTs are instrumental in supporting and shaping three alternate information practices—*situating*, *codification*, and *scaffolding*—that each serve the goals of direct democratic engagement. We also show how local activist communities engage in these three practices through their varied use of ICTs, including the ways they provide mechanisms for informal but politically significant—and legitimate—civic engagement.

Author Keywords

Community Computing; Civic Engagement; Public Participation

ACM Classification Keywords

K.4.3 Organizational Impacts

INTRODUCTION

There are multiple ways to construct a democratic society [47], and multiple ways one might participate in such a society. Whether through participating in elections, or becoming involved in different citizen organizations, or working outside the 'system' to effect change, each mode of citizenship brings with it different sets of challenges for interpreting and accomplishing work and establishing collaborative practices to accomplish what are often large-scale goals to shape policy and governance [30, 47, 18].

CSCW '15, March 14 – 18, 2015, Vancouver, BC, Canada.

ACM 978-1-4503-2922-4/15/03...$15.00.
http://dx.doi.org/10.1145/2675133.2675212

Within the broad and diverse milieu of civic engagement, we can find diverse scholarship on the role of Information and Communication Technologies (ICTs) as a public good [22, 33, 35]. In looking beyond the commercial development, consumption, and use of ICTs, researchers have engaged in a number public sites: studies of educational policy and development have gauged the efficacy of ICTs as a pedagogical tool [48]; international development scholars have incorporated ICTs into user-centered design processes in developing countries [5, 36, 37]; and sustainability studies have asked how we might incorporate ICTs into sustainable environmental and economic practices [24, 28].

Additionally, researchers have begun to look at the use of ICTs in different political contexts. For example, with the growing presence of ICTs in public spaces, there are concerns of privacy, security, and authority; concerns made ever-more present after revelations of wholesale surveillance by government agencies [1, 3]. There are also questions on how to best leverage ICTs to encourage civic participation: the capabilities of contemporary social computing present new opportunities for the kind of deliberative democracy around which western political processes are based [9, 15, 27].

Many of the efforts to explore the role of ICTs in civic engagement dwell on concepts of e-democracy or digital democracy, which aim to realize traditional political ideals through technology mediated interactions. These interactions are meant to complement more familiar in-person, or analogue, forms of democracy and typically focus on the translation of traditional political practices into online spaces, including but not limited to e-polling and online fora for supporting discourse to inform public opinion [47].

There is a need to expand upon the sites and goals that commonly dominate efforts under the umbrella of digital democracy. We need to interrogate how different kinds of civic engagement exist on digital platforms in spaces outside formal political and institutional channels. What would it mean to think of political participation outside traditional, "legitimate" means of interacting with government, such as voting, lobbying through interest groups, or engaging in public oversight? How might ICTs play a role in complementing—rather than replacing—existing civic activities that are by nature more grassroots and local?

By "legitimate" civic action, we refer to the mechanisms and processes available to citizens in order to influence change and decision-making on issues of concern. Such action often takes place through the channels of representative democracy, such as elections, public officials, and policy regulations, but there are many other ways one might legitimately interact with government. Beyond e-townhalls and Change.org petitions, how are ICTs used to support and coordinate concrete, 'on the ground' political work done outside established political institutions? How do we consider the impact of these technologies on issue advocacy and activist work?

To explore these particular and understudied questions, we conducted ethnographic fieldwork with a housing justice activist group. Our work gained insight into how the specific affordances of different ICTs supported their mission of confronting the social injustices connected with the recent—and on-going—housing crisis in the U.S. The affordances of the ICTs they used in their work highlight a number of issues and concerns that demonstrate how current technologies are not well suited to the particular practices of activist organizations. Whereas institutionally mediated participation might be considered legitimate civic engagement, the activists with whom we worked engaged in a range of political acts, information management practices, and ways of organizing labor that challenge notions of legitimate action and demonstrate the role that ICTs play in supporting alternate, illegitimate forms of civic action.

ICTS AND CIVIC PARTICIPATION

The historic role of ICTs in supporting different community goals is long and diverse. From systems that support public deliberation in urban planning processes [20], to systems set in international contexts to support post-civil war reconciliation [4], ICTs have been deployed to both bring people together and to mediate the impact of those collective voices. These implementations are based on different models and values of democracy, which in turn structure how the ICTs are situated within particular sociocultural systems.

Digital Democracy

The development of the personal computer and the Internet were both inextricably bound to, and informed by, the counter culture movements in the US [45]. These factors instigated a rise in techno-democratic discourse where civic engagement and public participation were recast in light of using ICTs to overcome the physical, temporal, and spatial limits of traditional democracy [34, 35, 47].

Though often sanguine and uncritical, these early narratives of digital democracy brought to light different principles of democracy that, ideally, ICTs could enable—equality, access, and accountability, among others. However, just as the constituents of a democracy are heterogeneous and diverse, ICTs have varied impacts and influences on political practices. van Dijk deconstructs the concept of digital democracy and puts forward a thoughtful analysis of the interplay between different forms of democracy and various ICT affordances that might support or hinder different outcomes. [47]. van Dijk's analysis is comprehensive, but for the purposes of this paper, we limit our analysis to the models of democracy most commonly associated with civil engagement and community participation in the west, those of direct (*i.e.* non-representative) democracy: *participatory*, *plebiscitary*, and *libertarian* democracy.

A *participatory* democracy focuses its attention on the development of citizenship through civic education, discussion, and debate as a primary response to distrust in a ruling establishment [47]. The goal is to amass a collective will of the people such that they can directly engage with political officials, rather than communicating via intermediary organizations or representatives. Examples of this kind of support include virtual town halls and teleconferences. The main concern regarding ICTs in this model is access: ICTs should not only cater to the social, intellectual, or economic elite, but should work to narrow the gap between the information rich and the information poor.

Building on the participatory model, a *plebiscitary* democracy seeks to amplify the voice of an informed citizenry [47]. ICT use emphasizes more direct citizen involvement, such as voter registration systems or tele-referenda. These systems are, ideally, maintained and informed by the citizenry to ensure that their interests are served and not coopted by the ruling establishment.

The *libertarian* model emerged with the rise of personal electronics and, more specifically, the Internet [47]. Like the previous models, the libertarian model conveys a distrust of institutions; governmental entities are presumed to be unable to solve constituents' problems and, as a result, citizens must be autonomous, engaging in politics through group association and the "horizontal communication capabilities" of ICTs. The libertarian model moves away from artifacts of e-democracy—like tele-polls—and instead emphasizes discourse among the citizens themselves through ICTs like chatrooms, discussion boards, and email.

In van Dijk's model, ICTs do different kinds of democratic work, but a common thread binding them is the importance of an educated populace who engages in debate. Informed citizens and discourse are also important for political legitimacy according to Saward [43], who writes that public deliberation is crucial because it enacts political legitimacy: citizens are informed and reason amongst themselves to reach consensus, which then forms the basis of legal rules and a stable political system; the foundation of deliberative democracy relies on civic participation as exercised within the boundaries of an institutional entity (*i.e.* government) [42]. Laird's interpretation of pluralism similarly necessitates participation from an engaged populace through the formation of interest groups who influence policy outcomes, not unlike the way libertarian democracy emphasizes free association with interest groups [30, 47]. The associations form around issues of concern and organize to ensure that officials in power make decisions for the good of the polity. Organized pluralist groups are also a mechanism for political legitimacy because they act as a safeguard to keep political officials in check, ensuring they act justly in service of their constituents. These actions of the pluralist groups can be seen as information management practices in the service of democracy.

Public Civic Service

Beyond the deployment of ICTs for the purpose of supporting governance, the introduction of ICTs as a public good has been explored through a variety of perspectives. In addition to contributions made to pedagogical and economic development domains [24, 28], ICTs also address various challenges faced by non-profit organizations to better address questions of accountability, transparency, and information flow [22, 33, 40, 41]. To this end, the function of ICTs in these public organizations is similar to their role in private organizations: they contribute to a more efficient organization, maximizing the use of resources and distributing them to best serve the needs of the organization as a whole. However, non-profit organizations face challenges unique from corporate contexts: *e.g.*, non-profit work relies heavily on the labor and efforts of a volunteer workforce, which typically entails a high staff turnover and varied training or educational backgrounds [23, 34, 39]. Organizations that rely on volunteer efforts also employ ICTs to create make-do structures to account for gaps in knowledge, training, or infrastructure. These solutions serve important organizational needs as ICTs become ways to bridge and coordinate efforts in resource- and labor-constrained environments [8, 13, 41].

In a similar vein, researchers have introduced ICTs into neighborhood contexts to equip residents or participants with particular skillsets with the aim of empowering the community to engage in civic participation [19]. The aim of this kind of civic work is to encourage critical thinking about common issues and concerns, develop engagement with a community's physical and lived environments, and coordinate efforts on multiple scales to improve services and local collaboration [13, 39, 41]. One of the particular challenges faced in these settings is knowledge transfer because working at the scale of small communities often means relying on specialized and local knowledge that either requires specific expertise or the implementation of systems (social or technical) to enable information transfer [8, 32].

The introduction of ICTs into more institutional or formalized environments also does not necessarily focus on developing skills or acquiring knowledge specific to a particular domain. Gordon incorporated virtual worlds into traditional planning practices (*i.e.* charrettes) to encourage empathy and understanding among residents of the same community [25, 26]. This expansion beyond more conventional planning tools offers researchers new ways to engage with various publics: Gordon's work created space for residents to better envision potential changes made in their neighborhood. The workshop also offered some transparency to previously inaccessible planning conversations and vocabularies. On a pragmatic level, ICTs can also offer new sources of data to incorporate into their analysis. Social media, for example, has the ability to broadcast information to a set audience, but also collect real-time data that can facilitate a connection between city departments and citizens [16, 17]. ICTs writ large offer channels of communication that can facilitate both formal (*e.g.* those aimed at organizational efficiency) and informal (*e.g.* those built to encourage empathy) modes of civic service to benefit the public.

Given the diverse ways ICTs have made their way into public life, there is a clear richness to ICTs as they facilitate different kinds of civic participation. ICTs also cater to a variety of democratic relations by enabling specific kinds of interactions through many different legitimate means: informed citizens can engage with each other, interest groups can influence policy decisions, and communities can contribute to urban planning practices. However, these forms of civic participation are mechanisms for *representative* democracy: elected officials have the agency to enforce change and ICTs can only ever act within predetermined processes.

Our fieldwork speaks to the boundaries of current systems by examining how activists use ICTs to serve the democratic ideals mentioned above, but through more direct and engaged tactics. Activist work stresses the need to explore how ICTs can support alternate democratic practices to beget different kinds of outcomes. Our ethnographic fieldwork suggests at least one avenue: while ICTs can, themselves, be vehicles through which democracy is practiced, our time spent with a local activist group showed the value of ICTs to coordinate and facilitate already existing political work on the ground. Through our observations, we developed insight into the particular strengths, needs, and limitations of activist groups who use different forms of ICTs to achieve a more inclusive and equitable society.

BACKGROUND, METHOD, PARTICIPANTS

In order to understand the particular needs and uses of ICTs by activist organizations, we conducted ethnographic fieldwork with a local issue-oriented community called Occupy Our Homes Atlanta (OOHA). The organization was an outgrowth of the Occupy movement that developed in 2011 to protest social and economic inequality. OOHA focused specifically on housing justice and provided foreclosure and eviction rights education. They were driven by a belief that decent housing is a universal human right, that disenfranchised communities have the right to self-autonomy, and that politicians should be held accountable to their constituents rather than to corporate stakeholders. The tactics that OOHA deployed were often antagonistic and attention-seeking, which created a complex relationship with supporters, the public, and private officials with whom they interacted. The group engaged in non-violent direct action, such as protests and sit-ins in public spaces. These activities were sometimes illegal, but were not always intended to break the law. This intentionality is important to distinguish from anarchists, who frequently operate under the guise of activism; OOHA, by contrast, only engaged in illegal activities strategically to forward political causes in the service of justice. OOHA's work was largely in resistance to established institutions that they saw as major players and responsible parties with respect to housing issues (*e.g.* banks, local authorities).

We spent over a year and a half deeply involved with OOHA, participating at least three hours a week in organization meetings and protest events. During this time we documented our observations and participation through extensive, field notes and memos [10, 13]. During our time with the organizations we hosted design workshops to explore specific questions of technology use [2]; we contributed administrative work (*e.g.* note taking, data entry); we attended major actions, such as marches, court auctions, and press events; and we helped creat internal documentation (*e.g.* by-laws, codes of conduct). The time spent with the group has offered insight into their organizational norms, motivations, and the activists' perceptions of their own work [2].

The group was a rich research site because of the unique role they serve: their strategies were deliberately enacted in what they refer to as "the public court." They conducted their work publicly, rather than through less visible services that might be directly provided to home owners at risk of foreclosure and eviction. This approach was based on a commitment to creating an infrastructure of engaged and informed citizens inspired to take action in instances where institutional politics had failed. In addition to embodied political action on the streets, much of OOHA's work dealt with information gathering and management: their protests were in direct response to exploitative—in many cases, illegal—and generally invisible actions taken by banks following the housing-market collapse [43]. The banks that OOHA confronted were large, established institutions, that had a vested interest in making invisible the knowledge about their unjust practices: it was the predatory practices of the banking industry in the late 2000's that motivated the group to engage in direct action.

While information practices—collecting and sharing data, documenting specific events—were part of the group's everyday work, knowledge gathering and analysis played a very particular role during protest actions. It was the specific information needs and information sharing practices that developed during a protest action that became particularly interesting as an under-explored venue of collaborative work. To illuminate the particular needs of activists engaged in protests, we focus on a four-hour window of a single day in August where OOHA organized a series of protest actions to support a resident who was forcibly evicted from his home that morning. This window of time is intentionally narrow in order to demonstrate the depth and intricacy of activist work. Our field notes, observations, and coding schemas resulted in the following analysis of activist activities and three categories of information practices. The described practices are emblematic of the group's ICT use under contingent, unpredictable circumstances, but also shine a light on the way in which the chosen systems operate in service of democratic principles.

ILLEGITIMACY IN ACTION

Over the course of the four-hour protest action, OOHA engaged with ICTs across three distinct sets of practices: situating, codification, and scaffolding. *Situating* was a process of revealing to the public the issues at hand and the consequences of those issues to which the group was trying to draw attention. *Codification* included acts of translation where one domain, issue, or body of knowledge was translated for different purposes within the organization. *Scaffolding* operationalized different bodies of knowledge in order to help recruit and marshal additional support from a wide range of loosely connected social justice groups, concerned community members, and neighbors. These three concepts are not mutually exclusive; practices situated in the moment of a protest action often connected to multiple categories of ICT use simultaneously. By discussing them separately, however, we want to draw attention to the labor, design, and organization that goes into each of these practices in order to accomplish the organization's civic-oriented goals while working in highly volatile contexts.

Situating

ICT use in the service of *situating* entails the strategic positioning of resources in order to broadcast information to audiences outside the housing justice group. Specifically, activists used ICTs to *situate* during the action to deliberately reveal hidden information; revealing this knowledge created an argument about the resident's individual eviction within the context of the larger housing crisis. Part of the group's work writ large was making transparent banking practices that were viewed as exploitative; this information sharing practice typically dealt with financial information from banks, deeds and related ownership documents, or internal organizational structures that could identify accountable parties.

Situating practices played a much more pointed role on the day of an eviction protest because it set the context for the action itself: ICTs were used to uncover and share what the group argued to be predatory banking practices, which showed what led to the eviction of the resident that day. The motivation behind this design was the hope that it would create a powerful statement and act as a compelling call to action for others to join the protest. Searching for information and making it public may resemble research practices in similar organizations, like advocacy or policy groups, but a key distinction was that OOHA activists believed institutions were deliberately hiding information; revealing these bodies of knowledge was what justified and legitimized the group's actions, which were commonly seen

Figure 1: The Home Defenders League Twitter feed shows tweets leading up to and on the day of the protest action.

as hostile or antagonistic. It was the severity of the hidden information—both the efforts in keeping it hidden and the gravity of the exploitative practices themselves—that directly informed why the group felt it necessary to take any action at all.

During the eviction protest we observed, the activists used Twitter to communicate general updates about the individual resident's eviction. The updates themselves were not a unique use of Twitter, but the group did take advantage of the affordances of the medium in order to craft a particular argument about the protest to other audiences. The rhetoric heavily relied on the Twitter feeds of affiliate housing justice groups, as well as an intimate knowledge of the content of affiliate group feeds.

The Home Defenders League (HDL) is one such affiliate group. HDL is a national organization working with smaller scale groups to offer strategies and tactics for defending homes. They can be seen as more of an advocacy group that deals in bureaucracy and policy changes rather than direct action. Figure 1 shows six tweets from the HDL feed leading up to and on the day of the eviction. The feed combined different kinds of knowledge around the same topic and incorporated different modes of information delivery, including Facebook pages, MSNBC video clips, New York Times news articles, economics blogs, and a widely used progressive hashtag (#P2). The use of the #P2 hashtag can itself be seen as a kind of situating practice, but one that is built into Twitter itself and does not deeply engage with the affordances of the medium. The HDL feed already participated in a process of revealing and informing; this is key to understanding the role of situating during the protest action.

Consider the tweets in Figure 1. The argument created through the tweets is through juxtaposition: the resident's eviction was framed as part of a national crisis, which was a direct result of the practices of large banking institutions. The rhetoric afforded by the Twitter feed is possible because the activist tweeting on the ground was intimately familiar with the HDL feed and its contents: by her own admission, posting on Twitter the day of the eviction was almost entirely driven by the certainty that it would be retweeted by HDL and similar groups. This did more than just boost the signal of communication going out from the protest: it leveraged online content strategically as a way to situate the resident's individual eviction within the larger context of housing justice. The on-the-ground updates showed some of the very material, embodied impacts of the crisis (images of personal belongings thrown on the lawn, crowds of supporters, etc.), but also the more factual, data-heavy tweets from affiliate organizations demonstrated the vast scale and magnitude at which housing injustices occur.

The situating process is not without its stipulations: when it is not made explicit what information can and cannot be shared, situating can fail and effectively work against the group. During the action, a non-member was present with a video camera livestreaming the day's events. It was discovered that he had posted sensitive, internal material online and energy had to be diverted to redact the information and do damage control. In that moment of re-covering, it demonstrated how important control was for this practice; situating can be counter-strategic if the group's boundaries are not closely and intentionally maintained. By the same token, it was because of OOHA's semi-opaque positioning that they were able to gather, uncover, and communicate information about exploitation in housing without larger banking institutions acting in retribution (*e.g.* taking legal recourse).

Codification

Codification refers to the ways group members tailored their communications to different audiences; this act of translation ensures that specific bodies of knowledge were directed to meet particular ends. While there were a few OOHA members who had participated in similar eviction actions previously, that knowledge still needed to be distributed in some capacity to the other volunteers and supporters. Codification made it such that people who were present learned practices that could then be adapted to best reach different recipients. On the day of the action, this took the form of political solidarity; volunteers recruited people to be physically present at the residence to offer support to the resident and to shame impending authorities into not carrying out the eviction.

Supporters at the eviction were given a standardized text message to send to their contacts and a general script for voice conversations to invite people to the residence. Beyond the script, however, there was some instruction as to the subtleties of recruiting: there were a number of factors that would impact how politically palatable the call would be, such as the strength of the relationship with the caller and the respondent's political persuasion, but the most influential factor was the selection of communication technology.

As seen in the previous section, Twitter was used to broadcast a blanket invitation that, when retweeted by affiliate groups, had a slim possibility of successfully convincing anyone to join the action. In order to achieve direct participation, the most widely used modes of communication were text messages and phone calls and the decision to use one over the other was complex. Some contacts preferred entirely text-based communication, so a phone call might potentially backfire, though some volunteers thought that, in this context, a phone call would impart a sense urgency, which would better garner political support. Some group members, having engaged in recruiting before, were familiar with rebuffs and shared with the group some tactics for preempting negative responses. Text messages might be more effective with people who were ideologically aligned, whereas phone calls were a medium better suited for having conversations, like explaining the unfairness of the eviction or the importance of having physical presence at the house.

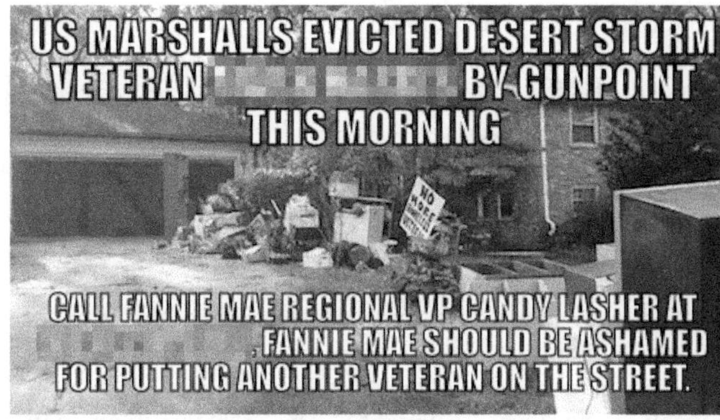

Figure 2: The Facebook macro uses both a visual image and text to try and encourage civic action.

In addition to phone calls and texts, volunteers were encouraged to share with their Facebook networks a member-created image macro, a short caption (typically white, bold, sans-serif text) superimposed on an image. The genre is typically humorous or witty, such as lolcats or Advice Animals, though the group had co-opted macros as a form of information broadcast, relying on irony or satire instead of humor.

The image offers another mode through which volunteers tried to recruit supporters at a different scale than phone calls or text messages as the posted image on Facebook reached a large audience at once. The image tactic spread a blanket message, like Twitter, but readers on Facebook have stronger relationships to the resident via the volunteers posting the image, and thus are more likely to engage in varying capacities (*i.e.* making a phone call, sharing the image, showing up at the residence). Activists and supporters sharing the image on Facebook relied on existing relationships with people—*i.e.* people who may be politically or ideologically aligned—to respond to the macro with some form of action.

The challenges of codification can be attributed to the speed of communication afforded by each technology: if a volunteer was prompted for more information than she had been given by a more experienced member of the group, the conversation falters and the communication structure begins to break down. This has severe implications when trying to build community support for the resident. If the distributed knowledge was not enough for the volunteer to be persuasive in a conversation, the entire action was impacted. A lack of information might demonstrate ignorance about the subject, lack of dedication to the cause, or—worse—might result in misinformation, defeating the driving force behind codification efforts entirely.

Scaffolding

Scaffolding refers to ICT use that creates space for non-group members to participate in an action without prior knowledge of or history with an activist group. The motivation behind this observed practice was to strategically distribute information via ICTs so that people who were politically aligned could participate in the group's actions without being physically present at the residence. Scaffolding harnessed the momentum of allies, community supporters, and affiliated social justice groups and allowed them to take action for and with the resident with minimal delay and through varying capacities.

The aforementioned image macro was not pre-planned, but was created at the residence after the action had already started. The creator of the macro stated that her intention was to broadcast eviction information to as many people as possible in hopes they would take up the call to action and help save the resident's home. She also explained that she opted to use a meme in spite of its reputation online (*i.e.* as a visual punchline) because "it worked." The creator explained the different ways in which Facebook, as a platform, offered the most opportunity for reach and visibility. Visually, the macro used a striking image, which was an effective hook into the textual content. A mundane 'like' on the image was meaningful to the resident and was seen as a form of emotional support or political solidarity. The image also communicated more than a text description of the event—it was affective as much as it was informative—which the creator hoped would lead to it to be shared more widely. She described the 'share' function as relatively user friendly and requiring minimal Facebook expertise. Scaffolding was incorporated into the image through multiple layers of invitations: as posted via Facebook, the image was a link to a wall post on OOHA's Facebook page that explained the details of the resident's eviction. The macro was also an invitation to multiple forms of action: in addition to Facebook's 'share' feature, there was a script provided in case someone called the Fannie Mae phone number. There were also links to the resident's online petition and various blogposts about his story leading up to the action, both of which could have been 'liked' or 'shared.'

The ultimate goal of using ICTs during the action was to draw out more people to support the resident in person during the eviction process. The scaffolded Facebook macro, however, provided some flexibility to allow for varying kinds of engagement: whereas the situated Facebook macro relied on existing resources (*i.e.* the strength and closeness of interpersonal relationships), the scaffolded image operated autonomously and allowed for supporters to participate in the action remotely without prior training or needing to be assigned tasks. The posted image on Facebook was a way to instrumentalize political support and resulted in a high post reach and an organized campaign to flood Fannie Mae with phone calls voicing support for the resident. To date, the macro reached 359 people and has 182 comments, 317 likes, and 2,893 shares, compared to the 50 or so people who were physically present the day of the eviction.

DISCUSSION

Metrics, Evaluation, and Success

Most of the ICT use we observed offered some degree of metrics; OOHA could tally Facebook shares and Twitter retweets after a protest action. However, it is unclear how the metrics would inform any further action or decisions within the group; there is no implicit meaning to a Facebook like or a favorite Tweet. Other tactics are even less legible. Other than physical bodies present at the residence, it is difficult to identify what qualifies as a success: a reclaimed home might only be temporary, and even the presence of supporters is ambiguous. A crowd could connote a network of allies, perhaps from affiliate groups, but supporters present at the residence may have their own motivation for participating (*e.g.* shared press, owed favors, recruiting for their own organization). This highlights a challenge for incorporating ICTs into activist practices: social computing technologies offer the allure of various metrics—such as number of retweets, email newsletter opens, or blogpost views—but they do not translate into any clear criteria for evaluation or directions for future action.

Due to the intersectionality of social justice work, it is often futile to connect a particular task with a goal; end goals are varied and interrelated, which can be at odds with design processes that are often oriented towards specific uses. Part of the challenge is assigning specific goals to particular actions. Consider the democratic models introduced earlier: it is clear how the Facebook macro is aligned with principles such as narrowing the information gap or informing a populace, but it becomes more complicated when tying the macro to a specific goal, such preventing someone's home from being foreclosed upon. As such, OOHA makes decisions to support the city-wide housing justice movement, but they are also oriented towards less specific but related objectives, such as progressive politics in the predominantly conservative Atlanta region or regaining local and community control in disenfranchised neighborhoods. Additionally, a particular protest action may try to address many goals simultaneously.

In the same way that OOHA is driven by a network of overarching objectives, the individual metrics of a specific use of ICT must be situated within a larger scale of impact. The Facebook macro might not have done any civic work in and of itself, but it resulted in a call-in campaign to the regional Fannie Mae office, which might have some immeasurable result in the future. There is some demonstrated impact, but there is no way to evaluate the role of the ICT itself; the group can infer that it was the number of likes that led to the phone calls, but it cannot validate that through the available tools. van Dijk suggests that particular ICTs are better suited for different kinds of civic work [47]; our analysis of the protest action discourages limiting a single goal or purpose to a particular use of an ICT. The Facebook macro could have made multiple impacts: it could have raised awareness, facilitated discourse, or instigated 'real world' action. However, the expectation that the use of or evaluation of an ICT for a single effect is to limit the potential impact it might have—to OOHA, its cause, and its members—more broadly.

We suggest a reframing: the question should not ask *how* ICTs could best measure success, but rather *should they*? Because of the difficulties inherent in activist work, morale and organizational motivation might suffer when actions are divided into successes and failures. This binary limits the activist group through over-engineering their work: by categorizing a protest action a success, it imposes goals, qualifiers, and consequences that do not translate well to the kind of immeasurable objectives that activists work toward, such as political support or educating uninformed audiences. Often, activists will refer to an action in terms of highlights, accomplishments, and progressions, which helps members feel empowered and motivated to continue the work. This is not to be interpreted as acts of denial or placation, but rather acts of sustainability and care to prevent burnout, fatigue, or disillusionment; community empowerment is another example of impact on activist work that ICTs can facilitate, but cannot measure. While ICTs are impactful in operationalizing activist work, they do not provide legible feedback that is appropriate for evaluation.

Design Orientations

In some ways, designing systems to support activism poses similar challenges as designing for traditional office work: practices are dynamic and emergent, environments are contingent, and plans must be tailored to the specificities of each use case. However, because of the unpredictability of housing justice work and activism writ large, OOHA faces unique challenges in trying to do their particular kind of democratic work. Returning to van Dijk, his participatory democracy model assumes that information is freely available for a polity to self-inform [47]. However, the situating example demonstrates that what constitutes 'knowledge' is contestable and can be interpreted to have different implications for civic work, such as the role the banks played in the housing crisis. It is not enough to design a system for activists that reveals information, but it must also be assembled and contextualized. Additionally, activist work relies on *ad hoc* practices and quick responses: the Facebook macro would not have been as impactful had it been posted the day after the eviction, for example. This environment of unpredictability refuses system designs that rely on stability and persistency.

Rather than try to force structure onto the inevitable uncertainties of activist work, designers of activist ICTs should embrace these inconsistencies. It would be more beneficial to design for existing activist practices instead of imposing design onto activist communities. This reorients the typical design process: instead of identifying particular activist-specific problems (*i.e.* to solve through design), how can we design infrastructures to support an activist context? We suggest a move away from artifact- and outcome-centric ways of thinking about designing systems for activists. We instead propose *flexibility* and *process* as two examples that do not prescribe specific solutions or artifacts, but suggest approaches that can better support activist work.

Flexibility affords a less rigid relationship between how something is *designed* to be used and how it *might* be used; designing towards flexibility is to cultivate more of a possibility space to encourage creativity and interpretation. Thinking beyond outcome-oriented design, Gmail's delegation feature is an example of a more flexible approach: one Gmail user can allow another access to their account such that the chosen delegate can view and send email from the delegator's email address. The delegation feature is specific or detailed enough to center on a particular goal or value— such as efficiency or collaboration— but caters to certain *circumstances* that might suggest how the feature is used, like constant absenteeism or distributed communication responsibilities.

We draw a parallel to Bill Gaver's work when designing for ambiguity [21]. Gaver argues that the design of artifacts can be intentionally vague to be provocative and engaging: a product can draw attention to inconsistencies, which resists a transparent or legible reading and in turn encourages users to be reflective and thoughtful. This approach would be beneficial to activists if there was a move away from the construction of artifacts and ambiguity was instead treated as a kind of design logic. Instead of an activist using ambiguity in a system to arrive at a conclusion or form their own interpretation, we would encourage ambiguity as a means to communicate an *argument*, much like the strategic use of Twitter and its retweet mechanism. We observed many instances of information gathering during the protest, but it was not until it was synthesized—that is, finding the ambiguities in the knowledge and leveraging them to create arguments—that the information became valuable and instrumental. In Gaver's work, ambiguity was an attribute designed to create particular interactions between the user and the artifact [21]. To design with flexibility in mind, we argue for ambiguity between different components or interactions, which creates space for activists to use a system for their own purposes, rather than a prescribed one.

Process refers to designs that operate more like a platform than a single, deterministic service. This approach emphasizes the relationships between and integrations of existing components, rather than individual components themselves. An existing example might be IFTTT (If This Then That), which links various services together: the platform relies on actions and triggers in order to connect and enable various web applications. For example, if a photo is posted to Instagram with a specific hashtag, that might trigger an automated post to Facebook and Twitter simultaneously, which would reduce labor spent on menial online updates when urgency is required elsewhere on the ground.

The emphasis on generative interactions invokes Björgvinsson, *et al*'s framework for participatory design: they argues that design should be a process of democratization by pursuing ways to "organize milieus for innovation" [6]. Activist work could benefit from specific services that afford them more agency and control, but the activities would still be confined to the parameters and constraints of the platform. This kind of logic could be seen through the use of the Facebook meme: the activist acknowledged the limitations of the platform in communicating the group's message, but was also savvy enough to leverage its different features (*e.g.* sharing, liking) to garner multiple kinds of support for the resident in a time of need, resulting in a dynamic that supported multiple forms of participation (*e.g.* political, emotional, organizational).

These two approaches might be at odds with particular values held by an organization—such as privacy concerns with flexible design—so they should not be applied indiscriminately. Instead, these approaches should be implemented within the context of a specific group's practices and values. We focus on process and flexibility as ways to better support activist work through *under*deterministic design. Dourish points out that people do not encounter technology as designed rather but situate them into practice [14]. Indeed, this appropriation is the basis of activist work and should inform the design work that is done with or for activist communities. When designing systems to support activism as a kind of collaborative work, didactic principles, guidelines, or frameworks are overly prescriptive and would not adapt well to the fluid nature of their work. We encourage thinking beyond deterministic outputs to reconsider how ICTs might better facilitate existing activist practices to work more towards democratic principles rather than explicit results.

CONCLUSION

We observed how OOHA used ICTs at a housing justice action, which allowed us to begin teasing out ways in which systems can be used to support more on-the-ground forms of civic engagement and might allow us to envision different kinds of political support, participation, and communication. We bring attention to and draw out the nuances of particular activist ICT uses as opportunities for the CSCW community to better reflect on system design to better cater to these kinds of political work and facilitate illegitimate civic participation as a valuable and significant means of practicing democracy.

ACKNOWLEDGMENTS

The authors would like to thank our community collaborators at OOHA for graciously accepting us into their communities and homes. We also owe much to Sarah Fox (UW), who contributed to early stages of this work. This research was supported by the Intel Science and Technology Center for Social Computing.

REFERENCES

[1] Agosto, D. and Abbas, J. High school seniors' social network and other ICT use preferences and concerns. *Proc. ASIS&T '10*, (2010), Article No. 65.

[2] Asad, M., Fox, S., & Le Dantec, C.A.. Speculative Activist Technologies. *Proc. iConference,* (2014), 229-243.

[3] Becker, T. Rating the Impact of New Technologies on Democracy. *Commun. ACM* 44, 1 (2001), 39–43.

[4] Best, M.L., Jones, K., Kondo, I., Thakur, D., Wornyo, E., and Yu, C. Post-conflict communications: The case of Liberia. *Commun. ACM* 50, 10 (2007), 33–39.

[5] Best, M. and Kumar, R. Sustainability failures of rural telecenters: Challenges from the sustainable access in rural india (sari) project. In *Information Technologies and International Development.* ACM, (2008), 31-45.

[6] Björgvinsson, E., Ehn, P., Hillgren, P.A. Participatory design and "democratizing innovation." *Proc. PDC.* (2010), 41-50.

[7] Caldeira, F., Monteiro, E., and Simões, P. Trust and reputation for information exchange in critical infrastructures. *Proc. CRITIS '10*, ACM, (2010), 140-152.

[8] Carlisle, P. Transferring, Translating and Transforming: An Integrative Relational Approach to Sharing and Assessing Knowledge across Boundaries. *Proc. CRITO.* (2004).

[9] Cohen, Joshua. "Deliberation and democratic legitimacy." *Debates in Contemporary Political Philosophy* (1989): 342-360.

[10] Dimond, J., Dye, M., Larose, D., and Bruckman, A. Hollaback!: the role of storytelling online in a social movement organization. *Proc. CSCW*, (2013), 477-490.

[11] DiSalvo, C., Light, A., Hirsch, T., Le Dantec, C., Goodman, E. and Hill, K. HCI, communities, and politics. In *CHI EA '10.* ACM, (2010), 3151-3154.

[12] DiSalvo, C., Nourbakhsh, I., Holstius, D., Akin, A. and Louw, M. The Neighborhood Networks Project: A Case Study of Critical Engagement and Creative Expression Through Participatory Design. *Proc. PDC.* ACM, (2008), 1975-1984.

[13] Dombrowski, L., Voida, A., Hayes, G.R. and Mazmanian, M. The labor practices of service mediation: a study of the work practices of food assistance outreach. *Proc CHI.* ACM, (2012), 1977–1986.

[14] Dourish, P. Implications for design. *Proc. CHI.* ACM, (2006), 541-550.

[15] Dowling, J. and Pfeffer, J. Organizational Legitimacy: Social Values and Organizational Behavior. In *The Pacific Sociological Review.* 18, 1 (Jan 1975), 122-136.

[16] Evans-Cowley, J. Planning in the age of Facebook: the role of social networking in planning processes. *GeoJournal.* 75, (2010), 407–420.

[17] Evans-Cowley, J. Planning in the Real-Time City: The Future of Mobile Technology. *Journal of Planning Literature.* 25, 2 (Nov. 2010), 136–149.

[18] Fiorino, D. Citizen participation and environmental risk: A survey of institutional mechanisms. *Science, Technology, and Human Values.* 15. (1990), 226-243.

[19] Fox, S. and Le Dantec, C.A. Community Historians: Scaffolding Community Engagement through Culture and Heritage. *Proc. DIS.* ACM, (2014), 785-794.

[20] Friedman, B., Borning, A., Davis, J.L., et al. Laying the Foundations for Public Participation and Value

Advocacy: Interaction Design for a Large Scale Urban Simulation. *Proc. dg.o.* ACM, (2008), 305-314.

[21] Gaver, W., Beaver, J., and Benford, S. Ambiguity as a resource for design. *Proc. CHI.* ACM, (2003), 233-240.

[22] Goecks, J., Voida, A., Voida, S. and Mynatt, E.D. Charitable Technologies: Opportunities for Collaborative Computing in Nonprofit Fundraising. *Proc. CSCW.* ACM, (2008), 689-698.

[23] Ghassan, A. and Blythe, M. On legitimacy: designer as minor scientist. In *CHI EA '13*. ACM, (2013), 2149-2158.

[24] Goldweber, M., Little, J.C., Cross, G., Davoli, R., Riedesel, C., von Konsky, B.R., and Walker, H. Enhancing the Social Issues Components in our Computing Curriculum: Computing for the Social Good. *Proc. ITiCSE-WGR.* ACM, (2010), 117-133.

[25] Gordon, E. and Schirra, S. Playing With Empathy: Digital Role-Playing Games in Public Meetings. *Proc. C&T.* ACM, (2011), 179-185.

[26] Gordon, E., Schirra, S. and Hollander, J. Immersive planning: a conceptual model for designing public participation with new technologies. *Environment and Planning B: Planning and Design.* 38, (2011), 509–519

[27] Habermas, J. *The Structural Transformation of the Public Sphere: An Inquiry into a Category of Bourgeois Society.* The MIT Press, 1991.

[28] Håkansson, M. and Sengers, P. Beyond being green: simple living families and ICT. *Proc. CHI.* ACM, (2013), 2725-2734.

[29] Hirsch, T. 2009. Learning from activists: lessons for designers. *interactions* 16, 3 (2009).

[30] Laird, F. Participatory Analysis, Democracy, and Technological Decision Making. *Science, Technology & Human Values.* 18, 3. (1993), 341-361.

[31] Le Dantec, C.A. Legitimacy at the Outskirts: Categories, Use, and Adoption in Marginal Communities. *Proc. UbiComp.* ACM, (2009), 341-361.

[32] Le Dantec, C.A., Farrell, R.G., Christensen, J.E., Bailey, M., Ellis, J.B., Kellogg, W.A. and Edwards, W.K. Publics in Practice: Ubiquitous Computing at a Shelter for Homeless Mothers. *Proc. CHI.* ACM, (2011), 1687–1696.

[33] Le Dantec, C.A. and Edwards, W.K. Across Boundaries of Influence and Accountability: The Multiple Scales of Public Sector Information Systems. *Proc. CHI.* ACM, (2010), 113–122.

[34] Le Dantec, C.A. and Edwards, W.K. The View from the Trenches: Organization, Power, and Technology at Two Nonprofit Homeless Outreach Centers. *Proc. CSCW.* ACM, (2008), 589–598.

[35] Le Dantec, C.A., Christensen, J.E., Bailey, M., Farrell, R.G., Ellis, J.B., Danis, C.M., Kellogg, W.A., Edwards, W.K. A tale of two publics: democratizing design at the margins. *Proc. DIS.* ACM, (2010), 11-20.

[36] Marsden, G. Designing Technology for the Developing World. *interactions* 13, 2 (2006).

[37] Marsden, G , Maunder, A. and Parker, M. People Are People, but Technology is Not Technology. *Philosophical Transactions of the Royal Society.* 366, (Jul. 2008), 3795–3804.

[38] McMillan, D.W. and Chavis, D.M. Sense of community: A definition and theory. *Journal of Community Psychology.* 14, (1986).

[39] McPhail, B., Costantino, T., Bruckmann, D., Barclay, R. and Clement, A. Caveat Exemplar: Participatory Design in a Non-Profit Volunteer Organisation. *Proc. CSCW.* ACM, (1998), 223–241.

[40] Merkel, C., Farooq, U., Xiao, L., Ganoe, C., Rosson, M.B. and Carroll, J.M. Managing Technology Use and Learning in Nonprofit Community Organizations: Methodological Challenges and Opportunities. *Proc. CHIMIT.* ACM, (2007), Article No. 8.

[41] Merkel, C.B., Xiao, L., Farooq, U., Ganoe, C.H., Lee, R., Carroll, J.M. and Rosson, M.B. Participatory Design in Community Computing Contexts: Tales from the Field. *Proc. PDC.* ACM, (2004), 1–10.

[42] Mouffe, C. *The Democratic Paradox.* Verso, London, UK, 2005.

[43] Saward, M. Less than meets the eye: democratic legitimacy and deliberative theory. *Democratic Innovation.* M. Saward, ed. Routledge, 2000, 66-77.

[44] Silver-Greenberg, J. and Protess, B. "JPMorgan Reveals It Faces Criminal and Civil Inquiries." In *The New York Times.* (August 2013). Web. <http://dealbook.nytimes.com/2013/08/07/jpmorgan-reveals-it-faces-civil-and-criminal-inquiries/?ref=business&_r=0&module=ArrowsNav&contentCollection=Business%20Day&action=keypress&region=FixedLeft&pgtype=Blogs>

[45] Snellen, I. ICTs, Bureaucracies, and the Future of Democracy. *Commun. ACM.* 44, 1 (2001), 45–48.

[46] Turner, F. *From Counterculture to Cyberculture: Stewart Brand, the Whole Earth Network, and the Rise of Digital Utopianism.* University Of Chicago Press, Chicago, IL, 2006.

[47] van Dijk, J. Models of Democracy and Concepts of Communication. *Digital Democracy: Issues of Theory and Practice.* K.L. Hacker and J. van Dijk, eds. SAGE Publications Ltd, 2000, 30–53.

[48] York, D. and Zhengzin, X. Sharing the knowledge. *Proc. CHI.* ACM, (2011), 1007-1012.

(Infra)structures of Volunteering

Amy Voida[1], Zheng Yao[2] & Matthias Korn[1]

[1]School of Informatics and Computing
Indiana University, IUPUI
{amyvoida, korn}@iupui.edu

[2]Department of Information Science
Cornell University
zy87@cornell.edu

ABSTRACT
We report on the results of a diary study of the everyday volunteering and help giving of individuals in the millennial generation. We describe the breadth of work structures implicated in volunteering, the social structures implicated in volunteering, and the interdependencies between the two. We analyze the roles that technology plays in volunteering with a particular focus on the forms of infrastructure that are constituted through the work and social structures of this philanthropic activity. Finally, we reflect on design opportunities for infrastructures where work and social structures meet to support more everyday, ubiquitous forms of volunteering.

Author Keywords
Volunteering; Infrastructure

ACM Classification Keywords
H.5.3. [Information Interfaces and Presentation]: Group and Organization Interfaces—Collaborative Computing

INTRODUCTION
One of the earliest challenges observed in the nascent domain of collaborative computing was that of the discrepancy of benefit—between those who did the work and those who benefited from the system [11]. From the beginning, then, the theoretical attention of the field was focused on understanding the additional work carried out (or not) by some individuals in order to make the system work. Many early systems, of course, were designed for the private sector; perhaps because of this, help given or requested without a clear personal benefit was observed to be a critical challenge in the adoption of collaborative computing systems. Who, after all, would want to take the time to do work that mostly or only benefited others?

As collaborative system design has moved beyond the private sector, the importance of unpaid help and the role of volunteers has increasingly been recognized and become the object of research in a variety of domains. Researchers, for example, have asked questions about how to motivate volunteers to contribute to online communities (e.g., [13, 17]), about how design might help to scaffold novice volunteer contributors toward more expert participation [5], and about how grassroots groups structure volunteering [24]. Researchers have also designed new infrastructures for supporting the participation of volunteers [25].

While research in collaborative computing has primarily explored infrastructures that support volunteering on a technology-by-technology basis (e.g., Wikipedia or Twitter)[1], we have yet to examine empirically the breadth of philanthropic activity that constitutes volunteering and the ways in which technology supports that breadth of work. Volunteering is a phenomenon that extends beyond any one system, transcends physical and virtual realms, and permeates the everyday lives of many civically engaged individuals and groups.

In this paper, we report on the results of a diary study of the everyday volunteering[2] of individuals in the millennial generation, aiming to better understand technology use as part of the *breadth of philanthropic activities* carried out by individuals. Following Lefebvre's call to uncover the order of everyday life [16], we describe the work structures implicated in volunteering, the social structures implicated in volunteering, and the interdependencies between the two. We analyze the role that technology plays in volunteering with a particular focus on the forms of infrastructure that are constituted through the work and social structures of this philanthropic activity. Finally, we reflect on design opportunities for infrastructures where work and social structures meet to support more everyday, ubiquitous forms of volunteering.

RELATED WORK
Our research draws from two different threads of scholarship: research about volunteerism from the domain of philanthropic studies and research about infrastructures from the domains of collaborative computing and science and technology studies.

CSCW 2015, March 14–18, 2015, Vancouver, BC, Canada.

ACM 978-1-4503-2922-4/15/03...$15.00.
http://dx.doi.org/10.1145/2675133.2675153

[1] See Starbird and Palen for a notable exception [24].

[2] In this paper, we use the terms 'volunteering,' 'volunteer work,' 'help giving,' and 'unpaid assistance' interchangeably. This language reflects the breadth of terminology that we used in consent forms and data collection instruments in order to encourage a broader spectrum of reporting than would have been likely if we had only used the term 'volunteering,' as it is often interpreted very narrowly in contemporary culture.

Volunteering

Research in philanthropic studies suggests that the construct of volunteering is too narrowly understood. Schervish and Havens emphasize that:

> *...in order to study the full temporal, spatial, and relational range of voluntary assistance, we need to unlearn the bias toward equating the measure of a caring society with the amount of formal giving and volunteering taking place, and learn to recognize the day-to-day giving of time and money that sojourns in the daily occasions for care surrounding work, family, friends, and community. [22]*

Schervish and Havens refer to this broader understanding of philanthropy as both "moral citizenship" and "caritas," drawing philosophically from multiple intellectual traditions (e.g., Aquinas [9] and de Tocqueville [8]). A more holistic perspective on volunteering—one validating the importance of everyday caritas—may also help foster more "formal" volunteering in the long-term, as one's self-identification as an empathic or philanthropic human being is a first step toward caring about the fate of more distant others:

> *...the informal and generally unrecognized assistance carried out in and around the community of one's family, friends, and associates, is where we first identify with the fate of others and learn to care for them, and the beginning of and the opening to a wider horizon of assistance. [22]*

An orientation to and appreciation for a breadth of volunteering practices, beyond hours volunteered for nonprofit organizations, is also increasingly important as scholars in philanthropic studies have come to recognize that a diversity of volunteering styles are increasingly "blended together into a personal volunteer cocktail" [12]. Hustinx and Lammertyn suggest that collective and reflexive styles of volunteerism co-exist in individuals—sometimes held in tension and sometimes enriching each other.

A collective style of volunteering is centered around the desire for the construction of group-based identity and motivated by a sense of obligation to the community [12]. Collective volunteerism "thrives" in the context of formal voluntary organizations, which are typically highly structured and membership based. For collective volunteers, involvement with the organization is a way of "reaffirming shared group identity" and they may be as much or more concerned about supporting the values and goals of the organization than they are with the specific work that they are doing. Collective volunteers typically offer a regular, long-term commitment to an organization.

A reflexive style of volunteering is centered around one's individual experiences and identity and motivated by personal goals and self-realization [12]. Reflexive volunteerism is more apt to be associated with "an expanding field of rather informal, self-organized, and decentralized initiatives" in which the volunteer participates, not for a sense of belonging, but for the sake of the work being done [12]. Reflexive volunteers typically offer irregular, ad hoc, or project-based commitments to organizations.

Fundamental in this distinction between collective and reflexive styles of volunteering are the interdependencies between the social structures of volunteering (group versus individual biographical frames of reference) and the structure of volunteer work (regular versus episodic, for example). These interdependencies play out in different ways depending on the particular style of volunteering and can be expected to play out in an even larger diversity of ways given each individual's "personal volunteer cocktail."

Infrastructure

> *An infrastructure occurs when local practices are afforded by a larger-scale technology which can then be used in a natural, ready-to-hand fashion. [23]*

Infrastructures are often most notable because they are typically *not* noted—characterized by their invisibility [23]. Yet researchers in science and technology studies and, more recently, collaborative computing and human–computer interaction, have sought to orient more analytic attention to this construct. Bowker, in particular, has argued for research to methodologically undertake "infrastructural inversion"—subverting the traditional figure/ground relationship which perpetuates the analytic invisibility of infrastructures and, instead, foregrounding them in studies of science and technology [2].

Infrastructures are mutually constituted of interdependent technological and social structures [15, 23]. They are fundamentally relational—embedded in social structures, learned as part of membership in social structures, and shaped by the conventions of social structures [23].

Infrastructures are also temporal, changing over time [23]. Questions of "when is infrastructure" have gained increasing primacy in the research literature, both to understand when infrastructure becomes visible (e.g., when breakdowns occur in either technology or work practices, rendering the infrastructure visible) [20, 23] as well as to emphasize an empowering shift toward supporting the appropriation, tailoring, and ongoing repair of infrastructures over time as opposed to perfecting or fixing them in advance at the point of design [14, 20].

But the research community's critical engagement with infrastructure has also found that the evolution of infrastructures, from which it has become increasingly difficult for people to opt out, can be experienced as "noisy," inviting nuisance and distraction [18]. Additionally, the full-service, at-hand nature of many infrastructures may also invite complacency or disempowerment [18], which could be particularly problematic in civically engaged domains like volunteering.

METHOD

Participants

We recruited 19 participants from a large university in the northeastern United States; participants responded to an advertisement posted on a university-sponsored research recruitment website. Participants ranged in ages from 18 to 22. All participants were undergraduate students from a breadth of (15 different) majors. Our choice to include a college-age sample in this research was motivated by research suggesting that a diversity of volunteering styles—a valuable breadth of data for exploratory research such as this—might be more present in individuals of the millennial generation [12]. Individuals in this generation hold civic engagement as a core value; for them, helping others is simply part of what it means to live in a community [26].

Participants included 12 females and 7 males. The skew in distribution toward female participants mirrors trends in the demographics of volunteers in the United States; in 2013, 58% of volunteers in the United States were female [6].

Data Collection

Participants kept a diary via a Google Docs Spreadsheet, logging all of the "unpaid help or assistance you provide to anyone outside of your immediate family" over the course of one month. The guidance provided to participants was based on language recommended by researchers in philanthropic studies [22] and aimed at eliciting a breadth of everyday caritas—beyond the organizationally sponsored activities typically associated with the term 'volunteering.' In their diaries, participants logged the following information: date, start and stop times, a brief description of the unpaid assistance, their location, whether the participant was alone or providing assistance with a group of volunteers, for what organization (if any) they were volunteering, what activities they were doing before and after, and what technology(-ies) were used to provide the unpaid assistance.

All diaries were shared with researchers for the duration of the study so that we could customize reminder emails based on the incoming data (or lack thereof). We required participants to log a minimum of 30 days of data to constitute a complete diary. If there were no instances of unpaid assistance to log on any given day, we asked participants to indicate that explicitly with a "N/A" entry, so that we could differentiate between days with no help giving and days during which participants forgot to log data.

We conducted semi-structured follow-up interviews with all 19 participants. The interview protocol was designed to explore the following areas of interest:

- Similarities and differences among the various instances of volunteering reported in each diary;
- Decision making processes and rationales surrounding the various instances of volunteering; and
- Role(s) of technology(-ies) in each relevant instance of volunteering.

Interviews lasted 24 minutes, on average. Different subsets of researchers conducted the various interviews; all researchers used the same interview protocol. A subset of researchers met weekly while collecting data to discuss the interview data and to revisit the protocol, where necessary, in light of each new interview.

Participants were compensated with a $10 gift card after the completion of their diary and another $10 gift card following the interview.

Data Analysis

The data from the diary spreadsheets were aggregated and cleaned. Some missing information subsequently solicited in the interviews was also added. We computed descriptive statistics to provide general characterizations of the nature of the everyday volunteering of the millennials in this study.

We also inductively coded data that participants entered in two of the fields in the diaries. Descriptions of the help given were coded based on the type of help and the participant's relationship with the beneficiary. Descriptions of the technologies used were coded based on the class of technology(-ies) that played a role in each instance of volunteering. In all cases, coding was done based on a synthesis of the diary content as well as the elaborations and reflections elicited in the interviews. These elaborations were particularly essential in understanding technology use, as participants frequently under-reported technology use in their diaries. Cellphones, in particular, were often rendered invisible to participants, for example:

> *This [diary entry] I guess I should probably put as cell phone. I don't even think like cell phone as a technology. So like, I don't know... 'cause she was there, so she called me. (P1)*

In addition, participants frequently reported technology-as-hardware instead of technology-as-application, so unpacking what participants meant by "laptop," "cellphone," or "internet" was critical.

All interviews were transcribed and analyzed using inductive coding and affinity diagramming techniques (e.g., [7]). Our initial round of analysis yielded a set of categories describing volunteering practices, including motivation, investment, visibility of impact, scope of impact, relationships, context, rhythms, structure, etc. As we moved into subsequent rounds of analysis, it became increasingly clear that the boundaries among these categories were messier than we had originally understood. We 'exploded' each category via affinity diagrams, focusing on the relationships among categories. Instead of each interview excerpt being coded under a particular category, most excerpts were situated as bridges among two or more categories (Figure 1). These interrelationships were

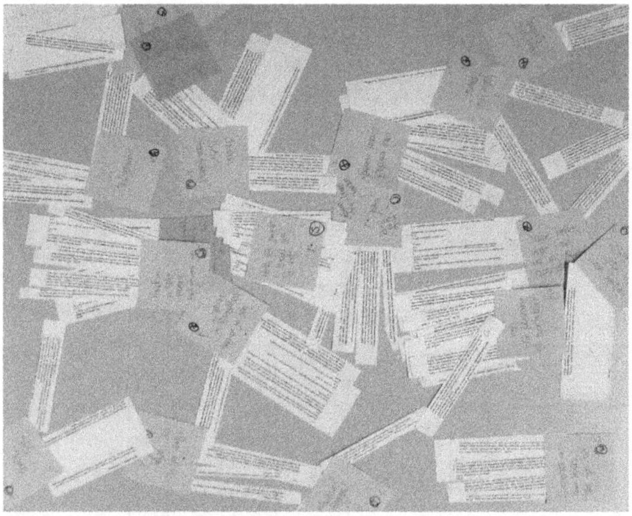

Figure 1. The interrelationships among dimensions led to new, bridging categories in our second round of data analysis.

highlighted by a new set of bridging categories including empathy and expertise, reciprocity and obligation, and impact. Reflecting on this shift in the analysis, we observed that many of these new coding categories bridged between data about the structure of volunteer work (i.e., the genres, temporality, and systematization of the work) and the social structures of volunteering (i.e., the role that social relationships play in arranging and carrying out the work). The interdependencies between work and social structures came to the foreground as we continued to work with and understand our data.

OVERVIEW OF RESULTS

Participants logged 380 instances of volunteering over the month-long study (an average of 20 instances of volunteering per participant). These instances lasted, on average, 63 minutes, and ranged in duration from a few seconds to 12.5 hours.

Participants collectively reported 183 instances of help giving (48%) during which they provided unpaid assistance alongside other volunteers; for the remainder of the unpaid assistance, then, they were the sole help giver. Participants also reported 105 instances of help giving (28%) that were affiliated with or coordinated through an organization (e.g., a nonprofit, sorority, or campus club); 71 of these organizational volunteering opportunities (68% of the organizational instances) were carried out alongside other volunteers, suggesting that organizationally-affiliated volunteering is more likely to be carried out alongside others than volunteering, more generally.

Participants collectively reported 169 instances of help giving (45%) in which technology was involved in some way. Participants appropriated a diversity of technologies for many different kinds of volunteer work (Table 1).[3] This ecosystem of technology used for philanthropic purposes ranges from cellphones to centrifuges, from search engines to stoves. The most frequently reported classes of technology include productivity software (16% of technologies reported), messaging (11%), email (10%), cellphone calls (7%), and vehicles (7%).

[3] Some participants noted multiple technologies used for particular instances of volunteering; because of this, numbers in the table do not add up to 169.

When single technologies are reported for an instance of help giving, they typically align more strongly with either the work or social structures of volunteering. That is, for many instances of help, participants reported using technology to *carry out* the volunteer work. In other instances of help giving, participants used technology to *activate* the social structures implicated in the volunteering.

When multiple technologies are used to support volunteering, the different technologies often support a combination of work and social structures. In these instances, participants shift between technologies—from a technology used to activate social structures to a technology used to support the work structures. This transition between technologies is similar to the "outeraction" observed by Nardi et al.—the work of negotiating availability for work at a later time, frequently arranged for a different medium [19]. P13, for example, exchanged text messages with a friend to coordinate and then met up with her later at a dorm, where she helped with a class assignment using productivity software.

Many technologies reported in this study seem to be infrastructural already: larger-scale technologies creatively appropriated for local volunteering practices. No participant reported using any technologies specifically designed for volunteer work, even in an organizational setting; this finding resonates with trends toward creative appropriation in previous studies of volunteer work from an organizational perspective [29]. Similar to the majority of homebrew databases in Voida et al.'s study, all infrastructures used by volunteers here are more general-purpose infrastructures (or at least they are not tailored for volunteering) that have been appropriated locally.

In what follows, we characterize the work structures of volunteering and the supporting technological infrastructures that have been appropriated. We then characterize the social structures implicated in volunteering and describe the supporting technological infrastructures that have been appropriated for this purpose. Finally, we describe some key interdependencies between work and social structures in volunteering and reflect on what it would mean for technological infrastructures to better support these interdependencies.

WORK STRUCTURES OF VOLUNTEERING

The structure of volunteer work is most saliently characterized by variations in its genre, its temporality, and the degree of pre-structuring and systematization of work activities. The diary entries reflect a diversity of genres or types of volunteer work including academic help (27% of

	Product. Software	Msg.	Email	Cellphone (Call)	Vehicle	Course Mgmt. System	Home Appliance	Sci. Equip.	Search Engine	Design Software	Nonprofit Website	E-Commerce	Web-Based Reference	A/V Equip.	Social Network Service	TV/ Stream. Video	Video Conf.	Online Survey	Printer	Scanners/ Swipe Cards	Software Dev. Tools	Total
Academic Help	20	7	2	2	5	11		8	8	2		1		1		1	2	3			2	**75**
Clerical Help	11	1	16	2						6				3					2	2	1	**44**
Householding & Errands		5		1	6		8					1										**21**
Small Courtesies		3		6	1		1					1			2					1		**15**
Information Help		2	1	1					1			1	4		2		1					**13**
Well-being		2		1				1			2	1				3	1					**11**
Lending		1	1		1		2	1					1						1			**8**
Financial Help											6	1										**7**
Total	**31**	**21**	**20**	**13**	**13**	**11**	**11**	**10**	**9**	**8**	**8**	**6**	**5**	**4**	**4**	**4**	**4**	**3**	**3**	**3**	**3**	**194**

Table 1. Instances of reported technology use and type of help given

	Product. Software	Msg.	Email	Cellphone (Call)	Vehicle	Course Mgmt. System	Home Appliance	Sci. Equip.	Search Engine	Design Software	Nonprofit Website	E-Commerce	Web-Based Reference	A/V Equip.	Social Network Service	TV/ Stream. Video	Video Conf.	Online Survey	Printer	Scanners/ Swipe Cards	Software Dev. Tools	Total
Helping Alone	12	12	13	9	2	6	7	2	5	2	7	3	5	1	4	3	3	3	2	1		**102**
Helping with Others	19	9	7	4	11	5	4	8	4	6	1	3		3		1	1		1	2	3	**92**
Total	**31**	**21**	**20**	**13**	**13**	**11**	**11**	**10**	**9**	**8**	**8**	**6**	**5**	**4**	**4**	**4**	**4**	**3**	**3**	**3**	**3**	**194**

Table 2. Instances of reported technology use when helping alone versus when helping alongside others

	Product. Software	Msg.	Email	Cellphone (Call)	Vehicle	Course Mgmt. System	Home Appliance	Sci. Equip.	Search Engine	Design Software	Nonprofit Website	E-Commerce	Web-Based Reference	A/V Equip.	Social Network Service	TV/ Stream. Video	Video Conf.	Online Survey	Printer	Scanners/ Swipe Cards	Software Dev. Tools	Total
No Org. Affiliate	21	20	6	11	8	10	9	5	9	2		5	5	2	3	4	4	2	2	1	2	**131**
Organizational Affiliate	10	1	14	2	5	1	2	5		6	8	1		2	1			1	1	2	1	**63**
Total	**31**	**21**	**20**	**13**	**13**	**11**	**11**	**10**	**9**	**8**	**8**	**6**	**5**	**4**	**4**	**4**	**4**	**3**	**3**	**3**	**3**	**194**

Table 3. Instances of reported technology use when help is and is not affiliated with an organization

all entries), clerical help (18%), household help and errands (18%), emotional and physical wellbeing (10%), financial help (8%), informational help (4%), and lending (4%). Many participants also reported small courtesies (11% of all entries) like holding open a door or giving up one's seat on the bus. This category is likely underreported in the data, however, as other participants were more hesitant to report small courtesies and explicitly told us this type of assistance should not 'count' as these behaviors are simply a reflection of how people ought to be treating each other rather than a type of help giving that should be reported.

In the interviews, participants portrayed a variety of structural characteristics that we describe on a spectrum from being planned and systematic on one end, to being spontaneous and unpredictable on the other end.

From Planned and Systematic...

At one extreme, activities may be scheduled in advance and have "a set time and a place" (P2); they may even take place repeatedly and at regular intervals with a "set time each week" (P2). As such, they are likely to be planned and "not just 'oh I randomly feel like going here'" (P2). Planned activities may also require aligning other activities to accommodate this schedule: "there's a specific time each week that I have to be there [so] I know I have to do it, [which] means that I have to plan other things around that" (P15). A scheduled activity also implies that one has made a commitment to the activity that would not be lightly retracted: "If, for instance, like one day, you are not really feeling up for it, you kind of already made that investment, like commitment, like you are certain you have to do it." (P2).

Besides being planned and scheduled in advance, volunteer work may not only be seen as "consistent" (P3) in terms of taking place regularly, but also consistent in terms of what has to be done. In that sense, the work may be "very systematic" (P3) and highly structured—i.e., the entity initiating the work activity may have laid out exactly what and how the work is to be conducted.

... to Spontaneous and Unpredictable

On the spontaneous side of the planned-to-spontaneous spectrum, volunteer work may be "more up in the air and spontaneous" (P3), e.g., "bump[ing] into" someone on the street or before class to help them find the way (P6), or when one considers picking up groceries for roommates at the store (P9). Spontaneous help can sometimes be "easier" (P11) because it doesn't have to be coordinated in advance. However, participants' willingness to help spontaneously does depend on what else they are doing and how much time they have, because one may be "more inclined to help someone else when I don't have like a lot going on" (P1). Hence, one may also have "to put [a request] on hold, tell someone, like, can you give me half an hour" (P2).

Although more spontaneous help may seem to signify a lack of structure, as in Lefebvre's analysis of everyday life, we find that it follows a different structural order [16]. The work structure of more spontaneous help seems to stem from a set of expectations derived from social structures—social relationships, personal motivations, and societal influences. There are expectations that, for some beneficiaries, one should drop everything in order to help. In addition, there is an expectation that more spontaneous help will have highly variable and uncertain durations (e.g., "the time is variable, like who knows how long you will have to be like devoting" (P2)) and this variability influences how and if one takes on spontaneous help.

The Evolution of Work Structure

Notably, the structures of volunteer work are not static; they frequently evolve over time. While some volunteers may enter into volunteer work after it has been heavily systematized, numerous participants noted changes in the structure of their volunteer work—either over the course of the one-month study or when reflecting on the historical trajectory of work structures leading to an instance of help giving reported in the diary. Most commonly, participants reported that a single instance of assistance evolved into a repeating pattern of help. With enough repetition, patterns of help may also become more institutionalized and those who help each other become a known "group":

> *Here is a group of girls that walk someone home.... We pick someone up. We come and get someone wherever they are.... A lot of us study at engineering quad [and] really don't want to walk home alone. (P3)*

Here, P3 describes a somewhat more institutionalized form of assistance in which a group of friends and classmates routinely make arrangements to pick each other up from the library or meet up to walk home safely together at night. This assistance has become so frequent among the students that it can be activated and made use of by members of the group at almost any time. Hence, the structure of volunteer work is also highly influenced by the social structures in which participants are embedded.

Technologies Foregrounding Work Structures

Different types of work are associated with different classes of technology. Among this student population, technology is, perhaps unsurprisingly, used to provide academic help more than any other type of help. And the technologies used to provide academic help are also more diverse than technology appropriated to provide any other type of help, ranging from productivity software to scientific equipment to vehicles to search engines to email (Table 1). Participants also appropriated many diverse classes of technology for clerical help and informational help; however, few classes of technology are appropriated to provide financial help.

Conversely, different classes of technology are also used for providing different types of help (Table 1). Messaging, cellphone calls and, more surprisingly, e-commerce, are used to provide numerous different types of help. Others, such as design software, are used for relatively few classes of help; in this case, for only academic and clerical help.

The planning and coordination of volunteer work are supported by email lists and productivity software, such as Google Docs' spreadsheets, documents, and forms (for polls and surveys).

> *A lot of planning and coordinating can go on in like Google Documents.... To put ideas of events, to sign up for shifts when we have a food fundraiser.... Sometimes we set up like duos for meeting polls. (P9)*

These infrastructures also support discussion and brainstorming about how to carry out the volunteer work as well as reflection about the work structure after the fact via shared meeting minutes.

Micro-coordination of volunteer work is supported by cellphone calls and messaging—both text messaging and Facebook messaging. These infrastructures are used to request spontaneous help, arrange meeting times and locations, confirm modes of transportation, etc. But they are also used to coordinate with and remind other volunteers closer to planned events:

> *Cellphone will be used just to coordinate volunteers.... If we've got an event going on and someone is not there for the shift they signed up for, I will send them a very polite text: "Hey, where are you? We need help!" (P9)*

In addition, a range of infrastructures (cellphones, laptops, internet) are seen to be convenient resources because they are available when needed, or in-the-moment, as was the case with many spontaneous instances of help giving:

> *I always use my laptop because it's really portable and [I] can take it wherever I am. I can just pull it out. So it's [a] more immediate vision of help, I guess.... My friend really needed help like right then... and I think technology was so useful for that. I was able to look stuff up and be talking to him online at the same time. (P2)*

All forms of volunteer work, then, are structured in some way or another and both the structures and structuring of this work are supported by technology. Yet, the work structure of volunteering is not influential in isolation, but through its interdependencies with the social structures implicated in volunteering.

SOCIAL STRUCTURES OF VOLUNTEERING

More, perhaps, than in most other types of work, social structures play a central role in how volunteer work is carried out—what kind of volunteer work is done, how it is done, and, in fact, whether volunteer work is done at all. In this research, two classes of social structures are influential:

- The nature of relationships between the help giver and beneficiaries—whom people help in what way and to what extent (see also [10] for a discussion of this relationship in the context of charitable giving).
- The nature of the relationships among volunteers, e.g., is one volunteering alone or with friends, with people who share similar interests and goals, under the purview of an organization, etc.

Note that we have scoped this paper to focus on the collaborative work that is predominant in volunteering. A few participants did acknowledge, however, that sometimes it is just "easier" to find ways to help others without the coordination overhead of working in groups (P3).

Relationships Between Volunteers and Beneficiaries

By far the largest group of beneficiaries of the help reported in the diaries is friends (57%), followed by volunteer organizations (17%), strangers (9%), and classmates (7%). All types of help, from academic help to help for physical and emotional wellbeing, are reported for beneficiaries who are friends. Help given to classmates, in contrast, was almost exclusively limited to academic help and lending; and the help given to strangers were predominantly instances of small courtesies. The interview data corroborates the importance of social structures and relationships as an indicator for the likelihood of help giving: "The biggest thing that might influence whether I choose to help someone out or not is how well I know them" (P4).

Even more, the closeness of the relationship also influences what types of help participants provided to others—particularly as it relates help that may require more of an emotional investment:

> *It will depend on how close I am with them, like what kind of assistance I give. [..] If it's like technical skill that I could help with, I would help like anyone with that, like doesn't matter how close I am. [..] But if it's something that requires more emotional investment, then it has to be someone that I'm close to. (P2)*

Relationships Among Volunteers

Participants also have preferences about whom (if anyone) they prefer to work with in providing assistance. Volunteering in conjunction with an organization was seen as more "fun" when done alongside others who share the same passion, whereas some things are just more effective if done alone:

> *Sometimes it's nice to have like another friend with you if it's an organization, 'cause it's like more fun that way. Just like feels good for both. But if it is like helping a friend, it's like one-on-one help is the best.... And also if I'm providing technical skills, any kind of skills, that's usually better alone, 'cause then I can just get it done. (P2)*

Social structures also served as critical bridges for introducing individuals to new organizations and to new volunteer opportunities within those organizations.

> *Holi [the Hindu festival of colors] is like one of my favorite holidays. One of my friends here... she's like, "Oh, let's volunteer." So I was just like, "Okay, let's do it...." I'm actually not [a member of the host organization]. I was just going to participate in Holi in either way.... I met a lot of people at Holi who were really great and I definitely see myself as joining that organization. (P19)*

In addition, some participants reported volunteering for organizations that support causes they do not strongly believe in, if it meant that they were helping a friend—i.e., they are only helping the organization for and because of the relationship to the friend:

> *I helped a friend with an event that I normally wouldn't have. And that's just because my friend wanted me to be there, support him and things like that.... I don't really feel like passionate about that.... I don't like not [to] support [them], but I wouldn't really go on my own. (P2)*

Hence, the social structure also influences the structure of the work—whether and how much someone is willing to help in a given way.

Technologies Foregrounding Social Structures

Participants reported a similar prevalence of help giving involving technology when helping alone (102 instances; 50% of all instances of solo volunteering) and when working alongside co-volunteers (92 instances; 52% of all volunteering with others) (Table 2). However, different social contexts of help giving are associated with different types of technology. Communication media, home appliances, and nonprofit websites are more commonly used when helping alone, whereas A/V equipment, design software, scientific equipment, software development tools, and vehicles are more commonly used when helping alongside others. Other technologies represented more diverse contexts of use, with course management systems, e-commerce, and search engines used for approximately the same number of instances of volunteering alone as when alongside others.

Participants also reported different patterns of technology use corresponding to the organizational affiliation of the volunteer work (Table 3). While there are fewer instances of organizationally affiliated help giving than non-affiliated help giving in the data, a larger percentage of the organizationally affiliated help giving involved technology—60% of organizationally affiliated help giving involved technology and 48% of non-organizationally affiliated help giving involved technology. Yet, the only classes of technology used more frequently for organizationally affiliated help are design software, email, and nonprofit websites. The only class of technology *not* used for non-organizationally affiliated volunteering in this study is nonprofit websites.

While communication media do contribute to supporting the coordination of work (as noted previously), they also, even more predominantly, foreground the social structures of volunteer work. Communication media take up the important function of helping people learn about volunteer opportunities and activating existing relationships for philanthropic purposes.

> *And also Facebook is really good about finding out causes.... And I feel like it's such an efficient way to get people involved. (P2)*

Often, these technologies function as broadcast channels where people send and receive help requests (see also [30] for similar evidence from an organizational perspective). In this sense, they present a way to tap into existing social networks. Prominent infrastructures appropriated for this include Facebook, group texting, and email listservs:

> *So people [in my sorority] are always like asking [for help]. You know, we have like a Facebook group that always posts like take the survey, like can you do this for me, or like can you come to this... (P1)*

> *'Cause we also had a big group text in our apartment, so people send things out like, "Oh, anyone going to the grocery store," like "Is anyone doing this?" Even if we talked in person about it, like that first, like initial, like the question, I need help with this... was through the cell phone. (P1)*

Yet these social structures require some form of an existing tie; Facebook groups and email listservs, in particular, require membership. In our data, volunteer work broadcast through these media only served beneficiaries who were part of that membership.

Social structures play key roles in initiating and motivating help. These structures influence and are influenced by both work structure and technology use. Indeed, it is the interdependencies among these constructs that provide the richest characterization of everyday volunteering.

INTERDEPENDENCIES BETWEEN WORK AND SOCIAL STRUCTURES

In introducing both the work and social structures of volunteering, we foreshadowed some of the basic interdependencies found in volunteer work. Here, we highlight three key interdependencies in more detail: expertise and empathy, reciprocity and obligation, and impact.

Expertise and Empathy

The structure of volunteer work is strongly influenced by the previous experiences and expertise of the volunteer. Participants valued giving help in areas where they had expertise. P2, for example, prefers to volunteer when "my knowledge can kind of benefit someone." P14 noted that expertise can extend beyond academic knowledge to practical hobbies such as baking, as well.

When this expertise was gained through hard work or personal struggle, participants suggested that they volunteered because they knew "I have been there and I know what you are going through" (P4). For the participants in this research—all students—empathic help often manifested in tutoring sessions for classmates who did not necessarily have strong pre-existing ties with the volunteer:

> *A lab was due for a CS class.... It was just like a large group of people there, working on it. I saw one person that basically just started to look at it and they really did not have a good feel. And I kind of have to empathize with them, because that's what I had a day or two before. And so I just kind of sat down with them, walk them through what kind of they have to do. (P4)*

The interrelationships between work and social structures come to the fore where empathy and expertise meet. Empathy fosters expert help where shared experiences are foregrounded, such as within a community of classmates. Empathy takes root in the social structure of volunteering whereas expertise is brought to bear as a resource for the tasks at hand, taking root in the work structure of volunteering.

Infrastructures of Expertise and Empathy

Participants in this study employed such a diverse set of technologies for their volunteer work, in large part, we believe, because of the diverse breadth of skills and expertise being developed by these undergraduate students. Technologies like centrifuges, incubators, specialized scientific calculators, design software, and software development tools all demand some degree of expertise in their use. Tools-of-the-trade, although diverse, individualized, and often-still-invisible, were a significant form of philanthropic infrastructure:

> *I never like think about [technology], but actually like as I was doing it, the computer is really useful. And then the Internet, for a lot of the skills that I could apply, like friends, I will take a lot of others' jobs like emailing. I helped like build this photo uploader and that all was kind of necessary. (P2)*

Collaborative computing has explored systems that provide expertise recommendation within given communities (e.g., [21]), crowdsourcing systems for complex tasks requiring skills and expertise (e.g., [27]), and social Q&A services for gathering expert knowledge (e.g., [28]). Systems that foster support among individuals with shared experiences, such as patientslikeme.com (e.g., [3]) are also relevant here. But part of what is striking in our data is the fluidity of social structures across which empathy and expertise extend. It is not simply existing friends or classmates whom one helps; expertise can function as an open call, leading volunteers to be introduced to new social structures and causes, enriching their "personal volunteer cocktail" based on this expertise [12]. For infrastructures supporting expertise and empathy, then, it will be fruitful to consider how expertise might be conveyed across existing (and even closed) communities, and how empathy can be extended to new social contexts.

Reciprocity and Obligation

Work and social structures interleave tightly where helping becomes reciprocal. Whether among housemates, friends, or sorority sisters, participants valued volunteering for people who they knew would "be there for [them], too" (P2):

> *Helping a friend... it just feels good. You will become closer to them. They are like opening up to you, you feel like reliable, stuff like that. And you also just have an implicit knowledge that they'll be there for you too, like if you did that. (P2)*

Giving reciprocal help not only builds closer relationships within a given social structure, it enables P2 to feel more reliable, a personality trait that has direct implications on the temporal structure of her volunteering. Being reliable implies that she will be available for others when needed.

Reciprocity also develops through the emergent structures of volunteer work. P3, for example, started walking home from campus with a few friends. After helping one another get home safely several times, they began to recognize the activity as a more structured, reciprocal form of volunteering:

> *We were like, "Okay, we are gonna pair assist." I like that a lot. [...] It feels good to know like, it's kind of like the girls there you are making a little family here. We all kind of watch out for each other. And I like that a lot. (P3)*

The reciprocity of help giving here also led to the development of closer, "family"-like relationships. Within some social structures, the assumption of reciprocity led to an even stronger interrelationship of obligation: "[There's] an obligation to help family members because they will always be there for one" (P2).

The obligation to provide help extended beyond family to both friends and organizations, but the social structures related to feelings of obligation varied among participants. P13, for example, felt a strong sense of obligation to help her friends: "Things that I do for friends, like out of that obligation of friendship..." (P13). In contrast, P12 reported feeling more of a sense of obligation for an organization than a friend: "[For the] individual, if I don't have time I would say no, but if I volunteer for an organization, I don't think... [I would say no]" (P12).

The sense of obligation also holds significant implications for the temporal structure of the volunteer work. For friends, the obligation can require a significant amount of time (e.g., "we did stay till 5 in the morning" (P2)) but this commitment is much more "variable" and "random" (P2).

In contrast, the obligation to organizations is not really "flexible":

> *So if, for instance like one day, you are not really feeling up for it. You kind of already made that investment, like commitment, like you are certain [you] have to do it. (P2)*

Yet, it is the interrelationships between work and social structures relating to both reciprocity and obligation that challenge beliefs about what 'counts' as volunteering. Numerous participants reacted against the idea that helping friends should 'count' for a study—even one that explicitly asked participants to report all instances of "unpaid help or assistance."

> *Well, the friend helping... I feel like that's just part of friendship, not really like assistance type of thing. Just like giving and taking relationship. They help me all the time and I help them.... With friendship that's kind of like an obligation.... This is weird. Want just to be a good person. (P13)*

Infrastructures of Reciprocity and Obligation

Although not mentioned by participants in this study, new infrastructures are emerging to support help giving practices reliant on reciprocity, such as timebanking [1]. However, Bellotti et al. find many challenges that have emerged in the infrastructuring of these practices. In particular, the overfixing of work structures in timebank systems may be crowding out the philanthropic goals of many participants and diminishing the potential for community building. Considering how to support not merely the work structures but the social structures within these technological infrastructures is likely key to sustaining their use.

As we reflect on infrastructures of reciprocity and obligation, it would also be prudent to heed the cautionary advice of Mainwaring et al. [18]. We need to better understand how to reflect obligation appropriately in infrastructuring—to balance between supporting the philanthropic work being done with the potential downside of increased infrastructural noise and distraction.

Impact

For nearly all participants, the work and social structures of volunteering were deeply tied to individual preferences about the kind of impact the individual wanted to make with his or her volunteering. Some individuals valued the scope of their impact while others valued its visibility.

For some individuals, the *scope of impact* was most important. These individuals valued "having more effect on other people's lives" (P8) and "making a huge difference" not simply doing a "small favor" (P11). They typically valued volunteer work more when it was coordinated though an organization:

> *I guess I feel better about the work I do with an organization. It's more actually community service. When it's just a friend, it made me feel good, but...I mean it's not bad that I'm doing a favor for my friend, but it's not like helping the world, anyway, for the community.... (P11)*

Part of the value of volunteering through an organization was the structure that it provided—not simply of the volunteer work being done—but the intentional, goal-driven nature of the work suggested a larger impact than when helping friends with everyday matters.

> *[Working with an organization] probably feels a little more significant.... Having more effect on other people's lives. I guess? 'Cause this seems like we required like specific dedications. None of these [instances of helping people I know] has any specific focus or particular goal I was trying to reach in helping people. (P8)*

When participants valued the scope of impact, they typically made connections between this impact and work that had been organized through the social structures of an organization. Similarly, P2 highlighted the benefit of volunteering with others who share the same mindset. Whether or not the volunteering was carried out within an organizational structure, working with a group that shares the same mindset may also suggest future possibilities for longer-term impact with that social cohort:

> *I also really like working with other volunteers too with same mindset. That's definitely a pro because people who share your interest, maybe in the future we could like work together on bigger things. (P2)*

For other individuals, the *visibility of impact* was of critical importance to their help giving; valuing the visibility of impact had different implications for the work and social structures of volunteering. When these participants knew the people they were helping, they had direct access to see the impact of their volunteer work. This direct access was meaningful for them:

> *Like sometimes when you are helping a friend it feels better than... helping for an organization. Because I know the person that I'm helping and I see the results. (P17)*

Even when the participant did not know the individual that was being helped, the direct nature of small courtesies helped provide the visibility of impact that was important.

> *Um yeah, I think the [helping by providing an] umbrella one stands out the most 'cuz it's just like... you really made a difference, like you saw that immediate difference as opposed to donating blood. Like I'm not gonna actually see the person who ends up getting blood or whatever. (P18)*

Those who valued visibility of impact rarely spoke about distributed help or virtual volunteering as being particularly meaningful. For these participants, visibility was always equated with co-presence.

And while most participants who valued the visibility of impact recalled work structures that were more sporadic and episodic, one participant, P2, did offer an example of a more structured or "formal" volunteering through a nonprofit organization in which she mentored elementary school-aged children directly. Here, the opportunity to build social relationships (as opposed to helping an individual within an existing social relationship) was of particular value.

> *I guess for the formal organization [tutoring children in an elementary school], it's just really good to know that I'm contributing to a cause that I feel good about. And like all of these causes involve helping people directly, which makes it feel even better because I wanted to [be] as helpful as I can.... You could really form formal relationships with them. You could see how you could benefit them. (P2)*

Infrastructures of Impact

We find little evidence in our data or from existing systems of technologies that serve as infrastructures of impact—either related to scope or visibility. The one instance we can point to of a technology providing consistent measures of impact was from a diary entry of P13, who knew, based on feedback from a 'quiz' website maintained by the United Nations World Food Programme, just how many grains of rice would be donated on her behalf as a result of quiz questions she had answered correctly: "Donated 1140 grains of rice through Freerice.com" (P13, diary entry).

However, the dearth of examples of infrastructures of impact is striking, particular given that impact is one of the most influential motivations for volunteering [4]. Previous research examining technologies used to support charitable donations also emphasized the need for technologies to provide better feedback about the impact of financial help [10]; our recommendation here is similar. Technological infrastructures are well positioned to track data about help given; tracing and visualizing trajectories of the impact of that help—across work and social structures—would be a compelling area for research.

INTEGRATING WORK AND SOCIAL STRUCTURES IN TECHNOLOGICAL INFRASTRUCTURES

Technology reflects and supports both the work and social structures of volunteering in a variety of ways. Yet, the strong interdependencies between work and social structures of volunteering that surface in the data from this study are not as clearly mirrored in technology use. Instead, we primarily see a diverse, ad hoc assemblage of different technologies supporting parts and pieces of volunteering—individual technologies that either primarily support work *or* social structures, but rarely both in a more integrated manner.

Certainly, some technologies can support both work and social structures. P5, for example, "talked with best friend back home about her depression and living situation"; to do this, she activated her social network via Skype and then provided emotional support in that medium, as well. Despite the few examples such as this, we believe it is useful to reflect on the more general disconnect between the integration of work and social structures observed in volunteering *practices*, on one hand, and the lack of integration of work and social structures in *technologies*, on the other. Not to suggest that all technologies should be all things in all contexts, but rather, as we reflect over the diverse set of technologies appropriated for philanthropic purposes, we see value in posing the questions, '*How might we be more attuned to the interdependencies between work and social structures in infrastructures of volunteering*?' and '*How might we imagine technologies that transect the space of volunteering—including dimensions of both work and social structures*?'

CONCLUSION

Lefebvre, in his seminal critique of everyday life, argues that everyday things are not "infantile" or "prelogic" [16]. They have an underlying order that is relevant, interesting, and uncoverable. Through our analysis of diary study and interview data about the everyday volunteering of millennials, we have sought to uncover the structures underlying this philanthropic activity.

We have provided empirical evidence of the diversity of everyday volunteering practices relative to more traditionally studied forms of organizationally affiliated volunteering. We also offer the first empirical study of technology use across this diversity of volunteer work. Our insights reinforce the crucial role that technology plays in an updated, expanded, and richer understanding of volunteering. In particular, we have made the following contributions:

- Characterized the prevalence and diversity of technologies used for volunteer work;
- Characterized the work structures of volunteering, noting, in particular, the spectrum from planned and systematic to unplanned and spontaneous volunteering as well as the evolution of these structures;
- Characterized the social structures implicated in volunteering, including the nature of relationships with other volunteers, organizations, and beneficiaries;
- Identified the interdependencies between work and social structures of volunteering as a key site for infrastructuring;
- Identified and characterized three key areas of interdependencies between the work and social structures of volunteering—expertise and empathy, reciprocity and obligation, and impact—and described implications for infrastructuring in each area; and

- Identified critical disconnects between the integration of work and social structures observed in volunteering *practices*, on one hand, and the lack of integration of work and social structures in *technologies*, on the other; nearly all technologies were either used to carry out volunteering work or to activate the social structures of volunteering, with little interplay between the two.

These findings have both methodological and design implications. Methodologically, we need to widen our analytic focus beyond technology-by-technology studies—exploring the broader ecosystem of philanthropic technology use. More mundane, everyday forms of volunteering are relatively pervasive and rely on an incredibly diverse ecology of technologies. These technologies need to be understood more holistically, as many of them serve as infrastructures already, pervading the everyday lives of many civically engaged individuals. From a design perspective, this research suggests that we need to explore infrastructuring that better integrates work and social structures, reflecting the highly interdependent nature of these structures in everyday volunteering.

Mainwaring, Cheng, and Anderson, in their study of individuals who have chosen to live beyond the boundaries of traditional infrastructures, remind us that...

> *Infrastructure, for all its benefits—indeed, because of all its ready-at-hand benefits—was seen to bring also complacency, stasis, vulnerability.... The challenge, then, as we see it, is for ubicomp systems that seek not to automate or even augment/amplify human skills but to exercise and celebrate them, to encourage active engagement, and provide resources to individuals and communities for continuous change.... [18]*

This study is an exploratory, formative step aimed at addressing this challenge. In it, we have sought to better understand those infrastructures that support active engagement and philanthropy. We have sought to bring the field of collaborative computing back to some of its earliest theoretical engagements, exploring the discrepancy of benefit in collaborative work. But instead of asking how to design systems to prevent some people from doing work from which they would not benefit, we ask what it would take to design the foundational infrastructures that provoke people to carry out work that *does* benefit others.

ACKNOWLEDGMENTS

Many thanks to Ellie Harmon for her feedback on early drafts of this paper. This material is based upon work supported by the National Science Foundation under Grant Number 1218051. Any opinions, findings, and conclusions or recommendations expressed in this material are those of the author(s) and do not necessarily reflect the views of the National Science Foundation.

REFERENCES

1. Bellotti, V.M.E., Cambridge, S., Hoy, K., Shih, P.C., Handalian, L.R., Han, K. & Carroll, J.M. (2014). Towards community-centered support for peer-to-peer service exchange: Rethinking the timebanking metaphor. In *Proc. CHI*. New York: ACM Press, 2975–2984.
2. Bowker, G. (1994). Information mythology: The world of/as information. In L. Bud-Frierman (Ed.), *Information acumen: The understanding and use of knowledge in modern business* (pp. 231–247). London: Routledge.
3. Brubaker, J.R., Lustig, C. & Hayes, G.R. (2010). Patients Like Me: Empowerment and representation in a patient centered social network. Presented at the CSCW Workshop on CSCW Research in Healthcare: Past, Present, and Future, Savannah, GA.
4. Brudney, J.L. (2010). Designing and managing volunteer programs. In D.O. Rentz (Ed.), *The Jossey-Bass Handbook of Nonprofit Leadership and Management* (pp. 753–793). San Francisco: Jossey-Bass.
5. Bryant, S.L., Forte, A. & Bruckman, A. (2005). Becoming Wikipedian: Transformation of participation in a collaborative online encyclopedia. In *Proc. GROUP*. New York: ACM Press, 1–10.
6. Bureau of Labor Statistics, US Department of Labor. (2013). *Volunteering in the United States—2013*. Retrieved 6 May 2014: http://www.bls.gov/news.release/volun.nr0.htm
7. Corbin, J. & Strauss, A. (2008). *Basics of qualitative research: Techniques and procedures for developing grounded theory* (3rd ed.). Los Angeles: Sage.
8. de Tocqueville, A. (2003). *Democracy in America*. I. Kramnick (Ed.). (G. Bevan, Trans.). London: Penguin. (Original work published 1835)
9. Gillemen, G.S.J. (1959). *The primacy of charity in moral theology*. Westminster, MD: Newman Press.
10. Goecks, J., Voida, A., Voida, S. & Mynatt, E.D. (2008). Charitable technologies: Opportunities for collaborative computing in nonprofit fundraising. In *Proc. CSCW*. New York: ACM Press, 689–698.
11. Grudin, J. (1994). Groupware and social dynamics: Eight challenges for developers. *Commun. ACM 37*(1), 92–105.
12. Hustinx, L. & Lammertyn, F. (2003). Collective and reflexive styles of volunteering: A sociological modernization perspective. *Voluntas: International Journal of Voluntary and Nonprofit Organizations 14*(2), 167–187.
13. Lampe, C., Wash, R., Velasquez, A. & Ozkaya, E. (2010). Motivations to participate in online communities. In *Proc. CHI*. New York: ACM Press, 1927–1936.

14. Le Dantec, C.A. & DiSalvo, C. (2013). Infrastructuring and the formation of publics in participatory design. *Social Studies of Science 43*(2), 241–264.

15. Lee, C.P., Dourish, P. & Mark, G. (2006). The human infrastructure of cyberinfrastructure. In *Proc. CSCW.* New York: ACM Press, 483–492.

16. Lefebvre, H. (2014). *Critique of everyday life.* London: Verso.

17. Ling, K., Beenen, G., Ludford, P., Wang, X., Chang, K., Li, X., Cosley, D., Frankowski, D., Terveen, L., Rashid, A., Resnick, P. & Kraut, R. (2005). Using social psychology to motivate contributions to online communities. *Journal of Computer-Mediated Communication 10*(4).

18. Mainwaring, S.D., Cheng, M.F., & Anderson, K. (2004). Infrastructures and their discontents: Implications for Ubicomp. In *Proc. Ubicomp*. Berlin: Springer, 418–432.

19. Nardi, B., Whittaker, S., & Bradner, E. (2000). Interaction and outeraction: Instant messaging in action. In *Proc CSCW*. New York: ACM Press, 79–88.

20. Pipek, V. & Wulf, V. 2009. Infrastructuring: Towards an integrated perspective on the design and use of information technology. *Journal of the Association of Information Systems 10*(5), 306–332.

21. Reichling, T., Veith, M. & Wulf, V. (2007). Expert recommender: Designing for a network organization. *Computer Supported Cooperative Work 16*(4-5), 431–465.

22. Schervish, P.G. & Havens, J.J. (2002). The Boston area diary study and the moral citizenship of care. *Voluntas: International Journal of Voluntary and Nonprofit Organizations 13*(1), 47–71.

23. Star, S.L. & Ruhleder, K. (1996). Steps toward an ecology of infrastructure: Design and access for large information. *Information Systems Research 7*(1), 111–134.

24. Starbird, K. & Palen, L. (2013). Working and sustaining the virtual disaster desk. *Proc. CSCW*. New York: ACM Press, 491–502.

25. Starbird, K. & Stamberger, J. (2010). Tweak the tweet: Leveraging microblogging proliferation with a prescriptive syntax to support citizen reporting. In *Proc. ISCRAM.*

26. Taylor, P. & Keeter, S. (Eds.). (2010). *Millennials: A portrait of Generation Next. Confident. Connected. Open to change*. Washington, D.C.: Pew Research Center. Online at: http://pewsocialtrends.org/assets/pdf/millennials-confident-connected-open-to-change.pdf

27. Teodoro, R., Ozturk, P., Naaman, M., Mason, W. & Lindqvist, J. (2014). The motivations and experiences of the on-demand mobile workforce. In *Proc. CSCW*. New York: ACM Press, 236–247.

28. Vasilescu, B., Serebrenik, A., Devanbu, P. & Filkov, V. (2014). How social Q&A sites are changing knowledge sharing in open source software communities. In *Proc. CSCW*. New York: ACM Press, 342–354.

29. Voida, A., Harmon, E. & Al-Ani, B. (2011). Homebrew databases: Complexities of everyday information management in nonprofit organizations. In *Proc. CHI*. New York: ACM Press, 915–924.

30. Voida, A., Harmon, E. & Al-Ani, B. (2012). Bridging between organizations and the public: Volunteer coordinators' uneasy relationship with social computing. In *Proc. CHI*. New York: ACM Press, 1967–1976.

Planning with Crowdsourced Data: Rhetoric and Representation in Transportation Planning

Christopher A. Le Dantec[1], Mariam Asad[1], Aditi Misra[2], Kari E. Watkins[2]

[1]School of Literature, Media, & Communication
Georgia Institute of Technology

[2]School of Civil and Environmental Engineering
Georgia Institute of Technology

ledantec@gatech.edu, missasad@gatech.edu, amisra7@gatech.edu, kari.watkins@ce.gatech.edu

ABSTRACT

We are in the midst of a new era of experimentation that blends social and mobile computing in support of digital democracy. These experiments will have potentially long lasting consequences on how the public is invited to participate in governance by elected as well as professional officials. In this paper, we look at how data from a purpose-built smartphone app we deployed were incorporated into a three-day urban planning event. The data collected were meant to help inform design decisions for new cycling infrastructure and to provide an alternate means for participating in the planning process. Through our analysis, we point to three distinct roles the data played at the event—as *authority*, as *evidence*, and as *ambivalent*. Each role demonstrates the challenge and potential for turning to crowdsourced data as a form of participation and as a resource for urban planning.

Author Keywords

Urban Informatics, Digital Democracy, Urban Planning, Public Participation

ACM Classification Keywords

K.4.3 Organizational Impacts: CSCW.

INTRODUCTION

Over the last 60 years, a number of social and technological processes have led to drastic and steady changes in how Americans interact with each other and engage in civic activities. While there are varying perspectives on why these changes are occurring—and on their overall effects in the long term—there is consensus that Americans are interacting less with each other and their various levels of local, state, and national government [6, 16, 41, 48]. This decline occurs at a time when a wealth of emerging social media technologies have brought about significant new forms of communication and interpersonal interaction, providing diverse new ways of documenting, sharing, and reflecting on the world.

CSCW '15, March 14 - 18 , 2015, Vancouver, BC, Canada.

ACM 978-1-4503-2922-4/15/03...$15.00
http://dx.doi.org/10.1145/2675133.2675212

The challenges in applying these new classes of digital technology to the milieu of civic engagement include re-locating technologies whose initial attractions was untethering people from places; encouraging broad participation across diverse constituencies; supporting robust engagement across both strong and weak social ties; and translating technology mediated action into direct impact on the "real world." Much recent research in this vein has looked at the mechanisms and opportunities for supporting citizen engagement in knowledge sharing and in public fora for planning and governance (*e.g.*, [12, 21, 44]). Less focus, however, has been given to the impact of these new forms of participation on planners and other government functionaries who must develop and implement policy.

To begin to understand how these new categories of public participation affect the development of policy, we have collaborated with planners and the current mayoral administration of Atlanta to develop and deploy a mobile computing system to collect route data from interested cyclists. The deployed system includes a smartphone app (for iOS and Android) and is supported by a backend web service to store data and facilitate analysis. By enlisting cyclists to record their route data via smartphone apps, city planners sought to enable new mechanisms for public participation in the planning process and to build a robust ground-truth model of how cyclists move through the city of Atlanta. The addition of crowdsourced data was meant to aid the development of plans for new cycling infrastructure that would more effectively respond to acute problems (traffic signals, pavement issues, and enforcement) as well as to systemic challenges in the existing street network (establishing bike lanes, cycle tracks, and synchronizing traffic signals).

The city's desire to make its planning process more data-driven through direct, digital participation raises a number of questions: How does the introduction of technology challenge existing modes of urban planning and development? How are different forms of data incorporated into public planning meetings? Who uses the collected data? To gain insight into these questions, we conducted ethnographic fieldwork at a three-day design and planning meeting called a charrette.

Growing out of a stated goal and commitment to enabling new forms of participation in the planning process, the charrette was a clear opportunity to systematically examine how professional planners were beginning to incorporate and make sense of new forms of data: answering for themselves how to interpret intentional acts of contributed data as a form of public participation and argument. At the charrette, we observed the ways in which the collected data served as an instrumental and discursive artifact, the ways they were used to marshal arguments about specific infrastructure proposals, and their role in brokering trust and commitment to real citizens.

Our analysis leads us to examine how the planners and participants at the charrette interpreted route data as a surrogate for direct participation in the public planning process. The ambiguity and heterogeneity of the data created opportunities for interpretation and this unevenness allowed the collected data to contribute to planning conversations in varied ways and to meet multiple ends. It is in this multiplicity and interpretability that we find opportunities for future programs of digital civic participation.

A TRIPTYCH OF DIGITAL DEMOCRATIC ENCOUNTERS

Starting at least as far back as the 1960's, researchers have argued for the potentially transformative nature of real-time systems and data analytics for achieving a more robust public good [46]. More broadly, there is a rich history within computing in considering the role of technology in supporting both public participation in democratic process (*e.g.*, [25, 28]) and the ways technology—and data in particular—might reconfigure the running of government and the production of different classes of public services (*e.g.*, [7, 50, 54]). More recently, the smart city movement marks a turn toward developing computing technology for critical urban infrastructures [17, 35, 36]. Following early visions of applying data to government services [46], the smart cities research agenda is to build the computing and data resources needed to make urban operation more efficient—from smart watershed management [11], to rationalized service information [37], to environmental sensing [26, 42].

While each of these areas apply computing technologies in different ways, they share a commitment to generating data that can be analyzed and used to improve the functioning of the city. In some cases, these data are generated through sensor networks and instrumented infrastructure [11, 40, 52], in others, data are produced through participatory sensing where citizens collect and contribute data for policy makers and government employees to interpret and act upon [10, 45, 47].

It is within this context of technology's potential transformation of government that we find recommendations at the highest levels of U.S. government for a serious engagement with the next era of digital democracy [43]. It is also within this context, and the contemporary trajectory of social and mobile computing, that we find new experiments in mediating democratic participation, sensing and data collection to connect to government services, and models for digital civic engagement.

Mediating Representation

In March 2013, then Newark mayor Cory Booker spoke at the South by Southwest Interactive conference and heralded the potential for digital democracy [2]. He called for more inclusive modes of communication between citizens and government, stating that "the future of government has to be getting to 2.0" [31]. Booker was known for his active participation on Twitter, most notably using it as personal liaison between citizens and city departments. His use of Twitter illustrates one way in which technologies can encourage movement towards digital democracy: Newark residents who had a Twitter account could reach out directly to the mayor in real time and inform him of problems in the city, thereby bypassing traditional bureaucratic mechanisms for interacting with city services.

By using Twitter to communicate with constituents directly, Booker created an online space for public discourse that offered a kind of transparency to his public interactions. That transparency came with an altered set of accountabilities, however, because it occurred outside the established channels for registering and responding to issues with city infrastructure. By shifting interactions away from established channels, Booker replicated the kind of shift in influence Kling documented over 35 years ago, noting that government officials who deploy computing systems are more likely gain influence and solidify organizational power through their use [25]. The subtleties that Kling pointed out in the relationship to elected officials, size of local agencies, and to the use of data track the complex interplay between different modes of democratic governance, the affordances of different classes of technology mediated communication, and the many accountabilities present in government agencies large and small [25, 53].

Sensing and the Smart City

Where Twitter created new direct channels of communication with elected officials, smartphones and sensors are enabling more direct interaction with public services. An example of how mobile sensing is changing public input into public services is the Street Bump app. Deployed in Boston, the app uses a smartphone's accelerometer to automate the detection and reporting of pavement issues around the city. When using the app, geo-located street quality data is automatically uploaded to the city and connected to Boston's processes for fixing potholes. One of the app developers referred to Street Bump as "a new kind of volunteerism," where it was not the citizens volunteering, but "the devices that are in [citizen's] pocket" [4]. Street Bump follows a model of public engagement with roots in the citizen-science movement where inexpert participants are enrolled in sometimes passive or low-skill sensing activities in order to collect and report environmental data [26].

In the context of digital democracy, environmental sensing projects like Street Bump help citizens become more self-aware of their relationship to their locales and act as catalysts to engage in conversations about community values and potentially initiate political and social change [26]. However, even as these new modes of sensing change the effort required to contribute toward the upkeep and improvement of urban infrastructure, they also privilege certain ways of knowing and acting in society [49]. The challenge is to both produce data that represent a diverse range of experience in the city as well as develop institutional responses that are sensitized to the limits of what kinds of knowledge the data enable. If part of the motivation for building these kinds of systems is to transform representative democratic practices into more direct participatory practices [1], then the question of who participates is paramount. However, asking "who participates" also means attending to how different kinds of participation are interpreted and integrated into the professional practices of developing and implementing policy [7, 50].

Models of Participation

Platforms beyond mobile- and sensor-based technologies can also offer ways of engaging in public discourse. In a project called Participatory Chinatown, citizens applied their local knowledge in an online world [20]. Physically co-present participants explored a virtual recreation of their neighborhood and could redesign the space to experience it from other perspectives. Each participant was given a character and quest to guide their experience, such as finding an apartment to rent, or securing a job. The social conditions of the neighborhood, including a high immigrant population and increasing gentrification, were also recreated to give social context to the virtual environment.

Between the detailed virtual model and the existing local knowledge, players could be in "both places at once;" embodying multiple perspectives in order to develop empathy and provide valuable planning feedback [20]. The project provided ways for planners to interpret local knowledge as they considered alternate strategies for redevelopment and it gave community residents a way to illustrate and experience the consequences of those alternatives.

These three examples illustrate how the affordances of different technology interventions lend themselves to different kinds of democratic relations [53]. Mayor Booker was able to create public and visible discourse using Twitter while also establishing a channel that allowed citizens to bypass established contact points with city services, creating a direct connection to an elected official and an opportunity to establish social ties and cultivate and use different forms of social capital [22]. Street Bump applied the sensing capabilities of smartphones to identify acute problems in road infrastructure, leveraging models of participation where citizens gather, collect, and produce spatial data for later action by professionals [12, 19, 24]. Participatory Chinatown was effective because players could draw on their knowledge of an existing, physical neighborhood to virtually explore alternative arrangements, visualizing proposed changes in a virtual world makes proposed planning projects easier to relate to and internalize [20].

Given the diverse transparencies, automation, and speculative futures that digital democracy can support, we have developed and deployed a smartphone app in order to experiment with empowering citizens by more directly connecting them to government. The app and the public initiative around the data collected via the app combines features of each of the systems described above: citizens provide geo-located data about cycling patterns, those data mediate interactions with city officials, and they provide an empirical basis for modeling and infrastructure design. The intersection of these capabilities, however, creates a set of unique challenges: where data become a proxy for discourse and not just empirical evidence of particular conditions; where civic participation and advocacy with city officials is mediated by data collection; and where local expertise and ways of knowing are imbedded both in the data and in the agency and intent of collecting the data.

To better understand how these features impact policy and urban planning, we focus on the ways in which the citizen-produced data were incorporated and interpreted within an on-going planning process. Mid-way through a year-long planning study to develop new cycling infrastructure, city planners gained access to the crowdsourced cycling data collected by our app. Just as new technologies evolve existing forms of civic labor—*e.g.*, collecting and contributing data—they also require a concomitant evolution in how existing institutions and professional practices act in response [12]. By focusing on the way new forms of data were used by city planners, we gain a better understanding of how different kinds of participation are represented and responded to in the development of specific infrastructure plans.

METHOD AND ANALYSIS

In order to understand how the contributed data were being used in the planning process, we conducted ethnographic fieldwork at a three-day planning and design session called a charrette. A charrette is particular kind of multi-day design workshop common in urban planning practice. The purpose of the charrette is to co-develop solutions and to create commitment and ownership of the plan by a diverse set of stakeholders. During the fieldwork, which took place in February of 2013, we paid particular attention how planners were using the collected data, how that data figured into conversations about design alternatives, and how the public was brought into the process, either directly via individuals present at the charrette, or via the data submitted through the apps.

The three-day charrette was run in stages: the first day was taken up with meetings with various stakeholders, such as other city departments and neighborhood representatives. The second day continued these consultations, but also offered a public forum in the evening to invite comment and feedback from the public at large. The third day included a ride through the city with planners and other stakeholders to experience specific corridors first-hand and to collect empirical data supporting the prior discussions about particular locations and facilities. The core personnel at the meeting included the assistant director of transportation planning for the city, contracted planners from a bicycle and pedestrian planning consultancy, key stakeholders from local bicycle advocacy groups, and representatives from central neighborhoods. Over the course of the three days, 85 people were involved with a core group of seven planners and city officials throughout the charrette. At any given time during the three days, about 15–20 people were in attendance as external stakeholders and other members of the public came and went from the event.

Our study data comprised audio recordings and their transcripts, field notes from observations, and a range of documents, maps, and planning manuals that were used and referenced during the charrette (*e.g*, [38]). Our data analysis was based on the fundamentals of qualitative data analysis [3, 33, 51]: field notes and observations were analyzed in an on-going manner to better inform the details to which we attended during the charrette and any follow-up questions we posed to meeting attendees. Transcripts were iteratively coded in an inductive manner, revealing key ways data—particularly from the app—were marshaled during the discussions. Design documents, maps, and manuals of best practice were referred to as source material to aid in triangulating observations with the professional practices of urban planning.

STUDY CONTEXT

Cycle Atlanta is the name of both the regional planning project and the smartphone app we developed for the planning department of our local government. The larger urban planning project began in late 2011 as part of a livable-centers initiative to promote particular kinds of development to enliven the urban center of our sprawling city. The initial plan identified a number of core roads crucial to providing robust bicycle infrastructure. These corridors were chosen for the access they provided to centers for healthcare, housing, employment, retail, and cultural arts.

In addition to identifying urban infrastructure projects to support a rich urban core, the regional planning organization wanted to support new modes of public participation as a complementary set of activities to strengthen the city. It was through this goal that the city reached out to our research team to build the digital tools for supporting alternate forms of public input into the process of developing plans for new cycling infrastructure.

Cycle Atlanta was launched in October 2012 and used the geo-locative capabilities of smartphones to record and upload cycling routes. Each recorded route provided a record of how the cyclist navigated the city, including the purpose of the trip and any rider-added notes. The app also included the ability to record specific locations with photos and text descriptions. These specific locations are classified as either issues (pavement issues, traffic signal, enforcement, etc.) or assets (bike parking, public restrooms, water fountains, etc.). Finally, the app collected optional demographic data including a self-assessment of cycling ability, cycling history, and current cycling frequency as indicators of comfort level to aid the eventual analysis of route data around an established taxonomy of urban cyclists [8].

We recruited cyclists to use our app by distributing postcards at local bike shops and community festivals. The recruitment

Figure 1 Charrette room with printed maps on central table and map of recorded ride data projected against wall.

specifically prompted cyclists to participate in improving cycling in the city by contributing data via the app. Our strategy was based on recognizing that many cyclists already use other kinds of tracking devices—smartphone apps like Strava (www.strava.com) or MapMyRide (www.mapmyride.com), or purpose-built cycling computers like those from Garmin, and so we focused on the value of sharing ride data with the city as a primary incentive. We also had a collective desire to connect cyclists using the app to an explicit form of civic engagement—we were not trying to displace other commercial products but to make it clear that our apps served the very specific purpose of providing data to planners who could then act on those data when developing plans for new cycling facilities. By focusing our app on civic engagement, the data recorded through our app became positioned in a particular way, more clearly demarcating it as an intentional act of civic participation (as opposed to a re-purposing of data resulting from fitness tracking).

PLANNING THROUGH DATA

The use of data is standard in urban planning processes—traffic counts, street widths, and other metrics anchor the process in the reality of the social and built environment [32]. Professional planning practice has a long history of working with these kinds of data, and with managing their messiness and imprecision. In addition to these familiar forms of data, the planners and stakeholders at the three-day charrette had access to a new kind of data: data contributed by cyclists through the app we had released four months earlier. At the time of the charrette, 535 cyclists had used the app, contributing 5386 rides. These new data exposed the specific routes of cyclists who had used the app and were a resource for making design decisions based on recorded cycling routes. The app data also posed a set of challenges for how the planners responded and reflected more generally

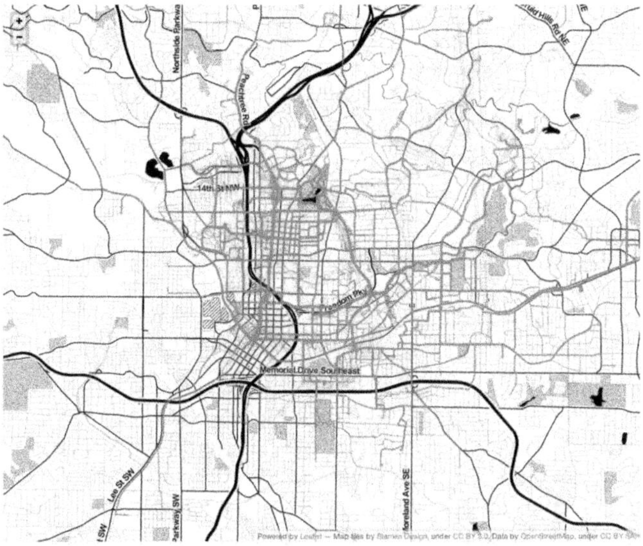

Figure 2 Detail of digital map showing trips recorded with our app.

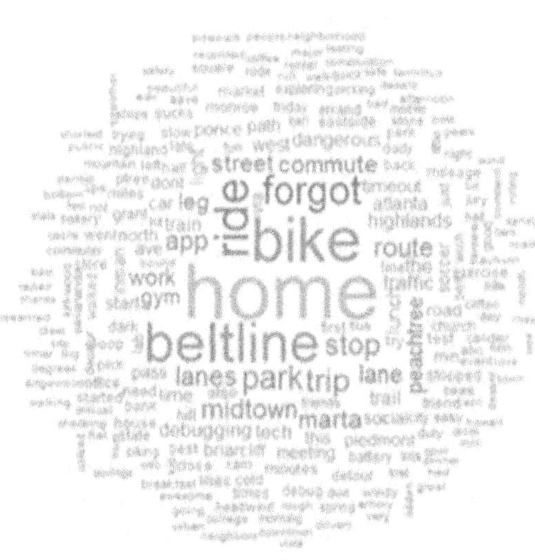

Figure 3 Comment word cloud showing occurrence of common terms in rider-submitted comments

on "data" as an objective measure versus as a curated and intentional form of participation.

In order to motivate how these different tensions arose during the charrette, it is necessary to understand that the concept of "data" was not homogenous. There were many sources of data that were used and referred to during discussion, each of which influenced the planning conversations in a different way. The first example came in the form of large printed maps produced by the city's planning office (see Figure 1). These maps showed the target corridors of the project, areas that themselves were the result of multiple data sources and considerable analysis in synthesizing which transportation links would most effectively connect residential areas with economic and cultural centers. Another example was the persistent use of Google Earth in discussions about specific locations. The interactivity of Google Earth enabled the participants at the charrette to ask probing questions about particular roads and intersections, to confirm street widths and distances, or find visual examples of traffic conditions. Finally, there was the group ride where the planners and other stakeholders rode their bicycles around key areas of the city. The group ride allowed the visiting planning consultants to develop a more visceral understanding of the city's infrastructure, its neighborhoods, and the natural and built environments in which proposed cycling facilities would be situated.

When compared to these other forms of data, however, the data collected via the smartphone apps played a different role in the design process. Broadly, the data were used for different rhetorical ends in both the framing of particular arguments and in the instrumental way arguments were constructed: throughout the charrette, the data were implicated in calls to authority, appeals to reason, or affective references to the aspirations of the larger planning initiative. As design alternatives were developed and discussed, the data were deployed in whatever way would best support the argument at hand: the data were a mutable and universal resource for supporting or refuting design moves by planners and participating stakeholders alike.

Initially, data from the app were presented in two material ways: as a map showing the accumulated trips recorded by cyclists (see Figure 2), and as a word cloud that displayed the most commonly used words in the user-submitted comments (see Figure 3). The map of route data clearly showed which roads were the most ridden in the urban core; the word cloud highlighted the experience cyclists had while traversing the city, presenting a visual way to reference rider sentiment about riding in the city (divorced from any one particular route). These two visualizations reflected dual uses of the recorded data, one as concrete and specific, tied to the geographic particulars of the city and the second as symbolic, reinforcing the connection between the map and the cyclists it represented.

The word cloud was less sophisticated than the empirical, geographic data, and was not used in constructing design arguments because any specificity that might have been gleaned from the rider comments was lost in the aggregate visualization of common terms. Despite this limitation, however, it played an important role in supporting the "hard" data by humanizing it and making present the cyclists who contributed to the recorded route data—connecting the data collected to the agency and intent of those collecting it. The open-house on the evening of the second day served a similar function insofar as it highlighted contributions from non-experts—students, parents, hobbyists, commuters—that pluralized interpretations of specific map corridors and locations. In this way the collected data extended the traditional means of public participation: some users showed up directly to the public open house, but many others were made present through their data.

Polysemic Data: Three Roles of Data in Planning

The map was the main data artifact referred to during the charrette (see Figures 1 and 2); it played the most visible role throughout the three days and was the primary reference for questions about the characteristics of cyclist travel through the city, including gaining a sense of traffic volume, preferred route, and network density. When the map was introduced, a member of the research team made clear that it was derived from "raw" data—the data had not been normalized or otherwise cleaned to account for duplicate trips or any other error or bias that might be present in the data. In spite of these limitations, participants at the charrette referred to the map with excitement and confidence.

Throughout the three-day meeting, the data played three distinct roles: as *authority*, as *evidence*, and as *ambivalent*. When referred to as authority, the map served a symbolic function: its mere presence served as an argument for the robustness of the process and demonstrated that planning decisions were being based in ground-truth reality of where cyclists were. As evidence, the data were used to defend or refute arguments being made about specific routes or corridors under consideration. Finally, when viewed as ambivalent, the data were acknowledged as potentially misleading or inaccurate; the veracity of the data was questioned but not its rhetorical power within the context of the charrette. These roles were multivalent such that as the charrette participants incorporated the data into their discussions, the data were frequently marshaled in multiple ways, crossing from authoritative, to evidentiary, and then qualified as ambivalent.

Data as Authority

As a source of *authority*, the data—and particularly the map—played an important role in the charrette. That role was composed of two characteristics. First, the data's authority was derived from its technical origins as computationally sensed and stored knowledge about the world. Second, and related, the data's authority was based in the way it afforded rhetorical weight both to specific points of discussion and to the overall process and the commitment to demonstrating a data-driven planning process.

Following these characteristics, the map was a testimonial object: it served as a resource for argumentation simply through its presence as an empirical backdrop to the charrette (see Figure 2). The fact that data had been collected for use in planning inspired some degree of trust in the results. This trust was buttressed by the notion that, because of its origins in a technical artifact, the data were simultaneously objective and transparent. The fact that traveling the route was the only way to generate the mapped data lent veracity and legitimacy to the rendering; it was not viewed as fallible as routes drawn from memory or from idealized preferences.

In a particular exchange, two of the consulting planners and the assistant director used the mapped data as an authoritative answer to where cyclists were moving against traffic through a particular area:

> *Planner 1: Now are people doing that out-of-direction movement already?*
>
> *Assistant Director: Probably not*
>
> *Planner 2: Let's see*
>
> *Planner 1: I mean, are people coming off of 10th to skip that section?*
>
> *Planner 2: Yeah, they're all using 12th*
>
> *Assistant Director: If you look at the Cycle Atlanta data, they're all using 12th [showing and gesturing to the map]*

Despite the specificity of the geo-located data, when the map was used as an authority it was more often done through gestures to larger areas rather than fine-grained examination of particular locations. Part of this was due to the format used to present the data. The map was interactive and participants at the charrette could zoom in to specific areas under consideration; however, there were no additional features available that would have supported more pointed questions such as the number of riders, demographic breakdown in particular regions, or other metadata about a given ride or collection of rides. By being limited to panning and zooming, the participants could only partially disambiguate popular routes. Zooming in would make it more clear how many line segments might be clustered in an area, but that assessment was ambiguous and created opportunities for alternate interpretation. Nonetheless, the map was still an authority as the presence of the "hard" data that it symbolized fed into the discussions throughout the three days.

Interestingly, the efficacy of the map as an artifact of authority did not derive from the data themselves, but rather from its representation of truth and fact. The map was emblematic of data collection practices that accredited and validated the planning conversations of the charrette. While there were other sources of data—the plotted maps from the planning office, Google Earth, and the fieldwork stemming from the group ride—the map of the recorded routes was a robust visual symbol of the legitimacy of the local process.

Data as Evidence

During the charrette, planners continually referred to the route data as *evidence* of a particular need for cycling infrastructure. This reference—and at times, deference—to the data came despite early qualifications that the data had yet to be rigorously normalized or analyzed, and that the map, as rendered, was open to conflicting interpretations. In spite of this, planners continually referred to activity along particular streets on the map as accurate representations—making calls to the legitimacy of the data.

As an example of how the mapped ride data was used as evidence, the assistant director referred to a section of the map to affirm a planning decision that had already been made as part of a prior project:

> *Assistant Director: I like to see all these people on Peachtree 'cause that means when we put facilities on Ju-*

niper and Piedmont, I think we're gonna see a lot of people using it.

This statement strengthened the planners' arguments for new bike facilities along the referenced busy street, even though the feasibility of those facilities being built during the current project was low. The street was a highly contested route because of the current car traffic it carried because commercial interests were unwilling to forfeit on-street parking for bike lanes due to fears of loss of business. The recorded data, however, provided evidence that considerable bicycle traffic was present and could be used to persuade local businesses that street-level changes would be a boost to business—as has been seen in other large cities [39].

The work the recorded data were doing here was different than other sources of data deployed in the meeting. Unlike traffic counts or road dimensions, the evidence being provided was less about the specific measure of cyclists on that particular road, and more about a simple visibility. Their presence via the recorded data was used as evidence of the need for facilities and as well as demonstrating a hope for how those facilities would be used. Much in the way a strong turnout at a public meeting becomes evidence of the importance of a particular issue, the mapped data became a stable representation of the presence of cyclists in the city, evidence that the current plans were tied to a real need.

Even in this more mutable role of evidence-as-visibility, the route data were continually deployed as evidence to corroborate and validate the creation of facilities on specific streets. Though potentially inaccurate, the presence of cyclists along corridors with planned improvements underway was used to motivate the current project by serving as a reminder that people, and potentially many people, would benefit. Moreover, as the above quote indicates, the role of data as future evidence was equally important: the data not only provided evidence for the activities at this charrette, but was also presumed to provide evidence for assessing the use of newly built facilities in future planning activities.

Data as Ambivalent

Despite the rhetorical weight conveyed by the route data, the limitations of the data and the particular representation of it via the map were both well understood. It was due to those limitations that the data were frequently used to alternately support and counter different design moves depending on the context of the conversation. Even though the data frequently served conflicting arguments, those arguments were developed as qualifications about how the data were *ambivalent* rather than as outright dismissal of the data as incorrect or unusable.

The conflicted use of the route data is best exemplified by an exchange where the assistant director invoked the data to make a case for a suggested facility along a busy street. The street in question had been consistently identified as the most important corridor in the study area and the map showed a concentration of lines along the street.

Planner 1: That looks like the strongest corridor.

Assistant Director: Well, again though, that's Georgia Tech, a lotta the people using the app are at Georgia Tech. It is one of the busiest corridors in the city.

In this exchange, the assistant director referred to a potential bias in the route data that may have skewed who was represented. Interestingly, the assistant director also immediately verified the same corridor as one of the city's busiest. This complicated the framing of the data in the conversation as it embodied paradoxical roles simultaneously: as it appeared on the map, the reliability of the data could be called into question because it showed substantial bicycle traffic on a busy street known to be unsafe for cyclists; however, when taken in context with other forms of knowledge about the street in question, its accuracy was accepted.

The main question that confronted the participants in the charrette was how to interpret the data. The ambiguity of why particular areas had, or did not have, apparent cycling traffic meant that there was constant interpretive work happening when participants at the charrette referred to the recorded data. This work treated the data simultaneously as factual and counterfactual: the data clearly demonstrated that cyclists were present, but that presence was followed with a qualification of what if the reason, or number, or sample of cyclists represented were not robust enough to justify the argument being made in relation to that apparent presence.

While these three roles—as authority, evidence, and ambivalence—were distinct, it was often the case that they were deployed within a single exchange as charrette participants discussed alternatives and worked through the trade-offs and rationales for particular design decisions. Returning to the example above demonstrating how the map data was used as authority, the conversation continued and can be seen to walk through these different roles:

Planner 1: I mean, are people coming off of 10th to skip that section?

Planner 2: Yeah, they're all using 12th

Assistant Director: If you look at the Cycle Atlanta data, they're all using 12th [showing and gesturing to the map]

Planner 1: This is a big movement too

Assistant Director: And it looks like they're using Charles Allen, Monroe, Virginia to 8th. See, 8th is easier to get to from [that street] if you're coming from Virginia Highland.

Planner 3: I'm surprised that there are so many people riding on 10th Street

Assistant Director: Yeah, me too... well, it looks like it's one guy going to, um,Turner [Broadcasting] everyday

In this extended exchange, the assistant director used the map data to serve the three different roles simultaneously: the data as *authority* ("If you look at the data..."), the data as *evidence* ("See, 8th is easier..."), and the data as *ambivalent*

("It looks like it's one guy..."). The interleaving of these roles demonstrates how route data was polysemic: its presence in the charrette introduced multiple challenges in assessing the data and multiple interpretations of how to apply the data.

The interpretability of the data also demonstrated the potential for multiple modes of participation in civic processes: uploaded routes allowed users to be "present" at planning activities they could not attend. This kind of data-driven participation authentically mirrors physically co-present interactions: in the same way that a participant's opinions and contributions can be complex and contradictory, so too was their digitally mediated presence. The recorded route data did not definitively answer questions about the habits and preferences of cyclists in the city, but it did make those cyclists visible and enlist them in the design process in new and complex ways.

DISCUSSION

Discourse that engages the multiple, polysemic voices of the citizenry is a crucial element to the civic engagement necessary for participatory democracy. The multiple roles the route data played in the charrette show the possibility for digital democracy to capture the same subtle, layered, and paradoxical dynamics of issue advocacy and public participation.

Within that participation, however, we need to attend to the fact that "not all forms of participation are equally democratic… and any amount of any type of participation" does not necessarily result in more democracy [28]. While cyclists had a unique way of participating in the planning process through their data, one that went beyond the public hearings, surveys, or negotiated rule making of established forms public consultation [15], the overall transparency of that participation was not apparent. Questions remain of how data-based participation was presented, who was represented, and by whom.

These questions are important to attend to as it is very different to invite individual participation mediated by data collection than to place it within formalized processes more common in public policy [15, 28]. While the city held traditional public meetings for comment and input—the charrette being one such public venue—there was a substantial difference in scale between the number of people who were present at public meetings and the number whose presence was felt through the inclusions of app-collected data. The consequence of this shift was a kind of authority without agency, where the intentions of cyclists who submitted data were subordinated by whatever in-person argument was being made with that very same data at the charrette.

We recognize that building out programs to dramatically increase the number of citizens who attend public planning meetings is difficult, and that new modes of participation that rely on social and mobile technologies are attractive. However, data-based participation shifts the focus to mobile phones and to sensors and leads to a different set of challenges for planners and citizens alike. These new kinds of participation and civic labor need to be understood and reflected on as they are incorporated into our democratic processes—whether used for communicating directly with elected officials, or for developing data-driven processes of planning.

Equity and Inclusion

Chief among the challenges to digital democratic endeavors are those focused on extending participation to those who typically lack access to ICTs due to existing socio-economic barriers [14, 27]. Where project like Street Bump can be reasonably criticized on the grounds that the volunteerism of the device excludes whole classes of people who either do not have such devices or who choose not to use them to sense their environment, similar critiques can likewise be leveled at our project where the means and the desire to record where one rides and contribute that data to the city for use in planning is a necessarily self-selected group: a group that most certainly does not equitably trace the larger contours of our urban population.

During the design charrette, it was clear that the planners and other participants understood the limits of the data—its authority was repeatedly contextualized and the ways the data were used as evidence were genuine and skeptical. Charrette participants recognized that what was represented on the map was not an accurate picture of all the ways people cycle around the city and that the data were not of the same quality normally selected for such purposes. The transportation surveys, or traffic counts, or other forms of data normally present in urban planning are produced and analyzed with specific protocols and methods for weighting and understanding bias and error and were treated differently but also less visibly in the charrette [32].

The presumption of objectivity affiliated with the app-collected data framed the public's involvement in a way that was problematic when compared to the way in which other publics were represented during the charrette. One challenge was the platform: because the vehicle for data collection was an application for smartphones, it inherently limited how certain groups were represented and made visible in the data. Confounding this fact, Atlanta has historically had—and continues to have—dramatic racial and socio-economic divides. In many cases, these divides are deeply rooted in neighborhoods that were currently under consideration as locations for key infrastructure corridors. Developing meaningful public input from some of these disenfranchised communities was acknowledged and understood by the city's personnel as an on-going issue; though this had not yet been well met by the new model of data-driven participation, and instead relied on existing strategies for accounting for under-represented groups.

The disconnect between the data collection and the need for innovation in alternate, non-digital modes of engagement demonstrates a gap in the digital democracy literature: the use of data in and of itself does not inherently create more participation, more public engagement, or more inclusive processes [28]. Taken at face value, the absence of recorded route data in parts of the city would suggest continued divestment rather than the significant improvements that were being considered. The reasons for those new projects were only partially captured during the charrette as they connected to alternate development narratives around re-connection and re-investment in some of the city's neglected historic communities.

Data as Disruption

The idea that more cyclists had participated in the formulation of the infrastructure plan was an important component to conveying the authority of the data in the charrette. One way to interpret the persistent reference to the recorded data, especially given the obvious and recognized limitations the data and the map had as instrumental tools for analysis, was that the planners treated the data as a form of surrogate participation by cyclists. It was deference to the individuals who contributed the data, not deference to the data itself.

One of the challenges planners need to overcome as they turn to social media and other computing platforms to enable participation is the difficulty in translating on-line affinities into real-world commitments to action [13]. There is some promise that adding additional avenues of participation may enlist more people into action—where tens of people attended the design charrette, hundreds contributed data via our app. However, that additional participation brings with it considerable disruption to professional practice and long-standing techniques for mitigating underrepresentation and equity in urban planning.

In particular, examining how data were interpreted as evidence, there was a difference between the data produced as part of professional practice, and those that were derived from personal contribution. In many respects, the ambivalence of the recorded ride data grew out of its decoupling from the context of production—the people and their intentions—which is a direct consequence of turning to sensed data to account for individual or collective agency. In our case, the data and mode of collection look, at first blush, very similar to data from projects like Street Bump where smartphones provide geo-located facts about the world. However, where Street Bump's data report the state of infrastructure as it currently is, the data from our app are being collected to advocate for how infrastructure might be created, taking on some of the speculative elements of systems like Participatory Chinatown. While these new forms of data-based civic labor can scaffold individual engagement by creating new and asynchronous modes of participation in governance—like Twitter enabled with Mayor Booker—they need to be carefully integrated into existing modes of governance, professional practice, and collective issue advocacy.

The focus on the individual interaction with government further evolves the kinds of challenges that arise from a desire for a more data-intensive model for planning and governing. When the project was launched at an event with the Mayor, the data collected by the apps were framed by a rhetoric of objectivity and transparency: the data simply show where cyclists are; and anyone could contribute. This was not unproblematic as a significant challenge to planners is how to infer cyclist intentions by looking at the produced map. If a cyclist uses a particular path to get from Point A to Point B, the transmitted geo-location data does not answer *why* she chose that particular route nor why she chose cycling as the mode of transportation. The collected data force us to think about how to disrupt the assumption of data objectivity and transparency, moving toward more nuanced engagements with forms of civic data that create room for interpretation and alternate analysis.

Data Collection as Rhetoric

Throughout the design charrette, city planners and other participants made arguments about infrastructure decisions by referring to or refuting the recorded route data. While the rhetorical utility of the data was made apparent through its deployment in multiple roles in the meeting, we should also consider the ways the production of that data is an act of advocacy. Consider the planning conversation about the visibility of one individual recording their daily commute. If it was indeed a single rider recording the same trip multiple times, then we might look at the ways that form of participation was an attempt at making an emphatic case about the need for infrastructure. While the route data used in the charrette was not normalized to account for an individual introducing bias, we might instead turn away from the notion of *bias* in the data to a notion of *persuasion* via the data. A future analysis of the data that removes duplicate trips from public representations strips away the ability for individuals to turn their participation through the smartphone app into a form of civic argument.

Data driven models of governance presume an empirical, objective, and dispassionate basis upon which to make policy decisions [25, 46]. Democratic participation, by contrast, is messy, subjective, and impassioned [5, 9, 34]. As we look at projects like ours that rely on participation through data production, we need to be able to acknowledge and account for civic participation not in the early Habermasian sense of rational discourse [23], but through conflicting, messy, agonistic models of public participation and design intervention [9, 29]. Our contention here is that the multiple trips from one cyclists should not be simply dismissed as bias, but internalized as a form of argument via the asynchronous, data-driven participation that collecting data via smartphone apps enabled.

Ultimately, we need to interrogate how data-driven public processes may overshadow alternate narratives of how we engage in democratic society and collective action [18, 53]. It is not simply a problem of access to the tools for data production, but of considering and integrating alternate ways of experiencing community, and of taking seriously the task of understanding how different socio-technical systems constitute and configure publics [30], engender participation, and achieved outcomes.

CONCLUSION

The endeavor of this project has been, in many important ways, a significant step and substantial success for the city's desire to adopt new methods of public participation: the cycling community had direct input into the planning process in new ways; new forms of data informed planning decisions and were integrated into existing planning processes; a dialogue between planners, elected officials, and the cycling public was created around what this kind of participation meant and how it would be carried forward into a number of planned projects around the longer-term livable-centers initiative.

While the project achieved a measure of success, the specifics of how the recorded data were used, the role they played in the planning process, and the kind of participation they afforded highlight more nuanced challenges that must be met as we move toward more digital democratic processes. These kinds of socio-technical undertakings can disrupt and reconfigure civic processes to redefine what it means to participate. The production of data can be viewed not as a means of fact-collection, but a space for discourse, discussion, and argumentation. Each of these introduce new kind of challenges to professional planners who must integrate multiple data sources into a coherent analysis and plan.

More critically, though, is the reflex to reduce all civic issues to problems in need of the right technology, the right data, and the right algorithm. However, by situating data into the larger socio-cultural context and treating it as a product of social relations, we can better understand how technology can catalyze conversations and actions that are more informed, better connected to existing civic processes, and—ultimately—more democratic.

ACKNOWLEDGMENTS

We thank the City of Atlanta and the Atlanta Regional Commission for their support and collaboration for this research. This research was supported by the Intel Science and Technology Center for Social Computing.

REFERENCES

[1] Becker, T. Rating the impact of new technologies on democracy. *Communications of the ACM 44*, 1 (2001), 39–43.

[2] Bella, T. Cory Booker"s Twitter Talk at SXSW Shows He"s Really an Old-School Pol. *The Atlantic*, 2013. http://www.theatlantic.com/politics/archive/2013/03/cory-bookers-twitter-talk-at-sxsw-shows-hes-really-an-old-school-pol/273914/.

[3] Bernard, H.R. *Research Methods in Anthropology: Qualitative and Quantitative Approaches*. AltaMira Press, 2005.

[4] Brown, M. "Street Bump" Android app detects and reports potholes. *Wired.co.uk*, 2011. http://www.wired.co.uk/news/archive/2011-02/14/street-bump-app.

[5] Callon, M., Lascoumes, P., and Barthe, Y. *Acting in an Uncertain World: An Essay on Technical Democracy*. MIT Press, 2009.

[6] Center for Information and Research on Civic Learning and Engagement. *The Youth Vote 2004 With a Historical Look at Youth Voting Patterns, 1972-2004*. 2005.

[7] Dawes, S.S. and Pardo, T.A. Maximizing Knowledge for Program Evaluation: Critical Issues and Practical Challenges of ICT Strategies. *4084/2006*, (2006), 58–69.

[8] Dill, J. and McNeil, N. Four Types of Cyclists? *Transportation Research Record: Journal of the Transportation Research Board 2387*, -1 (2014), 129–138.

[9] DiSalvo, C.F. *Adversarial Design*. The MIT Press, 2012.

[10] Doran, D., Gokhale, S., and Dagnino, A. Human Sensing for Smart Cities. *Proceedings of the 2013 IEEE/ACM International Conference on Advances in Social Networks Analysis and Mining*, ACM (2013), 1323–1330.

[11] Erickson, T., Podlaseck, M., Sahu, S., Dai, J.D., Chao, T., and Naphade, M. The Dubuque Water Portal: Evaluation of the Uptake, Use and Impact of Residential Water Consumption Feedback. *Proc. CHI*, ACM (2012), 675–684.

[12] Evans-Cowley, J. Planning in the Real-Time City: The Future of Mobile Technology. *Journal of Planning Literature 25*, 2 (2010), 136–149.

[13] Evans-Cowley, J. Planning in the age of Facebook: the role of social networking in planning processes. *GeoJournal 75*, (2010), 407–420.

[14] Fallis, D. Social Epistemology and the Digital Divide. *Computing and Philosophy Conference*, Australian Computer Society (2004), 79–84.

[15] Fiorino, D.J. Citizen Participation and Environmental Risk: A Survey of Institutional Mechanisms. *Science, Technology & Human Values 15*, 2 (1990), 226–243.

[16] Galston, W.A. Civic education and political participation. *Phi Kappa Phi Forum*, (2004).

[17] Gil-Garcia, J.R., Pardo, T.A., and Aldama-Nalda, A. Smart Cities and Smart Governments: Using Information Technologies to Address Urban Challenges. *Proc. Digital Gov. Research*, ACM (2013), 296–297.

[18] Gilbert, J. *Common Ground*. Pluto Press, 2013.

[19] Goodchild, M.F. Citizens as sensors: the world of volunteered geography. *GeoJournal 69*, 4 (2007), 211.

[20] Gordon, E. and Schirra, S. Playing With Empathy: Digital Role-Playing Games in Public Meetings. *Community Mental Health Journal*, (2011).

[21] Gordon, E., Schirra, S., and Hollander, J. Immersive planning: a conceptual model for designing public participation with new technologies. *Environment and Planning B: Planning and Design 38*, (2011), 509–519.

[22] Granovetter, M.S. The Strength of Weak Ties. *78*, 6 (1973), 1360–1380.

[23] Habermas, J. *The Structural Transformation of the Public Sphere: An Inquiry into a Category of Bourgeois Society*. MIT Press, 1991.

[24] Ho, S. and Rajabifard, A. Learning From The Crowd: The Role of Volunteered Geographic Information in Realising a Spatially Enabled Society. *Proc. Realising Spatially Enabled Societies*, (2010).

[25] Kling, R. Automated information systems as social resources in policy making. *ACM '78: Proceedings of the 1978 annual conference*, ACM (1978), 666–674.

[26] Kuznetsov, S. and Paulos, E. Participatory sensing in public spaces: activating urban surfaces with sensor probes. *Proc. DIS*, ACM Request Permissions (2010).

[27] Kvasny, L. and Keil, M. The Challenges of Redressing the Digital Divide: A Tale of Two Us Cities. *Information Systems Journal 16*, 1 (2006), 23–53.

[28] Laird, F.N. Participatory Analysis, Democracy, and Technological Decision Making. *Science, Technology & Human Values 18*, 3 (1993).

[29] Latour, B. and Weibel, P. *Making Things Public: Atmospheres of Democracy*. MIT Press, Cambridge, MA, 2005.

[30] Le Dantec, C.A. and DiSalvo, C.F. Infrastructuring and the Formation of Publics in Participatory Design. *Social Studies of Science 43*, 2 (2013), 241–264.

[31] McKenzie, H. Cory Booker calls for tech-empowered open democracy. 2013. http://pando.com/2013/03/10/cory-booker-calls-for-tech-empowered-open-democracy/.

[32] Meyer, M.D. and Miller, E.J. *Urban Transportation Planning: A Decision-Oriented Approach*. McGraw-Hill Higher Education, 2001.

[33] Miles, M.B. and Huberman, A.M. *Qualitative Data Analysis: An Expanded Sourcebook*. Sage, 1994.

[34] Mouffe, C. *The Democratic Paradox*. Verso, London, UK, 2005.

[35] Nam, T. and Pardo, T.A. Smart City As Urban Innovation: Focusing on Management, Policy, and Context. *Proc. Theory and Practice of E-Governance*, ACM (2011), 185–194.

[36] Nam, T. and Pardo, T.A. Conceptualizing Smart City with Dimensions of Technology, People, and Institutions. *Proc. Dig. Gov.*, ACM (2011), 282–291.

[37] Nam, T. and Pardo, T.A. Transforming City Government: A Case Study of Philly311. *Proceedings of the 6th International Conference on Theory and Practice of Electronic Governance*, ACM (2012), 310–319.

[38] National Association of City Transportation Officials. *Urban Bikeway Design Guide, Second Edition*. National Assoc of City Trans Officials, 2012.

[39] New York Department of Transportation. *Measuring the Street: New Metrics for the 21st Century Streets*. NYDOT, 2012.

[40] Olivares, T., Royo, F., and Ortiz, A.M. An Experimental Testbed for Smart Cities Applications. *Proc. Mobility Management and Wireless Access*, ACM (2013), 115–118.

[41] Pew Center Research Center for the People & the Press. *Cable and Internet loom large in fragmented political news universe*. Pew Internet and American Life Project, 2004.

[42] Pierce, J. and Paulos, E. Beyond Energy Monitors: Interaction, Energy, and Emerging Energy Systems. *Proc. CHI*, ACM (2012), 665–674.

[43] President's Council of Advisors on Science and Technology. Designing a Digital Future: Federally Funded Research and Development in Networking and Information Technology. (2010).

[44] Priedhorsky, R., Masli, M., and Terveen, L. Eliciting and focusing geographic volunteer work. *Proc. CSCW*, ACM Request Permissions (2010), 61–70.

[45] Roitman, H., Mamou, J., Mehta, S., Satt, A., and Subramaniam, L.V. Harnessing the Crowds for Smart City Sensing. *Proc. Multimodal Crowd Sensing*, ACM (2012), 17–18.

[46] Sackman, H. A public philosophy for real time information systems. *AFIPS '68 (Fall, part II): Proceedings of the December 9-11, 1968, fall joint computer conference, part II*, ACM (1968), 1491–1498.

[47] Shilton, K. Participatory Sensing: Building Empowering Surveillance. *Surveillance & Society 8*, 2 (2010), 131–150.

[48] Skocpol, T. and Fiorina, M.P. *Civic Engagement in American Democracy*. Brookings Institution Press, Washington D.C., 1999.

[49] Slee, T. Seeing Like a Geek. http://crookedtimber.org/2012/06/25/seeing-like-a-geek/.

[50] Snellen, I. ICTs, bureaucracies, and the future of democracy. *Communications of the ACM 44*, 1 (2001), 45–48.

[51] Strauss, A. and Corbin, J. *Basics of Qualitative Research: Techniques and Procedures for Developing Grounded Theory*. Sage, 1998.

[52] Vakali, A., Anthopoulos, L., and Krco, S. Smart Cities Data Streams Integration: Experimenting with Internet of Things and Social Data Flows. *Proc. WIMS*, ACM (2014), 60:1–60:5.

[53] van Dijk, J. Models of Democracy and Concepts of Communication. In K.L. Hacker and J. van Dijk, eds., *Digital Democracy: Issues of Theory and Practice*. SAGE Publications Ltd, 2000, 30–53.

[54] Weiss, J.A., Gruber, J.E., and Carver, R.H. Reflections on Value: Policy Makers Evaluate Federal Information Systems. *Public Administration Review 46*, 6 (1986), 497–505.

"I LOVE THIS SITE!" vs. "It's a little girly": Perceptions of and Initial User Experience with Pinterest

Hannah Miller, Shuo Chang, Loren Terveen
GroupLens Research
Dept. of Computer Science and Engineering
University of Minnesota
{hmiller, schang, terveen}@cs.umn.edu

ABSTRACT

Pinterest is a popular social networking site that lets people discover, collect, and share pictures of items from the Web. Among popular social media sites, Pinterest has by far the most skewed gender distribution: women are four times more likely than men to use it. To better understand this, we examined two factors that generally affect whether people try a social site and whether they continue using it: the external *perception* of a site (e.g., as conveyed in popular media) and the site's initial user experience. For the latter, we focused on the role of *social bootstrapping*, importing contacts from one social site to another. We conducted a survey study, finding that: perceptions of Pinterest among users and non-users of the site differed significantly; trying Pinterest led to substantial changes in user perceptions of the site; social bootstrapping affected users' initial impression of Pinterest, generally improving it for women and harming it for men. We present implications of our findings for design and research.

Author Keywords

Pinterest; social networks; social media; perception; social bootstrapping; gender

ACM Classification Keywords

H.1.2 User/Machine Systems

General Terms

Human Factors

INTRODUCTION

Pinterest is a popular social network site. It has been one of the fastest growing sites in the United States [15] and according to Pew Internet Research, now is the third largest social network site in the US [17], behind Facebook and LinkedIn and ahead of Twitter. Pinterest is built around the metaphor of a pin board. Users "pin" pictures with links to items they find on the web and organize them into boards representing interests like recipes, crafts, fashion, arts, etc. Like many other sites, users can follow each other: if you follow someone, their new pins show up in your home page's feed.

CSCW 2015, March 14–18, 2015, Vancouver, BC, Canada.

http://dx.doi.org/10.1145/2675133.2675269

One interesting aspect of Pinterest is that women make up a large majority of its users: the recent Pew report finds that women in the US are four times more likely than men to use Pinterest [19]. Quantitative research [2, 8, 15] has found a number of different behavioral patterns among female and male users.

Let us be clear: the fact that most Pinterest users are women is not a "problem." Indeed, one trend on the Web is sites that are not targeted toward "everyone" (unlike Facebook), but instead appeal to particular populations and interests.

However, we believe that it still is worth seeking out the *why* behind Pinterest's demographics and gender differences in its users' behavior for several reasons:

- Pinterest claims to want to reach everyone, so why is it much less appealing to men?
- Pinterest in fact contains an extremely broad range of content that should appeal to just about any interest that anyone, woman or man, might have.
- The appeal of a social network based around collecting pictures of and links to web items certainly is not limited to women; indeed, the success of Pinterest has inspired a host of copycat "Pinterest for men" sites [22].

Our own experience and prior research suggest two factors that likely play a role in creating and maintaining Pinterest's demographics and behavior patterns: (1) perceptions of the site, e.g., in the popular media, and (2) design affordances of the site, particularly those contributing to the initial experience of new users. If potential users of Pinterest see it as "for women" and about topics of interest to women, that certainly will influence who chooses to use it. And if the initial experience – the visual design and the content that is displayed – reinforces a "traditionally feminine" image, that will influence who chooses to continue using Pinterest.

In this research, we used an open-ended survey to study perceptions of Pinterest among users and non-users of the site, then directed the non-users to sign up and explore Pinterest, and finally surveyed these users to investigate their perceptions after their initial experience. We present findings showing differences in perceptions between users and non-users and between men and women. When studying the initial experience, we focused on the role of *social bootstrapping*, the importing of one's social contacts from one social site (e.g., Facebook) to another (e.g., Pinterest). This is the ever-so-familiar "Sign up with Facebook" (or any other source social network) option offered when signing up for a new social site. To the best of our knowledge, we are the first to study how this common practice actually affects users: we found it affects men and women differently.

In the rest of the paper, we survey related work, motivating the factors we chose to study and showing how we extend previous research; present our research questions and describe our study design and methods; present our results and conclude by discussing inspiration for future work.

RELATED WORK

We discuss how we frame gender in our research; survey prior work on people's perceptions of social media sites, the gender demographics of Pinterest and gender differences in Pinterest usage; discuss how social bootstrapping can influence a new users' initial impressions of a site; and then situate our work explicitly against previous research.

Gender and This Research

Our treatment of gender here follows that of our prior work [2]. Of the three positions for engaging with gender discussed by Rode [20], we identify our work with the approach that "takes the issue of gender differences seriously," treating "gender as a variable" that *might* have explanatory power. This is appropriate because – despite good reason for studying whether perception and social bootstrapping relate to the gender gap in Pinterest – we do not *know* that these are actually contributing factors. Therefore, we study various ways these factors might affect users, including being open to identifying any differences between men and women actually present. In discussing other related work, we further motivate our reasons for studying the factors we chose.

Perception: Who and What is a Site for?

People often have impressions of social media sites that they do not use: for example, the authors of this paper do not use Snapchat, but we have ideas of what it is like and the sort of people who use it, and these ideas influence the probability that we will try it out.

Antin [1] studied this issue in the context of Wikipedia to see if perceptions were contributing to the pattern of slowed growth of new contributors. He conducted interviews with Wikipedia readers and casual contributors to probe their perceptions of contributors to Wikipedia. He discovered a number of recurring perceptions; while these included positive attributes such as generosity and a love of knowledge, they also included negative stereotypes, notably that Wikipedia contributors were "solitary techno-geeks." He argued that these perceptions can constitute a barrier to participation: people are not likely to join a group when they cannot or do not want to identify with its members. Antin's work motivated our choice to study perception with respect to Pinterest, but we aimed to further identify whether gender plays a role in people's perceptions and whether this impacts men's and women's choice to participate in different ways.

Zarro et al. [26] did a qualitative study of Pinterest users. They presented a number of interesting findings, but most relevant to our concerns was that different Pinterest users had quite different perceptions of what Pinterest is for. For example, some of their participants perceived Pinterest in terms of *discovering* and *collecting content of interest* rather than primarily for social interaction.

Like this work, Chang et al. [2] investigated the role that gender plays in Pinterest. Their study used quantitative methods, finding that men and women differed significantly in the types and diversity of content they pinned. However, they also considered how gendered representations of Pinterest in popular media (see [13, 24, 25] for discussion) may shape perceptions of what Pinterest is and who it is for, and thus may influence who chooses to use – or not to use – Pinterest. In particular, it may encourage women and discourage men from trying the site. This point directly influenced our choice to study perceptions of Pinterest among both users and non-users of the site.

Social Influence and Social Bootstrapping

Chang et al. [2] also noted that since women dominate Pinterest, much of the content on the site appeals to "traditionally feminine" interests, such as crafts, fashion, and hair and beauty. While in reality Pinterest content is quite diverse, covering a broad range of topics, the Pinterest user interface tends to promote the display of content that is most popular among most users. According to the theory of social proof [4], this is likely to result in users re-pinning that content, thus creating a positive feedback loop further increasing its popularity. In fact, 80% of pins in Pinterest are re-pins of content already pinned by other users, and 92% of all pins are made by women [7]. This effect has been observed in other online social interactions, including rating movies [5] and tagging movies [21]. The cumulative effect of this is that it is plausible that men who try Pinterest are more likely to be exposed to content that they are not traditionally interested in. Crucially, this will be true during their initial experience, when they are forming first impressions and deciding whether to continue using the site.

Due to the resulting initial social context, this effect may be amplified by what Zhong et al. [27] termed "social bootstrapping" – "copying one's social ties or links from a source social network to a target social network." Zhong et al. did a quantitative study of large datasets representing Pinterest and Last.fm users who had "socially bootstrapped" using their Facebook accounts. They compared the subgraph of connections imported from Facebook to the subgraph formed by connections created within Pinterest and Last.fm over time. They found that the Facebook subgraph has a giant component, higher reciprocity and clustering and was useful for initiating social interaction in the target social networks.

This Research

To summarize, we build on Antin [1], Zarro et al. [26], and Chang et al. [2] by studying perceptions of both users and non-users of Pinterest concerning who Pinterest users are and what Pinterest is for. This previous work, particularly Antin and Chang et al., suggests that non-users of a site can have a biased impression of the site based on popular stereotypes; we thus directly compare the perceptions of Pinterest by users and non-users. Building on Chang et al. and Zhong et al. [27], we examine the initial context – both content and people – encountered by new users of Pinterest. We examine whether their initial context is gender-skewed, whether it changes their perceptions of Pinterest, and whether it affects their intention to continue using Pinterest. Finally, building upon all of this work, we explore both perception and initial context (social bootstrapping) as they may relate to the gender gap in Pinterest, something that is not explicitly done in any of the works cited.

RESEARCH QUESTIONS

We organize our research around the two main themes we have introduced: (1) *perceptions* of Pinterest and (2) the influence of *social bootstrapping* on people's initial experience of Pinterest.

Perceptions of Pinterest

How do Pinterest users perceive what the site is for, and who uses it? How do non-users perceive the site and its users, and are their perceptions significantly different than those of users? Do men and women differ in their perceptions, for example regarding the "femininity" of the site? Do non-users' perceptions change after they sign up?

Social Bootstrapping

How does social bootstrapping affect a user's social context on Pinterest? How does social bootstrapping affect users' initial experience with Pinterest, their perception of it, and their intention to continue using it? Are women and men affected differently by social bootstrapping?

STUDY DESIGN AND METHODS

We addressed our research questions with a three-part study:

1. We administered a survey on perceptions of Pinterest to a set of participants including both current Pinterest users and non-users.
2. We then instructed non-users to sign up for Pinterest; in one condition, they signed up with Facebook, in the other with email. We then instructed them to explore the site
3. We administered a second survey to these users about their initial impressions of Pinterest and whether they intended to continue to use Pinterest.

Our primary analytic method was qualitative coding of participant responses to the survey questions. We also collected basic descriptive statistics to better understand the context of social bootstrapping. Figure 1 gives a road-map of our study, including the number of participants for each condition. We elaborate on it in the following sections.

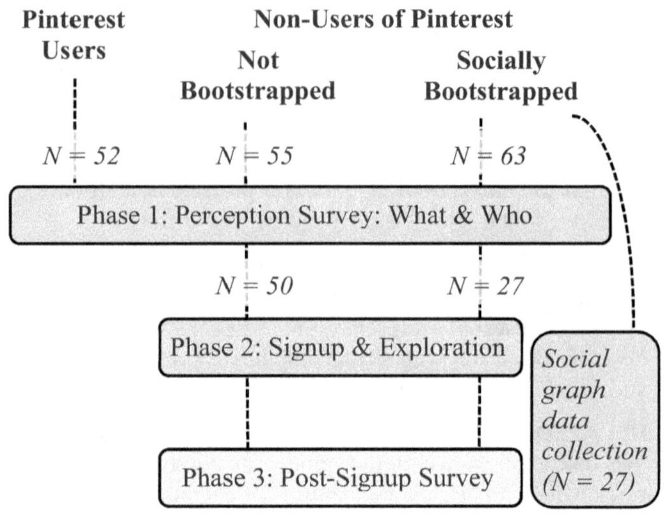

Figure 1: Overview of Study

Participants

We used Amazon Mechanical Turk to recruit participants. Participants were directed to a web-based survey that we hosted. We recruited one set of participants that had used Pinterest (N=52), and a second set that had not used Pinterest. For the second phase of the study, the non-user participants were divided into two groups: one signed up with Facebook (N=63) and the other with email (N=55). Not all participants completed the second phase: 50 of the 55 email participants, and 27 of the 63 Facebook participants did (see below for more discussion). Since participants in the different groups did different amounts of work, we paid different incentives to each: \$0.50 to Pinterest users, \$2.00 to the non-users who signed up with email, and \$3.00 to the non-users who signed up with Facebook.

The average age of participants was 32.4 (SD = 10.2; min = 19; max = 82). We also asked participants whether they used any of seven other social media sites, with the following results: 170 used Facebook[1], 130 used YouTube, 110 used Twitter, 78 used Google+, 71 used LinkedIn, 57 used Instagram, and 40 used Tumblr. The mean number of social media sites used was 3.9 (SD = 1.5). A majority of the Pinterest users (77%) were women, roughly consistent with general Pinterest demographics. A smaller majority of the non-users were men (57%).

We asked the Pinterest users how often they used the site. Of the 52 participants, 20 reported using it daily, 19 weekly, 9 monthly, and 4 less than monthly. We asked the non-users of Pinterest their attitude towards the site.

[1] We required all non-users of Pinterest to be on Facebook: in Phase 2 of the study, half of them would be assigned to sign up for Pinterest using their Facebook account, and we wanted all the participants to be eligible for this condition.

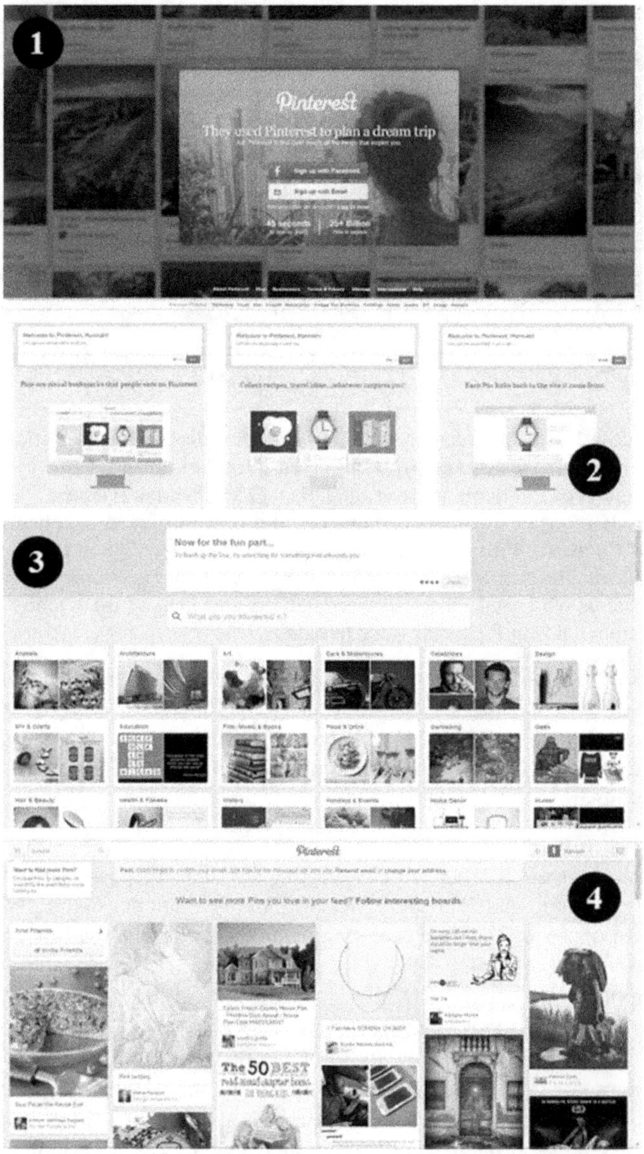

Figure 2: Screen sequence experienced by participants that signed up for Pinterest. (1) Pinterest.com screen to sign up. (2) A "quick tour" of Pinterest. (3) A prompt to search for something of interest with a display of example categories. (4) The Pinterest home feed.

Of the 118 participants, 59 reported that they had not tried Pinterest, but were interested in doing so; 51 said they had not tried, and were not interested; 5 said they had tried in the past, but had stopped; and 3 did not respond to this question.

Phase 1. Perception Survey

We asked participants in all three groups several open-ended questions regarding their perceptions of Pinterest and Pinterest users:

S1. How would you describe what you think Pinterest is and what it is used for?

S2. How would you describe a person that uses Pinterest? That is, when you think of a person that uses Pinterest, what comes to mind?

Phase 2. Signup and Exploration

After the non-users completed the perception survey, they were instructed to sign up for Pinterest. The instructions were delivered through a sequence of screens proceedings directly from the end of the perception survey. Thus, participants kept the instructions for our study open in one web browser window, while opening Pinterest in another window or tab.

As noted above, one group was directed to sign up with email and the other with Facebook; the latter is the social bootstrapping group. (We talk about the social bootstrapping process in more detail below.) Figure 2 shows the sequence of screens the participants saw as they went through the signup process:

1. The initial screen where participants choose to sign up with Facebook or Email.
2. A "quick tour" of Pinterest explaining how it works and what you can do.
3. A prompt to "search for something that interests" the user, with a variety of categories displayed for search inspiration.
4. The Pinterest home feed.

We instructed participants to observe the home feed:

> When you complete the sign up process and click "Finish," observe the initial screen you are provided with. Feel free to scroll down the page.

Phase 3. Post-Signup Survey

We then administered a second set of survey questions; operationally, participants now shifted their attention back to the web browser window containing our experimental instructions and survey questions. All the participants who signed up for Pinterest were asked the first question:

S3. Now that you have completed the signup process and observed the initial screen, what is your first impression of Pinterest? Does your first impression differ from what you thought before you signed up? Please explain.

The next question was only for social bootstrapping participants. They were instructed to look through the list of users they were following (i.e., the Facebook friends they imported), then were asked:

S4. What is your impression of the group of users that you are initially following? Do you like the group you are provided with? Why or why not?

Social bootstrapping participants also were instructed to make a count of the number of women and number of men they were following. We used this to compute descriptive statistics about the effect of social bootstrapping (see below).

All participants were asked a final survey question:

S5. At this point, would you continue using/exploring Pinterest? Why or why not?

Social Bootstrapping: Process and Descriptive Statistics

Social bootstrapping projects the social graph from one site (the origin) onto another site (the destination). In our study, Facebook is the origin and Pinterest the destination. For a given user, the social bootstrapping process begins with that user's Facebook friends as the source social graph. But the social graph narrows throughout the bootstrapping process: you only can follow your Facebook friends who actually are on Pinterest. The user controls which ones to follow once on the site, but Pinterest makes it easy to follow many of them at once during signup.

Given our research interests, we wondered whether narrowing the social graph also might skew it. In particular, we were interested in whether the gender composition of the social graph changed.

However, we first discuss why (as shown in Figure 1) only 27 of the participants assigned to the social bootstrapping condition completed the process, i.e., actually imported Facebook friends. Given that they were participating in a web-based process, we do not have an exact answer. Perhaps they did not have any Facebook friends who used Pinterest, maybe they dropped out[2], or perhaps there was an error in Pinterest's import process, but we cannot account for all the bootstrapping "failures." However, for our purposes we want to explore the effect of social bootstrapping precisely for those people who do have Facebook friends who use Pinterest and who do import them into Pinterest.

To understand the overall Facebook social graph of social bootstrapping participants, we instructed participants how to use Facebook features to gather the relevant data (they did this after completing question S5):

- The total number of Facebook friends, which is visible in one's Facebook profile.
- The percentage of Facebook friends who are female and who are male, available through the Friends & Profile Statistics app in Facebook.
- The number of female and male Facebook friends who use Pinterest, available by using Facebook Graph Search.

They entered these numbers to finish the survey.

Together with data about participants' Pinterest social graphs that they entered earlier, we can examine whether social bootstrapping skews social graphs. The data presented in Table 1 give an answer: the social context for bootstrapping users becomes predominantly female. In our sample, the typical user's Facebook friends were about 57% female. However, their initial Pinterest social graphs consisted of over 80% women (mean: 81%, median: 89%). Users might find this surprising. At the least, even though they imported from Facebook, the projection of their Facebook friends onto Pinterest results in a significantly different social context.

[2] Perhaps they were unwilling to pay the "social cost" of potentially bothering friends whom they included in their social graph or the "privacy cost" of giving Pinterest access to their social graph, so they gave up when they encountered this step.

Levels of Social Bootstrapping	Total		% female		
	mean	SD	mean	median	dist.
Facebook friends	276	288	57%	55%	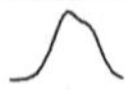
Facebook friends on Pinterest	54	58	83%	88%	
Pinterest following	50	54	81%	89%	

Table 1: Social bootstrapping and gender – descriptive statistics for the 27 participants who imported Facebook friends into Pinterest. Participants averaged over 275 Facebook friends, with about 54 of them on Pinterest, and they imported nearly all of them into Pinterest (mean of 50). On average, 57% of their Facebook friends were female, but 83% of their Facebook friends who used Pinterest were female, and 81% of the friends imported into Pinterest were female.

As we shall see, social bootstrapping played a large role in participants' initial perceptions of Pinterest and their intention to continue using Pinterest, and men's and women's reactions to social bootstrapping were more or less directly opposite.

Methods

We first qualitatively analyzed the raw data responses from the participants. The first two authors of this paper coded the responses to the five survey questions, generally taking an inductive approach as is described in [23]. This approach is appropriate because it "allow[s] research findings to emerge from the frequent, dominant, or significant themes inherent in raw data" [23]. Though this work was motivated by identifying likely contributing factors to the gender gap, the analysis conducted is sufficient for several reasons. First, we used the approach where we treated gender "as a variable," so we did not influence the participants' responses by directly asking gender-prompted questions in the survey. Further, as a result of the inductive approach, our findings are data-driven, coming from the content of the participants' responses *only*. In addition, prior to completing the coding, we prevented preconceived notions from biasing the results by randomly ordering the responses for each question and hiding the gender and experimental condition of participants. Finally, it is acceptable within the general inductive approach to have specific objectives that guide data collection and analysis [23].

Each researcher openly coded the first 20 percent of the responses to each question independently. We then discussed the results to agree on codes and definitions. We next revisited the original 20 percent of responses to confirm our understanding, and then finally coded the rest of the responses individually.

While coding the responses to S1 (What is Pinterest for?), we noticed that many responses touched on categories from the analysis of Pinterest in [26]. These categories were (illustrated with terms our participants used): *collecting* ("saving" and "organizing"), *discovering* ("searching" and "finding"), *publishing* ("sharing" and "posting"), and *interaction and identity* ("friends" and "social"). We thus included these categories in our code catalog.

We calculated a Kappa coefficient to evaluate inter-coder agreement and characterize the reliability of our results. Since we had a relatively small sample size and our data were sparse (due to having broad, open-ended questions), we calculated Kappa for each individual code. We then averaged the Kappa scores for each survey question: S1 – 0.850; S2 – 0.831; S3 – 0.786; S4 – 0.889; and S5 – 0.797. These results indicate that the coding was reliable: according to Cichetti [5], Kappa scores above 0.75 indicate "Excellent" agreement.

If only one of the coders assigned a code to a response, we decided at random (with 50% probability) whether to include that code for the response. Because of the high agreement between the coders, this did not happen often. Also, for each response there were some codes in the code catalog that were infrequently applied and for which the coders had low agreement. We did not use these codes in our analysis.

After the coding process was complete, we employed a more quantitative method for analyzing the coding result. This was appropriate due to the complexity and scale of our study:

- We had 170 total participants and associated responses in our study, which is much larger than most qualitative studies.
- Our study is a 2x2x2 design with Pinterest user versus non-user, male versus female, and social bootstrapping versus not variables.

In order to most effectively analyze the large number of responses with respect to each of the variables of interest, we examined aggregate response patterns. An example of such a pattern would be observing that a particular type of response was much more common among social bootstrapping users. Then, we performed statistical tests, specifically Fisher's Exact Test, to determine which differences in response patterns were significant. Finally, we identified particularly telling quotes from participants for each of the patterns identified. This mixed method analysis resulted in identifying three main themes.

RESULTS

We organize our results around three main themes:

1. How Pinterest users and non-users differ in their perceptions of *what Pinterest is for* and *who uses Pinterest* (survey questions S1 and S2).
2. Non-users' perceptions of Pinterest after their initial experience with Pinterest, including impressions of their social graph (survey questions S3 and S4).
3. The factors that influence new Pinterest users' intention to continue (or not) using Pinterest (survey question S5).

Each theme is broken down into more specific sub-themes. Sometimes female participants responded differently than male participants or social bootstrapping participants responded differently than non-bootstrapping participants; we report on these differences where relevant. We illustrate each theme through a combination of quotes from survey participants and aggregate responses of participants to the survey questions. Finally, we note whether differences in aggregate responses are statistically significant (and report p values if they are).

For ease of reference, Table 2 maps the research themes to the survey questions and participant information they are based on.

Research Theme & Corresponding Survey Questions	Pinterest users		Non-users of Pinterest			
			Email		Facebook	
	F	M	F	M	F	M
1. Perceptions: what/who Survey: S1 and S2	40	12	23	32	28	35
2. Post-signup perceptions Survey: S3 and S4	N/A		21	29	16	11
3. Intent to continue use Survey: S5						

Table 2: The survey questions and participant information used for each of our research themes. "F" indicates "Female," and "M" indicates "Male."

Perception of Pinterest: Users vs. Non-Users

We first report on how Pinterest users and non-users differ in their perceptions of what Pinterest is for and who uses it.

What is Pinterest for?

Figure 3 summarizes the codes resulting from our analysis of responses to the question "What is Pinterest for?" It shows the proportion of participants with a response assigned to each code, with responses from Pinterest users and non-users shown separately.

Discovering and Collecting Ideas vs. Publishing

The first difference we observed was that Pinterest users mentioned *collection* and *discovery* – activities done primarily for oneself – more frequently than non-Pinterest users. 40% and 25% of Pinterest user responses were coded for *collection* and *discovery*, respectively, compared to 25% and 11% for non-users.

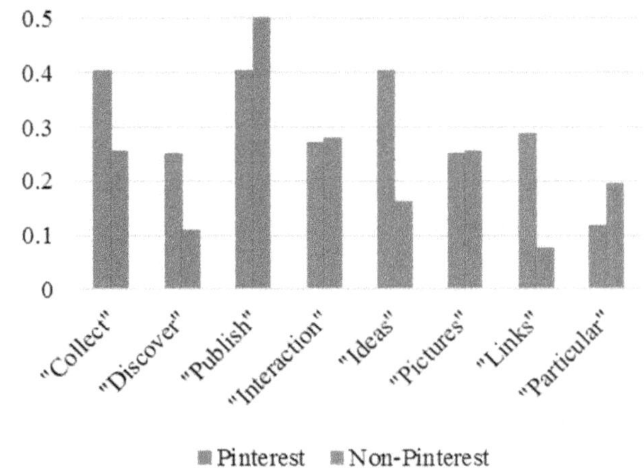

Figure 3: What is Pinterest for? Responses from Pinterest users and non-users (170 responses, 352 codes assigned).

These differences were significant ($p < 0.04$, $p = 0.02$ respectively). Two quotes from Pinterest users illustrate this:

> *Pinterest is a place where you can go and **browse** things that are of relevance and interest to you, such as recipes, fashion **ideas**, makeup tips, art, furniture, etc. When you see something you like, you are able to "pin" it to your own board, **saving** it for when you want to refer to it later.*

> *It's a site where I **collect** things that I like on a virtual pin board. I can **group** them and **share** with others. I can also look at other people's boards to **find** things that interest me and **save** them to my board.*

On the other hand, non-users mentioned *publishing* or *sharing* content with others 50% of the time, much more often than they mentioned discovering or collecting. Pinterest users also mentioned *publishing* (40%), but not as often as non-users, although this difference was not statistically significant. However, looking at the textual responses of non-users in more detail illustrated this perspective, as shown by two quotes from non-users:

> *It's a place you can **share pictures** with **friends**.*

> *I think it's a **photo sharing** thing…All I've seen are lots of different **photos** with captions.*

Thus, while Pinterest users see Pinterest as a place to *discover* and *collect information*, and *share it with others*, non-users see it more as just a place to *share* with others. This might help explain why some people choose not to use Pinterest: they do not see how to derive personal benefit from the site, but only that they would provide it to others.

A related observation is that users had a more developed notion of what one can discover, collect, and share on Pinterest, namely *ideas* – 40% of their responses were coded as mentioning *ideas*, compared to 16% of responses from non-users ($p < 0.01$). For example:

> *Pinterest is used to **find** new **ideas** for your household, wedding, children, etc. It is great for **finding** craft **ideas** and even meal recipes.*

> *Pinterest is for **sharing ideas** with your **friends** and for **bookmarking ideas** and **pictures** that you see and like.*

The "ideas" theme is consistent with the "everyday ideation" concept of Linder et al. [12]. They interviewed 20 Pinterest users, finding that they used items they found through Pinterest to develop ideas with practical and emotional value for their lives.

(Visual) Bookmarks vs. Pictures

Obviously, a prominent and compelling aspect of Pinterest is that pictures are front and center: every pin is depicted as a picture, and while textual comments are supported, there is relatively little annotation or discussion.

However, a pin also is a link to the external website from which the picture was collected. Participant responses showed that this was clear to Pinterest users – nearly 30% of their responses were coded as referring to a "link" (to content) – but not to non-users – less than 8% of their responses were so coded. This difference was significant ($p < 0.01$). For example, compare the two following quotes, the first from a Pinterest user and the second from a non-user:

> *Keeping **collections** of **images** of things you like, **images** that **link** to various things, from recipes to products you'd like to buy.*

> *I think I've seen Pinterest before. It seems to be like a **photo** blog. Kind of like twitter, but with **just photos.***

The Pinterest users understood that their actions on Pinterest were not just curating pictures, but actually managing visual representations of web content. Meanwhile, the non-user manifested a (literally) superficial understanding of Pinterest: it's just about pictures! A rough analogy is that Pinterest users see Pinterest as a visual *bookmarking* site, while non-users see it more as a photo-sharing site, like Instagram or "Twitter just with photos."

Who are Pinterest users?

Figure 4 summarizes the codes resulting from our analysis of responses to the question "Who uses Pinterest?" The first part of the figure shows the proportion of participants with a response assigned to each code, with responses from Pinterest users and non-users presented separately. In the second part of the figure we further divide responses by the gender of the respondent (female or male).

Creative and Crafty vs. Social

About 44% of responses from Pinterest users described users as *creative* (or "artistic" or "artsy") and about 40% described users as *crafty* or *Do-It-Yourselfers* ("DIY"). These characterizations were mentioned less frequently by non-users (about 25% for both codes). These differences were significant ($p < 0.02$, $p < 0.05$ respectively). Two users described Pinterest users as:

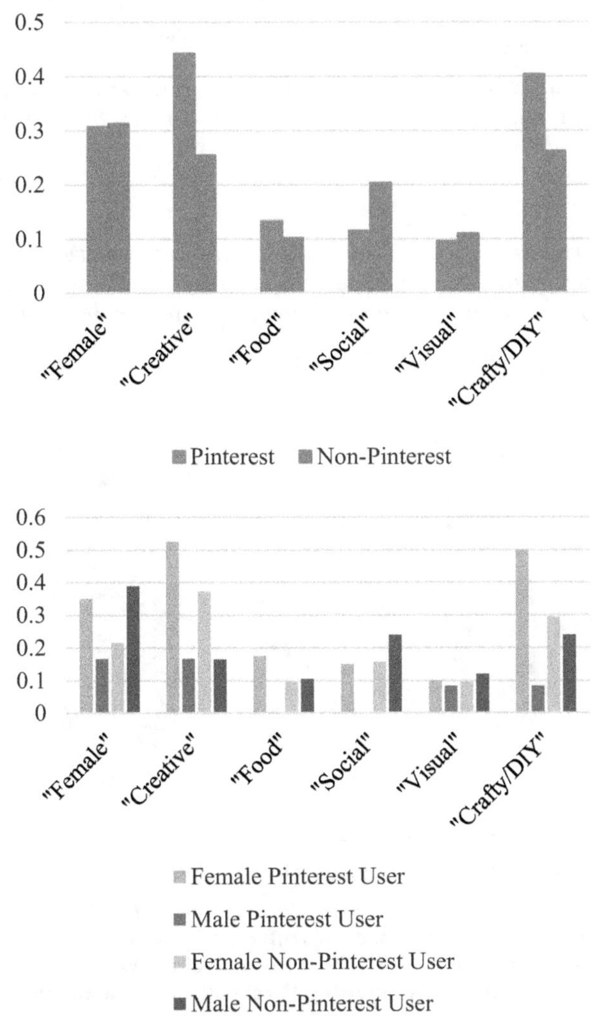

Figure 4: Who are Pinterest users? (170 responses, 225 codes assigned) Categories of responses by Pinterest users and non-users, then further divided by gender.

> ***Creative***, *resourceful*, ***DIY*** *person*, ***crafty***, *inspired.*

> *A* ***creative*** *person uses Pinterest. Someone who wants to try new things, and* ***do-it-yourself'ers***.

However, breaking down responses by gender lets us understand this pattern more clearly: women were significantly more likely to characterize Pinterest users as *creative* than men whether or not they used Pinterest ($p < 0.01$) Indeed, both the above quotes were from female users. Female participants also were significantly more likely to characterize Pinterest users as *crafty* ($p < 0.05$), although male users were more likely than male non-users to use this characterization. These results resonate with quantitative results from Chang et al.[2], who found that women pinned content to the "DIY & Crafts" category more often than men.

On the other hand, male non-users were more likely to describe Pinterest users as *social*, seeking to "share" or "connect" with others or just as active participants in social media. (Note that this is consistent with the previous finding that non-users were more likely to say that Pinterest was for publishing/sharing.) For example:

> *I think a person who loves to* ***connect*** *with others using visual images that they find appealing.*

> *A person who uses Pinterest is a person who wants to be* ***socially connected*** *to many people. They want to* ***share*** *many aspects about their life to the world...*

> *Just basically someone who uses all sorts of different* ***social media*** *platforms. They probably have a Google+, twitter & myspace too along with facebook and Pinterest. They are just a person who enjoys using* ***social media*** *as much as possible.*

The differences in perception between users and non-users regarding the role of "social" vs. "discovery" and "collection" deepens and extends the results of Zarro et al. [26]. Many of their participants emphasize the utility of Pinterest for finding and collecting information over its social features. Indeed, as one of our Pinterest users said:

> *The typical Pinterest user is someone who likes to make things but isn't very social necessarily. Someone who likes to catalog ideas.*

More generally, since Pinterest is part of the social media ecosystem, it may be that non-users – who are not familiar with Pinterest's unique affordances – perceive it more in terms of general stereotypes of a social media site. But people who begin using a site will learn about its unique affordances, thus refining their perception. For Pinterest, this can mean a shift from perceptions of it as a place for social interaction to a place for content discovery and curation.

Female(?)

Finally, about 30% of all responses to "Who are Pinterest users?" mentioned that they were *female,* or "women," "moms," or "girls":

> *I think of a* ***mom*** *with young kids, who uses it for decorating tips, recipes, kids projects, consumes, and similar. In my mind the typical Pinterest user is* ***female***.

> *Pinterest seems to be used mostly by* ***females***, *at least that's my perception of it.*

When we divide the responses only by user vs. non-user, the two groups mention *female* equally often. For non-users, this is the single most common response. However, breaking down the responses by gender, as shown in the second part of Figure 4, reveals a different and rather puzzling pattern. Female Pinterest users and male non-users are more likely to characterize users as female than male Pinterest users and female non-users.

We find this pattern striking. They may be related to Antin's observation about group identity: people will not want to belong to a group that they do not or do not want to identify with [1]. Based on this, we offer several speculations:

- Women who use Pinterest perceive it (accurately) as friendly to women and covering topics that many women are interested in. Women would be comfortable identifying with a "female site," so they are comfortable viewing Pinterest users as female. Indeed, the first quote above, with its description of a Pinterest user as a "mom with young kids," came from a female Pinterest user.

- Men who do not use Pinterest can come to perceive Pinterest as "for women," due to the gendered depiction of the site in popular and social media (see [2, 13, **Error! Reference source not found.**4, 25] for discussion). Men are less likely to identify with a site "for women," reinforcing a choice not to use Pinterest.
- Men who do use Pinterest obviously have overcome any such barrier. And to the extent that they identify with the community, it would make sense for them not to perceive Pinterest as a site "for women" or the typical Pinterest user as a "young mom."
- The most puzzling pattern is that women who did not use Pinterest did not strongly perceive Pinterest users as female. We do not have any speculation as to why this might be that we find plausible, so more in-depth study is required to see if this pattern is real, and if so, why.

Summary. We found a number of interesting results concerning perceptions of what Pinterest is for and who uses it, with noteworthy differences between users and non-users and between men and women. We now turn our attention to the initial experience on Pinterest for the participants who had not previously used the site.

Post-Signup Perceptions of Pinterest

After the non-user participants completed the sign up process, we instructed them to "look around Pinterest" and then administered the Post-Signup survey asking about their perceptions of Pinterest now that they had joined. We initially coded responses to see whether participants said that Pinterest was the *same* or *different* than they had expected. About half of the participants said it was the same, and about half said it was different. Perhaps not surprisingly, the participants who said it was the same did not elaborate or explain their impression much. Therefore, in subsequent analysis we focus on responses from subjects who said Pinterest was different than they had expected.

More Diverse

The most frequent specific reason that users viewed Pinterest as *different* than expected was that it was more *diverse:* there was a "bigger variety" and "many categories" of content. Just over 40% of users who had a different impression of Pinterest mentioned this reason. Illustrative quotes include:

> *There is a **wider variety** of things than I thought there would be.*

> ***Lots of categories** for many interests. I didn't know it covered so many things. I thought it was just people posting art and recipes.*

> *More than just fashion which I had thought it was. **It has everything** from art, food, fashion, history and more.*

These impressions are accurate: Pinterest *is* diverse, offering a broad range of content in over 33 different categories. But unless and until people experience Pinterest first-hand, their perception is based on fairly narrow stereotypes, such as "art," "recipes," and "fashion."

Social bootstrapping affects men and women differently…

We next broke down responses by two factors, the presence or absence of social bootstrapping, and the gender of the

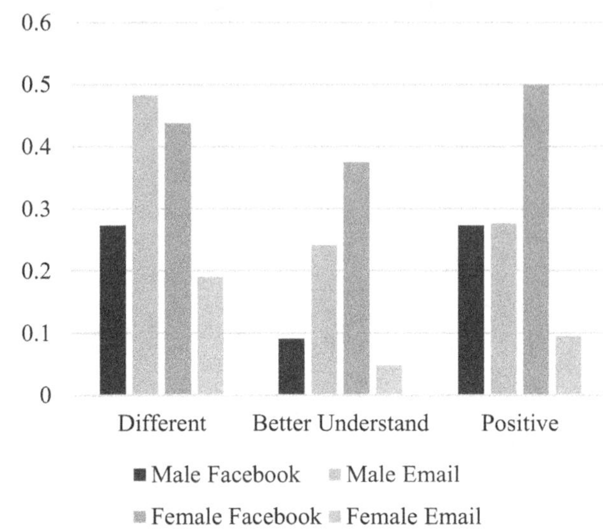

Figure 5: Changes in perception after signing up for Pinterest (77 responses, with 64 coded as "Different," "Better Understanding," or "Positive"). "Facebook" refers to participants who signed up using Facebook, and "Email" to those who signed up using Email.

participants. We found social bootstrapping affected men and women differently. First, Figure 5 suggests that social bootstrapping makes women more likely to have a different impression than expected, while the opposite is true for men. Though the difference in means looks large, neither of these differences were statistically significant, likely due to relatively small numbers of participants (see Figure 5).

… Bootstrapping increases women's understanding of Pinterest but not men's understanding

Another theme that emerged from our coding of this question was *better understanding* of Pinterest, for example that pins represent links to web sites, not just pictures:

> *It is a little **different** than I thought. I didn't know that all the pictures were **links**.*

> *I **didn't realize** that Pinterest was about **"pinning"** any **website** you find of interest. It's almost like having your **bookmarks** be public.*

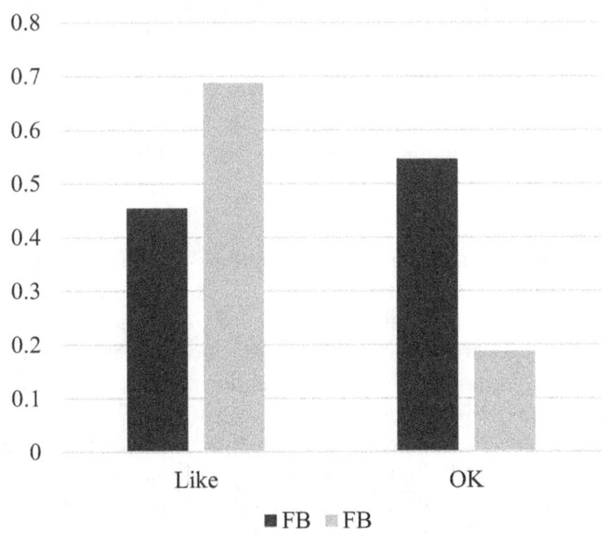

Figure 6: Do socially-bootstrapped users like their initial social graph? (28 responses, 27 were coded as either "Like" or "Just OK") Women are more likely to say that they like their social graph.

Social bootstrapping again affected women and men differently. Women who signed up with Facebook were significantly more likely than women who signed up with email to say that they understood Pinterest better ($p < 0.03$). For men, the opposite appears to be true, although this result was not statistically significant.

... Bootstrapping makes women more positive about Pinterest and men less positive

Another theme we coded for was *positive* remarks concerning participants' first impression of Pinterest. Some examples (all from women):

> *I am seeing some outfits I like, some I don't...I didn't realize I could browse purses on here!* ***Now, I'm excited!***
>
> ***I LOVE THIS SITE!!!!!!-*** *Generally few things impress me; however I was just nicely blown away. Anything and everything of possible interest is nicely categorized. It's set up like a great big collage. Again, very nice, not at all like what I had envisioned.*
>
> *I now* ***understand*** *I can pin something to make it available to me whenever I want. I can explore all kinds of things and can then pin them for my future use.* ***Pretty amazing.***

In contrast, several men in in the social bootstrapping condition remarked on the "girly" nature of the site:

> *It is a little girly and it looks well kept.*
>
> *Most of what I see is girly things pinned by female friends like clothes and jewelry, but I do see a few things pinned about food which caught my eye.*

Thus, social bootstrapping again affected men and women differently. Women in the Facebook condition were significantly more likely to make positive comments about their first impressions of Pinterest than women in the email condition ($p < 0.01$), while there was no effect for men.

... Women are more positive about their initial social graph than men

We also asked participants that bootstrapped to look at their initial Pinterest social graph – the users they were following – and give their impression of this group. Responses included:

> *My impression of the group is very pleased and yes, I do* ***like*** *the group they provided me with. I'm actually quite close to a bunch of the people.* (Female)
>
> *It's* ***OK****. It looks like it somehow linked in with my friends list on Facebook, and I am comfortable following all of these people.* (Male)

The aggregate responses in Figure 6 show that women generally were more likely than men to have a positive impression of their social graph, while men were more likely to say that it was just ok. These differences were not significant: again, this may be due to small N (11 men, 16 women; see Table 2).

Summary. Many users' first impression of Pinterest was different than they had expected. Second-hand stereotypes were replaced by first hand-experience: notably, content was more diverse than expected. Social bootstrapping had a powerful effect, and affected men and women differently. Its effect on women was uniformly positive, and on men negative or neutral.

Intent to continue using Pinterest

Our final survey question was whether participants intended to continue using Pinterest, and why or why not. 60% of men and 65% of women said that they would or possibly would continue using Pinterest.

Social bootstrapping affects men's and women's intention to continue differently.

Figure 7 shows that women who signed up with Facebook were more likely to express an intention to continue using Pinterest than women who signed up with email, while the opposite pattern held for men. This continues the pattern we saw in the analysis of the previous question, suggesting again that the social context created by social bootstrapping enhances the initial Pinterest experience for women, but harms it for men.

While these differences were not statistically significant, a more detailed look at responses revealed two interesting themes, one for participants who said they intended to continue, and another for those who said they did not.

Yes: Discovery

44% of participants who said they would continue using Pinterest mentioned Pinterest's support for *discovery* as a reason:

> ***Yes****, it could be cool* ***finding*** *new stuff.*
>
> *I think I* ***would continue*** *looking at Pinterest as it looks like I can* ***explore*** *most any area of interest. Can't do that on other social media as far as I can tell.*

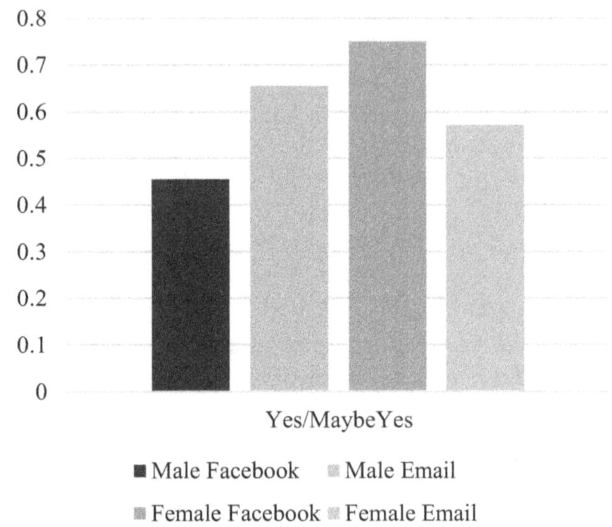

Figure 7: Intention to continue using Pinterest (77 responses, with 49 coded as "Yes" or "Maybe Yes"). A majority of all users say "yes," but social bootstrapping again affects women and men differently.

There is some evidence that this reaction was directly tied to the extent to which participants' perceptions of Pinterest were changed. Nearly all the participants who cited *discovery* as a reason for continuing to use Pinterest had not perceived Pinterest as a discovery tool prior to signing up.

No: Use other social media

The most common theme characterizing participants who did not intend to continue using Pinterest was that their social media "plate" already was "full" or that they did not see how Pinterest offered unique value compared to other sites. Such references to other social media appeared in over 30% of *not continuing* responses, for example:

> *I probably* ***would not****. It just seems like a lot more work than I am willing to invest right now. I feel like* ***my social media plate is already full*** *trying to keep up with Twitter, Instagram, and Facebook. Pinterest looks like a mediocre combination of those other three sites.*

> ***No****, it seems like I get the* ***same information*** *from twitter and instagram.*

> *I just do* ***not*** *see anything that I want to do with this site. Why does it think it is* ***different from anything else?*** *What can you accomplish here?*

Summary. Participants who intended to continue using Pinterest cited one of the distinguishing features of the site, namely that it supports *discovery*; and these new users had not been aware of this before. On the other hand, participants who did not intend to continue suggested that Pinterest did not offer sufficient unique value over other social media sites. Finally, social bootstrapping again was an influence, and again affected men and women differently.

SUMMARY OF CONTRIBUTIONS AND IMPLICATIONS

We presented many results from studying perceptions of and initial experience with Pinterest, but now we revisit the overarching question of why there is a gender gap. In treating gender as a variable, we wanted to see if perception and social bootstrapping produce gendered effects, ultimately finding that they do.

Perception

The strategy in researching perceptions of Pinterest and its users was to compare those of users with non-users to illuminate potential barriers to participation. Since we treated gender as a variable, we did not ask questions in the survey directly addressing if and how gender plays a role in their perceptions. Instead, we let it rise out of the data while finding multiple differences in perception between users and non-users that allude to reasons people do not participate in Pinterest. Ultimately, we discovered that gender *is* a factor in perceptions of Pinterest.

First, we found that Pinterest users tend to view Pinterest as a place to *discover* and *collect*, and *share with others*, while non-users view it more as just a place to *share* with others. This result lends itself to speculation that some people may choose not to use Pinterest because they perceive it as a place for providing benefit to others and do not see how to derive personal benefit from it—something that is generally well understood by users [12, 24]. Similarly, we found that non-users' mental models of the site affordances fall short in thinking that the site content is just a large collection of pictures, when really the site enables *linking* to other web content—represented by a picture. This superficial perception may be another barrier to participation because again it is unclear to some why a site full of pictures is useful to them, whereas users understand and enjoy the richness of curating actual content (not just pictures) [9, 12, 24]. Finally, after signing up and being asked about their first impression of Pinterest, many non-users reported that it was more diverse than they previously perceived. This implies yet another perception barrier for non-users: the impression that Pinterest does not contain diverse content, but instead likely contains a narrow range of topics.

Gender appeared in the "Who are Pinterest users?" survey question responses. In fact, 30% of all responses referred to users as being "female," "women," "moms," or "girls." However, when stratifying responses by users and non-users and male and female participants, we found that male non-users referred to users being female the most often. This finding together with Antin's insight [1] provides evidence for a gender gap-specific barrier to participation: men are less likely to (or less likely to want to) identify with a site that they perceive as being for women.

Social Bootstrapping

For the social bootstrapping factor, we first quantified the process by collecting, for each participant, the gender distribution at each level of the process: the source social graph (Facebook friends); the intersection of the source social graph and the destination user population (Facebook friends that use Pinterest); and the resulting destination social graph (initial users following in Pinterest). This process has not been illustrated level-by-level before, nor has it been analyzed with respect to gender. We showed that in the case of social bootstrapping one's Facebook social network into Pinterest, the process results in an overwhelmingly skewed initial social graph. As a result, both male and female new users are provided with predominantly female social graphs.

Then, based on responses to survey questions, we were able to identify patterns of how social bootstrapping, or not social bootstrapping, affects the initial experience of new users. In particular, we found that social bootstrapping affects men and women differently. Specifically, its effect on women was uniformly positive, and on men negative or neutral, compared to the control condition of not socially bootstrapping. We observed this general pattern in the following aspects of the initial user experience with Pinterest:

- Understanding the site after signing up
- Impression of / reaction to the site
- Degree of liking the initial social graph
- Intent to continue participation in the site

Though many of these results were not statistically significant due to our small sample size, the fact that the pattern was recurring in *all* of the initial user experience aspects identified gives us confidence in the pattern we detected.

By illustrating the skewed social bootstrapping process and recognizing an associated pattern of different impact on male and female users, we provide sufficient evidence that social bootstrapping is a factor of the gender gap in Pinterest. Designers of web sites that use social bootstrapping should consider these results carefully: social bootstrapping may not actually be producing desired social graphs for users, and may be helping or harming users in unintentional, but powerful, ways.

FUTURE WORK

Our results raise a number of possibilities for future research. We discuss three such possibilities that we find especially interesting and actionable.

Do rich studies of early user experiences of social sites

Our study showed the importance of early user experience with a site: for example, some participants changed their impressions of Pinterest substantially, and social bootstrapping played a major role, affecting women and men differently. However, since our study was web-based, we were limited in the data we could collect, the control we could exert over the process, and the duration of the study. An alternative study design could take us deeper into new users' thought process and impression formation. For example, in-person contextual interviews would yield richer observational data and deepen insights into issues around importing one's social graph (such as: Do people worry about bothering their friends? Do they have privacy concerns? Why are women and men affected differently?) Assigning open-ended at-home activities, followed by a second interview would yield data about actual use of the site, not just intention to use. Such a study would be particularly valuable to inform the next possibility.

Design smarter social bootstrapping techniques

Social bootstrapping is a common practice in current social sites. Our results illustrated its potential power, but also potential downsides. Can a site retain its virtues – giving new users immediate access to familiar contacts and content of (potential) interest – while avoiding the downsides? We think intelligent techniques that help users understand the effects of importing contacts have promise. For example, a "critiquing" approach [3] would let users select contacts to import and follow, then update their content feed in real time. If users don't like what they see in the feed, they could remove contacts. Or more fundamentally, perhaps basing the information feed around a social following model is a bad idea for a site like Pinterest. A content-based recommendation approach [17] might be a better fit for the primary site function of information discovery.

Study how people allocate time and attention across the social media ecosystem

When participants said they were not likely to continue using Pinterest, they often made reference to other social media; specifically they said that Pinterest did not give them anything they could not get elsewhere or that their "social media plate" already was full. This reminds us of an important point: people must decide how to allocate time and attention across a large range of social sites.

How do people do this? What factors drive these decisions? We are aware of very little research on this topic. Oeldorf-Hirsch et al. [14] did a lab experiment studying when users routed questions to search engines or their social network, but this was a very focused topic and thus did not get at the kinds of general factors we are interested in. Hargittai and Hsieh studied use of multiple social sites through analysis of survey data [10, 11], but did not look at why and how people divide their attention across sites. Research on this topic would be of significant practical and theoretical interest.

CONCLUSION

We deepened and expanded upon current research related to Pinterest by qualitatively exploring two factors that we believed to be likely contributors to the gender gap in Pinterest: perception and initial social context (social bootstrapping). We conducted a survey study to investigate perceptions of both Pinterest users and non-users, and to run a controlled experiment of having participants sign up for Pinterest with and without socially bootstrapping their social graph from Facebook. Using mixed methods of analysis, we found interesting insights into the role of perception and social bootstrapping, including evidence that both are contributing factors to the gender gap in Pinterest.

ACKNOWLEDGMENTS

We thank all the Mechanical Turk workers who participated in our study and the members of the GroupLens lab who helped us refine our survey. We also acknowledge our funding support, including from the National Science Foundation (IIS-0808692 and IIS-1210863) and the University of Minnesota Department of Computer Science and Engineering (through a GAANN Fellowship and a Block Grant Fellowship).

REFERENCES

1. Antin, J. My Kind of People? Perceptions about Wikipedia Contributors and Their Motivations. In *Proc. CHI 2011*, ACM (2011).
2. Chang, S., Kumar, V., Gilbert, E., & Terveen, L. G. Specialization, Homophily, and Gender in a Social Curation Site: Findings from Pinterest. In *Proc. CSCW 2014*, ACM (2014).
3. Chen, L. and Pu, P. Critiquing-based recommenders: survey and emerging trends. User Modeling and User-Adapted Interaction,22(1-2):125{150, 2012
4. Cialdini, Robert B. *Influence: Science and practice*. Boston, MA: Pearson education, 2009.
5. Cicchetti, D.V. Guidelines, criteria, and rules of thumb for evaluating normed and standardized assessment instruments in psychology, *Psychological Assessment*, Vol. 6, No. 4 (1994), p. 284.
6. Cosley, D., Lam, S.K., Albert, I., Konstan, J.A., and Riedl, J. Is Seeing Believing? How Recommender System Interfaces Affect Users' Opinions. In *Proc. CHI 2003,* ACM (2003).
7. Digital Marketing Ramblings. "By the Numbers: 140 Amazing Pinterest Statistics" (October 7, 2014) http://expandedramblings.com/index.php/pinterest-stats/5/#.VEn7ifnF-RI
8. Gilbert, E., Bakhshi, S., Chang, S., & Terveen, L. "I Need to Try This"? A Statistical Overview of Pinterest. In *Proc. CHI 2013*, ACM (2013).
9. Hall, C., & Zarro, M. Social curation on the website Pinterest.com. In *Proc. ASIST 2012*, ACM (2012).
10. Hargittai, E., & Hsieh, Y. L. P. (2010a). Predictors and consequences of differentiated practices on social network sites. *Information, Communication & Society*, *13*(4), 515-536.
11. Hargittai, E., & Hsieh, Y. L. P. (2010b). From dabblers to omnivores. In Papacharissi, Zizi, ed. *A networked self: Identity, community, and culture on social network sites*. Routledge, 2010.
12. Linder, R., Snodgrass, C., & Kerne, A. Everyday Ideation: All of My Ideas Are On Pinterest. In *Proc. CHI 2014*, ACM (2014).
13. Marcotte, A. A social network of one's own. The American Prospect (March 2 2012). http://prospect.org/article/social-network-ones-own.
14. Oeldorf-Hirsch, A., Hecht, B., Morris, M. R., Teevan, J., & Gergle, D. To search or to ask: the routing of information needs between traditional search engines and social networks. In *Proc. CSCW 2014,* ACM (2014).
15. Ottoni, R., Pesce, J. P., Casas, D. Las, Franciscani Jr., G., Meira Jr., W., Kumaraguru, P., & Almeida, V. Ladies first: Analyzing gender roles and behaviors in Pinterest. In *Proc. AAAI Conference on Weblogs and Social Media*, AAAI Publications (2013), 457-465.
16. P. Sloan. Pinterest: Crazy growth lands it as top 10 social site. http://news.cnet.com/8301-1023_3-57347187-93/pinterest-crazy-growth-lands-it-as-top-10-socialsite.
17. Pazzani, M. J., & Billsus, D. (2007). Content-based recommendation systems. In *The adaptive web* (pp. 325-341). Springer Berlin Heidelberg.
18. Pew Research Internet Project "Social Media Update 2013". http://www.pewinternet.org/2013/12/30/social-media-update-2013/.
19. Pew Research Internet Project. "Demographics of key social networking platforms". http://www.pewinternet.org/2013/12/30/demographics-of-key-social-networking-platforms/.
20. Rode, Jennifer A. "A theoretical agenda for feminist HCI." *Interacting with Computers* 23.5 (2011): 393-400.
21. Sen, S., Lam., S.K., Rashid, A.M., Cosley, D., Frankowski, D., Osterhouse, J., and Riedl, J. Tagging, communities, vocabulary, evolution. In *Proc. CSCW 2006*, ACM (2006).
22. Stevenson, S. Pinterest for dudes. slate.com (April 1, 2013). http://www.slate.com/articles/technology/technology/2013/04/gentlemint_manteresting_tapiture_is_it_sexist_to_create_a_pinterest_for.single.html.
23. Thomas, D.R. A General Inductive Approach for Analyzing Qualitative Evaluation Data, *American Journal of Evaluation*, Vol. 27, No. 2 (2006), p. 237-24
24. Wanenchak, S. Pinterest and playing gender. thesocietypages.org (April 5, 2013). http://thesocietypages.org/cyborgology/2013/04/05/pinterest-and-playing-gender/.
25. Williams, M. E. Pinterest's gender trouble. salon.com (May 2 2012). http://www.salon.com/2012/05/02/pinterests_gender_trouble/.
26. Zarro, M., Hall, C., & Forte, A. Wedding Dresses and Wanted Criminals: Pinterest.com as an Infrastructure for Repository Building. In *Proc. ICWSM 2013*, AAAI Publications (2013).
27. Zhong, C., Salehi, M., Shah, S., Cobzarenco, M., Sastry, N., & Cha, M. (2014). Social Bootstrapping : Developing Social Communities by Borrowing from Established Social Networks. In *Proc. WWW* 2014

The Diffusion of Support in an Online Social Movement: Evidence from the Adoption of Equal-Sign Profile Pictures

Bogdan State
bogdanstate@fb.com

Lada Adamic
ladamic@fb.com

Facebook Inc.
1 Hacker Way
Menlo Park, CA, U.S.

ABSTRACT

In March of 2013, 3 million Facebook users changed their profile picture to one of an equals sign to express support of same-sex marriage. We demonstrate that this action shows complex diffusion characteristics congruent with threshold models, with most users observing several of their friends changing their profile picture before taking the action themselves. While the number of friends played a role in the adoption dynamics, so did demographic characteristics and the general propensity of the individual to change their profile picture. We show via simulation that the adoption curve is consistent with a heterogeneous-threshold model, in which the probability of adoption depends on both the number of friends and the susceptibility of the individual.

Author Keywords

Online Social Movements; Diffusion Mechanisms;

ACM Classification Keywords

J.4 Social and Behavioral Sciences: Sociology

General Terms

Human Factors; Measurement

The online realm has emerged as a fertile domain for collective action. Online activism has played an important role in such diverse large-scale organizing efforts as Iran's Green Movement of 2009, the US-centered Occupy Movement or the "Arab Spring" uprisings [23]. Given that social movements – whether on- or offline – encounter the problem of collective action [29], it is widely believed that activism in social movements is governed by a process of *complex diffusion*, alternatively known as complex contagion. This is the process in which the likelihood to engage in activism increases with the observation of other individuals' activism – in contrast with the alternative *simple diffusion* process, in which the activism likelihood remains constant or decreases with multiple exposures.

CSCW 2015, March 14–18, 2015, Vancouver, BC, Canada.
ACM 978-1-4503-2922-4/15/03.
http://dx.doi.org/10.1145/2675133.2675290

It is easy to see why social proof obtained from multiple sources would be necessary for many individuals to show their support for a cause they believe in. Engaging in a behavior that challenges the status quo carries inherent risks, from the minute – a quarrel with one's otherwise-thinking friends – to the life-threatening, as experienced by activists in a political movement challenging a repressive regime. Additionally, action requires participants to bear the costs of mobilization [26], ranging from the time spent filling out a petition to the money spent on monetary donations to one's favorite campaigns to the lost wages due to strike activity.

We investigate here a case where both the risks and the costs associated with activism were low but nonetheless still discernible. In this paper we focus specifically on the demonstration of support for marriage equality by changing one's Facebook profile picture to an equal sign. The fact that we find support for the hypothesis of complex diffusion in social mobilization even in the case of lower-risk social movement activity bolsters the importance of this kind of diffusion process as a crucial avenue through which political behavior spreads.

The equal-sign movement on Facebook was precipitated by a post on March 25th by the Human Rights Campaign (HRC) Facebook page calling on its fans to change their profile picture in advance of the US Supreme Court's consideration of two cases involving marriage rights for gay and lesbian couples.

Figure 1: Example equal-sign profile pictures.

Within a week, an estimated 3 million Facebook users changed their profile picture to a form of the equals sign, making this the largest such single cascade on the site. In the months prior to the start of the diffusion, public opinion had shifted toward a majority support of marriage equality for gays and lesbians (58% vs 36%) [8], from roughly equal amounts of support and opposition just 3 years prior. This attitudinal shift came after two decades of much slower, positive change in attitudes towards LGBT individuals and same-sex marriage in the U.S. [33].

Arguably showing support for same-sex marriage still carried a level of perceived risk. Even though an opinion in favor of same-sex marriage had recently experienced a dramatic increase in popularity, individuals may not have been aware of the shift due to its recency. Moreover, it was also likely that at least some friends and acquaintances of potential supporters of same-sex marriage held the opposing view. Although in this case a political statement may be more effective – there is the potential for changing others' opinions – displaying an opinion that is unpopular (or at least thought to be as such) creates the risk for conflict and contention. Given the uncertainty surrounding the extent of support for same-sex marriage and the potential risks resulting from adoption, we expect that most individuals would only change their profile picture after observing several others doing so, a situation that gives a real-world, observational illustration of the afore-mentioned complex diffusion dynamics in online social movements.

LITERATURE REVIEW

Social activism is currently evolving in multitudinous and complex forms in the online environment, which presents a rich medium for understanding the micro-level dynamics of political mobilization [25, 16]. However, the analysis of online social movements is currently in its infancy. Several studies to date have examined political movements on Twitter [9, 10, 27]. They have examined different actor types, from mainstream media to the individual, from local to remote, and their roles in information diffusion. [9] find that the communication network of the Occupy Movement induced from Twitter was more localized than the general political communication network, likewise displaying a hierarchical, hub-and-spoke structure. Similar processes were observed in episodes of online mobilization in Spain in May 2011 [15], and Tunisia and Egypt in 2011 [23, 34]. Despite the continued role of social media in social movements, the impact of online mobilization has been questioned: [10] revealed the temporal dynamics of Occupy, finding no substantial long-term changes in the level of engagement of individuals who took part in Occupy activism during the movement's early days.

Although these studies have yielded interesting insights, Twitter dynamics are driven in large part by accounts representing public figures, journalists, or celebrities. It is unclear whether the movements would have spread purely from individual to individual. In contrast, in this paper, by studying mobilization on Facebook, we examine diffusion that occurs largely between individuals. The current paper focuses on a particular episode – the diffusion of equal sign profile pictures – in the larger political movement aimed at gaining equal recognition for same-sex marriage as compared to opposite-sex marriage. A prior example of a behavior that has spread from individual to individual on Facebook is that of voting. [4] showed that someone who is informed that their friends clicked the 'I voted' button is more likely to do the same, especially if the friend is a close tie. However, voting is a desirable and uncontroversial behavior in contrast to expressing a potentially-contentious opinion.

This study presents the opportunity of examining a large-scale and well-defined behavior – the adoption of an equal sign as one's profile picture – that has real meaning and involves real, though low-level risks. Prior work has considered how network structure and other factors may influence diffusion when there is some cost to adoption. Theoretical models have investigated how network topology [7] and a small committed minority [12] influence whether a behavior can spread through the network. There is increasing evidence that multiple exposures are most effective in determining the adoption of certain types of behaviors in the social realm, for instance in the adoption of health-related behavior [5, 6], use of political hashtags [31], product purchases [21], and joining groups [2]. Most of the above behaviors incur some cost, whether in terms of money (the purchase of a book), coordination (using the same hashtags as others), or time (reading a book or using a new health application).

In contrast to this complex model of diffusion, *simple contagion* – in which repeated exposures are progressively less effective in determining the adoption of a behavior – is the apparent driver of most online information diffusion [13], although the spread of a scientific rumor can be modeled as depending on the number of adopting friends [35, 11] and the community structure [36] in a non-trivial manner [11]. In this paper we present a novel model that accounts for both the increasing influence of multiple friends and variable susceptibility at the individual level, to produce adoption curves similar to those observed for the equal sign diffusion.

Furthermore, using an anonymized dataset that records both the timing of exposures and the demographics of the individuals exposed, we are able to formulate empirically the relationship between demographic attributes, exposure, and adoption probability.

DATASET DESCRIPTION

All analysis was performed on a de-identified version of already existing data, in accordance with Facebook's Statement of Rights and Responsibilities and Data Use Policy.

This de-identified dataset represented 3,232,827 profile pictures adopted by 3,054,327 users, 67.5% of whom were women, and 90.71% of whom were in the United States. Additionally, 106m users were exposed to equal-sign profile pictures, 104m of whom were in the United States.

Equal-Sign Picture Classifier

The first task is to identify profile photo changes that are related to the Equal Sign Movement. Using an internal classifier we pre-filtered 10 million pictures uploaded during the period 03/25 to 03/31 2013. The pre-filtering selected pictures rating highly on metrics for synthetic images and overlaid text. A separate audit was conducted on 500 randomly-selected images uploaded during the same period but which were not included in the candidate set. The audit revealed no picture related to LGBT rights in the random sample we extracted. For each image in the candidate set we generated a number of features using the ImageMagick software [19]. The features included the (log-transformed) file size, the minimum, maximum, mean and standard deviation of the image-level distribution for red, green and blue values, the aspect ratio and area of the image, the relative ratio between the mean RGB colors, as well as a number of internal image-classification metrics. Using a hand-labeled dataset of 10,000 randomly-selected images we trained a Random Forest [22] classifier to distinguish images related to LGBT rights or marriage equality (whether for or against) from images which were unrelated to the topic. We evaluated the classifier using ten-fold cross-validation. In this setting, the classifier achieved mean precision of 0.986 (range between 0.974 and 0.995) and mean recall of 0.956 (range between 0.928 and 0.976).[1]

Although our classifier was built to distinguish pictures related to same-sex marriage from those unrelated to the topic, the overwhelming majority of these pictures was in favor of same-sex marriage. An audit of over 4,000 randomly-selected, hand-coded pictures revealed 97.7% to be in favor of same-sex marriage and only 2.3% being opposed. As a result, we focus here on the main process of diffusion as indicative of displays of support for same-sex marriage, leaving the modelling of the dynamics of opposition to future research.

Adopter Characteristics.

We investigate the relationship between demographic and socio-economic characteristics and adoption patterns for U.S. Facebook users who were exposed to Facebook friends' adoption of the equal sign as a profile picture during the observation window.[2]

Age and Gender.

Table 1 shows the probability that a U.S. user with at least one adopting friend will themselves adopt varies with age and gender. As the results reveal, women were substantially more likely than men to change their profile picture (2.3% of women and 1.3% of men adopted the equal-sign picture), the likelihood of adoption peaking in the age group 25-34 for both genders. Women also received slightly more overall exposures than men (median of 4 for women and 3 for men). On balance, female adopters displayed an equal-sign picture after *fewer* exposures than male ones, with a median of 8 for women and 10 for men.

Education

Individuals who listed higher education were also more likely to display the equal sign picture than those individuals not listing education. Whereas .8% of individuals who did not list any education level adopted, 1.0% of high school graduates did so, the proportion increasing to 2.4% for users with college degrees and to 4.6% for users with graduate educations.

Age Group	Overall	Women	Men
13-17	0.009	0.012	0.008
18-24	0.016	0.020	0.011
25-34	0.026	0.035	0.017
35-44	0.023	0.029	0.017
45-54	0.016	0.019	0.014
55-64	0.010	0.012	0.008
65+	0.007	0.008	0.006

Table 1: Adoption Probability for Exposed Users, by Age and Gender

Same-Sex Interest

Individuals listing themselves as "Interested in" persons of the same gender as themselves were 8 times more likely (11.0%) to adopt the equal sign than individuals whose "Interested in" field indicated persons of the opposite gender (1.4%). Individuals reporting same-sex interest were exposed to a median of 6 equal-sign pictures, whereas those reporting opposite-sex interest received a median of 4 exposures. Furthermore, adopters reporting (exclusive) same-sex interest were exposed, at the median, to 12 equal sign pictures before adopting, compared to a median of 8 exposures for those adopters reporting (exclusive) opposite-sex interest.

Friends with Same-Sex Interest

Consistent with both the "contact hypothesis" [18] and with homophily based on attitudes [20], we expect individuals who have many friends indicating same-sex interest to be more likely to display the equal sign picture. This is indeed the case: as Figure 2 shows, the probability of adoption increases dramatically with the number of friends listing themselves as "interested in" individuals of the same sex.

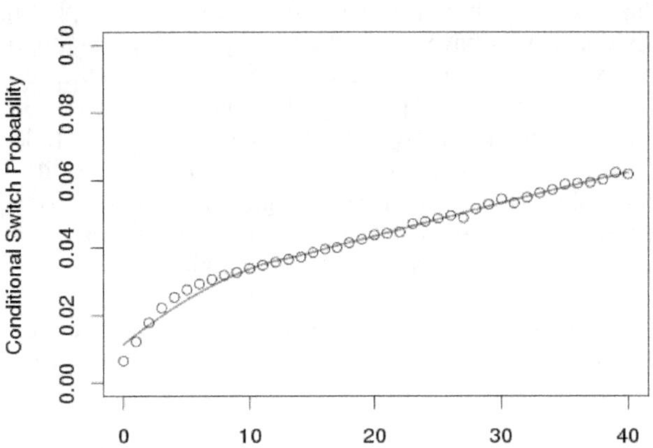

Figure 2: Adoption risk, by number of friends with same-sex interest.

[1] The lowest precision of 97.43% was achieved in a cross-validation run with 95.71% recall, whereas the lowest recall of 92.79% was achieved in a cross-validation run with 98.18% precision.

[2] We limit our analysis only to U.S. users given that the movement was overwhelmingly focused on the United States, and also due to the fact that the meaning of certain individual characteristics, such as religion, politics and education is highly dependent on national context.

Politics

Users who identified themselves as "very liberal" appear to be the most likely to adopt, 12.5% of those exposed having done so by the end of the observation window. The similar figure is 7.5% for liberal users, 5.1% for users identifying themselves as libertarian, 4.0% for moderates, 1.1% for "very conservative" users and 0.8% for conservative users. A potential explanation for the reversal seen between these last two categories has to do with the development of memes against same-sex marriage in response to the HRC campaign. While these memes are not prevalent in the overall population of Facebook users, it is plausible that very conservative individuals were more likely to be exposed to such counter-memes than individuals who listed themselves as conservative.

Religion

Religion has been recognized as a major factor in determining the support for same-sex marriage [28], and our results confirm its influence in shaping the probability of adoption of equal-sign profile pictures. Out of exposed U.S.-based users, 7.8% of persons identifying themselves as atheists and agnostics adopted the equal sign profile picture. The comparable figure is 2.3% for individuals indicating a religious affiliation, and 1.6% for individuals who listed no such affiliation.

HRC Followers

Because the Human Rights Campaign launched the equal-sign initiative, we expect individuals who were followers of the HRC Facebook page at the beginning of the observation window to have a higher probability of adoption. 32.5% of the 980 thousand US-based users who were followers of the HRC page at the start of the observation window came to display the equal sign, compared to 1.6% of non-followers. We also note 23.4% of U.S. users who adopted with no prior friends having adopted were followers of the HRC Facebook page, compared to 11.4% for individuals who adopted after their Facebook friends adopted.

Friends' Religion

Because individuals with similar political and religious affiliations tend to cluster together, we expect the counts of friends by affiliation to communicate more information about individuals with missing attributes. Additionally we expect that individuals who have more friends from a higher-adoption group would also be more likely to be exposed to the equal-sign meme, and to hold pro-same-sex marriage attitudes, both of which should make them more likely to adopt. Indeed, this is the case, as we see that the adoption probability increases sharply with the first few agnostic or atheist friends. the equal-sign picture (Figure 3). In contrast, we see a slower, linear increase with the number of religious friends – this may be a reflection of individuals with many friends (and thus more likely to use Facebook and participate in the campaign, see subsequent discussion) also having many religious friends.

Friends' Politics

The adoption probability increases dramatically with the number of very liberal friends, from around 0.8% for individuals who have no such friends to just under 12.2% for individuals with twenty Facebook friends who identify themselves as very liberal. The probability increases in a similar manner with the number of liberal and moderate friends and decreases slightly with the number of very conservative friends, as is apparent in Figure 4.

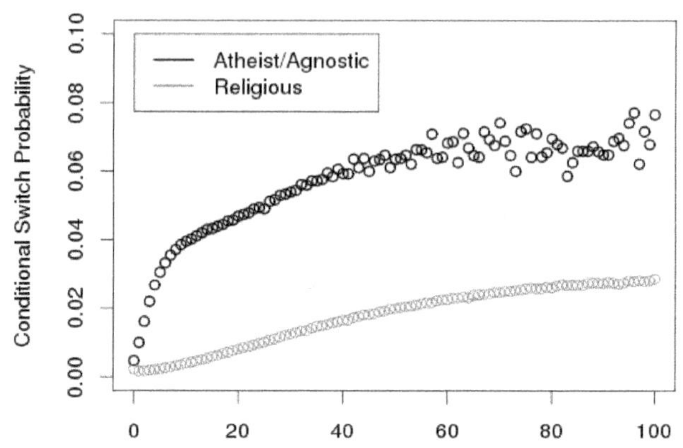

Figure 3: Adoption risk, by number of religious and atheist/agnostic friends.

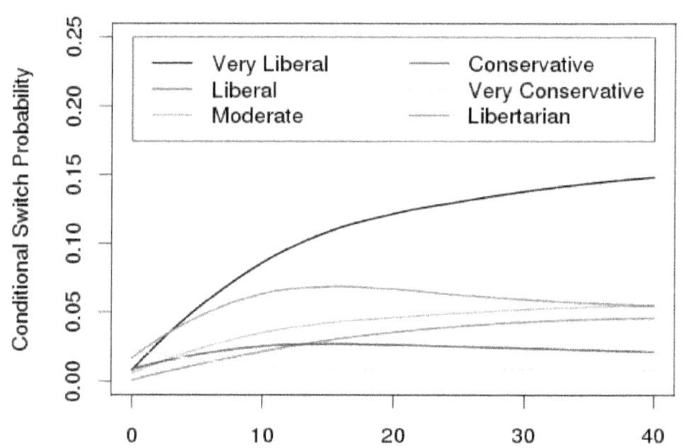

Figure 4: Adoption risk, by proportion of friends with political affiliation (LOESS regressions).

Profile Photo Change Frequency.

An important observation concerns the fact that, regardless of values and attitudes, some individuals will only change their profile picture seldom, or they will not change their profile picture to display a meme, no matter the cause. Figure 5 bolsters this hypothesis, showing a steep increase in the adoption probability with the number of profile picture changes during the six months prior to the observation window.

Number of Facebook Friends

Another metric for site usage concerns the number of Facebook friends that a person had in the beginning of the observation window, graphed against the adoption probability in the lower panel of Figure 5. The adoption probability peaks around 400 friends, and then decreases slowly with an increase in friends. It seems likely that two countervailing processes are captured by this variable. On the one hand, site usage is likely to increase as the number of Facebook friends increases. At the same time, as one accumulates friends, the salience of any friends' posting is reduced due to the increasing volume of information which the social networking platform delivers to the user.

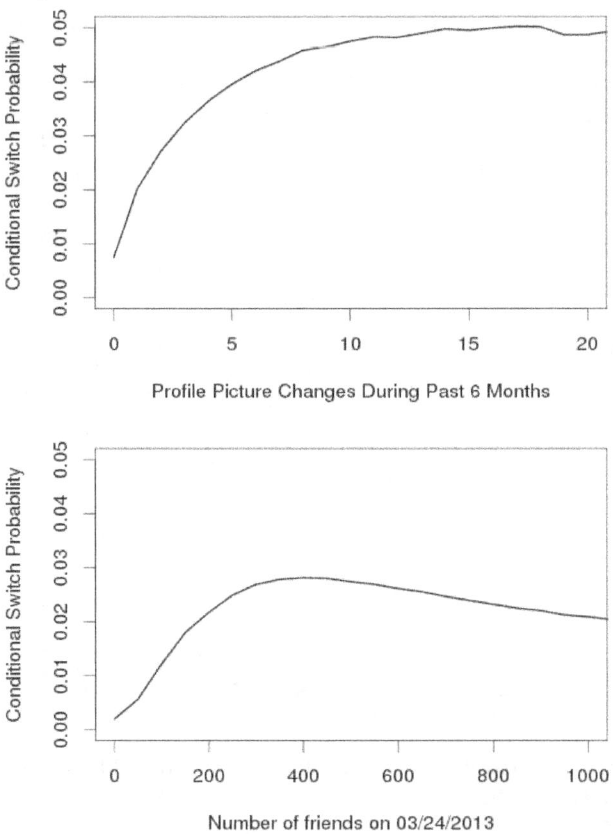

Figure 5: Adoption probability, by profile photo changes in the six months prior to March 24, 2013 and the number of friends on that date.

LOGISTIC MODEL FOR ADOPTION

As the prior statistics suggest, there are many variables that factor into the adoption of equal sign profile pictures. Many factors may be correlated however – religion and politics or education and age. To distinguish between the myriad variables at our disposal we use a logistic regression that predicts the probability of adopting the equal sign (Table 2). To avoid making any parametric assumptions about the function linking exposure to adoption, we used splines to measure the effect of each additional exposure starting from the first.

The complex diffusion hypothesis would have us expect a pattern of increased likelihood of adoption with each additional exposure. The model shows precisely this pattern, but only for the first six exposures (understood as the number of Facebook friends who adopted before ego). *Ceteris paribus,* the model estimates an increase in the odds ratio of adoption by a factor of $e^{.81} = 2.24$ for individuals who have received their first exposure, and of $e^{.5} = 1.64$ for individuals who have received their second exposure, the effect attributable to each exposure decreasing progressively to around the sixth exposure, where it becomes virtually flat. We also included a linear term for each additional exposure past the tenth – consistent with our prior findings the likelihood to adopt appears to decrease slightly with each additional exposure.

The results also reveal that the identified factors maintain their influence on the adoption probability, with a few exceptions. When factors such as politics and education are taken into account, both below-18 and 35-44 age groups appear more likely to adopt the equal sign. We also see that individuals who do not report a religious or political affiliation are rather unlikely to adopt the equal sign, even when a behavioral measure as direct as their previous profile photo change frequency is taken into account.

DIFFUSION AS COMPLEX CONTAGION

Measuring the contagion profile

A potentially confounding factor in measuring the influence of one's friends is the role of broadcast media in popularizing a certain action, in this case the change of one's profile picture to an equal sign. Unlike most memes spreading online, the equal-sign meme received ample coverage while it was diffusing. As such, it is perhaps not surprising that 58,111 individuals displayed the equal sign before any of their friends did. As Figure 6 shows, most of these "independent" adoptions occurred during March 26th, the first full day after the Equal Rights Campaign launched the original equal-sign picture.

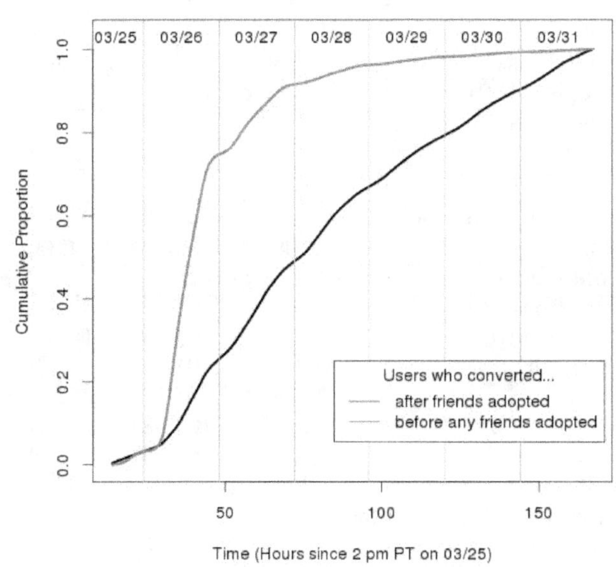

Figure 6: Cumulative Distribution Functions of users who first adopted equal sign with or without any friends having previously adopted.

Next we examine the marginal likelihood of adoption, given exposure to adoption by one's friends. Figure 8 (a) plots the

Table 2: Determinants of Adoption (Logistic Regression)

Independent Variable	Coef.	(S.E.)	Z-stat.
Prior Exposures			
Intercept	4.278***	(0.062)	68.821
... 1st exposure	0.811***	(0.025)	32.542
... 2nd exposure	0.500***	(0.028)	17.772
... 3rd exposure	0.317***	(0.029)	11.107
... 4th exposure	0.161***	(0.030)	5.439
... 5th exposure	0.097**	(0.031)	3.118
... 6th exposure	0.037	(0.033)	1.122
... 7th exposure	0.081*	(0.035)	2.324
... 9th exposure	-0.020	(0.037)	-0.552
... 10th exposure	0.012	(0.039)	0.312
... > 10 exposures	-0.018	(0.030)	-0.598
each exp. > 10	-0.007***	(0.000)	-25.680
Site Usage			
Profile pic. changes	0.407***	(0.006)	66.774
Number of friends†	-1.681***	(0.022)	-77.982
Age (ref.: 25-34 years old)			
... below 18	0.134***	(0.037)	3.664
... 18-24	-0.347***	(0.016)	-21.682
... 35-44	0.129***	(0.015)	8.357
... 45-54	-0.034	(0.019)	-1.758
... 55-64	-0.354***	(0.027)	-13.345
... above 65	-0.629***	(0.037)	-17.009
Female	0.575***	(0.012)	49.143
Education (ref.: none reported)			
High School	0.212***	(0.025)	8.604
College	0.360***	(0.022)	16.499
Graduate School	0.559***	(0.025)	22.190
Same-/Opposite-Sex Interest			
Same-Sex Interest (SSI)	0.515***	(0.033)	15.483
Opposite-Sex Interest	-1.380***	(0.066)	-20.947
No. Friends w/ SSI†	0.353***	(0.008)	45.472
Religious Affiliation (ref.: none reported)			
Atheism/Agnosticism	0.539***	(0.031)	17.217
Religious	0.033**	(0.012)	2.786
Friends' Religious Affiliation†			
No. Atheist/Agnostic†	0.295***	(0.009)	32.390
No. Religious†	0.100***	(0.023)	4.333
Political Affiliation (ref.: none reported)			
Very Conservative	-0.048	(0.153)	-0.310
Conservative	-0.641***	(0.034)	-18.964
Moderate	0.261***	(0.032)	8.140
Liberal	0.684***	(0.019)	35.853
Very Liberal	0.690***	(0.048)	14.518
Libertarian	0.320***	(0.064)	4.968
HRC fan	1.111***	(0.027)	40.820
Friends' Political Affiliation†			
Very Conservative	-0.150***	(0.012)	-12.515
Conservative	0.126***	(0.010)	12.712
Moderate	0.074***	(0.011)	6.692
Liberal	0.317***	(0.012)	25.615
Very Liberal	0.078***	(0.010)	7.848
Libertarian	0.045***	(0.010)	4.435

$***: p < .001; **: p < .01; *: p < .05$. Two-sided tests. N=200,000. Sample balanced on DV. † transformed using $f(x) = \ln(x+1)$.

empirically-observed adoption rate for each additional "re-exposure," defined there as the adoption of the equal sign picture by another friend. [3] The figure shows an increasing trend in the effectiveness of each additional re-exposure up to the eighth event, after which the trend reverses. The decline in effectiveness for individuals re-exposed to multiple equal sign pictures hints at an "immunity" some users had to the equal-sign campaign. We can imagine that some individuals are highly unlikely to display an equal-sign picture, either due to disagreement with the campaign's goals, or because they do not post any memes at all, or even due to inexperience with the Facebook interface.

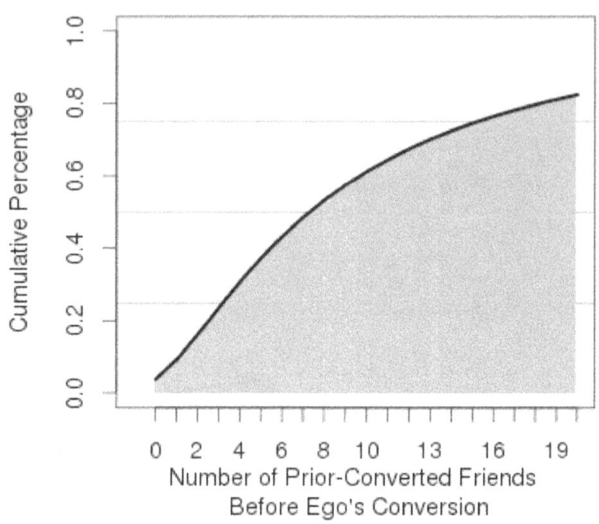

Figure 7: Probability of Conversion by number of friends previously adopting equal-sign (Cumulative Distribution Function).

An important nuance in our study concerns the definition of "exposure." Whereas the theoretical case presents exposure as easy to quantify, this concept's manifestation in the real world is considerably more complicated. A user may become only vaguely aware of a friend's adoption of the equal sign when the friend's new profile picture appears in the chat side bar. The impression's salience will arguably increase if the profile picture change generates a story in the user's Newsfeed. Furthermore, the user will become even more aware of their friend's decision if they click on such a story, and even more so if they engage with the story by "liking" it. In Figure 8 (b) we consider all these alternative measures of exposure, all of which show the same concave pattern with respect to the probability of adoption.[4]

[3]We only count re-exposures as valid at the first time when a user was known to have logged in to the Facebook platform. For instance, if at t_0 user u logged into Facebook and had $k = 3$ friends who had changed profile pictures, while at the time of u's next login (t_1) $k = 7$ friends had changed profile pictures, we will only count u as having "received" exposures with $k = 3$ and $k = 7$, since it was only at these values that u *could* have changed their profile picture.

[4]The choice of "liking" as a measure of exposure may seem bizarre, as liking seems to be more a measure of pre-existing ideological support for the campaign's goals than a "pure" measure of exposure. A

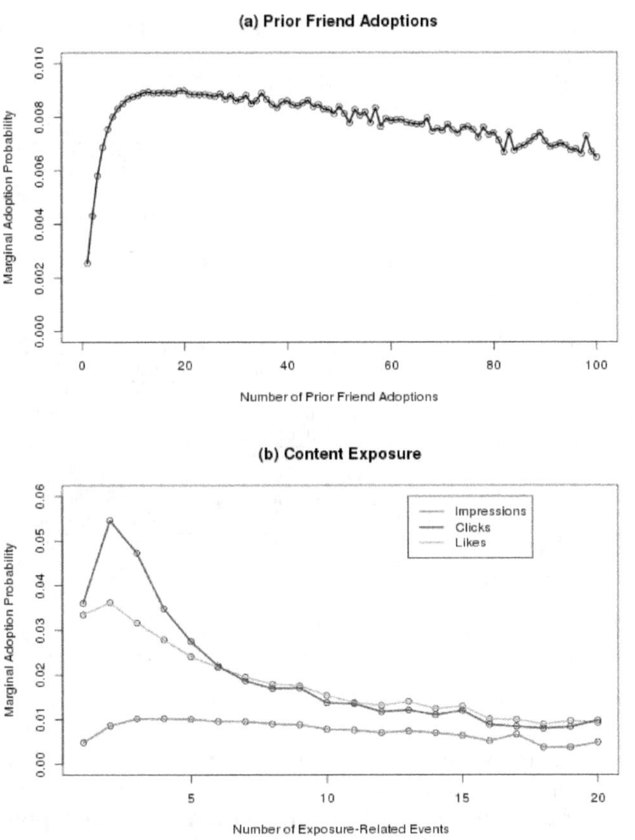

Figure 8: Marginal Adoption Probability as function of friends' adoption and of exposure to profile picture changes.

Distinguishing degrees of complexity in diffusion

The observed, complex diffusion curves for the equals sign stand in contrast to the simple contagion model, where contact with any one adopter carries a constant probability of spreading the diffusion to the susceptible individual. We expect diffusion processes on Facebook to vary between simple and complex according to the cost and benefit of adoption. The simplest contagion ought to occur when the individual has to expend very little time and effort to share content, e.g. simply replicating information. On Facebook, such simple diffusion occurs when a compelling image or message, appearing in a person's Newsfeed, is reshared by that person to her friends at the click of a button.[5] The effort expended is low and also the benefit of sharing the information does not depend on the number of friends who have shared it before. If anything, the image might be less appealing to share if everyone else has shared it already [24]. We therefore expect photo reshare cascades to be well-modeled by a process of simple contagion and include the three such photo cascades in July of 2013 which were the most reshared instances corresponding to known rumors [14]. Other items we might expect to diffuse through a more "complex" or threshold-like mechanism [17]. This may include expressing opinions for which one doesn't know that they are shared by a majority of one's social network, or taking risks such as making oneself vulnerable to ridicule or associating with a disease or condition [30]. In the case of the LGBT rights issue, we hypothesize social proof to be of paramount importance. Given the great level of contention in the same-sex marriage debate, taking a stance either for or against same-sex marriage potentially brings along important social risks to the actor.

We also expect complex diffusion to be more likely to occur when the effort of sharing information is greater than simply clicking a button. Prior to the existence of the reshare button, many ideas propagated when individuals copied others' status updates and pasted them into their own. This action required more effort than a click, and the message varied as well, allowing us to compare diffusion across different memes.

Figure 9 compares the average number of friends who have adopted before an individual does with the total size of the cascade for the three different kind of diffusion: the equal sign movement, three most reshared photo-reshares associated with rumors in July 2013, and 107 copy and paste memes active during 2009-2011. In general, in larger cascades it is more likely that many of one's friends posted first, simply because many people have posted. However, it is the deviations from this trend that reveal how the risk and effort in sharing correlate with seeing several friends post before taking action. As anticipated, the photo reshare cascades exhibit simple contagion – they are typically propagated as soon as 1.3 - 1.5 of one's friends have reshared, i.e. a single exposure is typically sufficient to pass on a rumor. In contrast, copy and paste memes are copied on average after several friends have first. Within these memes there are interesting differences in the extent of complex diffusion as shown in Table 3. High-threshold memes tend to expose the poster to potentially-negative social consequences: the actor risks embarrassment when promising to answer any question posed by their friends – as one such meme demands. By comparison, low-threshold memes deliver only benefits to the actor, as there is arguably little contention (at least comparatively) as to the desirability of appreciating teachers or family, or raising awareness of a security feature.

We observe that the equals sign diffusion is positioned among the higher threshold memes, some of which express political

division of online behavior into "passive" exposure and "active" engagement would be misguided however. A user's current friendship circle and, by extension, their current content stream is the result of prior decisions made by the user: the user decided whom to add as a friend and what kind of content to give feedback on. Thus we may think of liking an equal-sign profile picture change as a particularly strong exposure to the diffusion episode *and* as a manifestation of one's pre-existing ideological support for the movement. Similarly, one's friendship circle is not randomly-selected but its composition is influenced by homophily. Inasmuch as attitudes towards gay rights are one dimension of homophily, the fact that one has friends who support the marriage equality cause is likewise, partially, an indicator of active support for the cause. This entanglement between exposure and support is arguably nothing other than a ramification of the long-noticed confounding of homophily and social influence [1].

[5] It should be emphasized that in the case of profile picture there is no button allowing one to copy another's profile picture on Facebook. The other's profile picture must be downloaded and then re-uploaded to the site.

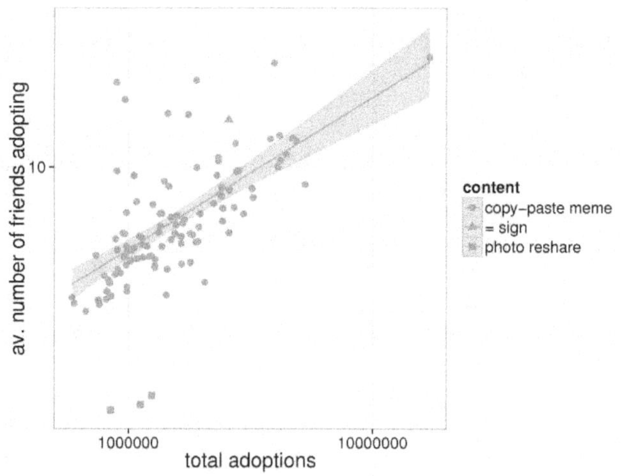

Figure 9: Comparison of the average number of friends previously adopting for three kinds of diffusion actions: changing one's profile to the equals sign, copying and pasting a status update meme, and resharing a photo embodying a rumor.

or religious opinions. With a mean of 14.4 and a median of 8 friends having switched before a given user (Figure 7)[6], the equal-sign movement appears to have required more social proof than most copy-and-paste memes, showing that most individuals need to observe several of their friends taking the action before social proof is sufficient to justify deciding to engage in the action themselves. This could be the result of effort (downloading the photo, and then re-uploading it takes several steps relative to a single click reshare), but also uncertainty about the meaning, importance and popularity of the initiative.

Simulation

We next present a simple model that can account for a range of complex diffusion curves. Prior complex contagion models typically assume that individuals have varying adoption thresholds [17], with the threshold expressed either in terms of the absolute number of friends who have adopted a behavior, or the proportion of friends who have. If such models were to hold, then observing more friends adopting a certain behavior should correspond to a higher likelihood of adoption. Instead, what we saw in Figure 8 and what has surfaced in prior studies [21], is that people who have many exposures, e.g. 40, are less likely to adopt than those who have had a moderate number. How is that possible? One workaround has been to specify the probability of adopting after k friends, $P(k)$, explicitly [31], but this fails to expose the fundamental ingredients of the diffusion process.

Here we propose a model with two separate, essential ingredients, which together produce adoption curves consistent with the complex diffusion model. First, each additional exposure presents an opportunity to adopt, but the marginal increase in adoption probability diminishes. That is, I will be more likely to adopt if a 5th friend adopts than when the 4th friend adopted, but the increase won't be as great as when two friends adopt vs. one., as we saw in the preceeding sections. Second, individuals' susceptibility is heterogeneous: some are more prone to the behavior or cause then others, regardless of the number of adopting friends. A model multiplying the two factors together can produce both the initial increase in probability with increasing numbers of exposures, as well as decreasing probabilities at high numbers of exposures – individuals who have not adopted by this point are very likely to have very low susceptibility and additional exposures are less likely to sway them. We simulate such a spreading process on the network of a small country with 810,923 Facebook users and 76,447,288 undirected edges. There are three main ingredients: (a) the overall infectiousness (virality) of the behavior v, (b) the susceptibility of the individual s_i, and (c) how the likelihood of adoption varies with the number of adopting friends k.

[6]Here we consider only the case of users who have switched after at least one of their friends, see discussion below for the role of broadcasting in getting users to display the picture.

Table 3: Examples of low- and high-threshold textual memes on Facebook.

Friends	Resid.	Normalized Meme Text
20.1	14.2	copy this as your status and see what people want from you 1 phone number 2 second chance 3 hangout 4 friendship ...
23.5	13.3	copy this into your status and see what people rate you 1 crazy 2 I'd marry you 3 talkative 4 sarcastic ...
15.4	8.3	i will be completely honest for 24 hours you can ask me one question only in my inbox any question no matter how crazy sinister or wrong it is i will answer ...
10.8	2.9	in america the homeless go without eating ... yet we donate billions to other countries before helping our own first ...
10.5	2.6	... easter is not about bunnies and chocolate eggs let s lift up god s name and make a statement
9.4	1.5	i am a handful unfortunately most women won t re post this i m strong willed independent a bit outspoken and i tell it like it is
8.3	-0.7	do any of us really know everybody on our friend list here is a task for you i want all my fb friends to comment on this status about how you met me
3.4	-2.3	it s national book week the rules grab the closest book to you go to page 56 copy the 5th sentence as your status ...
3.3	-2.4	a teacher somewhere in your neighborhood tonight is grading iand preparing lessons to teach your children while you are ...
3.5	-3.1	your brother is your first friend in life no one will ever understand your crazy family like your brother even if you ...
3.9	-3.6	attention while on fb look at your url address the very top box on on screen if u see http instead of https ...

Note: Friends: mean number of friends adopting prior to ego's adoption. Resid.: residual of Friends in linear regression (see Figure 9).

We assume that the susceptibility is distributed exponentially. A few people are quite susceptible but most are not. For most trends and fashions, this is likely a sensible assumption, where a few enthusiasts are readily converted, but most of the population is not eager to adopt.

$$p(s_i) = \lambda e^{-\lambda s_i} \quad (1)$$

Next, we model the influence of observing increasing numbers of friends. Seeing more friends should have more influence than seeing fewer, but there should be diminishing returns for each additional friend. We choose to model the probability of adoption as being proportional to the logarithm of k_i to capture this intuition. Finally, we combine all three factors to derive the probability of adoption $p(a_i)$ by individual i, with susceptibility s_i and k friends who have adopted so far:

$$p(a_i) = v s_i \log(k+1) \quad (2)$$

We run the simulation by increasing the virality v until occasional cascades occur starting from a randomly selected individual. Each individual who adopts has one chance to influence each of their friends. We then track k for each adoption and non-adoption after each exposure.

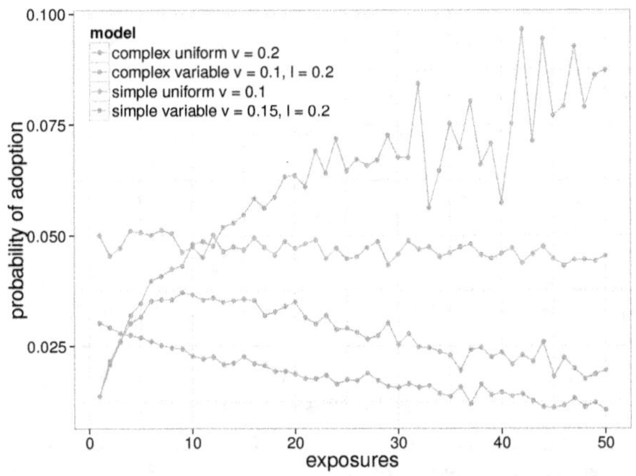

Figure 10: Infection rates of re-exposures (simulated).

In Figure 10 the simulation replicates the empirical diffusion trend from Figure 8 – a trend which is also consistent with the complex diffusion hypothesis. We note that both variable susceptibility and multiple exposures are key to obtaining the characteristic curve. For example, if everyone in the population is equally susceptible, and each exposure has equal likelihood of infection, then the curve is entirely flat. On the other hand, if susceptibility within the population is variable, but each additional exposure has the same probability of infection per individual, then the probability of adopting with each additional exposure drops, because the users who are left over after several exposures are the ones with a lower susceptibility.

Similarly, if the susceptibility is uniform, but observing more friends increases the probability of adoption, then greater k should correspond to strictly higher adoption probability, which is inconsistent with the empirical observation. Finally, if we incorporate both variable susceptibility, and increasing probability of adoption with more exposures, we replicate the empirically-observed pattern. There is an initial increase in adoption probability as more friends adopt and there are many relatively susceptible individuals who are becoming exposed. Those individuals who "survive" many exposures without adopting are likely to be quite resistant to adoption – an observation that serves to explain why the probability of adoption drops again after reaching a peak around a middling number of prior adopting friends.

The above simulation is overly simplistic and does not take into account the varying login rates of different users or the true distribution of susceptibilities. However, it does demonstrate that a few simple assumptions are sufficient to recreate the characteristics of adoption in this diffusion process.

CONCLUSION

In this paper we analyzed the behavior of a single, large social movement on Facebook. Millions of users changed their profile pictures in support of same-sex marriage. Although this was by no means the first large cascade on Facebook, it had a very distinct characteristic: most of these individuals changed their profile picture to a variant of the equal sign only after observing *several* of their friends doing so first. Relative to other types of diffusion on Facebook, the spread of memes in this context is consistent with the complex diffusion hypothesis.

In particular, our findings further bolster the observations made by Romero, Meeder and Kleinberg (2011), about the operation of complex contagion in activities perceived as higher-risk or requiring coordination on the Internet. However, our paper reveals a seemingly-peculiar adoption curve which climbs steeply to a peak level of the adoption probability as the number of adopting friends increases from zero, only to continue on a trajectory of slow decline beyond its maximum. This shape is markedly different from the concave, increasing graph often associated with theoretical understandings of complex diffusion (see the "complex uniform" graph in Figure 10 for an illustration). Our simulation results reveal that, indeed, a process of complex diffusion is very likely to be at work in the case of the equal-sign diffusion episode too. However, the important addendum is that actors in this case present a great degree of heterogeneity in their susceptibility to adoption, a situation which we expect to be the case in many cases involving political mobilization.

These findings are (unsurprisingly) consistent with the existence of different mean levels of susceptibility to adopting a politically-significant meme in various social groups, defined by age, gender, education, and political beliefs. These meso-level differences should not obscure the existence of large amounts of intra-group variation in each person's adoption probability as a function of number of friends adopting. Indeed, we see the same pattern of decline in the adoption probability persist even after accounting for a large number of factors related to social group membership (Table 2).

Hence, we not only provide additional evidence of this diffusion pattern in a different, broader setting, but also demonstrate how varying susceptibilities and multiple exposures can produce P(k) curves similar to those observed in this process. Rather than having to directly specify P(k) in the simulation [31], we make a more natural set of assumptions: susceptibility is highly skewed, and additional exposures have incremental but diminishing influence. Finally, by accounting for the timing and quantity of exposure doses, our work also highlights the robustness of the complex diffusion hypothesis to different measurements of exposure. Our analysis of the drivers of adoption revealed that, net of exposures and Facebook usage, there are important, socially-driven differences in the likelihood to adopt.

As always, there is an interesting confound because susceptibility is homophilous, so that someone who has many friends who have changed their profile picture is themselves likely to be the type of person who would change their profile picture. Previous work [3] has shown that additional exposures will have higher influence with diminishing returns relative to the individual not observing any social signal from their friends. However the relative effect of seeing one's friends is only partly measured through our observational study [32]. We believe that separating the relative importance of influence and susceptibility in these types of diffusion processes would be a fruitful direction for future research.

REFERENCES

1. Aral, S., Muchnik, L., and Sundararajan, A. Distinguishing influence-based contagion from homophily-driven diffusion in dynamic networks. *Proceedings of the National Academy of Sciences 106*, 51 (2009), 21544–21549.
2. Backstrom, L., Huttenlocher, D., Kleinberg, J., and Lan, X. Group formation in large social networks: membership, growth, and evolution. In *Proc. KDD'06*, ACM (2006), 44–54.
3. Bakshy, E., Rosenn, I., Marlow, C., and Adamic, L. The role of social networks in information diffusion. In *Proc. WWW'12*, ACM (2012), 519–528.
4. Bond, R. M., Fariss, C. J., Jones, J. J., Kramer, A. D., Marlow, C., Settle, J. E., and Fowler, J. H. A 61-million-person experiment in social influence and political mobilization. *Nature 489*, 7415 (2012), 295–298.
5. Centola, D. The spread of behavior in an online social network experiment. *Science 329*, 5996 (2010), 1194–1197.
6. Centola, D. An experimental study of homophily in the adoption of health behavior. *Science 334*, 6060 (2011), 1269–1272.
7. Centola, D., and Macy, M. Complex contagions and the weakness of long ties. *American Journal of Sociology 113*, 3 (2007), 702–734.
8. Cohen, J. Gay marriage support hits new high in post-abc poll. *Washington Post*, 18 March 2013. Available: http://www.washingtonpost.com/blogs/the-fix/wp/2013/03/18/gay-marriage-support-hits-new-high-in-post-abc-poll/ [Last accessed: 22 February 2014], March 2013.
9. Conover, M. D., Davis, C., Ferrara, E., McKelvey, K., Menczer, F., and Flammini, A. The geospatial characteristics of a social movement communication network. *PloS one 8*, 3 (2013), e55957.
10. Conover, M. D., Ferrara, E., Menczer, F., and Flammini, A. The digital evolution of occupy wall street. *PloS one 8*, 5 (2013), e64679.
11. De Domenico, M., Lima, A., Mougel, P., and Musolesi, M. The anatomy of a scientific rumor. *Scientific reports 3* (2013).
12. De Domenico, M., Lima, A., Mougel, P., and Musolesi, M. Role of committed minorities in times of crisis. *Scientific reports 3*, 1371 (2013).
13. Dow, P. A., Adamic, L. A., and Friggeri, A. The Anatomy of Large Facebook Cascades. In *Proc ICWSM'13* (2013).
14. Friggeri, A., Adamic, L. A., Eckles, D., and Cheng, J. Rumor Cascades. In *Proc ICWSM'14* (2014).
15. González-Bailón, S., Borge-Holthoefer, J., Rivero, A., and Moreno, Y. The dynamics of protest recruitment through an online network. *Scientific reports 1* (2011).
16. Gould, R. V. Multiple networks and mobilization in the paris commune, 1871. *American Sociological Review* (1991), 716–729.
17. Granovetter, M. Threshold models of collective behavior. *American journal of sociology* (1978), 1420–1443.
18. Herek, G. M., and Glunt, E. K. Interpersonal contact and heterosexuals' attitudes toward gay men: Results from a national survey. *The Journal of Sex Research 30*, 3 (August 1993), 239–244.
19. ImageMagick Studio, L. Imagemagick (version 6.8.7-2) [computer software], 2013.
20. Lazarsfeld, P. F., Merton, R. K., et al. Friendship as a social process: A substantive and methodological analysis. *Freedom and control in modern society 18*, 1 (1954), 18–66.
21. Leskovec, J., Adamic, L. A., and Huberman, B. A. The dynamics of viral marketing. *ACM Transactions on the Web (TWEB) 1*, 1 (2007), 5.
22. Liaw, A., and Wiener, M. Classification and regression by randomforest. *R News 2*, 3 (2002), 18–22.
23. Lotan, G., Graeff, E., Ananny, M., Gaffney, D., Pearce, I., and Boyd, D. The revolutions were tweeted: Information flows during the 2011 tunisian and egyptian revolutions. *International Journal of Communication 5* (2011), 1375–1405.
24. Macskassy, S. A., and Michelson, M. Why do people retweet? anti-homophily wins the day! In *Proc. ICWSM'11* (2011).
25. McAdam, D. Recruitment to high-risk activism: The case of freedom summer. *American Journal of Sociology* (1986), 64–90.
26. McCarthy, J. D., and Zald, M. N. Resource mobilization and social movements: A partial theory. *American journal of sociology* (1977), 1212–1241.
27. Mejova, Y., and Weber, I. Quantifying politics using online data: Introduction. *Social Science Computer Review* (2013), 0894439313506848.
28. Olson, L. R., Cadge, W., and Harrison, J. T. Religion and public opinion about same-sex marriage*. *Social Science Quarterly 87*, 2 (2006), 340–360.
29. Olson, M. *The logic of collective action: public goods and the theory of groups*. Harvard University Press, 1965.
30. Rao, H., Greve, H. R., and Davis, G. F. Fool's gold: Social proof in the initiation and abandonment of coverage by wall street analysts. *Administrative Science Quarterly 46*, 3 (2001), 502–526.
31. Romero, D. M., Meeder, B., and Kleinberg, J. Differences in the mechanics of information diffusion across topics: idioms, political hashtags, and complex contagion on twitter. In *Proc. WWW'11*, ACM (2011), 695–704.
32. Shalizi, C. R., and Thomas, A. C. Homophily and contagion are generically confounded in observational social network studies. *Sociological Methods & Research 40*, 2 (2011), 211–239.
33. Sherkat, D. E., Powell-Williams, M., Maddox, G., and De Vries, K. M. Religion, politics, and support for same-sex marriage in the united states, 1988–2008. *Social Science Research 40*, 1 (2011), 167–180.
34. Starbird, K., and Palen, L. (How) will the revolution be retweeted?: information diffusion and the 2011 Egyptian uprising. In *Proc. CSCSW'12* (2012), 7–16.
35. Ver Steeg, G., Ghosh, R., and Lerman, K. What stops social epidemics? In *Proc. ICWSM'11* (2011).
36. Weng, L., Menczer, F., and Ahn, Y.-Y. Virality prediction and community structure in social networks. *Scientific reports 3* (2013).

Do I Need To Follow You? Examining the Utility of The Pinterest Follow Mechanism

Bluma Gelley*
Computer Science and Engineering
New York University
Brooklyn, NY, USA
bgelley@nyu.edu

Ajita John
Avaya Labs
Basking Ridge, NJ, USA
ajita@avaya.com

ABSTRACT

Pinterest is a Social Network Site (SNS) centered around the curation and sharing of visual content. The site encourages users to form ties with (follow) other users based on mutual interests, and use these ties to discover and share content. In this work, we examine the efficacy and relevance of the Pinterest follow mechanism in driving content discovery and curation. We collect a sample of user activity and find that the vast majority (88%) of the unique users who interact with an average user's content are non-followers. Conversely, only 12.3% of a user's followers interact with any of their pins. Users who discover and repost content from outside their follow network also do not subsequently follow the contributors of that content. Our results strongly suggest that following is neither heavily utilized nor strongly effective for driving content discovery and sharing on Pinterest.

Author Keywords

Pinterest; Online Social Networks; Following; Social Browsing; Activity Graph; Tie formation

ACM Classification Keywords

H.3.5. Information Systems: Online Information Services—*Web-based Services*; J.4.3. Social and behavioral sciences

General Terms

Human Factors; Measurement

INTRODUCTION

The follow mechanism — the public articulation of links between users[1] [6] — is an essential part of a Social Network Site (SNS) [7]. According to boyd and Ellison [21], this mechanism is "the key differentiating feature of SNSs." Following is what connects users to the social graph maintained on the site and allows them access to the many benefits it provides [52, 65]. Follow links are the means by which users influence others [62, 2] and ideas and advertisements are spread through the network [65, 12, 13]. A user's follow network can even be used to target ads for the products and services that they may be likely to purchase [31]. As such, the follow mechanism is a crucial part of any social network site.

The act of following (or friending) another user can be understood as an example of the sociological concept of tie formation in social networks [27]. Various mechanisms for tie formation have been well-studied in the sociology and psychology literature, including homophily, friendship based on similarity or mutual interests [45]; triadic closure, connecting with friends of friends [57]; and preferential attachment, or the tendency of people to connect with others who already have many relationships [3]. People form ties on social network sites as well for similar reasons [57, 54, 8]. In the early days of the Internet, communities were formed by people who shared common interests; one example of this is Usenet newsgroups. Tie formation in those communities resulted from ***interest homophily*** [4] — connecting with others because of common interests. Those early communities, however, never gained the mainstream acceptance that later social network sites such as Facebook have [21]. These sites "signaled a shift from interest-driven to friendship-driven spaces" [21], generally depending on mechanisms other than interest homophily to build their networks. This shift is substantiated by the work of Bisgin and colleagues [4], who found that shared interests had only a weak influence on tie formation on several mainstream SNSs of varying types. On most modern social network sites, the majority of ties that are 'formed' are actually ones that already existed off the site. A Nielsen survey of Internet users showed that the top reason given by users for friending someone on Facebook was "knowing [them] in real life" [35]. The 2013 Surveying the Digital Future survey also found that most users had only a small number of friends whom they had met online [16]. This has been confirmed repeatedly for a number of social network sites: the majority of a user's connections are usually 'real life' friends and acquaintances who were simply transferred to the site as 'friends' [22, 39, 41, 32, 14, 23]. This transfer is often encouraged by the site: Facebook users are encouraged to use the site's search feature to find people they already know and add them as friends. LinkedIn takes this idea even further by

*A significant portion of this work was done while the author was at Avaya Labs.

[1]In this paper, for purposes of simplicity, we use the word 'follow' to refer to both unidirectional ('follow') and bidirectional ('friend') links on a social network site.

CSCW 2015, March 14–18, 2015, Vancouver, BC, Canada.

ACM 978 1 4503 2922 4/15/03 ...$15.00.
http://dx.doi.org/10.1145/2675133.2675209

allowing users to connect only with people they already know. Users attempting to add another user to their network are required to specify exactly how they are previously connected to the person; otherwise, they must provide the person's email address or ask to be introduced by a mutual acquaintance.

Recently, however, an SNS with a tie-formation strategy based on interest homophily has gained prominence: Pinterest. Pinterest is a social network site centered around the curation and sharing of visual content. Since its inception in 2010, it has grown extremely rapidly, reaching 10 million monthly unique visitors faster than any SNS ever[17] and boasting 70 million users by June 2013 [55]. A 2013 Pew Internet Survey [20] found that 21% of all Internet users in the US use Pinterest. By early 2014, Pinterest was driving 7.1% of all referrals to purchasing sites, second only to Facebook [19]. Pinterest has attracted much attention from marketers, due to its 'aspirational' nature [49, 47], with users using the site to find and share products and services that they would like to buy. The site uses the metaphor of virtual 'pinboards' on which images and other media (known as ***pins***) are 'pinned'. An example of a ***board*** (a collection of pins on a specific topic) is found in Figure 1.

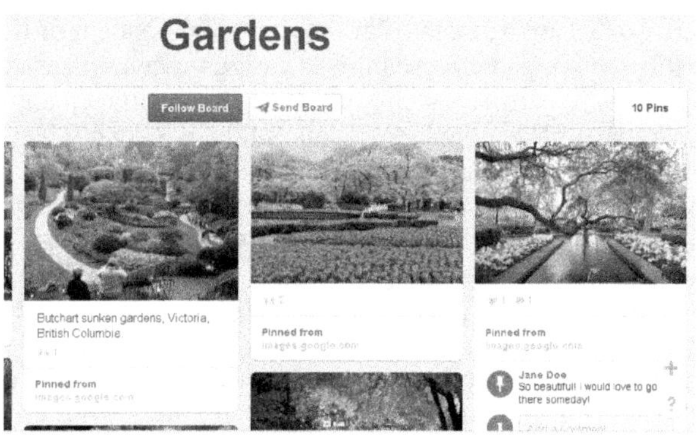

Figure 1: An example of a Pinterest board in the 'Gardening' category (see next section).

Hall and Zarro [29] use the term ***social curation*** to describe the activity on Pinterest. Users collect pins, sometimes from the boards of other Pinterest users, sometimes from elsewhere on the Internet, and arrange them into topical collections. This process of selection and categorization adds value to the individual pieces of the collection and is referred to as ***curation*** [58]. The social element is introduced through the publicly viewable nature of these collections and the ability of users to "view, favorite...copy, and comment" [29] each others' content. Pinterest's focus on the *curation* of others' content is what separates it from other content-focused SNSs like Flickr and YouTube, which center around the creation and sharing of user-created media [61, 46].

Like other social network sites, Pinterest is built around the concept of a social graph, allowing users — known as ***pinners*** — to ***follow*** other users and be shown the content they post. Pinterest uses the ***social awareness stream*** [51] mechanism popularized by sites like Facebook and Twitter, called the ***home feed*** on Pinterest, which shows users all new content posted by the users they follow as it is posted. This method of finding relevant content by browsing through the content posted by one's friends has been labeled ***social browsing*** by Lerman and Jones [42]. Follow links on Pinterest are unidirectional — users can follow other users who do not follow them.

Unlike the relationship-centered SNSs described earlier, Pinterest relies on interest homophily to build its social graph. The site is centered on content, with all activity revolving around pins. Users are encouraged to follow others whose content they find interesting, rather than people they know offline. In fact, the recommended follow mechanism on Pinterest is following just specific boards, rather than whole users.[2] In the words of a Pinterest user quoted by Zarro, Hall, and Forte [68], Pinterest is a "community of people who don't know each other." In this way, Pinterest is attempting to create a new social graph, based not on pre-existing offline connections, but on mutual interests. While Pinterest, like Facebook, does provide a mechanism to find people on the site whom a user already knows, Pinterest carefully limits this to "friend[s] who share your interests."[3] Facebook, on the other hand, suggests that users "send a friend request to any of your friends that already have a Facebook account" and even invite to the site those who don't.[4] Pinterest further cements its emphasis on content as a basis for following by asking new users what topics they are interested in and presenting them with a selection of relevant boards to follow, rather than users.

On the surface, the interest-homophily tie-formation model seems to be highly successful on Pinterest. We found that the median number of followers per user is 106, more than both Facebook and Twitter at a later stage of their growth [60, 2]. In addition, Chang et al. [11] report that there is indeed a high degree of interest homophily in the Pinterest follow network. However, a social graph has little value on its own; its success can only be measured by how well it advances the goals of the site and its users — in this case, discovering, curating, and sharing visual content [11]. To the best of our knowledge, no one has yet examined the effectiveness of the Pinterest follow mechanism in achieving these goals.

In this paper, we examine following on Pinterest, exploring some intriguing questions. How effective is the Pinterest follow model at fostering content discovery, the spread of ideas, and interaction based on common interests? Following is essential to Pinterest's success as a social network site, but is it essential to the average Pinterest user's experience with the site? Can a follow mechanism based on interest homophily succeed on a large-scale, mainstream SNS?

To answer these questions, we turn to the ***activity graph***, the hidden network formed by interactions between users. A large body of work has shown that the network formed by linking users with their followers — the ***follow graph*** — contains incomplete information about users and their relationships. Studies of Facebook [64], Twitter [33], and Cyworld

[2]Though in practice most users choose to follow whole users; see the next section.

[3]http://help.pinterest.com/en/articles/find-your-friends

[4]https://www.facebook.com/help/336320879782850/

[15] all found that the activity graph is very different from the follow graph. Specifically, users tend to interact with only a small subset of their friends and followers [44, 33]; thus, relationship strength, and in turn, strength of influence, are difficult to predict using the follow graph alone [10, 59, 56]. On Pinterest, activity takes the form of liking, commenting on, and repinning other users' pins. These actions are the means through which content is curated and shared. Repinning is a curation action — reposting desired content in the user's own space. Liking can be a curation action as well, since users often like pins to save them for later, as described in the next section. Comments have less of a curation dimension and are therefore rare; all three are indications that other users have seen and reacted to the content. Activity can thus be viewed as traces that users leave behind when they view content; it can be used to track user viewing patterns that would otherwise be invisible. We therefore sample the implicit activity graph on Pinterest and compare it to the follow graph to determine whether the follow mechanism - through the medium of social browsing - is successfully promoting content discovery, curation, and sharing. To guide our examination, we formulate the following research questions.

RQ1: What is the relationship between followers and activity?

If following is indeed successful at fostering activity, we would expect to find a strong relationship between a user's number of followers and the amount of activity done to their pins. Does such a correlation indeed exist? Do followers and activity follow similar patterns in their relationships with other metrics, such as a user's number of pins?

RQ2: How heavily do followers interact with their followees' content?

If the follow mechanism is heavily utilized for content discovery, we would also expect most of a user's followers to engage with at least some of their content. We therefore ask: are most followers active on their followees' boards? If so, to what extent?

RQ3: Do users find content from sources other than their followees?

Do users primarily utilize their home feeds when finding interesting content, and therefore only see (and curate) content from the users they follow? Or do they make use of other sources for pins as well?

RQ4: Do users follow the 'out-of-network' users or boards whose content they interact with?

Pinterest provides several mechanisms outside the home feed to help users discover content from pinners they do not follow, including search and featured content pages. The site encourages users to follow the boards or pinners where they found the content. This will allow them to see more, potentially similar, content from the user or board in the future. Do users avail themselves of this option?

The answers to these questions may shed some light on the importance of the follow mechanism for content discovery and curation.

We present the following results:

- Though following is supposed to be based on mutual interests, only a small percentage of a user's followers interact with the user's content or add any of it to their own collections. On average, only 12.3% of a user's followers like, comment, or repin any of their pins.
- A large majority (>70%) of the activity on a user's posts comes from users who are not their followers. Those followers who do interact, however, perform nearly 2.5 times more actions, on average, than non-followers. This suggests that users find content to curate in locations other than their home feeds or the boards of those they follow.

  Users who collect content from the Popular or Category pages do not generally proceed to follow the pinners of that content or their boards, though Pinterest encourages them to do so; an average Popular pin receives 673 likes, comments, and repins, but the user who posted it gains just one new follower for every 450 of these interactions; more than half gain no followers at all.
- Taken together, our results suggest that following is neither heavily utilized for nor strongly effective at promoting content discovery, curation, and sharing on Pinterest.In this way, Pinterest differs significantly from Flickr, another SNS focused on visual content, where following and the resultant social browsing has been shown to be important for content discovery [42].

The remainder of this paper is structured as follows. In the Background section, we provide an overview of Pinterest and define the terms we use in the rest of the paper. We then discuss related work. We devote the next section to describing our sampling and data collection methods, along with the resulting dataset. In the Data Analysis section, we report the results obtained from our analysis of the dataset; we then discuss their implications in a section entitled Discussion. Finally, we conclude and propose some ideas for future work.

BACKGROUND

Overview of Pinterest

Pinterest describes itself as "a place to discover ideas for all your projects and interests, hand-picked by people like you."[5] It's billed as a 'virtual pinboard' service, where users can easily 'pin' digital content they find interesting or useful and share it with others. The central entity on Pinterest is the ***pin***. A pin is an image or video, often accompanied by a caption. Pins can be uploaded by the user, but the vast majority are reposted from somewhere else on the Web [24]; these link back to the original source when clicked on. Users, or ***pinners***, ***pin*** content onto their ***boards*** — pages, usually organized around a specific theme, where pins are laid out in an informal style reminiscent of a physical pinboard. Pinterest's trademark layout is designed for maximum visual appeal: pins are displayed in neat rectangles of varying heights in a grid pattern that continuously loads new content as the viewer scrolls down. Clicking on a pin opens it on a separate

[5]https://about.pinterest.com/en

page with more detail. See Figure 1 in the Introduction for an example of a board.

User profiles on Pinterest are relatively basic: users can add a profile picture, a brief description, and their location, as well as links to Facebook, Twitter, and/or a personal website. Also displayed are the user's number of boards and pins and the number of pins they have liked, as well as the number of other users they follow (called 'following') and the number of followers they have. The rest of the profile page is devoted to the user's boards. Like pins, the board 'teasers' on a user's profile page are laid out as small rectangles in a grid, and display several images from the board. Every board on Pinterest belongs to a topical category (or 'Other'), and the pins on each board are supposed to fit that topic.

Pinterest users can connect with other users by ***following*** them. New pins from followed boards or users show up in a follower's ***home feed***, similar to a Facebook news feed, which they see when they open Pinterest. Follow edges in Pinterest are directed; pinners can follow other users who do not follow them back, and following someone does not require their permission. Since pinners often have boards on many different topics, users are encouraged to follow only those boards which interest them. However, Ottoni et al. found that in practice, users overwhelmingly (~90%) choose to follow other pinners entirely rather than single boards [53]. As well, despite the site's emphasis on following boards over users, board followers and followees are counted in the user's general follower and followee counts on his/her profile page. Users can also create and join group boards, some of which have thousands of pinners posting content to them. Each user is also allowed up to 3 secret boards, which are only visible to the owner(s).

There are three main types of interaction on Pinterest: likes, comments, and repins. According to the Pinterest help page, "Like a pin when you want to say Hey you! Neat idea!" When a user likes a pin, it is also saved to the 'Likes' page in her profile, so pinners will often like pins that they want to be easily able to find later. Users can also comment on a pin; comments are displayed beneath the pin on the board. Finally, users can repin a pin to one of their own boards. Since Pinterest's goal is primarily *curation* of content [25], rather than creation, repins are treated no differently than ordinary pins: they are displayed on the user's board and in her followers' home feeds without even an indication that they were originally pinned by someone else. We use the term post to include both pinning and repinning. Any logged-in user can like, comment on, or repin any other user's pins, without needing to follow the user or board. We visualize the Pinterest data model and the interactions between entities in Figure 2.

Pinterest provides several methods for content discovery besides the home feed. A continuously changing sample of pins from boards in each category are reposted on the Category pages, accessible from a drop-down menu on the site header. There is also a 'Popular' page, where popular pins from around the site are displayed, and a search box for finding pins, boards, or users matching a search term.

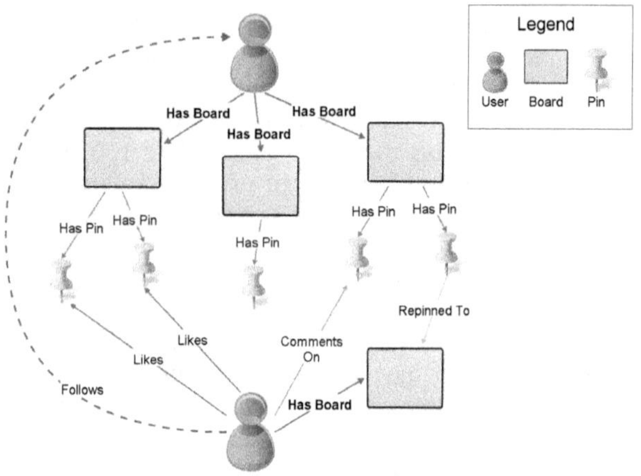

Figure 2: The Pinterest data model. Note that it is not necessary to follow a user in order to repin, like, or comment on their pins.

Definitions

In this section, we define some of the terms we use.

Follow graph: a graph representation of the users in a social network where vertices represent users and the edges between users are formed by users following (directed) or friending (undirected) each other

Activity graph: a graph representation of the users in a social network where the directed edges between users represent interactions between them. Two users A and B are connected in the activity graph if there was an interaction of some sort between them. ***Activity link***: an edge in the activity graph, formed by an interaction between the users at its ends.

Follow link: an edge in the follow graph, formed by a friend/follower relationship.

Pinterest activity link: a like, comment, or repin *received by* a user. Though the interaction is technically with the pin itself, it creates a link to the pin's owner. In this work, we calculate per-user statistics based on *incoming* activity — actions done *to* a user's content, rather than *by* the user.

Post: A pin or repin. These are not distinguished in Pinterest, but we use this term here for clarity.

RELATED WORK

Pinterest

Pinterest is a fairly new site, and its lack of an API has created an additional barrier to its study. A few analyses of Pinterest, however, have been published very recently. Gilbert et al. [25] attempt to determine what drives user behavior on Pinterest by calculating the contribution that various factors (such as the gender and nationality of the original pinner) have to the likelihood of a pin's being repinned and the number of followers a user attracts. They also compare the language used by the same users on Pinterest and on Twitter and determine that there are significant differences. Feng et al. [24] study user behavior on Pinterest, but they confine their analysis to the static follow graph; they also study the content and categories of pins, particularly popular ones. Mittal et al. analyze various aspects of Pinterest, including some user characteristics, the distribution of user locations, and pin sources. They also address privacy and copyright issues and find many instances of personal data leakage and copyright violations on Pinterest. Finally, they find that they can predict gender of Pinterest users with high accuracy [48]. Gender differences in Pinterest are a popular topic of study; Ottoni et al. [53] quantify the differences in Pinterest behavior between male and female users. Chang and colleagues [11] also study gender, specifically, the types of content favored by, and degree of specialization of, the two genders. They also report that homophily — here defined as similarity in interests — has a large influence on repinning, but a smaller one on following. Kamath et al. [36] build a model to automatically recommend boards that users might like. Zarro et al. [68] studied Pinterest from a qualitative perspective through user interviews. They found that users see Pinterest as a content provider rather than a social network. This was confirmed by the findings of Han et al. [30], who showed that repinning is mostly driven by the pin's content rather than user characteristics.

Activity Graph

The concept of the implicit activity network in an online social network and the fact that it differs from the explicit follow network was first proposed by [15], who analyzed the topographical characteristics of both the follow and activity networks of Cyworld, a Korean SNS. They found that the one-way interaction network had a similar topology to the follow network, but the reciprocal 'friends' network was quite different, more similar to known topologies of offline social networks than to the usual characteristics of online social networks. Ahn et al. [1] had previously made a similar observation about the testimonial network on Cyworld, but did not extend their results to the concept of the activity graph in general. Wilson and colleagues [64] performed a very similar analysis on Facebook, referring to the implicit network as the interaction graph.They found significant differences between the follow graph and the interaction graph, once again finding that the interaction graph displays the small-world properties typical of online social network graphs to a lesser extent than the follow graph does. Viswanath, et. al. [63] studied the evolution of activity links over time and discovered that Facebook activity links change over time, but many of the graph-theoretic properties of the activity graph did not. The Twitter interaction graph was studied by Huberman et al. [33], who found that most users interact closely with only a small subset of their followers. This disparity was confirmed in the case of Facebook by the Facebook Data Science team, who, with access to all of Facebook's user data, showed that the number of active reciprocal relationships per user was much smaller than the user's friend count [44].

Tie Formation and Homophily in Social Networks

A large body of research exists in sociology and psychology on tie formation and homophily, too numerous to cite here. We refer readers to McPherson et al.'s literature review on homophily [45], and Donath and boyd's discussion of some previous work on tie formation [18]. Here we briefly list research on homophily and tie formation in online social networks. Lauw et al. found that users on LiveJournal with similar interests were more likely to be friends [40], but the much larger study of Bisgin et al. found no evidence of interest homophily on several social network sites [4]. Macskassy and Michelson found that models that take homophily into account better fit retweet behavior on Twitter than those that don't [43]. Kivran-Swaine et al. [37], Quercia et al. [54], and Kwak et al. [38] studied the breaking of ties on social network sites. Romero and Kleinberg looked at the process of directed closure in social networks through the lens of follow links on Twitter [57]. There is also a large amount of work on modelling ties [67] and predicting link formation in SNSs, including [26, 34, 27].

DATA COLLECTION & DESCRIPTION

As discussed in the introduction, we concentrated on the activity graph rather than the follow graph. Instead of crawling follower edges, we followed activity links between users (though we did collect follow links as well for crawled users). As is common in social network analysis, analyzing the entire Pinterest graph was impractical; we therefore did our analyses on a sample of the network. Since unique ids on Pinterest are text-based, random sampling was difficult. In addition, Pinterest lacks an API, and employs various design techniques that make collecting all data for each user prohibitively expensive. We therefore used a modified Breadth-First Search (BFS) (that is, Snowball Sampling [28]) on the full graph to collect a sample of nodes and edges. We began the crawl from several randomly chosen seeds and moved outward by selecting a random subset of edge clusters and crawling all edges in each cluster. This is accomplished by randomly choosing 5 boards of each crawled user, and then crawling all activity links on each board. Likewise, we limited the number of pins collected per board to the first 300, since 90% of boards have 300 or fewer pins. On a similar SNS graph, Bonneau et al. [5] were able to estimate many graph properties using, as we do, a random sample of k edges from each node, even with very small k. Due to the extreme difficulty and expense of crawling large follower lists, we limited our analysis of activity from followers (see the end of the Data Analysis section) to users with 10,000 followers or fewer; this includes 99.96% of the users in our dataset.

We utilized a multithreaded crawler architecture for data collection. We ran the crawler for 5 weeks in December 2013 and January 2014 and collected the data described in Table 1. The first row consists of users whose incoming activity we sampled as described previously. For those users who liked or commented on one of the crawled pins, or followed one of the crawled users, we collected their real names, number of pins and number of followers (here denoted 'partial data'); 'users touched' includes the two categories above it, as well as users who repinned one of the pins in our dataset, for whom we have only their usernames. Boards are similar — we have full metadata, plus up to 350 pins, for the crawled boards, partial data (URL and number of pins) for an additional 2 million boards, and just the URL for the final ~2.9 million.

Dataset Details	
Crawled Users (with boards and pins)	31,644
Users (partial data)	4.5 million
Total Users touched	5.4 million
Crawled Boards	163,300
Boards (partial data)	2 million
Total Boards Touched	5.1 million
Total Pins Crawled	14 million
Total Repins	7 million
Total Likes	1.56 million
Total Comments	47,557

Table 1: Data Description

	Mean	Med.	Mode	Stdev	Max
Boards per User	30.1	19	12	41	2,310*
Pins per Board	138	39	1	563	100,228**
Followers per User	604	64	0	26,639	4,283,442

*All are group boards.
**This is the largest number of pins on a board with a single pinner. Group boards can have millions of pins.

Table 2: Statistics for the dataset. All mins are 0.

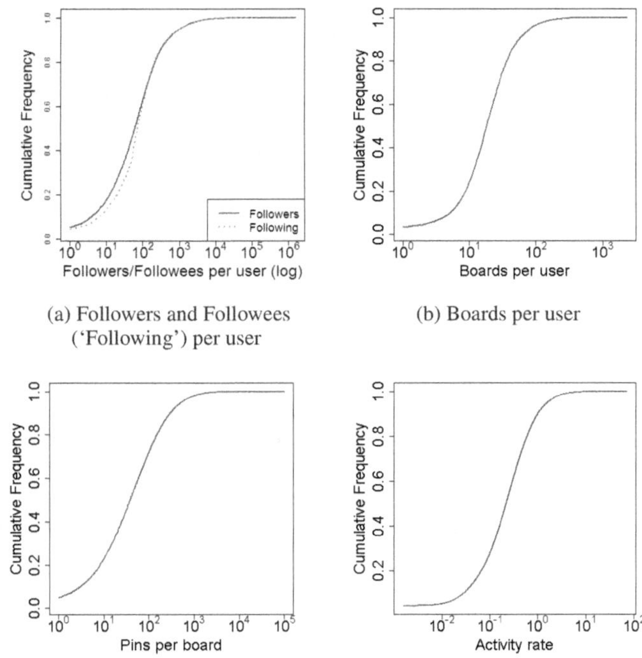

(a) Followers and Followees ('Following') per user

(b) Boards per user

(c) Pins per board

(d) Activity Rate per user

Figure 3: Cumulative frequency distributions of followers and followees (3a), boards (3b), and activity rate (3d) per user, and pins per board (3c), in log scale.

Descriptive Statistics

We first present some descriptive statistics about our dataset, including distribution of the three types of activity across users, boards, and pins. Table 2 contains basic statistics for numbers of boards, pins, and followers/following; corresponding distributions are shown in Figure 3.

Table 3 summarizes the activity links contained in our dataset. Figure 4 shows the distributions of likes, comments, and re-

	Mean	Med.	Stdev	Max
Activity per user	265.4	67	951.7	78,336
Activity per board	51.5	5	262.6	32,640
Repins per pin	0.47	0	4.4	1424
Likes per pin	0.11	0	1.5	755
Comments per pin	0.003	0	0.1	126

Table 3: Statistics for activity distribution. All mins and modes are 0.

pins across users, boards, and pins. While overall, there are 58 interactions (likes, comments, or repins) for every 100 pins, only 17.7% of pins have even a single interaction, due to the skew in the distribution of activity per pin. Repins are by far the most common type of activity, about 4 times more common than likes and nearly 150 times more than comments. They make up 81% of total activity recorded and, on average, 79% of activity on each board. Comments are extremely rare; just .3% of pins have even one comment. By contrast, 15.2% of the pins in our dataset were repinned at least once. We attribute this to the nature of Pinterest itself, where the primary goal is discovering and curating content (i.e. pins), with social interaction coming in a distant second. Comments by nature involve far more social interaction than repins; repinning just means that the repinner wants the content for herself, while commenting is usually a form of communication with others. In this aspect, Pinterest is different from Facebook, where liking is many times more common than resharing (even commenting is more common than resharing), and similar to Twitter, where resharing is more common than liking [50]. All of the distributions are very heavy-tailed, as is clear from the plots. The distribution of activity per pin is the most skewed; there are a few pins that seem to be more desirable or interesting, while others appear to be ignored. All of these distributions were so skewed that they had to be plotted on a log-log scale to be clearly visible.

Activity Rate

In this work, we use activity links as edges in the activity graph. When comparing activity between users, however, or even when comparing to the follow graph, the raw activity count is not a useful metric. Different users have different numbers of pins, so a large amount of activity may just be a function of having many pins. Activity (specifically reposting) per post is used as a measure of influence on Twitter by [59], and on Pinterest by [25]. We therefore use activity rate throughout this paper instead of raw activity

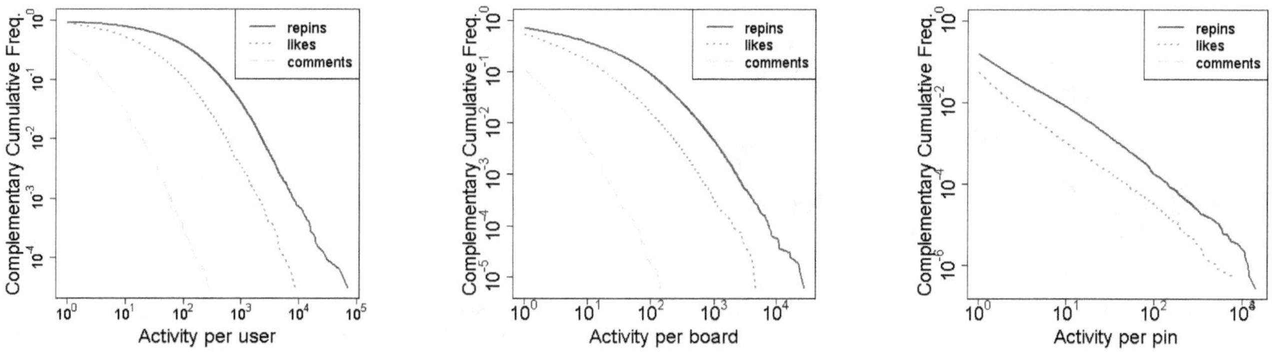

(a) Activity per user

(b) Activity per board

(c) Activity per pin. Comments were so rare that they did not show up in the plot, even in log-log scale.

Figure 4: Complementary cumulative frequency distributions of activity per: user (4a), board (4b), and pin (4c). The distributions are plotted on a log-log scale so that they can be shown on the same plot; despite this, the number of comments per pin is so small that the distribution line disappears off the side of even a log-log plot.

counts. As would be expected from the activity distributions shown above, activity rates vary widely. Some users have large amounts of activity per pin, while others have next to none: the minimum activity rate in our sample is 0, while the maximum belongs to the Pinterest account of the popular children's retailer Carter's — the brand averages 105 likes, repins, or comments per pin. The distribution of activity rate for the users in our sample is shown in Figure 3d.

DATA ANALYSIS

Followers and Activity — RQ1

We now begin to address our research questions, beginning with RQ1, the relationship between number of followers and activity rate. A strong relationship between followers and activity would suggest that users are engaged with the content of their followees. Figure 5a shows the number of followers per user plotted against the user's activity rate, both on a log scale so differences are clearly visible. Each hexagon represents multiple points, as shown on the key to the right of the plot, with lighter areas representing more data points. Spearman's ρ correlation coefficient between the number of followers and the activity rate is 0.55, and the R^2 goodness-of-fit is 0.26.[6] The above correlation includes users with many hundreds of thousands or millions of followers who bear little resemblance to 'ordinary' pinners; we therefore exclude the top 5% of users by follower count ($>$ 924 followers), as well as users with fewer than 5 followers. The scatterplot of followers and activity rate for these 'average' users is shown in Figure 5b. Here, the correlation is $\rho = 0.44$, with an R^2 of 0.19. These correlations are moderately high; we therefore continue to further analysis.

Pins, Followers, and Activity Links

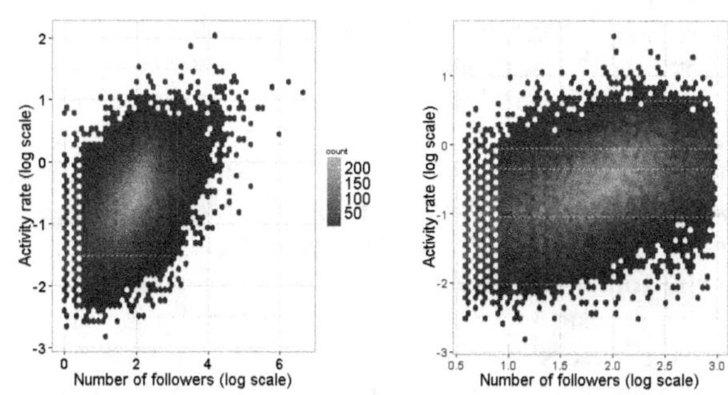

(a) Followers and activity rate for all users.

(b) Followers and activity rate for users with 5–924 followers.

Figure 5: Followers and Activity for: 5a) all users; 5b) the middle 85% of users by follower count. Each hexagon contains the amount of data points indicated by its color; lighter areas have more data points.

To shed more light on the relationship between following and activity rate, we compare each one with a third measure: pin count. If following and activity rate parallel each other closely, we would expect to see similar relationships between each of them and pin count. Figure 6a plots number of pins against follower count for each user in our sample. Spearman's ρ here is 0.78, and R^2 is 0.3. Figure 6b shows the activity rate plotted against the number of pins, using the same methodology as Figure 6a. Here, Spearman's ρ is 0.32, and R^2 is 0.06.

The relationship between pins and activity rate is much weaker than between pins and followers. This can be seen on the scatterplot; both the entire mass of data points and the lighter (denser) area are nearly circular, denoting a weak relationship between the two variables. This difference casts some doubt on the existence of a strong relationship between

[6] All correlations and R^2 values reported in this and the next subsections are statistically significant, $p < .0001$.

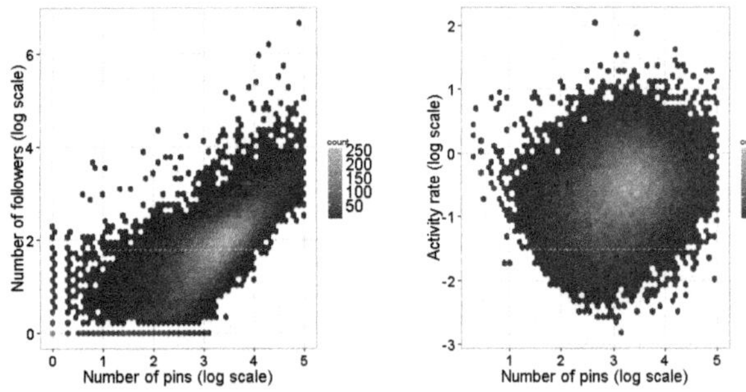

(a) Pins and followers. (b) Pins and activity rate.

Figure 6: Number of pins (x axis) plotted against edges in the follow graph (6a) and the activity graph (6b). (All axes are log scale.) Each hexagon contains the amount of data points indicated by its color; lighter areas have more data points.

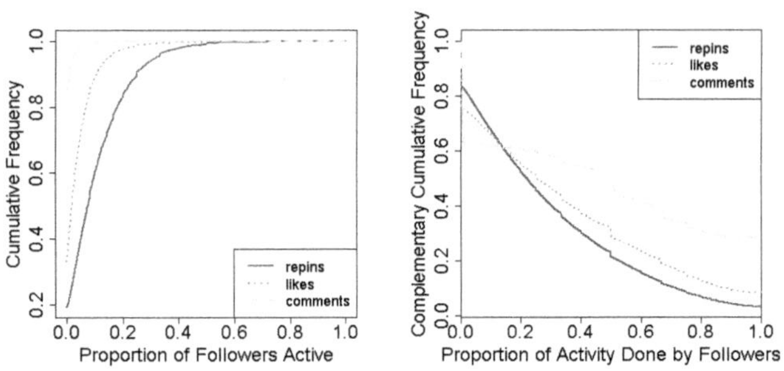

(a) Proportion of a user's followers who engaged in activity on the user's boards, by type of activity.

(b) Proportion of the activity on each user's boards done by their followers.

Figure 7: Activity by followers.

followers and activity. There does seem to be a relationship between pin count and follower count. It may be that people with more followers are more motivated to pin, or conversely, that users with more pins garner more followers. (Or there may be other factors causing both.) As for pins and activity rate, a correlation of 0.32 on SNS data is strong enough to confirm Wu et al.'s [66] finding of a positive feedback loop between feedback on posts and posting frequency. However, the relationship is clearly weaker than the correlation between pins and followers. Are pinners more motivated by follower count as a positive feedback measure than by activity? Or, perhaps, do users like following pinners with many pins but are less interested in acquiring (i.e. repinning) their content? These questions provide an intriguing base for further study.

Similar results have been reported for Twitter: Suh et al. [59] found a linear relationship between retweets and followers, but a lower correlation between numbers of tweets and retweets. For a direct comparison, we correlated just the repin rate with the number of pins, and found that the correlation between number of pins and repins was far lower ($\rho = 0.34$) than between the number of pins and followers, reported above.

Activity without Followers

We also examined the extreme end of our dataset: users who have no followers at all but nevertheless have activity on their pins. These users make up about 1.4% of our dataset, and strengthen the case for following being less than essential for content discovery; obviously, other users managed to find the content of these pinners, despite their having no followers.

Active Followers — RQ2

We now address RQ2, whether followers interact with their followees' content. Understanding the way users interact with the others they follow and those they don't is crucial to evaluating whether the follow mechanism is utilized for content discovery and sharing. It is well-known that only a small percentage of users' followers actively interact with them. This has been shown for Facebook, Twitter, and Cyworld (see the Related Work section). However, since following on Pinterest is supposed to be based on shared interests — a way to find new content to curate, and 'interactions' are mostly just a way of collecting content, we would expect users to receive interactions from a large percentage of their followers. We find, however, that this is not true: on average, only 12.3% of a user's followers have ever engaged in even a single action (like, comment, or repin) on any of the user's pins. The distributions of percentages of followers interacting for each user with any activity on the boards we crawled is shown in Figure 7a. Likes and comments once again have a more uneven distribution than repins; not only do those users who do interact comment and like much less than they repin, there are also *fewer* users who engage in either of the two activities than who repin. Even repins are only done by a small percentage of followers: only 19% of users have ever received even a single repin from more than 20% of their followers.

Content from Other Sources — RQ3

Unlike some SNSs, Pinterest is an open network — that is, users are not limited to interacting with their friends. Any user can like, comment on, or repin any other user's pins, without having to follow that user. This means that users can potentially find content for their 'collections' in places other than their home feeds or the boards of their followees. We wish to determine whether this capability is utilized by Pinterest users. Do they take content from users whom they don't follow? If so, how often? What percentage of activity does non-follower activity represent?

Figure 7b shows the distribution of the proportion of all repins, likes, and comments that are done by followers, for each user with at least one instance of the corresponding activity on their crawled boards. For the majority of users, only a small percentage of the interaction on their boards is from their followers (board or full-user) — the median is 24%. The remaining 76% are likes, comments, and repins done by non-followers. This is very different from Flickr, where between 47% and 71% (depending on photo visibility) of all interactions (comments) come from followers [42]. To confirm that these percentages were not skewed by a few prolific non-followers who engaged in a large amount of activity, we extracted the number of *unique* non-followers who interacted with each user's content. The median is 34, showing that most users have a significant number of non-followers interacting with their content; each non-follower contributes an average of just 1.4 actions. Non-following interacters make up a median of 88% of all unique users interacting with a user's pins.

These non-followers clearly discovered the content in this case somewhere other than their home feeds. (Since they are not following that user or board and therefore do not see the user's content in their home feed.) Yet they make up the vast majority of unique users interacting with the content. Together, these statistics strongly imply that users discover a great deal of the content they collect for themselves in places other than their home feeds, or their followers' boards.

Following as a result of content discovery — RQ4

Until now, we have discussed following as a driver of content discovery. In this section, we discuss following as a *result* of content discovery. As part of its mission to help users find content they like, Pinterest provides various mechanisms for content discovery besides the home feed. As we described previously, there are several pages containing a sampling of content from around the site. Among these are the Category pages, each with a sampling of pins from that category; and a Popular page, which hosts a continuous feed of pins with a large amount of activity. The pins remain on the boards of the users who posted them, but they can be interacted with from these 'sample' pages without visiting the original board; all activity done to a pin while on one of these pages is counted as part of the pin's activity as displayed on the original board. Users can browse these pages to find content and repin it to their own boards. They can also use the search feature to search for pins that match their keywords. Commensurate with its emphasis on following, Pinterest recommends that once a user finds and possibly interacts with new content, they should follow the board where the content was posted, or the entire pinner.[7] After all, if they liked this pin, they may like the other content on that board or pinned by that user as well. The idea that repins and likes on the Category or Popular pages are the gateway to new followers is frequently posited by Pinterest users and marketing experts [9].

We set out to investigate whether users do indeed go on to follow the users or boards whose pins they discover through search or the Category and Popular pages. The high proportion of non-follower activity that we reported in the previous section is the first indication we find that this behavior may not be very common. We assume that following that results from content discovery occurs within a fairly short time after the discovery and interaction. Thus, if the non-followers had indeed followed the user or board after interacting with the content, they would have been listed in our dataset as followers, since we crawled each board only once.[8] To further investigate, we compared the average number of actions contributed by each interacting follower of a user to the average number of interactions from each interacting non-follower. Each interacting non-follower contributes 1.4 interactions, on average, while the average interacting follower produces 3.4, almost almost two-and-a-half times as many (difference in means is significant, $p < .0001$). This difference suggests that non-followers, who have to find the board in some other way than viewing its pins in their home feed, seem to mostly find individual pins and do not interact with the rest of the pins on the board.

Being 'Popular' does not increase follower count

Lacking site usage data and search logs, we cannot trace the content that users found when searching. We do, however, have access to the Popular and Category pages. We therefore attempt to determine whether users who find interesting content on one of these pages go on to explore the rest of that pinner's content. We repeatedly visited the Popular page and collected a randomly-chosen single pin from the top row of pins (these are the most visible) as soon as it appeared on the page. We then crawled the board where each pin originated from,[9] once immediately and then again several hours later, after people had a chance to see the pin and possibly click through to, and follow, the board or user. We collected 1,013 Popular pins and found that, on average, each Popular pin had 673 likes, comments, and repins. (None had less than 111; 45% had over 500, and nearly a quarter had over 1,000.) In the vast majority of cases, the large amount of activity was clearly a result of being featured, since each popular pin had a median of 224 times more activity than an average pin on the same board. Despite all this activity, 60% of boards and 56% of users did not gain a single follower, and 80% gained 3 or fewer — a per-user average gain of one new follower for every 450 repins, likes, and comments — for those who gained at all. In addition, the majority of the 15% of users who did gain seven or more followers already had six or seven-digit numbers of followers; many are large retailers or successful bloggers with high visibility outside of Pinterest and multiple avenues for acquiring new followers. These factors mean that the additional followers they gained cannot be easily attributed to one of their pins being featured on the Popular page. Nor do users seem particularly interested in the other pins on the original board of a Popular pin; 70% of boards containing a Popular pin see no extra activity on their other pins after the pin is featured; those which do get some additional activity get a single repin, like, or comment on the non-featured pins for every 146 actions on the featured one.

It seems, then, that users do not go on to follow the 'out-of-network' users (or boards) whose content they discover and collect. After a pin is listed on the Popular page and receives high visibility and a large amount of additional activity, the number of followers of the user and board it belongs to barely change. We also found a wide disparity between the number of interactions on the Popular pins and the rest of the pins on the same board. This difference obviously cannot be accounted for by activity from the board's followers, since that

[7] http://help.pinterest.com/en/guide/following-and-your-home-feed

[8] Of course, there is always the small possibility that we managed to visit the page in the short time between when a user interacted with a pin and when they followed its pinner, but the chance of that happening is low enough that we assume that the number of pins affected, if any, is not significant.

[9] The first 100–300 pins; these are most likely to be looked at by a casual visitor.

should affect all pins. Nor can it be explained by differences in topic, since all pins on a board generally belong to the same category. It is likely that the additional activity came from non-followers who found the pin on the Popular page, but may not have even clicked through to the board. These users also do not appear to go on to follow the pinners who posted the content they enjoyed.

DISCUSSION

The results we present above show that the follow mechanism on Pinterest, and the resultant i.e. social browsing, does not seem to be very heavily utilized by users for content discovery and curation. The role of the home feed seems to be smaller than might be expected, given the site's emphasis on following as a driver of content discovery. We speculate that users see Pinterest as something of a 'mini-Web', an interlinked network of content that can be easily searched, browsed, and bookmarked.

Unlike Twitter and Facebook, for instance, Pinterest is not very time-bound; much of the content on it can still be relevant and engaging long after it was posted. The live-stream aspect of the home feed is therefore less essential. It is also (deliberately) centered around content, rather than people, which reduces the necessity for following: a status update about a friend's new baby is only interesting because you know the friend; a pin about a great recipe is useful even when it comes from a stranger. Pinterest may have hoped that this content-centrism would mean that people would follow others they didn't know solely for their content. What actually seems to be happening, however, is that people turn to other methods of content discovery, as discussed above. The many mechanisms that the site provides for finding desirable content means that users don't have to wait for their followees to post something interesting — they can look for it themselves.

Our findings have important implications for those who wish to promote goods or ideas on Pinterest. Rather than just seeking to maximize their number of followers, they will have to develop ways to engage with large numbers of users who have no interest in following them. These users may be very open, however, to repinning and otherwise engaging with their content.

Our results also add to the sparse existing knowledge on interest-based homophily on social network sites. While the example of Pinterest shows that it is possible to build a follow network based solely on common interests, it also shows that this network may not be robust enough to be heavily used by its members for content discovery when more attractive options are available.

CONCLUSION AND FUTURE WORK

In this paper, we study the effectiveness and utilization of the Pinterest follow mechanism for content discovery. Pinterest encourages users to form follow links on the site based on interest homophily, or similarity of interests. We sample user activity, in particular the curation and interaction actions of liking, commenting, and repinning, and examine it to determine whether or not users commonly use following and their home feeds as a way to find new content. We find that followers are not very active on the boards of their followees - on average, only 12.3% of a user's followers interact with any of the user's pins. Conversely, $> 75\%$ of the activity on an average user's boards is done by a large number of non-followers - 88% of all unique interacters on an average user's boards are non-followers. Users also do not seem to follow the boards or users that provide the content that they interact with, despite Pinterest's recommendation that they do so. Our results show that following seems to be a second-class mechanism for content discovery on Pinterest.

In this paper, we have mostly discussed characteristics of user interaction that can be extracted from the activity network. In the future, we would like to collect a larger, more fully connected dataset and examine various graph properties of the activity graph itself. We hope that this analysis will shed more light on Pinterest and the unique dynamics of user activity on a content-centered social network site. In particular, we are interested in the study of influence on Pinterest. Influence in social networks is an important topic of study because of the opportunities it presents for those who want to maximize the spread of ideas or advertising. Given the findings we present in this paper, we have reason to believe that the mechanisms of influence on Pinterest are both similar and different to those in other SNSs, and we would like to explore them in greater detail.

ACKNOWLEDGEMENTS

Bluma Gelley thanks Dan Pelleg, Mark Shovman, and Ido Guy for helpful discussions and valuable input. The authors thank Dorée Duncan Seligmann for her input in the preliminary stages of this work.

REFERENCES

1. Ahn, Y.-Y., et al. Analysis of topological characteristics of huge online social networking services. In *Proceedings of WWW 2007* (2007), 835–844.
2. Bakshy, E., et al. Everyone's an influencer: Quantifying influence on Twitter. In *Proceedings of WSDM 2011* (2011), 65–74.
3. Barabási, A.-L., and Albert, R. Emergence of scaling in random networks. *Science 286*, 5439 (1999), 509–512.
4. Bisgin, H., Agarwal, N., and Xu, X. Investigating homophily in online social networks. In *Proceedings of WI-IAT 2010*, vol. 1 (2010), 533–536.
5. Bonneau, J., et al. Eight friends are enough: Social graph approximation via public listings. In *Proceedings of WOSN 2009* (2009), 13–18.
6. boyd, d. Friendster and publicly articulated social networks. In *Proceedings of CHI 2004* (2004).
7. boyd, d., and Ellison, N. B. Social network sites: Definition, history, and scholarship. *Journal of Computer-Mediated Communication 13*, 1 (2007), 210–230.
8. Capocci, A., et al. Preferential attachment in the growth of social networks: The Internet encyclopedia Wikipedia. *Physical Review E 74*, 3 (2006), 036116.

9. Cario, J. E. *Pinterest Marketing: An Hour a Day*. John Wiley & Sons, 2012.
10. Cha, M., et al. Measuring user influence in Twitter: The million follower fallacy. In *Proceedings of ICWSM 2010*, vol. 10 (2010), 10–17.
11. Chang, S., et al. Specialization, homophily, and gender in a social curation site: Findings from Pinterest. In *Proceedings of CSCW 2014* (2014), 674–686.
12. Chen, W., Wang, C., and Wang, Y. Scalable influence maximization for prevalent viral marketing in large-scale social networks. In *Proceedings KDD 2010* (2010), 1029–1038.
13. Chen, W., Wang, Y., and Yang, S. Efficient influence maximization in social networks. In *Proceedings of KDD 2009* (2009), 199–208.
14. Choi, J. H.-j. Living in Cyworld: Contextualising Cy-ties in South Korea. In *Uses of Blogs*, A. Bruns and J. Jacobs, Eds. Peter Lang, New York, 2006, 173–186.
15. Chun, H., et al. Comparison of online social relations in volume vs interaction: A case study of Cyworld. In *Proceedings of IMC 2008* (2008), 57–70.
16. Cole, J., and Lebo, H. Surveying the digital future report. *USC Annenberg School Center for the Digital Future* (2013).
17. Constine, J. Pinterest hits 10 million u.s. monthly uniques faster than any standalone site ever -comscore. `http://techcrunch.com/2012/02/07/pinterest-monthly-uniques/`, 2012.
18. Donath, J., and boyd, d. Public displays of connection. *BT technology Journal 22*, 4 (2004), 71–82.
19. D'Onfro, J. This chart shows why pinterest is way more important than twitter or reddit for traffic referrals. `http://www.businessinsider.com/pinterest-advertising-big-deal-2014-4`, 2014.
20. Duggan, M., and Smith, A. Social media update 2013. *Pew Internet and American Life Project* (December 30, 2013).
21. Ellison, N. B., and boyd, d. Sociality through social network sites. *The Oxford handbook of Internet studies* (2013), 151.
22. Ellison, N. B., Steinfield, C., and Lampe, C. The benefits of Facebook"friends": Social capital and college students use of online social network sites. *Journal of Computer-Mediated Communication 12*, 4 (2007), 1143–1168.
23. Ellison, N. B., Steinfield, C., and Lampe, C. Connection strategies: Social capital implications of Facebook-enabled communication practices. *New Media & Society* (2011), 1461444810385389.
24. Feng, Z., et al. An empirical study of user behaviors on Pinterest social network. In *Proceedings of WI-IAT 2013*, vol. 1 (2013), 402–409.
25. Gilbert, E., et al. I need to try this?: A statistical overview of Pinterest. In *Proceedings of CHI 2013* (2013), 2427–2436.
26. Gilbert, E., and Karahalios, K. Predicting tie strength with social media. In *Proceedings of CHI 2009* (2009), 211–220.
27. Golder, S. A., and Yardi, S. Structural predictors of tie formation in Twitter: Transitivity and mutuality. In *Proceedings of SocialCom 2010* (2010), 88–95.
28. Goodman, L. A. Snowball sampling. *The Annals of Mathematical Statistics 32*, 1 (1961), 148–170.
29. Hall, C., and Zarro, M. Social curation on the website Pinterest.com. *Proceedings of the American Society for Information Science and Technology 49*, 1 (2012), 1–9.
30. Han, J., et al. Collecting, organizing, and sharing pins in Pinterest: Interest-driven or social-driven? In *Proceedings of SIGMETRICS 2014* (2014).
31. Henry, A. How Facebook is using you to annoy your friends (and how to stop it). `http://lifehacker.com/5987248/how-facebook-is-using-you-to-annoy-your-friends-and-how-to-stop-it`, 2013.
32. Hodkinson, P. Subcultural blogging? online journals and group involvement among UK Goths. In *Uses of blogs*, A. Bruns and J. Jacobs, Eds. Peter Lang, New York, 2006, 187–198.
33. Huberman, B., Romero, D. M., and Wu, F. Social networks that matter: Twitter under the microscope. *First Monday 14*, 1 (2008).
34. Hutto, C., Yardi, S., and Gilbert, E. A longitudinal study of follow predictors on Twitter. In *Proceedings of CHI 2013* (2013).
35. Incite, N. Friends & frenemies: Why we add and remove Facebook friends. *State of Social Media Survey* (2011).
36. Kamath, K. Y., Popescu, A.-M., and Caverlee, J. Board recommendation in Pinterest. In *Proceedings of UMAP Workshops 2013* (2013).
37. Kivran-Swaine, F., Govindan, P., and Naaman, M. The impact of network structure on breaking ties in online social networks: Unfollowing on Twitter. In *Proceedings of CHI 2011* (2011), 1101–1104.
38. Kwak, H., Moon, S. B., and Lee, W. More of a receiver than a giver: Why do people unfollow in Twitter? In *Proceedings of ICWSM 2012* (2012).
39. Lampe, C., Ellison, N., and Steinfield, C. A Face (book) in the crowd: Social searching vs. social browsing. In *Proceedings of CSCW 2006* (2006), 167–170.
40. Lauw, H. W., et al. Homophily in the digital world: A LiveJournal case study. *Internet Computing, IEEE 14*, 2 (2010), 15–23.

41. Lenhart, A., and Madden, M. Teens, privacy, and online social networks. *Pew Internet and American Life Project* (April 18,2007).

42. Lerman, K., and Jones, L. A. Social browsing on Flickr. In *Proceedings of ICWSM 2007* (2007).

43. Macskassy, S. A., and Michelson, M. Why do people retweet? Anti-homophily wins the day! In *Proceedings of ICWSM 2011* (2011).

44. Marlow, C., et al. Maintained relationships on Facebook. `http://overstated.net/2009/03/09/maintained-relationships-on-facebook`, 2009.

45. McPherson, M., Smith-Lovin, L., and Cook, J. M. Birds of a feather: Homophily in social networks. *Annual review of sociology* (2001), 415–444.

46. Miller, A. D., and Edwards, W. K. Give and take: A study of consumer photo-sharing culture and practice. In *Proceedings of CHI 2007* (2007), 347–356.

47. Minott, K. Is Pinterest an aspirational social network? `http://www.komverse.com/2013/04/04/is-pinterest-an-aspirational-social-network/`, 2013.

48. Mittal, S., et al. The pin-bang theory: Discovering the Pinterest world. *arXiv preprint arXiv:1307.4952* (2013).

49. Moore, R. J. Pinners be pinnin: How to justify Pinterests 3.8b valuation. `http://blog.rjmetrics.com/2014/05/07/pinners-be-pinnin-how-to-justify-pinterests-3-8b-valuation/`, 2014.

50. Motamedi, R., et al. Characterizing group-level user behavior in major online social networks. `http://onrg.cs.uoregon.edu/pub/CIS-TR-2013-09.pdf`, 2014.

51. Naaman, M., Boase, J., and Lai, C.-H. Is it really about me?: Message content in social awareness streams. In *Proceedings of CSCW 2010* (2010), 189–192.

52. Nogueira Cortimiglia, M., Ghezzi, A., and Renga, F. Social applications: Revenue models, delivery channels, and critical success factors-an exploratory study and evidence from the Spanish-speaking market. *Journal of theoretical and applied electronic commerce research 6*, 2 (2011), 108–122.

53. Ottoni, R., et al. Ladies first: Analyzing gender roles and behaviors in Pinterest. *Proceedings of ICWSM 2013* (2013), 457–465.

54. Quercia, D., Bodaghi, M., and Crowcroft, J. Losing friends on Facebook. In *Proceedings of WebSci 2012* (2012), 251–254.

55. report, S. Geolocation and activity analysis of Pinterest accounts by Semiocast. `http://semiocast.com/en/publications/2013_07_10_Pinterest_has_70_million_users`, 2013.

56. Romero, D. M., et al. Influence and passivity in social media. In *Machine learning and knowledge discovery in databases*. Springer, 2011, 18–33.

57. Romero, D. M., and Kleinberg, J. M. The directed closure process in hybrid social-information networks, with an analysis of link formation on Twitter. In *Proceedings of ICWSM 2010* (2010).

58. Seitzinger, J. Curate me! exploring online identity through social curation in networked learning. In *Proceedings of NLC 2014* (2014), 412–419.

59. Suh, B., et al. Want to be retweeted? Large scale analytics on factors impacting retweet in Twitter network. In *Proceedings of SocialCom 2010* (2010), 177–184.

60. Ugander, J., et al. The anatomy of the Facebook social graph. *arXiv preprint arXiv:1111.4503* (2011).

61. Van House, N. A. Flickr and public image-sharing: Distant closeness and photo exhibition. In *CHI'07 extended abstracts* (2007), 2717–2722.

62. Ver Steeg, G., and Galstyan, A. Information transfer in social media. In *Proceedings of WWW 2012* (2012), 509–518.

63. Viswanath, B., et al. On the evolution of user interaction in Facebook. In *Proceedings of WOSN 2009* (2009), 37–42.

64. Wilson, C., et al. User interactions in social networks and their implications. In *Proceedings of EuroSys 2009* (2009), 205–218.

65. Wirtz, B. W., Schilke, O., and Ullrich, S. Strategic development of business models: implications of the Web 2.0 for creating value on the Internet. *Long Range Planning 43*, 2 (2010), 272–290.

66. Wu, F., Wilkinson, D. M., and Huberman, B. A. Feedback loops of attention in peer production. In *Proceedings of CSE 2009*, vol. 4 (2009), 409–415.

67. Xiang, R., Neville, J., and Rogati, M. Modeling relationship strength in online social networks. In *Proceedings of WWW 2010* (2010), 981–990.

68. Zarro, M., Hall, C., and Forte, A. Wedding dresses and wanted criminals: Pinterest.com as an infrastructure for repository building. In *Proceedings of ICWSM 2013* (2013), 650–658.

Transition and Reflection in the Use of Health Information: The Case of Pediatric Bone Marrow Transplant Caregivers

Elizabeth Kaziunas[1], Ayse G. Buyuktur[1], Jasmine Jones[1], Sung W. Choi[2], David A. Hanauer[2,1], Mark S. Ackerman[1,3]

[1]School of Information, [2]Medical School, [3]EECS
University of Michigan, Ann Arbor
Ann Arbor, MI
{eskaziu, abuyuktu, jazzij, sungchoi, hanauer, ackerm}@umich.edu

ABSTRACT
The impact of health information on caregivers is of increasing interest to HCI/CSCW in designing systems to support the social and emotional dimensions of managing health. Drawing on an interview study, as well as corroborating data including a multi-year ethnography, we detail the practices of caregivers (particularly parents) in a bone marrow transplant (BMT) center. We examine the interconnections between information and emotion work performed by caregivers through a liminal lens, highlighting the BMT experience as a time of transition and reflection in which caregivers must quickly adapt to the new social world of the hospital and learn to manage a wide range of patient needs. The transition from parent to 'caregiver' is challenging, placing additional emotional burdens on the intensive information work for managing BMT. As a time of reflection, the BMT experience also provides an occasion for generative thinking and alternative approaches to health management. Our study findings call for health systems that reflect a design paradigm focused on 'transforming lives' rather than 'transferring information.'

Author Keywords
CSCW, health information, medical informatics, health informatics, caregiving, caregiver, pediatric, health and wellness, healthcare technology, reflection, social worlds.

ACM Classification Keywords : J.3 Life and Medical Sciences, Health, Medical Information Systems; H.5.2 User Interfaces, User-centered design; H.5.3 Group and organization Interfaces, Computer Supported Cooperative Work

General Terms
Design

http://dx.doi.org/10.1145/2675133.2675276

INTRODUCTION AND BACKGROUND
Bone marrow transplant (BMT) is used to treat a range of blood disorders and blood cell cancers such as leukemias and lymphomas. The procedure involves replacing unhealthy stem cells in the bone marrow with healthy ones harvested from the patient or a donor. BMT is often the only hope for a cure or for slowing down disease progress. It is an aggressive approach that takes a substantial toll on the patient's body.

Recipients constitute some of the most complex clinical cases due to the nature of the treatment and the serious risks it involves, the severity of the diseases for which transplant is done, and the heavy physical and psychosocial burdens. The BMT process is correspondingly challenging—clinically and emotionally—for patients and caregivers alike.

BMT, and especially pediatric BMT, is of considerable interest not only because the care process is so complex and difficult, but also because this setting offers critical insight into a number of wider sociotechnical healthcare issues being explored by the HCI and CSCW communities, such as supporting clinician-patient communication and managing chronic illness. As a growing number of specialized treatments are being developed for a range of health conditions, there is a need for patients and families (or in this case, parents and families), to access and understand clinical information in ways that are both expedient and meaningful. BMT differs from what is typically understood as chronic care in important ways – such as the amount of resources involved, including clinician time; however, it is similar in that BMT caregivers must collaborate closely with a team of healthcare professionals, learning the specialized language and the technical practices of medicine. Furthermore, as with many chronic illnesses, BMT intimately and profoundly shapes the everyday lives of patient, caregiver, and family.

In this study, we examined the lived experience for pediatric BMT caregivers. To do so, we considered the types of healthcare and interactional work caregivers and their families perform, and the meanings those activities hold for them. We found the high stakes of the pediatric

BMT process lead to considerable information work on the part of caregivers. Caregivers also engaged in a variety of emotion work to manage BMT. In documenting the interconnections between this information and emotion work, we found that the caregiving goals of families and clinical teams often misaligned, and that clinical information needed to be reconciled with the inclinations of a parent whose most pressing concerns may not necessarily coincide with the treatment protocol. The findings we present here therefore not only focus on the straight-forward information needs of caregivers, but also speak to the social tensions and emotional burdens that arise in managing a complex healthcare treatment.

We first discuss what is known in the CSCW and HCI literature about healthcare management at home, with children, and with caregivers (especially parents). We then discuss the framework we use in our analysis, that of Strauss et al.'s interaction work. We follow with a description of the site, our data collection, and the BMT process. Next, we present our findings about the information and emotion work parents do—detailed in terms of caregiving practices—as part of a process of moving from the social world of their everyday lives to a medical world and then back to a transformed everyday life. Finally, we explore the theoretical implications of the BMT caregiver experience, arguing that as people live amongst multiple social worlds, the relationship between clinical information and emotional inclinations needs to be understood as a negotiated activity, involving a form of labor that we call 'reflection work.'

RELATED WORK

Health Management in CSCW

There has been increasing interest in the CSCW/HCI communities to design systems that better support the social and emotional dimensions of managing a variety of health and wellness conditions [8, 9, 13, 14]. Furthermore, a number of studies in the CSCW/HCI literature have looked at the needs of parents in a variety of healthcare contexts as a space for technological support [6,12,19,20,23]. Although such studies have examined technologies to augment or facilitate consumer health, there are only a handful of caregiver-oriented ethnographic studies, especially of pediatric patients.

Important studies include Kientz [11], which examined the interactions between parents and pediatricians, describing tensions and challenges in this communication dynamic, including parents who had difficulty recalling and remembering details after consultation and asking questions of clinicians. Based on the study findings, Kientz recommended systems that help track information and include family members in shared health experiences via social media [11]. Toscos et al. [20] described how health-monitoring technology affects the parent-child relationship and highlighted the conflicts that can occur in the parent-child relationship in caregiving work. In a study of caregivers and high-risk infants, Liu et al. [12] noted that currently little has been done to design collaborative systems for parents of pediatric patients. In their discussion of information-sharing challenges, Liu et al. pointed to social isolation as a problem for parents of ill children and suggested social support tools for networks of friends, family members, and health professionals.

In this work, we draw heavily on the contributions of Chen [3], and in particular, Chen et al. [4], which presented a qualitative study of caregivers and highlighted the need in CSCW and HCI to better understand the situated practices of caregiving in people's everyday lives [4]. Drawing on Strauss, the authors discussed the 'identity work' caregivers engage in as they manage multiple 'selves' (e.g. physical, emotional, and social selves). Furthermore, the authors found that caregiving is both a collaborative and reflective endeavor calling attention to the need for management in 'social-emotion work' and reflective learning. We seek to extend Chen et al.'s [4] work through grappling with the specifics of contextualized caregiving work.

Framing Healthcare "Work"

In this paper, we draw upon the work of Anselm Strauss and colleagues for a general theoretical framing. Strauss contributed to many areas within health informatics and CSCW, the best known of which is articulation, or coordination, work. Strauss and colleagues [17, 18, 22], as well as Wiener et al. [22] and other related papers [17], described not only articulation work but also additional kinds of work in interaction and social activity in healthcare contexts. (For Strauss, and here in this paper, work is micro-interactional work, and is not necessarily conducted in formal workplace settings.)

Strauss largely analyzed the activities performed in medical settings by clinicians, such as safety work, or making sure that clinical processes wouldn't cause harm. As neither patients nor caregivers were the focus of Strauss' theoretical analysis, the two types of work in Strauss upon which we draw heavily for our analysis are 'patient-centered' in that they can also be performed by patients and/or caregivers. The first is sentimental work, also called emotion work; it is the intra- and inter-personal work involved in maintaining one's composure and self-control.

The second type is information work, which is generally under- theorized in Strauss et al. [18, 22]. Information work, as detailed in this writing, was premised on a conceptual model of straightforward information transfer that neglected to address social complexity. There has been a renewed interest in CSCW to articulate more contextually-situated understandings of information work [10, 15]. We follow these extensions of information work here, further contemplating the relationship between information and emotion work, in the intra-personal and inter-personal labor involved in making sense of different types of information that we term reflection work.

RESEARCH SITE AND STUDY METHODS

Our study was conducted at Hemphill Children's Hospital, a teaching hospital in the U.S. Midwest. Our specific site was the pediatric bone marrow transplant floor and clinic.

Data Collection

Our data include 10 semi-structured interviews with caregivers of pediatric BMT patients. These data were also informed by approximately 10 hours of observing hospital rounds and pre-BMT consults by the first author. Observations included attending meetings between caregivers, patients, and clinicians, as well as informal conversations held among BMT team members that included nurses, doctors, dieticians, pharmacists, and social workers. Observational data were recorded as fieldnotes and later transcribed. Additionally the analysis of blogs and social media sites maintained by interview participants added to our understanding of the pediatric BMT experience. Five distinct websites (with a total of 371 distinct posts), shared with us by interview participants, were analyzed and used to triangulate our interview and observational data.

The interviews were conducted with primary caregivers for BMT pediatric patients. Study participants were recruited through referrals from the BMT clinical team and included caregivers at varying stages of the BMT process, although all participants had experienced the transplant procedure and at the time of the interview were being treated in the outpatient clinic. Interviews were approximately an hour and were recorded and transcribed; children were recorded with the permission of their parents. These semi-structured interviews took place in a conference room at the pediatric BMT center. Semi-structured interviews explored (1) The participant's caregiver experience with BMT, (2) everyday caregiving practices, (3) the impact of BMT on family life, and (4) information needs in the BMT process.

Interview participants included 6 mothers, 3 fathers, and 1 grandmother who acted as caregivers. Participants came from a wide range of socio-economic backgrounds and family structures. Some participants were single parents working full-time to maintain insurance coverage, while other participants had the support of two full-time adult caregivers for the patient. Some participants were from intact, nuclear families; others were not. Age and education also varied as a number of caregivers had little or no higher education while others had several degrees and professional training in the sciences. We acknowledge that such demographic data shapes the BMT experience, and in this paper we have limited ourselves to reporting findings commonly articulated by caregivers across demographics.

During the interviews, additional family members and occasionally children going through the BMT process, would join the conversation and provide insight. While caregivers were the main focus of this study, we routinely observed an intimacy in the communication between children and their caregivers to the point where they would often finish one another's sentences. While acknowledging the child's role as a BMT patient as a unique experience unto itself (caregivers, in fact, often deferred to the patient's interpretations of medical events), it is also important to note that participants often spoke about the BMT experience in terms of "we" and "our family." This collective language perhaps points to the deep social impact of BMT and the close relationship between parent and child amplified by long days spent together in the hospital and clinic.

Our work has also been informed by a larger research project aimed at understanding the BMT experience. We also have conducted 3 focus groups of 26 individual participants involved in BMT that included 6 caregivers of BMT pediatric patients as part of a study (led by the fourth author), and a 2-year ethnographic study of adult BMT (by the second author). IRB approval for data collection was obtained along with participant consent.

Data Analysis

Our data analysis followed grounded theory [5,7] in that our data collection and analysis mutually informed one another. Four initial interviews were transcribed and analyzed using an open coding method by each researcher to identify significant concepts. These coded interviews were then discussed among four of the authors to ascertain main issues; for confidentiality reasons, only the non-medical researchers could see the raw data. During data analysis we collectively generated new codes as significant concepts were identified, compared, and revised. These codes were later used as probes in subsequent interviews. The second stage of data analysis with new data resulted in consistent themes and confirmed our findings. Fieldnotes and blog posts were read, coded, and analyzed in a similar manner during data analysis sessions. Analytical memos were also circulated and discussed among the group as theoretical insights emerged from the ongoing data collection.

BONE MARROW TRANSPLANT BACKGROUND

The BMT process can be viewed in three overarching stages: pre-transplant, transplant, and post-transplant. Patients are first admitted to the hospital for pre-transplant conditioning therapy, high doses of chemotherapy sometimes along with radiation therapy, in order to wipe out the patient's bone marrow and destroy diseased cells. During transplant (commonly referred to as "day 0") new cells are then used to rescue the marrow. Unlike solid organ transplants, a bone marrow transplant is not a surgical procedure; the stem cells are infused much like a blood transfusion and find their way to the patient's marrow spaces. The transplant is, in itself, painless and anti-climactic; the emotional and physical toll comes later.

Because chemotherapy wipes out the patient's bone marrow and blood counts become very low, for a while the patient is dependent on red blood cell and platelet transfusions. Since white blood cells are killed off, the patient is also at risk for infections that can be life threatening. The patient is placed on a strict regimen of antibacterial, antifungal, and antiviral medications to prevent potential infections. Patients remain in the hospital on average 2 to 4 weeks while they wait for the transplanted cells to grow and produce new blood cells. This process is called engraftment and is generally acknowledged as an anxious period of waiting for the patient, family, and clinicians alike.

The patient remains in the hospital at least until engraftment occurs. Absent complications, the patient is discharged from the hospital (often referred to as "day 30"). Since the patient is placed on anti-rejection medication for months, however, the risk for infections continues for much longer.

Clinical Challenges

The most feared complication from BMT is known as graft-versus-host disease (GVHD), which results from donor cells recognizing the patient's body as foreign and attacking it. Acute GVHD usually occurs within the first 100 days post-transplant, whereas chronic GVHD tends to emerge later and last longer, sometimes for the patient's lifetime. Although the location and severity of GVHD varies, acute GVHD commonly affects the skin, gut, and/or liver.

GVHD must be diagnosed and treated as early as possible in order to prevent it from getting rapidly out of control. Since GVHD results from the donor's immune cells attacking the patient's body, the standard treatment is steroids and/or other immunosuppressive drugs, sometimes in high doses. One of the main challenges is that the immunosuppressive medication used to prevent and treat GVHD also makes the patient more prone to infections.

In addition to infection risk, long-term steroid use can cause complications such as osteoporosis, high blood sugar, and adrenal insufficiency (where the body quits making a sufficient amount of steroids on its own), among others. Even short-term steroid use may have side effects (e.g. mood swings or high blood pressure). The side effects or adverse effects are managed using additional medications.

A BMT patient can often be on 15+ medications at a time, taking many of them several times a day, for many months. Side effects from medications and any co-morbidity that the patient has must be managed. The ultimate goal is to get the patient off all immunosuppressives and other medication that is not needed. The balancing act is challenging; and to the caregiver, at times it seems as much an art as science.

Given the need for close monitoring, if the family lives too far away, then the patient and a caregiver must find a temporary residence for the first few months as an outpatient (commonly until day 100) somewhere close to Hemphill. The BMT physician and clinical team see the patient and caregiver in the outpatient BMT clinic during this period as often as twice a week. The interval gradually increases based on the patient's progress, going to once a week, then every two weeks, and so on. The child is closely monitored by the team for at least 1 year, but often longer.

The BMT Care Team

At Hemphill, each patient remains under the care of one primary BMT physician throughout the transplant process, however, a large number of other clinicians and medical staff are also involved, first during the stay in the hospital and then again as outpatients in the clinic. During daily rounds in the hospital, for instance, parents and patients meet with a team of medical professionals that includes an arrangement of physicians, nurse practitioners and nurses, physical therapists, dieticians, pharmacists, and social workers, among others. Some of these clinicians remain constant through a family's stay in the hospital, while others rotate through the hospital ward every two weeks. In outpatient care, parents work with the primary BMT physician as well as other clinic staff such as physician assistants, nurse practitioners, and infusion nurses.

The BMT clinicians, both in the hospital and outpatient clinic, come to know the patients, caregivers, and often their extended families very well. We have been consistently impressed with the level of care and commitment that the BMT clinicians demonstrate. Several team members (including physicians) have noted how important it is for them to interact with their patients and their families on a personal, as well as clinical level.

Role of the Caregiver

It is significant to note that a parent, as caregiver, is required to stay with the patient, essentially 24/7, during the first 2 to 3 months following hospital discharge or as long as medically required by the BMT physician. In fact, in this hospital no transplant is approved without a satisfactory and formal caregiver plan. According to hospital policy, it is acceptable for the caregiver role to be fulfilled by multiple people; however, usually only 1 or 2 people (almost always a parent) perform these duties for pediatric patients.

In the first year of transplant, much of the caregiver's time is spent in clinical settings involving visits with the BMT team and other specialists, various tests and procedures, and blood transfusions or other infusions. Once the patient is discharged from the hospital following transplant, much of patient care falls to the caregiver. These include managing medications, infusions, and sometimes injections; following infection precautions and, adhering to dietary and lifestyle restrictions. Much of normal life is put on hold. Arrangements must be made with school and employers, and social life is severely limited.

In all, the transplant is an exhausting process physically and mentally. There are also significant emotional challenges with the BMT process. This is true not only for the patient but for the caregiver(s) as well. The treatment is highly technical and demanding, which brings with it anxieties about understanding critical health information and how well one will be able to cope with pressing day-to-day concerns. There is also much uncertainty about the future and fear associated with these unknowns.

INFORMATION AND EMOTIONAL CHALLENGES

We now turn to the caregiver experiences with information and emotion work during the BMT process. Throughout the BMT process—from hospital to home—caregivers engage in a wide range of information and emotion work that is necessary for the child's welfare. We note that although information work and emotion work can be analytically separated, in practice, these two types of work are often inextricably linked.

Clinical Information Work

Clinical information work includes tasks such as learning how to perform medical procedures, understanding and organizing medication regimens, tracking a child's diet, fluid intake, exercise, and bowel movements, interpreting blood counts, researching treatment options and medication side effects, and becoming adept at conversing with and questioning medical professionals.

Participants described "following protocol" in relation to the various medication and treatment regimens as generally "overwhelming," even in the best of times. For the majority of our participants, clinical protocols were viewed as important to understand and follow closely (often as a matter of life or death). A mother explained:

> *Everyday we're still very cautious about, you know, follow[ing] what they tell us to do to the "T" or we try to at least. We don't want any setbacks.[P-03]*

Participants expressed that this information work, especially in the initial weeks, took a great deal of attention, diligence, organizational skill, hands-on training and medical terminology so as to perform the necessary tasks.

Learning at the Hospital: Pharmaceuticals and Procedures

The weeks spent living at the hospital during the BMT procedure was spoken of by caregivers as a rich informational experience. It was during their hospital stay that they learned the skills and knowledge needed to do medical tasks. While there were varying levels of training offered to caregivers before discharge, our participants pointed to the informal education they received through watching and chatting with nurses day-to-day. One father discussed how he and his wife learned through careful observation of the BMT clinical team:

> *I pay attention to everything, and my wife is the same way, with what they are doing...You just learn by watching, it's just repetitive nature. [P-06]*

Participants also received more direct instruction from clinicians. For example, many caregivers in the study informed us that they learned proper line care, medication regimens, and wound care through promptings and encouragement by the nursing staff. A participant explained how nurses provided both her and her spouse with hands-on line care training at the bedside of their son who had a catheter inserted through the veins in his chest.

> *Like with flushing his lines and stuff like that; you know, cleaning when he had his NeoStar...When we were in the hospital, the nurses ... they were always asking, "Do you want to do this?" They'll watch you and train you like right there. Changing the bandages and stuff. [P-02]*

Another caregiver explained how nurses in the hospital trained him to administer his child's medication regimen so that he could continue to follow it when the family was discharged and returned home.

> *And as he [child] got further along through the process, they had you make sure--he had like six or seven oral medicines to take each day--and so, they made you do it, well, they give you the option. They ask the parents to do it.... We had to do it at a certain time each day. Some of the pills were time-sensitive; some of them just were day pills. So that routine is what we still follow. [P-08]*

Attending to the Child: Charting and Tracking

On leaving the hospital, caregivers are charged with tracking the patient's food, fluid, and even bodily emissions like urine and bowl movements. Parents also kept track of changes in a child's skin texture or color, sleep patterns, and energy levels. A participant explained about her son:

> *I pay attention to everything that is done with him, every movement ... Any bruise, any mark, you know, he doesn't even have to have labs done for me to tell you if his platelets are low. [P-09]*

This information is important, as the patient needs to maintain specific caloric and fluid intake not only to avoid malnutrition and dehydration, but also to prevent complications, such as GVHD. One participant explained that the high risks of complications associated after the BMT require hyper-attention and discipline in tracking:

> *People don't die from the transplant, I feel like. I think a lot of times it seems like they have like the secondary things that come with it, the infections and all those things. It's very, very hard to be...not that I'm tooting my own horn ... but it's hard to be disciplined in those things. [P-05]*

This type of discipline and training, though, begins in the hospital as caregivers are provided official forms to guide aspects of this work. For instance, one participant noted how he and his wife first started recording nutritional information for their child during the inpatient process:

> *We had to write down what they were eating, how much they drank ... In the hospital they dropped off a sheet every day, a nutrition sheet, and we just filled it out. [P-06]*

When they return home, the responsibility of tracking is left to the caregivers. One participant, a mother, noted that the labor involved with such detailed tracking is like a full-time job that she and her husband did together. They also noted that it became "a way of life":

> *It's almost like a job every day, because you're taking medicine four different times of the day, ... writing down what you eat every second, keeping track of, you know what I mean, everything! Even the water he had to drink, like two liters of water per day ... We needed to track and make sure that he was going to the bathroom enough ... It just becomes a way of life. [P-02]*

Sentimental/Emotion Work

Participants, not unexpectedly, experience a great deal of fear, anxiety, and stress throughout the BMT process due to the uncertainty of the procedure's success (e.g. child's ability to engraft new cells) and risk of potentially fatal complications (e.g. infections and GVHD).

All of our caregiver participants describe the frustration, anxiety, and even panic felt when trying to replicate medical regimens at home. One overarching concern was remembering how to do line care properly. Line care involves cleaning the lines of the child's implanted port or doing IV infusions. "It was nerve wracking!" was a common refrain among caregivers, especially in the first weeks at home. One participant noted the risk involved:

> *It's scary. That line goes right into your child's heart. ... I'm not a doctor or a nurse, but you have no choice, so you do it. [P-05]*

A grandmother, who acted as a caregiver for her grandson a few days a week, struggled to remember all of the steps involved in line care. During the interview she expressed feeling at times guilty and inadequate for not being able to remember these important details:

> *It was learning how to do all that IV stuff. I was nervous, very nervous ... I had a hard time remembering. It's like he [the grandchild] had to talk me through it ... [P-01]*

Another major challenge of caregiving described by our participants was dealing with the medication regimens. It was often difficult, for instance, for caregivers to keep track of the large number of medications prescribed to their child and the times at which each needed to be given. All the caregivers articulated designing elaborate organizational charts and routines to help them remember the ever-changing details of medication.

One often repeated difficulty was trying to get children to swallow the necessary large number of pills prescribed. Participants used expressions like "exhausting" and "hissy fits" to describe how time-consuming and emotionally draining these events were. For example, one father found his 7 year-old son hiding his pills because of the unpleasant taste and side effects.

> *So we actually have to physically watch him take his pills ... I don't blame him, I wouldn't really want to take them either ... They don't taste good ... I'm a blunt person, so I just told him, "You want to die? This is how serious it is." And he cried or whatever, but we still make sure we watch him take them and let him know how serious it is. [P-06]*

Another caregiver father echoed similar struggles with getting his 10 year-old child to take his medication. Unable to swallow pills, the family tried liquid versions unsuccessfully before eventually resorting to the placement of a Nasojejunal Tube, which runs from the nose into the intestines to inject the medication. He describes this as a "battle" that could last hours.

> *I mean, literally ... it would take 12 hours sometimes to get him to take his medicine, but he would always take it. And it sucked. It sucked really bad, really bad. You don't want to fight with your kid about anything. [P-08]*

All these daily trials appeared to feed into a constant anxiety for our participants, especially as they contemplated the uncertain outcome of the procedure. As one mother of a 5-year-old boy explained, caregivers must constantly navigate the "unknown."

> *The unknown. The most difficult part of the process, because it's a life or death process. That's the most difficult part. And do you want to subject your child to chemo? And will your child survive? What type of complications will he face? Is it worth it? Does the benefits outweigh the costs? That's the most difficult thing, is the unknown. [P-03]*

Along with concern about future outcomes and the day-to-day, the caregiver's near constant state of anxiety also needs to be managed. This is often dealt with by clinicians during rounds or clinic visits. Parents were often legitimately concerned about prescribed drugs or curious about alternative treatments, and look to clinicians for both information and assurance. Despite their best intentions, the medical staff cannot always provide the necessary time or offer the certainty that the anxious caregiver longs to hear.

Connecting Information and Emotional Work

Managing Burnout: Talking with Other Caregivers

Despite the BMT team's considerable efforts, the clinical process takes a heavy toll on the caregivers and on the family as a whole. Many participants noted they try to remain strong for their children and deal with their stress silently. When we asked one how she manages her life as a caregiver, she responded that she simply has not stopped 'going' since her son's diagnosis of leukemia 3 years ago:

> *I don't know how to answer that. I think God gives you the trials he gives you for a reason. This was just one I was made to handle. I mean honestly, [participant tears up and speaks in a distraught voice] I don't know ... there are other parents that have cried on my shoulder ... I just keep going. I don't know how or why ... I don't know. [P-02]*

Many participants echoed the need to "keep going" and "put one foot ahead of the other," but they also mentioned the connections and strength they drew from other BMT caregivers. At the hospital or clinic, caregivers chatted with each other in the halls or waiting rooms sharing stories and offering support to one another.

One participant, a father whose daughter had a bone marrow transplant, recounted his family's friendships with other BMT caregivers. One of these families became trusted guides that helped them adjust to life in the hospital:

> *They said, "Oh, this is how you can survive at the hospital." Because they had been here ... like buckets of toys by the windowsill. How do you survive the hospital room for months at a time? [P-08]*

Along with offering emotional support, caregivers also tried to help each other manage "the unknown" by sharing their experiences with particular medications or medical procedures. One participant spoke about the close relationships with other caregivers:

> *And even across diseases, making friends with families and knowing where they're at and their struggle ... you know everybody, and know who's dying and who's not dying ... And so while the kids play Legos, mom and dad sit and talk: "What drugs your kid on? Watch out for Reglan [type of drug]!" You know, "Don't ever let any family member get Reglan." "Why?" "Well the old docs love to prescribe it, but it can destroy your bladder." [P-07]*

Extreme Protocols and Creating Artifacts

Parents who were not socially inclined found other ways of coping. Sometimes this took the form of performing tasks that went past the already rigorous recommendations of the clinical protocol. A few participants, for example, spoke of doing extensive remodeling to their home. These families installed new flooring, repainted, and threw away furniture in an effort to eliminate germs, mold, and dander that might negatively impact their immune-suppressed child.

One participant, a mother of an 8-year-old patient, described her cleaning regimen as "extreme" noting that she and her husband researched extensively how to minimize risk of infection on the Internet and "ran with it."

> *We might be extremist... [We have] no carpet in our house, no fabric curtains. I mean, if there was anything that could be done, that's what we did.... And I think we took every bit of information that we found and we ran with it. You know, new furniture, nothing on the walls. I mean, I washed the walls every day; there was no dust. It was insane. [P-05]*

As the interview progressed, the same participant noted that this flurry for research and cleaning also reflected her family's emotional state, noting, *"Maybe that's how we coped ... I think it's probably a coping mechanism for us, now that I think about it." [P-05]*

There were many parents who took on the role of biographer of their child's medical experience. Along with capturing images and videos of their children visiting with relatives or celebrating a birthday in the hospital, caregivers also often took photographs related to medical procedures from transplant itself to routine line care activities to bags of blood and pill containers. Other common subjects included documenting potential medical problems like a rash on the skin. Many of our participants also noted how they routinely collected and shared clinical information artifacts, from photographs of a nurse's scribbled notations of a patient's blood work counts on a white board to a doctors' hand-drawn diagram of GVHD, through blog posts, Facebook page updates, and various social media.

Often these information artifacts were deeply meaningful to the caregivers and their families as testaments to particular moments of triumph or loss. These artifacts have a practical importance, but their symbolic nature is critical to our participants. Indeed, we have seen many small, ritual-like interactions with information artifacts in much of the caregiving work performed by parents.

So far, we have discussed a number of complex information and emotional challenges for BMT caregivers. Some of these difficulties are also encountered in a range of other health conditions, such as medication issues and the need to emulate clinical regimens. The nature of BMT, however, draws out the emotional issues and highlights ways in which information is often invested with additional symbolic meaning(s). These issues are, moreover, framed by two critically important contextual characteristics of BMT: the transitions between social worlds and engaging with a multiplicity of logics. We turn to this next.

Navigating Between Social Worlds

The first days at Hemphill Children's Hospital often elicit hopeful feelings among BMT caregivers. The transplant is often a last resort for treating terminally ill children and represents the chance for a healthy life for the admitted child. Many of the obstacles families have faced—from the child's chemo regimens to finding a willing and healthy donor match—have at this point finally been overcome.

This cautious optimism for most families, however, was quickly tempered by the pressing cognitive, physical, and emotional demands that come with their new reality of living day-to-day on the hospital floor. Due to the length of the inpatient stay, families are informed by BMT staff to expect considerable disruptions to family life. Caregivers are often separated from significant others and other children in order to stay in the hospital. This separation can last even longer if the caregiver needs to geographically relocate near the hospital while the child is an outpatient. At times, these household disruptions can be quite emotionally burdensome. A mother from out-of-state explained:

> *There's five in my household. ... We have two other kids, 17 and 15. So I'm leaving kids in the highlight of their high school year ... I miss my husband, my older son, and my youngest daughter ... Medical stuff ain't nothing. [P-02]*

It should also be noted that learning the "medical stuff" is far from trivial as it requires an in-depth knowledge of the healthcare system. Early on in their BMT hospital stay, all of our participants described challenges in their communications with doctors who relied upon technical medical language. During rounds, for instance, one participant noted that doctors would speak "book talk."

> *All the fellows [physicians] would be all like book talk. "Oh, your creatinine levels are at such and such." I'm like, "Excuse me?" They're like, "Liver is doing fine." [P-10]*

As caregivers lived on the hospital floor, they came to understand more medical terminology and gain confidence in communicating with and questioning clinicians. This confidence was especially important during rounds, a time when caregivers and patients met with the core BMT team to share information and get feedback on the child's status. During this brief daily interaction, caregivers felt the need to have questions formulated in advance in order to competently speak to the BMT clinical team. Participants likened this experience to preparing for class:

> *So I suppose it's a learning curve ... We didn't know Day 1 what to track. And there are times we are just dead wrong. We were talking about cholesterol when LDH is not cholesterol, it's acid created by your muscles when they are injured. At the time, I was thinking ... you know, one kind of cholesterol and then there is the other kind of cholesterol. Like, no, that is not what it is. [P-04]*

The life of having a sick child"

After transplant, caregivers began to adapt to their new daily existence of medication regimens, lack of sleep, and anxiety that make up their hospital life. Holidays, birthdays, and anniversaries come and go while in the hospital. A family whose child had severe GVHD described their "new normal" as a family disrupted:

> *This starts the sixth week of admission. The walk to the car is getting longer and the camaraderie with the nurses grows, because this is the new normal. The life of having a sick child, the life of a sick child. [P-07, blog entry]*

As caregivers adjusted to life on the floor, they found ways of bridging the space between social worlds. They talked to other parents over endless cups of coffee, connected to family with Skype, and learned the new routines and rhythms of the hospital.

The caregivers' experience of BMT is often quite different from that of the clinicians', even when medical work is collaborative in nature. This is reflected in the important routine of blood work, as caregivers wait for the daily blood counts to be returned from the lab to see if the BMT process is working (or not). To explain how significant blood work is on the hospital floor, a participant explained, *"Every person's day on 3North revolves around blood products." [P-07, blog entry]*

Caregivers collect blood count lab results verbally from the medical staff during rounds or from nurses on the floor. Observing rounds, we watched as parents asked eagerly about "the numbers" and waited with clasped hands for the answer. Blood counts for BMT patients can often go up and down significantly in a matter of days. If blood counts that day are "good" according to the doctor's interpretation, parents might clap and cheer, as a sign they might be discharged soon. If blood counts are lower than expected, the caregiver waits patiently for the next round of tests.

Blood work numbers are hand-recorded on a large calendar hung prominently in each room, individualized with the child's name across the top. Parents also routinely create their own information artifacts around blood work, posting updates and photographs through social media.

Going "Home"

When a child's blood counts rebound and the medical team deems the child ready to leave the hospital, it is cause for celebration. Due to the extensive follow-up outpatient appointments, however, families must remain located within commuting distance. Even local families, however, never really go 'home,' at least as existed pre-BMT. The child is now also a 'patient.'

As mentioned, the transition between hospital and home also heightens anxieties for caregivers as they take on the routine medical work once performed by nurses in the hospital. Many participants described this anxiety:

> *It's just like when you have your first child, and when you first leave the hospital, it's kind of scary, but you've got your in-laws or your parents usually to fall back on. Well, you ... don't have that. [P-06]*

Although caregivers are trained by medical staff to perform routine tasks like cleaning incisions and doing IV magnesium infusions, caregivers often still expressed being overwhelmed because the risks were so real. The sentiment in the following quote was echoed by many participants:

> *I was just scared...scared that you are going to do something wrong. Am I going to remember everything that ... that I have to do? What if I forget to do this and he gets sick, or I don't do it right? Those are the scary things. [P-04]*

Indeed, one mother told us she did not want to leave the hospital at first to go home, uncomfortable returning to her former life without the "backup" of the medical team.

Our participants reported that their family life changed dramatically. Children who had the BMT procedure often had to be kept away from friends for fear of infection. One 8 year-old girl recalled going home:

> *[C]ertain people could come in the room and everyone else had to stay out. They could talk to me through the screen door. "I love you from a distance." [P-12]*

The risk of contracting a cold or flu from others can leave the family isolated from their previous worlds. Another caretaker described how this isolation impacted her family:

> *And even when you go home you're kind of secluded because like we disinfected the whole house ... you don't really have visitors. You don't have family over because they could potentially have a cold or a virus that they don't even know of ... [I]t stays that way for like the first whole year. [P-04]*

The experience of being between social worlds may continue on going home as friends and extended family cannot grasp the new reality of the caregiver and patient.

Transformations: Engaging with Multiple Logics

Medical tasks require the BMT caregivers to collaborate closely with a team of clinicians, learning much of the specialized language of medicine and the technical practices of care. As our findings demonstrate, information in such a health context is never solely clinical. It is grounded in the moment of life and death choices, sleepless nights in the hospital, the frenzied washing of walls, and ritual archiving of blood counts. Clinical work sometimes combines a range of logics and is at times in tension with the other inclinations and concerns of a parent seeking to provide a child with a whole and happy life.

A common competing logic found in BMT is found in the attitudes and practices around alternative therapies, exemplified by 'June', a mother who pressed the BMT team for the inclusion of alternative therapies in her 11-year-old daughter's treatment regime. During rounds, June asked the physician about her daughter's blood cell counts. She worried about how long engraftment would take and the doctor told her they would just have to wait and see whether the cell counts grew. June looked anxious after this pronouncement and asked about supplements, such as mushroom teas. June explained to the medical staff:

> *I have special teas too. I know you doctors don't believe in all of this, but I see her every day and her energy level goes up. There is nothing you give us to build back the immune system, to strengthen the immune system.*

The pharmacist on the BMT team responded to June's queries with concern, explaining that mushrooms could cause fungal infections and other supplements might contain problematic ingredients such as human growth hormone. While a parent naturally wants to try anything to help build their child's immune system, many alternative treatments could be harmful immediately after transplant. The BMT team acknowledged they understood the caregiver's desire to try to find things that would help June's daughter, explaining:

> *We don't mind reviewing everything with you at clinic. Just bring in the box or package. We know that it can be important to the families. I don't have a problem with it; but, we just ask that before you take it, you talk to us first.*

Another important logic for caregivers in our study was tied to the experience of being a parent. Many of our participants, especially those who have had years in and out of medical facilities, spent considerable time reflecting upon how different treatments affect their child, not just medically, but as a human being. These caregivers weigh clinical information from the BMT team against their past experiences and insight from other families, often carefully deliberating treatment decisions with a range of more humanistic concerns, such as quality of life.

One of our caregiver participants, 'Martin', was a father whose 10-year-old son received multiple transplants. Martin started out full of optimism during the first BMT, learning complex medical terminology with enthusiasm and having high hopes for the procedure. His family strove to follow the clinical treatment protocol. After watching his son go through two rejections and spend multiple birthdays in the hospital, however, Martin found himself weighing clinical protocol against his son's deep desire for a "normal life". We recount his family's BMT story, one of three transplants and countless hard decisions:

> *The first two transplants were really, really difficult. We went through a lot to decide to do the third. He [Martin's son] was prepared to die. He knew the ramifications of not having the third transplant and would rather have died then go through that. But then he got a taste of school and wanted nothing more than to go back to school even if it was for a short period of time. And so we did the third transplant ...*
>
> *They told us we couldn't have pets because it would cause an immune system problem. But here you have a child who has a 6% chance at living, and the docs just sent him home and said, "You can't go to school and we don't know when you will be able to because you are so immune compromised." And so, what do Mom and Dad do? ... We got a beautiful German Shepherd dog ... He's just the best dog ever and my son's best friend ... And we haven't had any problems.*

Martin reflected on his BMT experience, noting that he has found himself engaging a range of different logics. The clinical information is always considered when making decisions about the management of his son's condition, but it does not necessarily trump being a father, as he noted:

> *But again, the human perspective versus the textbook perspective is two very, very different things.*

In this narrative, the daily trauma of being a caregiver, as expressed by this participant, is one of warring sensibilities between fighting for survival and easing suffering: Will my child's present pain be worth it?

These competing logics operate alongside, against, and with the logic of medicine. Practices like documenting blood work are grounded in a kind of embodied 'ritual logic' that may offer solace and hope. Other logics, such as those that argue for alternative therapies, make sense for parents, but perhaps not for clinicians. Information work and emotion work are understood by families within these logics.

DISCUSSION

Above, we presented the challenges for our BMT caregivers and described the important practices they adopted to fulfill their roles as caregivers. In summary:

- Our participants learned important caregiving practices from the members of the clinical team, especially nurses. Nonetheless, they often found themselves struggling to understand what they needed to know at different points in the BMT process.
- Our caregivers found themselves under intense psychosocial burdens, which include anxiety, stress, exhaustion, and isolation. The BMT process requires 24/7 care and at times is very stressful due to the high risks involved. It requires the caregiver learn a great deal about medical issues very quickly, and there is considerable anxiety about performing well. Furthermore, the caregivers are exhausted and socially isolated because of the demands of caregiving.
- For our participants, information often came in forms (and at times) that required emotional work. As well, emotionally critical times often fostered information needs. Information work and emotional work, then, were often intermingled, and were often not separable in actual practice.
- As a way of managing the challenges that come with the intermingling of information and emotional work, our participants developed coping strategies including interacting with other caregivers, creating symbolically rich information artifacts, and implementing extreme health management protocols.

In our analysis, these challenges, information work, and emotion work described by our participants appeared to be grounded in three central characteristics of the BMT caregiver experience: (1) the inherent connection of information and emotional work, (2) the transitions between the social worlds of hospital and home; and (3) the engagement with a multiplicity of logics from different social worlds needed to manage this health condition.

We now turn to unpacking the implications of these characteristics and discussing how such insights can help extend the design of health-related systems. First, as we have noted repeatedly, information and emotional work were not always separable in practice (e.g., [15]). Information work created emotional work, emotional work created information work, and often the two happened at the same time. Understanding how information transfer occurs in practice will be extremely important in creating useful and usable information sources for these patients.

Second, the hospital is its own social world [18], a community with its own roles, norms, language, and even rituals. Leaving home and moving into this new medicalized social world can be understood as a liminal experience, characterized by being transitional states or situations. Victor Turner and others have pointed to the social significance that transitions between social worlds (marked by rites like weddings, pilgrimage, coming of age ceremonies) have in people's lives. Turner's conceptualization of liminality, rooted in the study of rituals, highlights how that movement can be profoundly meaningful, and at times even transformative. Turner characterizes the liminal as a period of ambiguity and uncertainty (a place between and betwixt) in which people are not held to the norms of their other social worlds [21]. During ritual events, for instance, the liminal period is an essential stage in which people move from a state of the uninitiated to being transformed. For Turner then liminality is both a period of time and a process.

In our findings, we saw our participants, too, necessarily going through a transformative process. That is, our caregivers often did not start knowing medical jargon and procedures. (The exceptions were those caregivers whose children had been through chemo regimens already.) Our participants had to become 'caregivers' and as they did so, they lived in a space that was no longer of the everyday, but also was not a clinician's professional world.

The transformation into a formal caregiver is only one aspect of the BMT's liminality. Tuner noted that the liminal is also a period of reflection and generativity in which people are exposed to new ideas, question dominant knowledge paradigms, and reshape their understanding of the world. In this way, through documenting blood work, questioning clinicians, and talking to other families, we saw parents transition into caregivers, coming to understand 'medicine' and 'home' in new ways.

Understanding liminality as a process allows one to understand how information work and emotional work change for caregivers over time. The transition between the social world of everyday life and the social world of a family with a patient requires many transitions and stresses. Knowing the rhythms of these changes will be critical to understand.

This also extends the concept of social worlds. For Strauss and colleagues, people obviously move among social worlds. How they do so is not specified (although Charmaz [2] details some of this in her examination of how people come to understand themselves as having chronic conditions). This extension to social world theory will allow a better-grounded examination of the micro-details of the transition process, as well as the information and emotional work required for BMT. We believe this theoretical extension will also be valuable for caregivers and patients in a large range of chronic conditions.

Third, the theoretical framing of liminality makes visible the work involved in navigating the multiplicity of logics and counter-intuitive logics inherent in differing social worlds. What looks like intransigence or even anxiety on the part of caregivers may be better viewed as ongoing navigation, reconciliation, and even superimposition in progress. In this view, information work and emotion work in BMT are part of processes in which people make connections between differing logics (reconciling them) or generating alternatives (challenging or even rejecting a dominant logic). Indeed, from the viewpoint of Turner, being pushed outside of one's previous social world presents parents the opportunity to reconsider commonly held understandings and generate "novel configurations of ideas and relations." [21].

This is micro-interactional work in its own right. Drawing on the theoretical framings of Turner and Strauss, 'reflection work' can be seen as the labor involved in managing the utility of both information and emotional work when a person is confronted with differing social worlds. (We note that some of our caregivers were also confronted with viewpoints from alternative medicine, such as those believing in herbal remedies, or from faith-based beliefs.) Our findings point to the potential augmentation of this reflection work as a way to motivate and further the medical work, while maintaining a tie to the caregivers' other social worlds) in the design of health management tools and systems.

CONCLUSION

In this study, we tried to open the box of micro-interactional work to include both a nuanced view of information and emotional work. We believe this work offers several important contributions. At a theoretical level, it extends Strauss' theories about information work, and details how two important kinds of Straussian micro-interactional work (information and emotional) are related. Previous CSCW work has pointed towards that relationship and its importance to users (e.g., [14, 15, 16] and even [1]), but our work here points towards the centrality of how information work and emotional work was combined for our participants.

As well, we have pointed to Turner's liminality as process. We showed its usefulness in understanding how caregivers must both transition between social worlds and manage the differing logics among social worlds. Seeing information work and emotional work as part of a transition process will be helpful in demarking phases of patient and caregiver needs.

We have shown that some of the issues in BMT information work result from the medical disease and treatment. However, we also showed that a considerable amount is the result of participants' needing to navigate between different social worlds, some of which were unknown at first or even conflicting, in this liminality process. For example, we noted that understanding medical terms and the medical viewpoint requires considerable information work and can also require emotional work.

Our work also offers important implications at a practical level. Our basic goal was to understand how to support pediatric BMT caregivers in their role. In this paper we analyzed the caregiver role, following the lead of Chen, and we focused on their information and emotional work. We showed how information most needed by the pediatric BMT caregiver has to be contexualized and situationally understood (as has been found in many CSCW studies). It is almost impossible to do this by oneself, and caregiving tasks often require scaffolding and collaborative assistance. More importantly, since information and emotional work are intertwined, we believe that what might be understood as information transfer is secondary to supporting the processes of bringing people more comfortably into adopting very new life circumstances. The design of tools and support to do so will be critical. Our future work will extend the analysis presented here to new prototypes that incorporate these findings. We plan to carefully examine the kinds of scaffolding we can present to caregivers that combines information and emotional work. We also plan to examine the rhythms of the transition caregivers make to understand their new world.

ACKNOWLEDGMENTS

This work was funded in part by a fellowship by the National Science Foundation IGERT 0903629 (OpenData) as well as an NSF Graduate Fellowship. We would like to thank the other members of the SocialWorlds research group, as well as the clinicians and patients in the BMT clinic. We would also like to thank the anonymous reviewers, who substantially improved this paper.

REFERENCES

[1] Ackerman, M.S. Augmenting organizational memory: a field study of Answer Garden. *ACM Transactions on Information Systems*, 16, 3 (1998), 2013-224.

[2] Charmaz, K. *Good days, bad days: The self and chronic illness in time*. Rutgers, New Brunswick, NJ, 1991.

[3] Chen, Y. Health use in chronic care cycles. In *Proc. CSCW 2011*, 485-488.

[4] Chen, Y., Ngo, V., and Park, S.Y. Caring for caregivers: Designing for integrality. In *Proc. CSCW 2013*, 91-102.

[5] Corbin, J.M. and Strauss, A.C. *Basics of Qualitative Research*. Sage Publications, Inc., 1998.

[6] Farnham, S., Cheng, L., Stone, L., Zaner-Godsey, M., and Hibbeln, C. HutchWorld: Clinical study of computer-mediated social support for cancer patients and their caregivers. In *Proc. CHI 2002*, 375-382.

[7] Glaser, B.G. and Strauss, A.L. *The discovery of grounded theory*. Aldine, Hawthorne, NY, 1967.

[8] Grimes, A., Landry, B., and Grinter, R.E. Characteristics of shared health reflections in a local community. In *Proc. CSCW 2010*, 435-444.

[9] Huh, J., Patel, R. and Pratt, W. Tackling dilemmas in supporting "the whole person in online patient communities. In *Proc. CHI 2012*, , 923-926.

[10] Kaziunas, E., Ackerman, M.S. and Veinot, T.C.E. Localizing chronic disease management: Information work and health translations. In *Proc. ASIST 2013*, 1-10.

[11] Kientz., J.A. Understanding parent-pediatrician interactions for the design of health technologies. In *Proc. IHI'10*, 230-239.

[12] Liu, L.S., Hirano, S.H., Tentori, M., and Cheng, K.G. In *Proc. CHI 2002*, 1-8.

[13] Liu, L.S., Huh, J., Neogi, T., Inkpen, K. and Pratt, W. Health vlogger-viewed interaction in chronic illness management. *In Proc. CHI'13*, 49-58.

[14] Mamykina, L., Mynatt, E., Davidson, P.R., and Greenblatt, D. MAHI: Investigation of social scaffolding for reflection thinking in diabetes management. In *Proc. CHI'08*, 477-486.

[15] Mentis, H., Reddy, M., and Rosson, M.B. Invisible emotion: Information and interaction in an emergency room. In *Proc. CSCW 2010*, 311-320.

[16] Prilla, M., Degeling, M., and Herrmann, T. Collaborative reflection at work. In *Proc. GROUP 2012*, 55-64.

[17] Strauss, A., Fagerhaugh, S., Suczek, B. and Weiner, C. Sentimental work in the technologized hospital. *Sociology of Health and Illness*, 4,3 (1982), 255-278.

[18] Strauss, A. *Continual permutations of action*, Aldine Transaction, Chicago, IL, 1993.

[19] Tixier, M., Gaglio, G., and Lewkowicz, M. Translating social support practices into online services for family caregivers. In *Proc. GROUP 2009*, 71-80.

[20] Toscos, T., Connelly, K., and Rogers, Y. Best intentions: Health monitoring technology and children. In *Proc. CHI' 12*, 1431-1440.

[21] Turner, V. Betwixt and between: The liminal period in Rites de Passage. In *Proc. of the American Ethnological Society, Symposium on New Approaches to the Study of Religion*, 1964, 4-20.

[22] Weiner, C.L, Fagerhaugh, S., Suczek, B., and Strauss, A. *Social organization of medical work.* Transaction Publishers, New Brunswick, NJ, 1997.

[23] Yamashita, N., Kuzuoka, H., Hirata, K., and Kudo, T. Understanding the conflicting demands of family caregivers caring for depressed family members. In *Proc. CHI'13,* 2637-2646.

Spaceship Launch: Designing a Collaborative Exergame for Families

Herman Saksono[1], Ashwini Ranade[2], Geeta Kamarthi[2], Carmen Castaneda-Sceppa[2], Jessica A. Hoffman[2], Cathy Wirth[2], Andrea G. Parker[1,2]

[1]College of Computer and Information Science
Northeastern University
360 Huntington Ave. Boston, MA 02120
{saksono.h, ranade.as, kamarthi.g}@husky.neu.edu,

[2]Bouvé College of Health Sciences
Northeastern University
360 Huntington Ave. Boston, MA 02120
{c.sceppa, j.hoffman, c.wirth, a.parker}@neu.edu

ABSTRACT

Parents play a critical role in facilitating children's physical activity, as they are an important source of modeling and support. While Human-Computer Interaction (HCI) researchers have explored exergame design for children or adults separately, an important open area of work is identifying design guidelines for family exergames. One question that researchers have increasingly posed is, how can exergames be designed to avoid potential negative consequences of competition? To address these questions we designed Spaceship Launch, an exergame for parents and kids in lower income neighborhoods, where obesity is most prevalent. We describe our iterative design process: the formative study to identify design opportunities, our resulting system, and our field evaluation of the tool. Our findings highlight the impact of SL on physical activity intentions, and how parental preferences for in-game competition were aligned with the psychological needs of relatedness and competence. We conclude with design recommendations for future family-focused exergames.

Author Keywords

Exergames; serious games for health; physical activity; collaborative games; gamification; competition

ACM Classification Keywords

H.5.3 [Group and Organization Interfaces]: Computer-supported cooperative work

General Terms

Human Factors; Design

INTRODUCTION

Combating childhood obesity begins with the family. In this environment, preventive health behaviors such as physical activity (PA) can be modeled and supported [13]. Human-computer interaction (HCI) researchers have explored the use of interactive computing systems for promoting PA and reducing sedentary behavior, in the form of exercise games (*exergames*) [18,41], gamified PA visualizations [5,17], and social support systems [23,38]. However, very little work has explored how systems should account for familial influence, even though parental modeling is a strong predictor of children's PA behavior [8]. There is rich opportunity for HCI innovation in this space, given the barriers to modeling that families often face (*e.g.*, limited opportunities to exercise together).

The overarching question in our work is: how can parent-child interaction in a technology-based intervention facilitate PA promotion and what are design guidelines for creating such tools? To answer this question, we conducted an 8-month iterative design process. Our work began with a formative study examining parental attitudes towards, and perceptions of PA, as well as current PA behaviors. One key finding of this study is that while the parents provided support for their child to be physically active, they provided little PA modeling for their child, which research has shown to be important for increasing children's PA levels [21,24].

Using this finding as a starting point, we explored how an exergame could encourage PA modeling. Prior work has raised concerns about the negative impact that competition can have on user engagement in exergames [17,18,41]. As such, we attempted to avoid the potential negative effects of competition by designing a *collaborative* game environment. We developed Spaceship Launch (SL), a collaborative exergame for parents and young children, aged 3-8. Prior work in HCI has not extensively studied exergames in the context of the family unit. Informed by social cognitive theory (SCT) [2], SL was designed to encourage the parent and child to work together to be more physically active at a moderate or vigorous level. We conducted a three-week field study of SL with 13 families in a predominantly lower-income neighborhood in the northeast United States. This demographic was chosen due to the increased barriers to PA facing low-income families. To study use of and engagement with SL, we conducted interviews and participatory design workshops.

Through our inductive analysis, we found that while SL was a collaborative game, families had strong, yet nuanced desires for increased competitive game elements. Using self-

CSCW 2015, March 14–18, 2015, Vancouver, BC, Canada.

ACM 978-1-4503-2922-4/15/03…$15.00.
http://dx.doi.org/10.1145/2675133.2675159.

determination theory (SDT) [28] as an analytic lens, we further unpacked this value. Our findings suggest that parents' desire for competition was partially driven by the psychological needs and SDT constructs of relatedness and competence. Our results highlight the value of fulfilling this need as a means of nurturing exergame engagement.

We contribute to HCI research by providing a case study exploring how technology can promote increased PA in families. We report on our formative study, the design of SL, and our evaluation of this tool. As there has been limited work in this area, our findings can help motivate future research in this space. We further contribute to HCI by proposing four design implications for future work, specifically articulating the value of promoting family PA through a task-mastery exergame environment. Finally, prior work has not explored how the feeling of relatedness between family members affects exergame engagement and PA promotion. Our findings highlight theory and empirically based directions for future work.

RELATED WORK

Our work is motivated by public health research showing the importance of family-based PA interventions. We begin with an overview of this literature and then briefly overview self-determination theory, which helps characterize PA motivation. We conclude with a discussion of HCI research that has used games and *gamification* (game design elements used in non-game contexts [7]) to promote PA, focusing on competition in such systems.

Family-based Physical Activity Promotion

The family environment can have a profound influence on health behaviors through parental provision of modeling, support, and influence [30,35]. A ten-year study found that parental involvement in childhood obesity prevention efforts yields a higher rate of success [9]. Parental PA modeling has been cited as a predictor of children's PA [8,21] and there is a significant correlation between the time parents spend being active and children's PA [24]. However, the impact of parental modeling may be diminished if the child does not directly see how active their parent is [39]. Yet, PA modeling is challenging because families often face barriers to exercising together (*e.g.,* time constraints and differing physical capabilities) [36]. These barriers suggest opportunities for systems that facilitate PA modeling.

Prior HCI research has explored the design of *exergames* (*i.e.,* games in which play is driven by an individual's PA) [32] and activity sharing tools [4,15] for family health promotion. These systems often incorporate a social element, whereby intra- and inter-family performance is compared. While such comparisons can encourage higher system participation [4],.Grimes *et al.* [12] noted parental concerns regarding the impact of competitive design elements on children, for example, questioning how comparisons might impact the child's self-esteem. While this prior work suggests the potential of using technology to promote healthy behaviors in a family context, work in this area is just beginning to emerge, and little is known about how such systems can effectively engage family members.

Self-Determination Theory

Self-Determination Theory (SDT) explains how individuals are motivated to engage in various activities [28]. Within SDT, motivation is fostered by the satisfaction of psychological needs, including competence and relatedness. *Competence* is an individual's perceived capacity to complete a task. *Relatedness* is defined as the need to feel *connected* to others, to be *concerned* for them, and to feel *accepted* in a social environment. Prior work has shown the value of SDT in predicting PA engagement [22] as well as computer game engagement [29], suggesting its promise as a theoretical basis for exergame design and evaluation. Moreno *et al.* [22] examined two types of motivational environments: task-mastery climates (*i.e.,* the focus is on the task domain and personal improvement) and ego-involved motivational climates (*i.e.,* the focus is on comparisons with others). Their findings showed that a task-mastery climate positively predicted the fulfillment of the psychological needs posited by SDT, which in effect predicted enjoyment. On the other hand, an ego-involved climate predicted none. Motivational climates that emphasized cooperation and effort fulfilled the need of competence as it is "a self referenced criteria, which is far more controllable" [22]. A cooperative climate that avoids peer comparison also nurtured the feeling relatedness.

Competition in Exergames & Gamified PA Visualizations

Increasingly, HCI researchers have examined how games can encourage increased PA. As the goal of such serious games is not only to provide entertainment but also encourage a positive shift in behavior [27], it is critical that designers carefully examine ways of avoiding undesirable outcomes [26]. The potential negative effect of competition has been highlighted in child-focused exergame research. iFitQuest, designed for adolescents, is a set of two mini exergames with open-ended goals that players can freely choose [18]. The game mechanics are driven by players' runs in the real world. Similarly, the American Horsepower Challenge (AHPC) encourages school children to walk by comparing the aggregated step count of their school versus other schools. The school with the most steps wins [41]. Evaluations of iFitQuest and AHPC revealed that challenges emerged due to comparisons and competition. One iFitQuest player exercised in a separate area to be out of sight from peers and one player ridiculed others with lower scores [18]. One AHPC player was uncomfortable sharing his contributions to the game with peers, because he was concerned with not being sufficiently competent [41]. Research on gamified PA visualizations has also raised concerns about competition, with a participant in one study noting *"there is enough competition in real life"* [17].

To avoid undesired effects of competition in the context of family health monitoring tools, Grimes *et al.* [12] recommended that such tools be designed to facilitate collaboration between family members instead of competition. These systems can be designed by emphasizing, "how healthfully the family is living as a unit, rather than how each person is doing compared to other". This recommendation of avoiding an others-referenced climate resonates with prior research on PA [22,40], which argues that task-mastery climates are more effective for maintaining enjoyment. In summary, competition is clearly a design element that must be carefully considered and designed. Our study revealed important considerations around competition for family-based exergames.

IDENTIFYING DESIGN GUIDELINES

To begin exploring how technology might facilitate PA in families, we conducted a formative study with 13 parents. The study was conducted at a community gym that hosts a free program for families with young children (approximately aged 3-8) to be active together. The program is held in a predominantly lower income neighborhood in Boston, MA, United States, in an attempt to help families overcome barriers to exercise in this context (*e.g.,* limited access to safe play spaces [1]).

Formative Study Method

We used focus groups (n=13) to probe parental attitudes towards, and support for, their child's PA. There were two to six participants in each session. At this stage, we focused on parents (as opposed to their young children) as we felt they could more clearly express to us how much PA their family was getting, barriers to exercise, and the family's PA needs. Focus groups were audio-recorded and two researchers completed an iterative, inductive analysis of the transcripts, inspired by grounded theory analysis [33]. We independently coded the transcripts and met regularly to discuss and reconcile our codes. We then iteratively clustered codes into higher-level themes and identified relationships between themes through axial coding. Participants were first asked to complete a demographic survey at the start of the focus group. We administered a follow-up survey (n=10) using validated instruments to gain more insight about parental support for PA [20].

Formative Study Results

The focus group data suggests that parents provided support for their child to be active. This finding is somewhat unsurprising given that parents were recruited from a family-based PA program. Parents were informed about the importance of child PA and were actively seeking and providing PA opportunities. For example, P5 discussed how she seeks PA opportunities in an unconventional way:

> P5: When I'm driving around and I see someone playing soccer or something, I pull over and I ask more questions. I find out a little more… I feel like there's information out there.

Parents also discussed in detail the interplay of barriers that limit their ability to help their kids to be physically active. They also detailed their efforts to overcome the barriers and the disappointment of not being able to do so. The most apparent barriers were financial and informational; parents experienced difficulties finding PA programs (such as summer camps and soccer clubs) that were within their budget. P7 expressed her sense of helplessness:

Type of parental PA support or modeling (scale 1-5; 1: never, 5: daily)	**Avg**	**Stdev**	**Min**	**Max**
Encouraged PA	4.8	0.42	4	5
Provided transportation to PA	4.5	0.85	3	5
Watched kids' PA	4.1	0.87	3	5
Discuss the value of PA w/ kids	4.9	0.32	4	5
Engage in PA with kids	3.7	1.10	2	5

Table 1. Parental PA Support & Modeling in Formative Study

> P7: And I just feel like it's a catch 22, because you want quality childcare, and you know there's cost associated with that, but sometimes it feels like things are out of reach.

In some situations, financial and informational barriers were coupled with transportation and time barriers (having insufficient time to take their kids to PA opportunities). P5 summarized this interplay of barriers, implying her hopelessness in supporting her child to be active.

> P5: Some of the resources that are out there are either very far out and the drive is ridiculous just to get there, and I'm not driving to a situation where I come back to [local neighborhood] to go to work, or they're very, very expensive.

While parents made great efforts to support their child's PA, they rarely discuss exercising with their kids. This finding is further supported by the survey data: parents reported providing high levels of PA social support for their kids (*e.g.,* encouraging and watching kids do PA), but they less frequently engaged in "PA with kids" (Table 1). In addition, we used self-report height and weight data to calculate parental body mass index (BMI), and most parents were overweight or obese (n=11). A previous evaluation of the community gym showed that most parents rarely modeled moderate and vigorous physical activity during gym sessions [3]. Our results further elaborate on this prior work by shedding light on parental PA levels outside of the gym as well as their BMI data. Together these results characterize parents' limited PA levels and likely caloric imbalance.

These findings collectively suggest that parents are not engaged in recommended levels of PA (such as those articulated by the Centers for Disease Control and Prevention (CDC)), therefore minimizing the opportunity for modeling positive behaviors for their children. Going back to Thompson *et al.*'s [36] recommendation to design interventions accommodating the complex needs and demands of today's families (*e.g.,* the inability to exercise together), a potential design direction would be to develop a tool that helps parents and children to collectively pursue increased PA even if they do not exercise at the same physical location or at the same time.

SPACESHIP LAUNCH DESIGN AND EVALUATION

Based on our formative study findings that some parents do not or unable to model PA behavior for their children and that parents may not be engaging in recommended PA levels

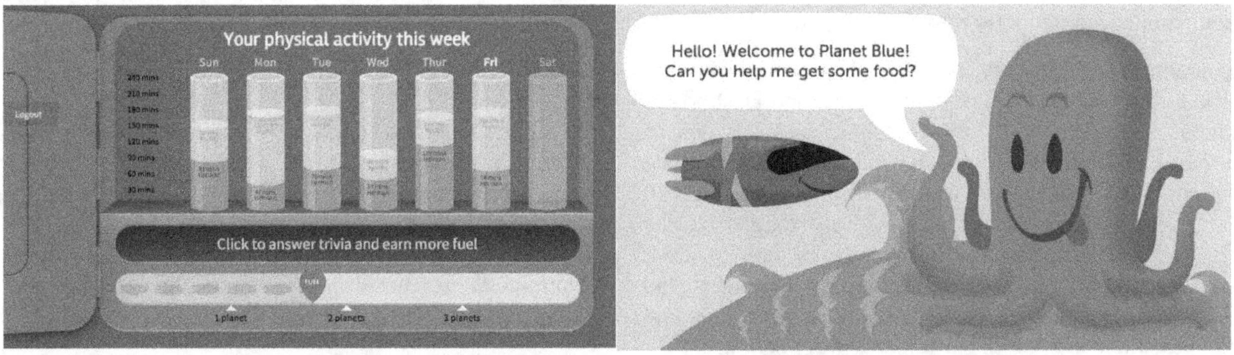

Figure 1. SL Dashboard (left) and Launch Game (right)

more generally, we designed Spaceship Launch (SL), a collaborative exergame for promoting PA in a family context. SL consists of two elements: the Dashboard and the Launch game. The goal of the Dashboard is to facilitate collaborative PA reflection between the parent and child, whereas the Launch game provides virtual rewards as the parent and child team achieve recommended PA levels.

Design Rationale

SL is a collaborative exergame, where the team of a parent and a child must work together to meet the game's objective: achieving the CDC's recommended PA levels[1] (150 minutes of moderate or 75 minutes of vigorous activity for adults each week; 60 minutes of moderate to vigorous activity for kids each day). Using Fitbit activity trackers worn by the parent and the child, the game tracks the weekly minutes that each player spends in moderate and vigorous PA (MVPA). Fitbit accuracy has been validated by prior studies, (*e.g.*, [34]). The more time the team spends in MVPA, the more fuel the child receives to launch their spaceship to planets in the game.

Drawing inspiration from Grimes *et al.*, [12] about the potential of cooperative social interactions over competition in the family context, we designed SL as a collaborative game. Zagal *et al.* [43] described the distinction between competitive, cooperative, and collaborative game. In a *competitive game*, the objective is to outdo the other player. The mechanics ensure that one player wins and the other loses. In a *cooperative game*, the mechanics require two players to work together to achieve a collective goal, even if the individual goals may be different. In contrast, a *collaborative game* has intrinsic mechanics that guarantees players who work together to complete a collective goal will always get an equal benefit. If one player loses, then the other player will lose. El-Nasr *et al.* [31] found that collective goals encourage players to help each other, work out problems together, and laugh together.

The objective of SL is to collect as many minutes as possible per week to meet CDC recommendation. The rewards in this game are the ability to launch the virtual spaceship to a planet in outer space and the experience of fantasy and discovery of the planet inhabitants and environments. The planets and overall game visuals are designed for kids aged 3-8, because they are expected to be a driving factor of parental engagement with SL.

The SL Dashboard is designed for the parent and child to monitor their PA levels during the week and their fuel progress. The rationale behind this design is that some families may not be able to be physically active together, though the parent may be physically active at work and the child may be active at school. Observational learning is a central element of social-cognitive theory (SCT) [2]; this construct suggests that increasing opportunities for kids to observe their parents engaged in PA may lead to increased PA for the kids themselves. Furthermore, the PA visualization is designed for self-monitoring, which affords self-regulation, another important element of SCT. Finally, in our formative study parents repeatedly discussed experiencing elevated positive emotions when observing their child being active. Therefore, the Dashboard may provide an additional incentive for the parent to engage.

The second element of SL, the Launch game, articulated the game's task (meet recommended MVPA levels to gain spaceship fuel). In the Launch game, players could: see how many planets they can launch to, select the planet to visit, observe the launching experience, land on the planet, and complete a mission. Both the Launch game and the Dashboard are accessible through home devices as well as a large interactive display deployed during the gym sessions.

SL was implemented as a web application. The frontend was developed using HTML and SVG, which is controlled using the JQuery and SVG.JS JavaScript libraries. The backend was developed using Laravel PHP Framework; it stores and retrieves users' minute-by-minute time series PA data from Fitbit's server.

Evaluation Method

We evaluated the use and impact of SL in a 3-week field study with 13 families. Participants were recruited from the same community gym as in the formative study. 29 people participated, including 15 caregivers and 14 children.

[1]cdc.gov/physicalactivity/everyone/guidelines/adults.html

Northeastern University's Human Subject Research Protection approved the IRB protocol for this work.

At the beginning of the study, we showed participants how to wear the Fitbits and how to use the SL game and Dashboard. Participants then completed demographic and surveys to assess baseline PA intention [6] and parental PA modeling and support [20]. Participants were then given access to SL for three weeks; their SL interactions were logged by the system. We asked participants to log into the game at least once every week and recommended they check the Dashboard as often as possible. If more than three days had passed since their last login, participants were sent an email or SMS reminder to use the system.

After they had used SL for three weeks, we conducted semi-structured interviews with eight parents to understand their experience with the game and to what extent it affected their intention to be physically active and their PA modeling behavior. Our findings from this initial examination will inform the design of future iterations of SL, which will be more closely evaluated from the child's perspective. At the conclusion of the study, parents repeated the PA intention survey that was administered at baseline.

In addition, we conducted participatory design workshops with four families: both caregivers (n=5) and their children (n=4) participated in the workshops, for a total of 9 participants. Participants were asked to redesign the SL Dashboard using a variety of art supplies (*e.g.,* colored papers, stickers, felt pens) so that the game better fit their needs. Each workshop included one to two families. Following the work of Yoo *et al.* [42], we encouraged iterative revision using prompting cards to elicit nuanced requirements and stories that are harder to attain in conventional interviews.

To help parents and children to iterate on the SL dashboard design, we gave each participant an instruction card that provided focused direction about what to design:

> "Redesign the SL dashboard so that you and your child could sit together and monitor your weekly physical activities."

After this first task was completed, we presented them with an envisioning card to help them revise their initial design:

> "Improve the way your dashboard works so that it fits better with your routine, your household, and your family's needs"

After families completed their revisions, we conducted interviews with them. We used their designs to probe deeper and better understand how the experience of using the game through the SL Dashboard affected their behavior and how it could be improved to encourage family fitness.

Type of parental PA support or modeling (scale 1-5; 1: never, 5: daily)	Avg.	Stdev.	Min	Max
Encouraged PA	3.40	1.06	1	5
Provided transportation to PA	3.33	1.18	1	5
Watched kids' PA	3.07	1.03	1	5
Discuss the value of PA w/kids	4.00	1.07	1	5
Engage in PA with kids	2.80	1.15	1	5

Table 2. Baseline PA Support & Modeling during Evaluation

We conducted an inductive analysis of the interview and design workshop transcripts. Our approach was inspired by grounded theory [33]: we inductively open-coded the transcripts, iteratively clustering codes to arrive at a set of emergent themes. We then conducted axial coding to examine the relationship between the themes.

Participant Overview

The majority of the participating caregivers were female (n=11) as well as the majority the children (n=10). This gender distribution reflects the general make up of gym attendees in which female caregivers are the majority (female=56.4%, male=35.9%, not reported=7.7%). Four caregivers also participated in the earlier formative study. Caregivers were mainly parents (n=13), but also included one grandparent, and an uncle. The median age of the caregivers was 39 and the median age of the children was 8. The BMI calculation indicated that most caregivers were obese (n=8) or overweight (n=3), with two in the healthy range (2 participants provided no data). The median household income was $20,000-$29,999 and the majority of the families lived in neighborhoods where the average household income is below the city's average (n=13).

Caregivers' intention to be physically activity appears to be low. Our baseline survey data indicated that the median number of times that caregivers intended to be physically active is a total of 5-8 times in the next 4 weeks. Similar to the findings in our formative study, our survey results suggest that caregiver support for child PA is moderate and the PA modeling is lower (Table 2). On average, caregivers self-reported that they sometimes exercised with their kids.

SPACESHIP LAUNCH EVALUATION RESULTS

Three themes emerged from our analysis. First, we found that the game seemed to help *increase PA intention.* Participant accounts helped us identify how they used SL as a motivational tool for exercise and to assess their PA. We also found that while SL was designed to be collaborative, most participants expressed nuanced preferences for competition. Finally, our results suggest that competition was desired because it was perceived as a catalyst for social interactions fulfilling the psychological need of relatedness.

Increased PA Intention

Having daily PA duration visualized through the SL dashboard and a target of game-defined PA duration seemed to affect most participants' *intention to be active.* Our PA intention survey showed that all but one participant intended to be at least as active as at the start of the study, if not more. Four participants reported an increase in intention; of the 6 that reported no change, 3 were already intending to be active at the maximum level (7 days/week) at the start of the study. These preliminary findings suggest the potential value of SL for helping encourage sustained and increased desire to be physically active.

Our interview data mirrors these findings, shedding more light on the impact that SL had on participants' pursuit of PA. All but one of our interviewees said that the game increased their intention to be physically active. Some (P3, P8) intended to exercise individually, whereas others (P9, P1) intended to exercise with their child. The participants also expressed varying levels of intention. For example, the game's PA target led P3 to *contemplate exercising* as her awareness of the need to be more active increased.

> P3: I'm thinking to exercise more. Because my fuels were low. And I know I could do, I know I could do better than that.

Other caregivers were more motivated to change by *preparing to exercise*. P8 and P9 expressed the intention to change through by *reminding themselves* to exercise. P9 also spoke with her child about exercising to accomplish the game's target.

> P8: [Using the game made me say to myself,] "*Oh, I got to get up. Got to get out of the house. Got to do something.*"

> P9: You know, you get your mindset. "*Okay, tomorrow I'm going to fill this tank up*" [...] My daughter and I, we said "*Okay, we're gonna work.*"

P1 went further in *preparing to exercise* by *identifying exercise opportunities* to earn game points. P1 also saw the need to earn game points *with* her child, and was expressed by her intention to *identify team exercise opportunities* that she and her child could participate in.

These varying intentions can be mapped to the Transtheoretical Model's stages of health behavior change [25]. Individuals who *contemplate exercising* may need further incentive to translate intentions into action, as traditional action-based programs may not be effective for them [25]. Participants who were *preparing to exercise* were making strides towards health behavior change, and the game provided them with a reason to exercise. However, unlike P1 who started to *identify exercise opportunities*, P8 and P9 did not explicitly do so. They may need ideas to proceed to action. While this could be supported through a database of PA ideas, it may be more sustainable if this is provided by other game participants. Stories from peers are potentially inspirational because they have been tried out by similar others [11].

Some participants translated these intentions into *actions to accomplish the game's objective* (*i.e.*, obtaining spaceship fuel by being physically active in a duration that meets the CDC's recommendation). Participants realized that the Fitbit tracks all kind of physical movement; therefore they come up with a diverse range of exercise opportunities. For example, P2 identified the relationship between the magnitude of her movement and the game points (spaceship fuel) that she will acquire. In the account below, after she *identified the exergame mechanics* she expressed her excitement when she shoveled the snow because she will get more spaceship fuel:

> P2: Oh, this is a good opportunity for me to get some, you know, points for my [spaceship]. So it helped to encourage me to want to go do Zumba and then with all the snow was there I was like, "*Oh, I'm shoveling!*"

Similarly, P15 expressed how the game encouraged him to *substitute the sedentariness* of sitting on a bus for a short ride, opting to walk instead. P1 also described how she substituted the sedentariness of taking the elevator: she deliberately took the stairs to get to the 7th floor to get water to earn more spaceship fuel. P1 also *planned exercise opportunities* that would help her succeed in the game, and she materialized the plan by exercising with her child:

> P1: So I got this tape, Shaun T. And it's a hip-hop moving tape. And I decided in the morning that's what we're going to do. So I did it, and it worked one day.

As SL recognized small PA efforts, game players started to *substitute sedentariness* with more physically involving activities such as walking or taking the stairs. This suggests that SL potentially increased the awareness of opportunistic exercise and helped reduce sitting. For participants who are aware of opportunistic exercise, the game provided reasons for them to do so, as suggested by the accounts from P1 and P2. For others, SL may provide an increased awareness of PA opportunities.

Nuanced Preferences Regarding Competition

As a collaborative game, SL was designed *not* to support competition. In a competitive game the mechanics guarantee that there is always a winner and a loser. In contrast, collaborative games have intrinsic mechanics that ensure two players who work together will either both win or both lose [43]. However, the interview data suggests that many participants desired competition. Five out of the eight participants we interviewed proposed competitive game elements even if we did not specifically ask them if they wanted competition. P1, for example noted that competition would make SL more fun and P3 noted that:

> P3: Sometime when you see that someone else is doing better, you want to do better.

It becomes evident that the notion of competition is multifaceted. While previous research has highlighted negative effects of competition [17,18,41] some form of competition may improve users' engagement with exergames. Our analysis highlighted the importance of understanding competition based upon the setting in which it takes place—*intra-family* and *inter-family*—and the relationships of the actors involved.

Intra-family Competition

While SL's game mechanics did not directly facilitate competition, such interactions between the parent and the child may have motivational value. P4, who initially stated that she was not motivated by the game, felt that competing with her child would be motivational for her. Parents further discussed how competition is desirable because it facilitates various forms of interaction with their kids. For example, two parents envisioned how competition would lead to collective assessment of their PA as well discussions of the experience of playing SL with their children. P9 suggested that reviewing and making comparison between her and her child's PA levels is an enjoyable experience:

> P9: It's fun [to have a competition] to see how much you've done [during] the day. Like... my daughter and I might say, *"Okay, which one of us were [higher]?"*

P15 was also comfortable comparing PA levels with his child. He emphasized that it is not a "real competition" but rather an opportunity to observe his child's PA and discuss their game experiences.

> P15: It doesn't bother me [to have a competition with my child]... We don't really have to make it like a competition, you know, she just be happy to get to the [gym session], to really see how much [spaceship] fuel she got. At the end of the [gym session], we just could sit back and discuss how much fuel she earned.

Parent-child competition can also be an opportunity to bond. P6 felt that PA comparisons between the parent and the child are an opportunity to influence behavior by giving motivation and building confidence.

> P6: If your child is, needs more exercise and the adult doesn't need as much, you're kind of helping, using this as a way to kind of bond with your kid. And build some confidence and encourage her to get in shape.

Parents did not express any uneasiness when they saw they were less active than their child. P1 actually suggested the game explicitly show that her son beat her:

> P1: [Make the game say:] "You're beating your mom today!" Or yeah, "You did this many steps, and you outdid your mom!" [...]
> *I: How would that affect you?*
> P1: It'll make me want to go beat him. [laughter]

P6 raised concerns about comparisons with younger children. He was concerned that if they do not perform well in the competition, they may feel incompetent and subsequently lose motivation to play the game:

> P6: There's people gonna feel bad [if they lose]. Especially little kids. Six, seven years old, they may say, *"Well, I'm not doing well. I don't want to do it anymore."*

In summary, parents discussed competition as being more than trying to win or be better than others. Their accounts suggest that parent-child competition in an exergame context may be valued as a means of catalyzing health-promoting social interaction, whereby the parent is able to help the child toward positive behaviors. These interactions may be in the form of observing, discussing, and encouraging PA. Our participants did not express any uneasiness when their PA was compared using the game. While our analysis focuses on the parental perspective, future work should examine children's reaction to their PA being compared with that of their parents.

While only discussed by one participant, an important area for further inquiry is the differing characteristics of individual families and how competition may have a motivational or de-motivational effect on different families. P6's remarks suggest that such competition may need to be cautiously designed to avoid negative consequences.

> P6: [The effect of competition] depends [on] if the family is very close. Sometimes having a competition can be fun. If the family is not really competitive type of family it can sometimes draw some people away. Because they'll feel like, "Oh, well. I don't want to bother doing this, because I'm not gonna win anyway."

P6 notes how the closeness of a family and their inherent competitiveness can impact how a competitive game is received. P6 went onto suggest that families be allowed to tailor competition to fit their unique characteristics.

> P6: I think within the game there should be a choice. You know, do you want to have a competition between members of your family. Or you guys want to monitor and just kind of keep track of each one. Without really put it in a competitive type of stance.

P6's quote suggests that the family environment and the relationship between family members may affect the outcome of competition in a family exergame.

Interfamily competition

Our participants also discussed the potential value of interfamily competition, distinguishing the place for competition between *familiar families* as compared to *new acquaintance families*. Two participants (P1 and P3) who are sisters imagined the value of family-to-family interactions that could emerge from competition:

> P1: We can compete against families. I think that would make it more fun... As long [as we]—*I guess*—sign a paper saying, *"No hard feelings."*

> P3: [In agreement with P1] we can play with different families or a household. [...] I have three girls and one boy. [P1] has her son and her boyfriend... We can be competing against each other and come over to the house on Saturday or take turns and see who won or something.

P1 was slightly more cautious by warning that families should have no hard feeling when they lose. This highlights that while parents may be comfortable with a competitive environment, they acknowledged the potential negative effects that such game elements can yield.

These parents also supported competition between *new-acquaintance families*. However, P2 emphasized the need to share characteristics with the other family. These characteristics may include parental structure (*i.e.,* single or dual-parent), number of children, or PA lifestyle.

> P2: I mean it'd be nice [to compete against], in my case, a single parent and two kids or somehow we would get paired

kind of like [by] family types. Because, I mean, obviously if it's somebody who exercises all the time, we never do.

Similar to P1 and P3, P2 envisioned the interactions that may emerge in family-to-family competition. She suggested that competing with another family would allow her to discuss PA levels and ideas. She also felt that by communicating with the other family, they would be able to meet and exercise together. Her desire to use the game to exchange PA ideas suggests an opportunity to overcome the informational barrier that participants discussed in our formative study. In her account, P2 suggested that by being able to see other families' activity level, she could ask:

P2: "*What did you do on day two when I see you were very active?*" It might give you some ideas that you didn't think of, things you could do. [...] You may end up doing it together.

P2's comments seem to contradict the notion of competition as the pursuit of outdoing others. It may be that she saw competition as simply a benchmark to assess competence or that SL's task-mastery climate encouraged her to focus less on peer-referenced comparison.

In conclusion, similar to parent-and-child competition, caregivers also envisioned how social interaction may emerge in competitions with a familiar family or new-acquaintance family. They described how such interactions can elevate the experience, for example, by increasing the game's entertainment level or facilitating opportunities to meet and discuss their game and PA experiences. These social interactions could potentially help families break the informational barrier to support their child to be active.

Competition: Seeking Social Interaction & Competency

As we analytically studied the emerging themes, it become clear that caregivers' preferences regarding competition aligned with the two constructs from Self-Determination Theory (SDT): relatedness and competence. As discussed previously, this theory helps explain individuals' motivation to be physically active. In SDT, *relatedness* is described as the need to feel connected to others and be concerned about them [28]. Relatedness is also manifested as a need to feel accepted in the social environment [28]. As such, caregivers' desire for competition between others with a shared tie (the parent and child, familiar families, or new acquaintance families who share similar characteristics), and their interest in using competition as a springboard for social interaction may be reflective of their desire for relatedness. Indeed, prior work has shown that PA enjoyment is bolstered when people feel a sense of relatedness with those they are being active with [22].

In parent-child competition and familiar-family competition, the feeling of relatedness may already be present. Therefore game-supported relatedness in this context may be desirable to nurture existing feelings of connectedness. On the other hand, P2's desire to share similar characteristics with new-acquaintance families suggests the need to feel accepted, which is associated with the construct of relatedness. Exergames for such families may need to help nurture relatedness and highlight ways that families share similar characteristics.

Caregivers' positive attitudes towards competition may be further explained as a pursuit of the psychological need of *competence*, as defined by SDT. Competence is described as the feeling of control over the outcome of a task. The primary objective of SL is helping players develop PA competency, that is, the ability to be more physically active. Our findings suggest that the pursuit of competence was an important driver of parents' acceptance of competition. For example, one parent said that parent-child comparison is acceptable if the end goal is to achieve PA competency.

P9: We compete with each other to see which one of us has moved more. So some days she moves a lot more than me. And some days we move equal. Some days I move more. But all positive, no negative. [...] I think competition's good. With each other. As long as they're competing for positive things.

Caregivers and kids also *collectively assessed their PA* using the SL Dashboard. P9 described this in the previous quote where she made PA comparisons with her child day by day. P1 also described a similar comparison, and sometimes used this data to motivate their child by using the Dashboard to provide positive feedback:

P1: After you see [the game's dashboard] and you'd be like, "*Oh, it's not enough.*" Or I'll be like, "*Oh, I did pretty good.*" Or "*We both did good.*" I'll be like, "*Oh, look [child name], this is how much you did.*"

These collective assessments suggest families' desire to assess their capacity to meet the game's objective of more competently engaging in PA.

In conclusion, the data suggests that for our participants, comparisons within a family-based exergame such as SL were seen as positive, in part, because they facilitate opportunities for social interactions that fulfill the need of relatedness. Caregivers indicated that the fulfillment of this feeling is important to maintain their engagement with SL. The caregivers described how they collectively assess their PA performance with the child, which suggests that their engagement with SL was also driven by the desire to feel competent in attaining a physically active lifestyle.

DISCUSSION

Our findings highlight the value of designing systems that help parents and kids to collectively increase PA and reduce prolonged sitting, even if they do not exercise at the same place or at the same time. In our formative study, we identified strong parental support for child activity, but parents were not very active themselves and they infrequently modeled PA—two endeavors correlated with increased child PA [8].We explored how an exergame could support the increase and modeling of PA in a family environment. Our evaluation of SL highlighted the value of exergames for impacting intentions to be physically active. Furthermore, our study identified forms of in-game competition that participants desired. Unlike competition that is focused on outdoing others, our participants desired comparison through competition. Comparisons were perceived to be motivational when the focus is being connected as a family and being competent in achieving wellness. These values resonate with the SDT's psychological needs of relatedness and competence, needs that are well-fostered in a task mastery climate [22].

Based upon our findings and using SDT as theoretical grounding [28], we suggest that future work explore the design of family-focused, task-mastery exergames. We propose a conceptual framework for designing such games (Figure 2); we hope that this rhetorical tool can motivate future work and highlight potential areas of inquiry. In this framework, game engagement (*i.e.*, the desire to play) is driven by two factors (additional factors are potentially salient, we highlight those that arose in our analysis). First, engagement is driven by the goal of being competent in attaining an active life. Our participants regularly monitored their competence by checking their SL dashboard to see how much fuel they acquired and how active they were. This system interaction suggests that the pursuit of competence contributed to participants' desire to use the system. Second, engagement is supported by the satisfaction of relatedness between family members or across families (*i.e.,* feeling connected to and accepted by others). Familial bonding may already be present and this may provide an incentive to play a game that further affirms this bonding. However, our participants also saw the potential of playing family-based exergames to spark family-centric interactions, which suggests the desire for increased bonding between family members. Our participants were in favor of parent-child competition in exergames in large part because they viewed it as a catalyst for family social interaction. Stated differently, they felt that competition could help fulfill their desire for relatedness—feeling connected to others.

When considering the design of exergames, opportunities for positive interactions within a family may be limited if the social environment places too much emphasis on egoistic victories. For example, if a game is designed such that one or more players will win *over* other players, someone in the family may be identified as the weaker player. With such a hierarchy, feelings of shame or disappointment could hinder positive interactions such as discussions about how the family can better achieve its PA.

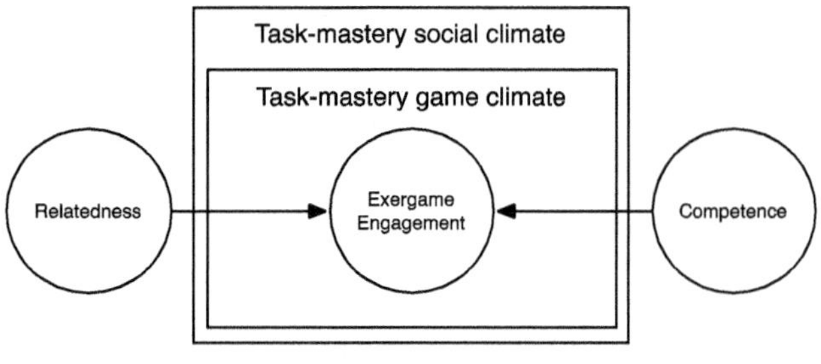

Figure 2. Task-mastery Exergame Framework

In support of this hypothesis, prior work has argued that a *task-mastery* PA climate (as opposed to an *ego climate* that focuses on winning over other players) helps nurture feelings of competence and relatedness, which are correlated with self-determination to engage in PA; ego climate is not correlated with increased self-determination [22]. Therefore, competition in exergames may be best facilitated in a task-mastery environment that nurtures relatedness and competence over outdoing others.

Given this prior work, we propose the design of exergames that help players focus on achieving the game task, versus beating others. Furthermore, given that the social dynamics of the family have important influences on behavior, we suggest that any game designed for play in this environment carefully consider the influence of the family social climate. Based upon this conceptualization, we suggest four design implications for family-based exergames.

Recognize individuals' efforts and value family as a unit

Our findings suggest that participants desired the satisfaction of relatedness and competence during SL game play. Within the SDT framework, a task-mastery climate values individual and group efforts rather than outdoing others, because it nurtures the feeling of relatedness and competence [22]. Therefore, we propose that family exergames should be designed such that the PA efforts of individual members are recognized and celebrated as positive pursuits of a healthier life. Such recognition may be a valuable way of nurturing the feeling of relatedness because it maintains the feeling of acceptance by not excluding the weaker players from the rest of the family. It can also help prevent the feeling of competence from being weakened by peer comparisons. Furthermore, the game should encourage family members to support one another, so that the family can be healthier as a unit, as proposed by Grimes *et. al* [12]. For example, when player's game performance is shared, a beneficial approach may be to emphasize family progress towards meeting the recommended PA level, rather than ranking who exercised the most. And, when individuals' PA is displayed comparatively, the game should highlight how family members could encourage one another to be healthier.

Exergames that leverage personal health monitoring could also be designed so that family members are made aware when others are physically active or meeting their target. For example, an activity tracker wristband might vibrate to let a parent know when their child is active. In turn, the parent could reply by sending a vibrating pulse to the child's wristband, conveying motivational support. Long-distance couples communicating through a similar tool felt the device facilitated stronger feelings of closeness [16].

Design competition that spurs social interaction

Given that a task-mastery environment prioritizes the accomplishment of the game task (*e.g.,* improving one's PA levels) and not beating other players, the inclusion of competitive features in such environments must be carefully considered. Our findings suggest that comparisons in a competition can be desirable if they promote increased social interaction. Future work should explore how competition can be framed not as a way of winning over others, but as a catalyst for positive social interaction and fulfilling the need of relatedness. This is a particularly important consideration for individuals who are motivated to exercise not because they find it intrinsically enjoyable, but when PA is "prompted, modeled, or valued by significant others to whom they feel (or want to feel) attached or related" [28]. Games may be designed to motivate these individuals by guiding players to discuss health topics and to engage in team-based physical activities, using comparisons solely as an outlet for such interactions. For example, in the next iteration of SL, when a parent's PA is lower than her child's (or vice versa), the game could help players imagine and implement creative ways of helping one another to be more active. Such prompting could motivate families to meet target PA levels.

Recognize the pursuit of relatedness

As discussed previously, task-mastery climate is correlated with the satisfaction of relatedness. Our participants preferred to play with individuals or families with whom the barriers to feeling related are reduced. They described wanting to play SL with their own family members, familiar families, and new-acquaintance families who share similar characteristics, such as a comparable family structure (*i.e.,* similar number of parents and child) and routines (*e.g.,* similar PA frequency). To implement this design implication, a feature could be added to the next iteration of SL so that two families with similar PA patterns are matched and their PA levels compared. When one family's PA level is low, the game could automatically encourage that family to ask the other family for PA ideas. This feature could promote health-oriented interactions and simultaneously satisfy the need for relatedness.

One of our participants also suggested that family-based PA tracking systems might be a valuable way to help families bond, even if they are constrained by time and work. These tools can help facilitate a beneficial outcome (bonding), even amidst the barriers to joint exercise that families face [36]. Presenting family members' PA time series data, for example, side by side can help them understand each other's routine. Such increased understanding may help families to form stronger bonds. To implement this design implication, the next iteration of SL could be expanded with a more detailed and child-friendly view of the family members' activities during the day. This detailed view could be made child friendly by dividing the daily timeline into time spans labeled "morning", "work/school", "lunch", "afternoon", etc. When the child's activity is low (or high) during a particular time span, the game could prompt the parent to ask the child what they were doing at that time. The same approach could be applied to the parent.

This type of system has the characteristics of a socially translucent system that supports visibility, awareness, and accountability [10]. In a socially translucent system, individuals become aware of their actions because socially significant data is visible to everyone, and as a result they are aware that other family members are apprised of the actions they choose [10]. In a PA tool that is socially translucent, family members may become aware that their physical activities are visible to others, and they are held accountable for their activity and inactivity. For example a parent might become encouraged to exercise during her lunch hour so that her children can see that she is physically active. Or, a parent who did housework during the day may feel the effort is recognized because his children and partner would be able to see his activity. Family members could also use the PA timeline as an impetus for sending motivational feedback. For example, when activity is low, families could send a caring message and offer support.

While these design ideas are common in social health monitoring tools, in a family setting they may cause a conflict of competing values, such as caring, openness, and modeling [12]. Prior work by Grimes *et al.* [12] suggested that while parents want to model healthy behaviors for their child, they are concerned that seeing their unhealthy behavior could cause the child to worry. Openness also raises privacy concerns. Parents and children may not feel comfortable having the entire family see their activity data, especially as viewers could potentially infer the kind of activity being done. As such, PA monitoring and information sharing in the family can quickly transition from health promotion to surveillance. This concern is supported by prior work emphasizing the need to balance "control over data versus the feeling of surveillance" [37]. Future work should examine how to balance the opportunities and potential benefits of collective PA monitoring as a means of fulfilling the relatedness need (through the enabling of support, nurturing, and bonding) with emergent privacy concerns.

Examine the interplay between family social context & exergame environment

One participant raised an important concern regarding how the particular social dynamics within a family could impact how competition is received. Indeed, prior work has argued that health interventions should be designed to reflect an understanding of household norms, practices, and attitudes [14]. This highlights how the effectiveness of, and reaction to a task-mastery game depend on the larger social family context in which the game resides. If a family places more emphasis on outdoing others, for example, then the task-mastery game climate may be weakened. To reinforce the that value of collaborative effort, SL could be expanded by providing motivational messages to remind family members that they are playing as a team. For example, when the family's PA is low, SL could encourage them with this message: "Your family is not as active as yesterday. Can you think of how you can become more active as a family?"

Future work should examine how exergames can promote task mastery within the encompassing social system. In particular, further research is needed to understand how variations in factors such as parenting style, communication norms, and household routines interact to support or inhibit PA promotion within exergames. For example, future work might explore how task-mastery environments can be designed for maximum effectiveness in families with an *authoritarian* parenting style (where parents prohibit and enforce activities, disregarding child preferences) versus an *authoritative* style (where activities are encouraged but the child is able to choose amongst presented options). One direction would be to design games that resonate with existing parenting styles; another would be to help parents consider alternative parenting approaches that research has shown more effectively encourage child wellness.

LIMITATIONS AND FUTURE WORK

Our work focused primarily on caregivers' perspectives on PA, SL, and the potential for family-based exergames. Exploring such perspectives is critical to the design of these tools; future work should further investigate the complimentary and equally important perspective of the child. It should also be noted that a majority of the participants are female, reflective of the demographics of the gym program we recruited from. However, future work should further examine the perspective of male caregivers to unpack potential gender differences in the context of family-centered exergames. Taking such a gender-sensitive approach will be critical for understanding how to effectively engage different family members in technology-based health interventions. In addition, we studied exergames in the context of a two-member team. Future work should examine how an entire family might work together in an exergame context. For example, researchers should carefully explore issues of sibling rivalry that may emerge, to help avoid potentially undesirable outcomes.

Our participants were community gym attendees who are informed about the value of PA. Future work should examine how systems can be designed for families who are in the pre-contemplative stage, that is, not yet thinking about increasing PA. Future work should also compare the efficacy of exergames to other health education efforts (such as informational workshops) in instilling healthy PA behavior. In addition, building on work by Mandryk *et al.*, [19], a potential direction for future work is to explore how family exergames can not only target MVPA (as in SL), but support anti-sedentary behavior more broadly. Finally, larger, longitudinal studies are needed to further validate our findings and explore how games like SL are used over time as well as their impact on behaviors.

CONCLUSION

Our work has explored how technology can promote PA in the family context, as prior work has shown the important influence of the family on behaviors. Through a formative study, we identified the opportunity for task-mastery exergames to facilitate increased parental modeling of PA. While we designed SL to be collaborative, participants expressed nuanced desires for comparison in competition, particularly as a means of achieving relatedness and competence. These findings suggest the value of a task-mastery climate for nurturing exergame engagement. Accordingly, we presented a set of design recommendations for future work on family exergames. In addition, our preliminary results point the potential efficacy of this game. Therefore, we encourage future work to examine how family-focused exergames can be designed as task-mastery environments. We hope that our design recommendations will spur further research in this area.

ACKNOWLEDGMENTS

We thank the community gym families and staff, and Dr. Magy Seif El-Nasr for supporting this work. This research was funded by a Northeastern University Tier 1 Grant.

REFERENCES

1. Addy, C.L., Wilson, D.K., Kirtland, K. a, Ainsworth, B.E., Sharpe, P., and Kimsey, D. Associations of perceived social and physical environmental supports with physical activity and walking behavior. *American Journal of Public Health 94*, 3 (2004), 440–3.
2. Bandura, A. Social cognitive theory: an agentic perspective. *Annual Review of Psychology 52*, (2001).
3. Castaneda-Sceppa, C., Hoffman, J.A., Thomas, J., et al. A Model to Promote Physical Activity for Families with Young Children. *Journal of Health Care for the Poor and Underserved*, (2014).
4. Colineau, N. and Paris, C. Motivating reflection about health within the family: the use of goal setting and tailored feedback. *User Modeling and User-Adapted Interaction 21*, 4-5 (2010), 341–376.
5. Consolvo, S., Mcdonald, D.W., Toscos, T., et al. Activity Sensing in the Wild: A Field Trial of UbiFit Garden. *CHI 2008*, (2008), 1797–1806.
6. Courneya, K.S. and Mcauley, E. Predicting Physical Activity From Intention: Conceptual and Methodological Issues. *Journal of Sport & Exercise Psychology 15*, (1993), 50–63.
7. Deterding, S. and Dixon, D. From Game Design Elements to Gamefulness: Defining "Gamification."*MindTrek '11*, (2011).
8. DiLorenzo, T. and Stuckyropp, R. Determinants of exercise among children. *Preventive medicine*, (1993).
9. Epstein, L.H., Valoski, A., Wing, R.R., and McCurley, J. Ten-year outcomes of behavioral family-based treatment for childhood obesity. *American Psychological Association 13*, 5 (1994), 373–83.
10. Erickson, T., Kellogg, W.A., and Watson, I.B.M.T.J. Social Translucence: An Approach to Designing Systems that Support Social Processes. *ACM Transactions on Computer-Human Interaction 7*, 1 (2000), 59–83.
11. Grimes, A., Bednar, M., Bolter, J.D., Grinter, R.E., and Atlanta, C.S. EatWell: Sharing Nutrition-Related

Memories in a Low-Income Community. *CSCW' 08*, (2008).

12. Grimes, A., Tan, D., and Morris, D. Toward Technologies that Support Family Reflections on Health. *GROUP '09*, ACM Press (2009), 311.
13. Gruber, K.J. and Haldeman, L.A. Using the family to combat childhood and adult obesity. *Preventing chronic disease 6*, 3 (2009), A106.
14. Kaufman, L. and Karpati, A. Understanding the sociocultural roots of childhood obesity: food practices among Latino families of Bushwick, Brooklyn. *Social science & medicine (1982) 64*, 11 (2007), 2177–88.
15. Kimani, S., Baghaei, N., Freyne, J., Berkovsky, S., Bhandari, D., and Smith, G. Gender and role differences in family-based healthy living networks. *International Conference on Human Factors in Computing Systems - CHI EA '10*, (2010), 4219.
16. Kowalski, R., Loehmann, S., and Hausen, D. cubble: A Multi-Device Hybrid Approach Supporting Communication in Long-Distance Relationships. *TEI 2013*, (2013), 201–204.
17. Lin, J.J., Mamykina, L., Lindtner, S., Delajoux, G., and Strub, H.B. Fish'n'Steps: Encouraging Physical Activity with an Interactive Computer Game. *Ubicomp 2006*, (2006), 261–278.
18. Macvean, A. and Robertson, J. iFitQuest: A School Based Study of a Mobile Location-Aware Exergame for Adolescents. *MobileHCI '12*, (2012), 359–368.
19. Mandryk, R.L., Gerling, K.M., and Stanley, K.G. Designing Games to Discourage Sedentary Behaviour. In A. Nijholt, ed., *Playful User Interfaces*. Springer Singapore, Singapore, 2014, 253–274.
20. McMinn, A.M., van Sluijs, E.M., Harvey, N.C., et al. Validation of a maternal questionnaire on correlates of physical activity in preschool children. *International Journal of Behavioral Nutrition and Physical Activity 6*, (2009), 81.
21. Moore, L.L., Lombardi, D.A., White, M.J., Campbell, J.L., Oliveria, S.A., and Ellison, R.C. Influence of parents' physical activity levels on activity levels of young children. *The Journal of Pediatrics 118*, (1991).
22. Moreno, J.A., López, M., Galindo, C.M., Alonso, N., and González-Cutre, D. Peers' influence on exercise enjoyment : A self-determination theory approach. *Journal of Sports Science and Medicine 7*, August 2007 (2008), 23–31.
23. O'Brien, S. and Mueller, F. "Floyd." Jogging the distance. *CHI 2007*, ACM Press (2007), 523.
24. Poest, C.A., Williams, J.R., Witt, D.D., and Atwood, M.E. Physical activity patterns of preschool children. *Early Childhood Research Quarterly 4*, 3 (1989).
25. Prochaska, J. and Velicer, W. The transtheoretical model of health behavior change. *American Journal of Health Promotion*, (1997).
26. Ratan, R. and Ritterfeld, U. Classifying Serious Games. In *Serious games: Mechanisms & Effects*. 2009, 10–24.
27. Ritterfeld, U., Cody, M., and Vorderer, P. *Serious Games: Mechanisms and Effects*. 2009.
28. Ryan, R.M. and Deci, E.L. Self-Determination Theory and the Facilitation of Intrinsic Motivation, Social Development, and Well-Being. *The American Psychologist 55*, (2000), 68–78.
29. Ryan, R.M., Rigby, C.S., and Przybylski, A. The Motivational Pull of Video Games: A Self-Determination Theory Approach. *Motivation and Emotion 30*, 4 (2006), 344–360.
30. Sallis, J. and Nader, P. Family determinants of health behaviors. In D. (Plenum P. Gochman, ed., *Health Behavior: Emerging Research Perspectives*. New York, 1988, 107–124.
31. Seif El-Nasr, M., Aghabeigi, B., Milam, D., et al. Understanding and evaluating cooperative games. *CHI 2010*, ACM Press (2010), 253.
32. Stanley, K.G., Livingston, I., Bandurka, A., Kapiszka, R., and Mandryk, R.L. PiNiZoRo: A GPS-based Exercise Game for Families. *FuturePlay*, (2010).
33. Strauss, A. and Corbin, J. *Basics of Qualitative Research: Grounded Theory Procedures and Techniques*. Sage, 2007.
34. Takacs, J., Pollock, C.L., Guenther, J.R., Bahar, M., Napier, C., and Hunt, M. a. Validation of the Fitbit One activity monitor device during treadmill walking. *Journal of Science and Medicine in Sport*, (2013), 1–5.
35. Taylor, W., Baranowski, T., and Young, D. Physical activity interventions in low-income, ethnic minority, and populations with disability. *American Journal of Preventive Medicine*, (1998).
36. Thompson, J.L., Jago, R., Brockman, R., Cartwright, K., Page, a S., and Fox, K.R. Physically active families - De-bunking the myth? *Child: care, health and development 36*, 2 (2010), 265–74.
37. Toscos, T. and Connelly, K. Best Intentions: Health Monitoring Technology & Children. *CHI 2012*, (2012).
38. Toscos, T. and Faber, A. Chick Clique: Persuasive Technology to Motivate Teenage Girls to Exercise. *CHI 2006, Student Design Competition*, (2006), 1873–1878.
39. Trost, S.G., Kerr, L.M., Ward, D.S., and Pate, R.R. Physical activity and determinants of physical activity in obese and non-obese children. *International Journal of Obesity 25*, 6 (2001), 822–9.
40. Whitehead, J. Physical activity and intrinsic motivation. *PCPFS Research Digest 1*, 2 (1993).
41. Xu, Y., Poole, E., and Miller, A. This is not a one-horse race: understanding player types in multiplayer pervasive health games for youth. *CSCW '12*, ACM (2012), 843–852.
42. Yoo, D., Huldtgren, A., Woelfer, J.P., Hendry, D.G., and Friedman, B. A Value Sensitive Action-Reflection Model: Evolving a Co-Design Space with Stakeholder and Designer Prompts. *CHI 2013*, ACM (2013).
43. Zagal, J.P. Collaborative games: Lessons learned from board games. *Simulation & Gaming 37*, 1 (2006).

Making "Safe": Community-Centered Practices in a Virtual World Dedicated to Children with Autism

Kathryn E. Ringland, Christine T. Wolf, Lynn Dombrowski, Gillian R. Hayes
Department of Informatics
University of California, Irvine
{kringlan, wolfct, ldombrow, hayesg}@uci.edu

ABSTRACT

The use of online games and virtual worlds is becoming increasingly prominent, particularly in children and young adults. Parents have concerns about risks their children might encounter in these online spaces. Parents dynamically manage the boundaries between safe and unsafe spaces online through both explicit and implicit means. In this work, we use empirical data gathered from a digital ethnography of a Minecraft server, Autcraft, to explore how parents of children with autism continually create a "safe" virtual world through both implicit and explicit means. In particular, we demonstrate how their actions in these spaces define and produce "safety," shedding light on our theoretical understanding of child safety in online spaces.

Author Keywords

Autism Spectrum Disorder; children; assistive technology; virtual worlds.

ACM Classification Keywords

K.4.2. Social Issues: Assistive technologies for persons with disabilities.

INTRODUCTION

As use of online games and virtual worlds becomes increasingly prominent, particularly for children and young adults, parents have concerns regarding their children's welfare. For example, parents worry that their children will come to harm through exposure to pornographic and violent content, cyberbullying [9,50,51], trolling [49], griefing (*i.e.,* intentionally breaking objects) [14,20], and sexual predators. Children with autism[1] are three times more likely to be bullied in school than their neurotypical peers (*i.e.,* those not diagnosed with autism) [3,16]. Given the tight correlation between school-based bullying and cyberbullying [4,34], it is reasonable to assume that children with autism are at great risk online. Particular attributes and behaviors of some children with autism that could lead them to be targeted by bullies include topic fixation, frequent meltdowns, and an inability to be flexible in social situations [16]. Prompted by the worry over bullying and child welfare more generally, some parents have taken action to create "safe" spaces in the online worlds their children frequent. By making "safe" spaces, parents appropriate available technological tools to create conditions that better align with the experiences they wish their children to have. These innovative appropriations augment our understanding of online safety practices, particularly with regards to children with special needs.

In this paper, we describe the results of an ethnographic study of an online multiplayer virtual world created specifically for children with autism and their friends and families. We show how this community has transformed a relatively open virtual world system into a highly structured space. We demonstrate how this community creates a "safe" space where the detailed, explicit structure of the system as well as implicit norms and routine experiences create expectations of safety and therefore freedom from fear of bullying. To create or render this space "safe", parents use practices of rule creation, structure within the virtual world, mentoring, and monitoring. Additionally, we examine these practices as a means to inform our theoretical understanding of safety in online spaces, particularly in light of the differences between how parents discuss online safety and how they make safe.

RELATED WORK

The CSCW community has a history of researching virtual worlds as a place of play (*e.g.,* [12,18,36]). The "work" of childhood is play [22], during which children learn to be appropriately social [21,39]. Children's play within virtual worlds often mimics and expands upon play in the physical world [32]. Specifically for children with autism, playing with technology as a way to scaffold the development of social skills has been an area of much research [26,47]. However, little work has specifically studied children with autism engaging with virtual worlds [38].

Parental concerns about safety shape the way in which their children play in online spaces. A child's context can be

[1] The term *autism* will be used throughout this paper to denote Autism Spectrum Disorder as well as Asperger's Syndrome as previously defined before the DSM-V changes [2].

CSCW 2015, March 14–18, 2015, Vancouver, BC, Canada.

http://dx.doi.org/10.1145/2675133.2675216

Figure 1. Home Office of researcher in-world.

shaped by fears imparted to them by their parents [11] and also by measures parents take to modify or restrict how their children interact in online spaces. Thus, in this section, we review related research focused on (cyber)bullying and children's online safety.

Risks

Concerns of parents and caregivers about online safety range from children viewing inappropriate content to sexual solicitation [10]. Government agencies and other entities, such as schools and community programs, have begun to educate parents and children about online safety [50,52]. Attempting to understand the scope of the problem, researchers have conducted large surveys assessing the risks that online activity poses for children. These studies have found that some youth are more at risk than others when using the Internet [29,48]. For instance, very young users in particular do not have the safety skills (*e.g.,* bookmarking websites so they can easily find a website again or blocking messages from unwanted people) necessary to use the Internet safely [29].

Researchers have examined the risks of children's exposure to inappropriate content, such as pornography, and ways (*e.g.,* technological tools) to protect children from being exposed in the first place [30,46]. For example, researchers have determined the effectiveness of spam filters and content blockers to reduce potential exposure of sexual content to children [46], finding that 42% of youth (ages 10-17) had been exposed to pornographic content within the last year and that filters and blockers did have some effect on reducing this exposure [46]. Findings from the Second Youth Internet Safety Survey show a decrease in the number of youth reported receiving passive sexual solicitation (*e.g.,* ads or spam) from 19% in 2000 to 13% in 2005 [48], with targeted sexual solicitation (*e.g.,* unwanted chat messages) remaining stable during this time period [35]. However, parents continue to worry about sexual predators online [9,10,17].

Bullying

In addition to fears about strangers or inappropriate content that their children might encounter online, parents also worry about what inappropriate content children might *generate.* There are always at least two people involved in any social aggression: the bullied and the bully. A national survey of parents found that children with autism were not only more likely to become victims of bullying, but also perpetrators [3]. Parents are concerned with both sides of bullying: they do not want their children to bully nor to be bullied [9].

Bullying in schools and other physical spaces has long been a concern. However, cyberbullying (*i.e.,* bullying that occurs online) has raised new worries for many parents and educators. There is no consistent definition of cyberbullying, other than it is very similar to physical world bullying [8,28,34]. Cyberbullying can consist of activities such as spreading rumors, making derogatory comments, and making threats [34]. Cyberbullying is more often perpetrated by individuals who are known to children in their offline world (*e.g.,* classmates) rather than strangers or individuals known only through online interactions [34].

Definitions of what behaviors count as bullying vary by community. Outsiders may view many forms of negative social behavior as cyberbullying, whereas members of a particular community may have distinct classifications for these same behaviors and practices [14,20,33]. Parents may also view some activities within virtual worlds—such as destruction of in-world property, harassment, and theft—as cyberbullying, while participants in these virtual world communities term it griefing [9,14,20]. In fact, children and adults who participate in these online communities differentiate between trolling, griefing, bullying, and drama [9,11,14,20,33]. However, parents who do not spend time in world tend not to differentiate between these different terms [11]. Because of the differing viewpoints about cyberbullying between parents and children, solutions to creating safe spaces can also differ.

There is an ongoing debate on how to stop or curb negative, aggressive behaviors in virtual worlds [14], with each virtual world adopting different strategies [7,37]. Most agree that cyberbullying is a problem that needs a solution to create a safer online experience for children [4,8,24]. We build on these related streams of research to demonstrate how a community of parents and players with autism create spaces believed to be safer online by creating structure in a normally open and free virtual world.

METHODS

As a part of an ongoing digital ethnography, we conducted observations in a Minecraft[2] virtual world dedicated to children with autism and their families, Autcraft. The digital ethnography includes immersive participant observations in

[2] http://minecraft.net

the virtual world [6,7,37], conducted by the first author. The first author has 2.5 years experience playing Minecraft recreationally, playing approximately 15 hours per month. The first author gained access to Autcraft via permission of the server's creator. In Autcraft, we have collected 30 hours of in-world observations and analyzed a myriad of digital artifacts surrounding the virtual world. This digital ethnographic study is structurally similar to others conducted with disability communities in virtual worlds, such as Irani *et al.'s* work in Second Life [25]. In-world observations include participating in activities on the server, recording dialogue as it appears in the chat, and writing extensive field notes on everyday practices and events as they occur in the virtual world. Researcher participation in the world also included building an in-world home office that acts as a home-base for in-world activities and enabled other players to visit and ask the researcher questions, as the researcher's presence and purpose were made clear to the community through announcements on Autcraft web forums and through in-world chat (See Figure 1). Observations occurred at various times during the day and evening, mostly during the afternoon and evening hours after North American children (*i.e.,* the bulk of the permitted players) would be home from school. However, as this is a global server, observations have also occurred at other times of the day as well, with approximately 10 hours occurring during the afternoon and evening for players in Australia (*e.g.,* where another large segment of the players live). One of the requirements for playing on the server is that all chat activities occur in English, meaning most players are located in English speaking countries.

In addition to conducting participant observation, researchers conducted two semi-structured expert interviews with

Figure 2. A player next to a pond in a forest in a Minecraft virtual world.

the creator of Autcraft and have analyzed digital artifacts (*e.g.,* community blog posts, web forum posts, and community website pages) collected over a period of six months in early 2014. These included reading approximately 500 forum threads (which included approximately 5,000 forum posts), as well as reading 15 blog posts created by players, parents, and administrators. The first author also participated in the forums, posting information about the research project and answering questions players had about the study. The interviews and all observations were recorded, transcribed, and inspected together.

We used an inductive approach to derive the emergent themes from our data, following techniques similar to those employed in grounded theory [13]. We conducted weekly meetings, during which observations and interviews were discussed, scrutinized, and written into analytic memos. We organized these memos initially through open coding. Through these preliminary codes, types of practices and meanings emerged, particularly patterns of common behaviors and situations around practices of safeguarding. Additionally, through directed coding around the theme of safeguarding behaviors, we identified the dimensions and degrees of variation around these behaviors (*e.g.,* the various *kinds* of safety these parents are making). We used affinity diagramming and axial coding to understand the relationship between, across, and within these codes.

RESEARCH SETTING

Minecraft is an open-ended, free-play style game through which players can interact in a virtual world with no particular goals or play requirements [19]. The open-endedness of Minecraft allows for an expression of individuality and creativity during play, which may make the game particularly compelling for players [19]. The graphics are intentionally pixelated and blocky (See Figure 2). Minecraft can be played as either a single or a multiplayer game. In a single player game, the player is alone in his or her own unique virtual world. This virtual world is procedurally generated at the outset of the initial play session creating a randomly unique world each time a new virtual world is started. As a multiplayer game, Minecraft allows players to interact with others and be as socially engaged as the individual player desires in a procedurally generated virtual world. One world could have each individual building on his or her own land plot, while another could have a communal space where everyone builds collaboratively.

Multiplayer Minecraft servers are virtual worlds that allow multiple players to interact with each other and objects in a shared space. The server in our study, Autcraft, is a semi-private server that currently has approximately 4,000 whitelisted players (*i.e.,* permitted players). Players can only be added to the whitelist if they attest to having autism or a friend or family member with autism who plays on the server. The community Facebook page states that Autcraft is *"[the] first Minecraft server dedicated to providing a safe, fun and learning environment for children on the au-*

tism spectrum and their families." Minecraft generally has no specific directed goals, unlike like a traditional 'game'. However, the Autcraft server does express the goal of allowing players to play without the fear of being bullied. As such, the server provides a supportive environment in which children can gain social skills while participating in an activity they enjoy (*e.g.*, creative play). A virtual world is well suited to the particular needs of children with autism (*e.g.,* the need for coaching in particular social situations and special accommodations for sensory needs, etc.) and can be a boon for parents who struggle to find appropriate, supportive social activities in which their children can participate. Another perceived benefit of the server may be the camaraderie from interacting with others experiencing autism. One parent even noted how her child said he was happy to have autism, because otherwise, he would not be able to play on the server.

While some players only play on Autcraft, others also play on other servers not specifically dedicated to autism. In addition to playing on these larger servers, many players also have their own private servers for their family or also play in single player games. In fact, while on Autcraft, players will discuss leaving the server to go play on a "normal" server or in their own game for a while, usually to come back later.

Unique Features

Autcraft has some unique features that make it different from other Minecraft servers. This includes how the virtual world is administered, unique spaces within the virtual world, and specialized events and activities. Many of these features are accomplished through "mods" (*i.e.,* additional software packages that modify the original game) to either the single player or multiplayer game. Using these mods, a server owner can customize the virtual world, gameplay, and objects within the virtual world (*e.g.,* add or modify existing objects found within the virtual world). Autcraft is set up with specific measures in place with the intention of creating a "fun, safe environment for children with autism". These safety measures include giving each player the ability to keep their items safe from other players, turning off violent monsters, and monitoring and logging of all activity by administrators, moderators, and add-on tools.

Administration

Autcraft's rules are enforced by administrators, junior helpers, and senior helpers. Administrators have the ability to be invisible in the game in order to monitor activity unobtrusively and to maintain the game without being bothered by other players. Helpers are both adults and children that have been selected by the administrators as being 'responsible enough' for the position. Junior helpers are children, while senior helpers are adults on the server. In the main area, there is a board with all the current junior helpers listed and a sign, which describes how junior helpers are selected. It reads:

> *"Jr. Helpers ~ Always helpful. Helpers are picked because they help others and they help the community. They also follow the rules. The [administrators] are always watching. Don't ask to become a helper. We will ask you when we think you are ready."*

Community Areas

In addition to special rules and roles, administrators have created unique spaces for players on the server. These spaces serve as meeting places, areas for building, and a means to go on adventures with other players.

Spawn. The area where players arrive when they first access the virtual world is the starting area, commonly referred to as the "spawn". This is the area where all the current administrators, helpers, and Player of the Week are displayed. Portals to all the other areas players can access in the virtual world are found in the spawn area, the entryway of the virtual world.

Mini-Games. Small, enclosed games or mini-games are group activities that players can choose to take part in within the virtual world. These games have their own arenas that players can access by teleporting through a portal found in the starting area. Mini-games include: Paint Ball, Hide & Seek, Wither Battles, Parkour, and Spleef. In each of these areas, when the player teleports to the arena, players are given the equipment they need in order to participate in the game.

One of the more popular mini-games is Hide & Seek, an extension of the classic "hide and seek" children's game. In this alternate version, hiders that have been caught by the seeker also become a seeker. This allows players to continue playing even after they have been found. In addition, players call out taunts (or hints) to the seeker as time begins to run out to give the seeker a sporting chance to win. For instance, a player might say, "I can't believe I haven't been found yet. I'm very near the rose bushes!"

Villages. Villages are large, public community sites. These can be used by everyone, but cannot be altered by players (*i.e.,* players cannot place or destroy structures in these spaces). Villages include many different kinds of buildings including: hotels, banks, schools, churches, libraries, reading spaces (including outdoor reading gardens), general stores, court houses, and jails. These serve as common meeting grounds for players to engage in various activities.

Player Activities

Players participate in a number of activities within the spaces created by administrators. These activities include building houses and other structures, participating in communal building projects, and socializing within these various spaces.

Player Houses. In the Peaceful Survival World (as opposed to other areas where building is not permitted or only temporary), players can build their houses anywhere outside of the administrator created village as long as they are at least

30 blocks away from other players' buildings. Administrators can "protect" player created houses. Once a house is protected, only designated players (*i.e.,* owners) can add or remove blocks in that house. This protection feature is not available in the original Minecraft software, but is a mod that the administration selected when creating the server.

Community Spaces. Players can also form groups to create their own community spaces. Players have made villages of their own where each member has a house and as a group, they have created other buildings, such as cafés or other places to be together. One player made a *"Hang Out Place"* with a dance floor, cooking area, horse swimming center, and lounge chairs. As noted on a sign left by the space's creator, *"No killing horses is magior,"* meaning that not killing horses was a "major" rule for that communal area. These places serve as spaces for community events to take place such as firework displays.

PARENTAL SAFETY CONCERNS AND "MAKING SAFE" PRACTICES

"Safety" is a thorny concept in any setting, but when considering children and online social spaces, it can become even more complicated. Children mature and learn continually, and not at a steady or predictable rate. Additionally, the children's in-world experiences are largely shaped by their parents and other adults, particularly in the case of Autcraft. Thus, in this research, we focused on the views of the parents, because they have the resources and control to set up and encourage or require their children to use "safe" spaces in online worlds. However, parenting approaches vary widely amongst and even within different cultures and geographies. In this section, we unpack the idea of "safety" as the parents described it in interviews and digital artifacts. We then compare this to the described and observed practices these parents undertake to make Autcraft "safe" for their children. A key finding of this work is that the parents' practices often do not align with their descriptions of safety. By examining both, we deepen our theoretical understanding of online safety, specifically in regard to three categories: emotional safety, physical safety, and social safety. These categories are deeply intertwined, as are the definitions and actions surrounding safety. Our analysis illustrates what families understand safety to mean online, even when they cannot always articulate that understanding.

Emotional Safety

In this section, we describe how parents understand emotional safety in the context of Autcraft and the different practices they engage in to keep their children from emotional harm. Parents define emotional safety in online spaces as securing the child's self esteem, sense of security, and identity acceptance. For parents, emotional safety is breeched when avoidable negative and/or inappropriate behaviors occur, including bullying, trolling, griefing, and sharing inappropriate content.

These risks come from behaviors enacted by an insensitive or cruel "other." On his blog[3], Stuart Duncan, Autcraft's founder, describes the prevalence of these negative experiences in both online and real world settings:

> *Most players come to us with tales of bullying and hate from other servers. Many of those same players experience the same thing from school and in other aspects of their life. They feel they have no friends, no one to talk to and they are angry.*

Bullying and negative social experiences could lead to children with autism viewing their differences (from neurotypical children) as a source of unhappiness [5]. Stuart Duncan explicitly praises avoiding judgment for differences as a feature of the server on his blog:

> *Just last night, a new player said 'this is the only server i have found without being judged for being 'different'.*

Those with disabilities often struggle with positive identity formation in the face of exclusion and negative social experiences [31]. In participating on this server, parents attempt to build a safe space in which players can develop positive self-image and find self-worth without fear of judgment from others.

Preventing Emotional Pain through Explicit Rules

Rude behavior, name-calling and bullying are explicitly prohibited by the community rules[4] of Autcraft:

> *No one likes to be called a name, no one likes it when someone is mean to them, and no one likes to be bullied.*

Explicit rules also regulate acceptable chat discourse, including the prohibition of chat spam or caps, swearing, name-calling, and bullying. These rules govern both the chat content (*e.g.,* dating, scary content, etc.) and the mechanisms by which the conversations may take place (*e.g.,* no bullying, spam, all caps, etc.).

For example, the community actively discourages and restricts potentially "scary" content by regulating avatar appearance and chat content. Given the wide age range of players, the community restricts the use or discussion of fictional monsters associated with the game, often referred to as the "no Herobrine[5]" rule, because such content may be intimidating and frightening for younger players. Justification of rules about content are explained by a parent on the community forum:

> *We want [this server] to be a safe, happy, comfortable place for all our players to enjoy no matter what they're afraid of or who they're talking to.*

This parental stance focused on protection, particularly for younger children, can lead to some resistance from the old-

[3] http://www.stuartduncan.name/

[4] http://www.autcraft.com/rules

[5] Herobrine is a fan fiction monster in Minecraft lore.

er players. For example, the "no dating" rule prohibits players "to talk about dating, or love, or marriage, or being a boyfriend/girlfriend" as well as "pretending to talk about these things…[including] role playing." These explicit rules engender meta-discussions among the players about dating via discourse around the rules themselves:

<matt_awesome>[6] `*hugging Candy3421sis*`

<matt_awesome> `This is just friendhugs`

<matt_awesome> `Dating is not allowed on autcraft`

<(Donator) babes4> `whats dating`

<Candy3421> `no plez`

<cryptic1200> `there are apparently a lot of things not allowed on autcraft`

<matt_awesome> `Dating is what you do with your girlfriend`

<(JrHelper) bb1135> `matt_awesome please stop`

<matt_awesome> `Ok sorry`

<matt_awesome> `I just told about the rules`

<cryptic1200> `we wouldn't want autistic people to breed, obviously...`

<cryptic1200> `that was sarcasm`

<matt_awesome> `Listen to bb1`

<(SrHelper) GlovedPlayer> `Hey, Cryptic, that's not the point and it's a mean thing to say, even if you're joking :/`

Of course, rules must be enforced to be effective. And, as we can see in this example, several types of players—junior helpers, senior helpers, and other players—may work together to stop someone from engaging in what has been deemed inappropriate discourse.

Monitoring and Enforcement

Administrators (*i.e.,* parents who have administrative power in-world), senior helpers (*i.e.,* select parents), and junior helpers (*i.e.,* select children) monitor all chat within the virtual world. In addition to administrative monitoring of chat, the players also monitor each other's chat and activities while in the virtual world. This evidences the extent to which the players have internalized and come to rely on the emotional security the world's predictability affords via rules. Players frequently chime in via chat that a rule is being broken. This behavior creates a self-sustaining safeguarding practice. It speaks to the way in which the rules created by the parents have become important to the children as an embodiment of safety. Below is an excerpt from field notes describing an incident in which players were all role-playing at another player's castle, "bellum", who happened to be offline at the time. One player, "piratescurse", was attempting to police these other players for not asking for permission to be in the castle and was in turn chastised for yelling:

> *The player, piratescurse, tells off some other players for being mean by going into another player's, bel's, castle without permission. Another player counters by saying that piratescurse is "taking over" the castle by policing it. Piratescurse insists that the players ask permission, this time with force, "guys ASK BEL FIRST." Another player chimes in to admonish piratescurse for the use of all caps. More arguing unfolds, with another player in the chat complaining that players are taking their things from the castle. Finally, one player calls for another player to be banned from the game. Piratescurse does not give up the fight easily, and begins calling for anyone to help him, "someone came into my [castle] without asking HELP HELP".*

In this instance, the argument ended when a senior helper stepped in and defused the situation. The most common activities that are policed are that of inappropriate language, use of caps, and spamming. As in the example above, when piratescurse first wrote in all caps, another player noted the rule breaking by reminding everyone in chat, *"caps piratescurse".*

By means of another mod, administrators are able to monitor all chats, including private messages sent from one player to another. This allows the administrators to see any bullying that may occur out of view from the public virtual world forum. Parents' fear about the emotional safety of their children is so great that curtailing the privacy of the players on Autcraft, even in spaces assumed to be private, may be an appropriate sacrifice.

One might imagine a "safe" emotional space in which actions and discussions can be practiced, sometimes with negative consequences, as a type of learning. However, by choosing rule enforcement and surveillance as the primary modes of addressing emotional safety, Autcraft parents implicitly signal that being "safe" means avoiding all risk through obedience to rules and enjoyment of benign activities. Players trust selected others to protect them rather than being provided the agency to learn to be safe themselves.

Enforcement Hierarchy

Beyond explicit rules, the Autcraft servers are set up in such a way as to reduce the potential for negative or inappropriate behaviors that might emerge over time. Parents explicitly control access, monitor and regulate chat communications, and restrict content they deem as potentially frightening to their children. These actions go beyond the definitions of emotional risk the parents provide in interviews, chat forums, and websites, which are largely focused on specific concerns around bullying, and move into a set of risks that are much harder to define and may vary from parent to parent (*e.g.,* content that is inappropriate for one age group of children, but not another).

[6] All player names are pseudonyms.

Tightly controlled access to Autcraft is key to its operation, because any given parent might view particular actions or content differently from another. For example, some sexual content might be viewed by one parent as a normal part of adolescence and by another as deeply inappropriate. Likewise, humor and jokes are highly contextual and person dependent: one person's joke is another's bullying or offensive behavior. Access to Autcraft is regulated through a vetting process, which culminates in individuals being placed on a whitelist, allowing players to access the game. This gatekeeping practice ensures that players have a connection to the autism community (*e.g.,* have autism or are a family member or friend of a player with autism). This personal connection to autism attempts to alleviate the stigma towards autism and reduce the likelihood that members of the group will victimize one another [15]. Typically, the vetting process occurs when individuals describe their connection to autism and agree to follow the rules of the community. Allowing only those with a direct connection to the autism community helps ensure safety by allowing players to express their differences without fear of repercussions such as stigma.

Additionally, server administrators provide individual players with greater access and responsibilities over time. This practice has the dual effect of taking some of the workload off the parents and empowering some more senior members of the community to develop greater social skills and confidence by becoming "helpers." Although most in-world policing occurs by players reminding one another of the rules, those who have been promoted to junior and senior helpers have the ability to mute and jail players who are breaking rules.

These policing functions help maintain the rules while requiring players with autism (*i.e.,* junior helpers) to police their friends. This can be quite a responsibility, as one young player referred to logging onto Autcraft as a junior helper as *"going back to work"*. On the one hand, peer enforcement may improve the in-world experience dramatically for both the helpers and the players they monitor—much like the traditional "hall monitor" in schools. On the other hand, however, by offloading the enforcement of rules developed by adults with particular concerns, parents may inadvertently be increasing the stress and social anxiety of their children, another kind of emotional risk.

Regardless, the inclusion—and exclusion—of particular players from the server or from the ranks of helpers implicitly demonstrates a key component of safety as enacted by the Autcraft server. Emotional safety, in light of this hierarchy, must be understood as an evolving boundary regulation process, much like privacy has been understood by others [1,40]. What might hurt another's feelings or cause emotional discomfort is under continuous negotiation. Meanwhile, the boundaries between safe and unsafe are tightly controlled. The administrators of Autcraft must navigate the tension between inclusion of those who need such a space with protection of the space from the general public who might want in. Likewise, they must balance the needs of developing emotional maturity—through questioning discourses and promoting helpers—with the need to protect those inside the boundaries of the safe space from emotional harm.

Physical Safety

Despite virtual worlds having no explicit physicality themselves, parents have substantial concerns that center on what we name *virtual physical safety*. This type of safety has two components: the transfer of risk from the *virtual* world into the *physical*, such as the risk that might be posed by sexual predators, and the risk to the *physical* elements of the avatar in the *virtual* world (*e.g.,* being killed in world, having a player's home or other buildings destroyed, and item theft).

Physical Risk Inside a Virtual World

Risks of all kinds in and surrounding Autcraft come under the label of bullying. Just as bullies in the physical world not only taunt, but also injure their victims, the same is true in the virtual world. Parents fear their children's avatars or property may come to harm at the hands of online bullies. In an interview with Stuart Duncan, he describes the physical risks inside a virtual world:

> *All of these people were telling the same stories, about how their children were bullied on every server they tried. Even on XBox, where you can only play with people you add as a "friend"... it was [nonstop] bullying. Either killing them all the time, stealing their things, destroying everything [they] build.*

Unsurprisingly, there are explicit rules from the Autcraft community website around both injury to the avatar and "griefing":

> *...building a trap of any sort for players, Trapping (blocking them in), break a block out from under someone or otherwise somehow find a way to kill another player will result in being jailed.*
>
> *If something was created, crafted, built, placed or simply owned by another player, it is not ok to take it or break it.*

Some rules regarding physical safety can be enforced in part through mods. Technology-assisted rule enforcement leaves little ambiguity. Player versus player damage is turned off in all areas of the virtual world except for a specific arena designated for combat. This means that players cannot attack and injure or kill one another outside the combat arena. Administrators can "protect" player created houses. Once a house is protected, only designated players (*i.e.,* owners) can add or remove blocks in that house. Property protection also safeguards players' virtual animals from harm from other players if they are fenced within the property.

Not all property can be protected automatically, however, and in practice, those rules that cannot be enforced automatically—primarily focused on "griefing"—are variably enforced. Although these rules are quite detailed in their wording, administrator actions provide insight into the actual meaning of avoidance of griefing in this space. For example, while the rule against destroying property is enforced for players who repeatedly inflict damage on other player's possessions, other players, especially younger players, typically are not punished for property destruction. In this case, parent and helper actions help us to see that learning to navigate the physical space—including through construction and destruction of property—is a value of a "safe" space.

Young and new players can make mistakes when interacting within the world. They may not understand the consequences of their actions, be new to interacting with the physics of the space, and so on. Additionally, there is recognition that having autism increases the likelihood that one might have poor executive functioning and anger management skills [23,41]. These infractions—particularly when they happen infrequently—then are handled by talking to the player about the problem in the chat window. Mentoring replaces punishment to privilege the emotional wellbeing of the perpetrator over the physical safety of others.

Virtual Risks to the Physical World

As parents have stated in other surveys [9,51], one of the biggest concerns about their children going online is the risk of strangers hurting them in some way in the offline world. To mitigate this risk, the Autcraft community website explicitly prohibits sharing of personal information:

> *The Internet is a scary place sometimes and not everyone is who they appear to be. As such, sometimes we even need to be protected from ourselves where this is concerned. No personal information other than your first name may be shared on the server, on our forums, on our Facebook page.*

Parents are worried about their children divulging information that strangers can use to harass them or even simply to locate them in the physical world. By creating such rigid regulation of information flow in this space, parents may actually prevent their children from learning how and when to disclose such information in a relatively safe experimental world. The child players, however, appear to bristle at these rules, recognizing that the risk is limited for some personal information that is technically prohibited, as is shown in the following excerpt from researcher field notes:

> *One player mentions that their school does not start for another week because they are in the state of New Mexico. Suddenly, several players are speaking up in chat comparing and discussing which state they live in. When one player asks what town players live in, another player says, "please be [careful] telling where you live, safety first". The first player says, "fine what county". A junior helper then also joins the chat, "guys please don't share where [you] live". This is retorted by the original player, "[it's] not like we are sharing our [address, it's] a state".*

In this example, as in the chat transcript in the emotional safety section, other players began enforcing the rules. By the end of the conversation, a junior helper advised players not to share personal information. Even in the face of such authority, however, the players respond with their own understanding of what it means to avoid risk and be safe, a more liberal definition than the rules provide but still fairly conservative from a general online community viewpoint. No one was punished for these infractions, and the situation was not deemed serious enough for intervention from a senior helper or administrators. This indicates that in context, the parents themselves may also see the wisdom of a more tempered approach regardless of what is explicitly stated and defined on the community's website.

Social Safety

Parents' actions demonstrate an important element to their working definition of safety: the ability to learn social skills and act as a community. Social safety is rarely spoken about within the community, but rather simply enacted through practices such as structure, role-playing, and mentoring.

Additional Social Structure

Neurotypical children often learn their social skills in classrooms, playgrounds, and virtual worlds like Minecraft through a lot of trial and error, watching, and mimicking [21,22,39]. These kind of free-form explorations of the social world are supported particularly well by Minecraft. However, as is described by Duncan in an interview, additional structures are often necessary to teach social skills to children with autism [42]:

> *Minecraft servers are everywhere but they're largely left free. That is to say, they let players do as they please. And rightly so really, considering Minecraft is a sandbox, a free to do as you please type of game. But that environment isn't great for those that may struggle socially.*

Autcraft seeks to be a place for children with autism to learn appropriate social skills and relationships with other children, and therefore, the administrators have created structured social skills interventions throughout the world.

Mods help support the basic social act of welcoming a new player. When a new player logs into the world for the first time, the chat window instructs all players online to welcome the new player:

```
<CHAT> slithytove joined the game.
<CHAT> Hello slithytove!! Welcome to Autcraft Spawn!
<-------------=[Autcraft]=---------------->
<CHAT> Welcome, slithytove!
<CHAT> Welcome slithytove to AutCraft!
```

Figure 3. A giant pony construction found in Ponyville.

<(Donator) MuffinMadness> Welcome

<KnightofAwesome> Hello slithytove

<(SrHelper)ParentMiner> hi tove :)

<mathman> Howdy tove.

<(YouTube) piratescurse> welcome slithy-tove

In addition, the chat window occasionally sends messages instructing players how to complete certain tasks (*e.g.,* how to protect a house when the player finishes building it). These built in instructions give the players cues on how to be supportive of one another.

Autcraft also gives structure and context to the players through the physical spaces within the virtual world. Administrators have sectioned off various areas within the virtual world and created distinct locations in these areas. For example, Peaceful Survival World, a location within the world of Autcraft, is the only area players are permitted to build their homes and other creations.

Parents often take the lead in large construction sites. For example, the community villages and themed zones such as Ponyville (See Figure 3) and Giantland (See Figure 4). Driven by the need to create a contextualized space for their children to play, parents run the risk of overreaching and not giving their children the freedom to build in Minecraft for himself or herself. However, this is sometimes balanced by having "build groups" consisting of parents and children who work on projects together, such as Doctor Who Island.

Individual players (both parents and children alike) create personal and public spaces in Autcraft. These spaces give the players context for various activities. An example of player created spaces is that for mourning of physical world people or pets. One such memorial is a large cross with flowers growing around its base. On a sign below the cross it reads *"R.I.P. Bubbles dad"*. Another player created a special memorial room in his community house for his deceased dog (See Figure 5) that can only be accessed with permission of the player. Inside the room are flowers, signs with inscriptions about the beloved pet, and an in-world dog that lives on in the virtual world. Parents strive to encourage children players to create both literal and metaphorical structure in the virtual world. For example, when a child complained of being lonely, a parent suggested building a clubhouse and inviting other players to come over and play.

Figure 4. Giant recreations of the Autcraft administrators overlooking Giantland.

Role Play

Children learn through play [39,45], and whether online or off, role-playing provides a means for trying on potential future careers, various social configurations, and so on. To facilitate role-playing, at the behest of a group of young players, the Autcraft parents created "Role Play Castle." As one parent posted about the benefits of role-playing on the community forum:

> *It allows people with autism the opportunity to play around with social interaction without the pressure of worrying about getting it wrong.*

Despite its recognized benefits [26,43,44], many of the adults on the server are conflicted about allowing role-playing. This activity can blur the rules of the server, potentially impacting the emotional and physical safety of players. For example, a lively sword fight could easily end in physical damage to a player's body. Likewise, playing "house" invariably leans toward discussions about dating, marriage, or future imagined children, and a fictitious daring spy mission might frighten young children. The positive nature of role-play—that it sparks potentially endless imagination—is the very thing that creates substantial risk. Thus, the very existence of Role Play Castle without substantial rules and regulations surrounding it demonstrates how conflicted the Autcraft community is around issues of safety as they are enacted in world. These parents recognize both the importance of play as a necessary aspect of socialization, important given the challenges children with autism experience around social skills, and the potential social risks associated with unregulated play spaces.

Learning through Mentoring

Administrators and peers teach players about fairness, work, and sharing. These community values are a part of the official community rules:

> *...we encourage everyone to be generous, to be nice and to help as much as you can. You don't have to give your stuff away but to just give someone a little help if they need it. And always do your best to remember to say "please" and "thank you".*

The server has its own monetary system with which players can purchase objects. In addition, players often barter items that they might need.

Players may share objects with others through community chests. People offer to trade or give away objects through the chat dialog. Players also will meet at the spawn to give away excess items, calling it a "drop party". This means they will just drop their items on the floor and if anyone wants them, they can pick them up. As one parent said on the community blog:

> *I wanted to say, my son is loving Autcraft. Another child gave him gifts today and he was shocked. A little while later he said to me, 'I didn't really want to, but I gave some gifts away to others. It makes me want to give things to people.' It is a new thing for him to want to share.*

Sharing is a community value, which is then taught to and encouraged in younger players through these activities. More experienced players engage in mentoring of other players to perpetuate sharing practices throughout the community.

Social safety is ambiguous and flexible, with risks that are hard to define. Parental actions in this venue indicate an interest in education over protection. Structures and rules are still heavily used, but they are conceived as tools for learning more so than regulations to be policed. These tightly controlled structures create a space in which children with autism can play collaboratively. However, they also restrict the kinds of relationships players can form with each other. They may also make it more difficult for the children to translate the social skills they learn in game to their lives outside of the game. This kind of generalization is a key goal for socials skills interventions but extremely challenging to meet.

DISCUSSION

Parents must balance the needs of their children to explore, learn, and grow with the potential risks such exploration inherently includes. Anyone who has watched a child take a first step, jump from a high height, or ask a crush on a date knows the anxiety that comes with these acts. When those children have special needs, this anxiety can become even

Figure 5. Player created memorial for a family dog.

more profound, leading parents to define and redefine their own thoughts about safety, independence, and even childhood itself through both their discussions and their actions. In this work, we explored how parents make "safe" spaces for their children online, a place that has both the potential for limitless learning and exploration, but also terrifying risks. Our results demonstrate that it is not enough to define safety based solely on what parents are able to articulate. Actions of the parents in the Autcraft community make safety through their monitoring and enforcement of rules through a variety of social and technological means. Safety is accomplished in these settings by actions that prioritize and balance risks and rewards and attempt to align viewpoints of various members of the community.

In this online community, there are several key complications associated with attempting to reduce risk. Reducing one risk can increase another. Actions to mitigate risk can infringe on a child's personal growth. The community has to prioritize certain risks over others due to resource constraints. Finally, children sometimes resist being controlled.

Members of the community—largely led by parent administrators but including child players, parent players, and helpers—collectively determine which risks to mitigate and how to resolve them (*e.g.*, through the mods to the software, rules, and so on). The prioritization of safety-related actions takes place through various channels. Parents negotiate with one another through forum and chat discussions, through social networking sites, and also through the software code. Throughout these processes, the outside world is consistently seen as threatening. It is perhaps unsurprising that such fear would exist amongst community members given the reason for Autcraft's creation in the first place. Parents with children of special needs have a unique set of lived experiences that may make the social world feel inherently unsafe. Parents who are accustomed to hearing about their children's deficits [27,31] are understandably more likely to fear the dangers that surround them. They may see a need to control not only dangers from the outside world, but also the danger of those found in the difference in their own child. However, at the same time, many parents of children with special needs regularly lament that their children can learn more, do more, and be more than the outside world allows. Thus, parents must balance the risk of harm from others with the risk of enabling enough control over the environment to allow their children to grow and mature. Safeguarding—keeping out the dangers of the outside world—can have the unintended consequence of reduced opportunities to learn and perhaps even infantilizing children as they grow into adolescents and adults.

In practice, parents must continually work to align themselves with the interests and actions of other parents as well as children on the Autcraft server. Without this alignment process, their efforts to make a safe space cannot be effective. Parents and their children must agree and enact the same practices to mitigate risk. This tension can be seen when children and young adults push back on their parents' control and create their own practices. Through this virtual world, parents have created the means by which their children can gain more responsibility in enforcement of rules through the junior helper role. This role, as well as informal policing by server members who are not officially designated as junior helpers, may help children learn self-regulation and how to read the social cues necessary to regulate others, important skills for children with autism. There is, however, a tension between the potential benefits from learning these types of regulating behaviors and their potential to create stress or social anxiety from the undue burden these types of responsibilities can create. As we see, 'play' begins to feel like 'work' for some children taking on these junior helper roles.

Parents must also find alignment between each other, determining not only for themselves what practices to employ and which risks to prioritize, but also aligning their beliefs and practices with other parents. Parents must agree on the "right" way to safeguard each other's children while in the online space. Meanwhile, administrators and players, parents and children, continually redefine the boundaries of "safe." Safety is never complete, can never really be achieved, because it is continually developed and produced.

Given the challenges parents face in their daily lives, the creation of Autcraft as a safe online space for children with autism to play is in itself rather astonishing. Parenting is an inherently fraught endeavor, with numerous schools of thought. From debates about co-sleeping or sleep training and cloth or paper diapers to the merits of a gluten free diet or ABA therapy, parents align with, judge, and argue with other parents in nearly every aspect of their child rearing. Thus, the very existence of Autcraft, a collective endeavor created by thousands, is impressive. Ultimately, the process of balancing and aligning views and actions allow a disparate community with a shared goal to make a safe space in the online world. At the same time, they are making a new concept of online safety. While parents readily label certain practices as *unsafe* (*e.g.*, bullying), an agreed upon, coherent definition of safety eludes parents' explicit discussions (*e.g.*, blogs, chats, forum posts, even posts about rules, etc.) and for good reason. Safety must be made, it cannot just be discussed. Any parental attempts at explicitly defining the practices that form safe conduct will have a limitation in that what is 'safe' cannot be universally applicable to all situations and contexts.

In the context of Autcraft, safety comes out of a continually negotiated process through which both parents and children strive for a balance between risk and autonomy in a given situation. Through both social and technological means, the concept of online safety emerges as one that is dynamic, contextual, rapidly shifting, and continually negotiated. Through their interactions, parents and children continually define and redefine the fluid boundaries between safe and unsafe, allowing for the evolution of both the technological platform's capacity to allow for safe practices and the inhabitant's social practices the platform is meant to guard. No static definition of safety can account for what we see in this work: safety is, in fact, a process.

CONCLUSION AND FUTURE WORK

The results of our work suggest that parents define and enact safety in complementary, but different ways. By examining both their production of safety through appropriation of the Minecraft platform and their discourse around safety, we can develop a deeper understanding of the evolving meaning of "safe" in online spaces. Three categories of risks emerge from our empirical work—emotional, physical, and social—but even these categories should be seen as evolving. This work therefore contributes to our greater understanding of online safety and collaboration by recasting safety as a process enacted by a community in online spaces.

Our work demonstrates how players—both parents and their children—continually manage the dynamic boundaries between safe and unsafe in an online virtual world, Autcraft. The production of a safe space is a feat unto itself, and the communal processes by which parents negotiate with one another to create this space is worth exploring in detail in future work. A deeper look at what happens when parents do not agree on what "safe" means and how they resolve that tension could illuminate further how safety is crafted in online spaces.

Additionally, this work has thus far privileged the parents—as indeed does the platform itself. Future work should explore these same experiences from the viewpoint of the children and the tensions between parents and children as safety is made in online spaces. More work is needed to examine how the children in these virtual worlds engage in safety practices, accept or reject safety measures imposed by their parents, and still fulfill their own needs and desires for socializing and fun in these online spaces.

By shifting to a view of safety as a process and recognizing that the discourse and actions of people in virtual worlds collectively make safety, we can push the field farther in terms of our understanding of collaborative online experiences. We can also strengthen our ability to create educational interventions for children about online safety and create additional supports for parents making safety in online spaces.

ACKNOWLEDGMENTS

We thank the members of Autcraft for the warm welcome to their community, in particular Stuart Duncan and other participants for their time and insights. We appreciate the thoughtful feedback from the members of the LUCI lab and STAR group at UCI. We also thank Paul Dourish, Melissa Mazmanian, and Jed Brubaker for helpful conversations during the formative stages of this paper. This work was supported in part by the Intel Science and Technology Center for Social Computing. We would also like to thank Robert and Barbara Kleist for their support. This work is covered by human subjects protocol #2014-1079 at the University of California, Irvine.

REFERENCES

1. Altman, I. Privacy regulation: culturally universal or culturally specific? *Journal of Social Issues 33*, 3 (1977), 66–84.
2. American Psychiatric Association. *Diagnostic and Statistical Manual of Mental Disorders*. 2013.
3. Anderson, C. IAN Research Report_ Bullying and Children with ASD _ Interactive Autism Network.pdf. *Interactive Autism Network*, 2012. http://www.iancommunity.org/cs/ian_research_reports/ian_research_report_bullying.
4. Aponte, D.F.G. and Richards, D. Managing cyberbullying in online educational virtual worlds. ACM Press (2013), 1–9.
5. Bagatell, N. Orchestrating voices: autism, identity and the power of discourse. *Disability & Society 22*, 4 (2007), 413–426.
6. Boellstorff, T., Nardi, B., Pearce, C., and Taylor, T.L. *Ethnography and Virtual Worlds: A Handbook of Method.* Princeton University Press, 2012.
7. Boellstorff, T. *Coming of Age in Second Life: An Anthropologist Explores the Virtually Human*. Princeton University Press, 2010.
8. Bowler, L., Mattern, E., and Knobel, C. Developing Design Interventions for Cyberbullying: A Narrative-Based Participatory Approach. iSchools (2014).
9. boyd, danah and Hargittai, E. Connected and concerned: Variation in parents' online safety concerns. *Policy & Internet 5*, 3 (2013), 245–269.
10. boyd, danah, Marwick, A., Aftab, P., and Koeltl, M. The Conundrum of Visibility: Youth safety and the Internet. *Journal of Children and Media 3*, 4 (2009), 410–419.
11. boyd, danah. *It's Complicated: the social lives of networked teens*. Yale University Press, 2014.
12. Brown, B. and Bell, M. CSCW at play:'there'as a collaborative virtual environment. *Proceedings of the 2004 ACM conference on Computer supported cooperative work*, ACM (2004), 350–359.
13. Charmaz, K. *Constructing Grounded Theory: A Practical Guide to Qualitative Analysis*. Sage Publications Ltd, 2006.
14. Chesney, T., Coyne, I., Logan, B., and Madden, N. Griefing in virtual worlds: causes, casualties and coping strategies. *Information Systems Journal 19*, 6 (2009), 525–548.
15. Collins, R.L., Wong, E.C., Cerully, J.L., Schultz, D., and Eberhart, N.K. *Interventions to Reduce Mental Health Stigma and Discrimination*. RAND Corporation, 2012.
16. Diament, M. Kids With Autism Bullied Three Times More - Disability Scoop.pdf. *Disability Scoop*, 2012. http://www.disabilityscoop.com/2012/03/26/kids-autism-bullied/15242/.
17. Dombrowski, S.C., Gischlar, K.L., and Durst, T. Safeguarding young people from cyber pornography and cyber sexual predation: a major dilemma of the internet. *Child Abuse Review 16*, 3 (2007), 153–170.
18. Dourish, P. Introduction: The state of play. *Computer Supported Cooperative Work (CSCW) 7*, 1 (1998), 1–7.
19. Duncan, S.C. Minecraft, beyond construction and survival. *Well Played: a journal on video games, value and meaning 1*, 1 (2011), 1–22.
20. Foo, C.Y. and Koivisto, E.M. Defining grief play in MMORPGs: player and developer perceptions. *Proceedings of the 2004 ACM SIGCHI International Conference on Advances in computer entertainment technology*, ACM (2004), 245–250.
21. Garvey, C. Some properties of social play. *Merrill-Palmer Quarterly of Behavior and Development*, (1974), 163–180.
22. Garvey, C. *Play*. Harvard University Press, Cambridge, MA, 1990.
23. Geurts, H.M., Verté, S., Oosterlaan, J., Roeyers, H., and Sergeant, J.A. How specific are executive functioning deficits in attention deficit hyperactivity disorder and autism? *Journal of child psychology and psychiatry 45*, 4 (2004), 836–854.
24. Hall, L., Jones, S., Paiva, A., and Aylett, R. FearNot!: providing children with strategies to cope with bullying. *Proceedings of the 8th International Conference on Interaction Design and Children*, ACM (2009), 276–277.

25. Irani, L.C., Hayes, G.R., and Dourish, P. Situated practices of looking: visual practice in an online world. *Proceedings of the 2008 ACM conference on Computer supported cooperative work*, ACM (2008), 187–196.

26. Jordan, R. Social Play and Autistic Spectrum Disorders: A Perspective on Theory, Implications and Educational Approaches. *Autism 7*, 4 (2003), 347–360.

27. Kras, J.F. The "Ransom Notes" Affair: When the Neurodiversity Movement Came of Age. *Disability Studies Quarterly 30*, 1 (2010).

28. Levy, N., Cortesi, S., Gasser, U., et al. Bullying in a Networked Era: A Literature Review. *Kinder & Braver World Project: Research Series*, (2012).

29. Livingstone, S., Haddon, L., Görzig, A., and Ólafsson, K. Risks and safety for children on the internet: the UK report. *Politics 6*, (2010), 1.

30. Livingstone, S. and Palmer, T. Identifying vulnerable children online and what strategies can help them. (2012).

31. Mankoff, J., Hayes, G.R., and Kasnitz, D. Disability studies as a source of critical inquiry for the field of assistive technology. *Proceedings of the 12th international ACM SIGACCESS conference on Computers and accessibility*, (2010), 3–10.

32. Marsh, J. young children's play in online virtual worlds. *Journal of Early Childhood Research 8*, 1 (2010), 23–39.

33. Marwick, A. and boyd, danah. 'It's just drama': teen perspectives on conflict and aggression in a networked era. *Journal of Youth Studies*, (2014), 1–18.

34. Mishna, F., Saini, M., and Solomon, S. Ongoing and online: Children and youth's perceptions of cyber bullying. *Children and Youth Services Review 31*, 12 (2009), 1222–1228.

35. Mitchell, K., Finkelhor, D., and Wolak, J. Youth Internet Users at Risk for the Most Serious Online Sexual Solicitations. *American Journal of Preventive Medicine 32*, 6 (2007), 532–537.

36. Nardi, B. and Harris, J. Strangers and friends: Collaborative play in World of Warcraft. *Proceedings of the 2006 20th anniversary conference on Computer supported cooperative work*, ACM (2006), 149–158.

37. Nardi, B. *My Life as a Night Elf Priest An Anthropological Account of World of Warcraft*. University of Michigan Press, 2010.

38. Newbutt, N. Representations of Self in Classroom Virtual Worlds: a case-study of pupils on the autism spectrum. (2012).

39. Nicolopoulou, A. Play, Cogntivie Development, and the Social World: Piaget, Vygotsky, and Beyond. *Human Development 36*, 1 (1993), 1–23.

40. Palen, L. and Dourish, P. Unpacking privacy for a networked world. *Proceedings of the SIGCHI conference on Human factors in computing systems*, ACM (2003), 129–136.

41. Sofronoff, K., Attwood, T., Hinton, S., and Levin, I. A Randomized Controlled Trial of a Cognitive Behavioural Intervention for Anger Management in Children Diagnosed with Asperger Syndrome. *Journal of Autism and Developmental Disorders 37*, 7 (2007), 1203–1214.

42. Strain, P.S. and Schwartz, I. ABA and the Development of Meaningful Social Relations for Young Children with Autism. *Focus on Autism and Other Developmental Disabilities 16*, 2 (2001), 120–128.

43. Tartaro, A. and Cassell, J. Playing with virtual peers: bootstrapping contingent discourse in children with autism. *Proceedings of the 8th international conference on International conference for the learning sciences-Volume 2*, International Society of the Learning Sciences (2008), 382–389.

44. Thorp, D.M., Stahmer, A.C., and Schreibman, L. Effects of sociodramatic play training on children with autism. *Journal of autism and developmental disorders 25*, 3 (1995), 265–282.

45. Vygotsky, L.S. *Mind in Society: The Development of Higher Psychological Processes*. Harvard University Press, Cambridge, MA, 1978.

46. Wolak, J., Mitchell, K., and Finkelhor, D. Unwanted and Wanted Exposure to Online Pornography in a National Sample of Youth Internet Users. *PEDIATRICS 119*, 2 (2007), 247–257.

47. Wolfberg, P., Bottema-Beutel, K., and DeWitt, M. Including Children with Autism in Social and Imaginary Play with Typical Peers. *American Journal of Play 5*, 1 (2012).

48. Ybarra, M.L., Mitchell, K.J., Wolak, J., and Finkelhor, D. Examining Characteristics and Associated Distress Related to Internet Harassment: Findings From the Second Youth Internet Safety Survey. *PEDIATRICS 118*, 4 (2006), e1169–e1177.

49. Your Kids are Being Trolled on Minecraft. *Ruby Red Bricks*, 2013. http://rubyredbricks.com/blog/2013/10/06/your-kids-are-being-trolled-on-minecraft/.

50. What is Cyberbullying. *stopbullying.gov*. stopbullying.gov.

51. Technology and Youth: Protecting your Child from Electronic Aggression. *Centers for Disease Control and Prevention*. www.cdc.gov.

52. A Parent's Guide to Internet Safety. *The FBI: Federal Bureau of Investigation*. http://www.fbi.gov/stats-services/publications/parent-guide.

The Effects of Pay-to-Quit Incentives on Crowdworker Task Quality

Christopher G. Harris
Department of Computer Science
SUNY Oswego
Oswego, NY 13126
christopher.harris@oswego.edu

ABSTRACT
Companies such as Zappos.com and Amazon.com provide financial incentives for newer employees to quit. The premise is that workers who will accept this offer are misaligned with their company culture, which will therefore negatively affect quality over time. Could this pay-to-quit incentive scheme align workers in online labor markets? We conduct five empirical experiments evaluating different pay-to-quit incentives with crowdworkers and evaluate their effects on mean task accuracy, retention rate, and improvement in mean task accuracy. We find that the number of times a user is prompted for the inducement, the type and frequency of performance feedback given to participants, the type of incentive, as well as the amount offered can help retain high-performing workers but encourage poor-performing workers to quit early. When we combine the best features from our experiments and examine their aggregate effectiveness, mean task accuracy is improved by 28.3%. Last, we also find that certain demographics contribute to the effectiveness of pay-to-quit incentives.

Author Keywords
Risk Aversion; Human Computation; Crowdsourcing, Relevance Assessment; Incentive Schemes; Pay-to-quit Incentives

ACM Classification Keywords
H.5.2 Information Interfaces and Presentation: Interaction Styles; J.4 Social and Behavioral Sciences: Economics

General Terms
Human Factors; Economics; Experimentation

http://dx.doi.org/10.1145/2675133.2675185

INTRODUCTION
Online labor markets have facilitated the performance of *microtasks* – concise, simple, and easily-defined tasks that humans can perform well but computers cannot, such as annotating images, performing relevance assessments, or validating common sense facts. These labor markets have demonstrated value, dramatically lowering costs, reducing task completion times and, provided the task is well explained and quality checks are in place, the results can be of high quality. For these reasons, online labor markets, such as Amazon Mechanical Turk (MTurk), have proliferated, serving as matchmaker between task requester and worker.

For centuries, economic theory has held that rational workers will choose to improve their outcome in response to incentives [22, 31]. Over the same period of time, techniques to enhance worker motivation have been discussed, such as in the writings of Industrial Age philosophers Robert Owen and Jeremy Brentham, as well as through experiments by behavioral psychologists such as Frederick Herzberg and B.F. Skinner. More recently, companies known for their service have using incentives early on to separate employees motivated by personal financial gain from those who are not, under the premise that the former will not provide the same commitment to corporate culture and loyalty than the latter. Zappos.com, a company regarded for its top-notch customer service, has provided a pay-to-quit incentive of $4,000 to newly-hired employees, called "The Offer" [21, 28]. This offer provides an opportunity for newbies to quit with no questions asked. However, this opportunity is rarely acted upon, with fewer than three percent of new employees accepting the offer. Other companies have offered similar incentives with varying results. In May, 2012, start-up wine seller L18.com offer employees pay-to-quit incentives of up to a month's salary with six of the company's 85 employees taking the offer [18]. Amazon also offers its employees $1,000 per year of employment, up to $5,000, as a pay-to-quit incentive [26]. In June 2014, Riot Games, maker of the popular "League of Legends" game, announced it would offer employees up to $25,000 to quit [3].

Many researchers that have examined workplace employment incentives have concluded they must work, since they are still being offered and these offers have expanded to new firms. This gives rise to some important questions: Can these same pay-to-quit incentives be structured for online labor markets to obtain similar increases in productivity? Also, which motivational techniques, such as financial incentives, can be used in online labor markets to improve work quality?

The study of incentive schemes, particularly those that attempt to discriminate between high-performing workers and poorly-performing workers, has received scant scholarly attention. Although there is a fair amount of theoretical guidance in the literature, remarkably few empirical studies have been conducted on incentive schemes. We offer the following contributions. First, using a game format, we conduct a series of experiments to see what factors may induce poorly-performing crowdworkers to quit before the end of the task, improving the mean crowdworker accuracy. Second, borrowing from game show design and established theories of economic behavior, we introduce pay-to-quit inducements and observe if they can encourage poorly-performing workers to withdraw from the tasks early while retaining the high-performing workers. This is the first empirical evaluation of the effects of pay-to-quit incentive schemes in crowdsourcing tasks. Third, as collaborative work continues its global expansion, an understanding of the role of these incentive schemes plays across demographics may influence how task designers develop incentive schemes that increase task quality. To this end, we examine worker demographics and examine their role in the performance of incentive schemes.

This paper is organized as follows. In the next section, we discuss the related work, background and motivation for our study. We then develop our research questions and explain our experimental design. Last, we discuss our findings and conclude and indicate planned future work.

BACKGROUND AND MOTIVATION

In this section, we discuss some of the elements involved in our work, and why they are important to our study.

Online Labor Markets

Online labor markets, such as MTurk, are crowdsourcing platforms in which requesters list tasks called HITs or "human intelligence tasks" along with the compensation to be provided. The compensation is usually in the range of a few cents per task. Individual workers (called crowdworkers or simply workers) can then elect to perform a task; upon completion workers are compensated by the task requester. Requesters also may provide additional incentives to workers in the form of a bonus payment.

Incentives

Under certain circumstances the provision of financial incentives can undermine "intrinsic motivation" (e.g. enjoyment, desire to help out), possibly leading to poor outcomes [11, 16]. Locke [24], presented evidence that it is not monetary incentives, time limits, or knowledge, but a person's intrinsic motivation (such as their goals and intentions) that have the largest effect on task performance. To this end, we examine the role of feedback in pay-to-quit inducements.

In crowdsourcing, Mason and Watts examined financial incentives on two MTurk tasks in [27]. They found that greater financial incentives increase the quantity, but not the quality, of work performed. The authors indicate this could be due to the result of the "anchoring" effect, where workers who were paid a small amount believed the value of their work to be greater, and were less motivated to produce quality than those doing it without compensation. Shaw, Horton and Chen examined the role of incentives on non-expert raters using controlled experiments on MTurk in [33]. They evaluated 14 incentive schemes designed to increase mean task accuracy. Two of these incentive structures significantly improved results. We use information from their study design as a foundation for our own experiments, expanding the number of treatment options on their "punish-agreement" incentive scheme. Harris examined various types of financial incentives (only positive, only negative, or both positive and negative incentives with MTurk in a resume evaluation task finding the hybrid scheme outperformed the other incentive schemes [14].

Risk Attitude

According to economic theory, risk attitude plays an essential role in evaluating incentives under uncertainty. Several studies provide insight on people's view of risk. Kahneman and Tversky investigated how risk is evaluated by people in decision-making events [20]. They found that people prefer avoiding losses to acquiring gains by a factor of nearly two-to-one. Recent studies by others have shown loss aversion does not occur as frequently as previously thought. Gal illustrated that loss aversion phenomena are more likely to result from inertia than from loss/gain asymmetry, but found that loss aversion may be more salient when people are in a competition [9]. Gil and Prowse [10] demonstrated that people are loss averse in a competitive environment that involves real effort. Holt and Laury examined risk aversion and the effects of incentives and found that when the payout was tangible (i.e., paid in cash), people became more risk averse [17]. Others have investigated risk and loss aversion in game show environments. Hartley *et. al.* and [15] Lam *et. al.* [23] examined risk attitude on the popular game show "Who Wants to Be a Millionaire." Each discovered that risk aversion is affected by the scale of the financial incentive at risk as well as the probability of success. We note that game show design typically involves a rapid increase in task difficulty as the game proceeds, making the amplified risk apparent to the player through various clues. Traditional online labor market task design, on the other hand, rarely provides an increasing level of difficulty or reward to the worker; however, as a worker proceeds through a set of tasks, their effects on task quality become magnified for the requester.

Pay-to-Quit Inducement Amounts

In the literature, most discussion regarding pay-to-quit inducements (also called *reservation* or *walk-away* amounts) comes from negotiation theory and game show risk attitude studies. Van Puocke and Beulens explain in [34] that a reserve amount is an indifference point where a negotiator should be indifferent between accepting the offer or ending the negotiation (i.e., accepting the walk away amount). It therefore represents the lowest outcome a negotiator is willing to accept. In this paper, we regard the pay-to-quit incentive as the compensation offered to a worker if they choose to quit before the completion of the task. This amount is typically a percentage of the cumulative pay + bonus earned by that worker. Since the inducement represents "certain compensation," the amount should be set so that highly-performing workers would be better off refusing the inducement and continuing with the task, while poorly-performing workers would be better off accepting it and quitting the task early.

RESEARCH QUESTIONS

Our objective in this study is to evaluate pay-to-quit incentives in online labor markets and evaluate how they affect non-expert worker quality. Specifically, we examine the following five research questions.

1. Does performance improve if participants are given explicit windows in which they can accept the pay-to-quit incentive, as Amazon.com does, or is permitting the right to leave with an incentive at any time the better approach? If explicit windows are the better choice, how many should be offered?
2. Understanding the participant's choice to keep playing or to take a pay-to-quit incentive involves rational decision-making, which works best with performance feedback. How frequent should this feedback be provided in order to discriminate the two groups? Does the information provided need to be truthful?
3. When requesters list a task on an online labor market, they often seek to maximize worker quality (with time and cost also being considerations). How should incentive bonus schemes be structured so that we only retain the highest-performing workers? Should it be additive (start with zero bonus and add to it for each successive correct answer) or subtractive (start with a large bonus and deduct for each incorrect answer)?
4. What amount should the bonus be to induce the poorly performing participants to quit but not the highly-performing participants?
5. Are there certain demographics that are more responsive to pay-to-quit incentives than others?

EXPERIMENTAL DESIGN

Beat the Clock or Walk

To evaluate the role of incentive structure in mean task accuracy, we used a game, "Beat the Clock, or Walk" (abbreviated BTCOW). In relevance assessment tasks, games have shown the ability to provide quality inputs with less spam and at lower cost than crowdsourcing [8]. Games with a purpose (GWAP) are often designed for repetitive tasks such as labeling images [35] or evaluating common sense facts [36]. Perhaps most importantly, the game format allows us to dynamically evaluate different bonus incentives with the crowd that would be difficult to accomplish through a standard crowdsourcing platform.

In each round of BTCOW, a worker is presented with an image or short movie description, along with five potential movie titles, with only one being a correct choice. The player (worker) is instructed to select the best choice. Figure 1 displays a screenshot from the BTCOW game.

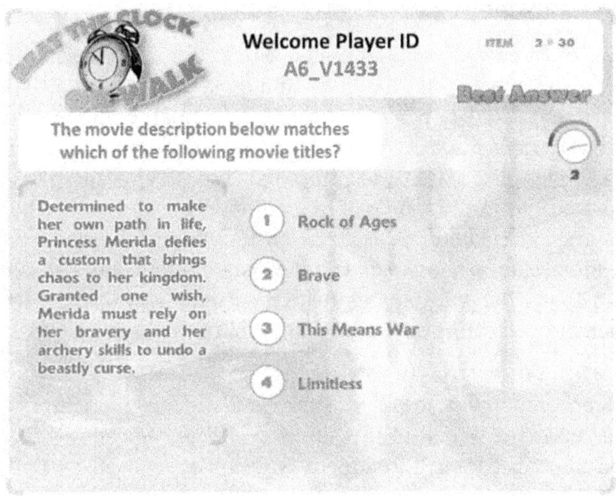

Figure 1. A screenshot from the BTCOW game

Participant Assignments

We recruited 1200 participants from MTurk. Experiments 1 through 4 used 60 participants for the control group and 60 for each treatment (some experiments have multiple treatments). Experiment 5, which applied the best features from each experiment against a baseline, used 120 participants for the baseline and 120 for the treatment group.

Participants were randomly assigned to a control condition or one of several treatment conditions. The same thirty questions and the answer choices for each question were randomly assigned to each user to avoid question order and position bias (each question is considered a *round;* all thirty questions comprise the *task*). Participants could only play the BTCOW game once; our game logged the MTurk User ID and the IP address of each participant. Only the participant's first attempt was evaluated; any suspected duplicate efforts were removed from our study and the task was relisted for other participants.

For each of the 30 rounds, workers have 15 seconds to make a selection. Three consecutive non-selections indicate abandonment of the game, this occurred in 116 (9.6%) of games played; when this occurred, the participant is considered to have withdrawn from the task, the data was not used, and the task was relisted. This time limit is provided to enhance *flow*, a concept introduced by Csikszentmihalyi [5] to describe the delicate balance between anxiety (due to a task that is too difficult) and boredom (due to a task that is too easy). In an earlier pilot task, we found that 80 percent of participants could make a comparable selection within 15 seconds. We believe that this, coupled with the financial incentive offered in the game, provide a sufficient ongoing balance of flow to a majority of participants. There is also an additional benefit to imposing a time limit: In the game, descriptions of movies are provided and participants must select the movie title to match the description; providing a time limit restricts the ability to do external searches and thus limits the ability for participants to cheat.

Participants were compensated \$0.30 for completing the task and answering the pre- and post-task surveys. This represents \$0.01 per question – a typical compensation offered on MTurk for this level of effort. The amounts that are under risk (\$0.30) are minimal, but as Gal and Prowe pointed out in [10], people in a competitive situation where payments are tangible (i.e., in cash) often make decisions without carefully considering the magnitude of their losses. We found our participants made decisions within the game that showed effort beyond the amount of money under risk.

Performance Measurements

Mean accuracy is the most appropriate quality indicator for this task; we therefore measure *mean accuracy* across the k participants for each treatment as follows.

$$Accuracy_i = \sum_{i=1}^{k} \frac{Correct_i}{Answered_i} \quad (1)$$

In order to evaluate the effects of removing those participants who accept our pay-to-quit incentive offer, we provide two different calculations for mean accuracy; one in which answers selected by participants accepting the incentive are removed, another where they are not removed. Answers selected by participants who withdraw from the game, but do not accept the offered incentive, are not considered.

The task was designed to be challenging to differentiate performance levels between participants. In order to evaluate the number of participants that complete the entire task, we also evaluate the *retention rate*, which is the percentage of participants who answer each question. Last, we look at the *gain* in mean accuracy between those that accept the pay-to-quit incentive and those that complete the task. A larger difference indicates the feature being tested is more effective to separate the two groups.

Demographic Survey of Participants

A brief survey of all participants was conducted, asking questions about gender, country of residence, income, experience with games, and if crowdsourcing was their primary source of income. Of the 1200 workers participating in our main study, all provided this information. Once the game was completed participants were given a three-question survey on the player's game experience. A total of 1153 workers provided this information. We asked if the time given to answer questions was sufficient, if the task was challenging enough, and for those players that chose to leave before the game's completion, we asked their reasons for doing so.

EXPERIMENTS

We conduct a series of four sequential experiments to evaluate our research questions, using the outputs of the earlier experiments as inputs to the later experiments.

Experiment 1 –The Role of Explicit Pay-to-Quit Offers

All participants are able to quit the task at any time; however, they are only able to receive \$0.01 per question if they leave when prompted by the game. How many pay-to-quit windows are appropriate? The number of windows is likely to affect flow; too many would be a distraction to the task's objective, too few would have participants finish the task that otherwise may be in their best interest to quit. Therefore, we want to determine how many were appropriate in a thirty-question task.

Participants (N=240, Female = 48%) were randomly assigned to either a control group (N = 60) or to one of three treatment groups (N = 60 each). The control group was provided a message before the task began indicating they could quit at any time and receive the \$0.01 per question, but did not provide any prompts during the task.

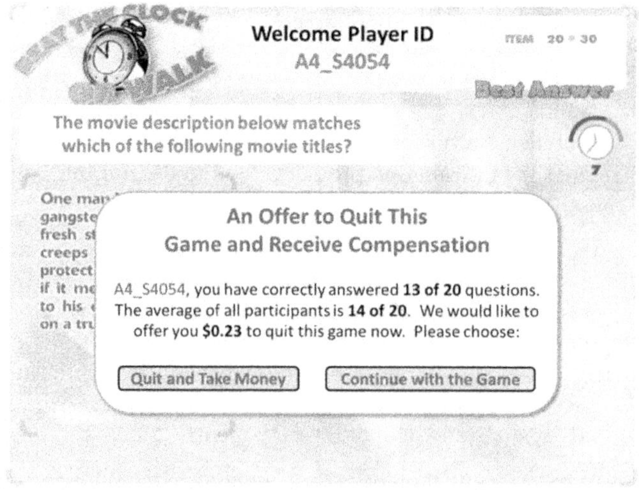

Figure 2. A screenshot of the pay-to-quit pop-up window, displaying the information participants see.

The first treatment group was provided a pop-up window after the 15th question (i.e., half-way through the task), requiring the participant to either accept or refuse the offer in order to proceed (see Figure 2 for a screenshot of the pay-to-quit incentive pop-up). The second treatment group was provided the same pop-up at one-third and two-thirds through the task (i.e., after the 10th and 20th questions). The third treatment group was offered an identical pop-up after the 7th, 14th and 21st questions. There was no time limit to accept/decline the pay-to-quit incentive. This addresses our first research question.

Experiment 2 – The Role of Performance Feedback

Participants (N =300, Female = 45%) are randomly assigned to a control group or one of four treatment groups. The control group is only provided feedback at the end of the task. Feedback consisted of the number of questions the participant got correct and the average number correctly chosen for all participants. Treatment group 1 is provided feedback during two pop-ups (after the 10th and 20th questions) and asked if they wanted to quit and receive an incentive. Treatment group 2 is accurately provided feedback after responding to each of the 30 questions. Treatment group 3 is provided correct feedback on the number correctly answered, but told they outperformed the average, regardless of their true performance, during two pay-to-quit pop-ups. Treatment group 4 is provided the opposite of Treatment group 3; they are told their performance was worse than the average, regardless of their true performance. This addresses our second research question.

Experiment 3 – The Role of Incentive Type

Participants (N = 180, Female = 47%) were randomly assigned into a control group or one of two treatment groups. The control group was not provided any additional pay-to-quit incentive, but at two pay-to-quit windows during the game, they are offered $0.01 for every question answered. Treatment group 1, modeled after Amazon.com's pay-to-quit incentive, is offered an *increasing* incentive during the two pay-to-quit windows; they are told that they would receive $0.01 per question answered plus $0.01 per question they got correct. Treatment group 2 is offered a *decreasing* incentive during the two pay-to-quit windows; they are offered n cents, with n defined as:

$$n = c * (30 + \#incorrect\ answers - \#answered) \quad (2)$$

where the magnitude constant, c, is 0.5 for this experiment. We believe this decreasing incentive will induce participants to quit early if they initially perform poorly. This addresses our third research question.

Experiment 4 – The Role of Incentive Size

Participants (N = 240, Female = 44%) are randomly assigned to a control group or one of three treatment groups. The control group is provided with $0.01 per question answered and no additional incentive. Treatment group 1 is offered a smaller *decreasing* incentive (i.e., c in Equation 2 is set to 0.5) in the two pay-to-quit pop-up windows that appear after the 10th and the 20th questions). Treatment group 2 is offered a moderate *decreasing* incentive (i.e., c = 0.75). Treatment group 3 is offered a larger *decreasing* incentive (i.e., c = 1). This addresses our fourth research question.

Experiment 5 – Putting it All Together

In this last experiment, we take the best strategies from each experiment and combine them into a single "best" strategy, and run them against a control group. The control group allows participants can quit at any time and receive payment of $0.01for each question attempted, but no other incentives are offered.

RESULTS AND DISCUSSION

Experiment 1 – The Role of Explicit Pay-to-Quit Offers

Mean accuracy for the control group and each of our 3 treatment groups is reported in Table 1. The mean and standard deviation for mean accuracy for *all participants* (the answers for quitters are not removed), for *finishers* (only those not taking the pay-to-quit incentives are included; the answers for quitters are removed), and for *quitters* is provided. A bolded mean value indicates the difference from the control group is statistically significant at $p<0.05$.

A two-tailed independent samples t-test was used to evaluate the effects of the number of prompts on mean accuracy. There was a significant difference between our control group at the $p<0.05$ level for the two-prompt condition, $t(118) = 2.138$, $p = 0.0346$, for the finishers, $t(91) = 3.100$, $p = 0.0024$, for the quitters, $t(25) = 2.426$, $p = 0.0168$. Cohen's d was 0.41, 0.63, and 0.51 for these three values, respectively, which indicates a moderate effect size. None of the other treatment groups provided a significant difference from the control group for mean accuracy.

Table 1. Mean accuracy and standard deviations for the control group (N=60) and three treatment groups (each N=60), each offering a different number of inducement prompts.

Group	Control		1 Prompt		2 Prompts		3 Prompts	
	M	SD	M	SD	M	SD	M	SD
All	.647	.175	.631	.187	**.708**	.135	.612	.165
Finishers	.653	.171	.639	.193	**.738**	.126	.610	.178
Quitters	.645	.194	.597	.164	**.575**	.111	.619	.095

In the control group, as well as in the three-prompt treatment, there was little difference between the mean accuracy for the participants that chose to accept the pay-to-quit incentive and those that refused it. This is surprising, as the rational choice for most high-performing participants would be to continue. There is a slight difference for the single-prompt treatment and a significant difference in the two-prompt treatment. In the single-prompt case, even the high-performing participants could obtain payment for half their work (since they were halfway through the task when the prompt appears) if they are risk-averse. In the three-prompt treatment, our data shows many of the poorly-performing participants did not take any of the three offers, even though they were consistently underperforming from the beginning. Having multiple opportunities to quit may downplay their significance more than if only one or two opportunities are offered. This indicates that of the four models explored, the two-prompt model appears to be the best at discriminating the highly-performing and the poor-performing participant groups.

Although Table 1 indicates how using two-prompt treatment is significantly better for both finishers and quitters than the control group, we are more interested to see if we can *discriminate* between the two cases; that is, see a large non-overlapping difference between the finishers and quitters in our treatment group. If the task finishers and task quitter groups are very distinct, it indicates that particular treatment is helpful for raising mean accuracy, since we can eliminate the results from the group with lower mean accuracy. Figure 3 illustrates the differences between the finishers (F) and quitters (Q) for the control and the two-prompt treatment groups. In both cases, as expected, the finishers outperform the quitters. Additionally, the amount of overlap between the two unshaded boxplots on the right (representing the two-prompt model) is smaller than the overlap between the two shaded ones on the left (representing the control group). This visually indicates our two-prompt treatment is effective to retain the better performers while eliminating the poorer performers.

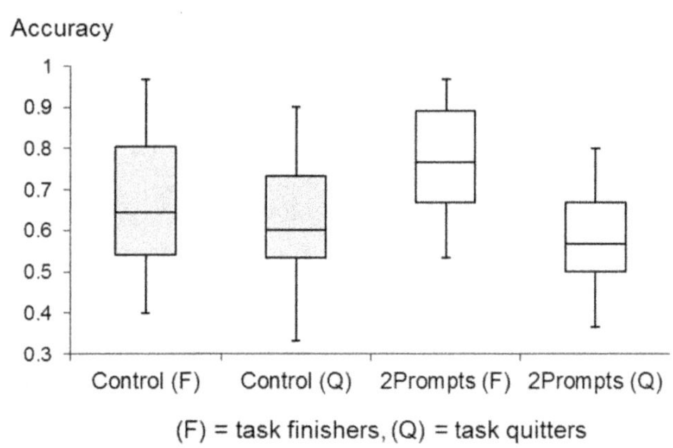

Figure 3. Box-plot comparison of mean accuracy between the control (light blue) and two-prompt group (unshaded)

We also examined the retention rate. Overall, our four groups for this experiment averaged a 79% retention rate, with the control group obtaining a 77% retention rate, and treatment groups 1 2, and 3 obtaining retention rates of 82%, 78% and 80% respectively. This consistency across groups indicates that as we offer a greater frequency of pay-to-quit incentive prompts, it does not encourage more participants to quit.

The gain in mean accuracy for the finishers as compared with all participants was -1.9%, 2.3%, 2.4% and 0.7% for our control group and each of our three treatment groups, respectively. Thus, the second treatment group, offering two prompts to accept the pay-to-quit incentive, provides the best discrimination power, with the one-prompt treatment group closely following. The control group actually eliminated its better-performing participants before the end of the game, lowering the overall mean accuracy score. We note going forward that the two-prompt treatment group with its higher mean accuracy scores, and better discriminatory power, is the best of these choices.

Experiment 2 – The Role of Performance Feedback

We report the mean accuracy for the control group and each of our 5 treatment groups in Tables 2 and 3. In each table, we report the mean and standard deviation for mean accuracy for all participants, for finishers and for quitters.

In Table 2, we compare the mean accuracy for those in the control group (where feedback is provided only once at the end of the task), Treatment group 1, where it is reported at the end of each question, and those in Treatment group 2, where feedback is reported thrice (after the 10th question, the 20th question, and at the end of the game). A bolded mean value indicates the difference from the control group is statistically significant at $p<0.05$. Boxplots to illustrate the differences between groups shown in Figure 4

Table 2. Mean accuracy and standard deviations for the control group (N=60) and two treatment groups (N=60), each offering a different frequency of feedback to the participant.

	Control		Each Round		Each Prompt	
Group	**M**	**SD**	**M**	**SD**	**M**	**SD**
All	.629	.159	.649	.176	**.686**	.153
Finishers	.636	.157	.668	.177	**.712**	.151
Quitters	.603	.167	.583	.171	.559	.159

A two-tailed independent samples t-test was used to evaluate the effects of the feedback frequency on mean accuracy. There was a significant difference between our control group at the $p<0.05$ level for the providing feedback at each pay-to-quit prompt condition for all participants, $t(118) = 2.001$, $p = 0.0477$ and for the finishers, , $t(96) = 2.631$, $p = 0.0096$. Cohen's *d* for these values were 0.37 and 0.49, respectively, indicating a moderate effect size. None of the other values provided a significant difference from the control group for mean accuracy.

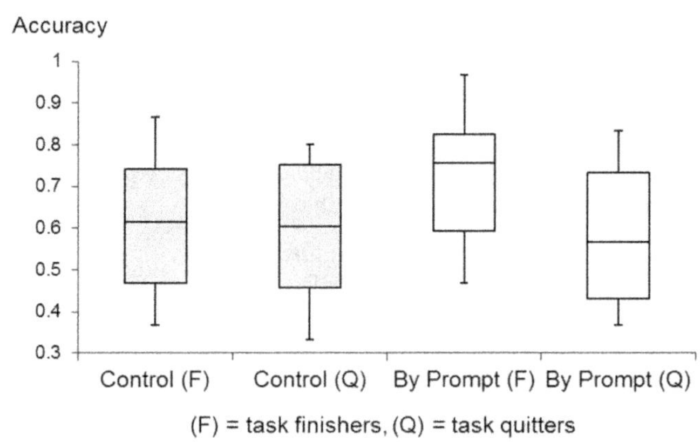

Figure 4. Box-plot comparison of mean accuracy between the control (light blue) and feedback after each prompt (unshaded).

The retention rate varied only slightly between the three treatment groups, with the accurate, feedback each round, and feedback each prompt treatment groups retaining 77%, 77%, and 73% respectively. The gain in mean accuracy for the finishers as compared with all participants was 0.9%, 2.3%, and 3.1% for each of our three treatment groups, respectively. The treatment the largest discrimination power is the feedback at each prompt treatment. We carry this forward to the next part of Experiment 2.

In Table 3, we evaluate the effects of feedback on *relative* performance on a participant's choice to accept a pay-to-quit incentive during two pay-to-quit prompts. We compare the group in which they are given an accurate indication of performance (Treatment group 2), those told that they are outperforming the group average (Treatment group 3) and those that are told they are underperforming the group average (Treatment group 4). A bolded mean value indicates the difference from Treatment group 2 is statistically significant at p<0.05.

Table 3. Mean accuracy and standard deviations for three treatment groups (each N=60), each providing a different feedback message during the pay-to-quit incentive prompt.

Group	Accurate		Outperform		Underperform	
	M	SD	M	SD	M	SD
All	.658	.153	**.717**	.157	.627	.151
Finishers	.712	.151	.727	.155	.695	.155
Quitters	.559	.159	**.698**	.167	.502	.143

A two-tailed independent samples t-test was used to evaluate the effects of the feedback type given to participants on mean accuracy. There was a significant difference between Treatment group 2, which provided accurate feedback, at the p<0.05 level for the outperform condition for all participants, t(118) = 2.08 , p = 0.039, and for those that chose to accept our pay-to-quit incentive, t(23) = 2.37 , p = 0.025. Cohen's *d* was 0.37 (a moderate effect) and 0.85 (a strong effect), for all participants and the quitters, respectively. None of the other treatment groups provided a significant difference in mean accuracy from Treatment group 2.

In Figure 5, we compare the finishers and quitters for those who receive accurate reporting of their performance (Treatment group 2) with those who are told they are outperforming the group average (Treatment group 3). The distinction between finishers and quitters is clear in both models, but more pronounced for Treatment group 3.

The retention rate varied between more these treatment groups than any other, with the accurate, outperform and underperform groups retaining 73%, 85%, and 65% respectively. This is a bit surprising, since all participants are paid based on their own performance, regardless of how they perform relative to other participants.

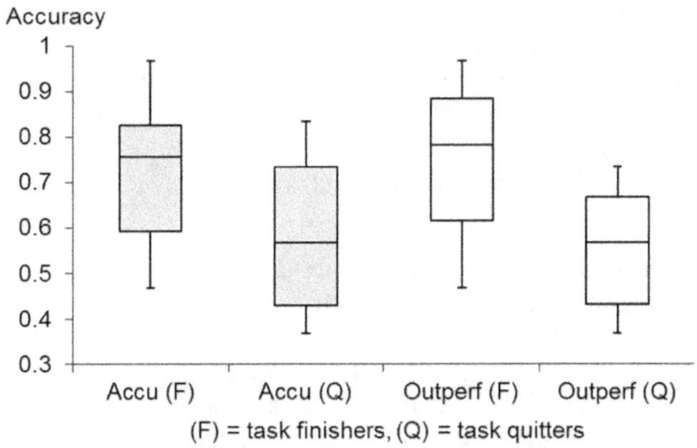

Figure 5. Box-plot comparison of mean accuracy between those accurately reporting task performance (light blue) and those told they are outperforming the group average (unshaded).

The difference between the mean accuracy for finishers and all participants was 5%, 1%, and 7% for each of our three treatment groups, respectively. Thus, the treatment the largest discrimination power is the under-encouraging treatment, with the policy of accurately providing feedback close behind. The 1% gain by providing over-encouraging feedback does not persuade the best performers to improve their performance any further, but the 7% gain by the underperforming feedback group weeds out many of the poorly-performing participants, leaving many of the stronger participants to complete the task.

Experiment 3 – The Role of Incentive Type

Mean accuracy for the control group and our two treatment groups is reported in Table 4. A bolded mean value indicates the difference from the control group is statistically significant at p<0.05.

Table 4. Mean accuracy and standard deviations for a control group (N=60) and two treatment groups (each N=60), each offering a different incentive type.

Group	Control		Increasing		Decreasing	
	M	SD	M	SD	M	SD
All	.648	.156	.682	.171	.653	.151
Finishers	.656	.152	.707	.172	.699	.149
Quitters	.618	.170	.573	.164	.525	.158

A two-tailed independent samples t-test was used to evaluate the effects of the frequency of feedback on mean accuracy. There were no a significant differences between our control group and the treatment groups at p<0.05. Neither the increasing nor the decreasing incentive types were significant, therefore we do not provide a box-plot comparison.

The retention rates for this experiment were 78%, 82%, and 72% for the control, increasing and decreasing incentives, respectively. This indicates that a greater number of participants (28%) chose to take the pay-to-quit incentive for the decreasing incentive, which we believe demonstrates its effectiveness.

The gain in mean accuracy for the finishers as compared with all participants was 0.8%, 2.5%, and 4.9% for the control group and two treatment groups, respectively. Thus, the decreasing incentive is the treatment with the largest discrimination power. Overall, the decreasing incentive is the most valuable to us, and therefore we use it in Experiments 4 and 5.

Experiment 4 – The Role of Incentive Size

Mean accuracy for the control group and our three treatment groups, which use a different value of our magnitude constant, *c*, to set our decreasing incentives, is reported in Table 5. Bolded mean values indicate the difference from the control group is significant at $p<0.05$.

A two-tailed independent samples t-test was used to evaluate the effects of the frequency of feedback on mean accuracy. There was a significant difference between our control group and finishers given the medium incentive, $t(91) = 2.181$, $p = 0.032$ and between our control group and finishers given the larger incentive, , $t(94) = 2.366$, $p = 0.020$, at the $p<0.05$ confidence level. Cohen's d was 0.57 and 0.63, respectively, indicating a moderate effect size. None of the other values provided a significant difference from the control group for mean accuracy.

Table 5. Mean accuracy and standard deviations for the control group (N=60) and two treatment groups, (each N=60), each offering a different incentive size.

	Control		Small (0.5)		Med (0.75)		Large (1.0)	
Group	**M**	**SD**	**M**	**SD**	**M**	**SD**	**M**	**SD**
All	.649	.154	.673	.159	.679	.141	.681	.139
Finishers	.651	.156	.691	.161	**.719**	.144	**.722**	.138
Quitters	.621	.146	.599	.149	.568	.131	.569	.142

In Figure 6, we look at the quitters and finishers for the control group, medium-sized incentive, and large incentive. We see that the medium-sized and large incentives have the best discriminatory power between finishers and quitters, with the large incentive treatment being slightly better.

The retention rate varied between more these treatment groups than any other, with the control, small incentive, medium incentive, and large incentive groups retaining 78%, 80%, 73% and 68% respectively. The gain in mean accuracy for the finishers as compared with all participants was 0.8%, 1.8%, 4.0% and 4.1% for these groups, respectively. Thus, the treatment with the largest discrimination power is the large incentive treatment, with the medium incentive treatment very close behind. The medium incentive, with nearly the same metrics as the large incentive, but it provides a higher retention rate and a lower cost; therefore it slightly edges out the larger incentive as the best treatment.

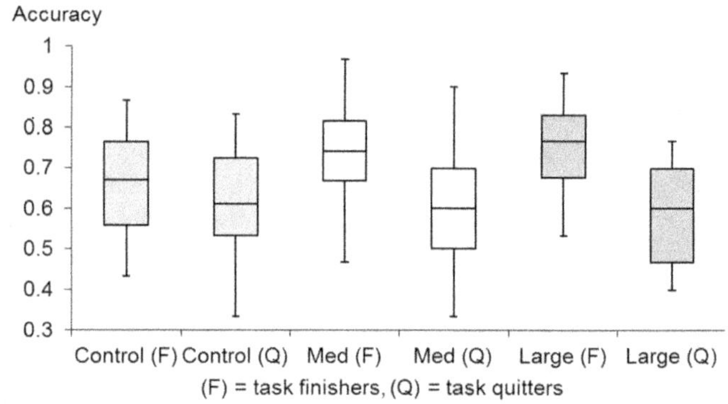

Figure 6. Box-plot comparison of mean accuracy between our control group (shaded light blue, on left), those offered a medium-sized incentive (unshaded, center), and those offered a large incentive (shaded orange, right).

Experiment 5 – Putting it All Together

Next, we compare the performance of our best model, which uses two pay-to-quit incentive prompts after the 10th and 20th questions, provides accurate feedback on performance during the prompt, and provides a decreasing incentive with the magnitude constant, c, at the moderate value of 0.75. For this experiment, we doubled the number of participants to 240. Participants were randomly assigned to the control group (N=120, Female = 46%) or the best strategy group (N=120, Female = 45%).

Mean accuracy for the control group and our treatment group is reported in Table 6. A bolded mean value indicates the difference from the control group is statistically significant at $p<0.05$.

A two-tailed independent samples t-test was used to evaluate the effects of the number of prompts on mean accuracy. There was a significant difference between our control group at the $p<0.05$ level for the two-prompt condition, $t(238) = 2.773$, $p = 0.006$, for finishers, $t(196) = 3.791$, $p = 0.002$. Cohen's d was 0.41 and 0.51 for these two values, respectively, which indicates a moderate effect size. None of the other treatment groups provided a significant difference from the control group for mean accuracy.

Table 6. Mean accuracy and standard deviations comparing a control group (N=120) and a treatment group (N=120) comprised of the best strategies from Experiments 1 through 4

	Control		Single Best Strategy	
Group	**M**	**SD**	**M**	**SD**
All	.637	.146	**.687**	.133
Finishers	.642	.145	**.717**	.133
Quitters	.618	.151	.578	.131

The retention rates for our control group and our best model were 78% and 73%, respectively. This indicates that more than a quarter of our participants (27%) chose to take the pay-to-quit incentive for the decreasing incentive, which we believe demonstrates its effectiveness.

The mean accuracy gain for the finishers as compared with all participants was 0.5% and 3.0% for the control group and the treatment group, respectively. Comparing the finishers of our *best* model compared with all users in the control group, a baseline representing a typical crowdsourcing study design is 8.0%, or a 28.3% gain in mean accuracy. Since it is highly unusual for crowdsourcing tasks to offer any incentives to quit early, we feel that comparing the finishers with our best treatments applied with all participants in the baseline represents an appropriate comparison.

Figure 7 shows box-plots for All (A), task finishers (F) and task quitters (Q) for the "Control" baseline group (shown in light blue shading) and the combination of treatments shown to provide the "Best" performance in Experiments 1-4 (shown in white). The distinction between the finishers and quitters is greatest in the "Best" model – this discrimination allows us to improve our score by comparing the "Best (F)" model with the "Control (A)" model resulting in the 28.3% reported earlier.

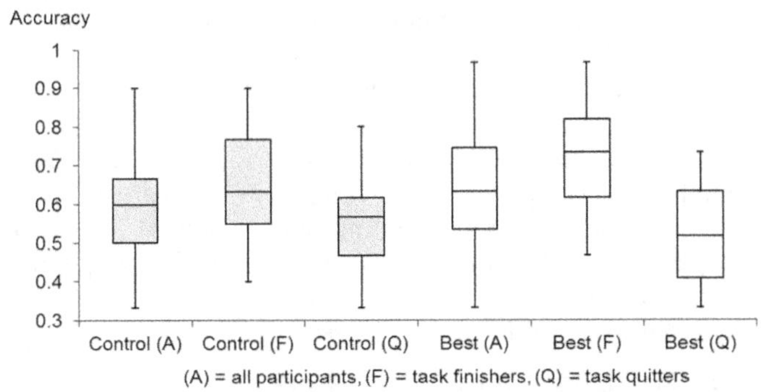

Figure 7. Box-plot comparison of mean accuracy between our baseline (Control) and the combination of treatments from Experiments 1 to 4 that provided the best performance (Best).

We also captured the time taken to answer each question. Based on the *sunk cost fallacy*, more time taken per question may suggest a greater investment in the process and therefore a greater commitment to the task. Conversely, just as with those employed by companies such as Amazon.com or Zappos.com, participants who rushed through the game may be enticed by some easy money to quit early. Thus, we wanted to see if participants who took more time per question were more likely to stay in the game. There was a significant positive correlation between average time taken per question and retention, $r(1200) = +0.489$, $p < .001$. This correlation indicates that participants who took more time to answer each question, on average, were more likely to refuse the offer to quit the game when provided with the pay-to-quit offer.

The Role of Demographics

We examined the demographic information reported in the 1200 pre-task and 1153 post-task surveys to see if any incentive-related patterns existed. We found that females, who comprised 46% of our study participants overall, were significantly more risk averse, accepting the pay-to-quit incentives in far greater frequency than men, despite providing nearly the same overall mean accuracy (two-tailed t-test, $p<0.001$). This may indicate that females are more sensitive to opportunity costs, or it may also indicate greater risk-aversion, as a number of other studies indicate (e.g., [6, 19, 32]). Likewise, Indian and "other South Asian" residents (together comprising 36% of our participants) were more likely to accept the pay-to-quit incentive than residents of other countries or regions (two-tailed t-test, $p = 0.012$), which implies the same aversion to risk [2] or awareness of greater opportunity cost of completing the entire task.

Workers who played games more than 5 hours per week (19% of participants), were significantly less likely to take the reserve bonus than those reporting fewer hours of gaming, even when they were performing poorly (two-tailed t-test, $p<0.001$). This may indicate a greater focus on the game's entertainment value than on the bonus, or it may be due to issues such as cognitive bias – experienced by people who begin to lose at a slot machine gambling and make an irrational attempt to win back their initial investment [12, 37]. Participants who relied on crowdsourcing as their primary source of income were less likely to take the reserve bonus than those who did not (two-tailed t-test, $p = 0.024$). Interestingly, workers in the highest reported income band (exceeding $40K per year) were more likely to take the reserve bonus than those whose reported income was in the lowest band (less than $10K year) (two-tailed t-test, $p = 0.017$). While we expect people to be risk-neutral when relatively small amounts of money are involved, this difference may be due to factors such as greater opportunity cost, competitiveness, or the entertainment value of the game itself.

ANALYSIS

Many of the experiments conducted here examine a few features of a single game for a small amount of compensation. Therefore, it would seem that the implications for pay-to-quit incentives are limited. However, as Experiment 5 illustrates, the value of proper design of incentives can encourage the high-performers to complete the task while encouraging the poor-performing participants to accept an inducement to quit early and is backed up by other research, e.g. [13]. We believe that applying these techniques on a larger scale, with more at risk for participants, is likely to magnify the effects of these treatments.

In Experiment 1, we note that two prompts appear to be the optimal number to offer for our thirty-question task. In Experiment 2, we identify that feedback at the time of a pay-to-quit incentive is important to the decision maker – and the relative performance matters as much as the absolute performance in the decision to accept the pay-to-quit incentive. In the short-term, we note that telling participants they are underperforming (e.g, performing worse than their peers) will help to discriminate the better performing workers from the poorly-performing ones. When a worker is aware they are underperforming, it normally can be rationally explained; when others mention it, it impacts the decision to continue with work. In the long-term, however, people are likely to be aware of the performance of others and the underperformance message is unlikely to carry as much weight. In an anonymous work environment, such as an online labor market, this façade is more difficult for workers to verify.

Experiment 3 illustrates the importance of designing the incentives so poorly-performing workers have a better incentive to leave. We note, however, that the decreasing incentive model that performed well in this study could be reverse engineered by workers over time, and a new model would need to be introduced. However, the underlying idea of providing enough compensation for the poorer performers to leave remains the same.

Many of the incentives we offered, including the large incentive in Experiment 4, produced a range of possible pay-to-quit incentives between $0.20 and $0.30 at the first prompt, and between $0.10 and $0.30 at the second prompt. The poorest-performing participants were offered larger incentives. Since all participants are aware the entire task is worth at most $0.30, and a poorly-performing participant who has played two-thirds of the game has a good idea of the maximum compensation they could receive at the game's conclusion, why wouldn't they take an incentive that provides a greater income than continuing to play?

Based on the feedback provided in the 1,153 completed post-hoc surveys, a few explanations come to mind. First, cognitive overload, often a problem in game design, could obfuscate the decision to be made at the prompt during a game designed to induce a stressful environment. Second, the participant may be less interested in the compensation than participating in the task. Third, because of the perception of a limited downside to the task, they could continue to play without giving the pay-to-quit incentive serious consideration. Fourth, it could be due to self-selection; the people who would benefit from the incentive are risk-seekers and want to continue to take a risk instead of take the "safe" incentive.

Each of these has important considerations for pay-to-quit inducements in online labor markets. First, because tasks in online labor markets are often simply designed and are known to serve as experimental test-beds for deception studies and other information gathering studies, participants may not consider an incentive to quit to be valid. They may rush through the prompt without giving it careful thought. This is backed up by studies on crowdsourcing that indicates even the most basic quality checks are frequently overlooked by workers [7]. Second, when tasks are designed as a game and advertised in online labor markets, the task requesters are looking for people to participate more than once, since more work is accomplished at no additional cost. The value of actual compensation offered then becomes secondary to task enjoyment [8]. This draws a certain type of worker, which is not representative of crowdworkers overall. It also has parallels to job-related employment in the real world.

Third, microtasks, through their anonymity, are often thought of as "disposable work", with little expectation for worker and requester to continue to work together in the future. Last, the type of people who are looking for work on MTurk may be more risk-seeking than the population as a whole [4, 30], affecting their decision to take an incentive to quit a task early. This type of risk-seeking behavior as a response to a run of bad luck has been studied in stock markets [25, 29] and in game shows [1], where frequently people make decisions that may seem irrational to others.

One may wonder if the better-performers are discouraged by being excluded from receiving pay-to-quit rewards. We believe this is not the case; the incentives offered by these firms as attempts to signal to customers, employees, and investors that top-notch customer service and dedicated employees are an essential part of their enterprise that is worth a sum of money to protect. This increases the likelihood that the better performers will see themselves as part of an exclusive group, which in turn will likely encourage them to maintain high performance. Similarly, the few hiring mistakes these companies make are corrected as early as possible, limiting any potential long-term negative effects. On a smaller scale, these same qualities are valuable to task requesters in online labor markets as well for many of the same reasons.

Implications for Collaborative Work

Incentive schemes, when properly designed and applied, can provide an important role in aligning the goals of workers and requesters alike. However, in our study, we demonstrate that not all incentive schemes can improve performance as expected. Most notably, a pay-to-quit incentive does not always discriminate between those that rationally should quit early and those that rationally should continue with the task. However, by taking steps to identify the features most relevant to the online labor market pool, we can discriminate between the high-performing and poor performing workers as companies like Zappos.com, Amazon.com and L18 have attempted to do.

Some workers continued with the task even though the most rational option would have been to quit and accept the incentive. Their reluctance to quit may be due to the "pseudo-certainty" effect, where people overestimate the likelihood of an uncertain event (in our case, obtaining more compensation at the game's conclusion).

In more diverse collaborative groups, an understanding of the group's collective view on risk may provide information on the most effective incentive to offer workers. Even in simple tasks with little at stake, such as with multiple-choice questions with the possible reward of $0.30, workers tend to demonstrate either risk-seeking or risk-averse behavior. We believe that future designers of crowdsourcing tasks will need to incorporate protocols that will be more complex, involve a more diverse set of workers with different attitudes and motivations towards work, and encompass incentives that are far more complex than are currently offered.

CONCLUSION

Companies known for hiring the best people, such as Zappos.com, have implemented pay-to-quit incentives to best align work attitudes towards corporate objectives. These companies have found that these incentives help enhance the corporate culture and increase productivity. In this study, we have observed the effects of different types of incentives on worker mean task accuracy through a game.

Through a series of five experiments, we examined different aspects of pay-to-quit incentive schemes in online labor markets. The first evaluated the frequency workers should be prompted with the pay-to-quit incentive and found that making offers every 10 questions (approximately every 5 minutes) appears to be correct in a 30-question task. The second experiment examined the amount of feedback to provide, and found that providing feedback at the time of the incentive offer worked best. This experiment also demonstrated that feedback on relative performance did matter, with poorly-performing workers who were told that they were underperforming accepted the incentive more often than groups that were provided accurate information or told that they were outperforming other workers.

The third experiment looked at incentive types based on performance, one providing incentives that increased based on performance and one that offered incentives that decreased based on performance. The latter provided the best incentives for the poorly performing workers to leave. Our fourth experiment looked at the size of the incentive, finding that the size of the incentive matters, but there is little difference between a moderately-sized incentive and a larger one. In our fifth experiment, we sought to validate our findings. We took the best strategies uncovered from each of the four earlier experiments and ran this experiment with a control group. The workers we retained provided an increase in mean task accuracy of 28.3% over the mean accuracy of all workers in our control group. We believe this represents a true measure of performance improvement over a task without the pay-to-quit incentives.

Given the increasingly multi-national scope of collaborative work, an understanding the worker pool demographics is essential. Examining our worker demographics, we observe that females, South Asian residents and people earning higher wages are more likely than other groups to accept the pay-to-quit incentive when offered, possibly indicating greater risk aversion or greater opportunity cost for their time. People who play games regularly, who depend on income from crowdsourcing, and workers in the lowest income band are less likely to accept the reserve bonus. Our results indicate that certain demographics may be more risk averse than other groups, and this can be explored through additional analysis.

One limitation to this study is we have only examined financial incentives. A number of studies, including the aforementioned one by Locke [21] have shown that financial incentives are less important to workers than other types of incentives, such as recognition of effort or achievement. This is particularly true in collaborative work environments. Financial incentives, coupled with other incentive types, are likely to further improve performance in collaborative environments.

To this end, we believe that this pay-to-quit incentive model can also be applied to non-financially rewarding crowdsourcing works, such as games. A participant in a war game, for example, may choose to quit at certain milestones in the game and keep their earned rewards if they get the feeling that a particular mission will not go well (or is not in their best interest). We also believe this model can apply even better to participant models that have different roles or levels, rather than a single level as we have explored in this study. Not only could we offer financial compensation as an incentive, but also the promotion/demotion between levels. For many, earning titles in Wikipedia, for example, such as steward, sysadmin or ombudsman, are coveted by those that devote considerable time in making Wikipedia edits; keeping (or promoting to) those titles incentivizes them to be aligned with Wikipedia's objectives, which parallels the incentives faced by employees at Zappos.com, Amazon.com and elsewhere.

In future work, we plan to continue our examination of incentives including an evaluation of non-financial incentives. Games provide numerous advantages over static tasks for applying treatments. We plan to examine this area in greater detail and provide participants with more complex tradeoffs in order to examine the decisions they make.

REFERENCES

1. Andersen, S., Harrison, G. W., Lau, M. I., & Rutström, E. E. (2008). *Risk aversion in game shows* (Vol. 12, pp. 359-404). Emerald Group Publishing Limited.
2. Binswanger, H. Attitudes toward risk: Experimental measurement in rural India. *American Journal of Agricultural Economics*, 62:3 1980, 395-407
3. Cavuto, N. (2014, June 24) *Pay to Go Away: Bribing Some Workers to Just…Disappear*. Retrieved from http://www.foxbusiness.com/economy-policy/ 2014/06/ 24/pay-to-go-away-bribing-some-workers-to-just-disappear/
4. Charness, G., Gneezy, U., & Kuhn, M. A. (2013). Experimental methods: Extra-laboratory experiments-

extending the reach of experimental economics. *Journal of Economic Behavior & Organization*, *91*, 93-100.

5. Csikszentmihalyi, M. Flow: The psychology of optimal experience. Harper Perennial, 1991.
6. Eckel, C. C. and Grossman, J. Men, women and risk aversion: Experimental evidence. *Handbook of experimental economics results*, 1, 2008, 1061-1073.
7. Eickhoff, C., & de Vries, A. (2011). How crowdsourcable is your task. *Proceedings of the workshop on crowdsourcing for search and data mining (CSDM)*, pp. 11-14.
8. Eickhoff, C., Harris, C. G., de Vries, A.P. and Srinivasan, P. Quality through Flow and Immersion: Gamifying Crowdsourced Relevance Assessments. *Proc. of SIGIR'12*, ACM, New York
9. Gal, D. A psychological law of inertia and the illusion of loss aversion. *Judgment and Decision Making*, 1, 1 2006. 23-32.
10. Gill, D. and Prowse, V. A structural analysis of disappointment aversion in a real effort competition. *The American economic review*, 102:1 2012, 469-503.
11. Gneezy, U. and Rustichini, A. Pay enough or don't pay at all. *Quarterly Jour. of Econ.,* 115:3 2000, 791-810.
12. Griffiths, M. D. (1994). The role of cognitive bias and skill in fruit machine gambling. *British Journal of Psychology*, *85*(3), 351-369.
13. Harinck, F., Van Dijk, E., Van Beest, I. and Mersmann, P. When gains loom larger than losses: reversed loss aversion for small amounts of money. *Psychological science,* 18:12, 2007, 1099-1113.
14. Harris, C. G. You're Hired! An Examination of Crowdsourcing Incentive Models in Human Resource Tasks. *Proc. WSDM 2011 Workshop on Crowdsourcing for Search and Data Mining (Hong Kong, China)* 2011.
15. Hartley, R., Lanot, G. and Walker, I. Who really wants to be a millionaire? Estimates of risk aversion from game show data. 2006. Working paper.
16. Heyman, J. and Ariely, D. Effort for payment a tale of two markets. *Psych Science*, 15, 11. 2004, 787-793.
17. Holt, C. A. and Laury, S. K. Risk aversion and incentive effects. *Amer. economic review*, 92:5. 2002, 1644-1655.
18. Jeffries, A. *Lot18 Is Straight-Up Paying Unhappy Employees to Quit*. https://betabeat.com/2012/05/lot18-founder-offered-to-pay-unhappy-employees-to-quit-today-and-six-of-them-did/
19. Jianakoplos, N. A. and Bernasek, A. Are Women More Risk Averse? *Economic Inquiry*, 36:4 1998, 620-630.
20. Kahneman, D. and Tversky, A. Prospect theory: An analysis of decision under risk. *Econometrica: Journal of the Econometric Society* 1979, 263-291.
21. Kopelman, R. E., Chiou, A. Y., Lipani, L. J., & Zhu, Z. (2012). Interpreting the success of Zappos. com, Four Seasons, and Nordstrom: Customer centricity is but one-third of the job. *Global Business and Organizational Excellence*, *31*(5), 20-35.
22. Laffont, J. J. The theory of incentives: the principal-agent model. *Princeton Univ Pr,* 2002.
23. Lam, S. K., Pennock, D. M., Cosley, D. and Lawrence, S. 1 Billion Pages= 1 Million Dollars? mining the web to play" who wants to be a millionaire?". *Morgan Kaufmann Publishers Inc*., New York, 2002.
24. Locke, E. A. Toward a theory of task motivation and incentives. *Organizational Behavior and Human Performance*, 3, 2 1968, 157-189.
25. March, J. and Shapira, Z. Managerial perspectives on risk and risk taking. *Mgmt science.* 1987, 1404-1418.
26. Martin, D. *Amazon Pays Employees $5,000 to Quit Their Jobs.* http://www.cbsnews.com/news/amazon-pays-employees-5000-to-quit/, 2014.
27. Mason, W. and Watts, D. J. Financial incentives and the performance of crowds. ACM. New York, USA, 2010.
28. McFarland, K. (2013). Why Zappos Offers New Hires $2,000 to Quit. *http://www.businessweek.com/stories/2008-09-16/why-zapposoffers-new-hires-2-000-to-quit*
29. Miller, E. M. Risk, uncertainty, and divergence of opinion. *Journal of finance*. 1977, 1151-1168.
30. Paolacci, G., Chandler, J., & Ipeirotis, P. G. (2010). Running experiments on amazon mechanical turk. *Judgment and Decision making*, *5*(5), 411-419.
31. Prendergast, C. The provision of incentives in firms. *Journal of economic literature*, 37, 1 1999, 7-63.
32. Schubert, R., Brown, M., Gysler, M. and Brachinger, H. W. Financial decision-making: are women really more risk-averse? *The American economic review*, 89:2 1999), 381-385
33. Shaw, A. D., Horton, J. J. and Chen, D. L. Designing incentives for inexpert human raters. *Proc. of the ACM 2011 conference on Computer supported cooperative work (Hangzhou, China*). ACM, New York, NY. 2011.
34. van Poucke, D. and Buelens, M. Predicting the outcome of a two-party price negotiation: Contribution of reservation price, aspiration price and opening offer. *Journal of Economic Psychology*, 23, 1 2002, 67-76.
35. von Ahn, L. and Dabbish, L. Labeling images with a computer game. ACM, New York, 2004.
36. von Ahn, L., Kedia, M. and Blum, M.Verbosity: a game for collecting common-sense facts. ACM New York 2006.
37. Walker, M. B. (1992). Irrational thinking among slot machine players.*Journal of Gambling studies*, *8*(3), 245-261

Motivating Multi-Generational Crowd Workers in Social-Purpose Work

Masatomo Kobayashi[1], Shoma Arita[2], Toshinari Itoko[1], Shin Saito[1], and Hironobu Takagi[1]

[1]IBM Research – Tokyo
5-6-52 Toyosu, Koto, Tokyo 135-8511, Japan
{mstm, itoko, shinsa, takagih}@jp.ibm.com

[2]The University of Tokyo
7-3-1 Hongo, Bunkyo, Tokyo 113-8656, Japan
arita@cyber.t.u-tokyo.ac.jp

ABSTRACT
Crowdsourcing for social goals (e.g., supporting public libraries or people with disabilities) is a promising area. However, little is known about how to develop active worker communities for such goals. First, we need reliable metrics for the workers' motivation. Second, the characteristics of senior crowd workers have rarely been studied, even though they often play a primary role in social-purpose work. This work introduces a four-quadrant worker motivation model for social-purpose crowdsourcing and describes a system based on that model. Then we investigate the outcomes from the system's operations for six months, which involved both young and senior workers, seeking better ways to build an active community of crowd workers. We analyzed the workers' activities based on the system logs, conducted a survey, assessed the correlations between the subjective values and actual behaviors, and then discuss the implications.

Author Keywords
Crowdsourcing; Motivation; Gamification; Assistive Services; GLAM; Accessibility; Senior Workforce.

ACM Classification Keywords
H.5.3 [Information Interfaces and Presentation]: Group and Organization Interfaces - Evaluation/methodology.

General Terms
Human Factors; Design; Measurement.

INTRODUCTION
Crowdsourcing [12] has been used in diverse areas such as content generation, transcription, image labeling, and Web research, and has proven its effectiveness. Social-purpose work such as assistive services for PwDs (People with Disabilities) [4] and GLAM (Galleries, Libraries, Archives, and Museums) [23] is one of the most promising application areas for crowdsourcing. These areas have a long history of community-driven work, which fits well with the crowdsourcing model in the Internet era.

CSCW 2015, March 14–18, 2015, Vancouver, BC, Canada.
Copyright © 2015 ACM 978-1-4503-2922-4/15/03...$15.00.
http://dx.doi.org/10.1145/2675133.2675255

However, for social-purpose crowdsourcing projects, particularly at early stages with relatively small numbers of workers, the sustainability of the worker community often becomes a serious challenge. Takagi et al. [26] reported that this kind of community easily falls into an inactive state, which suggests that we need better ways to encourage the workers. Unfortunately, there are no established metrics to assess the motivation of the workers in this area (of social-purpose crowdsourcing). Alam and Campbell [1] described several types of worker motivation in digitalizing historical newspapers, but they did not test the quantitative effects of each type of motivation. Some studies suggested that senior crowd workers could be more dedicated than younger workers [16][26], but there is little known about the actual effects of the differences among generations.

This study investigates ways to sustain the community of active crowds in social-purpose crowdsourcing, based on our experiences in hosting a volunteer-based, crowdsourced proofreading service for six months to create accessible digital books. This work helps people with print disabilities (such as visual impairments or dyslexia) who cannot effectively read printed materials. We introduce a four-quadrant worker motivation model for social-purpose crowdsourcing, which is primarily inspired by the model of Kaufmann et al. for general crowd workers [15]. Along with this model, we designed and deployed a system for crowd-based proofreading. During six months of active use, the size of the worker community gradually grew to 174 volunteers. We had an open participation policy, and about half of the volunteers were 60 or older.

In contrast to the similar previous efforts reported in [26], which often suffered from low "registration-contribution" and low "returnee" rates and thus failed to sustain worker communities of about a hundred contributors, our attempt sustained the participation of a diverse group of workers, from top contributors to long-tail participants, involving younger and older generations. As a result, the workers completed more than 2.5 million micro-tasks for proofreading during the six-month period. To investigate the success factors and future challenges for each cohort, we analyzed the system logs that include all of the results of the micro-tasks, conducted a questionnaire-based survey of the workers to assess their values, and considered the correlations between the reported values and their actual behaviors. The initial results of the first few months of this crowd-based proofreading project were reported in [14].

The goal of this work is to empirically find better ways to sustain the active participation of crowd workers in social-purpose crowdsourcing, by analyzing the results produced from long-term community activities on a system that has several features to motivate workers. To achieve the goal, we reorganized the known motivation factors found in the literature to provide structured metrics for better system design and analyses. The research questions include how to involve more highly dedicated workers (*Can senior citizens become dedicated crowd workers?*) and how to effectively motivate them (*What is the most important motivation factors?*). Even though the findings we report in this paper are based on a single project, our contributions (including the metrics) provide clues to design and investigate different types of projects in this area of social-purpose crowdsourcing.

This paper is organized as follows. In the next section, we summarize related work. Next we introduce our motivation model for social-purpose crowd workers, which is followed by an overview of the design of our system. Then we describe the method and results of our investigation. Finally we conclude with discussions on the implications of our investigations and the limitations of this work.

RELATED WORK

Crowdsourced Assistive Services for PwDs

Many studies and projects have used crowd workers to help people who have accessibility needs. HearSay [5] is a non-visual Web browser with special functions to assist people with visual impairments. It allows users to act as crowd workers to add landmark labels to webpages to help other users. The Social Accessibility project [27] asked volunteer workers to create patches to fix accessibility problems on websites, based on an "upon-request" policy. For the accessibility of videos, Dotsub [31] has an option for crowdsourced captioning. The DVX project [20] tried to crowdsource the creation of video descriptions (i.e., descriptive narrations for people with visual impairments).

For real-world accessibility, there are also several systems. VizWiz [3] is a smartphone application to allow people with visual impairments to ask visual questions to crowds on Amazon Mechanical Turk (MTurk) [29], to friends via email or Twitter, or to an image recognition engine. Hara, et al. proposed methods to use crowds to find accessibility problems on streets [9] and landmarks to locate bus stops [10], using Google Street View as an annotation interface. IBM Rota Acessível [32] allows crowd workers to report accessibility problems in their cities via a smartphone application to construct knowledge base about urban mobility issues, thus helping people with limited mobility.

The studies listed above introduced novel crowdsourcing mechanisms to help PwDs, but they gave little attention to mechanisms to sustain the motivation of the workers. Their motivations were not even assessed. As a result, little is known about the best ways to keep crowd workers active, even though these kinds of projects are likely to suffer when active participation declines, as reported in [26]. Our study aims to introduce a social-purpose crowdsourcing system equipped with built-in motivational features as well as to investigate the motivations of the workers in actual practice, including the effects of the motivational features.

Crowdsourced Tasks for GLAM

In GLAM scenarios, crowdsourcing has been used for a variety of purposes, such as "correction and transcription tasks", "contextualization", "complementing collection", "classification", "co-curation", and "crowdfunding" [23]. The correction and transcription area, for example, includes many projects that exploit the power of crowds to efficiently digitalize historical documents. Bookshare [30] is one of the largest projects in the intersection between PwD assistance and GLAM, and now houses more than 300,000 accessible books for people with print disabilities. Volunteer workers help scan printed books and proofread the resulting texts.

The Australian Newspaper Digitisation Program (ANDP) [11] of the National Library of Australia, uses a Web-based interface to ask crowd workers to correct errors produced by the optical character recognition (OCR) engine during the process of digitalizing historical newspapers. CONCERT [21] is a Web-based OCR error correction tool, developed in the IMPACT project, driven by national and regional libraries in Europe seeking to digitize massive amounts of historical text. For efficiency, this tool decomposes each task into several levels of sub-tasks and provides a special interface for each level. CONCERT was also used to digitize historical books archived in the National Diet Library of Japan [13].

Again, those projects did not focus much attention on the motivation of their crowds. Even though some of them elicited large amounts of participation, little was learned about how to manage these active crowds. Meanwhile, several projects have introduced interesting approaches to collect active participants. For example, reCAPTCHA [28] distributes small pieces of character recognition tasks that cannot be handled by OCR engines and uses human capabilities for CAPTCHA tests. Digitalkoot [7] proposed video-game-like interfaces to treat OCR error correction tasks as entertainment. These two systems introduced specific ways to (potentially) motivate crowds, but they did not quantitatively investigate the effects on the workers' motivations. We decided to investigate the motivations of crowds in the contexts of PwD assistance and GLAM.

	Intrinsic Motivations	Extrinsic Motivations
Personal Motivations	**Skill Fitness.** [8] If the difficulty of tasks matches the skill set of the worker, the motivation will increase. For novice workers, this may correspond to Simplicity [1]. **Task Identity.** [8] If the worker perceives the sense of accomplishment, the motivation will be stimulated. **Task Autonomy.** [8] The worker is motivated if more decisions on "when" and "what" are permitted. This also covers Trust [1]. **Direct Feedback from the Job.** [8] Seeing the results of task execution in a tangible form increases the motivation. This is feedback from the system, not from other persons. **Fun.** [1] The worker is motivated if the task and interactions are enjoyable. This also covers Addiction [6].	**Payment.** [18] Monetary remuneration for completing tasks increases the motivation. **Pastime.** [6] This motivation covers acting just to "kill time", avoiding boredom. **Signaling.** [18] The worker is motivated if their visibility is increased through the activities. **Human Capital Advancement.** [18] The worker is motivated if their skills are improved through the activities. This covers Learning New Knowledge [1]. **Personal Interest.** [1] If the activity matches the worker's existing interests, the motivation is stimulated. This corresponds to Action Significance by External Values in [8].
Social Motivations	**Community Identification.** [18] The motivation is stimulated by feelings of collective identities. This may depend on a Supportive Environment [1]. **Social Contribution.** The worker is motivated by feeling that task outcomes benefit target users. This is driven by Altruism [1] and can be stimulated by feedback from the users. **Community Reciprocity.** [22] The worker is motivated if the task outcomes directly benefit the worker.	**Social Contact.** [6] This motivation represents the willingness to connect with other people and the society. **External Obligations.** [8] This motivation is induced by people or organizations outside the community. This is driven by obligations, social norms, or sanctions. **Indirect Feedback from the Job.** [8] This motivation is encouraged when the community receives positive feedback from external people or organizations.

Table 1. Descriptions of sixteen types of motivation in four categories.

Motivation Models for Crowd Workers

For workers on general-purpose crowdsourcing platforms such as MTurk, Kaufmann et al. [15] proposed a motivation model based on Self-Determination Theory [25]. By combining a variety of factors introduced in relevant fields such as work motivation and education theories and studies on open source software (OSS) development communities (e.g., [6][8][18]), their model classifies motivation of crowd workers into two major categories: intrinsic and extrinsic. The former consists of enjoyment-based and community-based motivations. The latter consists of immediate payoffs, delayed payoffs, and social motivations. Their survey with MTurk workers found that extrinsic motivations have a strong effect on the time spent on the crowdsourcing platform, whereas they scored enjoyment-based motivations as more important. Since only a few senior workers participated in their survey (3.2% of the respondents were 60 or older), little was discovered about the characteristics of senior crowd workers.

For social-purpose crowdsourcing, the motivational trends can be different because of its nature. Many initiatives in this area use volunteer-based models rather than payment-based models. Also, they often try to develop their own community of dedicated workers instead of exploiting open crowds on an existing crowdsourcing platform. Alam and Campbell [1] investigated the motivations of text correctors in ANDP through interviews, and found that the workers placed more value on intrinsic motivations than extrinsic motivations. By adapting Kaufmann et al.'s framework to the findings from their interviews, they introduced a motivation model for crowd workers for GLAM tasks. In their model, the intrinsic motivations can be egoism-based (personal interest, supportive environment, etc.), community-based (altruism, collectivism, etc.), or enjoyment-based (fun, pastime, etc.). The extrinsic motivations represent social motivation such as acknowledgement and desire for recognition. Since their study was an interview-based qualitative investigation, it cannot be assessed as to what extent the workers rated each type of motivation and how the motivation affected the actual behavior of the workers. Olson and Rosacker [22] reviewed the literature to compare worker motivation in crowdsourcing and OSS projects, and found that the reciprocity is a minor factor in crowdsourcing, whereas it is a major motivation in OSS. We suppose that motivation in social-purpose crowdsourcing could be similar to that in OSS because of its community-based nature. Thus we decided to include the reciprocity in our model.

FOUR-QUADRANT MOTIVATION MODEL

As mentioned in the introduction, the primary goal of our motivation model is to provide structured metrics to assess workers' motivation in a social-purpose crowdsourcing community. Table 1 describes the framework. Overall, it has two criteria: *intrinsic* vs *extrinsic* and *personal* vs *social*.

We used Kaufmann et al.'s formulation of intrinsic and extrinsic motivations in crowdsourcing [15], which follows

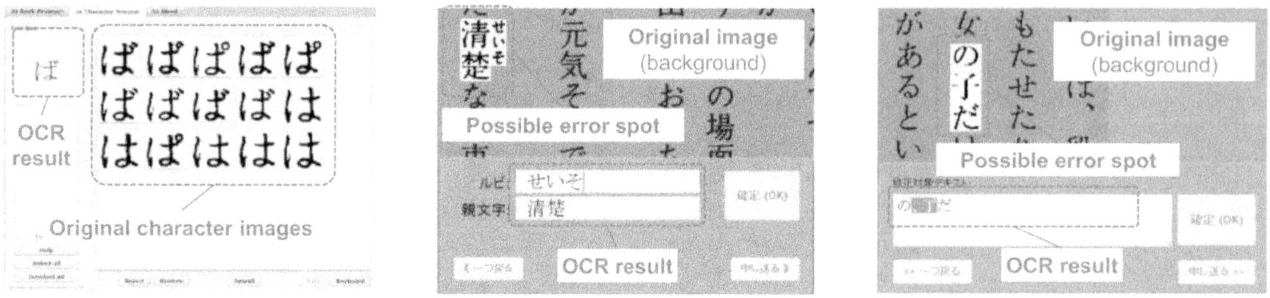

(a) Character (b) Ruby (c) Phrase

Figure 1. The proofreading system consists of three types of interfaces.

the classification in Self-Determination Theory [25]. The intrinsic motivations represent motivations "seeking for the fulfillment generated by the activity." For the extrinsic motivations, "the activity is just an instrument for achieving a certain desired outcome." In other words, for intrinsic, the reason to do a task exists within the work to achieve a specific goal (e.g., supporting a library for PwDs) while for extrinsic the reason exists outside of the activity. Based on this principle, Fun and Pastime are separated into the intrinsic and extrinsic categories, respectively, although they were classified in the same category in Alam and Campbell's work [1]. The worker will feel Fun if the task itself is enjoyable. Pastime represents that the worker has a desire to kill time before doing the task. Similarly, Personal Interest falls into the extrinsic category because it indicates that the worker has an interest in advance and doing the task is just an opportunity to gratify the interest.

We introduce another criterion to divide personal and social motivations. This aspect is emphasized because we assume that, for social-purpose crowdsourcing, motivation induced by the social relationships around the worker may have a primary role in addition to the motivations based on personal beliefs and enjoyment. The personal motivations represent motivations developed without requiring interactions with other individuals. The social motivations are motivation induced by interactions with others. In other words, the worker can feel personal motivations even if no other person actually participated in or contacted the community, whereas the worker could not feel social motivations without other people.

Based on these two dimensions, our motivation framework uses a four-quadrant model to structure motivations rather than a tree-based hierarchical model such as Kaufmann et al. used [14]. The four-quadrant model allows us to quantitatively compare the workers' motivations from multiple levels and perspectives. We can use rough binary criteria for each dimension (e.g., intrinsic vs extrinsic) as well as comparing the four quadrants. It is also possible to compare each small unit of a motivation within a category or between categories. Each quadrant has three to five sub-items. For example, the intrinsic-personal motivations include: Skill Fitness, Task Identity, Task Autonomy, Direct Feedback from the Job, and Fun. Those factors are based on [15] except for Fun, which is derived from [1]. Basically, we combined Kaufmann et al.'s [15] and Alam and Campbell's [1] frameworks and reorganized them so that they match the four-quadrant categories. The descriptions of all sub-items in the four quadrants are shown in Table 1. Note that the borders between the quadrants may be ambiguous because the motivational feelings may differ among individuals. For example, Social Contact may overlap Community Identification for those who desire connections with allies who achieve the same goal together. Note also that, even though the model considers Payment because some previous attempts in this area paid a certain amount of compensation, social-purpose crowdsourcing often depends on unpaid volunteers. Our model primarily targets social-purpose work such as PwD assistance and GLAM, but it may be applicable to broader types of crowdsourcing situations.

SYSTEM DESIGN

The system we deployed uses the Web-based proofreading (OCR error correction) interfaces shown in Figure 1. It is based on the same concepts as the systems used in [13] and [21], where each proofreading task was decomposed into multiple types of micro-tasks to make each micro-task simpler for efficient dispatch to crowd workers. We redesigned the interfaces to better handle OCR errors specific to Japanese text, since our system was for digitalizing Japanese books. There are three types of interfaces: (a) Character, (b) Ruby, and (c) Phrase. In each screen, the worker is presented with the original, scanned image of some text and the OCR results for the text, side by side. Then the worker is asked to determine if the OCR results are correct and, if wrong, to type the correct text.

The Character interface is the same as the carpet session interface proposed in [21]. Each worker sees a set of scanned thumbnail images of characters that were recognized by the OCR as a certain character. The character that the OCR recommended as a match is shown in the upper-left area of the screen. The worker is asked to choose and correctly identify any incorrectly recognized characters. The Ruby and Phrase interfaces show the worker a small piece of a scanned page and the recognized text in an

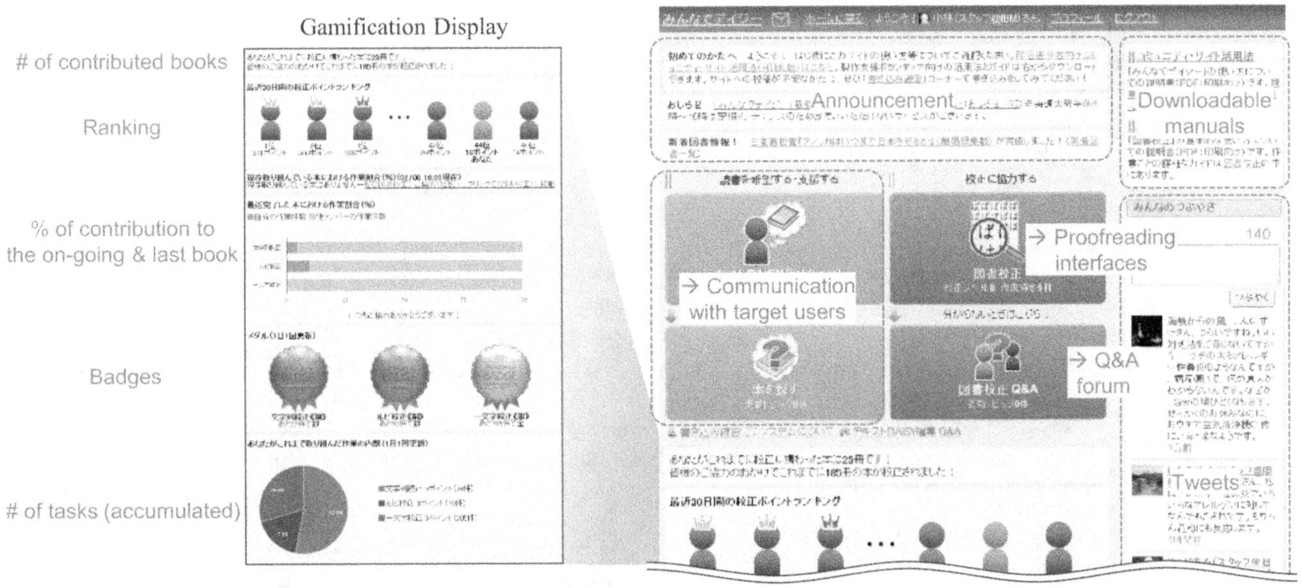

Figure 2. The community portal has a communication platform, instruction manuals, and a gamification display.

editable field, which may contain OCR errors. The worker is asked to correct any errors by editing the text. The difference between the two interfaces is that Ruby is designed to process a pair of base and ruby texts [33], while Phrase is designed for a simple line of text. Overall, the Character interface is relatively complicated and requires some technical skill, since it is designed to effectively process multiple errors in parallel. The other two interfaces mainly require linguistic and editorial knowledge rather than technical skills, since the designs of the interfaces are straightforward and easy to use.

Motivating Features

On the basis of the four-quadrant motivation framework, we added some features to encourage workers' motivation. More specifically, we developed the motivation framework and the system in parallel. We collected known motivation factors through literature reviews. Then we implemented the features describe below to stimulate the corresponding motivations while considering the categories of motivations, so that the system could cover motivations in all of the categories. In the following paragraphs, the corresponding motivations appear in parentheses.

Community Portal. The proofreading system is integrated with a communication platform, which also works as a portal page of the system, as shown in Figure 2. The communications between proofreaders, library staff members, and target users (people with print disabilities) provides a sense of Community Identification and Social Contribution, as well as Social Contact. The on-screen (Figure 3) and downloadable (Figure 4) manuals and the supplemental Q&A forum provide detailed instructions to workers, providing a sense of supportiveness (Community Identification). In addition, the Twitter-like chat widget allows workers to display their presence (Community Identification, Signaling).

Proofreading Interfaces. The interfaces are designed to allow workers to simply answer a series of "questions" displayed on the screen one after another. The worker is allowed to choose one of the three types of tasks that matches their skills and interests which will stimulate Skill Fitness. To provide a sense of completion, the series of tasks is not endless. Instead, it is segmented for each book (Task Identity). Also, it was reported that the question-answer interaction is enjoyable even for senior workers [16] (Fun). The workers may develop their technical, linguistic, or editorial skills through proofreading (Human Capital Advancement).

Gamification Display. The portal page shows some statistics about the tasks the worker has completed, which seeks to provide game-like feedback to the worker. The display includes: the number of books that the worker has worked on relative to the total number of books produced in this project (Social Contribution); the worker ranking based on the number of completed tasks (Community Identification); and charts and badges to show the percentages and accumulated total contributions (Task Identity, Direct Feedback from the Job). In detail, the charts and badges include the percentages of the worker's contributions for the ongoing and last-contributed books, badges and a pie chart based on the accumulated numbers of contributions for each type of task. Based on the suggestions of beta testers and library staff members, the worker ranks were anonymous, so the rank of each worker was not exposed to the other workers. Thus, in contrast to a typical "ranking" feature in other online social systems, it does not support Signaling. Also we did not assume that

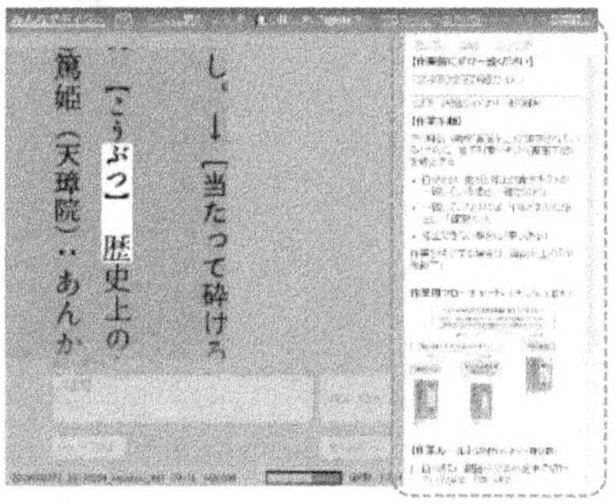

Figure 3. The on-screen manuals appear in the sidebar of the proofreading screens.

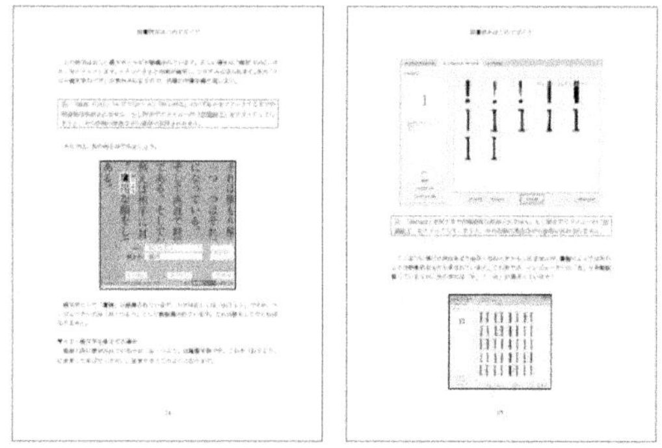

Figure 4. The downloadable manuals provide step-by-step, illustrated instructions.

this "gamification" feature directly supports Fun, since it does not gamify the task itself as in Digitalkoot [7].

Real-World Recruiting. To involve multi-generational workers (especially seniors), we asked for participation via offline media (words of mouth, handouts, etc.) as well as online media (the library website, Twitter, etc.). We provided seminars in offline classrooms to instruct them in each step of using the proofreading system (Figure 5). These efforts helped the workers choose their best-fit tasks, which will result in Skill Fitness, as well as in developing a sense of External Obligation.

Hybrid Task Requests. The system processes two types of tasks: user-requested books and library-requested books. The user-requested tasks occur each time a person who has a print disability requests a digitalized version of a printed book. This type of tasks is entered into the system on an on-demand basis, which creates a stronger sense of Social Contribution. However, the number of user-requested tasks fluctuated and tended to cause task shortages. In contrast, the library-requested tasks are queued into the system at regular intervals to increase the number of accessible books in the library's collection. These more regular tasks allow workers to find available tasks whenever they want to contribute, which leads to greater Task Autonomy.

Special Considerations

We assume that our system is a representative case of social-purpose crowdsourcing, since it is a hybrid of assistive services for PwDs and tasks to support GLAM. However there are several considerations in evaluating the system.

First, contrary to previous GLAM attempts that involved historical documents and aimed to produce open data (e.g., [11]), our target is available-for-sale, copyrighted books and private materials. Thus, by design, the system fragments scanned images into minimal-sized pieces. This can have serious negative impact on Task Identity and Direct Feedback from the Job, by preventing each worker from forming a comprehensive view of their own tasks. It may also reduce their Personal-Interest motivation, because workers cannot read the content even if the topic of the book is of interest to them. This leads to a research question: Can the gamification display and other design considerations compensate for these negative impacts?

Second, we provided more detailed manuals and classroom seminars than typical crowdsourcing projects. It is known that senior citizens prefer to have explicit instructions rather than using trial-and-error approaches for new information technologies [16][19]. We considered this fact since we wanted to involve senior workers, who had limited participation in earlier crowdsourcing projects.

Third, we have expert proofreaders who sample the crowd-proofread books to check for human errors made by the crowd and for OCR errors that cannot be resolved by the crowd. Their work can be taken as "gold standard" answers. Thus we can assess the accuracy of the crowd proofreaders by comparing their work with the experts' answers, at least for the sampled subset of their results. This is not a typical situation in crowdsourced proofreading, where the system has no knowledge about whether or not the crowd-corrected text is actually correct.

EVALUATION

We evaluated the system by analyzing the results from the six months of the experimental period to determine which motivation factors are the key drivers of community activities and whether there are differences between young and senior crowd workers. The use of the four-quadrant motivation model to define the metrics allowed us to conduct the evaluation systematically and quantitatively. The result will be comparable with future studies on different systems that use the same metrics.

Figure 5. Some workers attended classroom seminars. The majority of the attendees were seniors.

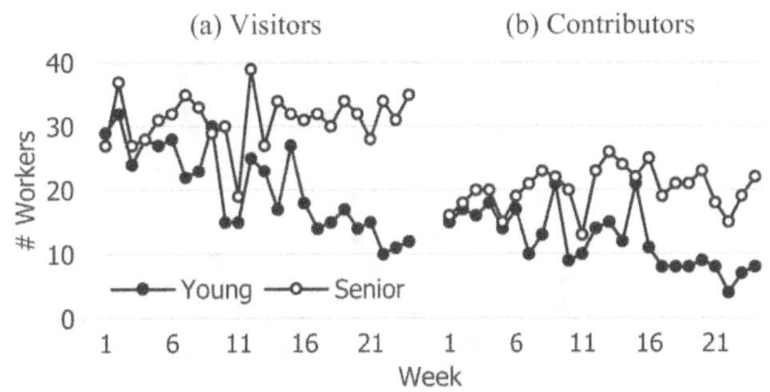

Figure 6. The numbers of workers who (a) visited the site and (b) contributed to work during Week 1 to Week 24.

Evaluation Method

Our system described in the previous section was deployed in a collaboration with a public library for people with print disabilities. For the first two months we had closed beta testing with selected volunteers, and then the system was officially launched, shifting to an open participation policy, where anyone who has an Internet connection can register as a volunteer and work as a proofreader at their favored times and locations. Six months (24 weeks) after the official launch, the worker community consisted of 174 volunteers (82 young, 92 senior), including the 33 beta testers. We label people who are 60 years old or older as "senior" while the others are "young", since 60 is a typical retirement age in Japan, and retirement is believed to be deeply related to the motivation to work as indicated in Kooij et al.'s study [17]. The volunteer proofreaders consisted of a broad range of ages from so-called millennials to people older than baby boomers, ranging from 19 to 84 years old. The average ages of the young and senior groups were 45.6 (SD = 9.6) and 68.5 (SD = 5.8), respectively. During the six months period, they completed a total of 2,514,161 micro-tasks. Since the gamification features were added in the middle of the period (at 12 weeks), we can compare the results before and after the introduction of gamification features.

For the evaluation, we first analyzed the system logs during the target period to find the trends in evolving worker activities for both young and senior workers. We also used a questionnaire-based survey of the workers with an online survey form. The questionnaire had four parts. The first part asked demographic questions (e.g., occupational status and familiarity with information technologies). The next part asked to what extent each motivating feature of the system was effective (e.g., "*Was the ranking interesting to you?*"). The third part directly asked about the levels of the stimulated motivations, such as to what extent the worker felt each type of motivation when using the system (e.g., "*When working on the system, did you feel a sense of accomplishment?*" for Task Identity). The last part asked about the levels of motivational values in a similar manner, i.e., to what extent did the worker rate each type of motivation, regardless of whether or not they used the system (e.g., "*When doing any work online, is it important that your skill can be improved though the activities?*" for Human Capital Advancement). All of the questions except for the demographic questions used a 7-level Likert scale. The respondents were also allowed to give free-text comments. Finally, we aligned the survey results with the system logs and tried to assess the effects of each type of motivation on the actual activities and performances of the workers.

Worker Activities and Performances

Figure 6 shows the evolving numbers of workers: (a) who accessed the site (visitors) and (b) who completed at least one task (contributors) for each age group, during the six-month period. On average, the system had steady participation from a number of workers. Approximately 50 workers visited the site and 30 performed micro-tasks each week. The comparison between the age groups shows an interesting trend. In the first half of the period, the numbers of visitors and contributors were similar for the two groups. In the second half, however, the young workers seemed to lose their interest while the numbers of senior visitors and contributors were slightly increased. This indicates that the senior workers showed more sustained activity, even when we adjusted for the number of registered senior workers being slightly larger than the number of young workers.

Figure 7 shows the evolving percentages of each worker's contribution relative to the total work for each week based on the time workers spent on tasks, emphasizing the values of the top ten contributors. To assess the contributions, we used the expended time instead of the number of completed tasks because the effort needed to complete a task was not the same for the three types of tasks. The time is expected to be fairly comparable regardless of the age, given that there was no significant effect of the age on the speeds in performing tasks ($p > .05$).

About half of the total work was completed by the top ten contributors, while the rest was done by the other (long-tail) workers. In other words, the results follow the famous Pareto principle [24], where 80% of the contributions come from 20% of the workers. Seven of the top contributors were 60 or older, including three who are 80 or older. In addition, as shown in the figure, there are different types of

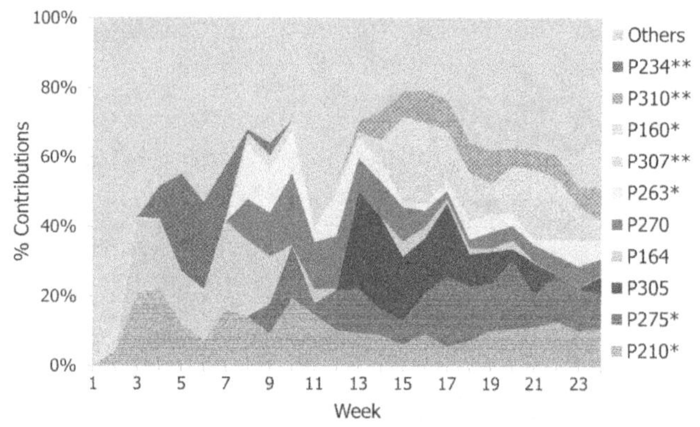

Figure 7. The percentages of each worker's contribution for each week (top ten contributors and others). The workers with * and ** are older than 60 and 80 years, respectively.

top contributors. We categorized them into three types: "constant active workers" (P210, P275, and P310), who steadily performed a certain number of tasks each week after they joined the community; "sprinters" (P305, P164, P270, P263, P307, and P234), who made most of their contributions in their first weeks; and "late bloomers" (P160), who became active a few months after joining. Note that most of sprinters were still working as long-tail workers at the end of the six-month period, and did not drop out of the community. Overall, the community seemed to evolve into a stable state in later months, where the accumulating work from diverse workers produced a constant flow of results.

Subjective Effectiveness and Motivations

In total, 55 volunteer proofreaders (20 young, 35 senior) answered the questionnaire. The young respondents include 9 full-time employees, 2 part-time employees, and 4 volunteers who also participated in other volunteer work. The senior respondents include 5 part-time employees and 16 volunteers. All respondents had at least five years of personal computer experience and most of them stated that they use computers every day. A total of 35 of the 55 respondents (11 young, 24 senior) had prior experience in assisting PwDs, while 16 (6 young, 10 senior) had prior experience in proofreading.

Figure 8 and 9 show the average scores for the stimulated motivations and the motivational ratings, respectively, along with standard deviations. To test the reliability of the four-quadrant motivation model, we calculated Cronbach's Alpha values for each quadrant based on the motivational ratings. The values were 0.843, 0.981, 0.963, and 0.972 for the intrinsic-personal, intrinsic-social, extrinsic-personal, and extrinsic-social quadrants, respectively, which indicate the model effectively categorizes the motivations. The gap between the stimulated motivations and the motivational ratings was relatively small (*mean* = 0.91, *SD* = 0.96), which suggests that the system design generally matched the respondents' motivational ratings.

The values in Figure 8 show that the respondents felt Social Contribution most strongly (*mean* = 6.04, *SD* = 0.98) when using the system. Overall, the respondents felt more intrinsic motivation except for Community Reciprocity, while they felt less extrinsic motivation except for Personal Interest. More specifically, the young respondents felt more intrinsic motivation than seniors even though seniors also felt more intrinsic motivation than extrinsic motivation. T-tests show that the age differences were significant for Skill Fitness ($p < .005$), Task Autonomy ($p < .01$), Fun ($p < .01$), and Social Contribution ($p < .05$).

The values in Figure 9 show that the respondents rated Task Autonomy most highly (*mean* = 6.04, *SD* = 0.74). Overall, they relatively rated intrinsic motivations more highly except for Community Reciprocity and less extrinsic motivations except for Personal Interest, which generally shows a similar trend to the values in Figure 8. The age differences were not significant except that the young respondents rated Human Capital Advancement more highly than the seniors ($p < .05$). The young respondents gave higher ratings to Signaling as well while the seniors rated External Obligations higher, but the differences were not significant ($p > .05$).

For the proofreading tasks and interfaces, the respondents answered that the three types of tasks were generally easy to perform. The average subjective levels of easiness were 4.83 (*SD* = 1.39), 5.43 (1.08), and 5.40 (1.21) for Character, Ruby, and Phrase tasks, respectively. In addition, the respondents stated that the more tasks there were in the queues, the more they felt encouraged (*mean* = 5.20, *SD* = 1.51), which supports the Alam and Campbell's result that indicated that more tasks increase motivation in crowdsourcing for GLAM [1]. Also the respondents stated that they were demotivated by the shortage of tasks (*mean* = 5.31, *SD* = 1.56), even though we used the hybrid approach to avoid the task-shortage problem [26]. For all of the values presented in this paragraph, there were no significant differences between the two age groups ($p > .05$).

For the subjective effectiveness of the instructions, the senior respondents rated the classroom seminars most highly (*mean* = 6.27), followed by the downloadable complete manuals (5.52), the Q&A forums (4.97), and the on-screen outline manuals (4.10). In contrast, the young respondents equally rated the four modalities of instructions (5.50–6.00). The age had significant effects on the effectiveness of the Q&A forum ($p < .005$) and on-screen manuals ($p < .001$). These results confirm the previous findings that senior citizens tend to prefer manuals and in-person instructions [16][19].

For the gamification display, the respondents' answers show that they found the number of books that contain the worker's contribution (*mean* = 4.16, *SD* = 1.53) and the total number of books produced in the project (*mean* = 4.65, *SD* = 1.56) more effective, while the worker ranking, charts, and badges were less effective (*mean* < 4 for all). There

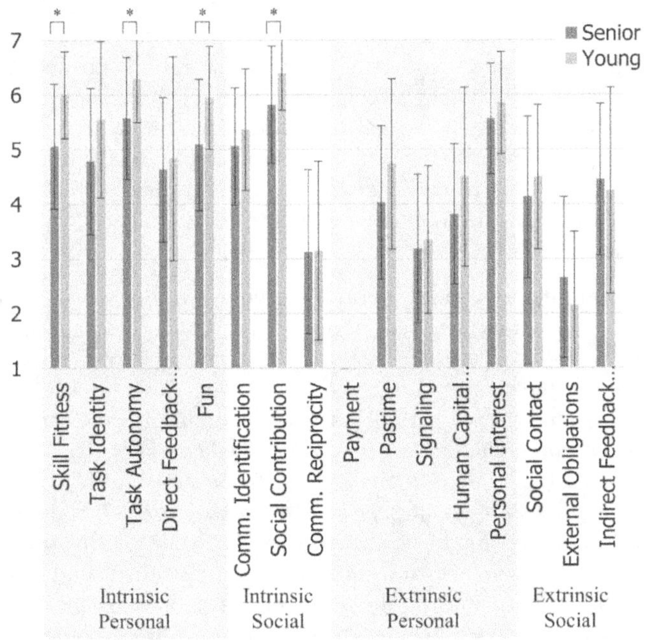

Figure 8. The average scores for 15 types of motivations the workers felt in using the system. (Payment was not tested because the system worked on an unpaid volunteer model.)

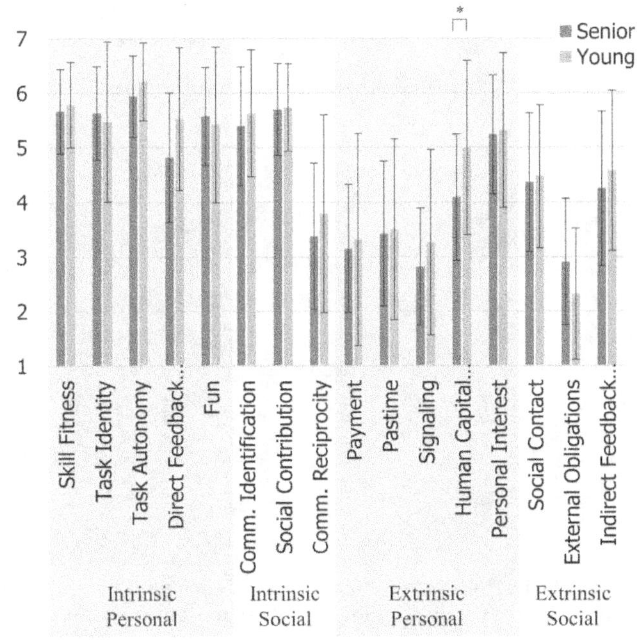

Figure 9. The average scores for the 16 types of motivations the workers valued.

were no significant differences between the two age groups ($p > .05$). The young respondents rated the Twitter-like chat widget more highly than the seniors (*mean* = 4.95 and 4.06 for youths and seniors, respectively), where the effect of the age was significant ($p < .05$).

Motivation Effects on Worker Performances

To investigate how motivation affects the actual performances of the workers, we analyzed their continuity, frequency, and accuracy in relation to their reported motivations. For the *continuity*, we defined *long-standing* workers as those who had worked for at least two weeks during the six months period and worked for a month after that period. We defined *dropped-out* workers as those who had worked for at least two weeks during the six months period and never worked after that period. Workers who had never worked for a two-week period were excluded from the continuity analysis. The *frequency* was defined as the average time per day that the worker expended in tasks. The *accuracy* was defined as the rate of correctly answered tasks, which was calculated based on the experts' answers we had for a subset of completed tasks. The target workers for this analysis consisted of those who answered the questionnaire and for whom the continuity, frequency, and accuracy could also be calculated.

For the continuity analysis, we had 21 long-standing workers and 22 dropped-out workers. As shown in Figure 10, the long-standing workers gave higher ratings to the gamification components in comparison to the dropped-out workers. In particular, the differences were significant for the number of books that the worker had contributed to ($p < .05$), the worker ranking ($p < .005$), and the badges based on the accumulated amount of contributions ($p < .05$). This indicates that the long-standing workers paid more attention to the feedback for their own accumulated work. In addition, the dropped-out workers stated that they tended to do specific types of tasks they preferred (*mean* = 4.68, *SD* = 1.32), while the long-standing workers tended to showed the opposite behavior (*mean* = 3.62, *SD* = 1.72), which indicates that they accepted the system's recommendations. The difference was significant ($p < .05$). Among the 16 types of motivations, Pastime ($p < .005$) and External Obligations ($p < .05$) had significant effects on the continuity. For Pastime, the average scores were 4.14 (*SD* = 1.24) and 2.80 (1.32) for the long-standing and dropped-out workers, respectively. For External Obligations, the values were 3.10 (*SD* = 1.04) and 2.33 (1.20). This result indicates that the workers who rated Pastime and External Obligation highly tended to be long-standing workers.

For the accuracy, the respondents generally performed well, where the mean rate of correct answers was 97.67% (*max* = 100%, *min* = 94.34%). The values for the young and senior groups were 97.66% and 97.69%, respectively. The overall accuracy was 97.72% (97.61% for youths, 97.78% for seniors), including the results from the workers who did not respond to the survey, which indicates that the survey respondents can be taken as representative of all of the workers. Note that we could obtain accuracy values for only 23 of the 55 respondents due to the methodological limitations.

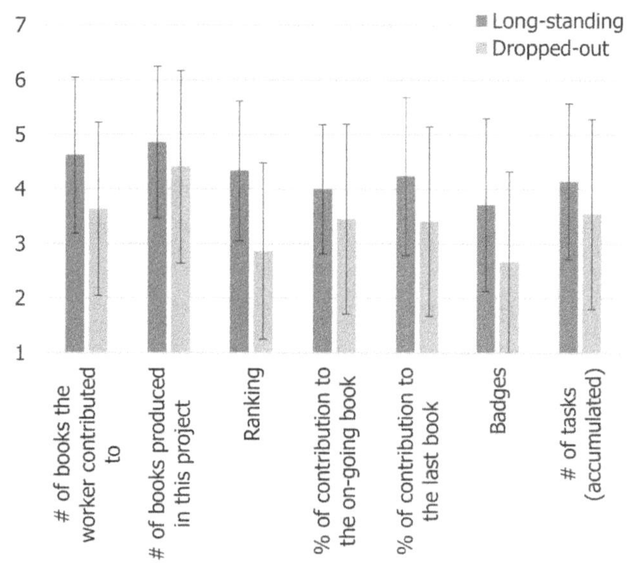

Figure 10. The subjective effectiveness of each gamification component for long-standing and dropped-out workers.

Among the 15 types of stimulated motivations, a logistic regression analysis showed a significant positive association between the continuity and Community Identification (*coeff* = .87, $p < .05$). A linear regression analysis showed a significant negative association between the frequency and External Obligations (*coeff* = –.45, $p < .05$) and Task Autonomy (*coeff* = –.56, $p < .05$). We failed to use a probit analysis to assess the association between the accuracy and motivation because we had too few samples. However, there seems to be a trend that personal motivations had positive effects on the accuracy while social motivations had negative effects. In those analyses, the missing values were replaced with average values.

DISCUSSION

Activity and Persistence of Senior Workers

In our evaluation, the senior workers were more active and persistent than the young workers, as shown in Figure 6. It is notable that three of the top ten contributors were 80 or older, which shows that even older senior workers could be quite active. Their performance was much better than a naïve prediction. This indicates the great potential of seniors to be core workers in social-purpose crowdsourcing, even though they have participated in little of this kind of work to date.

One question is what caused their activity and persistence. A possible reason is their lower values for Human Capital Advancement. Their strong motivation towards Social Contribution and lower desire for skill development would make them more satisfied with micro-tasks for proofreading, which may often be tedious and repetitive. Altruism alone could also explain this trend. It is known that senior citizens have strong interests in helping PwDs and in using their linguistic abilities [16]. Unfortunately, our evaluation found no evidence that the seniors had more relevant motivations than the young workers. Further research is needed to assess the detailed effects of altruism. Another simple explanation might be that the seniors had more free time, given that most of the seniors were unemployed while most of the young workers were full- or part-time employees, even though the motivation metrics did not clearly capture this aspect.

During the evaluation period, the young workers often left the community, even though they reported stronger motivations than the seniors. In contrast, once seniors joined the community, they were more likely to become long-standing workers. This result might confirm that the older workers tend to avoid trying new tasks [17]. The other side of this trait is that older workers rarely leave a task once they start it. Another possible reason for this apparent contradiction might be the existence of other motivational factors that our metrics did not cover. Also there might be an age-related bias on the answers in the Likert scale. This indicates we need to conduct more study of this problem.

Top Contributors vs. Long-Tail Workers

As shown in Figure 7, the top contributors and long-tail players had complementary outcomes. The long-tail workers may become top contributors over a long period, or vice versa, which indicates that the worker community needs to satisfy both top contributors and long-tail workers. The contribution of each long-tail worker is small, but their accumulated outcomes are comparable to those of the top contributors. Also, the presence of many long-tail workers encourages the top contributors by providing a sense of Community Identification. Some of the top contributors in our evaluation expressed concern about taking opportunities away from the other workers by completing all of the tasks in the system by themselves.

Effects of Gamification Mechanisms

Among the gamification components, the display of the number of books the community has produced was rated as most effective. This result suggests that a typical worker in social-purpose crowdsourcing pays more attention to the community's collective results rather than individual results. At the same time, as shown in Figure 10, long-standing workers were interested in the feedback about their personal results as well. In summary, the feedback for the collective results motivates general workers while the feedback for the individual results seems more effective for long-standing workers. The use of a combination of collective and individual feedback is a good approach, since both newcomers and long-standing workers are essential parts of a sustainable community.

In addition to the effect on the continuity of the workers, the comparison between the activities before and after the introduction of gamification revealed that it increased the number of accesses to the community portal page regardless of the age of the worker. During the first half of the target period, each worker accessed the page 12.9 times per week on average. During the second half, the value was 20.4 times per week. The access count itself does not directly contribute to the productivity, but this change appears to have positive effects on Community Identification by increasing the mutual exposure among volunteer workers, target users, and library staff members. In addition, the increase in the number of accesses leads to an increase in the number of available workers, which can improve the turnaround times for proofreading. This is a similar situation as with real-time crowdsourcing [2], where crowd workers are woken up in advance, before the system actually sends requests, so that the workers can more quickly respond to the requests.

Effects of Motivational Factors

Overall, what are the critical motivational factors in social-purpose crowdsourcing? In our evaluation, the workers particularly valued intrinsic motivations (except for Community Reciprocity) and Personal Interest. This result seems to support Alam and Campbell's work [1] which emphasized intrinsic motivations including Personal Interest for crowdsourcing in a GLAM context. In comparison with motivations for general crowdsourced work [15], the primary difference is that, in social-purpose crowdsourcing, workers do not care much about Payment. Also, senior workers place less value on Human Capital Advancement. In comparison with the case of OSS projects [22], one remarkable difference appears to be that Community Reciprocity is a primary factor in OSS projects. We expect that the reciprocity is also less important in other types of social-purpose crowdsourcing because the altruism seems to be the primary motivational factor. However it is unclear to what extent our findings can be generalized to other types of work, which remains as future work.

Our system did not give the workers a comprehensive view of their tasks due to copyright concerns. We regard this as having a negative impact on motivation. As expected, the Task Identity and Direct Feedback from the Job that the workers felt were slightly weaker than the other intrinsic motivations. This is confirmed by some of the free-text comments. A dropped-out worker reported leaving because of the frustration caused by this limitation. Another worker also wanted to see a comprehensive view of the system. Given the active and persistent participation of the workers, it might be concluded that those negative impacts could be successfully compensated by the other motivating features. We need further research to investigate better ways to alleviate and compensate for those kinds of negative impacts caused by task-specific restrictions. Another motivational factor we need to discuss is External Obligations. The average scores were relatively low, but some of the seniors valued this type of motivation, which indicates that External Obligations are an important factor for them to decide to join the community. Meanwhile, it was found that the long-standing workers felt this type of motivation less than the dropped-out workers (*mean* = 2.33 and 2.82, respectively). This might indicate that invitations from their friends or close relatives can be a motivation to *start* working, while other types of motivation are necessary to *continue* working.

CONCLUSION

We investigated workers' motivation in a social-purpose crowdsourcing project running for six months, which involved both young and senior volunteer workers, by introducing a four-quadrant system of metrics to assess their motivations for a crowd-based proofreading system that had several features designed to stimulate different motivations.

Our primary findings from the evaluation include:

- Senior citizens are promising candidates as dedicated crowd workers, at least for social-purpose work, even though this cohort has not been much involved in crowdsourcing so far. Any projects in this area should consider involving more senior workers. In contrast to the young group, the seniors prefer classroom and downloadable instructions rather than on-screen instructions. Also the seniors tend to put less value on Human Capital Advancement among the motivational factors.
- The intrinsic motivations are primary drivers of participation in social-purpose work. The sense of Social Contribution is the most important motivation. A feeling of Community Identification encourages continuous participation, while the feelings of Task Autonomy and External Obligations inhibit more frequent participation. The game-like feedback seems to be effective to increase the activity of workers. The visualization of the individual's contribution (e.g., ranking) is more attractive for long-standing workers, though the other workers are more interested in the collective outcomes of the community.

The findings confirm several known trends and anecdotal assumptions from previous studies. The contribution of our experiment is to quantitatively assess the effects based on structured metrics as well as to provide the metrics for future studies to produce comparable results.

ACKNOWLEDGMENTS

This research was partially supported by the Japan Science and Technology Agency (JST) under the Strategic Promotion of Innovative Research and Development Program. We thank Mr. Sawamura and other staff members of the Japan Braille Library for their support. We also thank all of the participants in our experiment.

REFERENCES

1. Alam, S.L. and Campbell, J. Crowdsourcing motivations in a not-for-profit GLAM context: the

Australian newspapers digitisation program. In *Proc. ACIS 2012*, 1–11.

2. Bernstein, M.S., Karger, D.R., Miller, R.C., and Brandt, J. Analytic methods for optimizing realtime crowdsourcing. *arXiv:1204.2995* (2012).
3. Bigham, J. P., Jayant, C., Ji, H., Little, G., Miller, A., Miller, R. C., Miller, R., Tatarowicz, A., White, B., White, S., and Yeh, T. VizWiz: nearly real-time answers to visual questions. In *Proc. UIST 2010*, 333–342.
4. Bigham, J.P., Ladner, R.E., and Borodin, Y. The design of human-powered access technology. In *Proc. ASSETS '11*, 3–10.
5. Borodin, Y., Bigham, J.P., Stent, A., and Ramakrishnan, I.V. Towards one world web with HearSay3. In *Proc. W4A '08*. pp, 130–131.
6. Brabham, D.C. Moving the crowd at Threadless: Motivations for participation in a crowdsourcing application. *Information, Communication & Society*, 13, 8 (2010), 1122–1145.
7. Chrons, O. and Sundell, S. Digitalkoot: making old archives accessible using crowdsourcing. In *Proc. HCOMP 2011*, 20–25.
8. Hackman J.R. and Oldham G.R. Work redesign. Addison-Wesley (1980).
9. Hara, K., Le, V., and Froehlich, J. Combining crowdsourcing and google street view to identify street-level accessibility problems. In *Proc. CHI '13*, 631–640.
10. Hara, K., Azenkot, S., Campbell, M., Bennett, C.L., Le, V., Pannella, S., Moore, R., Minckler, K., Ng, R.H., and Froehlich, J.E. Improving public transit accessibility for blind riders by crowdsourcing bus stop landmark locations with Google street view. In *Proc. ASSETS '13*, Article 16.
11. Holley, R. Many hands make light work: public collaborative OCR text correction in Australian historic newspapers. *National Library of Australia Staff Papers* (2009).
12. Howe, J. The rise of crowdsourcing. *Wired Magazine*, 14, 6 (2006).
13. Ishihara, T., Itoko, T., Sato, D., Tzadok, A., and Takagi, H. Transforming Japanese archives into accessible digital books. In *Proc. JCDL '12*, 91–100.
14. Itoko, T., Arita, S., Kobayashi, M., and Takagi, H. Involving senior workers in crowdsourced proofreading. In *Proc. HCII 2014*, 106-117.
15. Kaufmann, N., Schulze, T., and Veit, D. More than fun and money. Worker motivation in crowdsourcing – A study on Mechanical Turk. In *Proc. AMCIS 2011*, Paper 340.
16. Kobayashi, M., Ishihara, T., Kosugi, A., Takagi, H., and Asakawa, C. Question-answer cards for an inclusive micro-tasking framework for the elderly. In *Proc. INTERACT 2013*, 590–607.
17. Kooij, D., De Lange, A., Jansen, P., and Dikkers, J. Older workers' motivation to continue to work: five meanings of age: a conceptual review. *Journal of managerial psychology*, 23, 4 (2008), 364–394.
18. Lakhani, K.R., and Wolf, R.G. Why hackers do what they do: understanding motivation and effort in free/open source software projects. In *Perspectives on free and open source software*, MIT Press (2005).
19. Leung, R., Tang, C., Haddad, S., McGrenere, J., Graf, P., and Ingriany, V. How older adults learn to use mobile devices: survey and field investigations. *ACM Trans. Access. Comput.*, 4, 3 (2012), Article 11.
20. Miele, J. The descriptive video exchange: the technology and implications of crowd-sourced description. *CSUN 2012*.
21. Neudecker, C. and Tzadok, A. User collaboration for improving access to historical texts. *Liber Quarterly*, 20, 1 (2010), 119–128.
22. Olson, D.L. and Rosacker, K. Crowdsourcing and open source software participation. *Service Business*, 7, 4 (2013), 499–511.
23. Oomen J. and Aroyo, L. Crowdsourcing in the cultural heritage domain: opportunities and challenges. In *Proc. C&T '11*, 138–149.
24. Reed, W.J. The Pareto, Zipf and other power laws. *Economics Letters*, 74, 1 (2001), 15–19.
25. Ryan, R.M., and Deci, E.L. Self-determination theory and the facilitation of intrinsic motivation, social development, and well-being. *American psychologist*, 55, 1 (2000), 68.
26. Takagi, H., Harada, S., Sato, D., and Asakawa, C. Lessons learned from crowd accessibility services. In *Proc. INTERACT 2013*, 587–604.
27. Takagi, H., Kawanaka, S., Kobayashi, M., Itoh, T., and Asakawa, C. Social accessibility: achieving accessibility through collaborative metadata authoring. In *Proc. ASSETS '08*, 193–200.
28. von Ahn, L., Maurer, B., McMillen, C., Abraham, D., and Blum, M. reCAPTCHA: human-based character recognition via web security measures. *Science*, 321, 5895 (2008), 1465–1468.
29. Amazon Mechanical Turk, http://www.mturk.com/
30. Bookshare, http://www.bookshare.org/
31. Dotsub, http://dotsub.com/
32. IBM Rota Acessível, http://rotaacessivel.com/
33. Ruby Annotation, http://www.w3.org/TR/ruby/

Handheld or Handsfree? Remote Collaboration via Lightweight Head-Mounted Displays and Handheld Devices

Steven Johnson[1], **Madeleine Gibson**[2], **Bilge Mutlu**[1]
[1] Department of Computer Sciences
[2] Department of Industrial and Systems Engineering
University of Wisconsin–Madison
sjj@cs.wisc.edu; mcgibson2@wisc.edu; bilge@cs.wisc.edu

ABSTRACT
Emerging wearable and mobile communication technologies, such as lightweight head-mounted displays (HMDs) and handheld devices, promise support for everyday remote collaboration. Despite their potential for widespread use, their effectiveness as collaborative tools is unknown, particularly in physical tasks involving mobility. To better understand their impact on collaborative behaviors, perceptions, and performance, we conducted a two-by-two (technology type: HMD vs. tablet computer; task setting: static vs. dynamic) between-subjects study where participants ($n = 66$) remotely collaborated as "helper" and "worker" pairs in the construction of a physical object. Our results showed that, in the dynamic task, HMD use enabled helpers to offer more frequent directing commands and more proactive assistance, resulting in marginally faster task completion. In the static task, while tablet use helped convey subtle visual information, helpers and workers had conflicting perceptions of how the two technologies contributed to their success. Our findings offer strong design and research implications, underlining the importance of a consistent view of the shared workspace and the differential support collaborators with different roles receive from technologies.

ACM Classification Keywords
H.5.3 **Information Interfaces and Presentation**: Group and Organization Interfaces–*Collaborative computing, Computer-supported cooperative work, Evaluation/methodology*

General Terms
Human Factors; Performance; Experimentation

Author Keywords
Computer-supported cooperative work; remote collaboration; videoconferencing; head-mounted displays (HMDs); wearable computing; handheld devices; tablet computers

ACM 978-1-4503-2922-4/15/03...$15.00.
http://dx.doi.org/10.1145/2675133.2675176

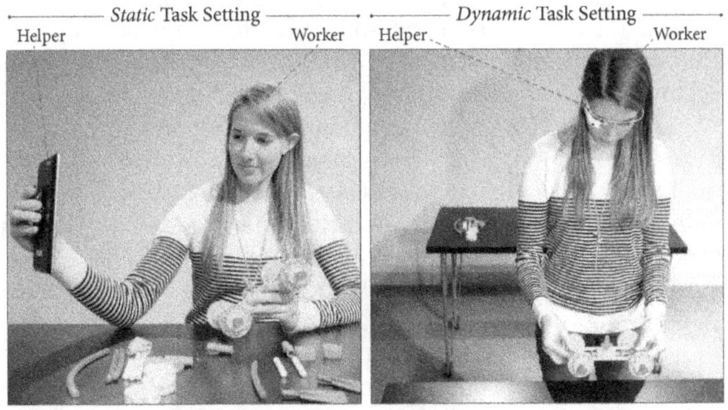

Figure 1. Participants remotely collaborated in pairs using either a tablet or an HMD in a construction task in one of two task settings: a *static* task setting, requiring low levels of mobility, or a *dynamic* task setting, requiring high levels of mobility.

INTRODUCTION
Collaborative work across many domains involves physical tasks. A team of doctors performing surgery, workers repairing machinery, and young adults learning how to cook from their parents are examples of hands-on activities where the level of expertise differs across members of the collaboration. Distributed physical tasks, in which not all members of the collaboration are collocated, have important roles in medical, industrial, and educational domains. With the rapid development of communication and collaboration technologies that enable remote workspace sharing, such as smartphones, tablets, and lightweight head-mounted displays (HMDs), remote collaboration for physical tasks has become more feasible than ever. These technologies promise easy assistance to users from their co-workers, family members, or friends who have expertise in their task—not just those individuals who are most geographically accessible.

While many technologies that support assistance in physical tasks are finding widespread use, little research has been conducted to evaluate their efficiency and effectiveness in these settings. One class of collaboration technologies are handheld mobile devices, such as smartphones and tablet computers, which are equipped with videoconferencing capabilities that can enhance collaboration [8]. Tablets are also becoming increasingly popular for both work and casual use [9]. The larger screen size of a tablet computer relative to the smartphone may also prove beneficial for supporting collaborative activities. One real-world example of tablet usage is a theatre company which provided each of its troupes with a tablet to hold video conferences with managers located at company headquarters, reducing the costs of emergency travel [21]. Other instances of tablet use involve the receipt of instructions by repair technicians in the field and the relay of video footage of furniture products from warehouse staff to purchasing agents to ensure product quality [32].

Lightweight HMDs constitute another class of technologies which hold promise for supporting remote physical collaboration. These devices are emerging as a commercially available family of products that people use for collaboration to link and work seamlessly with other mobile and wearable technologies. While the concept of a head-mounted display is not new [43], these emerging lightweight HMDs are designed to be smaller and less obtrusive relative to eariler immersive HMDs [12]. Lightweight HMDs are designed to provide information in a minimal fashion, which links them more closely to the physical environment than to a virtual environment [31]. This closer connection to the real environment while emphasizing less the augmentation of reality may make lightweight HMDs better suited than immersive HMDs to supporting communication and collaboration. Similar to smartphones and tablet computers, there is limited research evaluating the effectiveness of lightweight HMDs in supporting remote collaboration on physical tasks.

Given the growing availability of remote collaboration tools, a better understanding of how these tools support collaboration in physical tasks is required to inform the design of collaboration tools and to help predict collaborative outcomes. Furthermore, it is important to understand how these technologies impact collaborative outcomes under a variety of task conditions. One such condition is the level of *mobility*—the ability to physically move freely and easily—required by the task. Different tasks require different levels of mobility of the collaborators (see Figure 1). Repairing a large piece of machinery requires a worker to be very mobile, whereas performing surgery involves focused work with low mobility. We expect there to be tradeoffs involved with different technologies providing a better fit for collaborations with different goals and task requirements.

Prior work evaluating remote collaboration technologies has focused almost exclusively on tasks requiring low levels of mobility [13, 14, 29]. For example, Fussell et al. [14] compared a scene camera and a camera integrated in a bulky HMD and found that the scene-oriented display outperformed the HMD in a low-mobility task. However, whether these findings would generalize to handheld mobile devices or lightweight wearable devices is unclear. How these findings generalize to tasks requiring high levels of mobility also remains unexplored.

Our objective in this work is to begin to fill this gap by investigating how the design features of two different technologies, a handheld tablet computer and a lightweight HMD, affect collaborative outcomes for remote collaboration on physical tasks under task settings requiring differing levels of mobility. These technologies were chosen because mobile handheld computers have found widespread use in many domains [11, 22, 35], and lightweight HMDs are emerging as a handsfree alternative to handheld computers [47]. We seek to inform the design of future collaborative technologies and to highlight the strengths and weaknesses of the technology types in various collaborative settings, explaining these differences using concepts from prior work including shared visual space [13] and conversational grounding [5].

The next section provides an overview of related work on supporting remote physical collaboration and previous evaluations of technologies in similar collaboration settings. This section is followed by a description of our hypothesis and study design. We then present the results of our study and discuss our findings and their implications for the design and evaluation of future remote collaboration technologies.

RELATED WORK

In order to understand how different technologies can support collaborative outcomes, it is important to identify the aspects of collaboration that are most critical to its success. Prior work on supporting remote collaboration has focused on the importance of a *shared visual space*—the ability of collaborators to have simultaneous visual access to the task space being worked in—and on supporting *conversational grounding*—the process of establishing common ground to reach mutual understanding [3].

Shared Visual Space

Previous work identifies a shared visual space between collaborators as a key factor contributing to the success of their collaboration [14] because it provides an awareness of the task state [18]. The shared visual space can be divided into two categories: a shared view of the task space and a shared view of the collaborator.

Previous work found that participants perform better in side-by-side settings in which they share views of the workspace rather than when they use communication tools to complete a task [13, 15, 20, 28, 33]. Fussell et al. [13] conducted an experiment with collaborators working over an audio/video link or working side-by-side. They found that collocated pairs completed the task more quickly and accurately than pairs working remotely and cited the shared task space as a contributing factor to the difference. Prior work has found shared visual space to help collaborators understand the current state of their task and enable them to communicate more efficiently [28]. Daly-Jones et al. [8] compared videoconferencing to high-quality audio conferencing and identified a shared visual space as the most important resource for effective communication.

Research on videoconferencing and audio conferencing has also found that videoconferencing can enhance collaboration by providing a view of the collaborator to convey other visual information including gestures, posture, and facial expressions [25]. Tasks that rely heavily on social cues, such as situations of conflict, have been shown to be especially affected by the visual view of the collaborator [2, 16, 40]. This work suggests that technologies that provide support for the shared visual task space and view of the collaborator result in more effective collaboration than technologies that do not.

Conversational Grounding

Conversational grounding has been found to be a critical factor in many types of efficient collaborations [3]. Fussell et al. [15] found that communication is demonstrably more efficient when people share greater amounts of common ground. Studies of the process collaborators follow to establish common ground during physical tasks demonstrate the following pattern between a helper (the expert) and a worker [5, 6, 15, 19]. First, the collaborators use referential expressions to form common ground about the task steps. The helper next instructs the worker on how to manipulate the objects needed for the task and then verifies that they understood the instructions and are executing them correctly. These acts of conversational grounding build up a level of common ground that is necessary for the communication of beliefs and intentions [45].

How this grounding process takes place also depends on the communication medium itself. The chosen medium of communication imposes costs on the grounding process and shapes how conversations will be conducted over the medium [5]. Prior work has shown that mutual belief can be achieved much faster in face-to-face conversations compared with mediated ones [4]. Kraut et al. [29] argued that the medium affects how collaborators communicate and speak about the task, indicating that the choice of communication medium directly affects collaborators' ability to establish common ground and to communicate intentions.

Technological Support for Collaboration

A growing body of work has evaluated the effectiveness of emerging technologies to support collaboration. This work has examined collaborations employing a variety of new technologies, including large multi-touch displays [1, 27, 38] and tabletops [7, 24, 39]. Other work has examined remote collaborations using these technologies, studying how distributed tabletops may support gesture use [17], how virtually embodying users' arms affects coordination on distributed tabletops [10], and how design guidelines for non-distributed tabletop settings may extend to distributed tabletops [26]. These technologies are not mobile and generally necessitate user collocation around the display for collaboration. Furthermore, collaboration on large displays and tabletops primarily involves the manipulation of digital artifacts, providing little support for collaborations over physical artifacts.

Fewer studies have focused on understanding how emerging mobile technologies support remote collaboration in the context of physical tasks. Poelman et al. [34] examined how an immersive HMD allowed an expert to remotely assist a novice in a crime scene investigation task. Their system provided the remote expert and the novice with the ability to add and remove virtual artifacts from a map of the environment visible to the novice via the HMD. They found that their system supported mutual understanding of the task state between the collaborators. Similar work has explored supporting collaboration with other augmented reality techniques, such as projecting the expert's gestures into the worker's workspace [23, 41]. To study collaboration on shared geocaching over distance, Procyk et al. [36] used a system consisting of a wearable mobile video camera mounted on a pair of glasses and a smartphone on an armband for displaying live video from the other user's camera. They found that their mobile system was able to create an intimate shared experience with the remote partner. Rae et al. [37] studied the effects of mobility on the task performance of robotic telepresence users. They investigated whether the mobility of the system was more useful in tasks requiring higher levels of mobility. They found that mobility in general increased remote users' sense of presence but did not improve task performance, even impairing it in some cases due to the added burden of understanding spatial positioning in the remote environment. Fussell et al. [14] conducted an experiment in which dyads performed a collaborative task to determine the most effective medium to support remote collaboration among audio, scene video, head-mounted video, and combined scene and head-mounted video. They found that a scene camera achieved better results than a head-mounted camera because it provided a more consistent view of the shared visual space [8]. However, this work only considered static tasks (e.g., assembling a toy robot in a stationary position). Additionally, the authors noted that the HMD slipped off of participants' heads, and that HMDs at the time the study was conducted were not "robust enough for actual field applications" [14].

To bridge the gap in previous work examining the impact of task mobility on collaborative outcomes across communication technologies, our study compares the collaborative outcomes of users in a remote physical task using either of two emerging technologies—a tablet computer or a lightweight HMD—in tasks requiring either high or low levels of mobility.

HYPOTHESIS

Previous work found that a static camera achieved better results in a collaborative task than a head-mounted camera in static task settings, demonstrating the importance of providing collaborators a consistent view of the shared visual space [14]. Informed by this research, we formed our hypothesis on how communication technology and the mobility required by the task will affect collaborative outcomes—how collaborators behave, perceive the collaboration, and perform. We expect different technologies to be better suited to different task settings, to provide different degrees of consistency of the shared visual space, and to support collaboration differently in these settings. Specifically, we predict that the HMD will provide a more consistent view of the workspace during a dynamic task—a task requiring high levels of mobility—and that this increased view of the shared visual space will improve collaborative outcomes. Furthermore, we also predict that the tablet will provide a more consistent view of the worker's workspace in a static task setting—a task requiring low levels of mobility—which will lead to an increased view of the shared visual space and improve collaborative outcomes.

> **Hypothesis:** There will be a significant interaction effect of technology type and task setting on the behavioral, perceptual, and performance dimensions of collaboration. Specifically, the HMD will provide better support for these outcomes than the tablet in dynamic task settings, while the tablet will provide better support than the HMD in static task settings.

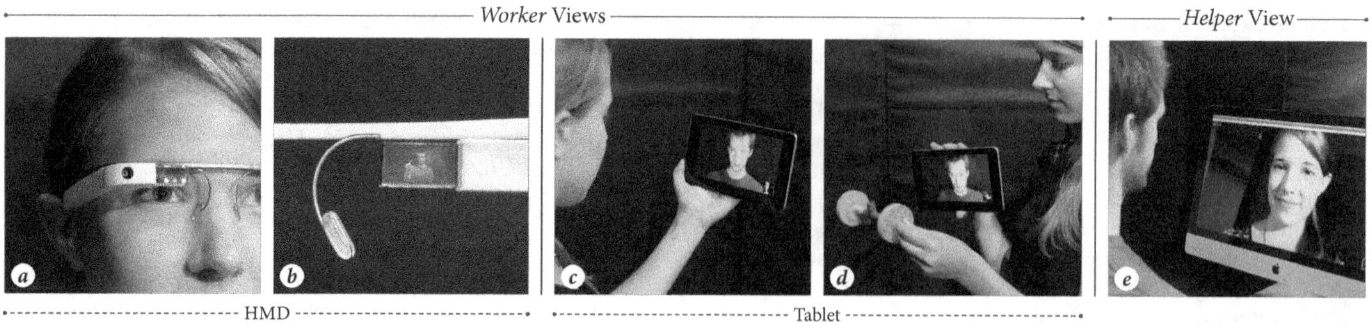

Figure 2. The capture (A) and display (B) using the HMD. The head-mounted camera on the HMD was used to provide live video to the remote helper, and the HMD display showed only the remote helper and no viewfinder. The display (C) and capture (D) using the tablet in two commonly used methods. Workers used the front-facing tablet camera to show the helper themselves or their workspace, and the tablet display showed the remote helper and a small viewfinder. The display (E) of the helper's computer, showing the worker.

METHOD

To test our hypothesis, we designed an experiment in which dyads worked together on a remote construction task similar to experimental tasks used in prior work (e.g., [14, 15, 29, 37]). In our study, participants were instructed to work together to make a toy cart. For each dyad, one participant played the role of the "worker," physically constructing the object with the assistance and guidance of another participant, the "helper," who was given a schematic detailing the cart's construction.

Participants

We recruited 66 participants (34 males and 32 females) to take part in the study. Participants were recruited in pairs and did not know each other before the study. All participants were native English speakers recruited from the University of Wisconsin–Madison campus. Participant ages ranged 18–35 ($M = 21.8$, $SD = 3.8$). Based on post-task questionnaire results, participants were overall comfortable using technology. On a five-point scale (1 = very uncomfortable, 5 = very comfortable), participants averaged 4.74 ($SD = 0.81$) on comfort using a laptop, 3.91 ($SD = 1.06$) on comfort using a tablet, and 4.03 ($SD = 0.81$) on comfort using videoconferencing software.

Study Design

We designed a two-by-two (technology type: HMD vs. tablet computer; task setting: static vs. dynamic) between-subjects study to examine the effects of technology type and task setting on measures of the behavioral, perceptual, and performance dimensions of collaboration.

The first independent variable we considered was technology type. Following prior approaches (e.g., [14]), we picked two devices designed for widespread use and investigated their support for collaboration at a system level, rather than using prototypes, the elements of which (camera, viewfinder, etc.) we could manipulate. Workers used either a *Google Nexus 7 tablet*[1] (7 in / 17.8 cm in screen size, 10.6 oz / 300 g in weight) in the *tablet* condition or wore *Google Glass*[2] (1.8 oz / 50 g in weight) in the *HMD* condition to collaborate with their partner. The Nexus 7 tablet was used because it is a representative example of modern tablet computers, and Google Glass was used because it is an example of an emerging commercially-available lightweight HMD. Because we wanted to examine differences in collaborative outcomes between mobile devices in mobile settings, no stand or propping device was provided with the tablet.

In each technology condition, the interaction took place using a browser-based videoconferencing application called *Google Hangouts*.[3] The use of the same videoconferencing software standardized the interface design for helpers and workers in both technology conditions. The helper used a 27" desktop computer equipped with a webcam and microphone for videoconferencing, regardless of the worker's device. Both the camera and display functionalities of the Nexus 7 tablet and Google Glass were used to support the videoconferencing interactions. Figure 2 shows the display and camera configurations for both devices and demonstrates how the videoconferencing user interface was shown on the devices. The tablet videoconferencing interface displayed a view of the remote collaborator and a small "viewfinder" pane, showing what the tablet camera was capturing. As shown in the bottom-right corner of the tablet images in Figure 2C and 2D, the tablet viewfinder pane was very small, measuring less than 2.2% of the area of the tablet screen. Additionally, as shown in Figure 2D, the screen of the tablet and the viewfinder in the interface were not always visible to workers during the task. The HMD interface displayed a view of the remote collaborator as well, but did not show a viewfinder pane. The helper's desktop interface displayed the video captured from the worker's device camera and a viewfinder pane.

The second independent variable we considered was the task setting. In the *static* setting, the necessary components to construct the object were separated into three groups located on a single workstation in the worker's room. In the *dynamic* setting, the component groups were placed on three workstations spaced several feet apart throughout the room. Participants were not allowed to carry more than one individual unconstructed piece between piles. This restriction ensured that participants did not treat the dynamic task as a static one by consolidating piles. Video recordings of the collaboration were reviewed to ensure the success of the task-setting manipulation. The dynamic setting represents many physical

[1] http://www.google.com/nexus/7/
[2] http://www.google.com/glass/
[3] http://www.google.com/hangouts/

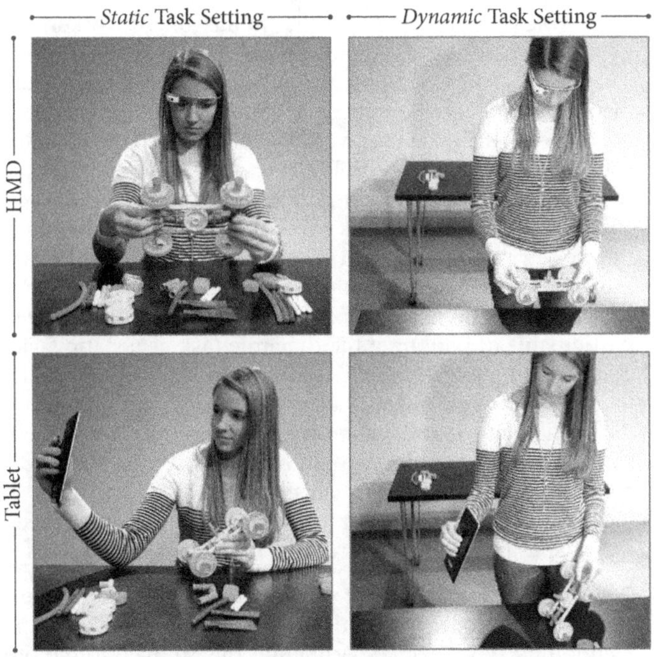

Figure 3. The worker's environment across the four conditions of our study. Participants collaborated using either an HMD (top row) or a tablet (bottom row) in a task setting requiring either low levels of mobility (left column) or high levels of mobility (right column).

collaboration settings where tools and parts are distributed throughout the environment, such as in a kitchen or a workshop. In both conditions, not all of the pieces in the piles were necessary to construct the object. Figure 3 illustrates the worker's environment across the four conditions.

Setup and Materials

The following paragraphs describe the construction task and the setup of the study.

Setup — Figure 4 shows the layout of the worker's and helper's rooms for each task setting. In both the static and dynamic task settings, the helper and worker were located in different rooms during the construction task. The setup for the helper, as illustrated in the center of Figure 4 and the left of Figure 5, was the same across all conditions. The setups for the worker in static and dynamic task settings are also depicted on the left and the right in Figure 4, respectively. In the static task setting, all of the components were located in three piles on a single workstation in the worker's room, whereas in the dynamic task setting, they were distributed between three workstations in the room. Each pile included parts for various components of the target object to increase the mobility required of the participants as they switched between piles during the task.

Task — The right side of Figure 5 shows the toy cart used as the basis for the construction task. The cart was selected for its moderate level of construction difficulty. The completed cart contained 48 components of various sizes and colors.

Schematic — A schematic showing three overarching construction steps and an image of the completed object was given to the helpers for use in guiding the workers to construct the cart. The schematic was printed in color and marked components which needed repeated construction, such as sections of the wheels and axles. Helpers were not allowed to show their partner any part of the schematic.

Measurement

To measure the behavioral, perceptual, and performance dimensions of collaboration during the task, we used a number of behavioral, subjective, and objective measures.

Collaborative Behavior — Participant pairs were video-recorded collaborating on the task, and the videos were coded for high-level conversational events, including:

- Helper proactive assistance
- Helper reactive assistance
- Helper high-level directing commands
- Helper view commands
- Helper questions about the task
- Worker questions about the task

These codes measured conversational acts of collaborators that constituted a majority of the speech acts occurring during the task. Many of these codes were selected for their use in prior work (e.g., [29]). We coded the videos for both proactive and reactive helper assistance, differentiated by whether or not the helper's description or statement was in response to a previous speech act of the worker. We also coded the recordings for high-level *directing* commands from the helper. These

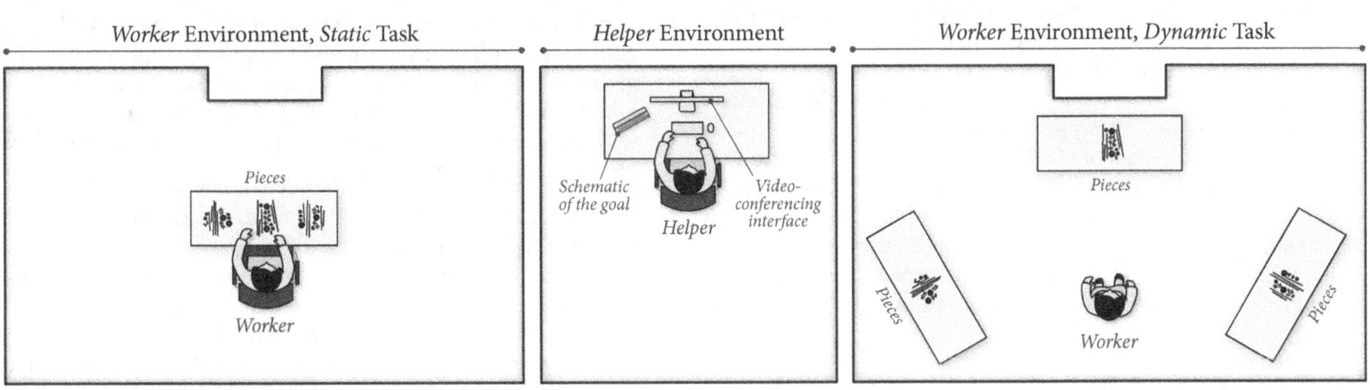

Figure 4. The physical arrangements of the worker's room in the static task condition (left), the helper's environment in both conditions (center), and the worker's room in the dynamic condition (right).

Figure 5. ***Left:*** **the helper at the remote workstation.** ***Right:*** **the completed cart.**

commands involved defining an objective, and often require subsequent sub-commands, clarifications, or other assistance to ensure that the action is properly executed. We also coded the videos for helper *view* commands, which are commands to the worker to adjust the orientation of their device to offer the helper a more desirable view of the workspace.

The coding process involved a single experimenter coding all videos and a second experimenter coding 10% of the videos in order to verify the reliability of the coding process. An inter-coder reliability analysis showed substantial agreement between the experimenters (87% agreement, Cohen's $\kappa = .79$).

Collaborative Performance — Two measures of task performance were considered during the experiment: completion time and error rate. To measure completion time, the the experimenter started a timer after instructing the participants to begin the task and then exiting the room. The timer was stopped when a participant knocked on the door or opened it and informed the experimenter that they believed they had finished the task. After the task was completed, the video was coded for errors. An error was counted if (1) a part that wasn't required for the construction was used or (2) a part required for the construction was used in the wrong place.

Collaborative Perceptions — Two questionnaires, one for each experimental role (helper and worker), were administered after the completion of the task. The questionnaires each contained 14 questions designed to capture participants' perceptions of the success of their collaboration. Items such as "I am confident we completed the task correctly" and "My partner and I worked well together on the task" were used to create a scale of the perceived overall success of the collaboration. Role-specific questions were also used. For instance, helpers were asked, "I could tell when my partner needed assistance." Correspondingly, workers were asked, "My partner could tell when I needed assistance." Responses to all items were measured on a five-point rating scale (1 = Strongly disagree, 5 = Strongly agree). Reliability tests for these scales are provided in the Analyses Section. Additionally, the questionnaires included a brief section collecting basic demographic information such as age, gender, and major/occupation and assessing participants' overall level of comfort with technology use.

Procedure

For this study, two participants were recruited at once to form dyads. An experimenter randomly assigned one participant to the role of helper and the other to the role of worker. Each dyad was randomly assigned to one of the four conditions. The experimenter then obtained informed consent and briefed the participants on the selected technology and the constraints of the task setting. If the dyad was assigned to the static task setting, the experimenter told the participants that the worker was required to remain seated at the workstation. If they were assigned to the dynamic task setting, participants were told that the worker was not allowed to move parts from a workstation unless the parts had already been assembled or the worker was carrying only a single piece. This restriction ensured that participants did not treat the dynamic task as a static task by consolidating piles of pieces. To provide participants with an incentive to work together efficiently, the experimenter told the participants that the team with the fastest task completion time of a correct object would each receive an extra dollar, similar to the incentive mechanism used by Rae et al. [37]. The participants were then separated into different rooms based on their experimental roles to receive individual instructions.

After the participants were separated, the experimenter gave the worker specific instructions on how to use their assigned technology type. The experimenter then moved to the other room, showed the helper the videoconferencing interface on the desktop computer, and gave the helper time to examine the schematic of the cart. The experimenter then enabled the videoconferencing connection between the participants, waited for a moment to ensure that the connection was stable, and told the participants that they could begin the task. Audio and video from the experiment were recorded for coding of behavioral measures. Once one of the participants opened the door to their experiment room and indicated that they finished the task, the experimenter re-entered the helper's room, turned off the timer, terminated the videoconferencing connection, and administered the post-task questionnaire. The experimenter then re-entered the worker's room and administered the post-task questionnaire. Upon the completion of the questionnaires, participants were debriefed together by the experimenter. Each session took approximately 30 minutes. Participants were each paid $5.00 USD for their time. Additionally, although participants were told that members of the fastest team would receive an extra dollar to incentivize them, all participants received the additional compensation.

Analyses

A two-way fixed-effects analysis of variance (ANOVA) was conducted with task setting and technology type as input variables and the behavioral, objective, and subjective measures as response variables. Following Wickens and Keppel [46], we calculated *a priori* contrast tests to make comparisons indicated by our hypothesis.

To construct scales from the items in our questionnaires, we conducted an exploratory factor analysis, which resulted in two factors—one for each participant role—that corresponded to scales of perceptions of overall collaborative success. The helpers' scale consisted of two items (Cronbach's $\alpha = .851$), and the workers' scale consisted of five items (Cronbach's $\alpha = .841$). Our analysis also included a single item for workers' ease of seeing the helper.

RESULTS

Guided by our hypothesis, our analysis primarily involved testing for interaction effects between technology type and task setting and for differences between technology types for each task setting across the behavioral, perceptual, and performance dimensions of collaboration that we measured. We also tested for main effects of technology type to better understand the overall effects these technologies had on collaboration. Our analyses used an alpha level of .05 for significance. We also report on marginal effects at an alpha level of .10 to illustrate trends in our data. Effect sizes are reported as eta-squared (η^2) values. To facilitate readability, the paragraphs below provide only a textual description of the results and a discussion of them in the context of our hypotheses and the specific characteristics of the study. The results for the statistical tests we conducted are provided in Table 1, and the results for the contrast tests are provided in Table 2.

Across the behavioral and perceptual dimensions of collaboration, our results revealed several interaction effects of technology type and task setting on measures of proactive assistance, reactive assistance, helpers' perceptions of collaborative success, and workers' perceptions of collaborative success, demonstrating that the task setting affected users of the technologies differently. We found that in the dynamic task setting, HMD use allowed helpers to offer faster directing commands and more proactive assistance, resulting in marginally faster task completion times. In the static task setting, tablet use helped convey subtle visual information, and helpers and workers had opposing perceptions of how the two technologies contributed to their success. These findings provide support for the first portion of our hypothesis, which predicted the interaction effects between technology type and task setting shown by our analyses.

Our hypothesis predicted that the HMD would outperform the tablet in measures of collaborative outcomes in dynamic task settings, and we found support for this prediction in the behavioral and performance dimensions of collaboration. Data from measures of proactive assistance, reactive assistance, rate of directing commands given, and task completion time provide support for the HMD improving these collaborative outcomes in dynamic task settings.

As illustrated on the left in Figure 6, our results showed that helpers offered significantly more proactive assistance in both static and dynamic task settings and marginally less reactive assistance in dynamic task settings when collaborating via the HMD compared to the tablet. There was no significant difference in the total amount of assistance between technologies in dynamic conditions. We believe that this shift from reactive to proactive assistance is potentially very beneficial. A greater amount of helper proactive assistance indicates that helpers are better able to see when their partner requires help and to ground their directing commands to assist them accordingly. A simultaneous reduction in the quantity of reactive assistance is also beneficial, as it again shows that assistance is being offered without the worker need to ask for it, further attesting to the superior view of the task space the HMD appears to provide in these settings. Because of this shift in the

Behavioral Measures

Amount of *Proactive* Assistance

Source of Variation	*Df*	*f*	*p*	η^2
Technology type	1	29.64	<.001***	0.488
Environment type	1	0.14	.711	0.002
Technology type × Environment type	1	2.95	.096†	0.048
Error	29			

Amount of *Reactive* Assistance

Source of Variation	*Df*	*f*	*p*	η^2
Technology type	1	0.01	.935	0.000
Environment type	1	0.01	.959	0.000
Technology type × Environment type	1	6.95	.013*	0.193
Error	29			

Helper *Directing* Commands/Minute

Source of Variation	*Df*	*f*	*p*	η^2
Technology type	1	4.05	.054†	0.102
Environment type	1	6.15	.019*	0.155
Technology type × Environment type	1	0.29	.595	0.007
Error	29			

Helper *View* Commands/Minute

Source of Variation	*Df*	*f*	*p*	η^2
Technology type	1	3.68	.065†	0.107
Environment type	1	1.56	.222	0.045
Technology type × Environment type	1	0.00	.996	0.000
Error	29			

Perceptual Measures

***Helper* Perceptions of Overall Success**

Source of Variation	*Df*	*f*	*p*	η^2
Technology type	1	1.31	.263	0.066
Environment type	1	4.66	.039*	0.118
Technology type × Environment type	1	4.66	.039*	0.118
Error	29			

***Worker* Perceptions of Overall Success**

Source of Variation	*Df*	*f*	*p*	η^2
Technology type	1	1.36	.254	0.035
Environment type	1	0.64	.430	0.017
Technology type × Environment type	1	7.78	.009**	0.201
Error	29			

Ease of Seeing Partner for *Worker*

Source of Variation	*Df*	*f*	*p*	η^2
Technology type	1	5.44	.028*	0.194
Environment type	1	0.01	.911	0.000
Technology type × Environment type	1	0.49	.492	0.014
Error	29			

Performance Measures

Task Completion Time

Source of Variation	*Df*	*f*	*p*	η^2
Technology type	1	2.81	.104	0.068
Environment type	1	8.45	.007**	0.203
Technology type × Environment type	1	0.79	.381	0.019
Error	29			

Error Rate

Source of Variation	*Df*	*f*	*p*	η^2
Technology type	1	0.00	.965	0.000
Environment type	1	0.04	.840	0.001
Technology type × Environment type	1	0.13	.719	0.005
Error	29			

Table 1. ANOVA test results for the behavioral, perceptual, and performance dimensions of collaboration.

Behavioral Measures

Measure Group A	Group B	Mean A	SD A	Mean B	SD B	p
Amount of *Proactive* Assistance						
Dynamic, HMD	Dynamic, Tablet	3.25	2.61	1.22	0.97	.011*
Static, HMD	Static, Tablet	4.38	1.30	0.50	0.54	<.001***
Amount of *Reactive* Assistance						
Dynamic, HMD	Dynamic, Tablet	3.25	2.32	5.78	2.49	.061†
Static, HMD	Static, Tablet	5.75	3.92	3.38	1.30	.086†
Amount of *Total* Assistance						
Dynamic, HMD	Dynamic, Tablet	6.50	4.00	7.00	2.78	.759
Static, HMD	Static, Tablet	10.13	4.26	3.88	1.64	<.001***
Helper *Directing* Commands/Minute						
Dynamic, HMD	Dynamic, Tablet	1.85	0.51	1.55	0.52	.294
Static, HMD	Static, Tablet	2.46	0.54	1.95	0.72	.084†
Helper *View* Commands/Minute						
Dynamic, HMD	Dynamic, Tablet	0.33	0.19	0.17	0.14	.180
Static, HMD	Static, Tablet	0.43	0.35	0.27	0.19	.190

Perceptual Measures

Measure Group A	Group B	Mean A	SD A	Mean B	SD B	p
***Helper* Perceptions of Overall Success**						
Dynamic, HMD	Dynamic, Tablet	4.75	0.38	4.50	0.50	.472
Static, HMD	Static, Tablet	3.69	0.46	4.50	1.19	.029*
***Worker* Perceptions of Overall Success**						
Dynamic, HMD	Dynamic, Tablet	4.13	0.60	4.53	0.40	.253
Static, HMD	Static, Tablet	4.63	0.31	3.63	1.23	.010*
Worker Ease of Seeing Partner						
Dynamic, HMD	Dynamic, Tablet	3.63	1.19	4.56	0.73	.039*
Static, HMD	Static, Tablet	3.88	0.99	4.38	0.52	.269

Performance Measures

Measure Group A	Group B	Mean A	SD A	Mean B	SD B	p
Task Completion Time						
Dynamic, HMD	Dynamic, Tablet	801.00	194.50	1004.56	321.90	.076†
Static, HMD	Static, Tablet	640.88	198.30	703.38	137.90	.587
Error Rate						
Dynamic, HMD	Dynamic, Tablet	1.88	2.23	1.56	2.79	.772
Static, HMD	Static, Tablet	1.75	1.98	2.00	1.77	.826

Table 2. Contrast test results for the behavioral, perceptual, and performance dimensions of collaboration.

type of the assistance offered, workers may not need to ask for verification of correctness as frequently during their tasks. These results suggest that HMD use, especially in dynamic task settings, may result in a more fluid collaboration and fewer interruptions for verification of task status.

Our results also showed that helpers gave directing commands at a marginally higher rate in HMD conditions than in tablet conditions, and there was no significant difference in the total number of directing commands given between conditions (see Figure 6, right). Furthermore, as is shown on the right in Figure 7, pairs collaborating using the HMD achieved marginally faster task completion times than those using a tablet in dynamic task settings. These results suggest that HMD use supports marginally more efficient collaborations than a tablet computer when the task requires higher levels of mobility. Based on these results, we predict HMDs to be more effective than tablets for achieving efficient and fluid collaboration in dynamic task settings, improving both collaborative behaviors and performance.

Our hypothesis also predicted that the tablet computer would outperform the HMD in measures of collaborative outcomes in static task settings. We found support for this prediction in the behavioral and perceptual dimensions of collaboration. Data from measures of rate of helpers' view commands, helpers' perceptions of collaborative success, and workers' ease of seeing their partner provide support for tablet use improving behavioral and subjective outcomes of collaboration.

As shown on the left in Figure 7, we found that helpers rated their perceptions of collaborative success significantly higher when their partner communicated with them using a tablet than an HMD in the static task setting. We believe that this difference results from the more consistent view of the current focus of the interaction that the tablet provided in the static setting. We observed workers using the tablet in the static condition working in two phases. In one phase, they sat the tablet on their workstation and constructed the cart. They performed the construction while either holding the components they were working with above the tablet such that the helper could observe their work or with the components outside of the helper's view. In the latter case, they sought verification by holding their work in front of the helper after completion. In the second phase, when searching for pieces, they picked the tablet up and held it such that the helper could see all of the piles of pieces at once or had the helper describe the piece needed and showed the helper pieces they thought matched the description. Pairs developed this workaround because they were unable to position the tablet such that it offered a complete and consistent view of their workspace. The tablet videoconferencing interface displayed a small view in the corner of the screen of what the helper was able to see from the tablet's camera, which allowed workers to ensure that the helper was able to see what they needed during both phases. These phases amount to the helper having two views and associated tasks to alternate between when using a tablet in the static setting—constructing and searching/describing. When their partner used an HMD in the static task setting, these two phases of the construction task were less distinct, possibly increasing helpers' cognitive load.

When pairs collaborated via the HMD, having the helper's view tied to the worker's head motions in the static task was at times detrimental. We found that helper commands to adjust the view were required marginally more frequently when using the HMD compared to the tablet, shown on the right in Figure 6. Unlike the tablet interface, the HMD interface offered no feedback to the worker regarding what the helper could see from their camera, requiring helpers to ask the workers to look down more when constructing the cart in static conditions because they were working with the object on the table too close to their body for the helper to see. Since workers were moving between stations in the dynamic condition, they held the cart more frequently during construction, providing helpers with more opportunities to see their work. We believe that the dependency of the camera view on the worker's head orientation combined with the lack of feedback given to the worker on what the helper could see when using an HMD led to helpers' reduced perceptions of success in static task settings. Tablet use may consequently improve aspects of collaborative perceptions in static task settings.

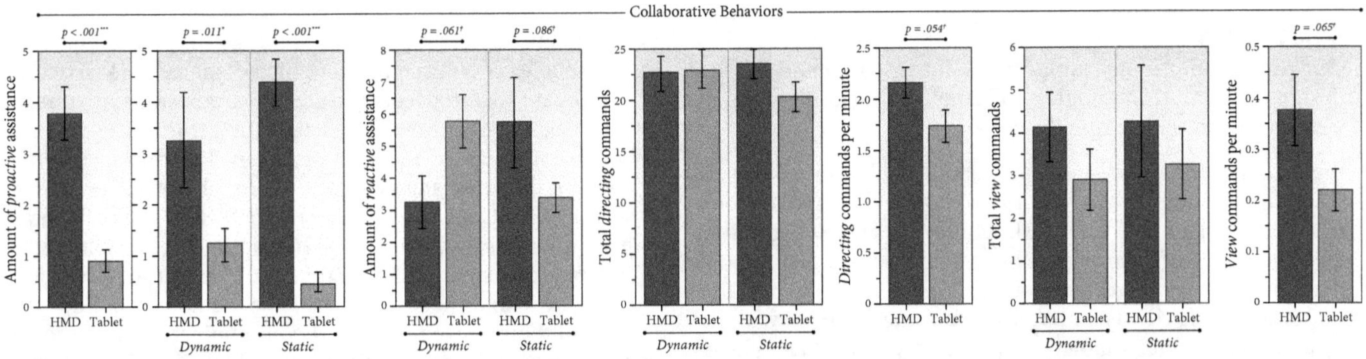

Figure 6. ***Left:*** **Amount of proactive and reactive assistance.** ***Right:*** **Data from coding of total directing commands, directing commands per minute, total view commands, and view commands per minute. (†), (*), and (***) denote $p < .10$, $p < .05$, and $p < .001$, respectively. Helpers gave significantly more proactive assistance in HMD conditions and marginally less reactive assistance when an HMD was used compared to when a tablet computer was used in dynamic task settings. Helpers also gave directing commands and view commands at a higher rate in HMD conditions than in tablet conditions. There were no significant differences in the total number of directing or view commands between conditions.**

Workers found it significantly easier to see their partner when using the tablet compared to the HMD (see Figure 7, left). This difference is likely due to the difference in the amount of visual information that is transferred between collaborators using the tablet compared with the HMD. Although the Google Glass display is closer to the worker, the Nexus 7 has a much larger screen than the Google Glass display. The Nexus 7's 1280 × 800 resolution display is also much more detailed than Google Glass' 640 × 360 display, and it is therefore likely a much better platform for conveying gestures, facial expressions, and other visual cues. We therefore anticipate that in situations where there is more than one expert providing assistance or when the worker would benefit from gestures or other visual cues from the expert, that a tablet, with its larger and more detailed display, will achieve better collaborative outcomes than an HMD or other devices with smaller screens.

Contrary to our hypothesis, we found that workers perceived their collaboration to be overall more successful when using the HMD compared to the tablet in the static task setting (see Figure 7, left). These perceptions could be explained by a novelty effect; when we gathered this data, Google Glass was not yet available to the public, so participants were especially enthusiastic to use the new technology. However, our results do not support this explanation, as we found no significant difference in workers' perceptions of overall success between the technologies in the dynamic task setting. Based on experimenter observations, we believe that workers perceived their collaboration as more successful when using the HMD during the static task because of the perceived "clunkiness" of their use of the tablet. As previously described, it was difficult for workers to place the tablet such that it offered a complete and consistent view of their workspace, so they alternated between the constructing and the searching/describing phases. While this method improved helpers' perceptions of the collaboration by offering them two views and associated tasks, it negatively affected workers' perceptions of task success by increasing the amount of work required to complete the task. This distinction suggests that technological workarounds during collaborative tasks may have a differential effect on the parties involved.

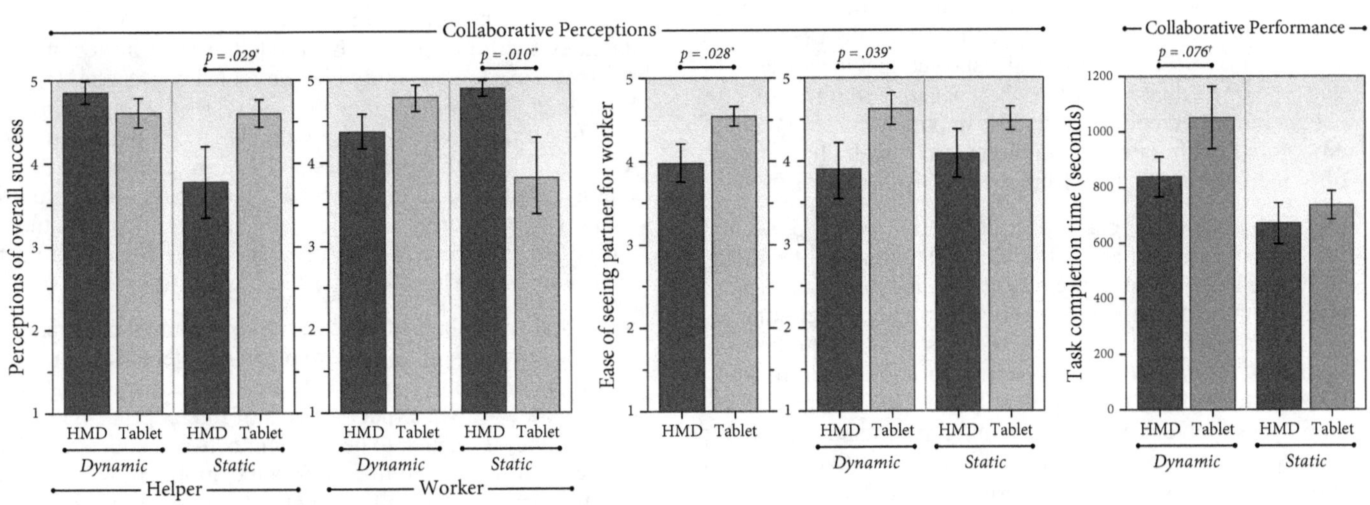

Figure 7. ***Left:*** **Mean scale responses of helpers' and workers' perceptions of the overall success of their collaboration and from workers' perception of the ease of seeing their partner.** ***Right:*** **Mean task completion times. (†), (*), and (**) denote $p < .10$, $p < .05$, and $p < .01$, respectively. In static task settings, helpers had significantly higher perceptions of collaborative success in the tablet condition, while workers had significantly higher perceptions of collaborative success in the HMD condition. Workers in tablet conditions had a significantly easier time seeing their partners, and pairs using an HMD completed the task marginally faster than pairs using a tablet in dynamic task settings.**

DISCUSSION

Our results offer many implications for research and for the design of future technologies for remote collaboration which we describe in the paragraphs below.

We found that helpers' perceptions of collaborative success were significantly lower when workers used an HMD compared to a tablet in the static task setting. This result highlights the importance of offering feedback to technology users about what their camera is capturing. This feedback is especially important for HMD users because the camera moves with its wearer's head. Many tablet, smartphone, and desktop videoconferencing interfaces offer a "viewfinder" showing what the device's camera is capturing. However, the HMD interface of Google Hangouts used in our study did not offer this feature. We speculate that this view was not included in the design of the HMD for three reasons. First, seeing a moving video as they move their head might be disruptive to the user's focus. Second, the only function for such a viewfinder would be to indicate to the wearer the extent of their camera view, of which wearers may build a mental model as they use the HMD for other purposes, such as recording videos. Third, because the resolution of the Google Glass display is relatively low (640 × 360 pixels), offering a large enough viewfinder that offers a similarly detailed view to other tablet or smartphone interfaces may be difficult. For these reasons, the videoconferencing interface was not replicated in the HMD conditions and the viewfinder was omitted.

To better allow remote helpers to gather the visual information they need, future HMD devices could be designed with a camera with a wider angle of view or with a camera whose orientation can be controlled by the remote collaborator. To offer a better view of the task space in static conditions, software could allow helpers to define the object of interest and to have the camera mounted on the HMD turn to keep that object in the field of view despite the wearer's head motions. Even without altering the hardware, it could also be beneficial to simply allow HMD users to alternate their display to show either their collaborator or the video feed from their camera to provide workers the necessary feedback to ensure that their helper can see what they need. As our results showed that the absence of this type of feedback may have had negative implications for collaborative perceptions, it will be important for designers of emerging collaborative technologies to consider how to best offer feedback to the user from their device's camera.

Our findings also suggest that collaborative technologies and their associated workarounds affect collaborative roles differently. We believe that future researchers and designers need to consider these differences when developing new technologies and interfaces for collaboration. For instance, when developing a new interface to support remote training of employees, one may be inclined to evaluate only how the interface affects employees' perceptions of the training experience. Given our finding that there may be tradeoffs in collaborative outcomes involved, it would also be important to evaluate how the interface affects the performance, behaviors, and perceptions of the remote trainers.

Our results confirm previous findings that highlight the importance of a consistent view of the shared task space as a significant factor affecting multiple dimensions of collaboration [8, 13, 28]. We found that the HMD offered a more consistent view of the task space in dynamic task settings and that this consistency improved collaborative behaviors by shifting assistance from reactive to proactive and collaborative performance by allowing pairs to complete the task marginally faster. Consistent with findings by Kraut et al. [28], our results show that the shared visual space helped collaborators ground their conversation and communicate more efficiently by marginally increasing the rate at which directing commands were given.

Our results demonstrate the importance of a consistent view of the shared task space. However, we believe that offering a view of the task space itself may not be enough to effectively support remote collaboration. Our results are from technology conditions where the view given to the remote helper also provides cues about the worker's current focus. The HMD closely ties the visual information given to the remote helper with the worker's focus by changing the view with the worker's head movements, which previous work has shown to be a reliable predictor of attention [30, 42]. Accordingly, as we chose to maintain the intended "mobile" characteristics of these devices and offered no stand or propping device for the tablet, the visual information given to the helper was the result of an intentional action of the worker picking up the tablet and specifically showing the helper their workspace and therefore provided cues for their focus. When seeking to disconnect the visual information provided to the remote helper from the worker's focus, such as when using a stand with a handheld device or when giving the remote user control of the camera mounted to an HMD, in addition to supporting the shared view of the workspace, providing remote helpers with other cues such as an indicator of worker focus may be important.

Limitations and Future Work

There are six key limitations of our study that reveal potential avenues for future research. First, the specific technology platforms used in our study likely affected our results. Using a lightweight HMD other than Google Glass may give different results. Similarly, we used a popular tablet computer, but using a larger tablet with a portable stand or a smaller mobile device that is easier to handle, such as a smartphone, might provide users with a different experience. Future replication studies with other platforms will inform us on whether or not these results are generalizable.

Second, the members of the dyads in our study were strangers, but collaborations often involve repeated interactions or established practices and rapport between collaborators. Based on prior work [44], we expect aspects of interactions, including how grounding occurs, to be different between colleagues than between strangers. Future work can examine how collaboration history affects the use and effectiveness of the communication medium across different task settings.

Third, our study examined how technology and task setting affected a single collaborative instance of a short duration.

People may change how they use technologies over time, discover additional workarounds, or find more effective ways of using them for their task. Future work can examine how technology supports repeated instances of collaboration or collaborations over time.

Fourth, the experts in our study were not true experts. They only had the schematic for the construction task. True experts will also know patterns in which people make errors, predict them during instruction, and offer more proactive suggestions and corrections. This difference may make a stronger case for HMD use, given our observation that it involved greater levels of proactive assistance.

Fifth, our experimental task was very tolerant to errors, and we only examined the total number of errors upon the completion of the task. Errors made during a task in an industrial setting could result in damages to expensive equipment. Similarly, errors in medical settings could result in loss of life. In such settings, measures of task performance other than total errors upon completion will be more relevant. Future work could use other task-specific measures of performance, such as errors made during the task or ranked errors that factor in the criticality of errors, to better represent how the technology supports collaboration in these settings.

Finally, our work took the Nexus 7 tablet computer and Google Glass as they were and used them as mobile systems that are designed for widespread use. This choice introduces limitations such as not being able to isolate the effects of the camera, display, or viewfinder. Future research might conduct more detailed investigations using modular prototype systems with which these specific elements can be manipulated. However, our study provides a first look at how these technologies support communication and collaboration at a system level.

CONCLUSION

Our work examined the effects of using two different emerging mobile and wearable computing technologies—a Google Nexus 7 tablet computer and Google Glass, a lightweight HMD—on collaborative behaviors, perceptions, and performance in tasks requiring differing levels of mobility. We examined these differences in a collaborative construction task in two task settings: a *static* condition, in which the components necessary for construction were located in a single workspace, and a *dynamic* condition, in which the components were distributed across multiple workspaces. We conducted a two-by-two (technology type: HMD vs. tablet computer; task setting: static vs. dynamic) between-participants study in which pairs of "helpers" and "workers" collaborated to construct an object. We found that in the dynamic task setting, HMD use allowed helpers to offer more frequent directing commands and more proactive assistance, resulting in marginally faster task completion times. In the static task setting, tablet use helped convey subtle visual information, and helpers and workers had opposing perceptions of how the two technologies contributed to their success. Our findings have implications for designers of collaborative systems, interfaces, and devices by highlighting the importance of offering a consistent view of the workspace and of providing feedback to technology users about the information they are giving to their remote collaborators. Our findings also demonstrate that the use of a collaborative technology and its associated workarounds affect collaborative roles differently, suggesting that future researchers and designers must consider these differences when developing new technologies or interfaces for collaborators.

ACKNOWLEDGMENTS

This research was supported by National Science Foundation award 1117652 and by a Google Glass Award. We would like to thank Brandi Hefty, Ross Luo, Ying Zheng, and Catherine Steffel for their help in our work.

REFERENCES

1. C. Ardito, R. Lanzilotti, M. F. Costabile, and G. Desolda. Integrating traditional learning and games on large displays: An experimental study. *Journal of Educational Technology & Society*, 16(1), 2013.
2. M. Argyle and M. Cook. *Gaze and Mutual Gaze.* Cambridge University Press, 1976.
3. M. Baker, T. Hansen, R. Joiner, and D. Traum. The role of grounding in collaborative learning tasks. *Collaborative learning: Cognitive and Computational Approaches*, pages 31–63, 1999.
4. S. E. Brennan. The grounding problem in conversations with and through computers. *Social and Cognitive Psychological Approaches to Interpersonal Communication*, pages 201–225, 1998.
5. H. H. Clark and S. E. Brennan. Grounding in communication. *Perspectives on Socially Shared Cognition*, 13:127–149, 1991.
6. H. H. Clark and D. Wilkes-Gibbs. Referring as a collaborative process. *Cognition*, 22(1):1–39, 1986.
7. A. Clayphan, J. Kay, and A. Weinberger. Scriptstorm: scripting to enhance tabletop brainstorming. *Personal and Ubiquitous Computing*, 18:1433–1453, 2014.
8. O. Daly-Jones, A. Monk, and L. Watts. Some advantages of video conferencing over high-quality audio conferencing: fluency and awareness of attentional focus. *International Journal of Human-Computer Studies*, 49(1):21–58, 1998.
9. P. D'Arcy. CIO strategies for consumerization: The future of enterprise mobile computing. *Dell CIO Insight Series*, 2011.
10. A. Doucette, C. Gutwin, R. L. Mandryk, M. Nacenta, and S. Sharma. Sometimes when we touch: how arm embodiments change reaching and collaboration on digital tables. In *Proceedings of the 2013 conference on Computer Supported Cooperative Work*, pages 193–202, 2013.
11. M. J. Farrell and L. Rose. Use of mobile handheld computers in clinical nursing education. *The Journal of Nursing Education*, 47(1):13–19, 2008.
12. R. Furlan. Build your own Google Glass. *IEEE Spectrum*, 50(1):20–21, 2013.
13. S. R. Fussell, R. E. Kraut, and J. Siegel. Coordination of communication: Effects of shared visual context on collaborative work. In *Proceedings of the 2000 conference on Computer Supported Cooperative Work*, pages 21–30, 2000.
14. S. R. Fussell, L. D. Setlock, and R. E. Kraut. Effects of head-mounted and scene-oriented video systems on remote collaboration on physical tasks. In *Proceedings of the SIGCHI conference on Human Factors in Computing Systems*, pages 513–520, 2003.
15. S. R. Fussell, L. D. Setlock, J. Yang, J. Ou, E. Mauer, and A. D. Kramer. Gestures over video streams to support remote collaboration on physical tasks. *Human-Computer Interaction*, 19(3):273–309, 2004.

16. W. W. Gaver, A. Sellen, C. Heath, and P. Luff. One is not enough: Multiple views in a media space. In *Proceedings of the INTERACT'93 and CHI'93 conference on Human Factors in Computing Systems*, pages 335–341, 1993.

17. A. M. Genest, C. Gutwin, A. Tang, M. Kalyn, and Z. Ivkovic. Kinectarms: a toolkit for capturing and displaying arm embodiments in distributed tabletop groupware. In *Proceedings of the 2013 conference on Computer Supported Cooperative Work*, pages 157–166, 2013.

18. D. Gergle. The value of shared visual space for collaborative physical tasks. In *CHI'05 extended abstracts on Human Factors in Computing Systems*, pages 1116–1117, 2005.

19. D. Gergle, R. E. Kraut, and S. R. Fussell. Using visual information for grounding and awareness in collaborative tasks. *Human–Computer Interaction*, 28(1):1–39, 2013.

20. C. Gutwin and S. Greenberg. A descriptive framework of workspace awareness for real-time groupware. In *Proceedings of 2002 conference on Computer Supported Cooperative Work*, pages 411–446, 2002.

21. J. Hamburg-Coplan. Don't run out of cash: 3 growth-company case studies. *Inc. Magazine*, Feb, 2014.

22. M. V. Hooft, S. Diaz, and K. Swan. Examining the potential of handheld computers: Findings from the ohio pep project. *Journal of Educational Computing Research*, 30(4):295–311, 2004.

23. W. Huang, L. Alem, and F. Tecchia. Handsin3d: augmenting the shared 3D visual space with unmediated hand gestures. In *SIGGRAPH Asia 2013 Emerging Technologies*, pages 1–3, 2013.

24. A. Ioannou, P. Zaphiris, F. Loizides, and C. Vasiliou. Let's talk about technology for peace: A systematic assessment of problem-based group collaboration around an interactive tabletop. *Interacting with Computers*, 2013.

25. E. A. Isaacs and J. C. Tang. What video can and cannot do for collaboration: A case study. *Multimedia Systems*, 2(2):63–73, 1994.

26. A. Kharrufa, R. Martinez-Maldonado, J. Kay, and P. Olivier. Extending tabletop application design to the classroom. In *Proceedings of the 2013 ACM International Conference on Interactive Tabletops and Surfaces*, pages 115–124, 2013.

27. H. Kim and S. Snow. Collaboration on a large-scale, multi-touch display: asynchronous interaction and multiple-input use. In *Proceedings of the 2013 conference on Computer Supported Cooperative Work Companion*, pages 165–168, 2013.

28. R. E. Kraut, D. Gergle, and S. R. Fussell. The use of visual information in shared visual spaces: Informing the development of virtual co-presence. In *Proceedings of the 2002 ACM conference on Computer Supported Cooperative Work*, pages 31–40, 2002.

29. R. E. Kraut, M. D. Miller, and J. Siegel. Collaboration in performance of physical tasks: Effects on outcomes and communication. In *Proceedings of the 1996 ACM conference on Computer Supported Cooperative Work*, pages 57–66, 1996.

30. S. R. Langton. The mutual influence of gaze and head orientation in the analysis of social attention direction. *The Quarterly Journal of Experimental Psychology: Section A*, 53(3):825–845, 2000.

31. P. Milgram, H. Takemura, A. Utsumi, and F. Kishino. Augmented reality: A class of displays on the reality-virtuality continuum. In *Photonics for Industrial Applications*, pages 282–292, 1995.

32. C. Murphy. 9 powerful business uses for tablet computers. http://www.informationweek.com/mobile/mobile-devices/9-powerful-business-uses-for-tablet-computers/d/d-id/1102752, 2012. [Online; accessed 9-May-2014].

33. B. A. Nardi, H. Schwarz, A. Kuchinsky, R. Leichner, S. Whittaker, and R. Sclabassi. Turning away from talking heads: The use of video-as-data in neurosurgery. In *Proceedings of the INTERACT'93 and CHI'93 conference on Human Factors in Computing Systems*, pages 327–334, 1993.

34. R. Poelman, O. Akman, S. Lukosch, and P. Jonker. As if being there: mediated reality for crime scene investigation. In *Proceedings of the ACM 2012 conference on Computer Supported Cooperative Work*, pages 1267–1276, 2012.

35. M. Prgomet, A. Georgiou, and J. I. Westbrook. The impact of mobile handheld technology on hospital physicians' work practices and patient care: a systematic review. *Journal of the American Medical Informatics Association*, 16(6):792–801, 2009.

36. J. Procyk, C. Neustaedter, C. Pang, A. Tang, and T. K. Judge. Exploring video streaming in public settings: Shared geocaching over distance using mobile video chat. In *Proceedings of the 2014 SIGCHI conference on Human Factors in Computing Systems*, pages 2163–2172. ACM, 2014.

37. I. Rae, B. Mutlu, and L. Takayama. Bodies in motion: mobility, presence, and task awareness in telepresence. In *Proceedings of the 32nd annual ACM conference on Human factors in computing systems*, pages 2153–2162. ACM, 2014.

38. M. Rittenbruch, A. Sorensen, J. Donovan, D. Polson, M. Docherty, and J. Jones. The cube: A very large-scale interactive engagement space. In *Proceedings of the 2013 ACM International Conference on Interactive Tabletops and Surfaces*, pages 1–10, 2013.

39. R. Shadiev, W.-Y. Hwang, Y.-S. Yang, and Y.-M. Huang. Investigating multi-touch tabletop technology: Facilitating collaboration, interaction and awareness. In *2013 International Joint Conference on Awareness Science and Technology and Ubi-Media Computing*, pages 701–707, 2013.

40. J. Short, E. Williams, and B. Christie. *The Social Psychology of Telecommunications*. John Wiley and Sons Ltd, 1976.

41. R. S. Sodhi, B. R. Jones, D. Forsyth, B. P. Bailey, and G. Maciocci. Bethere: 3D mobile collaboration with spatial input. In *Proceedings of the 2013 SIGCHI Conference on Human Factors in Computing Systems*, pages 179–188, 2013.

42. R. Stiefelhagen and J. Zhu. Head orientation and gaze direction in meetings. In *CHI'02 Extended Abstracts on Human Factors in Computing Systems*, pages 858–859. ACM, 2002.

43. I. E. Sutherland. A head-mounted three dimensional display. In *Proceedings of the December 9-11, 1968, Fall Joint Computer Conference, part I*, pages 757–764, 1968.

44. J. Svennevig. *Getting acquainted in conversation: a study of initial interactions*. John Benjamins Publishing, 2000.

45. D. R. Traum and J. F. Allen. A "speech acts" approach to grounding in conversation. In *In Proceedings of 1992 International Conference on Spoken Language Processing*, pages 137–140, 1992.

46. T. D. Wickens and G. Keppel. Design and analysis: a researchers handbook, 2004.

47. J. York and P. C. Pendharkar. Human–computer interaction issues for mobile computing in a variable work context. *International Journal of Human-Computer Studies*, 60(5):771–797, 2004.

A User-Powered American Sign Language Dictionary

Danielle Bragg Kyle Rector Richard E. Ladner

Computer Science & Engineering
DUB Group, University of Washington
Seattle, WA 98195 USA
{dkbragg,rectorky,ladner}@cs.washington.edu

ABSTRACT

Students learning American Sign Language (ASL) have trouble searching for the meaning of unfamiliar signs. ASL signs can be differentiated by a small set of simple *features* including hand shape, orientation, location, and movement. In a feature-based ASL-to-English dictionary, users search for a sign by providing a query, which is a set of observed features. Because there is natural variability in the way signs are executed, and observations are error-prone, an approach other than exact matching of features is needed. We propose ASL-Search, an ASL-to-English dictionary entirely powered by its users. ASL-Search utilizes Latent Semantic Analysis (LSA) on a database of feature-based user queries to account for variability. To demonstrate ASL-Search's viability, we created ASL-Flash, a learning tool that presents online flashcards to ASL students and provides query data. Our simulations on this data serve as a proof of concept, demonstrating that our dictionary's performance improves with use and performs well for users with varied levels of ASL experience.

Author Keywords

American Sign Language (ASL); Dictionary; Education; Crowdsourcing; Latent Semantic Analysis (LSA); Information Retrieval (IR)

ACM Classification Keywords

H.3.3. Information Storage and Retrieval: Information Search and Retrieval; H.5.0 Information Interfaces and Presentation (e.g., HCI): General; K.3.1 Computers and Education: Computer Uses in Education

INTRODUCTION

Second language acquisition is an important human activity supported in K-12, higher, and continuing education institutions. According to the Modern Language Association, more than 1.6 million higher education students were enrolled in foreign language classes in 2009 [10]. The most popular languages taught in higher education are Spanish, French, German, and American Sign Language (ASL), in that order. ASL has the fastest growing enrollment among the four (16% compared to less than 5% between 2006 and 2009). Dictionaries that translate words from known to unknown languages and vice versa are important tools in learning a new language. For example, one might hear or read a word in the new language, but not know what it means. A dictionary provides the resource to find that meaning. Since ASL is a visual language with no standard written form, ASL-to-English dictionaries must take a different form than a text-based dictionary.

Current ASL-to-English resources attempt to help people search for unfamiliar signs, but fall short. For instance, online web search resources[1] accept text input and return videos or images of signs. Forming search queries for signs is not intuitive, as they require a text description or guess of the English meaning. Other tools allow people to naturally express a sign by demonstration, via computer vision or worn sensors. However, there are no guarantees that a user will replicate the sign accurately, or that the system will recognize the sign. Instead of demonstrating the sign, feature-based ASL-to-English dictionaries allow for people to use *features* of a sign (e.g. hand shape or location) to find the English meaning. Unfortunately, a person must use the features expected by existing dictionaries, or they may not find the translation. The limitations of each approach demonstrate a need for a more intuitive and flexible dictionary system.

In this paper, we propose ASL-Search and ASL-Flash, depicted in Figure 1. ASL-Search (Figure 1a) is a feature-based ASL-to-English dictionary powered entirely by its own users. Users form queries for unfamiliar signs by selecting sets of features (hand shapes, orientations, locations, or movements) based on their observations. The dictionary is backed by a search engine that uses information retrieval techniques adapted for ASL. Specifically, the search engine uses Latent Semantic Analysis (LSA), which traditionally models relationships between words and documents, to model relationships between features and signs. ASL-Flash (Figure 1b) is a learning tool for ASL students that provides an additional source of user queries for ASL-Search. ASL-Flash shows visitors online flashcards of ASL signs. Before providing the user with the definition, ASL-Flash requests that the user acts as if he/she is searching for the sign using the ASL-Search interface. ASL-Flash utilizes an established corpus of online videos from SigningSavvy, an English-to-ASL online dictionary. We built and deployed ASL-Flash, and used the query data gathered with ASL-Flash to provide a proof of concept of ASL-Search.

[1] e.g. Google, Bing, YouTube, and online ASL video resources like SigningSavvy

CSCW 2015, March 14–18, 2015, Vancouver, BC, Canada.

ACM 978-1-4503-2922-4/15/03...$15.00.
http://dx.doi.org/10.1145/2675133.2675226

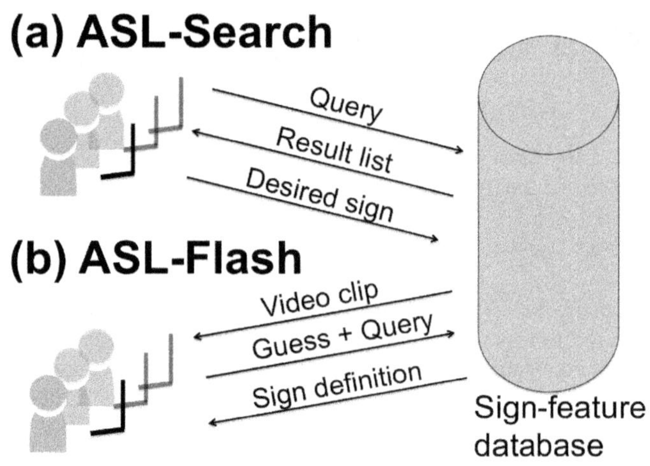

Figure 1: (a) ASL-Search: A feature-based dictionary that stores its users' queries in a database, and learns from that data to improve results. (b) ASL-Flash: An online learning tool that also contributes queries to the ASL-Search database. Users of both ASL-Search and ASL-Flash use the same query input interface, and contribute to the same database.

The core contributions of this work are:

- A survey of the methods that ASL students currently use to look up signs, and the difficulties they encounter.
- The design of ASL-Search, a user-powered ASL-to-English dictionary built by its users' queries.
- ASL-Flash, a learning tool for ASL students that serves as a source for user query data.
- ASL-Search proof of concept with data gathered from ASL-Flash.

BACKGROUND AND RELATED WORK

Computer-based sign language recognition, translation, and lookup systems accept two types of input: 1) a physical demonstration of the sign, or 2) a set of features describing the sign. Systems that require physical demonstrations often require expensive hardware, and rely on gesture recognition algorithms that cannot yet translate signs accurately. Accepting features as input simplifies the translation problem and gives users flexibility, but existing feature-based systems still do a poor job of matching input features to signs. Below, we explore existing sign language search methods further, describe their limitations, and how we improve upon their work by leveraging the crowd of users.

Search by Example

Some sign language recognition systems allow the user to search for a sign by demonstrating the motion of the sign. Video, the Microsoft Kinect, and sensory gloves have been used to record sign motions. These "search by example" systems rely on computer vision and gesture recognition to identify the sign.

Video Input

Recognizing signs from video recordings is difficult [7, 13, 26, 32, 38, 40]. Boston University [38] and Cooper et al. [7] have built systems that accept video as input and return lists of similar sign clips. Both perform well when trained and tested on the same users, but make no performance guarantees when trained and tested on different users. Other systems (e.g. [26]) attempt to recognize signs made by diverse users. While search results are accurate for small corpuses of signs, there are no guarantees about scalability. To recognize nuanced gestures, video-based systems often track pixel color (e.g. [13]), using Hidden Markov Models (e.g. [32]) or Time Delay Neural Networks (e.g. [40]). Researchers are actively working to improve these methods due to a conflict in visual perception; while humans perceive high-level features [30], features that computational methods extract from images and videos are typically low-level. Unlike these systems, ASL-Search accepts feature descriptions of signs from users and learns from these descriptions, making it both highly scalable and allowing for diverse search queries.

Kinect Input

More recently, the Kinect has been explored for sign language recognition [9, 41]. The Kinect supports Skeletal Tracking, and can be used to track 20 joints in 3 dimensions[2]. As in gesture recognition for video, HMMs are commonly used to model these skeletal gestures over time (e.g. [41]). While the Kinect provides a rich data source, accurate sign language translation for diverse users with a complete sign language vocabulary is still an open problem. Recent attempts have tackled the problem of generalizing to diverse users by extracting universally relevant features from the Kinect data (e.g. [9]). While the Kinect collects more data than video alone, processing that data is computationally expensive, and system performance still depends on the accuracy of the user's sign demonstration. Our system removes these difficulties by allowing users to choose which features they use to describe signs, both reducing the complexity of and increasing confidence in the data provided.

Glove and Sensor Input

Gloves and other arm and hand sensors have also been used to input signs to a computer [20, 39, 25, 21]. A rich literature on the use of gloves and other sensors to detect movements exists beyond the scope of this related work section. These systems support detection of nuanced hand movements and positions that can be meaningful to signs. For example, Kim et al. studied the use of sensory gloves for depth detection [20]. In addition to sensing finger movement directly, research efforts have studied how to track the movement of fingers through video capture of a glove with differently colored fingers and areas [39]. Unfortunately, these systems require specialized hardware that can be expensive and uncomfortable. ASL-Search removes the need for additional hardware by allowing users to interact directly with a website.

Search by Feature Selection

Feature-based ASL-to-English dictionaries avoid the computational problems of "search by example" by allowing users

[2]http://www.xbox.com/en-US/kinect

to input features describing a sign. The features used by these systems are supported by linguistic analysis of ASL.

Features Grounded in Linguistics

Linguists have developed several ASL notation systems. They are not widely used for communication between people; it is easier to communicate in English or to sign [5, 31]. Stokoe notation is the best known in the Deaf community, as it propelled ASL to be recognized as a true language [33]. It defines a grammar based on five feature types: hand shape, location, orientation, movement, and relative position.

Printed ASL-to-English dictionaries use features from these notation systems to organize signs. Stokoe published his seminal notation with an ASL-to-English Dictionary, which sorts signs first by location followed by hand shape [33]. The Gallaudet ASL Handshape Dictionary also sorts signs by hand shape [34]. When a hand shape can be identified, it narrows the set of possible English translations. However, users may need to sift through a lengthy list of possibilities. Our dictionary builds on this prior linguistic work by using features taken directly from Stokoe notation.

Feature-Based Electronic Dictionaries

Electronic feature-based ASL-to-English dictionaries allow the user to select features to describe a sign (e.g. Handspeak[3], Jinkle[4], and SLinto[5]). For example, one commercial resource, "The Ultimate ASL to English Dictionary," uses hand shape, location, orientation, and movement for search [36]. Possible matching English words are returned in an alphabetized list, which is undesirable because the target word may be late in the alphabetical ordering. Existing feature-based ASL-to-English dictionaries have several limitations:

1. Poor matching of features to signs.[6]
2. Requirements on features that the user must select.[7]
3. Lack of support for feature omissions.[8]
4. Cumbersome search interfaces.[9]

The design of ASL-Search seeks to address each of these issues with a front front end that gives the user freedom in feature selection, and a backend that learns from user queries. The search engine that drives ASL-Search stores past user queries in a feature-sign matrix, and uses LSA to identify meaningful dimensions in feature space before matching new queries to signs.

[3]http://www.handspeak.com

[4]http://asl.jinkle.com/lsearch.php

[5]http://slinto.com/us/

[6]These dictionaries do not seem to be fully functional, and do not publish the algorithms used for returning search results. Based on the authors' experience using these systems, it is likely that they find matching signs by executing a strict database search.

[7]Handspeak requires hand shape, movement, and location for *only* one unspecified hand; Jinkle requires the starting hand shape, orientation, location, and movement for *only* the dominant hand; and SLinto requires *only* hand shape and location for both hands.

[8]SLinto is the only tool to allow for missing features.

[9]For example, Handspeak and Jinkle afford feature selection through drop-down lists of English words, which are poor descriptors of visual cues.

Crowdsourcing for Language and Search Tools

Crowdsourcing has been explored as a resource for language analysis (e.g. [11, 23, 27, 28]). For example, lexical applications include translating text between languages (e.g. [28]) and disambiguating word meanings (e.g. [27]). Crowdsourcing has also been explored as a means for real-time captioning of spoken words into written form [23] and collaboratively translating rich literature like Shakespeare's plays [11]. However, to the best of our knowledge, crowdsourcing has not been used to gather data in support of a sign language dictionary.

Crowdsourcing has also been used to build Duolingo [37], a program that teaches written languages through a progression of written and spoken exercises. Instead of paying language experts to translate the phrases used in the exercises, a crowd of volunteers translates them. Duolingo also looks for patterns in the translations that its users provide, allowing it to build language models. Like Duolingo, our ASL-Search dictionary learns from its users' queries to form a model of language. Our ASL-Flash "game" helps crowdsource the dictionary, simultaneously providing value to users by reinforcing vocabulary, and enriching the set of queries used to train the ASL-Search dictionary. Unlike Duolingo, ASL-Flash and ASL-Search are built specifically for signed languages, provide a dictionary, and do not require language competency of any contributors.

Search tools have also attempted to use crowdsourcing to improve search results (e.g. [6, 19, 24, 29, 35]). As the data sources for information retrieval systems become increasingly large and diverse, it becomes more difficult to use an expert to evaluate the relevance of these resources [17]. Fortunately, crowdsourcing offers a flexible, scalable resource for relevance evaluation. Workers from scalable platforms like Amazon's Mechanical Turk have been used to evaluate relevance of documents and other search results (e.g. [3, 12, 18, 24]). In search engines, *social search* uses explicit feedback from previous users to inform search results for subsequent users (e.g. [2]). Implicit user feedback, like click data, has also been leveraged to refine results (e.g. [1, 15, 16, 29]). Users can also contribute content including tags, reviews, and comments to improve search results for web search (e.g. [6]), library systems (e.g. [35]), and book searches (e.g. [19]). The use of crowdsourcing to improve search results in other domains suggests the potential of users to contribute to sign language dictionary search methods, as we do with ASL-Search and ASL-Flash.

SURVEY OF SEARCH METHODS

In order to motivate our system, we conducted a survey with current ASL students to determine methods used to search for unfamiliar signs. The survey used multiple choice questions to ask about the frequency of use for the resources in Figure 2, and free-form responses to gather more information on the students' lookup processes. We recruited 28 participants, 3 male and 25 female. The average (mean) age was 21, with a range of 18-41. All participants were either learning or already knew ASL, with a mean of 1.46 years of ASL experience. Two participants had experience with one addi-

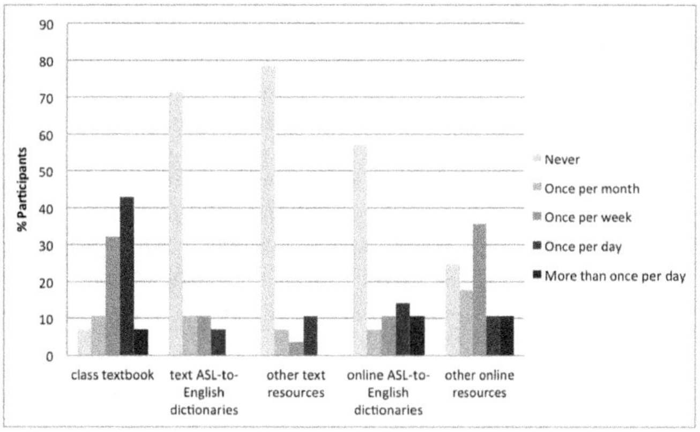

Figure 2: Use of existing sign search methods by ASL students.

tional sign language. The mean number of spoken languages including English was 1.89 per participant.

Despite the existence of online ASL-to-English dictionary resources, students predominantly did *not* use them. Each participant provided frequency of use for: 1) class textbook, 2) text ASL-to-English dictionaries, 3) other text resources, 4) online ASL-to-English dictionaries, and 5) other online resources. Examples of online resources that are not ASL-to-English dictionaries include YouTube videos, online English-to-ASL dictionaries, and search engines like Google or Bing. We found that the class textbook (92.86%) and non-dictionary online resources (75.00%) were the only resources used by the majority of students (see Figure 2). However, only 42.86% of the surveyed students used online ASL-to-English dictionaries. This disparity suggests that the internet is an appealing place for students to search for signs, but ASL-to-English dictionary performance or discoverability is not yet competitive with other online resources. Because most students use the internet to search for unfamiliar signs, it is possible that improved online dictionaries will provide benefit to those learning ASL.

Another valuable resource for inquiring about unfamiliar signs is to ask another person, but only 17 of the 28 participants used this method regularly (60.71%). One reason that fewer students ask others[10] is the lack of availability to do so. For example, it might be inconvenient or embarrassing to stop a conversation and ask, particularly in a social setting. In addition, there are other scenarios when it is never possible, like when viewing a video alone. The other 11 students (39.29%) who did not ask others relied on text[11], online resources[12], and guessing the English representation.

Text and online resources as they exist today are not a viable solution to the problem of looking up signs for many students. In fact, 8 (28.57%) students said if they saw an unfamiliar sign, and had no one available to ask, they had no idea what actions to take. One possible reason is the difficulty of expressing a sign in text. In the words of one participant, *"describing the hand motions for a particular sign in words isn't always the easiest thing to do."* Another possible reason is that students must guess the meaning of the unknown sign using context in order to use English-to-ASL dictionaries, many text resources, or online videos. Other issues emerge when using ASL-to-English dictionaries; in particular, one participant alluded to inconsistent performance, explaining, *"I compare different dictionaries to make sure that I understand how the sign is formed or possible variations on the sign."* These responses strongly suggest that there is a need and opportunity to improve upon text and online resources when an ASL signer is not available.

In the face of these difficulties while searching for signs in online and text resources, 13 participants (46.43%) forego them altogether. If nobody is around to ask, 2 students (7.14%) ask somebody later and repeat the sign from memory. However, this task may be difficult because people may forget the need to ask, let alone the sign. 2 other students (7.14%) admitted that they were content with ignorance. *"I'd probably be content with just not knowing what the sign is,"* admitted one, while the other elaborated, *"It's such a visual language that trying to 'look' up how to sign a word can be more confusing than not having known it ever existed."* Several participants described a lineup of resources that they use. One participant explained, *"I first check my class textbook in the section where they go over vocabulary for the chapter. If it's not there I ask my twin brother who took the ASL series two years ago to see if he knows. If none of those things work I wait till it comes up in class to try and gain some more context for the sign."* The students' use of lists of resources highlights the difficultly and unreliability of searching for signs.

Implications from survey

Our survey demonstrated that current ASL learners not only struggle to search for the meanings of ASL signs, but stop their efforts altogether due to a lack of resources or motivation. Text and online resources are not conducive to inputting signs, and current ASL-to-English dictionaries are not complete or strong in performance. Therefore, our survey suggests that a usable, reliable, online ASL-to-English dictionary may remove an educational barrier: difficulty of searching for signs independently.

ASL-SEARCH

We propose ASL-Search, an ASL-to-English dictionary that is entirely powered by its users. The dictionary allows users to search for a sign by selecting a set of features that describe the sign. The system stores queries from previous users in a matrix of feature frequencies for each sign. As each user enters a query into ASL-Search, the system learns and improves the strength of its results using Latent Semantic Analysis (LSA). While the system's search interface allows an ASL sign to be described with many features spanning hand shape, orientation, location, and movement, LSA reduces the number of features needed (or dimensionality) when comparing a query to our database. By reducing the dimensionality

[10] in comparison to using a textbook or online resource that is not a dictionary

[11] class textbook, and other ASL books

[12] Google, Bing, YouTube, and AslPro [4]

of the feature space, LSA reduces noise in data while leveraging trends in the previously entered queries. For a feature-based sign language dictionary, there are several sources of variability in queries: 1) difficulty to create a comprehensive, unambiguous, and intuitive set of features that fully describe a signed language, 2) natural variability between different signers, 3) differences in perceptions between viewers, and 4) distorted memory of a sign. Instead of suffering from these sources of confusion, ASL-Search uses LSA to identify patterns in query variability and improve search results.

Search Interface

In order to design our search interface, we used the five feature types identified by Stokoe [33]. To be comprehensive, we used the hand shapes from the American Sign Language Handshape Dictionary (ASLHD) [34], while the rest of the features come directly from Stokoe notation. The features we chose are well grounded in linguistics, but further refinement of the features is an area for research outside the scope of this paper. The ASL-Search backend also compensates for imperfect design of the feature set by performing dimension reduction on the feature space. Below, we present each feature type, and the means to input features in a search query.

1. *Hand shape* (40 total): **What is the configuration of the hand and fingers?** Hand shapes are selected by clicking on pictures of the hand shapes. The pictures are of a fluent signer and organized in morphologic order, as in ASLHD.
2. *Location* (10 total): **Where relative to the body is the hand located?** The locations are selected by clicking on discrete regions of a picture of a person's torso and head.
3. *Orientation* (10 total): **Which direction is the palm facing? Are the fingers pointing up or down?** The orientations are presented by a series of pictures of a hand facing in the appropriate directions.
4. *Movement* (22 total): **What is the change in position over the sign duration?** The movements are presented by ball-and-arrow diagrams of the hand movement. We also provide a video of a person making the movement on demand.
5. *Relative position* (7 Total): **If there are two hands, where are they located with respect to one another?** The relative positions are presented by images showing the relation between the two hands.

Our user interface allows for the selection of features to describe and search for a sign (as in Figure 3). We allow users to omit feature types, or to select multiple features within a single type. By giving the user freedom, the ASL-Search interface allows the user to describe the sign as he or she remembers. Next, we discuss how our backend uses LSA to compensate for the variability in search queries.

Backend

Latent Semantic Analysis (LSA) is traditionally used in Natural Language Processing to analyze the similarity between documents and words based on word counts [8]. In this domain, the data is represented as a matrix X. Each row represents a document, and each column represents a word. Item

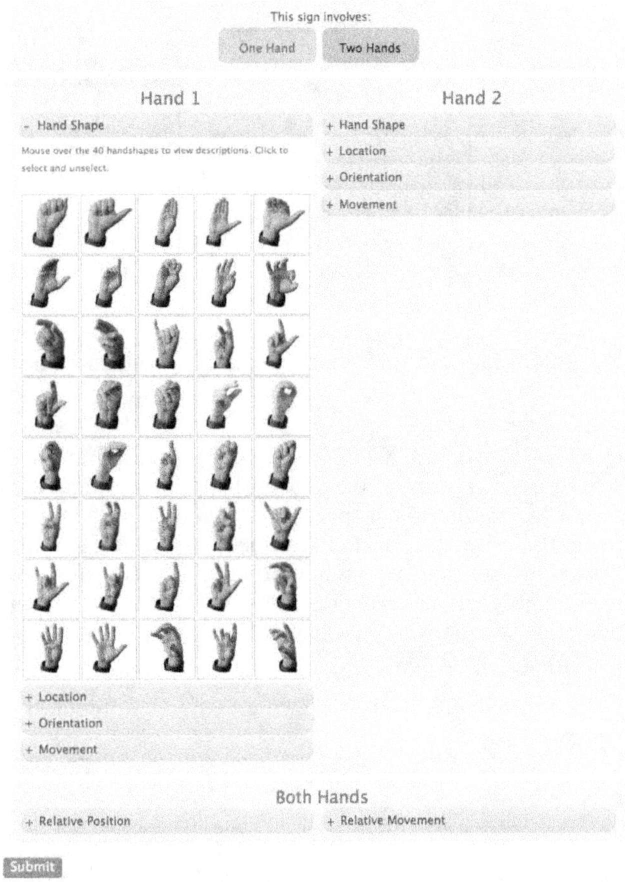

Figure 3: Screen shot of feature input interface as a user enters the hand shape for a two-handed sign. This interface is part of the ASL-Search design, and was deployed in ASL-Flash.

(i, j) thus contains the frequency of word j in document i. Instead of documents and words, our ASL dictionary has signs and features, as demonstrated in Figure 4. Each row of X represents a sign, and each column represents a feature. A query is represented as a vector of 0's and 1's, where a 1 indicates that a particular feature was entered as part of that query.

LSA utilizes Singular Value Decomposition (SVD) to factorize $X = U\Sigma V^T$, where U and V are orthogonal matrices, and Σ is a diagonal matrix. More specifically, U and V are matrices whose rows comprise the eigenvectors of XX^T and X^TX, respectively, while Σ contains the eigenvalues of XX^T (and also of X^TX). We can then select the k largest eigenvalues and corresponding eigenvectors to yield a rank-k approximation for X, $X_k = U_k\Sigma_kV_k^T$. This is an optimal approximation for X,[13] and can be used to map each feature (word) or sign (document) to an item in k-dimensional space.

To compute the similarity between an incoming query q and each sign in our database, we first project both q and X onto our lower-dimensional space as shown in Figure 5, yielding

[13]optimal by the Frobenius norm

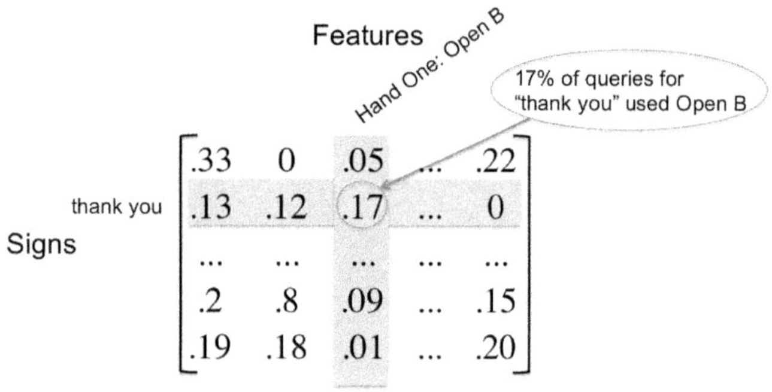

Figure 4: Matrix X of feature frequencies from user queries.

$q' = \Sigma_k^{-1} V_k^T q$ and $X' = \Sigma_k^{-1} V_k^T X$. We have now represented the query as well as each sign in our database as a vector in k-dimensional space. We want to identify the signs in our database that are closest to the query vector, so we take the angle between the incoming query and each sign vector in the space of reduced dimensionality. More specifically, we return the signs in our database sorted by cosine similarity with the incoming query, computed as $\frac{x' \cdot q'}{||x'|| ||q'||}$, where x' is a projected sign from our database and q' is the projected query.

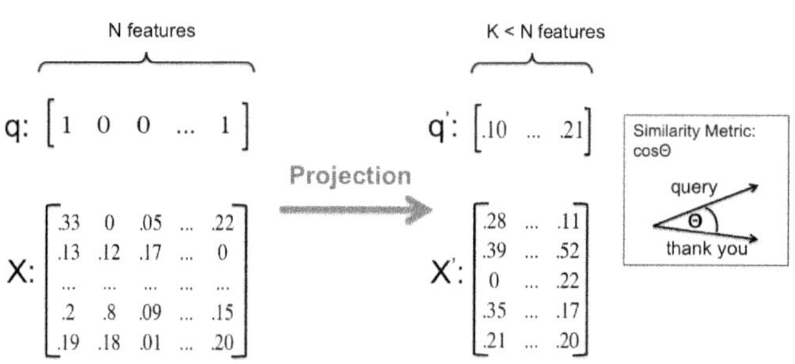

Figure 5: Dimension reduction from the original feature space to a lower-dimensional feature space.

We tailored the classic LSA algorithm for ASL-Search to account for ambiguity between hands. When entering a two-handed sign, each user determines which hand to input as "Hand 1" and which as "Hand 2" (as in Figure 3). Because people can make two choices, we replicate all entered data by switching "Hand 1" and "Hand 2." We store the flipped queries for each sign in a new row of the data matrix. A sign is a match for an incoming query when either the original or flipped row is a match. The intuition is that the flipped row more accurately represents the sign for users whose mental model of the two hands is opposite that of most users. By adding the flipped row, we can more accurately match queries for users who make the less popular hand choice.

ASL-FLASH

We also present ASL-Flash, a learning tool that teaches students ASL and contributes queries to the ASL-Search database. ASL-Flash presents a series of ASL "flashcards" to the user. The sign clips are taken with permission from SigningSavvy [14]. Each clip shows a single sign. Once the user views the clip, ASL-Flash presents a multiple choice question on the English meaning. Next, the person is instructed to use ASL-Search's interface as if they were searching for the sign. Finally, ASL-Flash provides the English meaning of the sign accompanied by the original sign video.

Query data collected by ASL-Flash has several uses: 1) it will provide seed data for ASL-Search when the dictionary is deployed, 2) it will provide ASL-Search with query data for new signs added to the dictionary and existing signs that are looked up infrequently, and 3) it can be used to demonstrate the viability of the ASL-Search design, as we do in this paper.

ASL-Flash Deployment

We used ASL-Flash to gather query data to verify ASL-Search. Because ASL-Search is of use to people learning ASL, we used signs from a textbook used in first-year ASL curricula [42]. The textbook contains 1101 signs, and we selected a random sample of 100 signs to use in our deployment. Each ASL-Flash user viewed 10 of these 100 signs, randomly selected[15] and ordered. Users were given the option to quit early, so some respondents completed fewer than 10. Overall, we collected 670 viable queries from 94 users: 52 (55.32%) female, 41 (43.62%) male, and 1 (1.06%) other. The mean age was 28.4 years, with a range of 14 to 67 years. Users had a wide range of ASL experience (9 with 0 years; 14 with 0-0.5 years; 18 with 0.5-1 years; 14 with 1-2 years; 6 with 2-3 years; 32 with over 3 years; 1 chose not to respond). The mean number of signed languages known was 1.7 with a standard deviation of 3.7. The mean number of spoken languages was 1.9 with a standard deviation of 1.4.

ASL-Flash is a sustainable source of query data for ASL-Search. The sustainability of ASL-Flash is important because we will use ASL-Flash to seed ASL-Search upon release, and to gather data for new or rare signs. 79.72% of users said they would use the system again (76.92% of those who answered all flash cards correctly, and 81.25% with at least one wrong answer). Regardless of the user's accuracy in identifying signs, the tool provides value in learning or reviewing signs.

A strong motivation for people to continue using ASL-Flash (and providing more data for ASL-Search) are the learning benefits. Out of users who incorrectly guessed at least one sign, 87.50% reported learning something new from ASL-Flash. In addition, those same users showed more activity viewing the sign videos that accompany the sign definitions on the answer pages. The count of video views was not normally distributed for those who guessed all signs correctly ($W = 0.4862$, p-value < 0.001) or their counterparts ($W = 0.7626$, p-value < 0.001). Users who made mistakes viewed videos significantly more times than those who guessed all of the signs correctly ($W = 158802$, p-value < 0.001, Mann-Whitney). This suggests the dual benefit of ASL-Flash users learning ASL, while providing valuable data for ASL-Search.

[14] http://www.signingsavvy.com

[15] from the least-viewed signs

During deployment, we asked users about their experience with the feature entry interface, which is identical to the interface proposed for ASL-Search. We found that our feature-based interface felt natural to most users. When asked the yes/no question: *"Did this survey give you a natural way to describe signs to look them up?"*, 75.68% said that the input mechanism was natural to use. Out of users who correctly guessed every sign, 73.08% found the interface intuitive; out of users who incorrectly guessed at least one sign, 77.08% agreed. This positive feedback suggests that the ASL-Search search interface will be suitable for looking up signs.

Feature Data from Experts

In addition to gathering features with ASL-Flash, we asked two experienced signers to provide features. They evaluated the same 100 signs used by ASL-Flash. Unlike in the ASL-Flash condition, we allowed the experts to replay the videos and complete the task in as much time as was needed. Their feature inputs were used to form baseline comparison search methods for ASL-Search.

The experts did not completely agree on the features present in the 100 signs. Though they agreed on the number of hands used for each sign, they entered slightly different feature sets for each of the 100 signs. On average (mean), they disagreed on 7.21 out of 164 features (4.40%). The lack of agreement between experts confirms the ambiguity inherent to sign executions and viewer perceptions. This ambiguity supports our choice of LSA for ASL-Search's backend, which extracts meaningful feature dimensions through dimension reduction.

The disagreement between experts also highlights the necessity of collaborative work in building a sign language dictionary. Even if the dictionary backend is constructed by experts (as in previous work), it would be inappropriate for a single expert to evaluate all signs; rather, a group of experts would be required. The tasks required of them would be time-consuming and tedious, and difficult to scale. Instead of dealing with these problems surrounding the collection and synthesis of expert input, our system supports the collaboration required to build an ASL dictionary effortlessly. The dictionary is built as it is used, by the users themselves.

PROOF OF CONCEPT FOR ASL-SEARCH ALGORITHM

We used the data gathered by ASL-Flash to form the database backend of ASL-Search and simulate its performance looking up signs. We formed baseline search methods that mimic existing ASL-to-English dictionaries using our expert feature evaluations. Our comparisons find that ASL-Search outperforms these baselines.

Metric

Discounted Cumulative Gain (DCG) is a standard metric used to evaluate the performance of search engines [14]. Let rel_i be the relevance of the i-th result. The score for a list of p ordered results is computed as $DCG_p = \sum_{i=1}^{p} \frac{2^{rel_i}-1}{log_2(i+1)}$. For our problem, we are searching for one particular sign, so the relevance of each sign in the result list is binary $rel_i \in \{0, 1\}$. Consequently, the DCG reduces to $\frac{1}{log_2(i+1)}$, where i is the placement of the desired sign in the result list.

Normalized Discounted Cumulative Gain (NDCG) normalizes DCG across queries, since the range of DCG scores that are possible varies for different queries. To do this, it divides the DCG for a given query by the maximal possible DCG for that query if results were returned in the optimal order. This means that NDCG will take a value in $[0, 1]$ for all queries. For our problem, because relevance is binary and $rel_i = 1$ for exactly one sign i in the returned list, DCG and NDCG are equivalent.

Overall Performance

To validate the design of ASL-Search, we simulated its use with the query data gathered from ASL-Flash, as demonstrated in Figure 6. In the Testing Phase, we use leave-one-out cross-validation. The single held-out test query represents an incoming user query for a sign. We generate the sorted list of results that ASL-Search would return, using the rest of the data as its database of previous queries, and evaluate the quality of those results using DCG. In the Training Phase, we simulate ASL-Search learning the dimensionality to be used for reduction in the LSA algorithm. We run 10-fold cross-validation, computing a list of results for each query in the held-out part of the database, and average the DCG scores for each dimensionality. The dimensionality $K_{optimal}$ with the highest average DCG is chosen and used to generate results for the incoming test query.

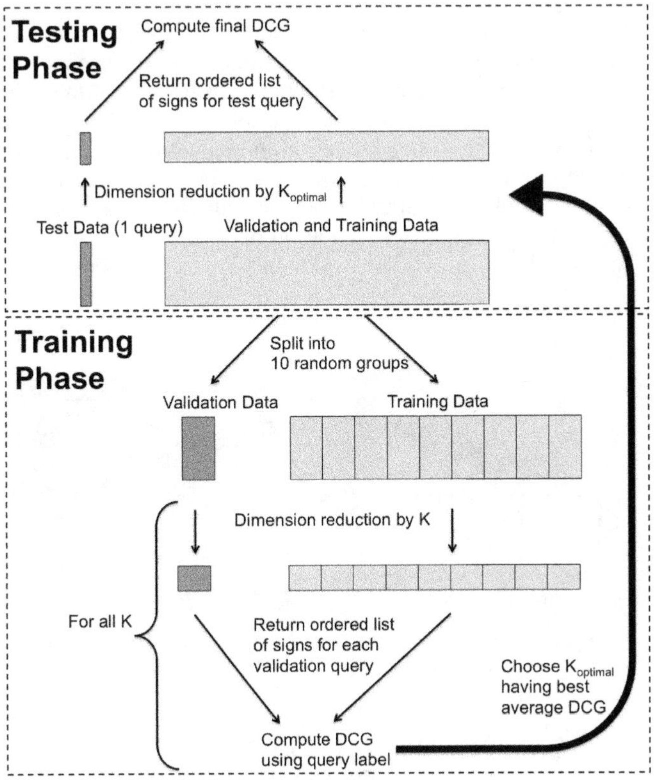

Figure 6: Simulated use and analysis of ASL-Search. The Training Phase replicates ASL-Search learning the dimensionality $K_{optimal}$ for reduction. The Testing Phase produces and evaluates the ordered list of signs that ASL-Search would return in response to incoming queries.

Because our online dictionary returns a sorted list of results, we can identify the position of the desired result in that list. Figure 7 provides a histogram of those placements for the Test Phase. 59.10% of the time, the desired result was the first result, and 84.93% of the time, it was in the top 10.

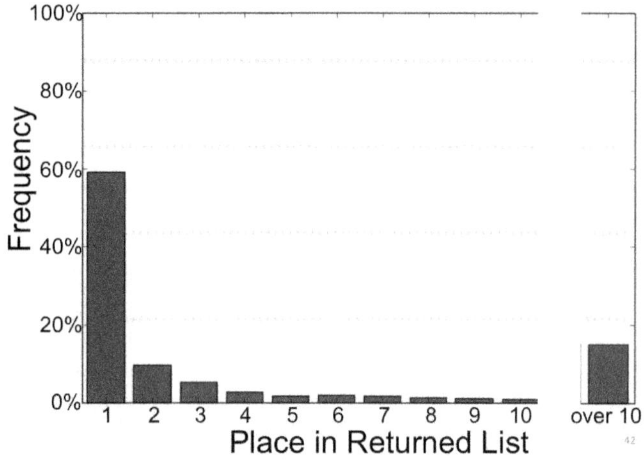

Figure 7: Place of desired result in the sorted result list. The "over 10" bucket summarizes the long tail of the distribution.

Tuning Dimensionality K

Choice of dimensionality to which the original feature space is reduced greatly impacts ASL-Search's performance, as demonstrated in Figure 8. Reducing to too few dimensions detracts from performance, as we lose meaningful information. Conversely, not reducing enough hurts performance, as we eliminate too little noise from the data. Because the choice of dimensionality impacts the quality of search results, ASL-Search uses cross-validation on the database of queries to learn the "best" choice of dimensionality for its users.

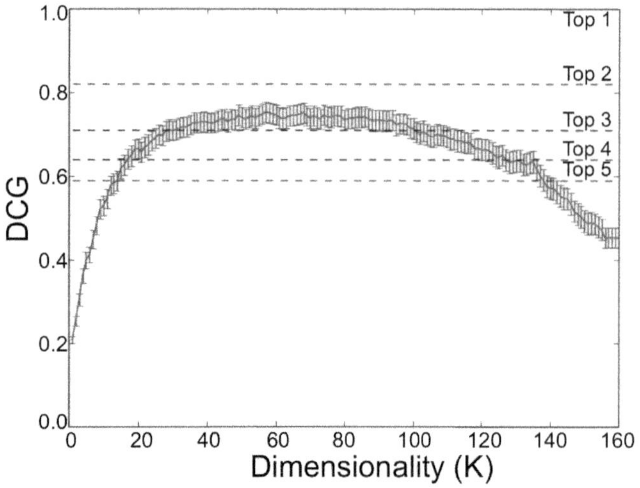

Figure 8: Effect of dimensionality K on performance, demonstrated by leave-one-out cross-validation on our entire dataset. The dotted lines show DCG when the desired sign is in the top 1, 2, 3, 4, or 5 results, with equal probability.

The dimensionality learned by the Training Phase was relatively stable throughout our simulation. Figure 9 shows the distribution of the chosen dimensionality. The mean optimal dimensionality found was 69.26. The feature dimensions produced by the dimension reduction are difficult to interpret intuitively. Each resulting dimension was a linear combination of all the original features.These results are characteristic of LSA, which is known to create dimensions that are difficult to interpret [22].

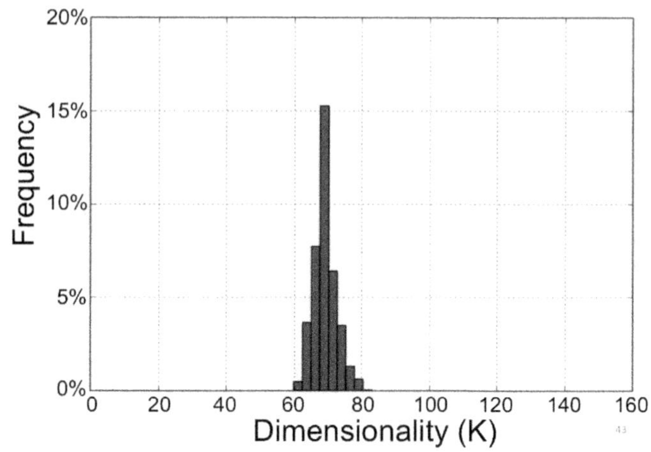

Figure 9: Dimensionality learned by ASL-Search ($K_{optimal}$ in Figure 6) from the database of past queries.

Baseline Methods

We compared ASL-Search to three baseline methods that return an ordered list of signs in response to a feature-based query. Because existing online ASL-to-English dictionaries do not seem to be fully functional and are not guaranteed to cover a vocabulary that matches the signs used in ASL-Flash, we generated our own baseline methods. These baselines are explained below:

- *Random*: Returns all signs in the dictionary in a completely random order.
- *Expert Or*: Compares the incoming query to the union (logical "or") of our expert feature vectors. It returns all signs for which the incoming features are a subset of the expert "or" vector, sorted by the number of matching features. We suspect that existing feature-based ASL-to-English electronic dictionaries use similar methods, since their results vary in length, and sometimes return no results at all. We chose the union of expert features, rather than their intersection (logical "and") because the union allows for more successful feature matches and better performance.
- *Expert Hamming*: Computes the hamming distance between the incoming query and the union (logical "or") of our expert feature vectors for each sign in the dictionary. It returns all signs in the dictionary, ordered by increasing Hamming distance so that the closest signs are returned first. *Expert Hamming* serves as a more robust alternative to *Expert Or*.

Performance as the ASL-Search Database Grows

The simulated longitudinal performance of our dictionary demonstrates that ASL-Search significantly outperforms existing baselines. ASL-Search improves as more users contribute data, suggesting that ASL-Search will further outpace other methods in the future.

We simulated the performance of our dictionary over time using the query data gathered by ASL-Flash. We repeated the following two steps 20 times: 1) We held out a set of 100 test queries, one chosen randomly for each of our 100 signs. 2) We simulated the growth of the database by incrementally adding queries to the database, and evaluated performance on the test queries. Specifically, we divided the remaining query data into 10 equal sized and random groups, and added each group to the database to simulate database growth. Performance after each addition was evaluated by computing the DCG for the results generated for the 100 test queries. Figure 10 displays the average DCG from the 20 trials, with error bars of the standard error over the 20 trials.

Perhaps surprisingly, *Random* and *Expert Or* had almost the same average performance, with *Expert Or* outperforming *Random* by less than 0.001. The average performance of *Expert Or* is comparable to *Random* because it fails to return the desired sign for some queries. *Expert Or* only returns signs that the experts have determined to have all features selected in the query. Because there is variation in the features that viewers perceive, some queries contain features that the experts considered absent from the desired sign. In these cases, *Expert Or* does not return the desired sign (and in fact might not return any results at all), and receives a DCG score of 0. For these queries, *Random* outperforms *Expert Or* since it always returns the desired sign at some position in the result list. Conversely, for queries whose features are considered to be present in the desired sign by the experts, *Expert Or* typically outperforms *Random*. While *Expert Or* is a weak baseline, it is representative of existing ASL-to-English dictionaries.

The *Expert Hamming* baseline better leverages the valuable signal in the expert data, and consequently outperforms *Expert Or*. Unlike *Expert Or*, *Expert Hamming* does not restrict the signs returned to those that possess all features present in the query. Instead, it uses Hamming distance to evaluate similarity between the incoming query and every expert evaluation of a sign in the dictionary. Using Hamming distance produces more nuanced comparisons, and allows *Expert Hamming* to always return the desired sign at some rank in the result list.

Overall, our system returned more accurate results than the *Random*, *Expert Or*, and *Expert Hamming* baseline methods. The crowd provides data that experts do not: the features commonly seen by real users who are unfamiliar with the signs they look up. ASL-Search's use of dimension reduction through LSA allows ASL-Search to leverage this signal. Furthermore, our system improves with additional data from users, which is not possible for *Random*, *Expert Or*, *Expert Hamming*, or variants of our baselines employed by existing online ASL-to-English dictionaries.

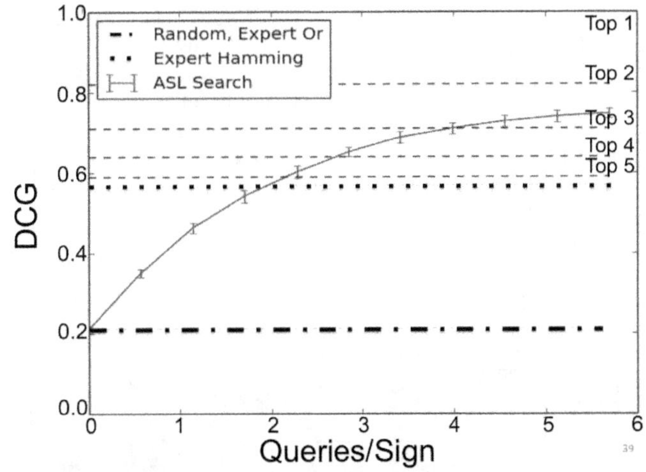

Figure 10: Performance of ASL-Search with use. Results were averaged over 20 simulations of dictionary growth.

Performance by ASL Experience

Our system performs well for target users with varying levels of ASL experience, as seen in Figure 11. To generate these results, we set the dimensionality to 70, which was the mean dimensionality chosen in the Training Phase, and held out one query at a time for testing. Our performance is relatively stable for target users of varying levels of ASL experience, but was slightly worse for those with absolutely no ASL experience. One possible reason for this lower performance is that brand new signers may have trouble identifying the visual queues in a sign. They may have suffered from fatigue as well, with decreased quality as they progressed through ASL-Flash's flash cards.

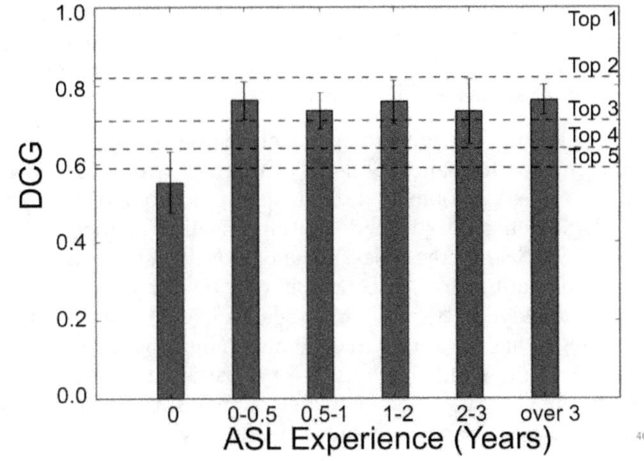

Figure 11: Performance for queries entered by users with varying ASL experience.

Our proposed system typically returned the most appropriate results when the English meaning of the sign was not known, as shown in Figure 12. For all levels of experience, except for users with 1-2 years of ASL, queries for unknown signs produced better results than those for known signs. Even for users with 1-2 years of ASL, the difference in performance is negligible. It is likely that LSA handles queries for unfamiliar signs better because these queries are characterized by feature variabilities that LSA expects and compensates for. Our results demonstrate that ASL-Search should fulfill its purpose of helping users to look up ASL signs, and especially unfamiliar ones.

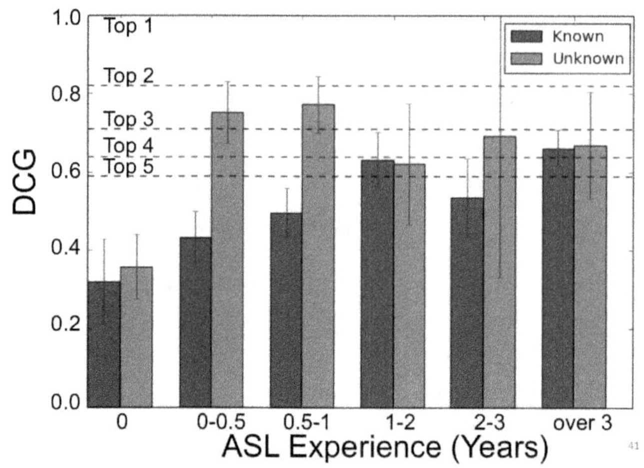

Figure 12: Performance for queries entered by target users with varying ASL experience, separated by whether or not the sign was known.

DISCUSSION AND FUTURE WORK

Our proof of concept for ASL-Search suggests that implementing our design will be effective. The survey we ran on existing lookup methods exposed difficulties that ASL students encounter when searching for a sign definition, and highlighted the need for a tool that allows users to easily and accurately look up ASL signs. Our proof of concept demonstrates that ASL-Search can accurately match its users' queries to signs and fill this need.

Furthermore, our proof of concept demonstrated that ASL-Search's performance will only improve with use. Even with a small amount of user data in our proof of concept, ASL-Search outperformed existing baseline methods. Unlike ASL-Search, these baseline methods do not improve with use, indicating that ASL-Search will further outpace them when deployed. Because ASL-Search learns from its users' queries, it has the ability to evolve with the language. For example, if the hand shape used for a particular sign changes over time, ASL-Search will detect that shift in its users' queries, and adapt its results accordingly. Because ASL-Search is built entirely upon input from the user community, its results are tailored to its users. Furthermore, because its users build the dictionary as they use it, crowdsourcing through ASL-Search happens effortlessly.

Our deployment of ASL-Flash with a small corpus of signs demonstrated that ASL-Flash is both a sustainable resource of supplementary data for ASL-Search, and a valuable learning tool in its own right. In our deployment, the majority of ASL-Flash users reported they would use ASL-Flash again, and that the flash cards helped them learn. Additionally, the majority of knowledgeable signers reported that they would use the tool again and that it helped them learn. We found that less knowledgeable signers devoted more attention to the answer videos. These results suggest that users of all experience levels can benefit from using ASL-Flash, and will likely continue to use it and provide data for ASL-Search.

ASL-Search can be adapted to solve problems besides sign language lookup, and serve communities of users in other domains. For example, a version of ASL-Search can be released to support bird watchers looking up the species of birds that they see. The bird can be described by a discrete set of features, like feather color and beak shape. Latent Semantic Analysis is well suited for this domain because the birds can be described by a set of features, and there will be natural variability in people's descriptions of the birds they see, just as there is natural variability in people's descriptions of signs. The ASL-Search design serves as a model for domains outside of sign language.

We are excited to explore a number of future directions. We plan to investigate improvements to the lookup algorithm. Alternative topic modeling methods could be used, like probabilistic latent semantic analysis (PLSA) or latent Dirichlet allocation (LDA), which would allow us to model the co-occurrence probability of queries and signs. Alternate feature-sign weights, like term frequency-inverse document frequency (TF-IDF), and other dimension reduction techniques, like principal component analysis (PCA) or group sparsity methods, could also be used. With or without dimensionality reduction, classification methods like decision trees, support vector machines (SVMs), and even multinomial logistic regression could also be used to determine the sign class for each incoming query, instead of LSA's cosine similarity. Unsupervised or semi-supervised methods could leverage unlabeled data, for example queries from ASL-Search where the user did not provide information about which sign they sought. Relevant methods can also be combined in various ways, for example by applying a sequence of operations, or weighting results from methods run in parallel. We also plan to investigate the scalability of these search methods as we expand the ASL-Search dictionary in preparation for release. We look forward to seeing the system deployed for public use.

Another interesting direction is to make the collaboration with other users more transparent. Our current ASL-Search design supports *implicit* cooperation between users. As the users enter their queries, they might be unaware of the fact that they are contributing to the success of the dictionary along with their fellow users. Making this collaboration more transparent may introduce future research questions to explore.

CONCLUSION

In this work, we present the design of ASL-Search, an ASL-to-English dictionary system entirely powered by its users. We motivated our system with a survey on methods used by ASL students to search for signs they do not understand. Our survey demonstrated the inadequacy of existing methods and the potential for our system to help mitigate this issue. ASL-Search's system design allows the user to search for a sign by entering visual features that describe the sign (such as hand shape and movement), and stores these queries in a database. Unlike existing systems, it novelly applies Latent Semantic Analysis (LSA) to match incoming queries to signs in the database, thereby mitigating noise in the data and accounting for observation variability.

We also built ASL-Flash, a learning tool that presents a series of ASL flashcards and simultaneously gathers additional query data for ASL-Search. We used ASL-Flash to gather query data from real users to demonstrate ASL-Search's performance in a proof of concept for the system design. The proof of concept demonstrates that ASL-Search outperforms comparable existing dictionaries, and will only improve over time with use.

This work supports learning ASL in two distinct but related ways: 1) through the design of ASL-Search, an electronic ASL-to-English dictionary that is both easy to use and accurate and 2) with the development of ASL-Flash, a set of online flash cards that help students learn ASL. The two systems work together to support the community of sign language learners. As ASL-Flash users reinforce and acquire ASL knowledge, they also contribute query data that improves the performance of the ASL-Search dictionary. ASL-Search has the potential to become a valuable resource for a large community, supporting sign language students and fluent signers alike.

When we look beyond ASL to other signed languages, the potential impact of ASL-Search and ASL-Flash grows. The difficulties encountered in learning ASL are not unique to ASL, but pervasive to all signed languages. Regardless of the language from which they come, signs are three-dimensional motions not easily described with written words, and there is natural variability in their execution and perception. ASL-Search can provide a dictionary resource for an international community of signers with releases in sign languages besides ASL and target languages other than English. Similarly, ASL-Flash can help students learn and reinforce sign meanings in other languages, and provide a sustainable datasource for the ASL-Search release in those languages.

ACKNOWLEDGMENTS

We thank SigningSavvy for granting us permission to use their sign videos in our deployment of ASL-Flash. This work is based in part upon work supported by the National Science Foundation under Grant No. 0915268. Any opinions, findings, and conclusions or recommendations expressed in this work are those of the authors and do not necessarily reflect the views of the National Science Foundation.

REFERENCES

1. Agichtein, E., Brill, E., and Dumais, S. Improving web search ranking by incorporating user behavior information. In *Proceedings of the 29th annual international ACM SIGIR conference on Research and development in information retrieval*, ACM (2006), 19–26.
2. Agrahri, A. K., Manickam, D. A. T., and Riedl, J. Can people collaborate to improve the relevance of search results? In *Proceedings of the 2008 ACM conference on Recommender systems*, ACM (2008), 283–286.
3. Alonso, O., Rose, D. E., and Stewart, B. Crowdsourcing for relevance evaluation. In *ACM SIGIR Forum*, vol. 42, ACM (2008), 9–15.
4. Aslpro, May 2014. `http://www.aslpro.com`.
5. Aslwrite - support american sign language through writing!, May 2013. `http://www.aslwrite.com/`.
6. Bao, S., Xue, G., Wu, X., Yu, Y., Fei, B., and Su, Z. Optimizing web search using social annotations. In *Proceedings of the 16th international conference on World Wide Web*, ACM (2007), 501–510.
7. Cooper, H., Pugeault, N., and Bowden, R. Reading the signs: A video based sign dictionary. In *Computer Vision Workshops (ICCV Workshops), 2011 IEEE International Conference on*, IEEE (2011), 914–919.
8. Deerwester, S. C., Dumais, S. T., Landauer, T. K., Furnas, G. W., and Harshman, R. A. Indexing by latent semantic analysis. *Journal of the Association for Information Science and Technology (JASIS) 41*, 6 (1990), 391–407.
9. Elliott, R., Cooper, H., Ong, E.-J., Glauert, J., Bowden, R., and Lefebvre-Albaret, F. Search-by-example in multilingual sign language databases. In *Procs. of Second International Workshop on Sign Language Translation and Avatar Technology (SLTAT)* (2011).
10. Furman, N., Goldberg, D., and Lusin, N. Enrollments in languages other than english in united states institutions of higher education, fall 2009. In *Modern Language Association*, ERIC (2010).
11. Giordano, T. *Toward a crowdsourced model for ASL translations of Shakespeare's works*. PhD thesis, California State University, 2013.
12. Grady, C., and Lease, M. Crowdsourcing document relevance assessment with mechanical turk. In *Proceedings of the NAACL HLT 2010 workshop on creating speech and language data with Amazon's mechanical turk*, Association for Computational Linguistics (2010), 172–179.
13. Imagawa, K., Lu, S., and Igi, S. Color-based hands tracking system for sign language recognition. In *Proceedings of the Third IEEE International Conference on Automatic Face and Gesture Recognition*, IEEE (1998), 462–467.
14. Järvelin, K., and Kekäläinen, J. Cumulated gain-based evaluation of ir techniques. *ACM Transactions on Information Systems (TOIS) 20*, 4 (2002), 422–446.
15. Joachims, T. Optimizing search engines using clickthrough data. In *Proceedings of the eighth ACM SIGKDD international conference on Knowledge discovery and data mining*, ACM (2002), 133–142.

16. Joachims, T., and Radlinski, F. Search engines that learn from implicit feedback. *IEEE Computer 40*, 8 (2007), 34–40.
17. Kamps, J., Geva, S., Peters, C., Sakai, T., Trotman, A., and Voorhees, E. Report on the sigir 2009 workshop on the future of ir evaluation. In *ACM SIGIR Forum*, vol. 43, ACM (2009), 13–23.
18. Kazai, G. In search of quality in crowdsourcing for search engine evaluation. In *Advances in information retrieval*, vol. 6611 of *Lecture Notes in Computer Science*. Springer, 2011, 165–176.
19. Kazai, G., Kamps, J., Koolen, M., and Milic-Frayling, N. Crowdsourcing for book search evaluation: impact of hit design on comparative system ranking. In *Proceedings of the 34th international ACM SIGIR conference on Research and development in Information Retrieval*, ACM (2011), 205–214.
20. Kim, J.-H., Thang, N. D., and Kim, T.-S. 3-d hand motion tracking and gesture recognition using a data glove. In *Industrial Electronics, 2009. ISIE 2009. IEEE International Symposium on*, IEEE (2009), 1013–1018.
21. Kim, J.-S., Jang, W., and Bien, Z. A dynamic gesture recognition system for the korean sign language (ksl). *Systems, Man, and Cybernetics, Part B: Cybernetics, IEEE Transactions on 26*, 2 (1996), 354–359.
22. Landauer, T. K., Foltz, P. W., and Laham, D. An introduction to latent semantic analysis. *Discourse processes 25*, 2-3 (1998), 259–284.
23. Lasecki, W., Miller, C., Sadilek, A., Abumoussa, A., Borrello, D., Kushalnagar, R., and Bigham, J. Real-time captioning by groups of non-experts. In *Proceedings of the 25th annual ACM symposium on User interface software and technology*, ACM (2012), 23–34.
24. Le, J., Edmonds, A., Hester, V., and Biewald, L. Ensuring quality in crowdsourced search relevance evaluation: The effects of training question distribution. In *SIGIR 2010 workshop on crowdsourcing for search evaluation* (2010), 21–26.
25. Liang, R.-H., and Ouhyoung, M. A real-time continuous gesture recognition system for sign language. In *Automatic Face and Gesture Recognition, 1998. Proceedings. Third IEEE International Conference on*, IEEE (1998), 558–567.
26. Ong, E.-J., Cooper, H., Pugeault, N., and Bowden, R. Sign language recognition using sequential pattern trees. In *Computer Vision and Pattern Recognition (CVPR), 2012 IEEE Conference on*, IEEE (2012), 2200–2207.
27. Parent, G., and Eskenazi, M. Clustering dictionary definitions using amazon mechanical turk. In *Proceedings of the NAACL HLT 2010 Workshop on Creating Speech and Language Data with Amazon's Mechanical Turk*, Association for Computational Linguistics (2010), 21–29.
28. Post, M., Callison-Burch, C., and Osborne, M. Constructing parallel corpora for six indian languages via crowdsourcing. In *Proceedings of the Seventh Workshop on Statistical Machine Translation*, Association for Computational Linguistics (2012), 401–409.
29. Radlinski, F., and Joachims, T. Query chains: learning to rank from implicit feedback. In *Proceedings of the eleventh ACM SIGKDD international conference on Knowledge discovery in data mining*, ACM (2005), 239–248.
30. Rui, Y., Huang, T. S., and Chang, S.-F. Image retrieval: Current techniques, promising directions, and open issues. *Journal of visual communication and image representation 10*, 1 (1999), 39–62.
31. Signwriting for sign languages, May 2013. `http://www.signwriting.org/`.
32. Starner, T., and Pentland, A. Real-time american sign language recognition from video using hidden markov models. In *Motion-Based Recognition*. Springer, 1997, 227–243.
33. Stokoe, W. C., Casterline, D. C., and Croneberg, C. G. *A dictionary of American Sign Language on linguistic principles*. Linstok Press Silver Spring, 1976.
34. Tennant, R. A., and Brown, M. G. *The American sign language handshape dictionary*. Gallaudet University Press, 1998.
35. Trainor, C. Open source, crowd source: harnessing the power of the people behind our libraries. *Program: electronic library and information systems 43*, 3 (2009), 288–298.
36. The ultimate american sign language dictionary, May 2013. `http://idrt.com/store/the-ultimate-american-sign-language-dictionary`.
37. von Ahn, L. Duolingo: learn a language for free while helping to translate the web. In *Proceedings of the 2013 international conference on Intelligent user interfaces (IUI)*, ACM Press (2013), 1–2.
38. Wang, H., Stefan, A., Moradi, S., Athitsos, V., Neidle, C., and Kamangar, F. A system for large vocabulary sign search. In *Trends and Topics in Computer Vision*. Springer, 2012, 342–353.
39. Wang, R. Y., and Popović, J. Real-time hand-tracking with a color glove. In *ACM Transactions on Graphics (TOG)*, vol. 28, ACM (2009), 63.
40. Yang, M.-H., and Ahuja, N. Recognizing hand gestures using motion trajectories. In *Face Detection and Gesture Recognition for Human-Computer Interaction*. Springer, 2001, 53–81.
41. Zafrulla, Z., Brashear, H., Starner, T., Hamilton, H., and Presti, P. American sign language recognition with the kinect. In *Proceedings of the 13th international conference on multimodal interfaces*, ACM (2011), 279–286.
42. Zinza, J. E. *Master ASL!* Sign Media Inc, 2006.

Enhancing Evaluation of Potential Dates Online Through Paired Collaborative Activities

Doug Zytko
New Jersey Institute of Technology
Newark, NJ
daz2@njit.edu

Guo Freeman
Indiana University
Bloomington, IN
guozhang@indiana.edu

Sukeshini A. Grandhi
Eastern Connecticut State University
Willimantic, CT
grandhis@easternct.edu

Susan Herring
Indiana University
Bloomington, IN
herring@indiana.edu

Quentin Jones
New Jersey Institute of Technology
Newark, NJ
qgjones@acm.org

ABSTRACT
Online dating systems are the most common way people meet their marriage partners online. Nevertheless, online daters struggle to evaluate personality traits of potential partners using profile pages and private messaging in these systems. Meanwhile, Multiplayer Online Games (MOGs) have emerged as a popular way young people find romantic partners for relationships in the physical world. We conducted two interview studies – one concerning evaluation behavior in online dating systems (n=41) and the other concerning collaborative activities in MOGs (n=35). Insights from these studies reveal the weaknesses in evaluation tools native to online dating and suggest that collaborative activities could potentially address evaluation challenges in online dating. The paper concludes with a discussion of a series of design concepts for online dating in order to improve users' abilities to evaluate their potential romantic partners for in-person meetings.

Author Keywords
Online dating systems; Multiplayer Online Games; collaboration; evaluation; personality traits

ACM Classification Keywords
H.5.2 [Information Interfaces and Presentation]: User Interfaces - Interaction styles

General Terms
Human Factors; Design; Measurement.

INTRODUCTION
Technology, spearheaded by online dating systems, has impacted how people seek romantic intimacy. As of 2013, one in 10 single Americans had used an online dating system, an increase from just one in 30 in 2008 [27]. Online daters largely share the desire to meet their potential romantic partners face-to-face and enjoy their relationships in the physical world [14]. To achieve this they spend their time on these systems evaluating other users for face-to-face meetings.

CSCW '15, March 14 – 18, 2015, Vancouver, BC, Canada.

ACM 978-1-4503-2922-4/15/03...$15.00.
http://dx.doi.org/10.1145/2675133.2675184

Within today's online dating systems, users employ two means to evaluate their potential partners: profile pages and private messaging. Research has indicated that online daters struggle to evaluate their potential partners [38, 39, 40], particularly the subjective and tacit personality traits that are vital to romantic attraction [10]. Previous research has suggested that first dates between online daters often go poorly because their personality trait evaluations are inaccurate [38, 39]. In this paper we explore how the evaluation capabilities in online dating can be enhanced.

To address this, we looked into other online contexts that facilitate romantic intimacy. A recent survey study [15] showed that online communities, which include Multiplayer Online Games (MOGs), are the second most popular way people meet their marriage partners online. MOGs are virtual game environments such as *World of Warcraft, Everquest*, *League of Legends*, *Final Fantasy, Star Wars Galaxies*, and *Audition*. MOG players typically need to collaborate with one another to complete tasks necessary for progressing through the game. However, these collaborations can also be romance-facilitating, with players using these collaborative activities to explore their romantic compatibility [36, 37]. As a result, in-game partnerships sometimes blossom into romantically intimate relationships in the physical world [24].

In this paper we draw insights from two studies concerning people's explicit and implicit attempts to find romantic partners in two contexts: online dating systems and romance-facilitating collaboration in MOGs. Findings from these two studies suggest that collaborative activities could help address evaluation deficiencies experienced by users of online dating systems. Based on these insights, we present and discuss a series of design concepts for incorporating collaborative activities into online dating environments that could improve users' abilities to evaluate their potential romantic partners for in-person meetings.

BACKGROUND

The research reviewed in this section revolves around the online evaluation of potential partners for romantically intimate relationships in the physical world. Moss and Schwebel describe romantic intimacy as being indicative of the "commitment and positive affective, cognitive, and physical closeness one experiences with a partner in a reciprocal relationship" [23]. Romantic intimacy, under this definition, comprises marriage and long-term romantic relationships between committed partners face-to-face.

Evaluation in Online Dating Systems

Online dating systems are "Internet services designed to facilitate interactions between potential romantic partners" [18]. The most common way people meet their marriage partners online is through online dating systems [15] – a trend facilitated by systems like *eHarmony* and *match.com*, which specialize in connecting potential marriage partners. Many online dating systems, like *OkCupid* and *Plenty of Fish*, also cater to a variety of other relationship goals such as short-term or casual dating and platonic friendships.

After discovering a potential partner in the online dating system, a user evaluates that person for a face-to-face meeting [14, 29]. Users evaluate two types of information about their potential partners: searchable attributes and experiential attributes [10]. Searchable attributes are objective, demographic qualities such as height, weight, and age, which can be unambiguously conveyed and verified. Experiential attributes, in contrast, are subjective and tacit, and are "aesthetic, holistic, emotive, and tied to the production of sensation" [10]. These include personality traits such as confidence and sense of humor. Because of their subjective nature, experiential attributes must be experienced personally in order to be evaluated (e.g., Mary may consider John's sense of humor to be funny and playful, but Samantha considers it childish).

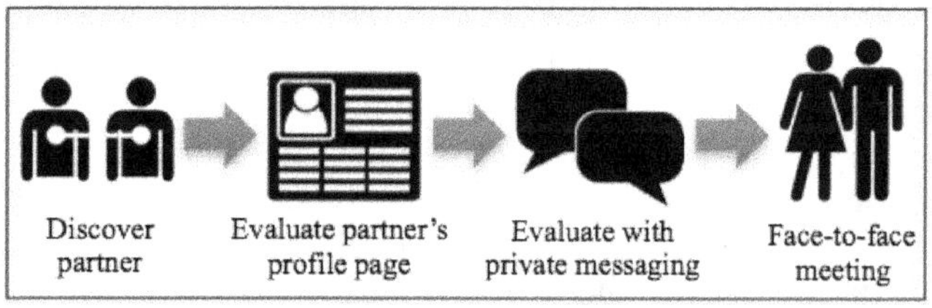

Figure 1: Online dating evaluation process

There are two standard components within an online dating system that users employ to evaluate each other. The first is public profile pages, and the second is private messaging. In most online dating systems, all users are required to have a profile page, which serves as the first source of information a user has about a potential partner. The content of profile pages can vary from system to system, but users are typically allowed to populate their profiles with pictures of themselves (profile pictures), searchable attributes, and answers to open-ended questions (such as "describe your ideal first date").

Pictures have been found to be the biggest determinant of attraction on profile pages [8, 16, 29, 32]. Searchable attributes, such as height, also factor into evaluations through profile pages [19, 34]. Research has indicated that online daters often exaggerate searchable attributes on their profile pages in an attempt to appear more attractive [7, 32]. Thus profile pages are often depictions of one's "ideal future self" instead of one's actual self, which may explain why online daters are wary that their fellow users lie [11].

Experiential attributes are integral to the evaluation of potential romantic partners [10, 14, 38, 39, 40], and open-ended questions on profile pages are often read to evaluate these traits. Women review open-ended answers to find men who are genuine, trustworthy, and extroverted, while men look for attributes such as femininity and self-esteem [8]. Previous research has shown, however, that users struggle with the evaluation of experiential traits through profile pages [10], leading to uncertainty in online evaluations.

After viewing each other's profile page, two users can engage in private messaging. This is the second opportunity for online daters to evaluate each other for a face-to-face meeting. Previous research on Warranting Theory has shown that online daters engage in private messaging as an interactive uncertainty reduction strategy to seek cues that they hope will "warrant" or authenticate information found in profile pages [6, 12]. Yet despite their warranting efforts, users still find it difficult to validate experiential attributes through private messaging [38, 39, 40]. This previous research [38, 39, 40] has found that:

1. Private messaging is more important than profile pages for evaluating experiential attributes, and is a required step before meeting another user in-person.
2. Online daters often do not trust their evaluations of experiential attributes, which leads some to meet other users faster than they are comfortable with.
3. Online daters usually find their impressions of experiential attributes to be incorrect once they meet the respective user in person.

This research shows that online daters struggle to evaluate experiential attributes through private messaging. However, it does not explain why private messaging fails to satisfy users' evaluation needs because such research focused on how users attempt to self-present and evaluate instead of how private messaging facilitates those attempts.

Evaluation in Multiplayer Online Games

Multiplayer Online Games (MOGs) – as a form of online communities – are the second most popular way married couples have met online in the past decade [15]. MOGs are computer games through which multiple geographically distributed users can engage and interact with one another in real time over the Internet [25], making them inherently social environments. The design of many of these games encourages players to work together or collaborate in teams – often called clans, tribes, or guilds – in order to progress through the game [28]. MOG players typically interact with one another using in-game multimodal communication channels such as voice chat, instant messaging, and in-game email. Research suggests that MOGs "have evolved into places for people to meet up, find romantic partners and maintain relationships" because of their collaboration and communication capabilities [20].

Several studies have investigated romantic intimacy in MOGs such as *World of Warcraft* and *MapleStory* [20, 24]. These studies depict MOGs as collaborative virtual environments where a player's actual self (versus their ideal self) naturally comes out through collaboration, coordination, and teamwork.

Collaboration in MOGs is often task-driven and functional at first [35], with players evaluating each other's potential utility: skills, weapons, and general advantages that a player could offer to increase chances of success in the game. Romantic intimacy is usually not a pre-existing goal for players.

However, task-driven collaboration can evolve into romance-driven collaboration in MOGs [20, 24, 37]. Task-driven collaboration can spark romantic attraction between players by developing trust and interdependence, and elucidating the ability to work together as a team [24, 36]. In many of these game environments players can explore any budding romantic feelings through in-game, non-competitive collaborative activities like having a picnic in a castle or building a virtual garden together [24, 37]. Continued participation in competitive and non-competitive collaborative activities can foster genuine emotional bonds between partners that often escalate outside the game and turn into face-to-face romantic relationships [20, 24, 37].

RESEARCH QUESTIONS

The overarching research questions for this paper are:

1. Why does private messaging fail to meet the evaluation needs of online daters?
2. How do MOG players evaluate the experiential attributes of their potential romantic partners online?
3. Can evaluation methods in MOGs be adapted to improve evaluations in online dating systems, and if so, how?

STUDY 1: EVALUATION BEHAVIOR IN ONLINE DATING

We conducted a semi-structured interview study with 41 users (20 male, 20 female) of a popular, free online dating system in the United States. The objective of this study was to understand how online daters attempt to evaluate and self-present experiential attributes within such systems. We searched for interview participants using the online dating system's search feature based on a combination of location (within 25 miles of the lead researcher's university), gender, and ethnicity. The online dating system had eight different ethnicity choices that users could identify with, which yielded 16 different combinations of search criteria (2 genders x 8 ethnicities).

We created a profile page on the system on which our research intent was clearly indicated, and sent a private message with an interview invitation to the top six profiles returned for each ethnicity/gender search combination every week for eight weeks. This led to 96 users (48 male, 48 female) being messaged each week, resulting in 864 unique users being private messaged with an interview invitation. Of these requests, 41 resulted in an interview. Twenty-eight interviews were conducted in-person at places such as coffee shops and restaurants, while 13 were conducted online using Skype video chat for logistical reasons. Participants mostly self-identified as heterosexual, with seven identifying themselves as gay or bisexual. Our participants were aged 19-37.

The interviews ranged from 22 to 72 minutes in length. All interviews were voice recorded and summarized in writing within 24 hours by the first author, who was also the interviewer for this study. A grounded theory approach [13] was used by the first author to code the interview data and identify emergent themes and concepts. The interview codebook underwent three iterations to reflect emergent themes from our open coding process. This research yielded three publications [38, 39, 40], showing that online daters struggle to evaluate experiential attributes through private messaging. However, these publications do not explain why private messaging does not satisfy users' evaluation needs. For this paper, we re-coded our interview data around concepts pertaining to private messaging as an evaluation tool. In this section we present new insights based on this re-coding to explain why private messaging is a deficient evaluation tool. Our findings are presented with interview quotes that illustrate themes identified during the re-coding process. Pseudonyms are used instead of participants' real names for the sake of their privacy.

1. Users distrust evaluations based on information explicitly provided by a potential partner

Private messaging allows participants to ask specific questions to potential partners for evaluation purposes. However, potential partners can consciously weigh their answers to these questions and give answers that they think will positively influence a user's evaluation of them. This made the participants unsure whether their private messaging partners were trying to have a genuine conversation or were merely saying things that they thought would make them appear more attractive.

Amanda, 19: *"Most of these guys [that I exchange private messages with], I'm wary of their intentions. I think they just want sexual favors."*

Janet, 23: *"Some guys try too hard to be funny. They end up just coming off as creepy."*

Most participants, especially men, reported that they did use private messaging to emphasize experiential qualities they thought were attractive, but they did not want to lie. Yet the ability to consciously engineer one's self-presentation through private messaging always made intentional deception plausible. As such, when participants discovered that they had misinterpreted experiential attributes about a partner, many assumed the misinterpretation was due to intentional deception.

Pamela, 23: *"Then you meet them and you find out they lied because they're not like you were expecting."*

Participants had little choice but to base their evaluations of experiential traits on information that a potential partner explicitly provided. They were unable to develop ways to consistently validate experiential attributes because no available information was immune to deception. This negatively affected the confidence they had in their evaluations.

Linda, 21: *"I'm not too confident [about my online evaluations]. A person online, you never know how they really are."*

2. Private messaging provides no opportunity for deception-free observation

The primary purpose of a private messaging conversation for our participants was either to evaluate a potential partner for an in-person meeting or to self-present in a way that would make a potential partner want to meet in-person. This made private messaging conversations feel awkward and inorganic because they were not natural conversations, per se, but rather thinly veiled attempts at evaluation and self-presentation. As a result, participants struggled to feel "*chemistry*" or romantic compatibility with a potential partner before meeting in-person.

Madhan, 25: *"I wouldn't even call it a 'conversation' anymore. My [private messaging] routine has become so specific. First, I'll start with a generic 'copy & paste' message that has gotten responses for me in the past. Then I'll include something personal about the girl to show that I've read her profile."*

Yvette, 30: *"[Before meeting in-person] I really have to vibe with you. That's by having a natural conversation, but it doesn't happen a lot."*

Several participants remarked how the online dating evaluation process is distinctively different from how they evaluate potential partners offline. In physical world settings – such as nightclubs, bars, and parties – evaluation of a potential romantic partner is never the primary or explicit activity. Evaluation of potential partners takes a secondary role to dancing, drinking, or socializing with friends – activities that enable people to plausibly deny that romantic evaluation is the purpose of their interactions. These activities provide an opportunity for deception-free evaluation through the observation of a potential partner without having to directly question and overtly evaluate them. Some participants explained that they feel overwhelmed by these physical world environments where music can be too loud and attention spans can be short. These participants believed online dating was an environment more conducive to expressing their personalities.

Ian, 37: *"I like fuller and deeper [private] messages. I don't want the interaction to feel like in a bar. My personality doesn't work well there."*

However, private messaging is a communication tool that makes self-presentation and evaluation too explicit in online dating systems. Because there are no additional activities or tasks to distract them from the pressures of overt romantic evaluation, male participants were less inclined to have a real conversation – in which personality traits may reveal themselves naturally – and more inclined to send premeditated private messages as a form of personalized advertisement of experiential traits. (Female interviewees were less likely to advertise themselves like this because they tended to receive many more messages than men.)

Edward, 24: *"Sure, I'll re-use messages that have worked in the past. I bring up Obama and politics a lot because it makes me look smart."*

This is not to say that people are completely truthful in offline dating or that daters in the physical world lie less than online daters. Rather, this finding emphasizes that offline social environments and private messaging differ substantially as evaluation methods. Bars, clubs, and parties offer a myriad of distractions that make evaluation of potential romantic partners less overt and thus less susceptible to manipulation. However, these distractions can overwhelm some people and stifle their willingness to express themselves. Private messaging, in contrast, alleviates the distractions that can feel overwhelming, but makes evaluation the primary focus and affords no opportunities for deception-free observation or information that users believe was not manipulated by the potential partner. There is currently no evaluation tool in online dating systems that can provide experiential attribute information that cannot be manipulated to engineer an intended impression.

3. Information richness does not improve evaluations

Private messaging relies on text alone to communicate. Text has been claimed to be a relatively impoverished medium, in that social cues such as facial expressions and tone of voice are lacking [5]. It is temping to conclude that the deficiencies of private messaging can be solved with more information-rich tools such as voice and video chat. Four of our participants mentioned that they require phone calls and/or Skype video chats before meeting a potential partner in-person as a way to acquire non-verbal cues that are lost through private messaging. However, a majority of our participants indicated reluctance to use voice and video chat because such tools invade their privacy and create awkward situations (such as awkward silences during conversations, or wearing pajamas during a video chat). Text messaging was the typical mode of communication after exchanging phone numbers.

Courtney, 27: *"We'll exchange [phone] numbers to arrange a date, but I'll only use text messaging. A phone call is just weird. Once I start talking I can go on and on and on. It's embarrassing."*

Marissa, 19: *"There's no way I'd do a video chat. I don't want them to see what I'm doing!"*

Furthermore, the few participants who engaged in communication through richer channels before meeting still found most of their evaluations to be inaccurate once validated in-person.

Jeremy, 30: *"I require three in-depth phone calls before meeting in-person. [...] But still, they're not exactly the person you were expecting."*

Limitations

Several limitations of this study should be noted. Most online daters are in their mid-20s to mid-40s [27], but our participants were mostly in their 20s and early 30s, meaning that older online daters were not represented in our sample. Furthermore, all participants were located in or near a large east coast city. Our findings may not be representative of online daters in other geographic areas. Moreover, an interview study alone is not sufficient to verify the validity of participants' responses, or to track how participants' thoughts and behavior change over time.

STUDY 2: EVALUATION BEHAVIOR IN MOGS

We conducted a semi-structured interview study with 35 players (25 female, 10 male) of the MOG *Audition*, which attracts more than 300 million players worldwide [26]. This is our first publication for this interview study. *Audition* is a non-violent dancing game in which players can pair up with a partner with an opposite sex avatar to perform "dance battles" against other player pairs by synchronizing their keyboard strokes. For example, during a dance battle (Figure 1), couples press the arrow keys and spacebar on their keyboards in accordance with arrows on the screen, which are synchronized to the rhythm of a song being played. The greater accuracy and coordination they exhibit in pressing the right keys with their partner, the higher their scores. Players find available dance partners in virtual "dance rooms" irrespective of their offline location, meaning partners are usually geographically dispersed and rarely know each other beforehand.

Romance is taken literally in *Audition* through an in-game marriage system. Two opposite sex avatars can formalize a long-term collaboration by getting "married" in the game. In-game "marriage" between same-sex avatars is not allowed, however some homosexual players use cross-gender play (e.g., a biologically male player creates a female avatar) as a way to circumvent this restriction. In-game marriage is a significant achievement in *Audition*, requiring prolonged collaboration to practice for and complete a "wedding party" dance task. Because it costs real money (at least $5.60) for the opportunity to complete this dance task, players often coordinate their real-world schedules so they can meet in the game and practice dancing together in preparation for this task.

Completion of this dance task is signified with traditional marriage artifacts such as a wedding party, a love license, and a virtual wedding ring (Figure 2). After a couple gets married in-game they can continue participating in dance battles together to achieve higher couple levels and amass more aesthetically pleasing virtual rings. Sometimes collaboration between dance partners extends beyond the game's dance theme and can cross the boundary between the game world and out-game worlds [37]. For example, a couple can build and decorate a virtual garden together in the "couple farm." Couples can also design matching clothes, poses, and accessories for their avatars in the "photo studio," another in-game location. Outside the game, couples usually collaborate to compose love stories and post them to online message boards, or work together to design their message board signature. These various collaborative activities (in-battle and out-battle, in-game and out-game) provide opportunities for evaluating multi-faceted experiential attributes.

Figure 2: A couple dance battle in *Audition*

Audition was chosen for this study for two reasons. First, collaboration in *Audition* is done only in pairs. Because research concerning MOGs has investigated collaboration primarily in groups (e.g., a *World of Warcraft* dungeon raid with as many as 40 teammates), little information is available regarding the dynamics of collaboration in pairs, such as in-game marriage partners, in MOGs. Second, in-game marriage is becoming popular in the MOG domain, but *Audition* is one of the only MOGs in which marriage is tied directly to progress or achievements in the game. *World of Warcraft* – the focal point of most intimacy-related MOG research – does not have an official marriage system, instead letting players role-play weddings independent of their progress through the game. *Audition* is one of the only MOGs to make marriage an actual achievement in the game, allowing it to seamlessly meld collaboration for utility and collaboration for virtual intimacy.

Figure 3: A wedding party (left), and a love license with ring (right) in *Audition*

We recruited our participants by posting a message on the two largest English-language message boards for *Audition* (forums.redbana.com and forums.jordantrudgett.com), inviting all players who had used the in-game marriage system to an interview. The interviews investigated players' motivations for getting "married" in *Audition* and the dynamics of their relationships with in-game marriage partners. Central questions during the interviews included "What does your *Audition* marriage mean to you?" and "How did collaboration influence your in-game marriage(s)?" We did not provide definitions of "marriage" or "collaboration" so as to encourage participants to narrate the meaning of *Audition* marriage in their own words. Several participants were in romantically intimate relationships with their in-game marriage partner, but this relationship status was not explicitly sought out in the recruitment process.

We interviewed all *Audition* players who responded to the message board posts within a month of their response to our invitation (N=35). Before being interviewed, all participants emailed us their informed consent. Semi-structured interviews were then conducted via text chat in Skype (which our participants preferred over voice or video chat). Forty-nine percent of all participants (N=17) had played *Audition* for 6 to 8 years, 46% (N=16) had played for 3 to 5 years, while 6% (N=2) had played for less than 2 years. On average, participants had married in *Audition* six times in five years. Thirty-one percent of all participants (N=11) had married 1 to 3 times, 52% (N=18) had married for 4 to 8 times, while 17% (N=6) had married more than 8 times. Of the 35 participants, 83% (N=29) self-identified as being in or having been in at least one "romantic relationship" with someone they met in *Audition*, but 18 of those had not met their partner in-person. Thus 11 out of those 29 satisfied our definition of a romantically intimate relationship, in that they had met their romantic partner face-to-face. Sixteen participants were aged 14-17 (46%), and 19 were aged 18-22 (54%). This age distribution is consistent with the general age distribution of *Audition* players, according to the age data that Redbana.com shared with us via an email request. Five participants self-identified as homosexual or bisexual. A majority of participants (N=31) were located in North America (U.S. and Canada).

A grounded theory approach was used for the qualitative analysis of the Skype interview chat logs [13]. Our findings from these interviews consisted of three main themes, which are illustrated below with representative quotes from the participants. The three themes explain how *Audition* players evaluate the experiential attributes of their potential romantic partners online via collaborative activities. Pseudonyms are used instead of participants' real names for the sake of their privacy.

1. Romance was not explicitly sought

Most participants reported that they did not have a pre-existing intention to meet a romantic partner through the game. Instead, romantic feelings for people they had met through *Audition* just "*came naturally*" (Samantha, 20) from spending time doing collaborative activities together in the game.

Rebecca, 19: *"We kind of just started off as a mutual goal for having the pretty rings and having the max ring [part of the level-up system in* Audition*]. Then we ended up talking a lot and flirting and it just sort of...happened."*

Matt, 19: *"I've never sought romance through playing this game. I just meet people then wind up liking them, and if they like me back a relationship starts."*

Even though the design of *Audition* is embedded with intimacy-related concepts like marriage, players had relatively little intention to construct a deliberate self-presentation in order to appear more romantically attractive. Because our participants used *Audition* just to have a fun, collaborative gaming experience, they had little motivation to present an "ideal" self. This allowed romantic compatibility between players to reveal itself naturally.

Cathy, 19: *"I don't use the game marriage to seek romance, the only reason I dated my [Audition partner] is because I was very close to him and I liked him as a real person."*

2. Collaborative activities let player pairs experience potential romantic compatibility

Our *Audition* players experienced a potential partner's personality traits via collaborative activities (e.g., dance battles) without having to consciously probe for experiential attribute information.

Tyler, 16: *"I believe what happens, happens. An in-game relationship should be like a real life one. You start out, get to know each other, dance together, solve problems together, fight, negotiate, and maybe fall in love. The coupling system allows you to learn about your partner."*

Emma, 19: *"[In-game marriage] is kind like online dating except more fun because you are in a game and there is actually stuff to do. It is like online dating but if you have nothing to do you can go on the game and be like let's dance together."*

Most of our participants did not consciously realize that they had been evaluating their dance partner as a potential romantic partner until romantic feelings had already formed. They enjoyed the act of collaboration through dance battles, and used such collaboration as an implicit way to "*learn about*," or evaluate, their dance battle partner as a potential romantic partner.

However, some participants did consciously recognize the value of collaborative activities for developing romantic relationships. In-game dance battles, especially, served as a venue for developing trust and revealing emotional compatibility.

Andrew, 19: *"I like to know my [in-game marriage partner] more, even if it was through a game. It is like giving trust and that bond can grow to becoming friends or lovers. Collaborating would make it easier for a couple to be closer or chill down."*

Samantha, 20: *"Whenever I marry in Audition I would try to get to know them and spend more time doing things together, even though it is not as serious as real life marriage. Maybe that's why I usually develop feelings toward my [in-game marriage partners], and why I usually trust them."*

3. Collaborative activities alone do not complete the evaluation process

In-game collaboration alone did not escalate *Audition* partnerships to romantically intimate relationships. Most participants employed external communication methods to interact with their *Audition* partners during and outside of game play. These methods ranged in information richness from instant/text messaging, to phone calls, to video chat.

Anna, 17: *"Well, we play in game together. But we're usually Skyping at the same time. I mean we can watch movies on Netflix together [too]."*

Many participants were not adverse to, and indeed preferred, richer communication modes like video chat after they had developed a sense of familiarity and closeness with their partner through in-game collaboration. Since *Audition* players are usually geographically dispersed, meeting in-person was sometimes impossible. Video chats were perceived as the best alternative in these cases.

Anna, 17: *"It's not ideal that you can't be together in person but you make the most out of what you have. I videochat a lot with my [partner], and use Whatsapp to text him. Sometimes, I do use Facebook to contact him too."*

Michelle, 16: *"On birthdays we would Skype chat with voice and video chat since we live far away from each other. It's important to talk to each other on those days. We did the same for Christmas, anniversaries, etc."*

Participants recounted using these external communication methods to maintain and strengthen their emotional bonds when they could not be together in person. They no longer viewed their partners as mere in-game collaborators, but as romantic partners – often before ever meeting face-to-face.

Chris, 21: *"On special occasions we try to make it a day where it's just us and we spend time and talk to only each other on Skype. So that we can focus all our attention into making the special day that much more."*

Cathy, 19: *"We talk on Skype about how our days have gone. [...] We make it a point to catch up and inform each other how everything in our lives are going."*

Limitations

Three limitations of this study should be noted. We studied only one MOG, *Audition*, and our findings may not generalize to other MOGs. *Audition* players are mostly in their teens and early 20s. The way these players view and define "romance" may differ significantly from older adults. As with study 1, follow-up research is needed to verify the validity of the participants' responses and to track if and how participants' thoughts change over time, especially for participants who were still transitioning from adolescence into adulthood. In addition, all participants were volunteers recruited from online forums. Thus, there is a potential bias in a self-selected convenience sample.

DISCUSSION OF STUDY FINDINGS

Study 1 brought to light two main limitations of private messaging as an online dating system evaluation tool. First, online daters base their evaluations during private messaging largely on information consciously provided by their messaging partner, which limits the information's "warranting value" [6, 12] and makes online daters wary of deception. As a result, online daters do not believe they can authenticate experiential attributes without an in-person meeting. Second, as the evaluation process for romantic intimacy is explicit, private message exchanges often become thinly veiled attempts at self-presentation and evaluation with little opportunity for deception-immune information to be conveyed. This makes it difficult for real personalities and romantic compatibility to be elucidated. Study 2, in contrast, revealed that *Audition* players form romantically intimate relationships with each other because collaborative activities within the game allow them to experience each other's personalities implicitly without the interference of conscious self-presentation attempts.

These results are understandable considering that romantic attraction is not predicated solely on demographic or definable attributes. External factors – the context in which two potential partners initially interact – also influence resultant attraction [1, 21]. Collaborative activities provide such contexts, and their merits for facilitating romantic attraction are supported not just by MOGs, but by encounters in the physical world. For example, Lewandowski and Aron [21] found that participation in an arousing activity with a stranger in a gym setting – such as running together with ankle weights on – significantly increased romantic attraction for the activity partner. Participating in challenging or "exciting" tasks – like physically intensive games – together with a stranger also increased romantic attraction [21].

Admittedly, the motivations of online daters differ from those of MOG players. Because MOG players are not looking for romance, they have relatively little motivation to deceive or otherwise attempt to manipulate their self-presentation. Yet the abovementioned studies, along with the findings reported in this paper, indicate that evaluation of potential romantic partners is influenced by the context or activities occurring during interactions, not just by the personalities of the potential partners. These observations suggest that online collaborative activities could be a promising introductory context for facilitating romantic attraction in online dating.

DESIGN CONCEPTS

In this section we consider how collaborative activities could be implemented as a supplemental evaluation tool for online daters. Such collaborative activities would not replace the traditional evaluation methods of profile pages and private messaging, but would serve as an additional tool for evaluation. Based on the relevant MOG literature and our second study, we identify what we call *paired collaborative activities*, or activities designed for collaboration between two potential romantic partners. A paired collaborative activity is a *shared experience* between two users (the users do it together); it involves a *common goal* (the two users are working with each other towards the same achievement, not against each other); and it requires *reciprocity* (the two users need to work together to achieve mutual success).

Paired collaborative activities as a private messaging supplement

Paired collaborative activities could be added to online dating systems as a complement to private messaging. This would allow online daters to experience tacit experiential attributes through a paired collaborative activity and then use them to guide conversations through private messaging. Conversely, paired collaborative activities could be used to validate evaluations of experiential attributes gathered through private messaging. Such activities would not necessarily be complex gaming environments like MOGs, but rather activities that are readily understood by all users.

One of the ways this could be implemented is through a drawing game akin to *Pictionary*. One partner would be given a secret word by the system that they have to draw. The other partner would then have to guess the secret word based on the drawing within a limited amount of time. For example, while collaborating in a *Pictionary*-like game Sally finds Bill's drawing of George Washington to be funny and clever because he drew the Washington Monument with George Washington's face on it. She experiences Bill's sense of humor through the paired collaborative activity, and then uses his drawing to spark a private messaging conversation about traveling ("ha ha the Washington Monument! Have you ever been to Washington D.C.?").

Paired collaborative activities with explicit incentives

MOG players are often motivated to work together to achieve specific goals or rewards [24], such as virtual rings in *Audition* and skill levels in *World of Warcraft*. These rewards are explicit incentives for collaborating. Explicit incentives could be used in online dating systems to distract from overt evaluation motives that often spur online daters to act unnaturally in an attempt to consciously engineer the way they are evaluated.

Research into Warranting Theory posits that "the less information is perceived to be controllable by the person to whom it refers, the more weight it will carry in shaping impressions" [6]. Information gathered through paired collaborative activities about a potential partner's experiential attributes is relatively uncontrollable compared to information gathered through private messaging. Explicit incentives would serve to encourage initial and prolonged participation in paired collaborative activities, which would be helpful to users who want to authenticate experiential attribute evaluations through extended participation in the activity. These incentives could come in the form of unlocked system features or physical world activities.

Online dating systems often use a "freemium" business model, meaning users have access to the system's core functions for free, but must pay a one-time or monthly fee to access additional features. *OkCupid*, for example, requires users to pay a monthly fee in order to view time stamps of when their private messages were read and to see which users found their profile page attractive. Under this design concept, such features could be unlocked through prolonged participation in a paired collaborative activity with the same partner. Users would thus have a plausible motivation to engage in a paired collaborative activity aside from overt evaluation.

Instead of (or in addition to) unlocked system features, designers could use physical world activities to incentivize prolonged participation in a paired collaborative activity and alleviate an awkward transition from private messaging to an in-person meeting. For example, prolonged participation in a paired collaborative activity with a partner could yield coupons for coffee shops or restaurants that the users can only redeem if they go together. This would extend collaboration to physical world settings in a seamless fashion that would help avoid the awkwardness that can ensue when online daters try to escalate their communication off the system [38, 39, 40]. Online daters would no longer have to risk rejection when trying to escalate to an in-person meeting because the system would be broaching the date idea, not the user.

Romance-driven MOGs

Currently romance is not a pre-existing goal or motivation for playing MOGs, yet our second study shows that players often develop romantic feelings for their collaboration partners nonetheless. This design concept for romance-driven MOGS would entail MOGs promoting romance as an explicit goal for playing the game. As demonstrated by

Frost [10], online daters typically do not enjoy their time in online dating systems and their only motivation for participation is the expectant reward of a romantic relationship in the physical world. MOGs, however, are built for enjoyment and fun. Introducing romance as a primary goal for participating in innately fun and enjoyable MOGs would encourage daters to spend more time in the game/system evaluating partners and letting those partners evaluate them, therefore lessening the chances of inaccurate evaluations once two daters meet in person.

MOGs enable people in geographically dispersed locations to collaborate together in-game, but they do not necessarily let players choose their collaborators based on geographic proximity. MOG players are often logistically unable to meet romantic partners they encounter through these games because they live far away from one another. A romance-driven MOG could better facilitate in-person meetings by emphasizing or suggesting in-game partners who are geographically nearby, similar to how the mobile dating app *Tinder* suggests potential partners based on spatial proximity (e.g., "6 miles away").

Romance-driven MOGs could also encourage in-person meetings by making them a paired collaborative activity. This could be facilitated through augmented reality [9] – an approach popularized by many iPhone and Android games in which the physical world and virtual world are melded into a cohesive gaming experience. For example, in the iPhone game *Zombies Everywhere!*, players use their smart phone's camera to see virtual zombies transposed into the physical world that they must defeat using virtual weapons. Some of these games also encourage collaboration between players in-person, such as *Find the Future,* which encourages library-goers to collaborate to find specific books in the New York Public Library.

A romance-driven MOG could use augmented reality to facilitate paired collaborative activities in the physical world. For example, potential romantic partners could go on a scavenger hunt together in which they use their smart phone's camera to see rare in-game items hidden in various physical world locations. Once an item is discovered, players can take a picture together at the location to confirm that they found the item.

CONCLUSION

Online dating systems are a leading tool for satisfying the need for romantic intimacy through technology [15], and they continue to grow in popularity as the social stigma surrounding their use has all but dissipated [27]. However, our first study showed several reasons why current system components like private messaging fail to satisfy users' evaluation needs. In contrast, our second study found that multiplayer online games (MOGs) facilitate meaningful personality trait evaluation because their collaborative activities serve as a prime mechanism for experiencing in-game partners without interference from conscious self-presentations. These collaborative experiences sometimes trigger romantic attraction between players, which can culminate in romantically intimate relationships in the physical world.

Inspired by our findings, we presented and discussed a series of design concepts for incorporating paired collaborative activities into online dating systems as novel evaluation tools. Our future work will involve implementing and testing how these design concepts influence evaluations and romantic attraction between online daters. Specifically, we are interested to see how overt romantic motivations affect use of collaborative activities, and what utility collaborative activities can provide online daters who have no prior experience with online games.

REFERENCES

1. Aron, A., Norman, C. C., Aron, E. N., McKenna, C., & Heyman, R. E. (2000). Couples' shared participation in novel and arousing activities and experienced relationship quality. In *Journal of Personality and Social Psychology*, 78 (2), 273-284.
2. Bardzell, J., Nichols, J., Pace, T., & Bardzell, S. (2012). Come meet me at Ulduar: progression raiding in World of Warcraft. In *Proc. CSCW 2012*. New York: ACM, 603-612.
3. Choi, B., Lee, I., Choi, D., & Kim, J. (2007). Collaborate and share: An experimental study of the effects of task and reward interdependencies in online games. *Cyber Psychology & Behavior*, *10*(4), 591-595.
4. Couch, D., & Liamputtong, P. (2008). Online dating and mating: The use of the internet to meet sexual partners *Qualitative Health Research*, *18*(2), 268-279.
5. Daft, R. L., & Lengel, R. H. (1983). Information richness. A new approach to managerial behavior and organization design (No. TR-ONR-DG-02). Texas A & M University Department of Management.
6. DeAndrea, D. C. (2014). Advancing Warranting Theory. *Communication Theory*, *24*(2), 186-204.
7. Ellison, N. B., Hancock, J. T., & Toma, C. L. (2012). Profile as promise: A framework for conceptualizing veracity in online dating self-presentations. *New Media & Society*, *14*(1), 45-62.
8. Fiore, A. T., Taylor, L. S., Mendelsohn, G. A., & Hearst, M. (2008). Assessing attractiveness in online dating profiles. In *Proc. CHI2008*. New York: ACM, 797-806.
9. Flintham, M., Benford, S., Anastasi, R., Hemmings, T., Crabtree, A., Greenhalgh, C., Tandavanitj, N., Adams, M., & Row-Farr, J. (2003). Where on-line meets on the streets: Experiences with mobile mixed reality games. In *Proc. CHI2003*. New York: ACM, 569-576.
10. Frost, J. H., Chance, Z., Norton, M. I., & Ariely, D., (2008). People are experience goods: Improving online

dating with virtual dates. *Journal of Interactive Marketing, 22*(1), 51-61.

11. Gibbs, J. L., Ellison, N. B., & Heino, R. D. (2006). Self-presentation in online personals the role of anticipated future interaction, self-disclosure, and perceived success in Internet dating. *Communication Research*, *33*(2), 152-177.
12. Gibbs, J. L., Ellison, N. B., & Lai, C. H. (2011). First comes love, then comes Google: An investigation of uncertainty reduction strategies and self-disclosure in online dating. *Communication Research*, *38*(1), 70-100.
13. Glaser, B., & Strauss, A. (1967). *The discovery of grounded theory: Strategies for qualitative research.* Aldine Transaction.
14. Guadagno, R. E., Okdie, B. M., & Kruse, S. A. (2012). Dating deception: Gender, online dating, and exaggerated self-presentation. *Computers in Human Behavior, 28*(2), 642-647.
15. Hall, J. A. (2014). First comes social networking, then comes marriage? Characteristics of Americans married 2005–2012 who met through social networking sites. *Cyberpsychology, Behavior, and Social Networking*, *17*(5), 322-326.
16. Hancock, J. T., Toma, C., & Ellison, N. (2007). The truth about lying in online dating profiles. In *Proc. CHI2007*. New York: ACM, 449-452.
17. Hassenzahl, M., Heidecker, S., Eckoldt, K., Diefenbach, S., & Hillmann, U. (2012). All you need is love: Current strategies of mediating intimate relationships through technology. *ACM Transactions on Computer-Human Interaction (TOCHI)*, *19*(4), article 30.
18. Heino, R. D., Ellison, N. B., & Gibbs, J. L. (2010). Relationshopping: Investigating the market metaphor in online dating. *Journal of Social and Personal Relationships, 27*(4), 427-447.
19. Hitsch, G. J., Hortaçsu, A., & Ariely, D. (2010). What makes you click? Mate preferences in online dating. *Quantitative Marketing and Economics*, *8*(4), 393-427.
20. Huynh, K. P., Lim, S. W., & Skoric, M. M. (2013). Stepping out of the magic circle: Regulation of play/life boundary in MMO-mediated romantic relationship. *Journal of Computer-Mediated Communication*, *18*(3), 251–264.
21. Lewandowski, G. W., & Aron, A. P. (2004). Distinguishing arousal from novelty and challenge in initial romantic attraction between strangers. In *Social Behavior and Personality: an international journal*, 32(4), 361-372.
22. Maslow, A. H. (1970). *Motivation and personality*. New York: Harper & Row.
23. Moss, B. F., & Schwebel, A. I. (1993). Defining intimacy in romantic relationships. *Family relations*, 31-37.
24. Pace, T., Bardzell, S., & Bardzell, J. (2010). The rogue in the lovely black dress: Intimacy in World of Warcraft. In *Proc. CHI 2010*. New York: ACM, 233-242.
25. Papargyris, A., & Poulymenakou, A. (2005). Learning to fly in persistent digital worlds: The case of massively multiplayer online role playing games. *ACM SIGGROUP Bulletin*, *25*(1), 41-49.
26. Redbana. Retrieved July 21, 2014. http://www.redbana.com/Pop/AboutRedbana.aspx
27. Smith, A., & Duggan, M. (October 21, 2013). Online Dating and Relationships. Retrieved February 12, 2014. http://www.pewinternet.org/2013/10/21/main-report/.
28. Sotamaa, O. (2005). Creative user-centered design practices: Lessons from game cultures. In L. Haddon, E. Mante, B. Sapio, K. H. Kommonen, L. Fortunati, & A. Kant (Eds.), *Everyday Innovators: Researching the role of users in shaping ICTs* (pp.104–116). Dordrecht, Netherlands: Springer.
29. Toma, C. L., & Hancock, J. T. (2010). Looks and lies: The role of physical attractiveness in online dating self-presentation and deception. *Communication Research*, *37*(3), 335-351.
30. Toma, C. L., Hancock, J. T., & Ellison, N. B. (2008). Separating fact from fiction: An examination of deceptive self-presentation in online dating profiles. *Personality and Social Psychology Bulletin*, *34*(8), 1023-1036.
31. Williams, D., Ducheneaut, N., Xiong, L., Zhang, Y., Yee, N., & Nickell, E. (2006). From tree house to barracks: The social life of guilds in World of Warcraft. *Games and Culture*, *1*(4), 338-361.
32. Whitty, M. T. (2008). Revealing the 'real'me, searching for the 'actual' you: Presentations of self on an internet dating site. *Computers in Human Behavior, 24*(4), 1707-1723.
33. Wu, W., Fore, S., Wang, X., & Ho, P. S. Y. (2007). Beyond virtual carnival and masquerade in-game marriage on the Chinese Internet. *Games and Culture*, *2*(1), 59-89.
34. Yancey, G., & Emerson, M. O. (2014). Does height matter? An examination of height preferences in romantic coupling. *Journal of Family Issues.* Published online January 21, doi: 10.1177/0192513X13519256
35. Yee, N. (2006). The psychology of massively multi-user online role-playing games: Motivations, emotional investment, relationships and problematic usage. In R. Schroder, & A. S. Axelsson (Eds.), *Avatars at work and*

play: Collaboration and interaction in shared virtual environments (pp. 187-207). London: Springer-Verlag.

36. Zhang, G. (2014). Can you marry me?: Conceptualizing in-game marriage as intimacy-mediated collaboration. In *Proc. CSCW 2014*. New York: ACM, 273-276.

37. Zhang, G., & Herring, S. C. (2013). In-game marriage and computer-mediated collaboration: An exploratory study of *Audition*. In *Proc. IR14*.

38. Zytko, D., Grandhi S.A., & Jones, Q. (2014). Impression management and formation in online dating systems. In *Proc. ECIS 2014*. AIS.

39. Zytko, D., Grandhi, S.A., & Jones, Q. (In press). Impression management struggles in online dating. In *Proc. GROUP 2014*. New York: ACM.

40. Zytko, D., Grandhi, S. A., & Jones, Q. G. (2014). Impression management through communication in online dating. In *Proc. CSCW 2014*. New York: ACM, 277-280.

Games for Crowds: A Crowdsourcing Game Platform for the Enterprise

Ido Guy*
Yahoo Labs, Israel
idoguy@acm.org

Anat Hashavit
IBM Research – Haifa, Israel
anath@il.ibm.com

Yaniv Corem*
MIT Media Lab, USA
yaniv.corem@media.mit.edu

ABSTRACT

In this paper, we present a crowdsourcing game platform that allows users to play, create, and share simple games that harness the collective intelligence of employees within the enterprise. The platform uses the wizard design pattern to guide users through the process of creating a game. We describe the platform in detail and report our findings from deploying it within a large global organization for a period of three months, in which 34 games were created by 25 employees and played by 339. We combine qualitative and quantitative analysis to understand the characteristics of the different games and their impact on popularity and engagement, to validate our design goals, and to suggest potential enhancements.

Author Keywords

Crowdsourcing; Games; Human Computation

ACM Classification Keywords

H.5.3 Group and Organizational Interfaces: *Computer-supported cooperative work*

INTRODUCTION

Crowdsourcing has come a long way since the days of Sir Francis Galton, who tried to estimate the weight of an ox at a county fair by averaging the individual estimates of people in the crowd [26]. In fact, various applications of crowdsourcing in recent years have shown, not only that crowdsourcing is a viable problem-solving technique, but that for some tasks under certain conditions, it can outperform an individual expert or computer algorithm [31,32,34]. Crowdsourcing is the act of taking a job traditionally performed by a designated agent and outsourcing it to an undefined, generally large group of people, in the form of an open call [16,24]. Among some of the more prominent applications of crowdsourcing are image tagging [31], text digitization [34], and translation [4]. Despite its conceptual simplicity, crowdsourcing presents many intrinsic challenges that ultimately determine its success. These challenges include recruiting and retaining participants, quality assurance, task assignment, aggregation of results, and more.

The benefits of crowdsourcing have not escaped the attention of large companies as they search for ways to harness the collective intelligence of employees to drive business. Several attempts have been made to apply crowdsourcing techniques within the enterprise to enrich the social graph [15], locate assets [35], or recommend bookmarks [11]. Despite the relative success of these initial attempts, enterprise crowdsourcing is still in its infancy and often remains an untapped resource due to challenges such as the entry barrier and employee engagement in a workplace setting.

In this work, we introduce a crowdsourcing game platform called "Games for Crowds" (G4C) that allows users to play, create, and share simple games that harness the collective intelligence of employees within the enterprise. G4C addresses the challenges of enterprise crowdsourcing in several ways: (1) it packages the crowdsourcing task as a game, making it more fun and engaging for users; (2) it not only allows users to play, but also enables them to create simple crowdsourcing games; and (3) it builds a community around players and game creators, making users feel more involved in the crowdsourcing tasks.

Creating crowdsourcing games in a simple and intuitive manner is a key aspect of G4C. To achieve this, we extract the game's DNA – goals, logic, rules, feedback system, and entities – and then use a wizard design pattern to guide users through the process of creating it. The wizard helps the user provide a set of parameters that are essential for creating the game. It includes three parts: general information, such as the name and description of the game; the topics and questions, which form the game's content; and advanced settings, such as the order of questions and topics and the reward mechanism. These parameters are used by the wizard to initialize a game that is similar in its look-and-feel to the GuessWho game [15], which the user can access and share with others through the platform.

G4C was deployed in a large global IT organization for a period of three months. During this period, 34 different games were created by 25 different employees and played by a total of 339 employees, who contributed a total of 28,374 answers. Our evaluation is based on data collected from the G4C database logs, as well as on interviews of 12

*Part of the research was conducted while working at IBM Research.

CSCW 2015, March 14–18, 2015, Vancouver, BC, Canada.

http://dx.doi.org/10.1145/2675133.2675189

creators and 12 players who played at least 3 games. We review the different games and their characteristics to give a sense of what kind of games employees are creating. We also try to understand what factors contribute to the popularity of a game and its players' contribution. Finally, our analysis aims at validating the G4C design goals and understanding what has worked well and what can be improved.

RELATED WORK

Crowdsourcing Games

One of the major challenges in crowdsourcing is engagement, i.e., motivating individuals within the crowd to complete a task [5]. Games have already been used to make crowdsourcing tasks more fun and engaging. Luis von Ahn coined the term *Games With A Purpose* (GWAP) [30] to define a type of crowdsourcing game that is (a) fun and engaging, (b) includes a task that can only be completed by humans, and (c) has a goal that is hidden from the player. The first GWAP, the ESP game [31], matched two players against each other and presented them with a random image they were asked to label with as many tags as possible. Whenever players' tags corresponded, both players would receive points. Following the success of the ESP game, other GWAP were created such as Peekaboom [33], a game for locating objects in an image and Verbosity [32], a game used to collect commonsense knowledge. These GWAP and others were later collected to form a game portal where users could play, and in the process, complete tasks. Similarly, G4C includes a portal of crowdsourcing games. However, G4C games are created by users, often without past experience in game creation or crowdsourcing, making its portal a community hub for game creators and players.

Crowdsourcing Platforms

With the rise of crowdsourcing, corresponding platforms and markets have become popular [6,10]. Amazon's Mechanical Turk (MTurk) is an increasingly popular web service for paying people (Turkers), typically a few cents, to carry out simple tasks, known as Human Intelligence Tasks (HITs), that would otherwise be extremely difficult, if not impossible, for computers to perform [17,19]. MTurk has been largely successful for conducting user studies [17], speech-to-text transcription [13], clustering [23], and more. However, the use of monetization as an incentive has sometimes been shown to have a negative effect on the completion time and quality of work produced by Turkers [5,7]. Quadrant of Euphoria is a crowdsourcing platform meant to address the problems of inaccuracy and cost when trying to assess the experience of multimedia end-users. Workers can be recruited either by payment or by publishing to online communities [8]. InnoCentive is an open innovation platform that broadcasts research and development problems for anyone to solve, granting cash awards for thc bcst solutions that meet the criteria [3,18]. In contrast, G4C uses game mechanics, such as leader-boards, to incentivize users to play, and awards points as compensation for completing micro-tasks.

Crowdsourcing and Games in the Enterprise

The most comprehensive work on crowdsourcing within the enterprise is by Vukovic [35], who presented a sample scenario for enterprise crowdsourcing in the software development domain, in order to derive requirements and a research agenda for a general-purpose crowdsourcing service in the cloud. Among the identified challenges were the task request model, the matchmaking process, the bid evaluation, and the quality of experience measurement. The paper did not focus on games as the incentive mechanism. In his work about video games, Gee [14] argues that the use of game technologies for learning skills in workplaces will become pervasive. Mollick and Rothbard [21] examined whether managerially-initiated games at work can provide the desired benefits for affect and performance. They found that the answer depends on the notion of "consent" – the degree to which employees actively cooperate with management initiatives.

Another body of research focuses on brainstorming at large scale through crowds in order to collect and evaluate ideas. This is often referred to as "crowdstorming" or "ideastroming". The Dell IdeaStrorm website [9] was launched in 2007 to help Dell promote innovation by collecting and measuring ideas. Crowdsourcing in this case went beyond the scope of the enterprise, reaching out to the company's end user community. In their recently published book, Abrahamson et al. [2] argue that enterprise crowdstorming tools focused on gathering, assessing, and understanding ideas, may be more beneficial for organizations than "traditional" enterprise social media tools. While some of the games created using G4C focused on idea gathering, others had different goals, such as building knowledge bases, collecting resources, or educating.

A few studies focused on specific enterprise crowdsourcing games. The Dogear game [11] drove employees to create and share bookmarks within the enterprise, while the GuessWho game [15] collected social network information from employees. The G4C system builds on some of the elements included in GuessWho, as described later in this work.

Human-Centered Game Creation Tools

The culture of Web 2.0 has made a significant impact on the video game industry [2,14]. The e-Adventure3D platform [28] was among the first to facilitate the rapid creation of 3D adventure games without any programming background. The popular Minecraft game [12] introduced a block-based editing paradigm where players can create their own games using a collection of meter-square blocks, from tree leaves to floating clouds. In Sony's Little Big Planet [36], players create the levels of the game by using an extensive inventory of game objects, from building materials to physical behavior. Additionally, algorithms

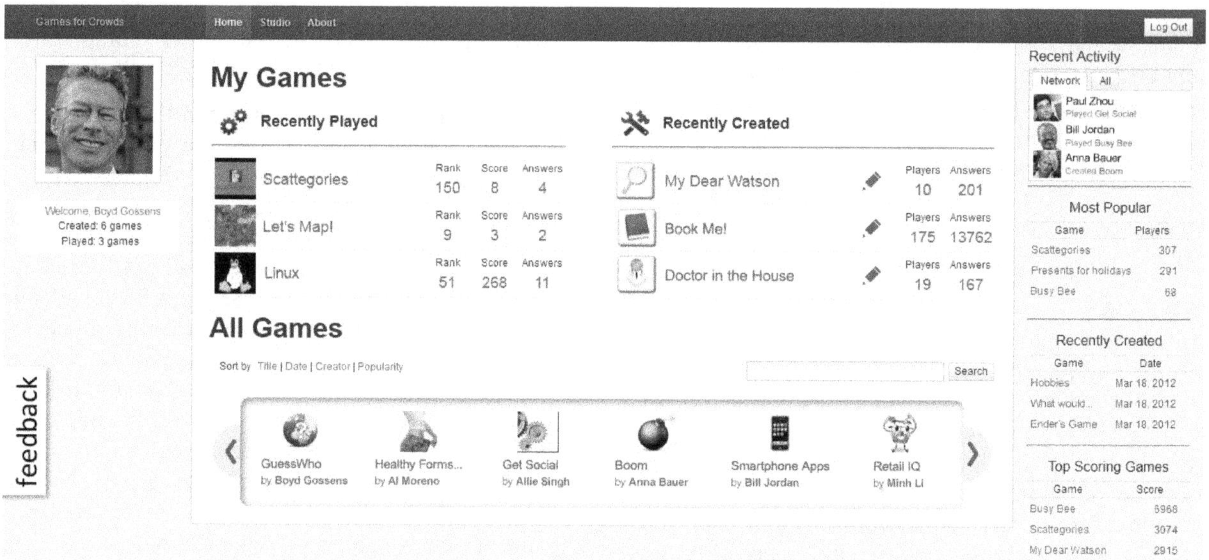

Figure 1. Personalized home screen.

have been widely used to automatically create levels in games [25]. Mehm et al. [20] provide an overview of state-of-the-art game authoring tools and suggest future directions, such as multiplayer authoring and automated model checking. These game authoring tools substantially lower the entry barrier, allowing novice authors without technical expertise to contribute. Analogously, G4C aims at lowering the entry barrier for creating human computation games, which unlike video games have the hidden agenda of collecting data from the crowd. Hence, more emphasis is put on the game's content and logic than on its UI. Game creators are provided with a predefined UI, in which they can control a limited set of parameters.

To the best of our knowledge, no other work provides a platform that brings together game authoring and crowdsourcing capabilities in the enterprise. We take a user-centered approach to crowdsourcing and extend the role of every individual from worker to "crowdsourcer", with the power to create crowdsourcing games in the workplace.

GAMES FOR CROWDS

Design Goals

G4C was designed to help users create games that leverage human computation, with the following goals in mind:

- Game lifecycle – provide users with a simple, intuitive, and fast way of creating and managing games
- Data and analytics – enable creators to collect game-generated data and analyze it to gain initial insight
- Engagement – create an entertaining and engaging user experience for players, to provide a crowd for creators
- Community – blur the lines between players and creators and allow them to work (and play) together.

The rest of this section describes G4C and its UI.

Home Screen

After logging in with their intranet ID and password, users are navigated to a personalized home screen (Figure 1), which includes three sections. The left sidebar displays the user's profile including a picture and the number of games played and created. The right sidebar displays four different widgets, which together provide a snapshot of game activity. The Recent Activity widget is a news feed that includes information organized into two tabs – Network and All – about users who recently created or played a game. The All feed includes any public activity from any G4C user, whereas the Network feed is limited to a user's social network (taken from the enterprise social network service). Under the Most Popular widget, users find the three most popular games by the total number of players in the last month. Similarly, the Recently Created widget provides the three games most recently created. Finally, the Top Scoring Games widget displays the three games with the overall top scoring player per game.

The home screen's central section shows the user's three most recently played games and three most recently created games. If no games have been played or created, a message is displayed to the user, prompting him to play or create games. The bottom part contains a library of all games created by the different users. Users can manually browse the library by horizontally scrolling through it; sort the library's games by title, date, creator, or popularity; and search for games using a free-text string.

Studio

G4C provides a studio for users who want to create a game. The left and right sidebars in the studio remain the same as in the home screen, displaying the profile information and gaming activity, respectively. The studio's middle section is shown in Figure 2. It allows the user to type a name and create a new game using the New Game wizard. It also displays all games created by the user and allows to toggle a game online or offline, delete a

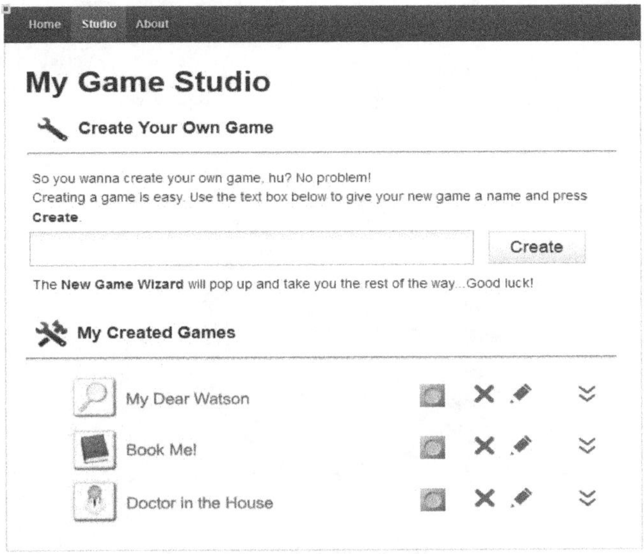

Figure 2. Studio screen.

game, edit game details, and view the game's statistics by clicking on the arrow at the end of each row.

New Game Wizard

The following section describes the process of creating a new game using the New Game wizard. One of our design goals was to provide users with a simple, intuitive, and fast way of creating games. Therefore, we decided to follow the wizard design pattern [27], which guides the user step-by-step through the process. The wizard, illustrated in Figure 3, includes three parts: (1) General Information (2) Topics and Questions, and (3) Advanced Settings.

General Information

The first step in the game creation process requires general information about the game such as name, description, playing instructions, and a representative thumbnail. If no thumbnail is provided, a default one is used. Some fields, such as Name and Description are marked with a red asterisk to indicate that they are mandatory.

Topics and Questions

The second step in the game creation process is to insert the content of the game, i.e., topics and questions. A topic and a question are presented to the player in each round of the game, which lasts one minute. Typically the question refers to the topic, for example, if the topic is *Research Division*, then the question can be *Name as many departments as you can under the Research Division*. The user needs to provide as many *good* answers as possible during the time allotted, where *good* is defined by the scoring function, which considers answers provided by other players to the same topic and question. Topics can be embedded within questions using the [topic] placeholder, which is replaced during game runtime by the current topic. In a simple embodiment, there is either one question that refers to many topics or one topic to which many questions refer. In a more advanced embodiment, there are multiple questions and topics. In this case, each question is paired with all topics. For example, the GuessWho game had two questions – *People related to [topic]* and *Tags related to [topic]* – and multiple topics representing different people's names. During the game, the [topic] placeholder was replaced with a person's name and the player's goal was to list as many related people or tags as possible [15].

The user must enter at least one topic and one question, while there is no upper limit on both. Topics and questions can be entered either manually or through an uploaded comma-separated value (CSV) file. Overall, in order to create a game, the user must enter a name, description, at least one topic, and at least one question.

Advanced Settings

The third and final step in the game creation process allows users to set several parameters that control the logic and behavior of the game. *Order* determines the order in which topics and questions are displayed, with three options to choose from: (1) Random – displays the topics and questions in random order (the way it was implemented for GuessWho [15]); (2) Fixed by question – displays a question and then loops through all topics (in a randomized order); (3) Fixed by topic – displays a topic and then loops through all questions (randomized order).

Access determines whether or not a game is available for everyone to play. If Public is selected, the game will

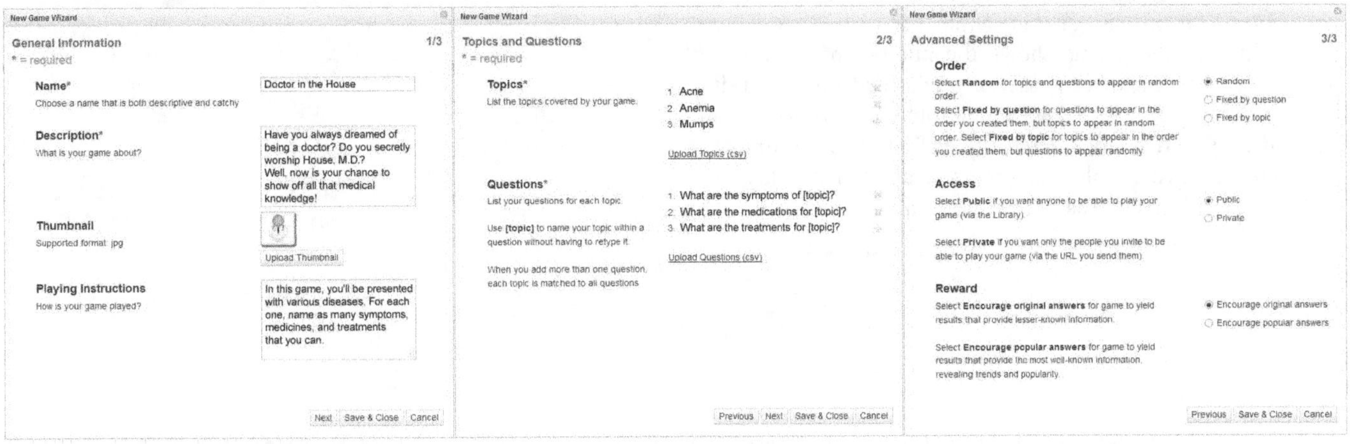

Figure 3. New Game wizard.

appear in the All Games library and various sidebar lists when relevant. If Private is selected, the game will only be accessible through a unique URL. The *Reward* section controls when and how points are awarded to a player for completing a task. If 'encourage popular answers' is selected, players will receive points based on the number of times an answer was already mentioned by other players. If 'encourage original answers' is selected, the score per player will increase for the first few players, up to a given cutoff threshold, and then decrease towards zero for answers that are already very popular. Figure 4 describes the scoring of a given answer as a function of the number of players who mentioned that answer for both types of reward mechanisms. In addition, for 'encourage original answers', dividend points [15] are used to reward the previous players who gave an answer with each subsequent mention of that answer by another player (up to a threshold). This mechanism aims at encouraging diverse yet valid answers (see [15] for more details).

The wizard produces a game (Figure 5) that is similar in its look-and-feel to the GuessWho game [15]. It uses the information provided by the game creator to propagate the various fields in the UI. For example, the current topic appears in the center circle of the game's visualization. The question, with the current topic highlighted in green, appears at the top of the UI. Answers already given by the user for this question and topic are highlighted in circles coming out of the central circle, while the small opaque circles denote answers given by other users for this pair of question and topic that the user has still not given. See [15] for more information about the type of games created using G4C and a detailed description of the UI.

Game Statistics Page

The game statistics page, reached from the studio page as described before, is shown in Figure 6. It includes details such as the total number of players and answers and a button for exporting the game-generated data to a CSV file, which can be processed further using external tools. The central part of the statistics page includes a graph showing the distribution of answers for a given topic-question pair. Figure 6, for example, shows data for the topic *Animals* and the question *Name as many Animals as you can.* The x-axis contains the answers sorted by popularity and the y-axis shows the number of mentions per answer. If an answer passed a predefined threshold, it is considered valid and appears in blue; otherwise it is colored gray and is considered unverified. The bottom of the page has two graphs showing the number of players and number of answers as a function of time.

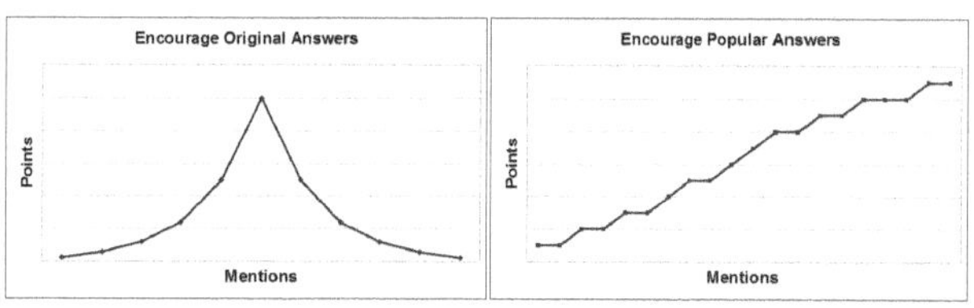

Figure 4. Scoring functions.

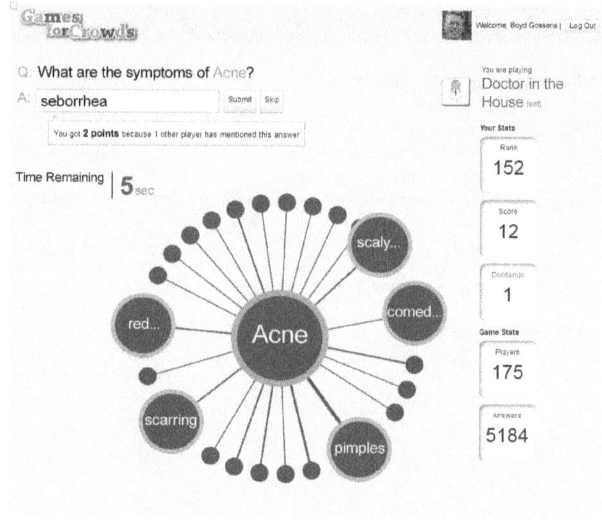

Figure 5. The generated game.

EVALUATION

Setup

G4C was deployed in our organization, a large global IT company, for a period of three months. For the evaluation, we examined the G4C server logs, which documented the details of each created game (name, creator, parameters, etc.) and the details of each answer provided by players in a game along with the player's username and a timestamp. We also conducted interviews with 12 game creators and 12 active players (who played at least 3 games), to get a better understanding of the user experience from both the creators' and players' perspectives. Interviews were semi-structured, conducted by phone, and lasted 30 minutes each. The creator interview template contained 17 questions covering the motivation for game creation, the game generation process, the dissemination and

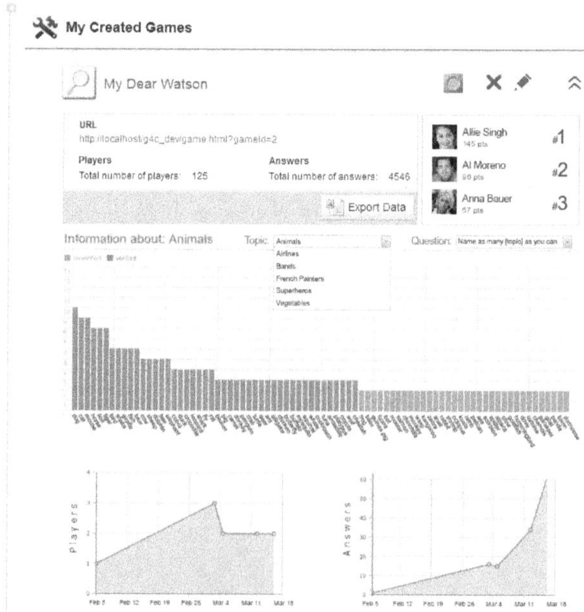

Figure 6. Game statistics screen.

management of the game, and the overall outcome of the game. The player template contained 15 questions regarding the motivation for playing games, the playing experience, the characteristics of engaging games, and the effect of games on the sense of community.

Our analysis provides an overview of the games created and the motivation for creating them, and then discusses each of the design goals, to what extent it was achieved, and how it could be improved. As part of the engagement design goal, we also discuss game characteristics that were found to influence its popularity and players' contribution.

Game Overview

During the three-month period, 25 employees from 7 different countries created 41 different public games. Only 4 additional games were defined private. Our analysis of the data collected from this period comes from 34 unique games, excluding 5 games that were created for testing purposes and 2 that included monetary rewards that were not part of the platform. On average, each game contained 23.15 questions (stdev: 42.32, max: 205, median: 8.5) and was played by 24.88 players (stdev: 35.35, max: 165, median: 11). Overall, 339 players from 31 countries played at least one game. Players spanned the different business units of our organization: 36.87% Services, 16.22% Software, 13.57% Research, 12.98% Sales, 5.6% Operations, 5.02% Headquarters, 4.72% Systems, and 5.02% others. These players contributed a total of 28,374 answers, distributed by the statistics described in Table 1.

Observing the games created, we distinguish between two types of games: business games (24 of 34), which relate to the creator's job, and leisure games, which relate to topics outside of work (10 of 34). For example, LotusHear is a business game, which included questions about a large annual business event, such as *Name influential keynote speakers;* My Dear Watson is an example of a leisure game that contained trivia questions, such as *Name as many whisky brands as you can.* Table 2 shows the 20 most popular games by number of their players. For each game, the following information is presented: (1) name, (2) reward mechanism ('P' for games that encouraged popular answers or 'O' for games that encouraged original answers), (3) type ('B' for business or 'L' for leisure), (4) the number of questions in the game, (5) the number of players who played the game, and (6) the total number of answers collected in the game.

Motivation for Creating Games

When asked about their reasons and motivations for creating games, many creators mentioned they wanted to gain or expand knowledge, often to address a challenge in their day-to-day work. Creator of Big Business Glossary said: "*through the game I was trying to build the business taxonomy for various domains in our organization [...] from water management to front office digitization.*" Creator of the Linux game noted: "*I wanted to expand my technical knowledge further in an area I'm already knowledgeable.*" The <Customer> Challenge game was built to collect information from salespeople about one of the company's main clients, asking about its brands, products, deals, and contact persons. Creator of Let's Map <Company> described: "*We were in a group meeting and my boss was explaining on the board all sorts of things about the organizational structure [...] he didn't always remember all the details [...] so it struck me I can create it using the crowd [...] every person would get a division name and would have to indicate its parents or children.*"

Other games sought to discover assets or ideas. Creator of the <Company> Cloud Seeding game explained: "*I used the game to inspect what resources people were using to find information about Cloud Computing*". Creator of Healthy Form of Exercises told us he created the game "*to get feedback and ideas of healthy forms of exercise, so that I can design exercise missions for health promotion programs.*" Volunteering game's creator described: "*I had two main purposes for the game: get new ideas from the crowd about volunteering projects for <Company> and get a sense of how 'real' this crowd is, the potential number of people who would actually volunteer*".

Teaching the crowd was also mentioned as a reason for game creation. Indeed, enhancing education and learning

	Avg	Stdev	Min	Max	Median
Answers per game	834.53	2,136.75	4	9,081	189
Answers per question	48.92	67.66	1	517	21
Answers per player	83.7	110.53	1	1,030	38

Table 1. Answer Statistics in G4C.

Name	Rewd	Type	Qust	Plyr	Answr
Scattegories	O	L	156	165	9001
My Dear Watson	O	L	44	125	9081
Doctor In The House	O	L	51	60	787
Let 's Map <Company>!	P	B	28	57	704
Boom	O	B	4	51	385
Linux	O	B	16	50	2637
Smarphone Apps	P	L	18	42	391
Learning on the Fast Track	O	B	3	38	588
Who wants to be a Socialite?	P	L	14	30	997
Healthy Forms of Exercise!	O	B	18	27	587
The <Customer> Challenge	P	B	4	21	272
Let's Map HRL!	P	B	40	19	281
LotusHear	O	B	7	19	246
Test your IQ	P	L	4	19	102
JavaScript Skill Test	P	B	7	16	83
Get Social Biznified	O	B	4	14	205
Volunteering	O	B	12	12	100
Big Business Glossary	O	B	9	10	129
Retail_IQ	O	B	25	9	145
All About SDG	O	B	24	9	521

Table 2. Twnety most popular games in G4C.

has already been pointed out as a key goal for computer games in the workplace [14]. Creator of the ISC Game told us: "*I was looking for a fun, interesting, and engaging way to teach our division about our strategy and products. I needed something that was competitive and that would get the team excited.*" Creator of Get Social Biznified said: "*I wanted to create a game that would quickly teach a group of top-level executives what Social Business is,*" and added: "*I also wanted to showcase the phenomenon and potential power of crowd games in the enterprise*".

Several creators mentioned they wanted to produce a fun and engaging experience that would increase excitement in their work environment. Finally, interest and curiosity about the game creation process and the capabilities of enterprise crowdsourcing were mentioned, for example, "*I was intrigued by the idea and wanted to see how easy it was to create a game and get people to play it.*"

Game Lifecycle

In our interviews with game creators, the simplicity of game creation was consistently mentioned as a primary advantage of G4C. Fast, easy, simple, intuitive, and convenient were among the commonly used adjectives to describe the game generation process. One creator said: "*I was able to get it up and running within a few minutes*" and another noted: "*The game was simple to put together [...] truthfully, if the process was more sophisticated, I wouldn't have tried it out [...] it should be simple enough so even non-techies like me can easily use it.*" Indeed, about half of the game creators (12 of 25) belonged to the non-technical divisions (Sales, Services, Operations), indicating that the creation process was intuitive enough for non-technical employees.

Several creators indicated they would like more control and flexibility when creating a game, for example, by being able to choose a color "theme" for the game, set the duration of a game round, or set the scoring function in a more flexible way. One creator said: "*The platform should be more tunable [...] support multiple-choice questions, allow spell-checking for inputs, or a single-answer mode*" and another suggested: "*support more complex types of games, like games with non-textual inputs [...] or allow using one game to validate the results of another.*" There is naturally a trade-off between the simplicity of game creation and the flexibility it allows. But this feedback suggests that crowdsourcing game platforms should offer more choices to advanced or experienced game creators, while keeping reasonable defaults that preserve the option of creating an initial game very quickly.

While the game creation process itself was simple, creators sometimes had to invest more time in framing their problem as a game: "*I had to change my view of the problem and look at it through the lens of a game [...] design questions whose answers can be easily compared for granting points.*" There were a few suggestions from creators to further facilitate game creation. Duplicating an existing game as a basis for creating a new one was mentioned by several creators. One of them said: "*I looked at other popular games to learn how to create my own [...] seeing a good game made me want to create a similar one*". Another interesting suggestion was to "*show game creators popular choices for created games. For example, indicating that it is common to ask 20 questions or write 5 sentences as instructions can help you understand the expectations and trust your game's ability to succeed*".

Our logs show that thumbnail images were provided for 28 of the 34 games (82.35%). This suggests that creators were willing to invest some time to make the game more attractive and unique. Of the 34 games, 24 (70.59%) provided additional instructions on top of the game's description, again pointing to creators' willingness to dedicate time to non-mandatory fields they perceive as important. Only five games used both multiple topics and multiple questions. Two examples are Scattegories, which used alphabetic letters as topics and contained questions such as *Name cities that start with [topic]* and Smartphone Apps, which defined smartphone application categories such as games, education, and lifestyle as topics and contained questions such as *Name good [topic] apps that cost less than 1$*. Several creators said they did not fully understand how the use of multiple topics and questions should work. Providing a concrete example or a simple UI to match topics with questions may help make this feature clearer and more accessible.

Almost all games (28 out of 34) were edited during the time period, with an average number of 3.52 revisions per game (stdev: 2.58, max: 15, median: 3). Creators reported using the game edit option to keep their game competitive. The creator of All About SDG told us: "*as the game progressed we added more and more questions, to make it tougher and more challenging.*" The creator of Let's Map HRL noted: "*I manually added departments that I got as answers as new questions to the game, to keep it fresh.*" A future G4C enhancement can allow converting answers to questions by certain rules to address similar needs.

Data and Analytics

Creators were generally satisfied with their game's ability to produce data quickly. "*It was amazing how much data you could get in a very short time*" said one and another noted: "*We got like 84 answers within 5 minutes.*" Inspecting the data created in different games indicates that indeed games collected a wide variety of data from the company's crowd. As a few anecdotal examples, 31 US presidents were mentioned in the game My Dear Watson (out of 43 in total); 168 countries were mentioned in Scattegories (out of 193 UN members); 21 departments were mentioned in Let's Map HRL (out of 40 in total); and 41 system calls were mentioned in the Linux game (out of 348).

In our interviews, 7 of 12 creators indicated they viewed the statistics page. "*The section that shows the distribution of answers per question was very handy"*, said one of them. Of these 7 creators, 5 said they exported the game's data into a spreadsheet and reported different uses. The creator of the Volunteering game said "*I got about 7 new ideas [...] The answers had a good mix of expected ones with a few surprising ones [...] You don't want to have all results surprising, as it indicates the crowd did not understand you, while you also don't want all answers to be expected, since you will not learn anything new.*" The creator of Healthy Forms of Exercise noted: "*The game provided extra input I could not find on the intranet [...] both brand new info and perception of existing info by people in the company.*" The creator of Smartphone Apps said: "*The export feature allowed me to share a spreadsheet with my colleagues and try to sort and make sense of the data together.*"

Apparently the data extraction feature was not visible enough for some creators. One said: "*the only difficulty I had was getting the report but then I sent you a mail and subsequently was able to go in and see what people really contributed.*" Another noted: "*finding how to get to the analysis page took me a while [...] I think it should be more prominent.*"

Creators suggested various enhancements to G4C's data analysis features. One proposed: "*more possible queries on the data [...] allow grouping or merging answers based on rules or categories*" and another commented: "*I was curious to see whether people in different geo's would mention different brands of <Customer> products.*" Another creator suggested using data visualization tools such as ManyEyes [29] to enhance data analysis capabilities.

Engagement

In our player interviews, crowdsourcing games appeared to serve as a form of escapism at work, providing a good alternative to take a break from work for a few minutes, without the guilt typically involved with going to external games, news sites, or social networks. One player noted: "*When I context-switch at work, I usually need a break to clean my head [...] the games provided me an interesting option for that*". Another player noted: "*I liked the games that related to different things internal to <Company>, such as divisions and products [...] gave me the feeling my playing is helpful and contributes something,*" and another said: "*I had a bad feeling since I was playing games while at work [...] if it's a kind of a brainstorm that worth something to <Company>, it would make me more easy.*"

Fun and challenge, sometimes mixed with the desire to learn, played a key role in players' engagement. One player explained: "*It was a way for me to quiz myself and learn more about the company I work for*" and another noted: "*the clock ticking down really added the element of challenge and excitement to the game.*" The gaming aspects were also intimidating for some employees, for example one player expressed her anxiety of not succeeding in a game within the enterprise: "*I felt stressed, worried I would look dumb [...] so I only played games I felt I had a good chance to know the answers.*" A similar point was made by one of the creators: "*One guy told me that he didn't play because he had too much work and he wasn't willing to be at the bottom with his name and picture displayed".*

Players' competitiveness did not escape the eyes of game creators. One of them said: "*The really competitive people were just going crazy [...] even my manager was playing over and over again."* G4C logs indicate that 3 managers created a game (12% of all game creators) and 57 managers played at least 1 game (16.8% of all players). These percentages are similar to the portion of managers in the organization (13%). Managers were insignificantly more successful than non-managerial employees in terms of their average rank per game (their average rank in a game divided by the total number of players in the game): 0.58 vs. 0.53 (one-tailed, unpaired t-test, $p=.16$).

The average duration of a game, from the first day it was played to the last, was a little over a month – 33.3 days (stdev: 27.9, max: 85, median: 30). Each game was played on average in 8.18 different days (stdev: 6.9, max: 28, median: 7). Games generally appeared to be a good mechanism to extract a significant amount of data in a short period of time, rather than serving as long-living applications. This is consistent with previous findings on crowdsourcing games in the enterprise [15].

Creators reported various means to publicize their games. Some relied on G4C's existing mechanisms, e.g.,: "*The fact that G4C shows newly created games helped a lot since I knew my game would be there at the top of the list for at least some time after it has been created.*" Others published the game via email, instant messaging, microblogging, and face-to-face meetings. More mechanisms should be added to G4C to support game diffusion and virality, such as distributing games to matching communities or sending update emails to players with teasers, such as the number of points needed to advance in the leader-board.

Game Popularity and Players' Contribution

We examined a variety of game characteristics and their influence on two measures of the game: (1) popularity, determined by the number of players who played a game; and (2) players' contribution, determined by the average number of answers per player per question in a game. We report the findings we discovered across four different game characteristics.

Business vs. Leisure. Leisure games were found to be significantly more popular than business games, with 40.28 players on average compared to 14.1, respectively (one-tailed, unpaired t-test, $p<.05$). On the other hand, in business games, players' contribution was significantly higher, with an average of 3.59 answers per player per question versus 1.41 for leisure games (one-tailed, unpaired t-test, $p<.05$). It appears that business games attract fewer players, but receive higher contribution from each. One of the creators explained: "*there is a tension between creating a closed game on a very specific topic, which would potentially attract domain experts and be highly interesting for them and creating a generic game that would attract anyone, but with less specific interest.*"

Reward Mechanism. Games that encouraged original answers (15 of 34) had an average of 32.16 players, while games that encouraged popular answers (19 of 34) had an average of 15.67 players. This difference was found statistically insignificant (one-tailed, unpaired t-test, $p=.073$). When playing a game rewarding originality, players provided an average of 3.41 answers per question, compared to 2.08 for games rewarding popularity. This difference too was found statistically insignificant (one-tailed unpaired t-test, $p=.16$). Overall, these findings suggest that there are no significant differences between the two reward mechanisms in terms of popularity and engagement. In our interviews, we noticed that the selection of a reward method often stems from the goal of the game. One creator who chose to encourage popular answers noted: *"The subject matter of the questions I was asking was trying to get to a common denominator [...] I was trying to identify what lots of people felt the same about."* On the other hand, another creator who chose to encourage original answers said: *"When I think about crowdsourcing and idea management [...] it works best when you have diverse insight and feedback [...] I wasn't looking for consensus."*

Instruction Length. The average instruction length per game was 16.31 words (stdev: 17.99, median: 11.5, max: 72). Since instructions were input through a free-text field, without providing any hints or auto-completion, their content and phrasing style was different for each game; no copying of instructions from one game to another occurred. Comparing players' contributions in games with instruction length of 10 words or less (15 of 34 games) to games with instruction length of more than 10 words (19 of 34) indicated no significant difference (one-tailed, unpaired t-test, $p>.05$). Further partitioning these groups into four in total, based on round borders and group size balance, revealed a significant effect, as summarized in Table 3. A one-way ANOVA indicated that players' contributions across the four groups were significantly different, $F(3,30)=4.415$, $p<.05$. Tukey post-hoc comparisons indicated that the mean for the third group, which had instruction length between 11 and 20 words, was significantly higher than the three other groups. This result implies that instructions should be neither too short nor too long. Presumably, instructions that are too short can fail to adequately explain the game and might also convey lack of attention or effort, while instructions that are too long can be tedious to read and hard to follow. For the game description, we did not observe a similar effect of its length on players' contribution.

Instruction Length	# Games	Mean	Stdev
None	10	1.56	1.30
1-10 words	5	1.73	1.06
11-20 words	7	**7.34**	7.91
Over 20 words	12	1.69	1.08

Table 3. Instruction length effect on players' contribution (number of answers per player per question).

Number of Questions. Comparing games with up to 8 questions and games with over 8 questions (17 games in both groups) shows that games with more than 8 questions were significantly more popular: they had 37.59 players on average, compared to 12.18 players for games with 8 questions or less (one-tailed, unpaired t-test, $p<.05$). The number of answers per player per question was, as could be expected, significantly higher for games with fewer questions, at 3.77 compared to 1.36 for games with more questions. It can also be seen that the four most popular games in Table 2 had a large number of questions – over 25 – and the most popular game, Scattegories, had a particularly large amount of questions – 156. One player noted: "*I got the same question many times, which was very discouraging [...] creators should be urged to upload more questions,*" and another said: "*If there was a game that had lots of questions I would probably assume that it is a well set up game or a game that's got more essence in it.*" Players also indicated that questions that required shorter answers were more appealing *"since the task was clearer and so was the scoring*", as one of them explained.

Community

Several games related to existing communities within the organization. The game All About SDG was created to support the Solution Development Group by "*communicating with our developers and analysts [...] the game experience, the competition, and different answers helped strengthen the community*". The creator of the Linux game attributed its success to "*the nature of the Linux community – all developers, technical, know their area very well and are passionate about Linux*". Game creators wished to have a way to easily connect a game to an online community [22], so it is exposed on the homepage of the community and accessible to is members. "*Online communities can be a great way to drive crowdsourcing games in the organization*", said one creator and another suggested: "*would be great if G4C can support competition between communities.*"

Aside from strengthening a specific community, both creators and players pointed out that G4C helped share knowledge and connect people that are not necessarily familiar with each other. One player said: *"It takes you out of the everyday race for a few minutes and makes you aware of other colleagues*" and another noted: *"The right panel with all gaming activity contributes to the sense of community among employees who play and create different games"*. Another player mentioned he would want more mechanisms to enhance the sense of community among players: "*promote more interactivity between players even if they are anonymous [...] show another player who answered a question while I was playing [...] or help discover players who are similar to me based on how they play different games*".

G4C logs show that players who also created a game (20 in total) played significantly more games than players who did not: 3.7 versus 1.56 (one-tailed, unpaired t-test, $p<.05$). In addition, game creators had significantly more members of their organizational social network play games: 1.85 versus 0.71 (one-tailed, unpaired t-test, $p<.05$). These findings indicate that game creators are more engaged as players, not just of their own games, and also engage their social environment. The mutuality between playing and creating a game was reflected in several employees creating a game after gaining some experience as players. One commented: *"After playing I saw how simple it can be to create a game. It removed the barrier"*. In other cases, creators mentioned they played other games after they created their own: *"playing other games taught me more ways to pose my questions"*.

DISCUSSION, LIMITATIONS, AND FUTURE WORK

We examined 34 games created along a three-month deployment period of G4C in our organization. Creators reported different motivations for creating games, from learning from the crowd and collecting knowledge, through experiencing with crowdsourcing in the enterprise, to producing fun and excitement in their teams. The game creation process was reported to be easy and intuitive, typically taking just a few minutes to complete. Creators did invest in non-mandatory fields to improve their game: most of them provided instructions in addition to the mandatory description and most also provided a thumbnail image to characterize their game. Most creators also revised their game multiple times after its initial creation. Together with its simplicity, the game creation process was often pointed out as not flexible enough. Future versions should provide more flexibility, such as supporting more complex game types that would allow framing more business problems as games; allowing the reuse of an existing game when creating a new one; and controlling more parameters such as round duration or colors of UI elements.

Games were created to gather different types of data, from ideas of volunteering or exercises at work, through knowledge resources about professional topics such as cloud computing, to items that help build knowledge bases, such as business glossaries and organizational charts, or expand the business knowledge around technical topics (Linux, Javascript), customers, or business events. Many creators used the statistics page to view their data and almost half chose to export the data into a spreadsheet. Creators' feedback also indicated that the prominence and integration of the statistics page into the game management process should be improved. Actively alerting creators about the status of their game's data can be one future direction to address this. Additionally, more advanced options should be provided to share the data with others and analyze it.

Both managers and employees, spanning all organizational divisions, including the non-technical ones, engaged in creating and playing games. Games appeared to be used as a guilt-reduced alternative for employees to escape work when they needed to take a break or make a context-switch, by challenging themselves, competing with colleagues, learning more about the business, and contributing knowledge. Future versions of G4C should provide integrated dissemination and engagement means, for instance through email updates or enterprise social media. Additionally, supporting mobile games would open more opportunities for employees to engage in games when they have spare time on the go.

We also saw that playing games at work can be difficult for some employees, both because they need to justify the allocated time and because some feel particularly pressured to succeed as their real identity is exposed alongside their score. In their work about "mandatory fun", Mollick and Rothbard [21] found that legitimacy plays a key role in employee's' consent to enterprise games. Crowdsourcing games should therefore convey to players their value to the business and give them the feeling they contribute each time they play.

Our findings from inspecting the characteristics of the 34 games indicate that games with more questions enjoy higher popularity; instructions that are not too short and not too long (11-20 words) yield higher players' contribution; and while leisure games enjoy higher popularity, business games yield higher players' contribution. Even though some of these factors must be determined by the specific needs of a game, the platform can aid creators by indicating the recommended length of instructions or encouraging uploading more questions. With regards to the instruction length, our findings are based on one specific group partitioning with some level of arbitrariness and thus the exact borders of the recommended range should be further validated.

G4C strives to create an ecosystem of creators, players, and games. We found that employees are willing to share their created games – only four of them were kept private. The gaming activity sidebar, presenting activity across different games by different criteria, was indicated to contribute to the sense of community. Several players created a game after learning how simple it can be from their playing experience. Other creators played others' games to compare with their own. More ideas were suggested to further promote the sense of community, for example by encouraging more interaction between users, allowing competition between groups, or recommending similar players.

G4C enables employees to create a certain type of human computation games. It provides them a ready-made user interface and thus spares them the need to become game designers, but rather focus on the content and rules of the game. Aarseth [1] defines three dimensions that characterize computer games, which may have different weights in different games: the gameplay (players' actions and strategies), the game structure (rules), and the game world (fictional content, level topology, textures). In our case, many of the game "world" elements are already provided for the authors, leaving more weight to the game's content and structure. In the video game domain, the concept of "modders" describes game moderators that contribute new content, such as skills, missions, scenarios, maps, or episodes, to a game. Gee [14] states that good games allow players to be producers and not just consumers. He argues that such players' actions co-create the game's world, which makes them as much designers of the game as the original creator. The role of a game creator in G4C has a lot in common with this role of "modder" or "contributor" in the video game field.

This work particularly contributes to the area of enterprise crowdsourcing. Its main novelty lies in brining together crowdsourcing and game creation capabilities in one platform deployed in a workplace setting. While G4C only enables the creation of one game type, we observed that this type on its own leads to the creation of different games with diverse purposes. We believe this is an important step in making enterprise crowdsourcing more accessible; many of the game creators in our study were non-technical employees and some of them indicated the low entry barrier as their key reason for "joining the club". We also pointed at design opportunities, stemming from the fact that such games are perceived as a "legitimate" way to take a break from work, which comes with its own challenges, such as the need to perform publicly in front of one's co-workers. We also found that many game creators invoked their social network within the organization to encourage play. This implies that giving certain employee, such as those with higher connectivity within the organizational network, a creative role with higher engagement, can help promote enterprise crowdsourcing.

Our study is influenced by the characteristics of the specific organization in which it was conducted. We believe that many of the games created using G4C address general challenges in large organizations, such as volunteer recruiting, org chart building, and education about a department or a customer. Still, culture changes from one organization to another and may substantially affect the way crowdsourcing games are created and played. Additionally, our study is based on a relatively modest dataset of 34 games and 339 players. While these provide a good initial sense of the created games' diversity and their characteristics, quantitative findings should be treated with care given the small number of analyzed games. Future research should further explore the concepts presented here, in other organizational environments and with more participants.

CONCLUSION

We presented Games for Crowds, a novel crowdsourcing game platform that facilitates the creation and playing of enterprise human-computation games. G4C creates a layer of abstraction over the game generation process by using the wizard design pattern and exposing a set of parameters needed to create a game. Our evaluation provides an overview of the platform's use in the enterprise and suggests future enhancements that can be applied in similar systems, as enterprise crowdsourcing is expected to grow and become more ubiquitous.

ACKNOWLEDGMENTS

We thank Artem Barger, Maya Barnea, Tal Daniel, Ohad Greenshpan, Michal Jacovi, Vladimir Soroka, and Itai Turbahn for their help in evolving and developing G4C over the years.

REFERENCES

1. Aarseth, E. 2003. Playing Research: Methodological approaches to game analysis. *Proc. DAC '03*, 28-29.
2. Abrahamson, S., Ryder, P., & Unterberg, B. 2013. Crowdstorm: the future of innovation, ideas, and problem solving. *John Wiley & Sons*.
3. Allio, R. J. 2004. CEO interview: the InnoCentive model of open innovation, *Strategy & Leadership* 32,4 (2004), 4–9.
4. Ambati, V., Vogel, S., & Carbonell J. 2010. Active learning and crowd-sourcing for machine translation. *Proc. LREC'10*.
5. Antin, J. & Shaw, A. 2012. Social desirability bias and self-reports of motivation: a study of Amazon Mechanical Turk in the US and India. *Proc. CHI '12*, 2925-2934.
6. Bernstein, M., Chi, E., Chilton, L., Hartmann, B., Kittur, A., & Miller, R. 2011. Crowdsourcing and human computation: systems, studies and platforms. *Proc. CHI EA '11*, 53-56.
7. Buhrmester M., Kwang T., & Gosling S.D. 2011. Amazon's Mechanical Turk: a new source of inexpensive, yet high-quality, data? *Perspectives on Psychological Science* (2011).
8. Chen, K., Chang, C., Wu, C., Chang, Y., & Lei, C. 2010. Quadrant of euphoria: a crowdsourcing platform for QoE assessment. Network, IEEE 24, 2 (March 2010), 28-35.
9. Di Gangi, P.M. & Wasko, M. 2009. Steal my idea! Organizational adoption of user innovations from a

user innovation community: a case study of Dell IdeaStorm. *Decision Support Systems*, 48(1), 303-312.

10. Doan, A., Ramakrishnan R., & Halevy, A. Y. 2011. Crowdsourcing systems on the world-wide web. *Commun. ACM* 54, 4 (2011), 86-96.

11. Dugan, C., Muller, M., Millen, D. R., Geyer, W., Brownholtz, B., & Moore, M. 2007. The dogear game: a social bookmark recommender system. *Proc. GROUP '07*, 387-390.

12. Duncan, S.C. 2011. Minecraft, beyond construction and survival. *Well Played Journal* 1(1), 1-22.

13. Evanini, K., Higgins, D., & Zechner, K. 2010. Using Amazon Mechanical Turk for transcription of non-native speech. *Proc. NAACL HLT '10*, 53-56.

14. Gee, J.P. 2003. What video games have to teach us about learning and literacy. *Computers in Entertainment*, *1*(1), 20.

15. Guy, I., Perer, A., Daniel, T., Greenshpan, O., & Turbahn, I. 2011. Guess who? enriching the social graph through a crowdsourcing game. *Proc. CHI '11*, 1373-1382.

16. Howe, J. 2006. The rise of crowdsourcing, *Wired* 14, 6 (June 2006).

17. Kittur, A., Chi, E. H., & Suh, B. 2008. Crowdsourcing user studies with Mechanical Turk. *Proc. CHI '08*, 453-456.

18. Lakhani, K. R., Jeppeson, L. B., Lohse, P. A. & Panetta, J. A. 2007. The value of openness in scientific problem solving. *HBS working paper* (Feb. 2007).

19. Little, G., Chilton, L. B., Goldman, M., & Miller, R. C. 2009. TurKit: Tools for iterative tasks on Mechanical Turk. *Proc. HCOMP '09*, 29-30.

20. Mehm, F., Reuter, C., Göbel, S., & Steinmetz, R. 2012. Future trends in game authoring tools. *Proc. ICEC '12*, 536-541.

21. Mollick, E.R. & Rothbard, N. 2013. Mandatory fun: gamification and the impact of games at work. *The Wharton School Research Paper Series*.

22. Muller, M., Ehrlich, K., Matthews, T., Perer, A., Ronen, I., & Guy, I. Diversity among enterprise online communities: collaborating, teaming, and innovating through social media. *Proc. CHI '12*, 2815-2824.

23. Parent, G. & Eskenazi, M. 2010. Clustering dictionary definitions using Amazon Mechanical Turk. *Proc. NAACL HLT '10*, 21-29.

24. Quinn, A. J. & Bederson, B. B. 2011. Human computation: a survey and taxonomy of a growing field. *Proc. CHI '11*, 1403-1412.

25. Sorenson, N. & Pasquier, P. Towards a generic framework for automated video game level creation. *Proc. EvoApplications*, 130–139.

26. Surowiecki, James. The wisdom of crowds. 2005. *Anchor Books*.

27. Tidwell, J. Designing interfaces. 2005. *O'Reilly*.

28. Torrente, J., Del Blanco, Á., Cañizal, G., Moreno-Ger, P., & Fernández-Manjón, B. 2008. < e-Adventure3D>: an open source authoring environment for 3D adventure games in education. *Proc. ACE '08*, 191-194.

29. Viegas, F.B, Wattenberg, M, Van Ham, F, Kriss, J., & McKeon, M. 2007. ManyEyes: a site for visualization at internet scale. *IEEE TVCG* 13, 6 (Nov. 2007), 1121-1128.

30. Von Ahn, L. & Dabbish, L. 2008. Designing games with a purpose. *Commun. ACM* 51, 8 (Aug. 2008), 58–67.

31. Von Ahn, L. & Dabbish, L. 2004. Labeling images with a computer game. *Proc. CHI '04*, 319-326.

32. Von Ahn, L., Kedia, M., & Blum, M. 2006. Verbosity: a game for collecting common-sense facts. *Proc. CHI '06*, 75-78.

33. Von Ahn, L., Liu, R., & Blum, M. 2006. Peekaboom: a game for locating objects in images. *Proc. CHI '06*, 55-64.

34. Von Ahn, L., Maurer, B., McMillen, C., Abraham, D., & Blum, M. 2008. Recaptcha: human-based character recognition via web security measures. *Science* 321, 5895 (2008), 1465–1468.

35. Vukovic, M. 2009. Crowdsourcing for enterprises. *Proc. Services '09*, 686–692.

36. Westecott, E. 2011. Crafting play: little big planet. *Loading* 5, (2011) 90–100.

Collective Intelligence or Group Think? Engaging Participation Patterns in *World without Oil*

Nassim JafariNaimi
School of Literature, Media, and Communication
Georgia Institute of Technology
85 5th ST NW, Atlanta, GA
nassim@gatech.edu

Eric M. Meyers
The iSchool@UBC
University of British Columbia
1961 East Mall, Vancouver, BC
eric.meyers@ubc.ca

ABSTRACT
This article presents an analysis of participation patterns in an Alternate Reality Game, World Without Oil. This game aims to bring people together in an online environment to reflect on how an oil crisis might affect their lives and communities as a way to both counter such a crisis and to build collective intelligence about responding to it. We present a series of participation profiles based on a quantitative analysis of 1554 contributions to the game narrative made by 322 players. We further qualitatively analyze a sample of these contributions. We outline the dominant themes, the majority of which engage the global oil crisis for its effects on commute options and present micro-sustainability solutions in response. We further draw on the quantitative and qualitative analysis of this space to discuss how the design of the game, specifically its framing of the problem, feedback mechanism, and absence of subject-matter expertise, counter its aim of generating collective intelligence, making it conducive to groupthink.

Author Keywords
Alternate Reality Games; Participation; Collective Intelligence; Groupthink

ACM Classification Keywords
H.5.m. Information interfaces and presentation (e.g., HCI): Miscellaneous.

INTRODUCTION
Alternate Reality Games (ARGs) are a specific set of games that are based on collaborative problem solving and storytelling. These games have been part of the gaming landscape since around 2001 as transmedia entertainment or promotional pieces for product launches [10, 13, 14]. Recently, a second wave of ARGs seeks to address societal issues (e.g., poverty and hunger) through widespread collaboration. It's been argued that such environments are a powerful means of engaging participants in awareness-building, collective intelligence, and participatory forms of learning [11, 16, 17].

CSCW '15, March 14 - 18, 2015, Vancouver, BC, Canada.

http://dx.doi.org/10.1145/2675133.2675258

However, much the current literature on the success of ARGs relies heavily on the observations of ARG designers and developers [e.g., 6, 17] as opposed to empirical evidence of player participation (with few exceptions such as [20, 23, 24]). If we are to take the claims of ARG proponents seriously, we need to address key questions, among them: what are the kinds of engagement fostered in these environments?; and are these engagements generative of collective intelligence and innovative problem solving?

This paper presents a study of one ARG, World Without Oil (WWO), seeking to address the above questions. Based on quantitative analysis of player responses, we put forward a set of participation profiles that characterize different levels of engagement. We further analyze a sample of these contributions by thematically coding their content. We outline the dominant themes, the majority of which engage the global oil crisis for its effects on commute options and present micro-sustainability solutions in response.

This paper's contribution is multifaceted. Through the case study of WWO, we critically engage one of the key arguments in support of ARGs: that they are environments generative of collective intelligence. Based on this study, we illustrate that the narrative is dominated by a limited set of themes and a small group of highly active participants including the designers of the game who refer to themselves as *puppet masters*. We further discuss the characteristics that run counter to the objective of collective intelligence, making the environment susceptible to groupthink. Based on this study, we highlight a set of design considerations that are key in success of ARGs if they are to avoid the problems related to groupthink, among them: balancing the number of players with different participation profiles; including the voice of subject matter experts; encouraging critical thinking alongside cooperative and collaborative practices; and provision of markers for players to distinguish reality from fiction and facts from misinformation. In doing so, we contribute to existing research on the social aspects of gaming as well as the larger scholarship on (mediated) group interactions and online communities.

BACKGROUND AND PREVIOUS WORK

ARGs are multi-player narratives that involve online and offline participation, using a variety of tasks, challenges, puzzles, and prompts to engage players in co-constructing a fictional scenario. One or more "puppet masters" guide the narrative and serve as architects of user participation, often drawing on player engagement to alter the narrative flow, encourage specific forms of participation, or redirect player efforts. As a kind of emergent, interactive problem-based story, the ARG genre combines elements of live action role-play, transmedia storytelling, and cooperative games. Gurzick and colleagues [9, 10] suggest that ARGs are a type of self-organizing collective, similar in some ways to Wikipedia and other open content development spaces. Analyzing the characteristics of ARGs may lend insights to the development of new gaming experiences as well as organizational groupware systems.

One of the key characteristics of ARGs is that they require players to perform tasks or act in the world and then document and report these actions in response to the fictional "situations" that are presented to them. The online and offline components constitute different kinds of engagement that may be considered a kind of "move". Some moves are public, as when a player documents or responds to the game through social media, a blog post, or a public action at the prompt of other players or the puppet masters. Some of these moves may be private, as when a player changes his awareness, behavior, or attitude concerning the topic of game play. The moves, in aggregate, constitute the narrative of the game. One can argue that multiple narratives are created in this process: the personal or private narrative, comprised of the individual's self-constructed "story" of the game and their part in it, and the social or public narrative, which is the combined effort of all the players including the puppet masters.

The interplay between these public and private narratives is where ARGs have the potential to be rich spaces for innovation and knowledge building. As players engage in reflection on their own moves and the moves of others, they are experiencing a form of learning through individual and collective storytelling and listening [5]. The quality of this learning depends on the level and quality of the participatory opportunities offered by the game narrative, and the extent to which players engage with the narrative and each other [12]. Thus, analyzing participation patterns in these collaborative narratives is an important aspect of understanding whether or not ARGs live up to dominant discourse, which presents them as sources of collective intelligence.

More specifically, the discourse around ARGs echoes one of the most dominant themes of social tools and web 2.0 celebrating the power and wisdom of the 'crowds' [e.g., 3, 27, 29]. ARGs present a specific interpretation of collective intelligence: collaborative and creative environments that bring people together to solve real-world problems [e.g., 4, 5]. Drawing on the work of Pierre Levy, Jane McGonigal, one of the prominent advocates of ARGs, argues that members of a collective intelligence *would work with the collected facts and viewpoints to actively author, discover and invent new, computer-fueled ways of thinking, strategizing, and coordinating* [18, 15, 17]. However, while the diversity and talents of group members can be a great resource for collaborative problem solving, such groups are susceptible to group think, *a mode of thinking that people engage in when they are deeply involved in a cohesive in-group, and members' strivings for unanimity override their motivation to realistically appraise alternative courses of action* [12]. In this study, we examine this challenge in WWO and discuss some of the design strategies that can potentially counter groupthink.

WORLD WITHOUT OIL

World Without Oil is a massively collaborative imagining of the first 32 weeks of a global oil crisis. Designed by Ken Eklund (Creative Director) and Jane McGonigal (Participation Architect), the game aims to bring people together around a shared concern, namely getting them to reflect and share insights about oil dependence with the aim of devising plausible and effective courses of action in response to an "oil shock" scenario. Two aims are central to the design of WWO: one, that individuals can initiate change if they are motivated; two, that difficult problems can be solved by a diverse group of people coming together to share their individual perspectives and come up with innovative solutions to encounter the situation, the sum of which leads to a kind of collective intelligence. In what follows we describe the design of the game in detail.

Design

Scenario

The game's main site of interaction is the website worldwithoutoil.org. As noted earlier, the game is built around the premise that an oil shock arrived on April 30, 2007. Starting with the initial news that "gas prices have risen to $7[1]," the puppet masters shared the day-to-day news of a global oil shock on the website. Each day of the game represented a week of the imagined crisis with the unfolding events simulating eight months of an imagined crisis. For the period of 32 days, the puppet masters, who also acted as game characters, shared fake but realistic news, stories, commentary, resources, and activities related to the unfolding of the oil shock. Players were challenged to respond in creative ways. They were asked to share stories about how their lives were affected and strategies they employed to confront the crisis. Their stories were incorporated into the narrative in concert with the ones created by the puppet masters, to which others players could react and respond.

[1] $7/gallon is roughly three times the average price of gasoline in the U.S. in 2007.

Participation
To facilitate various forms of contribution, the game environment did not set limitations on participation. Anyone could register to play and contribute to the collective narrative. There were also no limitations about entering or exiting the game or any requirements as to the intensity of participation such as a minimum or maximum number of entries. One could participate with one post, or a series of posts. Similarly, people could choose to participate through the communication method of their choice. As a result, some wrote on their weblogs or made videos or images. Others played by email or called a number to share their stories. Lastly, there were no rules about what people should say or do in relationship to the game.

One of the main features of the game is a series of missions designed to help players make actual changes and act in response to the simulated crisis. On the game's website, missions are described as *creative, real-world actions that respond to our new world without oil.* The game designers (i.e., its puppet masters), who also took part in the game as characters, assigned most of the missions. Players could also set up new missions to which other players and puppet masters could respond.

Interface
On the homepage, the game is explained in detail, including pages outlining its history and how-to play guides. The main areas that draw attention on the homepage are the *dashboard*, a white banner at the top of the site which details the oil prices of the day (representing a week of the crisis), followed by the first few sentences of the main scenario of the week, together with links for joining the game and reading the blog. On the left, there is a banner with the list of all the weeks' contributions, putting the highest-ranking posts on the top.

One webpage is dedicated to each day of the game. On this webpage we see an "update" of the news of that week posted by the designers. These stories set the theme for each day of the game. Following the updates, all the posts by the players are included in (seemingly) chronological order.

Feedback
The dashboard included responses from players in different regions based on the level of activity and whether responses are positive (e.g., positive forecasts, cooperative strategies, actively reducing daily oil consumption) or negative (e.g. reporting a darker turn of events, focusing on competition, or difficulties to adapt to low energy consumption) [16, p. 307]. Players are also ranked based on the frequency of their contributions and what appears to be a subjective rating of the quality of their contribution by the designers. The website explains:

> ***Scores:*** *The way people get a higher score depends on what they contribute, and how often.[...]*
>
> ***Areas:*** *The area rankings are based on a combination of how much and how cool is the stuff people in the area are doing, and how many people from the area are doing anything. [...]*
>
> *There is a certain amount of furry logic though, not to mention I suspect some of my colleagues will succumb to arm twisting and go in and fiddle with the scores :(*

Aim 1. Positive Behavior Change
The first concept central to the design of WWO is that individuals are creative and capable of initiating change. However, in real life they lack the motivation to take action. As a result, the game aims to provide motivation and remove the negative pressures associated with making changes in real life. According to McGonigal, real life can be "fixed" by creating scenarios and reward systems that motivate people to act in more positive ways. These scenarios can be applied to a range of tasks and activities ranging from household chores to "saving the world" [16].

Aim 2. Collective Intelligence
The second concept that is central to the design of WWO is the ability of a diverse group of people with different life experiences to devise innovative solutions to complex problems. Being experts in their own needs, it is individuals who can best imagine how their everyday practices might change in a hypothetical situation such as an oil crisis. By engaging in realistic scenarios and stories, players are contributing to a collective intelligence on the issue of oil dependence. Through their participation, players raise their awareness of environmental issues and devise innovative strategies to lessen their dependence on oil. At the same time, the entire community can learn from the players' responses because they present a diversity of ways that one might prepare for and/or survive in a world without oil. Summarized in the words of Jane McGonigal, "World without Oil would give players firsthand insight into a plausible future, help them prepare for, or even prevent, its worst outcomes. The game would create a collective record of how a real peak-oil scenario might play out — a kind of survival guide for the future, a record of tremendous value for educators, policy makers and organizations of all kinds."

METHOD
According to the WWO website, over 1,900 people signed up as players of WWO, and submitted over 1,500 stories with over 60,000 active observers [16]. However, these numbers tell us very little about the character of participation, and how individual contributors shaped the game narrative. To better understand participation patterns at a granular level, we constructed a database of participant contributions–an aggregate record of the game narrative–that we could explore quantitatively and qualitatively.

Basic metadata about participation in the game is hosted in two places: on the archived WWO site itself and an offsite archive set up by the game designers in partnership with the Internet Archive's Wayback Machine. While the WWO site still exists, many of the links to the original posts are no

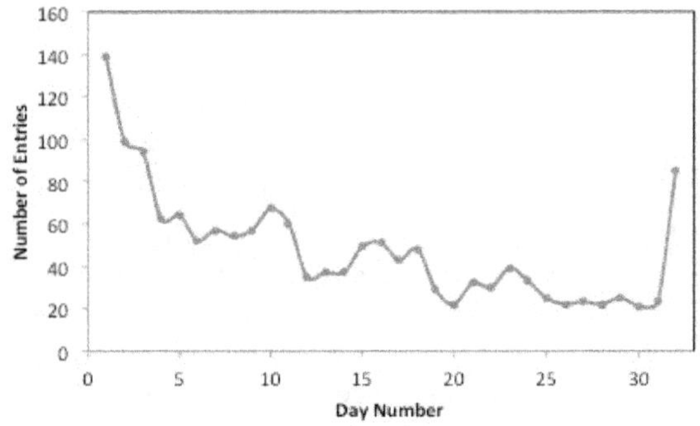

Figure 1: Total number of entries per day versus days passed

longer valid. The game archive captured 94% of the content from the posts made during the game's active period of 32 days (with some gaps most likely related to participants deleting their own posts prior to the construction of the archive). Our database includes 86 audio files, 1165 blog entries, 117 images, 114 emails, and 75 videos.

We used linked relational databases, MS Excel, and SPSS 22 to identify a set of participation profiles based on several criteria: post types, frequency of contribution, and distribution of contributions, both in relation to the game sequence and each other. We used contextual factors, including URLs, location IDs, and other trace data to identify, where possible, when the same person(s) made contributions with slightly different UserIDs. This quantitative analysis was complemented by a qualitative study of a random set of 232 entries from this set (15%). In what follows we describe these analyses in detail.

QUANTITATIVE ANALYSIS

It has been noted that WWO attracted 60,000 unique views, and over 1500 contributions from players across several continents [16]. At face value, these are impressive numbers. However, exploring the participation patterns in detail, we see that engaged participation was not as broad as these numbers might suggest. Furthermore, our analysis reveals high attrition rates among participants early in the simulation, and a small number of contributors authoring the majority of the narrative.

The overall trend in contributions shows a sharp decline at the beginning, with the first day being the highest participation rate, strong declines over the first five days, then steady decline in posting with a brief uptick at the end (Figure 1).

If we use contributions to the game narrative as one measure of engagement, we can identify three groups: limited, moderate and high engagement. We considered limited engagement 4 or fewer posts (an average of once per week of the simulation or less); 227 of the 308 participants (excluding WWO puppetmasters) fall into this category, accounting for 367 posts. Moderate engagement was set at 5–9 contributions to the game; 38 participants engaged at this level, accounting for 244 posts. There were 43 high-engagement players, those who submitted 10 or more posts (at least every third day of the simulation on average), accounting for 827 posts.

With an open game narrative like WWO, one would expect there to be more persons interested in observing the simulation than active players constructing the narrative. However, we see the ratio of contributing participants to lurkers even smaller than expected. The 30 most frequent participants (top 10% by number of posts) accounted for roughly 50% of contributions. The 60 most frequent participants (top 20%) accounted for roughly 67% of contributions. These ratios are slightly better than the Pareto Rule, a marketing maxim that suggests 20% of customers produce 80% of sales [26]. However, the number of unique hits on the site during the 32 days of the simulation numbered over 60,000. The number of contributors, then, is less than 1% of all those who expressed interest in the simulation itself. Furthermore, we see that the ratio of highly engaged participants to all participants is exceptionally small, with only a few dozen contributors accounting for most of the narrative, and over 50% attrition of active contributors at the midway point of the simulation. These numbers conform to the "1% rule," which states that 90% of participants in online communities lurk, 9% contribute intermittently, 1% account for nearly all the activity [19, 30]. ARGs, then, share similarities in participation patterns with crowd-sourced knowledge spaces like Wikipedia, as well as healthcare social network sites [21, 30].

Player Participation Profiles

Game participation patterns, when examined at the level of the individual contributor, reveal a number of "profiles" or clusters of participant behavior. These profiles provide insights as to how the game mechanics may have influenced user engagement, particularly maintaining participant interest over time. Narratively and in Table 1 we document the nature and frequency of these profiles.

Toe Dippers – these players posted a single contribution, or in 13 cases contributed two times on the same day, but thereafter did not contribute again. We identified 150 players as Toe Dippers, 46.6% of active contributors. The majority of Toe-dippers contributed early in the game; 57% contributed in the first five days; 87% prior to day 16.

Lurkers – these players also posted a single contribution to the game narrative, but on the final day of the simulation, and with some evidence in the post that they had been reading and engaging with the WWO story. We identified 18 lurkers, comprising 5.6% of contributors. We call out this group as they demonstrate the kind of summative reflection that may be overlooked by exploring the player profiles strictly algorithmically.

Drop-Outs – these players posted frequently in the early days of the simulation, then fell away by the middle, with no posts past the mid-way point of the game. We labeled 65 players as drop-outs, 20.2% of players. Of these, 24 players

Profile	Players		Posts	
Toe-dippers	150	46.6%	164	10.6%
Lurkers	18	5.6%	20	1.3%
Drop-outs	65	20.2%	395	25.4%
Late-comers	15	4.7%	114	7.3%
Regulars	39	12.1%	689	44.3%
Designers	14	4.3%	68	4.4%
No Profile	21	6.5%	56	3.6%
*Unidentified**			48	3.1%

Table 1: Participant profiles by frequency and their contribution to the game narrative.

posted 3 or more times in the first five days, but were not heard from again, suggesting initial excitement that did not lead to continued engagement.

Late-Comers – players who joined the game in the second half of the simulation, contributing regularly between days 20 and 32. Some of this later interest may have been driven by documentation of WWO on public radio, which partially funded the development of the game. The Late-Comers profile accounts for 15 players, only 4.7% of active contributors. This includes some participants who did not actively contribute to the game narrative until the final week.

Regulars – only 39 players (12.1% of active contributors) participated steadily throughout the game, posting 5 or more times (greater than once per week) including posts in the final days of the simulation. We used standard deviation to account for post spread to eliminate players who may have posted a flurry of contributions in the final week (distinguishing Late-Comers from Regulars). A subset of this group, the hyper-engaged, totaling 9 players, posted more than 25 times apiece. Although comprising 1/8 of the players, this group, along with the game designers, submitted nearly half the narrative content.

QUALITATIVE ANALYSIS

As we noted in the introductory sections, WWO has been praised as a space for collective intelligence as it focuses on *producing new discourse about a global energy crisis* [i.e., 4]. However, such arguments rely heavily on anecdotal evidence from designers or a small set of players [6, 17]. To understand the nature of participation by players, we thematically coded a selection of 230 posts from the database. This selection included a random set of 130 entries spanning various days during the game interval. We also randomly selected a set of another 100 entries that were listed as award winners, were posted by puppet masters, or included comments by the puppet masters.

Our analysis and thematic coding of entries was focused on our research question: are the scenarios and practices put forward by the players innovative in ways that would lead us to think of the WWO ARG as a space that is generative of innovative problem solving and collective intelligence? Our thematic analysis leads us to four themes related to short-term and long-term changes as described below:

Disruptions in Everyday Routines and Practices

One of the dominant themes among the responses (and perhaps an expected one give the scenario set by puppet masters) is that of the immediate disruption of everyday practices. The disruptions range from minor to major. The entries describe long lines at the gas stations; power outages; rationing of fuel or food; inability to pay for everyday necessities such as food or medicine; money and goods losing their value; job loss; being stranded at airports; breakdown of services such as healthcare or postal services; blackouts; or the inability of the public transportation infrastructure to bear the load. For example, player Cid Yama writes about the effect of fuel prices on the car market and purchasing power of individuals,

"Riding my bike to work has made me more aware of what's going on around town. More and more SUV's and Pick-Up's are up for sale "by owner". The dealerships are offering practically nothing for trade-ins on these vehicles.[...] Jobs up here are few and far between. Their paychecks have to be mostly going to gas to get to work. I can't even imagine." – Player Cid Yama (Regular)[2]

Micro-sustainability

In addition to recounting ongoing changes (i.e., disruptions in everyday life), players describe how they are coping. The dominant theme in these responses is micro sustainability, focusing on small individual actions. Subthemes include alternate commute (e.g., biking); alternate food (buying local food, starting a garden); alternate energy (e.g., investing in solar energy); or buying a fuel-efficient car. For example, *hideousallusion* writes:

"Workwise, I am in a position to help- both my jobs are poised to assist the alternative economy (one more than the other.) My regular job is Carpool Coordination and my other gig as at the Santa Cruz Farmers' Market, which I'm sure will be essential to regional operations in any serious crashlike scenario. I do worry about the farmers, and how they will get their goods to market if they are fuel-poor.

I need to get my 3-speed in working order soon, and get some tools and essentials together. I wish I knew some of my neighbors better and could get them hip to the situation- some of them have very large lots/fields around their houses that will be essential for times like this- communal composting toilets, community gardens, tent cities etc. [...]" –Player hideousallusion (Toe-dipper)[3]

---

[2] http://wayback.archive-it.org/690/20070511045848/http://cid-yama.livejournal.com/1285.html

[3] http://hideousallusion.livejournal.com/41737.html

Another set of entries under micro-sustainability focus on preparedness and acquiring new expertise, such as:

"[...]So if you're an accountant or website designer or social studies teacher- that's not enough. [...]. You may need these other skills both to earn cash or barter with others or for your own household. What sorts of skills? Well for starters, how about bike repair, carpentry, plumbing, knitting, sewing/repairs, bread baking, wildcrafting, cheesemaking or whatever else you find interesting or useful. Nobody can take these away from you- they're different than "stuff"." – Player blueski (Regular)[4]

On day 3 of the game, in an entry titled "It's time to start experimenting!", puppet master *mpathytest* puts forward the following: *This is what I believe: Shock helps solve problems we would otherwise ignore. Shock turns us into innovators. [...] When things get hard, when normal stops working, we will innovate. We will re-design our everyday lives. We will hack the way our neighborhoods work. We will re-engineer society.* Following this statement, she poses the following challenge to players:

And we need your brain to help us come up with completely original, maybe slightly crazy, ideas for banding together and living without as much oil as we're used to.

The responses to this challenge were of particular interest to us as we were interested in innovative strategies that emerged from the game. However, based on our analysis, the so-called *crazy ideas* put forward by players in response to this challenge also fall under the theme of micro-sustainability. The two entries below are representative:

"I threw up the question about how it is that those guys could transport larger items or large amounts of items. How did they get their flatpacks home from Ikea? So we had this pretty wacky brainwave of welding two bikes together with a large carrying basket in between the two. That way, not only could we have a way to move larger stuff around, with twice the power being applied to the vehicle, we could go a little faster too when we were unloaded." – Player drowned_saved (Drop-out)

"Although our supplies are weakening, we see hope and have taken up alternate means to survive.

Being in near perfect weather, with lots of plants growing, we started our garden. Although it is thriving, it is not fully operational. Will report more news on our garden soon.

We have started exploring the blocks around our home, looking for edible plants. We'll archive some spots in our neighborhood to eat for free, in the alleys and in the streets there may be enough to keep us going." –eek (Regular)[5]

[4] http://rdy2rte.livejournal.com/2239.html

[5] http://wayback.archive-it.org/690/20070511045852/http:/www.polka.com/worldwithoutoil/

Scenarios of Chaos, War, and Stress

In their responses to the game, players also engage with the long-term implications of an oil crisis. Some players' responses describe a world of chaos, war, and stress. Examples include new conflicts over resources such as news of the US military headed to Alberta borders to take over the oil reserves;[6] burning down gas stations;[7] assaults and gas theft.[8] For example, player *fabulareine (Drop-out)* asks,

Will we soon have drug mules crossing the Mexican border smuggling coffee beans instead of meth?[9]

Other players describe how the situation is leading to radical behaviors and personal choices such as the following:

"I've raped my existing customers, (who all trust me very deeply,) only staying somewhat true to my "bread and butter" client. For that client, I openly, honestly, and cheaply implemented systems that can allow the entire workforce to work from home. I even went as far as installing unlicensed software, as nobody is going to find out anyway. Yes, I still charged them for it. Lots.

[...]I am a one man source of disinformation, citing abiotic oil and every other anti-peak-oil reference I can find. I've convinced a good portion of my clients that this is temporary, turning around in 90-120 days. I've even done this with co-workers and friends. I've gone as far as writing fake news articles, and emailing them to those that aren't blood." –Player Fosedeitch (Drop-out)[10]

While we will discuss the lack of credibility and guidance later in this article, it is important to note here that the above post does not receive any dissenting comments and the troubling language in the post remains unchecked.

Scenarios of Hope, Community, and Return to Primitive Practices

In imagining the scenarios of a future without oil, and in contrast to the above, some players anticipate a return to primitive practices in tandem with the themes of hope, community, and individual resilience.

For example, player *lead_tag (Regular)* recommends that players take four items into the approaching twilight of our advanced age: an axe, an awl, a knife, and a file to survive. An axe is useful for instance as it is,

The oldest manufactured tool and the most useful, it can do most of the cutting tasks required by humans from the smallest to the most ambitious (think skinning a rabbit to felling a redwood). Cutting wood for fuel, the spark to light it when struck with a flint, the timbers for a shelter, protection as a weapon, a

[6] http://hideousallusion.livejournal.com/41737.html

[7] http://fallingintosin.livejournal.com/3311.html

[8] http://wayback.archive-it.org/690/20070511045847/http://midasmulligan.livejournal.com/998.html

[9] http://fabulareine.livejournal.com/2116.html

[10] http://fosedeitch.livejournal.com/1741.html

hammer to pound with using the poll, and should you care to abuse it, a tool to dig with, all this an axe can provide.

Anticipating a similar scenario, Player *Degaussed (Drop-out)* writes:

"Until my lifestyle becomes natural enough to gather, I've planted a garden. I've also spent some time on indian [sic] reservations, where the old ways are still sometimes practiced. Learning how to tan hides, how to make weapons, how to hunt your own food with your own tools. Things will be pretty messy for a while, but...

It will be for the best. This will all be for the best. Money won't be worth anything for much longer anyways, so I'm stocking up on sustainables [sic] and learning as much as I can." —player Degaussed[11]

In this scenario the absence of oil and the failure of infrastructures, organizations, and government is translated into messages of optimism, hope, self-reliance, and community. For example, player *the fiddler (Drop-out)* writes:

Aside from working together we are also sharing food. Every Sunday the whole community comes together to break bread potluck-style at someone's home. The atmosphere is both jovial and serious. We laugh at life's small mishaps and discuss how we can use our collective resources to everyone's advantage. Right now plans are being laid for a community garden to be set up on some of my unused land. The situation seems grim, for now, but my neighbors have really come together.

The puppet masters particularly celebrate this theme both throughout the game and toward its end. The following quotation, from puppet master *Bodi (Designer)* is an example:

We have this brilliance in our midst and maybe World Without Oil has got some way to empowering it. Including the voice in each of us that did not know how to begin speaking. We've been together for almost 9 months. So, what did we really just [?] and give birth to? ... that phone call made me realize that we've lived through something that defines us, that we cannot just walk away from. We are woven into each other's stories, and we resonate like harp strings into our collective future.[12]

The theme of community is particularly pronounced in later posts as players reflect on their experience of playing the game.

DISCUSSION

In this section, we go back to our research questions, specifically how the qualitative analysis of participation patterns begins to address the question: *What are the kinds of engagement are fostered in these environments and are these engagements generative of collective intelligence and innovative problem solving?* To do so, we first outline three main issues that are highlighted by the qualitative and quantitative analysis, namely the imbalance of participation profiles; the narrow framing of the problem; and limited guidance and emphasis on credibility of information. Based on these issues we discuss the challenge of groupthink specifically as it appears in WWO.

Imbalance of Participation Profiles

The five profiles outlined in the quantitative analysis, plus the 14 game designers who submitted content during the simulation, account for 93.6% of active contributors. High attrition rates, and the large percent of one-time contributors (170 of 331 active participants) suggest that the designers of the game might have planned the participation structures to better engage players over the long term.

At the most basic level we see a high drop in participation after the first few days raising the question of how varied mechanisms such as diverse storylines, feedback, or varied kinds of content may be used to sustain participation. For example, an important element in maintaining player interest in games is feedback. Ipsatic feedback (how you are doing relative to your own prior play) and normative feedback (how you are doing relative to all players) permit participants a richer understanding of the game and how their contributions construct the game narrative [28] Real-time feedback during the game, such as personalized reminders, return prompts, or other tools commonly employed by commercial sites and social networks to increase and sustain user engagement may also be used productively to sustain interest and engagement in the game.

The participation profiles outlined in the quantitative section enable a more detailed assessment of participation in WWO than has previously been possible. They also serve as an analytical tool to guide thinking about meaningful engagements in self-organizing collaborative environments. For example, we might consider the presence and contribution of "toe dippers" and "drop-outs" in the overall success of the game. These players are able to enter the space because of the low barrier to participation and no commitment requirements. Ease of entry to the game is arguably important for inviting people to try a novel experience; furthermore it helps create the excitement and sense of collective mission that is key to building momentum. At the same time, the initial high response rate may mislead more committed players and puppet masters regarding the game's overall success.

The hyper-engaged players pose a different but related challenge. These players' engagement and participation is important to the success of the game, as their frequent contributions keep the narrative fresh and moving. At the same time the intensity of their participation might dominate the flow and direction of the narrative at the expense of marginal voices. This goes against one of the central concepts of the ARG: their ability to bring together players with diverse backgrounds and experiences, thus enabling the entire player community to learn. Analysis of Wikipedia

[11] http://degausser618.livejournal.com/929.html

[12] http://dessum9.dl.hipcast.com/deluge/f8121e71-02df-81f4-086d-04b78d6dee62.mp3

contribution patterns have identified similar challenges: the contributions of less-frequent editors may be stifled by more regular users, those who set the norms of participation [21].

Future ARGs might employ the profiles developed from this exploration to balance the number of "toe dippers" and "drop-outs", increasing long-term engagement, and improving the likelihood of fostering learning from the game experience. While the algorithmic nature of the profiles may change to suit a particular game experience, the five profiles we propose can serve as patterns off of which participation designers can craft better game mechanics.

Problem Framing

In reading the contributions to World Without Oil, we were struck by the degree to which gasoline availability was a central focus of the narrative across all participant profiles. The game's daily update to the price of gasoline, positioned prominently in the upper left of the website layout during the simulation, was more than just a gentle reminder that fuel consumption is an important component of our sustainability discourse. It appears to have framed oil issues specifically in terms of oil consumption for transportation, both of people and material goods, even though this is only one of the areas where petroleum shortage would affect daily life. Other areas where petroleum directly or indirectly affects everyday activities, from the creation of plastics and petrochemicals, defense, or infrastructural uses of gasoline in public transit are less salient themes when they are touched upon at all. Strikingly absent from the discourse is a discussion of social justice and concern for those in the majority world, where an oil crisis might have a more significant impact not just on comforts like the single-occupancy vehicle, but on economic and physical survival.

Credibility and Guidance

In spite of the close connection established with reality, and the goal of the game to develop "firsthand insights," about a possible crisis and "a record of a real peak-oil scenario might play out," there are no mechanisms in the game to check the credibility of information and effectiveness of proposed changes, or evaluate the plausibility of the imagined scenarios.

The inability to distinguish factual and fictional information is further complicated by the subjective nature of feedback from the game. For example, a post about energy being a finite resource, citing data from the U.S. Energy Information Administration[13], and an amateur music video titled, "I choose to be positive," (submitted by one of the puppet masters) are both among the top posts on in their respective weeks.

Voices of knowledgeable individuals from environmental science, policy, or other related topics who can help players to see different sides of the issues and reason about the soundness and effectiveness of their proposals are missing. Similarly, the voices of experts who can help participants in their imagination of what the situation might entail (such as those who have first-hand experience of a similar situation) are not included [7]. There is no measure or attempt to check the imagined scenarios and actions against facts or actual scenarios.

There is little discussion of how the proposals might take hold in actuality considering the economic, political and cultural complexities and interdependences in a real world system.

For example, player *nitefoll (Drop-out)* rightly questions the practicality of his/her "crazy idea" of a community kitchen where people donate anything they can and in return they get a nutritious meal.

"Not sure about the long term ramifications/practicalities but people boarding themselves in their homes surviving on tinned beans is not the way to go. If nothing else for the prevention of malnutrition and health risks doing this causes."[14]

However, this question is not engaged and the entry is largely praised for being community-oriented by the puppet masters. In summary, while the game claims to simulate 'reality' there is no mechanism that would enable its participants to check it against reality.

The absence of outside perspectives, or other sources to encourage, support, or bring in critical points of view, together with the overall emphasis on members to adopt "positive" responses, can inadvertently undermine this diversity, motivating the members to conform.

The qualitative analysis thus highlights the challenges creating an environment that is cooperative and cultivates critical and creative engagement with issues at the same time. Based on our analyses, the design of the game creates a flexible space enabling participants to easily communicate and exchange ideas. The mechanics of the game, such as the challenges and rewards set by the designers, succeed in getting the participants to actively and imaginatively engage with the thought-experiment. This active engagement with the game and other participants creates a sense of commitment and accomplishment that manifests in players' reflections on the game.

At the same time, our sampling of players' responses indicates that while player contributions are colorful and imaginative in their details, the recurring themes (of disruption; micro-sustainability; scenarios of chaos; and scenarios of hope) are predictable and trite. These themes

---

13 http://ourfiniteworld.com/2007/04/22/our-world-is-finite-is-this-a-problem

14 http://wayback.archive-it.org/690/20070511045900/http:/nitefoll.livejournal.com/5366.html

broadly follow the arc of the narrative as put forward by the puppet masters in their daily updates that appear on the homepage of the game on each day.

Collective Intelligence or Groupthink

In our view, World Without Oil undermines diversity by reducing all entries to equally valid contributions and perspectives. This concern is closely related to concerns about the general inability of (young) people to assess or "read" games similar to texts that structure information with their own "aesthetic norms, genre conventions, ideological biases, and codes of representation" [13, p.15]. In his study of youth, media and learning, Henry Jenkins identifies this as a *transparency problem,* among the three main challenges for young people to effectively use and participate in media consumption and production. He defines the transparency problem as "the challenges young people face in learning to see clearly the ways that media shape perceptions of the world" [13, p. 15]. In the context of WWO, references to reality and supporting material such as factual data, real-life events, news, and stories complicate the scenario, making it more difficult for participants to distinguish the reality constructed by the game–and lived experience. Moreover, players do not question or critique the framework of the game itself or the challenges and scenarios set by the designers.

In summary, the theme of reality is an important aspect of WWO. However, there are no means available to the players or viewers to evaluate factual data, effectiveness of the proposals for change, or contrast the imagined scenarios against lived experience. Fiction, facts, and opinions are all woven together; creating a world that appears to be real but is distant from real world correlates.

In its emphasis to encourage diverse points of view, WWO relies upon a considerable degree of subjective involvement. Thus, the nature of individual contributions and the overall tone and substance of the collective depends on the experience and expertise of its participants, and their willingness and ability to engage with the issues critically. All actions and proposals for change are considered equally valid contributions to the "collective intelligence."

World Without Oil seeks to overcome the limitations of hierarchical structures and the rigidity and political nature of traditional organizations, replacing it with a non-hierarchical ad-hoc system for sharing knowledge and learning. In doing so it downplays the role and power of the game's structure, and the fact that stories that are added or highlighted by the designers in steering the direction of the game. Moreover, in its emphasis on openness, inclusiveness and a positive atmosphere, it (unintentionally) plays down reflection and resistance that are important modes of participation and real world problem solving.

CONCLUSION

Based on our discussion, we draw out the following design implications for ARGs that seek to cultivate diversity and engage players in creative problem solving. Foremost, it is important to give careful attention to problem framing and seed scenarios that guide players' responses and development of the narrative. It is also crucial to design feedback mechanisms that guide players and viewers in judging and evaluating the responses enabling them to parse out facts from fiction, and plausible scenarios and solutions from problematic or ineffective ones. To do so, ARGs that aim to cultivate diversity and creative problem solving need to involve puppet masters with subject matter expertise who can better guide the narrative and engage players toward scenarios that are both imaginative and plausible. Lastly, it such spaces should be more transparent about their limitations by acknowledging how their design and development are intertwined with the discourse that emerges within them so players can better judge and "read" the resulting narrative.

WWO provided a novel interactive space for people to engage with problems of genuine social import. While ARGs and other collective, narrative problem solving spaces hold tremendous potential for addressing these problems, they are not without their challenges. Designers of these spaces should be cognizant of different participant profiles, and how these patterns of contribution affect the flow of the game. Subsequent learning or anticipated individual behavior change is predicated on both the quantity and character of engagement with the problem space and other participants. Our approach to understanding ARGs such as WWO, using a reconstructed "searchable" game narrative and content analysis, provides unique "post mortem" insights that contribute to our assessment of the game's overall effects. It also serves as a pattern that might be replicated with other ARGs to further analyze learning outcomes. To be effective learning spaces, ARGs much provide feedback that facilitates richer modes of interaction, as well as game mechanics that promote diverse communities and reflection on a range of possible solutions. Our analysis suggests that WWO was too tightly scripted to the designers' own solutions and philosophy; the result is a flat conversation with little innovation and almost no productive dissent. As funding agencies such as the National Science Foundation have promoted the design of ARGs to facilitate learning, we can and should do much more to assess their validity and impact before, during and after the game, beyond anecdotal evidence from designers and puppet masters.

REFERENCES

1. Arthur C. 2006 Jul 20. What is the 1% rule? *The Guardian.* Accessed 20 July 2014 from: http://www.theguardian.com/technology/2006/jul/20/guardianweeklytechnologysection2
2. Benford, S. and Giannachi, G. 2011. *Performing Mixed Reality.* MIT Press, Cambridge, MA, USA.
3. Benkler, Y. 2006. *The Wealth of Networks: How Social Production Transforms Markets and Freedom.* New Haven, CT: Yale University Press.

4. Bogost, I., Ferrari S., and Schweizer, B. 2012. *Newsgames: Journalism at Play*. Cambridge, MA: MIT Press.

5. Bonsignore, B. 2012. Designing alternate reality games. In *CHI '12 Extended Abstracts on Human Factors in Computing Systems* (CHI EA '12). ACM, New York, NY, USA, 911–914.

6. Bonsignore, E., Hansen, D., Kraus, K., & Ruppel, M. (2012). Alternate reality games as platforms for practicing 21st-Century literacies. *International Journal of Learning and Media*, 4(1), 25–54.

7. Boskic, N., Dobson, T., and Rusnak, P. 2008. Play it seriously: juxtaposing AR and RW crises. In *Proceedings of the 2nd European Conference on Games Based Learning*. Barcelona, Spain.

8. Gee, J. P. 2004. *What Video Games Have to Teach Us about Learning and Literacy*. New York: Palgrave Macmillan.

9. Gurzick, D., Landry, B. M., and White, K. F. 2010. Alternate reality games and groupwork. In *Proceedings of the ACM 2010 International Conference on Supporting Group Work* (GROUP '10). ACM, New York, NY, USA, 303–4.

10. Gurzick, D., White, K. F., Lutters, W. J, Landry, B. M., Dombrowski, C, and Kim, J. Y. 2011. Designing the future of collaborative workplace systems: lessons learned from a comparison with alternate reality games. In *Proceedings of the 2011 iConference* (iConference '11). ACM, New York, NY, USA, 174–180.

11. Hayes, E. and Gee, J. P. 2011. Public pedagogy through video games. In (J. Sandlin, B. Schultz and J. Burdick, eds.) *Handbook of Public Pedagogy: Education and Learning beyond Schooling*. New York: Routledge.

12. Janis, I. L. 1982. *Groupthink: Psychological Studies of Policy Decisions and Fiascoes.* 2nd Edition. New York: Houghton Mifflin.

13. Jenkins, J. 2006. *Convergence Culture: Where Old and New Media Collide*. New York: NYU Press.

14. Kim, J., Allen, J. P., and Lee, E. 2008. Alternate reality gaming. *Communications of the ACM*, 51 (2), 36

15. Levy, P. 1997. *Collective Intelligence*. Trans. Robert Bononno. Cambridge: Perseus.

16. McGonigal, J. 2011. *Reality Is Broken: Why Games Make Us Better and How They Can Change the World*. NY: Penguin.

17. McGonigal, J. 2008. Why I love bees: a case study in collective intelligence gaming. In (Katie Salen, ed.) *The Ecology of Games: Connecting Youth, Games and Learning*, pp 199–228. Cambridge, MA: MIT Press.

18. McGonigal, J. 2010. Gaming can make a better world. *TED Talk: http://www. ted.com/talks/jane_mcgonigal_ gaming_can_ make_a_better_world.html.*

19. Nielsen J. 2006. Participation inequality: Lurkers vs. contributors in Internet communities. Accessed 20 July 2014 from: http://www.nngroup.com/articles/ participation-inequality/

20. O'Hara, K., Grian, H., and Williams, J. 2008. Participation, collaboration and spectatorship in an alternate reality game. In *Proceedings of the 20th Australasian Conference on Computer-Human Interaction: Designing for Habitus and Habitat* (OZCHI '08). ACM, New York, NY, USA, 130–139.

21. Panciera, K., Halfaker, A., and Terveen, L. 2009. Wikipedians are born, not made: A study of power editors on Wikipedia. In *Proceedings of the ACM 2009 International Conference on Supporting Group Work* (GROUP '09). ACM, New York, NY, USA, 51–60.

22. Pelletier, C. 2009 Games and learning: What's the connection? *International J. of Learning and Media* 1, 1, 83–101.

23. Peyton, T., Young, A.L., and Lutters, W. 2013. Playing with leadership and expertise: Military tropes and teamwork in an ARG. In *Proceedings of the SIGCHI Conference on Human Factors in Computing Systems.*

24. Rusnak, P., Dobson, T., and Boskic, N. 2008. Articulation of ecological values in Alternate Reality Gaming: A case study of World Without Oil. In *Proceedings of the 2nd European Conference on Games Based Learning.*

25. Salen, K. 2008. *The Ecology of Games: Connecting Youth, Games, and Learning*. The John D. and Catherine T. Macarthur Foundation Series on Digital Media and Learning. Cambridge, MA: MIT Press.

26. Sanders R. 1992. The Pareto Principle: Its use and abuse. *Journal of Product & Brand Management*, 1(2), 37–40.

27. Shirky, C. 2008. *Here Comes Everybody: The Power of Organizing without Organizations*. New York: Penguin Press.

28. Shute, V. J. 2008. Focus on formative feedback. *Review of Educational Research,* 78(1), 153–189.

29. Surowiecki, J. 2004. *The Wisdom of Crowds: Why the Many Are Smarter than the Few and How Collective Wisdom Shapes Business, Economies, Societies, and Nations.* New York: Doubleday.

30. van Mierlo T. 2014. The 1% Rule in four digital health social networks: An observational study. *J. Med Internet Res,* 16(2), e33, http://www.jmir.org/2014/2/ e33/

31. World Without Oil, http://worldwithoutoil.org

Understanding Student Motivation, Behaviors, and Perceptions in MOOCs

Saijing Zheng, Mary Beth Rosson, Patrick C. Shih, and John M. Carroll
The Pennsylvania State University, University Park, PA
{suz128, mrosson, patshih, carroll@ist.psu.edu}

ABSTRACT
Massive Open Online Courses (MOOCs) have recently experienced rapid development and garnered significant attention from various populations. Despite the wide recognition of MOOCs as an important opportunity within educational practices, there are still many questions as to how we might satisfy students' needs, as evidenced by very high dropout rates. Researchers lack a solid understanding of what student needs are being addressed by MOOCs, and how well MOOCs now address (or fail to address) these needs. To help in building such an understanding, we conducted in-depth interviews probing student motivations, learning perceptions and experiences towards MOOCs, paying special attention to the MOOC affordances and experiences that might lead to high drop rates. Our study identified learning motivations, learning patterns, and a number of factors that appear to influence student retention. We proposed that the issue of retention should be addressed from two perspectives: retention as a problem but also retention as an opportunity.

Author Keywords
Massive Open Online Courses; MOOCs; online learning; student retention; learning motivation; learning experiences

ACM Classification Keywords
H.5 [Information Interfaces and Presentation] (e.g. HCI); K.3.1 [Computer Uses in Education]: Distance Learning; J.4 [Social and Behavioral Sciences]

General Terms
Human Factors; Design

INTRODUCTION
Massive Open Online Courses (MOOCs) are a recent expansion in e-learning and distant education that have experienced rapid development and achieved substantial attention from a broad range of learners. Compared to traditional online courses, MOOCs are larger in scale and distributed worldwide across a variety of networks and platforms, with no limitations on individual involvement. MOOCs provide an opportunity to teach interesting or critical content to new groups of learners [18]; they also may have important impacts for online education practices in general, for instance allowing institutions to develop distinctive MOOC-centered missions [8]. As Siemens noted "even if the current generation of MOOCs spectacularly crash and fade into oblivion, the legacy of top tier university research and growing public awareness of online learning will be dramatic." [32]

Although MOOCs have been widely accepted, and are rightly viewed as an educational innovation, education researchers know very little about what student needs a MOOC may address, or how well they address those needs. In comparison to the more long-lived concept of a virtual learning environment (VLE), MOOCs are a relatively new phenomenon. They differ from VLEs from several ways including scale, students' level of control and flexibility, the relative roles of instructor and students, student motivation and outcomes. Although efforts have been made to understand user experiences (UX) of VLEs [21, 26, 35, 41], differences such as these can cause a misalignment of UX observations for VLEs situations. Thus, educators have called for a study of user experiences in the context of MOOCs [25, 12]. Milligan emphasized, "understanding the nature of learners and their engagement is critical to the success of any online education provision, especially those MOOCs where there is an expectation that the learners should self-motivate and self-direct their learning [25]."

Notably, MOOCs have been plagued by extremely high drop-out rates [1, 4, 9, 17, 19]. Although several studies have investigated students' retention and engagement issues, surprisingly little research attention has been directed to the population of students who do not finish the courses in which they register [1, 25]; as a result it is difficult to fully capture the user experiences tied to retention problems, and many important reflections are missed [30]. In recent years, some researchers have been using data mining method to investigate enrollment and retention within large datasets [13, 20, 16]. Nevertheless, even these researchers have called for qualitative studies that can complement and help to the quantitative trends and patterns mined from the online data [16]. It is essential to understand student motivations, learning perceptions and experiences towards MOOCs, and to understand how the

CSCW 2015, March 14–18, 2015, Vancouver, BC, Canada.

http://dx.doi.org/10.1145/2675133.2675217

affordances and experiences of MOOCs may lead to high drop rates.

Historically, MOOC designs have been of two different types: the connectivist MOOCs (cMOOC) applying the concepts of connectivist learning (e.g., an emphasis on connected, collaborative learning)[8, 31, 32]; and content-based extended MOOCs (xMOOCs), which emphasize a more traditional learning approach by video presentations that are complemented by short quizzes and other testing[8, 31, 32, 39]. Here we focus particularly on the more recent xMOOCs, as this is the style of MOOC that has grown so tremendously in scale and variety, gaining significant attention by students and institution, but without a solid understanding of the student experience and factors influencing retention and outcomes.

In this paper, we employ the grounded theory method in an in-depth interview study to investigate users' motivation to register for a particular course, their learning perceptions and behavior patterns, and potential reasons for not finishing courses. Using these interview data, we have identified four broad types of motivations for joining a MOOC, which we have labeled fulfilling current needs, prepare for the future, satisfying curiosity, and connecting with people. Also, five interesting learning behavior patterns emerged from our interviews, including the auditing of a MOOC, or joining MOOCs as part of a pre-existing cohort. We also recognized multiple factors as threats or opportunities affecting retention during online learning. Those interesting stories suggest that researchers should consider MOOCs as a new virtual organization that integrates educational content, technology and learners. We discuss design implications from these results as well. In general, our study provides actionable guidance for MOOCs and also fills the gap of current literature on retention problems. Our efforts will help improve MOOCs overall community and offer better opportunity for students to enjoy learning and occupy MOOCs.

LITERATURE REVIEW

MOOCs are a manifestation of the open education movement that emphasizes how open education resources and tools can improve the quality of education [14]. Open education platforms (i.e., Coursera, edX, Udacity, etc.) utilize technological innovations (e.g., interactive videos) to allow educators to provide MOOCs to massive number of students [11]. Meanwhile, this educational format allows students to overcome physical and financial barriers [33] and to freely pursue their own learning goals [2]. Not surprisingly, these opportunities have attracted significant attention from education and technology researchers and practitioners.

MOOCs may impact society in multiple ways. First, they may expand or enhance teaching practices, encouraging institutions to develop distinctive missions [8] and to provide an opportunity to develop new pedagogy. For instance, MOOCs can provide their students with better and more varied teaching than individual instructors might be able to develop by themselves [8]. Second, they may increase access to good teaching and interesting curriculum for new groups of learners, and help attract students into higher education who might otherwise not have ventured there [18]. The current focus on MOOCs is opportunity for researchers to engage with emerging pedagogical mode that is significantly under-theorized [18].

MOOCs and VLEs

We draw some research inspirations from existing online learning literature. Virtual Learning Environments (VLEs) have evolved from commercial course management systems (e.g., Blackboard) to current open source platforms (e.g., Moodle)[39, 21]. They have been widely adopted by higher education institutions (HEIs). In terms of technical features, VLEs and MOOCs platforms offer similar course content delivery and forum-based discussion features. However, in terms of pedagogical differences, MOOCs are designed and implemented very differently because of their *massiveness* and *openness*. Below we detail how MOOCs separate themselves from VLEs based on these characteristics.

First, the intention of MOOCs is to make course content available to as many people as possible. The number of students in MOOCs typically ranges from tens of thousands to hundreds of thousands. The scale of a VLE is typically much closer to that of traditional classrooms and is much smaller than MOOCs. MOOCs need to be designed differently to accommodate the large number of learners. Specifically, while the instructors are expected to play a hands-on role and to provide personal feedback in VLEs, the learners in MOOCs take a much greater role in shaping their own learning experiences [39]. For instance, in a MOOC, an instructor acts more as a facilitator [5, 23, 39] fostering a space for learning connections to occur. MOOCs instructors also often rely on automatic assessment and peer grading instead of providing personal feedback like the VLE instructors [18].

Second, a fundamental mission of MOOCs is to make the course materials *freely* and *openly accessible* to the general public, whereas VLEs are adopted by HEIs based on the traditional university course scheduling, format and registrations [21, 26]. For this reason, most MOOCs only offer a completion certificate, whereas students using VLEs are often earning credits for a formal degree. In this sense, participants in VLEs are a "captive audience" [21] wherein learners cannot choose a preferred VLE, but rather must use the online learning content and tools mandated by their institution. MOOC users have the freedom to adopt different learning platforms and content depending on their needs. The open nature of MOOCs creates a population that is self-selected to be engaged and passionate about this approach to learning [40].

Although research on VLE usability and UX [21, 26, 35, 41] can provide some insight for MOOCs, the pedagogical and sociotechnical differences in terms of MOOCs' *massiveness* and *openness* are likely to lead to distinctive considerations for the design of both systems and curricula. Therefore, it is necessary to fully investigate user experiences in MOOCs.

Recently, VLE providers have considered how they might expand services and features to accommodate MOOCs, facilitating more open access to VLE courses, as well as supporting advanced analytics, interactive multimedia, synchronous collaboration, and even integration with student support services [40]. Thus, the MOOC characteristics of size and open access may be integrated within existing VLEs [40]. If so, an understanding of UX for MOOCs may provide valuable input to these extended VLEs.

cMOOCs versus xMOOCs

The development of MOOCs is rooted within the ideals of openness in education, namely that knowledge should be shared freely, and that the desire to learn should be met without demographic, economic, or geographical constraints [24]. Historically, MOOCs have developed into two distinct directions: the connectivist MOOCs (cMOOCs) and extended MOOCs (xMOOCs). According to Siemens, cMOOCs focus on knowledge creation and generation while xMOOCs focus on "knowledge duplication" [8, 32].

cMOOCs, pioneered by Siemens and Stephen Downes with a first course "Connectivism and Connected Knowledge 2008" [8, 9], seek to embed online discussions and collaborations by which the networked community of learners will build knowledge and understanding. cMOOC participants are free to share material and collaborate using any technological tools they like [24]. While xMOOCs (edX, Coursera, Udacity, etc.) and cMOOCs share the notion of free worldwide participants in a course without credit, xMOOCs differ in that they employ a well-defined course management platform.

Here we focus on the more recent xMOOCs that have emerged quickly and at a tremendous scale, gaining rapid attention from students and institutions [8]. We hope to address the paucity of research examining xMOOC retention issues [4], especially using a qualitative methods. All subsequent mentions of 'MOOCs' in this paper refer to the xMOOCs.

Current Research on MOOCs

A large (massive) group of learners is an indispensable part of any given MOOCs' success [8, 40]. However, the learning experiences of these massive groups have been difficult to characterize. Milligan noted that "understanding the nature of learners and their engagement is critical to the success of any online education provision, especially those MOOCs where there is an expectation that the learners should self-motivate and self-direct their learning [25]." Haywood also pointed out that much more research is needed to understand MOOC learners, for instance how to design and deliver content successfully across a range of subjects and at a range of levels, ensuring that the MOOC experience is helpful to learners, and that learners get value from their certificates of completion [12].

A number of researchers have investigated issues that might improve the experience and success of MOOC courses. One stream of literature has examined on the role of discussion forums and how users utilize these during learning in MOOCs [6, 13, 20]. Other researchers have investigated the challenges of peer assessment [15, 27, 33]. Still others have worked at a more general level to characterize MOOCs and to call for improving the learner experience [5, 22].

One notable phenomenon in MOOC research is the very low retention rates in MOOCs [1, 4, 8, 9, 19, 16]. Researchers have attempted to investigate the observed retention and engagement issues and offered design insights that might better serve learners' needs [1, 16, 25]. For instance, Milligan et al. explored patterns of engagement in cMOOCs and uncovered three general patterns: active participant, lurker, and passive participant. They also found factors affecting engagement, including confidence, prior experience and motivation [25]. Adamopoulos identified teachers as the most important factor affecting retention. However, these studies have not yet attended to the population of students who drop out of MOOCs [1, 25]. As a result, the results of these earlier studies may be biased because they do not capture the experiences of users who engage little or not at all with the course [30].

Another set of researchers have been applying learning analytics to investigate retention issues [4, 13, 16, 20]. Clow proposed a model named "the funnel of participation" to describe MOOCs retention, in which learners would go through a four-stage funnel (i.e., awareness, registration, activity, and progress)[4]. Only some of them will achieve meaningful learning progress at the end; drop off at each stage is large. However, this work does not explain the *causes* of the drop offs and what we might do to encourage more learners to attain meaningful learning outcomes. Kizilcec et. al made a finer analysis of MOOC disengagement, and classified learners into four categories (i.e., auditing, completing, disengaging, and sampling), but again these results do not explain the rationales that led to student disengagement[16]. They call for qualitative study to more fully explore and complement their study that relies on quantitative data analysis [16].

Our study extends these prior studies and employs the methods of grounded theory in an in-depth interview study to investigate users' motivation to register for a particular course, their learning perceptions, behavioral patterns, and potential reasons for not finishing the MOOCs courses.

RESEARCH METHOD

Data and Data Collection

We posted a study recruitment announcement on research website of a large northeastern university. We also recruited participants using a snowball sampling method, through our social media accounts and personal friendship network.

At the beginning of the semi-structured interview, we gathered demographic information about each participant (e.g., gender, age, occupation). We then interviewed participants about their general MOOCs experiences (e.g., how many MOOCs they have taken, what are the topics of these MOOCs, the platforms used to access the online courses, how long they have been using MOOCs). Our particular focus was on the motivations for joining and continuing (or not) with a course.

Interviews ranged from approximately 35 minutes to 2 hours. All interviews were audio-recorded, annotated and transcribed for further data analysis. The interviews

#	Occupation	Gender	Age	Region	Interview	Citizenship	Completed Courses	Uncompleted Courses
P1	Student	M	20	U.S.	F2F	American	American History(C)	Game Theory(C)
P2	Student	F	25	China	Skype	Chinese	Social Network Analysis(C)	Networks: Friends, Money, and Bytes(C)
P3	Student	M	27	U.S.	F2F	Chinese	Machine Leaning(C) American History(C) Artificial Intelligence(E) Music in the 20th Century(E) Game Theory(C) Natural Language Processing(C)	Cryptography(C) Principles of Written English(E) Academic Writing(C) Mathematical Methods for Quantitative Finance(C)
P4	Employee	M	26	U.S.	Phone	American	Cryptography 1(C)	Cryptography 2(C); Creativity, Innovation, and Change(C)
P5	Student	M	20	U.S.	F2F	Italian	Java(U)	Computer Science101(C)
P6	Student	M	23	China	Skype	Chinese	HCI(C) Social Network Analysis(C) Introduction to Databases(C) Learn to Program: The Fundamentals(C) Statistics: Making Sense of Data(C)	Game Theory(C) Introduction to Data Science(C) The Fiction of Relationship(C) Design: Creation of Artifacts in Society(C) The Camera Never Lies(C)
P7	Student	M	25	U.S.	F2F	American	HCI(C) Personal Finance(C)	Networks: Friends, Money, and Bytes(C)
P8	Student	M	18	U.S.	F2F	Indian	Python (U)	Python (C)
P9	Student	F	26	U.S.	F2F	Chinese	Machine Leaning(C) Game Theory(C) Data Analysis and statistical inference(C) Networks: Friends, Money, and Bytes(C)	Statistics(C) Artificial Intelligence(E) Principles of Written English(E) The Ancient Greek Hero(E) Algorithms(U) Data Analysis(C)
P10	Student	M	24	U.S.	F2F	American	Web Development(U) How to Build a Startup(U)	Java(C)
P11	Student	F	26	U.S.	F2F	American	Maps and the Geospatial Revolution(C)	Statistics(C) Computing for Data Analysis(C)
P12	Student	F	22	China	Skype	Chinese	Algorithms(C)	Foundations of Computer Graphics(E)
P13	Engineer	F	36	U.S.	Tele	American	Introduction to Arts(C)	Renaissance Architecture in Italy(C)
P14	Manager	M	40	U.S.	Skype	American	--	Social Psychology(C) History of Chinese Architecture(E) How to Build a Startup
P15	Stay-at-home Parent	F	32	U.S.	F2F	American	Computer Science101(C) Introduction to Arts(C)	Calculus: Single Variable(C) Maps and the Geospatial Revolution(C)
P16	Parent	F	36	U.S.	F2F	Japanese	Statistics One(C) Music(C)	Algorithms, Part I(C) Introduction to Arts(C) Science & Cooking(E)
P17	Retire	M	62	U.S.	F2F	American	Guitar(C)	Songwriting(C)
P18	Ph.D	F	26	U.S.	Skype	Germany	Social Network Analysis(C)	Academic Writing(C) Core Concepts in Data Analysis(C) A History of the World since 1300(C)

Table 1. Demographics of Participants and MOOCs Usage. (C) for Coursera, (E) for edX, and (U) for Udacity.

produced a rich set of recollections and descriptions addressing many issues in the MOOC experience, which have been summarized as a number of emergent themes. The balance of this paper will focus on four categories of findings: 1) *motivations of registering for the particular course; 2) online learning perceptions and behaviors*; 3) *reasons for not finishing the course*; 4) *design reflections and suggestions to better fulfill their study needs.*

As summarized in Table 1, our 18 interviewees included undergraduate students, Masters students, Ph.D students, parents of high school students, a housewife, employees with almost 10 years work experience, and elderly people retired for several years. In the following discussion, we refer to individuals as relevant by participant number.

Data Analysis

We applied grounded theory in this interview study; this method emphasizes the simultaneous processes of data collection and analysis [7]. We conducted initial data analysis sessions after the first few interviews to identify core themes. Learner motivations, perceptions, and learning behaviors were identified as the key concepts from the first stage of analysis. When those main themes were identified, axial coding was used to identify categories. Themes and categories were further refined through an iterative coding process that involved all the authors. The results presented as a coding guideline were used to guide the next round of coding. When the second round of the analysis were not able to find a new concept and category, it demonstrate the saturation of the theory [7].

FINDINGS

Motivations to Join MOOCs

We identified four broad types of student motivations for joining MOOCs: fulfilling current needs, preparing for the future, satisfying curiosity, and connecting with people. Note that although the following discussion treats each of these themes separately, it is quite possible that a student might choose to join different MOOCs for different reasons, perhaps even at the same time.

Fulfilling Current Needs

Course Complement

A common motivation for students to enroll in a MOOC is to complement other courses they are currently taking. Two primary rationales underlie this motivation. First, students feel pressure to achieve a high GPA or at least to earn the credits for a school course. The course content is frequently challenging and fast-paced, which may make it difficult for a student to keep up. MOOCs that cover similar subject areas can provide a high level overview that helps to them grasp their school course content more quickly. As an example, P5 was taking a Java course. He found it difficult to fully understand the programming concepts within the standard class period. So he enrolled in an Udacity MOOC, "Java programming for beginners" to help him succeed:

"It worked very well. The professor explained the concepts very well and I was able to watch repeatedly until I understood the concepts. I also practiced programming following the instructions of the professor. [MOOC] gave me some basic knowledge that was missing in my school class. I finished this course when my school class ended, and I got high marks! " [P5]

Second, a school class usually cannot cover all the knowledge in a particular field and different instructors have their own perspectives on how to arrange the course content. Some student participants felt the content in a class did not meet their needs well enough and they desired to learn more. For instance, P6 took an HCI class at his university, but he also registered an HCI course on Coursera. He liked that the MOOC professor taught in a different way and covered different topics. This helped him broaden his perspective of HCI.

Professional Needs

Another motivation of interviewees was more typical of Ph.D students, Masters students and others who are seeking to gain knowledge that will allow them to better fulfill their current job responsibilities. For example, a new project or an innovative idea may require a new kind of skill or require use of a new tool to create specialized environments or conduct a detailed data analysis. Our participants see MOOCs as effective and efficient resources to gain knowledge for such performance-related needs.

Two rationales underlie this motivation. First, although students may opt to enroll in a regular class to gain needed knowledge, a traditional class requires a prescribed investment of time and energy investment. For instance, P9 needed new statistical knowledge to analyze her dissertation data. She enrolled in a statistics class, but gave up in the second week because the class met three times a week, and she needed to spend 40 minutes to commute to each session. After class, she needed to return to her home campus quickly to manage TA office hours and meetings. She was running out of time quickly, so she dropped the class and bought a book on statistics to learn on her own. Her friend recommended her to join a MOOC, where she was able to access the course content when she had time:

"Previously, I had to audit or take a class in school even though I didn't need credits and only wanted to learn something for my research. Now I can choose a MOOC based on my research needs and learn whenever I want. Many of my friends (they are also Ph.D. students) take MOOCs for their research. It's really cool!"[P9]

Indeed, all of our Ph.D. and Masters students interviewees had registered for at least one MOOC to meet their current research needs (e.g., machine learning, statistical classes, programing languages, etc.).

Interviewees who are working also took advantage of MOOCs to better fulfill their job responsibilities. P4 works in the security department of his company. He joined the company after he got his bachelor degree and received some training after starting the job, but this education only taught him how to monitor and solve security problems without providing the underlying rationales. He completed several security courses on Coursera, and now feels more confident about his work.

A second rationale in this category is that students tend to trust the quality of MOOC instruction. Because MOOCs are often created by professors who are renowned in the subject matter and employed by famous institutions, the participants believe that they will achieve equal or better education than they can get from classes at their own university:

"You definitely want to learn Machine Leaning with Professor Andrew [Ng] at Stanford. He is very famous in this field. I took his class last year on Coursera. I also recommended his class to my friends. It's a very helpful class for my research. " [P3]

Preparing for the Future

Impress Potential Employer

Many participants enroll in MOOCs to enhance their future employability. These individuals have strong wills to complete the course, because receiving the completion certificate vouches for satisfactory knowledge of the course content. Some participants (i.e. P3, P6, P9, P10) have the perception that the more MOOC certificates they receive, the more they will be able to impress their potential employers;

"If I only finished one course, a future employer would say 'the guy knows this knowledge.' But if I finished 10 courses and no one required me to do that, the future employer would probably think 'this guy has strong self motivation and persistence.' I might impress them this way". [P6]

At the same time, interviewees (P1, P6, P9, P11) were well aware that a MOOC certificate is not official and might not even be appropriate for inclusion on a resume. Alternatively, they might list their finished MOOCs on personal websites, for example connecting their certificates to a LinkedIn profile, because they believe that future employers might view their online profiles.

Shape a Goal for College Application

We interviewed two mothers (P15, P16) whose children are in high school and will apply for college next year. Their children are interested in several different majors, but they do not know what the majors are like and how difficult the courses will be. These parents enrolled their children in MOOCs as a test run to explore college courses. MOOCs provide an opportunity for high school students to experience different courses and instructors, and perhaps to identify emerging interests. Parents also encourage their children to finish the most interesting MOOCs and to include the certificates as a part of the support materials in their college applications:

"I am so happy I can help him...now he is taking Computer Science [101] offered by Stanford. He is enjoying the class so far. Hopefully he can find one [major] he truly loves." [P15]

Satisfying Curiosity

One common motivation to register for a particular course is personal interest. Most of our interviewees have taken at least three MOOCs, and several interviewees said the reason they took the first course was that they were very curious about what MOOCs look like (P1, P2, P3, P6, P9, P16). When they learned about MOOCs from friends, professors, or news media, they tried to learn more about MOOCs as well as to gain benefit from the free and high quality education resource:

"I learned about MOOCs from New York Times, and they sounded amazing. You know, they are free and offered by famous institutions. I was very curious about such kind of education format, so I went to Coursera and registered for a course about American history. I also registered for other courses later, but for the first one, it was just for my personal interest and curiosity." [P1]

Most interviewees thought that MOOCs opened a door for them, a door that allowed them to access valuable education resources they were always interested in but had found difficult to pursue in reality. For example, P13 has been a technical support in an insurance company for 10 years and described her reason for enrolling in a MOOC on art. She has always wanted to systematically learn art, but has not been able to find a suitable opportunity because she has never had spare time or the financial resources to attend classes. MOOCs matched all her needs perfectly: free, flexible and high quality:

"I was so excited when I learned about MOOCs from my friend. The fact was that I didn't believe it at the beginning. But when I opened an MOOC account on Coursera and registered for the art class, I realized my dream would become true. I finally could learn art just for my interest without any finical burdens and time constrains. The feeling was so amazing. Thank MOOCs!" [P13]

Connecting with People

One of our more surprising themes is that learners sometimes enroll in MOOCs to find peers with common interests. They found that meeting someone with mutual interests makes them feel happy and connected. P17 is 62 years old and has been retired for several years; he recently moved to a small town to live nearby his daughter. He felt lonely in a new environment. He had always liked playing music and was a part of a band when he was in college. When he learned about MOOCs from the newspaper, he enrolled in a Guitar class with the goal of meeting people who also enjoy music, even though he already knows how to play a guitar. He also planned to take future classes with the friends that he met in MOOCs.

"*I never thought I could find friends online. Although we don't meet face to face, I am very happy to share my thoughts with someone who knows music. Hopefully, our friendship can go beyond this class period and last for a long time.*" [P17]

P13 works remotely for an insurance company. After finishing her daily work at home, she feels very isolated. To increase her social life, she works twice a week as a volunteer in a Mcdonald's house. But she still has a lot of spare time. Finally, she finds MOOCs are worthy of joining, where she can find a lot of interesting classes and friends! She finished a personal finance course and was taking Renaissance Architecture in Italy when taking the interview.

"*Taking those classes has become part of my daily life. I know some friends there and we have some very interesting discussions which sometimes are related to courses but sometimes not. They do enrich my life.*" [P13]

How Students Learn from MOOCs

Because different participants may have different motivations for taking any given MOOC, many interesting learning patterns emerged from our interviews. Some participants treat MOOCs as regular school classes, following a self-mandated course schedule, while others seem to appropriate MOOCs based on their current needs. MOOCs are used at times as modularized resources, edutainment, and a motivation for study groups. Students also integrate online resources other than MOOCs.

MOOCs as Regular School Classes

One common way for students to study in a MOOC is as if the online resource is a standard school class. These participants follow a fixed course schedule week by week. They usually arrange a fixed time in each week to watch videos, take notes, complete quizzes and assignments, and participate in forums. For example, P2 took a Social Network Analysis on Coursera; she watched course lectures on Monday morning, did quizzes and assignments in the afternoon, and sometimes joined discussion forum if she encountered problems. She successfully finished this course and also achieved valuable research insights from it.

"*I was so excited to join this class. Although it is optional, I took it as a serious class and marked it on my calendar...I really treasured this opportunity to learn from such a famous professor. I also received useful comments from other students about my research. I felt happy when I watched the course videos, did assignments, and discussed with others every Monday*". [P2]

P7 is an undergraduate who took a personal finance course on Coursera that is unrelated to his major. He took four university courses and one from Coursera. He also inserted this online course into his class schedule, completing the MOOC at the same time as the semester finished.

MOOCs as Modularized Resources

In some cases, participants did not care whether they could complete a course or receive a certificate. Instead, they wanted to learn something based on specific needs, such as understanding basic concepts, complementing a school course, learning a particular algorithm, gaining a general picture of a topic, or simply learning new materials.

"*I just want to learn the basic rules of Java without doing any quizzes and assignments and participating in discussions. I learn it not because I am interested in it but I need to use it. So I just watch the lectures and get a general understanding of Java. That's it.*" [P10]

Some participants only focused on a few lectures that fulfilled their immediate needs and skipped others. For example, P11 just needed to learn linear regression to analyze her data, so she left the lessons on logistic regression unfinished in a statistics course.

MOOCs as Edutainment

Edutainment is content that is primarily educational but has incidental entertainment value. Our participants (P4, P6, P10, P14, P18) have appropriated some MOOCs (i.e., history, music, and art) for edutainment purposes. For these participants, they neither wanted to waste valuable time on watching videos purely for entertainment, nor invest long time periods to join regular courses that are unrelated to work or study. They chose to take advantage of the free and informative nature of MOOCs, treating them as edutainment videos to watch in their spare time (e.g., while eating breakfast, doing house chores, working out, resting, etc.). Typically, participants who treat MOOCs as edutainment only watch the lecture videos without completing quizzes and assignments.

"*I am taking a MOOC about American history. My wife and I watch the videos every morning when we eat breakfast and wash dishes. Our breakfast is fun and educational! We enjoy them very much!* [P14]

"*I also download videos on my phone and watch them when I work out. Previously I only listened to music, but now I find MOOCs videos are more attractive. You know, you can learn much unconsciously.*" [P4]

MOOCs as an Opportunity to Interact with Others

Some participants feel lonely when they study MOOCs on their own. Although MOOC platforms (e.g., Coursera, edX, and Udacity) provide discussion forums, the majority of participants felt that discussion forums failed to facilitate interactive communication. They also had a desire to study MOOCs with their friends rather than complete strangers. To solve this problem, some participants joined or organized local study groups. In a sense by doing this they converted *virtual courses* into *actual courses*. For example, P9 joined a MOOCs study group of 12 organized by her friend. Her friend organized the study group by sending emails that invited friends and classmates to join. The group consisted of graduate students from different departments, such as computer science, chemistry engineering and information sciences and technology. They created a mailing list to recommend and choose MOOCs to join as a group, and planned study events once a course had started. The group studied together once or twice a week at the university library. They watched lecture videos, worked on assignments and discussed problems together.

"We took Machine Learning together every week. That was a hard course, but studying with them was really beneficial to me. I don't think I was able to have finished the course without them." [P9]

In another example, P13 organized a learning group that included socializing as well as shared study. She recruited friends and colleagues to take a particular art MOOC. This class required students to make art crafts as assignments, so she invited her friends to meet at her home on Friday nights. They had dinner together while they watched the videos and then made crafts together. *"It's a kind of a party! But we also learn something."* [P13]

Going Beyond MOOCs to Support Learning

Many participants told us that they prefer to ask questions, search for answers, help others, or collaborate with group members via other tools or websites – that is they do not rely on the normal MOOC discussion forums. Because MOOCs involve many students and only a few course staff members or volunteers to provide answers, student posts to the forums are often ignored or not addressed in a timely manner.

Instead, participants often submitted questions to popular Q&A platforms like StackOverflow. Google Search is also a very common tool for finding answers to specific questions. As contributors our participants prefer answering questions via something like StackOverflow, which allows them to earn recognition points that might enhance their professional reputation. When students needed to collaborate, they used emails and Google Docs to work with online peers, primarily due to a lack of collaboration features in MOOC platforms:

"*When I run into a problem, I usually search for it on Google first. If no answer satisfies me, I will go to StackOverflow. I can always get a good answer there. I don't rely on discussion forum because you never know whether and when you can get an answer.*" [P3]

Factors Influencing Retention Rate

Many of our participants were disappointed that they retook the same MOOC multiple times but never finished it, despite high motivation; others were satisfied with their learning even when they did not complete the course. We attempted to understand this phenomena in our interviews, identifying eight factors associated with retention problems: high workload, challenging course content, lack of time, lack of pressure, lack of awareness features, social influence, long course start-up, and learning on demand.

High Workload

Our participants reported that some MOOCs required much more time than they had initially expected. Participants claimed that, although they were able to understand the course lectures, they could not fulfill their obligations related to the written assignments and peer assessments and had to drop out. For example, P18 enrolled in an academic writing course that required students to not only write critique articles based on the weekly readings but to also provide assessments for five other students' articles as well. This student spent at least 15 hours per week to complete the course requirements, which exceeded the 7 hours claimed by syllabus.

"*Maybe because I am a responsible person and I took the peer assessment seriously, I needed a lot of time to finish my essay and help others. So I only took two lectures and I quitted because I had other priorities, though the course was very helpful for my writing. I can tell even though I only took the class for two weeks.*" [P18]

Challenging Course Content

Participants left some courses because they were too difficult to follow. During online learning, participants had to slow down the video pace to half or even a quarter of the original pace to follow instructors, and also had to pause and rewind frequently to make sure they understood the point. This resulted in two significant consequences. First, they needed to spend double or triple the estimated time to finish a lecture, which resulted in falling behind the course schedule. Falling behind means they were unable to receive feedback from peers or teaching staff as the course progressed. Second, when they did not fully comprehend the course content, participants felt incompetent and discouraged, causing them to withdraw. For instance, P3 participant completed 6 of 10 MOOCs, but one of the unfinished courses was especially memorable to him:

"*I took Cryptography last semester. That was a very hard course. Even though I watched videos as half pace, I still need to pause and rewind very frequently! This really made me frustrated. I began to think 'is it the right course for me? Should I take an easier one?' ...You know, my progress was slow, but time was limited because I still had other priorities... I was two weeks behind the course schedule and I asked questions but no one answered, I guess they were not on the same page with me. So I had to give up. I may try another time. Who knows!* " [P3]

Lack of Time

Participants, especially student participants, perceived lack of time as a significant factor affecting their decision to withdraw. They would enroll in MOOCs during down times such as a winter break. The time available for their learning on MOOCs naturally decreased after school resumed. P1 enrolled in a Game Theory course during his vacation, but the new semester began after two weeks. New courses and new activities filled his time so he had to discontinue his online learning. Similar reasons like finding internships, travelling, and preparing for final exams during semester final weeks resulted in them giving up on MOOCs.

"I had taken Python twice but failed both times. The first time was because I needed to go back school and I suddenly had five courses to take care of. So I didn't have extra energy to learn it. The second time was because I went to a company as an intern, so I stopped again." [P8]

Lack of Pressure

Another reason for leaving a MOOC before finishing was that the absence of pressure or urgency to complete a free course. For instance, once enrolled, MOOC participants can usually access the course materials anytime, even after the course officially ends. They do not need to finish the course within the limited time if their goal is not to obtain a certificate. Many participants intended to complete the course in their spare time, but this did not always happen:

"*You know the videos won't disappear if you miss a deadline. You still have access to them. But the problem is I never went back after I stopped learning last year [laugh]*". [P7]

In addition, most participants chose to take MOOCs as optional work that had no influence on their school records or job evaluations, so they did not always push themselves to finish the course.

"No one keeps you accountable. You don't have a grade on the certificate. Even if it gets graded, it does not affect my GPA here. There is no consequence for doing poorly on it or doing nothing at all. The reward is just a certification at the end. So when I quit, I don't think it's a big deal. I might feel a little bit sorry because I didn't finish a thing that I started." [P1]

No Sense of Community or Awareness of Others

As previous literature has pointed out, feeling a sense of community can help students to be more engaged in a class, enhancing retention and learning outcomes [10]. In our case, we also found that a lack of community feeling may have affected retention. As P8 described: "*In a real classroom, when you answer a question correctly, the instructor will praise you. When you did an excellent job on assignments, the grade and comments will encourage you. When you have a smart idea and share in class, you will feel proud. When you do assignment, you have your classmates sitting together to discuss. But in MOOCs, you feel nothing. You are alone.*" [P8] In fact, most participants declared that they did not feel a sense of community while in a MOOC.

Our participants mentioned that it was difficult to get to know their MOOC peers, and that this affects their MOOC experience: "*In a classroom, you know the person sitting beside you is a real person. After you look over, you would have a feeling of how they would be, either friendly or not.*" [P12] Existing MOOC platform do not provide features to promote community awareness. Participants are unable to know how many students are studying online with them at any given point. *"I really wish I could see who they are, where they are from, and how many students are working with me when I study online. That might give me a feeling that I belong to this class and I had classmates."* [P11]

Some participants did try to browse the profiles of others who were enrolled in the same course, but they found most profiles to be incomplete, and there was no way to verify whether a name is fake or not. As a result, they also refused to provide their personal profile information: *"I don't provide any information and say hello in the forum. I don't know why. I guess I don't trust them just like they don't trust others, otherwise why would they not provide their own information?"* [P14]

It was also difficult for our participants to find suitable peers for group projects because the forum did not provide any useful student background. In many cases, they ended up completing the projects by themselves. "*This is a big problem for most of the MOOCs. They just want student to watch the videos and do the homework. They don't care about how you can find the right people to form a group.*" [P7]

Social Influence

We found that participants tended to take a MOOC more seriously if it had been recommended by a respected family member or friend. *"I definitely trust his recommendation! He is my best friend and is a genius in programing."* [P8] If a respected peer recommended the course, the students would try hard to finish the course to meet expectations:

"One of my upperclassmen recommended this course and he completed this with high marks. Actually he had taken 12 MOOCs and finished them all! So whenever I felt that it was hard to continue learning this course, I would think of him to gain inspiration." [P18]

"If he can finish the course, I can finish it too. Otherwise, I am just being too lazy, right?" [P11]

Social influence can also have negative effects. For example, if the person recommending a course did *not* finish it, participants would find excuses to not complete the course as well. *"[Did you finish the course?] No, I didn't. My friend didn't finish it either. Er... I mean maybe the course were not suitable for the both of us."* [P12]

Lengthy Course Start-Up

Another factor affecting retention was that participants sometimes needed to wait for a long time to access the course after registration. For example, P11 registered for a Coursera Data Science course in March but had to wait for the course to open in April. She wanted to view the course content immediately to complement her current school course. After one month, she was finally able to enter the course, but it only released the first week's materials. She left the course when she found out that she would need to wait for another three weeks to access the specific content she needed. *"I don't know whether I'll still need it after another three weeks so I left the course. I know I may lose a learning opportunity, but waiting really makes me frustrated. Why don't they put them [course materials] up all at once?"* [P11]

Learning on Demand

The participants in this case used MOOCs as modularized learning resources. They left the course once they had fulfilled their needs. *"I am only interested in the American history during the Cold War, I only studied those related lectures and skipped others. That was why I didn't finish the course. I have already reached my goal."* [P2]

DISCUSSION

In this study, we have identified a number of different learning motivations, summarized innovative approaches that students take when learning from MOOCs, and described multiple factors that seem to be threats or opportunities affecting retention during online learning. Although MOOCs are still in a developing stage, we believe that these educational offerings have great potential to help people improve their lives. As we suggested earlier, MOOCs can help high school students understand their interests; they can help to realize an expensive art dream with zero pennies; they can be edutainment products to make people's life nourishing and so forth. From our view, MOOCs are not merely education resources. They should be viewed as a flexible integration of educational content, technology support, and instructors' and learners' creations and activities. Our primary mission is to better understand learners' needs, and to use that understanding to fit the elements together in ways that meet many kinds of needs.

Decompose Motivation

We categorized learners' motivations into four broad types: fulfilling current needs, preparing for the future, satisfying curiosity, and connecting with people. Prior literature either does not focus on the learners' motivation [1, 4, 16, 25] or addresses them in a general way without careful consideration of rationale, making it difficult to inspire design implications. We have attempted to decompose the general notion of motivation into the many different rationales held by different kinds of students.

With respect to fulfilling current needs, we can see that MOOCs may evolve into a reliable learning channel to help individuals enrich professional knowledge. They can provide options for professional development beyond the more traditional selection of a book for self-learning or hiring a tutor. For students seeking to influence their future options, we saw that some participants believe that the more certificates they get, the larger chance they can impress the future employer. However, the real value of certificates on the job market has not yet been widely discussed. The developers of MOOCs need to carefully position the "value" of their certificates, and businesses must be persuaded to value them in kind.

Shaping a child's interests in preparation for college is a particularly interesting motivation for MOOC learning. MOOCs offer a convenient way for high school students to gain some appreciation of multiple disciplines or majors. One implication is that institutions might deliberately build MOOC-based introductory courses for high school students, supporting the transition into college-level instruction.

The desire for social interaction as part of MOOC learning was another interesting discovery. Some learners' primary motivation may come from connecting with people rather than learning specific material. It may be that learning-based social interactions are particularly meaningful for some individuals. Future work could explore this unique phenomenon.

What Learning Patterns Tell Us

Prior research has explored MOOCs learning patterns. For example, [16] clustered four learning patterns applying learning analytics on three computer sciences (CS) MOOCs, including auditing, completing, disengaging and sampling based on their completion status. Their findings are limited because 1) the courses they choose belong to the same type but learners may have different study strategies for different types of courses (i.e. CS VS. Arts.); and 2) completion status only reflects completion rate and cannot give us insight into *how* learners reached that status.

To fill the gap, we have used qualitative methods to present a vivid picture of learning patterns. Our data analysis yielded five patterns. Three are at the individual level, including taking MOOCs as regular school classes, taking MOOCs as modularized resources and taking MOOCs as edutainment. MOOCs as modularized resources are confirmed by auditing proposed by [16]'s and lurker generated by [25].

These patterns may provide guidance for future studies that rely on more systematic learning analytics. For example, the interaction logs of learners who take MOOCs as regular school classes may convey a regular pattern; in contrast, for students viewing a MOOC as a modular resource, the log activity may peak during specific weeks; learners who take MOOCs as edutainment may carry out a much more limited set of actions (e.g., video view only).

We also identified a collaboration pattern, in that learners may join MOOCs as part of a formal or informal study group that works on learning goals together. This finding suggests that MOOC builders should devote more attention to features that promote a sense of community and collaborative interaction, for instance building behavior visualizations that capture student interactions over time as well as when they are online working at the same time.

The last pattern described the use of external tools (e.g., Google Doc, Google Search, Facebook) to support MOOC learning. This finding exposes drawbacks of current MOOC platforms (e.g., ineffectiveness of discussion forums), while also pointing to future design work: how do users appropriate these other tools to support their study, and is it feasible and desirable for MOOCs to provide these features? If not, how might we better integrate the other platforms as part of a larger MOOC ecosystem?

Factors Affecting Retention

We identified eight factors associated with low MOOC retention rates: high workload, challenging course content, lack of time, lack of pressure, lack of awareness features, social influence, lengthy course start-up, and learning on demand. Our findings are in accordance with prior research on the factors of difficulty [38], workload [34], and lack of time [34] with respect to course retention in traditional educational settings. Factors of difficulty and workload are also consistent with other research on MOOCs [1, 36]. However, other factors are inconsistent with this earlier work. The possible explanations are that 1) [25] focuses on cMOOCs retention, which may be rather different from xMOOCs retention; 2) [25] focuses on a single cMOOC and does not include learners who left the course. Other factors, such as social influence, little or no awareness of other students, lengthy start-up time and learning on demand, may be unique to the MOOC context.

Retention Problem versus Retention Opportunity

As discussed earlier, previous studies have observed very low retention rates for MOOCs [1, 4, 8, 9, 16, 19]. We propose that once we achieve an in-depth understanding of MOOC participants' motivation and behavioral patterns, the issue of retention should be addressed from two perspectives: retention as a *problem* and retention as an *opportunity*. The rationale behind this proposal centers on the variety of conceptions about what counts as "finishing" a MOOC. For some students, the concept of finishing is a good match to what the instructor likely believes – in other words, watching all the lectures, completing all the quizzes and assignments, and receiving a certificate. In contrast, others seem to feel that they are finished once they satisfy a learning goal, which may be as specific as a lesson covering an important computer algorithm. Still others may take the MOOC with a more amorphous goal, for instance wishing to gain insight into a particular area of study, but not feeling it necessary to view all lessons or complete all assignments. Indeed, some of our students told us that interacting with other students who share interests was a primary goal, rather than the goal of learning assumed by educators (recall, for instance the older man who took a music MOOC just to meet others interested in the guitar). Therefore, when we discuss retention issues in MOOCs, we must begin with a solid understanding of participants' learning goals and the implications for corresponding views of what counts as being "finished". Students who learn what they want and leave the course in the middle are not evidence of a retention problem; instead they should be commended for taking advantage these free and easily accessed online resources. Drop-out cases like these should be viewed as retention opportunities. Of course we have also seen that many students do plan to finish all course content but give up during the learning process for a variety of reasons; these are the retention problems in need of attention.

Going back to prior literature on MOOC retention, Clow's [4] funnel model views learners as going through a four-stage process: awareness, registration, activity, and progress. Only some of them reach the fourth stage of meaningful learning. This model captures the problems of retention from a learning analytics perspective. However, we offer another interpretation: after gaining awareness of a MOOC opportunity and choosing to enroll, learners engage in activity that may lead them to drop off sooner or later with respect to the course structure. What counts as "meaningful learning" is a function or their learning goals, and the extent to which they are able to achieve those goals is a function of retention-related factors such as we discussed earlier. For example, some people register for a MOOC out of curiosity; their curiosity might be satisfied by quickly scanning some of the learning materials, causing them to drop out "early". In other cases, curiosity may also be a driving factor, but the MOOC is not set up for a quick browse of content, and the participant may drop out with a feeling of frustration. In short, the concept of "meaningful learning" is not defined by *time in the course* or *completion,* but rather by each participant's learning goals.

Our qualitative findings point to a need for future research on students who have "true" retention problems. It is not clear yet how such individuals can be identified, but it may be that pre-course surveys can provide a reasonable approximation. At the same time, we argue that educators and MOOC technology developers should direct at least some attention to the retention opportunities that inhere in the broad range of motivations that we have discussed. We turn now to the design implications of our findings.

IMPLICATIONS

Diversify Learning Modules to Support Diverse Goals

Because different participants bring different motivations to their MOOCs, they may benefit from different services. We propose two styles of modules based on the four general motivations we discussed: one style that is learning-driven and another that is certificate-driven. It is quite possible that the same content could be offered in both styles, allowing the MOOC to serve as many needs as possible.

For a learning-driven module, the MOOC schedule would be very flexible, without strict deadlines. In such a module, students could arrange their learning activities based on their own abilities, needs, and time. Such MOOCs should also be open to public at all times, allowing students who have immediate learning needs to access the course instantly and not wait for the next session being launched. This module could solve several problems raised in interviews such as lack of time, lack of pressure of falling behind schedule, lack of confidence, and unnecessary waiting. Of course we recognize that providing this level of flexibility might imply even less direct involvement by an instructor, who cannot be expected to constantly be available to different students who are interacting and progressing at different rates. Thus a MOOC of this sort would need to rely much more on self-study materials or to provide much more support for peer discovery and interactions.

In contrast, for a certificate-driven MOOC, students who are eager to prepare for some future job or other educational activity may be willing to work in a very structured fashion so as to earn a formal recognition at the end. These courses would be similar to most current MOOCs and traditional courses offered by universities and other educational institutions. The course schedule in this MOOC would be formal, and assignments would need to be followed up with valid assessments of student performance. This will allow a completion certificate to be more valuable and worthy of pursuit.

Facilitate Social Interaction

Although MOOCs are built upon a tradition of opening up the academy through recorded lectures, they also can be seen as a new form of online community. We found that participants often wanted better support for peer communications and interactions, including setting up their own ad hoc mechanisms to experience the value of collaborative learning and discussion. For example, some participants join MOOCs for social needs, others join MOOCs as part of a cohort. Some support should be provided by MOOC platforms to facilitate social interactions.

Utilize social influence to stimulate learning passion.

Participants were usually excited when they started a MOOC, but their passion gradually died out because of the factors identified in our interviews. Most participants found it difficult to motivate themselves in continuous learning. MOOC designers should consider strategies to stimulate students' initiative and encourage them to learn. For example, constructivist theory [37] emphasizes that learners should be active and not passive, and that collaborative learning is one way to increase engagement. Indeed, we found that social influence may play an important role in MOOC experiences and retention. For example, the system might provide comparisons of learning progress among students, perhaps even using a leaderboard to indicate how the top performers are performing and what they have accomplished so far.

Enhance Sense of Community. Research on community informatics has confirmed a central role of sub-networks in forming community [3]. Students vary enormously in their background, value systems, current situations, and personal objectives. The occurrence of subgroups enables this diversity to coalesce, emerge, shape and contribute to the richness and tenacity of a community. Subgroups offer opportunities for smaller-scale activates, such as idea sharing, brainstorming, and identity formation, which in turn benefit the larger community. Membership across groups will ultimately strengthen the overall community. MOOC designers might encourage subgroup formation by improving technology design, such as building virtual small-scale classrooms. This result is consistent with [16], who has suggested that MOOC platform designers consider building other community-oriented features to promote pro-social behavior, such as text or video chat, small-group projects, or facilitated discussions [16].

Provide Community Awareness Mechanisms. Community awareness mechanisms are one way to build community [3]. In other work we have talked with MOOC instructors and learned about related efforts for particular courses. For example, one instructor uses a map to emphasize how students are distributed throughout the world. This type of visualization not only raises awareness but also suggests a strategy for finding peers in the same geographic region. Another instructor developed a class roster that listed all registered students but then marked their performance with icons near their names. Participants from these two courses reported that the awareness of other students' performance gave them a better sense of how their learning community is doing. Even displaying the number of students online at any given moment might give them the sense that they are part of a larger collective with shared goals. Thus, future MOOCs should explore different community awareness mechanisms to create a more active and inter-connected learning context.

As Cormier and Siemens noted, "the actions of institutions like MIT suggest that the true benefit of the academy is the interaction, the access to the debate, to the negotiation of knowledge – not to the stale cataloging of content" [5]. When we better understand learners' needs for socializing, we can encourage communication and collaboration by leveraging the massive body of co-learners, and supporting interaction with appropriate technology, rather than solely focusing on content and delivery. There is a potential for a cMOOC and xMOOC hybrid concepts to emerge in the future, offering different balances of content delivery and conversational models of learning, to address a wider range of potential participants and topics.

LIMITATIONS AND RECOMMENDATIONS FOR FUTURE

Our interview study reveals a broad picture of learner motivations and learning patterns, as well as factors affecting retention in xMOOCs. While the study fills gaps in the literature and contributes a substantial body of new empirical data about the learning experience afforded by xMOOCs, some limitations must be acknowledged and considered. First, the sampling strategy used (snowball sampling) has likely produced a biased sample. We call for caution in generalizability of our results. Second, although we tried to reach out to a wide age range of participants, not all age groups are well represented. Third, learners in different geographic regions may present different motivations, and learning patterns. However, our samples mainly locate in U.S., which limit our understanding regarding this issue. A more systematic future study could avoid these limitations. Furthermore, a quantitative study with a more varied and larger population would be a useful complement for this qualitative, explorative study. A broad survey of xMOOC users would be helpful to confirm and further develop our findings.

CONCLUSION

In this study, we have examined student motivations for participating in MOOCs; presented innovative approaches they take to their use of MOOCs; and recognized multiple factors as threats or opportunities that seem to affect student retention in online courses. Interestingly, many participants who enroll in MOOCs never have the intention to finish them at all, in the sense of conventional courses, even when the online courses are organized and marketed as conventional offerings (e.g., lectures and exercises). Indeed, we have documented a wide range of motivations for using MOOCs; course completion and certification is only one of those. Our findings are important because the "retention problem" of MOOCs can now be elaborated in a more articulated way; namely, these online courses enable a diversity of motivations that simply were not possible or appropriate in earlier educational paradigms. Our study suggests that researchers should consider retention issues in MOOCs from two perspectives: retention as an *opportunity* and retention as a *problem*. Also, MOOCs should be considered as a new type of virtual organization that is composed by educational contents, technology and learners, rather than a simple combination of learning materials and platforms. Building a deep understanding of user needs is crucial for future evolution of MOOCs.

REFERENCES

1. Adamopoulos, P. (2013). What Makes a Great MOOC? An Interdisciplinary Analysis of Student Retention in Online Courses, In Proc. ICIS.
2. Armstrong, J.S. (2012). Natural Learning in Higher Education, in Encyclopedia of the Sciences of Learning, Springer, pages 2426-2433.
3. Carroll, J.M. (2012). The Neighborhood in the Internet: Design Research Projects in Community Informatics. Rutledge.
4. Clow, D. (2013). MOOCs and the Funnel of Participation, in: Proceedings of the Third International Conference on Learning Analytics and Knowledge, pages 185-189.
5. Cormier, D., and Siemens, G. (2010). The Open Course: Through the Open Door--Open Courses as Research, Learning, and Engagement, Educause Review (45:4), pages 30-32.
6. Coetzee, D., Fox, A., Hearst, M. A., & Hartmann, B. (2014). Should your MOOC forum use a reputation system?. In Proc. CSCW 2014, pages 1176-1187.
7. Corbin, J., and Strauss, A. (2007). Basics of Qualitative Research: Techniques and Procedures for Developing Grounded Theory. Sage Publications, Incorporated.
8. Daniel, J. (2012). Making Sense of MOOCs: Musings in a Maze of Myth, Paradox and Possibility. Journal of Interactive Media in Education.
9. Downes, S. (2010). Learning Networks and Connective Knowledge, Collective intelligence and e-learning (2), pages 1-26.
10. Du, H., Rosson, M.B., Carroll, J.M. & Ganoe, C. (2009). I felt like a contributing member of the class: Increasing class participation with Class Commons, In Proc. GROUP 2009, pages 233-242.
11. Fox, A., and Patterson, D. (2012). Crossing the Software Education Chasm, Communications of the Acm (55:5), pages 44-49.
12. Haywood, J. No such thing as a free MOOC. http://www.jisc.ac.uk/blog/no-such-thing-as-a-free-mooc-20-jul-2012
13. Huang, J., Dasgupta, A., Ghosh, A., Manning, J., & Sanders, M. (2014). Superposter behavior in MOOC forums, In Proc. L@S 2014, pages 117-126.
14. Iiyoshi, T., and Kumar, S.V. (2008). Opening up Education: The Collective Advancement of Education through Open Technology, Open Content, and Open Knowledge. Mit Press.
15. Joglekar, M., Garcia-Molina, H., and Parameswaran, A. (2013). Evaluating the Crowd with Confidence, In:Proc. SIGKDD 2013, pages 686-694.
16. Kizilcec, R. F., Piech, C., & Schneider, E. (2013). Deconstructing disengagement: analyzing learner subpopulations in massive open online courses. In Proceedings of the third international conference on learning analytics and knowledge, pages 170-179.
17. Knowledge@Wharton. (2013). MOOCs on the Move: How Coursera Is Disrupting the Traditional Classroom, Innovation and Entrepreneurship. Articles Retrieved from
18. Knox, J., Bayne, S., Macleod, H., Ross, J. & Sinclair, C. (2012). MOOC Pedagogy: the challenges of developing for Coursera.
19. Lewin, T. (2013). Universities Abroad Join Partnerships on the Web, in: The New York Times February 21, 2013, page A18.
20. Mak, S., Williams, R., & Mackness, J. (2010). Blogs and forums as communication and learning tools in a MOOC. In Networked Learing Conference, pages 275-285.
21. Martin, L.; Roldán Martinez, D.; Revilla, O.; Aguilar, M.J.; Santos, O.C.; Boticario, J.G. (2008). Usability in e-Learning Platforms: heuristics comparison between

Moodle, Sakai and dotLRN. In OpenACS and .LRN conference, pages 75-84.

22. Masters, K. (2011). A Brief Guide to Understanding Moocs, The Internet Journal of Medical Education (1:2).
23. McAuley, A., Stewart, B., Siemens, G. & Cormier, D. (2010). The MOOC Model for Digital Practice. Retrieved from http://www.elearnspace.org/Articles/MOOC_Final.pdf
24. Means, Barbara; Bakia, Marianne; Murphy, Robert (2014). Learning Online : What Research Tells Us About Whether, When and How. Retrieved from http://www.eblib.com
25. Milligan, C., Margaryan, A., & Littlejohn, A. (2013). Patterns of engagement in massive open online courses. Journal of Online Learning with Technology, 9(2). Online HTTP: http://jolt.merlot.org/vol9no2/milligan_0613.htm
26. Müller, D., Law, E.L., Strohmeier, S. (2010). Analysis of the Persuasiveness of User Experience Feedback on a Virtual Learning Environment. In Proc. I-UxSED pages 30-39.
27. Piech, C., Huang, J., Chen, Z., Do, C., Ng, A., and Koller, D. (2013). Tuned Models of Peer Assessment in Moocs, In 6th International Conference on Educational Data Mining.
28. Rosson, M.B.(2014), Building Community within Large Groups of Online Learners. In Proc. CHI 2014 Learning Workshop.
29. Russell, D.M., Klemmer, S., Fox, A., Latulipe, C., Duneier, M., and Losh, E. (2013). Will Massive Online Open Courses (Moocs) Change Education?, In Proc. CHI 2013 Extended Abstracts on Human Factors in Computing Systems, pages 2395-2398.
30. Satchell, C., & Dourish, P. (2009). Beyond the user: use and non-use in HCI. In Proceedings of the 21st Annual Conference of the Australian Computer-Human Interaction Special Interest Group: Design: Open 24/7, pages 9-16.
31. Siemens, G. (2011). The race to platform education. eLearnspace. http://www.elearnspace.org/blog/2011/10/13/the-race-to-platform-education/accessed 2012-09-21
32. Siemens, G. (2012). MOOCs are really a platform. eLearnspace. http://www.elearnspace.org/blog/2012/07/25/moocs-are-really-a-platform/accessed 2012-09-21
33. Singh, R., Gulwani, S., and Solar-Lezama, A. (2013). Automated Feedback Generation for Introductory Programming Assignments, SIGPLAN Not. (48:6), pages 15-26.
34. Tresman, S. (2002). Towards a Strategy for Improved Student Retention in Programmes of Open, Distance Education: A Case Study from the Open University Uk. The International Review of Research in Open and Distance Learning (3:1).
35. Van Schaik. (2009). Unified theory of acceptance and use for websites used by students in higher education. Technology Acceptance in Education, pages 159-181.
36. Vihavainen, A., Luukkainen, M., and Kurhila, J. (2012). Multi-Faceted Support for Mooc in Programming, In Proceedings of the 13th annual conference on Information technology education, pages 171-176.
37. Vygotsky, L.S. (1978). Mind in Society: The Development of Higher Psychological Processes (Translated by M. Cole, V. John- Steiner, S. Scribner & E. Souberman). Harvard University Press, Cambridge, MA.
38. Xenos, M., Pierrakeas, C., and Pintelas, P. (2002). A Survey on Student Dropout Rates and Dropout Causes Concerning the Students in the Course of Informatics of the Hellenic Open University. Computers & Education (39:4), pages 361-377.
39. Yuan, L., Powell, S., & CETIS, J. (2013). MOOCs and open education: Implications for higher education. Cetis White Paper.
40. Yuan, L., Powell, S., & Olivier, B. (2014). Beyond MOOCs: Sustainable Online Learning in Institutions. Cetis publications. Retrieved February, 8, 2014.
41. Zaharias, P., and Mehlenbacher, B. (2012). Exploring User Experience (UX) in virtual learning environments. Int. J. Human-Computer Studies, pages 475-477.

Open Education in the Wild: The Dynamics of Course Production in the Peer 2 Peer University

June Ahn[1,2], Sarah Webster[1], Brian S. Butler[1]
[1]College of Information Studies, [2]College of Education
University of Maryland, College Park
4105 Hornbake Building, South Wing, College Park, MD 20742
{juneahn, websters, bsbutler}@umd.edu

ABSTRACT
The Peer 2 Peer University (P2PU) is an online, open education platform where any user can create a course, contribute content, or join an existing course as a learner. P2PU represents an experiment in organizing the production of entirely user-generated, open education. However, the open model of P2PU rests on the critical assumption that members can successfully coordinate and produce a sufficient supply of courses and motivate others to join in. In this paper, we use log data from P2PU to describe the dynamics of organizers – members who try to produce and launch open courses – and explore the factors related to their ability to successfully create courses on this open platform. We find that a critical predictor of successful course development is quickly finding like-minded organizers to collaborate with, suggesting that creating new education *systems* based on open, social computing platforms requires facilitation of key aspects of social coordination beyond providing platform and content resources.

Author Keywords
Open learning; open education; social computing; computer supported cooperative work.

ACM Classification Keywords
H.5.2 [Information Interfaces and Presentation]: User Interfaces - Interaction styles.

General Terms
Human Factors; Design.

INTRODUCTION
The combination of the Internet and social computing platforms has engendered new forms of user-generated collaboration and production [27]. Crowdsourcing platforms aggregate contributions from individuals to enable scientific data collection and new discoveries through citizen science [32]. Open source software projects demonstrate how technical infrastructure and open license policies can be combined to create communities within which individuals can create, share, and remix code to create new software applications [11].

These technological components – social computing platforms, widely available Internet and mobile infrastructures, and open licenses – combined with a participatory culture of open sharing and production have also been implemented to address critical education challenges. The Open Education movement has largely focused on creating and disseminating open education resources (OERs) such as lesson content, curriculum, and learning tools [19,25,30]. Open learning platforms have recently garnered widespread attention as potential ways to deliver education. And while they vary significantly in their degree and conceptualization of "open", massive open online course (MOOC) platforms (e.g. Coursera, edX, Udacity etc.) where formal institutions such as universities create and deliver educational content to users have significantly increased in popularity and visibility [24].

Less well known are experiments in user-generated approaches that attempt to leverage social computing platforms to broaden participation in education. More than just increasing access, these efforts seek to use open, collaborative platforms to increase the size and scale of the community that is creating and providing educational content and experiences. The Peer 2 Peer University (P2PU) is one example of an organization that is experimenting with fostering learner-generated, peer-to-peer education. On P2PU's platform anyone can register as a member, create a course, contribute content, or join an existing course as a learner. This approach has the effect of opening up opportunities for both the use and creation of materials and courses.

However, for open platforms such as P2PU to function effectively, members must produce quality courses, contribute content, join courses, and participate actively to keep courses alive [10]. On the one hand, this need is similar to other online communities and social computing systems which are dependent on participants for content and support [9]. However, open education platforms require more from their participant populations than simple

CSCW '15, March 14 – 18, 2015, Vancouver, BC, Canada.

ACM 978-1-4503-2922-4/15/03…$15.00.
http://dx.doi.org/10.1145/2675133.2675292

provision of incremental content, active participation, or transactional social support. For these platforms to function, some member must take on the more extensive role of course organizers. In this study, we explore an issue that is critical to P2PU, and open education platforms more generally: understanding the experiences of organizers – or members who attempt to design and launch courses – to better support a supply of courses for the community.

In the following, we first articulate how this practical issue is also an interesting theoretical question of how to design and facilitate the computer supported cooperative work to orchestrate the necessary support for new *systems* of education delivery. Formal education institutions have complex sociotechnical systems to coordinate the work of providing education at societal scale. These systems include mechanisms such as policies that require and motivate student activity; infrastructure such as schools and classrooms; and the training and employment of compensated, certified, professionals such as teachers and administrators. User-driven, open education platforms are an emerging test bed to experiment with new ways to coordinate this work of orchestrating education at scale.

Second, we describe our analysis of log data from P2PU to explore the 3,028 members who have collectively attempted to create 3,347 courses over the history of the platform. Within this universe of potential courses, 426 courses (≈ 12%) were successfully launched on P2PU. In the presented analysis we examine how factors such as organizer experience, instructional design training, and peer collaboration relate to the likelihood of successful course production. Finally, we articulate design guidelines for the sociotechnical supports that are needed to guide the education production critical to open education systems, and suggest implications for future research.

RELATED WORK

Open education is one instantiation of the larger open movement. Others include citizen science, which leverages technology platforms to promote virtual collaboration between scientists and the general public [29,32], open source software projects that use technical platforms to manage the creation of openly available software [11], and popularly known platforms such as Wikipedia that coordinate individuals to create collective information repositories on global scale [8,12].

Adopting similar ideas and technical infrastructures, open education proponents worked to facilitate sharing and dissemination of open educational resources (OER) such as curriculum and learning tools. Early examples, such as the OpenCourseware initiative at MIT and Open Learning Initiative at Carnegie Mellon [1], have focused on freely disseminating syllabi and curriculum from university settings. Most recently, open education has received renewed interest with the growing availability of MOOCs. The current popular notion of MOOCs are free online courses, created by universities or affiliated organization, and delivered with high enrollment numbers through online platforms such as Coursera or edX. However, the original notion of a MOOC was not an institutionally driven delivery system, but rather a strategy to organize people online to share information and learn about a topic through a learner-generated process [23]. Different terms (such as xMOOC vs. cMOOC) have emerged to describe these differences in institutionally driven versus user-generated approaches for delivering educational experiences [3].

While these different approaches to open education undoubtedly have implications for students and learning [4,5,6], they also significantly change how the work of creating materials is performed. Open education platforms where technical and social infrastructures allow, at least theoretically, anyone to participate in the production of OERs, alter the roles, incentives, structures, and processes that underlie the provision of education content and experiences. Hence, the design and creation of these platforms is critically dependent on a strong understanding of the dynamics of production in open education environments.

Coordinating Cooperative Work: Policies, Infrastructure, and Social Participation

Although it hasn't been the focus of prior studies of open education platforms, existing research on other open communities has considered how policies, infrastructure, and social factors intersect to influence how members coordinate and perform work. These notions inform our understanding of the challenges associated with fostering production of open education resources. Butler, Joyce, and Pike [8] illuminate how an open platform such as Wikipedia is guided by policies that play various roles such as coordinating user behavior, developing meaning and identity for members, and providing signals for both members and outsiders about what is important in the community. Even within a class of open communities, the different intents and goals of a given community will likely shape user behavior and production. For example, Wiggins and Crowston [32] show how within citizen science projects there are very different goals in a given project, ranging from promoting Action, Conservation, Virtual Collaboration, or Education.

Policy signals guide member actions, shape how individuals govern themselves, and set norms that form the social and cultural setting of an online community [2,12,21]. Open licenses are another type of policy that allows individuals to create and disseminate artifacts (such as software code) for others to openly inspect, reuse, modify, and redistribute. Such policies have enabled a wide variety of collaborative production in areas such as software [11] and OERs [19].

In addition to a foundation of policy is a technological infrastructure. One clear innovation of social computing is the availability of technological platforms needed to broaden participation in a given activity. Wikipedia rests upon a technological platform where anyone can edit a webpage. From this simple, but powerful mechanism, organizations and individuals can create a broad array of collaborative interaction and production mechanisms [8]. Citizen science projects utilize technology to lower the floor for participation, so that individuals who may be hobbyists can collect observations (e.g. eBird), anyone with an interest in playing a video game can contribute to scientific research (e.g. FoldIt), or interested individuals can curate information (e.g. Encyclopedia of Life) [29]. Open source software development is enabled by collaborative platforms such as Sourceforge and Github that allow individuals and teams to easily share code, fork projects, and coordinate distributed activity [11].

The combination of open licenses, online communities, and technology has created situations where individuals can easily produce artifacts with technological tools and freely disseminate and collaborate around these artifacts. This idea of a participatory culture [16] has spread to the realm of education in various ways. For example, children can learn to code using programming environments such as Scratch, and upload, share, and remix these artifacts in their online communities [28]. In addition, the Open Education movement rests on the idea that anyone can create educational resources and share them widely [19,25,30].

Online communities research has shown that this vision of technology-mediated social participation is difficult to facilitate [26]. The vast majority of individuals never participate in a given online community and a small subset of members typically account for a substantial portion of site activity. These issues also arise in open online communities and researchers have examined how factors such as motivation to participate in citizen science activities predicts participation [29]. Prior research has shown that strategies to facilitate social interaction such as welcoming newcomers, coordinating and requesting actions to direct activity, and encouraging members to signal their identification with the community, are important to develop and sustain online communities [7,20]. This past research lays a foundation to help understand the unique issues facing an open education community such as P2PU.

P2PU and the Idiosyncrasies of Coordinating Education

Just as policy, infrastructure, and social participation help frame understanding of open, online communities, these factors also characterize education *systems*. For example, the United States public education system functions by combining policies, infrastructure, and teaching and learning practices. Policies such as mandatory attendance for youth under the age of 18 ensure some level of participation. Educational standards that spell out what students should learn, and in which grade levels, guide curriculum. Infrastructure and institutions organize a system of states, school districts, schools, and classrooms to orchestrate the delivery of educational materials and experiences. Colleges and universities create teacher education programs to train and certify professionals in skills such as instructional design and teaching strategies.

This framing helps to illuminate how P2PU is both an open, online community and an attempt at redesigning an education system. Issues of policy, infrastructure, and social participation also shape the interactions on the P2PU platform. The name Peer 2 Peer University communicates a foundational goal of promoting learner-generated, peer-to-peer education. This mission influences decisions about technology design. P2PU is built on a platform that allows anyone (not just designated teachers or other certified professionals) to design and launch courses, and permits anyone to join existing courses. All content in P2PU is shared under an entirely open, Creative Commons license. Technological features, open licenses, and the values of the open education movement combine to enable a platform like P2PU.

However, developing and sustaining this type of education system requires cooperative work that, for many who have experienced formal education, is largely ignored [10]. Someone needs to create courses, motivate others to join in, understand teaching strategies to guide learners along and engender participation, and design ways for learners to collaborate [4,17].

When one begins to understand these systemic issues, the particular challenges of open education production also become clear. The level of specialized knowledge required to design and launch a course is high. For example, one might need training in instructional design to organize the sequence of activities to effectively guide a novice learner through a topic. Course organizers need to grasp how to recruit and motivate other peers to join the course [17]. They also need to understand how to guide discussion and participation to sustain engagement [4]. In P2PU, anyone can create or join a course from a technological standpoint. However, there are open issues about how to help anyone facilitate and sustain vibrant learning groups. Research from educational psychologists and cognitive scientists cast doubts on whether novice learners are capable of understanding a topic area that they, by definition, know little about [18]. Similarly, there are open questions as to whether learners can generate their own learning experiences in an effective way. However, other experiments such as participatory MOOCs suggest that social computing platforms could aid in helping learners create their own learning paths [23].

Given this understanding of P2PU as both an online community and education system, we set out to examine a critical issue that has been a main area of interest to both P2PU, and more generally to online community researchers: the experience of organizers in creating courses for the community. Prior research on P2PU found that while 2,034 courses were started by organizers, only 368 courses were ever completed and launched publicly (about 18%) [3]. Such studies of P2PU have identified potential issues such as the small percentage of courses that ever successfully launch, but have not explored what factors might explain these patterns in any depth. We build on this prior work with an updated P2PU log dataset and delve deeper into the factors that may explain the successful launching of courses in the platform. In particular, we examine the following exploratory research questions:

R1: How do P2PU course organizers engage with the P2PU platform?

R2: What factors are correlated with the successful launching of courses in P2PU?

In R2, we specifically examine three hypotheses that are informed by the prior literature in online communities and salient aspects of P2PU's history over the past few years. First, online communities research suggests that the prior experience of participants in interacting with the online community plays a role in their future interactions [20]. In the context of P2PU, we examine whether the prior experience of organizers is correlated with the likelihood that they will successfully launch a course in the future:

H1: An organizer's prior experience including (a) how long they have been a member of P2PU, (b) how many courses they attempted to organize in the past, and (c) how many courses they participated in the past, will be correlated with the likelihood of successfully launching a course in the future.

For our second hypothesis, we drew upon knowledge of P2PU's history based on participant observation and informal discussion with P2PU's founders. P2PU was long aware of the issue of helping more organizers launch courses in order to sustain the community. In their efforts to help alleviate the high level of instructional design knowledge needed to create courses, they created their own initial course entitled "How do I Make a P2PU Course?" that guided new members in how to design participatory, peer-to-peer learning experiences. We utilized data that tracked when organizers took this instructional design course (if ever) to explore the following hypothesis:

H2: Organizers who took the P2PU Instructional Design course will be more likely to successfully launch a future course.

Finally, as noted earlier, a strong community mission for P2PU is to encourage and facilitate peer-to-peer, collaborative learning. Thus, the technology platform and interface allowed for multiple members to join together and collaboratively create courses. We were interested in exploring whether those organizers who decided to collaborate were more likely to successfully launch their courses than those members who worked alone:

H3: Organizers who worked with others to create courses will be more likely to successfully launch a course.

METHODOLOGY

To examine these questions, we obtained a MySQL database dump from P2PU that contained the entire database backend for the online platform from the appearance of the first course in March 2011 to September 2013. We wrote SQL scripts to extract and transform this raw data into a dataset suitable for statistical analysis. Specifically, our research questions examine the relationship between organizers and courses and we constructed a panel dataset that included the entire universe of courses started in P2PU over time, linked to the organizer of that course. Thus, the longitudinal, panel dataset includes multiple rows for a course, if that course had multiple organizers. We also collapsed this dataset by organizer in descriptive analyses that focused at the organizer level (see below).

Variables

Given the longitudinal, multidimensional nature of the dataset (e.g. course, organizer, time), we wrote scripts to extract and combine data from multiple database tables including *projects*, *users*, and *course* tables in the MySQL database. Scripts compared time-stamps of activity across tables to generate several variables with a time component. The following variables were used to create an analysis dataset that consisted of a set of records for each valid course / organizer pair:

Course ID: This was a unique ID that represented each course in the database. Of special note is a quirky detail of the P2PU database. In prior research on P2PU [3] course information was stored in a set of *projects* tables. Our dataset utilizes a more recent version of the P2PU database, and due to a redesign of the platform, new courses were represented in a new set of tables labeled *courses*. We wrote scripts to extract data from both the old course history (in *projects* tables) and the recent courses history (in the *courses* tables) to include the entire universe of courses in P2PU.

Launched: This binary flag indicated whether a given course was successfully designed and launched to the public in P2PU. This attribute was constructed from a combination of attributes in the courses and projects tables.

Organizer ID: This unique ID identified each member of P2PU who attempted to organize a course.

Weeks Elapsed since Joining P2PU: This variable utilized information about when the organizer first registered for P2PU and the date that they commenced creation of a given course. The time elapsed between these two dates was converted to weeks, and represents how long a given organizer was an active member of P2PU.

Prior Courses Organized: Using time-stamped information about course creation, this variable is a count of how many courses the organizer attempted to create **prior** to starting design of this current course (successfully launched or not).

	Mean	Standard Deviation	Min	Median	75th Percentile	Max
Courses Started	1.41	2.32	1.0	1.0	1.0	66.0
Courses Launched	0.37	1.28	0.0	0.0	0.0	24.0
Weeks Between Signup and 1st Course	5.87	18.79	0.0	0.0	0.16	178.63
Weeks Between Signup and last Course	7.89	23.17	0.0	0.0	0.67	179.80
Took Instructional Design Course at any point	0.05	0.21	0.0	--	--	1.0
Took Instructional Design Course Before creating another course	0.02	0.14	0.0	--	--	1.0
Number of others collaborated with on a course	6.66	18.89	1.0	1.0	1.0	98.0
Classes Participated Prior	0.29	1.28	0.0	0.0	0.0	25.0

N = 3,028

Table 1: Descriptive Statistics on All Potential Organizers in P2PU

Prior Courses Participated In: Using time-stamped information about course participation, this variable is a count of how many courses the organizer joined as a participant **prior** to starting design of the focal course.

Took Instructional Design: Using time-stamped information about course participation, this variable indicated whether the organizer took the P2PU instructional design course **prior** to starting design of the focal course.

Multiple Organizers: This binary flag indicated whether the focal course in the record had more than 1 organizer associated with it.

Organizer Count: This variable is a count of how many organizers were associated with the focal course.

Course Category: This variable indicated what type of course this was: study group, course, challenge, or new course. This variable was used as a control variable to account for the particular, idiosyncratic history of courses in P2PU.

In the beginning, P2PU encouraged individuals to create "study groups" and later changed the name of this structure to "courses". These courses were removed and closed after the group finished its activities and dispersed. P2PU then created a new course type "challenges" to represent courses that remained on the site persistently for anyone to take. A notable detail is that challenges came about around the same time as a few high-profile P2PU initiatives, such as a partnership with Mozilla to create a series of web development courses. Finally, "new courses" are challenges/courses that were created in P2PU recently as of February 2013. There is no substantive difference in these courses, but P2PU developers decided to store these courses in a separate table given other site redesign decisions. Study groups, courses, and challenges represent both idiosyncratic design changes in the history of the P2PU platform, and also unobserved factors related to the "eras" of P2PU's development. For example, it may be the case that challenges were more likely to be launched, but not due to any substantive reason except that the challenges course type came about at the same time as high profile initiatives such as Mozilla's web development courses. By including course type as a control variable, we are able to control for some unobserved factors in P2PU's evolution.

Analysis

To explore R1, we first present descriptive statistics for both organizers and courses in P2PU to glean insight into the characteristics, experiences, and dynamics of course organizers on the P2PU platform. To examine R2, we ran a logistic regression model predicting the probability that a given course was launched successfully (Launched) predicted by:

(a) Prior organizer experience – weeks as a member, prior courses organized, and prior course participated in

(b) Whether the organizer took the P2PU instructional design course prior to starting creation of a respective course

(c) Whether the organizer was part of a collaborative group that was designing the course together, or worked alone

(d) How many organizers were associated with the course

(e) Control Variable for type of course category for the course: study group, course, challenge, or new course

	Mean	Standard Deviation	Min	Median	75th Percentile	Max
Courses Started	2.18	4.04	1.0	1.0	2.0	66.0
Courses Launched	1.59	2.25	1.0	1.0	1.0	24.0
Weeks Between Signup and 1st Course	14.52	26.87	0.0	1.0	16.69	178.63
Weeks Between Signup and last Course	21.85	36.12	0.0	3.48	28.63	179.80
Took Instructional Design Course at any point	0.07	0.26	0.0	--	--	1.0
Took Instructional Design Course Before creating another course	0.04	0.17	0.0	--	--	1.0
Number of others collaborated with on a course	24.04	33.40	1.0	6.0	59.0	98.0
Classes Participated Prior	0.82	1.95	0.0	0.0	0.75	16.0

N = 711

Table 2: Descriptive Statistics on Organizers in P2PU Who Launched at Least 1 Course

The logistic model was used because the dependent variable (course launched) is binary. Using this model allows us to assess the observed impact of different factors on the probability of a course being successfully launched. The independent variables correspond to the three hypotheses we explore in the study. We note the inclusion of a fixed effect for multiple organizers (0/1 indicating whether a course had multiple organizers). When set to 0, we are examining the subset of courses that have a sole organizer (organizer count = 1). When set to 1, the analysis is examining the subset of courses that have an organizer count above 1.

FINDINGS

There were over 56,065 registered members in the P2PU community and 12,453 who returned to the site at least once after their initial registration visit. A smaller subset of 3,028 members ever began to organize a course and collectively this group attempted to create 3,347 courses over the history of P2PU. Of this universe of potential courses, 426 courses were completed and launched publicly on the site (about 12%). Table 1 provides descriptive statistics for the P2PU members who ever attempted to create a course (i.e. potential course organizers) (n = 3,028), and Table 2 describes the subset of members who successfully launched at least one course (n = 711).

Examining Table 1, we see notable characteristics of P2PU members who are potential course organizers. The variable Weeks Between Signup and 1st Course represents how long a member took between registering in P2PU and attempting to create their first course. The majority of members (at least 75%) attempted to create a course within 1 day of creating accounts in P2PU. At the 75th percentile, members took 1.12 days between registering for the site and attempting to create their first course. Furthermore, the vast majority of would-be organizers never participated in any courses before attempting to create their own course. Only about 5% of all potential organizers ever enrolled in the P2PU instructional design course, and only 2% took this course *before* creating a future course. Conversely, this statistic suggests that 3% took the instructional design course after attempting prior courses, and never created a future course thereafter.

These indicators suggest a particular dynamic for potential course organizers. It appears that these members join P2PU with an existing intent to create a course and jumpstart a learning group. Almost immediately after signing up for the community, they attempt to create a course. They do not participate in prior courses, and few took the P2PU instructional design course prior to attempting to start their own course design. Subsequently, the majority of courses were begun but never completely designed and launched publicly.

The experiences of course organizers that successfully launched at least one course were markedly different (see Table 2). Of the 3,028 members who attempted to start courses, 711 were successful in launching (about 24%). On average, these organizers attempted to start 2.18 courses and successfully launched 1.59. Half of all of these organizers (median) spent 1 week on the platform between first signing up and attempting to design their first course. At the 75th percentile, organizers took about 17 weeks in between signing up and joining their first course as an organizer.

A higher percentage of successful organizers took the P2PU instructional design course (7%, and 4% of whom took the instructional design course before creating a future course) and they were more apt to collaborate with peers to launch courses. The median number of peers that a successful

	B	S.E.	P-value	Odds Ratio
Weeks Elapsed since Joining P2PU	**0.007**	**0.002**	**0.00**	**1.01**
Prior Courses Organized	0.013	0.007	0.09	1.01
Prior Courses Participated In	**0.07**	**0.02**	**0.01**	**1.07**
Took Instructional Design	-0.17	0.20	0.40	0.845
Multiple Organizers	**2.30**	**0.13**	**0.00**	**11.01**
Organizer Count	**0.12**	**0.02**	**0.00**	**1.12**
Course Category [a]				
Course	0.01	0.14	0.95	1.01
Challenge	**0.66**	**0.13**	**0.00**	**1.93**
(New) Course	0.05	0.14	0.73	1.05

Dependent Variable: Launched (0/)
N = 4,262 Pseudo $R^2 = 0.42$
[a] Reference category = study group

Table 3: Logistic Regression Results Predicting Probability that a Course was Launched

organizer collaborated with was 6 people (Table 2). This contrasting profile suggests that successful organizers in P2PU spent more time on the platform between initial sign up and first attempt at a course. This time could be spent learning about the community, understanding how to best participate, or developing relationships with other members.

What Factors are Associated with Successful Course Launches?

The results of the logistic regression model are presented in Table 3. Our first hypothesis explored whether aspects of prior experience for organizers were related to the probability that they would launch a course successfully in the future. We expected that gaining prior experience on the platform would be positively associated with the probability of successfully launching a course in the future. In addition, our descriptive analysis of organizers suggested that successful organizers spent considerable more time on the platform prior to starting to create their own course.

Contrary to our expectations, and studies of other online communities, we found mixed results for prior experience. While weeks elapsed between signup on P2PU and the start of a course design (Weeks Elapsed) was a statistically significant variable, the relationship was very small (Odds Ratio = 1.01). Furthermore, experience with starting creation of prior courses (Prior Courses Organized) was not significantly associated with the probability of successfully launching a future course. The one significant experience variable was whether an organizer had participated (as a learner) in prior courses (Prior Courses Participated In). For each course that an organizer participated in the past, the odds that they would successfully launch a future course were 7% greater.

The second hypothesis examined whether participation in P2PU's instructional design course (Took Instructional Design) was correlated with the probability of successful, future course launch. Here we, and P2PU developers, expected that an instructional design course would have a positive relationship to the probability that organizers would successfully launch a course in the future. Contrary to our expectations and those of P2PU developers, taking this course had no significant relationship with the odds of launching a future course for organizers. Merely offering content, in the form of an introductory course, does not seem to be an effective intervention to promote course development in P2PU. Other factors are likely needed and we delve deeper into potential design needs in the following section.

Our third hypothesis suggested that collaborating with other peers in P2PU would be correlated with a higher likelihood of launching courses. The findings show that these variables had the strongest relationship to successful course launches (Table 3). For example, the odds of successfully launching a course were approximately *11 times greater* if the course had more than one course organizer (Multiple Organizers). Within the population of courses that had more than 1 organizer, the findings also suggest that for each additional organizer that collaborated on creating a course (Organizer Count), the odds that the course would be launched increased by 12% (Odds Ratio = 1.12).

DESIGN CONSIDERATIONS AND LIMITATIONS

Taken together, this analysis begins to identify some critical processes that may be salient for P2PU, and other learner-driven, open education platforms that are trying to promote production of OER and learning experiences online. In P2PU, members who become organizers register with at least a general intent to create courses. Most organizers attempt to create a course within a day of joining the community and the majority of these members fail in this activity. However, our findings suggest two design considerations for P2PU. We find that "successful" organizers tend to wait several days or a week before attempting their first course design. In addition, our findings point to specific ways that P2PU could encourage members to utilize this time between signup and starting one's course design. The most significant factors related to the probability of successful course launching were taking other courses and collaborating with other organizers. These patterns suggest that encouraging members to participate in other courses to gain experience, and finding like-minded peers to collaborate with, would be effective ways to promote course launching.

The findings also illuminate the affordances and limitations of open platforms. The combination of open licenses, a social computing platform that allows any member to create and produce, and the mission and values of open education that are instantiated in P2PU, creates a platform that encourages broad participation. Many individuals (over 3,000) attempted to participate in a highly complex task (designing courses for others) and this is a testament to the opportunities afforded in open communities. In reflecting on these findings, P2PU developer Dirk Uys commented to us that "Course creation has always been very easy and at the forefront [of the interface]. I think this resulted in lots of people creating a course simply to see what it is like." [31].

In response to the broadened participation, and low success rate of course launching, enabled by the P2PU platform, the developers created a formal instructional design course to help members. Contrary to our, and P2PU's, expectations the formal instructional design course that P2PU offered to new members had no correlation with successful course launching. These findings suggest that more than providing content and platform resources, careful thinking is required to better understand the social processes that are required to onboard, or acculturate, new members to truly understand how to organize and facilitate open, peer-to-peer learning. Some of this acculturation may likely happen by participating in already existing courses and observing how these learning groups function (Prior Courses Participated In), and also occurs effectively if a new member can find like-minded collaborators to create courses together.

There are several limitations of our analysis that also highlight the need for further research. First, if designing open educational experiences requires a high-level of expertise, it is likely the case that some organizers already possess instructional design training while others do not. Our regression models could not account for this factor and figuring out ways to capture this factor from digital trace data would be a needed step forward in future studies. Second, our analyses illuminated interesting relationships to successful course launching that were sometimes contradictory to our expectations. For example, the formal instructional design courses did not relate to course launching, and only particular forms of prior experience (e.g. taking courses and collaborating with others) were correlated with a higher probability of successful course organizing. However, descriptive studies are needed to better understand why these patterns may be important or how these processes play out in practice. Such limitations are common in studies that can only utilize trace data of already existing platforms [15]. Future qualitative studies of P2PU would be particularly helpful to understand the intricacies of organizers' experiences and pinpoint particular design interventions that would improve the supply of peer-generated learning.

While qualitative analysis was beyond the scope of this study, P2PU had conducted its own interviews with 11 successful course organizers as part of their own past design efforts. Their data confirm our findings and provide initial insight into some of the mechanisms that may be important for production of user-generated, open education [13]. For example, P2PU found that their most successful course organizers often took 2 weeks or more to develop courses, and that this task was intensive and required multiple iterations of design. In addition, successful organizers often had to collaborate with many other peers in co-designing courses given the complexity of this task. Taken together, our findings show that for future open education communities it is important to (a) utilize technologies, open infrastructures, and open policies to *allow* for wide participation, but (b) we need to draw lessons from research in both education and CSCW to focus on the critical social learning and acculturation practices that might enhance production in these platforms.

CONCLUSIONS

This study makes several contributions toward understanding the design and facilitation of open education communities such as P2PU. First, we show the importance of delineating how an open education platform such as P2PU is similar to other open, online communities but differ in critical ways. P2PU is built from a technical, policy, and social infrastructure that broadens participation in an activity, and in this vein is similar to other open communities. Open licenses, a social computing platform, and identification with the open education movement combine to enable P2PU as a community.

However, a key difference is the type and complexity of activity that is needed for P2PU to flourish. In Wikipedia or other information repositories such as Stack Exchange, the system functions by asking members to contribute facts or information (if they know them). In P2PU, the community can only function if individuals commit the needed time and energy to design courses and peer-learning experiences for others. The level of instructional design skills and personal commitment needed to produce educational experiences for others is non-trivial.

Haythornthwaite's [14] characterization of online peer production communities as light vs. heavyweight is a useful way to understand the factors critical to an open education community such as P2PU. Lightweight models of production can rely on micro-participation from many unconnected members. Heavyweight models require deeper commitment, collaboration, and interdependence between members in order to enable production. Our exploration into P2PU reminds us that producing education is fundamentally a heavyweight endeavor.

Second, our analysis builds from an understanding of this type of peer production model to clarify some critical design needs. If producing education is a heavyweight endeavor, our findings show that content-driven interventions (e.g. creating a course about instructional design) are not enough. P2PU will need to encourage potential course organizers to gain *specific experiences* by taking prior courses and connect with other *collaborators* when they begin creating their own courses.

Future studies are needed to unpack the local processes involved in peer-production of open education. Scholars of open education note that the field has done considerable work in defining open licenses, infrastructure, and creating systems to enable open production of OERs. However, research is now needed to understand how to implement these infrastructures and make use of OERs in effective ways to facilitate actual learning practices [19,25]. Research in CSCW and online communities is particularly helpful in this regard. Prior studies of online communities articulate how individuals can welcome others, acculturate new members, direct tasks, and coordinate social processes [9,12,14,20,21,26]. In addition, online communities researchers have also shown how interfaces and platform features help in acculturating members or directing behavior [2,22], or how policies and other structuring artifacts help create norms of online community interaction [8,21]. These dynamics are likely to be vital in efforts to help peers develop relationships, form teams, and build the requisite level of trust, interdependence, and commitment to engage in the production of open education. Future research is needed that can transfer and link online communities findings to the peer production model of open education.

Lessons could be drawn from research in formal education systems. For example, formal education settings have teacher education programs, a diverse array of degrees, systems of professional development, and complex academic disciplines and communities to train, acculturate, and develop educators (e.g. professors, teachers, teaching assistants etc.). There is a wide body of research literature to support different approaches and clearly articulate the intricacies of teaching and learning. However, it is an open question whether recreating these structures in open, online communities will yield the desired results of vibrant, learner-generated platforms. P2PU's attempt to create a relatively formal instructional design course showed little correlation with course organizers' success. However, CSCW researchers and open education practitioners may find ways to re-appropriate formal models of training and production that make sense in online communities. Future work that articulates unique designs and re-designs of education models would be particularly impactful.

Open education is an area where disparate fields of CSCW and education are uniquely positioned to inform one another and fill in critical gaps of understanding ranging from (1) the design and implementation of online communities, peer production systems, and open movements to (2) the intricacies of education production, teaching, and learning. This paper begins to build such bridges by considering peer production in an open, education platform, P2PU. As online learning and open education evolve, there will be a continuing need to develop theories of technology mediated social participation [26] as they relate to creating and facilitating learning. These theories must move beyond simple models of posting educational content for others to consume. Instead, future research is needed that build upon what we know about online organizing, socializing, and relationship development and link these findings to theories about how to train, acculturate, and facilitate collaboration between individuals as they create educational experiences, teach, and learn in open communities.

ACKNOWLEDGEMENTS

We thank Dirk Uys, Vanessa Gennarelli, Philipp Schmidt, and everyone at P2PU for their help with this research. This material is based upon work supported by the National Science Foundation under Award #1257347. Any opinions, findings, and conclusions or recommendations expressed in this material are those of the author(s) and do not necessarily reflect the views of the National Science Foundation or P2PU.

REFERENCES

1. Abelson, H. The Creation of OpenCourseWare at MIT. *Journal of Science Education and Technology 17*, 2 (2008), 164–174.
2. Ahn, J., Butler, B., Weng, C., and Webster, S. Learning to be a better q'er in social q&a sites: Social norms and information artifacts. *Proceedings of the Association for Information Science & Technology (ASIS&T)*, (2013).
3. Ahn, J., Butler, B.S., Alam, A., and Webster, S.A. Learner Participation and Engagement in Open Online Courses: Insights from the Peer 2 Peer University. *Journal of Online Learning & Teaching 9*, 2 (2013).
4. Ahn, J., Weng, C., and Butler, B.S. The Dynamics of Open, Peer-to-Peer Learning: What Factors Influence Participation in the P2P University? *Proceedings of the 46th Hawaii International Conference on System Sciences (HICSS)*, IEEE (2013), 3098–3107.
5. Bernard, R.M., Abrami, P.C., Borokhovski, E., et al. A meta-analysis of three types of interaction treatments in distance education. *Review of Educational Research 79*, 3 (2009), 1243–1289.
6. Bruckman, A. Learning in online communities. *The Cambridge handbook of the learning sciences*, (2006), 461–472.
7. Burke, M., Joyce, E., Kim, T., Anand, V., and Kraut, R. Introductions and requests: Rhetorical strategies that

elicit response in online communities. In *Communities and Technologies 2007*. Springer, 2007, 21–39.

8. Butler, B., Joyce, E., and Pike, J. Don't Look Now, but We've Created a Bureaucracy: The Nature and Roles of Policies and Rules in Wikipedia. *Proceedings of the SIGCHI Conference on Human Factors in Computing Systems*, ACM (2008), 1101–1110.
9. Butler, B., Kiesler, S., and Kraut, R. Community Effort in Online Groups: Who Does the Work and Why? *Leadership at a distance: Research in technologically-supported work*, (2013), 171.
10. Butler, B.S. and Ahn, J. Ecological perspectives on creating and sustaining open learning environments. *Proceedings of Computer Supported Cooperative Work, Workshop on CSCW and Education*, ACM (2013).
11. Crowston, K., Wei, K., Howison, J., and Wiggins, A. Free/Libre Open-source Software Development: What We Know and What We Do Not Know. *ACM Comput. Surv. 44*, 2 (2008), 7:1–7:35.
12. Forte, A. and Bruckman, A. Scaling consensus: Increasing decentralization in Wikipedia governance. *Hawaii International Conference on System Sciences, Proceedings of the 41st Annual*, IEEE (2008), 157–157.
13. Gennarelli, V. Personal Communication. 2014. http://www.slideshare.net/VanessaGennarelli/design-research-course-creation.
14. Haythornthwaite, C. Crowds and communities: Light and heavyweight models of peer production. *System Sciences, 2009. HICSS'09. 42nd Hawaii International Conference on*, IEEE (2009), 1–10.
15. Howison, J., Wiggins, A., and Crowston, Kevin. Validity issues in the use of social network analysis with digital trace data. *Journal of the Association for Information Systems 12*, 12 (2011), 767–797.
16. Jenkins, H. *Confronting the challenges of participatory culture: Media education for the 21st century*. The MIT Press, 2009.
17. Kafai, Y.B. and Peppler, K.A. Beyond small groups: New opportunities for research in computer-supported collective learning. *Proceedings of the 9th Conference of Computer Supported Collaborative Learning*, (2011).
18. Kirschner, P.A. and van Merriënboer, J.J.G. Do Learners Really Know Best? Urban Legends in Education. *Educational Psychologist 48*, 3 (2013), 169–183.
19. Knox, J. Five critiques of the Open Educational Resources movement. *Teaching in Higher Education 18*, 8 (2013), 821–832.
20. Kraut, R., Wang, X., Butler, B., Joyce, E., and Burke, M. Beyond information: Developing the relationship between the individual and the group in online communities. *Information Systems Research*, (under review).
21. Maloney-Krichmar, D. and Preece, J. A multilevel analysis of sociability, usability, and community dynamics in an online health community. *ACM Transactions on Computer-Human Interaction (TOCHI) 12*, 2 (2005), 201–232.
22. Mamykina, L., Manoim, B., Mittal, M., Hripcsak, G., and Hartmann, B. Design lessons from the fastest q&a site in the west. *Proceedings of the 2011 annual conference on Human factors in computing systems*, (2011), 2857–2866.
23. McAuley, A., Stewart, B., Siemens, G., and Cormier, D. *The MOOC model for digital practice*. 2010.
24. Pappano, L. Massive Open Online Courses Are Multiplying at a Rapid Pace. *The New York Times*, 2012. http://www.nytimes.com/2012/11/04/education/edlife/massive-open-online-courses-are-multiplying-at-a-rapid-pace.html.
25. Peter, S. and Deimann, M. On the role of openness in education: A historical reconstruction. *Open Praxis 5*, 1 (2013), 7–14.
26. Preece, J. and Shneiderman, B. The Reader-to-Leader Framework: Motivating Technology-Mediated Social Participation. *AIS Transactions on Human-Computer Interaction 1*, 1 (2009), 13–32.
27. Quinn, A.J. and Bederson, B.B. Human computation: a survey and taxonomy of a growing field. *Proceedings of the SIGCHI Conference on Human Factors in Computing Systems*, (2011), 1403–1412.
28. Resnick, M., Maloney, J., Monroy-Hernández, A., et al. Scratch: programming for all. *Communications of the ACM 52*, 11 (2009), 60–67.
29. Rotman, D., Preece, J., Hammock, J., et al. Dynamic Changes in Motivation in Collaborative Citizen-science Projects. *Proceedings of the ACM 2012 Conference on Computer Supported Cooperative Work*, ACM (2012), 217–226.
30. Seely Brown, J. and Adler, R.P. Open education, the long tail, and learning 2.0. *Educause review 43*, 1 (2008), 16–20.
31. Uys, D. Personal communication. 2014.
32. Wiggins, A. and Crowston, K. From Conservation to Crowdsourcing: A Typology of Citizen Science. *2011 44th Hawaii International Conference on System Sciences (HICSS)*, (2011), 1–10.

The Emergence of GitHub as a Collaborative Platform for Education

Alexey Zagalsky, Joseph Feliciano, Margaret-Anne Storey, Yiyun Zhao, Weiliang Wang
University of Victoria
Victoria, BC, Canada
{alexeyza, noelf, mstorey, evianz, weiliang}@uvic.ca

ABSTRACT

The software development community has embraced GitHub as an essential platform for managing their software projects. GitHub has created efficiencies and helped improve the way software professionals work. It not only provides a traceable project repository, but it acts as a social meeting place for interested parties, supporting communities of practice. Recently, educators have seen the potential in GitHub's collaborative features for managing and improving—perhaps even transforming—the learning experience.

In this study, we examine how GitHub is emerging as a collaborative platform for education. We aim to understand how environments such as GitHub—environments that provide social and collaborative features in conjunction with distributed version control—may improve (or possibly hinder) the educational experience for students and teachers. We conduct a qualitative study focusing on how GitHub is being used in education, and the motivations, benefits and challenges it brings.

Author Keywords

CSCW; CSCL; Learning; Education; GitHub; Social Media; Qualitative Methodology; Distributed Version Control

ACM Classification Keywords

K.3.1 Collaborative Learning: Computer Uses in Education

INTRODUCTION

GitHub is a popular Web-based social code sharing service that utilizes the Git distributed version control system. It has become an essential tool in technology areas that require collaboration, such as software development and technical writing [33]. It is also seeing widespread adoption in other areas[1], transforming how people collaborate over a shared repository [2]. One of GitHub's main strengths is in the awareness and transparency features it provides to team, project and community members [5]. These features positively influence how people contribute to projects [36].

In this paper we examine how GitHub is starting to emerge as a collaborative platform for education. We aim to understand how environments such as GitHub—environments that provide social and collaborative features in conjunction with distributed version control[2,3]—may improve (or possibly hinder) the educational experience for students and teachers.

Only a few years after GitHub's 2007 release, well-known computer science educator Greg Wilson suggested[4] that GitHub could be used for learning materials despite some limitations:

> *Would it be possible to create a "GitHub for education?" Right now, I think the answer is "no", because today's learning content formats make* ***merging hard****. Whatever a "GitHub for education" would look like, it would not be yet another repository of open learning materials. There are lots of those already, but almost all their content is write-once-and-upload, ... rather than* ***sharing course content in a reusable, remixable way****.*

In 2012, he further elaborated[5]:

> *"GitHub for Education" isn't necessarily, "Let's put educational materials in GitHub", but rather, "Let's* ***facilitate a culture of spontaneous-but-structured collaboration*** *and improvement."*

He recognized that the majority of learning management systems introduced friction for instructors trying to reuse and share course materials—the type of problem that the software development community solved through the use of tools such as GitHub [5]. Moreover, his comments echo the **participatory culture** that, according to Jenkins [17], results from the use of social media in education.

In an effort to promote GitHub to higher education, GitHub launched the GitHub Education Website[6] in 2014. In re-

[1] `http://www.wired.com/2013/09/github-for-anything/`

[2] `https://bitbucket.org/`

[3] `https://www.gitlab.com/`

[4] `http://software-carpentry.org/blog/2011/12/fork-merge-and-share.html`

[5] `http://software-carpentry.org/blog/2012/04/github-for-education.html`

[6] `https://education.github.com/`

CSCW '15, March 14–18 2015, Vancouver, BC, Canada
Copyright 2015 ACM 978-1-4503-2922-4/15/03$15.00
http://dx.doi.org/10.1145/2675133.2675284

sponse to this and other *ad hoc* opinions on the benefits of using GitHub for education, we conducted a first study to examine whether and how GitHub, with its powerful collaboration, social and awareness features, can be used for educational purposes. Specifically, we aimed to answer the following research questions:

RQ1: **How does GitHub support learning and teaching?**

RQ2: **What are the motivations for and benefits of using GitHub for education?**

RQ3: **What challenges are related to the use of GitHub for education?**

We conducted interviews with early adopters of GitHub for educational purposes and followed-up with a survey to validate our findings. Our findings indicate that GitHub not only supports the main learning features present in traditional Learning Management Systems, but it also provides additional features that educators and students can benefit from: revealing transparency of activity, encouraging participation and collaboration, and supporting reuse and sharing of course materials and knowledge. However, it also brings challenges, such as a difficult learning curve for students. We conclude with a discussion of our findings and recommendations for GitHub users.

BACKGROUND

Before discussing GitHub and how its unique features can support education, we present a brief overview on technology in education and the strong connection between education and Computer Supported Cooperative Work (CSCW).

CSCW and Education

In the mid-1990s, online learning was supported by the Internet, email and forums, and focused on interactions between the student and the computer. Currently, online learning focuses on computer-mediated communications and the formation of communities of practice [26], and uses technologies such as cloud computing [34], social media (e.g., Twitter [15, 31]), mobile devices [12] and Massive Open Online Courses (MOOCs) [28]. Technology has had a major influence on education and it will continue to do so (e.g., Khan Academy [35]). However, questioning if and how various technologies should be used to improve learning is non-trivial.

As described in the book "Technology in Education—Looking Toward 2020" [27], participants of the "2020 Panel" tried to envision the future of education and enrich people's understanding of technology's potential role in education, as well as opportunities, drawbacks and challenges. William Bossert, one of the panelists, proposed that technology should be used to encourage intellectual exchanges among students in the classroom. *"Appropriately designed computer programs would make possible the solution of complex problems by a group of students, while helping 'level the abilities' within a group so that less able students might take on tasks that would be viewed by others as meaningfully furthering the group activity."* Another panelist, Jim Minstrell, envisioned the classroom of the future as *"full with electronic aids for teachers, helping with organizational and management tasks such as: keeping track of appointments and deadlines."*

Moreover, a branch of CSCW—Computer Supported Collaborative Learning (CSCL)—describes the benefits of collaborative learning using technology. Creativity in a collaborative context, for example, can be aided by activity awareness, whereby each individual is aware of other collaborators' work and is cognizant of other people's plans and understandings [11]. Indeed, Web-based collaborative learning systems give learners more opportunities to participate, which may benefit both individual and team performance [23]. Our findings suggest that GitHub is one such system, as the use of its collaboration, social and awareness features provides benefits beyond traditional systems. This transforms the ecosystem of teachers, students and content into an open collaborative ecosystem (see Fig. 1).

Learning Management Systems

Typically, a learning management system (LMS) or course management system (CMS) (e.g., Blackboard, Moodle, Sakai) provides educators with course management features that allow grade tracking, file management, assignment hosting and real-time chat. Many of these are listed in Kumar *et al.*'s comparative study of different virtual learning management systems [20]. Malikowski *et al.* [25] developed a model that dissects the quality of LMS tools into five categories: (1) transmitting course content, (2) evaluating students, (3) evaluating courses and instructors, (4) creating class discussions, and (5) creating computer-based instruction. Their study shows that the most prominent use of an LMS is to transmit information to students, whereas the categories of creating class discussions and evaluating students receive moderate and low-to-moderate use, respectively.

In response to the popularity of Web 2.0 technologies, LMSs evolved to include features such as blogs and wikis [9]. However, learning systems are typically geared towards administrative purposes rather than fully supporting self-governed or collaborative learning activities [6], leading to interactive features being underutilized and students being less engaged [1]. We argue that GitHub can support much of what traditional learning systems do, as well as go beyond them by supporting collaborative activities.

What is GitHub?

GitHub offers several unique features to facilitate user collaboration. Its most important feature is the Pull Request (PR) mechanism which is a way to initiate discussion with other users and share or comment on the various artifacts in a project (typically changes to the project's content). The discussion may include code that is visible to everyone and it shows the exact changes that would be merged if the PR were accepted. A PR may involve other content (e.g., screenshots) to provide a background for the discussion, or include changes to other resources in the project. When a user wishes to contribute to someone else's project, they can *clone*[7] the project to create a full copy of the project in their

[7] `https://help.github.com/articles/duplicating-a-repository`

local environment, but where committed changes will still affect the original project. This is called a Shared Repository Model[8]: contributors can either commit changes directly into the shared repository or use PRs to start code reviews and conversations about proposed changes before the changes are merged into the master branch. Alternatively, a user can *fork*[9] the entire project to create a parallel project where committed changes do not directly affect the original project. This is called a Fork & Pull Model: PRs provide a way to notify the original project maintainers about the changes you would like them to consider.

Users can not only follow other users or projects of interest, but they can also broadcast their activities to their followers. Furthermore, users can discover new projects by using the *explore* feature, or share snippets using the *Gist* feature. GitHub also supports awareness by broadcasting updates to the user's news feed. The combination of these features facilitates *"a culture of spontaneous-but-structured collaboration."*[10] As an example, Dabbish *et al.* [5] describe GitHub as beneficial to the collaboration of a community because of transparency, where individual contributors can infer a collaborator's technical goals or be aware of what other users are paying close attention to.

GitHub is not just a prime example of CSCW, but it is also a good data source to study how people collaborate[11]. Wu *et al.* [38] analyzed rich GitHub timeline data and found that most of the *follow* activities on GitHub are not due to developers' collaborations on GitHub, but rather their interactions outside GitHub, such as through Twitter, Hacker News and Stack Overflow. Majumder *et al.* [24] conducted an investigation on how teams are formed in a social network based on millions of software repositories spanning a period of four years and hundreds of thousands of developers on GitHub. Tsay *et al.* [36] performed a quantitative analysis of project success of over 5,000 open source software projects hosted on GitHub. They used two measures for project success—**developer attention** and **work contribution**—and found that projects with a high level of developer multitasking tend to receive less developer attention, but greater work contribution.

Why GitHub for Education?

Software developers, sometimes described as the "prototype of the future knowledge worker"[12], are often the first to adopt new tools and new techniques. We predict that future knowledge workers will have to deal with more complex models for managing content than has been done in the past and how GitHub is being used for education is one example of that.

Up until recently, GitHub has focused on code and project management for software development; it is now being extended to other domains that involve collaborative work, such as education [14]. However, in this different context, teaching techniques may require adjustment while some of GitHub's features may require repurposing. Jim Baker, a senior developer and University of Colorado Computer Science lecturer, shared his experiences with GitHub:

> *"We had a great experience using GitHub to support a collaborative workflow for the 70+ students in each of the 2 semesters of my CS course."*

When asked for more details, he elaborated:

> *"Pull requests (PR) are the heart of the GitHub workflow, and we took advantage of PRs, including task lists so that students could report on their work in progress and get over initial humps. Any merged PR got extra credit(!). Because the course had been improved in some way—this seemed like an interesting standard for giving out extra credit. Consequently, we mostly didn't merge PRs for labs, except for bug fixes, but we were always on the lookout for* ***better solutions than ours****. PRs were also merged for extra credit, such as* ***corrections of my course notes****. Next fall we expect to have* ***autograding*** *implemented as a form of continuous integration, by running against the PRs through postcommit hooks."*

Several other educators have also introduced GitHub into their classrooms and shared their experiences. In 2010, Luis Felipe Borjas[13] posted about the use of GitHub organizations[14]—a way to simplify the management of group-owned repositories—to manage class projects. He also applied GitHub to exams: instead of waiting until the exam deadline to upload the exams, students could just *push*[15] as many times they wished and the last *push* they made before the deadline was going to be considered their final submission. He also strongly suggested teachers create exams or homework assignments that could translate into private *git repos* for students to push to.

In 2011, David Humphrey blogged[16] that he asked his students to use Git/GitHub and highly recommended other instructors use it in the classroom. He claimed that although it was a little painful to learn Git/GitHub at the beginning, the payoff would be huge. *"One of the great things about Git in an educational setting is that you don't need to rely on institutional IT, which, in my experience, is never agile enough to help you with revision control. You can put repos on laptops, use USB keys, use DropBox, use GitHub, etc. You don't have to wait for someone to set up a server and make you accounts, don't have to deal with permissions, or any other nonsense that comes with centralized revision control systems."*

Version control systems have been used in the classroom as a way of managing students and their work. Reid & Wilson [30] introduced the Concurrent Versions System (CVS)

[8] `https://guides.github.com/introduction/flow/`

[9] `https://help.github.com/articles/fork-a-repo`

[10] `http://software-carpentry.org/blog/2012/04/github-for-education.html`

[11] `http://www.gousios.gr/blog/The-triumph-of-online-collaboration`

[12] `http://allankelly.blogspot.ca/2014/04/the-prototype-of-future-knowledge.html`

[13] `http://lfborjas.com/2010/10/30/git-classroom-exams.html`

[14] `https://github.com/blog/674-introducing-organizations`

[15] `https://help.github.com/articles/pushing-to-a-remote`

[16] `http://vocamus.net/dave/?p=1358`

to a second-year computer science course. This provided the instructors with a simple way to manage student assignments, made it easier for students to work in pairs or groups, and gave the instructors a history of student work. Clifton, Kaczmarczyk & Mrozek [4] used Subversion, another version control system, to collaboratively develop and run introductory computer science courses. The ease of managing courses using Subversion allowed the instructors to free up time from administrative demands, allowing them to spend more time focusing on pedagogical issues. In 2013, Griffin & Seals used GitHub in the classroom as a version control tool, leveraging the *Branch* and *Merge* features [14]. When students worked on programming assignments, it was easy to *merge* back into the original project if their version worked, or abandon a branch without destroying the original project.

Apart from these testimonies of using *"raw GitHub"* and other similar, developer-focused tools in the classroom, there are also education targeted platforms based on the GitHub model. Created in 2013, Coursefork[17] is described as *"GitHub for course creation."*[18] It is a platform for open-sourcing and collaborating on educational material, where educators can upload course materials and allow others to create copies of courses and modify or share them.

These examples show that GitHub is generating interest as a powerful platform for education. Our research provides first insights into how GitHub can benefit education.

METHODOLOGY

To discover if and how GitHub is being used in education, our study used exploratory research methods [10, 32] and consisted of three phases of data collection (online methods [37], interviews, and a validation survey). Our methodology consisted of data collection and iterative phases of data analysis. In this section, we discuss our research questions, study design, study participants, data collection methods and data analysis approach.

Research Questions

This study strives to answer the following research questions:

How does GitHub support learning and teaching? We investigate how GitHub is used and for what purposes within the education domain. Our findings indicate that even though GitHub use in education mirrors the way traditional learning systems are used, the implications differ substantially.

What are the motivations and benefits of using GitHub for education? Based on testimonies from our study participants, we explore the motivations for GitHub use in education and the possible benefits it might bring to support learning. We also look at the specific features of GitHub that are being used to support learning.

What challenges are related to the use of GitHub for education? And finally, we examine the challenges educators and their students face when using GitHub to support learning and teaching. We provide specific examples based on interviews with educators, and later synthesize recommendations for educators wishing to use GitHub, as well as recommendations to the GitHub design team.

Study Design

In the first phase of our study, we used online research methods [37] and searched for resources (such as blog posts) that described the personal experiences of educators using GitHub to support learning or teaching. The results from this phase are presented in the Background section.

Through this exploratory phase, we found creative and successful examples of GitHub supporting teaching and learning in the classroom. We also found discussions on the challenges and difficulties of using GitHub. This allowed us to refine our research questions and guided us in the following phases of the study, such as shaping the questions to ask during interviews.

In the second phase of our study, we interviewed 15 participants, including one of the blog authors from the first phase. In this phase, we were able to thoroughly investigate the usefulness and potential of GitHub in education. Through iterative analysis of the data collected, several themes emerged around the motivations for and challenges of using GitHub to support learning.

These themes informed the third phase of our research: a follow-up survey sent to interviewees from the previous phase and to other educators using GitHub for education. The goal of this survey was to receive interviewee feedback on our interpretations, but also to gain additional perspectives from other educators that use GitHub.

Data Collection

For the interviews, we emailed invitations to lecturers and professors that use or have used GitHub to support teaching or learning. Potential participants were recruited in several ways: by contacting blog authors who shared their experiences of using GitHub in the classroom; by posting an invitation on Twitter[19]; and through snowball sampling, where interviewees could suggest other colleagues.

The interviews lasted 20-60 minutes and were conducted face to face or with Skype. Audio was recorded and the interviewer took notes. The interviews were semi-structured based on 18 guiding questions (our interview form is available online[20]), and the interviewer could *dig deeper* with additional questions as deemed appropriate. This supported the exploratory nature of our study and allowed us to examine interesting and unexpected insights.

We also interviewed John Britton, an education liaison from GitHub (this interview form is also available online[21]). This

[17] `http://coursefork.org/`

[18] `http://opensource.com/education/13/9/coursefork-education-tool`

[19] `https://twitter.com/alexeyzagalsky/status/465914075348619264`

[20] `https://drive.google.com/file/d/0B273SDwCaBm_Z3V1X1BtakpKVlk/edit?usp=sharing`

[21] `https://drive.google.com/file/d/0B273SDwCaBm_Z2toY0hBUWVjZ3c/edit?usp=sharing`

interview provided us with GitHub's corporate take on the use of its tool in education.

Participants

Our study targeted lecturers and professors in higher education who use or have used GitHub to support teaching and learning. As our study aimed to investigate diverse populations as well as GitHub's usefulness in non-technical courses, we wanted to hear from lecturers and professors across domains.

Interview Participants

Table 1 shows some details about the courses each of the interviewees taught using GitHub. For each course taught, we list a summary of the students' GitHub knowledge, the type of course, and the number of students enrolled.

Table 1. Information on courses taught by interview participants while using GitHub.

P#	Course Type	Knew GitHub	Course Size(s)
1	CS	Yes	55
2	CS	Yes	40
3	CS	Yes	85, 130
4	Humanities	No	11, 40
5	Humanities	No	17
6	CS	Yes	60, 100
7	CS	Yes	50-237
8	CS	Varies	60
9	Sciences	No	235
10	CS	Varies	450
11	CS	Varies	20, 40
12	Statistics	No	40
13	CS	No	20
14	CS	Yes	8
15	CS	No	30-32

The participants represent a broad list of universities: University of Victoria, University of British Colombia, McGill University, University of California at Berkeley, University of California at Davis, Columbia University, The City University of New York, Harvard University, The University of Texas at Austin, Federal University of Pernambuco, and Delft University of Technology. Furthermore, one of the participants was from a company that teaches code to entrepreneurs and CEOs in Paris.

Follow-up Survey Respondents

We sent a follow-up survey to the interviewees to get their feedback on our interpretation of the interview findings. We also publicly broadcasted the survey using social media[22] and used snowball sampling to garner responses from additional educators we had not interviewed. 8 of the interview participants and an additional 7 new respondents completed the survey, for a total of 15 responses.

Data Analysis

Our analysis of the interview data followed qualitative data analysis guidelines [21, 32] and included the following stages: (1) transcription of the data recorded; (2) organization of the data into easily retrievable sections; (3) familiarization by reading and re-reading the data, making memos and summaries; (4) reading the data and labeling segments, i.e., coding; and (5) identifying themes or emergent concepts through discussions among the researchers and engaging in re-coding to develop more well-defined categories. After refining and merging some of the themes, a list was compiled. This process was performed iteratively for each category.

[22] `https://twitter.com/alexeyzagalsky/status/471053256718692352`

FINDINGS

In this section, we address our research questions and present the themes that emerged from the interviews. To illustrate the different aspects of each theme, we provide selected quotes from the interviews, where each participant is identified by an anonymized identifier (P#).

RQ1: How does GitHub support learning and teaching?

There are two ways that our interviewees utilized GitHub in the classroom: as a submission platform, and as a way to host course content. These two basic uses mirror how teachers use typical learning management systems (e.g., Moodle and Sakai) [25]. However, the implications of how they use these features differ substantially. Figure 1 gives a high-level overview of the interactions that are possible between teachers, students and content, and shows the additional interactions that the use of GitHub natively supports over traditional learning environments. For example, as seen in the bottom-left quadrant of the figure, while traditional LMSs support students reading and accessing course material, GitHub also allows them to easily contribute to the course material.

Figure 1. The additional features GitHub provides in addition to the features provided by traditional LMSs.

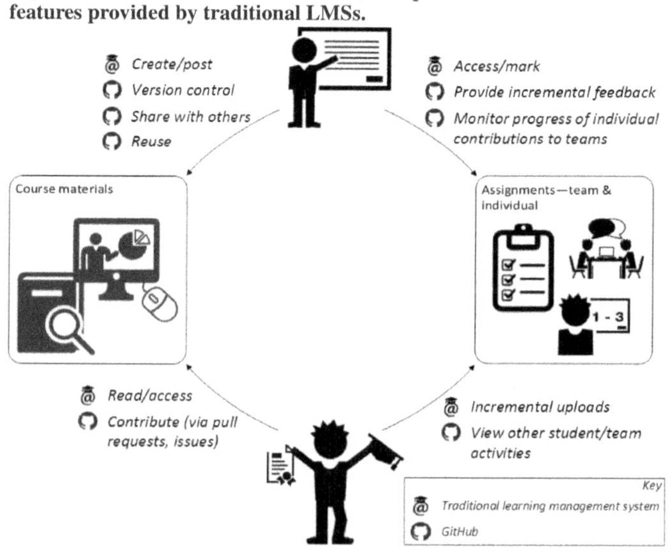

GitHub as a Submission Platform

Many of the interviewees used GitHub as a place for students to host their work and submit their course assignments and projects [P1, P2, P3, P4, P5, P6, P7, P11, P12, P13, P14, P15]. The benefits of using it as a submission platform are further discussed in the findings of RQ2.

Using GitHub as a submission platform was accomplished in one of two ways[23]. Some interviewees set up a base repository for the class and had each student fork it—everyone who forked the base repository could see all other forked repositories as well. This allowed students to cross-reference different solutions and encouraged student collaboration (e.g., by using PRs) and peer learning. *"When you do a pull, you can see what the others in the seminar are doing. For example, a student wrote a python script, and others want to use it, so they can just grab it and use it."*[P4]

Other interviewees set up private repositories for each student, and individual students could only see other repositories when explicitly given access. For P5's course, *"Students have separate repositories, and it's private so that people cannot see what they are working on."* With this option, repositories and permissions are manually set up, which may be difficult in courses with a large number of students.

Hosting Course Material

Many interviewees used GitHub to host and deliver course materials [P4, P5, P8, P9, P10, P11, P12, P13, P15], including syllabi, slides, notes, reading materials, exercises and homework. It was even used to host the actual course Website, making GitHub *"a bulletin board."*[P10] The basic mechanism to host course Websites is by using GitHub markdown files, or for more traditional Websites, by using GitHub Pages[24] which hosts the material directly from one's repository.

With course materials hosted on GitHub, students and other educators were able to suggest course improvements [P1, P10, P11, P12] by submitting an issue or a PR. *"Students would actually find corrections and things and they would send me Pull Requests... But there was some sense of a community that was at least, certainly invited to collaborate on the course material itself."*[P12] As such, interviewees were able to facilitate student contribution to the course material itself using GitHub, a use case and benefit that GitHub offers beyond many traditional systems.

RQ2: What are the motivations and benefits of using GitHub for education?

We explored why educators chose to use GitHub and how they (and their students) benefited from its use. While GitHub is still an emerging tool for education and many benefits have not yet been fully realized, we extracted several themes from our interviews.

Transparency of Activity

Using GitHub as a submission platform made it easy for our interviewees to monitor student progress, activity and participation. GitHub has numerous features that support transparency of student activities. For example, GitHub allows users to see the **history** of activities. As P1 mentioned, *"You really see the full history of how the document comes into being, including all the discussions, the former versions. And the groups can look at each others' documents and see them emerge. I can see how they are creating it, so I can monitor who's active, working in certain teams, which is also handy, practical."*

GitHub also provides a **graph view** that visualizes a summary of project activities. This allowed teachers to easily gain a high-level view of student activity. *"You can see who is doing what, you can see how people are sharing work because you have the commit history."*[P4] This same feature supported teachers in identifying outlier students that were not participating as expected. *"I would go into their team repository, and...they have some graphs in there that show you what's the activity level and who's most active. I would use that to get a sense for what was happening because inevitably, you would have one of the students...that's not doing anything and you want to get some hard data on exactly what he isn't doing."*[P6]

Furthermore, GitHub has **news feeds** that teachers used to keep up to date with activity. By watching the news feeds, they could catch problems early with how frequently students were participating in the course. *"Personally, what I did is that I subscribed to all [the students'] repositories and followed the feed of those repositories."*[P2]

However, GitHub allowed people to do more than just passively observe progress. Students **opened issues** and **tagged** them with the teacher's name to get the teacher's attention. *"You could watch the commits go by. They can ask for help by opening issues and tagging us, so that worked quite beautifully for monitoring and in some cases actively providing advice on group project work."*[P12] This kind of support encouraged a style of communication between the teacher and student that is not available in traditional learning management systems.

Encourage Participation

The transparency features discussed above allowed interviewees to encourage student course participation and contribution to the hosted course material. With traditional environments, students would need to contact the instructor directly to suggest changes to the materials. Using GitHub, a student could suggest changes by submitting an issue connected with the material. Or, they could make changes themselves and then submit a pull request, which the teacher, if they agreed with the changes, could simply accept. The history of these actions helped the teacher keep track of who participated, and by its visibility, also encouraged students as their actions were logged and possibly used to improve their grades.

P1 spoke about how these features helped to persist the effort that students put forth: *"Yes, [using GitHub encouraged student participation] because everything you do is also recorded. It stays there forever, it's persistent. So your comments are persistent, your activities are persistent. So you work, you get rewarded, and if you don't work it's visible... in GitHub it's a little more transparent."*

Some interviewees felt that using GitHub helped them encourage participation, even in indirect ways: *"I will use the logs [that students put on GitHub] as materials for discus-*

[23]`https://education.github.com/guide#4-set-up-the-repositories`

[24]`https://pages.github.com/`

sion in class. That can encourage participation because you know you are committing something that can be discussion material."[P5]

Although few mandated the use of GitHub's issue tracker for their classes and students' group projects, some found novel uses for this feature. P12 and P14 had students use it when they needed help, and otherwise used it as a simple communication method between students and markers. P1's students participated by discussing an issue they had with a deadline: *"the students didn't like [a deadline], so they opened an issue on GitHub: 'Can we move it?'... So everyone responded to that issue on GitHub, and then at the end I said, 'based on the discussion, it is going to be on Sunday."'* These features supported student/teacher discussions—communication was recorded and tied directly to the relevant course content.

Reuse and Sharing of Course Materials and Knowledge

Another important advantage GitHub provided our interviewees was the ease with which materials and knowledge could be shared and reused, by both students and course instructors.

Some of our interviewees' students shared work and material with each other. In P4's course, a student's python script was visible to others, and therefore, easily shared. The ability to make content either public, private amongst collaborators, or completely private, gave our interviewees' students an easy way to share with others or contribute to their work. For example, P1 noted that this visibility had the useful side effect that his students gave each other **feedback** on their pull requests and reports.

Moreover, our interviewees used GitHub to share courses and their associated materials with other educators. Although this is also a feature in many learning environments, they lack a way to visualize how a reused course has changed from the original one. Seeing when courses are **forked** and how they differ from one another is a key feature in GitHub. *"We were developing all the content from scratch... the various teaching staff had to collaborate and develop the material, and so GitHub was a nice fit for that... We had two repositories: we had a private one and a public one, and so we could sort of have private conversations among the staff to refine the content and then it was pretty easy to just migrate it over once it was ready.*"[P10]

GitHub's **access control** features allowed the instructors to **version** their material and choose who to share it with. *"Some of [the material] is shared with the world, and some of it is shared with other instructors of other universities. So for example, when we create new exam questions and stuff like that, we try to keep those [repositories] private for a little while so other instructors can use them. But we're versioning all of it.*"[P7]

Interestingly, unregistered students and other GitHub users would also visit these public repositories: *"We kept everything public from the beginning, so it ended up getting a lot of attention outside of the course. I think the repository has something like 200 stars on GitHub right now and as far as I can tell most of those stars are from people who didn't take the course.*"[P10]

Industry Relevance

As working with Git and GitHub are relevant skills for industry, this theme emerged as both a motivation to use GitHub in courses and a benefit of using the tool. This relevance to industry meant that some of our interviewees and their students had prior GitHub experience, and as a result, were motivated to use it in class. For example, P12 had already been using GitHub regularly and explained why they chose to use GitHub in their courses: *"... partially to unify what I'm doing in the research side of my life with what I do with the teaching side. Like once you've taken the trouble to learn [GitHub] and get it all set up, you start to see lots of areas of your life where this workflow would actually be very useful."*

Meanwhile, we saw some instances where students who had prior experience using GitHub encouraged their course instructors to use it for class. As P1 told us: *"So actually, some students came to me, and they said - you should watch this video on how GitHub uses GitHub to build GitHub."*

Learning to use Git and GitHub in a course is a significant benefit in certain fields, particularly in computer science and software engineering[25]. In fact, P12 felt that learning to use GitHub was required to progress within their field: *"To prepare this cohort of graduate students for computational work, they should know how to use these tools. This is very much what people do these days in [statistics], and so I actually consider it a completely valid pedagogical goal in it of itself."*

By using GitHub for course work, students further benefited by having an end product that could easily be shared with prospective employers. *"you can use it sort of as an online resume... GitHub allowed you the opportunity to convert [your class work] to a public project so that employers for example could see what code you've been writing.*"[P6]

Ease of Use

GitHub's administrative functions are relatively simple and easy to work with: getting students set up for the class, setting privacy options and creating repositories. *"I don't think it saved time at the beginning... because I was starting an entirely new approach to doing this. But once it was up and running, the next semester would have been quite simple to administer because I knew the process.*"[P6] Although GitHub has a definite learning curve, it can be mitigated by sharing practices among practitioners. *"I worked with [the next instructor of the course] a bit on explaining how it worked and what we did with it, so she found it pretty easy to get started too.*"[P6]

Despite the learning curve and some technical difficulties, several interviewees mentioned that GitHub was relatively easy to use and to administer, both on its own and compared to existing university systems. *"For me it was the ease of updating the class schedule and course notes. The class schedule is something that is extremely painful to update on the university Website... Each course is a little window and you have to click arrows to move them up and down to reorder them, or something really horrible like that. And [with GitHub] it*

[25] `http://techcrunch.com/2014/07/23/modernizing-computer-science-education`

was very easy to just go into a markdown, add a link, and hit push."[P9]

Free Academic Licenses

Generally, GitHub allows all users to create free public repositories. However, an additional benefit mentioned in the interviews [P3, P6, P7] is that GitHub provides free academic licenses. Students and educators can apply for a free micro plan that allows private repositories. Educators can also apply for a free organization account[26] that facilitates team management and administration. The implications of these free public accounts go beyond benefiting face-to-face instruction, allowing teachers to *scale-up* traditional education and create online courses that will benefit part-time and remote students.

Shared Space and Course Versioning

By hosting course materials on GitHub, students could easily share course notes, references or other material for the same class. From the aspect of teaching, educators could easily share [P13] or duplicate course resources. *"The simplest thing I've been using [GitHub for], especially from an instructor's view, is to duplicate the course Website for different semesters."*[P4] Therefore, when teaching the same course again, preparing the course materials was simple: participants used the same repository or forked it. *"If I improve the material in some way, I'd just keep it there...And if someone wants an older version of the repository, they just need to get it. However, if I did want to create a separate course with just part of the material of the original course, I would [fork the repository]."*[P11]

RQ3: What challenges are related to the use of GitHub for education?

We have grouped the challenges our analysis revealed into five themes: shared knowledge base of suggested practices, barriers to entry, support for additional formats, external restrictions, and large scale management.

Shared Knowledge Base of Suggested Practices

Interviewees showed a need for *a shared knowledge base* of suggested practices on how to use GitHub for educational purposes. P6 went into great detail about their struggles in this area: *"It's a different use in a team at some startup or what have you. And it's not clear how exactly you should, for example, enforce a methodology for the students for working. Should you use Pull Requests? When should you file issues? Divide up the repository, should you each have an individual repository as well and then fork the main project? There's a lot of good evidence and good data for how you should work in Git for your software development project, for commercial projects. For educational projects, they're quite different because they're short in duration, there's 4 or 5 people working on it that aren't very experienced with software development."*

Educators wished for easily accessible *how-to guides* or shared experiences by others on how they've used GitHub. *"Maybe some documentation on best practices or some kind of shared knowledge base that would say here's what so-and-so at UC Irvine is doing with GitHub."*[P6] Interestingly, the GitHub education Website contains a guide that could meet some basic needs, but our interviewees did not know of this relatively new feature.

Barriers to Entry

At its core, GitHub is a **Git-based** system, and while it provides a simple Web interface, tasks that involve collaboration require an understanding of Git and its command-line arguments. In particular, dealing with **merges and conflicts** can be challenging: *"To get the most out of GitHub, you need to understand Git. Even if you just use it to edit documents together, you will get conflicts once in a while. And if you want to use the review mechanism, then you want/should use the Pull Requests. That requires some pretty deep knowledge of Git still. If you use it the right way it is simple, but somehow with Git you end up with conflicts, and if you don't understand it, it's magic."*[P1]

Difficulties using Git are experienced by technical novices and software developers alike [29]. Our interviewees reinforced the need to improve **accessibility** for novice users or users with a limited technical background: *"Largely, the biggest challenge is to lower the learning curve, not on the high end, but the very low end for people who are new to it to have much gentler learning curve."*[P5]

Support for Additional Formats

GitHub's file and format support is another main challenge mentioned by the interviewees, specifically the lack of support for formats widely used in education, such as PDF and LaTeX. The ability to view or render these formats directly on GitHub, similar to Markdown rendering, would be very helpful. But more importantly, there is a need to support the powerful features Git has for text files: *diff* and review functionality, and the mechanism to add inline comments to a file without altering the original file. For example, when an instructor wishes to mark the students' assignments or reports, they are forced to download and comment on each file (e.g., using the comment feature in a PDF file) separately, which also alters the original file. Another option is to use the *issues* mechanism of GitHub to provide comments, however, this mechanism can't reference a specific place in the file and may be tedious if the instructor wants to add many small comments on a submission.

Poor support for slides was also mentioned: *"You can not easily view slides in GitHub, because the PDF is too large and you have to download it, it's a bit cumbersome... in a course you always have presentation material, so you want some sort of integration with slides here. They [GitHub] have Speaker Deck, so I want Speaker Deck integrated with GitHub."*[P1] Being able to *diff* slides is also important.

External Restrictions

Interviewees also mentioned external restrictions that limit or prevent them from using GitHub for education. External restrictions can be local restrictions (e.g., university policy) or global restrictions (e.g., regional publishing licenses). *"We*

[26] `https://help.github.com/articles/what-s-the-difference-between-user-and-organization-accounts`

have LMS systems that we use, and in a way it's very important to use them because they're authenticated by the university. So things like student's grades and stuff like that you don't (store on GitHub), because of the rules in the US. You cannot store it anywhere else."[P3] Another teacher also shared this concern: *"Ethically, I wish I could know where the server is, where I am pushing all my material."*[P4]

Knowing the server's location plays a significant role when educators decide whether to use GitHub. Not only from the **ethical aspects**, but also from **copyright aspects**. As P5 mentioned: *"Copyright is a big issue. For instance, we are working with a novel. In Canada, that novel is in public domain so it can be accessed online, but not in United States."*

Large-scale Management
Educators are challenged when managing courses with large numbers of students, teams, projects or issues. *"One thing I'm not so happy with, is the way group management [works]. So managing teams, different sizes, I have an organization for the students and the organization has 50 members and I need to create different groups, and different roles, and different access... I think that could be done... [in a] more convenient way."*[P1]

P6 further discusses the challenges with managing teams and repositories: *"The thing that I think was missing... was more management for the administrator: assigning people to teams, assigning teams to repositories, finer grained permission control, I think [that] is something that could have been useful."* However, the cause of these difficulties might not be an issue with GitHub, but perhaps the lack of *how-to guides* and suggested practices by others.

GitHub's Perspective
To gain insights into GitHub's perspective on the topic, we interviewed John Britton, an education liaison at GitHub and one of two engineers working full time to support educational uses of GitHub. GitHub's main goal in this regard is to make the tool easier to use, and to make sure users are aware of what resources are available to them to meet their needs and solve their challenges.

Regarding GitHub's benefits for education, John replied:

> *"We're working with students and teachers on using GitHub. It's essentially leveraging those tools in the classroom, so you can get a classroom experience that's more similar to what people in the industry are using, as software developers."*

However, there are challenges involved:

> *"When I first started, I definitely was targeting all forms of education. But I think that it's most applicable in computer science, software engineering, and technical fields. Maybe someday when the tools are easier to use and... require less technical knowledge upfront, it will be much more useful to non-technical fields, or to other types of educational stuff. But I think that Git as it stands requires a certain amount of basic knowledge of computing."*

He then elaborated:

> *"There's different groups. People who know Git and GitHub already and just want to use it in the classroom—they're totally on board with using Pull Requests right from the beginning. The group of people who's like, 'What's Git? What's GitHub?', they have a little bit harder time getting into the mindset of students submitting their code as a Pull Request. Rather than submitting an assignment with a zip file, you create a branch and make a Pull Request, and then grade the student on the Pull Request"*

John concluded by describing how GitHub plans to assist educators:

> *"I think we're going to do more of those [stories of existing use cases], along with technical documentation, or technical information on 'Here's what they're doing. Here's how you can do it too'. But as far as...we don't have a set, like, this is the way, right? There are multiple ways to use GitHub in the classroom, and it depends on what goal you're trying to achieve."*

The education use case is important for GitHub. While their focus remains on its use in software development, they provide dedicated support and resources for educators to take advantage of the tool.

Follow-up Survey
After conducting the interviews, we sent a follow-up survey to both interviewees and the public. We wanted to see if respondents agreed with our interpretation of the interview findings. However, the number of respondents (15) was too low to confidently validate our findings. Regardless, the survey supports many of our findings, with respondents mostly agreeing or strongly agreeing to many of the uses (as a submission platform and course material host) and benefits (simpler than current university systems, reuse and sharing of material, and facilitating collaboration). Interestingly, many respondents from this group of educators stated that they didn't struggle with the challenges that emerged in our interviews (e.g., technical difficulties limiting educator GitHub use, external restrictions, and managing large groups). However, while strongly disagreeing that technical difficulties limited their own use of GitHub, most respondents agreed that technical difficulties limited their student use of GitHub.

DISCUSSION
Our study uncovered how some educators use GitHub to support learning and teaching, while extending or even replacing traditional LMSs. However, the implications of our findings go beyond GitHub itself. The emergence of *"the GitHub way"* within education is transforming the traditional e-learning model (Figure 1) and will better support socio-collaborative learning environments [18] of the future.

Comparing GitHub to Traditional LMSs
GitHub was not designed as an LMS or a CMS, but our study shows it can be used as such. Judging the use of Git and GitHub based on LMS features [20], GitHub supports many

of the important learning features (e.g., assignment delivery and submission), but it also lacks certain features (e.g., grading management tools). In examining the model published by Malikowski *et al.* [25], we come to similar conclusions, where platforms like GitHub have the capability to support all five categories of the model. However, student and course evaluation may require additional work, as well as developing programs to detect and automatically grade student pushes.

Lane [22] discusses two sides of the CMS. From one side, CMS are a **toolbox** for educators, providing a default course structure, and managerial and administrative features. From the other side, integrated commercial CMS are a **trap** that limit faculty creativity, are difficult to customize (sometimes this involves additional cost), and they make it hard to accommodate individual teaching styles. As GitHub is adopted for more and more courses, it remains to be seen if it suffers from similar or different issues to mainstream CMSs.

Going Beyond Traditional LMSs
Beyond the features discussed above, GitHub provides a number of other tools and features that allow educators more novel possibilities.

Version Control
According to the interviewees that teach technical courses (such as computer science), students destined for careers in software and information technology benefit from learning to use version control systems [3]. This reflects the benefits mentioned in previous work on these types of systems [30]. At the same time, version control allows educators to see the final results as well as the processes students used to produce the results [13]. However, this is a double-edged sword as the technical aspects of version control, specifically Git, is one of the main challenges mentioned by interviewees.

Transparency & Awareness
Kreijns *et al.* [19] discuss the shortcomings of contemporary CSCL, particularly in group learning, social construction of knowledge, and the learning process itself. They link these problems to the impeded social interaction of CSCL environments caused by two major pitfalls: taking social interaction in groups for granted, and the lack of attention paid to the social psychological dimension of social interaction outside of the task context. **Transparency of activities** allows GitHub to address this by embedding **social affordances** and by supporting **group awareness**, as proposed by the suggested theoretical framework [18].

However, only a few of our participants mentioned using the **transparency** and **awareness** features to promote collaboration among students. If taken advantage of, GitHub's transparency could be beneficial for collaborating students [7], creating awareness of each others' activities that could, in turn, support collaborator creativity [11]. As such, GitHub is a good example of a transition from a space to a place, as it transitioned from a hosting service that provided space for projects, to a place where work, activities, ideas and discussion can be shared [8].

Student Engagement & Participation
GitHub enables students to contribute to course material or work done by other students with the use of the Pull Request mechanism—a novel way to participate in courses. GitHub provides more in-depth ways to communicate and collaborate and provides teachers and students with a way to gain social group awareness and get information about what group members are doing, who they are communicating with, and how they are contributing [16]. Thus, GitHub enables a participatory culture [17] where students can create, edit, and share in such a way that they feel their contributions matter.

Indeed, one of our interview questions asked whether the use of GitHub encouraged student participation. Impact on student engagement and participation came up several times by the interview participants. However, except for some specific examples, the interviewees didn't have any metrics to measure this. In that sense, our study is limited and leads to future work to investigate if GitHub encourages student participation.

Reusing and Remixing
Some interviewees described the ability to pull from other sources or old material as useful for creating and organizing course material. The main way to reuse materials as seen from our findings was to fork an old instance of a course. However, there were also instances of educators collaborating with each other to create course material, or sharing material with instructors in other universities so that material can be remixed as an instructor sees fit. With current learning management tools, as educators ourselves, we have noted it is extremely tedious to version and share course materials. We end up with each new course as a new entity, losing the history of where we got the materials and who contributed to them. GitHub mitigates this through the use of the *Blame* feature, which visualizes the providence of file changes. In time, we expect to see large networks of educators contributing to the same course, and know who contributed to the material and how.

Implications Beyond GitHub
Our findings go beyond GitHub and apply to related environments, such as BitBucket[27], that provide similar social and collaborative features. In fact, a few of our interviewees also mentioned using BitBucket and described similar experiences using that tool. The lessons learned can be applied to other social hosting tools as well.

Recommendations
A question that an educator might ask at this point is, *"is GitHub ready for 'prime-time,' or should it only be used by early adopters for now?"* We feel that the answer currently lies somewhere in between. From one aspect, GitHub's current platform is considered mature, supports many learning features, provides numerous benefits in the educational context, and is available to anyone wishing to try it out (for free). On the other hand, the use of GitHub involves several challenges (as reported in our Findings, but not repeated in the

[27]`https://bitbucket.org/`

follow-up survey), and currently, is not widely used among educators. As the environment evolves and educators learn and share more about using the platform, we expect that some of these challenges, such as the steep learning curve, may be mitigated.

Our recommendation to educators is to share their experiences and resources with other educators. This shared information should be organized in a shared knowledge base, created by GitHub, and maintained by the community. Furthermore, GitHub (or a third-party developer) can further resolve some of the challenges by tailoring the platform for educational purposes (e.g., providing support for additional file formats). Once these changes are made, we expect to see a rapid adoption of GitHub by educators.

Limitations

From the data collection aspect, we collected data from the educator's point of view only. However, the student's point of view is also crucial and may provide additional support to our findings or reveal new insights. Additionally, the participants of our study were recruited under the condition that they already use GitHub to support learning, where it may imply that their experience had to be (somewhat) successful. This means that our study may have missed the challenges faced by potential participants who failed to use GitHub to support teaching. Additionally, our participants used GitHub at different periods of time, thus their experiences may differ and this may affect our findings.

CONCLUSIONS

In this study, we found that GitHub can be a powerful learning management tool, and while it provides many benefits, there are challenges involved as well. Our findings indicate that various educators use GitHub differently, even in similar environments (e.g., technical background) and with similar requirements (e.g., class size, course type). In some cases, this may happen due to differences in requirements or personal preferences. However, in other cases, there are different uses because GitHub's potential in the context of education is still emerging and many educators aren't aware of the possible uses and advantages it may bring. In this sense, suggested practices should be formed and shared among educators to better utilize GitHub's capabilities as a collaboration platform.

The contribution of this research is fourfold: (1) insights into how GitHub is being used in educational contexts; (2) a list of the benefits that GitHub's content hosting and social features provide in education; (3) a description of the challenges and problems related to using GitHub for education; and, (4) recommendations and suggested practices for how GitHub could be used to support learning. The findings from this research shed light on the use of GitHub as a collaborative social learning platform, and show that tools such as GitHub have the potential to bring more collaboration and transparency to education.

Lastly, this is only the first step in investigating this phenomena. The next steps should be to investigate the student perspective in using GitHub to support learning, and to conduct in-depth case studies of how GitHub plays a role in specific courses.

ACKNOWLEDGMENTS

We thank Cassandra Petrachenko for her valuable comments and editing support. We are extremely grateful to all the interview and survey participants. We would also like to thank GitHub for their willingness to help with this study.

REFERENCES

1. Alhazmi, A., and Rahman, A. Why lms failed to support student learning in higher education institutions. In *E-Learning, E-Management and E-Services (IS3e), 2012 IEEE Symposium on* (2012), 1–5.

2. Begel, A., Bosch, J., and Storey, M.-A. Social networking meets software development: Perspectives from github, msdn, stack exchange, and topcoder. *Software, IEEE 30*, 1 (2013), 52–66.

3. Britton, J., and Berglund, T. Using version control in the classroom. In *Proceeding of the 44th ACM technical symposium on Computer science education*, ACM (2013), 753–753.

4. Clifton, C., Kaczmarczyk, L. C., and Mrozek, M. Subverting the fundamentals sequence: Using version control to enhance course management. *SIGCSE Bull. 39*, 1 (Mar. 2007), 86–90.

5. Dabbish, L., Stuart, C., Tsay, J., and Herbsleb, J. Social coding in github: Transparency and collaboration in an open software repository. In *Proceedings of the ACM 2012 Conference on Computer Supported Cooperative Work*, CSCW '12, ACM (New York, NY, USA, 2012), 1277–1286.

6. Dalsgaard, C. Social software: E-learning beyond learning management systems. *European Journal of Open, Distance and E-Learning 2006*, 2 (2006).

7. Dalsgaard, C., and Paulsen, M. F. Transparency in cooperative online education. *The International Review of Research in Open and Distance Learning 10*, 3 (2009).

8. Dourish, P., and Bellotti, V. Awareness and coordination in shared workspaces. In *Proceedings of the 1992 ACM conference on Computer-supported cooperative work*, ACM (1992), 107–114.

9. Downes, S. Feature: E-learning 2.0. *Elearn magazine 2005*, 10 (2005), 1.

10. Easterbrook, S., Singer, J., Storey, M.-A., and Damian, D. Selecting empirical methods for software engineering research. In *Guide to advanced empirical software engineering*. Springer, 2008, 285–311.

11. Farooq, U., Carroll, J. M., and Ganoe, C. H. Supporting creativity with awareness in distributed collaboration. In *Proceedings of the 2007 international ACM conference on Supporting group work*, ACM (2007), 31–40.

12. Gikas, J., and Grant, M. M. Mobile computing devices in higher education: Student perspectives on learning with cellphones, smartphones & social media. *The Internet and Higher Education 19* (2013), 18–26.
13. Glassy, L. Using version control to observe student software development processes. *Journal of Computing Sciences in Colleges 21*, 3 (2006), 99–106.
14. Griffin, T., and Seals, S. Github in the classroom: Not just for group projects. *J. Comput. Sci. Coll. 28*, 4 (Apr. 2013), 74–74.
15. Grosseck, G., and Holotescu, C. Can we use twitter for educational activities. In *4th international scientific conference, eLearning and software for education, Bucharest, Romania* (2008).
16. Janssen, J., and Bodemer, D. Coordinated computer-supported collaborative learning: Awareness and awareness tools. *Educational Psychologist 48*, 1 (2013), 40–55.
17. Jenkins, H., Clinton, K., Purushotma, R., Robison, A. J., and Weigel, M. Confronting the challenges of participatory culture: Media education for the 21st century, 2006.
18. Kreijns, K., Kirschner, P. A., and Jochems, W. The sociability of computer-supported collaborative learning environments. *Educational Technology & Society 5*, 1 (2002), 8–22.
19. Kreijns, K., Kirschner, P. A., and Vermeulen, M. Social aspects of cscl environments: A research framework. *Educational Psychologist 48*, 4 (2013), 229–242.
20. Kumar, S., Gankotiya, A., and Dutta, K. A comparative study of moodle with other e-learning systems. In *Electronics Computer Technology (ICECT), 2011 3rd International Conference on*, vol. 5 (April 2011), 414–418.
21. Lacey, A., and Luff, D. *Qualitative data analysis*. Trent Focus Sheffield, 2001.
22. Lane, L. M. Toolbox or trap? course management systems and pedagogy. *Educause Quarterly 31*, 2 (2008), 4.
23. Liaw, S.-S., Chen, G.-D., and Huang, H.-M. Users attitudes toward web-based collaborative learning systems for knowledge management. *Computers & Education 50*, 3 (2008), 950 – 961.
24. Majumder, A., Datta, S., and Naidu, K. Capacitated team formation problem on social networks. In *Proceedings of the 18th ACM SIGKDD International Conference on Knowledge Discovery and Data Mining*, KDD '12, ACM (New York, NY, USA, 2012), 1005–1013.
25. Malikowski, S. R., Thompson, M. E., and Theis, J. G. A model for research into course management systems: Bridging technology and learning theory. *Journal of educational computing research 36*, 2 (2007), 149–173.
26. McLure Wasko, M., and Faraj, S. it is what one does: Why people participate and help others in electronic communities of practice. *The Journal of Strategic Information Systems 9*, 2 (2000), 155–173.
27. Nickerson, R. S., and Zodhiates, P. P. *Technology in education: Looking toward 2020*. Routledge, 2013.
28. Pappano, L. The year of the mooc. *The New York Times 2*, 12 (2012), 2012.
29. Perez De Rosso, S., and Jackson, D. What's wrong with git?: a conceptual design analysis. In *Proceedings of the 2013 ACM international symposium on New ideas, new paradigms, and reflections on programming & software*, ACM (2013), 37–52.
30. Reid, K. L., and Wilson, G. V. Learning by doing: Introducing version control as a way to manage student assignments. *SIGCSE Bull. 37*, 1 (Feb. 2005), 272–276.
31. Reinhardt, W., Wheeler, S., and Ebner, M. All i need to know about twitter in education i learned in kindergarten. In *Key Competencies in the Knowledge Society*. Springer, 2010, 322–332.
32. Seaman, C. B. Qualitative methods in empirical studies of software engineering. *Software Engineering, IEEE Transactions on 25*, 4 (1999), 557–572.
33. Storey, M.-A., Singer, L., Cleary, B., Figueira Filho, F., and Zagalsky, A. The (r) evolution of social media in software engineering. In *Proceedings of the on Future of Software Engineering*, ACM (2014), 100–116.
34. Sultan, N. Cloud computing for education: A new dawn? *International Journal of Information Management 30*, 2 (2010), 109–116.
35. Thompson, C. How khan academy is changing the rules of education. *Wired Magazine 126* (2011).
36. Tsay, J. T., Dabbish, L., and Herbsleb, J. Social media and success in open source projects. In *Proceedings of the ACM 2012 Conference on Computer Supported Cooperative Work Companion*, CSCW '12, ACM (New York, NY, USA, 2012), 223–226.
37. Wakeford, N., and Cohen, K. Fieldnotes in public: using blogs for research. *The Sage handbook of online research methods* (2008), 307–326.
38. Wu, Y., Kropczynski, J., Shih, P. C., and Carroll, J. M. Exploring the ecosystem of software developers on github and other platforms. In *Proceedings of the Companion Publication of the 17th ACM Conference on Computer Supported Cooperative Work & Social Computing*, CSCW Companion '14, ACM (New York, NY, USA, 2014), 265–268.

Algorithms in our Midst: Information, Power and Choice when Software is Everywhere

Zeynep Tufekci
University of North Carolina, Chapel Hill
zeynep@unc.edu

Abstract

Our personal, financial and civic interactions are increasingly digitally mediated, and more and more objects come embedded with chips and sensors. As a result, a new layer of power has arisen: that of the algorithm. Software—human-constructed, often invisible and progressively pervasive—not only mediates our lives, it is increasingly used to make decisions in a diverse group areas ranging from sociality to employment to health to relationships. While automation's social, political and economic impacts have long been debated, there is now a new layer that requires consideration: algorithms, often aided by big data, now make decisions in subjective realms where there is no right decision, and no anchor with which to judge outcomes. What is good? What is relevant? What is important? Who is right? What is desirable? What is valuable? These questions with philosophical roots that go to beginning of civilization are now turned over to algorithms that bring about a new set of structural biases and issues. This new phase in pervasive computing raises significant questions and challenges, and important areas of research.

ACM Classification

K.4.0

Author Keywords: algorithms; big data; policy; internet of things; software

Short Bio

Zeynep Tufekci is an assistant professor at the University of North Carolina, Chapel Hill at the School of Information (SILS) with an affiliate appointment in the Department of Sociology. She's also a faculty associate at the Harvard Berkman Center for Internet and Society.

CSCW 2015, March 14–18, 2015, Vancouver, BC, Canada.
ACM 978-1-4503-2922-4/15/03.
http://dx.doi.org/10.1145/2675133.2697079

Zeynep was previously:

- a fellow at the Center for Information Technology Policy at Princeton University and I taught at the Woodrow Wilson School of Public Policy and International Affairs.
- a fellow at the Berkman Center for Internet and Society at Harvard University.
- an assistant professor of sociology at the University of Maryland, Baltimore County

Her research revolves around the interaction between technology and social, cultural and political dynamics with particular interested in collective action, civics, algorithms and big data, surveillance, privacy, and sociality. Zeynep believes that academic knowledge is crucial to significant issues facing us and besides carrying out her academic research, she tries to write at the intersection of academic knowledge and accessible and relevant content.

Author Index

www.ingramcontent.com/pod-product-compliance
Lightning Source LLC
LaVergne TN
LVHW080100011026
849160LV00013B/1004